Digest of Education Statistics 2018

54th Edition

Thomas D. Snyder
Cristobal de Brey
National Center for Education Statistics

Sally A. Dillow
American Institutes for Research

U.S Department of Education

National Center for Education Statistics

Institute of Education Sciences

- Staff employed and pupil/staff ratios in public elementary and secondary school systems, by type of assignment and locale (*web-only table 213.60*)
- Number and percentage distribution of public elementary and secondary charter schools and students, and charter schools and enrollment as a percentage of total public schools and enrollment, by locale (*web-only table 216.92*)
- Percentage of students ages 5 through 17 enrolled in kindergarten through grade 12 who took any school-related courses online and who took courses from various providers, by selected child, parent, and household characteristics (table 218.16)
- Public high school 4-year adjusted cohort graduation rate (ACGR), by selected student characteristics and locale (*web-only table 219.47*)
- Number of 16- to 24-year-old high school dropouts (status dropouts) and percentage of dropouts among persons 16 to 24 years old (status dropout rate), by race/ethnicity and racial/ethnic subgroup (*web-only table 219.82*)
- Average National Assessment of Educational Progress (NAEP) reading scale score, by percentage of students in school eligible for free or reduced-price lunch, grade, and school locale (*web-only table 221.25*)
- Average National Assessment of Educational Progress (NAEP) reading scale score and percentage distribution of 12th-graders, by whether student uses a computer at home, whether student has access to the Internet at home, and other selected characteristics (*web-only table 221.36*)
- Average National Assessment of Educational Progress (NAEP) reading scale score of 4th- and 8th-grade public school students, by school locale and state (*web-only table 221.72*)
- Average National Assessment of Educational Progress (NAEP) mathematics scale score, by percentage of students in school eligible for free or reduced-price lunch, grade, and school locale (*web-only table 222.25*)
- Average National Assessment of Educational Progress (NAEP) mathematics scale score of 4th- and 8th-grade public school students, by school locale and state (*web-only table 222.75*)
- Average National Assessment of Educational Progress (NAEP) science scale score, by percentage of students in school eligible for free or reduced-price lunch, grade, and school locale (*web-only table 223.17*)
- Average National Assessment of Educational Progress (NAEP) science scale score of 4th- and 8th-grade public school students, by school locale and state (*web-only table 223.23*)
- Among public schools with any of grades 9 to 12 (or ungraded equivalent), percentage of schools with students enrolled or classes offered in selected courses or programs, and percentage of 9th- to 12th-graders enrolled in these courses or programs, by locale (*web-only table 225.72*)
- Percentage of 4th-, 8th-, and 12th-graders whose school reported offering selected classes and percentage of 8th-graders whose school reported having students who take high school math classes, by selected student and school characteristics (*web-only table 225.75*)
- Percentage distribution of 4th-, 8th-, and 12th-graders, by number of days absent from school in the last month and school locale (*web-only table 227.52*)
- Number of active shooter incidents at educational institutions and number of casualties, by level of institution (*web-only table 228.15*)
- Number of active shooter incidents at educational institutions, number and type of guns used, and number and characteristics of shooters, by level of institution (*web-only table 228.16*)
- Percentage distribution of students in grades 9–12, by number of times they reported being threatened or injured with a weapon on school property during the previous 12 months and selected student characteristics (*web-only table 228.42*)
- Percentage of students ages 12–18 who reported that gangs were present at school during the school year, by grade, control of school, and urbanicity (*web-only table 230.20a*)
- Percentage of students ages 12–18 who reported being bullied at school during the school year, by type of bullying and selected student and school characteristics (*web-only table 230.45*)
- Percentage of students ages 12–18 who reported being bullied at school during the school year, percentage of bullied students reporting various types of power imbalances in favor of someone who bullied them, and percentage distribution of bullied students, by whether they thought the bullying would happen again and selected student and school characteristics (*web-only table 230.51*)
- Percentage of students ages 12–18 reporting that they were victimized, that they were in a physical fight, or that alcohol or illegal drugs were available or used at school, by school locale, type of victimization, number of times in a fight, and type of drug (*web-only table 230.85*)
- Percentages of 8th-, 10th-, and 12th-graders reporting use and availability of heroin and narcotics other than heroin, by grade and recency of use (*web-only table 232.65*)
- Percentages of 8th-, 10th-, and 12th-graders reporting use of heroin and narcotics other than heroin during past 12 months, by grade and selected student and family characteristics (*web-only table 232.65a*)

- Percentages of 8th-, 10th-, and 12th-graders who reported thinking that people are at great risk of harming themselves if they engage in activities related to use of heroin and narcotics other than heroin, by grade and type of activity (*web-only table 232.65b*)
- Unadjusted and geographically adjusted current expenditure per pupil in fall enrollment in public elementary and secondary schools, by locale, function, and district poverty level (*web-only table 236.85*)
- Percentage distribution of all 2009 9th-graders and those who ever attended a postsecondary institution, by socioeconomic status in 2009 and selected postsecondary outcomes (*web-only table 302.44*)
- Percentage distribution of all 2009 9th-graders and those who ever attended a postsecondary institution, by poverty status in 2009 and 2012 and selected postsecondary outcomes (*web-only table 302.45*)
- Percentage distribution of fall 2009 9th-graders, by high school locale in 2009, high school completion status, postsecondary enrollment and work status or plans, and postsecondary attainment status (*web-only table 302.46*)
- Total fall enrollment in private nonprofit degree-granting postsecondary institutions, by state or jurisdiction (table 304.21)
- Total fall enrollment in private for-profit degree-granting postsecondary institutions, by state or jurisdiction (table 304.22)
- Employees in degree-granting postsecondary institutions, by employment status, sex, control and level of institution, and primary occupation (*web-only table 314.35*)
- Employees in degree-granting postsecondary institutions, by race/ethnicity, sex, employment status, control and level of institution, and primary occupation (*web-only table 314.45*)
- Ratios of full-time-equivalent (FTE) students to FTE staff and FTE faculty in public degree-granting postsecondary institutions, by level of institution and state or jurisdiction (*web-only table 314.55*)
- Ratios of full-time-equivalent (FTE) students to FTE staff and FTE faculty in private degree-granting postsecondary institutions, by level of institution and state or jurisdiction (*web-only table 314.65*)
- Percentage distribution of first-time, full-time bachelor's degree-seeking students at 4-year postsecondary institutions 6 years after entry, by completion and enrollment status at first institution attended, sex, race/ethnicity, control of institution, and percentage of applications accepted (table 326.15)
- Percentage distribution of first-time, full-time degree/certificate-seeking students at 2-year postsecondary institutions 3 years after entry, by completion and enrollment status at first institution attended, sex, race/ethnicity, and control of institution (table 326.25)
- Number of degree/certificate-seeking undergraduate students entering a postsecondary institution and percentage of students 4, 6, and 8 years after entry, by completion and enrollment status at the same institution, institution level and control, attendance level and status, Pell Grant recipient status, and acceptance rate (*web-only table 326.27*)
- Average amount of aid awarded to part-time or part-year postbaccalaureate students receiving financial aid, by type of aid, level of study, and control and level of institution (*web-only table 332.42*)
- Percentage distribution of persons 25 to 64 years old, by labor force and employment status and earnings, educational attainment, and locale (*web-only table 501.45*)

Thomas D. Snyder
Supervisor
Annual Reports and Information Staff

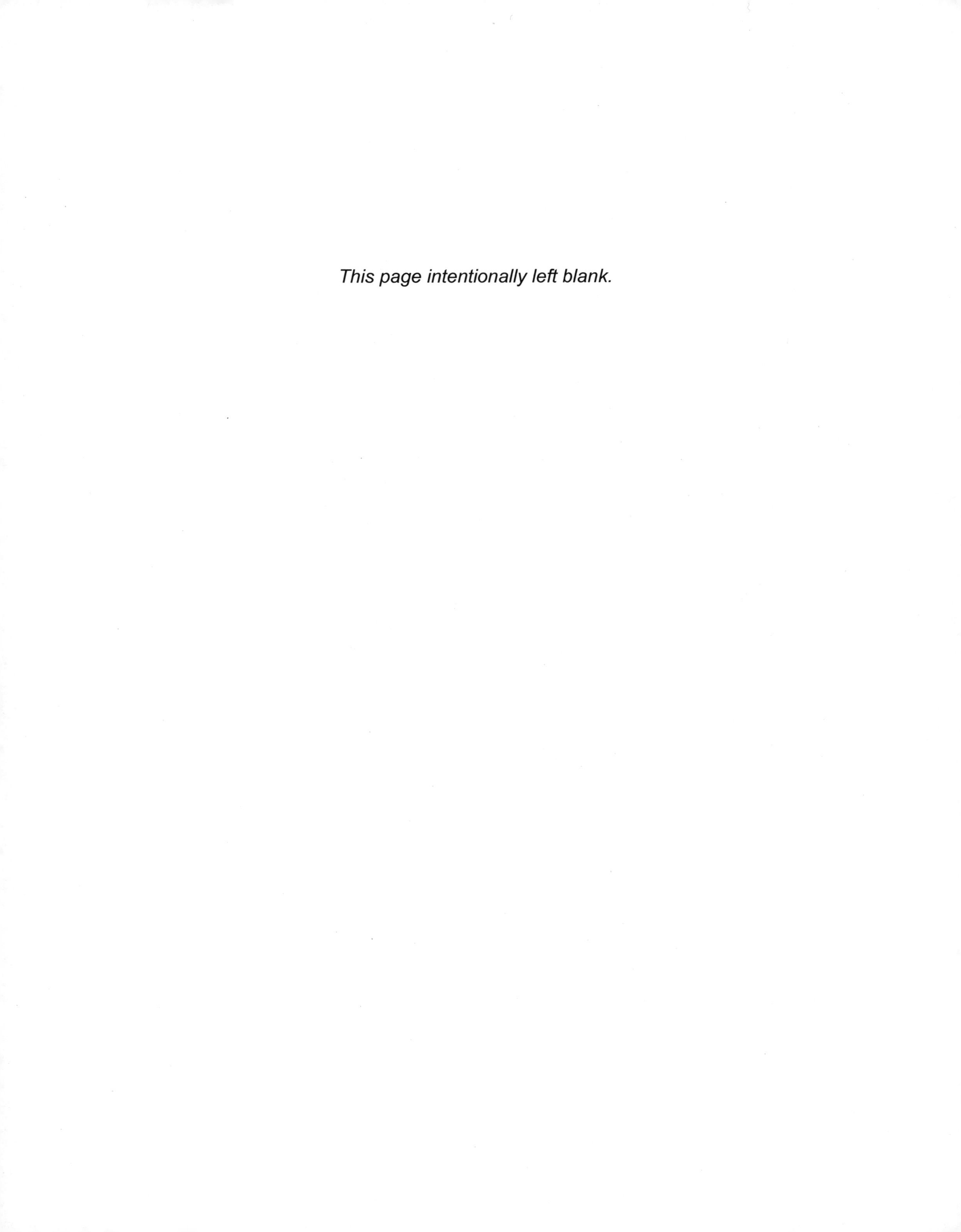

This page intentionally left blank.

CONTENTS

List of Figures

List of Text Tables

List of Reference Tables

Chapter 1. All Levels of Education **Page**

Population

Characteristics of Households With Children

Enrollment Rates

Educational Attainment

Summary of Enrollment, Teachers, and Schools

Summary of Finances

Chapter 2. Elementary and Secondary Education

Historical

Enrollment Status and Child Care Arrangements of Young Children

Enrollment in Public Schools

Participation in Public School Services

Private School Education

Homeschooling and School Choice

Large School Districts

Public Schools

School Facilities

Use of Computers and Technology

High School Completers and Dropouts

Skills of Young Children

Reading Achievement

Mathematics Achievement

Science Achievement

Achievement in Other Subjects

College Admission Tests

Student Activities, Homework, and Attendance

School Crime Victims

School Crime Incidents

School Environment

Fights and Weapons

Alcohol, Illicit Drugs, and Cigarettes

Discipline, Safety and Security, and Juvenile Justice

Chapter 3. Postsecondary Education

Overview and Historical

Enrollment Rates

Total Fall Enrollment—General

Total Fall Enrollment—State-Level

First-Time Students and Admissions

Enrollment of Racial/Ethnic Groups

Full-Time-Equivalent Fall Enrollment

Twelve-Month Enrollment

Student Residence and Migration

Study Abroad and Foreign Students

Programs and Courses

Large Institutions and Institutions Serving Specific Groups

Historically Black Colleges and Universities

Staff

Faculty and Instructional Staff

Faculty Salaries and Benefits

Institutions

Trends in Degrees by Field

Student Charges

Financial Aid for Undergraduates

Expenditures

Chapter 4. Federal Funds for Education and Related Activities

On-Budget and Off-Budget Support

Federal Obligations for Research and Development

Chapter 5. Outcomes of Education

Labor Force Status by Educational Attainment

Achievement, Instruction, and School Environment

Chapter 7. Libraries and Use of Technology

Libraries

Computer and Internet Use

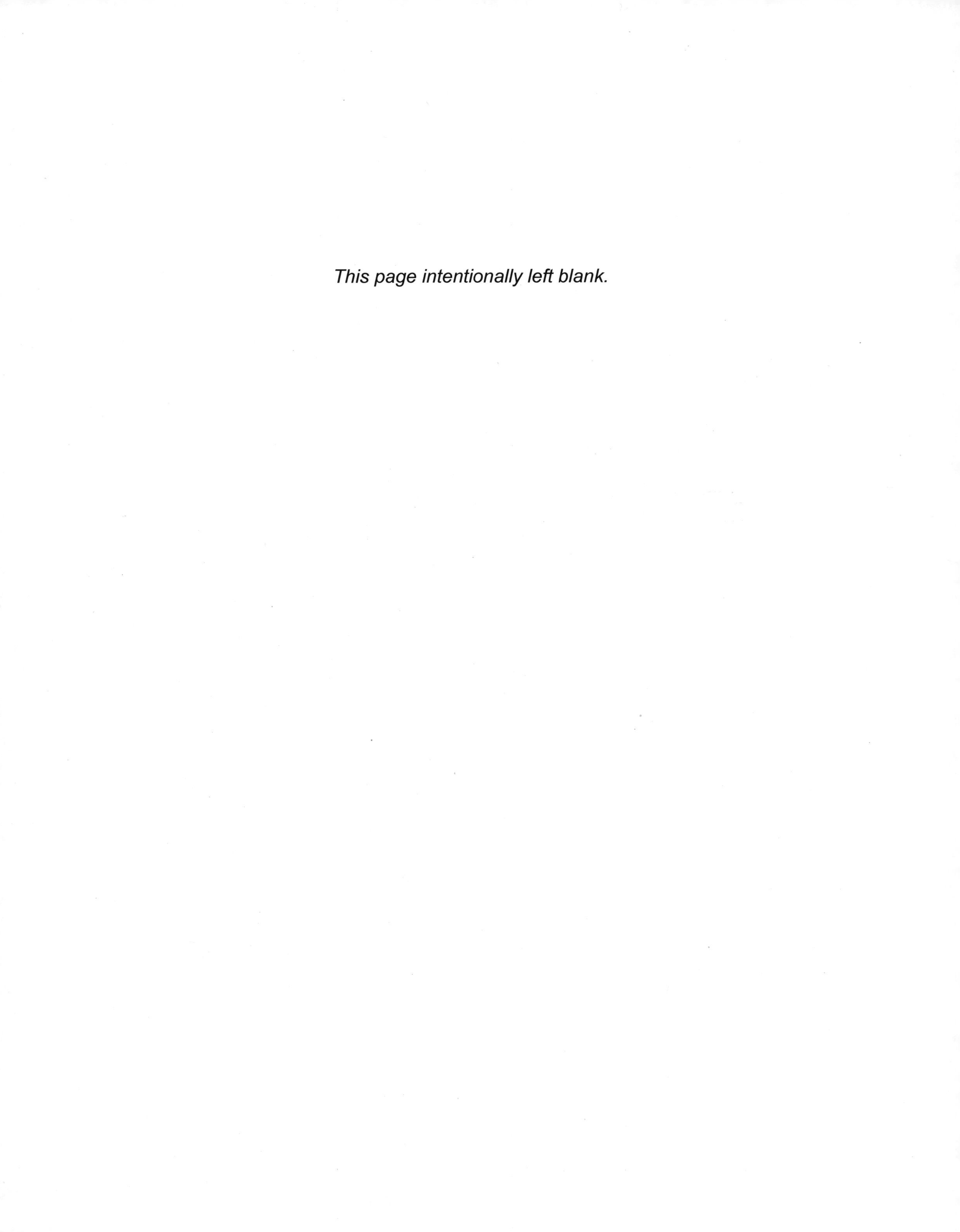

This page intentionally left blank.

READER'S GUIDE

Data Sources

The data in this edition of the *Digest of Education Statistics* were obtained from many different sources—including students and teachers, state education agencies, local elementary and secondary schools, and colleges and universities—using surveys and compilations of administrative records. Users should be cautious when comparing data from different sources. Differences in aspects such as procedures, timing, question phrasing, and interviewer training can affect the comparability of results across data sources.

Most of the tables present data from surveys conducted by the National Center for Education Statistics (NCES) or conducted by other agencies and organizations with support from NCES. Some tables also include other data published by federal and state agencies, private research organizations, or professional organizations. Totals reported in the *Digest* are for the 50 states and the District of Columbia unless otherwise noted. Brief descriptions of the surveys and other data sources used in this volume can be found in Appendix A: Guide to Sources. For each NCES and non-NCES data source, the Guide to Sources also provides information on where to obtain further details about that source.

Data are obtained primarily from two types of surveys: universe surveys and sample surveys. In universe surveys, information is collected from every member of the population. For example, in a survey regarding certain expenditures of public elementary and secondary schools, data would be obtained from each school district in the United States. When data from an entire population are available, estimates of the total population or a subpopulation are made by simply summing the units in the population or subpopulation. As a result, there is no sampling error, and observed differences are reported as true.

Since universe surveys are often expensive and time consuming, many surveys collect data from a sample of the population of interest (sample surveys). For example, the National Assessment of Educational Progress (NAEP) assesses a representative sample of students rather than the entire population of students. When a sample survey is used, statistical uncertainty is introduced, because the data come from only a portion of the entire population. This statistical uncertainty must be considered when reporting estimates and making comparisons. For information about how NCES accounts for statistical uncertainty when reporting sample survey results, see "Data Analysis and Interpretation," later in this Reader's Guide.

Common Measures and Indexes

Various types of statistics derived from universe and sample surveys are reported. Many tables report the size of a population or a subpopulation, and often the size of a subpopulation is expressed as a percentage of the total population.

In addition, the average (or *mean*) value of some characteristic of the population or subpopulation may be reported. The average is obtained by summing the values for all members of the population and dividing the sum by the size of the population. An example is the average annual salary of full-time instructional faculty at degree-granting postsecondary institutions. Another measure that is sometimes used is the *median*. The median is the midpoint value of a characteristic at or above which 50 percent of the population is estimated to fall, and at or below which 50 percent of the population is estimated to fall. An example is the median annual earnings of young adults who are full-time year-round workers. Some tables also present an *average per capita*, or per person, which represents an average computed for every person in a specified group or population. It is derived by dividing the total for an item (such as income or expenditures) by the number of persons in the specified population. An example is the per capita expenditure on education in each state.

Many tables report financial data in dollar amounts. Unless otherwise noted, all financial data are in *current dollars*, meaning not adjusted for changes in the purchasing power of the dollar over time due to inflation. For example, 1996–97 teacher salaries in current dollars are the amounts that the teachers earned in 1996–97, without any adjustments to account for inflation. *Constant dollar* adjustments attempt to remove the effects of price changes (inflation) from statistical series reported in dollars. For example, if teacher salaries over a 20-year period are adjusted to constant 2017–18 dollars, the salaries for all years are adjusted to the dollar values that presumably would exist if prices in each year were the same as in 2017–18 (in other words, as if the dollar had constant purchasing power over the entire period). Any changes in the constant dollar amounts would reflect only changes in real values. Constant dollar amounts are computed using *price indexes*. Price indexes for inflation adjustments can be found in *web-only table 106.70*. Each table that presents constant dollars includes a note indicating which index was used for the inflation adjustments; in most cases, the Consumer Price Index was used.

When presenting data for a time series, some tables include both *actual* and *projected* data. Actual data are data that have already been collected. Projected data can be used when data for a recent or future year are not yet available. Projections are estimates that are based on recent trends in relevant statistics and patterns associated with correlated variables. Unless otherwise noted, all data in this volume are actual.

Standard Errors

Using estimates calculated from data based on a sample of the population requires consideration of several factors before the estimates can be interpreted. When using data from a sample, some margin of error will always be present in estimations of characteristics of the total population or subpopulation because the data are available from only a portion of the total population. Consequently, data from samples can provide only an approximation of the true or actual value. The margin of error of an estimate, or the range of potential true or actual values, depends on several factors such as the amount of variation in the responses, the size and representativeness of the sample, and the size of the subgroup for which the estimate is computed. The magnitude of this margin of error is measured by what statisticians call the *standard error* of an estimate.

When data from sample surveys are reported, the standard error is calculated for each estimate. In the tables, the standard error for each estimate generally appears in parentheses next to the estimate to which it applies. In order to caution the reader when interpreting findings, estimates from sample surveys are flagged with a "!" when the standard error is between 30 and 50 percent of the estimate, and suppressed with a "‡" when the standard error is 50 percent of the estimate or greater. The term *coefficient of variation* (CV) refers to the ratio of the standard error to the estimate; for example, if an estimate has a CV of 30 percent, this means that the standard error is equal to 30 percent of the value of the estimate.

Nonsampling Errors

In addition to standard errors, which apply only to sample surveys, all surveys are subject to nonsampling errors. Nonsampling errors may arise when individual respondents or interviewers interpret questions differently; when respondents must estimate values, or when coders, keyers, and other processors handle answers differently; when people who should be included in the universe are not; or when people fail to respond, either totally or partially. Total nonresponse means that people do not respond to the survey at all, while partial nonresponse (or item nonresponse) means that people fail to respond to specific survey items. To compensate for nonresponse, adjustments are often made. For universe surveys, an adjustment made for either type of nonresponse, total or partial, is often referred to as an *imputation*, which is often a substitution of the "average" questionnaire response for the nonresponse. For universe surveys, imputations are usually made separately within various groups of sample members that have similar survey characteristics. For sample surveys, total nonresponse is handled through nonresponse adjustments to the sample weights. For sample surveys, imputation for item nonresponse is usually made by substituting for a missing item the response to that item of a respondent having characteristics that are similar to those of the nonrespondent. For additional general information about imputations, see the *NCES Statistical Standards* (NCES 2014-097). Appendix A: Guide to Sources includes some information about specific surveys' response rates, nonresponse adjustments, and other efforts to reduce nonsampling error. Although the magnitude of nonsampling error is frequently unknown, idiosyncrasies that have been identified are noted in the appropriate tables.

Data Analysis and Interpretation

When estimates are from a sample, caution is warranted when drawing conclusions about one estimate in comparison to another or about whether a time series of estimates is increasing, decreasing, or staying the same. Although one estimate may appear to be larger than another, a statistical test may find that the apparent difference between them is not reliably measurable due to the uncertainty around the estimates. In this case, the estimates will be described as having "no measurable difference," meaning that the difference between them is not statistically significant.

Whether differences in means or percentages are statistically significant can be determined using the standard errors of the estimates. In reports produced by NCES, when differences are statistically significant, the probability that the difference occurred by chance is less than 5 percent, according to NCES standards.

Data presented in the text do not investigate more complex hypotheses, account for interrelationships among variables, or support causal inferences. We encourage readers who are interested in more complex questions and in-depth analysis to explore other NCES resources, including publications, online data tools, and public- and restricted-use datasets at https://nces.ed.gov.

In text that reports estimates based on samples, differences between estimates (including increases and decreases) are stated only when they are statistically significant. To determine whether differences reported are statistically significant, two-tailed *t* tests at the .05 level are typically used. The *t* test formula for determining statistical significance is adjusted when the samples being compared are dependent. The *t* test formula is not adjusted for multiple comparisons, with the exception of statistical tests conducted using the NAEP Data Explorer (https://nces.ed.gov/nationsreportcard/naepdata/). When the variables to be tested are postulated to form a trend, the relationship may be tested using linear regression, logistic regression, or ANOVA trend analysis instead of a series of *t* tests. These alternate methods of analysis test for specific relationships (e.g., linear, quadratic, or cubic) among variables. For more information on data analysis, please see the NCES Statistical Standards, Standard 5-1, available at https://nces.ed.gov/statprog/2012/pdf/Chapter5.pdf.

A number of considerations influence the ultimate selection of the data years to include in the tables and to feature in the text. To make analyses as timely as possible, the latest year of available data is shown. The choice of comparison years is often also based on the need to show the earliest available survey year, as in the case of NAEP and the international assessment surveys. The text typically compares the most current year's data with those from the initial year and then with those from a more recent year. In the case of surveys with long time frames, such as surveys measuring enrollment, changes over the course of a decade may be noted in the text. Where applicable, the text may also note years in which the data begin to diverge from previous trends. In figures and tables, intervening years are selected in increments in order to show the general trend.

Rounding and Other Considerations

All calculations are based on unrounded estimates. Therefore, the reader may find that a calculation, such as a difference or a percentage change, cited in the text or a figure may not be identical to the calculation obtained by using the rounded values shown in the accompanying tables. Although values reported in the tables are generally rounded to one decimal place (e.g., 76.5 percent), values reported in the text are generally rounded to whole numbers (with any value of 0.50 or above rounded to the next highest whole number). Due to rounding, cumulative percentages may sometimes equal 99 or 101 percent rather than 100 percent.

Race and Ethnicity

The Office of Management and Budget (OMB) is responsible for the standards that govern the categories used to collect and present federal data on race and ethnicity. The OMB revised the guidelines on racial/ethnic categories used by the federal government in October 1997, with a January 2003 deadline for implementation. The revised standards require a minimum of these five categories for data on race: American Indian or Alaska Native, Asian, Black or African American, Native Hawaiian or Other Pacific Islander, and White. The standards also require the collection of data on the ethnicity categories Hispanic or Latino and Not Hispanic or Latino. It is important to note that Hispanic origin is an ethnicity rather than a race, and therefore persons of Hispanic origin may be of any race. Origin can be viewed as the heritage, nationality group, lineage, or country of birth of the person or the person's parents or ancestors before their arrival in the United States. The race categories White, Black, Asian, Native Hawaiian or Other Pacific Islander, and American Indian or Alaska Native exclude persons of Hispanic origin unless otherwise noted.

For a description of each racial/ethnic category, please see the "Racial/ethnic group" entry in Appendix B: Definitions. Some of the category labels are shortened for more concise presentation in text, tables, and figures. American Indian or Alaska Native is denoted as American Indian/Alaska Native (except when separate estimates are available for American Indians alone or Alaska Natives alone); Black or African American is shortened to Black; and Hispanic or Latino is shortened to Hispanic. When discussed separately from Asian estimates, Native Hawaiian or Other Pacific Islander is shortened to Pacific Islander.

Many of the data sources used for this volume are federal surveys that collect data using the OMB standards for racial/ethnic classification described above; however, some sources have not fully adopted the standards, and some tables include historical data collected prior to the adoption of the OMB standards. Asians and Pacific Islanders are combined into a single category for years in which the data were not collected separately for the two groups. The combined category can sometimes mask significant differences between the two subgroups. For example, prior to 2011, NAEP collected data that did not allow for separate reporting of estimates for Asians and Pacific Islanders. The population counts presented in table 101.20, based on the U.S. Census Bureau's Current Population Reports, indicate that 96 percent of all Asian/Pacific Islander 5- to 17-year-olds were Asian in 2010. Thus, the combined category for Asians/Pacific Islanders is more representative of Asians than of Pacific Islanders.

Some surveys give respondents the option of selecting more than one race category, an "other" race category, or a "Two or more races" or "more than one race" category. Where possible, tables present data on the "Two or more races" category; however, in some cases this category may not be separately shown because the information was not collected or due to other data issues. Some tables include the "other" category. Any comparisons made between persons of one racial/ethnic group and persons of "all other racial/ethnic groups" include only the racial/ethnic groups shown in the reference table. In some surveys, respondents are not given the option to select more than one race category and also are not given an option such as "other" or "more than one race." In these surveys, respondents of Two or more races must select a single race category. Any comparisons between data from surveys that give the option to select more than one race and surveys that do not offer such an option should take into account the fact that there is a potential for bias if members of one racial group are more likely than members of the others to identify themselves as "Two or more races."[1] For postsecondary data, foreign students are counted separately and are therefore not included in any racial/ethnic category.

[1] For discussion of such bias in responses to the 2000 Census, see Parker, J., et al. (2004). Bridging Between Two Standards for Collecting Information on Race and Ethnicity: An Application to Census 2000 and Vital Rates. *Public Health Reports, 119*(2): 192–205. Available at https://www.ncbi.nlm.nih.gov/pmc/articles/PMC1497618/.

In addition to the major racial/ethnic categories, several tables include Hispanic ancestry subgroups (such as Mexican, Puerto Rican, Cuban, Dominican, Salvadoran, Other Central American, and South American) and Asian ancestry subgroups (such as Asian Indian, Chinese, Filipino, Japanese, Korean, and Vietnamese). In addition, selected tables include "Two or more races" subgroups (such as White and Black, White and Asian, and White and American Indian/Alaska Native).

Limitations of the Data

Due to large standard errors, some differences that seem substantial are not statistically significant and, therefore, are not cited in the text. This situation often applies to estimates involving American Indians/Alaska Natives and Pacific Islanders. The relatively small sizes of these populations pose many measurement difficulties when conducting statistical analysis. Even in larger surveys, the numbers of American Indians/Alaska Natives and Pacific Islanders included in a sample are often small. Researchers studying data on these two populations often face small sample sizes that increase the size of standard errors and reduce the reliability of results. Readers should keep these limitations in mind when comparing estimates presented in the tables.

As mentioned, caution should be exercised when comparing data from different sources. Differences in sampling, data collection procedures, coverage of target population, timing, phrasing of questions, scope of nonresponse, interviewer training, and data processing and coding mean that results from different sources may not be strictly comparable. For example, the racial/ethnic categories presented to a respondent, and the way in which the question is asked, can influence the response, especially for individuals who consider themselves of more than one race or ethnicity. In addition, data on American Indians/Alaska Natives are often subject to inaccuracies that can result from respondents self-identifying their race/ethnicity. Research on the collection of race/ethnicity data suggests that the categorization of American Indian and Alaska Native is the least stable self-identification (for example, the same individual may identify as American Indian when responding to one survey but may not do so on a subsequent survey).[2]

[2] See U.S. Department of Labor, Bureau of Labor Statistics (1995). *A Test of Methods for Collecting Racial and Ethnic Information* (USDL 95-428). Washington DC: Author. Available at https://www.bls.gov/news.release/history/ethnic_102795.txt.

INTRODUCTION

The Introduction provides a brief overview of current trends in American education, highlighting key data that are presented in more detail later in this volume. Topics outlined include the participation of students, teachers, and faculty in U.S. educational institutions; the performance of U.S. elementary/secondary students overall and in comparison to students in other countries; the numbers of high school graduates and postsecondary degrees; and the amounts of expenditures on education at the elementary/secondary and postsecondary levels. Data on enrollments, teachers, and faculty are for fall of the given year.

In fall 2018, about 76.3 million people were enrolled in American schools and colleges (table 105.10). About 4.7 million people were employed as elementary and secondary school teachers or as college faculty, in full-time equivalents (FTE). Other professional, administrative, and support staff at educational institutions totaled 5.6 million FTE employees. All data for 2018 in this Introduction are projected, except for data on educational attainment. Some data for other years are projected or estimated as noted. In discussions of historical trends, different time periods and specific years are cited, depending on the timing of important changes as well as the availability of relevant data.

Elementary/Secondary Education

Enrollment

A pattern of annual increases in total public elementary and secondary school enrollment began in 1985, but enrollment remained at 49.3 million between 2006 and 2008, before beginning to increase again (table 105.30). Overall, public school enrollment rose 29 percent, from 39.4 million to 50.7 million, between 1985 and 2018. Private school enrollment fluctuated during this period, with the fall 2017 enrollment of 5.8 million being 4 percent higher than the fall 1985 enrollment of 5.6 million. About 10 percent of elementary and secondary school students were enrolled in private schools in 2018, reflecting a decrease from 12 percent in 1985.

In public schools between 1985 and 2018, there was a 31 percent increase in elementary enrollment (prekindergarten through grade 8), compared with a 23 percent increase in secondary enrollment (grades 9 through 12) (table 105.30). Part of the higher growth in public elementary school enrollment resulted from the expansion of prekindergarten enrollment (table 203.10). Between 1985 and 2018, enrollment in prekindergarten increased 837 percent, while enrollment in other elementary grades (including kindergarten through grade 8 and ungraded elementary programs) increased 27 percent. The number of children enrolled in prekindergarten increased from 0.2 million in 1985 to 1.4 million in 2018, and the number enrolled in other elementary grades increased from 26.9 million to 34.0 million. Public secondary school enrollment declined 8 percent from 1985 to 1990 but then increased 33 percent from 1990 to 2007. Over the most recent 10-year period (between 2008 and 2018), public school enrollment rose 3 percent. Elementary school enrollment increased 3 percent between 2008 and 2018, while secondary school enrollment increased 2 percent.

Since the enrollment rates of 5- and 6-year-olds, 7- to 13-year-olds, and 14- to 17-year-olds changed by fewer than 4 percentage points from 1985 to 2017, overall increases in public school enrollment primarily reflect increases in the number of children in these age groups (tables 101.10 and 103.20). For example, the enrollment rate of 7- to 13-year-olds decreased from 99 to 98 percent between 1985 and 2017, but the number of 7- to 13-year-olds increased 26 percent. Similarly, increases in public secondary school enrollment are more reflective of the 13 percent increase in the 14- to 17-year-old population between 1985 and 2017 than the enrollment rates for these years, which were not measurably different (about 95 to 96 percent for both years). The enrollment rate of 3- and 4-year-olds increased from 39 percent in 1985 to 54 percent in 2017, which contributed to the overall enrollment increase. Also, the number of children in this age group increased from 7.1 million in 1985 to 8.0 million in 2017.

The National Center for Education Statistics (NCES) projects record levels of total public elementary and secondary school enrollment from 2018 (50.7 million) through 2028 (51.4 million) (table 105.30). Public elementary school enrollment is projected to increase 2 percent between 2018 and 2028, while public secondary school enrollment is expected to be about 1 percent higher in 2028 than in 2018. Overall, total public school enrollment is expected to increase 1 percent between 2018 and 2028.

Teachers

About 3.7 million full-time-equivalent (FTE) elementary and secondary school teachers were engaged in classroom instruction in fall 2018 (table 105.40), which is about the same as the number of FTE teachers in fall 2008.

The 2018 number of FTE teachers includes 3.2 million public school teachers and 0.5 million private school teachers.

Public school enrollment was 3 percent higher in 2018 than in 2008, while the number of public school teachers was 1 percent lower (table 208.20). The number of public school pupils per teacher increased from 15.3 in 2008 to 16.0 in 2018.

The average salary for public school teachers in 2017–18 was $60,483 (table 211.50). In constant (i.e., inflation-adjusted) dollars, the average teacher salary was 1 percent lower in 2017–18 than in 1990–91.

Student Performance

National Comparisons

Most of the student performance data in the *Digest* are drawn from the National Assessment of Educational Progress (NAEP). The NAEP assessments have been conducted using three basic designs: the national main NAEP, state NAEP, and long-term trend NAEP. The national main NAEP and state NAEP provide current information about student performance in subjects including reading, mathematics, science, and writing, while long-term trend NAEP provides information on performance since the early 1970s in reading and mathematics only. Results from long-term trend NAEP are included in the discussion in chapter 2 of the *Digest*, while the information in this Introduction includes only selected results from the national main and state NAEP. Readers should keep in mind that comparisons of NAEP scores in the text (like all comparisons of estimates in the *Digest*) are based on statistical testing of unrounded values.

The main NAEP reports current information for the nation and specific geographic regions of the country. The assessment program includes students drawn from both public and private schools and reports results for student achievement at grades 4, 8, and 12. The main NAEP assessments follow the frameworks developed by the National Assessment Governing Board and use the latest advances in assessment methodology. The state NAEP is identical in content to the national main NAEP, but the state NAEP reports information only for public school students. Chapter 2 presents more information on the NAEP designs and methodology, and additional details appear in Appendix A: Guide to Sources.

NAEP Reading

The main NAEP reading assessment data are reported on a scale of 0 to 500. In 2017, the average reading score for 4th-grade students (222) was not measurably different from the 2015 score but was higher than the 1992 score (217) (table 221.10). At grade 4, the 2017 scores for White (232), Black (206), Hispanic (209), and Asian/Pacific Islander (239) students were not measurably different from the scores in 2015, but the score for each group was higher than in 1992 (224, 192, 197, and 216, respectively). In 2017, the average score for American Indian/Alaska Native 4th-graders (202) was not measurably different from the scores in 2015 and 1994 (1994 was the first year data were available for 4th-grade American Indian/Alaska Native students). For 8th-grade students, the score in 2017 (267) was higher than in 2015 (265) or 1992 (260). At grade 8, the 2017 scores for White (275), Black (249), Hispanic (255), and Asian/Pacific Islander (282) students were not measurably different from the scores in 2015. Consistent with the findings at grade 4, the scores for White, Black, Hispanic, and Asian/Pacific Islander 8th-grade students were higher in 2017 than in 1992. In 2017, the score for 8th-grade American Indian/Alaska Native students (253) was not measurably different from the scores in 2015 and in 1994 (1994 was the first year data were available for 8th-grade American Indian/Alaska Native students). For 12th-grade students, the most recent scores available are from 2015. The score in 2015 (287) was not measurably different from the score in 2013, but it was lower than the score in 1992 (292). At grade 12, the 2015 scores for White (295), Hispanic (276), and Asian/Pacific Islander (297) students were not measurably different from the scores in 2013 and in 1992. For Black students, the 2015 score (266) was lower than the 1992 score (273), but it was not measurably different from the 2013 score.

From 1992 through 2017, the average reading scores for White 4th- and 8th-grade students were higher than those of their Black and Hispanic peers (table 221.10). Although the White-Black and White-Hispanic achievement gaps did not change measurably from 2015 to 2017 at either grade 4 or 8, some of the racial/ethnic achievement gaps have narrowed since 1992. At grade 4, the White-Black gap narrowed from 32 points in 1992 to 26 points in 2017; at grade 8, the White-Hispanic gap narrowed from 26 points in 1992 to 19 points in 2017.

NAEP Mathematics

The main NAEP mathematics assessment data for 4th- and 8th-graders are reported on a scale of 0 to 500 (table 222.10). The average 4th-grade mathematics score in 2017 (240) was not measurably different from the score in 2015, but it was higher than the score in 1990 (213). At grade 4, the scores in 2017 for White (248), Black (223), Hispanic (229), and Asian/Pacific Islander (258) students were not measurably different from the 2015 scores, but the score for each group was higher than in 1990 (220, 188, 200, and 225, respectively). The 2017 score for 4th-grade American Indian/Alaska Native students (227) was not measurably different from the scores in 2015 and in 1996 (1996 was the first year data were available for 4th-grade American Indian/Alaska Native students). The 8th-grade score in

2017 (283) was not measurably different from the score in 2015, but it was higher than the score in 1990 (263). At grade 8, the scores for White (293), Black (260), Hispanic (269), and Asian/Pacific Islander (310) students in 2017 were not measurably different from the scores in 2015, but the score for each group was higher than in 1990 (270, 237, 246, and 275, respectively). In 2017, the score for 8th-grade American Indian/Alaska Native students (267) was not measurably different from the scores in 2015 and in 2000 (2000 was the first year data were available for 8th-grade American Indian/Alaska Native students). Due to changes in the 12th-grade mathematics assessment framework, a new trend line started in 2005, with scores reported on a scale of 0 to 300. The 12th-grade score in 2015 (152) was lower than the score in 2013 (153) but not measurably different from the score in 2005, the first year the revised assessment was administered.

From 1990 through 2017, the average mathematics scores for White students in grades 4 and 8 were higher than those of their Black and Hispanic peers (table 222.10). Although the 4th-grade White-Black and White-Hispanic achievement gaps did not change measurably from 2015 to 2017, the White-Black achievement gap narrowed from 32 points in 1990 to 25 points in 2017. The 4th-grade White-Hispanic gap in 2017 (19 points) was not measurably different from the White-Hispanic gap in 1990. The 8th-grade White-Black gap (32 points) and White-Hispanic gap (24 points) in 2017 were not measurably different from the gaps in 2015 or in 1990.

NAEP Science

NAEP has assessed the science abilities of students in grades 4, 8, and 12 in both public and private schools since 1996. As of 2009, however, NAEP science assessments are based on a new framework, so results from these assessments cannot be compared to results from earlier science assessments. Scores are based on a scale ranging from 0 to 300 (table 223.10). In 2015, the average 4th-grade science score (154) was higher than the score in 2009 (150). The 8th-grade score in 2015 (154) was higher than the scores in 2009 (150) and in 2011 (152). The 12th-grade score in 2015 (150) was not measurably different from the score in 2009. In addition, the 5-point gender gap between male and female 12th-graders in 2015 was not measurably different from the gap in 2009. While the scores for White 4th- and 8th-grade students remained higher than those of their Black and Hispanic peers in 2015, racial/ethnic achievement gaps in 2015 were smaller than in 2009. At grade 4, the White-Black achievement gap was 36 points in 2009 and 33 points in 2015, and the White-Hispanic achievement gap was 32 points in 2009 and 27 points in 2015. While the scores for White 12th-grade students remained higher than those of their Black and Hispanic peers in 2015, these racial/ethnic achievement gaps were not measurably different between 2009 and 2015.

International Comparisons

Trends in International Mathematics and Science Study (TIMSS)

The 2015 Trends in International Mathematics and Science Study (TIMSS) assessed students' mathematics and science performance at grades 4 and 8. Mathematics performance was assessed in 43 countries at grade 4 and in 34 countries at grade 8. Science performance was assessed in 42 countries at grade 4 and in 34 countries at grade 8. In addition, TIMSS Advanced data were collected by 9 countries from students in their final year of secondary school (grade 12 in the United States). At grades 4 and 8, several subnational entities also participated in TIMSS as separate education systems (e.g., Hong Kong and Chinese Taipei, the U.S. state of Florida, England and Northern Ireland within the United Kingdom). However, the following paragraphs include results only from countries, not from subnational entities. At all three grades, TIMSS scores are reported on a scale of 0 to 1,000, with a fixed scale centerpoint of 500.

In 2015, the average mathematics scores of U.S. 4th-graders (539) and 8th-graders (518) were higher than the TIMSS centerpoint of 500 (tables 602.20 and 602.30). At grade 4, the average U.S. mathematics score was higher than the average score in 30 of the 42 other countries participating at grade 4, lower than the average score in 6 countries, and not measurably different from the average score in the remaining 6 countries (table 602.20). The 6 countries that outperformed the United States in 4th-grade mathematics were Ireland, Japan, the Republic of Korea, Norway, the Russian Federation, and Singapore. At grade 8, the average U.S. mathematics score was higher than the average score in 21 of the 33 other participating countries, lower than the average score in 5 countries, and not measurably different from the average score in the remaining 7 countries (table 602.30). The 5 countries that outperformed the United States in eighth-grade mathematics were Canada, Japan, the Republic of Korea, the Russian Federation, and Singapore.

The average science scores of both U.S. 4th-graders (546) and U.S. 8th-graders (530) were higher than the TIMSS scale centerpoint of 500 in 2015 (tables 602.20 and 602.30). The average U.S. fourth-grade science score was higher than the average score in 30 of the 41 other countries participating in the science assessment at grade 4, lower than the average score in 5 countries, and not measurably different from the average score in the remaining 6 countries (table 602.20). The 5 countries that outperformed the United States in 4th-grade science were Finland, Japan, the Republic of Korea, the Russian Federation, and Singapore. At grade 8, the average U.S. science score was higher than the average score in 23 of the 33 other participating countries in 2015, lower than the average score in 5 countries, and not measurably different from the average score in the remaining 5 countries (table 602.30). The 5 countries that outperformed the United States in 8th-grade science were Japan, the Republic of Korea, the Russian Federation, Singapore, and Slovenia.

The TIMSS Advanced assessment measures the advanced mathematics and physics achievement of students in their final year of secondary school who are taking or have taken advanced courses (table 602.35). On TIMSS Advanced, the U.S. average advanced mathematics score (485) and physics score (437) in 2015 were lower than the TIMSS Advanced scale centerpoint of 500.

Program for International Student Assessment (PISA)

The Program for International Student Assessment (PISA), coordinated by the Organization for Economic Cooperation and Development (OECD), has measured the performance of 15-year-old students in reading, mathematics, and science literacy every 3 years since 2000. PISA assesses 15-year-old students' application of reading, mathematics, and science literacy to problems within a real-life context. In 2015, PISA assessed students in the 35 OECD countries as well as in a number of other education systems. Some subnational entities participated as separate education systems, including public school systems in the U.S. states of Massachusetts and North Carolina. Results for the participating U.S. states are included in the discussion in chapter 6, while this Introduction includes only results for the United States in comparison with other OECD countries. PISA scores are reported on a scale of 0 to 1,000. On the 2015 PISA assessment, U.S. 15-year-olds' average score in reading literacy was 497, which was not measurably different from the OECD average score of 493 (table 602.50). The average reading literacy score in the United States was lower than the average score in 11 of the 34 other OECD countries, higher than the average score in 13 OECD countries, and not measurably different from the average score in 10 OECD countries. In all countries, females outperformed males in reading literacy (table 602.40). The U.S. gender gap in reading (20 points) was not measurably different from the OECD average gap but was smaller than the gap in 12 other OECD countries.

In mathematics literacy, U.S. 15-year-olds' average score of 470 on the 2015 PISA assessment was lower than the OECD average score of 490 (table 602.60). The average mathematics literacy score in the United States was lower than the average score in 27 of the 34 other OECD countries, higher than the average score in 4 OECD countries, and not measurably different from the average score in 3 OECD countries. In 18 OECD countries, including the United States, males outperformed females in mathematics literacy (table 602.40). The U.S. gender gap in favor of males in mathematics (9 points) was not measurably different from the OECD average gap.

In science literacy, U.S. 15-year-olds' average score of 496 was not measurably different from the OECD average score of 493 (table 602.70). The average science literacy score in the United States was lower than the average score in 12 of the 34 other OECD countries, higher than the average score in 10 OECD countries, and not measurably different from the average score in 12 OECD countries. In 15 OECD countries, including the United States, males outperformed females in science literacy. In 4 OECD countries, females outperformed males in science literacy. The U.S. gender gap in favor of males in science (7 points) was not measurably different from the OECD average gap.

Progress in International Reading Literacy Study (PIRLS)

The Progress in International Reading Literacy Study (PIRLS) measures the reading knowledge and skills of 4th-graders over time. PIRLS scores are reported on a scale from 0 to 1,000, with the scale centerpoint set at 500. On the 2016 PIRLS, U.S. 4th-graders had an average reading literacy score of 549 (table 602.10). The U.S. average score in 2016 was 7 points lower than in 2011 but 10 points higher than in 2006. In all 4 assessment years, the U.S. average score was higher than the PIRLS scale centerpoint. In 2016, PIRLS assessed 4th-grade reading literacy in 43 countries. The average reading literacy score of 4th-graders in the United States was higher than the average score in 24 of the 42 other participating countries, lower than the average score in 7 countries, and not measurably different from the average score in the remaining 11 countries.

High School Graduates and Dropouts

About 3,650,000 high school students are expected to graduate during the 2019–20 school year (table 219.10), including 3,304,000 public school graduates and 347,000 private school graduates. High school graduates include only recipients of diplomas, not recipients of equivalency credentials. The 2019–20 projection of high school graduates is slightly lower than the prior record-high projection of 3,684,000 graduates in 2018–19, but it exceeds the baby boom era's high point in 1975–76, when 3,142,000 students earned diplomas. In 2016–17, about 85 percent of public high school students graduated with a regular diploma within 4 years of first starting 9th grade (table 219.46). This rate is known as the 4-year adjusted cohort graduation rate (ACGR).

The status dropout rate has decreased over the past several decades (table 219.70). The status dropout rate is the percentage of the civilian noninstitutionalized 16- to 24-year-old population who are not enrolled in school and who have not completed a high school program, regardless of when they left school. (People who left school but went on to receive a GED credential are not treated as dropouts.) Between 1990 and 2017, the status dropout rate declined from 12.1 to 5.8 percent. During this period, the status dropout rate for Black 16- to 24-year-olds declined from 13.2 percent to 5.7 percent, and the rate for Hispanic 16- to 24-year-olds declined from 32.4 to 9.5 percent. In 2017, the status dropout rate for White 16- to 24-year-olds (4.6 percent) was lower than the rate for Hispanic 16- to

24-year-olds, but it was not measurably different from the rate for Black 16- to 24-year-olds.

Postsecondary Education

Enrollment in Degree-Granting Institutions

College enrollment was 19.8 million in fall 2017, reflecting a 6 percent decrease from the record enrollment of 21.0 million in fall 2010 (table 105.30). College enrollment is expected to remain below the 2010 record through fall 2028, the last year for which NCES enrollment projections have been developed. Between fall 2017 and fall 2028, enrollment is expected to increase 3 percent. Despite decreases in the size of the traditional college-age population (18 to 24 years old) during the late 1980s and early 1990s, total enrollment increased during this period (tables 101.10 and 105.30). The traditional college-age population was 3 percent higher in 2017 than in 2007, and total college enrollment was 8 percent higher in 2017 than in 2007. The number of full-time students was 7 percent higher in 2017 than in 2007, while the number of part-time students was 10 percent higher (table 303.10). The number of male students enrolled was 10 percent higher in 2017 than in 2007, while the number of female students enrolled was 7 percent higher.

Faculty

In fall 2017, degree-granting institutions—defined as postsecondary institutions that grant an associate's or higher degree and are eligible for Title IV federal financial aid programs—employed 1.5 million faculty members, including 0.8 million full-time and 0.7 million part-time faculty (table 314.30). In addition, degree-granting institutions employed 0.4 million graduate assistants.

Degrees

During the 2018–19 academic year, postsecondary degrees conferred were projected to number 985,000 associate's degrees, 1,968,000 bachelor's degrees, 816,000 master's degrees, and 184,000 doctor's degrees (table 318.10). The doctor's degree total includes most degrees that were classified as first-professional prior to 2010–11, such as M.D.'s, D.D.S.'s, and law degrees. Between 2006–07 and 2016–17 (the last year of actual data), the number of degrees conferred increased at all levels. Between 2006–07 and 2016–17, the number of associate's degrees increased 38 percent, the number of bachelor's degrees increased 28 percent, the number of master's degrees increased 32 percent, and the number of doctor's degrees increased 25 percent.

Between 2006–07 and 2016–17, the number of bachelor's degrees awarded to male students increased 29 percent, while the number of bachelor's degrees awarded to female students increased 28 percent (table 318.10). Female students earned 57 percent of all bachelor's degrees in 2016–17, which was the same as the percentage in 2006–07. Between 2006–07 and 2016–17, the number of bachelor's degrees awarded to White students increased 9 percent, which was smaller than the increases for Black students (34 percent), Hispanic students (119 percent), and Asian/Pacific Islander students (37 percent) (table 322.20). The number of bachelor's degrees awarded to American Indian/Alaska Native students decreased 16 percent during this period. In 2016–17, White students earned 64 percent of all bachelor's degrees (compared with 74 percent in 2006–07), Black students earned 11 percent (compared with 10 percent in 2006–07), Hispanic students earned 14 percent (compared with 8 percent in 2006–07), and Asian/Pacific Islander students earned 8 percent (compared with 7 percent in 2006–07). American Indian/AlaskaNative students earned less than 1 percent of all bachelor's degrees in both years. In 2016–17, students of Two or more races earned 4 percent of all bachelor's degrees.

Undergraduate Prices

For the 2017–18 academic year, average annual prices for undergraduate tuition, fees, room, and board were estimated to be $17,797 at public institutions, $46,014 at private nonprofit institutions, and $26,261 at private for-profit institutions (table 330.10). Between 2007–08 and 2017–18, prices for undergraduate tuition, fees, room, and board at public institutions rose 31 percent, and prices at private nonprofit institutions rose 23 percent, after adjustment for inflation. Prices for total tuition, fees, room, and board at private for-profit institutions decreased 9 percent between 2007–08 and 2017–18.

Educational Attainment

The U.S. Census Bureau collects annual statistics on the educational attainment of the population. Between 2008 and 2018, the percentage of the adult population age 25 and over who had completed at least high school rose from 87 percent to 90 percent, and the percentage of adults with a bachelor's or higher degree increased from 29 percent to 35 percent (table 104.10). (High school completers include those who graduated from high school with a diploma as well as those who completed high school through equivalency programs.) Among adults age 25 and over who were employed, 41 percent had a bachelor's or higher degree in 2018, and about half (52 percent) had an associate's or higher degree (table 502.10). The percentage of 25- to 29-year-olds who had completed at least high school increased from 88 percent in 2008 to 93 percent in 2018 (table 104.20). The percentage of 25- to 29-year-olds who had completed a bachelor's or higher degree increased from 31 percent in 2008 to 37 percent in 2018. During this same period, the percentage of 25- to 29-year-olds who had completed a master's or higher degree increased from 7 to 9 percent.

Adult Literacy and Numeracy Skills

The Program for the International Assessment of Adult Competencies (PIAAC) assesses the cognitive skills of adults in three areas—literacy, numeracy, and problem solving in technology-rich environments—that are considered key to facilitating the social and economic participation of adults in advanced economies. The discussion below focuses on the areas of literacy and numeracy. PIAAC 2012 results are available for adults in 24 education systems, including 22 OECD education systems. The education systems that participated in the 2012 assessment were primarily countries, but also included 3 subnational education systems: Northern Ireland and England within the United Kingdom, and the Flemish community in Belgium. PIAAC literacy and numeracy scores are reported on a scale of 0 to 500.

In 2012, average scores on the PIAAC literacy scale for adults ages 25 to 65 ranged from 249 in Italy and 250 in Spain to 296 in Japan (table 604.10). U.S. 25- to 65-year-olds had an average PIAAC literacy score of 269, which was not measurably different from the OECD average score of 271. Across education systems, adults' average literacy scores generally increased with higher levels of educational attainment. In the United States, for example, 25- to 65-year-olds whose highest level of attainment was high school completion had an average literacy score of 259, compared with an average score of 302 for those who had a bachelor's or higher degree. The average literacy score for U.S. high school completers in the 25- to 65-year-old age group was lower than the OECD average score of 268 for high school completers in this age group, while the literacy score for U.S. 25- to 65-year-olds with a bachelor's or higher degree was not measurably different from the OECD average score of 302 for those with a bachelor's or higher degree.

On the PIAAC numeracy scale, 2012 average scores for adults ages 25 to 65 ranged from 245 in Spain and 246 in Italy to 289 in Japan. U.S. 25- to 65-year-olds had an average PIAAC numeracy score of 254, which was lower than the OECD average score of 268. Across education systems, adults' average numeracy scores generally increased with higher levels of educational attainment. In the United States, for example, 25- to 65-year-olds whose highest level of attainment was high school completion had an average numeracy score of 241, compared with an average score of 293 for those who had a bachelor's or higher degree. The average numeracy score for U.S. 25- to 65-year-olds who had completed only high school was lower than the OECD average score of 265 for those with the same level of educational attainment. Likewise, the average numeracy score for U.S. 25- to 65-year-olds with a bachelor's or higher degree was lower than the OECD average score of 303 for those with a bachelor's or higher degree.

Education Expenditures

U.S. expenditures for public and private education, from prekindergarten through graduate school (excluding postsecondary schools not awarding associate's or higher degrees), were an estimated $1.4 trillion for 2017–18 (table 106.10). Expenditures of elementary and secondary schools totaled an estimated $789 billion, while those of degree-granting postsecondary institutions totaled an estimated $608 billion. Total expenditures for education were an estimated 7.2 percent of the gross domestic product (GDP) in 2017–18. Education spending as a percentage of GDP peaked at 7.6 percent in 2009–10 but declined between 2009–10 and 2014–15 (7.1 percent).

CHAPTER 1
All Levels of Education

This chapter provides a broad overview of education in the United States. It brings together material from preprimary, elementary, secondary, and postsecondary education, as well as from the general population, to present a composite picture of the American education system. Tables feature data on the total number of people enrolled in school, the number of teachers, the number of schools, and the total expenditures for education at all levels. This chapter also includes statistics on education-related topics such as educational attainment, family characteristics, and population. Economic indicators and price indexes have been added to facilitate analyses.

Many of the statistics in this chapter are derived from the statistical activities of the National Center for Education Statistics (NCES). In addition, substantial contributions have been drawn from the work of other groups, both governmental and nongovernmental, as shown in the source notes of the tables. Information on survey methodologies is contained in Appendix A: Guide to Sources and in the publications cited in the table source notes.

The U.S. System of Education

The U.S. system of education can be described as having three levels of formal education: elementary, secondary, and postsecondary (figure 1). Students may spend 1 to 3 years in preprimary programs (prekindergarten [PK] and kindergarten [K]), which may be offered either in separate schools or in elementary schools that also offer higher grades. (In *Digest of Education Statistics* tables, prekindergarten and kindergarten are generally defined as a part of elementary education.) Following kindergarten, students ordinarily spend 6 to 8 years in elementary school. The elementary school program is followed by a 4- to 6-year program in secondary school. Students typically complete the entire program through grade 12 by age 18. Education at the elementary and secondary levels is provided in a range of institutional settings—including elementary schools (preprimary schools, middle schools, and schools offering broader ranges of elementary grades); secondary schools (junior high schools, high schools, and senior high schools); and combined elementary/secondary schools—that vary in structure from locality to locality.

High school graduates who decide to continue their education may enter a specialized career/technical institution, a 2-year community or junior college, or a 4-year college or university. A 2-year college typically offers the first 2 years of a standard 4-year college curriculum and a selection of terminal career and technical education programs. Academic courses completed at a 2-year college are usually transferable for credit at a 4-year college or university. A career/technical institution offers postsecondary technical training programs of varying lengths that lead to a specific career.

An associate's degree requires at least 2 years of postsecondary coursework, and a bachelor's degree typically requires 4 years of postsecondary coursework. At least 1 year of coursework beyond a bachelor's degree is necessary for a master's degree, while a doctor's degree usually requires a minimum of 3 or 4 years beyond a bachelor's degree.

Professional schools differ widely in admission requirements and program length. Medical students, for example, generally complete a bachelor's program of premedical studies at a college or university before they can enter the 4-year program at a medical school. Law programs typically involve 3 years of coursework beyond a bachelor's degree.

Enrollment

Total enrollment in public and private elementary and secondary schools (prekindergarten through grade 12) grew rapidly during the 1950s and 1960s, reaching a peak year in 1971 (table A, table 105.30, and figure 2). This enrollment rise reflected what is known as the "baby boom," a dramatic increase in births following World War II. Between 1971 and 1984, total elementary and secondary school enrollment decreased every year, reflecting a decline in the size of the school-age population over that period. After these years of decline, enrollment in elementary and secondary schools started increasing in fall 1985, began hitting new record levels in the mid-1990s, and continued to reach new record levels every year through 2006. After a period of slightly declining or stable enrollment from 2007 to 2012, enrollment began increasing again. Enrollments in fall 2013 (55.4 million) through fall 2016 (56.4 million) were higher than the fall 2006 record level of 55.3 million. A pattern of annual enrollment increases is projected to continue at least through fall 2028 (the last year for which NCES has projected school enrollment). Total elementary and secondary enrollment is projected to increase 2 percent between fall 2018 and fall 2028, when enrollment is expected to reach 57.4 million.

Table A. Total elementary and secondary school enrollment, by overall trends: Selected years, 1949–50 through fall 2028

Trend and year	Number of students (in millions)
"Baby boom" increases	
1949–50 school year	28.5
Fall 1959	40.9
Fall 1969	51.1
Fall 1971 (peak)	51.3
13 years with annual declines	
Fall 1972 (first year of decline)	50.7
Fall 1984 (final year of decline)	44.9
Annual increases from 1985 to 2006	
Fall 1985	45.0
Fall 1996 (new record highs begin)	51.5
Fall 2006 (final year of record highs)	55.3
Slight declines or stable enrollment	
Fall 2007	55.2
Fall 2010	54.9
Fall 2012	55.1
Annual increases with new record highs	
Fall 2013	55.4
Fall 2014	55.9
Fall 2015	56.2
Fall 2016 (projected)	56.4
Fall 2017 (projected)	56.5
Fall 2018 (projected)	56.5
Fall 2028 (projected)	57.4

SOURCE: U.S. Department of Education, National Center for Education Statistics, *Biennial Survey of Education in the United States*, 1949–50; *Statistics of Public Elementary and Secondary School Systems*, 1959 through 1972; Common Core of Data (CCD), 1984 through 2015; Private School Universe Survey (PSS), 1997–98 through 2015–16; and National Elementary and Secondary Enrollment Projection Model, 1972 through 2028.

Between 1985 and 2017, the total public and private elementary and secondary school enrollment rate for 5- and 6-year-olds decreased from 96 to 94 percent, and the enrollment rate for 7- to 13-year-olds decreased from 99 to 98 percent (table 103.20). In 2017, the enrollment rate for 14- to 17-year-olds (96 percent) was not measurably different from the rate in 1985. Since these enrollment rates changed by less than 4 percentage points between 1985 and 2017, increases in elementary and secondary school enrollment primarily reflect the larger increases in the number of children in these age groups. Between 1985 and 2017, the number of 5- and 6-year-olds increased by 16 percent, the number of 7- to 13-year-olds increased by 26 percent, and the number of 14- to 17-year-olds increased by 13 percent (table 101.10). Increases in the enrollment rate of prekindergarten-age children (ages 3 and 4), from 39 percent in 1985 to 54 percent in 2017 (table 103.20), and in the number of 3- and 4-year-olds, from 7.1 million to 8.0 million (table 101.10), also contributed to overall increases in prekindergarten through grade 12 enrollment.

Public school enrollment at the elementary level (prekindergarten through grade 8) rose from 29.9 million in fall 1990 to 34.2 million in fall 2003 (table 105.30). Public elementary school enrollment was less than 1 percent lower in fall 2004 than in fall 2003 and then generally increased to a projected total of 35.5 million for fall 2018. Public elementary school enrollment is projected to increase 2 percent between 2018 and 2028. Public school enrollment at the secondary level (grades 9 through 12) rose from 11.3 million in 1990 to 15.1 million in 2007 but then declined 2 percent to 14.7 million in 2011. Public secondary school enrollment is projected to increase 3 percent between 2011 and 2018. Public secondary school enrollment in 2028 is expected to be about 1 percent higher than in 2018. Total public elementary and secondary school enrollment is projected to increase in most years between 2018 to 2028.

The percentage of students in private elementary and secondary schools declined from 11.0 percent in fall 2005 to 10.2 percent in fall 2015 (table 105.30). In fall 2018, an estimated 5.8 million students were enrolled in private schools at the elementary and secondary levels.

Total enrollment in public and private degree-granting postsecondary institutions reached 14.5 million in fall 1992 but decreased every year through fall 1995 (table 105.30). Total enrollment increased 47 percent between 1995 and 2010 (to 21.0 million) but declined 6 percent between 2010 and 2017 (to 19.8 million). Total enrollment is expected to increase 3 percent between fall 2017 and fall 2028, reaching 20.3 million. The percentage of students who attended private institutions in fall 2017 (26 percent) was the same as the percentage in 2007. In fall 2017, about 5.2 million students attended private institutions, with 4.1 million in nonprofit institutions and 1.1 million in for-profit institutions (table 303.10).

Enrollment in degree-granting institutions in fall 2017 was 8 percent higher than in fall 2007 (table 105.30). This enrollment change was affected by changes in the enrollment rate and the population of 20- to 24-year-olds. The percentage of 18- and 19-year-olds enrolled in degree-granting postsecondary institutions in 2017 (48 percent) was not measurably different from the percentage in 2007 (49 percent). The number of 18- and 19-year-olds decreased 3 percent, from 8.7 million in 2007 to 8.5 million in 2017 (tables 101.10 and 103.20). In contrast, the number of 20- to 24-year-olds rose by 5 percent during this period, from 21.1 to 22.1 million. Also, the enrollment rate of 20- to 24-year-olds was higher in 2017 (39 percent) than in 2007 (36 percent).

Educational Attainment

The percentages of people 25 years old and over completing high school and higher education have been rising. Between 2008 and 2018, the percentage of people 25 years old and over who had completed at least high school increased from 87 to 90 percent, and the percentage who had completed a bachelor's or higher degree increased from 29 to 35 percent (table 104.10 and figure 3). In 2018, about 10 percent of people 25 years old and over held a master's degree as their highest degree and 3 percent held a doctor's or first-professional degree (table 104.30).

Among 25- to 29-year-olds, the percentage who had completed at least high school increased from 88 percent in 2008 to 93 percent in 2018 (table 104.20 and figure 4). The percentage of 25- to 29-year-olds who had completed a bachelor's or higher degree increased from 31 percent in

2008 to 37 percent in 2018. In 2018, about 7 percent of 25- to 29-year-olds held a master's degree as their highest degree and 2 percent held a doctor's or first-professional degree (table 104.30 and figure 5). Overall, the percentage of 25- to 29-year-olds who held a master's or higher degree rose from 7 percent in 2008 to 9 percent in 2018.

Between 2008 and 2018, changes in the educational attainment of 25- to 29-year-olds also occurred by race/ethnicity. During this period, the percentages of Hispanic, White, and Black 25- to 29-year-olds who had completed at least high school increased, but there was no measurable change in the percentage of Asian 25- to 29-year-olds (table 104.20 and figure 6). The percentage of Hispanic 25- to 29-year-olds who had completed at least high school rose from 68 percent in 2008 to 85 percent in 2018, an increase of 17 percentage points. During the same period, the percentage of White 25- to 29-year-olds who had completed at least high school rose from 94 to 96 percent. Since the increase for White 25- to 29-year-olds was smaller than the increase for Hispanic 25- to 29-year-olds, the gap between the high school completion percentages for these two groups decreased from 25 percentage points in 2008 to 10 percentage points in 2018. Between 2008 and 2018, the percentage of Black 25- to 29-year-olds who had completed high school increased from 88 to 92 percent. The gap between the White and Black high school completion percentages in 2018 (4 percentage points) was not measurably different from the gap in 2008. In 2018, the percentage of 25- to 29-year-olds who had completed at least high school was higher for those who were Asian (97 percent) and White (96 percent) than for those who were Black (92 percent), American Indian/Alaska Native (89 percent), and Hispanic (85 percent).

The percentage of bachelor's degree holders also varied among 25- to 29-year-olds of different racial/ethnic groups, with 71 percent of Asian 25- to 29-year-olds holding a bachelor's or higher degree in 2018, which was higher than the percentages for those who were White (44 percent), of Two or more races (27 percent), Black (23 percent), Hispanic (21 percent), American Indian/Alaska Native (16 percent), and Pacific Islander (15 percent) (table 104.20 and figure 6). Between 2008 and 2018, the percentages who had completed a bachelor's or higher degree increased for Asian, White, and Hispanic 25- to 29-year-olds but showed no measurable change for those who were Black, Pacific Islander, American Indian/Alaska Native, and of Two or more races. During this 10-year period, the percentages who held a bachelor's or higher degree increased from 37 to 44 percent among White 25- to 29-year-olds, from 12 to 21 percent among Hispanic 25- to 29-year-olds, and from 60 to 71 percent among Asian 25- to 29-year-olds. The gap in bachelor's degree attainment percentages between White and Black 25- to 29-year-olds in 2018 (21 percentage points) was not measurably different from the gap in 2008. Also, the gap between White and Hispanic 25- to 29-year-olds in 2018 (23 percentage points) was not measurably different from the gap in 2008.

Teachers and Faculty

A projected 3.7 million elementary and secondary school full-time-equivalent (FTE) teachers were engaged in classroom instruction in the fall of 2018 (table 105.40), which was less than 1 percent lower than in 2008. The number of FTE public elementary and secondary school teachers in 2018 was 3.2 million, and the number of FTE private elementary and secondary school teachers was 0.5 million. FTE faculty at degree-granting postsecondary institutions totaled a projected 1.1 million in 2018, including 0.7 million at public institutions and 0.4 million at private institutions (table 105.10).

Expenditures

Expenditures of educational institutions were an estimated $1.4 trillion for the 2017–18 school year (table 106.20 and figure 2). Elementary and secondary schools spent 56 percent of this total ($789 billion), and degree-granting postsecondary institutions spent the remaining 44 percent ($608 billion). After adjustment for inflation, total expenditures of all educational institutions rose by an estimated 13 percent between 2007–08 and 2017–18. Inflation-adjusted expenditures of degree-granting postsecondary institutions rose by an estimated 27 percent. Expenditures of public elementary and secondary schools were 4 percent higher in 2017–18 than in 2007–08. In 2017–18, expenditures of educational institutions were an estimated 7.2 percent of the gross domestic product (table 106.10).

Figure 1. The structure of education in the United States

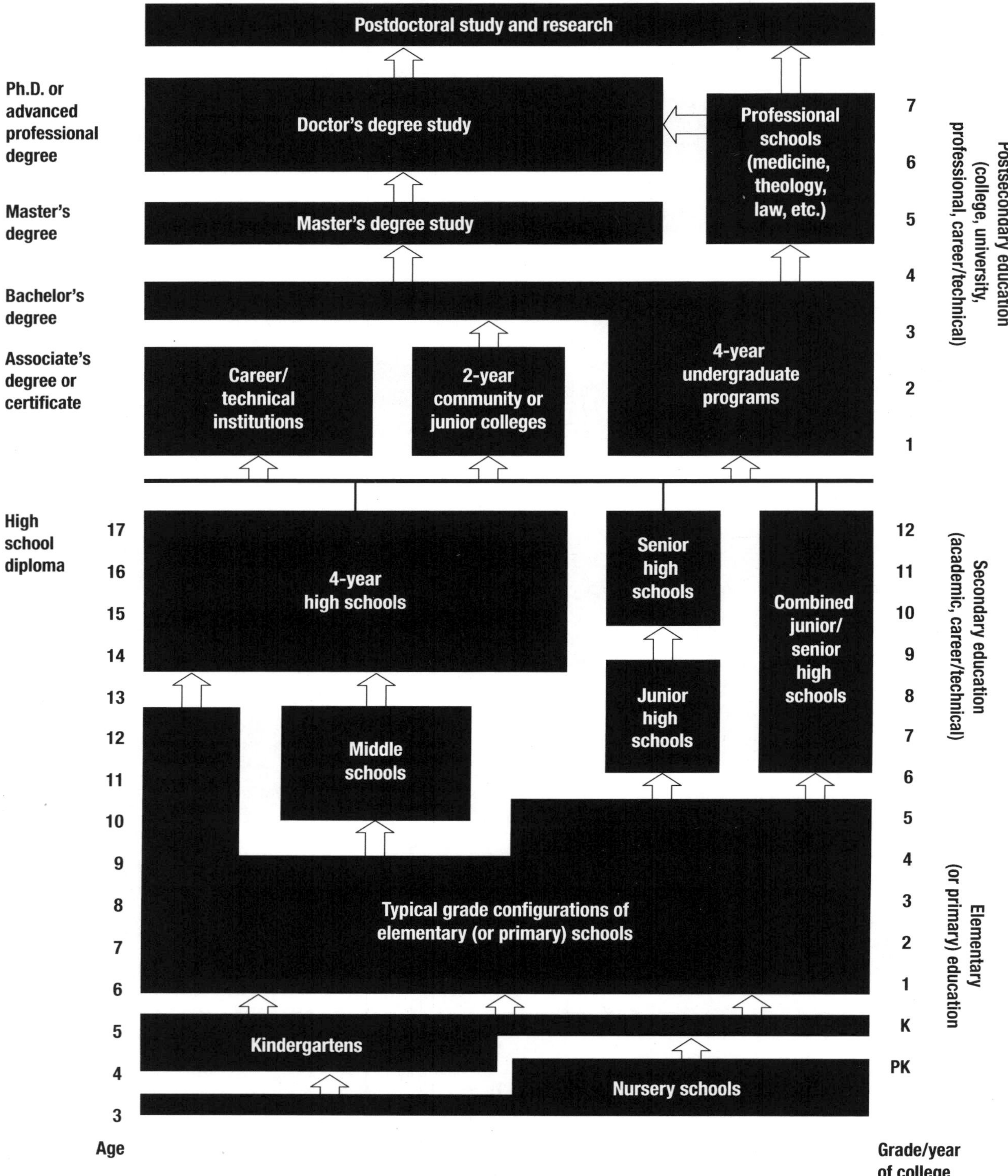

NOTE: Figure is not intended to show relative number of institutions nor relative size of enrollment for the different levels of education. Figure reflects typical patterns of progression rather than all possible variations. Adult education programs, while not separately delineated above, may provide instruction at the adult basic, adult secondary, or postsecondary education levels.
SOURCE: U.S. Department of Education, National Center for Education Statistics, Annual Reports Program.

Figure 2. Fall enrollment, total expenditures, and expenditures as a percentage of the gross domestic product (GDP), by level of education: Selected years, 1965–66 through 2017–18

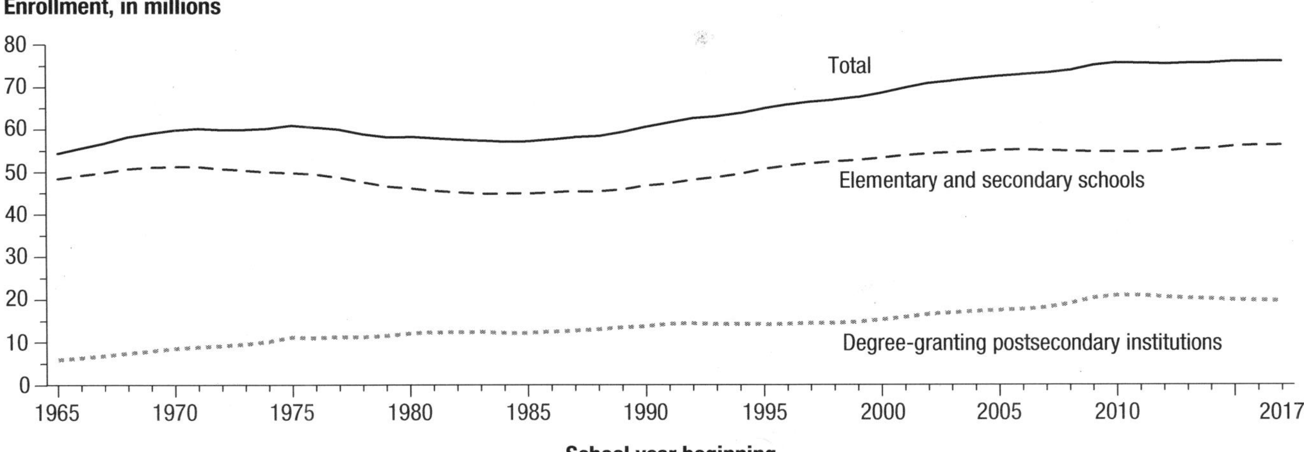

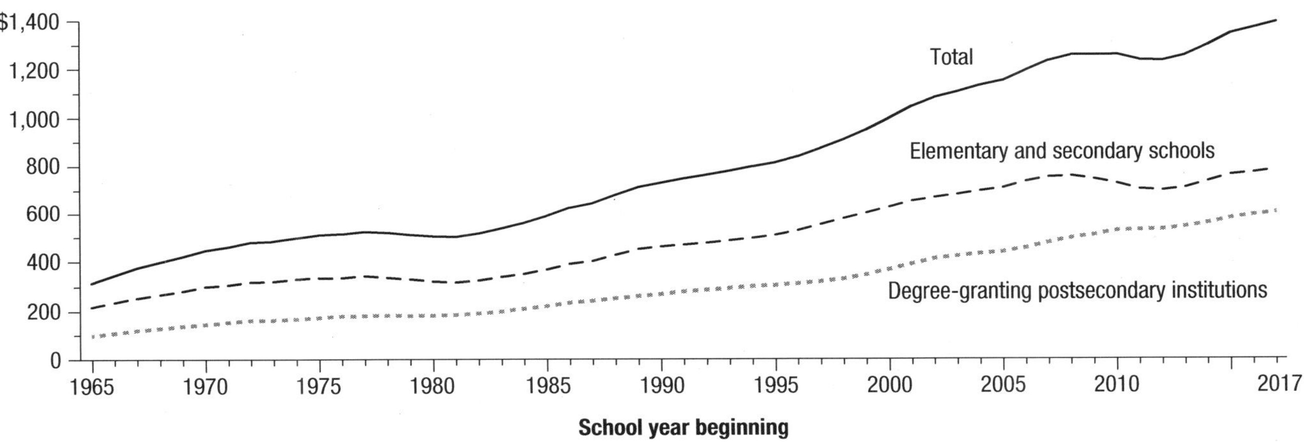

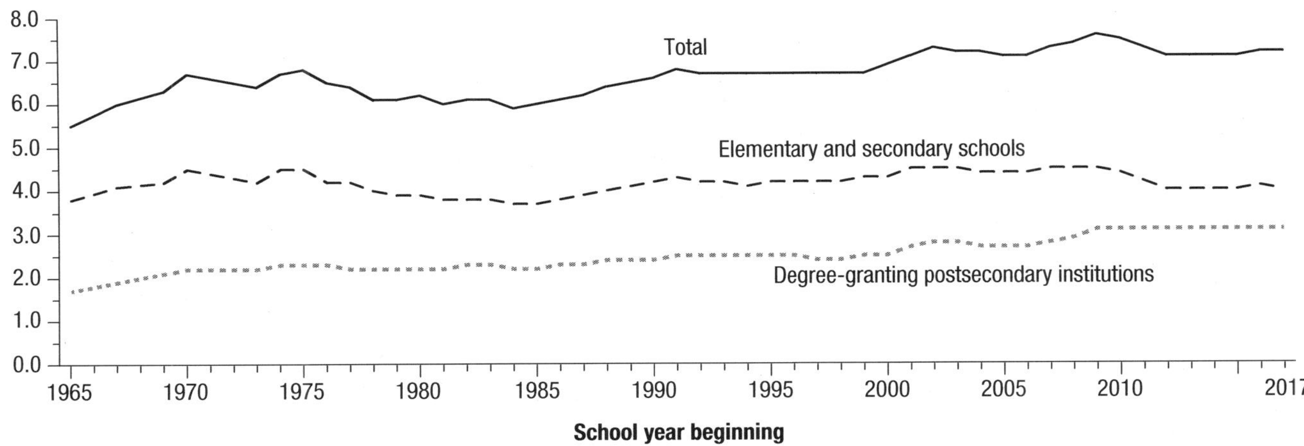

NOTE: Elementary and secondary enrollment data for school year 2017 (2017–18) are projected. Elementary and secondary expenditure data for school years 2016 and 2017 (2016–17 and 2017–18) are estimated. Postsecondary expenditure data for school year 2017 (2017–18) are estimated.
SOURCE: U.S. Department of Education, National Center for Education Statistics, *Statistics of State School Systems*, 1965–66 through 1969–70; *Statistics of Public Elementary and Secondary School Systems*, 1965 through 1980; *Revenues and Expenditures for Public Elementary and Secondary Education*, 1970–71 through 1986–87; Common Core of Data (CCD), "State Nonfiscal Survey of Public Elementary and Secondary Education," 1981–82 through 2016–17, and "National Public Education Financial Survey," 1987–88 through 2015–16; Private School Universe Survey (PSS), 1989–90 through 2015–16; National Elementary and Secondary Enrollment Projection Model, 1972 through 2028; Higher Education General Information Survey (HEGIS), "Fall Enrollment in Institutions of Higher Education" and "Financial Statistics of Institutions of Higher Education" surveys, 1965–66 through 1985–86; Integrated Postsecondary Education Data System (IPEDS), "Fall Enrollment Survey" (IPEDS-EF:86–99) and "Finance Survey" (IPEDS-F:FY87–99); and IPEDS Spring 2001 through Spring 2018, Enrollment and Finance components. U.S. Department of Commerce, Bureau of Economic Analysis, National Income and Product Accounts Tables, retrieved March 8, 2019, from https://apps.bea.gov/itable/index.cfm.

Figure 3. Percentage of persons 25 years old and over, by highest level of educational attainment: Selected years, 1940 through 2018

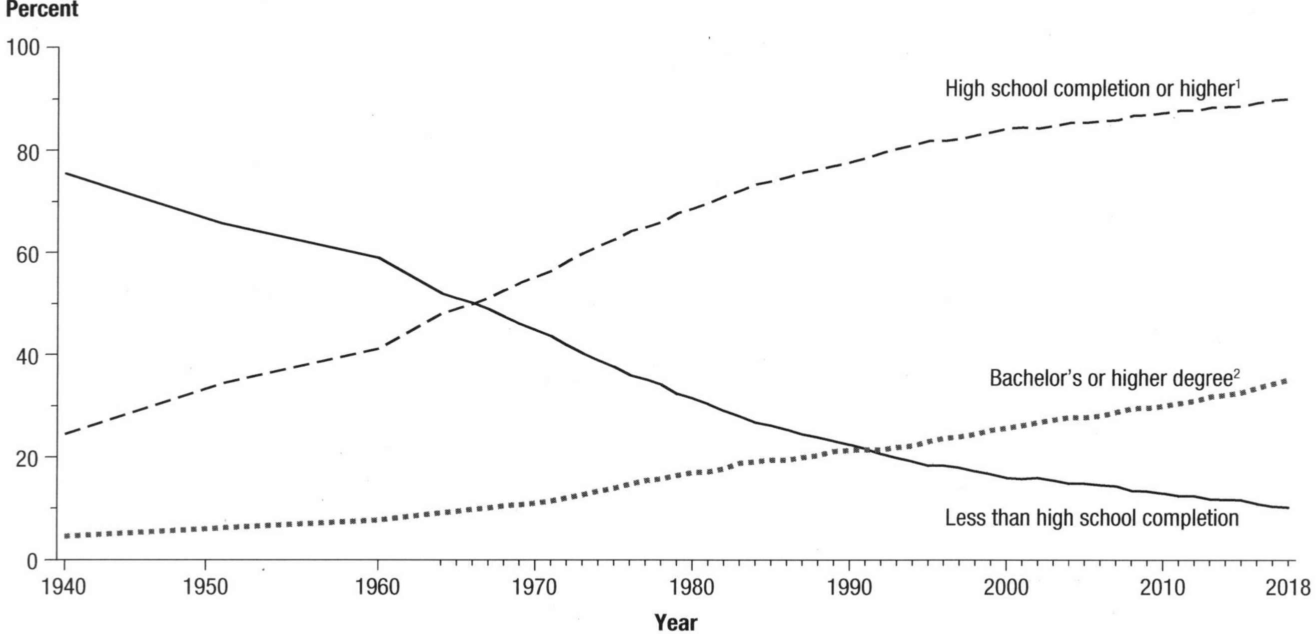

[1]Includes high school completion through equivalency programs, such as a GED program. For years prior to 1993, includes all persons with 4 or more years of high school.
[2]For years prior to 1993, includes all persons with 4 or more years of college.
SOURCE: U.S. Department of Commerce, Census Bureau, *U.S. Census of Population: 1960*, Vol. I, Part 1; J.K. Folger and C.B. Nam, *Education of the American Population* (1960 Census Monograph); Current Population Reports, Series P-20, various years; and Current Population Survey (CPS), Annual Social and Economic Supplement, 1961 through 2018.

Figure 4. Percentage of persons 25 through 29 years old, by highest level of educational attainment: Selected years, 1940 through 2018

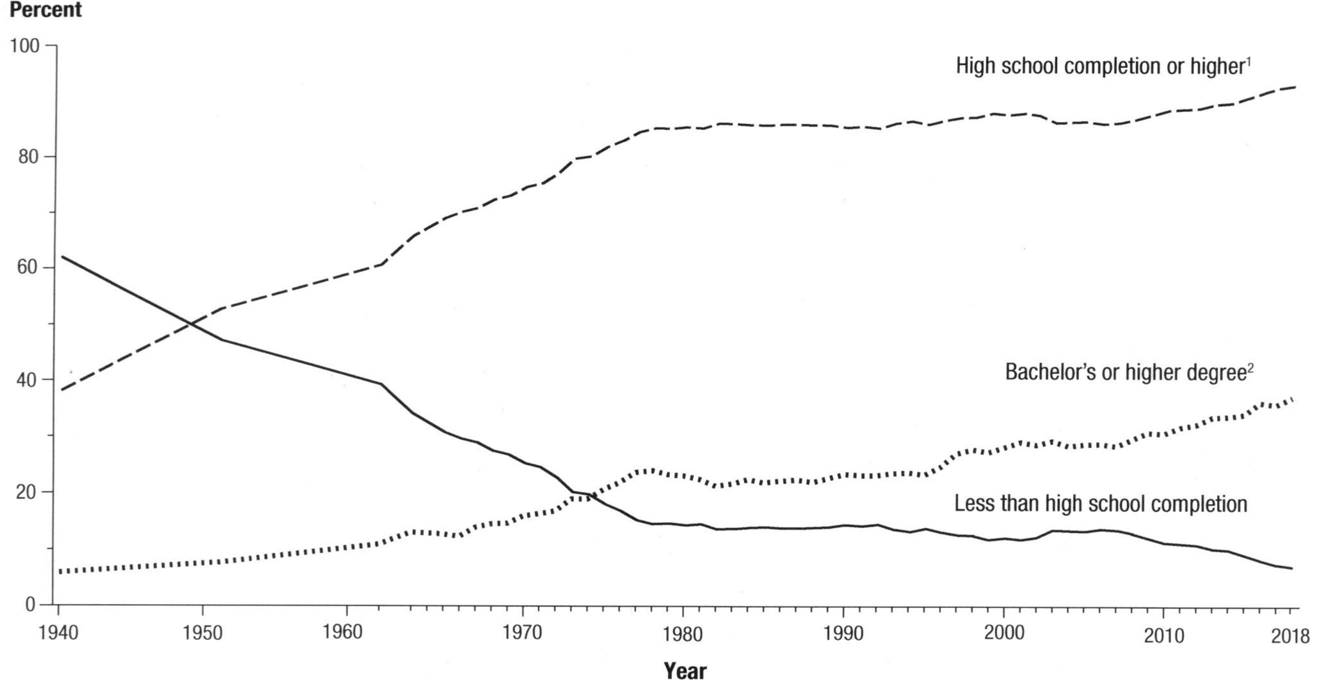

[1]Includes high school completion through equivalency programs, such as a GED program. For years prior to 1993, includes all persons with 4 or more years of high school.
[2]For years prior to 1993, includes all persons with 4 or more years of college.
SOURCE: U.S. Department of Commerce, Census Bureau, *U.S. Census of Population: 1960*, Vol. I, Part 1; J.K. Folger and C.B. Nam, *Education of the American Population* (1960 Census Monograph); Current Population Reports, Series P-20, various years; and Current Population Survey (CPS), Annual Social and Economic Supplement, 1961 through 2018.

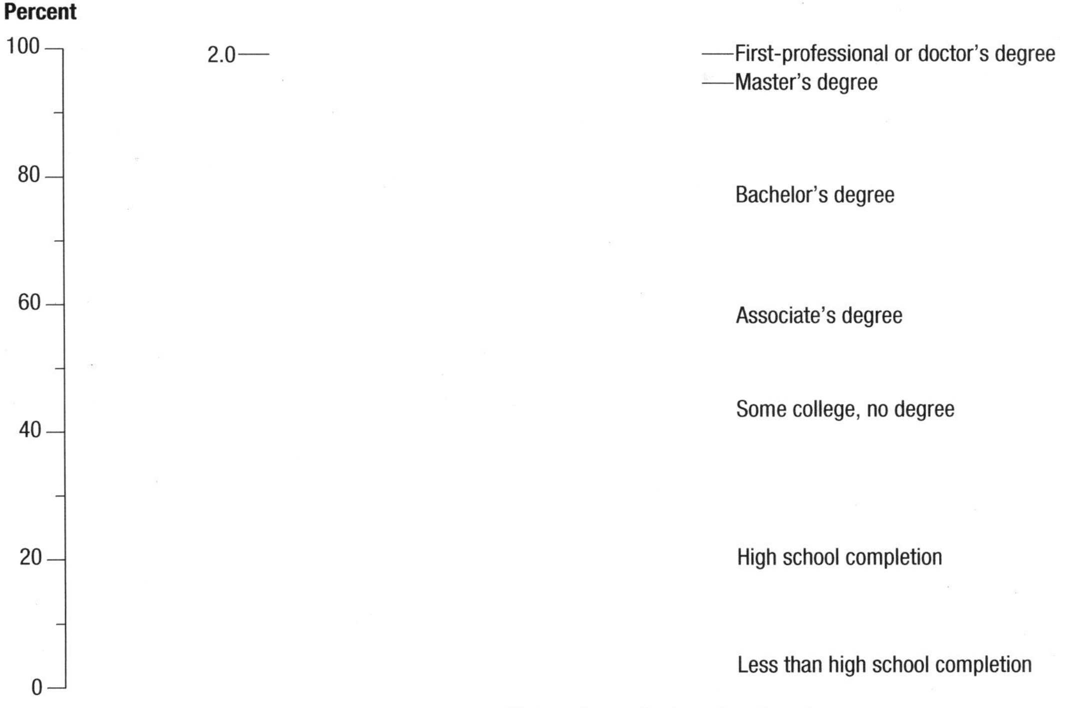
Percent
100
80
60
40
20
0
2.0
First-professional or doctor's degree
Master's degree
Bachelor's degree
Associate's degree
Some college, no degree
High school completion
Less than high school completion
Highest level of educational attainment

Table 101.10. Estimates of resident population, by age group: 1970 through 2018

[In thousands]

Year	Total, all ages	Total, 3 to 34 years old	3 and 4 years old	5 and 6 years old	7 to 13 years old	14 to 17 years old	18 and 19 years old	20 and 21 years old	22 to 24 years old	25 to 29 years old	30 to 34 years old
1	2	3	4	5	6	7	8	9	10	11	12
1970	205,052	109,592	6,961	7,703	28,969	15,924	7,510	7,210	9,992	13,736	11,587
1971	207,661	111,202	6,805	7,344	28,892	16,328	7,715	7,350	10,809	14,041	11,917
1972	209,896	112,807	6,789	7,051	28,628	16,639	7,923	7,593	10,560	15,240	12,383
1973	211,909	114,426	6,938	6,888	28,158	16,867	8,114	7,796	10,725	15,786	13,153
1974	213,854	116,075	7,117	6,864	27,600	17,035	8,257	8,003	10,972	16,521	13,704
1975	215,973	117,435	6,912	7,013	26,905	17,128	8,478	8,196	11,331	17,280	14,191
1976	218,035	118,474	6,436	7,195	26,321	17,119	8,659	8,336	11,650	18,274	14,485
1977	220,239	119,261	6,190	6,978	25,877	17,045	8,675	8,550	11,949	18,277	15,721
1978	222,585	119,833	6,208	6,500	25,594	16,946	8,677	8,730	12,216	18,683	16,280
1979	225,055	120,544	6,252	6,256	25,175	16,611	8,751	8,754	12,542	19,178	17,025
1980	227,225	121,132	6,366	6,291	24,800	16,143	8,718	8,669	12,716	19,686	17,743
1981	229,466	121,999	6,535	6,315	24,396	15,609	8,582	8,759	12,903	20,169	18,731
1982	231,664	121,823	6,658	6,407	24,121	15,057	8,480	8,768	12,914	20,704	18,714
1983	233,792	122,302	6,877	6,572	23,709	14,740	8,290	8,652	12,981	21,414	19,067
1984	235,825	122,254	7,045	6,694	23,367	14,725	7,932	8,567	12,962	21,459	19,503
1985	237,924	122,512	7,134	6,916	22,976	14,888	7,637	8,370	12,895	21,671	20,025
1986	240,133	122,688	7,187	7,086	22,992	14,824	7,483	8,024	12,720	21,893	20,479
1987	242,289	122,672	7,132	7,178	23,325	14,502	7,502	7,742	12,450	21,857	20,984
1988	244,499	122,713	7,176	7,238	23,791	14,023	7,701	7,606	12,048	21,739	21,391
1989	246,819	122,655	7,315	7,184	24,228	13,536	7,898	7,651	11,607	21,560	21,676
1990	249,623	122,787	7,359	7,244	24,785	13,329	7,702	7,886	11,264	21,277	21,939
1991	252,981	123,210	7,444	7,393	25,216	13,491	7,208	8,029	11,205	20,923	22,301
1992	256,514	123,722	7,614	7,447	25,752	13,775	6,949	7,797	11,391	20,503	22,494
1993	259,919	124,371	7,887	7,549	26,212	14,096	6,985	7,333	11,657	20,069	22,584
1994	263,126	124,976	8,089	7,725	26,492	14,637	7,047	7,071	11,585	19,740	22,590
1995	266,278	125,478	8,107	8,000	26,825	15,013	7,182	7,103	11,197	19,680	22,372
1996	269,394	125,924	8,022	8,206	27,168	15,443	7,399	7,161	10,715	19,864	21,945
1997	272,647	126,422	7,915	8,232	27,683	15,769	7,569	7,309	10,601	19,899	21,446
1998	275,854	126,939	7,841	8,152	28,302	15,829	7,892	7,520	10,647	19,804	20,953
1999	279,040	127,446	7,772	8,041	28,763	16,007	8,094	7,683	10,908	19,575	20,603
2000	282,162	128,041	7,724	7,972	29,082	16,144	8,199	7,995	11,122	19,280	20,524
2001	284,969	128,467	7,630	7,883	29,210	16,280	8,235	8,290	11,467	18,819	20,652
2002	287,625	128,955	7,617	7,750	29,251	16,506	8,237	8,342	11,902	18,691	20,658
2003	290,108	129,346	7,678	7,661	29,153	16,694	8,325	8,324	12,267	18,772	20,472
2004	292,805	129,965	7,885	7,652	28,806	17,054	8,457	8,312	12,534	19,107	20,160
2005	295,517	130,280	7,973	7,721	28,527	17,358	8,482	8,392	12,568	19,535	19,724
2006	298,380	130,754	7,937	7,942	28,327	17,549	8,567	8,507	12,529	20,110	19,285
2007	301,231	131,417	8,002	8,040	28,256	17,597	8,730	8,500	12,578	20,543	19,171
2008	304,094	132,269	8,033	8,012	28,426	17,395	9,014	8,555	12,626	20,903	19,305
2009	306,772	133,202	8,059	8,088	28,569	17,232	9,146	8,691	12,693	21,078	19,645
2010[1]	309,338	134,098	8,189	8,137	28,729	17,066	9,061	8,956	12,746	21,144	20,070
2011[1]	311,644	134,900	8,223	8,162	28,754	16,872	8,920	9,193	12,969	21,286	20,521
2012[1]	313,993	135,512	8,093	8,228	28,776	16,722	8,787	9,177	13,414	21,394	20,921
2013[1]	316,235	136,076	7,983	8,263	28,810	16,653	8,679	9,028	13,791	21,583	21,286
2014[1]	318,623	136,629	8,009	8,138	28,815	16,748	8,545	8,895	13,988	21,967	21,524
2015[1]	321,040	136,941	7,993	8,033	28,869	16,810	8,468	8,799	13,888	22,426	21,654
2016[1]	323,406	137,334	7,969	8,062	28,898	16,779	8,469	8,673	13,711	22,931	21,841
2017[1]	325,719	137,678	8,003	8,047	28,909	16,761	8,498	8,595	13,524	23,370	21,972
2018	328,033	138,036	8,059	8,023	28,892	16,700	8,602	8,596	13,358	23,619	22,186

[1]Revised from previously published figures.

NOTE: Resident population includes civilian population and armed forces personnel residing within the United States; it excludes armed forces personnel residing overseas. Detail may not sum to totals because of rounding. Population estimates as of July 1 of the indicated reference year.

SOURCE: U.S. Department of Commerce, Census Bureau, Current Population Reports, Series P-25, Nos. 1000, 1022, 1045, 1057, 1059, 1092, and 1095; 2000 through 2009 Population Estimates, retrieved August 14, 2012, from http://www.census.gov/popest/data/national/asrh/2011/index.html; and 2010 through 2018 Population Estimates, retrieved November 8, 2018, from https://www.census.gov/data/tables/2017/demo/popest/nation-detail.html. (This table was prepared November 2018.)

Table 101.20 Estimates of resident population, by race/ethnicity and age group: Selected years, 1980 through 2018

Year and age group	Number (in thousands)								Percentage distribution							
	Total	White	Black	Hispanic	Asian	Pacific Islander	American Indian/ Alaska Native	Two or more races	Total	White	Black	Hispanic	Asian	Pacific Islander	American Indian/ Alaska Native	Two or more races
1	2	3	4	5	6	7	8	9	10	11	12	13	14	15	16	17
Total																
1980	227,225	181,140	26,215	14,869	3,665	([1])	1,336	—	100.0	79.7	11.5	6.5	1.6	([1])	0.6	—
1990	249,623	188,725	29,439	22,573	7,092	([1])	1,793	—	100.0	75.6	11.8	9.0	2.8	([1])	0.7	—
1995	266,278	194,389	32,500	28,158	9,188	([1])	2,044	—	100.0	73.0	12.2	10.6	3.5	([1])	0.8	—
2000[2]	282,162	195,702	34,406	35,662	10,469	370	2,102	3,452	100.0	69.4	12.2	12.6	3.7	0.1	0.7	1.2
2005[2]	295,517	196,621	36,147	43,024	12,658	434	2,186	4,447	100.0	66.5	12.2	14.6	4.3	0.1	0.7	1.5
2008[2]	304,094	197,184	37,291	47,794	13,956	475	2,237	5,158	100.0	64.8	12.3	15.7	4.6	0.2	0.7	1.7
2010[2]	309,338	197,389	38,015	50,753	14,766	500	2,269	5,647	100.0	63.8	12.3	16.4	4.8	0.2	0.7	1.8
2013[2]	316,235	197,693	39,144	54,143	16,206	533	2,331	6,185	100.0	62.5	12.4	17.1	5.1	0.2	0.7	2.0
2014[2]	318,623	197,803	39,523	55,293	16,738	543	2,351	6,372	100.0	62.1	12.4	17.4	5.3	0.2	0.7	2.0
2015[2]	321,040	197,844	39,909	56,505	17,297	555	2,369	6,561	100.0	61.6	12.4	17.6	5.4	0.2	0.7	2.0
2016[2]	323,406	197,835	40,285	57,733	17,851	566	2,387	6,749	100.0	61.2	12.5	17.9	5.5	0.2	0.7	2.1
2017[2]	325,719	197,803	40,652	58,947	18,399	577	2,403	6,938	100.0	60.7	12.5	18.1	5.6	0.2	0.7	2.1
2018[2]	328,033	197,765	41,015	60,163	18,947	588	2,420	7,135	100.0	60.3	12.5	18.3	5.8	0.2	0.7	2.2
Under 5 years old																
1980	16,451	11,904	2,413	1,677	319	([1])	137	—	100.0	72.4	14.7	10.2	1.9	([1])	0.8	—
1990	18,856	12,757	2,825	2,497	593	([1])	184	—	100.0	67.7	15.0	13.2	3.1	([1])	1.0	—
1995	19,627	12,415	3,050	3,245	734	([1])	182	—	100.0	63.3	15.5	16.5	3.7	([1])	0.9	—
2000[2]	19,178	11,253	2,753	3,748	686	30	171	538	100.0	58.7	14.4	19.5	3.6	0.2	0.9	2.8
2005[2]	19,917	10,847	2,706	4,607	839	35	171	712	100.0	54.5	13.6	23.1	4.2	0.2	0.9	3.6
2008[2]	20,271	10,557	2,753	5,032	885	38	176	831	100.0	52.1	13.6	24.8	4.4	0.2	0.9	4.1
2010[2]	20,189	10,278	2,780	5,128	891	39	176	898	100.0	50.9	13.8	25.4	4.4	0.2	0.9	4.4
2013[2]	19,848	9,951	2,735	5,119	910	39	171	922	100.0	50.1	13.8	25.8	4.6	0.2	0.9	4.6
2014[2]	19,871	9,930	2,736	5,136	929	39	170	931	100.0	50.0	13.8	25.8	4.7	0.2	0.9	4.7
2015[2]	19,916	9,920	2,744	5,151	954	40	169	937	100.0	49.8	13.8	25.9	4.8	0.2	0.8	4.7
2016[2]	19,920	9,883	2,745	5,159	980	40	167	946	100.0	49.6	13.8	25.9	4.9	0.2	0.8	4.7
2017[2]	19,939	9,853	2,744	5,181	999	41	165	956	100.0	49.4	13.8	26.0	5.0	0.2	0.8	4.8
2018[2]	19,951	9,810	2,741	5,215	1,010	41	163	971	100.0	49.2	13.7	26.1	5.1	0.2	0.8	4.9
5 to 17 years old																
1980	47,232	35,220	6,840	4,005	790	([1])	377	—	100.0	74.6	14.5	8.5	1.7	([1])	0.8	—
1990	45,359	—	—	—	—	—	—	—	—	—	—	—	—	—	—	—
1995	49,838	—	—	—	—	—	—	—	—	—	—	—	—	—	—	—
2000[2]	53,198	33,008	7,994	8,700	1,829	85	522	1,059	100.0	62.0	15.0	16.4	3.4	0.2	1.0	2.0
2005[2]	53,606	31,379	7,987	10,207	2,047	92	499	1,396	100.0	58.5	14.9	19.0	3.8	0.2	0.9	2.6
2008[2]	53,833	30,226	7,813	11,346	2,227	98	483	1,641	100.0	56.1	14.5	21.1	4.1	0.2	0.9	3.0
2010[2]	53,932	29,496	7,644	12,057	2,350	101	475	1,809	100.0	54.7	14.2	22.4	4.4	0.2	0.9	3.4
2013[2]	53,726	28,587	7,450	12,638	2,502	103	465	1,981	100.0	53.2	13.9	23.5	4.7	0.2	0.9	3.7
2014[2]	53,700	28,289	7,432	12,826	2,549	104	463	2,037	100.0	52.7	13.8	23.9	4.7	0.2	0.9	3.8
2015[2]	53,713	28,007	7,413	13,030	2,601	105	462	2,094	100.0	52.1	13.8	24.3	4.8	0.2	0.9	3.9
2016[2]	53,739	27,745	7,398	13,240	2,647	105	459	2,144	100.0	51.6	13.8	24.6	4.9	0.2	0.9	4.0
2017[2]	53,717	27,474	7,383	13,407	2,699	106	457	2,190	100.0	51.1	13.7	25.0	5.0	0.2	0.9	4.1
2018[2]	53,616	27,185	7,352	13,533	2,750	107	454	2,234	100.0	50.7	13.7	25.2	5.1	0.2	0.8	4.2
18 to 24 years old																
1980	30,103	23,278	3,872	2,284	468	([1])	201	—	100.0	77.3	12.9	7.6	1.6	([1])	0.7	—
1990	26,853	—	—	—	—	—	—	—	—	—	—	—	—	—	—	—
1995	25,482	—	—	—	—	—	—	—	—	—	—	—	—	—	—	—
2000[2]	27,315	16,913	3,780	4,786	1,158	50	239	389	100.0	61.9	13.8	17.5	4.2	0.2	0.9	1.4
2005[2]	29,442	17,741	4,092	5,406	1,351	57	263	531	100.0	60.3	13.9	18.4	4.6	0.2	0.9	1.8
2008[2]	30,194	17,712	4,283	5,813	1,445	62	266	613	100.0	58.7	14.2	19.3	4.8	0.2	0.9	2.0
2010[2]	30,763	17,616	4,436	6,183	1,519	66	266	678	100.0	57.3	14.4	20.1	4.9	0.2	0.9	2.2
2013[2]	31,498	17,507	4,703	6,523	1,630	65	277	794	100.0	55.6	14.9	20.7	5.2	0.2	0.9	2.5
2014[2]	31,428	17,322	4,670	6,610	1,658	64	275	829	100.0	55.1	14.9	21.0	5.3	0.2	0.9	2.6
2015[2]	31,155	17,025	4,591	6,663	1,682	62	271	860	100.0	54.6	14.7	21.4	5.4	0.2	0.9	2.8
2016[2]	30,853	16,719	4,501	6,713	1,705	61	266	888	100.0	54.2	14.6	21.8	5.5	0.2	0.9	2.9
2017[2]	30,616	16,472	4,412	6,764	1,732	60	261	915	100.0	53.8	14.4	22.1	5.7	0.2	0.9	3.0
2018[2]	30,556	16,313	4,351	6,859	1,772	60	258	943	100.0	53.4	14.2	22.4	5.8	0.2	0.8	3.1
25 years old and over																
1980	133,438	110,737	13,091	6,903	2,088	([1])	620	—	100.0	83.0	9.8	5.2	1.6	([1])	0.5	—
1990	158,555	125,653	16,322	11,447	4,190	([1])	944	—	100.0	79.2	10.3	7.2	2.6	([1])	0.6	—
1995	171,332	131,839	18,250	14,519	5,628	([1])	1,096	—	100.0	76.9	10.7	8.5	3.3	([1])	0.6	—
2000[2]	182,471	134,529	19,879	18,427	6,796	205	1,170	1,465	100.0	73.7	10.9	10.1	3.7	0.1	0.6	0.8
2005[2]	192,551	136,655	21,361	22,804	8,421	250	1,253	1,808	100.0	71.0	11.1	11.8	4.4	0.1	0.7	0.9
2008[2]	199,795	138,689	22,441	25,603	9,400	277	1,312	2,074	100.0	69.4	11.2	12.8	4.7	0.1	0.7	1.0
2010[2]	204,454	140,000	23,155	27,386	10,006	294	1,352	2,262	100.0	68.5	11.3	13.4	4.9	0.1	0.7	1.1
2013[2]	211,162	141,648	24,255	29,863	11,164	326	1,418	2,488	100.0	67.1	11.5	14.1	5.3	0.2	0.7	1.2
2014[2]	213,623	142,262	24,685	30,722	11,602	337	1,442	2,575	100.0	66.6	11.6	14.4	5.4	0.2	0.7	1.2
2015[2]	216,257	142,891	25,160	31,661	12,059	348	1,467	2,670	100.0	66.1	11.6	14.6	5.6	0.2	0.7	1.2
2016[2]	218,894	143,488	25,641	32,621	12,519	359	1,494	2,772	100.0	65.6	11.7	14.9	5.7	0.2	0.7	1.3
2017[2]	221,447	144,003	26,113	33,595	12,969	370	1,520	2,878	100.0	65.0	11.8	15.2	5.9	0.2	0.7	1.3
2018[2]	223,911	144,458	26,570	34,556	13,416	380	1,544	2,987	100.0	64.5	11.9	15.4	6.0	0.2	0.7	1.3

—Not available.
[1]Included under Asian.
[2]Data on persons of Two or more races were collected beginning in 2000. Direct comparability of the data (other than Hispanic) prior to 2000 with the data for 2000 and later years is limited by the extent to which people reporting more than one race in later years had been reported in specific race groups in earlier years.
NOTE: Resident population includes civilian population and armed forces personnel residing within the United States; it excludes armed forces personnel residing overseas. Race categories exclude persons of Hispanic ethnicity. Detail may not sum to totals because of rounding. Some data have been revised from previously published figures. Population estimates as of July 1 of the indicated reference year.
SOURCE: U.S. Department of Commerce, Census Bureau, Current Population Reports, Series P-25, Nos. 1092 and 1095; 2000 through 2009 Population Estimates, retrieved August 14, 2012, from http://www.census.gov/popest/data/national/asrh/2011/index.html; and 2010 through 2018 Population Estimates, retrieved November 8, 2018, from https://www.census.gov/data/tables/2017/demo/popest/nation-detail.html. (This table was prepared November 2018.)

Table 102.10. Number and percentage distribution of family households, by family structure and presence of own children under 18: Selected years, 1970 through 2018

[Standard errors appear in parentheses]

Family structure and presence of own children	1970		1980		1990		2000		2010		2015		2016		2017		2018		Change, 2000 to 2010		Change, 2010 to 2018	
1	2		3		4		5		6		7		8		9		10		11		12	
	Number (in thousands)																		Percent change			
All families	**51,456**	**(257.3)**	**59,550**	**(271.4)**	**66,090**	**(307.8)**	**72,025**	**(311.6)**	**78,833**	**(241.0)**	**81,716**	**(267.6)**	**82,184**	**(268.0)**	**82,827**	**(268.6)**	**83,088**	**(268.8)**	**9.5**	**(0.58)**	**5.4**	**(0.47)**
Married-couple families	44,728	(243.6)	49,112	(252.7)	52,317	(283.3)	55,311	(289.5)	58,410	(218.6)	60,010	(243.1)	60,251	(243.5)	60,804	(244.2)	61,241	(244.8)	5.6	(0.68)	4.8	(0.57)
Without own children under 18	19,196	(168.7)	24,151	(187.3)	27,780	(218.1)	30,062	(230.5)	33,835	(176.1)	35,970	(199.4)	36,480	(200.6)	37,153	(202.1)	37,430	(202.7)	12.6	(1.04)	10.6	(0.83)
With own children under 18	25,532	(192.0)	24,961	(190.1)	24,537	(206.4)	25,248	(214.1)	24,575	(153.1)	24,040	(167.3)	23,772	(166.5)	23,651	(166.1)	23,812	(166.6)	-2.7!	(1.02)	-3.1	(0.91)
One own child under 18	8,163	(112.5)	9,671	(122.0)	9,583	(133.0)	9,402	(136.2)	9,567	(98.5)	9,163	(106.6)	9,131	(106.4)	9,206	(106.8)	9,205	(106.8)	‡	(†)	-3.8!	(1.49)
Two own children under 18	8,045	(111.7)	9,488	(120.9)	9,784	(134.3)	10,274	(142.1)	9,658	(98.9)	9,662	(109.3)	9,581	(108.9)	9,492	(108.4)	9,397	(107.9)	-6.0	(1.62)	‡	(†)
Three or more own children under 18	9,325	(119.9)	5,802	(95.3)	5,170	(98.5)	5,572	(105.9)	5,351	(74.3)	5,215	(81.0)	5,061	(79.8)	4,954	(79.0)	5,209	(81.0)	‡	(†)	‡	(†)
Families with male householder, no spouse present	1,228	(44.2)	1,733	(52.5)	2,884	(73.9)	4,028	(90.4)	5,580	(75.8)	6,162	(87.9)	6,310	(88.9)	6,452	(89.9)	6,424	(89.7)	38.5	(3.63)	15.1	(2.24)
Without own children under 18	887	(37.6)	1,117	(42.2)	1,731	(57.4)	2,242	(67.7)	3,356	(59.0)	3,774	(69.1)	3,838	(69.7)	4,057	(71.6)	3,939	(70.6)	49.7	(5.23)	17.4	(2.95)
With own children under 18	341	(23.3)	616	(31.3)	1,153	(46.9)	1,786	(60.5)	2,224	(48.2)	2,388	(55.1)	2,472	(56.1)	2,395	(55.2)	2,484	(56.2)	24.5	(5.01)	11.7	(3.50)
One own child under 18	179	(16.9)	374	(24.4)	723	(37.2)	1,131	(48.2)	1,375	(37.9)	1,433	(42.8)	1,487	(43.6)	1,403	(42.3)	1,339	(41.4)	21.6	(6.17)	‡	(†)
Two own children under 18	87	(11.8)	165	(16.2)	307	(24.2)	483	(31.6)	576	(24.6)	653	(28.9)	663	(29.2)	690	(29.7)	811	(32.2)	19.3!	(9.31)	40.8	(8.21)
Three or more own children under 18	75	(10.9)	77	(11.1)	123	(15.3)	171	(18.8)	273	(16.9)	302	(19.7)	322	(20.3)	302	(19.7)	335	(20.7)	59.6!	(20.15)	22.7!	(10.75)
Families with female householder, no spouse present	5,500	(92.8)	8,705	(116.0)	10,890	(141.4)	12,687	(156.9)	14,843	(121.4)	15,544	(137.0)	15,622	(137.3)	15,572	(137.1)	15,423	(136.5)	17.0	(1.73)	3.9!	(1.25)
Without own children under 18	2,642	(64.7)	3,261	(71.8)	4,290	(89.9)	5,116	(101.6)	6,424	(81.2)	6,993	(93.5)	7,097	(94.2)	7,326	(95.6)	7,267	(95.3)	25.6	(2.96)	13.1	(2.06)
With own children under 18	2,858	(67.2)	5,445	(92.3)	6,599	(111.0)	7,571	(122.8)	8,419	(92.6)	8,551	(103.1)	8,525	(102.9)	8,246	(101.3)	8,156	(100.7)	11.2	(2.18)	‡	(†)
One own child under 18	1,008	(40.1)	2,398	(61.6)	3,225	(78.1)	3,777	(87.6)	4,207	(66.0)	4,192	(72.8)	4,173	(72.6)	4,119	(72.2)	4,032	(71.4)	11.4	(3.12)	‡	(†)
Two own children under 18	810	(35.9)	1,817	(53.7)	2,173	(64.2)	2,458	(70.9)	2,714	(53.2)	2,844	(60.1)	2,794	(59.6)	2,620	(57.7)	2,534	(56.8)	10.4!	(3.85)	-6.6!	(2.78)
Three or more own children under 18	1,040	(40.7)	1,230	(44.2)	1,202	(47.9)	1,336	(52.4)	1,499	(39.6)	1,515	(44.0)	1,557	(44.6)	1,508	(43.9)	1,590	(45.1)	12.2!	(5.31)	‡	(†)
	Percentage distribution of all families																		Change in percentage points			
All families	**100.0**	**(†)**	**100.0**	**(†)**	**100.0**	**(†)**	**100.0**	**(†)**	**100.0**	**(†)**	**100.0**	**(†)**	**100.0**	**(†)**	**100.0**	**(†)**	**100.0**	**(†)**	**†**	**(†)**	**†**	**(†)**
Married-couple families	86.9	(0.19)	82.5	(0.20)	79.2	(0.22)	76.8	(0.23)	74.1	(0.16)	73.4	(0.18)	73.3	(0.17)	73.4	(0.17)	73.7	(0.17)	-2.7	(0.28)	‡	(†)
Without own children under 18	37.3	(0.27)	40.6	(0.25)	42.0	(0.27)	41.7	(0.26)	42.9	(0.18)	44.0	(0.20)	44.4	(0.20)	44.9	(0.20)	45.0	(0.20)	1.2	(0.32)	2.1	(0.27)
With own children under 18	49.6	(0.28)	41.9	(0.26)	37.1	(0.26)	35.1	(0.26)	31.2	(0.17)	29.4	(0.18)	28.9	(0.18)	28.6	(0.18)	28.7	(0.18)	-3.9	(0.31)	-2.5	(0.25)
One own child under 18	15.9	(0.20)	16.2	(0.19)	14.5	(0.19)	13.1	(0.18)	12.1	(0.12)	11.2	(0.13)	11.1	(0.12)	11.1	(0.12)	11.1	(0.12)	-0.9	(0.22)	-1.1	(0.17)
Two own children under 18	15.6	(0.20)	15.9	(0.19)	14.8	(0.19)	14.3	(0.19)	12.3	(0.12)	11.8	(0.13)	11.7	(0.13)	11.5	(0.13)	11.3	(0.12)	-2.0	(0.22)	-0.9	(0.17)
Three or more own children under 18	18.1	(0.21)	9.7	(0.15)	7.8	(0.14)	7.7	(0.14)	6.8	(0.09)	6.4	(0.10)	6.2	(0.10)	6.0	(0.09)	6.3	(0.10)	-0.9	(0.17)	-0.5	(0.13)
Families with male householder, no spouse present	2.4	(0.09)	2.9	(0.09)	4.4	(0.11)	5.6	(0.12)	7.1	(0.09)	7.5	(0.10)	7.7	(0.11)	7.8	(0.11)	7.7	(0.11)	1.5	(0.15)	0.7	(0.14)
Without own children under 18	1.7	(0.07)	1.9	(0.07)	2.6	(0.09)	3.1	(0.09)	4.3	(0.07)	4.6	(0.08)	4.7	(0.08)	4.9	(0.09)	4.7	(0.08)	1.1	(0.12)	0.5	(0.11)
With own children under 18	0.7	(0.05)	1.0	(0.05)	1.7	(0.07)	2.5	(0.08)	2.8	(0.06)	2.9	(0.07)	3.0	(0.07)	2.9	(0.07)	3.0	(0.07)	0.3!	(0.10)	‡	(†)
One own child under 18	0.3	(0.03)	0.6	(0.04)	1.1	(0.06)	1.6	(0.07)	1.7	(0.05)	1.8	(0.05)	1.8	(0.05)	1.7	(0.05)	1.6	(0.05)	0.2!	(0.08)	‡	(†)
Two own children under 18	0.2	(0.02)	0.3	(0.03)	0.5	(0.04)	0.7	(0.04)	0.7	(0.03)	0.8	(0.04)	0.8	(0.04)	0.8	(0.04)	1.0	(0.04)	‡	(†)	0.2	(0.05)
Three or more own children under 18	0.1	(0.02)	0.1	(0.02)	0.2	(0.02)	0.2	(0.03)	0.3	(0.02)	0.4	(0.02)	0.4	(0.02)	0.4	(0.02)	0.4	(0.02)	0.1!	(0.03)	‡	(†)
Families with female householder, no spouse present	10.7	(0.17)	14.6	(0.18)	16.5	(0.20)	17.6	(0.20)	18.8	(0.14)	19.0	(0.16)	19.0	(0.16)	18.8	(0.15)	18.6	(0.15)	1.2	(0.25)	‡	(†)
Without own children under 18	5.1	(0.12)	5.5	(0.12)	6.5	(0.13)	7.1	(0.14)	8.1	(0.10)	8.6	(0.11)	8.6	(0.11)	8.8	(0.11)	8.7	(0.11)	1.0	(0.17)	0.6	(0.15)
With own children under 18	5.6	(0.13)	9.1	(0.15)	10.0	(0.16)	10.5	(0.16)	10.7	(0.11)	10.5	(0.12)	10.4	(0.12)	10.0	(0.12)	9.8	(0.12)	‡	(†)	-0.9	(0.16)
One own child under 18	2.0	(0.08)	4.0	(0.10)	4.9	(0.12)	5.2	(0.12)	5.3	(0.08)	5.1	(0.09)	5.1	(0.09)	5.0	(0.09)	4.9	(0.08)	‡	(†)	-0.5	(0.12)
Two own children under 18	1.6	(0.07)	3.1	(0.09)	3.3	(0.10)	3.4	(0.10)	3.4	(0.07)	3.5	(0.07)	3.4	(0.07)	3.2	(0.07)	3.0	(0.07)	‡	(†)	-0.4	(0.09)
Three or more own children under 18	2.0	(0.08)	2.1	(0.07)	1.8	(0.07)	1.9	(0.07)	1.9	(0.05)	1.9	(0.05)	1.9	(0.05)	1.8	(0.05)	1.9	(0.05)	‡	(†)	‡	(†)

†Not applicable.
!Interpret data with caution. The coefficient of variation (CV) for this estimate is between 30 and 50 percent.
‡Reporting standards not met. The coefficient of variation (CV) for this estimate is 50 percent or greater.
NOTE: A family household consists of two or more people who are related by birth, marriage, or adoption and are residing together. Own children are never-married sons and daughters, including stepchildren and adopted children, of the householder or married couple. Detail may not sum to totals because of rounding.

SOURCE: U.S. Department of Commerce, Census Bureau, Current Population Reports, Series P20, *Household and Family Characteristics*, 1994 and 1995; and Current Population Survey (CPS), Annual Social and Economic Supplement, *America's Families and Living Arrangements* (F table series), 2000 and 2010–2018. 2018 data retrieved May 24, 2019, from https://www.census.gov/content/census/en/data/tables/2018/demo/families/cps-2018.html. (This table was prepared May 2019.)

Table 102.20. Number and percentage distribution of children under age 18 and under age 6, by living arrangements, race/ethnicity, and selected racial/ethnic subgroups: 2017

[Standard errors appear in parentheses]

Age and race/ethnicity	Number of children (in thousands)		Percentage distribution of children		Percentage distribution of children, by living arrangements: Total		Children living with parent(s) or related to householder[1]: Married-couple household		Female householder, no spouse present		Male householder, no spouse present		All other children[2]	
1	2		3		4		5		6		7		8	
All children under age 18														
Total	**73,564**	**(28.8)**	**100.0**	**(†)**	**100.0**	**(†)**	**63.7**	**(0.11)**	**26.3**	**(0.10)**	**7.9**	**(0.06)**	**2.1**	**(0.03)**
White	37,159	(8.7)	50.5	(0.02)	100.0	(†)	73.7	(0.14)	17.0	(0.11)	7.3	(0.07)	2.0	(0.04)
Black	9,870	(30.3)	13.4	(0.04)	100.0	(†)	33.8	(0.38)	55.0	(0.37)	8.7	(0.18)	2.6	(0.08)
Hispanic	18,528	(9.3)	25.2	(0.01)	100.0	(†)	57.3	(0.23)	31.3	(0.22)	9.5	(0.13)	1.9	(0.06)
Cuban	475	(11.1)	0.6	(0.02)	100.0	(†)	60.0	(1.21)	29.7	(1.12)	9.2	(0.66)	1.1	(0.20)
Dominican	596	(13.4)	0.8	(0.02)	100.0	(†)	44.4	(1.29)	46.9	(1.24)	7.3	(0.63)	1.4	(0.26)
Mexican	12,418	(31.9)	16.9	(0.04)	100.0	(†)	58.9	(0.31)	29.7	(0.28)	9.6	(0.16)	1.8	(0.07)
Puerto Rican	1,691	(23.2)	2.3	(0.03)	100.0	(†)	45.0	(0.70)	44.4	(0.77)	8.6	(0.44)	2.0	(0.16)
Spaniard	197	(9.1)	0.3	(0.01)	100.0	(†)	66.4	(1.77)	22.9	(1.66)	9.1	(1.18)	1.6	(0.43)
Central American[3]	1,668	(22.1)	2.3	(0.03)	100.0	(†)	55.3	(0.81)	30.9	(0.74)	11.2	(0.46)	2.6	(0.23)
Costa Rican	39	(3.7)	0.1	(#)	100.0	(†)	73.4	(3.28)	21.2	(2.95)	4.4!	(1.40)	1.0!	(0.48)
Guatemalan	462	(14.1)	0.6	(0.02)	100.0	(†)	57.9	(1.55)	26.1	(1.27)	13.0	(0.99)	2.9	(0.39)
Honduran	301	(11.8)	0.4	(0.02)	100.0	(†)	50.1	(1.81)	36.3	(1.62)	10.1	(1.08)	3.5	(0.61)
Nicaraguan	104	(6.4)	0.1	(0.01)	100.0	(†)	52.8	(2.94)	35.0	(2.66)	11.0	(2.01)	1.1!	(0.55)
Panamanian	49	(4.3)	0.1	(0.01)	100.0	(†)	54.7	(4.83)	32.9	(4.07)	9.2	(2.36)	‡	(†)
Salvadoran	700	(16.4)	1.0	(0.02)	100.0	(†)	55.0	(1.24)	31.5	(1.16)	11.2	(0.70)	2.3	(0.31)
South American	862	(17.1)	1.2	(0.02)	100.0	(†)	68.9	(0.93)	21.4	(0.79)	8.1	(0.52)	1.6	(0.23)
Chilean	36	(3.2)	#	(†)	100.0	(†)	71.8	(4.16)	17.2	(3.54)	8.9	(2.43)	2.1!	(0.97)
Colombian	272	(10.1)	0.4	(0.01)	100.0	(†)	67.0	(1.78)	23.8	(1.64)	7.2	(0.74)	2.1	(0.50)
Ecuadorian	198	(7.8)	0.3	(0.01)	100.0	(†)	61.4	(1.92)	25.7	(1.83)	10.7	(1.38)	2.2	(0.60)
Peruvian	155	(6.4)	0.2	(0.01)	100.0	(†)	70.1	(2.24)	19.2	(1.87)	10.1	(1.49)	0.6!	(0.24)
Venezuelan	95	(5.5)	0.1	(0.01)	100.0	(†)	75.7	(2.50)	18.1	(2.26)	4.9	(1.25)	1.3!	(0.47)
Other South American	107	(4.5)	0.1	(0.01)	100.0	(†)	78.8	(1.75)	14.9	(1.69)	5.5	(1.22)	0.8!	(0.30)
Other Hispanic	620	(13.5)	0.8	(0.02)	100.0	(†)	54.8	(1.06)	29.7	(1.02)	10.9	(0.83)	4.6	(0.36)
Asian	3,505	(16.7)	4.8	(0.02)	100.0	(†)	84.3	(0.32)	10.4	(0.25)	3.8	(0.15)	1.5	(0.09)
Chinese[4]	737	(12.5)	1.0	(0.02)	100.0	(†)	80.8	(0.84)	12.2	(0.60)	4.3	(0.35)	2.7	(0.26)
Filipino	439	(10.8)	0.6	(0.01)	100.0	(†)	78.6	(0.88)	14.9	(0.73)	4.9	(0.49)	1.6	(0.23)
Japanese	68	(4.5)	0.1	(0.01)	100.0	(†)	86.7	(1.62)	7.5	(1.30)	2.9	(0.85)	2.8	(0.80)
Korean	221	(7.6)	0.3	(0.01)	100.0	(†)	87.6	(1.03)	8.5	(0.83)	2.6	(0.53)	1.3	(0.28)
South Asian[5]	1,179	(13.6)	1.6	(0.02)	100.0	(†)	93.3	(0.35)	4.4	(0.25)	1.8	(0.20)	0.6	(0.09)
Asian Indian	941	(12.1)	1.3	(0.02)	100.0	(†)	94.4	(0.32)	3.7	(0.25)	1.4	(0.21)	0.5	(0.08)
Bangladeshi	47	(3.2)	0.1	(#)	100.0	(†)	87.0	(2.68)	7.5	(2.01)	3.9!	(1.34)	‡	(†)
Bhutanese	7	(1.6)	#	(†)	100.0	(†)	84.5	(6.27)	10.4!	(5.13)	‡	(†)	‡	(†)
Nepalese	46	(3.6)	0.1	(#)	100.0	(†)	84.3	(2.86)	10.3	(2.44)	4.4	(1.30)	‡	(†)
Pakistani	132	(7.1)	0.2	(0.01)	100.0	(†)	91.3	(1.23)	5.7	(0.97)	2.3	(0.61)	0.7!	(0.34)
Southeast Asian	652	(11.1)	0.9	(0.02)	100.0	(†)	75.3	(1.06)	16.6	(0.83)	6.4	(0.53)	1.7	(0.19)
Burmese	62	(4.6)	0.1	(0.01)	100.0	(†)	88.0	(2.77)	8.7	(2.54)	1.3!	(0.59)	2.0!	(0.95)
Cambodian	53	(3.9)	0.1	(0.01)	100.0	(†)	61.3	(4.08)	28.3	(3.62)	8.2	(1.98)	2.2!	(1.05)
Hmong	106	(6.1)	0.1	(0.01)	100.0	(†)	71.1	(2.88)	18.3	(2.19)	9.8	(1.93)	‡	(†)
Laotian	38	(3.2)	0.1	(#)	100.0	(†)	64.1	(4.44)	30.7	(4.51)	5.0	(1.44)	‡	(†)
Thai	26	(2.4)	#	(†)	100.0	(†)	65.0	(4.18)	16.2	(2.69)	12.5	(3.10)	6.3	(1.61)
Vietnamese	354	(8.7)	0.5	(0.01)	100.0	(†)	77.7	(1.30)	14.8	(1.09)	5.8	(0.60)	1.7	(0.20)
Other Southeast Asian[6]	14	(1.9)	#	(†)	100.0	(†)	90.8	(2.86)	‡	(†)	‡	(†)	‡	(†)
Other Asian	209	(7.0)	0.3	(0.01)	100.0	(†)	82.2	(1.45)	12.4	(1.19)	4.4	(0.81)	1.1	(0.29)
Pacific Islander	125	(5.5)	0.2	(0.01)	100.0	(†)	62.0	(2.74)	24.7	(2.60)	10.6	(1.73)	2.7	(0.58)
American Indian/Alaska Native	551	(7.0)	0.7	(0.01)	100.0	(†)	41.2	(1.10)	40.3	(1.10)	15.0	(0.67)	3.5	(0.31)
Some other race[7]	277	(8.8)	0.4	(0.01)	100.0	(†)	62.3	(1.76)	24.3	(1.47)	11.2	(1.28)	2.3	(0.45)
Two or more races	3,549	(28.0)	4.8	(0.04)	100.0	(†)	58.6	(0.42)	32.1	(0.43)	7.3	(0.22)	1.9	(0.11)
White and Black	1,505	(23.7)	2.0	(0.03)	100.0	(†)	43.0	(0.73)	46.8	(0.73)	7.5	(0.38)	2.7	(0.21)
White and Asian	992	(13.2)	1.3	(0.02)	100.0	(†)	82.8	(0.55)	11.0	(0.47)	5.3	(0.38)	0.9	(0.13)
White and American Indian/Alaska Native	382	(9.4)	0.5	(0.01)	100.0	(†)	61.7	(1.28)	26.9	(1.14)	9.7	(0.78)	1.7	(0.32)
Other Two or more races	669	(15.4)	0.9	(0.02)	100.0	(†)	56.1	(1.04)	33.4	(1.07)	8.5	(0.60)	2.0	(0.21)
Children under age 6														
Total	**23,559**	**(34.4)**	**100.0**	**(†)**	**100.0**	**(†)**	**64.0**	**(0.16)**	**26.0**	**(0.16)**	**8.3**	**(0.11)**	**1.7**	**(0.04)**
White	11,696	(19.2)	49.6	(0.08)	100.0	(†)	75.8	(0.18)	15.6	(0.15)	7.0	(0.12)	1.7	(0.05)
Black	3,095	(19.5)	13.1	(0.08)	100.0	(†)	32.5	(0.55)	56.5	(0.53)	9.1	(0.26)	1.9	(0.14)
Hispanic	6,056	(17.7)	25.7	(0.06)	100.0	(†)	54.9	(0.38)	32.2	(0.41)	11.2	(0.22)	1.7	(0.11)
Cuban	161	(5.7)	0.7	(0.02)	100.0	(†)	56.0	(2.12)	30.2	(1.87)	13.1	(1.45)	0.7!	(0.34)
Dominican	213	(6.9)	0.9	(0.03)	100.0	(†)	43.1	(2.05)	47.7	(2.04)	7.7	(0.94)	1.5	(0.44)
Mexican	4,012	(17.1)	17.0	(0.07)	100.0	(†)	56.1	(0.49)	30.9	(0.50)	11.5	(0.28)	1.5	(0.12)
Puerto Rican	556	(11.5)	2.4	(0.05)	100.0	(†)	43.0	(0.99)	45.9	(0.94)	9.2	(0.74)	1.9	(0.25)
Spaniard	61	(4.4)	0.3	(0.02)	100.0	(†)	70.3	(2.75)	21.2	(2.42)	8.4	(1.72)	‡	(†)
Central American[3]	573	(11.7)	2.4	(0.05)	100.0	(†)	53.3	(1.04)	30.0	(1.03)	13.8	(0.70)	2.8	(0.43)
Costa Rican	11	(1.7)	#	(†)	100.0	(†)	85.5	(3.54)	9.5!	(3.21)	‡	(†)	‡	(†)
Guatemalan	163	(6.8)	0.7	(0.03)	100.0	(†)	54.7	(2.16)	25.7	(1.50)	16.3	(1.67)	3.4	(0.69)
Honduran	107	(6.0)	0.5	(0.03)	100.0	(†)	48.7	(2.57)	34.7	(2.38)	13.7	(1.95)	2.9	(0.77)
Nicaraguan	37	(3.2)	0.2	(0.01)	100.0	(†)	54.2	(4.64)	34.9	(4.16)	9.8	(2.29)	‡	(†)
Panamanian	13	(1.6)	0.1	(0.01)	100.0	(†)	48.7	(6.25)	37.4	(6.79)	8.3!	(3.03)	5.6!	(2.79)
Salvadoran	236	(8.3)	1.0	(0.04)	100.0	(†)	53.0	(1.75)	30.5	(1.63)	13.9	(1.20)	2.6	(0.68)
South American	288	(9.4)	1.2	(0.04)	100.0	(†)	71.1	(1.40)	19.8	(1.32)	8.2	(0.73)	1.0	(0.25)
Chilean	15	(2.0)	0.1	(0.01)	100.0	(†)	83.7	(4.87)	10.0!	(3.84)	5.8!	(2.70)	‡	(†)
Colombian	86	(4.5)	0.4	(0.02)	100.0	(†)	68.6	(2.65)	24.1	(2.38)	6.3	(1.18)	‡	(†)
Ecuadorian	67	(4.3)	0.3	(0.02)	100.0	(†)	61.1	(2.97)	24.6	(2.93)	13.2	(2.31)	‡	(†)
Peruvian	52	(3.6)	0.2	(0.02)	100.0	(†)	69.4	(3.51)	21.1	(2.90)	8.5	(2.08)	‡	(†)
Venezuelan	34	(3.1)	0.1	(0.01)	100.0	(†)	82.0	(3.32)	10.7	(2.55)	6.0!	(2.22)	‡	(†)
Other South American	33	(2.9)	0.1	(0.01)	100.0	(†)	83.7	(2.96)	10.1	(2.54)	5.5!	(1.77)	‡	(†)
Other Hispanic	193	(6.9)	0.8	(0.03)	100.0	(†)	53.0	(1.75)	30.4	(1.71)	12.2	(1.26)	4.4	(0.57)

See notes at end of table.

Table 102.20. Number and percentage distribution of children under age 18 and under age 6, by living arrangements, race/ethnicity, and selected racial/ethnic subgroups: 2017—Continued

[Standard errors appear in parentheses]

Age and race/ethnicity	Number of children (in thousands)		Percentage distribution of children		Percentage distribution of children, by living arrangements									
							Children living with parent(s) or related to householder[1]							
					Total		Married-couple household		Female householder, no spouse present		Male householder, no spouse present		All other children[2]	
1	2		3		4		5		6		7		8	
Asian	1,118	(9.3)	4.7	(0.04)	100.0	(†)	86.7	(0.47)	8.9	(0.45)	3.6	(0.24)	0.8	(0.10)
Chinese[4]	219	(6.0)	0.9	(0.03)	100.0	(†)	84.9	(1.09)	10.4	(0.88)	3.9	(0.58)	0.7	(0.20)
Filipino	106	(4.2)	0.4	(0.02)	100.0	(†)	76.3	(1.57)	16.9	(1.53)	4.2	(0.67)	2.5	(0.61)
Japanese	25	(2.4)	0.1	(0.01)	100.0	(†)	90.4	(3.05)	5.5!	(2.68)	‡	(†)	2.2!	(0.99)
Korean	62	(3.6)	0.3	(0.02)	100.0	(†)	93.1	(1.47)	3.4	(1.00)	3.0!	(0.89)	‡	(†)
South Asian[5]	439	(7.8)	1.9	(0.03)	100.0	(†)	94.7	(0.47)	3.6	(0.38)	1.5	(0.21)	0.2!	(0.07)
Asian Indian	353	(7.0)	1.5	(0.03)	100.0	(†)	95.8	(0.40)	2.9	(0.37)	1.1	(0.19)	0.1!	(0.06)
Bangladeshi	16	(1.9)	0.1	(0.01)	100.0	(†)	89.3	(3.06)	5.8!	(2.52)	3.0!	(1.43)	‡	(†)
Bhutanese	‡	(†)	#	(†)	100.0	(†)	‡	(†)	‡	(†)	‡	(†)	‡	(†)
Nepalese	19	(2.3)	0.1	(0.01)	100.0	(†)	87.0	(3.77)	9.0!	(3.07)	4.1!	(1.65)	‡	(†)
Pakistani	45	(4.0)	0.2	(0.02)	100.0	(†)	92.4	(1.62)	5.5	(1.39)	2.0!	(0.90)	‡	(†)
Southeast Asian	188	(6.2)	0.8	(0.03)	100.0	(†)	74.2	(1.78)	16.7	(1.44)	7.9	(1.02)	1.3	(0.30)
Burmese	25	(2.5)	0.1	(0.01)	100.0	(†)	88.0	(3.87)	9.2!	(3.80)	‡	(†)	‡	(†)
Cambodian	18	(2.1)	0.1	(0.01)	100.0	(†)	62.8	(6.22)	22.9	(4.56)	13.4!	(4.69)	‡	(†)
Hmong	35	(2.7)	0.1	(0.01)	100.0	(†)	67.2	(4.47)	21.2	(3.41)	11.4	(2.70)	‡	(†)
Laotian	9	(1.2)	#	(†)	100.0	(†)	53.1	(6.99)	43.4	(6.82)	‡	(†)	‡	(†)
Thai	6	(1.1)	#	(†)	100.0	(†)	65.1	(7.12)	21.1!	(6.78)	‡	(†)	7.6!	(3.66)
Vietnamese	91	(4.3)	0.4	(0.02)	100.0	(†)	77.7	(2.27)	13.0	(1.81)	7.7	(1.38)	1.7!	(0.53)
Other Southeast Asian[6]	3	(0.7)	#	(†)	100.0	(†)	89.0	(6.66)	‡	(†)	‡	(†)	‡	(†)
Other Asian	78	(4.0)	0.3	(0.02)	100.0	(†)	83.9	(1.83)	10.8	(1.55)	4.8	(1.18)	‡	(†)
Pacific Islander	38	(2.6)	0.2	(0.01)	100.0	(†)	55.6	(3.63)	29.9	(3.92)	12.2	(2.21)	2.3!	(0.95)
American Indian/Alaska Native	178	(4.0)	0.8	(0.02)	100.0	(†)	36.5	(1.28)	44.8	(1.45)	15.5	(0.98)	3.1	(0.46)
Some other race[7]	95	(4.9)	0.4	(0.02)	100.0	(†)	61.1	(2.50)	25.4	(2.18)	10.7	(1.70)	2.8	(0.79)
Two or more races	1,282	(17.0)	5.4	(0.07)	100.0	(†)	60.2	(0.58)	30.7	(0.61)	7.7	(0.32)	1.4	(0.15)
White and Black	563	(11.4)	2.4	(0.05)	100.0	(†)	43.4	(0.97)	46.1	(1.03)	8.4	(0.60)	2.1	(0.31)
White and Asian	381	(7.1)	1.6	(0.03)	100.0	(†)	85.7	(0.78)	8.8	(0.71)	5.0	(0.49)	0.4	(0.12)
White and American Indian/Alaska Native	113	(4.4)	0.5	(0.02)	100.0	(†)	61.4	(1.97)	25.6	(1.51)	10.9	(1.31)	2.0	(0.59)
Other Two or more races	225	(7.5)	1.0	(0.03)	100.0	(†)	58.5	(1.63)	31.7	(1.64)	8.8	(0.83)	1.1	(0.23)

†Not applicable.
#Rounds to zero.
!Interpret data with caution. The coefficient of variation (CV) for this estimate is between 30 and 50 percent.
‡Reporting standards not met. Either there are too few cases for a reliable estimate or the coefficient of variation (CV) is 50 percent or greater.
[1]Includes all children who live either with their parent(s) or with a householder to whom they are related by birth, marriage, or adoption (except a child who is the spouse of the householder). Children are classified by their parents' marital status or, if no parents are present in the household, by the marital status of the householder who is related to the children. Living arrangements with only a "female householder" or "male householder" are those in which the parent or the householder who is related to the child does not have a spouse living in the household. The householder is the person (or one of the people) who owns or rents (maintains) the housing unit.
[2]Includes foster children, children in unrelated subfamilies, children living in group quarters, and children who were reported as the householder or spouse of the householder.
[3]Includes other Central American subgroups not shown separately.
[4]Includes Taiwanese.
[5]In addition to the subgroups shown, also includes Sri Lankan.
[6]Consists of Indonesian and Malaysian.
[7]Respondents who wrote in some other race that was not included as an option on the questionnaire.
NOTE: Data are based on sample surveys of the entire population residing within the United States, including both noninstitutionalized persons (e.g., those living in households, college housing, or military housing located within the United States) and institutionalized persons (e.g., those living in prisons, nursing facilities, or other healthcare facilities). Race categories exclude persons of Hispanic ethnicity. Detail may not sum to totals because of rounding.
SOURCE: U.S. Department of Commerce, Census Bureau, American Community Survey (ACS), 2017. (This table was prepared November 2018.)

Table 102.40 Poverty rates for all persons and poverty status of related children under age 18, by region and state: Selected years, 1990 through 2017

[Standard errors appear in parentheses]

Region and state	Percent of persons in poverty[1] 1990[3]	2000[4]	2010[5]	2015[5]	2017[5]	Poverty status of related children[2] under age 18: 1990,[3] percent in poverty	2000,[4] percent in poverty	2010,[5] percent in poverty	2015[5] Number in poverty (in thousands)	2015[5] Percent in poverty	2017[5] Number in poverty (in thousands)	2017[5] Percent in poverty
1	2	3	4	5	6	7	8	9	10	11	12	13
United States	**13.1**	**12.4**	**14.9 (0.06)**	**14.3 (0.06)**	**13.0 (0.05)**	**17.9 (0.02)**	**16.1 (0.01)**	**21.1 (0.13)**	**14,652 (109.9)**	**20.3 (0.15)**	**12,938 (91.6)**	**18.0 (0.12)**
Region												
Northeast	10.6	11.4	12.5 (0.09)	12.5 (0.09)	11.6 (0.09)	14.3 (0.54)	14.3 (0.39)	17.4 (0.20)	2,057 (25.4)	17.7 (0.22)	1,847 (23.6)	16.1 (0.20)
South	15.7	13.9	14.1 (0.10)	13.5 (0.12)	12.3 (0.10)	20.5 (0.90)	17.6 (0.64)	20.0 (0.24)	2,878 (41.4)	18.8 (0.27)	2,482 (35.9)	16.4 (0.23)
Midwest	12.0	10.2	16.5 (0.08)	15.6 (0.09)	14.3 (0.08)	14.9 (0.58)	12.0 (0.37)	23.8 (0.18)	6,291 (58.7)	22.7 (0.21)	5,691 (52.3)	20.4 (0.18)
West	12.6	13.0	15.0 (0.09)	14.4 (0.09)	12.6 (0.09)	16.2 (0.79)	16.2 (0.54)	20.6 (0.19)	3,425 (32.6)	19.6 (0.18)	2,919 (34.1)	16.7 (0.19)
Alabama	18.3	16.1	18.6 (0.39)	18.4 (0.37)	16.3 (0.35)	24.0 (0.14)	21.2 (0.10)	27.6 (0.86)	285 (8.7)	26.2 (0.79)	257 (9.0)	23.9 (0.83)
Alaska	9.0	9.4	10.6 (0.75)	9.9 (0.95)	11.3 (0.93)	10.9 (0.24)	11.2 (0.16)	13.5 (1.32)	27 (3.7)	14.7 (2.03)	24 (3.8)	13.5 (2.11)
Arizona	15.7	13.9	17.1 (0.35)	16.9 (0.31)	14.4 (0.27)	21.7 (0.13)	18.8 (0.10)	24.0 (0.74)	381 (10.8)	24.0 (0.67)	323 (9.8)	20.2 (0.60)
Arkansas	19.1	15.8	18.2 (0.41)	18.8 (0.44)	15.7 (0.43)	25.0 (0.17)	21.4 (0.11)	26.6 (1.00)	185 (6.7)	26.9 (0.97)	151 (7.1)	21.8 (1.02)
California	12.5	14.2	15.4 (0.13)	15.0 (0.12)	12.9 (0.14)	17.8 (0.05)	19.0 (0.04)	21.5 (0.28)	1,866 (25.4)	20.9 (0.28)	1,566 (26.7)	17.7 (0.30)
Colorado	11.7	9.3	12.8 (0.33)	11.3 (0.26)	10.1 (0.25)	15.0 (0.11)	10.8 (0.07)	16.6 (0.71)	177 (7.2)	14.3 (0.58)	146 (6.4)	11.9 (0.52)
Connecticut	6.8	7.9	9.6 (0.30)	9.9 (0.33)	9.1 (0.31)	10.4 (0.13)	10.0 (0.09)	12.3 (0.63)	100 (5.6)	13.4 (0.76)	88 (5.1)	12.0 (0.69)
Delaware	8.7	9.2	11.7 (0.73)	13.1 (0.87)	12.5 (0.74)	11.7 (0.23)	11.9 (0.20)	18.2 (1.59)	42 (4.4)	21.0 (2.19)	34 (3.3)	17.3 (1.64)
District of Columbia	16.9	20.2	18.3 (0.87)	15.5 (0.76)	15.5 (0.70)	25.0 (0.49)	31.1 (0.37)	29.3 (2.58)	29 (2.6)	25.4 (2.21)	32 (2.6)	25.8 (2.10)
Florida	12.7	12.5	16.2 (0.16)	15.3 (0.16)	13.7 (0.18)	18.3 (0.09)	17.2 (0.06)	23.2 (0.40)	917 (17.5)	22.9 (0.43)	820 (17.3)	19.9 (0.42)
Georgia	14.7	13.0	17.4 (0.27)	16.6 (0.22)	14.7 (0.30)	19.8 (0.12)	16.7 (0.07)	24.4 (0.46)	590 (12.3)	24.0 (0.50)	515 (16.5)	20.9 (0.67)
Hawaii	8.3	10.7	10.1 (0.50)	10.4 (0.52)	10.2 (0.51)	11.1 (0.21)	13.5 (0.16)	12.5 (1.29)	41 (3.8)	13.4 (1.24)	37 (3.9)	12.6 (1.33)
Idaho	13.3	11.8	15.0 (0.50)	13.8 (0.63)	12.9 (0.57)	15.8 (0.21)	13.8 (0.13)	17.5 (0.96)	66 (4.9)	15.6 (1.16)	66 (5.3)	15.2 (1.22)
Illinois	11.9	10.7	13.6 (0.19)	13.4 (0.21)	12.4 (0.20)	16.8 (0.07)	14.0 (0.04)	19.4 (0.41)	560 (14.7)	19.3 (0.50)	482 (13.8)	16.9 (0.48)
Indiana	10.7	9.5	14.9 (0.28)	14.6 (0.29)	13.1 (0.30)	13.9 (0.09)	11.7 (0.08)	21.7 (0.63)	332 (10.8)	21.6 (0.70)	269 (10.3)	17.6 (0.67)
Iowa	11.5	9.1	12.3 (0.41)	12.5 (0.47)	9.8 (0.34)	14.0 (0.13)	10.5 (0.08)	16.7 (0.94)	111 (7.5)	15.7 (1.07)	78 (5.5)	10.9 (0.76)
Kansas	11.5	9.9	12.7 (0.42)	12.6 (0.40)	11.6 (0.36)	13.9 (0.13)	11.5 (0.09)	17.4 (0.94)	123 (6.2)	17.5 (0.85)	99 (5.8)	14.3 (0.83)
Kentucky	19.0	15.8	18.1 (0.32)	17.6 (0.32)	16.8 (0.36)	24.5 (0.14)	20.4 (0.09)	25.4 (0.76)	245 (7.7)	25.0 (0.77)	220 (7.7)	22.3 (0.77)
Louisiana	23.6	19.6	17.9 (0.31)	18.8 (0.43)	19.4 (0.44)	31.2 (0.16)	26.3 (0.10)	26.9 (0.68)	303 (10.3)	27.6 (0.94)	304 (10.1)	27.9 (0.91)
Maine	10.8	10.9	13.3 (0.58)	12.5 (0.56)	11.1 (0.54)	13.2 (0.18)	13.0 (0.14)	18.3 (1.28)	35 (2.8)	14.3 (1.12)	32 (3.3)	13.0 (1.34)
Maryland	8.3	8.5	9.8 (0.25)	9.8 (0.28)	9.2 (0.26)	10.9 (0.10)	10.3 (0.08)	12.8 (0.51)	173 (8.5)	13.2 (0.64)	156 (8.1)	11.8 (0.62)
Massachusetts	8.9	9.3	11.0 (0.25)	10.9 (0.22)	10.1 (0.24)	12.9 (0.10)	11.6 (0.07)	13.7 (0.55)	194 (7.1)	14.2 (0.52)	180 (7.6)	13.4 (0.57)
Michigan	13.1	10.5	16.2 (0.24)	15.5 (0.28)	13.9 (0.23)	18.2 (0.08)	13.4 (0.05)	22.5 (0.52)	472 (13.3)	22.0 (0.62)	408 (10.7)	19.4 (0.50)
Minnesota	10.2	7.9	11.1 (0.32)	9.7 (0.26)	9.5 (0.25)	12.4 (0.09)	9.2 (0.06)	14.6 (0.72)	153 (7.9)	12.2 (0.62)	146 (6.9)	11.6 (0.54)
Mississippi	25.2	19.9	21.5 (0.51)	21.1 (0.51)	19.1 (0.37)	33.5 (0.18)	26.7 (0.11)	31.7 (1.05)	224 (7.7)	31.2 (1.07)	185 (6.0)	26.4 (0.84)
Missouri	13.3	11.7	15.1 (0.28)	14.2 (0.28)	12.9 (0.25)	17.4 (0.10)	15.3 (0.07)	20.6 (0.59)	266 (10.5)	19.6 (0.77)	237 (8.1)	17.6 (0.60)
Montana	16.1	14.6	14.1 (0.70)	14.2 (0.70)	12.3 (0.62)	19.9 (0.27)	18.4 (0.18)	19.8 (1.43)	41 (3.9)	18.5 (1.74)	31 (2.6)	14.2 (1.20)
Nebraska	11.1	9.7	12.7 (0.56)	12.2 (0.43)	10.3 (0.48)	13.5 (0.16)	11.8 (0.11)	18.2 (1.32)	71 (4.2)	15.4 (0.91)	64 (5.0)	13.9 (1.10)
Nevada	10.2	10.5	14.9 (0.49)	14.7 (0.46)	12.9 (0.44)	12.8 (0.22)	13.5 (0.14)	21.7 (0.97)	136 (7.3)	20.8 (1.11)	123 (6.7)	18.4 (1.00)
New Hampshire	6.4	6.5	8.0 (0.44)	7.7 (0.49)	7.2 (0.43)	7.0 (0.14)	7.3 (0.11)	9.8 (1.09)	26 (3.0)	9.9 (1.16)	25 (3.2)	9.8 (1.27)
New Jersey	7.6	8.5	10.0 (0.22)	10.4 (0.22)	9.5 (0.20)	11.0 (0.08)	10.8 (0.06)	14.0 (0.45)	293 (10.9)	14.9 (0.55)	258 (9.6)	13.3 (0.49)
New Mexico	20.6	18.4	19.9 (0.65)	20.4 (0.66)	19.1 (0.50)	27.5 (0.21)	24.6 (0.15)	29.5 (1.22)	150 (7.0)	30.5 (1.38)	123 (5.8)	25.7 (1.19)
New York	13.0	14.6	14.6 (0.19)	14.8 (0.17)	13.6 (0.16)	18.8 (0.07)	19.6 (0.05)	21.1 (0.36)	879 (17.8)	21.4 (0.43)	776 (14.0)	19.2 (0.35)
North Carolina	13.0	12.3	16.8 (0.24)	16.2 (0.23)	14.4 (0.24)	16.9 (0.09)	15.7 (0.06)	24.1 (0.52)	532 (11.7)	23.7 (0.51)	476 (12.5)	21.1 (0.55)
North Dakota	14.4	11.9	11.8 (0.77)	11.3 (0.57)	9.4 (0.56)	16.9 (0.26)	13.5 (0.15)	14.2 (1.92)	19 (2.2)	11.0 (1.28)	14 (1.8)	8.3 (1.02)
Ohio	12.5	10.6	15.4 (0.21)	14.5 (0.21)	13.5 (0.20)	17.6 (0.07)	14.0 (0.05)	22.9 (0.48)	552 (13.3)	21.5 (0.51)	495 (13.0)	19.5 (0.51)
Oklahoma	16.7	14.7	16.5 (0.39)	15.7 (0.38)	14.9 (0.44)	21.4 (0.14)	19.1 (0.09)	24.9 (0.98)	207 (8.3)	22.1 (0.88)	192 (8.8)	20.4 (0.94)
Oregon	12.4	11.6	15.6 (0.34)	14.8 (0.40)	13.0 (0.33)	15.2 (0.13)	14.0 (0.09)	21.0 (0.77)	165 (7.9)	19.7 (0.95)	134 (7.1)	15.7 (0.82)
Pennsylvania	11.1	11.0	12.8 (0.18)	12.5 (0.21)	12.1 (0.21)	15.4 (0.07)	14.3 (0.05)	18.2 (0.44)	480 (13.2)	18.3 (0.49)	438 (13.0)	16.8 (0.49)
Rhode Island	9.6	11.9	14.0 (0.59)	13.1 (0.61)	11.2 (0.60)	13.5 (0.26)	16.5 (0.22)	19.7 (1.49)	38 (3.3)	18.5 (1.56)	34 (3.0)	16.7 (1.48)
South Carolina	15.4	14.1	17.6 (0.33)	16.0 (0.32)	15.0 (0.30)	20.8 (0.16)	18.5 (0.10)	25.5 (0.73)	245 (7.6)	23.1 (0.70)	236 (7.8)	21.9 (0.72)
South Dakota	15.9	13.2	14.4 (0.89)	12.5 (0.69)	11.7 (0.64)	20.1 (0.28)	16.7 (0.19)	18.7 (1.97)	29 (3.2)	14.0 (1.51)	30 (2.6)	14.6 (1.24)
Tennessee	15.7	13.5	17.2 (0.30)	16.4 (0.31)	14.7 (0.29)	20.7 (0.12)	17.6 (0.09)	25.3 (0.67)	351 (10.9)	24.0 (0.74)	309 (8.7)	20.9 (0.59)
Texas	18.1	15.4	17.3 (0.16)	15.4 (0.17)	14.3 (0.14)	24.0 (0.08)	20.2 (0.05)	25.2 (0.31)	1,591 (25.1)	22.4 (0.35)	1,475 (25.1)	20.3 (0.34)
Utah	11.4	9.4	13.1 (0.46)	11.2 (0.43)	9.4 (0.40)	12.2 (0.14)	9.7 (0.08)	15.8 (0.87)	115 (6.9)	12.8 (0.77)	95 (6.4)	10.4 (0.71)
Vermont	9.9	9.4	11.4 (0.76)	9.2 (0.84)	10.7 (0.83)	11.5 (0.23)	10.7 (0.15)	14.8 (2.12)	14 (2.5)	11.7 (2.16)	15 (2.2)	13.6 (2.00)
Virginia	10.2	9.6	11.0 (0.18)	11.0 (0.22)	10.1 (0.22)	13.0 (0.10)	11.9 (0.07)	15.0 (0.42)	279 (8.7)	15.2 (0.47)	244 (9.0)	13.3 (0.49)
Washington	10.9	10.6	13.2 (0.27)	12.4 (0.25)	11.0 (0.23)	14.0 (0.09)	13.2 (0.08)	17.8 (0.58)	248 (9.8)	15.8 (0.62)	232 (9.3)	14.4 (0.58)
West Virginia	19.7	17.9	17.9 (0.54)	17.3 (0.55)	18.5 (0.53)	25.9 (0.21)	23.9 (0.15)	25.9 (1.37)	93 (5.4)	25.3 (1.44)	86 (4.2)	24.0 (1.13)
Wisconsin	10.7	8.7	12.7 (0.31)	11.3 (0.34)	10.6 (0.30)	14.6 (0.09)	10.8 (0.07)	18.1 (0.76)	191 (10.0)	15.2 (0.79)	160 (8.8)	12.8 (0.69)
Wyoming	11.9	11.4	10.4 (0.80)	9.9 (0.80)	11.5 (0.85)	14.1 (0.30)	13.8 (0.22)	13.4 (1.69)	15 (2.5)	10.9 (1.81)	18 (2.5)	13.5 (1.84)

[1]Data exclude institutionalized persons (e.g., those living in prisons or nursing homes) as well as persons living in most types of noninstitutional group quarters (e.g., college housing or military barracks). Data include noninstitutionalized persons living in households as well as those living in group homes and shelters.

[2]Related children in a family include all children in the household who are related to the householder by birth, marriage, or adoption (except a child who is the spouse of the householder). The householder is the person (or one of the people) who owns or rents (maintains) the housing unit. This table excludes unrelated children and householders who are themselves under the age of 18.

[3]Based on 1989 incomes and family sizes collected in the 1990 census.

[4]Based on 1999 incomes and family sizes collected in the 2000 census.

[5]Based on income and family size data from the American Community Survey (ACS). ACS respondents were interviewed throughout the given year and reported the income they received during the previous 12 months. Data are based on sample surveys of the entire population residing within the United States.

NOTE: Poverty status is determined by the Census Bureau using a set of money income thresholds that vary by family size and composition. For additional information about poverty status, see https://www.census.gov/topics/income-poverty/poverty/guidance/poverty-measures.html. Poverty estimates in this table may differ from table 102.50's official national poverty estimates, which are based on a different data source (the Current Population Survey). Detail may not sum to totals because of rounding.

SOURCE: U.S. Department of Commerce, Census Bureau, 1990 Summary Tape File 3 (STF 3), "Median Household Income in 1989" and "Poverty Status in 1989 by Family Type and Age"; Decennial Census, 1990, *Minority Economic Profiles*, unpublished data; Decennial Census, 2000, *Summary Social, Economic, and Housing Characteristics*; Census 2000 Summary File 4 (SF 4), "Poverty Status in 1999 of Related Children Under 18 Years by Family Type and Age"; and American Community Survey (ACS), 2010, 2015, and 2017. (This table was prepared October 2018.)

Table 102.62. Percentage of children under age 18 living in poverty, by parents' highest level of educational attainment, child's race/ethnicity, and selected racial/ethnic subgroups: 2010 and 2017

[Standard errors appear in parentheses]

Year and race/ethnicity	Percent in poverty, all children under age 18 who resided with at least one parent[1]	Percent of children in poverty, by highest level of education attained by any parent residing with child[1]							
						Bachelor's or higher degree			
		Less than high school completion	High school completion[2]	Some college, no degree	Associate's degree	Total	Bachelor's degree	Master's degree	Doctor's degree[3]
1	2	3	4	5	6	7	8	9	10
2010									
Total	**20.8 (0.13)**	**53.4 (0.33)**	**32.3 (0.25)**	**23.0 (0.22)**	**12.7 (0.27)**	**4.3 (0.08)**	**5.6 (0.12)**	**2.8 (0.10)**	**2.1 (0.13)**
White	12.5 (0.12)	48.8 (0.75)	24.6 (0.31)	17.1 (0.25)	8.8 (0.23)	3.2 (0.08)	4.1 (0.13)	2.1 (0.10)	1.5 (0.14)
Black	37.6 (0.39)	72.8 (0.76)	49.0 (0.65)	36.9 (0.72)	23.9 (0.99)	8.0 (0.37)	10.0 (0.51)	4.6 (0.57)	4.7 (1.12)
Hispanic	31.8 (0.23)	50.6 (0.42)	34.1 (0.44)	24.8 (0.50)	16.4 (0.68)	7.9 (0.33)	9.5 (0.45)	4.9 (0.55)	4.9 (0.73)
Cuban	18.6 (1.12)	52.3 (5.24)	27.0 (2.56)	21.9 (2.80)	11.4 (2.21)	6.7 (1.07)	9.5 (1.77)	2.2! (0.99)	3.4! (1.52)
Dominican	33.9 (1.22)	50.9 (3.29)	46.5 (2.73)	32.2 (2.61)	11.1 (2.60)	11.1 (1.91)	14.2 (2.60)	‡ (†)	‡ (†)
Mexican	33.8 (0.28)	50.7 (0.49)	34.4 (0.53)	24.9 (0.62)	15.8 (0.90)	8.1 (0.44)	9.1 (0.58)	5.7 (0.91)	5.9 (1.19)
Puerto Rican	33.3 (0.78)	68.6 (2.06)	38.7 (1.44)	29.0 (1.42)	23.7 (2.50)	7.9 (0.83)	9.9 (1.20)	5.1! (1.58)	‡ (†)
Spaniard	16.9 (1.58)	44.1 (8.89)	30.9 (4.83)	21.6 (3.34)	17.0! (5.73)	3.4! (1.05)	3.9! (1.28)	‡ (†)	‡ (†)
Central American[4]	26.8 (0.79)	40.0 (1.44)	26.8 (1.63)	19.7 (1.62)	10.0 (1.87)	9.5 (1.33)	11.8 (1.86)	4.4! (1.85)	8.1! (3.51)
Costa Rican	18.9 (3.67)	‡ (†)	28.7! (9.73)	29.7 (8.13)	‡ (†)	‡ (†)	‡ (†)	‡ (†)	‡ (†)
Guatemalan	31.2 (1.67)	50.2 (2.44)	27.4 (3.45)	22.4 (3.74)	11.0! (3.37)	8.3 (1.99)	11.5 (3.40)	‡ (†)	‡ (†)
Honduran	33.5 (2.15)	41.0 (3.44)	37.0 (4.44)	25.8 (4.58)	12.4! (5.46)	19.4 (4.59)	24.5 (6.06)	‡ (†)	‡ (†)
Nicaraguan	21.6 (2.96)	51.2 (7.70)	29.2 (5.70)	20.1 (5.13)	‡ (†)	‡ (†)	‡ (†)	‡ (†)	‡ (†)
Panamanian	15.5 (3.54)	‡ (†)	41.9! (17.94)	15.7! (5.31)	‡ (†)	8.9! (3.92)	18.3! (7.25)	‡ (†)	‡ (†)
Salvadoran	23.8 (1.09)	33.6 (2.28)	20.7 (2.13)	15.4 (2.26)	9.9 (2.87)	11.9 (2.65)	11.3 (2.71)	‡ (†)	‡ (†)
South American	17.0 (0.77)	41.7 (3.69)	25.7 (1.99)	18.4 (1.80)	16.5 (2.61)	7.4 (0.82)	9.8 (1.22)	3.6 (0.94)	5.1! (1.58)
Chilean	10.9 (3.02)	‡ (†)	13.2! (5.94)	23.0! (10.50)	‡ (†)	‡ (†)	‡ (†)	‡ (†)	‡ (†)
Colombian	13.8 (1.29)	37.1 (8.57)	24.6 (3.47)	16.3 (2.92)	10.2! (3.53)	6.0 (1.26)	7.5 (1.88)	3.2! (1.45)	‡ (†)
Ecuadorian	24.2 (2.05)	42.4 (4.95)	29.8 (4.40)	21.9 (4.73)	17.2 (4.90)	9.8 (2.85)	11.5! (4.06)	‡ (†)	‡ (†)
Peruvian	17.9 (2.17)	65.0 (11.70)	22.9 (4.15)	17.1 (4.07)	10.5! (4.43)	11.4 (2.43)	13.8 (2.98)	‡ (†)	‡ (†)
Venezuelan	17.1 (3.20)	‡ (†)	37.8! (12.96)	‡ (†)	61.0 (11.07)	7.3 (1.84)	8.3! (2.75)	‡ (†)	‡ (†)
Other South American	14.0 (1.89)	33.0 (8.91)	24.5 (6.93)	20.6 (4.29)	10.8! (5.38)	4.5! (1.40)	8.3! (2.85)	‡ (†)	‡ (†)
Other Hispanic	28.2 (1.18)	52.8 (3.10)	34.7 (2.38)	24.9 (2.09)	18.2 (3.39)	7.5 (1.25)	9.2 (1.79)	6.0! (2.32)	3.6! (1.52)
Asian	12.0 (0.30)	41.7 (1.71)	24.3 (1.26)	15.2 (0.99)	11.0 (1.09)	5.2 (0.27)	7.0 (0.43)	4.1 (0.37)	2.7 (0.35)
Chinese[5]	9.5 (0.53)	32.0 (2.77)	23.5 (2.60)	12.8 (2.11)	9.5 (2.17)	3.8 (0.39)	6.1 (0.92)	3.1 (0.66)	2.4 (0.56)
Filipino	5.2 (0.71)	10.6! (4.73)	12.4 (3.03)	9.1 (1.83)	7.6! (2.61)	2.8 (0.59)	2.9 (0.67)	‡ (†)	‡ (†)
Japanese	4.5 (1.14)	‡ (†)	26.9! (10.91)	‡ (†)	‡ (†)	2.7! (0.91)	3.7! (1.45)	‡ (†)	‡ (†)
Korean	12.9 (0.99)	‡ (†)	16.9 (4.85)	18.2 (5.18)	6.0! (2.17)	11.7 (1.16)	14.9 (1.66)	10.7 (1.70)	6.6 (1.86)
South Asian[6]	9.9 (0.63)	50.7 (4.76)	26.9 (3.38)	22.7 (3.92)	17.7 (3.66)	4.9 (0.49)	8.7 (1.16)	3.2 (0.53)	1.6! (0.50)
Asian Indian	7.6 (0.61)	49.2 (5.88)	25.0 (4.31)	22.9 (4.32)	13.0! (4.52)	3.6 (0.49)	7.4 (1.25)	1.9 (0.42)	0.9! (0.45)
Bangladeshi	30.0 (4.25)	79.5 (9.81)	‡ (†)	‡ (†)	‡ (†)	21.3 (4.96)	24.8! (7.93)	23.5! (8.18)	‡ (†)
Bhutanese	— (†)	— (†)	— (†)	— (†)	— (†)	— (†)	— (†)	— (†)	— (†)
Nepalese	— (†)	— (†)	— (†)	— (†)	— (†)	— (†)	— (†)	— (†)	— (†)
Pakistani	19.2 (2.33)	43.5 (10.91)	33.9 (6.31)	‡ (†)	30.5! (10.37)	11.1 (2.00)	12.2 (3.16)	12.0! (3.80)	‡ (†)
Southeast Asian	21.4 (0.91)	43.0 (2.51)	27.5 (2.04)	16.1 (1.74)	12.1 (2.36)	7.0 (1.07)	8.0 (1.32)	6.0 (1.55)	‡ (†)
Burmese	— (†)	— (†)	— (†)	— (†)	— (†)	— (†)	— (†)	— (†)	— (†)
Cambodian	27.2 (3.09)	57.0 (6.67)	31.3 (7.65)	19.3! (6.53)	‡ (†)	4.7! (2.22)	‡ (†)	‡ (†)	‡ (†)
Hmong	39.5 (3.68)	70.2 (6.78)	39.2 (6.62)	16.5! (5.47)	20.6! (8.76)	13.7! (6.32)	19.3! (8.84)	‡ (†)	‡ (†)
Laotian	19.0 (3.16)	27.7! (8.40)	26.7 (6.08)	14.4 (4.29)	‡ (†)	‡ (†)	‡ (†)	‡ (†)	‡ (†)
Thai	23.2 (6.73)	‡ (†)	‡ (†)	‡ (†)	‡ (†)	‡ (†)	‡ (†)	‡ (†)	‡ (†)
Vietnamese	15.9 (1.01)	28.2 (2.48)	22.9 (2.47)	15.7 (2.27)	10.1 (2.52)	5.2 (0.96)	5.9 (1.07)	‡ (†)	‡ (†)
Other Southeast Asian[7]	22.9 (5.69)	‡ (†)	‡ (†)	‡ (†)	‡ (†)	17.1! (5.22)	15.2! (7.06)	22.8! (8.78)	‡ (†)
Other Asian	15.9 (1.29)	54.3 (6.45)	23.8 (4.15)	21.1 (4.47)	12.1 (3.55)	5.6 (0.96)	6.1 (1.51)	6.3! (2.46)	3.4! (1.54)
Pacific Islander	22.4 (2.29)	68.3 (9.33)	23.6 (3.90)	18.7 (3.45)	21.8 (6.17)	11.7! (5.04)	13.5! (6.66)	‡ (†)	‡ (†)
American Indian/Alaska Native[8]	33.9 (1.16)	65.0 (2.96)	42.0 (2.30)	29.8 (1.88)	20.1 (2.76)	12.6 (2.24)	14.6 (3.03)	6.0! (2.77)	15.2! (5.64)
Amercian Indian	35.4 (1.24)	66.7 (2.92)	44.5 (2.58)	31.1 (2.16)	19.8 (2.96)	12.6 (2.63)	14.5 (3.55)	3.6! (1.81)	22.1! (8.12)
Alaska Native	25.3 (3.55)	61.6 (12.23)	32.1 (5.12)	15.8! (5.45)	‡ (†)	‡ (†)	‡ (†)	‡ (†)	‡ (†)
Some other race[9]	19.3 (1.63)	41.5 (6.50)	30.9 (4.30)	22.9 (4.49)	9.0! (4.28)	6.6! (2.05)	13.8! (4.15)	‡ (†)	‡ (†)
Two or more races	21.0 (0.49)	57.8 (2.04)	35.8 (1.38)	27.1 (0.77)	18.0 (1.38)	5.3 (0.39)	7.2 (0.60)	3.4 (0.45)	1.7! (0.52)
2017									
Total	**17.6 (0.12)**	**48.0 (0.39)**	**30.6 (0.25)**	**21.4 (0.25)**	**12.2 (0.28)**	**3.9 (0.07)**	**5.2 (0.12)**	**2.5 (0.10)**	**2.3 (0.14)**
White	10.4 (0.11)	45.3 (0.91)	23.9 (0.34)	16.2 (0.30)	8.2 (0.29)	2.7 (0.08)	3.6 (0.12)	1.6 (0.10)	1.7 (0.15)
Black	32.2 (0.35)	68.4 (1.16)	46.1 (0.68)	33.5 (0.82)	22.9 (0.98)	7.6 (0.41)	9.2 (0.62)	5.6 (0.55)	5.0 (0.96)
Hispanic	25.9 (0.25)	44.5 (0.51)	30.2 (0.46)	21.9 (0.52)	14.9 (0.69)	7.2 (0.27)	8.9 (0.34)	4.0 (0.46)	4.9 (0.70)
Cuban	17.9 (0.98)	47.5 (5.80)	31.5 (2.49)	17.8 (2.39)	16.6 (3.38)	6.5 (1.06)	8.6 (1.66)	3.7! (1.12)	‡ (†)
Dominican	28.6 (1.10)	47.5 (3.88)	37.1 (2.81)	29.0 (2.71)	20.3 (3.34)	12.5 (1.79)	14.1 (2.24)	9.5! (4.38)	7.1! (3.51)
Mexican	26.9 (0.34)	44.1 (0.65)	29.5 (0.59)	21.7 (0.67)	12.7 (0.84)	7.2 (0.39)	8.5 (0.50)	4.0 (0.64)	5.9 (1.19)
Puerto Rican	28.6 (0.84)	58.5 (2.56)	41.7 (1.79)	27.9 (1.54)	24.2 (2.29)	5.1 (0.64)	6.4 (0.92)	3.0! (1.08)	3.1! (1.40)
Spaniard	11.9 (1.22)	16.4! (5.71)	34.9 (4.80)	19.9 (3.93)	11.3! (4.26)	3.4 (0.92)	5.2! (1.77)	2.1! (0.91)	‡ (†)
Central American[3]	26.9 (0.71)	43.5 (1.55)	26.0 (1.61)	19.8 (1.55)	12.4 (2.15)	7.1 (0.83)	9.8 (1.18)	2.9! (1.15)	‡ (†)
Costa Rican	7.8 (2.12)	‡ (†)	‡ (†)	16.3! (6.77)	‡ (†)	‡ (†)	‡ (†)	‡ (†)	‡ (†)
Guatemalan	32.8 (1.56)	50.8 (2.64)	25.3 (2.54)	19.3 (3.35)	26.6 (7.56)	6.9! (2.08)	9.0! (2.94)	‡ (†)	‡ (†)
Honduran	34.0 (1.90)	50.7 (3.82)	29.9 (3.63)	27.6 (3.80)	11.3! (4.85)	15.6 (3.21)	18.8 (4.26)	10.8! (5.13)	‡ (†)
Nicaraguan	16.7 (2.18)	39.8! (12.64)	25.8 (5.05)	18.2 (4.58)	‡ (†)	5.0! (1.95)	5.3! (2.30)	‡ (†)	‡ (†)
Panamanian	14.4 (3.10)	‡ (†)	46.1 (9.12)	17.4! (5.97)	‡ (†)	‡ (†)	‡ (†)	‡ (†)	‡ (†)
Salvadoran	23.8 (1.08)	34.8 (2.32)	24.6 (2.22)	17.7 (2.44)	9.8! (3.50)	5.6 (1.23)	8.5 (1.85)	‡ (†)	‡ (†)
South American	13.4 (0.66)	32.1 (4.49)	20.4 (2.11)	11.9 (1.65)	13.8 (2.20)	8.6 (0.85)	11.3 (1.38)	4.6 (1.01)	5.4! (1.67)
Chilean	11.8! (3.55)	‡ (†)	‡ (†)	‡ (†)	‡ (†)	‡ (†)	‡ (†)	‡ (†)	‡ (†)
Colombian	11.4 (1.12)	26.4! (8.34)	22.8 (4.11)	13.2 (3.02)	13.2 (3.38)	5.6 (1.05)	7.5 (1.84)	2.1! (0.99)	4.7! (2.22)
Ecuadorian	15.6 (1.66)	30.9 (5.93)	19.2 (3.40)	8.9 (2.63)	19.5! (7.13)	6.1! (2.08)	9.4! (3.10)	‡ (†)	‡ (†)
Peruvian	11.0 (1.61)	49.4 (13.01)	19.6 (4.58)	8.1! (3.47)	9.4! (3.06)	6.2 (1.59)	7.5! (2.26)	5.1! (2.45)	‡ (†)
Venezuelan	23.2 (2.65)	‡ (†)	25.5 (7.59)	18.6! (6.04)	19.4! (7.95)	24.4 (3.73)	31.8 (5.78)	14.1! (5.49)	17.9! (7.99)
Other South American	9.6 (1.74)	39.7 (11.87)	13.7! (5.83)	13.2! (4.80)	‡ (†)	5.3! (2.17)	8.8! (3.82)	‡ (†)	‡ (†)
Other Hispanic	21.7 (1.04)	42.5 (3.28)	27.8 (2.59)	18.5 (1.86)	17.6 (3.62)	7.5 (1.49)	8.9 (2.31)	5.0! (1.79)	7.3! (3.63)

See notes at end of table.

Table 102.62. Percentage of children under age 18 living in poverty, by parents' highest level of educational attainment, child's race/ethnicity, and selected racial/ethnic subgroups: 2010 and 2017—Continued

[Standard errors appear in parentheses]

Year and race/ethnicity	Percent in poverty, all children under age 18 who resided with at least one parent[1]		Percent of children in poverty, by highest level of education attained by any parent residing with child[1]															
			Less than high school completion		High school completion[2]		Some college, no degree		Associate's degree		Bachelor's or higher degree							
											Total		Bachelor's degree		Master's degree		Doctor's degree[3]	
1	2		3		4		5		6		7		8		9		10	
Asian	10.1	(0.31)	36.8	(2.20)	21.9	(1.30)	15.5	(1.21)	13.4	(1.45)	4.6	(0.23)	6.3	(0.50)	3.7	(0.30)	2.7	(0.35)
Chinese[5]	11.6	(0.70)	36.4	(3.48)	21.8	(2.63)	13.2	(2.53)	21.7	(3.92)	5.8	(0.52)	7.4	(1.06)	6.0	(0.81)	4.0	(0.68)
Filipino	4.5	(0.54)	‡	(†)	11.8	(2.69)	7.9	(1.91)	4.0!	(1.56)	2.5	(0.48)	2.9	(0.61)	2.3!	(0.79)	‡	(†)
Japanese	3.9	(0.99)	‡	(†)	‡	(†)	‡	(†)	‡	(†)	3.1!	(1.26)	5.2!	(2.47)	‡	(†)	‡	(†)
Korean	8.7	(0.97)	‡	(†)	29.7	(6.96)	11.9!	(5.02)	‡	(†)	7.5	(1.04)	8.5	(1.60)	7.8	(1.66)	5.8!	(1.80)
South Asian[6]	7.9	(0.49)	37.0	(4.55)	26.1	(3.35)	23.2	(3.26)	23.4	(3.96)	3.9	(0.40)	8.3	(1.18)	2.4	(0.37)	1.4!	(0.46)
Asian Indian	4.7	(0.40)	20.0	(4.37)	19.0	(4.19)	16.4	(3.27)	25.5	(5.67)	2.6	(0.31)	6.1	(0.97)	1.4	(0.28)	0.9!	(0.44)
Bangladeshi	18.1	(2.87)	‡	(†)	36.0	(8.07)	17.0!	(7.44)	‡	(†)	9.4!	(3.18)	8.3!	(3.90)	12.1!	(4.95)	‡	(†)
Bhutanese	20.8!	(8.77)	‡	(†)	‡	(†)	‡	(†)	‡	(†)	‡	(†)	‡	(†)	‡	(†)	‡	(†)
Nepalese	25.2	(3.27)	51.0	(8.63)	42.9	(11.78)	‡	(†)	‡	(†)	5.0!	(1.73)	8.4!	(3.62)	‡	(†)	‡	(†)
Pakistani	20.8	(2.48)	43.4	(11.69)	33.3	(7.44)	42.7	(9.42)	32.4!	(10.20)	13.8	(2.90)	20.2	(5.80)	12.8	(3.54)	‡	(†)
Southeast Asian	18.0	(0.96)	39.5	(3.24)	22.9	(2.27)	17.5	(2.49)	9.7	(2.09)	6.0	(0.86)	6.0	(1.23)	6.8	(1.71)	‡	(†)
Burmese	35.9	(3.81)	46.3	(5.17)	27.0!	(8.88)	‡	(†)	‡	(†)	18.4!	(7.55)	‡	(†)	‡	(†)	‡	(†)
Cambodian	16.6	(3.49)	31.0!	(11.04)	19.1	(5.20)	27.4!	(10.45)	‡	(†)	‡	(†)	‡	(†)	‡	(†)	‡	(†)
Hmong	23.8	(3.17)	58.7	(10.67)	35.4	(7.31)	16.2	(3.87)	8.9!	(4.43)	4.1!	(1.89)	‡	(†)	‡	(†)	‡	(†)
Laotian	11.8	(2.97)	‡	(†)	20.7!	(7.25)	12.3!	(5.63)	‡	(†)	‡	(†)	‡	(†)	‡	(†)	‡	(†)
Thai	16.1	(3.99)	45.7	(12.39)	‡	(†)	‡	(†)	‡	(†)	‡	(†)	‡	(†)	‡	(†)	‡	(†)
Vietnamese	14.5	(1.13)	29.4	(3.46)	18.9	(2.97)	17.9	(3.29)	12.8	(3.00)	6.1	(1.13)	6.0	(1.61)	7.3!	(2.41)	‡	(†)
Other Southeast Asian[7]	8.9!	(3.44)	‡	(†)	‡	(†)	‡	(†)	‡	(†)	7.6!	(3.66)	‡	(†)	‡	(†)	‡	(†)
Other Asian	8.3	(0.92)	24.1	(6.50)	19.1	(5.03)	21.3	(4.37)	20.9!	(6.81)	2.9	(0.63)	4.1	(0.98)	2.8!	(1.10)	‡	(†)
Pacific Islander	26.1	(3.03)	51.4	(10.01)	40.3	(5.91)	20.3	(4.89)	9.4!	(4.23)	14.3!	(4.88)	20.9!	(7.61)	‡	(†)	‡	(†)
American Indian/Alaska Native[8]	31.1	(1.22)	60.1	(3.71)	44.0	(2.39)	28.6	(1.80)	22.7	(2.80)	8.6	(1.28)	10.6	(1.83)	5.6!	(1.69)	‡	(†)
Amercian Indian	32.3	(1.33)	60.6	(3.96)	46.1	(2.81)	30.3	(2.06)	23.9	(3.10)	8.7	(1.43)	10.6	(2.00)	5.8!	(1.87)	‡	(†)
Alaska Native	23.3	(2.68)	44.9	(9.27)	34.2	(4.71)	10.8!	(3.64)	31.8!	(12.21)	‡	(†)	‡	(†)	‡	(†)	‡	(†)
Some other race[9]	16.8	(1.64)	48.5	(6.97)	21.1	(3.46)	16.9	(2.92)	14.8!	(5.99)	7.1	(1.50)	8.8	(2.35)	4.9!	(2.23)	‡	(†)
Two or more races	17.1	(0.39)	62.0	(2.48)	32.7	(1.17)	25.2	(1.07)	14.9	(1.10)	4.1	(0.26)	5.9	(0.45)	2.5	(0.35)	1.9	(0.41)

—Not available.
†Not applicable.
!Interpret data with caution. The coefficient of variation (CV) for this estimate is between 30 and 50 percent.
‡Reporting standards not met. Either there are too few cases for a reliable estimate or the coefficient of variation (CV) is 50 percent or greater.
[1]Parents include adoptive and stepparents, but exclude parents not residing in the same household as their children.
[2]Includes parents who completed high school through equivalency programs, such as a GED program.
[3]Includes parents with professional degrees.
[4]Includes other Central American subgroups not shown separately.
[5]Includes Taiwanese.
[6]In addition to the subgroups shown, also includes Sri Lankan.
[7]Consists of Indonesian and Malaysian.
[8]Includes persons reporting American Indian alone, persons reporting Alaska Native alone, and persons from American Indian and/or Alaska Native tribes specified or not specified.
[9]Respondents who wrote in some other race that was not included as an option on the questionnaire.
NOTE: Table includes only children under the age of 18 who resided with at least one of their parents (including an adoptive or stepparent). Respondents were interviewed throughout the given year and reported the income they received during the previous 12 months. Data are based on sample surveys of the entire population residing within the United States. Poverty status is determined by the Census Bureau using a set of money income thresholds that vary by family size and composition. For additional information about poverty status, see https://www.census.gov/topics/income-poverty/poverty/guidance/poverty-measures.html. Race categories exclude persons of Hispanic ethnicity.
SOURCE: U.S. Department of Commerce, Census Bureau, American Community Survey (ACS), 2010 and 2017. (This table was prepared November 2018.)

Table 103.10. Percentage of the population 3 to 34 years old enrolled in school, by sex, race/ethnicity, and age group: Selected years, 1980 through 2017

[Standard errors appear in parentheses]

Year and age group	Total: Total	Total: White	Total: Black	Total: Hispanic	Male: Total	Male: White	Male: Black	Male: Hispanic	Female: Total	Female: White	Female: Black	Female: Hispanic
1	2	3	4	5	6	7	8	9	10	11	12	13
1980												
Total, 3 to 34 years old	**49.7** (0.21)	**48.8** (0.24)	**54.0** (0.69)	**49.8** (1.40)	**50.9** (0.30)	**50.0** (0.34)	**56.2** (0.99)	**49.9** (2.00)	**48.5** (0.30)	**47.7** (0.34)	**52.1** (0.95)	**49.8** (1.98)
3 and 4 years old	36.7 (0.95)	37.4 (1.12)	38.2 (2.85)	28.5 (5.13)	37.8 (1.34)	39.2 (1.59)	36.4 (3.98)	30.1 (7.03)	35.5 (1.35)	35.5 (1.59)	40.0 (4.08)	26.6 (7.48)
5 and 6 years old	95.7 (0.40)	95.9 (0.46)	95.5 (1.23)	94.5 (2.79)	95.0 (0.61)	95.4 (0.68)	94.1 (1.97)	94.0 (4.21)	96.4 (0.53)	96.5 (0.62)	97.0 (1.45)	94.9 (3.70)
7 to 9 years old	99.1 (0.15)	99.1 (0.18)	99.4 (0.36)	98.4 (1.19)	99.0 (0.22)	99.0 (0.26)	99.5 (0.46)	97.7 (2.05)	99.2 (0.20)	99.2 (0.24)	99.3 (0.55)	99.0 (1.29)
10 to 13 years old	99.4 (0.10)	99.4 (0.12)	99.4 (0.31)	99.7 (0.47)	99.4 (0.14)	99.4 (0.16)	99.4 (0.43)	99.4 (0.86)	99.4 (0.15)	99.3 (0.18)	99.3 (0.46)	99.9 (0.32)
14 and 15 years old	98.2 (0.22)	98.7 (0.22)	97.9 (0.73)	94.3 (2.46)	98.7 (0.27)	98.9 (0.28)	98.4 (0.89)	96.7 (2.74)	97.7 (0.36)	98.5 (0.34)	97.3 (1.16)	92.1 (3.91)
16 and 17 years old	89.0 (0.51)	89.2 (0.57)	90.7 (1.46)	81.8 (4.25)	89.1 (0.71)	89.4 (0.80)	90.7 (2.06)	81.5 (6.15)	88.8 (0.73)	89.0 (0.83)	90.6 (2.06)	82.2 (5.88)
18 and 19 years old	46.4 (0.80)	47.0 (0.91)	45.8 (2.58)	37.8 (5.16)	47.0 (1.15)	48.5 (1.30)	42.9 (3.76)	36.9 (7.12)	45.8 (1.12)	45.7 (1.27)	48.3 (3.55)	38.8 (7.47)
20 and 21 years old	31.0 (0.75)	33.0 (0.86)	23.3 (2.23)	19.5 (4.31)	32.6 (1.09)	34.8 (1.24)	22.8 (3.32)	21.4 (6.39)	29.5 (1.02)	31.3 (1.18)	23.7 (3.02)	17.6! (5.80)
22 to 24 years old	16.3 (0.49)	16.8 (0.56)	13.6 (1.54)	11.7 (2.96)	17.8 (0.73)	18.7 (0.84)	13.4 (2.31)	10.7! (4.11)	14.9 (0.66)	15.0 (0.75)	13.7 (2.07)	12.6! (4.25)
25 to 29 years old	9.3 (0.31)	9.4 (0.35)	8.8 (1.05)	6.9 (1.88)	9.8 (0.46)	9.8 (0.51)	10.6 (1.71)	6.8! (2.70)	8.8 (0.42)	9.1 (0.48)	7.5 (1.31)	6.9! (2.61)
30 to 34 years old	6.4 (0.27)	6.4 (0.30)	6.9 (1.01)	5.1! (1.77)	5.9 (0.38)	5.6 (0.40)	7.2 (1.56)	6.2! (2.72)	7.0 (0.39)	7.2 (0.45)	6.6 (1.33)	‡ (†)
1990												
Total, 3 to 34 years old	**50.2** (0.23)	**49.8** (0.27)	**52.2** (0.71)	**47.2** (1.06)	**50.9** (0.32)	**50.4** (0.38)	**54.3** (1.02)	**46.8** (1.48)	**49.5** (0.32)	**49.2** (0.38)	**50.3** (0.99)	**47.7** (1.52)
3 and 4 years old	44.4 (0.99)	47.2 (1.19)	41.8 (2.97)	30.7 (4.08)	43.9 (1.38)	47.9 (1.66)	38.1 (4.14)	28.0 (5.57)	44.9 (1.41)	46.6 (1.70)	45.5 (4.25)	33.6 (5.95)
5 and 6 years old	96.5 (0.37)	96.7 (0.43)	96.5 (1.05)	94.9 (1.96)	96.5 (0.51)	96.8 (0.59)	96.2 (1.53)	95.8 (2.48)	96.4 (0.53)	96.7 (0.62)	96.9 (1.43)	93.9 (3.05)
7 to 9 years old	99.7 (0.09)	99.7 (0.11)	99.8 (0.19)	99.5 (0.52)	99.7 (0.13)	99.7 (0.16)	99.9 (0.24)	99.5 (0.70)	99.6 (0.14)	99.7 (0.15)	99.8 (0.31)	99.4 (0.79)
10 to 13 years old	99.6 (0.09)	99.7 (0.10)	99.9 (0.15)	99.1 (0.64)	99.6 (0.13)	99.6 (0.14)	99.9 (0.19)	99.0 (0.93)	99.7 (0.12)	99.7 (0.13)	99.8 (0.24)	99.1 (0.87)
14 and 15 years old	99.0 (0.19)	99.0 (0.23)	99.4 (0.46)	99.0 (0.90)	99.1 (0.25)	99.2 (0.30)	99.7 (0.48)	99.1 (1.10)	98.9 (0.29)	98.9 (0.35)	99.1 (0.79)	98.8 (1.47)
16 and 17 years old	92.5 (0.52)	93.5 (0.58)	91.7 (1.59)	85.4 (3.22)	92.6 (0.72)	93.4 (0.82)	93.0 (2.09)	85.5 (4.39)	92.4 (0.74)	93.7 (0.81)	90.5 (2.41)	85.3 (4.73)
18 and 19 years old	57.2 (0.94)	59.1 (1.11)	55.0 (2.83)	44.0 (4.36)	58.2 (1.33)	59.7 (1.56)	60.4 (3.99)	40.7 (6.23)	56.3 (1.32)	58.5 (1.57)	49.8 (3.96)	47.2 (6.08)
20 and 21 years old	39.7 (0.92)	43.1 (1.10)	28.3 (2.56)	27.2 (3.82)	40.3 (1.32)	44.2 (1.59)	31.0 (3.81)	21.7 (4.94)	39.2 (1.28)	42.0 (1.53)	25.8 (3.45)	33.1 (5.79)
22 to 24 years old	21.0 (0.63)	21.9 (0.75)	19.7 (2.01)	9.9 (2.05)	22.3 (0.92)	23.7 (1.11)	19.3 (3.03)	11.2 (2.98)	19.9 (0.86)	20.3 (1.02)	20.0 (2.68)	8.4! (2.77)
25 to 29 years old	9.7 (0.33)	10.4 (0.39)	6.1 (0.87)	6.3 (1.29)	9.2 (0.46)	10.0 (0.55)	4.7 (1.14)	4.6! (1.55)	10.2 (0.47)	10.7 (0.56)	7.3 (1.27)	8.1 (2.05)
30 to 34 years old	5.8 (0.25)	6.2 (0.30)	4.5 (0.75)	3.6 (0.99)	4.8 (0.33)	5.0 (0.38)	2.3! (0.80)	4.0! (1.45)	6.9 (0.38)	7.4 (0.46)	6.3 (1.19)	3.1! (1.32)
2000												
Total, 3 to 34 years old	**55.9** (0.22)	**56.0** (0.27)	**59.3** (0.59)	**51.3** (0.63)	**55.8** (0.31)	**55.8** (0.38)	**59.7** (0.85)	**50.5** (0.88)	**56.0** (0.31)	**56.1** (0.38)	**59.0** (0.83)	**52.2** (0.89)
3 and 4 years old[1]	52.1 (0.93)	54.6 (1.19)	59.8 (2.50)	35.9 (2.36)	50.8 (1.30)	54.1 (1.66)	58.0 (3.53)	31.9 (3.23)	53.4 (1.32)	55.2 (1.70)	61.8 (3.55)	40.0 (3.43)
5 and 6 years old	95.6 (0.38)	95.5 (0.49)	96.7 (0.89)	94.3 (1.13)	95.1 (0.56)	94.5 (0.76)	96.0 (1.38)	95.4 (1.41)	96.1 (0.51)	96.4 (0.63)	97.5 (1.12)	93.1 (1.79)
7 to 9 years old	98.1 (0.20)	98.4 (0.24)	97.5 (0.61)	97.5 (0.65)	98.0 (0.29)	98.1 (0.36)	98.2 (0.72)	96.6 (1.09)	98.2 (0.28)	98.6 (0.32)	96.7 (1.01)	98.4 (0.74)
10 to 13 years old	98.3 (0.17)	98.5 (0.19)	98.5 (0.42)	97.4 (0.59)	98.3 (0.23)	98.2 (0.30)	98.8 (0.52)	98.4 (0.65)	98.3 (0.24)	98.8 (0.25)	98.1 (0.66)	96.4 (1.01)
14 and 15 years old	98.7 (0.20)	98.9 (0.22)	99.6 (0.30)	96.2 (0.99)	98.7 (0.27)	98.8 (0.33)	99.6 (0.42)	96.9 (1.26)	98.6 (0.29)	99.0 (0.31)	99.6 (0.42)	95.4 (1.54)
16 and 17 years old	92.8 (0.45)	94.0 (0.50)	91.7 (1.32)	87.0 (1.77)	92.7 (0.63)	94.7 (0.66)	88.9 (2.09)	85.7 (2.60)	92.9 (0.64)	93.3 (0.76)	94.6 (1.54)	88.3 (2.40)
18 and 19 years old	61.2 (0.84)	63.9 (1.02)	57.2 (2.34)	49.5 (2.47)	58.3 (1.19)	61.2 (1.46)	51.5 (3.45)	48.0 (3.40)	64.2 (1.16)	66.7 (1.42)	62.2 (3.14)	51.1 (3.59)
20 and 21 years old	44.1 (0.88)	49.2 (1.10)	37.4 (2.38)	26.1 (2.22)	41.0 (1.23)	45.8 (1.54)	31.3 (3.42)	24.2 (3.02)	47.3 (1.26)	52.7 (1.58)	42.3 (3.26)	28.1 (3.26)
22 to 24 years old	24.6 (0.63)	24.9 (0.78)	24.0 (1.76)	18.2 (1.64)	23.9 (0.88)	25.0 (1.12)	22.0 (2.46)	15.2 (2.08)	25.3 (0.89)	24.8 (1.09)	25.8 (2.51)	21.6 (2.55)
25 to 29 years old	11.4 (0.37)	11.1 (0.45)	14.5 (1.18)	7.4 (0.88)	10.0 (0.50)	10.5 (0.62)	11.6 (1.63)	5.1 (1.06)	12.7 (0.53)	11.8 (0.65)	16.7 (1.66)	9.5 (1.38)
30 to 34 years old	6.7 (0.27)	6.1 (0.32)	9.9 (0.97)	5.6 (0.75)	5.6 (0.36)	4.7 (0.41)	8.5 (1.34)	5.7 (1.06)	7.7 (0.41)	7.4 (0.50)	11.2 (1.39)	5.5 (1.05)
2005												
Total, 3 to 34 years old	**56.5** (0.20)	**57.6** (0.26)	**58.5** (0.57)	**50.9** (0.53)	**55.8** (0.28)	**57.1** (0.37)	**58.8** (0.82)	**48.4** (0.73)	**57.2** (0.29)	**58.0** (0.37)	**58.1** (0.80)	**53.7** (0.76)
3 and 4 years old[1]	53.6 (0.86)	58.5 (1.14)	52.4 (2.39)	43.0 (2.07)	52.8 (1.21)	56.8 (1.61)	54.8 (3.42)	43.0 (2.91)	54.4 (1.23)	60.3 (1.63)	50.1 (3.32)	43.0 (2.96)
5 and 6 years old	95.4 (0.37)	95.9 (0.47)	95.9 (0.97)	93.8 (1.06)	94.8 (0.54)	95.4 (0.68)	94.8 (1.50)	92.4 (1.62)	96.1 (0.50)	96.3 (0.63)	97.1 (1.18)	95.3 (1.34)
7 to 9 years old	98.6 (0.17)	99.0 (0.19)	98.7 (0.45)	97.4 (0.58)	98.2 (0.27)	98.9 (0.27)	98.0 (0.81)	96.0 (1.00)	99.0 (0.20)	99.0 (0.27)	99.5 (0.41)	98.8 (0.57)
10 to 13 years old	98.6 (0.14)	99.0 (0.16)	98.5 (0.40)	97.9 (0.46)	98.4 (0.22)	99.1 (0.21)	97.6 (0.70)	97.2 (0.72)	98.9 (0.18)	98.8 (0.24)	99.5 (0.33)	98.6 (0.54)
14 and 15 years old	98.0 (0.22)	98.6 (0.24)	96.1 (0.83)	97.3 (0.70)	97.5 (0.34)	98.4 (0.35)	93.3 (1.52)	97.8 (0.90)	98.4 (0.28)	98.7 (0.33)	98.8 (0.66)	96.7 (1.09)
16 and 17 years old	95.1 (0.33)	96.1 (0.38)	93.6 (1.05)	92.6 (1.14)	95.1 (0.47)	95.9 (0.55)	93.6 (1.51)	92.5 (1.61)	95.1 (0.47)	96.3 (0.53)	93.6 (1.47)	92.6 (1.60)
18 and 19 years old	67.6 (0.79)	71.6 (0.95)	62.0 (2.30)	54.3 (2.33)	66.5 (1.11)	69.8 (1.35)	66.9 (3.20)	51.8 (3.22)	68.8 (1.12)	73.5 (1.34)	57.4 (3.27)	57.2 (3.37)
20 and 21 years old	48.7 (0.80)	54.4 (1.01)	37.9 (2.25)	30.0 (1.96)	45.3 (1.11)	50.5 (1.42)	35.5 (3.12)	25.2 (2.56)	52.3 (1.15)	58.5 (1.43)	40.4 (3.23)	35.3 (2.99)
22 to 24 years old	27.3 (0.59)	27.8 (0.76)	28.6 (1.75)	19.5 (1.41)	25.2 (0.83)	26.4 (1.07)	24.0 (2.45)	17.5 (1.85)	29.2 (0.85)	29.1 (1.09)	32.5 (2.45)	21.8 (2.17)
25 to 29 years old	11.9 (0.34)	12.5 (0.45)	11.9 (1.00)	7.8 (0.70)	9.6 (0.43)	10.2 (0.58)	9.1 (1.32)	5.6 (0.82)	14.2 (0.51)	14.7 (0.67)	14.2 (1.47)	10.4 (1.19)
30 to 34 years old	6.9 (0.27)	6.9 (0.34)	9.8 (0.94)	4.2 (0.54)	5.9 (0.35)	6.5 (0.47)	6.3 (1.15)	2.6 (0.58)	7.9 (0.40)	7.4 (0.50)	12.7 (1.42)	6.1 (0.94)

See notes at end of table.

Table 103.10. Percentage of the population 3 to 34 years old enrolled in school, by sex, race/ethnicity, and age group: Selected years, 1980 through 2017—Continued

[Standard errors appear in parentheses]

Year and age group	Total: Total	Total: White	Total: Black	Total: Hispanic	Male: Total	Male: White	Male: Black	Male: Hispanic	Female: Total	Female: White	Female: Black	Female: Hispanic
1	2	3	4	5	6	7	8	9	10	11	12	13
2010												
Total, 3 to 34 years old	**56.6** (0.17)	**56.1** (0.25)	**58.7** (0.58)	**55.1** (0.35)	**55.9** (0.23)	**55.5** (0.29)	**58.4** (0.78)	**52.9** (0.45)	**57.4** (0.26)	**56.7** (0.36)	**58.9** (0.77)	**57.4** (0.49)
3 and 4 years old[1]	53.2 (0.89)	56.1 (1.17)	57.2 (2.78)	44.2 (1.84)	53.0 (1.21)	55.9 (1.64)	57.0 (3.79)	43.3 (2.60)	53.4 (1.27)	56.3 (1.53)	57.4 (3.79)	45.0 (2.68)
5 and 6 years old	94.5 (0.46)	94.2 (0.66)	94.1 (1.12)	94.3 (0.96)	93.7 (0.69)	93.3 (1.04)	93.5 (1.94)	93.4 (1.31)	95.3 (0.54)	95.2 (0.77)	94.7 (1.38)	95.2 (1.20)
7 to 9 years old	97.7 (0.25)	97.4 (0.37)	96.9 (0.77)	98.5 (0.37)	97.6 (0.36)	97.1 (0.54)	97.3 (0.88)	98.1 (0.60)	98.0 (0.35)	97.7 (0.53)	96.5 (1.23)	98.9 (0.40)
10 to 13 years old	98.2 (0.21)	98.3 (0.26)	99.2 (0.41)	97.3 (0.54)	97.9 (0.30)	97.7 (0.42)	99.6 (0.37)	96.9 (0.77)	98.6 (0.26)	98.9 (0.24)	98.8 (0.74)	97.7 (0.61)
14 and 15 years old	98.1 (0.25)	98.0 (0.37)	98.8 (0.58)	97.9 (0.69)	98.0 (0.37)	98.0 (0.52)	98.4 (0.92)	97.5 (0.98)	98.3 (0.34)	98.1 (0.49)	99.3 (0.46)	98.3 (0.85)
16 and 17 years old	96.1 (0.33)	96.2 (0.47)	95.7 (0.82)	96.0 (0.83)	94.9 (0.51)	94.7 (0.74)	93.7 (1.41)	96.0 (1.17)	97.3 (0.38)	97.8 (0.47)	97.6 (0.95)	96.0 (1.10)
18 and 19 years old	69.2 (0.92)	71.0 (1.28)	62.9 (2.42)	66.2 (2.03)	66.9 (1.25)	67.8 (1.63)	62.3 (3.88)	64.9 (3.02)	71.5 (1.38)	74.3 (2.01)	63.4 (3.44)	67.6 (2.78)
20 and 21 years old	52.4 (1.08)	55.5 (1.28)	51.1 (2.93)	37.0 (2.34)	49.2 (1.31)	52.1 (1.76)	45.7 (4.18)	34.0 (3.08)	56.0 (1.47)	59.2 (1.78)	56.0 (3.84)	40.5 (3.36)
22 to 24 years old	28.9 (0.79)	29.1 (1.01)	29.8 (2.13)	23.8 (1.57)	27.0 (1.15)	27.8 (1.44)	29.5 (3.12)	18.6 (2.08)	30.8 (1.10)	30.4 (1.46)	30.0 (2.99)	29.2 (2.16)
25 to 29 years old	14.6 (0.47)	14.6 (0.64)	16.5 (1.34)	11.4 (0.90)	13.5 (0.65)	13.8 (0.84)	13.9 (2.06)	9.6 (1.21)	15.8 (0.66)	15.4 (0.88)	18.8 (1.97)	13.6 (1.44)
30 to 34 years old	8.3 (0.39)	8.5 (0.50)	11.0 (1.14)	5.7 (0.65)	6.7 (0.44)	7.2 (0.62)	6.6 (1.20)	4.9 (0.87)	9.9 (0.58)	9.8 (0.77)	14.8 (1.80)	6.6 (0.95)
2015												
Total, 3 to 34 years old	**55.2** (0.20)	**54.4** (0.25)	**55.4** (0.63)	**55.8** (0.38)	**54.9** (0.26)	**54.1** (0.36)	**55.7** (0.75)	**54.4** (0.48)	**55.6** (0.28)	**54.6** (0.35)	**55.0** (0.83)	**57.3** (0.54)
3 and 4 years old[1]	52.7 (1.02)	56.0 (1.26)	53.7 (2.90)	44.1 (2.24)	53.6 (1.40)	57.1 (1.75)	52.4 (3.57)	44.3 (2.88)	51.8 (1.55)	54.8 (1.97)	55.3 (4.34)	44.0 (3.08)
5 and 6 years old	94.2 (0.46)	94.1 (0.64)	94.7 (1.41)	93.7 (1.00)	93.5 (0.69)	93.2 (0.92)	93.3 (1.93)	93.6 (1.48)	94.9 (0.64)	95.1 (0.92)	96.1 (1.62)	93.9 (1.38)
7 to 9 years old	97.3 (0.28)	97.5 (0.35)	94.9 (1.16)	97.9 (0.49)	97.5 (0.34)	97.8 (0.42)	95.4 (1.31)	97.5 (0.72)	97.2 (0.41)	97.2 (0.58)	94.4 (1.63)	98.4 (0.59)
10 to 13 years old	98.0 (0.19)	98.1 (0.25)	98.6 (0.47)	97.1 (0.46)	98.3 (0.23)	98.3 (0.29)	100.0[2] (#)	97.3 (0.67)	97.6 (0.28)	97.9 (0.36)	97.2 (0.94)	96.9 (0.66)
14 and 15 years old	98.0 (0.27)	98.3 (0.32)	98.6 (0.68)	96.7 (0.74)	97.9 (0.37)	98.3 (0.42)	99.5 (0.50)	96.0 (1.17)	98.1 (0.38)	98.4 (0.48)	97.6 (1.30)	97.4 (0.96)
16 and 17 years old	93.7 (0.49)	94.4 (0.61)	95.1 (0.94)	92.6 (1.10)	93.1 (0.71)	93.8 (0.85)	94.1 (1.49)	91.7 (1.66)	94.4 (0.58)	95.0 (0.83)	96.0 (1.24)	93.7 (1.42)
18 and 19 years old	68.5 (0.86)	70.1 (1.05)	64.1 (2.91)	65.2 (2.20)	65.7 (1.39)	67.2 (1.66)	63.3 (4.43)	59.9 (3.30)	71.4 (1.19)	73.1 (1.60)	64.8 (3.86)	70.1 (2.74)
20 and 21 years old	53.3 (1.14)	55.5 (1.46)	43.1 (2.92)	48.8 (2.46)	50.2 (1.61)	53.3 (2.20)	38.0 (3.92)	44.4 (3.13)	56.5 (1.52)	57.7 (1.93)	47.9 (4.26)	53.2 (3.54)
22 to 24 years old	28.8 (0.81)	28.9 (1.02)	27.4 (2.11)	25.2 (1.67)	27.5 (1.07)	26.9 (1.33)	30.5 (3.24)	24.2 (2.51)	30.1 (1.25)	30.9 (1.43)	24.5 (3.07)	26.3 (2.69)
25 to 29 years old	13.2 (0.50)	13.1 (0.60)	13.7 (1.29)	11.2 (1.03)	11.7 (0.67)	12.3 (0.83)	10.9 (1.69)	9.2 (1.25)	14.6 (0.72)	14.0 (0.89)	16.3 (2.02)	13.2 (1.47)
30 to 34 years old	6.6 (0.30)	6.5 (0.35)	8.6 (1.05)	4.6 (0.61)	5.5 (0.39)	5.9 (0.48)	4.8 (1.37)	3.3 (0.77)	7.7 (0.44)	7.1 (0.55)	11.9 (1.57)	5.9 (1.02)
2016												
Total, 3 to 34 years old	**55.2** (0.21)	**54.1** (0.27)	**54.8** (0.60)	**56.8** (0.40)	**54.8** (0.26)	**53.8** (0.37)	**55.3** (0.86)	**55.4** (0.53)	**55.6** (0.27)	**54.4** (0.35)	**54.2** (0.77)	**58.3** (0.59)
3 and 4 years old[1]	53.8 (1.04)	55.5 (1.43)	51.5 (3.47)	49.5 (2.10)	54.1 (1.43)	56.6 (1.96)	49.6 (4.53)	50.7 (2.66)	53.5 (1.51)	54.3 (1.60)	53.5 (4.64)	48.2 (3.61)
5 and 6 years old	93.3 (0.58)	93.9 (0.68)	93.6 (1.60)	93.0 (1.30)	92.7 (0.84)	94.2 (0.90)	91.8 (2.55)	91.8 (2.04)	93.8 (0.75)	93.5 (1.03)	95.6 (1.78)	94.2 (1.39)
7 to 9 years old	97.8 (0.29)	98.0 (0.37)	97.9 (0.69)	97.0 (0.87)	97.5 (0.37)	98.0 (0.48)	97.2 (1.15)	96.3 (1.11)	98.1 (0.35)	97.9 (0.49)	98.6 (0.58)	97.6 (0.93)
10 to 13 years old	98.5 (0.17)	98.5 (0.23)	98.4 (0.43)	98.4 (0.35)	98.3 (0.25)	98.3 (0.37)	98.4 (0.55)	98.1 (0.51)	98.7 (0.20)	98.8 (0.29)	98.4 (0.67)	98.8 (0.38)
14 and 15 years old	98.0 (0.27)	98.7 (0.29)	95.6 (1.48)	97.6 (0.62)	98.7 (0.35)	98.8 (0.50)	98.8 (1.15)	98.4 (0.68)	97.3 (0.46)	98.6 (0.36)	92.3 (2.70)	96.8 (1.05)
16 and 17 years old	93.0 (0.55)	92.2 (0.81)	94.7 (1.27)	93.6 (0.89)	92.7 (0.81)	91.9 (1.19)	95.8 (1.66)	93.4 (1.29)	93.3 (0.70)	92.5 (1.02)	93.6 (1.74)	93.9 (1.32)
18 and 19 years old	69.5 (1.05)	70.4 (1.32)	66.2 (3.05)	68.4 (2.04)	68.2 (1.36)	69.4 (1.50)	65.8 (3.95)	66.3 (2.94)	70.7 (1.59)	71.6 (1.98)	66.7 (4.37)	70.5 (2.96)
20 and 21 years old	55.5 (1.12)	57.3 (1.47)	48.6 (3.34)	51.7 (2.25)	51.4 (1.53)	52.8 (2.06)	47.0 (4.27)	46.0 (3.12)	59.7 (1.49)	62.0 (1.83)	50.4 (4.53)	57.5 (3.39)
22 to 24 years old	28.8 (0.85)	27.7 (1.14)	29.0 (2.14)	26.7 (1.79)	27.6 (1.08)	26.8 (1.40)	26.6 (3.23)	23.4 (2.39)	30.0 (1.15)	28.5 (1.59)	31.3 (3.04)	30.2 (2.43)
25 to 29 years old	13.2 (0.46)	13.3 (0.57)	12.7 (1.29)	11.3 (0.99)	11.8 (0.57)	11.7 (0.69)	12.6 (1.68)	9.3 (1.37)	14.7 (0.68)	14.9 (0.83)	12.8 (1.82)	13.3 (1.36)
30 to 34 years old	6.4 (0.31)	6.6 (0.40)	7.6 (1.10)	4.7 (0.65)	5.5 (0.45)	5.5 (0.57)	6.9 (1.59)	3.6 (0.80)	7.2 (0.49)	7.8 (0.60)	8.3 (1.48)	5.9 (1.01)
2017												
Total, 3 to 34 years old	**54.6** (0.19)	**53.2** (0.26)	**55.0** (0.60)	**56.4** (0.40)	**54.0** (0.28)	**52.8** (0.35)	**54.9** (0.79)	**55.0** (0.51)	**55.2** (0.25)	**53.6** (0.34)	**55.0** (0.77)	**57.8** (0.57)
3 and 4 years old[1]	53.8 (1.08)	56.0 (1.41)	59.0 (3.08)	47.9 (2.22)	53.4 (1.39)	54.3 (1.82)	62.3 (3.95)	47.1 (2.70)	54.1 (1.48)	57.8 (2.07)	55.3 (4.06)	48.8 (3.11)
5 and 6 years old	93.5 (0.54)	93.0 (0.78)	91.0 (1.69)	95.0 (1.10)	92.8 (0.71)	92.5 (0.94)	89.4 (2.43)	94.6 (1.45)	94.2 (0.78)	93.5 (1.06)	92.8 (2.19)	95.5 (1.42)
7 to 9 years old	97.1 (0.30)	97.0 (0.40)	96.9 (0.75)	97.0 (0.58)	97.1 (0.43)	97.2 (0.52)	96.3 (1.16)	97.5 (0.75)	97.0 (0.38)	96.8 (0.57)	97.5 (1.02)	96.5 (0.85)
10 to 13 years old	97.8 (0.21)	97.8 (0.29)	98.7 (0.47)	97.3 (0.44)	97.8 (0.28)	97.9 (0.41)	98.7 (0.70)	97.4 (0.59)	97.8 (0.32)	97.6 (0.42)	98.8 (0.64)	97.3 (0.69)
14 and 15 years old	98.2 (0.25)	98.5 (0.33)	96.3 (1.19)	98.4 (0.55)	98.2 (0.40)	98.6 (0.45)	95.1 (1.91)	98.2 (0.90)	98.3 (0.35)	98.4 (0.46)	97.5 (1.30)	98.6 (0.73)
16 and 17 years old	92.9 (0.55)	93.3 (0.65)	90.4 (1.54)	92.7 (1.17)	92.3 (0.73)	92.8 (0.88)	87.9 (2.11)	91.7 (1.68)	93.5 (0.68)	93.8 (0.86)	92.9 (2.11)	93.6 (1.46)
18 and 19 years old	68.2 (1.08)	67.8 (1.42)	67.8 (2.98)	67.2 (2.22)	65.1 (1.40)	65.4 (1.87)	65.3 (4.19)	63.3 (2.91)	71.3 (1.53)	70.3 (1.87)	70.2 (4.04)	71.1 (3.14)
20 and 21 years old	55.0 (1.13)	58.1 (1.53)	47.8 (2.87)	46.0 (2.57)	50.8 (1.63)	54.6 (2.12)	42.4 (4.23)	40.9 (3.39)	59.2 (1.45)	61.8 (2.02)	53.7 (4.16)	50.7 (3.07)
22 to 24 years old	28.4 (0.92)	27.2 (1.19)	28.1 (2.59)	25.9 (1.84)	26.8 (1.15)	25.9 (1.46)	24.7 (3.50)	23.0 (2.43)	30.0 (1.26)	28.4 (1.62)	30.9 (3.45)	29.2 (2.71)
25 to 29 years old	12.1 (0.45)	11.3 (0.57)	13.4 (1.33)	12.3 (0.92)	10.9 (0.64)	10.5 (0.81)	11.8 (2.01)	9.9 (1.28)	13.4 (0.63)	12.1 (0.74)	15.0 (1.87)	14.7 (1.51)
30 to 34 years old	5.9 (0.31)	5.8 (0.38)	7.7 (0.97)	4.8 (0.65)	5.2 (0.40)	5.0 (0.44)	6.3 (1.39)	5.0 (0.95)	6.5 (0.45)	6.6 (0.54)	8.9 (1.44)	4.6 (0.84)

†Not applicable.
#Rounds to zero.
!Interpret data with caution. The coefficient of variation (CV) for this estimate is between 30 and 50 percent.
‡Reporting standards not met. The coefficient of variation (CV) for this estimate is 50 percent or greater.
[1]Beginning in 1994, preprimary enrollment data were collected using new procedures. Data may not be comparable to figures for earlier years.
[2]Rounds to 100.0.
NOTE: Data are based on sample surveys of the civilian noninstitutionalized population, which excludes persons in the military and persons living in institutions (e.g., prisons or nursing facilities). Includes enrollment in any type of graded public, parochial, or other private schools. Includes nursery schools, preschools, kindergartens, elementary and secondary schools, colleges, universities, and professional schools. Attendance may be on either a full-time or part-time basis and during the day or night. Prior to 2010, standard errors were computed using generalized variance function methodology rather than the more precise replicate weight methodology used in later years. Total includes persons from other racial/ethnic groups not shown separately. Race categories exclude persons of Hispanic ethnicity.
SOURCE: U.S. Department of Commerce, Census Bureau, Current Population Survey (CPS), October, selected years, 1980 through 2017. (This table was prepared January 2019.)

Table 103.20. Percentage of the population 3 to 34 years old enrolled in school, by age group: Selected years, 1940 through 2017

[Standard errors appear in parentheses]

Year	Total, 3 to 34 years old	3 and 4 years old	5 and 6 years old	7 to 13 years old	14 to 17 years old: Total	14 to 17 years old: 14 and 15	14 to 17 years old: 16 and 17	18 and 19 years old: Total	18 and 19 years old: In secondary education	18 and 19 years old: In higher education	20 to 24 years old: Total	20 to 24 years old: 20 and 21	20 to 24 years old: 22 to 24	25 to 29 years old	30 to 34 years old
1	2	3	4	5	6	7	8	9	10	11	12	13	14	15	16
1940	— (†)	— (†)	— (†)	95.0 (—)	79.3 (—)	— (†)	— (†)	28.9 (—)	— (†)	— (†)	6.6 (—)	— (†)	— (†)	— (†)	— (†)
1945	— (†)	— (†)	— (†)	98.1 (—)	78.4 (—)	— (†)	— (†)	20.7 (—)	— (†)	— (†)	3.9 (—)	— (†)	— (†)	— (†)	— (†)
1947	— (†)	— (†)	73.8 (—)	98.5 (—)	79.3 (—)	91.6 (—)	67.6 (—)	24.3 (—)	— (†)	— (†)	10.2 (—)	— (†)	— (†)	3.0 (—)	1.0 (—)
1948	— (†)	— (†)	74.7 (—)	98.1 (—)	81.8 (—)	92.7 (—)	71.2 (—)	26.9 (—)	— (†)	— (†)	9.7 (—)	— (†)	— (†)	2.6 (—)	0.9 (—)
1949	— (†)	— (†)	76.2 (—)	98.6 (—)	81.6 (—)	93.5 (—)	69.5 (—)	25.3 (—)	— (†)	— (†)	9.2 (—)	— (†)	— (†)	3.8 (—)	1.1 (—)
1950	— (†)	— (†)	74.4 (—)	98.7 (—)	83.7 (—)	94.7 (—)	71.3 (—)	29.4 (—)	— (†)	— (†)	9.0 (—)	— (†)	— (†)	3.0 (—)	0.9 (—)
1951	— (†)	— (†)	73.6 (—)	99.1 (—)	85.2 (—)	94.8 (—)	75.1 (—)	26.2 (—)	— (†)	— (†)	8.6 (—)	— (†)	— (†)	2.5 (—)	0.7 (—)
1952	— (†)	— (†)	75.2 (—)	98.8 (—)	85.2 (—)	96.2 (—)	73.4 (—)	28.8 (—)	— (†)	— (†)	9.7 (—)	— (†)	— (†)	2.6 (—)	1.2 (—)
1953	— (†)	— (†)	78.6 (—)	99.4 (—)	85.9 (—)	96.5 (—)	74.7 (—)	31.2 (—)	— (†)	— (†)	11.1 (—)	— (†)	— (†)	2.9 (—)	1.7 (—)
1954	— (†)	— (†)	77.3 (—)	99.4 (—)	87.1 (—)	95.8 (—)	78.0 (—)	32.4 (—)	— (†)	— (†)	11.2 (—)	— (†)	— (†)	4.1 (—)	1.5 (—)
1955	— (†)	— (†)	78.1 (—)	99.2 (—)	86.9 (—)	95.9 (—)	77.4 (—)	31.5 (—)	— (†)	— (†)	11.1 (—)	— (†)	— (†)	4.2 (—)	1.6 (—)
1956	— (†)	— (†)	77.6 (—)	99.3 (—)	88.2 (—)	96.9 (—)	78.4 (—)	35.4 (—)	— (†)	— (†)	12.8 (—)	— (†)	— (†)	5.1 (—)	1.9 (—)
1957	— (†)	— (†)	78.6 (—)	99.5 (—)	89.5 (—)	97.1 (—)	80.5 (—)	34.9 (—)	— (†)	— (†)	14.0 (—)	— (†)	— (†)	5.5 (—)	1.8 (—)
1958	— (†)	— (†)	80.4 (—)	99.5 (—)	89.2 (—)	96.9 (—)	80.6 (—)	37.6 (—)	— (†)	— (†)	13.4 (—)	— (†)	— (†)	5.7 (—)	2.2 (—)
1959	— (†)	— (†)	80.0 (—)	99.4 (—)	90.2 (—)	97.5 (—)	82.9 (—)	36.8 (—)	— (†)	— (†)	12.7 (—)	18.8 (—)	8.6 (—)	5.1 (—)	2.2 (—)
1960	— (†)	— (†)	80.7 (—)	99.5 (—)	90.3 (—)	97.8 (—)	82.6 (—)	38.4 (—)	— (†)	— (†)	13.1 (—)	19.4 (—)	8.7 (—)	4.9 (—)	2.4 (—)
1961	— (†)	— (†)	81.7 (—)	99.3 (—)	91.4 (—)	97.6 (—)	83.6 (—)	38.0 (—)	— (†)	— (†)	13.7 (—)	21.5 (—)	8.4 (—)	4.4 (—)	2.0 (—)
1962	— (†)	— (†)	82.2 (—)	99.3 (—)	92.0 (—)	98.0 (—)	84.3 (—)	41.8 (—)	— (†)	— (†)	15.6 (—)	23.0 (—)	10.3 (—)	5.0 (—)	2.6 (—)
1963	— (†)	— (†)	82.7 (—)	99.3 (—)	92.9 (—)	98.4 (—)	87.1 (—)	40.9 (—)	10.9 (—)	29.8 (—)	17.3 (—)	25.0 (—)	11.4 (—)	4.9 (—)	2.5 (—)
1964[1]	— (†)	9.5 (—)	83.3 (—)	99.0 (—)	93.1 (—)	98.6 (—)	87.7 (—)	41.6 (—)	11.0 (—)	30.6 (—)	16.8 (—)	26.3 (—)	9.9 (—)	5.2 (—)	2.6 (—)
1965	55.5 (—)	10.6 (—)	84.9 (—)	99.4 (—)	93.2 (—)	98.9 (—)	87.4 (—)	46.3 (—)	11.2 (—)	35.0 (—)	19.0 (—)	27.6 (—)	13.2 (—)	6.1 (—)	3.2 (—)
1966	56.1 (—)	12.5 (—)	85.8 (—)	99.3 (—)	93.7 (—)	98.6 (—)	88.5 (—)	47.2 (—)	10.8 (—)	36.3 (—)	19.9 (—)	29.9 (—)	13.2 (—)	6.5 (—)	2.7 (—)
1967	56.6 (—)	14.2 (—)	87.4 (—)	99.3 (—)	93.7 (—)	98.2 (—)	88.8 (—)	47.6 (—)	11.7 (—)	36.0 (—)	22.0 (—)	33.3 (—)	13.6 (—)	6.6 (—)	4.0 (—)
1968	56.7 (—)	15.7 (—)	87.6 (—)	99.1 (—)	94.2 (—)	98.0 (—)	90.2 (—)	50.4 (—)	12.4 (—)	38.0 (—)	21.4 (—)	31.2 (—)	13.8 (—)	7.0 (—)	3.9 (—)
1969	57.0 (—)	16.1 (—)	88.4 (—)	99.2 (—)	94.0 (—)	98.1 (—)	89.7 (—)	50.2 (—)	11.2 (—)	39.0 (—)	23.0 (—)	34.1 (—)	15.4 (—)	7.9 (—)	4.8 (—)
1970	56.4 (0.22)	20.5 (0.74)	89.5 (0.54)	99.2 (0.08)	94.1 (0.27)	98.1 (0.22)	90.0 (0.50)	47.7 (0.87)	10.5 (0.53)	37.3 (0.84)	21.5 (0.48)	31.9 (0.87)	14.9 (0.53)	7.5 (0.33)	4.2 (0.27)
1971	56.2 (0.22)	21.2 (0.76)	91.6 (0.50)	99.1 (0.08)	94.5 (0.26)	98.6 (0.19)	90.2 (0.49)	49.2 (0.85)	11.5 (0.54)	37.7 (0.83)	21.9 (0.47)	32.2 (0.85)	15.4 (0.52)	8.0 (0.33)	4.9 (0.29)
1972	54.9 (0.22)	24.4 (0.81)	91.9 (0.51)	99.2 (0.08)	93.3 (0.28)	97.6 (0.24)	88.9 (0.51)	46.3 (0.84)	10.4 (0.51)	35.9 (0.81)	21.6 (0.46)	31.4 (0.81)	14.8 (0.51)	8.6 (0.34)	4.6 (0.28)
1973	53.5 (0.22)	24.2 (0.80)	92.5 (0.50)	99.2 (0.08)	92.9 (0.29)	97.5 (0.25)	88.3 (0.52)	42.9 (0.82)	10.0 (0.50)	32.9 (0.78)	20.8 (0.44)	30.1 (0.79)	14.5 (0.50)	8.5 (0.33)	4.5 (0.27)
1974	53.6 (0.22)	28.8 (0.85)	94.2 (0.44)	99.3 (0.08)	92.9 (0.29)	97.9 (0.23)	87.9 (0.52)	43.1 (0.81)	9.9 (0.49)	33.2 (0.77)	21.4 (0.45)	30.2 (0.77)	15.1 (0.51)	9.6 (0.34)	5.7 (0.29)
1975	53.7 (0.22)	31.5 (0.89)	94.7 (0.42)	99.3 (0.08)	93.6 (0.27)	98.2 (0.21)	89.0 (0.50)	46.9 (0.81)	10.2 (0.49)	36.7 (0.78)	22.4 (0.45)	31.2 (0.77)	16.2 (0.52)	10.1 (0.34)	6.6 (0.31)
1976	53.1 (0.21)	31.3 (0.91)	95.5 (0.38)	99.2 (0.09)	93.7 (0.27)	98.2 (0.21)	89.1 (0.50)	46.2 (0.80)	10.2 (0.49)	36.0 (0.77)	23.3 (0.45)	32.0 (0.77)	17.1 (0.52)	10.0 (0.33)	6.0 (0.29)
1977	52.5 (0.21)	32.0 (0.94)	95.8 (0.38)	99.4 (0.07)	93.7 (0.28)	98.5 (0.20)	88.9 (0.50)	46.2 (0.80)	10.4 (0.49)	35.7 (0.77)	22.9 (0.44)	31.8 (0.76)	16.5 (0.51)	10.8 (0.34)	6.9 (0.30)
1978	51.2 (0.21)	34.2 (0.95)	95.3 (0.42)	99.1 (0.09)	93.7 (0.28)	98.4 (0.20)	89.1 (0.50)	45.4 (0.80)	9.8 (0.48)	35.6 (0.77)	21.8 (0.43)	29.5 (0.74)	16.3 (0.50)	9.4 (0.32)	6.4 (0.28)
1979	50.3 (0.21)	35.1 (0.95)	95.8 (0.40)	99.2 (0.09)	93.6 (0.28)	98.1 (0.22)	89.2 (0.50)	45.0 (0.80)	10.3 (0.49)	34.6 (0.76)	21.7 (0.43)	30.2 (0.74)	15.8 (0.49)	9.6 (0.32)	6.4 (0.28)
1980	49.7 (0.21)	36.7 (0.95)	95.7 (0.40)	99.3 (0.09)	93.4 (0.29)	98.2 (0.22)	89.0 (0.51)	46.4 (0.80)	10.5 (0.49)	35.9 (0.77)	22.3 (0.43)	31.0 (0.75)	16.3 (0.49)	9.3 (0.31)	6.4 (0.27)
1981	48.9 (0.21)	36.0 (0.93)	94.0 (0.46)	99.2 (0.09)	94.1 (0.28)	98.0 (0.24)	90.6 (0.47)	49.0 (0.81)	11.5 (0.51)	37.5 (0.78)	22.5 (0.42)	31.6 (0.74)	16.5 (0.48)	9.0 (0.30)	6.9 (0.27)
1982	48.6 (0.22)	36.4 (0.97)	95.0 (0.45)	99.2 (0.10)	94.4 (0.29)	98.5 (0.22)	90.6 (0.51)	47.8 (0.86)	11.3 (0.54)	36.5 (0.83)	23.5 (0.45)	34.0 (0.81)	16.8 (0.51)	9.6 (0.32)	6.3 (0.28)
1983	48.4 (0.22)	37.5 (0.96)	95.4 (0.43)	99.2 (0.10)	95.0 (0.28)	98.3 (0.23)	91.7 (0.50)	50.4 (0.87)	12.8 (0.58)	37.6 (0.84)	22.7 (0.45)	32.5 (0.80)	16.6 (0.51)	9.6 (0.32)	6.4 (0.28)
1984	47.9 (0.22)	36.3 (0.94)	94.5 (0.46)	99.2 (0.10)	94.7 (0.29)	97.8 (0.26)	91.5 (0.51)	50.1 (0.89)	11.5 (0.57)	38.6 (0.87)	23.7 (0.46)	33.9 (0.82)	17.3 (0.52)	9.1 (0.30)	6.3 (0.27)
1985	48.3 (0.22)	38.9 (0.95)	96.1 (0.38)	99.2 (0.09)	94.9 (0.28)	98.1 (0.24)	91.7 (0.50)	51.6 (0.91)	11.2 (0.57)	40.4 (0.89)	24.0 (0.47)	35.3 (0.84)	16.9 (0.52)	9.2 (0.31)	6.1 (0.26)
1986	48.2 (0.22)	38.9 (0.95)	95.3 (0.41)	99.2 (0.10)	94.9 (0.28)	97.6 (0.28)	92.3 (0.48)	54.6 (0.91)	13.1 (0.62)	41.5 (0.90)	23.6 (0.47)	33.0 (0.84)	17.9 (0.54)	8.8 (0.30)	6.0 (0.25)
1987	48.6 (0.22)	38.3 (0.95)	95.1 (0.42)	99.5 (0.07)	95.0 (0.28)	98.6 (0.22)	91.7 (0.49)	55.6 (0.90)	13.1 (0.61)	42.5 (0.90)	25.5 (0.49)	38.7 (0.89)	17.5 (0.54)	9.0 (0.30)	5.8 (0.25)
1988	48.7 (0.24)	38.2 (1.02)	96.0 (0.41)	99.7 (0.07)	95.1 (0.31)	98.9 (0.22)	91.6 (0.55)	55.6 (0.98)	13.9 (0.68)	41.8 (0.97)	26.1 (0.54)	39.1 (0.98)	18.2 (0.60)	8.3 (0.32)	5.9 (0.27)
1989	49.0 (0.23)	39.1 (0.97)	95.2 (0.43)	99.3 (0.09)	95.7 (0.28)	98.8 (0.21)	92.7 (0.50)	56.0 (0.92)	14.4 (0.65)	41.6 (0.91)	27.0 (0.53)	38.5 (0.94)	19.9 (0.60)	9.3 (0.32)	5.7 (0.25)
1990	50.2 (0.23)	44.4 (0.99)	96.5 (0.37)	99.6 (0.06)	95.8 (0.28)	99.0 (0.19)	92.5 (0.52)	57.2 (0.94)	14.5 (0.67)	42.7 (0.94)	28.6 (0.54)	39.7 (0.92)	21.0 (0.63)	9.7 (0.33)	5.8 (0.25)
1991	50.7 (0.23)	40.5 (0.96)	95.4 (0.41)	99.6 (0.06)	96.0 (0.27)	98.8 (0.22)	93.3 (0.49)	59.6 (0.96)	15.6 (0.71)	44.0 (0.97)	30.2 (0.55)	42.0 (0.92)	22.2 (0.64)	10.2 (0.34)	6.2 (0.26)
1992	51.4 (0.23)	39.7 (0.95)	95.5 (0.41)	99.4 (0.08)	96.7 (0.25)	99.1 (0.18)	94.1 (0.46)	61.4 (0.96)	17.1 (0.74)	44.3 (0.98)	31.6 (0.56)	44.0 (0.95)	23.7 (0.65)	9.8 (0.34)	6.1 (0.26)
1993	51.8 (0.23)	40.4 (0.93)	95.4 (0.41)	99.5 (0.07)	96.5 (0.25)	98.9 (0.20)	94.0 (0.46)	61.6 (0.95)	17.2 (0.74)	44.4 (0.97)	30.8 (0.56)	42.7 (0.97)	23.6 (0.65)	10.2 (0.35)	5.9 (0.25)
1994	53.3 (0.23)	47.3[2] (0.94)	96.7 (0.34)	99.4 (0.08)	96.6 (0.24)	98.8 (0.20)	94.4 (0.43)	60.2 (0.94)	16.2 (0.70)	43.9 (0.95)	32.0 (0.55)	44.9 (0.95)	24.0 (0.64)	10.8 (0.36)	6.7 (0.27)

See notes at end of table.

Table 103.20. Percentage of the population 3 to 34 years old enrolled in school, by age group: Selected years, 1940 through 2017—Continued

[Standard errors appear in parentheses]

Year	Total, 3 to 34 years old	3 and 4 years old	5 and 6 years old	7 to 13 years old	14 to 17 years old			18 and 19 years old			20 to 24 years old			25 to 29 years old	30 to 34 years old
					Total	14 and 15	16 and 17	Total	In secondary education	In higher education	Total	20 and 21	22 to 24		
1	2	3	4	5	6	7	8	9	10	11	12	13	14	15	16
1995	53.7 (0.21)	48.7[2] (0.87)	96.0 (0.34)	98.9 (0.10)	96.3 (0.23)	98.9 (0.18)	93.6 (0.42)	59.4 (0.86)	16.3 (0.64)	43.1 (0.86)	31.5 (0.52)	44.9 (0.90)	23.2 (0.60)	11.6 (0.34)	5.9 (0.24)
1996	54.1 (0.22)	48.3[2] (0.91)	94.0 (0.43)	97.7 (0.15)	95.4 (0.26)	98.0 (0.24)	92.8 (0.45)	61.5 (0.87)	16.7 (0.67)	44.9 (0.89)	32.5 (0.55)	44.4 (0.93)	24.8 (0.65)	11.9 (0.36)	6.1 (0.25)
1997	55.6 (0.22)	52.6[2] (0.92)	96.5 (0.33)	99.1 (0.09)	96.6 (0.22)	98.9 (0.18)	94.3 (0.40)	61.5 (0.86)	16.7 (0.66)	44.7 (0.88)	34.3 (0.55)	45.9 (0.91)	26.4 (0.66)	11.8 (0.36)	5.7 (0.25)
1998	55.8 (0.22)	52.1[2] (0.92)	95.6 (0.37)	98.9 (0.10)	96.1 (0.24)	98.4 (0.22)	93.9 (0.41)	62.2 (0.84)	15.7 (0.63)	46.4 (0.86)	33.0 (0.54)	44.8 (0.91)	24.9 (0.65)	11.9 (0.36)	6.6 (0.27)
1999	56.0 (0.22)	54.2[2] (0.93)	96.0 (0.36)	98.7 (0.11)	95.8 (0.24)	98.2 (0.23)	93.6 (0.42)	60.6 (0.84)	16.5 (0.64)	44.1 (0.85)	32.8 (0.54)	45.3 (0.90)	24.5 (0.64)	11.1 (0.36)	6.2 (0.27)
2000	55.9 (0.22)	52.1[2] (0.93)	95.6 (0.38)	98.2 (0.13)	95.7 (0.25)	98.7 (0.20)	92.8 (0.45)	61.2 (0.84)	16.5 (0.64)	44.7 (0.85)	32.5 (0.53)	44.1 (0.88)	24.6 (0.63)	11.4 (0.37)	6.7 (0.27)
2001	56.4 (0.20)	52.4[2] (0.88)	95.3 (0.37)	98.3 (0.12)	95.8 (0.23)	98.1 (0.22)	93.4 (0.40)	61.1 (0.79)	17.1 (0.61)	44.0 (0.80)	34.1 (0.50)	46.1 (0.82)	25.5 (0.61)	11.8 (0.36)	6.9 (0.26)
2002	56.2 (0.20)	56.3[2] (0.89)	95.5 (0.37)	98.3 (0.12)	96.4 (0.21)	98.4 (0.20)	94.3 (0.37)	63.3 (0.79)	18.0 (0.63)	45.3 (0.82)	34.4 (0.50)	47.8 (0.83)	25.6 (0.59)	12.1 (0.35)	6.6 (0.25)
2003	56.2 (0.20)	55.1[2] (0.85)	94.5 (0.40)	98.3 (0.12)	96.2 (0.21)	97.5 (0.25)	94.9 (0.34)	64.5 (0.80)	17.9 (0.64)	46.6 (0.84)	35.6 (0.50)	48.3 (0.83)	27.8 (0.59)	11.8 (0.34)	6.8 (0.26)
2004	56.2 (0.20)	54.0[2] (0.85)	95.4 (0.37)	98.4 (0.12)	96.5 (0.21)	98.5 (0.19)	94.5 (0.36)	64.4 (0.80)	16.6 (0.62)	47.8 (0.83)	35.2 (0.49)	48.9 (0.82)	26.3 (0.58)	13.0 (0.35)	6.6 (0.26)
2005	56.5 (0.20)	53.6[2] (0.86)	95.4 (0.37)	98.6 (0.11)	96.5 (0.20)	98.0 (0.22)	95.1 (0.33)	67.6 (0.79)	18.3 (0.65)	49.3 (0.84)	36.1 (0.49)	48.7 (0.80)	27.3 (0.59)	11.9 (0.34)	6.9 (0.27)
2006	56.0 (0.20)	55.7[2] (0.86)	94.6 (0.39)	98.3 (0.12)	96.4 (0.21)	98.3 (0.21)	94.6 (0.36)	65.5 (0.77)	19.3 (0.64)	46.2 (0.81)	35.0 (0.49)	47.5 (0.81)	26.7 (0.58)	11.7 (0.33)	7.2 (0.27)
2007	56.1 (0.20)	54.5[2] (0.86)	94.7 (0.39)	98.4 (0.12)	96.4 (0.21)	98.7 (0.18)	94.3 (0.36)	66.8 (0.75)	17.9 (0.61)	48.9 (0.80)	35.7 (0.49)	48.4 (0.81)	27.3 (0.59)	12.4 (0.33)	7.2 (0.27)
2008	56.2 (0.20)	52.8[2] (0.85)	93.8 (0.42)	98.7 (0.11)	96.8 (0.20)	98.6 (0.19)	95.2 (0.34)	66.0 (0.75)	17.4 (0.60)	48.6 (0.79)	36.9 (0.49)	50.1 (0.81)	28.2 (0.59)	13.2 (0.34)	7.3 (0.27)
2009	56.5 (0.20)	52.4[2] (0.85)	94.1 (0.40)	98.2 (0.12)	96.3 (0.22)	98.0 (0.23)	94.6 (0.36)	68.9 (0.73)	19.1 (0.62)	49.8 (0.79)	38.7 (0.50)	51.7 (0.81)	30.4 (0.60)	13.5 (0.34)	8.1 (0.28)
2010	56.6 (0.17)	53.2[2] (0.89)	94.5 (0.46)	98.0 (0.16)	97.1 (0.21)	98.1 (0.25)	96.1 (0.33)	69.2 (0.92)	18.1 (0.71)	51.2 (1.05)	38.6 (0.71)	52.4 (1.08)	28.9 (0.79)	14.6 (0.47)	8.3 (0.39)
2011	56.8 (0.19)	52.4[2] (0.90)	95.1 (0.43)	98.3 (0.14)	97.1 (0.22)	98.6 (0.21)	95.7 (0.38)	71.1 (0.95)	21.0 (0.78)	50.1 (1.08)	39.9 (0.68)	52.7 (1.05)	31.1 (0.82)	14.8 (0.44)	7.7 (0.32)
2012	56.6 (0.22)	53.5[2] (1.11)	93.2 (0.49)	98.0 (0.17)	97.0 (0.28)	98.2 (0.31)	95.8 (0.40)	69.0 (0.98)	21.7 (0.77)	47.3 (0.96)	40.2 (0.72)	54.0 (1.04)	30.7 (0.84)	14.0 (0.48)	7.5 (0.33)
2013	55.8 (0.18)	54.9[2] (1.00)	93.8 (0.45)	98.1 (0.16)	96.1 (0.28)	98.4 (0.27)	93.7 (0.50)	67.1 (0.97)	20.5 (0.80)	46.6 (1.00)	38.7 (0.76)	52.8 (1.24)	29.7 (0.81)	13.3 (0.44)	6.7 (0.32)
2014	55.2 (0.21)	54.5[2] (0.98)	93.4 (0.53)	97.6 (0.19)	95.4 (0.29)	97.8 (0.26)	92.9 (0.51)	68.4 (0.92)	19.6 (0.79)	48.9 (1.09)	38.0 (0.76)	51.4 (1.24)	29.6 (0.80)	13.1 (0.44)	6.4 (0.31)
2015	55.2 (0.20)	52.7[2] (1.02)	94.2 (0.46)	97.7 (0.17)	95.9 (0.28)	98.0 (0.27)	93.7 (0.49)	68.5 (0.86)	19.8 (0.79)	48.8 (0.98)	38.5 (0.80)	53.3 (1.14)	28.8 (0.81)	13.2 (0.50)	6.6 (0.30)
2016	55.2 (0.21)	53.8[2] (1.04)	93.3 (0.58)	98.2 (0.15)	95.5 (0.30)	98.0 (0.27)	93.0 (0.55)	69.5 (1.05)	19.0 (0.76)	50.5 (1.15)	39.0 (0.78)	55.5 (1.12)	28.8 (0.85)	13.2 (0.46)	6.4 (0.31)
2017	54.6 (0.19)	53.8[2] (1.08)	93.5 (0.54)	97.5 (0.20)	95.5 (0.31)	98.2 (0.25)	92.9 (0.55)	68.2 (1.08)	20.2 (0.85)	48.0 (1.21)	38.8 (0.71)	55.0 (1.13)	28.4 (0.92)	12.1 (0.45)	5.9 (0.31)

—Not available.
†Not applicable.
[1]It is not possible to compute a 1964 enrollment percentage for the total 3- to 34-year-old population because, although enrollment percentages are available for each component age group, underlying data on population size are not available for 3- and 4-year-olds.
[2]Beginning in 1994, preprimary enrollment data were collected using new procedures. Data may not be comparable to figures for earlier years.
NOTE: Data for 1940 are for April. Data for all other years are as of October. Data are based on sample surveys of the civilian noninstitutionalized population, which excludes persons in the military and persons living in institutions (e.g., prisons or nursing facilities). Includes enrollment in any type of graded public, parochial, or other private schools. Includes nursery schools, kindergartens, elementary and secondary schools, colleges, universities, and professional schools. Attendance may be on either a full-time or part-time basis and during the day or night. Prior to 2010, standard errors were computed using generalized variance function methodology rather than the more precise replicate weight methodology used in later years.
SOURCE: U.S. Department of Commerce, Census Bureau, Historical Statistics of the United States, Colonial Times to 1970; Current Population Reports, Series P-20, various years; CPS Historical Time Series Tables on School Enrollment, retrieved June 6, 2012, from http://www.census.gov/hhes/school/data/cps/historical/index.html; and Current Population Survey (CPS), October, 1970 through 2017. (This table was prepared January 2019.)

Table 104.10. Rates of high school completion and bachelor's degree attainment among persons age 25 and over, by race/ethnicity and sex: Selected years, 1910 through 2018

[Standard errors appear in parentheses]

Sex, high school or bachelor's degree attainment, and year	Total, percent of all persons age 25 and over	White[1]	Black[1]	Hispanic	Asian/Pacific Islander: Total	Asian/Pacific Islander: Asian	Asian/Pacific Islander: Pacific Islander	American Indian/ Alaska Native	Two or more races
1	2	3	4	5	6	7	8	9	10
Total									
High school completion or higher[2]									
1910[3]	13.5 (—)	— (†)	— (†)	— (†)	— (†)	— (†)	— (†)	— (†)	— (†)
1920[3]	16.4 (—)	— (†)	— (†)	— (†)	— (†)	— (†)	— (†)	— (†)	— (†)
1930[3]	19.1 (—)	— (†)	— (†)	— (†)	— (†)	— (†)	— (†)	— (†)	— (†)
1940	24.5 (—)	26.1 (—)	7.7 (—)	— (†)	— (†)	— (†)	— (†)	— (†)	— (†)
1950	34.3 (—)	36.4 (—)	13.7 (—)	— (†)	— (†)	— (†)	— (†)	— (†)	— (†)
1960	41.1 (—)	43.2 (—)	21.7 (—)	— (†)	— (†)	— (†)	— (†)	— (†)	— (†)
1970	55.2 (—)	57.4 (—)	36.1 (—)	— (†)	— (†)	— (†)	— (†)	— (†)	— (†)
1975	62.5 (—)	65.8 (—)	42.6 (—)	38.5 (—)	— (†)	— (†)	— (†)	— (†)	— (†)
1980	68.6 (0.20)	71.9 (0.21)	51.4 (0.81)	44.5 (1.18)	— (†)	— (†)	— (†)	— (†)	— (†)
1985	73.9 (0.18)	77.5 (0.19)	59.9 (0.74)	47.9 (0.99)	— (†)	— (†)	— (†)	— (†)	— (†)
1986	74.7 (0.18)	78.2 (0.19)	62.5 (0.72)	48.5 (0.96)	— (†)	— (†)	— (†)	— (†)	— (†)
1987	75.6 (0.17)	79.0 (0.18)	63.6 (0.71)	50.9 (0.94)	— (†)	— (†)	— (†)	— (†)	— (†)
1988	76.2 (0.17)	79.8 (0.18)	63.5 (0.70)	51.0 (0.92)	— (†)	— (†)	— (†)	— (†)	— (†)
1989	76.9 (0.17)	80.7 (0.18)	64.7 (0.69)	50.9 (0.89)	82.3 (1.17)	— (†)	— (†)	— (†)	— (†)
1990	77.6 (0.17)	81.4 (0.17)	66.2 (0.67)	50.8 (0.88)	84.2 (1.09)	— (†)	— (†)	— (†)	— (†)
1991	78.4 (0.16)	82.4 (0.17)	66.8 (0.66)	51.3 (0.86)	84.2 (1.05)	— (†)	— (†)	— (†)	— (†)
1992	79.4 (0.16)	83.4 (0.16)	67.7 (0.65)	52.6 (0.85)	83.7 (1.02)	— (†)	— (†)	— (†)	— (†)
1993	80.2 (0.16)	84.1 (0.16)	70.5 (0.63)	53.1 (0.83)	84.2 (1.00)	— (†)	— (†)	— (†)	— (†)
1994	80.9 (0.15)	84.9 (0.16)	73.0 (0.61)	53.3 (0.78)	84.8 (0.98)	— (†)	— (†)	— (†)	— (†)
1995	81.7 (0.15)	85.9 (0.16)	73.8 (0.61)	53.4 (0.78)	83.8 (1.06)	— (†)	— (†)	— (†)	— (†)
1996	81.7 (0.16)	86.0 (0.16)	74.6 (0.53)	53.1 (0.68)	83.5 (0.82)	— (†)	— (†)	— (†)	— (†)
1997	82.1 (0.14)	86.3 (0.15)	75.3 (0.52)	54.7 (0.54)	85.2 (0.75)	— (†)	— (†)	— (†)	— (†)
1998	82.8 (0.14)	87.1 (0.14)	76.4 (0.50)	55.5 (0.53)	84.9 (0.74)	— (†)	— (†)	— (†)	— (†)
1999	83.4 (0.14)	87.7 (0.14)	77.4 (0.49)	56.1 (0.52)	84.7 (0.73)	— (†)	— (†)	— (†)	— (†)
2000	84.1 (0.13)	88.4 (0.14)	78.9 (0.48)	57.0 (0.51)	85.7 (0.71)	— (†)	— (†)	— (†)	— (†)
2001	84.3 (0.13)	88.7 (0.13)	79.5 (0.47)	56.5 (0.50)	87.8 (0.60)	— (†)	— (†)	— (†)	— (†)
2002	84.1 (0.09)	88.7 (0.10)	79.2 (0.34)	57.0 (0.34)	87.7 (0.44)	— (†)	— (†)	— (†)	— (†)
2003	84.6 (0.09)	89.4 (0.09)	80.3 (0.33)	57.0 (0.33)	87.8 (0.43)	87.8 (0.44)	88.2 (1.87)	77.2 (1.64)	86.1 (0.97)
2004	85.2 (0.09)	90.0 (0.09)	81.1 (0.32)	58.4 (0.32)	86.9 (0.43)	86.9 (0.44)	88.5 (1.91)	77.8 (1.61)	87.2 (0.91)
2005	85.2 (0.14)	90.1 (0.16)	81.4 (0.44)	58.5 (0.53)	87.8 (0.62)	87.7 (0.62)	90.1 (2.69)	75.6 (2.02)	88.6 (0.83)
2006	85.5 (0.15)	90.5 (0.15)	81.2 (0.43)	59.3 (0.58)	87.5 (0.71)	87.5 (0.71)	85.7 (2.51)	78.5 (2.11)	88.1 (0.90)
2007	85.7 (0.15)	90.6 (0.15)	82.8 (0.39)	60.3 (0.56)	88.0 (0.79)	87.9 (0.81)	88.6 (2.30)	80.3 (2.27)	89.3 (0.87)
2008	86.6 (0.15)	91.5 (0.15)	83.3 (0.40)	62.3 (0.58)	89.0 (0.62)	88.8 (0.64)	94.4 (1.00)	78.4 (2.74)	89.5 (1.12)
2009	86.7 (0.15)	91.6 (0.15)	84.2 (0.44)	61.9 (0.56)	88.4 (0.61)	88.3 (0.63)	90.8 (1.76)	81.5 (1.83)	87.4 (0.96)
2010	87.1 (0.13)	92.1 (0.14)	84.6 (0.41)	62.9 (0.53)	89.1 (0.67)	89.1 (0.68)	90.2 (1.95)	80.8 (1.76)	88.9 (0.90)
2011	87.6 (0.13)	92.4 (0.14)	84.8 (0.41)	64.3 (0.54)	88.8 (0.55)	88.7 (0.57)	90.4 (1.61)	82.3 (1.77)	89.4 (1.00)
2012	87.6 (0.15)	92.5 (0.14)	85.7 (0.40)	65.0 (0.59)	89.1 (0.59)	89.0 (0.61)	91.6 (1.33)	81.8 (1.69)	91.0 (0.89)
2013	88.2 (0.14)	92.9 (0.13)	85.9 (0.42)	66.2 (0.52)	90.2 (0.51)	90.2 (0.53)	89.5 (1.72)	82.2 (1.68)	92.6 (0.75)
2014	88.3 (0.15)	93.1 (0.17)	86.7 (0.45)	66.5 (0.57)	89.5 (0.62)	89.5 (0.64)	88.8 (2.15)	81.0 (2.01)	93.3 (0.88)
2015	88.4 (0.12)	93.3 (0.13)	87.7 (0.37)	66.7 (0.48)	88.9 (0.49)	89.1 (0.51)	85.1 (2.04)	83.8 (1.64)	91.6 (0.87)
2016	89.1 (0.13)	93.8 (0.13)	87.7 (0.34)	68.5 (0.48)	90.7 (0.49)	90.6 (0.51)	93.3 (1.38)	84.7 (1.35)	92.8 (0.83)
2017	89.6 (0.12)	94.1 (0.13)	88.1 (0.37)	70.5 (0.47)	90.9 (0.47)	90.9 (0.49)	89.3 (2.03)	85.3 (1.36)	93.4 (0.71)
2018	89.8 (0.12)	94.3 (0.13)	88.6 (0.33)	71.6 (0.40)	90.6 (0.40)	90.6 (0.41)	90.6 (1.77)	83.6 (1.32)	93.2 (0.61)
Bachelor's or higher degree[4]									
1910[3]	2.7 (—)	— (†)	— (†)	— (†)	— (†)	— (†)	— (†)	— (†)	— (†)
1920[3]	3.3 (—)	— (†)	— (†)	— (†)	— (†)	— (†)	— (†)	— (†)	— (†)
1930[3]	3.9 (—)	— (†)	— (†)	— (†)	— (†)	— (†)	— (†)	— (†)	— (†)
1940	4.6 (—)	4.9 (—)	1.3 (—)	— (†)	— (†)	— (†)	— (†)	— (†)	— (†)
1950	6.2 (—)	6.6 (—)	2.2 (—)	— (†)	— (†)	— (†)	— (†)	— (†)	— (†)
1960	7.7 (—)	8.1 (—)	3.5 (—)	— (†)	— (†)	— (†)	— (†)	— (†)	— (†)
1970	11.0 (—)	11.6 (—)	6.1 (—)	— (†)	— (†)	— (†)	— (†)	— (†)	— (†)
1975	13.9 (—)	14.9 (—)	6.4 (—)	6.6 (—)	— (†)	— (†)	— (†)	— (†)	— (†)
1980	17.0 (0.16)	18.4 (0.18)	7.9 (0.44)	7.6 (0.63)	— (†)	— (†)	— (†)	— (†)	— (†)
1985	19.4 (0.16)	20.8 (0.19)	11.1 (0.47)	8.5 (0.55)	— (†)	— (†)	— (†)	— (†)	— (†)
1986	19.4 (0.16)	20.9 (0.19)	10.9 (0.47)	8.4 (0.53)	— (†)	— (†)	— (†)	— (†)	— (†)
1987	19.9 (0.16)	21.4 (0.19)	10.8 (0.46)	8.6 (0.53)	— (†)	— (†)	— (†)	— (†)	— (†)
1988	20.3 (0.16)	21.8 (0.19)	11.2 (0.46)	10.0 (0.55)	— (†)	— (†)	— (†)	— (†)	— (†)
1989	21.1 (0.16)	22.8 (0.19)	11.7 (0.46)	9.9 (0.53)	41.5 (1.51)	— (†)	— (†)	— (†)	— (†)
1990	21.3 (0.16)	23.1 (0.19)	11.3 (0.45)	9.2 (0.51)	41.7 (1.47)	— (†)	— (†)	— (†)	— (†)
1991	21.4 (0.16)	23.3 (0.19)	11.5 (0.45)	9.7 (0.51)	40.3 (1.42)	— (†)	— (†)	— (†)	— (†)
1992	21.4 (0.16)	23.2 (0.19)	11.9 (0.45)	9.3 (0.49)	39.3 (1.35)	— (†)	— (†)	— (†)	— (†)
1993	21.9 (0.16)	23.8 (0.19)	12.2 (0.45)	9.0 (0.48)	42.1 (1.35)	— (†)	— (†)	— (†)	— (†)
1994	22.2 (0.16)	24.3 (0.19)	12.9 (0.46)	9.1 (0.45)	41.3 (1.34)	— (†)	— (†)	— (†)	— (†)
1995	23.0 (0.16)	25.4 (0.19)	13.3 (0.47)	9.3 (0.45)	38.5 (1.40)	— (†)	— (†)	— (†)	— (†)
1996	23.6 (0.17)	25.9 (0.20)	13.8 (0.42)	9.3 (0.40)	42.3 (1.09)	— (†)	— (†)	— (†)	— (†)
1997	23.9 (0.16)	26.2 (0.19)	13.3 (0.41)	10.3 (0.33)	42.6 (1.04)	— (†)	— (†)	— (†)	— (†)
1998	24.4 (0.16)	26.6 (0.19)	14.8 (0.42)	11.0 (0.33)	42.3 (1.02)	— (†)	— (†)	— (†)	— (†)
1999	25.2 (0.16)	27.7 (0.19)	15.5 (0.43)	10.9 (0.33)	42.4 (1.01)	— (†)	— (†)	— (†)	— (†)
2000	25.6 (0.16)	28.1 (0.19)	16.6 (0.44)	10.6 (0.32)	44.4 (1.00)	— (†)	— (†)	— (†)	— (†)
2001	26.1 (0.16)	28.6 (0.19)	16.1 (0.43)	11.2 (0.32)	48.0 (0.92)	— (†)	— (†)	— (†)	— (†)
2002	26.7 (0.11)	29.4 (0.14)	17.2 (0.31)	11.1 (0.21)	47.7 (0.66)	— (†)	— (†)	— (†)	— (†)
2003	27.2 (0.11)	30.0 (0.14)	17.4 (0.31)	11.4 (0.21)	48.8 (0.65)	50.0 (0.67)	27.0 (2.56)	12.6 (1.30)	22.0 (1.17)
2004	27.7 (0.11)	30.6 (0.14)	17.7 (0.31)	12.1 (0.21)	48.9 (0.64)	49.7 (0.66)	32.4 (2.81)	14.3 (1.36)	21.8 (1.13)
2005	27.7 (0.23)	30.6 (0.29)	17.6 (0.45)	12.0 (0.31)	49.3 (0.91)	50.4 (0.93)	24.6 (3.67)	14.5 (1.51)	23.2 (1.19)

See notes at end of table.

Table 104.10. Rates of high school completion and bachelor's degree attainment among persons age 25 and over, by race/ethnicity and sex: Selected years, 1910 through 2018—Continued

[Standard errors appear in parentheses]

Sex, high school or bachelor's degree attainment, and year	Total, percent of all persons age 25 and over	White[1]	Black[1]	Hispanic	Asian/Pacific Islander			American Indian/ Alaska Native	Two or more races
					Total	Asian	Pacific Islander		
1	2	3	4	5	6	7	8	9	10
2006	28.0 (0.20)	31.0 (0.25)	18.6 (0.47)	12.4 (0.32)	49.1 (1.04)	50.0 (1.06)	26.9 (3.42)	12.9 (1.60)	23.1 (1.28)
2007	28.7 (0.21)	31.8 (0.27)	18.7 (0.51)	12.7 (0.31)	51.2 (1.02)	52.5 (1.03)	23.8 (3.30)	13.1 (1.24)	23.7 (1.30)
2008	29.4 (0.21)	32.6 (0.26)	19.7 (0.51)	13.3 (0.29)	51.9 (0.95)	52.9 (0.97)	28.4 (2.86)	14.9 (1.52)	24.4 (1.36)
2009	29.5 (0.21)	32.9 (0.26)	19.4 (0.45)	13.2 (0.34)	51.6 (0.91)	52.8 (0.95)	28.3 (2.68)	17.5 (2.08)	25.5 (1.34)
2010	29.9 (0.19)	33.2 (0.24)	20.0 (0.51)	13.9 (0.31)	51.6 (1.04)	52.8 (1.09)	25.6 (2.89)	16.0 (1.77)	25.3 (1.30)
2011	30.4 (0.19)	34.0 (0.24)	20.2 (0.50)	14.1 (0.34)	49.5 (0.92)	50.8 (0.96)	22.1 (2.73)	16.1 (1.73)	27.4 (1.27)
2012	30.9 (0.21)	34.5 (0.27)	21.4 (0.53)	14.5 (0.35)	50.7 (0.92)	51.9 (0.94)	24.5 (2.75)	16.7 (1.82)	27.1 (1.34)
2013	31.7 (0.21)	35.2 (0.26)	22.0 (0.49)	15.1 (0.34)	52.5 (0.92)	53.9 (0.93)	25.6 (2.66)	15.4 (1.72)	30.6 (1.35)
2014	32.0 (0.27)	35.6 (0.35)	22.8 (0.66)	15.2 (0.39)	51.3 (1.00)	52.7 (1.02)	22.3 (3.27)	13.8 (1.43)	31.2 (1.81)
2015	32.5 (0.22)	36.2 (0.28)	22.9 (0.52)	15.5 (0.31)	52.9 (0.84)	54.4 (0.87)	22.8 (2.39)	19.8 (1.32)	30.6 (1.52)
2016	33.4 (0.24)	37.3 (0.31)	23.5 (0.46)	16.4 (0.40)	55.1 (0.87)	56.4 (0.89)	27.5 (2.92)	16.8 (1.39)	30.6 (1.52)
2017	34.2 (0.24)	38.1 (0.31)	24.3 (0.49)	17.2 (0.35)	53.9 (0.84)	55.4 (0.88)	25.1 (2.81)	20.5 (1.92)	32.6 (1.39)
2018	35.0 (0.26)	38.8 (0.34)	25.6 (0.53)	18.3 (0.37)	55.6 (0.81)	57.1 (0.80)	24.1 (2.34)	18.8 (1.72)	32.4 (1.40)
Males									
High school completion or higher[2]									
1940	22.7 (—)	24.2 (—)	6.9 (—)	— (†)	— (†)	— (†)	— (†)	— (†)	— (†)
1950	32.6 (—)	34.6 (—)	12.6 (—)	— (†)	— (†)	— (†)	— (†)	— (†)	— (†)
1960	39.5 (—)	41.6 (—)	20.0 (—)	— (†)	— (†)	— (†)	— (†)	— (†)	— (†)
1970	55.0 (—)	57.2 (—)	35.4 (—)	— (†)	— (†)	— (†)	— (†)	— (†)	— (†)
1980	69.2 (0.29)	72.4 (0.31)	51.2 (1.21)	44.9 (1.71)	— (†)	— (†)	— (†)	— (†)	— (†)
1990	77.7 (0.24)	81.6 (0.25)	65.8 (1.01)	50.3 (1.25)	86.0 (1.49)	— (†)	— (†)	— (†)	— (†)
1995	81.7 (0.22)	86.0 (0.22)	73.5 (0.91)	52.9 (1.11)	85.8 (1.46)	— (†)	— (†)	— (†)	— (†)
1996	81.9 (0.23)	86.1 (0.23)	74.6 (0.80)	53.0 (0.97)	86.2 (1.10)	— (†)	— (†)	— (†)	— (†)
1997	82.0 (0.21)	86.3 (0.21)	73.8 (0.79)	54.9 (0.76)	87.5 (1.00)	— (†)	— (†)	— (†)	— (†)
1998	82.8 (0.20)	87.1 (0.21)	75.4 (0.77)	55.7 (0.74)	87.9 (0.98)	— (†)	— (†)	— (†)	— (†)
1999	83.4 (0.20)	87.7 (0.20)	77.2 (0.74)	56.0 (0.75)	86.9 (1.00)	— (†)	— (†)	— (†)	— (†)
2000	84.2 (0.19)	88.5 (0.20)	79.1 (0.72)	56.6 (0.73)	88.4 (0.94)	— (†)	— (†)	— (†)	— (†)
2001	84.4 (0.19)	88.6 (0.19)	80.6 (0.69)	55.6 (0.72)	90.6 (0.78)	— (†)	— (†)	— (†)	— (†)
2002	83.8 (0.14)	88.5 (0.14)	79.0 (0.51)	56.1 (0.48)	89.8 (0.58)	— (†)	— (†)	— (†)	— (†)
2003	84.1 (0.13)	89.0 (0.14)	79.9 (0.50)	56.3 (0.46)	89.8 (0.58)	89.8 (0.59)	89.8 (2.61)	76.5 (2.33)	87.2 (1.36)
2004	84.8 (0.13)	89.9 (0.13)	80.8 (0.49)	57.3 (0.45)	88.8 (0.59)	88.8 (0.60)	88.9 (2.65)	77.1 (2.31)	87.8 (1.29)
2005	84.9 (0.19)	89.9 (0.20)	81.4 (0.60)	57.9 (0.69)	90.4 (0.65)	90.5 (0.66)	88.5 (3.62)	75.6 (2.57)	89.0 (1.19)
2006	85.0 (0.20)	90.2 (0.21)	80.7 (0.63)	58.5 (0.77)	89.5 (0.84)	89.7 (0.86)	85.8 (3.10)	78.1 (2.77)	88.0 (1.36)
2007	85.0 (0.21)	90.2 (0.22)	82.5 (0.55)	58.2 (0.80)	90.0 (0.81)	90.1 (0.82)	88.1 (2.75)	78.3 (3.58)	89.4 (1.28)
2008	85.9 (0.19)	91.1 (0.20)	82.1 (0.61)	60.9 (0.72)	91.0 (0.66)	90.8 (0.69)	95.8 (1.40)	77.3 (3.37)	89.6 (1.21)
2009	86.2 (0.19)	91.4 (0.20)	84.2 (0.60)	60.6 (0.72)	90.8 (0.66)	90.7 (0.68)	92.1 (2.18)	80.0 (2.33)	87.3 (1.26)
2010	86.6 (0.17)	91.8 (0.19)	84.2 (0.57)	61.4 (0.68)	91.4 (0.78)	91.5 (0.79)	89.3 (2.84)	78.9 (2.46)	88.1 (1.36)
2011	87.1 (0.18)	92.0 (0.17)	84.2 (0.55)	63.6 (0.71)	90.6 (0.68)	90.6 (0.69)	91.5 (2.22)	80.6 (2.35)	88.1 (1.40)
2012	87.3 (0.19)	92.2 (0.18)	85.1 (0.56)	64.0 (0.73)	90.6 (0.68)	90.5 (0.70)	93.3 (1.84)	81.8 (2.39)	90.2 (1.45)
2013	87.6 (0.17)	92.7 (0.17)	84.9 (0.62)	64.6 (0.66)	91.6 (0.57)	91.7 (0.57)	89.3 (2.48)	81.0 (2.11)	93.3 (1.03)
2014	87.7 (0.19)	92.5 (0.22)	86.3 (0.58)	65.1 (0.74)	91.8 (0.70)	91.9 (0.72)	90.0 (2.68)	80.2 (2.30)	93.8 (1.08)
2015	88.0 (0.16)	93.0 (0.16)	87.2 (0.48)	65.5 (0.63)	90.9 (0.56)	91.3 (0.58)	84.9 (2.83)	81.9 (2.12)	92.5 (1.23)
2016	88.5 (0.17)	93.4 (0.19)	87.0 (0.51)	67.2 (0.63)	92.3 (0.58)	92.2 (0.60)	94.9 (1.58)	84.1 (2.07)	92.8 (1.15)
2017	89.1 (0.16)	93.7 (0.18)	87.4 (0.53)	69.5 (0.59)	92.5 (0.55)	92.7 (0.55)	89.1 (2.77)	83.0 (1.96)	93.2 (1.15)
2018	89.4 (0.16)	93.9 (0.18)	88.3 (0.48)	70.7 (0.53)	92.8 (0.48)	92.9 (0.49)	92.2 (2.31)	79.3 (1.93)	92.5 (1.02)
Bachelor's or higher degree[4]									
1940	5.5 (—)	5.9 (—)	1.4 (—)	— (†)	— (†)	— (†)	— (†)	— (†)	— (†)
1950	7.3 (—)	7.9 (—)	2.1 (—)	— (†)	— (†)	— (†)	— (†)	— (†)	— (†)
1960	9.7 (—)	10.3 (—)	3.5 (—)	— (†)	— (†)	— (†)	— (†)	— (†)	— (†)
1970	14.1 (—)	15.0 (—)	6.8 (—)	— (†)	— (†)	— (†)	— (†)	— (†)	— (†)
1980	20.9 (0.26)	22.7 (0.29)	7.7 (0.65)	9.2 (0.99)	— (†)	— (†)	— (†)	— (†)	— (†)
1990	24.4 (0.25)	26.7 (0.28)	11.9 (0.69)	9.8 (0.74)	45.9 (2.14)	— (†)	— (†)	— (†)	— (†)
1995	26.0 (0.25)	28.9 (0.29)	13.7 (0.71)	10.1 (0.67)	42.3 (2.06)	— (†)	— (†)	— (†)	— (†)
1996	26.0 (0.26)	28.8 (0.30)	12.5 (0.61)	10.3 (0.59)	46.9 (1.59)	— (†)	— (†)	— (†)	— (†)
1997	26.2 (0.24)	29.0 (0.28)	12.5 (0.60)	10.6 (0.47)	48.0 (1.51)	— (†)	— (†)	— (†)	— (†)
1998	26.5 (0.24)	29.3 (0.28)	14.0 (0.62)	11.1 (0.47)	46.0 (1.50)	— (†)	— (†)	— (†)	— (†)
1999	27.5 (0.24)	30.6 (0.28)	14.3 (0.62)	10.7 (0.46)	46.3 (1.48)	— (†)	— (†)	— (†)	— (†)
2000	27.8 (0.24)	30.8 (0.28)	16.4 (0.65)	10.7 (0.45)	48.1 (1.47)	— (†)	— (†)	— (†)	— (†)
2001	28.0 (0.24)	30.9 (0.28)	15.9 (0.64)	11.1 (0.45)	52.9 (1.33)	— (†)	— (†)	— (†)	— (†)
2002	28.5 (0.17)	31.7 (0.20)	16.5 (0.47)	11.0 (0.30)	51.5 (0.96)	— (†)	— (†)	— (†)	— (†)
2003	28.9 (0.17)	32.3 (0.20)	16.8 (0.47)	11.2 (0.29)	52.8 (0.96)	54.2 (0.98)	25.7 (3.76)	13.1 (1.85)	21.9 (1.69)
2004	29.4 (0.17)	32.9 (0.20)	16.6 (0.46)	11.8 (0.30)	52.9 (0.93)	54.0 (0.95)	31.9 (3.94)	15.6 (1.99)	20.7 (1.60)
2005	28.9 (0.29)	32.4 (0.37)	16.0 (0.64)	11.8 (0.43)	53.0 (1.10)	54.3 (1.13)	25.1 (4.70)	17.0 (2.30)	23.1 (1.67)
2006	29.2 (0.24)	32.8 (0.31)	17.5 (0.63)	11.9 (0.40)	51.9 (1.33)	53.1 (1.35)	26.6 (4.67)	13.7 (2.07)	22.6 (1.75)
2007	29.5 (0.25)	33.2 (0.33)	18.1 (0.62)	11.8 (0.37)	54.2 (1.31)	55.8 (1.32)	19.2 (4.14)	12.7 (1.89)	21.5 (1.81)
2008	30.1 (0.25)	33.8 (0.33)	18.7 (0.67)	12.6 (0.39)	54.9 (1.24)	56.1 (1.24)	27.5 (3.64)	14.6 (2.15)	22.7 (1.62)
2009	30.1 (0.28)	33.9 (0.36)	17.9 (0.57)	12.5 (0.41)	54.8 (1.14)	56.5 (1.17)	23.0 (3.35)	16.1 (2.96)	24.4 (1.92)
2010	30.3 (0.23)	34.2 (0.30)	17.9 (0.59)	12.9 (0.37)	54.6 (1.26)	56.2 (1.30)	18.0 (3.74)	13.5 (2.61)	24.8 (1.86)
2011	30.8 (0.23)	35.0 (0.29)	18.4 (0.64)	13.1 (0.44)	52.4 (1.15)	54.0 (1.21)	19.1 (3.55)	14.1 (1.98)	25.7 (1.91)
2012	31.4 (0.27)	35.5 (0.33)	19.5 (0.62)	13.3 (0.45)	53.0 (1.26)	54.4 (1.29)	24.1 (3.34)	16.1 (2.27)	25.2 (1.85)
2013	32.0 (0.25)	36.0 (0.31)	20.2 (0.64)	13.9 (0.43)	55.1 (1.17)	56.9 (1.20)	23.1 (3.32)	14.0 (2.13)	29.0 (1.78)
2014	31.9 (0.32)	35.9 (0.41)	21.0 (0.88)	14.2 (0.51)	53.7 (1.33)	55.5 (1.34)	16.7 (3.42)	14.8 (2.46)	29.2 (2.56)
2015	32.3 (0.27)	36.3 (0.35)	21.1 (0.63)	14.3 (0.38)	55.6 (1.11)	57.3 (1.16)	24.4 (2.87)	18.1 (2.14)	27.2 (2.14)
2016	33.2 (0.29)	37.2 (0.37)	21.8 (0.62)	15.4 (0.48)	57.7 (1.05)	59.4 (1.10)	22.2 (3.65)	16.5 (1.87)	25.6 (2.06)
2017	33.7 (0.28)	37.8 (0.37)	22.6 (0.61)	15.8 (0.41)	55.7 (1.10)	57.2 (1.14)	26.2 (3.61)	17.7 (1.93)	30.3 (1.87)
2018	34.6 (0.30)	38.9 (0.40)	23.7 (0.73)	16.6 (0.45)	58.5 (1.01)	60.1 (1.02)	23.6 (3.59)	15.4 (1.78)	30.0 (2.05)

See notes at end of table.

Table 104.10. Rates of high school completion and bachelor's degree attainment among persons age 25 and over, by race/ethnicity and sex: Selected years, 1910 through 2018—Continued

[Standard errors appear in parentheses]

Sex, high school or bachelor's degree attainment, and year	Total, percent of all persons age 25 and over	White[1]	Black[1]	Hispanic	Asian/Pacific Islander: Total	Asian/Pacific Islander: Asian	Asian/Pacific Islander: Pacific Islander	American Indian/ Alaska Native	Two or more races
1	2	3	4	5	6	7	8	9	10
Females									
High school completion or higher[2]									
1940	26.3 (—)	28.1 (—)	8.4 (—)	— (†)	— (†)	— (†)	— (†)	— (†)	— (†)
1950	36.0 (—)	38.2 (—)	14.7 (—)	— (†)	— (†)	— (†)	— (†)	— (†)	— (†)
1960	42.5 (—)	44.7 (—)	23.1 (—)	— (†)	— (†)	— (†)	— (†)	— (†)	— (†)
1970	55.4 (—)	57.7 (—)	36.6 (—)	— (†)	— (†)	— (†)	— (†)	— (†)	— (†)
1980	68.1 (0.28)	71.5 (0.30)	51.5 (1.08)	44.2 (1.63)	— (†)	— (†)	— (†)	— (†)	— (†)
1990	77.5 (0.23)	81.3 (0.24)	66.5 (0.90)	51.3 (1.23)	82.5 (1.57)	— (†)	— (†)	— (†)	— (†)
1995	81.6 (0.21)	85.8 (0.22)	74.1 (0.81)	53.8 (1.09)	81.9 (1.54)	— (†)	— (†)	— (†)	— (†)
1996	81.6 (0.22)	85.9 (0.22)	74.6 (0.71)	53.3 (0.97)	81.0 (1.21)	— (†)	— (†)	— (†)	— (†)
1997	82.2 (0.20)	86.3 (0.20)	76.5 (0.68)	54.6 (0.76)	82.9 (1.11)	— (†)	— (†)	— (†)	— (†)
1998	82.9 (0.19)	87.1 (0.20)	77.1 (0.67)	55.3 (0.75)	82.3 (1.09)	— (†)	— (†)	— (†)	— (†)
1999	83.3 (0.19)	87.6 (0.19)	77.5 (0.66)	56.3 (0.73)	82.8 (1.06)	— (†)	— (†)	— (†)	— (†)
2000	84.0 (0.19)	88.4 (0.19)	78.7 (0.64)	57.5 (0.71)	83.4 (1.03)	— (†)	— (†)	— (†)	— (†)
2001	84.2 (0.18)	88.8 (0.19)	78.6 (0.64)	57.4 (0.70)	85.2 (0.91)	— (†)	— (†)	— (†)	— (†)
2002	84.4 (0.13)	88.9 (0.13)	79.4 (0.45)	57.9 (0.48)	85.7 (0.64)	— (†)	— (†)	— (†)	— (†)
2003	85.0 (0.13)	89.7 (0.13)	80.7 (0.44)	57.8 (0.46)	86.1 (0.62)	86.1 (0.64)	86.9 (2.63)	77.9 (2.30)	85.1 (1.38)
2004	85.4 (0.12)	90.1 (0.12)	81.2 (0.43)	59.5 (0.46)	85.3 (0.63)	85.1 (0.64)	88.1 (2.76)	78.6 (2.24)	86.5 (1.29)
2005	85.5 (0.15)	90.3 (0.18)	81.5 (0.53)	59.1 (0.63)	85.4 (0.76)	85.2 (0.78)	91.7 (2.46)	75.6 (2.29)	88.1 (1.12)
2006	85.9 (0.16)	90.8 (0.17)	81.5 (0.51)	60.1 (0.59)	85.6 (0.82)	85.6 (0.81)	85.7 (3.08)	78.9 (2.18)	88.2 (1.11)
2007	86.4 (0.15)	91.0 (0.16)	83.0 (0.49)	62.5 (0.56)	86.1 (0.93)	86.0 (0.97)	89.1 (2.40)	81.9 (1.91)	89.2 (1.22)
2008	87.2 (0.17)	91.8 (0.18)	84.2 (0.49)	63.7 (0.61)	87.2 (0.75)	87.0 (0.78)	93.0 (1.57)	79.2 (2.95)	89.5 (1.53)
2009	87.1 (0.16)	91.9 (0.17)	84.2 (0.48)	63.3 (0.59)	86.4 (0.73)	86.3 (0.75)	89.7 (2.33)	82.7 (1.96)	87.6 (1.16)
2010	87.6 (0.15)	92.3 (0.17)	85.0 (0.46)	64.4 (0.59)	87.2 (0.72)	87.1 (0.75)	90.9 (2.41)	82.5 (1.95)	89.7 (1.13)
2011	88.0 (0.15)	92.8 (0.16)	85.3 (0.50)	65.1 (0.57)	87.1 (0.64)	87.0 (0.66)	89.5 (2.25)	83.8 (2.00)	90.7 (1.22)
2012	88.0 (0.17)	92.7 (0.18)	86.1 (0.46)	66.0 (0.65)	87.9 (0.64)	87.8 (0.66)	90.1 (2.11)	81.8 (1.84)	91.6 (1.13)
2013	88.6 (0.16)	93.2 (0.16)	86.6 (0.46)	67.9 (0.55)	89.0 (0.61)	88.9 (0.63)	89.6 (2.01)	83.1 (2.16)	92.0 (0.95)
2014	88.9 (0.17)	93.7 (0.20)	87.0 (0.55)	67.9 (0.61)	87.4 (0.76)	87.4 (0.77)	87.8 (2.98)	81.6 (2.78)	92.8 (1.28)
2015	88.8 (0.14)	93.5 (0.15)	88.2 (0.43)	67.8 (0.53)	87.1 (0.60)	87.2 (0.62)	85.3 (2.46)	85.6 (2.10)	90.9 (1.14)
2016	89.6 (0.14)	94.3 (0.15)	88.3 (0.39)	69.7 (0.53)	89.3 (0.55)	89.2 (0.56)	91.8 (2.26)	85.2 (1.69)	92.8 (1.07)
2017	90.0 (0.14)	94.5 (0.14)	88.6 (0.43)	71.6 (0.52)	89.4 (0.54)	89.4 (0.56)	89.5 (2.20)	87.2 (1.52)	93.6 (0.92)
2018	90.2 (0.13)	94.7 (0.15)	88.7 (0.41)	72.5 (0.48)	88.6 (0.51)	88.6 (0.52)	89.1 (2.77)	87.4 (1.51)	93.7 (0.86)
Bachelor's or higher degree[4]									
1940	3.8 (—)	4.0 (—)	1.2 (—)	— (†)	— (†)	— (†)	— (†)	— (†)	— (†)
1950	5.2 (—)	5.4 (—)	2.4 (—)	— (†)	— (†)	— (†)	— (†)	— (†)	— (†)
1960	5.8 (—)	6.0 (—)	3.6 (—)	— (†)	— (†)	— (†)	— (†)	— (†)	— (†)
1970	8.2 (—)	8.6 (—)	5.6 (—)	— (†)	— (†)	— (†)	— (†)	— (†)	— (†)
1980	13.6 (0.20)	14.4 (0.23)	8.1 (0.59)	6.2 (0.79)	— (†)	— (†)	— (†)	— (†)	— (†)
1990	18.4 (0.21)	19.8 (0.25)	10.8 (0.59)	8.7 (0.69)	37.8 (2.01)	— (†)	— (†)	— (†)	— (†)
1995	20.2 (0.22)	22.1 (0.26)	13.0 (0.62)	8.4 (0.61)	35.0 (1.90)	— (†)	— (†)	— (†)	— (†)
1996	21.4 (0.23)	23.2 (0.27)	14.8 (0.58)	8.3 (0.53)	38.0 (1.50)	— (†)	— (†)	— (†)	— (†)
1997	21.7 (0.21)	23.7 (0.25)	14.0 (0.56)	10.1 (0.46)	37.4 (1.43)	— (†)	— (†)	— (†)	— (†)
1998	22.4 (0.21)	24.1 (0.25)	15.4 (0.58)	10.9 (0.47)	38.9 (1.39)	— (†)	— (†)	— (†)	— (†)
1999	23.1 (0.22)	25.0 (0.26)	16.5 (0.59)	11.0 (0.46)	39.0 (1.37)	— (†)	— (†)	— (†)	— (†)
2000	23.6 (0.22)	25.5 (0.26)	16.8 (0.59)	10.6 (0.44)	41.0 (1.37)	— (†)	— (†)	— (†)	— (†)
2001	24.3 (0.22)	26.5 (0.26)	16.3 (0.58)	11.3 (0.45)	43.4 (1.26)	— (†)	— (†)	— (†)	— (†)
2002	25.1 (0.15)	27.3 (0.19)	17.7 (0.42)	11.2 (0.31)	44.2 (0.91)	— (†)	— (†)	— (†)	— (†)
2003	25.7 (0.15)	27.9 (0.19)	18.0 (0.43)	11.6 (0.30)	45.3 (0.89)	46.3 (0.92)	28.0 (3.50)	12.2 (1.81)	22.2 (1.61)
2004	26.1 (0.15)	28.4 (0.19)	18.5 (0.43)	12.3 (0.31)	45.2 (0.88)	45.7 (0.90)	32.9 (4.01)	13.1 (1.84)	22.7 (1.59)
2005	26.5 (0.23)	28.9 (0.30)	18.9 (0.51)	12.1 (0.42)	46.0 (1.08)	46.8 (1.10)	24.1 (4.08)	12.2 (2.00)	23.3 (1.43)
2006	26.9 (0.22)	29.3 (0.28)	19.5 (0.55)	12.9 (0.39)	46.6 (1.11)	47.3 (1.15)	27.2 (4.03)	12.3 (1.81)	23.6 (1.70)
2007	28.0 (0.23)	30.6 (0.29)	19.2 (0.59)	13.7 (0.44)	48.6 (1.07)	49.5 (1.10)	27.9 (4.16)	13.4 (1.53)	25.8 (1.58)
2008	28.8 (0.24)	31.5 (0.29)	20.5 (0.58)	14.1 (0.37)	49.3 (0.99)	50.1 (1.02)	29.3 (3.82)	15.1 (1.75)	26.1 (1.92)
2009	29.1 (0.21)	31.9 (0.26)	20.6 (0.56)	14.0 (0.41)	48.8 (0.98)	49.7 (1.02)	32.9 (3.74)	18.8 (1.91)	26.6 (1.67)
2010	29.6 (0.21)	32.4 (0.26)	21.6 (0.63)	14.9 (0.42)	49.1 (1.12)	49.9 (1.19)	32.2 (4.11)	18.2 (1.83)	25.7 (1.59)
2011	30.1 (0.22)	33.1 (0.28)	21.7 (0.60)	15.2 (0.43)	47.0 (1.04)	48.0 (1.07)	24.7 (3.52)	17.9 (2.17)	28.9 (1.70)
2012	30.6 (0.23)	33.5 (0.30)	22.9 (0.61)	15.8 (0.45)	48.6 (0.93)	49.7 (0.94)	24.9 (3.70)	17.2 (2.13)	28.8 (1.88)
2013	31.4 (0.24)	34.4 (0.31)	23.4 (0.61)	16.2 (0.42)	50.2 (0.94)	51.3 (0.96)	28.0 (3.44)	16.6 (2.05)	32.0 (1.89)
2014	32.0 (0.32)	35.3 (0.42)	24.2 (0.75)	16.1 (0.50)	49.3 (1.12)	50.4 (1.15)	27.1 (4.38)	13.1 (1.92)	33.1 (2.08)
2015	32.7 (0.25)	36.1 (0.32)	24.3 (0.60)	16.6 (0.42)	50.4 (0.82)	51.8 (0.85)	21.3 (3.13)	21.3 (1.71)	33.4 (1.96)
2016	33.7 (0.27)	37.3 (0.32)	24.8 (0.54)	17.4 (0.47)	52.9 (0.96)	53.8 (0.97)	32.4 (3.94)	17.0 (1.78)	35.0 (2.17)
2017	34.6 (0.28)	38.3 (0.36)	25.7 (0.59)	18.6 (0.48)	52.3 (0.94)	53.8 (0.97)	24.2 (3.54)	22.9 (2.73)	34.6 (1.87)
2018	35.3 (0.30)	38.8 (0.37)	27.1 (0.63)	20.1 (0.47)	53.1 (0.90)	54.4 (0.88)	24.6 (3.34)	21.7 (2.26)	34.4 (1.84)

—Not available.
†Not applicable.
[1]Includes persons of Hispanic ethnicity for years prior to 1980.
[2]Data for years prior to 1993 are for persons with 4 or more years of high school. Data for later years are for high school completers—i.e., those persons who graduated from high school with a diploma as well as those who completed high school through equivalency programs, such as a GED program.
[3]Estimates based on Census Bureau reverse projection of 1940 census data on education by age.
[4]Data for years prior to 1993 are for persons with 4 or more years of college.

NOTE: Prior to 2005, standard errors were computed using generalized variance function methodology rather than the more precise replicate weight methodology used in later years. For 1960 and prior years, data were collected in April. For later years, data were collected in March. Race categories exclude persons of Hispanic ethnicity except where otherwise noted.
SOURCE: U.S. Department of Commerce, Census Bureau, *U.S. Census of Population: 1960*, Vol. I, Part 1; J.K. Folger and C.B. Nam, *Education of the American Population* (1960 Census Monograph); Current Population Reports, Series P-20, various years; and Current Population Survey (CPS), Annual Social and Economic Supplement, 1970 through 2018. (This table was prepared March 2019.)

Table 104.20. Percentage of persons 25 to 29 years old with selected levels of educational attainment, by race/ethnicity and sex: Selected years, 1920 through 2018

[Standard errors appear in parentheses]

Sex, selected level of educational attainment, and year	Total		White[1]		Black[1]		Hispanic		Asian/Pacific Islander: Total		Asian/Pacific Islander: Asian		Asian/Pacific Islander: Pacific Islander		American Indian/ Alaska Native		Two or more races	
1	2		3		4		5		6		7		8		9		10	
Total																		
High school completion or higher[2]																		
1920[3]	—	(†)	22.0	(—)	6.3	(—)	—	(†)	—	(†)	—	(†)	—	(†)	—	(†)	—	(†)
1940	38.1	(—)	41.2	(—)	12.3	(—)	—	(†)	—	(†)	—	(†)	—	(†)	—	(†)	—	(†)
1950	52.8	(—)	56.3	(—)	23.6	(—)	—	(†)	—	(†)	—	(†)	—	(†)	—	(†)	—	(†)
1960	60.7	(—)	63.7	(—)	38.6	(—)	—	(†)	—	(†)	—	(†)	—	(†)	—	(†)	—	(†)
1970	75.4	(—)	77.8	(—)	58.4	(—)	—	(†)	—	(†)	—	(†)	—	(†)	—	(†)	—	(†)
1980	85.4	(0.40)	89.2	(0.40)	76.7	(1.64)	58.0	(2.59)	—	(†)	—	(†)	—	(†)	—	(†)	—	(†)
1990	85.7	(0.38)	90.1	(0.37)	81.7	(1.37)	58.2	(1.94)	91.5	(2.09)	—	(†)	—	(†)	—	(†)	—	(†)
1995	86.8	(0.39)	92.5	(0.36)	86.7	(1.23)	57.1	(1.80)	90.8	(2.26)	—	(†)	—	(†)	81.5	(6.97)	—	(†)
2000	88.1	(0.37)	94.0	(0.33)	86.8	(1.13)	62.8	(1.22)	93.7	(1.27)	—	(†)	—	(†)	79.2	(5.19)	—	(†)
2005	86.2	(0.42)	92.8	(0.39)	87.0	(1.03)	63.3	(1.32)	95.6	(0.88)	95.5	(0.92)	99.5	(0.54)	80.2	(4.77)	91.4	(1.93)
2006	86.4	(0.36)	93.4	(0.35)	86.3	(1.09)	63.2	(1.17)	96.4	(0.88)	96.6	(0.86)	93.4	(3.70)	79.8	(5.19)	89.3	(2.70)
2007	87.0	(0.36)	93.5	(0.33)	87.7	(1.16)	65.0	(1.06)	96.8	(0.91)	97.5	(0.73)	86.2	(7.36)	84.5	(4.41)	90.5	(2.19)
2008	87.8	(0.36)	93.7	(0.38)	87.5	(1.29)	68.3	(1.16)	95.9	(0.86)	95.8	(0.91)	97.5	(2.09)	86.7	(3.36)	94.2	(1.72)
2009	88.6	(0.36)	94.6	(0.33)	88.9	(0.98)	68.9	(1.16)	95.4	(0.91)	95.8	(0.95)	91.6	(3.46)	81.1	(4.26)	88.5	(2.40)
2010	88.8	(0.32)	94.5	(0.31)	89.6	(0.93)	69.4	(1.22)	93.7	(1.18)	94.0	(1.24)	89.7	(5.05)	89.9	(2.98)	88.5	(2.76)
2011	89.0	(0.34)	94.4	(0.34)	88.1	(0.98)	71.5	(1.12)	95.4	(0.87)	95.3	(0.91)	98.3	(1.23)	84.9	(3.95)	90.7	(2.15)
2012	89.7	(0.38)	94.6	(0.37)	88.5	(0.96)	75.0	(1.16)	96.2	(0.73)	96.1	(0.77)	98.6	(0.83)	84.5	(3.94)	92.8	(2.22)
2013	89.9	(0.35)	94.1	(0.35)	90.3	(0.92)	75.8	(1.10)	95.4	(0.77)	95.4	(0.81)	95.5	(2.71)	84.7	(3.47)	97.4	(1.11)
2014	90.8	(0.39)	95.6	(0.41)	91.9	(0.93)	74.7	(1.31)	96.6	(0.76)	96.6	(0.79)	96.0	(2.19)	83.9	(4.67)	96.0	(2.01)
2015	91.2	(0.31)	95.4	(0.32)	92.5	(0.78)	77.1	(1.02)	95.3	(0.92)	95.8	(0.87)	87.2	(6.60)	86.7	(2.65)	94.9	(1.54)
2016	91.7	(0.34)	95.2	(0.33)	91.1	(0.92)	80.6	(1.01)	96.7	(0.68)	96.8	(0.68)	94.0	(3.90)	84.5	(4.13)	94.8	(1.49)
2017	92.5	(0.32)	95.6	(0.30)	92.3	(0.89)	82.7	(0.92)	96.4	(0.76)	96.8	(0.76)	90.1	(4.96)	84.6	(4.34)	94.8	(2.01)
2018	92.9	(0.32)	95.6	(0.37)	92.0	(0.86)	85.2	(0.89)	97.0	(0.70)	97.5	(0.71)	90.7	(3.86)	89.1	(3.06)	93.3	(1.68)
Associate's or higher degree																		
1995	33.0	(0.54)	38.3	(0.67)	22.5	(1.52)	13.0	(1.23)	51.1	(3.91)	—	(†)	—	(†)	11.6!	(5.75)	—	(†)
2000	37.7	(0.55)	43.7	(0.70)	26.0	(1.47)	15.4	(0.91)	60.8	(2.55)	—	(†)	—	(†)	29.7	(5.84)	—	(†)
2005	37.3	(0.56)	43.9	(0.77)	26.5	(1.43)	17.3	(0.91)	66.4	(2.14)	68.7	(2.17)	17.8!	(6.08)	24.4	(4.13)	36.8	(3.99)
2006	37.6	(0.51)	45.1	(0.75)	25.3	(1.48)	16.1	(0.77)	66.7	(2.27)	68.6	(2.33)	33.5	(8.26)	18.2	(5.17)	31.6	(3.67)
2007	38.6	(0.55)	45.8	(0.77)	27.3	(1.36)	18.1	(0.77)	66.2	(2.08)	68.0	(2.11)	37.1	(8.93)	14.6	(4.27)	35.3	(3.80)
2008	39.7	(0.55)	47.6	(0.72)	27.6	(1.39)	18.7	(0.90)	65.1	(2.21)	66.9	(2.19)	35.3	(7.53)	20.9	(3.60)	33.5	(3.84)
2009	39.3	(0.58)	47.1	(0.83)	27.8	(1.43)	18.4	(0.89)	63.0	(2.21)	66.7	(2.23)	20.9	(5.84)	20.8	(4.05)	35.6	(3.76)
2010	41.1	(0.51)	48.9	(0.69)	29.4	(1.41)	20.5	(0.99)	60.5	(2.33)	63.4	(2.45)	22.0!	(7.92)	28.9	(6.19)	36.9	(3.57)
2011	42.1	(0.65)	50.1	(0.85)	29.8	(1.50)	20.6	(0.87)	63.6	(2.36)	64.6	(2.35)	39.7	(9.75)	25.0	(4.52)	42.0	(4.33)
2012	42.8	(0.58)	49.9	(0.80)	31.6	(1.40)	22.7	(1.01)	66.3	(1.96)	68.3	(2.01)	32.4	(6.33)	23.6	(4.32)	47.6	(3.76)
2013	43.2	(0.57)	51.0	(0.79)	29.5	(1.42)	23.1	(0.87)	65.5	(1.93)	67.2	(1.96)	37.3	(7.84)	26.3	(5.70)	44.2	(3.81)
2014	44.1	(0.75)	51.9	(1.01)	32.0	(1.98)	23.4	(1.18)	67.8	(2.35)	70.3	(2.40)	‡	(†)	18.2	(4.23)	40.8	(4.46)
2015	45.7	(0.53)	54.0	(0.78)	31.1	(1.41)	25.7	(1.01)	68.9	(2.09)	71.7	(2.13)	24.9	(6.58)	22.3	(3.65)	38.4	(3.56)
2016	46.1	(0.62)	54.3	(0.82)	31.7	(1.46)	27.0	(1.19)	69.5	(2.07)	71.5	(2.15)	28.6	(8.03)	16.5	(3.47)	41.3	(4.10)
2017	46.1	(0.61)	53.5	(0.83)	32.7	(1.35)	27.7	(1.00)	68.0	(2.11)	69.9	(2.10)	35.8	(8.65)	27.1	(5.97)	45.6	(3.86)
2018	46.7	(0.65)	53.6	(0.89)	32.6	(1.54)	30.5	(1.17)	72.2	(1.90)	75.5	(1.83)	22.6	(5.98)	24.4	(4.14)	41.5	(3.50)
Bachelor's or higher degree[4]																		
1920[3]	—	(†)	4.5	(—)	1.2	(—)	—	(†)	—	(†)	—	(†)	—	(†)	—	(†)	—	(†)
1940	5.9	(—)	6.4	(—)	1.6	(—)	—	(†)	—	(†)	—	(†)	—	(†)	—	(†)	—	(†)
1950	7.7	(—)	8.2	(—)	2.8	(—)	—	(†)	—	(†)	—	(†)	—	(†)	—	(†)	—	(†)
1960	11.0	(—)	11.8	(—)	5.4	(—)	—	(†)	—	(†)	—	(†)	—	(†)	—	(†)	—	(†)
1970	16.4	(—)	17.3	(—)	10.0	(—)	—	(†)	—	(†)	—	(†)	—	(†)	—	(†)	—	(†)
1980	22.5	(0.47)	25.0	(0.55)	11.6	(1.24)	7.7	(1.39)	—	(†)	—	(†)	—	(†)	—	(†)	—	(†)
1990	23.2	(0.46)	26.4	(0.55)	13.4	(1.20)	8.1	(1.07)	43.0	(3.71)	—	(†)	—	(†)	—	(†)	—	(†)
1995	24.7	(0.49)	28.8	(0.62)	15.4	(1.31)	8.9	(1.04)	43.1	(3.87)	—	(†)	—	(†)	‡	(†)	—	(†)
2000	29.1	(0.52)	34.0	(0.67)	17.8	(1.28)	9.7	(0.75)	54.3	(2.60)	—	(†)	—	(†)	15.9	(4.68)	—	(†)
2005	28.8	(0.55)	34.5	(0.78)	17.6	(1.21)	11.2	(0.81)	60.0	(2.20)	62.1	(2.25)	17.0!	(6.01)	16.4	(3.56)	28.0	(3.79)
2006	28.4	(0.52)	34.3	(0.78)	18.7	(1.33)	9.5	(0.66)	59.6	(2.39)	61.9	(2.44)	20.7!	(6.70)	9.5!	(4.26)	23.3	(3.14)
2007	29.6	(0.54)	35.5	(0.75)	19.5	(1.21)	11.6	(0.61)	59.4	(2.24)	61.5	(2.26)	26.5!	(8.25)	6.4!	(2.99)	26.3	(3.44)
2008	30.8	(0.51)	37.1	(0.70)	20.4	(1.35)	12.4	(0.69)	57.9	(2.26)	60.2	(2.32)	20.2!	(6.75)	14.3	(3.17)	26.6	(3.75)
2009	30.6	(0.57)	37.2	(0.85)	18.9	(1.36)	12.2	(0.80)	56.4	(2.25)	60.3	(2.28)	12.5!	(4.44)	15.9	(3.73)	29.7	(3.84)
2010	31.7	(0.51)	38.6	(0.72)	19.4	(1.20)	13.5	(0.80)	52.5	(2.32)	55.8	(2.47)	10.0!	(4.40)	18.6	(4.80)	29.8	(3.22)
2011	32.2	(0.62)	39.2	(0.88)	20.1	(1.25)	12.8	(0.73)	56.0	(2.50)	57.2	(2.52)	28.8!	(9.04)	17.3	(4.45)	32.4	(3.85)
2012	33.5	(0.58)	39.8	(0.78)	23.2	(1.38)	14.8	(0.90)	59.6	(2.17)	61.7	(2.24)	25.5	(6.12)	10.4	(2.87)	32.9	(3.72)
2013	33.6	(0.55)	40.4	(0.77)	20.5	(1.38)	15.7	(0.82)	58.0	(2.16)	60.1	(2.18)	24.7!	(7.54)	16.6	(4.89)	29.6	(3.45)
2014	34.0	(0.75)	40.8	(1.05)	22.4	(1.82)	15.1	(0.97)	60.8	(2.44)	63.2	(2.50)	‡	(†)	5.6!	(2.24)	32.4	(4.12)
2015	35.6	(0.55)	43.0	(0.83)	21.3	(1.33)	16.4	(0.78)	62.8	(2.25)	66.0	(2.27)	11.4!	(4.64)	15.3	(3.21)	29.6	(3.62)
2016	36.1	(0.61)	42.9	(0.87)	22.7	(1.26)	18.7	(1.06)	63.5	(2.11)	65.6	(2.20)	20.4!	(6.62)	10.2	(2.57)	28.3	(3.76)
2017	35.7	(0.63)	42.1	(0.88)	22.8	(1.37)	18.5	(0.82)	60.6	(2.22)	62.7	(2.28)	25.3	(7.04)	16.3!	(5.22)	32.8	(3.84)
2018	37.0	(0.66)	43.5	(0.96)	22.6	(1.39)	20.7	(1.03)	67.1	(2.10)	70.5	(2.08)	15.1	(4.53)	15.5	(3.30)	26.9	(3.01)

See notes at end of table.

Table 104.20. Percentage of persons 25 to 29 years old with selected levels of educational attainment, by race/ethnicity and sex: Selected years, 1920 through 2018—Continued

[Standard errors appear in parentheses]

Sex, selected level of educational attainment, and year	Total	White[1]	Black[1]	Hispanic	Asian/Pacific Islander: Total	Asian/Pacific Islander: Asian	Asian/Pacific Islander: Pacific Islander	American Indian/ Alaska Native	Two or more races
1	2	3	4	5	6	7	8	9	10
Master's or higher degree									
1995	4.5 (0.24)	5.3 (0.31)	1.8 (0.48)	1.6 (0.46)	10.9 (2.43)	— (†)	— (†)	‡ (†)	— (†)
2000	5.4 (0.26)	5.8 (0.33)	3.7 (0.63)	2.1 (0.36)	15.5 (1.89)	— (†)	— (†)	‡ (†)	— (†)
2005	6.3 (0.31)	7.5 (0.45)	2.6 (0.44)	2.1 (0.38)	16.9 (1.93)	17.5 (2.01)	‡ (†)	‡ (†)	7.0! (2.49)
2006	6.4 (0.29)	7.5 (0.42)	3.2 (0.58)	1.5 (0.25)	20.1 (2.00)	21.1 (2.10)	‡ (†)	‡ (†)	7.1 (1.83)
2007	6.3 (0.30)	7.6 (0.42)	3.5 (0.59)	1.5 (0.25)	17.5 (1.84)	18.5 (1.93)	‡ (†)	‡ (†)	6.2! (2.38)
2008	7.0 (0.28)	8.2 (0.40)	4.4 (0.64)	2.0 (0.28)	19.9 (1.84)	21.0 (1.96)	‡ (†)	‡ (†)	6.9! (2.57)
2009	7.4 (0.30)	8.9 (0.45)	4.2 (0.54)	1.9 (0.26)	21.1 (1.98)	22.9 (2.16)	‡ (†)	‡ (†)	6.5! (2.02)
2010	6.8 (0.26)	7.7 (0.38)	4.7 (0.60)	2.5 (0.37)	17.9 (1.87)	19.2 (1.99)	‡ (†)	‡ (†)	5.3! (1.63)
2011	6.9 (0.32)	8.1 (0.45)	4.0 (0.52)	2.7 (0.37)	16.7 (1.78)	17.5 (1.85)	‡ (†)	‡ (†)	6.1 (1.59)
2012	7.2 (0.35)	8.2 (0.51)	5.1 (0.66)	2.7 (0.36)	17.8 (1.85)	18.9 (1.92)	‡ (†)	2.6! (1.28)	4.1! (1.49)
2013	7.4 (0.31)	8.6 (0.50)	3.3 (0.50)	3.0 (0.37)	20.6 (1.73)	21.8 (1.79)	‡ (†)	‡ (†)	4.8! (1.54)
2014	7.6 (0.41)	9.0 (0.58)	3.9 (0.77)	2.9 (0.43)	17.9 (1.84)	18.8 (1.92)	‡ (†)	‡ (†)	7.1! (2.32)
2015	8.7 (0.33)	10.1 (0.51)	5.0 (0.60)	3.2 (0.41)	21.6 (1.85)	22.8 (1.97)	‡ (†)	‡ (†)	7.8 (1.79)
2016	9.2 (0.33)	10.5 (0.52)	5.2 (0.69)	4.1 (0.49)	23.8 (1.95)	24.9 (2.01)	‡ (†)	2.1! (0.85)	5.3! (1.74)
2017	9.2 (0.34)	10.1 (0.55)	5.5 (0.71)	3.9 (0.40)	24.5 (1.76)	25.6 (1.89)	‡ (†)	‡ (†)	5.0! (1.72)
2018	9.0 (0.36)	10.1 (0.62)	4.5 (0.65)	3.4 (0.43)	27.5 (1.87)	29.2 (1.98)	‡ (†)	‡ (†)	2.9! (1.44)
Males									
High school completion or higher[2]									
1980	85.4 (0.49)	89.1 (0.48)	74.7 (1.97)	57.0 (3.45)	— (†)	— (†)	— (†)	— (†)	— (†)
1990	84.4 (0.56)	88.6 (0.57)	81.4 (2.03)	56.6 (2.69)	95.3 (1.78)	— (†)	— (†)	— (†)	— (†)
1995	86.3 (0.56)	92.0 (0.53)	88.4 (1.72)	55.7 (2.51)	90.5 (3.11)	— (†)	— (†)	83.6 (9.73)	— (†)
2000	86.7 (0.55)	92.9 (0.51)	87.6 (1.67)	59.2 (1.76)	92.1 (2.03)	— (†)	— (†)	68.5 (9.40)	— (†)
2005	85.0 (0.58)	91.8 (0.53)	86.6 (1.76)	63.2 (1.72)	96.8 (1.09)	96.7 (1.15)	99.1 (0.94)	73.0 (8.43)	89.1 (3.07)
2006	84.4 (0.54)	92.3 (0.52)	84.2 (2.02)	60.5 (1.64)	97.2 (1.01)	97.2 (1.06)	97.8 (1.60)	75.0 (6.34)	89.2 (3.81)
2007	84.9 (0.50)	92.7 (0.48)	87.4 (1.65)	60.5 (1.59)	95.9 (1.13)	96.3 (1.10)	‡ (†)	76.6 (8.90)	92.9 (2.64)
2008	85.8 (0.54)	92.6 (0.58)	85.7 (1.99)	65.6 (1.55)	95.6 (1.23)	95.4 (1.31)	100.0 (0.00)	90.5 (4.04)	92.7 (2.68)
2009	87.5 (0.51)	94.4 (0.46)	88.8 (1.56)	66.2 (1.54)	96.4 (1.17)	96.2 (1.25)	98.2 (1.81)	77.5 (8.59)	92.0 (3.01)
2010	87.4 (0.44)	94.6 (0.42)	87.9 (1.52)	65.7 (1.52)	93.8 (1.83)	93.5 (1.95)	98.2 (1.35)	93.2 (3.47)	87.9 (4.32)
2011	87.5 (0.49)	93.4 (0.48)	88.0 (1.43)	69.2 (1.62)	94.2 (1.30)	93.9 (1.36)	98.5 (1.46)	84.5 (5.28)	86.2 (4.41)
2012	88.4 (0.51)	93.8 (0.50)	86.2 (1.58)	73.3 (1.57)	96.1 (1.04)	96.0 (1.09)	97.3 (1.74)	82.8 (8.27)	91.0 (3.58)
2013	88.3 (0.52)	93.3 (0.53)	87.8 (1.60)	73.1 (1.64)	94.4 (1.12)	94.3 (1.21)	96.3 (3.04)	89.0 (3.25)	96.8 (1.77)
2014	90.1 (0.53)	95.4 (0.60)	93.5 (1.18)	72.4 (1.76)	96.1 (1.10)	96.1 (1.14)	‡ (†)	83.5 (7.17)	96.9 (2.02)
2015	90.5 (0.45)	95.1 (0.45)	91.8 (1.22)	75.7 (1.41)	95.9 (1.23)	97.1 (0.96)	75.8 (12.49)	83.2 (4.73)	98.0 (1.27)
2016	90.9 (0.46)	94.8 (0.44)	91.7 (1.19)	78.3 (1.34)	96.0 (1.06)	96.2 (1.05)	‡ (†)	84.4 (5.70)	98.1 (1.22)
2017	91.5 (0.48)	94.8 (0.46)	92.0 (1.19)	80.7 (1.31)	97.3 (0.77)	97.7 (0.75)	89.3 (6.87)	76.5 (8.11)	95.9 (2.38)
2018	91.9 (0.44)	95.0 (0.53)	90.7 (1.37)	83.4 (1.22)	97.1 (0.92)	97.6 (0.96)	89.3 (6.35)	82.9 (5.67)	92.8 (2.42)
Associate's or higher degree									
1995	32.1 (0.76)	37.1 (0.94)	23.5 (2.28)	11.6 (1.62)	49.8 (5.30)	— (†)	— (†)	‡ (†)	— (†)
2000	35.3 (0.78)	40.7 (0.98)	24.1 (2.16)	13.0 (1.20)	60.7 (3.68)	— (†)	— (†)	17.6! (7.71)	— (†)
2005	33.4 (0.74)	39.6 (1.05)	22.7 (1.77)	16.1 (1.12)	64.0 (3.16)	66.7 (3.19)	18.5! (7.78)	19.9! (7.06)	31.0 (5.10)
2006	33.8 (0.67)	41.5 (0.97)	21.3 (2.02)	12.8 (1.02)	65.4 (3.32)	67.9 (3.37)	25.6! (9.90)	18.9! (6.54)	28.4 (5.26)
2007	34.1 (0.76)	40.8 (1.01)	26.4 (2.06)	13.8 (0.96)	64.5 (3.04)	66.3 (3.12)	‡ (†)	14.9! (6.39)	30.8 (5.22)
2008	34.7 (0.72)	42.2 (0.98)	24.2 (2.16)	15.2 (1.05)	61.5 (3.23)	62.8 (3.21)	41.3 (11.71)	22.0! (6.95)	29.9 (4.62)
2009	34.5 (0.66)	41.8 (1.04)	21.9 (1.97)	15.9 (1.16)	63.0 (2.86)	66.6 (2.99)	17.4! (8.42)	17.1! (7.26)	31.7 (5.35)
2010	36.1 (0.68)	44.5 (0.98)	22.9 (2.16)	16.0 (1.20)	57.4 (3.12)	61.1 (3.27)	‡ (†)	30.1 (8.14)	31.5 (5.23)
2011	37.0 (0.88)	45.2 (1.17)	25.9 (2.24)	16.1 (1.18)	57.9 (3.40)	58.8 (3.48)	42.9 (12.13)	22.0 (5.29)	38.4 (7.04)
2012	38.2 (0.81)	44.8 (1.11)	25.3 (1.92)	20.6 (1.45)	63.4 (3.00)	65.5 (2.94)	28.8! (10.22)	15.7! (5.97)	46.3 (5.90)
2013	38.5 (0.69)	46.0 (1.03)	24.8 (1.76)	20.0 (1.20)	61.2 (2.74)	62.6 (2.80)	39.3 (11.03)	27.5 (7.59)	42.8 (5.00)
2014	39.4 (0.95)	47.4 (1.35)	28.9 (2.66)	18.2 (1.40)	63.5 (3.37)	66.0 (3.41)	‡ (†)	23.7! (8.06)	33.5 (6.67)
2015	41.3 (0.73)	49.3 (1.15)	24.6 (2.00)	22.7 (1.32)	67.1 (3.01)	69.5 (2.93)	26.0! (9.45)	17.7! (5.36)	37.7 (5.16)
2016	41.8 (0.87)	49.9 (1.19)	28.3 (2.21)	23.4 (1.56)	66.1 (2.83)	68.2 (2.90)	‡ (†)	13.7! (4.53)	27.7 (5.03)
2017	41.3 (0.86)	48.3 (1.22)	29.5 (2.22)	22.0 (1.33)	64.8 (2.85)	66.0 (2.88)	38.6! (11.88)	19.4! (7.61)	41.0 (5.82)
2018	42.0 (0.85)	47.8 (1.22)	29.1 (2.36)	27.3 (1.49)	71.2 (2.69)	74.1 (2.67)	21.2! (8.56)	15.6! (4.70)	34.9 (5.45)
Bachelor's or higher degree[4]									
1980	24.0 (0.59)	26.8 (0.69)	10.5 (1.39)	8.4 (1.94)	— (†)	— (†)	— (†)	— (†)	— (†)
1990	23.7 (0.65)	26.6 (0.79)	15.1 (1.87)	7.3 (1.41)	47.6 (4.19)	— (†)	— (†)	— (†)	— (†)
1995	24.5 (0.70)	28.4 (0.88)	17.4 (2.04)	7.8 (1.35)	42.0 (5.23)	— (†)	— (†)	‡ (†)	— (†)
2000	27.9 (0.73)	32.3 (0.93)	18.4 (1.96)	8.3 (0.98)	55.5 (3.74)	— (†)	— (†)	‡ (†)	— (†)
2005	25.5 (0.68)	30.7 (0.98)	14.2 (1.57)	10.2 (0.99)	58.5 (3.11)	61.0 (3.17)	17.2! (7.62)	14.5! (6.14)	24.5 (4.93)
2006	25.3 (0.67)	31.4 (0.98)	15.2 (1.66)	6.9 (0.70)	58.7 (3.46)	60.9 (3.52)	23.3! (9.77)	‡ (†)	20.8 (4.65)
2007	26.3 (0.72)	31.9 (0.98)	18.9 (1.86)	8.6 (0.71)	58.5 (3.45)	60.4 (3.54)	‡ (†)	‡ (†)	23.3 (4.88)
2008	26.8 (0.64)	32.6 (0.89)	19.0 (1.94)	10.0 (0.86)	54.1 (3.41)	55.8 (3.53)	26.1! (9.86)	17.7! (6.67)	25.7 (4.45)
2009	26.6 (0.66)	32.6 (1.04)	14.8 (1.82)	11.0 (1.04)	55.2 (3.07)	59.2 (3.24)	‡ (†)	15.2! (7.21)	24.6 (5.77)
2010	27.8 (0.68)	34.8 (0.96)	15.0 (1.72)	10.8 (1.06)	49.0 (3.12)	52.3 (3.31)	‡ (†)	18.9! (7.12)	24.9 (4.91)
2011	28.4 (0.82)	35.5 (1.16)	17.0 (1.83)	9.6 (0.90)	50.8 (3.42)	52.1 (3.55)	28.1! (11.40)	15.4! (4.80)	34.1 (6.62)
2012	29.8 (0.82)	36.0 (1.06)	19.1 (1.74)	12.5 (1.20)	55.0 (3.15)	56.9 (3.16)	24.3! (9.06)	‡ (†)	30.4 (5.43)
2013	30.2 (0.68)	37.1 (1.00)	17.4 (1.63)	13.1 (1.06)	53.0 (3.03)	55.1 (3.13)	19.0! (9.38)	16.8! (6.40)	29.3 (4.61)
2014	30.9 (0.93)	37.7 (1.36)	20.8 (2.40)	12.4 (1.22)	56.9 (3.55)	59.0 (3.59)	‡ (†)	‡ (†)	26.4 (6.13)
2015	32.4 (0.74)	39.5 (1.12)	17.6 (1.83)	14.5 (1.04)	60.9 (3.13)	63.8 (3.12)	‡ (†)	‡ (†)	26.7 (5.07)

See notes at end of table.

Table 104.20. Percentage of persons 25 to 29 years old with selected levels of educational attainment, by race/ethnicity and sex: Selected years, 1920 through 2018—Continued

[Standard errors appear in parentheses]

Sex, selected level of educational attainment, and year	Total	White[1]	Black[1]	Hispanic	Asian/Pacific Islander			American Indian/ Alaska Native	Two or more races
					Total	Asian	Pacific Islander		
1	2	3	4	5	6	7	8	9	10
2016	32.7 (0.80)	39.5 (1.20)	20.4 (1.87)	16.2 (1.31)	59.0 (2.86)	61.4 (2.98)	‡ (†)	7.8! (3.17)	19.7 (4.52)
2017	32.0 (0.81)	37.7 (1.19)	21.7 (1.79)	15.0 (1.13)	57.7 (2.92)	59.2 (3.00)	26.4! (10.58)	‡ (†)	26.1 (5.48)
2018	33.2 (0.85)	38.8 (1.32)	18.7 (1.95)	18.4 (1.34)	66.7 (2.97)	69.6 (2.97)	17.3! (8.00)	8.4! (3.50)	25.1 (4.93)
Master's or higher degree									
1995	4.9 (0.35)	5.6 (0.45)	2.2! (0.80)	2.0! (0.70)	12.6 (3.52)	— (†)	— (†)	‡ (†)	— (†)
2000	4.7 (0.34)	4.9 (0.43)	2.1! (0.72)	1.5 (0.43)	17.2 (2.85)	— (†)	— (†)	‡ (†)	— (†)
2005	5.2 (0.38)	6.2 (0.55)	1.1! (0.43)	1.7 (0.46)	19.7 (3.13)	20.5 (3.30)	‡ (†)	‡ (†)	‡ (†)
2006	5.1 (0.37)	5.8 (0.51)	1.7! (0.52)	1.1 (0.32)	20.5 (2.68)	21.8 (2.83)	‡ (†)	‡ (†)	5.9! (2.66)
2007	5.0 (0.39)	5.7 (0.50)	3.3 (0.99)	0.6! (0.19)	18.4 (2.89)	19.3 (3.00)	‡ (†)	‡ (†)	9.8! (4.28)
2008	5.3 (0.34)	5.9 (0.49)	3.4 (0.90)	1.2 (0.32)	20.9 (2.94)	22.1 (3.07)	‡ (†)	‡ (†)	7.8! (2.85)
2009	6.1 (0.37)	7.4 (0.60)	3.2 (0.73)	1.2 (0.28)	20.4 (2.48)	22.0 (2.69)	‡ (†)	‡ (†)	5.0! (2.38)
2010	5.2 (0.32)	6.3 (0.50)	2.9 (0.69)	1.5 (0.39)	15.0 (2.19)	16.2 (2.36)	‡ (†)	‡ (†)	‡ (†)
2011	5.1 (0.38)	5.9 (0.49)	1.9 (0.54)	1.8 (0.41)	18.0 (2.58)	19.1 (2.71)	‡ (†)	‡ (†)	‡ (†)
2012	5.6 (0.42)	6.3 (0.59)	2.7 (0.72)	2.4 (0.50)	16.2 (2.46)	17.2 (2.60)	‡ (†)	‡ (†)	‡ (†)
2013	5.7 (0.38)	6.3 (0.53)	1.5! (0.56)	2.1 (0.43)	20.8 (2.49)	22.1 (2.60)	‡ (†)	‡ (†)	5.9! (2.47)
2014	5.9 (0.51)	7.0 (0.72)	2.6! (0.82)	2.2 (0.52)	15.9 (2.56)	16.6 (2.65)	‡ (†)	‡ (†)	‡ (†)
2015	7.0 (0.40)	8.2 (0.62)	2.5 (0.75)	2.3 (0.56)	21.1 (2.65)	22.4 (2.78)	‡ (†)	‡ (†)	5.6! (2.37)
2016	7.2 (0.43)	8.7 (0.68)	3.9 (0.87)	2.1 (0.43)	19.7 (2.73)	20.6 (2.85)	‡ (†)	‡ (†)	‡ (†)
2017	7.8 (0.42)	8.5 (0.64)	3.9 (0.89)	2.8 (0.52)	24.3 (2.52)	25.4 (2.63)	‡ (†)	‡ (†)	‡ (†)
2018	7.3 (0.44)	7.7 (0.70)	2.8 (0.74)	3.1 (0.56)	27.0 (2.81)	28.6 (2.95)	‡ (†)	‡ (†)	‡ (†)
Females									
High school completion or higher[2]									
1980	85.5 (0.48)	89.2 (0.48)	78.3 (1.71)	58.9 (3.38)	— (†)	— (†)	— (†)	— (†)	— (†)
1990	87.0 (0.51)	91.7 (0.49)	82.0 (1.85)	59.9 (2.79)	85.1 (2.82)	— (†)	— (†)	— (†)	— (†)
1995	87.4 (0.54)	93.0 (0.50)	85.3 (1.75)	58.7 (2.60)	91.2 (3.28)	— (†)	— (†)	79.6 (9.88)	— (†)
2000	89.4 (0.49)	95.2 (0.43)	86.2 (1.53)	66.4 (1.69)	95.2 (1.55)	— (†)	— (†)	86.3 (5.68)	— (†)
2005	87.4 (0.44)	93.8 (0.47)	87.3 (1.22)	63.4 (1.54)	94.6 (1.36)	94.4 (1.41)	‡ (†)	87.1 (5.12)	94.2 (2.26)
2006	88.5 (0.44)	94.6 (0.41)	88.0 (1.14)	66.6 (1.41)	95.6 (1.44)	96.0 (1.31)	‡ (†)	83.3 (6.55)	89.4 (3.81)
2007	89.1 (0.45)	94.2 (0.44)	87.9 (1.46)	70.7 (1.30)	97.7 (1.05)	98.5 (0.68)	86.0 (8.19)	90.2 (4.49)	87.9 (3.82)
2008	89.9 (0.39)	94.7 (0.44)	89.2 (1.43)	71.9 (1.34)	96.1 (1.12)	96.2 (1.18)	95.2 (4.01)	84.2 (4.68)	95.9 (2.44)
2009	89.8 (0.41)	94.8 (0.44)	89.0 (1.12)	72.5 (1.34)	94.5 (1.20)	95.3 (1.18)	86.2 (5.92)	83.4 (4.81)	84.8 (3.57)
2010	90.2 (0.39)	94.4 (0.42)	91.1 (0.96)	74.1 (1.53)	93.6 (1.25)	94.5 (1.27)	81.2 (9.50)	86.8 (4.80)	89.1 (3.55)
2011	90.7 (0.36)	95.5 (0.42)	88.2 (1.24)	74.3 (1.26)	96.6 (0.89)	96.6 (0.92)	‡ (†)	85.3 (6.02)	94.0 (2.52)
2012	91.1 (0.44)	95.3 (0.46)	90.6 (1.11)	76.9 (1.39)	96.3 (0.98)	96.1 (1.04)	100.0 (0.00)	85.8 (4.53)	94.7 (2.35)
2013	91.5 (0.38)	94.9 (0.43)	92.5 (0.95)	78.8 (1.17)	96.2 (0.96)	96.3 (1.01)	94.8 (2.88)	82.0 (5.40)	98.2 (1.15)
2014	91.5 (0.50)	95.9 (0.54)	90.5 (1.62)	77.4 (1.56)	97.1 (0.96)	97.1 (0.99)	‡ (†)	84.1 (6.05)	95.2 (3.44)
2015	91.8 (0.39)	95.8 (0.41)	93.2 (0.90)	78.6 (1.34)	94.8 (1.18)	94.6 (1.25)	96.7 (1.86)	89.3 (3.52)	91.5 (2.99)
2016	92.5 (0.40)	95.7 (0.41)	90.7 (1.33)	83.2 (1.22)	97.4 (0.76)	97.4 (0.79)	‡ (†)	84.6 (5.34)	91.5 (2.76)
2017	93.4 (0.34)	96.4 (0.39)	92.6 (1.22)	84.8 (1.04)	95.5 (1.10)	95.8 (1.16)	90.7 (4.70)	90.9 (3.70)	94.0 (3.24)
2018	94.0 (0.39)	96.3 (0.44)	93.2 (0.95)	87.2 (1.13)	97.0 (0.91)	97.4 (0.85)	91.8 (6.23)	95.1 (2.18)	93.8 (2.49)
Associate's or higher degree									
1995	34.0 (0.77)	39.5 (0.95)	21.6 (2.03)	14.6 (1.86)	52.6 (5.77)	— (†)	— (†)	‡ (†)	— (†)
2000	40.1 (0.78)	46.6 (1.00)	27.5 (1.99)	17.7 (1.37)	60.8 (3.54)	— (†)	— (†)	37.7 (8.00)	— (†)
2005	41.3 (0.72)	48.2 (0.99)	29.8 (1.81)	18.8 (1.23)	68.5 (2.86)	70.4 (2.90)	‡ (†)	28.7 (6.96)	43.7 (6.04)
2006	41.5 (0.72)	48.8 (1.00)	28.8 (1.91)	20.3 (1.17)	68.0 (2.60)	69.4 (2.65)	‡ (†)	17.6! (6.91)	34.7 (5.09)
2007	43.2 (0.72)	50.8 (1.02)	28.0 (1.61)	23.5 (1.25)	67.7 (2.73)	69.6 (2.88)	42.5 (11.79)	14.5! (5.53)	40.2 (5.87)
2008	44.9 (0.77)	53.0 (1.00)	30.7 (1.79)	23.2 (1.43)	68.5 (2.80)	70.8 (2.82)	29.5! (9.83)	20.2 (4.14)	37.6 (5.73)
2009	44.4 (0.75)	52.5 (1.02)	33.0 (1.79)	21.7 (1.22)	63.0 (3.19)	66.8 (3.13)	23.6! (8.47)	23.3 (5.09)	39.8 (5.19)
2010	46.3 (0.71)	53.5 (0.92)	35.2 (1.77)	26.2 (1.48)	63.3 (2.68)	65.6 (2.80)	31.4! (13.43)	27.7 (8.27)	41.8 (5.08)
2011	47.4 (0.74)	55.2 (1.00)	33.3 (1.92)	26.2 (1.29)	69.1 (2.50)	70.2 (2.48)	‡ (†)	28.7 (7.46)	44.5 (5.08)
2012	47.4 (0.68)	55.0 (0.94)	37.0 (1.80)	25.1 (1.23)	69.1 (2.22)	71.0 (2.29)	36.1 (9.80)	29.2 (6.04)	49.0 (5.15)
2013	47.9 (0.77)	56.1 (0.99)	33.6 (1.99)	26.8 (1.30)	69.2 (2.29)	71.2 (2.33)	35.5 (10.28)	25.6 (7.48)	46.0 (6.22)
2014	48.9 (0.99)	56.5 (1.28)	34.8 (2.77)	29.4 (1.67)	71.5 (3.14)	74.1 (3.18)	‡ (†)	15.7! (5.27)	48.2 (6.06)
2015	50.1 (0.72)	58.7 (0.98)	36.9 (1.78)	29.0 (1.47)	70.7 (2.55)	73.8 (2.61)	24.0! (9.77)	25.8 (4.73)	39.2 (5.20)
2016	50.5 (0.71)	58.7 (0.95)	34.8 (1.73)	31.0 (1.51)	72.6 (2.49)	74.5 (2.56)	‡ (†)	18.9 (4.75)	54.5 (5.59)
2017	51.0 (0.73)	58.8 (1.04)	35.5 (1.69)	33.9 (1.34)	71.2 (2.77)	73.9 (2.71)	34.0! (10.51)	33.1 (7.83)	49.6 (5.82)
2018	51.5 (0.82)	59.6 (1.17)	35.8 (1.86)	34.2 (1.56)	73.1 (2.31)	76.9 (2.21)	23.6! (8.51)	32.8 (6.29)	48.2 (5.45)
Bachelor's or higher degree[4]									
1980	21.0 (0.56)	23.2 (0.65)	12.4 (1.36)	6.9 (1.74)	— (†)	— (†)	— (†)	— (†)	— (†)
1990	22.8 (0.64)	26.2 (0.78)	11.9 (1.56)	9.1 (1.64)	37.4 (3.83)	— (†)	— (†)	— (†)	— (†)
1995	24.9 (0.70)	29.2 (0.89)	13.7 (1.70)	10.1 (1.59)	44.5 (5.74)	— (†)	— (†)	‡ (†)	— (†)
2000	30.1 (0.73)	35.8 (0.96)	17.4 (1.69)	11.0 (1.12)	53.1 (3.62)	— (†)	— (†)	19.1! (6.48)	— (†)
2005	32.2 (0.75)	38.2 (1.00)	20.5 (1.68)	12.4 (1.07)	61.4 (3.06)	63.1 (3.11)	‡ (†)	18.2! (6.43)	32.1 (5.70)
2006	31.6 (0.70)	37.2 (0.99)	21.7 (1.77)	12.8 (1.05)	60.4 (2.76)	62.8 (2.82)	‡ (†)	‡ (†)	25.7 (4.72)
2007	33.0 (0.72)	39.2 (1.03)	20.0 (1.38)	15.4 (1.10)	60.3 (2.83)	62.5 (2.88)	32.1! (11.09)	‡ (†)	29.6 (5.17)
2008	34.9 (0.71)	41.7 (0.98)	21.6 (1.57)	15.5 (1.11)	61.6 (2.67)	64.4 (2.71)	‡ (†)	12.2! (3.69)	27.7 (5.57)
2009	34.8 (0.78)	42.0 (1.12)	22.6 (1.75)	13.8 (1.09)	57.6 (3.00)	61.3 (3.03)	18.2! (6.42)	16.3 (4.42)	35.0 (5.07)
2010	35.7 (0.68)	42.4 (0.96)	23.3 (1.72)	16.8 (1.20)	55.8 (2.93)	58.9 (3.00)	‡ (†)	18.4! (6.68)	34.0 (4.96)

See notes at end of table.

Table 104.20. Percentage of persons 25 to 29 years old with selected levels of educational attainment, by race/ethnicity and sex: Selected years, 1920 through 2018—Continued

[Standard errors appear in parentheses]

Sex, selected level of educational attainment, and year	Total	White[1]	Black[1]	Hispanic	Asian/Pacific Islander: Total	Asian/Pacific Islander: Asian	Asian/Pacific Islander: Pacific Islander	American Indian/ Alaska Native	Two or more races
1	2	3	4	5	6	7	8	9	10
2011	36.1 (0.71)	43.0 (1.03)	22.9 (1.62)	16.8 (1.10)	61.0 (2.74)	62.0 (2.75)	‡ (†)	19.7! (6.64)	31.2 (4.36)
2012	37.2 (0.69)	43.6 (0.97)	26.7 (1.78)	17.4 (1.10)	64.0 (2.38)	66.2 (2.45)	26.8! (9.73)	14.0! (4.55)	35.5 (5.50)
2013	37.0 (0.71)	43.8 (0.95)	23.2 (2.03)	18.6 (1.10)	62.4 (2.51)	64.3 (2.54)	29.7! (10.58)	16.4! (6.57)	30.0 (5.26)
2014	37.2 (1.00)	43.9 (1.36)	23.8 (2.61)	18.3 (1.40)	64.3 (3.23)	66.9 (3.29)	‡ (†)	‡ (†)	38.4 (5.96)
2015	38.9 (0.74)	46.6 (1.06)	24.6 (1.72)	18.5 (1.21)	64.5 (2.74)	68.1 (2.73)	‡ (†)	21.8 (4.51)	32.9 (5.20)
2016	39.5 (0.75)	46.3 (1.03)	24.9 (1.55)	21.5 (1.44)	67.7 (2.66)	69.6 (2.72)	‡ (†)	12.2! (4.00)	36.8 (5.55)
2017	39.3 (0.78)	46.5 (1.11)	23.8 (1.79)	22.4 (1.16)	63.5 (2.88)	66.3 (2.85)	24.6! (9.17)	18.7! (6.83)	38.5 (5.84)
2018	40.8 (0.84)	48.4 (1.24)	26.2 (1.81)	23.2 (1.43)	67.4 (2.60)	71.5 (2.55)	13.5! (6.42)	22.5 (5.87)	28.7 (4.34)
Master's or higher degree									
1995	4.1 (0.32)	5.0 (0.42)	1.4! (0.59)	1.2! (0.58)	8.9! (3.29)	— (†)	— (†)	‡ (†)	— (†)
2000	6.2 (0.38)	6.7 (0.50)	4.9 (0.96)	2.7 (0.58)	13.9 (2.51)	— (†)	— (†)	‡ (†)	— (†)
2005	7.3 (0.44)	8.8 (0.64)	4.0 (0.70)	2.6 (0.51)	14.4 (2.08)	15.0 (2.15)	‡ (†)	‡ (†)	10.0! (4.26)
2006	7.8 (0.42)	9.2 (0.63)	4.5 (0.93)	2.0 (0.41)	19.7 (2.33)	20.4 (2.44)	‡ (†)	‡ (†)	8.3! (2.89)
2007	7.6 (0.43)	9.4 (0.63)	3.7 (0.66)	2.6 (0.53)	16.5 (2.39)	17.7 (2.54)	‡ (†)	‡ (†)	‡ (†)
2008	8.7 (0.44)	10.4 (0.64)	5.2 (0.87)	2.9 (0.46)	18.9 (2.30)	19.9 (2.44)	‡ (†)	‡ (†)	‡ (†)
2009	8.8 (0.45)	10.4 (0.66)	5.1 (0.80)	2.7 (0.43)	21.7 (2.45)	23.7 (2.70)	‡ (†)	‡ (†)	7.9! (2.84)
2010	8.5 (0.39)	9.2 (0.56)	6.2 (0.94)	3.8 (0.56)	20.6 (2.60)	21.8 (2.75)	‡ (†)	‡ (†)	10.0! (3.06)
2011	8.8 (0.48)	10.4 (0.72)	5.8 (0.85)	3.8 (0.63)	15.4 (1.98)	15.9 (2.03)	‡ (†)	‡ (†)	9.9 (2.61)
2012	8.8 (0.45)	10.0 (0.67)	7.1 (1.00)	3.0 (0.45)	19.3 (2.23)	20.4 (2.31)	‡ (†)	‡ (†)	6.3! (2.49)
2013	9.2 (0.44)	10.8 (0.71)	4.8 (0.74)	4.0 (0.59)	20.4 (1.91)	21.6 (2.00)	‡ (†)	‡ (†)	3.3! (1.56)
2014	9.3 (0.56)	11.1 (0.84)	5.0 (1.17)	3.6 (0.63)	19.7 (2.33)	20.8 (2.47)	‡ (†)	‡ (†)	7.5! (3.00)
2015	10.4 (0.51)	12.0 (0.73)	7.2 (0.98)	4.1 (0.60)	22.0 (2.51)	23.2 (2.67)	‡ (†)	‡ (†)	10.2! (3.20)
2016	11.2 (0.51)	12.3 (0.74)	6.3 (1.02)	6.3 (0.89)	27.5 (2.51)	28.8 (2.58)	‡ (†)	‡ (†)	8.2! (3.17)
2017	10.5 (0.49)	11.8 (0.75)	6.8 (1.06)	5.0 (0.67)	24.8 (2.38)	25.8 (2.54)	‡ (†)	‡ (†)	5.4! (2.45)
2018	10.7 (0.50)	12.6 (0.83)	6.2 (1.02)	3.8 (0.54)	27.9 (2.40)	29.9 (2.56)	‡ (†)	‡ (†)	‡ (†)

—Not available.
†Not applicable.
!Interpret data with caution. The coefficient of variation (CV) for this estimate is between 30 and 50 percent.
‡Reporting standards not met. Either there are too few cases for a reliable estimate or the coefficient of variation (CV) is 50 percent or greater.
[1]Includes persons of Hispanic ethnicity for years prior to 1980.
[2]Data for years prior to 1993 are for persons with 4 or more years of high school. Data for later years are for high school completers—i.e., those persons who graduated from high school with a diploma as well as those who completed high school through equivalency programs, such as a GED program.
[3]Estimates based on Census Bureau reverse projection of 1940 census data on education by age.
[4]Data for years prior to 1993 are for persons with 4 or more years of college.

NOTE: Prior to 2005, standard errors were computed using generalized variance function methodology rather than the more precise replicate weight methodology used in later years. For 1960 and prior years, data were collected in April. For later years, data were collected in March. Data are based on sample surveys of the noninstitutionalized population, which excludes persons living in institutions (e.g., prisons or nursing facilities); data include military personnel who live in households with civilians, but exclude those who live in military barracks. Race categories exclude persons of Hispanic ethnicity except where otherwise noted.
SOURCE: U.S. Department of Commerce, Census Bureau, *U.S. Census of Population: 1960*, Vol. I, Part 1; J.K. Folger and C.B. Nam, *Education of the American Population* (1960 Census Monograph); Current Population Reports, Series P-20, various years; and Current Population Survey (CPS), Annual Social and Economic Supplement, 1970 through 2018. (This table was prepared October 2018.)

Table 104.30. Number of persons age 18 and over, by highest level of educational attainment, sex, race/ethnicity, and age: 2018

[Numbers in thousands. Standard errors appear in parentheses]

Sex, race/ethnicity, and age	Total	Elementary school (kindergarten–8th grade)	High school: 1 to 3 years	High school: 4 years, no completion	High school: Completion[1]	Postsecondary education: Some college, no degree	Postsecondary education: Associate's degree	Postsecondary education: Bachelor's degree	Postsecondary education: Master's degree	Postsecondary education: First-professional or doctor's degree
1	2	3	4	5	6	7	8	9	10	11
Total, 18 and over	**249,193 (122.2)**	**9,111 (165.9)**	**14,118 (203.2)**	**3,945 (120.7)**	**71,368 (477.0)**	**46,175 (335.8)**	**24,102 (257.0)**	**51,406 (422.1)**	**21,280 (273.2)**	**7,688 (173.1)**
18 and 19 years old	7,928 (96.0)	122 (26.0)	2,388 (73.3)	703 (37.8)	2,254 (76.3)	2,292 (77.7)	114 (18.6)	‡ (†)	‡ (†)	‡ (†)
20 to 24 years old	21,434 (27.7)	260 (33.6)	852 (53.4)	438 (41.2)	6,429 (130.9)	8,442 (139.4)	1,620 (74.5)	3,121 (106.7)	231 (25.0)	‡ (†)
25 years old and over	219,830 (56.4)	8,729 (155.7)	10,878 (176.8)	2,805 (102.4)	62,685 (447.6)	35,442 (294.4)	22,369 (237.3)	48,235 (402.3)	21,048 (269.7)	7,641 (172.9)
25 to 29 years old	23,160 (39.7)	397 (36.4)	929 (53.4)	308 (35.0)	6,162 (130.2)	4,543 (97.9)	2,256 (81.6)	6,478 (132.1)	1,618 (73.0)	467 (44.2)
30 to 34 years old	21,695 (47.0)	561 (40.7)	934 (52.6)	264 (31.3)	5,297 (118.7)	3,312 (80.0)	2,389 (76.1)	5,893 (116.7)	2,210 (77.0)	834 (49.6)
35 to 39 years old	21,269 (37.7)	740 (43.4)	1,020 (41.6)	308 (36.6)	5,049 (96.6)	3,295 (78.0)	2,246 (65.8)	5,308 (100.5)	2,494 (74.5)	810 (50.4)
40 to 49 years old	40,029 (53.9)	1,478 (57.3)	1,887 (65.0)	469 (35.3)	10,416 (142.2)	5,947 (108.9)	4,328 (100.2)	9,383 (144.1)	4,608 (95.3)	1,512 (55.9)
50 to 59 years old	42,521 (78.1)	1,570 (61.1)	2,083 (77.1)	617 (37.7)	13,022 (179.7)	6,645 (121.3)	4,679 (112.0)	8,817 (161.6)	3,731 (100.9)	1,356 (62.6)
60 to 64 years old	20,078 (145.5)	801 (42.5)	892 (44.9)	227 (25.5)	6,137 (126.0)	3,399 (92.1)	2,178 (75.2)	3,920 (97.3)	1,788 (71.4)	736 (51.0)
65 years old and over	51,080 (122.6)	3,182 (88.3)	3,132 (88.8)	612 (43.9)	16,601 (177.6)	8,300 (150.3)	4,292 (98.8)	8,436 (156.5)	4,597 (121.9)	1,927 (83.8)
Males, 18 and over	**120,705 (107.2)**	**4,453 (106.3)**	**7,174 (132.7)**	**2,133 (80.3)**	**36,274 (307.6)**	**22,096 (237.9)**	**10,489 (161.9)**	**24,379 (245.8)**	**9,294 (159.8)**	**4,415 (115.1)**
18 and 19 years old	4,034 (80.0)	55 (11.2)	1,295 (49.0)	376 (28.1)	1,208 (51.7)	1,010 (53.0)	69 (16.3)	‡ (†)	‡ (†)	‡ (†)
20 to 24 years old	10,809 (26.9)	141 (18.8)	416 (35.5)	280 (31.8)	3,741 (98.6)	4,105 (96.6)	733 (50.2)	1,283 (64.8)	76 (14.9)	‡ (†)
25 years old and over	105,862 (53.1)	4,256 (100.1)	5,463 (115.2)	1,476 (70.7)	31,325 (284.6)	16,981 (206.8)	9,687 (153.4)	23,080 (242.7)	9,217 (160.4)	4,376 (115.3)
25 to 29 years old	11,674 (40.3)	232 (24.0)	527 (42.7)	184 (25.7)	3,529 (99.8)	2,298 (81.9)	1,030 (56.0)	3,021 (90.6)	639 (44.3)	212 (26.5)
30 to 34 years old	10,816 (45.1)	295 (30.3)	553 (40.0)	167 (22.7)	3,001 (88.5)	1,651 (60.8)	1,067 (54.5)	2,813 (82.9)	848 (44.6)	421 (34.0)
35 to 39 years old	10,567 (37.4)	394 (32.1)	534 (33.7)	190 (32.3)	2,849 (71.2)	1,595 (56.6)	993 (45.7)	2,529 (65.0)	1,094 (46.6)	390 (31.7)
40 to 49 years old	19,627 (53.9)	754 (40.1)	968 (46.4)	247 (22.8)	5,648 (114.5)	2,982 (72.1)	1,938 (61.3)	4,306 (98.7)	2,014 (66.3)	769 (36.5)
50 to 59 years old	20,720 (58.7)	862 (40.8)	1,115 (57.8)	316 (25.8)	6,720 (121.2)	3,135 (85.7)	2,006 (78.4)	4,139 (101.3)	1,630 (65.8)	797 (47.2)
60 to 64 years old	9,399 (132.0)	352 (26.8)	415 (28.9)	117 (18.0)	2,877 (78.4)	1,603 (60.1)	865 (42.9)	1,892 (63.2)	830 (46.3)	447 (36.6)
65 years old and over	23,059 (122.6)	1,367 (55.3)	1,352 (54.5)	255 (25.1)	6,701 (119.3)	3,717 (92.3)	1,787 (66.8)	4,380 (101.6)	2,162 (75.0)	1,339 (62.0)
Females, 18 and over	**128,488 (70.3)**	**4,658 (99.8)**	**6,944 (129.1)**	**1,813 (73.8)**	**35,094 (296.5)**	**24,079 (201.0)**	**13,613 (177.2)**	**27,027 (274.6)**	**11,987 (175.7)**	**3,273 (104.0)**
18 and 19 years old	3,894 (67.9)	67 (18.7)	1,093 (51.2)	326 (23.4)	1,046 (49.7)	1,282 (53.9)	‡ (†)	‡ (†)	‡ (†)	‡ (†)
20 to 24 years old	10,625 (5.3)	119 (22.1)	436 (36.1)	158 (19.6)	2,687 (77.9)	4,337 (91.6)	886 (48.9)	1,838 (74.8)	154 (21.4)	‡ (†)
25 years old and over	113,969 (14.6)	4,472 (94.9)	5,415 (109.1)	1,328 (61.7)	31,360 (270.0)	18,461 (176.0)	12,682 (162.3)	25,155 (254.2)	11,831 (173.7)	3,265 (103.4)
25 to 29 years old	11,486 (9.7)	164 (22.4)	403 (29.0)	124 (19.1)	2,633 (75.2)	2,245 (68.9)	1,226 (57.7)	3,457 (84.1)	979 (51.6)	255 (28.6)
30 to 34 years old	10,878 (6.5)	266 (25.4)	381 (27.4)	97 (15.2)	2,297 (61.3)	1,661 (55.2)	1,322 (49.0)	3,080 (77.6)	1,362 (56.6)	412 (34.2)
35 to 39 years old	10,701 (6.1)	346 (24.6)	487 (25.3)	119 (14.8)	2,200 (60.8)	1,700 (50.6)	1,253 (48.3)	2,778 (65.5)	1,400 (52.9)	419 (30.3)
40 to 49 years old	20,402 (3.8)	724 (35.8)	919 (43.8)	221 (23.6)	4,768 (87.8)	2,966 (73.2)	2,390 (72.8)	5,077 (96.6)	2,594 (67.7)	743 (37.8)
50 to 59 years old	21,801 (49.8)	708 (37.3)	968 (40.7)	301 (27.4)	6,302 (112.3)	3,510 (85.8)	2,673 (71.0)	4,678 (105.2)	2,102 (75.2)	559 (37.3)
60 to 64 years old	10,679 (49.5)	449 (28.5)	477 (33.7)	110 (16.5)	3,260 (83.6)	1,797 (61.4)	1,313 (59.5)	2,029 (67.6)	958 (50.7)	288 (31.5)
65 years old and over	28,021 (0.9)	1,815 (55.2)	1,780 (66.2)	357 (31.5)	9,901 (122.5)	4,583 (105.0)	2,505 (71.0)	4,056 (102.8)	2,435 (81.0)	588 (47.1)
White, 18 and over	**158,209 (135.5)**	**2,170 (104.5)**	**6,645 (147.7)**	**1,601 (73.6)**	**44,442 (374.1)**	**29,281 (270.2)**	**16,530 (210.7)**	**36,568 (355.3)**	**15,350 (240.6)**	**5,622 (152.4)**
18 and 19 years old	4,211 (72.7)	72 (17.3)	1,321 (53.2)	316 (24.1)	1,175 (54.1)	1,225 (58.1)	65 (15.4)	‡ (†)	‡ (†)	‡ (†)
20 to 24 years old	11,578 (36.4)	95 (21.1)	316 (37.2)	167 (25.9)	3,257 (99.2)	4,653 (100.3)	907 (56.6)	2,021 (86.4)	132 (21.4)	‡ (†)
25 years old and over	142,420 (109.4)	2,003 (93.4)	5,007 (129.0)	1,118 (61.8)	40,010 (347.3)	23,403 (238.8)	15,558 (198.1)	34,513 (341.5)	15,217 (239.7)	5,590 (152.7)
25 to 29 years old	12,668 (45.6)	112 (24.0)	340 (33.4)	100 (19.6)	3,030 (86.2)	2,290 (78.4)	1,280 (66.9)	4,231 (109.6)	952 (66.8)	333 (40.5)
30 to 34 years old	12,269 (45.5)	87 (18.7)	311 (27.1)	68 (14.6)	2,737 (90.8)	1,847 (60.4)	1,453 (57.9)	3,825 (95.6)	1,401 (63.2)	540 (43.3)
35 to 39 years old	12,014 (39.0)	78 (13.9)	302 (25.6)	72 (13.9)	2,551 (66.5)	1,857 (59.4)	1,419 (49.5)	3,578 (80.4)	1,625 (59.9)	533 (40.0)
40 to 49 years old	23,584 (52.7)	199 (23.9)	641 (39.3)	134 (18.9)	5,648 (106.5)	3,617 (87.2)	2,864 (75.0)	6,401 (115.1)	3,085 (79.7)	994 (45.5)
50 to 59 years old	28,597 (62.9)	263 (27.6)	1,013 (59.8)	270 (25.1)	8,699 (157.4)	4,576 (109.2)	3,373 (104.0)	6,631 (139.6)	2,797 (88.5)	976 (56.0)
60 to 64 years old	14,157 (112.0)	149 (19.4)	428 (34.5)	106 (19.7)	4,346 (108.8)	2,481 (82.1)	1,643 (69.4)	2,987 (89.4)	1,429 (61.3)	589 (47.3)
65 years old and over	39,131 (120.0)	1,115 (61.8)	1,972 (73.3)	368 (36.8)	13,000 (172.4)	6,735 (141.7)	3,526 (97.3)	6,861 (146.8)	3,929 (119.8)	1,626 (80.3)
Black, 18 and over	**29,581 (86.9)**	**682 (48.3)**	**2,235 (76.2)**	**702 (48.2)**	**9,743 (159.6)**	**6,543 (143.7)**	**2,839 (90.9)**	**4,517 (115.1)**	**1,816 (68.4)**	**504 (36.7)**
18 and 19 years old	1,145 (43.8)	‡ (†)	340 (26.0)	95 (15.5)	367 (29.6)	292 (28.7)	‡ (†)	‡ (†)	‡ (†)	‡ (†)
20 to 24 years old	2,975 (26.1)	‡ (†)	154 (22.5)	70 (20.3)	1,069 (55.1)	1,157 (58.5)	181 (25.9)	305 (29.3)	‡ (†)	‡ (†)
25 years old and over	25,461 (72.7)	635 (43.1)	1,742 (66.9)	536 (40.7)	8,307 (140.1)	5,094 (120.4)	2,640 (84.3)	4,206 (109.2)	1,800 (67.6)	502 (36.6)
25 to 29 years old	3,279 (31.4)	‡ (†)	170 (21.8)	‡ (†)	1,097 (57.0)	850 (45.4)	329 (29.1)	592 (43.2)	112 (18.4)	‡ (†)
30 to 34 years old	2,713 (25.6)	‡ (†)	112 (18.3)	‡ (†)	771 (42.9)	574 (40.7)	319 (27.8)	597 (36.6)	189 (20.9)	69 (14.3)
35 to 39 years old	2,630 (23.1)	‡ (†)	146 (18.9)	‡ (†)	769 (49.6)	508 (37.2)	288 (26.6)	491 (34.5)	297 (27.5)	53 (12.4)
40 to 49 years old	4,953 (26.3)	‡ (†)	211 (21.9)	98 (14.8)	1,520 (50.4)	998 (45.4)	531 (37.3)	932 (45.0)	507 (34.1)	106 (16.2)
50 to 59 years old	4,983 (54.1)	96 (15.7)	341 (29.8)	132 (19.7)	1,786 (55.9)	944 (45.6)	560 (31.9)	740 (43.4)	295 (26.3)	89 (14.9)
60 to 64 years old	2,307 (59.5)	54 (11.7)	205 (20.8)	50 (10.6)	799 (41.9)	453 (31.0)	256 (24.1)	333 (23.4)	112 (15.7)	‡ (†)
65 years old and over	4,598 (38.5)	327 (24.4)	557 (30.2)	114 (15.2)	1,564 (44.7)	768 (36.1)	358 (25.3)	521 (27.3)	287 (22.9)	103 (13.3)

See notes at end of table.

Table 104.30. Number of persons age 18 and over, by highest level of educational attainment, sex, race/ethnicity, and age: 2018—Continued

[Numbers in thousands. Standard errors appear in parentheses]

Sex, race/ethnicity, and age	Total	Elementary school (kindergarten–8th grade)	High school			Postsecondary education				
			1 to 3 years	4 years, no completion	Completion[1]	Some college, no degree	Associate's degree	Bachelor's degree	Master's degree	First-professional or doctor's degree
1	2	3	4	5	6	7	8	9	10	11
Hispanic, 18 and over	**40,478 (43.6)**	**5,404 (107.7)**	**4,306 (101.4)**	**1,289 (68.3)**	**12,590 (173.3)**	**7,148 (117.6)**	**3,161 (92.1)**	**4,765 (107.5)**	**1,397 (55.9)**	**417 (32.3)**
18 and 19 years old	1,858 (41.0)	‡ (†)	552 (28.1)	199 (19.1)	547 (33.1)	510 (26.4)	‡ (†)	‡ (†)	‡ (†)	‡ (†)
20 to 24 years old	4,743 (4.6)	117 (21.3)	309 (28.9)	172 (23.5)	1,632 (61.3)	1,741 (60.5)	410 (30.0)	347 (27.6)	‡ (†)	‡ (†)
25 years old and over	33,877 (14.6)	5,263 (102.1)	3,445 (88.4)	918 (59.0)	10,412 (144.7)	4,897 (92.6)	2,729 (83.4)	4,414 (100.9)	1,385 (55.9)	414 (32.1)
25 to 29 years old	4,859 (32.4)	230 (23.3)	368 (31.4)	121 (19.8)	1,586 (61.1)	1,070 (39.8)	478 (34.8)	842 (45.3)	138 (19.0)	‡ (†)
30 to 34 years old	4,422 (34.3)	424 (34.1)	437 (34.8)	141 (22.1)	1,390 (51.1)	682 (36.3)	412 (32.6)	690 (38.7)	202 (23.2)	44 (9.9)
35 to 39 years old	4,483 (35.1)	598 (39.4)	514 (32.6)	183 (31.3)	1,337 (54.8)	634 (38.8)	363 (30.0)	605 (36.9)	201 (18.9)	47 (13.0)
40 to 49 years old	7,716 (49.5)	1,122 (46.4)	888 (44.5)	202 (23.2)	2,544 (67.4)	959 (46.2)	599 (34.6)	948 (44.4)	360 (25.6)	96 (13.6)
50 to 59 years old	5,873 (61.4)	1,068 (47.7)	586 (35.7)	146 (18.7)	1,767 (57.2)	781 (37.3)	471 (31.5)	706 (37.0)	247 (19.3)	101 (14.8)
60 to 64 years old	2,201 (47.6)	504 (29.0)	198 (18.1)	53 (9.7)	621 (35.7)	289 (22.4)	167 (17.4)	247 (25.5)	92 (14.6)	‡ (†)
65 years old and over	4,322 (8.4)	1,317 (41.2)	454 (28.1)	72 (12.2)	1,167 (44.6)	482 (29.4)	240 (21.6)	376 (22.5)	146 (15.0)	69 (11.1)
Asian, 18 and over	**15,035 (105.8)**	**731 (48.1)**	**478 (40.1)**	**234 (25.3)**	**2,757 (86.0)**	**1,857 (69.8)**	**920 (51.4)**	**4,578 (93.2)**	**2,442 (75.5)**	**1,039 (56.6)**
18 and 19 years old	372 (25.2)	‡ (†)	83 (13.5)	‡ (†)	60 (12.9)	173 (20.8)	‡ (†)	‡ (†)	‡ (†)	‡ (†)
20 to 24 years old	1,315 (34.7)	‡ (†)	‡ (†)	‡ (†)	177 (23.9)	587 (36.6)	58 (13.0)	358 (30.8)	68 (12.9)	‡ (†)
25 years old and over	13,349 (96.1)	707 (45.1)	378 (33.6)	170 (21.8)	2,519 (80.8)	1,097 (51.3)	859 (48.6)	4,215 (91.1)	2,374 (73.3)	1,029 (56.2)
25 to 29 years old	1,610 (36.0)	‡ (†)	‡ (†)	‡ (†)	202 (24.6)	152 (18.0)	80 (14.6)	665 (37.3)	406 (32.8)	65 (13.9)
30 to 34 years old	1,642 (37.1)	‡ (†)	‡ (†)	‡ (†)	212 (23.6)	109 (14.7)	110 (17.1)	627 (34.2)	377 (30.3)	161 (20.9)
35 to 39 years old	1,570 (37.2)	‡ (†)	‡ (†)	‡ (†)	231 (23.6)	159 (19.9)	103 (14.3)	534 (30.3)	327 (25.7)	154 (19.1)
40 to 49 years old	2,908 (50.8)	91 (14.6)	88 (14.4)	‡ (†)	478 (31.3)	214 (21.3)	221 (23.0)	920 (41.1)	571 (36.5)	299 (28.0)
50 to 59 years old	2,231 (53.1)	120 (19.6)	85 (14.9)	‡ (†)	513 (31.4)	174 (19.6)	159 (17.0)	616 (39.0)	348 (26.6)	171 (19.8)
60 to 64 years old	1,070 (37.7)	87 (17.7)	‡ (†)	‡ (†)	255 (24.3)	104 (14.4)	74 (13.1)	295 (25.2)	141 (17.8)	64 (11.7)
65 years old and over	2,318 (41.7)	363 (30.2)	101 (16.3)	‡ (†)	629 (35.9)	185 (19.6)	112 (15.6)	558 (32.5)	203 (21.7)	115 (16.4)

†Not applicable.
‡Reporting standards not met. Either there are too few cases for a reliable estimate or the coefficient of variation (CV) is 50 percent or greater.
[1]Includes completion of high school through equivalency programs, such as a GED program.

NOTE: Total includes other racial/ethnic groups not shown separately. Race categories exclude persons of Hispanic ethnicity. Detail may not sum to totals because of rounding.
SOURCE: U.S. Department of Commerce, Census Bureau, Current Population Survey (CPS), Annual Social and Economic Supplement, 2018. (This table was prepared February 2019.)

Table 104.50. Persons age 25 and over who hold a bachelor's or higher degree, by sex, race/ethnicity, age group, and field of bachelor's degree: 2017

[Standard errors appear in parentheses]

Field of bachelor's degree	Total	Sex: Male	Sex: Female	Race/ethnicity: White	Race/ethnicity: Black	Race/ethnicity: Hispanic	Race/ethnicity: Asian/Pacific Islander	Race/ethnicity: American Indian/Alaska Native	Age: 25 to 29 years old	Age: 30 to 49 years old	Age: 50 years old and over
1	2	3	4	5	6	7	8	9	10	11	12
Total population, 25 and over (in thousands)	**221,310 (21.0)**	**106,905 (24.7)**	**114,406 (21.0)**	**143,646 (27.3)**	**25,835 (9.8)**	**33,490 (8.9)**	**13,124 (9.2)**	**1,342 (1.3)**	**23,029 (10.1)**	**84,099 (23.7)**	**114,182 (19.8)**
Percent of population with bachelor's degree	**32.0 (0.07)**	**31.4 (0.08)**	**32.6 (0.07)**	**35.8 (0.08)**	**21.6 (0.12)**	**16.0 (0.11)**	**53.2 (0.20)**	**15.0 (0.36)**	**34.3 (0.18)**	**35.9 (0.10)**	**28.7 (0.06)**
Bachelor's degree holders	Number (in thousands)										
Total	**70,854 (164.9)**	**33,521 (87.4)**	**37,334 (87.7)**	**51,378 (110.8)**	**5,572 (31.1)**	**5,370 (39.3)**	**6,984 (27.5)**	**201 (5.5)**	**7,890 (42.2)**	**30,169 (84.5)**	**32,795 (76.3)**
Agriculture	715 (9.7)	468 (7.5)	247 (5.1)	598 (8.7)	24 (2.0)	35 (2.5)	47 (2.8)	‡ (†)	75 (3.5)	274 (6.3)	366 (6.0)
Architecture	507 (8.7)	340 (6.7)	167 (4.7)	339 (6.3)	26 (2.4)	63 (3.2)	68 (2.7)	‡ (†)	54 (3.6)	218 (6.1)	235 (5.8)
Business/management	14,355 (50.2)	7,912 (39.1)	6,443 (30.9)	10,231 (38.5)	1,300 (16.1)	1,225 (16.6)	1,313 (13.3)	41 (3.0)	1,381 (17.4)	6,378 (35.8)	6,596 (26.8)
Communications and communications technologies	2,737 (19.5)	1,129 (12.9)	1,608 (15.2)	2,087 (16.8)	244 (6.6)	213 (6.8)	133 (4.1)	6 (0.9)	427 (7.8)	1,424 (15.6)	886 (9.6)
Computer and information sciences	2,276 (20.1)	1,626 (16.4)	650 (9.4)	1,238 (12.3)	224 (7.0)	165 (5.6)	584 (9.8)	3 (0.6)	318 (8.6)	1,302 (15.0)	656 (9.8)
Criminal justice and fire protection	1,262 (15.1)	745 (10.1)	517 (10.5)	843 (11.6)	203 (6.4)	144 (5.3)	38 (2.5)	6 (0.9)	209 (6.4)	693 (10.9)	361 (6.4)
Education	8,973 (39.1)	2,129 (17.6)	6,844 (30.2)	7,255 (31.7)	677 (11.2)	577 (9.8)	325 (7.1)	35 (2.2)	559 (10.0)	2,775 (22.8)	5,639 (27.1)
Engineering and engineering technologies	6,357 (35.0)	5,359 (30.3)	998 (12.0)	4,076 (26.2)	310 (7.4)	548 (10.7)	1,294 (13.5)	11 (1.2)	705 (10.1)	2,657 (23.7)	2,995 (19.8)
English language and literature	2,254 (17.9)	762 (11.2)	1,492 (12.6)	1,807 (15.1)	124 (4.5)	110 (5.1)	162 (4.5)	4 (0.6)	217 (6.2)	920 (11.3)	1,117 (12.6)
Foreign languages, literatures, and linguistics	736 (10.7)	200 (5.2)	536 (9.9)	535 (9.6)	31 (2.8)	77 (3.5)	75 (2.9)	‡ (†)	75 (2.8)	291 (5.9)	369 (7.5)
Health sciences	5,365 (24.0)	954 (9.8)	4,411 (21.3)	3,792 (18.1)	482 (10.9)	356 (7.3)	622 (9.8)	18 (1.3)	618 (8.2)	2,252 (17.1)	2,496 (16.4)
Liberal arts and humanities	982 (12.7)	388 (7.9)	594 (9.3)	710 (10.1)	71 (3.4)	89 (3.6)	85 (3.7)	4 (0.9)	85 (3.6)	432 (7.8)	465 (7.1)
Mathematics/statistics	1,071 (12.2)	614 (8.3)	456 (8.1)	782 (10.0)	64 (3.1)	51 (3.1)	152 (4.6)	‡ (†)	107 (3.9)	375 (7.5)	589 (9.3)
Natural sciences (biological, environmental, and physical)	5,974 (40.0)	3,339 (25.7)	2,635 (23.0)	4,258 (28.0)	361 (9.3)	369 (7.4)	843 (10.2)	16 (1.5)	791 (13.3)	2,552 (25.9)	2,632 (18.0)
Philosophy/religion/theology	941 (13.5)	646 (10.1)	295 (6.8)	721 (10.4)	80 (3.8)	59 (3.1)	60 (3.2)	3 (0.6)	82 (3.7)	353 (7.6)	506 (7.7)
Psychology	3,403 (22.5)	1,024 (12.3)	2,380 (17.9)	2,462 (17.8)	333 (7.0)	312 (7.5)	201 (5.0)	10 (1.3)	482 (8.9)	1,607 (14.6)	1,314 (13.2)
Social sciences and history	6,638 (35.1)	3,701 (24.7)	2,937 (21.0)	4,990 (27.3)	485 (9.8)	471 (8.9)	528 (9.2)	16 (1.3)	743 (11.6)	2,767 (22.9)	3,129 (20.5)
Social work and public administration	1,005 (11.8)	220 (5.7)	785 (10.1)	652 (8.9)	182 (6.4)	97 (4.0)	48 (2.7)	6 (0.9)	115 (4.3)	437 (8.6)	453 (7.4)
Visual and performing arts	2,914 (21.0)	1,104 (13.8)	1,810 (16.7)	2,239 (18.1)	154 (6.0)	204 (5.9)	243 (6.5)	7 (1.0)	444 (9.7)	1,324 (16.8)	1,146 (11.6)
Other fields[1]	2,389 (18.6)	861 (11.3)	1,528 (13.0)	1,761 (15.2)	196 (6.5)	205 (5.1)	165 (4.9)	9 (1.1)	404 (9.1)	1,139 (14.6)	846 (11.5)
	Percentage distribution, by field										
Total	**100.0 (†)**	**100.0 (†)**	**100.0 (†)**	**100.0 (†)**	**100.0 (†)**	**100.0 (†)**	**100.0 (†)**	**100.0 (†)**	**100.0 (†)**	**100.0 (†)**	**100.0 (†)**
Agriculture	1.0 (0.01)	1.4 (0.02)	0.7 (0.01)	1.2 (0.02)	0.4 (0.04)	0.7 (0.05)	0.7 (0.04)	1.0 (0.25)	0.9 (0.04)	0.9 (0.02)	1.1 (0.02)
Architecture	0.7 (0.01)	1.0 (0.02)	0.4 (0.01)	0.7 (0.01)	0.5 (0.04)	1.2 (0.06)	1.0 (0.04)	0.4! (0.14)	0.7 (0.05)	0.7 (0.02)	0.7 (0.02)
Business/management	20.3 (0.06)	23.6 (0.10)	17.3 (0.08)	19.9 (0.06)	23.3 (0.26)	22.8 (0.28)	18.8 (0.17)	20.5 (1.30)	17.5 (0.19)	21.1 (0.12)	20.1 (0.07)
Communications and communications technologies	3.9 (0.03)	3.4 (0.04)	4.3 (0.04)	4.1 (0.03)	4.4 (0.12)	4.0 (0.12)	1.9 (0.06)	2.8 (0.45)	5.4 (0.10)	4.7 (0.05)	2.7 (0.03)
Computer and information sciences	3.2 (0.03)	4.9 (0.05)	1.7 (0.03)	2.4 (0.02)	4.0 (0.12)	3.1 (0.11)	8.4 (0.14)	1.7 (0.30)	4.0 (0.11)	4.3 (0.05)	2.0 (0.03)
Criminal justice and fire protection	1.8 (0.02)	2.2 (0.03)	1.4 (0.03)	1.6 (0.02)	3.7 (0.11)	2.7 (0.10)	0.5 (0.04)	3.2 (0.42)	2.6 (0.08)	2.3 (0.04)	1.1 (0.02)
Education	12.7 (0.04)	6.4 (0.05)	18.3 (0.06)	14.1 (0.05)	12.1 (0.20)	10.7 (0.17)	4.6 (0.10)	17.4 (0.97)	7.1 (0.12)	9.2 (0.07)	17.2 (0.06)
Engineering and engineering technologies	9.0 (0.04)	16.0 (0.08)	2.7 (0.03)	7.9 (0.05)	5.6 (0.13)	10.2 (0.18)	18.5 (0.18)	5.4 (0.60)	8.9 (0.12)	8.8 (0.07)	9.1 (0.05)
English language and literature	3.2 (0.02)	2.3 (0.03)	4.0 (0.03)	3.5 (0.03)	2.2 (0.08)	2.0 (0.09)	2.3 (0.06)	1.8 (0.28)	2.8 (0.08)	3.0 (0.04)	3.4 (0.04)
Foreign languages, literatures, and linguistics	1.0 (0.01)	0.6 (0.02)	1.4 (0.03)	1.0 (0.02)	0.6 (0.05)	1.4 (0.06)	1.1 (0.04)	0.7! (0.22)	1.0 (0.04)	1.0 (0.02)	1.1 (0.02)
Health sciences	7.6 (0.03)	2.8 (0.03)	11.8 (0.06)	7.4 (0.03)	8.7 (0.19)	6.6 (0.13)	8.9 (0.13)	9.2 (0.64)	7.8 (0.10)	7.5 (0.06)	7.6 (0.05)
Liberal arts and humanities	1.4 (0.02)	1.2 (0.02)	1.6 (0.02)	1.4 (0.02)	1.3 (0.06)	1.7 (0.07)	1.2 (0.05)	2.1 (0.46)	1.1 (0.05)	1.4 (0.03)	1.4 (0.02)
Mathematics/statistics	1.5 (0.02)	1.8 (0.02)	1.2 (0.02)	1.5 (0.02)	1.1 (0.05)	0.9 (0.06)	2.2 (0.07)	0.9! (0.27)	1.4 (0.05)	1.2 (0.02)	1.8 (0.03)
Natural sciences (biological, environmental, and physical)	8.4 (0.05)	10.0 (0.07)	7.1 (0.06)	8.3 (0.05)	6.5 (0.16)	6.9 (0.13)	12.1 (0.14)	8.0 (0.71)	10.0 (0.15)	8.5 (0.08)	8.0 (0.05)
Philosophy/religion/theology	1.3 (0.02)	1.9 (0.03)	0.8 (0.02)	1.4 (0.02)	1.4 (0.07)	1.1 (0.06)	0.9 (0.05)	1.4 (0.29)	1.0 (0.05)	1.2 (0.03)	1.5 (0.02)
Psychology	4.8 (0.03)	3.1 (0.04)	6.4 (0.04)	4.8 (0.03)	6.0 (0.12)	5.8 (0.13)	2.9 (0.07)	4.9 (0.63)	6.1 (0.11)	5.3 (0.05)	4.0 (0.04)
Social sciences and history	9.4 (0.04)	11.0 (0.07)	7.9 (0.05)	9.7 (0.05)	8.7 (0.17)	8.8 (0.15)	7.6 (0.13)	8.1 (0.64)	9.4 (0.13)	9.2 (0.07)	9.5 (0.06)
Social work and public administration	1.4 (0.02)	0.7 (0.02)	2.1 (0.03)	1.3 (0.02)	3.3 (0.11)	1.8 (0.07)	0.7 (0.04)	2.9 (0.43)	1.5 (0.06)	1.4 (0.03)	1.4 (0.02)
Visual and performing arts	4.1 (0.03)	3.3 (0.04)	4.8 (0.04)	4.4 (0.04)	2.8 (0.11)	3.8 (0.10)	3.5 (0.09)	3.4 (0.51)	5.6 (0.12)	4.4 (0.05)	3.5 (0.03)
Other fields[1]	3.4 (0.02)	2.6 (0.03)	4.1 (0.03)	3.4 (0.03)	3.5 (0.11)	3.8 (0.09)	2.4 (0.07)	4.3 (0.53)	5.1 (0.11)	3.8 (0.05)	2.6 (0.03)

†Not applicable.
!Interpret data with caution. The coefficient of variation (CV) for this estimate is between 30 and 50 percent.
‡Reporting standards not met (too few cases for a reliable estimate).
[1]Includes area, ethnic, and civilization studies; family and consumer sciences; library sciences; military sciences; multi/interdisciplinary studies; physical fitness, parks, recreation and leisure; precision production; transportation technologies; and other fields, not separately classified.
NOTE: Data are based on sample surveys of the entire population age 25 and over residing within the United States, including both noninstitutionalized persons (e.g., those living in households, college housing, or military housing located within the United States) and institutionalized persons (e.g., those living in prisons, nursing facilities, or other healthcare facilities). The first bachelor's degree major reported by respondents was used to classify their field of study, even though they were able to report a second bachelor's degree major and may possess advanced degrees in other fields. Totals include other racial/ethnic groups not separately shown. Race categories exclude persons of Hispanic ethnicity. Detail may not sum to totals because of rounding.
SOURCE: U.S. Department of Commerce, Census Bureau, American Community Survey (ACS), 2017. (This table was prepared May 2019.)

Table 104.80. Percentage of persons 18 to 24 years old and age 25 and over, by educational attainment and state: 2000 and 2017

[Standard errors appear in parentheses]

State	Percent of 18- to 24-year-olds who were high school completers[1]		Percent of population 25 years old and over, by educational attainment										
			2000					2017					
			Less than high school completion	High school completion[1] or higher	Bachelor's or higher degree			Less than high school completion	High school completion[1] or higher		Bachelor's or higher degree		
	2000	2017			Total	Bachelor's degree	Graduate degree		Total	High school only	Total	Bachelor's degree	Graduate degree
1	2	3	4	5	6	7	8	9	10	11	12	13	14
United States	**74.7 (0.02)**	**87.4 (0.08)**	**19.6 (0.01)**	**80.4 (0.01)**	**24.4 (0.01)**	**15.5 (0.01)**	**8.9 (#)**	**12.0 (0.04)**	**88.0 (0.04)**	**27.1 (0.06)**	**32.0 (0.07)**	**19.7 (0.05)**	**12.3 (0.04)**
Alabama	72.2 (0.15)	85.5 (0.71)	24.7 (0.06)	75.3 (0.06)	19.0 (0.05)	12.1 (0.04)	6.9 (0.03)	14.0 (0.26)	86.0 (0.26)	31.0 (0.38)	25.6 (0.26)	15.9 (0.22)	9.7 (0.18)
Alaska	76.9 (0.40)	83.0 (2.69)	11.7 (0.12)	88.3 (0.12)	24.7 (0.16)	16.1 (0.13)	8.6 (0.10)	8.4 (0.59)	91.6 (0.59)	27.3 (0.85)	29.0 (1.24)	18.7 (1.07)	10.3 (0.71)
Arizona	69.2 (0.19)	84.2 (0.60)	19.0 (0.06)	81.0 (0.06)	23.5 (0.07)	15.1 (0.06)	8.4 (0.04)	12.9 (0.20)	87.1 (0.20)	24.1 (0.22)	29.2 (0.27)	18.2 (0.22)	10.9 (0.17)
Arkansas	75.4 (0.19)	87.3 (0.78)	24.7 (0.07)	75.3 (0.07)	16.7 (0.06)	11.0 (0.05)	5.7 (0.04)	13.3 (0.28)	86.7 (0.28)	34.0 (0.42)	23.5 (0.39)	15.1 (0.30)	8.4 (0.22)
California	70.7 (0.07)	89.5 (0.20)	23.2 (0.03)	76.8 (0.03)	26.6 (0.03)	17.1 (0.02)	9.5 (0.02)	16.6 (0.09)	83.4 (0.09)	20.7 (0.10)	33.7 (0.13)	21.1 (0.11)	12.6 (0.08)
Colorado	75.1 (0.15)	88.6 (0.59)	13.1 (0.05)	86.9 (0.05)	32.7 (0.06)	21.6 (0.06)	11.1 (0.04)	8.3 (0.21)	91.7 (0.21)	21.4 (0.29)	41.2 (0.30)	25.9 (0.24)	15.3 (0.23)
Connecticut	78.2 (0.21)	89.6 (0.61)	16.0 (0.06)	84.0 (0.06)	31.4 (0.08)	18.1 (0.07)	13.3 (0.06)	9.5 (0.25)	90.5 (0.25)	27.3 (0.43)	38.4 (0.34)	21.3 (0.28)	17.1 (0.25)
Delaware	77.6 (0.41)	89.4 (1.38)	17.4 (0.14)	82.6 (0.14)	25.0 (0.16)	15.6 (0.14)	9.4 (0.11)	9.3 (0.60)	90.7 (0.60)	31.8 (0.86)	31.9 (0.80)	18.5 (0.60)	13.4 (0.57)
District of Columbia	79.4 (0.40)	90.1 (1.31)	22.2 (0.18)	77.8 (0.18)	39.1 (0.21)	18.1 (0.17)	21.0 (0.18)	9.4 (0.58)	90.6 (0.58)	17.1 (0.75)	57.2 (0.87)	23.5 (0.80)	33.7 (0.74)
Florida	71.7 (0.11)	84.9 (0.35)	20.1 (0.04)	79.9 (0.04)	22.3 (0.04)	14.2 (0.03)	8.1 (0.02)	11.6 (0.12)	88.4 (0.12)	28.8 (0.18)	29.6 (0.17)	18.9 (0.14)	10.7 (0.10)
Georgia	70.0 (0.15)	84.7 (0.46)	21.4 (0.05)	78.6 (0.05)	24.3 (0.05)	16.0 (0.05)	8.3 (0.04)	13.0 (0.17)	87.0 (0.17)	28.0 (0.26)	30.9 (0.22)	19.1 (0.19)	11.9 (0.17)
Hawaii	85.8 (0.25)	92.4 (1.02)	15.4 (0.10)	84.6 (0.10)	26.2 (0.12)	17.8 (0.10)	8.4 (0.08)	8.3 (0.42)	91.7 (0.42)	28.9 (0.65)	32.8 (0.74)	21.9 (0.59)	10.9 (0.40)
Idaho	77.3 (0.25)	88.0 (1.00)	15.3 (0.09)	84.7 (0.09)	21.7 (0.10)	14.9 (0.09)	6.8 (0.06)	8.8 (0.37)	91.2 (0.37)	28.5 (0.57)	26.8 (0.56)	18.6 (0.47)	8.2 (0.35)
Illinois	76.0 (0.09)	87.2 (0.48)	18.6 (0.03)	81.4 (0.03)	26.1 (0.03)	16.6 (0.03)	9.5 (0.02)	11.0 (0.15)	89.0 (0.15)	26.0 (0.22)	34.4 (0.21)	20.9 (0.17)	13.4 (0.15)
Indiana	76.5 (0.15)	84.9 (0.55)	17.9 (0.05)	82.1 (0.05)	19.4 (0.05)	12.2 (0.04)	7.2 (0.04)	11.2 (0.19)	88.8 (0.19)	33.0 (0.30)	26.9 (0.29)	17.1 (0.22)	9.8 (0.20)
Iowa	81.4 (0.16)	90.7 (0.67)	13.9 (0.06)	86.1 (0.06)	21.2 (0.07)	14.7 (0.06)	6.5 (0.04)	8.0 (0.27)	92.0 (0.27)	30.2 (0.44)	29.2 (0.47)	19.6 (0.37)	9.5 (0.30)
Kansas	78.3 (0.18)	88.2 (0.75)	14.0 (0.06)	86.0 (0.06)	25.8 (0.08)	17.1 (0.06)	8.7 (0.05)	9.0 (0.28)	91.0 (0.28)	25.4 (0.43)	33.9 (0.43)	21.2 (0.37)	12.7 (0.32)
Kentucky	74.9 (0.15)	88.4 (0.66)	25.9 (0.06)	74.1 (0.06)	17.1 (0.05)	10.2 (0.04)	6.9 (0.03)	13.5 (0.24)	86.5 (0.24)	33.5 (0.34)	23.9 (0.32)	14.1 (0.26)	9.8 (0.22)
Louisiana	72.3 (0.15)	82.1 (0.76)	25.2 (0.06)	74.8 (0.06)	18.7 (0.05)	12.2 (0.04)	6.5 (0.03)	15.0 (0.33)	85.0 (0.33)	33.6 (0.34)	23.9 (0.33)	15.5 (0.25)	8.4 (0.23)
Maine	78.9 (0.28)	89.5 (1.25)	14.6 (0.08)	85.4 (0.08)	22.9 (0.10)	15.0 (0.09)	7.9 (0.06)	7.3 (0.41)	92.7 (0.41)	30.6 (0.71)	32.9 (0.68)	20.5 (0.50)	12.3 (0.50)
Maryland	79.6 (0.16)	90.5 (0.43)	16.2 (0.05)	83.8 (0.05)	31.4 (0.07)	18.0 (0.06)	13.4 (0.05)	10.1 (0.21)	89.9 (0.21)	24.2 (0.22)	40.0 (0.31)	21.4 (0.24)	18.6 (0.24)
Massachusetts	82.2 (0.13)	88.8 (0.48)	15.2 (0.05)	84.8 (0.05)	33.2 (0.06)	19.5 (0.05)	13.7 (0.04)	9.2 (0.16)	90.8 (0.16)	24.3 (0.25)	43.6 (0.28)	24.0 (0.25)	19.6 (0.20)
Michigan	76.5 (0.10)	87.7 (0.38)	16.6 (0.03)	83.4 (0.03)	21.8 (0.04)	13.7 (0.03)	8.1 (0.02)	9.1 (0.15)	90.9 (0.15)	29.0 (0.22)	29.0 (0.23)	17.4 (0.20)	11.6 (0.16)
Minnesota	79.3 (0.13)	88.2 (0.60)	12.1 (0.04)	87.9 (0.04)	27.4 (0.06)	19.1 (0.05)	8.3 (0.03)	7.0 (0.18)	93.0 (0.18)	24.7 (0.31)	35.7 (0.36)	23.4 (0.31)	12.4 (0.24)
Mississippi	71.3 (0.18)	85.2 (0.92)	27.1 (0.08)	72.9 (0.08)	16.9 (0.06)	11.1 (0.05)	5.8 (0.04)	15.4 (0.38)	84.6 (0.38)	30.3 (0.44)	21.7 (0.43)	13.4 (0.34)	8.3 (0.26)
Missouri	76.5 (0.13)	87.3 (0.56)	18.7 (0.05)	81.3 (0.05)	21.6 (0.05)	14.0 (0.04)	7.6 (0.03)	10.4 (0.21)	89.6 (0.21)	30.3 (0.32)	29.0 (0.29)	17.8 (0.24)	11.2 (0.21)
Montana	78.6 (0.31)	88.5 (1.56)	12.8 (0.10)	87.2 (0.10)	24.4 (0.13)	17.2 (0.11)	7.2 (0.08)	7.4 (0.41)	92.6 (0.41)	27.8 (0.76)	31.4 (0.82)	20.7 (0.70)	10.7 (0.49)
Nebraska	80.0 (0.21)	88.5 (1.06)	13.4 (0.07)	86.6 (0.07)	23.7 (0.09)	16.4 (0.08)	7.3 (0.06)	8.6 (0.34)	91.4 (0.34)	26.8 (0.52)	31.2 (0.49)	20.7 (0.42)	10.5 (0.34)
Nevada	66.7 (0.32)	85.4 (0.95)	19.3 (0.10)	80.7 (0.10)	18.2 (0.10)	12.1 (0.08)	6.1 (0.06)	13.2 (0.33)	86.8 (0.33)	28.9 (0.40)	25.2 (0.38)	16.7 (0.30)	8.4 (0.24)
New Hampshire	77.8 (0.29)	91.0 (1.24)	12.6 (0.08)	87.4 (0.08)	28.7 (0.11)	18.7 (0.10)	10.0 (0.07)	6.8 (0.34)	93.2 (0.34)	28.0 (0.60)	37.1 (0.67)	22.6 (0.53)	14.5 (0.47)
New Jersey	76.3 (0.14)	89.6 (0.42)	17.9 (0.04)	82.1 (0.04)	29.8 (0.05)	18.8 (0.04)	11.0 (0.04)	9.8 (0.16)	90.2 (0.16)	27.3 (0.23)	39.7 (0.24)	24.2 (0.20)	15.5 (0.15)
New Mexico	70.5 (0.24)	83.9 (1.14)	21.1 (0.09)	78.9 (0.09)	23.5 (0.09)	13.7 (0.07)	9.8 (0.06)	14.1 (0.37)	85.9 (0.37)	26.6 (0.50)	27.3 (0.46)	15.3 (0.36)	12.0 (0.31)
New York	76.1 (0.09)	88.3 (0.34)	20.9 (0.03)	79.1 (0.03)	27.4 (0.04)	15.6 (0.03)	11.8 (0.03)	13.4 (0.13)	86.6 (0.13)	26.2 (0.14)	36.2 (0.17)	20.3 (0.15)	15.9 (0.12)
North Carolina	74.2 (0.11)	86.3 (0.44)	21.9 (0.04)	78.1 (0.04)	22.5 (0.04)	15.3 (0.04)	7.2 (0.03)	12.0 (0.16)	88.0 (0.16)	25.8 (0.23)	31.4 (0.22)	20.2 (0.18)	11.2 (0.14)
North Dakota	84.4 (0.24)	90.1 (1.61)	16.1 (0.10)	83.9 (0.10)	22.0 (0.12)	16.5 (0.10)	5.5 (0.06)	6.9 (0.50)	93.1 (0.50)	26.5 (0.82)	30.6 (0.84)	22.0 (0.77)	8.6 (0.45)
Ohio	76.8 (0.09)	87.0 (0.37)	17.0 (0.03)	83.0 (0.03)	21.1 (0.03)	13.7 (0.03)	7.4 (0.02)	9.7 (0.14)	90.3 (0.14)	33.1 (0.22)	28.0 (0.19)	17.4 (0.14)	10.6 (0.13)
Oklahoma	74.8 (0.16)	84.5 (0.85)	19.4 (0.06)	80.6 (0.06)	20.3 (0.06)	13.5 (0.05)	6.8 (0.04)	11.9 (0.28)	88.1 (0.28)	31.4 (0.42)	25.5 (0.38)	16.8 (0.31)	8.6 (0.26)
Oregon	74.2 (0.17)	84.9 (0.70)	14.9 (0.05)	85.1 (0.05)	25.1 (0.06)	16.4 (0.06)	8.7 (0.04)	9.1 (0.23)	90.9 (0.23)	23.3 (0.33)	33.7 (0.30)	21.0 (0.24)	12.7 (0.22)
Pennsylvania	79.8 (0.09)	88.2 (0.41)	18.1 (0.03)	81.9 (0.03)	22.4 (0.03)	14.0 (0.03)	8.4 (0.02)	9.5 (0.12)	90.5 (0.12)	34.7 (0.22)	31.7 (0.19)	19.1 (0.15)	12.5 (0.14)
Rhode Island	81.3 (0.32)	91.8 (1.09)	22.0 (0.13)	78.0 (0.13)	25.6 (0.14)	15.9 (0.12)	9.7 (0.10)	11.8 (0.50)	88.2 (0.50)	29.2 (0.66)	33.8 (0.63)	20.4 (0.58)	13.4 (0.54)
South Carolina	74.3 (0.18)	87.6 (0.67)	23.7 (0.07)	76.3 (0.07)	20.4 (0.07)	13.5 (0.06)	6.9 (0.04)	12.4 (0.22)	87.6 (0.22)	29.5 (0.33)	28.0 (0.29)	17.6 (0.24)	10.4 (0.19)
South Dakota	78.2 (0.33)	86.8 (1.48)	15.4 (0.12)	84.6 (0.12)	21.5 (0.13)	15.5 (0.12)	6.0 (0.08)	8.2 (0.50)	91.8 (0.50)	30.5 (0.94)	27.7 (0.75)	19.0 (0.73)	8.7 (0.48)
Tennessee	75.1 (0.16)	87.3 (0.59)	24.1 (0.06)	75.9 (0.06)	19.6 (0.06)	12.8 (0.05)	6.8 (0.03)	12.3 (0.21)	87.7 (0.21)	32.3 (0.31)	27.4 (0.28)	17.3 (0.21)	10.1 (0.19)
Texas	68.6 (0.08)	85.2 (0.32)	24.3 (0.03)	75.7 (0.03)	23.2 (0.03)	15.6 (0.03)	7.6 (0.02)	16.3 (0.11)	83.7 (0.11)	25.1 (0.16)	29.6 (0.14)	19.4 (0.13)	10.3 (0.09)
Utah	80.3 (0.16)	89.8 (0.63)	12.3 (0.07)	87.7 (0.07)	26.1 (0.09)	17.8 (0.08)	8.3 (0.06)	7.9 (0.29)	92.1 (0.29)	22.0 (0.48)	34.3 (0.47)	22.2 (0.40)	12.0 (0.30)
Vermont	83.0 (0.28)	86.4 (2.65)	13.6 (0.10)	86.4 (0.10)	29.4 (0.13)	18.3 (0.11)	11.1 (0.09)	7.6 (0.60)	92.4 (0.60)	29.7 (1.03)	37.2 (1.14)	22.6 (0.81)	14.6 (0.82)
Virginia	79.4 (0.13)	90.8 (0.47)	18.5 (0.05)	81.5 (0.05)	29.5 (0.06)	17.9 (0.05)	11.6 (0.04)	10.4 (0.18)	89.6 (0.18)	24.1 (0.22)	38.8 (0.28)	22.0 (0.24)	16.9 (0.19)
Washington	75.3 (0.16)	86.0 (0.64)	12.9 (0.05)	87.1 (0.05)	27.7 (0.06)	18.4 (0.05)	9.3 (0.04)	8.7 (0.17)	91.3 (0.17)	22.0 (0.25)	35.6 (0.29)	22.2 (0.23)	13.4 (0.17)
West Virginia	78.2 (0.22)	88.2 (1.00)	24.8 (0.09)	75.2 (0.09)	14.8 (0.07)	8.9 (0.06)	5.9 (0.05)	13.0 (0.46)	87.0 (0.46)	41.4 (0.50)	20.2 (0.42)	12.0 (0.35)	8.2 (0.26)
Wisconsin	78.9 (0.13)	88.6 (0.60)	14.9 (0.04)	85.1 (0.04)	22.4 (0.05)	15.2 (0.04)	7.2 (0.03)	7.5 (0.19)	92.5 (0.19)	30.8 (0.33)	30.5 (0.34)	20.0 (0.35)	10.5 (0.20)
Wyoming	79.0 (0.41)	85.6 (2.73)	12.1 (0.13)	87.9 (0.13)	21.9 (0.16)	14.9 (0.14)	7.0 (0.10)	6.9 (0.48)	93.1 (0.48)	29.5 (1.04)	27.6 (0.88)	17.2 (0.76)	10.3 (0.56)

#Rounds to zero.

[1]High school completers include those graduating from high school with a diploma as well as those completing high school through equivalency programs, such as a GED program.

NOTE: Data are based on sample surveys of the entire population in the given age range residing within the United States, including both noninstitutionalized persons (e.g., those living in households, college housing, or military housing located within the United States) and institutionalized persons (e.g., those living in prisons, nursing facilities, or other healthcare facilities). Detail may not sum to totals because of rounding.

SOURCE: U.S. Department of Commerce, Census Bureau, Census 2000 Summary File 3, retrieved October 11, 2006, from https://factfinder2.census.gov/faces/tableservices/jsf/pages/productview.xhtml?pid=DEC_00_SF3_QTP20&prodType=table; Census Briefs, *Educational Attainment: 2000*; and 2017 American Community Survey (ACS) 1-Year Public Use Microdata Sample (PUMS) data. (This table was prepared February 2019.)

Table 104.85. Rates of high school completion and bachelor's degree attainment among persons age 25 and over, by race/ethnicity and state: 2017

[Standard errors appear in parentheses]

State	Percent with high school completion[1] or higher						Percent with bachelor's or higher degree					
	Total[2]	White	Black	Hispanic	Asian	Two or more races	Total[2]	White	Black	Hispanic	Asian	Two or more races
1	2	3	4	5	6	7	8	9	10	11	12	13
United States	**88.0 (0.04)**	**92.9 (0.03)**	**86.1 (0.11)**	**68.8 (0.15)**	**87.0 (0.13)**	**91.9 (0.21)**	**32.0 (0.07)**	**35.8 (0.08)**	**21.6 (0.12)**	**16.0 (0.11)**	**54.1 (0.20)**	**34.9 (0.37)**
Alabama	86.0 (0.26)	88.4 (0.35)	82.6 (0.60)	60.5 (2.88)	83.6 (2.65)	87.1 (2.42)	25.6 (0.26)	28.8 (0.33)	17.0 (0.52)	15.9 (1.63)	45.8 (3.60)	29.0 (2.75)
Alaska	91.6 (0.59)	95.1 (0.66)	96.2 (2.03)	89.5 (3.01)	77.6 (4.29)	96.7 (1.17)	29.0 (1.24)	34.4 (1.44)	28.7! (10.43)	21.3 (4.94)	24.1 (3.84)	31.6 (5.04)
Arizona	87.1 (0.20)	94.6 (0.18)	91.1 (0.82)	68.8 (0.51)	88.7 (1.01)	93.4 (1.16)	29.2 (0.27)	35.6 (0.33)	23.5 (1.69)	12.6 (0.43)	58.7 (1.47)	34.1 (2.33)
Arkansas	86.7 (0.28)	89.6 (0.29)	83.6 (0.94)	57.0 (2.26)	80.2 (2.73)	88.8 (2.02)	23.5 (0.39)	25.4 (0.44)	15.6 (0.98)	11.3 (1.46)	48.2 (4.35)	21.2 (2.53)
California	83.4 (0.09)	95.0 (0.09)	89.8 (0.34)	65.1 (0.21)	87.7 (0.21)	93.3 (0.44)	33.7 (0.13)	43.8 (0.18)	25.7 (0.51)	13.1 (0.17)	52.6 (0.29)	41.0 (0.76)
Colorado	91.7 (0.21)	96.3 (0.14)	92.6 (0.92)	73.3 (0.93)	83.8 (1.64)	93.8 (1.29)	41.2 (0.30)	47.5 (0.36)	28.7 (1.65)	16.1 (0.59)	52.5 (1.71)	43.7 (2.06)
Connecticut	90.5 (0.25)	94.4 (0.20)	87.6 (0.97)	71.8 (1.31)	89.1 (1.34)	91.3 (2.02)	38.4 (0.34)	43.5 (0.41)	20.1 (1.24)	15.9 (0.86)	64.5 (1.92)	29.5 (3.45)
Delaware	90.7 (0.60)	93.1 (0.64)	91.6 (1.07)	65.6 (4.18)	92.3 (1.87)	90.7 (3.41)	31.9 (0.80)	34.9 (1.00)	22.9 (1.69)	10.0 (1.82)	69.5 (3.69)	22.9 (6.79)
District of Columbia	90.6 (0.58)	99.2 (0.20)	87.3 (1.05)	67.9 (3.85)	95.5 (1.68)	95.2 (3.92)	57.2 (0.87)	90.5 (0.84)	26.6 (1.59)	43.3 (3.23)	82.1 (3.16)	83.3 (5.35)
Florida	88.4 (0.12)	92.9 (0.11)	83.7 (0.42)	80.2 (0.33)	87.0 (0.71)	90.8 (0.99)	29.6 (0.17)	33.2 (0.21)	18.8 (0.42)	23.9 (0.32)	52.1 (1.00)	35.7 (1.37)
Georgia	87.0 (0.17)	90.9 (0.20)	86.1 (0.36)	60.9 (1.12)	87.5 (0.99)	89.8 (1.33)	30.9 (0.22)	35.0 (0.29)	23.1 (0.35)	16.8 (0.66)	55.4 (1.37)	37.2 (2.26)
Hawaii	91.7 (0.42)	97.1 (0.43)	97.3 (1.44)	87.7 (1.77)	89.4 (0.72)	94.1 (0.81)	32.8 (0.74)	47.4 (1.41)	40.1 (6.49)	20.4 (2.07)	33.5 (1.02)	22.9 (1.32)
Idaho	91.2 (0.37)	93.6 (0.31)	‡ (†)	69.8 (2.05)	87.9 (3.60)	94.0 (1.96)	26.8 (0.56)	28.3 (0.62)	‡ (†)	10.9 (1.38)	50.5 (5.70)	31.8 (4.90)
Illinois	89.0 (0.15)	94.2 (0.11)	87.2 (0.44)	66.2 (0.73)	90.6 (0.60)	91.1 (1.22)	34.4 (0.21)	38.8 (0.27)	21.1 (0.54)	14.1 (0.50)	64.4 (0.86)	41.3 (2.35)
Indiana	88.8 (0.19)	90.7 (0.20)	86.4 (0.78)	64.4 (1.04)	82.2 (2.42)	91.7 (1.53)	26.9 (0.29)	27.6 (0.33)	20.8 (1.02)	13.7 (1.03)	58.1 (2.50)	27.4 (2.53)
Iowa	92.0 (0.27)	94.1 (0.22)	81.5 (2.74)	60.4 (3.02)	77.0 (2.81)	94.0 (1.80)	29.2 (0.47)	30.0 (0.47)	20.0 (2.93)	10.6 (1.44)	41.4 (3.90)	29.0 (5.36)
Kansas	91.0 (0.28)	94.4 (0.23)	84.4 (1.84)	65.1 (1.65)	89.9 (1.46)	89.1 (2.39)	33.9 (0.43)	36.9 (0.50)	21.9 (1.82)	13.0 (1.17)	46.3 (3.65)	28.2 (3.06)
Kentucky	86.5 (0.24)	86.7 (0.26)	88.6 (0.81)	76.4 (2.44)	81.4 (2.76)	86.7 (2.26)	23.9 (0.32)	23.9 (0.34)	19.0 (1.39)	21.6 (1.98)	48.8 (3.27)	26.7 (3.02)
Louisiana	85.0 (0.33)	89.0 (0.31)	79.2 (0.68)	70.4 (1.64)	77.6 (2.61)	90.9 (1.70)	23.9 (0.33)	28.1 (0.39)	15.0 (0.58)	16.0 (1.17)	45.0 (2.77)	28.3 (3.15)
Maine	92.7 (0.41)	93.0 (0.41)	90.5 (4.84)	91.2 (3.57)	80.2 (4.89)	90.5 (2.74)	32.9 (0.68)	32.6 (0.68)	37.2 (7.06)	44.5 (6.29)	46.0 (5.90)	30.5 (5.90)
Maryland	89.9 (0.21)	93.6 (0.22)	90.0 (0.42)	64.6 (1.23)	90.5 (0.80)	94.3 (1.06)	40.0 (0.31)	45.5 (0.39)	29.2 (0.57)	22.1 (0.93)	62.8 (1.48)	46.0 (1.80)
Massachusetts	90.8 (0.16)	94.0 (0.18)	86.5 (0.85)	72.2 (0.94)	86.1 (0.85)	91.3 (1.58)	43.6 (0.28)	46.7 (0.31)	27.7 (1.12)	18.3 (0.69)	63.1 (1.14)	45.3 (2.72)
Michigan	90.9 (0.15)	92.6 (0.14)	85.9 (0.57)	73.4 (1.20)	90.4 (1.19)	90.5 (1.19)	29.0 (0.23)	30.3 (0.24)	16.8 (0.57)	17.5 (0.98)	64.0 (1.45)	32.7 (2.26)
Minnesota	93.0 (0.18)	95.7 (0.17)	82.4 (1.70)	65.1 (2.29)	82.2 (1.37)	92.3 (1.61)	35.7 (0.36)	37.1 (0.40)	24.4 (2.10)	17.1 (1.82)	45.1 (1.90)	29.6 (2.89)
Mississippi	84.6 (0.38)	87.7 (0.45)	80.2 (0.60)	68.7 (2.70)	82.2 (3.68)	86.6 (4.63)	21.7 (0.43)	25.3 (0.57)	15.2 (0.59)	15.5 (2.45)	37.4 (4.47)	38.1 (5.69)
Missouri	89.6 (0.21)	90.8 (0.21)	84.4 (0.80)	74.2 (2.00)	91.5 (1.17)	91.0 (1.42)	29.0 (0.29)	30.0 (0.32)	17.6 (0.77)	19.4 (1.41)	61.0 (2.18)	33.0 (3.30)
Montana	92.6 (0.41)	93.6 (0.40)	‡ (†)	73.9 (5.43)	79.3 (12.82)	94.9 (2.52)	31.4 (0.82)	32.9 (0.82)	‡ (†)	20.7 (4.51)	39.4! (12.40)	19.5 (4.18)
Nebraska	91.4 (0.34)	95.5 (0.27)	84.1 (2.50)	57.6 (2.54)	79.9 (3.73)	89.7 (3.22)	31.2 (0.49)	33.4 (0.55)	14.9 (2.53)	12.1 (1.45)	52.4 (4.12)	29.9 (5.93)
Nevada	86.8 (0.33)	94.1 (0.32)	88.8 (1.07)	66.3 (1.04)	91.1 (0.93)	96.1 (0.95)	25.2 (0.38)	30.4 (0.60)	18.3 (1.33)	10.4 (0.45)	39.9 (1.54)	26.5 (2.30)
New Hampshire	93.2 (0.34)	93.7 (0.33)	88.6 (4.39)	86.4 (3.92)	87.2 (2.77)	88.8 (3.92)	37.1 (0.67)	36.8 (0.70)	29.6 (5.14)	26.7 (3.12)	61.0 (4.61)	31.1 (5.70)
New Jersey	90.2 (0.16)	94.6 (0.15)	88.3 (0.56)	76.0 (0.59)	92.4 (0.41)	93.2 (1.04)	39.7 (0.24)	43.6 (0.34)	25.1 (0.74)	20.2 (0.50)	70.2 (0.71)	39.9 (2.35)
New Mexico	85.9 (0.37)	94.9 (0.37)	91.7 (2.27)	77.0 (0.83)	91.4 (2.35)	96.4 (1.55)	27.3 (0.46)	40.4 (0.69)	22.2 (4.66)	16.3 (0.80)	61.0 (5.31)	43.3 (5.14)
New York	86.6 (0.13)	93.4 (0.12)	84.4 (0.36)	69.7 (0.51)	78.2 (0.58)	89.7 (0.87)	36.2 (0.17)	42.8 (0.21)	24.6 (0.44)	18.5 (0.35)	44.9 (0.58)	41.4 (1.37)
North Carolina	88.0 (0.16)	91.6 (0.17)	86.1 (0.38)	60.5 (1.17)	86.5 (1.04)	89.5 (1.40)	31.4 (0.22)	35.1 (0.26)	21.4 (0.48)	15.4 (0.78)	58.8 (1.63)	33.1 (2.07)
North Dakota	93.1 (0.50)	94.1 (0.40)	88.5 (5.84)	82.1 (5.87)	83.5 (4.78)	88.2 (5.12)	30.6 (0.84)	31.4 (0.96)	26.4 (7.06)	6.3! (2.37)	74.0 (8.06)	27.5 (8.16)
Ohio	90.3 (0.14)	91.5 (0.14)	85.4 (0.51)	77.6 (1.14)	89.4 (1.30)	90.8 (1.18)	28.0 (0.19)	29.0 (0.21)	17.3 (0.65)	18.6 (1.06)	62.7 (1.94)	27.3 (1.75)
Oklahoma	88.1 (0.28)	90.9 (0.27)	89.6 (0.99)	64.5 (1.81)	79.8 (3.12)	90.1 (0.98)	25.5 (0.38)	28.2 (0.43)	21.0 (1.87)	10.5 (1.06)	38.8 (3.08)	22.8 (1.44)
Oregon	90.9 (0.23)	94.0 (0.21)	88.6 (2.30)	68.0 (1.35)	87.0 (1.36)	89.6 (1.41)	33.7 (0.30)	35.4 (0.36)	27.6 (2.63)	16.0 (0.79)	52.7 (2.12)	27.2 (2.21)
Pennsylvania	90.5 (0.12)	92.4 (0.11)	87.8 (0.51)	74.1 (1.02)	83.1 (0.88)	89.6 (1.48)	31.7 (0.19)	33.1 (0.22)	20.0 (0.73)	16.4 (0.74)	56.8 (1.24)	32.7 (2.11)
Rhode Island	88.2 (0.50)	90.4 (0.45)	86.0 (2.50)	76.0 (2.10)	85.2 (3.56)	93.4 (2.85)	33.8 (0.63)	36.5 (0.75)	25.6 (2.73)	14.2 (2.04)	57.4 (4.09)	31.5 (4.84)
South Carolina	87.6 (0.22)	90.9 (0.23)	82.1 (0.54)	68.2 (1.71)	84.7 (1.72)	92.0 (1.81)	28.0 (0.29)	33.3 (0.38)	15.0 (0.50)	15.3 (1.17)	47.4 (3.42)	28.6 (3.85)
South Dakota	91.8 (0.50)	94.0 (0.39)	94.3 (3.21)	71.6 (6.16)	95.2 (4.75)	94.0 (4.32)	27.7 (0.75)	29.5 (0.85)	17.7! (7.17)	18.5! (5.59)	48.7 (6.84)	20.9! (7.62)
Tennessee	87.7 (0.21)	88.9 (0.21)	87.3 (0.58)	63.6 (1.73)	89.2 (1.46)	90.2 (1.61)	27.4 (0.28)	28.7 (0.32)	20.4 (0.64)	15.6 (1.36)	58.1 (2.54)	29.2 (2.88)
Texas	83.7 (0.11)	94.0 (0.11)	89.9 (0.32)	66.2 (0.27)	88.5 (0.49)	92.9 (0.75)	29.6 (0.14)	38.6 (0.22)	24.7 (0.52)	14.3 (0.22)	59.8 (0.76)	36.8 (1.47)
Utah	92.1 (0.29)	95.5 (0.19)	86.7 (4.54)	69.9 (1.65)	90.7 (1.47)	92.3 (2.25)	34.3 (0.47)	36.8 (0.55)	31.1 (5.36)	14.8 (1.06)	53.8 (3.15)	35.5 (4.28)
Vermont	92.4 (0.60)	93.0 (0.59)	‡ (†)	83.2 (4.45)	62.9 (15.40)	95.2 (3.05)	37.2 (1.14)	37.3 (1.16)	‡ (†)	39.7 (8.19)	35.0! (15.03)	39.9 (8.36)
Virginia	89.6 (0.18)	92.7 (0.16)	85.8 (0.40)	70.9 (1.21)	91.2 (0.63)	92.2 (1.21)	38.8 (0.28)	42.1 (0.28)	24.6 (0.63)	25.3 (1.19)	60.9 (0.97)	42.1 (1.92)
Washington	91.3 (0.17)	94.9 (0.15)	89.9 (1.27)	66.3 (1.18)	88.3 (0.71)	93.2 (0.82)	35.6 (0.29)	37.0 (0.31)	25.9 (1.62)	16.8 (0.81)	51.7 (1.05)	33.5 (1.42)
West Virginia	87.0 (0.46)	86.9 (0.48)	91.1 (1.31)	84.3 (4.53)	91.7 (3.81)	86.2 (5.63)	20.2 (0.42)	20.0 (0.44)	18.0 (2.21)	20.2 (5.09)	53.9 (6.32)	28.4 (5.82)
Wisconsin	92.5 (0.19)	94.7 (0.17)	81.3 (1.46)	69.7 (2.04)	86.3 (1.84)	94.0 (1.60)	30.5 (0.34)	31.8 (0.35)	12.8 (1.05)	15.2 (1.42)	53.4 (2.73)	34.3 (3.46)
Wyoming	93.1 (0.48)	94.8 (0.46)	‡ (†)	73.6 (3.33)	95.1 (2.97)	96.0 (3.02)	27.6 (0.88)	28.8 (0.94)	‡ (†)	15.5 (2.93)	46.5 (11.41)	26.5! (8.10)

†Not applicable.
!Interpret data with caution. The coefficient of variation (CV) for this estimate is between 30 and 50 percent.
‡Reporting standards not met. Either there are too few cases for a reliable estimate or the coefficient of variation (CV) is 50 percent or greater.
[1]Includes completion of high school through equivalency programs, such as a GED program.
[2]Total includes racial/ethnic groups not shown separately.

NOTE: Data are based on sample surveys of the entire population in the given age range residing within the United States, including both noninstitutionalized persons (e.g., those living in households, college housing, or military housing located within the United States) and institutionalized persons (e.g., those living in prisons, nursing facilities, or other healthcare facilities). Race categories exclude persons of Hispanic ethnicity.
SOURCE: U.S. Department of Commerce, Census Bureau, 2017 American Community Survey (ACS) 1-Year Public Use Microdata Sample (PUMS) data. (This table was prepared February 2019.)

Table 105.10. Projected number of participants in educational institutions, by level and control of institution: Fall 2018

[In millions]

Participants	All levels (elementary, secondary, and degree-granting postsecondary)	Elementary and secondary schools			Degree-granting postsecondary institutions		
		Total	Public	Private	Total	Public	Private
1	2	3	4	5	6	7	8
Total	**86.7**	**63.9**	**57.2**	**6.7**	**22.8**	**16.6**	**6.3**
Enrollment	76.3	56.5	50.7	5.8	19.8	14.6	5.2
Teachers and faculty	4.7	3.7	3.2	0.5	1.1	0.7	0.4
Other professional, administrative, and support staff	5.6	3.7	3.3	0.4	1.9	1.3	0.7

NOTE: Includes enrollments in local public school systems and in most private schools (religiously affiliated and nonsectarian). Excludes federal Bureau of Indian Education schools and Department of Defense schools. Excludes private preprimary enrollment in schools that do not offer kindergarten or above. Degree-granting institutions grant associate's or higher degrees and participate in Title IV federal financial aid programs. Data for teachers and other staff in public and private elementary and secondary schools and colleges and universities are reported in terms of full-time equivalents. Detail may not sum to totals because of rounding.

SOURCE: U.S. Department of Education, National Center for Education Statistics, National Elementary and Secondary Enrollment Projection Model, 1972 through 2028; Enrollment in Degree-Granting Institutions Projection Model, 2000 through 2028; Elementary and Secondary Teacher Projection Model, 1973 through 2028; and unpublished projections and estimates. (This table was prepared April 2019.)

Table 105.20. Enrollment in elementary, secondary, and degree-granting postsecondary institutions, by level and control of institution, enrollment level, and attendance status and sex of student: Selected years, fall 1990 through fall 2028

[In thousands]

Level and control of institution, enrollment level, and attendance status and sex of student	Actual				Projected												
	1990	2000	2010	2016	2017	2018	2019	2020	2021	2022	2023	2024	2025	2026	2027	2028
1	2	3	4	5	6	7	8	9	10	11	12	13	14	15	16	17
All levels	**60,683**	**68,685**	**75,886**	**76,238**[1]	**76,242**	**76,346**	**76,476**	**76,606**	**76,675**	**76,856**	**77,013**	**77,126**	**77,206**	**77,308**	**77,471**	**77,693**
Elementary and secondary schools[2]	**46,864**	**53,373**	**54,867**	**56,391**[1]	**56,477**	**56,518**	**56,572**	**56,678**	**56,719**	**56,865**	**56,973**	**57,019**	**57,029**	**57,050**	**57,176**	**57,387**
Public	41,217	47,204	49,484	50,615[1]	50,695	50,728	50,770	50,857	50,892	51,012	51,098	51,124	51,119	51,123	51,228	51,419
Private	5,648[3]	6,169[3]	5,382[3]	5,776[4]	5,781	5,789	5,802	5,821	5,827	5,853	5,875	5,894	5,910	5,927	5,948	5,969
Prekindergarten to grade 8	34,388	38,592	38,708	39,779[1]	39,773	39,761	39,766	39,700	39,541	39,526	39,591	39,750	39,910	40,116	40,328	40,527
Public[5]	29,876	33,686	34,625	35,477[1]	35,473	35,465	35,457	35,384	35,231	35,189	35,235	35,376	35,519	35,703	35,894	36,073
Private	4,512[3]	4,906[3]	4,084[3]	4,301[4]	4,300	4,297	4,308	4,316	4,310	4,337	4,356	4,374	4,392	4,413	4,434	4,454
Grades 9 to 12	12,476	14,781	16,159	16,612	16,703	16,756	16,806	16,978	17,178	17,338	17,383	17,269	17,119	16,934	16,848	16,861
Public[5,6]	11,341	13,517	14,860	15,138	15,222	15,264	15,313	15,473	15,661	15,823	15,863	15,748	15,601	15,420	15,334	15,346
Private	1,136[3]	1,264[3]	1,299[3]	1,474[4]	1,481	1,492	1,494	1,505	1,517	1,515	1,520	1,521	1,518	1,514	1,514	1,515
Degree-granting post-secondary institutions	**13,819**	**15,312**	**21,019**	**19,847**	**19,766**[7]	**19,828**	**19,904**	**19,928**	**19,956**	**19,991**	**20,040**	**20,107**	**20,177**	**20,258**	**20,295**	**20,305**
Undergraduate	11,959	13,155	18,082	16,875	16,760[7]	16,813	16,877	16,897	16,920	16,949	16,990	17,047	17,106	17,175	17,206	17,214
Full-time	6,976	7,923	11,457	10,430	10,371[7]	10,393	10,421	10,418	10,415	10,416	10,428	10,457	10,493	10,531	10,538	10,528
Part-time	4,983	5,232	6,625	6,445	6,390[7]	6,421	6,456	6,478	6,506	6,533	6,562	6,590	6,613	6,644	6,668	6,686
Male	5,380	5,778	7,836	7,417	7,347[7]	7,372	7,399	7,407	7,412	7,422	7,440	7,463	7,488	7,520	7,536	7,539
Female	6,579	7,377	10,246	9,458	9,413[7]	9,441	9,478	9,490	9,508	9,527	9,551	9,584	9,618	9,655	9,670	9,675
2-year	5,240	5,948	7,684	6,092	5,942[7]	5,965	5,991	6,004	6,019	6,035	6,054	6,077	6,098	6,124	6,140	6,148
4-year	6,719	7,207	10,399	10,782	10,818[7]	10,849	10,885	10,893	10,902	10,914	10,936	10,970	11,008	11,050	11,066	11,066
Public	9,710	10,539	13,703	13,144	13,101[7]	13,144	13,195	13,213	13,234	13,259	13,293	13,338	13,385	13,439	13,465	13,474
Private	2,250	2,616	4,379	3,731	3,659[7]	3,669	3,682	3,684	3,686	3,690	3,697	3,709	3,722	3,736	3,741	3,740
Postbaccalaureate	1,860	2,157	2,937	2,972	3,005[7]	3,015	3,027	3,031	3,036	3,042	3,050	3,060	3,071	3,083	3,089	3,091
Full-time	845	1,087	1,630	1,695	1,707[7]	1,710	1,715	1,715	1,714	1,714	1,716	1,721	1,727	1,733	1,734	1,733
Part-time	1,015	1,070	1,307	1,277	1,299[7]	1,305	1,312	1,316	1,322	1,327	1,333	1,339	1,344	1,350	1,355	1,359
Male	904	944	1,209	1,222	1,220[7]	1,224	1,229	1,231	1,232	1,234	1,237	1,240	1,245	1,250	1,253	1,253
Female	955	1,213	1,728	1,751	1,785[7]	1,791	1,798	1,800	1,804	1,808	1,813	1,820	1,826	1,833	1,836	1,838

[1]Includes imputations for public school prekindergarten enrollment in California.
[2]Includes enrollments in local public school systems and in most private schools (religiously affiliated and nonsectarian). Excludes homeschooled children who were not also enrolled in public and private schools. Private elementary enrollment includes preprimary students in schools offering kindergarten or higher grades.
[3]Estimated.
[4]Projected.
[5]Includes prorated proportion of students classified as ungraded. The total ungraded counts of students were prorated to the elementary level (prekindergarten to grade 8) and the secondary level (grades 9 to 12) based on prior reports.
[6]In addition to students in grades 9 to 12 and ungraded secondary students, includes a small number of students reported as being enrolled in grade 13.
[7]Data are actual.

NOTE: Postsecondary data for 1990 are for institutions of higher education, while later data are for degree-granting institutions. Degree-granting institutions grant associate's or higher degrees and participate in Title IV federal financial aid programs. Detail may not sum to totals because of rounding. Some data have been revised from previously published figures.
SOURCE: U.S. Department of Education, National Center for Education Statistics, Common Core of Data (CCD), "State Nonfiscal Survey of Public Elementary and Secondary Education," 1990–91 through 2016–17; Private School Universe Survey (PSS), 1995–96 through 2015–16; National Elementary and Secondary Enrollment Projection Model, 1972 through 2028; Integrated Postsecondary Education Data System (IPEDS), "Fall Enrollment Survey" (IPEDS-EF:90–99); IPEDS Spring 2001 through Spring 2018, Fall Enrollment component; and Enrollment in Degree-Granting Institutions Projection Model, 2000 through 2028. (This table was prepared March 2019.)

Table 105.30. Enrollment in elementary, secondary, and degree-granting postsecondary institutions, by level and control of institution: Selected years, 1869–70 through fall 2028

[In thousands]

			Public elementary and secondary schools			Private elementary and secondary schools[1]			Degree-granting postsecondary institutions[2]		
Year	Total enrollment, all levels	Elementary and secondary, total	Total	Prekindergarten through grade 8	Grades 9 through 12	Total	Prekindergarten through grade 8	Grades 9 through 12	Total	Public	Private
1	2	3	4	5	6	7	8	9	10	11	12
1869–70	—	—	6,872	6,792	80	—	—	—	52	—	—
1879–80	—	—	9,868	9,757	110	—	—	—	116	—	—
1889–90	14,491	14,334	12,723	12,520	203	1,611	1,516	95	157	—	—
1899–1900	17,092	16,855	15,503	14,984	519	1,352	1,241	111	238	—	—
1909–10	19,728	19,372	17,814	16,899	915	1,558	1,441	117	355	—	—
1919–20	23,876	23,278	21,578	19,378	2,200	1,699	1,486	214	598	—	—
1929–30	29,430	28,329	25,678	21,279	4,399	2,651	2,310	341	1,101	—	—
1939–40	29,539	28,045	25,434	18,832	6,601	2,611	2,153	458	1,494	797	698
1949–50	31,151	28,492	25,111	19,387	5,725	3,380	2,708	672	2,659	1,355	1,304
Fall 1959	44,497	40,857	35,182	26,911	8,271	5,675	4,640	1,035	3,640	2,181	1,459
Fall 1969	59,055	51,050	45,550	32,513	13,037	5,500[3]	4,200[3]	1,300[3]	8,005	5,897	2,108
Fall 1985	57,226	44,979	39,422	27,034	12,388	5,557	4,195	1,362	12,247	9,479	2,768
Fall 1990	60,683	46,864	41,217	29,876	11,341	5,648[3]	4,512[3]	1,136[3]	13,819	10,845	2,974
Fall 1991	62,087	47,728	42,047	30,503	11,544	5,681	4,550	1,131	14,359	11,310	3,049
Fall 1992	63,181	48,694	42,823	31,086	11,737	5,870[3]	4,746[3]	1,125[3]	14,487	11,385	3,103
Fall 1993	63,837	49,532	43,465	31,502	11,963	6,067	4,950	1,118	14,305	11,189	3,116
Fall 1994	64,385	50,106	44,111	31,896	12,215	5,994[3]	4,856[3]	1,138[3]	14,279	11,134	3,145
Fall 1995	65,020	50,759	44,840	32,338	12,502	5,918	4,756	1,163	14,262	11,092	3,169
Fall 1996	65,911	51,544	45,611	32,762	12,849	5,933[3]	4,755[3]	1,178[3]	14,368	11,120	3,247
Fall 1997	66,574	52,071	46,127	33,071	13,056	5,944	4,759	1,185	14,502	11,196	3,306
Fall 1998	67,033	52,526	46,539	33,344	13,195	5,988[3]	4,776[3]	1,212[3]	14,507	11,138	3,369
Fall 1999	67,725	52,875	46,857	33,486	13,371	6,018	4,789	1,229	14,850	11,376	3,474
Fall 2000	68,685	53,373	47,204	33,686	13,517	6,169[3]	4,906[3]	1,264[3]	15,312	11,753	3,560
Fall 2001	69,920	53,992	47,672	33,936	13,736	6,320	5,023	1,296	15,928	12,233	3,695
Fall 2002	71,015	54,403	48,183	34,114	14,069	6,220[3]	4,915[3]	1,306[3]	16,612	12,752	3,860
Fall 2003	71,551	54,639	48,540	34,201	14,339	6,099	4,788	1,311	16,911	12,859	4,053
Fall 2004	72,154	54,882	48,795	34,178	14,618	6,087[3]	4,756[3]	1,331[3]	17,272	12,980	4,292
Fall 2005	72,674	55,187	49,113	34,204	14,909	6,073	4,724	1,349	17,487	13,022	4,466
Fall 2006	73,061	55,307	49,316	34,235	15,081	5,991[3]	4,631[3]	1,360[3]	17,754	13,175	4,579
Fall 2007	73,459	55,201	49,291	34,204	15,086	5,910	4,546	1,364	18,258	13,501	4,757
Fall 2008	74,055	54,973	49,266	34,286	14,980	5,707[3]	4,365[3]	1,342[3]	19,082	13,971	5,111
Fall 2009	75,163	54,849	49,361	34,409	14,952	5,488	4,179	1,309	20,314	14,811	5,503
Fall 2010	75,886	54,867	49,484	34,625	14,860	5,382[3]	4,084[3]	1,299[3]	21,019	15,142	5,877
Fall 2011	75,800	54,790	49,522	34,773	14,749	5,268	3,977	1,291	21,011	15,116	5,894
Fall 2012	75,748	55,104	49,771	35,018	14,753	5,333[3]	4,031[3]	1,302[3]	20,644	14,885	5,760
Fall 2013	75,817	55,440	50,045	35,251	14,794	5,396	4,084	1,312	20,377	14,747	5,630
Fall 2014	76,097	55,888	50,313	35,370	14,943	5,575[3]	4,202[3]	1,373[3]	20,209	14,655	5,554
Fall 2015	76,177[4]	56,189[4]	50,438[4]	35,388[4]	15,050	5,751	4,304	1,446	19,988	14,573	5,415
Fall 2016	76,238[5]	56,391[5]	50,615[5]	35,477[5]	15,138	5,776	4,301[6]	1,474[6]	19,847	14,586	5,261
Fall 2017[6]	76,242	56,477	50,695	35,473	15,222	5,781	4,300	1,481	19,766	14,560	5,205
Fall 2018[6]	76,346	56,518	50,728	35,465	15,264	5,789	4,297	1,492	19,828	14,608	5,220
Fall 2019[6]	76,476	56,572	50,770	35,457	15,313	5,802	4,308	1,494	19,904	14,665	5,239
Fall 2020[6]	76,606	56,678	50,857	35,384	15,473	5,821	4,316	1,505	19,928	14,685	5,243
Fall 2021[6]	76,675	56,719	50,892	35,231	15,661	5,827	4,310	1,517	19,956	14,708	5,248
Fall 2022[6]	76,856	56,865	51,012	35,189	15,823	5,853	4,337	1,515	19,991	14,736	5,255
Fall 2023[6]	77,013	56,973	51,098	35,235	15,863	5,875	4,356	1,520	20,040	14,774	5,266
Fall 2024[6]	77,126	57,019	51,124	35,376	15,748	5,894	4,374	1,521	20,107	14,824	5,283
Fall 2025[6]	77,206	57,029	51,119	35,519	15,601	5,910	4,392	1,518	20,177	14,876	5,301
Fall 2026[6]	77,308	57,050	51,123	35,703	15,420	5,927	4,413	1,514	20,258	14,936	5,321
Fall 2027[6]	77,471	57,176	51,228	35,894	15,334	5,948	4,434	1,514	20,295	14,965	5,329
Fall 2028[6]	77,693	57,387	51,419	36,073	15,346	5,969	4,454	1,515	20,305	14,975	5,330

—Not available.
[1]Beginning in fall 1985, data include estimates for an expanded universe of private schools. Therefore, direct comparisons with earlier years should be avoided.
[2]Data for 1869–70 through 1949–50 include resident degree-credit students enrolled at any time during the academic year. Beginning in 1959, data include all resident and extension students enrolled at the beginning of the fall term.
[3]Estimated.
[4]Includes imputations for public school prekindergarten enrollment in California and Oregon.
[5]Includes imputations for public school prekindergarten enrollment in California.
[6]Projected data. Fall 2017 data for degree-granting institutions are actual.
NOTE: Data for 1869–70 through 1949–50 reflect enrollment for the entire school year. Elementary and secondary enrollment includes students in local public school systems and in most private schools (religiously affiliated and nonsectarian), but generally excludes homeschooled children and students in subcollegiate departments of colleges and in federal schools. Excludes preprimary students in private schools that do not offer kindergarten or higher grades. Postsecondary data through 1995 are for institutions of higher education, while later data are for degree-granting institutions. Degree-granting institutions grant associate's or higher degrees and participate in Title IV federal financial aid programs. Some data have been revised from previously published figures. Detail may not sum to totals because of rounding.
SOURCE: U.S. Department of Education, National Center for Education Statistics, *Annual Report of the Commissioner of Education*, 1870 to 1910; *Biennial Survey of Education in the United States*, 1919–20 through 1949–50; *Statistics of Public Elementary and Secondary School Systems*, 1959 through 1979; *Statistics of Nonpublic Elementary and Secondary Schools*, 1959 through 1980; 1985–86 Private School Survey; Common Core of Data (CCD), "State Nonfiscal Survey of Public Elementary and Secondary Education," 1985–86 through 2016–17; Private School Universe Survey (PSS), 1991–92 through 2015–16; National Elementary and Secondary Enrollment Projection Model, 1972 through 2028; Opening (Fall) Enrollment in Higher Education, 1959; Higher Education General Information Survey (HEGIS), "Fall Enrollment in Institutions of Higher Education" surveys, 1969 and 1985; Integrated Postsecondary Education Data System (IPEDS), "Fall Enrollment Survey" (IPEDS-EF:90–99); IPEDS Spring 2001 through Spring 2018, Fall Enrollment component; and Enrollment in Degree-Granting Institutions Projection Model, 2000 through 2028. (This table was prepared March 2019.)

Table 105.40. Number of teachers in elementary and secondary schools, and faculty in degree-granting postsecondary institutions, by control of institution: Selected years, fall 1970 through fall 2028

[In thousands]

Year	All levels			Elementary and secondary teachers[1]			Degree-granting institutions instructional staff[2]		
	Total	Public	Private	Total	Public	Private	Total	Public	Private
1	2	3	4	5	6	7	8	9	10
1970	2,766	2,373	393	2,292	2,059	233	474	314	160
1975	3,081	2,641	440	2,453	2,198	255[3]	628	443	185
1980	3,171	2,679	492	2,485	2,184	301	686[3,4]	495[3,4]	191[3,4]
1981	3,145	2,636	509	2,440	2,127	313[3]	705	509	196
1982	3,168	2,639	529	2,458	2,133	325[3]	710[3,4]	506[3,4]	204[3,4]
1983	3,200	2,651	549	2,476	2,139	337	724	512	212
1984	3,225	2,673	552	2,508	2,168	340[3]	717[3,4]	505[3,4]	212[3,4]
1985	3,264	2,709	555	2,549	2,206	343	715[3,4]	503[3,4]	212[3,4]
1986	3,314	2,754	560	2,592	2,244	348[3]	722[3,4]	510[3,4]	212[3,4]
1987	3,424	2,832	592	2,631	2,279	352	793	553	240
1988	3,472	2,882	590	2,668	2,323	345	804[3]	559[3]	245[3]
1989	3,537	2,934	603	2,713	2,357	356	824	577	247
1990	3,577	2,972	604	2,759	2,398	361[3]	817[3]	574[3]	244[3]
1991	3,623	3,013	610	2,797	2,432	365	826	581	245
1992	3,700	3,080	621	2,823	2,459	364[3]	877[3]	621[3]	257[3]
1993	3,784	3,154	629	2,868	2,504	364	915	650	265
1994	3,846	3,205	640	2,922	2,552	370[3]	923[3]	653[3]	270[3]
1995	3,906	3,255	651	2,974	2,598	376	932	657	275
1996	4,006	3,339	666	3,051	2,667	384[3]	954[3]	672[3]	282[3]
1997	4,127	3,441	687	3,138	2,746	391	990	695	295
1998	4,230	3,527	703	3,230	2,830	400[3]	999[3]	697[3]	303[3]
1999	4,347	3,624	723	3,319	2,911	408	1,028	713	315
2000	4,432	3,683	750	3,366	2,941	424[3]	1,067[3]	741[3]	325[3]
2001	4,554	3,771	783	3,440	3,000	441	1,113	771	342
2002	4,631	3,829	802	3,476	3,034	442[3]	1,155[3]	794[3]	361[3]
2003	4,663	3,840	823	3,490	3,049	441	1,174	792	382
2004	4,773	3,909	863	3,536	3,091	445[3]	1,237[3]	818[3]	418[3]
2005	4,883	3,984	899	3,593	3,143	450	1,290	841	449
2006	4,944	4,020	924	3,622	3,166	456[3]	1,322[3]	853[3]	468[3]
2007	5,028	4,077	951	3,656	3,200	456	1,372	877	495
2008	5,063	4,106	957	3,670	3,222	448[3]	1,393[3]	884[3]	509[3]
2009	5,086	4,123	963	3,647	3,210	437	1,439	914	525
2010	5,022	4,044	978	3,512	3,099	413[3]	1,510[3]	945[3]	565[3]
2011	5,032	4,057	975	3,508	3,103	405	1,524	954	570
2012	5,049	4,067	981	3,517	3,109	408[3]	1,531[3]	958[3]	573[3]
2013	5,101	4,082	1,018	3,555	3,114	441	1,545	969	577
2014	5,146	4,102	1,044	3,594	3,132	461[3]	1,552[3]	970[3]	582[3]
2015	5,185	4,122	1,063	3,633	3,151	482	1,552	971	581
2016	5,201	4,144	1,057	3,655	3,169	485[3]	1,546	974	572
2017[5]	5,184	4,127	1,058	3,641	3,156	485	1,544	971	572
2018[6]	—	—	—	3,667	3,179	488	—	—	—
2019[6]	—	—	—	3,691	3,200	491	—	—	—
2020[6]	—	—	—	3,708	3,214	493	—	—	—
2021[6]	—	—	—	3,724	3,229	495	—	—	—
2022[6]	—	—	—	3,750	3,251	499	—	—	—
2023[6]	—	—	—	3,771	3,269	502	—	—	—
2024[6]	—	—	—	3,795	3,290	505	—	—	—
2025[6]	—	—	—	3,820	3,311	509	—	—	—
2026[6]	—	—	—	3,846	3,333	513	—	—	—
2027[6]	—	—	—	3,875	3,357	517	—	—	—
2028[6]	—	—	—	3,906	3,385	522	—	—	—

—Not available.
[1]Includes teachers in local public school systems and in most private schools (religiously affiliated and nonsectarian). Teachers are reported in terms of full-time equivalents.
[2]Data through 1995 are for institutions of higher education, while later data are for degree-granting institutions. Degree-granting institutions grant associate's or higher degrees and participate in Title IV federal financial aid programs. The degree-granting classification is very similar to the earlier higher education classification, but it includes more 2-year colleges and excludes a few higher education institutions that did not grant degrees. Includes full-time and part-time faculty with the rank of instructor or above in colleges, universities, professional schools, and 2-year colleges. Excludes teaching assistants.
[3]Estimated.
[4]Inclusion of institutions is not consistent with surveys for 1987 and later years.
[5]Data for elementary and secondary schools are projected; data for degree-granting institutions are actual.
[6]Projected.

NOTE: Detail may not sum to totals because of rounding. Some data have been revised from previously published figures. Headcounts are used to report data for degree-granting institutions faculty.
SOURCE: U.S. Department of Education, National Center for Education Statistics, *Statistics of Public Elementary and Secondary Day Schools*, 1970 and 1975; Common Core of Data (CCD), "State Nonfiscal Survey of Public Elementary/Secondary Education," 1980 through 2016; Private School Universe Survey (PSS), 1989–90 through 2015–16; Elementary and Secondary Teacher Projection Model, 1973 through 2028; Higher Education General Information Survey (HEGIS), "Fall Staff" survey, 1970 and 1975; Integrated Postsecondary Education Data System (IPEDS), "Fall Staff Survey" (IPEDS-S:87–99); IPEDS Winter 2001–02 through Winter 2011–12, Human Resources component, Fall Staff section; IPEDS Spring 2014 through Spring 2018, Human Resources component, Fall Staff section; U.S. Equal Opportunity Commission, EEO-6, 1981 and 1983; and unpublished data. (This table was prepared April 2019.)

Table 105.50. Number of educational institutions, by level and control of institution: Selected years, 1980–81 through 2016–17

Level and control of institution	1980–81	1990–91	1999–2000	2006–07	2007–08	2008–09	2009–10	2010–11	2011–12	2012–13	2013–14	2014–15	2015–16	2016–17
1	2	3	4	5	6	7	8	9	10	11	12	13	14	15
All institutions	—	—	**131,414**	—	**139,207**	—	**138,925**	—	**136,423**	—	**139,126**	—	**139,874**	—
Elementary and secondary schools	**106,746**	**109,228**	**125,007**	—	**132,656**	—	**132,183**	—	**129,189**	—	**131,890**	—	**132,853**	—
Elementary	72,659	74,716	86,433	—	88,982	—	88,565	—	86,386	—	89,543	—	88,665	—
Secondary	24,856	23,602	24,903	—	27,575	—	27,427	—	27,034	—	26,767	—	26,986	—
Combined	5,202	8,847	12,197	—	14,837	—	14,895	—	14,799	—	14,599	—	16,511	—
Other[1]	4,029	2,063	1,474	—	1,262	—	1,296	—	971	—	981	—	691	—
Public schools	85,982	84,538	92,012	98,793	98,916	98,706	98,817	98,817	98,328	98,454	98,271	98,176	98,277	98,158
Elementary	59,326	59,015	64,131	66,458	67,112	67,148	67,140	67,086	66,689	66,708	67,034	67,073	66,758	66,837
Secondary	22,619	21,135	22,365	23,920	24,643	24,348	24,651	24,544	24,357	24,294	24,067	24,181	24,040	23,814
Combined	1,743	2,325	4,042	5,984	5,899	5,623	5,730	6,137	6,311	6,329	6,189	6,347	6,788	6,783
Other[1]	2,294	2,063	1,474	2,431	1,262	1,587	1,296	1,050	971	1,123	981	575	691	724
Private schools[2]	20,764	24,690	32,995	—	33,740	—	33,366	—	30,861	—	33,619	—	34,576	—
Elementary	13,333	15,701	22,302	—	21,870	—	21,425	—	19,697	—	22,509	—	21,907	—
Schools with highest grade of kindergarten	†	†	5,952	—	5,522	—	5,275	—	4,658	—	5,255	—	5,147	—
Secondary	2,237	2,467	2,538	—	2,932	—	2,776	—	2,677	—	2,700	—	2,946	—
Combined	3,459	6,522	8,155	—	8,938	—	9,165	—	8,488	—	8,410	—	9,723	—
Other[1]	1,735	([3])	([3])	—	([3])	—	([3])	—	([3])	—	([3])	—	([3])	—
Postsecondary Title IV institutions	—	—	**6,407**	**6,536**	**6,551**	**6,632**	**6,742**	**7,021**	**7,234**	**7,253**	**7,236**	**7,151**	**7,021**	**6,606**
Public	—	—	2,078	2,009	2,004	1,997	1,989	2,015	2,011	1,981	1,980	1,964	1,965	1,958
Private	—	—	4,329	4,527	4,547	4,635	4,753	5,006	5,223	5,272	5,256	5,187	5,056	4,648
Nonprofit	—	—	1,936	1,848	1,815	1,809	1,809	1,812	1,830	1,820	1,834	1,827	1,859	1,823
For-profit	—	—	2,393	2,679	2,732	2,826	2,944	3,194	3,393	3,452	3,422	3,360	3,197	2,825
Title IV non-degree-granting institutions	—	—	2,323	2,222	2,199	2,223	2,247	2,422	2,528	2,527	2,512	2,524	2,438	2,246
Public	—	—	396	321	319	321	317	359	362	358	355	343	345	335
Private	—	—	1,927	1,901	1,880	1,902	1,930	2,063	2,166	2,169	2,157	2,181	2,093	1,911
Nonprofit	—	—	255	208	191	180	185	182	177	168	159	155	158	141
For-profit	—	—	1,672	1,693	1,689	1,722	1,745	1,881	1,989	2,001	1,998	2,026	1,935	1,770
Title IV degree-granting institutions	3,231	3,559	4,084	4,314	4,352	4,409	4,495	4,599	4,706	4,726	4,724	4,627	4,583	4,360
2-year colleges	1,274	1,418	1,721	1,685	1,677	1,690	1,721	1,729	1,738	1,700	1,685	1,616	1,579	1,528
Public	945	972	1,068	1,045	1,032	1,024	1,000	978	967	934	934	920	910	886
Private	329	446	653	640	645	666	721	751	771	766	751	696	669	642
Nonprofit	182	167	150	107	92	92	85	87	100	97	88	88	107	101
For-profit	147	279	503	533	553	574	636	664	671	669	663	608	562	541
4-year colleges	1,957	2,141	2,363	2,629	2,675	2,719	2,774	2,870	2,968	3,026	3,039	3,011	3,004	2,832
Public	552	595	614	643	653	652	672	678	682	689	691	701	710	737
Private	1,405	1,546	1,749	1,986	2,022	2,067	2,102	2,192	2,286	2,337	2,348	2,310	2,294	2,095
Nonprofit	1,387	1,482	1,531	1,533	1,532	1,537	1,539	1,543	1,553	1,555	1,587	1,584	1,594	1,581
For-profit	18	64	218	453	490	530	563	649	733	782	761	726	700	514

—Not available.
†Not applicable.
[1]Includes special education, alternative, and other schools not classified by grade span. Because of changes in survey definitions, figures for "other" schools are not comparable from year to year.
[2]Data for 1980–81 and 1990–91 include schools with first or higher grades. Data for later years include schools with kindergarten or higher grades.
[3]Included in the elementary, secondary, and combined categories.
NOTE: Postsecondary data for 1980–81 and 1990–91 are for institutions of higher education, while later data are for Title IV degree-granting and non-degree-granting institutions. Degree-granting institutions grant associate's or higher degrees and participate in Title IV federal financial aid programs. The degree-granting classification is very similar to the earlier higher education classification, but it includes more 2-year colleges and excludes a few higher education institutions that did not grant degrees.
SOURCE: U.S. Department of Education, National Center for Education Statistics, Common Core of Data (CCD), "Public Elementary/Secondary School Universe Survey," 1989-90 through 2016–17; *Private Schools in American Education*; *Statistics of Public Elementary and Secondary Day Schools*, 1980–81; Schools and Staffing Survey (SASS), "Private School Data File," 1990–91; Private School Universe Survey (PSS), 1995–96 through 2015–16; Higher Education General Information Survey (HEGIS), "Institutional Characteristics of Colleges and Universities" survey, 1980–81; Integrated Postsecondary Education Data System (IPEDS), "Institutional Characteristics Survey" (IPEDS-IC:90–99); and IPEDS Fall 2001 through Fall 2016, Institutional Characteristics component. (This table was prepared March 2019.)

Table 106.10. Expenditures of educational institutions related to the gross domestic product, by level of institution: Selected years, 1929–30 through 2017–18

Year	Gross domestic product (GDP) (in billions of current dollars)	School year	Expenditures for education in current dollars					
			All educational institutions		All elementary and secondary schools		All degree-granting postsecondary institutions	
			Amount (in millions)	As a percent of GDP	Amount (in millions)	As a percent of GDP	Amount (in millions)	As a percent of GDP
1	2	3	4	5	6	7	8	9
1929	$104.6	1929–30	—	—	—	—	$632	0.6
1939	93.4	1939–40	—	—	—	—	758	0.8
1949	272.5	1949–50	$8,494	3.1	$6,249	2.3	2,246	0.8
1959	521.7	1959–60	22,314	4.3	16,713	3.2	5,601	1.1
1961	562.2	1961–62	26,828	4.8	19,673	3.5	7,155	1.3
1963	637.5	1963–64	32,003	5.0	22,825	3.6	9,178	1.4
1965	742.3	1965–66	40,558	5.5	28,048	3.8	12,509	1.7
1967	860.0	1967–68	51,558	6.0	35,077	4.1	16,481	1.9
1969	1,017.6	1969–70	64,227	6.3	43,183	4.2	21,043	2.1
1970	1,073.3	1970–71	71,575	6.7	48,200	4.5	23,375	2.2
1971	1,164.9	1971–72	76,510	6.6	50,950	4.4	25,560	2.2
1972	1,279.1	1972–73	82,908	6.5	54,952	4.3	27,956	2.2
1973	1,425.4	1973–74	91,084	6.4	60,370	4.2	30,714	2.2
1974	1,545.2	1974–75	103,903	6.7	68,846	4.5	35,058	2.3
1975	1,684.9	1975–76	114,004	6.8	75,101	4.5	38,903	2.3
1976	1,873.4	1976–77	121,793	6.5	79,194	4.2	42,600	2.3
1977	2,081.8	1977–78	132,515	6.4	86,544	4.2	45,971	2.2
1978	2,351.6	1978–79	143,733	6.1	93,012	4.0	50,721	2.2
1979	2,627.3	1979–80	160,075	6.1	103,162	3.9	56,914	2.2
1980	2,857.3	1980–81	176,378	6.2	112,325	3.9	64,053	2.2
1981	3,207.0	1981–82	190,825	6.0	120,486	3.8	70,339	2.2
1982	3,343.8	1982–83	204,661	6.1	128,725	3.8	75,936	2.3
1983	3,634.0	1983–84	220,993	6.1	139,000	3.8	81,993	2.3
1984	4,037.6	1984–85	239,351	5.9	149,400	3.7	89,951	2.2
1985	4,339.0	1985–86	259,336	6.0	161,800	3.7	97,536	2.2
1986	4,579.6	1986–87	280,964	6.1	175,200	3.8	105,764	2.3
1987	4,855.2	1987–88	301,786	6.2	187,999	3.9	113,787	2.3
1988	5,236.4	1988–89	333,245	6.4	209,377	4.0	123,867	2.4
1989	5,641.6	1989–90	365,825	6.5	231,170	4.1	134,656	2.4
1990	5,963.1	1990–91	395,318	6.6	249,230	4.2	146,088	2.4
1991	6,158.1	1991–92	417,944	6.8	261,755	4.3	156,189	2.5
1992	6,520.3	1992–93	439,676	6.7	274,435	4.2	165,241	2.5
1993	6,858.6	1993–94	460,756	6.7	287,407	4.2	173,351	2.5
1994	7,287.2	1994–95	485,169	6.7	302,200	4.1	182,969	2.5
1995	7,639.7	1995–96	508,523	6.7	318,046	4.2	190,476	2.5
1996	8,073.1	1996–97	538,854	6.7	338,951	4.2	199,903[1]	2.5
1997	8,577.6	1997–98	570,471	6.7	361,615	4.2	208,856[1]	2.4
1998	9,062.8	1998–99	603,847	6.7	384,638	4.2	219,209	2.4
1999	9,630.7	1999–2000	649,322	6.7	412,538	4.3	236,784	2.5
2000	10,252.3	2000–01	705,017	6.9	444,811	4.3	260,206	2.5
2001	10,581.8	2001–02	752,780	7.1	472,064	4.5	280,715	2.7
2002	10,936.4	2002–03	795,691	7.3	492,807	4.5	302,884	2.8
2003	11,458.2	2003–04	830,293	7.2	513,542	4.5	316,751	2.8
2004	12,213.7	2004–05	875,988	7.2	540,969	4.4	335,019	2.7
2005	13,036.6	2005–06	925,249	7.1	571,669	4.4	353,580	2.7
2006	13,814.6	2006–07	984,048	7.1	608,495	4.4	375,553	2.7
2007	14,451.9	2007–08	1,054,901	7.3	646,414	4.5	408,487	2.8
2008	14,712.8	2008–09	1,089,683	7.4	658,926	4.5	430,757	2.9
2009	14,448.9	2009–10	1,100,897	7.6	654,418	4.5	446,479	3.1
2010	14,992.1	2010–11	1,124,352	7.5	652,356	4.4	471,997	3.1
2011	15,542.6	2011–12	1,136,876	7.3	648,794	4.2	488,083	3.1
2012	16,197.0	2012–13	1,153,874	7.1	655,013	4.0	498,861	3.1
2013	16,784.9	2013–14	1,192,886	7.1	675,818	4.0	517,067	3.1
2014	17,521.7	2014–15	1,241,626	7.1	706,135	4.0	535,491	3.1
2015	18,219.3	2015–16	1,296,307	7.1	736,841	4.0	559,466	3.1
2016	18,707.2	2016–17[2]	1,343,000	7.2	759,000	4.1	584,000	3.1
2017	19,485.4	2017–18[3]	1,397,000	7.2	789,000	4.0	608,000	3.1

—Not available.
[1]Estimated by the National Center for Education Statistics based on enrollment data for the given year and actual expenditures for prior years.
[2]Data for elementary and secondary education are estimated; data for degree-granting institutions are actual.
[3]Estimated by the National Center for Education Statistics based on teacher and enrollment data, and actual expenditures for prior years.
NOTE: Total expenditures for public elementary and secondary schools include current expenditures, interest on school debt, and capital outlay. Data for private elementary and secondary schools are estimated. Expenditures for colleges and universities in 1929–30 and 1939–40 include current-fund expenditures and additions to plant value. Public and private degree-granting institutions data for 1949–50 through 1995–96 are for current-fund expenditures. Data for private degree-granting institutions for 1996–97 and later years are for total expenditures. Data for public degree-granting institutions for 1996–97 through 2000–01 are for current expenditures; data for later years are for total expenditures. Postsecondary data through 1995–96 are for institutions of higher education, while later data are for degree-granting institutions. Degree-granting institutions grant associate's or higher degrees and participate in Title IV federal financial aid programs. Some data have been revised from previously published figures. Detail may not sum to totals because of rounding.
SOURCE: U.S. Department of Education, National Center for Education Statistics, *Biennial Survey of Education in the United States*, 1929–30 through 1949–50; *Statistics of State School Systems*, 1959–60 through 1969–70; *Revenues and Expenditures for Public Elementary and Secondary Education*, 1970–71 through 1986–87; Common Core of Data (CCD), "National Public Education Financial Survey," 1987–88 through 2015–16; Higher Education General Information Survey (HEGIS), Financial Statistics of Institutions of Higher Education, 1965–66 through 1985–86; Integrated Postsecondary Education Data System (IPEDS), "Finance Survey" (IPEDS-F:FY87–99); and IPEDS Spring 2001 through Spring 2018, Finance component. U.S. Department of Commerce, Bureau of Economic Analysis, National Income and Product Accounts Tables, retrieved March 8, 2019, from https://apps.bea.gov/itable/index.cfm. (This table was prepared March 2019.)

Table 106.20. Expenditures of educational institutions, by level and control of institution: Selected years, 1899–1900 through 2017–18

[In thousands]

School year	Current dollars							Constant 2017–18 dollars[1]			
		Elementary and secondary schools			Degree-granting postsecondary institutions				Elementary and secondary schools		Degree-granting postsecondary institutions
	Total	Total	Public	Private[2]	Total	Public	Private	Total	Total	Public	
1	2	3	4	5	6	7	8	9	10	11	12
1899–1900	—	—	$215	—	—	—	—	—	—	—	—
1909–10	—	—	426	—	—	—	—	—	—	—	—
1919–20	—	—	1,036	—	—	—	—	—	—	$13,490	—
1929–30	—	—	2,317	—	$632	$292	$341	—	—	33,584	$9,165
1939–40	—	—	2,344	—	758	392	367	—	—	41,619	13,466
1949–50	$8,494	$6,249	5,838	$411	2,246	1,154	1,092	$88,995	$65,467	61,161	23,528
1959–60	22,314	16,713	15,613	1,100	5,601	3,131	2,470	188,432	141,136	131,847	47,296
1969–70	64,227	43,183	40,683	2,500	21,043	13,250	7,794	421,874	283,651	267,230	138,222
1970–71	71,575	48,200	45,500	2,700	23,375	14,996	8,379	447,064	301,061	284,196	146,004
1971–72	76,510	50,950	48,050	2,900	25,560	16,484	9,075	461,339	307,220	289,733	154,119
1972–73	82,908	54,952	51,852	3,100	27,956	18,204	9,752	480,555	318,517	300,549	162,038
1973–74	91,084	60,370	56,970	3,400	30,714	20,336	10,377	484,725	321,275	303,181	163,450
1974–75	103,903	68,846	64,846	4,000	35,058	23,490	11,568	497,782	329,828	310,665	167,954
1975–76	114,004	75,101	70,601	4,500	38,903	26,184	12,719	510,067	336,009	315,876	174,058
1976–77	121,793	79,194	74,194	5,000	42,600	28,635	13,965	514,893	334,799	313,661	180,095
1977–78	132,515	86,544	80,844	5,700	45,971	30,725	15,246	524,970	342,853	320,272	182,117
1978–79	143,733	93,012	86,712	6,300	50,721	33,733	16,988	520,639	336,914	314,094	183,725
1979–80	160,075	103,162	95,962	7,200	56,914	37,768	19,146	511,623	329,719	306,707	181,904
1980–81	176,378	112,325	104,125	8,200	64,053	42,280	21,773	505,212	321,740	298,252	183,471
1981–82	190,825	120,486	111,186	9,300	70,339	46,219	24,120	503,132	317,674	293,154	185,458
1982–83	204,661	128,725	118,425	10,300	75,936	49,573	26,363	517,388	325,420	299,382	191,968
1983–84	220,993	139,000	127,500	11,500	81,993	53,087	28,907	538,736	338,853	310,819	199,883
1984–85	239,351	149,400	137,000	12,400	89,951	58,315	31,637	561,510	350,488	321,398	211,023
1985–86	259,336	161,800	148,600	13,200	97,536	63,194	34,342	591,341	368,939	338,840	222,402
1986–87	280,964	175,200	160,900	14,300	105,764	67,654	38,110	626,742	390,816	358,918	235,925
1987–88	301,786	187,999	172,699	15,300	113,787	72,641	41,145	646,407	402,681	369,910	243,725
1988–89	333,245	209,377	192,977	16,400	123,867	78,946	44,922	682,278	428,675	395,098	253,603
1989–90	365,825	231,170	212,770	18,400	134,656	85,771	48,885	714,871	451,736	415,780	263,135
1990–91	395,318	249,230	229,430	19,800	146,088	92,961	53,127	732,458	461,781	425,095	270,677
1991–92	417,944	261,755	241,055	20,700	156,189	98,847	57,342	750,338	469,931	432,768	280,408
1992–93	439,676	274,435	252,935	21,500	165,241	104,570	60,671	765,445	477,772	440,342	287,673
1993–94	460,757	287,407	265,307	22,100	173,351	109,310	64,041	781,892	487,721	450,218	294,171
1994–95	485,169	302,200	279,000	23,200	182,969	115,465	67,504	800,376	498,536	460,263	301,841
1995–96	508,523	318,046	293,646	24,400	190,476	119,525	70,952	816,684	510,781	471,594	305,903
1996–97	538,854	338,951	313,151	25,800	199,903[2]	125,978	73,925[2]	841,390	529,253	488,968	312,137[2]
1997–98	570,471	361,615	334,315	27,300	208,856[2]	132,846	76,010[2]	875,151	554,748	512,868	320,403[2]
1998–99	603,847	384,638	355,838	28,800	219,209	140,539	78,670	910,589	580,026	536,596	330,563
1999–2000	649,322	412,538	381,838	30,700	236,784	152,325	84,459	951,692	604,644	559,648	347,047
2000–01	705,017	444,811	410,811	34,000	260,206	170,345	89,861	999,092	630,350	582,168	368,742
2001–02	752,780	472,064	435,364	36,700	280,715	183,436	97,280	1,048,219	657,333	606,229	390,886
2002–03	795,691	492,807	454,907	37,900	302,884	197,026	105,858	1,084,146	671,460	619,820	412,686
2003–04	830,293	513,542	474,242	39,300	316,751	205,069	111,682	1,107,072	684,731	632,331	422,340
2004–05	875,988	540,969	499,569	41,400	335,019	215,794	119,225	1,133,878	700,230	646,641	433,648
2005–06	925,249	571,669	528,269	43,400	353,580	226,550	127,030	1,153,706	712,822	658,706	440,884
2006–07	984,048	608,495	562,195	46,300	375,553	238,829	136,724	1,196,092	739,614	683,337	456,478
2007–08	1,054,901	646,414	597,314	49,100	408,487	261,046	147,441	1,236,400	757,631	700,083	478,769
2008–09	1,089,683	658,926	610,326	48,600	430,757	273,019	157,739	1,259,579	761,661	705,484	497,918
2009–10	1,100,897	654,418	607,018	47,400	446,479	281,390	165,088	1,260,346	749,202	694,936	511,145
2010–11	1,124,352	652,356	604,356	48,000	471,997	296,863	175,134	1,261,861	732,139	678,269	529,722
2011–12	1,136,876	648,794	601,994	46,800	488,083	305,538	182,545	1,239,596	707,414	656,385	532,182
2012–13	1,153,874	655,013	606,813	48,200	498,861	311,421	187,439	1,237,535	702,505	650,810	535,030
2013–14	1,192,886	675,818	625,018	50,800	517,067	323,893	193,174	1,259,697	713,670	660,024	546,027
2014–15	1,241,626	706,135	651,135	55,000	535,491	335,630	199,861	1,301,688	740,294	682,633	561,394
2015–16	1,296,307	736,841	677,541	59,300	559,466	354,776	204,690	1,350,000	767,000	706,000	583,000
2016–17[3]	1,343,000	759,000	699,000	60,000	584,000	372,000	212,000	1,373,000	776,000	715,000	597,000
2017–18[4]	1,397,000	789,000	726,000	64,000	608,000	389,000	219,000	1,397,000	789,000	726,000	608,000

—Not available.
[1]Constant dollars based on the Consumer Price Index, prepared by the Bureau of Labor Statistics, U.S. Department of Labor, adjusted to a school-year basis.
[2]Estimated by the National Center for Education Statistics based on enrollment data for the given year and actual expenditures for prior years.
[3]Data for elementary and secondary education are estimated; data for degree-granting institutions are actual.
[4]Estimated by the National Center for Education Statistics based on teacher and enrollment data, and actual expenditures for prior years.
NOTE: Total expenditures for public elementary and secondary schools include current expenditures, interest on school debt, and capital outlay. Expenditures for public and private colleges and universities in 1929–30 and 1939–40 include current-fund expenditures and additions to plant value. Public and private degree-granting institutions data for 1949–50 through 1995–96 are for current-fund expenditures. Data for private degree-granting institutions for 1996–97 and later years are for total expenditures. Data for public degree-granting institutions for 1996–97 through 2000–01 are for current expenditures; data for later years are for total expenditures. Postsecondary data through 1995–96 are for institutions of higher education, while later data are for degree-granting institutions. Degree-granting institutions grant associate's or higher degrees and participate in Title IV federal financial aid programs. Some data have been revised from previously published figures. Detail may not sum to totals because of rounding.
SOURCE: U.S. Department of Education, National Center for Education Statistics, *Annual Report of the Commissioner of Education*, 1899–1900 and 1909–10; *Biennial Survey of Education in the United States*, 1919–20 through 1949–50; *Statistics of State School Systems*, 1959–60 and 1969–70; *Revenues and Expenditures for Public Elementary and Secondary Education*, 1970–71 through 1986–87; Common Core of Data (CCD), "National Public Education Financial Survey," 1987–88 through 2015–16; Higher Education General Information Survey (HEGIS), Financial Statistics of Institutions of Higher Education, 1965–66 through 1985–86; Integrated Postsecondary Education Data System (IPEDS), "Finance Survey," (IPEDS-F:FY87–99); IPEDS Spring 2001 through Spring 2018, Finance component; and unpublished tabulations. (This table was prepared March 2019.)

Table 106.30. Amount and percentage distribution of direct general expenditures of state and local governments, by function: Selected years, 1970–71 through 2015–16

Function	1970–71	1980–81	1990–91	2000–01	2010–11	2011–12	2012–13	2013–14	2014–15	2015–16
1	2	3	4	5	6	7	8	9	10	11
	Amount (in millions of current dollars)									
Total direct general expenditures	**$150,674**	**$407,449**	**$908,109**	**$1,621,757**	**$2,579,509**	**$2,588,308**	**$2,623,305**	**$2,710,967**	**$2,839,458**	**$2,944,651**
Education and public libraries	60,174	147,649	313,744	571,374	872,969	878,952	888,240	916,301	947,318	984,948
Education	59,413	145,784	309,302	563,572	862,271	867,508	877,059	905,213	935,754	972,906
Public libraries	761	1,865	4,442	7,802	10,699	11,444	11,181	11,088	11,564	12,042
Social services and income maintenance	30,376	92,555	214,919	396,086	729,846	732,192	765,511	805,538	883,060	922,654
Public welfare	18,226	54,121	130,402	257,380	490,645	485,342	515,296	543,511	614,553	637,644
Hospitals and health	11,205	36,101	81,110	134,010	233,018	240,895	244,290	256,553	263,420	279,752
Social insurance administration	945	2,276	3,250	4,359	5,256	5,116	4,901	4,415	4,114	3,905
Veterans' services	†	57	157	337	927	838	1,024	1,060	973	1,353
Transportation[1]	19,819	39,231	75,410	130,422	183,282	188,328	186,324	191,924	198,621	206,827
Public safety	9,416	31,233	79,932	146,544	225,202	225,607	228,400	235,042	241,787	249,805
Police and fire protection	7,531	21,283	46,568	84,554	138,147	139,306	141,308	145,952	151,011	156,986
Correction	1,885	7,393	27,356	52,370	73,243	72,725	73,040	74,943	77,058	78,017
Protective inspection and regulation	†	2,557	6,008	9,620	13,812	13,576	14,052	14,147	13,718	14,802
Environment and housing	11,832	35,223	76,167	124,203	200,491	196,120	190,321	190,175	193,912	203,197
Natural resources, parks, and recreation	5,191	13,239	28,505	50,082	67,053	66,397	65,472	65,544	68,358	72,807
Housing and community development	2,554	7,086	16,648	27,402	56,284	53,632	50,586	50,244	49,916	50,173
Sewerage and sanitation	4,087	14,898	31,014	46,718	77,154	76,091	74,263	74,387	75,638	80,217
Governmental administration	6,703	20,001	48,461	85,910	123,851	123,191	123,580	127,676	130,458	135,100
Financial administration	2,271	7,230	16,995	30,007	39,351	38,689	39,785	40,501	41,920	43,010
General control[2]	4,432	12,771	31,466	55,903	84,500	84,502	83,796	87,175	88,538	92,090
Interest on general debt	5,089	17,131	52,234	73,836	108,478	108,943	108,614	106,940	105,258	104,572
Other direct general expenditures	7,265	24,426	47,242	93,382	135,388	134,976	132,314	137,371	139,043	137,548
	Amount (in millions of constant 2017–18 dollars)[3]									
Total direct general expenditures	**$941,124**	**$1,167,084**	**$1,682,575**	**$2,298,221**	**$2,894,984**	**$2,822,167**	**$2,813,506**	**$2,862,804**	**$2,976,814**	**$3,066,418**
Education and public libraries	375,852	422,921	581,316	809,705	979,734	958,367	952,641	967,621	993,144	1,025,677
Education	371,099	417,579	573,085	798,648	967,727	945,889	940,650	955,912	981,020	1,013,137
Public libraries	4,753	5,342	8,230	11,056	12,007	12,478	11,991	11,709	12,124	12,540
Social services and income maintenance	189,731	265,112	398,209	561,300	819,107	798,347	821,014	850,655	925,778	960,808
Public welfare	113,841	155,023	241,613	364,738	550,651	529,194	552,658	573,952	644,281	664,012
Hospitals and health	69,987	103,407	150,283	189,908	261,517	262,661	262,002	270,922	276,163	291,320
Social insurance administration	5,903	6,519	6,022	6,177	5,899	5,578	5,256	4,662	4,313	4,066
Veterans' services	†	163	291	477	1,040	914	1,099	1,119	1,020	1,409
Transportation[1]	123,791	112,372	139,722	184,824	205,697	205,343	199,833	202,673	208,229	215,379
Public safety	58,813	89,463	148,101	207,671	252,744	245,991	244,960	248,206	253,483	260,134
Police and fire protection	47,039	60,962	86,283	119,823	155,042	151,892	151,554	154,126	158,316	163,477
Correction	11,774	21,176	50,686	74,215	82,201	79,296	78,336	79,141	80,785	81,243
Protective inspection and regulation	†	7,324	11,132	13,633	15,501	14,803	15,071	14,940	14,382	15,414
Environment and housing	73,904	100,892	141,125	176,010	225,011	213,840	204,120	200,826	203,292	211,600
Natural resources, parks, and recreation	32,423	37,921	52,815	70,973	75,254	72,396	70,219	69,215	71,665	75,818
Housing and community development	15,953	20,297	30,846	38,832	63,167	58,478	54,254	53,058	52,330	52,248
Sewerage and sanitation	25,528	42,673	57,464	66,205	86,590	82,966	79,647	78,553	79,297	83,534
Governmental administration	41,868	57,290	89,790	121,744	138,998	134,321	132,540	134,827	136,769	140,687
Financial administration	14,185	20,709	31,489	42,524	44,164	42,185	42,669	42,769	43,948	44,788
General control[2]	27,683	36,581	58,301	79,221	94,834	92,137	89,871	92,058	92,821	95,898
Interest on general debt	31,786	49,070	96,781	104,634	121,745	118,787	116,489	112,930	110,350	108,896
Other direct general expenditures	45,378	69,965	87,532	132,334	151,946	147,171	141,907	145,065	145,770	143,236
	Percentage distribution									
Total direct general expenditures	**100.0**	**100.0**	**100.0**	**100.0**	**100.0**	**100.0**	**100.0**	**100.0**	**100.0**	**100.0**
Education and public libraries	39.9	36.2	34.5	35.2	33.8	34.0	33.9	33.8	33.4	33.4
Education	39.4	35.8	34.1	34.8	33.4	33.5	33.4	33.4	33.0	33.0
Public libraries	0.5	0.5	0.5	0.5	0.4	0.4	0.4	0.4	0.4	0.4
Social services and income maintenance	20.2	22.7	23.7	24.4	28.3	28.3	29.2	29.7	31.1	31.3
Public welfare	12.1	13.3	14.4	15.9	19.0	18.8	19.6	20.0	21.6	21.7
Hospitals and health	7.4	8.9	8.9	8.3	9.0	9.3	9.3	9.5	9.3	9.5
Social insurance administration	0.6	0.6	0.4	0.3	0.2	0.2	0.2	0.2	0.1	0.1
Veterans' services	†	#	#	#	#	#	#	#	#	#
Transportation[1]	13.2	9.6	8.3	8.0	7.1	7.3	7.1	7.1	7.0	7.0
Public safety	6.2	7.7	8.8	9.0	8.7	8.7	8.7	8.7	8.5	8.5
Police and fire protection	5.0	5.2	5.1	5.2	5.4	5.4	5.4	5.4	5.3	5.3
Correction	1.3	1.8	3.0	3.2	2.8	2.8	2.8	2.8	2.7	2.6
Protective inspection and regulation	†	0.6	0.7	0.6	0.5	0.5	0.5	0.5	0.5	0.5
Environment and housing	7.9	8.6	8.4	7.7	7.8	7.6	7.3	7.0	6.8	6.9
Natural resources, parks, and recreation	3.4	3.2	3.1	3.1	2.6	2.6	2.5	2.4	2.4	2.5
Housing and community development	1.7	1.7	1.8	1.7	2.2	2.1	1.9	1.9	1.8	1.7
Sewerage and sanitation	2.7	3.7	3.4	2.9	3.0	2.9	2.8	2.7	2.7	2.7

See notes at end of table.

Table 106.30. Amount and percentage distribution of direct general expenditures of state and local governments, by function: Selected years, 1970–71 through 2015–16—Continued

Function	1970–71	1980–81	1990–91	2000–01	2010–11	2011–12	2012–13	2013–14	2014–15	2015–16
1	2	3	4	5	6	7	8	9	10	11
Governmental administration	4.4	4.9	5.3	5.3	4.8	4.8	4.7	4.7	4.6	4.6
Financial administration	1.5	1.8	1.9	1.9	1.5	1.5	1.5	1.5	1.5	1.5
General control[2]	2.9	3.1	3.5	3.4	3.3	3.3	3.2	3.2	3.1	3.1
Interest on general debt	3.4	4.2	5.8	4.6	4.2	4.2	4.1	3.9	3.7	3.6
Other direct general expenditures	4.8	6.0	5.2	5.8	5.2	5.2	5.0	5.1	4.9	4.7

†Not applicable.
#Rounds to zero.
[1]Includes highways, air transportation (airports), parking facilities, and sea and inland port facilities. For 2000–01 and earlier years, also includes transit subsidies.
[2]Includes judicial and legal expenditures, expenditures on general public buildings, and other governmental administration expenditures.
[3]Constant dollars based on the Consumer Price Index, prepared by the Bureau of Labor Statistics, U.S. Department of Labor, adjusted to a school-year basis.

NOTE: Excludes monies paid by states to the federal government. Some data have been revised from previously published figures. Detail may not sum to totals because of rounding.
SOURCE: U.S. Department of Commerce, Census Bureau, Governmental Finances. Retrieved October 22, 2018, from https://www.census.gov/data/datasets/2016/econ/local/public-use-datasets.html. (This table was prepared October 2018.)

Table 106.40. Direct general expenditures of state and local governments for all functions and for education, by level of education and state: 2014–15 and 2015–16

[In millions of current dollars. Standard errors appear in parentheses]

State	Direct general expenditures, 2014–15		Direct general expenditures, 2015–16								
				For education							
					Elementary and secondary education			Colleges and universities			
	Total[1]	For education	Total[1]	Total for education	Total for elementary and secondary	Current expenditure	Capital outlay	Total for colleges and universities	Current expenditure	Capital outlay	Other education[2]
1	2	3	4	5	6	7	8	9	10	11	12
United States	**$2,839,458 (1,703.7)**	**$935,754 (374.3)**	**$2,944,651 (1,472.3)**	**$972,906 (389.2)**	**$632,746 (379.6)**	**$574,425 (—)**	**$58,321 (—)**	**$287,813 (115.1)**	**$253,628 (—)**	**$34,186 (—)**	**$52,346 (0)**
Alabama	37,141 (85.4)	13,317 (9.3)	38,203 (84.0)	13,547 (9.5)	7,639 (9.9)	6,992 (—)	647 (—)	4,881 (#)	4,352 (—)	530 (—)	1,027 (0)
Alaska	14,820 (22.2)	3,660 (16.5)	13,665 (23.2)	3,541 (16.6)	2,365 (16.6)	2,103 (—)	262 (—)	1,093 (#)	731 (—)	361 (—)	83 (0)
Arizona	45,059 (76.6)	15,364 (#)	48,726 (87.7)	14,465 (#)	7,842 (#)	7,313 (—)	529 (—)	5,910 (#)	5,269 (—)	642 (—)	713 (0)
Arkansas	23,354 (35.0)	8,189 (#)	24,315 (43.8)	8,418 (#)	5,088 (#)	4,570 (—)	518 (—)	2,711 (#)	2,461 (—)	250 (—)	618 (0)
California	409,957 (819.9)	115,175 (126.7)	428,900 (900.7)	124,404 (136.8)	78,530 (133.5)	71,743 (—)	6,787 (—)	39,649 (#)	35,853 (—)	3,795 (—)	6,225 (0)
Colorado	44,709 (174.4)	15,180 (#)	46,981 (192.6)	16,075 (#)	9,410 (#)	8,530 (—)	880 (—)	5,921 (#)	4,992 (—)	928 (—)	743 (0)
Connecticut	37,240 (63.3)	13,052 (50.9)	38,425 (69.2)	13,563 (57.0)	9,441 (56.6)	8,806 (—)	635 (—)	3,367 (#)	2,774 (—)	594 (—)	755 (0)
Delaware	9,682 (#)	3,614 (#)	10,092 (#)	3,662 (#)	1,950 (#)	1,845 (—)	105 (—)	1,249 (#)	1,125 (—)	124 (—)	464 (0)
District of Columbia	12,388 (#)	2,724 (#)	12,771 (#)	2,766 (#)	2,607 (#)	2,292 (—)	315 (—)	159 (#)	141 (—)	18 (—)	— (0)
Florida	142,486 (270.7)	40,295 (#)	144,861 (304.2)	41,519 (#)	27,363 (2.7)	25,378 (—)	1,985 (—)	10,799 (#)	10,121 (—)	678 (—)	3,358 (0)
Georgia	67,103 (154.3)	25,665 (#)	68,697 (164.9)	26,726 (#)	18,917 (#)	17,082 (—)	1,835 (—)	5,721 (#)	5,004 (—)	717 (—)	2,088 (0)
Hawaii	13,579 (#)	3,233 (#)	13,627 (#)	3,386 (#)	2,118 (#)	1,876 (—)	242 (—)	1,110 (#)	987 (—)	123 (—)	158 (0)
Idaho	10,585 (16.9)	3,186 (#)	11,039 (26.5)	3,363 (#)	2,047 (#)	1,972 (—)	75 (—)	1,107 (#)	1,035 (—)	72 (—)	209 (0)
Illinois	113,904 (330.3)	37,950 (#)	111,434 (345.4)	37,733 (#)	26,537 (#)	24,522 (—)	2,016 (—)	9,495 (#)	8,864 (—)	631 (—)	1,701 (0)
Indiana	49,151 (127.8)	16,796 (#)	52,074 (135.4)	17,589 (#)	9,967 (#)	8,981 (—)	987 (—)	6,435 (#)	5,688 (—)	747 (—)	1,187 (0)
Iowa	30,223 (99.7)	10,833 (#)	30,894 (101.9)	10,996 (#)	6,584 (0.7)	5,695 (—)	890 (—)	3,918 (#)	3,336 (—)	583 (—)	493 (0)
Kansas	24,500 (83.3)	9,221 (#)	25,200 (93.2)	9,388 (#)	5,648 (#)	4,684 (—)	964 (—)	3,459 (#)	2,921 (—)	538 (—)	281 (0)
Kentucky	36,916 (44.3)	11,892 (#)	38,879 (46.7)	12,550 (#)	7,126 (#)	6,390 (—)	736 (—)	4,376 (#)	3,852 (—)	524 (—)	1,049 (0)
Louisiana	40,799 (24.5)	12,686 (#)	41,343 (28.9)	13,043 (#)	7,931 (#)	7,352 (—)	579 (—)	3,524 (#)	3,008 (—)	517 (—)	1,588 (0)
Maine	11,077 (26.6)	3,361 (16.1)	11,771 (27.1)	3,465 (15.6)	2,425 (15.8)	2,329 (—)	95 (—)	813 (#)	750 (—)	63 (—)	227 (0)
Maryland	58,041 (29.0)	19,521 (#)	58,618 (29.3)	20,006 (#)	12,842 (#)	11,787 (—)	1,056 (—)	6,364 (#)	5,523 (—)	840 (—)	800 (0)
Massachusetts	71,726 (150.6)	21,941 (105.3)	74,786 (142.1)	22,493 (108.0)	15,461 (108.2)	14,422 (—)	1,039 (—)	5,371 (#)	4,477 (—)	894 (—)	1,661 (0)
Michigan	79,778 (279.2)	28,932 (#)	82,786 (264.9)	29,997 (#)	16,951 (#)	15,888 (—)	1,063 (—)	11,720 (#)	10,115 (—)	1,605 (—)	1,326 (0)
Minnesota	52,384 (172.9)	16,991 (#)	56,956 (148.1)	18,292 (#)	12,230 (#)	10,520 (—)	1,710 (—)	5,082 (#)	4,666 (—)	417 (—)	979 (0)
Mississippi	25,143 (47.8)	7,822 (#)	26,105 (47.0)	8,322 (#)	4,581 (#)	4,246 (—)	335 (—)	3,172 (#)	2,755 (—)	417 (—)	569 (0)
Missouri	44,337 (88.7)	14,944 (#)	45,483 (118.3)	15,078 (#)	10,312 (#)	9,422 (—)	890 (—)	3,983 (#)	3,653 (—)	330 (—)	782 (0)
Montana	8,726 (9.6)	2,810 (#)	8,775 (15.8)	2,894 (#)	1,839 (#)	1,660 (—)	179 (—)	940 (#)	894 (—)	46 (—)	114 (0)
Nebraska	16,783 (67.1)	6,685 (#)	17,426 (68.0)	7,279 (#)	4,530 (#)	3,888 (—)	642 (—)	2,432 (#)	2,107 (—)	325 (—)	317 (0)
Nevada	20,152 (145.1)	5,998 (#)	20,500 (149.6)	6,133 (#)	4,203 (#)	3,978 (—)	224 (—)	1,420 (#)	1,319 (—)	101 (—)	510 (0)
New Hampshire	10,472 (9.4)	3,931 (#)	11,127 (14.5)	4,131 (8.3)	2,924 (8.5)	2,787 (—)	137 (—)	985 (#)	844 (—)	141 (—)	221 (0)
New Jersey	90,306 (162.6)	34,725 (27.8)	92,450 (231.1)	36,108 (43.3)	26,986 (43.2)	25,070 (—)	1,916 (—)	6,987 (#)	5,797 (—)	1,191 (—)	2,135 (0)
New Mexico	20,973 (21.0)	6,739 (#)	20,521 (12.3)	6,647 (#)	3,653 (#)	3,102 (—)	551 (—)	2,586 (#)	2,241 (—)	345 (—)	409 (0)
New York	257,320 (231.6)	79,664 (87.6)	268,376 (268.4)	82,511 (90.8)	66,106 (#)	61,447 (—)	4,658 (—)	14,287 (88.6)	12,387 (—)	1,900 (—)	2,119 (0)
North Carolina	74,509 (223.5)	24,801 (181.0)	77,209 (231.6)	25,447 (185.8)	13,801 (173.9)	12,878 (—)	923 (—)	9,727 (64.2)	8,975 (—)	752 (—)	1,919 (0)
North Dakota	9,051 (35.3)	2,941 (#)	9,577 (17.2)	3,187 (#)	1,873 (#)	1,461 (—)	412 (—)	1,220 (#)	1,053 (—)	167 (—)	93 (0)
Ohio	100,222 (300.7)	33,532 (100.6)	103,575 (310.7)	34,482 (110.3)	23,163 (111.2)	21,307 (—)	1,856 (—)	9,586 (#)	7,888 (—)	1,698 (—)	1,733 (0)
Oklahoma	28,566 (57.1)	10,147 (#)	29,146 (67.0)	10,629 (#)	5,915 (#)	5,273 (—)	642 (—)	4,053 (#)	3,542 (—)	511 (—)	661 (0)
Oregon	37,675 (75.3)	11,503 (#)	41,373 (91.0)	12,591 (#)	7,145 (#)	6,459 (—)	686 (—)	4,944 (#)	4,288 (—)	656 (—)	501 (0)
Pennsylvania	114,569 (229.1)	39,517 (4.0)	122,179 (207.7)	41,397 (4.1)	28,232 (2.8)	26,425 (—)	1,807 (—)	10,762 (#)	9,532 (—)	1,230 (—)	2,403 (0)
Rhode Island	10,080 (8.1)	3,275 (#)	10,220 (6.1)	3,409 (#)	2,411 (#)	2,340 (—)	71 (—)	683 (#)	673 (—)	9 (—)	316 (0)
South Carolina	39,092 (62.5)	13,742 (#)	40,888 (65.4)	14,353 (#)	8,756 (#)	7,667 (—)	1,089 (—)	4,179 (#)	3,743 (—)	436 (—)	1,418 (0)
South Dakota	6,567 (9.2)	2,245 (#)	6,991 (19.6)	2,456 (#)	1,431 (#)	1,239 (—)	192 (—)	881 (#)	696 (—)	185 (—)	144 (0)
Tennessee	44,027 (198.1)	14,164 (150.1)	44,974 (206.9)	13,977 (152.4)	9,274 (153.0)	8,763 (—)	512 (—)	3,713 (#)	3,288 (—)	425 (—)	990 (0)
Texas	205,921 (947.2)	80,073 (16.0)	215,064 (322.6)	83,062 (16.6)	52,800 (15.8)	44,466 (—)	8,334 (—)	27,959 (#)	24,242 (—)	3,717 (—)	2,303 (0)
Utah	21,903 (76.7)	8,684 (#)	23,285 (144.4)	9,752 (#)	4,817 (#)	4,108 (—)	709 (—)	4,402 (#)	3,784 (—)	618 (—)	533 (0)

See notes at end of table.

Table 106.40. Direct general expenditures of state and local governments for all functions and for education, by level of education and state: 2014–15 and 2015–16—Continued

[In millions of current dollars. Standard errors appear in parentheses]

State	Direct general expenditures, 2014–15		Direct general expenditures, 2015–16									
				For education								
					Elementary and secondary education			Colleges and universities				
	Total[1]	For education	Total[1]	Total for education	Total for elementary and secondary	Current expenditure	Capital outlay	Total for colleges and universities	Current expenditure	Capital outlay	Other education[2]
1	2	3	4	5	6	7	8	9	10	11	12
Vermont	6,830 (12.3)	2,539 (#)	7,031 (12.7)	2,678 (#)	1,608 (#)	1,566 (—)	43 (—)	872 (#)	782 (—)	90 (—)	198 (0)
Virginia	68,719 (247.4)	24,999 (127.5)	70,867 (255.1)	25,100 (150.6)	16,302 (150.0)	14,674 (—)	1,628 (—)	7,759 (#)	6,724 (—)	1,036 (—)	1,039 (0)
Washington	66,577 (213.0)	21,674 (36.8)	70,596 (211.8)	23,786 (38.1)	14,875 (37.2)	12,670 (—)	2,204 (—)	7,099 (#)	6,352 (—)	747 (—)	1,813 (0)
West Virginia	15,165 (12.1)	5,267 (#)	15,915 (25.5)	5,359 (#)	3,086 (#)	2,905 (—)	181 (—)	1,754 (#)	1,563 (—)	191 (—)	518 (0)
Wisconsin	50,786 (116.8)	17,679 (1.8)	51,177 (122.8)	18,030 (5.4)	11,084 (5.5)	9,991 (—)	1,093 (—)	6,295 (#)	5,702 (—)	593 (—)	651 (0)
Wyoming	8,385 (21.0)	2,876 (#)	8,777 (30.7)	3,119 (#)	2,015 (#)	1,561 (—)	454 (—)	898 (#)	759 (—)	139 (—)	206 (0)

—Not available.
#Rounds to zero.
[1]Includes state and local government expenditures for education and public libraries, social services and income maintenance, transportation, public safety, environment and housing, governmental administration, interest on general debt, and other direct general expenditures.
[2]Includes assistance and subsidies to individuals, private elementary and secondary schools, and private colleges and universities, as well as miscellaneous education expenditures. Does not include expenditures for public libraries.

NOTE: Current expenditure data in this table differ from figures appearing in other tables because of slightly varying definitions used in the Governmental Finances and Common Core of Data surveys. Detail may not sum to totals because of rounding. Some data have been revised from previously published figures.
SOURCE: U.S. Department of Commerce, Census Bureau, Governmental Finances. Retrieved January 23, 2019, from https://www.census.gov/data/datasets/2016/econ/local/public-use-datasets.html. (This table was prepared January 2019.)

Table 106.50. Direct general expenditures of state and local governments per capita for all functions and for education, by level of education and state: 2014–15 and 2015–16

[Amounts in current dollars]

State	Direct general expenditures, 2014–15			Direct general expenditures, 2015–16								
		For education			For education							
					All education		Elementary and secondary education		Colleges and universities		Other education[2]	
	Total amount per capita[1]	Amount per capita	As a percent of all functions	Total amount per capita[1]	Amount per capita	As a percent of all functions	Amount per capita	As a percent of all functions	Amount per capita	As a percent of all functions	Amount per capita	As a percent of all functions
1	2	3	4	5	6	7	8	9	10	11	12	13
United States	**$8,853**	**$2,917**	**33.0**	**$9,115**	**$3,011**	**33.0**	**$1,959**	**21.5**	**$891**	**9.8**	**$162**	**1.8**
Alabama	7,653	2,744	35.9	7,853	2,785	35.5	1,570	20.0	1,003	12.8	211	2.7
Alaska	20,094	4,963	24.7	18,429	4,776	25.9	3,190	17.3	1,474	8.0	112	0.6
Arizona	6,594	2,248	34.1	7,016	2,083	29.7	1,129	16.1	851	12.1	103	1.5
Arkansas	7,841	2,749	35.1	8,131	2,815	34.6	1,702	20.9	907	11.2	207	2.5
California	10,524	2,957	28.1	10,939	3,173	29.0	2,003	18.3	1,011	9.2	159	1.5
Colorado	8,200	2,784	34.0	8,479	2,901	34.2	1,698	20.0	1,069	12.6	134	1.6
Connecticut	10,380	3,638	35.0	10,737	3,790	35.3	2,638	24.6	941	8.8	211	2.0
Delaware	10,285	3,839	37.3	10,632	3,858	36.3	2,054	19.3	1,315	12.4	489	4.6
District of Columbia	18,346	4,035	22.0	18,600	4,028	21.7	3,797	20.4	232	1.2	—	—
Florida	7,045	1,992	28.3	7,022	2,013	28.7	1,326	18.9	523	7.5	163	2.3
Georgia	6,591	2,521	38.2	6,667	2,594	38.9	1,836	27.5	555	8.3	203	3.0
Hawaii	9,546	2,272	23.8	9,542	2,371	24.8	1,483	15.5	777	8.1	110	1.2
Idaho	6,410	1,929	30.1	6,560	1,998	30.5	1,216	18.5	658	10.0	124	1.9
Illinois	8,854	2,950	33.3	8,688	2,942	33.9	2,069	23.8	740	8.5	133	1.5
Indiana	7,438	2,542	34.2	7,850	2,652	33.8	1,503	19.1	970	12.4	179	2.3
Iowa	9,682	3,471	35.8	9,865	3,511	35.6	2,102	21.3	1,251	12.7	157	1.6
Kansas	8,421	3,169	37.6	8,656	3,225	37.3	1,940	22.4	1,188	13.7	96	1.1
Kentucky	8,341	2,687	32.2	8,760	2,828	32.3	1,606	18.3	986	11.3	236	2.7
Louisiana	8,746	2,719	31.1	8,837	2,788	31.5	1,695	19.2	753	8.5	339	3.8
Maine	8,338	2,530	30.3	8,841	2,603	29.4	1,821	20.6	611	6.9	170	1.9
Maryland	9,695	3,261	33.6	9,762	3,332	34.1	2,139	21.9	1,060	10.9	133	1.4
Massachusetts	10,554	3,229	30.6	10,956	3,295	30.1	2,265	20.7	787	7.2	243	2.2
Michigan	8,032	2,913	36.3	8,319	3,014	36.2	1,703	20.5	1,178	14.2	133	1.6
Minnesota	9,555	3,099	32.4	10,312	3,312	32.1	2,214	21.5	920	8.9	177	1.7
Mississippi	8,413	2,617	31.1	8,736	2,785	31.9	1,533	17.5	1,061	12.2	190	2.2
Missouri	7,302	2,461	33.7	7,472	2,477	33.2	1,694	22.7	654	8.8	129	1.7
Montana	8,467	2,727	32.2	8,430	2,780	33.0	1,767	21.0	903	10.7	110	1.3
Nebraska	8,873	3,534	39.8	9,143	3,819	41.8	2,377	26.0	1,276	14.0	166	1.8
Nevada	7,025	2,091	29.8	7,021	2,100	29.9	1,439	20.5	486	6.9	175	2.5
New Hampshire	7,836	2,942	37.5	8,289	3,077	37.1	2,178	26.3	734	8.9	165	2.0
New Jersey	10,180	3,914	38.5	10,417	4,069	39.1	3,041	29.2	787	7.6	241	2.3
New Mexico	10,034	3,224	32.1	9,806	3,176	32.4	1,746	17.8	1,235	12.6	195	2.0
New York	13,088	4,052	31.0	13,664	4,201	30.7	3,366	24.6	727	5.3	108	0.8
North Carolina	7,426	2,472	33.3	7,602	2,505	33.0	1,359	17.9	958	12.6	189	2.5
North Dakota	12,003	3,901	32.5	12,695	4,224	33.3	2,483	19.6	1,617	12.7	123	1.0
Ohio	8,627	2,886	33.5	8,902	2,964	33.3	1,991	22.4	824	9.3	149	1.7
Oklahoma	7,306	2,595	35.5	7,422	2,707	36.5	1,506	20.3	1,032	13.9	168	2.3
Oregon	9,379	2,864	30.5	10,112	3,077	30.4	1,746	17.3	1,208	11.9	123	1.2
Pennsylvania	8,961	3,091	34.5	9,558	3,238	33.9	2,208	23.1	842	8.8	188	2.0
Rhode Island	9,544	3,101	32.5	9,669	3,225	33.4	2,281	23.6	646	6.7	299	3.1
South Carolina	7,991	2,809	35.2	8,246	2,895	35.1	1,766	21.4	843	10.2	286	3.5
South Dakota	7,690	2,629	34.2	8,102	2,846	35.1	1,658	20.5	1,021	12.6	167	2.1
Tennessee	6,680	2,149	32.2	6,768	2,103	31.1	1,396	20.6	559	8.3	149	2.2
Texas	7,492	2,913	38.9	7,698	2,973	38.6	1,890	24.6	1,001	13.0	82	1.1
Utah	7,344	2,912	39.6	7,653	3,205	41.9	1,583	20.7	1,447	18.9	175	2.3
Vermont	10,924	4,062	37.2	11,274	4,295	38.1	2,579	22.9	1,398	12.4	317	2.8
Virginia	8,217	2,989	36.4	8,426	2,984	35.4	1,938	23.0	923	10.9	124	1.5
Washington	9,294	3,026	32.6	9,678	3,261	33.7	2,039	21.1	973	10.1	249	2.6
West Virginia	8,233	2,859	34.7	8,692	2,927	33.7	1,686	19.4	958	11.0	283	3.3
Wisconsin	8,815	3,068	34.8	8,865	3,123	35.2	1,920	21.7	1,090	12.3	113	1.3
Wyoming	14,317	4,910	34.3	15,022	5,339	35.5	3,449	23.0	1,537	10.2	353	2.3

—Not available.

[1]Includes state and local government expenditures for education and public libraries, social services and income maintenance, transportation, public safety, environment and housing, governmental administration, interest on general debt, and other direct general expenditures.

[2]Includes assistance and subsidies to individuals, private elementary and secondary schools, and private colleges and universities, as well as miscellaneous education expenditures. Does not include expenditures for public libraries.

NOTE: Per capita amounts for 2015–16 are based on population estimates for July 2016. Per capita amounts for 2014–15 are based on the latest population estimates for July 2015 and have been revised from previously published figures. Detail may not sum to totals because of rounding.

SOURCE: U.S. Department of Commerce, Census Bureau, Governmental Finances, retrieved November 27, 2018, from https://www.census.gov/data/datasets/2016/econ/local/public-use-datasets.html; and Population Estimates, retrieved April 9, 2019, from https://factfinder.census.gov/faces/tableservices/jsf/pages/productview.xhtml?pid=PEP_2018_PEPANNRES&src=pt. (This table was prepared April 2019).

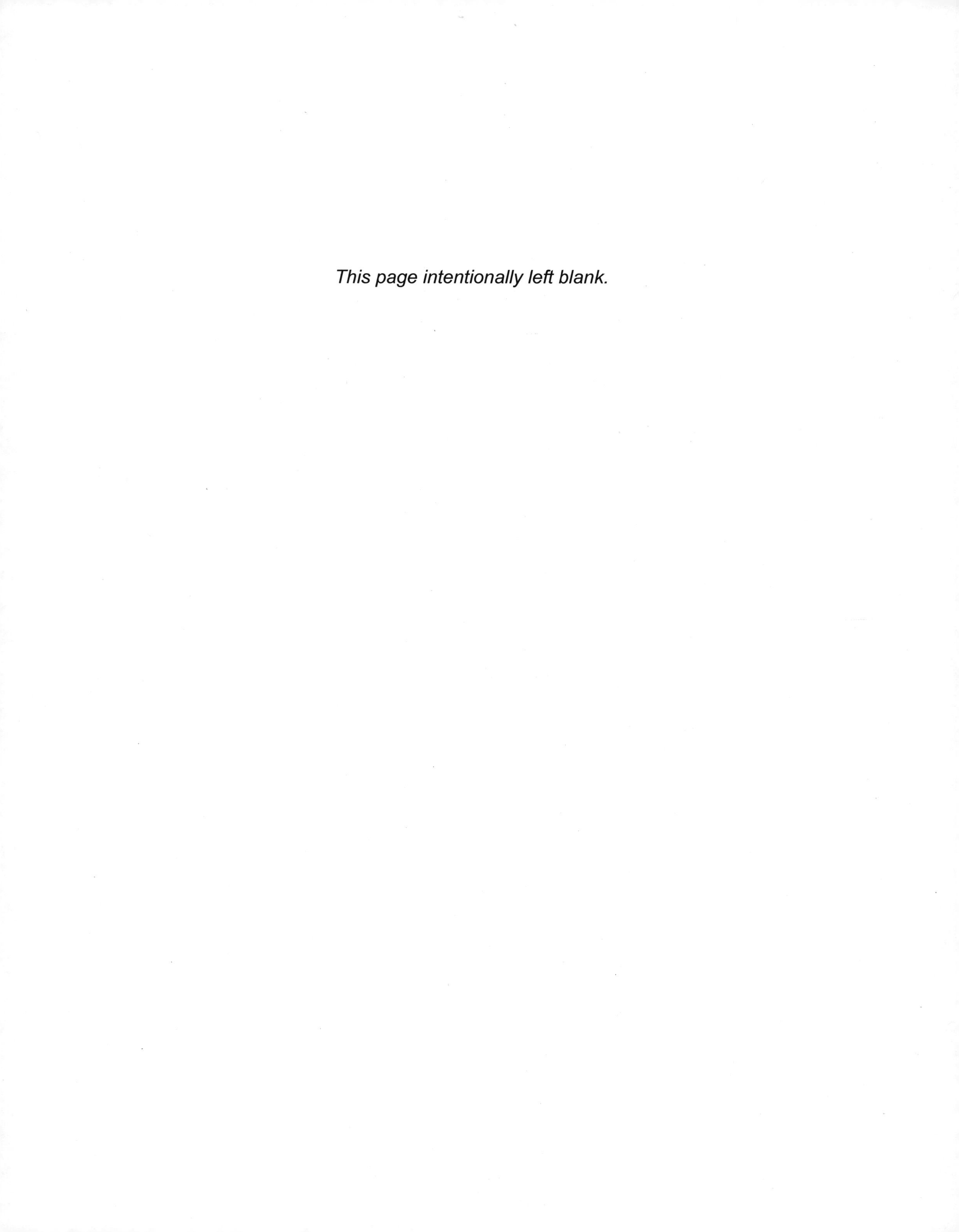

This page intentionally left blank.

CHAPTER 2
Elementary and Secondary Education

This chapter contains a variety of statistics on public and private elementary and secondary education. Data are presented for enrollments, teachers and other school staff, schools, dropouts, achievement, school violence, and revenues and expenditures. These data are derived from surveys, censuses, and administrative data collections conducted by the National Center for Education Statistics (NCES) and other public and private organizations. The information ranges from counts of students and schools to state graduation requirements. Public school enrollment data are for fall of the given year.

Enrollments

Public elementary and secondary school enrollment rose from 49.5 million in 2011 to 50.6 million in 2016, an increase of 2 percent (table 203.10 and figure 7). Public elementary enrollment increased 2 percent between 2011 and 2016 (from 34.8 million to 35.5 million), while public secondary enrollment increased 3 percent (from 14.7 million to 15.1 million).[1] Although public school enrollment increased overall between 2011 and 2016, there were enrollment decreases for some racial/ethnic groups and increases for others (table 203.50). Between 2011 and 2016, the enrollment of Hispanic students increased 13 percent and the enrollment of Asian students increased 10 percent. Also, the enrollment of Pacific Islander students was 3 percent higher in 2016 than in 2011. In contrast, the enrollment of American Indian/Alaska Native students decreased 7 percent, the enrollment of White students decreased 5 percent, and the enrollment of Black students decreased 1 percent. The reported number of students of Two or more races increased 45 percent between 2011 and 2016.

From 2011 to 2016, changes in public elementary and secondary school enrollment varied from state to state. Thirty-five states and the District of Columbia had higher enrollment in 2016 than in 2011, while 15 states had lower enrollment in 2016 than in 2010 (table 203.20 and figure 8). The largest public school enrollment increases occurred in the District of Columbia (16 percent), North Dakota (12 percent), and Utah (10 percent), and increases of 5 percent or more occurred in 11 other states (Nevada, Texas, Oregon, South Dakota, Idaho, South Carolina, Colorado, Nebraska, Delaware, Florida, and Washington). The largest decrease in public school enrollment occurred in New Hampshire (6 percent); decreases of 3 percent or more occurred in 3 other states (Maine, Connecticut, and West Virginia) (table 203.20).

Enrollment in private elementary and secondary schools in 2015 (5.8 million) was 5 percent lower than in 2005 (6.1 million), but 9 percent higher than in 2011 (5.3 million) (table 105.30). In 2015, private school students made up 10.2 percent of all elementary and secondary school students.

Sixty-four percent of 3- to 5-year-olds were enrolled in preprimary education (nursery school and kindergarten) in 2017, which was not measurably different from the percentage enrolled in 2005 (table 202.10 and figure 9). However, the percentage of these children enrolled in full-day programs increased from 58 percent in 2005 to 65 percent in 2017.

In 2016, a higher percentage of 3- to 5-year-old children not yet enrolled in kindergarten (49 percent) were cared for primarily in center-based programs than had no regular nonparental care (27 percent) or were cared for primarily in home-based settings by relatives (14 percent) or by nonrelatives (8 percent) (table 202.30). An earlier survey in 2005–06 found that there were differences in the average quality of care 4-year-old children received in these settings. A higher percentage of children in Head Start and other center-based programs (35 percent) received high-quality care than those in home-based relative and nonrelative care (9 percent), according to the ratings of trained observers (*web-only table 202.60*).

The Individuals with Disabilities Education Act (IDEA), enacted in 1975, mandates that children and youth ages 3–21 with disabilities be provided a free and appropriate public school education. The percentage of total public school enrollment that represents children served by federally supported special education programs increased from 8.3 percent to 13.8 percent between 1976–77 and 2004–05 (table 204.30 and *Digest of Education Statistics 2016*, table 204.30). Much of this overall increase can be attributed to a rise in the percentage of students identified as having specific learning disabilities from 1976–77 (1.8 percent) to 2004–05 (5.7 percent). The overall percentage of students being served in programs for those with disabilities was slightly lower in 2017–18 (13.7) than in

[1] Public elementary enrollment includes students in prekindergarten through grade 8 as well as elementary ungraded students. Public secondary enrollment includes students in grades 9 through 12 as well as secondary ungraded students and students reported as being enrolled in grade 13.

2004–05 (13.8 percent). However, there were different patterns of change in the percentages of students served with some specific conditions between 2004–05 and 2017–18. The percentage of children identified as having other health impairments (limited strength, vitality, or alertness due to chronic or acute health problems such as a heart condition, tuberculosis, rheumatic fever, nephritis, asthma, sickle cell anemia, hemophilia, epilepsy, lead poisoning, leukemia, or diabetes) rose from 1.1 to 2.0 percent of total public school enrollment; the percentage with autism rose from 0.4 to 1.4 percent; and the percentage with developmental delay rose from 0.7 to 0.9 percent. The percentage of children with specific learning disabilities declined from 5.7 percent to 4.6 percent of total public school enrollment during this period. In fall 2017, some 95 percent of 6- to 21-year-old students with disabilities were served in regular schools; 3 percent were served in a separate school for students with disabilities; 1 percent were placed in regular private schools by their parents; and less than 1 percent each were served in one of the following environments: in a separate residential facility, homebound or in a hospital, or in a correctional facility (*web-only table 204.60*).

Teachers and Other School Staff

During the 1970s and early 1980s, public school enrollment decreased while the number of teachers generally increased. For public schools, the number of pupils per teacher—that is, the pupil/teacher ratio[2]—declined from 22.3 in 1970 to 17.9 in 1985 (table 208.20 and figure 7). After enrollment started increasing in 1985, the public school pupil/teacher ratio continued to decline, reaching 17.2 in 1989. After a period of relative stability from the late 1980s through the mid-1990s, the ratio declined from 17.3 in 1995 to 15.3 in 2008. After 2008, the public school pupil/teacher ratio increased, reaching 16.0 in 2016. In comparison, the private school pupil/teacher ratio was 11.9 in 2015. The average class size in 2011–12 was 21.2 pupils for public elementary schools and 26.8 pupils for public secondary schools (table 209.30).

In 2011–12, some 76 percent of public school teachers were female, 44 percent were under age 40, and 56 percent had a master's or higher degree (*Digest of Education Statistics 2017,* table 209.10). Compared with public school teachers, a lower percentage of private school teachers had a master's or higher degree (43 percent).

Public school principals tend to be older and have more advanced credentials than public school teachers. In 2015–16, some 19 percent of public school principals were under age 40, and 98 percent had a master's or higher degree (table 212.08). In comparison, 43 percent of public school teachers were under age 40, and 57 percent had a master's or higher degree. A lower percentage of public school principals than of teachers were female: 54 percent of principals were female, compared with 77 percent of teachers.

From 1969–70 to 1980, there was an 8 percent increase in the number of public school teachers, compared with a 48 percent increase in the number of all other public school staff[3] (table B and table 213.10). Consequently, the percentage of staff who were teachers declined from 60 percent in 1969–70 to 52 percent in 1980. From 1980 to 2016, the number of teachers and the number of all other staff grew at more similar rates (45 and 67 percent, respectively) than they did in the 1970s. As a result, the proportion of teachers among total staff was 4 percentage points lower in 2016 than in 1980, in contrast to the decrease of 8 percentage points during the 1970s. The numbers of staff in two categories increased more than 100 percent between 1980 and 2016: the number of instructional aides rose 142 percent, and the number of instruction coordinators rose 339 percent. Taken together, the percentage of staff with direct instructional responsibilities (teachers and instructional aides) was higher in 2016 (61 percent) than in 1980 (60 percent). In 2016, there were 8 pupils per staff member (total staff) at public schools, compared with 10 pupils per staff member in 1980 (table 213.10). At private schools in 2011–12, the number of pupils per staff member was 6 (*web-only table 205.60*).

Table B. Number of public school staff, by selected categories: 1969–70, fall 1980, fall 2010, and fall 2016

[In thousands]

Selected staff category	1969–70	1980	2010	2016
Total	**3,361**	**4,168**	**6,195**	**6,485**
Teachers	2,016	2,184	3,099	3,169
Instructional aides	57	326	732	787
Instruction coordinators	32	21	69	90

SOURCE: U.S. Department of Education, National Center for Education Statistics, *Statistics of State School Systems, 1969–70*; *Statistics of Public Elementary and Secondary Schools, 1980*; and Common Core of Data (CCD), "State Nonfiscal Survey of Public Elementary/Secondary Education," 2010–11 and 2016–17.

In more recent years, the numbers of most types of staff have increased (table 213.10). Overall, the number of public school staff increased 5 percent between fall 2010 and fall 2016. The number of officials and administrators rose 9 percent during this period, and the number of principals and assistant principals rose 11 percent. Also, the number of instruction coordinators rose 30 percent, the number of instructional aides rose 8 percent, and the number of support staff rose 6 percent. The number of teachers rose 2 percent between fall 2010 and fall 2016, and the number of guidance counselors was 6 percent higher in fall 2016 than in fall 2010. In contrast, the number of librarians decreased by 15 percent during this period.

[2] The pupil/teacher ratio is based on all teachers—including teachers of students with disabilities and other special teachers—and all students enrolled in the fall of the school year. Unlike the pupil/teacher ratio, the average class size excludes students and teachers in classes that are exclusively for special education students. Class size averages are based on surveys of teachers reporting on the counts of students in their classes.

[3] "All other public school staff" includes administrative staff, principals, librarians, guidance counselors, secretaries, custodial staff, food service workers, school bus drivers, and other professional and nonprofessional staff.

Schools

During most of the last century, the trend of consolidating small schools brought declines in the total number of public schools in the United States. In 1929–30, there were approximately 248,000 public schools, compared with about 98,000 in 2015–16 (table 214.10). However, the number of public schools has increased in recent decades: Between 1988–89 and 2006–07, there was an increase of approximately 15,600 schools. Since 2006–07, the number of public schools has remained relatively stable, varying by fewer than 500 schools from year to year.

While the total number of public schools in the country has remained relatively stable in recent years, new schools have opened and some schools have closed. In 2016–17, there were 1,098 school closures (*web-only table 216.95*). The schools that closed had enrolled about 189,000 students in the prior school year (2015–16). Of the schools that closed, 738 were regular schools, 66 were special education schools, 10 were vocational schools, and 284 were alternative schools. Of these closed schools, 181 were classified as charter schools. The number of schools that closed in 2016–17 was lower than the number in 2000–01 (1,193); however, the number of annual school closures fluctuated during this period, ranging from 1,098 to 2,168. School closures do not necessarily reflect the number of school buildings that have been closed, since a school may share a building with another school, or one school may have multiple buildings.

Since the early 1970s, public school systems have been shifting away from junior high schools (schools consisting of either grades 7 and 8 or grades 7–9) and moving toward middle schools (a subset of elementary schools beginning with grade 4, 5, or 6 and ending with grade 6, 7, or 8) (table 216.10). The number of all public elementary schools (schools beginning with grade 6 or below and ending with grade 8 or below) increased 4 percent between 1970–71 and 2006–17 (64,000 and 66,800, respectively). In contrast, the number of middle schools increased by 537 percent (from 2,100 in 1970–71 to 13,300 in 2016–17). During the same period, the number of junior high schools declined by 67 percent (from 7,800 in 1970–71 to 2,500 in 2016–17). Compared over more recent years, the number of all elementary schools was less than 1 percent higher in 2016–17 than in 2006–07, while the subset of middle schools rose by 4 percent to 13,300. During the same period, the number of junior high schools declined by 19 percent to 2,500. The total number of secondary schools in 2016–17 (23,800) was slightly lower than the number in 2006–07 (23,900).

The average number of students in public elementary schools increased from 473 in 2006–07 to 483 in 2016–17 (table 216.45). In contrast, the average enrollment size of public secondary schools was lower in 2016–17 (708) than in 2006–07 (711). Also, the average size of regular public secondary schools—which exclude alternative, special education, and vocational education schools—was lower in 2016–17 (802) than in 2006–07 (818).

School Choice

Over the past two decades, the range of options that parents have for the education of their children has expanded. Private schools have been a traditional alternative to public school education, but there are now more options for parents to choose public charter schools, and more parents are also homeschooling their children. Between fall 1999 and fall 2015, enrollment in elementary and secondary private schools decreased from 6.0 million to 5.8 million, a decline of 0.3 million or 4 percent (table 105.30). Although private school enrollment declined through much of this period, it was higher in fall 2015 (5.8 million) than in fall 2011 (5.3 million). From fall 1999 to fall 2015, the percentage of students who were enrolled in private schools declined from 11.4 percent to 10.2 percent. In contrast, enrollment in public charter schools increased between fall 2000 and fall 2016, rising from 0.4 million to 3.0 million, an increase of 2.6 million students (table 216.20). During this period, the percentage of public elementary and secondary school students who were in charter schools increased from 0.7 percent to 6.0 percent. In addition, there has been an increase in the number and percentage of 5- to 17-year-olds who are homeschooled (table 206.10 and *web-only table 206.20*). About 1.7 million children were homeschooled in 2016, compared to 0.9 million in 1999.[4] Also, the percentage of 5- to 17-year-olds who were homeschooled in 2016 (3.3 percent) was higher than in 1999 (1.7 percent).

Charter schools are the typical form of school choice available to parents within the public education sector; however, there is also some opportunity for school choice among traditional public schools. In 2016, the parents of 41 percent of all students in grades 1–12 indicated that public school choice was available to them (*web-only table 206.40*). Also in 2016, some 20 percent of the students in grades 1–12 were enrolled in public schools chosen by their families (table 206.30). Some 71 percent of students attended an assigned public school and 9 percent attended a private school. There were differences by some characteristics in the percentages of students who attended public schools chosen by their parents and the percentages of students who attended private schools in 2016. For example, the percentage of students attending chosen public schools was higher for Black students (32 percent) and Hispanic students (25 percent) than for White students (14 percent). In contrast, the percentage attending private schools was higher for White students (11 percent) than for Black students (8 percent) and Hispanic students (6 percent).

[4] The number of homeschooled children in 1999 is from *Homeschooling in the United States: 1999* (NCES 2001-033), available at https://nces.ed.gov/pubsearch/pubsinfo.asp?pubid=2001033. While National Household Education Surveys Program (NHES) administrations prior to 2012 were administered via telephone with an interviewer, NHES:2016 used self-administered paper-and-pencil questionnaires that were mailed to respondents. Measurable differences in estimates between 1999 and 2016 could reflect actual changes in the population, or the changes could be due to the mode change from telephone to mail.

There were also some differences in the percentage of students in chosen public schools by different levels of parental educational attainment. A lower percentage of students whose parents had completed only a bachelor's degree (18 percent) were enrolled in chosen schools, compared to students whose parents had not completed high school (23 percent) or who had only completed high school (21 percent). In contrast, the percentage of students attending private schools was higher for students whose parents had a bachelor's degree (13 percent) or graduate degree (18 percent) than for students whose parents had less than a high school diploma (5 percent), only a high school diploma (4 percent), or only some college or a vocational degree (6 percent). The percentage of students attending chosen public schools was higher for students living in cities (31 percent) than for students in suburban areas (17 percent), towns (14 percent), and rural areas (11 percent).

Compared with students in assigned public schools, a higher percentage of students in chosen public schools had parents who were very satisfied with some elements of their children's education in 2016 (*web-only table 206.50*). Among students in grades 3 through 12, the percentage of students whose parents were very satisfied with their school was higher for students in chosen schools (60 percent) than for students in assigned schools (54 percent). Similarly, the percentage of students whose parents were very satisfied with their school's academic standards was higher for students in chosen schools (60 percent) than for students in assigned schools (53 percent). Also, higher percentages of students in chosen schools than in assigned schools had parents who were very satisfied with school order and discipline (57 vs. 53 percent) as well as with staff interaction with parents (51 vs. 47 percent). There was no measurable difference in the percentage of students who had parents who were highly satisfied with the teachers in their school, whether assigned or chosen.

High School Graduates and Dropouts

About 3,650,000 high school students are expected to graduate during the 2019–20 school year (table 219.10), including 3,304,000 public school graduates and 347,000 private school graduates. High school graduates include only recipients of diplomas, not recipients of equivalency credentials. The 2019–20 projection of high school graduates is slightly lower than the prior record high projection of 3,684,000 graduates for 2018–19, but it exceeds the baby boom era's high point in 1975–76, when 3,142,000 students earned diplomas. In 2016–17, about 85 percent of public high school students graduated with a regular diploma within 4 years of first starting 9th grade (table 219.46). This rate is known as the 4-year adjusted cohort graduation rate (ACGR).

The status dropout rate has decreased over the past two decades (table 219.70). The status dropout rate is the percentage of the civilian noninstitutionalized 16- to 24-year-old population who are not enrolled in school and who have not completed a high school program, regardless of when they left school. (People who left school but went on to receive a GED credential are not treated as dropouts.) Between 1990 and 2017, the status dropout rate declined from 12.1 to 5.8 percent. During this period, the status dropout rate for Black 16- to 24-year-olds declined from 13.2 percent to 5.7 percent and the rate for Hispanic 16- to 24-year-olds declined from 32.4 to 9.5 percent. In 2017, the status dropout rate for White 16- to 24-year-olds (4.6 percent) was lower than the rate for Hispanic 16- to 24-year-olds, but it was not measurably different from the rate for Black 16- to 24-year-olds.

Achievement

Most of the student performance data in the *Digest* are drawn from the National Assessment of Educational Progress (NAEP). The NAEP assessments have been conducted using three basic designs: the national main NAEP, state NAEP (which includes the Trial Urban District Assessment), and national long-term trend NAEP. The main NAEP reports current information for the nation and specific geographic regions of the country. The assessment program includes students drawn from both public and private schools and reports results for student achievement at grades 4, 8, and 12. The main NAEP assessments follow the frameworks developed by the National Assessment Governing Board and use the latest advances in assessment methodology. Because the assessment items reflect curricula associated with specific grade levels, the main NAEP uses samples of students at those grade levels.

Since 1990, NAEP assessments have also been conducted at the state level. Each participating state receives assessment results that report on the performance of students in that state. In its content, the state assessment is identical to the assessment conducted nationally. From 1990 through 2001, the national sample was a subset of the combined sample of students assessed in each participating state along with an additional sample from the states that did not participate in the state assessment. For mathematics, reading, science, and writing assessments since 2002, a combined sample of public schools has been selected for 4th- and 8th-grade national NAEP and state NAEP (including the Trial Urban District Assessment).

NAEP long-term trend assessments are designed to give information on the changes in the basic achievement level of America's youth since the early 1970s. They are administered nationally and report student performance in reading and mathematics at ages 9, 13, and 17. Measuring long-term trends of student achievement requires the precise replication of past procedures. For example, students of specific ages are sampled in order to maintain consistency with the original sample design. Similarly, the long-term trend instrument does not evolve based on changes in curricula or in educational practices. The differences in procedures between the main NAEP and the long-term trend NAEP mean that their results cannot be compared directly.

The following paragraphs discuss results for the national main NAEP, state NAEP, and long-term trend NAEP. Readers should keep in mind that comparisons of NAEP scores in the text (like all comparisons of estimates in the *Digest*) are based on statistical testing of unrounded values.

Reading

The main NAEP reading assessment data are reported on a scale of 0 to 500. In 2017, the average reading score for 4th-grade students (222) was not measurably different from the 2015 score but was higher than the 1992 score (217) (table 221.10). At grade 4, the 2017 scores for White (232), Black (206), Hispanic (209), and Asian/Pacific Islander (239) students were not measurably different from the scores in 2015, but the score for each group was higher than in 1992 (224, 192, 197, and 216, respectively). In 2017, the average score for American Indian/Alaska Native 4th-graders (202) was not measurably different from the scores in 2015 and 1994 (1994 was the first year data were available for 4th-grade American Indian/Alaska Native students). For 8th-grade students, the score in 2017 (267) was higher than in 2015 (265) or 1992 (260). At grade 8, the 2017 scores for White (275), Black (249), Hispanic (255), and Asian/Pacific Islander (282) students were not measurably different from the scores in 2015. Consistent with the findings at grade 4, the scores for White, Black, Hispanic, and Asian/Pacific Islander 8th-grade students were higher in 2017 than in 1992. In 2017, the score for 8th-grade American Indian/Alaska Native students (253) was not measurably different from the scores in 2015 and in 1994 (1994 was the first year data were available for 8th-grade American Indian/Alaska Native students). For 12th-grade students, the score in 2015 (287) was not measurably different from the score in 2013, but it was lower than the score in 1992 (292). At grade 12, the 2015 scores for White (295), Hispanic (276), and Asian/Pacific Islander (297) students were not measurably different from the scores in 2013 and in 1992. For Black students, the 2015 score (266) was lower than the 1992 score (273), but it was not measurably different from the 2013 score.

From 1992 through 2017, the average reading scores for White 4th- and 8th-grade students were higher than those of their Black and Hispanic peers (table 221.10). Although the White-Black and White-Hispanic achievement gaps did not change measurably from 2015 to 2017 at either grade 4 or 8, some of the racial/ethnic achievement gaps have narrowed since 1992. At grade 4, the White-Black gap narrowed from 32 points in 1992 to 26 points in 2017; at grade 8, the White-Hispanic gap narrowed from 26 points in 1992 to 19 points in 2017.

While there was no measurable change from 2015 to 2017 in the average reading score for 4th-grade public school students nationally, scores were lower in 2017 than in 2015 in 9 states (table 221.40). The 4th-grade scores in the District of Columbia and the remaining 41 states did not change measurably from 2015 to 2017. The scores for 8th-grade public school students were higher in 2017 than in 2015 nationally and in 9 states (table 221.60). However, 8th-grade students in Montana scored lower in 2017 than in 2015, and the scores in the remaining 40 states and the District of Columbia did not change measurably from 2015 to 2017.

Reported on a scale of 0 to 500, NAEP long-term trend results in reading are available for 13 assessment years going back to the first in 1971. The average reading score for 9-year-olds was higher in 2012 (221) than in assessment years prior to 2008, increasing 5 points since 2004 and 13 points since 1971 (*web-only table 221.85*). The score for 13-year-olds in 2012 (263) was higher than in all previous assessment years except for 1992. The score for 17-year-olds was higher in 2012 (287) than in 2004 (283), but it was not measurably different from the score in 1971 (285).

White, Black, and Hispanic 9-, 13-, and 17-year-old students all had higher average reading scores in 2012 than they did in the first assessment year (which was 1975 for Hispanic students because separate data for Hispanics were not collected in 1971). The scores were higher in 2012 than in 2004 for White, Black, and Hispanic students at all three ages (*web-only table 221.85*). Reading results for 2012 continued to show gaps in scores between White and Black students (ranging from 23 to 26 points, depending on age) and between White and Hispanic students (about 21 points at all three ages). The White-Black and White-Hispanic achievement gaps were smaller in 2012 than in the first assessment year at all three ages. For example, the White-Black reading gap for 17-year-olds was 53 points in 1971 compared with 26 points in 2012. Similarly, the White-Hispanic gap for 17-year-olds narrowed from 41 points in 1975 to 21 points in 2012.

In 2012, female 9-, 13-, and 17-year-old students continued to have higher average reading scores than male students at all three ages (*web-only table 221.85*). The gap between male and female 9-year-olds was 5 points in 2012; this was narrower than the gap in 1971 (13 points). The 8-point gender gap for 13-year-olds in 2012 was not measurably different from the gap in 1971. At age 17, the 8-point gap between males and females in 2012 was not measurably different from the gap in 1971.

Mathematics

The main NAEP mathematics assessment data for 4th- and 8th-graders are reported on a scale of 0 to 500 (table 222.10). The average 4th-grade mathematics score in 2017 (240) was not measurably different from the score in 2015, but it was higher than the score in 1990 (213). At grade 4, the scores in 2017 for White (248), Black (223), Hispanic (229), and Asian/Pacific Islander (258) students were not measurably different from the 2015 scores, but the score for each group was higher than in 1990 (220, 188, 200, and 225, respectively). The 2017 score for 4th-grade American Indian/Alaska Native students (227) was not measurably different from the scores in 2015 and in 1996 (1996 was the first year data were available for 4th-grade American Indian/Alaska Native students). The 8th-grade score in 2017 (283) was not measurably different from the score in 2015, but it was higher than the score in 1990 (263). At grade 8, the scores for White (293), Black (260), Hispanic (269), and Asian/Pacific Islander (310) students in 2017 were not measurably different from the scores in 2015, but the score for each group was higher than in 1990 (270, 237, 246, and 275, respectively). In 2017, the score for 8th-grade American Indian/Alaska Native students (267) was not measurably different from the scores in 2015 and in 2000 (2000 was the first year data were available for 8th-grade American Indian/Alaska Native students). Due to changes in the 12th-grade mathematics assessment framework, a new trend line started in 2005, with scores reported on a scale of 0 to 300. The 12th-grade score in 2015 (152) was lower than the score in 2013 (153) but not measurably different from the score in 2005, the first year the revised assessment was administered.

From 1990 through 2017, the average mathematics scores for White students in grades 4 and 8 were higher than those of their Black and Hispanic peers (table 222.10). Although the 4th-grade White-Black and White-Hispanic achievement gaps did not change measurably from 2015 to 2017, the White-Black achievement gap narrowed from 32 points in 1990 to 25 points in 2017. The 4th-grade White-Hispanic gap in 2017 (19 points) was not measurably different from the White-Hispanic gap in 1990. The 8th-grade White-Black gap (32 points) and White-Hispanic gap (24 points) in 2017 were not measurably different from the gaps in 2015 or in 1990.

While there was no measurable change from 2015 to 2017 in the average mathematics score for 4th-grade public school students nationally, the score was higher in 2017 than in 2015 in one state (Florida) (table 222.50). The mathematics scores for public school 4th-grade students were lower in 2017 than in 2015 in 10 states. For the remaining 39 states and the District of Columbia, scores in 2017 were not measurably different from the scores in 2015. At grade 8, the national average mathematics score for public school students in 2017 was not measurably different from the score in 2015 (table 222.60). In one state (Florida), the score for 8th-grade public school students was higher in 2017 than in 2015. In 3 states—Alaska, Rhode Island, and Vermont—the score for 8th-grade students in public schools was lower in 2017 than in 2015. The scores in the remaining 46 states and the District of Columbia showed no measurable difference between 2015 and 2017.

NAEP long-term trend mathematics results, reported on a scale of 0 to 500, are available for 12 assessment years, going back to the first in 1973. In 2012, the average mathematics score for 9-year-olds (244) was higher than in all previous assessment years prior to 2008 (*web-only table 222.85*). The score for 9-year-olds in 2012 was 5 points higher than in 2004 and 25 points higher than in 1973. The score for 13-year-olds in 2012 (285) was higher than in all previous assessment years. For 13-year-olds, the score in 2012 was 6 points higher than in 2004 and 19 points higher than in 1973. In contrast, the score for 17-year-olds in 2012 (306) was not measurably different from the scores in 2004 and in 1973.

White, Black, and Hispanic 9-, 13-, and 17-year-olds all had higher average mathematics scores in 2012 than in 1973 (*web-only table 222.85*). In comparison to 2004, scores were higher in 2012 for White 9- and 13-year-olds; Hispanic 13-year-olds; and Black 13-year-olds. Mathematics results for 2012 continued to show achievement gaps between White and Hispanic students (ranging from 17 to 21 points [based on unrounded scores], depending on age) and between White and Black students (ranging from 25 to 28 points). For 9-year-olds, the White-Black gap was lower in 2012 than in 1973. For 13- and 17-year-olds, both the White-Black and the White-Hispanic gaps were lower in 2012 than in 1973. For example, among 17-year-olds, the White-Black gap was 40 points in 1973 compared to 26 points in 2012, and the White-Hispanic gap was 33 points in 1973 compared to 19 points in 2012.

While there was no significant difference between the average mathematics scores of male and female 9- and 13-year-olds in 2012, male students did score higher than female students at age 17 (*web-only table 222.85*). At age 17, the 4-point gender score gap in 2012 was smaller than the gap in 1973 (8 points).

Science

NAEP has assessed the science abilities of students in grades 4, 8, and 12 in both public and private schools since 1996. As of 2009, however, NAEP science assessments are based on a new framework, so results from these assessments cannot be compared to results from earlier science assessments. Scores are based on a scale ranging from 0 to 300 (table 223.10). In 2015, the average 4th-grade science score (154) was higher than the score in 2009 (150). The 8th-grade score in 2015 (154) was higher than the scores in 2009 (150) and in 2011 (152). The 12th-grade score in 2015 (150) was not measurably different from the score in 2009. In addition, the 5-point gender gap between male and female 12th-graders in 2015 was not measurably different from the gap in 2009. While the scores for White 4th- and 8th-grade students remained higher than those of their Black and Hispanic peers in 2015, racial/ethnic achievement gaps in 2015 were smaller than in 2009. At grade 4, the White-Black achievement gap was 36 points in 2009 and 33 points in 2015, and the White-Hispanic achievement gap was 32 points in 2009 and 27 points in 2015. While the scores for White 12th-grade students remained higher than those of their Black and Hispanic peers in 2015, these racial/ethnic achievement gaps were not measurably different between 2009 and 2015.

Skills of Young Children

In addition to student performance data available through NAEP, the *Digest* presents data from other surveys to provide additional perspectives on student achievement. Differences among demographic groups in the acquisition of cognitive skills have been demonstrated at relatively early ages in the Early Childhood Longitudinal Study, Kindergarten Class of 2010–11 (ECLS-K:2011).

Children who enrolled in kindergarten for the first time in 2010–11 showed similar patterns of score differences by race/ethnicity and socioeconomic status (SES) (table 220.40 and *web-only table 220.41*). In fall 2010, average mathematics scores were higher for first-time kindergartners from high-SES families (43) than for those from low-SES families (29). White (39) and Asian (41) first-time kindergartners had higher mathematics scores than their Black (32), Hispanic (31), and American Indian/Alaska Native (33) peers. Similarly, average early reading scores in fall 2010 were higher for White (56) and Asian (59) first-time kindergartners than for their Black (53), Hispanic (51), and American Indian/Alaska Native (50) peers. High-SES children (61) had higher early reading scores than low-SES children (49). Most of these same patterns were observed among these children during 5th grade in spring 2016. White (125) and Asian (128) 5th-graders had higher mathematics scores than their Black (109), Hispanic (114), and American Indian/Alaska Native (119) peers. Mathematics scores were higher for 5th-graders from high-SES families (130) than for those from low-SES families (110). Reading scores were also higher for White (140) and Asian (141) 5th-graders than for their Black (130), Hispanic (132), and American Indian/Alaska Native (134) peers, and 5th-graders from high-SES families (145) had higher early reading scores than those from low-SES families (128).

School Violence

In 2015–16, some 69 percent of public schools reported one or more violent incidents, such as a serious violent incident, a physical attack, or a threat of a physical attack (table 229.10). This 2015–16 percentage was not measurably different from the percentage of schools reporting violent incidents in 1999–2000. Serious violent incidents is a subcategory of violent incidents that includes the crimes of rape, sexual assault, robbery, and aggravated assault. The percentage of schools reporting a serious violent incident in 2015–16 (15 percent) was lower than the percentage reporting a serious violent incident in 1999–2000 (20 percent). The percentage of schools reporting a physical attack or fight without a weapon in 2015–16 (65 percent) was not measurably different from the percentage in 1999–2000; however, the percentage of schools reporting a physical attack or fight with a weapon in 2015–16 (3 percent) was lower than the percentage in 1999–2000 (5 percent). Also, the percentage of schools reporting a threat of a physical attack without a weapon in 2015–16 (39 percent) was lower than the percentage in 1999–2000 (52 percent). Overall, schools reported 18 violent incidents per 1,000 students in 2015–16, which was lower than the 31 violent incidents per 1,000 students reported in 1999–2000 (*web-only table 229.20*).

On the National Crime Victimization Survey, students ages 12 to 18 reported a decrease in victimizations at school between 1992 and 2017 (*web-only table 228.20*). The total victimization rates for students ages 12 to 18 declined 82 percent, from 181 victimizations per 1,000 students in 1992 to 33 victimizations per 1,000 students in 2017. This pattern of decline in total victimization rates between 1992 and 2017 also held for thefts, violent victimizations, and serious violent victimizations. Thefts at school declined from a rate of 114 thefts per 1,000 students to 12 thefts per 1,000 students. The rate of violent victimization at school declined overall from 68 victimizations per 1,000 students in 1992 to 21 victimizations per 1,000 in 2017. Serious violent victimizations at school declined from 8 victimizations per 1,000 students in 1992 to 4 victimizations per 1,000 in 2017. The victimization rates for theft declined more rapidly than the victimization rates for violent crimes. In 1992, the victimization rates for theft were higher than the rates for violent crimes, but in 2017 the victimization rates for theft were lower than the rates for violent crimes.

Revenues and Expenditures

The federal share of public school revenues in 2015–16 (8.3 percent) was lower than in 2005–06 (9.1 percent) (figure 10). In contrast, the state share in 2015–16 (47.0 percent) was higher than in 2005–06 (46.5 percent). Also, the local share in 2015–16 (44.8 percent) was higher than in 2004–05 (44.4 percent).

After adjustment for inflation, current expenditures per student at public schools (based on fall enrollment) rose during the 1980s but remained stable during the first part of the 1990s (table 236.55 and figure 11). There was an increase of 37 percent from 1980–81 to 1990–91, followed by minor fluctuations from 1990–91 to 1994–95. Current expenditures per student increased 34 percent from 1994–95 to 2008–09 but declined 5 percent from 2008–09 to 2012–13. Current expenditures per student increased in 2013–14, 2014–15, and 2015–16, reaching $11,841 in unadjusted dollars. The expenditure for public school student transportation was $943 per student in 2015–16 (also in unadjusted dollars) (*web-only table 236.90*).

Figure 7. Enrollment, number of teachers, pupil/teacher ratio, and expenditures in public elementary and secondary schools: Selected years, 1960–61 through 2016–17

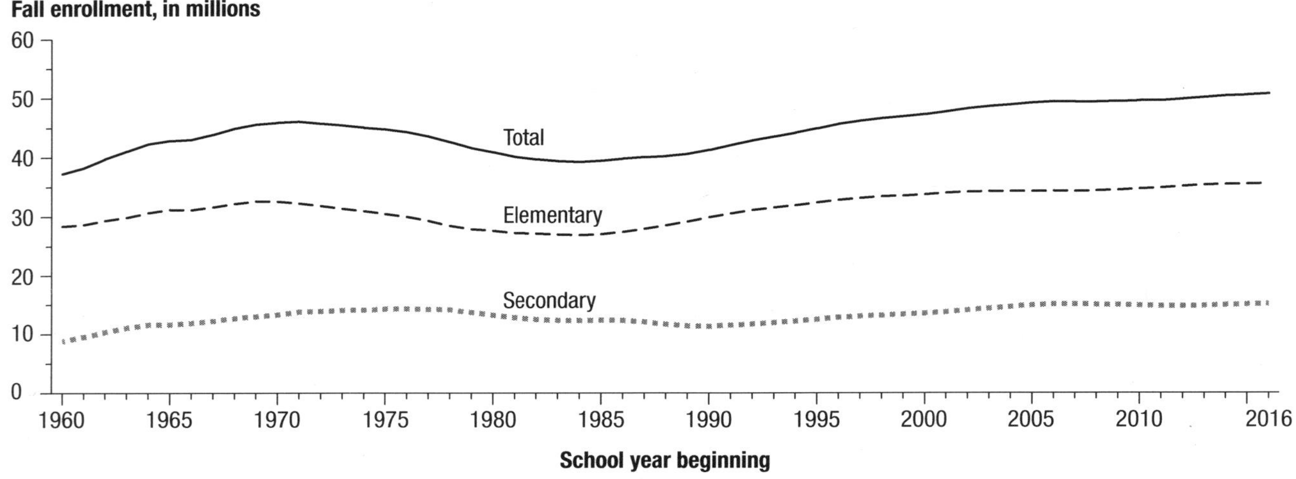

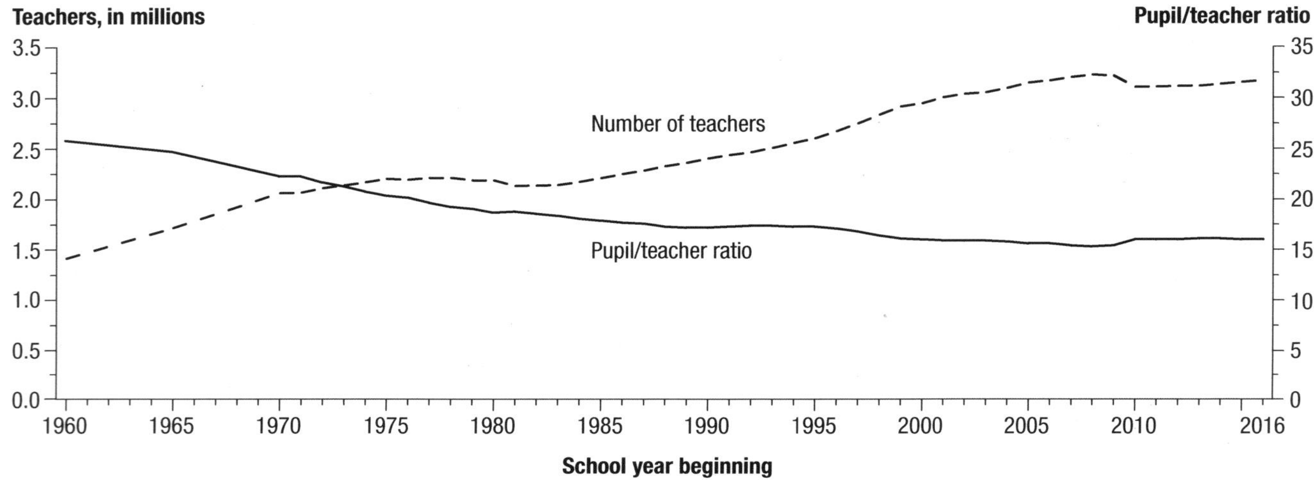

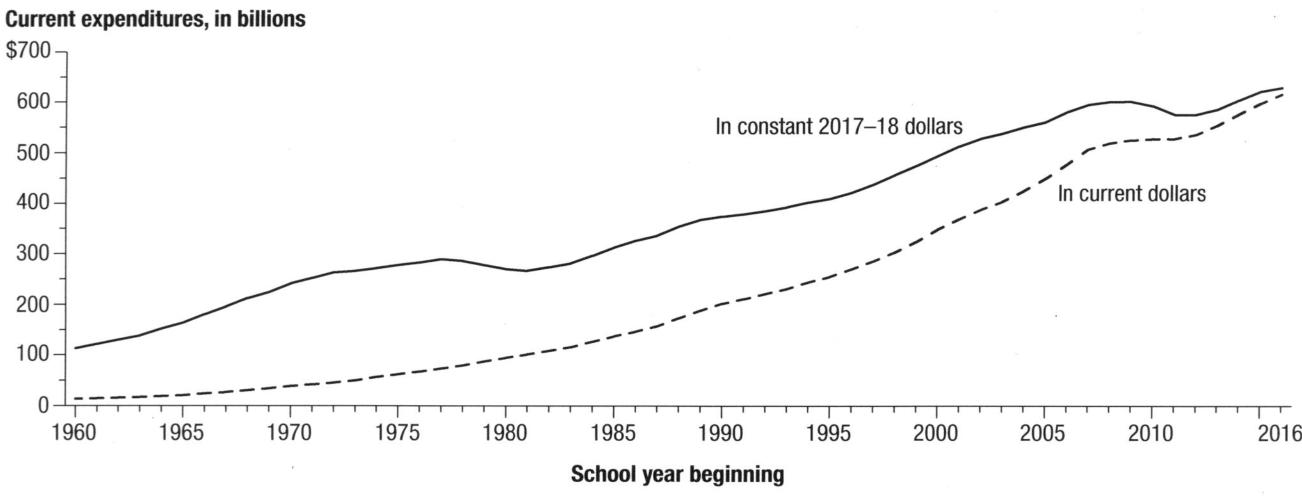

NOTE: Expenditure data for school year 2016 (2016–17) are projected.
SOURCE: U.S. Department of Education, National Center for Education Statistics, *Statistics of State School Systems*, 1959–60 through 1969–70; *Statistics of Public Elementary and Secondary Day Schools*, 1959–60 through 1980–81; *Revenues and Expenditures for Public Elementary and Secondary Education*, 1970–71 through 1980–81; and Common Core of Data (CCD), "State Nonfiscal Survey of Public Elementary/Secondary Education," 1981–82 through 2016–17; "National Public Education Financial Survey," 1989–90 through 2015–16; and Public Elementary and Secondary Education Current Expenditure Projection Model, 1973–74 through 2028–29.

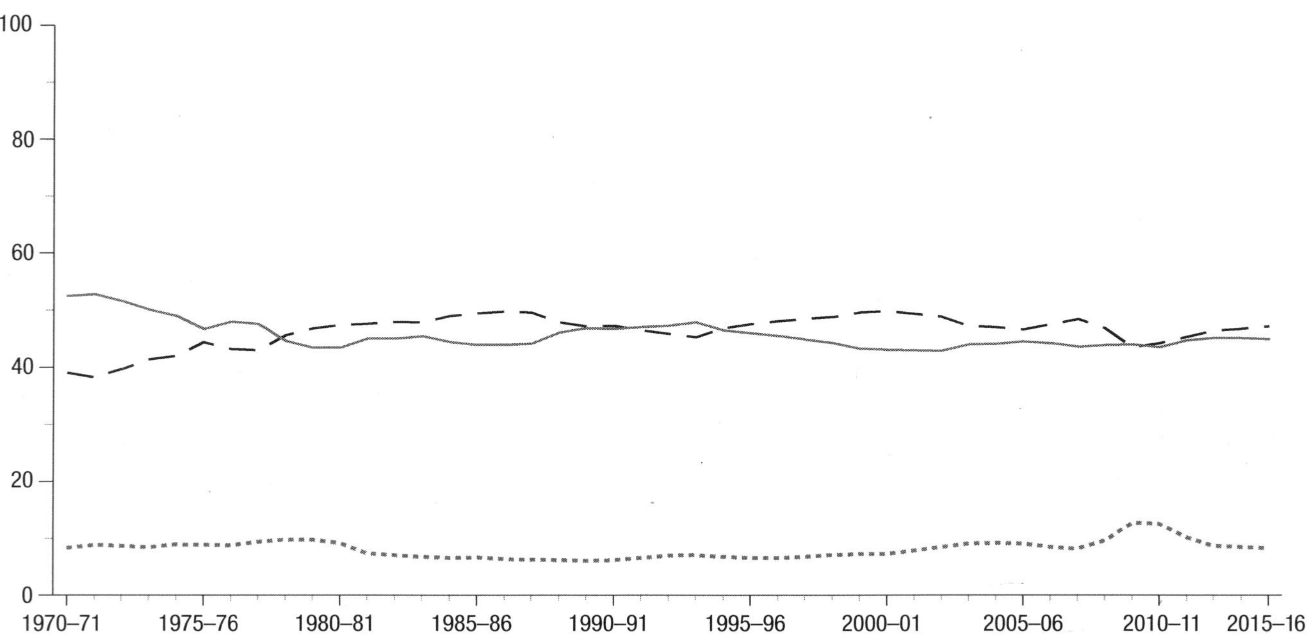

100
80
60
40
20
0
1970–71
1975–76
1980–81
1985–86
1990–91
1995–96
2000–01
2005–06
2010–11
2015–16

Table 201.10. Historical summary of public elementary and secondary school statistics: Selected years, 1869–70 through 2015–16

Selected characteristic	1869–70	1879–80	1889–90	1899–1900	1909–10	1919–20	1929–30	1939–40	1949–50	1959–60	1969–70	1979–80	1989–90	1999–2000	2009–10	2012–13	2013–14	2014–15	2015–16
1	2	3	4	5	6	7	8	9	10	11	12	13	14	15	16	17	18	19	20
Population, pupils, and instructional staff																			
Total population (in thousands)[1]	38,558	50,156	62,622	75,995	90,490	104,514	121,878	131,028	149,188	177,830	201,385	225,055	246,819	279,040	306,772	313,993	316,235	318,623	321,040
5- to 17-year-olds (in thousands)[1]	11,683	15,066	18,473	21,573	24,011	27,571	31,414	30,151	30,223	43,881	52,386	48,043	44,947	52,811	53,890	53,725	53,726	53,700	53,713
5- to 17-year-olds as a percent of total population	30.3	30.0	29.5	28.4	26.5	26.4	25.8	23.0	20.3	24.7	26.0	21.3	18.2	18.9	17.6	17.1	17.0	16.9	16.7
Total enrollment in elementary and secondary schools (in thousands)[2]	7,562[3]	9,867	12,723	15,503	17,814	21,578	25,678	25,434	25,112	36,087	45,550	41,651	40,543	46,857	49,361	49,771	50,045	50,313	50,438
Prekindergarten through grade 8 (in thousands)	7,481[3]	9,757	12,520	14,984	16,899	19,378	21,279	18,833	19,387	27,602	32,513	28,034	29,152	33,486	34,409	35,018	35,251	35,370	35,388
Grades 9–12 (in thousands)	80[3]	110	203	519	915	2,200	4,399	6,601	5,725	8,485	13,037	13,616	11,390	13,371	14,952	14,753	14,794	14,943	15,050
Enrollment as a percent of total population	19.6[3]	19.7	20.3	20.4	19.7	20.6	21.1	19.4	16.8	20.3	22.6	18.5	16.4	16.8	16.1	15.9	15.8	15.8	15.7
Enrollment as a percent of 5- to 17-year-olds	64.7[3]	65.5	68.9	71.9	74.2	78.3	81.7	84.4	83.1	82.2	87.0	86.7	90.2	88.7	91.6	92.6	93.1	93.7	93.9
Percent of total enrollment in grades 9–12	1.1[3]	1.1	1.6	3.3	5.1	10.2	17.1	26.0	22.8	23.5	28.6	32.7	28.1	28.5	30.3	29.6	29.6	29.7	29.8
High school graduates (in thousands)	—	—	22	62	111	231	592	1,143	1,063	1,627	2,589	2,748	2,320	2,554	3,128	3,169	—	—	—
Average daily attendance (in thousands)	4,077	6,144	8,154	10,633	12,827	16,150	21,265	22,042	22,284	32,477	41,934	38,289	37,799	43,807	45,919	46,554	46,830	47,064	47,248
Total number of days attended by pupils enrolled (in millions)	539	801	1,098	1,535	2,011	2,615	3,673	3,858	3,964	5,782	7,501	6,835[4]	—	7,858	8,199	8,354	8,404	8,434	8,461
Percent of enrolled pupils attending daily	59.3	62.3	64.1	68.6	72.1	74.8	82.8	86.7	88.7	90.0	90.4	90.1[4]	—	94.3	—	—	—	—	93.0
Average length of school term, in days	132.2	130.3	134.7	144.3	157.5	161.9	172.7	175.0	177.9	178.0	178.9	178.5[4]	—	179.4	178.6	179.5	179.5	179.2	179.1
Average number of days attended per pupil	78.4	81.1	86.3	99.0	113.0	121.2	143.0	151.7	157.9	160.2	161.7	160.8[4]	—	169.2	—	—	—	—	166.5
Total full-time-equivalent (FTE) instructional staff (in thousands)	—	—	—	—	—	678	880	912	963	1,457	2,286	2,406	2,986	3,819	4,279	4,158	4,167	4,205	4,250
Supervisors (in thousands)	—	—	—	—	—	7	7	5	—	—	—	—	—	—	—	—	—	—	—
Principals (in thousands)	—	—	—	—	—	14	31	32	43	64	91	106	126	137	168	169	168	175	182
Teachers, teacher aides, librarians, and guidance counselors (in thousands)[5]	201	287	364	423	523	657	843	875	920	1,393	2,195	2,300	2,860	3,682	4,111	3,989	3,999	4,030	4,068
Males (in thousands)	78	123	126	127	110	93	140	195	196	404[4]	711[4]	782[4]	—	—	—	—	—	—	—
Females (in thousands)	123	164	238	296	413	585	703	681	724	989[4]	1,484[4]	1,518[4]	—	—	—	—	—	—	—
Percent male	38.7	42.8	34.5	29.9	21.1	14.1	16.6	22.2	21.3	29.0[4]	32.4[4]	34.0[4]	—	—	—	—	—	—	—
	Amounts in current dollars																		
Total revenues and expenditures																			
Total revenue receipts (in millions)	—	—	$143	$220	$433	$970	$2,089	$2,261	$5,437	$14,747	$40,267	$96,881	$208,548	$372,944	$596,391	$603,770	$623,650	$647,679	$678,378
Federal government	—	—	—	—	—	2	7	40	156	652	3,220	9,504	12,701	27,098	75,998	55,861	54,506	55,003	55,981
State governments	—	—	—	—	—	160	354	684	2,166	5,768	16,063	45,349	98,239	184,613	258,864	273,215	288,637	301,530	318,573
Local sources, including intermediate	—	—	—	—	—	808	1,728	1,536	3,116	8,327	20,985	42,029	97,608	161,233	261,529	274,694	280,507	291,147	303,824
Percentage distribution of revenue receipts																			
Federal government	—	—	—	—	—	0.3	0.4	1.8	2.9	4.4	8.0	9.8	6.1	7.3	12.7	9.3	8.7	8.5	8.3
State governments	—	—	—	—	—	16.5	16.9	30.3	39.8	39.1	39.9	46.8	47.1	49.5	43.4	45.3	46.3	46.6	47.0
Local sources, including intermediate	—	—	—	—	—	83.2	82.7	68.0	57.3	56.5	52.1	43.4	46.8	43.2	43.9	45.5	45.0	45.0	44.8
Total expenditures for public schools (in millions)	$63	$78	$141	$215	$426	$1,036	$2,317	$2,344	$5,838	$15,613	$40,683	$95,962	$212,770	$381,838	$607,018	$606,813	$625,018	$651,135	$677,541
Current expenditures[6]	—	—	114	180	356	861	1,844	1,942	4,687	12,329[7]	34,218[7]	86,984[7]	188,229[7]	323,889[7]	524,715[7]	535,796[7]	553,501[7]	575,332[7]	596,136[7]
Capital outlay[8]	—	—	26	35	70	154	371	258	1,014	2,662	4,659	6,506	17,781	43,357	56,715	45,721	46,438	50,610	55,989
Interest on school debt	—	—	—	—	—	18	93	131	101	490	1,171	1,874	3,776	9,135	17,232	17,266	17,152	17,479	17,502
Other current expenditures[9]	—	—	—	—	—	3	10	13	36	133	636	598[10]	2,983	5,457	8,356	8,031	7,926	7,714	7,914
Percentage distribution of total expenditures																			
Current expenditures[6]	—	—	81.3	83.5	83.6	83.1	79.6	82.8	80.3	79.0[7]	84.1[7]	90.6[7]	88.5[7]	84.8[7]	86.4[7]	88.3[7]	88.6[7]	88.4[7]	88.0[7]
Capital outlay[8]	—	—	18.7	16.5	16.4	14.8	16.0	11.0	17.4	17.0	11.5	6.8	8.4	11.4	9.3	7.5	7.4	7.8	8.3
Interest on school debt	—	—	—	—	—	1.8	4.0	5.6	1.7	3.1	2.9	2.0	1.8	2.4	2.8	2.8	2.7	2.7	2.6
Other current expenditures[9]	—	—	—	—	—	0.3	0.4	0.6	0.6	0.8	1.6	0.6[10]	1.4	1.4	1.4	1.3	1.3	1.2	1.2

See notes at end of table.

Table 201.10. Historical summary of public elementary and secondary school statistics: Selected years, 1869–70 through 2015–16—Continued

Selected characteristic	1869–70	1879–80	1889–90	1899–1900	1909–10	1919–20	1929–30	1939–40	1949–50	1959–60	1969–70	1979–80	1989–90	1999–2000	2009–10	2012–13	2013–14	2014–15	2015–16
1	2	3	4	5	6	7	8	9	10	11	12	13	14	15	16	17	18	19	20
Teacher salaries; income and expenditures per pupil and per capita																			
Annual salary of classroom teachers[11]	$189	$195	$252	$325	$485	$871	$1,420	$1,441	$3,010	$4,995	$8,626	$15,970	$31,367	$41,807	$55,280	$56,173	$56,805	$57,754	$58,479
Personal income per member of labor force[1]	—	—	—	—	—	—	1,734	1,333	3,445	5,893	9,913	19,842	37,343	57,416	78,234	90,402	91,262	96,149	100,041
Total school expenditures per capita of total population	2	2	2	3	5	10	19	18	39	88	202	426	862	1,368	1,979	1,933	1,976	2,044	2,110
National income per capita[1]	—	—	—	—	—	—	773	629	1,607	2,580	4,455	9,954	19,286	29,710	39,206	44,889	45,835	47,848	49,162
Current expenditure per pupil in ADA[6,12,13]	—	—	14	17	28	53	87	88	210	375	816	2,272	4,980	7,394	11,427	11,509	11,819	12,224	12,617
Total expenditure per pupil in ADA[13,14]	16	13	17	20	33	64	108	106	260	471	955	2,491	5,547	8,589	13,035	12,859	13,174	13,668	14,170
National income per pupil in ADA[13]	—	—	—	—	—	—	4,430	3,738	10,757	14,127	21,396	58,510	125,931	189,249	261,921	302,762	309,519	323,929	334,049
Current expenditure per day per pupil in ADA[6,13,15]	—	—	0.10	0.12	0.18	0.33	0.50	0.50	1.17	2.11	4.56	12.73	—	41.22	64.00	64.13	65.86	68.22	70.46
Total expenditure per day per pupil in ADA[13]	0.12	0.10	0.13	0.14	0.21	0.40	0.63	0.60	1.46	2.65	5.34	13.95	—	47.90	73.02	71.67	73.43	76.29	79.14
	Amounts in constant 2017–18 dollars[16]																		
Annual salary of classroom teachers[11]	—	—	—	—	—	$11,340	$20,584	$25,585	$31,536	$42,180	$56,660	$51,042	$61,295	$61,275	$63,287	$60,246	$59,987	$60,548	$60,897
Personal income per member of labor force[1]	—	—	—	—	—	—	25,142	23,660	36,088	49,764	65,112	63,419	72,973	84,152	89,565	96,957	96,373	100,800	104,178
Total school expenditures per capita of total population	—	—	—	—	—	129	276	318	410	741	1,327	1,363	1,685	2,006	2,265	2,073	2,087	2,142	2,198
National income per capita[1]	—	—	—	—	—	—	11,204	11,166	16,833	21,787	29,264	31,816	37,687	43,546	44,884	48,143	48,402	50,163	51,195
Current expenditure per pupil in ADA[6,12,13]	—	—	—	—	—	694	1,257	1,564	2,204	3,168	5,360	7,261	9,731	10,837	13,082	12,344	12,481	12,816	13,139
Total expenditure per pupil in ADA[13,14]	—	—	—	—	—	833	1,573	1,877	2,728	3,978	6,273	7,960	10,840	12,589	14,923	13,791	13,912	14,329	14,756
National income per pupil in ADA[13]	—	—	—	—	—	—	64,214	66,374	112,697	119,295	140,537	187,008	246,086	277,377	299,856	324,713	326,855	339,599	347,863
Current expenditure per day per pupil in ADA[6,13,15]	—	—	—	—	—	4.3	7.2	8.9	12.3	17.8	30.0	40.7	—	60.4	73.3	68.8	69.6	71.5	73.4
Total expenditure per day per pupil in ADA[13]	—	—	—	—	—	5.2	9.1	10.7	15.3	22.4	35.1	44.6	—	70.2	83.6	76.9	77.5	80.0	82.4

—Not available.
[1]Data on population and labor force are from the Census Bureau, and data on personal income and national income are from the Bureau of Economic Analysis, U.S. Department of Commerce. Population data through 1900 are based on total population from the decennial census. From 1909–10 to 1959–60, population data are total population, including armed forces overseas, as of July 1. Data for later years are for resident population that excludes armed forces overseas.
[2]Data for 1869–70 through 1959–60 are school year enrollment. Data for later years are fall enrollment. Total counts of ungraded students were prorated to prekindergarten through grade 8 and grades 9 through 12 based on prior reports.
[3]Data for 1870–71.
[4]Estimated by the National Center for Education Statistics.
[5]Prior to 1919–20, data are for the number of different persons employed rather than number of positions.
[6]Prior to 1919–20, includes interest on school debt.
[7]Because of the modification of the scope of "current expenditures for elementary and secondary schools," data for 1959–60 and later years are not entirely comparable with prior years.
[8]Beginning in 1969–70, includes capital outlay by state and local school building authorities.
[9]Includes summer schools, community colleges, and adult education. Beginning in 1959–60, also includes community services, formerly classified with "current expenditures for elementary and secondary schools."
[10]Excludes community colleges and adult education.
[11]Prior to 1959–60, average includes supervisors, principals, teachers, and other nonsupervisory instructional staff. Data for 1959–60 and later years are estimated by the National Education Association.
[12]Excludes current expenditures not allocable to pupil costs.
[13]"ADA" means average daily attendance in elementary and secondary schools.
[14]Expenditure figure is the sum of current expenditures allocable to pupil costs, capital outlay, and interest on school debt.
[15]Per-day rates derived by dividing annual rates by average length of term.
[16]Constant dollars based on the Consumer Price Index, prepared by the Bureau of Labor Statistics, U.S. Department of Labor, adjusted to a school-year basis.
NOTE: Some data have been revised from previously published figures. Beginning in 1959–60, data include Alaska and Hawaii. Detail may not sum to totals because of rounding.
SOURCE: U.S. Department of Education, National Center for Education Statistics, *Annual Report of the United States Commissioner of Education*, 1869–70 through 1909–10; *Biennial Survey of Education in the United States*, 1919–20 through 1949–50; *Statistics of State School Systems*, 1959–60 and 1969–70; *Statistics of Public Elementary and Secondary School Systems, 1979–80*; *Revenues and Expenditures for Public Elementary and Secondary Education, FY 1980*; Schools and Staffing Survey (SASS), "Public School Questionnaire," 1999–2000, 2007–08, and 2011–12; and Common Core of Data (CCD), "State Nonfiscal Survey of Public Elementary/Secondary Education," 1989–90 through 2016–17; "National Public Education Financial Survey," 1989–90 through 2015–16; and "State Dropout and Completion Data File," 2012–13. U.S. Department of Commerce, Census Bureau, retrieved November 8, 2018, from https://www.census.gov/data/tables/2017/demo/popest/nation-detail.html. U.S. Department of Commerce, Bureau of Economic Analysis, retrieved March 29, 2019, from https://www.bea.gov/itable/. U.S. Department of Labor, Bureau of Labor Statistics, retrieved March 29, 2019, from https://stats.bls.gov/cps/tables.htm#empstat. (This table was prepared March 2019.)

Table 201.20. Enrollment in grades 9 through 12 in public and private schools compared with population 14 to 17 years of age: Selected years, 1889–90 through fall 2018

[In thousands]

Year	Enrollment, grades 9 to 12														Population 14 to 17 years of age[2]	Enrollment as a ratio of population 14 to 17 years of age[3]
		Public schools						Private schools								
	All schools	Total	9th grade	10th grade	11th grade	12th grade	Secondary ungraded[1]	Total	9th grade	10th grade	11th grade	12th grade	Secondary ungraded			
1	2	3	4	5	6	7	8	9	10	11	12	13	14	15	16
1889–90	298	203	—	—	—	—	—	95	—	—	—	—	—	5,355	5.6
1899–1900	630	519	—	—	—	—	—	111	—	—	—	—	—	6,152	10.2
1909–10	1,032	915	—	—	—	—	—	117	—	—	—	—	—	7,220	14.3
1919–20	2,414	2,200	917	576	396	312	0	214	—	—	—	—	—	7,736	31.2
1929–30	4,741	4,399	1,627	1,192	880	701	0	341[4]	—	—	—	—	—	9,341	50.7
1939–40	7,059	6,601	2,011	1,767	1,486	1,282	55	458[5]	—	—	—	—	—	9,720	72.6
1949–50	6,397	5,725	1,761	1,513	1,275	1,134	42	672	—	—	—	—	—	8,405	76.1
Fall 1959	9,306	8,271	—	—	—	—	—	1,035	—	—	—	—	—	11,155	83.4
Fall 1969	14,337	13,037	3,568	3,405	3,047	2,732	285	1,300[6]	—	—	—	—	—	15,549	92.2
Fall 1970	14,647	13,336	3,654	3,458	3,128	2,775	321	1,311	—	—	—	—	—	15,924	92.0
Fall 1971	15,053	13,753	3,781	3,571	3,200	2,864	337	1,300[6]	—	—	—	—	—	16,328	92.2
Fall 1972	15,148	13,848	3,779	3,648	3,248	2,873	299	1,300[6]	—	—	—	—	—	16,639	91.0
Fall 1973	15,344	14,044	3,801	3,650	3,323	2,918	352	1,300[6]	—	—	—	—	—	16,867	91.0
Fall 1974	15,403	14,103	3,832	3,675	3,302	2,955	339	1,300[6]	—	—	—	—	—	17,035	90.4
Fall 1975	15,604	14,304	3,879	3,723	3,354	2,986	362	1,300[6]	—	—	—	—	—	17,128	91.1
Fall 1976	15,656	14,314	3,825	3,738	3,373	3,015	363	1,342	—	—	—	—	—	17,119	91.5
Fall 1977	15,546	14,203	3,779	3,686	3,388	3,026	324	1,343	—	—	—	—	—	17,045	91.2
Fall 1978	15,441	14,088	3,726	3,610	3,312	3,023	416	1,353	—	—	—	—	—	16,946	91.1
Fall 1979	14,916	13,616	3,526	3,532	3,241	2,969	348	1,300[6]	—	—	—	—	—	16,611	89.8
Fall 1980	14,570	13,231	3,377	3,368	3,195	2,925	366	1,339	—	—	—	—	—	16,143	90.3
Fall 1981	14,164	12,764	3,286	3,218	3,039	2,907	314	1,400[6]	—	—	—	—	—	15,609	90.7
Fall 1982	13,805	12,405	3,248	3,137	2,917	2,787	315	1,400[6]	—	—	—	—	—	15,057	91.7
Fall 1983	13,671	12,271	3,330	3,103	2,861	2,678	299	1,400	—	—	—	—	—	14,740	92.7
Fall 1984	13,704	12,304	3,440	3,145	2,819	2,599	300	1,400[6]	—	—	—	—	—	14,725	93.1
Fall 1985	13,750	12,388	3,439	3,230	2,866	2,550	303	1,362	—	—	—	—	—	14,888	92.4
Fall 1986	13,669	12,333	3,256	3,215	2,954	2,601	308	1,336[6]	—	—	—	—	—	14,824	92.2
Fall 1987	13,323	12,076	3,143	3,020	2,936	2,681	296	1,247	—	—	—	—	—	14,502	91.9
Fall 1988	12,893	11,687	3,106	2,895	2,749	2,650	288	1,206[6]	—	—	—	—	—	14,023	91.9
Fall 1989	12,524	11,393	3,141	2,868	2,629	2,473	281	1,131	303	284	267	273	5	13,536	92.5
Fall 1990	12,476	11,341	3,169	2,896	2,612	2,381	284	1,136[6]	—	—	—	—	—	13,329	93.6
Fall 1991	12,675	11,544	3,313	2,915	2,645	2,392	278	1,131	309	286	272	260	4	13,491	94.0
Fall 1992	12,862	11,737	3,352	3,027	2,656	2,431	272	1,125[6]	—	—	—	—	—	13,775	93.4
Fall 1993	13,081	11,963	3,487	3,050	2,751	2,424	250	1,118	312	286	266	249	5	14,096	92.8
Fall 1994	13,354	12,215	3,604	3,131	2,748	2,488	244	1,138[6]	—	—	—	—	—	14,637	91.2
Fall 1995	13,665	12,502	3,704	3,237	2,826	2,487	247	1,163	325	304	276	255	2	15,013	91.0
Fall 1996	14,027	12,849	3,801	3,323	2,930	2,586	208	1,178[6]	—	—	—	—	—	15,443	90.8
Fall 1997	14,241	13,056	3,819	3,376	2,972	2,673	216	1,185	326	306	283	266	4	15,769	90.3
Fall 1998	14,407	13,195	3,856	3,382	3,021	2,722	214	1,212[6]	—	—	—	—	—	15,829	91.0
Fall 1999	14,600	13,371	3,935	3,415	3,034	2,782	205	1,229	336	313	295	280	5	16,007	91.2
Fall 2000	14,781	13,517	3,963	3,491	3,083	2,803	177	1,264[6]	—	—	—	—	—	16,144	91.6
Fall 2001	15,032	13,736	4,012	3,528	3,174	2,863	159	1,296	350	333	316	293	3	16,280	92.3
Fall 2002	15,374	14,069	4,105	3,584	3,229	2,990	161	1,306[6]	—	—	—	—	—	16,506	93.1
Fall 2003	15,651	14,339	4,190	3,675	3,277	3,046	150	1,311	351	334	317	304	5	16,694	93.8
Fall 2004	15,949	14,618	4,281	3,750	3,369	3,094	122	1,331[6]	—	—	—	—	—	17,054	93.5
Fall 2005	16,258	14,909	4,287	3,866	3,454	3,180	121	1,349							
Fall 2006	16,441	15,081	4,260	3,882	3,551	3,277	110	1,360[6]	—	—	—	—	—	17,549	93.7
Fall 2007	16,451	15,086	4,200	3,863	3,557	3,375	92	1,364	357	347	334	324	2	17,597	93.5
Fall 2008	16,322	14,980	4,123	3,822	3,548	3,400	87	1,342[6]	—	—	—	—	—	17,395	93.8
Fall 2009	16,261	14,952	4,080	3,809	3,541	3,432	90	1,309	333	330	324	319	3	17,232	94.4
Fall 2010	16,159	14,860	4,008	3,800	3,538	3,472	42	1,299[6]	—	—	—	—	—	17,066	94.7
Fall 2011	16,040	14,749	3,957	3,751	3,546	3,452	43	1,291	330	325	318	315	4	16,872	95.1
Fall 2012	16,055	14,753	3,975	3,730	3,528	3,477	43	1,302[6]	—	—	—	—	—	16,722	96.0
Fall 2013	16,106	14,794	3,980	3,761	3,526	3,476	52	1,312	334	331	325	320	3	16,653	96.7
Fall 2014	16,316	14,943	4,033	3,794	3,568	3,496	52	1,373[6]	—	—	—	—	—	16,748	97.4
Fall 2015	16,496	15,050	4,019	3,846	3,598	3,537	49	1,446	368	367	356	349	6	16,810	98.1
Fall 2016	16,612	15,138	3,986	3,860	3,669	3,571	52	1,474[6]	—	—	—	—	—	16,779	99.0
Fall 2017[7]	16,703	15,222	4,019	3,828	3,682	3,642	52	1,481	—	—	—	—	—	16,761	99.7
Fall 2018[7]	16,756	15,264	4,047	3,859	3,652	3,655	52	1,492	—	—	—	—	—	16,700	100.3

—Not available.
[1]Includes students reported as being enrolled in grade 13.
[2]Data for 1890 through 1950 are from the decennial censuses of population. Later data are Census Bureau estimates as of July 1 preceding the opening of the school year.
[3]Gross enrollment ratio (GER) based on school enrollment of all ages in grades 9 to 12 divided by the 14- to 17-year-old population. The GER allows for comparisons over time but is not intended to provide a precise measure of enrollment for any single year. Because some high school students are younger than 14 or older than 17, the GER is likely higher than the enrollment rate for the 14- to 17-year-old population. The GER differs from enrollment rates in other tables, which compare the population in a given age group with enrollment of persons in that age group only.
[4]Data are for 1927–28.
[5]Data are for 1940–41.
[6]Estimated.
[7]Projected.
NOTE: Includes enrollment in public schools that are a part of state and local school systems and also in most private schools, both religiously affiliated and nonsectarian. The enrollment for ungraded public school students was estimated based on the secondary proportion of ungraded students in prior years. The enrollment of ungraded private school students was estimated based on the secondary proportion of ungraded students in individual high schools. Some data have been revised from previously published figures. Detail may not sum to totals because of rounding.
SOURCE: U.S. Department of Education, National Center for Education Statistics, *Annual Report of the Commissioner of Education*, 1890 through 1910; *Biennial Survey of Education in the United States*, 1919–20 through 1949–50; *Statistics of State School Systems*, 1951–52 through 1957–58; *Statistics of Public Elementary and Secondary School Systems*, 1959 through 1980; *Statistics of Nonpublic Elementary and Secondary Schools*, 1959 through 1980; Common Core of Data (CCD), "State Nonfiscal Survey of Public Elementary/Secondary Education," 1981–82 through 2016–17; Schools and Staffing Survey, Private School Data File, 1987–88; Private School Universe Survey (PSS), 1989–90 through 2015–16; National Elementary and Secondary Enrollment Projection Model, 1972 through 2028; and unpublished data. U.S. Department of Commerce, Census Bureau, Current Population Reports, Series P-25, Nos. 1000, 1022, 1045, 1057, 1059, 1092, and 1095; 2000 through 2009 Population Estimates, retrieved August 14, 2012, from http://www.census.gov/popest/data/national/asrh/2011/index.html; and 2010 through 2018 Population Estimates, retrieved November 8, 2018, from https://www.census.gov/data/tables/2017/demo/popest/nation-detail.html. (This table was prepared January 2019.)

Table 202.10. Enrollment of 3-, 4-, and 5-year-old children in preprimary programs, by age of child, level of program, control of program, and attendance status: Selected years, 1970 through 2017

[Standard errors appear in parentheses]

Age of child, level and control of program, and attendance status	1970	1980	1990	1995[1]	2000[1]	2003[1]	2005[1]	2010[1]	2015[1]	2016[1]	2017[1]
1	2	3	4	5	6	7	8	9	10	11	12
3 to 5 years old[2]											
Total population (in thousands)	10,949 (131.4)	9,284 (121.0)	11,207 (145.5)	12,518 (153.7)	11,858 (155.3)	12,204 (149.6)	12,134 (149.1)	12,949 (80.4)	11,958 (79.8)	12,032 (113.7)	12,001 (133.4)
Enrollment of 3- to 5-year-olds (in thousands)											
Total	4,104 (78.9)	4,878 (75.0)	6,659 (88.8)	7,739 (86.4)	7,592 (86.2)	7,921 (82.6)	7,801 (82.7)	8,246 (107.3)	7,681 (107.3)	7,776 (103.5)	7,716 (117.0)
Level and attendance status											
Preschool	1,094 (48.9)	1,981 (61.5)	3,379 (83.0)	4,331 (84.6)	4,326 (86.5)	4,859 (84.7)	4,529 (83.4)	4,797 (94.5)	4,475 (96.9)	4,701 (116.0)	4,620 (141.8)
Full-day	291 (26.2)	681 (39.1)	1,150 (54.9)	1,951 (64.5)	2,049 (67.9)	2,479 (69.6)	2,275 (67.3)	2,297 (81.4)	2,264 (73.0)	2,544 (91.0)	2,584 (108.0)
Part-day	803 (42.5)	1,301 (52.1)	2,229 (72.2)	2,381 (69.8)	2,277 (70.8)	2,380 (68.5)	2,255 (67.1)	2,500 (75.4)	2,211 (81.3)	2,157 (86.7)	2,036 (90.2)
Kindergarten	3,010 (72.8)	2,897 (69.6)	3,280 (82.3)	3,408 (79.2)	3,266 (80.3)	3,062 (75.0)	3,272 (76.6)	3,449 (75.9)	3,207 (84.3)	3,075 (92.9)	3,097 (90.2)
Full-day	407 (30.9)	870 (43.8)	1,428 (60.3)	1,738 (61.5)	1,959 (66.7)	1,950 (63.4)	2,274 (67.3)	2,516 (69.7)	2,613 (77.3)	2,494 (86.7)	2,438 (83.4)
Part-day	2,603 (69.4)	2,026 (62.0)	1,853 (67.2)	1,670 (60.5)	1,307 (56.3)	1,112 (49.8)	998 (47.4)	932 (53.4)	594 (42.3)	581 (44.8)	659 (48.6)
Control											
Public	2,830 (71.4)	3,066 (70.6)	3,971 (86.5)	4,750 (86.3)	4,847 (88.3)	5,051 (85.2)	5,213 (85.4)	5,829 (105.5)	5,426 (95.6)	5,586 (98.7)	5,501 (105.4)
Private	1,274 (52.3)	1,812 (59.5)	2,688 (77.2)	2,989 (75.8)	2,745 (75.8)	2,870 (73.4)	2,588 (70.7)	2,417 (77.1)	2,255 (70.5)	2,190 (83.4)	2,216 (100.2)
Attendance status											
Full-day	698 (39.8)	1,551 (56.0)	2,577 (76.1)	3,689 (81.1)	4,008 (85.0)	4,429 (83.2)	4,548 (83.5)	4,813 (98.5)	4,877 (101.5)	5,038 (105.0)	5,022 (109.8)
Part-day	3,406 (75.5)	3,327 (72.0)	4,082 (87.0)	4,051 (83.2)	3,584 (82.5)	3,492 (78.2)	3,253 (76.4)	3,432 (88.5)	2,804 (91.6)	2,738 (87.7)	2,694 (93.9)
Percent of 3- to 5-year-olds enrolled											
Total	37.5 (0.72)	52.5 (0.81)	59.4 (0.79)	61.8 (0.69)	64.0 (0.73)	64.9 (0.68)	64.3 (0.68)	63.7 (0.66)	64.2 (0.79)	64.6 (0.81)	64.3 (0.77)
Full-day as a percent of total enrollment	17.0 (0.91)	31.8 (1.04)	38.7 (1.02)	47.7 (0.90)	52.8 (0.95)	55.9 (0.87)	58.3 (0.87)	58.4 (0.92)	63.5 (1.04)	64.8 (1.03)	65.1 (1.08)
Full-day preschool as a percent of total preschool enrollment	26.6 (2.08)	34.3 (1.66)	34.0 (1.39)	45.0 (1.20)	47.4 (1.25)	51.0 (1.12)	50.2 (1.16)	47.9 (1.31)	50.6 (1.34)	54.1 (1.45)	55.9 (1.51)
Full-day kindergarten as a percent of total kindergarten enrollment	13.5 (0.97)	30.0 (1.33)	43.5 (1.48)	51.0 (1.36)	60.0 (1.41)	63.7 (1.36)	69.5 (1.26)	73.0 (1.38)	81.5 (1.21)	81.1 (1.34)	78.7 (1.42)
3 and 4 years old											
Total population (in thousands)	7,135 (106.1)	6,215 (99.0)	7,415 (118.3)	8,294 (125.1)	7,869 (126.5)	8,336 (123.6)	8,179 (122.4)	8,850 (63.8)	7,971 (80.7)	7,971 (156.9)	8,030 (186.2)
Age											
3 years old	3,516 (74.4)	3,143 (70.4)	3,692 (83.5)	4,148 (88.5)	3,929 (89.4)	4,260 (88.4)	4,151 (87.2)	4,492 (59.4)	3,937 (92.3)	3,978 (71.2)	4,086 (81.1)
4 years old	3,620 (75.5)	3,072 (69.6)	3,723 (83.8)	4,145 (88.5)	3,940 (89.5)	4,076 (86.4)	4,028 (85.9)	4,358 (57.7)	4,034 (76.3)	3,993 (137.5)	3,943 (158.3)
Enrollment of 3- and 4-year-olds (in thousands)											
Total	1,461 (53.1)	2,280 (59.2)	3,292 (73.1)	4,043 (72.4)	4,097 (73.1)	4,590 (71.1)	4,383 (70.6)	4,706 (84.1)	4,203 (91.5)	4,289 (121.2)	4,319 (148.1)
Age											
3 years old	454 (31.0)	857 (38.9)	1,205 (48.7)	1,489 (49.1)	1,541 (50.5)	1,806 (50.5)	1,715 (49.7)	1,718 (59.5)	1,512 (70.2)	1,656 (63.8)	1,641 (76.5)
4 years old	1,007 (42.0)	1,423 (43.1)	2,087 (51.7)	2,553 (49.8)	2,556 (49.4)	2,785 (46.5)	2,668 (47.0)	2,988 (67.2)	2,691 (72.1)	2,633 (87.9)	2,678 (121.9)
Level and attendance status											
Preschool	1,003 (45.8)	1,889 (56.5)	3,026 (72.3)	3,720 (72.0)	3,762 (73.1)	4,198 (71.5)	4,024 (70.8)	4,245 (85.3)	3,855 (88.9)	4,034 (110.7)	3,966 (145.2)
Full-day	263 (24.8)	649 (37.6)	1,028 (50.8)	1,715 (58.6)	1,763 (61.0)	2,135 (62.4)	1,986 (60.7)	2,018 (70.6)	1,914 (70.3)	2,178 (81.4)	2,223 (106.3)
Part-day	741 (40.1)	1,240 (49.1)	1,998 (65.3)	2,006 (62.0)	1,999 (63.7)	2,063 (61.7)	2,038 (61.3)	2,226 (73.0)	1,941 (75.5)	1,856 (80.9)	1,742 (87.8)
Kindergarten	458 (32.3)	391 (29.8)	266 (27.3)	322 (28.0)	335 (29.6)	392 (30.3)	359 (29.0)	462 (44.6)	348 (36.5)	254 (32.0)	353 (34.3)
Full-day	110 (16.2)	139 (18.2)	135 (19.7)	144 (18.9)	181 (21.9)	245 (24.1)	247 (24.2)	247 (31.4)	253 (32.2)	202 (26.7)	216 (29.5)
Part-day	348 (28.3)	252 (24.2)	131 (19.4)	178 (21.0)	154 (20.3)	147 (18.8)	112 (16.5)	214 (28.5)	95 (17.4)	‡ (†)	137 (23.4)
Control											
Public	617 (37.0)	838 (42.0)	1,211 (54.4)	1,787 (59.5)	2,042 (64.2)	2,374 (64.5)	2,341 (64.0)	2,795 (82.2)	2,477 (80.6)	2,532 (86.5)	2,630 (111.8)
Private	844 (42.5)	1,441 (51.9)	2,081 (66.1)	2,256 (64.4)	2,055 (64.3)	2,216 (63.2)	2,042 (61.3)	1,911 (64.0)	1,726 (68.7)	1,757 (80.9)	1,689 (86.4)
Attendance status											
Full-day	373 (29.3)	788 (40.9)	1,163 (53.5)	1,858 (60.4)	1,944 (63.1)	2,380 (64.6)	2,233 (63.1)	2,265 (69.0)	2,167 (75.0)	2,381 (87.8)	2,439 (108.0)
Part-day	1,088 (47.3)	1,492 (52.5)	2,129 (66.6)	2,184 (63.8)	2,153 (65.3)	2,211 (63.1)	2,150 (62.4)	2,441 (76.5)	2,036 (75.3)	1,908 (83.3)	1,879 (91.8)

See notes at end of table.

Table 202.10. Enrollment of 3-, 4-, and 5-year-old children in preprimary programs, by age of child, level of program, control of program, and attendance status: Selected years, 1970 through 2017—Continued

[Standard errors appear in parentheses]

Age of child, level and control of program, and attendance status	1970	1980	1990	1995[1]	2000[1]	2003[1]	2005[1]	2010[1]	2015[1]	2016[1]	2017[1]
1	2	3	4	5	6	7	8	9	10	11	12
Percent of 3- and 4-year-olds enrolled											
Total	20.5 (1.65)	36.7 (1.57)	44.4 (1.48)	48.7 (1.25)	52.1 (1.29)	55.1 (1.15)	53.6 (1.18)	53.2 (0.89)	52.7 (1.02)	53.8 (1.04)	53.8 (1.08)
Age											
3 years old	12.9 (2.45)	27.3 (2.37)	32.6 (2.31)	35.9 (1.98)	39.2 (2.05)	42.4 (1.82)	41.3 (1.86)	38.2 (1.25)	38.4 (1.45)	41.6 (1.49)	40.2 (1.67)
4 years old	27.8 (2.20)	46.3 (2.06)	56.1 (1.86)	61.6 (1.53)	64.9 (1.56)	68.3 (1.38)	66.2 (1.43)	68.6 (1.25)	66.7 (1.32)	65.9 (1.50)	67.9 (1.35)
Full-day as a percent of total enrollment	25.5 (1.78)	34.5 (1.55)	35.3 (1.42)	46.0 (1.25)	47.4 (1.29)	51.8 (1.16)	50.9 (1.18)	48.1 (1.26)	51.6 (1.42)	55.5 (1.42)	56.5 (1.57)
Full-day preschool as a percent of total preschool enrollment	26.2 (2.16)	34.3 (1.70)	34.0 (1.47)	46.1 (1.30)	46.9 (1.34)	50.9 (1.21)	49.3 (1.23)	47.5 (1.36)	49.6 (1.49)	54.0 (1.49)	56.1 (1.64)
Full-day kindergarten as a percent of total kindergarten enrollment	24.0 (3.11)	35.6 (3.77)	50.8 (5.24)	44.6 (4.40)	54.0 (4.49)	62.4 (3.83)	68.8 (3.83)	53.6 (4.30)	72.8 (4.53)	79.6 (5.44)	61.2 (5.69)
5 years old[2]											
Total population (in thousands)	3,814 (77.5)	3,069 (69.6)	3,792 (84.6)	4,224 (89.3)	3,989 (90.1)	3,867 (84.2)	3,955 (85.1)	4,099 (57.9)	3,987 (73.9)	4,061 (90.5)	3,972 (100.6)
Enrollment of 5-year-olds (in thousands)											
Total	2,643 (44.4)	2,598 (31.1)	3,367 (33.2)	3,697 (34.1)	3,495 (34.3)	3,331 (33.7)	3,418 (33.7)	3,540 (56.2)	3,478 (74.8)	3,488 (96.5)	3,398 (90.4)
Level and attendance status											
Preschool	91 (14.7)	93 (14.8)	352 (30.5)	611 (36.3)	565 (36.3)	661 (36.7)	505 (32.9)	552 (35.8)	620 (46.1)	667 (45.3)	654 (48.1)
Full-day	28 (8.3)	32 (8.8)	122 (18.5)	236 (23.7)	286 (26.9)	344 (27.7)	289 (25.6)	279 (29.2)	350 (31.8)	366 (36.8)	361 (32.0)
Part-day	62 (12.2)	61 (12.0)	231 (25.2)	375 (29.4)	278 (26.6)	316 (26.7)	216 (22.4)	274 (26.9)	270 (32.1)	301 (31.2)	293 (36.5)
Kindergarten	2,552 (45.3)	2,505 (33.4)	3,015 (42.5)	3,086 (45.8)	2,931 (46.0)	2,670 (45.0)	2,913 (43.4)	2,987 (59.8)	2,859 (75.1)	2,821 (93.5)	2,744 (88.2)
Full-day	297 (25.8)	731 (36.8)	1,293 (49.9)	1,594 (50.1)	1,778 (51.8)	1,705 (48.4)	2,027 (49.2)	2,269 (60.2)	2,360 (70.9)	2,292 (85.3)	2,222 (77.4)
Part-day	2,255 (47.3)	1,774 (42.6)	1,722 (52.4)	1,492 (49.4)	1,152 (47.2)	965 (42.1)	886 (41.1)	718 (43.0)	499 (39.8)	529 (46.5)	522 (42.7)
Control											
Public	2,214 (47.5)	2,228 (38.5)	2,760 (46.8)	2,963 (47.3)	2,806 (47.6)	2,677 (45.0)	2,872 (43.9)	3,034 (57.8)	2,950 (70.7)	3,055 (89.2)	2,871 (90.7)
Private	429 (30.4)	370 (28.1)	607 (38.6)	733 (39.1)	690 (39.4)	654 (36.5)	546 (34.0)	506 (35.0)	529 (37.6)	433 (37.3)	527 (39.7)
Attendance status											
Full-day	326 (26.9)	763 (37.3)	1,414 (50.9)	1,830 (51.2)	2,065 (52.1)	2,050 (48.6)	2,316 (48.5)	2,548 (60.1)	2,710 (72.4)	2,657 (87.4)	2,583 (78.4)
Part-day	2,317 (47.0)	1,835 (42.3)	1,953 (52.6)	1,867 (51.3)	1,431 (50.0)	1,281 (45.8)	1,102 (44.2)	992 (44.6)	768 (51.7)	830 (52.5)	815 (56.2)
Percent of 5-year-olds enrolled											
Total	69.3 (1.16)	84.7 (1.01)	88.8 (0.88)	87.5 (0.81)	87.6 (0.86)	86.1 (0.87)	86.4 (0.85)	86.3 (0.92)	87.2 (0.95)	85.9 (1.05)	85.5 (1.08)
Full-day as a percent of total enrollment	12.3 (1.00)	29.4 (1.39)	42.0 (1.45)	49.5 (1.31)	59.1 (1.37)	61.5 (1.32)	67.7 (1.25)	72.0 (1.20)	77.9 (1.38)	76.2 (1.34)	76.0 (1.42)
Full-day preschool as a percent of total preschool enrollment	31.3 (7.58)	34.6 (7.70)	34.5 (4.33)	38.7 (3.13)	50.7 (3.47)	52.1 (3.04)	57.2 (3.45)	50.5 (3.90)	56.5 (3.60)	54.9 (3.82)	55.2 (3.76)
Full-day kindergarten as a percent of total kindergarten enrollment	11.6 (0.99)	29.2 (1.42)	42.9 (1.54)	51.7 (1.43)	60.7 (1.49)	63.9 (1.46)	69.6 (1.34)	76.0 (1.35)	82.6 (1.30)	81.2 (1.48)	81.0 (1.36)

†Not applicable.
‡Reporting standards not met. Either there are too few cases for a reliable estimate or the coefficient of variation (CV) is 50 percent or greater.
[1]Beginning in 1994, preprimary enrollment data were collected using new procedures. Data may not be comparable to figures for earlier years.
[2]Enrollment data for 5-year-olds include only those students in preprimary programs and do not include those enrolled in primary programs.

NOTE: Preprimary programs include kindergarten and preschool (or nursery school) programs. "Preschool," which was referred to as "nursery school" in previous versions of this table, is defined as a group or class that is organized to provide educational experiences for children during the year or years preceding kindergarten. Data are based on sample surveys of the civilian noninstitutionalized population, which excludes persons in the military and persons living in institutions (e.g., prisons or nursing facilities). Prior to 2010, standard errors were computed using generalized variance function methodology rather than the more precise replicate weight methodology used in later years. Detail may not sum to totals because of rounding.
SOURCE: U.S. Department of Commerce, Census Bureau, Current Population Survey (CPS), October, 1970 through 2017. (This table was prepared July 2018.)

Table 202.20. Percentage of 3-, 4-, and 5-year-old children enrolled in preprimary programs, by level of program, attendance status, and selected child and family characteristics: 2017

[Standard errors appear in parentheses]

Selected child or family characteristic	Total 3- to 5-year-old population (in thousands)	Total enrollment (in thousands)	Percent of 3- to 5-year-old population enrolled							Percentage distribution of enrollment	
				Preschool			Kindergarten				
			Total	Total	Full-day	Part-day	Total	Full-day	Part-day	Full-day	Part-day
1	2	3	4	5	6	7	8	9	10	11	12
Total	**12,001 (133.4)**	**7,716 (117.0)**	**64.3 (0.77)**	**38.5 (0.98)**	**21.5 (0.81)**	**17.0 (0.70)**	**25.8 (0.85)**	**20.3 (0.76)**	**5.5 (0.41)**	**65.1 (1.08)**	**34.9 (1.08)**
Sex											
Male	6,163 (118.1)	3,911 (90.1)	63.5 (1.03)	38.1 (1.24)	21.3 (1.09)	16.8 (0.92)	25.4 (1.20)	19.5 (1.03)	5.8 (0.61)	64.3 (1.62)	35.7 (1.62)
Female	5,839 (61.5)	3,806 (69.0)	65.2 (1.01)	38.9 (1.22)	21.8 (1.04)	17.1 (0.94)	26.3 (0.89)	21.1 (0.87)	5.1 (0.47)	65.8 (1.34)	34.2 (1.34)
Age of child											
3 and 4 years old	8,030 (186.2)	4,319 (148.1)	53.8 (1.08)	49.4 (1.11)	27.7 (1.05)	21.7 (0.91)	4.4 (0.43)	2.7 (0.38)	1.7 (0.29)	56.5 (1.57)	43.5 (1.57)
3 years old	4,086 (81.1)	1,641 (76.5)	40.2 (1.67)	38.6 (1.57)	21.8 (1.39)	16.8 (1.19)	1.6 (0.40)	1.0! (0.35)	0.5! (0.21)	56.8 (2.56)	43.2 (2.56)
4 years old	3,943 (158.3)	2,678 (121.9)	67.9 (1.35)	60.6 (1.43)	33.8 (1.45)	26.8 (1.33)	7.3 (0.84)	4.4 (0.67)	2.9 (0.54)	56.3 (1.85)	43.7 (1.85)
5 years old	3,972 (100.6)	3,398 (90.4)	85.5 (1.08)	16.5 (1.18)	9.1 (0.81)	7.4 (0.89)	69.1 (1.36)	55.9 (1.44)	13.1 (0.98)	76.0 (1.42)	24.0 (1.42)
Race/ethnicity of child											
White	5,885 (48.5)	3,894 (63.8)	66.2 (1.01)	41.4 (1.56)	21.6 (1.10)	19.8 (1.01)	24.8 (1.65)	19.6 (1.42)	5.1 (0.62)	62.3 (1.51)	37.7 (1.51)
Black	1,668 (74.1)	1,068 (65.3)	64.0 (2.43)	42.9 (2.52)	32.1 (2.31)	10.9 (1.73)	21.1 (1.83)	17.9 (1.78)	3.2 (0.81)	78.1 (3.04)	21.9 (3.04)
Hispanic	3,151 (49.3)	1,920 (57.8)	60.9 (1.61)	31.3 (1.69)	15.8 (1.46)	15.5 (1.34)	29.6 (1.21)	22.0 (1.21)	7.6 (0.98)	62.1 (2.36)	37.9 (2.36)
Asian	598 (35.1)	402 (31.8)	67.2 (3.55)	35.4 (3.63)	18.4 (3.01)	17.0 (2.81)	31.8 (3.10)	24.7 (2.93)	7.1 (1.85)	64.2 (4.23)	35.8 (4.23)
Pacific Islander	‡ (†)	‡ (†)	‡ (†)	‡ (†)	‡ (†)	‡ (†)	‡ (†)	‡ (†)	‡ (†)	‡ (†)	‡ (†)
American Indian/Alaska Native	131 (21.4)	72 (15.7)	54.8 (8.09)	34.3 (7.55)	23.1! (8.02)	11.2! (4.06)	20.5 (4.96)	20.2 (4.97)	‡ (†)	79.0 (7.69)	21.0! (7.69)
Two or more races	529 (35.8)	345 (32.7)	65.3 (3.79)	40.7 (4.14)	25.1 (3.79)	15.6 (3.04)	24.6 (3.45)	20.8 (3.25)	3.8! (1.65)	70.3 (5.06)	29.7 (5.06)
Number of parents or guardians in household											
One parent or guardian	3,427 (119.0)	2,178 (98.3)	63.6 (1.56)	36.4 (1.60)	23.4 (1.51)	13.0 (1.13)	27.2 (1.49)	21.8 (1.35)	5.4 (0.81)	71.0 (1.98)	29.0 (1.98)
Two parents or guardians	8,575 (130.4)	5,538 (116.5)	64.6 (0.94)	39.3 (1.21)	20.8 (0.87)	18.5 (0.92)	25.3 (1.01)	19.7 (0.92)	5.5 (0.48)	62.8 (1.35)	37.2 (1.35)
Mother's current employment status[1]											
Employed	7,010 (132.9)	4,740 (108.6)	67.6 (0.96)	40.6 (1.19)	24.1 (1.03)	16.5 (0.95)	27.0 (1.00)	21.2 (0.92)	5.8 (0.54)	67.0 (1.37)	33.0 (1.37)
Unemployed	324 (37.3)	201 (28.3)	62.2 (5.19)	39.2 (5.28)	30.9 (4.86)	8.4! (3.19)	23.0 (4.46)	19.3 (4.18)	3.6! (1.81)	80.7 (5.57)	19.3 (5.57)
Not in the labor force	4,109 (117.6)	2,414 (93.9)	58.8 (1.50)	35.5 (1.55)	16.5 (1.15)	19.0 (1.27)	23.3 (1.40)	18.5 (1.26)	4.8 (0.67)	59.6 (2.13)	40.4 (2.13)
No mother in household	559 (49.8)	361 (39.1)	64.6 (4.02)	33.7 (3.94)	21.2 (3.13)	12.5 (3.03)	30.9 (3.64)	23.2 (3.60)	7.7 (2.26)	68.7 (4.91)	31.3 (4.91)
Father's current employment status[1]											
Employed	8,318 (117.1)	5,375 (107.0)	64.6 (0.95)	39.0 (1.19)	20.9 (0.85)	18.1 (0.91)	25.6 (1.07)	20.1 (0.97)	5.5 (0.50)	63.5 (1.35)	36.5 (1.35)
Unemployed	215 (35.5)	130 (24.7)	60.5 (6.08)	33.7 (5.53)	16.8 (4.68)	16.9 (4.80)	26.8 (5.38)	18.3 (5.05)	8.5! (4.05)	57.9 (7.99)	42.1 (7.99)
Not in the labor force	601 (52.2)	394 (44.6)	65.6 (3.99)	41.1 (4.03)	21.2 (3.89)	19.9 (2.83)	24.5 (3.30)	17.7 (2.96)	6.8 (1.88)	59.3 (4.93)	40.7 (4.93)
No father in household	2,868 (109.6)	1,817 (87.5)	63.4 (1.71)	36.9 (1.77)	23.8 (1.60)	13.1 (1.24)	26.5 (1.55)	21.5 (1.37)	4.9 (0.82)	71.5 (2.10)	28.5 (2.10)
Every parent or guardian employed[1]	7,045 (129.5)	4,751 (106.9)	67.4 (0.98)	39.9 (1.10)	24.0 (1.01)	15.9 (0.89)	27.6 (1.01)	21.9 (0.93)	5.7 (0.53)	68.0 (1.31)	32.0 (1.31)
No parent or guardian employed[1]	1,295 (73.6)	760 (54.4)	58.7 (2.60)	34.3 (2.61)	21.2 (2.41)	13.1 (1.97)	24.4 (2.32)	20.1 (2.06)	4.3 (1.09)	70.3 (3.39)	29.7 (3.39)
Highest educational attainment of parents or guardians[1]											
Less than high school	1,044 (72.2)	546 (53.1)	52.3 (3.08)	25.9 (2.59)	12.9 (2.06)	13.0 (2.09)	26.4 (2.89)	20.9 (2.67)	5.5 (1.47)	64.7 (4.22)	35.3 (4.22)
High school completion[2]	2,499 (97.9)	1,481 (72.6)	59.3 (1.96)	33.1 (2.01)	18.9 (1.42)	14.2 (1.48)	26.2 (1.67)	21.2 (1.54)	5.0 (0.78)	67.7 (2.35)	32.3 (2.35)
Some college, no degree	2,012 (89.5)	1,251 (72.1)	62.2 (1.99)	34.1 (2.03)	20.2 (1.84)	13.9 (1.41)	28.1 (1.86)	20.8 (1.67)	7.3 (1.12)	65.8 (2.40)	34.2 (2.40)
Associate's degree	1,444 (82.5)	864 (56.2)	59.8 (2.44)	35.6 (2.39)	20.4 (1.90)	15.2 (1.77)	24.3 (2.23)	20.1 (2.00)	4.2 (1.13)	67.7 (3.08)	32.3 (3.08)
Bachelor's degree	2,665 (95.7)	1,849 (74.7)	69.4 (1.52)	46.9 (2.17)	26.1 (1.84)	20.8 (1.61)	22.5 (1.99)	17.6 (1.69)	4.9 (0.83)	62.9 (2.26)	37.1 (2.26)
Graduate or professional degree	2,337 (92.6)	1,726 (80.6)	73.8 (1.76)	46.0 (2.25)	24.9 (1.74)	21.1 (1.76)	27.8 (1.82)	21.9 (1.80)	5.9 (0.88)	63.4 (2.22)	36.6 (2.22)

†Not applicable.
!Interpret data with caution. The coefficient of variation (CV) for this estimate is between 30 and 50 percent.
‡Reporting standards not met. Either there are too few cases for a reliable estimate or the coefficient of variation (CV) is 50 percent or greater.
[1]Data pertain only to parents or guardians who live in the household with the child.
[2]Includes completion of high school through equivalency programs, such as a GED program.
NOTE: Preprimary programs include kindergarten and preschool (or nursery school) programs. "Preschool," which was referred to as "nursery school" in previous versions of this table, is defined as a group or class that is organized to provide educational experiences for children during the year or years preceding kindergarten. Enrollment data for 5-year-olds include only those students in preprimary programs and do not include those enrolled in primary programs. Race categories exclude persons of Hispanic ethnicity. Data are based on sample surveys of the civilian noninstitutionalized population, which excludes persons in the military and persons living in institutions (e.g., prisons or nursing facilities). Detail may not sum to totals because of rounding.
SOURCE: U.S. Department of Commerce, Census Bureau, Current Population Survey (CPS), October, 2017. (This table was prepared July 2018.)

Table 202.30. Number of children under 6 years old and not yet enrolled in kindergarten, percentage participating in center-based programs, average weekly hours in nonparental care, and percentage in various types of primary care arrangements, by selected child and family characteristics: 2016

[Standard errors appear in parentheses]

Selected child or family characteristic	Number of children under 6 years old (in thousands)	Percent participating in center-based programs[1]	Average hours per week in nonparental care[2]	Percentage distribution of children, by type of care: Parental care only	Nonparental care, by primary arrangement[3]: Center-based care	Nonrelative home-based care: Total	Nonrelative home-based care: In another home	Nonrelative home-based care: In child's home	Relative	Multiple arrangments[4]
1	2	3	4	5	6	7	8	9	10	11
Total children under 6 years old	**21,362 (54.2)**	**35.9 (0.79)**	**30.6 (0.38)**	**40.3 (0.94)**	**29.4 (0.73)**	**10.0 (0.42)**	**6.9 (0.37)**	**3.2 (0.26)**	**18.5 (0.72)**	**1.8 (0.21)**
Age										
Under 1 year old	4,724 (150.4)	13.2 (1.13)	33.0 (0.60)	52.6 (2.13)	10.7 (0.87)	11.8 (1.08)	8.0 (0.88)	3.7 (0.61)	23.2 (1.90)	1.6 (0.45)
1 to 2 years old	8,552 (176.3)	24.7 (1.18)	30.8 (0.74)	46.0 (1.34)	21.4 (1.16)	11.4 (0.77)	7.9 (0.66)	3.5 (0.45)	19.9 (1.09)	1.3 (0.28)
3 to 5 years old	8,087 (91.1)	60.9 (1.49)	29.5 (0.56)	27.1 (1.47)	48.7 (1.44)	7.6 (0.55)	5.1 (0.46)	2.5 (0.34)	14.4 (1.02)	2.3 (0.32)
Race/ethnicity of child and poverty status of household[5]										
White	10,731 (97.5)	38.5 (0.90)	30.5 (0.47)	37.8 (0.95)	31.4 (0.84)	12.4 (0.67)	8.5 (0.51)	3.9 (0.40)	16.4 (0.89)	2.0 (0.31)
Poor	1,182 (77.7)	23.4 (2.85)	27.4 (1.99)	59.3 (3.49)	19.7 (2.71)	4.7! (1.61)	2.6! (1.29)	2.1! (1.03)	14.8 (2.35)	‡ (†)
Near-poor	1,962 (89.7)	25.5 (2.17)	30.5 (1.53)	51.7 (2.53)	17.8 (1.50)	9.0 (1.51)	7.5 (1.30)	1.5! (0.57)	19.8 (2.31)	1.8! (0.80)
Nonpoor	7,586 (77.6)	44.2 (1.23)	30.7 (0.44)	30.9 (1.30)	36.7 (1.13)	14.5 (0.85)	9.6 (0.65)	4.8 (0.53)	15.8 (0.94)	2.1 (0.30)
Black	2,837 (0.0)	40.3 (3.37)	33.5 (1.29)	32.5 (3.38)	31.6 (3.07)	8.8 (1.70)	6.6 (1.62)	2.2! (0.71)	24.9 (2.54)	2.3! (0.75)
Poor	1,069 (40.7)	35.4 (4.70)	35.1 (2.83)	40.2 (5.63)	22.9 (4.24)	9.4! (3.29)	6.4! (2.99)	‡ (†)	25.1 (4.36)	‡ (†)
Near-poor	725 (47.3)	35.2 (8.13)	31.0 (2.42)	33.2 (6.61)	31.2 (8.12)	5.8! (2.79)	‡ (†)	‡ (†)	29.3 (6.15)	‡ (†)
Nonpoor	1,043 (32.9)	48.7 (4.75)	33.7 (1.81)	24.0 (4.32)	40.8 (4.57)	10.2 (2.76)	8.7! (2.67)	‡ (†)	21.6 (3.97)	3.4! (1.61)
Hispanic	5,418 (1.6)	28.3 (1.60)	28.1 (0.87)	48.5 (2.23)	23.1 (1.54)	7.2 (0.98)	4.9 (0.78)	2.3 (0.55)	19.7 (1.56)	1.5 (0.36)
Poor	1,443 (44.1)	21.8 (3.13)	27.8 (2.14)	60.1 (4.04)	17.1 (2.72)	3.9! (1.53)	3.0! (1.35)	‡ (†)	16.7 (2.88)	2.1! (0.84)
Near-poor	1,800 (91.8)	21.3 (2.63)	26.3 (2.00)	57.8 (4.08)	15.4 (2.12)	4.7 (1.40)	3.4! (1.10)	‡ (†)	20.5 (3.04)	1.6! (0.79)
Nonpoor	2,175 (80.2)	38.4 (2.71)	29.2 (1.06)	33.2 (3.05)	33.4 (2.68)	11.3 (1.89)	7.4 (1.50)	3.9 (1.11)	21.1 (2.37)	1.0! (0.46)
Asian/Pacific Islander	1,009 (69.7)	36.1 (2.75)	30.0 (1.68)	43.2 (3.66)	30.9 (2.60)	5.7 (1.32)	2.3! (0.77)	3.5! (1.15)	19.6 (3.31)	‡ (†)
Asian	995 (69.5)	35.9 (2.70)	30.3 (1.68)	43.1 (3.66)	30.6 (2.53)	5.8 (1.33)	2.3! (0.78)	3.5! (1.17)	19.9 (3.36)	‡ (†)
Pacific Islander	‡ (†)	‡ (†)	‡ (†)	‡ (†)	‡ (†)	‡ (†)	‡ (†)	‡ (†)	‡ (†)	‡ (†)
American Indian/Alaska Native	‡ (†)	‡ (†)	‡ (†)	‡ (†)	‡ (†)	‡ (†)	‡ (†)	‡ (†)	‡ (†)	‡ (†)
Two or more races	1,235 (77.7)	37.3 (3.56)	33.6 (1.40)	39.2 (3.62)	33.7 (3.37)	9.0 (1.68)	6.9 (1.59)	2.1! (0.73)	17.7 (2.43)	‡ (†)
Number of parents in the household[6]										
Two parents	16,428 (149.4)	35.8 (0.87)	29.3 (0.41)	42.9 (1.02)	30.0 (0.83)	9.8 (0.47)	6.5 (0.39)	3.3 (0.31)	15.5 (0.76)	1.8 (0.24)
One parent	4,449 (164.2)	36.5 (2.09)	34.2 (0.82)	32.3 (2.12)	27.5 (1.84)	11.5 (1.29)	8.7 (1.18)	2.8 (0.64)	27.1 (1.97)	1.7 (0.40)
Mother in household										
Yes	20,233 (99.4)	36.1 (0.81)	30.3 (0.36)	40.9 (0.98)	29.7 (0.79)	10.1 (0.45)	6.9 (0.37)	3.2 (0.28)	17.4 (0.74)	1.8 (0.22)
No	1,129 (80.9)	32.3 (3.39)	34.0 (1.85)	28.9 (3.90)	23.2 (2.73)	8.8 (2.50)	6.6! (2.23)	2.2! (0.96)	38.1 (4.13)	‡ (†)
Mother's employment status[7]										
Currently employed	12,154 (179.6)	45.5 (1.11)	33.2 (0.40)	21.1 (1.04)	36.5 (0.97)	15.2 (0.72)	10.9 (0.59)	4.3 (0.43)	24.6 (1.07)	2.6 (0.31)
35 or more hours per week	8,884 (159.5)	49.3 (1.31)	35.9 (0.45)	15.9 (1.08)	39.9 (1.14)	17.5 (0.87)	12.8 (0.71)	4.7 (0.52)	24.2 (1.14)	2.6 (0.36)
Less than 35 hours per week	3,270 (130.0)	35.2 (2.07)	23.6 (0.85)	35.3 (2.14)	27.2 (1.79)	9.1 (0.99)	5.8 (0.92)	3.2 (0.51)	25.9 (2.02)	2.5 (0.60)
Looking for work	795 (66.6)	22.2 (3.89)	22.0 (2.50)	59.9 (4.33)	15.4 (3.08)	5.6! (2.39)	‡ (†)	‡ (†)	16.9 (3.67)	‡ (†)
Not in labor force	7,811 (152.6)	22.7 (1.12)	20.6 (0.87)	69.0 (1.51)	20.4 (1.11)	2.3 (0.41)	0.8 (0.20)	1.5 (0.31)	7.9 (0.91)	0.4! (0.15)
Mother's highest education[7]										
Less than high school	2,716 (88.3)	20.9 (3.66)	27.6 (2.07)	60.4 (4.32)	18.0 (3.61)	5.5 (1.51)	3.9! (1.45)	1.7! (0.72)	15.4 (2.23)	‡ (†)
High school/GED	4,085 (86.0)	25.3 (1.66)	29.4 (1.10)	51.0 (2.40)	18.5 (1.54)	6.1 (1.08)	4.5 (0.90)	1.6! (0.62)	21.8 (2.23)	2.5 (0.61)
Vocational/technical or some college	3,698 (93.1)	33.7 (1.47)	28.8 (0.92)	41.1 (1.52)	27.6 (1.51)	9.2 (1.02)	7.8 (0.97)	1.4! (0.44)	20.9 (1.61)	1.2! (0.42)
Associate's degree	1,752 (94.1)	33.4 (2.49)	33.3 (1.35)	39.0 (2.81)	26.2 (2.02)	10.8 (1.84)	9.5 (1.53)	‡ (†)	22.1 (2.22)	1.9! (0.64)
Bachelor's degree	5,675 (126.7)	45.1 (1.40)	30.3 (0.61)	33.9 (1.52)	38.1 (1.42)	10.9 (0.74)	7.2 (0.69)	3.7 (0.52)	15.4 (1.17)	1.7 (0.35)
Graduate/professional degree	2,835 (49.7)	52.5 (1.71)	33.0 (0.76)	20.5 (1.51)	44.5 (1.61)	18.6 (1.45)	9.5 (0.98)	9.2 (1.03)	14.2 (1.37)	2.2 (0.47)
Language spoken most at home by mother[7]										
English	16,847 (167.2)	37.9 (0.78)	30.9 (0.40)	38.0 (0.91)	31.1 (0.72)	11.0 (0.54)	7.7 (0.44)	3.3 (0.28)	18.1 (0.80)	1.8 (0.25)
Non-English	2,640 (149.9)	26.4 (2.35)	28.0 (1.58)	52.4 (3.52)	22.5 (2.31)	6.7 (1.39)	4.0 (1.12)	2.7! (0.80)	16.6 (2.28)	1.8! (0.62)
English and another language equally	1,273 (85.0)	30.5 (2.97)	26.4 (1.57)	50.6 (3.68)	25.3 (2.82)	3.8! (1.43)	1.4! (0.53)	‡ (†)	19.7 (2.43)	‡ (†)
Mother's age when first became parent[7]										
Less than 18	1,237 (100.9)	26.0 (3.81)	32.2 (1.90)	50.4 (4.78)	20.1 (3.59)	6.5 (1.85)	5.4! (1.66)	‡ (†)	21.6 (3.61)	‡ (†)
18 or 19	2,476 (155.5)	25.7 (3.26)	31.7 (1.67)	47.0 (3.96)	21.0 (3.07)	8.4 (1.66)	6.3 (1.47)	2.2! (0.79)	22.2 (2.36)	1.3! (0.55)
20 or older	16,899 (176.1)	38.3 (0.86)	30.2 (0.39)	38.9 (1.00)	31.7 (0.81)	10.5 (0.50)	7.1 (0.41)	3.4 (0.30)	17.1 (0.81)	1.8 (0.23)
Household income										
$20,000 or less	3,049 (10.3)	30.5 (2.28)	31.3 (1.66)	52.3 (2.48)	22.5 (2.07)	5.7 (1.41)	3.8! (1.22)	1.9! (0.74)	17.4 (1.95)	2.2! (0.66)
$20,001 to $50,000	5,706 (53.6)	26.7 (1.87)	30.0 (0.85)	50.2 (2.03)	21.3 (1.88)	6.5 (0.75)	5.2 (0.67)	1.3 (0.34)	20.8 (1.48)	1.3 (0.31)
$50,001 to $75,000	3,821 (0.0)	27.7 (1.60)	29.1 (0.87)	43.9 (2.18)	21.6 (1.41)	11.6 (1.28)	9.5 (1.20)	2.1 (0.59)	21.0 (1.67)	1.9 (0.57)
$75,001 to $100,000	2,882 (0.0)	38.4 (2.39)	29.9 (0.96)	34.2 (2.16)	31.9 (2.14)	10.4 (1.28)	8.8 (1.23)	1.6 (0.39)	21.8 (2.21)	1.7 (0.42)
Over $100,000	5,904 (4.6)	51.5 (1.58)	31.7 (0.46)	25.3 (1.46)	44.6 (1.52)	14.5 (0.87)	7.4 (0.60)	7.1 (0.76)	13.8 (1.09)	1.9 (0.33)

See notes at end of table.

Table 202.30. Number of children under 6 years old and not yet enrolled in kindergarten, percentage participating in center-based programs, average weekly hours in nonparental care, and percentage in various types of primary care arrangements, by selected child and family characteristics: 2016—Continued

[Standard errors appear in parentheses]

Selected child or family characteristic	Number of children under 6 years old (in thousands)	Percent participating in center-based programs[1]	Average hours per week in nonparental care[2]	Percentage distribution of children, by type of care						
				Parental care only	Nonparental care, by primary arrangement[3]					
					Center-based care	Nonrelative home-based care			Relative	Multiple arrangments[4]
						Total	In another home	In child's home		
1	2	3	4	5	6	7	8	9	10	11
Poverty status of household[5]										
Poor	4,203 (92.6)	26.8 (1.98)	30.9 (1.27)	54.4 (2.53)	20.3 (1.81)	5.4 (1.10)	3.7 (0.96)	1.7! (0.58)	18.1 (1.93)	1.7 (0.49)
Near-poor	4,997 (156.1)	25.2 (1.82)	29.1 (0.91)	51.3 (2.16)	19.2 (1.74)	6.4 (0.76)	5.0 (0.65)	1.4 (0.38)	21.6 (1.67)	1.4 (0.42)
Nonpoor	12,162 (109.4)	43.4 (0.98)	30.9 (0.40)	30.9 (1.11)	36.7 (0.93)	13.1 (0.64)	8.7 (0.53)	4.4 (0.42)	17.4 (0.86)	1.9 (0.25)
Household size										
2 or 3 persons	5,109 (114.0)	41.1 (1.33)	33.7 (0.75)	32.3 (1.36)	34.5 (1.31)	12.2 (0.93)	8.5 (0.87)	3.7 (0.50)	18.6 (1.38)	2.2 (0.40)
4 persons	7,574 (116.9)	40.8 (1.42)	30.1 (0.55)	37.1 (1.49)	33.6 (1.27)	11.0 (0.92)	7.9 (0.78)	3.0 (0.50)	16.6 (1.00)	1.8 (0.39)
5 persons	4,610 (164.4)	33.3 (1.77)	28.7 (0.89)	44.1 (2.03)	27.0 (1.62)	8.5 (0.93)	5.1 (0.78)	3.4 (0.59)	19.2 (1.60)	1.3 (0.34)
6 or more persons	4,069 (166.3)	23.1 (1.64)	28.6 (1.11)	52.0 (2.60)	17.7 (1.53)	7.3 (1.06)	4.9 (0.97)	2.4 (0.63)	21.3 (2.05)	1.6 (0.44)
Locale										
City	7,246 (180.0)	36.4 (1.35)	30.8 (0.66)	40.2 (1.80)	29.6 (1.24)	9.7 (0.73)	5.9 (0.65)	3.8 (0.54)	18.8 (1.34)	1.7 (0.35)
Suburban	8,733 (203.4)	37.7 (1.30)	29.3 (0.61)	38.4 (1.39)	31.8 (1.18)	9.3 (0.69)	6.2 (0.61)	3.2 (0.42)	18.9 (1.09)	1.5 (0.25)
Town	1,931 (96.0)	31.2 (2.44)	30.3 (1.24)	44.2 (2.87)	24.3 (2.47)	10.5 (1.63)	7.7 (1.38)	2.8! (1.05)	19.0 (2.47)	‡ (†)
Rural	3,452 (141.6)	32.8 (2.02)	33.5 (1.19)	43.2 (2.22)	25.6 (1.81)	12.2 (1.23)	10.1 (1.01)	2.0 (0.49)	16.7 (1.94)	2.3 (0.63)

†Not applicable.
!Interpret data with caution. The coefficient of variation (CV) for this estimate is between 30 and 50 percent.
‡Reporting standards not met. Either there are too few cases for a reliable estimate or the coefficient of variation (CV) is 50 percent or greater.
[1]Center-based arrangements include day care centers, Head Start programs, preschools, prekindergartens, and other early childhood programs.
[2]Mean hours per week per child, among preschool children enrolled in any type of nonparental care arrangement. For children with more than one arrangement, the hours of each weekly arrangement were summed to calculate the total amount of time in child care per week.
[3]A child's primary arrangement is the regular nonparental care arrangement or early childhood education program in which the child spent the most time per week.
[4]Children who spent an equal number of hours per week in multiple nonparental care arrangements.
[5]Poor children are those whose family incomes were below the Census Bureau's poverty threshold in the year prior to data collection; near-poor children are those whose family incomes ranged from the poverty threshold to 199 percent of the poverty threshold; and nonpoor children are those whose family incomes were at or above 200 percent of the poverty threshold. The poverty threshold is a dollar amount that varies depending on a family's size and composition and is updated annually to account for inflation. In 2015, for example, the poverty threshold for a family of four with two children was $24,257. Survey respondents are asked to select the range within which their income falls, rather than giving the exact amount of their income; therefore, the measure of poverty status is an approximation.
[6]Excludes children living apart from their parents.
[7]Excludes children living in households with no mother or female guardian present.
NOTE: For the 2016 administration of the National Household Education Surveys Program (NHES), initial contact with all respondents was by mail, and the majority of respondents received paper-and-pencil questionnaires. However, as an experiment with web use, a small sample of NHES:2016 respondents received mailed invitations to complete the survey online. Race categories exclude persons of Hispanic ethnicity. Detail may not sum to totals because of rounding.
SOURCE: U.S. Department of Education, National Center for Education Statistics, Early Childhood Program Participation Survey of the National Household Education Surveys Program (ECPP-NHES:2016). (This table was prepared December 2017.)

Table 203.10. Enrollment in public elementary and secondary schools, by level and grade: Selected years, fall 1980 through fall 2028

[In thousands]

Year	All grades	Elementary												Secondary					
		Total	Pre-kinder-garten	Kinder-garten	1st grade	2nd grade	3rd grade	4th grade	5th grade	6th grade	7th grade	8th grade	Un-graded	Total	9th grade	10th grade	11th grade	12th grade	Un-graded[1]
1	2	3	4	5	6	7	8	9	10	11	12	13	14	15	16	17	18	19	20
1980	40,877	27,647	96	2,593	2,894	2,800	2,893	3,107	3,130	3,038	3,085	3,086	924	13,231	3,377	3,368	3,195	2,925	366
1985	39,422	27,034	151	3,041	3,239	2,941	2,895	2,771	2,776	2,789	2,938	2,982	511	12,388	3,439	3,230	2,866	2,550	303
1990	41,217	29,876	303	3,306	3,499	3,327	3,297	3,248	3,197	3,110	3,067	2,979	541	11,341	3,169	2,896	2,612	2,381	284
1991	42,047	30,503	375	3,311	3,556	3,360	3,334	3,315	3,268	3,239	3,181	3,020	542	11,544	3,313	2,915	2,645	2,392	278
1992	42,823	31,086	505	3,313	3,542	3,431	3,361	3,342	3,325	3,303	3,299	3,129	536	11,737	3,352	3,027	2,656	2,431	272
1993	43,465	31,502	545	3,377	3,529	3,429	3,437	3,361	3,350	3,356	3,355	3,249	513	11,963	3,487	3,050	2,751	2,424	250
1994	44,111	31,896	603	3,444	3,593	3,440	3,439	3,426	3,372	3,381	3,404	3,302	492	12,215	3,604	3,131	2,748	2,488	244
1995	44,840	32,338	637	3,536	3,671	3,507	3,445	3,431	3,438	3,395	3,422	3,356	500	12,502	3,704	3,237	2,826	2,487	247
1996	45,611	32,762	670	3,532	3,770	3,600	3,524	3,454	3,453	3,494	3,464	3,403	399	12,849	3,801	3,323	2,930	2,586	208
1997	46,127	33,071	695	3,503	3,755	3,689	3,597	3,507	3,458	3,492	3,520	3,415	440	13,056	3,819	3,376	2,972	2,673	216
1998	46,539	33,344	729	3,443	3,727	3,681	3,696	3,592	3,520	3,497	3,530	3,480	449	13,195	3,856	3,382	3,021	2,722	214
1999	46,857	33,486	751	3,397	3,684	3,656	3,691	3,686	3,604	3,564	3,541	3,497	415	13,371	3,935	3,415	3,034	2,782	205
2000	47,204	33,686	776	3,382	3,636	3,634	3,676	3,711	3,707	3,663	3,629	3,538	334	13,517	3,963	3,491	3,083	2,803	177
2001	47,672	33,936	865	3,379	3,614	3,593	3,653	3,695	3,727	3,769	3,720	3,616	304	13,736	4,012	3,528	3,174	2,863	159
2002	48,183	34,114	915	3,434	3,594	3,565	3,623	3,669	3,711	3,788	3,821	3,709	285	14,069	4,105	3,584	3,229	2,990	161
2003	48,540	34,201	950	3,503	3,613	3,544	3,611	3,619	3,685	3,772	3,841	3,809	255	14,339	4,190	3,675	3,277	3,046	150
2004	48,795	34,178	990	3,544	3,663	3,560	3,580	3,612	3,635	3,735	3,818	3,825	215	14,618	4,281	3,750	3,369	3,094	122
2005	49,113	34,204	1,036	3,619	3,691	3,606	3,586	3,578	3,633	3,670	3,777	3,802	205	14,909	4,287	3,866	3,454	3,180	121
2006	49,316	34,235	1,084	3,631	3,751	3,641	3,627	3,586	3,602	3,660	3,716	3,766	170	15,081	4,260	3,882	3,551	3,277	110
2007	49,291	34,204	1,081	3,609	3,750	3,704	3,659	3,624	3,600	3,628	3,700	3,709	139	15,086	4,200	3,863	3,557	3,375	92
2008	49,266	34,286	1,180	3,640	3,708	3,699	3,708	3,647	3,629	3,614	3,653	3,692	117	14,980	4,123	3,822	3,548	3,400	87
2009	49,361	34,409	1,223	3,678	3,729	3,665	3,707	3,701	3,652	3,644	3,641	3,651	119	14,952	4,080	3,809	3,541	3,432	90
2010	49,484	34,625	1,279	3,682	3,754	3,701	3,686	3,711	3,718	3,682	3,676	3,659	77	14,860	4,008	3,800	3,538	3,472	42
2011	49,522	34,773	1,291	3,746	3,773	3,713	3,703	3,672	3,699	3,724	3,696	3,679	77	14,749	3,957	3,751	3,546	3,452	43
2012	49,771	35,018	1,307	3,831	3,824	3,729	3,719	3,690	3,673	3,723	3,746	3,699	76	14,753	3,975	3,730	3,528	3,477	43
2013	50,045	35,251	1,328	3,834	3,885	3,791	3,738	3,708	3,697	3,684	3,748	3,753	85	14,794	3,980	3,761	3,526	3,476	52
2014	50,313	35,370	1,369	3,772	3,863	3,857	3,806	3,719	3,719	3,710	3,710	3,757	87	14,943	4,033	3,794	3,568	3,496	52
2015[2]	50,438	35,388	1,402	3,713	3,768	3,842	3,869	3,793	3,733	3,731	3,732	3,719	87	15,050	4,019	3,846	3,598	3,537	49
2016[3]	50,615	35,477	1,426	3,699	3,694	3,761	3,874	3,858	3,814	3,754	3,761	3,749	88	15,138	3,986	3,860	3,669	3,571	52
	Projected																		
2017	50,695	35,473	1,415	3,670	3,709	3,686	3,784	3,864	3,870	3,831	3,782	3,775	88	15,222	4,019	3,828	3,682	3,642	52
2018	50,728	35,465	1,417	3,678	3,680	3,700	3,709	3,774	3,876	3,888	3,859	3,796	88	15,264	4,047	3,859	3,652	3,655	52
2019	50,770	35,457	1,425	3,697	3,684	3,672	3,724	3,699	3,786	3,893	3,916	3,874	88	15,313	4,069	3,886	3,681	3,625	51
2020	50,857	35,384	1,430	3,712	3,704	3,676	3,695	3,714	3,710	3,803	3,922	3,931	88	15,473	4,153	3,907	3,707	3,654	51
2021	50,892	35,231	1,426	3,700	3,718	3,696	3,699	3,685	3,725	3,727	3,831	3,937	87	15,661	4,214	3,988	3,728	3,680	52
2022	51,012	35,189	1,457	3,782	3,706	3,710	3,719	3,689	3,696	3,742	3,755	3,846	87	15,823	4,220	4,047	3,804	3,700	52
2023	51,098	35,235	1,465	3,802	3,788	3,698	3,733	3,709	3,700	3,713	3,770	3,769	88	15,863	4,122	4,052	3,860	3,776	52
2024	51,124	35,376	1,473	3,821	3,809	3,780	3,721	3,723	3,720	3,717	3,740	3,784	88	15,748	4,040	3,958	3,866	3,832	52
2025	51,119	35,519	1,479	3,837	3,828	3,800	3,804	3,712	3,735	3,737	3,745	3,754	88	15,601	4,056	3,879	3,776	3,837	52
2026	51,123	35,703	1,484	3,851	3,844	3,819	3,824	3,794	3,723	3,752	3,765	3,759	89	15,420	4,025	3,895	3,701	3,748	51
2027	51,228	35,894	1,488	3,862	3,858	3,836	3,843	3,814	3,805	3,740	3,779	3,779	89	15,334	4,029	3,865	3,716	3,674	51
2028	51,419	36,073	1,492	3,871	3,869	3,850	3,860	3,833	3,826	3,823	3,767	3,794	90	15,346	4,051	3,869	3,687	3,688	51

[1]Includes students reported as being enrolled in grade 13.

[2]The prekindergarten, elementary total, and "all grades" counts include imputations for prekindergarten enrollment in California and Oregon.

[3]The prekindergarten, elementary total, and "all grades" counts include imputations for prekindergarten enrollment in California.

NOTE: Due to changes in reporting and imputation practices, prekindergarten enrollment for years prior to 1992 represent an undercount compared to later years. The total ungraded counts of students were prorated to the elementary and secondary levels based on prior reports. Detail may not sum to totals because of rounding.

SOURCE: U.S. Department of Education, National Center for Education Statistics, *Statistics of Public Elementary and Secondary School Systems*, 1980–81; Common Core of Data (CCD), "State Nonfiscal Survey of Public Elementary/Secondary Education," 1985–86 through 2016–17; and National Elementary and Secondary Enrollment Projection Model, 1972 through 2028. (This table was prepared March 2019.)

Table 203.20. Enrollment in public elementary and secondary schools, by region, state, and jurisdiction: Selected years, fall 1990 through fall 2028

Region, state, and jurisdiction	Actual total enrollment													Percent change in total enrollment, 2011 to 2016	Projected total enrollment						Percent change in total enrollment, 2016 to 2028
	Fall 1990	Fall 2000	Fall 2006	Fall 2007	Fall 2008	Fall 2009	Fall 2010	Fall 2011	Fall 2012	Fall 2013	Fall 2014	Fall 2015[1]	Fall 2016[2]		Fall 2017	Fall 2018	Fall 2019	Fall 2020	Fall 2021	Fall 2028	
1	2	3	4	5	6	7	8	9	10	11	12	13	14	15	16	17	18	19	20	21	22
United States	**41,216,683**	**47,203,539**	**49,315,842**	**49,290,559**	**49,265,572**	**49,360,982**	**49,484,181**	**49,521,669**	**49,771,118**	**50,044,522**	**50,312,581**	**50,438,043**	**50,615,189**	**2.2**	**50,695,200**	**50,728,400**	**50,770,000**	**50,857,100**	**50,891,900**	**51,418,700**	**1.6**
Region																					
Northeast	7,281,763	8,222,127	8,257,889	8,122,022	8,052,985	8,092,029	8,071,335	7,953,981	7,959,128	7,961,243	7,979,856	7,933,762	7,959,304	0.1	7,928,200	7,896,100	7,870,000	7,852,100	7,823,000	7,663,700	-3.7
Midwest	9,943,761	10,729,987	10,819,248	10,770,210	10,742,973	10,672,171	10,609,604	10,573,792	10,559,230	10,572,920	10,560,539	10,555,579	10,538,947	-0.3	10,514,400	10,485,600	10,457,400	10,443,900	10,417,300	10,316,100	-2.1
South	14,807,016	17,007,261	18,293,633	18,422,773	18,490,770	18,651,889	18,805,000	18,955,932	19,128,376	19,298,714	19,506,193	19,641,472	19,749,816	4.2	19,845,300	19,914,100	19,987,400	20,080,900	20,166,800	20,815,500	5.4
West	9,184,143	11,244,164	11,945,072	11,975,554	11,978,844	11,944,893	11,998,242	12,037,964	12,124,384	12,211,645	12,265,993	12,307,230	12,367,122	2.7	12,407,400	12,432,600	12,455,300	12,480,200	12,484,700	12,623,400	2.1
State																					
Alabama	721,806	739,992	743,632	742,919	745,668	748,889	755,552	744,621	744,637	746,204	744,164	743,789	744,930	#	739,400	734,200	732,200	732,300	732,700	740,900	-0.5
Alaska	113,903	133,356	132,608	131,029	130,662	131,661	132,104	131,167	131,489	130,944	131,176	132,477	132,737	1.2	133,700	134,300	135,100	136,200	137,400	144,400	8.8
Arizona	639,853	877,696	1,068,249	1,087,447	1,087,817	1,077,831	1,071,751	1,080,319	1,089,384	1,102,445	1,111,695	1,109,040	1,123,137	4.0	1,127,400	1,131,700	1,135,000	1,140,200	1,143,300	1,172,900	4.4
Arkansas	436,286	449,959	476,409	479,016	478,965	480,559	482,114	483,114	486,157	489,979	490,917	492,132	493,447	2.1	493,700	494,000	494,600	495,200	496,400	510,700	3.5
California	4,950,474	6,140,814	6,406,750	6,343,471	6,322,528	6,263,438	6,289,578	6,287,834	6,299,451	6,312,623	6,312,161	6,305,347	6,309,138	0.3	6,307,600	6,293,000	6,277,900	6,261,100	6,232,500	6,137,800	-2.7
Colorado	574,213	724,508	794,026	801,867	818,443	832,368	843,316	854,265	863,561	876,999	889,006	899,112	905,019	5.9	909,900	913,500	916,600	919,500	920,600	948,400	4.8
Connecticut	469,123	562,179	575,100	570,626	567,198	563,968	560,546	554,437	550,954	546,200	542,678	537,933	535,118	-3.5	528,100	521,400	514,600	508,800	501,700	471,100	-12.0
Delaware	99,658	114,676	122,254	122,574	125,430	126,801	129,403	128,946	129,026	131,687	134,042	134,847	136,264	5.7	137,400	138,300	139,100	139,800	140,300	141,000	3.5
District of Columbia	80,694	68,925	72,850	78,422	68,681	69,433	71,284	73,911	76,140	78,153	80,958	84,024	85,850	16.2	86,400	89,100	91,900	94,500	97,000	105,300	22.6
Florida	1,861,592	2,434,821	2,671,513	2,666,811	2,631,020	2,634,522	2,643,347	2,668,156	2,692,162	2,720,744	2,756,944	2,792,234	2,816,791	5.6	2,842,300	2,863,200	2,883,600	2,911,400	2,938,000	3,119,600	10.8
Georgia	1,151,687	1,444,937	1,629,157	1,649,589	1,655,792	1,667,685	1,677,067	1,685,016	1,703,332	1,723,909	1,744,437	1,757,237	1,764,346	4.7	1,769,500	1,772,800	1,776,000	1,781,000	1,785,900	1,814,200	2.8
Hawaii	171,708	184,360	180,728	179,897	179,478	180,196	179,601	182,706	184,760	186,825	182,384	181,995	181,550	-0.6	181,600	180,700	180,300	179,600	178,700	171,800	-5.4
Idaho	220,840	245,117	267,380	272,119	275,051	276,299	275,859	279,873	284,834	296,476	290,885	292,277	297,200	6.2	299,700	302,500	304,900	307,600	309,800	324,300	9.1
Illinois	1,821,407	2,048,792	2,118,276	2,112,805	2,119,707	2,104,175	2,091,654	2,083,097	2,072,880	2,066,990	2,050,239	2,041,779	2,026,718	-2.7	2,023,500	2,015,100	2,006,500	2,001,000	1,988,300	1,894,300	-6.5
Indiana	954,525	989,267	1,045,940	1,046,764	1,046,147	1,046,661	1,047,232	1,040,765	1,041,369	1,047,385	1,046,269	1,046,757	1,049,547	0.8	1,048,000	1,046,500	1,042,900	1,042,400	1,042,900	1,057,300	0.7
Iowa	483,652	495,080	483,122	485,115	487,559	491,842	495,775	495,870	499,825	502,964	505,311	508,014	509,831	2.8	511,700	514,000	516,700	519,500	521,500	535,400	5.0
Kansas	437,034	470,610	469,506	468,295	471,060	474,489	483,701	486,108	489,043	496,440	497,275	495,884	494,347	1.7	494,100	493,500	493,000	492,600	491,800	490,600	-0.8
Kentucky	636,401	665,850	683,152	666,225	670,030	680,089	673,128	681,987	685,167	677,389	688,640	686,598	684,017	0.3	682,400	680,000	678,100	677,200	676,200	682,200	-0.3
Louisiana	784,757	743,089	675,851	681,038	684,873	690,915	696,558	703,390	710,903	711,491	716,800	718,711	716,293	1.8	715,900	713,100	711,200	711,300	711,700	718,400	0.3
Maine	215,149	207,037	193,986	196,245	192,935	189,225	189,077	188,969	185,739	183,995	182,470	181,613	180,512	-4.5	179,100	177,900	176,700	175,900	175,100	171,600	-5.0
Maryland	715,176	852,920	851,640	845,700	843,861	848,412	852,211	854,086	859,638	866,169	874,514	879,601	886,221	3.8	893,500	898,900	904,700	909,000	911,900	914,100	3.1
Massachusetts	834,314	975,150	968,661	962,958	958,910	957,053	955,563	953,369	954,773	955,739	955,844	964,026	964,514	1.2	963,300	961,000	958,200	955,500	952,000	939,400	-2.6
Michigan	1,584,431	1,720,626	1,722,656	1,692,739	1,659,921	1,649,082	1,587,067	1,573,537	1,555,370	1,548,841	1,537,922	1,536,231	1,528,666	-2.9	1,511,400	1,493,500	1,478,300	1,465,100	1,451,500	1,400,700	-8.4
Minnesota	756,374	854,340	840,565	837,578	836,048	837,053	838,037	839,738	845,404	850,973	857,235	864,384	875,021	4.2	885,000	891,100	896,300	902,900	907,100	924,000	5.6
Mississippi	502,417	497,871	495,026	494,122	491,962	492,481	490,526	490,619	493,650	492,586	490,917	487,200	483,150	-1.5	478,600	473,400	469,000	465,400	462,400	441,600	-8.6
Missouri	816,558	912,744	920,353	917,188	917,871	917,982	918,710	916,584	917,900	918,288	917,785	919,234	915,040	-0.2	914,300	912,600	911,300	911,300	910,700	915,100	#
Montana	152,974	154,875	144,418	142,823	141,899	141,807	141,693	142,349	142,908	144,129	144,532	145,319	146,375	2.8	147,400	149,000	150,400	151,700	152,900	160,600	9.7
Nebraska	274,081	286,199	287,580	291,244	292,590	295,368	298,500	301,296	303,505	307,677	312,635	316,014	319,194	5.9	323,300	326,100	328,800	331,100	332,700	344,900	8.1
Nevada	201,316	340,706	424,766	429,362	433,371	428,947	437,149	439,634	445,707	451,831	459,189	467,527	473,744	7.8	479,300	485,400	490,900	496,000	501,000	527,800	11.4
New Hampshire	172,785	208,461	203,572	200,772	197,934	197,140	194,711	191,900	188,974	186,310	184,670	182,425	180,888	-5.7	178,600	176,300	174,200	172,000	170,000	161,000	-11.0
New Jersey	1,089,646	1,313,405	1,388,850	1,382,348	1,381,420	1,396,029	1,402,548	1,356,431	1,372,203	1,370,295	1,400,579	1,408,845	1,410,421	4.0	1,405,600	1,400,900	1,397,100	1,394,100	1,388,200	1,356,200	-3.8
New Mexico	301,881	320,306	328,220	329,040	330,245	334,419	338,122	337,225	338,220	339,244	340,365	335,694	336,263	-0.3	334,900	332,500	330,100	327,200	324,500	306,100	-9.0
New York	2,598,337	2,882,188	2,809,649	2,765,435	2,740,592	2,766,052	2,734,955	2,704,718	2,710,703	2,732,770	2,741,185	2,711,626	2,729,776	0.9	2,723,500	2,715,500	2,710,400	2,708,900	2,703,300	2,649,700	-2.9
North Carolina	1,086,871	1,293,638	1,444,481	1,489,492	1,488,645	1,483,397	1,490,605	1,507,864	1,518,465	1,530,857	1,548,895	1,544,934	1,550,062	2.8	1,554,200	1,554,500	1,555,100	1,559,300	1,563,300	1,612,600	4.0
North Dakota	117,825	109,201	96,670	95,059	94,728	95,073	96,323	97,646	101,111	103,947	106,586	108,644	109,706	12.4	108,700	110,700	112,600	114,600	116,400	127,400	16.1
Ohio	1,771,089	1,835,049	1,836,722	1,827,184	1,817,163	1,764,297	1,754,191	1,740,030	1,729,916	1,724,111	1,724,810	1,716,585	1,710,143	-1.7	1,695,900	1,686,500	1,676,400	1,669,000	1,661,500	1,637,400	-4.3
Oklahoma	579,087	623,110	639,391	642,065	645,108	654,802	659,911	666,120	673,483	681,848	688,511	692,878	693,903	4.2	697,000	698,400	700,100	702,100	703,400	721,600	4.0
Oregon	472,394	546,231	562,574	565,586	575,393	582,839	570,720	568,208	587,564	593,000	601,318	608,825	606,277	6.7	609,800	613,600	617,600	622,600	626,500	650,600	7.3
Pennsylvania	1,667,834	1,814,311	1,871,060	1,801,971	1,775,029	1,785,993	1,793,284	1,771,395	1,763,677	1,755,236	1,743,160	1,717,414	1,727,497	-2.5	1,721,000	1,715,200	1,712,300	1,712,000	1,709,400	1,698,600	-1.7
Rhode Island	138,813	157,347	151,612	147,629	145,342	145,118	143,793	142,854	142,481	142,008	141,959	142,014	142,150	-0.5	142,200	142,100	141,300	140,400	139,500	135,700	-4.5

See notes at end of table.

Table 203.20. Enrollment in public elementary and secondary schools, by region, state, and jurisdiction: Selected years, fall 1990 through fall 2028—Continued

Region, state, and jurisdiction	Actual total enrollment													Percent change in total enrollment, 2011 to 2016	Projected total enrollment						Percent change in total enrollment, 2016 to 2028
	Fall 1990	Fall 2000	Fall 2006	Fall 2007	Fall 2008	Fall 2009	Fall 2010	Fall 2011	Fall 2012	Fall 2013	Fall 2014	Fall 2015[1]	Fall 2016[2]		Fall 2017	Fall 2018	Fall 2019	Fall 2020	Fall 2021	Fall 2028	
1	2	3	4	5	6	7	8	9	10	11	12	13	14	15	16	17	18	19	20	21	22
South Carolina	622,112	677,411	708,021	712,317	718,113	723,143	725,838	727,186	735,998	745,657	756,523	763,533	771,250	6.1	776,700	781,600	786,900	792,700	798,300	822,000	6.6
South Dakota	129,164	128,603	121,158	121,606	126,429	123,713	126,128	128,016	130,471	130,890	133,040	134,253	136,302	6.5	137,600	139,100	140,800	142,400	143,900	151,000	10.8
Tennessee	824,595	909,161	978,368	964,259	971,950	972,549	987,422	999,693	993,496	993,556	995,475	1,001,235	1,001,562	0.2	1,002,200	1,001,300	1,002,000	1,004,700	1,007,600	1,044,400	4.3
Texas	3,382,887	4,059,619	4,599,509	4,674,832	4,752,148	4,850,210	4,935,715	5,000,470	5,077,659	5,153,702	5,233,765	5,301,477	5,360,849	7.2	5,414,700	5,462,600	5,506,400	5,549,800	5,587,800	5,861,300	9.3
Utah	446,652	481,485	523,386	576,244	559,778	571,586	585,552	598,832	613,279	625,461	635,577	647,870	659,801	10.2	667,400	674,600	681,600	688,000	693,000	732,400	11.0
Vermont	95,762	102,049	95,399	94,038	93,625	91,451	96,858	89,908	89,624	88,690	87,311	87,866	88,428	-1.6	86,700	85,900	85,100	84,500	83,800	80,400	-9.0
Virginia	998,601	1,144,915	1,220,440	1,230,857	1,235,795	1,245,340	1,251,440	1,257,883	1,265,419	1,273,825	1,280,381	1,283,590	1,287,026	2.3	1,290,400	1,291,200	1,292,100	1,293,600	1,295,100	1,316,200	2.3
Washington	839,709	1,004,770	1,026,774	1,030,247	1,037,018	1,035,347	1,043,788	1,045,453	1,051,694	1,058,936	1,073,638	1,087,030	1,101,711	5.4	1,115,200	1,128,400	1,141,700	1,157,300	1,171,600	1,253,600	13.8
West Virginia	322,389	286,367	281,939	282,535	282,729	282,662	282,879	282,870	283,044	280,958	280,310	277,452	273,855	-3.2	271,000	267,500	264,500	261,500	258,900	249,500	-8.9
Wisconsin	797,621	879,476	876,700	874,633	873,750	872,436	872,286	871,105	872,436	874,414	871,432	867,800	864,432	-0.8	860,700	856,900	853,700	851,800	848,900	837,900	-3.1
Wyoming	98,226	89,940	85,193	86,422	87,161	88,155	89,009	90,099	91,533	92,732	94,067	94,717	94,170	4.5	93,700	93,500	93,300	93,200	92,900	92,800	-1.4
Jurisdiction																					
Bureau of Indian Education	—	46,938	—	—	40,927	41,351	41,962	—	—	—	—	—	45,399	—	—	—	—	—	—	—	—
DoDEA[3]	—	107,755	87,522	84,795	84,781	—	—	—	—	—	—	74,970	—	—	—	—	—	—	—	—	—
Other jurisdictions																					
American Samoa	12,463	15,702	16,400	—	—	—	—	—	—	—	—	—	—	—	—	—	—	—	—	—	—
Guam	26,391	32,473	—	—	—	—	31,618	31,243	31,186	33,414	31,144	30,821	30,758	-1.6	—	—	—	—	—	—	—
Northern Marianas	6,449	10,004	11,695	11,299	10,913	10,961	11,105	11,011	10,646	10,638	—	—	—	—	—	—	—	—	—	—	—
Puerto Rico	644,734	612,725	544,138	526,565	503,635	493,393	473,735	452,740	434,609	423,934	410,950	379,818	365,181	-19.3	—	—	—	—	—	—	—
U.S. Virgin Islands	21,750	19,459	16,284	15,903	15,768	15,493	15,495	15,711	15,192	14,953	14,241	13,805	13,194	-16.0	—	—	—	—	—	—	—

—Not available.
#Rounds to zero.
[1]Includes imputations for prekindergarten enrollment in California and Oregon.
[2]Includes imputations for prekindergarten enrollment in California.
[3]DoDEA = Department of Defense Education Activity. Includes both domestic and overseas schools.

NOTE: Detail may not sum to totals because of rounding. Some data have been revised from previously published figures.
SOURCE: U.S. Department of Education, National Center for Education Statistics, Common Core of Data (CCD), "State Nonfiscal Survey of Public Elementary/Secondary Education," 1990–91 through 2016–17; and State Public Elementary and Secondary Enrollment Projection Model, 1980 through 2028. (This table was prepared March 2019.)

Table 203.40. Enrollment in public elementary and secondary schools, by level, grade, and state or jurisdiction: Fall 2016

State or jurisdiction	Total, all grades	Elementary												Secondary					
		Total	Prekindergarten	Kindergarten	Grade 1	Grade 2	Grade 3	Grade 4	Grade 5	Grade 6	Grade 7	Grade 8	Elementary ungraded	Total	Grade 9	Grade 10	Grade 11	Grade 12	Secondary ungraded[1]
1	2	3	4	5	6	7	8	9	10	11	12	13	14	15	16	17	18	19	20
United States	**50,615,189**	**35,477,332**	**1,425,654**	**3,699,159**	**3,693,847**	**3,760,772**	**3,874,023**	**3,858,436**	**3,813,738**	**3,753,910**	**3,761,002**	**3,748,905**	**87,886**	**15,137,857**	**3,986,172**	**3,859,678**	**3,669,059**	**3,571,441**	**51,507**
Alabama	744,930	522,292	14,755	55,474	56,577	57,608	58,554	57,945	55,798	55,256	55,270	55,055	0	222,638	58,792	57,037	54,489	52,320	0
Alaska	132,737	94,164	3,246	10,274	10,431	10,523	10,474	10,320	10,116	9,750	9,620	9,410	0	38,573	9,615	9,569	9,649	9,740	0
Arizona	1,123,137	783,905	9,704	79,760	82,115	85,620	88,897	89,184	88,101	87,055	86,762	86,312	395	339,232	85,960	85,327	80,948	86,960	37
Arkansas	493,447	350,297	16,181	36,917	37,251	37,759	38,586	38,598	35,930	36,055	36,515	36,351	154	143,150	38,327	36,829	35,048	32,881	65
California	6,309,138	4,367,509	80,903[2]	535,379	456,002	445,553	465,165	471,141	487,493	475,809	473,574	472,340	4,150	1,941,629	487,548	486,085	481,521	484,169	2,306
Colorado	905,019	639,519	32,452	64,011	65,380	67,480	69,225	69,376	68,757	67,638	67,541	67,659	0	265,500	68,476	66,463	64,317	66,244	0
Connecticut	535,118	368,843	18,536	36,621	36,877	37,815	38,651	39,859	39,417	39,820	40,119	41,128	0	166,275	43,024	41,741	40,679	40,831	0
Delaware	136,264	95,760	1,761	9,894	10,199	10,653	10,854	10,612	10,683	10,482	10,323	10,299	0	40,504	11,584	10,488	9,431	9,001	0
District of Columbia	85,850	66,798	12,544	7,574	7,138	6,825	6,590	6,295	5,596	5,024	4,655	4,557	0	19,052	6,501	4,607	4,144	3,800	0
Florida	2,816,791	1,969,010	60,332	201,060	205,870	213,263	232,380	212,595	217,601	209,332	208,241	208,336	0	847,781	218,689	220,866	210,345	197,881	0
Georgia	1,764,346	1,245,574	47,430	127,056	129,819	134,827	138,526	137,963	135,225	132,118	131,833	130,777	0	518,772	149,914	136,137	121,183	111,538	0
Hawaii	181,550	131,141	1,648	14,652	15,036	12,009	15,701	15,459	15,027	14,416	13,867	13,091	235	50,409	14,397	12,810	12,435	10,574	193
Idaho	297,200	208,561	2,536	21,085	22,102	22,724	23,592	23,765	23,209	23,563	23,167	22,818	0	88,639	23,108	22,689	21,695	21,084	63
Illinois	2,026,718	1,408,702	85,018	134,735	140,517	144,613	150,449	151,903	149,356	149,824	151,688	150,595	4	618,016	160,014	158,488	151,057	148,457	0
Indiana	1,049,547	725,811	18,882	76,874	77,100	77,930	82,108	78,034	78,511	77,690	79,373	78,029	1,280	323,736	82,040	83,417	80,776	77,503	0
Iowa	509,831	362,666	29,307	38,178	36,000	36,578	37,862	37,830	37,284	36,738	36,351	36,538	0	147,165	37,155	36,921	36,522	36,567	0
Kansas	494,347	351,447	19,302	35,750	36,675	36,794	37,498	37,692	36,894	36,066	36,120	35,948	2,708	142,900	37,185	35,989	34,923	33,784	1,019
Kentucky	684,017	485,275	26,902	48,888	50,987	51,602	52,291	52,487	51,290	50,186	50,148	50,098	396	198,742	53,529	51,678	48,704	44,668	163
Louisiana	716,293	516,206	27,974	53,103	55,067	56,039	56,546	56,267	53,558	53,103	52,937	51,612	0	200,087	58,085	51,852	47,718	42,432	0
Maine	180,512	124,938	5,437	12,650	12,661	13,102	13,249	13,561	13,424	13,630	13,724	13,500	0	55,574	13,823	14,045	13,838	13,868	0
Maryland	886,221	630,440	30,945	64,472	66,290	68,059	69,776	69,182	67,087	65,026	65,081	64,522	0	255,781	71,465	65,022	60,991	58,303	0
Massachusetts	964,514	669,178	29,633	66,249	68,327	70,079	72,167	72,481	71,399	71,121	72,454	72,576	2,692	295,336	77,287	74,452	72,595	71,002	0
Michigan	1,528,666	1,047,414	48,416	115,715	104,619	105,309	107,885	111,742	111,760	110,994	114,603	113,678	2,693	481,252	123,873	124,056	116,442	115,605	1,276
Minnesota	875,021	607,084	18,960	63,295	63,819	65,247	66,846	67,087	65,921	65,048	66,005	64,856	0	267,937	65,465	66,679	65,578	70,215	0
Mississippi	483,150	345,125	5,361	36,652	37,449	38,922	39,728	39,282	35,963	35,947	36,223	35,049	4,549	138,025	36,763	35,340	32,994	29,717	3,211
Missouri	915,040	647,307	31,808	66,052	67,198	68,602	70,499	70,736	69,159	68,141	67,834	67,278	0	267,733	69,279	68,496	66,214	63,744	0
Montana	146,375	104,337	1,066	11,678	11,149	11,546	11,990	11,687	11,764	11,186	11,227	11,044	0	42,038	11,336	10,802	10,081	9,819	0
Nebraska	319,194	226,051	16,467	22,283	23,400	24,019	24,026	22,378	23,525	23,168	23,607	23,178	0	93,143	23,348	23,276	22,922	23,597	0
Nevada	473,744	333,991	5,426	34,626	35,868	36,178	37,853	38,160	36,922	36,417	35,778	35,895	868	139,753	36,053	35,895	34,835	32,940	30
New Hampshire	180,888	123,602	3,965	11,430	12,460	12,907	13,325	13,644	13,747	13,771	14,186	14,167	0	57,286	15,316	14,473	13,989	13,502	6
New Jersey	1,410,421	990,740	62,149	91,197	95,812	98,025	100,139	101,704	99,427	98,545	100,625	100,200	42,917	419,681	103,145	101,373	99,872	98,490	16,801
New Mexico	336,263	236,407	7,430	24,301	24,703	26,112	26,528	26,358	25,692	25,409	24,973	24,901	0	99,856	29,185	26,105	23,143	21,423	0
New York	2,729,776	1,886,863	65,600	194,163	199,955	202,245	202,909	203,159	200,174	197,035	197,909	200,060	23,654	842,913	217,639	211,140	196,645	193,375	24,114
North Carolina	1,550,062	1,080,196	18,782	114,414	117,638	120,924	122,483	122,411	119,305	116,637	109,554	118,048	0	469,866	130,064	123,258	112,763	102,028	1,753
North Dakota	109,706	79,249	2,665	8,843	8,723	8,847	8,761	8,678	8,458	8,132	8,204	7,938	0	30,457	8,015	7,793	7,273	7,376	0
Ohio	1,710,143	1,190,358	36,148	122,516	124,598	127,317	132,576	129,706	128,995	126,726	130,737	131,039	0	519,785	142,344	136,286	119,688	121,467	0
Oklahoma	693,903	504,388	41,249	52,194	53,916	53,165	53,818	52,289	50,213	47,729	49,389	49,235	1,191	189,515	51,259	48,995	46,119	42,672	470
Oregon	606,277	425,768	27,330[3]	41,796	43,117	44,379	45,985	46,094	45,125	43,818	44,174	43,950	0	180,509	44,230	44,893	43,927	47,459	0
Pennsylvania	1,727,497	1,183,671	7,859	122,763	125,819	128,865	132,987	133,723	132,238	131,299	134,541	133,577	0	543,826	139,907	138,338	133,335	132,246	0
Rhode Island	142,150	98,871	2,498	10,059	10,231	10,490	10,891	11,055	10,933	10,788	11,087	10,839	0	43,279	11,826	11,199	10,210	10,044	0
South Carolina	771,250	547,928	25,613	55,424	57,152	60,004	60,403	60,797	58,277	57,346	56,736	56,176	0	223,322	64,797	57,792	52,476	48,257	0
South Dakota	136,302	98,712	3,290	11,643	10,518	10,635	10,840	10,866	10,574	10,503	10,115	9,728	0	37,590	10,326	9,584	8,972	8,708	0
Tennessee	1,001,562	708,027	27,987	74,667	74,356	74,699	77,792	78,472	77,105	74,948	74,290	73,711	0	293,535	76,802	75,428	72,453	68,852	0
Texas	5,360,849	3,835,671	248,116	372,019	395,816	408,841	412,782	411,117	400,196	398,196	396,167	392,421	0	1,525,178	432,402	395,697	364,110	332,969	0
Utah	659,801	471,213	15,280	48,264	49,951	51,045	52,473	52,802	51,404	50,232	50,264	49,498	0	188,588	48,596	47,912	46,803	45,277	0
Vermont	88,428	62,855	8,498	5,822	5,832	5,766	6,231	6,194	6,034	6,201	6,160	6,117	0	25,573	6,561	6,517	6,308	6,187	0
Virginia	1,287,026	897,696	33,281	90,800	94,000	96,570	99,022	99,258	97,165	95,956	96,410	95,234	0	389,330	104,051	99,936	94,843	90,500	0
Washington	1,101,711	762,362	13,933	81,102	82,224	84,872	86,566	86,114	83,639	81,483	81,390	81,039	0	339,349	81,927	83,512	83,265	90,645	0
West Virginia	273,855	194,413	14,949	19,869	19,570	19,840	20,178	20,324	19,608	19,936	20,208	19,931	0	79,442	22,065	20,289	18,933	18,155	0
Wisconsin	864,432	601,751	55,436	57,332	58,225	60,524	61,750	62,408	61,207	61,265	62,172	61,432	0	262,681	65,868	65,170	65,340	66,303	0
Wyoming	94,170	67,246	664	7,584	7,308	7,422	7,616	7,642	7,452	7,352	7,071	7,135	0	26,924	7,212	6,932	6,518	6,262	0

See notes at end of table.

Table 203.40. Enrollment in public elementary and secondary schools, by level, grade, and state or jurisdiction: Fall 2016—Continued

State or jurisdiction	Total, all grades	Elementary												Secondary					
		Total	Prekindergarten	Kindergarten	Grade 1	Grade 2	Grade 3	Grade 4	Grade 5	Grade 6	Grade 7	Grade 8	Elementary ungraded	Total	Grade 9	Grade 10	Grade 11	Grade 12	Secondary ungraded[1]
1	2	3	4	5	6	7	8	9	10	11	12	13	14	15	16	17	18	19	20
Bureau of Indian Education	45,399	34,132	—	4,330	3,942	3,823	3,944	3,762	3,736	3,705	3,508	3,382	—	11,267	3,335	2,936	2,575	2,421	—
DoDEA	—	—	—	—	—	—	—	—	—	—	—	—	—	—	—	—	—	—	—
Other jurisdictions																			
AmericanSamoa	—	—	—	—	—	—	—	—	—	—	—	—	—	—	—	—	—	—	—
Guam	30,758	20,621	585	1,976	2,174	2,244	2,377	2,355	2,268	2,187	2,273	2,182	—	10,137	3,135	2,892	2,454	1,656	—
Northern Marianas	—	—	—	—	—	—	—	—	—	—	—	—	—	—	—	—	—	—	—
Puerto Rico	365,181	251,197	2,876	23,599	26,777	26,477	26,294	26,859	26,916	27,649	27,953	27,279	8,518	113,984	27,576	28,466	27,507	25,830	4,605
U.S. Virgin Islands	13,194	9,037	—	886	956	1,051	1,061	1,030	1,048	1,022	1,030	953	—	4,157	1,401	973	911	872	—

—Not available.
[1]Includes students reported as being enrolled in grade 13.
[2]Estimated by the National Center for Education Statistics based on reports for prior years.
[3]Based on later data submissions not included in the published data file.

NOTE: DoDEA = Department of Defense Education Activity. The total ungraded counts of students were prorated to the elementary and secondary levels based on prior state reports of the percentage of elementary and of secondary ungraded students.
SOURCE: U.S. Department of Education, National Center for Education Statistics, Common Core of Data (CCD), "State Nonfiscal Survey of Public Elementary/Secondary Education," 2016–17. (This table was prepared September 2018.)

Table 203.50. Enrollment and percentage distribution of enrollment in public elementary and secondary schools, by race/ethnicity and region: Selected years, fall 1995 through fall 2028

Region and year	Enrollment (in thousands)								Percentage distribution							
	Total	White	Black	Hispanic	Asian	Pacific Islander	American Indian/ Alaska Native	Two or more races	Total	White	Black	Hispanic	Asian	Pacific Islander	American Indian/ Alaska Native	Two or more races
1	2	3	4	5	6	7	8	9	10	11	12	13	14	15	16	17
United States																
1995	44,840	29,044	7,551	6,072	1,668[1]	—	505	—	100.0	64.8	16.8	13.5	3.7[1]	—	1.1	—
2000	47,204	28,878	8,100	7,726	1,950[1]	—	550	—	100.0	61.2	17.2	16.4	4.1[1]	—	1.2	—
2001	47,672	28,735	8,177	8,169	2,028[1]	—	564	—	100.0	60.3	17.2	17.1	4.3[1]	—	1.2	—
2002	48,183	28,618	8,299	8,594	2,088[1]	—	583	—	100.0	59.4	17.2	17.8	4.3[1]	—	1.2	—
2003	48,540	28,442	8,349	9,011	2,145[1]	—	593	—	100.0	58.6	17.2	18.6	4.4[1]	—	1.2	—
2004	48,795	28,318	8,386	9,317	2,183[1]	—	591	—	100.0	58.0	17.2	19.1	4.5[1]	—	1.2	—
2005	49,113	28,005	8,445	9,787	2,279[1]	—	598	—	100.0	57.0	17.2	19.9	4.6[1]	—	1.2	—
2006	49,316	27,801	8,422	10,166	2,332[1]	—	595	—	100.0	56.4	17.1	20.6	4.7[1]	—	1.2	—
2007	49,291	27,454	8,392	10,454	2,396[1]	—	594	—	100.0	55.7	17.0	21.2	4.9[1]	—	1.2	—
2008	49,266	27,057	8,358	10,563	2,405	46	589	247[2]	100.0	54.9	17.0	21.4	4.9	0.1	1.2	0.5[2]
2009	49,361	26,702	8,245	10,991	2,435	49	601	338[2]	100.0	54.1	16.7	22.3	4.9	0.1	1.2	0.7[2]
2010	49,484	25,933	7,917	11,439	2,296	171	566	1,164	100.0	52.4	16.0	23.1	4.6	0.3	1.1	2.4
2011	49,522	25,602	7,827	11,759	2,334	179	547	1,272	100.0	51.7	15.8	23.7	4.7	0.4	1.1	2.6
2012	49,771	25,386	7,803	12,104	2,372	180	534	1,393	100.0	51.0	15.7	24.3	4.8	0.4	1.1	2.8
2013	50,045	25,160	7,805	12,452	2,417	176	523	1,511	100.0	50.3	15.6	24.9	4.8	0.4	1.0	3.0
2014	50,313	24,923	7,807	12,805	2,470	176	519	1,612	100.0	49.5	15.5	25.4	4.9	0.3	1.0	3.2
2015[3]	50,438	24,644	7,784	13,080	2,521	177	510	1,723	100.0	48.9	15.4	25.9	5.0	0.4	1.0	3.4
2016[4]	50,615	24,413	7,765	13,329	2,571	184	511	1,842	100.0	48.2	15.3	26.3	5.1	0.4	1.0	3.6
2017[5]	50,695	24,149	7,734	13,561	2,616	183	507	1,946	100.0	47.6	15.3	26.7	5.2	0.4	1.0	3.8
2018[5]	50,728	23,888	7,698	13,752	2,660	184	504	2,043	100.0	47.1	15.2	27.1	5.2	0.4	1.0	4.0
2019[5]	50,770	23,659	7,672	13,921	2,696	184	501	2,136	100.0	46.6	15.1	27.4	5.3	0.4	1.0	4.2
2020[5]	50,857	23,462	7,663	14,084	2,738	185	498	2,227	100.0	46.1	15.1	27.7	5.4	0.4	1.0	4.4
2021[5]	50,892	23,277	7,654	14,207	2,764	185	494	2,311	100.0	45.7	15.0	27.9	5.4	0.4	1.0	4.5
2022[5]	51,012	23,163	7,707	14,263	2,812	182	490	2,394	100.0	45.4	15.1	28.0	5.5	0.4	1.0	4.7
2023[5]	51,098	23,051	7,741	14,298	2,858	180	487	2,483	100.0	45.1	15.1	28.0	5.6	0.4	1.0	4.9
2024[5]	51,124	22,940	7,760	14,296	2,908	179	483	2,557	100.0	44.9	15.2	28.0	5.7	0.3	0.9	5.0
2025[5]	51,119	22,828	7,775	14,279	2,959	178	480	2,621	100.0	44.7	15.2	27.9	5.8	0.3	0.9	5.1
2026[5]	51,123	22,734	7,787	14,261	3,010	177	477	2,677	100.0	44.5	15.2	27.9	5.9	0.3	0.9	5.2
2027[5]	51,228	22,684	7,811	14,277	3,069	177	475	2,734	100.0	44.3	15.2	27.9	6.0	0.3	0.9	5.3
2028[5]	51,419	22,662	7,857	14,334	3,126	177	474	2,788	100.0	44.1	15.3	27.9	6.1	0.3	0.9	5.4
Northeast																
1995	7,894	5,497	1,202	878	295[1]	—	21	—	100.0	69.6	15.2	11.1	3.7[1]	—	0.3	—
2000	8,222	5,545	1,270	1,023	361[1]	—	24	—	100.0	67.4	15.4	12.4	4.4[1]	—	0.3	—
2005	8,240	5,317	1,282	1,189	425[1]	—	27	—	100.0	64.5	15.6	14.4	5.2[1]	—	0.3	—
2010	8,071	4,876	1,208	1,364	494	6	27	96	100.0	60.4	15.0	16.9	6.1	0.1	0.3	1.2
2013	7,961	4,593	1,158	1,492	526	6	28	158	100.0	57.7	14.5	18.7	6.6	0.1	0.3	2.0
2014	7,980	4,507	1,155	1,566	538	7	28	179	100.0	56.5	14.5	19.6	6.7	0.1	0.4	2.2
2015[3]	7,934	4,409	1,136	1,610	547	7	29	197	100.0	55.6	14.3	20.3	6.9	0.1	0.4	2.5
2016[4]	7,959	4,345	1,132	1,668	558	13	30	214	100.0	54.6	14.2	21.0	7.0	0.2	0.4	2.7
Midwest																
1995	10,512	8,335	1,450	438	197[1]	—	92	—	100.0	79.3	13.8	4.2	1.9[1]	—	0.9	—
2000	10,730	8,208	1,581	610	239[1]	—	92	—	100.0	76.5	14.7	5.7	2.2[1]	—	0.9	—
2005	10,819	7,950	1,654	836	283[1]	—	96	—	100.0	73.5	15.3	7.7	2.6[1]	—	0.9	—
2010	10,610	7,327	1,505	1,077	303	9	94	294	100.0	69.1	14.2	10.2	2.9	0.1	0.9	2.8
2013	10,573	7,111	1,464	1,212	330	11	87	358	100.0	67.3	13.8	11.5	3.1	0.1	0.8	3.4
2014	10,561	7,037	1,459	1,249	338	11	86	380	100.0	66.6	13.8	11.8	3.2	0.1	0.8	3.6
2015[3]	10,556	6,968	1,458	1,284	348	12	84	400	100.0	66.0	13.8	12.2	3.3	0.1	0.8	3.8
2016[4]	10,539	6,893	1,449	1,312	360	12	86	426	100.0	65.4	13.8	12.4	3.4	0.1	0.8	4.0
South																
1995	16,118	9,565	4,236	1,890	280[1]	—	148	—	100.0	59.3	26.3	11.7	1.7[1]	—	0.9	—
2000	17,007	9,501	4,516	2,468	352[1]	—	170	—	100.0	55.9	26.6	14.5	2.1[1]	—	1.0	—
2005	18,103	9,381	4,738	3,334	456[1]	—	194	—	100.0	51.8	26.2	18.4	2.5[1]	—	1.1	—
2010	18,805	8,869	4,545	4,206	533	22	207	424	100.0	47.2	24.2	22.4	2.8	0.1	1.1	2.3
2013	19,299	8,722	4,561	4,671	588	26	185	546	100.0	45.2	23.6	24.2	3.0	0.1	1.0	2.8
2014	19,506	8,681	4,577	4,846	613	28	184	579	100.0	44.5	23.5	24.8	3.1	0.1	0.9	3.0
2015[3]	19,641	8,601	4,583	4,994	637	29	181	615	100.0	43.8	23.3	25.4	3.2	0.1	0.9	3.1
2016[4]	19,750	8,513	4,571	5,142	665	30	177	652	100.0	43.1	23.1	26.0	3.4	0.2	0.9	3.3
West																
1995	10,316	5,648	662	2,866	896[1]	—	244	—	100.0	54.7	6.4	27.8	8.7[1]	—	2.4	—
2000	11,244	5,624	733	3,625	998[1]	—	264	—	100.0	50.0	6.5	32.2	8.9[1]	—	2.4	—
2005	11,951	5,356	771	4,428	1,115[1]	—	281	—	100.0	44.8	6.5	37.1	9.3[1]	—	2.4	—
2010	11,998	4,861	659	4,792	966	133	237	349	100.0	40.5	5.5	39.9	8.1	1.1	2.0	2.9
2013	12,212	4,733	623	5,077	973	133	224	449	100.0	38.8	5.1	41.6	8.0	1.1	1.8	3.7
2014	12,266	4,698	616	5,144	982	130	221	475	100.0	38.3	5.0	41.9	8.0	1.1	1.8	3.9
2015[3]	12,307	4,665	606	5,192	988	129	216	511	100.0	37.9	4.9	42.2	8.0	1.1	1.8	4.2
2016[4]	12,367	4,662	612	5,208	989	128	217	550	100.0	37.7	5.0	42.1	8.0	1.0	1.8	4.4

—Not available.
[1]Includes Pacific Islanders.
[2]For this year, data on Pacific Islanders and students of Two or more races were reported by only a small number of states. Therefore, the data are not comparable to figures for 2010 and later years.
[3]Includes imputations for prekindergarten enrollment in California and Oregon.
[4]Includes imputations for prekindergarten enrollment in California.
[5]Projected.

NOTE: Race categories exclude persons of Hispanic ethnicity. Enrollment data for students not reported by race/ethnicity were prorated by state and grade to match state totals. Prior to 2008, data on students of Two or more races were not collected. Some data have been revised from previously published figures. Detail may not sum to totals because of rounding.
SOURCE: U.S. Department of Education, National Center for Education Statistics, Common Core of Data (CCD), "State Nonfiscal Survey of Public Elementary and Secondary Education," 1995–96 through 2016–17; and National Elementary and Secondary Enrollment by Race/Ethnicity Projection Model, 1972 through 2028. (This table was prepared March 2019.)

Table 203.60. Enrollment and percentage distribution of enrollment in public elementary and secondary schools, by race/ethnicity and level of education: Fall 1999 through fall 2028

Level of education and year	Enrollment (in thousands)									Percentage distribution								
	Total	White	Black	His-panic	Asian/Pacific Islander			American Indian/ Alaska Native	Two or more races	Total	White	Black	His-panic	Asian/Pacific Islander			American Indian/ Alaska Native	Two or more races
					Total	Asian	Pacific Islander							Total	Asian	Pacific Islander		
1	2	3	4	5	6	7	8	9	10	11	12	13	14	15	16	17	18	19
Total																		
1999	46,857	29,035	8,066	7,327	1,887	—	—	542	—	100.0	62.0	17.2	15.6	4.0	†	†	1.2	†
2000	47,204	28,878	8,100	7,726	1,950	—	—	550	—	100.0	61.2	17.2	16.4	4.1	†	†	1.2	†
2001	47,672	28,735	8,177	8,169	2,028	—	—	564	—	100.0	60.3	17.2	17.1	4.3	†	†	1.2	†
2002	48,183	28,618	8,299	8,594	2,088	—	—	583	—	100.0	59.4	17.2	17.8	4.3	†	†	1.2	†
2003	48,540	28,442	8,349	9,011	2,145	—	—	593	—	100.0	58.6	17.2	18.6	4.4	†	†	1.2	†
2004	48,795	28,318	8,386	9,317	2,183	—	—	591	—	100.0	58.0	17.2	19.1	4.5	†	†	1.2	†
2005	49,113	28,005	8,445	9,787	2,279	—	—	598	—	100.0	57.0	17.2	19.9	4.6	†	†	1.2	†
2006	49,316	27,801	8,422	10,166	2,332	—	—	595	—	100.0	56.4	17.1	20.6	4.7	†	†	1.2	†
2007	49,291	27,454	8,392	10,454	2,396	—	—	594	—	100.0	55.7	17.0	21.2	4.9	†	†	1.2	†
2008	49,266	27,057	8,358	10,563	2,451	2,405	46	589	247[1]	100.0	54.9	17.0	21.4	5.0	4.9	0.1	1.2	0.5[1]
2009	49,361	26,702	8,245	10,991	2,484	2,435	49	601	338[1]	100.0	54.1	16.7	22.3	5.0	4.9	0.1	1.2	0.7[1]
2010	49,484	25,933	7,917	11,439	2,466	2,296	171	566	1,164	100.0	52.4	16.0	23.1	5.0	4.6	0.3	1.1	2.4
2011	49,522	25,602	7,827	11,759	2,513	2,334	179	547	1,272	100.0	51.7	15.8	23.7	5.1	4.7	0.4	1.1	2.6
2012	49,771	25,386	7,803	12,104	2,552	2,372	180	534	1,393	100.0	51.0	15.7	24.3	5.1	4.8	0.4	1.1	2.8
2013	50,045	25,160	7,805	12,452	2,593	2,417	176	523	1,511	100.0	50.3	15.6	24.9	5.2	4.8	0.4	1.0	3.0
2014	50,313	24,923	7,807	12,805	2,646	2,470	176	519	1,612	100.0	49.5	15.5	25.4	5.3	4.9	0.3	1.0	3.2
2015[2]	50,438	24,644	7,784	13,080	2,697	2,521	177	510	1,723	100.0	48.9	15.4	25.9	5.3	5.0	0.4	1.0	3.4
2016[3]	50,615	24,413	7,765	13,329	2,756	2,571	184	511	1,842	100.0	48.2	15.3	26.3	5.4	5.1	0.4	1.0	3.6
2017[4]	50,695	24,149	7,734	13,561	2,799	2,616	183	507	1,946	100.0	47.6	15.3	26.7	5.5	5.2	0.4	1.0	3.8
2018[4]	50,728	23,888	7,698	13,752	2,844	2,660	184	504	2,043	100.0	47.1	15.2	27.1	5.6	5.2	0.4	1.0	4.0
2019[4]	50,770	23,659	7,672	13,921	2,881	2,696	184	501	2,136	100.0	46.6	15.1	27.4	5.7	5.3	0.4	1.0	4.2
2020[4]	50,857	23,462	7,663	14,084	2,923	2,738	185	498	2,227	100.0	46.1	15.1	27.7	5.7	5.4	0.4	1.0	4.4
2021[4]	50,892	23,277	7,654	14,207	2,949	2,764	185	494	2,311	100.0	45.7	15.0	27.9	5.8	5.4	0.4	1.0	4.5
2022[4]	51,012	23,163	7,707	14,263	2,994	2,812	182	490	2,394	100.0	45.4	15.1	28.0	5.9	5.5	0.4	1.0	4.7
2023[4]	51,098	23,051	7,741	14,298	3,039	2,858	180	487	2,483	100.0	45.1	15.1	28.0	5.9	5.6	0.4	1.0	4.9
2024[4]	51,124	22,940	7,760	14,296	3,087	2,908	179	483	2,557	100.0	44.9	15.2	28.0	6.0	5.7	0.3	0.9	5.0
2025[4]	51,119	22,828	7,775	14,279	3,137	2,959	178	480	2,621	100.0	44.7	15.2	27.9	6.1	5.8	0.3	0.9	5.1
2026[4]	51,123	22,734	7,787	14,261	3,187	3,010	177	477	2,677	100.0	44.5	15.2	27.9	6.2	5.9	0.3	0.9	5.2
2027[4]	51,228	22,684	7,811	14,277	3,246	3,069	177	475	2,734	100.0	44.3	15.2	27.9	6.3	6.0	0.3	0.9	5.3
2028[4]	51,419	22,662	7,857	14,334	3,303	3,126	177	474	2,788	100.0	44.1	15.3	27.9	6.4	6.1	0.3	0.9	5.4
Prekindergarten through grade 8																		
1999	33,486	20,327	5,952	5,512	1,303	—	—	391	—	100.0	60.7	17.8	16.5	3.9	†	†	1.2	†
2000	33,686	20,130	5,981	5,830	1,349	—	—	397	—	100.0	59.8	17.8	17.3	4.0	†	†	1.2	†
2001	33,936	19,960	6,004	6,159	1,409	—	—	405	—	100.0	58.8	17.7	18.1	4.2	†	†	1.2	†
2002	34,114	19,764	6,042	6,446	1,447	—	—	415	—	100.0	57.9	17.7	18.9	4.2	†	†	1.2	†
2003	34,201	19,558	6,015	6,729	1,483	—	—	415	—	100.0	57.2	17.6	19.7	4.3	†	†	1.2	†
2004	34,178	19,368	5,983	6,909	1,504	—	—	413	—	100.0	56.7	17.5	20.2	4.4	†	†	1.2	†
2005	34,204	19,051	5,954	7,216	1,569	—	—	412	—	100.0	55.7	17.4	21.1	4.6	†	†	1.2	†
2006	34,235	18,863	5,882	7,465	1,611	—	—	414	—	100.0	55.1	17.2	21.8	4.7	†	†	1.2	†
2007	34,204	18,679	5,821	7,632	1,660	—	—	412	—	100.0	54.6	17.0	22.3	4.9	†	†	1.2	†
2008	34,286	18,501	5,793	7,689	1,705	1,674	31	410	187[1]	100.0	54.0	16.9	22.4	5.0	4.9	0.1	1.2	0.5[1]
2009	34,409	18,316	5,713	7,977	1,730	1,697	33	419	254[1]	100.0	53.2	16.6	23.2	5.0	4.9	0.1	1.2	0.7[1]
2010	34,625	17,823	5,495	8,314	1,711	1,589	122	394	887	100.0	51.5	15.9	24.0	4.9	4.6	0.4	1.1	2.6
2011	34,773	17,654	5,470	8,558	1,744	1,616	128	384	963	100.0	50.8	15.7	24.6	5.0	4.6	0.4	1.1	2.8
2012	35,018	17,535	5,473	8,804	1,773	1,644	129	375	1,057	100.0	50.1	15.6	25.1	5.1	4.7	0.4	1.1	3.0
2013	35,251	17,390	5,483	9,054	1,809	1,683	126	367	1,148	100.0	49.3	15.6	25.7	5.1	4.8	0.4	1.0	3.3
2014	35,370	17,193	5,471	9,273	1,842	1,718	124	363	1,227	100.0	48.6	15.5	26.2	5.2	4.9	0.4	1.0	3.5
2015[2]	35,388	16,972	5,448	9,424	1,878	1,754	124	356	1,311	100.0	48.0	15.4	26.6	5.3	5.0	0.4	1.0	3.7
2016[3]	35,477	16,823	5,440	9,544	1,914	1,784	129	358	1,399	100.0	47.4	15.3	26.9	5.4	5.0	0.4	1.0	3.9
2017[4]	35,473	16,641	5,434	9,643	1,930	1,802	128	355	1,470	100.0	46.9	15.3	27.2	5.4	5.1	0.4	1.0	4.1
2018[4]	35,465	16,468	5,437	9,721	1,957	1,829	128	352	1,530	100.0	46.4	15.3	27.4	5.5	5.2	0.4	1.0	4.3
2019[4]	35,457	16,335	5,441	9,771	1,976	1,850	126	350	1,584	100.0	46.1	15.3	27.6	5.6	5.2	0.4	1.0	4.5
2020[4]	35,384	16,193	5,428	9,789	2,004	1,878	126	346	1,624	100.0	45.8	15.3	27.7	5.7	5.3	0.4	1.0	4.6
2021[4]	35,231	16,056	5,394	9,766	2,021	1,896	126	342	1,651	100.0	45.6	15.3	27.7	5.7	5.4	0.4	1.0	4.7
2022[4]	35,189	16,008	5,413	9,692	2,059	1,935	124	339	1,678	100.0	45.5	15.4	27.5	5.9	5.5	0.4	1.0	4.8
2023[4]	35,235	15,989	5,431	9,661	2,101	1,978	124	336	1,717	100.0	45.4	15.4	27.4	6.0	5.6	0.4	1.0	4.9
2024[4]	35,376	16,007	5,474	9,667	2,141	2,018	123	335	1,751	100.0	45.2	15.5	27.3	6.1	5.7	0.3	0.9	5.0
2025[4]	35,519	16,019	5,516	9,669	2,191	2,068	123	334	1,790	100.0	45.1	15.5	27.2	6.2	5.8	0.3	0.9	5.0
2026[4]	35,703	16,031	5,561	9,705	2,236	2,113	123	333	1,837	100.0	44.9	15.6	27.2	6.3	5.9	0.3	0.9	5.1
2027[4]	35,894	16,037	5,606	9,757	2,273	2,151	122	333	1,888	100.0	44.7	15.6	27.2	6.3	6.0	0.3	0.9	5.3
2028[4]	36,073	16,022	5,648	9,813	2,316	2,194	122	333	1,941	100.0	44.4	15.7	27.2	6.4	6.1	0.3	0.9	5.4

See notes at end of table.

Table 203.60. Enrollment and percentage distribution of enrollment in public elementary and secondary schools, by race/ethnicity and level of education: Fall 1999 through fall 2028—Continued

Level of education and year	Enrollment (in thousands)									Percentage distribution								
					Asian/Pacific Islander			American Indian/ Alaska Native	Two or more races					Asian/Pacific Islander			American Indian/ Alaska Native	Two or more races
	Total	White	Black	His-panic	Total	Asian	Pacific Islander			Total	White	Black	His-panic	Total	Asian	Pacific Islander		
1	2	3	4	5	6	7	8	9	10	11	12	13	14	15	16	17	18	19
Grades 9 through 12																		
1999	13,371	8,708	2,114	1,815	584	—	—	151	—	100.0	65.1	15.8	13.6	4.4	†	†	1.1	†
2000	13,517	8,747	2,119	1,896	601	—	—	153	—	100.0	64.7	15.7	14.0	4.4	†	†	1.1	†
2001	13,736	8,774	2,173	2,011	619	—	—	159	—	100.0	63.9	15.8	14.6	4.5	†	†	1.2	†
2002	14,069	8,854	2,257	2,148	642	—	—	168	—	100.0	62.9	16.0	15.3	4.6	†	†	1.2	†
2003	14,339	8,884	2,334	2,282	663	—	—	177	—	100.0	62.0	16.3	15.9	4.6	†	†	1.2	†
2004	14,618	8,950	2,403	2,408	679	—	—	178	—	100.0	61.2	16.4	16.5	4.6	†	†	1.2	†
2005	14,909	8,954	2,490	2,570	709	—	—	186	—	100.0	60.1	16.7	17.2	4.8	†	†	1.2	†
2006	15,081	8,938	2,540	2,701	720	—	—	181	—	100.0	59.3	16.8	17.9	4.8	†	†	1.2	†
2007	15,086	8,775	2,571	2,821	736	—	—	183	—	100.0	58.2	17.0	18.7	4.9	†	†	1.2	†
2008	14,980	8,556	2,565	2,874	746	731	15	179	59[1]	100.0	57.1	17.1	19.2	5.0	4.9	0.1	1.2	0.4[1]
2009	14,952	8,385	2,532	3,014	754	738	16	182	84[1]	100.0	56.1	16.9	20.2	5.0	4.9	0.1	1.2	0.6[1]
2010	14,860	8,109	2,422	3,125	755	707	49	171	277	100.0	54.6	16.3	21.0	5.1	4.8	0.3	1.2	1.9
2011	14,749	7,948	2,357	3,202	769	719	50	163	309	100.0	53.9	16.0	21.7	5.2	4.9	0.3	1.1	2.1
2012	14,753	7,851	2,330	3,300	779	727	51	158	335	100.0	53.2	15.8	22.4	5.3	4.9	0.3	1.1	2.3
2013	14,794	7,770	2,322	3,398	784	733	51	156	363	100.0	52.5	15.7	23.0	5.3	5.0	0.3	1.1	2.5
2014	14,943	7,730	2,336	3,532	804	753	52	156	385	100.0	51.7	15.6	23.6	5.4	5.0	0.3	1.0	2.6
2015	15,050	7,672	2,336	3,656	819	767	52	154	412	100.0	51.0	15.5	24.3	5.4	5.1	0.3	1.0	2.7
2016	15,138	7,590	2,324	3,786	842	787	55	153	443	100.0	50.1	15.4	25.0	5.6	5.2	0.4	1.0	2.9
2017[4]	15,222	7,508	2,300	3,917	869	813	56	152	476	100.0	49.3	15.1	25.7	5.7	5.3	0.4	1.0	3.1
2018[4]	15,264	7,420	2,261	4,031	887	830	57	151	513	100.0	48.6	14.8	26.4	5.8	5.4	0.4	1.0	3.4
2019[4]	15,313	7,324	2,231	4,149	904	846	58	151	552	100.0	47.8	14.6	27.1	5.9	5.5	0.4	1.0	3.6
2020[4]	15,473	7,269	2,235	4,294	919	861	59	152	603	100.0	47.0	14.4	27.8	5.9	5.6	0.4	1.0	3.9
2021[4]	15,661	7,221	2,259	4,441	928	869	59	152	660	100.0	46.1	14.4	28.4	5.9	5.5	0.4	1.0	4.2
2022[4]	15,823	7,156	2,294	4,571	935	876	59	151	716	100.0	45.2	14.5	28.9	5.9	5.5	0.4	1.0	4.5
2023[4]	15,863	7,062	2,310	4,637	937	881	57	151	766	100.0	44.5	14.6	29.2	5.9	5.6	0.4	1.0	4.8
2024[4]	15,748	6,933	2,286	4,630	946	890	56	148	806	100.0	44.0	14.5	29.4	6.0	5.6	0.4	0.9	5.1
2025[4]	15,601	6,809	2,259	4,610	946	891	55	146	830	100.0	43.6	14.5	29.6	6.1	5.7	0.4	0.9	5.3
2026[4]	15,420	6,704	2,226	4,556	951	897	54	144	840	100.0	43.5	14.4	29.5	6.2	5.8	0.3	0.9	5.4
2027[4]	15,334	6,647	2,206	4,520	973	918	55	142	846	100.0	43.3	14.4	29.5	6.3	6.0	0.4	0.9	5.5
2028[4]	15,346	6,640	2,210	4,521	987	932	55	142	847	100.0	43.3	14.4	29.5	6.4	6.1	0.4	0.9	5.5

—Not available.
†Not applicable.
[1]For this year, data on students of Two or more races were reported by only a small number of states. Therefore, the data are not comparable to figures for 2010 and later years.
[2]Includes imputations for prekindergarten enrollment in California and Oregon.
[3]Includes imputations for prekindergarten enrollment in California.
[4]Projected.
NOTE: Race categories exclude persons of Hispanic ethnicity. Enrollment data for students not reported by race/ethnicity were prorated by state and grade to match state totals. Prior to 2008, data on students of Two or more races were not collected. Total counts of ungraded students were prorated to prekindergarten through grade 8 and grades 9 through 12 based on prior reports. Some data have been revised from previously published figures. Detail may not sum to totals because of rounding.
SOURCE: U.S. Department of Education, National Center for Education Statistics, Common Core of Data (CCD), "State Nonfiscal Survey of Public Elementary and Secondary Education," 1998–99 through 2016–17; and National Elementary and Secondary Enrollment by Race/Ethnicity Projection Model, 1972 through 2028. (This table was prepared March 2019.)

Table 203.70. Percentage distribution of enrollment in public elementary and secondary schools, by race/ethnicity and state or jurisdiction: Fall 2000 and fall 2016

State or jurisdiction	Percentage distribution, fall 2000						Percentage distribution, fall 2016							
	Total	White	Black	Hispanic	Asian/ Pacific Islander	American Indian/ Alaska Native	Total	White	Black	Hispanic	Asian	Pacific Islander	American Indian/ Alaska Native	Two or more races
1	2	3	4	5	6	7	8	9	10	11	12	13	14	15
United States	**100.0**	**61.2**	**17.2**	**16.3**	**4.1**	**1.2**	**100.0**	**48.2**	**15.3**	**26.4**	**5.1**	**0.4**	**1.0**	**3.6**
Alabama	100.0	60.8	36.5	1.3	0.7	0.7	100.0	54.9	33.0	7.4	1.4	0.1	0.9	2.2
Alaska	100.0	61.5	4.6	3.4	5.5	25.0	100.0	47.8	3.1	6.7	5.9	2.9	22.9	10.7
Arizona	100.0	52.8	4.6	33.9	2.1	6.6	100.0	38.8	5.3	45.2	2.8	0.4	4.6	2.9
Arkansas	100.0	71.7	23.3	3.6	0.9	0.5	100.0	61.3	20.6	12.7	1.6	0.7	0.6	2.4
California	100.0	36.1	8.5	43.4	11.1	0.9	100.0	23.6	5.6	54.2	11.4	0.5	0.5	4.1
Colorado	100.0	68.2	5.7	22.0	2.9	1.2	100.0	53.8	4.6	33.5	3.1	0.2	0.7	4.0
Connecticut	100.0	70.1	13.7	13.1	2.8	0.3	100.0	54.8	12.8	24.0	5.1	0.1	0.3	2.9
Delaware	100.0	60.7	30.8	6.0	2.3	0.3	100.0	45.1	30.3	16.8	3.7	0.1	0.4	3.5
District of Columbia	100.0	4.5	84.6	9.2	1.6	0.1	100.0	10.7	69.7	16.0	1.5	0.1	0.2	1.8
Florida	100.0	53.3	25.2	19.4	1.9	0.3	100.0	38.7	22.3	32.4	2.7	0.2	0.3	3.4
Georgia	100.0	54.7	38.2	4.8	2.2	0.2	100.0	40.3	36.8	15.2	3.9	0.1	0.2	3.5
Hawaii	100.0	20.4	2.3	4.5	72.3	0.4	100.0	12.6	1.8	13.2	29.4	29.5	0.3	13.2
Idaho	100.0	86.0	0.7	10.7	1.2	1.4	100.0	75.7	1.1	18.0	1.2	0.3	1.2	2.5
Illinois	100.0	59.8	21.3	15.4	3.4	0.2	100.0	48.5	17.0	25.7	4.9	0.1	0.4	3.4
Indiana	100.0	83.6	11.7	3.5	1.0	0.2	100.0	68.6	12.5	11.6	2.3	0.1	0.2	4.8
Iowa	100.0	90.2	4.0	3.6	1.7	0.5	100.0	76.6	5.9	10.6	2.5	0.2	0.4	3.8
Kansas	100.0	78.7	8.9	8.9	2.2	1.3	100.0	64.6	6.9	19.5	2.8	0.2	0.9	5.1
Kentucky	100.0	87.5	10.7	1.0	0.6	0.2	100.0	77.5	10.5	6.4	1.7	0.1	0.1	3.6
Louisiana	100.0	48.9	47.8	1.4	1.3	0.6	100.0	45.1	44.0	6.3	1.6	0.1	0.7	2.3
Maine	100.0	96.5	1.2	0.6	1.0	0.7	100.0	89.7	3.5	2.1	1.5	0.1	0.9	2.3
Maryland	100.0	53.4	37.1	4.8	4.4	0.4	100.0	38.2	34.1	16.5	6.4	0.1	0.3	4.4
Massachusetts	100.0	76.1	8.5	10.7	4.4	0.3	100.0	61.4	8.9	19.3	6.6	0.1	0.2	3.4
Michigan	100.0	73.8	19.8	3.5	1.8	1.0	100.0	66.6	18.0	7.7	3.3	0.1	0.6	3.7
Minnesota	100.0	82.9	6.6	3.4	5.1	2.0	100.0	67.5	10.7	9.0	6.7	0.1	1.7	4.4
Mississippi	100.0	47.3	51.1	0.8	0.7	0.1	100.0	44.4	48.9	3.6	1.1	0.1	0.2	1.8
Missouri	100.0	79.3	17.4	1.8	1.2	0.3	100.0	71.6	16.1	6.2	2.0	0.3	0.4	3.6
Montana	100.0	86.2	0.6	1.7	1.0	10.5	100.0	79.0	0.9	4.5	0.8	0.2	11.2	3.4
Nebraska	100.0	83.0	6.7	7.3	1.5	1.5	100.0	66.9	6.7	18.6	2.7	0.1	1.4	3.6
Nevada	100.0	56.7	10.2	25.7	5.7	1.7	100.0	33.2	10.8	42.1	5.5	1.4	0.9	6.1
New Hampshire	100.0	95.5	1.1	1.8	1.3	0.2	100.0	86.3	2.0	5.2	3.2	0.1	0.3	3.0
New Jersey	100.0	60.3	17.9	15.3	6.3	0.2	100.0	44.7	15.8	27.6	9.8	0.2	0.1	1.7
New Mexico	100.0	35.3	2.4	50.2	1.1	11.1	100.0	24.1	1.9	60.8	1.2	0.1	10.2	1.7
New York	100.0	54.9	20.2	18.5	6.0	0.4	100.0	43.9	17.4	26.5	9.1	0.3	0.7	2.2
North Carolina	100.0	61.0	31.3	4.4	1.9	1.5	100.0	48.9	25.6	16.9	3.2	0.1	1.3	4.0
North Dakota	100.0	89.4	1.0	1.2	0.8	7.6	100.0	78.1	4.5	4.7	1.5	0.3	8.7	2.2
Ohio	100.0	80.7	16.3	1.7	1.1	0.1	100.0	70.6	16.5	5.4	2.3	0.1	0.1	5.0
Oklahoma	100.0	64.9	10.8	6.0	1.4	16.9	100.0	49.4	8.8	16.8	2.0	0.3	13.9	8.8
Oregon	100.0	80.4	2.9	10.5	4.0	2.1	100.0	63.0	2.4	22.6	4.0	0.7	1.4	5.9
Pennsylvania	100.0	78.2	15.1	4.5	2.0	0.1	100.0	66.6	14.8	11.0	3.8	0.1	0.2	3.6
Rhode Island	100.0	74.3	7.9	14.0	3.3	0.5	100.0	58.7	8.4	24.7	3.2	0.2	0.7	4.0
South Carolina	100.0	54.9	42.1	1.9	1.0	0.2	100.0	51.2	34.0	9.0	1.5	0.1	0.3	3.8
South Dakota	100.0	86.5	1.2	1.2	0.9	10.1	100.0	74.6	3.1	5.5	1.8	0.1	11.2	3.7
Tennessee	100.0	72.4	24.5	1.8	1.1	0.2	100.0	63.5	22.2	9.7	1.9	0.1	0.2	2.5
Texas	100.0	42.0	14.4	40.6	2.7	0.3	100.0	28.1	12.6	52.4	4.2	0.1	0.4	2.2
Utah	100.0	85.8	1.0	8.9	2.8	1.6	100.0	74.9	1.4	16.9	1.7	1.6	1.1	2.5
Vermont	100.0	96.3	1.1	0.6	1.4	0.6	100.0	90.7	2.0	1.9	2.0	0.1	0.2	3.2
Virginia	100.0	63.6	27.1	4.9	4.1	0.3	100.0	49.7	22.6	15.1	6.8	0.2	0.3	5.3
Washington	100.0	74.4	5.3	10.2	7.3	2.7	100.0	55.3	4.4	22.8	7.5	1.1	1.3	7.7
West Virginia	100.0	94.7	4.3	0.4	0.5	0.1	100.0	90.4	4.3	1.6	0.6	#	0.1	2.8
Wisconsin	100.0	80.7	10.0	4.5	3.3	1.4	100.0	70.4	9.3	11.8	3.9	0.1	1.2	3.5
Wyoming	100.0	87.9	1.2	6.9	0.9	3.1	100.0	78.1	1.1	14.0	0.8	0.1	3.6	2.3
Bureau of Indian Education	100.0	0.0	0.0	0.0	0.0	100.0	100.0	0.0	0.0	0.0	0.0	0.0	100.0	0.0
DoDEA	100.0	56.9	23.1	11.4	7.9	0.8	—	—	—	—	—	—	—	—
Other jurisdictions														
American Samoa	100.0	0.0	0.0	0.0	100.0	0.0	—	—	—	—	—	—	—	—
Guam	100.0	1.7	0.3	0.2	97.7	0.1	100.0	0.0	0.1	0.8	22.5	74.5	#	2.0
Northern Marianas	100.0	0.3	#	0.0	99.7	0.0	—	—	—	—	—	—	—	—
Puerto Rico	100.0	0.0	0.0	100.0	0.0	0.0	100.0	0.1	#	99.8	#	#	0.1	0.0
U.S. Virgin Islands	100.0	0.8	85.8	13.1	0.2	0.1	100.0	1.6	77.3	20.1	0.4	0.1	0.2	0.3

—Not available.
#Rounds to zero.
NOTE: Percentage distribution based on students for whom race/ethnicity was reported, which may be less than the total number of students in the state. Race categories exclude persons of Hispanic ethnicity. DoDEA = Department of Defense Education Activity. Detail may not sum to totals because of rounding.

SOURCE: U.S. Department of Education, National Center for Education Statistics, Common Core of Data (CCD), "State Nonfiscal Survey of Public Elementary/Secondary Education," 2000–01 and 2016–17. (This table was prepared September 2018.)

Table 204.10. Number and percentage of public school students eligible for free or reduced-price lunch, by state: Selected years, 2000–01 through 2016–17

State	Number of students				Number of students eligible for free/reduced-price lunch				Percent of students eligible for free/reduced-price lunch			
	2000–01	2010–11	2015–16	2016–17	2000–01	2010–11	2015–16	2016–17	2000–01	2010–11	2015–16	2016–17
1	2	3	4	5	6	7	8	9	10	11	12	13
United States	**46,579,068**[1]	**48,941,267**	**49,753,676**	**49,944,748**	**17,839,867**[1]	**23,544,479**	**25,900,186**[1]	**26,113,604**[1]	**38.3**[1]	**48.1**	**52.1**[1]	**52.3**[1]
Alabama	728,351	730,427	742,919	744,809	335,143	402,386	379,554	384,199	46.0	55.1	51.1	51.6
Alaska	105,333	132,104	132,466	132,709	32,468	50,701	56,625	60,182	30.8	38.4	42.7	45.3
Arizona	877,696[2]	1,067,210	973,369	993,129	274,277[2]	482,044	488,182	566,549	31.2[2]	45.2	50.2	57.0
Arkansas	449,959	482,114	491,485	492,802	205,058	291,608	312,477	313,314[4]	45.6	60.5	63.6	63.6[4]
California	6,050,753	6,169,427	6,208,436	6,214,620	2,820,611	3,335,885	3,657,497	3,611,597	46.6	54.1	58.9	58.1
Colorado	724,349	842,864	899,008	904,798	195,148	336,426	376,162	381,537	26.9	39.9	41.8	42.2
Connecticut	562,179[2]	552,919	537,536	529,616	143,030[2]	190,554	203,774	188,877	25.4[2]	34.5	37.9	35.7
Delaware	114,676	128,342	133,792	136,217	37,766	61,564	50,459	65,563[5]	32.9	48.0	37.7	48.1[5]
District of Columbia	68,380	71,263	83,009	84,970	47,839	52,027	63,402	64,900[5]	70.0	73.0	76.4	76.4[5]
Florida	2,434,755	2,641,555	2,791,193	2,811,090	1,079,009	1,479,519	1,640,217	1,633,226	44.3	56.0	58.8	58.1
Georgia	1,444,937	1,676,419	1,756,579	1,763,540	624,511	961,954	1,096,426	1,092,777	43.2	57.4	62.4	62.0
Hawaii	184,357	179,601	181,991	181,550	80,657	84,106	90,298	86,376	43.8	46.8	49.6	47.6
Idaho	244,755	275,815	292,233	297,118	85,824	124,104	137,145	136,058	35.1	45.0	46.9	45.8
Illinois	2,048,792[2]	1,973,401	2,018,688	2,009,331	759,973[2]	921,471	1,006,936	1,008,830	37.1[2]	46.7	49.9	50.2
Indiana	977,219	1,038,817	1,045,235	1,048,952	285,267	485,728	504,787	502,844	29.2	46.8	48.3	47.9
Iowa	492,021	484,856	500,102	500,960	131,553	188,486	207,129	204,841	26.7	38.9	41.4	40.9
Kansas	462,594	479,953	488,568	489,706	154,693	228,852	240,209	235,849	33.4	47.7	49.2	48.2
Kentucky	626,723	673,128	686,113	683,844	298,334	380,773	407,754	401,614	47.6	56.6	59.4	58.7
Louisiana	741,162	695,772	683,839	716,248	433,068	460,546	419,284	451,173	58.4	66.2	61.3	63.0
Maine	198,532	183,477	176,400	175,383	60,162	78,915	81,172	79,819	30.3	43.0	46.0	45.5
Maryland	852,911	852,202	879,580	886,187	255,872	341,557	395,834	413,580	30.0	40.1	45.0	46.7
Massachusetts	979,590	955,301	953,423	953,693	237,871	326,849	380,636[3]	380,744[5]	24.3	34.2	39.9[3]	39.9[5]
Michigan	1,703,260	1,551,861	1,484,270	1,477,193	504,044	719,800	684,945	675,696	29.6	46.4	46.1	45.7
Minnesota	854,154	837,930	863,719	874,432	218,867	306,136	329,124	329,341	25.6	36.5	38.1	37.7
Mississippi	497,421	489,462	487,195	483,148	319,670	345,734	365,109	362,296	64.3	70.6	74.9	75.0
Missouri	912,247	902,375	917,862	913,838	315,608	406,358	460,004	481,683	34.6	45.0	50.1	52.7
Montana	154,438	140,497	140,868	146,213	47,415	57,836	65,095	66,649	30.7	41.2	46.2	45.6
Nebraska	286,138	298,276	316,009	319,147	87,045	127,114	139,569	142,555	30.4	42.6	44.2	44.7
Nevada	282,621	436,840	455,144	472,790	92,978	219,904	267,801	287,510	32.9	50.3	58.8	60.8
New Hampshire	206,919	194,001	181,307	179,762	31,212	48,904	51,343	49,058	15.1	25.2	28.3	27.3
New Jersey	1,312,983	1,356,882	1,368,639	1,370,824	357,728	444,735	514,386	519,298	27.2	32.8	37.6	37.9
New Mexico	320,303	335,810	334,061	332,184	174,939	227,077	239,540	237,331	54.6	67.6	71.7	71.4
New York	2,859,927	2,722,761	2,660,164	2,701,730	1,236,945	1,315,564	1,316,954	1,422,290	43.3	48.3	49.5	52.6
North Carolina	1,194,371	1,487,699	1,544,677	1,549,452	470,316	747,978	885,934	889,189	39.4	50.3	57.4	57.4
North Dakota	109,201	94,273	106,358	107,460	31,840	29,929	31,764	33,248	29.2	31.7	29.9	30.9
Ohio	1,745,237	1,747,851	1,707,833	1,707,469	494,829	745,121	766,460	757,120	28.4	42.6	44.9	44.3
Oklahoma	623,110	659,376	682,309	693,747	300,179	398,917	424,665	433,509	48.2	60.5	62.2	62.5
Oregon	535,617	553,468	549,322	552,350	186,203	280,174	282,506	279,145	34.8	50.6	51.4	50.5
Pennsylvania	1,798,977	1,742,608	1,665,328	1,572,026	510,121	686,641	802,045	747,388	28.4	39.4	48.2	47.5
Rhode Island	157,347	142,575	140,427	140,469	52,209	61,127	65,995	66,895	33.2	42.9	47.0	47.6
South Carolina	677,411	722,203	763,483	770,800	320,254	395,033	458,287	516,520	47.3	54.7	60.0	67.0
South Dakota	128,598	125,883	133,746	135,762	37,857	46,718	55,715	51,430	29.4	37.1	41.7	37.9
Tennessee	909,161[2]	987,078	974,752	997,148	436,298[2]	542,953	573,256	586,427[5]	48.0[2]	55.0	58.8	58.8[5]
Texas	4,059,353	4,916,401	5,300,136	5,360,055	1,823,029	2,471,212	3,123,844	3,159,896	44.9	50.3	58.9	59.0
Utah	470,265	585,552	647,843	645,030	135,428	223,943	235,644	235,042	28.8	38.2	36.4	36.4
Vermont	102,049	85,144	84,355	84,325	23,986	31,339	32,354	32,507	23.5	36.8	38.4	38.5
Virginia	1,067,710	1,250,206	1,271,067	1,273,127	320,233	458,879	523,972	525,022	30.0	36.7	41.2	41.2
Washington	1,004,770[2]	1,043,466	1,086,805	1,101,514	326,295[2]	418,065	493,019	480,171	32.5[2]	40.1	45.4	43.6
West Virginia	286,285	282,879	277,445	273,845	143,446	145,605	137,177	122,257	50.1	51.5	49.4	44.6
Wisconsin	859,276	872,164	857,907	863,557	219,276	342,660	342,247	323,368	25.5	39.3	39.9	37.4
Wyoming	89,895	88,779	94,681	94,079	43,483	32,968	35,473	36,314	48.4	37.1	37.5	38.6

[1]U.S. total includes imputation for nonreporting states.
[2]Imputation for survey nonresponse. State-level imputations for 2000–01 were based on the reported percentages for 2001–02 applied to the 2000–01 enrollments.
[3]Imputation for survey nonresponse. State-level imputations for 2015–16 were based on the reported percentages for 2014–15 applied to the 2015–16 enrollments.
[4]Imputation for survey nonresponse. State-level imputations for 2016–17 were based on the reported percentages for 2015–16 applied to the 2016–17 enrollments.
[5]For 2016–17, this state reported only the count of students who were eligible based on direct certification. Direct certification is the process by which children are certified for free meals based on household participation in one or more means-tested federal assistance programs—such as the Supplemental Nutrition Assistance Program (SNAP)—without the need for a household application.

NOTE: The National School Lunch Program (NSLP) is a federally assisted meal program. Table reflects counts of students enrolled in all schools for which both enrollment data and free/reduced-price lunch eligibility data were reported. Data for 2016–17 include students whose NSLP eligibility has been determined through direct certification.

SOURCE: U.S. Department of Education, National Center for Education Statistics, Common Core of Data (CCD), "Public Elementary/Secondary School Universe Survey," 2000–01, 2010–11, 2015–16, and 2016–17. (This table was prepared April 2019.)

Table 204.20. English language learner (ELL) students enrolled in public elementary and secondary schools, by state: Selected years, fall 2000 through fall 2016

State	Number of ELL students							Number of ELL students as a percent of total enrollment						
	2000	2005	2010	2013	2014	2015	2016	2000	2005	2010	2013	2014	2015	2016
1	2	3	4	5	6	7	8	9	10	11	12	13	14	15
United States	**3,793,764[1]**	**4,471,300[1]**	**4,455,860[1]**	**4,568,197[1]**	**4,670,356**	**4,794,994**	**4,858,377**	**8.1[1]**	**9.2[1]**	**9.0[1]**	**9.2[1]**	**9.3**	**9.5**	**9.6**
Alabama	7,226	16,550	17,559	17,457	18,651	20,228	20,725	1.0	2.3	2.4	2.3	2.5	2.7	2.8
Alaska	19,337	20,743	14,963	14,945	15,089	15,203	14,662	14.5	15.4	11.3	11.4	11.5	11.5	11.0
Arizona	131,933	174,856	76,320	69,636	67,389	67,195	70,546	15.0	18.2	7.3	6.3	6.1	6.1	6.3
Arkansas	11,850	20,709	31,537	35,961	37,799	38,376	41,482	2.6	4.6	6.8	7.3	7.7	7.8	8.4
California	1,479,819	1,571,463	1,474,250[2]	1,413,167	1,392,295	1,307,804	1,260,672	24.5	25.2	23.3[2]	22.7	22.3	21.0	20.2
Colorado	60,852	99,797	99,804	107,742	104,979	104,289	105,810	8.4	13.3	13.0	12.3	11.8	11.6	11.7
Connecticut	20,499	29,789	30,428	31,301	34,855	35,064	36,573	3.6	5.2	5.3	5.7	6.4	6.5	6.8
Delaware	2,081	5,919	6,858	8,212	8,482	9,704	10,831	1.8	5.1	5.8	6.2	6.3	7.2	7.9
District of Columbia	8,594	5,001	5,261	7,331	7,330	6,215	6,574	12.5	6.6	6.9	9.4	9.1	7.4	7.7
Florida	187,566	221,705	229,758	250,430	252,318	268,189	288,921	7.7	8.7	8.7	9.2	9.2	9.6	10.3
Georgia	54,444	86,615	81,409	90,563	97,768	112,006	114,427	3.8	5.8	5.2	5.3	5.6	6.4	6.5
Hawaii	12,718	18,106	19,092	15,949	14,425	13,619	12,658	6.9	9.8	10.4	8.5	7.9	7.5	7.0
Idaho	18,097	18,184	15,393	13,251	12,755	13,492	16,187	7.4	7.3	6.0	4.5	4.4	4.6	5.4
Illinois	126,475	172,049[3]	174,340	191,209	210,221	194,040	197,496	6.2	8.3[3]	8.3	9.3	10.3	9.5	9.8
Indiana	30,953	56,510	49,573	55,955	57,839	50,717	47,676	3.1	5.6	4.9	5.3	5.5	4.8	4.5
Iowa	11,253	15,156	21,733	23,137	25,875	27,300	28,659	2.3	3.1	4.5	4.6	5.1	5.4	5.6
Kansas	14,878	24,671	39,323	45,530	47,209	52,789	54,667	3.2	5.2	8.4	9.4	9.5	10.6	11.1
Kentucky	4,030	10,138	16,351	19,602	20,716	22,067	21,897	0.6	1.5	2.4	2.9	3.0	3.2	3.2
Louisiana	10,293	12,006	11,698	15,037	18,665	23,924	22,843	1.4	1.6	1.6	2.1	2.6	3.3	3.2
Maine	2,410[3]	3,353	4,792	5,201	5,177	5,091	5,295	1.1[3]	1.6	2.4	2.8	2.8	2.8	2.9
Maryland	24,213	31,416	45,500	56,047	60,705	63,349	69,079	2.8	3.6	5.3	6.5	6.9	7.2	7.8
Massachusetts	49,077	51,618	54,988	70,883	75,531	82,779	86,658	5.0	5.3	5.6	7.4	7.9	8.6	9.0
Michigan	49,279[3]	65,419	56,474	72,811	81,678	89,597	94,921	2.9[3]	3.7	3.2	4.7	5.3	5.8	6.2
Minnesota	44,360	57,831	48,428	64,377	66,934	71,162	72,128	5.2	6.8	5.8	7.6	7.8	8.2	8.2
Mississippi	2,176	2,859	5,620	6,574	7,773	9,588	13,042	0.4	0.6	1.1	1.3	1.6	2.0	2.7
Missouri	10,238	18,745	21,918	27,355	29,144	29,690	30,950	1.1	2.0	2.4	3.0	3.2	3.2	3.4
Montana	7,713[3]	6,711	3,300	3,311	3,299	3,202	3,000	5.0[3]	4.5	2.2	2.3	2.3	2.2	2.0
Nebraska	11,276	17,449	20,077	15,418	17,528	20,900	22,507	3.9	6.1	7.0	5.0	5.6	6.6	7.1
Nevada	38,301[3]	63,856	83,352	68,053	75,282	78,416	75,430	11.2[3]	17.3	20.8	15.1	16.4	16.8	15.9
New Hampshire	2,728	2,876[3]	3,965	3,513	3,605	4,116	4,321	1.3	1.4[3]	1.9	1.9	2.0	2.3	2.4
New Jersey	55,463[3]	50,515	52,771	61,151	66,748	68,725	70,941	4.2[3]	3.7	3.8	4.5	4.8	4.9	5.0
New Mexico	68,679	62,682	52,557	51,095	48,906	52,821	44,899	21.4	19.6	16.1	15.1	14.4	15.7	13.4
New York	230,625	194,123	208,125	184,562[2]	187,445	216,378	236,792	8.0	6.7	7.3	6.8[2]	6.8	8.0	8.7
North Carolina	44,165	73,634	103,249	94,810	94,093	102,090	92,388	3.4	5.5	7.5	6.3	6.1	6.6	6.0
North Dakota	925[3]	2,213[3]	2,788	2,749	3,111	3,171	3,198	0.8[3]	2.1[3]	2.8	2.7	3.0	3.0	2.9
Ohio	25,658[3]	29,804	37,116	43,502	46,766	51,441	56,945	1.4[3]	1.6	2.0	2.5	2.7	3.0	3.3
Oklahoma	38,042	47,381	41,812	48,318	49,102	46,831	46,396	6.1	7.6	6.6	7.1	7.1	6.8	6.7
Oregon	43,416	64,676	58,946	49,722	49,485	52,786	56,598	7.9	11.7	10.7	8.6	8.5	9.2	9.8
Pennsylvania	42,412[3]	42,795[3]	47,014	48,404	51,623	52,624	56,454	2.3[3]	2.4[3]	2.6	2.8	3.0	3.1	3.3
Rhode Island	10,245	7,468	7,655	9,319	10,066	10,550	11,057	6.5	4.7	4.9	6.6	7.1	7.4	7.8
South Carolina	5,121	14,388	36,379	40,340	42,480	42,574	44,301	0.8	2.1	5.2	5.4	5.6	5.6	5.7
South Dakota	4,270	5,110	4,383	4,254	4,679	4,598	4,678	3.3	4.0	3.5	3.3	3.5	3.4	3.4
Tennessee	26,452[3]	28,251[3]	29,681	34,397	36,398	40,637	43,277	3.0[3]	3.1[3]	3.2	3.5	3.7	4.1	4.3
Texas	570,453	711,737	738,663	798,071	814,945	892,082	922,012	14.1	16.7	16.8	15.5	15.6	16.8	17.2
Utah	38,998	49,973	42,804	34,409	38,543	42,815	41,339	8.2	10.3	8.7	5.5	6.1	6.6	6.3
Vermont	942	1,775	1,510	1,348	1,439	1,448	1,506	0.9	1.8	1.5	1.5	1.6	1.6	1.7
Virginia	36,802	72,420	88,033	94,496	97,871	109,104	100,814	3.2	6.2	7.3	7.4	7.6	8.5	7.8
Washington	70,431[3]	75,103	90,282	99,650	107,197	112,763	122,408	7.0[3]	7.4	8.9	9.4	10.0	10.4	11.1
West Virginia	920	1,944	1,788	1,879	2,707	2,812	2,546	0.3	0.7	0.6	0.7	1.0	1.0	0.9
Wisconsin	22,542	30,130	43,638	43,007	42,729	45,669	46,342	2.6	3.4	5.0	4.9	4.9	5.3	5.4
Wyoming	2,534	3,077	2,602	2,756	2,707	2,964	2,849	2.8	3.6	3.1	3.0	2.9	3.1	3.0

[1]U.S. total includes imputation for nonreporting states.
[2]Data are from U.S. Department of Education, National Center for Education Statistics, *EDFacts* file 046, Data Group 123, extracted October 25, 2017, from the *EDFacts* Data Warehouse (internal U.S. Department of Education source).
[3]Imputation for survey nonresponse. State-level imputations were based on the percentages reported by the state for other years applied to the enrollment for the given year.
NOTE: Data for 2014 and earlier years include only those ELL students who participated in ELL programs. Starting with 2015, data include all ELL students, regardless of program participation. Counts and percentages in this table are aggregated from data collected at the school district level and may differ from those in tables based on data collected at other levels.
SOURCE: U.S. Department of Education, National Center for Education Statistics, Common Core of Data (CCD), "Local Education Agency Universe Survey," 2000–01 through 2016–17. (This table was prepared October 2018.)

Table 204.30. Children 3 to 21 years old served under Individuals with Disabilities Education Act (IDEA), Part B, by type of disability: Selected years, 1976–77 through 2017–18

Type of disability	1976–77	1980–81	1990–91	2000–01	2007–08[1]	2008–09[1]	2009–10	2010–11	2011–12	2012–13	2013–14	2014–15	2015–16	2016–17[2,3]	2017–18[2,4]
1	2	3	4	5	6	7	8	9	10	11	12	13	14	15	16
	Number of children served (in thousands)														
All disabilities	**3,694**	**4,144**	**4,710**	**6,296**	**6,597**	**6,483**	**6,481**	**6,436**	**6,401**	**6,429**	**6,464**	**6,555**	**6,677**	**6,802**	**6,964**
Autism	—	—	—	93	296	336	378	417	455	498	538	576	617	661	710
Deaf-blindness	—	3	1	1	2	2	2	2	2	1	1	1	1	1	1
Developmental delay	—	—	—	213	357	354	368	382	393	402	410	419	434	446	461
Emotional disturbance	283	347	389	480	442	420	407	390	373	362	354	349	347	348	353
Hearing impairment	88	79	58	77	79	78	79	78	78	77	77	76	75	75	75
Intellectual disability	961	830	534	624	500	478	463	448	435	430	425	423	425	431	436
Multiple disabilities	—	68	96	131	138	130	131	130	132	133	132	132	131	132	132
Orthopedic impairment	87	58	49	82	67	70	65	63	61	59	56	52	47	42	41
Other health impairment[5]	141	98	55	303	641	659	689	716	743	779	817	862	909	955	1,002
Preschool disabled[6]	†	†	390	†	†	†	†	†	†	†	†	†	†	†	†
Specific learning disability	796	1,462	2,129	2,860	2,569	2,476	2,431	2,361	2,303	2,277	2,264	2,278	2,298	2,318	2,342
Speech or language impairment	1,302	1,168	985	1,388	1,454	1,426	1,416	1,396	1,373	1,356	1,334	1,332	1,337	1,337	1,357
Traumatic brain injury	—	—	—	16	25	26	25	26	26	26	26	26	27	27	27
Visual impairment	38	31	23	29	29	29	29	28	28	28	28	28	27	27	27
	Percentage distribution of children served														
All disabilities	**100.0**	**100.0**	**100.0**	**100.0**	**100.0**	**100.0**	**100.0**	**100.0**	**100.0**	**100.0**	**100.0**	**100.0**	**100.0**	**100.0**	**100.0**
Autism	—	—	—	1.5	4.5	5.2	5.8	6.5	7.1	7.8	8.3	8.8	9.2	9.7	10.2
Deaf-blindness	—	0.1	#	#	#	#	#	#	#	#	#	#	#	#	#
Developmental delay	—	—	—	3.4	5.4	5.5	5.7	5.9	6.1	6.2	6.3	6.4	6.5	6.6	6.6
Emotional disturbance	7.7	8.4	8.3	7.6	6.7	6.5	6.3	6.1	5.8	5.6	5.5	5.3	5.2	5.1	5.1
Hearing impairment	2.4	1.9	1.2	1.2	1.2	1.2	1.2	1.2	1.2	1.2	1.2	1.2	1.1	1.1	1.1
Intellectual disability	26.0	20.0	11.3	9.9	7.6	7.4	7.1	7.0	6.8	6.7	6.6	6.4	6.4	6.3	6.3
Multiple disabilities	—	1.6	2.0	2.1	2.1	2.0	2.0	2.0	2.1	2.1	2.0	2.0	2.0	1.9	1.9
Orthopedic impairment	2.4	1.4	1.0	1.3	1.0	1.1	1.0	1.0	1.0	0.9	0.9	0.8	0.7	0.6	0.6
Other health impairment[5]	3.8	2.4	1.2	4.8	9.7	10.2	10.6	11.1	11.6	12.1	12.6	13.2	13.6	14.0	14.4
Preschool disabled[6]	†	†	8.3	†	†	†	†	†	†	†	†	†	†	†	†
Specific learning disability	21.5	35.3	45.2	45.4	38.9	38.2	37.5	36.7	36.0	35.4	35.0	34.8	34.4	34.1	33.6
Speech or language impairment	35.2	28.2	20.9	22.0	22.0	22.0	21.8	21.7	21.4	21.1	20.6	20.3	20.0	19.7	19.5
Traumatic brain injury	—	—	—	0.2	0.4	0.4	0.4	0.4	0.4	0.4	0.4	0.4	0.4	0.4	0.4
Visual impairment	1.0	0.7	0.5	0.5	0.4	0.4	0.4	0.4	0.4	0.4	0.4	0.4	0.4	0.4	0.4
	Number of children served as a percent of total enrollment[7]														
All disabilities	**8.3**	**10.1**	**11.4**	**13.3**	**13.4**	**13.2**	**13.1**	**13.0**	**12.9**	**12.9**	**12.9**	**13.0**	**13.2**	**13.4**	**13.7**
Autism	—	—	—	0.2	0.6	0.7	0.8	0.8	0.9	1.0	1.1	1.1	1.2	1.3	1.4
Deaf-blindness	—	#	#	#	#	#	#	#	#	#	#	#	#	#	#
Developmental delay	—	—	—	0.5	0.7	0.7	0.7	0.8	0.8	0.8	0.8	0.8	0.9	0.9	0.9
Emotional disturbance	0.6	0.8	0.9	1.0	0.9	0.9	0.8	0.8	0.8	0.7	0.7	0.7	0.7	0.7	0.7
Hearing impairment	0.2	0.2	0.1	0.2	0.2	0.2	0.2	0.2	0.2	0.2	0.2	0.2	0.1	0.1	0.1
Intellectual disability	2.2	2.0	1.3	1.3	1.0	1.0	0.9	0.9	0.9	0.9	0.9	0.8	0.8	0.9	0.9
Multiple disabilities	—	0.2	0.2	0.3	0.3	0.3	0.3	0.3	0.3	0.3	0.3	0.3	0.3	0.3	0.3
Orthopedic impairment	0.2	0.1	0.1	0.2	0.1	0.1	0.1	0.1	0.1	0.1	0.1	0.1	0.1	0.1	0.1
Other health impairment[5]	0.3	0.2	0.1	0.6	1.3	1.3	1.4	1.4	1.5	1.6	1.6	1.7	1.8	1.9	2.0
Preschool disabled[6]	†	†	0.9	†	†	†	†	†	†	†	†	†	†	†	†
Specific learning disability	1.8	3.6	5.2	6.1	5.2	5.0	4.9	4.8	4.7	4.6	4.5	4.5	4.6	4.6	4.6
Speech or language impairment	2.9	2.9	2.4	2.9	2.9	2.9	2.9	2.8	2.8	2.7	2.7	2.6	2.7	2.6	2.7
Traumatic brain injury	—	—	—	#	0.1	0.1	0.1	0.1	0.1	0.1	0.1	0.1	0.1	0.1	0.1
Visual impairment	0.1	0.1	0.1	0.1	0.1	0.1	0.1	0.1	0.1	0.1	0.1	0.1	0.1	0.1	0.1

—Not available.
†Not applicable.
#Rounds to zero.
[1]Data do not include Vermont, for which 2007–08 and 2008–09 data were not available. In 2006–07, the total number of 3- to 21-year-olds served in Vermont was 14,010.
[2]Data in the 2016–17 and 2017–18 columns include 2015–16 data for 3- to 21-year-olds in Wisconsin because 2016–17 and 2017–18 data were not available for children served in Wisconsin.
[3]Data in the 2016–17 column include 2015–16 data for 3- to 5-year-olds in Nebraska because 2016–17 data were not available for children in that age group served in Nebraska.
[4]Data in the 2017–18 column include 2016–17 data for 3- to 5-year-olds in Minnesota and 6- to 21-year-olds in Maine and Vermont because 2017–18 data were not available for children in those age groups served in those states.
[5]Other health impairments include having limited strength, vitality, or alertness due to chronic or acute health problems such as a heart condition, tuberculosis, rheumatic fever, nephritis, asthma, sickle cell anemia, hemophilia, epilepsy, lead poisoning, leukemia, or diabetes.
[6]For 1990–91, preschool children are not included in the counts by disability condition but are separately reported. For other years, preschool children are included in the counts by disability condition.
[7]Based on total public school enrollment in prekindergarten through grade 12. For total public school enrollment, see table 203.20.

NOTE: Prior to October 1994, children and youth with disabilities were served under Chapter 1 of the Elementary and Secondary Education Act (ESEA) as well as under the Individuals with Disabilities Education Act (IDEA), Part B. Data reported in this table for years prior to 1994–95 include children ages 0–21 served under Chapter 1 of ESEA. Data are for the 50 states and the District of Columbia only. Increases since 1987–88 are due in part to new legislation enacted in fall 1986, which added a mandate for public school special education services for 3- to 5-year-old children with disabilities. Detail may not sum to totals because of rounding.

SOURCE: U.S. Department of Education, Office of Special Education Programs, *Annual Report to Congress on the Implementation of the Individuals with Disabilities Education Act*, selected years, 1979 through 2006; and Individuals with Disabilities Education Act (IDEA) database, retrieved December 21, 2018, from https://www2.ed.gov/programs/osepidea/618-data/state-level-data-files/index.html#bcc. National Center for Education Statistics, *Statistics of Public Elementary and Secondary School Systems*, 1977–78 and 1980–81; Common Core of Data (CCD), "State Nonfiscal Survey of Public Elementary/Secondary Education," 1990–91 through 2017–18; and National Elementary and Secondary Enrollment Projection Model, 1972 through 2028. (This table was prepared December 2018.)

Table 204.40. Children 3 to 21 years old served under Individuals with Disabilities Education Act (IDEA), Part B, by race/ethnicity and age group: 2000–01 through 2017–18

Age group and year	Total	White	Black	Hispanic	Asian[1]	Pacific Islander	American Indian/ Alaska Native	Two or more races
1	2	3	4	5	6	7	8	9
				Number of children served				
3 to 21 years old								
2000–01	6,295,709	3,957,589	1,259,348	877,655	121,044	—	80,073	—
2001–02	6,407,417	3,989,528	1,281,803	928,776	123,434	—	83,876	—
2002–03	6,522,977	4,014,340	1,311,270	980,590	130,252	—	86,525	—
2003–04	6,633,902	4,035,880	1,334,666	1,035,463	137,544	—	90,349	—
2004–05	6,718,630	4,044,491	1,355,550	1,081,697	144,339	—	92,553	—
2005–06	6,712,614	4,003,865	1,346,177	1,119,140	149,954	—	93,478	—
2006–07	6,686,386	3,948,853	1,335,870	1,154,217	153,265	—	94,181	—
2007–08[2]	6,574,368	3,833,922	1,307,462	1,181,130	158,623	—	93,231	—
2008–09[2]	6,461,938	3,725,896	1,273,996	1,200,290	162,630	—	93,672	5,454[3]
2009–10	6,461,226	3,659,194	1,262,799	1,252,493	167,144	—	92,646	26,950[3]
2010–11	6,435,141	3,518,169	1,214,849	1,310,031	145,896	19,581	91,258	135,357
2011–12[4]	6,401,238	3,436,105	1,196,679	1,352,435	147,697	19,203	88,665	160,458
2012–13[4]	6,429,331	3,396,135	1,189,148	1,406,540	150,913	20,343	86,884	180,268
2013–14[4]	6,464,096	3,356,261	1,191,817	1,469,282	155,668	19,606	86,307	185,274
2014–15[4]	6,555,291	3,350,084	1,199,743	1,531,923	161,250	20,227	86,226	205,980
2015–16[4]	6,676,974	3,366,701	1,208,510	1,602,140	167,263	20,408	87,870	224,911
2016–17[4,5,6]	6,802,402	3,374,045	1,219,376	1,679,626	174,486	20,525	87,724	247,278
2017–18[4,5,7,8]	6,964,424	3,409,308	1,234,609	1,758,498	184,409	20,807	88,870	268,565
3 to 5 years old								
2000–01	592,090	400,650	93,281	78,070	13,203	—	6,886	—
2010–11	723,793	416,034	102,097	153,033	23,189	2,159	9,141	18,140
2015–16[4]	746,499	400,073	101,724	177,529	27,340	1,811	8,285	29,782
2016–17[4,5,6]	765,820	406,236	102,618	185,344	29,546	1,792	8,322	31,997
2017–18[4,5,7]	793,039	416,222	104,229	195,242	32,242	1,964	8,775	34,378
6 to 21 years old								
2000–01	5,703,619	3,556,939	1,166,067	799,585	107,841	—	73,187	—
2010–11	5,711,348	3,102,135	1,112,752	1,156,998	122,707	17,422	82,117	117,217
2015–16[4]	5,930,475	2,966,628	1,106,786	1,424,611	139,923	18,597	79,585	195,129
2016–17[4,5]	6,036,582	2,967,809	1,116,758	1,494,282	144,940	18,733	79,402	215,281
2017–18[4,5,8]	6,171,385	2,993,086	1,130,380	1,563,256	152,167	18,843	80,095	234,187
				Percentage distribution of children served				
3 to 21 years old								
2000–01	100.0	62.9	20.0	13.9	1.9	—	1.3	—
2001–02	100.0	62.3	20.0	14.5	1.9	—	1.3	—
2002–03	100.0	61.5	20.1	15.0	2.0	—	1.3	—
2003–04	100.0	60.8	20.1	15.6	2.1	—	1.4	—
2004–05	100.0	60.2	20.2	16.1	2.1	—	1.4	—
2005–06	100.0	59.6	20.1	16.7	2.2	—	1.4	—
2006–07	100.0	59.1	20.0	17.3	2.3	—	1.4	—
2007–08[2]	100.0	58.3	19.9	18.0	2.4	—	1.4	—
2008–09[2]	100.0	57.7	19.7	18.6	2.5	—	1.4	0.1[3]
2009–10	100.0	56.6	19.5	19.4	2.6	—	1.4	0.4[3]
2010–11	100.0	54.7	18.9	20.4	2.3	0.3	1.4	2.1
2011–12	100.0	53.7	18.7	21.1	2.3	0.3	1.4	2.5
2012–13	100.0	52.8	18.5	21.9	2.3	0.3	1.4	2.8
2013–14	100.0	51.9	18.4	22.7	2.4	0.3	1.3	2.9
2014–15	100.0	51.1	18.3	23.4	2.5	0.3	1.3	3.1
2015–16	100.0	50.4	18.1	24.0	2.5	0.3	1.3	3.4
2016–17[5,6]	100.0	49.6	17.9	24.7	2.6	0.3	1.3	3.6
2017–18[5,7,8]	100.0	49.0	17.7	25.2	2.6	0.3	1.3	3.9
				Number of children served as a percent of total enrollment[9]				
3 to 21 years old								
2000–01	13.3	13.7	15.5	11.4	6.2	—	14.6	—
2001–02	13.4	13.9	15.7	11.4	6.1	—	14.9	—
2002–03	13.5	14.0	15.8	11.4	6.2	—	14.8	—
2003–04	13.7	14.2	16.0	11.5	6.4	—	15.2	—
2004–05	13.8	14.3	16.1	11.5	6.5	—	15.7	—
2005–06	13.7	14.3	15.9	11.4	6.6	—	15.6	—
2006–07	13.6	14.2	15.9	11.3	6.6	—	15.8	—
2007–08[2]	13.3	14.0	15.6	11.3	6.6	—	15.7	—
2008–09[2]	13.1	13.8	15.2	11.4	6.6	—	15.9	2.2[3]
2009–10	13.1	13.7	15.2	11.5	6.7	—	15.6	8.0[3]
2010–11	13.0	13.6	15.4	11.5	6.4	11.5	16.2	11.7
2011–12	12.9	13.4	15.3	11.5	6.4	10.8	16.2	12.6
2012–13	12.9	13.4	15.2	11.7	6.4	11.3	16.3	13.0
2013–14	12.9	13.4	15.3	11.8	6.5	11.2	16.5	12.3
2014–15	13.0	13.4	15.4	12.0	6.5	11.5	16.6	12.8
2015–16	13.2	13.7	15.5	12.2	6.6	11.6	17.2	13.0
2016–17[5,6]	13.4	13.8	15.7	12.6	6.8	11.1	17.2	13.4
2017–18[5,7,8]	13.7	14.1	16.0	13.0	7.1	10.9	17.5	13.8

—Not available.
[1]For years prior to 2010–11, Asian data include Pacific Islanders.
[2]Data do not include Vermont, for which 2007–08 and 2008–09 data were not available.
[3]For 2008–09 and 2009–10, data on children of Two or more races were reported by only a small number of states. Therefore, these data are not comparable to figures for later years.
[4]For 2011–12 and later years, the total column shows the overall counts of children as reported by the 50 states and the District of Columbia rather than the sum of counts reported for individual racial/ethnic groups. (Due to data limitations, summing the data for the racial/ethnic groups can result in overcounts. For 2016–17, summing these data would result in a total overcount of 35 children in the 3- to 5-year-old age group and 623 children in the 6- to 21-year-old age group. For 2017–18, summing these data would result in a total overcount of 13 children in the 3- to 5-year-old age group and 629 children in the 6- to 21-year-old age group.)
[5]Includes 2015–16 data for children served in Wisconsin. More recent data were not available for children in any age group served in Wisconsin.
[6]Includes 2015–16 data for 3- to 5-year-olds served in Nebraska because 2016–17 data were not available.
[7]Includes 2016–17 data for 3- to 5-year-olds served in Minnesota because 2017–18 data were not available.
[8]Includes 2016–17 data for 6- to 21-year-olds served in Maine and Vermont because 2017–18 data were not available.
[9]Based on total public school enrollment in prekindergarten through grade 12 by race/ethnicity. For total public school enrollment by race/ethnicity, see table 203.60.
NOTE: Data include only those children served for whom race/ethnicity was reported. Race categories exclude persons of Hispanic ethnicity. Detail may not sum to totals because of rounding.
SOURCE: U.S. Department of Education, Office of Special Education Programs, Individuals with Disabilities Education Act (IDEA) database, retrieved December 21, 2018, from https://www2.ed.gov/programs/osepidea/618-data/state-level-data-files/index.html#bcc. National Center for Education Statistics, Common Core of Data (CCD), "State Nonfiscal Survey of Public Elementary and Secondary Education," 2000–01 through 2017–18; and National Elementary and Secondary Enrollment Projection Model, 1972 through 2028. (This table was prepared December 2018.)

Table 204.70. Number and percentage of children served under Individuals with Disabilities Education Act (IDEA), Part B, by age group and state or jurisdiction: Selected years, 1990–91 through 2017–18

State or jurisdiction	3- to 21-year-olds served								3- to 5-year-olds served					
	1990–91	2000–01	2010–11	2015–16	2016–17[1]	2017–18[2]	As a percent of public school enrollment, 2017–18[3]	Percent change in number served, 2000–01 to 2017–18	1990–91	2000–01	2010–11	2015–16	2016–17[1]	2017–18[2]
1	2	3	4	5	6	7	8	9	10	11	12	13	14	15
United States	**4,710,089**	**6,295,816**	**6,434,916**	**6,676,974**	**6,802,402**	**6,964,424**	**13.7**	**10.6**	**389,751**	**592,087**	**723,738**	**746,499**	**765,820**	**793,039**
Alabama	94,601	99,828	82,286	84,278	86,922	90,319	12.2	-9.5	7,154	7,554	7,492	7,368	7,726	7,827
Alaska	14,390	17,691	18,048	18,390	18,711	19,148	14.3	8.2	1,458	1,637	2,104	2,115	2,221	2,430
Arizona	56,629	96,442	125,816	132,592	135,250	140,702	12.5	45.9	4,330	9,144	14,756	15,328	15,555	16,517
Arkansas	47,187	62,222	64,881	68,178	70,792	72,835	14.8	17.1	4,626	9,376	13,034	12,981	13,474	13,716
California	468,420	645,287	672,174	727,718	747,317	767,562	12.2	18.9	39,627	57,651	72,404	78,610	80,903	83,853
Colorado	56,336	78,715	84,710	95,101	98,031	102,240	11.2	29.9	4,128	8,202	11,797	12,774	13,485	14,293
Connecticut	63,886	73,886	68,167	75,030	77,519	79,758	15.1	7.9	5,466	7,172	7,933	8,691	9,086	9,120
Delaware	14,208	16,760	18,608	20,742	21,581	23,196	16.9	38.4	1,493	1,652	2,123	2,030	2,444	2,616
District of Columbia	6,290	10,559	11,947	12,258	12,811	13,399	15.5	26.9	411	374	957	1,471	1,675	1,789
Florida	234,509	367,335	368,808	372,476	382,870	389,626	13.7	6.1	14,883	30,660	36,027	39,359	40,412	39,862
Georgia	101,762	171,292	177,544	202,314	209,094	214,267	12.1	25.1	7,098	16,560	15,911	18,201	18,553	18,833
Hawaii	12,705	23,951	19,716	19,223	19,375	19,276	10.6	-19.5	809	1,919	2,398	2,444	2,491	2,469
Idaho	21,703	29,174	27,388	29,718	31,238	32,908	11.0	12.8	2,815	3,591	3,596	3,331	3,588	3,733
Illinois	236,060	297,316	302,830	296,784	294,150	295,066	14.6	-0.8	22,997	28,787	36,488	37,878	37,253	37,137
Indiana	112,949	156,320	166,073	171,368	173,293	176,104	16.8	12.7	7,243	15,101	18,725	18,049	18,108	18,644
Iowa	59,787	72,461	68,501	63,822	64,875	65,935	12.9	-9.0	5,421	5,580	7,378	6,226	6,591	6,976
Kansas	44,785	61,267	66,873	70,762	72,286	73,729	14.9	20.3	3,881	7,728	10,604	11,387	11,437	11,772
Kentucky	78,853	94,572	102,370	99,283	101,579	104,270	15.3	10.3	10,440	16,372	17,963	17,044	17,626	18,070
Louisiana	72,825	97,938	82,943	84,221	82,968	84,473	11.8	-13.7	6,703	9,957	10,427	10,430	10,019	9,885
Maine	27,987	35,633	32,261	32,531	33,125	33,004[4]	18.4	-7.4	2,895	3,978	3,824	3,512	3,505	3,384
Maryland	88,017	112,077	103,490	105,440	106,847	108,491	12.1	-3.2	7,163	10,003	12,875	13,473	13,885	14,300
Massachusetts	149,743	162,216	167,526	168,199	170,119	173,762	18.0	7.1	12,141	14,328	16,662	16,802	17,468	18,022
Michigan	166,511	221,456	218,957	197,316	197,965	198,751	13.1	-10.3	14,547	19,937	23,183	20,573	21,199	21,624
Minnesota	79,013	109,880	122,850	128,218	131,865	135,386[5]	15.3	23.2	8,646	11,522	15,076	15,843	16,586	16,586[5]
Mississippi	60,872	62,281	64,038	66,799	67,898	69,197	14.5	11.1	5,642	6,944	10,191	8,660	8,419	8,400
Missouri	101,166	137,381	127,164	126,328	128,623	131,114	14.3	-4.6	4,100	11,307	15,891	17,123	17,687	18,400
Montana	16,955	19,313	16,761	17,387	18,056	18,803	12.8	-2.6	1,751	1,635	1,656	1,592	1,697	1,660
Nebraska	32,312	42,793	44,299	47,795	48,700[6]	50,415	15.6	17.8	2,512	3,724	5,050	5,557	5,557[6]	6,217
Nevada	18,099	38,160	48,148	55,452	56,791	60,123	12.5	57.6	1,401	3,676	6,947	8,838	8,769	8,984
New Hampshire	19,049	30,077	29,920	28,806	28,935	29,233	16.4	-2.8	1,468	2,387	3,135	3,335	3,547	3,519
New Jersey	178,870	221,715	232,002	232,401	235,495	238,178	16.9	7.4	14,741	16,361	17,073	18,674	19,237	19,846
New Mexico	36,000	52,256	46,628	49,667	51,383	52,838	15.8	1.1	2,210	4,970	5,224	4,245	4,354	4,413
New York	307,366	441,333	454,542	499,551	505,414	522,221	19.2	18.3	26,266	51,665	64,923	67,067	66,317	71,893
North Carolina	122,942	173,067	185,107	198,808	199,512	200,905	12.9	16.1	10,516	17,361	18,433	19,070	19,211	19,899
North Dakota	12,294	13,652	13,170	13,953	14,407	15,153	13.9	11.0	1,164	1,247	1,714	1,972	2,012	2,189
Ohio	205,440	237,643	259,454	253,896	259,899	266,670	15.7	12.2	12,487	18,664	22,454	21,897	23,181	25,247
Oklahoma	65,457	85,577	97,250	108,459	109,391	112,080	16.1	31.0	5,163	6,393	8,298	9,023	9,450	9,751
Oregon	54,422	75,204	81,050	84,517	85,865	87,156	14.3	15.9	2,854	6,926	9,392	10,374	10,852	11,331
Pennsylvania	214,254	242,655	295,080	303,633	311,435	320,817	18.6	32.2	17,982	21,477	31,072	33,022	34,056	36,340
Rhode Island	20,646	30,727	25,332	23,515	23,296	23,748	16.7	-22.7	1,682	2,614	2,945	3,022	3,025	3,168
South Carolina	77,367	105,922	100,289	101,776	103,552	104,698	13.5	-1.2	7,948	11,775	11,083	9,432	9,631	9,568
South Dakota	14,726	16,825	18,026	19,527	20,312	21,190	15.4	25.9	2,105	2,286	2,738	2,627	2,748	2,941
Tennessee	104,853	125,863	120,263	129,386	128,936	129,319	12.9	2.7	7,487	10,699	13,096	12,905	13,480	13,950
Texas	344,529	491,642	442,019	463,238	477,526	498,588	9.2	1.4	24,848	36,442	41,494	43,787	46,652	49,681
Utah	46,606	53,921	70,278	79,932	81,956	84,196	12.6	56.1	3,424	5,785	8,990	10,007	10,516	10,731
Vermont	12,160	13,623	13,936	13,903	14,370	14,482[4]	16.7	6.3	1,097	1,237	1,762	1,774	1,893	2,005
Virginia	112,072	162,212	162,338	164,757	167,855	172,370	13.4	6.3	9,892	14,444	17,081	16,755	17,510	18,296
Washington	83,545	118,851	127,978	135,757	139,550	143,498	12.9	20.7	9,558	11,760	14,275	15,361	15,897	16,425
West Virginia	42,428	50,333	45,007	45,297	46,299	46,810	17.3	-7.0	2,923	5,445	5,607	5,004	5,376	5,219
Wisconsin	85,651	125,358	124,722	120,864	120,864[7]	120,864[7]	14.0	-3.6	10,934	14,383	16,079	16,089	16,089[7]	16,089[7]
Wyoming	10,852	13,154	15,348	15,608	15,499	15,551	16.6	18.2	1,221	1,695	3,398	3,367	3,367	3,419
Bureau of Indian Education	6,997	8,448	6,801	6,309	6,271	6,285	—	-25.6	1,092	338	396	266	240	250
Other jurisdictions	**38,986**	**70,670**	**131,847**	**128,268**	**123,710**	**110,613**	**—**	**56.5**	**3,892**	**8,168**	**14,505**	**16,743**	**15,206**	**12,840**
American Samoa	363	697	935	666	599	636	—	-8.8	48	48	142	50	29	37
Guam	1,750	2,267	2,003	2,036	2,018	2,015	—	-11.1	198	205	165	159	165	167
Northern Marianas	411	569	944	886	927	956	—	68.0	211	53	104	93	92	116
Palau	—	131	—	97	92	74	—	-43.5	—	10	—	6	6	3
Puerto Rico	35,129	65,504	126,560	123,376	118,882	105,827	—	61.6	3,345	7,746	13,952	16,303	14,794	12,391
U.S. Virgin Islands	1,333	1,502	1,405	1,207	1,192	1,105	—	-26.4	90	106	142	132	120	126

—Not available.
[1]Includes some data for 2015–16 due to unavailability of 2016–17 data for specific states, as noted below.
[2]Includes some data for 2015–16 or 2016–17 due to unavailability of 2017–18 data for specific states, as noted below.
[3]Based on total public school enrollment in prekindergarten through grade 12. For total public school enrollment, see table 203.40.
[4]Data for 6- to 21-year-olds are for 2016–17 instead of 2017–18 because 2017–18 data for this age group were not available for this state.
[5]Data for 3- to 5-year-olds are for 2016–17 instead of 2017–18 because 2017–18 data for this age group were not available for this state.
[6]Data for 3- to 5-year-olds are for 2015–16 instead of 2016–17 because 2016–17 data for this age group were not available for this state.
[7]Data are for 2015–16 because 2016–17 and 2017–18 data were not available for this state.

NOTE: Prior to October 1994, children and youth with disabilities were served under Chapter 1 of the Elementary and Secondary Education Act (ESEA) as well as under the Individuals with Disabilities Education Act (IDEA), Part B. Data reported in this table for 1990–91 include children ages 0–21 served under Chapter 1 of ESEA.

SOURCE: U.S. Department of Education, Office of Special Education Programs, *Annual Report to Congress on the Implementation of the Individuals with Disabilities Education Act*, selected years, 1992 through 2006; and Individuals with Disabilities Education Act (IDEA) database, retrieved December 31, 2018, from https://www2.ed.gov/programs/osepidea/618-data/state-level-data-files/index.html#bcc. National Center for Education Statistics, Common Core of Data (CCD), "State Nonfiscal Survey of Public Elementary/Secondary Education," 2017–18; and State Public Elementary and Secondary Enrollment Projection Model, 1980 through 2028. (This table was prepared December 2018.)

Table 204.75a. Homeless students enrolled in public elementary and secondary schools, by grade, primary nighttime residence, and selected student characteristics: 2009–10 through 2016–17

Grade, primary nighttime residence, or selected student characteristic	2009–10	2010–11	2011–12	2012–13	2013–14	2014–15[1]	2015–16	2016–17[2]
1	2	3	4	5	6	7	8	9
Total number of homeless students[3]	**910,439**	**1,047,397**	**1,128,503**	**1,216,117**	**1,285,641**	**1,260,721**	**1,301,238**	**1,351,120**
As a percent of total public school enrollment	1.8	2.1	2.3	2.4	2.6	2.5	2.6	2.7
Total number, by grade and nighttime residence								
Grade								
Prekindergarten[4]	28,871	32,966	32,866	38,281	47,976	39,381	42,580	43,333
Kindergarten	82,378	89,589	105,795	115,943	112,343	118,470	109,852	115,653
Grade 1	83,675	92,153	104,554	113,226	121,159	116,464	116,517	115,312
Grade 2	80,437	88,125	96,845	105,311	113,238	111,189	115,054	114,772
Grade 3	77,594	86,253	93,214	99,446	107,574	105,739	110,868	115,200
Grade 4	73,942	82,570	88,809	94,303	99,005	98,221	103,859	108,411
Grade 5	69,605	79,314	85,224	89,769	93,912	91,647	97,068	102,560
Grade 6	65,238	75,867	80,962	86,880	89,965	87,844	90,716	94,806
Grade 7	61,009	71,412	76,481	82,159	86,659	83,924	86,480	89,234
Grade 8	60,186	69,406	73,528	79,516	83,404	82,122	85,327	88,326
Grade 9	66,474	79,897	81,262	90,139	97,129	94,508	95,662	99,880
Grade 10	54,510	68,484	69,396	72,673	77,486	76,951	82,040	85,644
Grade 11	47,835	59,120	63,078	66,519	69,619	68,729	73,881	78,969
Grade 12	54,030	68,532	73,687	79,260	83,671	83,022	88,452	95,723
Ungraded[5]	4,655	3,709	2,802	2,692	2,501	2,510	2,882	3,297
Primary nighttime residence[6]								
Doubled-up or shared housing[7]	648,233	741,460	849,684	917,122	978,463	957,053	983,782	1,022,425
Hotels or motels	45,727	53,499	62,530	69,179	78,767	82,187	84,978	90,013
Shelters, transitional housing, or awaiting foster care placement	172,644	177,028	174,472	173,397	183,653	180,302	185,596	186,141
Unsheltered[8]	38,450	74,044	40,151	39,108	41,738	39,327	43,014	49,864
Number with selected characteristics								
Unaccompanied homeless youth[9]	—	—	—	78,654	88,390	94,800	111,720	118,362
English language learners[10]	—	—	—	174,821	190,256	181,764	201,099	216,245
Migrant students[11]	—	—	—	16,231	18,588	17,748	16,700	16,170
Students with disabilities[12]	—	—	—	190,050	217,048	215,630	232,764	245,130

—Not available.
[1]The decrease in homeless students in 2014–15 was caused in part by changes to California's data collection systems. For more information, see section 1.9.1.1 of California's 2014–15 *Consolidated State Performance Report*, available at https://www2.ed.gov/admins/lead/account/consolidated/sy14-15part1/ca.pdf.
[2]Includes imputed data for Kansas.
[3]The sum of counts by grade.
[4]Homeless children 3 to 5 years old who are not in kindergarten.
[5]Includes students reported as being enrolled in grade 13.
[6]Does not sum to the total number of homeless students because of missing data on primary nighttime residence. (Counts by primary nighttime residence differ from those shown in the total row by less than 2 percent for 2012–13 and less than 1 percent for all other years.)
[7]Refers to temporarily sharing the housing of other persons due to loss of housing, economic hardship, or other reasons (such as domestic violence).
[8]Includes living in cars, parks, campgrounds, temporary trailers—including Federal Emergency Management Agency (FEMA) trailers—or abandoned buildings.
[9]Youth who are not in the physical custody of a parent or guardian. Includes youth living on their own and youth living with a caregiver who is not their legal guardian.
[10]Students who met the definition of limited English proficient students as outlined in the ED*Facts* workbook. For more information, see https://www2.ed.gov/about/inits/ed/edfacts/eden-workbook.html.
[11]Students who met the definition of eligible migrant children as outlined in the ED*Facts* workbook. Such students are either migratory workers or the children or spouses of migratory workers and have moved within the preceding 36 months in order to obtain, or to accompany parents or spouses who moved in order to obtain, temporary or seasonal employment in agricultural or fishing work. For more information, see https://www2.ed.gov/about/inits/ed/edfacts/eden-workbook.html. Connecticut, the District of Columbia, Rhode Island, and West Virginia did not operate a migrant education program during the 2012–13, 2013–14, 2014–15, 2015–16, and 2016–17 school years and therefore had no data to provide on migrant homeless students.
[12]Includes only students with disabilities who were served under the Individuals with Disabilities Education Act (IDEA).
NOTE: Homeless students are defined as children/youth who lack a fixed, regular, and adequate nighttime residence. For more information, see "C118 - Homeless Students Enrolled" at https://www2.ed.gov/about/inits/ed/edfacts/sy-16-17-nonxml.html. Data include all homeless students enrolled at any time during the school year. Data exclude Puerto Rico and the Bureau of Indian Education. This table is based on state-level data unless otherwise noted.
SOURCE: U.S. Department of Education, National Center for Education Statistics, ED*Facts* file 118, Data Group 655, extracted June 5, 2019, from the ED*Facts* Data Warehouse (internal U.S. Department of Education Source); and Common Core of Data (CCD), "State Nonfiscal Survey of Public Elementary and Secondary Education," 2009–10 through 2016–17. (This table was prepared June 2019.)

Table 204.90. Percentage of public school students enrolled in gifted and talented programs, by sex, race/ethnicity, and state: Selected years, 2004 through 2013–14

[Standard errors appear in parentheses]

State	2004, total		2006, total		2011–12, total[1]	2013–14[1]									
						Total	Sex		Race/ethnicity						
							Male	Female	White	Black	Hispanic	Asian	Pacific Islander	American Indian/ Alaska Native	Two or more races
1	2		3		4	5	6	7	8	9	10	11	12	13	14
United States	**6.7**	**(0.05)**	**6.7**	**(0.04)**	**6.4**	**6.7**	**6.4**	**7.0**	**7.7**	**4.3**	**4.9**	**13.3**	**4.4**	**5.2**	**6.9**
Alabama	4.8	(0.11)	5.5	(0.06)	8.4	8.4	8.0	8.9	11.2	3.9	4.9	17.6	6.9	11.7	5.7
Alaska	4.1	(0.19)	4.1	(0.19)	4.7	4.9	4.7	5.2	6.8	3.0	4.3	6.3	2.3	0.9	6.5
Arizona	5.9	(0.17)	6.3	(0.11)	5.8	4.8	5.0	4.6	6.6	2.3	3.4	9.9	3.3	1.7	5.5
Arkansas	9.9	(0.65)	9.5	(0.43)	9.8	9.8	8.9	10.9	11.1	8.5	5.5	16.2	2.2	6.2	6.3
California	8.4	(0.18)	8.3	(0.21)	8.2	7.8	7.6	8.1	9.7	4.5	5.8	15.1	8.1	5.3	9.0
Colorado	6.7	(0.11)	6.8	(0.11)	6.5	7.7	7.9	7.5	9.6	4.1	4.4	12.8	6.4	4.3	9.0
Connecticut	3.0	(0.32)	3.8	(0.41)	2.3	2.2	2.0	2.4	2.7	1.1	1.0	4.6	0.5	1.1	2.4
Delaware	4.6[1]	(†)	5.6[1]	(†)	2.0	2.3	2.1	2.5	2.9	1.4	1.2	6.1	0.7–2.0	1.8	2.4
District of Columbia	—	(†)	—	(†)	0.1	#	#	#	0.1	#	#	0.1–0.3	0.0	0.0	0.0
Florida	4.5	(0.06)	4.7	(0.05)	5.4	5.8	5.6	5.9	7.6	2.3	5.3	13.3	4.1	4.3	6.2
Georgia	8.9	(0.30)	9.3	(0.35)	10.4	12.9	12.1	13.8	16.1	10.4	6.5	26.5	9.0	10.5	12.5
Hawaii	5.7	(0.57)	6.2[1]	(†)	1.4	3.0	2.4	3.5	4.4	2.1	1.6	4.2	1.7	4.2	2.5
Idaho	3.9	(0.23)	4.2	(0.20)	3.0	3.6	3.5	3.7	4.1	2.2	1.4	7.1	2.7	1.9	2.9
Illinois	5.4	(0.22)	5.8	(0.24)	3.5	6.8	6.5	7.1	5.7	7.7	6.7	15.4	10.9	6.4	7.1
Indiana	7.1	(0.49)	7.9	(0.40)	12.6	12.1	11.6	12.6	14.0	4.9	6.5	20.8	8.7	9.5	9.8
Iowa	8.5	(0.38)	8.2	(0.26)	9.3	9.4	9.2	9.7	10.5	3.2	4.2	13.9	4.4	4.1	7.9
Kansas	3.3	(0.11)	3.0	(0.12)	2.9	2.7	2.8	2.5	3.2	0.9	0.9	6.8	1.9	1.6	2.5
Kentucky	13.0	(0.54)	14.6	(0.50)	12.7	15.8	14.7	17.0	17.3	7.9	7.5	26.8	14.6	10.9	11.7
Louisiana	3.9	(0.32)	3.4	(0.13)	3.0	4.2	3.7	4.8	5.8	2.3	3.6	14.8	5.2	2.8	4.3
Maine	3.0	(0.36)	3.2	(0.19)	4.6	4.9	4.5	5.3	5.0	2.4	2.6	8.0	3.5	3.1	3.7
Maryland	13.8[1]	(†)	16.1[1]	(†)	15.8	16.0	14.7	17.4	17.5	11.1	14.0	39.4	10.1	10.2	17.2
Massachusetts	0.8	(0.13)	0.7	(0.10)	0.7	0.5	0.4	0.5	0.4	0.6	0.4	1.0	0.4	0.3	0.5
Michigan	3.9	(0.37)	3.4	(0.29)	1.9	1.3	1.2	1.4	1.5	0.7	0.6	3.0	1.6	1.0	0.7
Minnesota	8.1	(0.37)	8.8	(0.28)	8.0	7.2	7.1	7.4	7.2	6.0	4.7	14.9	4.6	2.5	5.8
Mississippi	6.0	(0.19)	6.1	(0.20)	6.7	6.7	6.3	7.1	10.2	3.5	5.7	14.7	10.7	3.3	4.8
Missouri	3.8	(0.12)	3.6	(0.11)	4.0	4.2	4.1	4.3	4.5	2.2	2.7	11.6	2.2	3.0	3.9
Montana	5.6	(0.28)	5.2	(0.20)	4.2	3.8	3.9	3.7	4.2	2.4	2.0	6.5	3.4	1.7	2.5
Nebraska	11.4	(0.31)	11.4	(0.24)	11.8	12.0	11.5	12.6	13.5	8.3	6.9	19.9	8.7	5.6	11.7
Nevada	1.9	(0.01)	1.9[1]	(†)	2.0	3.3	3.3	3.3	5.4	0.9	1.7	5.5	2.0	1.8	4.6
New Hampshire	2.3	(0.55)	2.6	(0.54)	1.4	1.2	1.2	1.2	1.2	0.4	0.3	1.6	0.0	0.7	1.1
New Jersey	6.9	(0.38)	7.0	(0.35)	6.5	5.9	5.4	6.5	7.1	3.1	2.9	11.9	7.5	2.9	4.6
New Mexico	10.7	(0.26)	4.0	(0.14)	4.6	4.5	4.6	4.3	8.2	3.3	3.1	13.4	5.7	2.6	5.8
New York	2.2	(0.18)	2.9	(0.13)	1.5	1.7	1.6	1.9	2.2	0.9	0.6	3.6	1.9	1.1	2.1
North Carolina	10.9	(0.83)	10.8	(0.42)	10.6	10.0	9.8	10.3	14.4	4.0	4.5	18.7	7.9	5.9	9.8
North Dakota	3.1	(0.30)	2.8	(0.18)	3.3	2.3	2.3	2.2	2.2	1.7	0.7	6.2	3.1	3.1	0.1–0.2
Ohio	7.4	(0.40)	7.3	(0.33)	3.7	4.3	4.2	4.3	4.9	1.4	1.9	11.2	1.8	3.5	3.5
Oklahoma	14.0	(0.45)	13.7	(0.39)	13.9	13.7	13.1	14.3	16.5	7.6	7.7	26.5	8.5	13.3	11.1
Oregon	7.1	(0.20)	6.9	(0.16)	6.8	6.5	6.7	6.3	7.4	3.1	2.6	16.6	3.0	2.5	7.6
Pennsylvania	4.8	(0.19)	4.5	(0.17)	3.8	3.7	3.7	3.7	4.4	1.0	1.2	8.8	3.3	2.0	2.7
Rhode Island	1.8	(0.38)	1.4	(0.21)	0.5	0.3	0.3	0.3	0.2	0.5	0.6	0.6	0.0	0.1–0.2	0.1
South Carolina	12.7	(0.98)	11.0	(0.57)	12.0	13.4	12.0	14.9	18.7	6.5	7.2	25.6	14.1	8.2	11.7
South Dakota	2.2	(0.20)	2.7	(0.17)	2.0	2.0	2.0	1.9	2.3	0.8	0.7	4.5	3.0	0.4	1.3
Tennessee	3.3	(0.18)	1.7	(0.10)	2.5	1.6	1.6	1.6	2.0	0.6	0.7	4.0	1.8	1.3	1.5
Texas	8.0	(0.10)	7.6	(0.07)	7.7	7.6	7.4	7.9	10.6	4.0	6.0	18.3	6.6	5.8	8.2
Utah	4.6	(0.29)	5.0	(0.05)	3.9	4.7	4.4	5.0	4.9	3.7	3.4	10.7	5.6	2.2	3.4
Vermont	0.8	(0.17)	0.8	(0.15)	0.3	0.4	0.4	0.4	0.4	0.3	0.1–0.3	0.6	0.9–2.6	0.2–0.6	0.1–0.2
Virginia	12.1	(0.38)	12.6	(0.32)	11.8	12.1	11.6	12.6	14.6	6.0	7.5	22.6	11.3	8.4	13.4
Washington	3.8	(0.10)	3.9	(0.13)	3.5	3.3	3.2	3.4	3.7	1.3	1.9	6.7	1.3	1.2	3.1
West Virginia	2.2	(0.19)	2.2	(0.21)	1.9	2.1	2.1	2.1	2.1	1.3	1.1	10.2	5.4	1.9	1.7
Wisconsin	6.8	(0.47)	6.4	(0.35)	6.0	6.2	6.0	6.4	6.5	5.2	4.7	8.8	3.0	2.1	5.5
Wyoming	3.2!	(1.04)	2.2	(0.35)	3.3	3.6	3.6	3.7	4.2	2.4	1.3	5.6	3.1	0.9	1.8

—Not available.
†Not applicable.
#Rounds to zero.
!Interpret data with caution. The coefficient of variation (CV) for this estimate is between 30 and 50 percent.
[1]Data are based on universe counts of schools and school districts; therefore, these figures do not have standard errors.

NOTE: Race categories exclude persons of Hispanic ethnicity. Percentages based on counts of between 1 and 3 gifted and talented students are displayed as ranges to protect student privacy.
SOURCE: U.S. Department of Education, Office for Civil Rights, Civil Rights Data Collection: 2004, 2006, 2011–12, and 2013–14. (This table was prepared June 2018.)

Table 205.10. Private elementary and secondary school enrollment and private enrollment as a percentage of total enrollment in public and private schools, by region and grade level: Selected years, fall 1995 through fall 2015

[Standard errors appear in parentheses]

Grade level and year	Total private enrollment		Private enrollment, by region							
			Northeast		Midwest		South		West	
	In thousands	Percent of total enrollment	In thousands	Percent of total enrollment in Northeast	In thousands	Percent of total enrollment in Midwest	In thousands	Percent of total enrollment in South	In thousands	Percent of total enrollment in West
1	2	3	4	5	6	7	8	9	10	11
Total, all grades										
1995	5,918 (31.8)	11.7 (0.06)	1,509 (18.8)	16.0 (0.20)	1,525 (14.2)	12.7 (0.12)	1,744 (12.8)	9.8 (0.07)	1,141 (11.5)	10.0 (0.10)
1997	5,944 (18.5)	11.4 (0.04)	1,496 (8.3)	15.6 (0.09)	1,528 (11.6)	12.5 (0.10)	1,804 (11.3)	9.8 (0.06)	1,116 (5.2)	9.4 (0.04)
1999	6,018 (30.2)	11.4 (0.06)	1,507 (7.9)	15.5 (0.08)	1,520 (10.3)	12.4 (0.09)	1,863 (26.7)	10.0 (0.14)	1,127 (5.4)	9.2 (0.04)
2001	6,320 (40.3)	11.7 (0.08)	1,581 (9.5)	16.1 (0.10)	1,556 (22.9)	12.6 (0.19)	1,975 (21.4)	10.3 (0.11)	1,208 (23.4)	9.6 (0.19)
2003	6,099 (41.2)	11.2 (0.08)	1,513 (25.8)	15.4 (0.27)	1,460 (15.1)	11.9 (0.12)	1,944 (21.0)	9.9 (0.11)	1,182 (19.1)	9.1 (0.15)
2005	6,073 (42.4)	11.0 (0.08)	1,430 (7.7)	14.8 (0.08)	1,434 (21.0)	11.7 (0.17)	1,976 (24.7)	9.8 (0.12)	1,234 (26.3)	9.4 (0.20)
2007	5,910 (28.4)	10.7 (0.05)	1,426 (11.0)	14.9 (0.12)	1,352 (8.3)	11.2 (0.07)	1,965 (21.5)	9.6 (0.11)	1,167 (12.3)	8.9 (0.09)
2009	5,488 (35.9)	10.0 (0.07)	1,310 (15.7)	14.0 (0.17)	1,296 (25.9)	10.8 (0.22)	1,842 (17.6)	9.1 (0.09)	1,041 (8.0)	8.0 (0.06)
2011	5,268 (24.9)	9.7 (0.04)	1,252 (18.0)	13.7 (0.17)	1,263 (17.1)	10.7 (0.13)	1,747 (2.6)	8.5 (0.01)	1,006 (0.4)	7.8 (#)
2013	5,396 (50.3)	9.8 (0.08)	1,201 (9.5)	13.2 (0.09)	1,326 (45.2)	11.2 (0.34)	1,840 (8.3)	8.7 (0.04)	1,028 (18.3)	7.9 (0.13)
2015	5,751 (85.7)	10.3 (0.14)	1,314 (37.3)	14.3 (0.35)	1,408 (54.5)	11.9 (0.40)	1,965 (53.2)	9.1 (0.22)	1,062 (12.5)	8.0 (0.09)
Prekindergarten through grade 8										
1995	4,756 (28.4)	12.8 (0.08)	1,174 (16.8)	17.2 (0.25)	1,238 (13.5)	14.3 (0.16)	1,413 (11.9)	10.7 (0.09)	931 (9.2)	11.1 (0.11)
1997	4,759 (17.3)	12.6 (0.05)	1,165 (8.3)	16.8 (0.12)	1,235 (11.0)	14.1 (0.13)	1,449 (10.0)	10.8 (0.07)	909 (4.4)	10.5 (0.05)
1999	4,789 (23.1)	12.5 (0.06)	1,168 (7.5)	16.7 (0.11)	1,222 (8.4)	13.9 (0.10)	1,487 (19.6)	10.9 (0.14)	913 (4.4)	10.4 (0.05)
2001	5,023 (36.1)	12.9 (0.09)	1,216 (9.4)	17.3 (0.14)	1,253 (21.2)	14.3 (0.24)	1,584 (17.8)	11.3 (0.13)	969 (21.2)	10.6 (0.23)
2003	4,788 (30.3)	12.3 (0.08)	1,131 (7.8)	16.4 (0.11)	1,167 (13.6)	13.5 (0.16)	1,547 (18.6)	10.9 (0.13)	944 (18.1)	10.2 (0.20)
2005	4,724 (33.0)	12.1 (0.09)	1,063 (6.6)	15.9 (0.10)	1,142 (19.3)	13.3 (0.23)	1,551 (21.2)	10.7 (0.15)	969 (15.0)	10.5 (0.16)
2007	4,546 (21.9)	11.7 (0.06)	1,047 (6.3)	16.0 (0.10)	1,065 (7.7)	12.6 (0.09)	1,525 (17.7)	10.4 (0.12)	909 (8.1)	9.9 (0.09)
2009	4,179 (33.2)	10.8 (0.09)	938 (12.6)	14.6 (0.20)	1,016 (25.1)	12.1 (0.30)	1,424 (16.2)	9.8 (0.11)	802 (7.2)	8.8 (0.08)
2011	3,977 (18.2)	10.3 (0.04)	898 (12.8)	14.1 (0.17)	967 (12.8)	11.7 (0.14)	1,337 (1.8)	9.0 (0.01)	774 (0.3)	8.6 (#)
2013	4,084 (42.4)	10.5 (0.10)	859 (8.8)	13.5 (0.12)	1,036 (37.9)	12.4 (0.40)	1,403 (7.9)	9.2 (0.05)	786 (15.0)	8.6 (0.15)
2015	4,304 (69.2)	10.9 (0.16)	932 (27.8)	14.6 (0.37)	1,099 (48.9)	13.1 (0.51)	1,471 (38.4)	9.5 (0.23)	802 (12.2)	8.7 (0.12)
Grades 9 through 12										
1995	1,163 (4.6)	8.5 (0.03)	335 (2.9)	13.0 (0.11)	287 (0.9)	8.6 (0.03)	331 (2.1)	7.1 (0.04)	209 (2.3)	6.8 (0.08)
1997	1,185 (2.4)	8.3 (0.02)	331 (0.5)	12.5 (0.02)	293 (0.7)	8.5 (0.02)	354 (1.7)	7.2 (0.03)	207 (1.2)	6.4 (0.04)
1999	1,229 (8.3)	8.4 (0.06)	340 (1.1)	12.6 (0.04)	299 (2.5)	8.6 (0.07)	376 (7.6)	7.5 (0.15)	215 (1.8)	6.3 (0.05)
2001	1,296 (6.7)	8.6 (0.04)	365 (0.8)	13.1 (0.03)	302 (2.0)	8.6 (0.06)	390 (4.4)	7.5 (0.08)	239 (4.5)	6.8 (0.13)
2003	1,311 (24.7)	8.4 (0.16)	382 (24.0)	13.1 (0.83)	294 (4.1)	8.2 (0.11)	397 (3.0)	7.4 (0.06)	238 (3.5)	6.4 (0.09)
2005	1,349 (18.1)	8.3 (0.11)	367 (1.7)	12.3 (0.06)	292 (5.0)	7.9 (0.14)	425 (7.2)	7.5 (0.13)	265 (15.7)	6.7 (0.40)
2007	1,364 (12.0)	8.3 (0.07)	379 (8.8)	12.7 (0.30)	287 (1.3)	7.8 (0.04)	440 (5.5)	7.6 (0.10)	257 (5.7)	6.5 (0.14)
2009	1,309 (6.5)	8.0 (0.04)	372 (5.7)	12.6 (0.20)	280 (2.2)	7.7 (0.06)	418 (1.7)	7.3 (0.03)	239 (1.1)	6.1 (0.03)
2011	1,291 (15.4)	8.1 (0.09)	353 (5.2)	12.6 (0.16)	295 (14.4)	8.4 (0.38)	411 (1.8)	7.1 (0.03)	232 (0.1)	5.9 (#)
2013	1,312 (14.9)	8.2 (0.09)	342 (0.8)	12.4 (0.03)	291 (13.1)	8.4 (0.35)	437 (1.3)	7.4 (0.02)	242 (7.0)	6.2 (0.17)
2015	1,446 (23.8)	8.8 (0.13)	382 (10.5)	13.7 (0.32)	309 (10.9)	8.8 (0.28)	494 (18.2)	8.0 (0.27)	261 (1.9)	6.6 (0.04)

#Rounds to zero.
NOTE: Includes enrollment in prekindergarten through grade 12 in schools that offer kindergarten or higher grade. Ungraded students are prorated into prekindergarten through grade 8 and grades 9 through 12. Detail may not sum to totals because of rounding.

SOURCE: U.S. Department of Education, National Center for Education Statistics, Private School Universe Survey (PSS), 1995–96 through 2015–16; and Common Core of Data (CCD), "State Nonfiscal Survey of Public Elementary/Secondary Education," 1995–96 through 2015–16. (This table was prepared June 2018.)

Table 205.15. Private elementary and secondary school enrollment, percentage distribution of private school enrollment, and private school enrollment as a percentage of total enrollment in public and private schools, by school orientation and grade: Selected years, fall 1999 through fall 2015

[Standard errors appear in parentheses]

Grade	1999		2005		2011		2013		2015							
									Total		Catholic		Other religious		Nonsectarian	
1	2		3		4		5		6		7		8		9	
	Enrollment															
Total, all grades	**6,018,280**	**(30,179)**	**6,073,240**	**(42,446)**	**5,268,090**	**(24,908)**	**5,395,740**	**(50,342)**	**5,750,520**	**(85,729)**	**2,082,660**	**(42,791)**	**2,268,820**	**(68,162)**	**1,399,030**	**(29,132)**
Prekindergarten through grade 8	**4,788,990**	**(23,055)**	**4,724,310**	**(33,034)**	**3,976,960**	**(18,241)**	**4,083,860**	**(42,441)**	**4,304,470**	**(69,171)**	**1,487,620**	**(42,646)**	**1,771,440**	**(47,422)**	**1,045,410**	**(27,611)**
Prekindergarten	763,790	(6,261)	926,430	(15,701)	773,240	(2,420)	819,320	(10,185)	846,920	(17,898)	181,190	(7,731)	336,000	(8,563)	329,730	(10,690)
Kindergarten	593,690	(4,053)	547,590	(4,887)	449,820	(2,989)	461,730	(5,429)	466,470	(8,411)	148,250	(4,592)	190,540	(4,799)	127,680	(4,513)
1st grade	472,110	(2,080)	421,120	(2,826)	348,730	(2,191)	357,860	(4,963)	373,850	(6,901)	141,450	(4,075)	165,900	(5,400)	66,510	(1,789)
2nd grade	449,090	(2,248)	405,470	(2,659)	340,230	(2,008)	344,520	(4,887)	368,450	(6,625)	144,700	(4,639)	159,360	(4,671)	64,390	(1,534)
3rd grade	436,730	(1,962)	398,120	(2,462)	336,150	(1,850)	338,840	(4,193)	364,290	(6,479)	144,160	(3,822)	156,890	(5,176)	63,240	(1,469)
4th grade	425,140	(1,956)	391,530	(2,297)	328,950	(1,921)	337,440	(4,508)	357,820	(6,202)	143,150	(4,268)	152,500	(4,499)	62,180	(1,144)
5th grade	407,590	(2,019)	389,720	(2,379)	330,390	(1,832)	337,950	(4,192)	354,710	(5,903)	143,180	(3,731)	148,220	(4,520)	63,310	(1,015)
6th grade	403,110	(2,094)	393,220	(2,280)	341,690	(1,766)	344,960	(4,820)	372,750	(7,276)	148,830	(4,623)	154,780	(5,440)	69,140	(980)
7th grade	384,140	(2,140)	390,550	(4,093)	336,770	(1,684)	343,370	(4,317)	367,920	(6,574)	144,190	(3,463)	151,970	(5,354)	71,760	(936)
8th grade	369,580	(2,285)	387,720	(4,024)	336,670	(1,951)	343,500	(3,717)	363,840	(7,047)	142,720	(3,446)	147,740	(5,919)	73,370	(1,228)
Elementary ungraded	84,000	(1,267)	72,830	(1,916)	54,300	(672)	54,380	(1,061)	67,440	(11,164)	5,810	(†)	7,540	(1,184)	54,090	(11,101)
Grades 9 through 12	**1,229,290**	**(8,260)**	**1,348,930**	**(18,073)**	**1,291,130**	**(15,396)**	**1,311,880**	**(14,936)**	**1,446,060**	**(23,777)**	**595,050**	**(2,166)**	**497,390**	**(23,622)**	**353,620**	**(5,530)**
9th grade	336,220	(2,131)	356,130	(4,333)	329,600	(3,875)	333,610	(3,612)	367,810	(6,279)	152,790	(606)	130,540	(6,197)	84,470	(1,463)
10th grade	313,310	(1,919)	348,190	(5,949)	324,540	(4,161)	330,710	(3,780)	367,250	(6,041)	151,290	(535)	126,220	(5,984)	89,740	(1,451)
11th grade	294,650	(2,193)	326,260	(4,456)	318,310	(3,647)	324,680	(3,850)	356,150	(5,906)	146,850	(485)	122,090	(5,881)	87,210	(1,327)
12th grade	280,380	(1,958)	315,290	(4,850)	314,500	(3,769)	319,720	(3,787)	348,600	(5,652)	143,830	(544)	116,950	(5,641)	87,820	(1,371)
Secondary ungraded	4,720	(1,404)	3,070	(†)	4,180	(92)	3,160	(14)	6,240	(†)	290	(†)	1,580	(†)	4,370	(†)
	Percentage distribution															
Total, all grades	**100.0**	**(†)**	**100.0**	**(†)**	**100.0**	**(†)**	**100.0**	**(†)**	**100.0**	**(†)**	**100.0**	**(†)**	**100.0**	**(†)**	**100.0**	**(†)**
Prekindergarten through grade 8	**79.6**	**(0.06)**	**77.8**	**(0.22)**	**75.5**	**(0.23)**	**75.7**	**(0.22)**	**74.9**	**(0.27)**	**71.4**	**(0.59)**	**78.1**	**(0.51)**	**74.7**	**(0.53)**
Prekindergarten	12.7	(0.08)	15.3	(0.21)	14.7	(0.08)	15.2	(0.15)	14.7	(0.22)	8.7	(0.21)	14.8	(0.34)	23.6	(0.42)
Kindergarten	9.9	(0.04)	9.0	(0.06)	8.5	(0.04)	8.6	(0.08)	8.1	(0.08)	7.1	(0.08)	8.4	(0.13)	9.1	(0.18)
1st grade	7.8	(0.02)	6.9	(0.03)	6.6	(0.02)	6.6	(0.05)	6.5	(0.07)	6.8	(0.07)	7.3	(0.17)	4.8	(0.08)
2nd grade	7.5	(0.01)	6.7	(0.03)	6.5	(0.02)	6.4	(0.05)	6.4	(0.06)	6.9	(0.09)	7.0	(0.09)	4.6	(0.07)
3rd grade	7.3	(0.02)	6.6	(0.03)	6.4	(0.02)	6.3	(0.04)	6.3	(0.05)	6.9	(0.05)	6.9	(0.08)	4.5	(0.07)
4th grade	7.1	(0.01)	6.4	(0.03)	6.2	(0.02)	6.3	(0.04)	6.2	(0.05)	6.9	(0.07)	6.7	(0.06)	4.4	(0.06)
5th grade	6.8	(0.01)	6.4	(0.04)	6.3	(0.02)	6.3	(0.04)	6.2	(0.05)	6.9	(0.05)	6.5	(0.08)	4.5	(0.06)
6th grade	6.7	(0.02)	6.5	(0.03)	6.5	(0.02)	6.4	(0.05)	6.5	(0.07)	7.1	(0.10)	6.8	(0.10)	4.9	(0.09)
7th grade	6.4	(0.02)	6.4	(0.04)	6.4	(0.02)	6.4	(0.05)	6.4	(0.06)	6.9	(0.06)	6.7	(0.10)	5.1	(0.09)
8th grade	6.1	(0.02)	6.4	(0.04)	6.4	(0.02)	6.4	(0.04)	6.3	(0.06)	6.9	(0.06)	6.5	(0.11)	5.2	(0.11)
Elementary ungraded	1.4	(0.02)	1.2	(0.03)	1.0	(0.01)	1.0	(0.02)	1.2	(0.19)	0.3	(0.01)	0.3	(0.05)	3.9	(0.74)
Grades 9 through 12	**20.4**	**(0.06)**	**22.2**	**(0.22)**	**24.5**	**(0.23)**	**24.3**	**(0.22)**	**25.1**	**(0.27)**	**28.6**	**(0.59)**	**21.9**	**(0.51)**	**25.3**	**(0.53)**
9th grade	5.6	(0.02)	5.9	(0.05)	6.3	(0.06)	6.2	(0.05)	6.4	(0.07)	7.3	(0.15)	5.8	(0.13)	6.0	(0.13)
10th grade	5.2	(0.01)	5.7	(0.08)	6.2	(0.06)	6.1	(0.06)	6.4	(0.07)	7.3	(0.15)	5.6	(0.13)	6.4	(0.14)
11th grade	4.9	(0.02)	5.4	(0.06)	6.0	(0.05)	6.0	(0.06)	6.2	(0.07)	7.1	(0.15)	5.4	(0.13)	6.2	(0.13)
12th grade	4.7	(0.02)	5.2	(0.07)	6.0	(0.06)	5.9	(0.06)	6.1	(0.07)	6.9	(0.14)	5.2	(0.12)	6.3	(0.13)
Secondary ungraded	0.1	(0.02)	0.1	(#)	0.1	(#)	0.1	(#)	0.1	(#)	#	(†)	0.1	(#)	0.3	(#)

See notes at end of table.

Table 205.15. Private elementary and secondary school enrollment, percentage distribution of private school enrollment, and private enrollment as a percentage of total enrollment in public and private schools, by school orientation and grade: Selected years, fall 1999 through fall 2015—Continued

[Standard errors appear in parentheses]

Grade	1999		2005		2011		2013		2015							
									Total		Catholic		Other religious		Nonsectarian	
1	2		3		4		5		6		7		8		9	
	Private enrollment as a percent of total enrollment															
Total, all grades	**11.4**	**(0.05)**	**11.0**	**(0.07)**	**9.7**	**(0.04)**	**9.8**	**(0.08)**	**10.3**	**(0.14)**	**4.0**	**(0.08)**	**4.3**	**(0.12)**	**2.7**	**(0.06)**
Prekindergarten through grade 8	**12.6**	**(0.05)**	**12.2**	**(0.07)**	**10.3**	**(0.04)**	**10.4**	**(0.10)**	**10.9**	**(0.16)**	**4.1**	**(0.11)**	**4.8**	**(0.12)**	**2.9**	**(0.07)**
Prekindergarten	55.4	(0.20)	52.3	(0.42)	40.4	(0.08)	41.5	(0.30)	41.6	(0.51)	13.2	(0.49)	22.0	(0.44)	21.7	(0.55)
Kindergarten	14.9	(0.09)	13.2	(0.10)	10.7	(0.06)	10.8	(0.11)	11.2	(0.18)	3.8	(0.11)	4.9	(0.12)	3.3	(0.11)
1st grade	11.4	(0.04)	10.2	(0.06)	8.5	(0.08)	8.4	(0.11)	9.0	(0.15)	3.6	(0.10)	4.2	(0.13)	1.7	(0.05)
2nd grade	10.9	(0.05)	10.1	(0.06)	8.4	(0.05)	8.3	(0.11)	8.8	(0.14)	3.6	(0.11)	4.0	(0.11)	1.6	(0.04)
3rd grade	10.6	(0.04)	10.0	(0.06)	8.3	(0.05)	8.3	(0.09)	8.6	(0.14)	3.6	(0.09)	3.9	(0.12)	1.6	(0.04)
4th grade	10.3	(0.04)	9.9	(0.05)	8.2	(0.04)	8.4	(0.10)	8.6	(0.14)	3.6	(0.10)	3.9	(0.11)	1.6	(0.03)
5th grade	10.2	(0.05)	9.7	(0.05)	8.2	(0.04)	8.4	(0.10)	8.7	(0.13)	3.7	(0.09)	3.8	(0.11)	1.7	(0.03)
6th grade	10.2	(0.05)	9.7	(0.05)	8.4	(0.04)	8.6	(0.11)	9.1	(0.16)	3.8	(0.11)	4.0	(0.13)	1.8	(0.03)
7th grade	9.8	(0.05)	9.4	(0.09)	8.4	(0.04)	8.4	(0.10)	9.0	(0.15)	3.7	(0.09)	3.9	(0.13)	1.9	(0.02)
8th grade	9.5	(0.05)	9.3	(0.09)	8.4	(0.04)	8.4	(0.08)	8.9	(0.16)	3.7	(0.09)	3.8	(0.15)	1.9	(0.03)
Elementary ungraded	16.8	(0.21)	22.8	(0.46)	40.3	(0.30)	38.6	(0.46)	46.9	(4.20)	7.1	(†)	9.0	(1.28)	41.4	(5.06)
Grades 9 through 12	**8.4**	**(0.05)**	**8.3**	**(0.10)**	**8.1**	**(0.09)**	**8.2**	**(0.09)**	**8.8**	**(0.13)**	**3.8**	**(0.01)**	**3.2**	**(0.15)**	**2.3**	**(0.04)**
9th grade	7.9	(0.05)	7.7	(0.09)	7.7	(0.08)	7.8	(0.08)	8.4	(0.13)	3.7	(0.01)	3.2	(0.14)	2.1	(0.03)
10th grade	8.4	(0.05)	8.3	(0.13)	8.0	(0.09)	8.1	(0.09)	8.7	(0.13)	3.8	(0.01)	3.2	(0.15)	2.3	(0.04)
11th grade	8.8	(0.06)	8.6	(0.11)	8.3	(0.09)	8.5	(0.09)	9.0	(0.14)	3.9	(0.01)	3.3	(0.15)	2.4	(0.04)
12th grade	9.1	(0.06)	9.0	(0.13)	8.4	(0.09)	8.5	(0.09)	9.0	(0.13)	3.9	(0.01)	3.2	(0.15)	2.4	(0.04)
Secondary ungraded	3.6	(1.03)	3.2	(†)	9.5	(0.19)	6.8	(0.03)	11.7	(†)	0.6	(†)	3.2	(†)	8.5	(†)

†Not applicable.
#Rounds to zero.
NOTE: Includes enrollment in prekindergarten through grade 12 in schools that offer kindergarten or higher grade. Ungraded students are prorated into prekindergarten through grade 8 and grades 9 through 12. Detail may not sum to totals because of rounding.

SOURCE: U.S. Department of Education, National Center for Education Statistics, Private School Universe Survey (PSS), 1999–2000 through 2015–16; and Common Core of Data (CCD), "Public Elementary/Secondary School Universe Survey," 1999–2000 through 2015–16. (This table was prepared June 2017.)

Table 205.20. Enrollment and percentage distribution of students enrolled in private elementary and secondary schools, by school orientation and grade level: Selected years, fall 1995 through fall 2015

[Standard errors appear in parentheses]

Grade level and year	Total private enrollment	Catholic				Other religious				Nonsectarian
		Total	Parochial	Diocesan	Private	Total	Conservative Christian	Affiliated[1]	Unaffiliated[1]	
1	2	3	4	5	6	7	8	9	10	11
	Enrollment									
Total, all grades										
1995	5,918,040 (31,815)	2,660,450 (6,878)	1,458,990 (2,079)	850,560 (5,674)	350,900 (1,176)	2,094,690 (16,956)	786,660 (8,815)	697,280 (4,886)	610,750 (11,831)	1,162,900 (18,443)
1997	5,944,320 (18,543)	2,665,630 (5,472)	1,438,860 (5,331)	873,780 (761)	352,990 (1,405)	2,097,190 (13,733)	823,610 (7,342)	646,500 (3,104)	627,080 (11,133)	1,181,510 (12,013)
1999	6,018,280 (30,179)	2,660,420 (4,831)	1,397,570 (4,421)	880,650 (†)	382,190 (1,945)	2,193,370 (27,176)	871,060 (4,827)	646,280 (4,894)	676,030 (24,593)	1,164,500 (8,156)
2001	6,319,650 (40,272)	2,672,650 (12,460)	1,309,890 (5,626)	979,050 (6,976)	383,710 (3,152)	2,328,160 (17,281)	937,420 (6,070)	663,190 (8,636)	727,550 (13,303)	1,318,840 (27,300)
2003	6,099,220 (41,219)	2,520,120 (10,580)	1,183,250 (9,937)	963,140 (4,754)	373,740 (3,996)	2,228,230 (19,674)	889,710 (8,852)	650,530 (5,860)	688,000 (14,805)	1,350,870 (29,197)
2005	6,073,240 (42,446)	2,402,800 (9,293)	1,062,950 (6,355)	956,610 (6,325)	383,230 (3,996)	2,303,330 (22,368)	957,360 (9,561)	696,910 (6,677)	649,050 (14,200)	1,367,120 (27,558)
2007	5,910,210 (28,363)	2,308,150 (6,083)	945,860 (5,361)	969,940 (1,788)	392,340 (3,432)	2,283,210 (20,628)	883,180 (6,616)	527,040 (3,512)	872,990 (18,217)	1,318,850 (18,235)
2009	5,488,490 (35,857)	2,160,220 (3,494)	856,440 (3,088)	909,010 (4,393)	394,770 (1,087)	2,076,220 (32,751)	737,020 (1,891)	516,310 (4,366)	822,890 (31,180)	1,252,050 (8,849)
2011	5,268,090 (24,908)	2,087,870 (14,426)	804,410 (3,686)	899,810 (14,320)	383,650 (459)	1,991,950 (21,814)	730,570 (4,721)	565,340 (2,990)	696,040 (20,419)	1,188,270 (5,376)
2013	5,395,740 (50,342)	2,055,140 (37,142)	739,850 (18,829)	936,320 (32,000)	378,970 (980)	2,030,930 (30,090)	707,100 (7,544)	565,490 (5,884)	758,350 (28,152)	1,309,670 (14,800)
2015	5,750,520 (85,729)	2,082,660 (42,791)	716,120 (24,336)	960,590 (22,533)	405,950 (14,453)	2,268,820 (68,162)	760,790 (53,772)	587,490 (23,414)	920,550 (45,692)	1,399,030 (29,132)
Prekindergarten through grade 8										
1995	4,755,540 (28,435)	2,041,990 (5,249)	1,368,340 (2,079)	575,190 (3,528)	98,460 (1,176)	1,752,510 (14,834)	651,050 (7,219)	574,820 (4,581)	526,630 (11,121)	961,040 (17,471)
1997	4,759,060 (17,323)	2,046,620 (5,469)	1,352,620 (5,331)	598,380 (761)	95,620 (1,393)	1,744,500 (12,194)	678,660 (5,957)	529,050 (2,504)	536,790 (10,120)	967,940 (11,050)
1999	4,788,990 (23,055)	2,033,900 (4,830)	1,317,300 (4,421)	607,860 (†)	108,740 (1,943)	1,818,260 (19,897)	713,020 (3,748)	529,280 (3,866)	575,970 (17,632)	936,820 (7,302)
2001	5,023,160 (36,096)	2,032,080 (10,751)	1,226,960 (4,494)	687,540 (6,976)	117,580 (2,978)	1,926,870 (15,459)	765,080 (5,110)	535,850 (7,370)	625,940 (12,240)	1,064,210 (24,703)
2003	4,788,070 (30,338)	1,886,530 (11,055)	1,108,320 (9,937)	670,910 (4,754)	107,300 (337)	1,835,930 (16,931)	722,460 (6,517)	519,310 (4,134)	594,160 (13,504)	1,065,620 (15,379)
2005	4,724,310 (33,034)	1,779,830 (9,318)	993,390 (6,355)	673,110 (6,286)	113,330 (2,896)	1,865,430 (19,380)	764,920 (8,028)	561,320 (5,730)	539,190 (12,633)	1,079,050 (15,497)
2007	4,545,910 (21,853)	1,685,220 (5,288)	878,830 (4,562)	688,260 (1,640)	118,130 (3,104)	1,833,540 (18,364)	698,930 (5,885)	417,610 (3,218)	717,000 (16,573)	1,027,150 (11,379)
2009	4,179,060 (33,168)	1,541,830 (3,250)	782,050 (3,085)	642,720 (846)	117,050 (578)	1,665,680 (30,216)	579,190 (1,685)	401,430 (3,952)	685,050 (28,928)	971,550 (8,113)
2011	3,976,960 (18,241)	1,481,620 (3,867)	737,090 (3,675)	630,970 (321)	113,560 (459)	1,583,610 (16,558)	568,150 (3,607)	443,780 (2,604)	571,690 (15,197)	911,730 (3,469)
2013	4,083,860 (42,441)	1,466,550 (27,646)	680,370 (18,826)	666,260 (20,228)	119,930 (843)	1,615,120 (29,311)	544,610 (5,638)	446,050 (5,316)	624,470 (27,948)	1,002,180 (11,849)
2015	4,304,470 (69,171)	1,487,620 (42,646)	662,670 (24,233)	677,540 (22,542)	147,410 (14,387)	1,771,440 (47,422)	576,570 (38,496)	445,620 (15,105)	749,250 (33,313)	1,045,410 (27,611)
Grades 9 through 12										
1995	1,162,500 (4,625)	618,460 (2,786)	90,650 (†)	275,370 (2,786)	252,440 (†)	342,180 (3,174)	135,610 (2,338)	122,460 (645)	84,120 (1,720)	201,860 (1,495)
1997	1,185,260 (2,374)	619,010 (96)	86,240 (†)	275,400 (†)	257,370 (96)	352,690 (2,261)	144,950 (1,660)	117,450 (848)	90,290 (1,221)	213,560 (1,860)
1999	1,229,290 (8,260)	626,520 (70)	80,270 (†)	272,790 (†)	273,460 (70)	375,100 (7,920)	158,040 (1,640)	117,000 (1,237)	100,060 (7,461)	227,670 (2,208)
2001	1,296,480 (6,669)	640,570 (2,317)	82,930 (2,293)	291,520 (†)	266,130 (338)	401,290 (3,527)	172,340 (2,633)	127,340 (1,625)	101,600 (1,852)	254,620 (4,465)
2003	1,311,150 (24,733)	633,590 (3,888)	74,930 (†)	292,230 (†)	266,430 (3,888)	392,310 (4,195)	167,250 (3,144)	131,220 (1,924)	93,840 (2,031)	285,250 (23,952)
2005	1,348,930 (18,073)	622,970 (1,538)	69,560 (†)	283,510 (700)	269,900 (1,341)	437,900 (6,541)	192,440 (3,404)	135,590 (1,493)	109,860 (5,190)	288,070 (16,551)
2007	1,364,300 (11,958)	622,930 (1,377)	67,030 (1,201)	281,680 (566)	274,210 (364)	449,680 (3,796)	184,260 (1,768)	109,430 (374)	156,000 (3,052)	291,700 (11,156)
2009	1,309,430 (6,480)	618,390 (4,409)	74,380 (42)	266,290 (4,311)	277,720 (920)	410,540 (4,285)	157,830 (362)	114,880 (1,074)	137,840 (4,111)	280,500 (1,880)
2011	1,291,130 (15,396)	606,250 (14,313)	67,320 (10)	268,840 (14,313)	270,090 (†)	408,330 (5,747)	162,420 (1,349)	121,560 (513)	124,350 (5,792)	276,550 (3,485)
2013	1,311,880 (14,936)	588,580 (13,452)	59,480 (358)	270,060 (13,416)	259,040 (905)	415,810 (2,774)	162,490 (1,942)	119,440 (1,862)	133,880 (1,762)	307,490 (6,938)
2015	1,446,060 (23,777)	595,050 (2,166)	53,450 (1,662)	283,050 (38)	258,550 (1,388)	497,390 (23,622)	184,220 (15,411)	141,870 (9,045)	171,300 (16,438)	353,620 (5,530)

See notes at end of table.

Table 205.20. Enrollment and percentage distribution of students enrolled in private elementary and secondary schools, by school orientation and grade level: Selected years, fall 1995 through fall 2015—Continued

[Standard errors appear in parentheses]

Grade level and year	Total private enrollment	Catholic				Other religious				Nonsectarian
		Total	Parochial	Diocesan	Private	Total	Conservative Christian	Affiliated[1]	Unaffiliated[1]	
1	2	3	4	5	6	7	8	9	10	11
	Percentage distribution									
Total, all grades										
1995	100.0 (†)	45.0 (0.19)	24.7 (0.13)	14.4 (0.08)	5.9 (0.03)	35.4 (0.19)	13.3 (0.12)	11.8 (0.08)	10.3 (0.18)	19.7 (0.23)
1997	100.0 (†)	44.8 (0.13)	24.2 (0.09)	14.7 (0.05)	5.9 (0.03)	35.3 (0.18)	13.9 (0.12)	10.9 (0.06)	10.5 (0.17)	19.9 (0.17)
1999	100.0 (†)	44.2 (0.24)	23.2 (0.14)	14.6 (0.07)	6.4 (0.04)	36.4 (0.28)	14.5 (0.09)	10.7 (0.08)	11.2 (0.36)	19.3 (0.11)
2001	100.0 (†)	42.3 (0.25)	20.7 (0.14)	15.5 (0.12)	6.1 (0.04)	36.8 (0.22)	14.8 (0.13)	10.5 (0.13)	11.5 (0.18)	20.9 (0.33)
2003	100.0 (†)	41.3 (0.27)	19.4 (0.17)	15.8 (0.14)	6.1 (0.07)	36.5 (0.25)	14.6 (0.13)	10.7 (0.10)	11.3 (0.22)	22.1 (0.36)
2005	100.0 (†)	39.6 (0.26)	17.5 (0.13)	15.8 (0.14)	6.3 (0.07)	37.9 (0.25)	15.8 (0.14)	11.5 (0.09)	10.7 (0.20)	22.5 (0.34)
2007	100.0 (†)	39.1 (0.20)	16.0 (0.11)	16.4 (0.09)	6.6 (0.06)	38.6 (0.25)	14.9 (0.12)	8.9 (0.06)	14.8 (0.26)	22.3 (0.25)
2009	100.0 (†)	39.4 (0.25)	15.6 (0.11)	16.6 (0.13)	7.2 (0.05)	37.8 (0.37)	13.4 (0.09)	9.4 (0.07)	15.0 (0.48)	22.8 (0.16)
2011	100.0 (†)	39.6 (0.25)	15.3 (0.09)	17.1 (0.25)	7.3 (0.04)	37.8 (0.28)	13.9 (0.09)	10.7 (0.08)	13.2 (0.34)	22.6 (0.15)
2013	100.0 (†)	38.1 (0.50)	13.7 (0.33)	17.4 (0.51)	7.0 (0.07)	37.6 (0.44)	13.1 (0.16)	10.5 (0.13)	14.1 (0.47)	24.3 (0.28)
2015	100.0 (†)	36.2 (0.66)	12.5 (0.38)	16.7 (0.40)	7.1 (0.24)	39.5 (0.80)	13.2 (0.85)	10.2 (0.39)	16.0 (0.73)	24.3 (0.51)
Prekindergarten through grade 8										
1995	100.0 (†)	42.9 (0.20)	28.8 (0.17)	12.1 (0.06)	2.1 (0.02)	36.9 (0.22)	13.7 (0.13)	12.1 (0.09)	11.1 (0.21)	20.2 (0.28)
1997	100.0 (†)	43.0 (0.15)	28.4 (0.12)	12.6 (0.05)	2.0 (0.03)	36.7 (0.20)	14.3 (0.13)	11.1 (0.06)	11.3 (0.19)	20.3 (0.19)
1999	100.0 (†)	42.5 (0.23)	27.5 (0.16)	12.7 (0.06)	2.3 (0.04)	38.0 (0.26)	14.9 (0.09)	11.1 (0.07)	12.0 (0.32)	19.6 (0.12)
2001	100.0 (†)	40.5 (0.27)	24.4 (0.17)	13.7 (0.14)	2.3 (0.05)	38.4 (0.25)	15.2 (0.15)	10.7 (0.14)	12.5 (0.20)	21.2 (0.37)
2003	100.0 (†)	39.4 (0.25)	23.1 (0.18)	14.0 (0.13)	2.2 (0.01)	38.3 (0.23)	15.1 (0.12)	10.8 (0.09)	12.4 (0.24)	22.3 (0.22)
2005	100.0 (†)	37.7 (0.25)	21.0 (0.14)	14.2 (0.15)	2.4 (0.06)	39.5 (0.21)	16.2 (0.16)	11.9 (0.09)	11.4 (0.22)	22.8 (0.23)
2007	100.0 (†)	37.1 (0.20)	19.3 (0.13)	15.1 (0.09)	2.6 (0.07)	40.3 (0.27)	15.4 (0.14)	9.2 (0.07)	15.8 (0.30)	22.6 (0.21)
2009	100.0 (†)	36.9 (0.29)	18.7 (0.15)	15.4 (0.12)	2.8 (0.03)	39.9 (0.43)	13.9 (0.11)	9.6 (0.10)	16.4 (0.57)	23.2 (0.20)
2011	100.0 (†)	37.3 (0.18)	18.5 (0.11)	15.9 (0.08)	2.9 (0.02)	39.8 (0.24)	14.3 (0.08)	11.2 (0.08)	14.4 (0.32)	22.9 (0.11)
2013	100.0 (†)	35.9 (0.53)	16.7 (0.42)	16.3 (0.44)	2.9 (0.04)	39.5 (0.52)	13.3 (0.17)	10.9 (0.15)	15.3 (0.59)	24.5 (0.31)
2015	100.0 (†)	34.6 (0.78)	15.4 (0.48)	15.7 (0.50)	3.4 (0.31)	41.2 (0.81)	13.4 (0.82)	10.4 (0.35)	17.4 (0.73)	24.3 (0.61)
Grades 9 through 12										
1995	100.0 (†)	53.2 (0.20)	7.8 (0.03)	23.7 (0.20)	21.7 (0.09)	29.4 (0.20)	11.7 (0.18)	10.5 (0.06)	7.2 (0.14)	17.4 (0.12)
1997	100.0 (†)	52.2 (0.10)	7.3 (0.01)	23.2 (0.05)	21.7 (0.04)	29.8 (0.16)	12.2 (0.13)	9.9 (0.08)	7.6 (0.10)	18.0 (0.14)
1999	100.0 (†)	51.0 (0.34)	6.5 (0.04)	22.2 (0.15)	22.2 (0.15)	30.5 (0.45)	12.9 (0.14)	9.5 (0.11)	8.1 (0.56)	18.5 (0.19)
2001	100.0 (†)	49.4 (0.26)	6.4 (0.17)	22.5 (0.12)	20.5 (0.10)	31.0 (0.19)	13.3 (0.17)	9.8 (0.12)	7.8 (0.13)	19.6 (0.28)
2003	100.0 (†)	48.3 (0.91)	5.7 (0.11)	22.3 (0.42)	20.3 (0.44)	29.9 (0.59)	12.8 (0.32)	10.0 (0.23)	7.2 (0.20)	21.8 (1.43)
2005	100.0 (†)	46.2 (0.60)	5.2 (0.07)	21.0 (0.28)	20.0 (0.27)	32.5 (0.52)	14.3 (0.28)	10.1 (0.16)	8.1 (0.37)	21.4 (0.97)
2007	100.0 (†)	45.7 (0.40)	4.9 (0.09)	20.6 (0.18)	20.1 (0.17)	33.0 (0.33)	13.5 (0.16)	8.0 (0.07)	11.4 (0.22)	21.4 (0.65)
2009	100.0 (†)	47.2 (0.25)	5.7 (0.03)	20.3 (0.27)	21.2 (0.12)	31.4 (0.25)	12.1 (0.06)	8.8 (0.08)	10.5 (0.28)	21.4 (0.15)
2011	100.0 (†)	47.0 (0.63)	5.2 (0.06)	20.8 (0.88)	20.9 (0.25)	31.6 (0.49)	12.6 (0.18)	9.4 (0.13)	9.6 (0.43)	21.4 (0.35)
2013	100.0 (†)	44.9 (0.64)	4.5 (0.06)	20.6 (0.83)	19.7 (0.24)	31.7 (0.42)	12.4 (0.19)	9.1 (0.17)	10.2 (0.19)	23.4 (0.47)
2015	100.0 (†)	41.1 (0.67)	3.7 (0.13)	19.6 (0.32)	17.9 (0.30)	34.4 (1.11)	12.7 (0.96)	9.8 (0.59)	11.8 (1.02)	24.5 (0.51)

†Not applicable.
[1]Affiliated schools belong to associations of schools with a specific religious orientation other than Catholic or conservative Christian. Unaffiliated schools have a religious orientation or purpose but are not classified as Catholic, conservative Christian, or affiliated.

NOTE: Includes enrollment in prekindergarten through grade 12 in schools that offer kindergarten or higher grade. Ungraded students are prorated into prekindergarten through grade 8 and grades 9 through 12. Detail may not sum to totals because of rounding.
SOURCE: U.S. Department of Education, National Center for Education Statistics, Private School Universe Survey (PSS), 1995–96 through 2015–16. (This table was prepared May 2017.)

Table 205.30. Percentage distribution of students enrolled in private elementary and secondary schools, by school orientation and selected characteristics: Selected years, fall 2005 through fall 2015

[Standard errors appear in parentheses]

Selected characteristic	2005	2009	2013	2015									
				Total	Catholic				Other religious				Nonsectarian
					Total	Parochial	Diocesan	Private	Total	Conservative Christian	Affiliated[1]	Unaffiliated[1]	
1	2	3	4	5	6	7	8	9	10	11	12	13	14
Total	**100.0 (†)**	**100.0 (†)**	**100.0 (†)**	**100.0 (†)**	**100.0 (†)**	**100.0 (†)**	**100.0 (†)**	**100.0 (†)**	**100.0 (†)**	**100.0 (†)**	**100.0 (†)**	**100.0 (†)**	**100.0 (†)**
School level[2]													
Elementary	56.8 (0.34)	53.5 (0.24)	52.8 (0.47)	50.3 (0.80)	66.5 (0.69)	89.7 (0.46)	66.4 (0.79)	26.1 (2.63)	37.9 (1.57)	21.1 (1.46)	42.1 (1.70)	49.1 (2.58)	46.2 (0.85)
Secondary	14.2 (0.34)	14.3 (0.11)	13.7 (0.19)	13.5 (0.20)	25.4 (0.53)	6.8 (0.38)	28.0 (0.66)	52.0 (1.85)	5.5 (0.28)	2.2 (0.18)	9.4 (0.46)	5.6 (0.50)	8.7 (0.26)
Combined	29.1 (0.29)	32.2 (0.21)	33.5 (0.48)	36.2 (0.88)	8.1 (0.17)	3.5 (0.12)	5.6 (0.14)	21.9 (0.78)	56.6 (1.76)	76.6 (1.62)	48.4 (2.06)	45.3 (2.86)	45.1 (0.73)
Student race/ethnicity[3]													
White	75.3 (0.10)	72.6 (0.20)	69.6 (0.31)	68.6 (0.34)	65.9 (0.50)	67.1 (1.04)	66.7 (0.51)	62.4 (0.68)	73.1 (0.73)	70.2 (1.32)	76.1 (0.79)	73.7 (1.79)	65.2 (0.21)
Black	9.6 (0.08)	9.2 (0.07)	9.3 (0.27)	9.3 (0.31)	7.8 (0.23)	6.9 (0.65)	7.5 (0.15)	10.0 (0.14)	10.6 (0.74)	10.6 (0.49)	8.2 (0.24)	12.2 (1.81)	9.3 (0.12)
Hispanic	9.2 (0.05)	9.4 (0.09)	10.2 (0.11)	10.4 (0.15)	15.6 (0.30)	16.2 (0.67)	15.2 (0.25)	15.6 (0.49)	6.6 (0.16)	8.1 (0.48)	6.6 (0.27)	5.4 (0.19)	8.0 (0.12)
Asian	4.1 (0.05)	5.1 (0.05)	5.9 (0.05)	6.2 (0.06)	5.2 (0.08)	4.9 (0.12)	5.0 (0.08)	6.3 (0.25)	5.4 (0.10)	6.2 (0.51)	5.4 (0.21)	4.7 (0.41)	9.4 (0.08)
Pacific Islander	— (†)	0.6 (0.02)	0.7 (0.01)	0.7 (0.02)	0.6 (0.01)	0.6 (0.02)	0.5 (#)	0.7 (0.02)	0.5 (0.03)	0.5 (0.04)	0.3 (0.01)	0.6 (0.08)	1.4 (0.02)
American Indian/Alaska Native	1.8 (0.01)	0.4 (#)	0.5 (0.01)	0.5 (0.01)	0.5 (0.01)	0.5 (0.02)	0.5 (0.01)	0.6 (0.04)	0.4 (0.03)	0.5 (0.04)	0.3 (0.01)	0.4 (0.06)	0.5 (0.01)
Two or more races	— (†)	2.7 (0.02)	3.9 (0.03)	4.3 (0.08)	4.3 (0.07)	3.9 (0.12)	4.5 (0.08)	4.4 (0.10)	3.3 (0.15)	3.9 (0.40)	3.1 (0.08)	2.9 (0.15)	6.2 (0.16)
School enrollment													
Less than 50	4.5 (0.10)	5.4 (0.39)	5.4 (0.47)	5.5 (0.39)	0.4 (0.05)	0.5! (0.21)	0.2 (0.01)	0.8 (0.10)	7.9 (0.95)	3.8 (0.31)	4.2 (1.21)	13.6 (1.94)	9.0 (0.56)
50 to 149	16.7 (0.17)	17.3 (0.18)	17.1 (0.23)	16.8 (0.40)	7.3 (0.58)	7.9 (1.18)	7.6 (0.85)	5.4 (0.42)	19.8 (0.85)	16.3 (1.31)	15.4 (0.66)	25.6 (1.48)	26.0 (0.56)
150 to 299	26.6 (0.18)	25.9 (0.17)	25.5 (0.29)	25.1 (0.49)	29.5 (0.50)	37.8 (1.47)	28.3 (0.71)	17.7 (2.53)	23.1 (1.01)	22.9 (1.65)	26.8 (2.79)	20.9 (1.11)	21.9 (0.81)
300 to 499	21.1 (0.20)	21.0 (0.19)	20.4 (0.21)	19.5 (0.49)	27.7 (0.90)	29.1 (1.01)	29.1 (1.54)	21.7 (1.54)	15.8 (0.86)	19.2 (2.05)	18.0 (0.72)	11.4 (0.62)	13.6 (0.46)
500 to 749	15.0 (0.31)	14.0 (0.09)	14.5 (0.24)	15.8 (0.97)	18.8 (1.01)	19.2 (3.19)	17.8 (0.42)	20.4 (0.73)	16.4 (2.26)	23.2 (5.15)	13.8 (0.55)	12.5 (3.28)	10.3 (0.24)
750 or more	16.1 (0.24)	16.3 (0.12)	17.0 (0.54)	17.3 (0.29)	16.3 (0.34)	5.4 (0.18)	17.0 (0.40)	34.0 (1.21)	17.0 (0.56)	14.5 (1.22)	21.7 (0.87)	16.0 (0.80)	19.3 (0.46)
Region													
Northeast	23.5 (0.19)	23.9 (0.26)	22.3 (0.25)	22.9 (0.59)	23.2 (0.51)	22.7 (0.86)	20.0 (0.47)	31.7 (1.15)	20.9 (1.40)	12.7! (4.49)	25.2 (1.03)	25.1 (1.43)	25.5 (0.88)
Midwest	23.6 (0.30)	23.6 (0.38)	24.6 (0.64)	24.5 (0.77)	36.5 (1.28)	41.0 (1.94)	36.8 (1.49)	27.9 (2.28)	21.0 (1.35)	21.8 (3.96)	17.5 (0.76)	22.6 (2.29)	12.3 (0.48)
South	32.5 (0.33)	33.6 (0.29)	34.1 (0.33)	34.2 (0.73)	23.3 (0.52)	21.0 (0.94)	26.0 (0.61)	21.2 (0.77)	42.0 (1.50)	42.1 (3.05)	42.8 (2.28)	41.5 (2.66)	37.6 (1.13)
West	20.3 (0.36)	19.0 (0.17)	19.1 (0.32)	18.5 (0.33)	16.9 (0.50)	15.3 (0.87)	17.2 (0.41)	19.1 (1.53)	16.0 (0.52)	23.5 (1.80)	14.5 (0.58)	10.9 (0.56)	24.7 (0.70)
School locale													
City	41.3 (0.26)	41.0 (0.31)	42.5 (0.50)	43.0 (0.77)	47.0 (1.03)	42.4 (1.48)	48.6 (1.21)	51.2 (1.83)	38.8 (1.44)	28.6 (2.12)	42.7 (1.71)	44.8 (2.59)	43.8 (0.91)
Sburban	40.0 (0.35)	39.0 (0.34)	41.0 (0.44)	40.2 (0.82)	41.4 (1.11)	45.5 (1.79)	39.4 (0.93)	38.9 (2.00)	37.7 (1.60)	44.8 (3.63)	40.0 (1.62)	30.3 (1.50)	42.3 (0.70)
Town	7.2 (0.13)	7.1 (0.17)	6.3 (0.33)	6.2 (0.56)	7.1 (0.18)	8.6 (0.42)	8.0 (0.19)	2.4 (0.09)	7.4 (1.40)	11.6! (4.00)	4.5 (0.18)	5.8 (0.45)	2.8 (0.07)
Rural	11.5 (0.37)	12.9 (0.42)	10.1 (0.47)	10.7 (0.57)	4.5 (0.34)	3.5 (0.20)	4.0 (0.09)	7.5 (1.66)	16.1 (1.31)	15.0 (1.12)	12.7 (3.46)	19.2 (2.01)	11.0 (0.46)

—Not available.
†Not applicable.
#Rounds to zero.
!Interpret data with caution. The coefficient of variation (CV) for this estimate is between 30 and 50 percent.
[1]Affiliated schools belong to associations of schools with a specific religious orientation other than Catholic or conservative Christian. Unaffiliated schools have a religious orientation or purpose but are not classified as Catholic, conservative Christian, or affiliated.
[2]Elementary schools have grade 6 or lower and no grade higher than 8. Secondary schools have no grade lower than 7. Combined schools include those that have grades lower than 7 and higher than 8, as well as those that do not classify students by grade level.
[3]Race/ethnicity was not collected for prekindergarten students (846,900 out of 5,750,520 students in 2015). Percentage distribution is based on the students for whom race/ethnicity was reported.
NOTE: Includes enrollment in prekindergarten through grade 12 in schools that offer kindergarten or higher grade. Prior to 2009, data on students of Two or more races and separate data for Pacific Islanders were not collected. Race categories exclude persons of Hispanic ethnicity. Detail may not sum to totals because of rounding.
SOURCE: U.S. Department of Education, National Center for Education Statistics, Private School Universe Survey (PSS), 2005–06 through 2015–16. (This table was prepared May 2017.)

Table 205.40. Number and percentage distribution of private elementary and secondary students, teachers, and schools, by orientation of school and selected characteristics: Fall 1999, fall 2009, and fall 2015

[Standard errors appear in parentheses]

Selected characteristic	Fall 1999, total number	Fall 2009, total number	Fall 2015							
			Total		Catholic		Other religious		Nonsectarian	
			Number	Percent	Number	Percent	Number	Percent	Number	Percent
1	2	3	4	5	6	7	8	9	10	11
Students[1]										
Total	**6,018,280 (30,179)**	**5,488,490 (35,857)**	**5,750,520 (85,729)**	**100.0 (†)**	**2,082,660 (42,791)**	**100.0 (†)**	**2,268,820 (68,162)**	**100.0 (†)**	**1,399,030 (29,132)**	**100.0 (†)**
School level[2]										
Elementary	3,595,020 (11,516)	2,937,090 (26,807)	2,892,010 (55,884)	50.3 (0.80)	1,385,930 (42,655)	66.5 (0.69)	860,380 (31,793)	37.9 (1.57)	645,690 (20,790)	46.2 (0.85)
Secondary	806,640 (2,395)	785,810 (4,810)	774,650 (6,323)	13.5 (0.20)	528,460 (2,721)	25.4 (0.53)	124,050 (5,926)	5.5 (0.28)	122,140 (3,735)	8.7 (0.26)
Combined	1,616,620 (23,949)	1,765,590 (15,909)	2,083,870 (69,011)	36.2 (0.88)	168,280 (90)	8.1 (0.17)	1,284,390 (68,103)	56.6 (1.76)	631,200 (14,155)	45.1 (0.73)
School enrollment										
Less than 50	238,980 (5,691)	296,000 (22,889)	313,960 (23,275)	5.5 (0.39)	9,340 (1,109)	0.4 (0.05)	179,260 (22,014)	7.9 (0.95)	125,360 (9,844)	9.0 (0.56)
50 to 149	939,110 (10,717)	950,050 (12,053)	964,910 (21,228)	16.8 (0.40)	151,700 (11,198)	7.3 (0.58)	449,980 (16,242)	19.8 (0.85)	363,230 (9,074)	26.0 (0.56)
150 to 299	1,615,970 (7,315)	1,423,220 (9,951)	1,445,000 (33,147)	25.1 (0.49)	614,000 (16,856)	29.5 (0.50)	524,220 (23,690)	23.1 (1.01)	306,770 (15,443)	21.9 (0.81)
300 to 499	1,419,360 (13,203)	1,154,950 (10,730)	1,123,450 (25,543)	19.5 (0.49)	576,110 (21,829)	27.7 (0.90)	357,560 (14,931)	15.8 (0.86)	189,780 (5,812)	13.6 (0.46)
500 to 749	917,670 (2,330)	768,540 (†)	908,080 (66,158)	15.8 (0.97)	391,340 (26,531)	18.8 (1.01)	373,070 (60,722)	16.4 (2.26)	143,660 (3,078)	10.3 (0.24)
750 or more	887,190 (18,232)	895,720 (6,538)	995,120 (8,094)	17.3 (0.29)	340,170 (†)	16.3 (0.34)	384,720 (5,766)	17.0 (0.56)	270,230 (5,680)	19.3 (0.46)
Student race/ethnicity[3]										
White	4,061,870 (24,242)	3,410,360 (31,067)	3,363,900 (58,435)	68.6 (0.34)	1,253,540 (30,813)	65.9 (0.50)	1,413,310 (48,831)	73.1 (0.73)	697,050 (15,024)	65.2 (0.21)
Black	494,530 (5,079)	430,970 (2,579)	453,590 (18,121)	9.3 (0.31)	149,000 (4,569)	7.8 (0.23)	204,780 (17,392)	10.6 (0.74)	99,810 (2,096)	9.3 (0.12)
Hispanic	435,890 (1,592)	443,290 (4,113)	510,400 (6,041)	10.4 (0.15)	296,770 (5,045)	15.6 (0.30)	128,400 (1,724)	6.6 (0.16)	85,220 (1,870)	8.0 (0.12)
Asian	239,510 (877)	239,320 (1,894)	304,440 (3,687)	6.2 (0.06)	99,330 (1,750)	5.2 (0.08)	104,500 (2,813)	5.4 (0.10)	100,610 (1,736)	9.4 (0.08)
Pacific Islander	[4] (†)	28,020 (884)	35,480 (678)	0.7 (0.02)	10,930 (155)	0.6 (0.01)	9,570 (610)	0.5 (0.03)	14,980 (241)	1.4 (0.02)
American Indian/ Alaska Native	22,690 (164)	21,080 (162)	24,030 (524)	0.5 (0.01)	9,940 (237)	0.5 (0.01)	8,500 (458)	0.4 (0.03)	5,590 (89)	0.5 (0.01)
Two or more races	— (†)	127,090 (781)	211,780 (3,749)	4.3 (0.08)	81,960 (676)	4.3 (0.07)	63,750 (3,351)	3.3 (0.15)	66,070 (1,911)	6.2 (0.16)
School locale										
City	— (†)	2,252,780 (12,708)	2,470,840 (53,027)	43.0 (0.77)	977,860 (26,785)	47.0 (1.03)	880,190 (36,303)	38.8 (1.44)	612,790 (21,658)	43.8 (0.91)
Suburban	— (†)	2,137,800 (20,891)	2,309,860 (57,410)	40.2 (0.82)	862,870 (33,018)	41.4 (1.11)	854,660 (41,909)	37.7 (1.60)	592,330 (12,780)	42.3 (0.70)
Town	— (†)	387,920 (9,565)	355,410 (34,093)	6.2 (0.56)	147,580 (2,341)	7.1 (0.18)	168,270 (34,003)	7.4 (1.40)	39,560 (815)	2.8 (0.07)
Rural	— (†)	709,990 (26,462)	614,410 (34,188)	10.7 (0.57)	94,350 (7,354)	4.5 (0.34)	365,700 (31,744)	16.1 (1.31)	154,350 (6,418)	11.0 (0.46)
Teachers[5]										
Total	**408,400 (2,977)**	**437,410 (3,222)**	**481,560 (7,265)**	**100.0 (†)**	**143,190 (1,958)**	**100.0 (0.00)**	**193,220 (6,433)**	**100.0 (†)**	**145,160 (2,801)**	**100.0 (†)**
School level[2]										
Elementary	200,910 (735)	194,480 (1,878)	202,630 (3,654)	42.1 (0.71)	88,570 (1,949)	61.9 (0.53)	62,860 (2,409)	32.5 (1.38)	51,200 (1,698)	35.3 (0.81)
Secondary	62,740 (229)	67,530 (553)	69,490 (703)	14.4 (0.23)	39,830 (208)	27.8 (0.39)	13,750 (657)	7.1 (0.37)	15,910 (486)	11.0 (0.30)
Combined	144,750 (2,682)	175,410 (1,853)	209,440 (6,315)	43.5 (0.84)	14,780 (24)	10.3 (0.15)	116,610 (6,181)	60.4 (1.63)	78,040 (1,656)	53.8 (0.70)
School enrollment										
Less than 50	25,970 (488)	34,120 (1,642)	38,330 (2,348)	8.0 (0.46)	1,290 (76)	0.9 (0.05)	20,770 (2,155)	10.7 (1.07)	16,270 (1,282)	11.2 (0.74)
50 to 149	70,800 (983)	82,460 (1,102)	87,710 (2,113)	18.2 (0.45)	13,980 (1,196)	9.8 (0.85)	40,460 (1,626)	20.9 (0.98)	33,270 (1,148)	22.9 (0.66)
150 to 299	102,240 (486)	107,490 (1,873)	114,470 (3,619)	23.8 (0.63)	42,120 (1,181)	29.4 (0.62)	42,770 (3,209)	22.1 (1.42)	29,580 (1,135)	20.4 (0.64)
300 to 499	90,010 (1,316)	86,850 (751)	87,750 (1,408)	18.2 (0.39)	37,640 (1,114)	26.3 (0.64)	29,080 (958)	15.1 (0.74)	21,030 (540)	14.5 (0.42)
500 to 749	57,930 (79)	56,920 (†)	72,080 (5,118)	15.0 (0.91)	24,930 (983)	17.4 (0.59)	30,390 (5,017)	15.7 (2.23)	16,760 (390)	11.5 (0.25)
750 or more	61,440 (2,143)	69,570 (566)	81,230 (746)	16.9 (0.29)	23,220 (†)	16.2 (0.22)	29,750 (416)	15.4 (0.54)	28,250 (620)	19.5 (0.41)
School locale										
City	— (†)	176,740 (799)	204,320 (4,101)	42.4 (0.77)	65,620 (1,539)	45.8 (0.71)	74,980 (3,031)	38.8 (1.52)	63,710 (1,996)	43.9 (0.95)
Suburban	— (†)	166,170 (2,463)	185,460 (3,848)	38.5 (0.75)	58,630 (1,148)	40.9 (0.69)	69,380 (3,235)	35.9 (1.57)	57,440 (1,273)	39.6 (0.79)
Town	— (†)	30,390 (663)	30,530 (3,366)	6.3 (0.66)	11,100 (186)	7.8 (0.16)	15,340 (3,358)	7.9 (1.62)	4,090 (138)	2.8 (0.09)
Rural	— (†)	64,120 (1,960)	61,260 (3,835)	12.7 (0.72)	7,840 (453)	5.5 (0.30)	33,510 (3,521)	17.3 (1.60)	19,910 (1,223)	13.7 (0.75)

See notes at end of table.

Table 205.40. Number and percentage distribution of private elementary and secondary students, teachers, and schools, by orientation of school and selected characteristics: Fall 1999, fall 2009, and fall 2015—Continued

[Standard errors appear in parentheses]

Selected characteristic	Fall 1999, total number		Fall 2009, total number		Fall 2015															
					Total				Catholic				Other religious				Nonsectarian			
					Number		Percent		Number		Percent		Number		Percent		Number		Percent	
1	2		3		4		5		6		7		8		9		10		11	
Schools																				
Total	**33,000**	**(301)**	**33,370**	**(834)**	**34,580**	**(953)**	**100.0**	**(†)**	**7,010**	**(121)**	**100.0**	**(0.00)**	**16,260**	**(871)**	**100.0**	**(†)**	**11,300**	**(424)**	**100.0**	**(†)**
School level[2]																				
Elementary	22,300	(242)	21,420	(745)	21,910	(831)	63.4	(1.08)	5,570	(130)	79.4	(0.50)	9,110	(806)	56.0	(2.42)	7,230	(282)	64.0	(1.16)
Secondary	2,540	(62)	2,780	(39)	2,950	(120)	8.5	(0.27)	990	(9)	14.2	(0.27)	990	(113)	6.1	(0.54)	960	(34)	8.5	(0.40)
Combined	8,150	(160)	9,160	(153)	9,720	(377)	28.1	(1.13)	450	(13)	6.4	(0.27)	6,160	(316)	37.9	(2.61)	3,110	(207)	27.5	(1.16)
School enrollment																				
Less than 50	9,160	(210)	11,070	(801)	11,800	(771)	34.1	(1.37)	320	(38)	4.5	(0.51)	6,900	(738)	42.4	(2.44)	4,580	(309)	40.5	(1.37)
50 to 149	10,260	(134)	10,470	(154)	10,670	(268)	30.9	(0.65)	1,430	(99)	20.4	(1.30)	5,000	(236)	30.7	(1.22)	4,240	(126)	37.5	(1.18)
150 to 299	7,440	(34)	6,690	(46)	6,800	(161)	19.7	(0.59)	2,790	(67)	39.9	(0.82)	2,490	(118)	15.3	(0.99)	1,520	(85)	13.4	(0.58)
300 to 499	3,730	(41)	3,010	(30)	2,930	(62)	8.5	(0.36)	1,480	(47)	21.2	(0.63)	950	(44)	5.8	(0.56)	500	(17)	4.4	(0.22)
500 to 749	1,530	(3)	1,280	(†)	1,500	(103)	4.3	(0.31)	650	(42)	9.3	(0.60)	610	(94)	3.7	(0.59)	240	(4)	2.1	(0.08)
750 or more	870	(20)	850	(7)	880	(7)	2.5	(0.07)	330	(†)	4.7	(0.08)	320	(5)	2.0	(0.11)	230	(4)	2.0	(0.08)
School locale																				
City	—	(†)	10,810	(171)	11,480	(398)	33.2	(1.04)	2,880	(107)	41.2	(0.94)	4,550	(205)	28.0	(1.56)	4,040	(277)	35.7	(1.71)
Suburban	—	(†)	11,610	(176)	12,660	(273)	36.6	(1.06)	2,690	(52)	38.4	(1.12)	4,600	(149)	28.3	(1.43)	5,370	(199)	47.5	(1.54)
Town	—	(†)	3,340	(154)	2,900	(216)	8.4	(0.60)	830	(8)	11.9	(0.23)	1,630	(213)	10.0	(1.20)	430	(36)	3.8	(0.30)
Rural	—	(†)	7,610	(799)	7,540	(725)	21.8	(1.64)	600	(55)	8.6	(0.69)	5,480	(705)	33.7	(2.79)	1,460	(150)	12.9	(1.14)

—Not available.
†Not applicable.
[1]Includes students in prekindergarten through grade 12 in schools that offer kindergarten or higher grade.
[2]Elementary schools have grade 6 or lower and no grade higher than 8. Secondary schools have no grade lower than 7. Combined schools include those that have grades lower than 7 and higher than 8, as well as those that do not classify students by grade level.
[3]Race/ethnicity was not collected for prekindergarten students (846,900 in fall 2015). Percentage distribution is based on the students for whom race/ethnicity was reported.
[4]For 1999, Pacific Islander students are included under Asian. Prior to 2009, data were not collected on Pacific Islander students as a separate category.
[5]Reported in full-time equivalents (FTE). Excludes teachers who teach only prekindergarten students.
NOTE: Tabulation includes schools that offer kindergarten or higher grade. Detail may not sum to totals because of rounding.
SOURCE: U.S. Department of Education, National Center for Education Statistics, Private School Universe Survey (PSS), 1999–2000, 2009–10, and 2015–16. (This table was prepared June 2017.)

Table 205.80. Private elementary and secondary schools, enrollment, teachers, and high school graduates, by state: Selected years, 2005 through 2015

[Standard errors appear in parentheses]

State	Schools, fall 2015		Enrollment in prekindergarten through grade 12												Teachers,[1] fall 2015		High school graduates, 2014–15	
			Fall 2005		Fall 2007		Fall 2009		Fall 2011		Fall 2013		Fall 2015					
1	2		3		4		5		6		7		8		9		10	
United States	**34,580**	**(953)**	**6,073,240**	**(42,446)**	**5,910,210**	**(28,363)**	**5,488,490**	**(35,857)**	**5,268,090**	**(24,908)**	**5,395,740**	**(50,342)**	**5,750,520**	**(85,729)**	**481,560**	**(7,265)**	**343,250**	**(6,331)**
Alabama	350	(†)	92,280	(5,892)	83,840	(103)	95,570	(11,745)	81,070	(49)	76,400	(295)	75,070	(†)	5,870	(†)	4,710	(†)
Alaska	50	(†)	7,500	(1,028)	4,990	(†)	7,510!	(2,740)	5,170	(†)	5,080	(†)	5,540	(†)	480	(†)	220	(†)
Arizona	320	(†)	66,840	(†)	64,910	(†)	55,390	(†)	53,120	(229)	55,070	(†)	56,610	(†)	4,110	(†)	3,030	(†)
Arkansas	330!	(134)	35,390	(5,858)	40,120	(11,961)	28,900	(1,371)	29,930	(1,245)	30,340	(1,496)	37,930	(6,108)	3,670	(1,019)	1,800	(134)
California	3,420	(58)	737,490	(15,529)	703,810	(6,129)	623,150	(4,185)	608,070	(69)	596,160	(3,500)	627,170	(10,231)	49,520	(1,001)	36,930	(544)
Colorado	600!	(183)	70,770	(1,160)	64,740	(†)	63,720	(3,486)	61,140	(148)	60,690	(4,498)	68,140	(9,589)	5,680	(1,172)	2,790	(†)
Connecticut	420	(61)	76,220	(1,619)	85,150	(9,241)	72,540	(464)	66,320	(142)	72,770	(8,293)	66,710	(2,671)	7,770	(410)	7,140	(632)
Delaware	100	(†)	29,830	(†)	32,520	(2,701)	26,640	(†)	25,090	(†)	23,640	(†)	19,660	(†)	1,650	(†)	1,180	(†)
District of Columbia	90!	(31)	19,880	(†)	19,640	(†)	17,810	(†)	16,950	(†)	19,790	(277)	17,110	(1,939)	2,050	(285)	1,500	(16)
Florida	2,200	(69)	396,790	(7,429)	391,660	(6,123)	343,990	(1,023)	340,960	(230)	372,790	(2,812)	389,310	(207)	30,520	(69)	22,770	(†)
Georgia	1,220	(308)	152,600	(10,394)	157,430	(9,185)	150,300	(6,251)	138,080	(†)	150,360	(2,250)	189,630	(27,662)	19,930	(3,722)	11,630	(1,556)
Hawaii	140	(11)	32,810	(†)	37,300	(290)	37,130	(†)	37,530	(†)	33,820	(32)	45,600	(7,730)	3,730	(662)	3,510	(660)
Idaho	260!	(113)	15,320	(2,518)	24,700!	(11,608)	18,680	(4,814)	13,670	(193)	18,580	(3,090)	20,230	(3,947)	1,420	(229)	640	(†)
Illinois	1,500	(51)	317,940	(4,263)	312,270	(6,638)	289,720	(9,237)	271,030	(1,289)	281,360	(6,026)	280,440	(19,662)	19,600	(922)	16,800	(132)
Indiana	1,660!	(678)	139,370	(17,870)	119,910	(2,284)	120,770	(5,919)	129,120	(12,177)	121,230	(3,928)	171,570	(4,510)	11,940	(774)	7,130	(1,024)
Iowa	510!	(180)	60,960	(8,311)	47,820	(†)	45,160	(†)	63,840	(14,665)	56,150	(9,338)	70,870	(16,178)	5,120	(999)	2,580	(20)
Kansas	210	(†)	47,130	(1,654)	47,780	(2,414)	44,680	(1,668)	43,100	(1,640)	41,520	(3,286)	42,270	(†)	3,210	(†)	2,550	(†)
Kentucky	330	(†)	78,880	(1,228)	76,140	(2,074)	70,590	(2,132)	69,410	(12)	74,750	(4,226)	70,090	(†)	5,670	(†)	4,520	(†)
Louisiana	580	(150)	138,270	(525)	137,460	(†)	147,040	(9,890)	125,720	(108)	129,720	(2,606)	166,560	(33,949)	12,640	(2,721)	11,420!	(3,620)
Maine	140	(†)	20,680	(337)	21,260	(143)	18,310	(†)	18,350	(†)	18,380	(272)	18,600	(†)	2,020	(†)	2,700	(0)
Maryland	760	(18)	170,350	(4,201)	165,760	(1,160)	145,690	(160)	137,450	(564)	143,530	(2,030)	142,630	(3,549)	13,810	(21)	9,130	(†)
Massachusetts	760	(43)	157,770	(3,273)	151,640	(2,516)	137,110	(1,169)	130,940	(1,596)	134,560	(943)	123,230	(865)	14,440	(242)	9,270	(†)
Michigan	890	(120)	166,950	(407)	159,100	(2,047)	153,230	(5,828)	135,580	(544)	141,590	(6,240)	172,130	(34,196)	13,550	(3,271)	10,960	(2,377)
Minnesota	470	(†)	104,730	(3,467)	101,740	(3,903)	89,530	(†)	87,620	(†)	85,260	(†)	75,630	(†)	5,860	(†)	4,430	(†)
Mississippi	180	(†)	57,930	(4,104)	55,270	(†)	54,650	(2,458)	52,060	(†)	50,330	(3,333)	43,580	(†)	3,530	(†)	2,700	(†)
Missouri	870	(173)	137,810	(10,580)	125,610	(3,685)	117,970	(2,065)	130,130	(8,715)	139,570	(25,980)	125,290	(8,723)	10,340	(935)	8,540	(811)
Montana	120	(†)	‡	(†)	15,030!	(5,465)	10,390	(1,221)	10,550	(†)	10,560	(521)	11,690	(†)	980	(†)	400	(†)
Nebraska	350!	(133)	42,420	(†)	40,320	(†)	39,040	(†)	40,750	(†)	42,300	(†)	48,960	(5,442)	3,120	(133)	2,460	(†)
Nevada	150	(†)	29,120	(†)	29,820	(2,009)	25,060	(†)	26,130	(†)	21,980	(†)	23,910	(†)	1,540	(†)	1,240	(†)
New Hampshire	260	(†)	33,220	(†)	30,920	(†)	26,470	(†)	27,350	(†)	26,700	(†)	25,330	(†)	2,670	(†)	2,430	(†)
New Jersey	1,270	(97)	256,160	(8,439)	253,250	(5,016)	232,020	(16,536)	210,220	(1,211)	211,150	(4,607)	213,170	(13,684)	19,170	(1,154)	14,320	(836)
New Mexico	170	(†)	25,030	(141)	27,290	(1,388)	23,730	(507)	22,680	(10)	21,750	(†)	22,230	(†)	2,010	(†)	1,440	(†)
New York	1,940	(88)	510,750	(3,596)	518,850	(7,196)	486,310	(5,211)	487,810	(19,574)	452,380	(901)	520,660	(16,620)	46,140	(1,834)	35,600	(3,485)
North Carolina	650	(†)	117,280	(11,681)	121,660	(2,226)	110,740	(1,851)	119,070	(†)	118,090	(492)	124,030	(†)	11,830	(†)	7,490	(†)
North Dakota	50	(†)	7,290	(†)	7,430	(†)	7,750	(†)	7,770	(†)	8,290	(†)	7,830	(†)	630	(†)	370	(†)
Ohio	1,360	(133)	254,530	(9,821)	239,520	(2,741)	246,250	(24,214)	213,990	(3,419)	238,620	(19,487)	255,690	(40,837)	18,380	(2,652)	12,920	(†)
Oklahoma	180	(27)	35,350	(1,194)	40,320	(5,032)	34,000	(716)	35,750	(847)	32,740	(†)	32,160	(1,061)	2,740	(53)	1,570	(212)
Oregon	410	(†)	69,620	(14,139)	66,260	(5,188)	56,820	(3,502)	53,200	(†)	58,830	(3,109)	57,310	(†)	4,210	(†)	3,470	(†)
Pennsylvania	2,740	(221)	332,740	(3,918)	324,020	(6,253)	301,640	(5,036)	276,300	(3,668)	253,800	(756)	315,830	(38,974)	26,350	(3,070)	19,640	(3,078)
Rhode Island	130	(19)	30,600	(†)	28,260	(1,096)	24,940	(†)	25,420	(†)	22,180	(†)	20,620	(2,711)	1,900	(218)	1,460	(†)
South Carolina	370	(†)	70,240	(1,797)	71,430	(1,043)	62,320	(311)	60,890	(†)	65,350	(4,447)	62,830	(†)	5,310	(†)	3,130	(†)
South Dakota	70	(†)	12,700	(†)	12,280	(†)	11,470	(†)	12,490	(†)	9,950	(†)	10,740	(†)	830	(†)	380	(†)
Tennessee	500	(†)	105,240	(2,531)	117,540	(12,851)	98,310	(4,176)	92,430	(34)	93,990	(3,210)	91,950	(†)	8,730	(†)	6,040	(†)
Texas	2,400	(373)	304,170	(20,453)	296,540	(4,132)	313,360	(11,968)	285,320	(2,046)	312,640	(5,896)	351,270	(26,334)	30,430	(1,644)	16,540	(851)
Utah	160	(†)	21,220	(†)	20,860	(†)	21,990	(1,558)	18,660	(55)	23,310	(†)	21,140	(†)	1,800	(†)	1,490	(†)
Vermont	110	(†)	11,530	(†)	12,600	(232)	10,350	(†)	9,030	(†)	8,890	(†)	10,040	(†)	1,280	(†)	1,080	(†)
Virginia	950	(119)	155,220	(14,290)	143,140	(7,988)	128,140	(2,581)	123,780	(82)	131,330	(1,828)	140,350	(12,832)	12,850	(921)	7,150	(†)
Washington	640	(24)	119,640	(13,187)	104,070	(3,054)	94,340	(625)	93,630	(234)	119,730	(17,349)	100,140	(479)	7,680	(48)	5,650	(†)
West Virginia	130	(†)	16,120	(†)	14,980	(†)	13,860	(†)	13,430	(1)	14,350	(†)	14,780	(†)	1,330	(†)	850	(†)
Wisconsin	1,050	(114)	142,280	(137)	138,290	(1,597)	130,510	(†)	127,250	(†)	160,650	(32,980)	144,020	(11,405)	11,310	(1,128)	5,540	(†)
Wyoming	40	(†)	2,310	(†)	2,930	(†)	2,910	(†)	2,740	(†)	2,780	(†)	2,240	(†)	220	(†)	30	(†)

†Not applicable.
!Interpret data with caution. The coefficient of variation (CV) for this estimate is between 30 and 50 percent.
‡Reporting standards not met. The coefficient of variation (CV) for this estimate is 50 percent or greater.
[1]Reported in full-time equivalents (FTE). Excludes teachers who teach only prekindergarten students.

NOTE: Includes special education, vocational/technical education, and alternative schools. Tabulation includes schools that offer kindergarten or higher grade. Includes enrollment of students in prekindergarten through grade 12 in schools that offer kindergarten or higher grade. Detail may not sum to totals because of rounding.
SOURCE: U.S. Department of Education, National Center for Education Statistics, Private School Universe Survey (PSS), 2005–06 through 2015–16. (This table was prepared June 2017.)

Table 206.10. Number and percentage of homeschooled students ages 5 through 17 with a grade equivalent of kindergarten through 12th grade, by selected child, parent, and household characteristics: Selected years, 1999 through 2016

[Standard errors appear in parentheses]

Selected child, parent, or household characteristic	1999				2003				2007				2012				2016			
	Number homeschooled[1] (in thousands)		Percent homeschooled[1]		Number homeschooled[1] (in thousands)		Percent homeschooled[1]		Number homeschooled[1] (in thousands)		Percent homeschooled[1]		Number homeschooled[1,2] (in thousands)		Percent homeschooled[1,2]		Number homeschooled[1] (in thousands)		Percent homeschooled[1]	
1		2		3		4		5		6		7		8		9		10		11
Total	**850**	**(71.1)**	**1.7**	**(0.14)**	**1,096**	**(92.3)**	**2.2**	**(0.18)**	**1,520**	**(118.0)**	**3.0**	**(0.23)**	**1,773**	**(115.7)**	**3.4**	**(0.23)**	**1,690**	**(118.4)**	**3.3**	**(0.23)**
Sex of child																				
Male	417	(43.9)	1.6	(0.17)	569	(61.9)	2.2	(0.24)	639	(75.1)	2.4	(0.28)	875	(73.7)	3.3	(0.28)	807	(79.2)	3.0	(0.30)
Female	434	(46.1)	1.8	(0.19)	527	(58.2)	2.1	(0.23)	881	(97.4)	3.5	(0.39)	898	(80.3)	3.6	(0.32)	882	(74.8)	3.5	(0.29)
Race/ethnicity of child																				
White	640	(62.3)	2.0	(0.19)	843	(77.5)	2.7	(0.25)	1,171	(102.2)	3.9	(0.34)	1,205	(95.7)	4.5	(0.35)	998	(92.6)	3.8	(0.35)
Black	84	(24.8)	1.0	(0.31)	103!	(33.9)	1.3!	(0.42)	61!	(21.2)	0.8!	(0.28)	140	(37.1)	2.0	(0.52)	132	(27.6)	1.9	(0.39)
Hispanic	77	(17.7)	1.1	(0.25)	59!	(21.1)	0.7	(0.26)	147	(27.5)	1.5	(0.29)	265	(41.1)	2.3	(0.35)	444	(62.2)	3.5	(0.50)
Asian/Pacific Islander	‡	(†)	‡	(†)	‡	(†)	‡	(†)	‡	(†)	‡	(†)	73!	(21.9)	2.8!	(0.90)	44	(12.6)	1.4	(0.40)
Asian	—	(†)	—	(†)	—	(†)	—	(†)	‡	(†)	‡	(†)	‡	(†)	‡	(†)	42	(12.0)	1.4	(0.40)
Pacific Islander	—	(†)	—	(†)	—	(†)	—	(†)	‡	(†)	‡	(†)	‡	(†)	‡	(†)	‡	(†)	‡	(†)
American Indian/Alaska Native	‡	(†)	‡	(†)	‡	(†)	‡	(†)	‡	(†)	‡	(†)	‡	(†)	‡	(†)	‡	(†)	‡	(†)
Other[3]	16!	(6.4)	1.6!	(0.62)	59!	(26.9)	4.9!	(2.13)	111	(29.5)	4.8	(1.30)	82	(16.3)	3.2	(0.61)	69	(15.2)	2.7	(0.62)
Grade equivalent[4]																				
Kindergarten through grade 5	428	(48.1)	1.8	(0.20)	472	(55.3)	1.9	(0.23)	717	(83.8)	3.0	(0.36)	833	(84.8)	3.2	(0.33)	767	(74.4)	3.0	(0.29)
Kindergarten	92	(19.7)	2.4	(0.52)	‡	(†)	‡	(†)	‡	(†)	‡	(†)	212	(47.3)	4.0	(0.90)	181	(40.7)	3.5	(0.80)
Grades 1 through 3	199	(36.7)	1.6	(0.29)	214	(33.3)	1.8	(0.28)	406	(64.5)	3.4	(0.54)	353	(50.9)	2.9	(0.42)	300	(34.1)	2.4	(0.28)
Grades 4 and 5	136	(22.5)	1.7	(0.28)	160	(30.1)	1.9	(0.35)	197	(41.4)	2.5	(0.52)	268	(44.2)	3.2	(0.52)	287	(51.8)	3.4	(0.62)
Grades 6 through 8	186	(28.0)	1.6	(0.24)	302	(44.9)	2.4	(0.36)	371	(65.3)	3.0	(0.53)	424	(49.0)	3.5	(0.41)	398	(49.1)	3.3	(0.41)
Grades 9 through 12	235	(33.3)	1.7	(0.24)	315	(47.0)	2.3	(0.33)	422	(58.2)	2.8	(0.38)	516	(53.6)	3.8	(0.39)	525	(55.9)	3.8	(0.40)
Number of children in the household																				
One child	132	(18.0)	1.3	(0.17)	110	(22.3)	1.4	(0.27)	197	(32.5)	2.3	(0.38)	418	(29.6)	3.4	(0.23)	338	(35.5)	2.7	(0.27)
Two children	248	(28.4)	1.3	(0.15)	306	(45.1)	1.5	(0.22)	414	(67.2)	2.0	(0.32)	493	(51.5)	2.5	(0.26)	475	(55.3)	2.3	(0.27)
Three or more children	470	(63.9)	2.3	(0.31)	679	(80.2)	3.1	(0.36)	909	(102.4)	4.1	(0.46)	862	(88.4)	4.5	(0.47)	877	(84.8)	4.7	(0.45)
Number of parents in the household																				
Two parents	683	(68.3)	2.1	(0.21)	886	(82.7)	2.5	(0.23)	1,357	(111.5)	3.6	(0.30)	1,354	(104.2)	3.8	(0.29)	1,358	(103.7)	3.7	(0.28)
One parent	142	(25.0)	0.9	(0.16)	196	(42.6)	1.5	(0.32)	118	(28.4)	1.0	(0.24)	342	(51.6)	2.5	(0.37)	293	(38.4)	2.3	(0.30)
Nonparental guardians	25!	(14.4)	‡	(†)	‡	(†)	‡	(†)	‡	(†)	‡	(†)	77!	(31.9)	4.0!	(1.60)	38	(9.9)	2.0	(0.54)
Parent participation in the labor force																				
Two parents—both in labor force	237	(39.8)	1.0	(0.17)	274	(44.1)	1.1	(0.18)	518	(76.2)	2.0	(0.29)	588	(63.5)	2.5	(0.27)	427	(56.5)	1.7	(0.23)
Two parents—one in labor force	444	(53.9)	4.6	(0.55)	594	(73.7)	5.6	(0.67)	808	(94.3)	7.5	(0.82)	719	(76.3)	6.2	(0.65)	935	(87.8)	7.2	(0.68)
One parent in labor force	98	(21.8)	0.7	(0.16)	174	(39.8)	1.4	(0.33)	127	(29.5)	1.3	(0.30)	247	(40.9)	2.2	(0.36)	189	(29.6)	1.8	(0.29)
No parent participation in labor force	71	(18.8)	1.9	(0.48)	‡	(†)	‡	(†)	‡	(†)	‡	(†)	130	(31.9)	4.8	(1.15)	139	(23.9)	4.0	(0.72)
Highest education level of parents																				
High school diploma or less	160	(26.5)	0.9	(0.15)	269	(51.6)	1.7	(0.32)	208	(35.5)	1.5	(0.24)	560	(81.7)	3.4	(0.50)	510	(66.1)	3.3	(0.43)
Vocational/technical, associate's degree, or some college	287	(37.3)	1.9	(0.24)	338	(57.7)	2.1	(0.36)	559	(77.5)	3.8	(0.52)	525	(45.6)	3.4	(0.29)	418	(49.2)	3.1	(0.36)
Bachelor's degree/some graduate school	213	(36.2)	2.6	(0.42)	309	(48.5)	2.8	(0.45)	444	(64.7)	3.9	(0.57)	434	(51.4)	3.7	(0.43)	501	(64.0)	3.6	(0.45)
Graduate/professional degree	190	(39.8)	2.3	(0.46)	180	(41.6)	2.3	(0.55)	309	(50.0)	2.9	(0.46)	255	(27.3)	3.3	(0.36)	260	(30.7)	3.0	(0.35)
Household income[5]																				
$20,000 or less	184	(35.2)	1.5	(0.28)	164	(38.9)	1.8	(0.43)	186	(42.1)	2.2	(0.50)	219	(41.8)	2.9	(0.56)	184	(29.0)	2.9	(0.46)
$20,001 to $50,000	356	(42.9)	1.8	(0.22)	430	(60.3)	2.6	(0.36)	420	(59.8)	3.1	(0.42)	528	(65.5)	3.8	(0.47)	483	(59.4)	3.7	(0.46)
$50,001 to $75,000	162	(25.5)	1.9	(0.30)	264	(51.1)	2.4	(0.46)	414	(58.8)	4.0	(0.57)	370	(48.9)	3.9	(0.53)	435	(58.6)	4.8	(0.65)
$75,001 to $100,000	148	(26.5)	1.5	(0.28)	169	(42.9)	2.6	(0.66)	264	(57.2)	3.8	(0.83)	288	(47.3)	4.2	(0.69)	268	(38.4)	3.8	(0.55)
Over $100,000	—	(†)	—	(†)	‡	(†)	‡	(†)	236	(57.5)	2.0	(0.49)	367	(42.8)	2.7	(0.31)	319	(39.0)	1.9	(0.24)
Locale																				
City	—	(†)	—	(†)	—	(†)	—	(†)	327	(40.4)	2.0	(0.26)	493	(59.5)	3.3	(0.40)	493	(56.0)	3.0	(0.33)
Suburban	—	(†)	—	(†)	—	(†)	—	(†)	503	(78.8)	2.6	(0.41)	601	(66.8)	3.1	(0.34)	651	(76.2)	2.9	(0.33)
Town	—	(†)	—	(†)	—	(†)	—	(†)	168	(37.1)	3.0	(0.65)	127	(30.8)	2.6	(0.63)	177	(30.0)	4.3	(0.70)
Rural	—	(†)	—	(†)	—	(†)	—	(†)	523	(75.9)	4.9	(0.71)	552	(68.2)	4.5	(0.55)	368	(45.1)	4.4	(0.54)

—Not available.
†Not applicable.
!Interpret data with caution. The coefficient of variation (CV) for this estimate is between 30 and 50 percent.
‡Reporting standards not met (too few cases for a reliable estimate).
[1]Excludes students who were enrolled in school for more than 25 hours a week. Also excludes students who were homeschooled only due to a temporary illness.
[2]The National Center for Education Statistics uses a statistical adjustment for estimates of homeschoolers in 2012. For more information about this adjustment, please see *Homeschooling in the United States: 2012* (NCES 2016-096REV).
[3]Includes Two or more races and race/ethnicity not reported.
[4]Students whose grade equivalent was "ungraded" were excluded from the grade analysis. The percentage of students with an "ungraded" grade equivalent was 0.02 percent in 2003 and 2007. There were no students with an "ungraded" grade equivalent in 2012.
[5]For 1999, estimates combine the "$75,001 to $100,000" and "Over $100,000" categories.

NOTE: While National Household Education Surveys Program (NHES) administrations prior to 2012 were administered via telephone with an interviewer, NHES:2012 and NHES:2016 used self-administered paper-and-pencil questionnaires that were mailed to respondents. Measurable differences between estimates for years prior to 2012 and estimates for later years could reflect actual changes in the population, or the changes could be due to the mode change from telephone to mail. Race categories exclude persons of Hispanic ethnicity. Detail may not sum to totals because of rounding. Some data have been revised from previously published figures.

SOURCE: U.S. Department of Education, National Center for Education Statistics, Parent Survey and Parent and Family Involvement in Education Survey of the National Household Education Surveys Program (Parent-NHES:1999 and PFI-NHES:2003, 2007, 2012, and 2016). (This table was prepared February 2018.)

Table 206.30. Percentage distribution of students enrolled in grades 1 through 12, by public school type and charter status, private school orientation, and selected child and household characteristics: 2016

[Standard errors appear in parentheses]

Selected child or household characteristic and public school type	Total, all schools		Public school, total		Public school type[1] Assigned		Public school type[1] Chosen		Public school charter status Traditional[2]		Public school charter status Charter		Private school, total		Private school orientation Religious		Private school orientation Nonsectarian	
1	2		3		4		5		6		7		8		9		10	
Percentage distribution of all enrolled students, by school type and charter status	**100.0**	**(†)**	**90.5**	**(0.32)**	**70.6**	**(0.61)**	**19.8**	**(0.52)**	**85.9**	**(0.44)**	**4.6**	**(0.31)**	**9.5**	**(0.32)**	**7.6**	**(0.32)**	**1.9**	**(0.18)**
Percentage distribution of students in schools of each type or status, by characteristic																		
Total, all students	**100.0**	**(†)**	**100.0**	**(†)**	**100.0**	**(†)**	**100.0**	**(†)**	**100.0**	**(†)**	**100.0**	**(†)**	**100.0**	**(†)**	**100.0**	**(†)**	**100.0**	**(†)**
Sex of child																		
Male	51.8	(0.67)	52.0	(0.72)	52.2	(0.87)	51.2	(1.69)	52.0	(0.78)	51.4	(3.38)	50.3	(1.92)	50.2	(2.18)	50.9	(5.01)
Female	48.2	(0.67)	48.0	(0.72)	47.8	(0.87)	48.8	(1.69)	48.0	(0.78)	48.6	(3.38)	49.7	(1.92)	49.8	(2.18)	49.1	(5.01)
Race/ethnicity of child																		
White	51.8	(0.41)	50.7	(0.44)	54.6	(0.57)	36.9	(1.19)	51.8	(0.47)	30.4	(2.85)	62.1	(1.85)	64.0	(2.15)	54.6	(5.02)
Black	14.3	(0.19)	14.5	(0.26)	12.1	(0.41)	23.2	(1.27)	13.9	(0.31)	26.2	(3.63)	12.2	(1.34)	12.3	(1.57)	11.6	(2.75)
Hispanic	23.8	(0.28)	24.7	(0.35)	23.3	(0.52)	29.9	(1.43)	24.1	(0.37)	36.0	(3.09)	15.0	(1.38)	15.4	(1.51)	13.5	(3.25)
Asian/Pacific Islander	5.7	(0.26)	5.6	(0.29)	5.6	(0.30)	5.7	(0.63)	5.6	(0.30)	4.7	(1.37)	6.3	(1.05)	4.4	(0.90)	13.7	(3.54)
Asian	5.4	(0.25)	5.3	(0.28)	5.3	(0.29)	5.3	(0.60)	5.4	(0.28)	4.0	(1.15)	6.0	(1.02)	4.1	(0.85)	13.7	(3.54)
Pacific Islander	0.3	(0.05)	0.3	(0.06)	0.2	(0.06)	0.4!	(0.19)	0.2	(0.05)	‡	(†)	‡	(†)	‡	(†)	‡	(†)
Other[3]	4.5	(0.26)	4.5	(0.29)	4.5	(0.33)	4.3	(0.49)	4.6	(0.30)	2.7	(0.71)	4.4	(0.63)	3.9	(0.64)	6.7	(1.85)
Disability status of child as reported by parent																		
Has a disability	16.9	(0.57)	17.3	(0.61)	17.4	(0.68)	17.0	(1.04)	17.3	(0.61)	15.9	(2.00)	13.3	(1.20)	12.7	(1.40)	15.8	(2.86)
Does not have a disability	83.1	(0.57)	82.7	(0.61)	82.6	(0.68)	83.0	(1.04)	82.7	(0.61)	84.1	(2.00)	86.7	(1.20)	87.3	(1.40)	84.2	(2.86)
Grade level																		
Grades 1 through 5	43.5	(0.33)	43.6	(0.35)	44.2	(0.51)	41.3	(1.15)	43.2	(0.40)	51.6	(3.23)	42.7	(1.89)	43.2	(2.14)	40.9	(4.79)
Grades 6 through 8	25.2	(0.33)	24.9	(0.34)	25.3	(0.52)	23.8	(1.11)	24.8	(0.37)	27.9	(2.89)	27.4	(1.55)	27.8	(1.74)	25.8	(3.80)
Grades 9 through 12	31.3	(0.27)	31.5	(0.32)	30.5	(0.44)	34.8	(1.09)	32.0	(0.35)	20.5	(2.13)	29.9	(1.60)	29.0	(1.84)	33.4	(3.54)
Number of parents in the household																		
Two parents	70.3	(0.51)	69.3	(0.57)	70.5	(0.72)	64.9	(1.34)	69.3	(0.57)	68.2	(3.61)	80.6	(1.52)	80.0	(1.71)	82.7	(2.59)
One parent	25.7	(0.55)	26.6	(0.62)	25.4	(0.73)	30.7	(1.29)	26.4	(0.62)	28.7	(3.43)	17.7	(1.46)	18.2	(1.67)	15.4	(2.46)
Nonparental guardians	3.9	(0.26)	4.2	(0.28)	4.1	(0.37)	4.5	(0.62)	4.2	(0.30)	3.0	(0.59)	1.8	(0.37)	1.8	(0.36)	‡	(†)
Highest education level of parents																		
Less than a high school diploma	10.7	(0.30)	11.3	(0.34)	10.9	(0.44)	12.4	(1.13)	11.0	(0.35)	17.1	(3.53)	5.5	(1.27)	5.8	(1.37)	‡	(†)
High school diploma or GED	20.0	(0.27)	21.3	(0.30)	21.3	(0.48)	21.4	(1.28)	21.5	(0.36)	17.7	(3.26)	8.0	(1.43)	8.9	(1.62)	‡	(†)
Vocational/technical, associate's degree, or some college	25.7	(0.44)	26.6	(0.45)	26.7	(0.58)	26.0	(1.07)	26.7	(0.47)	25.0	(2.57)	17.5	(1.57)	19.5	(1.76)	9.7	(2.46)
Bachelor's degree/some graduate school	26.7	(0.46)	25.6	(0.47)	26.0	(0.60)	24.2	(0.99)	25.8	(0.50)	22.8	(1.96)	37.2	(1.60)	38.2	(1.89)	33.1	(3.76)
Graduate/professional degree	16.8	(0.18)	15.2	(0.19)	15.0	(0.27)	16.0	(0.78)	15.1	(0.19)	17.4	(1.87)	31.8	(1.68)	27.5	(1.75)	49.0	(5.11)
Poverty status of household[4]																		
Poor	17.3	(0.42)	18.3	(0.47)	18.1	(0.50)	18.8	(1.26)	18.2	(0.46)	19.9	(2.80)	7.6	(1.36)	7.0	(1.38)	9.9!	(4.05)
Near-poor	21.4	(0.45)	22.2	(0.51)	21.3	(0.59)	25.6	(1.50)	21.9	(0.52)	28.2	(4.09)	13.1	(1.59)	14.9	(1.90)	6.0	(1.70)
Nonpoor	61.4	(0.46)	59.5	(0.49)	60.6	(0.66)	55.6	(1.33)	59.9	(0.51)	51.8	(3.60)	79.3	(1.79)	78.1	(2.07)	84.1	(3.83)
Locale																		
City	31.2	(0.74)	30.5	(0.79)	25.6	(0.80)	48.1	(1.58)	29.1	(0.74)	57.8	(3.20)	37.2	(1.76)	36.8	(2.02)	38.6	(3.24)
Suburban	44.5	(0.73)	44.1	(0.77)	46.0	(0.82)	37.7	(1.47)	44.6	(0.76)	34.8	(2.90)	48.1	(1.90)	47.9	(2.19)	48.6	(3.38)
Town	7.9	(0.37)	8.5	(0.40)	9.3	(0.47)	5.4	(0.56)	8.7	(0.42)	3.4	(0.95)	3.0	(0.42)	3.0	(0.49)	2.6!	(0.89)
Rural	16.4	(0.42)	16.9	(0.45)	19.1	(0.51)	8.7	(0.66)	17.5	(0.46)	4.0	(1.14)	11.8	(1.19)	12.2	(1.33)	10.2	(2.42)
Region																		
Northeast	19.9	(0.50)	19.3	(0.57)	20.8	(0.65)	13.8	(1.23)	19.4	(0.57)	16.8	(2.93)	26.1	(1.81)	25.0	(2.02)	30.4	(4.34)
South	23.9	(0.53)	24.0	(0.56)	23.2	(0.65)	26.8	(1.57)	24.4	(0.56)	16.7	(2.15)	23.3	(1.51)	21.8	(1.73)	29.2	(3.50)
Midwest	21.9	(0.55)	21.5	(0.60)	22.3	(0.66)	18.2	(1.42)	21.5	(0.58)	20.6	(3.61)	26.5	(1.65)	31.0	(1.83)	8.4	(1.65)
West	34.2	(0.63)	35.3	(0.68)	33.7	(0.79)	41.2	(1.73)	34.7	(0.71)	45.9	(3.25)	24.1	(1.59)	22.2	(1.82)	32.1	(3.71)
Public school type[1]																		
Assigned	70.6	(0.61)	78.0	(0.57)	100.0	(†)	†	(†)	82.1	(0.53)	100.0	(†)	†	(†)	†	(†)	†	(†)
Chosen	19.8	(0.52)	21.8	(0.58)	†	(†)	100.0	(†)	17.6	(0.54)	†	(†)	†	(†)	†	(†)	†	(†)

†Not applicable.

!Interpret data with caution. The coefficient of variation (CV) for this estimate is between 30 and 50 percent.

‡Reporting standards not met. The coefficient of variation (CV) for this estimate is 50 percent or greater.

[1]In 31 cases, questions about whether a student's school was assigned were not asked because parents reported the school as a private school, and it was only later identified as a public school based on administrative data. Due to the missing data on whether the school was assigned or chosen, these cases were included neither with assigned public schools nor with chosen public schools. These cases were included in the public school totals, however, and they could still be accurately classified as either traditional or charter schools based on administrative data.

[2]Includes all types of public noncharter schools.

[3]Includes American Indian/Alaska Native, Two or more races, and race/ethnicity not reported.

[4]Poor children are those whose family incomes were below the Census Bureau's poverty threshold in the year prior to data collection; near-poor children are those whose family incomes ranged from the poverty threshold to 199 percent of the poverty threshold; and nonpoor children are those whose family incomes were at or above 200 percent of the poverty threshold. The poverty threshold is a dollar amount that varies depending on a family's size and composition and is updated annually to account for inflation. In 2015, for example, the poverty threshold for a family of four with two children was $24,257. Survey respondents are asked to select the range within which their income falls, rather than giving the exact amount of their income; therefore, the measure of poverty status is an approximation.

NOTE: Data exclude homeschooled children. Race categories exclude persons of Hispanic ethnicity. Detail may not sum to totals because of rounding.

SOURCE: U.S. Department of Education, National Center for Education Statistics, Parent and Family Involvement in Education Survey of the National Household Education Surveys Program (PFI-NHES:2016). (This table was prepared February 2018.)

Table 207.10. Number of 3- to 5-year-olds not yet enrolled in kindergarten and percentage participating in home literacy activities with a family member, by type and frequency of activity and selected child and family characteristics: 2001, 2012, and 2016

[Standard errors appear in parentheses]

Selected child or family characteristic	Number of children (in thousands)			Percent of children participating in literacy activity with family member[1]														
				Read to by family member three or more times in past week			At least once in past week									Visited a library at least once in past month		
							Told a story by family member			Taught letters, words, or numbers			Did arts and crafts					
	2001	2012	2016	2001	2012	2016	2001	2012	2016	2001	2012	2016	2001	2012	2016	2001	2012	2016
1	2	3	4	5	6	7	8	9	10	11	12	13	14	15	16	17	18	19
Total	**8,551 (11.0)**	**8,244 (85.1)**	**8,087 (91.1)**	**84 (0.8)**	**83 (0.8)**	**81 (1.1)**	**84 (0.8)**	**83 (0.9)**	**84 (1.2)**	**94 (0.6)**	**98 (0.3)**	**97 (0.6)**	**79 (0.9)**	**86 (0.8)**	**87 (1.1)**	**36 (1.1)**	**42 (1.2)**	**41 (1.4)**
Age																		
3 years old	3,795 (91.4)	3,674 (89.8)	3,404 (123.0)	84 (1.1)	82 (1.3)	82 (1.7)	83 (1.2)	82 (1.4)	84 (1.6)	93 (1.0)	97 (0.5)	96 (1.1)	77 (1.3)	85 (1.1)	85 (1.7)	35 (1.9)	38 (1.6)	39 (2.1)
4 years old	3,861 (89.0)	3,508 (90.4)	3,379 (109.8)	85 (1.2)	84 (1.3)	81 (2.1)	84 (1.1)	85 (1.3)	85 (1.9)	95 (0.7)	98 (0.3)	96 (0.8)	82 (1.2)	87 (1.2)	89 (1.3)	37 (1.4)	43 (1.8)	40 (2.1)
5 years old	896 (47.0)	1,062 (59.6)	1,303 (84.9)	81 (2.7)	80 (2.7)	80 (3.3)	82 (2.4)	81 (2.6)	82 (3.8)	93 (1.8)	98 (0.7)	97 (1.0)	80 (2.4)	88 (1.9)	85 (3.9)	37 (3.4)	49 (3.8)	46 (3.6)
Sex																		
Male	4,292 (79.9)	4,251 (103.9)	4,184 (118.8)	82 (1.2)	82 (1.2)	80 (1.5)	82 (1.1)	82 (1.4)	82 (1.5)	94 (0.7)	97 (0.4)	96 (1.0)	76 (1.3)	84 (1.1)	85 (1.4)	35 (1.4)	41 (1.7)	40 (2.1)
Female	4,260 (79.6)	3,993 (104.2)	3,903 (117.5)	86 (1.0)	84 (1.4)	83 (1.9)	85 (1.0)	85 (1.0)	86 (1.9)	94 (0.8)	98 (0.4)	97 (0.6)	83 (1.3)	88 (1.1)	89 (1.7)	37 (1.6)	42 (1.4)	42 (2.0)
Race/ethnicity																		
White	5,313 (68.0)	4,062 (97.4)	4,003 (96.8)	89 (0.8)	90 (1.0)	88 (1.2)	86 (1.0)	87 (1.1)	86 (1.1)	95 (0.7)	98 (0.4)	96 (0.9)	85 (1.0)	90 (0.9)	90 (1.2)	39 (1.3)	44 (1.4)	44 (1.7)
Black	1,251 (55.1)	1,154 (63.4)	1,086 (67.4)	77 (2.6)	77 (3.3)	79 (3.3)	81 (2.1)	80 (2.3)	85 (3.0)	94 (1.8)	99 (0.6)	98 (1.2)	70 (3.1)	83 (2.8)	85 (3.2)	31 (2.6)	41 (3.8)	42 (4.5)
Hispanic	1,506 (43.5)	2,100 (76.1)	2,133 (84.9)	71 (1.9)	71 (2.0)	71 (3.4)	75 (2.0)	78 (2.2)	78 (3.6)	92 (1.1)	97 (0.7)	97 (1.0)	67 (2.2)	80 (1.9)	82 (2.7)	30 (2.0)	34 (2.2)	33 (3.0)
Asian/Pacific Islander[2]	202 (29.0)	420 (32.7)	400 (44.7)	87 (4.1)	77 (3.3)	74 (6.5)	81 (5.8)	85 (2.7)	88 (3.2)	96 (2.2)	98 (1.1)	98 (0.9)	74 (6.9)	86 (2.6)	79 (6.6)	47 (7.5)	55 (4.4)	49 (5.8)
Asian	— (†)	374 (30.3)	386 (43.4)	— (†)	75 (3.5)	74 (6.7)	— (†)	83 (3.0)	88 (3.2)	— (†)	98 (1.2)	98 (0.9)	— (†)	84 (2.9)	78 (6.7)	— (†)	55 (4.4)	49 (5.9)
Pacific Islander	— (†)	‡ (†)	‡ (†)	— (†)	‡ (†)	‡ (†)	— (†)	‡ (†)	‡ (†)	— (†)	‡ (†)	‡ (†)	— (†)	‡ (†)	‡ (†)	— (†)	‡ (†)	‡ (†)
American Indian/Alaska Native	‡ (†)	‡ (†)	‡ (†)	‡ (†)	‡ (†)	‡ (†)	‡ (†)	‡ (†)	‡ (†)	‡ (†)	‡ (†)	‡ (†)	‡ (†)	‡ (†)	‡ (†)	‡ (†)	‡ (†)	‡ (†)
Two or more races	240 (26.9)	463 (41.1)	418 (47.8)	84 (3.9)	87 (3.2)	81 (4.0)	92 (2.7)	83 (3.8)	83 (5.0)	93 (3.1)	99 (0.8)	97 (1.3)	86 (3.7)	88 (3.8)	90 (2.6)	31 (5.8)	44 (4.2)	38 (5.0)
Mother's highest level of education[3]																		
Less than high school	996 (54.5)	1,291 (71.9)	1,093 (90.7)	69 (2.8)	73 (3.1)	61 (5.9)	72 (2.7)	75 (3.5)	77 (6.1)	91 (2.0)	98 (0.8)	94 (2.9)	62 (3.0)	82 (2.6)	77 (5.4)	21 (2.4)	26 (3.1)	27 (4.1)
High school/GED	2,712 (89.0)	1,614 (64.0)	1,482 (87.1)	81 (1.6)	75 (2.5)	79 (2.7)	83 (1.3)	83 (1.8)	78 (2.9)	95 (0.9)	97 (0.9)	96 (1.4)	77 (1.8)	84 (1.8)	86 (2.3)	30 (1.9)	38 (2.8)	35 (4.4)
Vocational/technical or some college	1,833 (73.9)	1,663 (77.3)	1,400 (64.0)	85 (1.8)	85 (1.7)	80 (2.3)	85 (1.7)	83 (1.5)	83 (2.4)	94 (1.2)	97 (0.8)	97 (1.1)	81 (1.9)	86 (1.6)	88 (2.2)	38 (2.2)	40 (2.0)	38 (2.7)
Associate's degree	573 (40.9)	678 (50.0)	700 (53.7)	89 (2.5)	85 (2.3)	85 (2.7)	84 (2.7)	84 (2.2)	87 (2.4)	92 (2.3)	98 (0.7)	97 (1.3)	82 (3.2)	86 (2.3)	89 (2.2)	42 (4.3)	43 (3.9)	42 (3.2)
Bachelor's degree/some graduate school	1,553 (68.4)	1,870 (65.9)	2,078 (75.4)	93 (1.2)	92 (1.2)	90 (1.4)	88 (1.5)	90 (1.2)	89 (1.6)	95 (1.1)	99 (0.3)	98 (0.5)	89 (1.4)	92 (1.0)	89 (1.4)	46 (2.4)	49 (2.2)	47 (2.2)
Graduate/professional degree	685 (45.7)	680 (30.8)	1,036 (45.0)	96 (1.1)	95 (1.0)	91 (1.4)	89 (2.3)	89 (1.5)	89 (1.5)	95 (1.3)	97 (0.8)	97 (0.8)	86 (2.2)	91 (1.5)	91 (1.4)	55 (3.8)	64 (2.5)	56 (2.0)
Mother's employment status[3]																		
Employed	5,148 (84.2)	4,491 (88.6)	4,782 (116.5)	86 (1.0)	84 (1.1)	83 (1.4)	84 (1.0)	84 (1.2)	85 (1.3)	94 (0.7)	98 (0.3)	96 (0.8)	80 (1.2)	86 (0.9)	86 (1.3)	36 (1.2)	42 (1.5)	41 (1.8)
Unemployed	396 (36.9)	550 (52.0)	269 (37.7)	77 (5.0)	80 (4.4)	91 (3.9)	80 (4.7)	84 (3.5)	82 (6.5)	94 (3.3)	98 (1.1)	98 (1.8)	69 (5.5)	89 (4.0)	88 (5.4)	37 (4.8)	33 (4.2)	36 (7.6)
Not in labor force	2,809 (73.3)	2,756 (86.9)	2,737 (104.2)	83 (1.4)	84 (1.7)	79 (2.7)	82 (1.5)	84 (1.6)	82 (2.6)	94 (0.9)	97 (0.7)	97 (0.8)	80 (1.3)	87 (1.4)	87 (2.0)	38 (1.9)	43 (1.9)	41 (2.6)
Family income (in current dollars)																		
$20,000 or less	2,106 (58.4)	1,480 (60.3)	1,162 (63.5)	74 (2.1)	76 (2.3)	70 (3.1)	81 (1.6)	83 (1.9)	82 (2.9)	92 (1.5)	97 (0.9)	95 (2.1)	72 (2.2)	84 (1.6)	85 (2.5)	27 (2.0)	39 (2.5)	40 (3.9)
$20,001 to $50,000	2,934 (86.6)	2,372 (77.4)	2,211 (93.6)	83 (1.4)	78 (2.1)	76 (2.7)	83 (1.4)	82 (1.6)	83 (1.9)	95 (0.7)	98 (0.5)	96 (1.3)	79 (1.4)	83 (1.8)	85 (2.2)	35 (1.8)	40 (2.2)	35 (2.9)
$50,001 to $75,000	1,724 (74.4)	1,510 (67.2)	1,342 (84.5)	88 (1.4)	82 (2.3)	79 (4.0)	87 (1.6)	82 (2.4)	82 (4.4)	95 (1.1)	98 (0.6)	96 (0.9)	82 (1.7)	85 (2.3)	87 (2.4)	38 (2.3)	38 (2.5)	37 (3.4)
$75,001 to $100,000	879 (49.4)	1,082 (46.5)	1,047 (58.6)	91 (1.6)	86 (2.5)	88 (2.3)	85 (2.2)	89 (2.1)	83 (3.5)	93 (1.7)	98 (0.6)	98 (0.6)	87 (2.1)	91 (2.2)	87 (3.6)	47 (3.1)	44 (2.9)	41 (3.5)
Over $100,000	909 (43.2)	1,800 (66.3)	2,325 (70.0)	96 (1.2)	93 (1.0)	90 (1.5)	84 (2.3)	83 (2.0)	87 (1.7)	96 (1.2)	98 (0.7)	98 (0.6)	87 (2.1)	89 (1.4)	89 (1.4)	45 (2.7)	48 (2.4)	48 (2.2)

See notes at end of table.

Table 207.10. Number of 3- to 5-year-olds not yet enrolled in kindergarten and percentage participating in home literacy activities with a family member, by type and frequency of activity and selected child and family characteristics: 2001, 2012, and 2016—Continued

[Standard errors appear in parentheses]

Selected child or family characteristic	Number of children (in thousands)			Percent of children participating in literacy activity with family member[1]														
				Read to by family member three or more times in past week			At least once in past week									Visited a library at least once in past month		
							Told a story by family member			Taught letters, words, or numbers			Did arts and crafts					
	2001	2012	2016	2001	2012	2016	2001	2012	2016	2001	2012	2016	2001	2012	2016	2001	2012	2016
1	2	3	4	5	6	7	8	9	10	11	12	13	14	15	16	17	18	19
Number of parents in the household																		
Two parents	6,429 (75.0)	5,958 (95.6)	5,969 (117.0)	87 (0.8)	85 (0.9)	84 (1.3)	84 (0.9)	85 (1.0)	84 (1.3)	94 (0.6)	98 (0.3)	97 (0.7)	81 (0.9)	87 (0.9)	88 (1.2)	38 (1.2)	42 (1.4)	43 (1.6)
None or one parent	2,123 (75.0)	2,286 (81.1)	2,117 (91.9)	76 (2.0)	77 (1.8)	74 (2.6)	82 (1.6)	79 (1.5)	83 (2.0)	93 (1.3)	97 (0.7)	97 (1.0)	74 (2.3)	84 (1.6)	84 (2.3)	30 (2.1)	40 (2.3)	33 (2.6)
Poverty status[4]																		
Poor	2,008 (60.4)	1,958 (77.8)	1,536 (67.1)	74 (2.1)	74 (2.2)	71 (3.0)	81 (1.7)	82 (1.7)	83 (2.8)	92 (1.6)	96 (0.8)	94 (1.7)	73 (2.3)	83 (1.7)	85 (2.6)	27 (2.1)	39 (2.2)	38 (3.3)
Near-poor	1,782 (70.5)	1,960 (86.5)	1,984 (112.9)	81 (1.8)	81 (2.1)	75 (3.4)	82 (2.0)	81 (2.0)	82 (3.0)	95 (1.0)	98 (0.5)	97 (1.0)	76 (1.9)	82 (2.1)	86 (2.3)	33 (2.8)	38 (2.6)	36 (3.1)
Nonpoor	4,762 (71.9)	4,327 (87.6)	4,567 (108.9)	90 (0.9)	88 (1.0)	87 (1.0)	85 (1.0)	85 (1.2)	85 (1.4)	95 (0.6)	98 (0.4)	97 (0.4)	84 (1.0)	89 (1.0)	88 (1.3)	41 (1.4)	44 (1.5)	44 (1.7)

—Not available.
†Not applicable.
‡Reporting standards not met. Either there are too few cases for a reliable estimate or the coefficient of variation (CV) is 50 percent or greater.
[1]The respondent was the parent most knowledgeable about the child's care and education. Responding parents reported on their own activities and the activities of their spouse/other adults in the household.
[2]The 2001 questionnaire included a single item for "Asian or Pacific Islander," whereas questionnaires for later years included one item for Asian and a separate item for Pacific Islander.
[3]Excludes children living in households with no mother or female guardian present.
[4]Poor children are those whose family incomes were below the Census Bureau's poverty threshold in the year prior to data collection; near-poor children are those whose family incomes ranged from the poverty threshold to 199 percent of the poverty threshold; and nonpoor children are those whose family incomes were at or above 200 percent of the poverty threshold. The poverty threshold is a dollar amount that varies depending on a family's size and composition and is updated annually to account for inflation. In 2015, for example, the poverty threshold for a family of four with two children was $24,257. Survey respondents are asked to select the range within which their income falls, rather than giving the exact amount of their income; therefore, the measure of poverty status is an approximation.
NOTE: Prior to 2012, National Household Education Surveys Program (NHES) surveys were administered via telephone with an interviewer. NHES:2012 used self-administered paper-and-pencil questionnaires that were mailed to respondents. For NHES:2016, initial contact with all respondents was by mail, and the majority of respondents received paper-and-pencil questionnaires. However, as an experiment with web use, a small sample of NHES:2016 respondents received mailed invitations to complete the survey online. Race categories exclude persons of Hispanic ethnicity. Detail may not sum to totals because of rounding and suppression of estimates that did not meet reporting standards. Some data have been revised from previously published figures.
SOURCE: U.S. Department of Education, National Center for Education Statistics, Early Childhood Program Participation Survey of the National Household Education Surveys Program (ECPP-NHES:2001, 2012, and 2016). (This table was prepared October 2017.)

Table 207.30. Number of kindergartners through fifth-graders and percentage whose parents reported doing education-related activities with their children in the past week, by selected child, parent, and school characteristics: 2003, 2012, and 2016

[Standard errors appear in parentheses]

Selected child, parent, or school characteristic	Number of children (in thousands)			Percent of children whose parents reported doing education-related activities with them in the past week: Told child a story			Did arts and crafts			Discussed family history/ethnic heritage			Played board games or did puzzles		
	2003	2012	2016	2003	2012	2016	2003	2012	2016	2003	2012	2016	2003	2012	2016
1	2	3	4	5	6	7	8	9	10	11	12	13	14	15	16
Total	**23,887 (55.7)**	**25,331 (137.9)**	**25,085 (167.1)**	**74.9 (0.66)**	**68.8 (0.91)**	**72.0 (0.94)**	**74.9 (0.70)**	**67.0 (0.84)**	**68.8 (1.11)**	**53.1 (0.89)**	**49.4 (1.00)**	**50.8 (0.99)**	**72.9 (0.68)**	**64.0 (0.94)**	**67.4 (1.13)**
Sex of child															
Male	12,192 (215.7)	13,103 (241.4)	12,925 (281.3)	73.3 (0.86)	68.2 (1.27)	71.3 (1.59)	69.7 (0.98)	60.7 (1.19)	61.8 (1.62)	51.1 (1.16)	47.6 (1.10)	47.9 (1.49)	71.8 (0.92)	63.0 (1.20)	66.5 (1.73)
Female	11,695 (207.6)	12,228 (234.7)	12,160 (221.5)	76.6 (0.96)	69.5 (1.22)	72.8 (1.27)	80.2 (1.01)	73.8 (1.25)	76.3 (1.29)	55.1 (1.28)	51.2 (1.47)	53.9 (1.35)	74.1 (1.05)	65.2 (1.14)	68.2 (1.37)
Race/ethnicity of child															
White	14,419 (155.8)	12,600 (173.4)	12,190 (262.3)	76.0 (0.96)	71.9 (0.98)	72.8 (1.21)	75.4 (0.89)	67.5 (1.08)	68.3 (1.17)	44.7 (1.13)	37.3 (1.21)	36.7 (1.18)	73.8 (0.87)	66.6 (1.03)	68.2 (1.19)
Black	3,765 (111.4)	3,642 (107.8)	3,450 (136.5)	69.6 (2.00)	64.3 (2.40)	73.8 (2.41)	68.1 (2.14)	64.0 (2.76)	66.1 (3.01)	66.6 (2.45)	67.4 (2.44)	69.9 (3.10)	72.9 (1.92)	60.1 (2.94)	64.7 (3.83)
Hispanic	4,220 (98.3)	6,051 (126.3)	6,234 (183.7)	74.2 (1.55)	65.4 (2.15)	69.9 (1.99)	79.6 (1.45)	67.7 (1.69)	71.9 (2.22)	64.5 (1.71)	58.1 (2.09)	64.5 (2.14)	68.5 (1.82)	62.2 (1.88)	69.2 (1.99)
Asian/Pacific Islander[1]	709 (82.9)	1,398 (93.2)	1,735 (171.4)	75.8 (3.73)	69.2 (3.38)	66.8 (6.31)	70.9 (4.34)	63.4 (3.45)	63.0 (7.10)	68.2 (4.83)	69.8 (3.56)	56.2 (5.10)	77.0 (3.82)	61.5 (3.87)	60.4 (6.54)
Asian	— (†)	1,331 (88.9)	1,676 (172.0)	— (†)	68.0 (3.52)	66.6 (6.54)	— (†)	62.7 (3.52)	62.8 (7.33)	— (†)	68.8 (3.78)	55.3 (5.19)	— (†)	60.6 (3.94)	61.1 (6.87)
Pacific Islander	— (†)	‡ (†)	‡ (†)	— (†)	‡ (†)	‡ (†)	— (†)	‡ (†)	‡ (†)	— (†)	‡ (†)	‡ (†)	— (†)	‡ (†)	‡ (†)
American Indian/Alaska Native	171 (36.3)	228 (54.2)	‡ (†)	84.1 (7.22)	70.3 (11.26)	‡ (†)	77.9 (8.06)	76.5 (9.66)	‡ (†)	82.4 (6.82)	56.0 (12.17)	‡ (†)	72.6 (10.24)	49.7 (11.34)	‡ (†)
Two or more races	603 (62.8)	1,411 (93.6)	1,410 (124.7)	83.5 (5.40)	66.4 (3.35)	77.5 (3.58)	75.7 (3.86)	69.7 (2.91)	73.6 (3.47)	63.3 (5.82)	51.7 (3.79)	58.5 (4.64)	77.8 (4.54)	64.2 (3.93)	67.0 (4.08)
Grade of child															
Kindergarten and grade 1	7,823 (32.5)	9,219 (140.6)	9,130 (174.2)	84.5 (0.93)	78.0 (1.60)	79.1 (1.72)	89.3 (0.84)	81.2 (1.14)	79.2 (2.22)	47.7 (1.38)	44.4 (1.89)	43.9 (2.00)	77.5 (1.17)	69.3 (1.56)	71.9 (2.28)
Grades 2 and 3	7,696 (24.5)	7,965 (155.5)	7,922 (183.1)	74.5 (1.21)	66.9 (1.51)	72.6 (1.68)	74.0 (1.12)	66.7 (1.54)	69.3 (1.57)	54.7 (1.34)	52.1 (1.53)	52.5 (1.88)	72.7 (1.09)	65.5 (1.44)	68.1 (1.99)
Grades 4 and 5	8,368 (30.1)	8,146 (130.5)	8,033 (167.3)	66.4 (1.20)	60.2 (1.55)	63.4 (1.55)	62.2 (1.36)	51.2 (1.45)	56.6 (1.56)	56.5 (1.42)	52.3 (1.44)	56.9 (1.59)	68.9 (1.18)	56.6 (1.50)	61.4 (1.62)
Language spoken most at home by child[2]															
English	21,595 (104.8)	21,763 (198.7)	20,716 (269.5)	75.4 (0.73)	69.4 (1.00)	73.2 (0.92)	74.4 (0.72)	67.2 (0.81)	68.5 (1.11)	51.5 (0.93)	46.8 (1.13)	47.2 (1.06)	73.7 (0.73)	64.0 (1.06)	67.0 (1.08)
Spanish	1,272 (69.2)	1,145 (78.2)	1,438 (151.4)	65.6 (2.85)	56.4 (5.08)	62.3 (5.94)	81.7 (2.16)	70.7 (3.63)	66.5 (5.88)	60.2 (3.11)	64.7 (4.04)	70.9 (5.69)	58.1 (3.10)	60.2 (4.36)	69.7 (5.49)
English and Spanish equally	559 (47.9)	1,310 (104.9)	1,398 (117.1)	76.6 (3.83)	68.7 (4.01)	69.0 (4.54)	78.7 (3.88)	64.5 (4.01)	78.3 (3.78)	77.3 (4.18)	64.0 (3.84)	75.9 (4.22)	75.2 (3.73)	67.0 (3.51)	72.8 (4.14)
English and other language equally	‡ (†)	705 (60.9)	1,038 (176.8)	‡ (†)	74.6 (3.94)	66.0 (8.87)	‡ (†)	66.9 (4.78)	66.9 (9.27)	‡ (†)	72.2 (4.54)	63.3 (8.85)	‡ (†)	68.2 (3.67)	63.8 (8.86)
Other language	375 (60.5)	335 (68.9)	415 (91.7)	81.7 (6.95)	66.1 (9.93)	77.6 (7.42)	76.7 (4.81)	55.2 (10.98)	70.1 (7.17)	75.1 (6.13)	63.1 (11.51)	47.6 (8.04)	74.8 (7.43)	65.5 (11.12)	66.9 (10.08)
Highest education level of parents/guardians in the household[3]															
Less than a high school diploma	1,664 (120.3)	2,933 (115.7)	2,690 (173.3)	67.2 (3.16)	65.0 (3.19)	59.6 (5.53)	74.8 (3.20)	67.2 (3.32)	66.1 (4.93)	60.4 (2.98)	60.7 (3.45)	59.6 (5.02)	66.8 (3.16)	61.7 (3.09)	59.3 (5.46)
High school diploma/equivalent (e.g., GED)	5,604 (163.6)	4,898 (146.9)	4,819 (168.4)	71.3 (1.59)	65.7 (2.45)	72.4 (2.45)	75.5 (1.32)	70.3 (2.50)	71.4 (2.76)	54.9 (1.91)	50.8 (2.04)	56.1 (3.27)	73.2 (1.39)	64.8 (2.32)	68.8 (2.40)
Vocational/technical or some college	5,466 (189.4)	5,044 (129.5)	4,043 (166.7)	75.9 (1.54)	69.1 (1.56)	70.3 (2.32)	76.2 (1.51)	64.4 (1.87)	68.9 (2.33)	50.8 (1.75)	47.0 (1.90)	49.0 (2.44)	71.6 (1.58)	63.9 (1.72)	70.8 (2.05)
Associate's degree	2,320 (139.6)	2,617 (141.8)	2,392 (138.2)	76.0 (2.00)	67.0 (3.80)	71.6 (2.57)	73.6 (2.47)	66.0 (2.45)	72.2 (2.69)	50.9 (3.16)	44.6 (3.22)	51.5 (3.36)	70.1 (2.50)	57.9 (3.69)	67.1 (2.70)
Bachelor's degree/some graduate school	5,214 (179.1)	6,485 (152.8)	6,688 (198.9)	77.3 (1.60)	71.3 (1.37)	76.0 (1.47)	74.0 (1.48)	66.8 (1.47)	68.4 (1.72)	47.3 (1.74)	45.6 (1.49)	46.3 (1.98)	75.8 (1.27)	65.1 (1.67)	67.8 (1.76)
Graduate/professional degree	3,618 (149.8)	3,354 (69.8)	4,452 (110.9)	78.6 (1.64)	72.7 (1.41)	75.0 (1.64)	73.9 (1.72)	67.3 (1.41)	66.4 (1.66)	60.1 (2.16)	51.9 (1.74)	47.8 (1.76)	74.9 (1.82)	67.8 (1.39)	67.0 (1.87)
Family income (in current dollars)															
$20,000 or less	4,418 (150.4)	3,838 (112.7)	3,324 (160.2)	73.9 (1.61)	68.7 (1.81)	65.6 (3.67)	76.0 (1.87)	71.4 (2.08)	67.1 (3.82)	61.6 (2.05)	54.3 (2.17)	57.9 (3.38)	73.3 (1.70)	61.7 (2.22)	64.7 (3.81)
$20,001 to $50,000	7,857 (230.1)	7,166 (155.7)	6,535 (154.9)	74.0 (1.31)	68.6 (1.87)	70.6 (1.94)	75.3 (1.05)	68.1 (1.86)	70.3 (2.41)	53.5 (1.59)	53.6 (2.07)	55.4 (2.38)	72.3 (1.45)	63.6 (1.80)	67.4 (2.16)
$50,001 to $75,000	5,024 (187.5)	4,380 (123.2)	4,159 (140.3)	74.9 (1.53)	68.5 (2.31)	71.9 (2.17)	75.3 (1.55)	67.5 (1.86)	68.8 (2.31)	49.6 (1.99)	47.7 (2.35)	54.7 (3.01)	72.1 (1.51)	63.3 (2.35)	68.1 (2.64)
$75,001 to $100,000	3,044 (127.1)	3,279 (81.0)	3,277 (99.8)	74.7 (2.02)	68.4 (2.03)	75.1 (2.30)	71.2 (1.98)	64.7 (2.13)	68.4 (2.78)	48.8 (2.28)	46.3 (2.46)	46.4 (2.39)	73.3 (2.30)	65.6 (2.29)	65.8 (2.46)
Over $100,000	3,543 (139.6)	6,668 (133.0)	7,790 (166.4)	78.6 (1.52)	69.4 (1.35)	74.7 (1.48)	75.1 (1.87)	64.1 (1.62)	68.6 (1.53)	50.1 (1.93)	44.5 (1.48)	43.8 (1.58)	74.7 (1.81)	65.5 (1.50)	68.7 (1.39)

See notes at end of table.

Table 207.30. Number of kindergartners through fifth-graders and percentage whose parents reported doing education-related activities with their children in the past week, by selected child, parent, and school characteristics: 2003, 2012, and 2016—Continued

[Standard errors appear in parentheses]

Selected child, parent, or school characteristic	Number of children (in thousands)			Percent of children whose parents reported doing education-related activities with them in the past week											
				Told child a story			Did arts and crafts			Discussed family history/ethnic heritage			Played board games or did puzzles		
	2003	2012	2016	2003	2012	2016	2003	2012	2016	2003	2012	2016	2003	2012	2016
1	2	3	4	5	6	7	8	9	10	11	12	13	14	15	16
Poverty status[4]															
Poor	4,396 (162.4)	5,489 (157.3)	4,771 (191.4)	73.2 (1.67)	68.6 (2.15)	67.3 (2.87)	76.9 (1.85)	72.0 (2.01)	68.2 (2.85)	60.9 (2.13)	57.6 (2.64)	55.8 (2.72)	72.4 (1.88)	61.7 (2.29)	66.8 (3.08)
Near-poor	5,332 (218.0)	5,495 (162.0)	5,470 (231.4)	74.3 (1.30)	68.3 (1.88)	70.6 (2.37)	76.7 (1.24)	67.5 (1.63)	70.6 (2.44)	53.3 (1.79)	49.8 (2.18)	57.4 (2.73)	73.6 (1.85)	63.3 (1.71)	66.6 (2.68)
Nonpoor	14,159 (182.1)	14,346 (167.4)	14,843 (209.6)	75.7 (0.85)	69.0 (1.07)	74.1 (1.02)	73.6 (0.92)	64.9 (0.98)	68.4 (1.11)	50.6 (1.11)	46.1 (1.09)	46.8 (1.19)	72.8 (0.87)	65.2 (1.16)	67.8 (1.09)
Control of school															
Public	21,004 (140.8)	22,797 (186.8)	22,626 (195.3)	75.0 (0.68)	68.2 (1.04)	71.3 (1.00)	75.2 (0.72)	67.0 (0.89)	68.2 (1.25)	52.4 (0.98)	49.6 (1.07)	50.7 (1.06)	73.4 (0.74)	63.7 (1.04)	67.4 (1.24)
Private	2,882 (127.8)	2,534 (113.4)	2,389 (134.3)	74.2 (2.09)	73.7 (2.08)	78.7 (2.48)	72.1 (1.94)	67.0 (2.45)	75.3 (2.31)	58.1 (2.17)	47.0 (2.75)	51.3 (3.22)	69.1 (1.99)	67.2 (2.25)	66.8 (2.71)
Locale of household[5]															
City	— (†)	7,473 (195.8)	8,376 (308.6)	— (†)	68.7 (1.64)	73.2 (1.98)	— (†)	68.1 (1.55)	69.6 (2.23)	— (†)	54.8 (1.69)	57.0 (1.99)	— (†)	64.1 (1.72)	66.9 (2.33)
Suburban	— (†)	9,418 (211.3)	10,797 (275.6)	— (†)	72.1 (1.37)	72.6 (1.35)	— (†)	67.6 (1.23)	69.7 (1.36)	— (†)	49.9 (1.59)	52.5 (1.48)	— (†)	65.2 (1.44)	68.1 (1.26)
Town	— (†)	2,483 (167.3)	2,019 (128.8)	— (†)	64.8 (4.83)	71.0 (2.64)	— (†)	67.4 (3.35)	64.2 (3.70)	— (†)	48.5 (3.24)	42.8 (3.62)	— (†)	57.6 (3.38)	65.0 (3.20)
Rural	— (†)	5,956 (191.3)	3,893 (189.6)	— (†)	65.3 (1.45)	68.4 (2.45)	— (†)	64.7 (1.54)	67.3 (2.42)	— (†)	42.2 (1.75)	36.9 (2.28)	— (†)	64.8 (1.45)	67.4 (2.24)

—Not available.
†Not applicable.
‡Reporting standards not met. Either there are too few cases for a reliable estimate or the coefficient of variation (CV) is 50 percent or greater.
[1]The 2003 questionnaire included a single item for "Asian or Pacific Islander," whereas questionnaires for later years included one item for Asian and a separate item for Pacific Islander.
[2]The 2012 and 2016 questionnaires included an item specifying that the child was not able to speak. Children who were not able to speak are excluded from this analysis.
[3]In 2003, education level was not collected for the second parent in a same sex couple.
[4]Poor children are those whose family incomes were below the Census Bureau's poverty threshold in the year prior to data collection; near-poor children are those whose family incomes ranged from the poverty threshold to 199 percent of the poverty threshold; and nonpoor children are those whose family incomes were at or above 200 percent of the poverty threshold. The poverty threshold is a dollar amount that varies depending on a family's size and composition and is updated annually to account for inflation. In 2015, or example, the poverty threshold for a family of four with two children was $24,257. Survey respondents are asked to select the range within which their income falls, rather than giving the exact amount of their income; therefore, the measure of poverty status is an approximation.
[5]Based on zip code of the household.
NOTE: While National Household Education Surveys Program (NHES) administrations prior to 2012 were administered via telephone with an interviewer, NHES:2012 and NHES:2016 used self-administered paper-and-pencil questionnaires that were mailed to respondents. Measurable differences between estimates for years prior to 2012 and estimates for later years could reflect actual changes in the population, or the changes could be due to the mode change from telephone to mail. The respondent was the parent most knowledgeable about the child's education. Responding parents reported on their own activities and the activities of their spouse/other adults in the household. Unless otherwise noted, all information is based on parent reports. Excludes homeschooled children. Race categories exclude persons of Hispanic ethnicity. Some data have been revised from previously published figures.
SOURCE: U.S. Department of Education, National Center for Education Statistics, Parent and Family Involvement in Education Survey of the National Household Education Surveys Program (PFI-NHES:2003, 2012, and 2016). (This table was prepared April 2019.)

Table 207.40. Percentage of elementary and secondary school children whose parents were involved in school activities, by selected child, parent, and school characteristics: 2003, 2012, and 2016

[Standard errors appear in parentheses]

Selected child, parent, or school characteristic	Percent of children whose parents reported the following types of involvement in school activities											
	2003				2012				2016			
	Attended a general school or PTO/PTA[1] meeting	Attended a parent-teacher conference	Attended a class event	Volunteered at school	Attended a general school or PTO/PTA[1] meeting	Attended a parent-teacher conference	Attended a class event	Volunteered at school	Attended a general school or PTO/PTA[1] meeting	Attended a parent-teacher conference	Attended a class event	Volunteered at school
1	2	3	4	5	6	7	8	9	10	11	12	13
Total	**87.7 (0.37)**	**77.1 (0.42)**	**69.9 (0.42)**	**41.8 (0.61)**	**87.4 (0.41)**	**75.8 (0.43)**	**74.4 (0.45)**	**41.7 (0.49)**	**88.6 (0.47)**	**77.7 (0.53)**	**79.3 (0.54)**	**43.4 (0.67)**
Sex of child												
Male	87.4 (0.49)	77.7 (0.63)	67.4 (0.75)	41.2 (0.88)	87.1 (0.66)	76.4 (0.61)	72.3 (0.65)	40.0 (0.71)	87.5 (0.80)	78.6 (0.74)	77.2 (0.97)	41.9 (0.82)
Female	87.9 (0.56)	76.5 (0.63)	72.6 (0.62)	42.4 (0.83)	87.7 (0.50)	75.1 (0.61)	76.7 (0.68)	43.5 (0.88)	89.8 (0.56)	76.6 (0.76)	81.6 (0.60)	45.0 (0.87)
Race/ethnicity of child												
White	88.7 (0.50)	76.3 (0.62)	74.1 (0.65)	48.3 (0.82)	89.1 (0.50)	77.2 (0.56)	81.5 (0.54)	49.6 (0.72)	90.6 (0.52)	78.8 (0.67)	85.8 (0.63)	49.1 (0.83)
Black	88.7 (0.85)	78.7 (1.35)	63.3 (1.54)	31.9 (1.64)	85.0 (1.35)	76.1 (1.35)	68.0 (1.66)	30.3 (1.33)	87.2 (1.72)	78.9 (1.60)	72.2 (2.02)	33.9 (1.81)
Hispanic	82.6 (1.05)	78.1 (1.10)	60.9 (1.36)	27.7 (1.23)	85.7 (0.98)	72.8 (1.08)	64.0 (1.34)	31.7 (1.14)	86.7 (0.98)	74.6 (1.38)	71.3 (1.29)	35.9 (1.49)
Asian/Pacific Islander[2]	88.5 (2.14)	77.7 (3.03)	65.1 (3.65)	33.8 (2.69)	83.0 (1.72)	71.5 (2.01)	65.8 (2.21)	35.2 (2.22)	80.0 (3.59)	76.4 (2.25)	71.1 (2.49)	41.7 (2.96)
Asian	— (†)	— (†)	— (†)	— (†)	82.5 (1.80)	71.5 (2.03)	65.0 (2.30)	34.0 (2.33)	79.5 (3.71)	76.4 (2.36)	71.9 (2.57)	41.4 (3.07)
Pacific Islander	— (†)	— (†)	— (†)	— (†)	90.7 (3.96)	71.4 (8.97)	79.0 (6.32)	54.3 (11.37)	92.0 (5.24)	78.7 (10.09)	52.3 (11.66)	48.2 (10.95)
American Indian/Alaska Native	85.1 (5.22)	85.1 (6.68)	69.5 (7.37)	18.9 (5.57)	85.1 (4.91)	79.9 (6.85)	75.6 (6.61)	42.3 (8.61)	93.0 (3.05)	87.5 (4.36)	80.1 (7.45)	59.4 (10.56)
Two or more races	87.2 (2.45)	74.9 (3.63)	72.3 (2.84)	47.7 (3.79)	88.8 (1.30)	78.4 (2.31)	76.0 (2.52)	45.3 (2.57)	91.2 (1.37)	78.1 (2.29)	83.1 (2.07)	48.0 (3.17)
Highest education level of parents/guardians in the household[3]												
Less than a high school diploma	69.8 (2.04)	67.8 (2.50)	42.4 (2.42)	15.6 (2.04)	77.0 (1.79)	63.3 (1.88)	48.0 (2.04)	18.3 (1.72)	76.4 (2.98)	69.8 (2.74)	54.3 (2.75)	25.0 (2.70)
High school diploma or equivalent	83.8 (0.91)	75.4 (0.94)	62.1 (1.28)	30.3 (1.27)	82.1 (1.42)	72.2 (1.23)	62.3 (1.45)	27.6 (1.38)	82.2 (1.34)	73.1 (1.55)	69.5 (1.70)	26.5 (1.99)
Vocational/technical or some college	88.5 (0.67)	78.0 (1.02)	69.1 (0.94)	38.8 (1.25)	87.5 (0.62)	75.4 (1.02)	76.1 (0.99)	39.0 (1.14)	89.2 (0.75)	75.7 (1.08)	78.2 (1.21)	34.7 (1.20)
Associate's degree	88.6 (1.27)	76.6 (1.68)	73.0 (1.76)	39.7 (1.67)	88.9 (0.91)	79.5 (1.13)	80.5 (1.37)	44.9 (1.77)	90.2 (1.08)	77.6 (1.30)	83.4 (1.45)	44.8 (1.70)
Bachelor's degree/some graduate school	92.0 (0.73)	79.8 (0.89)	80.1 (0.94)	53.9 (1.30)	92.1 (0.53)	79.9 (0.62)	85.0 (0.63)	55.0 (1.11)	92.9 (0.57)	81.5 (0.96)	87.3 (0.71)	54.0 (1.18)
Graduate/professional degree	94.6 (0.74)	79.5 (1.00)	80.8 (1.10)	61.7 (1.57)	95.1 (0.47)	83.0 (0.68)	90.1 (0.59)	61.8 (1.30)	95.3 (0.47)	83.8 (0.75)	92.7 (0.60)	64.9 (1.05)
Family income (in current dollars)												
$20,000 or less	79.8 (1.43)	74.6 (1.33)	56.6 (1.42)	26.1 (1.45)	79.9 (1.15)	69.4 (1.36)	57.2 (1.31)	24.1 (1.18)	79.5 (2.18)	73.7 (1.89)	61.4 (1.98)	24.2 (1.78)
$20,001 to $50,000	85.1 (0.67)	77.3 (0.85)	66.2 (0.94)	34.6 (1.14)	84.3 (0.73)	74.5 (1.04)	67.2 (1.28)	31.1 (1.22)	85.0 (1.12)	76.0 (1.18)	70.2 (1.47)	31.9 (1.63)
$50,001 to $75,000	89.9 (0.79)	76.8 (0.96)	74.5 (1.03)	46.0 (1.26)	88.7 (0.97)	77.3 (1.23)	77.3 (1.19)	43.7 (1.40)	88.7 (1.02)	78.3 (1.13)	81.2 (1.35)	39.7 (1.65)
$75,001 to $100,000	94.0 (0.80)	79.4 (1.28)	77.6 (1.34)	51.5 (1.71)	89.9 (0.88)	77.3 (1.15)	81.9 (1.13)	47.8 (1.24)	91.4 (0.87)	75.9 (1.23)	83.5 (1.32)	49.2 (1.53)
Over $100,000	93.9 (0.71)	77.9 (1.21)	80.7 (1.03)	61.1 (1.19)	92.5 (0.92)	79.0 (0.80)	85.5 (0.96)	57.6 (1.05)	93.6 (0.62)	80.8 (0.95)	90.5 (0.70)	59.1 (0.99)
Poverty status[4]												
Poor	79.4 (1.55)	74.5 (1.37)	56.7 (1.57)	26.8 (1.55)	82.5 (1.08)	71.3 (1.29)	60.0 (1.52)	26.8 (1.28)	81.1 (1.68)	74.8 (1.90)	62.3 (1.78)	26.6 (1.77)
Near-poor	85.1 (0.89)	77.9 (1.05)	64.8 (0.98)	32.5 (1.31)	83.7 (0.78)	75.2 (0.97)	66.5 (1.22)	31.2 (1.35)	85.8 (1.14)	76.4 (1.24)	71.4 (1.42)	33.0 (1.86)
Nonpoor	91.0 (0.46)	77.6 (0.58)	75.7 (0.51)	49.5 (0.76)	90.4 (0.51)	77.5 (0.55)	82.2 (0.61)	50.6 (0.71)	91.7 (0.48)	78.9 (0.66)	86.9 (0.57)	51.7 (0.78)
Control of school and enrollment level of child												
Public school	86.7 (0.40)	75.9 (0.45)	68.0 (0.47)	38.5 (0.64)	86.5 (0.43)	74.8 (0.45)	72.9 (0.50)	39.0 (0.52)	88.2 (0.50)	76.7 (0.56)	77.8 (0.60)	40.3 (0.69)
Elementary (kindergarten to grade 8)	90.9 (0.40)	85.1 (0.42)	71.7 (0.57)	42.8 (0.75)	90.0 (0.42)	82.4 (0.47)	76.0 (0.64)	44.1 (0.69)	91.0 (0.59)	84.8 (0.62)	80.5 (0.70)	44.6 (0.89)
Secondary (grades 9 to 12)	76.9 (1.06)	54.8 (1.03)	59.4 (1.06)	28.5 (0.98)	77.8 (0.92)	55.5 (1.04)	65.1 (0.90)	26.2 (0.71)	81.2 (0.88)	56.1 (1.21)	71.0 (1.01)	29.4 (0.95)
Private school	95.8 (0.61)	86.6 (1.02)	85.8 (1.20)	68.6 (1.57)	96.2 (0.58)	86.9 (1.13)	90.1 (1.18)	69.5 (1.63)	92.2 (1.39)	87.3 (1.21)	93.5 (1.14)	72.6 (1.91)
Elementary (kindergarten to grade 8)	96.6 (0.70)	91.6 (0.93)	88.4 (1.23)	73.3 (1.91)	97.4 (0.63)	91.2 (1.47)	91.8 (1.39)	74.4 (1.87)	92.1 (1.76)	90.5 (1.51)	94.2 (1.41)	78.2 (2.27)
Secondary (grades 9 to 12)	93.3 (1.55)	72.3 (2.49)	78.3 (2.77)	54.8 (2.82)	92.5 (1.20)	73.6 (2.19)	84.9 (2.08)	54.6 (2.44)	92.5 (2.36)	78.7 (1.89)	91.5 (1.30)	57.5 (2.80)
Locale of household[5]												
City	— (†)	— (†)	— (†)	— (†)	86.1 (0.76)	74.9 (0.84)	68.4 (0.93)	36.3 (0.98)	86.4 (1.02)	78.7 (1.10)	75.5 (1.25)	42.2 (1.39)
Suburban	— (†)	— (†)	— (†)	— (†)	88.3 (0.63)	74.9 (0.74)	74.5 (0.76)	44.2 (0.83)	90.0 (0.65)	77.5 (0.88)	80.9 (0.79)	45.5 (0.88)
Town	— (†)	— (†)	— (†)	— (†)	87.3 (1.27)	76.9 (1.78)	76.5 (1.92)	37.3 (1.90)	87.4 (1.51)	77.0 (1.72)	76.3 (1.76)	34.9 (1.99)
Rural	— (†)	— (†)	— (†)	— (†)	87.6 (0.87)	78.0 (0.76)	81.0 (0.97)	46.1 (1.15)	89.8 (1.02)	76.3 (1.34)	84.2 (1.15)	44.0 (1.75)

See notes at end of table.

Table 207.40. Percentage of elementary and secondary school children whose parents were involved in school activities, by selected child, parent, and school characteristics: 2003, 2012, and 2016—Continued

[Standard errors appear in parentheses]

Selected child, parent, or school characteristic	Percent of children whose parents reported the following types of involvement in school activities											
	2003				2012				2016			
	Attended a general school or PTO/PTA[1] meeting	Attended a parent-teacher conference	Attended a class event	Volunteered at school	Attended a general school or PTO/PTA[1] meeting	Attended a parent-teacher conference	Attended a class event	Volunteered at school	Attended a general school or PTO/PTA[1] meeting	Attended a parent-teacher conference	Attended a class event	Volunteered at school
1	2	3	4	5	6	7	8	9	10	11	12	13
Enrollment level of child and locale of household												
Elementary												
City	— (†)	— (†)	— (†)	— (†)	88.9 (0.77)	81.1 (0.93)	71.7 (1.15)	40.4 (1.25)	88.8 (1.25)	86.9 (1.13)	78.3 (1.41)	46.4 (1.85)
Suburban	— (†)	— (†)	— (†)	— (†)	91.8 (0.62)	83.6 (0.71)	77.8 (0.97)	50.6 (0.96)	92.4 (0.75)	85.4 (0.95)	83.4 (0.96)	51.1 (1.13)
Town	— (†)	— (†)	— (†)	— (†)	91.2 (1.39)	83.4 (2.30)	77.9 (2.37)	41.2 (2.41)	90.9 (1.74)	84.8 (1.98)	79.5 (2.52)	37.4 (2.58)
Rural	— (†)	— (†)	— (†)	— (†)	91.0 (0.74)	85.0 (0.84)	84.1 (1.00)	51.6 (1.41)	92.4 (1.17)	82.2 (1.67)	86.1 (1.57)	47.5 (2.10)
Secondary												
City	— (†)	— (†)	— (†)	— (†)	78.0 (1.47)	57.2 (1.64)	59.1 (1.81)	24.8 (1.38)	79.6 (1.66)	55.6 (1.92)	67.3 (1.74)	30.4 (1.57)
Suburban	— (†)	— (†)	— (†)	— (†)	79.8 (1.47)	54.0 (1.58)	66.3 (1.55)	28.7 (1.35)	84.1 (1.18)	58.7 (1.61)	74.8 (1.35)	32.2 (1.26)
Town	— (†)	— (†)	— (†)	— (†)	76.6 (2.38)	59.2 (2.81)	72.6 (2.35)	26.6 (2.24)	78.1 (3.12)	55.9 (3.63)	67.8 (3.32)	28.1 (3.18)
Rural	— (†)	— (†)	— (†)	— (†)	79.2 (2.05)	60.6 (1.86)	73.5 (2.20)	32.7 (1.76)	83.6 (1.72)	61.9 (1.87)	79.7 (1.68)	35.5 (2.07)

—Not available.
†Not applicable.
[1]PTO stands for Parent Teacher Organization and PTA stands for Parent Teacher Association.
[2]The 2003 questionnaire included a single item for "Asian or Pacific Islander," whereas questionnaires for later years included one item for Asian and a separate item for Pacific Islander.
[3]In 2003, education level was not collected for the second parent in a same sex couple.
[4]Poor children are those whose family incomes were below the Census Bureau's poverty threshold in the year prior to data collection; near-poor children are those whose family incomes ranged from the poverty threshold to 199 percent of the poverty threshold; and nonpoor children are those whose family incomes were at or above 200 percent of the poverty threshold. The poverty threshold is a dollar amount that varies depending on a family's size and composition and is updated annually to account for inflation. In 2015, for example, the poverty threshold for a family of four with two children was $24,257. Survey respondents are asked to select the range within which their income falls, rather than giving the exact amount of their income; therefore, the measure of poverty status is an approximation.
[5]Based on zip code of the household.
NOTE: While National Household Education Surveys Program (NHES) administrations prior to 2012 were administered via telephone with an interviewer, NHES:2012 and NHES:2016 used self-administered paper-and-pencil questionnaires that were mailed to respondents. Measurable differences between estimates for years prior to 2012 and estimates for later years could reflect actual changes in the population, or the changes could be due to the mode change from telephone to mail. Includes children enrolled in kindergarten through grade 12 and ungraded students. Excludes homeschooled children. The respondent was the parent most knowledgeable about the child's education. Responding parents reported on their own activities and the activities of their spouse/other adults in the household. Race categories exclude persons of Hispanic ethnicity. Some data have been revised from previously published figures.
SOURCE: U.S. Department of Education, National Center for Education Statistics, Parent and Family Involvement in Education Survey of the National Household Education Surveys Program (PFI-NHES:2003, 2012, and 2016). (This table was prepared April 2019.)

Table 208.10. Public elementary and secondary pupil/teacher ratios, by selected school characteristics: Selected years, fall 1990 through fall 2016

Selected school characteristic	1990	1995	1998	1999	2000	2001	2002	2003	2004	2005	2006	2007	2008	2009	2010[1]	2011	2012	2013	2014	2015	2016
1	2	3	4	5	6	7	8	9	10	11	12	13	14	15	16	17	18	19	20	21	22
All schools	**17.4**	**17.8**	**16.9**	**16.6**	**16.4**	**16.3**	**16.2**	**16.4**	**16.2**	**16.0**	**15.8**	**15.7**	**15.7**	**16.0**	**16.4**	**16.3**	**16.4**	**16.3**	**16.2**	**16.2**	**16.2**
Enrollment size of school																					
Under 300	14.0	14.1	13.6	13.3	13.1	12.9	12.8	13.0	12.8	12.7	12.7	12.7	12.5	12.6	12.9	12.8	12.8	12.7	12.7	12.8	12.8
300 to 499	17.0	17.1	16.2	15.8	15.5	15.4	15.3	15.5	15.2	15.0	14.9	15.0	14.8	15.2	15.4	15.4	15.5	15.4	15.3	15.3	15.2
500 to 999	18.0	18.2	17.1	16.8	16.7	16.5	16.5	16.6	16.4	16.2	15.9	15.9	15.9	16.3	16.7	16.7	16.7	16.7	16.5	16.5	16.5
1,000 to 1,499	17.9	18.7	17.7	17.6	17.4	17.4	17.4	17.6	17.3	16.9	16.7	16.5	16.5	16.8	17.3	17.1	17.1	17.1	16.9	16.9	17.0
1,500 or more	19.2	20.0	19.3	19.3	19.1	19.0	18.9	19.2	19.1	18.8	18.6	18.1	18.3	18.7	19.5	19.0	19.0	19.1	19.0	19.0	18.9
Type																					
Regular schools	17.6	17.9	17.0	16.7	16.5	16.4	16.3	16.5	16.3	16.1	15.9	15.8	15.8	16.1	16.5	16.4	16.5	16.5	16.3	16.3	16.3
Alternative	14.2	16.6	16.4	15.8	15.2	14.9	14.9	15.0	14.4	14.0	14.7	13.5	14.2	14.3	14.8	14.7	14.8	14.3	14.5	14.4	14.4
Special education	6.5	7.2	7.3	7.2	7.0	6.4	7.0	7.3	7.4	6.2	6.6	7.1	6.8	7.1	6.9	7.1	7.2	6.6	7.0	7.4	7.2
Vocational	13.0	12.7	13.1	13.0	12.7	12.7	9.9	10.3	11.5	12.0	13.3	11.3	10.7	10.2	11.7	11.8	11.6	11.8	11.8	11.9	11.8
Percent of students eligible for free or reduced-price lunch																					
25 percent or less	—	—	—	16.9	16.7	16.7	16.6	16.8	16.8	16.5	16.4	16.3	16.1	16.5	16.8	16.9	16.5	16.5	16.4	16.5	16.5
26 percent to 50 percent	—	—	—	16.4	16.2	16.1	16.2	16.4	16.2	16.1	15.8	15.7	15.7	16.1	16.5	16.2	16.4	16.3	16.2	16.2	16.1
51 percent to 75 percent	—	—	—	16.2	16.1	16.0	16.0	16.0	15.9	15.6	15.3	15.2	15.4	15.8	16.2	15.8	16.2	16.1	16.0	16.0	15.9
More than 75 percent	—	—	—	16.3	16.1	16.0	16.0	16.1	15.9	15.5	15.4	15.0	15.1	15.6	16.0	15.5	16.3	16.5	16.4	16.4	16.4
Level and size																					
Elementary schools	18.1	18.1	17.0	16.7	16.5	16.3	16.2	16.3	16.0	15.8	15.6	15.6	15.5	15.9	16.3	16.3	16.4	16.3	16.1	16.1	16.1
Regular	18.2	18.1	17.0	16.7	16.5	16.3	16.2	16.3	16.0	15.8	15.6	15.6	15.5	15.9	16.3	16.3	16.4	16.4	16.2	16.1	16.1
Under 300	16.0	15.7	15.1	14.6	14.4	14.1	13.9	14.0	13.7	13.6	13.5	13.7	13.5	13.7	14.0	14.0	14.0	14.0	13.8	13.8	13.7
300 to 499	17.6	17.5	16.4	16.1	15.8	15.6	15.5	15.6	15.3	15.2	15.1	15.2	15.0	15.4	15.6	15.7	15.7	15.6	15.5	15.4	15.4
500 to 999	18.8	18.6	17.4	17.1	16.9	16.8	16.7	16.8	16.5	16.3	16.0	16.0	16.0	16.5	16.9	16.9	17.0	17.0	16.7	16.7	16.7
1,000 to 1,499	19.5	19.7	18.4	18.3	18.1	18.0	18.0	18.1	17.7	17.2	17.0	16.7	16.8	17.2	17.8	17.7	17.8	17.7	17.5	17.4	17.4
1,500 or more	19.9	20.9	19.9	20.0	20.5	20.2	20.3	20.8	20.5	19.6	19.4	18.0	18.1	18.5	19.3	19.0	18.9	19.1	19.0	18.8	18.6
Secondary schools	16.6	17.6	17.0	16.8	16.6	16.6	16.7	16.9	16.8	16.6	16.4	16.3	16.2	16.4	16.8	16.5	16.6	16.6	16.6	16.6	16.6
Regular	16.7	17.7	17.1	16.9	16.7	16.7	16.8	17.0	16.9	16.8	16.6	16.4	16.3	16.6	16.9	16.7	16.7	16.7	16.7	16.7	16.7
Under 300	12.3	12.8	12.5	12.0	12.0	11.9	12.0	12.3	12.0	12.2	12.0	12.1	11.9	11.9	12.2	12.0	12.1	12.1	11.9	12.1	12.2
300 to 499	14.9	15.7	15.1	14.6	14.5	14.4	14.4	14.7	14.7	14.6	14.4	14.4	14.3	14.3	14.6	14.6	14.5	14.4	14.6	14.6	14.5
500 to 999	16.1	16.9	16.2	16.0	15.8	15.7	15.8	16.0	15.9	15.8	15.6	15.4	15.4	15.6	15.8	15.7	15.7	15.7	15.7	15.7	15.8
1,000 to 1,499	17.2	18.0	17.2	17.1	16.8	16.8	16.9	17.2	17.0	16.8	16.5	16.5	16.3	16.6	16.9	16.6	16.6	16.6	16.5	16.5	16.6
1,500 or more	19.3	20.0	19.3	19.2	18.9	18.8	18.8	19.0	19.0	18.8	18.5	18.2	18.2	18.6	19.3	18.8	18.9	18.9	18.9	18.7	18.7
Combined schools	14.5	15.0	13.4	13.4	13.7	13.4	13.5	13.8	13.9	14.1	14.7	13.4	13.9	14.0	15.4	14.4	14.4	14.7	14.2	15.2	15.0
Under 300	8.9	9.0	8.9	9.1	9.2	9.1	9.1	9.5	9.2	9.5	10.1	9.2	8.9	9.1	9.2	9.4	9.3	9.1	9.2	9.6	9.7
300 to 499	14.2	14.7	13.6	13.8	13.5	13.1	13.1	14.4	13.4	13.9	14.3	13.7	13.9	13.8	13.6	13.3	13.3	13.5	13.6	14.3	14.0
500 to 999	16.3	16.6	15.5	14.9	15.8	15.6	16.0	15.4	15.8	15.9	16.0	15.2	15.6	15.8	16.9	15.6	15.5	15.5	15.1	16.3	15.9
1,000 to 1,499	17.8	18.2	16.9	16.9	17.5	18.1	17.7	17.5	17.4	16.4	17.3	15.9	16.7	17.9	19.2	18.1	17.8	17.9	17.3	17.5	17.3
1,500 or more	17.7	19.6	18.7	19.2	18.6	18.9	19.1	19.2	18.7	20.0	20.3	18.0	21.7	21.7	25.7	23.4	23.3	24.7	20.9	23.6	22.9
Ungraded	6.4	6.9	5.9	5.3	7.0	6.3	6.8	9.6	8.0	7.7	7.2	7.3	5.5	8.5	5.3	6.0	5.9	3.0	8.1	9.0	5.1
Level, type, and percent of students eligible for free or reduced-price lunch																					
Elementary, regular																					
25 percent or less	—	—	—	17.1	16.9	16.7	16.5	16.7	16.6	16.4	16.2	16.2	16.0	16.4	16.8	16.6	16.5	16.5	16.3	16.4	16.3
26 to 50 percent	—	—	—	16.5	16.3	16.2	16.1	16.2	16.0	15.8	15.5	15.6	15.6	16.0	16.4	16.3	16.4	16.3	16.1	16.1	16.0
51 to 75 percent	—	—	—	16.3	16.2	16.1	16.0	16.0	15.7	15.5	15.1	15.2	15.2	15.7	16.0	15.9	16.2	16.1	15.8	15.8	15.8
More than 75 percent	—	—	—	16.6	16.4	16.2	16.1	16.3	16.0	15.6	15.4	15.1	15.2	15.8	16.1	15.7	16.5	16.6	16.5	16.4	16.4
Secondary, regular																					
25 percent or less	—	—	—	17.0	16.9	16.9	16.9	17.2	17.5	17.0	16.9	16.8	16.6	16.8	17.1	17.4	16.7	16.8	16.7	16.9	16.8
26 to 50 percent	—	—	—	16.6	16.4	16.3	16.5	16.9	16.9	16.8	16.4	16.4	16.2	16.5	16.8	16.4	16.6	16.5	16.5	16.6	16.6
51 to 75 percent	—	—	—	16.8	16.6	16.6	16.6	17.0	16.9	16.7	16.3	16.1	16.4	16.5	17.1	16.1	16.7	16.8	16.9	16.9	16.8
More than 75 percent	—	—	—	16.8	16.5	16.5	16.3	16.6	16.2	16.7	16.2	15.7	15.9	16.0	16.5	15.5	16.6	17.0	17.0	17.1	17.1

—Not available.
[1]Includes imputations for California and Wyoming.
NOTE: Includes only schools that reported both enrollment and teacher data. Ratios are based on data reported by schools and may differ from data reported in other tables that reflect aggregate totals reported by states. Some data have been revised from previously published figures.

SOURCE: U.S. Department of Education, National Center for Education Statistics, Common Core of Data (CCD), "Public Elementary/Secondary School Universe Survey," 1990–91 through 2016–17. (This table was prepared April 2019.)

Table 208.20. Public and private elementary and secondary teachers, enrollment, pupil/teacher ratios, and new teacher hires: Selected years, fall 1955 through fall 2028

Year	Teachers (in thousands)			Enrollment (in thousands)			Pupil/teacher ratio			Number of new teacher hires (in thousands)[1]		
	Total	Public	Private	Total	Public	Private	Total	Public	Private	Total	Public	Private
1	2	3	4	5	6	7	8	9	10	11	12	13
1955	1,286	1,141	145[2]	35,280	30,680	4,600[2]	27.4	26.9	31.7[2]	—	—	—
1960	1,600	1,408	192[2]	42,181	36,281	5,900[2]	26.4	25.8	30.7[2]	—	—	—
1965	1,933	1,710	223	48,473	42,173	6,300	25.1	24.7	28.3	—	—	—
1970	2,292	2,059	233	51,257	45,894	5,363	22.4	22.3	23.0	—	—	—
1975	2,453	2,198	255[2]	49,819	44,819	5,000[2]	20.3	20.4	19.6[2]	—	—	—
1976	2,457	2,189	268	49,478	44,311	5,167	20.1	20.2	19.3	—	—	—
1977	2,488	2,209	279	48,717	43,577	5,140	19.6	19.7	18.4	—	—	—
1978	2,479	2,207	272	47,637	42,551	5,086	19.2	19.3	18.7	—	—	—
1979	2,461	2,185	276[2]	46,651	41,651	5,000[2]	19.0	19.1	18.1[2]	—	—	—
1980	2,485	2,184	301	46,208	40,877	5,331	18.6	18.7	17.7	—	—	—
1981	2,440	2,127	313[2]	45,544	40,044	5,500[2]	18.7	18.8	17.6[2]	—	—	—
1982	2,458	2,133	325[2]	45,166	39,566	5,600[2]	18.4	18.6	17.2[2]	—	—	—
1983	2,476	2,139	337	44,967	39,252	5,715	18.2	18.4	17.0	—	—	—
1984	2,508	2,168	340[2]	44,908	39,208	5,700[2]	17.9	18.1	16.8[2]	—	—	—
1985	2,549	2,206	343	44,979	39,422	5,557	17.6	17.9	16.2	—	—	—
1986	2,592	2,244	348[2]	45,205	39,753	5,452[2]	17.4	17.7	15.7[2]	—	—	—
1987	2,631	2,279	352	45,488	40,008	5,479	17.3	17.6	15.6	—	—	—
1988	2,668	2,323	345[2]	45,430	40,189	5,242[2]	17.0	17.3	15.2[2]	—	—	—
1989	2,713	2,357	356	46,141	40,543	5,599	17.0	17.2	15.7	—	—	—
1990	2,759	2,398	361[2]	46,864	41,217	5,648[2]	17.0	17.2	15.6[2]	—	—	—
1991	2,797	2,432	365	47,728	42,047	5,681	17.1	17.3	15.6	—	—	—
1992	2,823	2,459	364[2]	48,694	42,823	5,870[2]	17.2	17.4	16.1[2]	—	—	—
1993	2,868	2,504	364	49,532	43,465	6,067	17.3	17.4	16.7	—	—	—
1994	2,922	2,552	370[2]	50,106	44,111	5,994[2]	17.1	17.3	16.2[2]	—	—	—
1995	2,974	2,598	376	50,759	44,840	5,918	17.1	17.3	15.7	—	—	—
1996	3,051	2,667	384[2]	51,544	45,611	5,933[2]	16.9	17.1	15.5[2]	—	—	—
1997	3,138	2,746	391	52,071	46,127	5,944	16.6	16.8	15.2	—	—	—
1998	3,230	2,830	400[2]	52,526	46,539	5,988[2]	16.3	16.4	15.0[2]	—	—	—
1999	3,319	2,911	408	52,875	46,857	6,018	15.9	16.1	14.7	305	222	83
2000	3,366	2,941	424[2]	53,373	47,204	6,169[2]	15.9	16.0	14.5[2]	—	—	—
2001	3,440	3,000	441	53,992	47,672	6,320	15.7	15.9	14.3	—	—	—
2002	3,476	3,034	442[2]	54,403	48,183	6,220[2]	15.7	15.9	14.1[2]	—	—	—
2003	3,490	3,049	441	54,639	48,540	6,099	15.7	15.9	13.8	311	236	74
2004	3,536	3,091	445[2]	54,882	48,795	6,087[2]	15.5	15.8	13.7[2]	—	—	—
2005	3,593	3,143	450	55,187	49,113	6,073	15.4	15.6	13.5	—	—	—
2006	3,622	3,166	456[2]	55,307	49,316	5,991[2]	15.3	15.6	13.2[2]	—	—	—
2007	3,656	3,200	456	55,201	49,291	5,910	15.1	15.4	13.0	327	246	80
2008	3,670	3,222	448[2]	54,973	49,266	5,707[2]	15.0	15.3	12.8[2]	—	—	—
2009	3,647	3,210	437	54,849	49,361	5,488	15.0	15.4	12.5	—	—	—
2010	3,512	3,099	413[2]	54,867	49,484	5,382[2]	15.6	16.0	13.0[2]	—	—	—
2011	3,508	3,103	405	54,790	49,522	5,268	15.6	16.0	13.0	241	173	68
2012	3,517	3,109	408[2]	55,104	49,771	5,333[2]	15.7	16.0	13.1[2]	—	—	—
2013	3,555	3,114	441	55,440	50,045	5,396	15.6	16.1	12.2	—	—	—
2014	3,594	3,132	461[2]	55,888	50,313	5,575[2]	15.6	16.1	12.1[2]	—	—	—
2015	3,633	3,151	482	56,189	50,438	5,751	15.5	16.0	11.9	325	218	107
2016	3,655	3,169	485	56,391	50,615	5,776	15.4	16.0	11.9	351	257	94
2017[3]	3,641	3,156	485	56,477	50,695	5,781	15.5	16.1	11.9	318	227	92
2018[3]	3,667	3,179	488	56,518	50,728	5,789	15.4	16.0	11.9	356	262	95
2019[3]	3,691	3,200	491	56,572	50,770	5,802	15.3	15.9	11.8	355	260	95
2020[3]	3,708	3,214	493	56,678	50,857	5,821	15.3	15.8	11.8	351	257	94
2021[3]	3,724	3,229	495	56,719	50,892	5,827	15.2	15.8	11.8	353	258	94
2022[3]	3,750	3,251	499	56,865	51,012	5,853	15.2	15.7	11.7	363	266	96
2023[3]	3,771	3,269	502	56,973	51,098	5,875	15.1	15.6	11.7	360	263	97
2024[3]	3,795	3,290	505	57,019	51,124	5,894	15.0	15.5	11.7	363	266	97
2025[3]	3,820	3,311	509	57,029	51,119	5,910	14.9	15.4	11.6	367	269	98
2026[3]	3,846	3,333	513	57,050	51,123	5,927	14.8	15.3	11.6	370	271	99
2027[3]	3,875	3,357	517	57,176	51,228	5,948	14.8	15.3	11.5	376	276	100
2028[3]	3,906	3,385	522	57,387	51,419	5,969	14.7	15.2	11.4	381	280	101

—Not available.

[1]A teacher is considered to be a new hire for a public or private school if the teacher had not taught in that control of school in the previous year. A teacher who moves from a public to private or a private to public school is considered a new teacher hire, but a teacher who moves from one public school to another public school or one private school to another private school is not considered a new teacher hire.

[2]Estimated.

[3]Projected.

NOTE: Data for teachers are expressed in full-time equivalents (FTE). Counts of private school teachers and enrollment include prekindergarten through grade 12 in schools offering kindergarten or higher grades. Counts of public school teachers and enrollment include prekindergarten through grade 12. The pupil/teacher ratio includes teachers for students with disabilities and other special teachers, while these teachers are generally excluded from class size calculations. Ratios for public schools reflect totals reported by states and differ from totals reported for schools or school districts. Some data have been revised from previously published figures. Detail may not sum to totals because of rounding.

SOURCE: U.S. Department of Education, National Center for Education Statistics, *Statistics of Public Elementary and Secondary Day Schools*, 1955–56 through 1980–81; *Statistics of Nonpublic Elementary and Secondary Schools*, 1955 through 1980; 1983–84, 1985–86, and 1987–88 Private School Survey; Common Core of Data (CCD), "State Nonfiscal Survey of Public Elementary/Secondary Education," 1981–82 through 2016–17; Private School Universe Survey (PSS), 1989–90 through 2015–16; Schools and Staffing Survey (SASS), "Public School Teacher Data File" and "Private School Teacher Data File," 1999–2000 through 2011–12; National Teacher and Principal Survey (NTPS), 2015–16; Elementary and Secondary Teacher Projection Model, 1973 through 2028; and New Teacher Hires Projection Model, 1988 through 2028. (This table was prepared April 2019.)

Table 208.30. Public elementary and secondary teachers, by level and state or jurisdiction: Selected years, fall 2000 through fall 2016

[In full-time equivalents]

State or jurisdiction	Fall 2000	Fall 2005	Fall 2010	Fall 2013	Fall 2014	Fall 2015				Fall 2016			
						Total	Elementary	Secondary	Ungraded	Total	Elementary	Secondary	Ungraded
1	2	3	4	5	6	7	8	9	10	11	12	13	14
United States	**2,941,461**[1]	**3,143,003**[1]	**3,099,095**[1]	**3,113,764**[1]	**3,132,351**[1]	**3,151,497**[1]	**1,745,337**[1]	**1,220,166**[1]	**185,994**[1]	**3,169,499**[1]	**1,759,610**[1]	**1,232,805**[1]	**177,083**[1]
Alabama	48,194[2]	57,757	49,363	47,162	42,737	40,766	21,687	19,080	0	42,533	22,476	20,057	0
Alaska	7,880	7,912	8,171	7,898	7,759	7,832	4,325	3,507	0	7,825	4,070	3,754	0
Arizona	44,438	51,376	50,031	48,359	48,124	47,944	33,455	14,489	0	48,220	33,135	15,085	0
Arkansas	31,947	32,997	34,273	34,933	35,430	35,804	18,474	14,714	2,616	35,730	18,317	14,768	2,645
California	298,021[2]	309,222[2]	260,806[2]	259,506[2]	267,685[2]	263,475	176,192	84,322	2,960	271,287[2]	182,600[2]	86,140	2,547
Colorado	41,983	45,841	48,543	50,157	51,388	51,798	29,578	22,220	0	52,014	29,401	22,613	0
Connecticut	41,044	39,687	42,951	43,443	42,062	43,772	27,256	16,233	284	42,343	26,744	15,373	226
Delaware	7,469	7,998	8,933	9,388	9,649	8,962	4,524	4,438	0	9,208	4,678	4,530	0
District of Columbia	4,949	5,481[3]	5,925	5,991	6,565	6,789	4,185	2,551	54	6,727	3,990	2,713	24
Florida	132,030	158,962	175,609	177,853	180,442	182,586	76,722	67,248	38,616	186,339	76,301	67,849	42,190
Georgia	91,043	108,535	112,460	109,441	111,470	113,031	52,471	43,869	16,690	114,763	52,918	44,721	17,124
Hawaii	10,927	11,226	11,396	11,781	11,663	11,747	6,410	5,248	89	11,782	6,397	5,315	70
Idaho	13,714	14,521	15,673	15,002	15,609	15,656	7,438	8,218	0	16,204	7,648	8,556	0
Illinois	127,620	133,857	132,983	136,355[4]	132,456[4]	129,948	90,437	39,508	3	128,893	90,125	38,506	263
Indiana	59,226	60,592	58,121[2]	59,823	56,547	57,675	30,305	27,370	0	60,162	31,163	28,999	0
Iowa	34,636	35,181	34,642	35,397	35,684	35,687	25,011	10,677	0	35,808	25,205	10,603	0
Kansas	32,742	33,608	34,644	38,153	37,659	40,035	20,261	19,774	0	36,193	18,496	17,697	0
Kentucky	39,589	42,413	42,042	41,820	41,586	41,902	24,848	10,028	7,026	42,029	24,772	10,058	7,199
Louisiana	49,915	44,660	48,655	46,437	46,340	58,469	33,250	15,271	9,949	48,408	32,806	15,602	0
Maine	16,559	16,684	15,384	15,452	14,937	14,857	10,336	4,521	0	14,750	10,284	4,467	0
Maryland	52,433	56,685	58,428	58,611	59,194	59,414	36,196	23,218	0	59,703	36,442	23,261	0
Massachusetts	67,432	73,596	68,754	70,490	71,859	71,969	47,210	24,759	0	72,413	47,382	25,031	0
Michigan	97,031	98,069	88,615	85,786	85,038	84,181	34,885	33,107	16,190	83,597	34,756	32,785	16,057
Minnesota	53,457	51,107	52,672	54,413	55,690	55,985	30,149	24,014	1,822	56,715	30,555	24,270	1,889
Mississippi	31,006	31,433	32,255	32,292	32,311	32,175	15,112	13,181	3,882	31,924	14,907	13,196	3,822
Missouri	64,735	67,076	66,735	66,651	67,356	67,635	35,221	32,414	0	67,926	35,235	32,691	0
Montana	10,411	10,369	10,361	10,310	10,234	10,412	7,257	3,115	40	10,555	7,391	3,127	36
Nebraska	20,983	21,359	22,345	22,401	22,988	23,308	14,618	8,690	0	23,611	15,221	8,390	0
Nevada	18,293	21,744	21,839	21,921	21,656	22,702	10,978	8,316	3,408	23,705	11,422	8,486	3,797
New Hampshire	14,341	15,536	15,365	14,826	14,773	14,770	10,005	4,765	0	14,760	9,761	4,999	0
New Jersey	99,061	112,673	110,202	114,581	115,067	114,968	60,873	37,731	16,365	115,729	61,286	37,911	16,532
New Mexico	21,042	22,021	22,437	22,239	22,411	21,722	9,687	8,236	3,798	21,331	9,454	8,123	3,754
New York	206,961	218,989	211,606	206,693	203,781	206,086	103,618	92,579	9,889	209,151	105,341	93,792	10,018
North Carolina	83,680	95,664	98,357	99,327	99,320	99,355	68,977	29,550	828	100,220	69,663	29,741	816
North Dakota	8,141	8,003	8,417	8,805	9,049	9,195	6,058	3,137	0	9,265	6,122	3,143	0
Ohio	118,361	117,982	109,282	106,010	106,526[3]	101,742	56,898	41,212	3,632	102,600	57,122	41,128	4,350
Oklahoma	41,318	41,833	41,278	41,983	42,073	42,452	23,780	18,673	0	41,090	23,119	17,970	0
Oregon	28,094	28,346	28,109	26,733	27,850	29,086	20,642	8,444	0	29,756	21,089	8,667	0
Pennsylvania	116,963	122,397	129,911	121,330	122,030	120,893	58,033	52,606	10,253	122,552	58,732	52,965	10,855
Rhode Island	10,645	14,180[2]	11,212	9,824	9,471	10,631	5,983	4,648	0	10,689	5,965	4,724	0
South Carolina	45,380	48,212	45,210	48,151	49,475	50,237	35,293	14,943	0	50,789	35,712	15,078	0
South Dakota	9,397	9,129	9,512	9,510	9,618	9,638	6,274	2,483	881	9,777	6,364	2,499	914
Tennessee	57,164	59,596	66,558	65,847	65,341	66,488	45,314	18,972	2,203	64,270	45,296	18,975	0
Texas	274,826	302,425	334,997	334,580	342,257	347,329	171,673	148,168	27,488	352,809	175,290	153,142	24,377
Utah	22,008	22,993	25,677	27,247	27,374[3]	28,348[3]	14,008[3]	11,673[3]	2,668[3]	28,841	14,050	11,882	2,909
Vermont	8,414	8,851	8,382	8,375	8,276	8,338	3,332	2,893	2,113	8,187	3,326	2,736	2,124
Virginia	86,977[2]	103,944	70,947	90,098	89,968	90,255	42,373	47,882	0	91,628	42,155	49,473	0
Washington	51,098	53,508	53,934	54,867	59,555	57,942	31,333	24,898	1,712	58,815	32,242	24,507	2,067
West Virginia	20,930	19,940	20,338	19,978	20,029	19,664	9,362	10,278	25	19,356	9,168	10,167	21
Wisconsin	60,165	60,127	57,625	57,980	58,376[3]	58,185	28,911	28,761	513	59,011	29,429	29,125	457
Wyoming	6,783	6,706	7,127	7,350	7,615	7,653	4,123	3,531	0	7,506	4,089	3,417	0
Jurisdiction													
Bureau of Indian Education	—	—	—	—	—	—	—	—	—	—	—	—	—
DoDEA, overseas	5,105	5,726	—	—	—	—	—	—	—	—	—	—	—
DoDEA, domestic	2,399	2,033	—	—	—	—	—	—	—	—	—	—	—
Other jurisdictions													
American Samoa	820	989	—	—	—	—	—	—	—	—	—	—	—
Guam	1,975	1,804	1,843	2,291	2,286	2,336	1,192	1,144	0	2,289	1,154	1,135	0
Northern Marianas	526	614	607	417	—	—	—	—	—	—	—	—	—
Puerto Rico	37,620	42,036	36,506	33,412	31,186	30,438	13,018	11,754	5,666	28,899	13,097	10,140	5,661
U.S. Virgin Islands	1,511	1,434	1,457	1,082	1,131	1,106	520	565	21	1,154	546	593	15

—Not available.
[1]Includes imputed values for states.
[2]Includes imputations to correct for underreporting of prekindergarten teachers.
[3]Imputed.
[4]Includes imputations to correct for underreporting of prekindergarten, kindergarten, and ungraded teachers.

NOTE: Distribution of elementary and secondary teachers determined by reporting units. DoDEA = Department of Defense Education Activity.
SOURCE: U.S. Department of Education, National Center for Education Statistics, Common Core of Data (CCD), "State Nonfiscal Survey of Public Elementary/Secondary Education," 2000–01 through 2016–17. (This table was prepared September 2018.)

Table 208.40. Public elementary and secondary teachers, enrollment, and pupil/teacher ratios, by state or jurisdiction: Selected years, fall 2000 through fall 2016

State or jurisdiction	Pupil/teacher ratio				Fall 2014			Fall 2015			Fall 2016		
	Fall 2000	Fall 2005	Fall 2010	Fall 2013	Teachers	Enrollment	Pupil/ teacher ratio	Teachers	Enrollment	Pupil/ teacher ratio	Teachers	Enrollment	Pupil/ teacher ratio
1	2	3	4	5	6	7	8	9	10	11	12	13	14
United States	**16.0**[1]	**15.6**[1]	**16.0**[1]	**16.1**[1]	**3,132,351**[1]	**50,312,581**	**16.1**[1]	**3,151,497**[1]	**50,438,043**[1]	**16.0**[1]	**3,169,499**[1]	**50,615,189**[1]	**16.0**[1]
Alabama	15.4[2]	12.8	15.3	15.8	42,737	744,164	17.4	40,766	743,789	18.2	42,533	744,930	17.5
Alaska	16.9	16.8	16.2	16.6	7,759	131,176	16.9	7,832	132,477	16.9	7,825	132,737	17.0
Arizona	19.8	21.3	21.4	22.8	48,124	1,111,695	23.1	47,944	1,109,040	23.1	48,220	1,123,137	23.3
Arkansas	14.1	14.4	14.1	14.0	35,430	490,917	13.9	35,804	492,132	13.7	35,730	493,447	13.8
California	20.6[2]	20.8[2]	24.1[2]	24.3[2]	267,685[2]	6,312,161	23.6[2]	263,475	6,305,347[2]	23.9[2]	271,287[2]	6,309,138[2]	23.3[2]
Colorado	17.3	17.0	17.4	17.5	51,388	889,006	17.3	51,798	899,112	17.4	52,014	905,019	17.4
Connecticut	13.7	14.5	13.1	12.6	42,062	542,678	12.9	43,772	537,933	12.3	42,343	535,118	12.6
Delaware	15.4	15.1	14.5	14.0	9,649	134,042	13.9	8,962	134,847	15.0	9,208	136,264	14.8
District of Columbia	13.9	14.0[3]	12.0	13.0	6,565	80,958	12.3	6,789	84,024	12.4	6,727	85,850	12.8
Florida	18.4	16.8	15.1	15.3	180,442	2,756,944	15.3	182,586	2,792,234	15.3	186,339	2,816,791	15.1
Georgia	15.9	14.7	14.9	15.8	111,470	1,744,437	15.6	113,031	1,757,237	15.5	114,763	1,764,346	15.4
Hawaii	16.9	16.3	15.8	15.9	11,663	182,384	15.6	11,747	181,995	15.5	11,782	181,550	15.4
Idaho	17.9	18.0	17.6	19.8	15,609	290,885	18.6	15,656	292,277	18.7	16,204	297,200	18.3
Illinois	16.1	15.8	15.7	15.2[4]	132,456[4]	2,050,239	15.5[4]	129,948	2,041,779	15.7	128,893	2,026,718	15.7
Indiana	16.7	17.1	18.0[2]	17.5	56,547	1,046,269	18.5	57,675	1,046,757	18.1	60,162	1,049,547	17.4
Iowa	14.3	13.7	14.3	14.2	35,684	505,311	14.2	35,687	508,014	14.2	35,808	509,831	14.2
Kansas	14.4	13.9	14.0	13.0	37,659	497,275	13.2	40,035	495,884	12.4	36,193	494,347	13.7
Kentucky	16.8	16.0	16.0	16.2	41,586	688,640	16.6	41,902	686,598	16.4	42,029	684,017	16.3
Louisiana	14.9	14.7	14.3	15.3	46,340	716,800	15.5	58,469	718,711	12.3	48,408	716,293	14.8
Maine	12.5	11.7	12.3	11.9	14,937	182,470	12.2	14,857	181,613	12.2	14,750	180,512	12.2
Maryland	16.3	15.2	14.6	14.8	59,194	874,514	14.8	59,414	879,601	14.8	59,703	886,221	14.8
Massachusetts	14.5	13.2	13.9	13.6	71,859	955,844	13.3	71,969	964,026	13.4	72,413	964,514	13.3
Michigan	17.7[2]	17.8	17.9	18.1	85,038	1,537,922	18.1	84,181	1,536,231	18.2	83,597	1,528,666	18.3
Minnesota	16.0	16.4	15.9	15.6	55,690	857,235	15.4	55,985	864,384	15.4	56,715	875,021	15.4
Mississippi	16.1	15.7	15.2	15.3	32,311	490,917	15.2	32,175	487,200	15.1	31,924	483,150	15.1
Missouri	14.1	13.7	13.8	13.8	67,356	917,785	13.6	67,635	919,234	13.6	67,926	915,040	13.5
Montana	14.9	14.0	13.7	14.0	10,234	144,532	14.1	10,412	145,319	14.0	10,555	146,375	13.9
Nebraska	13.6	13.4	13.4	13.7	22,988	312,635	13.6	23,308	316,014	13.6	23,611	319,194	13.5
Nevada	18.6	19.0	20.0	20.6	21,656	459,189	21.2	22,702	467,527	20.6	23,705	473,744	20.0
New Hampshire	14.5	13.2	12.7	12.6	14,773	184,670	12.5	14,770	182,425	12.4	14,760	180,888	12.3
New Jersey	13.3	12.4	12.7	12.0	115,067	1,400,579	12.2	114,968	1,408,845	12.3	115,729	1,410,421	12.2
New Mexico	15.2	14.8	15.1	15.3	22,411	340,365	15.2	21,722	335,694	15.5	21,331	336,263	15.8
New York	13.9	12.9	12.9	13.2	203,781	2,741,185	13.5	206,086	2,711,626	13.2	209,151	2,729,776	13.1
North Carolina	15.5	14.8	15.2	15.4	99,320	1,548,895	15.6	99,355	1,544,934	15.5	100,220	1,550,062	15.5
North Dakota	13.4	12.3	11.4	11.8	9,049	106,586	11.8	9,195	108,644	11.8	9,265	109,706	11.8
Ohio	15.5	15.6	16.1	16.3	106,526[3]	1,724,810	16.2[3]	101,742	1,716,585	16.9	102,600	1,710,143	16.7
Oklahoma	15.1	15.2	16.0	16.2	42,073	688,511	16.4	42,452	692,878	16.3	41,090	693,903	16.9
Oregon	19.4	19.5	20.3	22.2	27,850	601,318	21.6	29,086	608,825[2]	20.9[2]	29,756	606,277[2]	20.4[2]
Pennsylvania	15.5	15.0	13.8	14.5	122,030	1,743,160	14.3	120,893	1,717,414	14.2	122,552	1,727,497	14.1
Rhode Island	14.8	10.8	12.8	14.5	9,471	141,959	15.0	10,631	142,014	13.4	10,689	142,150	13.3
South Carolina	14.9	14.6	16.1	15.5	49,475	756,523	15.3	50,237	763,533	15.2	50,789	771,250	15.2
South Dakota	13.7	13.4	13.3	13.8	9,618	133,040	13.8	9,638	134,253	13.9	9,777	136,302	13.9
Tennessee	15.9[2]	16.0	14.8	15.1	65,341	995,475	15.2	66,488	1,001,235	15.1	64,270	1,001,562	15.6
Texas	14.8	15.0	14.7	15.4	342,257	5,233,765	15.3	347,329	5,301,477	15.3	352,809	5,360,849	15.2
Utah	21.9	22.1	22.8	23.0	27,374[3]	635,577	23.2[3]	28,348[3]	647,870	22.9[3]	28,841[3]	659,801	22.9
Vermont	12.1	10.9	11.6	10.6	8,276	87,311	10.6	8,338	87,866	10.5	8,187	88,428	10.8
Virginia	13.2[2]	11.7	17.6	14.1	89,968	1,280,381	14.2	90,255	1,283,590	14.2	91,628	1,287,026	14.0
Washington	19.7	19.3	19.4	19.3	59,555	1,073,638	18.0	57,942	1,087,030	18.8	58,815	1,101,711	18.7
West Virginia	13.7	14.1	13.9	14.1	20,029	280,310	14.0	19,664	277,452	14.1	19,356	273,855	14.1
Wisconsin	14.6	14.6	15.1	15.1	58,376[3]	871,432	14.9[3]	58,185	867,800	14.9	59,011	864,432	14.6
Wyoming	13.3	12.6	11.5	12.5	7,555	92,732	12.3	7,615	94,067	12.4	7,653	94,717	12.5
Jurisdiction													
Bureau of Indian Education	—	—	—	—	—	—	—	—	—	—	—	45,399	—
DoDEA, overseas	14.4	10.9	—	—	—	—	—	—	74,970	—	—	—	—
DoDEA, domestic	14.2	13.9	—	—	—	—	—	—	—	—	—	—	—
Other jurisdictions													
American Samoa	19.1	16.6	—	—	—	—	—	—	—	—	—	—	—
Guam	16.4	—	17.2	14.6	2,286	31,144	13.6	2,336	30,821	13.2	2,289	30,758	13.4
Northern Marianas	19.0	19.1	18.3	25.5	—	—	—	—	—	—	—	—	—
Puerto Rico	16.3	13.4	13.0	12.7	31,186	410,950	13.2	30,438	379,818	12.5	28,899	365,181	12.6
U.S. Virgin Islands	12.9	11.7	10.6	13.8	1,131	14,241	12.6	1,106	13,805	12.5	1,154	13,194	11.4

—Not available.
[1]Includes imputed values for states.
[2]Includes imputations to correct for underreporting of prekindergarten teachers/enrollment.
[3]Imputed.
[4]Includes imputations to correct for underreporting of prekindergarten, kindergarten, and ungraded teachers.
NOTE: Teachers reported in full-time equivalents (FTE). DoDEA = Department of Defense Education Activity. The pupil/teacher ratio includes teachers for students with disabilities and other special teachers, while these teachers are generally excluded from class size calculations. Ratios reflect totals reported by states and differ from totals reported for schools or school districts.
SOURCE: U.S. Department of Education, National Center for Education Statistics, Common Core of Data (CCD), "State Nonfiscal Survey of Public Elementary/Secondary Education," 2000–01 through 2016–17. (This table was prepared September 2018.)

Table 209.30. Highest degree earned, years of full-time teaching experience, and average class size for teachers in public elementary and secondary schools, by state: 2011–12

[Standard errors appear in parentheses]

State	Total number of teachers (in thousands)		Percent of teachers, by highest degree earned: Less than bachelor's		Bachelor's		Master's		Education specialist[2] or doctor's		Percent of teachers, by years of full-time teaching experience: Less than 3		3 to 9		10 to 20		Over 20		Average class size, by level of instruction[1]: Elementary		Secondary	
1	2		3		4		5		6		7		8		9		10		11		12	
United States	**3,385.2**	**(41.42)**	**3.8**	**(0.24)**	**39.9**	**(0.52)**	**47.7**	**(0.57)**	**8.7**	**(0.28)**	**9.0**	**(0.29)**	**33.3**	**(0.52)**	**36.4**	**(0.51)**	**21.3**	**(0.54)**	**21.2**	**(0.18)**	**26.8**	**(0.22)**
Alabama	45.0	(2.61)	3.8!	(1.51)	34.5	(2.69)	52.8	(2.81)	8.9	(1.64)	8.0	(1.28)	30.9	(2.75)	39.2	(2.85)	21.9	(2.34)	19.2	(0.42)	27.4	(0.94)
Alaska	7.5	(0.70)	4.4!	(1.78)	45.6	(4.44)	41.9	(4.01)	8.2	(2.37)	12.9	(3.30)	30.8	(4.15)	39.6	(4.16)	16.7	(3.76)	18.3	(1.35)	18.7	(1.22)
Arizona	61.7	(2.61)	4.6	(1.16)	44.4	(3.67)	44.1	(3.49)	6.9	(1.71)	16.4	(2.29)	38.0	(2.75)	28.5	(2.60)	17.2	(2.02)	24.1	(0.67)	27.7	(0.96)
Arkansas	37.7	(2.01)	3.7!	(1.45)	54.7	(3.36)	35.0	(3.13)	6.6	(1.72)	11.5	(2.03)	28.9	(3.38)	32.3	(3.93)	27.3	(3.37)	20.4	(0.73)	25.4	(1.69)
California	285.5	(7.27)	4.8	(0.91)	43.4	(2.33)	39.2	(2.18)	12.7	(1.56)	9.4	(1.29)	29.1	(2.13)	42.3	(2.25)	19.1	(1.89)	25.0	(0.52)	32.0	(0.53)
Colorado	55.9	(3.14)	2.8!	(1.00)	36.1	(3.51)	49.9	(4.26)	11.2	(2.79)	10.8	(2.25)	33.4	(3.50)	42.9	(3.96)	12.9	(2.51)	22.8	(1.29)	29.1	(1.25)
Connecticut	44.9	(2.51)	‡	(†)	15.3	(1.86)	64.4	(3.01)	17.7	(2.37)	10.0	(1.43)	29.1	(2.66)	37.1	(2.43)	23.8	(3.34)	19.6	(0.68)	22.0	(0.71)
Delaware	9.3	(0.70)	4.0!	(1.50)	34.5	(4.36)	49.7	(4.55)	11.8	(2.85)	12.6	(3.31)	35.0	(3.59)	33.8	(4.04)	18.6	(2.75)	20.3	(0.82)	25.8	(2.09)
District of Columbia	‡	(†)	‡	(†)	‡	(†)	‡	(†)	‡	(†)	‡	(†)	‡	(†)	‡	(†)	‡	(†)	‡	(†)	‡	(†)
Florida	‡	(†)	‡	(†)	‡	(†)	‡	(†)	‡	(†)	‡	(†)	‡	(†)	‡	(†)	‡	(†)	‡	(†)	‡	(†)
Georgia	123.3	(3.97)	3.4!	(1.15)	29.5	(3.48)	43.5	(3.79)	23.6	(3.00)	6.3	(1.70)	34.2	(3.42)	39.8	(3.34)	19.7	(2.58)	21.0	(0.91)	27.5	(1.42)
Hawaii	‡	(†)	‡	(†)	‡	(†)	‡	(†)	‡	(†)	‡	(†)	‡	(†)	‡	(†)	‡	(†)	‡	(†)	‡	(†)
Idaho	16.3	(1.83)	4.6	(1.37)	55.6	(3.30)	35.3	(3.18)	4.4	(1.20)	10.4	(1.93)	30.4	(3.18)	35.2	(3.02)	24.0	(2.89)	24.5	(0.63)	25.4	(2.13)
Illinois	140.9	(9.09)	2.7!	(0.81)	32.6	(2.53)	57.8	(2.44)	7.0	(1.34)	9.3	(1.56)	36.4	(2.59)	34.4	(2.85)	20.0	(2.51)	22.9	(1.26)	27.7	(1.00)
Indiana	64.0	(2.98)	2.2	(0.52)	43.6	(3.04)	47.4	(3.29)	6.9	(1.45)	10.0	(1.92)	26.1	(2.42)	35.6	(3.01)	28.3	(3.02)	21.4	(0.45)	27.3	(1.07)
Iowa	36.1	(2.28)	3.5!	(1.22)	52.8	(3.89)	39.7	(3.60)	4.1!	(1.26)	8.8	(1.85)	29.0	(2.98)	33.0	(2.77)	29.2	(2.55)	20.3	(0.93)	27.4	(1.35)
Kansas	36.5	(2.27)	3.8	(0.83)	43.8	(3.52)	47.0	(3.66)	5.4	(1.38)	12.5	(2.98)	27.4	(3.00)	32.7	(3.15)	27.4	(2.83)	20.4	(0.86)	24.6	(1.21)
Kentucky	46.8	(2.51)	5.1	(1.22)	17.5	(2.24)	57.5	(2.58)	20.0	(2.11)	10.1	(1.83)	32.2	(2.82)	38.5	(2.81)	19.2	(2.02)	23.3	(1.92)	26.6	(1.09)
Louisiana	44.5	(2.39)	3.5!	(1.72)	61.9	(3.12)	27.0	(2.68)	7.6	(1.55)	8.6	(1.51)	31.2	(3.13)	33.4	(3.31)	26.8	(3.10)	19.0	(0.80)	23.4	(0.78)
Maine	18.4	(0.90)	4.9!	(1.60)	46.3	(3.41)	42.8	(3.30)	6.0	(1.36)	5.8	(1.47)	24.1	(2.57)	39.4	(3.32)	30.6	(2.81)	17.6	(0.64)	19.9	(1.76)
Maryland	‡	(†)	‡	(†)	‡	(†)	‡	(†)	‡	(†)	‡	(†)	‡	(†)	‡	(†)	‡	(†)	‡	(†)	‡	(†)
Massachusetts	79.2	(4.42)	3.9	(1.08)	21.8	(2.33)	67.5	(2.54)	6.8	(1.48)	12.4	(1.96)	33.4	(3.04)	36.8	(3.02)	17.4	(3.09)	19.9	(1.72)	24.5	(1.18)
Michigan	96.7	(3.73)	2.3	(0.55)	29.8	(2.50)	62.9	(2.52)	5.0	(1.40)	7.3	(1.00)	31.4	(2.68)	42.7	(2.44)	18.7	(2.12)	23.8	(0.93)	28.9	(0.81)
Minnesota	62.3	(2.99)	4.4	(0.77)	35.3	(2.06)	50.1	(1.87)	10.2	(1.40)	9.5	(1.20)	27.4	(2.05)	40.3	(2.14)	22.9	(2.00)	22.8	(0.70)	29.9	(0.86)
Mississippi	37.6	(2.11)	5.3	(1.45)	54.4	(3.87)	35.2	(3.57)	5.1	(1.51)	10.3	(1.97)	41.0	(3.45)	30.5	(3.35)	18.2	(3.18)	21.6	(1.01)	22.8	(1.15)
Missouri	68.7	(2.34)	4.4	(0.91)	33.3	(2.90)	57.5	(2.96)	4.8	(0.94)	10.4	(1.90)	35.3	(2.21)	35.2	(2.31)	19.2	(2.31)	20.2	(0.83)	26.8	(1.18)
Montana	12.4	(0.90)	6.4	(1.52)	55.2	(3.34)	34.6	(3.39)	3.8!	(1.66)	9.6	(2.33)	31.3	(3.17)	30.5	(3.04)	28.6	(3.65)	18.9	(0.80)	21.7	(1.81)
Nebraska	23.9	(1.73)	5.5	(1.31)	44.9	(3.29)	45.9	(3.15)	3.7	(0.98)	10.6	(1.74)	27.2	(2.52)	34.6	(2.63)	27.6	(2.54)	17.9	(0.72)	23.5	(0.99)
Nevada	25.2	(2.63)	4.5!	(1.85)	25.1	(3.92)	49.8	(4.26)	20.6	(3.23)	6.5!	(2.17)	39.0	(4.02)	36.2	(4.29)	18.2	(3.55)	25.3	(1.41)	34.5	(1.54)
New Hampshire	15.7	(1.05)	3.0!	(1.12)	40.2	(3.49)	48.7	(3.55)	8.1	(1.82)	8.1	(1.54)	32.8	(3.41)	31.5	(3.57)	27.5	(3.54)	20.4	(3.09)	21.7	(1.16)
New Jersey	125.2	(4.16)	3.0	(0.74)	48.5	(2.47)	40.8	(2.30)	7.6	(1.60)	7.3	(1.24)	35.4	(2.45)	37.4	(2.66)	20.0	(2.03)	18.5	(0.81)	23.9	(0.68)
New Mexico	21.7	(2.83)	4.3!	(2.01)	43.3	(3.80)	42.1	(3.72)	10.3	(2.82)	8.0!	(2.46)	30.9	(3.73)	40.3	(5.11)	20.8	(5.19)	19.8	(0.76)	23.7	(1.58)
New York	241.4	(14.58)	2.8!	(1.00)	4.4	(1.09)	84.2	(1.56)	8.6	(1.32)	5.3	(1.38)	30.0	(2.81)	45.5	(2.35)	19.1	(2.41)	20.7	(1.36)	25.1	(0.96)
North Carolina	104.3	(5.71)	4.1!	(1.57)	54.2	(3.16)	33.8	(2.80)	7.8	(1.84)	8.4	(1.52)	35.8	(3.13)	34.8	(3.05)	21.1	(2.74)	18.8	(0.65)	25.8	(1.25)
North Dakota	10.3	(0.74)	6.9	(1.63)	59.2	(3.08)	30.1	(2.60)	3.9	(1.13)	12.2	(2.09)	24.6	(3.06)	30.6	(3.28)	32.6	(3.45)	17.8	(0.60)	19.2	(1.41)
Ohio	122.1	(4.29)	5.3	(1.17)	24.0	(1.79)	64.5	(2.16)	6.2	(1.28)	7.1	(1.11)	28.8	(2.48)	40.8	(2.67)	23.3	(2.00)	21.3	(0.99)	26.7	(0.85)
Oklahoma	46.2	(2.49)	4.3	(1.04)	65.6	(2.66)	26.9	(2.56)	3.2!	(1.12)	9.8	(1.84)	30.1	(2.58)	36.9	(2.93)	23.3	(2.27)	20.7	(0.56)	23.7	(0.88)
Oregon	31.8	(1.28)	4.2!	(1.53)	26.3	(3.18)	59.8	(3.62)	9.7	(1.94)	7.2	(1.54)	37.0	(3.58)	35.6	(3.58)	20.2	(2.45)	26.4	(0.96)	30.0	(1.05)
Pennsylvania	148.8	(7.48)	4.5!	(1.94)	32.9	(2.52)	53.9	(3.34)	8.7	(1.77)	6.2	(1.78)	37.0	(2.55)	35.8	(2.17)	21.0	(2.30)	22.4	(0.99)	25.2	(0.96)
Rhode Island	‡	(†)	‡	(†)	‡	(†)	‡	(†)	‡	(†)	‡	(†)	‡	(†)	‡	(†)	‡	(†)	‡	(†)	‡	(†)
South Carolina	51.8	(1.76)	3.0!	(1.34)	28.8	(3.14)	57.9	(3.95)	10.3	(2.15)	8.4	(1.58)	30.5	(3.22)	32.3	(3.54)	28.9	(3.38)	19.1	(0.75)	26.0	(1.98)
South Dakota	10.8	(0.92)	2.3!	(0.73)	68.8	(3.52)	26.6	(3.13)	2.3!	(1.14)	8.8	(1.65)	24.6	(2.76)	32.9	(3.63)	33.7	(3.38)	20.4	(0.66)	22.3	(1.31)
Tennessee	76.5	(2.91)	4.4!	(1.52)	35.1	(3.54)	46.3	(3.44)	14.2	(2.83)	10.6	(1.80)	34.0	(3.66)	34.1	(3.48)	21.3	(3.28)	17.7	(0.52)	26.9	(1.60)
Texas	350.8	(22.99)	3.3	(0.65)	66.4	(2.09)	25.8	(2.12)	4.6	(0.77)	8.9	(0.95)	40.4	(2.05)	31.1	(1.88)	19.7	(1.74)	18.2	(0.82)	26.9	(1.07)
Utah	27.9	(1.67)	4.2	(1.10)	56.8	(3.96)	27.3	(3.88)	11.7!	(3.94)	15.0	(2.43)	39.9	(4.49)	25.6	(4.52)	19.5	(3.12)	27.4	(2.09)	31.5	(1.29)
Vermont	9.4	(0.34)	6.6	(1.46)	35.4	(2.78)	52.0	(2.87)	6.0	(1.59)	12.9	(1.60)	22.1	(2.38)	37.0	(2.56)	28.0	(2.73)	16.6	(0.40)	19.8	(1.25)
Virginia	88.5	(3.35)	3.3!	(1.07)	47.5	(3.08)	41.6	(3.17)	7.6	(1.26)	9.1	(1.68)	31.5	(3.20)	34.2	(2.73)	25.2	(2.43)	20.4	(1.27)	23.8	(0.90)
Washington	55.5	(3.15)	2.9	(0.59)	23.1	(2.61)	62.9	(2.92)	11.1	(1.96)	6.2	(1.45)	32.2	(3.00)	34.8	(2.82)	26.8	(3.03)	23.7	(0.60)	29.7	(0.99)
West Virginia	24.2	(0.79)	3.1	(0.90)	46.6	(4.82)	43.2	(4.71)	7.1	(1.73)	12.0	(2.26)	31.2	(4.12)	30.5	(3.82)	26.3	(3.24)	18.7	(1.00)	24.0	(1.65)
Wisconsin	66.8	(3.42)	2.7	(0.79)	36.7	(2.96)	55.1	(2.98)	5.5	(1.41)	10.5	(1.67)	26.2	(3.12)	42.1	(3.24)	21.3	(2.73)	20.8	(0.55)	27.9	(0.95)
Wyoming	8.5	(0.57)	7.0!	(3.08)	44.3	(4.47)	41.2	(4.18)	7.5!	(2.74)	7.6!	(2.62)	25.2	(4.09)	35.1	(3.73)	32.1	(4.30)	17.0	(1.05)	19.6	(1.22)

†Not applicable.
!Interpret data with caution. The coefficient of variation (CV) for this estimate is between 30 and 50 percent.
‡Reporting standards not met. Data may be suppressed because the response rate is under 50 percent, there are too few cases for a reliable estimate, or the coefficient of variation (CV) is 50 percent or greater.
[1]Elementary teachers are those who taught self-contained classes at the elementary level, and secondary teachers are those who taught departmentalized classes (e.g., science, art, social science, or other course subjects) at the secondary level. Teachers were classified as elementary or secondary on the basis of the grades they taught, rather than on the level of the school in which they taught. In general, elementary teachers include those teaching prekindergarten through grade 5 and those teaching multiple grades, with a preponderance of grades taught being kindergarten through grade 6. In general, secondary teachers include those teaching any of grades 7 through 12 and those teaching multiple grades, with a preponderance of grades taught being grades 7 through 12 and usually with no grade taught being lower than grade 5.
[2]Education specialist degrees or certificates are generally awarded for 1 year's work beyond the master's level. Includes certificate of advanced graduate studies.
NOTE: Data are based on a head count of all teachers rather than on the number of full-time-equivalent teachers appearing in other tables. Excludes prekindergarten teachers. Detail may not sum to totals because of rounding and cell suppression.
SOURCE: U.S. Department of Education, National Center for Education Statistics, Schools and Staffing Survey (SASS), "Public School Teacher Data File," 2011–12. (This table was prepared May 2013.)

Table 211.50. Estimated average annual salary of teachers in public elementary and secondary schools: Selected years, 1959–60 through 2017–18

School year	Current dollars					Average public school teachers' salary in constant 2017–18 dollars[1]		
	Average public school teachers' salary			Wage and salary accruals per full-time-equivalent (FTE) employee[2]	Ratio of average teachers' salary to accruals per FTE employee			
	All teachers	Elementary teachers[3]	Secondary teachers[4]			All teachers	Elementary teachers[3]	Secondary teachers[4]
1	2	3	4	5	6	7	8	9
1959–60	$4,995	$4,815	$5,276	$4,749	1.05	$42,180	$40,660	$44,553
1961–62	5,515	5,340	5,775	5,063	1.09	45,526	44,081	47,672
1963–64	5,995	5,805	6,266	5,478	1.09	48,230	46,702	50,410
1965–66	6,485	6,279	6,761	5,934	1.09	50,429	48,827	52,576
1967–68	7,423	7,208	7,692	6,533	1.14	54,159	52,590	56,122
1969–70	8,626	8,412	8,891	7,486	1.15	56,660	55,254	58,401
1970–71	9,268	9,021	9,568	7,998	1.16	57,889	56,346	59,763
1971–72	9,705	9,424	10,031	8,521	1.14	58,519	56,825	60,485
1972–73	10,174	9,893	10,507	9,056	1.12	58,971	57,342	60,901
1973–74	10,770	10,507	11,077	9,667	1.11	57,315	55,915	58,949
1974–75	11,641	11,334	12,000	10,411	1.12	55,770	54,299	57,490
1975–76	12,600	12,280	12,937	11,194	1.13	56,374	54,942	57,882
1976–77	13,354	12,989	13,776	11,971	1.12	56,455	54,912	58,239
1977–78	14,198	13,845	14,602	12,811	1.11	56,247	54,848	57,847
1978–79	15,032	14,681	15,450	13,807	1.09	54,450	53,179	55,964
1979–80	15,970	15,569	16,459	15,050	1.06	51,042	49,761	52,605
1980–81	17,644	17,230	18,142	16,461	1.07	50,539	49,353	51,965
1981–82	19,274	18,853	19,805	17,795	1.08	50,818	49,708	52,218
1982–83	20,695	20,227	21,291	18,873	1.10	52,318	51,134	53,824
1983–84	21,935	21,487	22,554	19,781	1.11	53,473	52,381	54,982
1984–85	23,600	23,200	24,187	20,694	1.14	55,365	54,426	56,742
1985–86	25,199	24,718	25,846	21,685	1.16	57,459	56,362	58,934
1986–87	26,569	26,057	27,244	22,700	1.17	59,267	58,125	60,773
1987–88	28,034	27,519	28,798	23,777	1.18	60,047	58,944	61,683
1988–89	29,564	29,022	30,218	24,752	1.19	60,529	59,419	61,868
1989–90	31,367	30,832	32,049	25,762	1.22	61,295	60,250	62,628
1990–91	33,084	32,490	33,896	26,935	1.23	61,299	60,199	62,804
1991–92	34,063	33,479	34,827	28,169	1.21	61,154	60,105	62,525
1992–93	35,029	34,350	35,880	29,245	1.20	60,983	59,801	62,465
1993–94	35,737	35,233	36,566	30,030	1.19	60,645	59,789	62,051
1994–95	36,675	36,088	37,523	30,857	1.19	60,502	59,534	61,901
1995–96	37,642	37,138	38,397	31,822	1.18	60,453	59,643	61,665
1996–97	38,443	38,039	39,184	33,058	1.16	60,027	59,396	61,184
1997–98	39,350	39,002	39,944	34,638	1.14	60,366	59,832	61,277
1998–99	40,544	40,165	41,203	36,280	1.12	61,140	60,568	62,133
1999–2000	41,807	41,306	42,546	38,144	1.10	61,275	60,541	62,358
2000–01	43,378	42,910	44,053	39,729	1.09	61,472	60,809	62,428
2001–02	44,655	44,177	45,310	40,600	1.10	62,180	61,515	63,093
2002–03	45,686	45,408	46,106	41,659	1.10	62,248	61,869	62,820
2003–04	46,542	46,187	46,976	43,303	1.07	62,057	61,583	62,636
2004–05	47,516	47,122	47,688	44,957	1.06	61,505	60,995	61,727
2005–06	49,086	48,573	49,496	46,690	1.05	61,206	60,566	61,717
2006–07	51,052	50,740	51,529	48,816	1.05	62,053	61,674	62,633
2007–08	52,800	52,385	53,262	50,649	1.04	61,884	61,398	62,426
2008–09	54,368	53,998	54,552	51,594	1.05	62,845	62,417	63,057
2009–10	55,280	54,918	55,595	52,512	1.05	63,287	62,872	63,647
2010–11	55,628	55,217	56,225	53,966	1.03	62,431	61,970	63,101
2011–12	55,497	54,704	56,226	55,391	1.00	60,511	59,647	61,306
2012–13	56,173	55,344	57,077	56,373	1.00	60,246	59,357	61,215
2013–14	56,805	56,395	56,886	57,509	0.99	59,987	59,554	60,072
2014–15	57,754	57,092	57,678	59,149	0.98	60,548	59,854	60,468
2015–16	58,479	58,225	58,385	60,371	0.97	60,897	60,633	60,799
2016–17	59,660	58,773	58,978	61,773	0.97	61,005	60,098	60,307
2017–18	60,483	—	—	—	—	60,483	—	—

—Not available.
[1]Constant dollars based on the Consumer Price Index, prepared by the Bureau of Labor Statistics, U.S. Department of Labor, adjusted to a school-year basis.
[2]The average monetary remuneration earned by FTE employees across all industries in a given year, including wages, salaries, commissions, tips, bonuses, voluntary employee contributions to certain deferred compensation plans, and receipts in kind that represent income. Calendar-year data from the U.S. Department of Commerce, Bureau of Economic Analysis, have been converted to a school-year basis by averaging the two appropriate calendar years in each case.
[3]Teachers at schools that are classified as elementary by state and local practice and composed of any span of grades not above grade 8. Preschool or kindergarten schools are included only if they are an integral part of an elementary school or a regularly established school system.
[4]Teachers at schools comprising any span of grades beginning with the next grade following an elementary or middle school (usually 7, 8, or 9) and ending with or below grade 12. Includes both junior high schools and senior high schools.
NOTE: Some data have been revised from previously published figures. Standard errors are not available for these estimates, which are based on state reports.
SOURCE: National Education Association, *Estimates of School Statistics*, 1959–60 through 2017–18; and unpublished tabulations. U.S. Department of Commerce, Bureau of Economic Analysis, National Income and Product Accounts, table 6.6D, retrieved September 12, 2018, from https://apps.bea.gov/iTable/iTable.cfm?reqid=19&step=2#reqid=19&step=2&isuri=1&1921=survey. (This table was prepared September 2018.)

Table 212.08. Number and percentage distribution of principals in public and private elementary and secondary schools, by selected characteristics: Selected years, 1993–94 through 2015–16

[Standard errors appear in parentheses]

Selected characteristic	Number of principals										Percentage distribution of principals									
	1993–94		1999–2000		2007–08		2011–12		2015–16		1993–94		1999–2000		2007–08		2011–12		2015–16	
1	2		3		4		5		6		7		8		9		10		11	
Public schools																				
Total	**79,620**	**(235)**	**83,790**	**(327)**	**90,470**	**(544)**	**89,810**	**(406)**	**90,410**	**(298)**	**100.0**	**(†)**	**100.0**	**(†)**	**100.0**	**(†)**	**100.0**	**(†)**	**100.0**	**(†)**
Sex																				
Male	52,110	(613)	47,130	(604)	44,950	(1,129)	43,450	(901)	41,380	(690)	65.5	(0.70)	56.2	(0.69)	49.7	(1.21)	48.4	(0.92)	45.8	(0.74)
Female	27,500	(542)	36,660	(598)	45,520	(1,129)	46,360	(801)	49,030	(672)	34.5	(0.70)	43.8	(0.69)	50.3	(1.21)	51.6	(0.92)	54.2	(0.74)
Race/ethnicity																				
White[1]	67,080	(540)	68,930	(579)	73,160	(1,008)	72,070	(723)	70,340	(541)	84.3	(0.54)	82.3	(0.57)	80.9	(0.92)	80.3	(0.66)	77.8	(0.52)
Black[1]	8,020	(351)	9,240	(321)	9,620	(659)	9,110	(394)	9,550	(354)	10.1	(0.45)	11.0	(0.39)	10.6	(0.73)	10.1	(0.43)	10.6	(0.39)
Hispanic[1]	3,270	(258)	4,330	(300)	5,870	(540)	6,130	(404)	7,430	(361)	4.1	(0.33)	5.2	(0.36)	6.5	(0.60)	6.8	(0.46)	8.2	(0.40)
Asian[1,2]	620	(109)	630	(124)	570	(146)	820	(154)	1,290	(192)	0.8	(0.14)	0.8	(0.15)	0.6	(0.16)	0.9	(0.17)	1.4	(0.21)
Pacific Islander	—	(†)	—	(†)	130!	(52)	‡	(†)	‡	(†)	—	(†)	—	(†)	0.1!	(0.06)	#	(†)	0.2	(0.06)
American Indian/Alaska Native[1]	630	(67)	660	(60)	620	(179)	650	(123)	620	(114)	0.8	(0.08)	0.8	(0.07)	0.7	(0.20)	0.7	(0.14)	0.7	(0.13)
Two or more races	—	(†)	—	(†)	490!	(155)	1,010	(183)	980	(131)	—	(†)	—	(†)	0.5!	(0.17)	1.1	(0.20)	1.1	(0.15)
Age																				
Under 40	5,940	(273)	8,440	(302)	17,290	(785)	18,040	(523)	17,360	(507)	7.5	(0.34)	10.1	(0.35)	19.1	(0.84)	20.1	(0.58)	19.2	(0.56)
40 to 44	14,570	(496)	10,510	(317)	13,330	(706)	17,650	(565)	19,150	(515)	18.3	(0.61)	12.5	(0.37)	14.7	(0.78)	19.7	(0.62)	21.2	(0.56)
45 to 49	25,430	(429)	19,600	(535)	13,690	(767)	14,700	(541)	19,460	(599)	31.9	(0.55)	23.4	(0.63)	15.1	(0.86)	16.4	(0.60)	21.5	(0.65)
50 to 54	18,870	(539)	27,120	(606)	17,570	(746)	15,060	(668)	13,910	(438)	23.7	(0.68)	32.4	(0.71)	19.4	(0.82)	16.8	(0.73)	15.4	(0.49)
55 or over	14,820	(441)	18,130	(500)	28,590	(1,000)	24,350	(655)	20,540	(631)	18.6	(0.55)	21.6	(0.60)	31.6	(1.06)	27.1	(0.74)	22.7	(0.70)
School level																				
Elementary	53,680[4]	(294)	60,110	(253)	62,340	(584)	61,250	(443)	62,090	(276)	71.9	(0.21)	71.7	(0.21)	68.9	(0.54)	68.2	(0.38)	68.7	(0.31)
Secondary	18,260[4]	(161)	20,450	(197)	21,550	(460)	20,470	(537)	20,280	(395)	24.4	(0.20)	24.4	(0.20)	23.8	(0.46)	22.8	(0.56)	22.4	(0.41)
Combined	2,750[4]	(143)	3,230	(146)	6,580	(364)	8,090	(658)	8,050	(332)	3.7	(0.19)	3.9	(0.17)	7.3	(0.40)	9.0	(0.74)	8.9	(0.37)
Highest degree earned																				
Bachelor's or less	1,150	(167)	1,540	(182)	1,320	(207)	1,960	(272)	2,030	(212)	1.4	(0.21)	1.8	(0.22)	1.5	(0.23)	2.2	(0.30)	2.2	(0.23)
Master's	50,470	(536)	45,440	(579)	55,250	(906)	55,420	(678)	55,390	(682)	63.4	(0.65)	54.2	(0.63)	61.1	(1.01)	61.7	(0.71)	61.3	(0.73)
Education specialist[3]	20,570	(459)	28,280	(493)	26,270	(930)	23,560	(492)	24,020	(570)	25.8	(0.57)	33.8	(0.60)	29.0	(0.97)	26.2	(0.54)	26.6	(0.62)
Doctor's or first professional	7,430	(263)	8,530	(386)	7,630	(512)	8,870	(442)	8,970	(415)	9.3	(0.33)	10.2	(0.46)	8.4	(0.57)	9.9	(0.49)	9.9	(0.46)
Number of years as a principal																				
3 or fewer	24,450	(451)	25,080	(513)	31,500	(1,033)	29,520	(758)	35,420	(644)	30.7	(0.56)	29.9	(0.60)	34.8	(1.11)	32.9	(0.84)	39.2	(0.71)
4 to 9	26,600	(548)	25,900	(524)	32,140	(989)	35,500	(886)	31,370	(618)	33.4	(0.68)	30.9	(0.61)	35.5	(1.09)	39.5	(0.96)	34.7	(0.67)
10 to 19	19,730	(412)	23,230	(525)	20,470	(926)	19,870	(634)	19,960	(533)	24.8	(0.52)	27.7	(0.62)	22.6	(1.01)	22.1	(0.70)	22.1	(0.58)
20 or more	8,840	(377)	9,580	(331)	6,350	(414)	4,920	(273)	3,670	(285)	11.1	(0.47)	11.4	(0.39)	7.0	(0.46)	5.5	(0.31)	4.1	(0.31)
Years of full- and part-time teaching experience prior to becoming a principal																				
3 or fewer	5,690	(251)	3,210	(186)	4,150	(384)	4,040	(264)	3,360	(235)	7.1	(0.31)	3.8	(0.22)	4.6	(0.42)	4.5	(0.30)	3.7	(0.26)
4 to 9	29,500	(516)	22,510	(491)	30,260	(958)	34,240	(792)	34,970	(639)	37.1	(0.63)	26.9	(0.57)	33.4	(1.03)	38.1	(0.84)	38.7	(0.69)
10 to 19	36,680	(558)	38,110	(597)	40,200	(992)	39,160	(752)	41,970	(710)	46.1	(0.70)	45.5	(0.69)	44.4	(1.09)	43.6	(0.82)	46.4	(0.77)
20 or more	7,740	(275)	19,960	(485)	15,850	(781)	12,380	(519)	10,110	(418)	9.7	(0.34)	23.8	(0.57)	17.5	(0.86)	13.8	(0.58)	11.2	(0.46)
School locale																				
City	—	(†)	20,100	(328)	21,560	(731)	23,440	(274)	24,770	(190)	27.4	(0.34)	24.0	(0.40)	23.8	(0.81)	26.1	(0.28)	27.4	(0.17)
Suburban	—	(†)	30,640	(440)	25,880	(921)	24,520	(356)	29,120	(180)	25.9	(0.45)	36.6	(0.53)	28.6	(1.01)	27.3	(0.36)	32.2	(0.17)
Town	—	(†)	10,860	(228)	13,860	(669)	12,330	(341)	12,360	(372)	22.0	(0.43)	13.0	(0.26)	15.3	(0.74)	13.7	(0.40)	13.7	(0.41)
Rural	—	(†)	22,200	(404)	29,170	(1,012)	29,520	(430)	24,170	(399)	24.7	(0.43)	26.5	(0.44)	32.2	(1.07)	32.9	(0.43)	26.7	(0.43)

See notes at end of table.

Table 212.08. Number and percentage distribution of principals in public and private elementary and secondary schools, by selected characteristics: Selected years, 1993–94 through 2015–16—Continued

[Standard errors appear in parentheses]

Selected characteristic	Number of principals										Percentage distribution of principals									
	1993–94		1999–2000		2007–08		2011–12		2015–16		1993–94		1999–2000		2007–08		2011–12		2015–16	
1	2		3		4		5		6		7		8		9		10		11	
Private schools																				
Total	**25,020**	**(198)**	**26,230**	**(259)**	**27,960**	**(328)**	**25,730**	**(605)**	**—**	**(†)**	**100.0**	**(†)**	**100.0**	**(†)**	**100.0**	**(†)**	**100.0**	**(†)**	**—**	**(†)**
Sex																				
Male	11,610	(301)	11,900	(308)	13,070	(457)	11,490	(501)	—	(†)	46.4	(1.10)	45.4	(1.06)	46.7	(1.38)	44.6	(1.48)	—	(†)
Female	13,410	(283)	14,330	(307)	14,890	(369)	14,240	(462)	—	(†)	53.6	(1.10)	54.6	(1.06)	53.3	(1.38)	55.4	(1.48)	—	(†)
Race/ethnicity																				
White[1]	23,130	(270)	23,320	(309)	24,400	(409)	22,470	(628)	—	(†)	92.5	(0.70)	88.9	(0.76)	87.3	(0.91)	87.3	(1.08)	—	(†)
Black[1]	1,060	(124)	1,570	(164)	1,820	(184)	1,750	(193)	—	(†)	4.2	(0.50)	6.0	(0.62)	6.5	(0.67)	6.8	(0.75)	—	(†)
Hispanic[1]	520	(91)	830	(135)	1,110	(149)	860	(141)	—	(†)	2.1	(0.37)	3.2	(0.52)	4.0	(0.52)	3.3	(0.56)	—	(†)
Asian[1,2]	‡	(†)	350	(64)	‡	(†)	‡	(†)	—	(†)	0.7	(0.17)	1.3	(0.25)	1.2	(0.28)	1.8	(0.38)	—	(†)
Pacific Islander	—	(†)	—	(†)	‡	(†)	‡	(†)	—	(†)	—	(†)	—	(†)	‡	(†)	‡	(†)	—	(†)
American Indian/Alaska Native[1]	‡	(†)	‡	(†)	‡	(†)	‡	(†)	—	(†)	0.5	(0.15)	0.6	(0.15)	‡	(†)	‡	(†)	—	(†)
Two or more races	—	(†)	—	(†)	200!	(62)	90!	(45)	—	(†)	—	(†)	—	(†)	0.7!	(0.22)	0.4!	(0.17)	—	(†)
Age																				
Under 40	4,790	(302)	3,750	(223)	4,750	(318)	4,360	(392)	—	(†)	19.2	(1.21)	14.3	(0.80)	17.0	(1.09)	16.9	(1.44)	—	(†)
40 to 44	4,400	(217)	3,450	(212)	3,250	(277)	3,130	(300)	—	(†)	17.6	(0.83)	13.2	(0.83)	11.6	(1.00)	12.2	(1.05)	—	(†)
45 to 49	5,140	(216)	5,210	(261)	3,420	(246)	2,630	(281)	—	(†)	20.6	(0.87)	19.9	(0.96)	12.2	(0.86)	10.2	(1.00)	—	(†)
50 to 54	4,120	(228)	5,840	(291)	4,390	(263)	3,480	(247)	—	(†)	16.5	(0.90)	22.3	(1.11)	15.7	(0.94)	13.5	(0.93)	—	(†)
55 or over	6,550	(043)	7,980	(276)	12,150	(77)	12,120	(101)	—	(†)	26.2	(0.17)	30.4	(1.01)	43.5	(0.28)	47.1	(0.38)	—	(†)
School level																				
Elementary	13,350[4]	(244)	15,810	(245)	16,110	(297)	14,510	(505)	—	(†)	59.5	(0.74)	60.3	(0.85)	57.6	(0.81)	56.4	(0.90)	—	(†)
Secondary	2,300[4]	(115)	2,630	(133)	2,930	(168)	2,660	(138)	—	(†)	10.3	(0.52)	10.0	(0.51)	10.5	(0.59)	10.3	(0.57)	—	(†)
Combined	6,770[4]	(174)	7,800	(265)	8,920	(271)	8,570	(210)	—	(†)	30.2	(0.77)	29.7	(0.89)	31.9	(0.88)	33.3	(0.71)	—	(†)
Highest degree earned																				
Bachelor's or less	8,590	(337)	8,050	(334)	9,120	(427)	7,990	(570)	—	(†)	34.3	(1.23)	30.7	(1.16)	32.6	(1.37)	31.0	(1.73)	—	(†)
Master's	12,900	(292)	13,370	(288)	14,030	(344)	12,800	(363)	—	(†)	51.6	(1.28)	51.0	(1.09)	50.2	(1.20)	49.7	(1.49)	—	(†)
Education specialist[3]	2,050	(103)	2,600	(159)	2,800	(203)	2,610	(200)	—	(†)	8.2	(0.41)	9.9	(0.60)	10.0	(0.75)	10.1	(0.80)	—	(†)
Doctor's or first professional	1,480	(138)	2,220	(167)	2,010	(177)	2,340	(224)	—	(†)	5.9	(0.54)	8.5	(0.64)	7.2	(0.63)	9.1	(0.87)	—	(†)
Number of years as a principal																				
3 or fewer	8,270	(341)	7,540	(327)	9,190	(351)	7,100	(516)	—	(†)	33.1	(1.32)	28.7	(1.19)	32.9	(1.20)	27.6	(1.74)	—	(†)
4 to 9	7,080	(269)	6,990	(320)	7,230	(345)	6,750	(415)	—	(†)	28.3	(1.03)	26.6	(1.16)	25.9	(1.19)	26.2	(1.45)	—	(†)
10 to 19	6,950	(310)	7,340	(250)	6,430	(298)	6,910	(350)	—	(†)	27.8	(1.23)	28.0	(0.93)	23.0	(1.04)	26.8	(1.33)	—	(†)
20 or more	2,710	(189)	4,360	(230)	5,110	(260)	4,970	(318)	—	(†)	10.8	(0.77)	16.6	(0.90)	18.3	(0.91)	19.3	(1.27)	—	(†)
Years of full- and part-time teaching experience prior to becoming a principal																				
3 or fewer	6,290	(335)	3,610	(241)	7,850	(381)	6,820	(473)	—	(†)	25.2	(1.27)	13.8	(0.87)	28.1	(1.24)	26.5	(1.48)	—	(†)
4 to 9	6,940	(268)	5,560	(244)	7,030	(287)	6,810	(363)	—	(†)	27.8	(1.05)	21.2	(0.88)	25.1	(1.00)	26.5	(1.36)	—	(†)
10 to 19	9,240	(251)	9,070	(260)	8,510	(306)	7,790	(403)	—	(†)	36.9	(1.03)	34.6	(1.04)	30.4	(1.09)	30.3	(1.50)	—	(†)
20 or more	2,540	(136)	7,990	(265)	4,580	(247)	4,310	(249)	—	(†)	10.1	(0.54)	30.4	(0.98)	16.4	(0.89)	16.7	(0.99)	—	(†)
School locale																				
City	—	(†)	11,250	(226)	9,610	(268)	8,590	(267)	—	(†)	—	(†)	42.9	(0.78)	34.4	(0.90)	33.4	(1.28)	—	(†)
Suburban	—	(†)	9,190	(229)	9,510	(229)	8,110	(298)	—	(†)	—	(†)	35.0	(0.80)	34.0	(0.83)	31.5	(1.27)	—	(†)
Town	—	(†)	3,250	(190)	2,780	(205)	2,630	(323)	—	(†)	—	(†)	12.4	(0.73)	10.0	(0.72)	10.2	(1.16)	—	(†)
Rural	—	(†)	2,540	(211)	6,060	(296)	6,390	(510)	—	(†)	—	(†)	9.7	(0.78)	21.7	(0.95)	24.8	(1.57)	—	(†)

—Not available.
†Not applicable.
#Rounds to zero.
!Interpret data with caution. The coefficient of variation (CV) for this estimate is between 30 and 50 percent.
‡Reporting standards not met. Either there are too few cases for a reliable estimate or the coefficient of variation (CV) is 50 percent or greater.
[1]Data for 1993–94 and 1999–2000 are only roughly comparable to data for later years, because the new category of Two or more races was introduced in 2003–04.
[2]Includes Pacific Islander for 1993–94 and 1999–2000.
[3]Education specialist degrees or certificates are generally awarded for 1 year's work beyond the master's level. Includes certificate of advanced graduate studies.
[4]Excludes data for 4,930 public and 2,690 private school principals whose school level could not be determined.
NOTE: Data are based on a head count of full-time and part-time principals rather than on the number of full-time-equivalent principals reported in other tables. Detail may not sum to totals because of rounding and cell suppression. Race categories exclude persons of Hispanic ethnicity.
SOURCE: U.S. Department of Education, National Center for Education Statistics, Schools and Staffing Survey (SASS), "Public School Principal Data File" and "Private School Principal Data File," 1993–94, 1999–2000, 2007–08, and 2011–12; "Charter School Principal Data File," 1999–2000; and National Teacher and Principal Survey (NTPS), "Public School Principal Data File," 2015–16. (This table was prepared December 2017.)

Table 213.10. Staff employed in public elementary and secondary school systems, by type of assignment: Selected years, 1949–50 through fall 2016

[In full-time equivalents]

School year	Total	School district administrative staff: Total	School district administrative staff: Officials and administrators	School district administrative staff: Instruction coordinators	Instructional staff: Total	Instructional staff: Principals and assistant principals	Instructional staff: Teachers	Instructional staff: Instructional aides	Instructional staff: Librarians	Instructional staff: Guidance counselors	Support staff[1]
1	2	3	4	5	6	7	8	9	10	11	12
					Number						
1949–50[2]	1,300,031	33,642	23,868	9,774	956,808	43,137	913,671	([3])	([3])	([3])	309,582
1959–60[2]	2,089,283	42,423	28,648	13,775	1,448,931	63,554	1,353,372	([3])	17,363	14,643	597,929
1969–70[2]	3,360,763	65,282	33,745	31,537	2,255,707	90,593	2,016,244	57,418	42,689	48,763	1,039,774
Fall 1980[2]	4,168,286	78,784	58,230	20,554	2,729,023	107,061	2,184,216	325,755	48,018	63,973	1,360,479
Fall 1990	4,494,076	75,868	—	—	3,051,404	127,417	2,398,169	395,959	49,909	79,950	1,366,804
Fall 2000	5,709,753	97,270	57,837	39,433	3,876,628	141,792	2,941,461	641,392	54,246	97,737	1,735,855
Fall 2001	5,904,195	109,526	63,517	46,009	3,989,211	160,543	2,999,528	674,741	54,350	100,049	1,805,458
Fall 2002	5,954,661	110,777	62,781	47,996	4,016,963	164,171	3,034,123	663,552	54,205	100,912	1,826,921
Fall 2003	5,953,667	107,483	63,418	44,065	4,052,739	165,233	3,048,652	685,118	54,349	99,387	1,793,445
Fall 2004	6,058,174	111,832	64,101	47,731	4,120,063	165,657	3,090,925	707,514	54,145	101,822	1,826,279
Fall 2005	6,130,686	121,164	62,464	58,700	4,151,236	156,454	3,143,003	693,792	54,057	103,930	1,858,286
Fall 2006	6,153,735	118,707	53,722	64,985	4,186,968	153,673	3,166,391	709,715	54,444	102,745	1,848,060
Fall 2007	6,232,911	130,044	59,361	70,683	4,235,238	157,539	3,199,995	717,806	54,386	105,512	1,867,629
Fall 2008	6,326,702	135,706	62,153	73,553	4,277,674	159,897	3,222,154	734,010	53,805	107,808	1,913,322
Fall 2009	6,351,157	138,471	63,969	74,502	4,279,488	168,450	3,209,672	741,337	52,545	107,484	1,933,198
Fall 2010	6,195,207	133,833	64,597	69,236	4,151,225	165,047	3,099,095	731,705	50,300	105,079	1,910,150
Fall 2011	6,138,890	130,595	62,884	67,711	4,133,767	166,416	3,103,263	710,335	48,402	105,351	1,874,528
Fall 2012	6,181,238	136,387	65,420	70,967	4,158,000	169,240	3,109,101	729,756	46,685	103,218	1,886,851
Fall 2013	6,187,901	139,667	66,732	72,935	4,167,118	168,101	3,113,764	738,226	45,106	101,920	1,881,116
Fall 2014	6,258,543	148,229	68,962	79,267	4,205,088	174,664	3,132,351	749,143	44,624	104,306	1,905,226
Fall 2015	6,373,406	155,273	67,778	87,495	4,249,784	182,006	3,151,497	764,537	43,368	108,376	1,968,350
Fall 2016	6,484,723	160,540	70,357	90,183	4,294,185	183,671	3,169,499	786,773	42,964	111,278	2,029,998
					Percentage distribution						
1949–50[2]	100.0	2.6	1.8	0.8	73.6	3.3	70.3	([3])	([3])	([3])	23.8
1959–60[2]	100.0	2.0	1.4	0.7	69.4	3.0	64.8	([3])	0.8	0.7	28.6
1969–70[2]	100.0	1.9	1.0	0.9	67.1	2.7	60.0	1.7	1.3	1.5	30.9
Fall 1980[2]	100.0	1.9	1.4	0.5	65.5	2.6	52.4	7.8	1.2	1.5	32.6
Fall 1990	100.0	1.7	—	—	67.9	2.8	53.4	8.8	1.1	1.8	30.4
Fall 2000	100.0	1.7	1.0	0.7	67.9	2.5	51.5	11.2	1.0	1.7	30.4
Fall 2001	100.0	1.9	1.1	0.8	67.6	2.7	50.8	11.4	0.9	1.7	30.6
Fall 2002	100.0	1.9	1.1	0.8	67.5	2.8	51.0	11.1	0.9	1.7	30.7
Fall 2003	100.0	1.8	1.1	0.7	68.1	2.8	51.2	11.5	0.9	1.7	30.1
Fall 2004	100.0	1.8	1.1	0.8	68.0	2.7	51.0	11.7	0.9	1.7	30.1
Fall 2005	100.0	2.0	1.0	1.0	67.7	2.6	51.3	11.3	0.9	1.7	30.3
Fall 2006	100.0	1.9	0.9	1.1	68.0	2.5	51.5	11.5	0.9	1.7	30.0
Fall 2007	100.0	2.1	1.0	1.1	67.9	2.5	51.3	11.5	0.9	1.7	30.0
Fall 2008	100.0	2.1	1.0	1.2	67.6	2.5	50.9	11.6	0.9	1.7	30.2
Fall 2009	100.0	2.2	1.0	1.2	67.4	2.7	50.5	11.7	0.8	1.7	30.4
Fall 2010	100.0	2.2	1.0	1.1	67.0	2.7	50.0	11.8	0.8	1.7	30.8
Fall 2011	100.0	2.1	1.0	1.1	67.3	2.7	50.6	11.6	0.8	1.7	30.5
Fall 2012	100.0	2.2	1.1	1.1	67.3	2.7	50.3	11.8	0.8	1.7	30.5
Fall 2013	100.0	2.3	1.1	1.2	67.3	2.7	50.3	11.9	0.7	1.6	30.4
Fall 2014	100.0	2.4	1.1	1.3	67.2	2.8	50.0	12.0	0.7	1.7	30.4
Fall 2015	100.0	2.4	1.1	1.4	66.7	2.9	49.4	12.0	0.7	1.7	30.9
Fall 2016	100.0	2.5	1.1	1.4	66.2	2.8	48.9	12.1	0.7	1.7	31.3
					Pupils per staff member						
1949–50[2]	19.3	746.4	1,052.1	2,569.2	26.2	582.1	27.5	([3])	([3])	([3])	81.1
1959–60[2]	16.8	829.3	1,228.1	2,554.1	24.3	553.6	26.0	([3])	2,026.3	2,402.7	58.8
1969–70[2]	13.6	697.7	1,349.8	1,444.3	20.2	502.8	22.6	793.3	1,067.0	934.1	43.8
Fall 1980[2]	9.8	518.9	702.0	1,988.8	15.0	381.8	18.7	125.5	851.3	639.0	30.0
Fall 1990	9.2	543.3	—	—	13.5	323.5	17.2	104.1	825.8	515.5	30.2
Fall 2000	8.3	485.3	816.1	1,197.1	12.2	332.9	16.0	73.6	870.2	483.0	27.2
Fall 2001	8.1	435.3	750.5	1,036.1	12.0	296.9	15.9	70.7	877.1	476.5	26.4
Fall 2002	8.1	435.0	767.5	1,003.9	12.0	293.5	15.9	72.6	888.9	477.5	26.4
Fall 2003	8.2	451.6	765.4	1,101.6	12.0	293.8	15.9	70.8	893.1	488.4	27.1
Fall 2004	8.1	436.3	761.2	1,022.3	11.8	294.6	15.8	69.0	901.2	479.2	26.7
Fall 2005	8.0	405.3	786.3	836.7	11.8	313.9	15.6	70.8	908.5	472.6	26.4
Fall 2006	8.0	415.4	918.0	758.9	11.8	320.9	15.6	69.5	905.8	480.0	26.7
Fall 2007	7.9	379.0	830.4	697.3	11.6	312.9	15.4	68.7	906.3	467.2	26.4
Fall 2008	7.8	363.0	792.6	669.8	11.5	308.1	15.3	67.1	915.6	457.0	25.7
Fall 2009	7.8	356.5	771.6	662.5	11.5	293.0	15.4	66.6	939.4	459.2	25.5
Fall 2010	8.0	369.7	766.0	714.7	11.9	299.8	16.0	67.6	983.8	470.9	25.9
Fall 2011	8.1	379.2	787.5	731.4	12.0	297.6	16.0	69.7	1,023.1	470.1	26.4
Fall 2012	8.1	364.9	760.8	701.3	12.0	294.1	16.0	68.2	1,066.1	482.2	26.4
Fall 2013	8.1	358.3	749.9	686.2	12.0	297.7	16.1	67.8	1,109.5	491.0	26.6
Fall 2014	8.0	339.4	729.6	634.7	12.0	288.1	16.1	67.2	1,127.5	482.4	26.4
Fall 2015	7.9	324.8	744.2	576.5	11.9	277.1	16.0	66.0	1,163.0	465.4	25.6
Fall 2016	7.8	315.3	719.4	561.2	11.8	275.6	16.0	64.3	1,178.1	454.9	24.9

—Not available.
[1]Includes school district administrative support staff, school and library support staff, student support staff, and other support services staff.
[2]Because of classification revisions, categories other than teachers, principals, librarians, and guidance counselors are only roughly comparable to figures for years after 1980.
[3]Data included in column 8.

NOTE: Data for 1949–50 through 1969–70 are cumulative for the entire school year, rather than counts as of the fall of the year. Detail may not sum to totals because of rounding. Some data have been revised from previously published figures.
SOURCE: U.S. Department of Education, National Center for Education Statistics, *Statistics of State School Systems*, various years; *Statistics of Public Elementary and Secondary Schools*, various years; and Common Core of Data (CCD), "State Nonfiscal Survey of Public Elementary/Secondary Education," 1986–87 through 2016–17. (This table was prepared March 2019.)

Table 213.20. Staff employed in public elementary and secondary school systems, by type of assignment and state or jurisdiction: Fall 2016

[In full-time equivalents]

State or jurisdiction	Total	School district staff: Officials and adminis-trators	School district staff: Adminis-trative support staff	School district staff: Instruction coordinators	School staff: Principals and assistant principals	School staff: School and library support staff	School staff: Teachers	School staff: Instruc-tional aides	School staff: Guidance counselors	School staff: Librarians	Student support staff	Other support services staff
1	2	3	4	5	6	7	8	9	10	11	12	13
United States[1]	**6,478,617**	**70,357**	**196,157**	**90,183**	**183,671**	**285,093**	**3,169,499**	**780,668**	**111,278**	**42,964**	**343,227**	**1,205,522**
Alabama[2]	87,251	1,184	2,369	127	4,416	2,942	42,533	6,873	1,786	1,193	3,045	20,784
Alaska	17,231	641	801	0	640	1,142	7,825	2,602	324	142	659	2,455
Arizona	104,170	1,379	4,128	613	2,438	3,932	48,220	15,694	1,241	421	11,784	14,321
Arkansas	73,599	624	2,610	1,007	1,832	3,075	35,730	9,025	1,296	948	7,577	9,875
California[3]	599,786	3,767	21,240	25,916	17,761	34,677	271,287	81,369	9,522	196	20,037	114,013
Colorado	111,293	1,359	4,645	3,127	3,498	5,932	52,014	17,039	2,482	579	6,904	13,713
Connecticut[4]	96,047	2,156	1,639	4,966	2,246	3,471	42,343	16,565	1,165	754	3,934	16,808[4]
Delaware	17,142	84	107	332	505	395	9,208	2,349	330	120	811	2,902
District of Columbia	13,402	476	960	84	194	2,213	6,727	1,786	168	17	676	102
Florida	351,531	2,247	15,296	662	8,842	17,306	186,339	33,038	5,824	1,988	11,843	68,146
Georgia	228,523	2,533	2,644	3,701	6,436	10,254	114,763	24,943	3,784	2,089	8,470	48,907
Hawaii[3]	22,598	301	692	610	694	994	11,782	2,556	634	149	1,695	2,493
Idaho	28,079	133	641	235	716	1,203	16,204	3,131	553	50	533	4,680
Illinois	259,560	3,411	7,129	1,573	6,851	11,555	128,893	27,787	2,955	1,534	37,183	30,688
Indiana	144,997	603	760	4,374	3,441	7,822	60,162	17,272	2,112	688	9,031	38,733
Iowa	73,495	1,767	1,912	823	1,722	2,718	35,808	12,501	1,239	414	4,481	10,110
Kansas[4]	68,847	443	1,360	935	1,854	2,695	36,193	8,950	1,041	587	4,293	10,496[4]
Kentucky	97,694	954	2,281	1,593	3,496	5,605	42,029	12,958	1,552	1,054	3,218	22,954
Louisiana[4]	97,152	101	472	1,339	3,786	4,446	48,408	13,577	1,822	1,227	4,227	17,748[4]
Maine	35,607	639	704	477	921	1,661	14,750	5,983	563	193	4,243	5,473
Maryland[4]	117,750	3,708	2,060	1,939	3,592	6,126	59,703	11,150	2,376	1,178	5,009	20,907[4]
Massachusetts[4]	130,732	2,569	2,898	448	4,899	6,662	72,413	26,108	2,349	666	10,079	1,642[4]
Michigan	181,556	4,209	1,115	1,312	6,603	11,498	83,597	20,097	2,063	429	14,223	36,410
Minnesota	118,632	2,366	2,235	1,730	2,531	4,615	56,715	19,621	1,328	567	13,823	13,103
Mississippi	67,583	993	2,068	709	2,001	2,520	31,924	8,172	1,116	809	3,265	14,005
Missouri	124,666	888	6,162	1,423	3,293	337	67,926	13,572	2,645	1,386	5,412	21,623
Montana[3]	21,233	441	752	183	520	772	10,555	2,680	475	366	687	3,801
Nebraska[3]	47,979	656	1,286	809	1,092	1,913	23,611	7,006	837	542	1,599	8,629
Nevada[2,5]	29,772	37	88	49	1,176	1,928	23,705	—	975	310	391	1,116
New Hampshire[2,6,7]	31,622	752	747	273	517	739	14,760	6,980	822	324	715	4,994
New Jersey	237,561	1,467	5,465	3,878	5,234	9,897	115,729	37,852	3,824	1,382	13,516	39,317
New Mexico	36,506	201	32	375	1,138	2,060	21,331	5,666	699	223	1,351	3,432
New York	386,801	3,062	20,319	1,876	11,138	9,452	209,151	44,763	7,525	2,336	11,651	65,528
North Carolina	193,031	1,685	5,673	1,193	5,903	7,313	100,220	22,410	4,212	2,128	11,077	31,216
North Dakota	18,412	504	285	233	493	775	9,265	2,735	361	190	910	2,662
Ohio	325,387	2,571	14,365	2,524	5,381	13,961	102,600	22,053	3,822	830	27,110	130,170
Oklahoma	84,115	851	3,065	318	2,236	4,323	41,090	9,950	1,582	924	4,662	15,115
Oregon[4]	68,089	486	2,586	531	1,716	4,873	29,756	11,178	1,162	162	2,853	12,785[4]
Pennsylvania	247,299	2,481	7,401	1,673	5,195	10,941	122,552	31,759	4,534	1,671	9,323	49,769
Rhode Island	20,233	287	553	202	552	715	10,689	2,567	340	202	2,100	2,027
South Carolina	87,314	808	2,332	1,480	3,207	2,528	50,789	11,385	2,147	1,078	3,704	7,856
South Dakota	19,732	737	367	170	453	647	9,777	2,711	353	99	1,036	3,382
Tennessee	128,323	258	1,282	812	3,665	5,239	64,270	17,001	2,992	1,509	3,193	28,101
Texas	707,173	6,891	26,098	3,845	26,172	28,295	352,809	68,211	12,123	4,606	28,011	150,111
Utah	59,325	914	1,649	2,171	1,525	2,675	28,841	9,934	1,019	227	2,060	8,310
Vermont	18,048	131	473	254	493	828	8,187	4,044	438	211	988	2,002
Virginia	180,091	1,867	4,358	1,907	4,270	8,651	91,628	18,616	3,563	1,807	4,968	38,458
Washington[4]	94,685	1,282	3,269	3,401	3,371	4,886	58,815	10,608	2,207	1,127	3,487	2,233
West Virginia	36,885	918	1,378	410	30	484	19,356	3,596	729	271	1,160	8,556
Wisconsin	113,145	1,140	2,920	1,207	2,606	4,419	59,011	9,844	1,992	958	9,362	19,686
Wyoming	16,933	395	489	355	379	989	7,506	2,403	275	107	860	3,176
Bureau of Indian Education	—	—	—	—	—	—	—	—	—	—	—	—
DoDEA, overseas	—	—	—	—	—	—	—	—	—	—	—	—
DoDEA, domestic	—	—	—	—	—	—	—	—	—	—	—	—
Other jurisdictions												
American Samoa	—	—	—	—	—	—	—	—	—	—	—	—
Guam	3,954	44	259	131	96	176	2,289	615	85	40	123	96
Northern Marianas	—	—	—	—	—	—	—	—	—	—	—	—
Puerto Rico[3]	41,012	386	1,152	466	1,257	1,018	28,899	69	639	761	1,725	4,640
U.S. Virgin Islands	2,377	17	87	35	78	163	1,154	287	62	0	63	431

—Not available.
[1]Includes imputations to correct for undercounts in states as designated in footnotes 2 through 7.
[2]Includes imputations for school and library support staff.
[3]Includes imputations for teachers.
[4]Includes staff not reported by type of assignment.
[5]Includes imputations for school district administrative support staff.
[6]Includes imputations for school district instructional coordinators.
[7]Includes imputations for principals and assistant principals.
NOTE: DoDEA = Department of Defense Education Activity.
SOURCE: U.S. Department of Education, National Center for Education Statistics, Common Core of Data (CCD), "State Nonfiscal Survey of Public Elementary/Secondary Education," 2016–17. (This table was prepared September 2018.)

Table 213.40. Staff, teachers, and teachers as a percentage of staff in public elementary and secondary school systems, by state or jurisdiction: Selected years, fall 2000 through fall 2016

[In full-time equivalents]

State or jurisdiction	Teachers as a percent of staff						Fall 2014			Fall 2015			Fall 2016		
	Fall 2000	Fall 2005	Fall 2010	Fall 2011	Fall 2012	Fall 2013	All staff	Teachers	Teachers as a percent of staff	All staff	Teachers	Teachers as a percent of staff	All staff	Teachers	Teachers as a percent of staff
1	2	3	4	5	6	7	8	9	10	11	12	13	14	15	16
United States[1]	**51.5**	**51.3**	**50.0**	**50.6**	**50.3**	**50.3**	**6,258,543**	**3,132,351**	**50.0**	**6,373,406**	**3,151,497**	**49.4**	**6,484,723**	**3,169,499**	**48.9**
Alabama	53.7[2]	55.7	51.9	51.7	53.8[2]	51.4	87,454	42,737	48.9	71,628[2]	40,766	56.9[2]	87,251	42,533	48.7
Alaska	49.3[2]	44.1[2]	45.1[2]	45.6[2]	44.9[2]	46.1[2]	17,088[2]	7,759	45.4[2]	16,982	7,832	46.1	17,231	7,825	45.4
Arizona	49.3	51.3	51.8	51.5	47.3	46.8	102,383	48,124	47.0	103,175	47,944	46.5	104,170	48,220	46.3
Arkansas	50.6	46.7	47.5	46.8	47.9	49.6	74,107	35,430	47.8	73,658	35,804	48.6	73,599	35,730	48.5
California	54.1[2]	53.4[2]	49.2[2]	49.1[2]	48.9[2]	47.9[2]	571,389[2]	267,685[2]	46.8[2]	577,836	263,475	45.6	599,786[2]	271,287[2]	45.2[2]
Colorado	50.7	49.2	47.9	47.9	47.7	48.2	108,671	51,388	47.3	111,939	51,798	46.3	111,293	52,014	46.7
Connecticut	50.0	46.9	46.1	47.1	48.1	46.1	94,058	42,062	44.7	98,166	43,772	44.6	96,047[2]	42,343	44.1[2]
Delaware	59.2	51.7	54.2	55.6	52.7	51.4	18,553	9,649	52.0	17,097	8,962	52.4	17,142	9,208	53.7
District of Columbia	46.2	44.3[2]	52.1	54.4	47.5	52.5	13,617	6,565	48.2	14,106	6,789	48.1	13,402	6,727	50.2
Florida	47.8	50.6	52.7	53.2	52.7	53.1	341,440	180,442	52.8	345,645	182,586	52.8	351,531	186,339	53.0
Georgia	49.2	49.6	49.5	49.6	49.6	50.2	221,926	111,470	50.2	224,488	113,031	50.4	228,523	114,763	50.2
Hawaii	59.5	53.3	52.5	51.9	52.2	52.5	22,424	11,663	52.0	22,596	11,747	52.0	22,598[2]	11,782[2]	52.1[2]
Idaho	56.2	55.8	56.4	57.0	55.3[2]	63.0[2]	27,451	15,609	56.9	27,186	15,656	57.6	28,079	16,204	57.7
Illinois	51.1[2]	53.2[2]	61.6[2]	61.7[2]	51.5[2]	51.1[2]	261,922	132,456	50.6	260,463	129,948	49.9	259,560	128,893	49.7
Indiana	46.7	45.5	41.9[2]	41.5	40.5	41.4	139,587	56,547	40.5	143,417	57,675	40.2	144,997	60,162	41.5
Iowa	51.1	50.9	49.8	49.6	49.3	49.5	72,129	35,684	49.5	72,887	35,687	49.0	73,495	35,808	48.7
Kansas	50.9	51.3	51.1	53.0	56.5	53.0	71,175	37,659	52.9	73,272	40,035	54.6	68,847[2]	36,193	52.6[2]
Kentucky	44.1	43.3	42.4	45.4	43.1	42.8	97,269	41,586	42.8	97,712	41,902	42.9	97,694	42,029	43.0
Louisiana	49.3	48.2	48.2	48.2	48.6	48.5	85,371	46,340	54.3	107,600	58,469	54.3	97,152[2]	48,408	49.8[2]
Maine	49.7	47.3	47.3	37.3[2]	46.3	45.1	32,225	14,937	46.4	35,241	14,857	42.2	35,607	14,750	41.4
Maryland	54.3	51.0	50.6	50.8	51.0	50.9	117,238	59,194	50.5	115,517	59,414	51.4	117,750[2]	59,703	50.7[2]
Massachusetts	55.1	53.0[2]	56.3	56.4	56.4	55.5	128,723	71,859	55.8	128,291	71,969	56.1	130,732[2]	72,413	55.4[2]
Michigan	46.1	47.9[2]	45.8	46.2	46.3	46.6	183,722	85,038	46.3	181,468	84,181	46.4	181,556	83,597	46.0
Minnesota	51.6[2]	48.9	48.3	48.4	48.2	48.3	115,999	55,690	48.0	117,236	55,985	47.8	118,632	56,715	47.8
Mississippi	47.9	46.5	47.5	47.2	47.8	47.3	68,000	32,311	47.5	67,757	32,175	47.5	67,583	31,924	47.2
Missouri	53.2	52.1	52.0	50.1	52.2	54.0	127,062	67,356	53.0	128,938	67,635	52.5	124,666	67,926	54.5
Montana	53.5[2]	52.9[2]	53.8[2]	54.0[2]	54.0[2]	49.4[2]	20,456[2]	10,234	50.0[2]	21,330	10,412	48.8	21,233[2]	10,555[2]	49.7[2]
Nebraska	52.6	51.9	49.1	49.0	48.7	48.8	46,931	22,988	49.0	47,292	23,308	49.3	47,979[2]	23,611[2]	49.2[2]
Nevada	58.6	67.2[2]	65.4[2]	65.0[2]	63.3[2]	64.5[2]	33,749[2]	21,656	64.2[2]	26,430	22,702	85.9	35,878	23,705	66.1
New Hampshire	51.1	48.5	46.6	47.1	47.0	46.6	31,851	14,773	46.4	31,980	14,770	46.2	31,622	14,760	46.7
New Jersey	53.4	53.2[2]	54.4[2]	54.1[2]	49.7[2]	49.6[2]	235,231[2]	115,067	48.9[2]	236,558	114,968	48.6	237,561	115,729	48.7
New Mexico	46.8	45.9	48.2	47.8	48.0	47.9	46,921	22,411	47.8	37,573	21,722	57.8	36,506	21,331	58.4
New York	49.7	58.6	51.1	51.5	55.9	57.5	356,055	203,781	57.2	372,692	206,086	55.3	386,801	209,151	54.1
North Carolina	51.5	52.5	51.0	51.6	51.4	51.6	191,323	99,320	51.9	190,855	99,355	52.1	193,031	100,220	51.9
North Dakota	53.9	52.9	51.8	52.0	51.9	51.7	17,599	9,049	51.4	17,983	9,195	51.1	18,412	9,265	50.3
Ohio	53.1	49.4	45.3	44.3	43.7	42.7	250,106[2]	106,526[2]	42.6[2]	322,611	101,742	31.5	325,387	102,600	31.5
Oklahoma	55.0	51.1	50.2	50.0	49.5	49.3	85,835	42,073	49.0	85,915	42,452	49.4	84,115	41,090	48.8
Oregon	50.0	47.0	44.2	44.1	44.2	44.7	62,956	27,850	44.2	65,928	29,086	44.1	68,089[2]	29,756	43.7[2]
Pennsylvania	52.2	50.9	48.7	49.0	48.8	49.9[2]	243,290	122,030	50.2	241,548	120,893	50.0	247,299	122,552	49.6
Rhode Island	60.0	58.4[2]	60.2	60.9	58.3	56.7	15,716	9,471	60.3	19,483	10,631	54.6	20,233	10,689	52.8
South Carolina	65.7[2]	70.9[2]	69.0	67.5	66.3	66.5	75,718	49,475	65.3	78,108	50,237	64.3	87,314	50,789	58.2
South Dakota	52.0	48.0	48.7	48.5	48.8	49.5	19,326	9,618	49.8	19,543	9,638	49.3	19,732	9,777	49.5
Tennessee	52.1	52.2	51.9	51.9	52.0	52.5	127,043	65,341	51.4	128,469	66,488	51.8	128,323	64,270	50.1
Texas	50.6	50.5	50.3	50.7	50.8	50.8	675,112	342,257	50.7	690,077	347,329	50.3	707,173	352,809	49.9
Utah	54.1	50.2	49.1	49.9	49.5	49.6	55,355[2]	27,374[2]	49.5[2]	56,146[2]	28,348[2]	50.5[2]	59,325	28,841	48.6
Vermont	47.3	46.5	45.3	45.5	45.6	45.8	18,130	8,276	45.6	18,183	8,338	45.9	18,048	8,187	45.4
Virginia	54.1[2]	44.4	35.3	50.4	50.4	50.6	177,733	89,968	50.6	178,551	90,255	50.5	180,091	91,628	50.9
Washington	52.3	47.0	52.0	52.1	52.4	52.1	111,696	59,555	53.3	94,883[2]	57,942	61.1[2]	94,685	58,815	62.1
West Virginia	54.3	52.3	51.8[2]	51.4[2]	51.2[2]	51.1[2]	39,272[2]	20,029	51.0[2]	38,452	19,664	51.1	36,885	19,356	52.5
Wisconsin	56.3	57.0	55.5	55.4	56.6	56.6	103,208[2]	58,376[2]	56.6[2]	101,250	58,185	57.5	113,145	59,011	52.2
Wyoming	48.6	46.2	43.4	45.8	44.3	44.6	16,946	7,615	44.9	17,269	7,653	44.3	16,933	7,506	44.3
Bureau of Indian Education	—	—	—	—	42.9[3]	—	—	—	—	—	—	—	—	—	—
DoDEA, overseas	66.0	62.9	—	—	—	—	—	—	—	—	—	—	—	—	—
DoDEA, domestic	59.2	55.4	—	—	—	—	—	—	—	—	—	—	—	—	—
Other jurisdictions															
American Samoa	50.0	68.4	—	—	—	—	—	—	—	—	—	—	—	—	—
Guam	51.5	52.2	54.5	58.4	58.4	58.4	3,938	2,286	58.0	4,019	2,336	58.1	3,954	2,289	57.9
Northern Marianas	50.2	49.8	50.0	47.6	45.9	47.6	—	—	—	—	—	—	—	—	—
Puerto Rico	54.4	56.0	61.6	59.3	57.0	61.4	50,099	31,186	62.2	48,820	30,438	62.3	41,012[2]	28,899[2]	70.5[2]
U.S. Virgin Islands	52.1	53.8	49.9	50.9	51.1	49.9	2,212	1,131	51.1	2,284	1,106	48.4	2,377	1,154	48.5

—Not available.

[1]U.S. totals include imputations for underreporting and nonreporting states.

[2]Includes imputations to correct for underreporting.

[3]Total staff count excludes officials and administrators and administrative support staff, so computed percentage of teachers may be overstated.

NOTE: DoDEA = Department of Defense Education Activity. Some data have been revised from previously published figures.

SOURCE: U.S. Department of Education, National Center for Education Statistics, Common Core of Data (CCD), "State Nonfiscal Survey of Public Elementary/Secondary Education," 2000–01 through 2016–17. (This table was prepared March 2019.)

Table 213.50. Staff, enrollment, and pupil/staff ratios in public elementary and secondary school systems, by state or jurisdiction: Selected years, fall 2000 through fall 2016

State or jurisdiction	Pupil/staff ratio						Fall 2014			Fall 2015			Fall 2016		
	Fall 2000	Fall 2005	Fall 2010	Fall 2011	Fall 2012	Fall 2013	Staff	Enrollment	Pupil/staff ratio	Staff	Enrollment	Pupil/staff ratio	Staff	Enrollment	Pupil/staff ratio
1	2	3	4	5	6	7	8	9	10	11	12	13	14	15	16
United States[1]	**8.3**	**8.0**	**8.0**	**8.1**	**8.1**	**8.1**	**6,258,543**	**50,312,581**	**8.0**	**6,373,406**	**50,438,043**	**7.9**	**6,484,723**	**50,615,189**	**7.8**
Alabama	8.2[2]	7.1	7.9	8.1	7.7[2]	8.1	87,454	744,164	8.5	71,628[2]	743,789	10.4[2]	87,251	744,930	8.5
Alaska	8.3[2]	7.4[2]	7.3[2]	7.4[2]	7.7[2]	7.6[2]	17,088[2]	131,176	7.7[2]	16,982	132,477	7.8	17,231	132,737	7.7
Arizona	9.7	10.9	11.1	10.9	10.6	10.7	102,383	1,111,695	10.9	103,175	1,109,040	10.7	104,170	1,123,137	10.8
Arkansas	7.1	6.7	6.7	6.6	6.8	7.0	74,107	490,917	6.6	73,658	492,132	6.7	73,599	493,447	6.7
California	11.1[2]	11.1[2]	11.9[2]	11.5[2]	11.6[2]	11.7[2]	571,389[2]	6,312,161	11.0[2]	577,836	6,305,347	10.9	599,786	6,309,138	10.5
Colorado	8.7	8.4	8.3	8.5	8.4	8.4	108,671	889,006	8.2	111,939	899,112	8.0	111,293	905,019	8.1
Connecticut	6.8	6.8	6.0	6.0	6.0	5.8	94,058	542,678	5.8	98,166	537,933	5.5	96,047[2]	535,118	5.6[2]
Delaware	9.1	7.8	7.9	8.3	7.4	7.2	18,553	134,042	7.2	17,097	134,847	7.9	17,142	136,264	7.9
District of Columbia	6.4	6.2[3]	6.3	6.4	6.1	6.9	13,617	80,958	5.9	14,106	84,024	6.0	13,402	85,850	6.4
Florida	8.8	8.5	7.9	8.1	8.0	8.1	341,440	2,756,944	8.1	345,645	2,792,234	8.1	351,531	2,816,791	8.0
Georgia	7.8	7.3	7.4	7.5	7.7	7.9	221,926	1,744,437	7.9	224,488	1,757,237	7.8	228,523	1,764,346	7.7
Hawaii	10.0	8.7	8.3	8.3	8.3	8.3	22,424	182,384	8.1	22,596	181,995	8.1	22,598	181,550	8.0
Idaho	10.1	10.1	9.9	10.0	10.8[2]	12.5[2]	27,451	290,885	10.6	27,186	292,277	10.8	28,079	297,200	10.6
Illinois	8.2[2]	8.4[2]	9.7[2]	9.8[2]	7.9[2]	7.8[2]	261,922	2,050,239	7.8	260,463	2,041,779	7.8	259,560	2,026,718	7.8
Indiana	7.8	7.8	7.5[2]	6.9	7.0	7.3	139,587	1,046,269	7.5	143,417	1,046,757	7.3	144,997	1,049,547	7.2
Iowa	7.3	7.0	7.1	7.1	7.0	7.0	72,129	505,311	7.0	72,887	508,014	7.0	73,495	509,831	6.9
Kansas	7.3	7.1	7.1	6.9	6.7	6.9	71,175	497,275	7.0	73,272	495,884	6.8	68,847[2]	494,347	7.2[2]
Kentucky	7.4	6.9	6.8	7.4	6.9	6.9	97,269	688,640	7.1	97,712	686,598	7.0	97,694	684,017	7.0
Louisiana	7.3	7.1	6.9	7.0	7.4	7.4	85,371	716,800	8.4	107,600	718,711	6.7	97,152[2]	716,293	7.4[2]
Maine	6.2	5.5	5.8	4.7[2]	5.7	5.4	32,225	182,470	5.7	35,241	181,613	5.2	35,607	180,512	5.1
Maryland	8.8	7.7	7.4	7.5	7.6	7.5	117,238	874,514	7.5	115,517	879,601	7.6	117,750[2]	886,221	7.5[2]
Massachusetts	8.0	7.0[2]	7.8	7.8	7.6	7.5	128,723	955,844	7.4	128,291	964,026	7.5	130,732[2]	964,514	7.4[2]
Michigan	8.2[2]	8.5[2]	8.2	8.4	8.4	8.4	183,722	1,537,922	8.4	181,468	1,536,231	8.5	181,556	1,528,666	8.4
Minnesota	8.2[2]	8.0	7.7	7.7	7.6	7.5	115,999	857,235	7.4	117,236	864,384	7.4	118,632	875,021	7.4
Mississippi	7.7	7.3	7.2	7.2	7.2	7.2	68,000	490,917	7.2	67,757	487,200	7.2	67,583	483,150	7.1
Missouri	7.5	7.1	7.2	6.9	7.2	7.4	127,062	917,785	7.2	128,938	919,234	7.1	124,666	915,040	7.3
Montana	8.0[2]	7.4[2]	7.4[2]	7.6[2]	7.6[2]	6.9[2]	20,456[2]	144,532	7.1[2]	21,330	145,319	6.8	21,233	146,375	6.9
Nebraska	7.2	7.0	6.6	6.7	6.7	6.7	46,931	312,635	6.7	47,292	316,014	6.7	47,979	319,194	6.7
Nevada	10.9	12.7[2]	13.1[2]	13.5[2]	13.6[2]	13.3[2]	33,749[2]	459,189	13.6[2]	26,430	467,527	17.7	35,878	473,744	13.2
New Hampshire	7.4	6.4	5.9	6.0	6.0	5.9	31,851	184,670	5.8	31,980	182,425	5.7	31,622	180,888	5.7
New Jersey	7.1	6.6[2]	6.9[2]	6.7[2]	6.1[2]	5.9[2]	235,231[2]	1,400,579	6.0[2]	236,558	1,408,845	6.0	237,561	1,410,421	5.9
New Mexico	7.1	6.8	7.3	7.3	7.3	7.3	46,921	340,365	7.3	37,573	335,694	8.9	36,506	336,263	9.2
New York	6.9	7.5	6.6	6.7	7.3	7.6	356,055	2,741,185	7.7	372,692	2,711,626	7.3	386,801	2,729,776	7.1
North Carolina	8.0	7.8	7.7	8.0	7.9	8.0	191,323	1,548,895	8.1	190,855	1,544,934	8.1	193,031	1,550,062	8.0
North Dakota	7.2	6.5	5.9	6.0	6.0	6.1	17,599	106,586	6.1	17,983	108,644	6.0	18,412	109,706	6.0
Ohio	8.2	7.7	7.3	7.1	7.1	6.9	250,106[3]	1,724,810	6.9[3]	322,611	1,716,585	5.3	325,387	1,710,143	5.3
Oklahoma	8.3	7.8	8.0	8.1	8.0	8.0	85,835	688,511	8.0	85,915	692,878	8.1	84,115	693,903	8.2
Oregon	9.7	9.2	9.0	9.4	9.8	9.9	62,956	601,318	9.6	65,928	608,825	9.2	68,089[2]	606,277	8.9[2]
Pennsylvania	8.1	7.6	6.7	7.0	7.0	7.2[2]	243,290	1,743,160	7.2	241,548	1,717,414	7.1	247,299	1,727,497	7.0
Rhode Island	8.9	6.3[2]	7.7	7.6	8.4	8.2	15,716	141,959	9.0	19,483	142,014	7.3	20,233	142,150	7.0
South Carolina	9.8[2]	10.3[2]	11.1	10.5	10.2	10.3	75,718	756,523	10.0	78,108	763,533	9.8	87,314	771,250	8.8
South Dakota	7.1	6.4	6.5	6.7	6.8	6.8	19,326	133,040	6.9	19,543	134,253	6.9	19,732	136,302	6.9
Tennessee	8.3[2]	8.4	7.7	7.8	7.8	7.9	127,043	995,475	7.8	128,469	1,001,235	7.8	128,323	1,001,562	7.8
Texas	7.5	7.6	7.4	7.8	7.9	7.8	675,112	5,233,765	7.8	690,077	5,301,477	7.7	707,173	5,360,849	7.6
Utah	11.8	11.1	11.2	11.5	11.4	11.4	55,355[3]	635,577	11.5[3]	56,146[3]	647,870	11.5[3]	59,325	659,801	11.1
Vermont	5.7	5.1	5.2	4.9	4.9	4.8	18,130	87,311	4.8	18,183	87,866	4.8	18,048	88,428	4.9
Virginia	7.1[2]	5.2	6.2	7.0	7.1	7.1	177,733	1,280,381	7.2	178,551	1,283,590	7.2	180,091	1,287,026	7.1
Washington	10.3	9.1	10.1	10.3	10.3	10.1	111,696	1,073,638	9.6	94,883[2]	1,087,030	11.5[2]	94,685	1,101,711	11.6
West Virginia	7.4	7.4	7.2[2]	7.2[2]	7.2[2]	7.2[2]	39,272[2]	280,310	7.1[2]	38,452	277,452	7.2	36,885	273,855	7.4
Wisconsin	8.2	8.3	8.4	8.6	8.6	8.5	103,208[3]	871,432	8.4[3]	101,250	867,800	8.6	113,145	864,432	7.6
Wyoming	6.4	5.8	5.4	5.3	5.5	5.5	16,946	94,067	5.6	17,269	94,717	5.5	16,933	94,170	5.6
Bureau of Indian Education	—	—	—	—	—	—	—	—	—	—	—	—	—	45,399	—
DoDEA, overseas	9.5	6.9	—	—	—	—	—	—	—	—	74,970	—	—	—	—
DoDEA, domestic	8.4	7.7	—	—	—	—	—	—	—	—	—	—	—	—	—
Other jurisdictions															
American Samoa	9.6	11.4	—	—	—	—	—	—	—	—	—	—	—	—	—
Guam	8.5	9.0	9.3	8.0	7.9	8.5	3,938	31,144	7.9	4,019	30,821	7.7	3,954	30,758	7.8
Northern Marianas	9.6	9.5	9.1	10.6	11.9	12.1	—	—	—	—	—	—	—	—	—
Puerto Rico	8.9	7.5	8.0	8.1	8.0	7.8	50,099	410,950	8.2	48,820	379,818	7.8	41,012	365,181	8.9
U.S. Virgin Islands	6.7	6.3	5.3	6.6	6.9	6.9	2,212	14,241	6.4	2,284	13,805	6.0	2,377	13,194	5.6

—Not available.
[1]U.S. totals include imputations for underreporting and nonreporting states.
[2]Includes imputations to correct for underreporting.
[3]Staff data imputed based on prior year's report.

NOTE: Staff reported in full-time equivalents. DoDEA = Department of Defense Education Activity. Some data have been revised from previously published figures.
SOURCE: U.S. Department of Education, National Center for Education Statistics, Common Core of Data (CCD), "State Nonfiscal Survey of Public Elementary/Secondary Education," 2000–01 through 2016–17. (This table was prepared March 2019.)

Table 214.10. Number of public school districts and public and private elementary and secondary schools: Selected years, 1869–70 through 2016–17

School year	Regular public school districts[1]	Total, all public and private schools	Public schools[2]: Total, all public schools[4]	Public schools: Total, schools with reported grade spans[5]	Public schools: Schools with elementary grades: Total	Public schools: Schools with elementary grades: One-teacher[6]	Public schools: Schools with secondary grades	Private schools[2,3]: Total, all private schools[4]	Private schools: Schools with elementary grades	Private schools: Schools with secondary grades
1	2	3	4	5	6	7	8	9	10	11
1869–70	—	—	116,312	—	—	—	—	—	—	—
1879–80	—	—	178,122	—	—	—	—	—	—	—
1889–90	—	—	224,526	—	—	—	—	—	—	—
1899–1900	—	—	248,279	—	—	—	—	—	—	—
1909–10	—	—	265,474	—	—	212,448	—	—	—	—
1919–20	—	—	271,319	—	—	187,948	—	—	—	—
1929–30	—	—	248,117	—	238,306	148,712	23,930	—	9,275[7]	3,258[7]
1939–40	117,108[8]	—	226,762	—	—	113,600	—	—	11,306[7]	3,568[7]
1949–50	83,718[8]	—	—	—	128,225	59,652	24,542	—	10,375[7]	3,331[7]
1959–60	40,520[8]	—	—	—	91,853	20,213	25,784	—	13,574[7]	4,061[7]
1961–62	35,676[8]	125,634	107,260	—	81,910	13,333	25,350	18,374	14,762[7]	4,129[7]
1963–64	31,705[8]	—	104,015	—	77,584	9,895	26,431	—	—	4,451[7]
1965–66	26,983[8]	117,662	99,813	—	73,216	6,491	26,597	17,849[7]	15,340[7]	4,606[7]
1967–68	22,010[8]	—	—	94,197	70,879	4,146	27,011	—	—	—
1970–71	17,995[8]	—	—	89,372	65,800	1,815	25,352	—	14,372[7]	3,770[7]
1973–74	16,730[8]	—	—	88,655	65,070	1,365	25,906	—	—	—
1975–76	16,376[8]	—	88,597	87,034	63,242	1,166	25,330	—	—	—
1976–77	16,271[8]	—	—	86,501	62,644	1,111	25,378	19,910[7]	16,385[7]	5,904[7]
1978–79	16,014[8]	—	—	84,816	61,982	1,056	24,504	19,489[7]	16,097[7]	5,766[7]
1979–80	15,944[8]	—	87,004	—	—	—	—	—	—	—
1980–81	15,912[8]	106,746	85,982	83,688	61,069	921	24,362	20,764[7]	16,792[7]	5,678[7]
1982–83	15,824[8]	—	84,740	82,039	59,656	798	23,988	—	—	—
1983–84	15,747[8]	111,872	84,178	81,418	59,082	838	23,947	27,694	20,872	7,862
1984–85	—	—	84,007	81,147	58,827	825	23,916	—	—	—
1985–86	—	—	—	—	—	—	—	25,616	20,252	7,387
1986–87	15,713	—	83,421	82,316	60,811	763	23,481	—	—	—
1987–88	15,577	110,055	83,248	81,416	59,754	729	23,841	26,807	22,959	8,418
1988–89	15,376	—	83,165	81,579	60,176	583	23,638	—	—	—
1989–90	15,367	110,137	83,425	81,880	60,699	630	23,461	26,712	24,221	10,197
1990–91	15,358	109,228	84,538	82,475	61,340	617	23,460	24,690	22,223	8,989
1991–92	15,173	110,576	84,578	82,506	61,739	569	23,248	25,998	23,523	9,282
1992–93	15,025	—	84,497	82,896	62,225	430	23,220	—	—	—
1993–94	14,881	111,486	85,393	83,431	62,726	442	23,379	26,093	23,543	10,555
1994–95	14,772	—	86,221	84,476	63,572	458	23,668	—	—	—
1995–96	14,766	121,519	87,125	84,958	63,961	474	23,793	34,394	32,401	10,942
1996–97	14,841	—	88,223	86,092	64,785	487	24,287	—	—	—
1997–98	14,805	123,403	89,508	87,541	65,859	476	24,802	33,895	31,408	10,779
1998–99	14,891	—	90,874	89,259	67,183	463	25,797	—	—	—
1999–2000	14,928	125,007	92,012	90,538	68,173	423	26,407	32,995	30,457	10,693
2000–01	14,859	—	93,273	91,691	69,697	411	27,090	—	—	—
2001–02	14,559	130,007	94,112	92,696	70,516	408	27,468	35,895	33,191	11,846
2002–03	14,465	—	95,615	93,869	71,270	366	28,151	—	—	—
2003–04	14,383	130,407	95,726	93,977	71,195	376	28,219	34,681	31,988	11,188
2004–05	14,205	—	96,513	95,001	71,556	338	29,017	—	—	—
2005–06	14,166	132,436	97,382	95,731	71,733	326	29,705	35,054	32,127	12,184
2006–07	13,856	—	98,793	96,362	72,442	313	29,904	—	—	—
2007–08	13,838	132,656	98,916	97,654	73,011	288	30,542	33,740	30,808	11,870
2008–09	13,809	—	98,706	97,119	72,771	237	29,971	—	—	—
2009–10	13,625	132,183	98,817	97,521	72,870	217	30,381	33,366	30,590	11,941
2010–11	13,588	—	98,817	97,767	73,223	224	30,681	—	—	—
2011–12	13,567	129,189	98,328	97,357	73,000	205	30,668	30,861	28,184	11,165
2012–13	13,515	—	98,454	97,331	73,037	196	30,623	—	—	—
2013–14	13,491	131,890	98,271	97,290	73,223	193	30,256	33,619	30,919	11,110
2014–15	13,601	—	98,176	97,601	73,420	165	30,528	—	—	—
2015–16	13,584	132,853	98,277	97,586	73,546	197	30,828	34,576	31,630	12,669
2016–17	13,598	—	98,158	97,434	73,620	203	30,597	—	—	—

—Not available.
[1]Regular districts exclude regional education service agencies and supervisory union administrative centers, state-operated agencies, federally operated agencies, and other types of local education agencies, such as independent charter schools.
[2]Schools with both elementary and secondary grades are included under elementary schools and also under secondary schools.
[3]Data for most years prior to 1976–77 are partly estimated. Prior to 1995–96, excludes schools with highest grade of kindergarten.
[4]Includes schools not classified by grade span, which are not shown separately.
[5]Includes elementary, secondary, and combined elementary/secondary schools.
[6]Excludes alternative schools, academies, hospitals, virtual schools, prisons, and juvenile detention facilities.
[7]These data cannot be compared directly with the data for years after 1980–81.
[8]Because of expanded survey coverage, data are not directly comparable with figures after 1983–84.

SOURCE: U.S. Department of Education, National Center for Education Statistics, *Annual Report of the Commissioner of Education*, 1870 through 1910; *Biennial Survey of Education in the United States*, 1919–20 through 1949–50; *Statistics of State School Systems*, 1951–52 through 1967–68; *Statistics of Public Elementary and Secondary School Systems*, 1970–71 through 1980–81; *Statistics of Public and Nonpublic Elementary and Secondary Day Schools, 1968–69*; *Statistics of Nonpublic Elementary and Secondary Schools*, 1970–71; *Private Schools in American Education*; Schools and Staffing Survey (SASS), "Private School Questionnaire," 1987–88 and 1990–91; Private School Universe Survey (PSS), 1989–90 through 2015–16; and Common Core of Data (CCD), "Local Education Agency Universe Survey" and "Public Elementary/Secondary School Universe Survey," 1982–83 through 2016–17. (This table was prepared April 2019.)

Table 214.20. Number and percentage distribution of regular public school districts and students, by enrollment size of district: Selected years, 1979–80 through 2016–17

Year	Enrollment size of district									
	Total	25,000 or more	10,000 to 24,999	5,000 to 9,999	2,500 to 4,999	1,000 to 2,499	600 to 999	300 to 599	1 to 299	Size not reported
1	2	3	4	5	6	7	8	9	10	11
	Number of districts									
1979–80[1]	15,944	181	478	1,106	2,039	3,475	1,841	2,298	4,223	303
1989–90	15,367	179	479	913	1,937	3,547	1,801	2,283	3,910	318
1999–2000	14,928	238	579	1,036	2,068	3,457	1,814	2,081	3,298	357
2004–05	14,205	264	589	1,056	2,018	3,391	1,739	1,931	2,881	336
2005–06	14,166	269	594	1,066	2,015	3,335	1,768	1,895	2,857	367
2006–07	13,856	275	598	1,066	2,006	3,334	1,730	1,898	2,685	264
2007–08	13,838	281	589	1,062	2,006	3,292	1,753	1,890	2,692	273
2008–09	13,809	280	594	1,049	1,995	3,272	1,766	1,886	2,721	246
2009–10	13,625	284	598	1,044	1,985	3,242	1,750	1,891	2,707	124
2010–11	13,588	282	600	1,052	1,975	3,224	1,738	1,887	2,687	143
2011–12	13,567	286	592	1,044	1,952	3,222	1,755	1,911	2,676	129
2012–13	13,515	290	588	1,048	1,924	3,227	1,751	1,908	2,678	101
2013–14	13,491	286	596	1,046	1,920	3,186	1,791	1,894	2,668	104
2014–15	13,601	288	609	1,046	1,898	3,221	1,766	1,880	2,687	206
2015–16	13,584	287	613	1,040	1,888	3,214	1,782	1,909	2,643	208
2016–17	13,598	287	613	1,044	1,908	3,236	1,776	1,926	2,647	161
	Percentage distribution of districts									
1979–80[1]	100.0	1.1	3.0	6.9	12.8	21.8	11.5	14.4	26.5	1.9
1989–90	100.0	1.2	3.1	5.9	12.6	23.1	11.7	14.9	25.4	2.1
1999–2000	100.0	1.6	3.9	6.9	13.9	23.2	12.2	13.9	22.1	2.4
2004–05	100.0	1.9	4.1	7.4	14.2	23.9	12.2	13.6	20.3	2.4
2005–06	100.0	1.9	4.2	7.5	14.2	23.5	12.5	13.4	20.2	2.6
2006–07	100.0	2.0	4.3	7.7	14.5	24.1	12.5	13.7	19.4	1.9
2007–08	100.0	2.0	4.3	7.7	14.5	23.8	12.7	13.7	19.5	2.0
2008–09	100.0	2.0	4.3	7.6	14.4	23.7	12.8	13.7	19.7	1.8
2009–10	100.0	2.1	4.4	7.7	14.6	23.8	12.8	13.9	19.9	0.9
2010–11	100.0	2.1	4.4	7.7	14.5	23.7	12.8	13.9	19.8	1.1
2011–12	100.0	2.1	4.4	7.7	14.4	23.7	12.9	14.1	19.7	1.0
2012–13	100.0	2.1	4.4	7.8	14.2	23.9	13.0	14.1	19.8	0.7
2013–14	100.0	2.1	4.4	7.8	14.2	23.6	13.3	14.0	19.8	0.8
2014–15	100.0	2.1	4.5	7.7	14.0	23.7	13.0	13.8	19.8	1.5
2015–16	100.0	2.1	4.5	7.7	13.9	23.7	13.1	14.1	19.5	1.5
2016–17	100.0	2.1	4.5	7.7	14.0	23.8	13.1	14.2	19.5	1.2
	Number of students									
1979–80[1]	41,882,000	11,415,000	7,004,000	7,713,000	7,076,000	5,698,000	1,450,000	1,005,000	521,000	†
1989–90	40,069,756	11,209,889	7,107,362	6,347,103	6,731,334	5,763,282	1,402,623	997,434	510,729	†
1999–2000	46,318,635	14,886,636	8,656,672	7,120,704	7,244,407	5,620,962	1,426,280	911,127	451,847	†
2004–05	47,800,967	16,182,672	8,980,096	7,346,960	7,134,861	5,533,156	1,368,546	851,455	403,221	†
2005–06	48,013,931	16,376,213	9,055,547	7,394,010	7,114,942	5,442,588	1,391,314	835,430	403,887	†
2006–07	48,105,666	16,496,573	9,083,944	7,395,889	7,092,532	5,433,770	1,363,287	840,032	399,639	†
2007–08	48,096,140	16,669,611	8,946,432	7,408,553	7,103,274	5,358,492	1,381,342	834,295	394,141	†
2008–09	48,033,126	16,634,807	9,043,665	7,324,565	7,079,061	5,329,406	1,392,110	832,262	397,250	†
2009–10	48,021,335	16,788,789	9,053,144	7,265,111	7,034,640	5,266,945	1,381,415	835,035	396,256	†
2010–11	48,059,830	16,803,247	9,150,912	7,318,413	6,973,720	5,215,389	1,372,759	833,764	391,626	†
2011–12	47,973,834	16,934,369	9,031,528	7,266,770	6,907,658	5,218,533	1,381,289	842,134	391,553	†
2012–13	48,033,002	17,101,040	8,967,874	7,300,285	6,817,724	5,232,487	1,377,490	841,150	394,952	†
2013–14	48,124,386	17,125,416	9,128,194	7,270,070	6,792,172	5,169,748	1,412,987	832,091	393,708	†
2014–15	48,390,432	17,267,232	9,275,438	7,270,961	6,740,298	5,214,007	1,393,249	831,703	397,544	†
2015–16	48,413,211	17,301,641	9,347,240	7,223,779	6,693,454	5,202,470	1,405,851	844,470	394,306	†
2016–17	48,599,865	17,353,942	9,363,219	7,274,211	6,748,580	5,214,673	1,397,636	851,548	396,056	†
	Percentage distribution of students									
1979–80[1]	100.0	27.3	16.7	18.4	16.9	13.6	3.5	2.4	1.2	†
1989–90	100.0	28.0	17.7	15.8	16.8	14.4	3.5	2.5	1.3	†
1999–2000	100.0	32.1	18.7	15.4	15.6	12.1	3.1	2.0	1.0	†
2004–05	100.0	33.9	18.8	15.4	14.9	11.6	2.9	1.8	0.8	†
2005–06	100.0	34.1	18.9	15.4	14.8	11.3	2.9	1.7	0.8	†
2006–07	100.0	34.3	18.9	15.4	14.7	11.3	2.8	1.7	0.8	†
2007–08	100.0	34.7	18.6	15.4	14.8	11.1	2.9	1.7	0.8	†
2008–09	100.0	34.6	18.8	15.2	14.7	11.1	2.9	1.7	0.8	†
2009–10	100.0	35.0	18.9	15.1	14.6	11.0	2.9	1.7	0.8	†
2010–11	100.0	35.0	19.0	15.2	14.5	10.9	2.9	1.7	0.8	†
2011–12	100.0	35.3	18.8	15.1	14.4	10.9	2.9	1.8	0.8	†
2012–13	100.0	35.6	18.7	15.2	14.2	10.9	2.9	1.8	0.8	†
2013–14	100.0	35.6	19.0	15.1	14.1	10.7	2.9	1.7	0.8	†
2014–15	100.0	35.7	19.2	15.0	13.9	10.8	2.9	1.7	0.8	†
2015–16	100.0	35.7	19.3	14.9	13.8	10.7	2.9	1.7	0.8	†
2016–17	100.0	35.7	19.3	15.0	13.9	10.7	2.9	1.8	0.8	†

†Not applicable.

[1]Because of expanded survey coverage, data for 1979–89 are not directly comparable with figures for later years.

NOTE: Size not reported (column 11) includes school districts reporting enrollment of zero and school districts whose enrollment counts were suppressed because they failed data quality edits. Regular districts exclude regional education service agencies and supervisory union administrative centers, state-operated agencies, federally operated agencies, and other types of local education agencies, such as independent charter schools. Enrollment totals differ from other tables because this table represents data reported by regular school districts rather than states or schools. Detail may not sum to totals because of rounding.

SOURCE: U.S. Department of Education, National Center for Education Statistics, Common Core of Data (CCD), "Local Education Agency Universe Survey," 1979–80 through 2016–17. (This table was prepared April 2019.)

Table 214.30. Number of public elementary and secondary education agencies, by type of agency and state or jurisdiction: 2015–16 and 2016–17

			Type of agency											
	Total agencies		Regular school districts[1]		Regional education service agencies and supervisory union administrative centers		State-operated agencies		Federally operated agencies		Independent charter schools		Other agencies[2]	
State or jurisdiction	2015–16	2016–17	2015–16	2016–17	2015–16	2016–17	2015–16	2016–17	2015–16	2016–17	2015–16	2016–17	2015–16	2016–17
1	2	3	4	5	6	7	8	9	10	11	12	13	14	15
United States	**18,321**	**18,343**	**13,584**	**13,598**	**1,377**	**1,350**	**261**	**254**	**4**	**4**	**2,959**	**2,998**	**136**	**139**
Alabama	180	178	134	134	0	0	46	43	0	0	0	1	0	0
Alaska	54	54	53	53	0	0	1	1	0	0	0	0	0	0
Arizona	692	699	234	226	8	16	9	9	0	0	427	434	14	14
Arkansas	289	292	233	234	15	15	5	5	0	0	23	25	13	13
California	1,163	1,159	1,058	1,057	76	73	4	4	0	0	25	25	0	0
Colorado	265	267	178	178	81	83	4	4	0	0	2	2	0	0
Connecticut	205	205	169	169	6	6	6	6	0	0	24	24	0	0
Delaware	50	49	19	19	1	1	2	2	0	0	28	27	0	0
District of Columbia	59	61	1	1	0	0	1	1	0	0	57	59	0	0
Florida	75	76	67	67	0	0	2	2	0	0	1	2	5	5
Georgia	223	226	180	180	16	16	7	7	0	0	20	23	0	0
Hawaii	1	1	1	1	0	0	0	0	0	0	0	0	0	0
Idaho	159	160	115	115	2	2	3	3	0	0	39	40	0	0
Illinois	1,052	1,057	854	854	186	187	5	6	0	0	5	8	2	2
Indiana	418	423	294	294	30	30	4	4	0	0	88	93	2	2
Iowa	345	342	336	333	9	9	0	0	0	0	0	0	0	0
Kansas	317	317	307	307	0	0	10	10	0	0	0	0	0	0
Kentucky	186	186	173	173	9	9	4	3	0	0	0	0	0	1
Louisiana	179	185	69	69	0	0	6	6	0	0	99	105	5	5
Maine	267	268	248	249	8	8	4	2	0	0	7	9	0	0
Maryland	25	25	24	24	0	0	1	1	0	0	0	0	0	0
Massachusetts	408	431	239	326	87	26	1	1	0	0	81	78	0	0
Michigan	902	901	542	540	56	56	5	4	0	0	299	301	0	0
Minnesota	564	567	332	332	63	65	4	4	0	0	165	166	0	0
Mississippi	157	158	144	144	0	0	11	11	0	0	2	3	0	0
Missouri	567	566	518	518	0	0	6	6	0	0	39	38	4	4
Montana	490	487	404	401	77	77	4	4	0	0	0	0	5	5
Nebraska	284	284	245	245	34	34	5	5	0	0	0	0	0	0
Nevada	19	19	18	18	0	0	0	0	0	0	1	1	0	0
New Hampshire	299	301	180	180	95	97	0	0	0	0	24	24	0	0
New Jersey	694	678	601	565	0	20	4	4	0	0	89	88	0	1
New Mexico	158	157	89	89	0	0	6	6	0	0	63	62	0	0
New York[3]	989	999	690	689	37	37	6	6	0	0	256	267	0	0
North Carolina	297	306	115	115	1	1	4	4	3	3	158	167	16	16
North Dakota	222	226	175	178	44	45	3	3	0	0	0	0	0	0
Ohio	1,103	1,088	622	620	104	102	4	4	0	0	373	362	0	0
Oklahoma	605	600	516	513	0	0	3	3	0	0	32	31	54	53
Oregon	221	221	179	179	19	19	5	5	0	0	18	18	0	0
Pennsylvania	784	789	500	500	102	102	6	7	0	0	175	179	1	1
Rhode Island	64	63	32	32	4	4	9	8	0	0	19	19	0	0
South Carolina	102	101	84	84	11	11	3	3	0	0	2	1	2	2
South Dakota	168	167	150	150	14	14	4	3	0	0	0	0	0	0
Tennessee	146	146	146	146	0	0	0	0	0	0	0	0	0	0
Texas	1,232	1,228	1,026	1,025	20	20	3	3	0	0	183	180	0	0
Utah	152	156	41	41	4	4	3	3	0	0	104	108	0	0
Vermont	356	342	291	278	62	63	1	1	0	0	0	0	2	0
Virginia	222	222	130	130	71	71	20	20	1	1	0	0	0	0
Washington	330	332	301	299	9	10	0	0	0	0	9	8	11	15
West Virginia	57	57	55	55	0	0	2	2	0	0	0	0	0	0
Wisconsin	465	461	424	421	16	17	3	3	0	0	22	20	0	0
Wyoming	60	60	48	48	0	0	12	12	0	0	0	0	0	0
Jurisdiction														
Bureau of Indian Education	196	174	174	0	22	174	0	0	0	0	0	0	0	0
DoDEA	14	8	0	0	0	0	0	0	14	8	0	0	0	0
Other jurisdictions														
American Samoa	1	1	1	1	0	0	0	0	0	0	0	0	0	0
Guam	1	1	1	1	0	0	0	0	0	0	0	0	0	0
Northern Marianas	—	—	—	—	—	—	—	—	—	—	—	—	—	—
Puerto Rico	1	1	1	1	0	0	0	0	0	0	0	0	0	0
U.S. Virgin Islands	2	2	2	2	0	0	0	0	0	0	0	0	0	0

—Not available.
[1]Regular school districts include both independent districts and those that are a dependent segment of a local government. Also includes components of supervisory unions that operate schools, but share superintendent services with other districts.
[2]Includes public agencies that provide education but are not school districts, such as juvenile correctional institutions, sheriff's offices, hospitals, residential treatment centers, or university lab schools.
[3]New York City counted as one school district.
NOTE: DoDEA = Department of Defense Education Activities.
SOURCE: U.S. Department of Education, National Center for Education Statistics, Common Core of Data (CCD), "Local Education Agency Universe Survey," 2015–16 and 2016–17. (This table was prepared April 2019.)

Table 214.40. Public elementary and secondary school enrollment, number of schools, and other selected characteristics, by locale: Fall 2013 through fall 2016

Enrollment, number of schools, and other characteristics	Total	City				Suburban				Town				Rural				Locale unknown
		Total	Large[1]	Mid-size[2]	Small[3]	Total	Large[4]	Mid-size[5]	Small[6]	Total	Fringe[7]	Distant[8]	Remote[9]	Total	Fringe[10]	Distant[11]	Remote[12]	
1	2	3	4	5	6	7	8	9	10	11	12	13	14	15	16	17	18	19
Fall 2013																		
Enrollment (in thousands)	49,777	15,136	8,039	3,397	3,699	19,794	16,986	1,823	985	5,691	1,438	2,509	1,744	9,156	5,225	2,899	1,032	†
Percentage distribution of enrollment, by race/ethnicity	100.0	100.0	100.0	100.0	100.0	100.0	100.0	100.0	100.0	100.0	100.0	100.0	100.0	100.0	100.0	100.0	100.0	†
White	50.3	30.0	20.7	33.1	47.3	51.5	49.7	61.4	65.1	64.7	68.6	65.6	60.4	72.4	67.8	80.1	73.7	†
Black	15.6	23.9	26.5	24.6	17.7	13.6	14.3	10.3	8.3	10.1	7.0	11.7	10.4	9.3	10.9	7.5	6.9	†
Hispanic	24.9	35.1	41.5	32.3	23.9	24.8	25.6	20.3	19.5	18.4	18.3	17.1	20.4	12.2	15.2	7.7	9.3	†
Asian	4.8	6.7	7.6	5.4	6.0	6.0	6.5	3.0	3.2	1.3	1.5	1.0	1.5	1.4	2.1	0.5	0.5	†
Pacific Islander	0.4	0.4	0.4	0.4	0.4	0.4	0.4	0.5	0.2	0.4	0.4	0.1	0.9	0.2	0.2	0.1	0.3	†
American Indian/Alaska Native	1.0	0.7	0.7	0.6	0.8	0.5	0.4	0.7	0.7	2.2	1.2	1.7	3.8	2.1	1.1	2.0	7.4	†
Two or more races	3.0	3.2	2.7	3.7	3.8	3.2	3.1	3.9	3.1	2.8	3.0	2.8	2.7	2.4	2.7	2.1	2.0	†
Students participating in English language learner (ELL) programs (in thousands)[13]	4,568	2,159	1,368	450	342	1,816	1,637	114	65	340	76	151	112	253	156	59	39	†
ELL program participants as a percent of enrollment[13]	9.2	13.7	16.1	12.4	9.5	8.5	8.9	5.9	6.8	6.0	5.9	6.0	6.1	3.5	4.4	2.2	3.9	†
Schools	98,271	26,581	13,910	5,916	6,755	30,941	25,795	3,224	1,922	13,485	2,962	5,893	4,630	27,264	10,333	10,442	6,489	†
Average school size[14]	525	590	592	605	574	657	676	582	536	446	501	450	403	347	527	286	164	†
Pupil/teacher ratio[15]	16.3	17.0	17.3	17.1	16.3	16.7	16.7	16.3	17.0	15.8	16.5	15.7	15.4	14.9	15.9	14.3	12.5	†
Enrollment (percentage distribution)	100.0	30.4	16.2	6.8	7.4	39.8	34.1	3.7	2.0	11.4	2.9	5.0	3.5	18.4	10.5	5.8	2.1	†
Schools (percentage distribution)	100.0	27.0	14.2	6.0	6.9	31.5	26.2	3.3	2.0	13.7	3.0	6.0	4.7	27.7	10.5	10.6	6.6	†
Fall 2014																		
Enrollment (in thousands)	50,010	15,235	8,042	3,319	3,874	19,882	17,072	1,821	989	5,680	1,436	2,694	1,549	9,213	5,310	2,881	1,022	†
Percentage distribution of enrollment, by race/ethnicity	100.0	100.0	100.0	100.0	100.0	100.0	100.0	100.0	100.0	100.0	100.0	100.0	100.0	100.0	100.0	100.0	100.0	†
White	49.6	29.5	20.4	32.5	45.8	50.6	48.7	60.7	64.4	64.2	67.8	65.4	58.9	71.6	66.9	79.6	73.3	†
Black	15.5	23.7	26.1	25.0	17.5	13.7	14.4	10.1	8.4	10.0	7.0	11.6	10.1	9.4	10.9	7.5	6.8	†
Hispanic	25.4	35.6	42.0	32.1	25.4	25.4	26.2	21.0	19.8	18.9	19.0	17.3	21.6	12.7	15.9	8.1	9.5	†
Asian	4.9	6.8	7.6	5.5	6.2	6.1	6.6	3.0	3.2	1.3	1.5	1.0	1.6	1.4	2.1	0.5	0.5	†
Pacific Islander	0.3	0.4	0.4	0.4	0.4	0.4	0.4	0.5	0.2	0.4	0.4	0.1	0.9	0.2	0.2	0.1	0.3	†
American Indian/Alaska Native	1.0	0.7	0.7	0.6	0.8	0.5	0.4	0.7	0.7	2.2	1.2	1.6	4.1	2.1	1.1	2.0	7.5	†
Two or more races	3.2	3.4	2.9	3.9	4.0	3.4	3.3	4.1	3.4	3.0	3.1	3.0	2.8	2.6	2.9	2.2	2.1	†
Students participating in English language learner (ELL) programs (in thousands)[13]	4,670	2,186	1,358	441	387	1,879	1,696	116	67	352	79	160	113	255	159	61	35	†
ELL program participants as a percent of enrollment[13]	9.3	13.8	16.2	12.2	10.2	8.8	9.1	6.2	6.7	6.2	5.9	5.9	6.8	3.5	4.5	2.2	3.6	†
Schools	98,176	26,560	13,870	5,745	6,945	31,099	25,966	3,217	1,916	13,391	2,949	6,299	4,143	27,126	10,422	10,315	6,389	†
Average school size[14]	525	591	593	599	579	655	673	579	537	445	500	448	398	350	528	286	165	†
Pupil/teacher ratio[15]	16.2	16.9	17.1	17.0	16.3	16.5	16.5	16.2	16.9	15.8	16.4	15.6	15.5	14.9	15.9	14.2	12.5	†
Enrollment (percentage distribution)	100.0	30.5	16.1	6.6	7.7	39.8	34.1	3.6	2.0	11.4	2.9	5.4	3.1	18.4	10.6	5.8	2.0	†
Schools (percentage distribution)	100.0	27.1	14.1	5.9	7.1	31.7	26.4	3.3	2.0	13.6	3.0	6.4	4.2	27.6	10.6	10.5	6.5	†
Fall 2015																		
Enrollment (in thousands)	50,112	15,276	8,276	3,368	3,632	19,903	17,095	1,819	989	5,630	1,422	2,670	1,538	9,303	5,434	2,855	1,014	3
Percentage distribution of enrollment, by race/ethnicity	100.0	100.0	100.0	100.0	100.0	100.0	100.0	100.0	100.0	100.0	100.0	100.0	100.0	100.0	100.0	100.0	100.0	100.0
White	48.9	29.1	20.2	32.6	46.0	49.7	47.8	59.9	63.6	63.6	67.1	64.8	58.3	70.8	65.9	79.3	73.1	48.7
Black	15.4	23.4	25.7	24.2	17.4	13.7	14.4	10.2	8.4	10.0	7.0	11.5	10.1	9.4	11.0	7.3	6.6	11.5
Hispanic	25.9	36.0	42.4	32.4	24.8	25.9	26.7	21.5	20.3	19.4	19.5	17.8	22.1	13.2	16.4	8.4	9.7	30.1
Asian	5.0	6.8	7.6	5.6	6.4	6.3	6.8	3.0	3.2	1.3	1.5	1.0	1.6	1.5	2.3	0.5	0.5	5.5
Pacific Islander	0.4	0.4	0.4	0.4	0.4	0.4	0.4	0.5	0.2	0.4	0.4	0.1	0.9	0.2	0.2	0.1	0.3	0.2
American Indian/Alaska Native	1.0	0.7	0.7	0.6	0.8	0.4	0.4	0.6	0.7	2.1	1.1	1.5	4.0	2.1	1.1	2.0	7.5	0.3
Two or more races	3.4	3.6	3.0	4.2	4.3	3.6	3.5	4.4	3.6	3.2	3.3	3.2	3.0	2.8	3.1	2.4	2.3	3.6

See notes at end of table.

Table 214.40. Public elementary and secondary school enrollment, number of schools, and other selected characteristics, by locale: Fall 2013 through fall 2016—Continued

Enrollment, number of schools, and other characteristics	Total	City				Suburban				Town				Rural				Locale unknown
		Total	Large[1]	Mid-size[2]	Small[3]	Total	Large[4]	Mid-size[5]	Small[6]	Total	Fringe[7]	Distant[8]	Remote[9]	Total	Fringe[10]	Distant[11]	Remote[12]	
1	2	3	4	5	6	7	8	9	10	11	12	13	14	15	16	17	18	19
Number of English language learner (ELL) students (in thousands)[13]	4,795	2,217	1,402	452	363	1,941	1,754	119	68	365	81	164	120	272	173	64	36	#
ELL students as a percent of enrollment[13]	9.5	14.0	16.3	12.4	10.0	9.1	9.5	6.5	6.7	6.5	6.2	6.1	7.4	3.6	4.5	2.4	3.7	0.9
Schools	98,277	26,636	14,214	5,828	6,594	31,081	25,963	3,209	1,909	13,307	2,922	6,279	4,106	27,146	10,546	10,262	6,338	107
Average school size[14]	526	591	595	598	575	657	675	582	538	445	500	447	401	354	535	285	165	26
Pupil/teacher ratio[15]	16.2	16.8	17.1	16.8	16.3	16.5	16.5	16.4	16.8	15.8	16.3	15.7	15.4	14.9	15.9	14.3	12.5	11.8
Enrollment (percentage distribution)	100.0	30.5	16.5	6.7	7.2	39.7	34.1	3.6	2.0	11.2	2.8	5.3	3.1	18.6	10.8	5.7	2.0	#
Schools (percentage distribution)	100.0	27.1	14.5	5.9	6.7	31.6	26.4	3.3	1.9	13.5	3.0	6.4	4.2	27.6	10.7	10.4	6.4	0.1
Fall 2016																		
Enrollment (in thousands)	50,283	15,316	8,356	3,386	3,573	19,918	17,107	1,822	989	5,560	1,415	2,631	1,513	9,489	5,635	2,845	1,010	†
Percentage distribution of enrollment, by race/ethnicity	100.0	100.0	100.0	100.0	100.0	100.0	100.0	100.0	100.0	100.0	100.0	100.0	100.0	100.0	100.0	100.0	100.0	†
White	48.2	28.7	20.1	32.2	45.3	48.7	46.9	58.9	62.8	63.1	66.4	64.2	58.0	69.9	64.9	78.9	72.8	†
Black	15.3	23.2	25.3	23.9	17.4	13.6	14.3	10.3	8.3	9.9	7.0	11.3	10.0	9.4	11.0	7.2	6.4	†
Hispanic	26.4	36.4	42.5	33.3	25.0	26.5	27.3	22.1	20.8	19.8	19.9	18.3	22.2	13.8	17.2	8.7	9.8	†
Asian	5.1	6.9	7.8	5.2	6.4	6.4	7.0	3.1	3.3	1.3	1.5	1.0	1.6	1.6	2.4	0.5	0.5	†
Pacific Islander	0.4	0.4	0.4	0.4	0.4	0.4	0.4	0.4	0.2	0.4	0.4	0.1	0.9	0.2	0.3	0.1	0.3	†
American Indian/Alaska Native	1.0	0.7	0.7	0.6	0.8	0.4	0.4	0.6	0.6	2.1	1.1	1.6	4.1	2.0	1.0	2.0	7.7	†
Two or more races	3.6	3.8	3.2	4.4	4.6	3.9	3.8	4.7	3.9	3.4	3.6	3.4	3.2	3.0	3.3	2.6	2.5	†
Number of English language learner (ELL) students (in thousands)[13]	4,857	2,238	1,420	459	360	1,974	1,795	111	68	358	80	160	118	286	187	64	35	†
ELL students as a percent of enrollment[13]	9.6	14.0	16.2	12.4	10.1	9.3	9.7	6.3	6.9	6.5	6.4	6.0	7.4	3.8	4.7	2.4	3.6	†
Number of students with disabilities (in thousands)[13]	6,448	1,978	1,082	435	462	2,694	2,332	236	125	746	166	370	210	1,030	526	367	137	†
Students with disabilities as a percent of enrollment[13]	13.5	13.6	14.1	12.6	13.4	13.2	13.1	13.8	13.6	14.0	13.7	14.2	13.9	13.9	13.7	13.9	14.7	†
Schools	98,169	26,658	14,315	5,865	6,478	31,068	25,950	3,218	1,900	13,148	2,912	6,205	4,031	27,295	10,791	10,193	6,311	†
Average school size[14]	528	591	596	597	574	656	674	580	538	444	500	446	399	358	541	285	165	†
Pupil/teacher ratio[15]	16.2	16.8	16.9	16.8	16.3	16.5	16.5	16.3	17.0	15.8	16.3	15.7	15.5	15.0	15.9	14.3	12.6	†
Enrollment (percentage distribution)	100.0	30.5	16.6	6.7	7.1	39.6	34.0	3.6	2.0	11.1	2.8	5.2	3.0	18.9	11.2	5.7	2.0	†
Schools (percentage distribution)	100.0	27.2	14.6	6.0	6.6	31.6	26.4	3.3	1.9	13.4	3.0	6.3	4.1	27.8	11.0	10.4	6.4	†

†Not applicable.
#Rounds to zero.
[1]Located inside an urbanized area and inside a principal city with a population of 250,000 or more.
[2]Located inside an urbanized area and inside a principal city with a population of at least 100,000, but less than 250,000.
[3]Located inside an urbanized area and inside a principal city with a population less than 100,000.
[4]Located inside an urbanized area and outside a principal city with a population of 250,000 or more.
[5]Located inside an urbanized area and outside a principal city with a population of at least 100,000, but less than 250,000.
[6]Located inside an urbanized area and outside a principal city with a population less than 100,000.
[7]Located inside an urban cluster that is 10 miles or less from an urbanized area.
[8]Located inside an urban cluster that is more than 10 but less than or equal to 35 miles from an urbanized area.
[9]Located inside an urban cluster that is more than 35 miles from an urbanized area.
[10]Located outside any urbanized area or urban cluster, but 5 miles or less from an urbanized area or 2.5 miles or less from an urban cluster.
[11]Located outside any urbanized area or urban cluster and more than 5 miles but less than or equal to 25 miles from an urbanized area, or more than 2.5 miles but less than or equal to 10 miles from an urban cluster.
[12]Located outside any urbanized area or urban cluster, more than 25 miles from an urbanized area, and more than 10 miles from an urban cluster.
[13]Data are based on locales of school districts rather than locales of schools as in the rest of the table. ELL data include imputations for New York in 2013. Data for 2014 and earlier years include only those ELL students who participated in ELL programs. Starting with 2015, data include all ELL students, regardless of program participation.
[14]Average for schools reporting enrollment. Enrollment data were available for 94,876 out of 98,271 schools in 2013–14, 95,230 out of 98,176 schools in 2014–15, 95,240 out of 98,277 schools in 2015–16, and 95,306 out of 98,169 schools in 2016–17.
[15]Ratio for schools reporting both full-time-equivalent teachers and fall enrollment data.
NOTE: Detail may not sum to totals because of rounding. Race categories exclude persons of Hispanic ethnicity. Enrollment and ratios are based on data reported by schools and may differ from data reported in other tables that reflect aggregate totals reported by states.
SOURCE: U.S. Department of Education, National Center for Education Statistics, Common Core of Data (CCD), "Public Elementary/Secondary School Universe Survey," 2013–14, 2014–15, 2015–16, and 2016–17; and "Local Education Agency Universe Survey," 2013–14, 2014–15, 2015–16, and 2016–17. (This table was prepared October 2018.)

Table 215.30. Enrollment, poverty, and federal funds for the 120 largest school districts, by enrollment size in 2016: 2015–16 and fiscal year 2018

Name of district	State	Rank order	Enrollment, fall 2016	5- to 17-year-old population, 2016	5- to 17-year-olds in poverty, 2016[1]	Poverty rate of 5- to 17-year-olds, 2016[1]	Revenues by source of funds, 2015–16: Total (in thousands)	Federal (in thousands)	Federal as a percent of total	Federal revenue per student[3]	Revenue from selected federal programs (in thousands), 2015–16: Title I	School lunch	Individuals with Disabilities Education Act (IDEA)	Eisenhower math and science	Vocational education	Drug-free schools	Federal Title I allocations (in thousands), federal fiscal year 2018[2]: Total	Basic Grants	Concentration Grants	Targeted Grants	Education Finance Incentive Grants
1	2	3	4	5	6	7	8	9	10	11	12	13	14	15	16	17	18	19	20	21	22
New York City	NY	1	984,462	1,245,611	328,553	26.4	$27,448,356	$1,739,101	6.3	$1,772	$656,226	$442,300	$291,052	$0	$13,209	$0	$786,291	$263,726	$63,591	$244,742	$214,232
Los Angeles Unified	CA	2	633,621	715,436	194,823	27.2	10,329,380	1,091,400	10.6	1,707	356,168	368,564	125,629	38,351	7,877	0	426,351	128,870	31,074	128,537	137,870
City of Chicago (SD 299)	IL	3	378,199	408,677	108,558	26.6	5,272,668	792,420	15.0	2,046	307,138	204,737	93,483	34,208	6,117	0	283,988	86,598	20,881	83,464	93,045
Dade	FL	4	357,249	394,651	93,050	23.6	3,590,773	431,519	12.0	1,207	129,923	139,474	72,402	11,474	5,233	0	147,913	49,168	11,856	46,767	40,123
Clark County	NV	5	326,953	367,926	69,496	18.9	3,220,684	277,628	8.6	852	93,953	105,672	43,115	5,706	4,008	0	106,449	36,988	8,919	34,145	26,398
Broward	FL	6	271,852	295,468	48,843	16.5	2,607,068	278,292	10.7	1,034	63,140	83,798	57,031	9,849	2,872	0	74,139	25,870	6,238	22,623	19,409
Houston ISD	TX	7	216,106	248,155	76,878	31.0	2,480,131	293,958	11.9	1,363	82,708	109,055	38,873	12,489	2,917	0	125,571	40,694	9,812	37,986	37,079
Hillsborough	FL	8	214,386	228,744	43,271	18.9	2,098,358	308,427	14.7	1,455	70,281	84,928	45,151	8,465	2,883	0	65,509	23,144	5,581	19,798	16,986
Orange	FL	9	200,674	213,379	44,506	20.9	2,253,016	219,981	9.8	1,117	62,310	80,993	39,806	7,004	2,499	0	66,586	23,484	5,663	20,151	17,288
Palm Beach	FL	10	192,721	205,311	35,926	17.5	2,038,576	187,376	9.2	990	50,544	64,971	39,110	0	1,875	0	52,555	19,053	4,594	15,559	13,348
Fairfax County	VA	11	187,467	197,292	13,070	6.6	2,733,933	126,061	4.6	678	18,754	34,053	33,107	2,445	1,710	0	23,210	8,290	1,999	5,983	6,938
Hawaii Department of Education	HI	12	181,550	216,481	21,877	10.1	3,030,519	261,131	8.6	1,435	51,530	59,215	42,338	466	2,538	280	49,811	18,618	4,325	13,470	13,399
Gwinnett County	GA	13	178,214	185,631	28,329	15.3	1,893,150	142,728	7.5	811	37,832	65,091	27,303	2,613	1,134	0	42,282	14,995	3,616	11,973	11,697
Wake County	NC	14	160,467	190,315	19,440	10.2	1,380,356	109,144	7.9	691	26,914	30,191	31,734	2,757	0	0	28,950	10,336	2,491	7,944	8,179
Montgomery County	MD	15	159,010	177,421	14,769	8.3	2,898,647	112,717	3.9	721	21,826	36,008	32,390	3,759	1,138	0	31,766	11,782	2,841	8,710	8,432
Dallas ISD	TX	16	157,886	195,691	59,579	30.4	1,896,322	287,161	15.1	1,811	78,862	100,100	23,695	8,585	2,215	0	95,531	31,561	7,610	28,520	27,840
Charlotte-Mecklenburg	NC	17	147,428	183,372	31,461	17.2	1,389,280	146,058	10.5	999	45,987	51,195	29,782	1,163	0	0	47,686	16,590	4,000	13,351	13,746
Philadelphia City	PA	18	133,929	238,855	86,599	36.3	3,030,964	271,369	9.0	2,024	112,879	79,478	0	6,723	4,257	0	231,909	70,377	16,970	66,654	77,908
Prince George's County	MD	19	130,814	144,242	17,574	12.2	2,206,548	145,009	6.6	1,125	36,153	56,104	28,191	4,257	39	0	38,354	14,023	3,381	10,645	10,305
Duval	FL	20	129,479	147,336	28,913	19.6	1,211,671	150,524	12.4	1,165	39,064	47,889	36,787	5,070	1,294	0	42,289	15,701	3,750	12,292	10,546
San Diego Unified	CA	21	128,040	138,882	25,011	18.0	1,790,524	151,427	8.5	1,170	35,955	49,465	24,725	8,279	1,103	0	44,091	15,904	3,835	12,565	11,788
Cypress-Fairbanks ISD	TX	22	114,868	118,190	16,982	14.4	1,175,118	83,219	7.1	730	16,187	33,897	16,667	1,081	932	0	24,569	8,989	2,168	6,787	6,625
Cobb County	GA	23	113,151	124,723	15,084	12.1	1,239,449	87,739	7.1	778	23,154	30,628	20,596	1,965	730	0	21,883	8,077	1,948	5,999	5,860
Baltimore County	MD	24	112,139	130,717	13,929	10.7	1,782,381	102,256	5.7	920	26,382	31,245	25,992	3,425	941	0	30,632	11,397	2,748	8,377	8,110
Shelby County	TN	25	111,403	132,312	44,897	33.9	1,218,671	212,572	17.4	1,857	64,329	79,600	26,140	0	2,068	1,155	70,761	23,816	5,743	20,494	20,708
Northside ISD	TX	26	106,145	107,911	16,239	15.0	1,118,501	103,429	9.2	984	18,084	31,320	18,178	1,853	877	0	23,773	8,719	2,102	6,554	6,397
Pinellas	FL	27	102,905	116,901	19,940	17.1	1,036,722	115,587	11.1	1,117	26,409	39,243	29,343	4,110	1,408	0	28,617	10,694	2,579	8,259	7,085
Polk	FL	28	102,295	110,382	26,477	24.0	962,439	123,726	12.9	1,217	30,574	45,015	18,896	5,450	1,340	0	38,121	14,034	3,384	11,143	9,560
DeKalb County	GA	29	101,284	115,181	28,144	24.4	1,194,250	121,738	10.2	1,201	40,696	43,005	28,170	3,544	1,093	0	42,484	15,064	3,632	12,033	11,755
Jefferson County	KY	30	99,813	122,586	23,365	19.1	1,323,404	155,985	11.8	1,548	41,698	53,236	24,511	4,786	1,171	0	40,995	13,652	3,292	10,737	13,314
Fulton County	GA	31	96,122	113,312	18,050	15.9	1,196,919	76,288	6.4	798	24,177	26,120	18,206	1,886	628	0	26,268	9,564	2,306	7,283	7,115
Lee	FL	32	92,686	96,845	19,529	20.2	929,289	111,503	12.0	1,221	27,563	37,927	16,881	2,332	1,176	0	27,676	10,363	2,499	7,973	6,840
Denver	CO	33	91,138	96,455	19,503	20.2	1,271,873	128,902	10.1	1,429	33,242	36,083	17,173	4,525	1,676	0	32,442	10,873	2,622	8,382	10,565
Albuquerque	NM	34	90,651	112,667	23,996	21.3	1,021,201	102,693	10.1	1,134	29,733	22	17,787	0	1,535	0	38,271	13,083	3,155	10,322	11,712
Prince William County	VA	35	89,345	90,603	7,770	8.6	1,110,691	60,078	5.4	684	10,645	27,010	13,587	733	728	0	12,391	4,917	1,186	3,076	3,212
Fort Worth ISD	TX	36	87,428	94,508	28,946	30.6	963,004	136,873	14.2	1,572	39,262	41,590	14,267	5,880	1,047	0	43,144	15,291	3,687	12,229	11,937
Jefferson County, No. R1	CO	37	86,371	86,109	6,117	7.1	929,179	50,952	5.5	587	11,256	13,650	15,592	2,058	405	0	9,015	3,577	862	2,196	2,381
Davidson County	TN	38	85,163	98,704	22,632	22.9	1,004,078	114,198	11.4	1,334	31,282	47,021	21,049	0	1,296	1,136	33,968	12,068	2,910	9,446	9,544
Austin ISD	TX	39	83,067	102,363	17,478	17.1	1,238,622	107,568	8.7	1,286	27,145	27,731	15,124	1,973	880	0	25,984	9,691	2,308	7,077	6,908
Baltimore City	MD	40	82,354	89,009	27,470	30.9	1,420,023	160,881	11.3	1,923	52,749	49,872	22,568	5,999	1,487	0	62,633	22,279	5,372	17,775	17,207
Anne Arundel County	MD	41	81,379	92,347	7,809	8.5	1,206,658	55,404	4.6	689	10,300	16,659	17,759	1,943	599	0	15,320	6,190	1,493	3,881	3,757
Alpine	UT	42	78,957	87,585	6,253	7.1	603,204	32,485	5.4	422	5,589	9,595	11,011	957	633	0	8,565	3,367	804	2,047	2,347
Loudoun County	VA	43	78,348	82,840	2,610	3.2	1,089,781	21,500	2.0	282	1,674	7,562	9,077	559	437	0	1,703	1,703	0	0	0
Greenville, 01	SC	44	76,918	86,981	12,159	14.0	855,902	72,818	8.5	954	25,419	23,153	15,853	1,796	1,100	0	19,288	6,910	1,666	4,932	5,780
Long Beach Unified	CA	45	76,428	84,056	19,563	23.3	1,075,291	110,337	10.3	1,418	29,141	30,867	14,964	5,325	728	0	34,261	12,576	3,032	9,691	8,962

See notes at end of table.

Table 215.30. Enrollment, poverty, and federal funds for the 120 largest school districts, by enrollment size in 2016: 2015–16 and fiscal year 2018—Continued

							Revenues by source of funds, 2015–16				Revenue from selected federal programs (in thousands), 2015–16						Federal Title I allocations (in thousands), federal fiscal year 2018[2]				
Name of district	State	Rank order	Enroll-ment, fall 2016	5- to 17-year-old population, 2016	5- to 17-year-olds in poverty, 2016[1]	Poverty rate of 5- to 17-year-olds, 2016[1]	Total (in thousands)	Federal (in thousands)	Federal as a percent of total	Federal revenue per student[3]	Title I	School lunch	Individuals with Disabilities Education Act (IDEA)	Eisen-hower math and science	Voca-tional education	Drug-free schools	Total	Basic Grants	Concen-tration Grants	Targeted Grants	Education Finance Incentive Grants
1	2	3	4	5	6	7	8	9	10	11	12	13	14	15	16	17	18	19	20	21	22
Milwaukee	WI	46	76,206	110,915	37,495	33.8	1,186,209	178,749	15.1	2,360	70,414	46,720	17,438	0	1,883	0	75,912	24,378	5,878	20,158	25,497
Katy ISD	TX	47	75,428	67,757	6,399	9.4	835,819	45,898	5.5	629	5,952	11,582	11,340	529	404	0	7,879	3,396	374	2,079	2,030
Fort Bend ISD	TX	48	74,146	90,019	9,879	11.0	758,885	45,181	6.0	618	9,526	11,481	11,907	1,367	548	0	13,753	5,320	1,283	3,618	3,532
Brevard	FL	49	73,444	79,542	14,998	18.9	724,781	75,416	10.4	1,037	18,228	20,825	17,175	2,267	691	0	20,885	7,977	1,923	5,912	5,072
Fresno Unified	CA	50	73,356	80,662	34,739	43.1	998,861	120,771	12.1	1,644	42,155	47,235	15,069	5,671	1,315	0	62,692	22,201	5,353	18,003	17,134
Guilford County	NC	51	73,059	86,576	20,490	23.7	692,064	88,862	12.8	1,215	24,519	33,352	14,679	1,698	0	0	30,451	10,833	2,612	8,379	8,627
Davis	UT	52	72,987	81,884	4,983	6.1	565,357	44,924	7.9	626	4,678	11,810	10,508	1,203	566	0	6,515	2,644	539	1,560	1,772
Pasco	FL	53	72,493	77,344	12,760	16.5	698,805	72,438	10.4	1,027	14,751	24,279	16,635	1,836	607	0	17,529	6,798	1,639	4,894	4,199
Aldine ISD	TX	54	69,768	66,271	22,388	33.8	758,420	101,027	13.3	1,435	26,952	40,183	12,975	2,260	770	0	33,002	11,851	2,857	9,258	9,037
Granite	UT	55	69,580	83,404	10,403	12.5	557,620	62,079	11.1	886	14,342	23,182	11,924	2,087	1,026	0	15,286	5,505	1,327	3,777	4,677
Virginia Beach City	VA	56	69,085	72,563	7,721	10.6	792,261	58,564	7.4	839	10,445	16,100	15,403	2,254	741	0	12,431	4,933	1,189	3,086	3,223
Seminole	FL	57	67,808	72,393	8,965	12.4	636,054	54,132	8.5	808	11,828	19,604	12,698	1,841	556	0	11,756	4,769	1,150	3,142	2,695
North East ISD	TX	58	67,531	79,190	11,312	14.3	733,799	55,786	7.6	823	12,479	18,888	11,459	1,254	642	0	15,974	6,074	1,465	4,269	4,167
Douglas County, No. RE1	CO	59	67,470	70,114	1,750	2.5	682,388	18,449	2.7	276	1,657	3,796	8,616	529	147	0	984	984	0	0	0
Washoe County	NV	60	66,671	72,321	10,876	15.0	661,369	71,496	10.8	1,075	16,928	16,893	10,280	1,946	699	12	14,085	5,885	1,419	4,106	2,675
Mesa Unified	AZ	61	63,444	83,390	18,730	22.5	542,277	64,742	11.9	1,021	20,039	23,835	8,155	2,083	855	190	28,945	10,289	2,481	7,909	8,266
Elk Grove Unified	CA	62	63,061	69,369	12,093	17.4	736,543	58,357	7.9	930	16,027	20,710	10,684	1,601	527	0	19,966	7,736	1,865	5,511	4,853
Osceola	FL	63	63,031	61,371	13,740	22.4	602,465	72,832	12.1	1,177	18,837	28,752	11,568	2,027	812	0	18,771	7,234	1,744	5,271	4,522
Volusia	FL	64	63,028	68,964	12,608	18.3	624,595	66,211	10.6	1,052	22,403	20,722	13,802	2,428	713	0	18,179	7,105	1,697	5,059	4,317
Arlington ISD	TX	65	62,181	70,756	15,923	22.5	666,458	75,712	11.4	1,198	20,870	24,499	9,707	1,387	685	0	22,844	8,404	2,027	6,281	6,132
Knox County	TN	66	60,372	70,385	11,257	16.0	538,759	54,877	10.2	910	16,672	20,849	13,830	0	837	0	16,158	6,086	1,468	4,280	4,324
San Francisco Unified	CA	67	60,133	78,037	9,639	12.4	1,019,158	53,514	5.3	909	12,391	17,704	0	2,756	14	26	15,200	6,123	1,476	4,118	3,483
Chesterfield County	VA	68	60,060	61,383	5,299	8.6	718,087	33,520	4.7	562	5,608	9,875	10,986	952	651	0	7,438	3,367	0	2,005	2,066
Conroe ISD	TX	69	59,764	62,420	6,769	10.8	591,849	35,023	5.9	601	6,756	10,415	10,658	1,055	354	0	8,920	3,625	874	2,237	2,184
El Paso ISD	TX	70	59,424	61,880	18,527	29.9	643,516	111,553	17.3	1,858	26,988	27,403	11,730	4,661	918	0	26,847	9,762	2,354	7,454	7,276
Garland ISD	TX	71	57,133	62,916	11,977	19.0	597,799	54,476	9.1	947	12,978	21,297	9,602	1,107	620	0	16,749	6,337	1,528	4,496	4,388
Mobile County	AL	72	56,628	66,870	19,514	29.2	564,939	78,217	13.8	1,358	24,171	31,594	15,858	3,753	960	443	29,181	10,344	2,494	7,957	8,385
Pasadena ISD	TX	73	56,282	58,306	14,385	24.7	607,584	71,419	11.8	1,275	16,072	26,155	8,728	1,616	754	0	20,516	7,615	1,836	5,599	5,466
Frisco ISD	TX	74	55,923	43,248	1,579	3.7	574,629	12,497	2.2	234	1,099	4,146	4,122	121	222	0	842	842	0	0	0
Howard County	MD	75	55,626	58,873	3,342	5.7	949,631	27,394	2.9	499	4,741	6,766	9,530	1,058	322	0	5,462	2,649	0	1,430	1,384
Winston-Salem/Forsyth County	NC	76	55,228	64,492	14,495	22.5	503,819	62,956	12.5	1,145	18,949	18,960	14,749	1,388	0	0	21,021	7,741	1,849	5,632	5,799
Cherry Creek, No. 5	CO	77	54,852	57,432	4,192	7.3	623,750	27,612	4.4	505	5,732	7,789	9,005	756	244	0	5,100	2,337	0	1,339	1,424
Santa Ana Unified	CA	78	54,505	53,184	12,085	22.7	784,643	83,062	10.6	1,486	21,717	32,398	11,733	3,206	543	0	19,855	7,699	1,856	5,479	4,821
Clayton County	GA	79	54,345	57,722	16,816	29.1	542,286	71,543	13.2	1,322	22,083	34,087	9,990	1,963	530	0	24,350	8,914	2,149	6,721	6,566
Seattle	WA	80	54,215	66,075	6,627	10.0	881,789	52,833	6.0	991	14,410	9,378	13,585	486	360	0	11,812	4,455	1,074	2,747	3,536
Plano ISD	TX	81	54,173	69,733	4,898	7.0	707,660	31,851	4.5	584	5,018	8,870	8,404	786	408	0	5,698	2,632	0	1,551	1,514
Boston	MA	82	53,640	75,249	21,309	28.3	1,481,699	77,195	5.2	1,433	26,828	18,497	16,457	0	1,273	0	52,759	17,169	4,140	13,362	18,088
Capistrano Unified	CA	83	53,613	61,792	4,019	6.5	556,213	23,256	4.2	432	4,739	4,943	9,604	912	287	0	5,138	2,561	0	1,449	1,127
Jordan	UT	84	53,416	61,711	3,495	5.7	411,232	25,095	6.1	474	2,912	8,488	9,226	819	420	0	4,047	1,875	0	1,029	1,143
Lewisville ISD	TX	85	53,257	64,833	5,137	7.9	615,597	32,773	5.3	613	4,076	11,054	8,383	591	376	0	5,928	2,729	0	1,619	1,580
Corona-Norco Unified	CA	86	53,157	55,845	6,664	11.9	647,344	36,976	5.7	693	8,246	12,794	9,398	1,142	314	0	10,101	4,300	1,037	2,651	2,112
San Bernardino City Unified	CA	87	53,152	55,421	20,868	37.7	716,242	72,318	10.1	1,357	28,113	26,990	8,698	2,787	647	0	37,081	13,530	3,263	10,515	9,773
San Antonio ISD	TX	88	52,514	61,265	20,582	33.6	650,765	136,019	20.9	2,563	31,579	43,297	10,585	4,393	836	0	30,764	11,091	2,674	8,602	8,397
Omaha	NE	89	52,344	65,240	11,932	18.3	687,093	96,897	14.1	1,865	34,778	24,842	14,695	4,336	1,047	0	27,444	9,529	2,276	6,827	8,812
Atlanta	GA	90	51,927	58,615	19,520	33.3	903,489	82,444	9.1	1,601	38,069	24,030	9,512	6,372	597	0	28,811	10,484	2,557	7,977	7,793

See notes at end of table.

Table 215.30. Enrollment, poverty, and federal funds for the 120 largest school districts, by enrollment size in 2016: 2015–16 and fiscal year 2018—Continued

Name of district	State	Rank order	Enroll-ment, fall 2016	5- to 17-year-old population, 2016	5- to 17-year-olds in poverty, 2016[1]	Poverty rate of 5- to 17-year-olds, 2016[1]	Revenues by source of funds, 2015–16: Total (in thousands)	Federal (in thousands)	Federal as a percent of total	Federal revenue per student[3]	Revenue from selected federal programs (in thousands), 2015–16: Title I	School lunch	Individuals with Disabilities Education Act (IDEA)	Eisen-hower math and science	Voca-tional education	Drug-free schools	Federal Title I allocations (in thousands), federal fiscal year 2018[2]: Total	Basic Grants	Concen-tration Grants	Targeted Grants	Education Finance Incentive Grants
1	2	3	4	5	6	7	8	9	10	11	12	13	14	15	16	17	18	19	20	21	22
Klein ISD	TX	91	51,810	51,259	7,382	14.4	535,140	35,016	6.5	692	6,938	11,428	6,983	627	372	0	9,658	3,908	942	2,433	2,375
Henrico County	VA	92	51,425	55,420	6,171	11.1	533,398	29,242	5.5	567	5,580	12,425	7,636	729	1,064	0	9,638	3,929	836	2,393	2,481
Cumberland County	NC	93	51,194	54,197	14,042	25.9	436,794	65,548	15.0	1,281	14,115	21,149	9,872	2,481	0	0	20,743	7,591	1,830	5,579	5,744
Wichita	KS	94	50,600	57,497	12,758	22.2	666,255	73,972	11.1	1,452	24,904	21,355	0	0	0	0	22,266	7,636	1,832	5,524	7,273
Columbus City	OH	95	50,331	72,743	25,484	35.0	840,528	94,651	11.3	1,892	36,397	28,886	13,602	0	2,270	0	51,861	16,984	4,095	13,483	17,299
Oakland Unified	CA	96	49,760	58,151	12,817	22.0	688,124	65,125	9.5	1,326	18,473	16,544	9,277	4,386	500	0	21,151	8,137	1,962	5,858	5,194
San Juan Unified	CA	97	49,255	50,227	9,810	19.5	610,436	47,157	7.7	951	11,709	10,688	10,828	2,053	397	0	15,652	6,276	1,513	4,250	3,613
Manatee	FL	98	48,884	52,635	9,982	19.0	491,872	55,102	11.2	1,140	14,734	19,598	10,650	23	803	0	13,236	5,289	1,275	3,591	3,081
Jefferson Parish	LA	99	48,668	67,943	16,141	23.8	611,400	72,132	11.8	1,491	21,535	20,304	14,540	2,914	704	895	27,519	9,923	2,393	7,429	7,774
Charleston, 01	SC	100	48,551	55,211	11,106	20.1	763,748	71,926	9.4	1,496	18,158	18,457	10,812	2,380	591	0	17,246	6,278	1,514	4,387	5,068
District of Columbia	DC	101	48,462	77,386	21,997	28.4	1,329,719	154,922	11.7	3,205	29,450	25,496	9,053	6,185	2,358	321	50,946	18,434	4,445	14,455	13,611
Round Rock ISD	TX	102	48,321	54,846	3,278	6.0	519,574	31,087	6.0	650	3,400	8,089	7,941	435	319	0	3,689	1,783	0	965	942
Anchorage	AK	103	48,238	52,309	4,634	8.9	758,779	78,331	10.3	1,621	14,868	18,567	12,311	3,181	1,167	0	14,157	5,104	984	4,025	4,044
Portland, SD1J	OR	104	48,173	56,467	7,235	12.8	697,501	54,051	7.7	1,118	12,975	11,191	14,185	2,743	470	0	12,164	4,560	1,100	2,838	3,667
Tucson Unified	AZ	105	47,366	72,242	20,437	28.3	449,642	67,416	15.0	1,424	30,025	17,423	7,795	1,091	1,003	2,936	31,940	11,266	2,717	8,753	9,205
Brownsville ISD	TX	106	46,880	46,381	18,449	39.8	555,104	102,330	18.4	2,143	26,320	38,949	8,357	2,629	787	0	28,135	10,275	2,454	7,825	7,581
Sacramento City Unified	CA	107	46,815	52,925	13,719	25.9	645,019	76,733	11.9	1,638	18,414	21,969	9,811	3,458	1,222	0	23,040	8,777	2,116	6,410	5,737
Collier	FL	108	46,416	47,497	8,103	17.1	571,140	53,751	9.4	1,169	17,122	17,171	9,553	1,429	575	0	10,460	4,311	1,036	2,758	2,354
Alief ISD	TX	109	46,376	54,698	17,289	31.6	514,485	69,453	13.5	1,469	21,037	22,624	7,455	851	758	0	25,047	9,152	2,207	6,927	6,762
Forsyth County	GA	110	46,238	48,680	2,654	5.5	471,715	16,236	3.4	367	2,675	4,912	6,180	427	206	0	2,850	1,428	0	719	703
Socorro ISD	TX	111	45,927	42,950	10,640	24.8	439,467	46,901	10.7	1,036	10,623	20,712	6,156	1,147	521	0	14,541	5,588	1,347	3,849	3,757
Detroit Public Schools	MI	112	45,455	124,278	57,539	46.3	838,553	193,905	23.1	4,160	98,109	42,071	9,804	0	1,269	0	127,607	39,342	10,027	33,634	44,604
Hamilton County	TN	113	44,446	54,365	9,860	18.1	428,237	49,774	11.6	1,121	16,511	18,971	9,568	0	709	566	13,823	5,302	1,278	3,602	3,640
Chandler Unified	AZ	114	44,352	46,562	4,932	10.6	350,971	20,423	5.8	480	5,173	6,564	5,070	609	419	0	5,687	2,684	0	1,588	1,415
Garden Grove Unified	CA	115	44,223	49,336	9,904	20.1	647,198	51,880	8.0	1,146	12,985	18,669	8,870	2,137	510	230	15,752	6,309	1,521	4,279	3,642
Rutherford County	TN	116	44,149	44,849	4,910	10.9	378,876	25,534	6.7	593	4,778	10,427	7,945	0	650	0	5,737	2,626	0	1,547	1,564
Horry, 01	SC	117	43,991	44,231	11,581	26.2	543,802	42,444	7.8	983	14,500	15,036	9,301	1,290	633	0	17,971	6,502	1,568	4,580	5,321
Killeen ISD	TX	118	43,782	42,827	7,806	18.2	439,981	102,083	23.2	2,360	8,054	14,527	6,063	1,054	446	0	10,655	4,270	1,020	2,725	2,640
United ISD	TX	119	43,660	42,326	14,052	33.2	461,411	56,597	12.3	1,295	14,542	23,506	7,305	1,050	603	0	19,870	7,395	1,783	5,410	5,281
Marion	FL	120	43,032	47,672	12,175	25.5	418,762	59,188	14.1	1,383	16,300	22,792	11,194	1,980	646	0	16,605	6,473	1,561	4,613	3,958

[1]Poverty is defined based on the number of persons and related children in the family and their income. For information on poverty thresholds, see https://www.census.gov/data/tables/time-series/demo/income-poverty/historical-poverty-thresholds.html.
[2]Fiscal year 2018 Department of Education funds available for spending by school districts in the 2018–19 school year.
[3]Federal revenue per student is based on fall enrollment collected through the "Local Education Agency (School District) Finance Survey (F33)."

NOTE: Detail may not sum to totals because of rounding. ISD = independent school district.
SOURCE: U.S. Department of Education, National Center for Education Statistics, Common Core of Data (CCD), "Local Education Agency Universe Survey," 2016–17; "Local Education Agency (School District) Finance Survey (F33)," 2015–16; and unpublished Department of Education budget data. U.S. Department of Commerce, Census Bureau, Small Area Income and Poverty Estimates (SAIPE) Program, 2016 Poverty Estimates for School Districts. (This table was prepared May 2019.)

Table 216.10. Public elementary and secondary schools, by level of school: Selected years, 1967–68 through 2016–17

		Schools with reported grade spans											
			Elementary schools				Secondary schools						
Year	Total, all public schools	Total	Total[3]	Middle schools[4]	One-teacher schools	Other elementary schools	Total[5]	Junior high[6]	3-year or 4-year high schools	5-year or 6-year high schools	Other secondary schools	Combined elementary/secondary schools[2]	Other schools[1]
1	2	3	4	5	6	7	8	9	10	11	12	13	14
1967–68	—	94,197	67,186	—	4,146	63,040	23,318	7,437	10,751	4,650	480	3,693	—
1970–71	—	89,372	64,020	2,080	1,815	60,125	23,572	7,750	11,265	3,887	670	1,780	—
1972–73	—	88,864	62,942	2,308	1,475	59,159	23,919	7,878	11,550	3,962	529	2,003	—
1974–75	—	87,456	61,759	3,224	1,247	57,288	23,837	7,690	11,480	4,122	545	1,860	—
1975–76	88,597	87,034	61,704	3,916	1,166	56,622	23,792	7,521	11,572	4,113	586	1,538	1,563
1976–77	—	86,501	61,123	4,180	1,111	55,832	23,857	7,434	11,658	4,130	635	1,521	—
1978–79	—	84,816	60,312	5,879	1,056	53,377	22,834	6,282	11,410	4,429	713	1,670	—
1980–81	85,982	83,688	59,326	6,003	921	52,402	22,619	5,890	10,758	4,193	1,778	1,743	2,294
1982–83	84,740	82,039	58,051	6,875	798	50,378	22,383	5,948	11,678	4,067	690	1,605	2,701
1983–84	84,178	81,418	57,471	6,885	838	49,748	22,336	5,936	11,670	4,046	684	1,611	2,760
1984–85	84,007	81,147	57,231	6,893	825	49,513	22,320	5,916	11,671	4,021	712	1,596	2,860
1986–87	83,421	82,316	58,835	7,483	763	50,589	21,505	5,109	11,430	4,196	770	1,976	1,105[7]
1987–88	83,248	81,416	57,575	7,641	729	49,205	21,662	4,900	11,279	4,048	1,435	2,179	1,832[7]
1988–89	83,165	81,579	57,941	7,957	583	49,401	21,403	4,687	11,350	3,994	1,372	2,235	1,586[7]
1989–90	83,425	81,880	58,419	8,272	630	49,517	21,181	4,512	11,492	3,812	1,365	2,280	1,545[7]
1990–91	84,538	82,475	59,015	8,545	617	49,853	21,135	4,561	11,537	3,723	1,314	2,325	2,063
1991–92	84,578	82,506	59,258	8,829	569	49,860	20,767	4,298	11,528	3,699	1,242	2,481	2,072
1992–93	84,497	82,896	59,676	9,152	430	50,094	20,671	4,115	11,651	3,613	1,292	2,549	1,601
1993–94	85,393	83,431	60,052	9,573	442	50,037	20,705	3,970	11,858	3,595	1,282	2,674	1,962
1994–95	86,221	84,476	60,808	9,954	458	50,396	20,904	3,859	12,058	3,628	1,359	2,764	1,745
1995–96	87,125	84,958	61,165	10,205	474	50,486	20,997	3,743	12,168	3,621	1,465	2,796	2,167
1996–97	88,223	86,092	61,805	10,499	487	50,819	21,307	3,707	12,424	3,614	1,562	2,980	2,131
1997–98	89,508	87,541	62,739	10,944	476	51,319	21,682	3,599	12,734	3,611	1,738	3,120	1,967
1998–99	90,874	89,259	63,462	11,202	463	51,797	22,076	3,607	13,457	3,707	1,305	3,721	1,615
1999–2000	92,012	90,538	64,131	11,521	423	52,187	22,365	3,566	13,914	3,686	1,199	4,042	1,474
2000–01	93,273	91,691	64,601	11,696	411	52,494	21,994	3,318	13,793	3,974	909	5,096	1,582
2001–02	94,112	92,696	65,228	11,983	408	52,837	22,180	3,285	14,070	3,917	908	5,288	1,416
2002–03	95,615	93,869	65,718	12,174	366	53,178	22,599	3,263	14,330	4,017	989	5,552	1,746
2003–04	95,726	93,977	65,758	12,341	376	53,041	22,782	3,251	14,595	3,840	1,096	5,437	1,749
2004–05	96,513	95,001	65,984	12,530	338	53,116	23,445	3,250	14,854	3,945	1,396	5,572	1,512
2005–06	97,382	95,731	66,026	12,545	326	53,155	23,998	3,249	15,103	3,910	1,736	5,707	1,651
2006–07	98,793	96,362	66,458	12,773	313	53,372	23,920	3,112	15,043	4,048	1,717	5,984	2,431
2007–08	98,916	97,654	67,112	13,014	288	53,810	24,643	3,117	16,146	3,981	1,399	5,899	1,262
2008–09	98,706	97,119	67,148	13,060	237	53,851	24,348	3,037	16,246	3,761	1,304	5,623	1,587
2009–10	98,817	97,521	67,140	13,163	217	53,760	24,651	2,953	16,706	3,778	1,214	5,730	1,296
2010–11	98,817	97,767	67,086	13,045	224	53,817	24,544	2,855	16,321	4,047	1,321	6,137	1,050
2011–12	98,328	97,357	66,689	12,963	205	53,521	24,357	2,865	16,586	3,899	1,007	6,311	971
2012–13	98,454	97,331	66,708	13,064	196	53,448	24,294	2,816	16,393	3,875	1,210	6,329	1,123
2013–14	98,271	97,290	67,034	13,324	193	53,517	24,067	2,721	16,704	3,467	1,175	6,189	981
2014–15	98,176	97,601	67,073	13,250	165	53,658	24,181	2,706	16,603	3,585	1,287	6,347	575
2015–16	98,277	97,586	66,758	13,022	197	53,539	24,040	2,594	16,243	3,995	1,208	6,788	691
2016–17	98,158	97,434	66,837	13,253	203	53,381	23,814	2,527	16,514	3,523	1,250	6,783	724

—Not available.
[1]Includes special education, alternative, and other schools not reported by grade span.
[2]Includes schools beginning with grade 6 or below and ending with grade 9 or above.
[3]Includes schools beginning with grade 6 or below and with no grade higher than 8.
[4]Includes schools with grade spans beginning with 4, 5, or 6 and ending with 6, 7, or 8.
[5]Includes schools with no grade lower than 7.
[6]Includes schools with grades 7 and 8 or grades 7 through 9.
[7]Because of revision in data collection procedures, figures not comparable to data for other years.

SOURCE: U.S. Department of Education, National Center for Education Statistics, *Statistics of State School Systems*, 1967–68 and 1975–76; *Statistics of Public Elementary and Secondary Day Schools*, 1970–71, 1972–73, 1974–75, and 1976–77 through 1980–81; and Common Core of Data (CCD), "Public Elementary/Secondary School Universe Survey," 1982–83 through 2016–17. (This table was prepared November 2018.)

Table 216.20. Number and enrollment of public elementary and secondary schools, by school level, type, and charter, magnet, and virtual status: Selected years, 1990–91 through 2016–17

School level, type, and charter, magnet, or virtual status	Number of schools										Fall enrollment									
	1990–91	2000–01	2005–06	2010–11	2011–12	2012–13	2013–14	2014–15	2015–16	2016–17	1990–91	2000–01	2005–06	2010–11	2011–12	2012–13	2013–14	2014–15	2015–16	2016–17
1	2	3	4	5	6	7	8	9	10	11	12	13	14	15	16	17	18	19	20	21
Total, all schools	**84,538**	**93,273**	**97,382**	**98,817**	**98,328**	**98,454**	**98,271**	**98,176**	**98,277**	**98,158**	**41,141,366**	**47,060,714**	**48,912,085**	**49,177,617**	**49,256,120**	**49,519,559**	**49,777,410**	**50,009,771**	**50,115,178**	**50,274,747**
School type																				
Regular	80,395	85,422	87,585	88,929	88,663	89,031	89,183	89,386	89,501	89,527	40,599,943	46,194,730	47,957,375	48,259,245	48,273,539	48,583,049	48,863,752	49,178,890	49,313,134	49,468,870
Special education	1,932	2,008	2,128	2,206	2,087	2,034	2,010	1,954	2,005	1,991	209,145	174,577	222,497	190,910	195,161	198,626	214,611	186,269	180,155	184,261
Vocational	1,060	1,025	1,221	1,485	1,434	1,403	1,380	1,387	1,396	1,391	198,117	199,669	217,621	164,013	159,905	160,207	148,447	147,550	146,321	146,601
Alternative[1]	1,151	4,818	6,448	6,197	6,144	5,986	5,698	5,449	5,375	5,249	134,161	491,738	514,592	563,449	627,515	577,677	550,600	497,062	475,568	475,015
School level and type																				
Elementary[2]	59,015	64,601	66,026	67,086	66,689	66,708	67,034	67,073	66,758	66,837	26,503,677	30,673,453	31,104,018	31,581,751	31,724,573	31,918,613	32,226,881	32,225,908	32,035,708	32,132,682
Regular	58,440	63,674	64,996	65,874	65,461	65,572	65,948	66,036	65,734	65,853	26,400,740	30,582,610	31,003,942	31,441,027	31,545,886	31,772,432	32,083,759	32,116,995	31,930,363	32,034,365
Special education	419	496	508	587	544	541	543	578	568	551	58,204	42,127	49,652	58,987	58,844	59,826	62,596	54,161	50,508	43,555
Vocational	31	8	8	16	17	15	7	6	5	5	17,686	2,409	1,713	3,495	4,558	3,734	1,791	1,749	1,729	1,960
Alternative[1]	125	423	514	609	667	580	536	453	451	428	27,047	46,307	48,711	78,242	115,285	82,621	78,735	53,003	53,108	52,802
Secondary[3]	21,135	21,994	23,998	24,544	24,357	24,294	24,067	24,181	24,040	23,814	13,569,787	15,038,171	16,219,309	15,692,610	15,708,815	15,670,275	15,640,128	15,731,561	15,748,184	15,798,446
Regular	19,459	18,456	19,252	19,449	19,441	19,479	19,411	19,441	19,325	19,264	13,313,097	14,567,969	15,685,032	15,197,786	15,194,153	15,161,226	15,167,671	15,270,834	15,296,173	15,355,391
Special education	165	219	368	359	339	333	331	339	313	316	11,913	12,607	42,696	27,990	27,905	28,235	28,312	24,729	21,929	21,700
Vocational	1,010	997	1,185	1,387	1,349	1,324	1,311	1,318	1,329	1,332	174,105	193,981	209,762	154,088	154,187	154,610	144,066	144,042	142,611	142,332
Alternative[1]	501	2,322	3,193	3,349	3,228	3,158	3,014	3,083	3,073	2,902	70,672	263,614	281,819	312,746	332,570	326,204	300,079	291,956	287,471	279,023
Combined elementary/secondary[4]	2,325	5,096	5,707	6,137	6,311	6,329	6,189	6,347	6,788	6,783	925,887	1,266,778	1,526,186	1,897,712	1,818,020	1,926,786	1,898,252	2,049,039	2,329,346	2,335,618
Regular	1,784	2,780	3,121	3,363	3,435	3,558	3,446	3,713	4,236	4,236	855,814	1,007,368	1,263,952	1,620,031	1,533,002	1,649,010	1,611,918	1,790,208	2,085,918	2,078,659
Special education	376	715	735	964	970	935	940	935	923	907	43,992	86,253	91,966	99,120	104,344	107,295	111,958	106,500	107,658	112,826
Vocational	19	20	28	82	68	64	62	63	62	54	6,326	3,279	6,146	6,430	1,160	1,863	2,590	1,759	1,981	2,309
Alternative[1]	146	1,581	1,823	1,728	1,838	1,772	1,741	1,636	1,567	1,586	19,755	169,878	164,122	172,131	179,514	168,618	171,786	150,572	133,789	141,824
Other (not classified by grade span)	2,063	1,582	1,651	1,050	971	1,123	981	575	691	724	142,015	82,312	62,572	5,544	4,712	3,885	12,149	3,263	1,940	8,001
Regular	712	512	216	243	326	422	378	196	206	174	30,292	36,783	4,449	401	498	381	404	853	680	455
Special education	972	578	517	296	234	225	196	102	201	217	95,036	33,590	38,183	4,813	4,068	3,270	11,745	879	60	6,180
Vocational	0	0	0	0	0	0	0	0	0	0	0	0	0	0	0	0	0	0	0	0
Alternative[1]	379	492	918	511	411	476	407	277	284	333	16,687	11,939	19,940	330	146	234	0	1,531	1,200	1,366
Charter status and level																				
All charter schools[5]	—	1,993	3,780	5,274	5,696	6,079	6,465	6,747	6,855	7,011	—	448,343	1,012,906	1,787,091	2,057,599	2,269,435	2,522,022	2,721,786	2,845,322	3,010,287
Elementary[2]	—	1,011	1,969	2,866	3,127	3,388	3,634	3,851	3,854	3,934	—	249,101	532,217	905,575	1,045,492	1,156,075	1,288,568	1,405,015	1,448,523	1,511,812
Secondary[3]	—	467	1,057	1,368	1,418	1,465	1,522	1,563	1,576	1,618	—	79,588	219,627	341,534	386,482	399,921	443,423	467,231	482,296	504,301
Combined elementary/secondary[4]	—	448	704	1,027	1,112	1,204	1,268	1,330	1,406	1,454	—	117,377	259,837	539,653	625,429	713,073	789,883	848,875	914,110	994,021
Other (not classified by grade span)	—	67	50	13	39	22	41	3	19	5	—	2,277	1,225	329	196	366	148	665	393	153
Magnet status and level																				
All magnet schools[5]	—	1,469	2,736	2,722	2,949	3,151	3,254	3,285	3,237	3,164	—	1,213,976	2,103,013	2,055,133	2,248,177	2,478,531	2,556,644	2,609,104	2,604,145	2,537,011
Elementary[2]	—	1,111	1,994	1,849	2,012	2,150	2,164	2,216	2,135	2,087	—	704,763	1,186,160	1,035,288	1,158,405	1,287,771	1,300,317	1,312,571	1,281,873	1,266,076
Secondary[3]	—	328	643	746	802	862	939	911	884	853	—	484,684	869,010	944,434	1,015,267	1,118,574	1,178,272	1,207,248	1,188,316	1,141,181
Combined elementary/secondary[4]	—	29	80	103	116	121	133	142	203	205	—	24,529	47,509	75,411	74,505	72,148	78,055	89,277	133,956	129,752
Other (not classified by grade span)	—	1	19	24	19	18	18	16	15	19	—	0	334	0	0	38	0	8	0	2
Virtual status and level																				
All virtual schools[5,6]	—	—	—	—	—	—	477	576	592	562	—	—	—	—	—	—	200,343	229,608	234,148	212,311
Elementary[2]	—	—	—	—	—	—	65	77	74	68	—	—	—	—	—	—	14,277	19,341	19,064	14,669
Secondary[3]	—	—	—	—	—	—	100	132	144	132	—	—	—	—	—	—	18,625	29,303	32,535	23,355
Combined elementary/secondary[4]	—	—	—	—	—	—	310	366	373	361	—	—	—	—	—	—	167,441	180,964	182,549	174,287
Other (not classified by grade span)	—	—	—	—	—	—	2	1	1	1	—	—	—	—	—	—	0	0	0	0

—Not available.
[1]Includes schools that provide nontraditional education, address needs of students that typically cannot be met in regular schools, serve as adjuncts to regular schools, or fall outside the categories of regular, special education, or vocational education.
[2]Includes schools beginning with grade 6 or below and with no grade higher than 8.
[3]Includes schools with no grade lower than 7.
[4]Includes schools beginning with grade 6 or below and ending with grade 9 or above.
[5]Magnet, charter, and virtual schools are also included under regular, special education, vocational, or alternative schools as appropriate.
[6]Virtual schools are defined as having instruction during which students and teachers are separated by time and/or location and interact via internet-connected computers or other electronic devices.
SOURCE: U.S. Department of Education, National Center for Education Statistics, Common Core of Data (CCD), "Public Elementary/Secondary School Universe Survey," 1990–91 through 2016–17. (This table was prepared June 2019.)

Table 216.30. Number and percentage distribution of public elementary and secondary students and schools, by traditional or charter school status and selected characteristics: Selected years, 2000–01 through 2016–17

Selected characteristic	2000–01			2005–06			2010–11			2016–17		
	Total, all public schools	Traditional (non-charter) schools	Charter schools	Total, all public schools	Traditional (non-charter) schools	Charter schools	Total, all public schools	Traditional (non-charter) schools	Charter schools	Total, all public schools	Traditional (non-charter) schools	Charter schools
1	2	3	4	5	6	7	8	9	10	11	12	13
Fall enrollment (in thousands)	47,061	46,612	448	48,912	47,899	1,013	49,178	47,391	1,787	50,275	47,264	3,010
Percentage distribution of students												
Sex	100.0	100.0	100.0	100.0	100.0	100.0	100.0	100.0	100.0	100.0	100.0	100.0
Male	51.4	51.4	51.2	51.4	51.4	49.9	51.4	51.4	49.5	51.4	51.5	49.6
Female	48.6	48.6	48.8	48.6	48.6	50.1	48.6	48.6	50.5	48.6	48.5	50.4
Race/ethnicity	100.0	100.0	100.0	100.0	100.0	100.0	100.0	100.0	100.0	100.0	100.0	100.0
White	61.0	61.2	42.7	57.1	57.4	40.5	52.5	53.1	36.2	48.2	49.2	32.2
Black	17.0	16.9	33.2	17.2	16.9	32.1	16.0	15.5	28.9	15.3	14.6	26.5
Hispanic	16.6	16.6	19.4	19.8	19.8	22.4	23.1	22.9	27.3	26.4	26.0	32.6
Asian/Pacific Islander	4.2	4.2	2.9	4.6	4.6	3.6	5.0	5.0	3.7	5.5	5.5	4.4
American Indian/Alaska Native	1.2	1.2	1.8	1.2	1.2	1.4	1.1	1.1	0.9	1.0	1.0	0.7
Two or more races	—	—	—	—	—	—	2.4	2.3	2.9	3.6	3.6	3.6
Percent of students eligible for free or reduced-price lunch program[1]	100.0	100.0	100.0	100.0	100.0	100.0	100.0	100.0	100.0	100.0	100.0	100.0
0 to 25.0	34.3	34.3	39.3	32.9	32.9	36.1	23.9	23.8	26.7	21.2	21.2	20.2
25.1 to 50.0	24.7	24.8	12.7	29.1	29.4	15.9	28.9	29.2	18.9	28.3	28.9	19.4
50.1 to 75.0	16.0	16.1	14.9	21.0	21.0	17.4	26.6	26.8	20.4	25.7	25.9	21.5
More than 75.0	12.4	12.4	14.7	15.9	15.8	22.0	20.1	19.7	30.7	24.2	23.5	33.8
Missing/school does not participate	12.5	12.4	18.4	1.0	0.9	8.6	0.5	0.4	3.2	0.7	0.4	5.1
Number of teachers[2]	2,747,649	2,729,033	18,616	3,057,723	3,008,581	49,142	3,001,994	2,910,869	91,126	3,096,459	2,942,705	153,754
Pupil/teacher ratio[2]	16.4	16.4	18.2	16.0	16.0	17.3	16.4	16.4	18.0	16.2	16.1	17.8
Total number of schools	93,273	91,280	1,993	97,382	93,602	3,780	98,817	93,543	5,274	98,158	91,147	7,011
Percentage distribution of schools												
School level	100.0	100.0	100.0	100.0	100.0	100.0	100.0	100.0	100.0	100.0	100.0	100.0
Elementary[3]	69.3	69.7	50.7	67.8	68.4	52.1	67.9	68.7	54.3	68.1	69.0	56.1
Secondary[4]	23.6	23.6	23.4	24.6	24.5	28.0	24.8	24.8	25.9	24.3	24.4	23.1
Combined[5]	5.5	5.1	22.5	5.9	5.3	18.6	6.2	5.5	19.5	6.9	5.8	20.7
Other	1.7	1.7	3.4	1.7	1.7	1.3	1.1	1.1	0.2	0.7	0.8	0.1
Size of enrollment	100.0	100.0	100.0	100.0	100.0	100.0	100.0	100.0	100.0	100.0	100.0	100.0
Less than 300	31.9	31.0	75.2	32.3	30.7	69.6	30.9	29.3	59.0	30.0	28.7	46.8
300 to 499	26.5	26.8	12.7	26.7	27.1	16.5	27.8	28.1	22.3	27.8	28.0	25.4
500 to 999	32.0	32.5	9.7	31.2	32.1	10.9	32.3	33.4	14.8	32.8	33.7	21.6
1,000 or more	9.6	9.8	2.4	9.8	10.1	3.0	9.0	9.3	3.9	9.3	9.6	6.2
Racial/ethnic concentration												
More than 50 percent White	70.2	70.6	51.6	65.4	66.2	46.5	60.4	61.7	38.4	55.6	57.4	33.3
More than 50 percent Black	11.1	10.8	25.1	11.6	10.9	26.4	10.7	9.8	25.4	9.8	8.8	23.1
More than 50 percent Hispanic	9.2	9.1	11.5	11.9	11.7	15.1	14.5	14.1	20.8	17.0	16.3	25.8
Percent of students eligible for free or reduced-price lunch program[1]	100.0	100.0	100.0	100.0	100.0	100.0	100.0	100.0	100.0	100.0	100.0	100.0
0 to 25.0	29.9	29.8	33.1	28.3	28.1	32.7	23.2	22.9	27.7	18.0	17.9	18.3
25.1 to 50.0	25.0	25.3	11.5	27.9	28.4	15.2	26.9	27.4	17.4	27.0	27.6	18.6
50.1 to 75.0	16.8	16.9	11.1	21.6	21.8	16.9	26.4	26.8	20.1	25.8	26.0	22.0
More than 75.0	12.2	12.2	13.1	16.6	16.4	22.7	21.3	20.7	33.1	24.7	23.9	35.9
Missing/school does not participate	16.2	15.8	31.1	5.6	5.3	12.5	2.2	2.3	1.7	4.6	4.5	5.3
Locale	—	—	—	100.0	100.0	100.0	100.0	100.0	100.0	100.0	100.0	100.0
City	—	—	—	25.0	24.0	52.5	26.2	24.5	55.5	27.2	24.9	56.0
Suburban	—	—	—	28.2	28.4	22.2	27.4	27.8	21.3	31.7	32.1	26.2
Town	—	—	—	15.3	15.5	9.4	14.0	14.4	7.6	13.4	13.9	6.4
Rural	—	—	—	31.5	32.1	16.0	32.3	33.3	15.6	27.8	29.1	11.3
Region	100.0	100.0	100.0	100.0	100.0	100.0	100.0	100.0	100.0	100.0	100.0	100.0
Northeast	16.2	16.3	10.9	15.7	16.0	9.0	15.5	15.9	9.5	15.5	15.9	10.1
Midwest	28.7	28.8	23.3	27.9	27.9	27.4	26.4	26.6	23.1	25.8	26.2	20.5
South	33.1	33.2	27.5	33.8	34.1	26.5	34.7	35.0	29.5	34.8	35.0	32.9
West	22.0	21.6	38.3	22.6	22.0	37.2	23.4	22.5	37.9	23.9	22.9	36.6

—Not available.
[1]The National School Lunch Program (NSLP) is a federally assisted meal program. To be eligible for free lunch under the program, a student must be from a household with an income at or below 130 percent of the poverty threshold; to be eligible for reduced-price lunch, a student must be from a household with an income between 130 percent and 185 percent of the poverty threshold. Data for 2016–17 include students whose NSLP eligibility has been determined through direct certification.
[2]Pupil/teacher ratio based on schools that reported both enrollment and teacher data.
[3]Includes schools beginning with grade 6 or below and with no grade higher than 8.
[4]Includes schools with no grade lower than 7.
[5]Includes schools beginning with grade 6 or below and ending with grade 9 or above.
NOTE: Detail may not sum to totals because of rounding. Race categories exclude persons of Hispanic ethnicity.
SOURCE: U.S. Department of Education, National Center for Education Statistics, Common Core of Data (CCD), "Public Elementary/Secondary School Universe Survey," 2000–01 through 2016–17. (This table was prepared February 2019.)

Table 216.40. Number and percentage distribution of public elementary and secondary schools and enrollment, by level, type, and enrollment size of school: 2014–15, 2015–16, and 2016–17

Enrollment size of school	Number and percentage distribution of schools, by level and type						Enrollment totals and percentage distribution, by level and type of school[1]					
			Secondary[4]						Secondary[4]			
	Total[2]	Elementary[3]	All schools	Regular schools[7]	Combined elementary/ secondary[5]	Other[6]	Total[2]	Elementary[3]	All schools	Regular schools[7]	Combined elementary/ secondary[5]	Other[6]
1	2	3	4	5	6	7	8	9	10	11	12	13
2014–15												
Total	98,176	67,073	24,181	19,441	6,347	575	50,009,771	32,225,908	15,731,561	15,270,834	2,049,039	3,263
Percent[8]	**100.00**	**100.00**	**100.00**	**100.00**	**100.00**	**100.00**	**100.00**	**100.00**	**100.00**	**100.00**	**100.00**	**100.00**
Under 100	10.16	5.29	17.68	9.37	36.65	68.00	0.87	0.55	1.08	0.65	4.22	13.39
100 to 199	9.01	7.71	11.17	10.22	15.58	16.00	2.56	2.42	2.35	1.90	6.31	17.16
200 to 299	10.89	11.54	9.14	9.60	10.17	4.00	5.23	6.08	3.26	3.01	7.09	7.08
300 to 399	13.43	15.74	8.09	8.88	7.83	8.00	8.96	11.44	4.06	3.91	7.73	20.59
400 to 499	13.93	16.98	6.99	7.89	5.93	0.00	11.90	15.80	4.51	4.47	7.51	0.00
500 to 599	11.83	14.41	5.87	6.61	5.45	0.00	12.32	16.33	4.62	4.58	8.40	0.00
600 to 699	8.61	10.29	4.82	5.43	4.15	0.00	10.61	13.79	4.50	4.46	7.61	0.00
700 to 799	6.10	7.02	4.04	4.65	3.54	0.00	8.66	10.85	4.35	4.39	7.48	0.00
800 to 999	6.82	7.09	6.78	7.85	3.94	0.00	11.50	12.96	8.71	8.85	9.98	0.00
1,000 to 1,499	5.52	3.63	11.45	13.23	4.22	4.00	12.55	8.68	20.26	20.55	14.21	41.77
1,500 to 1,999	2.04	0.28	7.41	8.61	1.40	0.00	6.73	0.97	18.51	18.87	6.78	0.00
2,000 to 2,999	1.39	0.03	5.59	6.53	0.62	0.00	6.20	0.12	18.91	19.41	4.16	0.00
3,000 or more	0.27	#	0.98	1.13	0.52	0.00	1.90	0.01	4.89	4.96	8.53	0.00
Average enrollment[8]	525	483	694	791	354	131	525	483	694	791	354	131
2015–16												
Total	98,277	66,758	24,040	19,325	6,788	691	50,115,178	32,035,708	15,748,184	15,296,173	2,329,346	1,940
Percent[8]	**100.00**	**100.00**	**100.00**	**100.00**	**100.00**	**100.00**	**100.00**	**100.00**	**100.00**	**100.00**	**100.00**	**100.00**
Under 100	10.14	5.32	17.94	9.39	33.11	88.89	0.86	0.55	1.07	0.64	3.57	18.87
100 to 199	8.91	7.62	11.04	10.15	15.03	0.00	2.53	2.40	2.32	1.88	5.76	0.00
200 to 299	10.94	11.59	9.28	9.75	10.06	0.00	5.25	6.10	3.31	3.05	6.64	0.00
300 to 399	13.48	15.88	7.84	8.61	8.24	5.56	8.97	11.56	3.92	3.77	7.64	20.26
400 to 499	14.11	17.13	7.15	8.13	7.03	0.00	12.02	15.95	4.58	4.56	8.40	0.00
500 to 599	11.63	14.21	5.71	6.46	5.65	0.00	12.10	16.12	4.48	4.44	8.23	0.00
600 to 699	8.67	10.32	4.85	5.51	4.98	0.00	10.66	13.84	4.51	4.48	8.62	0.00
700 to 799	6.10	7.02	3.96	4.56	4.02	0.00	8.65	10.87	4.24	4.28	7.99	0.00
800 to 999	6.73	6.91	6.69	7.75	4.97	0.00	11.31	12.63	8.55	8.68	11.77	0.00
1,000 to 1,499	5.53	3.67	11.28	13.03	4.53	5.56	12.54	8.79	19.86	20.09	14.44	60.88
1,500 to 1,999	2.05	0.28	7.46	8.71	1.34	0.00	6.72	0.95	18.52	18.93	6.17	0.00
2,000 to 2,999	1.42	0.04	5.72	6.70	0.58	0.00	6.36	0.19	19.30	19.79	3.62	0.00
3,000 or more	0.29	#	1.07	1.25	0.45	0.00	2.03	0.04	5.34	5.41	7.16	0.00
Average enrollment[8]	526	482	698	797	376	108	526	482	698	797	376	108
2016–17												
Total	98,158	66,837	23,814	19,264	6,783	724	50,274,747	32,132,682	15,798,446	15,355,391	2,335,618	8,001
Percent[8]	**100.00**	**100.00**	**100.00**	**100.00**	**100.00**	**100.00**	**100.00**	**100.00**	**100.00**	**100.00**	**100.00**	**100.00**
Under 100	10.02	5.25	17.22	9.38	33.67	81.74	0.85	0.54	1.05	0.64	3.61	48.09
100 to 199	8.93	7.60	11.11	10.06	15.24	14.78	2.54	2.40	2.32	1.87	5.92	28.52
200 to 299	10.95	11.59	9.23	9.60	10.42	1.74	5.24	6.10	3.25	2.98	7.03	5.36
300 to 399	13.68	16.05	8.04	8.80	8.79	0.87	9.09	11.66	3.97	3.84	8.27	3.97
400 to 499	14.12	17.10	7.14	8.02	7.55	0.00	12.00	15.89	4.51	4.47	9.08	0.00
500 to 599	11.57	14.08	5.94	6.70	5.32	0.00	12.01	15.96	4.60	4.58	7.88	0.00
600 to 699	8.62	10.36	4.71	5.32	4.24	0.00	10.58	13.88	4.32	4.31	7.44	0.00
700 to 799	6.03	6.99	3.95	4.50	3.38	0.00	8.54	10.81	4.18	4.20	6.85	0.00
800 to 999	6.72	6.96	6.82	7.86	4.04	0.00	11.28	12.71	8.61	8.76	9.70	0.00
1,000 to 1,499	5.54	3.69	11.33	12.97	4.67	0.87	12.54	8.85	19.69	19.89	15.02	14.05
1,500 to 1,999	2.02	0.28	7.38	8.54	1.40	0.00	6.59	0.98	18.04	18.42	6.40	0.00
2,000 to 2,999	1.49	0.04	6.04	7.01	0.78	0.00	6.66	0.18	20.11	20.62	4.87	0.00
3,000 or more	0.29	0.01	1.08	1.24	0.51	0.00	2.08	0.04	5.35	5.42	7.93	0.00
Average enrollment[8]	528	483	708	802	371	70	528	483	708	802	371	70

#Rounds to zero.
[1]Because the data reflect reports by schools, totals differ from those in tables based on reports by states or school districts. Percentage distribution and average enrollment calculations exclude data for schools not reporting enrollment.
[2]Includes elementary, secondary, combined elementary/secondary, and other schools.
[3]Includes schools beginning with grade 6 or below and with no grade higher than 8.
[4]Includes schools with no grade lower than 7.
[5]Includes schools beginning with grade 6 or below and ending with grade 9 or above.
[6]Includes special education, alternative, and other schools not reported by grade span.
[7]Excludes special education schools, vocational schools, and alternative schools.
[8]Data are for schools reporting enrollments greater than zero. Enrollments greater than zero were reported for 95,230 out of 98,176 schools in 2014–15, 95,240 out of 98,277 in 2015–16, and 95,283 out of 98,158 in 2016–17.
NOTE: Detail may not sum to totals because of rounding. Some data have been revised from previously published figures.
SOURCE: U.S. Department of Education, National Center for Education Statistics, Common Core of Data (CCD), "Public Elementary/Secondary School Universe Survey," 2014–15, 2015–16, and 2016–17. (This table was prepared November 2018.)

Table 216.45. Average enrollment and percentage distribution of public elementary and secondary schools, by level, type, and enrollment size: Selected years, 1982–83 through 2016–17

Year	Average enrollment in schools, by level and type						Percentage distribution of schools, by enrollment size							
	Total[1]	Elementary[2]	Secondary[3]: All schools	Secondary[3]: Regular schools[6]	Combined elementary/ secondary[4]	Other[5]	Under 200	200 to 299	300 to 399	400 to 499	500 to 599	600 to 699	700 to 999	1,000 or more
1	2	3	4	5	6	7	8	9	10	11	12	13	14	15
1982–83	478	399	719	—	478	142	21.9	13.8	15.5	13.1	10.2	7.1	10.2	8.3
1983–84	480	401	720	—	475	145	21.7	13.7	15.5	13.2	10.2	7.1	10.3	8.3
1984–85	482	403	721	—	476	146	21.5	13.6	15.5	13.2	10.3	7.1	10.4	8.4
1986–87	489	416	707	714	426	118	21.1	13.1	15.0	13.5	10.8	7.5	10.7	8.1
1987–88	490	424	695	711	420	122	20.3	12.9	14.9	13.8	11.1	7.8	11.2	8.0
1988–89	494	433	689	697	412	142	20.0	12.5	14.7	13.8	11.4	8.0	11.6	8.0
1989–90	493	441	669	689	402	142	19.8	12.2	14.5	13.7	11.5	8.3	12.0	7.9
1990–91	497	449	663	684	398	150	19.7	11.9	14.2	13.6	11.7	8.5	12.3	8.1
1991–92	507	458	677	717	407	152	19.1	11.7	14.1	13.5	11.8	8.6	12.8	8.5
1992–93	513	464	688	733	423	135	18.6	11.6	13.9	13.5	11.9	8.7	13.1	8.7
1993–94	518	468	693	748	418	136	18.6	11.5	13.6	13.5	11.7	8.8	13.3	9.0
1994–95	520	471	696	759	412	131	18.6	11.4	13.6	13.4	11.8	8.7	13.3	9.2
1995–96	525	476	703	771	401	136	18.5	11.2	13.5	13.4	11.8	8.8	13.4	9.4
1996–97	527	478	703	777	387	135	18.7	11.3	13.2	13.2	11.8	8.8	13.6	9.5
1997–98	525	478	699	779	374	121	19.3	11.2	13.1	13.3	11.6	8.6	13.4	9.6
1998–99	524	478	707	786	290	135	19.6	11.2	13.1	13.2	11.5	8.5	13.3	9.6
1999–2000	521	477	706	785	282	123	20.0	11.3	13.3	13.2	11.2	8.4	13.1	9.5
2000–01	519	477	714	795	274	136	20.4	11.4	13.2	13.3	11.0	8.2	12.9	9.6
2001–02	520	477	718	807	270	138	20.5	11.5	13.3	13.1	10.9	8.1	12.7	9.7
2002–03	519	476	720	813	265	136	20.7	11.6	13.4	13.0	10.9	8.1	12.4	9.8
2003–04	521	476	722	816	269	142	20.7	11.6	13.5	13.2	10.8	8.0	12.3	9.9
2004–05	521	474	713	815	298	143	20.7	11.6	13.5	13.2	10.8	8.1	12.2	9.9
2005–06	521	473	709	819	318	128	20.7	11.5	13.6	13.2	11.0	8.1	12.2	9.8
2006–07	521	473	711	818	325	138	20.3	11.5	13.8	13.4	11.0	8.2	12.2	9.6
2007–08	516	469	704	816	292	136	20.4	11.5	13.9	13.6	11.1	8.1	12.0	9.3
2008–09	517	470	704	807	308	177	20.0	11.4	13.8	13.9	11.3	8.3	12.2	9.1
2009–10	516	473	692	796	300	191	20.0	11.3	13.7	13.9	11.4	8.5	12.3	9.0
2010–11	517	475	684	790	343	57	19.8	11.0	13.9	13.9	11.5	8.5	12.5	9.0
2011–12	520	479	690	788	322	84	19.4	11.0	13.8	13.9	11.7	8.6	12.7	9.0
2012–13	522	481	689	785	337	84	19.3	10.9	13.6	13.9	11.7	8.6	12.8	9.1
2013–14	525	483	693	788	340	238	19.2	10.9	13.4	13.9	11.8	8.7	13.0	9.1
2014–15	525	483	694	791	354	131	19.2	10.9	13.4	13.9	11.8	8.6	12.9	9.2
2015–16	526	482	698	797	376	108	19.0	10.9	13.5	14.1	11.6	8.7	12.8	9.3
2016–17	528	483	708	802	371	70	19.0	11.0	13.7	14.1	11.6	8.6	12.8	9.3

—Not available.
[1]Includes elementary, secondary, combined elementary/secondary, and other schools.
[2]Includes schools beginning with grade 6 or below and with no grade higher than 8.
[3]Includes schools with no grade lower than 7.
[4]Includes schools beginning with grade 6 or below and ending with grade 9 or above.
[5]Includes special education, alternative, and other schools not reported by grade span.
[6]Excludes special education schools, vocational schools, and alternative schools.

NOTE: Data reflect reports by schools rather than by states or school districts. Percentage distribution and average enrollment calculations include data only for schools reporting enrollments greater than zero. Enrollments greater than zero were reported for 95,283 out of 98,158 schools in 2016–17. Detail may not sum to totals because of rounding.
SOURCE: U.S. Department of Education, National Center for Education Statistics, Common Core of Data (CCD), "Public Elementary/Secondary School Universe Survey," 1982–83 through 2016–17. (This table was prepared November 2018.)

Table 216.50. Number and percentage distribution of public elementary and secondary school students, by percentage of minority enrollment in the school and student's racial/ethnic group: Selected years, fall 1995 through fall 2016

Year and racial/ethnic group	Number of students in racial/ethnic group, by percent minority enrollment in the school							Percentage distribution of students in racial/ethnic group, by percent minority enrollment in the school						
	Total	Less than 10 percent	10 to 24 percent	25 to 49 percent	50 to 74 percent	75 to 89 percent	90 percent or more	Total	Less than 10 percent	10 to 24 percent	25 to 49 percent	50 to 74 percent	75 to 89 percent	90 percent or more
1	2	3	4	5	6	7	8	9	10	11	12	13	14	15
Total, 1995	**44,424,467**	**14,508,573**	**8,182,484**	**8,261,110**	**5,467,784**	**2,876,302**	**5,128,214**	**100.0**	**32.7**	**18.4**	**18.6**	**12.3**	**6.5**	**11.5**
White	28,736,961	13,939,633	6,812,196	5,246,785	2,094,440	499,884	144,023	100.0	48.5	23.7	18.3	7.3	1.7	0.5
Minority	15,687,506	568,940	1,370,288	3,014,325	3,373,344	2,376,418	4,984,191	100.0	3.6	8.7	19.2	21.5	15.1	31.8
Black	7,510,678	198,386	598,716	1,588,850	1,622,448	941,335	2,560,943	100.0	2.6	8.0	21.2	21.6	12.5	34.1
Hispanic	6,016,293	174,140	415,761	932,949	1,289,184	1,099,109	2,105,150	100.0	2.9	6.9	15.5	21.4	18.3	35.0
Asian/Pacific Islander	1,656,787	142,886	259,335	367,888	379,110	297,680	209,888	100.0	8.6	15.7	22.2	22.9	18.0	12.7
American Indian/Alaska Native	503,748	53,528	96,476	124,638	82,602	38,294	108,210	100.0	10.6	19.2	24.7	16.4	7.6	21.5
Total, 2000	**46,120,425**	**12,761,478**	**8,736,252**	**8,760,300**	**6,013,131**	**3,472,083**	**6,377,181**	**100.0**	**27.7**	**18.9**	**19.0**	**13.0**	**7.5**	**13.8**
White	28,146,613	12,218,862	7,271,285	5,566,681	2,303,106	596,478	190,201	100.0	43.4	25.8	19.8	8.2	2.1	0.7
Minority	17,973,812	542,616	1,464,967	3,193,619	3,710,025	2,875,605	6,186,980	100.0	3.0	8.2	17.8	20.6	16.0	34.4
Black	7,854,032	178,185	561,488	1,485,130	1,652,393	1,043,907	2,932,929	100.0	2.3	7.1	18.9	21.0	13.3	37.3
Hispanic	7,649,728	181,685	505,612	1,121,809	1,542,982	1,432,639	2,865,001	100.0	2.4	6.6	14.7	20.2	18.7	37.5
Asian/Pacific Islander	1,924,875	132,813	295,437	441,769	423,175	353,395	278,286	100.0	6.9	15.3	23.0	22.0	18.4	14.5
American Indian/Alaska Native	545,177	49,933	102,430	144,911	91,475	45,664	110,764	100.0	9.2	18.8	26.6	16.8	8.4	20.3
Total, 2005	**48,584,980**	**10,711,307**	**9,283,783**	**9,865,121**	**6,839,850**	**4,149,802**	**7,735,117**	**100.0**	**22.0**	**19.1**	**20.3**	**14.1**	**8.5**	**15.9**
White	27,742,612	10,208,608	7,720,632	6,259,485	2,604,846	707,603	241,438	100.0	36.8	27.8	22.6	9.4	2.6	0.9
Minority	20,842,368	502,699	1,563,151	3,605,636	4,235,004	3,442,199	7,493,679	100.0	2.4	7.5	17.3	20.3	16.5	36.0
Black	8,366,722	162,455	560,928	1,513,020	1,752,207	1,176,649	3,201,463	100.0	1.9	6.7	18.1	20.9	14.1	38.3
Hispanic	9,638,712	182,039	581,533	1,388,496	1,873,877	1,803,567	3,809,200	100.0	1.9	6.0	14.4	19.4	18.7	39.5
Asian/Pacific Islander	2,242,628	115,084	319,524	543,952	496,515	406,788	360,765	100.0	5.1	14.2	24.3	22.1	18.1	16.1
American Indian/Alaska Native	594,306	43,121	101,166	160,168	112,405	55,195	122,251	100.0	7.3	17.0	27.0	18.9	9.3	20.6
Total, 2010	**49,212,031**	**7,395,549**	**9,177,649**	**11,236,328**	**7,904,340**	**4,718,126**	**8,780,039**	**100.0**	**15.0**	**18.6**	**22.8**	**16.1**	**9.6**	**17.8**
White	25,801,021	6,987,898	7,614,557	7,097,284	3,003,599	808,637	289,046	100.0	27.1	29.5	27.5	11.6	3.1	1.1
Minority	23,411,010	407,651	1,563,092	4,139,044	4,900,741	3,909,489	8,490,993	100.0	1.7	6.7	17.7	20.9	16.7	36.3
Black	7,873,809	95,108	415,807	1,335,674	1,697,727	1,236,333	3,093,160	100.0	1.2	5.3	17.0	21.6	15.7	39.3
Hispanic	11,367,157	142,927	583,019	1,654,084	2,238,071	2,063,492	4,685,564	100.0	1.3	5.1	14.6	19.7	18.2	41.2
Asian	2,281,908	63,974	259,910	585,447	552,633	390,731	429,213	100.0	2.8	11.4	25.7	24.2	17.1	18.8
Pacific Islander	169,678	4,958	13,772	27,478	32,241	41,652	49,577	100.0	2.9	8.1	16.2	19.0	24.5	29.2
American Indian/Alaska Native	561,126	26,066	77,990	157,300	116,787	58,476	124,507	100.0	4.6	13.9	28.0	20.8	10.4	22.2
Two or more races	1,157,332	74,618	212,594	379,061	263,282	118,805	108,972	100.0	6.4	18.4	32.8	22.7	10.3	9.4
Total, 2014	**50,009,771**	**5,741,083**	**9,011,877**	**11,661,644**	**8,756,197**	**5,324,763**	**9,514,207**	**100.0**	**11.5**	**18.0**	**23.3**	**17.5**	**10.6**	**19.0**
White	24,786,411	5,400,298	7,465,449	7,348,390	3,335,168	909,871	327,235	100.0	21.8	30.1	29.6	13.5	3.7	1.3
Minority	24,665,533	359,845	1,544,204	4,280,403	5,253,163	4,287,640	8,940,278	100.0	1.5	6.3	17.4	21.3	17.4	36.2
Black	7,759,943	62,983	342,668	1,225,416	1,697,167	1,335,814	3,095,895	100.0	0.8	4.4	15.8	21.9	17.2	39.9
Hispanic	12,716,373	126,800	612,981	1,780,885	2,539,142	2,355,996	5,300,569	100.0	1.0	4.8	14.0	20.0	18.5	41.7
Asian	2,454,856	42,901	231,503	606,496	647,976	444,359	481,621	100.0	1.7	9.4	24.7	26.4	18.1	19.6
Pacific Islander	174,834	3,928	13,146	28,596	35,634	39,266	54,264	100.0	2.2	7.5	16.4	20.4	22.5	31.0
American Indian/Alaska Native	514,123	16,971	58,319	139,443	109,437	62,654	127,299	100.0	3.3	11.3	27.1	21.3	12.2	24.8
Two or more races	1,603,231	87,202	287,811	532,418	391,673	176,803	127,324	100.0	5.4	18.0	33.2	24.4	11.0	7.9
Total, 2015	**50,115,178**	**5,396,946**	**8,879,198**	**11,705,331**	**9,039,153**	**5,397,826**	**9,696,724**	**100.0**	**10.8**	**17.7**	**23.4**	**18.0**	**10.8**	**19.3**
White	24,505,632	5,072,523	7,350,271	7,372,017	3,444,117	927,072	339,632	100.0	20.7	30.0	30.1	14.1	3.8	1.4
Minority	25,609,546	324,423	1,528,927	4,333,314	5,595,036	4,470,754	9,357,092	100.0	1.3	6.0	16.9	21.8	17.5	36.5
Black	7,731,426	57,618	326,861	1,195,388	1,705,877	1,334,427	3,111,255	100.0	0.7	4.2	15.5	22.1	17.3	40.2
Hispanic	12,982,345	121,565	612,478	1,800,949	2,628,585	2,392,367	5,426,401	100.0	0.9	4.7	13.9	20.2	18.4	41.8
Asian	2,504,848	38,098	222,680	606,969	685,774	458,658	492,669	100.0	1.5	8.9	24.2	27.4	18.3	19.7
Pacific Islander	175,646	3,654	13,358	28,769	37,209	36,554	56,102	100.0	2.1	7.6	16.4	21.2	20.8	31.9
American Indian/Alaska Native	504,365	15,229	54,626	136,002	109,499	58,998	130,011	100.0	3.0	10.8	27.0	21.7	11.7	25.8
Two or more races	1,710,916	88,259	298,924	565,237	428,092	189,750	140,654	100.0	5.2	17.5	33.0	25.0	11.1	8.2
Total, 2016	**50,274,747**	**5,022,678**	**8,774,358**	**11,786,119**	**9,298,054**	**5,573,066**	**9,820,472**	**100.0**	**10.0**	**17.5**	**23.4**	**18.5**	**11.1**	**19.5**
White	24,237,835	4,718,110	7,259,945	7,417,761	3,541,807	953,713	346,499	100.0	19.5	30.0	30.6	14.6	3.9	1.4
Minority	26,036,912	304,568	1,514,413	4,368,358	5,756,247	4,619,353	9,473,973	100.0	1.2	5.8	16.8	22.1	17.7	36.4
Black	7,698,283	51,649	309,819	1,168,994	1,714,844	1,360,977	3,092,000	100.0	0.7	4.0	15.2	22.3	17.7	40.2
Hispanic	13,262,558	114,844	615,713	1,823,154	2,708,043	2,475,126	5,525,678	100.0	0.9	4.6	13.7	20.4	18.7	41.7
Asian	2,560,906	32,890	213,564	612,963	720,640	472,524	508,325	100.0	1.3	8.3	23.9	28.1	18.5	19.8
Pacific Islander	183,415	3,708	13,567	29,378	38,580	38,780	59,402	100.0	2.0	7.4	16.0	21.0	21.1	32.4
American Indian/Alaska Native	502,152	13,441	51,288	133,381	108,048	62,795	133,199	100.0	2.7	10.2	26.6	21.5	12.5	26.5
Two or more races	1,829,598	88,036	310,462	600,488	466,092	209,151	155,369	100.0	4.8	17.0	32.8	25.5	11.4	8.5

NOTE: Data reflect racial/ethnic data reported by schools. Because some schools do not report complete racial/ethnic data, totals may differ from figures in other tables. Excludes 1995 data for Idaho and 2000 data for Tennessee because racial/ethnic data were not reported. Race categories exclude persons of Hispanic ethnicity. Detail may not sum to totals because of rounding.

SOURCE: U.S. Department of Education, National Center for Education Statistics, Common Core of Data (CCD), "Public Elementary/Secondary School Universe Survey," 1995–96 through 2016–17. (This table was prepared November 2018.)

Table 216.55. Number and percentage distribution of public elementary and secondary school students, by percentage of student's racial/ethnic group enrolled in the school and student's racial/ethnic group: Selected years, fall 1995 through fall 2016

Year and racial/ethnic group	Number of students in each racial/ethnic group, by percent of that racial/ethnic group in the school							Percentage distribution of students in each racial/ethnic group, by percent of that racial/ethnic group in the school						
	Total	Less than 10 percent	10 to 24 percent	25 to 49 percent	50 to 74 percent	75 to 89 percent	90 percent or more	Total	Less than 10 percent	10 to 24 percent	25 to 49 percent	50 to 74 percent	75 to 89 percent	90 percent or more
1	2	3	4	5	6	7	8	9	10	11	12	13	14	15
1995														
White	28,736,961	143,787	498,649	2,084,689	5,244,015	6,813,804	13,952,017	100.0	0.5	1.7	7.3	18.2	23.7	48.6
Black	7,510,678	657,403	1,119,556	1,873,303	1,386,802	811,898	1,661,716	100.0	8.8	14.9	24.9	18.5	10.8	22.1
Hispanic	6,016,293	646,364	847,792	1,359,649	1,360,020	874,878	927,590	100.0	10.7	14.1	22.6	22.6	14.5	15.4
Asian/Pacific Islander	1,656,787	703,101	435,495	301,984	135,001	67,558	13,648	100.0	42.4	26.3	18.2	8.1	4.1	0.8
American Indian/Alaska Native	503,748	223,244	75,019	63,070	39,200	15,084	88,131	100.0	44.3	14.9	12.5	7.8	3.0	17.5
2000														
White	28,146,613	189,779	595,137	2,294,232	5,556,108	7,279,301	12,232,056	100.0	0.7	2.1	8.2	19.7	25.9	43.5
Black	7,854,032	735,459	1,199,865	1,899,982	1,366,363	871,399	1,780,964	100.0	9.4	15.3	24.2	17.4	11.1	22.7
Hispanic	7,649,728	738,509	1,054,396	1,696,944	1,739,038	1,134,466	1,286,375	100.0	9.7	13.8	22.2	22.7	14.8	16.8
Asian/Pacific Islander	1,924,875	799,220	524,279	331,576	171,739	81,461	16,600	100.0	41.5	27.2	17.2	8.9	4.2	0.9
American Indian/Alaska Native	545,177	251,983	81,119	75,831	39,944	15,363	80,937	100.0	46.2	14.9	13.9	7.3	2.8	14.8
2005														
White	27,742,612	240,614	705,300	2,596,310	6,256,109	7,718,175	10,226,104	100.0	0.9	2.5	9.4	22.6	27.8	36.9
Black	8,366,722	849,399	1,396,670	2,004,856	1,453,759	884,663	1,777,375	100.0	10.2	16.7	24.0	17.4	10.6	21.2
Hispanic	9,638,712	848,160	1,316,558	2,071,303	2,218,616	1,545,322	1,638,753	100.0	8.8	13.7	21.5	23.0	16.0	17.0
Asian/Pacific Islander	2,242,628	925,411	616,762	363,562	214,304	100,845	21,744	100.0	41.3	27.5	16.2	9.6	4.5	1.0
American Indian/Alaska Native	594,306	276,846	86,978	84,665	43,272	21,275	81,270	100.0	46.6	14.6	14.2	7.3	3.6	13.7
2010														
White	25,801,021	288,136	807,107	2,991,928	7,090,581	7,620,071	7,003,198	100.0	1.1	3.1	11.6	27.5	29.5	27.1
Black	7,873,809	904,777	1,453,068	1,907,158	1,328,164	859,843	1,420,799	100.0	11.5	18.5	24.2	16.9	10.9	18.0
Hispanic	11,367,157	896,796	1,603,546	2,473,080	2,657,108	1,791,161	1,945,466	100.0	7.9	14.1	21.8	23.4	15.8	17.1
Asian	2,281,908	944,657	633,149	431,446	219,381	43,509	9,766	100.0	41.4	27.7	18.9	9.6	1.9	0.4
Pacific Islander	169,678	104,646	15,170	27,558	14,860	5,146	2,298	100.0	61.7	8.9	16.2	8.8	3.0	1.4
American Indian/Alaska Native	561,126	276,859	76,874	78,978	38,349	21,156	68,910	100.0	49.3	13.7	14.1	6.8	3.8	12.3
Two or more races	1,157,332	996,181	128,813	15,347	6,709	3,286	6,996	100.0	86.1	11.1	1.3	0.6	0.3	0.6
2014														
White	24,786,411	326,391	906,861	3,321,959	7,347,405	7,467,279	5,416,516	100.0	1.3	3.7	13.4	29.6	30.1	21.9
Black	7,759,943	916,247	1,495,510	1,925,536	1,350,373	874,182	1,198,095	100.0	11.8	19.3	24.8	17.4	11.3	15.4
Hispanic	12,716,373	917,811	1,815,981	2,766,817	3,013,933	2,057,591	2,144,240	100.0	7.2	14.3	21.8	23.7	16.2	16.9
Asian	2,454,856	958,881	677,894	500,886	252,293	48,914	15,988	100.0	39.1	27.6	20.4	10.3	2.0	0.7
Pacific Islander	174,834	113,812	15,541	27,772	12,828	4,786	95	100.0	65.1	8.9	15.9	7.3	2.7	0.1
American Indian/Alaska Native	514,123	251,476	70,266	72,766	33,205	21,219	65,191	100.0	48.9	13.7	14.2	6.5	4.1	12.7
Two or more races	1,603,231	1,370,555	220,692	8,815	1,482	1,062	625	100.0	85.5	13.8	0.5	0.1	0.1	#
2015														
White	24,505,632	338,854	925,174	3,433,953	7,370,748	7,349,746	5,087,157	100.0	1.4	3.8	14.0	30.1	30.0	20.8
Black	7,731,426	926,749	1,501,089	1,921,738	1,359,513	867,967	1,154,370	100.0	12.0	19.4	24.9	17.6	11.2	14.9
Hispanic	12,982,345	917,357	1,853,764	2,853,336	3,113,283	2,063,469	2,181,136	100.0	7.1	14.3	22.0	24.0	15.9	16.8
Asian	2,504,848	958,423	688,104	525,789	264,939	51,494	16,099	100.0	38.3	27.5	21.0	10.6	2.1	0.6
Pacific Islander	175,646	115,753	16,543	26,626	12,225	4,398	101	100.0	65.9	9.4	15.2	7.0	2.5	0.1
American Indian/Alaska Native	504,365	244,771	70,672	70,002	31,830	20,554	66,536	100.0	48.5	14.0	13.9	6.3	4.1	13.2
Two or more races	1,710,916	1,441,131	257,234	9,985	1,644	915	7	100.0	84.2	15.0	0.6	0.1	0.1	#
2016														
White	24,237,835	345,391	951,004	3,526,424	7,414,830	7,269,692	4,730,494	100.0	1.4	3.9	14.5	30.6	30.0	19.5
Black	7,698,283	934,011	1,525,821	1,918,536	1,370,443	847,520	1,101,952	100.0	12.1	19.8	24.9	17.8	11.0	14.3
Hispanic	13,262,558	915,163	1,908,509	2,959,009	3,184,219	2,112,281	2,183,377	100.0	6.9	14.4	22.3	24.0	15.9	16.5
Asian	2,560,906	957,860	699,521	554,255	277,419	56,823	15,028	100.0	37.4	27.3	21.6	10.8	2.2	0.6
Pacific Islander	183,415	124,482	18,105	25,524	12,050	3,142	112	100.0	67.9	9.9	13.9	6.6	1.7	0.1
American Indian/Alaska Native	502,152	243,356	69,973	70,719	32,069	21,969	64,066	100.0	48.5	13.9	14.1	6.4	4.4	12.8
Two or more races	1,829,598	1,510,009	301,306	15,955	808	1,074	446	100.0	82.5	16.5	0.9	0.0	0.1	#

#Rounds to zero.
NOTE: Data reflect racial/ethnic data reported by schools. Because some schools do not report complete racial/ethnic data, totals may differ from figures in other tables. Excludes 1995 data for Idaho and 2000 data for Tennessee because racial/ethnic data were not reported. Race categories exclude persons of Hispanic ethnicity. Detail may not sum to totals because of rounding.

SOURCE: U.S. Department of Education, National Center for Education Statistics, Common Core of Data (CCD), "Public Elementary/Secondary School Universe Survey," 1995–96 through 2016–17. (This table was prepared November 2018.)

Table 216.60. Number and percentage distribution of public school students, by percentage of students in school who are eligible for free or reduced-price lunch, school level, locale, and student race/ethnicity: Fall 2016

School level, locale, and student race/ethnicity	Number of students, by percent of students in school eligible for free or reduced-price lunch						Percentage distribution of students, by percent of students in school eligible for free or reduced-price lunch					
	Total[1]	0 to 25.0 percent	25.1 to 50.0 percent	50.1 to 75.0 percent	More than 75.0 percent	Missing/ school does not participate	Total[1]	0 to 25.0 percent	25.1 to 50.0 percent	50.1 to 75.0 percent	More than 75.0 percent	Missing/ school does not participate
1	2	3	4	5	6	7	8	9	10	11	12	13
Total	**50,274,747**	**10,647,925**	**14,244,477**	**12,908,098**	**12,144,248**	**329,999**	**100.0**	**21.2**	**28.3**	**25.7**	**24.2**	**0.7**
White	24,237,835	7,479,431	9,034,058	5,641,781	1,917,558	165,007	100.0	30.9	37.3	23.3	7.9	0.7
Black	7,698,283	566,614	1,415,020	2,273,153	3,388,185	55,311	100.0	7.4	18.4	29.5	44.0	0.7
Hispanic	13,262,558	1,097,634	2,403,084	3,780,174	5,911,620	70,046	100.0	8.3	18.1	28.5	44.6	0.5
Asian	2,560,906	1,006,812	655,202	513,457	370,770	14,665	100.0	39.3	25.6	20.0	14.5	0.6
Pacific Islander	183,415	22,231	51,793	63,877	44,559	955	100.0	12.1	28.2	34.8	24.3	0.5
American Indian/Alaska Native	502,152	39,173	113,145	143,376	193,324	13,134	100.0	7.8	22.5	28.6	38.5	2.6
Two or more races	1,829,598	436,030	572,175	492,280	318,232	10,881	100.0	23.8	31.3	26.9	17.4	0.6
School level[2]												
Elementary[3]	32,132,682	6,360,172	8,204,059	8,333,876	9,099,671	134,904	100.0	19.8	25.5	25.9	28.3	0.4
White	15,089,181	4,416,375	5,246,851	3,867,876	1,498,374	59,705	100.0	29.3	34.8	25.6	9.9	0.4
Black	4,951,958	302,001	762,785	1,343,414	2,517,005	26,753	100.0	6.1	15.4	27.1	50.8	0.5
Hispanic	8,754,451	656,865	1,362,115	2,318,389	4,386,700	30,382	100.0	7.5	15.6	26.5	50.1	0.3
Asian	1,631,133	661,213	378,372	320,928	265,305	5,315	100.0	40.5	23.2	19.7	16.3	0.3
Pacific Islander	113,870	12,589	26,890	39,697	34,269	425	100.0	11.1	23.6	34.9	30.1	0.4
American Indian/Alaska Native	310,544	20,234	59,744	87,508	135,935	7,123	100.0	6.5	19.2	28.2	43.8	2.3
Two or more races	1,281,545	290,895	367,302	356,064	262,083	5,201	100.0	22.7	28.7	27.8	20.5	0.4
Secondary[4]	15,798,446	3,837,261	5,452,290	3,941,038	2,452,708	115,149	100.0	24.3	34.5	24.9	15.5	0.7
White	7,993,766	2,753,288	3,408,526	1,453,828	317,392	60,732	100.0	34.4	42.6	18.2	4.0	0.8
Black	2,312,355	227,853	592,193	809,283	668,152	14,874	100.0	9.9	25.6	35.0	28.9	0.6
Hispanic	3,958,417	389,455	943,604	1,315,794	1,282,119	27,445	100.0	9.8	23.8	33.2	32.4	0.7
Asian	849,389	319,790	256,056	177,640	91,901	4,002	100.0	37.6	30.1	20.9	10.8	0.5
Pacific Islander	61,083	8,214	22,639	21,730	8,229	271	100.0	13.4	37.1	35.6	13.5	0.4
American Indian/Alaska Native	156,347	15,336	47,659	46,411	41,706	5,235	100.0	9.8	30.5	29.7	26.7	3.3
Two or more races	467,089	123,325	181,613	116,352	43,209	2,590	100.0	26.4	38.9	24.9	9.3	0.6
School locale												
City	15,316,001	1,947,874	3,191,372	3,914,467	6,139,113	123,175	100.0	12.7	20.8	25.6	40.1	0.8
White	4,391,156	1,124,033	1,524,083	1,090,833	613,150	39,057	100.0	25.6	34.7	24.8	14.0	0.9
Black	3,547,372	147,882	481,436	956,626	1,925,691	35,737	100.0	4.2	13.6	27.0	54.3	1.0
Hispanic	5,569,038	267,433	743,093	1,397,573	3,125,653	35,286	100.0	4.8	13.3	25.1	56.1	0.6
Asian	1,055,087	287,018	247,675	259,602	253,999	6,793	100.0	27.2	23.5	24.6	24.1	0.6
Pacific Islander	66,285	5,856	15,258	21,985	22,809	377	100.0	8.8	23.0	33.2	34.4	0.6
American Indian/Alaska Native	105,533	8,621	23,973	28,995	42,089	1,855	100.0	8.2	22.7	27.5	39.9	1.8
Two or more races	581,530	107,031	155,854	158,853	155,722	4,070	100.0	18.4	26.8	27.3	26.8	0.7
Suburban	19,917,509	6,450,792	5,561,185	4,251,982	3,518,550	135,000	100.0	32.4	27.9	21.3	17.7	0.7
White	9,708,972	4,529,749	3,183,594	1,460,317	453,279	82,033	100.0	46.7	32.8	15.0	4.7	0.8
Black	2,713,931	332,830	638,770	866,008	859,580	16,743	100.0	12.3	23.5	31.9	31.7	0.6
Hispanic	5,282,012	659,386	1,105,897	1,502,145	1,991,403	23,181	100.0	12.5	20.9	28.4	37.7	0.4
Asian	1,279,758	638,653	333,779	203,930	96,574	6,822	100.0	49.9	26.1	15.9	7.5	0.5
Pacific Islander	73,702	13,225	22,779	23,851	13,502	345	100.0	17.9	30.9	32.4	18.3	0.5
American Indian/Alaska Native	88,237	17,343	28,352	23,579	18,028	935	100.0	19.7	32.1	26.7	20.4	1.1
Two or more races	770,897	259,606	248,014	172,152	86,184	4,941	100.0	33.7	32.2	22.3	11.2	0.6
Town	5,555,569	502,817	1,968,836	1,968,313	1,093,032	22,571	100.0	9.1	35.4	35.4	19.7	0.4
White	3,504,174	420,815	1,537,730	1,212,185	322,002	11,442	100.0	12.0	43.9	34.6	9.2	0.3
Black	548,226	14,680	85,837	178,156	268,835	718	100.0	2.7	15.7	32.5	49.0	0.1
Hispanic	1,098,351	37,674	218,594	430,914	406,217	4,952	100.0	3.4	19.9	39.2	37.0	0.5
Asian	72,120	9,449	28,125	23,685	10,728	133	100.0	13.1	39.0	32.8	14.9	0.2
Pacific Islander	23,424	809	7,923	9,972	4,668	52	100.0	3.5	33.8	42.6	19.9	0.2
American Indian/Alaska Native	118,794	4,120	26,316	38,811	44,778	4,769	100.0	3.5	22.2	32.7	37.7	4.0
Two or more races	190,480	15,270	64,311	74,590	35,804	505	100.0	8.0	33.8	39.2	18.8	0.3
Rural	9,485,668	1,746,442	3,523,084	2,773,336	1,393,553	49,253	100.0	18.4	37.1	29.2	14.7	0.5
White	6,633,533	1,404,834	2,788,651	1,878,446	529,127	32,475	100.0	21.2	42.0	28.3	8.0	0.5
Black	888,754	71,222	208,977	272,363	334,079	2,113	100.0	8.0	23.5	30.6	37.6	0.2
Hispanic	1,313,157	133,141	335,500	449,542	388,347	6,627	100.0	10.1	25.5	34.2	29.6	0.5
Asian	153,941	71,692	45,623	26,240	9,469	917	100.0	46.6	29.6	17.0	6.2	0.6
Pacific Islander	20,004	2,341	5,833	8,069	3,580	181	100.0	11.7	29.2	40.3	17.9	0.9
American Indian/Alaska Native	189,588	9,089	34,504	51,991	88,429	5,575	100.0	4.8	18.2	27.4	46.6	2.9
Two or more races	286,691	54,123	103,996	86,685	40,522	1,365	100.0	18.9	36.3	30.2	14.1	0.5

[1]Includes students enrolled in schools that did not report free or reduced-price lunch eligibility.
[2]Combined elementary/secondary schools and schools not reported by grade span are not shown separately.
[3]Includes schools beginning with grade 6 or below and with no grade higher than 8.
[4]Includes schools with no grade lower than 7.
NOTE: Students with household incomes under 185 percent of the poverty threshold are eligible for free or reduced-price lunch under the National School Lunch Program (NSLP). In addition, some groups of children—such as foster children, children participating in the Head Start and Migrant Education programs, and children receiving services under the Runaway and Homeless Youth Act—are assumed to be categorically eligible to participate in the NSLP. Data include students whose NSLP eligibility has been determined through direct certification. Also, under the Community Eligibility option, some nonpoor children who attend school in a low-income area may participate if the district decides that it would be more efficient to provide free lunch to all children in the school. For more information, see http://www.fns.usda.gov/nslp/national-school-lunch-program-nslp. Race categories exclude persons of Hispanic ethnicity. Detail may not sum to totals because of rounding.
SOURCE: U.S. Department of Education, National Center for Education Statistics, Common Core of Data (CCD), "Public Elementary/Secondary School Universe Survey," 2016–17. (This table was prepared February 2019.)

Table 216.70. Public elementary and secondary schools, by level, type, and state or jurisdiction: 1990–91, 2000–01, 2010–11, and 2016–17

State or jurisdiction	Total, all schools, 1990–91	Total, all schools, 2000–01	Total, all schools, 2010–11	Schools by level, 2016–17								Selected types of schools, 2016–17		
				Total, all schools	Elementary[1]	Secondary[2]	Combined elementary/secondary[3]				Other[4]	Alternative[5]	Special education[5]	One-teacher schools[5]
							Total	Prekindergarten, kindergarten, or grade 1 to grade 12	Other schools ending with grade 12	Other combined schools				
1	2	3	4	5	6	7	8	9	10	11	12	13	14	15
United States	**84,538**	**93,273**	**98,817**	**98,158**	**66,837**	**23,814**	**6,783**	**3,471**	**2,736**	**576**	**724**	**5,249**	**1,991**	**203**
Alabama	1,297	1,517	1,600	1,513	925	406	159	105	48	6	23	83	34	0
Alaska	498	515	509	507	196	79	232	217	15	0	0	23	3	7
Arizona	1,049	1,724	2,265	2,308	1,377	750	165	89	58	18	16	59	20	2
Arkansas	1,098	1,138	1,110	1,089	697	374	18	4	9	5	0	5	4	0
California	7,913	8,773	10,124	10,286	7,037	2,509	625	477	140	8	115	1,103	150	34
Colorado	1,344	1,632	1,796	1,888	1,320	401	167	79	79	9	0	98	7	0
Connecticut	985	1,248	1,157	1,250	919	297	34	13	18	3	0	21	156	0
Delaware	173	191	214	228	168	38	17	10	5	2	5	6	18	0
District of Columbia	181	198	228	223	177	36	10	2	5	3	0	4	2	0
Florida	2,516	3,316	4,131	4,178	2,845	675	657	279	352	26	1	392	171	4
Georgia	1,734	1,946	2,449	2,300	1,775	453	66	15	37	14	6	41	19	0
Hawaii	235	261	289	290	212	52	26	22	3	1	0	1	1	1
Idaho	582	673	748	745	460	202	83	41	39	3	0	74	11	11
Illinois	4,239	4,342	4,361	4,173	3,048	894	131	19	102	10	100	141	110	0
Indiana	1,915	1,976	1,936	1,921	1,371	469	62	25	34	3	19	8	22	0
Iowa	1,588	1,534	1,436	1,328	939	348	41	4	37	0	0	18	3	2
Kansas	1,477	1,430	1,378	1,318	923	340	52	16	36	0	3	1	4	0
Kentucky	1,400	1,526	1,554	1,539	975	417	146	41	101	4	1	184	8	0
Louisiana	1,533	1,530	1,471	1,404	973	280	151	99	45	7	0	5	32	0
Maine	747	714	631	605	445	146	14	10	4	0	0	0	1	4
Maryland	1,220	1,383	1,449	1,424	1,125	241	45	20	22	3	13	44	37	0
Massachusetts	1,842	1,905	1,829	1,856	1,419	373	58	19	32	7	6	21	8	0
Michigan	3,313	3,998	3,877	3,458	1,744	864	827	477	340	10	23	323	180	6
Minnesota	1,590	2,362	2,392	2,513	1,357	857	298	144	144	10	1	500	306	0
Mississippi	972	1,030	1,083	1,066	619	329	45	37	7	1	73	66	1	0
Missouri	2,199	2,368	2,410	2,424	1,620	628	156	75	81	0	20	59	53	0
Montana	900	879	827	820	492	328	0	0	0	0	0	4	2	58
Nebraska	1,506	1,326	1,096	1,095	731	302	12	11	0	1	50	49	27	3
Nevada	354	511	645	657	479	125	53	18	28	7	0	33	13	14
New Hampshire	439	526	480	490	381	109	0	0	0	0	0	0	0	0
New Jersey	2,272	2,410	2,607	2,590	1,950	543	74	44	23	7	23	90	63	0
New Mexico	681	765	862	869	601	229	33	12	18	3	6	26	5	1
New York	4,010	4,336	4,757	4,798	3,273	1,121	401	180	167	54	3	56	131	0
North Carolina	1,955	2,207	2,567	2,624	1,919	546	158	72	62	24	1	73	25	0
North Dakota	663	579	516	519	305	181	0	0	0	0	33	0	32	5
Ohio	3,731	3,916	3,758	3,591	2,399	1,006	180	42	70	68	6	0	51	0
Oklahoma	1,880	1,821	1,785	1,792	1,225	558	8	1	6	1	1	5	4	0
Oregon	1,199	1,273	1,296	1,243	885	273	85	56	26	3	0	32	1	15
Pennsylvania	3,260	3,252	3,233	3,004	2,124	785	95	43	43	9	0	6	4	0
Rhode Island	309	328	317	315	239	70	6	5	1	0	0	2	1	0
South Carolina	1,097	1,127	1,214	1,252	931	281	40	11	22	7	0	12	8	0
South Dakota	802	769	710	697	438	243	16	6	10	0	0	33	12	12
Tennessee	1,543	1,624	1,784	1,774	1,343	345	86	30	43	13	0	18	16	0
Texas	5,991	7,519	8,732	8,909	6,122	2,092	695	280	239	176	0	932	11	1
Utah	714	793	1,016	1,037	674	282	81	44	6	31	0	28	59	6
Vermont	397	393	320	312	229	65	18	11	7	0	0	1	0	1
Virginia	1,811	1,969	2,175	2,134	1,493	436	35	25	10	0	170	125	53	0
Washington	1,936	2,305	2,338	2,436	1,563	656	217	140	69	8	0	314	95	2
West Virginia	1,015	840	757	739	548	120	69	45	24	0	2	33	3	0
Wisconsin	2,018	2,182	2,238	2,256	1,579	559	114	43	65	6	4	91	11	5
Wyoming	415	393	360	371	248	101	22	13	4	5	0	6	3	9
Jurisdiction														
Bureau of Indian Education	—	189	173	174	112	19	43	37	5	1	0	0	0	0
DoDEA[6]	—	227	191	—	—	—	—	—	—	—	—	—	—	—
Other jurisdictions														
American Samoa	30	31	28	28	22	6	0	0	0	0	0	0	0	0
Guam	35	38	40	41	34	7	0	0	0	0	0	1	0	0
Northern Marianas	26	29	30	—	—	—	—	—	—	—	—	—	—	—
Puerto Rico	1,619	1,543	1,473	1,283	932	251	73	5	15	53	27	10	19	0
U.S. Virgin Islands	33	36	32	28	19	9	0	0	0	0	0	0	0	0

—Not available.
[1]Includes schools beginning with grade 6 or below and with no grade higher than 8.
[2]Includes schools with no grade lower than 7.
[3]Includes schools beginning with grade 6 or below and ending with grade 9 or above.
[4]Includes schools not reported by grade span.
[5]Schools are also included under elementary, secondary, combined, or other as appropriate.
[6]DoDEA = Department of Defense Education Activity. Includes both domestic and overseas schools.
SOURCE: U.S. Department of Education, National Center for Education Statistics, Common Core of Data (CCD), "Public Elementary/Secondary School Universe Survey," 1990–91, 2000–01, 2010–11, and 2016–17. (This table was prepared November 2018.)

Table 216.75. Public elementary schools, by grade span, average school enrollment, and state or jurisdiction: 2016–17

State or jurisdiction	Total, all elementary schools	Total, all regular elementary schools[1]	Schools, by grade span: Prekindergarten, kindergarten, or grade 1 to grade 3 or 4	Prekindergarten, kindergarten, or grade 1 to grade 5	Prekindergarten, kindergarten, or grade 1 to grade 6	Prekindergarten, kindergarten, or grade 1 to grade 8	Grade 4, 5, or 6 to grade 6, 7, or 8	Other grade spans	Average school enrollment[2]: All elementary schools	Regular elementary schools[1]
1	2	3	4	5	6	7	8	9	10	11
United States	**66,837**	**65,853**	**4,949**	**25,714**	**9,569**	**6,664**	**13,253**	**6,688**	**483**	**488**
Alabama	925	915	92	293	143	59	218	120	497	499
Alaska	196	196	0	38	98	22	24	14	337	337
Arizona	1,377	1,360	51	240	364	476	170	76	512	514
Arkansas	697	694	133	144	155	7	156	102	441	442
California	7,037	6,881	119	2,545	2,057	1,073	1,065	178	550	558
Colorado	1,320	1,316	24	634	194	131	243	94	439	439
Connecticut	919	824	98	291	66	106	170	188	371	411
Delaware	168	159	15	78	4	9	38	24	550	566
District of Columbia	177	177	20	73	1	30	33	20	364	364
Florida	2,845	2,785	36	1,669	125	307	573	135	670	682
Georgia	1,775	1,774	34	1,066	19	41	464	151	683	684
Hawaii	212	212	1	86	85	10	28	2	539	539
Idaho	460	449	35	159	130	29	81	26	395	403
Illinois	3,048	3,033	282	773	288	645	577	483	432	434
Indiana	1,371	1,369	159	478	303	50	262	119	473	474
Iowa	939	938	120	324	133	10	226	126	352	352
Kansas	923	921	73	368	178	52	191	61	347	347
Kentucky	975	963	33	471	102	76	198	95	474	480
Louisiana	973	972	74	307	112	135	203	142	477	477
Maine	445	445	48	95	55	81	80	86	266	266
Maryland	1,125	1,111	10	685	59	98	222	51	553	558
Massachusetts	1,419	1,415	175	487	116	101	289	251	433	434
Michigan	1,744	1,711	186	627	159	218	324	230	418	420
Minnesota	1,357	1,187	112	431	242	82	268	222	425	466
Mississippi	619	619	72	140	85	36	157	129	497	497
Missouri	1,620	1,612	148	509	293	112	327	231	374	375
Montana	492	489	17	73	189	110	69	34	194	195
Nebraska	731	728	46	200	243	20	108	114	293	293
Nevada	479	470	8	270	74	20	93	14	636	645
New Hampshire	381	381	51	114	39	54	83	40	316	316
New Jersey	1,950	1,934	259	564	129	287	364	347	458	461
New Mexico	601	597	18	261	107	35	128	52	362	364
New York	3,273	3,262	279	1,291	355	285	719	344	517	518
North Carolina	1,919	1,907	83	1,102	56	123	466	89	531	534
North Dakota	305	305	9	86	99	68	34	9	240	240
Ohio	2,399	2,378	352	618	334	198	526	371	437	440
Oklahoma	1,225	1,221	80	299	163	276	252	155	388	389
Oregon	885	882	27	410	113	126	177	32	417	418
Pennsylvania	2,124	2,124	306	665	327	193	420	213	491	491
Rhode Island	239	238	36	100	18	3	48	34	396	397
South Carolina	931	928	44	479	31	45	229	103	562	564
South Dakota	438	428	26	128	59	94	104	27	216	220
Tennessee	1,343	1,334	174	523	56	182	317	91	503	505
Texas	6,122	6,003	594	2,916	432	146	1,368	666	570	578
Utah	674	638	10	117	420	35	43	49	547	568
Vermont	229	229	15	24	98	63	17	12	240	240
Virginia	1,493	1,493	47	841	148	12	308	137	576	576
Washington	1,563	1,481	58	694	285	85	295	146	455	471
West Virginia	548	547	67	254	33	39	113	42	347	348
Wisconsin	1,579	1,571	168	609	120	152	341	189	359	360
Wyoming	248	247	25	65	75	17	44	22	233	233
Jurisdiction										
Bureau of Indian Education	112	112	6	7	27	64	4	4	212	212
DoDEA[3]	—	—	—	—	—	—	—	—	—	—
Other jurisdictions										
American Samoa	22	22	0	0	0	22	0	0	—	—
Guam	34	34	0	24	0	0	8	2	607	607
Northern Marianas	—	—	—	—	—	—	—	—	—	—
Puerto Rico	932	931	18	325	324	146	97	22	233	234
U.S. Virgin Islands	19	19	1	1	14	1	2	0	398	398

—Not available.
[1]Excludes special education and alternative schools.
[2]Average for schools reporting enrollment data. Enrollment data were available for 66,556 out of 66,837 public elementary schools in 2016–17.
[3]DoDEA = Department of Defense Education Activity. Includes both domestic and overseas schools.

NOTE: Includes schools beginning with grade 6 or below and with no grade higher than 8. Excludes schools not reported by grade level, such as some special education schools for students with disabilities.
SOURCE: U.S. Department of Education, National Center for Education Statistics, Common Core of Data (CCD), "Public Elementary/Secondary School Universe Survey," 2016–17. (This table was prepared November 2018.)

Table 216.80. Public secondary schools, by grade span, average school enrollment, and state or jurisdiction: 2016–17

State or jurisdiction	Total, all secondary schools	Total, all regular secondary schools[1]	Schools, by grade span: Grades 7 to 8 and 7 to 9	Grades 7 to 12	Grades 8 to 12	Grades 9 to 12	Grades 10 to 12	Other spans ending with grade 12	Other grade spans	Vocational schools[2]	Average school enrollment[3]: All secondary schools	Regular secondary schools[1]
1	2	3	4	5	6	7	8	9	10	11	12	13
United States	**23,814**	**19,264**	**2,527**	**2,972**	**551**	**16,014**	**500**	**326**	**924**	**1,391**	**708**	**802**
Alabama	406	315	40	76	10	244	28	1	7	68	718	729
Alaska	79	61	12	20	1	42	2	1	1	3	456	543
Arizona	750	476	63	65	24	576	6	2	14	246	688	748
Arkansas	374	345	53	118	11	137	33	1	21	24	513	519
California	2,509	1,654	356	279	10	1,769	62	22	11	68	870	1,213
Colorado	401	336	38	42	4	297	4	1	15	8	658	744
Connecticut	297	208	35	12	2	200	7	36	5	17	589	783
Delaware	38	32	1	1	8	25	0	0	3	6	999	960
District of Columbia	36	32	0	0	1	33	0	0	2	0	439	474
Florida	675	509	15	33	34	563	7	21	2	35	1,274	1,573
Georgia	453	420	15	10	8	388	5	1	26	0	1,134	1,219
Hawaii	52	51	12	7	0	33	0	0	0	0	1,125	1,145
Idaho	202	144	28	36	1	127	8	0	2	14	507	637
Illinois	894	823	121	71	11	652	9	20	10	0	736	788
Indiana	469	438	75	80	9	261	3	8	33	28	821	827
Iowa	348	331	33	69	1	228	10	0	7	0	462	481
Kansas	340	337	34	96	3	205	1	1	0	0	456	460
Kentucky	417	233	26	35	6	226	2	0	122	121	700	862
Louisiana	280	258	29	41	80	109	13	1	7	12	740	769
Maine	146	118	8	15	2	93	0	0	28	27	457	461
Maryland	241	188	4	6	4	201	1	7	18	25	1,107	1,268
Massachusetts	373	322	29	37	15	285	2	4	1	38	813	825
Michigan	864	638	31	132	39	655	0	4	3	4	554	688
Minnesota	857	442	33	271	35	425	39	46	8	8	387	611
Mississippi	329	238	30	42	1	153	4	2	97	91	630	630
Missouri	628	551	57	173	3	367	13	8	7	63	540	542
Montana	328	325	157	0	0	171	0	0	0	0	156	157
Nebraska	302	291	23	158	2	112	1	6	0	0	381	381
Nevada	125	111	14	4	2	100	1	4	0	0	1,113	1,228
New Hampshire	109	109	14	0	0	92	1	0	2	0	554	554
New Jersey	543	417	56	38	10	408	8	4	19	58	828	1,009
New Mexico	229	209	34	29	1	145	9	0	11	0	475	503
New York	1,121	1,033	62	145	22	856	7	5	24	21	720	746
North Carolina	546	516	23	6	4	485	2	8	18	8	850	885
North Dakota	181	168	3	88	0	75	0	1	14	13	205	205
Ohio	1,006	927	125	156	47	625	21	13	19	74	594	605
Oklahoma	558	554	87	5	0	436	22	0	8	0	387	390
Oregon	273	252	26	41	4	200	1	1	0	0	643	685
Pennsylvania	785	696	99	152	11	500	14	1	8	84	810	818
Rhode Island	70	59	5	1	1	53	0	0	10	10	698	706
South Carolina	281	228	19	2	1	244	7	4	4	42	930	973
South Dakota	243	220	61	1	0	177	1	3	0	3	169	182
Tennessee	345	328	11	27	18	255	7	12	15	4	817	856
Texas	2,092	1,532	260	138	43	1,370	42	33	206	0	796	1,050
Utah	282	250	91	46	6	71	54	1	13	6	923	993
Vermont	65	49	7	17	0	41	0	0	0	15	477	486
Virginia	436	343	33	6	25	281	1	0	90	89	1,194	1,208
Washington	656	446	70	51	25	450	27	24	9	19	611	825
West Virginia	120	106	1	20	2	95	1	0	1	33	661	714
Wisconsin	559	494	51	60	3	410	13	19	3	6	496	543
Wyoming	101	101	17	14	1	68	1	0	0	0	329	329
Jurisdiction												
Bureau of Indian Education	19	19	1	4	2	12	0	0	0	0	339	339
DoDEA[4]	—	—	—	—	—	—	—	—	—	—	—	—
Other jurisdictions												
American Samoa	6	5	0	0	0	6	0	0	0	1	—	—
Guam	7	6	0	0	0	7	0	0	0	0	1,448	1,664
Northern Marianas	—	—	—	—	—	—	—	—	—	—	—	—
Puerto Rico	251	218	59	15	1	139	25	0	12	32	483	457
U.S. Virgin Islands	9	8	4	0	0	5	0	0	0	1	703	703

—Not available.
[1]Excludes vocational, special education, and alternative schools.
[2]Vocational schools are also included under appropriate grade span.
[3]Average for schools reporting enrollment data. Enrollment data were available for 22,318 out of 23,814 public secondary schools in 2016–17.
[4]DoDEA = Department of Defense Education Activity. Includes both domestic and overseas schools.

NOTE: Includes schools with no grade lower than 7. Excludes schools not reported by grade level, such as some special education schools for students with disabilities.
SOURCE: U.S. Department of Education, National Center for Education Statistics, Common Core of Data (CCD), "Public Elementary/Secondary School Universe Survey," 2016–17. (This table was prepared November 2018.)

Table 216.90. Public elementary and secondary charter schools and enrollment, and charter schools and enrollment as a percentage of total public schools and total enrollment in public schools, by state: Selected years, 2000–01 through 2016–17

State	Number of charter schools					Fall enrollment in charter schools					Charter schools as a percent of total public schools				Charter school enrollment as a percent of total fall enrollment in public schools			
	2000–01	2005–06	2010–11	2015–16	2016–17	2000–01	2005–06	2010–11	2015–16	2016–17	2000–01	2005–06	2010–11	2016–17	2000–01	2005–06	2010–11	2016–17
1	2	3	4	5	6	7	8	9	10	11	12	13	14	15	16	17	18	19
United States	**1,993**	**3,780**	**5,274**	**6,855**	**7,011**	**448,343**	**1,012,906**	**1,787,091**	**2,845,322**	**3,010,287**	**2.1**	**3.9**	**5.3**	**7.1**	**1.0**	**2.1**	**3.6**	**6.0**
Alabama	0	0	0	0	1	0	0	0	0	—	0.0	0.0	0.0	0.1	0.0	0.0	0.0	—
Alaska	19	23	27	28	28	2,594	4,660	5,751	6,343	6,677	3.7	4.6	5.3	5.5	1.9	3.5	4.4	5.0
Arizona	313	501	519	552	550	45,596	90,597	124,467	176,894	185,588	18.2	24.1	22.9	23.8	5.4	8.3	11.6	16.6
Arkansas	3	19	40	65	75	708	4,006	10,209	24,182	27,896	0.3	1.7	3.6	6.9	0.2	0.8	2.1	5.7
California	302	543	908	1,224	1,248	115,582	195,876	363,916	568,774	602,837	3.4	5.6	9.0	12.1	1.9	3.1	5.9	9.7
Colorado	77	121	168	226	238	20,155	44,254	74,685	108,793	114,694	4.7	7.1	9.4	12.6	2.8	5.7	8.9	12.7
Connecticut	16	14	18	24	24	2,429	2,927	5,139	9,132	9,573	1.3	1.3	1.6	1.9	0.4	0.5	0.9	1.8
Delaware	7	13	19	28	27	2,716	6,566	9,525	13,622	14,722	3.7	5.9	8.9	11.8	2.4	5.4	7.4	10.8
District of Columbia	33	52	97	109	110	—	17,260	26,910	35,798	37,151	16.7	22.7	42.5	49.3	—	22.5	37.8	43.7
Florida	148	342	458	653	655	26,893	92,335	154,703	270,953	283,560	4.5	9.2	11.1	15.7	1.1	3.5	5.9	10.1
Georgia	30	58	67	82	84	20,066	26,440	41,981	72,170	66,905	1.5	2.4	2.7	3.7	1.4	1.7	2.5	3.8
Hawaii	6	27	31	34	34	1,343	6,498	8,289	10,444	10,669	2.3	9.5	10.7	11.7	0.7	3.5	4.6	5.9
Idaho	9	26	40	54	57	1,083	8,003	15,330	19,381	20,579	1.3	3.7	5.3	7.7	0.4	3.1	5.6	6.9
Illinois	20	29	50	64	63	7,552	16,968	43,049	64,108	65,169	0.5	0.7	1.1	1.5	0.4	0.8	2.1	3.2
Indiana	0	29	60	88	93	0	7,409	22,472	39,671	43,079	0.0	1.5	3.1	4.8	0.0	0.7	2.2	4.1
Iowa	0	6	7	3	3	0	520	298	430	398	0.0	0.4	0.5	0.2	0.0	0.1	0.1	0.1
Kansas	1	26	25	10	10	67	1,914	4,618	3,186	3,159	0.1	1.8	1.8	0.8	#	0.4	1.0	0.6
Kentucky	0	0	0	0	0	0	0	0	0	0	0.0	0.0	0.0	0.0	0.0	0.0	0.0	0.0
Louisiana	19	26	78	138	151	3,212	8,315	29,199	74,030	79,022	1.2	1.9	5.3	10.8	0.4	1.3	4.2	11.0
Maine	1	0	0	7	9	154	0	0	1,518	1,955	0.1	0.0	0.0	1.5	0.1	0.0	0.0	1.1
Maryland	0	15	44	50	49	0	3,363	14,492	20,988	22,366	0.0	1.0	3.0	3.4	0.0	0.4	1.7	2.5
Massachusetts	41	59	63	81	78	13,712	21,958	28,422	40,199	42,596	2.2	3.1	3.4	4.2	1.4	2.3	3.0	4.5
Michigan	205	264	300	370	376	54,751	91,384	111,344	145,483	147,061	5.1	6.5	7.7	10.9	3.3	5.3	7.2	10.0
Minnesota	73	161	176	216	220	9,395	20,603	37,253	50,812	54,211	3.1	6.1	7.4	8.8	1.1	2.5	4.4	6.2
Mississippi	1	1	0	2	3	367	374	0	226	523	0.1	0.1	0.0	0.3	0.1	0.1	0.0	0.1
Missouri	21	23	53	70	72	7,061	10,972	20,076	21,619	22,803	0.9	1.0	2.2	3.0	0.8	1.2	2.2	2.5
Montana	0	0	0	0	0	0	0	0	0	0	0.0	0.0	0.0	0.0	0.0	0.0	0.0	0.0
Nebraska	0	0	0	0	0	0	0	0	0	0	0.0	0.0	0.0	0.0	0.0	0.0	0.0	0.0
Nevada	8	19	34	47	49	1,255	4,818	14,127	35,130	40,074	1.6	3.4	5.3	7.5	0.4	1.2	3.2	8.5
New Hampshire	0	6	14	31	31	0	200	983	3,011	3,422	0.0	1.3	2.9	6.3	0.0	0.1	0.5	1.9
New Jersey	53	54	76	89	88	10,179	14,937	24,591	41,026	46,274	2.2	2.2	2.9	3.4	0.8	1.1	1.8	3.4
New Mexico	10	53	81	99	99	1,335	8,595	15,290	22,079	25,139	1.3	6.2	9.4	11.4	0.4	2.6	4.6	7.6
New York	38	79	170	256	267	0	21,539	54,443	117,710	128,784	0.9	1.7	3.6	5.6	0.0	0.8	2.0	4.8
North Carolina	90	99	99	158	167	15,523	27,441	42,141	82,521	92,281	4.1	4.2	3.9	6.4	1.2	1.9	2.8	6.0
North Dakota	0	0	0	0	0	0	0	0	0	0	0.0	0.0	0.0	0.0	0.0	0.0	0.0	0.0
Ohio	66	316	339	373	362	14,745	68,679	96,669	118,603	116,279	1.7	7.9	9.0	10.1	0.8	3.7	5.5	6.8
Oklahoma	6	14	18	45	48	1,208	4,081	6,585	19,893	24,248	0.3	0.8	1.0	2.7	0.2	0.6	1.0	3.5
Oregon	12	54	108	126	124	559	5,192	20,372	30,728	32,323	0.9	4.3	8.3	10.0	0.1	1.0	3.7	5.7
Pennsylvania	65	116	145	175	179	18,981	55,630	90,613	130,940	132,979	2.0	3.6	4.5	6.0	1.0	3.0	5.1	7.8
Rhode Island	3	11	16	29	30	557	2,571	3,971	7,310	8,137	0.9	3.3	5.0	9.5	0.4	1.7	2.8	5.8
South Carolina	8	27	44	68	70	484	4,104	16,390	29,470	32,343	0.7	2.3	3.6	5.6	0.1	0.6	2.3	4.2
South Dakota	0	0	0	0	0	0	0	0	0	0	0.0	0.0	0.0	0.0	0.0	0.0	0.0	0.0
Tennessee	0	12	29	100	104	0	1,685	6,517	29,274	34,984	0.0	0.7	1.6	5.9	0.0	0.2	0.7	3.5
Texas	201	319	561	702	753	37,978	70,895	164,940	284,617	310,846	2.7	3.7	6.4	8.5	1.0	1.6	3.3	5.8
Utah	8	36	78	117	124	537	11,439	39,862	67,398	71,417	1.0	3.8	7.7	12.0	0.1	2.2	6.8	10.8
Vermont	0	0	0	0	0	0	0	0	0	0	0.0	0.0	0.0	0.0	0.0	0.0	0.0	0.0
Virginia	2	3	4	7	8	55	210	348	1,001	1,176	0.1	0.1	0.2	0.4	#	#	#	0.1
Washington	0	0	0	9	8	0	0	0	1,225	1,676	0.0	0.0	0.0	0.3	0.0	0.0	0.0	0.2
West Virginia	0	0	0	0	0	0	0	0	0	0	0.0	0.0	0.0	0.0	0.0	0.0	0.0	0.0
Wisconsin	78	181	207	242	237	9,511	27,450	36,863	44,162	44,209	3.6	8.1	9.2	10.5	1.1	3.1	4.2	5.1
Wyoming	0	3	3	4	5	0	238	258	468	503	0.0	0.8	0.8	1.3	0.0	0.3	0.3	0.5

—Not available.
#Rounds to zero.

SOURCE: U.S. Department of Education, National Center for Education Statistics, Common Core of Data (CCD), "Public Elementary/Secondary School Universe Survey," 2000–01 through 2016–17. (This table was prepared December 2018.)

Table 218.16. Percentage of students ages 5 through 17 enrolled in kindergarten through grade 12 who took any school-related courses online and, among those taking courses online, percentage who took courses from various providers, by selected child, parent, and household characteristics: 2016

[Standard errors appear in parentheses]

Selected child, parent, or household characteristic	Percent who took any school-related courses online		Among those taking school-related courses online, percent taking courses from various providers[1]									
			Local public school		State		Charter school, another public school, or private school		College, community college, or university		Someplace else	
1	2		3		4		5		6		7	
Total	**3.1**	**(0.20)**	**55.3**	**(2.96)**	**11.6**	**(1.62)**	**16.0**	**(2.80)**	**13.9**	**(1.64)**	**13.6**	**(2.33)**
Sex of child												
Male	3.0	(0.26)	55.9	(4.74)	10.0	(2.25)	19.4	(4.16)	10.5	(2.11)	15.3	(3.27)
Female	3.3	(0.29)	54.7	(3.96)	13.2	(2.64)	12.7	(3.51)	17.3	(2.91)	11.9	(2.89)
Race/ethnicity of child												
White	2.5	(0.21)	50.6	(3.90)	10.1	(1.80)	12.8	(2.40)	23.7	(3.25)	11.1	(2.48)
Black	4.5	(0.74)	61.2	(8.91)	7.1!	(3.12)	27.6!	(9.89)	‡	(†)	12.1!	(4.98)
Hispanic	2.8	(0.47)	51.4	(5.96)	17.4	(5.02)	18.5	(5.53)	‡	(†)	18.0!	(5.83)
Asian/Pacific Islander	5.9	(1.04)	52.7	(8.08)	18.7!	(6.92)	9.5!	(3.53)	13.7!	(4.92)	18.8!	(5.70)
Asian	5.6	(0.99)	55.6	(8.52)	12.6!	(5.41)	8.8!	(3.46)	15.2!	(5.40)	20.9	(6.19)
Pacific Islander	‡	(†)	‡	(†)	‡	(†)	‡	(†)	‡	(†)	‡	(†)
American Indian/Alaska Native	‡	(†)	‡	(†)	‡	(†)	‡	(†)	‡	(†)	‡	(†)
Two or more races	3.2!	(1.10)	‡	(†)	‡	(†)	‡	(†)	‡	(†)	‡	(†)
Grade equivalent												
Kindergarten through grade 5	2.1	(0.27)	66.5	(6.17)	‡	(†)	21.1!	(6.59)	‡	(†)	17.5	(4.93)
Kindergarten and grade 1	1.7	(0.47)	‡	(†)	‡	(†)	‡	(†)	‡	(†)	‡	(†)
Grades 2 and 3	2.3	(0.48)	76.7	(8.55)	‡	(†)	‡	(†)	‡	(†)	18.1!	(7.57)
Grades 4 and 5	2.3	(0.55)	66.1	(12.02)	‡	(†)	31.2!	(13.53)	‡	(†)	‡	(†)
Grades 6 through 8	1.6	(0.30)	55.0	(9.85)	‡	(†)	16.0!	(5.85)	‡	(†)	25.9	(7.66)
Grades 9 through 12	6.6	(0.43)	48.8	(3.48)	16.0	(2.29)	13.0	(2.44)	23.2	(2.56)	8.7	(2.02)
Number of children in the household												
One child	4.0	(0.29)	46.5	(4.00)	15.4	(2.46)	16.3	(2.73)	17.7	(2.55)	14.1	(2.98)
Two children	3.3	(0.29)	58.8	(4.70)	14.3	(3.45)	10.6	(2.11)	12.1	(2.58)	14.2	(3.52)
Three or more children	2.4	(0.42)	60.1	(8.50)	‡	(†)	23.8!	(9.37)	12.4!	(4.23)	12.1!	(4.53)
Number of parents in the household												
Two parents	3.4	(0.24)	53.9	(3.53)	11.2	(1.84)	17.4	(3.71)	15.3	(1.98)	13.2	(2.63)
One parent	2.7	(0.36)	58.9	(5.75)	12.6	(2.91)	12.1!	(3.75)	8.2!	(2.64)	15.5	(4.10)
Nonparental guardians	2.3	(0.66)	‡	(†)	‡	(†)	‡	(†)	‡	(†)	‡	(†)
Highest education level of parents/guardians in the household												
Less than a high school diploma	2.9	(0.72)	67.6	(12.15)	‡	(†)	‡	(†)	‡	(†)	‡	(†)
High school diploma/equivalent (e.g., GED)	2.2	(0.48)	54.4	(9.62)	14.6!	(7.13)	15.1!	(7.33)	11.7!	(4.48)	17.1!	(7.31)
Vocational/technical, associate's degree, or some college	2.9	(0.38)	63.9	(6.24)	10.1	(2.91)	18.9!	(6.22)	7.3	(2.05)	8.1!	(2.84)
Bachelor's degree/some graduate school	3.8	(0.41)	46.4	(4.88)	13.0	(2.99)	12.7	(3.18)	19.0	(3.36)	15.7	(3.45)
Graduate/professional degree	3.7	(0.43)	54.1	(6.42)	9.9	(2.89)	13.1	(3.83)	17.1	(3.55)	17.7	(4.12)
Household income												
$20,000 or less	3.0	(0.59)	72.8	(7.06)	‡	(†)	13.8!	(5.42)	8.0!	(2.68)	‡	(†)
$20,001 to $50,000	2.9	(0.46)	59.7	(8.71)	10.2!	(3.23)	16.1!	(6.62)	‡	(†)	18.7!	(6.38)
$50,001 to $75,000	2.9	(0.47)	49.6	(7.06)	15.0!	(5.30)	18.2!	(7.04)	10.3!	(4.10)	14.2!	(5.65)
$75,001 to $100,000	3.5	(0.68)	44.3	(9.74)	9.8!	(3.48)	33.6!	(11.93)	16.3!	(5.44)	8.4!	(3.78)
Over $100,000	3.4	(0.33)	53.8	(4.30)	11.2	(2.08)	8.2	(2.07)	20.4	(3.33)	14.9	(3.25)
Locale												
City	2.9	(0.35)	47.1	(5.73)	11.0	(2.58)	26.4	(6.33)	7.1	(1.89)	19.2	(4.44)
Suburban	3.5	(0.30)	56.5	(3.74)	12.6	(2.48)	10.5	(2.35)	15.1	(2.73)	14.5	(3.26)
Town	2.6	(0.58)	43.8	(13.06)	‡	(†)	‡	(†)	33.1!	(13.40)	‡	(†)
Rural	3.0	(0.50)	71.6	(6.45)	8.7!	(3.26)	‡	(†)	14.7	(4.03)	‡	(†)

†Not applicable.
!Interpret data with caution. The coefficient of variation (CV) for this estimate is between 30 and 50 percent.
‡Reporting standards not met. Either there are too few cases for a reliable estimate or the coefficient of variation (CV) is 50 percent or greater.
[1]One student could take courses from more than one provider. Therefore, the percentages sum to more than 100.

NOTE: Excludes homeschooled students and any enrolled students whose parents filled out the questionnaire that was intended for homeschooled students. Race categories exclude persons of Hispanic ethnicity. Detail may not sum to totals because of rounding.
SOURCE: U.S. Department of Education, National Center for Education Statistics, Parent and Family Involvement in Education Survey of the National Household Education Surveys Program (PFI-NHES:2016). (This table was prepared April 2019.)

Table 219.10. High school graduates, by sex and control of school; public high school averaged freshman graduation rate (AFGR); and total graduates as a ratio of 17-year-old population: Selected years, 1869–70 through 2028–29

School year	High school graduates							Public school AFGR[3]	Population 17 years old[4]	Graduates as a ratio of 17-year-old population[5]
		Sex		Control						
				Public[2]						
	Total[1]	Males	Females	Total	Males	Females	Private, total			
1	2	3	4	5	6	7	8	9	10	11
1869–70	16,000	7,064	8,936	—	—	—	—	—	815,000	2.0
1879–80	23,634	10,605	13,029	—	—	—	—	—	946,026	2.5
1889–90	43,731	18,549	25,182	21,882	—	—	21,849[6]	—	1,259,177	3.5
1899–1900	94,883	38,075	56,808	61,737	—	—	33,146[6]	—	1,489,146	6.4
1909–10	156,429	63,676	92,753	111,363	—	—	45,066[6]	—	1,786,240	8.8
1919–20	311,266	123,684	187,582	230,902	—	—	80,364[6]	—	1,855,173	16.8
1929–30	666,904	300,376	366,528	591,719	—	—	75,185[6]	—	2,295,822	29.0
1939–40	1,221,475	578,718	642,757	1,143,246	538,273	604,973	78,229[6]	—	2,403,074	50.8
1949–50	1,199,700	570,700	629,000	1,063,444	505,394	558,050	136,256[6]	—	2,034,450	59.0
1959–60	1,858,023	895,000	963,000	1,627,050	791,426	835,624	230,973	—	2,672,000	69.5
1969–70	2,888,639	1,430,000	1,459,000	2,588,639	1,285,895	1,302,744	300,000[6]	78.7	3,757,000	76.9
1975–76	3,142,120	1,552,000	1,590,000	2,837,129	1,401,064	1,436,065	304,991	74.9	4,272,000	73.6
1979–80	3,042,214	1,503,000	1,539,000	2,747,678	—	—	294,536	71.5	4,262,000	71.4
1980–81	3,020,285	1,492,000	1,528,000	2,725,285	—	—	295,000[6]	72.2	4,212,000	71.7
1981–82	2,994,758	1,479,000	1,515,000	2,704,758	—	—	290,000[6]	72.9	4,134,000	72.4
1982–83	2,887,604	1,426,000	1,461,000	2,597,604	—	—	290,000[6]	73.8	3,962,000	72.9
1983–84	2,766,797	—	—	2,494,797	—	—	272,000[6]	74.5	3,784,000	73.1
1984–85	2,676,917	—	—	2,413,917	—	—	263,000[6]	74.2	3,699,000	72.4
1985–86	2,642,616	—	—	2,382,616	—	—	260,000[6]	74.3	3,670,000	72.0
1986–87	2,693,803	—	—	2,428,803	—	—	265,000[6]	74.3	3,754,000	71.8
1987–88	2,773,020	—	—	2,500,020	—	—	273,000[6]	74.2	3,849,000	72.0
1988–89	2,743,743	—	—	2,458,800	—	—	284,943	73.4	3,842,000	71.4
1989–90[7]	2,574,162	—	—	2,320,337	—	—	253,825[8]	73.6	3,505,000	73.4
1990–91	2,492,988	—	—	2,234,893	—	—	258,095	73.7	3,417,913	72.9
1991–92	2,480,399	—	—	2,226,016	—	—	254,383[8]	74.2	3,398,884	73.0
1992–93	2,480,519	—	—	2,233,241	—	—	247,278	73.8	3,449,143	71.9
1993–94	2,463,849	—	—	2,220,849	—	—	243,000[6]	73.1	3,442,521	71.6
1994–95	2,519,084	—	—	2,273,541	—	—	245,543	71.8	3,635,803	69.3
1995–96	2,518,109	—	—	2,273,109	—	—	245,000[6]	71.0	3,640,132	69.2
1996–97	2,611,988	—	—	2,358,403	—	—	253,585	71.3	3,792,207	68.9
1997–98	2,704,050	—	—	2,439,050	1,187,647	1,251,403	265,000[6]	71.3	4,008,416	67.5
1998–99	2,758,655	—	—	2,485,630	1,212,924	1,272,706	273,025	71.1	3,917,885	70.4
1999–2000	2,832,844	—	—	2,553,844	1,241,631	1,312,213	279,000[6]	71.7	4,056,639	69.8
2000–01	2,847,973	—	—	2,569,200	1,251,931	1,317,269	278,773	71.7	4,023,686	70.8
2001–02	2,906,534	—	—	2,621,534	1,275,813	1,345,721	285,000[6]	72.6	4,023,968	72.2
2002–03	3,015,735	—	—	2,719,947	1,330,973	1,388,974	295,788	73.9	4,125,087	73.1
2003–04[7,9]	3,054,438	—	—	2,753,438	1,347,800	1,405,638	301,000[6]	74.3	4,113,074	74.3
2004–05	3,106,499	—	—	2,799,250	1,369,749	1,429,501	307,249	74.7	4,120,073	75.4
2005–06[7]	3,122,544	—	—	2,815,544	1,376,458	1,439,086	307,000[6]	73.4	4,200,554	74.3
2006–07	3,199,650	—	—	2,893,045	1,414,069	1,478,976	306,605	73.9	4,297,239	74.5
2007–08	3,312,337	—	—	3,001,337	1,467,180	1,534,157	311,000[6]	74.7	4,436,955	74.7
2008–09[7]	3,347,828	—	—	3,039,015	1,490,317	1,548,698	308,813	75.5	4,336,950	77.2
2009–10	3,435,022	—	—	3,128,022	1,542,684[10]	1,585,338[10]	307,000[6]	78.2	4,311,831	79.8
2010–11	3,449,940	—	—	3,144,100	1,552,981	1,591,113	305,840	79.6	4,367,891	79.0
2011–12	3,455,405	—	—	3,149,185	1,558,489	1,590,694	306,220[6]	80.8	4,294,530	80.5
2012–13	3,478,027	—	—	3,169,257	1,569,675	1,599,579	308,770	81.9	4,256,553	81.7
2013–14[11]	3,479,930	—	—	3,168,450	—	—	311,480	83.1	4,185,547	83.1
2014–15[12]	3,530,250	—	—	3,187,000	—	—	343,250	—	4,171,850	84.6
2015–16[11]	3,563,750	—	—	3,224,140	—	—	339,620	—	4,206,222	84.7
2016–17[11]	3,599,700	—	—	3,255,320	—	—	344,380	—	4,221,958	85.3
2017–18[11]	3,672,200	—	—	3,319,760	—	—	352,440	—	4,297,191	85.5
2018–19[11]	3,683,540	—	—	3,331,520	—	—	352,020	—	4,230,390	87.1
2019–20[11]	3,650,460	—	—	3,303,890	—	—	346,580	—	—	—
2020–21[11]	3,682,230	—	—	3,330,840	—	—	351,390	—	—	—
2021–22[11]	3,717,110	—	—	3,354,240	—	—	362,870	—	—	—
2022–23[11]	3,726,140	—	—	3,372,640	—	—	353,500	—	—	—
2023–24[11]	3,799,480	—	—	3,441,920	—	—	357,560	—	—	—
2024–25[11]	3,855,370	—	—	3,492,860	—	—	362,520	—	—	—
2025–26[11]	3,859,130	—	—	3,497,750	—	—	361,380	—	—	—
2026–27[11]	3,774,260	—	—	3,416,680	—	—	357,580	—	—	—
2027–28[11]	3,707,210	—	—	3,348,520	—	—	358,690	—	—	—
2028–29[11]	3,722,010	—	—	3,361,890	—	—	360,120	—	—	—

—Not available.
[1]Includes graduates of public and private schools.
[2]Includes estimates for states not reporting counts of graduates by sex. Data for 1929–30 and preceding years are from *Statistics of Public High Schools* and exclude graduates from high schools that failed to report to the Office of Education.
[3]The averaged freshman graduation rate provides an estimate of the percentage of students who receive a regular diploma within 4 years of entering ninth grade. The rate uses aggregate student enrollment data to estimate the size of an incoming freshman class and aggregate counts of the number of diplomas awarded 4 years later. Averaged freshman graduation rates in this table are based on reported totals of enrollment by grade and high school graduates, rather than on details reported by race/ethnicity.
[4]Derived from Current Population Reports, Series P-25. For years 1869–70 through 1989–90, 17-year-old population is an estimate of the October 17-year-old population based on July data. Data for 1990–91 and later years are October resident population estimates prepared by the Census Bureau.
[5]Based on persons of all ages graduating from high school in a given year divided by the 17-year-old population in the same year. This ratio allows for comparisons over time but does not provide a measure of graduation rates for incoming freshmen who form a cohort (or class) that is scheduled to graduate 4 years later. The ratio of high school graduates to the 17-year-old population differs from measures such as the AFGR (shown in column 9), which are designed to estimate high school cohort graduation rates.
[6]Estimated.
[7]Includes imputations for nonreporting states.
[8]Projected by private schools responding to the Private School Universe Survey.
[9]Includes estimates for public schools in New York and Wisconsin. Without estimates for these two states, the averaged freshman graduation rate for the remaining 48 states and the District of Columbia is 75.0 percent.
[10]Includes estimate for Connecticut, which did not report graduates by sex.
[11]Projected by NCES.
[12]Public school data are projected by NCES; private school data are actual.
NOTE: Includes graduates of regular day school programs. Excludes graduates of other programs, when separately reported, and recipients of high school equivalency certificates. Some data have been revised from previously published figures. Detail may not sum to totals because of rounding and adjustments to protect student privacy.
SOURCE: U.S. Department of Education, National Center for Education Statistics, *Annual Report of the Commissioner of Education*, 1870 through 1910; *Biennial Survey of Education in the United States*, 1919–20 through 1949–50; *Statistics of Public Elementary and Secondary School Systems*, 1958–59 through 1980–81; *Statistics of Nonpublic Elementary and Secondary Schools*, 1959 through 1980; Common Core of Data (CCD), "State Nonfiscal Survey of Public Elementary/Secondary Education," 1981–82 through 2009–10; "State Dropout and Completion Data File," 2005–06 through 2012–13; *Public School Graduates and Dropouts from the Common Core of Data*, 2007–08 and 2008–09; Private School Universe Survey (PSS), 1989 through 2015; and National High School Graduates Projection Model, 1972–73 through 2028–29. U.S. Department of Commerce, Census Bureau, Current Population Reports, Series P-25, Nos. 1000, 1022, 1045, 1057, 1059, 1092, and 1095; 2000 through 2009 Population Estimates, retrieved August 14, 2012, from http://www.census.gov/popest/data/national/asrh/2011/index.html; and 2010 through 2017 Population Estimates, retrieved November 8, 2018, from https://www.census.gov/data/tables/2017/demo/popest/nation-detail.html. (This table was prepared March 2019.)

Table 219.20. Public high school graduates, by region, state, and jurisdiction: Selected years, 1980–81 through 2028–29

Region, state, and jurisdiction	Actual data							Projected data				
	1980–81	1989–90	1999–2000	2009–10	2010–11	2011–12	2012–13	2013–14	2014–15	2015–16	2016–17	2017–18
1	2	3	4	5	6	7	8	9	10	11	12	13
United States	**2,725,285**	**2,320,337**[1]	**2,553,844**	**3,128,022**	**3,144,100**	**3,149,185**	**3,169,257**	**3,168,450**	**3,187,000**	**3,224,140**	**3,255,320**	**3,319,760**
Region												
Northeast	593,727	446,045	453,814	556,400	556,611	554,705	555,202	546,910	543,080	545,820	551,480	554,810
Midwest	784,071	616,700	648,020	726,844	718,779	716,072	713,662	705,550	708,240	714,040	719,240	723,280
South	868,068	796,385	861,498	1,104,770	1,119,414	1,121,400	1,138,965	1,145,570	1,162,950	1,189,220	1,211,650	1,252,210
West	479,419	461,207	590,512	740,008	749,296	757,008	761,428	770,420	772,720	775,060	772,950	789,460
State												
Alabama	44,894	40,485	37,819	43,166	46,035	45,394	44,233	44,540	45,420	46,070	47,560	48,260
Alaska	5,343	5,386	6,615	8,245	8,064	7,989	7,860	7,720	7,860	7,840	7,910	8,050
Arizona	28,416	32,103	38,304	61,145	64,472	63,208	62,208	66,700	67,200	67,120	68,770	69,560
Arkansas	29,577	26,475	27,335	28,276	28,205	28,419	28,928	29,610	30,350	30,290	30,750	31,020
California	242,172	236,291	309,866	404,987	410,467	418,664	422,125	424,080	422,830	419,190	411,710	420,500
Colorado	35,897	32,967	38,924	49,321	50,122	50,087	50,968	51,310	51,450	53,310	54,060	56,050
Connecticut	38,369	27,878	31,562	34,495	38,854	38,681	38,722	37,860	37,160	37,420	37,890	37,130
Delaware	7,349	5,550	6,108	8,133	8,043	8,247	8,070	8,240	8,390	8,480	8,690	8,930
District of Columbia[2]	4,848	3,626	2,695	3,602	3,477	3,860	3,961	3,880	3,990	4,510	4,430	4,200
Florida	88,755	88,934	106,708	156,130	155,493	151,964	158,029	158,440	163,740	166,540	170,820	176,160
Georgia	62,963	56,605	62,563	91,561	92,338	90,582	92,416	94,380	97,420	100,070	102,050	105,890
Hawaii	11,472	10,325	10,437	10,998	10,716	11,360	10,790	11,050	10,760	10,860	10,690	11,130
Idaho	12,679	11,971	16,170	17,793	17,525	17,568	17,198	19,120	18,050	18,230	19,130	19,280
Illinois	136,795	108,119	111,835	139,035	134,956	139,575	139,228	137,640	140,520	140,850	141,250	143,510
Indiana	73,381	60,012	57,012	64,551	66,133	65,667	66,595	67,560	66,750	66,720	68,970	69,640
Iowa	42,635	31,796	33,926	34,462	33,853	33,230	32,548	32,590	32,450	32,700	32,850	33,390
Kansas	29,397	25,367	29,102	31,642	31,370	31,898	31,922	32,150	31,900	32,790	32,900	33,470
Kentucky	41,714	38,005	36,830	42,664	43,031	42,642	42,888	42,400	42,530	43,280	43,280	44,330
Louisiana	46,199	36,053	38,430	36,573	35,844	36,675	37,508	38,180	37,720	38,790	39,380	41,970
Maine	15,554	13,839	12,211	14,069	13,653	13,473	13,170	12,730	12,560	12,790	12,640	12,470
Maryland	54,050	41,566	47,849	59,078	58,745	58,811	58,896	58,120	57,650	57,490	57,290	59,040
Massachusetts	74,831	55,941[3]	52,950	64,462	64,724	65,157	66,360	65,200	65,790	68,630	68,610	69,320
Michigan	124,372	93,807	97,679	110,682	106,017	105,446	104,210	102,520	102,020	100,800	101,570	102,440
Minnesota	64,166	49,087	57,372	59,667	59,357	57,501	58,255	56,370	56,800	56,640	57,250	58,370
Mississippi	28,083	25,182	24,232	25,478	27,321	26,158	26,502	26,650	26,260	26,770	26,900	28,050
Missouri	60,359	48,957	52,848	63,994	62,994	61,313	61,407	60,900	60,590	61,600	60,890	61,700
Montana	11,634	9,370	10,903	10,075	9,732	9,750	9,369	9,470	9,390	9,320	9,380	9,210
Nebraska	21,411	17,664	20,149	19,370	20,331	20,464	20,442	20,580	20,650	21,090	21,130	21,960
Nevada	9,069	9,477	14,551	20,956	21,182	21,891	23,038	22,720	23,040	23,190	23,780	24,170
New Hampshire	11,552	10,766	11,829	15,034	14,495	14,426	14,262	13,790	13,520	13,600	13,160	13,160
New Jersey	93,168	69,824	74,420	96,225	95,186	93,819	96,490	95,220	95,250	97,130	97,990	98,330
New Mexico	17,915	14,884	18,031	18,595	19,352	20,315	19,232	18,590	19,530	19,480	19,770	20,190
New York	198,465	143,318	141,731	183,826	182,759	180,806	180,351	178,810	179,110	178,260	181,790	185,630
North Carolina	69,395	64,782	62,140	88,704	89,892	93,977	94,339	96,210	97,020	98,970	101,710	105,280
North Dakota	9,924	7,690	8,606	7,155	7,156	6,942	6,900	6,960	7,040	7,020	6,940	6,570
Ohio	143,503	114,513	111,668	123,437	124,229	123,135	122,491	119,520	120,940	125,050	126,590	122,380
Oklahoma	38,875	35,606	37,646	38,503	37,744	37,305	37,033	37,260	38,420	39,690	40,230	41,170
Oregon	28,729	25,473	30,151	34,671	34,723	34,261	33,899	34,440	34,800	35,650	34,700	35,380
Pennsylvania	144,645	110,527	113,959	131,182	130,284	131,733	129,777	127,200	123,560	121,840	123,990	123,190
Rhode Island	10,719	7,825	8,477	9,908	9,724	9,751	9,579	9,730	9,900	10,050	9,390	9,660
South Carolina	38,347	32,483	31,617	40,438	40,708	41,442	42,246	41,720	42,650	43,840	45,090	46,640
South Dakota	10,385	7,650	9,278	8,162	8,248	8,196	8,239	7,960	8,140	8,080	8,160	8,280
Tennessee	50,648	46,094	41,568	62,408	61,862	62,454	61,323	60,970	62,010	63,480	63,710	66,310
Texas	171,665	172,480	212,925	280,894	290,470	292,531	301,390	304,360	309,280	318,660	327,690	339,950
Utah	19,886	21,196	32,501	31,481	30,888	31,157	33,186	33,400	34,070	35,400	36,560	37,690
Vermont	6,424	6,127	6,675	7,199	6,932	6,859	6,491	6,360	6,240	6,090	6,010	5,930
Virginia	67,126	60,605	65,596	81,511	82,895	83,336	83,279	83,100	82,680	84,640	84,720	87,490
Washington	50,046	45,941	57,597	66,046	66,453	65,205	66,066	66,240	68,200	69,770	70,840	72,500
West Virginia	23,580	21,854	19,437	17,651	17,311	17,603	17,924	17,510	17,460	17,640	17,370	17,540
Wisconsin	67,743	52,038	58,545	64,687	64,135	62,705	61,425	60,810	60,460	60,710	60,740	61,560
Wyoming	6,161	5,823	6,462	5,695	5,600	5,553	5,489	5,590	5,550	5,700	5,660	5,740
Jurisdiction												
Bureau of Indian Education	—	—	—	—	—	—	—	—	—	—	—	—
DoDEA[4]	—	—	3,202	—	—	—	—	—	—	—	—	—
Other jurisdictions												
American Samoa	—	703	698	—	—	—	—	—	—	—	—	—
Guam	—	1,033	1,406	—	—	—	—	—	—	—	—	—
Northern Marianas	—	227	360	—	—	—	—	—	—	—	—	—
Puerto Rico	—	29,049	30,856	25,514	26,231	25,720	—	—	—	—	—	—
U.S. Virgin Islands	—	1,260	1,060	958	1,014	1,046	897	—	—	—	—	—

See notes at end of table.

Table 219.20. Public high school graduates, by region, state, and jurisdiction: Selected years, 1980–81 through 2028–29—Continued

Region, state, and jurisdiction	Projected data											Percent change, 2012–13 to 2028–29
	2018–19	2019–20	2020–21	2021–22	2022–23	2023–24	2024–25	2025–26	2026–27	2027–28	2028–29	
1	14	15	16	17	18	19	20	21	22	23	24	25
United States	**3,331,520**	**3,303,890**	**3,330,840**	**3,354,240**	**3,372,640**	**3,441,920**	**3,492,860**	**3,497,750**	**3,416,680**	**3,348,520**	**3,361,890**	**6.1**
Region												
Northeast	548,330	540,460	545,870	546,630	543,610	549,770	558,550	554,750	544,040	534,770	535,430	-3.6
Midwest	724,260	712,420	719,140	726,350	719,070	732,220	742,610	740,420	722,430	703,170	704,090	-1.3
South	1,264,620	1,255,800	1,258,750	1,267,480	1,286,540	1,316,310	1,350,670	1,361,840	1,337,760	1,296,070	1,307,060	14.8
West	794,300	795,210	807,090	813,780	823,430	843,620	841,020	840,740	812,450	814,520	815,300	7.1
State												
Alabama	45,740	44,070	43,490	43,380	43,600	43,870	45,410	45,810	44,770	42,960	43,610	-1.4
Alaska	8,030	7,840	7,830	7,930	8,030	8,320	8,580	8,740	8,780	8,660	8,690	10.6
Arizona	70,710	69,610	71,070	70,940	72,200	74,230	76,480	77,540	75,780	72,450	72,560	16.6
Arkansas	31,060	31,320	30,800	30,960	30,940	30,780	32,990	33,030	32,140	31,350	31,460	8.7
California	420,780	421,890	427,540	430,350	434,120	444,030	429,550	425,400	408,150	418,160	416,950	-1.2
Colorado	57,030	57,760	59,150	59,290	59,790	61,090	61,990	62,170	60,930	59,170	59,040	15.8
Connecticut	37,040	35,980	36,640	35,810	35,670	35,220	35,550	34,450	33,720	32,860	32,610	-15.8
Delaware	9,010	9,080	9,260	9,280	9,500	9,880	9,920	10,240	10,060	9,740	9,800	21.4
District of Columbia[2]	4,290	4,270	4,320	4,310	4,630	4,970	5,520	5,550	5,550	5,640	6,020	51.9
Florida	179,520	175,370	176,380	179,930	182,780	192,590	190,040	197,900	192,690	187,880	190,410	20.5
Georgia	106,920	105,660	104,900	106,500	107,710	110,270	112,930	113,710	111,370	107,750	108,130	17.0
Hawaii	10,540	10,820	10,830	11,010	11,210	11,290	11,510	11,580	8,780	10,890	10,670	-1.1
Idaho	19,720	19,440	19,830	20,340	21,040	21,090	21,850	21,960	21,400	21,010	21,320	23.9
Illinois	142,800	139,490	144,730	146,850	144,610	147,870	152,340	149,530	146,040	138,960	138,790	-0.3
Indiana	71,980	69,520	68,320	69,820	68,920	70,120	70,340	71,660	69,740	68,530	68,580	3.0
Iowa	33,310	33,390	33,890	33,930	34,700	35,460	36,120	36,390	35,350	35,090	35,110	7.9
Kansas	33,410	33,330	33,490	33,680	33,660	34,200	34,870	34,670	33,910	33,560	33,500	5.0
Kentucky	44,420	43,760	43,830	43,840	43,930	44,930	45,890	45,440	44,540	42,610	42,660	-0.5
Louisiana	41,720	40,430	39,810	40,380	40,360	41,590	42,410	42,570	41,560	39,600	40,130	7.0
Maine	12,430	12,100	12,050	12,250	12,300	12,160	12,340	12,080	11,960	11,600	11,580	-12.1
Maryland	58,560	60,180	60,920	61,640	61,990	63,770	65,820	66,930	65,550	64,340	64,550	9.6
Massachusetts	69,810	69,790	70,020	70,360	69,700	70,020	71,160	71,310	69,390	67,880	68,390	3.1
Michigan	99,910	98,170	97,790	97,500	94,870	96,260	96,030	92,560	90,060	88,840	88,680	-14.9
Minnesota	59,350	58,510	60,360	61,810	61,920	63,460	65,100	65,520	64,560	63,320	63,910	9.7
Mississippi	27,390	26,680	25,990	26,300	26,180	25,950	28,040	27,280	26,330	24,560	24,850	-6.2
Missouri	61,770	60,750	60,800	61,170	61,590	62,280	63,600	63,560	61,920	60,470	60,440	-1.6
Montana	9,430	9,610	9,660	9,870	9,890	10,430	10,430	10,800	10,530	10,200	10,380	10.8
Nebraska	22,270	22,750	23,240	23,800	23,640	24,050	22,970	24,790	24,890	24,450	24,420	19.5
Nevada	24,880	25,150	25,190	25,410	26,270	27,270	28,460	28,610	27,590	27,520	27,770	20.5
New Hampshire	12,950	12,960	12,780	12,810	12,540	12,550	12,500	12,290	11,910	11,490	11,380	-20.2
New Jersey	97,120	96,210	97,920	98,540	97,370	98,540	100,920	99,270	97,620	96,130	96,020	-0.5
New Mexico	20,300	20,780	20,410	20,430	20,800	20,820	21,380	21,510	20,920	19,510	19,290	0.3
New York	182,480	179,160	180,970	180,070	180,320	183,830	186,510	185,690	183,510	180,560	181,140	0.4
North Carolina	107,590	104,770	104,820	97,640	104,440	107,090	110,400	110,430	108,930	105,400	106,280	12.7
North Dakota	6,800	6,850	7,050	7,330	7,450	7,910	8,140	8,240	8,270	8,000	8,190	18.7
Ohio	123,350	121,250	120,550	120,190	117,580	120,240	121,250	122,090	117,540	114,030	114,690	-6.4
Oklahoma	41,370	41,640	41,920	41,960	40,480	42,640	44,270	44,080	43,800	42,440	42,720	15.4
Oregon	35,610	35,190	35,790	36,200	36,320	37,570	38,690	38,920	37,850	37,360	37,620	11.0
Pennsylvania	120,390	118,130	119,550	120,570	119,610	121,370	123,220	123,420	120,520	118,990	119,130	-8.2
Rhode Island	10,240	10,390	10,250	10,510	10,300	10,420	10,540	10,390	9,990	9,780	9,740	1.7
South Carolina	46,890	46,620	46,480	47,070	48,120	49,580	52,080	52,000	51,900	49,310	50,000	18.4
South Dakota	8,190	8,380	8,500	8,820	9,200	9,350	9,610	9,660	9,470	9,380	9,470	14.9
Tennessee	65,660	64,430	64,190	64,540	65,250	67,010	68,260	67,850	65,050	64,230	64,670	5.5
Texas	349,360	352,500	357,190	363,530	370,780	374,490	387,420	390,110	387,360	374,920	377,680	25.3
Utah	38,350	39,140	40,300	41,230	41,670	42,770	44,030	44,070	43,120	42,500	42,650	28.5
Vermont	5,880	5,750	5,680	5,730	5,800	5,660	5,810	5,860	5,420	5,490	5,440	-16.2
Virginia	87,860	87,800	87,670	89,310	89,250	90,680	92,690	92,530	90,310	88,120	88,820	6.6
Washington	73,160	72,220	73,530	74,900	75,990	78,500	81,790	83,300	82,670	81,360	82,790	25.3
West Virginia	17,270	17,230	16,790	16,920	16,600	16,220	16,600	16,370	15,850	15,230	15,270	-14.8
Wisconsin	61,130	60,040	60,420	61,450	60,940	61,020	62,250	61,750	60,700	58,540	58,330	-5.0
Wyoming	5,770	5,770	5,950	5,880	6,130	6,200	6,290	6,170	5,960	5,720	5,590	1.8
Jurisdiction												
Bureau of Indian Education	—	—	—	—	—	—	—	—	—	—	—	—
DoDEA[4]	—	—	—	—	—	—	—	—	—	—	—	—
Other jurisdictions												
American Samoa	—	—	—	—	—	—	—	—	—	—	—	—
Guam	—	—	—	—	—	—	—	—	—	—	—	—
Northern Marianas	—	—	—	—	—	—	—	—	—	—	—	—
Puerto Rico	—	—	—	—	—	—	—	—	—	—	—	—
U.S. Virgin Islands	—	—	—	—	—	—	—	—	—	—	—	—

—Not available.
[1]U.S. total includes estimates for nonreporting states.
[2]Beginning in 1989–90, graduates from adult programs are excluded.
[3]Projected data from NCES 91-490, *Projections of Education Statistics to 2002*.
[4]DoDEA = Department of Defense Education Activity. Includes both domestic and overseas schools.
NOTE: Data include regular diploma recipients, but exclude students receiving a certificate of attendance and persons receiving high school equivalency certificates. Some data have been revised from previously published figures. Detail may not sum to totals because of rounding.
SOURCE: U.S. Department of Education, National Center for Education Statistics, Common Core of Data (CCD), "State Nonfiscal Survey of Public Elementary/Secondary Education," 1981–82 through 2005–06; "State Dropout and Completion Data File," 2005–06 through 2012–13; and State High School Graduates Projection Model, 1980–81 through 2028–29. (This table was prepared March 2019.)

Table 219.30. Public high school graduates, by race/ethnicity: 1998–99 through 2028–29

Year	Number of high school graduates							Percentage distribution of graduates						
	Total	White	Black	Hispanic	Asian/ Pacific Islander	American Indian/ Alaska Native	Two or more races	Total	White	Black	Hispanic	Asian/ Pacific Islander	American Indian/ Alaska Native	Two or more races
1	2	3	4	5	6	7	8	9	10	11	12	13	14	15
1998–99	2,485,630	1,749,561	325,708	270,836	115,216	24,309	—	100.0	70.4	13.1	10.9	4.6	1.0	†
1999–2000	2,553,844	1,778,370	338,116	289,139	122,344	25,875	—	100.0	69.6	13.2	11.3	4.8	1.0	†
2000–01	2,569,200	1,775,036	339,578	301,740	126,465	26,381	—	100.0	69.1	13.2	11.7	4.9	1.0	†
2001–02	2,621,534	1,796,110	348,969	317,197	132,182	27,076	—	100.0	68.5	13.3	12.1	5.0	1.0	†
2002–03	2,719,947	1,856,454	359,920	340,182	135,588	27,803	—	100.0	68.3	13.2	12.5	5.0	1.0	†
2003–04	2,753,438	1,829,177	383,443	374,492	137,496	28,830	—	100.0	66.4	13.9	13.6	5.0	1.0	†
2004–05	2,799,250	1,855,198	385,987	383,714	143,729	30,622	—	100.0	66.3	13.8	13.7	5.1	1.1	†
2005–06	2,815,544	1,838,765	399,406	396,820	150,925	29,628	—	100.0	65.3	14.2	14.1	5.4	1.1	†
2006–07	2,893,045	1,868,056	418,113	421,036	154,837	31,003	—	100.0	64.6	14.5	14.6	5.4	1.1	†
2007–08	3,001,337	1,898,367	429,840	448,887	159,410	32,036	32,797[1]	100.0	63.3	14.3	15.0	5.3	1.1	1.1[1]
2008–09	3,039,015	1,883,382	451,384	481,698	163,575	32,213	26,763[1]	100.0	62.0	14.9	15.9	5.4	1.1	0.9[1]
2009–10	3,128,022	1,871,980	472,261	545,518	167,840	34,131	36,292[1]	100.0	59.8	15.1	17.4	5.4	1.1	1.2[1]
2010–11	3,144,100	1,835,332	471,461	583,907	168,875	32,768	51,748	100.0	58.4	15.0	18.6	5.4	1.0	1.6
2011–12	3,149,185	1,807,528	467,932	608,726	173,835	32,450	58,703	100.0	57.4	14.9	19.3	5.5	1.0	1.9
2012–13	3,169,257	1,791,147	461,919	640,413	179,101	31,100	65,569	100.0	56.5	14.6	20.2	5.7	1.0	2.1
2013–14[2]	3,168,450	1,769,050	454,270	661,020	181,900	30,180	72,030	100.0	55.8	14.3	20.9	5.7	1.0	2.3
2014–15[2]	3,187,000	1,750,350	459,300	685,900	185,170	30,060	76,220	100.0	54.9	14.4	21.5	5.8	0.9	2.4
2015–16[2]	3,224,140	1,746,430	465,320	713,740	185,070	30,230	83,350	100.0	54.2	14.4	22.1	5.7	0.9	2.6
2016–17[2]	3,255,320	1,742,040	468,970	736,760	186,830	30,190	90,520	100.0	53.5	14.4	22.6	5.7	0.9	2.8
2017–18[2]	3,319,760	1,738,760	477,200	774,750	200,730	30,060	98,270	100.0	52.4	14.4	23.3	6.0	0.9	3.0
2018–19[2]	3,331,520	1,717,950	472,450	805,450	200,850	29,220	105,600	100.0	51.6	14.2	24.2	6.0	0.9	3.2
2019–20[2]	3,303,890	1,676,320	459,460	824,330	203,680	28,620	111,480	100.0	50.7	13.9	25.0	6.2	0.9	3.4
2020–21[2]	3,330,840	1,669,020	451,510	847,770	212,240	29,190	121,110	100.0	50.1	13.6	25.5	6.4	0.9	3.6
2021–22[2]	3,354,240	1,659,320	445,420	869,910	217,940	29,560	132,100	100.0	49.5	13.3	25.9	6.5	0.9	3.9
2022–23[2]	3,372,640	1,632,870	447,270	904,420	217,310	29,040	141,730	100.0	48.4	13.3	26.8	6.4	0.9	4.2
2023–24[2]	3,441,920	1,629,570	460,740	945,420	218,260	29,310	158,630	100.0	47.3	13.4	27.5	6.3	0.9	4.6
2024–25[2]	3,492,860	1,627,540	469,950	971,900	220,650	29,430	173,390	100.0	46.6	13.5	27.8	6.3	0.8	5.0
2025–26[2]	3,497,750	1,603,120	474,420	981,800	225,280	29,100	184,030	100.0	45.8	13.6	28.1	6.4	0.8	5.3
2026–27[2]	3,416,680	1,552,660	463,790	963,620	220,040	28,710	187,860	100.0	45.4	13.6	28.2	6.4	0.8	5.5
2027–28[2]	3,348,520	1,513,160	444,520	941,360	226,210	27,540	195,730	100.0	45.2	13.3	28.1	6.8	0.8	5.8
2028–29[2]	3,361,890	1,514,110	448,170	955,040	221,040	27,670	195,860	100.0	45.0	13.3	28.4	6.6	0.8	5.8

—Not available.
†Not applicable.
[1]Data on students of Two or more races were not reported by all states; therefore, the data are not comparable to figures for 2010–11 and later years.
[2]Projected.
NOTE: Race categories exclude persons of Hispanic ethnicity. Prior to 2007–08, data on students of Two or more races were not collected separately. Some data have been revised from previously published figures. Detail may not sum to totals because of rounding and statistical methods used to prevent the identification of individual students.
SOURCE: U.S. Department of Education, National Center for Education Statistics, Common Core of Data (CCD), "State Nonfiscal Survey of Public Elementary/Secondary Education," 1981–82 through 2005–06; "State Dropout and Completion Data File," 2005–06 through 2012–13; and National Public High School Graduates by Race/Ethnicity Projections Model, 1995–96 through 2028–29. (This table was prepared March 2019.)

Table 219.46. Public high school 4-year adjusted cohort graduation rate (ACGR), by selected student characteristics and state: 2010–11 through 2016–17

State	Total, ACGR for all students							ACGR for students with selected characteristics,[1] 2016–17										
								Race/ethnicity										
											Asian/Pacific Islander[5]							
	2010–11	2011–12	2012–13	2013–14	2014–15	2015–16	2016–17	White	Black	Hispanic	Total	Asian	Pacific Islander	American Indian/ Alaska Native	Two or more races	Students with disabilities[2]	Limited English proficient[3]	Economically disadvantaged[4]
1	2	3	4	5	6	7	8	9	10	11	12	13	14	15	16	17	18	19
United States	**79**[6]	**80**[6]	**81**[7]	**82**	**83**	**84**	**85**	**89**	**78**	**80**	**91**	**—**	**—**	**72**[8]	**—**	**67**[8]	**66**[8]	**78**[8]
Alabama[9]	72	75	80	86	89	87	89	91	87	88	95	—	—	—	91	—	—	—
Alaska	68	70	72	71	76	76	78	82	74	77	84	88	77	69	75	59	58	72
Arizona	78	76	75	76	77	80	78	83	74	75	89	—	—	67	—	66	30	72
Arkansas	81	84	85	87	85	87	88	90	83	86	86	92	69	89	86	84	82	85
California	76	79	80	81	82	83	83	87	73	80	93	93	91	68	70	65	67	79
Colorado	74	75	77	77	77	79	79	84	72	71	89	90	77	64	80	57	65	69
Connecticut	83	85	86	87	87	87	88	93	80	78	95	95	81	88	88	67	68	78
Delaware	78	80	80	87	86	86	87	90	83	82	95	96	>=50	76	91	69	69	78
District of Columbia	59	59	62	61	69	69	73	85	72	72	78	‡	‡	‡	>=90	53	63	73
Florida	71	75	76	76	78	81	82	86	75	81	93	93	87	80	83	66	67	77
Georgia	67	70	72	73	79	79	81	84	78	74	91	—	—	79	82	59	59	76
Hawaii	80	81	82	82	82	83	83	80	79	80	84	—	—	79	—	65	69	78
Idaho	—	—	—	77	79	80	80	81	70	75	85	86	78	66	76	61	75	72
Illinois	84	82	83	86	86	86	87	91	79	84	95	95	82	81	86	71	74	79
Indiana	86	86	87	88	87	87	84	88	71	76	80	81	70	76	82	71	50	80
Iowa	88	89	90	91	91	91	91	93	82	82	91	93	77	83	85	74	80	84
Kansas	83	85	86	86	86	86	87	89	78	81	93	94	75	81	84	78	80	79
Kentucky	—	—	86	88	88	89	90	91	82	84	92	93	76	77	87	74	67	87
Louisiana	71	72	74	75	78	79	78	84	73	67	90	91	77	81	82	53	36	73
Maine	84	85	86	87	88	87	87	87	83	89	89	88	>=50	71	79	73	81	79
Maryland	83	84	85	86	87	88	88	93	85	74	96	96	89	86	91	68	45	79
Massachusetts	83	85	85	86	87	88	88	93	80	74	94	94	78	81	85	73	63	79
Michigan	74	76	77	79	80	80	80	84	69	73	91	91	85	68	75	57	69	68
Minnesota	77	78	80	81	82	82	83	88	65	66	85	86	63	51	71	61	65	69
Mississippi	75	75	76	78	81	82	83	87	79	81	91	91	>=80	80	79	36	67	80
Missouri	81	84	86	87	88	89	88	91	76	84	91	—	—	84	89	77	67	80
Montana	82	84	84	85	86	86	86	89	81	80	91	94	83	69	—	77	63	77
Nebraska	86	88	89	90	89	89	89	93	81	82	82	82	85	70	86	71	50	82
Nevada	62	63	71	70	71	74	81	84	68	80	91	93	82	74	81	65	82	77
New Hampshire	86	86	87	88	88	88	89	90	79	76	93	93	>=50	75	85	74	78	78
New Jersey	83	86	88	89	90	90	91	95	83	84	97	97	>=95	92	92	79	76	84
New Mexico	63	70	70	69	69	71	71	76	68	71	85	—	—	61	—	62	68	66
New York	77	77	77	78	79	80	82	90	72	71	88	88	77	67	83	55	31	75
North Carolina	78	80	83	84	86	86	87	89	84	81	94	—	—	84	84	70	58	82
North Dakota	86	87	88	87	87	88	87	91	75	76	80	80	—	68	—	66	69	74
Ohio	80	81	82	82	81	84	84	88	69	74	88	—	—	76	79	71	55	73
Oklahoma	—	—	85	83	83	82	83	84	80	79	86	86	84	83	83	77	57	77
Oregon	68	68	69	72	74	75	77	78	68	73	86	89	69	59	77	59	55	70
Pennsylvania	83	84	86	85	85	86	87	91	74	74	92	92	90	73	79	74	65	80
Rhode Island	77	77	80	81	83	83	84	88	81	76	88	89	68	73	79	63	72	76
South Carolina	74	75	78	80	80	83	84	85	81	81	93	—	—	76	—	54	77	85
South Dakota	83	83	83	83	84	84	84	90	78	71	85	‡	‡	50	78	60	59	67
Tennessee	86	87	86	87	88	89	90	93	84	84	94	94	93	89	—	73	74	85
Texas	86	88	88	88	89	89	90	94	86	88	96	96	89	86	92	77	76	87
Utah	76	80	83	84	85	85	86	88	73	77	87	89	86	74	87	69	67	77
Vermont	87	88	87	88	88	88	89	90	77	90	82	‡	‡	‡	83	76	66	81
Virginia	82	83	85	85	86	87	87	91	83	73	93	94	91	83	90	60	57	78
Washington	76	77	76	78	78	80	79	82	72	73	85	88	68	62	80	59	58	70
West Virginia	78	79	81	85	87	90	89	90	87	92	95	95	>=50	>=80	83	76	‡	87
Wisconsin	87	88	88	89	88	88	89	93	67	80	91	91	85	79	84	68	65	77
Wyoming	80	79	77	79	79	80	86	88	83	80	84	81	>=50	59	79	68	77	65

—Not available.
‡Reporting standards not met (too few cases).
[1]The time when students are identified as having certain characteristics varies by state. Depending on the state, a student may be included in a category if the relevant characteristic is reported in 9th-grade data, if the characteristic is reported in 12th-grade data, or if it is reported at any point during the student's high school years.
[2]Students identified as children with disabilities under the Individuals with Disabilities Education Act (IDEA).
[3]Students who met the definition of limited English proficient students as outlined in the ED*Facts* workbook. For more information, see http://www2.ed.gov/about/inits/ed/edfacts/eden-workbook.html.
[4]Students who met the state criteria for classification as economically disadvantaged.
[5]States either report data for a combined "Asian/Pacific Islander" group or report the "Asian" and "Pacific Islander" groups separately. Total represents either a single value reported by the state for "Asian/Pacific Islander" or an aggregation of separate values reported for "Asian" and "Pacific Islander." "Pacific Islander" includes the "Filipino" group, which only California reports separately.
[6]Includes imputed data for Idaho, Kentucky, and Oklahoma. Data were not available for these states because they had not yet started reporting ACGR data in 2010–11 and 2011–12.
[7]Includes imputed data for Idaho. Data were not available for Idaho because this state had not yet started reporting ACGR data in 2012–13.
[8]Includes estimated data for Alabama because Alabama did not report data for this subgroup. Estimated Alabama data were based on data published on the Alabama State Education Agency website.
[9]Use data with caution. The Alabama State Department of Education has indicated that their ACGR data for some years was misstated. For more information, please see the following press release issued by the state: https://www.alsde.edu/sec/comm/News%20Releases/12-08-2016%20Graduation%20Rate%20Review.pdf.
NOTE: The adjusted cohort graduation rate (ACGR) is the percentage of public high school freshmen who graduate with a regular diploma within 4 years of starting 9th grade. Students who are entering 9th grade for the first time form a cohort for the graduating class. This cohort is "adjusted" by adding any students who subsequently transfer into the cohort and subtracting any students who subsequently transfer out, emigrate to another country, or die. Values preceded by the ">=" symbol have been "blurred" (rounded) to protect student privacy. Race categories exclude persons of Hispanic ethnicity.
SOURCE: U.S. Department of Education, Office of Elementary and Secondary Education, Consolidated State Performance Report, 2010–11 through 2016–17. (This table was prepared December 2018.)

Table 219.55. Among 15- to 24-year-olds enrolled in grades 10 through 12, percentage who dropped out (event dropout rate), by sex and race/ethnicity: 1972 through 2017

[Standard errors appear in parentheses]

Year	Event dropout rate[1]											
			Sex				Race/ethnicity					
	Total[2]		Male		Female		White		Black		Hispanic	
1	2		3		4		5		6		7	
1972	6.1	(0.34)	5.9	(0.47)	6.3	(0.49)	5.3	(0.35)	9.6	(1.36)	11.2!	(3.70)
1973	6.3	(0.34)	6.8	(0.50)	5.7	(0.46)	5.5	(0.35)	10.0	(1.39)	10.0!	(3.50)
1974	6.7	(0.35)	7.4	(0.52)	6.0	(0.47)	5.8	(0.36)	11.6	(1.44)	9.9!	(3.34)
1975	5.8	(0.32)	5.4	(0.45)	6.1	(0.47)	5.1	(0.34)	8.7	(1.28)	10.9!	(3.30)
1976	5.9	(0.33)	6.6	(0.49)	5.2	(0.44)	5.6	(0.36)	7.4	(1.18)	7.3!	(2.71)
1977	6.5	(0.34)	6.9	(0.49)	6.1	(0.47)	6.1	(0.37)	8.6	(1.21)	7.8!	(2.79)
1978	6.7	(0.35)	7.5	(0.52)	5.9	(0.46)	5.8	(0.36)	10.2	(1.32)	12.3	(3.60)
1979	6.7	(0.35)	6.8	(0.50)	6.7	(0.49)	6.1	(0.37)	10.0	(1.34)	9.8!	(3.20)
1980	6.1	(0.33)	6.7	(0.49)	5.5	(0.45)	5.3	(0.35)	8.3	(1.22)	11.7	(3.36)
1981	5.9	(0.33)	6.0	(0.47)	5.8	(0.46)	4.9	(0.34)	9.7	(1.30)	10.7	(3.00)
1982	5.5	(0.34)	5.8	(0.50)	5.2	(0.47)	4.8	(0.37)	7.8	(1.23)	9.2!	(3.04)
1983	5.2	(0.34)	5.8	(0.50)	4.7	(0.46)	4.4	(0.36)	7.0	(1.20)	10.1!	(3.18)
1984	5.1	(0.34)	5.5	(0.50)	4.8	(0.47)	4.5	(0.37)	5.8	(1.08)	11.1	(3.28)
1985	5.3	(0.35)	5.4	(0.51)	5.1	(0.49)	4.4	(0.37)	7.8	(1.29)	9.8	(2.58)
1986	4.7	(0.33)	4.7	(0.46)	4.7	(0.46)	3.8	(0.34)	5.5	(1.08)	11.9	(2.70)
1987	4.1	(0.31)	4.4	(0.45)	3.8	(0.42)	3.6	(0.33)	6.4	(1.16)	5.6!	(1.94)
1988	4.8	(0.37)	5.4	(0.55)	4.6	(0.53)	4.4	(0.42)	6.3	(1.28)	11.0	(3.08)
1989	4.5	(0.35)	4.6	(0.50)	4.6	(0.50)	3.6	(0.37)	8.2	(1.40)	8.1	(2.43)
1990	4.0	(0.33)	4.2	(0.49)	4.1	(0.49)	3.5	(0.37)	5.2	(1.17)	8.4	(2.41)
1991	4.0	(0.33)	3.9	(0.47)	4.4	(0.51)	3.3	(0.37)	6.4	(1.27)	7.8	(2.33)
1992	4.4	(0.35)	3.9	(0.46)	4.9	(0.53)	3.7	(0.38)	5.0	(1.09)	8.2	(2.23)
1993	4.5	(0.36)	4.6	(0.51)	4.3	(0.50)	3.9	(0.40)	5.8	(1.20)	6.7!	(2.02)
1994	5.3	(0.37)	5.2	(0.51)	5.4	(0.53)	4.2	(0.40)	6.6	(1.21)	10.0	(2.18)
1995	5.7	(0.35)	6.2	(0.51)	5.3	(0.48)	4.5	(0.38)	6.4	(1.01)	12.4	(1.62)
1996	5.0	(0.34)	5.0	(0.48)	5.1	(0.49)	4.1	(0.38)	6.7	(1.05)	9.0	(1.49)
1997	4.6	(0.32)	5.0	(0.47)	4.1	(0.43)	3.6	(0.35)	5.0	(0.91)	9.5	(1.45)
1998	4.8	(0.33)	4.6	(0.45)	4.9	(0.47)	3.9	(0.36)	5.2	(0.91)	9.4	(1.46)
1999	5.0	(0.33)	4.6	(0.44)	5.4	(0.49)	4.0	(0.36)	6.5	(0.99)	7.8	(1.27)
2000	4.8	(0.33)	5.5	(0.49)	4.1	(0.43)	4.1	(0.37)	6.1	(1.00)	7.4	(1.24)
2001	5.0	(0.32)	5.6	(0.46)	4.3	(0.42)	4.1	(0.35)	6.3	(0.96)	8.8	(1.31)
2002	3.5	(0.27)	3.7	(0.39)	3.4	(0.37)	2.6	(0.28)	4.9	(0.87)	5.8	(1.01)
2003	4.0	(0.28)	4.2	(0.40)	3.8	(0.38)	3.2	(0.31)	4.8	(0.85)	7.1	(1.06)
2004	4.7	(0.30)	5.1	(0.44)	4.3	(0.41)	3.7	(0.34)	5.7	(0.94)	8.9	(1.20)
2005	3.8	(0.27)	4.2	(0.40)	3.4	(0.36)	2.8	(0.29)	7.3	(1.03)	5.0	(0.87)
2006	3.8	(0.27)	4.1	(0.39)	3.4	(0.36)	2.9	(0.30)	3.8	(0.77)	7.0	(1.01)
2007	3.5	(0.26)	3.7	(0.37)	3.3	(0.35)	2.2	(0.26)	4.5	(0.80)	6.0	(0.98)
2008	3.5	(0.26)	3.1	(0.34)	4.0	(0.39)	2.3	(0.27)	6.4	(0.94)	5.3	(0.85)
2009	3.4	(0.25)	3.5	(0.36)	3.4	(0.35)	2.4	(0.28)	4.8	(0.83)	5.8	(0.87)
2010	3.0	(0.26)	3.0	(0.36)	2.9	(0.35)	2.3	(0.29)	3.6	(0.88)	4.1	(0.73)
2011	3.4	(0.30)	3.6	(0.43)	3.1	(0.37)	2.7	(0.38)	4.4	(0.87)	4.6	(0.81)
2012	3.4	(0.32)	3.6	(0.48)	3.3	(0.49)	1.6	(0.24)	6.8	(1.35)	5.4	(0.93)
2013	4.7	(0.40)	4.8	(0.53)	4.5	(0.55)	4.3	(0.51)	5.8	(1.17)	5.7	(0.95)
2014	5.2	(0.38)	5.4	(0.58)	5.0	(0.53)	4.7	(0.43)	5.7	(1.21)	7.9	(1.05)
2015	4.9	(0.43)	5.1	(0.60)	4.6	(0.57)	3.8	(0.47)	6.8	(1.37)	6.2	(1.12)
2016	4.8	(0.36)	5.4	(0.57)	4.1	(0.52)	4.5	(0.45)	5.9	(1.19)	4.7	(0.76)
2017	4.7	(0.37)	5.4	(0.52)	3.9	(0.49)	3.9	(0.43)	5.5	(1.16)	6.5	(0.98)

!Interpret data with caution. The coefficient of variation (CV) for this estimate is between 30 and 50 percent.

[1]The event dropout rate is the percentage of 15- to 24-year-olds in grades 10 through 12 who dropped out between one October and the next (e.g., the 2017 data refer to 10th- through 12th-graders who were enrolled in October 2016 but had dropped out by October 2017). Dropping out is defined as leaving school without a high school diploma or alternative credential such as a GED certificate.

[2]Includes other racial/ethnic groups not separately shown.

NOTE: Data are based on sample surveys of the civilian noninstitutionalized population, which excludes persons in the military and persons living in institutions (e.g., prisons or nursing facilities). Because of changes in data collection procedures, data for 1992 and later years may not be comparable with figures for prior years. Prior to 2010, standard errors were computed using generalized variance function methodology rather than the more precise replicate weight methodology used in later years. Race categories exclude persons of Hispanic ethnicity. Detail may not sum to totals because of rounding.

SOURCE: U.S. Department of Commerce, Census Bureau, Current Population Survey (CPS), October, 1972 through 2017. (This table was prepared November 2018.)

Table 219.57. Among 15- to 24-year-olds enrolled in grades 10 through 12, percentage who dropped out (event dropout rate), and number and percentage distribution of 15- to 24-year-olds in grades 10 through 12, by selected characteristics: Selected years, 2007 through 2017

[Standard errors appear in parentheses]

Selected characteristic	Event dropout rate (percent)[1]								2017: Number of 15- to 24-year-olds enrolled in grades 10 through 12 (in thousands)				2017: Percentage distribution of 15- to 24-year-olds enrolled in grades 10 through 12			
	2007		2012		2016		2017		Total population[2]		Event dropouts only[3]		Total population[2]		Event dropouts only[3]	
1	2		3		4		5		6		7		8		9	
Total	**3.5**	**(0.26)**	**3.4**	**(0.32)**	**4.8**	**(0.36)**	**4.7**	**(0.37)**	**11,138**	**(121.5)**	**523**	**(41.6)**	**100.0**	**(†)**	**100.0**	**(†)**
Sex																
Male	3.7	(0.37)	3.6	(0.48)	5.4	(0.57)	5.4	(0.52)	5,669	(83.0)	307	(29.5)	50.9	(0.49)	58.8	(3.69)
Female	3.3	(0.35)	3.3	(0.49)	4.1	(0.52)	3.9	(0.49)	5,469	(80.7)	215	(26.9)	49.1	(0.49)	41.2	(3.69)
Race/ethnicity																
White	2.2	(0.26)	1.6	(0.24)	4.5	(0.45)	3.9	(0.43)	5,988	(88.8)	235	(25.8)	53.8	(0.64)	44.9	(4.20)
Black	4.5	(0.80)	6.8	(1.35)	5.9	(1.19)	5.5	(1.16)	1,533	(54.8)	85	(18.2)	13.8	(0.48)	16.2	(3.18)
Hispanic	6.0	(0.98)	5.4	(0.93)	4.7	(0.76)	6.5	(0.98)	2,482	(70.4)	161	(24.9)	22.3	(0.57)	30.8	(3.68)
Asian	7.9	(2.14)	3.6!	(1.15)	3.6!	(1.53)	4.7!	(1.53)	609	(37.8)	‡	(†)	5.5	(0.32)	5.5!	(1.74)
Pacific Islander	‡	(†)	‡	(†)	‡	(†)	‡	(†)	‡	(†)	‡	(†)	0.4	(0.11)	‡	(†)
American Indian/Alaska Native	20.8!	(6.40)	‡	(†)	17.3!	(6.10)	4.4!	(1.86)	123	(19.4)	‡	(†)	1.1	(0.17)	1.0!	(0.43)
Two or more races	‡	(†)	4.5!	(2.25)	‡	(†)	‡	(†)	365	(31.6)	‡	(†)	3.3	(0.28)	‡	(†)
Age[4]																
15 and 16	3.2	(0.45)	2.2	(0.42)	5.3	(0.74)	4.5	(0.64)	3,091	(70.8)	138	(20.2)	27.7	(0.60)	26.4	(3.44)
17	2.1	(0.34)	1.9	(0.36)	3.8	(0.56)	4.1	(0.55)	3,813	(56.8)	155	(21.2)	34.2	(0.51)	29.7	(3.62)
18	4.0	(0.54)	3.2	(0.71)	5.2	(0.78)	5.2	(0.79)	2,912	(62.6)	150	(23.1)	26.1	(0.51)	28.7	(3.72)
19	4.1	(1.01)	8.2	(1.74)	4.5	(1.31)	6.1!	(1.89)	924	(54.9)	‡	(†)	8.3	(0.46)	10.8	(3.09)
20 to 24	20.3	(3.60)	14.9	(3.61)	7.4!	(2.55)	5.8!	(2.31)	399	(44.1)	‡	(†)	3.6	(0.38)	4.4!	(1.89)
Recency of immigration[5]																
Born outside the United States																
Hispanic	10.6	(2.67)	10.7	(2.44)	3.1!	(1.50)	5.9!	(2.27)	306	(34.9)	‡	(†)	2.8	(0.31)	3.5!	(1.46)
Non-Hispanic	5.8!	(2.00)	2.7!	(1.25)	6.7!	(2.26)	9.6	(2.53)	386	(43.1)	‡	(†)	3.5	(0.38)	7.1	(1.93)
First generation																
Hispanic	3.3!	(1.11)	5.5	(1.50)	5.3	(1.12)	4.7	(1.17)	1,201	(63.9)	‡	(†)	10.8	(0.57)	10.8	(2.55)
Non-Hispanic	3.1	(0.88)	1.9!	(0.86)	3.3!	(1.09)	3.5	(1.04)	943	(57.3)	‡	(†)	8.5	(0.50)	6.4	(1.87)
Second or later generation																
Hispanic	6.5	(1.71)	2.3!	(0.88)	4.7	(1.41)	8.8	(1.93)	974	(55.8)	‡	(†)	8.7	(0.49)	16.5	(3.19)
Non-Hispanic	2.9	(0.27)	3.0	(0.36)	4.8	(0.46)	4.0	(0.40)	7,327	(108.0)	291	(29.5)	65.8	(0.75)	55.7	(4.03)
Disability status[6]																
With a disability	—	(†)	10.0	(2.81)	6.7!	(2.17)	6.2!	(2.10)	413	(33.5)	‡	(†)	3.7	(0.30)	4.9!	(1.69)
Without a disability	—	(†)	3.2	(0.33)	4.7	(0.36)	4.6	(0.39)	10,725	(125.9)	497	(41.7)	96.3	(0.30)	95.1	(1.69)
Region																
Northeast	2.9	(0.52)	3.3	(0.67)	4.2	(0.87)	4.9	(1.01)	1,729	(73.5)	‡	(†)	15.5	(0.63)	16.4	(3.18)
Midwest	3.1	(0.48)	2.7	(0.56)	4.4	(0.72)	3.2	(0.63)	2,508	(79.2)	81	(15.6)	22.5	(0.68)	15.6	(2.75)
South	3.6	(0.47)	3.7	(0.60)	5.2	(0.62)	5.2	(0.62)	4,229	(107.2)	219	(27.9)	38.0	(0.88)	41.9	(4.01)
West	4.2	(0.62)	3.8	(0.76)	4.8	(0.73)	5.1	(0.73)	2,672	(85.7)	137	(19.9)	24.0	(0.72)	26.2	(3.35)

—Not available.
†Not applicable.
!Interpret data with caution. The coefficient of variation (CV) for this estimate is between 30 and 50 percent.
‡Reporting standards not met. Either there are too few cases for a reliable estimate or the coefficient of variation (CV) is 50 percent or greater.
[1]The event dropout rate is the percentage of 15- to 24-year-olds in grades 10 through 12 who dropped out between one October and the next (e.g., the 2017 data refer to 10th- through 12th-graders who were enrolled in October 2016 but had dropped out by October 2017). Dropping out is defined as leaving school without a high school diploma or alternative credential such as a GED certificate.
[2]Includes all 15- to 24-year-olds who were enrolled in grades 10 through 12 in October 2016.
[3]Includes only those 15- to 24-year-olds who dropped out of grades 10 through 12 between October 2016 and October 2017. Dropping out is defined as leaving school without a high school diploma or alternative credential such as a GED certificate.
[4]Age at the time of data collection. A person's age at the time of dropping out may be 1 year younger, because the dropout event could occur at any time over the previous 12-month period.
[5]United States refers to the 50 states, the District of Columbia, Puerto Rico, American Samoa, Guam, the U.S. Virgin Islands, and the Northern Marianas. Children born abroad to U.S.-citizen parents are counted as born in the United States. Individuals defined as "first generation" were born in the United States, but one or both of their parents were born outside the United States. Individuals defined as "second generation or higher" were born in the United States, as were both of their parents.
[6]Individuals identified as having a disability reported difficulty with at least one of the following: hearing, seeing even when wearing glasses, walking or climbing stairs, dressing or bathing, doing errands alone, concentrating, remembering, or making decisions.
NOTE: Data are based on sample surveys of the civilian noninstitutionalized population, which excludes persons in the military and persons living in institutions (e.g., prisons or nursing facilities). Race categories exclude persons of Hispanic ethnicity. Detail may not sum to totals because of rounding. Prior to 2010, standard errors were computed using generalized variance function methodology rather than the more precise replicate weight methodology used in later years.
SOURCE: U.S. Department of Commerce, Census Bureau, Current Population Survey (CPS), October, 2007 through 2017. (This table was prepared November 2018.)

Table 219.65. High school completion rate of 18- to 24-year-olds not enrolled in high school (status completion rate), by sex and race/ethnicity: 1972 through 2017

[Standard errors appear in parentheses]

	Status completion rate[1]						
		Sex		Race/ethnicity			
Year	Total	Male	Female	White	Black	Hispanic	Asian[2]
1	2	3	4	5	6	7	8
1972	82.8 (0.36)	83.0 (0.52)	82.7 (0.49)	86.0 (0.36)	72.1 (1.45)	56.2 (3.67)	— (†)
1973	83.7 (0.34)	84.0 (0.50)	83.4 (0.48)	87.0 (0.35)	71.6 (1.42)	58.7 (3.68)	— (†)
1974	83.6 (0.34)	83.4 (0.50)	83.8 (0.47)	86.7 (0.35)	72.9 (1.41)	60.1 (3.40)	— (†)
1975	83.8 (0.34)	84.1 (0.48)	83.6 (0.47)	87.2 (0.34)	70.2 (1.43)	62.2 (3.45)	— (†)
1976	83.5 (0.33)	83.0 (0.49)	84.0 (0.46)	86.4 (0.34)	73.5 (1.36)	60.3 (3.36)	— (†)
1977	83.6 (0.33)	82.8 (0.49)	84.4 (0.45)	86.7 (0.34)	73.9 (1.34)	58.6 (3.50)	— (†)
1978	83.6 (0.33)	82.8 (0.48)	84.2 (0.45)	86.9 (0.34)	73.4 (1.33)	58.8 (3.21)	— (†)
1979	83.1 (0.33)	82.1 (0.49)	84.0 (0.45)	86.5 (0.34)	72.6 (1.33)	58.5 (3.15)	— (†)
1980	83.9 (0.32)	82.3 (0.48)	85.3 (0.43)	87.5 (0.33)	75.2 (1.28)	57.1 (2.99)	— (†)
1981	83.8 (0.32)	82.0 (0.48)	85.4 (0.43)	87.1 (0.33)	76.7 (1.22)	59.1 (2.90)	— (†)
1982	83.8 (0.34)	82.7 (0.50)	84.9 (0.46)	87.0 (0.35)	76.4 (1.28)	60.9 (2.61)	— (†)
1983	83.9 (0.34)	82.1 (0.51)	85.6 (0.45)	87.4 (0.35)	76.8 (1.27)	59.4 (3.13)	— (†)
1984	84.7 (0.34)	83.3 (0.50)	85.9 (0.45)	87.5 (0.35)	80.3 (1.19)	63.7 (3.03)	— (†)
1985	85.4 (0.34)	84.0 (0.50)	86.7 (0.45)	88.2 (0.35)	81.0 (1.20)	66.6 (2.40)	— (†)
1986	85.5 (0.34)	84.2 (0.51)	86.7 (0.45)	88.8 (0.35)	81.8 (1.19)	63.5 (2.30)	— (†)
1987	84.7 (0.35)	83.6 (0.52)	85.8 (0.47)	87.7 (0.37)	81.9 (1.20)	65.1 (2.24)	— (†)
1988	84.5 (0.39)	83.2 (0.58)	85.8 (0.52)	88.6 (0.40)	80.9 (1.35)	58.2 (2.56)	— (†)
1989	84.7 (0.37)	83.2 (0.55)	86.2 (0.49)	89.0 (0.38)	81.9 (1.25)	59.4 (2.29)	89.3 (2.46)
1990	85.6 (0.36)	85.1 (0.53)	86.0 (0.50)	89.6 (0.37)	83.2 (1.22)	59.1 (2.35)	94.2 (1.72)
1991	84.9 (0.37)	83.8 (0.55)	85.9 (0.51)	89.4 (0.38)	82.5 (1.26)	56.5 (2.32)	95.2 (1.42)
1992	86.4 (0.36)	85.3 (0.53)	87.4 (0.49)	90.7 (0.36)	82.0 (1.26)	62.1 (2.32)	93.1 (1.73)
1993	86.2 (0.36)	85.4 (0.53)	86.9 (0.50)	90.1 (0.37)	81.9 (1.27)	64.4 (2.26)	93.9 (1.66)
1994	85.8 (0.36)	84.5 (0.53)	87.0 (0.49)	90.7 (0.36)	83.3 (1.19)	61.8 (2.06)	92.4 (1.83)
1995	85.0 (0.34)	84.3 (0.50)	85.7 (0.47)	89.5 (0.36)	84.1 (1.01)	62.6 (1.40)	94.8 (1.43)
1996	86.2 (0.35)	85.7 (0.50)	86.8 (0.48)	91.5 (0.34)	83.0 (1.08)	61.9 (1.49)	93.5 (1.24)
1997	85.9 (0.35)	84.6 (0.51)	87.2 (0.47)	90.5 (0.36)	82.0 (1.10)	66.7 (1.42)	90.6 (1.58)
1998	84.8 (0.36)	82.6 (0.53)	87.0 (0.47)	90.2 (0.36)	81.4 (1.11)	62.8 (1.37)	94.2 (1.22)
1999	85.9 (0.34)	84.8 (0.50)	87.0 (0.46)	91.2 (0.34)	83.5 (1.04)	63.4 (1.39)	94.0 (1.19)
2000	86.5 (0.33)	84.9 (0.49)	88.1 (0.44)	91.8 (0.33)	83.7 (1.01)	64.1 (1.36)	94.6 (1.13)
2001	86.5 (0.31)	84.6 (0.47)	88.3 (0.41)	91.1 (0.32)	85.7 (0.92)	65.7 (1.24)	96.1 (0.91)
2002	86.6 (0.31)	84.8 (0.46)	88.4 (0.41)	91.8 (0.31)	84.7 (0.95)	67.3 (1.15)	95.7 (0.89)
2003	87.1 (0.30)	85.1 (0.46)	89.2 (0.40)	91.9 (0.31)	85.0 (0.96)	69.2 (1.15)	94.8 (1.06)
2004	86.9 (0.30)	84.9 (0.46)	88.8 (0.40)	91.7 (0.31)	83.5 (0.98)	69.9 (1.12)	95.2 (1.00)
2005	87.6 (0.30)	85.4 (0.45)	89.8 (0.38)	92.3 (0.30)	86.0 (0.91)	70.3 (1.12)	96.0 (0.93)
2006	87.8 (0.29)	86.5 (0.43)	89.2 (0.39)	92.6 (0.30)	84.9 (0.93)	70.9 (1.11)	95.8 (0.95)
2007	89.0 (0.28)	87.4 (0.42)	90.6 (0.37)	93.5 (0.28)	88.8 (0.80)	72.7 (1.07)	92.8 (1.23)
2008	89.9 (0.27)	89.3 (0.39)	90.5 (0.37)	94.2 (0.26)	86.9 (0.86)	75.5 (1.03)	95.5 (1.01)
2009	89.8 (0.27)	88.3 (0.40)	91.2 (0.35)	93.8 (0.27)	87.1 (0.84)	76.8 (1.00)	97.6 (0.72)
2010	90.4 (0.35)	89.2 (0.53)	91.6 (0.38)	93.7 (0.38)	89.2 (1.08)	79.4 (1.21)	95.3 (1.26)
2011	90.8 (0.35)	89.9 (0.50)	91.8 (0.46)	93.8 (0.39)	90.1 (0.98)	82.2 (1.04)	94.1 (1.48)
2012	91.3 (0.33)	90.3 (0.47)	92.3 (0.45)	94.6 (0.38)	90.0 (1.01)	82.8 (1.02)	95.3 (1.24)
2013	92.0 (0.35)	91.4 (0.47)	92.6 (0.45)	94.3 (0.38)	91.5 (1.13)	85.0 (0.98)	96.3 (1.27)
2014	92.4 (0.32)	91.8 (0.46)	93.1 (0.38)	94.2 (0.40)	91.7 (0.91)	87.1 (0.88)	98.8 (0.47)
2015	93.0 (0.33)	92.5 (0.44)	93.4 (0.45)	94.7 (0.36)	91.9 (0.91)	88.4 (0.93)	97.3 (0.75)
2016	92.9 (0.32)	91.6 (0.46)	94.3 (0.37)	94.5 (0.36)	92.2 (1.02)	89.1 (0.81)	96.8 (0.75)
2017	93.3 (0.33)	92.3 (0.44)	94.3 (0.41)	94.8 (0.38)	93.8 (0.84)	88.3 (0.90)	98.6 (0.51)

—Not available.
†Not applicable.
[1]The status completion rate is the number of 18- to 24-year-olds who are high school completers as a percentage of the total number of 18- to 24-year-olds who are not enrolled in high school or a lower level of education. High school completers include those with a high school diploma, as well as those with an alternative credential, such as a GED.
[2]Prior to 2003, Asian data include Pacific Islanders.
NOTE: Data are based on sample surveys of the civilian noninstitutionalized population, which excludes persons in the military and persons living in institutions (e.g., prisons or nursing facilities). Because of changes in data collection procedures, data for 1992 and later years may not be comparable with figures for prior years. Prior to 2010, standard errors were computed using generalized variance function methodology rather than the more precise replicate weight methodology used in later years. Race categories exclude persons of Hispanic ethnicity. Totals include other racial/ethnic groups not separately shown.
SOURCE: U.S. Department of Commerce, Census Bureau, Current Population Survey (CPS), October, 1972 through 2017. (This table was prepared November 2018.)

Table 219.67. Number and high school completion rate of 18- to 24-year-olds not enrolled in high school (status completion rate), by selected characteristics: Selected years, 2007 through 2017

[Standard errors appear in parentheses]

Selected characteristic	Status completion rate[1]								2017							
									Number of 18- to 24-year-olds not enrolled in high school (in thousands)				Percentage distribution of 18- to 24-year-olds not enrolled in high school			
	2007		2012		2016		2017		Total population[2]		Status completers only[3]		Total population[2]		Status completers only[3]	
1	2		3		4		5		6		7		8		9	
Total	**89.0**	**(0.28)**	**91.3**	**(0.33)**	**92.9**	**(0.32)**	**93.3**	**(0.33)**	**27,603**	**(119.1)**	**25,766**	**(142.3)**	**100.0**	**(†)**	**100.0**	**(†)**
Sex																
Male	87.4	(0.42)	90.3	(0.47)	91.6	(0.46)	92.3	(0.44)	13,715	(72.4)	12,665	(86.4)	49.7	(0.19)	49.2	(0.23)
Female	90.6	(0.37)	92.3	(0.45)	94.3	(0.37)	94.3	(0.41)	13,888	(85.0)	13,101	(98.9)	50.3	(0.19)	50.8	(0.23)
Race/ethnicity																
White	93.5	(0.28)	94.6	(0.38)	94.5	(0.36)	94.8	(0.38)	14,999	(87.3)	14,213	(96.7)	54.3	(0.32)	55.2	(0.37)
Black	88.8	(0.80)	90.0	(1.01)	92.2	(1.02)	93.8	(0.84)	3,791	(63.8)	3,555	(66.0)	13.7	(0.20)	13.8	(0.22)
Hispanic	72.7	(1.07)	82.8	(1.02)	89.1	(0.81)	88.3	(0.90)	6,161	(66.6)	5,441	(86.6)	22.3	(0.25)	21.1	(0.31)
Asian	92.8	(1.23)	95.3	(1.24)	96.8	(0.75)	98.6	(0.51)	1,605	(71.1)	1,583	(70.9)	5.8	(0.25)	6.1	(0.27)
Pacific Islander	97.7	(2.80)	89.6	(4.73)	83.6	(7.71)	89.2	(7.65)	99	(21.3)	88	(19.4)	0.4	(0.08)	0.3	(0.08)
American Indian/Alaska Native	77.9	(4.67)	79.0	(6.77)	75.3	(4.48)	86.3	(3.21)	274	(36.0)	236	(33.4)	1.0	(0.13)	0.9	(0.13)
Two or more races	90.4	(2.16)	91.9	(2.07)	96.2	(1.35)	96.4	(1.28)	676	(47.6)	651	(48.0)	2.4	(0.17)	2.5	(0.19)
Race/ethnicity by sex																
Male																
White	92.3	(0.42)	94.1	(0.51)	93.8	(0.47)	94.3	(0.51)	7,507	(62.6)	7,079	(63.8)	54.7	(0.38)	55.9	(0.44)
Black	89.0	(1.15)	88.2	(1.57)	88.7	(1.64)	92.1	(1.48)	1,820	(56.3)	1,677	(58.5)	13.3	(0.39)	13.2	(0.44)
Hispanic	68.1	(1.55)	80.8	(1.48)	86.8	(1.41)	85.9	(1.22)	3,077	(51.8)	2,644	(61.9)	22.4	(0.38)	20.9	(0.46)
Asian	93.5	(1.70)	97.0	(1.10)	97.4	(0.93)	99.3	(0.41)	815	(32.4)	809	(33.1)	5.9	(0.23)	6.4	(0.26)
Pacific Islander	‡	(†)	‡	(†)	‡	(†)	‡	(†)	‡	(†)	‡	(†)	0.4	(0.10)	0.4	(0.10)
American Indian/Alaska Native	74.5	(7.43)	81.3	(7.98)	70.3	(6.53)	85.8	(5.00)	142	(22.6)	122	(21.1)	1.0	(0.16)	1.0	(0.17)
Two or more races	90.1	(3.20)	88.3	(3.57)	95.3	(2.40)	95.1	(2.14)	305	(30.7)	290	(30.2)	2.2	(0.22)	2.3	(0.24)
Female																
White	94.6	(0.36)	95.2	(0.48)	95.1	(0.47)	95.2	(0.49)	7,492	(59.0)	7,134	(66.3)	53.9	(0.45)	54.5	(0.53)
Black	88.7	(1.12)	91.7	(1.34)	95.5	(1.02)	95.3	(0.96)	1,970	(40.6)	1,878	(43.3)	14.2	(0.28)	14.3	(0.31)
Hispanic	77.6	(1.44)	84.8	(1.34)	91.3	(0.99)	90.7	(1.16)	3,084	(46.6)	2,797	(60.5)	22.2	(0.30)	21.3	(0.39)
Asian	92.2	(1.76)	93.6	(2.11)	96.2	(1.16)	97.9	(0.90)	790	(62.0)	774	(61.3)	5.7	(0.43)	5.9	(0.45)
Pacific Islander	‡	(†)	‡	(†)	‡	(†)	‡	(†)	‡	(†)	‡	(†)	0.4	(0.09)	0.3	(0.09)
American Indian/Alaska Native	80.4	(5.93)	77.2	(8.41)	79.8	(5.71)	87.0	(5.29)	131	(20.8)	114	(19.7)	0.9	(0.15)	0.9	(0.15)
Two or more races	90.7	(2.93)	95.6	(2.11)	97.1	(1.31)	97.4	(1.41)	371	(29.2)	361	(30.1)	2.7	(0.21)	2.8	(0.23)
Age																
18 and 19	89.8	(0.53)	89.9	(0.74)	91.4	(0.66)	90.6	(0.70)	6,560	(78.4)	5,945	(86.7)	23.8	(0.22)	23.1	(0.26)
20 and 21	89.5	(0.50)	92.8	(0.56)	93.3	(0.56)	94.2	(0.54)	8,108	(183.4)	7,640	(172.4)	29.4	(0.65)	29.7	(0.65)
22 to 24	88.2	(0.43)	91.0	(0.51)	93.5	(0.42)	94.2	(0.41)	12,935	(172.4)	12,181	(169.4)	46.9	(0.64)	47.3	(0.66)
Recency of immigration[4]																
Born outside the United States																
Hispanic	54.3	(1.87)	67.4	(2.52)	79.8	(1.99)	78.1	(2.25)	1,378	(77.9)	1,076	(64.1)	5.0	(0.28)	4.2	(0.25)
Non-Hispanic	89.3	(1.39)	93.7	(1.53)	94.4	(1.16)	94.7	(1.23)	1,447	(80.7)	1,370	(79.0)	5.2	(0.28)	5.3	(0.30)
First generation																
Hispanic	87.3	(1.47)	88.6	(1.36)	92.0	(1.09)	91.7	(1.18)	2,624	(95.3)	2,405	(93.4)	9.5	(0.35)	9.3	(0.36)
Non-Hispanic	96.8	(0.64)	96.0	(0.82)	96.7	(0.82)	97.9	(0.64)	1,983	(98.4)	1,941	(98.6)	7.2	(0.35)	7.5	(0.38)
Second generation or higher																
Hispanic	83.4	(1.63)	87.1	(1.61)	92.2	(1.23)	90.8	(1.37)	2,159	(89.0)	1,959	(85.5)	7.8	(0.32)	7.6	(0.33)
Non-Hispanic	92.3	(0.28)	93.3	(0.38)	93.7	(0.37)	94.5	(0.37)	18,012	(140.8)	17,014	(150.3)	65.3	(0.46)	66.0	(0.51)
Disability[5]																
With a disability	—	(†)	81.5	(2.16)	83.8	(2.00)	84.8	(2.28)	927	(60.5)	786	(52.4)	3.4	(0.22)	3.0	(0.20)
Without a disability	—	(†)	91.7	(0.35)	93.3	(0.33)	93.6	(0.34)	26,677	(124.7)	24,981	(144.1)	96.6	(0.22)	97.0	(0.20)
Region																
Northeast	92.1	(0.54)	91.3	(0.79)	95.0	(0.64)	94.9	(0.64)	4,845	(137.5)	4,596	(131.8)	17.6	(0.49)	17.8	(0.51)
Midwest	91.4	(0.51)	92.6	(0.70)	92.6	(0.75)	93.3	(0.73)	5,842	(138.7)	5,452	(136.8)	21.2	(0.51)	21.2	(0.54)
South	87.2	(0.52)	91.1	(0.56)	92.0	(0.56)	92.8	(0.56)	10,181	(175.4)	9,445	(176.8)	36.9	(0.63)	36.7	(0.66)
West	87.1	(0.66)	90.5	(0.80)	93.1	(0.61)	93.1	(0.71)	6,736	(167.5)	6,273	(169.8)	24.4	(0.58)	24.3	(0.62)

—Not available.
†Not applicable.
‡Reporting standards not met (too few cases for a reliable estimate).
[1]The status completion rate is the number of 18- to 24-year-olds who are high school completers as a percentage of the total number of 18- to 24-year-olds who are not enrolled in high school or a lower level of education. High school completers include those with a high school diploma, as well as those with an alternative credential, such as a GED.
[2]Includes all 18- to 24-year-olds who are not enrolled in high school or a lower level of education.
[3]Status completers are 18- to 24-year-olds who are not enrolled in high school or a lower level of education and who also are high school completers—that is, have either a high school diploma or an alternative credential, such as a GED.
[4]United States refers to the 50 states, the District of Columbia, Puerto Rico, American Samoa, Guam, the U.S. Virgin Islands, and the Northern Marianas. Children born abroad to U.S.-citizen parents are counted as born in the United States. Individuals defined as "first generation" were born in the United States, but one or both of their parents were born outside the United States. Individuals defined as "second generation or higher" were born in the United States, as were both of their parents.
[5]Individuals identified as having a disability reported difficulty in at least one of the following: hearing, seeing even when wearing glasses, walking or climbing stairs, dressing or bathing, doing errands alone, concentrating, remembering, or making decisions.
NOTE: Data are based on sample surveys of the civilian noninstitutionalized population, which excludes persons in the military and persons living in institutions (e.g., prisons or nursing facilities). Race categories exclude persons of Hispanic ethnicity. Detail may not sum to totals because of rounding and the suppression of cells that do not meet National Center for Education Statistics reporting standards.
SOURCE: U.S. Department of Commerce, Census Bureau, Current Population Survey (CPS), October, 2007 through 2017. (This table was prepared November 2018.)

Table 219.70. Percentage of high school dropouts among persons 16 to 24 years old (status dropout rate), by sex and race/ethnicity: Selected years, 1960 through 2017

[Standard errors appear in parentheses]

Year	Total								Male								Female							
	All races/ ethnicities[1]		White		Black		Hispanic		All races/ ethnicities[1]		White		Black		Hispanic		All races/ ethnicities[1]		White		Black		Hispanic	
1	2		3		4		5		6		7		8		9		10		11		12		13	
1960[2]	27.2	(—)	—	(†)	—	(†)	—	(†)	27.8	(—)	—	(†)	—	(†)	—	(†)	26.7	(—)	—	(†)	—	(†)	—	(†)
1967[3]	17.0	(—)	15.4	(—)	28.6	(—)	—	(†)	16.5	(—)	14.7	(—)	30.6	(—)	—	(†)	17.3	(—)	16.1	(—)	26.9	(—)	—	(†)
1968[3]	16.2	(—)	14.7	(—)	27.4	(—)	—	(†)	15.8	(—)	14.4	(—)	27.1	(—)	—	(†)	16.5	(—)	15.0	(—)	27.6	(—)	—	(†)
1969[3]	15.2	(—)	13.6	(—)	26.7	(—)	—	(†)	14.3	(—)	12.6	(—)	26.9	(—)	—	(†)	16.0	(—)	14.6	(—)	26.7	(—)	—	(†)
1970[3]	15.0	(0.30)	13.2	(0.30)	27.9	(1.25)	—	(†)	14.2	(0.42)	12.2	(0.43)	29.4	(1.87)	—	(†)	15.7	(0.42)	14.1	(0.43)	26.6	(1.69)	—	(†)
1971[3]	14.7	(0.29)	13.4	(0.30)	24.0	(1.17)	—	(†)	14.2	(0.41)	12.6	(0.42)	25.5	(1.74)	—	(†)	15.2	(0.41)	14.2	(0.42)	22.6	(1.58)	—	(†)
1972	14.6	(0.28)	12.3	(0.29)	21.3	(1.09)	34.3	(2.93)	14.1	(0.40)	11.6	(0.41)	22.3	(1.63)	33.7	(4.26)	15.1	(0.40)	12.8	(0.42)	20.5	(1.48)	34.8	(4.03)
1973	14.1	(0.28)	11.6	(0.28)	22.2	(1.09)	33.5	(2.96)	13.7	(0.39)	11.5	(0.40)	21.5	(1.57)	30.4	(4.17)	14.5	(0.39)	11.8	(0.40)	22.8	(1.51)	36.4	(4.18)
1974	14.3	(0.28)	11.9	(0.28)	21.2	(1.07)	33.0	(2.74)	14.2	(0.39)	12.0	(0.41)	20.1	(1.55)	33.8	(3.94)	14.3	(0.39)	11.8	(0.40)	22.1	(1.49)	32.2	(3.82)
1975	13.9	(0.27)	11.4	(0.28)	22.9	(1.08)	29.2	(2.67)	13.3	(0.38)	11.0	(0.39)	23.0	(1.60)	26.7	(3.75)	14.5	(0.38)	11.8	(0.39)	22.9	(1.48)	31.6	(3.78)
1976	14.1	(0.27)	12.0	(0.28)	20.5	(1.03)	31.4	(2.66)	14.1	(0.39)	12.1	(0.40)	21.2	(1.53)	30.3	(3.88)	14.2	(0.38)	11.8	(0.39)	19.9	(1.39)	32.3	(3.64)
1977	14.1	(0.27)	11.9	(0.28)	19.8	(1.00)	33.0	(2.65)	14.5	(0.39)	12.6	(0.41)	19.5	(1.47)	31.6	(3.79)	13.8	(0.37)	11.2	(0.38)	20.0	(1.38)	34.3	(3.71)
1978	14.2	(0.27)	11.9	(0.28)	20.2	(1.01)	33.3	(2.62)	14.6	(0.39)	12.2	(0.40)	22.5	(1.54)	33.6	(3.77)	13.9	(0.37)	11.6	(0.39)	18.3	(1.32)	33.1	(3.65)
1979	14.6	(0.27)	12.0	(0.28)	21.1	(1.02)	33.8	(2.60)	15.0	(0.39)	12.6	(0.40)	22.4	(1.53)	33.0	(3.71)	14.2	(0.37)	11.5	(0.39)	20.0	(1.36)	34.5	(3.63)
1980	14.1	(0.27)	11.4	(0.27)	19.1	(0.98)	35.2	(2.47)	15.1	(0.39)	12.3	(0.40)	20.8	(1.48)	37.2	(3.57)	13.1	(0.36)	10.5	(0.37)	17.7	(1.29)	33.2	(3.42)
1981	13.9	(0.26)	11.3	(0.27)	18.4	(0.94)	33.2	(2.36)	15.1	(0.39)	12.5	(0.40)	19.9	(1.41)	36.0	(3.42)	12.8	(0.35)	10.2	(0.37)	17.1	(1.25)	30.4	(3.25)
1982	13.9	(0.28)	11.4	(0.29)	18.4	(0.99)	31.7	(2.51)	14.5	(0.40)	12.0	(0.43)	21.2	(1.52)	30.5	(3.57)	13.3	(0.38)	10.8	(0.40)	15.9	(1.28)	32.8	(3.53)
1983	13.7	(0.28)	11.1	(0.29)	18.0	(0.98)	31.6	(2.51)	14.9	(0.41)	12.2	(0.43)	19.9	(1.48)	34.3	(3.71)	12.5	(0.38)	10.1	(0.40)	16.2	(1.30)	29.1	(3.41)
1984	13.1	(0.28)	11.0	(0.29)	15.5	(0.93)	29.8	(2.49)	14.0	(0.41)	11.9	(0.43)	16.8	(1.39)	30.6	(3.62)	12.3	(0.38)	10.1	(0.40)	14.3	(1.24)	29.0	(3.42)
1985	12.6	(0.28)	10.4	(0.29)	15.2	(0.93)	27.6	(1.93)	13.4	(0.40)	11.1	(0.43)	16.1	(1.39)	29.9	(2.77)	11.8	(0.37)	9.8	(0.40)	14.3	(1.25)	25.2	(2.68)
1986	12.2	(0.27)	9.7	(0.29)	14.2	(0.91)	30.1	(1.88)	13.1	(0.40)	10.3	(0.42)	15.0	(1.36)	32.8	(2.67)	11.4	(0.37)	9.1	(0.39)	13.5	(1.23)	27.2	(2.64)
1987	12.6	(0.28)	10.4	(0.30)	14.1	(0.92)	28.6	(1.85)	13.2	(0.41)	10.8	(0.43)	15.0	(1.37)	29.1	(2.58)	12.1	(0.39)	10.0	(0.41)	13.3	(1.23)	28.1	(2.65)
1988	12.9	(0.31)	9.6	(0.32)	14.5	(1.01)	35.8	(2.17)	13.5	(0.45)	10.3	(0.47)	15.0	(1.50)	36.0	(3.02)	12.2	(0.42)	8.9	(0.43)	14.0	(1.38)	35.4	(3.13)
1989	12.6	(0.30)	9.4	(0.31)	13.9	(0.94)	33.0	(1.92)	13.6	(0.43)	10.3	(0.45)	14.9	(1.41)	34.4	(2.70)	11.7	(0.40)	8.5	(0.41)	13.0	(1.27)	31.6	(2.73)
1990	12.1	(0.29)	9.0	(0.30)	13.2	(0.94)	32.4	(1.91)	12.3	(0.42)	9.3	(0.44)	11.9	(1.30)	34.3	(2.71)	11.8	(0.41)	8.7	(0.42)	14.4	(1.34)	30.3	(2.70)
1991	12.5	(0.30)	8.9	(0.31)	13.6	(0.95)	35.3	(1.93)	13.0	(0.43)	8.9	(0.44)	13.5	(1.37)	39.2	(2.74)	11.9	(0.41)	8.9	(0.43)	13.7	(1.31)	31.1	(2.70)
1992[4]	11.0	(0.28)	7.7	(0.29)	13.7	(0.95)	29.4	(1.86)	11.3	(0.41)	8.0	(0.42)	12.5	(1.31)	32.1	(2.67)	10.7	(0.39)	7.4	(0.40)	14.8	(1.35)	26.6	(2.56)
1993[4]	11.0	(0.28)	7.9	(0.29)	13.6	(0.94)	27.5	(1.79)	11.2	(0.40)	8.2	(0.42)	12.6	(1.32)	28.1	(2.54)	10.9	(0.40)	7.6	(0.41)	14.4	(1.34)	26.9	(2.51)
1994[4]	11.4	(0.28)	7.7	(0.29)	12.6	(0.89)	30.0	(1.66)	12.3	(0.41)	8.0	(0.41)	14.1	(1.34)	31.6	(2.30)	10.6	(0.38)	7.5	(0.40)	11.3	(1.17)	28.1	(2.38)
1995[4]	12.0	(0.27)	8.6	(0.28)	12.1	(0.75)	30.0	(1.15)	12.2	(0.38)	9.0	(0.40)	11.1	(1.05)	30.0	(1.59)	11.7	(0.37)	8.2	(0.39)	12.9	(1.06)	30.0	(1.66)
1996[4]	11.1	(0.27)	7.3	(0.27)	13.0	(0.80)	29.4	(1.19)	11.4	(0.38)	7.3	(0.38)	13.5	(1.18)	30.3	(1.67)	10.9	(0.38)	7.3	(0.39)	12.5	(1.08)	28.3	(1.69)
1997[4]	11.0	(0.27)	7.6	(0.28)	13.4	(0.80)	25.3	(1.11)	11.9	(0.39)	8.5	(0.41)	13.3	(1.16)	27.0	(1.55)	10.1	(0.36)	6.7	(0.37)	13.5	(1.11)	23.4	(1.59)
1998[4]	11.8	(0.27)	7.7	(0.28)	13.8	(0.81)	29.5	(1.12)	13.3	(0.40)	8.6	(0.41)	15.5	(1.23)	33.5	(1.59)	10.3	(0.36)	6.9	(0.37)	12.2	(1.05)	25.0	(1.56)
1999[4]	11.2	(0.26)	7.3	(0.27)	12.6	(0.77)	28.6	(1.11)	11.9	(0.38)	7.7	(0.39)	12.1	(1.10)	31.0	(1.58)	10.5	(0.36)	6.9	(0.37)	13.0	(1.08)	26.0	(1.54)
2000[4]	10.9	(0.26)	6.9	(0.26)	13.1	(0.78)	27.8	(1.08)	12.0	(0.38)	7.0	(0.37)	15.3	(1.20)	31.8	(1.56)	9.9	(0.35)	6.9	(0.37)	11.1	(1.00)	23.5	(1.48)
2001[4]	10.7	(0.24)	7.3	(0.25)	10.9	(0.68)	27.0	(1.01)	12.2	(0.36)	7.9	(0.37)	13.0	(1.06)	31.6	(1.47)	9.3	(0.32)	6.7	(0.34)	9.0	(0.86)	22.1	(1.35)
2002[4]	10.5	(0.24)	6.5	(0.24)	11.3	(0.70)	25.7	(0.93)	11.8	(0.35)	6.7	(0.35)	12.8	(1.07)	29.6	(1.32)	9.2	(0.32)	6.3	(0.34)	9.9	(0.91)	21.2	(1.27)
2003[4,5]	9.9	(0.23)	6.3	(0.24)	10.9	(0.69)	23.5	(0.90)	11.3	(0.34)	7.1	(0.35)	12.5	(1.05)	26.7	(1.29)	8.4	(0.30)	5.6	(0.32)	9.5	(0.89)	20.1	(1.23)
2004[4,5]	10.3	(0.23)	6.8	(0.24)	11.8	(0.70)	23.8	(0.89)	11.6	(0.34)	7.1	(0.35)	13.5	(1.08)	28.5	(1.30)	9.0	(0.31)	6.4	(0.34)	10.2	(0.92)	18.5	(1.18)
2005[4,5]	9.4	(0.22)	6.0	(0.23)	10.4	(0.66)	22.4	(0.87)	10.8	(0.33)	6.6	(0.34)	12.0	(1.02)	26.4	(1.26)	8.0	(0.29)	5.3	(0.31)	9.0	(0.86)	18.1	(1.16)
2006[4,5]	9.3	(0.22)	5.8	(0.23)	10.7	(0.66)	22.1	(0.86)	10.3	(0.33)	6.4	(0.33)	9.7	(0.91)	25.7	(1.25)	8.3	(0.30)	5.3	(0.31)	11.7	(0.96)	18.1	(1.15)
2007[4,5]	8.7	(0.21)	5.3	(0.22)	8.4	(0.59)	21.4	(0.83)	9.8	(0.32)	6.0	(0.32)	8.0	(0.82)	24.7	(1.22)	7.7	(0.29)	4.5	(0.28)	8.8	(0.84)	18.0	(1.13)
2008[4,5]	8.0	(0.20)	4.8	(0.21)	9.9	(0.63)	18.3	(0.78)	8.5	(0.30)	5.4	(0.30)	8.7	(0.85)	19.9	(1.12)	7.5	(0.28)	4.2	(0.28)	11.1	(0.93)	16.7	(1.08)
2009[4,5]	8.1	(0.20)	5.2	(0.21)	9.3	(0.61)	17.6	(0.76)	9.1	(0.31)	6.3	(0.33)	10.6	(0.93)	19.0	(1.10)	7.0	(0.27)	4.1	(0.27)	8.1	(0.80)	16.1	(1.06)
2010[4,5]	7.4	(0.27)	5.1	(0.30)	8.0	(0.76)	15.1	(0.87)	8.5	(0.40)	5.9	(0.42)	9.5	(1.11)	17.3	(1.24)	6.3	(0.28)	4.2	(0.35)	6.7	(0.85)	12.8	(0.97)
2011[4,5]	7.1	(0.26)	5.0	(0.31)	7.3	(0.67)	13.6	(0.78)	7.7	(0.36)	5.4	(0.41)	8.3	(0.98)	14.6	(1.09)	6.5	(0.34)	4.6	(0.38)	6.4	(0.94)	12.4	(0.97)
2012[4,5]	6.6	(0.25)	4.3	(0.31)	7.5	(0.76)	12.7	(0.72)	7.3	(0.36)	4.8	(0.40)	8.1	(1.15)	13.9	(1.04)	5.9	(0.33)	3.8	(0.37)	7.0	(1.01)	11.3	(1.00)
2013[4,5]	6.8	(0.28)	5.1	(0.31)	7.3	(0.87)	11.7	(0.74)	7.2	(0.37)	5.5	(0.39)	8.2	(1.11)	12.6	(1.01)	6.3	(0.34)	4.7	(0.36)	6.6	(1.07)	10.8	(0.98)
2014[4,5]	6.5	(0.25)	5.2	(0.32)	7.4	(0.74)	10.6	(0.68)	7.1	(0.37)	5.7	(0.42)	7.1	(1.02)	11.8	(1.04)	5.9	(0.29)	4.8	(0.41)	7.7	(1.02)	9.3	(0.84)
2015[4,5]	5.9	(0.26)	4.6	(0.29)	6.5	(0.70)	9.2	(0.71)	6.3	(0.37)	5.0	(0.40)	6.4	(1.04)	9.9	(0.93)	5.4	(0.33)	4.1	(0.37)	6.5	(0.98)	8.4	(0.97)
2016[4,5]	6.1	(0.27)	5.2	(0.31)	6.2	(0.80)	8.6	(0.64)	7.1	(0.38)	5.8	(0.42)	8.2	(1.22)	10.1	(1.06)	5.1	(0.31)	4.6	(0.39)	4.3	(0.84)	7.0	(0.76)
2017[4,5]	5.8	(0.26)	4.6	(0.30)	5.7	(0.66)	9.5	(0.67)	6.6	(0.36)	5.0	(0.43)	7.0	(1.08)	11.5	(0.95)	5.0	(0.31)	4.3	(0.36)	4.4	(0.78)	7.4	(0.83)

—Not available.
†Not applicable.
[1]Includes other racial/ethnic groups not separately shown.
[2]Based on the April 1960 decennial census.
[3]For 1967 through 1971, White and Black include persons of Hispanic ethnicity.
[4]Because of changes in data collection procedures, data may not be comparable with figures for years prior to 1992.
[5]White and Black exclude persons of Two or more races.
NOTE: Status dropouts are 16- to 24-year-olds who are not enrolled in school and who have not completed a high school program, regardless of when they left school. People who have received equivalency credentials, such as the GED, are counted as high school completers. All data except for 1960 are based on October counts. Data are based on sample surveys of the civilian noninstitutionalized population, which excludes persons in the military and persons living in institutions (e.g., prisons or nursing facilities). Prior to 2010, standard errors were computed using generalized variance function methodology rather than the more precise replicate weight methodology used in later years. Race categories exclude persons of Hispanic ethnicity except where otherwise noted.
SOURCE: U.S. Department of Commerce, Census Bureau, Current Population Survey (CPS), October, 1967 through 2017. (This table was prepared November 2018.)

Table 219.75. Percentage of high school dropouts among persons 16 to 24 years old (status dropout rate) and percentage distribution of status dropouts, by labor force status and years of school completed: Selected years, 1970 through 2017

[Standard errors appear in parentheses]

Year	Status dropout rate	Percentage distribution of status dropouts, by labor force status[1]				Percentage distribution of status dropouts, by years of school completed				
		Total	In labor force		Not in labor force	Total	Less than 9 years	9 years	10 years	11 or 12 years
			Employed[2]	Unemployed						
1	2	3	4	5	6	7	8	9	10	11
1970	15.0 (0.30)	100.0 (†)	49.8 (1.08)	10.3 (0.66)	39.9 (1.06)	100.0 (†)	28.5 (0.98)	20.6 (0.87)	26.8 (0.96)	24.0 (0.92)
1975	13.9 (0.27)	100.0 (†)	46.0 (1.04)	15.6 (0.76)	38.4 (1.02)	100.0 (†)	23.5 (0.89)	21.1 (0.85)	27.5 (0.93)	27.9 (0.94)
1976	14.1 (0.27)	100.0 (†)	48.8 (1.03)	16.0 (0.75)	35.2 (0.98)	100.0 (†)	24.3 (0.88)	20.1 (0.82)	27.8 (0.92)	27.8 (0.92)
1977	14.1 (0.27)	100.0 (†)	52.9 (1.02)	13.6 (0.70)	33.6 (0.97)	100.0 (†)	24.3 (0.88)	21.7 (0.84)	27.3 (0.91)	26.6 (0.91)
1978	14.2 (0.27)	100.0 (†)	54.3 (1.01)	12.4 (0.67)	33.3 (0.96)	100.0 (†)	22.9 (0.85)	20.2 (0.81)	28.2 (0.91)	28.8 (0.92)
1979	14.6 (0.27)	100.0 (†)	54.0 (1.00)	12.7 (0.67)	33.3 (0.94)	100.0 (†)	22.6 (0.84)	21.0 (0.82)	28.6 (0.90)	27.8 (0.90)
1980	14.1 (0.27)	100.0 (†)	50.4 (1.02)	17.0 (0.77)	32.6 (0.95)	100.0 (†)	23.6 (0.86)	19.7 (0.81)	29.8 (0.93)	27.0 (0.90)
1981	13.9 (0.26)	100.0 (†)	49.8 (1.01)	18.3 (0.78)	31.9 (0.94)	100.0 (†)	24.3 (0.87)	18.6 (0.79)	30.2 (0.93)	26.9 (0.90)
1982	13.9 (0.28)	100.0 (†)	45.2 (1.08)	21.1 (0.88)	33.7 (1.02)	100.0 (†)	22.9 (0.91)	20.8 (0.88)	28.8 (0.98)	27.6 (0.97)
1983	13.7 (0.28)	100.0 (†)	48.4 (1.10)	18.2 (0.85)	33.4 (1.04)	100.0 (†)	23.0 (0.92)	19.3 (0.87)	28.8 (0.99)	28.8 (0.99)
1984	13.1 (0.28)	100.0 (†)	49.7 (1.13)	17.3 (0.86)	32.9 (1.06)	100.0 (†)	23.6 (0.96)	21.4 (0.93)	27.5 (1.01)	27.5 (1.01)
1985	12.6 (0.28)	100.0 (†)	50.1 (1.17)	17.5 (0.89)	32.4 (1.09)	100.0 (†)	23.9 (1.00)	21.0 (0.95)	27.9 (1.05)	27.2 (1.04)
1986	12.2 (0.27)	100.0 (†)	51.1 (1.19)	16.4 (0.88)	32.5 (1.12)	100.0 (†)	25.4 (1.04)	21.5 (0.98)	25.7 (1.04)	27.4 (1.07)
1987	12.6 (0.28)	100.0 (†)	52.4 (1.18)	13.6 (0.81)	34.0 (1.12)	100.0 (†)	25.9 (1.04)	20.7 (0.96)	26.0 (1.04)	27.5 (1.06)
1988	12.9 (0.31)	100.0 (†)	52.9 (1.29)	— (†)	— (†)	100.0 (†)	28.9 (1.17)	19.3 (1.02)	25.1 (1.12)	26.8 (1.14)
1989	12.6 (0.30)	100.0 (†)	53.2 (1.25)	13.8 (0.86)	33.0 (1.18)	100.0 (†)	29.4 (1.14)	20.8 (1.02)	24.9 (1.08)	25.0 (1.09)
1990	12.1 (0.29)	100.0 (†)	52.5 (1.29)	13.3 (0.88)	34.2 (1.23)	100.0 (†)	28.6 (1.17)	20.9 (1.05)	24.4 (1.11)	26.1 (1.14)
1991	12.5 (0.30)	100.0 (†)	47.5 (1.28)	15.8 (0.93)	36.7 (1.23)	100.0 (†)	28.6 (1.15)	20.5 (1.03)	26.1 (1.12)	24.9 (1.10)
1992[3]	11.0 (0.28)	100.0 (†)	47.6 (1.36)	15.0 (0.97)	37.4 (1.32)	100.0 (†)	21.6 (1.12)	17.5 (1.04)	24.4 (1.17)	36.5 (1.31)
1993[3]	11.0 (0.28)	100.0 (†)	48.7 (1.37)	12.8 (0.91)	38.5 (1.33)	100.0 (†)	20.5 (1.10)	16.6 (1.02)	24.1 (1.17)	38.8 (1.33)
1994[3]	11.4 (0.28)	100.0 (†)	49.5 (1.30)	13.0 (0.88)	37.5 (1.26)	100.0 (†)	23.9 (1.11)	16.2 (0.96)	20.3 (1.05)	39.6 (1.28)
1995[3]	12.0 (0.27)	100.0 (†)	48.9 (1.19)	14.2 (0.83)	37.0 (1.15)	100.0 (†)	22.2 (0.99)	17.0 (0.89)	22.5 (0.99)	38.3 (1.16)
1996[3]	11.1 (0.27)	100.0 (†)	47.3 (1.28)	15.0 (0.91)	37.7 (1.24)	100.0 (†)	20.3 (1.03)	17.7 (0.98)	22.6 (1.07)	39.4 (1.25)
1997[3]	11.0 (0.27)	100.0 (†)	53.3 (1.27)	13.2 (0.86)	33.5 (1.21)	100.0 (†)	19.9 (1.02)	15.7 (0.93)	22.3 (1.06)	42.1 (1.26)
1998[3]	11.8 (0.27)	100.0 (†)	55.1 (1.22)	10.3 (0.74)	34.6 (1.17)	100.0 (†)	21.0 (1.00)	14.9 (0.87)	21.4 (1.00)	42.6 (1.21)
1999[3]	11.2 (0.26)	100.0 (†)	55.6 (1.23)	10.0 (0.74)	34.4 (1.18)	100.0 (†)	22.2 (1.03)	16.3 (0.92)	22.5 (1.04)	39.0 (1.21)
2000[3]	10.9 (0.26)	100.0 (†)	56.9 (1.24)	12.3 (0.82)	30.8 (1.16)	100.0 (†)	21.5 (1.03)	15.3 (0.90)	23.1 (1.06)	40.0 (1.23)
2001[3]	10.7 (0.24)	100.0 (†)	58.3 (1.17)	14.8 (0.85)	26.9 (1.05)	100.0 (†)	18.4 (0.92)	16.8 (0.89)	23.8 (1.01)	40.9 (1.17)
2002[3]	10.5 (0.24)	100.0 (†)	57.4 (1.18)	13.3 (0.81)	29.2 (1.09)	100.0 (†)	22.8 (1.00)	17.1 (0.90)	21.3 (0.98)	38.9 (1.17)
2003[3]	9.9 (0.23)	100.0 (†)	53.5 (1.22)	13.7 (0.84)	32.9 (1.15)	100.0 (†)	21.2 (1.00)	18.2 (0.94)	20.7 (0.99)	40.0 (1.20)
2004[3]	10.3 (0.23)	100.0 (†)	53.0 (1.19)	14.3 (0.83)	32.7 (1.12)	100.0 (†)	21.4 (0.97)	15.9 (0.87)	22.5 (0.99)	40.3 (1.17)
2005[3]	9.4 (0.22)	100.0 (†)	56.9 (1.23)	11.9 (0.80)	31.2 (1.15)	100.0 (†)	18.9 (0.97)	16.8 (0.93)	21.4 (1.02)	42.9 (1.23)
2006[3]	9.3 (0.22)	100.0 (†)	56.4 (1.23)	11.7 (0.80)	32.0 (1.16)	100.0 (†)	22.1 (1.03)	13.4 (0.85)	20.7 (1.01)	43.9 (1.23)
2007[3]	8.7 (0.21)	100.0 (†)	55.5 (1.27)	11.2 (0.80)	33.3 (1.20)	100.0 (†)	21.2 (1.04)	16.9 (0.96)	22.9 (1.07)	39.0 (1.24)
2008[3]	8.0 (0.20)	100.0 (†)	46.8 (1.33)	16.3 (0.98)	36.9 (1.28)	100.0 (†)	18.4 (1.03)	15.2 (0.96)	23.8 (1.13)	42.6 (1.32)
2009[3]	8.1 (0.20)	100.0 (†)	43.2 (1.31)	19.9 (1.06)	36.9 (1.28)	100.0 (†)	17.7 (1.01)	13.6 (0.91)	24.4 (1.14)	44.3 (1.32)
2010[3]	7.4 (0.27)	100.0 (†)	45.8 (1.64)	18.7 (1.38)	35.5 (1.70)	100.0 (†)	19.2 (1.48)	13.1 (1.07)	22.5 (1.59)	45.2 (1.89)
2011[3]	7.1 (0.26)	100.0 (†)	49.8 (1.77)	16.0 (1.33)	34.2 (1.69)	100.0 (†)	18.1 (1.72)	12.9 (1.15)	21.2 (1.39)	47.7 (1.87)
2012[3]	6.6 (0.25)	100.0 (†)	44.8 (2.07)	18.1 (1.49)	37.1 (1.83)	100.0 (†)	18.3 (1.76)	10.2 (1.21)	21.9 (1.57)	49.6 (2.20)
2013[3]	6.8 (0.28)	100.0 (†)	41.1 (2.01)	16.8 (1.58)	42.1 (1.84)	100.0 (†)	18.3 (1.70)	13.3 (1.34)	21.1 (1.63)	47.4 (2.31)
2014[3]	6.5 (0.25)	100.0 (†)	44.7 (1.84)	17.0 (1.41)	38.3 (1.61)	100.0 (†)	15.0 (1.58)	13.7 (1.28)	21.3 (1.56)	50.0 (1.94)
2015[3]	5.9 (0.26)	100.0 (†)	41.7 (2.10)	14.2 (1.48)	44.1 (2.10)	100.0 (†)	14.5 (1.67)	13.9 (1.40)	21.3 (1.65)	50.2 (2.00)
2016[3]	6.1 (0.27)	100.0 (†)	46.6 (1.99)	13.9 (1.31)	39.6 (1.90)	100.0 (†)	17.6 (1.91)	10.8 (1.14)	21.9 (1.64)	49.7 (2.22)
2017[3]	5.8 (0.26)	100.0 (†)	46.7 (1.91)	8.3 (1.09)	44.9 (1.98)	100.0 (†)	21.0 (2.14)	9.8 (1.22)	20.3 (1.76)	49.0 (2.41)

—Not available.
†Not applicable.
[1]Data are not comparable to employment and unemployment rate data produced by the Bureau of Labor Statistics, because the percentage distributions presented here include persons who are not in the labor force. The labor force consists of those who are employed and those who are unemployed (i.e., seeking employment); persons who are neither employed nor seeking employment are not in the labor force.
[2]Includes persons who were employed but not at work during the survey week.
[3]Because of changes in data collection procedures, data may not be comparable with figures for years prior to 1992.

NOTE: Status dropouts are 16- to 24-year-olds who are not enrolled in school and who have not completed a high school program, regardless of when they left school. People who have received equivalency credentials, such as the GED, are counted as high school completers. Data are based on sample surveys of the civilian noninstitutionalized population, which excludes persons in the military and persons living in institutions (e.g., prisons or nursing facilities). Prior to 2010, standard errors were computed using generalized variance function methodology rather than the more precise replicate weight methodology used in later years. Detail may not sum to totals because of rounding.
SOURCE: U.S. Department of Commerce, Census Bureau, Current Population Survey (CPS), October, 1970 through 2017. (This table was prepared November 2018.)

Table 219.90. Number and percentage distribution of 14- through 21-year-old students served under Individuals with Disabilities Education Act (IDEA), Part B, who exited school, by exit reason, sex, race/ethnicity, age, and type of disability: 2015–16 and 2016–17

Year, sex, race/ethnicity, age, and type of disability	Exited school						Transferred to regular education[4]	Moved, known to be continuing[5]
	Total	Graduated with regular diploma	Received alternative certificate[1]	Reached maximum age[2]	Dropped out[3]	Died		
1	2	3	4	5	6	7	8	9
2015–16								
Total number	**403,466**	**283,638**	**42,765**	**5,391**	**70,188**	**1,484**	**58,610**	**164,945**
Percentage distribution of total	100.0	69.4	11.1	1.3	17.8	0.4	†	†
Number by sex								
Male	262,228	181,764	27,329	3,569	48,529	1,037	38,470	109,237
Female	141,238	101,874	15,436	1,822	21,659	447	20,140	55,708
Number by race/ethnicity								
White	200,305	149,284	19,210	2,447	28,650	714	33,316	76,814
Black	85,699	53,795	12,156	1,051	18,315	382	8,227	42,181
Hispanic	92,585	63,306	9,101	1,425	18,477	276	12,640	34,757
Asian	7,216	5,411	905	297	562	41	1,699	1,760
Pacific Islander	1,564	1,072	124	27	326	15	309	487
American Indian/Alaska Native	6,066	4,022	255	43	1,729	17	801	3,224
Two or more races	10,031	6,748	1,014	101	2,129	39	1,618	5,722
Number by age[6]								
14	3,334	28	1	†	3,100	205	15,748	37,665
15	5,829	70	40	†	5,453	266	13,965	38,395
16	16,825	4,493	438	†	11,624	270	13,378	37,390
17	165,894	133,888	12,204	0	19,499	303	9,944	29,506
18	146,099	112,002	15,834	0	18,054	209	4,003	14,959
19	35,476	21,866	5,505	11	7,989	105	914	4,704
20	17,182	7,792	4,744	1,320	3,240	86	443	1,660
21	12,827	3,499	3,999	4,060	1,229	40	215	666
Number by type of disability								
Autism	26,370	18,307	5,117	1,117	1,739	90	2,391	7,545
Deaf-blindness	73	42	17	5	6	3	8	29
Emotional disturbance	37,448	21,553	2,556	258	12,970	111	4,822	25,930
Hearing impairment	4,513	3,651	398	60	393	11	627	1,473
Intellectual disability	34,692	14,876	12,140	2,095	5,376	205	1,256	12,354
Multiple disabilities	8,528	4,053	2,584	585	1,011	295	350	2,796
Orthopedic impairment	2,974	1,925	535	172	276	66	399	756
Other health impairment[7]	67,107	50,121	4,821	311	11,557	297	9,671	30,160
Specific learning disability	206,204	156,497	13,732	620	35,006	349	28,070	77,550
Speech or language impairment	11,079	9,214	384	35	1,433	13	10,532	5,206
Traumatic brain injury	2,713	1,928	357	85	311	32	268	657
Visual impairment	1,765	1,471	124	48	110	12	216	489
2016–17								
Total number	**413,353**	**293,096**	**42,857**	**5,219**	**70,636**	**1,545**	**64,962**	**157,645**
Percentage distribution of total	100.0	70.9	10.4	1.3	17.1	0.4	†	†
Number by sex								
Male	268,210	187,865	27,314	3,433	48,518	1,080	42,570	103,784
Female	145,140	105,229	15,543	1,786	22,117	465	22,392	53,860
Number by race/ethnicity								
White	203,362	151,159	19,663	2,357	29,433	750	36,414	72,481
Black	86,180	54,857	11,714	984	18,258	367	9,584	40,169
Hispanic	96,796	68,017	9,114	1,448	17,907	310	12,932	34,662
Asian	7,365	5,634	885	252	559	35	1,629	1,724
Pacific Islander	1,736	1,205	110	37	372	12	353	513
American Indian/Alaska Native	6,511	4,449	271	35	1,726	30	1,817	2,381
Two or more races	11,403	7,775	1,100	106	2,381	41	2,233	5,715
Number by age[6]								
14	3,468	18	2	†	3,236	211	16,805	36,133
15	5,989	64	40	†	5,647	238	15,302	36,814
16	18,179	4,876	455	†	12,536	312	15,179	36,156
17	172,682	141,114	11,815	1	19,428	324	11,406	27,703
18	149,070	115,314	15,630	1	17,919	206	4,601	14,061
19	34,341	20,738	5,735	10	7,730	128	1,006	4,414
20	16,986	7,563	5,037	1,242	3,062	82	457	1,686
21	12,638	3,409	4,143	3,964	1,078	44	206	678

See notes at end of table.

Table 219.90. Number and percentage distribution of 14- through 21-year-old students served under Individuals with Disabilities Education Act (IDEA), Part B, who exited school, by exit reason, sex, race/ethnicity, age, and type of disability: 2015–16 and 2016–17—Continued

Year, sex, race/ethnicity, age, and type of disability	Exited school						Transferred to regular education[4]	Moved, known to be continuing[5]
	Total	Graduated with regular diploma	Received alternative certificate[1]	Reached maximum age[2]	Dropped out[3]	Died		
1	2	3	4	5	6	7	8	9
Number by type of disability								
Autism	29,295	20,568	5,596	1,083	1,985	63	2,966	7,972
Deaf-blindness	77	42	19	9	4	3	3	34
Emotional disturbance	37,891	22,017	2,355	250	13,128	141	5,844	23,402
Hearing impairment	4,667	3,734	468	52	404	9	733	1,293
Intellectual disability	35,338	15,180	12,446	2,069	5,407	236	1,773	12,313
Multiple disabilities	8,506	3,878	2,684	649	969	326	404	2,671
Orthopedic impairment	2,697	1,730	562	149	198	58	246	528
Other health impairment[7]	71,481	53,396	4,940	279	12,558	308	11,463	30,029
Specific learning disability	207,649	159,563	12,910	540	34,282	354	31,558	73,438
Speech or language impairment	11,314	9,600	388	30	1,283	13	9,473	4,898
Traumatic brain injury	2,641	1,933	317	74	295	22	282	645
Visual impairment	1,797	1,455	172	35	123	12	217	422

†Not applicable.
[1]Received a certificate of completion, modified diploma, or some similar document, but did not meet the same standards for graduation as those for students without disabilities.
[2]Each state determines its maximum age to receive special education services. At the time these data were collected, the maximum age across states generally ranged from 20 to 22 years old.
[3]"Dropped out" is defined as the total who were enrolled at some point in the reporting year, were not enrolled at the end of the reporting year, and did not exit for any of the other reasons described. Includes students previously categorized as "moved, not known to continue."
[4]"Transferred to regular education" was previously labeled "no longer receives special education."
[5]"Moved, known to be continuing" is the total number of students who moved out of the administrative area or transferred to another district and are known to be continuing in an educational program.
[6]Age data are as of fall of the school year, so some students may have been 1 year older at the time they exited school.
[7]Other health impairments include having limited strength, vitality, or alertness due to chronic or acute health problems such as a heart condition, tuberculosis, rheumatic fever, nephritis, asthma, sickle cell anemia, hemophilia, epilepsy, lead poisoning, leukemia, or diabetes.
NOTE: Data are for the 50 states, the District of Columbia, the Bureau of Indian Education, American Samoa, the Federated States of Micronesia, Guam, the Northern Marianas, Puerto Rico, the Republic of Palau, the Republic of the Marshall Islands, and the U.S. Virgin Islands. Race categories exclude persons of Hispanic ethnicity. Detail may not sum to totals because of reporting anomalies and rounding.
SOURCE: U.S. Department of Education, Office of Special Education Programs, Individuals with Disabilities Education Act (IDEA) Section 618 Data Products: State Level Data Files. Retrieved January 8, 2019, from http://www2.ed.gov/programs/osepidea/618-data/state-level-data-files/index.html. (This table was prepared January 2019.)

Table 220.40. Fall 2010 first-time kindergartners' reading scale scores and standard deviations through spring of fifth grade, by selected child, family, and school characteristics during the kindergarten year: Fall 2010 and spring 2011 through spring 2016

[Standard errors appear in parentheses]

Selected child, family, or school characteristic during the kindergarten year	Kindergarten				First grade, spring 2012		Second grade, spring 2013		Third grade, spring 2014		Fourth grade, spring 2015		Fifth grade, spring 2016	
	Fall 2010		Spring 2011											
1	2		3		4		5		6		7		8	
	Mean reading score[1]													
Total	**54.5**	**(0.24)**	**69.3**	**(0.34)**	**95.3**	**(0.40)**	**112.8**	**(0.37)**	**121.4**	**(0.32)**	**129.7**	**(0.28)**	**136.8**	**(0.30)**
Sex of child														
Male	54.0	(0.30)	68.6	(0.41)	93.7	(0.45)	111.1	(0.44)	119.8	(0.40)	128.8	(0.34)	136.1	(0.36)
Female	55.0	(0.26)	70.1	(0.39)	97.0	(0.48)	114.5	(0.42)	123.0	(0.37)	130.7	(0.32)	137.5	(0.36)
Age of child at kindergarten entry, fall 2010														
Less than 5 years old	50.7	(0.62)	63.8	(0.96)	87.9	(1.40)	107.1	(1.22)	117.3	(1.02)	126.2	(0.98)	134.0	(1.07)
5 years old to 5 1/2 years old	53.0	(0.32)	67.7	(0.41)	93.5	(0.48)	111.3	(0.40)	119.8	(0.38)	128.7	(0.35)	135.6	(0.37)
More than 5 1/2 years old to 6 years old	55.5	(0.30)	70.6	(0.37)	96.9	(0.52)	114.1	(0.49)	122.6	(0.41)	130.6	(0.36)	137.8	(0.38)
More than 6 years old	57.9	(0.45)	73.1	(0.63)	99.6	(0.74)	115.9	(0.74)	124.0	(0.61)	131.9	(0.68)	138.4	(0.74)
Race/ethnicity of child														
White	56.1	(0.33)	71.4	(0.45)	98.6	(0.50)	116.1	(0.43)	124.8	(0.38)	132.8	(0.32)	140.0	(0.35)
Black	53.0	(0.44)	66.5	(0.58)	91.0	(0.90)	107.7	(0.80)	115.3	(0.62)	123.8	(0.68)	130.5	(0.57)
Hispanic	50.8	(0.32)	65.3	(0.33)	89.2	(0.52)	107.1	(0.61)	116.0	(0.56)	125.0	(0.56)	132.0	(0.53)
Asian	59.2	(0.66)	74.4	(0.82)	100.4	(1.00)	117.1	(0.88)	125.2	(0.70)	134.3	(0.81)	141.3	(0.76)
Pacific Islander	52.7	(2.00)	69.9	(2.96)	97.7	(2.87)	115.4	(2.82)	123.2	(2.61)	131.3	(1.87)	138.8	(2.09)
American Indian/Alaska Native	50.3	(0.61)	64.2	(1.08)	91.3	(1.39)	107.5	(1.33)	117.6	(1.21)	126.7	(1.33)	134.0	(1.59)
Two or more races	56.2	(0.74)	70.8	(1.01)	97.0	(1.12)	114.6	(1.08)	123.6	(0.82)	132.0	(0.84)	139.2	(0.82)
How often child exhibited positive learning behaviors, fall 2010[2]														
Never	45.6	(0.81)	55.3	(1.41)	71.8	(1.86)	91.5	(2.15)	103.4	(1.89)	113.9	(1.75)	119.8	(1.97)
Sometimes	49.9	(0.35)	63.5	(0.38)	87.0	(0.59)	105.1	(0.54)	114.4	(0.46)	123.8	(0.48)	130.7	(0.47)
Often	54.3	(0.26)	69.5	(0.43)	96.4	(0.48)	114.0	(0.41)	122.5	(0.38)	130.7	(0.35)	137.9	(0.39)
Very often	59.2	(0.45)	75.4	(0.62)	103.0	(0.62)	119.4	(0.60)	127.3	(0.49)	134.8	(0.46)	141.8	(0.44)
Primary type of nonparental care arrangement prior to kindergarten entry[3]														
No regular nonparental arrangement	52.1	(0.34)	67.1	(0.43)	92.0	(0.61)	109.6	(0.59)	118.9	(0.54)	127.3	(0.46)	135.0	(0.45)
Home-based care														
Relative care	52.4	(0.37)	68.0	(0.40)	93.8	(0.54)	111.4	(0.57)	119.9	(0.49)	128.8	(0.42)	135.2	(0.46)
Nonrelative care	54.7	(0.62)	70.3	(0.82)	98.4	(0.78)	115.3	(0.74)	123.6	(0.71)	132.2	(0.58)	139.5	(0.64)
Center-based care	56.0	(0.28)	70.5	(0.42)	96.7	(0.50)	114.1	(0.41)	122.5	(0.37)	130.6	(0.35)	137.7	(0.38)
Multiple arrangements	55.1	(0.61)	70.8	(0.82)	96.5	(1.05)	114.2	(1.08)	121.2	(1.00)	130.8	(0.92)	137.4	(0.94)
Household type, fall 2010[4]														
Two-parent household	55.6	(0.27)	70.8	(0.38)	97.3	(0.45)	114.8	(0.40)	123.3	(0.35)	131.6	(0.31)	138.7	(0.34)
Mother-only household	51.7	(0.32)	65.6	(0.44)	90.4	(0.60)	108.0	(0.53)	116.9	(0.51)	125.3	(0.49)	132.1	(0.50)
Father-only household	51.6	(0.69)	65.6	(1.01)	89.0	(1.30)	107.0	(1.22)	115.4	(1.06)	123.8	(1.20)	132.2	(1.24)
Other household type	49.4	(0.83)	63.5	(0.86)	87.0	(1.79)	103.5	(1.51)	112.6	(1.57)	120.8	(1.86)	127.0	(1.53)
Primary home language														
English	55.3	(0.25)	70.3	(0.39)	96.8	(0.42)	114.1	(0.37)	122.6	(0.33)	130.8	(0.26)	137.8	(0.29)
Non-English	49.9	(0.44)	63.9	(0.55)	87.4	(0.81)	105.5	(0.72)	115.0	(0.63)	124.1	(0.63)	131.2	(0.68)
Primary language not identified[5]	51.6	(1.24)	66.8	(1.52)	91.0	(1.96)	107.5	(2.22)	115.6	(1.68)	126.2	(1.95)	131.3	(1.81)
Parents' highest level of education[6]														
Less than high school	47.5	(0.43)	61.4	(0.48)	83.5	(0.80)	101.0	(0.81)	110.6	(0.67)	119.2	(0.70)	126.0	(0.67)
High school completion	50.3	(0.31)	64.5	(0.33)	88.7	(0.53)	106.1	(0.51)	115.6	(0.44)	124.3	(0.41)	131.2	(0.44)
Some college/vocational	53.4	(0.27)	68.1	(0.39)	94.3	(0.42)	111.7	(0.41)	120.1	(0.42)	128.7	(0.36)	135.9	(0.36)
Bachelor's degree	57.6	(0.34)	73.1	(0.48)	100.3	(0.58)	118.1	(0.40)	126.2	(0.35)	134.3	(0.35)	141.5	(0.35)
Any graduate education	61.1	(0.51)	76.8	(0.60)	104.7	(0.52)	122.2	(0.41)	130.0	(0.41)	137.8	(0.39)	144.7	(0.36)
Poverty status, spring 2011[7]														
Below poverty threshold	50.0	(0.30)	63.7	(0.37)	86.6	(0.58)	104.4	(0.58)	113.6	(0.56)	122.3	(0.49)	129.4	(0.51)
100 to 199 percent of poverty threshold	53.0	(0.31)	67.9	(0.53)	93.8	(0.64)	111.0	(0.58)	119.9	(0.55)	128.3	(0.55)	135.5	(0.55)
200 percent or more of poverty threshold	57.7	(0.31)	73.0	(0.41)	100.7	(0.44)	118.2	(0.36)	126.3	(0.35)	134.4	(0.27)	141.5	(0.30)
Two risk factors[8]														
Both risk factors: No parent completed high school[9] and family below poverty threshold[7]	47.4	(0.50)	61.2	(0.63)	83.2	(0.99)	101.0	(0.98)	110.2	(0.82)	118.8	(0.87)	125.7	(0.90)
One risk factor: No parent completed high school	49.0	(0.81)	62.4	(0.77)	85.6	(1.09)	103.8	(1.20)	113.3	(1.09)	122.9	(1.05)	130.2	(1.21)
One risk factor: Family below poverty threshold	50.7	(0.33)	64.5	(0.41)	87.6	(0.58)	105.4	(0.65)	114.6	(0.62)	123.4	(0.55)	130.5	(0.57)
Neither risk factor	56.4	(0.27)	71.7	(0.40)	99.0	(0.41)	116.4	(0.36)	124.6	(0.33)	132.8	(0.27)	140.0	(0.30)
Socioeconomic status[10]														
Lowest 20 percent	48.8	(0.35)	62.4	(0.38)	85.0	(0.60)	102.8	(0.58)	112.2	(0.54)	120.9	(0.52)	127.8	(0.51)
Middle 60 percent	54.0	(0.22)	69.0	(0.34)	95.4	(0.37)	112.7	(0.34)	121.2	(0.29)	129.7	(0.27)	136.9	(0.28)
Highest 20 percent	61.0	(0.46)	76.7	(0.58)	104.6	(0.54)	122.0	(0.45)	130.1	(0.40)	137.9	(0.33)	144.8	(0.32)
School control, fall 2010														
Public	54.1	(0.27)	68.9	(0.38)	94.8	(0.44)	112.1	(0.41)	120.7	(0.37)	129.1	(0.32)	136.1	(0.34)
Private	57.4	(0.66)	72.4	(1.06)	99.6	(1.25)	118.5	(0.90)	126.5	(0.86)	134.8	(0.76)	141.9	(0.68)
	Standard deviation of the reading score													
Total	10.5	(0.22)	13.2	(0.26)	16.5	(0.25)	15.6	(0.26)	14.0	(0.24)	13.3	(0.25)	14.0	(0.24)

See notes at end of table.

Table 220.40. Fall 2010 first-time kindergartners' reading scale scores and standard deviations through spring of fifth grade, by selected child, family, and school characteristics during the kindergarten year: Fall 2010 and spring 2011 through spring 2016—Continued

[1]Reflects performance on questions measuring basic skills (e.g., word recognition); vocabulary knowledge; and reading comprehension, including identifying information specifically stated in text (e.g., definitions, facts, and supporting details), making complex inferences from texts, and considering the text objectively and judging its appropriateness and quality. Possible scores for the reading assessment range from 0 to 167.
[2]Derived from child's approaches to learning scale score in fall of the kindergarten year. This score is based on teachers' reports on how often students exhibit positive learning behaviors in seven areas: attentiveness, task persistence, eagerness to learn, learning independence, ability to adapt easily to changes in routine, organization, and ability to follow classroom rules. Possible scores range from 1 to 4, with higher scores indicating that a child exhibits positive learning behaviors more often. Fall 2010 scores were categorized into the four anchor points on the original scale—1 (never), 2 (sometimes), 3 (often), and 4 (very often)—by rounding the mean score to the nearest whole number.
[3]The type of nonparental care in which the child spent the most hours. "Multiple arrangements" refers to children who spent an equal amount of time in each of two or more arrangements.
[4]A two-parent household may have two biological parents, two adoptive parents, or one biological/adoptive parent and one other parent/partner. A mother-only or father-only household has one biological or adoptive parent only, without another parent/partner. In other household types, which do not include biological or adoptive parents, the guardian or guardians may be related or unrelated to the child.
[5]Two or more languages (which could include English) were spoken in the child's home, and the parent respondent was unable to specify which language was the primary one (the one spoken most of the time).
[6]Parents' highest level of education is the highest level of education achieved by either of the parents or guardians in a two-parent household, by the only parent in a single-parent household, or by any guardian in a household with no parents.
[7]Poverty status is based on preliminary U.S. Census income thresholds for 2010, which identify incomes determined to meet household needs, given family size and composition. For example, a family of three with one child was below the poverty threshold if its income was less than $17,552 in 2010.
[8]Includes only children for whom information about both risk factors is available. Excludes children with missing information about parental education or poverty status.
[9]High school not completed by any parent or guardian living with the child.
[10]Socioeconomic status (SES) was measured by a composite score based on parental education and occupations and household income during the child's kindergarten year.
NOTE: Estimates weighted by W9C9P_20. Estimates pertain to a sample of children who were enrolled in kindergarten for the first time in the 2010–11 school year. The same children were assessed in spring 2012 (when the majority were in first grade), spring 2013 (when the majority were in second grade), spring 2014 (when the majority were in third grade), spring 2015 (when the majority were in fourth grade), and spring 2016 (when the majority were in fifth grade). Estimates differ from previously published figures because reading scale scores were recalculated to represent the kindergarten through fifth-grade assessment item pools and because weights were adjusted to account for survey nonresponse at each data collection wave, including the latest round of data collection (spring 2016). Race categories exclude persons of Hispanic ethnicity.
SOURCE: U.S. Department of Education, National Center for Education Statistics, Early Childhood Longitudinal Study, Kindergarten Class of 2010–11 (ECLS-K:2011), Kindergarten–Fifth Grade Restricted-Use Data File. (This table was prepared March 2019.)

Table 221.10. Average National Assessment of Educational Progress (NAEP) reading scale score, by sex, race/ethnicity, and grade: Selected years, 1992 through 2017

[Standard errors appear in parentheses]

Grade and year	All students	Sex: Average reading scale score: Male	Sex: Average reading scale score: Female	Sex: Gap between female and male score	Race/ethnicity: Average reading scale score: White	Black	Hispanic	Asian/Pacific Islander: Total	Asian/Pacific Islander: Asian[1]	Asian/Pacific Islander: Pacific Islander[1]	American Indian/ Alaska Native	Two or more races[1]	Gap between White and Black score	Gap between White and Hispanic score
1	2	3	4	5	6	7	8	9	10	11	12	13	14	15
Grade 4														
1992[2]	217 (0.9)	213 (1.2)	221 (1.0)	8 (1.6)	224 (1.2)	192 (1.7)	197 (2.6)	216 (2.9)	— (†)	— (†)	‡ (†)	— (†)	32 (2.1)	27 (2.9)
1994[2]	214 (1.0)	209 (1.3)	220 (1.1)	10 (1.7)	224 (1.3)	185 (1.8)	188 (3.4)	220 (3.8)	— (†)	— (†)	211 (6.6)	— (†)	38 (2.2)	35 (3.6)
1998	215 (1.1)	212 (1.3)	217 (1.3)	5 (1.8)	225 (1.0)	193 (1.9)	193 (3.2)	215 (5.6)	— (†)	— (†)	‡ (†)	— (†)	32 (2.2)	32 (3.3)
2000	213 (1.3)	208 (1.3)	219 (1.4)	11 (1.9)	224 (1.1)	190 (1.8)	190 (2.9)	225 (5.2)	— (†)	— (†)	214 (6.0)	— (†)	34 (2.1)	35 (3.1)
2002	219 (0.4)	215 (0.4)	222 (0.5)	6 (0.7)	229 (0.3)	199 (0.5)	201 (1.3)	224 (1.6)	— (†)	— (†)	207 (2.0)	— (†)	30 (0.6)	28 (1.4)
2003	218 (0.3)	215 (0.3)	222 (0.3)	7 (0.5)	229 (0.2)	198 (0.4)	200 (0.6)	226 (1.2)	— (†)	— (†)	202 (1.4)	— (†)	31 (0.5)	28 (0.6)
2005	219 (0.2)	216 (0.2)	222 (0.3)	6 (0.4)	229 (0.2)	200 (0.3)	203 (0.5)	229 (0.7)	— (†)	— (†)	204 (1.3)	— (†)	29 (0.4)	26 (0.5)
2007	221 (0.3)	218 (0.3)	224 (0.3)	7 (0.4)	231 (0.2)	203 (0.4)	205 (0.5)	232 (1.0)	— (†)	— (†)	203 (1.2)	— (†)	27 (0.5)	26 (0.6)
2009	221 (0.3)	218 (0.3)	224 (0.3)	7 (0.4)	230 (0.3)	205 (0.5)	205 (0.5)	235 (1.0)	— (†)	— (†)	204 (1.3)	— (†)	26 (0.6)	25 (0.6)
2011	221 (0.3)	218 (0.3)	225 (0.3)	7 (0.5)	231 (0.2)	205 (0.5)	206 (0.5)	235 (1.2)	236 (1.3)	216 (1.9)	202 (1.3)	227 (1.2)	25 (0.5)	24 (0.6)
2013	222 (0.3)	219 (0.3)	225 (0.3)	7 (0.5)	232 (0.3)	206 (0.5)	207 (0.5)	235 (1.1)	237 (1.1)	212 (2.5)	205 (1.3)	227 (1.0)	26 (0.6)	25 (0.6)
2015	223 (0.4)	219 (0.4)	226 (0.4)	7 (0.6)	232 (0.3)	206 (0.5)	208 (0.8)	239 (1.4)	241 (1.6)	215 (2.9)	205 (1.5)	227 (1.2)	26 (0.6)	24 (0.9)
2017	222 (0.3)	219 (0.3)	225 (0.3)	6 (0.4)	232 (0.3)	206 (0.5)	209 (0.5)	239 (0.9)	241 (1.0)	212 (2.7)	202 (1.8)	227 (0.9)	26 (0.6)	23 (0.5)
Grade 8														
1992[2]	260 (0.9)	254 (1.1)	267 (1.0)	13 (1.5)	267 (1.1)	237 (1.7)	241 (1.6)	268 (3.9)	— (†)	— (†)	‡ (†)	— (†)	30 (2.0)	26 (2.0)
1994[2]	260 (0.8)	252 (1.0)	267 (1.0)	15 (1.4)	267 (1.0)	236 (1.8)	243 (1.2)	265 (3.0)	— (†)	— (†)	248 (4.7)	— (†)	30 (2.1)	24 (1.5)
1998	263 (0.8)	256 (1.0)	270 (0.8)	14 (1.3)	270 (0.9)	244 (1.2)	243 (1.7)	264 (7.1)	— (†)	— (†)	‡ (†)	— (†)	26 (1.5)	27 (1.9)
2000	— (†)	— (†)	— (†)	— (†)	— (†)	— (†)	— (†)	— (†)	— (†)	— (†)	— (†)	— (†)	— (†)	— (†)
2002	264 (0.4)	260 (0.5)	269 (0.5)	9 (0.7)	272 (0.4)	245 (0.7)	247 (0.8)	267 (1.7)	— (†)	— (†)	250 (3.5)	— (†)	27 (0.9)	26 (0.9)
2003	263 (0.3)	258 (0.3)	269 (0.3)	11 (0.4)	272 (0.2)	244 (0.5)	245 (0.7)	270 (1.1)	— (†)	— (†)	246 (3.0)	— (†)	28 (0.5)	27 (0.7)
2005	262 (0.2)	257 (0.2)	267 (0.2)	10 (0.3)	271 (0.2)	243 (0.4)	246 (0.4)	271 (0.8)	— (†)	— (†)	249 (1.4)	— (†)	28 (0.5)	25 (0.5)
2007	263 (0.2)	258 (0.3)	268 (0.3)	10 (0.4)	272 (0.2)	245 (0.4)	247 (0.4)	271 (1.1)	— (†)	— (†)	247 (1.2)	— (†)	27 (0.4)	25 (0.5)
2009	264 (0.3)	259 (0.3)	269 (0.3)	9 (0.5)	273 (0.2)	246 (0.4)	249 (0.6)	274 (1.1)	— (†)	— (†)	251 (1.2)	— (†)	26 (0.5)	24 (0.7)
2011	265 (0.2)	261 (0.3)	270 (0.2)	9 (0.4)	274 (0.2)	249 (0.5)	252 (0.5)	275 (1.0)	277 (1.0)	254 (2.2)	252 (1.2)	269 (1.2)	25 (0.5)	22 (0.5)
2013	268 (0.3)	263 (0.3)	273 (0.3)	10 (0.4)	276 (0.3)	250 (0.4)	256 (0.5)	280 (0.9)	282 (0.9)	259 (2.6)	251 (1.0)	271 (0.9)	26 (0.5)	21 (0.5)
2015	265 (0.2)	261 (0.2)	270 (0.3)	10 (0.4)	274 (0.2)	248 (0.5)	253 (0.4)	280 (1.3)	281 (1.3)	255 (2.4)	252 (1.7)	269 (1.1)	26 (0.5)	21 (0.5)
2017	267 (0.3)	262 (0.3)	272 (0.4)	10 (0.5)	275 (0.3)	249 (0.5)	255 (0.5)	282 (1.0)	284 (1.0)	255 (2.5)	253 (1.3)	272 (1.1)	25 (0.6)	19 (0.6)
Grade 12														
1992[2]	292 (0.6)	287 (0.7)	297 (0.7)	10 (1.0)	297 (0.6)	273 (1.4)	279 (2.7)	290 (3.2)	— (†)	— (†)	‡ (†)	— (†)	24 (1.5)	19 (2.7)
1994[2]	287 (0.7)	280 (0.8)	294 (0.8)	14 (1.2)	293 (0.7)	265 (1.6)	270 (1.7)	278 (2.4)	— (†)	— (†)	274 (5.8)	— (†)	29 (1.8)	23 (1.9)
1998	290 (0.6)	282 (0.8)	298 (0.8)	16 (1.1)	297 (0.7)	269 (1.4)	275 (1.5)	287 (2.7)	— (†)	— (†)	‡ (†)	— (†)	27 (1.6)	22 (1.6)
2000	— (†)	— (†)	— (†)	— (†)	— (†)	— (†)	— (†)	— (†)	— (†)	— (†)	— (†)	— (†)	— (†)	— (†)
2002	287 (0.7)	279 (0.9)	295 (0.7)	16 (1.1)	292 (0.7)	267 (1.3)	273 (1.5)	286 (2.0)	— (†)	— (†)	‡ (†)	— (†)	25 (1.5)	20 (1.6)
2003	— (†)	— (†)	— (†)	— (†)	— (†)	— (†)	— (†)	— (†)	— (†)	— (†)	— (†)	— (†)	— (†)	— (†)
2005	286 (0.6)	279 (0.8)	292 (0.7)	13 (1.1)	293 (0.7)	267 (1.2)	272 (1.2)	287 (1.9)	— (†)	— (†)	279 (6.3)	— (†)	26 (1.4)	21 (1.4)
2007	— (†)	— (†)	— (†)	— (†)	— (†)	— (†)	— (†)	— (†)	— (†)	— (†)	— (†)	— (†)	— (†)	— (†)
2009	288 (0.7)	282 (0.7)	294 (0.8)	12 (1.1)	296 (0.6)	269 (1.1)	274 (1.0)	298 (2.4)	— (†)	— (†)	283 (3.7)	— (†)	27 (1.3)	22 (1.2)
2011	— (†)	— (†)	— (†)	— (†)	— (†)	— (†)	— (†)	— (†)	— (†)	— (†)	— (†)	— (†)	— (†)	— (†)
2013	288 (0.6)	284 (0.6)	293 (0.7)	10 (0.9)	297 (0.6)	268 (0.9)	276 (0.9)	296 (1.9)	296 (2.0)	289 (6.0)	277 (3.5)	291 (2.5)	30 (1.0)	22 (1.0)
2015	287 (0.5)	282 (0.6)	292 (0.7)	10 (1.0)	295 (0.7)	266 (1.1)	276 (0.9)	297 (2.1)	297 (2.1)	‡ (†)	279 (6.2)	295 (2.9)	30 (1.3)	20 (1.1)
2017	— (†)	— (†)	— (†)	— (†)	— (†)	— (†)	— (†)	— (†)	— (†)	— (†)	— (†)	— (†)	— (†)	— (†)

—Not available.
†Not applicable.
‡Reporting standards not met. Either there are too few cases for a reliable estimate or the coefficient of variation (CV) is 50 percent or greater.
[1]Prior to 2011, separate data for Asian students, Pacific Islander students, and students of Two or more races were not collected.
[2]Accommodations were not permitted for this assessment.
NOTE: Scale ranges from 0 to 500. Includes public and private schools. For 1998 and later years, includes students tested with accommodations (1 to 13 percent of all students, depending on grade level and year); excludes only those students with disabilities and English language learners who were unable to be tested even with accommodations (2 to 6 percent of all students). Data on race/ethnicity are based on school reports. Race categories exclude persons of Hispanic ethnicity.
SOURCE: U.S. Department of Education, National Center for Education Statistics, National Assessment of Educational Progress (NAEP), 1992, 1994, 1998, 2000, 2002, 2003, 2005, 2007, 2009, 2011, 2013, 2015, and 2017 Reading Assessments, retrieved March 13, 2018, from the Main NAEP Data Explorer (http://nces.ed.gov/nationsreportcard/naepdata/). (This table was prepared March 2018.)

Table 221.20. Percentage of students at or above selected National Assessment of Educational Progress (NAEP) reading achievement levels, by grade and selected student characteristics: Selected years, 2003 through 2017

[Standard errors appear in parentheses]

Grade and selected student characteristic	2003		2005		2007		2009		2011		2013		2015		2017	
	At or above *Basic*[1]	At or above *Proficient*[2]	At or above *Basic*[1]	At or above *Proficient*[2]	At or above *Basic*[1]	At or above *Proficient*[2]	At or above *Basic*[1]	At or above *Proficient*[2]	At or above *Basic*[1]	At or above *Proficient*[2]	At or above *Basic*[1]	At or above *Proficient*[2]	At or above *Basic*[1]	At or above *Proficient*[2]	At or above *Basic*[1]	At or above *Proficient*[2]
1	2	3	4	5	6	7	8	9	10	11	12	13	14	15	16	17
4th grade, all students	**63 (0.3)**	**31 (0.3)**	**64 (0.3)**	**31 (0.2)**	**67 (0.3)**	**33 (0.3)**	**67 (0.3)**	**33 (0.4)**	**67 (0.3)**	**34 (0.4)**	**68 (0.3)**	**35 (0.3)**	**69 (0.4)**	**36 (0.4)**	**68 (0.3)**	**37 (0.3)**
Sex																
Male	60 (0.4)	28 (0.3)	61 (0.4)	29 (0.3)	64 (0.4)	30 (0.3)	64 (0.3)	30 (0.4)	64 (0.4)	31 (0.4)	65 (0.3)	32 (0.4)	66 (0.5)	33 (0.5)	65 (0.4)	34 (0.4)
Female	67 (0.4)	35 (0.4)	67 (0.3)	34 (0.3)	70 (0.3)	36 (0.4)	70 (0.4)	36 (0.4)	71 (0.4)	37 (0.5)	72 (0.4)	38 (0.4)	72 (0.4)	39 (0.5)	71 (0.4)	39 (0.4)
Race/ethnicity																
White	75 (0.3)	41 (0.4)	76 (0.3)	41 (0.3)	78 (0.3)	43 (0.4)	78 (0.3)	42 (0.4)	78 (0.3)	44 (0.4)	79 (0.3)	46 (0.4)	79 (0.3)	46 (0.5)	78 (0.3)	47 (0.4)
Black	40 (0.5)	13 (0.4)	42 (0.5)	13 (0.3)	46 (0.6)	14 (0.4)	48 (0.8)	16 (0.5)	49 (0.6)	17 (0.5)	50 (0.6)	18 (0.5)	52 (0.6)	18 (0.5)	51 (0.8)	20 (0.5)
Hispanic	44 (0.7)	15 (0.5)	46 (0.7)	16 (0.5)	50 (0.6)	17 (0.6)	49 (0.7)	17 (0.5)	51 (0.8)	18 (0.5)	53 (0.6)	20 (0.6)	55 (1.0)	21 (0.7)	54 (0.6)	23 (0.5)
Asian/Pacific Islander	70 (1.5)	38 (1.4)	73 (0.9)	42 (0.9)	77 (1.0)	46 (1.4)	80 (1.0)	49 (1.3)	80 (1.2)	49 (1.7)	80 (1.0)	51 (1.2)	82 (1.3)	55 (1.8)	82 (0.9)	56 (1.4)
Asian	— (†)	— (†)	— (†)	— (†)	— (†)	— (†)	— (†)	— (†)	81 (1.2)	50 (1.7)	82 (1.0)	53 (1.2)	84 (1.4)	57 (2.0)	84 (0.9)	59 (1.4)
Pacific Islander	— (†)	— (†)	— (†)	— (†)	— (†)	— (†)	— (†)	— (†)	61 (2.4)	28 (3.2)	57 (3.2)	27 (3.0)	60 (3.7)	28 (3.7)	58 (3.7)	27 (3.5)
American Indian/Alaska Native	47 (2.0)	16 (1.5)	48 (1.5)	18 (1.0)	49 (1.4)	18 (1.1)	50 (1.7)	20 (1.4)	47 (1.7)	18 (1.4)	51 (1.6)	21 (1.4)	52 (2.1)	21 (1.9)	48 (2.3)	20 (1.9)
Two or more races	— (†)	— (†)	— (†)	— (†)	— (†)	— (†)	— (†)	— (†)	50 (1.7)	20 (1.4)	73 (1.2)	40 (1.4)	73 (1.4)	40 (1.6)	73 (1.3)	42 (1.3)
Eligibility for free or reduced-price lunch																
Eligible	45 (0.4)	15 (0.3)	46 (0.4)	16 (0.3)	50 (0.4)	17 (0.3)	51 (0.4)	17 (0.3)	52 (0.4)	18 (0.3)	53 (0.4)	20 (0.3)	56 (0.5)	21 (0.4)	54 (0.4)	22 (0.3)
Not eligible	76 (0.3)	42 (0.5)	77 (0.2)	42 (0.3)	79 (0.3)	44 (0.4)	80 (0.3)	45 (0.4)	82 (0.3)	48 (0.5)	83 (0.3)	51 (0.5)	83 (0.3)	52 (0.6)	82 (0.3)	52 (0.4)
Unknown	76 (0.9)	43 (1.1)	77 (1.1)	45 (1.4)	80 (1.3)	46 (1.8)	81 (1.9)	50 (1.9)	82 (1.0)	48 (1.3)	83 (1.6)	51 (2.1)	81 (1.3)	52 (1.8)	80 (1.5)	51 (1.7)
8th grade, all students	**74 (0.3)**	**32 (0.3)**	**73 (0.2)**	**31 (0.2)**	**74 (0.2)**	**31 (0.2)**	**75 (0.3)**	**32 (0.4)**	**76 (0.3)**	**34 (0.3)**	**78 (0.3)**	**36 (0.3)**	**76 (0.3)**	**34 (0.3)**	**76 (0.3)**	**36 (0.3)**
Sex																
Male	69 (0.3)	27 (0.3)	68 (0.3)	26 (0.3)	69 (0.4)	26 (0.3)	71 (0.4)	28 (0.4)	72 (0.4)	29 (0.3)	74 (0.4)	31 (0.4)	72 (0.3)	29 (0.4)	72 (0.4)	31 (0.4)
Female	79 (0.3)	38 (0.3)	78 (0.2)	36 (0.3)	79 (0.3)	36 (0.3)	79 (0.4)	37 (0.5)	80 (0.3)	38 (0.4)	82 (0.3)	42 (0.4)	80 (0.3)	39 (0.5)	81 (0.4)	41 (0.5)
Race/ethnicity																
White	83 (0.2)	41 (0.3)	82 (0.2)	39 (0.3)	84 (0.3)	40 (0.3)	84 (0.2)	41 (0.4)	85 (0.2)	43 (0.4)	86 (0.2)	46 (0.4)	85 (0.2)	44 (0.4)	84 (0.3)	45 (0.4)
Black	54 (0.6)	13 (0.4)	52 (0.6)	12 (0.4)	55 (0.6)	13 (0.4)	57 (0.6)	14 (0.5)	59 (0.7)	15 (0.5)	61 (0.6)	17 (0.5)	58 (0.7)	16 (0.5)	60 (0.6)	18 (0.5)
Hispanic	56 (0.9)	15 (0.6)	56 (0.6)	15 (0.4)	58 (0.5)	15 (0.4)	61 (0.8)	17 (0.6)	64 (0.8)	19 (0.5)	68 (0.7)	22 (0.6)	66 (0.6)	21 (0.5)	67 (0.6)	23 (0.6)
Asian/Pacific Islander	79 (1.2)	40 (1.6)	80 (0.8)	40 (1.2)	80 (1.1)	41 (1.1)	83 (1.1)	45 (1.7)	83 (1.0)	47 (1.4)	86 (0.7)	52 (1.3)	86 (1.0)	52 (1.8)	86 (0.9)	55 (1.5)
Asian	— (†)	— (†)	— (†)	— (†)	— (†)	— (†)	— (†)	— (†)	84 (1.0)	49 (1.5)	87 (0.7)	54 (1.3)	87 (1.0)	54 (1.9)	87 (0.9)	57 (1.5)
Pacific Islander	— (†)	— (†)	— (†)	— (†)	— (†)	— (†)	— (†)	— (†)	63 (2.7)	24 (3.2)	70 (3.5)	27 (3.7)	66 (3.3)	24 (3.0)	65 (3.9)	23 (3.3)
American Indian/Alaska Native	57 (3.3)	17 (1.7)	59 (2.1)	17 (1.7)	56 (1.9)	18 (1.3)	62 (2.0)	21 (1.2)	63 (1.4)	22 (1.7)	62 (1.8)	19 (1.6)	63 (2.2)	22 (1.8)	63 (1.8)	22 (2.1)
Two or more races	— (†)	— (†)	— (†)	— (†)	— (†)	— (†)	— (†)	— (†)	79 (1.7)	39 (1.5)	81 (1.1)	40 (1.4)	79 (1.2)	38 (1.6)	82 (1.2)	42 (1.4)
Eligibility for free or reduced-price lunch																
Eligible	57 (0.5)	16 (0.3)	57 (0.4)	15 (0.3)	58 (0.4)	15 (0.2)	60 (0.5)	16 (0.3)	63 (0.5)	18 (0.3)	66 (0.4)	20 (0.2)	64 (0.4)	20 (0.4)	65 (0.4)	21 (0.3)
Not eligible	82 (0.3)	40 (0.4)	81 (0.3)	39 (0.2)	83 (0.3)	40 (0.4)	85 (0.3)	42 (0.5)	86 (0.3)	45 (0.4)	87 (0.3)	48 (0.4)	87 (0.3)	47 (0.5)	86 (0.3)	48 (0.5)
Unknown	81 (0.9)	42 (1.2)	84 (1.0)	45 (1.3)	86 (1.0)	48 (1.6)	89 (1.3)	51 (1.8)	90 (0.8)	54 (1.4)	92 (0.9)	59 (2.4)	89 (0.9)	53 (1.5)	87 (1.1)	52 (1.8)
12th grade, all students	**— (†)**	**— (†)**	**73 (0.8)**	**35 (0.7)**	**— (†)**	**— (†)**	**74 (0.6)**	**38 (0.8)**	**— (†)**	**— (†)**	**75 (0.6)**	**38 (0.7)**	**72 (0.5)**	**37 (0.6)**	**— (†)**	**— (†)**
Sex																
Male	— (†)	— (†)	67 (0.9)	29 (0.9)	— (†)	— (†)	69 (0.8)	32 (0.9)	— (†)	— (†)	70 (0.7)	33 (0.7)	68 (0.6)	33 (0.7)	— (†)	— (†)
Female	— (†)	— (†)	78 (0.9)	41 (0.9)	— (†)	— (†)	80 (0.6)	43 (1.0)	— (†)	— (†)	79 (0.7)	42 (0.9)	76 (0.8)	42 (0.9)	— (†)	— (†)
Race/ethnicity																
White	— (†)	— (†)	79 (0.8)	43 (0.9)	— (†)	— (†)	81 (0.5)	46 (0.8)	— (†)	— (†)	83 (0.6)	47 (0.8)	79 (0.7)	46 (0.9)	— (†)	— (†)
Black	— (†)	— (†)	54 (1.5)	16 (1.2)	— (†)	— (†)	57 (1.3)	17 (1.2)	— (†)	— (†)	56 (1.2)	16 (0.9)	52 (1.5)	17 (1.0)	— (†)	— (†)
Hispanic	— (†)	— (†)	60 (1.9)	20 (1.3)	— (†)	— (†)	61 (1.1)	22 (1.3)	— (†)	— (†)	64 (1.2)	23 (1.0)	63 (1.1)	25 (1.0)	— (†)	— (†)
Asian/Pacific Islander	— (†)	— (†)	74 (2.3)	36 (2.3)	— (†)	— (†)	81 (1.5)	49 (2.9)	— (†)	— (†)	80 (1.8)	47 (2.5)	79 (1.7)	48 (3.0)	— (†)	— (†)
Asian	— (†)	— (†)	— (†)	— (†)	— (†)	— (†)	— (†)	— (†)	— (†)	— (†)	80 (1.9)	48 (2.6)	80 (1.8)	49 (3.0)	— (†)	— (†)
Pacific Islander	— (†)	— (†)	— (†)	— (†)	— (†)	— (†)	— (†)	— (†)	— (†)	— (†)	75 (8.2)	39 (8.4)	‡ (†)	‡ (†)	— (†)	— (†)
American Indian/Alaska Native	— (†)	— (†)	67 (10.1)	26 (8.6)	— (†)	— (†)	70 (6.4)	29 (5.5)	— (†)	— (†)	65 (5.0)	26 (4.8)	65 (8.6)	28 (6.0)	— (†)	— (†)
Two or more races	— (†)	— (†)	— (†)	— (†)	— (†)	— (†)	— (†)	— (†)	— (†)	— (†)	77 (2.9)	38 (3.4)	79 (3.0)	45 (3.4)	— (†)	— (†)

—Not available.
†Not applicable.
‡Reporting standards not met (too few cases for a reliable estimate).
[1]*Basic* denotes partial mastery of the knowledge and skills that are fundamental for proficient work at a given grade.
[2]*Proficient* represents solid academic performance. Students reaching this level have demonstrated competency over challenging subject matter.
NOTE: Includes public and private schools. Includes students tested with accommodations (1 to 13 percent of all students, depending on grade level and year); excludes only those students with disabilities and English language learners who were unable to be tested even with accommodations (2 to 6 percent of all students). Race categories exclude persons of Hispanic ethnicity. Prior to 2011, separate data for Asian students, Pacific Islander students, and students of Two or more races were not collected.
SOURCE: U.S. Department of Education, National Center for Education Statistics, National Assessment of Educational Progress (NAEP), 2003, 2005, 2007, 2009, 2011, 2013, 2015, and 2017 Reading Assessments, retrieved May 8, 2018, from the Main NAEP Data Explorer (http://nces.ed.gov/nationsreportcard/naepdata/). (This table was prepared May 2018.)

Table 221.40. Average National Assessment of Educational Progress (NAEP) reading scale score of 4th-grade public school students, by state: Selected years, 1992 through 2017

[Standard errors appear in parentheses]

State	1992[1]		1994[1]		1998		2002		2003		2005		2007		2009		2011		2013		2015		2017	
1	2		3		4		5		6		7		8		9		10		11		12		13	
United States	**215**	**(1.0)**	**212**	**(1.1)**	**213**	**(1.2)**	**217**	**(0.5)**	**216**	**(0.3)**	**217**	**(0.2)**	**220**	**(0.3)**	**220**	**(0.3)**	**220**	**(0.3)**	**221**	**(0.3)**	**221**	**(0.4)**	**221**	**(0.2)**
Alabama	207	(1.7)	208	(1.5)	211	(1.9)	207	(1.4)	207	(1.7)	208	(1.2)	216	(1.3)	216	(1.2)	220	(1.3)	219	(1.2)	217	(1.4)	216	(1.2)
Alaska	—	(†)	—	(†)	—	(†)	—	(†)	212	(1.6)	211	(1.4)	214	(1.0)	211	(1.2)	208	(1.1)	209	(1.0)	213	(1.3)	207	(1.2)
Arizona	209	(1.2)	206	(1.9)	206	(1.4)	205	(1.5)	209	(1.2)	207	(1.6)	210	(1.6)	210	(1.2)	212	(1.2)	213	(1.4)	215	(1.3)	215	(1.5)
Arkansas	211	(1.2)	209	(1.7)	209	(1.6)	213	(1.4)	214	(1.4)	217	(1.1)	217	(1.2)	216	(1.1)	217	(1.0)	219	(0.9)	218	(1.1)	216	(1.2)
California[2,3]	202	(2.0)	197	(1.8)	202	(2.5)	206	(2.5)	206	(1.2)	207	(0.7)	209	(1.0)	210	(1.5)	211	(1.8)	213	(1.2)	213	(1.7)	215	(1.3)
Colorado	217	(1.1)	213	(1.3)	220	(1.4)	—	(†)	224	(1.2)	224	(1.1)	224	(1.1)	226	(1.2)	223	(1.3)	227	(1.0)	224	(1.6)	225	(1.5)
Connecticut	222	(1.3)	222	(1.6)	230	(1.6)	229	(1.1)	228	(1.1)	226	(1.0)	227	(1.3)	229	(1.1)	227	(1.3)	230	(0.9)	229	(1.1)	228	(1.2)
Delaware[4]	213	(0.6)	206	(1.1)	207	(1.7)	224	(0.6)	224	(0.7)	226	(0.8)	225	(0.7)	226	(0.5)	225	(0.7)	226	(0.8)	224	(0.8)	221	(0.8)
District of Columbia	188	(0.8)	179	(0.9)	179	(1.2)	191	(0.9)	188	(0.9)	191	(1.0)	197	(0.9)	202	(1.0)	201	(0.8)	206	(0.9)	212	(0.9)	213	(0.8)
Florida	208	(1.2)	205	(1.7)	206	(1.4)	214	(1.4)	218	(1.1)	219	(0.9)	224	(0.8)	226	(1.0)	225	(1.1)	227	(1.1)	227	(1.0)	228	(1.1)
Georgia	212	(1.5)	207	(2.4)	209	(1.4)	215	(1.0)	214	(1.3)	214	(1.2)	219	(0.9)	218	(1.1)	221	(1.1)	222	(1.1)	222	(1.2)	220	(1.2)
Hawaii	203	(1.7)	201	(1.7)	200	(1.5)	208	(0.9)	208	(1.4)	210	(1.0)	213	(1.1)	211	(1.0)	214	(1.0)	215	(1.0)	215	(1.0)	216	(1.0)
Idaho	219	(0.9)	‡	(†)	—	(†)	220	(1.1)	218	(1.0)	222	(0.9)	223	(0.8)	221	(0.9)	221	(0.8)	219	(0.9)	222	(1.0)	223	(1.0)
Illinois	—	(†)	—	(†)	‡	(†)	‡	(†)	216	(1.6)	216	(1.2)	219	(1.2)	219	(1.4)	219	(1.1)	219	(1.4)	222	(1.2)	220	(1.2)
Indiana	221	(1.3)	220	(1.3)	—	(†)	222	(1.4)	220	(1.0)	218	(1.1)	222	(0.9)	223	(1.1)	221	(0.9)	225	(1.0)	227	(1.1)	226	(1.1)
Iowa[2,3]	225	(1.1)	223	(1.3)	220	(1.6)	223	(1.1)	223	(1.1)	221	(0.9)	225	(1.1)	221	(1.2)	221	(0.8)	224	(1.1)	224	(1.1)	222	(1.2)
Kansas[2,3]	—	(†)	—	(†)	221	(1.4)	222	(1.4)	220	(1.2)	220	(1.3)	225	(1.1)	224	(1.3)	224	(1.0)	223	(1.3)	221	(1.5)	223	(1.2)
Kentucky	213	(1.3)	212	(1.6)	218	(1.5)	219	(1.1)	219	(1.3)	220	(1.1)	222	(1.1)	226	(1.1)	225	(1.0)	224	(1.2)	228	(1.2)	224	(1.1)
Louisiana	204	(1.2)	197	(1.3)	200	(1.6)	207	(1.7)	205	(1.4)	209	(1.3)	207	(1.6)	207	(1.1)	210	(1.4)	210	(1.3)	216	(1.5)	212	(1.4)
Maine[4]	227	(1.1)	228	(1.3)	225	(1.4)	225	(1.1)	224	(0.9)	225	(0.9)	226	(0.9)	224	(0.9)	222	(0.7)	225	(0.9)	224	(0.9)	221	(1.1)
Maryland	211	(1.6)	210	(1.5)	212	(1.6)	217	(1.5)	219	(1.4)	220	(1.3)	225	(1.1)	226	(1.4)	231	(0.9)	232	(1.3)	223	(1.3)	225	(1.3)
Massachusetts[2]	226	(0.9)	223	(1.3)	223	(1.4)	234	(1.1)	228	(1.2)	231	(0.9)	236	(1.1)	234	(1.1)	237	(1.0)	232	(1.1)	235	(1.0)	236	(1.1)
Michigan	216	(1.5)	‡	(†)	216	(1.5)	219	(1.1)	219	(1.2)	218	(1.5)	220	(1.4)	218	(1.0)	219	(1.2)	217	(1.4)	216	(1.3)	218	(1.5)
Minnesota[2,3]	221	(1.2)	218	(1.4)	219	(1.7)	225	(1.1)	223	(1.1)	225	(1.3)	225	(1.1)	223	(1.3)	222	(1.2)	227	(1.2)	223	(1.3)	225	(1.3)
Mississippi	199	(1.3)	202	(1.6)	203	(1.3)	203	(1.3)	205	(1.3)	204	(1.3)	208	(1.0)	211	(1.1)	209	(1.2)	209	(0.9)	214	(1.0)	215	(1.2)
Missouri	220	(1.2)	217	(1.5)	216	(1.3)	220	(1.3)	222	(1.2)	221	(0.9)	221	(1.1)	224	(1.1)	220	(0.9)	222	(1.0)	223	(1.1)	223	(1.1)
Montana[2,3,5]	—	(†)	222	(1.4)	225	(1.5)	224	(1.8)	223	(1.2)	225	(1.1)	227	(1.0)	225	(0.8)	225	(0.6)	223	(0.8)	225	(0.8)	222	(0.9)
Nebraska[4,5]	221	(1.1)	220	(1.5)	—	(†)	222	(1.5)	221	(1.0)	221	(1.2)	223	(1.3)	223	(1.0)	223	(1.0)	223	(1.0)	227	(1.1)	224	(1.2)
Nevada	—	(†)	—	(†)	206	(1.8)	209	(1.2)	207	(1.2)	207	(1.2)	211	(1.2)	211	(1.1)	213	(1.0)	214	(1.1)	214	(1.2)	215	(1.6)
New Hampshire[2,4,5]	228	(1.2)	223	(1.5)	226	(1.7)	—	(†)	228	(1.0)	227	(0.9)	229	(0.9)	229	(1.0)	230	(0.8)	232	(0.9)	232	(1.0)	229	(1.0)
New Jersey[4]	223	(1.4)	219	(1.2)	—	(†)	—	(†)	225	(1.2)	223	(1.3)	231	(1.2)	229	(0.9)	231	(1.2)	229	(1.3)	229	(1.4)	233	(1.2)
New Mexico	211	(1.5)	205	(1.7)	205	(1.4)	208	(1.6)	203	(1.5)	207	(1.3)	212	(1.3)	208	(1.4)	208	(1.0)	206	(1.1)	207	(1.0)	208	(1.1)
New York[2,3,4]	215	(1.4)	212	(1.4)	215	(1.6)	222	(1.5)	222	(1.1)	223	(1.0)	224	(1.0)	224	(1.0)	222	(1.1)	224	(1.2)	223	(1.1)	222	(1.3)
North Carolina	212	(1.1)	214	(1.5)	213	(1.6)	222	(1.0)	221	(1.0)	217	(1.0)	218	(0.9)	219	(1.1)	221	(1.2)	222	(1.1)	226	(1.1)	224	(1.0)
North Dakota[3]	226	(1.1)	225	(1.2)	—	(†)	224	(1.0)	222	(0.9)	225	(0.7)	226	(0.9)	226	(0.8)	226	(0.5)	224	(0.5)	225	(0.7)	222	(0.8)
Ohio	217	(1.3)	—	(†)	—	(†)	222	(1.3)	222	(1.2)	223	(1.4)	226	(1.1)	225	(1.1)	224	(1.0)	224	(1.2)	225	(1.2)	225	(1.0)
Oklahoma	220	(0.9)	—	(†)	219	(1.2)	213	(1.2)	214	(1.2)	214	(1.1)	217	(1.1)	217	(1.1)	215	(1.1)	217	(1.1)	222	(1.1)	217	(1.1)
Oregon	—	(†)	—	(†)	212	(1.8)	220	(1.4)	218	(1.3)	217	(1.4)	215	(1.4)	218	(1.2)	216	(1.1)	219	(1.3)	220	(1.4)	218	(1.4)
Pennsylvania[5]	221	(1.3)	215	(1.6)	—	(†)	221	(1.2)	219	(1.3)	223	(1.3)	226	(1.0)	224	(1.4)	227	(1.2)	226	(1.3)	227	(1.8)	225	(1.1)
Rhode Island[5]	217	(1.8)	220	(1.3)	218	(1.4)	220	(1.2)	216	(1.3)	216	(1.2)	219	(1.0)	223	(1.1)	222	(0.8)	223	(0.9)	225	(0.9)	223	(1.0)
South Carolina	210	(1.3)	203	(1.4)	209	(1.4)	214	(1.3)	215	(1.3)	213	(1.3)	214	(1.2)	216	(1.1)	215	(1.2)	214	(1.2)	218	(1.4)	213	(1.2)
South Dakota	—	(†)	—	(†)	—	(†)	—	(†)	222	(1.2)	222	(0.5)	223	(1.0)	222	(0.6)	220	(0.9)	218	(1.0)	220	(0.9)	222	(1.0)
Tennessee[3,5]	212	(1.4)	213	(1.7)	212	(1.4)	214	(1.2)	212	(1.6)	214	(1.4)	216	(1.2)	217	(1.2)	215	(1.1)	220	(1.4)	219	(1.4)	219	(1.1)
Texas	213	(1.6)	212	(1.9)	214	(1.9)	217	(1.7)	215	(1.0)	219	(0.8)	220	(0.9)	219	(1.2)	218	(1.5)	217	(1.1)	218	(1.7)	215	(1.1)
Utah	220	(1.1)	217	(1.3)	216	(1.2)	222	(1.0)	219	(1.0)	221	(1.0)	221	(1.2)	219	(1.0)	220	(1.0)	223	(1.1)	226	(1.1)	225	(1.1)
Vermont	—	(†)	—	(†)	—	(†)	227	(1.1)	226	(0.9)	227	(0.9)	228	(0.8)	229	(0.8)	227	(0.6)	228	(0.6)	230	(0.8)	226	(0.8)
Virginia	221	(1.4)	213	(1.5)	217	(1.2)	225	(1.3)	223	(1.5)	226	(0.8)	227	(1.1)	227	(1.2)	226	(1.1)	229	(1.3)	229	(1.7)	228	(1.5)
Washington[3]	—	(†)	213	1.5	218	(1.4)	224	(1.2)	221	(1.1)	223	(1.1)	224	(1.4)	221	(1.2)	221	(1.1)	225	(1.4)	226	(1.5)	223	(1.4)
West Virginia	216	(1.3)	213	(1.1)	216	(1.7)	219	(1.2)	219	(1.0)	215	(0.8)	215	(1.1)	215	(1.0)	214	(0.8)	215	(0.8)	216	(1.2)	217	(1.2)
Wisconsin[2,5]	224	(1.0)	224	(1.1)	222	(1.1)	‡	(†)	221	(0.8)	221	(1.0)	223	(1.2)	220	(1.1)	221	(0.8)	221	(1.6)	223	(1.1)	220	(0.9)
Wyoming	223	(1.1)	221	(1.2)	218	(1.5)	221	(1.0)	222	(0.8)	223	(0.7)	225	(0.5)	223	(0.7)	224	(0.8)	226	(0.6)	228	(0.7)	227	(0.9)
Department of Defense dependents schools[6]	—	(†)	—	(†)	220	(0.7)	224	(0.4)	224	(0.5)	226	(0.6)	229	(0.5)	228	(0.5)	229	(0.5)	232	(0.6)	234	(0.7)	234	(0.6)

—Not available.
†Not applicable.
‡Reporting standards not met (too few cases for a reliable estimate).
[1]Accommodations were not permitted for this assessment.
[2]Did not meet one or more of the guidelines for school participation in 1998. Data are subject to appreciable nonresponse bias.
[3]Did not meet one or more of the guidelines for school participation in 2002. Data are subject to appreciable nonresponse bias.
[4]Did not meet one or more of the guidelines for school participation in 1992. Data are subject to appreciable nonresponse bias.
[5]Did not meet one or more of the guidelines for school participation in 1994. Data are subject to appreciable nonresponse bias.
[6]Prior to 2005, NAEP divided the Department of Defense (DoD) schools into two jurisdictions, domestic and overseas. In 2005, NAEP began combining the DoD domestic and overseas schools into a single jurisdiction. Data shown in this table for years prior to 2005 were recalculated for comparability.

NOTE: Scale ranges from 0 to 500. State-level data for 2000 are not available. For 1998 and later years, includes public school students who were tested with accommodations; excludes only those students with disabilities (SD) and English language learners (ELL) who were unable to be tested even with accommodations. SD and ELL populations, accommodation rates, and exclusion rates vary from state to state.

SOURCE: U.S. Department of Education, National Center for Education Statistics, National Assessment of Educational Progress (NAEP), 1992, 1994, 1998, 2002, 2003, 2005, 2007, 2009, 2011, 2013, 2015, and 2017 Reading Assessments, retrieved March 13, 2018, from the Main NAEP Data Explorer (http://nces.ed.gov/nationsreportcard/naepdata/). (This table was prepared March 2018.)

Table 221.60. Average National Assessment of Educational Progress (NAEP) reading scale score of 8th-grade public school students, by state: Selected years, 1998 through 2017

[Standard errors appear in parentheses]

State	1998		2002		2003		2005		2007		2009		2011		2013		2015		2017	
1	2		3		4		5		6		7		8		9		10		11	
United States	**261**	**(0.8)**	**263**	**(0.5)**	**261**	**(0.2)**	**260**	**(0.2)**	**261**	**(0.2)**	**262**	**(0.3)**	**264**	**(0.2)**	**266**	**(0.2)**	**264**	**(0.2)**	**265**	**(0.3)**
Alabama	255	(1.4)	253	(1.3)	253	(1.5)	252	(1.4)	252	(1.0)	255	(1.1)	258	(1.5)	257	(1.2)	259	(1.1)	258	(1.0)
Alaska	—	(†)	—	(†)	256	(1.1)	259	(0.9)	259	(1.0)	259	(0.9)	261	(0.9)	261	(0.8)	260	(1.1)	258	(0.8)
Arizona	260	(1.1)	257	(1.3)	255	(1.4)	255	(1.0)	255	(1.2)	258	(1.2)	260	(1.2)	260	(1.1)	263	(1.2)	263	(0.9)
Arkansas	256	(1.3)	260	(1.1)	258	(1.3)	258	(1.1)	258	(1.0)	258	(1.2)	259	(0.9)	262	(1.1)	259	(1.2)	260	(0.8)
California[1,2]	252	(1.6)	250	(1.8)	251	(1.3)	250	(0.6)	251	(0.8)	253	(1.2)	255	(1.0)	262	(1.2)	259	(1.2)	263	(1.2)
Colorado	264	(1.0)	—	(†)	268	(1.2)	265	(1.1)	266	(1.0)	266	(0.8)	271	(1.4)	271	(1.1)	268	(1.4)	270	(1.3)
Connecticut	270	(1.0)	267	(1.2)	267	(1.1)	264	(1.3)	267	(1.6)	272	(0.9)	275	(0.9)	274	(1.0)	273	(1.1)	273	(0.9)
Delaware	254	(1.3)	267	(0.5)	265	(0.7)	266	(0.6)	265	(0.6)	265	(0.7)	266	(0.6)	266	(0.7)	263	(0.8)	263	(0.8)
District of Columbia	236	(2.1)	240	(0.9)	239	(0.8)	238	(0.9)	241	(0.7)	242	(0.9)	242	(0.9)	248	(0.9)	248	(1.0)	247	(1.0)
Florida	255	(1.4)	261	(1.6)	257	(1.3)	256	(1.2)	260	(1.2)	264	(1.2)	262	(1.0)	266	(1.1)	263	(1.0)	267	(1.1)
Georgia	257	(1.4)	258	(1.0)	258	(1.1)	257	(1.3)	259	(1.0)	260	(1.0)	262	(1.1)	265	(1.2)	262	(1.3)	266	(1.1)
Hawaii	249	(1.0)	252	(0.9)	251	(0.9)	249	(0.9)	251	(0.8)	255	(0.6)	257	(0.7)	260	(0.8)	257	(0.9)	261	(0.8)
Idaho	—	(†)	266	(1.1)	264	(0.9)	264	(1.1)	265	(0.9)	265	(0.9)	268	(0.7)	270	(0.8)	269	(0.9)	270	(0.9)
Illinois	‡	(†)	‡	(†)	266	(1.0)	264	(1.0)	263	(1.0)	265	(1.2)	266	(0.8)	267	(1.0)	267	(1.0)	267	(1.1)
Indiana	—	(†)	265	(1.3)	265	(1.0)	261	(1.1)	264	(1.1)	266	(1.0)	265	(1.0)	267	(1.2)	268	(1.1)	272	(1.0)
Iowa	—	(†)	—	(†)	268	(0.8)	267	(0.9)	267	(0.9)	265	(0.9)	265	(1.0)	269	(0.8)	268	(1.0)	268	(1.1)
Kansas[1,2]	268	(1.4)	269	(1.3)	266	(1.5)	267	(1.0)	267	(0.8)	267	(1.1)	267	(1.0)	267	(1.0)	267	(1.2)	267	(1.0)
Kentucky	262	(1.4)	265	(1.0)	266	(1.3)	264	(1.1)	262	(1.0)	267	(0.9)	269	(0.8)	270	(0.8)	268	(1.0)	265	(0.8)
Louisiana	252	(1.4)	256	(1.5)	253	(1.6)	253	(1.6)	253	(1.1)	253	(1.6)	255	(1.5)	257	(1.0)	255	(1.2)	257	(1.5)
Maine[4]	271	(1.2)	270	(0.9)	268	(1.0)	270	(1.0)	270	(0.8)	268	(0.7)	270	(0.8)	269	(0.8)	268	(0.9)	269	(0.9)
Maryland[1]	261	(1.8)	263	(1.7)	262	(1.4)	261	(1.2)	265	(1.2)	267	(1.1)	271	(1.2)	274	(1.1)	268	(1.1)	267	(1.0)
Massachusetts	269	(1.4)	271	(1.3)	273	(1.0)	274	(1.0)	273	(1.0)	274	(1.2)	275	(1.0)	277	(1.0)	274	(1.1)	278	(1.1)
Michigan	—	(†)	265	(1.6)	264	(1.8)	261	(1.2)	260	(1.2)	262	(1.4)	265	(0.9)	266	(1.0)	264	(1.2)	265	(1.1)
Minnesota[1]	265	(1.4)	‡	(†)	268	(1.1)	268	(1.2)	268	(0.9)	270	(1.0)	270	(1.0)	271	(1.0)	270	(1.1)	269	(1.0)
Mississippi	251	(1.2)	255	(0.9)	255	(1.4)	251	(1.3)	250	(1.1)	251	(1.0)	254	(1.2)	253	(1.0)	252	(1.0)	256	(0.7)
Missouri	262	(1.3)	268	(1.0)	267	(1.0)	265	(1.0)	263	(1.0)	267	(1.0)	267	(1.1)	267	(1.1)	267	(1.1)	266	(1.2)
Montana[1,2]	271	(1.3)	270	(1.0)	270	(1.0)	269	(0.7)	271	(0.8)	270	(0.6)	273	(0.6)	272	(0.8)	270	(0.8)	267	(0.8)
Nebraska	—	(†)	270	(0.9)	266	(0.9)	267	(0.9)	267	(0.9)	267	(0.9)	268	(0.7)	269	(0.8)	269	(0.9)	269	(0.7)
Nevada	258	(1.0)	251	(0.8)	252	(0.8)	253	(0.9)	252	(0.8)	254	(0.9)	258	(0.9)	262	(0.7)	259	(0.9)	260	(0.8)
New Hampshire	—	(†)	—	(†)	271	(0.9)	270	(1.2)	270	(0.9)	271	(1.0)	272	(0.7)	274	(0.8)	275	(0.9)	275	(0.9)
New Jersey	—	(†)	—	(†)	268	(1.2)	269	(1.2)	270	(1.1)	273	(1.3)	275	(1.2)	276	(1.1)	271	(1.0)	275	(1.1)
New Mexico	258	(1.2)	254	(1.0)	252	(0.9)	251	(1.0)	251	(0.8)	254	(1.2)	256	(0.9)	256	(0.8)	253	(0.9)	256	(0.9)
New York[1,2]	265	(1.5)	264	(1.5)	265	(1.3)	265	(1.0)	264	(1.1)	264	(1.2)	266	(1.1)	266	(1.1)	263	(1.4)	264	(1.0)
North Carolina	262	(1.1)	265	(1.1)	262	(1.0)	258	(0.9)	259	(1.1)	260	(1.2)	263	(0.9)	265	(1.1)	261	(1.3)	263	(1.2)
North Dakota[2]	—	(†)	268	(0.8)	270	(0.8)	270	(0.6)	268	(0.7)	269	(0.6)	269	(0.7)	268	(0.6)	267	(0.6)	265	(0.8)
Ohio	—	(†)	268	(1.6)	267	(1.3)	267	(1.3)	268	(1.2)	269	(1.3)	268	(1.1)	269	(1.0)	266	(1.5)	268	(1.9)
Oklahoma	265	(1.2)	262	(0.8)	262	(0.9)	260	(1.1)	260	(0.8)	259	(0.9)	260	(1.1)	262	(0.9)	263	(1.3)	261	(1.0)
Oregon[2]	266	(1.5)	268	(1.3)	264	(1.2)	263	(1.1)	266	(0.9)	265	(1.0)	264	(0.9)	268	(0.9)	268	(1.3)	266	(1.2)
Pennsylvania	—	(†)	265	(1.0)	264	(1.2)	267	(1.3)	268	(1.2)	271	(0.8)	268	(1.3)	272	(1.0)	269	(1.5)	270	(1.1)
Rhode Island	264	(0.9)	262	(0.8)	261	(0.7)	261	(0.7)	258	(0.9)	260	(0.6)	265	(0.7)	267	(0.6)	265	(0.7)	266	(0.8)
South Carolina	255	(1.1)	258	(1.1)	258	(1.3)	257	(1.1)	257	(0.9)	257	(1.2)	260	(0.9)	261	(1.0)	260	(1.2)	260	(1.0)
South Dakota	—	(†)	—	(†)	270	(0.8)	269	(0.6)	270	(0.7)	270	(0.5)	269	(0.8)	268	(0.8)	267	(1.0)	267	(0.7)
Tennessee[2]	258	(1.2)	260	(1.4)	258	(1.2)	259	(0.9)	259	(1.0)	261	(1.1)	259	(1.0)	265	(1.1)	265	(1.4)	262	(1.1)
Texas	261	(1.4)	262	(1.4)	259	(1.1)	258	(0.6)	261	(0.9)	260	(1.1)	261	(1.0)	264	(1.1)	261	(1.0)	260	(1.2)
Utah	263	(1.0)	263	(1.1)	264	(0.8)	262	(0.8)	262	(1.0)	266	(0.8)	267	(0.8)	270	(0.9)	269	(1.0)	269	(0.9)
Vermont	—	(†)	272	(0.9)	271	(0.8)	269	(0.7)	273	(0.8)	272	(0.6)	274	(0.9)	274	(0.7)	274	(0.8)	273	(0.8)
Virginia	266	(1.1)	269	(1.0)	268	(1.1)	268	(1.0)	267	(1.1)	266	(1.1)	267	(1.2)	268	(1.3)	267	(1.2)	268	(1.3)
Washington[2]	264	(1.2)	268	(1.2)	264	(0.9)	265	(1.3)	265	(0.9)	267	(1.1)	268	(1.0)	272	(1.0)	267	(1.2)	272	(1.4)
West Virginia	262	(1.0)	264	(1.0)	260	(1.0)	255	(1.2)	255	(1.0)	255	(0.9)	256	(0.9)	257	(0.9)	260	(0.9)	259	(0.9)
Wisconsin[1]	265	(1.8)	‡	(†)	266	(1.3)	266	(1.1)	264	(1.0)	266	(1.0)	267	(0.9)	268	(0.9)	270	(1.1)	269	(1.0)
Wyoming	263	(1.3)	265	(0.7)	267	(0.5)	268	(0.7)	266	(0.7)	268	(1.0)	270	(1.0)	271	(0.6)	269	(0.7)	269	(0.7)
Department of Defense dependents schools[3]	269	(1.3)	273	(0.5)	272	(0.6)	271	(0.7)	273	(1.0)	272	(0.7)	272	(0.7)	277	(0.7)	277	(0.7)	280	(0.8)

—Not available.
†Not applicable.
‡Reporting standards not met. Participation rates fell below the required standards for reporting.
[1]Did not meet one or more of the guidelines for school participation in 1998. Data are subject to appreciable nonresponse bias.
[2]Did not meet one or more of the guidelines for school participation in 2002. Data are subject to appreciable nonresponse bias.
[3]Prior to 2005, NAEP divided the Department of Defense (DoD) schools into two jurisdictions, domestic and overseas. In 2005, NAEP began combining the DoD domestic and overseas schools into a single jurisdiction. Data shown in this table for years prior to 2005 were recalculated for comparability.

NOTE: Scale ranges from 0 to 500. State-level data for 1992 and 1994 are not available. Includes public school students who were tested with accommodations; excludes only those students with disabilities (SD) and English language learners (ELL) who were unable to be tested even with accommodations. SD and ELL populations, accommodation rates, and exclusion rates vary from state to state.
SOURCE: U.S. Department of Education, National Center for Education Statistics, National Assessment of Educational Progress (NAEP), 1998, 2002, 2003, 2005, 2007, 2009, 2011, 2013, 2015, and 2017 Reading Assessments, retrieved March 13, 2018, from the Main NAEP Data Explorer (http://nces.ed.gov/nationsreportcard/naepdata/). (This table was prepared March 2018.)

Table 222.10. Average National Assessment of Educational Progress (NAEP) mathematics scale score, by sex, race/ethnicity, and grade: Selected years, 1990 through 2017

[Standard errors appear in parentheses]

Grade and year	All students	Sex: Average mathematics scale score: Male	Sex: Average mathematics scale score: Female	Sex: Gap between female and male score	Race/ethnicity: Average mathematics scale score: White	Black	Hispanic	Asian/Pacific Islander: Total	Asian/Pacific Islander: Asian[1]	Asian/Pacific Islander: Pacific Islander[1]	American Indian/ Alaska Native	Two or more races[1]	Gap between White and Black score	Gap between White and Hispanic score
1	2	3	4	5	6	7	8	9	10	11	12	13	14	15
Grade 4														
1990[2]	213 (0.9)	214 (1.2)	213 (1.1)	-1 (1.7)	220 (1.0)	188 (1.8)	200 (2.2)	225 (4.1)	— (†)	— (†)	‡ (†)	— (†)	32 (2.0)	20 (2.4)
1992[2]	220 (0.7)	221 (0.8)	219 (1.0)	-2 (1.2)	227 (0.8)	193 (1.4)	202 (1.5)	231 (2.1)	— (†)	— (†)	‡ (†)	— (†)	35 (1.6)	25 (1.7)
1996	224 (1.0)	224 (1.1)	223 (1.1)	# (†)	232 (1.0)	198 (1.6)	207 (1.9)	229 (4.2)	— (†)	— (†)	217 (5.6)	— (†)	34 (1.8)	25 (2.1)
2000	226 (0.9)	227 (1.0)	224 (0.9)	-3 (1.4)	234 (0.8)	203 (1.2)	208 (1.5)	‡ (†)	— (†)	— (†)	208 (3.5)	— (†)	31 (1.5)	27 (1.7)
2003	235 (0.2)	236 (0.3)	233 (0.2)	-3 (0.3)	243 (0.2)	216 (0.4)	222 (0.4)	246 (1.1)	— (†)	— (†)	223 (1.0)	— (†)	27 (0.4)	22 (0.5)
2005	238 (0.1)	239 (0.2)	237 (0.2)	-3 (0.2)	246 (0.1)	220 (0.3)	226 (0.3)	251 (0.7)	— (†)	— (†)	226 (0.9)	— (†)	26 (0.3)	20 (0.3)
2007	240 (0.2)	241 (0.2)	239 (0.2)	-2 (0.3)	248 (0.2)	222 (0.3)	227 (0.3)	253 (0.8)	— (†)	— (†)	228 (0.7)	— (†)	26 (0.4)	21 (0.4)
2009	240 (0.2)	241 (0.3)	239 (0.3)	-2 (0.4)	248 (0.2)	222 (0.3)	227 (0.4)	255 (1.0)	— (†)	— (†)	225 (0.9)	— (†)	26 (0.4)	21 (0.5)
2011	241 (0.2)	241 (0.2)	240 (0.2)	-1 (0.3)	249 (0.2)	224 (0.4)	229 (0.3)	256 (1.0)	257 (1.0)	236 (2.1)	225 (0.9)	245 (0.6)	25 (0.4)	20 (0.4)
2013	242 (0.2)	242 (0.3)	241 (0.2)	-1 (0.4)	250 (0.2)	224 (0.3)	231 (0.4)	258 (0.8)	259 (0.8)	236 (2.0)	227 (1.1)	245 (0.7)	26 (0.4)	19 (0.5)
2015	240 (0.3)	241 (0.3)	239 (0.3)	-2 (0.4)	248 (0.3)	224 (0.4)	230 (0.5)	257 (1.2)	259 (1.2)	231 (2.3)	227 (1.0)	245 (0.8)	24 (0.5)	18 (0.5)
2017	240 (0.2)	241 (0.3)	239 (0.2)	-2 (0.4)	248 (0.2)	223 (0.5)	229 (0.4)	258 (1.1)	260 (1.0)	229 (2.7)	227 (1.3)	245 (0.8)	25 (0.5)	19 (0.5)
Grade 8														
1990[2]	263 (1.3)	263 (1.6)	262 (1.3)	-1 (2.1)	270 (1.3)	237 (2.7)	246 (4.3)	275 (5.0)	— (†)	— (†)	‡ (†)	— (†)	33 (3.0)	24 (4.5)
1992[2]	268 (0.9)	268 (1.1)	269 (1.0)	1 (1.5)	277 (1.0)	237 (1.3)	249 (1.2)	290 (5.9)	— (†)	— (†)	‡ (†)	— (†)	40 (1.7)	28 (1.5)
1996	270 (0.9)	271 (1.1)	269 (1.1)	-2 (1.5)	281 (1.1)	240 (1.9)	251 (1.7)	‡ (†)	— (†)	— (†)	‡ (†)	— (†)	41 (2.2)	30 (2.0)
2000	273 (0.8)	274 (0.9)	272 (0.9)	-2 (1.3)	284 (0.8)	244 (1.2)	253 (1.3)	288 (3.5)	— (†)	— (†)	259 (7.5)	— (†)	40 (1.5)	31 (1.6)
2003	278 (0.3)	278 (0.3)	277 (0.3)	-2 (0.4)	288 (0.3)	252 (0.5)	259 (0.6)	291 (1.3)	— (†)	— (†)	263 (1.8)	— (†)	35 (0.6)	29 (0.7)
2005	279 (0.2)	280 (0.2)	278 (0.2)	-2 (0.3)	289 (0.2)	255 (0.4)	262 (0.4)	295 (0.9)	— (†)	— (†)	264 (0.9)	— (†)	34 (0.4)	27 (0.5)
2007	281 (0.3)	282 (0.3)	280 (0.3)	-2 (0.4)	291 (0.3)	260 (0.4)	265 (0.4)	297 (0.9)	— (†)	— (†)	264 (1.2)	— (†)	32 (0.5)	26 (0.5)
2009	283 (0.3)	284 (0.3)	282 (0.4)	-2 (0.5)	293 (0.3)	261 (0.5)	266 (0.6)	301 (1.2)	— (†)	— (†)	266 (1.1)	— (†)	32 (0.5)	26 (0.6)
2011	284 (0.2)	284 (0.3)	283 (0.2)	-1 (0.4)	293 (0.2)	262 (0.5)	270 (0.5)	303 (1.0)	305 (1.1)	269 (2.4)	265 (0.9)	288 (1.3)	31 (0.5)	23 (0.5)
2013	285 (0.3)	285 (0.3)	284 (0.3)	-1 (0.4)	294 (0.3)	263 (0.4)	272 (0.5)	306 (1.1)	309 (1.1)	275 (2.3)	269 (1.2)	288 (1.2)	31 (0.5)	22 (0.5)
2015	282 (0.3)	282 (0.3)	282 (0.4)	# (†)	292 (0.3)	260 (0.5)	270 (0.5)	306 (1.5)	307 (1.5)	276 (2.9)	267 (1.3)	285 (1.1)	32 (0.6)	22 (0.6)
2017	283 (0.3)	283 (0.3)	282 (0.3)	-1 (0.4)	293 (0.3)	260 (0.5)	269 (0.5)	310 (1.5)	312 (1.5)	274 (2.2)	267 (1.4)	287 (1.1)	32 (0.6)	24 (0.6)
Grade 12														
1990[2]	[3] (†)	[3] (†)	[3] (†)	[3] (†)	[3] (†)	[3] (†)	[3] (†)	[3] (†)	[3] (†)	[3] (†)	[3] (†)	[3] (†)	[3] (†)	[3] (†)
1992[2]	[3] (†)	[3] (†)	[3] (†)	[3] (†)	[3] (†)	[3] (†)	[3] (†)	[3] (†)	[3] (†)	[3] (†)	[3] (†)	[3] (†)	[3] (†)	[3] (†)
1996	[3] (†)	[3] (†)	[3] (†)	[3] (†)	[3] (†)	[3] (†)	[3] (†)	[3] (†)	[3] (†)	[3] (†)	[3] (†)	[3] (†)	[3] (†)	[3] (†)
2000	[3] (†)	[3] (†)	[3] (†)	[3] (†)	[3] (†)	[3] (†)	[3] (†)	[3] (†)	[3] (†)	[3] (†)	[3] (†)	[3] (†)	[3] (†)	[3] (†)
2003	— (†)	— (†)	— (†)	— (†)	— (†)	— (†)	— (†)	— (†)	— (†)	— (†)	— (†)	— (†)	— (†)	— (†)
2005	150 (0.6)	151 (0.7)	149 (0.7)	-3 (1.0)	157 (0.6)	127 (1.1)	133 (1.3)	163 (2.0)	— (†)	— (†)	134 (4.1)	— (†)	31 (1.2)	24 (1.4)
2007	— (†)	— (†)	— (†)	— (†)	— (†)	— (†)	— (†)	— (†)	— (†)	— (†)	— (†)	— (†)	— (†)	— (†)
2009	153 (0.7)	155 (0.9)	152 (0.7)	-3 (1.1)	161 (0.6)	131 (0.8)	138 (0.8)	175 (2.7)	— (†)	— (†)	144 (2.8)	— (†)	30 (1.0)	23 (1.0)
2011	— (†)	— (†)	— (†)	— (†)	— (†)	— (†)	— (†)	— (†)	— (†)	— (†)	— (†)	— (†)	— (†)	— (†)
2013	153 (0.5)	155 (0.6)	152 (0.6)	-3 (0.9)	162 (0.6)	132 (0.8)	141 (0.8)	172 (1.3)	174 (1.3)	151 (2.8)	142 (3.2)	155 (1.7)	30 (1.0)	21 (1.0)
2015	152 (0.5)	153 (0.7)	150 (0.6)	-3 (0.9)	160 (0.6)	130 (1.0)	139 (0.8)	170 (2.0)	171 (1.9)	‡ (†)	138 (2.8)	157 (2.2)	30 (1.2)	22 (1.0)
2017	— (†)	— (†)	— (†)	— (†)	— (†)	— (†)	— (†)	— (†)	— (†)	— (†)	— (†)	— (†)	— (†)	— (†)

—Not available.
†Not applicable.
#Rounds to zero.
‡Reporting standards not met. Either there are too few cases for a reliable estimate or the coefficient of variation (CV) is 50 percent or greater.
[1]Prior to 2011, separate data for Asian students, Pacific Islander students, and students of Two or more races were not collected.
[2]Accommodations were not permitted for this assessment.
[3]Because of major changes to the framework and content of the grade 12 assessment, scores from 2005 and later assessment years cannot be compared with scores from earlier assessment years. Therefore, this table does not include scores from the earlier grade 12 assessment years (1990, 1992, 1996, and 2000). For data pertaining to scale score comparisons between earlier years, see the *Digest of Education Statistics 2009*, table 138 (http://nces.ed.gov/programs/digest/d09/tables/dt09_138.asp).

NOTE: For the grade 4 and grade 8 assessments, the scale ranges from 0 to 500. For the grade 12 assessment, the scale ranges from 0 to 300. Includes public and private schools. For 1996 and later years, includes students tested with accommodations (1 to 14 percent of all students, depending on grade level and year); excludes only those students with disabilities and English language learners who were unable to be tested even with accommodations (1 to 4 percent of all students). Race categories exclude persons of Hispanic ethnicity.
SOURCE: U.S. Department of Education, National Center for Education Statistics, National Assessment of Educational Progress (NAEP), 1990, 1992, 1996, 2000, 2003, 2005, 2007, 2009, 2011, 2013, 2015, and 2017 Mathematics Assessments, retrieved March 13, 2018, from the Main NAEP Data Explorer (http://nces.ed.gov/nationsreportcard/naepdata/). (This table was prepared March 2018.)

Table 222.20. Percentage of students at or above selected National Assessment of Educational Progress (NAEP) mathematics achievement levels, by grade and selected student characteristics: Selected years, 2003 through 2017

[Standard errors appear in parentheses]

Grade and selected student characteristic	2003		2005		2007		2009		2011		2013		2015		2017	
	At or above *Basic*[1]	At or above *Proficient*[2]	At or above *Basic*[1]	At or above *Proficient*[2]	At or above *Basic*[1]	At or above *Proficient*[2]	At or above *Basic*[1]	At or above *Proficient*[2]	At or above *Basic*[1]	At or above *Proficient*[2]	At or above *Basic*[1]	At or above *Proficient*[2]	At or above *Basic*[1]	At or above *Proficient*[2]	At or above *Basic*[1]	At or above *Proficient*[2]
1	2	3	4	5	6	7	8	9	10	11	12	13	14	15	16	17
4th grade, all students	**77 (0.3)**	**32 (0.3)**	**80 (0.2)**	**36 (0.2)**	**82 (0.2)**	**39 (0.3)**	**82 (0.3)**	**39 (0.3)**	**82 (0.2)**	**40 (0.3)**	**83 (0.2)**	**42 (0.3)**	**82 (0.3)**	**40 (0.4)**	**80 (0.3)**	**40 (0.4)**
Sex																
Male	78 (0.4)	35 (0.4)	81 (0.2)	38 (0.2)	82 (0.2)	41 (0.3)	82 (0.3)	41 (0.4)	83 (0.3)	42 (0.4)	82 (0.3)	43 (0.4)	82 (0.4)	42 (0.5)	80 (0.4)	42 (0.4)
Female	76 (0.3)	30 (0.3)	80 (0.2)	34 (0.3)	82 (0.2)	37 (0.4)	82 (0.3)	37 (0.4)	82 (0.3)	39 (0.4)	83 (0.2)	41 (0.4)	82 (0.3)	38 (0.5)	80 (0.3)	38 (0.4)
Race/ethnicity																
White	87 (0.2)	43 (0.3)	90 (0.2)	47 (0.2)	91 (0.2)	51 (0.4)	91 (0.2)	51 (0.4)	91 (0.2)	52 (0.4)	91 (0.2)	54 (0.4)	90 (0.3)	51 (0.5)	88 (0.3)	51 (0.4)
Black	54 (0.6)	10 (0.3)	60 (0.5)	13 (0.3)	64 (0.6)	15 (0.4)	64 (0.6)	16 (0.5)	66 (0.6)	17 (0.5)	66 (0.6)	18 (0.5)	65 (0.7)	19 (0.6)	63 (0.8)	19 (0.6)
Hispanic	62 (0.7)	16 (0.5)	68 (0.5)	19 (0.3)	70 (0.5)	22 (0.4)	71 (0.7)	22 (0.4)	72 (0.5)	24 (0.5)	73 (0.7)	26 (0.6)	73 (0.6)	26 (0.7)	71 (0.5)	26 (0.6)
Asian/Pacific Islander	87 (0.8)	48 (1.9)	90 (0.5)	55 (1.1)	91 (0.7)	58 (1.3)	92 (0.6)	60 (1.5)	91 (0.6)	62 (1.6)	91 (0.6)	64 (1.2)	91 (0.8)	62 (1.7)	90 (0.8)	64 (1.4)
Asian	— (†)	— (†)	— (†)	— (†)	— (†)	— (†)	— (†)	— (†)	93 (0.5)	64 (1.6)	92 (0.6)	66 (1.2)	93 (0.7)	65 (1.7)	92 (0.7)	67 (1.4)
Pacific Islander	— (†)	— (†)	— (†)	— (†)	— (†)	— (†)	— (†)	— (†)	77 (2.7)	34 (3.2)	77 (3.1)	33 (3.2)	68 (4.0)	30 (2.8)	71 (3.7)	29 (3.5)
American Indian/Alaska Native	64 (1.7)	17 (1.2)	68 (1.5)	21 (1.2)	70 (1.2)	25 (1.1)	66 (1.6)	21 (1.2)	66 (1.2)	22 (1.2)	68 (1.7)	23 (1.4)	69 (1.8)	23 (1.7)	69 (2.0)	24 (1.9)
Two or more races	— (†)	— (†)	— (†)	— (†)	— (†)	— (†)	— (†)	— (†)	87 (0.7)	45 (1.2)	85 (1.0)	46 (1.4)	86 (0.9)	45 (1.3)	85 (0.9)	45 (1.3)
Eligibility for free or reduced-price lunch																
Eligible	62 (0.5)	15 (0.3)	67 (0.3)	19 (0.2)	70 (0.4)	22 (0.3)	70 (0.4)	22 (0.3)	72 (0.3)	24 (0.3)	73 (0.4)	25 (0.4)	72 (0.4)	24 (0.4)	69 (0.4)	25 (0.3)
Not eligible	88 (0.3)	45 (0.4)	90 (0.2)	49 (0.3)	91 (0.2)	53 (0.4)	91 (0.3)	54 (0.4)	92 (0.2)	57 (0.4)	93 (0.2)	59 (0.4)	92 (0.3)	58 (0.6)	91 (0.3)	57 (0.5)
Unknown	84 (0.9)	41 (1.2)	87 (0.7)	45 (1.2)	90 (0.9)	48 (1.5)	88 (1.3)	47 (1.7)	90 (0.8)	52 (1.4)	90 (1.0)	52 (2.2)	89 (1.2)	50 (1.7)	87 (1.1)	49 (1.7)
8th grade, all students	**68 (0.3)**	**29 (0.3)**	**69 (0.2)**	**30 (0.2)**	**71 (0.3)**	**32 (0.3)**	**73 (0.3)**	**34 (0.3)**	**73 (0.2)**	**35 (0.2)**	**74 (0.3)**	**35 (0.3)**	**71 (0.3)**	**33 (0.3)**	**70 (0.3)**	**34 (0.3)**
Sex																
Male	69 (0.4)	30 (0.4)	70 (0.3)	31 (0.3)	72 (0.3)	34 (0.4)	73 (0.3)	36 (0.4)	73 (0.4)	36 (0.3)	74 (0.3)	36 (0.4)	71 (0.4)	34 (0.4)	70 (0.3)	35 (0.4)
Female	67 (0.4)	27 (0.3)	69 (0.3)	28 (0.3)	71 (0.3)	30 (0.3)	72 (0.4)	32 (0.4)	73 (0.2)	34 (0.3)	74 (0.4)	35 (0.4)	72 (0.4)	33 (0.4)	70 (0.3)	33 (0.5)
Race/ethnicity																
White	80 (0.3)	37 (0.4)	80 (0.2)	39 (0.3)	82 (0.3)	42 (0.3)	83 (0.3)	44 (0.4)	84 (0.3)	44 (0.3)	84 (0.2)	45 (0.4)	82 (0.3)	43 (0.4)	80 (0.3)	44 (0.4)
Black	39 (0.8)	7 (0.3)	42 (0.5)	9 (0.3)	47 (0.7)	11 (0.3)	50 (0.6)	12 (0.5)	51 (0.6)	13 (0.4)	52 (0.7)	14 (0.5)	48 (0.9)	13 (0.5)	47 (0.7)	13 (0.5)
Hispanic	48 (0.8)	12 (0.5)	52 (0.6)	13 (0.4)	55 (0.7)	15 (0.4)	57 (0.8)	17 (0.6)	61 (0.7)	20 (0.6)	62 (0.6)	21 (0.5)	60 (0.7)	19 (0.6)	57 (0.7)	20 (0.5)
Asian/Pacific Islander	78 (1.1)	43 (1.3)	81 (0.8)	47 (1.2)	83 (0.8)	50 (1.1)	85 (1.0)	54 (1.8)	86 (1.0)	55 (1.2)	87 (0.8)	60 (1.3)	87 (0.9)	59 (1.7)	87 (0.9)	62 (1.5)
Asian	— (†)	— (†)	— (†)	— (†)	— (†)	— (†)	— (†)	— (†)	88 (0.9)	58 (1.3)	89 (0.8)	63 (1.3)	88 (0.9)	61 (1.7)	88 (0.9)	64 (1.6)
Pacific Islander	— (†)	— (†)	— (†)	— (†)	— (†)	— (†)	— (†)	— (†)	59 (4.7)	22 (1.9)	67 (3.5)	24 (2.9)	63 (4.2)	29 (3.9)	64 (2.8)	25 (3.3)
American Indian/Alaska Native	52 (2.7)	15 (1.7)	53 (1.3)	14 (1.2)	53 (1.8)	16 (1.2)	56 (1.5)	18 (1.3)	55 (1.5)	17 (1.2)	59 (1.7)	21 (1.5)	57 (1.8)	20 (1.7)	56 (1.6)	18 (1.8)
Two or more races	— (†)	— (†)	— (†)	— (†)	— (†)	— (†)	— (†)	— (†)	78 (1.1)	39 (1.7)	76 (1.2)	38 (1.4)	74 (1.5)	36 (1.3)	73 (1.3)	37 (1.4)
Eligibility for free or reduced-price lunch																
Eligible	48 (0.5)	12 (0.4)	51 (0.4)	13 (0.2)	55 (0.5)	15 (0.3)	57 (0.5)	17 (0.3)	59 (0.4)	19 (0.3)	60 (0.4)	20 (0.3)	58 (0.4)	18 (0.3)	55 (0.4)	18 (0.3)
Not eligible	79 (0.3)	37 (0.4)	79 (0.2)	39 (0.3)	81 (0.3)	42 (0.4)	83 (0.3)	45 (0.4)	84 (0.2)	47 (0.4)	86 (0.3)	49 (0.4)	84 (0.3)	48 (0.5)	82 (0.3)	48 (0.4)
Unknown	75 (1.1)	36 (1.2)	79 (1.1)	40 (1.4)	81 (1.7)	43 (1.7)	83 (1.3)	48 (1.9)	85 (0.9)	48 (1.5)	84 (1.3)	50 (2.6)	81 (1.5)	46 (1.9)	83 (1.1)	47 (1.8)
12th grade, all students	**— (†)**	**— (†)**	**61 (0.8)**	**23 (0.7)**	**— (†)**	**— (†)**	**64 (0.8)**	**26 (0.8)**	**— (†)**	**— (†)**	**65 (0.7)**	**26 (0.6)**	**62 (0.8)**	**25 (0.7)**	**— (†)**	**— (†)**
Sex																
Male	— (†)	— (†)	62 (0.9)	25 (1.0)	— (†)	— (†)	65 (0.9)	28 (1.0)	— (†)	— (†)	66 (0.8)	28 (0.8)	63 (1.0)	26 (0.7)	— (†)	— (†)
Female	— (†)	— (†)	60 (1.0)	21 (0.8)	— (†)	— (†)	63 (0.8)	24 (0.8)	— (†)	— (†)	64 (0.9)	24 (0.7)	61 (0.9)	23 (0.7)	— (†)	— (†)
Race/ethnicity																
White	— (†)	— (†)	70 (0.8)	29 (0.8)	— (†)	— (†)	75 (0.7)	33 (0.8)	— (†)	— (†)	75 (0.8)	33 (0.8)	73 (0.9)	32 (0.9)	— (†)	— (†)
Black	— (†)	— (†)	30 (1.7)	6 (0.8)	— (†)	— (†)	37 (1.2)	6 (0.6)	— (†)	— (†)	38 (1.5)	7 (0.6)	36 (1.6)	7 (0.7)	— (†)	— (†)
Hispanic	— (†)	— (†)	40 (2.1)	8 (1.0)	— (†)	— (†)	45 (1.1)	11 (0.8)	— (†)	— (†)	50 (1.3)	12 (0.7)	47 (1.3)	12 (0.7)	— (†)	— (†)
Asian/Pacific Islander	— (†)	— (†)	73 (2.6)	36 (3.0)	— (†)	— (†)	84 (1.9)	52 (3.4)	— (†)	— (†)	81 (1.4)	47 (2.0)	78 (2.1)	46 (2.6)	— (†)	— (†)
Asian	— (†)	— (†)	— (†)	— (†)	— (†)	— (†)	— (†)	— (†)	— (†)	— (†)	83 (1.5)	49 (2.0)	79 (2.0)	47 (2.5)	— (†)	— (†)
Pacific Islander	— (†)	— (†)	— (†)	— (†)	— (†)	— (†)	— (†)	— (†)	— (†)	— (†)	65 (7.3)	16 (6.0)	‡ (†)	‡ (†)	— (†)	— (†)
American Indian/Alaska Native	— (†)	— (†)	42 (8.6)	6 (2.9)	— (†)	— (†)	56 (5.4)	12 (3.3)	— (†)	— (†)	54 (5.8)	12 (4.0)	46 (4.6)	10 (3.3)	— (†)	— (†)
Two or more races	— (†)	— (†)	— (†)	— (†)	— (†)	— (†)	— (†)	— (†)	— (†)	— (†)	67 (3.0)	26 (2.7)	67 (3.2)	31 (3.1)	— (†)	— (†)

—Not available.
†Not applicable.
‡Reporting standards not met (too few cases for a reliable estimate).
[1]*Basic* denotes partial mastery of the knowledge and skills that are fundamental for proficient work at a given grade.
[2]*Proficient* represents solid academic performance. Students reaching this level have demonstrated competency over challenging subject matter.
NOTE: Includes public and private schools. Includes students tested with accommodations (1 to 14 percent of all students, depending on grade level and year); excludes only those students with disabilities and English language learners who were unable to be tested even with accommodations (1 to 4 percent of all students). Race categories exclude persons of Hispanic ethnicity. Prior to 2011, separate data for Asian students, Pacific Islander students, and students of Two or more races were not collected.
SOURCE: U.S. Department of Education, National Center for Education Statistics, National Assessment of Educational Progress (NAEP), 2003, 2005, 2007, 2009, 2011, 2013, 2015, and 2017 Mathematics Assessments, retrieved July 2, 2018, from the Main NAEP Data Explorer (http://nces.ed.gov/nationsreportcard/naepdata/). (This table was prepared July 2018.)

Table 222.50. Average National Assessment of Educational Progress (NAEP) mathematics scale score of 4th-grade public school students, by state: Selected years, 1992 through 2017

[Standard errors appear in parentheses]

State	1992[1]		1996[2]		2000		2003		2005		2007		2009		2011		2013		2015		2017	
1	2		3		4		5		6		7		8		9		10		11		12	
United States	**219**	**(0.8)**	**222**	**(1.0)**	**224**	**(1.0)**	**234**	**(0.2)**	**237**	**(0.2)**	**239**	**(0.2)**	**239**	**(0.2)**	**240**	**(0.2)**	**241**	**(0.2)**	**240**	**(0.3)**	**239**	**(0.2)**
Alabama	208	(1.6)	212	(1.2)	217	(1.2)	223	(1.2)	225	(0.9)	229	(1.3)	228	(1.1)	231	(1.0)	233	(1.0)	231	(0.9)	232	(1.0)
Alaska[3]	—	(†)	224	(1.3)	—	(†)	233	(0.8)	236	(1.0)	237	(1.0)	237	(0.9)	236	(0.9)	236	(0.8)	236	(1.1)	230	(0.9)
Arizona	215	(1.1)	218	(1.7)	219	(1.3)	229	(1.1)	230	(1.1)	232	(1.0)	230	(1.1)	235	(1.1)	240	(1.2)	238	(1.0)	234	(1.1)
Arkansas[3]	210	(0.9)	216	(1.5)	216	(1.1)	229	(0.9)	236	(0.9)	238	(1.1)	238	(0.9)	238	(0.8)	240	(0.9)	235	(0.8)	234	(0.9)
California[4]	208	(1.6)	209	(1.8)	213	(1.6)	227	(0.9)	230	(0.6)	230	(0.7)	232	(1.2)	234	(1.4)	234	(1.2)	232	(1.4)	232	(1.2)
Colorado	221	(1.0)	226	(1.0)	—	(†)	235	(1.0)	239	(1.1)	240	(1.0)	243	(1.0)	244	(0.9)	247	(0.8)	242	(1.0)	241	(1.1)
Connecticut	227	(1.1)	232	(1.1)	234	(1.1)	241	(0.8)	242	(0.8)	243	(1.1)	245	(1.0)	242	(1.3)	243	(0.9)	240	(0.9)	239	(1.1)
Delaware	218	(0.8)	215	(0.6)	—	(†)	236	(0.5)	240	(0.5)	242	(0.4)	239	(0.5)	240	(0.6)	243	(0.7)	239	(0.6)	236	(0.8)
District of Columbia	193	(0.5)	187	(1.1)	192	(1.1)	205	(0.7)	211	(0.8)	214	(0.8)	219	(0.7)	222	(0.7)	229	(0.7)	231	(0.6)	231	(0.7)
Florida	214	(1.5)	216	(1.2)	—	(†)	234	(1.1)	239	(0.7)	242	(0.8)	242	(1.0)	240	(0.8)	242	(0.8)	243	(1.0)	246	(0.7)
Georgia	216	(1.2)	215	(1.5)	219	(1.1)	230	(1.0)	234	(1.0)	235	(0.8)	236	(0.9)	238	(0.7)	240	(1.0)	236	(1.2)	236	(1.1)
Hawaii	214	(1.3)	215	(1.5)	216	(1.0)	227	(1.0)	230	(0.8)	234	(0.8)	236	(1.1)	239	(0.7)	243	(0.8)	238	(0.9)	238	(0.8)
Idaho[4]	222	(1.0)	—	(†)	224	(1.4)	235	(0.7)	242	(0.7)	241	(0.7)	241	(0.8)	240	(0.6)	241	(0.9)	239	(0.9)	240	(0.9)
Illinois[4]	—	(†)	—	(†)	223	(1.9)	233	(1.1)	233	(1.0)	237	(1.1)	238	(1.0)	239	(1.1)	239	(1.2)	237	(1.2)	238	(1.0)
Indiana[4]	221	(1.0)	229	(1.0)	233	(1.1)	238	(0.9)	240	(0.8)	245	(0.8)	243	(0.9)	244	(1.0)	249	(0.9)	248	(1.1)	247	(1.1)
Iowa[3,4]	230	(1.0)	229	(1.1)	231	(1.2)	238	(0.7)	240	(0.7)	243	(0.8)	243	(0.8)	243	(0.8)	246	(0.9)	243	(0.9)	243	(1.1)
Kansas[4]	—	(†)	—	(†)	232	(1.6)	242	(1.0)	246	(1.0)	248	(0.9)	245	(1.0)	246	(0.9)	246	(0.8)	241	(1.0)	241	(0.9)
Kentucky	215	(1.0)	220	(1.1)	219	(1.4)	229	(1.1)	231	(0.9)	235	(0.9)	239	(1.1)	241	(0.8)	241	(0.9)	242	(1.1)	239	(0.9)
Louisiana	204	(1.5)	209	(1.1)	218	(1.4)	226	(1.0)	230	(0.9)	230	(1.0)	229	(1.0)	231	(1.0)	231	(1.2)	234	(1.1)	229	(1.2)
Maine[4]	232	(1.0)	232	(1.0)	230	(1.0)	238	(0.7)	241	(0.8)	242	(0.8)	244	(0.8)	244	(0.7)	246	(0.7)	242	(0.8)	240	(0.9)
Maryland	217	(1.3)	221	(1.6)	222	(1.2)	233	(1.3)	238	(1.0)	240	(0.9)	244	(0.9)	247	(0.9)	245	(1.3)	239	(1.0)	241	(1.1)
Massachusetts	227	(1.2)	229	(1.3)	233	(1.2)	242	(0.8)	247	(0.8)	252	(0.8)	252	(0.9)	253	(0.8)	253	(1.0)	251	(1.2)	249	(1.0)
Michigan[3,4]	220	(1.7)	226	(1.3)	229	(1.6)	236	(0.9)	238	(1.2)	238	(1.3)	236	(1.0)	236	(1.1)	237	(1.1)	236	(1.2)	236	(1.3)
Minnesota[4]	228	(0.9)	232	(1.1)	234	(1.3)	242	(0.9)	246	(1.0)	247	(1.0)	249	(1.1)	249	(0.9)	253	(1.1)	250	(1.2)	249	(1.2)
Mississippi	202	(1.1)	208	(1.2)	211	(1.1)	223	(1.0)	227	(0.9)	228	(1.0)	227	(1.0)	230	(0.9)	231	(0.7)	234	(0.9)	235	(0.8)
Missouri	222	(1.2)	225	(1.1)	228	(1.2)	235	(0.9)	235	(0.9)	239	(0.9)	241	(1.2)	240	(0.9)	240	(0.8)	239	(0.9)	240	(1.1)
Montana[3,4]	—	(†)	228	(1.2)	228	(1.7)	236	(0.8)	241	(0.8)	244	(0.8)	244	(0.7)	244	(0.6)	244	(0.6)	241	(0.7)	241	(0.8)
Nebraska	225	(1.2)	228	(1.2)	225	(1.8)	236	(0.8)	238	(0.9)	238	(1.1)	239	(1.0)	240	(1.0)	243	(1.0)	244	(0.9)	246	(0.9)
Nevada[3]	—	(†)	218	(1.3)	220	(1.0)	228	(0.8)	230	(0.8)	232	(0.9)	235	(0.9)	237	(0.8)	236	(0.8)	234	(1.1)	232	(1.2)
New Hampshire	230	(1.2)	—	(†)	—	(†)	243	(0.9)	246	(0.8)	249	(0.8)	251	(0.8)	252	(0.6)	253	(0.8)	249	(0.8)	245	(0.9)
New Jersey[3]	227	(1.5)	227	(1.5)	—	(†)	239	(1.1)	244	(1.1)	249	(1.1)	247	(1.0)	248	(0.9)	247	(1.1)	245	(1.2)	248	(1.3)
New Mexico	213	(1.4)	214	(1.8)	213	(1.5)	223	(1.1)	224	(0.8)	228	(0.9)	230	(1.0)	233	(0.8)	233	(0.7)	231	(0.8)	230	(0.8)
New York[3,4]	218	(1.2)	223	(1.2)	225	(1.4)	236	(0.9)	238	(0.9)	243	(0.8)	241	(0.7)	238	(0.8)	240	(1.0)	237	(0.9)	236	(1.0)
North Carolina	213	(1.1)	224	(1.2)	230	(1.1)	242	(0.8)	241	(0.9)	242	(0.8)	244	(0.8)	245	(0.7)	245	(0.9)	244	(1.0)	241	(1.0)
North Dakota	229	(0.8)	231	(1.2)	230	(1.2)	238	(0.7)	243	(0.5)	245	(0.5)	245	(0.6)	245	(0.4)	246	(0.5)	245	(0.5)	244	(0.7)
Ohio[4]	219	(1.2)	—	(†)	230	(1.5)	238	(1.0)	242	(1.0)	245	(1.0)	244	(1.1)	244	(0.8)	246	(1.1)	244	(1.2)	241	(1.0)
Oklahoma	220	(1.0)	—	(†)	224	(1.0)	229	(1.0)	234	(1.0)	237	(0.8)	237	(0.9)	237	(0.8)	239	(0.7)	240	(1.0)	237	(0.9)
Oregon[4]	—	(†)	223	(1.4)	224	(1.8)	236	(0.9)	238	(0.8)	236	(1.0)	238	(0.9)	237	(0.9)	240	(1.3)	238	(1.1)	233	(1.1)
Pennsylvania[3]	224	(1.3)	226	(1.2)	—	(†)	236	(1.1)	241	(1.2)	244	(0.8)	244	(1.1)	246	(1.1)	244	(1.0)	243	(1.4)	242	(1.0)
Rhode Island	215	(1.5)	220	(1.4)	224	(1.1)	230	(1.0)	233	(0.9)	236	(0.9)	239	(0.8)	242	(0.7)	241	(0.8)	238	(0.7)	238	(0.7)
South Carolina[3]	212	(1.1)	213	(1.3)	220	(1.4)	236	(0.9)	238	(0.9)	237	(0.8)	236	(0.9)	237	(1.0)	237	(1.0)	237	(1.1)	234	(1.0)
South Dakota	—	(†)	—	(†)	—	(†)	237	(0.7)	242	(0.5)	241	(0.7)	242	(0.5)	241	(0.6)	241	(0.5)	240	(0.7)	242	(0.8)
Tennessee	211	(1.4)	219	(1.4)	220	(1.4)	228	(1.0)	232	(1.2)	233	(0.9)	232	(1.1)	233	(0.9)	240	(0.9)	241	(1.1)	237	(1.0)
Texas	218	(1.2)	229	(1.4)	231	(1.1)	237	(0.9)	242	(0.6)	242	(0.7)	240	(0.7)	241	(1.1)	242	(0.9)	244	(1.3)	241	(1.2)
Utah	224	(1.0)	227	(1.2)	227	(1.3)	235	(0.8)	239	(0.8)	239	(0.9)	240	(1.0)	243	(0.8)	243	(0.9)	243	(1.0)	242	(1.0)
Vermont[3,4]	—	(†)	225	(1.2)	232	(1.6)	242	(0.8)	244	(0.5)	246	(0.5)	248	(0.4)	247	(0.5)	248	(0.6)	243	(0.7)	241	(0.7)
Virginia	221	(1.3)	223	(1.4)	230	(1.0)	239	(1.1)	240	(0.9)	244	(0.9)	243	(1.0)	245	(0.8)	246	(1.1)	247	(1.3)	248	(1.0)
Washington	—	(†)	225	(1.2)	—	(†)	238	(1.0)	242	(0.9)	243	(1.0)	242	(0.8)	243	(0.9)	246	(1.1)	245	(1.3)	242	(1.3)
West Virginia	215	(1.1)	223	(1.0)	223	(1.3)	231	(0.8)	231	(0.7)	236	(0.9)	233	(0.8)	235	(0.7)	237	(0.8)	235	(0.8)	236	(1.0)
Wisconsin	229	(1.1)	231	(1.0)	‡	(†)	237	(0.9)	241	(0.9)	244	(0.9)	244	(0.9)	245	(0.8)	245	(1.0)	243	(1.1)	240	(0.9)
Wyoming	225	(0.9)	223	(1.4)	229	(1.1)	241	(0.6)	243	(0.6)	244	(0.5)	242	(0.6)	244	(0.4)	247	(0.4)	247	(0.6)	248	(0.6)
Department of Defense dependents schools[5]	—	(†)	224	(0.6)	227	(0.6)	237	(0.4)	239	(0.5)	240	(0.4)	240	(0.5)	241	(0.4)	245	(0.4)	248	(0.5)	249	(0.5)

—Not available.
†Not applicable.
‡Reporting standards not met. Participation rates fell below the required standards for reporting.
[1]Accommodations were not permitted for this assessment.
[2]The 1996 data in this table do not include students who were tested with accommodations. Data for students tested with accommodations are not available at the state level for 1996.
[3]Did not meet one or more of the guidelines for school participation in 1996. Data are subject to appreciable nonresponse bias.
[4]Did not meet one or more of the guidelines for school participation in 2000. Data are subject to appreciable nonresponse bias.
[5]Prior to 2005, NAEP divided the Department of Defense (DoD) schools into two jurisdictions, domestic and overseas. In 2005, NAEP began combining the DoD domestic and overseas schools into a single jurisdiction. Data shown in this table for years prior to 2005 were recalculated for comparability.
NOTE: Scale ranges from 0 to 500. State-level data for 1990 are not available. For 2000 and later years, includes public school students who were tested with accommodations; excludes only those students with disabilities (SD) and English language learners (ELL) who were unable to be tested even with accommodations. SD and ELL populations, accommodation rates, and exclusion rates vary from state to state.
SOURCE: U.S. Department of Education, National Center for Education Statistics, National Assessment of Educational Progress (NAEP), 1992, 1996, 2000, 2003, 2005, 2007, 2009, 2011, 2013, 2015, and 2017 Mathematics Assessments, retrieved March 13, 2018, from the Main NAEP Data Explorer (http://nces.ed.gov/nationsreportcard/naepdata/). (This table was prepared March 2018.)

Table 222.60. Average National Assessment of Educational Progress (NAEP) mathematics scale score of 8th-grade public school students, by state: Selected years, 1990 through 2017

[Standard errors appear in parentheses]

State	1990[1]		1992[1]		1996[2]		2000		2003		2005		2007		2009		2011		2013		2015		2017	
1	2		3		4		5		6		7		8		9		10		11		12		13	
United States	**262**	**(1.4)**	**267**	**(1.0)**	**271**	**(1.2)**	**272**	**(0.9)**	**276**	**(0.3)**	**278**	**(0.2)**	**280**	**(0.3)**	**282**	**(0.3)**	**283**	**(0.2)**	**284**	**(0.2)**	**281**	**(0.3)**	**282**	**(0.3)**
Alabama	253	(1.1)	252	(1.7)	257	(2.1)	264	(1.8)	262	(1.5)	262	(1.5)	266	(1.5)	269	(1.2)	269	(1.4)	269	(1.3)	267	(1.2)	268	(1.3)
Alaska[3]	—	(†)	—	(†)	278	(1.8)	—	(†)	279	(0.9)	279	(0.8)	283	(1.1)	283	(1.0)	283	(0.8)	282	(0.9)	280	(1.0)	277	(0.9)
Arizona[4]	260	(1.3)	265	(1.3)	268	(1.6)	269	(1.8)	271	(1.2)	274	(1.1)	276	(1.2)	277	(1.4)	279	(1.2)	280	(1.2)	283	(1.4)	282	(1.1)
Arkansas[3]	256	(0.9)	256	(1.2)	262	(1.5)	257	(1.5)	266	(1.2)	272	(1.2)	274	(1.1)	276	(1.1)	279	(1.0)	278	(1.1)	275	(1.4)	274	(1.0)
California[4]	256	(1.3)	261	(1.7)	263	(1.9)	260	(2.1)	267	(1.2)	269	(0.6)	270	(0.8)	270	(1.3)	273	(1.2)	276	(1.2)	275	(1.3)	277	(1.2)
Colorado	267	(0.9)	272	(1.0)	276	(1.1)	—	(†)	283	(1.1)	281	(1.2)	286	(0.9)	287	(1.4)	292	(1.1)	290	(1.2)	286	(1.5)	286	(1.4)
Connecticut	270	(1.0)	274	(1.1)	280	(1.1)	281	(1.3)	284	(1.2)	281	(1.4)	282	(1.5)	289	(1.0)	287	(1.1)	285	(1.1)	284	(1.2)	284	(0.9)
Delaware	261	(0.9)	263	(1.0)	267	(0.9)	—	(†)	277	(0.7)	281	(0.6)	283	(0.6)	284	(0.5)	283	(0.7)	282	(0.7)	280	(0.7)	278	(0.7)
District of Columbia	231	(0.9)	235	(0.9)	233	(1.3)	235	(1.1)	243	(0.8)	245	(0.9)	248	(0.9)	254	(0.9)	260	(0.7)	265	(0.9)	263	(0.9)	266	(0.9)
Florida	255	(1.2)	260	(1.5)	264	(1.8)	—	(†)	271	(1.5)	274	(1.1)	277	(1.3)	279	(1.1)	278	(0.8)	281	(0.8)	275	(1.4)	279	(1.1)
Georgia	259	(1.3)	259	(1.2)	262	(1.6)	265	(1.2)	270	(1.2)	272	(1.1)	275	(1.0)	278	(0.9)	278	(1.0)	279	(1.2)	279	(1.2)	281	(1.4)
Hawaii	251	(0.8)	257	(0.9)	262	(1.0)	262	(1.4)	266	(0.8)	266	(0.7)	269	(0.8)	274	(0.7)	278	(0.7)	281	(0.8)	279	(0.8)	277	(0.8)
Idaho[4]	271	(0.8)	275	(0.7)	—	(†)	277	(1.0)	280	(0.9)	281	(0.9)	284	(0.9)	287	(0.8)	287	(0.8)	286	(0.7)	284	(0.9)	284	(1.2)
Illinois[4]	261	(1.7)	—	(†)	—	(†)	275	(1.7)	277	(1.2)	278	(1.1)	280	(1.1)	282	(1.2)	283	(1.1)	285	(1.0)	282	(1.3)	282	(1.2)
Indiana[4]	267	(1.2)	270	(1.1)	276	(1.4)	281	(1.4)	281	(1.1)	282	(1.0)	285	(1.1)	287	(0.9)	285	(1.0)	288	(1.1)	287	(1.2)	288	(1.3)
Iowa[3]	278	(1.1)	283	(1.0)	284	(1.3)	—	(†)	284	(0.8)	284	(0.9)	285	(0.9)	284	(1.0)	285	(0.9)	285	(0.9)	286	(1.2)	286	(0.9)
Kansas[4]	—	(†)	—	(†)	—	(†)	283	(1.7)	284	(1.3)	284	(1.0)	290	(1.1)	289	(1.0)	290	(0.9)	290	(1.0)	284	(1.3)	285	(1.0)
Kentucky	257	(1.2)	262	(1.1)	267	(1.1)	270	(1.3)	274	(1.2)	274	(1.2)	279	(1.1)	279	(1.1)	282	(0.9)	281	(0.9)	278	(0.9)	278	(1.0)
Louisiana	246	(1.2)	250	(1.7)	252	(1.6)	259	(1.5)	266	(1.5)	268	(1.4)	272	(1.1)	272	(1.6)	273	(1.2)	273	(0.9)	268	(1.4)	267	(1.3)
Maine[4]	—	(†)	279	(1.0)	284	(1.3)	281	(1.1)	282	(0.9)	281	(0.8)	286	(0.8)	286	(0.7)	289	(0.8)	289	(0.7)	285	(0.7)	284	(0.9)
Maryland[3]	261	(1.4)	265	(1.3)	270	(2.1)	272	(1.7)	278	(1.0)	278	(1.1)	286	(1.2)	288	(1.1)	288	(1.2)	287	(1.1)	283	(1.2)	281	(1.1)
Massachusetts	—	(†)	273	(1.0)	278	(1.7)	279	(1.5)	287	(0.9)	292	(0.9)	298	(1.3)	299	(1.3)	299	(0.8)	301	(0.9)	297	(1.4)	297	(1.1)
Michigan[3,4]	264	(1.2)	267	(1.4)	277	(1.8)	277	(1.9)	276	(2.0)	277	(1.5)	277	(1.4)	278	(1.6)	280	(1.4)	280	(1.3)	278	(1.3)	280	(1.2)
Minnesota[4]	275	(0.9)	282	(1.0)	284	(1.3)	287	(1.4)	291	(1.1)	290	(1.2)	292	(1.0)	294	(1.0)	295	(1.0)	295	(1.0)	294	(1.0)	294	(1.5)
Mississippi	—	(†)	246	(1.2)	250	(1.2)	254	(1.1)	261	(1.1)	262	(1.2)	265	(0.8)	265	(1.2)	269	(1.4)	271	(0.9)	271	(1.1)	271	(0.9)
Missouri	—	(†)	271	(1.2)	273	(1.4)	271	(1.5)	279	(1.1)	276	(1.3)	281	(1.0)	286	(1.0)	282	(1.1)	283	(1.0)	281	(1.2)	281	(1.1)
Montana[3,4]	280	(0.9)	—	(†)	283	(1.3)	285	(1.4)	286	(0.8)	286	(0.7)	287	(0.7)	292	(0.9)	293	(0.6)	289	(0.9)	287	(0.8)	286	(0.8)
Nebraska	276	(1.0)	278	(1.1)	283	(1.0)	280	(1.2)	282	(0.9)	284	(1.0)	284	(1.0)	284	(1.1)	283	(0.8)	285	(0.9)	286	(0.8)	288	(1.0)
Nevada	—	(†)	—	(†)	‡	(†)	265	(0.8)	268	(0.8)	270	(0.8)	271	(0.8)	274	(0.7)	278	(0.8)	278	(0.7)	275	(0.7)	275	(0.7)
New Hampshire	273	(0.9)	278	(1.0)	‡	(†)	—	(†)	286	(0.8)	285	(0.8)	288	(0.7)	292	(0.9)	292	(0.7)	296	(0.8)	294	(0.9)	293	(0.8)
New Jersey	270	(1.1)	272	(1.6)	‡	(†)	—	(†)	281	(1.1)	284	(1.4)	289	(1.2)	293	(1.4)	294	(1.2)	296	(1.1)	293	(1.2)	292	(1.0)
New Mexico	256	(0.7)	260	(0.9)	262	(1.2)	259	(1.3)	263	(1.0)	263	(0.9)	268	(0.9)	270	(1.1)	274	(0.8)	273	(0.7)	271	(1.0)	269	(1.0)
New York[3,4]	261	(1.4)	266	(2.1)	270	(1.7)	271	(2.2)	280	(1.1)	280	(0.9)	280	(1.2)	283	(1.2)	280	(0.9)	282	(0.9)	280	(1.4)	282	(1.2)
North Carolina	250	(1.1)	258	(1.2)	268	(1.4)	276	(1.3)	281	(1.0)	282	(0.9)	284	(1.1)	284	(1.3)	286	(1.0)	286	(1.1)	281	(1.6)	282	(1.2)
North Dakota	281	(1.2)	283	(1.1)	284	(0.9)	282	(1.1)	287	(0.8)	287	(0.6)	292	(0.7)	293	(0.7)	292	(0.6)	291	(0.5)	288	(0.7)	288	(0.8)
Ohio	264	(1.0)	268	(1.5)	—	(†)	281	(1.6)	282	(1.3)	283	(1.1)	285	(1.2)	286	(1.0)	289	(1.0)	290	(1.1)	285	(1.6)	288	(2.0)
Oklahoma	263	(1.3)	268	(1.1)	—	(†)	270	(1.3)	272	(1.1)	271	(1.0)	275	(0.9)	276	(1.0)	279	(1.0)	276	(1.0)	275	(1.3)	275	(1.1)
Oregon[4]	271	(1.0)	—	(†)	276	(1.5)	280	(1.5)	281	(1.3)	282	(1.0)	284	(1.1)	285	(1.0)	283	(1.0)	284	(1.1)	283	(1.2)	282	(1.2)
Pennsylvania	266	(1.6)	271	(1.5)	—	(†)	—	(†)	279	(1.1)	281	(1.5)	286	(1.1)	288	(1.3)	286	(1.2)	290	(1.0)	284	(1.5)	286	(1.2)
Rhode Island	260	(0.6)	266	(0.7)	269	(0.9)	269	(1.3)	272	(0.7)	272	(0.8)	275	(0.7)	278	(0.8)	283	(0.5)	284	(0.6)	281	(0.7)	277	(0.8)
South Carolina[3]	—	(†)	261	(1.0)	261	(1.5)	265	(1.5)	277	(1.3)	281	(0.9)	282	(1.0)	280	(1.3)	281	(1.1)	280	(1.1)	276	(1.3)	275	(1.0)
South Dakota	—	(†)	—	(†)	—	(†)	—	(†)	285	(0.8)	287	(0.6)	288	(0.8)	291	(0.5)	291	(0.5)	287	(0.7)	285	(0.9)	286	(0.7)
Tennessee	—	(†)	259	(1.4)	263	(1.4)	262	(1.5)	268	(1.8)	271	(1.1)	274	(1.1)	275	(1.4)	274	(1.2)	278	(1.3)	278	(1.8)	279	(1.2)
Texas	258	(1.4)	265	(1.3)	270	(1.4)	273	(1.6)	277	(1.1)	281	(0.6)	286	(1.0)	287	(1.3)	290	(0.9)	288	(1.0)	284	(1.2)	282	(1.4)
Utah	—	(†)	274	(0.7)	277	(1.0)	274	(1.2)	281	(1.0)	279	(0.7)	281	(0.9)	284	(0.9)	283	(0.8)	284	(0.9)	286	(1.1)	287	(0.9)
Vermont[3,4]	—	(†)	—	(†)	279	(1.0)	281	(1.5)	286	(0.8)	287	(0.7)	291	(0.7)	293	(0.6)	294	(0.7)	295	(0.7)	290	(0.7)	288	(0.7)
Virginia	264	(1.5)	268	(1.2)	270	(1.6)	275	(1.3)	282	(1.3)	284	(1.1)	288	(1.1)	286	(1.1)	289	(1.1)	288	(1.2)	288	(1.2)	290	(1.5)
Washington	—	(†)	—	(†)	276	(1.3)	—	(†)	281	(0.9)	285	(1.0)	285	(1.0)	289	(1.0)	288	(1.0)	290	(1.0)	287	(1.3)	289	(1.4)
West Virginia	256	(1.0)	259	(1.0)	265	(1.0)	266	(1.2)	271	(1.2)	269	(1.0)	270	(1.0)	270	(1.0)	273	(0.7)	274	(0.9)	271	(0.9)	273	(0.9)
Wisconsin[3]	274	(1.3)	278	(1.5)	283	(1.5)	‡	(†)	284	(1.3)	285	(1.1)	286	(1.1)	288	(0.9)	289	(1.0)	289	(0.9)	289	(1.3)	288	(1.0)
Wyoming	272	(0.7)	275	(0.9)	275	(0.9)	276	(1.0)	284	(0.7)	282	(0.7)	287	(0.7)	286	(0.6)	288	(0.6)	288	(0.5)	287	(0.7)	289	(0.7)
Department of Defense dependents schools[5]	—	(†)	—	(†)	274	(0.9)	277	(1.1)	285	(0.7)	284	(0.7)	285	(0.8)	287	(0.9)	288	(0.8)	290	(0.8)	291	(0.7)	293	(0.7)

—Not available.
†Not applicable.
‡Reporting standards not met. Participation rates fell below the required standards for reporting.
[1]Accommodations were not permitted for this assessment.
[2]The 1996 data in this table do not include students who were tested with accommodations. Data for students tested with accommodations are not available at the state level for 1996.
[3]Did not meet one or more of the guidelines for school participation in 1996. Data are subject to appreciable nonresponse bias.
[4]Did not meet one or more of the guidelines for school participation in 2000. Data are subject to appreciable nonresponse bias.
[5]Prior to 2005, NAEP divided the Department of Defense (DoD) schools into two jurisdictions, domestic and overseas. In 2005, NAEP began combining the DoD domestic and overseas schools into a single jurisdiction. Data shown in this table for years prior to 2005 were recalculated for comparability.
NOTE: Scale ranges from 0 to 500. For 2000 and later years, includes public school students who were tested with accommodations; excludes only those students with disabilities (SD) and English language learners (ELL) who were unable to be tested even with accommodations. SD and ELL populations, accommodation rates, and exclusion rates vary from state to state.
SOURCE: U.S. Department of Education, National Center for Education Statistics, National Assessment of Educational Progress (NAEP), 1990, 1992, 1996, 2000, 2003, 2005, 2007, 2009, 2011, 2013, 2015, and 2017 Mathematics Assessments, retrieved March 13, 2018, from the Main NAEP Data Explorer (http://nces.ed.gov/nationsreportcard/naepdata/). (This table was prepared March 2018.)

Table 223.10. Average National Assessment of Educational Progress (NAEP) science scale score, standard deviation, and percentage of students attaining science achievement levels, by grade level, selected student and school characteristics, and percentile: 2009, 2011, and 2015

[Standard errors appear in parentheses]

Selected characteristic, percentile, and achievement level	Grade 4			Grade 8			Grade 12		
	2009	2011	2015	2009	2011	2015	2009	2011	2015
1	2	3	4	5	6	7	8	9	10
	Average science scale score[1]								
All students	**150 (0.3)**	**— (†)**	**154 (0.3)**	**150 (0.3)**	**152 (0.3)**	**154 (0.3)**	**150 (0.8)**	**— (†)**	**150 (0.6)**
Sex									
Male	151 (0.3)	— (†)	154 (0.4)	152 (0.4)	154 (0.3)	155 (0.3)	153 (0.9)	— (†)	153 (0.8)
Female	149 (0.3)	— (†)	154 (0.3)	148 (0.3)	149 (0.3)	152 (0.4)	147 (0.9)	— (†)	148 (0.7)
Gap between male and female score	1 (0.4)	— (†)	1 (0.5)	4 (0.5)	5 (0.5)	3 (0.5)	6 (1.3)	— (†)	5 (1.0)
Race/ethnicity									
White	163 (0.2)	— (†)	166 (0.3)	162 (0.2)	163 (0.2)	166 (0.3)	159 (0.7)	— (†)	160 (0.7)
Black	127 (0.4)	— (†)	133 (0.4)	126 (0.4)	129 (0.5)	132 (0.5)	125 (1.2)	— (†)	125 (1.5)
Hispanic	131 (0.5)	— (†)	139 (0.7)	132 (0.6)	137 (0.5)	140 (0.5)	134 (1.3)	— (†)	136 (1.0)
Asian/Pacific Islander	160 (1.2)	— (†)	167 (1.4)	160 (1.0)	159 (1.3)	164 (0.9)	164 (3.0)	— (†)	166 (2.3)
Asian	— (†)	— (†)	169 (1.4)	— (†)	161 (1.3)	166 (0.9)	— (†)	— (†)	167 (2.3)
Pacific Islander	— (†)	— (†)	143 (2.2)	— (†)	139 (1.9)	138 (2.5)	— (†)	— (†)	‡ (†)
American Indian/Alaska Native	135 (1.3)	— (†)	139 (1.5)	137 (1.4)	141 (1.4)	139 (1.6)	144 (3.7)	— (†)	135 (5.3)
Two or more races[2]	154 (1.1)	— (†)	158 (1.0)	151 (1.2)	156 (1.3)	159 (1.3)	151 (3.7)	— (†)	156 (2.5)
Gap between White and Black score	36 (0.4)	— (†)	33 (0.5)	36 (0.5)	35 (0.6)	34 (0.5)	34 (1.4)	— (†)	36 (1.6)
Gap between White and Hispanic score	32 (0.6)	— (†)	27 (0.7)	30 (0.6)	27 (0.6)	26 (0.6)	25 (1.5)	— (†)	24 (1.2)
English language learner (ELL) status									
ELL	114 (0.8)	— (†)	121 (1.0)	103 (1.0)	106 (1.2)	110 (1.1)	104 (2.4)	— (†)	105 (2.7)
Non-ELL	154 (0.2)	— (†)	158 (0.3)	153 (0.3)	154 (0.2)	157 (0.3)	151 (0.8)	— (†)	152 (0.5)
Gap between ELL and non-ELL score	39 (0.8)	— (†)	36 (1.0)	49 (1.0)	48 (1.3)	46 (1.2)	47 (2.6)	— (†)	47 (2.7)
Disability status[3]									
Identified as student with disability (SD)	129 (0.6)	— (†)	131 (0.6)	123 (0.5)	124 (0.6)	124 (0.6)	121 (1.8)	— (†)	124 (1.8)
Not identified as SD	153 (0.3)	— (†)	157 (0.3)	153 (0.3)	155 (0.3)	158 (0.3)	153 (0.8)	— (†)	153 (0.6)
Gap between SD and non-SD score	23 (0.7)	— (†)	26 (0.7)	31 (0.6)	31 (0.7)	34 (0.7)	31 (2.0)	— (†)	29 (1.9)
Highest education level of either parent									
Did not finish high school	— (†)	— (†)	— (†)	131 (0.6)	132 (0.7)	137 (0.7)	131 (1.4)	— (†)	131 (1.4)
Graduated high school	— (†)	— (†)	— (†)	139 (0.4)	140 (0.4)	142 (0.5)	138 (1.2)	— (†)	136 (1.2)
Some education after high school	— (†)	— (†)	— (†)	152 (0.4)	153 (0.4)	155 (0.5)	147 (0.9)	— (†)	148 (0.9)
Graduated college	— (†)	— (†)	— (†)	161 (0.4)	162 (0.3)	165 (0.3)	161 (0.7)	— (†)	162 (0.7)
Percent of students in school eligible for free or reduced-price lunch									
0–25 percent eligible (low poverty)	167 (0.4)	— (†)	172 (0.6)	165 (0.5)	167 (0.4)	170 (0.6)	163 (1.2)	— (†)	165 (1.1)
26–50 percent eligible	155 (0.5)	— (†)	161 (0.7)	154 (0.5)	157 (0.5)	161 (0.5)	148 (1.1)	— (†)	154 (1.0)
51–75 percent eligible	144 (0.5)	— (†)	151 (0.7)	141 (0.6)	146 (0.5)	150 (0.6)	136 (1.7)	— (†)	143 (1.1)
76–100 percent eligible (high poverty)	126 (0.6)	— (†)	134 (0.6)	124 (0.7)	129 (0.7)	134 (0.8)	124 (2.1)	— (†)	126 (1.7)
Gap between low- and high-poverty score	41 (0.8)	— (†)	38 (0.8)	41 (0.9)	38 (0.8)	36 (1.0)	38 (2.5)	— (†)	39 (2.0)
School locale									
City	142 (0.6)	— (†)	148 (0.6)	142 (0.6)	144 (0.6)	148 (0.6)	146 (1.8)	— (†)	145 (1.2)
Suburban	154 (0.4)	— (†)	157 (0.6)	154 (0.5)	155 (0.5)	158 (0.4)	154 (1.4)	— (†)	153 (1.0)
Town	150 (0.6)	— (†)	153 (0.8)	149 (1.0)	153 (0.7)	154 (0.7)	150 (1.2)	— (†)	150 (2.1)
Rural	155 (0.5)	— (†)	157 (0.7)	154 (0.4)	156 (0.5)	156 (0.6)	150 (1.2)	— (†)	152 (1.3)
Percentile[4]									
10th	104 (0.6)	— (†)	108 (0.6)	103 (0.6)	106 (0.5)	109 (0.6)	104 (1.2)	— (†)	103 (1.0)
25th	128 (0.4)	— (†)	132 (0.4)	128 (0.4)	131 (0.4)	133 (0.5)	126 (0.8)	— (†)	126 (0.9)
50th	153 (0.3)	— (†)	157 (0.4)	153 (0.3)	155 (0.3)	157 (0.4)	151 (1.1)	— (†)	151 (0.6)
75th	175 (0.3)	— (†)	178 (0.3)	175 (0.2)	176 (0.4)	178 (0.4)	174 (1.0)	— (†)	176 (0.6)
90th	192 (0.3)	— (†)	196 (0.4)	192 (0.3)	193 (0.4)	195 (0.3)	194 (1.0)	— (†)	196 (0.6)
	Standard deviation of the science scale score[5]								
All students	35 (0.2)	— (†)	35 (0.2)	35 (0.2)	34 (0.2)	34 (0.2)	35 (0.4)	— (†)	36 (0.4)
	Percent of students attaining science achievement levels								
Achievement level									
Below *Basic*	28 (0.3)	— (†)	24 (0.3)	37 (0.4)	35 (0.3)	32 (0.4)	40 (1.0)	— (†)	40 (0.7)
At or above *Basic*[6]	72 (0.3)	— (†)	76 (0.3)	63 (0.4)	65 (0.3)	68 (0.4)	60 (1.0)	— (†)	60 (0.7)
At or above *Proficient*[7]	34 (0.3)	— (†)	38 (0.4)	30 (0.3)	32 (0.4)	34 (0.4)	21 (0.8)	— (†)	22 (0.6)
At *Advanced*[8]	1 (0.1)	— (†)	1 (0.1)	2 (0.1)	2 (0.1)	2 (0.1)	1 (0.2)	— (†)	2 (0.2)

—Not available.
†Not applicable.
‡Reporting standards not met (too few cases for a reliable estimate).
[1]Scale ranges from 0 to 300 for all three grades, but scores cannot be compared across grades. For example, the average score of 166 for White 4th-graders in 2015 does not denote higher performance than the score of 160 for White 12th-graders.
[2]Prior to 2011, students in the "Two or more races" category were categorized as "Unclassified."
[3]The student with disability (SD) variable used in this table includes students who have a 504 plan, even if they do not have an Individualized Education Plan (IEP).
[4]The percentile represents a specific point on the percentage distribution of all students ranked by their science score from low to high. For example, 10 percent of students scored at or below the 10th percentile score, while 90 percent of students scored above it.
[5]The standard deviation provides an indication of how much the test scores varied. The lower the standard deviation, the closer the scores were clustered around the average score. About two-thirds of the student scores can be expected to fall within the range of one standard deviation above and one standard deviation below the average score. In 2015, for example, the average score for all 4th-graders was 154, and the standard deviation was 35. This means that one would expect about two-thirds of the students to have scores between 189 (one standard deviation above the average) and 119 (one standard deviation below). Standard errors also must be taken into account when making comparisons of these ranges.
[6]*Basic* denotes partial mastery of the knowledge and skills that are fundamental for proficient work.
[7]*Proficient* represents solid academic performance. Students reaching this level have demonstrated competency over challenging subject matter.
[8]*Advanced* signifies superior performance.
NOTE: In 2011, only 8th-grade students were assessed in science. Includes students tested with accommodations (7 to 14 percent of all students, depending on grade level and year); excludes only those students with disabilities and English language learners who were unable to be tested even with accommodations (1 to 3 percent of all students). Race categories exclude persons of Hispanic ethnicity.
SOURCE: U.S. Department of Education, National Center for Education Statistics, National Assessment of Educational Progress (NAEP), 2009, 2011, and 2015 Science Assessments, retrieved January 10, 2017, from the Main NAEP Data Explorer (http://nces.ed.gov/nationsreportcard/naepdata/). (This table was prepared January 2017.)

Table 224.10. Average National Assessment of Educational Progress (NAEP) music and visual arts scale scores of 8th-graders, percentage distribution by frequency of instruction at their school, and percentage participating in selected musical activities in school, by selected characteristics: 2016

[Standard errors appear in parentheses]

Selected characteristic	Average scale score[1]		Percentage distribution of students by school-reported frequency of instruction[2]										Percent of students reporting participation in musical activities in school		
			Music					Visual arts							
	Music[3]	Visual arts[4]	Subject not offered	Less than once a week	Once or twice a week	3 or 4 times a week	Every day	Subject not offered	Less than once a week	Once or twice a week	3 or 4 times a week	Every day	Play in band	Play in orchestra	Sing in chorus or choir
1	2	3	4	5	6	7	8	9	10	11	12	13	14	15	16
All students	**147 (1.0)**	**149 (0.9)**	**8 (1.7)**	**5 (1.4)**	**23 (3.0)**	**19 (3.0)**	**45 (3.4)**	**14 (3.0)**	**7 (1.8)**	**24 (3.1)**	**18 (2.9)**	**37 (3.5)**	**17 (0.8)**	**5 (0.6)**	**16 (1.0)**
Sex															
Male	140 (1.1)	142 (1.1)	7 (1.6)	5 (1.4)	24 (3.2)	19 (3.0)	45 (3.3)	14 (3.0)	7 (1.8)	24 (3.2)	18 (2.8)	37 (3.4)	18 (1.0)	5 (0.7)	8 (0.9)
Female	155 (1.1)	156 (1.0)	9 (1.9)	5 (1.3)	22 (2.8)	19 (3.1)	45 (3.5)	14 (3.0)	7 (1.8)	23 (3.1)	19 (2.9)	37 (3.7)	16 (1.2)	6 (0.7)	24 (1.3)
Race/ethnicity															
White	158 (1.2)	158 (1.1)	8 (2.2)	4 (1.6)	27 (4.2)	19 (4.2)	42 (4.2)	13 (3.9)	8 (2.6)	28 (4.2)	17 (3.5)	34 (4.4)	19 (1.3)	5 (0.9)	19 (1.5)
Black	129 (2.0)	128 (2.0)	9 (3.8)	10 (3.7)	21 (4.2)	16 (4.2)	43 (5.0)	20 (5.5)	7 (2.9)	17 (3.7)	19 (4.5)	37 (4.9)	12 (1.6)	4 (1.0)	16 (1.5)
Hispanic	135 (1.2)	139 (1.3)	9 (2.5)	4 (1.6)	17 (3.0)	17 (3.3)	53 (3.8)	15 (3.5)	5 (1.7)	18 (3.1)	17 (3.3)	44 (3.9)	15 (1.2)	5 (0.8)	10 (1.1)
Asian	163 (2.5)	167 (2.6)	2 (1.2)	4 (2.4)	22 (5.4)	34 (6.2)	38 (6.2)	4 (1.7)	6 (2.5)	26 (5.6)	32 (5.8)	32 (5.5)	17 (2.5)	15 (2.5)	13 (2.3)
Pacific Islander	‡ (†)	‡ (†)	‡ (†)	‡ (†)	‡ (†)	‡ (†)	‡ (†)	‡ (†)	‡ (†)	‡ (†)	‡ (†)	‡ (†)	‡ (†)	‡ (†)	‡ (†)
American Indian/Alaska Native	‡ (†)	‡ (†)	‡ (†)	‡ (†)	‡ (†)	‡ (†)	‡ (†)	‡ (†)	‡ (†)	‡ (†)	‡ (†)	‡ (†)	‡ (†)	‡ (†)	‡ (†)
Two or more races	149 (3.3)	155 (4.5)	4 (2.1)	6 (2.2)	14 (3.0)	20 (4.4)	56 (5.9)	9 (3.2)	3 (1.9)	26 (4.8)	25 (7.0)	37 (6.6)	21 (4.1)	3 (1.9)	24 (3.6)
Free or reduced-price lunch eligibility															
Eligible	134 (1.1)	137 (1.2)	9 (2.1)	5 (1.7)	20 (3.3)	17 (3.2)	48 (4.0)	18 (3.8)	5 (1.6)	18 (3.4)	17 (3.1)	42 (4.5)	15 (1.0)	4 (0.7)	14 (1.2)
Not eligible	160 (1.1)	159 (1.2)	6 (1.8)	4 (1.7)	22 (3.5)	22 (4.3)	47 (4.2)	12 (3.9)	9 (2.8)	24 (4.0)	20 (3.9)	36 (3.8)	19 (1.4)	7 (1.1)	18 (1.5)
Unknown	157 (3.1)	161 (3.7)	13 (8.0)	8 (†)	49 (11.1)	12 (6.3)	17 (7.9)	2 (†)	12 (7.0)	57 (10.0)	16 (7.3)	12 (7.8)	16 (2.7)	4 (0.9)	18 (3.4)
Control of school															
Public	146 (1.0)	148 (0.9)	8 (1.7)	5 (1.4)	20 (3.1)	20 (3.2)	48 (3.6)	15 (3.2)	6 (1.9)	21 (3.4)	19 (3.0)	39 (3.7)	17 (0.9)	6 (0.7)	15 (1.0)
Private	160 (2.6)	164 (3.2)	14 (8.5)	8 (†)	59 (10.8)	8 (4.5)	10 (†)	5 (†)	17 (8.2)	61 (10.2)	11 (5.8)	6 (1.3)	16 (2.9)	3 (0.8)	23 (4.3)
School location															
City	140 (1.9)	145 (1.8)	7 (2.8)	6 (2.8)	25 (4.4)	18 (4.7)	43 (5.1)	13 (3.6)	2 (1.7)	29 (4.1)	19 (4.6)	36 (4.6)	13 (1.1)	6 (0.9)	14 (1.4)
Suburban	153 (1.5)	152 (1.6)	4 (1.7)	3 (1.7)	26 (4.2)	18 (4.2)	49 (5.1)	11 (2.0)	9 (2.9)	21 (3.9)	21 (4.8)	38 (5.3)	16 (1.3)	7 (1.1)	16 (1.3)
Town	143 (4.4)	147 (3.6)	25 (11.3)	4 (0.7)	8 (1.8)	31 (12.1)	32 (9.2)	26 (12.9)	8 (5.2)	19 (9.4)	12 (7.8)	34 (9.0)	22 (5.2)	1 (0.4)	19 (4.2)
Rural	149 (2.1)	148 (2.0)	14 (5.7)	7 (3.6)	18 (4.8)	18 (6.7)	43 (7.6)	17 (8.5)	9 (5.6)	24 (7.8)	13 (5.7)	37 (8.3)	21 (2.0)	2 (0.8)	19 (2.8)
Region															
Northeast	152 (2.3)	160 (1.4)	3 (0.4)	9 (5.4)	61 (11.2)	25 (8.3)	2 (1.1)	8 (1.0)	11 (5.9)	54 (8.8)	22 (6.1)	4 (†)	17 (1.8)	8 (2.8)	24 (2.7)
Midwest	152 (2.2)	148 (2.2)	9 (4.3)	4 (†)	23 (5.1)	27 (8.9)	37 (9.4)	11 (3.6)	11 (5.2)	31 (7.9)	19 (6.3)	29 (8.8)	20 (2.5)	6 (1.3)	20 (3.7)
South	146 (1.6)	146 (1.7)	10 (3.6)	6 (1.9)	15 (4.4)	11 (3.5)	58 (5.8)	16 (6.6)	6 (2.7)	14 (5.2)	12 (4.0)	52 (6.1)	17 (1.3)	5 (0.5)	14 (0.9)
West	143 (1.6)	148 (1.4)	7 (2.3)	2 (0.1)	11 (3.4)	23 (5.2)	57 (5.1)	17 (5.1)	3 (†)	12 (3.0)	27 (6.3)	42 (5.5)	14 (1.2)	5 (0.8)	11 (1.4)
Frequency of instruction[2,5]															
Subject not offered	133 (3.3)	139 (2.6)	† (†)	† (†)	† (†)	† (†)	† (†)	† (†)	† (†)	† (†)	† (†)	† (†)	13 (2.9)	# (†)	13 (3.4)
Less than once a week	145 (5.9)	153 (5.5)	† (†)	† (†)	† (†)	† (†)	† (†)	† (†)	† (†)	† (†)	† (†)	† (†)	14 (2.7)	3 (1.2)	19 (5.0)
Once or twice a week	151 (2.1)	155 (2.5)	† (†)	† (†)	† (†)	† (†)	† (†)	† (†)	† (†)	† (†)	† (†)	† (†)	18 (1.7)	6 (1.7)	20 (2.2)
3 or 4 times a week	152 (3.4)	150 (2.5)	† (†)	† (†)	† (†)	† (†)	† (†)	† (†)	† (†)	† (†)	† (†)	† (†)	18 (3.0)	8 (1.3)	16 (2.0)
Every day	147 (1.7)	149 (1.7)	† (†)	† (†)	† (†)	† (†)	† (†)	† (†)	† (†)	† (†)	† (†)	† (†)	17 (1.2)	5 (0.6)	14 (1.1)

†Not applicable.
#Rounds to zero.
‡Reporting standards not met (too few cases for a reliable estimate).
[1]Scale ranges from 0 to 300 for both music and visual arts.
[2]Based on principals' responses to the following question: "How often does a typical eighth-grade student in your school receive instruction in each of the following subjects?"
[3]Students were asked to analyze, interpret, or critique a piece of music that they listened to or to describe the social, historical, or cultural context of a piece of music.
[4]Students were asked to analyze, describe, or judge works of art and design to show understanding of form, aesthetics, and cultural or historical context.
[5]For columns 2, 14, 15, and 16, refers to music instruction. For column 3, refers to visual arts instruction.

NOTE: Includes students tested with accommodations (10 percent of all 8th-graders for visual arts and 11 percent for music); excludes only those students with disabilities and English language learners who were unable to be tested even with accommodations (2 percent of all 8th-graders both for visual arts and for music). Detail may not sum to totals because of rounding. Race categories exclude persons of Hispanic ethnicity.

SOURCE: U.S. Department of Education, National Center for Education Statistics, National Assessment of Educational Progress (NAEP), 2016 Arts Assessment, retrieved May 11, 2017, from the Main NAEP Data Explorer (http://nces.ed.gov/nationsreportcard/naepdata/). (This table was prepared May 2017.)

Table 224.70. Average National Assessment of Educational Progress (NAEP) technology and engineering literacy (TEL) overall and content area scale scores of 8th-graders and percentage of 8th-graders attaining TEL achievement levels, by selected student and school characteristics: 2018

[Standard errors appear in parentheses]

Selected student or school characteristic	Average scale score[1]								Percent attaining TEL achievement levels[2]											
			Content area								At or above *Basic*[3]									
															At or above *Proficient*[4]					
	Overall TEL score		Technology and society		Design and systems		Information and communication technology		Below *Basic*[3]		Total at or above *Basic*[3]		At *Basic*[3]		Total at or above *Proficient*[4]		At *Proficient*[4]		At *Advanced*[5]	
1	2		3		4		5		6		7		8		9		10		11	
All students	**152**	**(0.6)**	**152**	**(0.7)**	**153**	**(0.8)**	**153**	**(0.7)**	**16**	**(0.6)**	**84**	**(0.6)**	**38**	**(0.7)**	**46**	**(0.8)**	**42**	**(0.7)**	**5**	**(0.3)**
Sex																				
Male	150	(0.7)	151	(0.7)	152	(0.9)	149	(0.7)	18	(0.7)	82	(0.7)	38	(0.8)	44	(0.9)	40	(0.9)	4	(0.4)
Female	155	(0.8)	154	(0.8)	154	(0.9)	156	(0.9)	14	(0.6)	86	(0.6)	37	(0.8)	49	(1.0)	44	(1.0)	5	(0.4)
Race/ethnicity																				
White	163	(0.7)	163	(0.7)	164	(1.0)	162	(0.8)	8	(0.6)	92	(0.6)	33	(0.9)	59	(1.0)	52	(1.0)	7	(0.5)
Black	132	(1.1)	132	(1.1)	131	(1.3)	133	(1.3)	32	(1.4)	68	(1.4)	44	(1.4)	23	(1.3)	23	(1.2)	1	(0.3)
Hispanic	139	(0.8)	139	(0.9)	141	(1.0)	140	(0.9)	24	(0.9)	76	(0.9)	45	(1.0)	31	(1.0)	29	(1.0)	2	(0.3)
Asian	169	(2.0)	167	(2.4)	168	(2.4)	172	(2.7)	8	(1.0)	92	(1.0)	25	(2.7)	66	(2.8)	53	(2.4)	13	(1.4)
Pacific Islander	‡	(†)	‡	(†)	‡	(†)	‡	(†)	‡	(†)	‡	(†)	‡	(†)	‡	(†)	‡	(†)	‡	(†)
American Indian/Alaska Native	133	(6.2)	135	(6.4)	135	(5.7)	131	(5.0)	33	(6.6)	67	(6.6)	38	(4.2)	29	(5.8)	27	(5.6)	2	(†)
Two or more races	157	(1.9)	157	(2.2)	156	(2.7)	157	(2.0)	13	(1.9)	87	(1.9)	34	(2.9)	53	(3.2)	48	(3.3)	5	(1.2)
English language learner (ELL) status																				
ELL	106	(1.3)	109	(1.4)	106	(1.8)	106	(1.5)	61	(2.1)	39	(2.1)	34	(2.1)	5	(0.9)	5	(0.9)	#	(†)
Non-ELL	155	(0.6)	155	(0.7)	156	(0.8)	156	(0.7)	13	(0.6)	87	(0.6)	38	(0.7)	49	(0.8)	44	(0.7)	5	(0.3)
Disability status[6]																				
Identified as student with a disability (SD)	118	(1.1)	120	(1.1)	120	(1.4)	117	(1.3)	48	(1.4)	52	(1.4)	39	(1.5)	13	(1.2)	13	(1.1)	1	(0.2)
Not identified as SD	157	(0.6)	157	(0.6)	158	(0.8)	158	(0.7)	11	(0.5)	89	(0.5)	37	(0.7)	51	(0.8)	46	(0.7)	5	(0.3)
Access to desktop or laptop computer at home																				
Yes	156	(0.6)	155	(0.6)	156	(0.8)	156	(0.7)	13	(0.5)	87	(0.5)	37	(0.7)	50	(0.8)	44	(0.7)	5	(0.3)
No	134	(1.1)	134	(1.1)	134	(1.4)	134	(1.0)	31	(1.5)	69	(1.5)	43	(1.5)	26	(1.4)	25	(1.4)	1	(0.4)
Access to Internet at home																				
Yes	153	(0.7)	153	(0.6)	154	(0.8)	154	(0.7)	15	(0.6)	85	(0.6)	37	(0.7)	47	(0.8)	42	(0.7)	5	(0.3)
No	127	(2.0)	128	(2.2)	129	(2.9)	126	(2.2)	38	(3.0)	62	(3.0)	41	(3.4)	21	(2.8)	21	(2.9)	1	(†)
Highest education level of either parent[7]																				
Did not finish high school	138	(1.3)	138	(1.3)	138	(1.5)	140	(1.5)	24	(1.9)	76	(1.9)	47	(2.3)	29	(1.9)	28	(1.9)	1	(0.4)
Graduated high school	138	(1.0)	138	(1.0)	139	(1.3)	138	(1.0)	26	(1.4)	74	(1.4)	45	(1.6)	29	(1.2)	28	(1.2)	1	(0.4)
Some education after high school	151	(1.1)	151	(1.2)	152	(1.5)	152	(1.2)	14	(0.9)	86	(0.9)	42	(1.4)	44	(1.7)	41	(1.6)	3	(0.7)
Graduated college	163	(0.7)	163	(0.7)	163	(1.0)	163	(0.8)	9	(0.5)	91	(0.5)	32	(0.8)	59	(0.9)	51	(0.9)	7	(0.5)
Percent of students in school eligible for free or reduced-price lunch[8]																				
0 to 25 percent eligible	170	(1.4)	169	(1.8)	169	(1.8)	170	(1.7)	6	(0.8)	94	(0.8)	27	(1.7)	67	(2.0)	57	(1.8)	10	(1.2)
26 to 50 percent eligible	157	(1.3)	157	(1.5)	159	(1.7)	157	(1.4)	12	(0.9)	88	(0.9)	37	(1.4)	51	(1.9)	46	(1.5)	5	(0.7)
51 to 75 percent eligible	148	(1.0)	148	(0.9)	148	(1.2)	148	(1.1)	17	(1.1)	83	(1.1)	42	(1.3)	41	(1.5)	39	(1.4)	2	(0.4)
76 to 100 percent eligible	134	(1.2)	135	(1.3)	134	(1.5)	135	(1.4)	30	(1.4)	70	(1.4)	45	(1.2)	26	(1.2)	25	(1.1)	1	(0.3)
School control[9]																				
Public	151	(0.7)	151	(0.7)	151	(0.8)	151	(0.7)	17	(0.6)	83	(0.6)	38	(0.7)	45	(0.9)	40	(0.8)	4	(0.3)
Private	‡	(†)	‡	(†)	‡	(†)	‡	(†)	‡	(†)	‡	(†)	‡	(†)	‡	(†)	‡	(†)	‡	(†)
School locale																				
City	147	(1.4)	148	(1.3)	148	(1.6)	148	(1.5)	21	(1.2)	79	(1.2)	38	(1.2)	42	(1.8)	37	(1.5)	4	(0.5)
Suburb	156	(0.8)	156	(1.0)	156	(0.9)	157	(0.9)	13	(0.7)	87	(0.7)	36	(1.0)	51	(1.2)	45	(1.1)	6	(0.5)
Town	153	(2.6)	153	(2.3)	156	(2.8)	153	(2.6)	14	(2.4)	86	(2.4)	41	(1.8)	46	(3.1)	42	(2.4)	4	(1.1)
Rural	152	(1.7)	153	(2.0)	153	(2.5)	152	(1.8)	15	(1.2)	85	(1.2)	40	(1.5)	45	(2.1)	41	(1.7)	4	(0.8)

†Not applicable.
#Rounds to zero.
‡Reporting standards not met (too few cases for a reliable estimate) or the standard error could not be accurately determined.
[1]Scale ranges from 0 to 300.
[2]TEL achievement levels are for performance on the TEL assessment overall, rather than performance on any specific content area.
[3]*Basic* denotes partial mastery of the knowledge and skills that are fundamental for proficient work at a given grade.
[4]*Proficient* represents solid academic performance. Students reaching this level have demonstrated competency over challenging subject matter.
[5]*Advanced* signifies superior performance.
[6]In addition to students with an Individualized Education Program (IEP), also includes students with a 504 plan.
[7]These data are based on students' responses to questions about their parents' education level. Data for students whose parents have an unknown level of education are included in table totals, but not shown separately.
[8]Nonresponse rate for this item was greater than 15 percent but not greater than 50 percent.
[9]Bureau of Indian Education and Department of Defense schools are excluded from the Public category but included elsewhere in this table. The Private category includes Catholic and Other private schools.
NOTE: Includes students tested with accommodations (11 percent of all 8th-graders); excludes only those students with disabilities and English language learners who were unable to be tested even with accommodations (2 percent of all 8th-graders). Race categories exclude persons of Hispanic ethnicity. Detail may not sum to totals because of rounding.
SOURCE: U.S. Department of Education, National Center for Education Statistics, National Assessment of Educational Progress (NAEP), 2018 Technology and Engineering Literacy (TEL) Assessment, retrieved February 12, 2019, from the Main NAEP Data Explorer (http://nces.ed.gov/nationsreportcard/naepdata/). (This table was prepared February 2019.)

Table 225.10. Average number of Carnegie units earned by public high school graduates in various subject fields, by sex and race/ethnicity: Selected years, 1982 through 2009

[Standard errors appear in parentheses]

Graduation year, sex, and race/ethnicity	Total	English	History/ social studies	Mathematics	Science					Foreign languages	Arts	Career/ technical (occupational) education[1]	Labor market, family, and consumer education[2]	Personal use[3]
					Total	Biology	Chemistry	Physics	Other science[4]					
1	2	3	4	5	6	7	8	9	10	11	12	13	14	15
1982 graduates	**21.58 (0.090)**	**3.93 (0.022)**	**3.16 (0.028)**	**2.63 (0.022)**	**2.20 (0.025)**	**0.94 (0.014)**	**0.34 (0.010)**	**0.17 (0.008)**	**0.73 (0.016)**	**0.99 (0.029)**	**1.47 (0.035)**	**— (†)**	**— (†)**	**2.58 (0.048)**
Sex														
Male	21.40 (0.108)	3.88 (0.026)	3.16 (0.034)	2.71 (0.030)	2.27 (0.031)	0.91 (0.016)	0.36 (0.014)	0.23 (0.012)	0.76 (0.018)	0.80 (0.030)	1.29 (0.044)	— (†)	— (†)	2.69 (0.056)
Female	21.75 (0.101)	3.98 (0.026)	3.15 (0.029)	2.57 (0.024)	2.13 (0.029)	0.97 (0.017)	0.33 (0.013)	0.12 (0.008)	0.71 (0.017)	1.17 (0.036)	1.63 (0.044)	— (†)	— (†)	2.48 (0.049)
Race/ethnicity														
White	21.69 (0.107)	3.90 (0.025)	3.19 (0.032)	2.68 (0.026)	2.27 (0.029)	0.97 (0.015)	0.38 (0.013)	0.20 (0.010)	0.73 (0.017)	1.06 (0.033)	1.53 (0.042)	— (†)	— (†)	2.52 (0.052)
Black	21.15 (0.169)	4.08 (0.050)	3.08 (0.054)	2.61 (0.043)	2.06 (0.049)	0.90 (0.033)	0.26 (0.023)	0.09 (0.011)	0.81 (0.033)	0.72 (0.067)	1.26 (0.063)	— (†)	— (†)	2.60 (0.094)
Hispanic	21.23 (0.122)	3.94 (0.037)	3.00 (0.037)	2.33 (0.040)	1.80 (0.038)	0.81 (0.025)	0.16 (0.012)	0.07 (0.007)	0.75 (0.026)	0.77 (0.042)	1.29 (0.054)	— (†)	— (†)	2.87 (0.081)
Asian/Pacific Islander	22.46 (0.216)	4.01 (0.091)	3.16 (0.094)	3.15 (0.095)	2.64 (0.125)	1.11 (0.048)	0.61 (0.046)	0.42 (0.048)	0.51 (0.061)	1.79 (0.105)	1.31 (0.124)	— (†)	— (†)	3.05 (0.146)
American Indian/ Alaska Native	21.45 (0.330)	3.98 (0.114)	3.25 (0.207)	2.35 (0.129)	2.04 (0.090)	0.84 (0.124)	0.42 (0.087)	0.12! (0.039)	0.67 (0.087)	0.48 (0.117)	1.72 (0.338)	— (†)	— (†)	2.84 (0.128)
1987 graduates	**23.00 (0.157)**	**4.12 (0.022)**	**3.32 (0.037)**	**3.01 (0.029)**	**2.55 (0.046)**	**1.10 (0.020)**	**0.47 (0.015)**	**0.21 (0.011)**	**0.76 (0.033)**	**1.35 (0.049)**	**1.44 (0.044)**	**— (†)**	**— (†)**	**2.67 (0.073)**
Sex														
Male	22.88 (0.162)	4.08 (0.021)	3.29 (0.037)	3.05 (0.029)	2.59 (0.049)	1.05 (0.021)	0.47 (0.016)	0.26 (0.013)	0.79 (0.032)	1.16 (0.051)	1.24 (0.046)	— (†)	— (†)	2.83 (0.081)
Female	23.12 (0.156)	4.15 (0.026)	3.35 (0.041)	2.96 (0.030)	2.52 (0.048)	1.14 (0.022)	0.47 (0.017)	0.17 (0.012)	0.74 (0.035)	1.53 (0.051)	1.63 (0.050)	— (†)	— (†)	2.51 (0.069)
Race/ethnicity														
White	23.11 (0.189)	4.08 (0.028)	3.29 (0.045)	3.01 (0.034)	2.61 (0.058)	1.12 (0.025)	0.50 (0.020)	0.23 (0.012)	0.75 (0.040)	1.38 (0.055)	1.50 (0.055)	— (†)	— (†)	2.60 (0.082)
Black	22.40 (0.251)	4.22 (0.038)	3.34 (0.073)	2.99 (0.060)	2.33 (0.060)	1.01 (0.036)	0.31 (0.021)	0.10 (0.012)	0.90 (0.051)	1.08 (0.094)	1.20 (0.064)	— (†)	— (†)	2.73 (0.120)
Hispanic	22.84 (0.162)	4.30 (0.055)	3.22 (0.061)	2.81 (0.056)	2.24 (0.045)	1.07 (0.028)	0.29 (0.015)	0.10 (0.013)	0.78 (0.028)	1.25 (0.071)	1.34 (0.056)	— (†)	— (†)	3.19 (0.096)
Asian/Pacific Islander	24.47 (0.332)	4.37 (0.076)	3.65 (0.163)	3.71 (0.094)	3.14 (0.116)	1.17 (0.027)	0.87 (0.069)	0.50 (0.045)	0.59 (0.048)	2.07 (0.105)	1.18 (0.077)	— (†)	— (†)	3.23 (0.185)
American Indian/ Alaska Native	23.23 (0.153)	4.22 (0.033)	3.18 (0.044)	2.98 (0.113)	2.44 (0.104)	1.22 (0.073)	0.32 (0.035)	0.09! (0.027)	0.81 (0.041)	0.75 (0.138)	1.68 (0.112)	— (†)	— (†)	3.06 (0.050)
1990 graduates	**23.53 (0.127)**	**4.19 (0.034)**	**3.47 (0.040)**	**3.15 (0.028)**	**2.75 (0.028)**	**1.14 (0.019)**	**0.53 (0.014)**	**0.23 (0.010)**	**0.85 (0.026)**	**1.54 (0.041)**	**1.55 (0.045)**	**— (†)**	**— (†)**	**2.68 (0.073)**
Sex														
Male	23.35 (0.130)	4.13 (0.035)	3.45 (0.041)	3.16 (0.028)	2.78 (0.033)	1.11 (0.021)	0.52 (0.017)	0.28 (0.012)	0.88 (0.027)	1.33 (0.040)	1.31 (0.047)	— (†)	— (†)	2.87 (0.077)
Female	23.69 (0.132)	4.25 (0.036)	3.50 (0.041)	3.14 (0.033)	2.73 (0.027)	1.17 (0.019)	0.53 (0.014)	0.19 (0.010)	0.83 (0.027)	1.72 (0.045)	1.76 (0.050)	— (†)	— (†)	2.51 (0.072)
Race/ethnicity														
White	23.54 (0.133)	4.12 (0.036)	3.46 (0.045)	3.13 (0.032)	2.80 (0.033)	1.15 (0.020)	0.55 (0.016)	0.25 (0.011)	0.84 (0.022)	1.58 (0.049)	1.61 (0.056)	— (†)	— (†)	2.61 (0.076)
Black	23.40 (0.255)	4.34 (0.044)	3.49 (0.058)	3.20 (0.064)	2.68 (0.061)	1.11 (0.042)	0.42 (0.024)	0.16 (0.020)	0.98 (0.068)	1.20 (0.075)	1.34 (0.052)	— (†)	— (†)	2.74 (0.124)
Hispanic	23.83 (0.210)	4.51 (0.139)	3.42 (0.071)	3.13 (0.058)	2.50 (0.046)	1.10 (0.034)	0.42 (0.034)	0.14 (0.016)	0.83 (0.041)	1.57 (0.060)	1.48 (0.072)	— (†)	— (†)	3.10 (0.103)
Asian/Pacific Islander	24.07 (0.236)	4.50 (0.117)	3.70 (0.126)	3.52 (0.060)	2.97 (0.114)	1.12 (0.085)	0.74 (0.057)	0.42 (0.047)	0.68 (0.080)	2.06 (0.150)	1.29 (0.084)	— (†)	— (†)	2.96 (0.221)
American Indian/ Alaska Native	22.64 (0.267)	4.08 (0.092)	3.34 (0.083)	3.04 (0.152)	2.48 (0.175)	1.09 (0.090)	0.42 (0.072)	0.15 (0.039)	0.83 (0.090)	1.15 (0.188)	1.11 (0.126)	— (†)	— (†)	2.81 (0.148)
1994 graduates	**24.17 (0.144)**	**4.29 (0.028)**	**3.55 (0.041)**	**3.33 (0.021)**	**3.04 (0.028)**	**1.26 (0.018)**	**0.62 (0.013)**	**0.28 (0.011)**	**0.88 (0.024)**	**1.71 (0.033)**	**1.66 (0.041)**	**— (†)**	**— (†)**	**2.63 (0.077)**
Sex														
Male	23.79 (0.146)	4.26 (0.028)	3.51 (0.041)	3.32 (0.022)	3.03 (0.030)	1.20 (0.020)	0.59 (0.015)	0.32 (0.014)	0.91 (0.026)	1.49 (0.034)	1.43 (0.038)	— (†)	— (†)	2.83 (0.081)
Female	24.11 (0.147)	4.32 (0.030)	3.59 (0.041)	3.34 (0.023)	3.06 (0.028)	1.31 (0.018)	0.64 (0.014)	0.24 (0.010)	0.86 (0.024)	1.93 (0.034)	1.87 (0.051)	— (†)	— (†)	2.44 (0.078)
Race/ethnicity														
White	24.08 (0.183)	4.23 (0.035)	3.56 (0.049)	3.36 (0.023)	3.13 (0.032)	1.29 (0.022)	0.65 (0.014)	0.30 (0.014)	0.89 (0.030)	1.76 (0.039)	1.74 (0.049)	— (†)	— (†)	2.61 (0.096)
Black	23.28 (0.132)	4.36 (0.034)	3.51 (0.039)	3.23 (0.030)	2.80 (0.042)	1.21 (0.036)	0.49 (0.028)	0.17 (0.013)	0.92 (0.051)	1.35 (0.052)	1.36 (0.066)	— (†)	— (†)	2.69 (0.101)
Hispanic	23.71 (0.131)	4.61 (0.075)	3.45 (0.046)	3.28 (0.041)	2.69 (0.046)	1.19 (0.027)	0.49 (0.047)	0.17 (0.021)	0.83 (0.058)	1.73 (0.062)	1.51 (0.046)	— (†)	— (†)	2.93 (0.086)
Asian/Pacific Islander	23.84 (0.256)	4.60 (0.091)	3.66 (0.097)	3.66 (0.082)	3.35 (0.131)	1.22 (0.042)	0.81 (0.062)	0.48 (0.058)	0.80 (0.034)	2.09 (0.085)	1.32 (0.121)	— (†)	— (†)	2.78 (0.123)
American Indian/ Alaska Native	23.40 (0.541)	4.27 (0.113)	3.57 (0.201)	3.11 (0.038)	2.82 (0.073)	1.28 (0.069)	0.50 (0.065)	0.13 (0.039)	0.91 (0.057)	1.30 (0.150)	2.01 (0.351)	— (†)	— (†)	3.12 (0.355)
1998 graduates	**25.14 (0.162)**	**4.25 (0.037)**	**3.74 (0.038)**	**3.40 (0.024)**	**3.12 (0.026)**	**1.26 (0.021)**	**0.66 (0.015)**	**0.31 (0.015)**	**0.89 (0.024)**	**1.85 (0.039)**	**1.90 (0.079)**	**— (†)**	**— (†)**	**2.89 (0.076)**
Sex														
Male	24.64 (0.162)	4.19 (0.038)	3.68 (0.040)	3.37 (0.024)	3.09 (0.028)	1.20 (0.021)	0.62 (0.014)	0.33 (0.018)	0.93 (0.026)	1.62 (0.040)	1.61 (0.072)	— (†)	— (†)	3.12 (0.079)
Female	25.04 (0.166)	4.31 (0.039)	3.80 (0.036)	3.42 (0.025)	3.17 (0.029)	1.32 (0.023)	0.70 (0.018)	0.28 (0.015)	0.87 (0.023)	2.06 (0.041)	2.15 (0.094)	— (†)	— (†)	2.67 (0.080)
Race/ethnicity														
White	24.87 (0.178)	4.19 (0.049)	3.77 (0.046)	3.40 (0.028)	3.18 (0.028)	1.28 (0.025)	0.69 (0.017)	0.33 (0.019)	0.87 (0.027)	1.90 (0.049)	2.00 (0.078)	— (†)	— (†)	2.80 (0.088)
Black	24.37 (0.250)	4.28 (0.045)	3.69 (0.050)	3.42 (0.042)	3.03 (0.064)	1.24 (0.038)	0.58 (0.025)	0.22 (0.022)	0.97 (0.045)	1.58 (0.062)	1.57 (0.152)	— (†)	— (†)	2.94 (0.080)
Hispanic	24.69 (0.218)	4.51 (0.055)	3.60 (0.051)	3.28 (0.041)	2.81 (0.054)	1.13 (0.026)	0.50 (0.036)	0.20 (0.020)	0.97 (0.042)	1.78 (0.055)	1.78 (0.113)	— (†)	— (†)	3.36 (0.121)
Asian/Pacific Islander	24.67 (0.195)	4.37 (0.068)	3.92 (0.086)	3.62 (0.029)	3.43 (0.079)	1.26 (0.027)	0.83 (0.037)	0.51 (0.036)	0.81 (0.041)	2.29 (0.129)	1.52 (0.056)	— (†)	— (†)	2.95 (0.208)
American Indian/ Alaska Native	23.81 (0.350)	4.18 (0.082)	3.67 (0.093)	3.10 (0.081)	2.68 (0.081)	1.07 (0.056)	0.49 (0.038)	0.15 (0.024)	0.98 (0.070)	1.45 (0.132)	1.94 (0.146)	— (†)	— (†)	3.40 (0.212)

See notes at end of table.

Table 225.10. Average number of Carnegie units earned by public high school graduates in various subject fields, by sex and race/ethnicity: Selected years, 1982 through 2009—Continued

[Standard errors appear in parentheses]

Graduation year, sex, and race/ethnicity	Total	English	History/ social studies	Mathematics	Science					Foreign languages	Arts	Career/ technical (occupational) education[1]	Labor market, family, and consumer education[2]	Personal use[3]
					Total	Biology	Chemistry	Physics	Other science[4]					
1	2	3	4	5	6	7	8	9	10	11	12	13	14	15
2000 graduates	**26.15 (0.204)**	**4.26 (0.037)**	**3.89 (0.036)**	**3.62 (0.029)**	**3.20 (0.038)**	**1.28 (0.028)**	**0.71 (0.020)**	**0.37 (0.018)**	**0.84 (0.030)**	**2.01 (0.045)**	**2.03 (0.054)**	**2.86 (0.105)**	**1.35 (0.044)**	**3.49 (0.071)**
Sex														
Male	26.01 (0.210)	4.18 (0.036)	3.83 (0.036)	3.60 (0.032)	3.15 (0.039)	1.20 (0.030)	0.67 (0.020)	0.42 (0.020)	0.87 (0.029)	1.77 (0.045)	1.75 (0.051)	3.24 (0.133)	1.35 (0.049)	3.76 (0.079)
Female	26.26 (0.204)	4.34 (0.040)	3.95 (0.038)	3.64 (0.028)	3.24 (0.041)	1.36 (0.030)	0.74 (0.022)	0.33 (0.018)	0.81 (0.031)	2.25 (0.050)	2.29 (0.065)	2.48 (0.086)	1.34 (0.047)	3.22 (0.068)
Race/ethnicity														
White	26.31 (0.256)	4.26 (0.037)	3.93 (0.042)	3.63 (0.032)	3.24 (0.038)	1.30 (0.034)	0.72 (0.024)	0.39 (0.021)	0.83 (0.033)	1.98 (0.054)	2.11 (0.068)	2.97 (0.136)	1.37 (0.055)	3.37 (0.080)
Black	25.85 (0.233)	4.36 (0.078)	3.81 (0.068)	3.57 (0.046)	3.12 (0.059)	1.25 (0.041)	0.66 (0.030)	0.30 (0.027)	0.91 (0.043)	1.71 (0.070)	1.94 (0.134)	2.74 (0.143)	1.54 (0.075)	3.60 (0.134)
Hispanic	25.59 (0.358)	4.29 (0.125)	3.84 (0.076)	3.48 (0.069)	2.86 (0.112)	1.18 (0.068)	0.58 (0.055)	0.25 (0.026)	0.84 (0.044)	2.22 (0.063)	1.76 (0.062)	2.64 (0.152)	1.20 (0.082)	3.95 (0.173)
Asian/Pacific Islander	26.23 (0.332)	4.12 (0.060)	3.80 (0.055)	4.01 (0.108)	3.70 (0.162)	1.35 (0.066)	0.97 (0.050)	0.67 (0.042)	0.71 (0.086)	2.90 (0.089)	1.78 (0.085)	1.99 (0.149)	0.81 (0.050)	3.52 (0.221)
American Indian/ Alaska Native	25.24 (0.342)	4.08 (0.069)	3.82 (0.102)	3.35 (0.117)	2.88 (0.086)	1.25 (0.080)	0.45 (0.045)	0.19 (0.042)	0.98 (0.038)	1.41 (0.105)	1.99 (0.220)	3.23 (0.380)	1.60 (0.151)	3.60 (0.365)
2005 graduates	**26.88 (0.102)**	**4.33 (0.022)**	**4.08 (0.027)**	**3.80 (0.018)**	**3.35 (0.019)**	**1.28 (0.016)**	**0.75 (0.011)**	**0.37 (0.012)**	**0.95 (0.019)**	**2.07 (0.022)**	**2.06 (0.035)**	**2.64 (0.045)**	**1.38 (0.030)**	**3.83 (0.047)**
Sex														
Male	26.70 (0.107)	4.26 (0.024)	4.01 (0.030)	3.78 (0.021)	3.29 (0.023)	1.19 (0.016)	0.71 (0.012)	0.41 (0.014)	0.98 (0.019)	1.87 (0.025)	1.71 (0.035)	3.01 (0.050)	1.36 (0.032)	4.17 (0.055)
Female	27.05 (0.104)	4.39 (0.022)	4.16 (0.028)	3.83 (0.018)	3.41 (0.019)	1.37 (0.017)	0.79 (0.012)	0.33 (0.012)	0.92 (0.020)	2.25 (0.023)	2.38 (0.045)	2.29 (0.049)	1.41 (0.033)	3.52 (0.050)
Race/ethnicity														
White	27.06 (0.127)	4.30 (0.030)	4.12 (0.030)	3.80 (0.022)	3.44 (0.021)	1.31 (0.018)	0.77 (0.014)	0.39 (0.012)	0.96 (0.021)	2.03 (0.025)	2.17 (0.043)	2.75 (0.059)	1.39 (0.036)	3.64 (0.059)
Black	26.76 (0.151)	4.50 (0.028)	4.10 (0.054)	3.86 (0.036)	3.22 (0.035)	1.27 (0.025)	0.69 (0.017)	0.28 (0.025)	0.99 (0.037)	1.77 (0.041)	1.77 (0.056)	2.58 (0.074)	1.56 (0.065)	4.32 (0.096)
Hispanic	26.18 (0.147)	4.33 (0.026)	3.88 (0.052)	3.64 (0.034)	2.93 (0.036)	1.11 (0.021)	0.64 (0.022)	0.25 (0.017)	0.94 (0.031)	2.39 (0.047)	1.78 (0.055)	2.41 (0.086)	1.30 (0.046)	4.44 (0.100)
Asian/Pacific Islander	26.58 (0.183)	4.28 (0.043)	4.02 (0.048)	4.08 (0.051)	3.65 (0.057)	1.31 (0.035)	0.98 (0.028)	0.59 (0.036)	0.77 (0.061)	2.70 (0.066)	1.80 (0.076)	1.94 (0.116)	0.98 (0.052)	3.53 (0.122)
American Indian/ Alaska Native	26.66 (0.454)	4.42 (0.136)	4.15 (0.151)	3.60 (0.175)	3.00 (0.075)	1.27 (0.061)	0.52 (0.053)	0.17 (0.036)	1.04 (0.063)	1.55 (0.125)	2.45 (0.179)	2.45 (0.208)	1.70 (0.184)	4.24 (0.294)
2009 graduates	**27.15 (0.100)**	**4.37 (0.013)**	**4.19 (0.027)**	**3.91 (0.017)**	**3.47 (0.022)**	**1.35 (0.014)**	**0.78 (0.011)**	**0.42 (0.013)**	**0.92 (0.017)**	**2.21 (0.027)**	**2.12 (0.036)**	**2.47 (0.059)**	**1.11 (0.030)**	**3.86 (0.059)**
Sex														
Male	26.98 (0.111)	4.30 (0.015)	4.13 (0.028)	3.88 (0.018)	3.46 (0.027)	1.27 (0.014)	0.74 (0.012)	0.48 (0.017)	0.96 (0.017)	2.01 (0.028)	1.76 (0.034)	2.77 (0.068)	1.13 (0.036)	4.18 (0.070)
Female	27.31 (0.095)	4.42 (0.014)	4.25 (0.027)	3.93 (0.018)	3.49 (0.020)	1.43 (0.015)	0.82 (0.011)	0.37 (0.012)	0.88 (0.019)	2.40 (0.028)	2.46 (0.046)	2.19 (0.055)	1.10 (0.028)	3.57 (0.060)
Race/ethnicity														
White	27.30 (0.151)	4.32 (0.016)	4.23 (0.037)	3.91 (0.021)	3.55 (0.026)	1.37 (0.015)	0.80 (0.013)	0.44 (0.016)	0.94 (0.022)	2.19 (0.032)	2.26 (0.042)	2.55 (0.071)	1.16 (0.040)	3.70 (0.075)
Black	27.42 (0.141)	4.56 (0.039)	4.26 (0.036)	4.02 (0.035)	3.31 (0.027)	1.33 (0.025)	0.68 (0.022)	0.30 (0.019)	1.00 (0.028)	1.87 (0.044)	1.87 (0.067)	2.72 (0.127)	1.21 (0.052)	4.29 (0.102)
Hispanic	26.47 (0.194)	4.43 (0.024)	4.04 (0.040)	3.70 (0.029)	3.13 (0.028)	1.24 (0.019)	0.70 (0.015)	0.32 (0.015)	0.87 (0.024)	2.34 (0.034)	1.85 (0.046)	2.31 (0.101)	1.04 (0.040)	4.26 (0.095)
Asian/Pacific Islander	26.94 (0.190)	4.19 (0.039)	4.13 (0.083)	4.16 (0.052)	4.06 (0.091)	1.56 (0.077)	1.08 (0.035)	0.75 (0.033)	0.68 (0.063)	2.98 (0.090)	1.99 (0.065)	1.63 (0.074)	0.62 (0.054)	3.47 (0.100)
American Indian/ Alaska Native	26.17 (0.409)	4.39 (0.085)	4.11 (0.083)	3.76 (0.125)	3.20 (0.070)	1.38 (0.062)	0.50 (0.051)	0.24 (0.046)	1.09 (0.066)	1.56 (0.097)	2.19 (0.157)	2.35 (0.188)	1.20 (0.117)	4.54 (0.370)

—Not available.
†Not applicable.
!Interpret data with caution. The coefficient of variation (CV) for this estimate is between 30 and 50 percent.
[1]Includes occupational education in agriculture; business and marketing; communications and design; computer and information sciences; construction and architecture; engineering technologies; health sciences; manufacturing; repair and transportation; and personal, public, and legal services. Does not include general labor market preparation courses and family and consumer sciences education courses.
[2]Includes general labor market preparation courses and family and consumer sciences education courses.
[3]Includes general skills, personal health and physical education, religion, military sciences, special education, and other courses not included in other academic subject fields. Some personal-use courses are also included in the Career/technical (occupational) education column and the Labor market, family, and consumer education column.
[4]Includes all science credits earned outside of biology, chemistry, and physics.
NOTE: The Carnegie unit is a standard of measurement that represents one credit for the completion of a 1-year course. Data differ slightly from figures appearing in other NCES reports because of differences in taxonomies and case exclusion criteria. Race categories exclude persons of Hispanic ethnicity. Totals include other racial/ethnic groups not separately shown. Detail may not sum to totals because of rounding.
SOURCE: U.S. Department of Education, National Center for Education Statistics, High School and Beyond Longitudinal Study of 1980 Sophomores (HS&B-So:80/82), "High School Transcript Study"; and 1987, 1990, 1994, 1998, 2000, 2005, and 2009 High School Transcript Study (HSTS). (This table was prepared September 2011.)

Table 225.30. Percentage of public and private high school graduates taking selected mathematics and science courses in high school, by sex and race/ethnicity: Selected years, 1982 through 2009

[Standard errors appear in parentheses]

Course (Carnegie units)	1982	1990	1994	1998	2000	2005	2009							
								Sex		Race/ethnicity				
							Total	Male	Female	White	Black	Hispanic	Asian/Pacific Islander	American Indian/Alaska Native
1	2	3	4	5	6	7	8	9	10	11	12	13	14	15
Mathematics[1]														
Any mathematics (≥10)	98.5 (0.21)	99.6 (0.07)	99.5 (0.07)	99.9 (0.05)	99.8 (0.05)	99.9 (0.02)	100.0 (†)	100.0 (†)	100.0 (†)	100.0 (†)	100.0 (†)	100.0 (†)	100.0 (†)	100.0 (†)
Algebra I (≥10)[2]	55.2 (1.01)	64.5 (1.55)	66.9 (1.33)	63.4 (1.44)	66.5 (1.75)	68.4 (0.99)	68.9 (0.94)	68.5 (0.98)	69.3 (1.01)	67.0 (1.09)	77.2 (1.26)	75.4 (1.60)	53.3 (3.52)	74.8 (5.85)
Geometry (≥10)	47.1 (0.99)	64.1 (1.33)	70.6 (1.25)	75.3 (1.06)	78.3 (1.08)	83.8 (0.63)	88.3 (0.53)	86.6 (0.75)	89.9 (0.54)	88.8 (0.73)	88.4 (1.07)	87.0 (0.96)	86.1 (1.47)	81.6 (4.09)
Algebra II (≥05)[3]	39.9 (0.93)	48.8 (1.39)	61.5 (1.38)	61.7 (1.77)	67.6 (1.43)	70.3 (1.01)	75.5 (0.92)	73.5 (1.09)	77.6 (0.91)	77.1 (1.09)	70.5 (1.68)	71.1 (1.83)	82.8 (2.57)	66.3 (4.12)
Trigonometry (≥05)	8.1 (0.54)	18.2 (1.28)	11.8 (1.16)	8.9 (1.06)	7.9 (1.33)	8.4 (0.88)	6.1 (0.77)	5.8 (0.78)	6.4 (0.81)	7.1 (1.01)	3.2 (0.55)	3.6 (0.69)	8.5 (1.96)	6.5 (1.84)
Analysis/precalculus (≥05)	6.2 (0.46)	13.4 (0.95)	17.4 (0.87)	23.2 (1.44)	26.6 (1.40)	29.4 (0.98)	35.3 (0.84)	33.8 (1.02)	36.6 (0.89)	37.9 (0.98)	22.7 (1.29)	26.5 (1.36)	60.5 (2.88)	18.5 (2.98)
Statistics/probability (≥05)	1.0 (0.16)	1.0 (0.21)	2.0 (0.33)	3.7 (0.54)	5.7 (0.85)	7.7 (0.53)	10.8 (0.49)	10.7 (0.51)	10.9 (0.58)	11.6 (0.64)	7.9 (1.04)	7.5 (0.77)	17.6 (1.69)	5.9! (2.07)
Calculus (≥10)	5.0 (0.43)	6.5 (0.46)	9.4 (0.56)	11.0 (0.85)	11.6 (0.72)	13.6 (0.53)	15.9 (0.66)	16.1 (0.75)	15.7 (0.69)	17.5 (0.69)	6.1 (0.59)	8.6 (0.64)	42.2 (3.11)	6.3 (1.60)
AP/honors calculus (≥10)[4]	1.6 (0.26)	4.2 (0.44)	7.0 (0.54)	6.8 (0.49)	7.8 (0.58)	9.2 (0.44)	11.0 (0.55)	11.3 (0.65)	10.7 (0.54)	11.5 (0.52)	4.0 (0.37)	6.3 (0.46)	34.8 (2.77)	4.9 (1.44)
Science[1]														
Any science (≥10)	96.4 (0.39)	99.4 (0.13)	99.5 (0.09)	99.5 (0.10)	99.4 (0.12)	99.7 (0.05)	99.9 (0.02)	99.8 (0.04)	99.9 (0.02)	99.9 (0.03)	99.9 (0.04)	99.8 (0.06)	100.0 (†)	100.0 (†)
Biology (≥10)	77.4 (0.87)	91.3 (0.98)	93.7 (0.98)	92.9 (0.68)	91.1 (1.01)	92.5 (0.60)	95.6 (0.40)	94.9 (0.45)	96.2 (0.43)	95.6 (0.51)	96.3 (0.56)	94.8 (0.67)	95.8 (0.95)	94.5 (1.64)
AP/honors biology (≥10)[4]	10.0 (0.64)	5.0 (0.76)	12.0 (0.93)	16.3 (1.32)	16.3 (1.45)	16.0 (0.83)	22.4 (0.78)	19.7 (0.76)	25.0 (0.89)	24.2 (0.88)	14.1 (0.80)	16.1 (0.88)	39.7 (3.58)	15.4 (3.38)
Chemistry (≥10)	32.1 (0.84)	49.2 (1.22)	56.1 (1.01)	60.5 (1.29)	61.8 (1.48)	66.4 (0.94)	70.4 (0.75)	67.4 (0.95)	73.4 (0.76)	71.5 (0.87)	65.3 (1.80)	65.7 (1.41)	84.8 (1.72)	44.5 (4.78)
AP/honors chemistry (≥10)[4]	3.0 (0.33)	3.5 (0.47)	3.9 (0.53)	4.8 (0.50)	5.7 (0.84)	7.6 (0.53)	5.9 (0.43)	6.1 (0.52)	5.8 (0.39)	6.5 (0.47)	2.5 (0.46)	2.6 (0.35)	17.0 (2.36)	3.4! (1.39)
Physics (≥10)	15.0 (0.62)	21.3 (0.84)	24.8 (0.86)	28.8 (1.49)	31.3 (1.16)	32.9 (0.91)	36.1 (1.01)	39.2 (1.29)	33.0 (0.92)	37.6 (1.24)	26.9 (1.72)	28.6 (1.33)	61.1 (2.35)	19.8 (3.89)
AP/honors physics (≥10)[4]	1.2 (0.17)	2.0 (0.38)	2.7 (0.34)	3.0 (0.37)	3.9 (0.60)	5.3 (0.33)	5.7 (0.46)	7.7 (0.63)	3.7 (0.38)	6.1 (0.54)	2.5 (0.39)	3.4 (0.39)	15.1 (2.51)	‡ (†)
Engineering (≥10)	1.2 (0.21)	0.1 (0.04)	4.5 (0.80)	6.7 (1.76)	4.1 (0.98)	4.8 (0.56)	8.2 (0.93)	9.0 (1.02)	7.4 (0.93)	8.2 (1.18)	10.1 (1.75)	7.1 (1.06)	6.4 (1.17)	9.0! (3.15)
Astronomy (≥05)	1.2 (0.24)	1.2 (0.31)	1.7 (0.50)	1.9 (0.46)	2.8 (0.59)	2.8 (0.37)	3.3 (0.40)	3.9 (0.51)	2.7 (0.33)	4.0 (0.57)	1.8 (0.38)	2.0 (0.36)	1.9 (0.43)	5.3! (2.51)
Geology/earth science (≥05)	13.6 (1.04)	25.3 (2.47)	23.1 (2.44)	20.9 (2.35)	18.5 (1.92)	24.7 (1.43)	27.7 (1.70)	28.9 (1.88)	26.5 (1.66)	28.2 (2.04)	30.1 (2.57)	27.1 (2.15)	19.1 (2.38)	26.0 (5.25)
Biology and chemistry (≥20)[5]	29.3 (0.83)	47.8 (1.23)	53.8 (1.18)	59.1 (1.22)	59.2 (1.50)	64.3 (0.97)	68.3 (0.77)	65.0 (0.91)	71.4 (0.84)	68.9 (0.93)	64.3 (1.74)	64.2 (1.45)	82.7 (1.93)	43.9 (4.77)
Biology, chemistry, and physics (≥30)[5]	11.2 (0.51)	18.7 (0.71)	21.4 (0.83)	25.6 (1.34)	25.0 (1.10)	27.4 (0.89)	30.1 (0.87)	31.9 (1.08)	28.3 (0.85)	31.4 (1.04)	21.9 (1.48)	22.7 (1.19)	54.4 (2.77)	13.6 (2.87)

†Not applicable.
!Interpret data with caution. The coefficient of variation (CV) for this estimate is between 30 and 50 percent.
‡Reporting standards not met. The coefficient of variation (CV) for this estimate is 50 percent or greater.
[1]For each course category, percentages include only students who earned at least the number of credits shown in parentheses.
[2]Excludes prealgebra.
[3]Includes courses where trigonometry or geometry has been combined with algebra II.
[4]For 2000 and later years, includes International Baccalaureate (IB) courses in addition to Advanced Placement (AP) and honors courses.
[5]Percentages include only students who earned at least one credit in each of the indicated courses.

NOTE: For a transcript to be included in the analyses, it had to meet three requirements: (1) the student graduated with either a standard or honors diploma, (2) the student's transcript contained 16 or more Carnegie units, and (3) the student's transcript contained more than 0 Carnegie units in English courses. The Carnegie unit is a standard of measurement that represents one credit for the completion of a 1-year course (0.5 = one semester; 1.0 = one academic year). Data differ slightly from figures appearing in other National Center for Education Statistics reports because of differences in taxonomies and case exclusion criteria. Race categories exclude persons of Hispanic ethnicity. Totals include other racial/ethnic groups not separately shown. Some data have been revised from previously published figures.
SOURCE: U.S. Department of Education, National Center for Education Statistics, High School and Beyond Longitudinal Study of 1980 Sophomores (HS&B-So:80/82), "High School Transcript Study"; and 1990, 1994, 1998, 2000, 2005, and 2009 High School Transcript Study (HSTS). (This table was prepared October 2012.)

Table 225.70. Number and percentage of high school graduates who took foreign language courses in high school and average number of credits earned, by language and number of credits: 2000, 2005, and 2009

[Standard errors appear in parentheses]

Language and number of credits	2000			2005			2009		
	Number of graduates (in thousands)	Percent of graduates	Average credits[1]	Number of graduates (in thousands)	Percent of graduates	Average credits[1]	Number of graduates (in thousands)	Percent of graduates	Average credits[1]
1	2	3	4	5	6	7	8	9	10
All foreign languages									
Any credit	**2,487 (33.8)**	**84.0 (0.92)**	**2.5 (0.03)**	**2,295 (51.1)**	**85.7 (0.49)**	**2.5 (0.02)**	**2,599 (52.7)**	**88.5 (0.45)**	**2.6 (0.02)**
Spanish									
Any credit	1,780 (31.9)	60.1 (0.90)	2.2 (0.03)	1,705 (42.2)	63.7 (0.66)	2.2 (0.02)	2,032 (45.0)	69.2 (0.70)	2.3 (0.02)
2 or more credits	1,369 (32.2)	46.2 (1.04)	2.6 (0.03)	1,344 (35.9)	50.2 (0.67)	2.6 (0.01)	1,638 (39.2)	55.8 (0.73)	2.6 (0.02)
3 or more credits	554 (26.3)	18.7 (0.90)	3.4 (0.03)	531 (20.1)	19.8 (0.57)	3.4 (0.01)	721 (30.2)	24.5 (0.78)	3.4 (0.02)
French									
Any credit	528 (21.5)	17.8 (0.73)	2.3 (0.05)	414 (14.1)	15.5 (0.49)	2.3 (0.03)	411 (16.1)	14.0 (0.47)	2.4 (0.04)
2 or more credits	398 (17.8)	13.4 (0.61)	2.7 (0.04)	309 (11.1)	11.5 (0.38)	2.7 (0.03)	314 (14.1)	10.7 (0.42)	2.8 (0.03)
3 or more credits	190 (12.1)	6.4 (0.42)	3.5 (0.04)	143 (7.2)	5.4 (0.25)	3.5 (0.03)	167 (10.6)	5.7 (0.32)	3.5 (0.03)
German									
Any credit	142 (17.2)	4.8 (0.57)	2.3 (0.08)	139 (10.0)	5.2 (0.36)	2.3 (0.04)	122 (8.6)	4.2 (0.29)	2.3 (0.06)
2 or more credits	104 (14.6)	3.5 (0.49)	2.8 (0.07)	102 (8.2)	3.8 (0.29)	2.8 (0.04)	91 (7.8)	3.1 (0.27)	2.8 (0.05)
3 or more credits	55 (8.6)	1.8 (0.29)	3.5 (0.06)	53 (4.7)	2.0 (0.17)	3.5 (0.04)	46 (5.3)	1.6 (0.18)	3.5 (0.03)
Latin									
Any credit	120 (15.3)	4.0 (0.52)	2.1 (0.08)	106 (10.4)	4.0 (0.36)	2.1 (0.05)	108 (10.6)	3.7 (0.35)	2.2 (0.07)
Italian									
Any credit	29 (5.5)	1.0 (0.19)	2.2 (0.20)	29 (5.3)	1.1 (0.20)	2.4 (0.16)	36 (7.0)	1.2 (0.23)	2.3 (0.18)
Japanese									
Any credit	36 (7.3)	1.2 (0.25)	2.3 (0.15)	30 (4.4)	1.1 (0.16)	2.1 (0.12)	28 (4.3)	1.0 (0.15)	2.5 (0.12)
Chinese									
Any credit	12 (3.1)	0.4 (0.10)	2.4 (0.20)	8 (2.1)	0.3 (0.08)	2.1 (0.23)	20 (4.1)	0.7 (0.14)	1.9 (0.13)
Arabic									
Any credit	‡ (†)	‡ (†)	‡ (†)	‡ (†)	‡ (†)	‡ (†)	‡ (†)	‡ (†)	2.8 (0.36)
Russian									
Any credit	10 (2.7)	0.3 (0.09)	1.9 (0.24)	5 (1.3)	0.2 (0.05)	1.5 (0.17)	3! (1.3)	0.1! (0.04)	2.4 (0.14)
Other foreign languages									
Any credit	106 (12.0)	3.6 (0.40)	2.5 (0.17)	89 (5.9)	3.3 (0.23)	2.8 (0.10)	105 (10.6)	3.6 (0.37)	2.5 (0.18)
AP/IB/honors foreign languages									
Any credit	183 (23.9)	6.2 (0.81)	1.2 (0.04)	157 (10.3)	5.9 (0.38)	1.2 (0.02)	233 (15.9)	7.9 (0.52)	1.2 (0.02)

†Not applicable.
!Interpret data with caution. The coefficient of variation (CV) for this estimate is between 30 and 50 percent.
‡Reporting standards not met. Either there are too few cases for a reliable estimate or the coefficient of variation (CV) is 50 percent or greater.
[1]Average credits earned are shown only for those graduates who earned any credit in the specified language while in high school. For these students, however, credits earned include both courses taken in high school and courses taken prior to entering high school.

Credits are shown in Carnegie units. The Carnegie unit is a standard unit of measurement that represents one credit for the completion of a 1-year course.
NOTE: For a transcript to be included in the analyses, it had to meet three requirements: (1) the graduate received either a standard or honors diploma, (2) the graduate's transcript contained 16 or more Carnegie credits, and (3) the graduate's transcript contained more than 0 Carnegie credits in English courses.
SOURCE: U.S. Department of Education, National Center for Education Statistics, 2000, 2005, and 2009 High School Transcript Study (HSTS). (This table was prepared April 2014.)

Table 225.80. Percentage distribution of elementary and secondary school children, by average grades and selected child and school characteristics: 2003, 2012, and 2016

[Standard errors appear in parentheses]

Selected child or school characteristic	Percentage distribution of children, by parental reports of average grades in all subjects											
	2003				2012				2016			
	Mostly A's	Mostly B's	Mostly C's	Mostly D's or F's	Mostly A's	Mostly B's	Mostly C's	Mostly D's or F's	Mostly A's	Mostly B's	Mostly C's	Mostly D's or F's
1	2	3	4	5	6	7	8	9	10	11	12	13
All students	**43.6 (0.62)**	**37.0 (0.58)**	**15.9 (0.52)**	**3.6 (0.24)**	**49.2 (0.53)**	**35.6 (0.57)**	**12.8 (0.37)**	**2.5 (0.21)**	**49.2 (0.60)**	**34.6 (0.69)**	**13.0 (0.56)**	**3.2 (0.30)**
Sex of child												
Male	36.4 (0.72)	38.6 (0.86)	19.8 (0.74)	5.2 (0.40)	42.9 (0.74)	37.7 (0.78)	16.1 (0.58)	3.3 (0.34)	42.8 (0.97)	36.8 (1.08)	16.0 (0.86)	4.3 (0.50)
Female	51.0 (0.84)	35.3 (0.76)	11.9 (0.61)	1.9 (0.24)	55.9 (0.82)	33.3 (0.80)	9.3 (0.51)	1.5 (0.22)	56.1 (0.95)	32.1 (0.95)	9.7 (0.70)	2.1 (0.23)
Race/ethnicity of child												
White	47.8 (0.86)	35.2 (0.75)	14.0 (0.63)	3.1 (0.25)	53.6 (0.74)	33.5 (0.77)	10.8 (0.48)	2.1 (0.22)	55.3 (0.82)	32.0 (0.87)	10.3 (0.59)	2.4 (0.29)
Black	34.5 (1.75)	39.5 (1.65)	20.9 (1.33)	5.0 (0.82)	37.0 (1.88)	39.7 (1.97)	19.9 (1.19)	3.4 (0.75)	36.7 (2.18)	37.6 (1.99)	20.4 (1.51)	5.3 (1.40)
Hispanic	34.9 (1.14)	42.3 (1.24)	18.6 (1.03)	4.2 (0.48)	43.2 (1.09)	39.9 (1.05)	14.3 (0.83)	2.6 (0.41)	40.2 (1.37)	40.5 (1.58)	15.2 (1.40)	4.1 (0.60)
Asian/Pacific Islander[1]	62.0 (3.47)	25.5 (2.76)	11.3 (3.06)	‡ (†)	60.9 (2.74)	32.5 (2.83)	5.9 (0.98)	0.7! (0.28)	64.6 (4.52)	23.7 (2.54)	10.9! (4.81)	‡ (†)
Asian	— (†)	— (†)	— (†)	— (†)	63.2 (2.82)	31.8 (2.86)	4.6 (0.98)	0.4! (0.20)	64.9 (4.64)	23.3 (2.42)	11.2! (5.02)	‡ (†)
Pacific Islander	— (†)	— (†)	— (†)	— (†)	23.7! (7.70)	43.4 (10.65)	27.5! (8.38)	‡ (†)	59.2 (12.85)	32.3! (13.31)	‡ (†)	‡ (†)
American Indian/Alaska Native	29.5 (6.53)	53.3 (6.42)	12.1! (4.90)	5.1! (2.54)	54.6 (8.07)	28.2 (6.56)	16.3! (5.26)	‡ (†)	36.5 (9.40)	45.8 (10.14)	‡ (†)	‡ (†)
Two or more races[2]	41.4 (4.34)	36.2 (3.91)	18.8 (2.81)	3.5! (1.38)	55.7 (2.79)	28.2 (2.68)	11.1 (1.68)	5.0! (2.28)	53.7 (3.55)	33.9 (4.00)	8.6 (1.53)	3.8 (1.07)
Highest education level of parents/guardians in the household[3]												
Less than high school	27.8 (2.17)	41.6 (2.05)	22.7 (2.27)	7.8 (1.46)	39.5 (2.25)	39.7 (2.02)	16.8 (1.73)	4.0 (0.93)	30.2 (2.46)	36.3 (2.75)	26.0 (3.28)	7.5 (1.88)
High school/GED	32.1 (1.20)	41.4 (1.23)	21.7 (1.12)	4.8 (0.57)	37.7 (1.51)	40.8 (1.62)	17.6 (1.31)	4.0 (0.71)	35.3 (1.91)	43.0 (1.96)	17.1 (1.63)	4.6 (0.64)
Vocational/technical or some college	39.8 (1.34)	38.3 (1.36)	17.2 (0.95)	4.7 (0.58)	43.5 (1.07)	38.1 (1.05)	15.6 (0.87)	2.8 (0.32)	41.5 (1.59)	38.0 (1.62)	16.2 (1.25)	4.3 (0.68)
Associate's degree	46.7 (2.13)	34.5 (1.94)	16.4 (1.51)	2.4 (0.57)	47.0 (1.82)	34.9 (1.78)	15.4 (1.29)	2.7 (0.52)	49.4 (1.89)	35.0 (1.98)	12.6 (1.32)	3.0 (0.62)
Bachelor's degree/some graduate school	53.0 (1.26)	34.2 (1.29)	11.1 (0.85)	1.7 (0.28)	60.1 (1.05)	31.4 (1.02)	7.5 (0.53)	1.0 (0.19)	60.2 (1.04)	31.1 (0.94)	7.6 (0.69)	1.2 (0.21)
Graduate/professional degree	61.9 (1.71)	30.5 (1.75)	6.7 (0.67)	0.9 (0.24)	68.1 (1.04)	27.3 (1.04)	4.2 (0.36)	0.5 (0.10)	69.4 (1.07)	25.0 (0.98)	4.7 (0.39)	0.9 (0.24)
Family income (in current dollars)												
$20,000 or less	33.1 (1.53)	38.9 (1.56)	22.0 (1.30)	6.0 (0.85)	37.2 (1.35)	40.2 (1.19)	18.3 (1.04)	4.4 (0.59)	31.4 (2.04)	36.4 (2.32)	25.8 (2.49)	6.5 (1.03)
$20,001 to $50,000	37.8 (1.20)	40.0 (1.19)	17.7 (0.85)	4.5 (0.42)	41.3 (1.22)	38.9 (1.19)	16.7 (0.90)	3.1 (0.44)	37.6 (1.41)	40.9 (1.61)	16.6 (1.15)	4.9 (0.90)
$50,001 to $75,000	48.0 (1.29)	35.0 (1.22)	14.0 (0.81)	3.0 (0.45)	49.3 (1.45)	35.8 (1.37)	12.9 (1.07)	1.9 (0.32)	48.6 (1.84)	34.7 (1.85)	13.5 (1.25)	3.2 (0.59)
$75,001 to $100,000	51.8 (1.66)	33.7 (1.45)	13.3 (1.23)	1.3 (0.32)	53.7 (1.64)	33.5 (1.42)	10.6 (1.03)	2.3 (0.50)	54.3 (1.70)	33.4 (1.73)	9.8 (0.98)	2.5 (0.55)
Over $100,000	55.8 (1.74)	33.9 (1.72)	9.1 (1.09)	1.2 (0.24)	61.8 (1.15)	30.4 (1.19)	6.6 (0.61)	1.1! (0.41)	63.9 (1.09)	29.2 (1.12)	6.0 (0.63)	0.9 (0.23)
Poverty status[4]												
Poor	33.1 (1.61)	39.4 (1.65)	21.9 (1.39)	5.6 (0.91)	39.1 (1.39)	38.9 (1.33)	17.8 (1.06)	4.2 (0.54)	32.7 (1.78)	37.0 (1.83)	24.5 (2.07)	5.8 (0.78)
Near-poor	34.8 (1.39)	42.0 (1.26)	18.2 (1.08)	5.0 (0.59)	40.1 (1.19)	40.3 (1.07)	17.0 (0.93)	2.7 (0.45)	38.5 (1.57)	40.8 (1.44)	15.2 (1.08)	5.5 (1.00)
Nonpoor	49.9 (0.83)	34.5 (0.76)	13.2 (0.54)	2.4 (0.23)	56.0 (0.75)	32.7 (0.75)	9.5 (0.45)	1.8 (0.25)	57.9 (0.75)	31.6 (0.79)	8.8 (0.42)	1.7 (0.20)
Control of school and enrollment level of child												
Public school	41.8 (0.64)	37.5 (0.62)	16.8 (0.57)	3.8 (0.26)	47.9 (0.55)	36.0 (0.60)	13.5 (0.39)	2.6 (0.23)	47.4 (0.64)	35.4 (0.77)	13.6 (0.61)	3.5 (0.33)
Elementary (kindergarten to grade 8)	46.1 (0.80)	35.9 (0.84)	14.6 (0.74)	3.4 (0.32)	52.9 (0.69)	34.2 (0.73)	11.0 (0.49)	1.8 (0.22)	50.5 (0.83)	34.6 (1.00)	11.9 (0.76)	3.0 (0.41)
Secondary (grades 9 to 12)	34.6 (0.96)	40.2 (0.97)	20.6 (0.94)	4.6 (0.46)	37.5 (0.83)	39.7 (1.03)	18.4 (0.84)	4.4 (0.54)	41.1 (0.99)	37.2 (1.20)	17.1 (1.01)	4.5 (0.50)
Private school	57.6 (1.72)	33.0 (1.68)	8.1 (0.91)	1.3! (0.45)	63.4 (1.63)	30.8 (1.51)	5.4 (0.68)	0.4! (0.20)	66.4 (1.81)	26.2 (1.49)	7.0 (1.17)	0.4! (0.14)
Elementary (kindergarten to grade 8)	61.6 (2.39)	30.3 (2.28)	7.3 (1.03)	0.8! (0.28)	67.8 (1.95)	28.2 (1.91)	3.5 (0.61)	‡ (†)	71.2 (2.45)	22.4 (2.11)	6.1 (1.52)	‡ (†)
Secondary (grades 9 to 12)	48.8 (3.22)	38.9 (2.94)	10.0 (1.77)	‡ (†)	52.8 (2.70)	37.2 (2.58)	9.9 (1.60)	‡ (†)	55.6 (2.76)	34.6 (2.42)	9.0 (1.95)	0.7! (0.32)

—Not available.
†Not applicable.
!Interpret data with caution. The coefficient of variation (CV) for this estimate is between 30 and 50 percent.
‡Reporting standards not met. Either there are too few cases for a reliable estimate or the coefficient of variation (CV) is 50 percent or greater.
[1]The 2003 questionnaire included a single item for "Asian or Pacific Islander," whereas questionnaires for later years included one item for Asian and a separate item for Pacific Islander.
[2]For 2003, the "Two or more races" row also includes children whose race was reported as "Other." The "Other" race category was not included on the 2012 and 2016 questionnaires.
[3]In 2003, education level was not collected for the second parent in a same sex couple.
[4]Poor children are those whose family incomes were below the Census Bureau's poverty threshold in the year prior to data collection; near-poor children are those whose family incomes ranged from the poverty threshold to 199 percent of the poverty threshold; and nonpoor children are those whose family incomes were at or above 200 percent of the poverty threshold. The poverty threshold is a dollar amount that varies depending on a family's size and composition and is updated annually to account for inflation. In 2015, for example, the poverty threshold for a family of four with two children was $24,257. Survey respondents are asked to select the range within which their income falls, rather than giving the exact amount of their income; therefore, the measure of poverty status is an approximation.
NOTE: While National Household Education Surveys Program (NHES) administrations prior to 2012 were administered via telephone with an interviewer, NHES:2012 and NHES:2016 used self-administered paper-and-pencil questionnaires that were mailed to respondents. Measurable differences between estimates for years prior to 2012 and estimates for later years could reflect actual changes in the population, or the changes could be due to the mode change from telephone to mail. Excludes children whose programs have no classes with lettered grades. Race categories exclude persons of Hispanic ethnicity. Detail may not sum to totals because of rounding. Some data have been revised from previously published figures.
SOURCE: U.S. Department of Education, National Center for Education Statistics, Parent and Family Involvement in Education Survey of the National Household Education Surveys Program (PFI-NHES:2003, 2012, and 2016). (This table was prepared June 2018.)

Table 228.30. Percentage of students ages 12–18 who reported criminal victimization at school during the previous 6 months, by type of victimization and selected student and school characteristics: Selected years, 1995 through 2017

[Standard errors appear in parentheses]

Type of victimization and student or school characteristic	1995	2001	2003	2005	2007	2009	2011	2013	2015	2017
1	2	3	4	5	6	7	8	9	10	11
Total	**9.1 (0.33)**	**5.5 (0.31)**	**5.1 (0.24)**	**4.3 (0.31)**	**4.3 (0.29)**	**3.9 (0.28)**	**3.5 (0.28)**	**3.0 (0.25)**	**2.7 (0.25)**	**2.2 (0.22)**
Sex										
Male	9.6 (0.44)	6.1 (0.41)	5.3 (0.33)	4.6 (0.43)	4.5 (0.43)	4.6 (0.40)	3.7 (0.35)	3.2 (0.40)	2.6 (0.35)	2.6 (0.34)
Female	8.5 (0.45)	4.9 (0.39)	4.8 (0.36)	3.9 (0.38)	3.9 (0.38)	3.2 (0.35)	3.4 (0.38)	2.8 (0.34)	2.8 (0.38)	1.8 (0.28)
Race/ethnicity[1]										
White	9.4 (0.36)	5.7 (0.40)	5.4 (0.32)	4.6 (0.36)	4.2 (0.38)	3.9 (0.37)	3.6 (0.35)	3.0 (0.32)	2.9 (0.36)	2.2 (0.27)
Black	9.6 (1.02)	6.1 (0.78)	5.1 (0.78)	3.9 (0.80)	4.3 (0.83)	4.4 (0.74)	4.6 (0.89)	3.2 (0.71)	2.2! (0.77)	2.6 (0.52)
Hispanic	7.1 (0.96)	4.6 (0.64)	3.9 (0.50)	3.9 (0.70)	3.6 (0.54)	3.9 (0.75)	2.9 (0.47)	3.2 (0.46)	2.3 (0.47)	2.0 (0.45)
Asian/Pacific Islander	8.3 (1.63)	3.7 (1.08)	3.2 (0.93)	1.4! (0.64)	3.4! (1.33)	‡ (†)	2.3! (1.13)	2.4! (0.99)	‡ (†)	2.1! (1.02)
Asian	— (†)	— (†)	3.3! (1.00)	1.5! (0.69)	3.6! (1.38)	‡ (†)	2.5! (1.23)	2.6! (1.08)	‡ (†)	2.1! (1.05)
Pacific Islander	— (†)	— (†)	‡ (†)	‡ (†)	‡ (†)	‡ (†)	‡ (†)	‡ (†)	‡ (†)	‡ (†)
American Indian/Alaska Native	9.6! (3.27)	‡ (†)	‡ (†)	‡ (†)	‡ (†)	‡ (†)	‡ (†)	‡ (†)	‡ (†)	11.1! (4.80)
Two or more races	— (†)	— (†)	9.8 (2.85)	‡ (†)	10.1 (2.59)	‡ (†)	4.9! (1.77)	3.0! (1.46)	6.5! (2.24)	‡ (†)
Grade										
6th	8.8 (0.92)	5.9 (0.90)	3.8 (0.77)	4.6 (0.83)	3.9 (0.86)	3.7 (0.91)	3.8 (0.85)	4.1 (0.92)	3.1 (0.79)	3.1 (0.75)
7th	10.6 (0.79)	5.8 (0.67)	6.3 (0.74)	5.4 (0.71)	4.7 (0.69)	3.4 (0.70)	3.1 (0.61)	2.5 (0.51)	3.4 (0.70)	2.6 (0.60)
8th	10.1 (0.76)	4.3 (0.61)	5.2 (0.65)	3.6 (0.63)	4.4 (0.63)	3.8 (0.78)	3.8 (0.67)	2.3 (0.52)	2.3 (0.57)	1.8 (0.51)
9th	11.4 (0.86)	7.9 (0.81)	6.3 (0.70)	4.7 (0.69)	5.3 (0.75)	5.3 (0.85)	5.1 (0.83)	4.1 (0.76)	3.0 (0.62)	2.7 (0.67)
10th	8.7 (0.73)	6.5 (0.77)	4.7 (0.63)	4.3 (0.71)	4.4 (0.67)	4.2 (0.79)	3.0 (0.58)	3.3 (0.57)	1.6 (0.47)	2.7 (0.49)
11th	7.0 (0.72)	4.8 (0.62)	5.0 (0.69)	3.6 (0.51)	4.0 (0.75)	4.7 (0.88)	3.1 (0.65)	3.3 (0.65)	4.4 (1.04)	1.4 (0.40)
12th	5.8 (0.73)	2.9 (0.52)	3.6 (0.71)	3.7 (0.85)	2.7 (0.70)	2.0 (0.52)	2.9 (0.68)	2.0! (0.67)	1.3! (0.45)	1.4 (0.41)
Urbanicity[2]										
Urban	8.6 (0.59)	5.9 (0.58)	6.0 (0.58)	5.3 (0.66)	4.5 (0.58)	4.2 (0.56)	4.3 (0.56)	3.3 (0.47)	3.3 (0.51)	2.7 (0.45)
Suburban	9.9 (0.48)	5.6 (0.41)	4.7 (0.32)	4.2 (0.34)	4.1 (0.38)	4.0 (0.36)	3.3 (0.34)	3.2 (0.35)	2.8 (0.35)	2.1 (0.25)
Rural	8.1 (0.78)	4.7 (0.93)	4.7 (0.75)	2.8 (0.69)	4.4 (0.55)	3.1 (0.66)	2.8 (0.57)	2.0 (0.58)	1.5 (0.37)	1.6! (0.49)
Control of school										
Public	9.3 (0.37)	5.7 (0.34)	5.1 (0.26)	4.4 (0.32)	4.5 (0.32)	4.1 (0.30)	3.7 (0.29)	3.1 (0.27)	2.8 (0.26)	2.3 (0.23)
Private	6.2 (0.89)	3.4 (0.72)	4.9 (0.79)	2.7 (0.77)	1.1! (0.50)	1.8! (0.76)	1.9! (0.68)	2.8! (0.89)	‡ (†)	‡ (†)
Theft	**7.0 (0.28)**	**4.2 (0.24)**	**4.0 (0.20)**	**3.1 (0.27)**	**3.0 (0.23)**	**2.8 (0.23)**	**2.6 (0.23)**	**1.9 (0.20)**	**1.9 (0.22)**	**1.5 (0.17)**
Sex										
Male	7.0 (0.37)	4.5 (0.34)	3.9 (0.27)	3.1 (0.34)	3.0 (0.34)	3.4 (0.36)	2.6 (0.29)	2.0 (0.30)	1.7 (0.26)	1.6 (0.27)
Female	7.0 (0.41)	3.8 (0.33)	4.1 (0.31)	3.2 (0.36)	3.0 (0.32)	2.1 (0.28)	2.6 (0.33)	1.8 (0.28)	2.0 (0.34)	1.3 (0.24)
Race/ethnicity[1]										
White	7.3 (0.32)	4.1 (0.31)	4.3 (0.28)	3.4 (0.32)	3.1 (0.29)	2.9 (0.31)	2.5 (0.28)	1.6 (0.22)	2.0 (0.28)	1.3 (0.20)
Black	6.9 (0.87)	5.0 (0.68)	3.8 (0.64)	2.7 (0.66)	3.1 (0.70)	2.5 (0.61)	3.7 (0.78)	2.7 (0.67)	1.3! (0.63)	1.8 (0.51)
Hispanic	5.7 (0.79)	3.7 (0.69)	3.0 (0.41)	3.1 (0.64)	2.2 (0.47)	3.0 (0.63)	2.0 (0.41)	1.8 (0.39)	1.6 (0.39)	1.4 (0.36)
Asian/Pacific Islander	6.4 (1.47)	3.5 (1.03)	3.2 (0.93)	‡ (†)	3.0! (1.27)	‡ (†)	2.3! (1.13)	2.4! (0.99)	‡ (†)	2.1! (1.02)
Asian	— (†)	— (†)	3.3! (1.00)	‡ (†)	3.2! (1.32)	‡ (†)	2.5! (1.23)	2.6! (1.08)	‡ (†)	2.1! (1.05)
Pacific Islander	— (†)	— (†)	‡ (†)	‡ (†)	‡ (†)	‡ (†)	‡ (†)	‡ (†)	‡ (†)	‡ (†)
American Indian/Alaska Native	7.2! (3.04)	‡ (†)	‡ (†)	‡ (†)	‡ (†)	‡ (†)	‡ (†)	‡ (†)	‡ (†)	7.2! (3.37)
Two or more races	— (†)	— (†)	8.3! (2.72)	‡ (†)	5.3! (2.01)	‡ (†)	3.7! (1.56)	‡ (†)	4.3! (1.80)	‡ (†)
Grade										
6th	5.4 (0.66)	4.0 (0.70)	2.2 (0.63)	2.8 (0.75)	2.6 (0.75)	1.3! (0.52)	2.7 (0.70)	1.4! (0.57)	1.6! (0.65)	1.0! (0.42)
7th	8.1 (0.72)	3.4 (0.51)	4.8 (0.67)	2.9 (0.50)	2.7 (0.54)	2.1 (0.57)	1.9 (0.44)	1.4 (0.38)	1.6! (0.54)	1.3! (0.39)
8th	7.8 (0.72)	3.3 (0.50)	4.1 (0.57)	2.4 (0.53)	2.5 (0.54)	2.0 (0.55)	2.0 (0.48)	1.0! (0.33)	1.8 (0.50)	1.1! (0.41)
9th	8.8 (0.76)	6.2 (0.76)	5.2 (0.63)	3.7 (0.61)	4.6 (0.70)	4.9 (0.80)	4.4 (0.78)	2.7 (0.58)	2.1 (0.52)	2.4 (0.60)
10th	7.6 (0.70)	5.7 (0.72)	3.7 (0.59)	3.8 (0.66)	3.6 (0.63)	3.5 (0.72)	2.1 (0.50)	2.6 (0.48)	1.4! (0.43)	2.1 (0.39)
11th	5.4 (0.66)	3.8 (0.57)	4.1 (0.64)	2.8 (0.45)	2.6 (0.61)	3.3 (0.74)	2.7 (0.58)	2.3 (0.50)	3.4 (0.85)	1.1! (0.36)
12th	4.5 (0.67)	2.3 (0.45)	3.1 (0.68)	3.4 (0.84)	1.9 (0.55)	1.5 (0.44)	2.4 (0.62)	1.6! (0.62)	1.0! (0.40)	1.2! (0.42)
Urbanicity[2]										
Urban	6.4 (0.51)	4.5 (0.52)	4.5 (0.46)	3.6 (0.52)	2.8 (0.48)	2.9 (0.45)	3.0 (0.45)	2.4 (0.44)	2.3 (0.45)	1.8 (0.39)
Suburban	7.5 (0.40)	4.3 (0.32)	3.8 (0.26)	3.2 (0.31)	3.0 (0.31)	2.8 (0.32)	2.5 (0.30)	1.9 (0.27)	1.8 (0.30)	1.4 (0.18)
Rural	6.8 (0.66)	3.4 (0.65)	3.9 (0.66)	2.2! (0.68)	3.2 (0.46)	2.3 (0.59)	2.0 (0.47)	0.8 (0.24)	1.2 (0.32)	0.9! (0.35)
Control of school										
Public	7.2 (0.31)	4.4 (0.26)	4.0 (0.22)	3.3 (0.28)	3.2 (0.25)	2.9 (0.25)	2.7 (0.24)	1.9 (0.21)	1.9 (0.22)	1.6 (0.19)
Private	4.9 (0.73)	2.4 (0.67)	4.0 (0.77)	1.3! (0.48)	1.1! (0.50)	‡ (†)	1.2! (0.52)	2.0! (0.76)	‡ (†)	‡ (†)
Violent	**2.5 (0.19)**	**1.8 (0.19)**	**1.3 (0.15)**	**1.2 (0.15)**	**1.6 (0.18)**	**1.4 (0.17)**	**1.1 (0.15)**	**1.2 (0.15)**	**0.9 (0.15)**	**0.7 (0.12)**
Sex										
Male	3.0 (0.26)	2.1 (0.26)	1.7 (0.23)	1.6 (0.25)	1.7 (0.26)	1.6 (0.25)	1.2 (0.21)	1.3 (0.23)	1.0 (0.21)	1.0 (0.20)
Female	2.0 (0.22)	1.4 (0.24)	0.9 (0.16)	0.8 (0.15)	1.4 (0.23)	1.1 (0.21)	0.9 (0.17)	1.1 (0.23)	0.9 (0.19)	0.5 (0.14)
Race/ethnicity[1]										
White	2.5 (0.21)	2.0 (0.24)	1.4 (0.17)	1.3 (0.21)	1.5 (0.22)	1.2 (0.21)	1.2 (0.17)	1.5 (0.24)	1.0 (0.22)	0.9 (0.19)
Black	3.0 (0.57)	1.3! (0.40)	1.5 (0.41)	1.3! (0.47)	1.6! (0.50)	2.3 (0.62)	1.1! (0.42)	‡ (†)	0.9! (0.44)	0.8! (0.31)
Hispanic	2.0 (0.47)	1.5 (0.41)	1.1 (0.28)	0.9 (0.24)	1.4 (0.42)	1.3! (0.40)	1.0 (0.28)	1.5 (0.26)	0.6! (0.23)	0.5! (0.23)
Asian/Pacific Islander	2.2! (0.98)	‡ (†)	‡ (†)	‡ (†)	‡ (†)	‡ (†)	‡ (†)	‡ (†)	‡ (†)	‡ (†)
Asian	— (†)	— (†)	‡ (†)	‡ (†)	‡ (†)	‡ (†)	‡ (†)	‡ (†)	‡ (†)	‡ (†)
Pacific Islander	— (†)	— (†)	‡ (†)	‡ (†)	‡ (†)	‡ (†)	‡ (†)	‡ (†)	‡ (†)	‡ (†)
American Indian/Alaska Native	‡ (†)	‡ (†)	‡ (†)	‡ (†)	‡ (†)	‡ (†)	‡ (†)	‡ (†)	‡ (†)	‡ (†)
Two or more races	— (†)	— (†)	‡ (†)	‡ (†)	5.3! (1.90)	‡ (†)	‡ (†)	‡ (†)	3.6! (1.64)	‡ (†)

See notes at end of table.

Table 228.30. Percentage of students ages 12–18 who reported criminal victimization at school during the previous 6 months, by type of victimization and selected student and school characteristics: Selected years, 1995 through 2017—Continued

[Standard errors appear in parentheses]

Type of victimization and student or school characteristic	1995	2001	2003	2005	2007	2009	2011	2013	2015	2017
1	2	3	4	5	6	7	8	9	10	11
Grade										
6th	4.3 (0.68)	2.6 (0.66)	1.9 (0.53)	1.9 (0.55)	1.5! (0.54)	2.6! (0.83)	1.3! (0.49)	2.7 (0.73)	1.6! (0.65)	2.1 (0.60)
7th	3.1 (0.50)	2.6 (0.46)	1.7 (0.43)	2.6 (0.53)	2.4 (0.50)	1.2! (0.42)	1.2! (0.41)	1.2! (0.38)	1.9 (0.47)	1.4! (0.45)
8th	2.7 (0.39)	1.3 (0.34)	1.4 (0.34)	1.4 (0.39)	2.1 (0.47)	2.0 (0.60)	2.1 (0.50)	1.4 (0.42)	0.6! (0.30)	0.7! (0.29)
9th	2.9 (0.47)	2.4 (0.46)	1.5 (0.31)	1.0 (0.29)	1.2! (0.37)	0.9! (0.37)	1.1! (0.35)	1.4! (0.44)	0.8! (0.34)	‡ (†)
10th	1.8 (0.35)	1.2 (0.31)	1.3 (0.36)	0.5! (0.24)	1.2! (0.39)	1.0! (0.37)	0.9! (0.34)	1.0! (0.35)	‡ (†)	0.7! (0.32)
11th	1.6 (0.35)	1.6 (0.39)	0.9! (0.32)	0.7! (0.31)	1.5 (0.46)	1.5! (0.51)	‡ (†)	1.0! (0.43)	1.3! (0.49)	‡ (†)
12th	1.6 (0.36)	0.9! (0.31)	0.5! (0.26)	‡ (†)	0.8! (0.35)	‡ (†)	‡ (†)	‡ (†)	‡ (†)	‡ (†)
Urbanicity[2]										
Urban	2.6 (0.34)	1.7 (0.29)	1.8 (0.31)	1.8 (0.34)	2.0 (0.35)	1.8 (0.41)	1.4 (0.31)	0.9 (0.21)	1.0 (0.27)	0.9 (0.21)
Suburban	3.0 (0.29)	1.7 (0.20)	1.2 (0.19)	1.1 (0.18)	1.3 (0.23)	1.3 (0.23)	0.9 (0.16)	1.4 (0.21)	1.0 (0.20)	0.6 (0.17)
Rural	1.5 (0.27)	2.0! (0.64)	0.9! (0.31)	0.6! (0.26)	1.7 (0.36)	0.8! (0.32)	1.0! (0.31)	1.1! (0.46)	0.5! (0.22)	0.7! (0.33)
Control of school										
Public	2.6 (0.19)	1.8 (0.20)	1.4 (0.15)	1.2 (0.15)	1.7 (0.20)	1.4 (0.19)	1.1 (0.15)	1.2 (0.16)	1.0 (0.15)	0.8 (0.12)
Private	1.6 (0.44)	1.0! (0.32)	0.9! (0.39)	1.4! (0.60)	‡ (†)	‡ (†)	‡ (†)	‡ (†)	‡ (†)	‡ (†)
Serious violent[3]	**0.5 (0.08)**	**0.4 (0.08)**	**0.2 (0.05)**	**0.3 (0.07)**	**0.4 (0.08)**	**0.3 (0.09)**	**0.1! (0.05)**	**0.2! (0.07)**	**0.2! (0.07)**	**0.2! (0.06)**
Sex										
Male	0.7 (0.12)	0.5 (0.11)	0.3! (0.09)	0.3! (0.10)	0.5! (0.14)	0.6 (0.16)	0.2! (0.08)	0.2! (0.10)	0.2! (0.12)	0.2! (0.10)
Female	0.3 (0.08)	0.4! (0.12)	‡ (†)	0.3 (0.07)	0.2! (0.08)	‡ (†)	‡ (†)	0.2! (0.10)	‡ (†)	0.2! (0.08)
Race/ethnicity[1]										
White	0.5 (0.08)	0.4 (0.08)	0.2! (0.07)	0.3! (0.09)	0.2! (0.08)	0.3! (0.10)	0.2! (0.07)	0.2! (0.09)	0.3! (0.10)	0.3! (0.11)
Black	0.8! (0.28)	0.5! (0.25)	‡ (†)	‡ (†)	‡ (†)	‡ (†)	‡ (†)	‡ (†)	‡ (†)	‡ (†)
Hispanic	0.4! (0.18)	0.8! (0.33)	0.4! (0.18)	0.4! (0.16)	0.8! (0.32)	‡ (†)	‡ (†)	0.4! (0.17)	‡ (†)	‡ (†)
Asian/Pacific Islander	‡ (†)	‡ (†)	‡ (†)	‡ (†)	‡ (†)	‡ (†)	‡ (†)	‡ (†)	‡ (†)	‡ (†)
Asian	— (†)	— (†)	‡ (†)	‡ (†)	‡ (†)	‡ (†)	‡ (†)	‡ (†)	‡ (†)	‡ (†)
Pacific Islander	— (†)	— (†)	‡ (†)	‡ (†)	‡ (†)	‡ (†)	‡ (†)	‡ (†)	‡ (†)	‡ (†)
American Indian/Alaska Native	‡ (†)	‡ (†)	‡ (†)	‡ (†)	‡ (†)	‡ (†)	‡ (†)	‡ (†)	‡ (†)	‡ (†)
Two or more races	— (†)	— (†)	‡ (†)	‡ (†)	‡ (†)	‡ (†)	‡ (†)	‡ (†)	‡ (†)	‡ (†)
Grade										
6th	1.2! (0.38)	‡ (†)	‡ (†)	‡ (†)	‡ (†)	‡ (†)	‡ (†)	0.8! (0.42)	‡ (†)	‡ (†)
7th	0.5! (0.19)	0.6! (0.24)	‡ (†)	‡ (†)	0.4! (0.20)	‡ (†)	0.5! (0.23)	‡ (†)	‡ (†)	‡ (†)
8th	0.6! (0.19)	0.3! (0.14)	‡ (†)	‡ (†)	‡ (†)	‡ (†)	# (†)	‡ (†)	‡ (†)	‡ (†)
9th	0.5! (0.19)	0.8! (0.31)	0.6! (0.21)	‡ (†)	‡ (†)	‡ (†)	‡ (†)	‡ (†)	‡ (†)	‡ (†)
10th	0.2! (0.11)	0.4! (0.18)	‡ (†)	‡ (†)	‡ (†)	‡ (†)	# (†)	‡ (†)	‡ (†)	‡ (†)
11th	0.3! (0.16)	‡ (†)	‡ (†)	‡ (†)	0.6! (0.27)	‡ (†)	# (†)	‡ (†)	‡ (†)	‡ (†)
12th	‡ (†)	‡ (†)	‡ (†)	‡ (†)	‡ (†)	‡ (†)	# (†)	‡ (†)	‡ (†)	‡ (†)
Urbanicity[2]										
Urban	0.9 (0.20)	0.5 (0.15)	0.3! (0.14)	0.4! (0.17)	0.7! (0.23)	0.6! (0.22)	‡ (†)	0.3! (0.16)	‡ (†)	‡ (†)
Suburban	0.4 (0.10)	0.4 (0.09)	0.1! (0.05)	0.3! (0.08)	0.2! (0.09)	0.3! (0.11)	‡ (†)	0.2! (0.08)	0.3! (0.12)	0.2! (0.09)
Rural	0.2! (0.09)	0.5! (0.24)	‡ (†)	‡ (†)	‡ (†)	‡ (†)	‡ (†)	‡ (†)	‡ (†)	‡ (†)
Control of school										
Public	0.5 (0.08)	0.5 (0.09)	0.2 (0.06)	0.3 (0.06)	0.4 (0.09)	0.4 (0.10)	0.1! (0.06)	0.2! (0.08)	0.2! (0.08)	0.2! (0.07)
Private	‡ (†)	‡ (†)	‡ (†)	‡ (†)	‡ (†)	‡ (†)	# (†)	‡ (†)	‡ (†)	‡ (†)

—Not available.
†Not applicable.
#Rounds to zero.
!Interpret data with caution. The coefficient of variation (CV) for this estimate is between 30 and 50 percent.
‡Reporting standards not met. Either there are too few cases for a reliable estimate or the coefficient of variation (CV) is 50 percent or greater.
[1]Race categories exclude persons of Hispanic ethnicity. Prior to 2003, separate data for Asian students, Pacific Islander students, and students of Two or more races were not collected.
[2]Refers to the Standard Metropolitan Statistical Area (MSA) status of the respondent's household as defined by the U.S. Census Bureau. Categories include "central city of an MSA (Urban)," "in MSA but not in central city (Suburban)," and "not MSA (Rural)."
[3]Serious violent victimization is also included in violent victimization.

NOTE: "Total victimization" includes theft and violent victimization. A single student could report more than one type of victimization. In the total victimization section, students who reported both theft and violent victimization are counted only once. "Theft" includes attempted and completed purse-snatching, completed pickpocketing, and all attempted and completed thefts, with the exception of motor vehicle thefts. Theft does not include robbery, which involves the threat or use of force and is classified as a violent crime. "Serious violent victimization" includes the crimes of rape, sexual assault, robbery, and aggravated assault. "Violent victimization" includes the serious violent crimes as well as simple assault. "At school" includes in the school building, on school property, on a school bus, and, from 2001 onward, going to and from school. Some data have been revised from previously published figures.
SOURCE: U.S. Department of Justice, Bureau of Justice Statistics, School Crime Supplement (SCS) to the National Crime Victimization Survey, 1995 through 2017. (This table was prepared September 2018.)

Table 229.10. Percentage of public schools recording incidents of crime at school and reporting incidents to police, number of incidents, and rate per 1,000 students, by type of crime: Selected years, 1999–2000 through 2015–16

[Standard errors appear in parentheses]

Type of crime recorded or reported to police	Percent of schools						2015–16		
	1999–2000	2003–04	2005–06	2007–08	2009–10	2013–14[1]	Percent of schools	Number of incidents	Rate per 1,000 students
1	2	3	4	5	6	7	8	9	10
Recorded incidents									
Total	**86.4 (1.23)**	**88.5 (0.85)**	**85.7 (1.07)**	**85.5 (0.87)**	**85.0 (1.07)**	**— (†)**	**78.9 (1.28)**	**1,381,200 (42,660)**	**28.0 (0.90)**
Violent incidents	**71.4 (1.37)**	**81.4 (1.05)**	**77.7 (1.11)**	**75.5 (1.09)**	**73.8 (1.07)**	**65.0 (1.46)**	**68.9 (1.30)**	**864,900 (42,950)**	**17.5 (0.89)**
Serious violent incidents	19.7 (0.98)	18.3 (0.99)	17.1 (0.91)	17.2 (1.06)	16.4 (0.94)	13.1 (1.00)	15.5 (0.93)	40,800 (3,460)	0.8 (0.07)
Rape or attempted rape	0.7 (0.10)	0.8 (0.17)	0.3 (0.07)	0.8 (0.17)	0.5 (0.10)	0.2! (0.10)	0.9 (0.19)	1,100 (190)	# (†)
Sexual assault other than rape[2]	2.5 (0.33)	3.0 (0.32)	2.8 (0.24)	2.5 (0.33)	2.3 (0.34)	1.7 (0.37)	3.4 (0.38)	6,100 (1,360)	0.1 (0.03)
Physical attack or fight with a weapon	5.2 (0.60)	4.0 (0.46)	3.0 (0.38)	3.0 (0.33)	3.9 (0.48)	1.8 (0.34)	2.6 (0.38)	5,300 (1,280)	0.1 (0.03)
Threat of physical attack with a weapon	11.1 (0.70)	8.6 (0.71)	8.8 (0.66)	9.3 (0.77)	7.7 (0.72)	8.7 (0.78)	8.5 (0.79)	18,300 (2,420)	0.4 (0.05)
Robbery with a weapon	0.5! (0.15)	0.6 (0.15)	0.4 (0.12)	0.4! (0.14)	0.2 (0.05)	‡ (†)	0.5! (0.16)	600 (160)	# (†)
Robbery without a weapon	5.3 (0.56)	6.3 (0.60)	6.4 (0.59)	5.2 (0.56)	4.4 (0.49)	2.5 (0.42)	2.7 (0.36)	9,500 (1,440)	0.2 (0.03)
Physical attack or fight without a weapon	63.7 (1.52)	76.7 (1.21)	74.3 (1.20)	72.7 (1.07)	70.5 (1.11)	57.5 (1.43)	64.9 (1.28)	567,000 (36,780)	11.5 (0.75)
Threat of physical attack without a weapon	52.2 (1.47)	53.0 (1.34)	52.2 (1.27)	47.8 (1.19)	46.4 (1.33)	47.1 (1.50)	39.4 (1.48)	257,000 (15,630)	5.2 (0.33)
Theft[3]	**45.6 (1.37)**	**46.0 (1.29)**	**46.0 (1.07)**	**47.3 (1.29)**	**44.1 (1.31)**	**— (†)**	**38.7 (1.29)**	**166,000 (5,190)**	**3.4 (0.11)**
Other incidents[4]	**72.7 (1.30)**	**64.0 (1.27)**	**68.2 (1.07)**	**67.4 (1.13)**	**68.1 (1.12)**	**— (†)**	**58.5 (1.68)**	**350,400 (10,710)**	**7.1 (0.22)**
Possession of a firearm/explosive device	5.5 (0.44)	6.1 (0.49)	7.2 (0.60)	4.7 (0.38)	4.7 (0.52)	— (†)	4.0 (0.50)	10,500! (3,220)	0.2! (0.06)
Possession of a knife or sharp object	42.6 (1.28)	— (†)	42.8 (1.23)	40.6 (1.10)	39.7 (1.06)	— (†)	38.4 (1.26)	70,600 (3,210)	1.4 (0.07)
Distribution of illegal drugs[5]	12.3 (0.50)	12.9 (0.55)	— (†)	— (†)	— (†)	— (†)	— (†)	— (†)	— (†)
Possession or use of alcohol or illegal drugs[5]	26.6 (0.72)	29.3 (0.87)	— (†)	— (†)	— (†)	— (†)	— (†)	— (†)	— (†)
Distribution, possession, or use of illegal drugs[6]	— (†)	— (†)	25.9 (0.68)	23.2 (0.68)	24.6 (0.57)	— (†)	24.9 (0.85)	112,100 (4,250)	2.3 (0.09)
Inappropriate distribution, possession, or use of prescription drugs[7]	— (†)	— (†)	— (†)	— (†)	12.1 (0.47)	— (†)	9.5 (0.55)	20,100 (1,580)	0.4 (0.03)
Distribution, possession, or use of alcohol[6]	— (†)	— (†)	16.2 (0.68)	14.9 (0.57)	14.1 (0.50)	— (†)	13.3 (0.50)	29,900 (1,620)	0.6 (0.03)
Sexual harassment	36.3 (1.26)	— (†)	— (†)	— (†)	— (†)	— (†)	— (†)	— (†)	— (†)
Vandalism	51.4 (1.61)	51.4 (1.17)	50.5 (1.17)	49.3 (1.16)	45.8 (1.12)	— (†)	33.4 (1.25)	107,200 (7,040)	2.2 (0.14)
Reported incidents to police									
Total	**62.5 (1.37)**	**65.2 (1.35)**	**60.9 (1.15)**	**62.0 (1.24)**	**60.0 (1.58)**	**— (†)**	**47.4 (1.54)**	**448,900 (13,330)**	**9.1 (0.27)**
Violent incidents	**36.0 (0.82)**	**43.6 (1.15)**	**37.7 (1.09)**	**37.8 (1.16)**	**39.9 (1.13)**	**— (†)**	**32.7 (1.13)**	**195,600 (9,620)**	**4.0 (0.20)**
Serious violent incidents	14.8 (0.10)	13.3 (0.88)	12.6 (0.70)	12.6 (0.86)	10.4 (0.62)	— (†)	10.0 (0.68)	20,000 (1,700)	0.4 (0.04)
Rape or attempted rape	0.6 (0.34)	0.8 (0.17)	0.3 (0.07)	0.8 (0.17)	0.5 (0.10)	— (†)	0.7 (0.14)	900 (160)	# (†)
Sexual assault other than rape[2]	2.3 (0.50)	2.6 (0.28)	2.6 (0.26)	2.1 (0.29)	1.4 (0.20)	— (†)	2.7 (0.28)	3,600 (490)	0.1 (0.01)
Physical attack or fight with a weapon	3.9 (0.59)	2.8 (0.38)	2.2 (0.27)	2.1 (0.27)	2.2 (0.32)	— (†)	1.3 (0.24)	2,500! (830)	0.1! (0.02)
Threat of physical attack with a weapon	8.5 (0.09)	6.0 (0.55)	5.9 (0.49)	5.7 (0.59)	4.5 (0.43)	— (†)	5.3 (0.53)	7,500 (770)	0.2 (0.02)
Robbery with a weapon	0.3! (0.41)	0.6 (0.15)	0.4 (0.12)	0.4! (0.14)	0.2 (0.05)	— (†)	0.3! (0.13)	400! (140)	# (†)
Robbery without a weapon	3.4 (0.91)	4.2 (0.51)	4.9 (0.48)	4.1 (0.42)	3.5 (0.40)	— (†)	1.9 (0.28)	5,000 (690)	0.1 (0.01)
Physical attack or fight without a weapon	25.8 (0.94)	35.6 (0.98)	29.2 (1.00)	28.2 (0.90)	34.3 (0.90)	— (†)	25.1 (1.03)	121,500 (8,560)	2.5 (0.18)
Threat of physical attack without a weapon	18.9 (0.94)	21.0 (0.82)	19.7 (0.69)	19.5 (0.76)	15.2 (0.79)	— (†)	12.9 (0.65)	54,200 (3,680)	1.1 (0.07)

See notes at end of table.

Table 229.10. Percentage of public schools recording incidents of crime at school and reporting incidents to police, number of incidents, and rate per 1,000 students, by type of crime: Selected years, 1999–2000 through 2015–16—Continued

[Standard errors appear in parentheses]

Type of crime recorded or reported to police	Percent of schools												2015–16					
	1999–2000		2003–04		2005–06		2007–08		2009–10		2013–14[1]		Percent of schools		Number of incidents		Rate per 1,000 students	
1		2		3		4		5		6		7		8		9		10
Theft[3]	**28.5**	**(1.04)**	**30.5**	**(1.17)**	**27.9**	**(0.97)**	**31.0**	**(1.12)**	**25.4**	**(1.01)**	**—**	**(†)**	**18.1**	**(0.80)**	**71,600**	**(3,280)**	**1.5**	**(0.07)**
Other incidents[4]	**52.0**	**(1.14)**	**50.0**	**(1.18)**	**50.6**	**(1.00)**	**48.7**	**(1.17)**	**46.3**	**(1.23)**	**—**	**(†)**	**33.5**	**(1.15)**	**181,700**	**(5,500)**	**3.7**	**(0.11)**
Possession of a firearm/explosive device	4.5	(0.41)	4.9	(0.44)	5.5	(0.51)	3.6	(0.32)	3.1	(0.39)	—	(†)	1.9	(0.29)	7,500!	(2,760)	0.2!	(0.06)
Possession of a knife or sharp object	23.0	(0.84)	—	(†)	25.0	(1.00)	23.3	(0.69)	20.0	(0.88)	—	(†)	15.8	(0.66)	27,700	(1,330)	0.6	(0.03)
Distribution of illegal drugs[5]	11.4	(0.48)	12.4	(0.57)	—	(†)	—	(†)	—	(†)	—	(†)	—	(†)	—	(†)	—	(†)
Possession or use of alcohol or illegal drugs[5]	22.2	(0.67)	26.0	(0.76)	—	(†)	—	(†)	—	(†)	—	(†)	—	(†)	—	(†)	—	(†)
Distribution, possession, or use of illegal drugs[6]	—	(†)	—	(†)	22.8	(0.62)	20.7	(0.60)	21.4	(0.57)	—	(†)	19.9	(0.71)	82,200	(3,300)	1.7	(0.07)
Inappropriate distribution, possession, or use of prescription drugs[7]	—	(†)	—	(†)	—	(†)	—	(†)	9.6	(0.42)	—	(†)	7.4	(0.56)	15,100	(1,270)	0.3	(0.03)
Distribution, possession, or use of alcohol[6]	—	(†)	—	(†)	11.6	(0.61)	10.6	(0.55)	10.0	(0.41)	—	(†)	8.6	(0.41)	17,800	(1,330)	0.4	(0.03)
Sexual harassment	14.7	(0.78)	—	(†)	—	(†)	—	(†)	—	(†)	—	(†)	—	(†)	—	(†)	—	(†)
Vandalism	32.7	(1.10)	34.3	(1.06)	31.9	(1.02)	30.8	(1.18)	26.8	(1.09)	—	(†)	12.9	(0.86)	31,600	(2,370)	0.6	(0.05)

—Not available.
†Not applicable.
#Rounds to zero.
!Interpret data with caution. The coefficient of variation (CV) for this estimate is between 30 and 50 percent.
‡Reporting standards not met. Either there are too few cases for a reliable estimate or the coefficient of variation (CV) is 50 percent or greater.
[1]Data for 2013–14 were collected using the Fast Response Survey System (FRSS), while data for all other years were collected using the School Survey on Crime and Safety (SSOCS). The 2013–14 FRSS survey was designed to allow comparisons with SSOCS data. However, respondents to the 2013–14 survey could choose either to complete the survey on paper (and mail it back) or to complete the survey online, whereas respondents to SSOCS did not have the option of completing the survey online. The 2013–14 survey also relied on a smaller sample. The smaller sample size and difference in survey administration may have impacted the 2013–14 results.
[2]Prior to 2015–16, the wording of the survey item was "sexual battery other than rape."
[3]Theft/larceny (taking things worth over $10 without personal confrontation) was defined for respondents as "the unlawful taking of another person's property without personal confrontation, threat, violence, or bodily harm." This includes pocket picking, stealing a purse or backpack (if left unattended or no force was used to take it from owner), theft from a building, theft from a motor vehicle or motor vehicle parts or accessories, theft of a bicycle, theft from a vending machine, and all other types of thefts.
[4]Caution should be used when making direct comparisons of "Other incidents" between years because the survey questions about alcohol and drugs changed, as outlined in footnotes 5, 6, and 7.
[5]The survey items "Distribution of illegal drugs" and "Possession or use of alcohol or illegal drugs" appear only on the 1999–2000 and 2003–04 questionnaires. Different alcohol- and drug-related survey items were used on the SSOCS questionnaires for later years.
[6]The survey items "Distribution, possession, or use of illegal drugs" and "Distribution, possession, or use of alcohol" appear only on the SSOCS questionnaires for 2005-06 and later years.
[7]The survey item "Inappropriate distribution, possession, or use of prescription drugs" appears only on the 2009–10 and 2015–16 questionnaires.
NOTE: Responses were provided by the principal or the person most knowledgeable about crime and safety issues at the school. "At school" was defined to include activities that happen in school buildings, on school grounds, on school buses, and at places that hold school-sponsored events or activities. Respondents were instructed to include incidents that occurred before, during, and after normal school hours or when school activities or events were in session. Detail may not sum to totals because of rounding and because schools that recorded or reported more than one type of crime incident were counted only once in the total percentage of schools recording or reporting incidents.
SOURCE: U.S. Department of Education, National Center for Education Statistics, 1999–2000, 2003–04, 2005–06, 2007–08, 2009–10, and 2015–16 School Survey on Crime and Safety (SSOCS), 2000, 2004, 2006, 2008, 2010, and 2016; and Fast Response Survey System (FRSS), "School Safety and Discipline: 2013–14," FRSS 106, 2014. (This table was prepared September 2017.)

Table 230.10. Percentage of public schools reporting selected discipline problems that occurred at school, by frequency and selected school characteristics: Selected years, 1999–2000 through 2015–16

[Standard errors appear in parentheses]

Year and school characteristic	Happens at least once a week[1]							Happens at all[2]	
	Student racial/ ethnic tensions[3]	Student bullying[4]	Student sexual harassment of other students	Student harassment of other students based on sexual orientation or gender identity[5]	Student verbal abuse of teachers	Widespread disorder in classrooms	Student acts of disrespect for teachers other than verbal abuse	Gang activities	Cult or extremist group activities
1	2	3	4	5	6	7	8	9	10
All schools									
1999–2000	3.4 (0.41)	29.3 (1.21)	— (†)	— (†)	12.5 (0.69)	3.1 (0.44)	— (†)	18.7 (0.85)	6.7 (0.46)
2003–04	2.1 (0.28)	26.8 (1.09)	4.0 (0.40)	— (†)	10.7 (0.80)	2.8 (0.39)	— (†)	16.7 (0.78)	3.4 (0.35)
2005–06	2.8 (0.31)	24.5 (1.14)	3.5 (0.40)	— (†)	9.5 (0.61)	2.3 (0.24)	— (†)	16.9 (0.76)	3.7 (0.41)
2007–08	3.7 (0.49)	25.3 (1.11)	3.0 (0.39)	— (†)	6.0 (0.48)	4.0 (0.45)	10.5 (0.71)	19.8 (0.88)	2.6 (0.36)
2009–10	2.8 (0.39)	23.1 (1.12)	3.2 (0.55)	2.5 (0.41)	4.8 (0.49)	2.5 (0.37)	8.6 (0.67)	16.4 (0.84)	1.7 (0.31)
2013–14[6]	1.4 (0.31)	15.7 (1.12)	1.4 (0.26)	0.8 (0.19)	5.1 (0.54)	2.3 (0.45)	8.6 (0.74)	— (†)	— (†)
2015–16									
All schools	**1.7 (0.33)**	**11.9 (0.79)**	**1.0 (0.19)**	**0.6 (0.13)**	**4.8 (0.51)**	**2.3 (0.38)**	**10.3 (0.80)**	**10.4 (0.62)**	**— (†)**
School level[7]									
Primary	1.2! (0.48)	8.1 (1.04)	‡ (†)	‡ (†)	3.6 (0.74)	1.6! (0.59)	8.8 (1.27)	2.7 (0.66)	— (†)
Middle	3.2 (0.69)	21.8 (1.59)	2.1 (0.44)	1.2! (0.40)	8.2 (1.13)	4.9 (0.67)	15.9 (1.28)	19.4 (1.33)	— (†)
High school	2.3 (0.64)	14.7 (1.37)	2.5 (0.55)	2.2 (0.59)	7.6 (1.24)	2.6 (0.52)	12.1 (1.47)	30.6 (1.70)	— (†)
Combined	‡ (†)	11.0 (3.17)	‡ (†)	‡ (†)	‡ (†)	‡ (†)	4.3! (1.89)	7.2! (2.85)	— (†)
Enrollment size									
Less than 300	‡ (†)	6.4 (1.58)	‡ (†)	‡ (†)	3.6! (1.31)	‡ (†)	6.4 (1.62)	6.0 (1.52)	— (†)
300 to 499	‡ (†)	9.6 (1.72)	0.7! (0.32)	0.4! (0.19)	3.4 (1.00)	1.3 (0.37)	9.1 (1.87)	6.5 (1.17)	— (†)
500 to 999	2.3 (0.62)	14.0 (1.40)	1.4 (0.32)	0.7! (0.27)	6.0 (0.85)	3.8 (0.91)	12.4 (1.25)	9.3 (0.79)	— (†)
1,000 or more	2.6 (0.64)	22.1 (1.81)	2.4! (0.74)	1.5! (0.49)	7.0 (0.89)	3.8 (0.78)	14.4 (1.74)	35.0 (1.82)	— (†)
Locale									
City	1.8! (0.77)	12.9 (1.45)	0.9! (0.36)	0.9! (0.36)	9.6 (1.58)	4.9 (1.22)	15.3 (1.90)	17.9 (1.79)	— (†)
Suburban	2.3 (0.67)	10.3 (1.12)	0.9! (0.29)	0.3! (0.13)	3.3 (0.74)	1.9 (0.47)	8.1 (1.04)	8.7 (0.79)	— (†)
Town	‡ (†)	18.3 (2.77)	1.2! (0.62)	‡ (†)	5.4 (1.62)	1.5! (0.53)	14.5 (2.93)	8.8 (1.45)	— (†)
Rural	0.9! (0.38)	9.7 (1.58)	1.2 (0.37)	0.8! (0.29)	1.3! (0.54)	‡ (†)	5.9 (1.31)	5.7 (0.99)	— (†)
Percent combined enrollment of Black, Hispanic, Asian, Pacific Islander, and American Indian/Alaska Native students, and students of Two or more races									
Less than 5 percent	‡ (†)	15.6 (4.31)	‡ (†)	‡ (†)	‡ (†)	‡ (†)	‡ (†)	‡ (†)	— (†)
5 percent to less than 20 percent	1.0! (0.38)	10.8 (1.61)	1.4! (0.46)	‡ (†)	2.1! (0.80)	0.8! (0.36)	6.5 (1.39)	1.9 (0.44)	— (†)
20 percent to less than 50 percent	1.4! (0.54)	11.0 (1.42)	0.9 (0.26)	0.9! (0.28)	3.6 (0.83)	1.1 (0.31)	9.9 (1.81)	7.7 (0.92)	— (†)
50 percent or more	2.6 (0.67)	12.5 (1.23)	1.0 (0.30)	0.7! (0.24)	7.9 (1.05)	4.3 (0.86)	13.7 (1.46)	18.6 (1.33)	— (†)
Percent of students eligible for free or reduced-price lunch									
0 to 25 percent	‡ (†)	9.5 (1.67)	1.1! (0.49)	‡ (†)	‡ (†)	‡ (†)	3.5 (0.98)	2.5 (0.47)	— (†)
26 to 50 percent	1.2! (0.37)	10.0 (1.22)	1.3 (0.35)	0.6! (0.22)	3.1! (0.97)	1.5! (0.60)	8.8 (1.58)	5.8 (0.58)	— (†)
51 to 75 percent	1.8! (0.53)	11.8 (1.65)	0.9 (0.26)	0.7! (0.27)	5.0 (1.05)	2.4 (0.68)	9.5 (1.38)	11.0 (0.94)	— (†)
76 to 100 percent	3.1! (1.01)	15.3 (1.91)	‡ (†)	‡ (†)	8.9 (1.39)	4.4 (1.16)	16.7 (1.90)	19.2 (2.10)	— (†)

See notes at end of table.

Table 230.10. Percentage of public schools reporting selected discipline problems that occurred at school, by frequency and selected school characteristics: Selected years, 1999–2000 through 2015–16—Continued

[Standard errors appear in parentheses]

Year and school characteristic	Happens at least once a week[1]							Happens at all[2]	
	Student racial/ethnic tensions[3]	Student bullying[4]	Student sexual harassment of other students	Student harassment of other students based on sexual orientation or gender identity[5]	Student verbal abuse of teachers	Widespread disorder in classrooms	Student acts of disrespect for teachers other than verbal abuse	Gang activities	Cult or extremist group activities
1	2	3	4	5	6	7	8	9	10
Student/teacher ratio[8]									
Less than 12	‡ (†)	9.2 (2.45)	‡ (†)	‡ (†)	2.5! (0.79)	2.7! (1.06)	4.5 (1.25)	4.4 (0.86)	— (†)
12 to 16	1.1! (0.34)	9.1 (1.10)	0.9! (0.32)	0.6! (0.30)	5.8 (1.09)	2.9 (0.83)	12.1 (1.52)	9.4 (1.17)	— (†)
More than 16	2.6 (0.60)	14.5 (1.16)	1.0 (0.21)	0.7 (0.17)	4.7 (0.65)	1.8 (0.38)	10.6 (1.07)	12.7 (1.08)	— (†)
Prevalence of violent incidents[9] at school during school year									
No violent incidents	‡ (†)	3.3! (1.02)	‡ (†)	‡ (†)	‡ (†)	‡ (†)	4.6 (1.16)	2.5! (0.99)	— (†)
Any violent incidents	2.2 (0.44)	15.8 (1.11)	1.4 (0.26)	0.9 (0.19)	6.7 (0.68)	3.3 (0.54)	12.9 (1.07)	13.9 (0.87)	— (†)

—Not available.
†Not applicable.
!Interpret data with caution. The coefficient of variation (CV) for this estimate is between 30 and 50 percent.
‡Reporting standards not met. Either there are too few cases for a reliable estimate or the coefficient of variation (CV) is 50 percent or greater.
[1]Includes schools that reported the activity happens either at least once a week or daily.
[2]Includes schools that reported the activity happens at all at their school during the school year. In the 1999–2000 survey administration, the questionnaire specified "undesirable" gang activities and "undesirable" cult or extremist group activities. The 2013–14 and 2015–16 questionnaires did not ask about cult or extremist group activities.
[3]Prior to the 2007–08 survey administration, the questionnaire wording was "student racial tensions."
[4]The 2015–16 questionnaire defined bullying as "any unwanted aggressive behavior(s) by another youth or group of youths who are not siblings or current dating partners that involves an observed or perceived power imbalance and is repeated multiple times or is highly likely to be repeated." The term was not defined for respondents in previous survey administrations.
[5]Prior to 2015–16, the questionnaire asked about "student harassment of other students based on sexual orientation or gender identity (i.e., lesbian, gay, bisexual, transgender, questioning)" in one single item. The 2015–16 questionnaire had one item asking about "student harassment of other students based on sexual orientation," followed by a separate item on "student harassment of other students based on gender identity." For 2015–16, schools are included in this column if they responded "daily" or "at least once a week" to either or both of these items; each school is counted only once, even if it indicated daily/weekly frequency for both items. The 2015–16 questionnaire provided definitions for sexual orientation—"one's emotional or physical attraction to the same and/or opposite sex"—and gender identity—"one's inner sense of one's own gender, which may or may not match the sex assigned at birth. Different people choose to express their gender identity differently..." These terms were not defined for respondents in previous survey administrations.
[6]Data for 2013–14 were collected using the Fast Response Survey System (FRSS), while data for all other years were collected using the School Survey on Crime and Safety (SSOCS). The 2013–14 FRSS survey was designed to allow comparisons with SSOCS data. However, respondents to the 2013–14 survey could choose either to complete the survey on paper (and mail it back) or to complete the survey online, whereas respondents to SSOCS did not have the option of completing the survey online. The 2013–14 survey also relied on a smaller sample. The smaller sample size and difference in survey administration may have impacted the 2013–14 results.
[7]Primary schools are defined as schools in which the lowest grade is not higher than grade 3 and the highest grade is not higher than grade 8. Middle schools are defined as schools in which the lowest grade is not lower than grade 4 and the highest grade is not higher than grade 9. High schools are defined as schools in which the lowest grade is not lower than grade 9 and the highest grade is not higher than grade 12. Combined schools include all other combinations of grades, including K–12 schools.
[8]Student/teacher ratio was calculated by dividing the total number of students enrolled in the school, as reported on SSOCS, by the total number of full-time-equivalent (FTE) teachers. Information regarding the total number of FTE teachers was obtained from the Common Core of Data (CCD), the sampling frame for SSOCS.
[9]"Violent incidents" include rape or attempted rape, sexual assault other than rape, physical attack or fight with or without a weapon, threat of physical attack or fight with or without a weapon, and robbery with or without a weapon. Respondents were instructed to include violent incidents that occurred before, during, or after normal school hours or when school activities or events were in session.
NOTE: Responses were provided by the principal or the person most knowledgeable about crime and safety issues at the school. "At school" was defined for respondents to include activities that happen in school buildings, on school grounds, on school buses, and at places that hold school-sponsored events or activities. Respondents were instructed to respond only for those times that were during normal school hours or when school activities or events were in session, unless the survey specified otherwise.
SOURCE: U.S. Department of Education, National Center for Education Statistics, 1999–2000, 2003–04, 2005–06, 2007–08, 2009–10, and 2015–16 School Survey on Crime and Safety (SSOCS), 2000, 2004, 2006, 2008, 2010, and 2016; and Fast Response Survey System (FRSS), "School Safety and Discipline: 2013–14," FRSS 106, 2014. (This table was prepared August 2017.)

Table 230.40. Percentage of students ages 12–18 who reported being bullied at school during the school year, by selected student and school characteristics: Selected years, 2005 through 2017

[Standard errors appear in parentheses]

Student or school characteristic	2005[1]		2007		2009		2011		2013		2015		2017	
1	2		3		4		5		6		7		8	
Total	**28.5**	**(0.70)**	**31.7**	**(0.74)**	**28.0**	**(0.83)**	**27.8**	**(0.76)**	**21.5**	**(0.66)**	**20.8**	**(0.99)**	**20.2**	**(0.71)**
Sex														
Male	27.5	(0.90)	30.3	(0.96)	26.6	(1.04)	24.5	(0.91)	19.5	(0.81)	18.8	(1.31)	16.7	(0.87)
Female	29.7	(0.85)	33.2	(0.99)	29.5	(1.08)	31.4	(0.99)	23.7	(0.98)	22.8	(1.39)	23.8	(1.01)
Race/ethnicity														
White	30.3	(0.85)	34.1	(0.97)	29.3	(1.03)	31.5	(1.07)	23.7	(0.93)	21.6	(1.43)	22.8	(1.02)
Black	29.2	(2.23)	30.4	(2.18)	29.1	(2.29)	27.2	(1.97)	20.3	(1.81)	24.7	(3.29)	22.9	(1.98)
Hispanic	22.3	(1.29)	27.3	(1.53)	25.5	(1.71)	21.9	(1.07)	19.2	(1.30)	17.2	(1.58)	15.7	(1.12)
Asian/Pacific Islander	20.8	(2.61)	17.2	(2.47)	17.8	(2.79)	13.8	(2.48)	9.3	(1.67)	19.4	(4.45)	7.3	(1.54)
Asian	20.9	2.7	18.1	(2.60)	17.3	(3.01)	14.9	(2.70)	9.2	(1.67)	15.6	(4.02)	7.3	(1.56)
Pacific Islander	‡	(†)	‡	(†)	‡	(†)	‡	(†)	‡	(†)	‡	(†)	‡	(†)
American Indian/Alaska Native	‡	(†)	29.8	(7.40)	‡	(†)	21.1!	(6.72)	24.3!	(9.87)	‡	(†)	27.2	(5.93)
Two or more races	34.6	(4.44)	38.2	(3.95)	27.3	(5.56)	26.9	(4.30)	27.6	(4.50)	17.7	(3.96)	23.2	(3.03)
Grade														
6th	37.0	(2.06)	42.7	(2.23)	39.4	(2.60)	37.0	(2.17)	27.8	(2.31)	31.0	(3.53)	29.5	(2.79)
7th	35.1	(1.70)	35.6	(1.78)	33.1	(1.87)	30.3	(1.64)	26.4	(1.65)	25.1	(2.48)	24.4	(1.60)
8th	31.3	(1.60)	36.9	(1.84)	31.7	(1.85)	30.7	(1.68)	21.7	(1.42)	22.2	(2.41)	25.3	(1.69)
9th	28.3	(1.59)	30.6	(1.72)	28.0	(1.90)	26.5	(1.66)	23.0	(1.42)	19.0	(2.11)	19.3	(1.52)
10th	25.1	(1.42)	27.7	(1.44)	26.6	(1.71)	28.0	(1.56)	19.5	(1.48)	21.2	(2.13)	18.9	(1.67)
11th	23.5	(1.62)	28.5	(1.48)	21.1	(1.69)	23.8	(1.72)	20.0	(1.50)	15.8	(2.24)	14.7	(1.45)
12th	20.8	(1.83)	23.0	(1.60)	20.4	(1.63)	22.0	(1.34)	14.1	(1.51)	14.9	(2.18)	12.2	(1.34)
Urbanicity[2]														
Urban	26.2	(1.32)	30.7	(1.36)	27.4	(1.25)	24.8	(1.28)	20.7	(1.10)	21.5	(1.84)	18.3	(1.32)
Suburban	29.4	(0.80)	31.2	(1.07)	27.5	(1.06)	29.0	(1.07)	22.0	(0.90)	21.1	(1.22)	19.7	(0.80)
Rural	29.5	(1.97)	35.2	(1.73)	30.7	(1.99)	29.7	(1.82)	21.4	(1.86)	18.2	(2.86)	26.7	(2.13)
Control of school[3]														
Public	29.0	(0.74)	32.0	(0.76)	28.8	(0.88)	28.4	(0.82)	21.5	(0.67)	21.1	(1.06)	20.6	(0.73)
Private	23.3	(2.16)	29.1	(2.10)	18.9	(2.16)	21.5	(1.91)	22.4	(2.71)	16.1	(3.40)	16.0	(2.39)

†Not applicable.
!Interpret data with caution. The coefficient of variation (CV) for this estimate is between 30 and 50 percent.
‡Reporting standards not met. Either there are too few cases for a reliable estimate or the coefficient of variation (CV) is 50 percent or greater.
[1]In 2005, the period covered by the survey question was "during the last 6 months," whereas the period was "during this school year" beginning in 2007. Cognitive testing showed that estimates for 2005 are comparable to those for 2007 and later years.
[2]Refers to the Standard Metropolitan Statistical Area (MSA) status of the respondent's household as defined by the U.S. Census Bureau. Categories include "central city of an MSA (Urban)," "in MSA but not in central city (Suburban)," and "not MSA (Rural)." These data by metropolitan status were based on the location of households and differ from those published in *Student Reports of Bullying: Results From the 2015 School Crime Supplement to the National Crime Victimization Survey*, which were based on the urban-centric measure of the location of the school that the child attended.
[3]Control of school as reported by the respondent. These data differ from those based on a matching of the respondent-reported school name to the Common Core of Data's Public Elementary/Secondary School Universe Survey or the Private School Survey, as reported in *Student Reports of Bullying: Results From the 2015 School Crime Supplement to the National Crime Victimization Survey*.
NOTE: "At school" includes in the school building, on school property, on a school bus, and going to and from school. Race categories exclude persons of Hispanic ethnicity. Some data have been revised from previously published figures.
SOURCE: U.S. Department of Justice, Bureau of Justice Statistics, School Crime Supplement (SCS) to the National Crime Victimization Survey, selected years, 2005 through 2017. (This table was prepared September 2018.)

Table 231.10. Percentage of students in grades 9–12 who reported having been in a physical fight at least one time during the previous 12 months, by location and selected student characteristics: Selected years, 1993 through 2017

[Standard errors appear in parentheses]

Location and student characteristic	1993	1997	1999	2001	2003	2005	2007	2009	2011	2013	2015	2017
1	2	3	4	5	6	7	8	9	10	11	12	13
Anywhere (including on school property)[1]												
Total	**41.8 (0.99)**	**36.6 (1.01)**	**35.7 (1.17)**	**33.2 (0.71)**	**33.0 (0.99)**	**35.9 (0.77)**	**35.5 (0.77)**	**31.5 (0.70)**	**32.8 (0.65)**	**24.7 (0.74)**	**22.6 (0.87)**	**23.6 (0.97)**
Sex												
Male	51.2 (1.05)	45.5 (1.07)	44.0 (1.27)	43.1 (0.84)	40.5 (1.32)	43.4 (1.01)	44.4 (0.89)	39.3 (1.20)	40.7 (0.74)	30.2 (1.10)	28.4 (1.04)	30.0 (1.14)
Female	31.7 (1.19)	26.0 (1.26)	27.3 (1.70)	23.9 (0.95)	25.1 (0.85)	28.1 (0.94)	26.5 (0.99)	22.9 (0.74)	24.4 (0.92)	19.2 (0.72)	16.5 (1.04)	17.2 (1.01)
Race/ethnicity												
White	40.3 (1.13)	33.7 (1.29)	33.1 (1.45)	32.2 (0.95)	30.5 (1.11)	33.1 (0.88)	31.7 (0.96)	27.8 (0.88)	29.4 (0.74)	20.9 (0.70)	20.1 (1.13)	20.8 (0.82)
Black	49.5 (1.82)	43.0 (1.92)	41.4 (3.12)	36.5 (1.60)	39.7 (1.23)	43.1 (1.74)	44.7 (1.33)	41.1 (1.71)	39.1 (1.52)	34.7 (1.67)	32.4 (2.11)	33.2 (2.49)
Hispanic	43.2 (1.58)	40.7 (1.68)	39.9 (1.65)	35.8 (0.91)	36.1 (0.98)	41.0 (1.64)	40.4 (1.25)	36.2 (0.95)	36.8 (1.44)	28.4 (1.15)	23.0 (1.10)	25.7 (1.85)
Asian[2]	— (†)	— (†)	22.7 (2.71)	22.3 (2.73)	25.9 (2.99)	21.6 (2.43)	24.3 (3.50)	18.9 (1.72)	18.4 (1.87)	16.1 (1.87)	14.7 (1.12)	11.0 (1.61)
Pacific Islander[2]	— (†)	— (†)	50.7 (3.42)	51.7 (6.25)	30.0 (5.21)	34.4 (5.58)	42.6 (7.74)	32.6 (3.50)	43.0 (5.14)	22.0 (4.95)	29.2 (7.98)	22.6 (2.47)
American Indian/Alaska Native	49.8 (4.79)	54.7 (5.75)	48.7 (6.78)	49.2 (6.58)	46.6 (6.53)	44.2 (3.40)	36.0 (1.49)	42.4 (5.23)	42.4 (2.12)	32.1 (7.39)	29.9 (5.07)	34.7 (6.36)
Two or more races[2]	— (†)	— (†)	40.2 (2.76)	39.6 (2.85)	38.2 (3.64)	46.9 (4.16)	47.8 (3.30)	34.2 (3.51)	45.0 (2.60)	28.5 (2.31)	27.6 (2.58)	25.5 (2.30)
Sexual orientation[3]												
Heterosexual	— (†)	— (†)	— (†)	— (†)	— (†)	— (†)	— (†)	— (†)	— (†)	— (†)	21.7 (0.78)	23.2 (0.95)
Gay, lesbian, or bisexual	— (†)	— (†)	— (†)	— (†)	— (†)	— (†)	— (†)	— (†)	— (†)	— (†)	28.4 (2.34)	27.9 (1.66)
Not sure	— (†)	— (†)	— (†)	— (†)	— (†)	— (†)	— (†)	— (†)	— (†)	— (†)	34.5 (4.44)	19.8 (2.83)
Grade												
9th	50.4 (1.54)	44.8 (1.98)	41.1 (1.96)	39.5 (1.27)	38.6 (1.38)	43.5 (1.15)	40.9 (1.16)	37.0 (1.21)	37.7 (1.11)	28.3 (1.17)	27.9 (1.51)	28.3 (1.53)
10th	42.2 (1.45)	40.2 (1.91)	37.7 (2.11)	34.7 (1.37)	33.5 (1.20)	36.6 (1.09)	36.2 (1.34)	33.5 (1.19)	35.3 (1.35)	26.4 (1.42)	23.4 (1.46)	26.2 (1.14)
11th	40.5 (1.52)	34.2 (1.72)	31.3 (1.55)	29.1 (1.10)	30.9 (1.38)	31.6 (1.44)	34.8 (1.36)	28.6 (0.93)	29.7 (1.14)	24.0 (1.04)	20.5 (1.23)	20.4 (0.91)
12th	34.8 (1.56)	28.8 (1.36)	30.4 (1.91)	26.5 (1.01)	26.5 (1.08)	29.1 (1.26)	28.0 (1.42)	24.9 (0.99)	26.9 (0.95)	18.8 (1.19)	17.4 (1.23)	17.8 (1.52)
Urbanicity[4]												
Urban	— (†)	38.2 (2.00)	37.0 (2.66)	36.8 (1.53)	35.5 (2.17)	— (†)	— (†)	— (†)	— (†)	— (†)	— (†)	— (†)
Suburban	— (†)	36.7 (1.59)	35.0 (1.56)	31.3 (0.80)	33.1 (1.23)	— (†)	— (†)	— (†)	— (†)	— (†)	— (†)	— (†)
Rural	— (†)	32.9 (2.91)	36.6 (2.14)	33.8 (2.58)	29.7 (1.61)	— (†)	— (†)	— (†)	— (†)	— (†)	— (†)	— (†)
On school property[5]												
Total	**16.2 (0.59)**	**14.8 (0.64)**	**14.2 (0.62)**	**12.5 (0.49)**	**12.8 (0.76)**	**13.6 (0.56)**	**12.4 (0.48)**	**11.1 (0.54)**	**12.0 (0.39)**	**8.1 (0.35)**	**7.8 (0.54)**	**8.5 (0.53)**
Sex												
Male	23.5 (0.71)	20.0 (1.04)	18.5 (0.66)	18.0 (0.74)	17.1 (0.92)	18.2 (0.93)	16.3 (0.60)	15.1 (1.05)	16.0 (0.58)	10.7 (0.55)	10.3 (0.79)	11.6 (0.62)
Female	8.6 (0.73)	8.6 (0.78)	9.8 (0.95)	7.2 (0.47)	8.0 (0.70)	8.8 (0.52)	8.5 (0.62)	6.7 (0.42)	7.8 (0.43)	5.6 (0.38)	5.0 (0.45)	5.6 (0.54)
Race/ethnicity												
White	15.0 (0.68)	13.3 (0.84)	12.3 (0.86)	11.2 (0.60)	10.0 (0.73)	11.6 (0.66)	10.2 (0.56)	8.6 (0.58)	9.9 (0.51)	6.4 (0.45)	5.6 (0.35)	6.5 (0.64)
Black	22.0 (1.39)	20.7 (1.20)	18.7 (1.51)	16.8 (1.26)	17.1 (1.30)	16.9 (1.39)	17.6 (1.10)	17.4 (0.99)	16.4 (0.89)	12.8 (0.84)	12.6 (1.96)	15.3 (1.45)
Hispanic	17.9 (1.75)	19.0 (1.50)	15.7 (0.91)	14.1 (0.89)	16.7 (1.14)	18.3 (1.62)	15.5 (0.81)	13.5 (0.82)	14.4 (0.79)	9.4 (0.44)	8.9 (0.87)	9.4 (0.90)
Asian[2]	— (†)	— (†)	10.4 (0.95)	10.8 (1.92)	13.1 (2.26)	5.9 (1.53)	8.5 (1.99)	7.7 (1.09)	6.2 (1.06)	5.5 (1.39)	6.3 (1.63)	3.7 (1.00)
Pacific Islander[2]	— (†)	— (†)	25.3 (4.60)	29.1 (7.63)	22.2 (4.82)	24.5 (5.60)	9.6! (3.47)	14.8 (2.37)	20.9 (4.41)	7.1! (2.58)	20.9! (7.11)	14.2 (3.58)
American Indian/Alaska Native	18.6 (2.74)	18.9 (5.55)	16.2! (5.23)	18.2 (4.41)	24.2 (5.03)	22.0 (3.16)	15.0 (1.12)	20.7 (3.73)	12.0 (1.77)	10.7 (3.13)	13.2 (3.54)	8.6! (3.74)
Two or more races[2]	— (†)	— (†)	16.9 (2.40)	14.7 (1.97)	20.2 (3.83)	15.8 (2.61)	19.6 (2.39)	12.4 (2.19)	16.6 (1.41)	10.0 (1.04)	9.3 (1.49)	9.2 (1.36)
Sexual orientation[3]												
Heterosexual	— (†)	— (†)	— (†)	— (†)	— (†)	— (†)	— (†)	— (†)	— (†)	— (†)	7.1 (0.51)	8.3 (0.56)
Gay, lesbian, or bisexual	— (†)	— (†)	— (†)	— (†)	— (†)	— (†)	— (†)	— (†)	— (†)	— (†)	11.2 (1.22)	9.6 (1.16)
Not sure	— (†)	— (†)	— (†)	— (†)	— (†)	— (†)	— (†)	— (†)	— (†)	— (†)	14.6 (2.38)	11.8 (2.25)
Grade												
9th	23.1 (1.55)	21.3 (1.29)	18.6 (1.02)	17.3 (0.77)	18.0 (1.24)	18.9 (0.93)	17.0 (0.67)	14.9 (0.98)	16.2 (0.77)	10.9 (0.78)	11.6 (0.82)	12.3 (1.05)
10th	17.2 (1.07)	17.0 (1.67)	17.2 (1.23)	13.5 (0.88)	12.8 (0.89)	14.4 (1.08)	11.7 (0.86)	12.1 (0.83)	12.8 (0.86)	8.3 (0.61)	7.3 (0.76)	9.6 (0.74)
11th	13.8 (1.27)	12.5 (0.87)	10.8 (1.01)	9.4 (0.71)	10.4 (0.89)	10.4 (0.75)	11.0 (0.73)	9.5 (0.63)	9.2 (0.55)	7.5 (0.53)	6.5 (0.83)	6.0 (0.66)
12th	11.4 (0.66)	9.5 (0.73)	8.1 (1.00)	7.5 (0.56)	7.3 (0.70)	8.5 (0.70)	8.6 (0.62)	6.6 (0.59)	8.8 (0.69)	4.9 (0.63)	4.5 (0.51)	5.0 (0.61)
Urbanicity[4]												
Urban	— (†)	15.8 (1.50)	14.4 (1.08)	14.8 (0.90)	14.8 (1.31)	— (†)	— (†)	— (†)	— (†)	— (†)	— (†)	— (†)
Suburban	— (†)	14.2 (0.95)	13.7 (0.86)	11.0 (0.75)	12.8 (1.23)	— (†)	— (†)	— (†)	— (†)	— (†)	— (†)	— (†)
Rural	— (†)	14.7 (2.09)	16.3 (2.33)	13.8 (1.10)	10.0 (1.36)	— (†)	— (†)	— (†)	— (†)	— (†)	— (†)	— (†)

—Not available.
†Not applicable.
!Interpret data with caution. The coefficient of variation (CV) for this estimate is between 30 and 50 percent.
[1]The term "anywhere" is not used in the Youth Risk Behavior Survey (YRBS) questionnaire; students were simply asked how many times in the past 12 months they had been in a physical fight.
[2]Before 1999, Asian students and Pacific Islander students were not categorized separately, and students could not be classified as Two or more races. Because the response categories changed in 1999, caution should be used in comparing data on race from 1993 and 1997 with data from later years.
[3]Students were asked which sexual orientation—"heterosexual (straight)," "gay or lesbian," "bisexual," or "not sure"—best described them.
[4]Refers to the Standard Metropolitan Statistical Area (MSA) status of the respondent's household as defined by the U.S. Census Bureau. Categories include "central city of an MSA (Urban)," "in MSA but not in central city (Suburban)," and "not MSA (Rural)."
[5]In the question asking students about physical fights at school, "on school property" was not defined for survey respondents.
NOTE: Race categories exclude persons of Hispanic ethnicity.
SOURCE: Centers for Disease Control and Prevention, Division of Adolescent and School Health, Youth Risk Behavior Surveillance System (YRBSS), 1993 through 2017. (This table was prepared July 2018.)

Table 232.10. Percentage of students in grades 9–12 who reported using alcohol at least 1 day during the previous 30 days, by location and selected student characteristics: Selected years, 1993 through 2017

[Standard errors appear in parentheses]

Location and student characteristic	1993	1997	1999	2001	2003	2005	2007	2009	2011	2013	2015	2017
1	2	3	4	5	6	7	8	9	10	11	12	13
Anywhere (including on school property)[1]												
Total	**48.0 (1.06)**	**50.8 (1.43)**	**50.0 (1.30)**	**47.1 (1.11)**	**44.9 (1.21)**	**43.3 (1.38)**	**44.7 (1.15)**	**41.8 (0.80)**	**38.7 (0.75)**	**34.9 (1.08)**	**32.8 (1.18)**	**29.8 (1.27)**
Sex												
Male	50.1 (1.23)	53.3 (1.22)	52.3 (1.47)	49.2 (1.42)	43.8 (1.31)	43.8 (1.40)	44.7 (1.39)	40.8 (1.11)	39.5 (0.93)	34.4 (1.30)	32.2 (0.89)	27.6 (1.24)
Female	45.9 (1.32)	47.8 (1.99)	47.7 (1.45)	45.0 (1.11)	45.8 (1.29)	42.8 (1.56)	44.6 (1.42)	42.9 (0.85)	37.9 (0.91)	35.5 (1.39)	33.5 (1.89)	31.8 (1.57)
Race/ethnicity												
White	49.9 (1.26)	54.0 (1.51)	52.5 (1.62)	50.4 (1.12)	47.1 (1.51)	46.4 (1.84)	47.3 (1.67)	44.7 (1.16)	40.3 (0.97)	36.3 (1.63)	35.2 (2.00)	32.4 (1.73)
Black	42.5 (1.82)	36.9 (1.46)	39.9 (4.07)	32.7 (2.33)	37.4 (1.67)	31.2 (1.05)	34.5 (1.65)	33.4 (1.45)	30.5 (1.40)	29.6 (1.65)	23.8 (2.82)	20.8 (2.27)
Hispanic	50.8 (2.82)	53.9 (1.96)	52.8 (2.41)	49.2 (1.52)	45.6 (1.39)	46.8 (1.39)	47.6 (1.80)	42.9 (1.43)	42.3 (1.38)	37.5 (2.11)	34.4 (1.28)	31.3 (1.53)
Asian[2]	— (†)	— (†)	25.7 (2.24)	28.4 (3.22)	27.5 (3.47)	21.5 (1.98)	25.4 (2.17)	18.3 (1.60)	25.6 (2.90)	21.7 (1.80)	13.1 (1.83)	12.2 (1.74)
Pacific Islander[2]	— (†)	— (†)	60.8 (5.11)	52.3 (8.54)	40.0 (7.04)	38.7 (8.43)	48.8 (6.58)	34.8 (4.36)	38.4 (6.40)	26.8 (5.84)	36.9 (10.62)	18.7 (3.17)
American Indian/Alaska Native	45.3 (7.18)	57.6 (3.79)	49.4 (6.43)	51.4 (3.97)	51.9 (5.29)	57.4 (4.13)	34.5 (1.77)	42.8 (5.43)	44.9 (2.26)	33.4 (5.13)	46.0 (8.12)	31.8 (8.15)
Two or more races[2]	— (†)	— (†)	51.1 (3.98)	45.4 (4.11)	47.1 (3.59)	39.0 (3.59)	46.2 (2.89)	44.3 (2.42)	36.9 (3.08)	36.1 (2.87)	39.6 (2.68)	32.7 (2.50)
Sexual orientation[3]												
Heterosexual	— (†)	— (†)	— (†)	— (†)	— (†)	— (†)	— (†)	— (†)	— (†)	— (†)	32.1 (1.30)	29.7 (1.02)
Gay, lesbian, or bisexual	— (†)	— (†)	— (†)	— (†)	— (†)	— (†)	— (†)	— (†)	— (†)	— (†)	40.5 (2.07)	37.4 (2.39)
Not sure	— (†)	— (†)	— (†)	— (†)	— (†)	— (†)	— (†)	— (†)	— (†)	— (†)	34.6 (2.81)	21.5 (2.77)
Grade												
9th	40.5 (1.79)	44.2 (3.12)	40.6 (2.17)	41.1 (1.82)	36.2 (1.43)	36.2 (1.23)	35.7 (1.15)	31.5 (1.28)	29.8 (1.35)	24.4 (1.13)	23.4 (1.28)	18.8 (1.23)
10th	44.0 (2.00)	47.2 (2.19)	49.7 (1.89)	45.2 (1.29)	43.5 (1.66)	42.0 (1.95)	41.8 (1.68)	40.6 (1.42)	35.7 (1.37)	30.9 (1.84)	29.0 (2.49)	27.0 (1.60)
11th	49.7 (1.73)	53.2 (1.49)	50.9 (1.98)	49.3 (1.70)	47.0 (2.08)	46.0 (1.98)	49.0 (1.83)	45.7 (2.05)	42.7 (1.28)	39.2 (1.52)	38.0 (1.68)	34.4 (1.68)
12th	56.4 (1.35)	57.3 (2.50)	61.7 (2.25)	55.2 (1.53)	55.9 (1.65)	50.8 (2.12)	54.9 (2.09)	51.7 (1.37)	48.4 (1.29)	46.8 (1.85)	42.4 (2.00)	40.8 (1.92)
Urbanicity[4]												
Urban	— (†)	48.9 (2.07)	46.5 (2.75)	45.2 (1.97)	41.5 (1.48)	— (†)	— (†)	— (†)	— (†)	— (†)	— (†)	— (†)
Suburban	— (†)	50.5 (2.11)	51.4 (1.32)	47.6 (1.26)	46.5 (2.10)	— (†)	— (†)	— (†)	— (†)	— (†)	— (†)	— (†)
Rural	— (†)	55.4 (5.36)	52.2 (4.51)	50.2 (1.91)	45.3 (2.35)	— (†)	— (†)	— (†)	— (†)	— (†)	— (†)	— (†)
On school property[5]												
Total	**5.2 (0.39)**	**5.6 (0.34)**	**4.9 (0.39)**	**4.9 (0.28)**	**5.2 (0.46)**	**4.3 (0.30)**	**4.1 (0.32)**	**4.5 (0.29)**	**5.1 (0.33)**	**— (†)**	**— (†)**	**— (†)**
Sex												
Male	6.2 (0.39)	7.2 (0.66)	6.1 (0.54)	6.1 (0.43)	6.0 (0.61)	5.3 (0.39)	4.6 (0.35)	5.3 (0.41)	5.4 (0.43)	— (†)	— (†)	— (†)
Female	4.2 (0.54)	3.6 (0.37)	3.6 (0.39)	3.8 (0.39)	4.2 (0.41)	3.3 (0.32)	3.6 (0.37)	3.6 (0.34)	4.7 (0.35)	— (†)	— (†)	— (†)
Race/ethnicity												
White	4.6 (0.44)	4.8 (0.42)	4.8 (0.55)	4.2 (0.26)	3.9 (0.45)	3.8 (0.38)	3.2 (0.35)	3.3 (0.27)	4.0 (0.38)	— (†)	— (†)	— (†)
Black	6.9 (0.98)	5.6 (0.72)	4.3 (0.52)	5.3 (0.65)	5.8 (0.80)	3.2 (0.45)	3.4 (0.63)	5.4 (0.59)	5.1 (0.50)	— (†)	— (†)	— (†)
Hispanic	6.8 (0.84)	8.2 (0.96)	7.0 (0.88)	7.0 (0.71)	7.6 (1.08)	7.7 (1.04)	7.5 (0.86)	6.9 (0.70)	7.3 (0.68)	— (†)	— (†)	— (†)
Asian[2]	— (†)	— (†)	2.0 (0.42)	6.8 (1.42)	5.6 (1.55)	1.3! (0.62)	4.4 (1.17)	2.9 (0.65)	3.5! (1.21)	— (†)	— (†)	— (†)
Pacific Islander[2]	— (†)	— (†)	6.7 (1.59)	12.4 (3.50)	8.5! (3.29)	‡ (†)	‡ (†)	10.0 (2.34)	8.3! (3.61)	— (†)	— (†)	— (†)
American Indian/Alaska Native	6.7! (3.06)	8.6! (4.15)	‡ (†)	8.2 (1.69)	7.1! (2.61)	6.2! (2.05)	5.0 (0.89)	4.3! (1.58)	20.9 (4.15)	— (†)	— (†)	— (†)
Two or more races[2]	— (†)	— (†)	5.2 (1.09)	7.0! (2.36)	13.3 (2.93)	3.5 (1.02)	5.4 (1.25)	6.7 (1.37)	5.8 (1.32)	— (†)	— (†)	— (†)
Grade												
9th	5.2 (0.38)	5.9 (0.83)	4.4 (0.60)	5.3 (0.47)	5.1 (0.69)	3.7 (0.48)	3.4 (0.43)	4.4 (0.37)	5.4 (0.56)	— (†)	— (†)	— (†)
10th	4.7 (0.43)	4.6 (0.71)	5.0 (0.67)	5.1 (0.45)	5.6 (0.60)	4.5 (0.45)	4.1 (0.50)	4.8 (0.46)	4.4 (0.51)	— (†)	— (†)	— (†)
11th	5.2 (0.80)	6.0 (0.86)	4.7 (0.57)	4.7 (0.45)	5.0 (0.57)	4.0 (0.47)	4.2 (0.54)	4.6 (0.44)	5.2 (0.56)	— (†)	— (†)	— (†)
12th	5.5 (0.64)	5.9 (0.66)	5.0 (0.89)	4.3 (0.44)	4.5 (0.68)	4.8 (0.57)	4.8 (0.55)	4.1 (0.44)	5.1 (0.48)	— (†)	— (†)	— (†)
Urbanicity[4]												
Urban	— (†)	6.4 (0.85)	5.0 (0.60)	5.4 (0.61)	6.1 (0.94)	— (†)	— (†)	— (†)	— (†)	— (†)	— (†)	— (†)
Suburban	— (†)	5.2 (0.43)	4.6 (0.61)	4.9 (0.37)	4.8 (0.54)	— (†)	— (†)	— (†)	— (†)	— (†)	— (†)	— (†)
Rural	— (†)	5.3 (0.55)	5.6 (0.67)	4.0 (0.83)	4.7 (0.49)	— (†)	— (†)	— (†)	— (†)	— (†)	— (†)	— (†)

—Not available.
†Not applicable.
!Interpret data with caution. The coefficient of variation (CV) for this estimate is between 30 and 50 percent.
‡Reporting standards not met. The coefficient of variation (CV) for this estimate is 50 percent or greater.
[1]The term "anywhere" is not used in the Youth Risk Behavior Survey (YRBS) questionnaire; students were simply asked how many days during the previous 30 days they had at least one drink of alcohol.
[2]Before 1999, Asian students and Pacific Islander students were not categorized separately, and students could not be classified as Two or more races. Because the response categories changed in 1999, caution should be used in comparing data on race from 1993 and 1997 with data from later years.
[3]Students were asked which sexual orientation—"heterosexual (straight)," "gay or lesbian," "bisexual," or "not sure"—best described them.
[4]Refers to the Standard Metropolitan Statistical Area (MSA) status of the respondent's household as defined by the U.S. Census Bureau. Categories include "central city of an MSA (Urban)," "in MSA but not in central city (Suburban)," and "not MSA (Rural)."
[5]In the question about drinking alcohol at school, "on school property" was not defined for survey respondents. Data on alcohol use at school were not collected from 2013 onward.
NOTE: Race categories exclude persons of Hispanic ethnicity.
SOURCE: Centers for Disease Control and Prevention, Division of Adolescent and School Health, Youth Risk Behavior Surveillance System (YRBSS), 1993 through 2017. (This table was prepared July 2018.)

Table 232.40. Percentage of students in grades 9–12 who reported using marijuana at least one time during the previous 30 days, by location and selected student characteristics: Selected years, 1993 through 2017

[Standard errors appear in parentheses]

Location and student characteristic	1993	1997	1999	2001	2003	2005	2007	2009	2011	2013	2015	2017
1	2	3	4	5	6	7	8	9	10	11	12	13
Anywhere (including on school property)[1]												
Total	**17.7 (1.22)**	**26.2 (1.11)**	**26.7 (1.30)**	**23.9 (0.77)**	**22.4 (1.09)**	**20.2 (0.84)**	**19.7 (0.97)**	**20.8 (0.70)**	**23.1 (0.80)**	**23.4 (1.08)**	**21.7 (1.22)**	**19.8 (0.84)**
Sex												
Male	20.6 (1.61)	30.2 (1.46)	30.8 (1.92)	27.9 (0.81)	25.1 (1.25)	22.1 (0.98)	22.4 (1.02)	23.4 (0.80)	25.9 (1.01)	25.0 (1.14)	23.2 (1.46)	20.0 (0.89)
Female	14.6 (1.02)	21.4 (1.04)	22.6 (0.96)	20.0 (0.87)	19.3 (0.96)	18.2 (0.99)	17.0 (1.13)	17.9 (0.87)	20.1 (0.95)	21.9 (1.28)	20.1 (1.33)	19.6 (1.14)
Race/ethnicity												
White	17.3 (1.41)	25.0 (1.56)	26.4 (1.59)	24.4 (1.04)	21.7 (1.20)	20.3 (1.11)	19.9 (1.28)	20.7 (0.93)	21.7 (1.09)	20.4 (1.36)	19.9 (1.67)	17.7 (1.12)
Black	18.6 (1.84)	28.2 (1.67)	26.4 (3.49)	21.8 (2.12)	23.9 (1.58)	20.4 (1.11)	21.5 (1.64)	22.2 (1.44)	25.1 (1.35)	28.9 (1.30)	27.1 (1.57)	25.3 (1.24)
Hispanic	19.4 (1.33)	28.6 (2.06)	28.2 (2.29)	24.6 (0.81)	23.8 (1.16)	23.0 (1.22)	18.5 (1.41)	21.6 (1.04)	24.4 (1.27)	27.6 (1.50)	24.5 (1.49)	23.4 (1.85)
Asian[2]	— (†)	— (†)	13.5 (2.04)	10.9 (2.12)	9.5 (2.21)	6.7 (1.64)	9.4 (1.63)	7.5 (1.40)	13.6 (3.75)	16.4 (2.99)	8.2 (1.58)	7.3 (1.79)
Pacific Islander[2]	— (†)	— (†)	33.8 (4.11)	21.9 (4.07)	28.1 (6.47)	12.4! (3.87)	28.7 (6.14)	24.8 (5.50)	31.1 (7.08)	23.4! (7.35)	17.4 (4.88)	16.1 (4.08)
American Indian/Alaska Native	17.4 (4.77)	44.2 (4.31)	36.2 (6.55)	36.4 (5.48)	32.8 (5.29)	30.3 (4.36)	27.4 (3.50)	31.6 (5.26)	47.4 (3.20)	35.5 (6.37)	26.9 (5.20)	29.7 (6.30)
Two or more races[2]	— (†)	— (†)	29.1 (4.00)	31.8 (3.22)	28.3 (5.57)	16.9 (2.43)	20.5 (2.73)	21.7 (2.33)	26.8 (2.10)	28.8 (2.55)	23.5 (2.18)	20.3 (2.27)
Sexual orientation[3]												
Heterosexual	— (†)	— (†)	— (†)	— (†)	— (†)	— (†)	— (†)	— (†)	— (†)	— (†)	20.7 (1.29)	19.1 (0.83)
Gay, lesbian, or bisexual	— (†)	— (†)	— (†)	— (†)	— (†)	— (†)	— (†)	— (†)	— (†)	— (†)	32.0 (1.64)	30.6 (1.68)
Not sure	— (†)	— (†)	— (†)	— (†)	— (†)	— (†)	— (†)	— (†)	— (†)	— (†)	26.0 (2.28)	18.9 (2.76)
Grade												
9th	13.2 (1.10)	23.6 (1.95)	21.7 (1.84)	19.4 (1.25)	18.5 (1.52)	17.4 (1.16)	14.7 (1.02)	15.5 (0.97)	18.0 (1.11)	17.7 (1.13)	15.2 (0.98)	13.1 (1.07)
10th	16.5 (1.79)	25.0 (1.29)	27.8 (2.21)	24.8 (1.12)	22.0 (1.47)	20.2 (1.27)	19.3 (1.12)	21.1 (1.11)	21.6 (1.15)	23.5 (1.89)	20.0 (1.87)	18.7 (0.93)
11th	18.4 (1.77)	29.3 (1.81)	26.7 (2.47)	25.8 (1.33)	24.1 (1.56)	21.0 (1.24)	21.4 (1.49)	23.2 (1.52)	25.5 (1.44)	25.5 (1.37)	24.8 (1.27)	22.6 (1.23)
12th	22.0 (1.40)	26.6 (2.09)	31.5 (2.81)	26.9 (1.77)	25.8 (1.19)	22.8 (1.23)	25.1 (1.96)	24.6 (1.49)	28.0 (1.08)	27.7 (1.58)	27.6 (1.93)	25.7 (1.43)
Urbanicity[4]												
Urban	— (†)	26.8 (1.50)	27.5 (2.32)	25.6 (1.23)	23.4 (1.65)	— (†)	— (†)	— (†)	— (†)	— (†)	— (†)	— (†)
Suburban	— (†)	27.0 (1.05)	26.1 (1.60)	22.5 (0.96)	22.8 (1.90)	— (†)	— (†)	— (†)	— (†)	— (†)	— (†)	— (†)
Rural	— (†)	21.9 (3.23)	28.0 (4.36)	26.2 (2.49)	19.9 (2.80)	— (†)	— (†)	— (†)	— (†)	— (†)	— (†)	— (†)
On school property[5]												
Total	**5.6 (0.65)**	**7.0 (0.52)**	**7.2 (0.73)**	**5.4 (0.37)**	**5.8 (0.68)**	**4.5 (0.32)**	**4.5 (0.46)**	**4.6 (0.35)**	**5.9 (0.39)**	**— (†)**	**— (†)**	**— (†)**
Sex												
Male	7.8 (0.83)	9.0 (0.68)	10.1 (1.30)	8.0 (0.54)	7.6 (0.88)	6.0 (0.44)	5.9 (0.61)	6.3 (0.54)	7.5 (0.56)	— (†)	— (†)	— (†)
Female	3.3 (0.48)	4.6 (0.56)	4.4 (0.40)	2.9 (0.28)	3.7 (0.48)	3.0 (0.31)	3.0 (0.39)	2.8 (0.32)	4.1 (0.32)	— (†)	— (†)	— (†)
Race/ethnicity												
White	5.0 (0.72)	5.8 (0.69)	6.5 (0.84)	4.8 (0.45)	4.5 (0.66)	3.8 (0.41)	4.0 (0.63)	3.8 (0.38)	4.5 (0.42)	— (†)	— (†)	— (†)
Black	7.3 (1.23)	9.1 (1.07)	7.2 (1.10)	6.1 (0.60)	6.6 (0.89)	4.9 (0.65)	5.0 (0.73)	5.6 (0.64)	6.7 (0.77)	— (†)	— (†)	— (†)
Hispanic	7.5 (1.10)	10.4 (1.03)	10.7 (1.21)	7.4 (0.58)	8.2 (0.72)	7.7 (0.76)	5.4 (0.80)	6.5 (0.76)	7.7 (0.54)	— (†)	— (†)	— (†)
Asian[2]	— (†)	— (†)	4.3 (0.71)	4.7! (1.56)	4.3! (1.38)	‡ (†)	2.7! (1.06)	2.0 (0.54)	4.5 (1.34)	— (†)	— (†)	— (†)
Pacific Islander[2]	— (†)	— (†)	11.0 (3.21)	6.4! (2.46)	9.1! (3.17)	‡ (†)	13.4! (5.38)	9.0 (2.40)	12.5! (4.94)	— (†)	— (†)	— (†)
American Indian/Alaska Native	‡ (†)	16.2! (5.56)	‡ (†)	21.5! (6.55)	11.4! (4.42)	9.2 (1.85)	8.2 (2.30)	2.9! (1.25)	20.9 (4.05)	— (†)	— (†)	— (†)
Two or more races[2]	— (†)	— (†)	7.8 (1.81)	5.2 (1.24)	11.4! (5.49)	3.6 (0.91)	3.6! (1.08)	5.4 (1.34)	8.1 (1.79)	— (†)	— (†)	— (†)
Grade												
9th	4.4 (0.40)	8.1 (0.90)	6.6 (0.97)	5.5 (0.62)	6.6 (1.03)	5.0 (0.59)	4.0 (0.52)	4.3 (0.38)	5.4 (0.65)	— (†)	— (†)	— (†)
10th	6.5 (0.94)	6.4 (0.73)	7.6 (1.14)	5.8 (0.51)	5.2 (0.70)	4.6 (0.54)	4.8 (0.60)	4.6 (0.50)	6.2 (0.63)	— (†)	— (†)	— (†)
11th	6.5 (1.07)	7.9 (1.17)	7.0 (0.72)	5.1 (0.48)	5.6 (0.71)	4.1 (0.49)	4.1 (0.73)	5.0 (0.55)	6.2 (0.70)	— (†)	— (†)	— (†)
12th	5.1 (0.78)	5.7 (0.61)	7.3 (1.14)	4.9 (0.71)	5.0 (0.75)	4.1 (0.45)	5.1 (0.73)	4.6 (0.49)	5.4 (0.39)	— (†)	— (†)	— (†)
Urbanicity[4]												
Urban	— (†)	8.0 (1.11)	8.5 (1.03)	6.8 (0.56)	6.8 (1.05)	— (†)	— (†)	— (†)	— (†)	— (†)	— (†)	— (†)
Suburban	— (†)	7.0 (0.67)	6.4 (1.03)	4.7 (0.46)	6.0 (1.03)	— (†)	— (†)	— (†)	— (†)	— (†)	— (†)	— (†)
Rural	— (†)	4.9! (2.02)	8.1 (1.57)	5.3 (0.93)	3.9 (0.64)	— (†)	— (†)	— (†)	— (†)	— (†)	— (†)	— (†)

—Not available.
†Not applicable.
!Interpret data with caution. The coefficient of variation (CV) for this estimate is between 30 and 50 percent.
‡Reporting standards not met. The coefficient of variation (CV) for this estimate is 50 percent or greater.
[1]The term "anywhere" is not used in the Youth Risk Behavior Survey (YRBS) questionnaire; students were simply asked how many times during the previous 30 days they had used marijuana.
[2]Before 1999, Asian students and Pacific Islander students were not categorized separately, and students could not be classified as Two or more races. Because the response categories changed in 1999, caution should be used in comparing data on race from 1993, 1995, and 1997 with data from later years.
[3]Students were asked which sexual orientation—"heterosexual (straight)," "gay or lesbian," "bisexual," or "not sure"—best described them.
[4]Refers to the Standard Metropolitan Statistical Area (MSA) status of the respondent's household as defined by the U.S. Census Bureau. Categories include "central city of an MSA (Urban)," "in MSA but not in central city (Suburban)," and "not MSA (Rural)."
[5]In the question about using marijuana at school, "on school property" was not defined for survey respondents. Data on marijuana use at school were not collected from 2013 onward.
NOTE: Race categories exclude persons of Hispanic ethnicity.
SOURCE: Centers for Disease Control and Prevention, Division of Adolescent and School Health, Youth Risk Behavior Surveillance System (YRBSS), 1993 through 2017. (This table was prepared August 2018.)

Table 233.40. Percentage of students suspended and expelled from public elementary and secondary schools, by sex, race/ethnicity, and state: 2013–14

State	Percent receiving out-of-school suspensions[1]										Percent expelled[2]									
	Total	Sex		Race/ethnicity[3]							Total	Sex		Race/ethnicity[3]						
		Male	Female	White	Black	Hispanic	Asian	Pacific Islander[4]	American Indian/ Alaska Native	Two or more races		Male	Female	White	Black	Hispanic	Asian	Pacific Islander	American Indian/ Alaska Native	Two or more races
1	2	3	4	5	6	7	8	9	10	11	12	13	14	15	16	17	18	19	20	21
United States	**5.28**	**7.25**	**3.20**	**3.43**	**13.68**	**4.54**	**1.11**	**4.53**	**6.74**	**5.26**	**0.22**	**0.32**	**0.12**	**0.20**	**0.44**	**0.15**	**0.03**	**0.12**	**0.37**	**0.31**
Alabama	7.98	10.50	5.30	4.51	15.25	2.97	1.58	4.03	3.87	5.90	0.19	0.28	0.09	0.09	0.36	0.06	0.00	0.14–0.43	0.02–0.05	0.49
Alaska	5.06	7.24	2.72	3.47	8.81	4.80	2.03	6.49	8.48	4.82	0.08	0.13	0.03	0.05	0.21	0.16	0.00	0.03–0.09	0.12	0.11
Arizona	5.18	7.45	2.78	3.90	11.54	5.50	1.54	4.81	8.90	5.02	0.04	0.06	0.02	0.04	0.07	0.04	0.00–0.01	0.10	0.04	0.05
Arkansas	7.00	9.63	4.25	4.47	17.87	3.82	1.45	3.11	4.83	4.34	0.18	0.25	0.09	0.17	0.23	0.10	0.07	0.04–0.11	0.46	0.10
California	3.99	5.74	2.14	3.25	11.24	4.03	1.18	4.80	7.11	3.43	0.14	0.22	0.06	0.13	0.35	0.14	0.04	0.13	0.26	0.12
Colorado	4.41	6.27	2.45	3.13	11.04	5.84	1.35	3.64	6.80	4.87	0.15	0.24	0.06	0.11	0.41	0.18	0.06	0.35	0.38	0.15
Connecticut	3.94	5.23	2.57	1.99	9.02	6.61	0.82	([4])	6.23	3.31	0.22	0.36	0.08	0.16	0.49	0.27	0.04	0.00	0.26	0.16
Delaware	8.48	10.72	6.05	4.43	15.64	5.83	1.68	6.08	9.18	6.25	0.09	0.12	0.05	0.06	0.15	0.06	0.00	0.00	0.00	0.03–0.09
District of Columbia	12.44	15.52	9.37	0.90	15.98	4.26	1.52	10.00	9.86	3.83	0.15	0.18	0.12	0.01–0.04	0.19	0.04	0.00	0.00	1.41–4.23	0.00
Florida	5.04	7.06	2.90	3.67	9.89	3.86	1.00	2.92	4.65	4.91	0.01	0.01	#	#	0.01	#	0.00	0.00	0.01–0.03	0.01
Georgia	7.29	9.86	4.59	3.52	13.38	4.46	1.28	6.53	4.57	6.71	0.16	0.23	0.08	0.11	0.26	0.06	0.02	0.86	0.19	0.19
Hawaii	3.47	4.76	2.06	2.54	4.53	2.96	2.05	5.58	6.16	2.22	#	0.01	#	0.00	0.00	0.01–0.02	0.00–0.01	0.00–0.01	0.00	0.00
Idaho	2.57	3.82	1.25	2.37	3.61	3.43	1.27	2.38	4.66	2.33	0.06	0.09	0.02	0.05	0.13	0.10	0.03–0.08	0.00	0.22	0.02–0.05
Illinois	6.83	9.02	4.51	2.88	21.91	5.45	0.87	3.56	4.57	5.78	0.13	0.18	0.08	0.11	0.35	0.05	0.02	0.00	0.18	0.19
Indiana	6.79	9.35	4.09	4.50	20.58	6.21	1.44	2.78	5.93	10.00	0.51	0.69	0.31	0.38	1.26	0.53	0.10	0.70	0.63	0.53
Iowa	2.60	3.68	1.45	1.96	11.03	2.99	1.08	2.57	4.27	4.66	0.04	0.06	0.01	0.03	0.09	0.04	0.01–0.03	0.00	0.00	0.03
Kansas	4.04	5.73	2.24	2.82	14.03	4.40	1.22	3.41	6.21	5.51	0.16	0.24	0.08	0.13	0.34	0.16	0.05	0.12–0.35	0.32	0.29
Kentucky	4.87	6.91	2.71	4.08	12.21	3.08	0.90	3.12	5.67	5.82	0.05	0.08	0.02	0.05	0.06	0.04	0.00	0.00	0.12–0.35	0.06
Louisiana	8.38	11.08	5.54	4.70	12.61	4.22	1.83	5.68	6.44	5.90	0.62	0.89	0.34	0.31	1.00	0.17	0.07	0.22–0.66	0.49	0.36
Maine	3.45	4.96	1.84	3.36	6.62	4.56	1.26	2.08	3.51	2.75	0.11	0.16	0.05	0.11	0.14	0.14	0.00	0.00	0.00	0.25
Maryland	5.19	6.95	3.34	2.89	9.26	3.34	0.76	2.69	5.86	4.56	0.09	0.13	0.05	0.02	0.20	0.03	0.00–0.01	0.08–0.24	0.16	0.04
Massachusetts	4.28	5.92	2.55	2.61	10.46	8.60	1.26	2.13	5.94	5.34	0.03	0.05	0.02	0.03	0.06	0.04	0.00–0.01	0.00	0.04–0.13	0.09
Michigan	7.34	9.91	4.62	4.51	19.23	6.60	1.69	3.22	7.96	7.48	0.14	0.21	0.07	0.12	0.27	0.14	0.04	0.00	0.12	0.12
Minnesota	3.30	4.57	1.95	2.00	12.29	4.04	1.11	2.69	9.50	4.00	0.10	0.15	0.05	0.08	0.21	0.10	0.03	0.00	0.20	0.17
Mississippi	9.67	12.83	6.35	4.77	14.80	4.08	1.76	3.85	6.03	3.77	0.29	0.42	0.14	0.15	0.43	0.06	0.12	0.00	0.09–0.27	0.45
Missouri	5.74	7.86	3.48	3.87	17.02	4.38	1.62	2.90	5.96	5.33	0.35	0.45	0.23	0.34	0.37	0.51	0.01–0.02	0.41	0.47	0.45
Montana	3.66	5.12	2.10	2.54	4.44	2.85	1.14	1.99	11.84	2.26	0.14	0.19	0.09	0.07	0.07–0.21	0.11	0.00	0.00	0.52	0.61
Nebraska	4.27	5.95	2.48	2.88	16.20	4.68	1.83	3.26	9.23	6.82	0.30	0.43	0.17	0.17	1.37	0.35	0.17	0.00	0.64	0.54
Nevada	4.60	6.38	2.70	3.52	10.87	4.42	1.55	3.33	6.47	4.41	0.42	0.61	0.21	0.22	1.23	0.43	0.14	0.24	0.31	0.38
New Hampshire	4.88	6.95	2.67	4.29	19.21	14.21	2.22	7.51	7.30	3.71	0.02	0.03	0.01	0.02	0.00	0.00	0.00	0.00	0.00	0.00
New Jersey	4.44	5.95	2.84	2.21	12.79	5.59	0.80	1.26	3.70	3.10	0.01	0.02	0.01	0.01	0.04	0.01	#	0.00	0.00	0.03
New Mexico	6.25	8.20	4.19	4.82	10.22	6.78	2.83	2.52	6.03	8.55	0.58	0.80	0.35	0.36	1.24	0.69	0.33	0.00	0.29	1.13
New York	3.22	4.36	2.01	2.68	7.05	2.29	0.49	1.20	4.00	4.23	0.09	0.13	0.05	0.11	0.13	0.05	0.01	0.00	0.13	0.14
North Carolina	6.67	9.19	4.00	3.77	13.42	4.92	1.17	4.68	11.57	7.01	0.06	0.08	0.03	0.03	0.11	0.04	0.01	0.06–0.17	0.09	0.08
North Dakota	2.21	3.09	1.27	1.49	5.21	2.50	0.74	0.31–0.93	8.13	0.50	0.09	0.13	0.04	0.03	0.61	0.17	0.00	0.00	0.41	0.00
Ohio	7.14	9.71	4.42	4.68	18.70	6.79	1.47	3.47	7.73	9.24	1.76	2.49	0.99	1.53	2.83	1.31	0.28	1.84	2.58	2.23
Oklahoma	5.64	7.86	3.29	4.33	16.99	5.75	1.22	4.22	4.42	4.29	1.07	1.46	0.65	0.72	3.68	0.98	0.12	0.63	0.84	1.29
Oregon	4.12	6.03	2.11	3.86	9.24	4.46	1.22	4.18	6.45	4.52	0.20	0.31	0.09	0.20	0.26	0.22	0.04	0.23	0.45	0.21
Pennsylvania	5.62	7.52	3.61	3.01	17.13	7.53	1.28	4.23	4.43	7.30	0.11	0.16	0.06	0.08	0.19	0.18	0.01	0.08–0.23	0.21	0.17
Rhode Island	6.24	8.57	3.75	4.28	12.41	9.29	2.93	4.69	9.33	6.95	0.04	0.06	0.03	0.04	0.04	0.05	0.00	0.00	0.08–0.23	0.11

See notes at end of table.

Table 233.40. Percentage of students suspended and expelled from public elementary and secondary schools, by sex, race/ethnicity, and state: 2013–14—Continued

State	Percent receiving out-of-school suspensions[1]										Percent expelled[2]									
	Total	Sex		Race/ethnicity[3]							Total	Sex		Race/ethnicity[3]						
		Male	Female	White	Black	Hispanic	Asian	Pacific Islander[4]	American Indian/ Alaska Native	Two or more races		Male	Female	White	Black	Hispanic	Asian	Pacific Islander	American Indian/ Alaska Native	Two or more races
1	2	3	4	5	6	7	8	9	10	11	12	13	14	15	16	17	18	19	20	21
South Carolina	10.29	13.68	6.72	6.17	17.88	5.88	1.94	5.43	9.22	8.56	0.38	0.57	0.19	0.23	0.68	0.15	0.09	0.00	0.65	0.28
South Dakota	2.70	3.77	1.55	1.93	7.03	3.95	1.43	0.76–2.27	6.20	2.88	0.03	0.04	0.01	0.01	0.11	0.02–0.05	0.00	0.76–2.27	0.09	0.00
Tennessee	6.70	8.97	4.30	3.55	17.10	4.22	1.69	2.87	5.19	4.52	0.43	0.63	0.22	0.25	1.01	0.29	0.08	0.40	0.22	0.34
Texas	4.77	6.53	2.91	2.49	12.14	4.57	0.91	3.60	4.38	3.51	0.15	0.23	0.07	0.12	0.30	0.14	0.03	0.11	0.36	0.12
Utah	1.70	2.53	0.82	1.32	4.29	3.00	1.19	2.52	5.17	1.72	0.02	0.04	0.01	0.02	0.05	0.04	0.07	0.01–0.03	0.07	0.01–0.02
Vermont	3.88	5.48	2.17	3.79	6.59	3.49	0.68	0.90–2.70	12.60	2.83	0.05	0.08	0.03	0.05	0.27	0.00	0.00	0.00	0.00	0.00
Virginia	5.68	7.80	3.43	3.74	12.72	3.40	0.82	3.81	4.65	4.95	0.06	0.10	0.03	0.05	0.11	0.07	0.01	0.05–0.16	0.15	0.08
Washington	4.58	6.68	2.34	3.89	10.52	5.35	1.44	6.42	9.31	5.34	0.33	0.49	0.15	0.26	0.55	0.45	0.11	0.48	0.84	0.39
West Virginia	7.30	10.27	4.12	7.11	13.60	4.35	1.04	3.60	4.53	5.72	0.17	0.27	0.06	0.17	0.33	0.15	0.05–0.16	0.00	0.32–0.97	0.07
Wisconsin	3.96	5.46	2.36	2.27	17.03	4.22	0.76	3.01	6.53	4.82	0.12	0.18	0.06	0.08	0.53	0.11	0.02	0.00	0.21	0.07
Wyoming	3.12	4.61	1.51	2.92	6.05	3.79	1.69	3.17	5.18	3.03	0.11	0.19	0.03	0.10	0.09–0.28	0.15	0.00	0.00	0.24	0.06–0.17

#Rounds to zero.

[1]An out-of-school suspension is an instance in which a student is temporarily removed from his or her regular school for disciplinary purposes for at least half a day (but less than the remainder of the school year) to another setting (e.g., home or behavior center).

[2]Expulsions are actions taken by a local education agency that result in the removal of a student from his or her regular school for disciplinary purposes, with or without the continuation of educational services, for the remainder of the school year or longer in accordance with local education agency policy. Expulsions also include removals resulting from violations of the Gun Free Schools Act that are modified to less than 365 days.

[3]Data by race/ethnicity exclude students with disabilities served only under Section 504 (not receiving services under IDEA).

[4]Connecticut Pacific Islander data are suppressed and excluded from the Pacific Islander U.S. total pending further data quality review.

NOTE: The percentage of students receiving a disciplinary action is calculated by dividing the cumulative number of students receiving that type of disciplinary action for the entire 2013–14 school year by the student enrollment based on a count of students taken on a single day between September 27 and December 31. Percentages based on suspension or expulsion counts of between 1 and 3 students are displayed as ranges to protect student privacy. Race categories exclude persons of Hispanic ethnicity.

SOURCE: U.S. Department of Education, Office for Civil Rights, Civil Rights Data Collection, "2013–14 Discipline Estimations by Discipline Type" and "2013–14 Estimations for Enrollment." (This table was prepared January 2018.)

Table 233.50. Percentage of public schools with various safety and security measures: Selected years, 1999–2000 through 2015–16

[Standard errors appear in parentheses]

School safety and security measures	1999–2000		2003–04		2005–06		2007–08		2009–10		2013–14[1]		2015–16	
1	2		3		4		5		6		7		8	
Controlled access during school hours														
Buildings (e.g., locked or monitored doors)	74.6	(1.35)	83.0	(1.04)	84.9	(0.89)	89.5	(0.80)	91.7	(0.80)	93.3	(0.95)	94.1	(0.64)
Grounds (e.g., locked or monitored gates)	33.7	(1.26)	36.2	(1.08)	41.1	(1.25)	42.6	(1.41)	46.0	(1.26)	42.7	(1.53)	49.9	(1.53)
Visitors required to sign or check in	96.6	(0.54)	98.3	(0.40)	97.6	(0.42)	98.7	(0.37)	99.3	(0.27)	98.6	(0.49)	93.5	(0.69)
Classrooms equipped with locks so that doors can be locked from inside	—	(†)	—	(†)	—	(†)	—	(†)	—	(†)	—	(†)	66.7	(1.34)
Student dress, IDs, and school supplies														
Required students to wear uniforms	11.8	(0.82)	13.8	(0.85)	13.8	(0.78)	17.5	(0.70)	18.9	(1.02)	20.4	(1.27)	21.5	(1.36)
Enforced a strict dress code	47.4	(1.50)	55.1	(1.24)	55.3	(1.18)	54.8	(1.20)	56.9	(1.56)	58.5	(1.60)	53.1	(1.22)
Required students to wear badges or picture IDs	3.9	(0.32)	6.4	(0.64)	6.2	(0.47)	7.6	(0.60)	6.9	(0.57)	8.9	(0.81)	7.0	(0.53)
Required faculty and staff to wear badges or picture IDs	25.4	(1.39)	48.0	(1.21)	47.9	(1.12)	58.3	(1.37)	62.9	(1.14)	68.0	(1.65)	67.9	(1.36)
Required clear book bags or banned book bags on school grounds	5.9	(0.50)	6.2	(0.63)	6.4	(0.43)	6.0	(0.48)	5.5	(0.53)	6.3	(0.81)	3.9	(0.44)
Provided school lockers to students	46.5	(1.07)	49.5	(1.24)	50.5	(1.08)	48.9	(1.17)	52.1	(1.10)	49.9	(1.35)	50.4	(1.24)
Drug testing														
Athletes	—	(†)	4.2	(0.44)	5.0	(0.46)	6.4	(0.48)	6.0	(0.52)	6.6	(0.59)	7.2	(0.55)
Students in extracurricular activities (other than athletes)	—	(†)	2.6	(0.37)	3.4	(0.32)	4.5	(0.51)	4.6	(0.47)	4.3	(0.47)	6.0	(0.53)
Any other students	—	(†)	—	(†)	3.0	(0.34)	3.0	(0.42)	3.0	(0.26)	3.5	(0.44)	—	(†)
Metal detectors, dogs, and sweeps														
Random metal detector checks on students	7.2	(0.54)	5.6	(0.55)	4.9	(0.40)	5.3	(0.37)	5.2	(0.42)	4.2	(0.48)	4.5	(0.48)
Students required to pass through metal detectors daily	0.9	(0.16)	1.1	(0.16)	1.1	(0.18)	1.3	(0.20)	1.4	(0.24)	2.0	(0.40)	1.8	(0.32)
Random dog sniffs to check for drugs	20.6	(0.75)	21.3	(0.77)	23.0	(0.79)	21.5	(0.59)	22.9	(0.71)	24.1	(0.97)	24.6	(0.85)
Random sweeps[2] for contraband (e.g., drugs or weapons)	11.8	(0.54)	12.8	(0.58)	13.1	(0.76)	11.4	(0.71)	12.1	(0.68)	11.4	(0.86)	11.9	(0.78)
Communication systems and technology														
Provided telephones in most classrooms	44.6	(1.80)	60.8	(1.48)	66.9	(1.30)	71.6	(1.16)	74.0	(1.13)	78.7	(1.34)	79.3	(1.14)
Provided electronic notification system for schoolwide emergency	—	(†)	—	(†)	—	(†)	43.2	(1.26)	63.1	(1.40)	81.6	(1.12)	73.0	(1.35)
Provided structured anonymous threat reporting system[3]	—	(†)	—	(†)	—	(†)	31.2	(1.22)	35.9	(1.19)	46.5	(1.63)	43.9	(1.58)
Had silent alarms directly connected to law enforcement	—	(†)	—	(†)	—	(†)	—	(†)	—	(†)	—	(†)	27.1	(1.23)
Used security cameras to monitor the school	19.4	(0.88)	36.0	(1.28)	42.8	(1.29)	55.0	(1.37)	61.1	(1.16)	75.1	(1.31)	80.6	(0.96)
Provided two-way radios to any staff	—	(†)	71.2	(1.18)	70.9	(1.22)	73.1	(1.15)	73.3	(1.33)	74.2	(1.42)	73.3	(1.22)
Limited access to social networking sites from school computers	—	(†)	—	(†)	—	(†)	—	(†)	93.4	(0.59)	91.9	(0.80)	89.1	(0.88)
Prohibited use of cell phones and text messaging devices	—	(†)	—	(†)	—	(†)	—	(†)	90.9	(0.67)	75.9	(1.07)	65.8	(1.36)

—Not available.
†Not applicable.
[1]Data for 2013–14 were collected using the Fast Response Survey System (FRSS), while data for all other years were collected using the School Survey on Crime and Safety (SSOCS). The 2013–14 FRSS survey was designed to allow comparisons with SSOCS data. However, respondents to the 2013–14 survey could choose either to complete the survey on paper (and mail it back) or to complete the survey online, whereas respondents to SSOCS did not have the option of completing the survey online. The 2013–14 survey also relied on a smaller sample. The smaller sample size and difference in survey administration may have impacted the 2013–14 results.
[2]Does not include random dog sniffs.
[3]For example, a system for reporting threats through online submission, telephone hotline, or written submission via drop box.
NOTE: Responses were provided by the principal or the person most knowledgeable about crime and safety issues at the school.
SOURCE: U.S. Department of Education, National Center for Education Statistics, 1999–2000, 2003–04, 2005–06, 2007–08, 2009–10, and 2015–16 School Survey on Crime and Safety (SSOCS), 2000, 2004, 2006, 2008, 2010, and 2016; and Fast Response Survey System (FRSS), "School Safety and Discipline: 2013–14," FRSS 106, 2014. (This table was prepared September 2017.)

Table 234.10. Age range for compulsory school attendance and special education services, and policies on year-round schools and kindergarten programs, by state: Selected years, 2000 through 2018

State	Compulsory attendance							Compulsory special education services, 2004[1]	Year-round schools, 2008		Kindergarten programs, 2018		
	2000	2002	2004	2006	2010	2015	2017		Has policy on year-round schools	Has districts with year-round schools	School districts required to offer: Program	School districts required to offer: Full-day program	Attendance required
1	2	3	4	5	6	7	8	9	10	11	12	13	14
Alabama	7 to 16	7 to 16	7 to 16[2]	7 to 16	7 to 17	6 to 17[3]	6 to 17[3]	6 to 21		Yes	X	X	
Alaska	7 to 16	7 to 16	7 to 16[2]	7 to 16	7 to 16	7 to 16[2]	7 to 16[2]	3 to 22		Yes			
Arizona	6 to 16[2]	6 to 16[2]	6 to 16[2]	6 to 16[2]	6 to 16[2]	6 to 16[2]	6 to 16[2]	3 to 21	—	—	X		
Arkansas	5 to 17[2,3]	5 to 17[2,3]	5 to 17[2,3]	5 to 17[2,3]	5 to 17[2,3]	5 to 18	5 to 18	5 to 21	X	Yes	X	X	X
California	6 to 18[2]	6 to 18	6 to 18	6 to 18	6 to 18	6 to 18	6 to 18	Birth to 21[4]	X	Yes	X		
Colorado	—	—	7 to 16	7 to 16	6 to 17	6 to 17	6 to 17	3 to 21		Yes	X		
Connecticut	7 to 16	7 to 18[2]	7 to 18[2]	5 to 18[3]	5 to 18[3]	5 to 18[3]	5 to 18[3]	3 to 21		—	X		X
Delaware	5 to 16	5 to 16	5 to 16[2]	5 to 16	5 to 16	5 to 16	5 to 16	Birth to 20		Yes	X	X	X
District of Columbia	—	5 to 18	5 to 18	5 to 18	5 to 18	5 to 18	5 to 18	—	—	—	X	X	X
Florida	6 to 16[5]	6 to 16[5]	6 to 16[5]	6 to 16[5]	6 to 16[5]	6 to 16	6 to 16	3 to 21	X	Yes	X		
Georgia	6 to 16	6 to 16	6 to 16	6 to 16	6 to 16	6 to 16	6 to 16	Birth to 21[6]		Yes	X		
Hawaii	6 to 18	6 to 18	6 to 18	6 to 18	6 to 18	5 to 18	5 to 18	Birth to 19		([7])	X	X	X
Idaho	7 to 16	7 to 16	7 to 16	7 to 16	7 to 16	7 to 16	7 to 16	3 to 21		Yes			
Illinois	7 to 16	7 to 16	7 to 17	7 to 17	7 to 17	6 to 17	6 to 17	3 to 21	X	Yes	X	([8])	
Indiana	7 to 16	7 to 16	7 to 16	7 to 18[2]	7 to 18[2]	7 to 18	7 to 18	3 to 22		Yes	X		
Iowa	6 to 16[2]	6 to 16[2]	6 to 16	6 to 16	6 to 16	6 to 16[9]	6 to 16[9]	Birth to 21	X	Yes	X		([10])
Kansas	7 to 18[2]	7 to 18[2]	7 to 18[2]	7 to 18[2]	7 to 18[2]	7 to 18	7 to 18	3 to 21[11]		—	X		
Kentucky	6 to 16	6 to 16	6 to 16[2]	6 to 16	6 to 16	6 to 18[12]	6 to 18	Birth to 21		Yes	X		
Louisiana	7 to 17	7 to 17	7 to 17[2]	7 to 18[2]	7 to 18[2]	7 to 18	7 to 18	3 to 21[13]		Yes	X	X	X[14]
Maine	7 to 17	7 to 17	7 to 17[2]	7 to 17[2]	7 to 17[2]	7 to 17	7 to 17	5 to 19[13,15]		—	X		([10])
Maryland	5 to 16	5 to 16	5 to 16	5 to 16	5 to 16[3]	5 to 17	5 to 18	Birth to 21	X	—	X	X	X
Massachusetts	6 to 16	6 to 16	6 to 16	6 to 16[2]	6 to 16[2]	6 to 16	6 to 16[16]	3 to 21[6]	([17])	—	X		([10])
Michigan	6 to 16	6 to 16	6 to 16	6 to 16	6 to 18	6 to 18	6 to 18	Birth to 25	X	Yes			
Minnesota	7 to 18[2]	7 to 16	7 to 16	7 to 16[2]	7 to 16[2]	7 to 17	7 to 17	Birth to 21	X	Yes			
Mississippi	6 to 17	6 to 17	6 to 16	6 to 16	6 to 17	6 to 17	6 to 17	Birth to 20		—	X	X	([10])
Missouri	7 to 16	7 to 16	7 to 16	7 to 16	7 to 17	7 to 17[2,3]	7 to 17[2,3]	Birth to 20		Yes[18]	X		
Montana	7 to 16[2]	7 to 16[2]	7 to 16[2]	7 to 16[2]	7 to 16[2]	7 to 16[2]	7 to 16[2]	3 to 18[13]		—	X	([8])	
Nebraska	7 to 16	7 to 16	7 to 16	6 to 18	6 to 18	6 to 18	6 to 18	Birth to 20		Yes	X		
Nevada	7 to 17	7 to 17	7 to 17	7 to 17	7 to 18[2]	7 to 18	7 to 18	Birth to 21[4]		Yes	X		X[14]
New Hampshire	6 to 16	6 to 16	6 to 16	6 to 16	6 to 18	6 to 18	6 to 18	3 to 21		—			
New Jersey	6 to 16	6 to 16	6 to 16	6 to 16	6 to 16	6 to 16	6 to 16	5 to 21		—		([19])	([19])
New Mexico	5 to 18	5 to 18	5 to 18[2]	5 to 18[2]	5 to 18[2]	5 to 18	5 to 18	3 to 21	X	Yes	X		X
New York	6 to 16[2]	6 to 16	6 to 16	6 to 16[20]	6 to 16[20]	6 to 16[20]	6 to 16[20]	Birth to 20		—		([20])	([20])
North Carolina	7 to 16	7 to 16	7 to 16	7 to 16	7 to 16	7 to 16	7 to 16	5 to 20	X	Yes	X	X	
North Dakota	7 to 16	7 to 16	7 to 16	7 to 16	7 to 16	7 to 16	7 to 16	3 to 21		No	X		
Ohio	6 to 18	6 to 18	6 to 18	6 to 18	6 to 18	6 to 18	6 to 18	3 to 21	X	—	X		X
Oklahoma	5 to 18	5 to 18	5 to 18	5 to 18	5 to 18	5 to 18	5 to 18	Birth to 21[13]		Yes	X	X	X
Oregon	7 to 18	7 to 18	7 to 18[2]	7 to 18	7 to 18	7 to 18	6 to 18	3 to 20		Yes	X		
Pennsylvania	8 to 17	8 to 17	8 to 17[2]	8 to 17[2]	8 to 17[2]	8 to 17	8 to 17	6 to 21	X[18]	—[18]			
Rhode Island	6 to 16	6 to 16	6 to 16	6 to 16	6 to 16	6 to 18[2]	5 to 18[2]	3 to 21		—	X	X	X
South Carolina	5 to 16	5 to 16	5 to 16	5 to 17[3]	5 to 17[3]	5 to 17	5 to 17	3 to 21[21]		—	X	X	X
South Dakota	6 to 16	6 to 16	6 to 16	6 to 16	6 to 18[2]	6 to 18[2]	6 to 18[2]	Birth to 21	X	—	X		X[22]
Tennessee	6 to 17	6 to 17	6 to 17	6 to 17[3]	6 to 17[3]	6 to 18	6 to 18	3 to 21[4]	X	Yes	X	X	X
Texas	6 to 18	6 to 18	6 to 18	6 to 18	6 to 18	6 to 18	6 to 19	3 to 21	X	Yes	X		
Utah	6 to 18	6 to 18	6 to 18	6 to 18	6 to 18	6 to 18	6 to 18	3 to 22		Yes	X		
Vermont	7 to 16	6 to 16	6 to 16	6 to 16[2]	6 to 16[2]	6 to 16[2]	6 to 16[2]	3 to 21		—[18]	X		
Virginia	5 to 18	5 to 18	5 to 18	5 to 18[2]	5 to 18[2,3]	5 to 18	5 to 18	2 to 21	X	Yes	X		X
Washington	8 to 17[2]	8 to 17[2]	8 to 16[2]	8 to 18	8 to 18	8 to 18	8 to 18	3 to 21[21]		Yes	X	X	
West Virginia	6 to 16	6 to 16	6 to 16	6 to 16	6 to 17	6 to 17	6 to 17	5 to 21[23]	X	Yes	X	X	X
Wisconsin	6 to 18	6 to 18	6 to 18	6 to 18	6 to 18	6 to 18	6 to 18	3 to 21		Yes	X		X[24]
Wyoming	6 to 16[2]	6 to 16[2]	7 to 16[2]	7 to 16[2]	7 to 16[2]	7 to 16[2]	7 to 16[2]	3 to 21		—	X	([25])	([10])

—Not available.
X Denotes that the state has a policy. A blank denotes that the state does not have a policy.
[1]Most states have a provision whereby education is provided up to a certain age or completion of secondary school, whichever comes first.
[2]Child may be exempted from compulsory attendance if he/she meets state requirements for early withdrawal with or without meeting conditions for a diploma or equivalency.
[3]Parent/guardian may delay child's entry until a later age per state law/regulation.
[4]Student may continue in the program if 22nd birthday falls before the end of the school year.
[5]Attendance is compulsory until age 18 for Manatee County students, unless they earn a high school diploma prior to reaching their 18th birthday.
[6]Through age 21 or until child graduates with a high school or special education diploma or equivalent.
[7]Some schools operate on a multitrack system; the schools are open year round, but different cohorts start and end at different times.
[8]District must offer either a half-day or full-day program.
[9]Children enrolled in preschool programs (who must be 4 years old on or before September 15) are considered to be of compulsory school attendance age.
[10]Not specified in statute, rules, or regulations.
[11]To be determined by rules and regulations adopted by the state board.
[12]All districts adopted a policy to raise the upper compulsory school age from 16 to 18. The policy took effect for most districts in the 2015–16 school year.
[13]Children from birth through age 2 are eligible for additional services.
[14]Attendance is required unless the student otherwise satisfactorily passes an academic readiness screening upon enrollment in grade 1.
[15]Must be age 5 before October 15 and not age 20 before start of school year.
[16]Each school committee is permitted to establish its own minimum age for school attendance, provided that it is not older than the mandatory minimum age established by the state.
[17]Policies about year-round schools are decided locally.
[18]State did not participate in 2008 online survey. Data are from 2006.
[19]Abbott Districts are required to offer full-day kindergarten and students are required to attend.
[20]Local boards of education can require school attendance until age 17 unless employed. In Syracuse, New York City, Rochester, Utica, Buffalo, Cohoes, Watervliet, and Yonkers, districts are required to offer full-day kindergarten and children are required to attend full-day kindergarten.
[21]Student may complete school year if 21st birthday occurs while attending school.
[22]All children must attend kindergarten before age 7.
[23]Children with severe disabilities may begin receiving services at age 3.
[24]Children must attend in districts that offer kindergarten.
[25]School districts must establish and maintain relationships with a district that offers full-day kindergarten.
NOTE: The Education of the Handicapped Act (EHA) Amendments of 1986 make it mandatory for all states receiving EHA funds to serve all 3- to 18-year-old disabled children.
SOURCE: Council of Chief State School Officers, *Key State Education Policies on PK–12 Education*, 2000, 2002, 2004, 2006, and 2008; Education Commission of the States (ECS), ECS StateNotes, *Compulsory School Age Requirements*, retrieved August 9, 2010, from http://www.ecs.org/clearinghouse/86/62/8662.pdf; ECS StateNotes, *Special Education: State Special Education Definitions, Ages Served*, retrieved August 9, 2010, from http://www.ecs.org/clearinghouse/52/29/5229.pdf; ECS StateNotes, *Compulsory School Age Requirements*, retrieved May 19, 2015, from http://www.ecs.org/clearinghouse/01/18/68/11868.pdf; ECS StateNotes, *Age Requirements for Free and Compulsory Education*, retrieved July 2, 2018, from https://www.ecs.org/age-requirements-for-free-and-compulsory-education/; ESC StateNotes, *Does the state require the district to offer kindergarten and if so, full day or half day? What exemptions exist for districts?*, retrieved July 2, 2018, from http://ecs.force.com/mbdata/MBQuest2RTanw?rep=KK3Q1805; ESC StateNotes, *Does the state require children to attend kindergarten?*, retrieved July 2, 2018, from http://ecs.force.com/mbdata/MBQuest2RTanw?rep=KK3Q1804; and supplemental information retrieved from various state websites. (This table was prepared July 2018.)

Table 234.20. Minimum amount of instructional time per year and policies on textbooks, by state: Selected years, 2000 through 2018

State	Minimum amount of instructional time per year						Policies on textbooks, 2014		
	In days					In hours	Textbook selection level		Free textbooks provided to students
	2000	2006	2011	2014	2018	2018	State	Local education agency	
1	2	3	4	5	6	7	8	9	10
Alabama	175	175	180	180[1]	180[1]	1,080	X		X
Alaska	180	180	170[2]	180[3]	180[1]	740 (K–3); 900 (4–12)		X	X
Arizona	—	180	180[1]	180[1]	180	356 (K); 712 (1–3); 890 (4–6); 1,000 (7–8); 720[4] (9–12)		X	X[5]
Arkansas	178	178	178[2]	178[3]	178[3]	†		X[6]	X
California	175	180	180/175[7]	180/175[7]	180[8]	600 (K); 840 (1–3); 900 (4–8); 1,080 (9–12)	X[9]		X
Colorado	[10]	160	160	160	160	435/870[2] (K); 968[2] (1–5); 1,056[2] (6–12)		X	
Connecticut	180	180	180	180	180	450/900 (K); 900 (1–12)		X	X
Delaware	[10]	†	†	†	†	1,060 (K–11); 1,032 (12)		X	X
District of Columbia	180[11]	180	178	180	180	†			X
Florida	180	180	180	180	180[1]	720 (K–3); 900 (4–12)	X		X
Georgia	180[11]	180	180	180	180	†	X		X
Hawaii	184	179	180[12]	180[12]	180[2,12]	1,080[12]	X		X[13]
Idaho	180	†	†	†	†	450[3] (K); 810[3] (1–3); 900[3] (4–8); 990[3] (9–12)	X		X
Illinois	180[14]	176	176	180[3]	180[3]	†		X	[15]
Indiana	180	180	180	180	180	†		X	
Iowa	180	180	180	180	180[1]	1,080		X	
Kansas	186	186 (K–11); 181 (12)	186 (K–11); 181 (12)	186 (K–11); 181 (12)	186 (K–11); 181 (12)[1]	465 (K); 1,116 (1–11); 1,086 (12)		X	
Kentucky	175	175	175[2]	170[2]	170[2]	1,062	X		X[16]
Louisiana	175	177	177[2]	177[2,17]	177[1,17]	1,062	X		X
Maine	175	175	175[2]	175[2]	175[17]	†		X	X
Maryland	180	180	180	180	180	1,080; 1,170 (9–12)		X	X
Massachusetts	180	180	180	180	180	425 (K); 900 (1–5); 990 (6–12)		X	X
Michigan	180	†	165	175	180	1,098		X	X[18]
Minnesota	[10]	[10]	†	†	165 (1–11)	425/850 (K); 935 (1–6); 1,020 (7–12)		X	X
Mississippi	180	180	180	180	180	†	X		X
Missouri	174	174	174/142[19]	174/142[19]	174/142[19]	522 (K); 1,044 (1–12)		X	X
Montana	180	90 (K); 180 (K–12)	†	†	†	360/720[3] (K); 720[3] (1–3); 1,080[3,17] (4–12)		X	X
Nebraska	[10]	†	†	†	†	400 (K); 1,032 (1–8); 1,080 (9–12)		X	X
Nevada	180	180	180	180	180	†	X		X[13]
New Hampshire	180	180	180	180	180[1,17]	450 (K); 945 (Elementary); 990 (Middle); 990[17] (High)		X	X
New Jersey	180	180	180	180	180	†		X	X
New Mexico	180	180	180	†	†	450/990 (K); 990 (1–6); 1,080 (7–12)	X		X
New York	180[11]	180	180	180	180	†		X	X
North Carolina	180	180	180	185	185[1]	1,025	X		X
North Dakota	173	173	175[2]	175[2]	175[2]	†		X	X[18]
Ohio	182	182	182[3]	†	†	455/910 (K); 910 (1–6); 1,001 (7–12)		X	X
Oklahoma	180	180	180[3]	180	180[1]	1,080[3]	X		X
Oregon	[10]	†	†	†	†	450/900 (K); 900 (1–8); 990 (9–11); 966 (12)	X		X
Pennsylvania	180	180	180	180	180[1]	450 (K); 900 (1–8); 990 (9–12)		X	X
Rhode Island	180	180	180	180	180[1]	1,080		X	X[18]
South Carolina	180	180	180[2]	180[2]	180[2]	†	X		
South Dakota	—	†	†	†	†	437.5 (K); 875 (1–5); 962.5[17] (6–12)		X	X
Tennessee	180	180	180[2]	180[2]	180[2]	†	X		X
Texas	187	180	180	180	†	1,260	X		X
Utah	180	180	180	180	180[3]	450 (K); 810 (1); 990 (2–12)	X	[20]	

See notes at end of table.

Table 234.20. Minimum amount of instructional time per year and policies on textbooks, by state: Selected years, 2000 through 2018—Continued

State	Minimum amount of instructional time per year						Policies on textbooks, 2014		
	In days					In hours	Textbook selection level		Free textbooks provided to students
	2000	2006	2011	2014	2018	2018	State	Local education agency	
1	2	3	4	5	6	7	8	9	10
Vermont	175	175	175	175	175[2]	†		X	X
Virginia	180	180	180	180	180[1]	540 (K); 990 (1–12)	X		X
Washington	180[14]	180	180	180	180	1,000 (K–8); 1,080 (9–12)		X	[21]
West Virginia	180	180	180	180	180	†	X		X
Wisconsin	180	180	180	†	†	437 (K); 1,050 (1–6); 1,137 (7–12)		X	
Wyoming	175	175	180	175	175	450 (K); 900 (Elementary); 1,050 (Middle/Jr. High); 1,100 (Secondary)		X	X

—Not available.
†Not applicable.
X Denotes that the state has a policy. A blank denotes that the state does not have a policy.
[1]Or an equivalent number of hours or minutes of instruction per year.
[2]Does not include time for in-service or staff development or parent-teacher conferences.
[3]Includes time for in-service or staff development or parent-teacher conferences.
[4]Students must enroll in at least four subjects in addition to meeting the hour requirement.
[5]Fees permitted at the high school level for nonrequired or supplementary textbooks.
[6]State Department of Education prepares a list of suggestions, but the districts choose.
[7]Through 2014–15, districts were allowed to shorten the 180-day instructional year to 175 days without fiscal penalty.
[8]Charter schools and select districts are required to have 175 days.
[9]Statewide textbook adoption is only at the elementary level. Adoption practices have been suspended until the 2015–16 school year.
[10]No statewide policy; varies by district.
[11]1996 data.
[12]Does not apply to charter and multitrack schools.
[13]Fees for lost or damaged books permitted.
[14]1998 data.
[15]Fees permitted, but if 5 percent or more of the voters in a district petition the school board, a majority of the district's voters may decide to furnish free textbooks to students.
[16]Fees permitted for students in grades 9–12, but students who qualify for free or reduced-price lunch are exempted.
[17]Instructional time for graduating seniors may be reduced.
[18]Refundable or security deposits permitted.
[19]174 days required for a 5-day week; 142 days required for a 4-day week.
[20]Local districts may select textbooks not on the state recommended list provided the textbooks meet specific criteria and the selection is based on recommendations by the district's curriculum materials review committee.
[21]A district may provide free textbooks to students when, in its judgment, the best interests of the district will be served.
NOTE: Minimum number of instructional days refers to the actual number of days that pupils have contact with a teacher. Some states allow for different types of school calendars by setting instructional time in both days and hours, while others use only days or only hours. For states in which the number of days or hours varies by grade, the relevant grade(s) appear in parentheses. For states that specify minimum hours both for part-day kindergarten and for full-day kindergarten, a slash separates the part-day hours from the full-day hours.
SOURCE: Council of Chief State School Officers, *Key State Education Policies on PK–12 Education*, 2000 and 2006; Education Commission of the States, StateNotes, *Number of Instructional Days/Hours in the School Year* (August 2011 and October 2014 revisions), retrieved September 22, 2011, from http://www.ecs.org/clearinghouse/95/05/9505.pdf and May 19, 2015, from http://www.ecs.org/clearinghouse/01/15/05/11505.pdf; *State Textbook Adoption* (September 2013 edition), retrieved May 19, 2015, from http://www.ecs.org/clearinghouse/01/09/23/10923.pdf; *Minimum number of days or hours per school year*, retrieved July 2, 2018, from http://ecs.force.com/mbdata/mbquest2ci?rep=IT1801-2; and supplemental information retrieved from various state websites. (This table was prepared July 2018.)

Table 235.10. Revenues for public elementary and secondary schools, by source of funds: Selected years, 1919–20 through 2015–16

[Standard errors appear in parentheses]

School year	Revenues (in thousands)							Revenues per pupil						
				Local (including intermediate sources below the state level)							Local (including intermediate sources below the state level)			
	Total	Federal	State	Total	Property taxes	Other public revenue	Private[1]	Total	Federal	State	Total	Property taxes	Other public revenue	Private[1]
1	2	3	4	5	6	7	8	9	10	11	12	13	14	15
							Current dollars							
1919–20	$970,121	$2,475	$160,085	$807,561	—	—	—	$45	#	$7	$37	—	—	—
1929–30	2,088,557	7,334	353,670	1,727,553	—	—	—	81	#	14	67	—	—	—
1939–40	2,260,527	39,810	684,354	1,536,363	—	—	—	89	$2	27	60	—	—	—
1949–50	5,437,044	155,848	2,165,689	3,115,507	—	—	—	217	6	86	124	—	—	—
1959–60	14,746,618	651,639	5,768,047	8,326,932	—	—	—	419	19	164	237	—	—	—
1969–70	40,266,922	3,219,557	16,062,776	20,984,589	—	—	—	884	71	353	461	—	—	—
1979–80	96,881,164	9,503,537	45,348,814	42,028,813	—	—	—	2,326	228	1,089	1,009	—	—	—
1989–90	208,547,573	12,700,784	98,238,633	97,608,157	$74,867,627	$17,084,494	$5,656,036	5,144	313	2,423	2,408	$1,847	$421	$140
1994–95	273,149,449	18,582,157	127,729,576	126,837,717	97,978,129	21,560,162	7,299,425	6,192	421	2,896	2,875	2,221	489	165
1995–96	287,702,844	19,104,019	136,670,754	131,928,071	101,785,858	22,522,345	7,619,869	6,416	426	3,048	2,942	2,270	502	170
1996–97	305,065,192	20,081,287	146,435,584	138,548,321	106,545,881	24,288,693	7,713,747	6,688	440	3,211	3,038	2,336	533	169
1997–98	325,925,708	22,201,965	157,645,372	146,078,370	111,184,150	26,676,244	8,217,977	7,066	481	3,418	3,167	2,410	578	178
1998–99	347,377,993	24,521,817	169,298,232	153,557,944	119,483,487	25,348,879	8,725,578	7,464	527	3,638	3,300	2,567	545	187
1999–2000	372,943,802	27,097,866	184,613,352	161,232,584	124,735,516	27,628,923	8,868,145	7,959	578	3,940	3,441	2,662	590	189
2000–01	401,356,120	29,100,183	199,583,097	172,672,840	132,575,925	30,889,273	9,207,643	8,503	616	4,228	3,658	2,809	654	195
2001–02	419,501,976	33,144,633	206,541,793	179,815,551	141,095,685	28,924,825	9,795,041	8,800	695	4,333	3,772	2,960	607	205
2002–03	440,111,653	37,515,909	214,277,407	188,318,337	148,511,786	29,579,240	10,227,310	9,134	779	4,447	3,908	3,082	614	212
2003–04	462,026,099	41,923,435	217,384,191	202,718,474	160,602,055	31,651,489	10,464,930	9,518	864	4,478	4,176	3,309	652	216
2004–05	487,753,525	44,809,532	228,553,579	214,390,414	167,909,883	35,433,486	11,047,044	9,996	918	4,684	4,394	3,441	726	226
2005–06	520,621,788	47,553,778	242,151,076	230,916,934	178,279,408	41,111,066	11,526,460	10,600	968	4,930	4,702	3,630	837	235
2006–07	555,710,762	47,150,608	263,608,741	244,951,413	188,287,298	44,806,422	11,857,694	11,281	957	5,351	4,972	3,822	910	241
2007–08	584,683,686	47,788,467	282,622,523	254,272,697	196,521,569	45,314,965	12,436,163	11,879	971	5,742	5,166	3,993	921	253
2008–09	592,422,033	56,670,261	276,525,603	259,226,169	205,821,844	41,195,313	12,209,012	12,032	1,151	5,616	5,265	4,180	837	248
2009–10	596,390,664	75,997,858	258,863,973	261,528,833	210,837,095	38,771,186	11,920,551	12,089	1,540	5,247	5,301	4,274	786	242
2010–11	604,228,585	75,549,471	266,786,402	261,892,711	211,649,523	38,558,755	11,684,433	12,218	1,528	5,395	5,296	4,280	780	236
2011–12	597,885,111	60,921,462	269,043,077	267,920,572	215,830,316	40,290,007	11,800,249	12,075	1,230	5,434	5,411	4,359	814	238
2012–13	603,769,917	55,860,888	273,215,485	274,693,545	221,970,384	41,129,568	11,593,592	12,137	1,123	5,492	5,522	4,462	827	233
2013–14	623,649,738	54,505,981	288,637,122	280,506,635	227,019,185	41,943,022	11,544,428	12,469	1,090	5,771	5,608	4,539	839	231
2014–15	647,679,130	55,002,853	301,529,692	291,146,585	235,870,943	43,978,246	11,297,396	12,884	1,094	5,998	5,792	4,692	875	225
2015–16	678,378,476	55,981,180	318,572,978	303,824,317	246,997,299	45,300,714	11,526,305	13,474	1,112	6,328	6,035	4,906	900	229
							Constant 2017–18 dollars[2]							
1919–20	$12,630,509	$32,223	$2,084,230	$10,514,056	—	—	—	$585	$1	$97	$487	—	—	—
1929–30	30,275,474	106,313	5,126,758	25,042,403	—	—	—	1,179	4	200	975	—	—	—
1939–40	40,135,637	706,826	12,150,699	27,278,111	—	—	—	1,578	28	478	1,073	—	—	—
1949–50	56,963,728	1,632,814	22,689,851	32,641,063	—	—	—	2,268	65	904	1,300	—	—	—
1959–60	124,528,446	5,502,793	48,708,520	70,317,133	—	—	—	3,540	156	1,384	1,999	—	—	—
1969–70	264,494,250	21,147,738	105,508,732	137,837,780	—	—	—	5,807	464	2,316	3,026	—	—	—
1979–80	309,645,843	30,374,643	144,941,195	134,330,005	—	—	—	7,434	729	3,480	3,225	—	—	—
1989–90	407,529,633	24,819,017	191,971,325	190,739,292	$146,301,279	$33,385,369	$11,052,644	10,052	612	4,735	4,705	$3,609	$823	$273
1994–95	450,610,873	30,654,728	210,713,717	209,242,429	161,633,166	35,567,502	12,041,761	10,215	695	4,777	4,743	3,664	806	273
1995–96	462,048,905	30,680,931	219,492,346	211,875,628	163,467,429	36,170,740	12,237,460	10,304	684	4,895	4,725	3,646	807	273
1996–97	476,342,322	31,355,812	228,651,016	216,335,494	166,365,465	37,925,443	12,044,587	10,444	687	5,013	4,743	3,647	831	264
1997–98	499,997,787	34,059,705	241,841,424	224,096,658	170,565,953	40,923,629	12,607,076	10,840	738	5,243	4,858	3,698	887	273
1998–99	523,838,971	36,978,403	255,298,301	231,562,267	180,178,676	38,225,596	13,157,995	11,256	795	5,486	4,976	3,872	821	283
1999–2000	546,612,089	39,716,497	270,582,027	236,313,565	182,820,952	40,494,850	12,997,763	11,666	848	5,775	5,043	3,902	864	277
2000–01	568,768,925	41,238,388	282,832,771	244,697,765	187,875,711	43,773,740	13,048,315	12,049	874	5,992	5,184	3,980	927	276
2001–02	584,141,529	46,152,718	287,602,074	250,386,736	196,470,706	40,276,786	13,639,244	12,253	968	6,033	5,252	4,121	845	286
2002–03	599,661,432	51,116,219	291,957,497	256,587,715	202,350,449	40,302,340	13,934,926	12,445	1,061	6,059	5,325	4,200	836	289
2003–04	616,043,075	55,898,664	289,849,481	270,294,930	214,138,949	42,202,553	13,953,427	12,691	1,152	5,971	5,568	4,412	869	287

See notes at end of table.

Table 235.10. Revenues for public elementary and secondary schools, by source of funds: Selected years, 1919–20 through 2015–16—Continued

[Standard errors appear in parentheses]

	Revenues (in thousands)							Revenues per pupil						
				Local (including intermediate sources below the state level)							Local (including intermediate sources below the state level)			
School year	Total	Federal	State	Total	Property taxes	Other public revenue	Private[1]	Total	Federal	State	Total	Property taxes	Other public revenue	Private[1]
1	2	3	4	5	6	7	8	9	10	11	12	13	14	15
2004–05	631,347,845	58,001,429	295,839,603	277,506,812	217,342,444	45,865,082	14,299,287	12,939	1,189	6,063	5,687	4,454	940	293
2005–06	649,170,830	59,295,493	301,941,675	287,933,661	222,299,170	51,261,982	14,372,510	13,218	1,207	6,148	5,863	4,526	1,044	293
2006–07	675,456,253	57,310,700	320,411,596	297,733,956	228,859,761	54,461,385	14,412,810	13,711	1,163	6,504	6,044	4,646	1,106	293
2007–08	685,280,367	56,010,624	331,248,623	298,021,120	230,333,727	53,111,548	14,575,845	13,923	1,138	6,730	6,055	4,680	1,079	296
2008–09	684,788,404	65,505,898	319,639,575	299,642,931	237,912,172	47,618,203	14,112,557	13,908	1,330	6,492	6,086	4,832	967	287
2009–10	682,769,418	87,005,073	296,356,759	299,407,586	241,373,867	44,386,644	13,647,074	13,840	1,764	6,007	6,069	4,893	900	277
2010–11	678,125,905	84,789,192	299,414,452	293,922,261	237,534,317	43,274,502	13,113,443	13,713	1,715	6,055	5,944	4,803	875	265
2011–12	651,905,351	66,425,850	293,351,713	292,127,787	235,331,062	43,930,298	12,866,428	13,166	1,342	5,925	5,900	4,753	887	260
2012–13	647,545,794	59,911,039	293,024,765	294,609,990	238,064,177	44,111,636	12,434,177	13,017	1,204	5,890	5,922	4,786	887	250
2013–14	658,579,177	57,558,758	304,803,139	296,217,279	239,734,099	44,292,171	12,191,009	13,167	1,151	6,094	5,922	4,793	886	244
2014–15	679,009,924	57,663,558	316,115,873	305,230,494	247,280,951	46,105,647	11,843,895	13,507	1,147	6,288	6,072	4,919	917	236
2015–16	706,430,597	58,296,099	331,746,521	316,387,977	257,211,064	47,173,976	12,002,937	14,032	1,158	6,589	6,284	5,109	937	238
	Percentage distribution													
1919–20	100.0	0.3	16.5	83.2	—	—	—	100.0	0.3	16.5	83.2	—	—	—
1929–30	100.0	0.4	16.9	82.7	—	—	—	100.0	0.4	16.9	82.7	—	—	—
1939–40	100.0	1.8	30.3	68.0	—	—	—	100.0	1.8	30.3	68.0	—	—	—
1949–50	100.0	2.9	39.8	57.3	—	—	—	100.0	2.9	39.8	57.3	—	—	—
1959–60	100.0	4.4	39.1	56.5	—	—	—	100.0	4.4	39.1	56.5	—	—	—
1969–70	100.0	8.0	39.9	52.1	—	—	—	100.0	8.0	39.9	52.1	—	—	—
1979–80	100.0	9.8	46.8	43.4	—	—	—	100.0	9.8	46.8	43.4	—	—	—
1989–90	100.0	6.1	47.1	46.8	35.9	8.2	2.7	100.0	6.1	47.1	46.8	35.9	8.2	2.7
1994–95	100.0	6.8	46.8	46.4	35.9	7.9	2.7	100.0	6.8	46.8	46.4	35.9	7.9	2.7
1995–96	100.0	6.6	47.5	45.9	35.4	7.8	2.6	100.0	6.6	47.5	45.9	35.4	7.8	2.6
1996–97	100.0	6.6	48.0	45.4	34.9	8.0	2.5	100.0	6.6	48.0	45.4	34.9	8.0	2.5
1997–98	100.0	6.8	48.4	44.8	34.1	8.2	2.5	100.0	6.8	48.4	44.8	34.1	8.2	2.5
1998–99	100.0	7.1	48.7	44.2	34.4	7.3	2.5	100.0	7.1	48.7	44.2	34.4	7.3	2.5
1999–2000	100.0	7.3	49.5	43.2	33.4	7.4	2.4	100.0	7.3	49.5	43.2	33.4	7.4	2.4
2000–01	100.0	7.3	49.7	43.0	33.0	7.7	2.3	100.0	7.3	49.7	43.0	33.0	7.7	2.3
2001–02	100.0	7.9	49.2	42.9	33.6	6.9	2.3	100.0	7.9	49.2	42.9	33.6	6.9	2.3
2002–03	100.0	8.5	48.7	42.8	33.7	6.7	2.3	100.0	8.5	48.7	42.8	33.7	6.7	2.3
2003–04	100.0	9.1	47.1	43.9	34.8	6.9	2.3	100.0	9.1	47.1	43.9	34.8	6.9	2.3
2004–05	100.0	9.2	46.9	44.0	34.4	7.3	2.3	100.0	9.2	46.9	44.0	34.4	7.3	2.3
2005–06	100.0	9.1	46.5	44.4	34.2	7.9	2.2	100.0	9.1	46.5	44.4	34.2	7.9	2.2
2006–07	100.0	8.5	47.4	44.1	33.9	8.1	2.1	100.0	8.5	47.4	44.1	33.9	8.1	2.1
2007–08	100.0	8.2	48.3	43.5	33.6	7.8	2.1	100.0	8.2	48.3	43.5	33.6	7.8	2.1
2008–09	100.0	9.6	46.7	43.8	34.7	7.0	2.1	100.0	9.6	46.7	43.8	34.7	7.0	2.1
2009–10	100.0	12.7	43.4	43.9	35.4	6.5	2.0	100.0	12.7	43.4	43.9	35.4	6.5	2.0
2010–11	100.0	12.5	44.2	43.3	35.0	6.4	1.9	100.0	12.5	44.2	43.3	35.0	6.4	1.9
2011–12	100.0	10.2	45.0	44.8	36.1	6.7	2.0	100.0	10.2	45.0	44.8	36.1	6.7	2.0
2012–13	100.0	9.3	45.3	45.5	36.8	6.8	1.9	100.0	9.3	45.3	45.5	36.8	6.8	1.9
2013–14	100.0	8.7	46.3	45.0	36.4	6.7	1.9	100.0	8.7	46.3	45.0	36.4	6.7	1.9
2014–15	100.0	8.5	46.6	45.0	36.4	6.8	1.7	100.0	8.5	46.6	45.0	36.4	6.8	1.7
2015–16	100.0	8.3	47.0	44.8	36.4	6.7	1.7	100.0	8.3	47.0	44.8	36.4	6.7	1.7

—Not available.
#Rounds to zero.
[1]Includes revenues from gifts, and tuition and fees from patrons.
[2]Constant dollars based on the Consumer Price Index, prepared by the Bureau of Labor Statistics, U.S. Department of Labor, adjusted to a school-year basis.

NOTE: Beginning in 1989–90, revenues for state education agencies were excluded and new survey collection procedures were initiated; data may not be entirely comparable with figures for earlier years. Detail may not sum to totals because of rounding.
SOURCE: U.S. Department of Education, National Center for Education Statistics, *Biennial Survey of Education in the United States*, 1919–20 through 1949–50; *Statistics of State School Systems*, 1959–60 and 1969–70; *Revenues and Expenditures for Public Elementary and Secondary Education, 1979–80*; and Common Core of Data (CCD), "National Public Education Financial Survey," 1989–90 through 2015–16. (This table was prepared September 2018.)

Table 235.20. Revenues for public elementary and secondary schools, by source of funds and state or jurisdiction: 2015–16

[In current dollars]

State or jurisdiction	Total (in thousands)	Federal			State		Local (including intermediate sources below the state level)					
									Property taxes		Private[2]	
		Amount (in thousands)	Per pupil	Percent of total	Amount (in thousands)	Percent of total	Amount (in thousands)[1]	Percent of total	Amount (in thousands)	Percent of total	Amount (in thousands)	Percent of total
1	2	3	4	5	6	7	8	9	10	11	12	13
United States	**$678,378,476**	**$55,981,180**	**$1,112**	**8.3**	**$318,572,978**	**47.0**	**$303,824,317**	**44.8**	**$246,997,299**	**36.4**	**$11,526,305**	**1.7**
Alabama	7,586,636	846,066	1,138	11.2	4,148,799	54.7	2,591,770	34.2	1,180,586	15.6	336,395	4.4
Alaska	2,497,340	309,593	2,337	12.4	1,614,053	64.6	573,693	23.0	315,349	12.6	18,950	0.8
Arizona	10,225,235	1,292,800	1,175	12.6	4,694,392	45.9	4,238,042	41.4	3,050,055	29.8	239,647	2.3
Arkansas	5,383,382	624,286	1,269	11.6	2,750,455	51.1	2,008,641	37.3	1,734,495	32.2	155,758	2.9
California	85,779,627	7,269,632	1,153	8.5	50,967,666	59.4	27,542,328	32.1	22,245,864	25.9	381,615	0.4
Colorado	10,237,008	722,600	804	7.1	4,475,646	43.7	5,038,762	49.2	4,136,015	40.4	370,648	3.6
Connecticut	11,697,383	504,641	938	4.3	4,718,878	40.3	6,473,865	55.3	6,319,778	54.0	88,414	0.8
Delaware	2,190,905	182,544	1,354	8.3	1,257,941	57.4	750,420	34.3	470,779	21.5	13,874	0.6
District of Columbia	2,274,302	226,209	2,692	9.9	†	†	2,048,093	90.1	674,087	29.6	11,205	0.5
Florida	27,929,250	3,230,709	1,157	11.6	10,963,798	39.3	13,734,743	49.2	11,469,114	41.1	910,541	3.3
Georgia	19,617,068	1,867,232	1,063	9.5	8,993,752	45.8	8,756,085	44.6	5,796,092	29.5	469,418	2.4
Hawaii	3,031,312	261,130	1,435	8.6	2,711,156	89.4	59,026	1.9	0	0.0	29,856	1.0
Idaho	2,413,672	256,288	877	10.6	1,576,287	65.3	581,097	24.1	493,347	20.4	32,417	1.3
Illinois	27,704,831	2,332,394	1,142	8.4	6,687,655	24.1	18,684,782	67.4	16,511,399	59.6	483,316	1.7
Indiana	12,437,534	999,058	954	8.0	6,909,225	55.6	4,529,251	36.4	2,974,623	23.9	330,352	2.7
Iowa	6,657,857	484,041	953	7.3	3,583,116	53.8	2,590,700	38.9	2,099,098	31.5	144,446	2.2
Kansas	6,297,498	530,976	1,071	8.4	3,976,653	63.1	1,789,870	28.4	1,085,804	17.2	150,278	2.4
Kentucky	7,634,758	887,650	1,293	11.6	4,179,014	54.7	2,568,095	33.6	1,902,851	24.9	91,822	1.2
Louisiana	8,930,136	1,135,961	1,581	12.7	3,883,978	43.5	3,910,197	43.8	1,665,949	18.7	58,402	0.7
Maine	2,809,790	197,509	1,088	7.0	1,106,375	39.4	1,505,907	53.6	1,432,495	51.0	35,805	1.3
Maryland	14,420,623	841,914	957	5.8	6,334,951	43.9	7,243,758	50.2	3,530,471	24.5	112,895	0.8
Massachusetts	17,962,854	899,926	934	5.0	6,788,790	37.8	10,274,138	57.2	9,605,910	53.5	251,583	1.4
Michigan	19,835,653	1,761,671	1,147	8.9	11,937,148	60.2	6,136,833	30.9	5,264,843	26.5	268,971	1.4
Minnesota	12,725,423	714,029	826	5.6	8,506,328	66.8	3,505,065	27.5	2,281,970	17.9	337,833	2.7
Mississippi	4,712,456	691,584	1,420	14.7	2,412,932	51.2	1,607,939	34.1	1,347,859	28.6	110,007	2.3
Missouri	11,147,752	961,637	1,046	8.6	3,676,108	33.0	6,510,008	58.4	5,077,976	45.6	346,984	3.1
Montana	1,781,468	224,601	1,546	12.6	850,640	47.7	706,227	39.6	458,776	25.8	60,363	3.4
Nebraska	4,351,337	361,692	1,145	8.3	1,438,008	33.0	2,551,637	58.6	2,279,210	52.4	158,136	3.6
Nevada	4,683,088	416,596	891	8.9	1,668,136	35.6	2,598,356	55.5	1,164,070	24.9	32,133	0.7
New Hampshire	3,055,956	173,966	954	5.7	1,005,148	32.9	1,876,842	61.4	1,789,048	58.5	46,015	1.5
New Jersey	29,671,607	1,246,800	885	4.2	12,666,167	42.7	15,758,639	53.1	14,899,431	50.2	572,986	1.9
New Mexico	3,987,279	547,463	1,631	13.7	2,792,814	70.0	647,002	16.2	529,255	13.3	54,050	1.4
New York	65,776,757	3,312,702	1,245	5.0	27,460,780	41.7	35,003,275	53.2	32,234,178	49.0	309,184	0.5
North Carolina	14,072,129	1,635,705	1,059	11.6	8,735,404	62.1	3,701,020	26.3	3,142,297	22.3	177,705	1.3
North Dakota	1,705,036	155,462	1,431	9.1	985,340	57.8	564,234	33.1	386,975	22.7	67,024	3.9
Ohio	24,956,848	1,925,720	1,122	7.7	11,202,038	44.9	11,829,089	47.4	9,708,788	38.9	645,070	2.6
Oklahoma	6,270,084	721,312	1,041	11.5	3,030,336	48.3	2,518,436	40.2	1,902,720	30.3	286,976	4.6
Oregon	7,377,456	563,698	978	7.6	3,861,421	52.3	2,952,336	40.0	2,419,040	32.8	140,728	1.9
Pennsylvania	29,892,129	2,037,997	1,187	6.8	11,238,423	37.6	16,615,708	55.6	13,187,328	44.1	389,443	1.3
Rhode Island	2,485,803	191,437	1,348	7.7	1,029,125	41.4	1,265,241	50.9	1,223,469	49.2	26,271	1.1
South Carolina	9,442,258	894,762	1,172	9.5	4,505,718	47.7	4,041,777	42.8	3,054,687	32.4	247,121	2.6
South Dakota	1,461,886	201,311	1,499	13.8	444,457	30.4	816,118	55.8	698,961	47.8	43,037	2.9
Tennessee	9,596,867	1,100,272	1,099	11.5	4,434,856	46.2	4,061,738	42.3	1,948,690	20.3	406,834	4.2
Texas	58,954,734	6,223,101	1,174	10.6	24,104,698	40.9	28,626,935	48.6	26,193,418	44.4	1,022,964	1.7
Utah	5,447,070	454,465	701	8.3	2,975,371	54.6	2,017,234	37.0	1,567,901	28.8	226,293	4.2
Vermont	1,724,527	114,588	1,304	6.6	1,540,670	89.3	69,270	4.0	166	#	23,895	1.4
Virginia	15,927,348	1,058,006	824	6.6	6,297,600	39.5	8,571,742	53.8	5,214,229	32.7	237,672	1.5
Washington	14,830,244	1,098,846	1,011	7.4	9,218,360	62.2	4,513,039	30.4	3,841,555	25.9	312,653	2.1
West Virginia	3,433,438	356,760	1,286	10.4	1,906,257	55.5	1,170,422	34.1	1,080,075	31.5	23,133	0.7
Wisconsin	11,309,921	808,271	931	7.1	5,150,347	45.5	5,351,302	47.3	4,881,439	43.2	219,070	1.9
Wyoming	2,042,925	123,566	1,305	6.0	1,175,770	57.6	743,590	36.4	524,783	25.7	16,118	0.8
Other jurisdictions												
American Samoa	70,851	61,430	—	86.7	9,199	13.0	221	0.3	0	0.0	11	#
Guam	321,973	65,316	2,119	20.3	0	0.0	256,658	79.7	0	0.0	200	0.1
Northern Marianas	74,136	34,561	—	46.6	38,718	52.2	856	1.2	0	0.0	403	0.5
Puerto Rico	2,876,676	952,863	2,509	33.1	1,923,752	66.9	62	#	0	0.0	62	#
U.S. Virgin Islands	186,961	26,986	1,955	14.4	0	0.0	159,975	85.6	0	0.0	16	#

—Not available.
†Not applicable.
#Rounds to zero.
[1]Includes other categories of revenue not separately shown.
[2]Includes revenues from gifts, and tuition and fees from patrons.

NOTE: Excludes revenues for state education agencies. Detail may not sum to totals because of rounding.
SOURCE: U.S. Department of Education, National Center for Education Statistics, Common Core of Data (CCD), "National Public Education Financial Survey," 2015–16. (This table was prepared September 2018.)

Table 235.40. Public elementary and secondary revenues and expenditures, by locale, source of revenue, and purpose of expenditure: 2015–16

Source of revenue and purpose of expenditure	Total	City, large	City, midsize	City, small	Suburban, large	Suburban, midsize	Suburban, small	Town, fringe	Town, distant	Town, remote	Rural, fringe	Rural, distant	Rural, remote
1	2	3	4	5	6	7	8	9	10	11	12	13	14
Revenue amounts (in millions of current dollars)													
Total revenue[1]	$685,009	$127,233	$47,847	$48,255	$258,440	$23,581	$12,831	$16,562	$32,934	$19,941	$48,682	$34,316	$14,275
Federal	55,603	12,880	4,906	4,327	15,953	1,716	936	1,287	3,136	2,225	3,798	2,848	1,571
Title I	14,010	4,018	1,215	1,088	3,519	412	216	275	808	531	859	709	360
Child Nutrition Act	16,120	3,693	1,348	1,223	4,718	542	278	366	981	556	1,152	900	362
Children with disabilities (IDEA)	11,174	1,873	953	885	4,095	384	217	265	584	356	844	517	198
Impact aid	1,325	135	87	75	162	23	9	64	48	205	125	100	293
Bilingual education	335	95	35	29	120	8	6	6	11	7	12	4	2
Indian education	94	11	3	3	7	2	3	2	10	14	6	9	26
Math, science, and professional development	1,465	312	136	122	364	52	28	32	100	70	106	93	51
Safe and drug-free schools	82	18	5	7	13	2	1	2	7	7	8	8	5
Vocational and technical education	543	114	43	44	165	18	12	12	33	25	44	23	10
Other and unclassified	10,454	2,612	1,081	850	2,790	274	167	264	555	455	642	487	264
State	322,657	57,828	23,802	24,041	111,980	11,893	6,457	8,732	17,807	10,345	24,131	18,552	7,059
Special education programs	19,838	3,621	1,585	1,383	7,971	668	295	459	875	483	1,392	815	290
Compensatory and basic skills	5,215	934	405	462	1,828	260	78	96	268	127	383	266	105
Bilingual education	1,116	105	57	69	709	61	10	5	31	12	43	10	4
Gifted and talented	1,151	38	71	76	704	38	9	11	33	9	128	27	6
Vocational education	1,236	49	82	86	469	53	25	23	95	59	169	92	34
Other	294,100	53,080	21,603	21,964	100,299	10,814	6,040	8,137	16,505	9,655	22,017	17,343	6,620
Local[1]	306,749	56,525	19,139	19,888	130,506	9,972	5,438	6,543	11,991	7,372	20,752	12,915	5,645
Property tax[2]	195,662	27,471	11,816	12,839	89,594	5,599	3,791	4,602	8,375	5,391	13,132	9,003	4,047
Parent government contribution[2]	54,056	18,364	3,241	2,644	20,955	2,565	556	501	814	175	2,954	938	308
Private (fees from individuals)	14,694	1,476	873	887	6,471	566	276	415	746	439	1,293	885	363
Other[1]	42,337	9,215	3,209	3,518	13,485	1,242	815	1,025	2,057	1,367	3,374	2,089	927
Percentage distribution of revenue													
Total revenue	100.0	100.0	100.0	100.0	100.0	100.0	100.0	100.0	100.0	100.0	100.0	100.0	100.0
Federal	8.1	10.1	10.3	9.0	6.2	7.3	7.3	7.8	9.5	11.2	7.8	8.3	11.0
State	47.1	45.5	49.7	49.8	43.3	50.4	50.3	52.7	54.1	51.9	49.6	54.1	49.5
Local	44.8	44.4	40.0	41.2	50.5	42.3	42.4	39.5	36.4	37.0	42.6	37.6	39.5
Expenditure amounts (in millions of current dollars)													
Total expenditures	$692,508	$130,695	$48,294	$48,768	$259,390	$23,567	$12,834	$17,061	$33,704	$20,108	$48,902	$34,386	$14,628
Current expenditures for schools	585,806	107,526	40,771	41,192	220,825	20,452	11,242	14,265	28,602	16,979	42,057	29,628	12,156
Instruction	355,892	67,500	23,844	24,704	135,354	12,289	6,762	8,609	17,085	10,034	25,210	17,514	6,969
Support services, students	33,699	5,011	2,643	2,602	13,902	1,224	687	786	1,527	969	2,395	1,403	543
Support services, instructional staff	27,768	4,810	2,492	2,208	10,376	1,049	505	623	1,342	797	1,833	1,191	525
Administration	44,598	7,502	3,099	3,038	16,195	1,485	870	1,174	2,411	1,473	3,362	2,749	1,230
Operation and maintenance	52,814	9,713	3,551	3,705	19,673	1,852	1,025	1,296	2,614	1,617	3,811	2,738	1,214
Transportation	24,796	4,141	1,541	1,479	9,346	867	489	640	1,230	649	2,149	1,647	615
Food service	23,254	4,279	1,721	1,685	7,609	831	446	595	1,395	828	1,820	1,441	604
Other	22,986	4,572	1,879	1,771	8,368	855	459	541	999	611	1,477	945	457
Other current expenditures	30,175	7,864	2,060	1,985	10,689	801	400	649	1,129	704	1,871	1,260	710
Interest on school debt	18,263	4,330	1,210	1,179	6,955	554	321	498	740	355	1,230	693	197
Capital outlay	58,263	10,975	4,253	4,412	20,922	1,761	871	1,649	3,233	2,071	3,744	2,806	1,565
Percentage distribution of current expenditures for schools													
All current expenditures for schools	100.0	100.0	100.0	100.0	100.0	100.0	100.0	100.0	100.0	100.0	100.0	100.0	100.0
Instruction	60.8	62.8	58.5	60.0	61.3	60.1	60.1	60.4	59.7	59.1	59.9	59.1	57.3
Support services	10.5	9.1	12.6	11.7	11.0	11.1	10.6	9.9	10.0	10.4	10.1	8.8	8.8
Administration	7.6	7.0	7.6	7.4	7.3	7.3	7.7	8.2	8.4	8.7	8.0	9.3	10.1
Operation and maintenance	9.0	9.0	8.7	9.0	8.9	9.1	9.1	9.1	9.1	9.5	9.1	9.2	10.0
Transportation	4.2	3.9	3.8	3.6	4.2	4.2	4.3	4.5	4.3	3.8	5.1	5.6	5.1
Food service and other	7.9	8.2	8.8	8.4	7.2	8.2	8.1	8.0	8.4	8.5	7.8	8.1	8.7
Per student amounts (in current dollars)													
Current expenditure per student	$11,669	$12,509	$11,212	$11,469	$11,960	$11,069	$11,181	$11,055	$10,609	$10,438	$11,081	$11,010	$12,645
Instruction expenditure per student	7,089	7,853	6,557	6,878	7,331	6,651	6,725	6,672	6,337	6,169	6,642	6,508	7,249

[1]Excludes revenues from other in-state school systems.
[2]Property tax and parent government contributions are determined on the basis of independence or dependence of the local school system and are mutually exclusive.
NOTE: Total includes data for some school districts not identified by locale. Detail may not sum to totals because of rounding.

SOURCE: U.S. Department of Education, National Center for Education Statistics, Common Core of Data (CCD), "Local Education Agency (School District) Finance Survey (F33)," 2015–16; and Education Demographic and Geographic Estimates (EDGE), "Public School File," 2015–16. (This table was prepared May 2019.)

Table 236.10. Summary of expenditures for public elementary and secondary education and other related programs, by purpose: Selected years, 1919–20 through 2015–16

School year	Total expenditures	Current expenditures for public elementary and secondary education: Total	Administration	Instruction	Plant operation	Plant maintenance	Fixed charges	Other school services[3]	Current expenditures for other programs[1]	Capital outlay[2]	Interest on school debt
1	2	3	4	5	6	7	8	9	10	11	12
	Amounts in thousands of current dollars										
1919–20	$1,036,151	$861,120	$36,752	$632,556	$115,707	$30,432	$9,286	$36,387	$3,277	$153,543	$18,212
1929–30	2,316,790	1,843,552	78,680	1,317,727	216,072	78,810	50,270	101,993	9,825	370,878	92,536
1939–40	2,344,049	1,941,799	91,571	1,403,285	194,365	73,321	50,116	129,141	13,367	257,974	130,909
1949–50	5,837,643	4,687,274	220,050	3,112,340	427,587	214,164	261,469	451,663	35,614	1,014,176	100,578
1959–60	15,613,254	12,329,388	528,408	8,350,738	1,085,036	422,586	909,323	1,033,297	132,566	2,661,786	489,514
1969–70	40,683,429	34,217,773	1,606,646	23,270,158	2,537,257	974,941	3,266,920	2,561,856	635,803	4,659,072	1,170,782
1979–80	95,961,561	86,984,142	4,263,757	53,257,937	9,744,785	(4)	11,793,934	7,923,729	597,585	6,506,167	1,873,666
1989–90	212,769,564	188,229,359	16,346,991[5]	113,550,405[5]	20,261,415[5]	(4)	—	38,070,548[5]	2,982,543	17,781,342	3,776,321
1999–2000	381,838,155	323,888,508	25,079,298[5]	199,968,138[5]	31,190,295[5]	(4)	—	67,650,776[5]	5,457,015	43,357,186	9,135,445
2000–01	410,811,185	348,360,841	26,689,182[5]	214,333,003[5]	34,034,158[5]	(4)	—	73,304,498[5]	6,063,700	46,220,704	10,165,940
2005–06	528,268,772	449,131,342	34,197,083[5]	273,760,798[5]	44,313,835[5]	(4)	—	96,859,626[5]	7,415,575	57,375,299	14,346,556
2006–07	562,194,807	476,814,206	36,213,814[5]	290,678,482[5]	46,828,916[5]	(4)	—	103,092,995[5]	7,804,253	62,863,465	14,712,882
2007–08	597,313,726	506,884,219	38,203,341[5]	308,238,664[5]	49,362,661[5]	(4)	—	111,079,554[5]	8,307,720	66,426,299	15,695,488
2008–09	610,326,007	518,922,842	38,811,325[5]	316,075,710[5]	50,559,027[5]	(4)	—	113,476,779[5]	8,463,793	65,890,367	17,049,004
2009–10	607,018,292	524,715,242	38,972,700[5]	321,213,401[5]	50,023,919[5]	(4)	—	114,505,223[5]	8,355,761	56,714,992	17,232,297
2010–11	604,355,852	527,291,339	39,154,833[5]	322,536,983[5]	50,214,709[5]	(4)	—	115,384,813[5]	8,161,474	50,968,815	17,934,224
2011–12	601,993,584	527,207,246	39,491,926[5]	320,994,474[5]	49,834,165[5]	(4)	—	116,886,681[5]	8,188,640	48,793,436	17,804,262
2012–13	606,813,352	535,795,823	40,349,598[5]	325,682,380[5]	50,674,499[5]	(4)	—	119,089,346[5]	8,031,416	45,720,570	17,265,542
2013–14	625,018,277	553,501,209	41,538,042[5]	336,426,927[5]	53,051,141[5]	(4)	—	122,485,100[5]	7,926,285	46,438,323	17,152,459
2014–15	651,135,383	575,331,825	43,328,198[5]	349,453,258[5]	54,200,172[5]	(4)	—	128,350,197[5]	7,713,966	50,610,125	17,479,466
2015-16	677,541,010	596,135,643	45,247,664[5]	363,047,760[5]	55,045,308[5]	(4)	—	132,794,911[5]	7,913,839	55,989,047	17,502,481
	Amounts in thousands of constant 2017–18 dollars[6]										
1919–20	$13,490,188	$11,211,369	$478,493	$8,235,575	$1,506,450	$396,210	$120,899	$473,741	$42,665	$1,999,056	$237,111
1929–30	33,583,913	26,723,911	1,140,536	19,101,614	3,132,154	1,142,420	728,708	1,478,478	142,422	5,376,203	1,341,391
1939–40	41,618,569	34,476,624	1,625,842	24,915,313	3,450,949	1,301,814	889,809	2,292,897	237,331	4,580,326	2,324,288
1949–50	61,160,791	49,108,403	2,305,457	32,607,882	4,479,815	2,243,789	2,739,402	4,732,058	373,127	10,625,488	1,053,752
1959–60	131,846,791	104,116,044	4,462,164	70,518,164	9,162,633	3,568,546	7,678,817	8,725,721	1,119,459	22,477,566	4,133,722
1969–70	267,230,086	224,760,301	10,553,293	152,850,595	16,666,034	6,403,924	21,458,843	16,827,613	4,176,287	30,603,227	7,690,310
1979–80	306,706,662	278,013,567	13,627,568	170,219,866	31,145,705	(4)	37,695,074	25,325,354	1,909,966	20,794,626	5,988,500
1989–90	415,779,963	367,825,146	31,944,190[5]	221,892,560[5]	39,593,494[5]	(4)	—	74,394,903[5]	5,828,285	34,747,102	7,379,432
1999–2000	559,648,264	474,713,276	36,757,944[5]	293,087,058[5]	45,714,641[5]	(4)	—	99,153,631[5]	7,998,177	63,547,275	13,389,537
2000–01	582,167,867	493,668,371	37,821,716[5]	303,735,126[5]	48,230,414[5]	(4)	—	103,881,113[5]	8,592,978	65,500,185	14,406,334
2005–06	658,705,965	560,028,360	42,640,837[5]	341,356,295[5]	55,255,561[5]	(4)	—	120,775,667[5]	9,246,588	71,542,089	17,888,928
2006–07	683,337,490	579,558,934	44,017,228[5]	353,314,370[5]	56,919,689[5]	(4)	—	125,307,647[5]	9,485,927	76,409,390	17,883,239
2007–08	700,083,445	594,095,255	44,776,347[5]	361,272,102[5]	57,855,663[5]	(4)	—	130,191,143[5]	9,737,089	77,855,154	18,395,947
2008–09	705,483,843	599,829,724	44,862,520[5]	365,356,062[5]	58,441,844[5]	(4)	—	131,169,298[5]	9,783,410	76,163,540	19,707,168
2009–10	694,936,308	600,712,825	44,617,344[5]	367,736,619[5]	57,269,176[5]	(4)	—	131,089,686[5]	9,565,975	64,929,356	19,728,152
2010–11	678,268,736	591,779,212	43,943,480[5]	361,983,344[5]	56,355,982[5]	(4)	—	129,496,407[5]	9,159,624	57,202,315	20,127,585
2011–12	656,385,033	574,841,584	43,060,109[5]	349,997,034[5]	54,336,791[5]	(4)	—	127,447,651[5]	8,928,501	53,202,031	19,412,917
2012–13	650,809,890	574,643,290	43,275,115[5]	349,295,732[5]	54,348,615[5]	(4)	—	127,723,828[5]	8,613,728	49,035,505	18,517,367
2013–14	660,024,365	584,501,762	43,864,509[5]	355,269,561[5]	56,022,434[5]	(4)	—	129,345,258[5]	8,370,222	49,039,246	18,113,135
2014–15	682,633,369	603,162,894	45,424,154[5]	366,357,691[5]	56,822,048[5]	(4)	—	134,559,002[5]	8,087,121	53,058,336	18,325,017
2015–16	705,558,501	620,786,882	47,118,733[5]	378,060,412[5]	57,321,527[5]	(4)	—	138,286,210[5]	8,241,090	58,304,291	18,226,238
	Percentage distribution										
1919–20	100.0	83.1	3.5	61.0	11.2	2.9	0.9	3.5	0.3	14.8	1.8
1929–30	100.0	79.6	3.4	56.9	9.3	3.4	2.2	4.4	0.4	16.0	4.0
1939–40	100.0	82.8	3.9	59.9	8.3	3.1	2.1	5.5	0.6	11.0	5.6
1949–50	100.0	80.3	3.8	53.3	7.3	3.7	4.5	7.7	0.6	17.4	1.7
1959–60	100.0	79.0	3.4	53.5	6.9	2.7	5.8	6.6	0.8	17.0	3.1
1969–70	100.0	84.1	3.9	57.2	6.2	2.4	8.0	6.3	1.6	11.5	2.9
1979–80	100.0	90.6	4.4	55.5	10.2	(4)	12.3	8.3	0.6	6.8	2.0
1989–90	100.0	88.5	7.7[5]	53.4[5]	9.5[5]	(4)	—	17.9[5]	1.4	8.4	1.8
1999–2000	100.0	84.8	6.6[5]	52.4[5]	8.2[5]	(4)	—	17.7[5]	1.4	11.4	2.4
2000–01	100.0	84.8	6.5[5]	52.2[5]	8.3[5]	(4)	—	17.8[5]	1.5	11.3	2.5
2005–06	100.0	85.0	6.5[5]	51.8[5]	8.4[5]	(4)	—	18.3[5]	1.4	10.9	2.7
2006–07	100.0	84.8	6.4[5]	51.7[5]	8.3[5]	(4)	—	18.3[5]	1.4	11.2	2.6
2007–08	100.0	84.9	6.4[5]	51.6[5]	8.3[5]	(4)	—	18.6[5]	1.4	11.1	2.6
2008–09	100.0	85.0	6.4[5]	51.8[5]	8.3[5]	(4)	—	18.6[5]	1.4	10.8	2.8
2009–10	100.0	86.4	6.4[5]	52.9[5]	8.2[5]	(4)	—	18.9[5]	1.4	9.3	2.8
2010–11	100.0	87.2	6.5[5]	53.4[5]	8.3[5]	(4)	—	19.1[5]	1.4	8.4	3.0
2011–12	100.0	87.6	6.6[5]	53.3[5]	8.3[5]	(4)	—	19.4[5]	1.4	8.1	3.0
2012–13	100.0	88.3	6.6[5]	53.7[5]	8.4[5]	(4)	—	19.6[5]	1.3	7.5	2.8
2013–14	100.0	88.6	6.6[5]	53.8[5]	8.5[5]	(4)	—	19.6[5]	1.3	7.4	2.7
2014–15	100.0	88.4	6.7[5]	53.7[5]	8.3[5]	(4)	—	19.7[5]	1.2	7.8	2.7
2015–16	100.0	88.0	6.7[5]	53.6[5]	8.1[5]	(4)	—	19.6[5]	1.2	8.3	2.6

—Not available.
[1]Includes expenditures for summer schools, adult education, community colleges, and community services.
[2]Prior to 1969–70, excludes capital outlay by state and local school housing authorities.
[3]Prior to 1959–60, items included under "other school services" were listed under "auxiliary services," a more comprehensive classification that also included community services.
[4]Plant operation also includes plant maintenance.
[5]Data not comparable to figures prior to 1989–90.
[6]Constant dollars based on the Consumer Price Index, prepared by the Bureau of Labor Statistics, U.S. Department of Labor, adjusted to a school-year basis.

NOTE: Beginning in 1959–60, includes Alaska and Hawaii. Beginning in 1989–90, state administration expenditures were excluded from both "total" and "current" expenditures. Beginning in 1989–90, extensive changes were made in the data collection procedures. Detail may not sum to totals because of rounding.
SOURCE: U.S. Department of Education, National Center for Education Statistics, *Biennial Survey of Education in the United States*, 1919–20 through 1949–50; *Statistics of State School Systems*, 1959–60 and 1969–70; *Revenues and Expenditures for Public Elementary and Secondary Education, 1979–80*; and Common Core of Data (CCD), "National Public Education Financial Survey," 1989–90 through 2015–16. (This table was prepared September 2018.)

Table 236.15. Current expenditures and current expenditures per pupil in public elementary and secondary schools: 1989–90 through 2028–29

School year	Current expenditures in unadjusted dollars[1]			Current expenditures in constant 2017–18 dollars[2]					
				Total current expenditures		Per pupil in fall enrollment		Per pupil in average daily attendance (ADA)	
	Total, in billions	Per pupil in fall enrollment	Per pupil in average daily attendance (ADA)	In billions	Annual percentage change	Per pupil enrolled	Annual percentage change	Per pupil in ADA	Annual percentage change
1	2	3	4	5	6	7	8	9	10
1989–90	$188.2	$4,643	$4,980	$367.8	3.8	$9,073	2.9	$9,731	2.3
1990–91	202.0	4,902	5,258	374.3	1.8	9,082	0.1	9,742	0.1
1991–92	211.2	5,023	5,421	379.2	1.3	9,018	-0.7	9,733	-0.1
1992–93	220.9	5,160	5,584	384.7	1.4	8,982	-0.4	9,721	-0.1
1993–94	231.5	5,327	5,767	392.9	2.1	9,040	0.6	9,787	0.7
1994–95	243.9	5,529	5,989	402.3	2.4	9,121	0.9	9,880	0.9
1995–96	255.1	5,689	6,147	409.7	1.8	9,137	0.2	9,872	-0.1
1996–97	270.2	5,923	6,393	421.9	3.0	9,249	1.2	9,982	1.1
1997–98	285.5	6,189	6,676	438.0	3.8	9,495	2.7	10,241	2.6
1998–99	302.9	6,508	7,013	456.7	4.3	9,814	3.4	10,576	3.3
1999–2000	323.9	6,912	7,394	474.7	3.9	10,131	3.2	10,837	2.5
2000–01	348.4	7,380	7,904	493.7	4.0	10,458	3.2	11,200	3.4
2001–02	368.4	7,727	8,259	513.0	3.9	10,760	2.9	11,500	2.7
2002–03	387.6	8,044	8,610	528.1	3.0	10,960	1.9	11,731	2.0
2003–04	403.4	8,310	8,900	537.9	1.8	11,081	1.1	11,867	1.2
2004–05	425.0	8,711	9,316	550.2	2.3	11,275	1.8	12,059	1.6
2005–06	449.1	9,145	9,778	560.0	1.8	11,403	1.1	12,193	1.1
2006–07	476.8	9,679	10,336	579.6	3.5	11,765	3.2	12,563	3.0
2007–08	506.9	10,298	10,982	594.1	2.5	12,070	2.6	12,871	2.5
2008–09	518.9	10,540	11,239	599.8	1.0	12,183	0.9	12,991	0.9
2009–10	524.7	10,636	11,427	600.7	0.1	12,177	-0.1	13,082	0.7
2010–11	527.3	10,663	11,433	591.8	-1.5	11,967	-1.7	12,832	-1.9
2011–12	527.2	10,648	11,362	574.8	-2.9	11,610	-3.0	12,389	-3.5
2012–13	535.8	10,771	11,509	574.6	#	11,552	-0.5	12,344	-0.4
2013–14	553.5	11,066	11,819	584.5	1.7	11,686	1.2	12,481	1.1
2014–15	575.3	11,445	12,224	603.2	3.2	11,998	2.7	12,816	2.7
2015–16	596.1	11,841	12,617	620.8	2.9	12,330	2.8	13,139	2.5
2016–17[3]	614.7	12,140	12,990	628.5	1.2	12,420	0.7	13,280	1.1
2017–18[3]	638.4	12,590	13,470	638.4	1.6	12,590	1.4	13,470	1.4
2018–19[3]	661.5	13,040	13,940	647.2	1.4	12,760	1.3	13,640	1.3
2019–20[3]	680.1	13,440	14,370	650.2	0.5	12,850	0.7	13,740	0.7
2020–21[3]	702.1	13,860	14,820	657.3	1.1	12,970	1.0	13,870	1.0
2021–22[3]	725.3	14,300	15,300	663.5	0.9	13,090	0.9	13,990	0.9
2022–23[3]	748.0	14,740	15,770	668.8	0.8	13,180	0.7	14,090	0.7
2023–24[3]	770.5	15,180	16,230	673.1	0.6	13,260	0.6	14,180	0.6
2024–25[3]	792.5	15,620	16,700	676.8	0.6	13,340	0.6	14,260	0.6
2025–26[3]	815.1	16,080	17,200	681.3	0.7	13,440	0.8	14,380	0.8
2026–27[3]	839.3	16,580	17,730	686.8	0.8	13,560	0.9	14,510	0.9
2027–28[3]	867.4	17,110	18,300	694.4	1.1	13,700	1.0	14,650	1.0
2028–29[3]	890.2	17,520	18,730	700.9	0.9	13,790	0.7	14,750	0.7

#Rounds to zero.
[1]Unadjusted (or "current") dollars have not been adjusted to compensate for inflation.
[2]Constant dollars based on the Consumer Price Index, prepared by the Bureau of Labor Statistics, U.S. Department of Labor, adjusted to a school-year basis.
[3]Projected.
NOTE: Current expenditures include instruction, support services, food services, and enterprise operations. Some data have been revised from previously published figures.

SOURCE: U.S. Department of Education, National Center for Education Statistics, Common Core of Data (CCD), "National Public Education Financial Survey," 1989–90 through 2016–17; National Elementary and Secondary Enrollment Projection Model, 1972 through 2028; and Public Elementary and Secondary Education Current Expenditure Projection Model, 1973–74 through 2028–29. (This table was prepared April 2019.)

Table 236.20. Total expenditures for public elementary and secondary education and other related programs, by function and subfunction: Selected years, 1990–91 through 2015–16

Function and subfunction	Expenditures (in thousands of current dollars)								Percentage distribution of current expenditures for public schools							
	1990–91	2000–01	2005–06	2010–11	2012–13	2013–14	2014–15	2015–16	1990–91	2000–01	2005–06	2010–11	2012–13	2013–14	2014–15	2015–16
1	2	3	4	5	6	7	8	9	10	11	12	13	14	15	16	17
Total expenditures	**$229,429,715**	**$410,811,185**	**$528,268,772**	**$604,355,852**	**$606,813,352**	**$625,018,277**	**$651,135,383**	**$677,541,000**	†	†	†	†	†	†	†	†
Current expenditures for public schools	202,037,752	348,360,841	449,131,342	527,291,339	535,795,823	553,501,209	575,331,825	596,135,643	100.00	100.00	100.00	100.00	100.00	100.00	100.00	100.00
Salaries	132,730,931[1]	224,305,806	273,142,308	311,541,792	311,649,709	318,705,822	328,252,700	339,723,532	65.70	64.39	60.82	59.08	58.17	57.58	57.05	56.99
Employee benefits	33,954,456[1]	57,976,490	87,888,909	111,750,200	117,974,476	123,655,529	130,868,877	136,790,632	16.81	16.64	19.57	21.19	22.02	22.34	22.75	22.95
Purchased services	16,380,643[1]	31,778,754	43,195,665	53,498,786	55,789,458	58,171,703	61,118,818	64,571,862	8.11	9.12	9.62	10.15	10.41	10.51	10.62	10.83
Tuition	1,192,505[1]	2,458,366	3,828,079	4,988,203	5,097,767	5,296,241	5,572,087	5,743,719	0.59	0.71	0.85	0.95	0.95	0.96	0.97	0.96
Supplies	14,805,956[1]	28,262,078	36,637,037	40,417,163	40,662,095	42,895,737	43,793,547	43,716,529	7.33	8.11	8.16	7.67	7.59	7.75	7.61	7.33
Other	2,973,261[1]	3,579,347	4,439,345	5,095,195	4,622,319	4,776,178	5,725,796	5,589,370	1.47	1.03	0.99	0.97	0.86	0.86	1.00	0.94
Instruction	122,223,362	214,333,003	273,760,798	322,536,983	325,682,380	336,426,927	349,453,258	363,047,760	60.50	61.53	60.95	61.17	60.78	60.78	60.74	60.90
Salaries	90,742,284	154,512,089	186,905,065	212,998,609	212,563,444	217,274,753	223,044,251	230,473,355	44.91	44.35	41.61	40.39	39.67	39.25	38.77	38.66
Employee benefits	22,347,524	39,522,678	59,032,817	75,248,811	79,502,797	83,946,609	88,840,559	92,810,720	11.06	11.35	13.14	14.27	14.84	15.17	15.44	15.57
Purchased services	2,722,639	6,430,708	10,083,561	14,694,620	14,757,780	15,177,204	16,559,278	18,047,613	1.35	1.85	2.25	2.79	2.75	2.74	2.88	3.03
Tuition	1,192,505	2,458,366	3,828,079	4,988,203	5,097,767	5,296,241	5,572,087	5,743,719	0.59	0.71	0.85	0.95	0.95	0.96	0.97	0.96
Supplies	4,584,754	10,377,554	12,731,138	13,135,284	12,415,970	13,344,523	14,060,733	14,547,019	2.27	2.98	2.83	2.49	2.32	2.41	2.44	2.44
Textbooks	—	—	2,537,332	2,324,846	2,129,590	2,321,424	2,438,331	2,540,299	—	—	0.56	0.44	0.40	0.42	0.42	0.43
Other	633,656	1,031,608	1,180,138	1,471,457	1,344,623	1,387,596	1,376,350	1,425,335	0.31	0.30	0.26	0.28	0.25	0.25	0.24	0.24
Student support[2]	8,926,010	17,292,756	23,336,224	29,368,646	29,916,535	30,754,056	32,363,375	34,014,096	4.42	4.96	5.20	5.57	5.58	5.56	5.63	5.71
Salaries	6,565,965	12,354,464	15,833,312	19,367,865	19,331,709	19,823,136	20,658,101	21,598,398	3.25	3.55	3.53	3.67	3.61	3.58	3.59	3.62
Employee benefits	1,660,082	3,036,037	4,859,310	6,533,691	7,062,770	7,315,689	7,872,711	8,360,300	0.82	0.87	1.08	1.24	1.32	1.32	1.37	1.40
Purchased services	455,996	1,328,600	1,958,934	2,583,714	2,790,029	2,850,087	3,024,871	3,202,463	0.23	0.38	0.44	0.49	0.52	0.51	0.53	0.54
Supplies	191,482	421,838	497,201	521,729	536,040	564,419	599,269	628,105	0.09	0.12	0.11	0.10	0.10	0.10	0.10	0.11
Other	52,485	151,817	187,468	361,647	195,987	200,727	208,422	224,831	0.03	0.04	0.04	0.07	0.04	0.04	0.04	0.04
Instructional staff services[3]	8,467,142	15,926,856	21,923,223	24,893,140	24,940,915	25,354,104	26,953,637	28,014,688	4.19	4.57	4.88	4.72	4.65	4.58	4.68	4.70
Salaries	5,560,129	9,790,767	13,005,332	14,490,521	14,478,409	14,685,427	15,490,102	16,082,232	2.75	2.81	2.90	2.75	2.70	2.65	2.69	2.70
Employee benefits	1,408,217	2,356,440	3,898,171	4,933,118	5,098,479	5,234,451	5,640,401	5,898,941	0.70	0.68	0.87	0.94	0.95	0.95	0.98	0.99
Purchased services	622,487	2,003,598	2,944,703	3,438,979	3,484,764	3,444,243	3,659,324	3,942,599	0.31	0.58	0.66	0.65	0.65	0.62	0.64	0.66
Supplies	776,863	1,566,954	1,867,878	1,810,950	1,666,377	1,786,877	1,950,698	1,875,189	0.38	0.45	0.42	0.34	0.31	0.32	0.34	0.31
Other	99,445	209,097	207,139	219,573	212,886	203,106	213,112	215,727	0.05	0.06	0.05	0.04	0.04	0.04	0.04	0.04
General administration	5,791,253	7,108,291	8,920,041	10,494,526	10,825,907	11,117,393	11,535,748	12,051,604	2.87	2.04	1.99	1.99	2.02	2.01	2.01	2.02
Salaries	2,603,562	3,351,554	3,860,883	4,401,697	4,472,689	4,622,952	4,746,838	4,882,609	1.29	0.96	0.86	0.83	0.83	0.84	0.83	0.82
Employee benefits	777,381	1,000,698	1,479,556	1,856,221	1,951,275	1,915,512	2,036,756	2,089,012	0.38	0.29	0.33	0.35	0.36	0.35	0.35	0.35
Purchased services	1,482,427	2,099,032	2,735,714	3,236,857	3,450,629	3,585,418	3,735,708	4,037,141	0.73	0.60	0.61	0.61	0.64	0.65	0.65	0.68
Supplies	172,898	206,137	225,230	228,417	232,774	237,184	249,401	265,647	0.09	0.06	0.05	0.04	0.04	0.04	0.04	0.04
Other	754,985	450,870	618,657	771,334	718,540	756,327	767,045	777,195	0.37	0.13	0.14	0.15	0.13	0.14	0.13	0.13
School administration	11,695,344	19,580,890	25,277,042	28,660,307	29,523,691	30,420,650	31,792,450	33,196,060	5.79	5.62	5.63	5.44	5.51	5.50	5.53	5.57
Salaries	8,935,903	14,817,213	18,181,910	20,191,545	20,574,974	21,132,933	21,921,938	22,757,965	4.42	4.25	4.05	3.83	3.84	3.82	3.81	3.82
Employee benefits	2,257,783	3,689,689	5,622,342	6,972,708	7,426,690	7,718,180	8,194,129	8,633,445	1.12	1.06	1.25	1.32	1.39	1.39	1.42	1.45
Purchased services	247,750	611,638	862,664	931,765	944,190	973,307	1,067,751	1,158,928	0.12	0.18	0.19	0.18	0.18	0.18	0.19	0.19
Supplies	189,711	369,257	474,816	426,864	432,107	435,766	443,385	474,181	0.09	0.11	0.11	0.08	0.08	0.08	0.08	0.08
Other	64,197	93,093	135,311	137,426	145,730	160,463	165,248	171,541	0.03	0.03	0.03	0.03	0.03	0.03	0.03	0.03
Operation and maintenance	21,290,655	34,034,158	44,313,835	50,214,709	50,674,499	53,051,141	54,200,172	55,045,308	10.54	9.77	9.87	9.52	9.46	9.58	9.42	9.23
Salaries	8,849,559	13,461,242	16,021,701	17,604,634	17,468,535	17,846,272	18,205,576	18,735,694	4.38	3.86	3.57	3.34	3.26	3.22	3.16	3.14
Employee benefits	2,633,075	3,778,520	5,840,665	7,195,927	7,473,129	7,694,270	8,024,419	8,293,959	1.30	1.08	1.30	1.36	1.39	1.39	1.39	1.39
Purchased services	5,721,125	9,642,217	11,913,734	13,351,922	14,015,338	15,022,138	15,514,037	15,895,813	2.83	2.77	2.65	2.53	2.62	2.71	2.70	2.67
Supplies	3,761,738	6,871,845	10,147,971	11,638,187	11,349,828	12,078,609	12,047,041	11,728,035	1.86	1.97	2.26	2.21	2.12	2.18	2.09	1.97
Other	325,157	280,334	389,764	424,039	367,669	409,852	409,098	391,807	0.16	0.08	0.09	0.08	0.07	0.07	0.07	0.07
Student transportation	8,678,954	14,052,654	18,850,234	22,370,807	23,237,941	23,845,036	23,961,692	24,325,894	4.30	4.03	4.20	4.24	4.34	4.31	4.16	4.08
Salaries	3,285,127	5,406,092	6,701,455	7,527,611	7,525,466	7,683,616	7,897,110	8,198,056	1.63	1.55	1.49	1.43	1.40	1.39	1.37	1.38
Employee benefits	892,985	1,592,127	2,535,296	3,124,937	3,249,580	3,296,150	3,412,883	3,599,972	0.44	0.46	0.56	0.59	0.61	0.60	0.59	0.60
Purchased services	3,345,232	5,767,462	7,547,730	9,153,621	9,580,324	9,926,270	10,063,360	10,392,864	1.66	1.66	1.68	1.74	1.79	1.79	1.75	1.74
Supplies	961,447	1,159,350	1,867,495	2,370,182	2,656,230	2,695,508	2,356,982	1,886,842	0.48	0.33	0.42	0.45	0.50	0.49	0.41	0.32
Other	194,163	127,623	198,259	194,456	226,340	243,492	231,357	248,160	0.10	0.04	0.04	0.04	0.04	0.04	0.04	0.04

See notes at end of table.

Table 236.20. Total expenditures for public elementary and secondary education and other related programs, by function and subfunction: Selected years, 1990–91 through 2015–16—Continued

Function and subfunction	Expenditures (in thousands of current dollars)								Percentage distribution of current expenditures for public schools							
	1990–91	2000–01	2005–06	2010–11	2012–13	2013–14	2014–15	2015–16	1990–91	2000–01	2005–06	2010–11	2012–13	2013–14	2014–15	2015–16
1	2	3	4	5	6	7	8	9	10	11	12	13	14	15	16	17
Other support services[4]	5,587,837	11,439,134	14,463,815	17,246,807	18,054,249	19,034,045	20,885,114	21,595,076	2.77	3.28	3.22	3.27	3.37	3.44	3.63	3.62
Salaries	2,900,394	5,521,381	6,577,129	8,139,084	8,323,191	8,618,767	9,104,041	9,565,073	1.44	1.58	1.46	1.54	1.55	1.56	1.58	1.60
Employee benefits	980,859	1,594,540	2,483,366	3,295,052	3,497,220	3,694,720	3,912,721	4,061,910	0.49	0.46	0.55	0.62	0.65	0.67	0.68	0.68
Purchased services	798,922	2,783,176	3,455,292	3,876,650	4,317,682	4,671,337	4,853,416	5,120,351	0.40	0.80	0.77	0.74	0.81	0.84	0.84	0.86
Supplies	294,527	626,889	793,997	876,293	964,937	1,097,951	1,163,493	1,241,221	0.15	0.18	0.18	0.17	0.18	0.20	0.20	0.21
Other	613,135	913,148	1,154,031	1,059,728	951,218	951,270	1,851,443	1,606,520	0.30	0.26	0.26	0.20	0.18	0.17	0.32	0.27
Food services	8,430,490	13,816,635	17,263,582	20,394,768	21,835,757	22,342,085	23,064,706	23,643,250	4.17	3.97	3.84	3.87	4.08	4.04	4.01	3.97
Salaries	—	4,966,092	5,841,522	6,482,085	6,607,619	6,699,499	6,873,015	7,098,376	—	1.43	1.30	1.23	1.23	1.21	1.19	1.19
Employee benefits	—	1,381,923	2,061,344	2,492,673	2,609,835	2,731,484	2,818,033	2,923,479	—	0.40	0.46	0.47	0.49	0.49	0.49	0.49
Purchased services	—	923,091	1,464,511	2,058,018	2,270,476	2,335,017	2,460,967	2,566,875	—	0.26	0.33	0.39	0.42	0.42	0.43	0.43
Supplies	—	6,420,201	7,727,182	9,118,886	10,110,849	10,333,931	10,628,481	10,753,015	—	1.84	1.72	1.73	1.89	1.87	1.85	1.80
Other	—	125,327	169,023	243,105	236,978	242,155	284,209	301,505	—	0.04	0.04	0.05	0.04	0.04	0.05	0.05
Enterprise operations[5]	946,705	776,463	1,022,549	1,110,646	1,103,949	1,155,773	1,121,673	1,201,907	0.47	0.22	0.23	0.21	0.21	0.21	0.19	0.20
Salaries	—	124,913	213,999	338,141	303,674	318,467	311,727	331,775	—	0.04	0.05	0.06	0.06	0.06	0.05	0.06
Employee benefits	—	23,837	76,042	97,063	102,699	108,464	116,266	118,893	—	0.01	0.02	0.02	0.02	0.02	0.02	0.02
Purchased services	—	189,230	228,823	172,641	178,246	186,682	180,106	207,215	—	0.05	0.05	0.03	0.03	0.03	0.03	0.03
Supplies	—	242,052	304,129	290,372	296,981	320,969	294,064	317,276	—	0.07	0.07	0.06	0.06	0.06	0.05	0.05
Other	—	196,430	199,556	212,430	222,349	221,191	219,510	226,748	—	0.06	0.04	0.04	0.04	0.04	0.04	0.04
Current expenditures for other programs	3,295,717	6,063,700	7,415,575	8,161,474	8,031,416	7,926,285	7,713,966	7,913,839	†	†	†	†	†	†	†	†
Community services	964,370	2,426,189	3,015,207	3,269,802	3,132,422	3,187,692	3,279,485	3,426,859	†	†	†	†	†	†	†	†
Private school programs	527,609	1,026,695	1,389,204	1,427,539	1,471,013	1,431,807	1,590,684	1,662,359	†	†	†	†	†	†	†	†
Adult education	1,365,523	1,838,265	2,001,459	2,013,156	1,829,564	1,804,646	1,815,963	1,946,215	†	†	†	†	†	†	†	†
Community colleges	5,356	351	0	34,045	30,107	30,906	28,238	29,113	†	†	†	†	†	†	†	†
Other	432,858	772,200	1,009,704	1,416,931	1,568,310	1,471,234	999,597	849,293	†	†	†	†	†	†	†	†
Capital outlay[6]	19,771,478	46,220,704	57,375,299	50,968,815	45,720,570	46,438,323	50,610,125	55,989,047	†	†	†	†	†	†	†	†
Public schools	19,655,496	46,078,494	57,281,425	50,888,951	45,555,651	46,297,257	50,448,404	55,841,130	†	†	†	†	†	†	†	†
Other current expenditures	115,982	142,210	93,874	79,864	164,919	141,066	161,722	147,917	†	†	†	†	†	†	†	†
Interest on school debt	4,324,768	10,165,940	14,346,556	17,934,224	17,265,542	17,152,459	17,479,466	17,502,481	†	†	†	†	†	†	†	†

—Not available.
†Not applicable.
[1]Includes estimated data for subfunctions of food services and enterprise operations.
[2]Includes expenditures for guidance, health, attendance, and speech pathology services.
[3]Includes expenditures for curriculum development, staff training, libraries, and media and computer centers.
[4]Includes business support services concerned with paying, transporting, exchanging, and maintaining goods and services for local education agencies; central support services, including planning, research, evaluation, information, staff, and data processing services; and other support services.
[5]Includes expenditures for operations funded by sales of products or services (e.g., school bookstore or computer time). Includes very small amounts for direct program support made by state education agencies for local school districts.
[6]Includes expenditures for property and for buildings and alterations completed by school district staff or contractors.
NOTE: Excludes expenditures for state education agencies. Detail may not sum to totals because of rounding.
SOURCE: U.S. Department of Education, National Center for Education Statistics, Common Core of Data (CCD), "National Public Education Financial Survey," 1990–91 through 2015–16. (This table was prepared September 2018.)

Table 236.25. Current expenditures for public elementary and secondary education, by state or jurisdiction: Selected years, 1969–70 through 2015–16

[In thousands of current dollars]

State or jurisdiction	1969–70	1979–80	1989–90	1999–2000	2004–05	2005–06	2006–07	2007–08	2008–09	2009–10	2010–11	2011–12	2012–13	2013–14	2014–15	2015–16
1	2	3	4	5	6	7	8	9	10	11	12	13	14	15	16	17
United States	**$34,217,773**	**$86,984,142**	**$188,229,359**	**$323,888,508**	**$425,047,565**	**$449,131,342**	**$476,814,206**	**$506,884,219**	**$518,922,842**	**$524,715,242**	**$527,291,339**	**$527,207,246**	**$535,795,823**	**$553,501,209**	**$575,331,825**	**$596,135,643**
Alabama	422,730	1,146,713	2,275,233	4,176,082	5,164,406	5,699,076	6,245,031	6,832,439	6,683,843	6,670,517	6,592,925	6,386,517	6,532,358	6,742,829	6,806,467	6,885,677
Alaska	81,374	377,947	828,051	1,183,499	1,442,269	1,529,645	1,634,316	1,918,375	2,007,319	2,084,019	2,201,270	2,292,205	2,395,354	2,418,000	2,648,552	2,319,662
Arizona	281,941	949,753	2,258,660	4,288,739	6,579,957	7,130,341	7,815,720	8,403,221	8,726,755	8,482,552	8,340,211	7,976,089	8,164,529	8,187,607	8,370,884	8,551,673
Arkansas	235,083	666,949	1,404,545	2,380,331	3,546,999	3,808,011	3,997,701	4,156,368	4,240,839	4,459,910	4,578,136	4,606,995	4,637,169	4,778,074	4,813,321	4,872,214
California	3,831,595	9,172,158	21,485,782	38,129,479	50,918,654	53,436,103	57,352,599	61,570,555	60,080,929	58,248,662	57,526,835	57,975,189	58,323,458	61,050,894	65,953,946	72,003,129
Colorado	369,218	1,243,049	2,451,833	4,401,010	5,994,440	6,368,289	6,579,053	7,338,766	7,187,267	7,429,302	7,409,462	7,341,585	7,506,978	7,924,319	8,260,461	8,648,369
Connecticut	588,710	1,227,892	3,444,520	5,402,836	7,080,396	7,517,025	7,855,459	8,336,789	8,708,294	8,853,337	9,094,036	9,344,999	9,543,010	10,050,439	10,321,511	10,551,327
Delaware	108,747	269,108	520,953	937,630	1,299,349	1,405,465	1,437,707	1,489,594	1,518,786	1,549,812	1,613,304	1,751,143	1,761,559	1,816,383	1,860,732	1,941,408
District of Columbia	141,138	298,448	639,983	780,192	1,067,500	1,057,166	1,130,006	1,282,437	1,352,905	1,451,870	1,482,202	1,466,888	1,557,117	1,605,030	1,668,528	1,775,833
Florida	961,273	2,766,468	8,228,531	13,885,988	19,042,877	20,897,327	22,887,024	24,224,114	23,328,028	23,349,314	23,870,090	22,732,752	23,214,634	24,363,817	25,123,548	25,621,239
Georgia	599,371	1,608,028	4,505,962	9,158,624	12,528,856	13,739,263	14,828,715	16,030,039	15,976,945	15,730,409	15,527,907	15,623,633	15,536,733	15,921,673	16,530,506	17,283,295
Hawaii	141,324	351,889	700,012	1,213,695	1,648,086	1,805,521	2,045,198	2,122,779	2,225,438	2,136,144	2,141,561	2,187,480	2,178,284	2,316,586	2,344,496	2,502,117
Idaho	103,107	313,927	627,794	1,302,817	1,618,215	1,694,827	1,777,491	1,891,505	1,957,740	1,961,857	1,881,746	1,854,556	1,925,676	1,949,963	2,015,654	2,097,992
Illinois	1,896,067	4,579,355	8,125,493	14,462,773	18,658,428	19,244,908	20,326,591	21,874,484	23,495,271	24,695,773	24,554,467	25,012,915	25,783,911	27,289,963	28,545,089	29,253,457
Indiana	809,105	1,851,292	4,074,578	7,110,930	9,108,931	9,241,986	9,497,077	9,281,709	9,680,895	9,921,243	9,687,949	9,978,491	9,811,166	9,841,337	9,970,350	10,144,064
Iowa	527,086	1,186,659	2,004,742	3,264,336	3,808,200	4,039,389	4,231,932	4,499,236	4,731,463	4,794,308	4,855,871	4,971,944	5,143,771	5,354,843	5,526,877	5,663,444
Kansas	362,593	830,133	1,848,302	2,971,814	3,718,153	4,039,417	4,339,477	4,633,517	4,806,603	4,731,676	4,741,372	4,871,381	4,895,863	5,083,374	5,136,532	5,065,968
Kentucky	353,265	1,054,459	2,134,011	3,837,794	4,812,591	5,213,620	5,424,621	5,822,550	5,886,890	6,091,814	6,211,453	6,360,799	6,354,306	6,375,119	6,583,287	6,750,052
Louisiana	503,217	1,303,902	2,838,283	4,391,189	5,554,766	5,554,278	6,040,368	6,814,455	7,276,651	7,393,452	7,522,098	7,544,782	7,492,539	7,721,469	7,960,448	8,027,058
Maine	155,907	385,492	1,048,195	1,604,438	2,056,266	2,119,408	2,258,764	2,308,071	2,350,447	2,370,085	2,377,878	2,330,842	2,357,739	2,441,064	2,538,313	2,579,299
Maryland	721,794	1,783,056	3,894,644	6,545,135	8,682,586	9,381,613	10,210,303	11,211,176	11,591,965	11,883,677	11,885,333	11,850,634	12,108,546	12,314,446	12,620,036	12,774,063
Massachusetts	907,341	2,638,734	4,760,390	8,564,039	11,357,857	11,747,010	12,383,447	13,182,987	13,937,097	13,356,373	13,962,366	14,151,659	14,627,898	15,183,018	15,723,617	16,374,676
Michigan	1,799,945	4,642,847	8,025,621	13,994,294	16,353,921	16,681,981	17,013,259	17,053,521	17,217,584	17,227,515	16,786,444	16,485,178	16,354,807	16,493,575	16,849,135	16,977,163
Minnesota	781,243	1,786,768	3,474,398	6,140,442	7,310,284	7,686,638	8,060,410	8,426,264	9,182,281	8,927,288	8,944,867	9,053,021	9,354,376	9,723,759	10,222,017	10,687,048
Mississippi	262,760	756,018	1,472,710	2,510,376	3,243,888	3,550,261	3,692,358	3,898,401	3,967,232	3,990,876	3,887,981	3,972,787	4,006,798	4,071,006	4,145,632	4,234,977
Missouri	642,030	1,504,988	3,288,738	5,655,531	7,115,207	7,592,485	7,957,705	8,526,641	8,827,224	8,923,448	8,691,887	8,719,925	8,905,756	9,125,949	9,390,061	9,545,816
Montana	127,176	358,118	641,345	994,770	1,193,182	1,254,360	1,320,112	1,392,449	1,436,062	1,498,252	1,518,818	1,504,531	1,523,696	1,576,937	1,601,097	1,652,848
Nebraska	231,612	581,615	1,233,431	1,926,500	2,512,914	2,672,629	2,825,608	2,970,323	3,053,575	3,213,646	3,345,530	3,462,575	3,563,939	3,654,376	3,805,871	3,911,805
Nevada	87,273	281,901	712,898	1,875,467	2,722,264	2,959,728	3,311,471	3,515,004	3,606,035	3,592,994	3,676,997	3,574,233	3,577,346	3,738,777	3,880,472	4,092,457
New Hampshire	101,370	295,400	821,671	1,418,503	2,021,144	2,139,113	2,246,692	2,399,330	2,490,623	2,576,956	2,637,911	2,643,256	2,655,077	2,720,225	2,764,233	2,833,893
New Jersey	1,343,564	3,638,533	8,119,336	13,327,645	19,669,576	20,869,993	22,448,262	24,357,079	23,446,911	24,261,392	23,639,281	24,391,278	25,417,320	25,733,921	25,993,208	26,825,114
New Mexico	183,736	515,451	1,020,148	1,890,274	2,554,638	2,729,707	2,904,474	3,057,061	3,186,252	3,217,328	3,127,463	3,039,461	3,099,308	3,189,842	3,309,622	3,343,152
New York	4,111,839	8,760,500	18,090,978	28,433,240	38,866,853	41,149,457	43,679,908	46,443,426	48,635,363	50,251,461	51,574,134	52,460,494	52,938,586	55,080,662	56,862,010	59,161,439
North Carolina	676,193	1,880,862	4,342,826	7,713,293	9,835,550	10,476,056	11,248,336	11,482,912	12,598,382	12,200,362	12,322,555	12,303,426	12,666,607	12,685,461	13,210,839	13,466,942
North Dakota	97,895	228,483	459,391	638,946	832,157	857,774	838,221	886,317	928,528	1,000,095	1,049,772	1,098,090	1,174,364	1,287,133	1,373,266	1,451,309
Ohio	1,639,805	3,836,576	7,994,379	12,974,575	17,167,866	17,829,599	18,251,361	18,892,374	19,387,318	19,801,670	19,988,921	19,701,810	19,506,123	19,714,149	20,231,423	20,484,182
Oklahoma	339,105	1,055,844	1,905,332	3,382,581	4,161,024	4,406,002	4,750,536	4,932,913	5,082,062	5,192,124	5,036,031	5,170,978	5,329,897	5,451,048	5,560,047	5,606,044
Oregon	403,844	1,126,812	2,297,944	3,896,287	4,458,028	4,773,751	5,039,632	5,409,630	5,529,831	5,401,667	5,430,888	5,389,273	5,395,742	5,647,470	5,969,321	6,238,574
Pennsylvania	1,912,644	4,584,320	9,496,788	14,120,112	18,711,100	19,631,006	20,404,304	21,157,430	21,831,816	22,733,518	23,485,203	23,190,198	23,712,931	24,264,551	25,109,991	26,045,127
Rhode Island	145,443	362,046	801,908	1,393,143	1,825,900	1,934,429	2,039,633	2,134,609	2,139,317	2,136,582	2,149,366	2,167,450	2,121,403	2,182,976	2,242,486	2,283,927
South Carolina	367,689	997,984	2,322,618	4,087,355	5,312,739	5,696,629	6,023,043	6,453,817	6,626,763	6,566,165	6,465,486	6,619,072	6,950,410	7,163,995	7,437,182	7,669,725
South Dakota	109,375	238,332	447,074	737,998	916,563	948,671	977,006	1,037,875	1,080,054	1,115,861	1,126,503	1,100,100	1,125,929	1,182,721	1,211,080	1,253,268
Tennessee	473,226	1,319,303	2,790,808	4,931,734	6,446,691	6,681,445	6,975,099	7,540,306	7,768,063	7,894,661	8,225,374	8,345,584	8,531,675	8,606,624	8,736,367	8,886,994
Texas	1,518,181	4,997,689	12,763,954	25,098,703	31,919,107	33,851,773	36,105,784	39,033,235	40,688,181	42,621,886	42,864,291	41,067,619	42,066,035	44,330,579	47,527,971	49,577,688
Utah	179,981	518,251	1,130,135	2,102,655	2,627,022	2,778,236	2,987,810	3,444,936	3,638,775	3,635,085	3,704,133	3,779,760	3,944,736	4,094,074	4,290,876	4,539,291
Vermont	78,921	189,811	546,901	870,198	1,177,478	1,237,442	1,300,149	1,356,165	1,413,329	1,432,683	1,424,507	1,497,093	1,549,228	1,602,256	1,638,720	1,671,433
Virginia	704,677	1,881,519	4,621,071	7,757,598	10,705,162	11,470,735	12,465,858	13,125,666	13,505,290	13,193,633	12,968,457	13,403,576	13,868,587	13,955,249	14,384,705	14,677,698
Washington	699,984	1,825,782	3,550,819	6,399,885	7,870,979	8,239,716	8,752,007	9,331,539	9,940,325	9,832,913	10,040,312	10,040,607	10,216,676	10,911,929	11,470,245	12,483,668
West Virginia	249,404	678,386	1,316,637	2,086,937	2,527,767	2,651,491	2,742,344	2,841,962	2,998,657	3,328,177	3,388,294	3,275,246	3,188,181	3,194,770	3,226,918	3,169,684
Wisconsin	777,288	1,908,523	3,929,920	6,852,178	8,435,359	8,745,195	9,029,660	9,366,134	9,696,228	9,966,244	10,333,016	9,704,932	9,758,650	9,920,370	10,054,346	10,122,041
Wyoming	69,584	226,067	509,084	683,918	863,423	965,350	1,124,564	1,191,736	1,268,407	1,334,655	1,398,444	1,432,216	1,439,041	1,466,579	1,509,532	1,556,321
Other jurisdictions																
American Samoa	—	—	21,838	42,395	58,163	58,539	57,093	63,105	65,436	70,305	75,355	80,105	65,039	71,709	63,693	58,675
Guam	16,652	—	101,130	—	—	210,119	219,881	229,243	235,711	235,639	266,952	290,575	279,077	286,844	293,713	309,238
Northern Marianas	—	—	20,476	49,832	58,400	57,694	55,048	51,241	62,787	62,210	84,657	68,775	61,029	62,502	65,304	75,562
Puerto Rico	—	—	1,045,407	2,086,414	2,865,945	3,082,295	3,268,200	3,433,229	3,502,757	3,464,044	3,519,547	3,351,423	3,676,880	3,510,706	3,247,136	2,970,386
U.S. Virgin Islands	—	—	128,065	135,174	137,793	146,872	157,446	196,533	201,326	220,234	204,932	183,333	161,955	175,022	158,652	160,559

—Not available.

NOTE: Current expenditures include instruction, support services, food services, and enterprise operations. Beginning in 1989–90, expenditures for state administration are excluded. Data are not adjusted for changes in the purchasing power of the dollar due to inflation. Detail may not sum to totals because of rounding.

SOURCE: U.S. Department of Education, National Center for Education Statistics, *Statistics of State School Systems, 1969–70*; *Revenues and Expenditures for Public Elementary and Secondary Education, 1979–80*; and Common Core of Data (CCD), "National Public Education Financial Survey," 1989–90 through 2015–16. (This table was prepared September 2018.)

Table 236.30. Total expenditures for public elementary and secondary education and other related programs, by function and state or jurisdiction: 2015–16

[In thousands of current dollars]

State or jurisdiction	Total expenditures															
		Current expenditures for elementary and secondary programs														
				Support services												
	Total	Elementary/secondary current expenditures, total	Instruction	Support services, total	Student support[4]	Instructional staff[5]	General administration	School administration	Operation and maintenance	Student transportation	Other support services	Food services	Enterprise operations[3]	Current expenditures for other programs[1]	Capital outlay[2]	Interest on school debt
1	2	3	4	5	6	7	8	9	10	11	12	13	14	15	16	17
United States	**$677,541,010**	**$596,135,643**	**$363,047,760**	**$208,242,726**	**$34,014,096**	**$28,014,688**	**$12,051,604**	**$33,196,060**	**$55,045,308**	**$24,325,894**	**$21,595,076**	**$23,643,250**	**$1,201,907**	**$7,913,839**	**$55,989,047**	**$17,502,481**
Alabama	7,856,051	6,885,677	3,919,656	2,475,754	421,961	292,758	178,814	426,114	649,901	352,271	153,937	490,267	0	124,414	668,290	177,670
Alaska	2,620,322	2,319,662	1,251,726	983,880	181,082	181,634	32,821	142,072	275,954	76,143	94,174	74,113	9,944	7,484	255,045	38,131
Arizona	9,997,061	8,551,673	4,596,134	3,493,628	645,612	419,285	168,755	476,477	1,046,981	360,351	376,167	460,670	1,240	88,287	1,127,031	230,069
Arkansas	5,572,087	4,872,214	2,734,078	1,871,259	260,137	406,672	124,677	254,517	496,288	178,775	150,193	261,194	5,683	29,441	539,198	131,234
California	82,409,982	72,003,129	42,606,846	26,391,879	4,214,535	4,519,905	844,317	4,755,681	7,170,206	1,566,446	3,320,789	2,820,626	183,777	834,963	6,851,854	2,720,037
Colorado	10,037,994	8,648,369	4,872,737	3,431,287	452,660	523,542	145,684	629,144	792,313	249,626	638,317	297,862	46,483	76,878	893,515	419,232
Connecticut	11,738,548	10,551,327	6,654,475	3,571,233	677,863	332,539	234,445	614,056	912,979	526,161	273,190	236,847	88,773	149,930	919,215	118,075
Delaware	2,128,885	1,941,408	1,217,984	657,149	81,493	37,224	29,701	120,669	206,701	95,464	85,896	66,275	0	50,772	113,368	23,337
District of Columbia	2,352,758	1,775,833	984,313	725,257	79,734	61,941	150,447	120,929	137,502	117,401	57,304	63,880	2,383	42,862	393,478	140,585
Florida	28,897,234	25,621,239	15,763,102	8,586,268	1,140,143	1,626,893	237,029	1,423,931	2,508,146	967,758	682,369	1,271,869	0	569,722	1,983,369	722,904
Georgia	19,355,863	17,283,295	10,690,729	5,599,235	830,729	876,666	207,874	1,078,367	1,285,541	789,287	530,771	942,532	50,798	31,444	1,842,276	198,848
Hawaii	2,733,092	2,502,117	1,468,044	901,508	240,765	80,451	17,736	168,086	268,754	67,598	58,118	132,566	0	14,326	216,649	0
Idaho	2,429,358	2,097,992	1,244,728	744,678	117,285	109,587	50,993	120,489	197,121	94,036	55,167	108,513	73	4,873	269,299	57,193
Illinois	32,479,656	29,253,457	18,155,294	10,322,927	2,003,953	1,080,972	1,115,078	1,496,218	2,334,267	1,282,111	1,010,328	775,237	0	166,268	2,160,045	899,886
Indiana	11,669,049	10,144,064	5,831,669	3,819,141	513,635	402,497	218,024	650,556	1,164,296	611,214	258,919	493,254	0	160,818	1,058,051	306,115
Iowa	6,722,070	5,663,444	3,431,757	1,974,496	331,962	326,435	146,620	323,122	476,397	198,311	171,649	251,204	5,987	36,062	895,778	126,786
Kansas	6,285,438	5,065,968	3,027,649	1,792,129	317,618	211,087	141,621	294,252	490,787	201,331	135,433	246,190	0	4,417	989,773	225,280
Kentucky	7,725,201	6,750,052	3,909,722	2,398,596	325,340	371,904	155,325	393,334	594,814	380,277	177,602	424,641	17,093	76,160	717,626	181,362
Louisiana	8,776,666	8,027,058	4,518,231	3,072,282	484,084	406,831	234,294	508,399	745,495	457,123	236,055	436,157	387	41,437	595,689	112,482
Maine	2,736,938	2,579,299	1,516,283	956,620	175,215	136,138	86,258	136,806	261,276	127,171	33,756	106,085	312	27,897	82,730	47,012
Maryland	14,098,518	12,774,063	8,028,897	4,373,888	602,547	664,711	95,845	860,159	1,112,998	662,195	375,433	371,278	0	34,569	1,132,311	157,576
Massachusetts	17,133,936	16,374,676	10,492,714	5,435,668	1,196,664	732,437	255,630	709,066	1,399,278	731,142	411,450	446,294	0	64,378	460,085	234,797
Michigan	19,310,076	16,977,163	9,766,683	6,582,559	1,326,828	870,792	377,305	940,568	1,479,551	693,596	893,918	627,921	0	281,606	1,229,437	821,870
Minnesota	13,293,413	10,687,048	6,949,478	3,235,010	303,588	529,703	395,803	427,535	724,037	588,106	266,240	456,441	46,119	481,685	1,769,854	354,826
Mississippi	4,565,341	4,234,977	2,414,582	1,561,278	219,997	199,156	143,287	255,440	438,972	195,144	109,282	258,863	254	24,616	256,520	49,229
Missouri	11,040,542	9,545,816	5,651,864	3,444,594	427,176	439,181	343,589	559,116	954,453	485,917	235,163	449,358	0	246,346	906,207	342,173
Montana	1,870,966	1,652,848	970,897	603,092	109,494	60,592	52,103	92,120	166,220	76,673	45,889	73,657	5,203	10,581	185,847	21,690
Nebraska	4,603,453	3,911,805	2,486,681	1,158,242	178,618	130,421	115,046	182,607	329,957	116,152	105,442	165,719	101,164	1,849	601,757	88,042
Nevada	4,518,144	4,092,457	2,398,324	1,531,850	217,928	238,758	64,303	301,486	396,992	161,444	150,937	162,050	232	21,440	234,840	169,407
New Hampshire	3,019,784	2,833,893	1,804,284	959,722	218,076	92,490	100,114	158,416	230,448	125,507	34,669	69,887	0	6,681	137,225	41,986
New Jersey	29,093,257	26,825,114	16,132,662	9,839,684	2,746,074	853,808	539,639	1,336,945	2,615,120	1,112,664	635,434	602,924	249,844	242,549	1,377,448	648,146
New Mexico	3,879,350	3,343,152	1,902,034	1,276,925	345,700	88,942	78,728	202,151	348,475	106,794	106,134	161,916	2,276	2,008	534,031	159
New York	64,011,611	59,161,439	41,924,498	16,048,444	1,855,207	1,505,823	946,473	2,207,977	4,935,741	2,921,798	1,675,426	1,188,496	0	1,677,937	2,164,480	1,007,755
North Carolina	14,432,888	13,466,942	8,395,193	4,335,770	655,787	460,175	245,991	860,517	1,118,188	549,873	445,239	735,980	0	63,132	887,583	15,231
North Dakota	1,879,094	1,451,309	869,633	474,505	58,233	49,903	62,190	74,523	124,394	60,011	45,252	68,714	38,458	10,791	391,521	25,473
Ohio	23,319,945	20,484,182	11,954,341	7,838,117	1,385,266	838,277	649,307	1,177,890	1,785,591	970,927	1,030,859	690,598	1,126	436,360	1,844,170	555,234
Oklahoma	6,328,465	5,606,044	3,125,438	2,067,921	387,298	236,415	164,843	313,641	597,342	173,861	194,521	355,212	57,473	26,158	643,052	53,211
Oregon	7,297,297	6,238,574	3,650,480	2,362,984	460,542	247,660	87,416	400,070	491,601	272,635	403,061	222,206	2,903	29,711	686,106	342,906
Pennsylvania	29,492,243	26,045,127	16,083,136	8,984,548	1,442,409	880,455	795,951	1,166,707	2,412,682	1,301,027	985,316	868,478	108,965	600,230	1,905,689	941,197
Rhode Island	2,505,425	2,283,927	1,393,738	827,947	234,930	88,121	34,437	110,772	176,142	95,485	88,061	61,320	922	62,020	117,460	42,018
South Carolina	9,146,055	7,669,725	4,236,976	3,001,124	592,084	471,858	81,022	501,042	757,833	291,335	305,950	411,392	20,233	65,863	1,077,812	332,655
South Dakota	1,485,135	1,253,268	730,833	446,851	69,685	46,304	43,009	61,431	131,206	45,306	49,910	69,227	6,357	7,270	192,658	31,938
Tennessee	9,755,925	8,886,994	5,465,563	2,928,706	394,133	522,178	197,776	543,295	730,030	334,240	207,053	492,725	0	83,091	560,285	225,555
Texas	61,451,166	49,577,688	28,970,556	17,774,316	2,428,238	2,531,483	720,361	2,833,825	5,209,183	1,408,117	2,643,108	2,832,816	0	341,350	8,305,503	3,226,626
Utah	5,424,995	4,539,291	2,868,057	1,418,789	167,486	182,472	46,476	291,624	415,902	133,624	181,205	230,305	22,139	18,005	716,217	151,483

See notes at end of table.

Table 236.30. Total expenditures for public elementary and secondary education and other related programs, by function and state or jurisdiction: 2015–16—Continued

[In thousands of current dollars]

State or jurisdiction	Total expenditures															
		Current expenditures for elementary and secondary programs												Current expenditures for other programs[1]	Capital outlay[2]	Interest on school debt
				Support services												
	Total	Elementary/ secondary current expenditures, total	Instruction	Support services, total	Student support[4]	Instructional staff[5]	General administration	School administration	Operation and maintenance	Student transportation	Other support services	Food services	Enterprise operations[3]			
1	2	3	4	5	6	7	8	9	10	11	12	13	14	15	16	17
Vermont	1,735,331	1,671,433	1,061,379	563,594	128,615	72,186	35,162	107,192	129,284	54,367	36,788	44,914	1,546	10,540	43,357	10,001
Virginia	16,028,532	14,677,698	8,944,628	5,164,697	746,367	973,858	237,216	869,099	1,340,453	762,128	235,577	565,773	2,599	75,142	1,161,318	114,373
Washington	15,163,088	12,483,668	7,211,513	4,779,816	862,959	854,021	245,289	746,560	1,068,272	461,461	541,256	371,910	120,428	49,143	2,194,714	435,564
West Virginia	3,421,900	3,169,684	1,824,705	1,143,057	160,783	133,100	55,143	170,886	332,389	232,043	58,712	201,923	0	46,952	190,082	15,182
Wisconsin	11,690,833	10,122,041	6,018,974	3,724,119	502,608	525,980	290,818	512,271	930,911	427,186	534,344	378,863	85	346,566	1,054,892	167,334
Wyoming	2,020,051	1,556,321	923,865	585,703	92,971	88,469	30,820	87,907	145,943	76,281	63,312	46,107	647	6,816	454,305	2,608
Other jurisdictions																
American Samoa	67,309	58,675	29,612	11,233	34	4,302	936	4,118	0	568	1,275	17,830	0	1,800	6,833	0
Guam	329,509	309,238	142,690	148,333	29,188	17,080	4,853	17,750	48,055	8,306	23,099	18,215	0	0	10,519	9,752
Northern Marianas	78,783	75,562	36,419	26,183	6,861	6,428	1,972	3,725	4,536	1,330	1,330	12,960	0	2,850	371	0
Puerto Rico	3,071,992	2,970,386	1,188,311	1,389,070	325,798	174,241	84,598	130,663	512,128	82,140	79,501	393,005	0	76,403	25,203	0
U.S. Virgin Islands	162,386	160,559	94,624	55,611	13,814	3,461	7,458	8,885	7,407	7,175	7,411	10,172	152	1,394	433	0

[1]Includes expenditures for adult education, community colleges, private school programs funded by local and state education agencies, and community services.
[2]Includes expenditures for property and for buildings and alterations completed by school district staff or contractors.
[3]Includes expenditures for operations funded by sales of products or services (e.g., school bookstore or computer time). Also includes small amounts for direct program support made by state education agencies for local school districts.
[4]Includes expenditures for guidance, health, attendance, and speech pathology services.
[5]Includes expenditures for curriculum development, staff training, libraries, and media and computer centers.
NOTE: Excludes expenditures for state education agencies. Detail may not sum to totals because of rounding.
SOURCE: U.S. Department of Education, National Center for Education Statistics, Common Core of Data (CCD), "National Public Education Financial Survey," 2015–16. (This table was prepared September 2018.)

Table 236.50. Expenditures for instruction in public elementary and secondary schools, by subfunction and state or jurisdiction: 2014–15 and 2015–16

[In thousands of current dollars]

State or jurisdiction	2014–15						2015–16					
	Total	Salaries	Employee benefits	Purchased services[1]	Supplies	Tuition and other	Total	Salaries	Employee benefits	Purchased services[1]	Supplies	Tuition and other
1	2	3	4	5	6	7	8	9	10	11	12	13
United States	**$349,453,258**	**$223,044,251**	**$88,840,559**	**$16,559,278**	**$14,060,733**	**$6,948,438**	**$363,047,760**	**$230,473,355**	**$92,810,720**	**$18,047,613**	**$14,547,019**	**$7,169,054**
Alabama	3,872,177	2,486,747	964,905	144,100	257,225	19,200	3,919,656	2,477,404	965,949	169,353	285,000	21,950
Alaska	1,489,304	693,933	666,738	57,105	60,744	10,784	1,251,726	711,182	414,485	58,577	56,348	11,134
Arizona	4,487,506	3,040,265	916,617	297,427	199,391	33,805	4,596,134	3,126,187	934,003	309,608	194,855	31,482
Arkansas	2,701,703	1,829,292	518,679	121,267	197,297	35,168	2,734,078	1,846,357	524,988	126,960	197,711	38,062
California	39,213,957	25,433,552	8,958,204	1,959,137	2,035,673	827,392	42,606,846	27,148,052	10,154,297	2,228,377	2,185,023	891,098
Colorado	4,665,976	3,222,468	898,454	117,985	300,310	126,758	4,872,737	3,348,613	953,906	133,253	304,275	132,690
Connecticut	6,526,503	3,833,099	1,862,292	207,769	114,555	508,789	6,654,475	3,909,375	1,885,230	220,157	112,589	527,124
Delaware	1,149,485	705,383	352,172	13,330	49,110	29,490	1,217,984	732,116	382,812	13,611	55,002	34,444
District of Columbia	900,908	623,929	130,180	41,453	22,667	82,679	984,313	687,092	139,236	41,723	24,852	91,410
Florida	15,420,047	9,093,724	2,711,823	2,930,569	579,077	104,853	15,763,102	9,227,638	2,794,944	3,131,946	487,810	120,763
Georgia	10,213,889	6,689,671	2,494,344	366,574	606,976	56,324	10,690,729	6,932,398	2,674,848	399,785	625,381	58,319
Hawaii	1,377,713	894,305	338,738	51,694	71,774	21,202	1,468,044	948,100	381,962	55,103	73,434	9,444
Idaho	1,198,556	820,405	288,933	43,961	43,767	1,491	1,244,728	850,063	299,870	45,633	47,744	1,418
Illinois	17,612,116	9,965,876	5,858,828	1,002,755	419,835	364,823	18,155,294	10,057,461	6,270,188	1,024,980	444,020	358,645
Indiana	5,735,162	3,574,920	1,859,846	101,594	190,184	8,619	5,831,669	3,622,089	1,893,369	104,080	202,779	9,352
Iowa	3,367,129	2,357,489	779,276	92,699	104,785	32,880	3,431,757	2,414,681	786,969	90,387	104,827	34,894
Kansas	3,077,236	2,175,821	647,283	94,674	135,740	23,719	3,027,649	2,153,182	624,906	89,900	135,838	23,823
Kentucky	3,788,481	2,597,950	995,038	59,334	121,763	14,396	3,909,722	2,653,544	1,049,594	61,715	130,899	13,970
Louisiana	4,488,043	2,742,976	1,331,045	135,515	225,173	53,334	4,518,231	2,781,019	1,326,846	144,108	206,561	59,697
Maine	1,491,376	937,483	406,804	25,823	32,386	88,881	1,516,283	964,407	394,300	39,953	36,233	81,389
Maryland	7,882,693	4,940,005	2,221,890	232,136	200,822	287,840	8,028,897	5,029,476	2,283,910	250,071	187,431	278,008
Massachusetts	10,009,583	6,415,874	2,478,063	89,398	254,192	772,055	10,492,714	6,656,111	2,641,926	95,886	277,803	820,988
Michigan	9,686,774	5,259,496	3,242,438	906,122	259,632	19,087	9,766,683	5,176,562	3,368,889	947,726	254,201	19,306
Minnesota	6,619,067	4,499,275	1,503,059	339,174	197,255	80,303	6,949,478	4,641,312	1,642,237	367,612	207,138	91,179
Mississippi	2,357,120	1,624,328	541,001	64,756	106,373	20,663	2,414,582	1,667,459	552,238	72,636	102,866	19,384
Missouri	5,542,173	3,826,042	1,146,422	172,822	366,253	30,634	5,651,864	3,890,461	1,178,624	191,790	358,768	32,221
Montana	942,042	625,968	188,777	56,859	65,515	4,923	970,897	643,783	195,581	58,266	68,008	5,259
Nebraska	2,430,511	1,588,320	574,865	128,546	118,079	20,701	2,486,681	1,637,339	583,658	131,445	112,253	21,987
Nevada	2,255,867	1,480,410	583,389	42,110	145,680	4,276	2,398,324	1,565,794	640,137	47,619	140,144	4,631
New Hampshire	1,756,353	1,060,633	472,500	47,213	36,592	139,415	1,804,284	1,070,727	499,636	48,479	35,651	149,791
New Jersey	15,639,896	9,543,271	4,256,870	601,928	478,059	759,768	16,132,662	9,674,517	4,594,280	636,802	455,518	771,545
New Mexico	1,890,194	1,278,415	440,845	66,080	104,541	313	1,902,034	1,284,541	443,881	67,436	105,846	331
New York	39,941,146	23,422,021	13,181,503	1,954,045	691,050	692,527	41,924,498	24,955,914	13,224,238	2,330,671	729,050	684,624
North Carolina	8,219,015	5,685,089	1,878,685	265,190	390,051	0	8,395,193	5,810,078	1,895,980	284,479	404,208	449
North Dakota	817,363	555,689	204,526	23,076	28,840	5,232	869,633	590,288	221,357	23,072	28,732	6,183
Ohio	11,824,870	7,488,983	2,725,876	711,778	449,802	448,431	11,954,341	7,526,394	2,775,349	725,767	459,953	466,877
Oklahoma	3,063,208	2,141,680	679,060	65,286	164,994	12,188	3,125,438	2,163,799	696,168	59,181	193,959	12,330
Oregon	3,480,025	2,010,753	1,128,280	122,514	178,334	40,145	3,650,480	2,144,702	1,138,171	130,150	197,142	40,315
Pennsylvania	15,439,796	9,105,193	4,836,293	678,116	491,423	328,771	16,083,136	9,192,617	5,305,250	783,388	474,936	326,944
Rhode Island	1,376,735	857,109	410,935	13,317	22,128	73,246	1,393,738	870,708	420,972	11,913	23,693	66,453
South Carolina	4,103,458	2,774,511	983,740	160,296	161,416	23,495	4,236,976	2,842,958	1,027,856	174,223	168,222	23,717
South Dakota	708,499	475,667	144,489	28,944	47,056	12,342	730,833	492,308	148,723	28,656	48,482	12,665
Tennessee	5,369,137	3,581,742	1,206,926	122,743	447,399	10,326	5,465,563	3,665,541	1,205,593	127,147	454,033	13,249
Texas	27,490,783	21,014,720	3,509,535	924,910	1,719,679	321,939	28,970,556	22,035,575	3,664,960	1,003,668	1,928,691	337,661
Utah	2,710,146	1,662,727	762,359	89,796	181,827	13,437	2,868,057	1,748,837	810,108	101,254	192,319	15,539
Vermont	1,037,584	594,644	282,120	57,925	20,459	82,435	1,061,379	599,678	291,342	61,557	21,518	87,283
Virginia	8,755,906	5,911,978	2,320,287	179,955	334,467	9,219	8,944,628	6,054,755	2,366,965	188,634	321,229	13,045
Washington	6,603,006	4,371,176	1,526,690	386,895	259,107	59,138	7,211,513	4,685,619	1,732,671	445,329	284,788	63,107
West Virginia	1,845,599	1,138,412	554,776	39,552	108,143	4,716	1,824,705	1,122,269	526,003	39,033	131,236	6,164
Wisconsin	5,978,996	3,812,581	1,632,340	90,694	220,874	222,507	6,018,974	3,856,289	1,623,439	90,922	225,236	223,087
Wyoming	898,443	578,250	241,819	32,338	42,260	3,776	923,865	585,983	257,877	33,597	42,785	3,623
Other jurisdictions												
American Samoa	30,680	20,784	4,335	940	1,005	3,616	29,612	21,780	4,591	450	985	1,806
Guam	146,165	106,308	38,700	926	230	0	142,690	105,474	36,814	166	236	0
Northern Marianas	30,646	21,544	4,447	2,872	308	1,474	36,419	25,031	4,666	3,424	2,054	1,244
Puerto Rico	1,330,000	999,279	237,820	74,461	17,972	468	1,188,311	886,323	240,157	44,651	16,900	280
U.S. Virgin Islands	94,478	63,964	25,586	2,142	2,787	0	94,624	63,079	26,493	2,136	2,915	0

[1]Includes purchased professional services of teachers or others who provide instruction for students.

NOTE: Excludes expenditures for state education agencies. Detail may not sum to totals because of rounding.

SOURCE: U.S. Department of Education, National Center for Education Statistics, Common Core of Data (CCD), "National Public Education Financial Survey," 2014–15 and 2015–16. (This table was prepared September 2018.)

Table 236.55. Total and current expenditures per pupil in public elementary and secondary schools: Selected years, 1919–20 through 2015–16

School year	Expenditure per pupil in average daily attendance				Expenditure per pupil in fall enrollment[1]				
	Unadjusted dollars[2]		Constant 2017–18 dollars[3]		Unadjusted dollars[2]		Constant 2017–18 dollars[3]		
	Total expenditure[4]	Current expenditure	Total expenditure[4]	Current expenditure	Total expenditure[4]	Current expenditure	Total expenditure[4]	Current expenditure	Annual percent change in current expenditure
1	2	3	4	5	6	7	8	9	10
1919–20	$64	$53	$833	$694	$48	$40	$623	$520	—
1929–30	108	87	1,573	1,257	90	72	1,302	1,041	—
1931–32	97	81	1,667	1,395	82	69	1,411	1,181	—
1933–34	76	67	1,428	1,264	65	57	1,213	1,074	—
1935–36	88	74	1,588	1,342	74	63	1,343	1,135	—
1937–38	100	84	1,727	1,453	86	72	1,482	1,247	—
1939–40	106	88	1,877	1,564	92	76	1,627	1,356	—
1941–42	110	98	1,751	1,565	94	84	1,499	1,340	—
1943–44	125	117	1,775	1,666	105	99	1,496	1,404	—
1945–46	146	136	1,984	1,855	124	116	1,690	1,581	—
1947–48	205	181	2,182	1,933	179	158	1,905	1,688	—
1949–50	260	210	2,728	2,204	231	187	2,421	1,956	—
1951–52	314	246	2,969	2,323	275	215	2,599	2,034	—
1953–54	351	265	3,238	2,443	312	236	2,880	2,173	—
1955–56	387	294	3,572	2,716	354	269	3,265	2,482	—
1957–58	447	341	3,888	2,964	408	311	3,546	2,703	—
1959–60	471	375	3,978	3,168	440	350	3,716	2,959	—
1961–62	517	419	4,269	3,459	485	393	4,006	3,245	—
1963–64	559	460	4,495	3,703	520	428	4,184	3,447	—
1965–66	654	538	5,084	4,181	607	499	4,720	3,882	—
1967–68	786	658	5,738	4,803	732	612	5,338	4,468	—
1969–70	955	816	6,273	5,360	879	751	5,775	4,934	—
1970–71	1,049	911	6,555	5,691	970	842	6,060	5,261	6.6
1971–72	1,128	990	6,800	5,968	1,034	908	6,237	5,473	4.0
1972–73	1,211	1,077	7,017	6,242	1,117	993	6,473	5,758	5.2
1973–74	1,364	1,207	7,258	6,424	1,244	1,101	6,618	5,858	1.7
1974–75	1,545	1,365	7,401	6,537	1,423	1,257	6,818	6,022	2.8
1975–76	1,697	1,504	7,594	6,727	1,563	1,385	6,992	6,195	2.9
1976–77	1,816	1,638	7,678	6,923	1,674	1,509	7,076	6,379	3.0
1977–78	2,002	1,823	7,933	7,221	1,842	1,677	7,296	6,642	4.1
1978–79	2,210	2,020	8,005	7,319	2,029	1,855	7,351	6,721	1.2
1979–80	2,491	2,272	7,960	7,261	2,290	2,088	7,318	6,675	-0.7
1980–81	2,742[5]	2,502	7,855[5]	7,166	2,529[5]	2,307	7,245[5]	6,609	-1.0
1981–82	2,973[5]	2,726	7,840[5]	7,187	2,754[5]	2,525	7,262[5]	6,657	0.7
1982–83	3,203[5]	2,955	8,098[5]	7,471	2,966[5]	2,736	7,499[5]	6,918	3.9
1983–84	3,471[5]	3,173	8,462[5]	7,736	3,216[5]	2,940	7,839[5]	7,167	3.6
1984–85	3,722[5]	3,470	8,731[5]	8,141	3,456[5]	3,222	8,107[5]	7,559	5.5
1985–86	4,020[5]	3,756	9,166[5]	8,563	3,724[5]	3,479	8,492[5]	7,934	5.0
1986–87	4,308[5]	3,970	9,610[5]	8,857	3,995[5]	3,682	8,911[5]	8,213	3.5
1987–88	4,654[5]	4,240	9,969[5]	9,082	4,310[5]	3,927	9,232[5]	8,411	2.4
1988–89	5,108	4,645	10,458	9,509	4,737	4,307	9,698	8,818	4.8
1989–90	5,547	4,980	10,840	9,731	5,172	4,643	10,106	9,073	2.9
1990–91	5,882	5,258	10,898	9,742	5,484	4,902	10,160	9,082	0.1
1991–92	6,072	5,421	10,901	9,733	5,626	5,023	10,101	9,018	-0.7
1992–93	6,279	5,584	10,932	9,721	5,802	5,160	10,102	8,982	-0.4
1993–94	6,489	5,767	11,012	9,787	5,994	5,327	10,171	9,040	0.6
1994–95	6,723	5,989	11,091	9,880	6,206	5,529	10,238	9,121	0.9
1995–96	6,959	6,147	11,177	9,872	6,441	5,689	10,344	9,137	0.2
1996–97	7,297	6,393	11,394	9,982	6,761	5,923	10,558	9,249	1.2
1997–98	7,701	6,676	11,813	10,241	7,139	6,189	10,952	9,495	2.7
1998–99	8,115	7,013	12,238	10,576	7,531	6,508	11,357	9,814	3.4
1999–2000	8,589	7,394	12,589	10,837	8,030	6,912	11,769	10,131	3.2
2000–01	9,180	7,904	13,009	11,200	8,572	7,380	12,147	10,458	3.2
2001–02	9,611	8,259	13,383	11,500	8,993	7,727	12,522	10,760	2.9
2002–03	9,950	8,610	13,557	11,731	9,296	8,044	12,666	10,960	1.9
2003–04	10,308	8,900	13,744	11,867	9,625	8,310	12,834	11,081	1.1
2004–05	10,779	9,316	13,952	12,059	10,078	8,711	13,045	11,275	1.8
2005–06	11,338	9,778	14,137	12,193	10,603	9,145	13,221	11,403	1.1
2006–07	12,015	10,336	14,604	12,563	11,252	9,679	13,676	11,765	3.2
2007–08	12,759	10,982	14,954	12,871	11,965	10,298	14,023	12,070	2.6
2008–09	13,033	11,239	15,065	12,991	12,222	10,540	14,128	12,183	0.9
2009–10	13,035	11,427	14,923	13,082	12,133	10,636	13,890	12,177	-0.1
2010–11	12,926	11,433	14,506	12,832	12,054	10,663	13,528	11,967	-1.7
2011–12	12,796	11,362	13,952	12,389	11,991	10,648	13,075	11,610	-3.0
2012–13	12,859	11,509	13,791	12,344	12,033	10,771	12,906	11,552	-0.5
2013–14	13,174	11,819	13,912	12,481	12,335	11,066	13,026	11,686	1.2
2014–15	13,668	12,224	14,329	12,816	12,796	11,445	13,415	11,998	2.7
2015–16	14,170	12,617	14,756	13,139	13,298	11,841	13,847	12,330	2.8

—Not available.
[1]Data for 1919–20 to 1953–54 are based on school-year enrollment.
[2]Unadjusted (or "current") dollars have not been adjusted to compensate for inflation.
[3]Constant dollars based on the Consumer Price Index, prepared by the Bureau of Labor Statistics, U.S. Department of Labor, adjusted to a school-year basis.
[4]Excludes "Other current expenditures," such as community services, private school programs, adult education, and other programs not allocable to expenditures per student at public schools.
[5]Estimated.
NOTE: Beginning in 1980–81, state administration expenditures are excluded from both "total" and "current" expenditures. Current expenditures include instruction, support services, food services, and enterprise operations. Total expenditures include current expenditures, capital outlay, and interest on debt. Beginning in 1988–89, extensive changes were made in the data collection procedures.
SOURCE: U.S. Department of Education, National Center for Education Statistics, *Biennial Survey of Education in the United States*, 1919–20 through 1955–56; *Statistics of State School Systems*, 1957–58 through 1969–70; *Revenues and Expenditures for Public Elementary and Secondary Education*, 1970–71 through 1986–87; and Common Core of Data (CCD), "National Public Education Financial Survey," 1987–88 through 2015–16. (This table was prepared September 2018.)

Table 236.60. Total and current expenditures per pupil in fall enrollment in public elementary and secondary schools, by function and subfunction: Selected years, 1990–91 through 2015–16

Function and subfunction	Expenditures per pupil in current dollars									Expenditures per pupil in constant 2017–18 dollars[1]								
	1990–91	2000–01	2005–06	2010–11	2011–12	2012–13	2013–14	2014–15	2015–16	1990–91	2000–01	2005–06	2010–11	2011–12	2012–13	2013–14	2014–15	2015–16
1	2	3	4	5	6	7	8	9	10	11	12	13	14	15	16	17	18	19
Total expenditures	**$5,484**	**$8,572**	**$10,603**	**$12,054**	**$11,991**	**$12,033**	**$12,335**	**$12,796**	**$13,298**	**$10,160**	**$12,147**	**$13,221**	**$13,528**	**$13,075**	**$12,906**	**$13,026**	**$13,415**	**$13,847**
Current expenditures for public schools	4,902	7,380	9,145	10,663	10,648	10,771	11,066	11,445	11,841	9,082	10,458	11,403	11,967	11,610	11,552	11,686	11,998	12,330
Salaries	3,220[2]	4,752	5,561	6,300	6,233	6,265	6,372	6,530	6,748	5,967[2]	6,734	6,935	7,070	6,796	6,719	6,729	6,846	7,027
Employee benefits	824[2]	1,228	1,790	2,260	2,309	2,372	2,472	2,603	2,717	1,526[2]	1,741	2,231	2,536	2,518	2,543	2,611	2,729	2,829
Purchased services	397[2]	673	880	1,082	1,097	1,121	1,163	1,216	1,283	736[2]	954	1,097	1,214	1,197	1,203	1,228	1,275	1,336
Tuition	29[2]	52	78	101	101	102	106	111	114	54[2]	74	97	113	110	110	112	116	119
Supplies	359[2]	599	746	817	809	817	858	871	868	666[2]	848	930	917	883	877	906	913	904
Other	72[2]	76	90	103	98	93	95	114	111	134[2]	107	113	116	107	100	101	119	116
Instruction	2,965	4,541	5,574	6,522	6,483	6,547	6,726	6,951	7,211	5,494	6,435	6,950	7,320	7,069	7,022	7,103	7,288	7,509
Salaries	2,202	3,273	3,806	4,307	4,256	4,273	4,344	4,437	4,578	4,079	4,639	4,745	4,834	4,641	4,583	4,587	4,652	4,767
Employee benefits	542	837	1,202	1,522	1,554	1,598	1,678	1,767	1,843	1,005	1,187	1,499	1,708	1,695	1,714	1,772	1,853	1,920
Purchased services	66	136	205	297	294	297	303	329	358	122	193	256	333	320	318	320	345	373
Tuition	29	52	78	101	101	102	106	111	114	54	74	97	113	110	110	112	116	119
Supplies	111	220	259	266	251	250	267	280	289	206	312	323	298	274	268	282	293	301
Textbooks	—	—	—	47	44	43	46	49	50	—	—	—	53	48	46	49	51	53
Other	15	22	24	30	27	27	28	27	28	28	31	30	33	29	29	29	29	29
Student support[3]	217	366	475	594	589	601	615	644	676	401	519	592	667	642	645	649	675	704
Salaries	159	262	322	392	383	389	396	411	429	295	371	402	440	418	417	419	431	447
Employee benefits	40	64	99	132	137	142	146	157	166	75	91	123	148	149	152	154	164	173
Purchased services	11	28	40	52	54	56	57	60	64	20	40	50	59	59	60	60	63	66
Supplies	5	9	10	11	10	11	11	12	12	9	13	13	12	11	12	12	12	13
Other	1	3	4	7	4	4	4	4	4	2	5	5	8	5	4	4	4	5
Instructional staff services[4]	205	337	446	503	498	501	507	536	556	381	478	557	565	543	538	535	562	579
Salaries	135	207	265	293	289	291	294	308	319	250	294	330	329	316	312	310	323	333
Employee benefits	34	50	79	100	100	102	105	112	117	63	71	99	112	110	110	111	118	122
Purchased services	15	42	60	70	69	70	69	73	78	28	60	75	78	75	75	73	76	82
Supplies	19	33	38	37	35	33	36	39	37	35	47	47	41	38	36	38	41	39
Other	2	4	4	4	4	4	4	4	4	4	6	5	5	5	5	4	4	4
General administration	141	151	182	212	213	218	222	229	239	260	213	226	238	233	233	235	241	249
Salaries	63	71	79	89	88	90	92	94	97	117	101	98	100	96	96	98	99	101
Employee benefits	19	21	30	38	39	39	38	41	41	35	30	38	42	42	42	40	42	43
Purchased services	36	44	56	65	67	69	72	74	80	67	63	69	73	73	74	76	78	84
Supplies	4	4	5	5	5	5	5	5	5	8	6	6	5	5	5	5	5	5
Other	18	10	13	16	15	14	15	15	15	34	14	16	18	16	15	16	16	16
School administration	284	415	515	580	584	593	608	632	659	526	588	642	650	637	637	642	663	687
Salaries	217	314	370	408	408	414	423	436	452	402	445	462	458	445	444	446	457	471
Employee benefits	55	78	114	141	145	149	154	163	171	101	111	143	158	158	160	163	171	179
Purchased services	6	13	18	19	20	19	19	21	23	11	18	22	21	21	20	21	22	24
Supplies	5	8	10	9	9	9	9	9	9	9	11	12	10	9	9	9	9	10
Other	2	2	3	3	3	3	3	3	3	3	3	3	3	3	3	3	3	4
Operation and maintenance	517	721	902	1,015	1,006	1,019	1,061	1,078	1,093	957	1,022	1,125	1,140	1,097	1,093	1,120	1,130	1,139
Salaries	215	285	326	356	352	351	357	362	372	398	404	407	400	384	377	377	380	388
Employee benefits	64	80	119	146	148	150	154	160	165	118	113	148	163	161	161	162	167	172
Purchased services	139	204	243	270	271	282	300	309	316	257	289	302	303	296	302	317	324	329
Supplies	91	146	207	235	227	228	241	240	233	169	206	258	264	248	245	255	251	243
Other	8	6	8	9	8	7	8	8	8	15	8	10	10	9	8	9	9	8

See notes at end of table.

Table 236.60. Total and current expenditures per pupil in fall enrollment in public elementary and secondary schools, by function and subfunction: Selected years, 1990–91 through 2015–16—Continued

Function and subfunction	Expenditures per pupil in current dollars									Expenditures per pupil in constant 2017–18 dollars[1]								
	1990–91	2000–01	2005–06	2010–11	2011–12	2012–13	2013–14	2014–15	2015–16	1990–91	2000–01	2005–06	2010–11	2011–12	2012–13	2013–14	2014–15	2015–16
1	2	3	4	5	6	7	8	9	10	11	12	13	14	15	16	17	18	19
Student transportation	211	298	384	452	463	467	477	477	483	390	422	479	508	505	501	503	500	503
Salaries	80	115	136	152	151	151	154	157	163	148	162	170	171	165	162	162	165	170
Employee benefits	22	34	52	63	64	65	66	68	72	40	48	64	71	70	70	70	71	74
Purchased services	81	122	154	185	190	193	198	200	206	150	173	192	208	207	207	210	210	215
Supplies	23	25	38	48	53	53	54	47	37	43	35	47	54	58	57	57	49	39
Other	5	3	4	4	5	5	5	5	5	9	4	5	4	5	5	5	5	5
Other support services[5]	136	242	294	349	361	363	381	415	429	251	343	367	391	393	389	402	436	447
Salaries	70	117	134	165	165	167	172	181	190	130	166	167	185	180	179	182	190	198
Employee benefits	24	34	51	67	69	70	74	78	81	44	48	63	75	75	75	78	82	84
Purchased services	19	59	70	78	85	87	93	97	102	36	84	88	88	93	93	99	101	106
Supplies	7	13	16	18	19	19	22	23	25	13	19	20	20	20	21	23	24	26
Other	15	19	23	21	23	19	19	37	32	28	27	29	24	25	21	20	39	33
Food services	205	293	352	412	428	439	447	459	470	379	415	438	463	467	471	472	481	489
Salaries	—	105	119	131	133	133	134	137	141	—	149	148	147	145	142	141	143	147
Employee benefits	—	29	42	50	51	52	55	56	58	—	41	52	57	56	56	58	59	60
Purchased services	—	20	30	42	44	46	47	49	51	—	28	37	47	48	49	49	51	53
Supplies	—	136	157	184	196	203	207	211	214	—	193	196	207	213	218	218	222	222
Other	—	3	3	5	5	5	5	6	6	—	4	4	6	5	5	5	6	6
Enterprise operations[6]	23	16	21	22	22	22	23	22	24	43	23	26	25	24	24	24	23	25
Salaries	—	3	4	7	6	6	6	6	7	—	4	5	8	7	7	7	7	7
Employee benefits	—	1	2	2	2	2	2	2	2	—	1	2	2	2	2	2	2	2
Purchased services	—	4	5	3	4	4	4	4	4	—	6	6	4	4	4	4	4	4
Supplies	—	5	6	6	6	6	6	6	6	—	7	8	7	6	6	7	6	7
Other	—	4	4	4	4	4	4	4	5	—	6	5	5	5	5	5	5	5
Capital outlay[7]	477	976	1,166	1,029	984	916	926	1,004	1,109	884	1,383	1,454	1,155	1,073	982	977	1,052	1,155
Interest on school debt	105	215	292	363	360	347	343	348	348	194	305	364	407	392	372	362	365	362

—Not available.
[1]Constant dollars based on the Consumer Price Index, prepared by the Bureau of Labor Statistics, U.S. Department of Labor, adjusted to a school-year basis.
[2]Includes estimated data for subfunctions of food services and enterprise operations.
[3]Includes expenditures for guidance, health, attendance, and speech pathology services.
[4]Includes expenditures for curriculum development, staff training, libraries, and media and computer centers.
[5]Includes business support services concerned with paying, transporting, exchanging, and maintaining goods and services for local education agencies; central support services, including planning, research, evaluation, information, staff, and data processing services; and other support services.
[6]Includes expenditures for operations funded by sales of products or services (e.g., school bookstore or computer time).
[7]Includes expenditures for property and for buildings and alterations completed by school district staff or contractors.
NOTE: Excludes expenditures for state education agencies. Detail may not sum to totals because of rounding.
SOURCE: U.S. Department of Education, National Center for Education Statistics, Common Core of Data (CCD), "National Public Education Financial Survey," 1990–91 through 2015–16. (This table was prepared September 2018.)

Table 236.65. Current expenditure per pupil in fall enrollment in public elementary and secondary schools, by state or jurisdiction: Selected years, 1969–70 through 2015–16

State or jurisdiction	Unadjusted dollars[1]														
	1969–70	1979–80	1989–90	1999–2000	2005–06	2006–07	2007–08	2008–09	2009–10	2010–11	2011–12	2012–13	2013–14	2014–15	2015–16
1	2	3	4	5	6	7	8	9	10	11	12	13	14	15	16
United States	**$751**	**$2,088**	**$4,643**	**$6,912**	**$9,145**	**$9,679**	**$10,298**	**$10,540**	**$10,636**	**$10,663**	**$10,648**	**$10,771**	**$11,066**	**$11,445**	**$11,841**
Alabama	512	1,520	3,144	5,638	7,683	8,398	9,197	8,964	8,907	8,726	8,577	8,773	9,036	9,146	9,258
Alaska	1,059	4,267	7,577	8,806	11,476	12,324	14,641	15,363	15,829	16,663	17,475	18,217	18,466	20,191	17,510
Arizona	674	1,865	3,717	5,030	6,515	7,316	7,727	8,022	7,870	7,782	7,383	7,495	7,427	7,590	7,772
Arkansas	511	1,472	3,229	5,277	8,030	8,391	8,677	8,854	9,281	9,496	9,536	9,538	9,752	9,805	9,900
California	833	2,227	4,502	6,314	8,301	8,952	9,706	9,503	9,300	9,146	9,220	9,258	9,671	10,449	11,420
Colorado	686	2,258	4,357	6,215	8,166	8,286	9,152	8,782	8,926	8,786	8,594	8,693	9,036	9,292	9,619
Connecticut	911	2,167	7,463	9,753	13,072	13,659	14,610	15,353	15,698	16,224	16,855	17,321	18,401	19,020	19,615
Delaware	833	2,587	5,326	8,310	11,621	11,760	12,153	12,109	12,222	12,467	13,580	13,653	13,793	13,882	14,397
District of Columbia	947	2,811	7,872	10,107	13,752	15,511	16,353	19,698	20,910	20,793	19,847	20,451	20,537	20,610	21,135
Florida	683	1,834	4,597	5,831	7,812	8,567	9,084	8,867	8,863	9,030	8,520	8,623	8,955	9,113	9,176
Georgia	539	1,491	4,000	6,437	8,595	9,102	9,718	9,649	9,432	9,259	9,272	9,121	9,236	9,476	9,835
Hawaii	792	2,086	4,130	6,530	9,876	11,316	11,800	12,400	11,855	11,924	11,973	11,790	12,400	12,855	13,748
Idaho	573	1,548	2,921	5,315	6,469	6,648	6,951	7,118	7,100	6,821	6,626	6,761	6,577	6,929	7,178
Illinois	816	2,241	4,521	7,133	9,113	9,596	10,353	11,097	11,739	11,742	12,011	12,443	13,213	13,935	14,327
Indiana	661	1,708	4,270	7,192	8,929	9,080	8,867	9,254	9,479	9,251	9,588	9,421	9,396	9,529	9,691
Iowa	798	2,164	4,190	6,564	8,355	8,791	9,520	9,704	9,748	9,795	10,027	10,291	10,647	10,938	11,148
Kansas	699	1,963	4,290	6,294	8,640	9,243	9,894	10,204	9,972	9,802	10,021	10,011	10,240	10,329	10,216
Kentucky	502	1,557	3,384	5,921	7,668	7,941	8,740	8,786	8,957	9,228	9,327	9,274	9,411	9,560	9,831
Louisiana	589	1,629	3,625	5,804	8,486	8,937	10,006	10,625	10,701	10,799	10,726	10,539	10,853	11,106	11,169
Maine	649	1,692	4,903	7,667	10,841	11,644	11,761	12,183	12,525	12,576	12,335	12,694	13,267	13,976	14,202
Maryland	809	2,293	5,573	7,731	10,909	11,989	13,257	13,737	14,007	13,946	13,875	14,086	14,217	14,431	14,523
Massachusetts	791	2,548	5,766	8,816	12,087	12,784	13,690	14,534	13,956	14,612	14,844	15,321	15,886	16,450	16,986
Michigan	841	2,495	5,090	8,110	9,575	9,876	10,075	10,373	10,447	10,577	10,477	10,515	10,649	10,956	11,051
Minnesota	855	2,296	4,698	7,190	9,159	9,589	10,060	10,983	10,665	10,674	10,781	11,065	11,427	11,924	12,364
Mississippi	457	1,568	2,934	5,014	7,173	7,459	7,890	8,064	8,104	7,926	8,097	8,117	8,265	8,445	8,692
Missouri	596	1,724	4,071	6,187	8,273	8,848	9,532	9,617	9,721	9,461	9,514	9,702	9,938	10,231	10,385
Montana	728	2,264	4,240	6,314	8,626	9,191	9,786	10,120	10,565	10,719	10,569	10,662	10,941	11,078	11,374
Nebraska	700	2,025	4,553	6,683	9,324	10,068	10,565	10,846	11,339	11,704	11,492	11,743	11,877	12,174	12,379
Nevada	706	1,908	3,816	5,760	7,177	7,796	8,187	8,321	8,376	8,411	8,130	8,026	8,275	8,451	8,753
New Hampshire	666	1,732	4,786	6,860	10,396	11,036	11,951	12,583	13,072	13,548	13,774	14,050	14,601	14,969	15,535
New Jersey	924	2,825	7,546	10,337	14,954	16,163	17,620	16,973	17,379	16,855	17,982	18,523	18,780	18,559	19,041
New Mexico	665	1,870	3,446	5,825	8,354	8,849	9,291	9,648	9,621	9,250	9,013	9,164	9,403	9,724	9,959
New York	1,194	2,950	7,051	9,846	14,615	15,546	16,794	17,746	18,167	18,857	19,396	19,529	20,156	20,744	22,231
North Carolina	570	1,635	4,018	6,045	7,396	7,878	7,798	8,463	8,225	8,267	8,160	8,342	8,287	8,529	8,717
North Dakota	662	1,941	3,899	5,667	8,728	8,671	9,324	9,802	10,519	10,898	11,246	11,615	12,383	12,884	13,358
Ohio	677	1,894	4,531	7,065	9,692	9,937	10,340	10,669	11,224	11,395	11,323	11,276	11,434	11,730	11,933
Oklahoma	554	1,810	3,293	5,395	6,941	7,430	7,683	7,878	7,929	7,631	7,763	7,914	7,995	8,075	8,091
Oregon	843	2,412	4,864	7,149	8,645	8,958	9,565	9,611	9,268	9,516	9,485	9,572	9,959	10,457	10,823
Pennsylvania	815	2,328	5,737	7,772	10,723	10,905	11,741	12,299	12,729	13,096	13,091	13,445	13,824	14,405	15,165
Rhode Island	807	2,340	5,908	8,904	12,609	13,453	14,459	14,719	14,723	14,948	15,172	14,889	15,372	15,797	16,082
South Carolina	567	1,597	3,769	6,130	8,120	8,507	9,060	9,228	9,080	8,908	9,102	9,444	9,608	9,831	10,045
South Dakota	656	1,781	3,511	5,632	7,775	8,064	8,535	8,543	9,020	8,931	8,593	8,630	9,036	9,103	9,335
Tennessee	531	1,523	3,405	5,383	7,004	7,129	7,820	7,992	8,117	8,330	8,348	8,588	8,662	8,776	8,876
Texas	551	1,740	3,835	6,288	7,480	7,850	8,350	8,562	8,788	8,685	8,213	8,285	8,602	9,081	9,352
Utah	595	1,556	2,577	4,378	5,464	5,709	5,978	6,612	6,452	6,440	6,312	6,432	6,546	6,751	7,006
Vermont	790	1,930	5,770	8,323	12,805	13,629	14,421	15,096	15,666	14,707	16,651	17,286	18,066	18,769	19,023
Virginia	654	1,824	4,690	6,841	9,452	10,214	10,664	10,928	10,594	10,363	10,656	10,960	10,955	11,235	11,435
Washington	853	2,387	4,382	6,376	7,984	8,524	9,058	9,585	9,497	9,619	9,604	9,714	10,305	10,684	11,484
West Virginia	621	1,749	4,020	7,152	9,440	9,727	10,059	10,606	11,774	11,978	11,579	11,264	11,371	11,512	11,424
Wisconsin	793	2,225	5,020	7,806	9,993	10,372	10,791	11,183	11,507	11,947	11,233	11,186	11,345	11,538	11,664
Wyoming	805	2,369	5,239	7,425	11,437	13,266	13,856	14,628	15,232	15,815	15,988	15,815	15,903	16,047	16,431
Other jurisdictions															
American Samoa	—	—	1,781	2,739	3,561	3,481	—	—	—	—	—	—	—	—	—
Guam	766	—	3,817	—	6,781	—	—	—	—	8,443	9,300	8,949	8,585	9,431	10,033
Northern Marianas	—	—	3,356	5,120	4,924	4,707	4,535	5,753	5,676	7,623	6,246	5,733	5,875	—	—
Puerto Rico	—	—	1,605	3,404	5,470	6,006	6,520	6,955	7,021	7,429	7,403	8,460	8,281	7,902	7,821
U.S. Virgin Islands	—	—	6,043	6,478	8,768	9,669	12,358	12,768	14,215	13,226	11,669	10,661	11,705	11,141	11,631

See notes at end of table.

Table 236.65. Current expenditure per pupil in fall enrollment in public elementary and secondary schools, by state or jurisdiction: Selected years, 1969–70 through 2015–16—Continued

State or jurisdiction	Constant 2017–18 dollars[2]														
	1969–70	1979–80	1989–90	1999–2000	2005–06	2006–07	2007–08	2008–09	2009–10	2010–11	2011–12	2012–13	2013–14	2014–15	2015–16
1	17	18	19	20	21	22	23	24	25	26	27	28	29	30	31
United States	**$4,934**	**$6,675**	**$9,073**	**$10,131**	**$11,403**	**$11,765**	**$12,070**	**$12,183**	**$12,177**	**$11,967**	**$11,610**	**$11,552**	**$11,686**	**$11,998**	**$12,330**
Alabama	3,361	4,860	6,143	8,263	9,580	10,208	10,779	10,361	10,197	9,793	9,352	9,409	9,542	9,589	9,640
Alaska	6,957	13,638	14,807	12,907	14,310	14,980	17,160	17,758	18,121	18,701	19,054	19,538	19,500	21,168	18,234
Arizona	4,430	5,961	7,264	7,372	8,124	8,893	9,057	9,273	9,010	8,734	8,050	8,038	7,843	7,957	8,094
Arkansas	3,356	4,704	6,310	7,735	10,013	10,199	10,170	10,235	10,625	10,657	10,398	10,230	10,298	10,279	10,310
California	5,474	7,116	8,798	9,255	10,351	10,881	11,376	10,984	10,647	10,265	10,053	9,930	10,213	10,954	11,893
Colorado	4,506	7,217	8,514	9,109	10,183	10,071	10,727	10,151	10,218	9,861	9,371	9,323	9,542	9,741	10,017
Connecticut	5,982	6,926	14,583	14,294	16,299	16,603	17,124	17,747	17,972	18,208	18,378	18,577	19,431	19,940	20,426
Delaware	5,475	8,267	10,408	12,179	14,491	14,294	14,244	13,997	13,993	13,992	14,807	14,643	14,566	14,553	14,992
District of Columbia	6,220	8,986	15,382	14,813	17,147	18,854	19,167	22,770	23,939	23,336	21,640	21,933	21,687	21,607	22,009
Florida	4,484	5,862	8,983	8,546	9,741	10,413	10,646	10,249	10,146	10,135	9,290	9,248	9,456	9,554	9,555
Georgia	3,539	4,766	7,816	9,435	10,718	11,063	11,390	11,154	10,799	10,391	10,110	9,783	9,753	9,935	10,242
Hawaii	5,202	6,668	8,071	9,571	12,315	13,755	13,830	14,333	13,572	13,382	13,054	12,645	13,094	13,477	14,317
Idaho	3,765	4,949	5,708	7,790	8,067	8,080	8,147	8,227	8,129	7,656	7,225	7,251	6,946	7,265	7,475
Illinois	5,358	7,163	8,834	10,455	11,364	11,664	12,135	12,827	13,439	13,178	13,096	13,345	13,953	14,609	14,920
Indiana	4,343	5,459	8,345	10,541	11,133	11,037	10,393	10,697	10,852	10,382	10,454	10,105	9,922	9,990	10,092
Iowa	5,243	6,917	8,187	9,621	10,418	10,686	11,157	11,217	11,159	10,992	10,933	11,037	11,243	11,467	11,609
Kansas	4,590	6,274	8,383	9,224	10,773	11,234	11,597	11,795	11,416	11,001	10,927	10,737	10,813	10,829	10,638
Kentucky	3,297	4,977	6,612	8,678	9,562	9,652	10,243	10,156	10,255	10,356	10,170	9,947	9,938	10,022	10,238
Louisiana	3,872	5,206	7,083	8,507	10,581	10,863	11,728	12,281	12,251	12,120	11,695	11,304	11,460	11,643	11,631
Maine	4,264	5,408	9,582	11,238	13,518	14,153	13,785	14,082	14,339	14,114	13,449	13,614	14,010	14,653	14,789
Maryland	5,315	7,328	10,891	11,331	13,602	14,572	15,538	15,879	16,036	15,652	15,129	15,107	15,013	15,129	15,123
Massachusetts	5,194	8,143	11,268	12,921	15,071	15,539	16,046	16,800	15,977	16,399	16,185	16,432	16,776	17,246	17,688
Michigan	5,527	7,976	9,946	11,886	11,939	12,004	11,808	11,990	11,960	11,871	11,423	11,277	11,245	11,486	11,508
Minnesota	5,615	7,340	9,180	10,538	11,421	11,656	11,791	12,695	12,210	11,979	11,755	11,867	12,067	12,501	12,875
Mississippi	3,000	5,013	5,733	7,348	8,944	9,066	9,247	9,321	9,277	8,896	8,829	8,705	8,727	8,853	9,052
Missouri	3,915	5,510	7,954	9,068	10,316	10,754	11,172	11,116	11,129	10,618	10,373	10,406	10,495	10,726	10,814
Montana	4,779	7,235	8,285	9,254	10,756	11,172	11,470	11,698	12,096	12,030	11,524	11,435	11,554	11,614	11,844
Nebraska	4,596	6,471	8,897	9,795	11,626	12,238	12,382	12,537	12,981	13,135	12,531	12,594	12,543	12,762	12,890
Nevada	4,636	6,099	7,456	8,442	8,949	9,476	9,595	9,618	9,590	9,440	8,865	8,608	8,738	8,860	9,115
New Hampshire	4,375	5,536	9,352	10,054	12,963	13,414	14,007	14,545	14,965	15,205	15,019	15,069	15,418	15,693	16,177
New Jersey	6,068	9,030	14,746	15,151	18,647	19,646	20,652	19,619	19,896	18,916	19,607	19,866	19,832	19,457	19,828
New Mexico	4,368	5,978	6,734	8,538	10,417	10,756	10,889	11,152	11,014	10,381	9,828	9,828	9,929	10,194	10,371
New York	7,845	9,430	13,778	14,431	18,224	18,896	19,684	20,513	20,798	21,164	21,148	20,945	21,284	21,747	23,150
North Carolina	3,746	5,227	7,852	8,860	9,222	9,575	9,140	9,782	9,416	9,278	8,897	8,947	8,751	8,942	9,077
North Dakota	4,351	6,205	7,620	8,306	10,883	10,539	10,928	11,330	12,043	12,231	12,262	12,457	13,076	13,507	13,911
Ohio	4,444	6,055	8,854	10,354	12,085	12,078	12,119	12,332	12,849	12,789	12,346	12,093	12,075	12,297	12,427
Oklahoma	3,637	5,784	6,435	7,907	8,655	9,031	9,005	9,106	9,078	8,565	8,464	8,488	8,442	8,466	8,426
Oregon	5,539	7,710	9,506	10,478	10,780	10,888	11,210	11,109	10,610	10,680	10,342	10,266	10,516	10,963	11,271
Pennsylvania	5,355	7,442	11,211	11,392	13,371	13,255	13,761	14,217	14,572	14,698	14,274	14,420	14,598	15,102	15,792
Rhode Island	5,299	7,480	11,545	13,051	15,722	16,352	16,947	17,014	16,855	16,776	16,543	15,969	16,233	16,561	16,747
South Carolina	3,726	5,105	7,366	8,985	10,125	10,340	10,619	10,667	10,395	9,997	9,925	10,128	10,146	10,306	10,460
South Dakota	4,310	5,691	6,861	8,255	9,695	9,802	10,003	9,875	10,326	10,024	9,370	9,255	9,542	9,543	9,721
Tennessee	3,487	4,868	6,654	7,889	8,734	8,666	9,165	9,238	9,293	9,349	9,102	9,210	9,148	9,201	9,243
Texas	3,620	5,560	7,494	9,216	9,327	9,541	9,786	9,897	10,060	9,747	8,955	8,885	9,083	9,520	9,738
Utah	3,910	4,973	5,036	6,417	6,814	6,939	7,007	7,643	7,387	7,228	6,882	6,899	6,912	7,078	7,296
Vermont	5,186	6,169	11,276	12,198	15,967	16,565	16,903	17,449	17,935	16,506	18,156	18,539	19,078	19,677	19,809
Virginia	4,299	5,831	9,164	10,027	11,785	12,415	12,499	12,632	12,129	11,630	11,618	11,754	11,569	11,778	11,908
Washington	5,604	7,629	8,564	9,345	9,956	10,361	10,616	11,080	10,873	10,796	10,472	10,419	10,882	11,200	11,959
West Virginia	4,082	5,589	7,855	10,482	11,771	11,823	11,789	12,260	13,480	13,443	12,625	12,081	12,008	12,069	11,897
Wisconsin	5,209	7,111	9,809	11,442	12,460	12,607	12,648	12,927	13,174	13,408	12,248	11,997	11,981	12,096	12,146
Wyoming	5,288	7,572	10,238	10,883	14,260	16,125	16,240	16,909	17,438	17,749	17,432	16,961	16,794	16,824	17,111
Other jurisdictions															
American Samoa	—	—	3,481	4,015	4,441	4,231	—	—	—	—	—	—	—	—	—
Guam	5,035	—	7,459	—	8,455	—	—	—	—	9,476	10,141	9,598	9,065	9,887	10,448
Northern Marianas	—	—	6,559	7,505	6,139	5,721	5,315	6,650	6,498	8,556	6,810	6,148	6,204	—	—
Puerto Rico	—	—	3,137	4,988	6,821	7,300	7,642	8,039	8,038	8,338	8,071	9,074	8,745	8,284	8,144
U.S. Virgin Islands	—	—	11,808	9,495	10,934	11,752	14,485	14,759	16,274	14,843	12,723	11,433	12,360	11,679	12,111

—Not available.

[1]Unadjusted (or "current") dollars have not been adjusted to compensate for inflation.

[2]Constant dollars based on the Consumer Price Index (CPI), prepared by the Bureau of Labor Statistics, U.S. Department of Labor, adjusted to a school-year basis. The CPI does not account for differences in inflation rates from state to state.

NOTE: Current expenditures include instruction, support services, food services, and enterprise operations. Expenditures for state administration are excluded in all years except 1969–70 and 1979–80. Beginning in 1989–90, extensive changes were made in the data collection procedures.

SOURCE: U.S. Department of Education, National Center for Education Statistics, *Statistics of State School Systems*, 1969–70; *Revenues and Expenditures for Public Elementary and Secondary Schools, 1979–80*; and Common Core of Data (CCD), "National Public Education Financial Survey," 1989–90 through through 2015–16. (This table was prepared September 2018.)

Table 236.70. Current expenditure per pupil in average daily attendance in public elementary and secondary schools, by state or jurisdiction: Selected years, 1969–70 through 2015–16

State or jurisdiction	Unadjusted dollars[1]														
	1969–70	1979–80	1989–90	1999–2000	2005–06	2006–07	2007–08	2008–09	2009–10	2010–11	2011–12	2012–13	2013–14	2014–15	2015–16
1	2	3	4	5	6	7	8	9	10	11	12	13	14	15	16
United States	**$816**	**$2,272**	**$4,980**	**$7,394**	**$9,778**	**$10,336**	**$10,982**	**$11,239**	**$11,427**	**$11,433**	**$11,362**	**$11,509**	**$11,819**	**$12,224**	**$12,617**
Alabama	544	1,612	3,327	5,758	7,980	8,743	9,345	9,385	9,554	9,296	8,927	9,486	9,543	9,690	9,870
Alaska	1,123	4,728	8,431	9,668	12,537	13,508	16,002	16,822	17,350	18,352	19,134	19,982	20,254	22,161	19,242
Arizona	720	1,971	4,053	5,478	7,637	8,038	8,630	8,732	8,756	8,646	8,224	8,388	8,278	8,426	8,572
Arkansas	568	1,574	3,485	5,628	8,748	9,152	9,460	9,651	10,237	10,332	10,397	9,853	10,622	10,756	10,837
California	867	2,268	4,391	6,401	8,416	9,029	9,673	9,439	9,680	9,540	9,608	9,686	10,094	10,924	11,937
Colorado	738	2,421	4,720	6,702	8,938	9,110	9,977	9,611	9,747	9,709	9,415	9,572	9,924	10,349	10,619
Connecticut	951	2,420	7,837	10,122	13,461	14,143	15,063	15,840	16,133	16,932	17,472	17,859	19,029	19,731	20,380
Delaware	900	2,861	5,799	8,809	12,330	12,612	12,789	12,753	12,928	13,228	14,253	14,129	14,203	14,556	15,150
District of Columbia	1,018	3,259	8,955	11,935	17,877	18,285	20,807	19,766	21,283	21,304	20,399	20,333	21,629	21,362	22,260
Florida	732	1,889	4,997	6,383	8,376	9,055	9,711	9,452	9,363	9,394	8,825	8,925	9,189	9,295	9,337
Georgia	588	1,625	4,275	6,903	9,164	9,615	10,263	10,178	9,855	9,577	9,492	9,437	9,529	9,809	10,185
Hawaii	841	2,322	4,448	7,090	10,747	12,364	12,774	13,397	12,887	12,603	12,735	12,585	13,219	13,849	14,728
Idaho	603	1,659	3,078	5,644	6,861	7,074	7,402	7,567	7,481	7,155	7,041	7,273	7,215	7,409	7,607
Illinois	909	2,587	5,118	8,084	10,282	10,816	11,624	12,489	13,083	13,180	13,459	13,808	14,682	15,473	15,909
Indiana	728	1,882	4,606	7,652	9,558	9,727	9,569	9,946	10,160	9,924	10,220	10,037	10,078	10,202	10,379
Iowa	844	2,326	4,453	6,925	8,460	8,789	9,128	10,482	10,524	10,565	10,748	10,915	11,359	11,698	11,846
Kansas	771	2,173	4,752	6,962	9,905	10,280	11,065	11,485	10,859	10,700	10,712	10,789	11,180	11,106	10,815
Kentucky	545	1,701	3,745	6,784	8,975	9,303	9,940	10,054	10,376	10,469	10,700	10,269	10,248	10,659	10,912
Louisiana	648	1,792	3,903	6,256	8,568	9,650	10,797	11,410	11,492	11,500	11,352	11,118	11,415	11,697	11,775
Maine	692	1,824	5,373	8,247	11,760	12,628	13,177	13,558	14,090	14,406	14,000	14,347	14,926	15,839	16,060
Maryland	918	2,598	6,275	8,273	11,719	12,836	14,122	14,612	14,937	14,876	14,746	15,010	15,109	15,403	15,478
Massachusetts	859	2,819	6,237	9,375	12,629	13,263	14,373	15,249	14,632	15,334	15,607	16,111	16,646	17,311	18,026
Michigan	904	2,640	5,546	8,886	10,598	10,932	11,155	11,493	11,661	11,560	11,462	11,495	11,678	12,048	12,243
Minnesota	904	2,387	4,971	7,499	9,761	10,185	10,663	11,602	11,366	11,368	11,424	11,754	12,140	12,707	13,169
Mississippi	501	1,664	3,094	5,356	7,699	7,988	8,448	8,610	8,670	8,436	8,623	8,685	8,926	9,129	9,380
Missouri	709	1,936	4,507	6,764	8,834	9,266	10,007	10,341	10,468	10,348	10,370	10,555	10,764	11,079	11,233
Montana	782	2,476	4,736	6,990	9,653	10,244	10,541	10,881	11,463	11,599	11,290	11,493	11,840	11,999	12,379
Nebraska	736	2,150	4,842	7,360	10,170	10,711	11,217	11,457	11,920	12,324	12,114	12,374	12,502	12,825	13,700
Nevada	769	2,088	4,117	6,148	7,720	8,372	8,891	8,865	8,869	9,035	8,677	8,525	8,734	8,939	9,233
New Hampshire	723	1,916	5,304	7,082	10,698	11,347	12,280	12,912	13,424	13,964	14,215	14,463	15,013	15,380	15,934
New Jersey	1,016	3,191	8,139	10,903	15,362	16,650	18,174	17,466	18,060	17,654	18,197	19,020	19,282	19,296	20,055
New Mexico	707	2,034	3,515	5,835	8,426	8,876	9,377	9,727	9,716	9,356	9,069	9,230	9,546	9,891	9,954
New York	1,327	3,462	8,062	10,957	16,095	17,182	18,423	19,373	19,965	20,517	20,881	21,172	22,048	22,771	23,678
North Carolina	612	1,754	4,290	6,505	7,940	8,373	8,415	9,167	8,930	8,943	8,828	9,041	8,948	9,245	9,347
North Dakota	690	1,920	4,189	6,078	9,239	9,203	9,637	10,113	10,976	11,356	11,643	12,090	12,952	13,552	14,002
Ohio	730	2,075	5,045	7,816	10,306	10,792	11,374	11,905	12,307	12,484	12,271	12,284	12,447	12,285	12,488
Oklahoma	604	1,926	3,508	5,770	7,449	7,968	8,270	8,423	8,511	8,165	8,281	8,450	8,526	8,633	8,624
Oregon	925	2,692	5,474	8,129	9,294	9,762	10,487	10,673	10,476	10,497	10,386	10,370	10,739	11,356	11,856
Pennsylvania	882	2,535	6,228	8,380	11,530	11,995	12,493	12,989	13,678	14,072	13,973	14,378	14,789	15,405	15,997
Rhode Island	891	2,601	6,368	9,646	13,917	14,674	15,843	16,211	16,243	16,346	16,498	16,187	16,702	17,151	17,332
South Carolina	613	1,752	4,082	6,545	8,795	9,226	9,823	10,007	9,887	9,735	9,823	10,200	10,408	10,670	10,829
South Dakota	690	1,908	3,731	6,037	8,273	8,506	9,047	9,457	9,683	9,431	9,095	9,138	9,539	9,637	9,897
Tennessee	566	1,635	3,664	5,837	7,580	7,843	8,459	8,676	8,810	9,146	9,235	9,370	9,431	9,549	9,719
Texas	624	1,916	4,150	6,771	8,085	8,484	9,029	9,260	9,528	9,418	8,862	8,951	9,273	9,789	10,067
Utah	626	1,657	2,764	4,692	5,809	6,116	6,841	7,081	6,877	6,851	6,787	7,023	7,156	7,375	7,659
Vermont	807	1,997	6,227	8,799	13,377	14,219	15,089	16,073	16,586	16,661	17,575	18,372	19,032	19,793	20,196
Virginia	708	1,970	4,672	6,491	10,046	10,913	11,410	11,696	11,383	11,123	11,385	11,748	11,716	11,810	12,022
Washington	915	2,568	4,702	6,914	8,702	9,233	9,846	10,423	10,242	10,402	10,413	10,553	11,199	11,648	12,533
West Virginia	670	1,920	4,360	7,637	9,756	10,080	10,605	11,122	12,378	12,505	11,982	11,665	11,800	12,414	12,299
Wisconsin	883	2,477	5,524	8,299	10,484	10,813	11,370	11,773	12,194	12,515	11,750	11,768	11,963	12,227	12,312
Wyoming	856	2,527	5,577	7,944	12,415	14,219	14,936	15,658	16,535	17,126	17,228	17,135	17,165	17,445	17,796
Other jurisdictions															
American Samoa	—	—	1,908	2,807	3,842	3,909	4,309	4,468	4,881	4,877	5,154	4,870	5,504	5,120	5,235
Guam	820	—	4,234	—	7,095	7,450	8,084	8,264	8,393	9,280	10,112	9,431	9,914	10,120	10,335
Northern Marianas	—	—	3,007	5,720	5,307	5,356	5,162	6,397	6,284	8,495	7,068	6,381	6,548	6,921	8,127
Puerto Rico	—	—	1,750	3,859	5,897	6,152	6,937	7,329	7,426	8,560	7,798	8,701	8,822	8,025	8,124
U.S. Virgin Islands	—	—	6,767	7,238	9,637	10,548	12,358	12,768	14,215	13,014	11,669	10,661	14,372	14,849	15,087

See notes at end of table.

Table 236.70. Current expenditure per pupil in average daily attendance in public elementary and secondary schools, by state or jurisdiction: Selected years, 1969–70 through 2015–16—Continued

State or jurisdiction	Constant 2017–18 dollars[2]														
	1969–70	1979–80	1989–90	1999–2000	2005–06	2006–07	2007–08	2008–09	2009–10	2010–11	2011–12	2012–13	2013–14	2014–15	2015–16
1	17	18	19	20	21	22	23	24	25	26	27	28	29	30	31
United States	**$5,360**	**$7,261**	**$9,731**	**$10,837**	**$12,193**	**$12,563**	**$12,871**	**$12,991**	**$13,082**	**$12,832**	**$12,389**	**$12,344**	**$12,481**	**$12,816**	**$13,139**
Alabama	3,573	5,152	6,502	8,440	9,950	10,627	10,952	10,848	10,937	10,433	9,734	10,174	10,078	10,159	10,278
Alaska	7,374	15,110	16,476	14,170	15,633	16,419	18,755	19,444	19,863	20,596	20,863	21,431	21,389	23,233	20,037
Arizona	4,730	6,299	7,921	8,029	9,523	9,769	10,115	10,094	10,024	9,703	8,967	8,996	8,742	8,834	8,926
Arkansas	3,728	5,032	6,810	8,249	10,909	11,124	11,088	11,155	11,719	11,595	11,336	10,567	11,217	11,277	11,285
California	5,696	7,248	8,580	9,381	10,494	10,975	11,337	10,910	11,082	10,707	10,476	10,388	10,659	11,452	12,431
Colorado	4,847	7,737	9,224	9,822	11,145	11,073	11,694	11,109	11,159	10,897	10,266	10,266	10,480	10,850	11,058
Connecticut	6,248	7,735	15,314	14,835	16,785	17,191	17,655	18,309	18,469	19,002	19,051	19,154	20,095	20,686	21,222
Delaware	5,912	9,144	11,332	12,911	15,375	15,330	14,990	14,741	14,801	14,846	15,540	15,154	14,999	15,260	15,777
District of Columbia	6,689	10,416	17,499	17,493	22,291	22,225	24,386	22,847	24,366	23,909	22,242	21,808	22,840	22,395	23,180
Florida	4,810	6,038	9,765	9,355	10,445	11,007	11,382	10,926	10,719	10,543	9,623	9,572	9,704	9,745	9,724
Georgia	3,862	5,194	8,353	10,118	11,426	11,686	12,029	11,765	11,282	10,748	10,349	10,121	10,063	10,283	10,606
Hawaii	5,521	7,421	8,693	10,392	13,400	15,028	14,972	15,485	14,753	14,144	13,886	13,497	13,959	14,518	15,337
Idaho	3,962	5,303	6,014	8,272	8,556	8,598	8,676	8,747	8,565	8,030	7,678	7,800	7,619	7,767	7,921
Illinois	5,974	8,267	10,001	11,848	12,821	13,147	13,624	14,436	14,978	14,792	14,675	14,809	15,504	16,221	16,567
Indiana	4,782	6,017	9,001	11,215	11,918	11,823	11,215	11,497	11,632	11,138	11,144	10,765	10,643	10,695	10,809
Iowa	5,545	7,436	8,701	10,150	10,548	10,682	10,698	12,116	12,048	11,857	11,719	11,706	11,995	12,264	12,336
Kansas	5,064	6,945	9,285	10,204	12,351	12,495	12,969	13,276	12,432	12,008	11,680	11,571	11,806	11,643	11,262
Kentucky	3,581	5,437	7,319	9,943	11,190	11,308	11,650	11,621	11,879	11,749	11,667	11,014	10,822	11,174	11,363
Louisiana	4,256	5,728	7,628	9,169	10,684	11,730	12,654	13,189	13,156	12,907	12,377	11,924	12,055	12,263	12,262
Maine	4,549	5,828	10,499	12,087	14,664	15,349	15,444	15,672	16,130	16,167	15,265	15,387	15,762	16,605	16,725
Maryland	6,032	8,303	12,263	12,126	14,612	15,601	16,552	16,890	17,101	16,695	16,078	16,099	15,955	16,148	16,118
Massachusetts	5,643	9,011	12,188	13,741	15,747	16,121	16,846	17,626	16,752	17,209	17,017	17,279	17,579	18,148	18,772
Michigan	5,937	8,439	10,838	13,024	13,215	13,288	13,074	13,285	13,350	12,974	12,497	12,328	12,332	12,631	12,750
Minnesota	5,935	7,629	9,713	10,991	12,171	12,379	12,498	13,411	13,012	12,758	12,456	12,607	12,820	13,321	13,713
Mississippi	3,290	5,318	6,045	7,849	9,600	9,709	9,901	9,952	9,925	9,467	9,402	9,315	9,426	9,571	9,768
Missouri	4,654	6,189	8,807	9,914	11,016	11,262	11,728	11,954	11,984	11,613	11,306	11,320	11,367	11,615	11,698
Montana	5,135	7,915	9,256	10,245	12,036	12,451	12,354	12,577	13,123	13,017	12,310	12,326	12,503	12,579	12,891
Nebraska	4,837	6,872	9,461	10,787	12,681	13,019	13,147	13,243	13,647	13,831	13,208	13,271	13,203	13,445	14,267
Nevada	5,054	6,674	8,046	9,011	9,626	10,176	10,420	10,247	10,154	10,140	9,461	9,143	9,223	9,371	9,615
New Hampshire	4,749	6,123	10,365	10,381	13,340	13,792	14,393	14,925	15,368	15,671	15,499	15,512	15,854	16,124	16,593
New Jersey	6,675	10,200	15,905	15,979	19,155	20,237	21,301	20,189	20,675	19,813	19,842	20,399	20,362	20,229	20,884
New Mexico	4,644	6,500	6,868	8,552	10,506	10,788	10,990	11,244	11,123	10,500	9,888	9,900	10,081	10,369	10,366
New York	8,715	11,066	15,753	16,059	20,069	20,884	21,593	22,393	22,857	23,026	22,768	22,707	23,283	23,873	24,657
North Carolina	4,022	5,607	8,384	9,534	9,901	10,178	9,863	10,597	10,224	10,037	9,626	9,697	9,449	9,693	9,734
North Dakota	4,530	6,137	8,186	8,908	11,520	11,186	11,295	11,690	12,566	12,745	12,695	12,967	13,677	14,207	14,581
Ohio	4,795	6,631	9,858	11,456	12,850	13,117	13,331	13,761	14,089	14,011	13,380	13,175	13,144	12,879	13,004
Oklahoma	3,970	6,157	6,855	8,456	9,288	9,685	9,693	9,736	9,744	9,164	9,030	9,063	9,003	9,051	8,981
Oregon	6,074	8,604	10,697	11,914	11,589	11,865	12,292	12,337	11,993	11,781	11,324	11,122	11,341	11,905	12,346
Pennsylvania	5,792	8,101	12,170	12,283	14,377	14,580	14,642	15,014	15,660	15,793	15,236	15,421	15,617	16,150	16,659
Rhode Island	5,854	8,313	12,443	14,138	17,353	17,836	18,569	18,739	18,596	18,345	17,988	17,361	17,637	17,981	18,048
South Carolina	4,023	5,600	7,976	9,593	10,967	11,215	11,513	11,567	11,319	10,926	10,710	10,940	10,991	11,186	11,276
South Dakota	4,531	6,097	7,291	8,848	10,316	10,339	10,603	10,931	11,085	10,584	9,917	9,800	10,073	10,103	10,306
Tennessee	3,718	5,227	7,159	8,555	9,452	9,533	9,914	10,029	10,086	10,264	10,069	10,049	9,959	10,011	10,121
Texas	4,100	6,123	8,110	9,925	10,082	10,312	10,583	10,704	10,908	10,570	9,663	9,600	9,792	10,262	10,483
Utah	4,113	5,295	5,401	6,878	7,244	7,434	8,018	8,185	7,873	7,689	7,401	7,532	7,557	7,732	7,976
Vermont	5,302	6,383	12,168	12,897	16,679	17,283	17,685	18,579	18,988	18,698	19,163	19,704	20,098	20,751	21,032
Virginia	4,649	6,296	9,129	9,514	12,527	13,264	13,374	13,520	13,031	12,483	12,414	12,600	12,373	12,382	12,519
Washington	6,012	8,208	9,189	10,133	10,851	11,223	11,540	12,048	11,725	11,675	11,354	11,318	11,826	12,211	13,051
West Virginia	4,401	6,138	8,521	11,193	12,165	12,253	12,429	12,856	14,171	14,034	13,064	12,511	12,461	13,014	12,808
Wisconsin	5,798	7,916	10,794	12,163	13,072	13,143	13,326	13,609	13,961	14,046	12,812	12,621	12,633	12,818	12,821
Wyoming	5,622	8,076	10,899	11,643	15,480	17,283	17,506	18,099	18,930	19,221	18,785	18,377	18,127	18,289	18,532
Other jurisdictions															
American Samoa	—	—	3,728	4,114	4,791	4,751	5,050	5,164	5,588	5,473	5,620	5,223	5,812	5,368	5,452
Guam	5,384	—	8,275	—	8,846	9,055	9,475	9,553	9,609	10,415	11,026	10,115	10,470	10,610	10,762
Northern Marianas	—	—	5,877	8,384	6,618	6,511	6,050	7,394	7,194	9,534	7,706	6,844	6,915	7,256	8,463
Puerto Rico	—	—	3,419	5,656	7,354	7,477	8,131	8,472	8,501	9,607	8,502	9,332	9,316	8,414	8,460
U.S. Virgin Islands	—	—	13,224	10,608	12,016	12,821	14,485	14,759	16,274	14,606	12,723	11,433	15,177	15,568	15,711

—Not available.

[1]Unadjusted (or "current") dollars have not been adjusted to compensate for inflation.

[2]Constant dollars based on the Consumer Price Index (CPI), prepared by the Bureau of Labor Statistics, U.S. Department of Labor, adjusted to a school-year basis. The CPI does not account for differences in inflation rates from state to state.

NOTE: Current expenditures include instruction, support services, food services, and enterprise operations. Expenditures for state administration are excluded in all years except 1969–70 and 1979–80. Beginning in 1989–90, extensive changes were made in the data collection procedures. There are discrepancies in average daily attendance reporting practices from state to state.

SOURCE: U.S. Department of Education, National Center for Education Statistics, *Statistics of State School Systems, 1969–70*; *Revenues and Expenditures for Public Elementary and Secondary Education, 1979–80*; and Common Core of Data (CCD), "National Public Education Financial Survey," 1989–90 through 2015–16. (This table was prepared September 2018.)

Table 236.75. Total and current expenditures per pupil in fall enrollment in public elementary and secondary schools, by function and state or jurisdiction: 2015–16

State or jurisdiction	Current expenditures, capital expenditures, and interest on school debt per pupil														
		Current expenditures													
				Support services											
	Total[1]	Total	Instruction	Total	Student support[4]	Instructional staff[5]	General adminis-tration	School adminis-tration	Operation and maintenance	Student transpor-tation	Other support services	Food services	Enterprise operations[3]	Capital outlay[2]	Interest on school debt
1	2	3	4	5	6	7	8	9	10	11	12	13	14	15	16
United States	**$13,298**	**$11,841**	**$7,211**	**$4,136**	**$676**	**$556**	**$239**	**$659**	**$1,093**	**$483**	**$429**	**$470**	**$24**	**$1,109**	**$348**
Alabama	10,395	9,258	5,270	3,329	567	394	240	573	874	474	207	659	0	898	239
Alaska	19,723	17,510	9,449	7,427	1,367	1,371	248	1,072	2,083	575	711	559	75	1,925	288
Arizona	9,004	7,772	4,177	3,175	587	381	153	433	952	328	342	419	1	1,023	209
Arkansas	11,262	9,900	5,556	3,802	529	826	253	517	1,008	363	305	531	12	1,095	267
California	12,938	11,420	6,758	4,186	668	717	134	754	1,137	248	527	447	29	1,087	431
Colorado	11,078	9,619	5,419	3,816	503	582	162	700	881	278	710	331	52	992	466
Connecticut	21,542	19,615	12,370	6,639	1,260	618	436	1,142	1,697	978	508	440	165	1,707	219
Delaware	15,411	14,397	9,032	4,873	604	276	220	895	1,533	708	637	491	0	841	173
District of Columbia	27,476	21,135	11,715	8,632	949	737	1,791	1,439	1,636	1,397	682	760	28	4,668	1,673
Florida	10,145	9,176	5,645	3,075	408	583	85	510	898	347	244	456	0	710	259
Georgia	10,997	9,835	6,084	3,186	473	499	118	614	732	449	302	536	29	1,048	113
Hawaii	14,938	13,748	8,066	4,953	1,323	442	97	924	1,477	371	319	728	0	1,190	0
Idaho	8,295	7,178	4,259	2,548	401	375	174	412	674	322	189	371	0	921	196
Illinois	15,825	14,327	8,892	5,056	981	529	546	733	1,143	628	495	380	0	1,057	441
Indiana	10,992	9,691	5,571	3,649	491	385	208	621	1,112	584	247	471	0	1,009	292
Iowa	13,161	11,148	6,755	3,887	653	643	289	636	938	390	338	494	12	1,763	250
Kansas	12,666	10,216	6,106	3,614	641	426	286	593	990	406	273	496	0	1,996	454
Kentucky	11,140	9,831	5,694	3,493	474	542	226	573	866	554	259	618	25	1,044	264
Louisiana	12,154	11,169	6,287	4,275	674	566	326	707	1,037	636	328	607	1	829	157
Maine	14,916	14,202	8,349	5,267	965	750	475	753	1,439	700	186	584	2	455	259
Maryland	15,989	14,523	9,128	4,973	685	756	109	978	1,265	753	427	422	0	1,287	179
Massachusetts	17,706	16,986	10,884	5,639	1,241	760	265	736	1,451	758	427	463	0	477	244
Michigan	12,386	11,051	6,358	4,285	864	567	246	612	963	451	582	409	0	799	535
Minnesota	14,816	12,364	8,040	3,743	351	613	458	495	838	680	308	528	53	2,042	410
Mississippi	9,319	8,692	4,956	3,205	452	409	294	524	901	401	224	531	1	526	101
Missouri	11,740	10,385	6,148	3,747	465	478	374	608	1,038	529	256	489	0	983	372
Montana	12,801	11,374	6,681	4,150	753	417	359	634	1,144	528	316	507	36	1,278	149
Nebraska	14,561	12,379	7,869	3,665	565	413	364	578	1,044	368	334	524	320	1,904	279
Nevada	9,618	8,753	5,130	3,276	466	511	138	645	849	345	323	347	0	502	362
New Hampshire	16,516	15,535	9,891	5,261	1,195	507	549	868	1,263	688	190	383	0	751	230
New Jersey	20,478	19,041	11,451	6,984	1,949	606	383	949	1,856	790	451	428	177	977	460
New Mexico	11,550	9,959	5,666	3,804	1,030	265	235	602	1,038	318	316	482	7	1,591	0
New York	23,419	22,231	15,754	6,031	697	566	356	830	1,855	1,098	630	447	0	809	379
North Carolina	9,301	8,717	5,434	2,806	424	298	159	557	724	356	288	476	0	574	10
North Dakota	17,196	13,358	8,004	4,368	536	459	572	686	1,145	552	417	632	354	3,603	234
Ohio	13,310	11,933	6,964	4,566	807	488	378	686	1,040	566	601	402	1	1,054	323
Oklahoma	9,096	8,091	4,511	2,985	559	341	238	453	862	251	281	513	83	928	77
Oregon	12,608	10,823	6,333	4,100	799	430	152	694	853	473	699	386	5	1,190	595
Pennsylvania	16,821	15,165	9,365	5,231	840	513	463	679	1,405	758	574	506	63	1,108	548
Rhode Island	16,734	16,082	9,814	5,830	1,654	621	242	780	1,240	672	620	432	6	356	296
South Carolina	11,892	10,045	5,549	3,931	775	618	106	656	993	382	401	539	26	1,411	436
South Dakota	11,008	9,335	5,444	3,328	519	345	320	458	977	337	372	516	47	1,435	238
Tennessee	9,660	8,876	5,459	2,925	394	522	198	543	729	334	207	492	0	559	225
Texas	11,526	9,352	5,465	3,353	458	478	136	535	983	266	499	534	0	1,566	609
Utah	8,345	7,006	4,427	2,190	259	282	72	450	642	206	280	355	34	1,105	234
Vermont	19,629	19,023	12,080	6,414	1,464	822	400	1,220	1,471	619	419	511	18	493	114
Virginia	12,428	11,435	6,968	4,024	581	759	185	677	1,044	594	184	441	2	904	89
Washington	13,904	11,484	6,634	4,397	794	786	226	687	983	425	498	342	111	2,019	401
West Virginia	12,161	11,424	6,577	4,120	579	480	199	616	1,198	836	212	728	0	682	55
Wisconsin	13,070	11,664	6,936	4,291	579	606	335	590	1,073	492	616	437	0	1,213	193
Wyoming	21,254	16,431	9,754	6,184	982	934	325	928	1,541	805	668	487	7	4,795	28
Other jurisdictions															
American Samoa	—	—	—	—	—	—	—	—	—	—	—	—	—	—	—
Guam	10,691	10,033	4,630	4,813	947	554	157	576	1,559	270	749	591	0	341	316
Northern Marianas	—	—	—	—	—	—	—	—	—	—	—	—	—	—	—
Puerto Rico	7,884	7,821	3,129	3,657	858	459	223	344	1,348	216	209	1,035	0	63	0
U.S. Virgin Islands	11,662	11,631	6,854	4,028	1,001	251	540	644	537	520	537	737	11	31	0

—Not available.
[1]Excludes "Other current expenditures," such as community services, private school programs, adult education, and other programs not allocable to expenditures per pupil in public schools.
[2]Includes expenditures for property and for buildings and alterations completed by school district staff or contractors.
[3]Includes expenditures for operations funded by sales of products or services (e.g., school bookstore or computer time).
[4]Includes expenditures for guidance, health, attendance, and speech pathology services.
[5]Includes expenditures for curriculum development, staff training, libraries, and media and computer centers.
NOTE: Excludes expenditures for state education agencies. "0" indicates none or less than $0.50. Detail may not sum to totals because of rounding.
SOURCE: U.S. Department of Education, National Center for Education Statistics, Common Core of Data (CCD), "National Public Education Financial Survey," 2015–16. (This table was prepared September 2018.)

This page intentionally left blank.

CHAPTER 3
Postsecondary Education

Postsecondary education includes academic, career and technical, and continuing professional education programs after high school. American colleges and universities and career/technical institutions offer a diverse array of postsecondary educational experiences. For example, a community college normally offers the first 2 years of a standard college curriculum as well as a selection of terminal career and technical education programs. A university typically offers a full undergraduate course of study leading to a bachelor's degree, as well as programs leading to advanced degrees. A specialized career/technical institution offers training programs of varying lengths that are designed to prepare students for specific careers.

This chapter provides an overview of the latest statistics on postsecondary education, including data on various types of postsecondary institutions and programs. However, to maintain comparability over time, most of the data in the *Digest* are for degree-granting institutions, which are defined as postsecondary institutions that grant an associate's or higher degree and whose students are eligible to participate in Title IV federal financial aid programs.[1] Degree-granting institutions include almost all 2- and 4-year colleges and universities; they exclude institutions offering only career and technical programs of less than 2 years' duration and continuing education programs. The degree-granting institution classification currently used by the National Center for Education Statistics (NCES) includes approximately the same set of institutions as the higher education institution classification that was used by NCES prior to 1996–97.[2] This chapter highlights historical data that enable the reader to observe long-range trends in college education in America.

Other chapters provide related information on postsecondary education. Data on price indexes and on the number of degrees held by the general population are shown in chapter 1. Chapter 4 contains tabulations on federal funding for postsecondary education. Information on employment outcomes for college graduates is shown in chapter 5. Chapter 7 contains data on college libraries. Further information on survey methodologies is presented in Appendix A: Guide to Sources and in the publications cited in the table source notes. See chapter 5 for information on adults' participation in nonpostsecondary education, such as adult secondary education classes (e.g., to prepare for the GED test) or English as a Second Language (ESL) classes.

Enrollment

Fall enrollment in degree-granting postsecondary institutions increased 26 percent between 1997 and 2007 (table 303.10 and figure 12). Fall enrollment in degree-granting postsecondary institutions was 8 percent higher in 2017 (19.8 million) than in 2007 (18.3 million). The overall change between 2007 and 2017 reflects an increase of 15 percent between 2007 and 2010, followed by a decrease of 6 percent between 2010 and 2017. Similarly, the number of full-time students was higher in 2010 than 2007, but then fell 8 percent from 2010 to 2017. The number of part-time students rose 15 percent from 2007 to 2011, and then fell 4 percent from 2011 to 2017. The number of female students was 7 percent higher in 2017 than in 2007, while the number of male students was 10 percent higher. Although male enrollment increased by a larger percentage than female enrollment between 2007 and 2017, the majority (57 percent) of students in 2017 were female. Male and female enrollments were both higher in 2017 than in 2007, but there were increases during the early part of this period followed by decreases during the most recent part of the period (a decrease of 5 percent for males and 6 percent for females from 2010 to 2017). In addition to the students enrolled in degree-granting institutions, about 373,000 students attended non-degree-granting, Title IV eligible postsecondary institutions in fall 2017 (table 303.20). These institutions are postsecondary institutions that do not award associate's or higher degrees; they include, for example, institutions that offer only career and technical programs of less than 2 years' duration.

Enrollment trends can be affected both by changes in population and by changing rates of enrollment. The number of 18- to 24-year-olds in the population was 30.6 million in 2017, about 3 percent higher than in 2007

[1] Title IV programs, which are administered by the U.S. Department of Education, provide financial aid to postsecondary students.

[2] Included in the current degree-granting classification are some institutions (primarily 2-year colleges) that were not previously designated as higher education institutions. Excluded from the current degree-granting classification are a few institutions that were previously designated as higher education institutions even though they did not award an associate's or higher degree. The former higher education classification was defined as including institutions that were accredited by an agency or association that was recognized by the U.S. Department of Education or recognized directly by the Secretary of Education. The former higher education institutions offered courses that led to an associate's or higher degree or were accepted for credit toward a degree.

(table 101.10). The percentage of 18- to 24-year-olds enrolled in degree-granting postsecondary institutions was 40 percent in 2017, which was higher than the percentage in 2007 (39 percent) (table 302.60). The 2017 enrollment rates for female 18- to 24-year-olds (44 percent) was higher than for their male peers (37 percent), but neither of their rates were measurably different from their respective 2007 rates. The enrollment rate for Hispanic 18- to 24-year-olds rose from 27 percent in 2007 to 36 percent in 2017. In 2017, the enrollment rate for White 18- to 24-year-olds was 41 percent, and the enrollment rate for Black 18- to 24-year-olds was 36 percent; neither of these rates was measurably different from the corresponding rate in 2007.

Like enrollment in degree-granting institutions for the United States as a whole, the number of students enrolled in degree-granting institutions located within individual states generally has been lower in recent years (table 304.10 and figure 13). Overall, fall enrollment in degree-granting institutions declined 4 percent between 2012 and 2017. Similarly, fall 2017 enrollment was lower than fall 2012 enrollment in the majority of states (42). The largest declines were in Iowa (-28 percent) and Arizona (-20 percent). In contrast, enrollment was higher in 2017 than in 2012 in eight states and the District of Columbia. The largest increases were in New Hampshire (80 percent),[3] followed by Utah (24 percent), Idaho (22 percent), District of Columbia (6 percent), and Texas (6 percent). The enrollment declines in Iowa and Arizona between 2012 and 2017 resulted primarily from declines among private for-profit institutions, while the enrollment increases in New Hampshire, Utah, and Idaho during the same period resulted primarily from increases among private nonprofit institutions (tables 304.15, 304.21, and 304.22).

Between fall 2007 and fall 2017, the percentage increase in the number of students enrolled in degree-granting institutions was higher for students under age 25 than for older students; and this pattern is expected to continue in the coming years (table 303.40 and figure 14). The enrollment of students under age 25 was 11 percent higher in 2017 than in 2007, while the enrollment of those age 25 and over was 5 percent higher. NCES projects that enrollment for students under age 25 will be 6 percent higher in 2028 than in 2017, while the enrollment of students age 25 and over will be 2 percent lower.

Enrollment trends have differed at the undergraduate and postbaccalaureate levels. Undergraduate enrollment increased 47 percent between fall 1970 and fall 1983, when it reached 10.8 million (table 303.70).[4] Undergraduate enrollment dipped to 10.6 million in 1984 and 1985, but then increased each year from 1985 to 1992, rising 18 percent before stabilizing between 1992 and 1998. Undergraduate enrollment increased every year between 1998 and 2007. Undergraduate enrollment was 7 percent higher in 2017 (16.8 million) than in 2007 (15.6 million). This overall change reflects a 16 percent increase in undergraduate enrollment between 2007 and 2010 (when undergraduate enrollment reached 18.1 million), followed by a 7 percent decrease between 2010 and 2017. Postbaccalaureate enrollment increased 34 percent between 1970 and 1984, with most of this increase occurring in the early and mid-1970s (table 303.80). Postbaccalaureate enrollment increased from 1985 to 2017, rising a total of 82 percent. During the last decade of this period, between 2007 and 2017, postbaccalaureate enrollment rose 14 percent, from 2.6 million to 3.0 million. Unlike undergraduate enrollment, which was lower in 2017 than in 2010, postbaccalaureate enrollment was higher in 2017 than in 2010.

Since fall 1988, the number of female students in postbaccalaureate programs has exceeded the number of male students (table 303.80). Between 2007 and 2017, the number of full-time male postbaccalaureate students increased by 17 percent, compared with a 21 percent increase in the number of full-time female postbaccalaureate students. Among part-time postbaccalaureate students, the number of males enrolled in 2017 was 5 percent higher than in 2007, while the number of females was 8 percent higher.

Nineteen percent of undergraduates in 2015–16 reported having a disability (table 311.10). In 2015–16, the percentage of undergraduates who reported having a disability was 19 percent for male students and 20 percent for female students. There were some differences in the percentages of undergraduates with disabilities by characteristics such as veteran status, age, dependency status, and race/ethnicity. For example, 26 percent of undergraduates who were veterans reported having a disability, compared with 19 percent of undergraduates who were not veterans. The percentage of undergraduates having a disability was higher among those age 30 and over (23 percent) than among 15- to 23-year-olds (18 percent). Among dependent undergraduates, 17 percent reported having a disability, which was lower than the percentages for independent undergraduates who were married (21 percent) or unmarried (24 percent). A lower percentage of Asian undergraduates (15 percent) had a disability than White, Hispanic, and Black undergraduates (21, 18, and 17 percent, respectively). The percentage of postbaccalaureate students who reported having a disability (12 percent) was lower than the percentage for undergraduates (19 percent).

The percentage of American college students who are Hispanic, Asian/Pacific Islander, and Black has been increasing (table 306.30). From fall 1976 to fall 2017, the percentage of Hispanic students rose from 4 percent to 19 percent of all U.S. residents enrolled in degree-granting postsecondary institutions, and the percentage of Asian/

[3] Enrollment growth in New Hampshire was primarily driven by increases in online enrollment at Southern New Hampshire University.

[4] Fall 1983 and fall 1984 data on undergraduate enrollment are not included in the current version of table 303.70. For the fall 1983 and fall 1984 data, see the *Digest of Education Statistics 2016* version of table 303.70, available at https://nces.ed.gov/programs/digest/d16/tables/dt16_303.70.asp.

Pacific Islander students rose from 2 percent to 7 percent. The percentage of Black students increased from 10 percent in 1976 to 14 percent in 2017, but the 2017 percentage reflects a decrease since 2011, when Black students made up 15 percent of all enrolled U.S. residents. The percentage of American Indian/Alaska Native students in 2017 (0.7 percent) was about the same as in 1976 (0.7 percent). During the same period, the percentage of White students fell from 84 percent to 56 percent. About 4 percent of students in 2017 were of Two or more races. Race/ethnicity is not reported for nonresident aliens, who made up 5 percent of total enrollment in 2017 (table 306.10).

Of the 19.8 million students enrolled in degree-granting postsecondary institutions in fall 2017, some 18 percent took at least one distance education course as part of a program that included a mix of in-person and distance education courses (table 311.15). In addition, 16 percent of students took their college program exclusively through distance education courses. The remaining 66 percent of students took no distance education courses. About 11 percent of students at public institutions took their coursework exclusively through distance education courses, compared with 19 percent of students at private nonprofit institutions and 60 percent of students at private for-profit institutions. About 13 percent of undergraduates took their coursework exclusively through distance education courses, compared with 29 percent of postbaccalaureate students.

Despite the sizable numbers of small degree-granting colleges, most students attend larger colleges and universities. In fall 2017, some 42 percent of institutions had fewer than 1,000 students; however, these campuses enrolled 3 percent of all college students (table 317.40). While 13 percent of campuses enrolled 10,000 or more students, they accounted for 61 percent of total college enrollment.

In fall 2017, the five institutions with the highest enrollment (including distance education as well as in-person enrollment) were University of Phoenix, with 104,000 students; Western Governors University, with 98,600 students; Southern New Hampshire University with 91,000 students; Grand Canyon University, with 83,300 students; and Ivy Tech Community College, with 75,500 students (table 312.10). Enrollments in the four largest universities were primarily students enrolled in distance learning only.

Faculty, Staff, and Salaries

Approximately 3.9 million people were employed in degree-granting postsecondary institutions in fall 2017, including 1.5 million faculty, 0.4 million graduate assistants, and 2.0 million other staff (table 314.20). Out of the 1.5 million faculty in 2017, 0.8 million were full-time and 0.7 million were part-time faculty. From 2007 to 2017, the proportion of staff who were faculty rose about one percentage point to 39 percent. During the same period, the proportion of staff who were graduate assistants increased from 9 to 10 percent. The proportion of staff who were not engaged in teaching—that is, staff in any occupational category except the faculty and graduate assistant categories—decreased from 52 percent in 2007 to 51 percent in 2017. The full-time-equivalent (FTE) student/FTE staff ratio at degree-granting institutions in 2017 (5.0) was lower than in 2009 (5.4) (table 314.10 and figure 15). Also, the FTE student/FTE faculty ratio was lower in 2017 (14.0) than in 2009 (15.9).

Degree-granting postsecondary institutions differ in their practices of employing part-time and full-time staff. In fall 2017, some 48 percent of the employees at public 2-year institutions were employed full time, compared with 68 percent at public 4-year institutions, 69 percent at private nonprofit 4-year institutions, and 71 percent at private nonprofit 2-year institutions (table 314.30). The percentage of faculty employed full time was higher at public 4-year institutions (66 percent) than at private nonprofit 4-year institutions (55 percent), private for-profit 4-year institutions (16 percent), private nonprofit 2-year institutions (47 percent), private for-profit 2-year institutions (36 percent), and public 2-year institutions (32 percent). In recent years, the number of full-time staff has been growing at a faster rate than the number of part-time staff (table 314.20). Between 2007 and 2017, the number of full-time staff increased by 11 percent, while the number of part-time staff was 8 percent higher in 2017 than in 2007. Most of the increase in part-time staff was due to increases in the number of part-time faculty (8 percent) and graduate assistants (17 percent) during this time period.

In fall 2017, some 8 percent of faculty at degree-granting institutions were Black (based on a faculty count that excludes nonresident aliens and other persons whose race/ethnicity was unknown), 8 percent were Asian, 5 percent were Hispanic, 0.5 percent were American Indian/Alaska Native, 1 percent were of Two or more races, and 0.2 percent were Pacific Islander (table 314.40). About 77 percent of all faculty were White; 39 percent were White males and 38 percent were White females. Staff who were Black, Hispanic, Asian, Pacific Islander, American Indian/Alaska Native, or of Two or more races made up 29 percent of graduate assistants and 31 percent of other staff in nonfaculty positions in 2017. The proportion of total staff who were Black, Hispanic, Asian, Pacific Islander, American Indian/Alaska Native, and of Two or more races was similar at public 4-year institutions (28 percent), public 2-year institutions (28 percent), and private nonprofit 4-year institutions (26 percent), but the proportion was higher at private for-profit 4-year institutions (33 percent), private nonprofit 2-year institutions (37 percent), and private for-profit 2-year institutions (43 percent).

On average, full-time faculty and instructional staff spent 58 percent of their time teaching in 2003 (*web-only table 315.30*). Research and scholarship accounted for

20 percent of their time, and 22 percent was spent on other activities (administration, professional growth, etc.).

Faculty salaries generally lost purchasing power during the 1970s. In constant 2017–18 dollars, average salaries for faculty on 9-month contracts declined by 16 percent during the period from 1970–71 ($79,400 in constant 2017–18 dollars) to 1980–81 ($66,700) (table 316.10). During the 1980s, average salaries rose and recouped most of the losses. Between 1990–91 and 2017–18, there was a further increase in average faculty salaries, resulting in an average salary in 2017–18 ($86,700) that was 9 percent higher than the average salary in 1970–71. The average salary for male faculty in 2017–18 ($94,200) was 4 percent higher than in 2007–08 ($90,200). The average salary for female faculty in 2017–18 ($78,100) was 5 percent higher than the salary in 2007–08 ($74,300). The average salary for male faculty was higher than the average salary for female faculty in all years for which data are available. In 2017–18, average salaries for male faculty were 21 percent higher than for female faculty, the same percentage as in 2007–08.

The percentage of faculty with tenure has declined since 1993–94. Of those faculty at institutions with tenure systems, 46 percent of full-time faculty had tenure in 2017–18, compared with 56 percent in 1993–94 (table 316.80). The percentage of institutions with tenure systems in 2017–18 (55 percent) was lower than in 1993–94 (63 percent). Part of this change was due to the expansion in the number of for-profit institutions (table 317.10), relatively few of which have tenure systems (1.6 percent in 2017–18) (table 316.80). This pattern among institutions has shifted in more recent years. The percent of institutions with tenure systems increased from 49 percent in 2007–08 to 55 percent in 2017–18. The percentage of public institutions with a tenure system increased from 71 percent in 2007–08 to 75 percent in 2017–18. At institutions with tenure systems, there were differences between males and females in the percentage of full-time instructional faculty having tenure: 54 percent of males had tenure in 2017–18, compared with 41 percent of females. In 2017–18, about 50 percent of full-time instructional faculty had tenure at public institutions with tenure systems, compared with 44 percent at private nonprofit institutions with tenure systems and 18 percent at private for-profit institutions with tenure systems.

Degrees

During the 2017–18 academic year, 4,313 accredited institutions offered degrees at the associate's level or above (table 317.10). These included 1,626 public institutions, 1,689 private nonprofit institutions, and 998 private for-profit institutions. Of the 4,313 degree-granting institutions, 2,828 were 4-year institutions that awarded degrees at the bachelor's or higher level, and 1,485 were 2-year institutions that offered associate's degrees as their highest award. In 2016–17, associate's degrees were awarded by 2,701 institutions, bachelor's degrees by 2,445 institutions, master's degrees by 1,924 institutions, and doctor's degrees by 1,016 institutions (table 318.60). In addition to degree-granting institutions, 2,189 non-degree-granting institutions offered postsecondary education in 2017–18 but did not grant degrees at the associate's or higher level (*web-only table 317.30*).

Growing numbers of people are completing postsecondary degrees. Between 2006–07 and 2016–17, the number of associate's, bachelor's, master's, and doctor's degrees that were conferred rose (table 318.10). During this period, the number of associate's degrees increased by 38 percent from 728,000 to 1,006,000, the number of bachelor's degrees increased by 28 percent from 1,525,000 to 1,956,000, the number of master's degrees increased by 32 percent from 611,000 to 805,000, and the number of doctor's degrees increased by 25 percent from 145,000 to 181,000. The doctor's degree total includes most degrees formerly classified as first-professional, such as M.D. (medical), D.D.S. (dental), and J.D. (law) degrees. In addition to degrees awarded at the associate's and higher levels, 945,000 certificates were awarded by postsecondary institutions participating in federal Title IV financial aid programs in 2016–17 (table 320.20).

Since the mid-1980s, more females than males have earned associate's, bachelor's, and master's degrees (table 318.10). Beginning in 2005–06, the number of females earning doctor's degrees has also exceeded the number of males. Between 2006–07 and 2016–17, the number of associate's, bachelor's, and master's degrees awarded to males increased at a higher rate than the number awarded to females. The number of associate's degrees awarded to males increased by 43 percent during this period, while the number awarded to females increased by 35 percent. The number of bachelor's degrees awarded to males increased by 29 percent (from 650,000 to 836,000, an increase of 186,000 degrees), while the number of bachelor's degrees awarded to females increased by 28 percent (from 875,000 to 1,120,000, an increase of 245,000 degrees). The number of master's degrees awarded to males increased by 35 percent, while the number awarded to females increased by 30 percent. In contrast, the number of doctor's degrees increased at a higher rate for females than males between 2006–07 and 2016–17. The number of females earning doctor's degrees increased 32 percent, while the number of males earning doctor's degrees increased 19 percent.

Of the 1,956,000 bachelor's degrees conferred in 2016–17, the greatest numbers of degrees were conferred in the fields of business (381,000), health professions and related programs (238,000), social sciences and history (159,000), psychology (117,000), biological and biomedical sciences (117,000), engineering (116,000), communication, journalism, and related programs (94,000), and visual and performing arts (91,000) (table 322.10). At the master's degree level, the greatest numbers of degrees were conferred in the fields of business (187,000), education (146,000), and health professions and related programs (119,000) (table 323.10). At the doctor's degree level, the greatest numbers of degrees were conferred in the fields of health professions and related programs (77,700), legal professions and studies (35,100), education (12,700), engineering (10,400), biological and biomedical sciences (8,100), psychology (6,700), and physical sciences and science technologies (6,000) (table 324.10).

In recent years, the numbers of bachelor's degrees conferred have followed patterns that differed significantly by field of study. While the number of bachelor's degrees conferred increased by 28 percent overall between 2006–07 and 2016–17, there was substantial variation among the different fields of study, as well as shifts in the patterns of change during this time period (table 322.10 and figure 16). For example, the number of degrees conferred in foreign languages increased 7 percent between 2006–07 and 2011–12, but then decreased 19 percent between 2011–12 and 2016–17. Also, the number of degrees in social sciences and history increased by 9 percent between 2006–07 and 2011–12, but then decreased 11 percent between 2011–12 and 2016–17. In a number of other major fields, the number of bachelor's degrees increased by higher percentages in the second half of the 10-year period than in the first half. The number of bachelor's degrees conferred in the combined fields of engineering and engineering technologies increased 21 percent between 2006–07 and 2011–12, and then increased a further 36 percent between 2011–12 and 2016–17. Computer and information sciences was 12 percent higher in 2011–12 than in 2006–07, and then increased 51 percent between 2011–12 and 2016–17. Some other major fields had smaller increases between 2011–12 and 2016–17 than between 2006–07 and 2011–12. For example, the number of degrees conferred in agriculture and natural resources increased by 34 percent between 2006–07 and 2011–12 and then by 22 percent between 2011–12 and 2016–17. The number of degrees conferred in health professions and related programs increased by 61 percent between 2006–07 and 2011–12 and then by 45 percent between 2011–12 and 2016–17. Also, the number of degrees conferred in public administration and social services increased by 28 percent between 2006–07 and 2011–12 and then by 19 percent between 2011–12 and 2016–17. Other fields with large numbers of degrees (over 10,000 in 2016–17) that showed increases of 25 percent or more between 2011–12 and 2016–17 included parks, recreation, leisure, and fitness studies (37 percent), and mathematics and statistics (28 percent). Some other fields with sizable numbers of degrees did not have increases during the 2011–12 to 2016–17 period. For example, the number of degrees in philosophy and religious studies decreased 23 percent between 2011–12 and 2016–17. Also, the number of degrees in English language and literature/letters decreased 23 percent; the number of degrees in education decreased 19 percent; and the number of degrees in liberal arts and sciences, general studies, and humanities decreased 7 percent. The number of degrees in visual and performing arts was 5 percent lower in 2016–17 than in 2011–12.

Among first-time students who were seeking a bachelor's degree or its equivalent and attending a 4-year institution full time in 2011, about 42 percent completed a bachelor's degree or its equivalent at that institution within 4 years, while 57 percent did so within 5 years, and 60 percent did so within 6 years (*web-only table 326.10*). These graduation rates were calculated as the total number of completers within the specified time to degree attainment divided by the cohort of students who first enrolled at that institution in 2011. Graduation rates were higher at private nonprofit institutions than at public or private for-profit institutions. For example, the 6-year graduation rate for the 2011 cohort at private nonprofit institutions was 66 percent, compared with 60 percent at public institutions and 21 percent at private for-profit institutions. Graduation rates also varied by race/ethnicity. At 4-year institutions overall, the 6-year graduation rate for Asian students in the 2011 cohort was 74 percent, compared with 64 percent for Whites, 57 percent for students of Two or more races, 55 percent for Hispanics, 49 percent for Pacific Islanders, 40 percent for Blacks, and 38 percent for American Indians/Alaska Natives.

Finances and Financial Aid

For the 2017–18 academic year, annual current dollar prices for undergraduate tuition, fees, room, and board were estimated to be $17,797 at public institutions, $46,014 at private nonprofit institutions, and $26,261 at private for-profit institutions (table 330.10). Between 2007–08 and 2017–18, prices for undergraduate tuition, fees, room, and board at public institutions rose 31 percent, and prices at private nonprofit institutions rose 23 percent, after adjustment for inflation. The price for undergraduate tuition, fees, room, and board at private for-profit institutions decreased 9 percent between 2007–08 and 2017–18, after adjustment for inflation.

In 2015–16, about 86 percent of full-time undergraduate students received financial aid (grants, loans, work-study, or aid of multiple types) (table 331.10). About 70 percent of full-time undergraduates received federal financial aid in 2015–16, and 67 percent received aid from nonfederal sources. (Many students receive aid from both federal and nonfederal sources.) Section 484(r) of the Higher Education Act of 1965, as amended, suspends a student's eligibility for Title IV federal financial aid if the student is convicted of certain drug-related offenses that were committed while the student was receiving Title IV aid. For 2016–17, less than 0.01 percent of postsecondary students had their eligibility to receive aid suspended due to a conviction (table C).

Table C. Suspension of eligibility for Title IV federal student financial aid due to a drug-related conviction or failure to report conviction status on aid application form: 2007–08 through 2016–17

Award year	No suspension of eligibility	Suspension of eligibility: For part of award year	For full award year: Due to conviction	For full award year: Due to failure to report
2007–08				
Number	14,610,371	361	2,832	2,433
Percent	99.96	#	0.02	0.02
2008–09				
Number	16,410,285	398	1,064	724
Percent	99.99	#	0.01	#
2009–10				
Number	19,487,370	666	1,751	879
Percent	99.98	#	0.01	#
2010–11				
Number	21,114,404	606	1,284	406
Percent	99.99	#	0.01	#
2011–12				
Number	21,947,204	404	968	732
Percent	99.99	#	#	#
2012–13				
Number	21,803,176	322	778	432
Percent	99.99	#	#	#
2013–14				
Number	21,192,389	257	572	535
Percent	99.99	#	#	#
2014–15				
Number	20,560,709	242	474	504
Percent	99.99	#	#	#
2015–16				
Number	19,756,619	273	564	308
Percent	99.99	#	#	#
2016–17				
Number	18,739,769	254	657	375
Percent	99.99	#	#	#

#Rounds to zero.
NOTE: It is not possible to determine whether a student who lost eligibility due to a drug conviction otherwise would have received Title IV aid, since there are other reasons why an applicant may not receive aid. Detail may not sum to totals because of rounding.
SOURCE: U.S. Department of Education, Federal Student Aid, Free Application for Federal Student Aid (FAFSA), unpublished data.

In 2016–17, total revenue was $391 billion at public institutions, $243 billion at private nonprofit institutions, and $16 billion at private for-profit institutions (tables 333.10, 333.40, and 333.55 and figures 17, 18, and 19). The category of student tuition and fees typically accounts for a significant percentage of total revenue and was the largest single revenue source at both private nonprofit and for-profit institutions in 2016–17 (30 and 91 percent, respectively). Tuition and fees accounted for 20 percent of revenue at public institutions in 2016–17. Public institutions typically report Pell grants as revenue from federal grants, while private institutions report Pell grants as revenue from tuition and fees; this difference in reporting contributes to the smaller percentage of revenue reported as tuition and fees at public institutions compared with private institutions. At public institutions, the share of revenue from tuition and fees in 2016–17 (20 percent) was higher than the share from state appropriations (18 percent), while the share from state appropriations in 2007–08 (25 percent) was higher than that from tuition and fees (18 percent) (table 333.10). In 2016–17, tuition and fees constituted the largest revenue category at private nonprofit 2-year and 4-year institutions, private for-profit 2- and 4-year institutions, and public 4-year institutions (tables 333.10, 333.40, and 333.55). At public 2-year institutions, tuition and fees constituted the third-largest revenue category, below state and local appropriations.

Average total expenditures per full-time-equivalent (FTE) student in 2016–17—shown in constant 2017–18 dollars throughout this paragraph—varied by institution control and level, as did changes in average total expenditures per FTE student between 2009–10 and 2016–17 (after adjustment for inflation). In 2016–17, average total expenditures per full-time-equivalent (FTE) student at public degree-granting institutions were $35,900 (table 334.10). These 2016–17 total expenditures per FTE student were 20 percent higher than in 2009–10. In 2016–17, public 4-year institutions had average total expenditures per FTE student of $45,000, compared with $16,500 at public 2-year institutions. At private nonprofit institutions, total expenditures per FTE student in 2016–17 ($58,300) were 11 percent higher than in 2009–10 (table 334.30). In 2016–17, total expenditures per FTE student at private nonprofit institutions averaged $58,800 at 4-year institutions and $21,100 at 2-year institutions. The expenditures per FTE student at private for-profit institutions in 2016–17 ($16,800) were 9 percent higher than in 2009–10 (table 334.50). In 2016–17, total expenditures per FTE student at private for-profit institutions averaged $16,500 at 4-year institutions and $18,000 at 2-year institutions. This difference in expenditures per FTE student between 4-year and 2-year private for-profit institutions was relatively small compared with the differences between 4-year and 2-year institutions in the public and private nonprofit sectors.

At the end of fiscal year 2017, the market value of the endowment funds of colleges and universities was $598 billion, reflecting an increase of 10 percent compared with the beginning of the fiscal year, when the total was $544 billion (*web-only table 333.90*). At the end of fiscal year 2017, the 120 institutions with the largest endowments accounted for $443 billion, or about three-fourths of the national total. The five institutions with the largest endowments in 2017 were Harvard University ($37 billion), Yale University ($27 billion), the University of Texas System ($26 billion), Stanford University ($25 billion), and Princeton University ($23 billion).

Figure 12. Enrollment, degrees conferred, and expenditures in degree-granting postsecondary institutions: 1960–61 through 2017–18

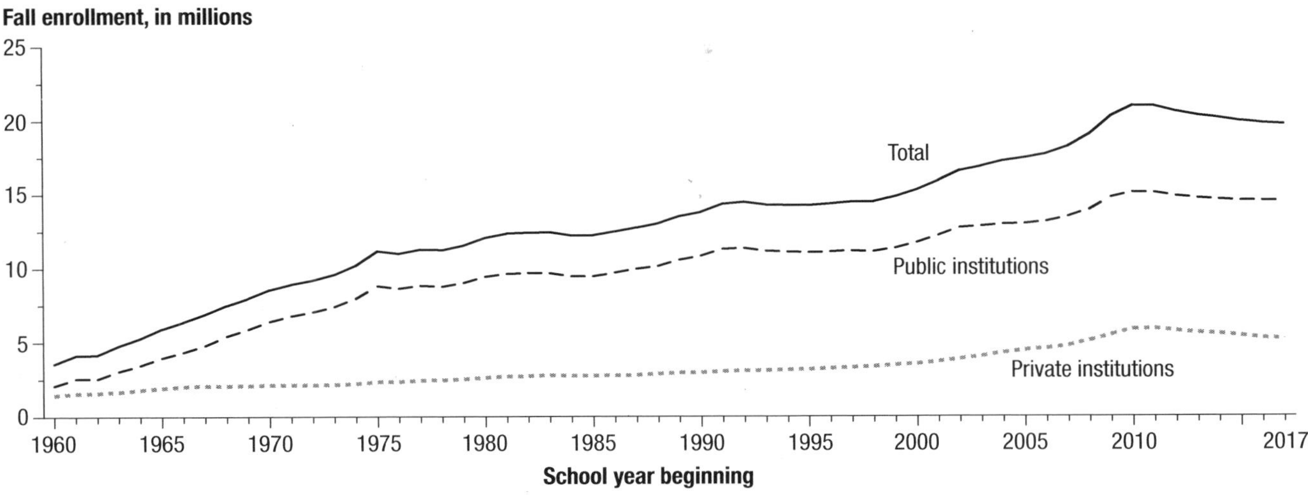

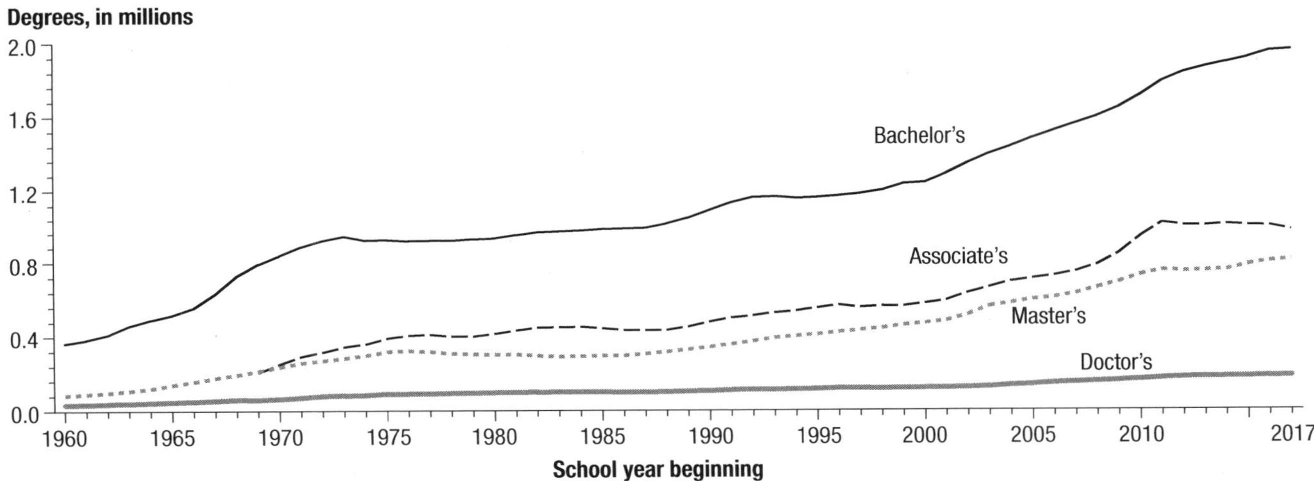

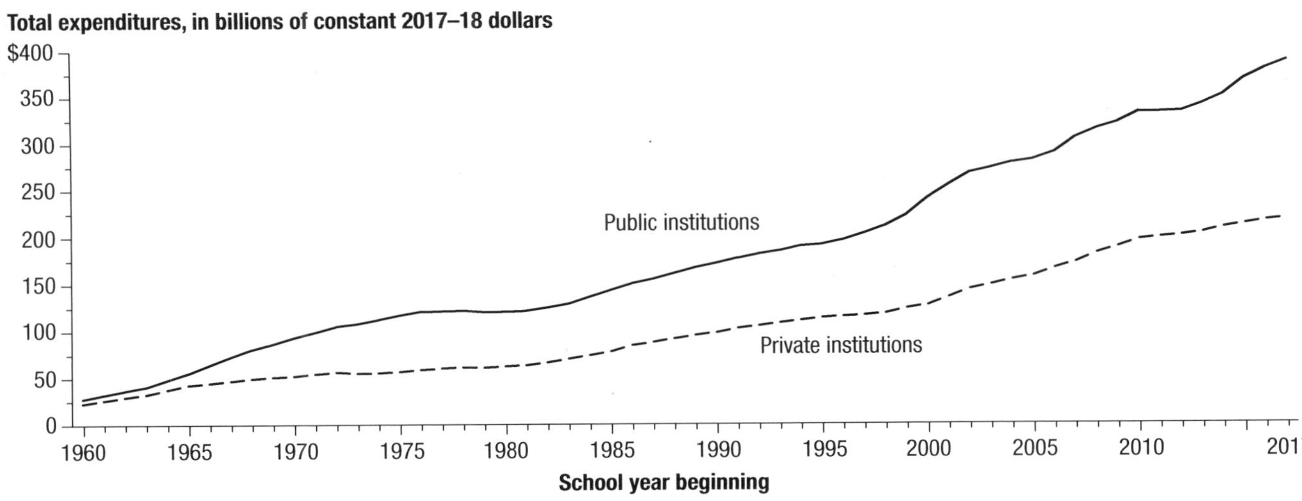

NOTE: Expenditure data for the school year beginning in 2017 (2017–18) are estimated. Degree data for the school year beginning in 2017 are projected. Doctor's degrees include Ph.D., Ed.D., and comparable degrees at the doctoral level, as well as such degrees as M.D., D.D.S., and law degrees that were classified as first-professional degrees prior to 2010–11.
SOURCE: U.S. Department of Education, National Center for Education Statistics, *Opening Fall Enrollment in Higher Education*, 1960 through 1965; *Financial Statistics of Higher Education*, 1959–60 through 1964–65; *Earned Degrees Conferred*, 1959–60 through 1964–65; Degrees Conferred Projection Model, 1980–81 through 2028–29; Higher Education General Information Survey (HEGIS), "Fall Enrollment in Institutions of Higher Education," "Degrees and Other Formal Awards Conferred," and "Financial Statistics of Institutions of Higher Education" surveys, 1965–66 through 1985–86; Integrated Postsecondary Education Data System (IPEDS), "Fall Enrollment Survey" (IPEDS-EF:86–99), "Completions Survey" (IPEDS-C:87–99), and "Finance Survey" (IPEDS-F:FY87–99); IPEDS Fall 2000 through Fall 2017, Completions component; and IPEDS Spring 2001 through Spring 2018, Fall Enrollment and Finance components.

Figure 15. Ratio of full-time-equivalent (FTE) students to total FTE staff and to FTE faculty in degree-granting postsecondary institutions, by control of institution: 1999, 2009, and 2017

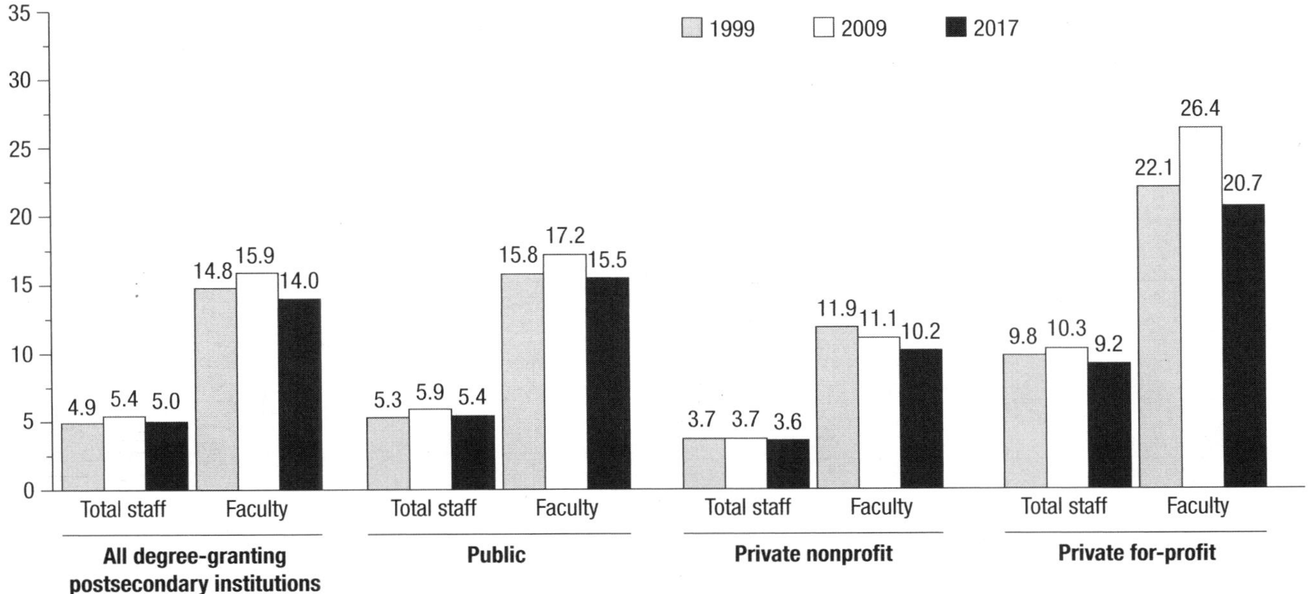

NOTE: Graphic display was generated using unrounded data.
SOURCE: U.S. Department of Education, National Center for Education Statistics, Integrated Postsecondary Education Data System (IPEDS), "Fall Enrollment Survey" (IPEDS-EF:99) and "Fall Staff Survey" (IPEDS-S:99); IPEDS Spring 2010 and Spring 2018, Fall Enrollment component; IPEDS Winter 2009–10, Human Resources component, Fall Staff section; and IPEDS Spring 2018, Human Resources component, Fall Staff section.

Figure 16. Number of bachelor's degrees conferred by postsecondary institutions in selected fields of study: 2006–07, 2011–12, and 2016–17

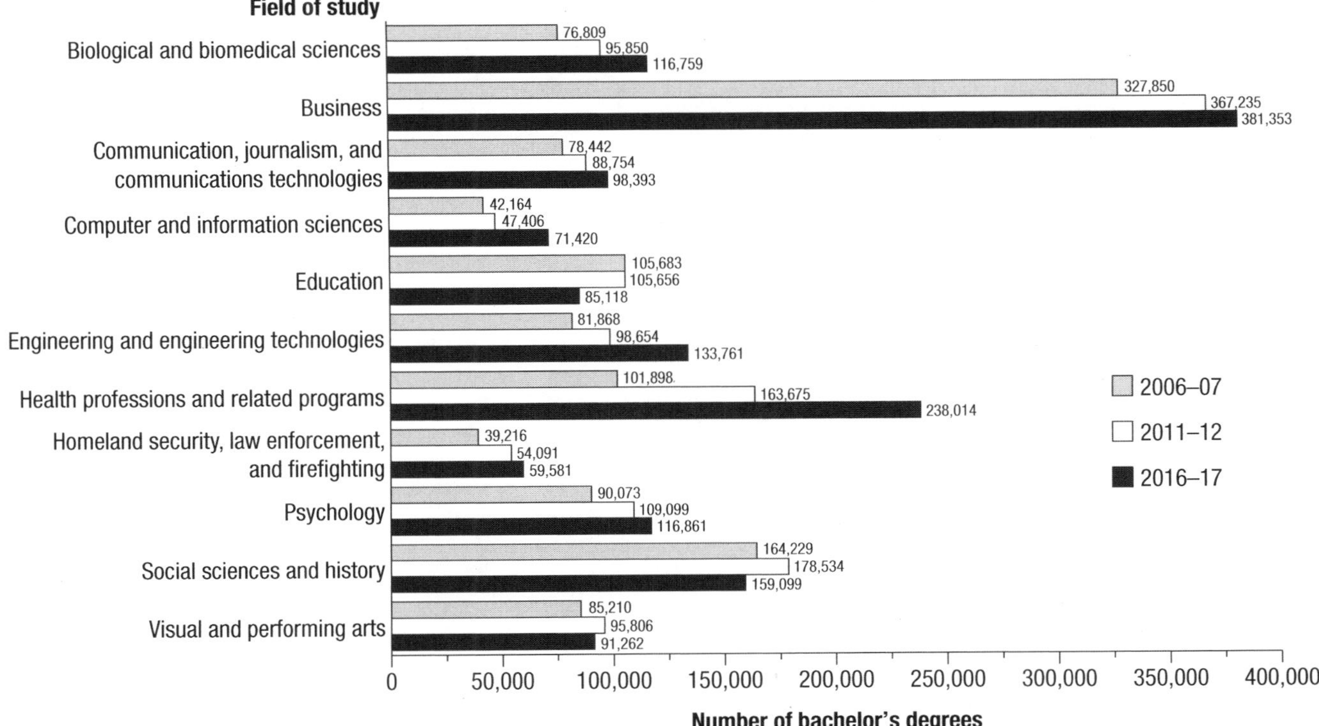

SOURCE: U.S. Department of Education, National Center for Education Statistics, Integrated Postsecondary Education Data System (IPEDS), Fall 2007, Fall 2012, and Fall 2017, Completions component.

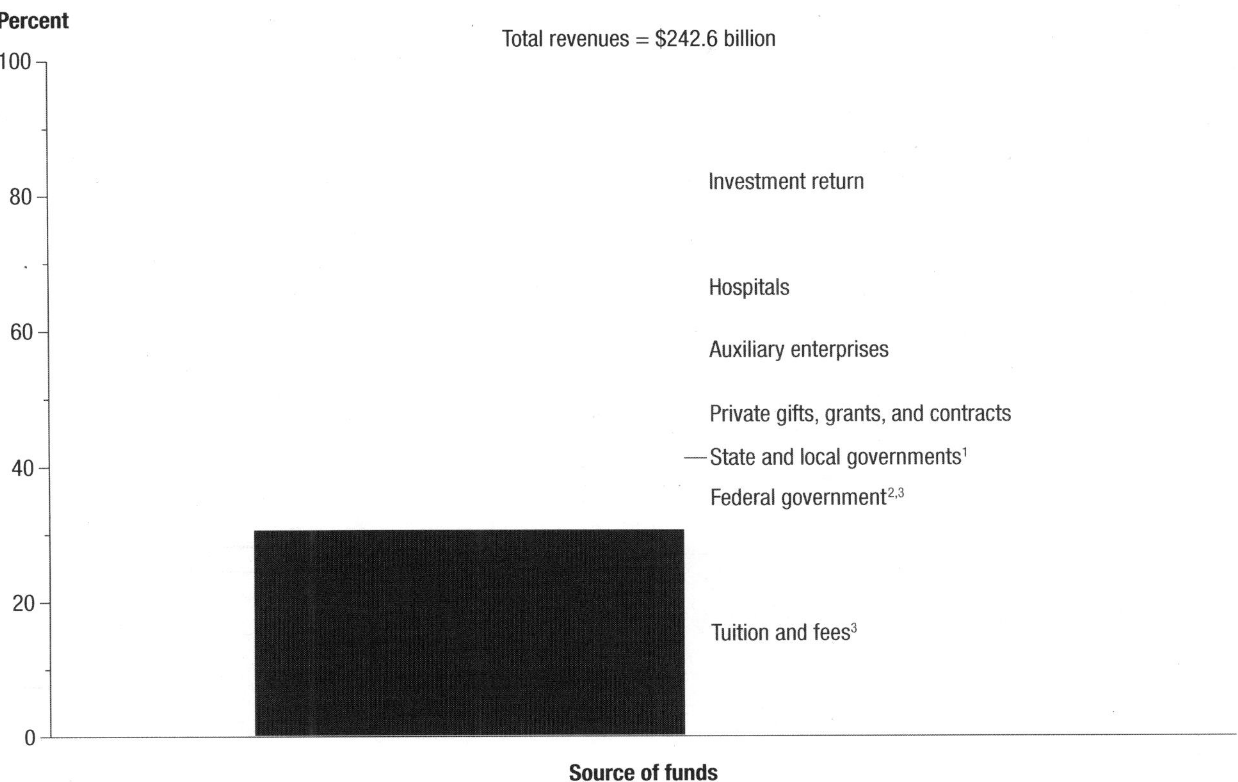
Percent
Total revenues = $242.6 billion
100
80
60
40
20
0
Investment return
Hospitals
Auxiliary enterprises
Private gifts, grants, and contracts
State and local governments[1]
Federal government[2,3]
Tuition and fees[3]
Source of funds

Table 301.10. Enrollment, staff, and degrees/certificates conferred in degree-granting and non-degree-granting postsecondary institutions, by control and level of institution, sex of student, type of staff, and level of degree: Fall 2017 and 2016–17

Level of institution, sex of student, type of staff, and level of degree	Total[1]	Degree-granting institutions					Non-degree-granting institutions				
				Private					Private		
		Total	Public	Total	Nonprofit	For-profit	Total	Public	Total	Nonprofit	For-profit
1	2	3	4	5	6	7	8	9	10	11	12
Enrollment, fall 2017											
Total	**20,138,477**	**19,765,598**	**14,560,155**	**5,205,443**	**4,106,477**	**1,098,966**	**372,879**	**109,399**	**263,480**	**16,813**	**246,667**
4-year institutions	13,823,919	13,823,640	8,853,477	4,970,163	4,058,087	912,076	279	5	274	274	0
Males	6,004,627	6,004,570	3,988,930	2,015,640	1,707,724	307,916	57	4	53	53	0
Females	7,819,292	7,819,070	4,864,547	2,954,523	2,350,363	604,160	222	1	221	221	0
2-year institutions	6,057,268	5,941,958	5,706,678	235,280	48,390	186,890	115,310	60,129	55,181	5,696	49,485
Males	2,623,571	2,563,062	2,488,990	74,072	12,716	61,356	60,509	35,196	25,313	1,493	23,820
Females	3,433,697	3,378,896	3,217,688	161,208	35,674	125,534	54,801	24,933	29,868	4,203	25,665
Less-than-2-year institutions	257,290	†	†	†	†	†	257,290	49,265	208,025	10,843	197,182
Males	79,776	†	†	†	†	†	79,776	23,954	55,822	3,838	51,984
Females	177,514	†	†	†	†	†	177,514	25,311	152,203	7,005	145,198
Staff, fall 2017											
Total	**3,976,901**	**3,914,542**	**2,564,974**	**1,349,568**	**1,209,311**	**140,257**	**62,359**	**22,290**	**40,069**	**3,885**	**36,184**
Faculty (instruction/research/public service)	1,575,699	1,543,569	971,183	572,386	486,183	86,203	32,130	11,912	20,218	1,706	18,512
Instruction	1,457,188	1,425,058	896,737	528,321	442,256	86,065	32,130	11,912	20,218	1,706	18,512
Research	89,445	89,445	54,731	34,714	34,620	94	†	†	†	†	†
Public service	29,066	29,066	19,715	9,351	9,307	44	†	†	†	†	†
Graduate assistants	377,156	377,156	295,798	81,358	80,946	412	†	†	†	†	†
Librarians, curators, and archivists	41,668	41,497	23,608	17,889	16,874	1,015	171	44	127	52	75
Student and academic affairs and other education services	187,318	181,731	119,178	62,553	51,128	11,425	5,587	2,496	3,091	378	2,713
Management	265,913	259,986	149,283	110,703	100,152	10,551	5,927	1,264	4,663	436	4,227
Business and financial operations	217,145	214,461	144,115	70,346	65,006	5,340	2,684	545	2,139	143	1,996
Computer, engineering, and science	236,232	235,674	161,842	73,832	71,728	2,104	558	345	213	32	181
Community, social service, legal, arts, design, entertainment, sports, and media	185,158	184,650	111,867	72,783	67,294	5,489	508	304	204	44	160
Healthcare practitioners and technicians	110,470	109,889	74,699	35,190	34,909	281	581	385	196	78	118
Service occupations	244,162	241,200	161,481	79,719	77,576	2,143	2,962	1,540	1,422	473	949
Sales and related occupations	15,231	13,210	4,755	8,455	4,386	4,069	2,021	83	1,938	75	1,863
Office and administrative support	426,485	418,537	278,567	139,970	129,505	10,465	7,948	2,618	5,330	428	4,902
Natural resources, construction, and maintenance	74,977	74,000	54,501	19,499	18,938	561	977	507	470	27	443
Production, transportation, and material moving	19,287	18,982	14,097	4,885	4,686	199	305	247	58	13	45
Degrees/certificates conferred, 2016–17											
Total	**4,892,714**	**4,643,736**	**3,172,249**	**1,471,487**	**1,087,671**	**383,816**	**248,978**	**61,386**	**187,592**	**12,344**	**175,248**
Less-than-1-year and 1- to less-than-4-year certificates	944,940	696,019	568,715	127,304	22,832	104,472	248,921	61,386	187,535	12,344	175,191
4-year institutions	140,313	140,266	98,273	41,993	11,514	30,479	47	5	42	42	0
Males	60,517	60,507	47,651	12,856	4,451	8,405	10	4	6	6	0
Females	79,796	79,759	50,622	29,137	7,063	22,074	37	1	36	36	0
2-year institutions	620,449	555,753	470,442	85,311	11,318	73,993	64,696	33,109	31,587	2,585	29,002
Males	288,741	258,691	232,379	26,312	3,524	22,788	30,050	16,188	13,862	794	13,068
Females	331,708	297,062	238,063	58,999	7,794	51,205	34,646	16,921	17,725	1,791	15,934
Less-than-2-year institutions	184,178	†	†	†	†	†	184,178	28,272	155,906	9,717	146,189
Males	55,455	†	†	†	†	†	55,455	11,344	44,111	3,735	40,376
Females	128,723	†	†	†	†	†	128,723	16,928	111,795	5,982	105,813
Associate's degrees	1,005,706	1,005,649	861,859	143,790	56,563	87,227	57	0	57	0	57
4-year institutions	291,497	291,497	191,928	99,569	44,868	54,701	0	0	0	0	0
Males	111,294	111,294	76,345	34,949	17,079	17,870	0	0	0	0	0
Females	180,203	180,203	115,583	64,620	27,789	36,831	0	0	0	0	0
2-year institutions	714,152	714,152	669,931	44,221	11,695	32,526	0	0	0	0	0
Males	282,865	282,865	267,971	14,894	2,877	12,017	0	0	0	0	0
Females	431,287	431,287	401,960	29,327	8,818	20,509	0	0	0	0	0
Less-than-2-year institutions	57	†	†	†	†	†	57	0	57	0	57
Males	3	†	†	†	†	†	3	0	3	0	3
Females	54	†	†	†	†	†	54	0	54	0	54
Bachelor's degrees	1,956,032	1,956,032	1,275,756	680,276	566,379	113,897	0	0	0	0	0
Males	836,045	836,045	559,822	276,223	232,487	43,736	0	0	0	0	0
Females	1,119,987	1,119,987	715,934	404,053	333,892	70,161	0	0	0	0	0
Master's degrees	804,684	804,684	374,387	430,297	360,352	69,945	0	0	0	0	0
Males	326,892	326,892	159,463	167,429	145,315	22,114	0	0	0	0	0
Females	477,792	477,792	214,924	262,868	215,037	47,831	0	0	0	0	0
Doctor's degrees	181,352	181,352	91,532	89,820	81,545	8,275	0	0	0	0	0
Males	84,646	84,646	44,169	40,477	37,639	2,838	0	0	0	0	0
Females	96,706	96,706	47,363	49,343	43,906	5,437	0	0	0	0	0

†Not applicable.
[1]Includes both degree-granting and non-degree-granting institutions.
NOTE: Data are for postsecondary institutions participating in Title IV federal financial aid programs. Degree-granting institutions grant degrees at the associate's or higher level, while non-degree-granting institutions grant only awards below that level. The non-degree-granting classification includes some institutions transitioning to higher level program offerings, though still classified at a lower level; therefore, a small number of associate's degrees are shown as awarded by non-degree-granting institutions.
SOURCE: U.S. Department of Education, National Center for Education Statistics, Integrated Postsecondary Education Data System (IPEDS), Spring 2018, Fall Enrollment component; Spring 2018, Human Resources component; and Fall 2017, Completions component. (This table was prepared April 2019.)

Table 301.20. Historical summary of faculty, enrollment, degrees conferred, and finances in degree-granting postsecondary institutions: Selected years, 1869–70 through 2016–17

Selected characteristic	1869–70	1879–80	1889–90	1899–1900	1909–10	1919–20	1929–30	1939–40	1949–50	1959–60	1969–70	1979–80	1989–90	1999–2000	2009–10	2016–17
1	2	3	4	5	6	7	8	9	10	11	12	13	14	15	16	17
Total institutions[1]	563	811	998	977	951	1,041	1,409	1,708	1,851	2,004	2,525	3,152	3,535	4,084	4,495	4,360
Total faculty[2]	5,553[3]	11,522[3]	15,809	23,868	36,480	48,615	82,386	146,929	246,722	380,554	450,000[4]	675,000[4]	824,220[5]	1,027,830[5]	1,439,074[5]	1,546,081[5]
Males	4,887[3]	7,328[3]	12,704[3]	19,151	29,132	35,807	60,017	106,328	186,189	296,773	346,000[4]	479,000[4]	534,254[5]	602,469[5]	761,002[5]	783,495[5]
Females	666[3]	4,194[3]	3,105[3]	4,717	7,348	12,808	22,369	40,601	60,533	83,781	104,000[4]	196,000[4]	289,966[5]	425,361[5]	678,072[5]	762,586[5]
Total fall enrollment[6]	52,286	115,817	156,756	237,592	355,213	597,880	1,100,737	1,494,203	2,444,900	3,639,847	8,004,660	11,569,899	13,538,560	14,791,224	20,313,594	19,846,904
Males	41,160[3]	77,972[3]	100,453[3]	152,254	214,648[3]	314,938	619,935	893,250	1,721,572	2,332,617	4,746,201	5,682,877	6,190,015	6,490,646	8,732,953	8,638,422
Females	11,126[3]	37,845[3]	56,303[3]	85,338	140,565[3]	282,942	480,802	600,953	723,328	1,307,230	3,258,459	5,887,022	7,348,545	8,300,578	11,580,641	11,208,482
Degrees conferred																
Associate's, total	—	—	—	—	—	—	—	—	—	—	206,023	400,910	455,102	564,933	848,856	1,005,649
Males	—	—	—	—	—	—	—	—	—	—	117,432	183,737	191,195	224,721	322,747	394,159
Females	—	—	—	—	—	—	—	—	—	—	88,591	217,173	263,907	340,212	526,109	611,490
Bachelor's, total[7]	9,371	12,896	15,539	27,410	37,199	48,622	122,484	186,500	432,058	392,440	792,316	929,417	1,051,344	1,237,875	1,649,919	1,956,032
Males	7,993	10,411	12,857	22,173	28,762	31,980	73,615	109,546	328,841	254,063	451,097	473,611	491,696	530,367	706,660	836,045
Females	1,378	2,485	2,682	5,237	8,437	16,642	48,869	76,954	103,217	138,377	341,219	455,806	559,648	707,508	943,259	1,119,987
Master's, total[8]	—	879	1,015	1,583	2,113	4,279	14,969	26,731	58,183	74,435	213,589	305,196	330,152	463,185	693,313	804,684
Males	—	868	821	1,280	1,555	2,985	8,925	16,508	41,220	50,898	130,799	156,882	158,052	196,129	275,317	326,892
Females	—	11	194	303	558	1,294	6,044	10,223	16,963	23,537	82,790	148,314	172,100	267,056	417,996	477,792
Doctor's, total[9]	1	54	149	382	443	615	2,299	3,290	6,420	9,829	59,486	95,631	103,508	118,736	158,590	181,352
Males	1	51	147	359	399	522	1,946	2,861	5,804	8,801	53,792	69,526	63,963	64,930	76,610	84,646
Females	0	3	2	23	44	93	353	429	616	1,028	5,694	26,105	39,545	53,806	81,980	96,706
	In thousands of current dollars															
Finances																
Revenue[10]	—	—	—	—	$76,883	$199,922	$554,511	$715,211	$2,374,645	$5,785,537	$21,515,242	$58,519,982	$139,635,477	$282,261,000	$496,720,000	$649,151,000
Educational and general income	—	—	$21,464	$35,084	67,917	172,929	483,065	571,288	1,833,845	4,688,352	16,486,177	—	—	—	—	—
Expenditures[11]	—	—	—	—	—	—	507,142	674,688	2,245,661	5,601,376	21,043,113	56,913,588	134,655,571	236,784,000	446,479,000	583,575,000
Value of physical property	—	—	95,426	253,599	457,594	747,333	2,065,049	2,753,780[12]	4,799,964	13,548,548	42,093,580	83,733,387	164,635,000	—	—	—
Market value of endowment funds	—	—	78,788[13]	194,998[13]	323,661[13]	569,071[13]	1,372,068[13]	1,686,283[13]	2,601,223[13]	5,322,080[13]	11,206,632	20,743,045	67,978,726	—	355,910,203	598,295,000
	In thousands of constant 2017–18 dollars[14]															
Finances																
Revenue[10]	—	—	—	—	—	—	$8,038,126	$12,698,565	$24,879,076	$48,856,215	$141,323,387	$187,038,103	$272,866,252	$413,702,000	$568,662,000	$663,784,000
Educational and general income	—	—	—	—	—	—	7,002,453	10,143,213	19,213,133	39,590,989	108,289,852	—	—	—	—	—
Expenditures[11]	—	—	—	—	—	—	7,351,470	11,979,079	23,527,715	47,301,059	138,222,196	181,903,842	263,134,855	347,047,000	511,145,000	596,730,000
Value of physical property	—	—	—	—	—	—	29,934,705	48,893,339[12]	50,289,063	114,411,293	276,492,697	267,623,696	321,718,638	—	—	—
Market value of endowment funds	—	—	—	—	—	—	19,889,335[13]	29,939,940[13]	27,252,926[13]	44,942,532[13]	73,611,033	66,297,693	132,839,452	—	407,458,764	611,782,000

—Not available.
[1]Prior to 1979–80, excludes branch campuses.
[2]Total number of different individuals (not reduced to full-time equivalent). Beginning in 1959-60, data are for the first term of the academic year.
[3]Estimated.
[4]Estimated number of senior instructional staff based on actual enrollment data for the designated year and enrollment/staff ratios for the prior staff survey. Excludes graduate assistants.
[5]Because of revised survey procedures, data may not be directly comparable with figures prior to 1989–90. Excludes graduate assistants.
[6]Data for 1869–70 to 1939–40 are for resident degree-credit students who enrolled at any time during the academic year.
[7]From 1869–70 to 1959–60, bachelor's degrees include degrees formerly classified as first-professional, such as M.D., D.D.S., and law degrees.
[8]Figures for years prior to 1969–70 are not precisely comparable with later data.
[9]Includes Ph.D., Ed.D., and comparable degrees at the doctoral level. Includes most degrees formerly classified as first-professional, such as M.D., D.D.S., and law degrees.
[10]Data for 1929–30 through 1989–90 are current-fund revenues only. Data for 1999–2000 include total revenues for private institutions and current-fund revenues for public institutions. Data for later years are for total revenues.
[11]Data for 1929–30 and 1939–40 include current-fund expenditures and additions to plant value. Data for 1949–50 through 1989–90 are current-fund expenditures only. Data for 1999–2000 include total expenditures for private institutions and current-fund expenditures for public institutions. Data for later years are for total expenditures.
[12]Includes unexpended plant funds.
[13]Book value. Includes other nonexpendable funds.
[14]Constant dollars based on the Consumer Price Index, prepared by the Bureau of Labor Statistics, U.S. Department of Labor, adjusted to a school-year basis.
NOTE: Data through 1989–90 are for institutions of higher education, while later data are for degree-granting institutions. Degree-granting institutions grant associate's or higher degrees and participate in Title IV federal financial aid programs. The degree-granting classification is very similar to the earlier higher education classification, but it includes more 2-year colleges and excludes a few higher education institutions that did not grant degrees. Detail may not sum to totals because of rounding.
SOURCE: U.S. Department of Education, National Center for Education Statistics, *Biennial Survey of Education in the United States*; *Education Directory, Colleges and Universities*; *Faculty and Other Professional Staff in Institutions of Higher Education*; *Fall Enrollment in Colleges and Universities*; *Earned Degrees Conferred*; *Financial Statistics of Institutions of Higher Education*; Higher Education General Information Survey (HEGIS), "Fall Enrollment in Institutions of Higher Education," "Degrees and Other Formal Awards Conferred," and "Financial Statistics of Institutions of Higher Education" surveys; Integrated Postsecondary Education Data System (IPEDS), "Fall Enrollment Survey" (IPEDS-EF:89–99), "Fall Staff Survey" (IPEDS-S:89–99), "Finance Survey" (IPEDS-F:FY90–00), "Completions Survey" (IPEDS-C:90–00), and "Institutional Characteristics Survey" (IPEDS-IC:89–99); IPEDS Winter 2009–10 and Spring 2017, Human Resources component, Fall Staff section; IPEDS Spring 2010 and Spring 2017, Fall Enrollment component; IPEDS Fall 2010 and Fall 2017, Completions component; and IPEDS Spring 2011 and Spring 2018, Finance component. (This table was prepared April 2019.)

Table 302.10. Recent high school completers and their enrollment in college, by sex and level of institution: 1960 through 2017

[Standard errors appear in parentheses]

Year	Number of high school completers[1] (in thousands)			Percent of recent high school completers[1] enrolled in college[2]								
				Total			Males			Females		
	Total	Males	Females	Total	2-year college	4-year college or university	Total	2-year college	4-year college or university	Total	2-year college	4-year college or university
1	2	3	4	5	6	7	8	9	10	11	12	13
1960	1,679 (44.5)	756 (32.3)	923 (30.1)	45.1 (2.16)	— (†)	— (†)	54.0 (3.23)	— (†)	— (†)	37.9 (2.85)	— (†)	— (†)
1961	1,763 (46.7)	790 (33.7)	973 (31.8)	48.0 (2.12)	— (†)	— (†)	56.3 (3.14)	— (†)	— (†)	41.3 (2.81)	— (†)	— (†)
1962	1,838 (44.3)	872 (32.0)	966 (30.4)	49.0 (2.08)	— (†)	— (†)	55.0 (3.00)	— (†)	— (†)	43.5 (2.84)	— (†)	— (†)
1963	1,741 (44.9)	794 (32.6)	947 (30.5)	45.0 (2.12)	— (†)	— (†)	52.3 (3.16)	— (†)	— (†)	39.0 (2.82)	— (†)	— (†)
1964	2,145 (43.6)	997 (32.3)	1,148 (28.9)	48.3 (1.92)	— (†)	— (†)	57.2 (2.79)	— (†)	— (†)	40.7 (2.58)	— (†)	— (†)
1965	2,659 (48.5)	1,254 (35.7)	1,405 (32.5)	50.9 (1.73)	— (†)	— (†)	57.3 (2.49)	— (†)	— (†)	45.3 (2.37)	— (†)	— (†)
1966	2,612 (45.7)	1,207 (34.4)	1,405 (29.5)	50.1 (1.74)	— (†)	— (†)	58.7 (2.53)	— (†)	— (†)	42.7 (2.35)	— (†)	— (†)
1967	2,525 (38.5)	1,142 (28.9)	1,383 (24.7)	51.9 (1.44)	— (†)	— (†)	57.6 (2.12)	— (†)	— (†)	47.2 (1.95)	— (†)	— (†)
1968	2,606 (38.0)	1,184 (28.7)	1,422 (24.2)	55.4 (1.41)	— (†)	— (†)	63.2 (2.04)	— (†)	— (†)	48.9 (1.93)	— (†)	— (†)
1969	2,842 (36.6)	1,352 (27.3)	1,490 (24.2)	53.3 (1.36)	— (†)	— (†)	60.1 (1.93)	— (†)	— (†)	47.2 (1.88)	— (†)	— (†)
1970	2,758 (38.1)	1,343 (26.6)	1,415 (27.3)	51.7 (1.38)	— (†)	— (†)	55.2 (1.97)	— (†)	— (†)	48.5 (1.93)	— (†)	— (†)
1971	2,875 (38.7)	1,371 (27.1)	1,504 (27.6)	53.5 (1.35)	— (†)	— (†)	57.6 (1.94)	— (†)	— (†)	49.8 (1.87)	— (†)	— (†)
1972	2,964 (38.5)	1,423 (27.5)	1,542 (26.9)	49.2 (1.33)	— (†)	— (†)	52.7 (1.92)	— (†)	— (†)	46.0 (1.84)	— (†)	— (†)
1973	3,058 (37.7)	1,460 (28.0)	1,599 (25.0)	46.6 (1.31)	14.9 (0.94)	31.6 (1.22)	50.0 (1.90)	14.6 (1.34)	35.4 (1.82)	43.4 (1.80)	15.2 (1.30)	28.2 (1.63)
1974	3,101 (39.3)	1,491 (28.2)	1,611 (27.3)	47.6 (1.30)	15.2 (0.94)	32.4 (1.22)	49.4 (1.88)	16.6 (1.40)	32.8 (1.77)	45.9 (1.80)	13.9 (1.25)	32.0 (1.69)
1975	3,185 (39.3)	1,513 (27.8)	1,672 (27.7)	50.7 (1.29)	18.2 (0.99)	32.6 (1.21)	52.6 (1.86)	19.0 (1.47)	33.6 (1.76)	49.0 (1.78)	17.4 (1.35)	31.6 (1.65)
1976	2,986 (40.5)	1,451 (29.4)	1,535 (27.8)	48.8 (1.33)	15.6 (0.96)	33.3 (1.25)	47.2 (1.90)	14.5 (1.34)	32.7 (1.79)	50.3 (1.85)	16.6 (1.38)	33.8 (1.75)
1977	3,141 (41.0)	1,483 (29.8)	1,659 (27.9)	50.6 (1.30)	17.5 (0.98)	33.1 (1.22)	52.1 (1.88)	17.2 (1.42)	35.0 (1.80)	49.3 (1.78)	17.8 (1.36)	31.5 (1.66)
1978	3,163 (40.0)	1,485 (29.4)	1,677 (26.8)	50.1 (1.29)	17.0 (0.97)	33.1 (1.22)	51.1 (1.88)	15.6 (1.37)	35.5 (1.80)	49.3 (1.77)	18.3 (1.37)	31.0 (1.64)
1979	3,160 (40.3)	1,475 (29.4)	1,685 (27.4)	49.3 (1.29)	17.5 (0.98)	31.8 (1.20)	50.4 (1.89)	16.9 (1.42)	33.5 (1.79)	48.4 (1.77)	18.1 (1.36)	30.3 (1.63)
1980	3,088 (39.6)	1,498 (28.5)	1,589 (27.5)	49.3 (1.31)	19.4 (1.03)	29.9 (1.20)	46.7 (1.87)	17.1 (1.41)	29.7 (1.71)	51.8 (1.82)	21.6 (1.50)	30.2 (1.67)
1981	3,056 (42.4)	1,491 (30.6)	1,565 (29.3)	53.9 (1.31)	20.5 (1.06)	33.5 (1.24)	54.8 (1.87)	20.9 (1.53)	33.9 (1.78)	53.1 (1.83)	20.1 (1.47)	33.0 (1.73)
1982	3,100 (41.0)	1,509 (29.4)	1,592 (28.6)	50.6 (1.38)	19.1 (1.09)	31.5 (1.28)	49.1 (1.98)	17.5 (1.50)	31.6 (1.84)	52.0 (1.93)	20.6 (1.56)	31.4 (1.79)
1983	2,963 (42.2)	1,389 (30.8)	1,573 (28.6)	52.7 (1.41)	19.2 (1.11)	33.5 (1.33)	51.9 (2.06)	20.2 (1.66)	31.7 (1.92)	53.4 (1.93)	18.4 (1.50)	35.1 (1.85)
1984	3,012 (37.0)	1,429 (29.1)	1,584 (22.2)	55.2 (1.39)	19.4 (1.11)	35.8 (1.34)	56.0 (2.02)	17.7 (1.55)	38.4 (1.98)	54.5 (1.92)	21.0 (1.57)	33.5 (1.82)
1985	2,668 (40.7)	1,287 (29.1)	1,381 (28.3)	57.7 (1.47)	19.6 (1.18)	38.1 (1.45)	58.6 (2.11)	19.9 (1.71)	38.8 (2.09)	56.8 (2.05)	19.3 (1.63)	37.5 (2.00)
1986	2,786 (39.2)	1,332 (28.9)	1,454 (26.4)	53.8 (1.45)	19.2 (1.15)	34.5 (1.39)	55.8 (2.09)	21.3 (1.73)	34.5 (2.00)	51.9 (2.02)	17.3 (1.53)	34.6 (1.92)
1987	2,647 (41.5)	1,278 (30.2)	1,369 (28.4)	56.8 (1.48)	18.9 (1.17)	37.9 (1.45)	58.3 (2.12)	17.3 (1.63)	41.0 (2.12)	55.3 (2.07)	20.3 (1.67)	35.0 (1.98)
1988	2,673 (47.7)	1,334 (34.6)	1,339 (32.8)	58.9 (1.60)	21.9 (1.34)	37.1 (1.57)	57.1 (2.27)	21.3 (1.88)	35.8 (2.20)	60.7 (2.24)	22.4 (1.91)	38.3 (2.23)
1989	2,450 (44.8)	1,204 (31.7)	1,246 (31.7)	59.6 (1.58)	20.7 (1.30)	38.9 (1.57)	57.6 (2.27)	18.3 (1.77)	39.3 (2.24)	61.6 (2.19)	23.1 (1.90)	38.5 (2.20)
1990	2,362 (43.0)	1,173 (30.6)	1,189 (30.2)	60.1 (1.60)	20.1 (1.31)	40.0 (1.61)	58.0 (2.29)	19.6 (1.85)	38.4 (2.26)	62.2 (2.24)	20.6 (1.87)	41.6 (2.28)
1991	2,276 (41.1)	1,140 (29.0)	1,136 (29.0)	62.5 (1.62)	24.9 (1.44)	37.7 (1.62)	57.9 (2.33)	22.9 (1.98)	35.0 (2.25)	67.1 (2.22)	26.8 (2.09)	40.3 (2.32)
1992	2,397 (40.5)	1,216 (29.1)	1,180 (28.1)	61.9 (1.58)	23.0 (1.37)	38.9 (1.59)	60.0 (2.24)	22.1 (1.89)	37.8 (2.21)	63.8 (2.23)	23.9 (1.98)	40.0 (2.27)
1993	2,342 (41.4)	1,120 (30.6)	1,223 (27.7)	62.6 (1.59)	22.8 (1.38)	39.8 (1.61)	59.9 (2.33)	22.9 (2.00)	37.0 (2.30)	65.2 (2.17)	22.8 (1.91)	42.4 (2.25)
1994	2,517 (41.1)	1,244 (30.1)	1,273 (27.9)	61.9 (1.54)	21.0 (1.29)	40.9 (1.56)	60.6 (2.21)	23.0 (1.90)	37.5 (2.19)	63.2 (2.15)	19.1 (1.75)	44.1 (2.22)
1995	2,599 (41.0)	1,238 (30.0)	1,361 (27.7)	61.9 (1.41)	21.5 (1.19)	40.4 (1.43)	62.6 (2.04)	25.3 (1.83)	37.4 (2.04)	61.3 (1.96)	18.1 (1.55)	43.2 (1.99)
1996	2,660 (40.5)	1,297 (29.5)	1,363 (27.7)	65.0 (1.42)	23.1 (1.26)	41.9 (1.47)	60.1 (2.09)	21.5 (1.76)	38.5 (2.08)	69.7 (1.91)	24.6 (1.79)	45.1 (2.07)
1997	2,769 (41.8)	1,354 (31.0)	1,415 (27.9)	67.0 (1.37)	22.8 (1.23)	44.3 (1.45)	63.6 (2.01)	21.4 (1.71)	42.2 (2.06)	70.3 (1.87)	24.1 (1.75)	46.2 (2.04)
1998	2,810 (43.9)	1,452 (31.0)	1,358 (31.0)	65.6 (1.38)	24.4 (1.25)	41.3 (1.43)	62.4 (1.96)	24.4 (1.73)	38.0 (1.96)	69.1 (1.93)	24.3 (1.79)	44.8 (2.08)
1999	2,897 (41.5)	1,474 (29.9)	1,423 (28.8)	62.9 (1.38)	21.0 (1.16)	41.9 (1.41)	61.4 (1.95)	21.0 (1.63)	40.5 (1.97)	64.4 (1.95)	21.1 (1.66)	43.3 (2.02)
2000	2,756 (45.3)	1,251 (33.6)	1,505 (29.7)	63.3 (1.41)	21.4 (1.20)	41.9 (1.45)	59.9 (2.13)	23.1 (1.83)	36.8 (2.10)	66.2 (1.88)	20.0 (1.59)	46.2 (1.98)
2001	2,549 (44.1)	1,277 (32.0)	1,273 (30.3)	61.8 (1.41)	19.6 (1.15)	42.1 (1.43)	60.1 (2.00)	18.6 (1.59)	41.4 (2.01)	63.5 (1.97)	20.6 (1.66)	42.8 (2.02)
2002	2,796 (42.7)	1,412 (31.3)	1,384 (29.0)	65.2 (1.31)	21.6 (1.14)	43.6 (1.37)	62.1 (1.88)	20.4 (1.57)	41.7 (1.92)	68.4 (1.82)	22.8 (1.65)	45.6 (1.95)
2003	2,677 (42.2)	1,306 (29.9)	1,372 (29.7)	63.9 (1.35)	21.5 (1.16)	42.5 (1.39)	61.2 (1.97)	21.9 (1.67)	39.3 (1.97)	66.5 (1.86)	21.0 (1.61)	45.5 (1.96)
2004	2,752 (40.0)	1,327 (29.1)	1,425 (27.3)	66.7 (1.31)	22.4 (1.16)	44.2 (1.38)	61.4 (1.95)	21.8 (1.65)	39.6 (1.96)	71.5 (1.74)	23.1 (1.63)	48.5 (1.93)
2005	2,675 (40.8)	1,262 (31.5)	1,414 (24.9)	68.6 (1.31)	24.0 (1.21)	44.6 (1.40)	66.5 (1.94)	24.7 (1.77)	41.8 (2.03)	70.4 (1.77)	23.4 (1.64)	47.0 (1.94)
2006	2,692 (44.6)	1,328 (32.7)	1,363 (30.1)	66.0 (1.33)	24.7 (1.21)	41.3 (1.39)	65.8 (1.90)	24.9 (1.73)	40.9 (1.97)	66.1 (1.87)	24.5 (1.70)	41.7 (1.95)
2007	2,955 (42.6)	1,511 (30.0)	1,444 (30.3)	67.2 (1.26)	24.1 (1.15)	43.1 (1.33)	66.1 (1.78)	22.7 (1.57)	43.4 (1.86)	68.3 (1.79)	25.5 (1.67)	42.8 (1.90)
2008	3,151 (42.8)	1,640 (29.6)	1,511 (30.9)	68.6 (1.21)	27.7 (1.16)	40.9 (1.28)	65.9 (1.71)	24.9 (1.56)	41.0 (1.77)	71.6 (1.69)	30.6 (1.73)	40.9 (1.85)
2009	2,937 (45.0)	1,407 (32.8)	1,531 (30.6)	70.1 (1.23)	27.7 (1.21)	42.4 (1.33)	66.0 (1.84)	25.1 (1.69)	40.9 (1.91)	73.8 (1.64)	30.1 (1.71)	43.8 (1.85)
2010	3,160 (91.8)	1,679 (64.6)	1,482 (58.4)	68.1 (1.49)	26.7 (1.52)	41.4 (1.61)	62.8 (1.88)	28.5 (2.03)	34.3 (1.97)	74.0 (2.31)	24.6 (2.32)	49.5 (2.59)
2011	3,079 (88.3)	1,611 (60.6)	1,468 (58.4)	68.2 (1.45)	25.9 (1.49)	42.3 (1.44)	64.7 (2.16)	24.7 (1.79)	40.0 (2.10)	72.2 (1.98)	27.3 (2.17)	44.9 (2.37)
2012	3,203 (96.2)	1,622 (70.1)	1,581 (54.0)	66.2 (1.59)	28.8 (1.57)	37.5 (1.60)	61.3 (2.17)	26.9 (2.20)	34.4 (2.15)	71.3 (2.11)	30.7 (2.09)	40.6 (2.21)
2013	2,977 (84.4)	1,524 (62.9)	1,453 (57.0)	65.9 (1.58)	23.8 (1.44)	42.1 (1.76)	63.5 (2.20)	24.5 (2.14)	39.0 (2.48)	68.4 (2.17)	23.0 (2.15)	45.3 (2.21)
2014	2,868 (78.5)	1,423 (58.1)	1,445 (57.5)	68.4 (1.67)	24.6 (1.56)	43.7 (1.81)	64.0 (2.32)	21.2 (2.07)	42.8 (2.69)	72.6 (2.50)	28.0 (2.35)	44.6 (2.57)
2015	2,965 (87.5)	1,448 (64.6)	1,516 (56.6)	69.2 (1.54)	25.2 (1.48)	44.0 (1.61)	65.8 (2.27)	24.3 (2.00)	41.5 (2.27)	72.5 (2.18)	26.2 (2.08)	46.4 (2.42)
2016	3,137 (102.3)	1,517 (70.6)	1,620 (66.7)	69.8 (1.64)	23.7 (1.56)	46.0 (1.85)	67.5 (2.12)	25.3 (2.26)	42.2 (2.47)	71.9 (2.40)	22.3 (1.99)	49.6 (2.46)
2017	2,870 (95.9)	1,345 (60.2)	1,525 (71.3)	66.7 (1.68)	22.6 (1.50)	44.2 (1.83)	61.1 (2.57)	23.9 (2.36)	37.2 (2.32)	71.7 (2.29)	21.4 (2.09)	50.3 (2.70)

—Not available.
†Not applicable.
[1]Individuals ages 16 to 24 who graduated from high school or completed a GED or other high school equivalency credential.
[2]Enrollment in college as of October of each year for individuals ages 16 to 24 who had completed high school earlier in the calendar year.
NOTE: Data are based on sample surveys of the civilian noninstitutionalized population. High school completion data in this table differ from figures appearing in other tables because of varying survey procedures and coverage. Prior to 2010, standard errors were computed using generalized variance function methodology rather than the more precise replicate weight methodology used in later years. Detail may not sum to totals because of rounding.
SOURCE: American College Testing Program, unpublished tabulations, derived from statistics collected by the Census Bureau, 1960 through 1969. U.S. Department of Commerce, Census Bureau, Current Population Survey (CPS), October, 1970 through 2017. (This table was prepared July 2018.)

Table 302.20. Percentage of recent high school completers enrolled in college, by race/ethnicity: 1960 through 2017

[Standard errors appear in parentheses]

Year	Percent of recent high school completers[1] enrolled in college[2] (annual data)					3-year moving averages[3]: Percent of recent high school completers[1] enrolled in college[2]					3-year moving averages[3]: Difference between percent enrolled		
	Total	White	Black	Hispanic	Asian[4]	Total	White	Black	Hispanic	Asian[4]	White-Black	White-Hispanic	White-Asian[4]
1	2	3	4	5	6	7	8	9	10	11	12	13	14
1960[5]	45.1 (2.16)	45.8 (2.24)	— (†)	— (†)	— (†)	46.6 (1.52)	47.7 (1.58)	— (†)	— (†)	— (†)	— (†)	— (†)	— (†)
1961[5]	48.0 (2.12)	49.5 (2.22)	— (†)	— (†)	— (†)	47.4 (1.22)	48.7 (1.28)	— (†)	— (†)	— (†)	— (†)	— (†)	— (†)
1962[5]	49.0 (2.08)	50.6 (2.19)	— (†)	— (†)	— (†)	47.4 (1.22)	48.6 (1.27)	— (†)	— (†)	— (†)	— (†)	— (†)	— (†)
1963[5]	45.0 (2.12)	45.6 (2.21)	— (†)	— (†)	— (†)	47.5 (1.18)	48.5 (1.23)	— (†)	— (†)	— (†)	— (†)	— (†)	— (†)
1964[5]	48.3 (1.92)	49.2 (2.01)	— (†)	— (†)	— (†)	48.5 (1.10)	49.2 (1.15)	— (†)	— (†)	— (†)	— (†)	— (†)	— (†)
1965[5]	50.9 (1.73)	51.7 (1.81)	— (†)	— (†)	— (†)	49.9 (1.03)	51.0 (1.08)	— (†)	— (†)	— (†)	— (†)	— (†)	— (†)
1966[5]	50.1 (1.74)	51.7 (1.82)	— (†)	— (†)	— (†)	51.0 (1.01)	52.1 (1.06)	— (†)	— (†)	— (†)	— (†)	— (†)	— (†)
1967[5]	51.9 (1.44)	53.0 (1.52)	— (†)	— (†)	— (†)	52.5 (0.82)	53.8 (0.87)	— (†)	— (†)	— (†)	— (†)	— (†)	— (†)
1968[5]	55.4 (1.41)	56.6 (1.50)	— (†)	— (†)	— (†)	53.6 (0.81)	55.0 (0.86)	— (†)	— (†)	— (†)	— (†)	— (†)	— (†)
1969[5]	53.3 (1.36)	55.2 (1.43)	— (†)	— (†)	— (†)	53.5 (0.80)	54.6 (0.85)	— (†)	— (†)	— (†)	— (†)	— (†)	— (†)
1970[5]	51.7 (1.38)	52.0 (1.46)	— (†)	— (†)	— (†)	52.9 (0.79)	53.8 (0.83)	— (†)	— (†)	— (†)	— (†)	— (†)	— (†)
1971[5]	53.5 (1.35)	54.0 (1.42)	— (†)	— (†)	— (†)	51.5 (0.78)	51.9 (0.83)	— (†)	— (†)	— (†)	— (†)	— (†)	— (†)
1972	49.2 (1.33)	49.7 (1.45)	44.6 (4.74)	45.0 (12.85)	— (†)	49.7 (0.77)	50.5 (0.83)	38.4 (3.26)	49.9 (8.76)	— (†)	12.1 (3.36)	‡ (†)	— (†)
1973	46.6 (1.31)	47.8 (1.43)	32.5 (4.40)	54.1 (11.89)	— (†)	47.8 (0.76)	48.2 (0.83)	41.4 (2.68)	48.8 (7.04)	— (†)	6.8! (2.81)	‡ (†)	— (†)
1974	47.6 (1.30)	47.2 (1.42)	47.2 (4.69)	46.9 (11.79)	— (†)	48.3 (0.75)	48.7 (0.82)	40.5 (2.69)	53.1 (6.72)	— (†)	8.3! (2.82)	‡ (†)	— (†)
1975	50.7 (1.29)	51.1 (1.40)	41.7 (4.81)	58.0 (11.14)	— (†)	49.1 (0.75)	49.1 (0.82)	44.5 (2.78)	52.7 (6.44)	— (†)	‡ (†)	‡ (†)	— (†)
1976	48.8 (1.33)	48.8 (1.45)	44.4 (4.94)	52.7 (10.52)	— (†)	50.1 (0.75)	50.3 (0.82)	45.3 (2.78)	53.6 (6.18)	— (†)	‡ (†)	‡ (†)	— (†)
1977	50.6 (1.30)	50.8 (1.42)	49.5 (4.70)	50.8 (10.43)	— (†)	49.9 (0.75)	50.1 (0.83)	46.8 (2.73)	48.8 (6.18)	— (†)	‡ (†)	‡ (†)	— (†)
1978	50.1 (1.29)	50.5 (1.42)	46.4 (4.55)	42.0 (11.06)	— (†)	50.0 (0.75)	50.4 (0.82)	47.5 (2.69)	46.1 (6.14)	— (†)	‡ (†)	‡ (†)	— (†)
1979	49.3 (1.29)	49.9 (1.42)	46.7 (4.73)	45.0 (10.37)	— (†)	49.6 (0.75)	50.1 (0.82)	45.2 (2.65)	46.3 (6.32)	— (†)	‡ (†)	‡ (†)	— (†)
1980	49.3 (1.31)	49.8 (1.44)	42.7 (4.48)	52.3 (11.39)	— (†)	50.8 (0.75)	51.5 (0.83)	44.0 (2.64)	49.6 (6.25)	— (†)	7.5! (2.76)	‡ (†)	— (†)
1981	53.9 (1.31)	54.9 (1.45)	42.7 (4.48)	52.1 (10.73)	— (†)	51.3 (0.76)	52.4 (0.84)	40.3 (2.53)	48.7 (6.13)	— (†)	12.2 (2.66)	‡ (†)	— (†)
1982	50.6 (1.38)	52.7 (1.54)	35.8 (4.39)	43.2 (10.37)	— (†)	52.4 (0.80)	54.2 (0.90)	38.8 (2.61)	49.4 (6.44)	— (†)	15.4 (2.76)	‡ (†)	— (†)
1983	52.7 (1.41)	55.0 (1.57)	38.2 (4.41)	54.2 (11.69)	— (†)	52.8 (0.81)	55.5 (0.90)	38.0 (2.50)	46.7 (6.16)	— (†)	17.5 (2.66)	‡ (†)	— (†)
1984	55.2 (1.39)	59.0 (1.57)	39.8 (4.21)	44.3 (10.00)	— (†)	55.1 (0.82)	57.9 (0.92)	39.9 (2.58)	49.3 (6.38)	— (†)	18.0 (2.74)	‡ (†)	— (†)
1985	57.7 (1.47)	60.1 (1.64)	42.2 (4.86)	51.0 (9.79)	— (†)	55.5 (0.83)	58.6 (0.93)	39.5 (2.59)	46.1 (5.20)	— (†)	19.1 (2.75)	12.5! (5.28)	— (†)
1986	53.8 (1.45)	56.8 (1.64)	36.9 (4.44)	44.0 (8.88)	— (†)	56.1 (0.85)	58.5 (0.96)	43.5 (2.75)	42.3 (5.21)	— (†)	15.0 (2.91)	16.2! (5.30)	— (†)
1987	56.8 (1.48)	58.6 (1.68)	52.2 (4.90)	33.5 (8.28)	— (†)	56.5 (0.85)	58.8 (0.96)	44.2 (2.69)	45.0 (5.06)	— (†)	14.6 (2.86)	13.8! (5.15)	— (†)
1988	58.9 (1.60)	61.1 (1.82)	44.4 (4.98)	57.1 (9.60)	— (†)	58.4 (0.94)	60.1 (1.07)	49.7 (3.02)	48.5 (5.67)	— (†)	10.4! (3.20)	11.6! (5.77)	— (†)
1989	59.6 (1.58)	60.7 (1.79)	53.4 (5.07)	55.1 (9.21)	81.1 (10.23)	59.5 (0.90)	61.6 (1.02)	48.0 (2.87)	52.7 (5.54)	81.4 (6.36)	13.6 (3.04)	‡ (†)	-19.8! (6.44)
1990	60.1 (1.60)	63.0 (1.80)	46.8 (5.08)	42.7 (10.82)	81.7 (8.12)	60.7 (0.92)	63.0 (1.04)	48.9 (2.97)	52.5 (5.70)	81.4 (6.36)	14.0 (3.14)	‡ (†)	-18.5! (6.44)
1991	62.5 (1.62)	65.4 (1.82)	46.4 (5.24)	57.2 (9.57)	78.9 (9.04)	61.5 (0.92)	64.2 (1.05)	47.2 (2.93)	52.6 (5.52)	80.6 (5.21)	17.0 (3.11)	11.7! (5.62)	-16.3! (5.31)
1992	61.9 (1.58)	64.3 (1.84)	48.2 (4.91)	55.0 (8.50)	81.7 (7.00)	62.3 (0.92)	64.2 (1.06)	50.0 (2.97)	58.2 (5.04)	80.9 (4.58)	14.2 (3.16)	‡ (†)	-16.7 (4.70)
1993	62.6 (1.59)	62.9 (1.86)	55.6 (5.27)	62.2 (8.21)	86.2 (6.63)	62.1 (0.91)	63.9 (1.04)	51.3 (2.96)	55.7 (4.97)	82.5 (4.30)	12.6 (3.14)	‡ (†)	-18.6 (4.42)
1994	61.9 (1.54)	64.5 (1.74)	50.8 (5.20)	49.1 (9.00)	78.3 (8.55)	62.1 (0.89)	64.0 (1.03)	52.4 (2.97)	55.0 (4.63)	82.2 (4.25)	11.5 (3.14)	‡ (†)	-18.2 (4.37)
1995	61.9 (1.41)	64.3 (1.65)	51.2 (4.22)	53.7 (4.94)	83.0 (6.94)	63.0 (0.81)	65.4 (0.94)	52.9 (2.40)	51.6 (3.19)	82.7 (4.47)	12.5 (2.58)	13.8 (3.33)	-17.3 (4.57)
1996	65.0 (1.42)	67.4 (1.66)	56.0 (4.03)	50.8 (5.79)	85.3 (5.21)	64.7 (0.82)	66.6 (0.97)	55.4 (2.41)	57.6 (2.96)	82.7 (3.59)	11.3 (2.60)	9.0! (3.11)	-16.0 (3.72)
1997	67.0 (1.37)	68.2 (1.64)	58.5 (4.11)	65.6 (4.52)	80.5 (6.09)	65.9 (0.80)	68.1 (0.94)	58.8 (2.35)	55.3 (2.93)	83.0 (3.49)	9.3 (2.53)	12.8 (3.08)	-15.0 (3.62)
1998	65.6 (1.38)	68.5 (1.61)	61.9 (4.04)	47.4 (4.92)	85.5 (5.71)	65.2 (0.80)	67.7 (0.94)	59.8 (2.31)	51.9 (2.79)	83.8 (3.28)	7.9! (2.49)	15.7 (2.94)	-16.1 (3.41)
1999	62.9 (1.38)	66.3 (1.63)	58.9 (3.85)	42.3 (4.76)	78.3 (5.73)	64.0 (0.80)	66.8 (0.94)	58.6 (2.31)	47.4 (2.84)	81.1 (3.40)	8.3! (2.50)	19.5 (2.99)	-14.3 (3.53)
2000	63.3 (1.41)	65.7 (1.66)	54.9 (4.10)	52.9 (5.03)	81.0 (6.29)	62.7 (0.82)	65.4 (0.96)	56.4 (2.33)	48.6 (2.96)	81.3 (3.44)	9.1 (2.52)	16.9 (3.11)	-15.8 (3.57)
2001	61.8 (1.41)	64.3 (1.63)	55.0 (3.96)	51.7 (5.33)	73.8 (8.71)	63.5 (0.78)	66.3 (0.92)	56.4 (2.26)	52.8 (2.78)	78.4 (3.87)	10.0 (2.44)	13.5 (2.93)	-12.0! (3.97)
2002	65.2 (1.31)	69.1 (1.55)	59.4 (3.90)	53.6 (4.46)	63.7 (6.51)	63.7 (0.78)	66.5 (0.92)	57.3 (2.33)	54.8 (2.75)	71.9 (4.05)	9.3 (2.50)	11.7 (2.90)	‡ (†)
2003[6]	63.9 (1.35)	66.2 (1.61)	57.5 (4.25)	58.6 (4.61)	84.1 (5.10)	65.3 (0.77)	68.0 (0.91)	59.9 (2.29)	57.7 (2.66)	74.2 (3.51)	8.1! (2.46)	10.3 (2.81)	‡ (†)
2004[6]	66.7 (1.31)	68.8 (1.57)	62.5 (3.77)	61.8 (4.76)	75.6 (6.13)	66.4 (0.77)	69.4 (0.91)	58.8 (2.34)	57.7 (2.60)	81.6 (3.37)	10.6 (2.51)	11.7 (2.75)	-12.2 (3.49)
2005[6]	68.6 (1.31)	73.2 (1.52)	55.7 (4.15)	54.0 (4.18)	86.7 (5.99)	67.1 (0.76)	70.2 (0.90)	58.2 (2.35)	57.5 (2.52)	80.9 (3.64)	12.0 (2.52)	12.6 (2.67)	-10.7! (3.75)
2006[6]	66.0 (1.33)	68.5 (1.60)	55.5 (4.33)	57.9 (4.18)	82.3 (5.32)	67.2 (0.75)	70.4 (0.89)	55.6 (2.35)	58.5 (2.43)	85.1 (3.64)	14.7 (2.51)	11.9 (2.59)	-14.7 (3.74)
2007[6]	67.2 (1.26)	69.5 (1.49)	55.7 (3.78)	64.0 (4.22)	88.8 (6.26)	67.3 (0.73)	70.0 (0.87)	55.7 (2.27)	62.0 (2.33)	85.8 (3.45)	14.3 (2.43)	8.0! (2.48)	-15.8 (3.56)
2008[6]	68.6 (1.21)	71.7 (1.44)	55.7 (3.78)	63.9 (3.72)	88.4 (5.08)	68.6 (0.71)	70.8 (0.86)	60.3 (2.15)	62.3 (2.25)	90.1 (3.01)	10.5 (2.31)	8.6 (2.41)	-19.2 (3.13)
2009[6]	70.1 (1.23)	71.3 (1.53)	69.5 (3.51)	59.3 (3.80)	92.1 (3.90)	68.9 (0.70)	71.2 (0.86)	62.4 (2.09)	60.9 (2.14)	88.1 (2.85)	8.8 (2.26)	10.3 (2.31)	-16.9 (2.98)
2010[6]	68.1 (1.49)	70.5 (1.68)	62.0 (4.81)	59.7 (4.18)	84.7 (5.27)	68.8 (0.71)	70.1 (0.90)	66.1 (2.01)	62.3 (2.01)	87.4 (2.78)	‡ (†)	7.8 (2.21)	-17.3 (2.92)
2011[6]	68.2 (1.45)	68.3 (1.86)	67.1 (4.01)	66.6 (3.50)	86.1 (4.25)	67.5 (0.89)	68.2 (1.03)	62.1 (2.86)	66.1 (2.17)	83.9 (2.79)	6.1! (3.04)	‡ (†)	-15.7 (2.97)
2012[6]	66.2 (1.59)	65.7 (1.94)	56.4 (4.84)	70.3 (3.22)	81.5 (5.15)	66.8 (0.94)	67.6 (1.12)	60.5 (2.64)	65.9 (1.99)	82.3 (3.59)	7.1! (2.87)	‡ (†)	-14.7 (3.76)
2013[6]	65.9 (1.58)	68.8 (1.90)	56.7 (5.59)	59.8 (3.62)	80.1 (6.52)	66.8 (0.98)	67.4 (1.26)	60.7 (3.09)	65.5 (2.06)	83.6 (3.20)	6.7! (3.34)	‡ (†)	-16.2 (3.44)
2014[6]	68.4 (1.67)	67.7 (2.25)	70.2 (4.56)	65.2 (4.08)	90.9 (3.91)	67.8 (1.00)	69.3 (1.17)	60.6 (3.40)	64.7 (2.16)	84.2 (3.16)	8.8! (3.59)	‡ (†)	-14.9 (3.37)
2015[6]	69.2 (1.54)	71.3 (1.74)	55.6 (5.69)	68.9 (3.64)	83.2 (4.65)	69.1 (1.07)	69.6 (1.32)	60.8 (3.41)	69.0 (2.05)	88.5 (2.48)	8.8! (3.66)	‡ (†)	-18.9 (2.81)
2016[6]	69.8 (1.64)	69.7 (2.34)	57.3 (6.11)	72.0 (3.24)	91.9 (3.65)	68.6 (1.02)	70.1 (1.28)	57.5 (3.44)	67.6 (2.20)	85.7 (2.60)	12.6 (3.67)	‡ (†)	-15.7 (2.90)
2017[6]	66.7 (1.68)	69.1 (2.09)	59.4 (4.79)	61.0 (3.98)	82.7 (5.20)	68.3 (1.22)	69.4 (1.60)	58.4 (3.94)	67.1 (2.69)	87.0 (3.22)	11.0! (4.26)	‡ (†)	-17.6 (3.60)

—Not available.
†Not applicable.
!Interpret data with caution. The coefficient of variation (CV) for this estimate is between 30 and 50 percent.
‡Reporting standards not met. The coefficient of variation (CV) for this estimate is 50 percent or greater.
[1]Individuals ages 16 to 24 who graduated from high school or completed a GED or other high school equivalency credential.
[2]Enrollment in college as of October of each year for individuals ages 16 to 24 who had completed high school earlier in the calendar year.
[3]A 3-year moving average is a weighted average of the year indicated, the year immediately preceding, and the year immediately following. For the first and final years of available data, a 2-year moving average is used: The moving average for 1960 reflects an average of 1960 and 1961; for Black and Hispanic data, the moving average for 1972 reflects an average of 1972 and 1973; for Asian data, the moving average for 2003 reflects an average of 2003 and 2004; and the moving average for 2017 reflects an average of 2016 and 2017. Moving averages are used to produce more stable estimates.
[4]Prior to 2003, Asian data include Pacific Islanders.
[5]Prior to 1972, White data include persons of Hispanic ethnicity.
[6]After 2002, White, Black, and Asian data exclude persons of Two or more races.
NOTE: Data are based on sample surveys of the civilian noninstitutionalized population. Includes enrollment in 2-year colleges and in 4-year colleges and universities. Race categories exclude persons of Hispanic ethnicity except where otherwise noted. Total includes persons of other racial/ethnic groups not separately shown. Prior to 2010, standard errors were computed using generalized variance function methodology rather than the more precise replicate weight methodology used in later years. Some data have been revised from previously published figures.
SOURCE: American College Testing Program, unpublished tabulations, derived from statistics collected by the Census Bureau, 1960 through 1969. U.S. Department of Commerce, Census Bureau, Current Population Survey (CPS), October, 1970 through 2017. (This table was prepared July 2018.)

Table 302.40. Number of high schools with 12th-graders and percentage of high school graduates attending 4-year colleges, by selected high school characteristics: Selected years, 1998–99 through 2011–12

[Standard errors appear in parentheses]

Selected high school characteristic	Number of high schools with 12th-graders				Graduation rate of 12th-graders in 2010–11[1]	Percent of graduates attending 4-year colleges			
	1998–99	2002–03	2006–07	2010–11		1998–99 graduates attending in 1999–2000	2002–03 graduates attending in 2003–04	2006–07 graduates attending in 2007–08	2010–11 graduates attending in 2011–12
1	2	3	4	5	6	7	8	9	10
Public high schools	**20,000 (230)**	**22,500 (400)**	**24,100 (540)**	**23,300 (330)**	**88.7 (0.90)**	**35.4 (0.43)**	**35.0 (0.61)**	**39.5 (0.91)**	**39.4 (0.59)**
Percent of students who are Black, Hispanic, Asian, Pacific Islander, American Indian/Alaska Native, or of Two or more races									
Less than 5 percent	6,400 (170)	6,100 (220)	5,200 (270)	3,600 (140)	94.7 (1.19)	41.3 (0.67)	42.6 (0.96)	46.8 (1.54)	43.9 (1.40)
5 to 19 percent	4,800 (180)	5,200 (270)	5,400 (320)	5,700 (310)	92.4 (2.55)	36.6 (0.88)	38.0 (1.77)	48.4 (2.06)	44.9 (1.02)
20 to 49 percent	4,000 (170)	4,700 (180)	6,200 (440)	5,900 (270)	91.2 (1.14)	32.5 (0.92)	34.1 (1.27)	35.0 (1.89)	39.6 (1.31)
50 percent or more	4,800 (150)	6,500 (280)	7,300 (430)	8,100 (320)	81.7 (1.58)	28.7 (0.89)	25.8 (1.43)	30.8 (2.00)	33.0 (1.17)
Percent of students approved for free or reduced-price lunch									
School does not participate	2,400 (130)	2,400 (230)	2,800 (320)	1,900 (250)	72.8 (7.11)	30.0 (1.75)	23.2 (2.26)	25.4 (4.12)	27.6 (5.24)
0 to 25 percent	8,600 (180)	6,800 (230)	6,700 (360)	5,100 (220)	93.3 (1.02)	42.6 (0.67)	46.9 (0.78)	52.1 (1.63)	50.7 (1.42)
26 to 50 percent	4,800 (160)	6,700 (220)	7,300 (350)	6,800 (230)	92.8 (0.91)	33.4 (0.81)	36.7 (1.08)	41.5 (1.44)	42.5 (1.00)
51 to 75 percent	2,300 (140)	4,000 (270)	4,100 (290)	5,100 (260)	90.3 (1.06)	29.1 (1.57)	27.3 (1.58)	33.2 (1.91)	35.8 (1.35)
76 to 100 percent	2,000 (100)	2,600 (260)	3,300 (360)	4,300 (230)	82.3 (1.93)	22.2 (1.35)	20.7 (2.79)	26.0 (2.93)	29.1 (1.66)
School locale									
City	— (†)	4,500 (240)	4,800 (300)	5,100 (220)	81.3 (3.11)	— (†)	32.5 (1.61)	36.1 (2.73)	38.6 (1.53)
Suburb	— (†)	4,800 (200)	5,400 (360)	4,800 (160)	86.1 (1.50)	— (†)	40.3 (1.11)	41.2 (2.35)	42.2 (1.42)
Town	— (†)	3,700 (200)	3,900 (310)	3,300 (260)	89.9 (2.21)	— (†)	31.1 (1.65)	35.2 (2.28)	35.3 (1.76)
Rural	— (†)	9,500 (390)	10,000 (460)	10,100 (260)	93.4 (0.67)	— (†)	35.2 (1.28)	41.9 (1.47)	39.8 (0.88)
Private high schools	**7,600 (240)**	**8,200 (260)**	**8,900 (280)**	**8,900 (310)**	**92.4 (1.34)**	**55.6 (1.74)**	**56.2 (1.77)**	**66.5 (1.57)**	**64.3 (2.10)**
Percent of students who are Black, Hispanic, Asian, Pacific Islander, American Indian/Alaska Native, or of Two or more races									
Less than 5 percent	2,700 (150)	2,500 (180)	2,100 (160)	1,600 (190)	96.1 (1.72)	53.3 (2.85)	54.4 (3.31)	68.2 (3.81)	58.0 (6.31)
5 to 19 percent	2,500 (130)	2,900 (170)	3,500 (200)	3,100 (230)	95.1 (1.90)	63.6 (2.37)	64.2 (2.71)	70.3 (2.24)	67.9 (3.40)
20 to 49 percent	1,400 (100)	1,700 (140)	2,000 (190)	2,200 (200)	90.4 (2.33)	55.3 (3.29)	56.7 (3.70)	58.7 (3.39)	69.4 (3.89)
50 percent or more	1,000 (110)	1,100 (140)	1,400 (130)	1,900 (190)	87.1 (3.49)	41.6 (5.34)	38.3 (4.52)	65.3 (3.37)	57.6 (5.18)
Percent of students approved for free or reduced-price lunch									
School does not participate	6,700 (230)	7,100 (250)	7,300 (280)	7,400 (280)	93.3 (1.27)	57.0 (1.74)	56.2 (2.00)	68.3 (1.77)	66.5 (2.29)
0 to 25 percent	700 (70)	600 (80)	700 (100)	600 (80)	96.8 (2.45)	53.8 (5.69)	66.2 (4.35)	73.2 (4.64)	74.6 (5.23)
26 to 100 percent	‡ (†)	400 (80)	1,000 (130)	900 (140)	83.0 (5.65)	‡ (†)	38.9 (6.70)	46.7 (6.86)	37.8 (8.06)
School locale									
City	— (†)	— (†)	3,100 (170)	‡ (†)	‡ (†)	— (†)	— (†)	71.8 (2.62)	‡ (†)
Suburb	— (†)	— (†)	2,800 (180)	‡ (†)	‡ (†)	— (†)	— (†)	67.0 (2.99)	‡ (†)
Town	— (†)	— (†)	1,000 (150)	‡ (†)	‡ (†)	— (†)	— (†)	63.8 (5.02)	‡ (†)
Rural	— (†)	— (†)	2,000 (190)	‡ (†)	‡ (†)	— (†)	— (†)	58.9 (3.54)	‡ (†)

—Not available.
†Not applicable.
‡Reporting standards not met. Data may be suppressed because the response rate is under 50 percent, there are too few cases for a reliable estimate, or the coefficient of variation (CV) is 50 percent or greater.
[1] The 12th-grade graduation rate is the number of students who graduated from grade 12 with a diploma during the 2010–11 school year divided by 12th-grade enrollment in October 2010.

NOTE: Data are based on a sample survey and may not be strictly comparable with data reported elsewhere. Includes all schools, including combined schools, with students enrolled in the 12th grade. Some data have been revised from previously published figures. Detail may not sum to totals because of rounding.
SOURCE: U.S. Department of Education, National Center for Education Statistics, Schools and Staffing Survey (SASS), "Public School Teacher Data File" and "Private School Teacher Data File," 1999–2000, 2003–04, 2007–08, and 2011–12; and "Charter School Teacher Data File," 1999–2000. (This table was prepared April 2014.)

Table 302.50. Estimated rate of 2011–12 high school graduates attending degree-granting postsecondary institutions, by state: 2012

State	Number of graduates from high schools located in the state			Number of fall 2012 first-time freshmen graduating from high school in the previous 12 months		Estimated rate of high school graduates going to college	
	Total[1]	Public, 2011–12	Private, 2012–13	State residents enrolled in institutions in any state[2]	State residents enrolled in institutions in their home state[3]	In any state	In their home state
1	2	3	4	5	6	7	8
United States	**3,457,955**	**3,149,185**	**308,770**	**2,132,264** [4]	**1,729,792**	**61.7**	**50.0**
Alabama	50,164	45,394	4,770	29,728	26,567	59.3	53.0
Alaska	8,189	7,989	200	3,732	2,413	45.6	29.5
Arizona	66,218	63,208	3,010	35,181	31,132	53.1	47.0
Arkansas	30,019	28,419	1,600	20,185	18,244	67.2	60.8
California	451,364	418,664	32,700	263,843	231,215	58.5	51.2
Colorado	52,607	50,087	2,520	31,139	23,268	59.2	44.2
Connecticut	44,751	38,681	6,070	31,662	17,396	70.8	38.9
Delaware	10,037	8,247	1,790	6,500	4,632	64.8	46.1
District of Columbia[5]	5,680	3,860	1,820	2,463	450	43.4	7.9
Florida	171,404	151,964	19,440	107,716	94,985	62.8	55.4
Georgia	99,952	90,582	9,370	66,494	55,399	66.5	55.4
Hawaii	13,970	11,360	2,610	9,040	6,091	64.7	43.6
Idaho	18,238	17,568	670	8,782	6,179	48.2	33.9
Illinois	153,605	139,575	14,030	92,394	63,610	60.2	41.4
Indiana	70,767	65,667	5,100	44,612	38,812	63.0	54.8
Iowa	41,550	33,230	2,400	23,488	20,340	56.5	49.0
Kansas	34,078	31,898	2,180	22,239	19,058	65.3	55.9
Kentucky	47,442	42,642	4,800	29,830	26,624	62.9	56.1
Louisiana	44,575	36,675	7,900	28,831	26,024	64.7	58.4
Maine	16,103	13,473	2,630	8,681	5,829	53.9	36.2
Maryland	67,781	58,811	8,970	41,033	25,773	60.5	38.0
Massachusetts	76,177	65,157	11,020	53,836	36,132	70.7	47.4
Michigan	115,256	105,446	9,810	70,843	63,296	61.5	54.9
Minnesota	61,891	57,501	4,390	43,264	30,237	69.9	48.9
Mississippi	29,748	26,158	3,590	23,436	21,752	78.8	73.1
Missouri	69,053	61,313	7,740	42,762	35,648	61.9	51.6
Montana	10,140	9,750	390	5,907	4,598	58.3	45.3
Nebraska	22,844	20,464	2,380	14,750	11,969	64.6	52.4
Nevada	22,731	21,891	840	12,288	9,310	54.1	41.0
New Hampshire	16,886	14,426	2,460	10,418	5,618	61.7	33.3
New Jersey	106,919	93,819	13,100	72,631	41,204	67.9	38.5
New Mexico	21,375	20,315	1,060	14,831	12,903	69.4	60.4
New York	209,216	180,806	28,410	146,458	117,960	70.0	56.4
North Carolina	101,097	93,977	7,120	62,531	55,578	61.9	55.0
North Dakota	7,322	6,942	380	4,751	3,527	64.9	48.2
Ohio	135,885	123,135	12,750	81,428	69,039	59.9	50.8
Oklahoma	39,295	37,305	1,990	22,667	20,207	57.7	51.4
Oregon	37,301	34,261	3,040	17,509	13,343	46.9	35.8
Pennsylvania	146,493	131,733	14,760	87,075	70,625	59.4	48.2
Rhode Island	11,501	9,751	1,750	7,715	5,056	67.1	44.0
South Carolina	44,452	41,442	3,010	29,023	26,154	65.3	58.8
South Dakota	8,456	8,196	260	5,825	4,443	68.9	52.5
Tennessee	67,964	62,454	5,510	41,027	34,318	60.4	50.5
Texas	306,591	292,531	14,060	176,871	156,566	57.7	51.1
Utah	32,757	31,157	1,600	16,650	15,101	50.8	46.1
Vermont	7,789	6,859	930	4,142	2,040	53.2	26.2
Virginia	89,866	83,336	6,530	58,035	47,582	64.6	52.9
Washington	71,165	65,205	5,960	34,168	25,854	48.0	36.3
West Virginia	18,383	17,603	780	10,241	9,110	55.7	49.6
Wisconsin	71,225	62,705	8,520	41,715	33,972	58.6	47.7
Wyoming	5,603	5,553	50	3,170	2,426	56.6	43.3

[1]Total includes public high school graduates for 2011–12 and private high school graduates for 2012–13. Data on private high school graduates are not available for 2011–12.
[2]All U.S. resident students living in a particular state when admitted to an institution in any state. Students may be enrolled in any state.
[3]Students who attend institutions in their home state. Total includes 183 students attending U.S. Service Academies in their home state, not shown separately.
[4]U.S. total includes some U.S. residents whose home state is unknown.
[5]A percentage of the private high school graduates are not residents of the District of Columbia.

NOTE: Degree-granting institutions grant associate's or higher degrees and participate in Title IV federal financial aid programs. Detail may not sum to totals because of rounding.
SOURCE: U.S. Department of Education, National Center for Education Statistics, Common Core of Data (CCD), "NCES Common Core of Data State Dropout and Completion Data File," 2011–12; Private School Universe Survey (PSS), 2013–14; and Integrated Postsecondary Education Data System (IPEDS), Spring 2013, Fall Enrollment component. (This table was prepared January 2016.)

Table 302.60. Percentage of 18- to 24-year-olds enrolled in college, by level of institution and sex and race/ethnicity of student: 1970 through 2017

[Standard errors appear in parentheses]

Year	Total, all students	Level of institution: 2-year college	Level of institution: 4-year college or university	Sex: Male	Sex: Female	Race/ethnicity: White	Race/ethnicity: Black	Race/ethnicity: Hispanic	Race/ethnicity: Asian[1]	Race/ethnicity: Pacific Islander	Race/ethnicity: American Indian/ Alaska Native	Race/ethnicity: Two or more races	White: Male	White: Female	Black: Male	Black: Female	Hispanic: Male	Hispanic: Female
1	2	3	4	5	6	7	8	9	10	11	12	13	14	15	16	17	18	19
1970[2]	25.7 (0.42)	— (†)	— (†)	32.1 (0.67)	20.3 (0.53)	27.1 (0.46)	15.5 (1.18)	— (†)	— (†)	— (†)	— (†)	— (†)	— (†)	— (†)	— (†)	— (†)	— (†)	— (†)
1971[2]	26.2 (0.42)	— (†)	— (†)	32.5 (0.65)	20.8 (0.53)	27.2 (0.45)	18.2 (1.22)	— (†)	— (†)	— (†)	— (†)	— (†)	— (†)	— (†)	— (†)	— (†)	— (†)	— (†)
1972	25.5 (0.40)	— (†)	— (†)	30.2 (0.62)	21.2 (0.52)	27.2 (0.46)	18.3 (1.20)	13.4 (2.42)	— (†)	— (†)	— (†)	— (†)	32.3 (0.69)	22.5 (0.60)	21.1 (1.87)	15.9 (1.55)	15.1 (3.77)	12.0 (3.13)
1973	24.0 (0.39)	6.9 (0.23)	17.1 (0.34)	27.7 (0.59)	20.5 (0.51)	25.5 (0.44)	15.9 (1.11)	16.1 (2.66)	— (†)	— (†)	— (†)	— (†)	29.6 (0.67)	21.8 (0.58)	18.7 (1.75)	13.5 (1.42)	16.7 (3.88)	15.5 (3.66)
1974	24.6 (0.39)	7.6 (0.24)	17.0 (0.34)	27.7 (0.59)	21.7 (0.52)	25.8 (0.44)	17.6 (1.17)	18.0 (2.57)	— (†)	— (†)	— (†)	— (†)	28.9 (0.66)	22.9 (0.59)	19.8 (1.82)	15.9 (1.51)	19.7 (3.85)	16.5 (3.44)
1975	26.3 (0.39)	9.0 (0.26)	17.3 (0.34)	29.0 (0.58)	23.7 (0.53)	27.4 (0.44)	20.4 (1.21)	20.4 (2.75)	— (†)	— (†)	— (†)	— (†)	30.7 (0.66)	24.3 (0.60)	19.9 (1.78)	20.8 (1.65)	21.4 (4.10)	19.5 (3.71)
1976	26.7 (0.39)	6.4 (0.22)	20.2 (0.36)	28.2 (0.57)	25.2 (0.53)	27.6 (0.44)	22.5 (1.23)	20.0 (2.64)	— (†)	— (†)	— (†)	— (†)	29.3 (0.64)	26.1 (0.61)	22.0 (1.82)	22.9 (1.68)	21.3 (4.02)	18.8 (3.48)
1977	26.1 (0.39)	6.8 (0.22)	19.4 (0.35)	28.1 (0.57)	24.3 (0.52)	27.2 (0.44)	21.1 (1.19)	17.2 (2.45)	— (†)	— (†)	— (†)	— (†)	29.4 (0.64)	25.1 (0.60)	20.3 (1.74)	21.9 (1.63)	18.3 (3.66)	16.3 (3.28)
1978	25.3 (0.38)	6.6 (0.22)	18.7 (0.34)	27.1 (0.56)	23.6 (0.52)	26.5 (0.43)	20.1 (1.16)	15.2 (2.28)	— (†)	— (†)	— (†)	— (†)	28.4 (0.63)	24.6 (0.59)	19.7 (1.72)	20.4 (1.57)	16.1 (3.42)	14.3 (3.05)
1979	25.0 (0.38)	6.3 (0.21)	18.7 (0.34)	25.9 (0.55)	24.2 (0.52)	26.3 (0.43)	19.8 (1.14)	16.7 (2.31)	— (†)	— (†)	— (†)	— (†)	27.1 (0.62)	25.5 (0.60)	19.1 (1.69)	20.3 (1.55)	18.3 (3.47)	15.2 (3.08)
1980	25.7 (0.38)	7.1 (0.22)	18.6 (0.34)	26.4 (0.55)	25.0 (0.52)	27.3 (0.44)	19.4 (1.13)	16.1 (2.15)	— (†)	— (†)	— (†)	— (†)	28.4 (0.63)	26.3 (0.60)	17.5 (1.62)	20.9 (1.57)	15.9 (3.05)	16.2 (3.04)
1981	26.1 (0.38)	7.5 (0.22)	18.6 (0.33)	27.1 (0.54)	25.2 (0.52)	27.7 (0.43)	19.9 (1.10)	16.6 (2.14)	— (†)	— (†)	— (†)	— (†)	28.7 (0.62)	26.6 (0.60)	18.9 (1.60)	20.7 (1.52)	16.6 (3.08)	16.7 (2.97)
1982	26.6 (0.40)	7.7 (0.24)	18.9 (0.35)	27.2 (0.58)	26.0 (0.56)	28.1 (0.46)	19.9 (1.16)	16.8 (2.30)	— (†)	— (†)	— (†)	— (†)	28.9 (0.67)	27.4 (0.64)	18.7 (1.66)	21.0 (1.61)	14.9 (3.19)	18.6 (3.29)
1983	26.2 (0.40)	7.4 (0.24)	18.8 (0.36)	27.3 (0.58)	25.1 (0.55)	27.9 (0.47)	19.2 (1.14)	17.3 (2.31)	— (†)	— (†)	— (†)	— (†)	29.4 (0.67)	26.5 (0.64)	18.1 (1.63)	20.1 (1.59)	15.6 (3.21)	18.8 (3.31)
1984	27.1 (0.41)	7.3 (0.24)	19.8 (0.37)	28.6 (0.59)	25.6 (0.56)	28.9 (0.48)	20.3 (1.16)	17.9 (2.35)	— (†)	— (†)	— (†)	— (†)	30.8 (0.69)	27.1 (0.66)	20.3 (1.70)	20.3 (1.60)	16.1 (3.27)	19.6 (3.35)
1985	27.8 (0.42)	7.4 (0.24)	20.4 (0.38)	28.4 (0.60)	27.2 (0.58)	30.0 (0.49)	19.6 (1.17)	16.9 (1.85)	— (†)	— (†)	— (†)	— (†)	30.9 (0.71)	29.2 (0.68)	20.2 (1.74)	19.1 (1.58)	14.9 (2.46)	18.9 (2.75)
1986	27.9 (0.42)	7.6 (0.25)	20.3 (0.38)	28.2 (0.61)	27.6 (0.59)	29.7 (0.50)	21.9 (1.23)	17.6 (1.77)	— (†)	— (†)	— (†)	— (†)	30.6 (0.73)	28.8 (0.69)	20.0 (1.75)	23.4 (1.72)	16.7 (2.37)	18.7 (2.65)
1987	29.6 (0.44)	8.1 (0.26)	21.5 (0.39)	30.6 (0.63)	28.7 (0.60)	31.9 (0.52)	22.8 (1.26)	17.5 (1.74)	— (†)	— (†)	— (†)	— (†)	33.0 (0.75)	30.8 (0.72)	22.6 (1.86)	22.9 (1.72)	18.5 (2.47)	16.5 (2.44)
1988	30.3 (0.48)	8.8 (0.30)	21.5 (0.43)	30.2 (0.69)	30.4 (0.67)	33.2 (0.58)	21.2 (1.35)	17.0 (1.90)	— (†)	— (†)	— (†)	— (†)	33.4 (0.83)	33.0 (0.80)	18.5 (1.90)	23.5 (1.91)	16.5 (2.60)	17.6 (2.77)
1989	30.9 (0.46)	8.0 (0.27)	22.9 (0.42)	30.2 (0.66)	31.6 (0.65)	34.2 (0.56)	23.4 (1.32)	16.1 (1.66)	46.1 (3.77)	— (†)	15.7! (5.13)	— (†)	34.1 (0.80)	34.4 (0.79)	19.7 (1.82)	26.7 (1.89)	14.6 (2.23)	17.6 (2.47)
1990	32.0 (0.47)	8.7 (0.28)	23.3 (0.43)	32.3 (0.68)	31.8 (0.66)	35.1 (0.57)	25.4 (1.37)	15.8 (1.67)	56.9 (3.56)	— (†)	15.8! (5.07)	— (†)	35.5 (0.82)	34.7 (0.80)	26.0 (2.03)	24.8 (1.85)	15.3 (2.31)	16.4 (2.42)
1991	33.3 (0.48)	9.7 (0.30)	23.6 (0.43)	32.8 (0.68)	33.6 (0.67)	36.8 (0.58)	23.5 (1.34)	17.9 (1.72)	57.1 (3.19)	— (†)	15.9! (5.45)	— (†)	36.5 (0.83)	37.0 (0.82)	23.2 (1.95)	23.8 (1.84)	14.0 (2.15)	22.2 (2.70)
1992	34.4 (0.49)	9.9 (0.31)	24.4 (0.44)	32.7 (0.68)	36.0 (0.69)	37.3 (0.59)	25.2 (1.36)	21.3 (1.87)	58.4 (3.27)	— (†)	18.5! (6.17)	— (†)	36.2 (0.83)	38.3 (0.83)	21.3 (1.87)	28.8 (1.96)	17.8 (2.47)	24.7 (2.80)
1993	34.0 (0.49)	9.8 (0.30)	24.2 (0.44)	33.6 (0.69)	34.4 (0.68)	36.8 (0.59)	24.5 (1.35)	21.7 (1.88)	61.2 (3.26)	— (†)	18.9 (5.65)	— (†)	36.5 (0.84)	37.1 (0.83)	22.9 (1.92)	26.0 (1.90)	19.7 (2.59)	23.7 (2.71)
1994	34.6 (0.48)	9.1 (0.29)	25.5 (0.44)	33.1 (0.67)	36.0 (0.68)	38.1 (0.59)	27.7 (1.38)	18.8 (1.58)	62.7 (3.31)	— (†)	29.4 (6.65)	— (†)	37.0 (0.84)	39.2 (0.84)	25.6 (1.95)	29.5 (1.94)	16.5 (2.04)	21.5 (2.44)
1995	34.3 (0.45)	8.9 (0.27)	25.4 (0.41)	33.1 (0.63)	35.5 (0.63)	37.9 (0.55)	27.5 (1.18)	20.7 (1.13)	54.6 (3.11)	— (†)	27.6 (6.16)	— (†)	37.0 (0.78)	38.8 (0.78)	26.0 (1.72)	28.7 (1.63)	18.7 (1.50)	23.0 (1.72)
1996	35.5 (0.47)	9.5 (0.29)	26.1 (0.43)	34.1 (0.66)	37.0 (0.67)	39.5 (0.59)	27.4 (1.23)	20.1 (1.18)	53.9 (2.47)	— (†)	30.3 (5.24)	— (†)	38.3 (0.83)	40.6 (0.84)	25.7 (1.77)	28.8 (1.70)	16.5 (1.52)	24.0 (1.81)
1997	36.8 (0.47)	9.9 (0.29)	27.0 (0.43)	35.0 (0.66)	38.7 (0.67)	40.6 (0.59)	29.8 (1.25)	22.4 (1.21)	55.1 (2.60)	— (†)	27.1 (4.62)	— (†)	39.3 (0.82)	41.8 (0.84)	25.4 (1.75)	33.7 (1.77)	19.2 (1.56)	26.1 (1.88)
1998	36.5 (0.46)	10.2 (0.29)	26.3 (0.42)	34.5 (0.65)	38.6 (0.66)	40.6 (0.59)	29.8 (1.24)	20.4 (1.11)	60.4 (2.49)	— (†)	20.3 (4.90)	— (†)	39.4 (0.82)	41.9 (0.84)	26.1 (1.76)	32.9 (1.73)	16.4 (1.41)	24.9 (1.73)
1999	35.6 (0.46)	9.1 (0.27)	26.5 (0.42)	34.1 (0.64)	37.0 (0.65)	39.4 (0.58)	30.4 (1.24)	18.7 (1.08)	55.7 (2.42)	— (†)	19.5 (4.70)	— (†)	38.3 (0.81)	40.6 (0.82)	28.9 (1.81)	31.6 (1.69)	15.8 (1.41)	21.9 (1.65)
2000	35.5 (0.45)	9.4 (0.27)	26.0 (0.41)	32.6 (0.62)	38.4 (0.65)	38.7 (0.57)	30.5 (1.21)	21.7 (1.12)	55.9 (2.42)	— (†)	15.9 (4.30)	— (†)	36.2 (0.79)	41.3 (0.81)	25.1 (1.67)	35.2 (1.72)	18.5 (1.45)	25.4 (1.71)
2001	36.3 (0.43)	9.8 (0.26)	26.6 (0.39)	33.6 (0.59)	39.0 (0.61)	39.5 (0.54)	31.4 (1.15)	21.7 (1.04)	61.3 (2.23)	— (†)	23.3 (4.07)	— (†)	37.2 (0.75)	41.9 (0.77)	26.7 (1.62)	35.5 (1.62)	17.4 (1.35)	26.1 (1.58)
2002	36.7 (0.43)	9.7 (0.26)	27.0 (0.39)	33.7 (0.59)	39.7 (0.61)	40.9 (0.55)	31.9 (1.18)	19.9 (0.94)	60.9 (2.10)	— (†)	23.6 (3.96)	— (†)	38.9 (0.77)	42.8 (0.78)	26.3 (1.63)	36.9 (1.68)	16.2 (1.17)	24.4 (1.51)
2003[3]	37.8 (0.43)	10.2 (0.27)	27.7 (0.39)	34.3 (0.59)	41.3 (0.61)	41.6 (0.55)	32.3 (1.20)	23.5 (1.02)	61.2 (2.27)	43.3 (9.97)	17.7 (4.45)	41.6 (3.58)	38.5 (0.77)	44.5 (0.78)	28.2 (1.68)	36.0 (1.69)	18.3 (1.27)	29.4 (1.60)
2004[3]	38.0 (0.42)	9.4 (0.25)	28.6 (0.39)	34.7 (0.59)	41.2 (0.61)	41.7 (0.55)	31.8 (1.18)	24.7 (1.02)	60.6 (2.24)	55.8 (8.99)	24.4 (4.52)	36.8 (3.44)	38.4 (0.76)	45.0 (0.78)	26.5 (1.63)	36.6 (1.67)	21.7 (1.33)	28.2 (1.56)
2005[3]	38.9 (0.43)	9.6 (0.26)	29.2 (0.40)	35.3 (0.59)	42.5 (0.61)	42.8 (0.55)	33.1 (1.18)	24.8 (1.02)	61.0 (2.26)	50.6 (10.95)	27.8 (4.88)	41.8 (3.48)	39.4 (0.76)	46.1 (0.79)	28.2 (1.64)	37.6 (1.69)	20.7 (1.31)	29.5 (1.58)
2006[3]	37.3 (0.42)	9.6 (0.25)	27.8 (0.39)	34.1 (0.58)	40.6 (0.60)	41.0 (0.54)	32.6 (1.16)	23.6 (0.99)	58.3 (2.28)	39.1 (8.36)	26.2 (5.18)	38.5 (3.51)	37.9 (0.75)	44.1 (0.78)	28.1 (1.60)	36.9 (1.65)	20.0 (1.29)	27.6 (1.52)
2007[3]	38.8 (0.42)	10.9 (0.27)	27.9 (0.39)	35.5 (0.58)	42.1 (0.60)	42.6 (0.54)	33.1 (1.15)	26.6 (1.02)	57.2 (2.28)	37.1 (9.07)	24.7 (4.63)	39.2 (3.48)	39.6 (0.76)	45.7 (0.78)	32.2 (1.63)	34.0 (1.61)	20.7 (1.29)	33.0 (1.57)
2008[3]	39.6 (0.42)	11.8 (0.28)	27.8 (0.38)	37.0 (0.58)	42.3 (0.60)	44.2 (0.54)	32.1 (1.13)	25.8 (1.01)	59.3 (2.32)	27.3! (8.92)	21.9 (4.22)	45.7 (3.55)	41.7 (0.76)	46.9 (0.78)	29.7 (1.61)	34.2 (1.59)	23.0 (1.35)	28.9 (1.50)
2009[3]	41.3 (0.42)	11.7 (0.27)	29.6 (0.39)	38.4 (0.59)	44.2 (0.60)	45.0 (0.55)	37.7 (1.17)	27.5 (1.01)	65.2 (2.17)	33.4 (7.45)	29.8 (5.10)	39.3 (3.32)	42.3 (0.76)	47.7 (0.78)	33.2 (1.64)	41.9 (1.64)	24.2 (1.35)	31.0 (1.50)
2010[3]	41.2 (0.57)	12.9 (0.36)	28.2 (0.53)	38.3 (0.78)	44.1 (0.84)	43.3 (0.81)	38.4 (1.66)	31.9 (1.15)	63.6 (2.70)	36.0 (8.36)	41.4 (6.60)	38.3 (4.38)	40.6 (1.00)	46.1 (1.17)	35.2 (2.13)	41.4 (2.16)	27.9 (1.57)	36.1 (1.60)
2011[3]	42.0 (0.59)	12.0 (0.35)	30.0 (0.58)	39.1 (0.80)	44.9 (0.80)	44.7 (0.77)	37.1 (1.53)	34.8 (1.20)	60.1 (2.45)	37.8 (7.93)	23.5 (5.30)	38.8 (3.60)	42.4 (0.96)	47.1 (1.08)	34.0 (2.29)	39.9 (1.90)	31.0 (1.63)	39.4 (1.58)
2012[3]	41.0 (0.62)	12.7 (0.38)	28.3 (0.58)	37.6 (0.79)	44.5 (0.86)	42.1 (0.83)	36.4 (1.62)	37.5 (1.18)	59.8 (2.61)	50.3 (9.60)	27.8 (4.43)	39.4 (3.64)	38.3 (1.06)	46.0 (1.08)	33.9 (2.04)	38.7 (2.33)	33.5 (1.58)	41.7 (1.73)
2013[3]	39.9 (0.63)	11.6 (0.36)	28.3 (0.57)	36.6 (0.85)	43.3 (0.80)	41.6 (0.90)	34.2 (1.58)	33.8 (1.24)	62.3 (2.62)	32.9 (8.26)	31.8 (5.58)	44.7 (3.99)	38.1 (1.11)	45.3 (1.11)	30.6 (2.13)	37.6 (2.18)	29.1 (1.72)	38.8 (1.58)
2014[3]	40.0 (0.65)	10.6 (0.40)	29.4 (0.61)	37.3 (0.89)	42.8 (0.79)	42.2 (0.87)	32.6 (1.48)	34.7 (1.21)	65.2 (2.27)	41.0 (11.29)	35.4 (4.63)	31.6 (3.20)	40.2 (1.28)	44.2 (0.99)	28.5 (1.95)	36.6 (2.04)	30.3 (1.65)	39.4 (1.70)
2015[3]	40.5 (0.70)	10.6 (0.35)	29.9 (0.69)	37.8 (0.91)	43.2 (0.93)	41.8 (0.88)	34.9 (1.54)	36.6 (1.31)	62.6 (2.65)	24.1! (7.29)	23.0 (4.45)	38.3 (3.86)	39.1 (1.16)	44.5 (1.10)	34.1 (2.21)	35.7 (2.17)	32.8 (1.76)	40.5 (1.91)
2016[3]	41.2 (0.71)	10.1 (0.36)	31.1 (0.64)	38.6 (0.83)	43.9 (0.91)	42.1 (0.88)	36.2 (1.69)	39.2 (1.28)	57.6 (2.17)	20.7! (8.02)	18.6 (3.72)	42.3 (3.64)	39.8 (1.09)	44.5 (1.12)	33.0 (2.18)	39.4 (2.51)	34.9 (1.67)	43.6 (1.76)
2017[3]	40.4 (0.66)	10.0 (0.37)	30.4 (0.64)	36.8 (0.84)	44.0 (0.91)	41.0 (0.76)	36.5 (1.71)	36.2 (1.50)	64.7 (2.49)	32.6! (10.94)	20.1 (4.47)	41.5 (3.66)	37.8 (1.05)	44.4 (1.12)	33.1 (2.45)	39.6 (2.18)	31.1 (1.82)	41.4 (2.02)

—Not available.
†Not applicable.
!Interpret data with caution. The coefficient of variation (CV) for this estimate is between 30 and 50 percent.
[1]Prior to 2003, Asian data include Pacific Islanders.
[2]Prior to 1972, White and Black data include persons of Hispanic ethnicity.
[3]After 2002, data for individual race categories exclude persons of Two or more races.

NOTE: Data are based on sample surveys of the civilian noninstitutionalized population. Totals include other racial/ethnic groups not separately shown. Race categories exclude persons of Hispanic ethnicity except where otherwise noted. Prior to 2010, standard errors were computed using generalized variance function methodology rather than the more precise replicate weight methodology used in later years.
SOURCE: U.S. Department of Commerce, Census Bureau, Current Population Survey (CPS), October, 1970 through 2017. (This table was prepared July 2018.)

Table 303.10. Total fall enrollment in degree-granting postsecondary institutions, by attendance status, sex of student, and control of institution: Selected years, 1947 through 2028

Year	Total enrollment	Attendance status			Sex of student			Control of institution			
									Private		
		Full-time	Part-time	Percent part-time	Male	Female	Percent female	Public	Total	Nonprofit	For-profit
1	2	3	4	5	6	7	8	9	10	11	12
1947[1]	2,338,226	—	—	—	1,659,249	678,977	29.0	1,152,377	1,185,849	—	—
1948[1]	2,403,396	—	—	—	1,709,367	694,029	28.9	1,185,588	1,217,808	—	—
1949[1]	2,444,900	—	—	—	1,721,572	723,328	29.6	1,207,151	1,237,749	—	—
1950[1]	2,281,298	—	—	—	1,560,392	720,906	31.6	1,139,699	1,141,599	—	—
1951[1]	2,101,962	—	—	—	1,390,740	711,222	33.8	1,037,938	1,064,024	—	—
1952[1]	2,134,242	—	—	—	1,380,357	753,885	35.3	1,101,240	1,033,002	—	—
1953[1]	2,231,054	—	—	—	1,422,598	808,456	36.2	1,185,876	1,045,178	—	—
1954[1]	2,446,693	—	—	—	1,563,382	883,311	36.1	1,353,531	1,093,162	—	—
1955[1]	2,653,034	—	—	—	1,733,184	919,850	34.7	1,476,282	1,176,752	—	—
1956[1]	2,918,212	—	—	—	1,911,458	1,006,754	34.5	1,656,402	1,261,810	—	—
1957	3,323,783	—	—	—	2,170,765	1,153,018	34.7	1,972,673	1,351,110	—	—
1959	3,639,847	2,421,016	1,218,831[2]	33.5	2,332,617	1,307,230	35.9	2,180,982	1,458,865	—	—
1961	4,145,065	2,785,133	1,359,932[2]	32.8	2,585,821	1,559,244	37.6	2,561,447	1,583,618	—	—
1963	4,779,609	3,183,833	1,595,776[2]	33.4	2,961,540	1,818,069	38.0	3,081,279	1,698,330	—	—
1964	5,280,020	3,573,238	1,706,782[2]	32.3	3,248,713	2,031,307	38.5	3,467,708	1,812,312	—	—
1965	5,920,864	4,095,728	1,825,136[2]	30.8	3,630,020	2,290,844	38.7	3,969,596	1,951,268	—	—
1966	6,389,872	4,438,606	1,951,266[2]	30.5	3,856,216	2,533,656	39.7	4,348,917	2,040,955	—	—
1967	6,911,748	4,793,128	2,118,620[2]	30.7	4,132,800	2,778,948	40.2	4,816,028	2,095,720	2,074,041	21,679
1968	7,513,091	5,210,155	2,302,936	30.7	4,477,649	3,035,442	40.4	5,430,652	2,082,439	2,061,211	21,228
1969	8,004,660	5,498,883	2,505,777	31.3	4,746,201	3,258,459	40.7	5,896,868	2,107,792	2,087,653	20,139
1970	8,580,887	5,816,290	2,764,597	32.2	5,043,642	3,537,245	41.2	6,428,134	2,152,753	2,134,420	18,333
1971	8,948,644	6,077,232	2,871,412	32.1	5,207,004	3,741,640	41.8	6,804,309	2,144,335	2,121,913	22,422
1972	9,214,860	6,072,389	3,142,471	34.1	5,238,757	3,976,103	43.1	7,070,635	2,144,225	2,123,245	20,980
1973	9,602,123	6,189,493	3,412,630	35.5	5,371,052	4,231,071	44.1	7,419,516	2,182,607	2,148,784	33,823
1974	10,223,729	6,370,273	3,853,456	37.7	5,622,429	4,601,300	45.0	7,988,500	2,235,229	2,200,963	34,266
1975	11,184,859	6,841,334	4,343,525	38.8	6,148,997	5,035,862	45.0	8,834,508	2,350,351	2,311,448	38,903
1976	11,012,137	6,717,058	4,295,079	39.0	5,810,828	5,201,309	47.2	8,653,477	2,358,660	2,314,298	44,362
1977	11,285,787	6,792,925	4,492,862	39.8	5,789,016	5,496,771	48.7	8,846,993	2,438,794	2,386,652	52,142
1978	11,260,092	6,667,657	4,592,435	40.8	5,640,998	5,619,094	49.9	8,785,893	2,474,199	2,408,331	65,868
1979	11,569,899	6,794,039	4,775,860	41.3	5,682,877	5,887,022	50.9	9,036,822	2,533,077	2,461,773	71,304
1980	12,096,895	7,097,958	4,998,937	41.3	5,874,374	6,222,521	51.4	9,457,394	2,639,501	2,527,787	111,714[3]
1981	12,371,672	7,181,250	5,190,422	42.0	5,975,056	6,396,616	51.7	9,647,032	2,724,640	2,572,405	152,235[3]
1982	12,425,780	7,220,618	5,205,162	41.9	6,031,384	6,394,396	51.5	9,696,087	2,729,693	2,552,739	176,954[3]
1983	12,464,661	7,261,050	5,203,611	41.7	6,023,725	6,440,936	51.7	9,682,734	2,781,927	2,589,187	192,740
1984	12,241,940	7,098,388	5,143,552	42.0	5,863,574	6,378,366	52.1	9,477,370	2,764,570	2,574,419	190,151
1985	12,247,055	7,075,221	5,171,834	42.2	5,818,450	6,428,605	52.5	9,479,273	2,767,782	2,571,791	195,991
1986	12,503,511	7,119,550	5,383,961	43.1	5,884,515	6,618,996	52.9	9,713,893	2,789,618	2,572,479	217,139[4]
1987	12,766,642	7,231,085	5,535,557	43.4	5,932,056	6,834,586	53.5	9,973,254	2,793,388	2,602,350	191,038[4]
1988	13,055,337	7,436,768	5,618,569	43.0	6,001,896	7,053,441	54.0	10,161,388	2,893,949	2,673,567	220,382
1989	13,538,560	7,660,950	5,877,610	43.4	6,190,015	7,348,545	54.3	10,577,963	2,960,597	2,731,174	229,423
1990	13,818,637	7,820,985	5,997,652	43.4	6,283,909	7,534,728	54.5	10,844,717	2,973,920	2,760,227	213,693
1991	14,358,953	8,115,329	6,243,624	43.5	6,501,844	7,857,109	54.7	11,309,563	3,049,390	2,819,041	230,349
1992	14,487,359	8,162,118	6,325,241	43.7	6,523,989	7,963,370	55.0	11,384,567	3,102,792	2,872,523	230,269
1993	14,304,803	8,127,618	6,177,185	43.2	6,427,450	7,877,353	55.1	11,189,088	3,115,715	2,888,897	226,818
1994	14,278,790	8,137,776	6,141,014	43.0	6,371,898	7,906,892	55.4	11,133,680	3,145,110	2,910,107	235,003
1995	14,261,781	8,128,802	6,132,979	43.0	6,342,539	7,919,242	55.5	11,092,374	3,169,407	2,929,044	240,363
1996	14,367,520	8,302,953	6,064,567	42.2	6,352,825	8,014,695	55.8	11,120,499	3,247,021	2,942,556	304,465
1997	14,502,334	8,438,062	6,064,272	41.8	6,396,028	8,106,306	55.9	11,196,119	3,306,215	2,977,614	328,601
1998	14,506,967	8,563,338	5,943,629	41.0	6,369,265	8,137,702	56.1	11,137,769	3,369,198	3,004,925	364,273
1999	14,849,691	8,803,139	6,046,552	40.7	6,515,164	8,334,527	56.1	11,375,739	3,473,952	3,055,029	418,923
2000	15,312,289	9,009,600	6,302,689	41.2	6,721,769	8,590,520	56.1	11,752,786	3,559,503	3,109,419	450,084
2001	15,927,987	9,447,502	6,480,485	40.7	6,960,815	8,967,172	56.3	12,233,156	3,694,831	3,167,330	527,501
2002	16,611,711	9,946,359	6,665,352	40.1	7,202,116	9,409,595	56.6	12,751,993	3,859,718	3,265,476	594,242
2003	16,911,481	10,326,133	6,585,348	38.9	7,260,264	9,651,217	57.1	12,858,698	4,052,783	3,341,048	711,735
2004	17,272,044	10,610,177	6,661,867	38.6	7,387,262	9,884,782	57.2	12,980,112	4,291,932	3,411,685	880,247
2005	17,487,475	10,797,011	6,690,464	38.3	7,455,925	10,031,550	57.4	13,021,834	4,465,641	3,454,692	1,010,949
2006	17,754,230	10,957,538	6,796,692	38.3	7,572,265	10,181,965	57.3	13,175,350	4,578,880	3,512,929	1,065,951
2007	18,258,138	11,270,929	6,987,209	38.3	7,819,938	10,438,200	57.2	13,500,894	4,757,244	3,571,395	1,185,849
2008	19,081,686	11,734,636	7,347,050	38.5	8,177,714	10,903,972	57.1	13,970,862	5,110,824	3,660,827	1,449,997
2009	20,313,594	12,605,355	7,708,239	37.9	8,732,953	11,580,641	57.0	14,810,768	5,502,826	3,767,672	1,735,154
2010	21,019,438	13,087,182	7,932,256	37.7	9,045,759	11,973,679	57.0	15,142,171	5,877,267	3,854,482	2,022,785
2011	21,010,590	13,002,531	8,008,059	38.1	9,034,256	11,976,334	57.0	15,116,303	5,894,287	3,926,819	1,967,468
2012	20,644,478	12,734,404	7,910,074	38.3	8,919,006	11,725,472	56.8	14,884,667	5,759,811	3,951,388	1,808,423
2013	20,376,677	12,596,610	7,780,067	38.2	8,861,197	11,515,480	56.5	14,746,848	5,629,829	3,971,390	1,658,439
2014	20,209,092	12,454,464	7,754,628	38.4	8,797,530	11,411,562	56.5	14,654,660	5,554,432	3,997,249	1,557,183

See notes at end of table.

Table 303.10. Total fall enrollment in degree-granting postsecondary institutions, by attendance status, sex of student, and control of institution: Selected years, 1947 through 2028—Continued

Year	Total enrollment	Attendance status			Sex of student			Control of institution			
									Private		
		Full-time	Part-time	Percent part-time	Male	Female	Percent female	Public	Total	Nonprofit	For-profit
1	2	3	4	5	6	7	8	9	10	11	12
2015	19,988,204	12,287,512	7,700,692	38.5	8,723,819	11,264,385	56.4	14,572,843	5,415,361	4,065,891	1,349,470
2016	19,846,904	12,125,314	7,721,590	38.9	8,638,422	11,208,482	56.5	14,585,840	5,261,064	4,078,956	1,182,108
2017	19,765,598	12,077,304	7,688,294	38.9	8,567,632	11,197,966	56.7	14,560,155	5,205,443	4,106,477	1,098,966
2018[5]	19,828,000	12,103,000	7,725,000	39.0	8,596,000	11,232,000	56.6	14,608,000	5,220,000	—	—
2019[5]	19,904,000	12,135,000	7,768,000	39.0	8,628,000	11,276,000	56.7	14,665,000	5,239,000	—	—
2020[5]	19,928,000	12,133,000	7,795,000	39.1	8,637,000	11,291,000	56.7	14,685,000	5,243,000	—	—
2021[5]	19,956,000	12,129,000	7,828,000	39.2	8,644,000	11,312,000	56.7	14,708,000	5,248,000	—	—
2022[5]	19,991,000	12,131,000	7,860,000	39.3	8,656,000	11,335,000	56.7	14,736,000	5,255,000	—	—
2023[5]	20,040,000	12,145,000	7,895,000	39.4	8,676,000	11,364,000	56.7	14,774,000	5,266,000	—	—
2024[5]	20,107,000	12,178,000	7,929,000	39.4	8,703,000	11,404,000	56.7	14,824,000	5,283,000	—	—
2025[5]	20,177,000	12,220,000	7,957,000	39.4	8,733,000	11,444,000	56.7	14,876,000	5,301,000	—	—
2026[5]	20,258,000	12,264,000	7,994,000	39.5	8,770,000	11,488,000	56.7	14,936,000	5,321,000	—	—
2027[5]	20,295,000	12,272,000	8,023,000	39.5	8,788,000	11,507,000	56.7	14,965,000	5,329,000	—	—
2028[5]	20,305,000	12,261,000	8,044,000	39.6	8,792,000	11,513,000	56.7	14,975,000	5,330,000	—	—

—Not available.
[1]Degree-credit enrollment only.
[2]Includes part-time resident students and all extension students (students attending courses at sites separate from the primary reporting campus). In later years, part-time student enrollment was collected as a distinct category.
[3]Large increases are due to the addition of schools accredited by the Accrediting Commission of Career Schools and Colleges of Technology.
[4]Because of imputation techniques, data are not consistent with figures for other years.
[5]Projected.
NOTE: Data through 1995 are for institutions of higher education, while later data are for degree-granting institutions. Degree-granting institutions grant associate's or higher degrees and participate in Title IV federal financial aid programs. The degree-granting classification is very similar to the earlier higher education classification, but it includes more 2-year colleges and excludes a few higher education institutions that did not grant degrees. Some data have been revised from previously published figures.
SOURCE: U.S. Department of Education, National Center for Education Statistics, *Biennial Survey of Education in the United States; Opening Fall Enrollment in Higher Education*, 1963 through 1965; Higher Education General Information Survey (HEGIS), "Fall Enrollment in Colleges and Universities" surveys, 1966 through 1985; Integrated Postsecondary Education Data System (IPEDS), "Fall Enrollment Survey" (IPEDS-EF:86–99); IPEDS Spring 2001 through Spring 2018, Fall Enrollment component; and Enrollment in Degree-Granting Institutions Projection Model, 2000 through 2028. (This table was prepared March 2019.)

Table 303.20. Total fall enrollment in all postsecondary institutions participating in Title IV programs and annual percentage change in enrollment, by degree-granting status and control of institution: 1995 through 2017

Year	All Title IV institutions[1]				Degree-granting institutions[2]					Non-degree-granting institutions[3]			
			Private				Private					Private	
	Total	Public	Nonprofit	For-profit	Total	Public	Total	Nonprofit	For-profit	Total	Public	Nonprofit	For-profit
1	2	3	4	5	6	7	8	9	10	11	12	13	14
							Enrollment						
1995	14,836,338	11,312,491	2,977,794	546,053	14,261,781	11,092,374	3,169,407	2,929,044	240,363	574,557	220,117	48,750	305,690
1996	14,809,897	11,312,775	2,976,850	520,272	14,367,520	11,120,499	3,247,021	2,942,556	304,465	442,377	192,276	34,294	215,807
1997	14,900,416	11,370,755	3,012,106	517,555	14,502,334	11,196,119	3,306,215	2,977,614	328,601	398,082	174,636	34,492	188,954
1998	14,923,839	11,330,811	3,040,251	552,777	14,506,967	11,137,769	3,369,198	3,004,925	364,273	416,872	193,042	35,326	188,504
1999	15,262,888	11,556,731	3,088,233	617,924	14,849,691	11,375,739	3,473,952	3,055,029	418,923	413,197	180,992	33,204	199,001
2000	15,701,409	11,891,450	3,137,108	672,851	15,312,289	11,752,786	3,559,503	3,109,419	450,084	389,120	138,664	27,689	222,767
2001	16,334,134	12,370,079	3,198,354	765,701	15,927,987	12,233,156	3,694,831	3,167,330	527,501	406,147	136,923	31,024	238,200
2002	17,035,027	12,883,071	3,299,094	852,862	16,611,711	12,751,993	3,859,718	3,265,476	594,242	423,316	131,078	33,618	258,620
2003	17,330,775	12,965,502	3,372,647	992,626	16,911,481	12,858,698	4,052,783	3,341,048	711,735	419,294	106,804	31,599	280,891
2004	17,710,798	13,081,358	3,440,559	1,188,881	17,272,044	12,980,112	4,291,932	3,411,685	880,247	438,754	101,246	28,874	308,634
2005	17,921,804	13,115,177	3,484,013	1,322,614	17,487,475	13,021,834	4,465,641	3,454,692	1,010,949	434,329	93,343	29,321	311,665
2006	18,198,370	13,276,881	3,543,064	1,378,425	17,754,230	13,175,350	4,578,880	3,512,929	1,065,951	444,140	101,531	30,135	312,474
2007	18,677,469	13,603,772	3,595,466	1,478,231	18,258,138	13,500,894	4,757,244	3,571,395	1,185,849	419,331	102,878	24,071	292,382
2008	19,553,784	14,090,863	3,684,190	1,778,731	19,081,686	13,970,862	5,110,824	3,660,827	1,449,997	472,098	120,001	23,363	328,734
2009	20,853,423	14,936,402	3,793,751	2,123,270	20,313,594	14,810,768	5,502,826	3,767,672	1,735,154	539,829	125,634	26,079	388,116
2010	21,591,742	15,279,455	3,881,630	2,430,657	21,019,438	15,142,171	5,877,267	3,854,482	2,022,785	572,304	137,284	27,148	407,872
2011	21,573,798	15,251,185	3,954,173	2,368,440	21,010,590	15,116,303	5,894,287	3,926,819	1,967,468	563,208	134,882	27,354	400,972
2012	21,148,181	15,000,302	3,973,422	2,174,457	20,644,478	14,884,667	5,759,811	3,951,388	1,808,423	503,703	115,635	22,034	366,034
2013	20,848,050	14,856,309	3,990,858	2,000,883	20,376,677	14,746,848	5,629,829	3,971,390	1,658,439	471,373	109,461	19,468	342,444
2014	20,664,180	14,764,741	4,016,240	1,883,199	20,209,092	14,654,660	5,554,432	3,997,249	1,557,183	455,088	110,081	18,991	326,016
2015	20,400,164	14,682,321	4,088,450	1,629,393	19,988,204	14,572,843	5,415,361	4,065,891	1,349,470	411,960	109,478	22,559	279,923
2016	20,230,012	14,695,538	4,097,022	1,437,452	19,846,904	14,585,840	5,261,064	4,078,956	1,182,108	383,108	109,698	18,066	255,344
2017	20,138,477	14,669,554	4,123,290	1,345,633	19,765,598	14,560,155	5,205,443	4,106,477	1,098,966	372,879	109,399	16,813	246,667
							Annual percentage change						
1995 to 1996	-0.2	#	#	-4.7	0.7	0.3	2.4	0.5	26.7	-23.0	-12.6	-29.7	-29.4
1996 to 1997	0.6	0.5	1.2	-0.5	0.9	0.7	1.8	1.2	7.9	-10.0	-9.2	0.6	-12.4
1997 to 1998	0.2	-0.4	0.9	6.8	#	-0.5	1.9	0.9	10.9	4.7	10.5	2.4	-0.2
1998 to 1999	2.3	2.0	1.6	11.8	2.4	2.1	3.1	1.7	15.0	-0.9	-6.2	-6.0	5.6
1999 to 2000	2.9	2.9	1.6	8.9	3.1	3.3	2.5	1.8	7.4	-5.8	-23.4	-16.6	11.9
2000 to 2001	4.0	4.0	2.0	13.8	4.0	4.1	3.8	1.9	17.2	4.4	-1.3	12.0	6.9
2001 to 2002	4.3	4.1	3.1	11.4	4.3	4.2	4.5	3.1	12.7	4.2	-4.3	8.4	8.6
2002 to 2003	1.7	0.6	2.2	16.4	1.8	0.8	5.0	2.3	19.8	-1.0	-18.5	-6.0	8.6
2003 to 2004	2.2	0.9	2.0	19.8	2.1	0.9	5.9	2.1	23.7	4.6	-5.2	-8.6	9.9
2004 to 2005	1.2	0.3	1.3	11.2	1.2	0.3	4.0	1.3	14.8	-1.0	-7.8	1.5	1.0
2005 to 2006	1.5	1.2	1.7	4.2	1.5	1.2	2.5	1.7	5.4	2.3	8.8	2.8	0.3
2006 to 2007	2.6	2.5	1.5	7.2	2.8	2.5	3.9	1.7	11.2	-5.6	1.3	-20.1	-6.4
2007 to 2008	4.7	3.6	2.5	20.3	4.5	3.5	7.4	2.5	22.3	12.6	16.6	-2.9	12.4
2008 to 2009	6.6	6.0	3.0	19.4	6.5	6.0	7.7	2.9	19.7	14.3	4.7	11.6	18.1
2009 to 2010	3.5	2.3	2.3	14.5	3.5	2.2	6.8	2.3	16.6	6.0	9.3	4.1	5.1
2010 to 2011	-0.1	-0.2	1.9	-2.6	#	-0.2	0.3	1.9	-2.7	-1.6	-1.7	0.8	-1.7
2011 to 2012	-2.0	-1.6	0.5	-8.2	-1.7	-1.5	-2.3	0.6	-8.1	-10.6	-14.3	-19.4	-8.7
2012 to 2013	-1.4	-1.0	0.4	-8.0	-1.3	-0.9	-2.3	0.5	-8.3	-6.4	-5.3	-11.6	-6.4
2013 to 2014	-0.9	-0.6	0.6	-5.9	-0.8	-0.6	-1.3	0.7	-6.1	-3.5	0.6	-2.5	-4.8
2014 to 2015	-1.3	-0.6	1.8	-13.5	-1.1	-0.6	-2.5	1.7	-13.3	-9.5	-0.5	18.8	-14.1
2015 to 2016	-0.8	0.1	0.2	-11.8	-0.7	0.1	-2.8	0.3	-12.4	-7.0	0.2	-19.9	-8.8
2016 to 2017	-0.5	-0.2	0.6	-6.4	-0.4	-0.2	-1.1	0.7	-7.0	-2.7	-0.3	-6.9	-3.4

#Rounds to zero.
[1]Includes degree-granting and non-degree-granting institutions.
[2]Data for 1995 are for institutions of higher education, while later data are for degree-granting institutions. Degree-granting institutions grant associate's or higher degrees and participate in Title IV federal financial aid programs. The degree-granting classification is very similar to the earlier higher education classification, but it includes more 2-year colleges and excludes a few higher education institutions that did not grant degrees.
[3]Data are for institutions that did not offer accredited 4-year or 2-year programs, but were participating in Title IV federal financial aid programs. Includes some institutions transitioning to higher level program offerings, though still classified at a lower level.
NOTE: Some data have been revised from previously published figures.
SOURCE: U.S. Department of Education, National Center for Education Statistics, Integrated Postsecondary Education Data System (IPEDS), "Fall Enrollment Survey" (IPEDS-EF:95–99); and IPEDS Spring 2001 through Spring 2018, Fall Enrollment component. (This table was prepared October 2018.)

Table 303.25. Total fall enrollment in degree-granting postsecondary institutions, by control and level of institution: 1970 through 2017

Year	All institutions			Public institutions			Private institutions								
							All private institutions			Nonprofit			For-profit		
	Total	4-year	2-year	Total	4-year	2-year	Total	4-year	2-year	Total	4-year	2-year	Total	4-year	2-year
1	2	3	4	5	6	7	8	9	10	11	12	13	14	15	16
1970	8,580,887	6,261,502	2,319,385	6,428,134	4,232,722	2,195,412	2,152,753	2,028,780	123,973	2,134,420	2,021,121	113,299	18,333	7,659	10,674
1971	8,948,644	6,369,355	2,579,289	6,804,309	4,346,990	2,457,319	2,144,335	2,022,365	121,970	2,121,913	2,011,682	110,231	22,422	10,683	11,739
1972	9,214,860	6,458,674	2,756,186	7,070,635	4,429,696	2,640,939	2,144,225	2,028,978	115,247	2,123,245	2,019,380	103,865	20,980	9,598	11,382
1973	9,602,123	6,590,023	3,012,100	7,419,516	4,529,895	2,889,621	2,182,607	2,060,128	122,479	2,148,784	2,045,804	102,980	33,823	14,324	19,499
1974	10,223,729	6,819,735	3,403,994	7,988,500	4,703,018	3,285,482	2,235,229	2,116,717	118,512	2,200,963	2,098,599	102,364	34,266	18,118	16,148
1975	11,184,859	7,214,740	3,970,119	8,834,508	4,998,142	3,836,366	2,350,351	2,216,598	133,753	2,311,448	2,198,451	112,997	38,903	18,147	20,756
1976	11,012,137	7,128,816	3,883,321	8,653,477	4,901,691	3,751,786	2,358,660	2,227,125	131,535	2,314,298	2,206,457	107,841	44,362	20,668	23,694
1977	11,285,787	7,242,845	4,042,942	8,846,993	4,945,224	3,901,769	2,438,794	2,297,621	141,173	2,386,652	2,277,072	109,580	52,142	20,549	31,593
1978	11,260,092	7,231,625	4,028,467	8,785,893	4,912,203	3,873,690	2,474,199	2,319,422	154,777	2,408,331	2,299,132	109,199	65,868	20,290	45,578
1979	11,569,899	7,353,233	4,216,666	9,036,822	4,980,012	4,056,810	2,533,077	2,373,221	159,856	2,461,773	2,351,364	110,409	71,304	21,857	49,447
1980	12,096,895	7,570,608	4,526,287	9,457,394	5,128,612	4,328,782	2,639,501	2,441,996	197,505[1]	2,527,787	2,413,693	114,094	111,714	28,303	83,411[1]
1981	12,371,672	7,655,461	4,716,211	9,647,032	5,166,324	4,480,708	2,724,640	2,489,137	235,503[1]	2,572,405	2,453,239	119,166	152,235	35,898	116,337[1]
1982	12,425,780	7,654,074	4,771,706	9,696,087	5,176,434	4,519,653	2,729,693	2,477,640	252,053[1]	2,552,739	2,437,763	114,976	176,954	39,877	137,077[1]
1983	12,464,661	7,741,195	4,723,466	9,682,734	5,223,404	4,459,330	2,781,927	2,517,791	264,136	2,589,187	2,472,894	116,293	192,740	44,897	147,843
1984	12,241,940	7,711,167	4,530,773	9,477,370	5,198,273	4,279,097	2,764,570	2,512,894	251,676	2,574,419	2,466,172	108,247	190,151	46,722	143,429
1985	12,247,055	7,715,978	4,531,077	9,479,273	5,209,540	4,269,733	2,767,782	2,506,438	261,344	2,571,791	2,463,000	108,791	195,991	43,438	152,553
1986	12,503,511	7,823,963	4,679,548	9,713,893	5,300,202	4,413,691	2,789,618	2,523,761	265,857[2]	2,572,479	2,470,981	101,498	217,139	52,780	164,359[2]
1987	12,766,642	7,990,420	4,776,222	9,973,254	5,432,200	4,541,054	2,793,388	2,558,220	235,168[2]	2,602,350	2,512,248	90,102	191,038	45,972	145,066[2]
1988	13,055,337	8,180,182	4,875,155	10,161,388	5,545,901	4,615,487	2,893,949	2,634,281	259,668	—	—	—	—	—	—
1989	13,538,560	8,387,671	5,150,889	10,577,963	5,694,303	4,883,660	2,960,597	2,693,368	267,229	—	—	—	—	—	—
1990	13,818,637	8,578,554	5,240,083	10,844,717	5,848,242	4,996,475	2,973,920	2,730,312	243,608	2,760,227	2,671,069	89,158	213,693	59,243	154,450
1991	14,358,953	8,707,053	5,651,900	11,309,563	5,904,748	5,404,815	3,049,390	2,802,305	247,085	2,819,041	2,729,752	89,289	230,349	72,553	157,796
1992	14,487,359	8,764,969	5,722,390	11,384,567	5,900,012	5,484,555	3,102,792	2,864,957	237,835	2,872,523	2,789,235	83,288	230,269	75,722	154,547
1993	14,304,803	8,738,936	5,565,867	11,189,088	5,851,760	5,337,328	3,115,715	2,887,176	228,539	2,888,897	2,802,540	86,357	226,818	84,636	142,182
1994	14,278,790	8,749,080	5,529,710	11,133,680	5,825,213	5,308,467	3,145,110	2,923,867	221,243	2,910,107	2,824,500	85,607	235,003	99,367	135,636
1995	14,261,781	8,769,252	5,492,529	11,092,374	5,814,545	5,277,829	3,169,407	2,954,707	214,700	2,929,044	2,853,890	75,154	240,363	100,817	139,546
1996	14,367,520	8,804,193	5,563,327	11,120,499	5,806,036	5,314,463	3,247,021	2,998,157	248,864	2,942,556	2,867,181	75,375	304,465	130,976	173,489
1997	14,502,334	8,896,765	5,605,569	11,196,119	5,835,433	5,360,686	3,306,215	3,061,332	244,883	2,977,614	2,905,820	71,794	328,601	155,512	173,089
1998	14,506,967	9,017,653	5,489,314	11,137,769	5,891,806	5,245,963	3,369,198	3,125,847	243,351	3,004,925	2,939,055	65,870	364,273	186,792	177,481
1999	14,849,691	9,196,160	5,653,531	11,375,739	5,977,678	5,398,061	3,473,952	3,218,482	255,470	3,055,029	2,991,728	63,301	418,923	226,754	192,169
2000	15,312,289	9,363,858	5,948,431	11,752,786	6,055,398	5,697,388	3,559,503	3,308,460	251,043	3,109,419	3,050,575	58,844	450,084	257,885	192,199
2001	15,927,987	9,677,408	6,250,579	12,233,156	6,236,455	5,996,701	3,694,831	3,440,953	253,878	3,167,330	3,119,781	47,549	527,501	321,172	206,329
2002	16,611,711	10,082,332	6,529,379	12,751,993	6,481,613	6,270,380	3,859,718	3,600,719	258,999	3,265,476	3,218,389	47,087	594,242	382,330	211,912
2003	16,911,481	10,417,247	6,494,234	12,858,698	6,649,441	6,209,257	4,052,783	3,767,806	284,977	3,341,048	3,297,180	43,868	711,735	470,626	241,109
2004	17,272,044	10,726,181	6,545,863	12,980,112	6,736,536	6,243,576	4,291,932	3,989,645	302,287	3,411,685	3,369,435	42,250	880,247	620,210	260,037
2005	17,487,475	10,999,420	6,488,055	13,021,834	6,837,605	6,184,229	4,465,641	4,161,815	303,826	3,454,692	3,411,170	43,522	1,010,949	750,645	260,304
2006	17,754,230	11,240,678	6,513,552	13,175,350	6,955,221	6,220,129	4,578,880	4,285,457	293,423	3,512,929	3,473,773	39,156	1,065,951	811,684	254,267
2007	18,258,138	11,628,893	6,629,245	13,500,894	7,164,759	6,336,135	4,757,244	4,464,134	293,110	3,571,395	3,537,903	33,492	1,185,849	926,231	259,618
2008	19,081,686	12,110,487	6,971,199	13,970,862	7,330,682	6,640,180	5,110,824	4,779,805	331,019	3,660,827	3,625,469	35,358	1,449,997	1,154,336	295,661
2009	20,313,594	12,791,012	7,522,582	14,810,768	7,709,198	7,101,570	5,502,826	5,081,814	421,012	3,767,672	3,732,900	34,772	1,735,154	1,348,914	386,240
2010	21,019,438	13,335,841	7,683,597	15,142,171	7,924,108	7,218,063	5,877,267	5,411,733	465,534	3,854,482	3,821,799	32,683	2,022,785	1,589,934	432,851
2011	21,010,590	13,499,440	7,511,150	15,116,303	8,048,145	7,068,158	5,894,287	5,451,295	442,992	3,926,819	3,886,964	39,855	1,967,468	1,564,331	403,137
2012	20,644,478	13,476,638	7,167,840	14,884,667	8,092,602	6,792,065	5,759,811	5,384,036	375,775	3,951,388	3,913,690	37,698	1,808,423	1,470,346	338,077
2013	20,376,677	13,406,033	6,970,644	14,746,848	8,120,437	6,626,411	5,629,829	5,285,596	344,233	3,971,390	3,939,199	32,191	1,658,439	1,346,397	312,042
2014	20,209,092	13,494,414	6,714,678	14,654,660	8,257,108	6,397,552	5,554,432	5,237,306	317,126	3,997,249	3,966,873	30,376	1,557,183	1,270,433	286,750
2015	19,988,204	13,488,743	6,499,461	14,572,843	8,348,539	6,224,304	5,415,361	5,140,204	275,157	4,065,891	4,015,882	50,009	1,349,470	1,124,322	225,148
2016	19,846,904	13,754,486	6,092,418	14,585,840	8,742,931	5,842,909	5,261,064	5,011,555	249,509	4,078,956	4,028,401	50,555	1,182,108	983,154	198,954
2017	19,765,598	13,823,640	5,941,958	14,560,155	8,853,477	5,706,678	5,205,443	4,970,163	235,280	4,106,477	4,058,087	48,390	1,098,966	912,076	186,890

—Not available.
[1]Large increases are due to the addition of schools accredited by the Accrediting Commission of Career Schools and Colleges of Technology.
[2]Because of imputation techniques, data are not consistent with figures for other years.
NOTE: Data through 1995 are for institutions of higher education, while later data are for degree-granting institutions. Degree-granting institutions grant associate's or higher degrees and participate in Title IV federal financial aid programs. The degree-granting classification is very similar to the earlier higher education classification, but it includes more 2-year colleges and excludes a few higher education institutions that did not grant degrees. Some data have been revised from previously published figures.
SOURCE: U.S. Department of Education, National Center for Education Statistics, Higher Education General Information Survey (HEGIS), "Fall Enrollment in Institutions of Higher Education" surveys, 1970 through 1985; Integrated Postsecondary Education Data System (IPEDS), "Fall Enrollment Survey" (IPEDS-EF:86–99); and IPEDS Spring 2001 through Spring 2018, Fall Enrollment component. (This table was prepared October 2018.)

Table 303.30. Total fall enrollment in degree-granting postsecondary institutions, by level and control of institution, attendance status, and sex of student: Selected years, 1970 through 2028

Level and control of institution, attendance status, and sex of student	Actual													
	1970	1975	1980[1]	1985	1990	1995	2000	2005	2010	2013	2014	2015	2016	2017
1	2	3	4	5	6	7	8	9	10	11	12	13	14	15
Total	**8,580,887**	**11,184,859**	**12,096,895**	**12,247,055**	**13,818,637**	**14,261,781**	**15,312,289**	**17,487,475**	**21,019,438**	**20,376,677**	**20,209,092**	**19,988,204**	**19,846,904**	**19,765,598**
Full-time	5,816,290	6,841,334	7,097,958	7,075,221	7,820,985	8,128,802	9,009,600	10,797,011	13,087,182	12,596,610	12,454,464	12,287,512	12,125,314	12,077,304
Males	3,504,095	3,926,753	3,689,244	3,607,720	3,807,752	3,807,392	4,111,093	4,803,388	5,838,383	5,682,322	5,619,778	5,558,447	5,472,798	5,424,575
Females	2,312,195	2,914,581	3,408,714	3,467,501	4,013,233	4,321,410	4,898,507	5,993,623	7,248,799	6,914,288	6,834,686	6,729,065	6,652,516	6,652,729
Part-time	2,764,597	4,343,525	4,998,937	5,171,834	5,997,652	6,132,979	6,302,689	6,690,464	7,932,256	7,780,067	7,754,628	7,700,692	7,721,590	7,688,294
Males	1,539,547	2,222,244	2,185,130	2,210,730	2,476,157	2,535,147	2,610,676	2,652,537	3,207,376	3,178,875	3,177,752	3,165,372	3,165,624	3,143,057
Females	1,225,050	2,121,281	2,813,807	2,961,104	3,521,495	3,597,832	3,692,013	4,037,927	4,724,880	4,601,192	4,576,876	4,535,320	4,555,966	4,545,237
4-year	**6,261,502**	**7,214,740**	**7,570,608**	**7,715,978**	**8,578,554**	**8,769,252**	**9,363,858**	**10,999,420**	**13,335,841**	**13,406,033**	**13,494,414**	**13,488,743**	**13,754,486**	**13,823,640**
Full-time	4,587,379	5,080,256	5,344,163	5,384,614	5,937,023	6,151,755	6,792,551	8,150,209	9,721,803	9,760,336	9,793,357	9,776,828	9,815,967	9,849,327
Males	2,732,796	2,891,192	2,809,528	2,781,412	2,926,360	2,929,177	3,115,252	3,649,622	4,355,153	4,402,528	4,419,130	4,414,743	4,414,959	4,410,727
Females	1,854,583	2,189,064	2,534,635	2,603,202	3,010,663	3,222,578	3,677,299	4,500,587	5,366,650	5,357,808	5,374,227	5,362,085	5,401,008	5,438,600
Part-time	1,674,123	2,134,484	2,226,445	2,331,364	2,641,531	2,617,497	2,571,307	2,849,211	3,614,038	3,645,697	3,701,057	3,711,915	3,938,519	3,974,313
Males	936,189	1,092,461	1,017,813	1,034,804	1,124,780	1,084,753	1,047,917	1,125,935	1,424,721	1,460,229	1,484,380	1,491,001	1,586,069	1,593,843
Females	737,934	1,042,023	1,208,632	1,296,560	1,516,751	1,532,744	1,523,390	1,723,276	2,189,317	2,185,468	2,216,677	2,220,914	2,352,450	2,380,470
Public 4-year	4,232,722	4,998,142	5,128,612	5,209,540	5,848,242	5,814,545	6,055,398	6,837,605	7,924,108	8,120,437	8,257,108	8,348,539	8,742,931	8,853,477
Full-time	3,086,491	3,469,821	3,592,193	3,623,341	4,033,654	4,084,711	4,371,218	5,021,745	5,811,214	5,934,886	6,011,908	6,081,177	6,236,018	6,310,488
Males	1,813,584	1,947,823	1,873,397	1,863,689	1,982,369	1,951,140	2,008,618	2,295,456	2,707,307	2,772,514	2,806,792	2,833,998	2,894,232	2,911,737
Females	1,272,907	1,521,998	1,718,796	1,759,652	2,051,285	2,133,571	2,362,600	2,726,289	3,103,907	3,162,372	3,205,116	3,247,179	3,341,786	3,398,751
Part-time	1,146,231	1,528,321	1,536,419	1,586,199	1,814,588	1,729,834	1,684,180	1,815,860	2,112,894	2,185,551	2,245,200	2,267,362	2,506,913	2,542,989
Males	609,422	760,469	685,051	693,115	764,248	720,402	683,100	724,375	860,968	911,023	941,104	955,658	1,065,112	1,077,193
Females	536,809	767,852	851,368	893,084	1,050,340	1,009,432	1,001,080	1,091,485	1,251,926	1,274,528	1,304,096	1,311,704	1,441,801	1,465,796
Private 4-year	2,028,780	2,216,598	2,441,996	2,506,438	2,730,312	2,954,707	3,308,460	4,161,815	5,411,733	5,285,596	5,237,306	5,140,204	5,011,555	4,970,163
Full-time	1,500,888	1,610,435	1,751,970	1,761,273	1,903,369	2,067,044	2,421,333	3,128,464	3,910,589	3,825,450	3,781,449	3,695,651	3,579,949	3,538,839
Males	919,212	943,369	936,131	917,723	943,991	978,037	1,106,634	1,354,166	1,647,846	1,630,014	1,612,338	1,580,745	1,520,727	1,498,990
Females	581,676	667,066	815,839	843,550	959,378	1,089,007	1,314,699	1,774,298	2,262,743	2,195,436	2,169,111	2,114,906	2,059,222	2,039,849
Part-time	527,892	606,163	690,026	745,165	826,943	887,663	887,127	1,033,351	1,501,144	1,460,146	1,455,857	1,444,553	1,431,606	1,431,324
Males	326,767	331,992	332,762	341,689	360,532	364,351	364,817	401,560	563,753	549,206	543,276	535,343	520,957	516,650
Females	201,125	274,171	357,264	403,476	466,411	523,312	522,310	631,791	937,391	910,940	912,581	909,210	910,649	914,674
Nonprofit 4-year	2,021,121	2,198,451	2,413,693	2,463,000	2,671,069	2,853,890	3,050,575	3,411,170	3,821,799	3,939,199	3,966,873	4,015,882	4,028,401	4,058,087
Full-time	1,494,625	1,596,074	1,733,014	1,727,707	1,859,124	1,989,457	2,226,028	2,534,793	2,864,640	2,957,476	2,981,188	3,009,240	3,019,342	3,041,196
Males	914,020	930,842	921,253	894,080	915,100	931,956	996,113	1,109,075	1,259,638	1,301,864	1,313,286	1,320,947	1,318,323	1,318,203
Females	580,605	665,232	811,761	833,627	944,024	1,057,501	1,229,915	1,425,718	1,605,002	1,655,612	1,667,902	1,688,293	1,701,019	1,722,993
Part-time	526,496	602,377	680,679	735,293	811,945	864,433	824,547	876,377	957,159	981,723	985,685	1,006,642	1,009,059	1,016,891
Males	325,693	329,662	327,986	336,168	352,106	351,874	332,814	339,572	366,735	378,324	379,513	385,942	385,008	389,521
Females	200,803	272,715	352,693	399,125	459,839	512,559	491,733	536,805	590,424	603,399	606,172	620,700	624,051	627,370
For-profit 4-year	7,659	18,147	28,303	43,438	59,243	100,817	257,885	750,645	1,589,934	1,346,397	1,270,433	1,124,322	983,154	912,076
2-year	**2,319,385**	**3,970,119**	**4,526,287**	**4,531,077**	**5,240,083**	**5,492,529**	**5,948,431**	**6,488,055**	**7,683,597**	**6,970,644**	**6,714,678**	**6,499,461**	**6,092,418**	**5,941,958**
Full-time	1,228,911	1,761,078	1,753,795	1,690,607	1,883,962	1,977,047	2,217,049	2,646,802	3,365,379	2,836,274	2,661,107	2,510,684	2,309,347	2,227,977
Males	771,299	1,035,561	879,716	826,308	881,392	878,215	995,841	1,153,766	1,483,230	1,279,794	1,200,648	1,143,704	1,057,839	1,013,848
Females	457,612	725,517	874,079	864,299	1,002,570	1,098,832	1,221,208	1,493,036	1,882,149	1,556,480	1,460,459	1,366,980	1,251,508	1,214,129
Part-time	1,090,474	2,209,041	2,772,492	2,840,470	3,356,121	3,515,482	3,731,382	3,841,253	4,318,218	4,134,370	4,053,571	3,988,777	3,783,071	3,713,981
Males	603,358	1,129,783	1,167,317	1,175,926	1,351,377	1,450,394	1,562,759	1,526,602	1,782,655	1,718,646	1,693,372	1,674,371	1,579,555	1,549,214
Females	487,116	1,079,258	1,605,175	1,664,544	2,004,744	2,065,088	2,168,623	2,314,651	2,535,563	2,415,724	2,360,199	2,314,406	2,203,516	2,164,767
Public 2-year	2,195,412	3,836,366	4,328,782	4,269,733	4,996,475	5,277,829	5,697,388	6,184,229	7,218,063	6,626,411	6,397,552	6,224,304	5,842,909	5,706,678
Full-time	1,129,165	1,662,621	1,595,493	1,496,905	1,716,843	1,840,590	2,000,008	2,387,016	2,950,024	2,532,530	2,385,023	2,272,769	2,091,361	2,017,585
Males	720,440	988,701	811,871	742,673	810,664	818,605	891,282	1,055,029	1,340,820	1,177,901	1,107,410	1,062,633	983,567	946,208
Females	408,725	673,920	783,622	754,232	906,179	1,021,985	1,108,726	1,331,987	1,609,204	1,354,629	1,277,613	1,210,136	1,107,794	1,071,377
Part-time	1,066,247	2,173,745	2,733,289	2,772,828	3,279,632	3,437,239	3,697,380	3,797,213	4,268,039	4,093,881	4,012,529	3,951,535	3,751,548	3,689,093
Males	589,439	1,107,680	1,152,268	1,138,011	1,317,730	1,417,488	1,549,407	1,514,363	1,769,737	1,707,629	1,683,249	1,665,373	1,571,824	1,542,782
Females	476,808	1,066,065	1,581,021	1,634,817	1,961,902	2,019,751	2,147,973	2,282,850	2,498,302	2,386,252	2,329,280	2,286,162	2,179,724	2,146,311
Private 2-year	123,973	133,753	197,505	261,344	243,608	214,700	251,043	303,826	465,534	344,233	317,126	275,157	249,509	235,280
Full-time	99,746	98,457	158,302	193,702	167,119	136,457	217,041	259,786	415,355	303,744	276,084	237,915	217,986	210,392
Males	50,859	46,860	67,845	83,635	70,728	59,610	104,559	98,737	142,410	101,893	93,238	81,071	74,272	67,640
Females	48,887	51,597	90,457	110,067	96,391	76,847	112,482	161,049	272,945	201,851	182,846	156,844	143,714	142,752
Part-time	24,227	35,296	39,203	67,642	76,489	78,243	34,002	44,040	50,179	40,489	41,042	37,242	31,523	24,888
Males	13,919	22,103	15,049	37,915	33,647	32,906	13,352	12,239	12,918	11,017	10,123	8,998	7,731	6,432
Females	10,308	13,193	24,154	29,727	42,842	45,337	20,650	31,801	37,261	29,472	30,919	28,244	23,792	18,456
Nonprofit 2-year	113,299	112,997	114,094	108,791	89,158	75,154	58,844	43,522	32,683	32,191	30,376	50,009	50,555	48,390
Full-time	91,514	82,158	83,009	76,547	62,003	54,033	46,670	28,939	23,127	24,097	22,789	36,027	39,513	41,090
Males	46,030	40,548	34,968	30,878	25,946	23,265	21,950	12,086	9,944	9,478	9,074	11,972	11,950	10,793
Females	45,484	41,610	48,041	45,669	36,057	30,768	24,720	16,853	13,183	14,619	13,715	24,055	27,563	30,297
Part-time	21,785	30,839	31,085	32,244	27,155	21,121	12,174	14,583	9,556	8,094	7,587	13,982	11,042	7,300
Males	12,097	18,929	11,445	10,786	7,970	6,080	4,499	3,566	2,585	2,373	2,198	2,707	2,547	1,923
Females	9,688	11,910	19,640	21,458	19,185	15,041	7,675	11,017	6,971	5,721	5,389	11,275	8,495	5,377
For-profit 2-year	10,674	20,756	83,411	152,553	154,450	139,546	192,199	260,304	432,851	312,042	286,750	225,148	198,954	186,890

See notes at end of table.

Table 303.30. Total fall enrollment in degree-granting postsecondary institutions, by level and control of institution, attendance status, and sex of student: Selected years, 1970 through 2028—Continued

Level and control of institution, attendance status, and sex of student	Projected										
	2018	2019	2020	2021	2022	2023	2024	2025	2026	2027	2028
1	16	17	18	19	20	21	22	23	24	25	26
Total	**19,828,000**	**19,904,000**	**19,928,000**	**19,956,000**	**19,991,000**	**20,040,000**	**20,107,000**	**20,177,000**	**20,258,000**	**20,295,000**	**20,305,000**
Full-time	12,103,000	12,135,000	12,133,000	12,129,000	12,131,000	12,145,000	12,178,000	12,220,000	12,264,000	12,272,000	12,261,000
Males	5,434,000	5,447,000	5,444,000	5,437,000	5,434,000	5,439,000	5,453,000	5,472,000	5,493,000	5,499,000	5,494,000
Females	6,669,000	6,689,000	6,689,000	6,691,000	6,696,000	6,706,000	6,725,000	6,748,000	6,770,000	6,773,000	6,767,000
Part-time	7,725,000	7,768,000	7,795,000	7,828,000	7,860,000	7,895,000	7,929,000	7,957,000	7,994,000	8,023,000	8,044,000
Males	3,163,000	3,181,000	3,193,000	3,207,000	3,222,000	3,237,000	3,250,000	3,261,000	3,276,000	3,289,000	3,298,000
Females	4,563,000	4,588,000	4,602,000	4,621,000	4,639,000	4,658,000	4,678,000	4,696,000	4,718,000	4,734,000	4,746,000
4-year	**13,864,000**	**13,912,000**	**13,924,000**	**13,938,000**	**13,956,000**	**13,985,000**	**14,030,000**	**14,079,000**	**14,134,000**	**14,155,000**	**14,157,000**
Full-time	9,870,000	9,897,000	9,895,000	9,891,000	9,893,000	9,904,000	9,932,000	9,966,000	10,001,000	10,008,000	9,999,000
Males	4,418,000	4,429,000	4,427,000	4,421,000	4,419,000	4,423,000	4,434,000	4,449,000	4,467,000	4,471,000	4,467,000
Females	5,452,000	5,468,000	5,468,000	5,470,000	5,474,000	5,482,000	5,498,000	5,517,000	5,535,000	5,537,000	5,532,000
Part-time	3,993,000	4,016,000	4,029,000	4,046,000	4,063,000	4,081,000	4,098,000	4,113,000	4,132,000	4,147,000	4,158,000
Males	1,604,000	1,613,000	1,619,000	1,626,000	1,634,000	1,641,000	1,648,000	1,653,000	1,661,000	1,668,000	1,673,000
Females	2,390,000	2,403,000	2,410,000	2,420,000	2,430,000	2,440,000	2,450,000	2,459,000	2,471,000	2,479,000	2,486,000
Public 4-year	8,879,000	8,910,000	8,918,000	8,926,000	8,938,000	8,957,000	8,986,000	9,017,000	9,052,000	9,066,000	9,067,000
Full-time	6,324,000	6,341,000	6,339,000	6,337,000	6,338,000	6,345,000	6,363,000	6,385,000	6,408,000	6,412,000	6,406,000
Males	2,917,000	2,924,000	2,922,000	2,919,000	2,917,000	2,920,000	2,927,000	2,937,000	2,949,000	2,952,000	2,949,000
Females	3,407,000	3,417,000	3,417,000	3,419,000	3,421,000	3,426,000	3,436,000	3,448,000	3,459,000	3,460,000	3,457,000
Part-time	2,555,000	2,570,000	2,578,000	2,589,000	2,600,000	2,612,000	2,623,000	2,632,000	2,644,000	2,654,000	2,661,000
Males	1,084,000	1,090,000	1,094,000	1,099,000	1,104,000	1,109,000	1,114,000	1,117,000	1,123,000	1,127,000	1,130,000
Females	1,471,000	1,479,000	1,484,000	1,490,000	1,496,000	1,502,000	1,509,000	1,514,000	1,521,000	1,527,000	1,531,000
Private 4-year	4,984,000	5,002,000	5,006,000	5,011,000	5,018,000	5,029,000	5,045,000	5,062,000	5,082,000	5,090,000	5,090,000
Full-time	3,546,000	3,556,000	3,555,000	3,554,000	3,555,000	3,559,000	3,569,000	3,581,000	3,594,000	3,596,000	3,593,000
Males	1,502,000	1,505,000	1,504,000	1,502,000	1,502,000	1,503,000	1,507,000	1,512,000	1,518,000	1,520,000	1,518,000
Females	2,045,000	2,051,000	2,051,000	2,052,000	2,053,000	2,056,000	2,062,000	2,069,000	2,076,000	2,077,000	2,075,000
Part-time	1,438,000	1,446,000	1,451,000	1,457,000	1,463,000	1,469,000	1,476,000	1,481,000	1,488,000	1,493,000	1,497,000
Males	520,000	523,000	525,000	527,000	530,000	532,000	534,000	536,000	539,000	541,000	542,000
Females	918,000	923,000	926,000	930,000	934,000	937,000	941,000	945,000	949,000	953,000	955,000
Nonprofit 4-year	—	—	—	—	—	—	—	—	—	—	—
Full-time	—	—	—	—	—	—	—	—	—	—	—
Males	—	—	—	—	—	—	—	—	—	—	—
Females	—	—	—	—	—	—	—	—	—	—	—
Part-time	—	—	—	—	—	—	—	—	—	—	—
Males	—	—	—	—	—	—	—	—	—	—	—
Females	—	—	—	—	—	—	—	—	—	—	—
For-profit 4-year	—	—	—	—	—	—	—	—	—	—	—
2-year	**5,965,000**	**5,991,000**	**6,004,000**	**6,019,000**	**6,035,000**	**6,054,000**	**6,077,000**	**6,098,000**	**6,124,000**	**6,140,000**	**6,148,000**
Full-time	2,233,000	2,239,000	2,238,000	2,237,000	2,238,000	2,240,000	2,247,000	2,254,000	2,262,000	2,264,000	2,262,000
Males	1,016,000	1,018,000	1,018,000	1,016,000	1,016,000	1,017,000	1,019,000	1,023,000	1,027,000	1,028,000	1,027,000
Females	1,217,000	1,221,000	1,221,000	1,221,000	1,222,000	1,224,000	1,227,000	1,232,000	1,236,000	1,236,000	1,235,000
Part-time	3,732,000	3,753,000	3,766,000	3,781,000	3,797,000	3,814,000	3,830,000	3,844,000	3,862,000	3,876,000	3,886,000
Males	1,559,000	1,568,000	1,574,000	1,581,000	1,588,000	1,596,000	1,602,000	1,607,000	1,615,000	1,621,000	1,626,000
Females	2,173,000	2,185,000	2,192,000	2,201,000	2,209,000	2,219,000	2,228,000	2,237,000	2,247,000	2,255,000	2,260,000
Public 2-year	5,729,000	5,755,000	5,767,000	5,782,000	5,798,000	5,817,000	5,839,000	5,859,000	5,884,000	5,900,000	5,908,000
Full-time	2,022,000	2,027,000	2,027,000	2,026,000	2,026,000	2,029,000	2,034,000	2,041,000	2,049,000	2,050,000	2,048,000
Males	948,000	950,000	950,000	948,000	948,000	949,000	951,000	954,000	958,000	959,000	958,000
Females	1,074,000	1,077,000	1,077,000	1,078,000	1,078,000	1,080,000	1,083,000	1,087,000	1,090,000	1,091,000	1,090,000
Part-time	3,707,000	3,728,000	3,740,000	3,756,000	3,772,000	3,789,000	3,805,000	3,818,000	3,836,000	3,850,000	3,860,000
Males	1,552,000	1,561,000	1,567,000	1,574,000	1,581,000	1,589,000	1,595,000	1,600,000	1,608,000	1,614,000	1,619,000
Females	2,155,000	2,166,000	2,173,000	2,182,000	2,191,000	2,200,000	2,209,000	2,218,000	2,228,000	2,235,000	2,241,000
Private 2-year	236,000	237,000	237,000	237,000	237,000	237,000	238,000	239,000	240,000	240,000	240,000
Full-time	211,000	211,000	211,000	211,000	211,000	212,000	212,000	213,000	214,000	214,000	214,000
Males	68,000	68,000	68,000	68,000	68,000	68,000	68,000	68,000	68,000	69,000	69,000
Females	143,000	144,000	144,000	144,000	144,000	144,000	144,000	145,000	145,000	145,000	145,000
Part-time	25,000	25,000	25,000	25,000	25,000	26,000	26,000	26,000	26,000	26,000	26,000
Males	6,000	7,000	7,000	7,000	7,000	7,000	7,000	7,000	7,000	7,000	7,000
Females	19,000	19,000	19,000	19,000	19,000	19,000	19,000	19,000	19,000	19,000	19,000
Nonprofit 2-year	—	—	—	—	—	—	—	—	—	—	—
Full-time	—	—	—	—	—	—	—	—	—	—	—
Males	—	—	—	—	—	—	—	—	—	—	—
Females	—	—	—	—	—	—	—	—	—	—	—
Part-time	—	—	—	—	—	—	—	—	—	—	—
Males	—	—	—	—	—	—	—	—	—	—	—
Females	—	—	—	—	—	—	—	—	—	—	—
For-profit 2-year	—	—	—	—	—	—	—	—	—	—	—

—Not available.
[1]Large increase in private 2-year institutions in 1980 is due to the addition of schools accredited by the Accrediting Commission of Career Schools and Colleges of Technology.
NOTE: Data through 1995 are for institutions of higher education, while later data are for degree-granting institutions. Degree-granting institutions grant associate's or higher degrees and participate in Title IV federal financial aid programs. The degree-granting classification is very similar to the earlier higher education classification, but it includes more 2-year colleges and excludes a few higher education institutions that did not grant degrees. Some data have been revised from previously published figures.

SOURCE: U.S. Department of Education, National Center for Education Statistics, Higher Education General Information Survey (HEGIS), "Fall Enrollment in Colleges and Universities" surveys, 1970 through 1985; Integrated Postsecondary Education Data System (IPEDS), "Fall Enrollment Survey" (IPEDS-EF:90–99); IPEDS Spring 2001 through Spring 2018, Fall Enrollment component; and Enrollment in Degree-Granting Institutions Projection Model, 2000 through 2028. (This table was prepared March 2019.)

Table 303.40. Total fall enrollment in degree-granting postsecondary institutions, by attendance status, sex, and age: Selected years, 1970 through 2028

[In thousands]

Attendance status, sex, and age	1970	1980	1990	2000	2005	2008	2009	2010	2011	2012	2013	2014	2015	2016	2017	Projected 2018	2019	2020	2028
1	2	3	4	5	6	7	8	9	10	11	12	13	14	15	16	17	18	19	20
All students	**8,581**	**12,097**	**13,819**	**15,312**	**17,487**	**19,082**	**20,314**	**21,019**	**21,011**	**20,644**	**20,377**	**20,209**	**19,988**	**19,847**	**19,766**	**19,828**	**19,904**	**19,928**	**20,305**
14 to 17 years old	263	257	153	131	187	195	215	202	221	242	256	239	214	214	221	227	224	226	226
18 and 19 years old	2,579	2,852	2,777	3,258	3,444	3,808	4,009	4,057	3,956	3,782	3,720	3,720	3,732	3,738	3,749	4,028	4,055	3,996	3,978
20 and 21 years old	1,885	2,395	2,593	3,005	3,563	3,645	3,916	4,103	4,269	4,235	4,183	4,163	4,148	4,204	4,166	4,464	4,476	4,529	4,589
22 to 24 years old	1,469	1,947	2,202	2,600	3,114	3,440	3,571	3,759	3,793	3,951	3,964	3,910	3,785	3,736	3,750	3,764	3,731	3,719	3,776
25 to 29 years old	1,091	1,843	2,083	2,044	2,469	2,837	3,082	3,254	3,272	3,155	3,050	3,084	3,165	3,192	3,188	3,065	3,076	3,051	2,969
30 to 34 years old	527	1,227	1,384	1,333	1,438	1,607	1,735	1,805	1,788	1,684	1,606	1,586	1,600	1,589	1,560	1,388	1,413	1,441	1,473
35 years old and over	767	1,577	2,627	2,942	3,272	3,550	3,785	3,840	3,712	3,597	3,597	3,507	3,344	3,174	3,131	2,893	2,928	2,966	3,295
Males	**5,044**	**5,874**	**6,284**	**6,722**	**7,456**	**8,178**	**8,733**	**9,046**	**9,034**	**8,919**	**8,861**	**8,798**	**8,724**	**8,638**	**8,568**	**8,596**	**8,628**	**8,637**	**8,792**
14 to 17 years old	125	106	66	58	68	92	103	94	104	119	125	117	94	83	74	84	83	84	84
18 and 19 years old	1,355	1,368	1,298	1,464	1,523	1,702	1,795	1,820	1,782	1,707	1,661	1,673	1,684	1,688	1,666	1,731	1,742	1,714	1,707
20 and 21 years old	1,064	1,219	1,259	1,411	1,658	1,693	1,866	1,948	1,985	1,960	1,955	1,960	1,954	1,945	1,914	2,025	2,031	2,056	2,079
22 to 24 years old	1,004	1,075	1,129	1,222	1,410	1,553	1,599	1,723	1,769	1,864	1,846	1,789	1,746	1,739	1,731	1,761	1,743	1,736	1,759
25 to 29 years old	796	983	1,024	908	1,057	1,221	1,378	1,410	1,404	1,353	1,356	1,379	1,382	1,366	1,358	1,325	1,333	1,324	1,282
30 to 34 years old	333	564	605	581	591	690	707	731	700	661	634	643	655	670	660	613	625	638	657
35 years old and over	366	559	902	1,077	1,149	1,227	1,285	1,320	1,290	1,255	1,283	1,237	1,208	1,148	1,164	1,057	1,071	1,086	1,226
Females	**3,537**	**6,223**	**7,535**	**8,591**	**10,032**	**10,904**	**11,581**	**11,974**	**11,976**	**11,725**	**11,515**	**11,412**	**11,264**	**11,208**	**11,198**	**11,232**	**11,276**	**11,291**	**11,513**
14 to 17 years old	137	151	87	73	119	102	113	108	116	123	131	121	120	131	147	143	142	142	142
18 and 19 years old	1,224	1,484	1,479	1,794	1,920	2,107	2,214	2,237	2,173	2,074	2,059	2,047	2,049	2,050	2,082	2,297	2,313	2,282	2,271
20 and 21 years old	821	1,177	1,334	1,593	1,905	1,952	2,050	2,155	2,284	2,276	2,228	2,203	2,194	2,259	2,252	2,439	2,445	2,473	2,511
22 to 24 years old	464	871	1,073	1,378	1,704	1,887	1,972	2,036	2,024	2,087	2,118	2,122	2,038	1,997	2,019	2,002	1,988	1,983	2,017
25 to 29 years old	296	859	1,059	1,136	1,413	1,616	1,704	1,844	1,868	1,802	1,694	1,706	1,783	1,826	1,831	1,739	1,743	1,727	1,687
30 to 34 years old	194	663	779	752	847	917	1,028	1,074	1,088	1,022	972	943	945	919	900	775	788	803	816
35 years old and over	401	1,018	1,725	1,865	2,123	2,323	2,500	2,520	2,422	2,341	2,314	2,270	2,136	2,026	1,967	1,836	1,857	1,880	2,069
Full-time	**5,816**	**7,098**	**7,821**	**9,010**	**10,797**	**11,735**	**12,605**	**13,087**	**13,003**	**12,734**	**12,597**	**12,454**	**12,288**	**12,125**	**12,077**	**12,103**	**12,135**	**12,133**	**12,261**
14 to 17 years old	246	231	134	121	152	168	179	170	185	207	210	200	182	186	188	178	176	177	177
18 and 19 years old	2,374	2,544	2,471	2,823	3,026	3,356	3,481	3,496	3,351	3,226	3,199	3,174	3,188	3,161	3,206	3,314	3,335	3,285	3,272
20 and 21 years old	1,649	2,007	2,137	2,452	2,976	3,039	3,241	3,364	3,427	3,386	3,327	3,326	3,290	3,365	3,350	3,592	3,602	3,646	3,693
22 to 24 years old	904	1,181	1,405	1,714	2,122	2,345	2,511	2,585	2,580	2,603	2,650	2,597	2,568	2,502	2,500	2,401	2,382	2,374	2,411
25 to 29 years old	426	641	791	886	1,174	1,368	1,506	1,605	1,600	1,555	1,528	1,525	1,519	1,478	1,471	1,363	1,368	1,357	1,320
30 to 34 years old	113	272	383	418	547	571	657	745	763	711	664	626	601	583	558	519	528	539	550
35 years old and over	104	221	500	596	800	889	1,030	1,122	1,096	1,047	1,018	1,005	941	852	805	736	745	754	838
Males	**3,504**	**3,689**	**3,808**	**4,111**	**4,803**	**5,227**	**5,632**	**5,838**	**5,793**	**5,708**	**5,682**	**5,620**	**5,558**	**5,473**	**5,425**	**5,434**	**5,447**	**5,444**	**5,494**
14 to 17 years old	121	95	55	51	53	73	77	71	85	102	106	100	81	71	64	61	60	61	61
18 and 19 years old	1,261	1,219	1,171	1,252	1,339	1,514	1,570	1,574	1,510	1,461	1,423	1,402	1,414	1,416	1,427	1,438	1,447	1,423	1,417
20 and 21 years old	955	1,046	1,035	1,156	1,398	1,405	1,536	1,586	1,586	1,537	1,542	1,549	1,546	1,552	1,535	1,658	1,663	1,684	1,702
22 to 24 years old	686	717	768	834	982	1,104	1,169	1,215	1,217	1,254	1,270	1,236	1,208	1,173	1,160	1,134	1,123	1,119	1,134
25 to 29 years old	346	391	433	410	506	596	661	715	727	728	734	732	709	689	683	650	654	650	629
30 to 34 years old	77	142	171	186	225	248	279	301	299	278	257	242	251	253	251	221	226	231	238
35 years old and over	58	80	174	222	300	287	341	376	369	349	351	360	349	320	305	271	274	278	314
Females	**2,312**	**3,409**	**4,013**	**4,899**	**5,994**	**6,508**	**6,973**	**7,249**	**7,210**	**7,026**	**6,914**	**6,835**	**6,729**	**6,653**	**6,653**	**6,669**	**6,689**	**6,689**	**6,767**
14 to 17 years old	125	136	78	70	98	95	102	99	100	105	104	101	101	115	125	117	116	116	116
18 and 19 years old	1,113	1,325	1,300	1,571	1,687	1,841	1,911	1,922	1,842	1,765	1,776	1,773	1,774	1,745	1,779	1,876	1,889	1,863	1,854
20 and 21 years old	693	961	1,101	1,296	1,578	1,634	1,705	1,778	1,840	1,849	1,785	1,777	1,744	1,813	1,815	1,934	1,939	1,962	1,991
22 to 24 years old	218	464	638	880	1,140	1,241	1,343	1,370	1,364	1,349	1,380	1,362	1,359	1,329	1,339	1,267	1,259	1,256	1,278
25 to 29 years old	80	250	358	476	668	771	845	891	873	827	794	793	810	789	788	712	714	707	691
30 to 34 years old	37	130	212	232	322	322	378	444	464	433	408	384	350	330	307	298	302	308	313
35 years old and over	46	141	326	374	500	602	690	746	727	698	667	645	592	532	500	465	470	476	524
Part-time	**2,765**	**4,999**	**5,998**	**6,303**	**6,690**	**7,347**	**7,708**	**7,932**	**8,008**	**7,910**	**7,780**	**7,755**	**7,701**	**7,722**	**7,688**	**7,725**	**7,768**	**7,795**	**8,044**
14 to 17 years old	16	26	19	10	36	27	36	32	36	35	47	38	32	28	33	49	48	49	49
18 and 19 years old	205	308	306	435	417	453	528	561	604	556	521	546	545	577	543	714	720	710	706
20 and 21 years old	236	388	456	553	586	606	675	738	842	850	855	836	858	839	816	872	874	883	897
22 to 24 years old	564	765	796	886	992	1,095	1,059	1,174	1,212	1,348	1,314	1,313	1,217	1,235	1,250	1,362	1,350	1,344	1,365
25 to 29 years old	665	1,202	1,291	1,158	1,296	1,469	1,576	1,648	1,672	1,600	1,522	1,560	1,646	1,715	1,718	1,702	1,708	1,694	1,649
30 to 34 years old	414	954	1,001	915	891	1,036	1,079	1,060	1,025	973	942	960	1,000	1,006	1,002	869	885	902	922
35 years old and over	663	1,356	2,127	2,345	2,472	2,661	2,754	2,718	2,616	2,550	2,579	2,502	2,404	2,322	2,327	2,157	2,184	2,212	2,457
Males	**1,540**	**2,185**	**2,476**	**2,611**	**2,653**	**2,951**	**3,101**	**3,207**	**3,241**	**3,211**	**3,179**	**3,178**	**3,165**	**3,166**	**3,143**	**3,163**	**3,181**	**3,193**	**3,298**
14 to 17 years old	4	12	11	7	15	20	25	23	20	17	20	18	13	12	11	23	23	23	23
18 and 19 years old	94	149	127	212	184	188	226	245	273	246	239	271	270	272	239	293	296	291	289
20 and 21 years old	108	172	224	255	260	288	330	362	398	423	413	411	408	393	379	367	368	372	377
22 to 24 years old	318	359	361	388	428	449	430	508	552	610	576	553	538	566	571	627	620	617	625
25 to 29 years old	450	592	591	498	551	624	718	695	677	625	622	646	673	677	674	675	679	674	653
30 to 34 years old	257	422	435	395	365	442	428	430	401	383	377	401	405	417	409	391	399	408	420
35 years old and over	309	479	728	855	850	940	944	944	921	906	932	877	859	829	859	786	797	808	912
Females	**1,225**	**2,814**	**3,521**	**3,692**	**4,038**	**4,396**	**4,607**	**4,725**	**4,767**	**4,699**	**4,601**	**4,577**	**4,535**	**4,556**	**4,545**	**4,563**	**4,588**	**4,602**	**4,746**
14 to 17 years old	12	14	9	3	21	7	11	9	16	18	27	20	19	16	22	26	26	26	26
18 and 19 years old	112	159	179	223	233	265	303	316	332	310	283	274	275	305	303	421	425	419	417
20 and 21 years old	128	216	233	298	327	318	345	377	444	427	443	425	450	446	437	505	506	511	520
22 to 24 years old	246	407	435	497	564	646	629	666	660	738	738	760	679	668	679	735	729	727	740
25 to 29 years old	216	609	700	660	745	845	859	953	995	975	900	913	973	1,037	1,043	1,027	1,029	1,020	996
30 to 34 years old	158	532	567	520	526	595	651	630	624	589	565	559	595	589	593	478	485	495	503
35 years old and over	354	876	1,399	1,491	1,623	1,721	1,810	1,774	1,695	1,643	1,647	1,625	1,544	1,493	1,467	1,371	1,387	1,404	1,545

NOTE: Distributions by age are estimates based on samples of the civilian noninstitutionalized population from the U.S. Census Bureau's Current Population Survey. Data through 1995 are for institutions of higher education, while later data are for degree-granting institutions. Degree-granting institutions grant associate's or higher degrees and participate in Title IV federal financial aid programs. The degree-granting classification is very similar to the earlier higher education classification, but it includes more 2-year colleges and excludes a few higher education institutions that did not grant degrees. Some data have been revised from previously published figures. Detail may not sum to totals because of rounding.

SOURCE: U.S. Department of Education, National Center for Education Statistics, Higher Education General Information Survey (HEGIS), "Fall Enrollment in Colleges and Universities" surveys, 1970 and 1980; Integrated Postsecondary Education Data System (IPEDS), "Fall Enrollment Survey" (IPEDS-EF:90–99); IPEDS Spring 2001 through Spring 2018, Fall Enrollment component; and Enrollment in Degree-Granting Institutions Projection Model, 2000 through 2028. U.S. Department of Commerce, Census Bureau, Current Population Survey (CPS), October, selected years, 1970 through 2017. (This table was prepared March 2019.)

Table 303.45. Total fall enrollment in degree-granting postsecondary institutions, by level of enrollment, sex, attendance status, and age of student: 2013, 2015, and 2017

Attendance status and age of student	Fall 2013	Fall 2015			Fall 2017								
	All levels	All levels			All levels			Undergraduate			Postbaccalaureate		
	Total	Total	Males	Females	Total	Males	Females	Total	Males	Females	Total	Males	Females
1	2	3	4	5	6	7	8	9	10	11	12	13	14
All students	**20,376,677**	**19,988,204**	**8,723,819**	**11,264,385**	**19,765,598**	**8,567,632**	**11,197,966**	**16,760,331**	**7,347,438**	**9,412,893**	**3,005,267**	**1,220,194**	**1,785,073**
Under 18	878,766	1,053,854	435,452	618,402	1,230,419	505,272	725,147	1,230,274	505,211	725,063	145	61	84
18 and 19	4,265,916	4,341,382	1,954,795	2,386,587	4,445,555	1,993,633	2,451,922	4,444,557	1,993,324	2,451,233	998	309	689
20 and 21	4,086,686	4,078,990	1,849,082	2,229,908	4,096,516	1,844,860	2,251,656	4,060,204	1,832,005	2,228,199	36,312	12,855	23,457
22 to 24	3,431,880	3,324,891	1,540,990	1,783,901	3,203,272	1,470,664	1,732,608	2,542,471	1,208,997	1,333,474	660,801	261,667	399,134
25 to 29	2,856,287	2,778,912	1,227,002	1,551,910	2,692,386	1,167,425	1,524,961	1,729,875	751,827	978,048	962,511	415,598	546,913
30 to 34	1,641,631	1,511,847	644,424	867,423	1,420,422	597,540	822,882	944,490	389,185	555,305	475,932	208,355	267,577
35 to 39	1,033,809	973,402	384,395	589,007	932,331	366,423	565,908	633,621	245,676	387,945	298,710	120,747	177,963
40 to 49	1,346,668	1,190,153	428,681	761,472	1,088,176	388,820	699,356	725,529	259,807	465,722	362,647	129,013	233,634
50 to 64	717,355	627,528	214,632	412,896	559,156	191,846	367,310	371,156	128,129	243,027	188,000	63,717	124,283
65 and over	66,202	66,683	28,234	38,449	67,037	28,485	38,552	53,499	22,676	30,823	13,538	5,809	7,729
Age unknown	51,477	40,562	16,132	24,430	30,328	12,664	17,664	24,655	10,601	14,054	5,673	2,063	3,610
Full-time	12,596,610	12,287,512	5,558,447	6,729,065	12,077,304	5,424,575	6,652,729	10,370,665	4,683,665	5,687,000	1,706,639	740,910	965,729
Under 18	185,285	206,770	83,135	123,635	220,615	86,145	134,470	220,568	86,120	134,448	47	25	22
18 and 19	3,549,171	3,612,294	1,612,557	1,999,737	3,694,625	1,643,721	2,050,904	3,693,798	1,643,481	2,050,317	827	240	587
20 and 21	3,245,703	3,241,515	1,470,848	1,770,667	3,267,248	1,475,119	1,792,129	3,234,486	1,463,359	1,771,127	32,762	11,760	21,002
22 to 24	2,240,365	2,156,073	1,033,642	1,122,431	2,068,941	983,363	1,085,578	1,539,873	769,542	770,331	529,068	213,821	315,247
25 to 29	1,497,997	1,442,151	681,881	760,270	1,373,147	637,181	735,966	761,146	353,711	407,435	612,001	283,470	328,531
30 to 34	724,235	649,695	296,410	353,285	592,027	266,736	325,291	361,656	156,144	205,512	230,371	110,592	119,779
35 to 39	408,932	368,319	151,776	216,543	338,942	139,040	199,902	221,706	87,573	134,133	117,236	51,467	65,769
40 to 49	483,716	403,959	151,610	252,349	350,641	129,828	220,813	228,966	83,439	145,527	121,675	46,389	75,286
50 to 64	226,402	177,157	64,530	112,627	148,810	53,926	94,884	91,789	33,202	58,587	57,021	20,724	36,297
65 and over	9,105	10,556	4,747	5,809	8,979	3,957	5,022	5,176	2,322	2,854	3,803	1,635	2,168
Age unknown	25,699	19,023	7,311	11,712	13,329	5,559	7,770	11,501	4,772	6,729	1,828	787	1,041
Part-time	7,780,067	7,700,692	3,165,372	4,535,320	7,688,294	3,143,057	4,545,237	6,389,666	2,663,773	3,725,893	1,298,628	479,284	819,344
Under 18	693,481	847,084	352,317	494,767	1,009,804	419,127	590,677	1,009,706	419,091	590,615	98	36	62
18 and 19	716,745	729,088	342,238	386,850	750,930	349,912	401,018	750,759	349,843	400,916	171	69	102
20 and 21	840,983	837,475	378,234	459,241	829,268	369,741	459,527	825,718	368,646	457,072	3,550	1,095	2,455
22 to 24	1,191,515	1,168,818	507,348	661,470	1,134,331	487,301	647,030	1,002,598	439,455	563,143	131,733	47,846	83,887
25 to 29	1,358,290	1,336,761	545,121	791,640	1,319,239	530,244	788,995	968,729	398,116	570,613	350,510	132,128	218,382
30 to 34	917,396	862,152	348,014	514,138	828,395	330,804	497,591	582,834	233,041	349,793	245,561	97,763	147,798
35 to 39	624,877	605,083	232,619	372,464	593,389	227,383	366,006	411,915	158,103	253,812	181,474	69,280	112,194
40 to 49	862,952	786,194	277,071	509,123	737,535	258,992	478,543	496,563	176,368	320,195	240,972	82,624	158,348
50 to 64	490,953	450,371	150,102	300,269	410,346	137,920	272,426	279,367	94,927	184,440	130,979	42,993	87,986
65 and over	57,097	56,127	23,487	32,640	58,058	24,528	33,530	48,323	20,354	27,969	9,735	4,174	5,561
Age unknown	25,778	21,539	8,821	12,718	16,999	7,105	9,894	13,154	5,829	7,325	3,845	1,276	2,569
	Percentage distribution of students with known age[1]												
All students	**100.0**	**100.0**	**100.0**	**100.0**	**100.0**	**100.0**	**100.0**	**100.0**	**100.0**	**100.0**	**100.0**	**100.0**	**100.0**
Under 18	4.3	5.3	5.0	5.5	6.2	5.9	6.5	7.4	6.9	7.7	#	#	#
18 and 19	21.0	21.8	22.4	21.2	22.5	23.3	21.9	26.6	27.2	26.1	#	#	#
20 and 21	20.1	20.4	21.2	19.8	20.8	21.6	20.1	24.3	25.0	23.7	1.2	1.1	1.3
22 to 24	16.9	16.7	17.7	15.9	16.2	17.2	15.5	15.2	16.5	14.2	22.0	21.5	22.4
25 to 29	14.1	13.9	14.1	13.8	13.6	13.6	13.6	10.3	10.2	10.4	32.1	34.1	30.7
30 to 34	8.1	7.6	7.4	7.7	7.2	7.0	7.4	5.6	5.3	5.9	15.9	17.1	15.0
35 to 39	5.1	4.9	4.4	5.2	4.7	4.3	5.1	3.8	3.3	4.1	10.0	9.9	10.0
40 to 49	6.6	6.0	4.9	6.8	5.5	4.5	6.3	4.3	3.5	5.0	12.1	10.6	13.1
50 to 64	3.5	3.1	2.5	3.7	2.8	2.2	3.3	2.2	1.7	2.6	6.3	5.2	7.0
65 and over	0.3	0.3	0.3	0.3	0.3	0.3	0.3	0.3	0.3	0.3	0.5	0.5	0.4
Full-time	100.0	100.0	100.0	100.0	100.0	100.0	100.0	100.0	100.0	100.0	100.0	100.0	100.0
Under 18	1.5	1.7	1.5	1.8	1.8	1.6	2.0	2.1	1.8	2.4	#	#	#
18 and 19	28.2	29.4	29.0	29.8	30.6	30.3	30.9	35.7	35.1	36.1	#	#	0.1
20 and 21	25.8	26.4	26.5	26.4	27.1	27.2	27.0	31.2	31.3	31.2	1.9	1.6	2.2
22 to 24	17.8	17.6	18.6	16.7	17.1	18.1	16.3	14.9	16.4	13.6	31.0	28.9	32.7
25 to 29	11.9	11.8	12.3	11.3	11.4	11.8	11.1	7.3	7.6	7.2	35.9	38.3	34.1
30 to 34	5.8	5.3	5.3	5.3	4.9	4.9	4.9	3.5	3.3	3.6	13.5	14.9	12.4
35 to 39	3.3	3.0	2.7	3.2	2.8	2.6	3.0	2.1	1.9	2.4	6.9	7.0	6.8
40 to 49	3.8	3.3	2.7	3.8	2.9	2.4	3.3	2.2	1.8	2.6	7.1	6.3	7.8
50 to 64	1.8	1.4	1.2	1.7	1.2	1.0	1.4	0.9	0.7	1.0	3.3	2.8	3.8
65 and over	0.1	0.1	0.1	0.1	0.1	0.1	0.1	#	#	0.1	0.2	0.2	0.2
Part-time	100.0	100.0	100.0	100.0	100.0	100.0	100.0	100.0	100.0	100.0	100.0	100.0	100.0
Under 18	8.9	11.0	11.2	10.9	13.2	13.4	13.0	15.8	15.8	15.9	#	#	#
18 and 19	9.2	9.5	10.8	8.6	9.8	11.2	8.8	11.8	13.2	10.8	#	#	#
20 and 21	10.8	10.9	12.0	10.2	10.8	11.8	10.1	12.9	13.9	12.3	0.3	0.2	0.3
22 to 24	15.4	15.2	16.1	14.6	14.8	15.5	14.3	15.7	16.5	15.1	10.2	10.0	10.3
25 to 29	17.5	17.4	17.3	17.5	17.2	16.9	17.4	15.2	15.0	15.3	27.1	27.6	26.7
30 to 34	11.8	11.2	11.0	11.4	10.8	10.5	11.0	9.1	8.8	9.4	19.0	20.5	18.1
35 to 39	8.1	7.9	7.4	8.2	7.7	7.3	8.1	6.5	5.9	6.8	14.0	14.5	13.7
40 to 49	11.1	10.2	8.8	11.3	9.6	8.3	10.6	7.8	6.6	8.6	18.6	17.3	19.4
50 to 64	6.3	5.9	4.8	6.6	5.3	4.4	6.0	4.4	3.6	5.0	10.1	9.0	10.8
65 and over	0.7	0.7	0.7	0.7	0.8	0.8	0.7	0.8	0.8	0.8	0.8	0.9	0.7

#Rounds to zero.
[1]Percentage distributions exclude students whose age is unknown.
NOTE: Degree-granting institutions grant associate's or higher degrees and participate in Title IV federal financial aid programs. Detail may not sum to totals because of rounding.
Some data have been revised from previously published figures.
SOURCE: U.S. Department of Education, National Center for Education Statistics, Integrated Postsecondary Education Data System (IPEDS), Spring 2014, 2016, and 2018, Fall Enrollment component. (This table was prepared October 2018.)

Table 303.50. Total fall enrollment in degree-granting postsecondary institutions, by level of enrollment, control and level of institution, attendance status, and age of student: 2017

Attendance status and age of student	Undergraduate										Postbaccalaureate			
		Public			Private nonprofit			Private for-profit						
	Total	Total	4-year	2-year	Total	4-year	2-year	Total	4-year	2-year	Total	Public	Private nonprofit	Private for-profit
1	2	3	4	5	6	7	8	9	10	11	12	13	14	15
All students	**16,760,331**	**13,100,953**	**7,394,275**	**5,706,678**	**2,817,017**	**2,768,627**	**48,390**	**842,361**	**655,471**	**186,890**	**3,005,267**	**1,459,202**	**1,289,460**	**256,605**
Under 18	1,230,274	1,128,680	377,282	751,398	96,905	96,246	659	4,689	3,577	1,112	145	42	100	3
18 and 19	4,444,557	3,526,056	2,172,387	1,353,669	859,887	852,686	7,201	58,614	36,724	21,890	998	448	522	28
20 and 21	4,060,204	3,132,761	2,172,028	960,733	846,904	841,486	5,418	80,539	54,176	26,363	36,312	19,738	16,113	461
22 to 24	2,542,471	2,063,678	1,295,451	768,227	362,734	355,690	7,044	116,059	83,076	32,983	660,801	358,850	289,071	12,880
25 to 29	1,729,875	1,336,473	630,442	706,031	209,884	200,225	9,659	183,518	143,558	39,960	962,511	492,268	423,618	46,625
30 to 34	944,490	672,970	282,854	390,116	134,719	128,676	6,043	136,801	113,317	23,484	475,932	234,930	196,011	44,991
35 to 39	633,621	431,135	172,504	258,631	103,076	98,888	4,188	99,410	83,806	15,604	298,710	134,919	121,428	42,363
40 to 49	725,529	485,482	185,088	300,394	128,763	123,616	5,147	111,284	94,468	16,816	362,647	146,384	150,379	65,884
50 to 64	371,156	261,608	88,680	172,928	62,437	59,709	2,728	47,111	39,701	7,410	188,000	66,195	81,772	40,033
65 and over	53,499	47,262	13,342	33,920	4,426	4,211	215	1,811	1,465	346	13,538	5,013	5,720	2,805
Age unknown	24,655	14,848	4,217	10,631	7,282	7,194	88	2,525	1,603	922	5,673	415	4,726	532
Full-time	10,370,665	7,516,055	5,498,470	2,017,585	2,299,345	2,258,255	41,090	555,265	385,963	169,302	1,706,639	812,018	782,941	111,680
Under 18	220,568	184,668	103,439	81,229	33,761	33,495	266	2,139	1,052	1,087	47	18	28	1
18 and 19	3,693,798	2,811,170	1,981,161	830,009	830,031	823,198	6,833	52,597	31,598	20,999	827	404	405	18
20 and 21	3,234,486	2,355,461	1,921,933	433,528	813,321	808,612	4,709	65,704	41,208	24,496	32,762	17,969	14,457	336
22 to 24	1,539,873	1,163,070	926,697	236,373	293,606	287,792	5,814	83,197	53,351	29,846	529,068	285,767	235,523	7,778
25 to 29	761,146	515,230	320,767	194,463	124,780	116,648	8,132	121,136	85,274	35,862	612,001	302,645	286,497	22,859
30 to 34	361,656	208,214	112,576	95,638	69,388	64,320	5,068	84,054	63,177	20,877	230,371	107,172	103,883	19,316
35 to 39	221,706	114,384	57,328	57,056	48,999	45,511	3,488	58,323	44,432	13,891	117,236	46,241	53,207	17,788
40 to 49	228,966	109,930	51,968	57,962	57,122	52,825	4,297	61,914	47,086	14,828	121,675	37,517	57,618	26,540
50 to 64	91,789	44,192	18,734	25,458	23,804	21,547	2,257	23,793	17,549	6,244	57,021	13,449	27,963	15,609
65 and over	5,176	3,296	1,022	2,274	954	776	178	926	623	303	3,803	752	1,909	1,142
Age unknown	11,501	6,440	2,845	3,595	3,579	3,531	48	1,482	613	869	1,828	84	1,451	293
Part-time	6,389,666	5,584,898	1,895,805	3,689,093	517,672	510,372	7,300	287,096	269,508	17,588	1,298,628	647,184	506,519	144,925
Under 18	1,009,706	944,012	273,843	670,169	63,144	62,751	393	2,550	2,525	25	98	24	72	2
18 and 19	750,759	714,886	191,226	523,660	29,856	29,488	368	6,017	5,126	891	171	44	117	10
20 and 21	825,718	777,300	250,095	527,205	33,583	32,874	709	14,835	12,968	1,867	3,550	1,769	1,656	125
22 to 24	1,002,598	900,608	368,754	531,854	69,128	67,898	1,230	32,862	29,725	3,137	131,733	73,083	53,548	5,102
25 to 29	968,729	821,243	309,675	511,568	85,104	83,577	1,527	62,382	58,284	4,098	350,510	189,623	137,121	23,766
30 to 34	582,834	464,756	170,278	294,478	65,331	64,356	975	52,747	50,140	2,607	245,561	127,758	92,128	25,675
35 to 39	411,915	316,751	115,176	201,575	54,077	53,377	700	41,087	39,374	1,713	181,474	88,678	68,221	24,575
40 to 49	496,563	375,552	133,120	242,432	71,641	70,791	850	49,370	47,382	1,988	240,972	108,867	92,761	39,344
50 to 64	279,367	217,416	69,946	147,470	38,633	38,162	471	23,318	22,152	1,166	130,979	52,746	53,809	24,424
65 and over	48,323	43,966	12,320	31,646	3,472	3,435	37	885	842	43	9,735	4,261	3,811	1,663
Age unknown	13,154	8,408	1,372	7,036	3,703	3,663	40	1,043	990	53	3,845	331	3,275	239
	Percentage distribution of students with known age[1]													
All students	**100.0**	**100.0**	**100.0**	**100.0**	**100.0**	**100.0**	**100.0**	**100.0**	**100.0**	**100.0**	**100.0**	**100.0**	**100.0**	**100.0**
Under 18	7.4	8.6	5.1	13.2	3.4	3.5	1.4	0.6	0.5	0.6	#	#	#	#
18 and 19	26.6	26.9	29.4	23.8	30.6	30.9	14.9	7.0	5.6	11.8	#	#	#	#
20 and 21	24.3	23.9	29.4	16.9	30.1	30.5	11.2	9.6	8.3	14.2	1.2	1.4	1.3	0.2
22 to 24	15.2	15.8	17.5	13.5	12.9	12.9	14.6	13.8	12.7	17.7	22.0	24.6	22.5	5.0
25 to 29	10.3	10.2	8.5	12.4	7.5	7.3	20.0	21.9	22.0	21.5	32.1	33.7	33.0	18.2
30 to 34	5.6	5.1	3.8	6.8	4.8	4.7	12.5	16.3	17.3	12.6	15.9	16.1	15.3	17.6
35 to 39	3.8	3.3	2.3	4.5	3.7	3.6	8.7	11.8	12.8	8.4	10.0	9.2	9.5	16.5
40 to 49	4.3	3.7	2.5	5.3	4.6	4.5	10.7	13.3	14.4	9.0	12.1	10.0	11.7	25.7
50 to 64	2.2	2.0	1.2	3.0	2.2	2.2	5.6	5.6	6.1	4.0	6.3	4.5	6.4	15.6
65 and over	0.3	0.4	0.2	0.6	0.2	0.2	0.4	0.2	0.2	0.2	0.5	0.3	0.4	1.1
Full-time	100.0	100.0	100.0	100.0	100.0	100.0	100.0	100.0	100.0	100.0	100.0	100.0	100.0	100.0
Under 18	2.1	2.5	1.9	4.0	1.5	1.5	0.6	0.4	0.3	0.6	#	#	#	#
18 and 19	35.7	37.4	36.0	41.2	36.2	36.5	16.6	9.5	8.2	12.5	#	#	0.1	#
20 and 21	31.2	31.4	35.0	21.5	35.4	35.9	11.5	11.9	10.7	14.5	1.9	2.2	1.8	0.3
22 to 24	14.9	15.5	16.9	11.7	12.8	12.8	14.2	15.0	13.8	17.7	31.0	35.2	30.1	7.0
25 to 29	7.3	6.9	5.8	9.7	5.4	5.2	19.8	21.9	22.1	21.3	35.9	37.3	36.7	20.5
30 to 34	3.5	2.8	2.0	4.7	3.0	2.9	12.3	15.2	16.4	12.4	13.5	13.2	13.3	17.3
35 to 39	2.1	1.5	1.0	2.8	2.1	2.0	8.5	10.5	11.5	8.2	6.9	5.7	6.8	16.0
40 to 49	2.2	1.5	0.9	2.9	2.5	2.3	10.5	11.2	12.2	8.8	7.1	4.6	7.4	23.8
50 to 64	0.9	0.6	0.3	1.3	1.0	1.0	5.5	4.3	4.6	3.7	3.3	1.7	3.6	14.0
65 and over	#	#	#	0.1	#	#	0.4	0.2	0.2	0.2	0.2	0.1	0.2	1.0
Part-time	100.0	100.0	100.0	100.0	100.0	100.0	100.0	100.0	100.0	100.0	100.0	100.0	100.0	100.0
Under 18	15.8	16.9	14.5	18.2	12.3	12.4	5.4	0.9	0.9	0.1	#	#	#	#
18 and 19	11.8	12.8	10.1	14.2	5.8	5.8	5.1	2.1	1.9	5.1	#	#	#	#
20 and 21	12.9	13.9	13.2	14.3	6.5	6.5	9.8	5.2	4.8	10.6	0.3	0.3	0.3	0.1
22 to 24	15.7	16.2	19.5	14.4	13.4	13.4	16.9	11.5	11.1	17.9	10.2	11.3	10.6	3.5
25 to 29	15.2	14.7	16.3	13.9	16.6	16.5	21.0	21.8	21.7	23.4	27.1	29.3	27.2	16.4
30 to 34	9.1	8.3	9.0	8.0	12.7	12.7	13.4	18.4	18.7	14.9	19.0	19.8	18.3	17.7
35 to 39	6.5	5.7	6.1	5.5	10.5	10.5	9.6	14.4	14.7	9.8	14.0	13.7	13.6	17.0
40 to 49	7.8	6.7	7.0	6.6	13.9	14.0	11.7	17.3	17.6	11.3	18.6	16.8	18.4	27.2
50 to 64	4.4	3.9	3.7	4.0	7.5	7.5	6.5	8.2	8.2	6.6	10.1	8.2	10.7	16.9
65 and over	0.8	0.8	0.7	0.9	0.7	0.7	0.5	0.3	0.3	0.2	0.8	0.7	0.8	1.1

#Rounds to zero.
[1]Percentage distributions exclude students whose age is unknown.
NOTE: Degree-granting institutions grant associate's or higher degrees and participate in Title IV federal financial aid programs. Detail may not sum to totals because of rounding.

SOURCE: U.S. Department of Education, National Center for Education Statistics, Integrated Postsecondary Education Data System (IPEDS), Spring 2018, Fall Enrollment component. (This table was prepared October 2018.)

Table 303.55. Total fall enrollment in degree-granting postsecondary institutions, by control and level of institution, attendance status, and age of student: 2017

Attendance status and age of student	All institutions			Public institutions			Private (nonprofit and for-profit) institutions						
								Nonprofit institutions			For-profit institutions		
	Total	4-year	2-year	Total	4-year	2-year	Total	Total	4-year	2-year	Total	4-year	2-year
1	2	3	4	5	6	7	8	9	10	11	12	13	14
All students	**19,765,598**	**13,823,640**	**5,941,958**	**14,560,155**	**8,853,477**	**5,706,678**	**5,205,443**	**4,106,477**	**4,058,087**	**48,390**	**1,098,966**	**912,076**	**186,890**
Under 18	1,230,419	477,250	753,169	1,128,722	377,324	751,398	101,697	97,005	96,346	659	4,692	3,580	1,112
18 and 19	4,445,555	3,062,795	1,382,760	3,526,504	2,172,835	1,353,669	919,051	860,409	853,208	7,201	58,642	36,752	21,890
20 and 21	4,096,516	3,104,002	992,514	3,152,499	2,191,766	960,733	944,017	863,017	857,599	5,418	81,000	54,637	26,363
22 to 24	3,203,272	2,395,018	808,254	2,422,528	1,654,301	768,227	780,744	651,805	644,761	7,044	128,939	95,956	32,983
25 to 29	2,692,386	1,936,736	755,650	1,828,741	1,122,710	706,031	863,645	633,502	623,843	9,659	230,143	190,183	39,960
30 to 34	1,420,422	1,000,779	419,643	907,900	517,784	390,116	512,522	330,730	324,687	6,043	181,792	158,308	23,484
35 to 39	932,331	653,908	278,423	566,054	307,423	258,631	366,277	224,504	220,316	4,188	141,773	126,169	15,604
40 to 49	1,088,176	765,819	322,357	631,866	331,472	300,394	456,310	279,142	273,995	5,147	177,168	160,352	16,816
50 to 64	559,156	376,090	183,066	327,803	154,875	172,928	231,353	144,209	141,481	2,728	87,144	79,734	7,410
65 and over	67,037	32,556	34,481	52,275	18,355	33,920	14,762	10,146	9,931	215	4,616	4,270	346
Age unknown	30,328	18,687	11,641	15,263	4,632	10,631	15,065	12,008	11,920	88	3,057	2,135	922
Full-time	12,077,304	9,849,327	2,227,977	8,328,073	6,310,488	2,017,585	3,749,231	3,082,286	3,041,196	41,090	666,945	497,643	169,302
Under 18	220,615	138,033	82,582	184,686	103,457	81,229	35,929	33,789	33,523	266	2,140	1,053	1,087
18 and 19	3,694,625	2,836,784	857,841	2,811,574	1,981,565	830,009	883,051	830,436	823,603	6,833	52,615	31,616	20,999
20 and 21	3,267,248	2,804,515	462,733	2,373,430	1,939,902	433,528	893,818	827,778	823,069	4,709	66,040	41,544	24,496
22 to 24	2,068,941	1,796,908	272,033	1,448,837	1,212,464	236,373	620,104	529,129	523,315	5,814	90,975	61,129	29,846
25 to 29	1,373,147	1,134,690	238,457	817,875	623,412	194,463	555,272	411,277	403,145	8,132	143,995	108,133	35,862
30 to 34	592,027	470,444	121,583	315,386	219,748	95,638	276,641	173,271	168,203	5,068	103,370	82,493	20,877
35 to 39	338,942	264,507	74,435	160,625	103,569	57,056	178,317	102,206	98,718	3,488	76,111	62,220	13,891
40 to 49	350,641	273,554	77,087	147,447	89,485	57,962	203,194	114,740	110,443	4,297	88,454	73,626	14,828
50 to 64	148,810	114,851	33,959	57,641	32,183	25,458	91,169	51,767	49,510	2,257	39,402	33,158	6,244
65 and over	8,979	6,224	2,755	4,048	1,774	2,274	4,931	2,863	2,685	178	2,068	1,765	303
Age unknown	13,329	8,817	4,512	6,524	2,929	3,595	6,805	5,030	4,982	48	1,775	906	869
Part-time	7,688,294	3,974,313	3,713,981	6,232,082	2,542,989	3,689,093	1,456,212	1,024,191	1,016,891	7,300	432,021	414,433	17,588
Under 18	1,009,804	339,217	670,587	944,036	273,867	670,169	65,768	63,216	62,823	393	2,552	2,527	25
18 and 19	750,930	226,011	524,919	714,930	191,270	523,660	36,000	29,973	29,605	368	6,027	5,136	891
20 and 21	829,268	299,487	529,781	779,069	251,864	527,205	50,199	35,239	34,530	709	14,960	13,093	1,867
22 to 24	1,134,331	598,110	536,221	973,691	441,837	531,854	160,640	122,676	121,446	1,230	37,964	34,827	3,137
25 to 29	1,319,239	802,046	517,193	1,010,866	499,298	511,568	308,373	222,225	220,698	1,527	86,148	82,050	4,098
30 to 34	828,395	530,335	298,060	592,514	298,036	294,478	235,881	157,459	156,484	975	78,422	75,815	2,607
35 to 39	593,389	389,401	203,988	405,429	203,854	201,575	187,960	122,298	121,598	700	65,662	63,949	1,713
40 to 49	737,535	492,265	245,270	484,419	241,987	242,432	253,116	164,402	163,552	850	88,714	86,726	1,988
50 to 64	410,346	261,239	149,107	270,162	122,692	147,470	140,184	92,442	91,971	471	47,742	46,576	1,166
65 and over	58,058	26,332	31,726	48,227	16,581	31,646	9,831	7,283	7,246	37	2,548	2,505	43
Age unknown	16,999	9,870	7,129	8,739	1,703	7,036	8,260	6,978	6,938	40	1,282	1,229	53
	Percentage distribution of students with known age[1]												
All students	**100.0**	**100.0**	**100.0**	**100.0**	**100.0**	**100.0**	**100.0**	**100.0**	**100.0**	**100.0**	**100.0**	**100.0**	**100.0**
Under 18	6.2	3.5	12.7	7.8	4.3	13.2	2.0	2.4	2.4	1.4	0.4	0.4	0.6
18 and 19	22.5	22.2	23.3	24.2	24.6	23.8	17.7	21.0	21.1	14.9	5.4	4.0	11.8
20 and 21	20.8	22.5	16.7	21.7	24.8	16.9	18.2	21.1	21.2	11.2	7.4	6.0	14.2
22 to 24	16.2	17.3	13.6	16.7	18.7	13.5	15.0	15.9	15.9	14.6	11.8	10.5	17.7
25 to 29	13.6	14.0	12.7	12.6	12.7	12.4	16.6	15.5	15.4	20.0	21.0	20.9	21.5
30 to 34	7.2	7.2	7.1	6.2	5.9	6.8	9.9	8.1	8.0	12.5	16.6	17.4	12.6
35 to 39	4.7	4.7	4.7	3.9	3.5	4.5	7.1	5.5	5.4	8.7	12.9	13.9	8.4
40 to 49	5.5	5.5	5.4	4.3	3.7	5.3	8.8	6.8	6.8	10.7	16.2	17.6	9.0
50 to 64	2.8	2.7	3.1	2.3	1.8	3.0	4.5	3.5	3.5	5.6	8.0	8.8	4.0
65 and over	0.3	0.2	0.6	0.4	0.2	0.6	0.3	0.2	0.2	0.4	0.4	0.5	0.2
Full-time	100.0	100.0	100.0	100.0	100.0	100.0	100.0	100.0	100.0	100.0	100.0	100.0	100.0
Under 18	1.8	1.4	3.7	2.2	1.6	4.0	1.0	1.1	1.1	0.6	0.3	0.2	0.6
18 and 19	30.6	28.8	38.6	33.8	31.4	41.2	23.6	27.0	27.1	16.6	7.9	6.4	12.5
20 and 21	27.1	28.5	20.8	28.5	30.8	21.5	23.9	26.9	27.1	11.5	9.9	8.4	14.5
22 to 24	17.1	18.3	12.2	17.4	19.2	11.7	16.6	17.2	17.2	14.2	13.7	12.3	17.7
25 to 29	11.4	11.5	10.7	9.8	9.9	9.7	14.8	13.4	13.3	19.8	21.6	21.8	21.3
30 to 34	4.9	4.8	5.5	3.8	3.5	4.7	7.4	5.6	5.5	12.3	15.5	16.6	12.4
35 to 39	2.8	2.7	3.3	1.9	1.6	2.8	4.8	3.3	3.3	8.5	11.4	12.5	8.2
40 to 49	2.9	2.8	3.5	1.8	1.4	2.9	5.4	3.7	3.6	10.5	13.3	14.8	8.8
50 to 64	1.2	1.2	1.5	0.7	0.5	1.3	2.4	1.7	1.6	5.5	5.9	6.7	3.7
65 and over	0.1	0.1	0.1	#	#	0.1	0.1	0.1	0.1	0.4	0.3	0.4	0.2
Part-time	100.0	100.0	100.0	100.0	100.0	100.0	100.0	100.0	100.0	100.0	100.0	100.0	100.0
Under 18	13.2	8.6	18.1	15.2	10.8	18.2	4.5	6.2	6.2	5.4	0.6	0.6	0.1
18 and 19	9.8	5.7	14.2	11.5	7.5	14.2	2.5	2.9	2.9	5.1	1.4	1.2	5.1
20 and 21	10.8	7.6	14.3	12.5	9.9	14.3	3.5	3.5	3.4	9.8	3.5	3.2	10.6
22 to 24	14.8	15.1	14.5	15.6	17.4	14.4	11.1	12.1	12.0	16.9	8.8	8.4	17.9
25 to 29	17.2	20.2	14.0	16.2	19.6	13.9	21.3	21.8	21.9	21.0	20.0	19.9	23.4
30 to 34	10.8	13.4	8.0	9.5	11.7	8.0	16.3	15.5	15.5	13.4	18.2	18.3	14.9
35 to 39	7.7	9.8	5.5	6.5	8.0	5.5	13.0	12.0	12.0	9.6	15.2	15.5	9.8
40 to 49	9.6	12.4	6.6	7.8	9.5	6.6	17.5	16.2	16.2	11.7	20.6	21.0	11.3
50 to 64	5.3	6.6	4.0	4.3	4.8	4.0	9.7	9.1	9.1	6.5	11.1	11.3	6.6
65 and over	0.8	0.7	0.9	0.8	0.7	0.9	0.7	0.7	0.7	0.5	0.6	0.6	0.2

#Rounds to zero.
[1]Percentage distributions exclude students whose age is unknown.
NOTE: Degree-granting institutions grant associate's or higher degrees and participate in Title IV federal financial aid programs. Detail may not sum to totals because of rounding.

SOURCE: U.S. Department of Education, National Center for Education Statistics, Integrated Postsecondary Education Data System (IPEDS), Spring 2018, Fall Enrollment component. (This table was prepared October 2018.)

Table 303.60. Total fall enrollment in degree-granting postsecondary institutions, by level of enrollment, sex of student, and other selected characteristics: 2017

Level and control of institution and attendance status of student	Total			Undergraduate			Postbaccalaureate		
	Total	Males	Females	Total	Males	Females	Total	Males	Females
1	2	3	4	5	6	7	8	9	10
Total	**19,765,598**	**8,567,632**	**11,197,966**	**16,760,331**	**7,347,438**	**9,412,893**	**3,005,267**	**1,220,194**	**1,785,073**
Full-time	12,077,304	5,424,575	6,652,729	10,370,665	4,683,665	5,687,000	1,706,639	740,910	965,729
Part-time	7,688,294	3,143,057	4,545,237	6,389,666	2,663,773	3,725,893	1,298,628	479,284	819,344
4-year	**13,823,640**	**6,004,570**	**7,819,070**	**10,818,373**	**4,784,376**	**6,033,997**	**3,005,267**	**1,220,194**	**1,785,073**
Full-time	9,849,327	4,410,727	5,438,600	8,142,688	3,669,817	4,472,871	1,706,639	740,910	965,729
Part-time	3,974,313	1,593,843	2,380,470	2,675,685	1,114,559	1,561,126	1,298,628	479,284	819,344
2-year	**5,941,958**	**2,563,062**	**3,378,896**	**5,941,958**	**2,563,062**	**3,378,896**	†	†	†
Full-time	2,227,977	1,013,848	1,214,129	2,227,977	1,013,848	1,214,129	†	†	†
Part-time	3,713,981	1,549,214	2,164,767	3,713,981	1,549,214	2,164,767	†	†	†
Public	**14,560,155**	**6,477,920**	**8,082,235**	**13,100,953**	**5,860,399**	**7,240,554**	**1,459,202**	**617,521**	**841,681**
Full-time	8,328,073	3,857,945	4,470,128	7,516,055	3,492,447	4,023,608	812,018	365,498	446,520
Part-time	6,232,082	2,619,975	3,612,107	5,584,898	2,367,952	3,216,946	647,184	252,023	395,161
Public 4-year	8,853,477	3,988,930	4,864,547	7,394,275	3,371,409	4,022,866	1,459,202	617,521	841,681
Full-time	6,310,488	2,911,737	3,398,751	5,498,470	2,546,239	2,952,231	812,018	365,498	446,520
Part-time	2,542,989	1,077,193	1,465,796	1,895,805	825,170	1,070,635	647,184	252,023	395,161
Public 2-year	5,706,678	2,488,990	3,217,688	5,706,678	2,488,990	3,217,688	†	†	†
Full-time	2,017,585	946,208	1,071,377	2,017,585	946,208	1,071,377	†	†	†
Part-time	3,689,093	1,542,782	2,146,311	3,689,093	1,542,782	2,146,311	†	†	†
Private	**5,205,443**	**2,089,712**	**3,115,731**	**3,659,378**	**1,487,039**	**2,172,339**	**1,546,065**	**602,673**	**943,392**
Full-time	3,749,231	1,566,630	2,182,601	2,854,610	1,191,218	1,663,392	894,621	375,412	519,209
Part-time	1,456,212	523,082	933,130	804,768	295,821	508,947	651,444	227,261	424,183
Private 4-year	4,970,163	2,015,640	2,954,523	3,424,098	1,412,967	2,011,131	1,546,065	602,673	943,392
Full-time	3,538,839	1,498,990	2,039,849	2,644,218	1,123,578	1,520,640	894,621	375,412	519,209
Part-time	1,431,324	516,650	914,674	779,880	289,389	490,491	651,444	227,261	424,183
Private 2-year	235,280	74,072	161,208	235,280	74,072	161,208	†	†	†
Full-time	210,392	67,640	142,752	210,392	67,640	142,752	†	†	†
Part-time	24,888	6,432	18,456	24,888	6,432	18,456	†	†	†
Nonprofit	4,106,477	1,720,440	2,386,037	2,817,017	1,192,312	1,624,705	1,289,460	528,128	761,332
Full-time	3,082,286	1,328,996	1,753,290	2,299,345	990,585	1,308,760	782,941	338,411	444,530
Part-time	1,024,191	391,444	632,747	517,672	201,727	315,945	506,519	189,717	316,802
Nonprofit 4-year	4,058,087	1,707,724	2,350,363	2,768,627	1,179,596	1,589,031	1,289,460	528,128	761,332
Full-time	3,041,196	1,318,203	1,722,993	2,258,255	979,792	1,278,463	782,941	338,411	444,530
Part-time	1,016,891	389,521	627,370	510,372	199,804	310,568	506,519	189,717	316,802
Nonprofit 2-year	48,390	12,716	35,674	48,390	12,716	35,674	†	†	†
Full-time	41,090	10,793	30,297	41,090	10,793	30,297	†	†	†
Part-time	7,300	1,923	5,377	7,300	1,923	5,377	†	†	†
For-profit	1,098,966	369,272	729,694	842,361	294,727	547,634	256,605	74,545	182,060
Full-time	666,945	237,634	429,311	555,265	200,633	354,632	111,680	37,001	74,679
Part-time	432,021	131,638	300,383	287,096	94,094	193,002	144,925	37,544	107,381
For-profit 4-year	912,076	307,916	604,160	655,471	233,371	422,100	256,605	74,545	182,060
Full-time	497,643	180,787	316,856	385,963	143,786	242,177	111,680	37,001	74,679
Part-time	414,433	127,129	287,304	269,508	89,585	179,923	144,925	37,544	107,381
For-profit 2-year	186,890	61,356	125,534	186,890	61,356	125,534	†	†	†
Full-time	169,302	56,847	112,455	169,302	56,847	112,455	†	†	†
Part-time	17,588	4,509	13,079	17,588	4,509	13,079	†	†	†

†Not applicable.

NOTE: Degree-granting institutions grant associate's or higher degrees and participate in Title IV federal financial aid programs.

SOURCE: U.S. Department of Education, National Center for Education Statistics, Integrated Postsecondary Education Data System (IPEDS), Spring 2018, Fall Enrollment component. (This table was prepared October 2018.)

Table 303.70. Total undergraduate fall enrollment in degree-granting postsecondary institutions, by attendance status, sex of student, and control and level of institution: Selected years, 1970 through 2028

Level and year	Total	Full-time	Part-time	Males	Females	Males		Females		Public	Private		
						Full-time	Part-time	Full-time	Part-time		Total	Nonprofit	For-profit
1	2	3	4	5	6	7	8	9	10	11	12	13	14
Total, all levels													
1970	7,368,644	5,280,064	2,088,580	4,249,702	3,118,942	3,096,371	1,153,331	2,183,693	935,249	5,620,255	1,748,389	1,730,133	18,256
1975	9,679,455	6,168,396	3,511,059	5,257,005	4,422,450	3,459,328	1,797,677	2,709,068	1,713,382	7,826,032	1,853,423	1,814,844	38,579
1980	10,475,055	6,361,744	4,113,311	5,000,177	5,474,878	3,226,857	1,773,320	3,134,887	2,339,991	8,441,955	2,033,100	1,926,703	106,397
1985	10,596,674	6,319,592	4,277,082	4,962,080	5,634,594	3,156,446	1,805,634	3,163,146	2,471,448	8,477,125	2,119,549	1,928,996	190,553
1986	10,797,975	6,352,073	4,445,902	5,017,505	5,780,470	3,146,330	1,871,175	3,205,743	2,574,727	8,660,716	2,137,259	1,928,294	208,965
1987	11,046,235	6,462,549	4,583,686	5,068,457	5,977,778	3,163,676	1,904,781	3,298,873	2,678,905	8,918,589	2,127,646	1,939,942	187,704
1988	11,316,548	6,642,428	4,674,120	5,137,644	6,178,904	3,206,442	1,931,202	3,435,986	2,742,918	9,103,146	2,213,402	—	—
1989	11,742,531	6,840,696	4,901,835	5,310,990	6,431,541	3,278,647	2,032,343	3,562,049	2,869,492	9,487,742	2,254,789	—	—
1990	11,959,106	6,976,030	4,983,076	5,379,759	6,579,347	3,336,535	2,043,224	3,639,495	2,939,852	9,709,596	2,249,510	2,043,407	206,103
1991	12,439,287	7,221,412	5,217,875	5,571,003	6,868,284	3,435,526	2,135,477	3,785,886	3,082,398	10,147,957	2,291,330	2,072,354	218,976
1992	12,537,700	7,244,442	5,293,258	5,582,936	6,954,764	3,424,739	2,158,197	3,819,703	3,135,061	10,216,297	2,321,403	2,101,721	219,682
1993	12,323,959	7,179,482	5,144,477	5,483,682	6,840,277	3,381,997	2,101,685	3,797,485	3,042,792	10,011,787	2,312,172	2,099,197	212,975
1994	12,262,608	7,168,706	5,093,902	5,422,113	6,840,495	3,341,591	2,080,522	3,827,115	3,013,380	9,945,128	2,317,480	2,100,465	217,015
1995	12,231,719	7,145,268	5,086,451	5,401,130	6,830,589	3,296,610	2,104,520	3,848,658	2,981,931	9,903,626	2,328,093	2,104,693	223,400
1996	12,326,948	7,298,839	5,028,109	5,420,672	6,906,276	3,339,108	2,081,564	3,959,731	2,946,545	9,935,283	2,391,665	2,112,318	279,347
1997	12,450,587	7,418,598	5,031,989	5,468,532	6,982,055	3,379,597	2,088,935	4,039,001	2,943,054	10,007,479	2,443,108	2,139,824	303,284
1998	12,436,937	7,538,711	4,898,226	5,446,133	6,990,804	3,428,161	2,017,972	4,110,550	2,880,254	9,950,212	2,486,725	2,152,655	334,070
1999	12,739,445	7,753,548	4,985,897	5,584,234	7,155,211	3,524,586	2,059,648	4,228,962	2,926,249	10,174,228	2,565,217	2,185,290	379,927
2000	13,155,393	7,922,926	5,232,467	5,778,268	7,377,125	3,588,246	2,190,022	4,334,680	3,042,445	10,539,322	2,616,071	2,213,180	402,891
2001	13,715,610	8,327,640	5,387,970	6,004,431	7,711,179	3,768,630	2,235,801	4,559,010	3,152,169	10,985,871	2,729,739	2,257,718	472,021
2002	14,257,077	8,734,252	5,522,825	6,192,390	8,064,687	3,934,168	2,258,222	4,800,084	3,264,603	11,432,855	2,824,222	2,306,091	518,131
2003	14,480,364	9,045,253	5,435,111	6,227,372	8,252,992	4,048,682	2,178,690	4,996,571	3,256,421	11,523,103	2,957,261	2,346,673	610,588
2004	14,780,630	9,284,336	5,496,294	6,340,048	8,440,582	4,140,628	2,199,420	5,143,708	3,296,874	11,650,580	3,130,050	2,389,366	740,684
2005	14,963,964	9,446,430	5,517,534	6,408,871	8,555,093	4,200,863	2,208,008	5,245,567	3,309,526	11,697,730	3,266,234	2,418,368	847,866
2006	15,179,591	9,571,349	5,608,242	6,511,198	8,668,393	4,264,722	2,246,476	5,306,627	3,361,766	11,842,625	3,336,966	2,448,250	888,716
2007	15,613,540	9,841,973	5,771,567	6,731,561	8,881,979	4,397,402	2,334,159	5,444,571	3,437,408	12,147,744	3,465,796	2,470,463	995,333
2008	16,344,592	10,244,174	6,100,418	7,055,640	9,288,952	4,570,913	2,484,727	5,673,261	3,615,691	12,589,947	3,754,645	2,535,789	1,218,856
2009	17,464,179	11,038,275	6,425,904	7,563,176	9,901,003	4,942,120	2,621,056	6,096,155	3,804,848	13,386,375	4,077,804	2,595,171	1,482,633
2010	18,082,427	11,457,040	6,625,387	7,836,282	10,246,145	5,118,975	2,717,307	6,338,065	3,908,080	13,703,000	4,379,427	2,652,993	1,726,434
2011	18,077,303	11,365,175	6,712,128	7,822,992	10,254,311	5,070,553	2,752,439	6,294,622	3,959,689	13,694,899	4,382,404	2,718,923	1,663,481
2012	17,735,638	11,097,092	6,638,546	7,714,938	10,020,700	4,984,389	2,730,549	6,112,703	3,907,997	13,478,100	4,257,538	2,744,400	1,513,138
2013	17,476,304	10,939,276	6,537,028	7,660,140	9,816,164	4,950,210	2,709,930	5,989,066	3,827,098	13,348,292	4,128,012	2,755,463	1,372,549
2014	17,294,136	10,784,392	6,509,744	7,586,299	9,707,837	4,877,531	2,708,768	5,906,861	3,800,976	13,244,533	4,049,603	2,772,065	1,277,538
2015	17,046,673	10,603,030	6,443,643	7,502,254	9,544,419	4,809,098	2,693,156	5,793,932	3,750,487	13,150,823	3,895,850	2,822,122	1,073,728
2016	16,874,649	10,430,068	6,444,581	7,416,859	9,457,790	4,725,510	2,691,349	5,704,558	3,753,232	13,143,979	3,730,670	2,813,742	916,928
2017	16,760,331	10,370,665	6,389,666	7,347,438	9,412,893	4,683,665	2,663,773	5,687,000	3,725,893	13,100,953	3,659,378	2,817,017	842,361
2018[1]	16,813,000	10,393,000	6,421,000	7,372,000	9,441,000	4,692,000	2,680,000	5,701,000	3,740,000	13,144,000	3,669,000	—	—
2019[1]	16,877,000	10,421,000	6,456,000	7,399,000	9,478,000	4,703,000	2,696,000	5,718,000	3,761,000	13,195,000	3,682,000	—	—
2020[1]	16,897,000	10,418,000	6,478,000	7,407,000	9,490,000	4,701,000	2,706,000	5,718,000	3,772,000	13,213,000	3,684,000	—	—
2021[1]	16,920,000	10,415,000	6,506,000	7,412,000	9,508,000	4,695,000	2,718,000	5,720,000	3,788,000	13,234,000	3,686,000	—	—
2022[1]	16,949,000	10,416,000	6,533,000	7,422,000	9,527,000	4,692,000	2,730,000	5,724,000	3,803,000	13,259,000	3,690,000	—	—
2023[1]	16,990,000	10,428,000	6,562,000	7,440,000	9,551,000	4,696,000	2,743,000	5,732,000	3,818,000	13,293,000	3,697,000	—	—
2024[1]	17,047,000	10,457,000	6,590,000	7,463,000	9,584,000	4,708,000	2,755,000	5,749,000	3,835,000	13,338,000	3,709,000	—	—
2025[1]	17,106,000	10,493,000	6,613,000	7,488,000	9,618,000	4,725,000	2,763,000	5,769,000	3,850,000	13,385,000	3,722,000	—	—
2026[1]	17,175,000	10,531,000	6,644,000	7,520,000	9,655,000	4,743,000	2,777,000	5,788,000	3,867,000	13,439,000	3,736,000	—	—
2027[1]	17,206,000	10,538,000	6,668,000	7,536,000	9,670,000	4,748,000	2,788,000	5,790,000	3,880,000	13,465,000	3,741,000	—	—
2028[1]	17,214,000	10,528,000	6,686,000	7,539,000	9,675,000	4,744,000	2,795,000	5,785,000	3,890,000	13,474,000	3,740,000	—	—
2-year institutions[2]													
1970	2,318,956	1,228,909	1,090,047	1,374,426	944,530	771,298	603,128	457,611	486,919	2,194,983	123,973	113,299	10,674
1975	3,965,726	1,761,009	2,204,717	2,163,604	1,802,122	1,035,531	1,128,073	725,478	1,076,644	3,831,973	133,753	112,997	20,756
1980	4,525,097	1,753,637	2,771,460	2,046,642	2,478,455	879,619	1,167,023	874,018	1,604,437	4,327,592	197,505	114,094	83,411
1985	4,531,077	1,690,607	2,840,470	2,002,234	2,528,843	826,308	1,175,926	864,299	1,664,544	4,269,733	261,344	108,791	152,553
1986	4,679,548	1,696,261	2,983,287	2,060,932	2,618,616	824,551	1,236,381	871,710	1,746,906	4,413,691	265,857	101,498	164,359
1987	4,776,222	1,708,669	3,067,553	2,072,823	2,703,399	820,167	1,252,656	888,502	1,814,897	4,541,054	235,168	90,102	145,066
1988	4,875,155	1,743,592	3,131,563	2,089,689	2,785,466	818,593	1,271,096	924,999	1,860,467	4,615,487	259,668	—	—
1989	5,150,889	1,855,701	3,295,188	2,216,800	2,934,089	869,688	1,347,112	986,013	1,948,076	4,883,660	267,229	—	—
1990	5,240,083	1,883,962	3,356,121	2,232,769	3,007,314	881,392	1,351,377	1,002,570	2,004,744	4,996,475	243,608	89,158	154,450
1991	5,651,900	2,074,530	3,577,370	2,401,910	3,249,990	961,397	1,440,513	1,113,133	2,136,857	5,404,815	247,085	89,289	157,796
1992	5,722,349	2,080,005	3,642,344	2,413,266	3,309,083	951,816	1,461,450	1,128,189	2,180,894	5,484,514	237,835	83,288	154,547
1993	5,565,561	2,043,319	3,522,242	2,345,396	3,220,165	928,216	1,417,180	1,115,103	2,105,062	5,337,022	228,539	86,357	142,182
1994	5,529,609	2,031,713	3,497,896	2,323,161	3,206,448	911,589	1,411,572	1,120,124	2,086,324	5,308,366	221,243	85,607	135,636
1995	5,492,098	1,977,046	3,515,052	2,328,500	3,163,598	878,215	1,450,285	1,098,831	2,064,767	5,277,398	214,700	75,154	139,546
1996	5,562,780	2,072,215	3,490,565	2,358,792	3,203,988	916,452	1,442,340	1,155,763	2,048,225	5,314,038	248,742	75,253	173,489
1997	5,605,569	2,095,171	3,510,398	2,389,711	3,215,858	931,394	1,458,317	1,163,777	2,052,081	5,360,686	244,883	71,794	173,089
1998	5,489,314	2,085,906	3,403,408	2,333,334	3,155,980	936,421	1,396,913	1,149,485	2,006,495	5,245,963	243,351	65,870	177,481
1999	5,653,256	2,167,242	3,486,014	2,413,322	3,239,934	979,203	1,434,119	1,188,039	2,051,895	5,397,786	255,470	63,301	192,169
2000	5,948,104	2,217,044	3,731,060	2,558,520	3,389,584	995,839	1,562,681	1,221,205	2,168,379	5,697,061	251,043	58,844	192,199
2001	6,250,529	2,374,490	3,876,039	2,675,193	3,575,336	1,066,281	1,608,912	1,308,209	2,267,127	5,996,651	253,878	47,549	206,329
2002	6,529,198	2,556,032	3,973,166	2,753,405	3,775,793	1,135,669	1,617,736	1,420,363	2,355,430	6,270,199	258,999	47,087	211,912
2003	6,493,862	2,650,337	3,843,525	2,689,928	3,803,934	1,162,555	1,527,373	1,487,782	2,316,152	6,208,885	284,977	43,868	241,109
2004	6,545,570	2,683,489	3,862,081	2,697,507	3,848,063	1,166,554	1,530,953	1,516,935	2,331,128	6,243,344	302,226	42,250	259,976
2005	6,487,826	2,646,763	3,841,063	2,680,299	3,807,527	1,153,759	1,526,540	1,493,004	2,314,523	6,184,000	303,826	43,522	260,304
2006	6,513,303	2,643,162	3,870,141	2,701,970	3,811,333	1,159,733	1,542,237	1,483,429	2,327,904	6,219,880	293,423	39,156	254,267
2007	6,628,936	2,694,608	3,934,328	2,775,166	3,853,770	1,191,058	1,584,108	1,503,550	2,350,220	6,335,826	293,110	33,492	259,618
2008	6,970,947	2,832,412	4,138,535	2,935,799	4,035,148	1,250,063	1,685,736	1,582,349	2,452,799	6,639,928	331,019	35,358	295,661
2009	7,522,581	3,243,952	4,278,629	3,197,338	4,325,243	1,446,372	1,750,966	1,797,580	2,527,663	7,101,569	421,012	34,772	386,240

See notes at end of table.

Table 303.70. Total undergraduate fall enrollment in degree-granting postsecondary institutions, by attendance status, sex of student, and control and level of institution: Selected years, 1970 through 2028—Continued

Level and year	Total	Full-time	Part-time	Males	Females	Males		Females		Public	Private		
						Full-time	Part-time	Full-time	Part-time		Total	Nonprofit	For-profit
1	2	3	4	5	6	7	8	9	10	11	12	13	14
2010	7,683,597	3,365,379	4,318,218	3,265,885	4,417,712	1,483,230	1,782,655	1,882,149	2,535,563	7,218,063	465,534	32,683	432,851
2011	7,511,150	3,170,207	4,340,943	3,175,803	4,335,347	1,391,183	1,784,620	1,779,024	2,556,323	7,068,158	442,992	39,855	403,137
2012	7,167,840	2,941,797	4,226,043	3,046,093	4,121,747	1,305,657	1,740,436	1,636,140	2,485,607	6,792,065	375,775	37,698	338,077
2013	6,970,644	2,836,274	4,134,370	2,998,440	3,972,204	1,279,794	1,718,646	1,556,480	2,415,724	6,626,411	344,233	32,191	312,042
2014	6,714,678	2,661,107	4,053,571	2,894,020	3,820,658	1,200,648	1,693,372	1,460,459	2,360,199	6,397,552	317,126	30,376	286,750
2015	6,499,461	2,510,684	3,988,777	2,818,075	3,681,386	1,143,704	1,674,371	1,366,980	2,314,406	6,224,304	275,157	50,009	225,148
2016	6,092,418	2,309,347	3,783,071	2,637,394	3,455,024	1,057,839	1,579,555	1,251,508	2,203,516	5,842,909	249,509	50,555	198,954
2017	5,941,958	2,227,977	3,713,981	2,563,062	3,378,896	1,013,848	1,549,214	1,214,129	2,164,767	5,706,678	235,280	48,390	186,890
2018[1]	5,965,000	2,233,000	3,732,000	2,574,000	3,390,000	1,016,000	1,559,000	1,217,000	2,173,000	5,729,000	236,000	—	—
2019[1]	5,991,000	2,239,000	3,753,000	2,586,000	3,406,000	1,018,000	1,568,000	1,221,000	2,185,000	5,755,000	237,000	—	—
2020[1]	6,004,000	2,238,000	3,766,000	2,591,000	3,412,000	1,018,000	1,574,000	1,221,000	2,192,000	5,767,000	237,000	—	—
2021[1]	6,019,000	2,237,000	3,781,000	2,597,000	3,422,000	1,016,000	1,581,000	1,221,000	2,201,000	5,782,000	237,000	—	—
2022[1]	6,035,000	2,238,000	3,797,000	2,604,000	3,431,000	1,016,000	1,588,000	1,222,000	2,209,000	5,798,000	237,000	—	—
2023[1]	6,054,000	2,240,000	3,814,000	2,612,000	3,442,000	1,017,000	1,596,000	1,224,000	2,219,000	5,817,000	237,000	—	—
2024[1]	6,077,000	2,247,000	3,830,000	2,621,000	3,456,000	1,019,000	1,602,000	1,227,000	2,228,000	5,839,000	238,000	—	—
2025[1]	6,098,000	2,254,000	3,844,000	2,630,000	3,468,000	1,023,000	1,607,000	1,232,000	2,237,000	5,859,000	239,000	—	—
2026[1]	6,124,000	2,262,000	3,862,000	2,642,000	3,483,000	1,027,000	1,615,000	1,236,000	2,247,000	5,884,000	240,000	—	—
2027[1]	6,140,000	2,264,000	3,876,000	2,649,000	3,491,000	1,028,000	1,621,000	1,236,000	2,255,000	5,900,000	240,000	—	—
2028[1]	6,148,000	2,262,000	3,886,000	2,653,000	3,495,000	1,027,000	1,626,000	1,235,000	2,260,000	5,908,000	240,000	—	—
4-year institutions													
1970	5,049,688	4,051,155	998,533	2,875,276	2,174,412	2,325,073	550,203	1,726,082	448,330	3,425,272	1,624,416	1,616,834	7,582
1975	5,713,729	4,407,387	1,306,342	3,093,401	2,620,328	2,423,797	669,604	1,983,590	636,738	3,994,059	1,719,670	1,701,847	17,823
1980	5,949,958	4,608,107	1,341,851	2,953,535	2,996,423	2,347,238	606,297	2,260,869	735,554	4,114,363	1,835,595	1,812,609	22,986
1985	6,065,597	4,628,985	1,436,612	2,959,846	3,105,751	2,330,138	629,708	2,298,847	806,904	4,207,392	1,858,205	1,820,205	38,000
1986	6,118,427	4,655,812	1,462,615	2,956,573	3,161,854	2,321,779	634,794	2,334,033	827,821	4,247,025	1,871,402	1,826,796	44,606
1987	6,270,013	4,753,880	1,516,133	2,995,634	3,274,379	2,343,509	652,125	2,410,371	864,008	4,377,535	1,892,478	1,849,840	42,638
1988	6,441,393	4,898,836	1,542,557	3,047,955	3,393,438	2,387,849	660,106	2,510,987	882,451	4,487,659	1,953,734	—	—
1989	6,591,642	4,984,995	1,606,647	3,094,190	3,497,452	2,408,959	685,231	2,576,036	921,416	4,604,082	1,987,560	—	—
1990	6,719,023	5,092,068	1,626,955	3,146,990	3,572,033	2,455,143	691,847	2,636,925	935,108	4,713,121	2,005,902	1,954,249	51,653
1991	6,787,387	5,146,882	1,640,505	3,169,093	3,618,294	2,474,129	694,964	2,672,753	945,541	4,743,142	2,044,245	1,983,065	61,180
1992	6,815,351	5,164,437	1,650,914	3,169,670	3,645,681	2,472,923	696,747	2,691,514	954,167	4,731,783	2,083,568	2,018,433	65,135
1993	6,758,398	5,136,163	1,622,235	3,138,286	3,620,112	2,453,781	684,505	2,682,382	937,730	4,674,765	2,083,633	2,012,840	70,793
1994	6,732,999	5,136,993	1,596,006	3,098,952	3,634,047	2,430,002	668,950	2,706,991	927,056	4,636,762	2,096,237	2,014,858	81,379
1995	6,739,621	5,168,222	1,571,399	3,072,630	3,666,991	2,418,395	654,235	2,749,827	917,164	4,626,228	2,113,393	2,029,539	83,854
1996	6,764,168	5,226,624	1,537,544	3,061,880	3,702,288	2,422,656	639,224	2,803,968	898,320	4,621,245	2,142,923	2,037,065	105,858
1997	6,845,018	5,323,427	1,521,591	3,078,821	3,766,197	2,448,203	630,618	2,875,224	890,973	4,646,793	2,198,225	2,068,030	130,195
1998	6,947,623	5,452,805	1,494,818	3,112,799	3,834,824	2,491,740	621,059	2,961,065	873,759	4,704,249	2,243,374	2,086,785	156,589
1999	7,086,189	5,586,306	1,499,883	3,170,912	3,915,277	2,545,383	625,529	3,040,923	874,354	4,776,442	2,309,747	2,121,989	187,758
2000	7,207,289	5,705,882	1,501,407	3,219,748	3,987,541	2,592,407	627,341	3,113,475	874,066	4,842,261	2,365,028	2,154,336	210,692
2001	7,465,081	5,953,150	1,511,931	3,329,238	4,135,843	2,702,349	626,889	3,250,801	885,042	4,989,220	2,475,861	2,210,169	265,692
2002	7,727,879	6,178,220	1,549,659	3,438,985	4,288,894	2,798,499	640,486	3,379,721	909,173	5,162,656	2,565,223	2,259,004	306,219
2003	7,986,502	6,394,916	1,591,586	3,537,444	4,449,058	2,886,127	651,317	3,508,789	940,269	5,314,218	2,672,284	2,302,805	369,479
2004	8,235,060	6,600,847	1,634,213	3,642,541	4,592,519	2,974,074	668,467	3,626,773	965,746	5,407,236	2,827,824	2,347,116	480,708
2005	8,476,138	6,799,667	1,676,471	3,728,572	4,747,566	3,047,104	681,468	3,752,563	995,003	5,513,730	2,962,408	2,374,846	587,562
2006	8,666,288	6,928,187	1,738,101	3,809,228	4,857,060	3,104,989	704,239	3,823,198	1,033,862	5,622,745	3,043,543	2,409,094	634,449
2007	8,984,604	7,147,365	1,837,239	3,956,395	5,028,209	3,206,344	750,051	3,941,021	1,087,188	5,811,918	3,172,686	2,436,971	735,715
2008	9,373,645	7,411,762	1,961,883	4,119,841	5,253,804	3,320,850	798,991	4,090,912	1,162,892	5,950,019	3,423,626	2,500,431	923,195
2009	9,941,598	7,794,323	2,147,275	4,365,838	5,575,760	3,495,748	870,090	4,298,575	1,277,185	6,284,806	3,656,792	2,560,399	1,096,393
2010	10,398,830	8,091,661	2,307,169	4,570,397	5,828,433	3,635,745	934,652	4,455,916	1,372,517	6,484,937	3,913,893	2,620,310	1,293,583
2011	10,566,153	8,194,968	2,371,185	4,647,189	5,918,964	3,679,370	967,819	4,515,598	1,403,366	6,626,741	3,939,412	2,679,068	1,260,344
2012	10,567,798	8,155,295	2,412,503	4,668,845	5,898,953	3,678,732	990,113	4,476,563	1,422,390	6,686,035	3,881,763	2,706,702	1,175,061
2013	10,505,660	8,103,002	2,402,658	4,661,700	5,843,960	3,670,416	991,284	4,432,586	1,411,374	6,721,881	3,783,779	2,723,272	1,060,507
2014	10,579,458	8,123,285	2,456,173	4,692,279	5,887,179	3,676,883	1,015,396	4,446,402	1,440,777	6,846,981	3,732,477	2,741,689	990,788
2015	10,547,212	8,092,346	2,454,866	4,684,179	5,863,033	3,665,394	1,018,785	4,426,952	1,436,081	6,926,519	3,620,693	2,772,113	848,580
2016	10,782,231	8,120,721	2,661,510	4,779,465	6,002,766	3,667,671	1,111,794	4,453,050	1,549,716	7,301,070	3,481,161	2,763,187	717,974
2017	10,818,373	8,142,688	2,675,685	4,784,376	6,033,997	3,669,817	1,114,559	4,472,871	1,561,126	7,394,275	3,424,098	2,768,627	655,471
2018[1]	10,849,000	8,160,000	2,689,000	4,797,000	6,051,000	3,676,000	1,122,000	4,484,000	1,567,000	7,415,000	3,433,000	—	—
2019[1]	10,885,000	8,182,000	2,704,000	4,813,000	6,073,000	3,685,000	1,128,000	4,497,000	1,576,000	7,441,000	3,445,000	—	—
2020[1]	10,893,000	8,180,000	2,713,000	4,815,000	6,078,000	3,683,000	1,132,000	4,497,000	1,581,000	7,446,000	3,447,000	—	—
2021[1]	10,902,000	8,177,000	2,724,000	4,816,000	6,086,000	3,678,000	1,137,000	4,499,000	1,587,000	7,452,000	3,450,000	—	—
2022[1]	10,914,000	8,179,000	2,736,000	4,819,000	6,095,000	3,676,000	1,142,000	4,502,000	1,593,000	7,461,000	3,453,000	—	—
2023[1]	10,936,000	8,188,000	2,748,000	4,828,000	6,108,000	3,680,000	1,148,000	4,508,000	1,600,000	7,476,000	3,460,000	—	—
2024[1]	10,970,000	8,211,000	2,759,000	4,842,000	6,129,000	3,689,000	1,153,000	4,522,000	1,607,000	7,499,000	3,471,000	—	—
2025[1]	11,008,000	8,239,000	2,769,000	4,858,000	6,150,000	3,702,000	1,156,000	4,537,000	1,613,000	7,525,000	3,483,000	—	—
2026[1]	11,050,000	8,268,000	2,782,000	4,878,000	6,172,000	3,716,000	1,162,000	4,552,000	1,620,000	7,554,000	3,496,000	—	—
2027[1]	11,066,000	8,274,000	2,792,000	4,887,000	6,179,000	3,720,000	1,166,000	4,554,000	1,626,000	7,565,000	3,501,000	—	—
2028[1]	11,066,000	8,267,000	2,800,000	4,887,000	6,180,000	3,717,000	1,170,000	4,550,000	1,630,000	7,566,000	3,501,000	—	—

—Not available.
[1]Projected.
[2]Beginning in 1980, 2-year institutions include schools accredited by the Accrediting Commission of Career Schools and Colleges of Technology.
NOTE: Data through 1995 are for institutions of higher education, while later data are for degree-granting institutions. Degree-granting institutions grant associate's or higher degrees and participate in Title IV federal financial aid programs. The degree-granting classification is very similar to the earlier higher education classification, but it includes more 2-year colleges and excludes a few higher education institutions that did not grant degrees. Some data have been revised from previously published figures.
SOURCE: U.S. Department of Education, National Center for Education Statistics, Higher Education General Information Survey (HEGIS), "Fall Enrollment in Colleges and Universities" surveys, 1970 through 1985; Integrated Postsecondary Education Data System (IPEDS), "Fall Enrollment Survey" (IPEDS-EF:86–99); IPEDS Spring 2001 through Spring 2018, Fall Enrollment component; and Enrollment in Degree-Granting Institutions Projection Model, 2000 through 2028. (This table was prepared March 2019.)

Table 303.80. Total postbaccalaureate fall enrollment in degree-granting postsecondary institutions, by attendance status, sex of student, and control of institution: 1970 through 2028

Year	Total	Full-time	Part-time	Males	Females	Males		Females		Public	Private		
						Full-time	Part-time	Full-time	Part-time		Total	Nonprofit	For-profit
1	2	3	4	5	6	7	8	9	10	11	12	13	14
1970	1,212,243	536,226	676,017	793,940	418,303	407,724	386,216	128,502	289,801	807,879	404,364	404,287	77
1971	1,204,390	564,236	640,154	789,131	415,259	428,167	360,964	136,069	279,190	796,516	407,874	407,804	70
1972	1,272,421	583,299	689,122	810,164	462,257	436,533	373,631	146,766	315,491	848,031	424,390	424,278	112
1973	1,342,452	610,935	731,517	833,453	508,999	444,219	389,234	166,716	342,283	897,104	445,348	445,205	143
1974	1,425,001	643,927	781,074	856,847	568,154	454,706	402,141	189,221	378,933	956,770	468,231	467,950	281
1975	1,505,404	672,938	832,466	891,992	613,412	467,425	424,567	205,513	407,899	1,008,476	496,928	496,604	324
1976	1,577,546	683,825	893,721	904,551	672,995	459,286	445,265	224,539	448,456	1,033,115	544,431	541,064	3,367
1977	1,569,084	698,902	870,182	891,819	677,265	462,038	429,781	236,864	440,401	1,004,013	565,071	561,384	3,687
1978	1,575,693	704,831	870,862	879,931	695,762	458,865	421,066	245,966	449,796	998,608	577,085	573,563	3,522
1979	1,571,922	714,624	857,298	862,754	709,168	456,197	406,557	258,427	450,741	989,991	581,931	578,425	3,506
1980	1,621,840	736,214	885,626	874,197	747,643	462,387	411,810	273,827	473,816	1,015,439	606,401	601,084	5,317
1981	1,617,150	732,182	884,968	866,785	750,365	452,364	414,421	279,818	470,547	998,669	618,481	613,557	4,924
1982	1,600,718	736,813	863,905	860,890	739,828	453,519	407,371	283,294	456,534	983,014	617,704	613,350	4,354
1983	1,618,666	747,016	871,650	865,425	753,241	455,540	409,885	291,476	461,765	985,616	633,050	628,111	4,939
1984	1,623,869	750,735	873,134	856,761	767,108	452,579	404,182	298,156	468,952	983,879	639,990	634,109	5,881
1985	1,650,381	755,629	894,752	856,370	794,011	451,274	405,096	304,355	489,656	1,002,148	648,233	642,795	5,438
1986	1,705,536	767,477	938,059	867,010	838,526	452,717	414,293	314,760	523,766	1,053,177	652,359	644,185	8,174
1987	1,720,407	768,536	951,871	863,599	856,808	447,212	416,387	321,324	535,484	1,054,665	665,742	662,408	3,334
1988	1,738,789	794,340	944,449	864,252	874,537	455,337	408,915	339,003	535,534	1,058,242	680,547	—	—
1989	1,796,029	820,254	975,775	879,025	917,004	461,596	417,429	358,658	558,346	1,090,221	705,808	—	—
1990	1,859,531	844,955	1,014,576	904,150	955,381	471,217	432,933	373,738	581,643	1,135,121	724,410	716,820	7,590
1991	1,919,666	893,917	1,025,749	930,841	988,825	493,849	436,992	400,068	588,757	1,161,606	758,060	746,687	11,373
1992	1,949,659	917,676	1,031,983	941,053	1,008,606	502,166	438,887	415,510	593,096	1,168,270	781,389	770,802	10,587
1993	1,980,844	948,136	1,032,708	943,768	1,037,076	508,574	435,194	439,562	597,514	1,177,301	803,543	789,700	13,843
1994	2,016,182	969,070	1,047,112	949,785	1,066,397	513,592	436,193	455,478	610,919	1,188,552	827,630	809,642	17,988
1995	2,030,062	983,534	1,046,528	941,409	1,088,653	510,782	430,627	472,752	615,901	1,188,748	841,314	824,351	16,963
1996	2,040,572	1,004,114	1,036,458	932,153	1,108,419	512,100	420,053	492,014	616,405	1,185,216	855,356	830,238	25,118
1997	2,051,747	1,019,464	1,032,283	927,496	1,124,251	510,845	416,651	508,619	615,632	1,188,640	863,107	837,790	25,317
1998	2,070,030	1,024,627	1,045,403	923,132	1,146,898	505,492	417,640	519,135	627,763	1,187,557	882,473	852,270	30,203
1999	2,110,246	1,049,591	1,060,655	930,930	1,179,316	508,930	422,000	540,661	638,655	1,201,511	908,735	869,739	38,996
2000	2,156,896	1,086,674	1,070,222	943,501	1,213,395	522,847	420,654	563,827	649,568	1,213,464	943,432	896,239	47,193
2001	2,212,377	1,119,862	1,092,515	956,384	1,255,993	531,260	425,124	588,602	667,391	1,247,285	965,092	909,612	55,480
2002	2,354,634	1,212,107	1,142,527	1,009,726	1,344,908	566,930	442,796	645,177	699,731	1,319,138	1,035,496	959,385	76,111
2003	2,431,117	1,280,880	1,150,237	1,032,892	1,398,225	589,190	443,702	691,690	706,535	1,335,595	1,095,522	994,375	101,147
2004	2,491,414	1,325,841	1,165,573	1,047,214	1,444,200	598,727	448,487	727,114	717,086	1,329,532	1,161,882	1,022,319	139,563
2005	2,523,511	1,350,581	1,172,930	1,047,054	1,476,457	602,525	444,529	748,056	728,401	1,324,104	1,199,407	1,036,324	163,083
2006	2,574,639	1,386,189	1,188,450	1,061,067	1,513,572	614,706	446,361	771,483	742,089	1,332,725	1,241,914	1,064,679	177,235
2007	2,644,598	1,428,956	1,215,642	1,088,377	1,556,221	632,619	455,758	796,337	759,884	1,353,150	1,291,448	1,100,932	190,516
2008	2,737,094	1,490,462	1,246,632	1,122,074	1,615,020	656,213	465,861	834,249	780,771	1,380,915	1,356,179	1,125,038	231,141
2009	2,849,415	1,567,080	1,282,335	1,169,777	1,679,638	689,977	479,800	877,103	802,535	1,424,393	1,425,022	1,172,501	252,521
2010	2,937,011	1,630,142	1,306,869	1,209,477	1,727,534	719,408	490,069	910,734	816,800	1,439,171	1,497,840	1,201,489	296,351
2011	2,933,287	1,637,356	1,295,931	1,211,264	1,722,023	722,265	488,999	915,091	806,932	1,421,404	1,511,883	1,207,896	303,987
2012	2,908,840	1,637,312	1,271,528	1,204,068	1,704,772	724,017	480,051	913,295	791,477	1,406,567	1,502,273	1,206,988	295,285
2013	2,900,373	1,657,334	1,243,039	1,201,057	1,699,316	732,112	468,945	925,222	774,094	1,398,556	1,501,817	1,215,927	285,890
2014	2,914,956	1,670,072	1,244,884	1,211,231	1,703,725	742,247	468,984	927,825	775,900	1,410,127	1,504,829	1,225,184	279,645
2015	2,941,531	1,684,482	1,257,049	1,221,565	1,719,966	749,349	472,216	935,133	784,833	1,422,020	1,519,511	1,243,769	275,742
2016	2,972,255	1,695,246	1,277,009	1,221,563	1,750,692	747,288	474,275	947,958	802,734	1,441,861	1,530,394	1,265,214	265,180
2017	3,005,267	1,706,639	1,298,628	1,220,194	1,785,073	740,910	479,284	965,729	819,344	1,459,202	1,546,065	1,289,460	256,605
2018[1]	3,015,000	1,710,000	1,305,000	1,224,000	1,791,000	742,000	482,000	968,000	823,000	1,464,000	1,551,000	—	—
2019[1]	3,027,000	1,715,000	1,312,000	1,229,000	1,798,000	744,000	485,000	971,000	827,000	1,470,000	1,557,000	—	—
2020[1]	3,031,000	1,715,000	1,316,000	1,231,000	1,800,000	744,000	487,000	971,000	830,000	1,472,000	1,559,000	—	—
2021[1]	3,036,000	1,714,000	1,322,000	1,232,000	1,804,000	743,000	489,000	971,000	833,000	1,474,000	1,562,000	—	—
2022[1]	3,042,000	1,714,000	1,327,000	1,234,000	1,808,000	742,000	491,000	972,000	836,000	1,477,000	1,565,000	—	—
2023[1]	3,050,000	1,716,000	1,333,000	1,237,000	1,813,000	743,000	494,000	973,000	840,000	1,481,000	1,569,000	—	—
2024[1]	3,060,000	1,721,000	1,339,000	1,240,000	1,820,000	745,000	496,000	976,000	843,000	1,486,000	1,574,000	—	—
2025[1]	3,071,000	1,727,000	1,344,000	1,245,000	1,826,000	747,000	497,000	980,000	847,000	1,491,000	1,579,000	—	—
2026[1]	3,083,000	1,733,000	1,350,000	1,250,000	1,833,000	750,000	500,000	983,000	850,000	1,497,000	1,586,000	—	—
2027[1]	3,089,000	1,734,000	1,355,000	1,253,000	1,836,000	751,000	502,000	983,000	853,000	1,500,000	1,589,000	—	—
2028[1]	3,091,000	1,733,000	1,359,000	1,253,000	1,838,000	750,000	503,000	982,000	856,000	1,501,000	1,590,000	—	—

—Not available.
[1]Projected.
NOTE: Data include unclassified graduate students. Data through 1995 are for institutions of higher education, while later data are for degree-granting institutions. Degree-granting institutions grant associate's or higher degrees and participate in Title IV federal financial aid programs. The degree-granting classification is very similar to the earlier higher education classification, but it includes more 2-year colleges and excludes a few higher education institutions that did not grant degrees. Some data have been revised from previously published figures.

SOURCE: U.S. Department of Education, National Center for Education Statistics, Higher Education General Information Survey (HEGIS), "Fall Enrollment in Colleges and Universities" surveys, 1970 through 1985; Integrated Postsecondary Education Data System (IPEDS), "Fall Enrollment Survey" (IPEDS-EF:86–99); IPEDS Spring 2001 through Spring 2018, Fall Enrollment component; and Enrollment in Degree-Granting Institutions Projection Model, 2000 through 2028. (This table was prepared March 2019.)

Table 303.90. Fall enrollment and number of degree-granting postsecondary institutions, by control and religious affiliation of institution: Selected years, 1980 through 2017

Control and religious affiliation of institution	Total enrollment						Enrollment, fall 2017					Number of institutions[1]				
								Full-time		Part-time						
	Fall 1980	Fall 1990	Fall 2000	Fall 2010	Fall 2015	Fall 2016	Total	Males	Females	Males	Females	Fall 1980	Fall 1990	Fall 2000	Fall 2010	Fall 2017
1	2	3	4	5	6	7	8	9	10	11	12	13	14	15	16	17
All institutions	**12,096,895**	**13,818,637**	**15,312,289**	**21,019,438**	**19,988,204**	**19,846,904**	**19,765,598**	**5,424,575**	**6,652,729**	**3,143,057**	**4,545,237**	**3,226**	**3,501**	**4,056**	**4,589**	**4,298**
Public institutions	9,457,394	10,844,717	11,752,786	15,142,171	14,572,843	14,585,840	14,560,155	3,857,945	4,470,128	2,619,975	3,612,107	1,493	1,548	1,676	1,652	1,626
Federal	50,989	50,669	16,917	21,610	19,700	19,804	20,171	12,744	5,788	547	1,092	12	17	12	14	14
State	([2])	7,181,380	9,548,090	12,364,881	12,045,013	12,089,310	12,103,676	3,410,243	3,980,128	1,972,380	2,740,925	([2])	978	1,355	1,331	1,314
Local	([2])	3,508,941	2,078,090	2,542,044	2,309,275	2,276,473	2,235,556	383,815	423,708	611,337	816,696	([2])	523	277	261	257
Other public	9,406,405	103,727	109,689	213,636	198,855	200,253	200,752	51,143	60,504	35,711	53,394	1,481	30	32	46	41
Private institutions	2,639,501	2,973,920	3,559,503	5,877,267	5,415,361	5,261,064	5,205,443	1,566,630	2,182,601	523,082	933,130	1,733	1,953	2,380	2,937	2,672
Independent nonprofit	1,521,614	1,474,818	1,577,242	1,994,900	2,171,490	2,190,233	2,220,512	739,359	945,141	207,109	328,903	795	709	729	736	809
For-profit	111,714	213,693	450,084	2,022,785	1,349,470	1,182,108	1,098,966	237,634	429,311	131,638	300,383	164	322	724	1,310	985
Religiously affiliated[3]	1,006,173	1,285,409	1,532,177	1,859,582	1,894,401	1,888,723	1,885,965	589,637	808,149	184,335	303,844	774	922	927	891	878
Advent Christian Church	143	—	—	—	—	—	—	—	—	—	—	1	—	—	—	—
African Methodist Episcopal Zion Church	1,091	88	34	1,536	1,579	1,547	1,462	741	685	22	14	3	1	1	3	3
African Methodist Episcopal	4,541	3,220	5,980	2,674	4,359	5,379	5,887	1,382	1,505	1,362	1,638	6	5	6	5	6
American Baptist	6,131	10,800	15,410	15,120	13,397	12,801	12,500	4,049	5,356	1,063	2,032	11	15	17	18	17
American Evangelical Lutheran Church	—	—	743	1,340	1,373	1,295	1,394	646	690	22	36	—	—	1	1	1
American Lutheran and Lutheran Church in America	3,092	—	1,460	—	—	—	—	—	—	—	—	3	—	1	—	—
American Lutheran	21,608	—	—	—	—	—	—	—	—	—	—	13	—	—	—	—
Assemblies of God Church	7,814	8,307	14,272	15,806	16,599	17,780	19,241	5,848	7,756	2,510	3,127	10	11	14	16	13
Baptist	38,231	99,510	107,610	174,538	108,717	111,744	111,158	34,438	46,988	12,762	16,970	33	69	68	69	64
Brethren Church	3,925	958	2,088	8,506	8,227	9,135	8,627	2,712	3,282	1,438	1,195	3	3	3	3	2
Brethren in Christ Church	1,301	2,239	2,797	—	—	—	—	—	—	—	—	1	1	1	—	—
Christian and Missionary Alliance Church	1,705	2,519	5,278	6,455	5,916	6,094	6,122	1,771	2,280	825	1,246	3	4	4	4	4
Christian Church (Disciples of Christ)	14,913	30,397	35,984	52,839	46,157	47,970	46,260	13,629	20,046	5,256	7,329	12	18	16	18	17
Christian Churches and Churches of Christ	1,342	2,263	7,277	10,074	10,183	10,061	9,970	3,560	3,450	1,366	1,594	7	8	18	18	17
Christian Methodist Episcopal	2,486	2,174	1,502	4,817	4,102	4,207	4,062	2,090	1,775	95	102	4	4	1	3	3
Christian Reformed Church	5,408	4,488	5,999	5,625	5,748	5,710	5,714	2,486	2,628	317	283	3	2	3	3	3
Church of Christ (Scientist)	2,773	2,557	—	—	—	—	—	—	—	—	—	6	8	—	—	—
Church of God of Prophecy	—	249	—	—	—	—	—	—	—	—	—	—	1	—	—	—
Church of God	6,082	5,627	12,540	16,731	17,745	17,768	16,962	4,857	7,655	1,997	2,453	9	9	7	7	9
Church of New Jerusalem	170	—	—	—	—	—	—	—	—	—	—	1	—	—	—	—
Church of the Brethren	8,482	4,463	4,187	6,154	6,379	6,484	6,401	2,649	3,166	247	339	6	5	4	5	6
Church of the Nazarene	11,716	10,779	16,661	21,144	21,726	22,572	23,267	6,290	9,880	2,398	4,699	10	9	12	10	10
Churches of Christ	9,343	14,611	30,140	35,538	35,701	36,299	36,136	11,731	16,119	3,219	5,067	9	19	19	17	18
Cumberland Presbyterian	594	746	1,112	4,652	6,585	6,142	6,007	1,947	2,349	646	1,065	2	2	2	2	2
Episcopal Church, Reformed	67	—	—	—	1,282	1,242	1,286	70	320	111	785	1	—	—	—	2
Evangelical Christian	—	—	—	—	80,494	77,375	76,649	16,333	23,045	15,267	22,004	—	—	—	—	3
Evangelical Congregational Church	80	88	148	153	124	120	111	20	10	55	26	1	1	1	1	1
Evangelical Covenant Church of America	1,401	1,035	2,387	3,233	3,225	3,122	3,011	754	1,265	318	674	1	1	1	1	2
Evangelical Free Church of America	833	2,355	4,022	2,926	2,490	2,391	2,409	705	421	773	510	1	2	3	2	2
Evangelical Lutheran Church	743	49,210	49,085	56,162	50,249	49,863	49,960	19,577	25,487	1,716	3,180	3	33	34	33	27
Free Methodist	5,543	5,902	7,323	12,270	11,978	11,324	10,965	3,040	5,912	626	1,387	5	3	4	5	5
Free Will Baptist Church	1,132	1,177	2,378	528	693	713	704	281	238	91	94	4	3	4	3	3
Friends United Meeting	1,109	—	—	—	—	—	—	—	—	—	—	1	—	—	—	—
Friends	5,157	5,844	10,898	13,876	11,651	11,636	11,356	4,173	5,039	858	1,286	5	6	8	7	7
General Baptist	—	—	—	—	1,450	1,469	1,303	293	357	290	363	—	—	—	—	1

See notes at end of table.

Table 303.90. Fall enrollment and number of degree-granting postsecondary institutions, by control and religious affiliation of institution: Selected years, 1980 through 2017—Continued

Control and religious affiliation of institution	Total enrollment						Enrollment, fall 2017					Number of institutions[1]				
								Full-time		Part-time						
	Fall 1980	Fall 1990	Fall 2000	Fall 2010	Fall 2015	Fall 2016	Total	Males	Females	Males	Females	Fall 1980	Fall 1990	Fall 2000	Fall 2010	Fall 2017
1	2	3	4	5	6	7	8	9	10	11	12	13	14	15	16	17
General Conference Mennonite Church	820	1,243	1,059	—	—	—	—	—	—	—	—	2	2	1	—	—
Greek Orthodox	204	148	132	220	193	195	170	116	46	6	2	1	1	1	1	1
Interdenominational	1,254	11,103	9,788	33,778	41,813	41,113	41,173	12,680	17,305	5,346	5,842	4	17	14	31	34
Jewish	5,738	12,217	14,182	12,755	14,758	13,846	14,064	10,203	2,523	383	955	24	63	62	36	34
Latter-Day Saints	39,172	42,274	44,680	53,514	82,143	84,046	91,403	25,222	26,066	17,013	23,102	4	4	4	4	4
Lutheran Church—Missouri Synod	11,727	13,827	18,866	28,255	38,050	36,542	36,263	8,331	14,513	4,429	8,990	15	14	13	12	12
Lutheran Church in America	23,877	5,796	4,322	8,240	8,613	8,708	8,181	3,224	4,171	266	520	20	5	2	3	3
Mennonite Brethren Church	1,344	1,864	2,390	4,136	4,071	4,291	4,875	1,146	2,271	420	1,038	3	3	3	3	2
Mennonite Church	4,008	2,859	3,553	4,263	4,193	4,131	3,886	1,269	1,819	255	543	6	5	5	6	6
Missionary Church Inc	487	699	1,647	2,152	1,719	1,639	1,513	426	657	127	303	1	1	1	1	1
Moravian Church	2,434	2,511	2,939	3,095	3,348	3,513	3,430	788	1,834	178	630	2	2	2	2	2
Multiple Protestant denominations	5,526	211	4,690	5,350	4,881	4,758	4,766	1,120	1,546	1,206	894	8	1	7	6	6
North American Baptist	155	—	124	120	201	207	229	13	14	142	60	1	—	1	1	1
Original Free Will Baptist	—	—	—	3,855	3,371	3,430	3,451	625	916	558	1,352	—	—	—	1	1
Pentecostal Holiness Church	767	566	976	1,272	1,630	1,684	1,623	751	629	110	133	3	3	2	3	2
Presbyterian	—	—	—	—	2,988	2,965	3,080	1,024	1,510	175	371	—	—	—	—	3
Presbyterian U.S.A.	47,144	77,700	78,950	85,719	84,218	82,215	80,867	29,485	38,324	3,983	9,075	57	70	64	58	56
Presbyterian Church in America	—	1,877	4,499	2,071	1,637	1,611	1,585	639	607	198	141	—	1	5	2	2
Protestant Episcopal	5,396	4,559	5,479	5,006	3,523	3,687	3,719	1,706	1,717	150	146	12	9	12	11	8
Protestant, other	4,072	38,136	30,116	13,450	18,380	19,342	19,215	5,534	7,348	2,772	3,561	11	44	34	23	26
Reformed Church in America	2,713	5,525	6,002	6,555	6,291	6,205	6,125	2,304	3,074	281	466	4	4	5	5	5
Reformed Presbyterian Church	2,014	1,556	2,355	2,982	2,561	2,585	2,393	1,049	967	214	163	4	2	2	3	3
Reorganized Latter-Day Saints Church	4,274	4,793	3,390	—	—	—	—	—	—	—	—	2	1	2	—	—
Roman Catholic	422,842	530,585	636,336	751,091	729,936	720,808	711,948	217,734	322,129	57,644	114,441	229	239	239	237	229
Russian Orthodox	47	38	106	60	77	75	89	66	5	16	2	1	1	1	1	1
Seventh-Day Adventists	19,168	15,771	19,223	25,430	24,277	23,914	23,602	7,461	10,885	1,844	3,412	11	11	13	14	13
Southern Baptist	85,281	49,493	54,275	49,936	54,955	55,308	59,959	17,091	21,038	9,803	12,027	54	29	32	22	22
Undenominational	—	6,758	23,573	27,748	33,487	35,365	36,005	8,180	12,702	5,966	9,157	—	14	16	16	20
Unitarian Universalist	87	82	132	166	183	181	178	31	85	19	43	2	2	2	2	2
United Brethren Church	545	601	938	1,260	1,252	1,295	1,321	427	648	94	152	1	1	1	1	1
United Church of Christ	14,169	20,175	23,709	20,537	16,248	15,641	15,324	5,082	6,234	1,318	2,690	16	18	18	17	14
United Methodist	127,099	148,851	171,109	206,744	200,314	200,792	200,277	72,160	95,274	12,079	20,764	91	96	100	96	94
Wesleyan Church	3,583	5,311	11,128	20,670	19,726	19,240	18,608	5,158	10,342	1,019	2,089	5	4	4	6	8
Wisconsin Evangelical Lutheran Synod	808	931	1,660	1,677	2,088	2,051	2,095	781	895	202	217	1	3	2	2	2
Other religiously affiliated	462	5,743	2,534	4,778	5,147	5,097	5,624	1,739	2,351	469	1,065	1	9	4	11	12

—Not available.
[1]Counts of institutions in this table may be lower than reported in other tables, because counts in this table include only institutions reporting separate enrollment data.
[2]Included under "Other public."
[3]Religious affiliation as reported by institution.
NOTE: Data for 1980 and 1990 are for institutions of higher education, while later data are for degree-granting institutions. Degree-granting institutions grant associate's or higher degrees and participate in Title IV federal financial aid programs. The degree-granting classification is very similar to the earlier higher education classification, but it includes more 2-year colleges and excludes a few higher education institutions that did not grant degrees. Some data have been revised from previously published figures.
SOURCE: U.S. Department of Education, National Center for Education Statistics, Higher Education General Information Survey (HEGIS), "Fall Enrollment in Institutions of Higher Education" and "Institutional Characteristics" surveys, 1980; Integrated Postsecondary Education Data System (IPEDS), "Fall Enrollment Survey" (IPEDS-EF:90) and "Institutional Characteristics Survey" (IPEDS-IC:90); and IPEDS Spring 2001 through Spring 2018, Fall Enrollment component. (This table was prepared April 2019.)

Table 304.10. Total fall enrollment in degree-granting postsecondary institutions, by state or jurisdiction: Selected years, 1970 through 2017

State or jurisdiction	1970	1980	1990	2000	2010	2012	2014	2015	2016	2017	Percent change, 2012 to 2017
1	2	3	4	5	6	7	8	9	10	11	12
United States	**8,580,887**	**12,096,895**	**13,818,637**	**15,312,289**	**21,019,438**	**20,644,478**	**20,209,092**	**19,988,204**	**19,846,904**	**19,765,598**	**-4.3**
Alabama	103,936	164,306	218,589	233,962	327,606	310,311	305,028	302,959	304,052	306,822	-1.1
Alaska	9,471	21,296	29,833	27,953	34,799	32,797	34,331	31,373	28,436	26,905	-18.0
Arizona	109,619	202,716	264,148	342,490	793,871	736,465	674,746	650,422	608,086	591,626	-19.7
Arkansas	52,039	77,347	90,425	115,172	175,848	176,458	169,571	168,402	167,235	164,082	-7.0
California	1,257,245	1,791,088	1,808,740	2,256,708	2,714,699	2,621,606	2,697,168	2,687,410	2,700,445	2,714,051	3.5
Colorado	123,395	162,916	227,131	263,872	369,450	363,170	353,949	348,159	352,255	360,236	-0.8
Connecticut	124,700	159,632	168,604	161,243	199,384	201,658	201,928	199,666	198,010	197,534	-2.0
Delaware	25,260	32,939	42,004	43,897	55,258	58,127	60,437	60,392	61,139	60,338	3.8
District of Columbia	77,158	86,675	79,551	72,689	91,992	90,150	90,053	93,972	93,040	95,999	6.5
Florida	235,525	411,891	588,086	707,684	1,124,778	1,154,506	1,111,018	1,083,570	1,075,527	1,071,484	-7.2
Georgia	126,511	184,159	251,786	346,204	568,916	545,360	530,963	530,711	533,073	538,124	-1.3
Hawaii	36,562	49,009	56,436	60,182	78,073	78,456	73,505	69,332	65,843	64,125	-18.3
Idaho	34,567	43,018	51,881	65,594	85,201	108,008	118,953	121,109	123,796	131,803	22.0
Illinois	452,146	645,288	729,246	743,918	906,845	866,893	825,002	802,211	777,720	757,002	-12.7
Indiana	192,668	247,253	284,832	314,334	459,493	447,263	436,455	426,364	419,284	398,804	-10.8
Iowa	108,902	140,449	170,515	188,974	381,867	361,189	282,518	275,106	266,513	260,954	-27.8
Kansas	102,485	136,605	163,733	179,968	214,849	213,855	226,290	219,994	215,832	213,962	0.1
Kentucky	98,591	143,066	177,852	188,341	291,104	281,133	264,197	255,722	255,062	258,498	-8.1
Louisiana	120,728	160,058	186,840	223,800	263,676	258,846	245,938	245,305	239,278	242,065	-6.5
Maine	34,134	43,264	57,186	58,473	72,406	73,095	71,750	71,719	72,116	71,811	-1.8
Maryland	149,607	225,180	259,700	273,745	377,967	374,496	365,597	364,225	366,809	364,207	-2.7
Massachusetts	303,809	418,415	417,833	421,142	507,753	514,119	511,060	510,512	505,722	503,508	-2.1
Michigan	392,726	520,131	569,803	567,631	697,765	663,703	619,962	601,462	583,034	558,053	-15.9
Minnesota	160,788	206,691	253,789	293,445	465,449	451,661	433,948	430,466	422,793	412,966	-8.6
Mississippi	73,967	102,364	122,883	137,389	179,995	176,618	170,724	174,183	172,588	171,751	-2.8
Missouri	183,930	233,378	289,899	321,348	444,750	441,186	419,935	409,999	401,098	383,489	-13.1
Montana	30,062	35,177	35,876	42,240	53,282	53,254	51,942	50,799	50,918	50,642	-4.9
Nebraska	66,915	89,488	112,831	112,117	144,692	139,558	135,825	136,091	136,098	135,864	-2.6
Nevada	13,669	40,455	61,728	87,893	129,360	118,300	119,205	116,101	116,030	117,574	-0.6
New Hampshire	29,400	46,794	59,510	61,718	75,539	82,678	106,559	123,508	133,159	149,184	80.4
New Jersey	216,121	321,610	324,286	335,945	444,092	439,966	436,249	423,759	421,386	419,037	-4.8
New Mexico	44,461	58,629	85,500	110,739	162,552	156,424	146,246	138,248	134,607	129,494	-17.2
New York	806,479	992,349	1,048,286	1,043,395	1,305,151	1,309,684	1,298,972	1,285,406	1,273,634	1,260,240	-3.8
North Carolina	171,925	287,537	352,138	404,652	585,792	578,265	569,955	562,442	561,415	563,831	-2.5
North Dakota	31,495	34,069	37,878	40,248	56,903	55,242	54,048	53,834	54,203	53,749	-2.7
Ohio	376,267	488,938	557,690	549,553	745,115	710,379	680,558	664,623	658,043	649,687	-8.5
Oklahoma	110,155	160,295	173,221	178,016	230,560	228,492	215,410	211,117	208,333	202,051	-11.6
Oregon	122,177	157,458	165,741	183,065	251,708	254,926	245,547	240,649	236,851	229,936	-9.8
Pennsylvania	411,044	507,716	604,060	609,521	804,640	777,350	750,376	736,163	725,682	717,289	-7.7
Rhode Island	45,898	66,869	78,273	75,450	85,110	83,952	83,499	82,292	83,348	82,766	-1.4
South Carolina	69,518	132,476	159,302	185,931	257,064	259,617	254,629	249,655	246,563	246,388	-5.1
South Dakota	30,639	32,761	34,208	43,221	58,360	56,058	53,961	53,664	53,683	53,620	-4.3
Tennessee	135,103	204,841	226,238	263,910	351,762	343,478	326,623	323,869	321,752	323,157	-5.9
Texas	442,225	701,391	901,437	1,033,973	1,535,864	1,544,524	1,556,288	1,579,614	1,605,498	1,630,516	5.6
Utah	81,687	92,159	121,303	163,776	255,653	267,309	274,926	292,995	311,450	332,334	24.3
Vermont	22,209	30,628	36,398	35,489	45,572	44,697	43,980	43,865	44,719	43,855	-1.9
Virginia	151,915	280,504	353,442	381,893	577,922	588,708	577,911	569,752	557,444	554,212	-5.9
Washington	183,544	303,603	263,384	320,840	388,116	365,529	365,186	364,844	366,547	367,944	0.7
West Virginia	63,153	81,973	84,790	87,888	152,431	162,182	157,052	150,897	146,608	142,963	-11.9
Wisconsin	202,058	269,086	299,774	307,179	384,181	369,738	358,924	350,255	341,717	340,770	-7.8
Wyoming	15,220	21,147	31,326	30,004	38,298	37,812	35,461	34,205	33,365	33,015	-12.7
U.S. Service Academies[1]	17,079	49,808	48,692	13,475	15,925	15,227	14,734	14,812	15,065	15,281	0.4
Other jurisdictions	**67,237**	**137,749**	**164,618**	**194,633**	**264,240**	**259,975**	**255,837**	**247,886**	**241,896**	**192,406**	**-26.0**
American Samoa	0	976	1,219	297	2,193	1,795	1,276	1,285	1,253	1,095	-39.0
Federated States of Micronesia	0	224	975	1,576	2,699	2,744	2,344	2,215	2,090	2,022	-26.3
Guam	2,719	3,217	4,741	5,215	6,188	5,955	6,488	6,395	6,084	6,027	1.2
Marshall Islands	0	0	0	328	869	1,123	1,087	995	978	1,032	-8.1
Northern Marianas	0	0	661	1,078	1,137	1,178	1,186	1,157	1,038	1,216	3.2
Palau	0	0	491	581	694	680	604	627	587	532	-21.8
Puerto Rico	63,073	131,184	154,065	183,290	247,727	244,077	240,572	232,891	227,496	178,312	-26.9
U.S. Virgin Islands	1,445	2,148	2,466	2,268	2,733	2,423	2,280	2,321	2,370	2,170	-10.4

[1]Data for 2000 and later years reflect a substantial reduction in the number of Department of Defense institutions included in the IPEDS survey.

NOTE: Data through 1990 are for institutions of higher education, while later data are for degree-granting institutions. Degree-granting institutions grant associate's or higher degrees and participate in Title IV federal financial aid programs. The degree-granting classification is very similar to the earlier higher education classification, but it includes more 2-year colleges and excludes a few higher education institutions that did not grant degrees. Some data have been revised from previously published figures.

SOURCE: U.S. Department of Education, National Center for Education Statistics, Higher Education General Information Survey (HEGIS), "Fall Enrollment in Colleges and Universities" surveys, 1970 and 1980; Integrated Postsecondary Education Data System (IPEDS), "Fall Enrollment Survey" (IPEDS-EF:90); and IPEDS Spring 2001 through Spring 2018, Fall Enrollment component. (This table was prepared December 2018.)

Table 304.15. Total fall enrollment in public degree-granting postsecondary institutions, by state or jurisdiction: Selected years, 1970 through 2017

State or jurisdiction	1970	1980	1990	2000	2010	2012	2014	2015	2016	2017	Percent change, 2012 to 2017
1	2	3	4	5	6	7	8	9	10	11	12
United States	**6,428,134**	**9,457,394**	**10,844,717**	**11,752,786**	**15,142,171**	**14,884,667**	**14,654,660**	**14,572,843**	**14,585,840**	**14,560,155**	**-2.2**
Alabama	87,884	143,674	195,939	207,435	267,083	251,045	246,989	247,450	251,038	254,071	1.2
Alaska	8,563	20,561	27,792	26,559	32,303	30,595	29,892	28,429	27,352	25,850	-15.5
Arizona	107,315	194,034	248,213	284,522	366,976	359,229	354,997	360,976	361,400	366,787	2.1
Arkansas	43,599	66,068	78,645	101,775	155,780	157,224	151,399	150,165	149,298	146,697	-6.7
California	1,123,529	1,599,838	1,594,710	1,927,771	2,223,163	2,129,152	2,167,818	2,202,258	2,228,592	2,246,844	5.5
Colorado	108,562	145,598	200,653	217,897	269,433	272,444	268,041	265,828	272,668	278,909	2.4
Connecticut	73,391	97,788	109,556	101,027	127,194	124,952	122,303	119,766	117,345	116,090	-7.1
Delaware	21,151	28,325	34,252	34,194	39,935	41,113	41,012	40,611	41,816	42,321	2.9
District of Columbia	12,194	13,900	11,990	5,499	5,840	5,476	5,115	5,118	4,587	4,529	-17.3
Florida	189,450	334,349	489,081	556,912	790,027	804,693	795,628	794,390	797,048	798,045	-0.8
Georgia	101,900	140,158	196,413	271,755	436,047	422,189	413,711	417,860	422,159	428,586	1.5
Hawaii	32,963	43,269	45,728	44,579	60,090	60,295	57,052	55,756	53,418	51,674	-14.3
Idaho	27,072	34,491	41,315	53,751	64,204	78,781	76,806	72,339	74,667	75,792	-3.8
Illinois	315,634	491,274	551,333	534,155	585,515	556,890	529,462	509,104	492,578	478,042	-14.2
Indiana	136,739	189,224	223,953	240,023	337,705	333,769	328,442	321,501	319,581	301,562	-9.6
Iowa	68,390	97,454	117,834	135,008	177,781	173,558	169,896	171,005	171,075	170,427	-1.8
Kansas	88,215	121,987	149,117	159,976	185,623	183,914	183,084	179,532	180,170	179,856	-2.2
Kentucky	77,240	114,884	147,095	151,973	229,725	223,100	213,043	205,908	205,431	202,266	-9.3
Louisiana	101,127	136,703	158,290	189,213	224,811	220,971	210,943	212,098	208,254	210,691	-4.7
Maine	25,405	31,878	41,500	40,662	50,903	50,555	48,354	47,408	47,763	46,999	-7.0
Maryland	118,988	195,051	220,783	223,797	309,779	310,503	305,156	303,849	306,892	303,640	-2.2
Massachusetts	116,127	183,765	186,035	183,248	224,542	228,178	226,213	222,243	218,465	213,389	-6.5
Michigan	339,625	454,147	487,359	467,861	562,448	540,242	514,712	501,411	492,771	478,735	-11.4
Minnesota	130,567	162,379	199,211	218,617	276,176	272,290	259,695	256,187	253,239	249,385	-8.4
Mississippi	64,968	90,661	109,038	125,355	161,493	157,995	152,092	155,334	153,082	152,319	-3.6
Missouri	132,540	165,179	200,093	201,509	256,030	257,430	252,980	248,516	244,921	235,540	-8.5
Montana	27,287	31,178	31,865	37,387	48,231	48,333	47,024	45,935	46,262	46,002	-4.8
Nebraska	51,454	73,509	94,614	88,531	107,979	104,166	99,821	100,030	101,032	101,038	-3.0
Nevada	13,576	40,280	61,242	83,120	113,103	103,619	106,028	104,418	106,196	107,864	4.1
New Hampshire	15,979	24,119	32,163	35,870	44,077	43,289	42,904	42,628	41,170	39,761	-8.1
New Jersey	145,373	247,028	261,601	266,921	358,256	356,457	351,357	339,722	337,099	334,597	-6.1
New Mexico	40,795	55,077	83,403	101,450	150,844	146,792	138,311	131,343	129,038	125,280	-14.7
New York	449,437	563,251	616,884	583,417	723,500	722,274	721,850	709,243	700,875	697,458	-3.4
North Carolina	123,761	228,154	285,405	329,422	475,064	465,950	455,100	448,055	450,080	454,632	-2.4
North Dakota	30,192	31,709	34,690	36,014	48,904	48,929	48,292	48,191	47,964	47,574	-2.8
Ohio	281,099	381,765	427,613	411,161	547,551	524,973	510,244	501,677	501,146	497,473	-5.2
Oklahoma	91,438	137,188	151,073	153,699	197,641	195,118	182,449	179,008	177,629	174,140	-10.8
Oregon	108,483	140,102	144,427	154,756	208,001	212,541	201,645	197,948	197,819	192,334	-9.5
Pennsylvania	232,982	292,499	343,478	339,229	432,923	425,890	413,591	408,522	406,346	400,943	-5.9
Rhode Island	25,527	35,052	42,350	38,458	43,224	43,204	42,765	41,320	41,369	41,018	-5.1
South Carolina	47,101	107,683	131,134	155,519	205,080	209,023	205,756	202,487	200,295	200,622	-4.0
South Dakota	23,936	24,328	26,596	34,857	44,569	44,185	44,132	44,254	44,305	44,630	1.0
Tennessee	98,897	156,835	175,049	202,530	242,486	235,010	224,033	223,411	221,288	223,179	-5.0
Texas	365,522	613,552	802,314	896,534	1,334,110	1,352,060	1,365,664	1,388,266	1,423,205	1,448,385	7.1
Utah	49,588	59,598	86,108	123,046	179,061	171,001	167,716	170,689	175,308	180,034	5.3
Vermont	12,536	17,984	20,910	20,021	27,524	26,501	25,643	25,383	25,736	25,300	-4.5
Virginia	123,279	246,500	291,286	313,780	409,004	409,753	399,359	394,210	389,446	389,249	-5.0
Washington	162,718	276,028	227,632	273,928	330,853	311,497	312,523	313,964	315,356	318,336	2.2
West Virginia	51,363	71,228	74,108	76,136	96,104	93,017	87,842	86,342	85,099	83,895	-9.8
Wisconsin	170,374	235,179	253,529	249,737	301,259	293,416	286,726	282,250	278,300	279,533	-4.7
Wyoming	15,220	21,121	30,623	28,715	36,292	35,859	34,316	33,693	32,802	32,551	-9.2
U.S. Service Academies[1]	17,079	49,808	48,692	13,475	15,925	15,227	14,734	14,812	15,065	15,281	0.4
Other jurisdictions	**46,680**	**60,692**	**66,244**	**84,464**	**83,719**	**78,400**	**77,716**	**80,129**	**81,479**	**37,419**	**-52.3**
American Samoa	0	976	1,219	297	2,193	1,795	1,276	1,285	1,253	1,095	-39.0
Federated States of Micronesia	0	224	975	1,576	2,699	2,744	2,344	2,215	2,090	2,022	-26.3
Guam	2,719	3,217	4,741	5,215	6,103	5,878	6,416	6,325	6,017	5,972	1.6
Marshall Islands	0	0	0	328	869	1,123	1,087	995	978	1,032	-8.1
Northern Marianas	0	0	661	1,078	1,137	1,178	1,186	1,157	1,038	1,216	3.2
Palau	0	0	491	581	694	680	604	627	587	532	-21.8
Puerto Rico	42,516	54,127	55,691	73,121	67,291	62,579	62,523	65,204	67,146	23,380	-62.6
U.S. Virgin Islands	1,445	2,148	2,466	2,268	2,733	2,423	2,280	2,321	2,370	2,170	-10.4

[1]Data for 2000 and later years reflect a substantial reduction in the number of Department of Defense institutions included in the IPEDS survey.

NOTE: Data through 1990 are for institutions of higher education, while later data are for degree-granting institutions. Degree-granting institutions grant associate's or higher degrees and participate in Title IV federal financial aid programs. The degree-granting classification is very similar to the earlier higher education classification, but it includes more 2-year colleges and excludes a few higher education institutions that did not grant degrees. Some data have been revised from previously published figures.

SOURCE: U.S. Department of Education, National Center for Education Statistics, Higher Education General Information Survey (HEGIS), "Fall Enrollment in Colleges and Universities" surveys, 1970 and 1980; Integrated Postsecondary Education Data System (IPEDS), "Fall Enrollment Survey" (IPEDS-EF:90); and IPEDS Spring 2001 through Spring 2018, Fall Enrollment component. (This table was prepared December 2018.)

Table 304.21. Total fall enrollment in private nonprofit degree-granting postsecondary institutions, by state or jurisdiction: Selected years, 1980 through 2017

State or jurisdiction	1980	1990	2000	2010	2012	2013	2014	2015	2016	2017	Percent change, 2012 to 2017
1	2	3	4	5	6	7	8	9	10	11	12
United States	**2,527,787**	**2,760,227**	**3,109,419**	**3,854,482**	**3,951,388**	**3,971,390**	**3,997,249**	**4,065,891**	**4,078,956**	**4,106,477**	**3.9**
Alabama	19,233	20,421	22,649	25,136	26,109	25,239	26,032	25,967	24,956	26,149	0.2
Alaska	735	1,647	908	732	715	764	693	621	660	625	-12.6
Arizona	2,949	7,184	11,092	8,817	9,187	9,150	9,854	9,606	9,802	9,935	8.1
Arkansas	9,557	10,078	12,640	16,654	17,152	16,919	16,995	17,554	17,446	17,009	-0.8
California	183,700	201,222	252,449	285,898	297,250	306,964	307,516	304,296	304,789	309,256	4.0
Colorado	16,156	19,254	27,548	32,938	33,765	34,530	34,372	35,400	34,269	34,081	0.9
Connecticut	61,457	58,346	58,444	66,750	67,765	68,779	70,396	71,715	72,344	72,360	6.8
Delaware	4,614	7,752	9,703	14,833	16,627	18,245	19,090	19,455	19,022	17,697	6.4
District of Columbia	70,894	64,645	64,212	78,215	79,000	78,908	78,502	79,276	78,938	81,099	2.7
Florida	73,767	87,476	113,580	162,311	179,935	180,611	181,931	207,518	205,323	203,259	13.0
Georgia	39,122	46,297	64,123	71,134	73,235	73,395	73,262	74,106	76,263	78,855	7.7
Hawaii	5,740	10,708	13,727	14,273	14,292	13,087	11,969	10,586	9,799	10,159	-28.9
Idaho	8,527	10,133	11,167	18,185	26,749	31,489	40,662	47,651	48,492	55,503	107.5
Illinois	147,269	165,669	184,856	227,482	227,880	224,127	222,651	221,310	218,283	215,251	-5.5
Indiana	54,641	56,929	67,307	88,928	88,916	88,834	90,580	90,752	91,604	89,985	1.2
Iowa	42,693	51,851	51,625	57,430	56,221	56,283	56,114	54,078	53,475	52,870	-6.0
Kansas	14,618	14,518	19,522	25,212	26,004	26,693	26,057	25,249	23,058	22,910	-11.9
Kentucky	22,326	26,084	28,015	37,554	40,223	39,830	39,025	39,483	41,332	47,958	19.2
Louisiana	22,980	26,183	29,963	27,667	28,881	28,065	27,052	26,345	25,676	26,436	-8.5
Maine	10,258	14,348	16,837	19,578	21,121	21,329	21,394	22,424	22,737	23,468	11.1
Maryland	30,035	38,557	46,529	54,894	54,917	53,856	52,822	53,063	53,881	54,647	-0.5
Massachusetts	234,007	231,232	236,050	275,565	278,907	280,088	280,138	284,065	284,513	287,987	3.3
Michigan	65,984	82,444	96,669	124,307	114,676	108,166	98,367	95,107	87,297	76,764	-33.1
Minnesota	42,292	51,502	62,870	73,504	71,446	71,366	71,004	70,666	70,356	70,653	-1.1
Mississippi	10,556	12,034	11,625	15,398	16,058	16,046	16,376	16,873	17,856	17,576	9.5
Missouri	66,440	86,202	109,784	153,918	154,169	152,442	149,771	147,328	146,452	139,898	-9.3
Montana	3,482	4,011	4,853	5,051	4,921	4,926	4,918	4,864	4,621	4,603	-6.5
Nebraska	15,979	17,885	21,608	32,940	32,783	33,400	33,707	34,233	33,747	33,854	3.3
Nevada	175	339	586	3,370	3,421	3,546	3,762	4,214	4,057	4,266	24.7
New Hampshire	20,783	24,900	21,939	26,566	35,681	46,681	61,412	79,388	91,989	109,423	206.7
New Jersey	73,757	59,011	62,049	75,980	74,391	73,483	73,908	73,636	73,822	73,693	-0.9
New Mexico	3,552	1,796	4,258	1,120	1,334	1,503	1,568	1,617	1,658	1,590	19.2
New York	407,101	406,510	424,379	526,357	535,236	533,749	528,729	530,798	530,938	524,187	-2.1
North Carolina	55,729	64,859	74,640	92,031	94,023	96,072	96,500	97,684	97,322	97,163	3.3
North Dakota	2,360	3,188	4,123	6,234	5,313	5,348	4,963	5,040	5,690	5,648	6.3
Ohio	95,918	109,749	124,718	146,389	146,179	142,502	141,357	138,542	138,327	136,807	-6.4
Oklahoma	21,149	18,492	21,094	22,657	24,032	25,117	24,740	25,996	26,227	23,919	-0.5
Oregon	17,192	20,353	25,289	32,811	33,370	35,289	37,256	37,533	35,429	34,623	3.8
Pennsylvania	207,975	223,478	239,128	298,997	296,704	294,767	292,276	292,166	291,914	294,802	-0.6
Rhode Island	31,817	35,923	36,768	41,886	40,748	40,674	40,734	40,972	41,979	41,748	2.5
South Carolina	21,868	26,734	29,655	35,089	34,601	34,195	34,552	34,606	35,106	34,137	-1.3
South Dakota	8,433	6,188	5,660	9,044	7,273	7,153	7,137	7,221	7,223	7,060	-2.9
Tennessee	44,711	47,344	55,809	77,764	82,816	83,912	83,412	83,352	84,426	84,459	2.0
Texas	86,001	92,672	120,123	131,485	136,187	136,077	137,171	140,057	142,266	142,736	4.8
Utah	32,561	34,387	35,986	61,310	81,270	85,599	100,548	117,009	131,527	147,610	81.6
Vermont	12,644	15,488	15,131	17,433	17,679	17,222	17,915	18,103	18,683	18,411	4.1
Virginia	33,269	57,142	50,979	110,720	128,323	130,794	134,602	135,037	132,850	132,988	3.6
Washington	27,087	32,145	41,415	43,702	43,177	43,222	43,162	44,568	43,992	42,861	-0.7
West Virginia	10,440	9,822	9,800	12,952	7,683	8,505	8,679	8,665	8,809	8,583	11.7
Wisconsin	33,254	45,095	55,535	65,281	63,043	62,427	61,556	59,584	57,168	58,452	-7.3
Wyoming	0	0	0	0	0	22	60	512	563	464	†
Other jurisdictions	**70,702**	**164,618**	**194,633**	**137,375**	**138,661**	**134,587**	**131,649**	**127,194**	**122,016**	**118,286**	**-14.7**
American Samoa	0	1,219	297	0	0	0	0	0	0	0	†
Federated States of Micronesia	0	975	1,576	0	0	0	0	0	0	0	†
Guam	0	4,741	5,215	85	77	79	72	70	67	55	-28.6
Marshall Islands	0	0	328	0	0	0	0	0	0	0	†
Northern Marianas	0	661	1,078	0	0	0	0	0	0	0	†
Palau	0	491	581	0	0	0	0	0	0	0	†
Puerto Rico	70,702	154,065	183,290	137,290	138,584	134,508	131,577	127,124	121,949	118,231	-14.7
U.S. Virgin Islands	0	2,466	2,268	0	0	0	0	0	0	0	†

†Not applicable.

NOTE: Data through 1990 are for institutions of higher education, while later data are for degree-granting institutions. Degree-granting institutions grant associate's or higher degrees and participate in Title IV federal financial aid programs. The degree-granting classification is very similar to the earlier higher education classification, but it includes more 2-year colleges and excludes a few higher education institutions that did not grant degrees.

SOURCE: U.S. Department of Education, National Center for Education Statistics, Higher Education General Information Survey (HEGIS), "Fall Enrollment in Colleges and Universities" survey, 1980; Integrated Postsecondary Education Data System (IPEDS), "Fall Enrollment Survey" (IPEDS-EF:90); and IPEDS Spring 2001 through Spring 2018, Fall Enrollment component. (This table was prepared December 2018.)

Table 304.22. Total fall enrollment in private for-profit degree-granting postsecondary institutions, by state or jurisdiction: Selected years, 1980 through 2017

State or jurisdiction	1980	1990	2000	2010	2012	2013	2014	2015	2016	2017	Percent change, 2012 to 2017
1	2	3	4	5	6	7	8	9	10	11	12
United States	**111,714**	**213,693**	**450,084**	**2,022,785**	**1,808,423**	**1,658,439**	**1,557,183**	**1,349,470**	**1,182,108**	**1,098,966**	**-39.2**
Alabama	1,399	2,229	3,878	35,387	33,157	32,282	32,007	29,542	28,058	26,602	-19.8
Alaska	0	394	486	1,764	1,487	2,526	3,746	2,323	424	430	-71.1
Arizona	5,733	8,751	46,876	418,078	368,049	330,079	309,895	279,840	236,884	214,904	-41.6
Arkansas	1,722	1,702	757	3,414	2,082	1,615	1,177	683	491	376	-81.9
California	7,550	12,808	76,488	205,638	195,204	182,846	221,834	180,856	167,064	157,951	-19.1
Colorado	1,162	7,224	18,427	67,079	56,961	52,577	51,536	46,931	45,318	47,246	-17.1
Connecticut	387	702	1,772	5,440	8,941	9,156	9,229	8,185	8,321	9,084	1.6
Delaware	0	0	0	490	387	378	335	326	301	320	-17.3
District of Columbia	1,881	2,916	2,978	7,937	5,674	5,002	6,436	9,578	9,515	10,371	82.8
Florida	3,775	11,529	37,192	172,440	169,878	149,401	133,459	81,662	73,156	70,180	-58.7
Georgia	4,879	9,076	10,326	61,735	49,936	46,324	43,990	38,745	34,651	30,683	-38.6
Hawaii	0	0	1,876	3,710	3,869	4,406	4,484	2,990	2,626	2,292	-40.8
Idaho	0	433	676	2,812	2,478	1,645	1,485	1,119	637	508	-79.5
Illinois	6,745	12,244	24,907	93,848	82,123	72,278	72,889	71,797	66,859	63,709	-22.4
Indiana	3,388	3,950	7,004	32,860	24,578	19,652	17,433	14,111	8,099	7,257	-70.5
Iowa	302	830	2,341	146,656	131,410	114,811	56,508	50,023	41,963	37,657	-71.3
Kansas	0	98	470	4,014	3,937	5,087	17,149	15,213	12,604	11,196	184.4
Kentucky	5,856	4,673	8,353	23,825	17,810	14,771	12,129	10,331	8,299	8,274	-53.5
Louisiana	375	2,367	4,624	11,198	8,994	8,169	7,943	6,862	5,348	4,938	-45.1
Maine	1,128	1,338	974	1,925	1,419	1,481	2,002	1,887	1,616	1,344	-5.3
Maryland	94	360	3,419	13,294	9,076	8,278	7,619	7,313	6,036	5,920	-34.8
Massachusetts	643	566	1,844	7,646	7,034	5,623	4,709	4,204	2,744	2,132	-69.7
Michigan	0	0	3,101	11,010	8,785	7,664	6,883	4,944	2,966	2,554	-70.9
Minnesota	2,020	3,076	11,958	115,769	107,925	103,831	103,249	103,613	99,198	92,928	-13.9
Mississippi	1,147	1,811	409	3,104	2,565	2,672	2,256	1,976	1,650	1,856	-27.6
Missouri	1,759	3,604	10,055	34,802	29,587	31,354	17,184	14,155	9,725	8,051	-72.8
Montana	517	0	0	0	0	0	0	0	35	37	†
Nebraska	0	332	1,978	3,773	2,609	2,650	2,297	1,828	1,319	972	-62.7
Nevada	0	147	4,187	12,887	11,260	10,654	9,415	7,469	5,777	5,444	-51.7
New Hampshire	1,892	2,447	3,909	4,896	3,708	3,048	2,243	1,492	0	0	-100.0
New Jersey	825	3,674	6,975	9,856	9,118	10,634	10,984	10,401	10,465	10,747	17.9
New Mexico	0	301	5,031	10,588	8,298	7,571	6,367	5,288	3,911	2,624	-68.4
New York	21,997	24,892	35,599	55,294	52,174	50,424	48,393	45,365	41,821	38,595	-26.0
North Carolina	3,654	1,874	590	18,697	18,292	18,823	18,355	16,703	14,013	12,036	-34.2
North Dakota	0	0	111	1,765	1,000	964	793	603	549	527	-47.3
Ohio	11,255	20,328	13,674	51,175	39,227	34,371	28,957	24,404	18,570	15,407	-60.7
Oklahoma	1,958	3,656	3,223	10,262	9,342	8,702	8,221	6,113	4,477	3,992	-57.3
Oregon	164	961	3,020	10,896	9,015	7,481	6,646	5,168	3,603	2,979	-67.0
Pennsylvania	7,242	37,104	31,164	72,720	54,756	50,958	44,509	35,475	27,422	21,544	-60.7
Rhode Island	0	0	224	0	0	0	0	0	0	0	†
South Carolina	2,925	1,434	757	16,895	15,993	15,932	14,321	12,562	11,162	11,629	-27.3
South Dakota	0	1,424	2,704	4,747	4,600	3,704	2,692	2,189	2,155	1,930	-58.0
Tennessee	3,295	3,845	5,571	31,512	25,652	24,983	19,178	17,106	16,038	15,519	-39.5
Texas	1,838	6,451	17,316	70,269	56,277	55,712	53,453	51,291	40,027	39,395	-30.0
Utah	0	808	4,744	15,282	15,038	7,987	6,662	5,297	4,615	4,690	-68.8
Vermont	0	0	337	615	517	462	422	379	300	144	-72.1
Virginia	735	5,014	17,134	58,198	50,632	47,046	43,950	40,505	35,148	31,975	-36.8
Washington	488	3,607	5,497	13,561	10,855	9,963	9,501	6,312	7,199	6,747	-37.8
West Virginia	305	860	1,952	43,375	61,482	58,667	60,531	55,890	52,700	50,485	-17.9
Wisconsin	653	1,150	1,907	17,641	13,279	12,333	10,642	8,421	6,249	2,785	-79.0
Wyoming	26	703	1,289	2,006	1,953	1,462	1,085	0	0	0	-100.0
Other jurisdictions	**6,355**	**164,618**	**194,633**	**43,146**	**42,914**	**41,820**	**46,472**	**40,563**	**38,401**	**36,701**	**-14.5**
American Samoa	0	1,219	297	0	0	0	0	0	0	0	†
Federated States of Micronesia	0	975	1,576	0	0	0	0	0	0	0	†
Guam	0	4,741	5,215	0	0	0	0	0	0	0	†
Marshall Islands	0	0	328	0	0	0	0	0	0	0	†
Northern Marianas	0	661	1,078	0	0	0	0	0	0	0	†
Palau	0	491	581	0	0	0	0	0	0	0	†
Puerto Rico	6,355	154,065	183,290	43,146	42,914	41,820	46,472	40,563	38,401	36,701	-14.5
U.S. Virgin Islands	0	2,466	2,268	0	0	0	0	0	0	0	†

†Not applicable.

NOTE: Data through 1990 are for institutions of higher education, while later data are for degree-granting institutions. Degree-granting institutions grant associate's or higher degrees and participate in Title IV federal financial aid programs. The degree-granting classification is very similar to the earlier higher education classification, but it includes more 2-year colleges and excludes a few higher education institutions that did not grant degrees.

SOURCE: U.S. Department of Education, National Center for Education Statistics, Higher Education General Information Survey (HEGIS), "Fall Enrollment in Colleges and Universities" survey, 1980; Integrated Postsecondary Education Data System (IPEDS), "Fall Enrollment Survey" (IPEDS-EF:90); and IPEDS Spring 2001 through Spring 2018, Fall Enrollment component. (This table was prepared December 2018.)

Table 304.30. Total fall enrollment in degree-granting postsecondary institutions, by attendance status, sex, and state or jurisdiction: 2016 and 2017

State or jurisdiction	2016					2017					Percent change, 2016 to 2017
	Total	Full-time		Part-time		Total	Full-time		Part-time		
		Males	Females	Males	Females		Males	Females	Males	Females	
1	2	3	4	5	6	7	8	9	10	11	12
United States	**19,846,904**	**5,472,798**	**6,652,516**	**3,165,624**	**4,555,966**	**19,765,598**	**5,424,575**	**6,652,729**	**3,143,057**	**4,545,237**	**-0.4**
Alabama	304,052	91,869	117,075	39,134	55,974	306,822	91,971	118,876	39,522	56,453	0.9
Alaska	28,436	5,804	6,749	5,764	10,119	26,905	5,485	6,705	5,409	9,306	-5.4
Arizona	608,086	149,953	217,019	90,974	150,140	591,626	141,890	196,826	94,483	158,427	-2.7
Arkansas	167,235	45,947	59,049	24,338	37,901	164,082	44,881	58,763	23,410	37,028	-1.9
California	2,700,445	661,370	818,752	558,869	661,454	2,714,051	665,826	828,188	555,106	664,931	0.5
Colorado	352,255	94,597	106,882	61,370	89,406	360,236	95,560	109,193	64,269	91,214	2.3
Connecticut	198,010	58,734	70,068	26,240	42,968	197,534	58,447	70,992	25,363	42,732	-0.2
Delaware	61,139	16,446	21,321	8,069	15,303	60,338	15,918	21,376	7,965	15,079	-1.3
District of Columbia	93,040	25,872	36,932	11,713	18,523	95,999	25,965	38,178	12,279	19,577	3.2
Florida	1,075,527	264,513	341,417	187,775	281,822	1,071,484	265,029	349,640	182,683	274,132	-0.4
Georgia	533,073	145,625	197,781	72,421	117,246	538,124	144,085	194,698	75,754	123,587	0.9
Hawaii	65,843	16,281	22,044	10,942	16,576	64,125	15,659	21,771	10,376	16,319	-2.6
Idaho	123,796	28,030	31,668	25,865	38,233	131,803	27,695	32,239	29,016	42,853	6.5
Illinois	777,720	208,187	240,800	128,548	200,185	757,002	201,415	235,665	123,824	196,098	-2.7
Indiana	419,284	123,798	144,506	63,918	87,062	398,804	121,301	142,262	57,894	77,347	-4.9
Iowa	266,513	75,093	81,293	42,315	67,812	260,954	73,515	79,679	41,613	66,147	-2.1
Kansas	215,832	60,837	65,313	38,191	51,491	213,962	59,848	64,465	37,810	51,839	-0.9
Kentucky	255,062	68,400	90,220	40,013	56,429	258,498	66,423	89,574	43,704	58,797	1.3
Louisiana	239,278	67,137	92,613	29,644	49,884	242,065	66,521	94,282	29,526	51,736	1.2
Maine	72,116	19,652	24,327	9,782	18,355	71,811	19,554	24,020	9,644	18,593	-0.4
Maryland	366,809	88,209	102,926	75,132	100,542	364,207	87,127	101,742	74,525	100,813	-0.7
Massachusetts	505,722	160,457	191,157	58,698	95,410	503,508	161,236	192,429	57,419	92,424	-0.4
Michigan	583,034	162,283	182,908	101,248	136,595	558,053	157,319	176,794	95,590	128,350	-4.3
Minnesota	422,793	97,358	128,040	68,513	128,882	412,966	94,227	125,640	66,074	127,025	-2.3
Mississippi	172,588	53,766	76,226	15,251	27,345	171,751	53,079	75,495	15,406	27,771	-0.5
Missouri	401,098	110,500	132,952	63,196	94,450	383,489	105,983	129,698	58,390	89,418	-4.4
Montana	50,918	17,921	18,148	5,860	8,989	50,642	17,412	17,980	5,869	9,381	-0.5
Nebraska	136,098	40,770	47,377	19,743	28,208	135,864	40,250	47,186	20,028	28,400	-0.2
Nevada	116,030	26,799	35,043	22,651	31,537	117,574	26,886	36,078	22,872	31,738	1.3
New Hampshire	133,159	30,734	40,043	21,604	40,778	149,184	29,337	38,914	28,460	52,473	12.0
New Jersey	421,386	131,275	143,003	61,159	85,949	419,037	131,377	143,515	59,872	84,273	-0.6
New Mexico	134,607	30,230	37,689	26,360	40,328	129,494	28,160	35,756	25,983	39,595	-3.8
New York	1,273,634	403,885	489,740	151,476	228,533	1,260,240	404,517	491,225	146,062	218,436	-1.1
North Carolina	561,415	157,142	203,545	76,389	124,339	563,831	156,315	203,030	77,730	126,756	0.4
North Dakota	54,203	19,126	18,456	7,617	9,004	53,749	18,770	18,292	7,512	9,175	-0.8
Ohio	658,043	195,593	222,299	95,433	144,718	649,687	192,586	220,051	94,259	142,791	-1.3
Oklahoma	208,333	62,983	73,602	28,604	43,144	202,051	60,325	70,638	27,791	43,297	-3.0
Oregon	236,851	67,340	79,757	40,403	49,351	229,936	64,710	78,544	38,723	47,959	-2.9
Pennsylvania	725,682	245,330	281,239	74,586	124,527	717,289	242,814	279,991	72,263	122,221	-1.2
Rhode Island	83,348	27,555	34,499	8,057	13,237	82,766	27,742	34,659	7,682	12,683	-0.7
South Carolina	246,563	74,791	96,087	26,722	48,963	246,388	74,099	97,014	26,898	48,377	-0.1
South Dakota	53,683	16,215	16,747	7,920	12,801	53,620	16,227	16,723	7,984	12,686	-0.1
Tennessee	321,752	100,433	129,035	35,473	56,811	323,157	100,053	130,691	35,515	56,898	0.4
Texas	1,605,498	385,277	453,885	316,371	449,965	1,630,516	387,682	465,777	318,677	458,380	1.6
Utah	311,450	98,987	124,668	42,284	45,511	332,334	103,652	139,032	43,211	46,439	6.7
Vermont	44,719	15,803	16,459	4,942	7,515	43,855	15,396	16,407	4,724	7,328	-1.9
Virginia	557,444	153,600	187,260	87,620	128,964	554,212	153,205	188,215	86,818	125,974	-0.6
Washington	366,547	115,231	136,553	49,439	65,324	367,944	115,274	138,436	49,055	65,179	0.4
West Virginia	146,608	35,486	39,744	38,763	32,615	142,963	34,776	39,523	36,927	31,737	-2.5
Wisconsin	341,717	99,088	114,556	51,372	76,701	340,770	96,688	112,670	54,310	77,102	-0.3
Wyoming	33,365	9,072	9,416	6,833	8,044	33,015	8,931	9,364	6,760	7,960	-1.0
U.S. Service Academies	15,065	11,414	3,628	20	3	15,281	11,432	3,828	18	3	1.4
Other jurisdictions	**241,896**	**81,322**	**111,694**	**19,749**	**29,131**	**192,406**	**62,737**	**85,872**	**17,983**	**25,814**	**-20.5**
American Samoa	1,253	240	462	171	380	1,095	205	410	164	316	-12.6
Federated States of Micronesia	2,090	613	857	259	361	2,022	639	815	257	311	-3.3
Guam	6,084	1,653	2,268	938	1,225	6,027	1,695	2,237	886	1,209	-0.9
Marshall Islands	978	322	350	165	141	1,032	331	336	196	169	5.5
Northern Marianas	1,038	335	493	77	133	1,216	354	559	124	179	17.1
Palau	587	186	175	82	144	532	168	196	70	98	-9.4
Puerto Rico	227,496	77,475	106,084	17,812	26,125	178,312	58,863	80,439	16,056	22,954	-21.6
U.S. Virgin Islands	2,370	498	1,005	245	622	2,170	482	880	230	578	-8.4

NOTE: Degree-granting institutions grant associate's or higher degrees and participate in Title IV federal financial aid programs. Some data have been revised from previously published figures.

SOURCE: U.S. Department of Education, National Center for Education Statistics, Integrated Postsecondary Education Data System (IPEDS), Spring 2017 and Spring 2018, Fall Enrollment component. (This table was prepared December 2018.)

Table 304.35. Total fall enrollment in public degree-granting postsecondary institutions, by attendance status, sex, and state or jurisdiction: 2016 and 2017

State or jurisdiction	2016					2017					Percent change, 2016 to 2017
	Total	Full-time		Part-time		Total	Full-time		Part-time		
		Males	Females	Males	Females		Males	Females	Males	Females	
1	2	3	4	5	6	7	8	9	10	11	12
United States	**14,585,840**	**3,877,799**	**4,449,580**	**2,636,936**	**3,621,525**	**14,560,155**	**3,857,945**	**4,470,128**	**2,619,975**	**3,612,107**	**-0.2**
Alabama	251,038	73,274	94,720	32,974	50,070	254,071	74,204	96,245	32,969	50,653	1.2
Alaska	27,352	5,581	6,175	5,653	9,943	25,850	5,289	6,133	5,306	9,122	-5.5
Arizona	361,400	91,062	96,225	73,547	100,566	366,787	90,375	98,218	75,047	103,147	1.5
Arkansas	149,298	39,189	50,847	23,199	36,063	146,697	38,360	50,747	22,243	35,347	-1.7
California	2,228,592	510,644	592,774	520,618	604,556	2,246,844	516,544	605,663	517,870	606,767	0.8
Colorado	272,668	73,900	76,952	51,478	70,338	278,909	74,706	78,038	54,672	71,493	2.3
Connecticut	117,345	32,624	36,421	19,610	28,690	116,090	32,653	36,476	18,798	28,163	-1.1
Delaware	41,816	12,761	17,104	4,268	7,683	42,321	12,727	17,222	4,488	7,884	1.2
District of Columbia	4,587	1,053	1,140	858	1,536	4,529	1,050	1,206	830	1,443	-1.3
Florida	797,048	178,700	222,720	159,494	236,134	798,045	181,640	227,474	155,578	233,353	0.1
Georgia	422,159	114,823	146,092	63,671	97,573	428,586	115,084	146,935	66,216	100,351	1.5
Hawaii	53,418	12,462	16,004	9,795	15,157	51,674	12,080	15,581	9,201	14,812	-3.3
Idaho	74,667	19,081	20,371	14,057	21,158	75,792	18,453	20,740	14,690	21,909	1.5
Illinois	492,578	126,935	133,953	98,944	132,746	478,042	122,250	129,588	96,430	129,774	-3.0
Indiana	319,581	88,510	98,074	57,463	75,534	301,562	87,402	96,787	51,562	65,811	-5.6
Iowa	171,075	52,072	51,292	30,256	37,455	170,427	51,200	50,396	30,355	38,476	-0.4
Kansas	180,170	50,679	54,294	31,582	43,615	179,856	49,807	53,755	31,850	44,444	-0.2
Kentucky	205,431	55,491	69,530	34,317	46,093	202,266	53,145	68,233	34,491	46,397	-1.5
Louisiana	208,254	58,079	76,449	27,875	45,851	210,691	57,500	77,266	27,979	47,946	1.2
Maine	47,763	12,392	13,397	8,150	13,824	46,999	12,283	13,326	7,845	13,545	-1.6
Maryland	306,892	71,715	81,254	67,254	86,669	303,640	70,761	79,773	66,368	86,738	-1.1
Massachusetts	218,465	59,944	64,631	36,135	57,755	213,389	59,644	64,619	34,183	54,943	-2.3
Michigan	492,771	137,344	153,275	87,285	114,867	478,735	133,968	150,110	83,964	110,693	-2.8
Minnesota	253,239	67,902	73,858	46,439	65,040	249,385	66,561	73,545	45,331	63,948	-1.5
Mississippi	153,082	49,098	68,416	13,187	22,381	152,319	48,572	67,568	13,299	22,880	-0.5
Missouri	244,921	69,207	81,029	38,147	56,538	235,540	66,018	78,943	36,025	54,554	-3.8
Montana	46,262	16,312	15,903	5,640	8,407	46,002	15,834	15,819	5,648	8,701	-0.6
Nebraska	101,032	29,765	31,843	17,027	22,397	101,038	29,570	31,906	17,199	22,363	#
Nevada	106,196	23,511	29,822	22,234	30,629	107,864	23,908	30,673	22,445	30,838	1.6
New Hampshire	41,170	13,150	15,405	4,995	7,620	39,761	12,907	15,160	4,447	7,247	-3.4
New Jersey	337,099	99,715	110,235	53,544	73,605	334,597	99,889	110,370	52,439	71,899	-0.7
New Mexico	129,038	28,698	34,838	25,998	39,504	125,280	27,085	33,394	25,768	39,033	-2.9
New York	700,875	214,562	247,231	97,252	141,830	697,458	215,895	248,886	95,192	137,485	-0.5
North Carolina	450,080	118,527	152,094	69,573	109,886	454,632	118,178	152,668	71,232	112,554	1.0
North Dakota	47,964	17,235	15,433	7,102	8,194	47,574	16,888	15,366	7,032	8,288	-0.8
Ohio	501,146	142,011	156,078	82,578	120,479	497,473	140,358	154,832	82,121	120,162	-0.7
Oklahoma	177,629	50,380	59,789	26,778	40,682	174,140	48,723	58,189	26,112	41,116	-2.0
Oregon	197,819	55,457	59,223	38,068	45,071	192,334	53,352	58,974	36,449	43,559	-2.8
Pennsylvania	406,346	134,191	143,773	50,927	77,455	400,943	132,492	142,340	49,690	76,421	-1.3
Rhode Island	41,369	10,296	14,187	6,191	10,695	41,018	10,563	14,628	5,775	10,052	-0.8
South Carolina	200,295	60,169	74,345	23,705	42,076	200,622	59,898	74,953	24,044	41,727	0.2
South Dakota	44,305	14,131	13,706	6,610	9,858	44,630	14,200	13,520	6,747	10,163	0.7
Tennessee	221,288	67,395	81,726	28,603	43,564	223,179	67,470	83,070	28,797	43,842	0.9
Texas	1,423,205	323,662	371,683	300,137	427,723	1,448,385	326,483	381,540	303,580	436,782	1.8
Utah	175,308	47,485	46,038	39,143	42,642	180,034	48,153	48,276	40,039	43,566	2.7
Vermont	25,736	7,736	9,386	2,856	5,758	25,300	7,565	9,503	2,667	5,565	-1.7
Virginia	389,446	109,813	126,682	64,134	88,817	389,249	109,603	127,093	64,099	88,454	-0.1
Washington	315,356	98,720	111,310	45,825	59,501	318,336	99,257	113,978	45,683	59,418	0.9
West Virginia	85,099	29,530	32,365	8,628	14,576	83,895	28,668	32,107	8,647	14,473	-1.4
Wisconsin	278,300	80,843	86,504	46,279	64,674	279,533	78,796	85,139	49,755	65,843	0.4
Wyoming	32,802	8,569	9,356	6,833	8,044	32,551	8,502	9,329	6,760	7,960	-0.8
U.S. Service Academies	15,065	11,414	3,628	20	3	15,281	11,432	3,828	18	3	1.4
Other jurisdictions	**81,479**	**30,260**	**39,434**	**5,037**	**6,748**	**37,419**	**14,492**	**15,929**	**3,141**	**3,857**	**-54.1**
American Samoa	1,253	240	462	171	380	1,095	205	410	164	316	-12.6
Federated States of Micronesia	2,090	613	857	259	361	2,022	639	815	257	311	-3.3
Guam	6,017	1,630	2,243	930	1,214	5,972	1,673	2,217	880	1,202	-0.7
Marshall Islands	978	322	350	165	141	1,032	331	336	196	169	5.5
Northern Marianas	1,038	335	493	77	133	1,216	354	559	124	179	17.1
Palau	587	186	175	82	144	532	168	196	70	98	-9.4
Puerto Rico	67,146	26,436	33,849	3,108	3,753	23,380	10,640	10,516	1,220	1,004	-65.2
U.S. Virgin Islands	2,370	498	1,005	245	622	2,170	482	880	230	578	-8.4

#Rounds to zero.
NOTE: Degree-granting institutions grant associate's or higher degrees and participate in Title IV federal financial aid programs. Some data have been revised from previously published figures.

SOURCE: U.S. Department of Education, National Center for Education Statistics, Integrated Postsecondary Education Data System (IPEDS), Spring 2017 and Spring 2018, Fall Enrollment component. (This table was prepared December 2018.)

Table 304.60. Total fall enrollment in degree-granting postsecondary institutions, by control and level of institution and state or jurisdiction: 2016 and 2017

State or jurisdiction	2016						2017					
	Public 4-year	Public 2-year	Private 4-year		Private 2-year		Public 4-year	Public 2-year	Private 4-year		Private 2-year	
			Nonprofit	For-profit	Nonprofit	For-profit			Nonprofit	For-profit	Nonprofit	For-profit
1	2	3	4	5	6	7	8	9	10	11	12	13
United States	**8,742,931**	**5,842,909**	**4,028,401**	**983,154**	**50,555**	**198,954**	**8,853,477**	**5,706,678**	**4,058,087**	**912,076**	**48,390**	**186,890**
Alabama	170,003	81,035	24,570	26,069	386	1,989	173,335	80,736	26,149	24,841	0	1,761
Alaska	27,164	188	581	0	79	424	25,850	0	551	0	74	430
Arizona	173,528	187,872	9,802	226,853	0	10,031	180,262	186,525	9,935	204,381	0	10,523
Arkansas	100,926	48,372	16,268	372	1,178	119	100,048	46,649	15,713	323	1,296	53
California	947,302	1,281,290	303,187	136,533	1,602	30,531	1,013,168	1,233,676	307,759	131,822	1,497	26,129
Colorado	200,109	72,559	34,004	38,415	265	6,903	212,011	66,898	33,730	39,861	351	7,385
Connecticut	66,797	50,548	72,344	8,321	0	0	66,710	49,380	72,360	9,084	0	0
Delaware	41,816	0	18,852	301	170	0	42,321	0	17,554	320	143	0
District of Columbia	4,587	0	78,938	9,036	0	479	4,529	0	81,099	9,984	0	387
Florida	767,650	29,398	187,138	54,757	18,185	18,399	770,419	27,626	183,113	50,604	20,146	19,576
Georgia	310,456	111,703	74,282	27,653	1,981	6,998	314,455	114,131	77,092	24,084	1,763	6,599
Hawaii	28,003	25,415	9,799	2,109	0	517	27,535	24,139	10,159	1,670	0	622
Idaho	52,474	22,193	48,492	197	0	440	52,432	23,360	55,503	79	0	429
Illinois	188,405	304,173	217,912	61,812	371	5,047	184,631	293,411	214,830	59,655	421	4,054
Indiana	240,671	78,910	91,022	5,560	582	2,539	226,076	75,486	89,437	4,403	548	2,854
Iowa	80,266	90,809	53,475	41,703	0	260	80,185	90,242	52,870	37,550	0	107
Kansas	100,613	79,557	23,058	11,321	0	1,283	100,731	79,125	22,910	10,154	0	1,042
Kentucky	126,021	79,410	41,332	7,668	0	631	124,710	77,556	47,958	7,272	0	1,002
Louisiana	142,238	66,016	25,308	852	368	4,496	144,430	66,261	25,955	56	481	4,882
Maine	30,510	17,253	22,517	1,315	220	301	30,040	16,959	23,226	1,096	242	248
Maryland	182,456	124,436	53,881	3,997	0	2,039	184,521	119,119	54,647	3,511	0	2,409
Massachusetts	125,983	92,482	283,391	2,180	1,122	564	125,770	87,619	286,894	1,914	1,093	218
Michigan	335,074	157,697	87,297	1,845	0	1,121	327,750	150,985	76,764	1,411	0	1,143
Minnesota	133,441	119,798	70,279	98,811	77	387	132,119	117,266	70,563	92,658	90	270
Mississippi	82,010	71,072	17,856	322	0	1,328	80,730	71,589	17,576	359	0	1,497
Missouri	154,208	90,713	145,598	4,948	854	4,777	148,708	86,832	139,725	4,929	173	3,122
Montana	37,884	8,378	4,196	0	425	35	38,116	7,886	4,228	0	375	37
Nebraska	61,079	39,953	33,597	1,161	150	158	60,740	40,298	33,822	903	32	69
Nevada	95,323	10,873	3,770	2,589	287	3,188	97,144	10,720	3,994	1,862	272	3,582
New Hampshire	27,726	13,444	91,808	0	181	0	27,308	12,453	109,300	0	123	0
New Jersey	186,622	150,477	73,822	7,426	0	3,039	187,735	146,862	73,693	6,894	0	3,853
New Mexico	59,951	69,087	1,658	2,484	0	1,427	58,250	67,030	1,590	1,283	0	1,341
New York	397,019	303,856	528,364	28,828	2,574	12,993	400,971	296,487	521,496	27,825	2,691	10,770
North Carolina	228,524	221,556	96,635	10,553	687	3,460	232,872	221,760	96,539	8,919	624	3,117
North Dakota	40,986	6,978	5,690	549	0	0	40,368	7,206	5,648	527	0	0
Ohio	330,959	170,187	137,058	7,271	1,269	11,299	326,542	170,931	135,388	6,098	1,419	9,309
Oklahoma	119,452	58,177	25,033	2,405	1,194	2,072	117,915	56,225	23,338	1,464	581	2,528
Oregon	104,572	93,247	35,429	2,620	0	983	104,604	87,730	34,589	2,209	34	770
Pennsylvania	279,720	126,626	284,077	11,295	7,837	16,127	277,568	123,375	288,749	8,544	6,053	13,000
Rhode Island	26,268	15,101	41,979	0	0	0	26,260	14,758	41,748	0	0	0
South Carolina	112,900	87,395	34,115	7,981	991	3,181	114,569	86,053	33,347	7,883	790	3,746
South Dakota	37,769	6,536	7,223	2,155	0	0	37,897	6,733	7,060	1,930	0	0
Tennessee	136,357	84,931	83,744	7,637	682	8,401	136,810	86,369	83,777	7,698	682	7,821
Texas	726,130	697,075	140,325	18,833	1,941	21,194	737,542	710,843	140,815	18,175	1,921	21,220
Utah	145,407	29,901	129,408	4,223	2,119	392	150,414	29,620	145,565	4,200	2,045	490
Vermont	19,873	5,863	18,683	300	0	0	19,796	5,504	18,411	144	0	0
Virginia	216,171	173,275	132,103	30,871	747	4,277	219,880	169,369	132,410	28,331	578	3,644
Washington	253,984	61,372	42,479	5,281	1,513	1,918	282,316	36,020	41,473	5,044	1,388	1,703
West Virginia	67,455	17,644	8,809	49,660	0	3,040	67,188	16,707	8,583	47,715	0	2,770
Wisconsin	190,658	87,642	57,168	6,082	0	167	189,518	90,015	58,452	2,407	0	378
Wyoming	12,366	20,436	45	0	518	0	12,397	20,154	0	0	464	0
U.S. Service Academies	15,065	0	†	†	†	†	15,281	0	†	†	†	†
Other jurisdictions	**72,839**	**8,640**	**121,212**	**18,876**	**804**	**19,525**	**29,524**	**7,895**	**117,928**	**18,879**	**358**	**17,822**
American Samoa	1,253	0	0	0	0	0	1,095	0	0	0	0	0
Federated States of Micronesia	0	2,090	0	0	0	0	0	2,022	0	0	0	0
Guam	3,875	2,142	67	0	0	0	3,917	2,055	55	0	0	0
Marshall Islands	0	978	0	0	0	0	0	1,032	0	0	0	0
Northern Marianas	1,038	0	0	0	0	0	1,216	0	0	0	0	0
Palau	0	587	0	0	0	0	0	532	0	0	0	0
Puerto Rico	64,303	2,843	121,145	18,876	804	19,525	21,126	2,254	117,873	18,879	358	17,822
U.S. Virgin Islands	2,370	0	0	0	0	0	2,170	0	0	0	0	0

†Not applicable.

NOTE: Degree-granting institutions grant associate's or higher degrees and participate in Title IV federal financial aid programs. Some data have been revised from previously published figures.

SOURCE: U.S. Department of Education, National Center for Education Statistics, Integrated Postsecondary Education Data System (IPEDS), Spring 2017 and Spring 2018, Fall Enrollment component. (This table was prepared December 2018.)

Table 305.10. Total fall enrollment of first-time degree/certificate-seeking students in degree-granting postsecondary institutions, by attendance status, sex of student, and level and control of institution: 1960 through 2028

Year	Total	Full-time	Part-time	Males			Females			4-year		2-year	
				Total	Full-time	Part-time	Total	Full-time	Part-time	Public	Private	Public	Private
1	2	3	4	5	6	7	8	9	10	11	12	13	14
1960[1]	923,069	—	—	539,512	—	—	383,557	—	—	395,884[2]	313,209[2]	181,860[2]	32,116[2]
1961[1]	1,018,361	—	—	591,913	—	—	426,448	—	—	438,135[2]	336,449[2]	210,101[2]	33,676[2]
1962[1]	1,030,554	—	—	598,099	—	—	432,455	—	—	445,191[2]	324,923[2]	224,537[2]	35,903[2]
1963[1]	1,046,424	—	—	604,282	—	—	442,142	—	—	—	—	—	—
1964[1]	1,224,840	—	—	701,524	—	—	523,316	—	—	539,251[2]	363,348[2]	275,413[2]	46,828[2]
1965[1]	1,441,822	—	—	829,215	—	—	612,607	—	—	642,233[2]	398,792[2]	347,788[2]	53,009[2]
1966	1,554,337	—	—	889,516	—	—	664,821	—	—	626,472[2]	382,889[2]	478,459[2]	66,517[2]
1967	1,640,936	1,335,512	305,424	931,127	761,299	169,828	709,809	574,213	135,596	644,525	368,300	561,488	66,623
1968	1,892,849	1,470,653	422,196	1,082,367	847,005	235,362	810,482	623,648	186,834	724,377	378,052	718,562	71,858
1969	1,967,104	1,525,290	441,814	1,118,269	876,280	241,989	848,835	649,010	199,825	699,167	391,508	814,132	62,297
1970	2,063,397	1,587,072	476,325	1,151,960	896,281	255,679	911,437	690,791	220,646	717,449	395,886	890,703	59,359
1971	2,119,018	1,606,036	512,982	1,170,518	895,715	274,803	948,500	710,321	238,179	704,052	384,695	971,295	58,976
1972	2,152,778	1,574,197	578,581	1,157,501	858,254	299,247	995,277	715,943	279,334	680,337	380,982	1,036,616	54,843
1973	2,226,041	1,607,269	618,772	1,182,173	867,314	314,859	1,043,868	739,955	303,913	698,777	378,994	1,089,182	59,088
1974	2,365,761	1,673,333	692,428	1,243,790	896,077	347,713	1,121,971	777,256	344,715	745,637	386,391	1,175,759	57,974
1975	2,515,155	1,763,296	751,859	1,327,935	942,198	385,737	1,187,220	821,098	366,122	771,725	395,440	1,283,523	64,467
1976	2,347,014	1,662,333	684,681	1,170,326	854,597	315,729	1,176,688	807,736	368,952	717,373	413,961	1,152,944	62,736
1977	2,394,426	1,680,916	713,510	1,155,856	839,848	316,008	1,238,570	841,068	397,502	737,497	404,631	1,185,648	66,650
1978	2,389,627	1,650,848	738,779	1,141,777	817,294	324,483	1,247,850	833,554	414,296	736,703	406,669	1,173,544	72,711
1979	2,502,896	1,706,732	796,164	1,179,846	840,315	339,531	1,323,050	866,417	456,633	760,119	415,126	1,253,854	73,797
1980	2,587,644	1,749,928	837,716	1,218,961	862,458	356,503	1,368,683	887,470	481,213	765,395	417,937	1,313,591	90,721[3]
1981	2,595,421	1,737,714	857,707	1,217,680	851,833	365,847	1,377,741	885,881	491,860	754,007	419,257	1,318,436	103,721[3]
1982	2,505,466	1,688,620	816,846	1,199,237	837,223	362,014	1,306,229	851,397	454,832	730,775	404,252	1,254,193	116,246[3]
1983	2,443,703	1,678,071	765,632	1,159,049	824,609	334,440	1,284,654	853,462	431,192	728,244	403,882	1,189,869	121,708
1984	2,356,898	1,613,185	743,713	1,112,303	786,099	326,204	1,244,595	827,086	417,509	713,790	402,959	1,130,311	109,838
1985	2,292,222	1,602,038	690,184	1,075,736	774,858	300,878	1,216,486	827,180	389,306	717,199	398,556	1,060,275	116,192
1986	2,219,208	1,589,451	629,757	1,046,527	768,856	277,671	1,172,681	820,595	352,086	719,974	391,673	990,973	116,588
1987	2,246,359	1,626,719	619,640	1,046,615	779,226	267,389	1,199,744	847,493	352,251	757,833	405,113	979,820	103,593
1988	2,378,803	1,698,927	679,876	1,100,026	807,319	292,707	1,278,777	891,608	387,169	783,358	425,907	1,048,914	120,624
1989	2,341,035	1,656,594	684,441	1,094,750	791,295	303,455	1,246,285	865,299	380,986	762,217	413,836	1,048,529	116,453
1990	2,256,624	1,617,118	639,506	1,045,191	771,372	273,819	1,211,433	845,746	365,687	727,264	400,120	1,041,097	88,143
1991	2,277,920	1,652,983	624,937	1,068,433	798,043	270,390	1,209,487	854,940	354,547	717,697	392,904	1,070,048	97,271
1992	2,184,113	1,603,737	580,376	1,013,058	760,290	252,768	1,171,055	843,447	327,608	697,393	408,306	993,074	85,340
1993	2,160,710	1,608,274	552,436	1,007,647	762,240	245,407	1,153,063	846,034	307,029	702,273	410,688	973,545	74,204
1994	2,133,205	1,603,106	530,099	984,558	751,081	233,477	1,148,647	852,025	296,622	709,042	405,917	952,468	65,778
1995	2,168,831	1,646,812	522,019	1,001,052	767,185	233,867	1,167,779	879,627	288,152	731,836	419,025	954,595	63,375
1996	2,274,319	1,739,852	534,467	1,046,662	805,982	240,680	1,227,657	933,870	293,787	741,164	427,442	989,536	116,177
1997	2,219,255	1,733,512	485,743	1,026,058	806,054	220,004	1,193,197	927,458	265,739	755,362	442,397	923,954	97,542
1998	2,212,593	1,775,412	437,181	1,022,656	825,577	197,079	1,189,937	949,835	240,102	792,772	460,948	858,417	100,456
1999	2,357,590	1,849,741	507,849	1,094,539	865,545	228,994	1,263,051	984,196	278,855	819,503	474,223	955,499	108,365
2000	2,427,551	1,918,093	509,458	1,123,948	894,432	229,516	1,303,603	1,023,661	279,942	842,228	498,532	952,175	134,616
2001	2,497,078	1,989,179	507,899	1,152,837	926,393	226,444	1,344,241	1,062,786	281,455	866,619	508,030	988,726	133,703
2002	2,570,611	2,053,065	517,546	1,170,609	945,938	224,671	1,400,002	1,107,127	292,875	886,297	517,621	1,037,267	129,426
2003	2,591,754	2,102,394	489,360	1,175,856	965,075	210,781	1,415,898	1,137,319	278,579	918,602	537,726	1,004,428	130,998
2004	2,630,243	2,147,546	482,697	1,190,268	981,591	208,677	1,439,975	1,165,955	274,020	925,249	562,485	1,009,082	133,427
2005	2,657,338	2,189,884	467,454	1,200,055	995,610	204,445	1,457,283	1,194,274	263,009	953,903	606,712	977,224	119,499
2006	2,707,205	2,220,184	487,021	1,228,703	1,015,786	212,917	1,478,502	1,204,398	274,104	990,077	598,266	1,013,419	105,443
2007	2,777,168	2,295,518	481,650	1,268,137	1,053,375	214,762	1,509,031	1,242,143	266,888	1,023,789	633,772	1,016,636	102,971
2008	3,022,736	2,425,987	596,749	1,388,441	1,114,724	273,717	1,634,295	1,311,263	323,032	1,053,829	672,372	1,186,640	109,895
2009	3,156,882	2,534,440	622,442	1,464,424	1,177,119	287,305	1,692,458	1,357,321	335,137	1,090,980	658,808	1,275,974	131,120
2010	3,156,727	2,533,636	623,091	1,461,016	1,171,090	289,926	1,695,711	1,362,546	333,165	1,110,601	674,573	1,238,491	133,062
2011	3,091,496	2,479,155	612,341	1,424,140	1,140,843	283,297	1,667,356	1,338,312	329,044	1,131,091	656,864	1,195,083	108,458
2012	2,994,187	2,408,063	586,124	1,387,316	1,115,266	272,050	1,606,871	1,292,797	314,074	1,128,344	642,716	1,137,927	85,200
2013	2,985,366	2,415,969	569,397	1,383,852	1,117,525	266,327	1,601,514	1,298,444	303,070	1,144,102	633,184	1,126,978	81,102
2014	2,925,998	2,383,328	542,670	1,355,164	1,100,005	255,159	1,570,834	1,283,323	287,511	1,170,639	612,162	1,070,625	72,572
2015	2,882,949	2,368,283	514,666	1,338,853	1,096,976	241,877	1,544,096	1,271,307	272,789	1,190,206	599,242	1,031,117	62,384
2016	2,882,991	2,369,021	513,970	1,333,598	1,093,968	239,630	1,549,393	1,275,053	274,340	1,259,214	581,098	981,029	61,650
2017	2,880,171	2,377,035	503,136	1,323,424	1,091,425	231,999	1,556,747	1,285,610	271,137	1,285,506	588,659	951,618	54,388
2018[4]	2,889,000	—	—	1,327,000	—	—	1,561,000	—	—	—	—	—	—
2019[4]	2,900,000	—	—	1,332,000	—	—	1,568,000	—	—	—	—	—	—
2020[4]	2,903,000	—	—	1,334,000	—	—	1,570,000	—	—	—	—	—	—
2021[4]	2,907,000	—	—	1,335,000	—	—	1,572,000	—	—	—	—	—	—
2022[4]	2,912,000	—	—	1,337,000	—	—	1,576,000	—	—	—	—	—	—
2023[4]	2,919,000	—	—	1,340,000	—	—	1,580,000	—	—	—	—	—	—
2024[4]	2,929,000	—	—	1,344,000	—	—	1,585,000	—	—	—	—	—	—
2025[4]	2,939,000	—	—	1,348,000	—	—	1,591,000	—	—	—	—	—	—
2026[4]	2,951,000	—	—	1,354,000	—	—	1,597,000	—	—	—	—	—	—
2027[4]	2,956,000	—	—	1,357,000	—	—	1,599,000	—	—	—	—	—	—
2028[4]	2,958,000	—	—	1,358,000	—	—	1,600,000	—	—	—	—	—	—

—Not available.

[1]Excludes first-time degree/certificate-seeking students in occupational programs not creditable towards a bachelor's degree.

[2]Data for 2-year branches of 4-year college systems are aggregated with the 4-year institutions.

[3]Large increases are due to the addition of schools accredited by the Accrediting Commission of Career Schools and Colleges of Technology.

[4]Projected.

NOTE: Data through 1995 are for institutions of higher education, while later data are for degree-granting institutions. Degree-granting institutions grant associate's or higher degrees and participate in Title IV federal financial aid programs. The degree-granting classification is very similar to the earlier higher education classification, but it includes more 2-year colleges and excludes a few higher education institutions that did not grant degrees. Alaska and Hawaii are included in all years. Some data have been revised from previously published figures.

SOURCE: U.S. Department of Education, National Center for Education Statistics, *Biennial Survey of Education in the United States*; *Opening Fall Enrollment in Higher Education*, 1963 through 1965; Higher Education General Information Survey (HEGIS), "Fall Enrollment in Colleges and Universities" surveys, 1966 through 1985; Integrated Postsecondary Education Data System (IPEDS), "Fall Enrollment Survey" (IPEDS-EF:86–99); IPEDS Spring 2001 through Spring 2018, Fall Enrollment component; and First-Time Freshmen Projection Model, 1980 through 2028. (This table was prepared March 2019.)

Table 305.20. Total fall enrollment of first-time degree/certificate-seeking students in degree-granting postsecondary institutions, by attendance status, sex of student, control of institution, and state or jurisdiction: Selected years, 2000 through 2017

State or jurisdiction	Total, fall 2000	Total, fall 2010	Total, fall 2014	Total, fall 2015	Total, fall 2016	Fall 2017									
						Total	Full-time			Part-time			Public	Private
							Total	Males	Females	Total	Males	Females		
1	2	3	4	5	6	7	8	9	10	11	12	13	14	15
United States	**2,427,551**	**3,156,727**	**2,925,998**	**2,882,949**	**2,882,991**	**2,880,171**	**2,377,035**	**1,091,425**	**1,285,610**	**503,136**	**231,999**	**271,137**	**2,237,124**	**643,047**
Alabama	43,411	52,990	51,148	50,151	50,108	50,295	44,750	19,695	25,055	5,545	2,684	2,861	44,773	5,522
Alaska	2,432	5,400	4,562	3,849	3,049	3,234	2,477	1,053	1,424	757	312	445	2,910	324
Arizona	46,646	76,832	72,960	67,751	65,784	62,844	46,669	20,626	26,043	16,175	7,218	8,957	49,369	13,475
Arkansas	22,695	29,321	27,407	27,388	27,276	26,781	24,361	10,889	13,472	2,420	1,023	1,397	23,166	3,615
California	246,128	402,832	391,838	383,920	394,845	388,587	271,120	123,444	147,676	117,467	60,396	57,071	345,024	43,563
Colorado	43,201	54,594	44,275	43,349	43,832	45,436	37,552	17,915	19,637	7,884	3,417	4,467	37,992	7,444
Connecticut	24,212	32,719	31,550	31,398	31,741	31,804	26,958	12,354	14,604	4,846	2,050	2,796	19,232	12,572
Delaware	7,636	8,947	9,526	9,352	9,727	10,051	8,309	3,543	4,766	1,742	669	1,073	8,445	1,606
District of Columbia	9,150	10,747	9,978	11,075	9,012	10,617	9,822	3,531	6,291	795	272	523	526	10,091
Florida	109,931	176,040	157,545	157,687	158,956	160,518	122,913	52,613	70,300	37,605	15,944	21,661	119,162	41,356
Georgia	67,616	100,140	84,387	86,071	84,932	85,736	70,423	30,717	39,706	15,313	6,602	8,711	70,684	15,052
Hawaii	8,931	10,740	9,613	8,851	8,398	8,691	7,072	2,707	4,365	1,619	683	936	7,035	1,656
Idaho	10,669	12,668	12,373	14,179	14,520	15,233	13,044	5,670	7,374	2,189	948	1,241	9,799	5,434
Illinois	107,592	114,467	99,519	95,852	93,994	92,738	78,960	37,987	40,973	13,778	6,318	7,460	63,693	29,045
Indiana	59,320	82,406	68,495	66,876	64,028	62,696	55,955	25,968	29,987	6,741	3,271	3,470	46,101	16,595
Iowa	39,564	47,257	40,690	37,851	38,130	37,996	31,849	16,458	15,391	6,147	2,290	3,857	27,727	10,269
Kansas	31,424	33,544	33,797	32,268	32,597	32,450	27,419	13,807	13,612	5,031	2,252	2,779	27,037	5,413
Kentucky	34,140	43,735	39,048	37,623	36,378	37,257	32,643	14,284	18,359	4,614	2,087	2,527	30,445	6,812
Louisiana	45,383	43,144	40,871	40,740	40,261	39,753	35,385	15,022	20,363	4,368	1,819	2,549	33,951	5,802
Maine	9,231	12,203	11,253	11,357	11,727	11,597	10,420	5,034	5,386	1,177	483	694	7,771	3,826
Maryland	35,552	51,104	46,143	44,767	47,084	44,394	34,507	16,286	18,221	9,887	4,382	5,505	37,485	6,909
Massachusetts	66,044	76,857	74,982	73,189	72,432	73,369	65,651	30,463	35,188	7,718	3,350	4,368	34,780	38,589
Michigan	84,998	101,063	89,320	89,224	86,314	83,053	66,761	31,632	35,129	16,292	7,595	8,697	72,879	10,174
Minnesota	63,893	55,723	46,249	45,323	45,102	44,662	38,767	18,682	20,085	5,895	2,647	3,248	33,851	10,811
Mississippi	30,356	37,034	31,376	31,185	32,088	30,407	28,683	12,768	15,915	1,724	788	936	28,281	2,126
Missouri	48,639	64,381	57,716	54,660	53,824	51,779	45,696	20,714	24,982	6,083	2,801	3,282	38,320	13,459
Montana	7,771	9,959	8,887	8,749	8,959	8,770	7,600	3,807	3,793	1,170	524	646	7,890	880
Nebraska	19,027	19,284	18,372	18,092	18,423	17,883	16,309	7,944	8,365	1,574	678	896	14,365	3,518
Nevada	10,490	18,572	16,337	15,917	16,112	17,169	13,006	5,490	7,516	4,163	1,917	2,246	15,995	1,174
New Hampshire	13,143	13,613	15,378	17,097	15,728	18,388	12,485	5,560	6,925	5,903	2,158	3,745	7,867	10,521
New Jersey	52,233	71,296	67,144	65,232	65,178	65,109	57,303	27,651	29,652	7,806	3,549	4,257	53,708	11,401
New Mexico	15,261	22,353	17,311	18,045	19,085	18,375	14,247	6,383	7,864	4,128	1,792	2,336	17,755	620
New York	168,181	197,849	189,419	187,059	185,714	187,756	179,352	84,938	94,414	8,404	3,944	4,460	113,459	74,297
North Carolina	69,343	92,627	92,331	88,995	88,547	88,257	72,872	32,289	40,583	15,385	6,787	8,598	68,379	19,878
North Dakota	8,929	9,073	8,565	8,606	8,709	8,874	8,522	4,533	3,989	352	169	183	7,874	1,000
Ohio	98,823	123,063	102,731	100,029	101,393	99,539	87,318	41,570	45,748	12,221	5,563	6,658	74,688	24,851
Oklahoma	35,094	39,107	36,170	36,371	36,266	35,259	28,860	13,644	15,216	6,399	2,632	3,767	30,218	5,041
Oregon	26,946	35,442	29,640	30,765	31,324	31,432	25,085	11,436	13,649	6,347	3,016	3,331	26,601	4,831
Pennsylvania	125,578	144,184	131,493	126,933	125,063	122,225	108,661	50,864	57,797	13,564	5,762	7,802	72,306	49,919
Rhode Island	13,789	15,698	15,447	15,004	14,942	14,602	13,742	6,330	7,412	860	351	509	6,664	7,938
South Carolina	32,353	47,535	47,164	46,080	45,173	46,448	40,531	17,795	22,736	5,917	2,586	3,331	37,482	8,966
South Dakota	8,597	10,074	8,372	8,473	8,316	8,622	8,053	4,168	3,885	569	210	359	7,273	1,349
Tennessee	43,327	59,279	53,074	56,498	56,605	58,399	54,714	23,979	30,735	3,685	1,432	2,253	42,477	15,922
Texas	181,813	228,503	238,283	234,131	235,197	242,911	177,626	80,519	97,107	65,285	30,355	34,930	213,055	29,856
Utah	24,953	35,126	28,221	31,884	32,141	34,898	29,337	12,367	16,970	5,561	2,782	2,779	25,825	9,073
Vermont	6,810	8,242	7,525	7,202	7,474	7,393	6,789	3,289	3,500	604	201	403	4,421	2,972
Virginia	52,661	83,166	81,473	80,362	79,020	79,355	66,565	30,846	35,719	12,790	5,774	7,016	63,125	16,230
Washington	36,287	41,124	42,543	46,370	47,853	48,447	42,521	19,291	23,230	5,926	2,604	3,322	40,094	8,353
West Virginia	15,659	23,020	22,357	18,866	18,874	18,068	16,047	7,535	8,512	2,021	1,162	859	14,347	3,721
Wisconsin	53,662	61,249	52,467	50,978	51,423	50,764	42,889	20,141	22,748	7,875	3,422	4,453	41,738	9,026
Wyoming	4,209	6,042	4,681	5,210	5,227	5,104	4,289	2,119	2,170	815	328	487	4,934	170
U.S. Service Academies	3,818	4,359	3,992	4,065	4,106	4,146	4,146	3,075	1,071	0	0	0	4,146	†
Other jurisdictions	**39,609**	**52,222**	**50,781**	**43,746**	**48,706**	**31,584**	**28,939**	**13,137**	**15,802**	**2,645**	**1,152**	**1,493**	**7,879**	**23,705**
American Samoa	297	657	450	382	392	381	268	102	166	113	47	66	381	0
Federated States of Micronesia	786	653	558	708	760	647	572	274	298	75	38	37	647	0
Guam	770	1,043	813	1,101	985	1,275	922	375	547	353	161	192	1,272	3
Marshall Islands	199	240	342	327	303	279	249	112	137	30	17	13	279	0
Northern Marianas	333	360	302	290	305	336	287	118	169	49	29	20	336	0
Palau	147	114	164	200	148	142	131	60	71	11	4	7	142	0
Puerto Rico	36,773	48,672	47,759	40,347	45,468	28,216	26,230	11,986	14,244	1,986	850	1,136	4,514	23,702
U.S. Virgin Islands	304	483	393	391	345	308	280	110	170	28	6	22	308	0

†Not applicable.
NOTE: Degree-granting institutions grant associate's or higher degrees and participate in Title IV federal financial aid programs. Some data have been revised from previously published figures.
SOURCE: U.S. Department of Education, National Center for Education Statistics, Integrated Postsecondary Education Data System (IPEDS), Spring 2001 through Spring 2018, Fall Enrollment component. (This table was prepared March 2019.)

Table 305.40. Acceptance rates; number of applications, admissions, and enrollees; and enrollees' SAT and ACT scores for degree-granting postsecondary institutions with first-year undergraduates, by control and level of institution: 2017–18

Acceptance rates, applications, admissions, enrollees, and SAT and ACT scores	All institutions			Public institutions			Private institutions								
										Nonprofit			For-profit		
	Total	4-year	2-year	Total	4-year	2-year	Total	4-year	2-year	Total	4-year	2-year	Total	4-year	2-year
1	2	3	4	5	6	7	8	9	10	11	12	13	14	15	16
Number of institutions reporting application data[1]	3,844	2,384	1,460	1,584	709	875	2,260	1,675	585	1,379	1,287	92	881	388	493
Percentage distribution of institutions by their acceptance of applications	100.0	100.0	100.0	100.0	100.0	100.0	100.0	100.0	100.0	100.0	100.0	100.0	100.0	100.0	100.0
No application criteria	51.8	27.2	91.9	65.0	23.7	98.4	42.5	28.7	82.2	18.3	14.7	69.6	80.4	75.0	84.6
90.0 percent or more accepted	7.4	10.8	1.8	4.2	9.3	0.1	9.6	11.4	4.4	12.1	12.4	7.6	5.7	8.0	3.9
75.0 to 89.9 percent accepted	12.1	17.8	2.7	11.9	26.1	0.3	12.2	14.3	6.2	16.5	16.8	12.0	5.6	6.2	5.1
50.0 to 74.9 percent accepted	19.6	30.3	2.2	14.0	30.2	0.8	23.6	30.4	4.3	35.5	37.5	7.6	5.1	7.0	3.7
25.0 to 49.9 percent accepted	7.1	10.8	1.1	4.2	9.2	0.2	9.1	11.5	2.4	13.0	13.8	1.1	3.1	3.6	2.6
10.0 to 24.9 percent accepted	1.6	2.4	0.3	0.6	1.3	0.1	2.3	2.9	0.5	3.6	3.7	2.2	0.2	0.3	0.2
Less than 10.0 percent accepted	0.4	0.7	0.0	0.1	0.3	0.0	0.7	0.9	0.0	1.1	1.2	0.0	0.0	0.0	0.0
Number of applications (in thousands)	10,690	10,625	65	6,022	5,993	28	4,669	4,632	37	4,580	4,560	20	89	72	17
Percentage distribution of admissions by institutions' acceptance of applications	100.0	100.0	100.0	100.0	100.0	100.0	100.0	100.0	100.0	100.0	100.0	100.0	100.0	100.0	100.0
No application criteria	†	†	†	†	†	†	†	†	†	†	†	†	†	†	†
90.0 percent or more accepted	4.8	4.8	16.9	5.5	5.5	21.4	4.0	3.9	13.4	3.8	3.8	5.0	10.0	6.8	23.5
75.0 to 89.9 percent accepted	19.0	19.0	17.3	22.6	22.6	8.6	14.4	14.3	23.8	14.4	14.4	14.7	13.3	8.3	34.8
50.0 to 74.9 percent accepted	39.1	39.1	35.0	41.0	40.9	59.5	36.7	36.8	16.5	36.1	36.2	10.3	67.1	77.3	24.0
25.0 to 49.9 percent accepted	25.3	25.3	30.2	25.9	25.9	9.9	24.6	24.4	45.5	24.9	24.7	69.8	9.3	7.6	16.2
10.0 to 24.9 percent accepted	7.8	7.8	0.7	4.6	4.6	0.6	11.9	11.9	0.7	12.1	12.1	0.1	0.3	#	1.5
Less than 10.0 percent accepted	4.0	4.0	0.0	0.5	0.5	0.0	8.5	8.6	0.0	8.7	8.7	0.0	0.0	0.0	0.0
Number of admissions (in thousands)	6,024	5,983	40	3,656	3,637	19	2,367	2,346	21	2,307	2,298	9	60	48	12
Percentage distribution of admissions by institutions' acceptance of applications	100.0	100.0	100.0	100.0	100.0	100.0	100.0	100.0	100.0	100.0	100.0	100.0	100.0	100.0	100.0
No application criteria	†	†	†	†	†	†	†	†	†	†	†	†	†	†	†
90.0 percent or more accepted	8.1	7.9	26.7	8.6	8.4	31.4	7.3	7.2	22.4	7.1	7.1	11.0	13.9	9.7	30.5
75.0 to 89.9 percent accepted	27.5	27.5	22.9	30.3	30.4	10.3	23.1	23.0	34.1	23.3	23.3	27.8	16.1	10.3	38.7
50.0 to 74.9 percent accepted	44.1	44.2	34.8	42.7	42.7	52.8	46.4	46.6	18.5	45.9	46.0	14.5	64.7	75.9	21.3
25.0 to 49.9 percent accepted	17.4	17.4	15.5	17.0	17.0	5.2	18.1	18.0	24.7	18.4	18.3	46.7	5.2	4.2	9.2
10.0 to 24.9 percent accepted	2.4	2.4	0.2	1.4	1.4	0.2	3.9	3.9	0.2	4.0	4.0	0.0	0.1	#	0.3
Less than 10.0 percent accepted	0.5	0.5	0.0	0.1	0.1	0.0	1.2	1.3	0.0	1.3	1.3	0.0	0.0	0.0	0.0
Number of enrollees (in thousands)	1,604	1,586	18	1,078	1,069	9	526	517	9	506	503	3	21	14	7
Percentage distribution of admissions by institutions' acceptance of applications	100.0	100.0	100.0	100.0	100.0	100.0	100.0	100.0	100.0	100.0	100.0	100.0	100.0	100.0	100.0
No application criteria	†	†	†	†	†	†	†	†	†	†	†	†	†	†	†
90.0 percent or more accepted	8.3	8.1	24.6	8.6	8.5	27.4	7.7	7.4	22.0	7.2	7.2	15.5	18.4	15.5	24.5
75.0 to 89.9 percent accepted	27.5	27.5	28.4	31.0	31.2	13.3	20.4	20.0	42.9	20.2	20.1	43.2	24.6	16.1	42.8
50.0 to 74.9 percent accepted	42.3	42.4	36.9	42.4	42.3	52.2	42.1	42.5	22.2	41.9	42.0	23.3	48.6	61.1	21.7
25.0 to 49.9 percent accepted	16.8	16.9	9.9	15.7	15.8	7.0	19.2	19.3	12.7	19.7	19.7	17.9	8.3	7.3	10.6
10.0 to 24.9 percent accepted	3.6	3.7	0.2	2.0	2.0	0.2	6.9	7.1	0.2	7.2	7.3	0.1	0.1	0.0	0.3
Less than 10.0 percent accepted	1.3	1.4	0.0	0.2	0.2	0.0	3.6	3.7	0.0	3.8	3.8	0.0	0.0	0.0	0.0
SAT scores of enrollees															
Evidence-based reading and writing (ERW), 25th percentile[2]	511	512	441	505	506	453	515	515	424	515	515	424	506	506	—
ERW, 75th percentile[2]	609	610	548	602	603	553	614	614	542	614	614	542	609	609	—
Mathematics, 25th percentile[2]	506	506	453	501	502	446	508	509	463	509	509	463	493	493	—
Mathematics, 75th percentile[2]	606	606	547	601	602	539	609	609	558	609	609	558	588	588	—
ACT scores of enrollees															
Composite, 25th percentile[2]	20.5	20.6	15.6	20.0	20.1	16.0	20.9	20.9	15.2	20.9	20.9	15.2	20.4	20.4	—
Composite, 75th percentile[2]	25.8	25.9	20.9	25.4	25.4	20.9	26.1	26.1	21.0	26.1	26.1	21.0	26.0	26.0	—
English, 25th percentile[2]	19.6	19.7	12.8	19.0	19.1	14.0	20.0	20.1	11.2	20.0	20.1	11.2	20.3	20.3	—
English, 75th percentile[2]	26.1	26.1	19.0	25.5	25.6	19.7	26.5	26.5	18.0	26.5	26.5	18.0	26.8	26.8	—
Mathematics, 25th percentile[2]	19.4	19.5	14.4	19.2	19.2	15.6	19.6	19.7	12.8	19.6	19.7	12.8	18.8	18.8	—
Mathematics, 75th percentile[2]	25.4	25.5	18.8	25.2	25.2	20.1	25.6	25.6	16.8	25.6	25.6	16.8	25.0	25.0	—

—Not available.
†Not applicable.
#Rounds to zero.
[1]The total on this table differs slightly from other counts of institutions with first-year undergraduates because approximately 1.0 percent of these institutions did not report application information.
[2]Data are only for institutions that require test scores for admission. Relatively few 2-year institutions require test scores for admission. The SAT evidence-based reading and writing (ERW) and mathematics scales range from 200 to 800. The ACT composite, English, and mathematics scales range from 1 to 36.

NOTE: Degree-granting institutions grant associate's or higher degrees and participate in Title IV federal financial aid programs. Excludes institutions not enrolling any first-time degree/certificate-seeking undergraduates. Detail may not sum to totals because of rounding.
SOURCE: U.S. Department of Education, National Center for Education Statistics, Integrated Postsecondary Education Data System (IPEDS), Winter 2017–18, Admissions component. (This table was prepared December 2018.)

Table 306.10. Total fall enrollment in degree-granting postsecondary institutions, by level of enrollment, sex, attendance status, and race/ethnicity or nonresident alien status of student: Selected years, 1976 through 2017

Level of enrollment, sex, attendance status, and race/ethnicity or nonresident alien status of student	Fall enrollment (in thousands)											Percentage distribution of U.S. resident students (excludes nonresident aliens)										
	1976	1980	1990	2000	2010	2012	2013	2014	2015	2016	2017	1976	1980	1990	2000	2010	2012	2013	2014	2015	2016	2017
1	2	3	4	5	6	7	8	9	10	11	12	13	14	15	16	17	18	19	20	21	22	23
All students, total	**10,985.6**	**12,086.8**	**13,818.6**	**15,312.3**	**21,019.4**	**20,644.5**	**20,376.7**	**20,209.1**	**19,988.2**	**19,846.9**	**19,765.6**	**100.0**	**100.0**	**100.0**	**100.0**	**100.0**	**100.0**	**100.0**	**100.0**	**100.0**	**100.0**	**100.0**
White	9,076.1	9,833.0	10,722.5	10,462.1	12,720.8	11,982.2	11,589.4	11,239.3	10,939.2	10,716.6	10,510.8	84.3	83.5	79.9	70.8	62.6	60.3	59.3	58.3	57.6	56.9	56.0
Total, selected races/ethnicities	1,690.8	1,948.8	2,704.7	4,321.5	7,591.0	7,878.7	7,947.1	8,052.0	8,066.7	8,132.2	8,254.1	15.7	16.5	20.1	29.2	37.4	39.7	40.7	41.7	42.4	43.1	44.0
Black	1,033.0	1,106.8	1,247.0	1,730.3	3,039.0	2,962.4	2,872.0	2,792.8	2,681.0	2,589.4	2,545.9	9.6	9.4	9.3	11.7	15.0	14.9	14.7	14.5	14.1	13.7	13.6
Hispanic	383.8	471.7	782.4	1,461.8	2,748.8	2,980.3	3,093.2	3,191.9	3,297.7	3,428.0	3,540.6	3.6	4.0	5.8	9.9	13.5	15.0	15.8	16.5	17.4	18.2	18.9
Asian/Pacific Islander	197.9	286.4	572.4	978.2	1,281.6	1,258.2	1,259.7	1,272.2	1,284.3	1,306.7	1,329.7	1.8	2.4	4.3	6.6	6.3	6.3	6.4	6.6	6.8	6.9	7.1
Asian	—	—	—	—	1,217.6	1,194.7	1,198.7	1,213.8	1,229.0	1,253.5	1,277.7	—	—	—	—	6.0	6.0	6.1	6.3	6.5	6.7	6.8
Pacific Islander	—	—	—	—	64.0	63.5	61.0	58.5	55.3	53.2	52.0	—	—	—	—	0.3	0.3	0.3	0.3	0.3	0.3	0.3
American Indian/Alaska Native	76.1	83.9	102.8	151.2	196.2	173.0	162.2	152.9	146.1	142.3	137.6	0.7	0.7	0.8	1.0	1.0	0.9	0.8	0.8	0.8	0.8	0.7
Two or more races	—	—	—	—	325.4	504.8	560.0	642.2	657.6	665.8	700.2	—	—	—	—	1.6	2.5	2.9	3.3	3.5	3.5	3.7
Nonresident alien[1]	218.7	305.0	391.5	528.7	707.7	783.6	840.2	917.8	982.3	998.1	1,000.7	†	†	†	†	†	†	†	†	†	†	†
Male	5,794.4	5,868.1	6,283.9	6,721.8	9,045.8	8,919.0	8,861.2	8,797.5	8,723.8	8,638.4	8,567.6	100.0	100.0	100.0	100.0	100.0	100.0	100.0	100.0	100.0	100.0	100.0
White	4,813.7	4,772.9	4,861.0	4,634.6	5,605.8	5,285.3	5,132.4	4,974.3	4,848.5	4,736.1	4,629.2	85.3	84.4	80.5	72.1	64.7	62.2	61.1	60.0	59.3	58.6	57.8
Total, selected races/ethnicities	826.6	884.4	1,176.6	1,789.8	3,060.3	3,208.6	3,268.7	3,313.4	3,326.8	3,346.7	3,386.6	14.7	15.6	19.5	27.9	35.3	37.8	38.9	40.0	40.7	41.4	42.2
Black	469.9	463.7	484.7	635.3	1,089.0	1,079.1	1,064.9	1,035.1	998.9	959.5	940.9	8.3	8.2	8.0	9.9	12.6	12.7	12.7	12.5	12.2	11.9	11.7
Hispanic	209.7	231.6	353.9	627.1	1,157.6	1,254.6	1,307.7	1,348.2	1,389.2	1,439.3	1,477.4	3.7	4.1	5.9	9.8	13.4	14.8	15.6	16.3	17.0	17.8	18.4
Asian/Pacific Islander	108.4	151.3	294.9	465.9	600.6	593.1	594.3	599.1	602.9	610.1	618.5	1.9	2.7	4.9	7.3	6.9	7.0	7.1	7.2	7.4	7.5	7.7
Asian	—	—	—	—	572.1	564.7	567.1	573.0	577.8	586.4	595.3	—	—	—	—	6.6	6.6	6.8	6.9	7.1	7.3	7.4
Pacific Islander	—	—	—	—	28.5	28.4	27.2	26.1	25.1	23.7	23.3	—	—	—	—	0.3	0.3	0.3	0.3	0.3	0.3	0.3
American Indian/Alaska Native	38.5	37.8	43.1	61.4	78.7	68.7	64.7	61.3	58.2	56.3	53.9	0.7	0.7	0.7	1.0	0.9	0.8	0.8	0.7	0.7	0.7	0.7
Two or more races	—	—	—	—	134.4	213.2	237.1	269.7	277.6	281.7	295.9	—	—	—	—	1.6	2.5	2.8	3.3	3.4	3.5	3.7
Nonresident alien[1]	154.1	210.8	246.3	297.3	379.6	425.1	460.1	509.9	548.6	555.6	551.8	†	†	†	†	†	†	†	†	†	†	†
Female	5,191.2	6,218.7	7,534.7	8,590.5	11,973.7	11,725.5	11,515.5	11,411.6	11,264.4	11,208.5	11,198.0	100.0	100.0	100.0	100.0	100.0	100.0	100.0	100.0	100.0	100.0	100.0
White	4,262.4	5,060.1	5,861.5	5,827.5	7,115.0	6,696.8	6,457.0	6,265.0	6,090.7	5,980.5	5,881.6	83.1	82.6	79.3	69.7	61.1	58.9	58.0	56.9	56.2	55.6	54.7
Total, selected races/ethnicities	864.2	1,064.4	1,528.1	2,531.7	4,530.7	4,670.1	4,678.4	4,738.6	4,739.9	4,785.4	4,867.5	16.9	17.4	20.7	30.3	38.9	41.1	42.0	43.1	43.8	44.4	45.3
Black	563.1	643.0	762.3	1,095.0	1,949.9	1,883.3	1,807.1	1,757.7	1,682.1	1,630.0	1,605.0	11.0	10.5	10.3	13.1	16.7	16.6	16.2	16.0	15.5	15.1	14.9
Hispanic	174.1	240.1	428.5	834.7	1,591.2	1,725.7	1,785.5	1,843.7	1,908.5	1,988.7	2,063.2	3.4	3.9	5.8	10.0	13.7	15.2	16.0	16.8	17.6	18.5	19.2
Asian/Pacific Islander	89.4	135.2	277.5	512.3	681.0	665.1	665.4	673.1	681.5	696.6	711.2	1.7	2.2	3.8	6.1	5.8	5.9	6.0	6.1	6.3	6.5	6.6
Asian	—	—	—	—	645.5	630.0	631.6	640.7	651.3	667.1	682.5	—	—	—	—	5.5	5.5	5.7	5.8	6.0	6.2	6.3
Pacific Islander	—	—	—	—	35.5	35.1	33.7	32.4	30.2	29.5	28.8	—	—	—	—	0.3	0.3	0.3	0.3	0.3	0.3	0.3
American Indian/Alaska Native	37.6	46.1	59.7	89.7	117.5	104.4	97.5	91.6	88.0	86.0	83.8	0.7	0.8	0.8	1.1	1.0	0.9	0.9	0.8	0.8	0.8	0.8
Two or more races	—	—	—	—	191.0	291.6	322.9	372.5	379.9	384.1	404.3	—	—	—	—	1.6	2.6	2.9	3.4	3.5	3.6	3.8
Nonresident alien[1]	64.6	94.2	145.2	231.4	328.0	358.5	380.1	407.9	433.7	442.5	448.9	†	†	†	†	†	†	†	†	†	†	†
Full-time	6,703.6	7,088.9	7,821.0	9,009.6	13,087.2	12,734.4	12,596.6	12,454.5	12,287.5	12,125.3	12,077.3	100.0	100.0	100.0	100.0	100.0	100.0	100.0	100.0	100.0	100.0	100.0
White	5,512.6	5,717.0	6,016.5	6,231.1	8,053.5	7,484.4	7,237.7	6,983.3	6,784.0	6,611.4	6,481.6	84.2	83.4	79.9	72.5	64.3	61.9	60.8	59.7	59.1	58.5	57.6
Total, selected races/ethnicities	1,030.9	1,137.5	1,514.9	2,368.5	4,468.5	4,608.1	4,663.7	4,708.6	4,690.3	4,686.0	4,770.7	15.8	16.6	20.1	27.5	35.7	38.1	39.2	40.3	40.9	41.5	42.4
Black	659.2	685.6	718.3	982.6	1,811.3	1,719.9	1,669.0	1,600.4	1,537.3	1,469.5	1,452.5	10.1	10.0	9.5	11.4	14.5	14.2	14.0	13.7	13.4	13.0	12.9
Hispanic	211.1	247.0	394.7	710.3	1,501.0	1,631.7	1,701.8	1,747.9	1,786.2	1,843.3	1,915.2	3.2	3.6	5.2	8.3	12.0	13.5	14.3	14.9	15.6	16.3	17.0
Asian/Pacific Islander	117.7	162.0	347.4	591.2	820.8	814.6	821.2	832.1	843.8	857.4	871.5	1.8	2.4	4.6	6.9	6.6	6.7	6.9	7.1	7.4	7.6	7.7
Asian	—	—	—	—	783.0	777.7	785.5	798.1	812.2	826.9	842.0	—	—	—	—	6.3	6.4	6.6	6.8	7.1	7.3	7.5
Pacific Islander	—	—	—	—	37.8	36.9	35.7	34.0	31.6	30.4	29.5	—	—	—	—	0.3	0.3	0.3	0.3	0.3	0.3	0.3
American Indian/Alaska Native	43.0	43.0	54.4	84.4	118.3	102.1	94.2	88.0	82.8	80.5	76.2	0.7	0.6	0.7	1.0	0.9	0.8	0.8	0.8	0.7	0.7	0.7
Two or more races	—	—	—	—	217.2	339.7	377.5	440.3	440.2	435.4	455.4	—	—	—	—	1.7	2.8	3.2	3.8	3.8	3.9	4.0
Nonresident alien[1]	160.0	234.4	289.6	410.0	565.2	641.9	695.2	762.6	813.2	827.9	825.0	†	†	†	†	†	†	†	†	†	†	†
Part-time	4,282.1	4,997.9	5,997.7	6,302.7	7,932.3	7,910.1	7,780.1	7,754.6	7,700.7	7,721.6	7,688.3	100.0	100.0	100.0	100.0	100.0	100.0	100.0	100.0	100.0	100.0	100.0
White	3,563.5	4,116.0	4,706.0	4,231.0	4,667.3	4,497.7	4,351.7	4,256.0	4,155.1	4,105.2	4,029.2	84.4	83.5	79.8	68.4	59.9	57.9	57.0	56.0	55.2	54.4	53.6
Total, selected races/ethnicities	659.9	811.3	1,189.8	1,953.0	3,122.5	3,270.6	3,283.4	3,343.4	3,376.4	3,446.2	3,483.4	15.6	16.5	20.2	31.6	40.1	42.1	43.0	44.0	44.8	45.6	46.4
Black	373.8	421.2	528.7	747.7	1,227.7	1,242.5	1,203.0	1,192.5	1,143.7	1,119.9	1,093.5	8.9	8.5	9.0	12.1	15.8	16.0	15.8	15.7	15.2	14.8	14.6
Hispanic	172.7	224.8	387.7	751.5	1,247.9	1,348.6	1,391.4	1,444.0	1,511.5	1,584.7	1,625.4	4.1	4.6	6.6	12.2	16.0	17.4	18.2	19.0	20.1	21.0	21.6
Asian/Pacific Islander	80.2	124.4	225.1	387.1	460.8	443.7	438.5	440.2	440.5	449.3	458.3	1.9	2.5	3.8	6.3	5.9	5.7	5.7	5.8	5.8	5.9	6.1
Asian	—	—	—	—	434.6	417.0	413.2	415.7	416.9	426.5	435.7	—	—	—	—	5.6	5.4	5.4	5.5	5.5	5.6	5.8
Pacific Islander	—	—	—	—	26.2	26.7	25.3	24.4	23.6	22.8	22.5	—	—	—	—	0.3	0.3	0.3	0.3	0.3	0.3	0.3
American Indian/Alaska Native	33.1	40.9	48.4	66.8	78.0	70.9	68.0	64.9	63.3	61.9	61.4	0.8	0.8	0.8	1.1	1.0	0.9	0.9	0.9	0.8	0.8	0.8
Two or more races	—	—	—	—	108.2	165.0	182.5	201.9	217.4	230.4	244.9	—	—	—	—	1.4	2.1	2.4	2.7	2.9	3.1	3.3
Nonresident alien[1]	58.7	70.6	101.8	118.7	142.5	141.7	145.0	155.2	169.1	170.2	175.7	†	†	†	†	†	†	†	†	†	†	†

See notes at end of table.

Table 306.10. Total fall enrollment in degree-granting postsecondary institutions, by level of enrollment, sex, attendance status, and race/ethnicity or nonresident alien status of student: Selected years, 1976 through 2017—Continued

Level of enrollment, sex, attendance status, and race/ethnicity or nonresident alien status of student	Fall enrollment (in thousands)											Percentage distribution of U.S. resident students (excludes nonresident aliens)										
	1976	1980	1990	2000	2010	2012	2013	2014	2015	2016	2017	1976	1980	1990	2000	2010	2012	2013	2014	2015	2016	2017
1	2	3	4	5	6	7	8	9	10	11	12	13	14	15	16	17	18	19	20	21	22	23
Undergraduate, total	**9,419.0**	**10,469.1**	**11,959.1**	**13,155.4**	**18,082.4**	**17,735.6**	**17,476.3**	**17,294.1**	**17,046.7**	**16,874.6**	**16,760.3**	**100.0**	**100.0**	**100.0**	**100.0**	**100.0**	**100.0**	**100.0**	**100.0**	**100.0**	**100.0**	**100.0**
White	7,740.5	8,480.7	9,272.6	8,983.5	10,895.9	10,249.1	9,898.1	9,582.5	9,303.8	9,085.6	8,876.9	83.4	82.7	79.0	69.8	61.6	59.3	58.2	57.2	56.4	55.7	54.8
Total, selected races/ethnicities	1,535.3	1,778.5	2,467.7	3,884.0	6,788.1	7,036.0	7,094.6	7,182.3	7,177.8	7,218.9	7,308.4	16.6	17.3	21.0	30.2	38.4	40.7	41.8	42.8	43.6	44.3	45.2
Black	943.4	1,018.8	1,147.2	1,548.9	2,677.1	2,593.2	2,504.7	2,426.7	2,316.5	2,226.4	2,180.5	10.2	9.9	9.8	12.0	15.1	15.0	14.7	14.5	14.1	13.7	13.5
Hispanic	352.9	433.1	724.6	1,351.0	2,551.0	2,767.7	2,872.2	2,962.4	3,055.0	3,168.3	3,265.6	3.8	4.2	6.2	10.5	14.4	16.0	16.9	17.7	18.5	19.4	20.2
Asian/Pacific Islander	169.3	248.7	500.5	845.5	1,087.3	1,062.8	1,064.5	1,074.9	1,084.0	1,100.3	1,114.9	1.8	2.4	4.3	6.6	6.1	6.1	6.3	6.4	6.6	6.7	6.9
Asian	—	—	—	—	1,029.8	1,006.2	1,010.3	1,022.9	1,034.8	1,053.2	1,068.8	—	—	—	—	5.8	5.8	5.9	6.1	6.3	6.5	6.6
Pacific Islander	—	—	—	—	57.5	56.6	54.1	52.1	49.2	47.1	46.1	—	—	—	—	0.3	0.3	0.3	0.3	0.3	0.3	0.3
American Indian/Alaska Native	69.7	77.9	95.5	138.5	179.1	157.6	147.4	138.6	132.2	128.6	124.0	0.8	0.8	0.8	1.1	1.0	0.9	0.9	0.8	0.8	0.8	0.8
Two or more races	—	—	—	—	293.7	454.7	505.8	579.6	590.1	595.2	623.4	—	—	—	—	1.7	2.6	3.0	3.5	3.6	3.7	3.9
Nonresident alien[1]	143.2	209.9	218.7	288.0	398.4	450.6	483.6	529.3	565.1	570.2	575.0	†	†	†	†	†	†	†	†	†	†	†
Male	4,896.8	4,997.4	5,379.8	5,778.3	7,836.3	7,714.9	7,660.1	7,586.3	7,502.3	7,416.9	7,347.4	100.0	100.0	100.0	100.0	100.0	100.0	100.0	100.0	100.0	100.0	100.0
White	4,052.2	4,054.9	4,184.4	4,010.1	4,861.0	4,572.7	4,438.9	4,299.0	4,188.1	4,087.0	3,987.8	84.4	83.5	79.6	71.3	63.7	61.2	60.0	58.9	58.2	57.5	56.7
Total, selected races/ethnicities	748.2	802.7	1,069.3	1,618.0	2,773.8	2,905.0	2,962.7	3,000.4	3,007.0	3,020.2	3,049.9	15.6	16.5	20.4	28.7	36.3	38.8	40.0	41.1	41.8	42.5	43.3
Black	430.7	428.2	448.0	577.0	982.9	969.4	955.3	924.9	888.4	849.4	830.5	9.0	8.8	8.5	10.3	12.9	13.0	12.9	12.7	12.3	12.0	11.8
Hispanic	191.7	211.2	326.9	582.6	1,082.9	1,173.7	1,224.1	1,261.8	1,298.3	1,343.5	1,377.0	4.0	4.3	6.2	10.4	14.2	15.7	16.5	17.3	18.0	18.9	19.6
Asian/Pacific Islander	91.1	128.5	254.5	401.9	513.4	505.3	507.5	511.7	515.0	520.6	526.2	1.9	2.6	4.8	7.1	6.7	6.8	6.9	7.0	7.2	7.3	7.5
Asian	—	—	—	—	487.4	479.7	482.9	488.1	492.3	499.2	505.2	—	—	—	—	6.4	6.4	6.5	6.7	6.8	7.0	7.2
Pacific Islander	—	—	—	—	26.0	25.6	24.5	23.5	22.7	21.4	21.0	—	—	—	—	0.3	0.3	0.3	0.3	0.3	0.3	0.3
American Indian/Alaska Native	34.8	34.8	39.9	56.4	72.3	63.0	59.4	56.1	53.2	51.5	49.2	0.7	0.7	0.8	1.0	0.9	0.8	0.8	0.8	0.7	0.7	0.7
Two or more races	—	—	—	—	122.3	193.6	216.6	245.9	252.1	255.2	266.9	—	—	—	—	1.6	2.6	2.9	3.4	3.5	3.6	3.8
Nonresident alien[1]	96.4	139.8	126.1	150.2	201.5	237.2	258.5	286.8	307.2	309.6	309.7	†	†	†	†	†	†	†	†	†	†	†
Female	4,522.1	5,471.7	6,579.3	7,377.1	10,246.1	10,020.7	9,816.2	9,707.8	9,544.4	9,457.8	9,412.9	100.0	100.0	100.0	100.0	100.0	100.0	100.0	100.0	100.0	100.0	100.0
White	3,688.3	4,425.8	5,088.2	4,973.3	6,035.0	5,676.3	5,459.2	5,283.5	5,115.7	4,998.6	4,889.1	82.4	81.9	78.4	68.7	60.1	57.9	56.9	55.8	55.1	54.3	53.4
Total, selected races/ethnicities	787.0	975.8	1,398.5	2,266.0	4,014.3	4,131.0	4,131.8	4,181.9	4,170.8	4,198.7	4,258.5	17.6	18.1	21.6	31.3	39.9	42.1	43.1	44.2	44.9	45.7	46.6
Black	512.7	590.6	699.2	971.9	1,694.2	1,623.8	1,549.4	1,501.7	1,428.2	1,376.9	1,349.9	11.5	10.9	10.8	13.4	16.9	16.6	16.2	15.9	15.4	15.0	14.8
Hispanic	161.2	221.8	397.6	768.4	1,468.1	1,594.0	1,648.1	1,700.6	1,756.7	1,824.9	1,888.6	3.6	4.1	6.1	10.6	14.6	16.3	17.2	18.0	18.9	19.8	20.6
Asian/Pacific Islander	78.2	120.2	246.0	443.6	573.9	557.5	557.0	563.2	569.0	579.7	588.7	1.7	2.2	3.8	6.1	5.7	5.7	5.8	6.0	6.1	6.3	6.4
Asian	—	—	—	—	542.4	526.5	527.4	534.7	542.5	554.0	563.7	—	—	—	—	5.4	5.4	5.5	5.6	5.8	6.0	6.2
Pacific Islander	—	—	—	—	31.5	31.0	29.6	28.5	26.5	25.7	25.1	—	—	—	—	0.3	0.3	0.3	0.3	0.3	0.3	0.3
American Indian/Alaska Native	34.9	43.1	55.5	82.1	106.8	94.6	88.0	82.6	79.1	77.1	74.8	0.8	0.8	0.9	1.1	1.1	1.0	0.9	0.9	0.9	0.8	0.8
Two or more races	—	—	—	—	171.3	261.1	289.2	333.7	337.9	340.0	356.5	—	—	—	—	1.7	2.7	3.0	3.5	3.6	3.7	3.9
Nonresident alien[1]	46.8	70.1	92.6	137.8	196.9	213.4	225.1	242.5	257.9	260.5	265.3	†	†	†	†	†	†	†	†	†	†	†
Postbaccalaureate, total	**1,566.6**	**1,617.7**	**1,859.5**	**2,156.9**	**2,937.0**	**2,908.8**	**2,900.4**	**2,915.0**	**2,941.5**	**2,972.3**	**3,005.3**	**100.0**	**100.0**	**100.0**	**100.0**	**100.0**	**100.0**	**100.0**	**100.0**	**100.0**	**100.0**	**100.0**
White	1,335.6	1,352.4	1,449.8	1,478.6	1,824.9	1,733.1	1,691.3	1,656.7	1,635.4	1,631.0	1,633.9	89.6	88.8	86.0	77.2	69.4	67.3	66.5	65.6	64.8	64.1	63.3
Total, selected races/ethnicities	155.5	170.3	237.0	437.5	802.8	842.8	852.5	869.7	888.9	913.3	945.7	10.4	11.2	14.0	22.8	30.6	32.7	33.5	34.4	35.2	35.9	36.7
Black	89.7	87.9	99.8	181.4	361.9	369.2	367.3	366.2	364.5	363.0	365.4	6.0	5.8	5.9	9.5	13.8	14.3	14.4	14.5	14.4	14.3	14.2
Hispanic	30.9	38.6	57.9	110.8	197.8	212.6	221.0	229.4	242.7	259.6	275.0	2.1	2.5	3.4	5.8	7.5	8.3	8.7	9.1	9.6	10.2	10.7
Asian/Pacific Islander	28.6	37.7	72.0	132.7	194.3	195.4	195.2	197.3	200.3	206.3	214.8	1.9	2.5	4.3	6.9	7.4	7.6	7.7	7.8	7.9	8.1	8.3
Asian	—	—	—	—	187.8	188.5	188.4	190.9	194.3	200.3	208.9	—	—	—	—	7.1	7.3	7.4	7.6	7.7	7.9	8.1
Pacific Islander	—	—	—	—	6.5	6.9	6.8	6.4	6.1	6.1	5.9	—	—	—	—	0.2	0.3	0.3	0.3	0.2	0.2	0.2
American Indian/Alaska Native	6.4	6.0	7.3	12.6	17.1	15.4	14.8	14.3	13.9	13.7	13.6	0.4	0.4	0.4	0.7	0.7	0.6	0.6	0.6	0.6	0.5	0.5
Two or more races	—	—	—	—	31.7	50.1	54.2	62.6	67.5	70.6	76.8	—	—	—	—	1.2	1.9	2.1	2.5	2.7	2.8	3.0
Nonresident alien[1]	75.5	95.1	172.7	240.7	309.3	333.0	356.5	388.5	417.2	428.0	425.7	†	†	†	†	†	†	†	†	†	†	†
Male	897.6	870.7	904.2	943.5	1,209.5	1,204.1	1,201.1	1,211.2	1,221.6	1,221.6	1,220.2	100.0	100.0	100.0	100.0	100.0	100.0	100.0	100.0	100.0	100.0	100.0
White	761.6	718.1	676.6	624.5	744.9	712.6	693.5	675.2	660.3	649.0	641.4	90.7	89.8	86.3	78.4	72.2	70.1	69.4	68.3	67.4	66.5	65.6
Total, selected races/ethnicities	78.4	81.7	107.4	171.9	286.5	303.6	306.0	313.0	319.8	326.5	336.7	9.3	10.2	13.7	21.6	27.8	29.9	30.6	31.7	32.6	33.5	34.4
Black	39.2	35.5	36.7	58.3	106.1	109.7	109.6	110.2	110.5	110.0	110.4	4.7	4.4	4.7	7.3	10.3	10.8	11.0	11.1	11.3	11.3	11.3
Hispanic	18.1	20.4	27.0	44.5	74.7	80.9	83.6	86.4	90.9	95.8	100.4	2.2	2.5	3.4	5.6	7.2	8.0	8.4	8.7	9.3	9.8	10.3
Asian/Pacific Islander	17.4	22.8	40.4	64.0	87.2	87.8	86.9	87.4	87.8	89.5	92.3	2.1	2.8	5.2	8.0	8.5	8.6	8.7	8.8	9.0	9.2	9.4
Asian	—	—	—	—	84.7	85.0	84.2	84.9	85.5	87.2	90.1	—	—	—	—	8.2	8.4	8.4	8.6	8.7	8.9	9.2
Pacific Islander	—	—	—	—	2.5	2.8	2.7	2.5	2.3	2.3	2.2	—	—	—	—	0.2	0.3	0.3	0.3	0.2	0.2	0.2
American Indian/Alaska Native	3.7	3.0	3.2	5.0	6.4	5.7	5.3	5.3	5.0	4.8	4.6	0.4	0.4	0.4	0.6	0.6	0.6	0.5	0.5	0.5	0.5	0.5
Two or more races	—	—	—	—	12.0	19.6	20.6	23.7	25.5	26.5	29.1	—	—	—	—	1.2	1.9	2.1	2.4	2.6	2.7	3.0
Nonresident alien[1]	57.7	71.0	120.2	147.1	178.2	187.9	201.6	223.0	241.4	246.0	242.1	†	†	†	†	†	†	†	†	†	†	†

See notes at end of table.

Table 306.10. Total fall enrollment in degree-granting postsecondary institutions, by level of enrollment, sex, attendance status, and race/ethnicity or nonresident alien status of student: Selected years, 1976 through 2017—Continued

Level of enrollment, sex, attendance status, and race/ethnicity or nonresident alien status of student	Fall enrollment (in thousands)											Percentage distribution of U.S. resident students (excludes nonresident aliens)										
	1976	1980	1990	2000	2010	2012	2013	2014	2015	2016	2017	1976	1980	1990	2000	2010	2012	2013	2014	2015	2016	2017
1	2	3	4	5	6	7	8	9	10	11	12	13	14	15	16	17	18	19	20	21	22	23
Female	669.1	747.0	955.4	1,213.4	1,727.5	1,704.8	1,699.3	1,703.7	1,720.0	1,750.7	1,785.1	100.0	100.0	100.0	100.0	100.0	100.0	100.0	100.0	100.0	100.0	100.0
White	574.1	634.3	773.2	854.1	1,080.0	1,020.5	997.8	981.5	975.0	982.0	992.5	88.1	87.7	85.6	76.3	67.7	65.4	64.6	63.8	63.1	62.6	62.0
Total, selected races/ethnicities	77.2	88.6	129.6	265.7	516.4	539.1	546.5	556.8	569.2	586.8	608.9	11.9	12.3	14.4	23.7	32.3	34.6	35.4	36.2	36.9	37.4	38.0
Black	50.5	52.4	63.1	123.1	255.8	259.5	257.7	256.0	254.0	253.0	255.1	7.7	7.2	7.0	11.0	16.0	16.6	16.7	16.6	16.4	16.1	15.9
Hispanic	12.8	18.3	30.9	66.3	123.1	131.8	137.4	143.1	151.8	163.8	174.6	2.0	2.5	3.4	5.9	7.7	8.4	8.9	9.3	9.8	10.4	10.9
Asian/Pacific Islander	11.2	15.0	31.5	68.7	107.0	107.6	108.3	109.9	112.5	116.9	122.5	1.7	2.1	3.5	6.1	6.7	6.9	7.0	7.1	7.3	7.5	7.6
Asian	—	—	—	—	103.1	103.5	104.2	106.0	108.8	113.1	118.8	—	—	—	—	6.5	6.6	6.7	6.9	7.0	7.2	7.4
Pacific Islander	—	—	—	—	3.9	4.1	4.1	3.9	3.7	3.8	3.7	—	—	—	—	0.2	0.3	0.3	0.3	0.2	0.2	0.2
American Indian/Alaska Native	2.7	3.0	4.1	7.6	10.7	9.8	9.5	9.0	8.9	8.9	9.0	0.4	0.4	0.5	0.7	0.7	0.6	0.6	0.6	0.6	0.6	0.6
Two or more races	—	—	—	—	19.7	30.5	33.6	38.8	42.0	44.1	47.7	—	—	—	—	1.2	2.0	2.2	2.5	2.7	2.8	3.0
Nonresident alien[1]	17.8	24.1	52.5	93.6	131.1	145.1	155.0	165.5	175.8	182.0	183.6	†	†	†	†	†	†	†	†	†	†	†

—Not available.
†Not applicable.
[1]Race/ethnicity not collected.
NOTE: Race categories exclude persons of Hispanic ethnicity. Because of underreporting and nonreporting of racial/ethnic data, some figures are slightly lower than corresponding data in other tables. Data through 1990 are for institutions of higher education, while later data are for degree-granting institutions. Degree-granting institutions grant associate's or higher degrees and participate in Title IV federal financial aid programs. The degree-granting classification is very similar to the earlier higher education classification, but it includes more 2-year colleges and excludes a few higher education institutions that did not grant degrees. Some data have been revised from previously published figures. Detail may not sum to totals because of rounding.
SOURCE: U.S. Department of Education, National Center for Education Statistics, Higher Education General Information Survey (HEGIS), "Fall Enrollment in Colleges and Universities" surveys, 1976 and 1980; Integrated Postsecondary Education Data System (IPEDS), "Fall Enrollment Survey" (IPEDS-EF:90); and IPEDS Spring 2001 through Spring 2018, Fall Enrollment component. (This table was prepared October 2018.)

Table 306.20. Total fall enrollment in degree-granting postsecondary institutions, by level and control of institution and race/ethnicity or nonresident alien status of student: Selected years, 1976 through 2017

Level and control of institution and race/ethnicity or nonresident alien status of student	Fall enrollment (in thousands)											Percentage distribution of U.S. resident students (excludes nonresident aliens)										
	1976	1980	1990	2000	2010	2012	2013	2014	2015	2016	2017	1976	1980	1990	2000	2010	2012	2013	2014	2015	2016	2017
1	2	3	4	5	6	7	8	9	10	11	12	13	14	15	16	17	18	19	20	21	22	23
All students, total	**10,985.6**	**12,086.8**	**13,818.6**	**15,312.3**	**21,019.4**	**20,644.5**	**20,376.7**	**20,209.1**	**19,988.2**	**19,846.9**	**19,765.6**	**100.0**	**100.0**	**100.0**	**100.0**	**100.0**	**100.0**	**100.0**	**100.0**	**100.0**	**100.0**	**100.0**
White	9,076.1	9,833.0	10,722.5	10,462.1	12,720.8	11,982.2	11,589.4	11,239.3	10,939.2	10,716.6	10,510.8	84.3	83.5	79.9	70.8	62.6	60.3	59.3	58.3	57.6	56.9	56.0
Total, selected races/ethnicities	1,690.8	1,948.8	2,704.7	4,321.5	7,591.0	7,878.7	7,947.1	8,052.0	8,066.7	8,132.2	8,254.1	15.7	16.5	20.1	29.2	37.4	39.7	40.7	41.7	42.4	43.1	44.0
Black	1,033.0	1,106.8	1,247.0	1,730.3	3,039.0	2,962.4	2,872.0	2,792.8	2,681.0	2,589.4	2,545.9	9.6	9.4	9.3	11.7	15.0	14.9	14.7	14.5	14.1	13.7	13.6
Hispanic	383.8	471.7	782.4	1,461.8	2,748.8	2,980.3	3,093.2	3,191.9	3,297.7	3,428.0	3,540.6	3.6	4.0	5.8	9.9	13.5	15.0	15.8	16.5	17.4	18.2	18.9
Asian/Pacific Islander	197.9	286.4	572.4	978.2	1,281.6	1,258.2	1,259.7	1,272.2	1,284.3	1,306.7	1,329.7	1.8	2.4	4.3	6.6	6.3	6.3	6.4	6.6	6.8	6.9	7.1
Asian	—	—	—	—	1,217.6	1,194.7	1,198.7	1,213.8	1,229.0	1,253.5	1,277.7	—	—	—	—	6.0	6.0	6.1	6.3	6.5	6.7	6.8
Pacific Islander	—	—	—	—	64.0	63.5	61.0	58.5	55.3	53.2	52.0	—	—	—	—	0.3	0.3	0.3	0.3	0.3	0.3	0.3
American Indian/Alaska Native	76.1	83.9	102.8	151.2	196.2	173.0	162.2	152.9	146.1	142.3	137.6	0.7	0.7	0.8	1.0	1.0	0.9	0.8	0.8	0.8	0.8	0.7
Two or more races	—	—	—	—	325.4	504.8	560.0	642.2	657.6	665.8	700.2	—	—	—	—	1.6	2.5	2.9	3.3	3.5	3.5	3.7
Nonresident alien[1]	218.7	305.0	391.5	528.7	707.7	783.6	840.2	917.8	982.3	998.1	1,000.7	†	†	†	†	†	†	†	†	†	†	†
Public	8,641.0	9,456.4	10,844.7	11,752.8	15,142.2	14,884.7	14,746.8	14,654.7	14,572.8	14,585.8	14,560.2	100.0	100.0	100.0	100.0	100.0	100.0	100.0	100.0	100.0	100.0	100.0
White	7,094.5	7,656.1	8,385.4	7,963.4	9,182.1	8,636.4	8,363.3	8,119.6	7,910.7	7,787.3	7,641.2	83.5	82.7	79.2	69.8	62.5	60.0	58.8	57.7	56.7	55.8	54.8
Total, selected races/ethnicities	1,401.2	1,596.2	2,199.2	3,446.3	5,507.1	5,748.8	5,849.1	5,947.5	6,035.3	6,165.0	6,294.0	16.5	17.3	20.8	30.2	37.5	40.0	41.2	42.3	43.3	44.2	45.2
Black	831.2	876.1	976.4	1,319.2	1,988.8	1,937.6	1,886.5	1,840.2	1,775.1	1,739.6	1,722.8	9.8	9.5	9.2	11.6	13.5	13.5	13.3	13.1	12.7	12.5	12.4
Hispanic	336.8	406.2	671.4	1,229.3	2,163.8	2,366.8	2,479.4	2,580.4	2,694.5	2,819.5	2,923.7	4.0	4.4	6.3	10.8	14.7	16.5	17.4	18.3	19.3	20.2	21.0
Asian/Pacific Islander	165.7	239.7	461.0	770.5	968.7	942.6	944.9	955.9	970.1	990.5	1,008.7	2.0	2.6	4.4	6.8	6.6	6.6	6.6	6.8	7.0	7.1	7.2
Asian	—	—	—	—	924.8	901.2	905.7	918.5	934.3	955.9	975.1	—	—	—	—	6.3	6.3	6.4	6.5	6.7	6.9	7.0
Pacific Islander	—	—	—	—	43.9	41.4	39.2	37.4	35.8	34.6	33.6	—	—	—	—	0.3	0.3	0.3	0.3	0.3	0.2	0.2
American Indian/Alaska Native	67.5	74.2	90.4	127.3	150.8	131.8	124.4	117.8	113.7	110.7	107.9	0.8	0.8	0.9	1.1	1.0	0.9	0.9	0.8	0.8	0.8	0.8
Two or more races	—	—	—	—	235.0	370.0	414.0	453.2	482.0	504.8	530.8	—	—	—	—	1.6	2.6	2.9	3.2	3.5	3.6	3.8
Nonresident alien[1]	145.3	204.2	260.0	343.1	453.0	499.5	534.5	587.6	626.8	633.5	624.9	†	†	†	†	†	†	†	†	†	†	†
Private	2,344.6	2,630.4	2,973.9	3,559.5	5,877.3	5,759.8	5,629.8	5,554.4	5,415.4	5,261.1	5,205.4	100.0	100.0	100.0	100.0	100.0	100.0	100.0	100.0	100.0	100.0	100.0
White	1,981.6	2,176.9	2,337.0	2,498.7	3,538.7	3,345.7	3,226.1	3,119.7	3,028.5	2,929.3	2,869.5	87.3	86.1	82.2	74.1	62.9	61.1	60.6	59.7	59.9	59.8	59.4
Total, selected races/ethnicities	289.6	352.7	505.5	875.2	2,083.9	2,130.0	2,098.0	2,104.5	2,031.4	1,967.2	1,960.1	12.7	13.9	17.8	25.9	37.1	38.9	39.4	40.3	40.1	40.2	40.6
Black	201.8	230.7	270.6	411.1	1,050.2	1,024.9	985.6	952.7	906.0	849.8	823.1	8.9	9.1	9.5	12.2	18.7	18.7	18.5	18.2	17.9	17.4	17.0
Hispanic	47.0	65.6	111.0	232.5	585.0	613.5	613.8	611.4	603.2	608.5	616.8	2.1	2.6	3.9	6.9	10.4	11.2	11.5	11.7	11.9	12.4	12.8
Asian/Pacific Islander	32.2	46.7	111.5	207.7	312.8	315.6	314.8	316.4	314.2	316.2	321.0	1.4	1.8	3.9	6.2	5.6	5.8	5.9	6.1	6.2	6.5	6.6
Asian	—	—	—	—	292.7	293.5	293.0	295.3	294.7	297.6	302.6	—	—	—	—	5.2	5.4	5.5	5.7	5.8	6.1	6.3
Pacific Islander	—	—	—	—	20.1	22.2	21.8	21.1	19.5	18.6	18.4	—	—	—	—	0.4	0.4	0.4	0.4	0.4	0.4	0.4
American Indian/Alaska Native	8.6	9.7	12.4	23.9	45.5	41.3	37.8	35.1	32.5	31.7	29.7	0.4	0.4	0.4	0.7	0.8	0.8	0.7	0.7	0.6	0.6	0.6
Two or more races	—	—	—	—	90.4	134.7	146.0	189.0	175.6	161.0	169.4	—	—	—	—	1.6	2.5	2.7	3.6	3.5	3.3	3.5
Nonresident alien[1]	73.4	100.8	131.4	185.6	254.7	284.1	305.7	330.2	355.5	364.6	375.8	†	†	†	†	†	†	†	†	†	†	†
4-year, total	**7,106.5**	**7,565.4**	**8,578.6**	**9,363.9**	**13,335.8**	**13,476.6**	**13,406.0**	**13,494.4**	**13,488.7**	**13,754.5**	**13,823.6**	**100.0**	**100.0**	**100.0**	**100.0**	**100.0**	**100.0**	**100.0**	**100.0**	**100.0**	**100.0**	**100.0**
White	5,999.0	6,274.5	6,768.1	6,658.0	8,399.5	8,143.2	7,954.2	7,829.1	7,713.4	7,715.0	7,637.6	86.6	85.7	82.0	74.6	66.0	63.7	62.8	61.8	61.2	60.0	59.2
Total, selected races/ethnicities	931.0	1,049.9	1,486.1	2,266.1	4,328.0	4,643.5	4,703.8	4,843.0	4,897.2	5,135.5	5,274.4	13.4	14.3	18.0	25.4	34.0	36.3	37.2	38.2	38.8	40.0	40.8
Black	603.7	634.3	722.8	995.4	1,840.0	1,845.6	1,799.2	1,778.7	1,740.5	1,724.0	1,703.2	8.7	8.7	8.8	11.2	14.5	14.4	14.2	14.0	13.8	13.4	13.2
Hispanic	173.6	216.6	358.2	617.9	1,355.9	1,532.6	1,599.6	1,670.8	1,742.1	1,932.5	2,034.6	2.5	3.0	4.3	6.9	10.7	12.0	12.6	13.2	13.8	15.0	15.8
Asian/Pacific Islander	118.7	162.1	357.2	576.3	818.5	834.3	843.7	864.8	882.5	929.6	959.6	1.7	2.2	4.3	6.5	6.4	6.5	6.7	6.8	7.0	7.2	7.4
Asian	—	—	—	—	782.5	795.6	806.1	827.5	847.1	893.9	924.3	—	—	—	—	6.1	6.2	6.4	6.5	6.7	7.0	7.2
Pacific Islander	—	—	—	—	36.0	38.7	37.6	37.3	35.4	35.7	35.3	—	—	—	—	0.3	0.3	0.3	0.3	0.3	0.3	0.3
American Indian/Alaska Native	35.0	36.9	47.9	76.5	109.0	98.1	91.4	87.0	83.4	83.6	81.8	0.5	0.5	0.6	0.9	0.9	0.8	0.7	0.7	0.7	0.7	0.6
Two or more races	—	—	—	—	204.6	332.9	369.8	441.7	448.8	465.7	495.2	—	—	—	—	1.6	2.6	2.9	3.5	3.6	3.6	3.8
Nonresident alien[1]	176.5	240.9	324.3	439.7	608.3	689.9	748.0	822.4	878.1	904.0	911.6	†	†	†	†	†	†	†	†	†	†	†
Public	4,892.9	5,127.6	5,848.2	6,055.4	7,924.1	8,092.6	8,120.4	8,257.1	8,348.5	8,742.9	8,853.5	100.0	100.0	100.0	100.0	100.0	100.0	100.0	100.0	100.0	100.0	100.0
White	4,120.2	4,243.0	4,605.6	4,311.2	5,069.6	4,952.3	4,867.1	4,833.9	4,790.3	4,879.3	4,851.6	86.1	85.1	81.5	74.4	67.0	64.4	63.4	62.3	61.2	59.5	58.3
Total, selected races/ethnicities	666.7	740.8	1,046.2	1,486.4	2,496.8	2,732.0	2,808.6	2,928.6	3,032.7	3,321.1	3,463.5	13.9	14.9	18.5	25.6	33.0	35.6	36.6	37.7	38.8	40.5	41.7
Black	421.8	438.2	495.1	627.8	912.6	922.5	909.0	914.8	916.0	950.9	956.2	8.8	8.8	8.8	10.8	12.1	12.0	11.8	11.8	11.7	11.6	11.5
Hispanic	129.3	156.4	262.5	420.0	869.5	1,007.0	1,063.4	1,133.0	1,199.5	1,379.5	1,471.0	2.7	3.1	4.6	7.2	11.5	13.1	13.9	14.6	15.3	16.8	17.7
Asian/Pacific Islander	87.5	117.2	250.6	381.3	522.8	535.0	544.7	563.1	579.4	623.7	648.4	1.8	2.4	4.4	6.6	6.9	7.0	7.1	7.3	7.4	7.6	7.8
Asian	—	—	—	—	504.7	516.1	526.1	544.3	562.0	605.2	630.2	—	—	—	—	6.7	6.7	6.9	7.0	7.2	7.4	7.6
Pacific Islander	—	—	—	—	18.1	19.0	18.6	18.7	17.4	18.5	18.3	—	—	—	—	0.2	0.2	0.2	0.2	0.2	0.2	0.2
American Indian/Alaska Native	28.2	29.0	38.0	57.2	69.5	61.3	58.1	56.0	54.6	55.3	55.1	0.6	0.6	0.7	1.0	0.9	0.8	0.8	0.7	0.7	0.7	0.7
Two or more races	—	—	—	—	122.4	206.2	233.4	261.9	283.2	311.6	332.8	—	—	—	—	1.6	2.7	3.0	3.4	3.6	3.8	4.0
Nonresident alien[1]	106.0	143.8	196.4	257.8	357.8	408.2	444.8	494.6	525.6	542.6	538.3	†	†	†	†	†	†	†	†	†	†	†
Private	2,213.6	2,437.8	2,730.3	3,308.5	5,411.7	5,384.0	5,285.6	5,237.3	5,140.2	5,011.6	4,970.2	100.0	100.0	100.0	100.0	100.0	100.0	100.0	100.0	100.0	100.0	100.0
White	1,878.8	2,031.5	2,162.5	2,346.9	3,330.0	3,190.9	3,087.1	2,995.2	2,923.1	2,835.7	2,786.0	87.7	86.8	83.1	75.1	64.5	62.5	62.0	61.0	61.1	61.0	60.6
Total, selected races/ethnicities	264.3	309.2	439.8	779.7	1,831.2	1,911.4	1,895.2	1,914.3	1,864.5	1,814.4	1,810.9	12.3	13.2	16.9	24.9	35.5	37.5	38.0	39.0	38.9	39.0	39.4
Black	182.0	196.1	227.7	367.6	927.4	923.1	890.3	864.0	824.5	773.1	747.0	8.5	8.4	8.7	11.8	18.0	18.1	17.9	17.6	17.2	16.6	16.3
Hispanic	44.3	60.2	95.7	197.9	486.3	525.6	536.2	537.8	542.7	553.0	563.6	2.1	2.6	3.7	6.3	9.4	10.3	10.8	11.0	11.3	11.9	12.3
Asian/Pacific Islander	31.2	44.9	106.6	195.0	295.7	299.3	299.0	301.7	303.0	305.9	311.2	1.5	1.9	4.1	6.2	5.7	5.9	6.0	6.1	6.3	6.6	6.8
Asian	—	—	—	—	277.8	279.5	280.0	283.1	285.1	288.7	294.2	—	—	—	—	5.4	5.5	5.6	5.8	6.0	6.2	6.4
Pacific Islander	—	—	—	—	17.9	19.8	19.0	18.6	18.0	17.2	17.0	—	—	—	—	0.3	0.4	0.4	0.4	0.4	0.4	0.4
American Indian/Alaska Native	6.8	7.9	9.9	19.3	39.6	36.8	33.3	31.0	28.8	28.3	26.7	0.3	0.3	0.4	0.6	0.8	0.7	0.7	0.6	0.6	0.6	0.6
Two or more races	—	—	—	—	82.2	126.7	136.4	179.8	165.6	154.1	162.4	—	—	—	—	1.6	2.5	2.7	3.7	3.5	3.3	3.5
Nonresident alien[1]	70.5	97.1	127.9	181.9	250.6	281.7	303.2	327.8	352.5	361.5	373.2	†	†	†	†	†	†	†	†	†	†	†

See notes at end of table.

Table 306.20. Total fall enrollment in degree-granting postsecondary institutions, by level and control of institution and race/ethnicity or nonresident alien status of student: Selected years, 1976 through 2017—Continued

Level and control of institution and race/ethnicity or nonresident alien status of student	Fall enrollment (in thousands)											Percentage distribution of U.S. resident students (excludes nonresident aliens)										
	1976	1980	1990	2000	2010	2012	2013	2014	2015	2016	2017	1976	1980	1990	2000	2010	2012	2013	2014	2015	2016	2017
1	2	3	4	5	6	7	8	9	10	11	12	13	14	15	16	17	18	19	20	21	22	23
2-year, total	**3,879.1**	**4,521.4**	**5,240.1**	**5,948.4**	**7,683.6**	**7,167.8**	**6,970.6**	**6,714.7**	**6,499.5**	**6,092.4**	**5,942.0**	**100.0**	**100.0**	**100.0**	**100.0**	**100.0**	**100.0**	**100.0**	**100.0**	**100.0**	**100.0**	**100.0**
White	3,077.1	3,558.5	3,954.3	3,804.1	4,321.3	3,838.9	3,635.2	3,410.2	3,225.8	3,001.6	2,873.2	80.2	79.8	76.4	64.9	57.0	54.3	52.8	51.5	50.4	50.0	49.1
Total, selected races/ethnicities	759.8	898.9	1,218.6	2,055.4	3,263.0	3,235.3	3,243.3	3,209.1	3,169.5	2,996.7	2,979.7	19.8	20.2	23.6	35.1	43.0	45.7	47.2	48.5	49.6	50.0	50.9
Black	429.3	472.5	524.3	734.9	1,198.9	1,116.9	1,072.8	1,014.1	940.5	865.5	842.7	11.2	10.6	10.1	12.5	15.8	15.8	15.6	15.3	14.7	14.4	14.4
Hispanic	210.2	255.1	424.2	843.9	1,393.0	1,447.7	1,493.5	1,521.1	1,555.6	1,495.4	1,506.0	5.5	5.7	8.2	14.4	18.4	20.5	21.7	23.0	24.3	24.9	25.7
Asian/Pacific Islander	79.2	124.3	215.2	401.9	463.1	424.0	416.0	407.5	401.9	377.1	370.1	2.1	2.8	4.2	6.9	6.1	6.0	6.0	6.2	6.3	6.3	6.3
Asian	—	—	—	—	435.1	399.1	392.6	386.3	381.9	359.6	353.4	—	—	—	—	5.7	5.6	5.7	5.8	6.0	6.0	6.0
Pacific Islander	—	—	—	—	28.0	24.8	23.4	21.2	19.9	17.5	16.7	—	—	—	—	0.4	0.4	0.3	0.3	0.3	0.3	0.3
American Indian/Alaska Native	41.2	47.0	54.9	74.7	87.2	74.9	70.8	66.0	62.8	58.7	55.8	1.1	1.1	1.1	1.3	1.1	1.1	1.0	1.0	1.0	1.0	1.0
Two or more races	—	—	—	—	120.8	171.9	190.2	200.5	208.7	200.0	205.0	—	—	—	—	1.6	2.4	2.8	3.0	3.3	3.3	3.5
Nonresident alien[1]	42.2	64.1	67.1	89.0	99.3	93.7	92.1	95.4	104.2	94.1	89.1	†	†	†	†	†	†	†	†	†	†	†
Public	3,748.1	4,328.8	4,996.5	5,697.4	7,218.1	6,792.1	6,626.4	6,397.6	6,224.3	5,842.9	5,706.7	100.0	100.0	100.0	100.0	100.0	100.0	100.0	100.0	100.0	100.0	100.0
White	2,974.3	3,413.1	3,779.8	3,652.2	4,112.5	3,684.1	3,496.2	3,285.7	3,120.4	2,908.0	2,789.6	80.2	80.0	76.6	65.1	57.7	55.0	53.5	52.1	51.0	50.6	49.6
Total, selected races/ethnicities	734.5	855.4	1,153.0	1,959.9	3,010.3	3,016.7	3,040.5	3,018.9	3,002.6	2,844.0	2,830.5	19.8	20.0	23.4	34.9	42.3	45.0	46.5	47.9	49.0	49.4	50.4
Black	409.5	437.9	481.4	691.4	1,076.1	1,015.0	977.5	925.4	859.0	788.7	766.7	11.0	10.3	9.8	12.3	15.1	15.1	15.0	14.7	14.0	13.7	13.6
Hispanic	207.5	249.8	408.9	809.2	1,294.3	1,359.8	1,415.9	1,447.5	1,495.1	1,439.9	1,452.7	5.6	5.9	8.3	14.4	18.2	20.3	21.7	23.0	24.4	25.0	25.8
Asian/Pacific Islander	78.2	122.5	210.3	389.2	445.9	407.6	400.2	392.8	390.7	366.8	360.3	2.1	2.9	4.3	6.9	6.3	6.1	6.1	6.2	6.4	6.4	6.4
Asian	—	—	—	—	420.2	385.2	379.6	374.2	372.3	350.7	344.9	—	—	—	—	5.9	5.7	5.8	5.9	6.1	6.1	6.1
Pacific Islander	—	—	—	—	25.7	22.4	20.6	18.7	18.4	16.1	15.4	—	—	—	—	0.4	0.3	0.3	0.3	0.3	0.3	0.3
American Indian/Alaska Native	39.3	45.2	52.4	70.1	81.3	70.4	66.3	61.9	59.1	55.3	52.8	1.1	1.1	1.1	1.2	1.1	1.1	1.0	1.0	1.0	1.0	0.9
Two or more races	—	—	—	—	112.7	163.8	180.6	191.3	198.8	193.2	198.0	—	—	—	—	1.6	2.4	2.8	3.0	3.2	3.4	3.5
Nonresident alien[1]	39.2	60.3	63.6	85.2	95.2	91.3	89.7	93.0	101.3	91.0	86.6	†	†	†	†	†	†	†	†	†	†	†
Private	131.0	192.6	243.6	251.0	465.5	375.8	344.2	317.1	275.2	249.5	235.3	100.0	100.0	100.0	100.0	100.0	100.0	100.0	100.0	100.0	100.0	100.0
White	102.8	145.4	174.5	151.8	208.8	154.8	139.0	124.5	105.4	93.6	83.6	80.3	77.0	72.7	61.4	45.2	41.5	40.7	39.6	38.7	38.0	35.9
Total, selected races/ethnicities	25.3	43.5	65.6	95.5	252.7	218.5	202.8	190.2	166.8	152.7	149.1	19.7	23.0	27.3	38.6	54.8	58.5	59.3	60.4	61.3	62.0	64.1
Black	19.8	34.6	42.9	43.5	122.8	101.8	95.3	88.7	81.5	76.8	76.1	15.5	18.3	17.9	17.6	26.6	27.3	27.9	28.2	29.9	31.2	32.7
Hispanic	2.6	5.3	15.3	34.7	98.7	87.9	77.6	73.6	60.5	55.5	53.3	2.1	2.8	6.4	14.0	21.4	23.5	22.7	23.4	22.2	22.5	22.9
Asian/Pacific Islander	0.9	1.8	4.9	12.7	17.2	16.4	15.7	14.7	11.2	10.3	9.8	0.7	1.0	2.0	5.1	3.7	4.4	4.6	4.7	4.1	4.2	4.2
Asian	—	—	—	—	14.9	13.9	13.0	12.1	9.6	8.9	8.4	—	—	—	—	3.2	3.7	3.8	3.9	3.5	3.6	3.6
Pacific Islander	—	—	—	—	2.2	2.4	2.8	2.5	1.5	1.4	1.4	—	—	—	—	0.5	0.6	0.8	0.8	0.6	0.6	0.6
American Indian/Alaska Native	1.8	1.8	2.5	4.5	5.9	4.5	4.5	4.1	3.7	3.4	3.0	1.4	1.0	1.1	1.8	1.3	1.2	1.3	1.3	1.4	1.4	1.3
Two or more races	—	—	—	—	8.1	8.0	9.7	9.2	10.0	6.8	7.0	—	—	—	—	1.8	2.1	2.8	2.9	3.7	2.8	3.0
Nonresident alien[1]	3.0	3.7	3.5	3.8	4.1	2.4	2.5	2.4	2.9	3.1	2.6	†	†	†	†	†	†	†	†	†	†	†

—Not available.
†Not applicable.
[1]Race/ethnicity not collected.
NOTE: Race categories exclude persons of Hispanic ethnicity. Because of underreporting and nonreporting of racial/ethnic data, some figures are slightly lower than corresponding data in other tables. Data through 1990 are for institutions of higher education, while later data are for degree-granting institutions. Degree-granting institutions grant associate's or higher degrees and participate in Title IV federal financial aid programs. The degree-granting classification is very similar to the earlier higher education classification, but it includes more 2-year colleges and excludes a few higher education institutions that did not grant degrees. Some data have been revised from previously published figures. Detail may not sum to totals because of rounding.
SOURCE: U.S. Department of Education, National Center for Education Statistics, Higher Education General Information Survey (HEGIS), "Fall Enrollment in Colleges and Universities" surveys, 1976 and 1980; Integrated Postsecondary Education Data System (IPEDS), "Fall Enrollment Survey" (IPEDS-EF:90); and IPEDS Spring 2001 through Spring 2018, Fall Enrollment component. (This table was prepared October 2018.)

Table 306.30. Fall enrollment of U.S. residents in degree-granting postsecondary institutions, by race/ethnicity: Selected years, 1976 through 2028

	Enrollment (in thousands)									Percentage distribution								
					Asian/Pacific Islander									Asian/Pacific Islander				
Year	Total	White	Black	Hispanic	Total	Asian	Pacific Islander	American Indian/ Alaska Native	Two or more races	Total	White	Black	Hispanic	Total	Asian	Pacific Islander	American Indian/ Alaska Native	Two or more races
1	2	3	4	5	6	7	8	9	10	11	12	13	14	15	16	17	18	19
1976	10,767	9,076	1,033	384	198	—	—	76	—	100.0	84.3	9.6	3.6	1.8	—	—	0.7	—
1980	11,782	9,833	1,107	472	286	—	—	84	—	100.0	83.5	9.4	4.0	2.4	—	—	0.7	—
1990	13,427	10,722	1,247	782	572	—	—	103	—	100.0	79.9	9.3	5.8	4.3	—	—	0.8	—
1994	13,823	10,427	1,449	1,046	774	—	—	127	—	100.0	75.4	10.5	7.6	5.6	—	—	0.9	—
1995	13,807	10,311	1,474	1,094	797	—	—	131	—	100.0	74.7	10.7	7.9	5.8	—	—	1.0	—
1996	13,901	10,264	1,506	1,166	828	—	—	138	—	100.0	73.8	10.8	8.4	6.0	—	—	1.0	—
1997	14,037	10,266	1,551	1,218	859	—	—	142	—	100.0	73.1	11.0	8.7	6.1	—	—	1.0	—
1998	14,063	10,179	1,583	1,257	900	—	—	144	—	100.0	72.4	11.3	8.9	6.4	—	—	1.0	—
1999	14,361	10,329	1,649	1,324	914	—	—	146	—	100.0	71.9	11.5	9.2	6.4	—	—	1.0	—
2000	14,784	10,462	1,730	1,462	978	—	—	151	—	100.0	70.8	11.7	9.9	6.6	—	—	1.0	—
2001	15,363	10,775	1,850	1,561	1,019	—	—	158	—	100.0	70.1	12.0	10.2	6.6	—	—	1.0	—
2002	16,021	11,140	1,979	1,662	1,074	—	—	166	—	100.0	69.5	12.4	10.4	6.7	—	—	1.0	—
2003	16,314	11,281	2,068	1,716	1,076	—	—	173	—	100.0	69.1	12.7	10.5	6.6	—	—	1.1	—
2004	16,682	11,423	2,165	1,810	1,109	—	—	176	—	100.0	68.5	13.0	10.8	6.6	—	—	1.1	—
2005	16,903	11,495	2,215	1,882	1,134	—	—	176	—	100.0	68.0	13.1	11.1	6.7	—	—	1.0	—
2006	17,158	11,568	2,280	1,964	1,165	—	—	181	—	100.0	67.4	13.3	11.4	6.8	—	—	1.1	—
2007	17,635	11,761	2,384	2,081	1,218	—	—	190	—	100.0	66.7	13.5	11.8	6.9	—	—	1.1	—
2008	18,421	12,075	2,580	2,271	1,303	—	—	193	—	100.0	65.5	14.0	12.3	7.1	—	—	1.0	—
2009	19,631	12,669	2,884	2,537	1,335	—	—	206	—	100.0	64.5	14.7	12.9	6.8	—	—	1.0	—
2010	20,312	12,721	3,039	2,749	1,282	1,218	64	196	325	100.0	62.6	15.0	13.5	6.3	6.0	0.3	1.0	1.6
2011	20,270	12,402	3,079	2,893	1,277	1,211	66	186	433	100.0	61.2	15.2	14.3	6.3	6.0	0.3	0.9	2.1
2012	19,861	11,982	2,962	2,980	1,258	1,195	64	173	505	100.0	60.3	14.9	15.0	6.3	6.0	0.3	0.9	2.5
2013	19,537	11,589	2,872	3,093	1,260	1,199	61	162	560	100.0	59.3	14.7	15.8	6.4	6.1	0.3	0.8	2.9
2014	19,291	11,239	2,793	3,192	1,272	1,214	58	153	642	100.0	58.3	14.5	16.5	6.6	6.3	0.3	0.8	3.3
2015	19,006	10,939	2,681	3,298	1,284	1,229	55	146	658	100.0	57.6	14.1	17.4	6.8	6.5	0.3	0.8	3.5
2016	18,849	10,717	2,589	3,428	1,307	1,253	53	142	666	100.0	56.9	13.7	18.2	6.9	6.7	0.3	0.8	3.5
2017	18,765	10,511	2,546	3,541	1,330	1,278	52	138	700	100.0	56.0	13.6	18.9	7.1	6.8	0.3	0.7	3.7
2018[1]	18,815	10,525	2,610	3,542	1,300	—	—	135	702	100.0	55.9	13.9	18.8	6.9	—	—	0.7	3.7
2019[1]	18,853	10,507	2,623	3,578	1,307	—	—	134	703	100.0	55.7	13.9	19.0	6.9	—	—	0.7	3.7
2020[1]	18,844	10,434	2,636	3,628	1,309	—	—	133	703	100.0	55.4	14.0	19.3	6.9	—	—	0.7	3.7
2021[1]	18,837	10,365	2,649	3,674	1,314	—	—	132	703	100.0	55.0	14.1	19.5	7.0	—	—	0.7	3.7
2022[1]	18,834	10,303	2,658	3,717	1,320	—	—	132	703	100.0	54.7	14.1	19.7	7.0	—	—	0.7	3.7
2023[1]	18,844	10,244	2,671	3,765	1,329	—	—	131	703	100.0	54.4	14.2	20.0	7.1	—	—	0.7	3.7
2024[1]	18,868	10,193	2,684	3,817	1,340	—	—	130	704	100.0	54.0	14.2	20.2	7.1	—	—	0.7	3.7
2025[1]	18,892	10,142	2,697	3,872	1,348	—	—	129	705	100.0	53.7	14.3	20.5	7.1	—	—	0.7	3.7
2026[1]	18,928	10,090	2,716	3,933	1,354	—	—	128	706	100.0	53.3	14.4	20.8	7.2	—	—	0.7	3.7
2027[1]	18,921	10,009	2,734	3,988	1,357	—	—	126	706	100.0	52.9	14.4	21.1	7.2	—	—	0.7	3.7
2028[1]	18,886	9,913	2,748	4,036	1,359	—	—	125	705	100.0	52.5	14.5	21.4	7.2	—	—	0.7	3.7

—Not available.
[1]Projected.
NOTE: Race categories exclude persons of Hispanic ethnicity. Prior to 2010, institutions were not required to report separate data on Asians, Pacific Islanders, and students of Two or more races. Projections for Asian and Pacific Islander enrollment are not available due to the limited amount of historical data available upon which to base a projection model. Data through 1995 are for institutions of higher education, while later data are for degree-granting institutions. Degree-granting institutions grant associate's or higher degrees and participate in Title IV federal financial aid programs. The degree-granting classification is very similar to the earlier higher education classification, but it includes more 2-year colleges and excludes a few higher education institutions that did not grant degrees. Detail may not sum to totals because of rounding. Some data have been revised from previously published figures.
SOURCE: U.S. Department of Education, National Center for Education Statistics, Higher Education General Information Survey (HEGIS), "Fall Enrollment in Colleges and Universities" surveys, 1976 and 1980; Integrated Postsecondary Education Data System (IPEDS), "Fall Enrollment Survey" (IPEDS-EF:90–99); IPEDS Spring 2001 through Spring 2018, Fall Enrollment component; and Enrollment in Degree-Granting Institutions by Race/Ethnicity Projection Model, 1980 through 2028. (This table was prepared March 2019.)

Table 306.50. Total fall enrollment in degree-granting postsecondary institutions, by control and classification of institution, level of enrollment, and race/ethnicity of student: 2017

Level of enrollment and race/ethnicity of student	Total, all institutions	Public institutions									Nonprofit institutions									For-profit institutions		
			4-year									4-year										
		Total	Total	Research university, very high[1]	Research university, high[2]	Doctoral/research university[3]	Master's[4]	Baccalaureate[5]	Special focus[6]	2-year	Total	Total	Research university, very high[1]	Research university, high[2]	Doctoral/research university[3]	Master's[4]	Baccalaureate[5]	Special focus[6]	2-year	Total	4-year	2-year
1	2	3	4	5	6	7	8	9	10	11	12	13	14	15	16	17	18	19	20	21	22	23
All students, total	**19,765,598**	**14,560,155**	**8,853,477**	**2,844,803**	**1,366,233**	**628,300**	**2,487,434**	**1,433,586**	**93,121**	**5,706,678**	**4,106,477**	**4,058,087**	**633,342**	**326,266**	**442,414**	**1,596,806**	**668,707**	**390,552**	**48,390**	**1,098,966**	**912,076**	**186,890**
White	10,510,784	7,641,235	4,851,639	1,545,924	829,505	313,999	1,415,455	697,155	49,601	2,789,596	2,401,698	2,381,969	282,619	189,168	255,240	1,009,164	421,408	224,370	19,729	467,851	404,019	63,832
Black	2,545,916	1,722,844	956,178	191,913	155,682	98,998	322,938	176,565	10,082	766,666	496,597	478,492	39,329	31,940	61,196	198,393	102,012	45,622	18,105	326,475	268,530	57,945
Hispanic	3,540,584	2,923,743	1,470,999	379,476	179,395	127,155	403,977	372,166	8,830	1,452,744	432,741	427,308	60,809	32,929	50,561	193,582	54,654	34,773	5,433	184,100	136,281	47,819
Asian	1,277,733	975,098	630,151	297,200	63,173	36,995	142,669	79,124	10,990	344,947	259,523	258,337	85,861	21,900	29,897	65,658	21,011	34,010	1,186	43,112	35,857	7,255
Pacific Islander	52,015	33,622	18,250	4,376	2,012	928	5,511	5,286	137	15,372	10,537	10,297	669	643	1,037	5,140	1,734	1,074	240	7,856	6,743	1,113
American Indian/Alaska Native	137,632	107,889	55,089	9,690	9,048	2,284	16,096	10,187	7,784	52,800	19,578	18,682	1,208	932	1,838	7,951	3,023	3,730	896	10,165	8,047	2,118
Two or more races	700,212	530,836	332,836	110,418	50,851	21,560	90,294	57,557	2,156	198,000	134,224	132,462	22,779	10,089	13,085	48,374	24,426	13,709	1,762	35,152	29,893	5,259
Nonresident alien[7]	1,000,722	624,888	538,335	305,806	76,567	26,381	90,494	35,546	3,541	86,553	351,579	350,540	140,068	38,665	29,560	68,544	40,439	33,264	1,039	24,255	22,706	1,549
Undergraduate	16,760,331	13,100,953	7,394,275	2,160,020	1,104,197	522,304	2,144,761	1,427,893	35,100	5,706,678	2,817,017	2,768,627	305,582	209,878	272,366	1,147,851	635,351	197,599	48,390	842,361	655,471	186,890
White	8,876,872	6,823,692	4,034,096	1,187,296	670,482	256,102	1,210,698	692,732	16,786	2,789,596	1,699,556	1,679,827	141,945	131,053	161,248	732,397	398,371	114,813	19,729	353,624	289,792	63,832
Black	2,180,467	1,588,382	821,716	150,648	130,866	84,109	274,967	176,068	5,058	766,666	350,970	332,865	19,687	18,243	33,252	139,215	97,584	24,884	18,105	241,115	183,170	57,945
Hispanic	3,265,599	2,786,825	1,334,081	323,972	157,479	112,222	365,160	371,980	3,268	1,452,744	319,380	313,947	36,346	20,526	34,499	150,716	52,511	19,349	5,433	159,394	111,575	47,819
Asian	1,068,832	879,728	534,781	246,133	51,415	31,289	125,373	78,994	1,577	344,947	158,605	157,419	50,456	14,316	18,635	42,455	19,880	11,677	1,186	30,499	23,244	7,255
Pacific Islander	46,090	31,921	16,549	3,627	1,748	813	5,017	5,273	71	15,372	7,875	7,635	332	450	640	3,930	1,671	612	240	6,294	5,181	1,113
American Indian/Alaska Native	124,019	101,033	48,233	7,249	7,591	1,864	14,021	10,126	7,382	52,800	14,811	13,915	656	598	1,121	5,733	2,871	2,936	896	8,175	6,057	2,118
Two or more races	623,409	493,152	295,152	91,677	44,658	18,971	81,717	57,473	656	198,000	102,263	100,501	14,584	7,302	9,588	37,694	23,804	7,529	1,762	27,994	22,735	5,259
Nonresident alien[7]	575,043	396,220	309,667	149,418	39,958	16,934	67,808	35,247	302	86,553	163,557	162,518	41,576	17,390	13,383	35,711	38,659	15,799	1,039	15,266	13,717	1,549
Postbaccalaureate	3,005,267	1,459,202	1,459,202	684,783	262,036	105,996	342,673	5,693	58,021	†	1,289,460	1,289,460	327,760	116,388	170,048	448,955	33,356	192,953	†	256,605	256,605	†
White	1,633,912	817,543	817,543	358,628	159,023	57,897	204,757	4,423	32,815	†	702,142	702,142	140,674	58,115	93,992	276,767	23,037	109,557	†	114,227	114,227	†
Black	365,449	134,462	134,462	41,265	24,816	14,889	47,971	497	5,024	†	145,627	145,627	19,642	13,697	27,944	59,178	4,428	20,738	†	85,360	85,360	†
Hispanic	274,985	136,918	136,918	55,504	21,916	14,933	38,817	186	5,562	†	113,361	113,361	24,463	12,403	16,062	42,866	2,143	15,424	†	24,706	24,706	†
Asian	208,901	95,370	95,370	51,067	11,758	5,706	17,296	130	9,413	†	100,918	100,918	35,405	7,584	11,262	23,203	1,131	22,333	†	12,613	12,613	†
Pacific Islander	5,925	1,701	1,701	749	264	115	494	13	66	†	2,662	2,662	337	193	397	1,210	63	462	†	1,562	1,562	†
American Indian/Alaska Native	13,613	6,856	6,856	2,441	1,457	420	2,075	61	402	†	4,767	4,767	552	334	717	2,218	152	794	†	1,990	1,990	†
Two or more races	76,803	37,684	37,684	18,741	6,193	2,589	8,577	84	1,500	†	31,961	31,961	8,195	2,787	3,497	10,680	622	6,180	†	7,158	7,158	†
Nonresident alien[7]	425,679	228,668	228,668	156,388	36,609	9,447	22,686	299	3,239	†	188,022	188,022	98,492	21,275	16,177	32,833	1,780	17,465	†	8,989	8,989	†
	Percentage distribution of U.S. resident students (excludes nonresident aliens)																					
U.S. resident students, total	**100.0**	**100.0**	**100.0**	**100.0**	**100.0**	**100.0**	**100.0**	**100.0**	**100.0**	**100.0**	**100.0**	**100.0**	**100.0**	**100.0**	**100.0**	**100.0**	**100.0**	**100.0**	**100.0**	**100.0**	**100.0**	**100.0**
White	56.0	54.8	58.3	60.9	64.3	52.2	59.1	49.9	55.4	49.6	64.0	64.2	57.3	65.8	61.8	66.0	67.1	62.8	41.7	43.5	45.4	34.4
Black	13.6	12.4	11.5	7.6	12.1	16.4	13.5	12.6	11.3	13.6	13.2	12.9	8.0	11.1	14.8	13.0	16.2	12.8	38.2	30.4	30.2	31.3
Hispanic	18.9	21.0	17.7	14.9	13.9	21.1	16.9	26.6	9.9	25.8	11.5	11.5	12.3	11.4	12.2	12.7	8.7	9.7	11.5	17.1	15.3	25.8
Asian	6.8	7.0	7.6	11.7	4.9	6.1	6.0	5.7	12.3	6.1	6.9	7.0	17.4	7.6	7.2	4.3	3.3	9.5	2.5	4.0	4.0	3.9
Pacific Islander	0.3	0.2	0.2	0.2	0.2	0.2	0.2	0.4	0.2	0.3	0.3	0.3	0.1	0.2	0.3	0.3	0.3	0.3	0.5	0.7	0.8	0.6
American Indian/Alaska Native	0.7	0.8	0.7	0.4	0.7	0.4	0.7	0.7	8.7	0.9	0.5	0.5	0.2	0.3	0.4	0.5	0.5	1.0	1.9	0.9	0.9	1.1
Two or more races	3.7	3.8	4.0	4.3	3.9	3.6	3.8	4.1	2.4	3.5	3.6	3.6	4.6	3.5	3.2	3.2	3.9	3.8	3.7	3.3	3.4	2.8
Undergraduate	100.0	100.0	100.0	100.0	100.0	100.0	100.0	100.0	100.0	100.0	100.0	100.0	100.0	100.0	100.0	100.0	100.0	100.0	100.0	100.0	100.0	100.0
White	54.8	53.7	56.9	59.1	63.0	50.7	58.3	49.7	48.2	49.6	64.1	64.5	53.8	68.1	62.3	65.9	66.8	63.2	41.7	42.8	45.2	34.4
Black	13.5	12.5	11.6	7.5	12.3	16.6	13.2	12.6	14.5	13.6	13.2	12.8	7.5	9.5	12.8	12.5	16.4	13.7	38.2	29.2	28.5	31.3
Hispanic	20.2	21.9	18.8	16.1	14.8	22.2	17.6	26.7	9.4	25.8	12.0	12.0	13.8	10.7	13.3	13.6	8.8	10.6	11.5	19.3	17.4	25.8
Asian	6.6	6.9	7.5	12.2	4.8	6.2	6.0	5.7	4.5	6.1	6.0	6.0	19.1	7.4	7.2	3.8	3.3	6.4	2.5	3.7	3.6	3.9
Pacific Islander	0.3	0.3	0.2	0.2	0.2	0.2	0.2	0.4	0.2	0.3	0.3	0.3	0.1	0.2	0.2	0.4	0.3	0.3	0.5	0.8	0.8	0.6
American Indian/Alaska Native	0.8	0.8	0.7	0.4	0.7	0.4	0.7	0.7	21.2	0.9	0.6	0.5	0.2	0.3	0.4	0.5	0.5	1.6	1.9	1.0	0.9	1.1
Two or more races	3.9	3.9	4.2	4.6	4.2	3.8	3.9	4.1	1.9	3.5	3.9	3.9	5.5	3.8	3.7	3.4	4.0	4.1	3.7	3.4	3.5	2.8

See notes at end of table.

Table 306.50. Total fall enrollment in degree-granting postsecondary institutions, by control and classification of institution, level of enrollment, and race/ethnicity of student: 2017—Continued

Level of enrollment and race/ethnicity of student	Total, all institutions	Public institutions									Nonprofit institutions									For-profit institutions		
		Total	4-year							2-year	Total	4-year							2-year	Total	4-year	2-year
			Total	Research university, very high[1]	Research university, high[2]	Doctoral/research university[3]	Master's[4]	Baccalaureate[5]	Special focus[6]			Total	Research university, very high[1]	Research university, high[2]	Doctoral/research university[3]	Master's[4]	Baccalaureate[5]	Special focus[6]				
1	2	3	4	5	6	7	8	9	10	11	12	13	14	15	16	17	18	19	20	21	22	23
Postbaccalaureate	100.0	100.0	100.0	100.0	100.0	100.0	100.0	100.0	100.0	†	100.0	100.0	100.0	100.0	100.0	100.0	100.0	100.0	†	100.0	100.0	†
White	63.3	66.4	66.4	67.9	70.5	60.0	64.0	82.0	59.9	†	63.7	63.7	61.4	61.1	61.1	66.5	73.0	62.4	†	46.1	46.1	†
Black	14.2	10.9	10.9	7.8	11.0	15.4	15.0	9.2	9.2	†	13.2	13.2	8.6	14.4	18.2	14.2	14.0	11.8	†	34.5	34.5	†
Hispanic	10.7	11.1	11.1	10.5	9.7	15.5	12.1	3.4	10.2	†	10.3	10.3	10.7	13.0	10.4	10.3	6.8	8.8	†	10.0	10.0	†
Asian	8.1	7.8	7.8	9.7	5.2	5.9	5.4	2.4	17.2	†	9.2	9.2	15.4	8.0	7.3	5.6	3.6	12.7	†	5.1	5.1	†
Pacific Islander	0.2	0.1	0.1	0.1	0.1	0.1	0.2	0.2	0.1	†	0.2	0.2	0.1	0.2	0.3	0.3	0.2	0.3	†	0.6	0.6	†
American Indian/Alaska Native	0.5	0.6	0.6	0.5	0.6	0.4	0.6	1.1	0.7	†	0.4	0.4	0.2	0.4	0.5	0.5	0.5	0.5	†	0.8	0.8	†
Two or more races	3.0	3.1	3.1	3.5	2.7	2.7	2.7	1.6	2.7	†	2.9	2.9	3.6	2.9	2.3	2.6	2.0	3.5	†	2.9	2.9	†

†Not applicable.
[1]Research universities with a very high level of research activity.
[2]Research universities with a high level of research activity.
[3]Institutions that award at least 20 research/scholarship doctor's degrees per year, but did not have a high level of research activity.
[4]Institutions that award at least 50 master's degrees and fewer than 20 doctor's degrees per year.
[5]Institutions that primarily emphasize undergraduate education. In addition to institutions that primarily award bachelor's degrees, also includes institutions classified as 4-year in the IPEDS system, but classified as 2-year baccalaureate/associate's colleges in the Carnegie Classification system because they primarily award associate's degrees.
[6]Four-year institutions that award degrees primarily in single fields of study, such as medicine, business, fine arts, theology, and engineering.
[7]Race/ethnicity not collected.
NOTE: Relative levels of research activity for research universities were determined by an analysis of research and development expenditures, science and engineering research staffing, and doctoral degrees conferred, by field. Further information on the research index ranking may be obtained from http://carnegieclassifications.iu.edu/. Includes imputed Carnegie classifications for institutions with missing data. Degree-granting institutions grant associate's or higher degrees and participate in Title IV federal financial aid programs. Race categories exclude persons of Hispanic ethnicity.
SOURCE: U.S. Department of Education, National Center for Education Statistics, Integrated Postsecondary Education Data System (IPEDS), Spring 2018, Fall Enrollment component. (This table was prepared October 2018.)

Table 306.60. Total fall enrollment in degree-granting postsecondary institutions, by race/ethnicity of student and state or jurisdiction: 2017

State or jurisdiction	Fall enrollment									Percentage distribution of U.S. resident students (excludes nonresident aliens)							
	Total	White	Black	Hispanic	Asian	Pacific Islander	American Indian/ Alaska Native	Two or more races	Nonresident alien	Total	White	Black	Hispanic	Asian	Pacific Islander	American Indian/ Alaska Native	Two or more races
1	2	3	4	5	6	7	8	9	10	11	12	13	14	15	16	17	18
United States	**19,765,598**	**10,510,784**	**2,545,916**	**3,540,584**	**1,277,733**	**52,015**	**137,632**	**700,212**	**1,000,722**	**100.0**	**56.0**	**13.6**	**18.9**	**6.8**	**0.3**	**0.7**	**3.7**
Alabama	306,822	190,307	80,781	11,270	5,914	337	1,945	7,323	8,945	100.0	63.9	27.1	3.8	2.0	0.1	0.7	2.5
Alaska	26,905	16,061	784	2,188	1,674	210	2,768	2,663	557	100.0	61.0	3.0	8.3	6.4	0.8	10.5	10.1
Arizona	591,626	288,582	74,989	146,506	22,452	2,862	13,976	22,059	20,200	100.0	50.5	13.1	25.6	3.9	0.5	2.4	3.9
Arkansas	164,082	112,495	25,995	9,947	2,825	156	1,281	5,687	5,696	100.0	71.0	16.4	6.3	1.8	0.1	0.8	3.6
California	2,714,051	762,119	170,689	1,086,402	400,209	12,573	10,996	123,058	148,005	100.0	29.7	6.7	42.3	15.6	0.5	0.4	4.8
Colorado	360,236	224,785	26,561	63,006	13,323	997	3,287	15,828	12,449	100.0	64.6	7.6	18.1	3.8	0.3	0.9	4.6
Connecticut	197,534	112,966	25,378	30,437	10,714	233	476	5,959	11,371	100.0	60.7	13.6	16.3	5.8	0.1	0.3	3.2
Delaware	60,338	33,116	12,710	5,344	2,148	78	330	1,676	4,936	100.0	59.8	22.9	9.6	3.9	0.1	0.6	3.0
District of Columbia	95,999	42,086	24,312	8,740	6,604	133	246	2,953	10,925	100.0	49.5	28.6	10.3	7.8	0.2	0.3	3.5
Florida	1,071,484	468,181	190,395	289,233	37,862	2,458	3,158	33,831	46,366	100.0	45.7	18.6	28.2	3.7	0.2	0.3	3.3
Georgia	538,124	258,774	168,240	41,389	28,802	729	1,674	15,535	22,981	100.0	50.2	32.7	8.0	5.6	0.1	0.3	3.0
Hawaii	64,125	10,767	1,452	7,441	19,614	4,270	162	16,466	3,953	100.0	17.9	2.4	12.4	32.6	7.1	0.3	27.4
Idaho	131,803	98,363	1,392	11,835	2,046	546	1,020	5,633	10,968	100.0	81.4	1.2	9.8	1.7	0.5	0.8	4.7
Illinois	757,002	402,561	96,301	140,366	52,456	1,069	1,673	20,017	42,559	100.0	56.3	13.5	19.6	7.3	0.1	0.2	2.8
Indiana	398,804	283,949	37,927	25,004	12,732	388	886	12,616	25,302	100.0	76.0	10.2	6.7	3.4	0.1	0.2	3.4
Iowa	260,954	189,357	23,366	19,683	7,403	494	1,339	6,580	12,732	100.0	76.3	9.4	7.9	3.0	0.2	0.5	2.7
Kansas	213,962	143,990	18,912	21,463	6,050	338	2,761	7,704	12,744	100.0	71.6	9.4	10.7	3.0	0.2	1.4	3.8
Kentucky	258,498	202,919	21,834	9,742	4,627	259	610	7,814	10,693	100.0	81.9	8.8	3.9	1.9	0.1	0.2	3.2
Louisiana	242,065	132,477	75,005	13,014	6,104	266	1,647	6,307	7,245	100.0	56.4	31.9	5.5	2.6	0.1	0.7	2.7
Maine	71,811	59,882	2,915	2,219	1,947	81	637	2,559	1,571	100.0	85.3	4.2	3.2	2.8	0.1	0.9	3.6
Maryland	364,207	163,824	101,313	33,357	27,511	914	1,006	14,554	21,728	100.0	47.8	29.6	9.7	8.0	0.3	0.3	4.2
Massachusetts	503,508	285,179	44,160	56,481	40,870	443	956	15,308	60,111	100.0	64.3	10.0	12.7	9.2	0.1	0.2	3.5
Michigan	558,053	387,756	65,541	28,630	23,204	554	3,152	18,514	30,702	100.0	73.5	12.4	5.4	4.4	0.1	0.6	3.5
Minnesota	412,966	272,607	61,165	22,466	22,816	645	3,007	14,115	16,145	100.0	68.7	15.4	5.7	5.7	0.2	0.8	3.6
Mississippi	171,751	95,346	63,244	4,070	2,118	123	791	2,816	3,243	100.0	56.6	37.5	2.4	1.3	0.1	0.5	1.7
Missouri	383,489	272,568	45,688	20,180	12,620	628	1,850	12,274	17,681	100.0	74.5	12.5	5.5	3.4	0.2	0.5	3.4
Montana	50,642	40,419	463	2,043	804	103	3,566	1,751	1,493	100.0	82.2	0.9	4.2	1.6	0.2	7.3	3.6
Nebraska	135,864	99,576	7,207	13,783	4,213	266	960	4,112	5,747	100.0	76.5	5.5	10.6	3.2	0.2	0.7	3.2
Nevada	117,574	51,278	9,016	32,580	12,642	1,230	852	7,625	2,351	100.0	44.5	7.8	28.3	11.0	1.1	0.7	6.6
New Hampshire	149,184	107,305	18,209	11,623	4,159	475	882	3,193	3,338	100.0	73.6	12.5	8.0	2.9	0.3	0.6	2.2
New Jersey	419,037	198,753	58,925	88,996	39,666	1,007	1,083	8,879	21,728	100.0	50.0	14.8	22.4	10.0	0.3	0.3	2.2
New Mexico	129,494	41,941	3,807	62,026	2,659	294	12,337	2,942	3,488	100.0	33.3	3.0	49.2	2.1	0.2	9.8	2.3
New York	1,260,240	597,970	170,655	224,315	122,028	2,266	4,280	30,624	108,102	100.0	51.9	14.8	19.5	10.6	0.2	0.4	2.7
North Carolina	563,831	326,741	126,761	45,274	19,895	918	6,164	18,566	19,512	100.0	60.0	23.3	8.3	3.7	0.2	1.1	3.4
North Dakota	53,749	42,807	1,811	1,941	763	80	2,186	1,649	2,512	100.0	83.5	3.5	3.8	1.5	0.2	4.3	3.2
Ohio	649,687	473,502	74,489	27,370	18,515	521	1,742	21,438	32,110	100.0	76.7	12.1	4.4	3.0	0.1	0.3	3.5
Oklahoma	202,051	116,375	16,837	18,000	6,066	311	14,828	19,554	10,080	100.0	60.6	8.8	9.4	3.2	0.2	7.7	10.2
Oregon	229,936	148,479	6,949	30,433	14,020	1,523	2,392	13,944	12,196	100.0	68.2	3.2	14.0	6.4	0.7	1.1	6.4
Pennsylvania	717,289	473,072	80,264	52,367	40,612	763	1,435	21,587	47,189	100.0	70.6	12.0	7.8	6.1	0.1	0.2	3.2
Rhode Island	82,766	53,749	6,036	10,873	3,899	73	302	2,996	4,838	100.0	69.0	7.7	14.0	5.0	0.1	0.4	3.8
South Carolina	246,388	155,107	60,910	11,756	4,527	302	880	7,756	5,150	100.0	64.3	25.2	4.9	1.9	0.1	0.4	3.2
South Dakota	53,620	43,295	1,813	1,716	698	54	2,836	1,292	1,916	100.0	83.7	3.5	3.3	1.3	0.1	5.5	2.5
Tennessee	323,157	219,394	60,449	14,818	8,522	314	963	9,632	9,065	100.0	69.9	19.2	4.7	2.7	0.1	0.3	3.1
Texas	1,630,516	592,772	204,325	612,280	99,677	2,494	5,897	43,065	70,006	100.0	38.0	13.1	39.2	6.4	0.2	0.4	2.8
Utah	332,334	250,132	14,924	33,929	9,361	2,429	2,536	11,752	7,271	100.0	76.9	4.6	10.4	2.9	0.7	0.8	3.6

See notes at end of table.

Table 306.60. Total fall enrollment in degree-granting postsecondary institutions, by race/ethnicity of student and state or jurisdiction: 2017—Continued

State or jurisdiction	Fall enrollment									Percentage distribution of U.S. resident students (excludes nonresident aliens)							
	Total	White	Black	Hispanic	Asian	Pacific Islander	American Indian/ Alaska Native	Two or more races	Non-resident alien	Total	White	Black	Hispanic	Asian	Pacific Islander	American Indian/ Alaska Native	Two or more races
1	2	3	4	5	6	7	8	9	10	11	12	13	14	15	16	17	18
Vermont	43,855	34,851	1,619	2,443	1,219	41	210	1,576	1,896	100.0	83.1	3.9	5.8	2.9	0.1	0.5	3.8
Virginia	554,212	315,195	108,854	47,665	36,743	1,282	2,014	22,761	19,698	100.0	59.0	20.4	8.9	6.9	0.2	0.4	4.3
Washington	367,944	211,575	16,629	47,538	35,092	2,384	4,144	27,081	23,501	100.0	61.4	4.8	13.8	10.2	0.7	1.2	7.9
West Virginia	142,963	107,463	14,124	8,637	2,462	604	609	4,750	4,314	100.0	77.5	10.2	6.2	1.8	0.4	0.4	3.4
Wisconsin	340,770	261,365	18,209	23,089	13,437	356	2,358	9,788	12,168	100.0	79.5	5.5	7.0	4.1	0.1	0.7	3.0
Wyoming	33,015	26,652	390	3,007	331	71	452	1,061	1,051	100.0	83.4	1.2	9.4	1.0	0.2	1.4	3.3
U.S. Service Academies	15,281	9,999	1,192	1,669	1,078	70	90	989	194	100.0	66.3	7.9	11.1	7.1	0.5	0.6	6.6
Other jurisdictions	**192,406**	**748**	**1,869**	**177,673**	**3,328**	**8,090**	**121**	**177**	**400**	**100.0**	**0.4**	**1.0**	**92.5**	**1.7**	**4.2**	**0.1**	**0.1**
American Samoa	1,095	4	0	0	9	980	0	0	102	100.0	0.4	0.0	0.0	0.9	98.7	0.0	0.0
Federated States of Micronesia	2,022	0	0	0	1	2,021	0	0	0	100.0	0.0	0.0	0.0	#	100.0	0.0	0.0
Guam	6,027	184	50	34	2,713	3,002	5	2	37	100.0	3.1	0.8	0.6	45.3	50.1	0.1	#
Marshall Islands	1,032	1	0	0	1	1,030	0	0	0	100.0	0.1	0.0	0.0	0.1	99.8	0.0	0.0
Northern Marianas	1,216	14	2	1	488	512	0	139	60	100.0	1.2	0.2	0.1	42.2	44.3	0.0	12.0
Palau	532	0	0	0	8	524	0	0	0	100.0	0.0	0.0	0.0	1.5	98.5	0.0	0.0
Puerto Rico	178,312	394	189	177,433	94	20	110	22	50	100.0	0.2	0.1	99.5	0.1	#	0.1	#
U.S. Virgin Islands	2,170	151	1,628	205	14	1	6	14	151	100.0	7.5	80.6	10.2	0.7	#	0.3	0.7

#Rounds to zero.
NOTE: Race categories exclude persons of Hispanic ethnicity. Degree-granting institutions grant associate's or higher degrees and participate in Title IV federal financial aid programs. Detail may not sum to totals because of rounding.

SOURCE: U.S. Department of Education, National Center for Education Statistics, Integrated Postsecondary Education Data System (IPEDS), Spring 2018, Fall Enrollment component. (This table was prepared October 2018.)

Table 307.10. Full-time-equivalent fall enrollment in degree-granting postsecondary institutions, by control and level of institution: 1967 through 2028

Year	All institutions			Public institutions			Private institutions						
								4-year			2-year		
	Total	4-year	2-year	Total	4-year	2-year	Total	Total	Nonprofit	For-profit	Total	Nonprofit	For-profit
1	2	3	4	5	6	7	8	9	10	11	12	13	14
1967	5,499,360	4,448,302	1,051,058	3,777,701	2,850,432	927,269	1,721,659	1,597,870	—	—	123,789	—	—
1968	5,977,768	4,729,522	1,248,246	4,248,639	3,128,057	1,120,582	1,729,129	1,601,465	—	—	127,664	—	—
1969	6,333,357	4,899,034	1,434,323	4,577,353	3,259,323	1,318,030	1,756,004	1,639,711	—	—	116,293	—	—
1970	6,737,819	5,145,422	1,592,397	4,953,144	3,468,569	1,484,575	1,784,675	1,676,853	—	—	107,822	—	—
1971	7,148,558	5,357,647	1,790,911	5,344,402	3,660,626	1,683,776	1,804,156	1,697,021	—	—	107,135	—	—
1972	7,253,757	5,406,833	1,846,924	5,452,854	3,706,238	1,746,616	1,800,903	1,700,595	—	—	100,308	—	—
1973	7,453,463	5,439,230	2,014,233	5,629,563	3,721,037	1,908,526	1,823,900	1,718,193	—	—	105,707	—	—
1974	7,805,452	5,606,247	2,199,205	5,944,799	3,847,543	2,097,256	1,860,653	1,758,704	—	—	101,949	—	—
1975	8,479,698	5,900,408	2,579,290	6,522,319	4,056,502	2,465,817	1,957,379	1,843,906	—	—	113,473	—	—
1976	8,312,502	5,848,001	2,464,501	6,349,903	3,998,450	2,351,453	1,962,599	1,849,551	—	—	113,048	—	—
1977	8,415,339	5,935,076	2,480,263	6,396,476	4,039,071	2,357,405	2,018,863	1,896,005	—	—	122,858	—	—
1978	8,348,482	5,932,357	2,416,125	6,279,199	3,996,126	2,283,073	2,069,283	1,936,231	—	—	133,052	—	—
1979	8,487,317	6,016,072	2,471,245	6,392,617	4,059,304	2,333,313	2,094,700	1,956,768	—	—	137,932	—	—
1980	8,819,013	6,161,372	2,657,641	6,642,294	4,158,267	2,484,027	2,176,719	2,003,105	—	—	173,614[1]	—	—
1981	9,014,521	6,249,847	2,764,674	6,781,300	4,208,506	2,572,794	2,233,221	2,041,341	—	—	191,880[1]	—	—
1982	9,091,648	6,248,923	2,842,725	6,850,589	4,220,648	2,629,941	2,241,059	2,028,275	—	—	212,784[1]	—	—
1983	9,166,398	6,325,222	2,841,176	6,881,479	4,265,807	2,615,672	2,284,919	2,059,415	—	—	225,504	—	—
1984	8,951,695	6,292,711	2,658,984	6,684,664	4,237,895	2,446,769	2,267,031	2,054,816	—	—	212,215	—	—
1985	8,943,433	6,294,339	2,649,094	6,667,781	4,239,622	2,428,159	2,275,652	2,054,717	—	—	220,935	—	—
1986	9,064,165	6,360,325	2,703,842	6,778,045	4,295,494	2,482,551	2,286,122	2,064,831	—	—	221,291[2]	—	—
1987	9,229,736	6,486,504	2,743,230	6,937,690	4,395,728	2,541,961	2,292,045	2,090,776	—	—	201,269[2]	—	—
1988	9,464,271	6,664,146	2,800,125	7,096,905	4,505,774	2,591,131	2,367,366	2,158,372	—	—	208,994	—	—
1989	9,780,881	6,813,602	2,967,279	7,371,590	4,619,828	2,751,762	2,409,291	2,193,774	—	—	215,517	—	—
1990	9,983,436	6,968,008	3,015,428	7,557,982	4,740,049	2,817,933	2,425,454	2,227,959	2,177,668	50,291	197,495	72,785	124,710
1991	10,360,606	7,081,454	3,279,152	7,862,845	4,795,704	3,067,141	2,497,761	2,285,750	2,223,463	62,287	212,011	72,545	139,466
1992	10,436,776	7,129,379	3,307,397	7,911,701	4,797,884	3,113,817	2,525,075	2,331,495	2,267,373	64,122	193,580	66,647	126,933
1993	10,351,415	7,120,921	3,230,494	7,812,394	4,765,983	3,046,411	2,539,021	2,354,938	2,282,643	72,295	184,083	70,469	113,614
1994	10,348,072	7,137,341	3,210,731	7,784,396	4,749,524	3,034,872	2,563,676	2,387,817	2,301,063	86,754	175,859	69,578	106,281
1995	10,334,956	7,172,844	3,162,112	7,751,815	4,757,223	2,994,592	2,583,141	2,415,621	2,328,730	86,891	167,520	62,416	105,104
1996	10,481,886	7,234,541	3,247,345	7,794,895	4,767,117	3,027,778	2,686,991	2,467,424	2,353,561	113,863	219,567	63,954	155,613
1997	10,615,028	7,338,794	3,276,234	7,869,764	4,813,849	3,055,915	2,745,264	2,524,945	2,389,627	135,318	220,319	61,761	158,558
1998	10,698,775	7,467,828	3,230,947	7,880,135	4,868,857	3,011,278	2,818,640	2,598,971	2,436,188	162,783	219,669	56,834	162,835
1999	10,974,519	7,634,247	3,340,272	8,059,240	4,949,851	3,109,389	2,915,279	2,684,396	2,488,140	196,256	230,883	53,956	176,927
2000	11,267,025	7,795,139	3,471,886	8,266,932	5,025,588	3,241,344	3,000,093	2,769,551	2,549,676	219,875	230,542	51,503	179,039
2001	11,765,945	8,087,980	3,677,965	8,639,154	5,194,035	3,445,119	3,126,791	2,893,945	2,612,833	281,112	232,846	41,037	191,809
2002	12,331,319	8,439,064	3,892,255	9,061,411	5,406,283	3,655,128	3,269,908	3,032,781	2,699,702	333,079	237,127	40,110	197,017
2003	12,687,597	8,744,188	3,943,409	9,240,724	5,557,680	3,683,044	3,446,873	3,186,508	2,776,850	409,658	260,365	36,815	223,550
2004	13,000,994	9,018,024	3,982,970	9,348,081	5,640,650	3,707,431	3,652,913	3,377,374	2,837,251	540,123	275,539	34,202	241,337
2005	13,200,790	9,261,634	3,939,156	9,390,216	5,728,327	3,661,889	3,810,574	3,533,307	2,878,354	654,953	277,267	34,729	242,538
2006	13,401,696	9,456,480	3,945,216	9,502,028	5,824,962	3,677,066	3,899,668	3,631,518	2,936,261	695,257	268,150	31,203	236,947
2007	13,786,735	9,768,388	4,018,347	9,744,001	5,992,611	3,751,390	4,042,734	3,775,777	2,993,901	781,876	266,957	26,140	240,817
2008	14,377,990	10,153,074	4,224,916	10,061,076	6,138,686	3,922,390	4,316,914	4,014,388	3,058,910	955,478	302,526	28,072	274,454
2009	15,379,473	10,695,816	4,683,657	10,746,637	6,452,414	4,294,223	4,632,836	4,243,402	3,153,294	1,090,108	389,434	27,964	361,470
2010	15,947,474	11,129,239	4,818,235	11,018,756	6,635,799	4,382,957	4,928,718	4,493,440	3,235,149	1,258,291	435,278	26,920	408,358
2011	15,892,792	11,261,845	4,630,947	10,954,754	6,734,116	4,220,638	4,938,038	4,527,729	3,285,711	1,242,018	410,309	34,267	376,042
2012	15,593,434	11,229,774	4,363,660	10,781,798	6,764,184	4,017,614	4,811,636	4,465,590	3,309,242	1,156,348	346,046	32,684	313,362
2013	15,410,058	11,183,239	4,226,819	10,697,939	6,790,930	3,907,009	4,712,119	4,392,309	3,337,799	1,054,510	319,810	27,313	292,497
2014	15,263,179	11,238,618	4,024,561	10,624,163	6,891,984	3,732,179	4,639,016	4,346,634	3,363,101	983,533	292,382	25,808	266,574
2015	15,078,504	11,226,353	3,852,151	10,569,574	6,970,121	3,599,453	4,508,930	4,256,232	3,399,283	856,949	252,698	41,579	211,119
2016	14,937,939	11,356,540	3,581,399	10,572,028	7,221,134	3,350,894	4,365,911	4,135,406	3,410,337	725,069	230,505	43,900	186,605
2017	14,880,079	11,403,660	3,476,419	10,565,751	7,309,604	3,256,147	4,314,328	4,094,056	3,435,169	658,887	220,272	43,990	176,282
2018[3]	14,919,000	11,432,000	3,487,000	10,594,000	7,328,000	3,266,000	4,325,000	4,104,000	—	—	221,000	—	—
2019[3]	14,967,000	11,467,000	3,500,000	10,629,000	7,350,000	3,279,000	4,338,000	4,117,000	—	—	221,000	—	—
2020[3]	14,975,000	11,471,000	3,504,000	10,635,000	7,352,000	3,283,000	4,340,000	4,118,000	—	—	221,000	—	—
2021[3]	14,982,000	11,474,000	3,509,000	10,641,000	7,354,000	3,287,000	4,341,000	4,119,000	—	—	221,000	—	—
2022[3]	14,996,000	11,482,000	3,514,000	10,652,000	7,359,000	3,293,000	4,344,000	4,122,000	—	—	222,000	—	—
2023[3]	15,023,000	11,501,000	3,522,000	10,672,000	7,371,000	3,301,000	4,351,000	4,129,000	—	—	222,000	—	—
2024[3]	15,069,000	11,535,000	3,534,000	10,705,000	7,393,000	3,312,000	4,364,000	4,141,000	—	—	222,000	—	—
2025[3]	15,121,000	11,575,000	3,546,000	10,742,000	7,419,000	3,323,000	4,379,000	4,156,000	—	—	223,000	—	—
2026[3]	15,178,000	11,618,000	3,560,000	10,783,000	7,446,000	3,336,000	4,395,000	4,171,000	—	—	224,000	—	—
2027[3]	15,197,000	11,630,000	3,567,000	10,797,000	7,455,000	3,342,000	4,400,000	4,176,000	—	—	224,000	—	—
2028[3]	15,194,000	11,626,000	3,568,000	10,796,000	7,452,000	3,344,000	4,398,000	4,174,000	—	—	224,000	—	—

—Not available.

[1]Large increases are due to the addition of schools accredited by the Accrediting Commission of Career Schools and Colleges of Technology.

[2]Because of imputation techniques, data are not consistent with figures for other years.

[3]Projected.

NOTE: Full-time-equivalent enrollment is the number of full-time students enrolled, plus the full-time equivalent of the part-time students. Data through 1995 are for institutions of higher education, while later data are for degree-granting institutions. Degree-granting institutions grant associate's or higher degrees and participate in Title IV federal financial aid programs. The degree-granting classification is very similar to the earlier higher education classification, but it includes more 2-year colleges and excludes a few higher education institutions that did not grant degrees. Some data have been revised from previously published figures. Detail may not sum to totals because of rounding.

SOURCE: U.S. Department of Education, National Center for Education Statistics, Higher Education General Information Survey (HEGIS), "Fall Enrollment in Colleges and Universities" surveys, 1967 through 1985; Integrated Postsecondary Education Data System (IPEDS), "Fall Enrollment Survey" (IPEDS-EF:86–99); IPEDS Spring 2001 through Spring 2018, Fall Enrollment component; and Enrollment in Degree-Granting Institutions Projection Model, 2000 through 2028. (This table was prepared March 2019.)

Table 309.10. Residence and migration of all first-time degree/certificate-seeking undergraduates in degree-granting postsecondary institutions, by state or jurisdiction: Fall 2016

State or jurisdiction	Total first-time enrollment in institutions located in the state	State residents enrolled in institutions		Ratio of in-state students		Migration of students		
		In any state[1]	In their home state	To first-time enrollment (col. 4/col. 2)	To residents enrolled in any state (col. 4/col. 3)	Out of state (col. 3 - col. 4)	Into state[2] (col. 2 - col. 4)	Net (col. 8 - col. 7)
1	2	3	4	5	6	7	8	9
United States	**2,882,991**	**2,780,087**	**2,263,966**	**0.79**	**0.81**	**516,121**	**619,025**	**102,904**
Alabama	50,108	40,930	35,567	0.71	0.87	5,363	14,541	9,178
Alaska	3,049	4,642	2,802	0.92	0.60	1,840	247	-1,593
Arizona	65,784	50,827	45,187	0.69	0.89	5,640	20,597	14,957
Arkansas	27,276	23,816	20,632	0.76	0.87	3,184	6,644	3,460
California	394,845	391,236	348,909	0.88	0.89	42,327	45,936	3,609
Colorado	43,832	42,380	32,304	0.74	0.76	10,076	11,528	1,452
Connecticut	31,741	36,288	20,790	0.65	0.57	15,498	10,951	-4,547
Delaware	9,727	8,426	5,781	0.59	0.69	2,645	3,946	1,301
District of Columbia	9,012	3,292	760	0.08	0.23	2,532	8,252	5,720
Florida	158,956	146,310	127,268	0.80	0.87	19,042	31,688	12,646
Georgia	84,932	88,264	70,974	0.84	0.80	17,290	13,958	-3,332
Hawaii	8,398	10,366	6,473	0.77	0.62	3,893	1,925	-1,968
Idaho	14,520	11,899	8,741	0.60	0.73	3,158	5,779	2,621
Illinois	93,994	113,160	77,641	0.83	0.69	35,519	16,353	-19,166
Indiana	64,028	52,731	45,399	0.71	0.86	7,332	18,629	11,297
Iowa	38,130	26,849	23,412	0.61	0.87	3,437	14,718	11,281
Kansas	32,597	27,087	22,928	0.70	0.85	4,159	9,669	5,510
Kentucky	36,378	33,520	28,704	0.79	0.86	4,816	7,674	2,858
Louisiana	40,261	38,764	34,042	0.85	0.88	4,722	6,219	1,497
Maine	11,727	10,492	7,445	0.63	0.71	3,047	4,282	1,235
Maryland	47,084	53,634	36,416	0.77	0.68	17,218	10,668	-6,550
Massachusetts	72,432	64,752	43,591	0.60	0.67	21,161	28,841	7,680
Michigan	86,314	84,957	74,952	0.87	0.88	10,005	11,362	1,357
Minnesota	45,102	49,999	35,204	0.78	0.70	14,795	9,898	-4,897
Mississippi	32,088	27,600	24,520	0.76	0.89	3,080	7,568	4,488
Missouri	53,824	50,783	41,179	0.77	0.81	9,604	12,645	3,041
Montana	8,959	7,340	5,824	0.65	0.79	1,516	3,135	1,619
Nebraska	18,423	16,906	13,823	0.75	0.82	3,083	4,600	1,517
Nevada	16,112	18,299	14,090	0.87	0.77	4,209	2,022	-2,187
New Hampshire	15,728	11,351	6,221	0.40	0.55	5,130	9,507	4,377
New Jersey	65,178	93,783	58,978	0.90	0.63	34,805	6,200	-28,605
New Mexico	19,085	18,988	16,036	0.84	0.84	2,952	3,049	97
New York	185,714	176,804	144,077	0.78	0.81	32,727	41,637	8,910
North Carolina	88,547	84,392	72,738	0.82	0.86	11,654	15,809	4,155
North Dakota	8,709	5,991	4,450	0.51	0.74	1,541	4,259	2,718
Ohio	101,393	95,021	80,533	0.79	0.85	14,488	20,860	6,372
Oklahoma	36,266	30,875	27,417	0.76	0.89	3,458	8,849	5,391
Oregon	31,324	26,686	21,893	0.70	0.82	4,793	9,431	4,638
Pennsylvania	125,063	108,247	88,578	0.71	0.82	19,669	36,485	16,816
Rhode Island	14,942	8,424	5,491	0.37	0.65	2,933	9,451	6,518
South Carolina	45,173	39,488	34,137	0.76	0.86	5,351	11,036	5,685
South Dakota	8,316	6,697	5,129	0.62	0.77	1,568	3,187	1,619
Tennessee	56,605	54,577	45,794	0.81	0.84	8,783	10,811	2,028
Texas	235,197	246,392	218,655	0.93	0.89	27,737	16,542	-11,195
Utah	32,141	24,713	22,451	0.70	0.91	2,262	9,690	7,428
Vermont	7,474	4,405	2,229	0.30	0.51	2,176	5,245	3,069
Virginia	79,020	73,514	60,098	0.76	0.82	13,416	18,922	5,506
Washington	47,853	49,707	39,068	0.82	0.79	10,639	8,785	-1,854
West Virginia	18,874	13,168	11,446	0.61	0.87	1,722	7,428	5,706
Wisconsin	51,423	48,561	39,362	0.77	0.81	9,199	12,061	2,862
Wyoming	5,227	4,684	3,576	0.68	0.76	1,108	1,651	543
U.S. Service Academies	4,106	†	251[3]	0.06	†	-251	3,855	4,106
State unknown[4]	†	18,070	†	†	†	18,070	†	-18,070
Other jurisdictions	**48,706**	**49,552**	**47,792**	**0.98**	**0.96**	**1,760**	**914**	**-846**
American Samoa	392	457	392	1.00	0.86	65	0	-65
Federated States of Micronesia	760	861	760	1.00	0.88	101	0	-101
Guam	985	1,157	931	0.95	0.80	226	54	-172
Marshall Islands	303	300	287	0.95	0.96	13	16	3
Northern Marianas	305	388	305	1.00	0.79	83	0	-83
Palau	148	144	122	0.82	0.85	22	26	4
Puerto Rico	45,468	45,592	44,661	0.98	0.98	931	807	-124
U.S. Virgin Islands	345	653	334	0.97	0.51	319	11	-308
Foreign countries	†	87,022	†	†	†	87,022	†	-87,022
Residence unknown	†	15,036	†	†	†	15,036	†	-15,036

†Not applicable.
[1]Students residing in a particular state when admitted to an institution anywhere—either in their home state or another state.
[2]Includes students coming to U.S. institutions from foreign countries and other jurisdictions.
[3]Students whose residence is in the same state as the service academy.
[4]Institution unable to determine student's home state.

NOTE: Includes all first-time postsecondary students enrolled at reporting institutions. Degree-granting institutions grant associate's or higher degrees and participate in Title IV federal financial aid programs. Some data have been revised from previously published figures.
SOURCE: U.S. Department of Education, National Center for Education Statistics, Integrated Postsecondary Education Data System (IPEDS), Spring 2017, Fall Enrollment component. (This table was prepared January 2019.)

Table 309.20. Residence and migration of all first-time degree/certificate-seeking undergraduates in degree-granting postsecondary institutions who graduated from high school in the previous 12 months, by state or jurisdiction: Fall 2016

State or jurisdiction	Total first-time enrollment in institutions located in the state	State residents enrolled in institutions		Ratio of in-state students		Migration of students		
		In any state[1]	In their home state	To first-time enrollment (col. 4/col. 2)	To residents enrolled in any state (col. 4/col. 3)	Out of state (col. 3 - col. 4)	Into state[2] (col. 2 - col. 4)	Net (col. 8 - col. 7)
1	2	3	4	5	6	7	8	9
United States	**2,221,870**	**2,166,518**	**1,737,094**	**0.78**	**0.80**	**429,424**	**484,776**	**55,352**
Alabama	41,568	32,801	29,007	0.70	0.88	3,794	12,561	8,767
Alaska	2,186	3,321	2,005	0.92	0.60	1,316	181	-1,135
Arizona	43,832	36,307	31,782	0.73	0.88	4,525	12,050	7,525
Arkansas	23,181	19,504	17,361	0.75	0.89	2,143	5,820	3,677
California	262,996	274,782	237,493	0.90	0.86	37,289	25,503	-11,786
Colorado	33,359	33,290	24,499	0.73	0.74	8,791	8,860	69
Connecticut	25,456	30,743	16,388	0.64	0.53	14,355	9,068	-5,287
Delaware	8,017	6,705	4,501	0.56	0.67	2,204	3,516	1,312
District of Columbia	7,938	2,470	454	0.06	0.18	2,016	7,484	5,468
Florida	110,896	110,525	95,001	0.86	0.86	15,524	15,895	371
Georgia	66,942	67,760	55,339	0.83	0.82	12,421	11,603	-818
Hawaii	6,395	8,264	4,852	0.76	0.59	3,412	1,543	-1,869
Idaho	10,822	8,626	6,295	0.58	0.73	2,331	4,527	2,196
Illinois	72,358	91,993	59,562	0.82	0.65	32,431	12,796	-19,635
Indiana	53,377	43,908	37,967	0.71	0.86	5,941	15,410	9,469
Iowa	31,471	23,007	20,012	0.64	0.87	2,995	11,459	8,464
Kansas	25,655	22,302	18,819	0.73	0.84	3,483	6,836	3,353
Kentucky	31,128	27,714	24,310	0.78	0.88	3,404	6,818	3,414
Louisiana	33,716	31,762	28,452	0.84	0.90	3,310	5,264	1,954
Maine	9,771	8,518	5,837	0.60	0.69	2,681	3,934	1,253
Maryland	34,490	42,057	26,822	0.78	0.64	15,235	7,668	-7,567
Massachusetts	61,644	54,960	35,528	0.58	0.65	19,432	26,116	6,684
Michigan	69,530	67,904	59,683	0.86	0.88	8,221	9,847	1,626
Minnesota	37,219	42,353	28,720	0.77	0.68	13,633	8,499	-5,134
Mississippi	27,825	22,612	21,018	0.76	0.93	1,594	6,807	5,213
Missouri	42,021	40,137	32,046	0.76	0.80	8,091	9,975	1,884
Montana	6,918	5,322	4,138	0.60	0.78	1,184	2,780	1,596
Nebraska	16,027	14,719	12,012	0.75	0.82	2,707	4,015	1,308
Nevada	12,058	13,509	10,182	0.84	0.75	3,327	1,876	-1,451
New Hampshire	10,703	9,665	4,973	0.46	0.51	4,692	5,730	1,038
New Jersey	47,311	74,952	42,814	0.90	0.57	32,138	4,497	-27,641
New Mexico	14,006	13,849	11,781	0.84	0.85	2,068	2,225	157
New York	151,418	145,443	116,195	0.77	0.80	29,248	35,223	5,975
North Carolina	70,797	65,702	57,385	0.81	0.87	8,317	13,412	5,095
North Dakota	7,443	4,842	3,680	0.49	0.76	1,162	3,763	2,601
Ohio	84,313	77,791	66,016	0.78	0.85	11,775	18,297	6,522
Oklahoma	28,334	23,929	21,302	0.75	0.89	2,627	7,032	4,405
Oregon	22,631	18,858	14,774	0.65	0.78	4,084	7,857	3,773
Pennsylvania	101,538	85,937	69,151	0.68	0.80	16,786	32,387	15,601
Rhode Island	13,200	7,054	4,412	0.33	0.63	2,642	8,788	6,146
South Carolina	36,904	30,642	27,154	0.74	0.89	3,488	9,750	6,262
South Dakota	7,299	5,722	4,347	0.60	0.76	1,375	2,952	1,577
Tennessee	48,022	46,153	39,047	0.81	0.85	7,106	8,975	1,869
Texas	178,980	190,086	167,542	0.94	0.88	22,544	11,438	-11,106
Utah	22,388	17,220	15,605	0.70	0.91	1,615	6,783	5,168
Vermont	6,743	3,719	1,808	0.27	0.49	1,911	4,935	3,024
Virginia	63,938	60,624	49,432	0.77	0.82	11,192	14,506	3,314
Washington	34,423	35,830	27,062	0.79	0.76	8,768	7,361	-1,407
West Virginia	14,306	10,518	9,352	0.65	0.89	1,166	4,954	3,788
Wisconsin	41,357	38,682	30,573	0.74	0.79	8,109	10,784	2,675
Wyoming	3,736	3,228	2,408	0.64	0.75	820	1,328	508
U.S. Service Academies	3,284	†	196[3]	0.06	†	-196	3,088	3,284
State unknown[4]	†	8,197	†	†	†	8,197	†	-8,197
Other jurisdictions	**37,596**	**38,835**	**37,382**	**0.99**	**0.96**	**1,453**	**214**	**-1,239**
American Samoa	316	357	316	1.00	0.89	41	0	-41
Federated States of Micronesia	557	638	557	1.00	0.87	81	0	-81
Guam	655	801	617	0.94	0.77	184	38	-146
Marshall Islands	258	263	253	0.98	0.96	10	5	-5
Northern Marianas	250	317	250	1.00	0.79	67	0	-67
Palau	122	120	102	0.84	0.85	18	20	2
Puerto Rico	35,176	35,843	35,032	1.00	0.98	811	144	-667
U.S. Virgin Islands	262	496	255	0.97	0.51	241	7	-234
Foreign countries	†	54,076	†	†	†	54,076	†	-54,076
Residence unknown	†	37	†	†	†	37	†	-37

†Not applicable.
[1]Students residing in a particular state when admitted to an institution anywhere—either in their home state or another state.
[2]Includes students coming to U.S. institutions from foreign countries and other jurisdictions.
[3]Students whose residence is in the same state as the service academy.
[4]Institution unable to determine student's home state.

NOTE: Includes all first-time postsecondary students who graduated from high school in the previous 12 months and were enrolled at reporting institutions. Degree-granting institutions grant associate's or higher degrees and participate in Title IV federal financial aid programs. Some data have been revised from previously published figures.
SOURCE: U.S. Department of Education, National Center for Education Statistics, Integrated Postsecondary Education Data System (IPEDS), Spring 2017, Fall Enrollment component. (This table was prepared January 2019.)

Table 309.30. Residence and migration of all first-time degree/certificate-seeking undergraduates in 4-year degree-granting postsecondary institutions who graduated from high school in the previous 12 months, by state or jurisdiction: Fall 2016

State or jurisdiction	Total first-time enrollment in institutions located in the state	State residents enrolled in institutions		Ratio of in-state students		Migration of students		
		In any state[1]	In their home state	To first-time enrollment (col. 4/col. 2)	To residents enrolled in any state (col. 4/col. 3)	Out of state (col. 3 - col. 4)	Into state[2] (col. 2 - col. 4)	Net (col. 8 - col. 7)
1	2	3	4	5	6	7	8	9
United States	**1,607,730**	**1,556,453**	**1,148,695**	**0.71**	**0.74**	**407,758**	**459,035**	**51,277**
Alabama	28,063	19,531	16,175	0.58	0.83	3,356	11,888	8,532
Alaska	2,115	3,137	1,935	0.91	0.62	1,202	180	-1,022
Arizona	27,211	19,852	15,612	0.57	0.79	4,240	11,599	7,359
Arkansas	17,491	13,713	11,846	0.68	0.86	1,867	5,645	3,778
California	152,534	166,430	129,902	0.85	0.78	36,528	22,632	-13,896
Colorado	27,047	26,866	18,659	0.69	0.69	8,207	8,388	181
Connecticut	19,303	24,444	10,269	0.53	0.42	14,175	9,034	-5,141
Delaware	7,942	6,623	4,483	0.56	0.68	2,140	3,459	1,319
District of Columbia	7,926	2,291	448	0.06	0.20	1,843	7,478	5,635
Florida	109,554	108,239	93,739	0.86	0.87	14,500	15,815	1,315
Georgia	56,733	57,577	45,941	0.81	0.80	11,636	10,792	-844
Hawaii	3,910	5,699	2,488	0.64	0.44	3,211	1,422	-1,789
Idaho	8,894	6,618	4,542	0.51	0.69	2,076	4,352	2,276
Illinois	46,414	65,595	34,007	0.73	0.52	31,588	12,407	-19,181
Indiana	46,240	36,589	31,090	0.67	0.85	5,499	15,150	9,651
Iowa	20,979	13,621	10,872	0.52	0.80	2,749	10,107	7,358
Kansas	15,284	13,349	10,100	0.66	0.76	3,249	5,184	1,935
Kentucky	23,774	20,358	17,154	0.72	0.84	3,204	6,620	3,416
Louisiana	24,935	22,842	19,905	0.80	0.87	2,937	5,030	2,093
Maine	7,659	6,493	3,864	0.50	0.60	2,629	3,795	1,166
Maryland	19,401	27,571	12,670	0.65	0.46	14,901	6,731	-8,170
Massachusetts	50,916	44,404	25,199	0.49	0.57	19,205	25,717	6,512
Michigan	52,957	51,272	43,458	0.82	0.85	7,814	9,499	1,685
Minnesota	25,326	30,839	17,837	0.70	0.58	13,002	7,489	-5,513
Mississippi	13,124	8,566	7,094	0.54	0.83	1,472	6,030	4,558
Missouri	29,328	27,140	19,734	0.67	0.73	7,406	9,594	2,188
Montana	6,208	4,440	3,484	0.56	0.78	956	2,724	1,768
Nebraska	11,901	10,454	8,250	0.69	0.79	2,204	3,651	1,447
Nevada	10,798	11,988	8,951	0.83	0.75	3,037	1,847	-1,190
New Hampshire	8,439	7,234	2,814	0.33	0.39	4,420	5,625	1,205
New Jersey	29,875	57,262	25,576	0.86	0.45	31,686	4,299	-27,387
New Mexico	7,121	7,360	5,547	0.78	0.75	1,813	1,574	-239
New York	110,369	104,891	76,136	0.69	0.73	28,755	34,233	5,478
North Carolina	48,778	43,853	35,929	0.74	0.82	7,924	12,849	4,925
North Dakota	6,366	3,870	3,029	0.48	0.78	841	3,337	2,496
Ohio	69,364	63,038	51,763	0.75	0.82	11,275	17,601	6,326
Oklahoma	19,642	15,681	13,427	0.68	0.86	2,254	6,215	3,961
Oregon	15,744	12,355	8,447	0.54	0.68	3,908	7,297	3,389
Pennsylvania	83,714	68,216	52,094	0.62	0.76	16,122	31,620	15,498
Rhode Island	11,707	5,522	2,968	0.25	0.54	2,554	8,739	6,185
South Carolina	24,791	18,902	15,609	0.63	0.83	3,293	9,182	5,889
South Dakota	6,088	4,578	3,355	0.55	0.73	1,223	2,733	1,510
Tennessee	30,353	28,637	21,828	0.72	0.76	6,809	8,525	1,716
Texas	108,148	120,213	98,693	0.91	0.82	21,520	9,455	-12,065
Utah	19,318	14,064	12,658	0.66	0.90	1,406	6,660	5,254
Vermont	6,483	3,382	1,566	0.24	0.46	1,816	4,917	3,101
Virginia	43,571	40,895	30,062	0.69	0.74	10,833	13,509	2,676
Washington	30,723	31,955	23,532	0.77	0.74	8,423	7,191	-1,232
West Virginia	12,270	8,341	7,433	0.61	0.89	908	4,837	3,929
Wisconsin	36,162	33,170	25,582	0.71	0.77	7,588	10,580	2,992
Wyoming	1,453	1,467	743	0.51	0.51	724	710	-14
U.S. Service Academies	3,284	†	196[3]	0.06	†	-196	3,088	3,284
State unknown[4]	†	5,026	†	†	†	5,026	†	-5,026
Other jurisdictions	**29,271**	**30,354**	**29,098**	**0.99**	**0.96**	**1,256**	**173**	**-1,083**
American Samoa	316	352	316	1.00	0.90	36	0	-36
Federated States of Micronesia	†	39	†	†	†	39	0	-39
Guam	437	576	399	0.91	0.69	177	38	-139
Marshall Islands	†	9	†	†	†	9	0	-9
Northern Marianas	250	310	250	1.00	0.81	60	0	-60
Palau	†	10	†	†	†	10	0	-10
Puerto Rico	28,006	28,574	27,878	1.00	0.98	696	128	-568
U.S. Virgin Islands	262	484	255	0.97	0.53	229	7	-222
Foreign countries	†	50,157	†	†	†	50,157	†	-50,157
Residence unknown	†	37	†	†	†	37	†	-37

†Not applicable.
[1]Students residing in a particular state when admitted to an institution anywhere—either in their home state or another state.
[2]Includes students coming to U.S. institutions from foreign countries and other jurisdictions.
[3]Students whose residence is in the same state as the service academy.
[4]Institution unable to determine student's home state.

NOTE: Includes all first-time postsecondary students who graduated from high school in the previous 12 months and were enrolled at reporting institutions. Degree-granting institutions grant associate's or higher degrees and participate in Title IV federal financial aid programs. Some data have been revised from previously published figures.
SOURCE: U.S. Department of Education, National Center for Education Statistics, Integrated Postsecondary Education Data System (IPEDS), Spring 2017, Fall Enrollment component. (This table was prepared January 2019.)

Table 310.10. Number of U.S. students studying abroad and percentage distribution, by sex, race/ethnicity, and other selected characteristics: Selected years, 2000–01 through 2016–17

Sex, race/ethnicity, and other selected characteristics	2000–01	2006–07	2007–08	2008–09	2009–10	2010–11	2011–12	2012–13	2013–14	2014–15	2015–16	2016–17	From 2006–07 to 2016–17
1	2	3	4	5	6	7	8	9	10	11	12	13	14
	Number of students												Percentage change in number of students
Total	**154,168**	**241,791**	**262,416**	**260,327**	**270,604**	**273,996**	**283,332**	**289,408**	**304,467**	**313,415**	**325,339**	**332,727**	**37.6**
	Percentage distribution of students												Percentage-point change in distribution of students
Sex	100.0	100.0	100.0	100.0	100.0	100.0	100.0	100.0	100.0	100.0	100.0	100.0	†
Male	35.0	34.9	34.9	35.8	36.5	35.6	35.2	34.7	34.7	33.4	33.5	32.7	-2.2
Female	65.0	65.1	65.1	64.2	63.5	64.4	64.8	65.3	65.3	66.6	66.5	67.3	2.2
Race/ethnicity	100.0	100.0	100.0	100.0	100.0	100.0	100.0	100.0	100.0	100.0	100.0	100.0	†
White	84.3	81.9	81.8	80.5	78.7	77.8	76.4	76.3	74.3	72.9	71.6	70.8	-11.1
Black	3.5	3.8	4.0	4.2	4.7	4.8	5.3	5.3	5.6	5.6	5.9	6.1	2.3
Hispanic	5.4	6.0	5.9	6.0	6.4	6.9	7.6	7.6	8.3	8.8	9.7	10.2	4.2
Asian/Pacific Islander	5.4	6.7	6.6	7.3	7.9	7.9	7.7	7.3	7.7	8.1	8.4	8.2	1.5
American Indian/Alaska Native	0.5	0.5	0.5	0.5	0.5	0.5	0.5	0.5	0.5	0.5	0.5	0.4	-0.1
Two or more races	0.9	1.2	1.2	1.6	1.9	2.1	2.5	3.0	3.6	4.1	3.9	4.3	3.1
Academic level	100.0	100.0	100.0	100.0	100.0	100.0	100.0	100.0	100.0	100.0	100.0	100.0	†
Freshman	3.1	3.3	3.5	3.4	3.5	3.3	3.3	3.8	3.9	3.9	3.6	4.0	0.7
Sophomore	14.0	12.9	13.1	13.9	13.2	12.6	13.0	13.7	13.1	13.1	12.7	13.2	0.3
Junior	38.9	36.6	35.9	36.8	35.8	35.8	36.0	34.7	33.9	33.1	32.9	33.0	-3.6
Senior	20.0	21.3	21.3	21.6	21.8	23.4	24.4	24.7	25.3	26.4	27.7	27.4	6.1
Associate's students	0.9	2.7	2.2	1.1	0.1	0.2	1.1	1.1	1.7	1.8	1.7	1.7	-1.0
Bachelor's, unspecified	13.5	12.5	13.4	11.3	11.0	10.3	8.4	8.4	9.1	9.3	9.1	8.6	-3.9
Master's level or higher	8.3	10.5	10.5	11.8	14.0	13.5	13.5	13.5	12.7	12.1	12.1	12.3	1.8
Other academic level	1.1	#	0.1	#	1.0	0.9	0.3	0.1	0.3	0.3	0.2	0.2	0.2
Host region	100.0	100.0	100.0	100.0	100.0	100.0	100.0	100.0	100.0	100.0	100.0	100.0	†
Sub-Saharan Africa[1]	2.5	3.5	3.6	4.2	4.2	4.3	4.5	4.6	4.4	3.4	3.9	4.0	0.5
Asia[2]	6.0	10.3	11.1	11.4	12.0	11.7	12.4	12.4	11.9	11.4	11.1	11.6	1.3
Europe[3]	63.3	57.4	56.3	54.5	53.5	54.6	53.3	53.3	53.3	54.5	54.4	54.4	-3.0
Latin America[4]	14.5	15.0	15.3	15.4	15.0	14.6	15.8	15.7	16.2	16.0	16.3	15.5	0.5
Middle East and North Africa[1,3]	1.6	1.8	2.2	2.5	3.1	2.6	2.5	2.2	2.1	2.2	1.9	2.1	0.3
North America[4,5]	0.7	0.6	0.4	0.5	0.7	0.5	0.6	0.5	0.5	0.5	0.6	0.5	-0.1
Oceania	6.0	5.7	5.3	5.5	5.0	4.8	4.5	4.0	3.9	4.0	4.2	4.4	-1.3
Multiple destinations	5.6	5.6	5.7	6.0	6.5	6.8	6.4	7.3	7.7	7.9	7.6	7.5	1.9
Duration of stay	100.0	100.0	100.0	100.0	100.0	100.0	100.0	100.0	100.0	100.0	100.0	100.0	†
Summer term	33.7	38.7	38.1	35.8	37.8	37.7	37.1	37.8	38.1	39.0	38.0	38.5	-0.2
One semester	38.5	36.3	35.5	37.3	35.8	34.5	35.0	33.6	31.9	31.8	31.9	30.7	-5.6
8 weeks or less during academic year	7.4	9.8	11.0	11.7	11.9	13.3	14.4	15.3	16.5	16.7	17.4	18.8	9.0
January term	7.0	6.8	7.2	7.0	6.9	7.1	7.0	7.1	7.5	7.4	7.4	7.1	0.3
Academic year	7.3	4.3	4.1	4.1	3.8	3.7	3.2	3.1	2.9	2.5	2.3	2.2	-2.1
One quarter	4.1	3.4	3.4	3.3	3.1	3.0	2.5	2.4	2.4	2.2	2.3	2.2	-1.2
Two quarters	0.6	0.5	0.6	0.5	0.4	0.5	0.4	0.3	0.6	0.3	0.3	0.2	-0.3
Calendar year	0.6	0.1	0.1	0.1	0.1	0.1	0.1	0.1	0.1	0.1	0.1	0.1	#
Other	0.8	0.1	#	0.2	0.1	0.1	0.3	0.3	#	0.1	0.4	0.2	0.1

†Not applicable.
#Rounds to zero.
[1]North Africa was combined with the Middle East to create the "Middle East and North Africa" category as of 2011–12, and the former "Africa" category was replaced by "Sub-Saharan Africa" (which excludes North Africa). Data for years prior to 2011–12 have been revised for comparability.
[2]Asia excludes the Middle Eastern countries (Bahrain, Iran, Iraq, Israel, Jordan, Kuwait, Lebanon, Oman, the Palestinian Territories, Qatar, Saudi Arabia, Syria, the United Arab Emirates, and Yemen).
[3]Cyprus and Turkey were classified as being in the Middle East prior to 2004–05 but in Europe for 2004–05 and later years. Data for 2000–01 have been revised for comparability.
[4]Mexico and Central America are included in Latin America, not in North America.
[5]Includes Antarctica from 2002-03 onward.
NOTE: Detail may not sum to totals because of rounding. Race categories exclude persons of Hispanic ethnicity.
SOURCE: Institute of International Education, *Open Doors: Report on International Educational Exchange*, 2018. (This table was prepared November 2018.)

Table 310.20. Foreign students enrolled in institutions of higher education in the United States, by continent, region, and selected countries of origin: Selected years, 1980–81 through 2017–18

Continent, region, and selected countries of origin	1980–81		1985–86		1990–91		1995–96		2000–01		2005–06		2010–11		2015–16		2017–18	
	Number	Percent	Number	Percent	Number	Percent	Number	Percent	Number	Percent	Number	Percent	Number	Percent	Number	Percent	Number	Percent
1	2	3	4	5	6	7	8	9	10	11	12	13	14	15	16	17	18	19
Total	**311,880**	**100.0**	**343,780**	**100.0**	**407,272**	**100.0**	**453,787**	**100.00**	**547,873**	**100.0**	**564,766**	**100.0**	**723,249**	**100.0**	**1,043,839**	**100.0**	**1,094,792**	**100.0**
Sub-Saharan Africa[1]	30,870	9.9	28,210	8.2	19,262	4.7	17,422	3.8	29,033	5.3	32,538	5.8	31,470	4.4	35,364	3.4	39,479	3.6
East Africa	6,260	2.0	6,730	2.0	7,592	1.9	7,596	1.7	13,516	2.5	13,635	2.4	8,863	1.2	7,690	0.7	9,093	0.8
Central Africa	1,130	0.4	1,540	0.4	1,647	0.4	1,346	0.3	1,859	0.3	2,825	0.5	2,831	0.4	3,311	0.3	3,562	0.3
Southern Africa	1,480	0.5	2,360	0.7	2,835	0.7	2,657	0.6	3,304	0.6	2,232	0.4	5,330	0.7	6,263	0.6	6,429	0.6
West Africa	22,000	7.1	17,580	5.1	7,178	1.8	5,818	1.3	10,346	1.9	13,846	2.5	14,446	2.0	18,100	1.7	20,395	1.9
Nigeria	17,350	5.6	13,710	4.0	3,714	0.9	2,093	0.5	3,820	0.7	6,192	1.1	7,148	1.0	10,674	1.0	12,693	1.2
Asia	94,640	30.3	156,830	45.6	229,825	56.4	259,893	57.3	302,058	55.1	327,785	58.0	461,790	63.8	689,525	66.1	758,076	69.2
East Asia	51,650	16.6	80,720	23.5	146,017	35.9	166,717	36.7	189,371	34.6	197,576	35.0	286,925	39.7	439,702	42.1	468,304	42.8
China	2,770	0.9	13,980	4.1	39,597	9.7	39,613	8.7	59,939	10.9	62,582	11.1	157,558	21.8	328,547	31.5	363,341	33.2
Hong Kong	9,660	3.1	10,710	3.1	12,625	3.1	12,018	2.6	7,627	1.4	7,849	1.4	8,136	1.1	7,923	0.8	7,162	0.7
Japan	13,500	4.3	13,360	3.9	36,611	9.0	45,531	10.0	46,497	8.5	38,712	6.9	21,290	2.9	19,060	1.8	18,753	1.7
South Korea	6,150	2.0	18,660	5.4	23,362	5.7	36,231	8.0	45,685	8.3	59,022	10.5	73,351	10.1	61,007	5.8	54,555	5.0
Taiwan	19,460	6.2	23,770	6.9	33,531	8.2	32,702	7.2	28,566	5.2	27,876	4.9	24,818	3.4	21,127	2.0	22,454	2.1
South and Central Asia	14,540	4.7	25,800	7.5	42,366	10.4	45,401	10.0	71,765	13.1	94,965	16.8	128,845	17.8	195,135	18.7	231,661	21.2
Bangladesh	1,180	0.4	1,930	0.6	2,533	0.6	3,360	0.7	4,114	0.8	2,581	0.5	2,873	0.4	6,513	0.6	7,496	0.7
India	9,250	3.0	16,070	4.7	28,857	7.1	31,743	7.0	54,664	10.0	76,503	13.5	103,895	14.4	165,918	15.9	196,271	17.9
Nepal	250	0.1	390	0.1	670	0.2	1,219	0.3	2,618	0.5	6,061	1.1	10,301	1.4	9,662	0.9	13,270	1.2
Pakistan	2,990	1.0	5,440	1.6	7,725	1.9	6,427	1.4	6,948	1.3	5,759	1.0	5,045	0.7	6,141	0.6	7,537	0.7
Southeast Asia	28,450	9.1	50,310	14.6	41,441	10.2	47,774	10.5	40,916	7.5	35,244	6.2	46,020	6.4	54,688	5.2	58,111	5.3
Indonesia	3,250	1.0	8,210	2.4	9,524	2.3	12,820	2.8	11,625	2.1	7,575	1.3	6,942	1.0	8,727	0.8	8,650	0.8
Malaysia	6,010	1.9	23,020	6.7	13,606	3.3	14,015	3.1	7,795	1.4	5,515	1.0	6,735	0.9	7,834	0.8	8,271	0.8
Singapore	1,320	0.4	3,930	1.1	4,495	1.1	4,098	0.9	4,166	0.8	3,909	0.7	4,316	0.6	4,865	0.5	4,575	0.4
Thailand	6,550	2.1	6,940	2.0	7,092	1.7	12,165	2.7	11,187	2.0	8,765	1.6	8,236	1.1	7,113	0.7	6,636	0.6
Vietnam	6,490	2.1	3,270	1.0	1,396	0.3	922	0.2	2,022	0.4	4,597	0.8	14,888	2.1	21,403	2.1	24,325	2.2
Europe[2]	28,650	9.2	38,910	11.3	55,422	13.6	76,855	16.9	93,784	17.1	84,697	15.0	84,296	11.7	91,915	8.8	92,655	8.5
France	2,570	0.8	3,680	1.1	5,633	1.4	5,710	1.3	7,273	1.3	6,640	1.2	8,098	1.1	8,764	0.8	8,802	0.8
Germany[3]	3,310	1.1	4,730	1.4	7,003	1.7	9,017	2.0	10,128	1.8	8,829	1.6	9,458	1.3	10,145	1.0	10,042	0.9
Italy	1,250	0.4	1,890	0.5	2,393	0.6	2,780	0.6	3,490	0.6	3,224	0.6	4,308	0.6	5,155	0.5	5,789	0.5
Russia[4]	630	0.2	83	#	1,206	0.3	5,589	1.2	6,858	1.3	4,801	0.9	4,692	0.6	5,444	0.5	5,518	0.5
Spain	950	0.3	1,740	0.5	4,304	1.1	4,809	1.1	4,156	0.8	3,455	0.6	4,330	0.6	6,640	0.6	7,489	0.7
Sweden	1,020	0.3	1,400	0.4	2,029	0.5	3,889	0.9	4,598	0.8	3,212	0.6	3,236	0.4	4,297	0.4	3,543	0.3
Turkey[2]	2,600	0.8	2,460	0.7	4,078	1.0	7,678	1.7	10,983	2.0	11,622	2.1	12,184	1.7	10,691	1.0	10,520	1.0
United Kingdom	4,440	1.4	5,940	1.7	7,298	1.8	7,799	1.7	8,139	1.5	8,274	1.5	8,947	1.2	11,599	1.1	11,460	1.0
Latin America	49,810	16.0	45,480	13.2	47,318	11.6	47,253	10.4	63,634	11.6	64,769	11.5	64,169	8.9	84,908	8.1	79,920	7.3
Caribbean	10,650	3.4	11,100	3.2	12,349	3.0	10,737	2.4	14,423	2.6	13,855	2.5	11,644	1.6	11,042	1.1	11,289	1.0
Central America	12,970	4.2	12,740	3.7	15,949	3.9	14,220	3.1	16,764	3.1	19,709	3.5	20,361	2.8	24,983	2.4	24,002	2.2
Mexico	6,730	2.2	5,460	1.6	6,739	1.7	8,687	1.9	10,670	1.9	13,931	2.5	13,713	1.9	16,733	1.6	15,468	1.4
South America	26,190	8.4	21,640	6.3	19,019	4.7	22,296	4.9	32,447	5.9	31,205	5.5	32,164	4.4	48,883	4.7	44,629	4.1
Brazil	2,870	0.9	2,840	0.8	3,898	1.0	5,497	1.2	8,846	1.6	7,009	1.2	8,777	1.2	19,370	1.9	14,620	1.3
Colombia	3,930	1.3	4,010	1.2	3,183	0.8	3,462	0.8	6,765	1.2	6,835	1.2	6,456	0.9	7,815	0.7	7,976	0.7
Venezuela	11,750	3.8	7,040	2.0	2,894	0.7	4,456	1.0	5,217	1.0	4,792	0.8	5,491	0.8	8,267	0.8	8,371	0.8
Middle East and North Africa[1]	88,700	28.4	54,100	15.7	32,177	7.9	24,488	5.4	28,842	5.3	21,576	3.8	47,963	6.6	108,227	10.4	91,375	8.3
Middle East[2]	81,390	26.1	48,120	14.0	27,636	6.8	21,066	4.6	23,658	4.3	17,806	3.2	42,543	5.9	100,926	9.7	84,107	7.7
Iran	47,550	15.2	14,210	4.1	6,262	1.5	2,628	0.6	1,844	0.3	2,420	0.4	5,626	0.8	12,269	1.2	12,783	1.2
Kuwait	2,990	1.0	3,810	1.1	1,624	0.4	3,035	0.7	3,045	0.6	1,703	0.3	2,998	0.4	9,772	0.9	10,190	0.9
Saudi Arabia	10,440	3.3	6,900	2.0	3,584	0.9	4,191	0.9	5,273	1.0	3,448	0.6	22,704	3.1	61,287	5.9	44,432	4.1
North Africa[1]	7,310	2.3	5,980	1.7	4,541	1.1	3,422	0.8	5,184	0.9	3,770	0.7	5,420	0.7	7,301	0.7	7,268	0.7
Egypt	1,860	0.6	2,270	0.7	1,777	0.4	1,490	0.3	2,255	0.4	1,509	0.3	2,181	0.3	3,442	0.3	3,701	0.3
North America[5]	14,790	4.7	16,030	4.7	18,949	4.7	23,644	5.2	25,888	4.7	28,699	5.1	27,941	3.9	26,973	2.6	25,909	2.4
Canada	14,320	4.6	15,410	4.5	18,350	4.5	23,005	5.1	25,279	4.6	28,202	5.0	27,546	3.8	26,973	2.6	25,909	2.4
Oceania	4,180	1.3	4,030	1.2	4,230	1.0	4,202	0.9	4,624	0.8	4,702	0.8	5,610	0.8	6,917	0.7	7,372	0.7
Australia	1,530	0.5	1,530	0.4	1,906	0.5	2,244	0.5	2,645	0.5	2,806	0.5	3,777	0.5	4,752	0.5	4,908	0.4
Unidentified[6]	240	0.1	190	0.1	89	#	30	#	10	#	#	#	10	#	10	#	6	#

#Rounds to zero.
[1]North Africa was combined with the Middle East to create the "Middle East and North Africa" category as of 2012–13, and the former "Africa" category was replaced by "Sub-Saharan Africa" (which excludes North Africa). Data for years prior to 2012–13 have been revised for comparability.
[2]Cyprus and Turkey were classified as being in the Middle East prior to 2004–05 but in Europe for 2004–05 and later years. Data for years prior to 2004–05 have been revised for comparability.
[3]Data for 1980–81 and 1985–86 are for West Germany (Federal Republic of Germany before unification).
[4]Data for 1980–81, 1985–86, and 1990–91 are for the former U.S.S.R.
[5]Excludes Mexico and Central America, which are included in Latin America.
[6]Place of origin unknown or undeclared.
NOTE: Includes foreign students enrolled in American Samoa, Guam, Puerto Rico, and the U.S. Virgin Islands. Totals and subtotals include other countries not shown separately. Region totals may not sum to continent totals because some continent totals include students who are not classified by country or region. Data are for "nonimmigrants" (i.e., students who have not migrated to the United States). Detail may not sum to totals because of rounding. Some data have been revised from previously published figures.
SOURCE: Institute of International Education, *Open Doors: Report on International Educational Exchange*, selected years, 1981 through 2018. (This table was prepared December 2018.)

Table 311.10. Number and percentage distribution of students enrolled in postsecondary institutions, by level, disability status, and selected student characteristics: 2015–16

[Standard errors appear in parentheses]

Selected student characteristic	Undergraduate						Postbaccalaureate					
	All students		Students with disabilities[1]		Students without disabilities		All students		Students with disabilities[1]		Students without disabilities	
1	2		3		4		5		6		7	
Number of students (in thousands)	19,308	(—)	3,755	(—)	15,554	(—)	3,547	(—)	423	(—)	3,124	(—)
Percentage distribution of students												
Total	**100.0**	**(†)**	**19.4**	**(0.21)**	**80.6**	**(0.21)**	**100.0**	**(†)**	**11.9**	**(0.45)**	**88.1**	**(0.45)**
Sex												
Male	100.0	(†)	19.2	(0.33)	80.8	(0.33)	100.0	(†)	9.9	(0.57)	90.1	(0.57)
Female	100.0	(†)	19.6	(0.26)	80.4	(0.26)	100.0	(†)	13.3	(0.57)	86.7	(0.57)
Race/ethnicity of student												
White	100.0	(†)	20.8	(0.31)	79.2	(0.31)	100.0	(†)	13.0	(0.59)	87.0	(0.59)
Black	100.0	(†)	17.2	(0.50)	82.8	(0.50)	100.0	(†)	10.3	(0.94)	89.7	(0.94)
Hispanic	100.0	(†)	18.3	(0.47)	81.7	(0.47)	100.0	(†)	14.3	(1.53)	85.7	(1.53)
Asian	100.0	(†)	15.2	(0.69)	84.8	(0.69)	100.0	(†)	6.2	(0.88)	93.8	(0.88)
Pacific Islander	100.0	(†)	23.6	(4.44)	76.4	(4.44)	100.0	(†)	14.9 !	(6.07)	85.1	(6.07)
American Indian/Alaska Native	100.0	(†)	27.8	(2.71)	72.2	(2.71)	100.0	(†)	11.8 !	(4.60)	88.2	(4.60)
Two or more races	100.0	(†)	22.1	(1.25)	77.9	(1.25)	100.0	(†)	19.7	(3.61)	80.3	(3.61)
Age												
15 to 23	100.0	(†)	17.6	(0.27)	82.4	(0.27)	100.0	(†)	8.1	(1.13)	91.9	(1.13)
24 to 29	100.0	(†)	21.6	(0.55)	78.4	(0.55)	100.0	(†)	11.3	(0.67)	88.7	(0.67)
30 or older	100.0	(†)	22.6	(0.48)	77.4	(0.48)	100.0	(†)	13.5	(0.66)	86.5	(0.66)
Attendance status[2]												
Full-time, full-year	100.0	(†)	17.3	(0.28)	82.7	(0.28)	100.0	(†)	12.0	(0.67)	88.0	(0.67)
Part-time or part-year	100.0	(†)	20.8	(0.28)	79.2	(0.28)	100.0	(†)	11.9	(0.57)	88.1	(0.57)
Student housing status												
On-campus	100.0	(†)	15.8	(0.49)	84.2	(0.49)	—	(†)	—	(†)	—	(†)
Off-campus	100.0	(†)	20.6	(0.31)	79.4	(0.31)	—	(†)	—	(†)	—	(†)
With parents or relatives	100.0	(†)	19.5	(0.45)	80.5	(0.45)	—	(†)	—	(†)	—	(†)
Attended more than one institution	100.0	(†)	18.7	(0.55)	81.3	(0.55)	—	(†)	—	(†)	—	(†)
Dependency status												
Dependent	100.0	(†)	17.2	(0.28)	82.8	(0.28)	—	(†)	—	(†)	—	(†)
Independent, unmarried	100.0	(†)	23.9	(0.55)	76.1	(0.55)	100.0	(†)	11.5	(0.61)	88.5	(0.61)
Independent, married	100.0	(†)	20.5	(1.07)	79.5	(1.07)	100.0	(†)	10.3	(1.12)	89.7	(1.12)
Independent with dependents	100.0	(†)	20.3	(0.41)	79.7	(0.41)	100.0	(†)	13.4	(0.74)	86.6	(0.74)
Veteran status												
Veteran	100.0	(†)	25.8	(0.98)	74.2	(0.98)	100.0	(†)	17.1	(1.09)	82.9	(1.09)
Not veteran	100.0	(†)	19.1	(0.22)	80.9	(0.22)	100.0	(†)	11.6	(0.47)	88.4	(0.47)
Field of study												
Business/management	100.0	(†)	17.7	(0.46)	82.3	(0.46)	100.0	(†)	9.9	(0.97)	90.1	(0.97)
Education	100.0	(†)	17.9	(0.92)	82.1	(0.92)	100.0	(†)	12.5	(1.25)	87.5	(1.25)
Engineering/computer science/mathematics	100.0	(†)	19.6	(0.75)	80.4	(0.75)	100.0	(†)	6.8	(0.90)	93.2	(0.90)
Health	100.0	(†)	18.3	(0.40)	81.7	(0.40)	100.0	(†)	12.2	(0.90)	87.8	(0.90)
Humanities	100.0	(†)	21.5	(0.60)	78.5	(0.60)	100.0	(†)	14.1	(1.72)	85.9	(1.72)
Law	—	(†)	—	(†)	—	(†)	100.0	(†)	15.0	(2.33)	85.0	(2.33)
Life/physical sciences	100.0	(†)	17.9	(0.74)	82.1	(0.74)	100.0	(†)	11.6	(1.81)	88.4	(1.81)
Social/behavioral sciences	100.0	(†)	21.8	(0.82)	78.2	(0.82)	100.0	(†)	17.5	(1.90)	82.5	(1.90)
Vocational/technical	100.0	(†)	21.6	(1.36)	78.4	(1.36)	—	(†)	—	(†)	—	(†)
Undeclared	100.0	(†)	21.7	(1.55)	78.3	(1.55)	—	(†)	—	(†)	—	(†)
Other	100.0	(†)	20.2	(0.64)	79.8	(0.64)	100.0	(†)	12.5	(1.29)	87.5	(1.29)

—Not available.
†Not applicable.
!Interpret data with caution. The coefficient of variation (CV) for this estimate is between 30 and 50 percent.
[1]Students with disabilities are those who reported having deafness or serious difficulty hearing; blindness or serious difficulty seeing; serious difficulty concentrating, remembering, or making decisions because of a physical, mental, or emotional condition; or serious difficulty walking or climbing stairs. For 2015–16, the question about difficulty concentrating, remembering, or making decisions was expanded to include examples of relevant conditions. Specifically, students were instructed to "consider conditions including, but not limited to, a serious learning disability, depression, ADD, or ADHD." The percentage of students reporting difficulty concentrating, remembering, or making decisions was 17 percent in 2015–16 (after the examples were added) and 8 percent in 2011–12 (before the examples were added). Due to addition of the examples, estimates of the percentage of students with this type of disability in 2015–16 and of the overall percentage of students with disabilities in 2015–16 cannot be compared to estimates of the percentages in earlier years.
[2]Full-time, full-year includes students enrolled full time for 9 or more months. Part-time or part-year includes students enrolled part time for 9 or more months and students enrolled less than 9 months either part time or full time.
NOTE: Data are based on a sample survey of students who enrolled at any time during the school year. Data exclude students attending institutions in Puerto Rico. Detail may not sum to totals because of rounding. Race categories exclude persons of Hispanic ethnicity.
SOURCE: U.S. Department of Education, National Center for Education Statistics, 2015–16 National Postsecondary Student Aid Study (NPSAS:16). (This table was prepared May 2018.)

Table 311.15. Number and percentage of students enrolled in degree-granting postsecondary institutions, by distance education participation, location of student, level of enrollment, and control and level of institution: Fall 2016 and fall 2017

Year, level of enrollment, and control and level of institution	Number of students: Total	Number: No distance education courses	Number: Taking any distance education course(s): Total, any distance education course(s)	Number: At least one, but not all, of student's courses	Number: Exclusively distance education courses, by location of student: Total	Number: Same state	Number: Different state	Number: State not known	Number: Outside of the United States	Number: Location unknown	Percent of students: Total	Percent: No distance education courses	Percent: Taking any distance education course(s): Total, any distance education course(s)	Percent: At least one, but not all, of student's courses	Percent: Exclusively distance education courses, by location of student: Total	Percent: Same state	Percent: Different state	Percent: State not known	Percent: Outside of the United States	Percent: Location unknown
1	2	3	4	5	6	7	8	9	10	11	12	13	14	15	16	17	18	19	20	21
Fall 2016																				
All students, total	**19,846,904**	**13,541,976**	**6,304,928**	**3,326,965**	**2,977,963**	**1,681,115**	**1,215,684**	**15,611**	**42,621**	**22,932**	**100.0**	**68.2**	**31.8**	**16.8**	**15.0**	**8.5**	**6.1**	**0.1**	**0.2**	**0.1**
Public	14,585,840	10,202,578	4,383,262	2,835,550	1,547,712	1,303,698	202,598	9,893	16,250	15,273	100.0	69.9	30.1	19.4	10.6	8.9	1.4	0.1	0.1	0.1
Private	5,261,064	3,339,398	1,921,666	491,415	1,430,251	377,417	1,013,086	5,718	26,371	7,659	100.0	63.5	36.5	9.3	27.2	7.2	19.3	0.1	0.5	0.1
Nonprofit	4,078,956	2,980,222	1,098,734	368,772	729,962	263,812	442,332	3,443	14,331	6,044	100.0	73.1	26.9	9.0	17.9	6.5	10.8	0.1	0.4	0.1
For-profit	1,182,108	359,176	822,932	122,643	700,289	113,605	570,754	2,275	12,040	1,615	100.0	30.4	69.6	10.4	59.2	9.6	48.3	0.2	1.0	0.1
Fall 2017																				
All students, total	**19,765,598**	**13,114,062**	**6,651,536**	**3,548,036**	**3,103,500**	**1,771,852**	**1,155,197**	**15,539**	**142,841**	**18,071**	**100.0**	**66.3**	**33.7**	**18.0**	**15.7**	**9.0**	**5.8**	**0.1**	**0.7**	**0.1**
4-year	13,823,640	9,104,456	4,719,184	2,388,821	2,330,363	1,070,036	1,095,665	11,430	139,343	13,889	100.0	65.9	34.1	17.3	16.9	7.7	7.9	0.1	1.0	0.1
2-year	5,941,958	4,009,606	1,932,352	1,159,215	773,137	701,816	59,532	4,109	3,498	4,182	100.0	67.5	32.5	19.5	13.0	11.8	1.0	0.1	0.1	0.1
Public	14,560,155	9,869,414	4,690,741	3,033,556	1,657,185	1,390,179	225,567	11,280	17,578	12,581	100.0	67.8	32.2	20.8	11.4	9.5	1.5	0.1	0.1	0.1
4-year	8,853,477	6,039,424	2,814,053	1,900,127	913,926	694,501	189,249	7,224	14,112	8,840	100.0	68.2	31.8	21.5	10.3	7.8	2.1	0.1	0.2	0.1
2-year	5,706,678	3,829,990	1,876,688	1,133,429	743,259	695,678	36,318	4,056	3,466	3,741	100.0	67.1	32.9	19.9	13.0	12.2	0.6	0.1	0.1	0.1
Private	5,205,443	3,244,648	1,960,795	514,480	1,446,315	381,673	929,630	4,259	125,263	5,490	100.0	62.3	37.7	9.9	27.8	7.3	17.9	0.1	2.4	0.1
Nonprofit	4,106,477	2,925,915	1,180,562	392,155	788,407	273,120	394,339	3,158	114,932	2,858	100.0	71.3	28.7	9.5	19.2	6.7	9.6	0.1	2.8	0.1
4-year	4,058,087	2,901,355	1,156,732	388,046	768,686	270,201	377,541	3,157	114,930	2,857	100.0	71.5	28.5	9.6	18.9	6.7	9.3	0.1	2.8	0.1
2-year	48,390	24,560	23,830	4,109	19,721	2,919	16,798	1	2	1	100.0	50.8	49.2	8.5	40.8	6.0	34.7	#	#	#
For-profit	1,098,966	318,733	780,233	122,325	657,908	108,553	535,291	1,101	10,331	2,632	100.0	29.0	71.0	11.1	59.9	9.9	48.7	0.1	0.9	0.2
4-year	912,076	163,677	748,399	100,648	647,751	105,334	528,875	1,049	10,301	2,192	100.0	17.9	82.1	11.0	71.0	11.5	58.0	0.1	1.1	0.2
2-year	186,890	155,056	31,834	21,677	10,157	3,219	6,416	52	30	440	100.0	83.0	17.0	11.6	5.4	1.7	3.4	#	#	0.2
Undergraduate	**16,760,331**	**11,251,714**	**5,508,617**	**3,273,825**	**2,234,792**	**1,394,756**	**716,977**	**9,546**	**98,321**	**15,192**	**100.0**	**67.1**	**32.9**	**19.5**	**13.3**	**8.3**	**4.3**	**0.1**	**0.6**	**0.1**
4-year	10,818,373	7,242,108	3,576,265	2,114,610	1,461,655	692,940	657,445	5,437	94,823	11,010	100.0	66.9	33.1	19.5	13.5	6.4	6.1	0.1	0.9	0.1
2-year	5,941,958	4,009,606	1,932,352	1,159,215	773,137	701,816	59,532	4,109	3,498	4,182	100.0	67.5	32.5	19.5	13.0	11.8	1.0	0.1	0.1	0.1
Public	13,100,953	8,878,747	4,222,206	2,888,930	1,333,276	1,175,665	128,505	7,140	10,587	11,379	100.0	67.8	32.2	22.1	10.2	9.0	1.0	0.1	0.1	0.1
4-year	7,394,275	5,048,757	2,345,518	1,755,501	590,017	479,987	92,187	3,084	7,121	7,638	100.0	68.3	31.7	23.7	8.0	6.5	1.2	#	0.1	0.1
2-year	5,706,678	3,829,990	1,876,688	1,133,429	743,259	695,678	36,318	4,056	3,466	3,741	100.0	67.1	32.9	19.9	13.0	12.2	0.6	0.1	0.1	0.1
Private	3,659,378	2,372,967	1,286,411	384,895	901,516	219,091	588,472	2,406	87,734	3,813	100.0	64.8	35.2	10.5	24.6	6.0	16.1	0.1	2.4	0.1
Nonprofit	2,817,017	2,082,341	734,676	275,000	459,676	137,490	236,605	1,583	82,643	1,355	100.0	73.9	26.1	9.8	16.3	4.9	8.4	0.1	2.9	#
4-year	2,768,627	2,057,781	710,846	270,891	439,955	134,571	219,807	1,582	82,641	1,354	100.0	74.3	25.7	9.8	15.9	4.9	7.9	0.1	3.0	#
2-year	48,390	24,560	23,830	4,109	19,721	2,919	16,798	1	2	1	100.0	50.8	49.2	8.5	40.8	6.0	34.7	#	#	#
For-profit	842,361	290,626	551,735	109,895	441,840	81,601	351,867	823	5,091	2,458	100.0	34.5	65.5	13.0	52.5	9.7	41.8	0.1	0.6	0.3
4-year	655,471	135,570	519,901	88,218	431,683	78,382	345,451	771	5,061	2,018	100.0	20.7	79.3	13.5	65.9	12.0	52.7	0.1	0.8	0.3
2-year	186,890	155,056	31,834	21,677	10,157	3,219	6,416	52	30	440	100.0	83.0	17.0	11.6	5.4	1.7	3.4	#	#	0.2
Postbaccalaureate	**3,005,267**	**1,862,348**	**1,142,919**	**274,211**	**868,708**	**377,096**	**438,220**	**5,993**	**44,520**	**2,879**	**100.0**	**62.0**	**38.0**	**9.1**	**28.9**	**12.5**	**14.6**	**0.2**	**1.5**	**0.1**
Public	1,459,202	990,667	468,535	144,626	323,909	214,514	97,062	4,140	6,991	1,202	100.0	67.9	32.1	9.9	22.2	14.7	6.7	0.3	0.5	0.1
Private	1,546,065	871,681	674,384	129,585	544,799	214,514	97,062	4,140	6,991	1,202	100.0	56.4	43.6	8.4	35.2	13.9	6.3	0.3	0.5	0.1
Nonprofit	1,289,460	843,574	445,886	117,155	328,731	135,630	157,734	1,575	32,289	1,503	100.0	65.4	34.6	9.1	25.5	10.5	12.2	0.1	2.5	0.1
For-profit	256,605	28,107	228,498	12,430	216,068	26,952	183,424	278	5,240	174	100.0	11.0	89.0	4.8	84.2	10.5	71.5	0.1	2.0	0.1

#Rounds to zero.
NOTE: Degree-granting institutions grant associate's or higher degrees and participate in Title IV federal financial aid programs. Some data have been revised from previously published figures.

SOURCE: U.S. Department of Education, National Center for Education Statistics, Integrated Postsecondary Education Data System (IPEDS), Spring 2017 and Spring 2018, Fall Enrollment component. (This table was prepared January 2019.)

Table 311.22. Number and percentage of undergraduate students enrolled in distance education or online classes and degree programs, by selected characteristics: Selected years, 2003–04 through 2015–16

[Standard errors appear in parentheses]

Selected characteristic	Percent of undergraduate students taking distance education or online classes												2015–16					
	2003–04				2007–08				2011–12				Number of undergraduate students (in thousands)		Percent of undergraduate students taking online classes			
	Total, any distance education classes		Entire degree program through distance education[1]		Total, any distance education classes		Entire degree program through distance education[1]		Total, any online classes		Entire degree program is online[1]		Total, all students	Number taking any online classes	Total, any online classes		Entire degree program is online[1]	
1	2		3		4		5		6		7		8	9	10		11	
Total	**15.6**	**(0.29)**	**4.9**	**(0.17)**	**20.6**	**(0.23)**	**3.8**	**(0.16)**	**32.0**	**(0.33)**	**6.5**	**(0.18)**	**19,308**	**8,319**	**43.1**	**(0.31)**	**10.8**	**(0.21)**
Sex																		
Male	13.6	(0.31)	4.3	(0.19)	18.8	(0.31)	3.4	(0.16)	28.5	(0.45)	4.9	(0.24)	8,406	3,340	39.7	(0.42)	9.2	(0.27)
Female	17.0	(0.40)	5.4	(0.23)	21.9	(0.28)	4.2	(0.22)	34.5	(0.39)	7.7	(0.21)	10,903	4,979	45.7	(0.42)	12.1	(0.28)
Race/ethnicity																		
White	16.2	(0.33)	5.0	(0.19)	21.9	(0.29)	3.9	(0.19)	33.5	(0.41)	6.8	(0.21)	10,276	4,671	45.5	(0.39)	11.1	(0.27)
Black	14.9	(0.59)	4.9	(0.37)	19.9	(0.66)	5.1	(0.48)	32.7	(0.70)	9.1	(0.56)	3,006	1,278	42.5	(0.72)	14.9	(0.47)
Hispanic	13.4	(0.54)	4.1	(0.27)	16.5	(0.53)	2.7	(0.23)	27.9	(0.57)	4.3	(0.24)	3,723	1,431	38.4	(0.68)	7.7	(0.32)
Asian	14.0	(0.92)	5.2	(0.58)	18.1	(0.86)	2.9	(0.40)	26.0	(1.06)	2.9	(0.35)	1,399	544	38.9	(1.10)	7.8	(0.63)
Pacific Islander	19.1	(2.37)	6.9	(1.69)	17.0	(1.89)	1.2 !	(0.53)	29.9	(3.18)	3.1 !	(1.29)	83	35	42.2	(4.02)	12.0	(2.44)
American Indian/Alaska Native	15.5	(1.85)	6.2	(1.41)	21.9	(2.41)	1.8 !	(0.55)	32.6	(2.56)	7.0	(1.43)	160	76	47.5	(3.08)	12.2	(1.71)
Two or more races	16.5	(1.33)	5.1	(1.16)	20.4	(1.08)	3.6	(0.86)	30.6	(1.48)	5.5	(0.69)	661	283	42.8	(1.39)	10.4	(0.89)
Age																		
15 to 23	11.7	(0.26)	3.1	(0.13)	15.2	(0.22)	1.4	(0.09)	26.5	(0.36)	3.2	(0.13)	11,368	4,157	36.6	(0.38)	3.5	(0.13)
24 to 29	18.4	(0.46)	6.7	(0.41)	25.7	(0.56)	5.6	(0.45)	36.5	(0.67)	8.0	(0.41)	3,536	1,793	50.7	(0.69)	17.5	(0.52)
30 or older	22.4	(0.65)	8.3	(0.42)	30.0	(0.55)	9.0	(0.40)	40.9	(0.64)	13.0	(0.50)	4,404	2,369	53.8	(0.58)	24.9	(0.58)
Attendance status																		
Full-time, full-year[2]	12.7	(0.32)	3.8	(0.20)	16.7	(0.33)	3.2	(0.29)	28.8	(0.41)	6.5	(0.20)	7,239	2,789	38.5	(0.44)	6.0	(0.28)
Part-time only, for only part of year	18.7	(0.46)	6.9	(0.32)	24.8	(0.39)	5.2	(0.22)	35.3	(0.62)	7.4	(0.38)	5,059	2,398	47.4	(0.62)	14.7	(0.44)
Mixed attendance status[3]	17.4	(0.53)	4.7	(0.23)	22.5	(0.42)	2.9	(0.20)	35.0	(0.62)	5.0	(0.28)	7,010	3,131	44.7	(0.47)	13.2	(0.38)
Undergraduate field of study																		
Business/management	18.7	(0.58)	7.0	(0.43)	24.2	(0.55)	6.4	(0.45)	39.3	(0.75)	11.4	(0.45)	2,973	1,525	51.3	(0.72)	17.0	(0.67)
Computer/information science	19.5	(0.96)	7.2	(0.71)	26.9	(1.53)	8.4	(1.17)	40.8	(1.37)	9.8	(0.81)	852	415	48.6	(1.60)	16.1	(1.10)
Education	17.1	(0.89)	4.6	(0.45)	22.8	(0.81)	3.2	(0.33)	33.8	(1.17)	6.4	(0.59)	841	384	45.7	(1.35)	9.7	(0.81)
Engineering	12.1	(0.83)	3.3	(0.40)	16.1	(0.77)	2.3	(0.36)	23.2	(0.93)	2.3	(0.48)	1,140	380	33.3	(0.91)	5.1	(0.51)
Health	17.4	(0.48)	5.6	(0.30)	21.9	(0.60)	4.2	(0.33)	33.3	(0.67)	6.7	(0.43)	3,438	1,547	45.0	(0.72)	13.3	(0.53)
Humanities	14.0	(0.53)	3.9	(0.26)	19.7	(0.53)	2.6	(0.22)	30.8	(0.65)	4.1	(0.33)	3,083	1,274	41.3	(0.66)	7.8	(0.40)
Life sciences	11.0	(0.81)	2.7	(0.39)	15.8	(0.68)	1.8	(0.21)	26.7	(0.92)	3.3	(0.37)	1,413	540	38.2	(0.91)	5.0	(0.53)
Mathematics	12.8	(2.48)	3.8 !	(1.42)	15.1	(2.51)	‡	(†)	20.4	(3.02)	2.2 !	(1.05)	118	50	42.2	(3.98)	9.7	(2.80)
Physical sciences	9.8	(2.02)	0.9 !	(0.41)	12.8	(1.56)	0.3 !	(0.16)	22.1	(1.93)	1.2 !	(0.46)	214	70	32.8	(2.45)	2.0 !	(0.67)
Social/behavioral sciences	12.5	(0.63)	3.4	(0.33)	17.1	(0.68)	2.3	(0.31)	31.8	(0.93)	7.0	(0.48)	1,323	556	42.0	(1.05)	9.1	(0.54)
Vocational/technical	13.1	(0.96)	4.2	(0.60)	18.5	(1.26)	3.3	(0.50)	22.3	(1.54)	2.8	(0.59)	594	188	31.7	(1.67)	6.0	(0.75)
Undeclared/no major	15.0	(0.61)	4.6	(0.34)	20.5	(0.56)	3.1	(0.45)	27.6	(1.16)	5.2	(0.81)	449	148	33.0	(1.71)	9.5	(1.12)
Other	14.4	(0.68)	4.3	(0.29)	19.0	(0.69)	3.9	(0.38)	30.5	(0.83)	6.9	(0.50)	2,279	983	43.1	(0.93)	11.4	(0.55)
Had job during academic year[4]																		
Yes	16.8	(0.34)	5.5	(0.22)	22.2	(0.25)	4.2	(0.16)	36.2	(0.42)	7.6	(0.24)	11,812	5,563	47.1	(0.39)	12.9	(0.28)
No	11.9	(0.32)	3.3	(0.17)	15.8	(0.37)	2.8	(0.25)	24.9	(0.42)	4.8	(0.20)	7,496	2,756	36.8	(0.44)	7.6	(0.25)
Dependency status																		
Dependent	11.1	(0.24)	2.9	(0.13)	14.4	(0.24)	1.0	(0.08)	25.5	(0.36)	2.7	(0.12)	9,772	3,428	35.1	(0.37)	1.9	(0.10)
Independent, no dependents, not married[5]	15.6	(0.50)	5.1	(0.37)	23.6	(0.56)	4.8	(0.30)	33.6	(0.64)	6.7	(0.33)	3,978	1,840	46.2	(0.69)	14.9	(0.45)
Independent, no dependents, married	19.6	(0.78)	6.9	(0.52)	28.6	(0.96)	7.2	(0.84)	37.4	(1.22)	10.1	(0.72)	953	528	55.4	(1.30)	20.8	(1.09)
Independent, with dependents, not married[5]	20.5	(0.70)	6.9	(0.49)	25.3	(0.61)	7.4	(0.52)	38.2	(0.67)	10.7	(0.45)	2,618	1,375	52.5	(0.80)	22.9	(0.74)
Independent, with dependents, married	25.1	(0.79)	9.7	(0.53)	32.9	(0.71)	9.4	(0.51)	44.9	(0.92)	14.7	(0.75)	1,987	1,148	57.8	(0.89)	27.1	(0.84)
Control and level of institution																		
Public	16.2	(0.35)	4.7	(0.18)	21.5	(0.25)	2.7	(0.11)	33.2	(0.39)	4.0	(0.16)	14,491	6,362	43.9	(0.37)	6.3	(0.21)
4-year	13.5	(0.54)	3.8	(0.23)	18.4	(0.41)	2.2	(0.19)	32.7	(0.51)	4.3	(0.24)	6,786	2,956	43.6	(0.50)	6.1	(0.40)
2-year	18.2	(0.43)	5.4	(0.25)	23.9	(0.33)	3.1	(0.16)	33.9	(0.54)	3.8	(0.24)	7,640	3,400	44.5	(0.58)	6.6	(0.25)
Less-than-2-year	11.8	(1.19)	3.0	(0.66)	8.1	(1.66)	1.9 !	(0.73)	11.3	(2.24)	‡	(†)	66	6	9.4	(1.89)	‡	(†)
Private nonprofit	12.3	(0.79)	4.1	(0.46)	14.3	(0.43)	2.9	(0.23)	21.0	(0.85)	4.5	(0.57)	2,955	1,060	35.9	(0.68)	17.8	(0.54)
4-year	12.3	(0.83)	4.1	(0.48)	14.2	(0.44)	2.8	(0.23)	21.3	(0.87)	4.6	(0.59)	2,857	1,033	36.2	(0.65)	17.7	(0.47)
2-year	11.2	(2.20)	3.1 !	(1.11)	19.4	(2.30)	5.9	(1.02)	12.7	(3.26)	0.5 !	(0.22)	95	26	27.5 !	(8.33)	21.2 !	(8.99)
Less-than-2-year	17.2	(2.63)	8.1	(1.35)	15.6 !	(4.69)	2.7	(0.66)	13.6 !	(5.68)	#	(†)	4	1	28.6	(1.46)	17.0	(2.97)
Private for-profit	15.3	(1.08)	8.6	(1.06)	21.7	(1.18)	12.8	(1.24)	35.5	(0.83)	21.6	(0.82)	1,861	896	48.1	(0.94)	33.5	(1.22)
4-year	26.3	(2.25)	15.6	(2.26)	29.1	(1.95)	19.1	(1.92)	53.0	(1.26)	33.3	(1.30)	1,102	816	74.0	(1.38)	55.0	(1.96)
2-year	12.1	(1.64)	6.3	(1.25)	17.6	(1.49)	8.0	(1.34)	8.4	(1.28)	2.9 !	(1.01)	420	59	14.1	(1.05)	3.0	(0.46)
Less-than-2-year	5.4	(0.26)	1.9	(0.13)	6.2	(0.40)	1.8	(0.28)	3.9	(0.77)	‡	(†)	340	21	6.2	(0.70)	1.1	(0.22)

†Not applicable.
#Rounds to zero.
!Interpret data with caution. The coefficient of variation (CV) for this estimate is between 30 and 50 percent.
‡Reporting standards not met. Either there are too few cases for a reliable estimate or the coefficient of variation (CV) is 50 percent or greater.
[1]Excludes students not in a degree or certificate program.
[2]Includes only students enrolled full-time for a full academic year (defined as 9 or more months).
[3]Includes students enrolled part-time for a full academic year, as well as, students enrolled full-time, but for only part of an academic year.
[4]Excludes work study/assistantships.
[5]Includes separated.

NOTE: In 2011–12 and 2015–16, students were asked whether they took classes that were taught entirely online and, if so, whether their entire degree program was online. In 2003–04 and 2007–08, students were asked about distance education, which was defined in 2007–08 as "primarily delivered using live, interactive audio or videoconferencing, pre-recorded instructional videos, webcasts, CD-ROM, or DVD, or computer-based systems delivered over the Internet." The 2003–04 definition was very similar, with only minor differences in wording. In both years, distance education did not include correspondence courses. Data exclude students attending institutions in Puerto Rico. Detail may not sum to totals because of rounding. Race categories exclude persons of Hispanic ethnicity.
SOURCE: U.S. Department of Education, National Center for Education Statistics, 2003–04, 2007–08, 2011–12, and 2015–16 National Postsecondary Student Aid Study (NPSAS:04, NPSAS:08, NPSAS:12, and NPSAS:16). (This table was prepared May 2018.)

Table 311.32. Number and percentage of graduate students enrolled in distance education or online classes and degree programs, by selected characteristics: Selected years, 2003–04 through 2015–16

[Standard errors appear in parentheses]

Selected characteristic	Percent of graduate students taking distance education classes												2015–16					
	2003–04				2007–08				2011–12				Number of graduate students (in thousands)		Percent of graduate students taking online classes			
	Total, any distance education classes		Entire degree program through distance education[1]		Total, any distance education classes		Entire degree program through distance education[1]		Total, any online classes		Entire degree program is online[1]		Total, all graduate students	Number taking any online classes	Total, any online classes		Entire degree program is online[1]	
1	2		3		4		5		6		7		8	9	10		11	
Total	**16.5**	**(0.76)**	**6.1**	**(0.58)**	**22.8**	**(0.76)**	**9.5**	**(0.68)**	**36.0**	**(0.74)**	**18.2**	**(0.63)**	**3,547**	**1,617**	**45.6**	**(0.72)**	**27.3**	**(0.75)**
Sex																		
Male	15.4	(1.17)	4.9	(0.74)	20.6	(1.17)	7.8	(1.07)	31.5	(1.17)	15.9	(1.06)	1,446	591	40.8	(0.95)	24.6	(1.02)
Female	17.3	(1.00)	7.0	(0.74)	24.2	(0.99)	10.6	(0.77)	39.0	(0.97)	19.8	(0.78)	2,101	1,026	48.9	(0.91)	29.3	(0.85)
Race/ethnicity																		
White	17.7	(0.88)	6.7	(0.74)	23.6	(0.99)	9.6	(0.95)	36.9	(0.98)	18.2	(0.88)	2,105	942	44.8	(0.93)	26.0	(0.90)
Black	19.2	(2.44)	7.5	(1.72)	25.8	(2.94)	11.5	(2.11)	48.8	(2.12)	31.4	(1.66)	504	315	62.5	(2.22)	45.3	(2.17)
Hispanic	13.1	(1.81)	5.0	(1.26)	23.7	(3.09)	9.4 !	(2.85)	34.6	(2.73)	17.9	(2.53)	326	161	49.5	(2.03)	31.2	(2.12)
Asian	9.4	(1.40)	3.0 !	(1.01)	12.8	(1.10)	4.5	(0.68)	19.4	(1.67)	6.0	(1.13)	500	138	27.5	(1.71)	10.8	(1.33)
Pacific Islander	‡	(†)	‡	(†)	31.1 !	(9.43)	13.5 !	(6.20)	44.2	(11.10)	‡	(†)	8	5	64.1	(11.99)	33.4 !	(11.23)
American Indian/Alaska Native	8.7 !	(3.54)	‡	(†)	16.7 !	(6.78)	‡	(†)	55.1	(12.39)	43.4 !	(15.26)	17	8	43.9	(9.31)	33.1	(7.59)
Two or more races	17.1	(4.46)	4.8 !	(2.33)	27.7 !	(8.38)	21.3 !	(9.56)	40.4	(4.24)	18.4	(3.84)	88	49	55.6	(4.48)	33.8	(4.20)
Age																		
15 to 23	11.1	(1.73)	3.7	(0.77)	16.6	(2.64)	1.6	(0.40)	19.5	(1.45)	4.3	(0.76)	466	130	27.9	(1.82)	8.0	(1.32)
24 to 29	13.6	(0.82)	3.6	(0.43)	16.1	(0.79)	5.7	(0.54)	30.8	(1.05)	14.4	(0.91)	1,387	525	37.8	(0.96)	16.8	(0.87)
30 or older	20.2	(1.21)	9.0	(1.06)	29.5	(1.39)	14.5	(1.31)	44.3	(1.21)	24.9	(1.01)	1,695	962	56.8	(1.02)	41.6	(1.00)
Attendance status																		
Full-time, full-year[2]	12.0	(1.00)	3.4	(0.72)	16.4	(1.35)	6.5	(1.24)	31.7	(1.16)	17.4	(0.98)	1,279	408	31.9	(0.96)	15.2	(0.81)
Part-time only, for only part of year	20.0	(1.01)	8.8	(0.97)	28.1	(1.17)	13.3	(1.07)	41.0	(1.21)	19.5	(1.21)	850	453	53.3	(1.54)	36.7	(1.72)
Mixed attendance status[3]	15.6	(1.89)	4.1	(0.71)	23.6	(2.15)	6.8	(0.95)	36.9	(1.98)	17.9	(1.66)	1,418	756	53.3	(1.09)	33.1	(1.06)
Graduate field of study																		
Business/management	22.6	(2.30)	10.3	(1.98)	27.6	(2.90)	13.9	(2.68)	40.0	(2.09)	25.1	(1.82)	592	320	54.1	(1.65)	36.7	(1.84)
Education	20.7	(1.74)	8.2	(1.29)	28.3	(1.67)	9.9	(1.36)	48.9	(1.65)	23.7	(1.47)	605	352	58.2	(1.73)	34.3	(1.82)
Health	12.6	(1.23)	3.9	(0.79)	22.0	(1.59)	8.9	(1.33)	36.5	(1.42)	16.5	(1.00)	694	325	46.8	(1.58)	26.6	(1.45)
Humanities	12.9	(2.43)	2.9 !	(0.87)	15.7	(1.72)	3.1	(0.65)	28.1	(3.13)	12.1	(2.88)	281	99	35.3	(2.76)	18.2	(2.32)
Law	5.6	(1.15)	‡	(†)	6.1	(0.87)	1.7 !	(0.54)	10.3	(1.46)	2.5	(0.65)	132	21	15.9	(2.09)	8.0	(1.63)
Life and physical sciences	—	(†)	—	(†)	—	(†)	—	(†)	13.9	(1.49)	5.3	(1.21)	197	39	19.9	(2.06)	9.1	(1.77)
Life sciences	12.4	(2.51)	6.9 !	(2.14)	14.0	(2.15)	4.3	(1.14)	—	(†)	—	(†)	—	—	—	(†)	—	(†)
Mathematics, engineering, and computer science	12.0	(2.03)	4.6 !	(1.48)	19.7	(3.06)	9.4 !	(2.96)	25.5	(1.78)	13.3	(1.42)	374	135	36.0	(1.87)	19.9	(1.56)
Social/behavioral sciences	8.5	(1.42)	3.4 !	(1.11)	21.3	(3.66)	12.7	(3.68)	36.6	(2.22)	21.7	(1.89)	245	112	45.7	(2.98)	29.0	(3.28)
Other[4]	19.0	(1.56)	4.6	(1.08)	22.2	(1.49)	9.4	(1.49)	38.6	(2.03)	19.2	(2.29)	427	214	50.2	(2.00)	32.7	(2.14)
Had job during academic year[5]																		
Yes	19.6	(0.97)	7.7	(0.78)	27.2	(0.89)	11.9	(0.79)	43.7	(0.91)	24.1	(0.79)	2,354	1,274	54.1	(0.90)	34.4	(0.98)
No	9.0	(0.81)	2.7	(0.41)	10.0	(1.36)	2.8 !	(1.27)	19.9	(1.12)	6.2	(0.78)	1,193	342	28.7	(1.08)	13.5	(0.75)
Dependency status																		
Dependent	—	(†)	—	(†)	—	(†)	—	(†)	—	(†)	—	(†)	—	—	—	(†)	—	(†)
Independent, no dependents, not married[6]	12.1	(0.75)	3.7	(0.39)	16.6	(0.90)	5.2	(0.59)	28.1	(0.88)	11.8	(0.67)	1,901	674	35.5	(0.90)	16.9	(0.86)
Independent, no dependents, married	15.5	(1.22)	5.0	(0.77)	22.3	(1.67)	10.1	(1.56)	36.1	(1.75)	19.5	(1.64)	503	247	49.1	(1.78)	27.6	(1.53)
Independent, with dependents, not married[6]	21.3	(3.18)	9.4	(2.21)	26.8	(3.23)	10.8	(1.86)	52.0	(2.49)	32.5	(2.54)	312	198	63.5	(2.06)	45.7	(2.05)
Independent, with dependents, married	24.2	(1.72)	10.8	(1.46)	34.2	(1.76)	17.5	(2.14)	45.6	(1.60)	25.1	(1.52)	831	498	59.9	(1.48)	44.4	(1.52)
Control of institution																		
Public	15.2	(0.68)	4.8	(0.39)	23.1	(0.99)	8.9	(0.95)	32.8	(0.93)	11.8	(0.69)	1,665	708	42.5	(0.99)	21.2	(1.07)
Private nonprofit	16.3	(1.25)	6.7	(1.03)	18.5	(0.74)	6.0	(0.41)	28.5	(1.16)	12.3	(1.03)	1,514	618	40.8	(1.17)	23.7	(1.11)
Private for-profit	35.3	(8.12)	18.6 !	(6.64)	41.6	(5.47)	29.9	(5.89)	74.1	(2.09)	62.5	(2.49)	368	290	78.9	(1.26)	68.5	(1.99)

—Not available.
†Not applicable.
!Interpret data with caution. The coefficient of variation (CV) for this estimate is between 30 and 50 percent.
‡Reporting standards not met. Either there are too few cases for a reliable estimate or the coefficient of variation (CV) is 50 percent or greater.
[1]Excludes students not in a degree or certificate program.
[2]Includes only students enrolled full time for a full academic year (defined as 9 or more months).
[3]Includes students enrolled part time for a full academic year as well as students enrolled full time, but for only part of an academic year.
[4]Includes students who are not in a degree program or have not declared a major. For 2003–04 and 2007–08, includes physical sciences.
[5]Excludes work study/assistantships.
[6]Includes separated.
NOTE: In 2011–12 and 2015–16, students were asked whether they took classes that were taught entirely online and, if so, whether their entire degree program was online. In 2003–04 and 2007–08, students were asked about distance education, which was defined in 2007–08 as "primarily delivered using live, interactive audio or videoconferencing, prerecorded instructional videos, webcasts, CD-ROM, or DVD, or computer-based systems delivered over the Internet." The 2003–04 definition was very similar, with only minor differences in wording. In both years, distance education did not include correspondence courses. Data exclude students attending institutions in Puerto Rico. Detail may not sum to totals because of rounding. Race categories exclude persons of Hispanic ethnicity.
SOURCE: U.S. Department of Education, National Center for Education Statistics, 2003–04, 2007–08, 2011–12, and 2015–16 National Postsecondary Student Aid Study (NPSAS:04, NPSAS:08, NPSAS:12, and NPSAS:16). (This table was prepared May 2018.)

Table 311.33. Selected statistics for degree-granting postsecondary institutions that primarily offer online programs, by control of institution and selected characteristics: Fall 2017 and 2016–17

Selected characteristic	All institutions	Primarily online institutions[1]					Other institutions[1]			
		Total	Percent of all institutions	Public	Nonprofit	For-profit	Total	Public	Nonprofit	For-profit
1	2	3	4	5	6	7	8	9	10	11
Number of institutions, fall 2017[2]	**4,298**	**103**	**2.4**	**9**	**31**	**63**	**4,195**	**1,617**	**1,656**	**922**
Fall 2017 enrollment										
Total enrollment	19,765,598	823,068	4.2	75,669	270,107	477,292	18,942,530	14,484,486	3,836,370	621,674
Full-time	12,077,304	428,223	3.5	19,269	158,580	250,374	11,649,081	8,308,804	2,923,706	416,571
Males	5,424,575	139,413	2.6	7,408	49,523	82,482	5,285,162	3,850,537	1,279,473	155,152
Females	6,652,729	288,810	4.3	11,861	109,057	167,892	6,363,919	4,458,267	1,644,233	261,419
Part-time	7,688,294	394,845	5.1	56,400	111,527	226,918	7,293,449	6,175,682	912,664	205,103
Males	3,143,057	145,369	4.6	25,978	44,158	75,233	2,997,688	2,593,997	347,286	56,405
Females	4,545,237	249,476	5.5	30,422	67,369	151,685	4,295,761	3,581,685	565,378	148,698
Undergraduate	16,760,331	580,744	3.5	57,715	212,461	310,568	16,179,587	13,043,238	2,604,556	531,793
Full-time	10,370,665	311,200	3.0	16,421	124,013	170,766	10,059,465	7,499,634	2,175,332	384,499
Part-time	6,389,666	269,544	4.2	41,294	88,448	139,802	6,120,122	5,543,604	429,224	147,294
Postbaccalaureate	3,005,267	242,324	8.1	17,954	57,646	166,724	2,762,943	1,441,248	1,231,814	89,881
Full-time	1,706,639	117,023	6.9	2,848	34,567	79,608	1,589,616	809,170	748,374	32,072
Part-time	1,298,628	125,301	9.6	15,106	23,079	87,116	1,173,327	632,078	483,440	57,809
White	10,510,784	455,265	4.3	49,940	172,455	232,870	10,055,519	7,591,295	2,229,243	234,981
Black	2,545,916	211,886	8.3	6,742	50,546	154,598	2,334,030	1,716,102	446,051	171,877
Hispanic	3,540,584	86,705	2.4	11,401	26,227	49,077	3,453,879	2,912,342	406,514	135,023
Asian	1,277,733	23,625	1.8	3,143	7,524	12,958	1,254,108	971,955	251,999	30,154
Pacific Islander	52,015	4,889	9.4	283	1,383	3,223	47,126	33,339	9,154	4,633
American Indian/Alaska Native	137,632	6,648	4.8	556	1,913	4,179	130,984	107,333	17,665	5,986
Two or more races	700,212	28,100	4.0	2,866	8,949	16,285	672,112	527,970	125,275	18,867
Nonresident alien	1,000,722	5,950	0.6	738	1,110	4,102	994,772	624,150	350,469	20,153
4-year institutions	13,823,640	800,346	5.8	75,195	251,544	473,607	13,023,294	8,778,282	3,806,543	438,469
Full-time	9,849,327	408,638	4.1	19,060	140,969	248,609	9,440,689	6,291,428	2,900,227	249,034
Part-time	3,974,313	391,708	9.9	56,135	110,575	224,998	3,582,605	2,486,854	906,316	189,435
2-year institutions	5,941,958	22,722	0.4	474	18,563	3,685	5,919,236	5,706,204	29,827	183,205
Full-time	2,227,977	19,585	0.9	209	17,611	1,765	2,208,392	2,017,376	23,479	167,537
Part-time	3,713,981	3,137	0.1	265	952	1,920	3,710,844	3,688,828	6,348	15,668
Earned degrees conferred, 2016–17										
Associate's	1,005,649	25,951	2.6	743	4,888	20,320	979,698	861,116	51,675	66,907
Males	394,159	10,363	2.6	448	1,772	8,143	383,796	343,868	18,184	21,744
Females	611,490	15,588	2.5	295	3,116	12,177	595,902	517,248	33,491	45,163
Bachelor's	1,956,032	91,230	4.7	8,957	25,691	56,582	1,864,802	1,266,799	540,688	57,315
Males	836,045	33,607	4.0	3,793	8,941	20,873	802,438	556,029	223,546	22,863
Females	1,119,987	57,623	5.1	5,164	16,750	35,709	1,062,364	710,770	317,142	34,452
Master's	804,684	62,305	7.7	4,425	15,301	42,579	742,379	369,962	345,051	27,366
Males	326,892	19,787	6.1	1,795	5,505	12,487	307,105	157,668	139,810	9,627
Females	477,792	42,518	8.9	2,630	9,796	30,092	435,274	212,294	205,241	17,739
Doctor's[3]	181,352	4,991	2.8	48	221	4,722	176,361	91,484	81,324	3,553
Males	84,646	1,661	2.0	7	60	1,594	82,985	44,162	37,579	1,244
Females	96,706	3,330	3.4	41	161	3,128	93,376	47,322	43,745	2,309
First-time students' rates of graduation from and retention at first institution attended										
Among full-time bachelor's degree-seekers starting at 4-year institutions in 2011, percent earning bachelor's degree										
Within 4 years after start	41.6	6.5	†	10.3	38.4	4.0	42.0	36.9	54.3	19.5
Within 5 years after start	56.5	10.6	†	19.2	43.1	8.0	57.1	55.0	64.2	24.1
Within 6 years after start	60.4	12.0	†	20.5	43.9	9.5	61.0	59.7	66.5	26.2
Among full-time degree/certificate-seekers starting at 2-year institutions in 2014, percent completing credential within 150 percent of normal time	31.6	‡	†	29.8	64.8	37.1	30.6	25.1	57.3	61.2
Among degree-seekers starting in 2016, percent returning in 2017										
Full-time entrants	75.5	47.5	†	74.5	61.3	33.8	75.6	74.3	81.3	65.3
Part-time entrants	45.4	43.9	†	50.8	43.4	42.5	45.4	45.6	44.4	38.1

†Not applicable.
‡Reporting standards not met (too few cases for a reliable estimate).
[1]Primarily online institutions have more than 90 percent of their students attending classes exclusively online. Other institutions may have some online offerings, but they are not primarily online.
[2]Includes only institutions reporting enrollment data in fall 2017.
[3]Includes Ph.D., Ed.D., and comparable degrees at the doctoral level, as well as such degrees as M.D., D.D.S., and law degrees that were classified as first-professional degrees prior to 2010–11.

NOTE: Degree-granting institutions grant associate's or higher degrees and participate in Title IV federal financial aid programs. Race categories exclude persons of Hispanic ethnicity.
SOURCE: U.S. Department of Education, National Center for Education Statistics, Integrated Postsecondary Education Data System (IPEDS), Spring 2018, Fall Enrollment component; IPEDS, Fall 2017, Completions component; and IPEDS, Winter 2017–18, Graduation Rates component. (This table was prepared May 2019.)

Table 311.40. Percentage of first-year undergraduate students who reported taking remedial education courses, by selected student and institution characteristics: Selected years, 2003–04 through 2015–16

[Standard errors appear in parentheses]

Selected student or institution characteristic	Percent of 2003–04 first-year undergraduates[1] who took any remedial courses		Percent of 2007–08 first-year undergraduates[1] who took any remedial courses		Percent of 2011–12 first-year undergraduates[1] who took any remedial courses		2015–16 first-year undergraduates[1]					
							Total number of students[2] (in thousands)	Students who took any remedial courses			Percent who took specific remedial courses in 2015–16	
	Ever	In 2003–04	Ever	In 2007–08	Ever	In 2011–12		Percent who ever took	Percent who took in 2015–16 (in thousands)	Percent who took in 2015–16	Mathematics	Reading/writing
1	2	3	4	5	6	7	8	9	10	11	12	13
Total	**34.8 (0.36)**	**19.2 (0.30)**	**36.2 (0.38)**	**20.0 (0.35)**	**32.6 (0.42)**	**19.7 (0.36)**	**7,706**	**43.0 (0.58)**	**1,482**	**19.2 (0.43)**	**14.0 (0.36)**	**8.8** (0.28)
Sex												
Male	33.0 (0.53)	18.4 (0.46)	33.0 (0.53)	19.3 (0.51)	30.8 (0.61)	19.9 (0.55)	3,364	40.7 (0.82)	643	19.1 (0.67)	13.9 (0.58)	8.5 (0.38)
Female	36.2 (0.54)	19.8 (0.39)	38.7 (0.51)	20.6 (0.46)	34.0 (0.52)	19.7 (0.46)	4,342	44.8 (0.66)	839	19.3 (0.50)	14.1 (0.41)	8.9 (0.36)
Race/ethnicity												
White	31.7 (0.42)	17.8 (0.35)	31.3 (0.46)	17.7 (0.41)	29.4 (0.51)	17.7 (0.47)	3,683	38.3 (0.76)	620	16.8 (0.48)	12.6 (0.42)	7.0 (0.33)
Black	41.2 (1.00)	22.4 (0.76)	45.1 (0.99)	24.4 (0.86)	37.6 (0.89)	22.2 (0.75)	1,419	48.7 (1.05)	292	20.6 (0.78)	15.0 (0.74)	10.2 (0.62)
Hispanic	38.5 (0.91)	21.5 (0.72)	43.7 (1.12)	23.3 (0.84)	35.8 (0.99)	22.4 (0.81)	1,726	47.7 (0.97)	397	23.0 (0.98)	16.7 (0.82)	10.7 (0.60)
Asian	39.6 (1.72)	17.6 (1.56)	38.9 (2.05)	20.0 (1.90)	37.6 (2.25)	23.0 (1.75)	490	45.4 (1.83)	97	19.8 (1.48)	13.9 (1.28)	10.4 (1.11)
Pacific Islander	40.8 (5.11)	22.4 (4.55)	39.9 (4.63)	19.1 (3.90)	33.4 (5.16)	15.2 (3.50)	37	43.7 (6.07)	‡	21.8 (5.04)	12.0 ! (3.73)	10.6 ! (4.44)
American Indian/Alaska Native	44.8 (4.34)	23.7 (3.10)	47.9 (4.66)	29.7 (3.88)	34.9 (4.11)	19.8 (2.79)	79	50.1 (5.64)	19	23.8 (4.98)	12.0 (3.30)	13.9 (4.10)
Two or more races	33.9 (2.02)	20.9 (1.80)	32.3 (2.29)	20.4 (2.06)	29.8 (2.02)	19.0 (1.68)	271	41.1 (2.28)	49	18.1 (1.79)	12.8 (1.55)	8.4 (1.35)
Other	31.1 (2.78)	17.3 (2.34)	35.2 (6.00)	21.7 (5.11)	— (†)	— (†)	—	— (†)	—	— (†)	— (†)	— (†)
Age												
15 to 23	33.7 (0.41)	21.5 (0.39)	34.5 (0.46)	22.0 (0.43)	31.0 (0.49)	21.1 (0.38)	4,678	41.0 (0.70)	912	19.5 (0.52)	14.5 (0.46)	9.8 (0.37)
24 to 29	35.0 (0.99)	16.0 (0.78)	39.7 (0.98)	19.5 (0.86)	34.4 (1.12)	17.2 (0.91)	1,332	47.4 (1.17)	252	18.9 (0.94)	13.9 (0.82)	6.6 (0.52)
30 or older	37.6 (0.87)	15.6 (0.52)	38.1 (0.84)	15.2 (0.68)	35.4 (0.94)	18.4 (0.82)	1,696	45.1 (1.06)	318	18.8 (0.81)	13.0 (0.66)	7.5 (0.56)
Attendance status												
Full-time, full-year[3]	31.4 (0.45)	19.1 (0.37)	31.4 (0.52)	19.4 (0.46)	28.1 (0.48)	17.6 (0.41)	3,254	36.7 (0.78)	550	16.9 (0.58)	12.5 (0.48)	8.5 (0.43)
Part-time only, for only part of year	37.5 (0.65)	17.9 (0.51)	39.8 (0.71)	19.0 (0.59)	37.4 (0.81)	21.3 (0.78)	3,033	47.7 (0.92)	616	20.3 (0.74)	14.5 (0.63)	8.1 (0.46)
Mixed attendance status[4]	41.1 (0.97)	23.7 (0.85)	42.6 (0.98)	26.3 (0.93)	37.0 (0.95)	23.4 (0.74)	1,419	47.4 (0.97)	316	22.2 (0.83)	16.4 (0.69)	10.8 (0.59)
Student housing status												
On-campus	24.5 (0.70)	16.8 (0.56)	23.2 (0.84)	17.1 (0.76)	17.9 (0.78)	14.1 (0.67)	921	24.7 (1.26)	120	13.0 (0.89)	9.7 (0.82)	6.8 (0.64)
Off-campus	35.9 (0.58)	17.0 (0.40)	37.2 (0.57)	17.8 (0.49)	34.0 (0.65)	19.6 (0.63)	3,810	45.9 (0.78)	720	18.9 (0.58)	13.6 (0.50)	8.2 (0.39)
With parents or relatives	37.9 (0.59)	24.5 (0.61)	39.6 (0.78)	25.2 (0.66)	35.3 (0.78)	22.2 (0.61)	2,293	47.6 (1.04)	545	23.7 (0.79)	17.7 (0.69)	11.2 (0.51)
Attended more than one institution	36.5 (1.18)	18.3 (0.98)	36.1 (1.11)	20.2 (0.97)	32.7 (1.09)	17.0 (0.95)	682	36.0 (1.07)	97	14.2 (0.81)	9.9 (0.59)	6.4 (0.49)
Dependency status												
Dependent	33.4 (0.45)	22.1 (0.41)	34.4 (0.51)	22.8 (0.46)	31.2 (0.53)	22.0 (0.42)	3,843	39.5 (0.77)	749	19.5 (0.55)	14.4 (0.50)	9.7 (0.41)
Independent	36.4 (0.61)	16.1 (0.39)	38.1 (0.59)	17.1 (0.51)	33.9 (0.57)	17.6 (0.52)	3,863	46.5 (0.76)	732	19.0 (0.55)	13.7 (0.47)	7.8 (0.36)
Veteran status												
Veteran	35.9 (2.33)	13.2 (1.52)	35.8 (2.36)	17.1 (2.08)	31.4 (2.21)	17.4 (1.74)	363	43.9 (2.08)	62	17.1 (1.53)	12.2 (1.38)	6.7 (0.99)
Not veteran	34.8 (0.38)	19.4 (0.31)	36.2 (0.38)	20.1 (0.36)	32.7 (0.42)	19.8 (0.37)	7,343	43.0 (0.58)	1,420	19.3 (0.43)	14.1 (0.37)	8.9 (0.30)
Field of study[5]												
Business/management	36.4 (1.00)	19.6 (0.97)	37.0 (1.13)	21.7 (1.06)	32.7 (1.11)	19.8 (0.85)	996	42.6 (1.37)	182	18.2 (0.95)	13.8 (0.86)	9.2 (0.70)
Computer science	33.7 (1.59)	19.2 (1.39)	34.7 (2.28)	19.8 (1.77)	29.3 (1.69)	17.4 (1.40)	329	41.0 (2.14)	64	19.4 (1.78)	14.8 (1.58)	8.9 (1.24)
Education	41.5 (1.61)	23.1 (1.14)	40.3 (1.90)	23.0 (1.48)	36.0 (1.84)	21.6 (1.53)	289	46.6 (2.33)	64	22.1 (1.91)	18.2 (1.81)	8.8 (1.37)
Engineering	30.9 (1.79)	16.6 (1.41)	33.0 (1.81)	19.0 (1.57)	33.1 (1.88)	20.9 (1.63)	394	38.6 (2.02)	70	17.8 (1.66)	13.7 (1.54)	9.0 (1.11)
Health	37.0 (0.83)	19.7 (0.68)	38.6 (2.49)	18.9 (4.49)	34.6 (0.74)	18.8 (0.70)	1,531	46.5 (1.09)	293	19.1 (0.87)	14.7 (0.75)	9.2 (0.68)
Humanities	34.0 (1.29)	18.8 (0.94)	31.2 (1.94)	20.5 (1.77)	36.6 (1.03)	23.9 (0.91)	1,421	46.8 (1.13)	292	20.5 (0.97)	14.4 (0.84)	9.0 (0.64)
Life sciences	31.2 (1.81)	19.7 (1.72)	31.2 (6.21)	20.5 ! (8.64)	26.7 (1.71)	17.9 (1.11)	386	36.4 (2.03)	69	18.0 (1.56)	14.0 (1.53)	8.2 (1.16)
Mathematics	23.0 (5.55)	11.0 ! (4.43)	41.1 (6.31)	15.6 ! (5.20)	14.3 ! (4.57)	8.4 ! (2.81)	29	36.4 (7.45)	‡	13.2 ! (4.85)	12.1 ! (4.68)	‡ (†)
Physical sciences	24.0 (4.39)	12.9 (3.49)	24.5 (4.31)	15.7 (3.92)	29.2 (4.72)	24.7 (4.59)	62	37.2 (6.96)	‡	15.4 (3.50)	9.2 (2.47)	7.6 (2.27)
Social/behavioral sciences	33.2 (2.08)	19.4 (1.57)	35.0 (2.16)	23.4 (1.94)	27.7 (1.87)	19.8 (1.38)	341	42.4 (2.23)	66	19.2 (1.61)	13.9 (1.40)	9.6 (1.30)
Vocational/technical	38.5 (2.11)	18.3 (1.60)	31.1 (1.93)	15.7 (1.78)	26.9 (1.94)	15.7 (1.59)	336	33.0 (2.32)	51	15.3 (1.64)	11.3 (1.41)	8.4 (1.16)
Undeclared	33.6 (0.67)	19.2 (0.59)	35.8 (1.29)	20.0 (1.14)	31.8 (2.10)	22.0 (1.86)	297	45.0 (2.56)	77	25.8 (2.15)	18.4 (1.97)	11.6 (1.57)
Other	33.3 (1.49)	18.0 (1.06)	34.6 (1.23)	18.5 (0.97)	29.3 (0.94)	16.7 (0.77)	930	42.6 (1.36)	174	18.7 (1.01)	12.8 (0.94)	8.0 (0.67)

See notes at end of table.

Table 311.40. Percentage of first-year undergraduate students who reported taking remedial education courses, by selected student and institution characteristics: Selected years, 2003–04 through 2015–16—Continued

[Standard errors appear in parentheses]

Selected student or institution characteristic	Percent of 2003–04 first-year undergraduates[1] who took any remedial courses: Ever		Percent of 2003–04 first-year undergraduates[1] who took any remedial courses: In 2003–04		Percent of 2007–08 first-year undergraduates[1] who took any remedial courses: Ever		Percent of 2007–08 first-year undergraduates[1] who took any remedial courses: In 2007–08		Percent of 2011–12 first-year undergraduates[1] who took any remedial courses: Ever		Percent of 2011–12 first-year undergraduates[1] who took any remedial courses: In 2011–12		2015–16 first-year undergraduates[1]: Total number of students[2] (in thousands)	2015–16: Students who took any remedial courses: Percent who ever took		2015–16: Students who took any remedial courses: Percent who took in 2015–16 (in thousands)	2015–16: Students who took any remedial courses: Percent who took in 2015–16		2015–16: Percent who took specific remedial courses in 2015–16: Mathematics		2015–16: Percent who took specific remedial courses in 2015–16: Reading/writing	
1	2		3		4		5		6		7		8	9		10	11		12		13	
Control and level of institution																						
Public less-than-2-year	30.6	(1.85)	10.9	(1.09)	31.9	(1.99)	9.0	(0.89)	30.2	(6.13)	12.2 !	(3.86)	55	33.0	(3.85)	‡	10.9	(1.54)	8.4	(1.61)	6.9	(0.93)
Public 2-year	41.4	(0.59)	23.0	(0.47)	41.8	(0.54)	23.7	(0.48)	40.3	(0.67)	25.6	(0.64)	4,275	52.5	(0.76)	1,082	25.3	(0.63)	18.6	(0.53)	10.8	(0.42)
Public 4-year nondoctorate	34.2	(1.77)	21.4	(1.12)	38.9	(1.24)	25.4	(1.14)	37.8	(2.12)	24.3	(1.30)	692	44.4	(1.92)	125	18.1	(1.28)	13.9	(1.09)	7.8	(0.77)
Public 4-year doctorate	25.7	(1.11)	16.3	(0.64)	25.0	(1.03)	17.8	(0.86)	21.9	(0.84)	15.6	(0.80)	819	26.2	(1.35)	96	11.7	(0.93)	9.0	(0.75)	5.7	(0.72)
Private nonprofit less-than-4-year	31.3	(2.06)	12.9	(1.89)	30.3	(3.75)	10.2	(2.81)	22.3	(4.25)	9.4 !	(3.42)	76	23.7	(1.86)	4	5.7 !	(2.02)	5.1 !	(2.05)	4.1 !	(2.06)
Private nonprofit 4-year nondoctorate	26.0	(1.16)	14.7	(0.78)	25.5	(1.74)	16.6	(1.46)	24.4	(1.66)	15.3	(1.23)	344	28.3	(1.88)	39	11.3	(0.93)	7.6	(0.91)	6.7	(0.71)
Private nonprofit 4-year doctorate	18.3	(1.67)	11.6	(1.39)	22.1	(1.70)	12.6	(1.38)	14.6	(1.85)	9.6	(1.24)	396	21.8	(1.71)	36	9.2	(1.07)	5.0	(0.97)	6.2	(0.93)
Private for-profit less-than-2-year	24.1	(0.50)	7.8	(0.23)	26.5	(1.02)	5.5	(0.51)	16.7	(0.74)	3.8	(0.56)	288	25.0	(1.10)	12	4.2	(0.69)	2.5	(0.49)	2.0	(0.50)
Private for-profit 2 years or more	25.4	(1.63)	11.7	(1.04)	28.8	(1.46)	11.3	(1.20)	20.9	(0.74)	8.2	(0.37)	761	33.9	(1.61)	82	10.7	(0.70)	7.5	(0.58)	6.7	(0.54)

—Not available.
†Not applicable.
!Interpret data with caution. The coefficient of variation (CV) for this estimate is between 30 and 50 percent.
‡Reporting standards not met. The coefficient of variation (CV) for this estimate is 50 percent or greater.
[1]First-year student status was determined by accumulation of credits. Students attending postsecondary education part time, or not completing the credit accumulation requirements for second-year status, could be considered first-year students for more than one year.
[2]Numbers may not equal those reported in other tables, since these data are based on a sample survey of students who enrolled at any time during the academic year.
[3]Includes only students enrolled full time for a full academic year (defined as 9 or more months).
[4]Includes students enrolled part time for a full academic year as well as students enrolled full time, but for only part of an academic year.
[5]Excludes students not in a degree or certificate program.
NOTE: Percentages of students who took remedial courses are based on student reports. Data exclude students attending institutions in Puerto Rico. Detail may not sum to totals because of survey item nonresponse and rounding. Race categories exclude persons of Hispanic ethnicity.
SOURCE: U.S. Department of Education, National Center for Education Statistics, 2003–04, 2007–08, 2011–12, and 2015–16 National Postsecondary Student Aid Study (NPSAS:04, NPSAS:08, NPSAS:12, and NPSAS:16). (This table was prepared June 2018.)

Table 311.60. Enrollment in postsecondary education, by level of enrollment, level of institution, student age, and major field of study: 2015–16

[Standard errors appear in parentheses]

Major field of study[1]	Undergraduate: All students: Total (in thousands)	Undergraduate: All students: Percentage distribution, by age: Under 25	Undergraduate: All students: Percentage distribution, by age: 25 to 35	Undergraduate: All students: Percentage distribution, by age: Over 35	Undergraduate: 2-year and less-than-2-year institutions[2]: Total (in thousands)	Undergraduate: 2-year and less-than-2-year institutions[2]: Percentage distribution, by age: Under 25	Undergraduate: 2-year and less-than-2-year institutions[2]: Percentage distribution, by age: 25 to 35	Undergraduate: 2-year and less-than-2-year institutions[2]: Percentage distribution, by age: Over 35	Undergraduate: 4-year institutions: Total (in thousands)	Undergraduate: 4-year institutions: Percentage distribution, by age: Under 25	Undergraduate: 4-year institutions: Percentage distribution, by age: 25 to 35	Undergraduate: 4-year institutions: Percentage distribution, by age: Over 35	Post-baccalaureate: Total (in thousands)
1	2	3	4	5	6	7	8	9	10	11	12	13	14
Total	**19,308**	**63.3 (0.32)**	**23.3 (0.26)**	**13.4 (0.23)**	**9,650**	**57.2 (0.56)**	**26.9 (0.45)**	**15.9 (0.37)**	**9,658**	**69.3 (0.40)**	**19.8 (0.32)**	**10.9 (0.26)**	**3,547**
Agriculture and related sciences	159	74.8 (3.22)	16.5 (2.56)	8.6 (1.91)	78	60.1 (5.38)	24.9 (4.62)	15.0 (3.49)	81	88.9 (2.10)	8.6 (1.72)	2.5 ! (0.99)	17
Anthropology	48	70.3 (5.64)	19.6 (5.01)	10.1! (4.77)	12	59.7 (17.51)	‡ (†)	‡ (†)	36	73.8 (5.28)	18.6 (4.93)	7.6 ! (3.42)	11
Architecture and related services	58	80.5 (4.08)	11.7 (3.14)	7.7! (3.50)	16	71.2 (8.57)	‡ (†)	14.9 ! (7.32)	42	84.1 (4.48)	10.9 ! (3.30)	‡ (†)	23
Area, ethnic, and gender studies	38	76.5 (5.27)	10.1! (3.05)	13.4! (4.93)	11	68.8 (13.23)	‡ (†)	‡ (†)	27	79.6 (4.89)	12.1 ! (3.74)	8.2 ! (3.74)	10
Biological and biomedical sciences	686	87.3 (1.03)	10.4 (0.88)	2.4 (0.52)	203	80.0 (2.03)	14.6 (1.56)	5.3 (1.59)	484	90.3 (1.05)	8.6 (1.01)	1.1 (0.30)	106
Business, management, and marketing	2,973	59.1 (0.79)	24.7 (0.61)	16.2 (0.56)	1,190	55.1 (1.61)	26.7 (1.34)	18.2 (0.94)	1,783	61.7 (1.00)	23.4 (0.75)	14.9 (0.71)	592
Communication and journalism	370	85.5 (1.23)	10.9 (1.11)	3.6 (0.56)	84	77.7 (3.16)	17.2 (2.84)	5.1 (1.39)	286	87.8 (1.30)	9.1 (1.14)	3.1 (0.67)	40
Communications technologies/technicians	97	68.9 (3.18)	20.8 (2.93)	10.2 (1.99)	50	63.0 (5.03)	23.5 (4.80)	13.5 (3.15)	47	75.1 (3.65)	18.0 (3.31)	6.8 ! (2.12)	‡
Computer and information sciences	852	53.0 (1.46)	29.5 (1.26)	17.4 (1.00)	396	50.8 (2.24)	28.6 (2.06)	20.6 (1.67)	456	55.0 (1.76)	30.3 (1.43)	14.7 (1.13)	131
Construction trades	85	41.6 (4.62)	41.5 (5.45)	16.9 (4.22)	74	40.2 (4.84)	41.3 (5.58)	18.5 (4.59)	11	50.6 (14.55)	43.0 ! (15.65)	‡ (†)	‡
Criminology	35	76.8 (4.92)	19.6 (4.64)	‡ (†)	9	70.1 (9.57)	26.6 ! (9.21)	‡ (†)	26	79.0 (5.99)	17.2 ! (5.55)	‡ (†)	‡
Economics	113	91.7 (2.13)	8.2 (2.11)	‡ (†)	17	76.8 (9.97)	23.2 ! (9.96)	‡ (†)	96	94.4 (1.44)	5.5 (1.41)	‡ (†)	16
Education	841	66.6 (1.16)	20.5 (0.96)	12.8 (0.90)	365	56.6 (2.21)	26.7 (1.81)	16.7 (1.75)	475	74.4 (1.25)	15.8 (1.12)	9.9 (0.90)	605
Engineering	799	82.6 (0.98)	13.2 (0.84)	4.2 (0.46)	244	70.9 (2.22)	21.8 (2.05)	7.3 (1.02)	555	87.7 (0.99)	9.5 (0.81)	2.8 (0.47)	188
Engineering technologies/technicians	341	49.0 (2.33)	31.8 (2.08)	19.2 (1.89)	222	46.5 (3.21)	32.0 (2.78)	21.5 (2.63)	120	53.5 (3.36)	31.3 (3.46)	15.2 (2.41)	26
English language and literature/letters	199	72.6 (4.22)	15.8 (1.93)	11.6 (3.23)	60	51.5 (9.53)	18.4 (3.70)	30.1 (7.76)	138	81.9 (2.55)	14.7 (2.31)	3.4 ! (1.06)	40
Family and consumer/human sciences	193	61.3 (2.83)	20.5 (1.93)	18.2 (2.31)	99	52.1 (4.35)	23.8 (3.25)	24.1 (3.89)	94	71.1 (3.12)	17.0 (2.35)	11.9 (2.47)	12
Foreign languages and literatures	84	74.8 (3.95)	15.9 (3.40)	9.3 (2.50)	28	58.7 (8.24)	25.4 (7.04)	15.9 ! (6.35)	55	83.0 (3.78)	11.1 ! (3.40)	5.9 ! (1.94)	11
Geography	20	61.6 (8.55)	22.4! (6.76)	‡ (†)	‡	‡ (†)	‡ (†)	‡ (†)	13	63.2 (7.94)	29.7 (8.31)	7.1 ! (2.78)	‡
Health professions and related sciences	3,438	50.0 (0.68)	32.0 (0.52)	18.0 (0.52)	2,067	48.0 (0.86)	33.7 (0.72)	18.3 (0.66)	1,371	53.0 (1.14)	29.5 (0.85)	17.5 (0.83)	694
History	112	71.8 (2.97)	21.0 (3.06)	7.2 (1.81)	27	70.5 (7.07)	27.3 (7.19)	2.2 ! (1.01)	85	72.2 (3.05)	19.0 (2.93)	8.8 (2.28)	25
International relations and affairs	38	89.2 (3.32)	9.2! (2.99)	‡ (†)	‡	‡ (†)	‡ (†)	‡ (†)	33	87.5 (3.71)	10.7 ! (3.39)	‡ (†)	12
Legal professions and studies	128	47.6 (3.84)	25.0 (2.84)	27.4 (3.80)	64	47.0 (5.95)	22.9 (4.54)	30.2 (6.45)	64	48.2 (5.31)	27.2 (3.43)	24.6 (5.15)	132
Liberal arts, sciences and humanities	1,915	66.4 (0.86)	21.6 (0.83)	12.0 (0.64)	1,426	64.7 (1.12)	23.0 (1.06)	12.2 (0.74)	490	71.3 (1.35)	17.5 (1.37)	11.2 (1.24)	31
Library science	‡	‡ (†)	‡ (†)	‡ (†)	‡	‡ (†)	‡ (†)	‡ (†)	‡	‡ (†)	‡ (†)	‡ (†)	11
Mathematics and statistics	118	83.5 (2.55)	13.0 (2.20)	3.5! (1.39)	35	78.2 (6.66)	14.8 ! (5.35)	‡ (†)	83	85.7 (2.42)	12.3 (2.37)	2.0 ! (0.79)	29
Mechanic and repair technologies	272	54.2 (2.77)	28.7 (1.93)	17.1 (2.00)	240	54.8 (2.94)	27.9 (2.02)	17.3 (2.19)	32	50.0 (9.84)	34.6 (8.02)	15.4 ! (4.90)	‡
Military technologies	‡	‡ (†)	‡ (†)	‡ (†)	‡	‡ (†)	‡ (†)	‡ (†)	‡	‡ (†)	‡ (†)	‡ (†)	‡
Multi/interdisciplinary studies	259	66.8 (2.32)	22.2 (1.87)	11.1 (1.62)	117	63.9 (3.61)	25.5 (3.10)	10.6 (2.07)	142	69.2 (2.77)	19.4 (2.26)	11.4 (2.34)	29
Natural resources and conservation	97	73.0 (3.38)	23.5 (3.47)	3.5! (1.07)	29	73.6 (5.57)	20.8 (5.23)	5.6 ! (2.61)	68	72.7 (4.13)	24.6 (4.31)	2.6 ! (1.24)	17
Parks, recreation, and fitness studies	302	84.7 (1.69)	11.7 (1.43)	3.6 (0.93)	98	75.9 (3.76)	15.5 (2.84)	8.6 ! (2.65)	204	88.9 (1.58)	9.9 (1.56)	1.2 (0.36)	26
Personal and culinary services	305	54.3 (2.18)	31.3 (1.78)	14.4 (1.49)	261	54.3 (2.36)	32.2 (1.97)	13.5 (1.66)	44	54.3 (4.94)	26.1 (3.76)	19.6 (3.63)	‡
Philosophy and religious studies	56	58.5 (7.65)	19.6 (4.71)	21.9! (7.00)	8	80.3 (11.32)	‡ (†)	‡ (†)	48	54.8 (8.39)	20.7 (5.36)	24.5 ! (7.93)	19
Physical sciences	214	82.1 (2.19)	14.7 (1.97)	3.3 (0.93)	76	75.1 (4.42)	19.8 (3.57)	5.0 ! (2.24)	139	85.9 (2.41)	11.9 (2.29)	2.3 ! (0.74)	46
Political science and government	144	85.7 (1.87)	10.5 (1.68)	3.7 (1.11)	28	86.0 (4.13)	8.7 ! (3.26)	5.3 ! (2.26)	116	85.6 (2.14)	11.0 (1.96)	3.4 ! (1.23)	25
Precision production	102	49.4 (4.74)	30.8 (4.57)	19.8 (3.37)	89	49.2 (5.31)	34.4 (4.84)	16.4 (3.00)	‡	‡ (†)	‡ (†)	‡ (†)	‡
Psychology	684	70.8 (1.41)	20.3 (1.27)	8.9 (0.79)	207	68.2 (2.96)	22.6 (2.84)	9.2 (1.46)	477	71.9 (1.59)	19.3 (1.41)	8.8 (0.89)	169
Public administration and social services	231	51.3 (2.58)	26.2 (2.23)	22.5 (1.77)	90	47.9 (4.91)	32.0 (4.06)	20.0 (2.61)	141	53.5 (2.56)	22.5 (2.28)	24.0 (2.28)	138
Science technologies/technicians	29	57.5 (7.71)	26.2 (6.66)	16.4 (4.50)	23	62.5 (8.59)	23.5 ! (7.40)	14.0 ! (5.26)	‡	‡ (†)	‡ (†)	‡ (†)	‡
Security and protective services	726	63.4 (1.38)	23.8 (1.13)	12.8 (0.96)	395	63.1 (1.97)	24.7 (1.77)	12.2 (1.50)	331	63.8 (1.75)	22.7 (1.31)	13.5 (1.27)	47

See notes at end of table.

Table 311.60. Enrollment in postsecondary education, by level of enrollment, level of institution, student age, and major field of study: 2015–16—Continued

[Standard errors appear in parentheses]

Major field of study[1]	Undergraduate: All students: Total (in thousands)	All students: Percentage distribution, by age: Under 25		25 to 35		Over 35		2-year and less-than-2-year institutions[2]: Total (in thousands)	Percentage distribution, by age: Under 25		25 to 35		Over 35		4-year institutions: Total (in thousands)	Percentage distribution, by age: Under 25		25 to 35		Over 35		Postbaccalaureate: Total (in thousands)
1	2	3		4		5		6	7		8		9		10	11		12		13		14
Social sciences, other	85	62.5	(4.62)	20.6	(4.01)	16.9	(3.27)	52	55.9	(6.83)	22.7	(6.28)	21.4	(5.12)	34	72.7	(5.43)	17.4	(4.31)	9.9 !	(3.15)	5
Sociology	147	67.6	(2.97)	23.5	(3.08)	8.8	(1.53)	51	53.7	(6.80)	36.8	(7.05)	9.5	(2.84)	97	75.0	(2.80)	16.6	(2.36)	8.4	(1.67)	12
Theology and religious vocations	46	55.5	(8.71)	16.1	(3.77)	28.4!	(9.31)	‡	‡	(†)	‡	(†)	‡	(†)	43	53.8	(9.05)	16.1	(3.97)	30.1 !	(9.66)	73
Transportation and materials moving	72	53.5	(5.59)	28.9	(6.36)	17.7	(4.22)	45	44.8	(6.85)	34.8	(8.85)	20.4 !	(7.16)	27	68.0	(5.41)	18.9	(5.20)	13.1	(2.80)	‡
Visual and performing arts	745	75.4	(1.14)	17.9	(1.09)	6.7	(0.71)	283	69.9	(2.12)	20.3	(1.81)	9.8	(1.56)	462	78.8	(1.32)	16.4	(1.36)	4.8	(0.58)	72
Undecided	449	70.4	(1.99)	17.4	(1.60)	12.2	(1.47)	274	66.0	(2.58)	20.1	(2.25)	13.9	(2.08)	175	77.3	(2.62)	13.2	(1.88)	9.5	(1.77)	†

†Not applicable.
!Interpret data with caution. The coefficient of variation (CV) for this estimate is between 30 and 50 percent.
‡Reporting standards not met. Either there are too few cases for a reliable estimate or the coefficient of variation (CV) is 50 percent or greater.
[1]For undergraduate students, the field of study categories include students who had already declared a major as well as students who had decided on, but not yet declared, an intended major. The "Undecided" category consists of undergraduate students who had neither declared nor decided on a major.
[2]Also includes students attending more than one institution.
NOTE: Because of different survey editing and processing procedures, enrollment data in this table may differ from those appearing in other tables. Includes students who enrolled at any time during the 2015–16 academic year. Data exclude Puerto Rico. Data have been revised from previously published figures. Detail may not sum to totals because of rounding.
SOURCE: U.S. Department of Education, National Center for Education Statistics, 2015–16 National Postsecondary Student Aid Study (NPSAS:16). (This table was prepared May 2018.)

Table 312.10. Enrollment of the 120 largest degree-granting college and university campuses, by selected characteristics and institution: Fall 2017

Institution	State	Rank[1]	Control[2]	Level	Total enrollment	Institution	State	Rank[1]	Control[2]	Level	Total enrollment
1	2	3	4	5	6	1	2	3	4	5	6
University of Phoenix, Arizona	AZ	1	PrivFp	4-year	103,975	George Mason University	VA	61	Public	4-year	35,984
Western Governors University	UT	2	PrivNp	4-year	98,627	Kennesaw State University	GA	62	Public	4-year	35,846
Southern New Hampshire University	NH	3	PrivNp	4-year	90,955	San Jose State University	CA	63	Public	4-year	35,835
Grand Canyon University	AZ	4	PrivFp	4-year	83,284	University of California, San Diego	CA	64	Public	4-year	35,772
Ivy Tech Community College	IN	5	Public	2-year	75,486	University of Colorado, Boulder	CO	65	Public	4-year	35,338
Liberty University	VA	6	PrivNp	4-year	75,044	University of California, Irvine	CA	66	Public	4-year	35,242
Lone Star College System	TX	7	Public	2-year	72,336	San Diego State University	CA	67	Public	4-year	35,158
Texas A & M University, College Station	TX	8	Public	4-year	67,929	University of South Carolina, Columbia	SC	68	Public	4-year	34,731
University of Central Florida	FL	9	Public	4-year	66,059	East Los Angeles College	CA	69	Public	2-year	34,578
Ohio State University, Main Campus	OH	10	Public	4-year	59,837	Virginia Polytechnic Institute and State University	VA	70	Public	4-year	34,440
University of Maryland, University College	MD	11	Public	4-year	59,379	North Carolina State University at Raleigh	NC	71	Public	4-year	34,432
Houston Community College	TX	12	Public	2-year	57,120	Brigham Young University, Provo	UT	72	PrivNp	4-year	34,334
Florida International University	FL	13	Public	4-year	56,718	Excelsior College	NY	73	PrivNp	4-year	34,022
Miami Dade College	FL	14	Public	4-year	56,001	College of Southern Nevada	NV	74	Public	4-year	33,914
Tarrant County College District	TX	15	Public	2-year	52,957	Boston University	MA	75	PrivNp	4-year	33,355
University of Florida	FL	16	Public	4-year	52,669	Kaplan University, Davenport Campus	IA	76	PrivFp	4-year	33,287
Brigham Young University, Idaho	ID	17	PrivNp	4-year	51,881	Colorado State University, Fort Collins	CO	77	Public	4-year	33,083
University of Minnesota, Twin Cities	MN	18	Public	4-year	51,848	Georgia State University	GA	78	Public	4-year	32,816
University of Texas at Austin	TX	19	Public	4-year	51,525	University of Utah	UT	79	Public	4-year	32,800
Northern Virginia Community College	VA	20	Public	2-year	51,190	University of Iowa	IA	80	Public	4-year	32,166
Arizona State University, Tempe	AZ	21	Public	4-year	51,164	American River College	CA	81	Public	2-year	31,858
New York University	NY	22	PrivNp	4-year	51,123	Arizona State University, Skysong	AZ	82	Public	4-year	31,702
Michigan State University	MI	23	Public	4-year	50,019	Collin County Community College District	TX	83	Public	2-year	31,609
Walden University	MN	24	PrivFp	4-year	49,680	South Texas College	TX	84	Public	4-year	31,321
Rutgers University, New Brunswick	NJ	25	Public	4-year	49,577	California State University, Sacramento	CA	85	Public	4-year	31,255
University of Illinois at Urbana-Champaign	IL	26	Public	4-year	48,216	Harvard University	MA	86	PrivNp	4-year	31,120
Pennsylvania State University, Main Campus	PA	27	Public	4-year	47,119	Northern Arizona University	AZ	87	Public	4-year	31,051
University of Texas at Arlington	TX	28	Public	4-year	46,497	Oregon State University	OR	88	Public	4-year	30,896
American Public University System	WV	29	PrivFp	4-year	46,420	Louisiana State U. and Agricultural & Mechanical	LA	89	Public	4-year	30,861
University of Washington, Seattle Campus	WA	30	Public	4-year	46,166	University of Missouri, Columbia	MO	90	Public	4-year	30,844
University of Michigan, Ann Arbor	MI	31	Public	4-year	46,002	University of Texas at San Antonio	TX	91	Public	4-year	30,768
University of Southern California	CA	32	PrivNp	4-year	45,687	Virginia Commonwealth University	VA	92	Public	4-year	30,675
University of Houston	TX	33	Public	4-year	45,364	University at Buffalo	NY	93	Public	4-year	30,648
Valencia College	FL	34	Public	4-year	44,834	Washington State University	WA	94	Public	4-year	30,614
University of California, Los Angeles	CA	35	Public	4-year	44,027	University of Illinois at Chicago	IL	95	Public	4-year	30,539
University of Arizona	AZ	36	Public	4-year	43,751	San Jacinto Community College	TX	96	Public	2-year	30,509
Indiana University, Bloomington	IN	37	Public	4-year	43,710	University of Nevada, Las Vegas	NV	97	Public	4-year	30,471
University of South Florida, Main Campus	FL	38	Public	4-year	43,540	Columbia University in the City of New York	NY	98	PrivNp	4-year	30,454
University of Wisconsin, Madison	WI	39	Public	4-year	42,977	University of Massachusetts, Amherst	MA	99	Public	4-year	30,340
Purdue University, Main Campus	IN	40	Public	4-year	42,699	Florida Atlantic University	FL	100	Public	4-year	30,208
University of California, Berkeley	CA	41	Public	4-year	41,891	Palm Beach State College	FL	101	Public	4-year	30,052
Florida State University	FL	42	Public	4-year	41,362	Mount San Antonio College	CA	102	Public	2-year	29,960
California State University, Northridge	CA	43	Public	4-year	41,319	University of North Carolina at Chapel Hill	NC	103	Public	4-year	29,911
California State University, Fullerton	CA	44	Public	4-year	40,905	Indiana University-Purdue University, Indianapolis	IN	104	Public	4-year	29,791
Austin Community College District	TX	45	Public	2-year	40,803	Auburn University	AL	105	Public	4-year	29,776
Broward College	FL	46	Public	4-year	40,754	Santa Monica College	CA	106	Public	4-year	29,760
University of Maryland, College Park	MD	47	Public	4-year	40,521	San Francisco State University	CA	107	Public	4-year	29,758
Temple University	PA	48	Public	4-year	39,967	Salt Lake Community College	UT	108	Public	2-year	29,620
Texas State University	TX	49	Public	4-year	38,666	Saint Petersburg College	FL	109	Public	4-year	29,548
University of Alabama	AL	50	Public	4-year	38,563	University of Kentucky	KY	110	Public	4-year	29,465
University of North Texas	TX	51	Public	4-year	38,276	Georgia Institute of Technology, Main Campus	GA	111	Public	4-year	29,376
California State University, Long Beach	CA	52	Public	4-year	37,622	Ohio University, Main Campus	OH	112	Public	4-year	29,369
University of Georgia	GA	53	Public	4-year	37,606	University of North Carolina at Charlotte	NC	113	Public	4-year	29,317
University of California, Davis	CA	54	Public	4-year	37,380	East Carolina University	NC	114	Public	4-year	29,131
Utah Valley University	UT	55	Public	4-year	37,282	Kent State University at Kent	OH	115	Public	4-year	28,972
University of Cincinnati, Main Campus	OH	56	Public	4-year	37,155	El Paso Community College	TX	116	Public	2-year	28,750
Texas Tech University	TX	57	Public	4-year	36,996	University of Pittsburgh, Pittsburgh Campus	PA	117	Public	4-year	28,642
Ashford University	CA	58	PrivFp	4-year	36,453	California State University, Los Angeles	CA	118	Public	4-year	28,531
Capella University	MN	59	PrivFp	4-year	36,284	University of Oklahoma, Norman Campus	OK	119	Public	4-year	28,527
Iowa State University	IA	60	Public	4-year	36,158	West Virginia University	WV	120	Public	4-year	28,406

[1]College and university campuses ranked by fall 2017 enrollment data.
[2]"PrivNp" stands for private nonprofit. "PrivFp" stands for private for-profit.
NOTE: Degree-granting institutions grant associate's or higher degrees and participate in Title IV federal financial aid programs. Includes online and distance education courses.

SOURCE: U.S. Department of Education, National Center for Education Statistics, Integrated Postsecondary Education Data System (IPEDS), Spring 2018, Fall Enrollment component. (This table was prepared May 2019.)

Table 312.50. Fall enrollment and degrees conferred in degree-granting tribally controlled postsecondary institutions, by state and institution: Selected years, fall 2000 through fall 2017, and 2015–16 and 2016–17

State and institution	Level and control[1]	Total fall enrollment											Degrees awarded to American Indians/Alaska Natives			
		2000								2017			Associate's		Bachelor's	
		Total	Total American Indian/Alaska Native	Percent American Indian/Alaska Native	2005	2010	2013	2015	2016	Total	Total American Indian/Alaska Native	Percent American Indian/Alaska Native	2015–16	2016–17	2015–16	2016–17
1	2	3	4	5	6	7	8	9	10	11	12	13	14	15	16	17
Tribally controlled institutions	**†**	**13,680**	**11,459**	**83.8**	**17,167**	**21,179**	**18,264**	**17,089**	**16,822**	**16,424**	**12,897**	**78.5**	**1,299**	**1,135**	**301**	**341**
Alaska																
Ilisagvik College	1	322	174	54.0	278	288	257	193	188	111	79	71.2	9	7	0	0
Arizona																
Diné College	1	1,712	1,645	96.1	1,825	2,033	1,489	1,490	1,396	1,465	1,445	98.6	187	129	17	10
Tohono O'odham Community College	2	—	—	—	270	207	243	212	276	400	359	89.8	12	17	†	†
Kansas																
Haskell Indian Nations University	1	918	918	100.0	918	958	742	799	820	806	806	100.0	115	93	86	102
Michigan																
Bay Mills Community College	2	360	228	63.3	406	607	531	541	467	448	248	55.4	22	21	†	†
Keweenaw Bay Ojibwa Community College	2	—	—	—	—	—	106	102	104	98	52	53.1	5	6	†	†
Saginaw Chippewa Tribal College	2	—	—	—	123	153	117	116	141	154	114	74.0	10	15	†	†
Minnesota																
Fond du Lac Tribal and Community College	2	999	221	22.1	1,981	2,339	2,272	2,227	2,101	1,946	163	8.4	25	22	†	†
Leech Lake Tribal College	2	240	228	95.0	189	235	348	348	286	181	161	89.0	40	39	†	†
White Earth Tribal and Community College	4	—	—	—	61	117	60	68	77	90	60	66.7	14	9	†	†
Montana																
Aaniiih Nakoda College	2	295	266	90.2	175	214	139	219	149	122	110	90.2	15	28	†	†
Blackfeet Community College	4	299	288	96.3	485	473	450	442	425	375	343	91.5	83	71	†	†
Chief Dull Knife College	2	461	365	79.2	554	433	201	218	168	186	169	90.9	35	20	†	†
Fort Peck Community College	2	400	338	84.5	408	452	405	321	385	358	320	89.4	13	20	†	†
Little Big Horn College	2	320	303	94.7	259	380	329	248	225	243	232	95.5	40	21	†	†
Salish Kootenai College	3	1,042	881	84.5	1,142	1,158	840	784	859	809	579	71.6	53	55	33	30
Stone Child College	1	38	38	100.0	344	332	404	540	544	554	487	87.9	7	17	0	0
Nebraska																
Little Priest Tribal College	2	141	121	85.8	109	148	144	132	132	141	118	83.7	8	10	†	†
Nebraska Indian Community College	2	170	146	85.9	107	177	199	158	175	180	174	96.7	13	4	†	†
New Mexico																
Institute of American Indian and Alaska Native Culture and Arts Development	1	139	139	100.0	113	313	422	493	582	659	438	66.5	6	4	24	19
Navajo Technical University	1	841	841	100.0	333	1,019	1,956	1,686	1,675	1,772	1,706	96.3	63	48	16	22
Southwestern Indian Polytechnic Institute	2	304	304	100.0	614	531	530	402	367	366	366	100.0	62	71	†	†
North Dakota																
Cankdeska Cikana Community College	2	9	8	88.9	198	220	254	188	178	242	220	90.9	15	22	†	†
Nueta Hidatsa Sahnish College	1	50	47	94.0	241	215	203	229	268	228	185	81.1	24	6	2	1
Sitting Bull College	1	22	20	90.9	287	314	246	261	282	317	285	89.9	32	23	8	6
Turtle Mountain Community College	3	686	608	88.6	615	969	602	555	584	567	544	95.9	75	62	10	9
United Tribes Technical College	3	204	186	91.2	885	600	505	391	483	315	257	81.6	41	25	14	18
Oklahoma																
College of the Muscogee Nation	2	—	—	—	—	—	191	202	213	227	190	83.7	17	26	†	†
South Dakota																
Oglala Lakota College	1	1,174	1,077	91.7	1,302	1,830	1,551	1,366	1,301	1,246	1,181	94.8	63	70	44	53
Sinte Gleska University	3	900	757	84.1	1,123	2,473	689	581	568	581	521	89.7	39	28	12	19
Sisseton Wahpeton College	2	250	192	76.8	290	261	194	132	142	197	162	82.2	8	9	†	†
Washington																
Northwest Indian College	1	524	440	84.0	495	626	681	641	579	544	434	79.8	78	86	33	47
Wisconsin																
College of the Menominee Nation	3	371	283	76.3	532	615	661	433	394	285	233	81.8	28	27	2	5
Lac Courte Oreilles Ojibwa Community College	2	489	397	81.2	505	489	303	371	288	211	156	73.9	42	24	†	†

—Not available.
†Not applicable.
[1]1 = 4-year public; 2 = 2-year public; 3 = 4-year private nonprofit; and 4 = 2-year private nonprofit.
NOTE: This table only includes institutions that were in operation during the 2017–18 academic year. They are all members of the American Indian Higher Education Consortium and, with few exceptions, are tribally controlled and located on reservations. Degree-granting institutions grant associate's or higher degrees and participate in Title IV federal financial aid programs. Totals include persons of other racial/ethnic groups not separately identified. Some data have been revised from previously published figures.
SOURCE: U.S. Department of Education, National Center for Education Statistics, Integrated Postsecondary Education Data System (IPEDS), Spring 2001 through Spring 2018, Fall Enrollment component; and Fall 2016 and Fall 2017, Completions component. (This table was prepared November 2018.)

Table 313.10. Fall enrollment, degrees conferred, and expenditures in degree-granting historically Black colleges and universities, by institution: 2016, 2017, and 2016–17

Institution	State	Level and control[1]	Total enrollment, fall 2016	Enrollment, fall 2017: Total	Enrollment, fall 2017: Black enrollment	Full-time-equivalent enrollment, fall 2017	Degrees conferred, 2016–17: Associate's	Bachelor's	Master's	Doctor's[2]	Total expenditures, 2016–17 (in thousands of current dollars)[3]
1	2	3	4	5	6	7	8	9	10	11	12
Total	†	†	**292,083**	**298,138**	**226,843**	**255,865**	**5,511**	**33,500**	**7,966**	**2,490**	**$7,871,667**
Alabama A&M University[4]	AL	1	5,859	6,001	5,543	5,590	0	453	351	9	149,506
Alabama State University	AL	1	5,318	4,760	4,399	4,411	0	743	139	29	140,342
Bishop State Community College	AL	2	3,028	3,233	1,992	2,120	269	†	†	†	34,764
Concordia College, Alabama	AL	3	340	389	352	372	37	36	0	0	9,784
Gadsden State Community College	AL	2	5,109	4,979	952	3,309	638	†	†	†	50,356
H. Councill Trenholm State Technical College	AL	2	1,661	1,845	1,259	1,169	172	†	†	†	21,972
J.F. Drake State Community and Technical College	AL	2	829	752	394	496	98	†	†	†	10,851
Lawson State Community College, Birmingham Campus	AL	2	3,128	3,248	2,623	2,237	263	†	†	†	46,769
Miles College	AL	3	1,820	1,650	1,585	1,592	0	223	0	0	31,453
Oakwood University	AL	3	1,794	1,711	1,493	1,629	2	362	7	0	51,255
Selma University	AL	3	172	324	315	269	8	15	5	0	4,078
Shelton State Community College	AL	2	4,810	4,607	1,774	2,936	494	†	†	†	42,014
Stillman College	AL	3	628	677	612	601	0	104	0	0	13,889
Talladega College	AL	3	675	782	693	770	0	103	0	0	15,616
Tuskegee University[4]	AL	3	2,851	3,289	3,162	3,182	0	453	106	80	124,884
Arkansas Baptist College	AR	3	878	593	553	534	67	29	0	0	15,785
Philander Smith College	AR	3	765	891	845	863	0	103	0	0	19,867
Shorter College	AR	4	446	521	284	417	51	†	†	†	5,102
University of Arkansas at Pine Bluff[4]	AR	1	2,821	2,612	2,378	2,468	7	405	36	2	79,149
Delaware State University[4]	DE	1	4,328	4,352	3,082	4,041	0	581	80	28	139,592
Howard University	DC	3	8,966	9,392	7,948	8,932	0	1,355	308	482	794,802
University of the District of Columbia[4]	DC	1	4,318	4,247	2,781	2,974	239	387	110	0	141,861
Bethune-Cookman University	FL	3	3,934	4,143	3,669	3,983	0	498	44	0	97,090
Edward Waters College	FL	3	3,062	3,443	1,956	1,870	0	147	0	0	23,484
Florida A&M University[4]	FL	1	9,619	9,913	8,253	9,071	48	1,555	252	327	281,562
Florida Memorial University	FL	3	1,339	1,250	992	1,185	0	191	23	0	35,573
Albany State University	GA	1	3,041	6,615	4,767	5,103	898	556	158	0	112,665
Clark Atlanta University	GA	3	3,884	3,992	3,618	3,779	0	430	244	43	92,813
Fort Valley State University[4]	GA	1	2,679	2,752	2,518	2,441	0	366	104	0	77,225
Interdenominational Theological Center	GA	3	280	295	289	179	0	0	39	12	7,731
Morehouse College	GA	3	2,108	2,202	2,099	2,134	0	286	0	0	88,719
Morehouse School of Medicine	GA	3	480	520	400	505	0	0	46	70	158,643
Paine College	GA	3	502	426	384	366	0	79	0	0	14,347
Savannah State University	GA	1	4,955	4,429	3,654	4,051	11	580	75	0	102,627
Spelman College	GA	3	2,125	2,137	2,071	2,106	0	450	0	0	96,384
Kentucky State University[4]	KY	1	1,736	1,926	1,024	1,501	43	315	40	0	72,596
Simmons College of Kentucky	KY	3	203	216	209	172	18	7	0	0	2,910
Dillard University	LA	3	1,261	1,290	1,250	1,235	0	172	0	0	45,519
Grambling State University	LA	1	4,863	5,191	4,723	4,478	0	550	261	9	94,123
Southern University and A&M College[4]	LA	1	5,877	6,118	5,659	5,439	0	735	296	19	141,334
Southern University at New Orleans	LA	1	2,430	2,546	2,372	2,098	14	324	189	0	41,116
Southern University at Shreveport	LA	2	3,240	3,088	2,793	2,096	249	†	†	†	31,646
Xavier University of Louisiana	LA	3	2,997	3,044	2,194	2,947	0	324	50	143	108,577
Bowie State University	MD	1	5,669	6,148	5,167	5,320	0	713	313	9	105,670
Coppin State University	MD	1	2,939	2,893	2,275	2,353	0	421	78	2	88,737
Morgan State University	MD	1	7,689	7,747	5,956	7,173	0	970	306	54	238,528
University of Maryland, Eastern Shore[4]	MD	1	3,904	3,490	2,440	3,181	0	514	50	108	123,897
Alcorn State University[4]	MS	1	3,420	3,716	3,362	3,324	7	451	192	0	93,852
Coahoma Community College	MS	2	2,064	1,954	1,858	1,611	273	†	†	†	34,557
Hinds Community College, Utica Campus	MS	2	693	688	657	656	84	†	†	†	—
Jackson State University	MS	1	9,811	8,558	7,628	7,426	0	942	391	91	207,509
Mississippi Valley State University	MS	1	2,455	2,385	2,270	2,023	0	322	91	0	54,445
Rust College	MS	3	1,004	860	840	819	9	116	0	0	17,454
Tougaloo College	MS	3	860	809	786	789	0	123	6	0	24,087
Harris-Stowe State University	MO	1	1,464	1,442	1,226	1,276	0	156	0	0	33,626
Lincoln University[4]	MO	1	2,738	2,619	1,279	2,154	67	266	46	0	56,068
Bennett College	NC	3	474	493	449	437	0	73	0	0	15,898
Elizabeth City State University	NC	1	1,357	1,411	1,022	1,281	0	259	17	0	57,997
Fayetteville State University	NC	1	6,223	6,226	3,904	5,097	0	1,001	150	17	117,705
Johnson C. Smith University	NC	3	1,428	1,483	1,363	1,433	0	224	54	0	43,534
Livingstone College	NC	3	1,204	1,150	1,074	1,144	2	151	0	0	29,486
North Carolina A&T State University[4]	NC	1	11,177	11,877	9,527	10,879	0	1,516	395	63	272,955
North Carolina Central University	NC	1	8,094	8,097	6,231	7,204	0	1,120	481	177	202,753
Saint Augustine's College	NC	3	944	974	926	966	0	137	0	0	29,793
Shaw University	NC	3	1,844	1,660	1,465	1,590	0	183	24	0	48,269
Winston-Salem State University	NC	1	5,151	5,098	3,805	4,644	0	1,131	101	26	145,185
Central State University	OH	1	1,741	1,784	1,672	1,740	0	219	9	0	54,833
Wilberforce University	OH	3	645	627	605	546	0	99	9	0	16,907
Langston University[4]	OK	1	2,420	2,219	1,564	2,056	12	232	62	14	63,336
Cheyney University of Pennsylvania	PA	1	746	755	655	719	0	148	16	0	39,331
Lincoln University	PA	1	2,092	2,266	2,038	2,118	0	279	126	0	55,131

See notes at end of table.

Table 313.10. Fall enrollment, degrees conferred, and expenditures in degree-granting historically Black colleges and universities, by institution: 2016, 2017, and 2016–17—Continued

				Enrollment, fall 2017			Degrees conferred, 2016–17				
Institution	State	Level and control[1]	Total enroll-ment, fall 2016	Total	Black enroll-ment	Full-time-equivalent enroll-ment, fall 2017	Asso-ciate's	Bachelor's	Master's	Doctor's[2]	Total expenditures, 2016–17 (in thousands of current dollars)[3]
1	2	3	4	5	6	7	8	9	10	11	12
Allen University	SC	3	600	590	572	574	0	66	0	0	13,768
Benedict College	SC	3	2,281	2,090	1,999	2,082	0	318	0	0	54,645
Claflin University	SC	3	1,978	2,129	1,957	2,067	0	339	29	0	48,520
Clinton College	SC	3	200	170	169	170	22	7	0	0	3,575
Denmark Technical College	SC	2	632	523	467	374	46	†	†	†	12,192
Morris College	SC	3	754	747	731	737	0	111	0	0	19,114
South Carolina State University[4]	SC	1	2,905	2,942	2,800	2,683	0	357	97	7	73,594
Voorhees College	SC	3	415	475	462	468	0	84	0	0	12,655
American Baptist College	TN	3	139	115	114	100	4	15	0	0	4,257
Fisk University	TN	3	761	701	633	681	0	115	21	0	27,646
Lane College	TN	3	1,427	1,420	1,391	1,390	1	163	0	0	24,560
Le Moyne-Owen College	TN	3	959	863	843	807	0	144	0	0	17,341
Meharry Medical College	TN	3	831	826	662	826	0	0	59	160	146,992
Tennessee State University[4]	TN	1	8,760	8,177	5,518	6,914	101	1,063	440	73	190,120
Huston-Tillotson University	TX	3	1,012	1,102	697	1,045	47	135	4	0	21,253
Jarvis Christian College	TX	3	868	909	741	864	8	76	0	0	18,538
Paul Quinn College	TX	3	436	519	387	503	0	26	0	0	10,217
Prairie View A&M University[4]	TX	1	8,782	9,219	7,581	8,392	0	1,108	469	15	231,081
Saint Philip's College	TX	2	11,604	12,050	1,130	5,109	998	†	†	†	78,771
Southwestern Christian College	TX	3	147	159	147	155	17	3	0	0	4,888
Texas College	TX	3	960	992	864	960	24	94	0	0	16,547
Texas Southern University	TX	1	8,862	10,237	7,839	9,094	0	1,002	361	287	210,191
Wiley College	TX	3	1,279	1,323	1,115	1,241	0	272	0	0	25,722
Hampton University	VA	3	4,646	4,618	4,265	4,393	0	621	130	99	184,308
Norfolk State University	VA	1	5,421	5,303	4,559	4,782	3	889	174	8	146,626
Virginia State University[4]	VA	1	4,584	4,713	3,212	4,449	0	828	106	8	140,285
Virginia Union University	VA	3	1,815	1,674	1,615	1,603	0	177	129	13	37,499
Virginia University of Lynchburg	VA	3	370	304	297	246	33	19	8	6	4,639
Bluefield State College	WV	1	1,362	1,379	117	1,212	91	199	0	0	20,786
West Virginia State University[4]	WV	1	3,514	3,879	374	2,654	0	358	11	0	53,199
University of the Virgin Islands[4]	VI	1	2,370	2,170	1,628	1,680	36	228	48	0	76,227

—Not available.
†Not applicable.
[1] 1 = 4-year public; 2 = 2-year public; 3 = 4-year private nonprofit; and 4 = 2-year private nonprofit.
[2] Includes Ph.D., Ed.D., and comparable degrees at the doctoral level, as well as such degrees as M.D., D.D.S., and law degrees that were classified as first-professional degrees prior to 2010–11.
[3] Includes private and some public institutions reporting total expenses and deductions under Financial Accounting Standards Board (FASB) reporting standards and public institutions reporting total expenses and deductions under Governmental Accounting Standards Board (GASB) 34/35 reporting standards.
[4] Land-grant institution.

NOTE: Degree-granting institutions grant associate's or higher degrees and participate in Title IV federal financial aid programs. Excludes historically Black colleges and universities that are not participating in Title IV programs. Historically Black colleges and universities are degree-granting institutions established prior to 1964 with the principal mission of educating Black Americans. Federal regulations, 20 U.S. Code, Section 1061 (2), allow for certain exceptions to the founding date. Totals include persons of other racial/ethnic groups not separately identified. Detail may not sum to totals because of rounding.
SOURCE: U.S. Department of Education, National Center for Education Statistics, Integrated Postsecondary Education Data System (IPEDS), Fall 2017, Completions component; Spring 2017 and Spring 2018, Fall Enrollment component; and Spring 2018, Finance component. (This table was prepared December 2018.)

Table 313.20. Fall enrollment in degree-granting historically Black colleges and universities, by sex of student and level and control of institution: Selected years, 1976 through 2017

Year	Total enrollment	Males	Females	4-year	2-year	Public			Private		
						Total	4-year	2-year	Total	4-year	2-year
1	2	3	4	5	6	7	8	9	10	11	12
						All students					
1976	222,613	104,669	117,944	206,676	15,937	156,836	143,528	13,308	65,777	63,148	2,629
1980	233,557	106,387	127,170	218,009	15,548	168,217	155,085	13,132	65,340	62,924	2,416
1982	228,371	104,897	123,474	212,017	16,354	165,871	151,472	14,399	62,500	60,545	1,955
1984	227,519	102,823	124,696	212,844	14,675	164,116	151,289	12,827	63,403	61,555	1,848
1986	223,275	97,523	125,752	207,231	16,044	162,048	147,631	14,417	61,227	59,600	1,627
1988	239,755	100,561	139,194	223,250	16,505	173,672	158,606	15,066	66,083	64,644	1,439
1990	257,152	105,157	151,995	240,497	16,655	187,046	171,969	15,077	70,106	68,528	1,578
1992	279,541	114,622	164,919	261,089	18,452	204,966	188,143	16,823	74,575	72,946	1,629
1993	282,856	116,397	166,459	262,430	20,426	208,197	189,032	19,165	74,659	73,398	1,261
1994	280,071	114,006	166,065	259,997	20,074	206,520	187,735	18,785	73,551	72,262	1,289
1995	278,725	112,637	166,088	259,409	19,316	204,726	186,278	18,448	73,999	73,131	868
1996	273,018	109,498	163,520	253,654	19,364	200,569	182,063	18,506	72,449	71,591	858
1997	269,167	106,865	162,302	248,860	20,307	194,674	175,297	19,377	74,493	73,563	930
1998	273,472	108,752	164,720	248,931	24,541	198,603	174,776	23,827	74,869	74,155	714
1999	274,321	108,301	166,020	249,156	25,165	199,826	175,364	24,462	74,495	73,792	703
2000	275,680	108,164	167,516	250,710	24,970	199,725	175,404	24,321	75,955	75,306	649
2001	289,985	112,874	177,111	260,547	29,438	210,083	181,346	28,737	79,902	79,201	701
2002	299,041	115,466	183,575	269,020	30,021	218,433	189,183	29,250	80,608	79,837	771
2003	306,727	117,795	188,932	274,326	32,401	228,096	196,077	32,019	78,631	78,249	382
2004	308,939	118,129	190,810	276,136	32,803	231,179	198,810	32,369	77,760	77,326	434
2005	311,768	120,023	191,745	272,666	39,102	235,875	197,200	38,675	75,893	75,466	427
2006	308,774	118,865	189,909	272,770	36,004	234,505	198,676	35,829	74,269	74,094	175
2007	306,742	118,672	188,070	270,554	36,188	234,034	197,939	36,095	72,708	72,615	93
2008	313,491	121,874	191,617	274,568	38,923	235,824	197,025	38,799	77,667	77,543	124
2009	322,860	125,728	197,132	280,133	42,727	246,595	204,016	42,579	76,265	76,117	148
2010	326,614	127,437	199,177	283,099	43,515	249,146	205,774	43,372	77,468	77,325	143
2011	323,648	126,160	197,488	281,150	42,498	246,685	204,363	42,322	76,963	76,787	176
2012	312,438	121,719	190,719	273,033	39,405	237,782	198,568	39,214	74,656	74,465	191
2013	303,191	119,299	183,892	264,454	38,737	230,325	191,918	38,407	72,866	72,536	330
2014	294,316	115,837	178,479	256,936	37,380	222,876	185,899	36,977	71,440	71,037	403
2015	293,304	115,818	177,486	256,295	37,009	221,276	184,503	36,773	72,028	71,792	236
2016	292,083	114,705	177,378	254,839	37,244	220,292	183,494	36,798	71,791	71,345	446
2017	298,138	115,324	182,814	260,650	37,488	225,179	188,212	36,967	72,959	72,438	521
						Black students					
1976	190,305	84,492	105,813	179,848	10,457	129,770	121,851	7,919	60,535	57,997	2,538
1980	190,989	81,818	109,171	181,237	9,752	131,661	124,236	7,425	59,328	57,001	2,327
1982	182,639	78,874	103,765	171,942	10,697	126,368	117,562	8,806	56,271	54,380	1,891
1984	180,803	76,819	103,984	171,401	9,402	124,445	116,845	7,600	56,358	54,556	1,802
1986	178,628	74,276	104,352	167,971	10,657	123,555	114,502	9,053	55,073	53,469	1,604
1988	194,151	78,268	115,883	183,402	10,749	133,786	124,438	9,348	60,365	58,964	1,401
1990	208,682	82,897	125,785	198,237	10,445	144,204	134,924	9,280	64,478	63,313	1,165
1992	228,963	91,949	137,014	217,614	11,349	159,585	149,754	9,831	69,378	67,860	1,518
1993	231,198	93,110	138,088	219,431	11,767	161,444	150,867	10,577	69,754	68,564	1,190
1994	230,162	91,908	138,254	218,565	11,597	161,098	150,682	10,416	69,064	67,883	1,181
1995	229,418	91,132	138,286	218,379	11,039	159,925	149,661	10,264	69,493	68,718	775
1996	224,201	88,306	135,895	213,309	10,892	156,851	146,753	10,098	67,350	66,556	794
1997	222,331	86,641	135,690	210,741	11,590	153,039	142,326	10,713	69,292	68,415	877
1998	223,745	87,163	136,582	211,822	11,923	154,244	142,985	11,259	69,501	68,837	664
1999	226,592	87,987	138,605	213,779	12,813	156,292	144,166	12,126	70,300	69,613	687
2000	227,239	87,319	139,920	215,172	12,067	156,706	145,277	11,429	70,533	69,895	638
2001	238,638	90,718	147,920	224,417	14,221	164,354	150,831	13,523	74,284	73,586	698
2002	247,292	93,538	153,754	231,834	15,458	172,203	157,507	14,696	75,089	74,327	762
2003	253,257	95,703	157,554	236,753	16,504	180,104	163,977	16,127	73,153	72,776	377
2004	257,545	96,750	160,795	241,030	16,515	184,708	168,619	16,089	72,837	72,411	426
2005	256,584	96,891	159,693	238,030	18,554	186,047	167,916	18,131	70,537	70,114	423
2006	255,144	96,507	158,637	238,440	16,704	185,894	169,365	16,529	69,250	69,075	175
2007	253,241	96,214	157,027	236,571	16,670	185,170	168,592	16,578	68,071	67,979	92
2008	258,402	98,633	159,769	240,132	18,270	186,446	168,299	18,147	71,956	71,833	123
2009	264,092	100,590	163,502	243,956	20,136	194,088	174,099	19,989	70,004	69,857	147
2010	265,908	101,605	164,303	245,158	20,750	193,840	173,233	20,607	72,068	71,925	143
2011	263,435	100,526	162,909	242,881	20,554	192,042	171,664	20,378	71,393	71,217	176
2012	251,527	96,079	155,448	232,897	18,630	183,018	164,578	18,440	68,509	68,319	190
2013	241,485	92,491	148,994	223,491	17,994	175,308	157,640	17,668	66,177	65,851	326
2014	231,889	88,469	143,420	214,631	17,258	167,246	150,383	16,863	64,643	64,248	395
2015	228,062	86,857	141,205	211,698	16,364	163,508	147,376	16,132	64,554	64,322	232
2016	223,512	84,153	139,359	207,379	16,133	160,053	144,176	15,877	63,459	63,203	256
2017	226,843	83,921	142,922	210,660	16,183	162,701	146,802	15,899	64,142	63,858	284

NOTE: Historically Black colleges and universities are degree-granting institutions established prior to 1964 with the principal mission of educating Black Americans. Federal regulations, 20 U.S. Code, Section 1061 (2), allow for certain exceptions to the founding date. Data through 1995 are for institutions of higher education, while later data are for degree-granting institutions. Degree-granting institutions grant associate's or higher degrees and participate in Title IV federal financial aid programs. The degree-granting classification is very similar to the earlier higher education classification, but it includes more 2-year colleges and excludes a few higher education institutions that did not grant degrees. Some data have been revised from previously published figures.

SOURCE: U.S. Department of Education, National Center for Education Statistics, Higher Education General Information Survey (HEGIS), "Fall Enrollment in Colleges and Universities," 1976 through 1985 surveys; Integrated Postsecondary Education Data System (IPEDS), "Fall Enrollment Survey" (IPEDS-EF:86–99); and IPEDS Spring 2001 through Spring 2018, Fall Enrollment component. (This table was prepared December 2018.)

Table 313.30. Selected statistics on degree-granting historically Black colleges and universities, by control and level of institution: Selected years, 1990 through 2017

		Public			Private		
Selected statistics	Total	Total	4-year	2-year	Total	4-year	2-year
1	2	3	4	5	6	7	8
Number of institutions, fall 2017	**102**	**51**	**40**	**11**	**51**	**50**	**1**
Fall enrollment							
Total enrollment, fall 1990	257,152	187,046	171,969	15,077	70,106	68,528	1,578
Males	105,157	76,541	70,220	6,321	28,616	28,054	562
Males, Black	82,897	57,255	54,041	3,214	25,642	25,198	444
Females	151,995	110,505	101,749	8,756	41,490	40,474	1,016
Females, Black	125,785	86,949	80,883	6,066	38,836	38,115	721
Total enrollment, fall 2000	275,680	199,725	175,404	24,321	75,955	75,306	649
Males	108,164	78,186	68,322	9,864	29,978	29,771	207
Males, Black	87,319	60,029	56,017	4,012	27,290	27,085	205
Females	167,516	121,539	107,082	14,457	45,977	45,535	442
Females, Black	139,920	96,677	89,260	7,417	43,243	42,810	433
Total enrollment, fall 2010	326,614	249,146	205,774	43,372	77,468	77,325	143
Males	127,437	95,883	78,528	17,355	31,554	31,482	72
Males, Black	101,605	72,629	65,512	7,117	28,976	28,904	72
Females	199,177	153,263	127,246	26,017	45,914	45,843	71
Females, Black	164,303	121,211	107,721	13,490	43,092	43,021	71
Total enrollment, fall 2017	298,138	225,179	188,212	36,967	72,959	72,438	521
Males	115,324	86,251	70,905	15,346	29,073	28,802	271
Males, Black	83,921	59,075	53,189	5,886	24,846	24,709	137
Females	182,814	138,928	117,307	21,621	43,886	43,636	250
Females, Black	142,922	103,626	93,613	10,013	39,296	39,149	147
Full-time enrollment, fall 2017	230,753	165,509	150,903	14,606	65,244	64,895	349
Males	90,440	64,724	58,253	6,471	25,716	25,536	180
Females	140,313	100,785	92,650	8,135	39,528	39,359	169
Part-time enrollment, fall 2017	67,385	59,670	37,309	22,361	7,715	7,543	172
Males	24,884	21,527	12,652	8,875	3,357	3,266	91
Females	42,501	38,143	24,657	13,486	4,358	4,277	81
Earned degrees conferred, 2016–17							
Associate's	5,511	5,161	1,577	3,584	350	299	51
Males	1,931	1,774	384	1,390	157	143	14
Males, Black	730	591	144	447	139	125	14
Females	3,580	3,387	1,193	2,194	193	156	37
Females, Black	1,773	1,601	556	1,045	172	138	34
Bachelor's	33,500	24,242	24,242	†	9,258	9,258	†
Males	11,949	8,614	8,614	†	3,335	3,335	†
Males, Black	9,273	6,415	6,415	†	2,858	2,858	†
Females	21,551	15,628	15,628	†	5,923	5,923	†
Females, Black	17,802	12,446	12,446	†	5,356	5,356	†
Master's	7,966	6,621	6,621	†	1,345	1,345	†
Males	2,536	2,080	2,080	†	456	456	†
Males, Black	1,595	1,258	1,258	†	337	337	†
Females	5,430	4,541	4,541	†	889	889	†
Females, Black	4,001	3,286	3,286	†	715	715	†
Doctor's[1]	2,490	1,382	1,382	†	1,108	1,108	†
Males	936	529	529	†	407	407	†
Males, Black	535	264	264	†	271	271	†
Females	1,554	853	853	†	701	701	†
Females, Black	1,004	508	508	†	496	496	†
Financial statistics, 2016–17[2]	In thousands of current dollars						
Total revenue	$8,341,989	$5,324,964	$4,954,777	$370,187	$3,017,025	$3,011,199	$5,826
Student tuition and fees	1,929,697	1,004,729	961,280	43,449	924,968	922,429	2,539
Federal government[3]	1,893,492	1,200,772	1,069,488	131,285	692,720	691,315	1,406
State governments	2,029,053	1,933,657	1,803,068	130,589	95,396	95,396	0
Local governments	115,404	85,381	42,276	43,105	30,023	29,870	153
Private gifts and grants[4]	338,656	99,439	90,283	9,156	239,217	238,672	546
Investment return (gain or loss)	390,202	67,368	66,927	441	322,834	322,834	0
Auxiliary (essentially self-supporting) enterprises	962,867	602,739	597,036	5,703	360,128	359,615	513
Hospitals and other sources	682,617	330,879	324,419	6,460	351,738	351,069	669
Total expenditures	7,871,667	5,091,253	4,727,363	363,891	2,780,413	2,775,312	5,102
Instruction	2,326,854	1,599,945	1,454,073	145,872	726,909	725,220	1,689
Research	481,571	318,668	318,668	0	162,904	162,904	0
Academic support	652,979	463,748	435,472	28,276	189,231	188,800	431
Institutional support	1,422,110	740,462	673,533	66,929	681,649	679,760	1,889
Auxiliary (essentially self-supporting) enterprises	1,094,600	769,776	762,686	7,090	324,824	323,929	895
Other expenditures	1,893,552	1,198,655	1,082,931	115,724	694,897	694,699	198

†Not applicable.

[1]Includes Ph.D., Ed.D., and comparable degrees at the doctoral level, as well as such degrees as M.D., D.D.S., and law degrees that were classified as first-professional degrees prior to 2010–11.

[2]Totals (column 2) of public and private institutions together are approximate because public and private nonprofit institutions fill out different survey forms with different accounting concepts.

[3]Includes independent operations.

[4]Includes contributions from affiliated entities.

NOTE: Degree-granting institutions grant associate's or higher degrees and participate in Title IV federal financial aid programs. Historically Black colleges and universities are degree-granting institutions established prior to 1964 with the principal mission of educating Black Americans. Federal regulations, 20 U.S. Code, Section 1061 (2), allow for certain exceptions to the founding date. Federal, state, and local governments revenue includes appropriations, grants, and contracts. Totals include persons of other racial/ethnic groups not separately identified. Detail may not sum to totals because of rounding.

SOURCE: U.S. Department of Education, National Center for Education Statistics, Integrated Postsecondary Education Data System (IPEDS), "Fall Enrollment Survey" (IPEDS-EF:90); IPEDS Spring 2001, Spring 2011, and Spring 2018, Fall Enrollment component; IPEDS Spring 2018, Finance component; and IPEDS Fall 2017, Completions component. (This table was prepared December 2018.)

Table 314.10. Total and full-time-equivalent (FTE) staff and FTE student/FTE staff ratios in postsecondary institutions participating in Title IV programs, by degree-granting status, control of institution, and primary occupation: Fall 1999, fall 2009, and fall 2017

Degree-granting status, control of institution, and primary occupation	Fall 1999				Fall 2009				Fall 2017			
	Total		Full-time-equivalent (FTE)		Total		Full-time-equivalent (FTE)		Total		Full-time-equivalent (FTE)	
	Number	Percent	Total	FTE students per FTE staff	Number	Percent	Total	FTE students per FTE staff	Number	Percent	Total	FTE students per FTE staff
1	2	3	4	5	6	7	8	9	10	11	12	13
All postsecondary institutions	**2,964,535**	**100.0**	**2,299,290**	**4.9**	**3,795,744**	**100.0**	**2,885,823**	**5.5**	**3,976,901**	**100.0**	**3,036,815**	**5.0**
Faculty (instruction/research/ public service)	1,072,202	36.2	765,284	14.8	1,476,716	38.9	992,148	16.0	1,575,699	39.6	1,084,046	14.0
Graduate assistants	242,525	8.2	80,842	139.8	343,204	9.0	114,401	138.6	377,156	9.5	125,719	120.8
Other staff	1,649,808	55.7	1,453,164	7.8	1,975,824	52.1	1,779,273	8.9	2,024,046	50.9	1,827,051	8.3
Degree-granting institutions[1]												
Total	**2,902,479**	**100.0**	**2,252,050**	**4.9**	**3,724,661**	**100.0**	**2,829,757**	**5.4**	**3,914,542**	**100.0**	**2,988,567**	**5.0**
Faculty (instruction/research/ public service)	1,037,529	35.7	741,426	14.8	1,439,074	38.6	965,793	15.9	1,543,569	39.4	1,061,968	14.0
Graduate assistants	240,995	8.3	80,332	136.6	343,204	9.2	114,401	134.4	377,156	9.6	125,719	118.4
Other staff	1,623,955	56.0	1,430,292	7.7	1,942,383	52.1	1,749,563	8.8	1,993,817	50.9	1,800,880	8.3
Public	1,999,704	100.0	1,524,881	5.3	2,442,693	100.0	1,832,312	5.9	2,564,974	100.0	1,941,114	5.4
Faculty (instruction/research/ public service)	718,585	35.9	511,400	15.8	913,788	37.4	623,675	17.2	971,183	37.9	680,510	15.5
Graduate assistants	201,611	10.1	67,204	119.9	275,878	11.3	91,959	116.9	295,798	11.5	98,599	107.2
Other staff	1,079,508	54.0	946,277	8.5	1,253,027	51.3	1,116,678	9.6	1,297,993	50.6	1,162,004	9.1
Private nonprofit	847,615	100.0	688,914	3.7	1,074,042	100.0	856,067	3.7	1,209,311	100.0	956,840	3.6
Faculty (instruction/research/ public service)	288,663	34.1	213,130	11.9	408,382	38.0	287,116	11.1	486,183	40.2	341,153	10.2
Graduate assistants	37,421	4.4	12,474	203.8	67,057	6.2	22,352	142.3	80,946	6.7	26,982	128.9
Other staff	521,531	61.5	463,310	5.5	598,603	55.7	546,599	5.8	642,182	53.1	588,705	5.9
Private for-profit	55,160	100.0	38,255	9.8	207,926	100.0	141,378	10.3	140,257	100.0	90,613	9.2
Faculty (instruction/research/ public service)	30,281	54.9	16,896	22.1	116,904	56.2	55,002	26.4	86,203	61.5	40,305	20.7
Graduate assistants	1,963	3.6	654	570.3	269	0.1	90	16,188.6	412	0.3	137	6,081.3
Other staff	22,916	41.5	20,705	18.0	90,753	43.6	86,286	16.8	53,642	38.2	50,171	16.6
Non-degree-granting institutions[2]												
Total	**62,056**	**100.0**	**47,239**	**6.9**	**71,083**	**100.0**	**56,066**	**8.5**	**62,359**	**100.0**	**48,248**	**6.5**
Faculty (instruction/research/ public service)	34,673	55.9	23,858	13.7	37,642	53.0	26,355	18.1	32,130	51.5	22,077	14.2
Graduate assistants	1,530	2.5	510	641.0	0	0.0	0	†	0	0.0	0	†
Other staff	25,853	41.7	22,872	14.3	33,441	47.0	29,710	16.1	30,229	48.5	26,171	11.9
Public	29,220	100.0	21,583	5.8	21,599	100.0	15,728	6.0	22,290	100.0	16,200	4.6
Faculty (instruction/research/ public service)	18,085	61.9	12,040	10.4	13,266	61.4	8,510	11.0	11,912	53.4	7,546	9.9
Graduate assistants	487	1.7	162	774.0	0	0.0	0	†	0	0.0	0	†
Other staff	10,648	36.4	9,380	13.4	8,333	38.6	7,218	13.0	10,378	46.6	8,654	8.7
Private nonprofit	4,712	100.0	3,677	6.4	5,087	100.0	4,141	5.7	3,885	100.0	3,082	5.2
Faculty (instruction/research/ public service)	2,365	50.2	1,674	14.0	2,442	48.0	1,834	12.8	1,706	43.9	1,225	13.2
Graduate assistants	78	1.7	26	902.1	0	0.0	0	†	0	0.0	0	†
Other staff	2,269	48.2	1,976	11.9	2,645	52.0	2,307	10.2	2,179	56.1	1,857	8.7
Private for-profit	28,124	100.0	21,980	8.1	44,397	100.0	36,197	9.9	36,184	100.0	28,966	7.6
Faculty (instruction/research/ public service)	14,223	50.6	10,143	17.5	21,934	49.4	16,011	22.5	18,512	51.2	13,306	16.6
Graduate assistants	965	3.4	322	552.8	0	0.0	0	†	0	0.0	0	†
Other staff	12,936	46.0	11,515	15.4	22,463	50.6	20,186	17.8	17,672	48.8	15,660	14.1

†Not applicable.
[1]Degree-granting institutions grant associate's or higher degrees and participate in Title IV federal financial aid programs.
[2]Data are for institutions that did not offer accredited 4-year or 2-year degree programs, but were participating in Title IV federal financial aid programs. Includes some institutions transitioning to higher level program offerings, though still classified at a lower level.
NOTE: Full-time-equivalent staff is the full-time staff, plus the full-time equivalent of the part-time staff. Data for 2009 and 2017 include institutions with fewer than 15 full-time employees; these institutions did not report staff data prior to 2007. By definition, all graduate assistants are part time. Detail may not sum to totals because of rounding.
SOURCE: U.S. Department of Education, National Center for Education Statistics, Integrated Postsecondary Education Data System (IPEDS), "Fall Enrollment Survey" (IPEDS-EF:99) and "Fall Staff Survey" (IPEDS-S:99); IPEDS Spring 2010 and Spring 2018, Fall Enrollment component; IPEDS Winter 2009–10, Human Resources Component, Fall Staff Section; and IPEDS Spring 2018, Human Resources component, Fall Staff section. (This table was prepared November 2018.)

Table 314.20. Employees in degree-granting postsecondary institutions, by sex, employment status, control and level of institution, and primary occupation: Selected years, fall 1991 through fall 2017

Sex, employment status, control and level of institution, and primary occupation	1991	1995	1997	1999	2001	2003	2005	2007	2009	2011	2013	2015	2016	2017	Percent change, 2007 to 2017
1	2	3	4	5	6	7	8	9	10	11	12	13	14	15	16
All institutions	**2,545,235**	**2,662,075**	**2,752,504**	**2,902,479**	**3,083,353**	**3,187,907**	**3,379,087**	**3,561,730**	**3,724,661**	**3,841,819**	**3,896,053**	**3,914,284**	**3,906,240**	**3,914,542**	**9.9**
Executive/administrative/managerial	144,755	147,445	151,363	160,793	152,038	184,913	196,324	217,039	230,438	238,677	([1])	([1])	([1])	([1])	†
Faculty (instruction/research/public service)	826,252	931,706	989,813	1,037,529	1,113,183	1,173,593	1,290,426	1,371,587	1,439,074	1,524,469	1,545,381	1,552,256	1,546,081	1,543,569	12.5
Graduate assistants	197,751	215,909	222,724	240,995	261,136	292,061	317,141	329,001	343,204	355,916	363,416	366,868	375,204	377,156	14.6
Other	1,376,477	1,367,015	1,388,604	1,463,162	1,556,996	1,537,340	1,575,196	1,644,103	1,711,945	1,722,757	1,987,256	1,995,160	1,984,955	1,993,817	†
Males	**1,227,591**	**1,274,676**	**1,315,311**	**1,375,114**	**1,451,773**	**1,496,867**	**1,581,498**	**1,650,641**	**1,710,021**	**1,754,919**	**1,772,803**	**1,776,928**	**1,775,229**	**1,773,654**	**7.5**
Executive/administrative/managerial	85,423	82,127	81,931	84,425	79,348	91,604	95,223	102,066	106,842	109,336	([1])	([1])	([1])	([1])	†
Faculty (instruction/research/public service)	525,599	562,893	587,420	608,007	644,514	663,723	714,453	744,047	761,002	789,567	791,971	789,405	783,495	777,821	4.5
Graduate assistants	119,125	123,962	125,873	133,066	142,120	156,881	167,529	173,128	181,328	188,305	191,501	193,202	196,170	196,077	13.3
Other	497,444	505,694	520,087	549,616	585,791	584,659	604,293	631,400	660,849	667,711	789,331	794,321	795,564	799,756	†
Females	**1,317,644**	**1,387,399**	**1,437,193**	**1,527,365**	**1,631,580**	**1,691,040**	**1,797,589**	**1,911,089**	**2,014,640**	**2,086,900**	**2,123,250**	**2,137,356**	**2,131,011**	**2,140,888**	**12.0**
Executive/administrative/managerial	59,332	65,318	69,432	76,368	72,690	93,309	101,101	114,973	123,596	129,341	([1])	([1])	([1])	([1])	†
Faculty (instruction/research/public service)	300,653	368,813	402,393	429,522	468,669	509,870	575,973	627,540	678,072	734,902	753,410	762,851	762,586	765,748	22.0
Graduate assistants	78,626	91,947	96,851	107,929	119,016	135,180	149,612	155,873	161,876	167,611	171,915	173,666	179,034	181,079	16.2
Other	879,033	861,321	868,517	913,546	971,205	952,681	970,903	1,012,703	1,051,096	1,055,046	1,197,925	1,200,839	1,189,391	1,194,061	†
Full-time	**1,812,912**	**1,801,371**	**1,828,507**	**1,926,836**	**2,043,208**	**2,083,142**	**2,179,864**	**2,281,516**	**2,382,305**	**2,435,988**	**2,472,434**	**2,507,787**	**2,506,784**	**2,525,579**	**10.7**
Executive/administrative/managerial	139,116	140,990	144,529	154,584	146,523	178,691	190,078	209,812	222,143	231,559	([1])	([1])	([1])	([1])	†
Faculty (instruction/research/public service)	535,623	550,822	568,719	593,375	617,868	630,092	675,624	703,757	729,152	762,114	791,378	807,109	813,978	821,168	16.7
Other	1,138,173	1,109,559	1,115,259	1,178,877	1,278,817	1,274,359	1,314,162	1,367,947	1,431,010	1,442,315	1,681,056	1,700,678	1,692,806	1,704,411	†
Part-time	**732,323**	**860,704**	**923,997**	**975,643**	**1,040,145**	**1,104,765**	**1,199,223**	**1,280,214**	**1,342,356**	**1,405,831**	**1,423,619**	**1,406,497**	**1,399,456**	**1,388,963**	**8.5**
Executive/administrative/managerial	5,639	6,455	6,834	6,209	5,515	6,222	6,246	7,227	8,295	7,118	([1])	([1])	([1])	([1])	†
Faculty (instruction/research/public service)	290,629	380,884	421,094	444,154	495,315	543,501	614,802	667,830	709,922	762,355	754,003	745,147	732,103	722,401	8.2
Graduate assistants	197,751	215,909	222,724	240,995	261,136	292,061	317,141	329,001	343,204	355,916	363,416	366,868	375,204	377,156	14.6
Other	238,304	257,456	273,345	284,285	278,179	262,981	261,034	276,156	280,935	280,442	306,200	294,482	292,149	289,406	†
Public 4-year	**1,341,914**	**1,383,476**	**1,418,661**	**1,474,830**	**1,558,576**	**1,569,870**	**1,656,709**	**1,742,370**	**1,804,332**	**1,843,314**	**1,884,854**	**1,925,674**	**1,966,008**	**1,987,634**	**14.1**
Executive/administrative/managerial	63,674	60,590	61,984	64,479	60,245	70,397	74,241	81,162	84,214	84,918	([1])	([1])	([1])	([1])	†
Faculty (instruction/research/public service)	358,376	384,399	404,109	418,500	438,459	450,123	486,691	518,930	539,946	575,624	601,126	622,283	646,584	654,601	26.1
Graduate assistants	144,344	178,342	182,481	196,802	218,260	239,600	257,578	266,451	275,878	285,905	287,839	291,770	293,954	295,783	11.0
Other	775,520	760,145	770,087	795,049	841,612	809,750	838,199	875,827	904,294	896,867	995,889	1,011,621	1,025,470	1,037,250	†
Private 4-year	**734,509**	**770,004**	**786,634**	**865,434**	**912,924**	**988,895**	**1,073,764**	**1,158,196**	**1,230,409**	**1,297,376**	**1,318,760**	**1,323,899**	**1,308,587**	**1,313,563**	**13.4**
Executive/administrative/managerial	57,148	62,314	62,580	70,082	65,739	84,306	90,415	102,906	111,616	118,220	([1])	([1])	([1])	([1])	†
Faculty (instruction/research/public service)	232,893	262,660	278,541	300,756	325,713	364,166	430,305	473,455	498,403	540,018	550,512	558,262	550,073	552,420	16.7
Graduate assistants	23,989	33,853	36,064	38,757	41,611	52,101	59,147	62,550	67,326	70,011	75,537	75,079	81,241	81,351	30.1
Other	420,479	411,177	409,449	455,839	479,861	488,322	493,897	519,285	553,064	569,127	692,711	690,558	677,273	679,792	†
Public 2-year	**441,414**	**482,454**	**512,086**	**524,874**	**578,394**	**593,466**	**610,978**	**619,455**	**638,361**	**642,455**	**642,430**	**622,754**	**591,066**	**577,340**	**-6.8**
Executive/administrative/managerial	20,772	21,806	22,822	21,699	22,566	25,872	26,770	27,363	27,827	27,562	([1])	([1])	([1])	([1])	†
Faculty (instruction/research/public service)	222,532	272,434	290,451	300,085	332,665	341,643	354,497	357,596	373,842	378,535	367,608	348,708	327,655	316,582	-11.5
Graduate assistants	29,216	3,401	3,561	4,809	1,215	323	374	0	0	0	13	13	9	15	†
Other	168,894	184,813	195,252	198,281	221,948	225,628	229,337	234,496	236,692	236,358	274,809	274,033	263,402	260,743	†
Private 2-year	**27,398**	**26,141**	**35,123**	**37,341**	**33,459**	**35,676**	**37,636**	**41,709**	**51,559**	**58,674**	**50,009**	**41,957**	**40,579**	**36,005**	**-13.7**
Executive/administrative/managerial	3,161	2,735	3,977	4,533	3,488	4,338	4,898	5,608	6,781	7,977	([1])	([1])	([1])	([1])	†
Faculty (instruction/research/public service)	12,451	12,213	16,712	18,188	16,346	17,661	18,933	21,606	26,883	30,292	26,135	23,003	21,769	19,966	-7.6
Graduate assistants	202	313	618	627	50	37	42	0	0	0	27	6	0	7	†
Other	11,584	10,880	13,816	13,993	13,575	13,640	13,763	14,495	17,895	20,405	23,847	18,948	18,810	16,032	†

†Not applicable.
[1]Included in other. Primary occupations were reclassified as of fall 2013; only the faculty and graduate assistant categories are comparable with data from earlier years.
NOTE: Data through 1995 are for institutions of higher education, while later data are for degree-granting institutions. Degree-granting institutions grant associate's or higher degrees and participate in Title IV federal financial aid programs. The degree-granting classification is very similar to the earlier higher education classification, but it includes more 2-year colleges and excludes a few higher education institutions that did not grant degrees. Beginning in 2007, includes institutions with fewer than 15 full-time employees; these institutions did not report staff data prior to 2007. By definition, all graduate assistants are part time. Some data have been revised from previously published figures.
SOURCE: U.S. Department of Education, National Center for Education Statistics, Integrated Postsecondary Education Data System (IPEDS), "Fall Staff Survey" (IPEDS-S:91–99); IPEDS Winter 2001–02 through Winter 2011–12, Human Resources component, Fall Staff section; and IPEDS Spring 2014 through Spring 2018, Human Resources component, Fall Staff section. (This table was prepared November 2018.)

Table 314.30. Employees in degree-granting postsecondary institutions, by employment status, sex, control and level of institution, and primary occupation: Fall 2017

Control and level of institution and primary occupation	Full-time and part-time: Total: Number	Full-time and part-time: Total: Percentage distribution	Full-time and part-time: Males	Full-time and part-time: Females: Number	Full-time and part-time: Females: Percent of all employees	Full-time: Total: Number	Full-time: Total: Percent of all employees	Full-time: Males	Full-time: Females	Part-time: Total	Part-time: Males	Part-time: Females
1	2	3	4	5	6	7	8	9	10	11	12	13
All institutions	**3,914,542**	**100.0**	**1,773,654**	**2,140,888**	**54.7**	**2,525,579**	**64.5**	**1,129,426**	**1,396,153**	**1,388,963**	**644,228**	**744,735**
Faculty (instruction/research/public service)	1,543,569	39.4	777,821	765,748	49.6	821,168	53.2	440,842	380,326	722,401	336,979	385,422
Instruction	1,425,058	36.4	712,123	712,935	50.0	724,060	50.8	385,907	338,153	700,998	326,216	374,782
Research	89,445	2.3	51,680	37,765	42.2	75,668	84.6	44,304	31,364	13,777	7,376	6,401
Public service	29,066	0.7	14,018	15,048	51.8	21,440	73.8	10,631	10,809	7,626	3,387	4,239
Graduate assistants	377,156	9.6	196,077	181,079	48.0	†	†	†	†	377,156	196,077	181,079
Librarians, curators, and archivists	41,497	1.1	12,358	29,139	70.2	35,460	85.5	10,752	24,708	6,037	1,606	4,431
Student and academic affairs and other education services	181,731	4.6	58,563	123,168	67.8	123,003	67.7	36,250	86,753	58,728	22,313	36,415
Management	259,986	6.6	113,571	146,415	56.3	253,115	97.4	110,861	142,254	6,871	2,710	4,161
Business and financial operations	214,461	5.5	58,083	156,378	72.9	200,946	93.7	54,492	146,454	13,515	3,591	9,924
Computer, engineering, and science	235,674	6.0	142,683	92,991	39.5	216,282	91.8	133,963	82,319	19,392	8,720	10,672
Community, social service, legal, arts, design, entertainment, sports, and media	184,650	4.7	82,419	102,231	55.4	149,906	81.2	65,670	84,236	34,744	16,749	17,995
Healthcare practitioners and technicians	109,889	2.8	32,999	76,890	70.0	90,729	82.6	27,824	62,905	19,160	5,175	13,985
Service occupations	241,200	6.2	139,878	101,322	42.0	199,942	82.9	117,473	82,469	41,258	22,405	18,853
Sales and related occupations	13,210	0.3	4,600	8,610	65.2	10,756	81.4	3,958	6,798	2,454	642	1,812
Office and administrative support	418,537	10.7	71,079	347,458	83.0	339,319	81.1	49,681	289,638	79,218	21,398	57,820
Natural resources, construction, and maintenance	74,000	1.9	67,993	6,007	8.1	69,686	94.2	64,883	4,803	4,314	3,110	1,204
Production, transportation, and material moving	18,982	0.5	15,530	3,452	18.2	15,267	80.4	12,777	2,490	3,715	2,753	962
Public 4-year	**1,987,634**	**100.0**	**919,911**	**1,067,723**	**53.7**	**1,349,439**	**67.9**	**618,585**	**730,854**	**638,195**	**301,326**	**336,869**
Faculty (instruction/research/public service)	654,601	32.9	343,275	311,326	47.6	432,308	66.0	239,316	192,992	222,293	103,959	118,334
Instruction	583,627	29.4	304,378	279,249	47.8	372,703	63.9	206,171	166,532	210,924	98,207	112,717
Research	54,622	2.7	31,172	23,450	42.9	45,958	84.1	26,659	19,299	8,664	4,513	4,151
Public service	16,352	0.8	7,725	8,627	52.8	13,647	83.5	6,486	7,161	2,705	1,239	1,466
Graduate assistants	295,783	14.9	153,220	142,563	48.2	†	†	†	†	295,783	153,220	142,563
Librarians, curators, and archivists	18,397	0.9	5,630	12,767	69.4	16,914	91.9	5,229	11,685	1,483	401	1,082
Student and academic affairs and other education services	69,106	3.5	21,797	47,309	68.5	52,913	76.6	15,783	37,130	16,193	6,014	10,179
Management	117,602	5.9	52,983	64,619	54.9	114,265	97.2	51,616	62,649	3,337	1,367	1,970
Business and financial operations	127,318	6.4	34,345	92,973	73.0	118,576	93.1	31,952	86,624	8,742	2,393	6,349
Computer, engineering, and science	146,092	7.4	87,926	58,166	39.8	133,892	91.6	82,783	51,109	12,200	5,143	7,057
Community, social service, legal, arts, design, entertainment, sports, and media	88,375	4.4	37,351	51,024	57.7	76,796	86.9	32,467	44,329	11,579	4,884	6,695
Healthcare practitioners and technicians	73,122	3.7	22,371	50,751	69.4	61,985	84.8	19,666	42,319	11,137	2,705	8,432
Service occupations	128,423	6.5	70,502	57,921	45.1	110,287	85.9	61,428	48,859	18,136	9,074	9,062
Sales and related occupations	2,908	0.1	1,044	1,864	64.1	2,222	76.4	862	1,360	686	182	504
Office and administrative support	204,688	10.3	34,178	170,510	83.3	172,438	84.2	25,391	147,047	32,250	8,787	23,463
Natural resources, construction, and maintenance	48,451	2.4	44,741	3,710	7.7	45,927	94.8	42,882	3,045	2,524	1,859	665
Production, transportation, and material moving	12,768	0.6	10,548	2,220	17.4	10,916	85.5	9,210	1,706	1,852	1,338	514
Public 2-year	**577,340**	**100.0**	**245,506**	**331,834**	**57.5**	**279,745**	**48.5**	**113,404**	**166,341**	**297,595**	**132,102**	**165,493**
Faculty (instruction/research/public service)	316,582	54.8	144,896	171,686	54.2	102,866	32.5	46,222	56,644	213,716	98,674	115,042
Instruction	313,110	54.2	143,550	169,560	54.2	102,280	32.7	46,028	56,252	210,830	97,522	113,308
Research	109	#	45	64	58.7	100	91.7	42	58	9	3	6
Public service	3,363	0.6	1,301	2,062	61.3	486	14.5	152	334	2,877	1,149	1,728
Graduate assistants	15	#	9	6	40.0	†	†	†	†	15	9	6
Librarians, curators, and archivists	5,211	0.9	1,172	4,039	77.5	3,544	68.0	820	2,724	1,667	352	1,315
Student and academic affairs and other education services	50,072	8.7	17,698	32,374	64.7	21,415	42.8	6,366	15,049	28,657	11,332	17,325
Management	31,681	5.5	12,963	18,718	59.1	30,578	96.5	12,541	18,037	1,103	422	681
Business and financial operations	16,797	2.9	4,301	12,496	74.4	15,026	89.5	3,780	11,246	1,771	521	1,250
Computer, engineering, and science	15,750	2.7	10,568	5,182	32.9	13,265	84.2	9,088	4,177	2,485	1,480	1,005
Community, social service, legal, arts, design, entertainment, sports, and media	23,492	4.1	8,959	14,533	61.9	16,000	68.1	5,739	10,261	7,492	3,220	4,272
Healthcare practitioners and technicians	1,577	0.3	534	1,043	66.1	767	48.6	311	456	810	223	587
Service occupations	33,058	5.7	22,960	10,098	30.5	22,902	69.3	16,552	6,350	10,156	6,408	3,748
Sales and related occupations	1,847	0.3	481	1,366	74.0	973	52.7	289	684	874	192	682
Office and administrative support	73,879	12.8	14,420	59,459	80.5	46,331	62.7	6,115	40,216	27,548	8,305	19,243
Natural resources, construction, and maintenance	6,050	1.0	5,498	552	9.1	5,329	88.1	4,957	372	721	541	180
Production, transportation, and material moving	1,329	0.2	1,047	282	21.2	749	56.4	624	125	580	423	157
Private nonprofit 4-year	**1,201,512**	**100.0**	**548,797**	**652,715**	**54.3**	**825,095**	**68.7**	**370,333**	**454,762**	**376,417**	**178,464**	**197,953**
Faculty (instruction/research/public service)	482,640	40.2	251,373	231,267	47.9	266,963	55.3	147,010	119,953	215,677	104,363	111,314
Instruction	438,734	36.5	225,987	212,747	48.5	230,145	52.5	125,453	104,692	208,589	100,534	108,055
Research	34,608	2.9	20,424	14,184	41.0	29,523	85.3	17,569	11,954	5,085	2,855	2,230
Public service	9,298	0.8	4,962	4,336	46.6	7,295	78.5	3,988	3,307	2,003	974	1,029
Graduate assistants	80,939	6.7	42,676	38,263	47.3	†	†	†	†	80,939	42,676	38,263
Librarians, curators, and archivists	16,763	1.4	5,277	11,486	68.5	14,258	85.1	4,522	9,736	2,505	755	1,750
Student and academic affairs and other education services	49,705	4.1	15,240	34,465	69.3	37,049	74.5	10,801	26,248	12,656	4,439	8,217
Management	99,373	8.3	42,831	56,542	56.9	97,129	97.7	41,985	55,144	2,244	846	1,398
Business and financial operations	64,790	5.4	17,835	46,955	72.5	62,047	95.8	17,206	44,841	2,743	629	2,114
Computer, engineering, and science	71,596	6.0	42,483	29,113	40.7	67,000	93.6	40,471	26,529	4,596	2,012	2,584
Community, social service, legal, arts, design, entertainment, sports, and media	67,088	5.6	33,817	33,271	49.6	51,965	77.5	25,466	26,499	15,123	8,351	6,772
Healthcare practitioners and technicians	34,878	2.9	9,979	24,899	71.4	27,792	79.7	7,760	20,032	7,086	2,219	4,867
Service occupations	77,381	6.4	44,893	32,488	42.0	65,230	84.3	38,486	26,744	12,151	6,407	5,744
Sales and related occupations	3,898	0.3	1,375	2,523	64.7	3,226	82.8	1,178	2,048	672	197	475
Office and administrative support	128,908	10.7	19,993	108,915	84.5	111,056	86.2	15,995	95,061	17,852	3,998	13,854
Natural resources, construction, and maintenance	18,876	1.6	17,250	1,626	8.6	17,912	94.9	16,620	1,292	964	630	334
Production, transportation, and material moving	4,677	0.4	3,775	902	19.3	3,468	74.2	2,833	635	1,209	942	267

See notes at end of table.

Table 314.30. Employees in degree-granting postsecondary institutions, by employment status, sex, control and level of institution, and primary occupation: Fall 2017—Continued

Control and level of institution and primary occupation	Full-time and part-time					Full-time				Part-time		
	Total			Females		Total						
	Number	Percentage distribution	Males	Number	Percent of all employees	Number	Percent of all employees	Males	Females	Total	Males	Females
1	2	3	4	5	6	7	8	9	10	11	12	13
Private nonprofit 2-year	**7,799**	**100.0**	**2,922**	**4,877**	**62.5**	**5,509**	**70.6**	**1,979**	**3,530**	**2,290**	**943**	**1,347**
Faculty (instruction/research/public service)	3,543	45.4	1,394	2,149	60.7	1,675	47.3	626	1,049	1,868	768	1,100
Instruction	3,522	45.2	1,389	2,133	60.6	1,660	47.1	623	1,037	1,862	766	1,096
Research	12	0.2	3	9	75.0	9	75.0	1	8	3	2	1
Public service	9	0.1	2	7	77.8	6	66.7	2	4	3	0	3
Graduate assistants	7	0.1	6	1	14.3	†	†	†	†	7	6	1
Librarians, curators, and archivists	111	1.4	30	81	73.0	70	63.1	20	50	41	10	31
Student and academic affairs and other education services	1,423	18.2	423	1,000	70.3	1,356	95.3	399	957	67	24	43
Management	779	10.0	351	428	54.9	759	97.4	340	419	20	11	9
Business and financial operations	216	2.8	62	154	71.3	186	86.1	57	129	30	5	25
Computer, engineering, and science	132	1.7	106	26	19.7	123	93.2	98	25	9	8	1
Community, social service, legal, arts, design, entertainment, sports, and media	206	2.6	109	97	47.1	164	79.6	83	81	42	26	16
Healthcare practitioners and technicians	31	0.4	5	26	83.9	12	38.7	3	9	19	2	17
Service occupations	195	2.5	153	42	21.5	116	59.5	91	25	79	62	17
Sales and related occupations	488	6.3	144	344	70.5	483	99.0	143	340	5	1	4
Office and administrative support	597	7.7	81	516	86.4	507	84.9	71	436	90	10	80
Natural resources, construction, and maintenance	62	0.8	52	10	16.1	54	87.1	46	8	8	6	2
Production, transportation, and material moving	9	0.1	6	3	33.3	4	44.4	2	2	5	4	1
Private for-profit 4-year	**112,051**	**100.0**	**46,244**	**65,807**	**58.7**	**49,740**	**44.4**	**19,412**	**30,328**	**62,311**	**26,832**	**35,479**
Faculty (instruction/research/public service)	69,780	62.3	30,389	39,391	56.5	11,373	16.3	5,141	6,232	58,407	25,248	33,159
Instruction	69,689	62.2	30,351	39,338	56.4	11,322	16.2	5,121	6,201	58,367	25,230	33,137
Research	62	0.1	21	41	66.1	47	75.8	18	29	15	3	12
Public service	29	#	17	12	41.4	4	13.8	2	2	25	15	10
Graduate assistants	412	0.4	166	246	59.7	†	†	†	†	412	166	246
Librarians, curators, and archivists	781	0.7	193	588	75.3	526	67.3	127	399	255	66	189
Student and academic affairs and other education services	9,223	8.2	2,842	6,381	69.2	8,304	90.0	2,412	5,892	919	430	489
Management	7,958	7.1	3,386	4,572	57.5	7,838	98.5	3,340	4,498	120	46	74
Business and financial operations	4,413	3.9	1,321	3,092	70.1	4,268	96.7	1,287	2,981	145	34	111
Computer, engineering, and science	1,880	1.7	1,421	459	24.4	1,811	96.3	1,373	438	69	48	21
Community, social service, legal, arts, design, entertainment, sports, and media	4,623	4.1	1,892	2,731	59.1	4,232	91.5	1,684	2,548	391	208	183
Healthcare practitioners and technicians	174	0.2	68	106	60.9	127	73.0	58	69	47	10	37
Service occupations	1,688	1.5	1,087	601	35.6	1,196	70.9	787	409	492	300	192
Sales and related occupations	2,744	2.4	1,103	1,641	59.8	2,675	97.5	1,081	1,594	69	22	47
Office and administrative support	7,821	7.0	1,948	5,873	75.1	6,931	88.6	1,757	5,174	890	191	699
Natural resources, construction, and maintenance	373	0.3	288	85	22.8	338	90.6	265	73	35	23	12
Production, transportation, and material moving	181	0.2	140	41	22.7	121	66.9	100	21	60	40	20
Private for-profit 2-year	**28,206**	**100.0**	**10,274**	**17,932**	**63.6**	**16,051**	**56.9**	**5,713**	**10,338**	**12,155**	**4,561**	**7,594**
Faculty (instruction/research/public service)	16,423	58.2	6,494	9,929	60.5	5,983	36.4	2,527	3,456	10,440	3,967	6,473
Instruction	16,376	58.1	6,468	9,908	60.5	5,950	36.3	2,511	3,439	10,426	3,957	6,469
Research	32	0.1	15	17	53.1	31	96.9	15	16	1	0	1
Public service	15	0.1	11	4	26.7	2	13.3	1	1	13	10	3
Graduate assistants	0	0.0	0	0	†	†	†	†	†	†	†	†
Librarians, curators, and archivists	234	0.8	56	178	76.1	148	63.2	34	114	86	22	64
Student and academic affairs and other education services	2,202	7.8	563	1,639	74.4	1,966	89.3	489	1,477	236	74	162
Management	2,593	9.2	1,057	1,536	59.2	2,546	98.2	1,039	1,507	47	18	29
Business and financial operations	927	3.3	219	708	76.4	843	90.9	210	633	84	9	75
Computer, engineering, and science	224	0.8	179	45	20.1	191	85.3	150	41	33	29	4
Community, social service, legal, arts, design, entertainment, sports, and media	866	3.1	291	575	66.4	749	86.5	231	518	117	60	57
Healthcare practitioners and technicians	107	0.4	42	65	60.7	46	43.0	26	20	61	16	45
Service occupations	455	1.6	283	172	37.8	211	46.4	129	82	244	154	90
Sales and related occupations	1,325	4.7	453	872	65.8	1,177	88.8	405	772	148	48	100
Office and administrative support	2,644	9.4	459	2,185	82.6	2,056	77.8	352	1,704	588	107	481
Natural resources, construction, and maintenance	188	0.7	164	24	12.8	126	67.0	113	13	62	51	11
Production, transportation, and material moving	18	0.1	14	4	22.2	9	50.0	8	1	9	6	3

†Not applicable.
#Rounds to zero.
NOTE: Degree-granting institutions grant associate's or higher degrees and participate in Title IV federal financial aid programs. By definition, all graduate assistants are part time. Detail may not sum to totals because of rounding.

SOURCE: U.S. Department of Education, National Center for Education Statistics, Integrated Postsecondary Education Data System (IPEDS), Spring 2018, Human Resources component, Fall Staff section. (This table was prepared November 2018.)

Table 314.40. Employees in degree-granting postsecondary institutions, by race/ethnicity, sex, employment status, control and level of institution, and primary occupation: Fall 2017

Sex, employment status, control and level of institution, and primary occupation	Total	White	Black, Hispanic, Asian, Pacific Islander, American Indian/Alaska Native, and Two or more races								Race/ ethnicity unknown	Non-resident alien[2]
			Total	Percent[1]	Black	Hispanic	Asian	Pacific Islander	American Indian/ Alaska Native	Two or more races		
1	2	3	4	5	6	7	8	9	10	11	12	13
All institutions	**3,914,542**	**2,564,739**	**987,131**	**27.8**	**374,922**	**288,989**	**246,696**	**8,167**	**20,111**	**48,246**	**163,809**	**198,863**
Faculty (instruction/research/public service)	1,543,569	1,086,081	325,133	23.0	106,836	77,168	116,394	2,879	7,041	14,815	76,747	55,608
Instruction	1,425,058	1,024,678	298,782	22.6	102,511	72,290	100,900	2,758	6,691	13,632	71,684	29,914
Research	89,445	41,001	19,305	32.0	2,113	3,377	12,658	79	200	878	4,158	24,981
Public service	29,066	20,402	7,046	25.7	2,212	1,501	2,836	42	150	305	905	713
Graduate assistants	377,156	170,799	71,084	29.4	15,711	20,773	25,693	657	941	7,309	20,541	114,732
Librarians, curators, and archivists	41,497	31,800	8,207	20.5	3,022	2,274	2,051	63	258	539	1,186	304
Student and academic affairs and other education services	181,731	119,554	53,174	30.8	23,307	17,259	7,694	644	1,461	2,809	6,823	2,180
Management	259,986	195,243	57,173	22.7	26,515	15,864	10,343	475	1,248	2,728	6,356	1,214
Business and financial operations	214,461	144,492	61,447	29.8	23,699	18,886	14,344	448	1,092	2,978	6,923	1,599
Computer, engineering, and science	235,674	153,776	61,227	28.5	14,933	15,995	25,761	394	1,057	3,087	7,636	13,035
Community, social service, legal, arts, design, entertainment, sports, and media	184,650	129,920	45,990	26.1	21,151	14,582	5,821	575	1,030	2,831	7,415	1,325
Healthcare practitioners and technicians	109,889	69,154	32,053	31.7	11,348	7,892	11,047	156	399	1,211	5,582	3,100
Service occupations	241,200	127,136	103,048	44.8	52,460	36,820	8,530	683	1,919	2,636	8,918	2,098
Sales and related occupations	13,210	7,924	4,752	37.5	2,331	1,561	460	53	93	254	495	39
Office and administrative support	418,537	262,962	140,271	34.8	62,882	50,873	16,616	949	2,743	6,208	12,054	3,250
Natural resources, construction, and maintenance	74,000	53,737	17,528	24.6	7,661	6,994	1,423	149	653	648	2,421	314
Production, transportation, and material moving	18,982	12,161	6,044	33.2	3,066	2,048	519	42	176	193	712	65
Males	**1,773,654**	**1,166,570**	**410,580**	**26.0**	**140,429**	**120,843**	**117,761**	**3,548**	**8,669**	**19,330**	**77,293**	**119,211**
Faculty (instruction/research/public service)	777,821	550,559	154,990	22.0	42,302	37,917	63,721	1,192	3,378	6,480	37,740	34,532
Instruction	712,123	517,879	141,537	21.5	40,591	35,604	55,025	1,134	3,243	5,940	35,083	17,624
Research	51,680	22,750	10,221	31.0	872	1,601	7,235	34	80	399	2,208	16,501
Public service	14,018	9,930	3,232	24.6	839	712	1,461	24	55	141	449	407
Graduate assistants	196,077	82,866	32,998	28.5	6,138	9,538	13,269	390	397	3,266	10,483	69,730
Librarians, curators, and archivists	12,358	9,640	2,226	18.8	714	772	518	18	58	146	370	122
Student and academic affairs and other education services	58,563	38,522	16,642	30.2	6,901	5,728	2,476	229	474	834	2,421	978
Management	113,571	87,899	22,202	20.2	9,637	6,233	4,505	254	525	1,048	2,879	591
Business and financial operations	58,083	40,493	14,924	26.9	5,254	4,927	3,575	123	285	760	2,106	560
Computer, engineering, and science	142,683	96,504	33,642	25.8	8,040	9,596	13,266	266	629	1,845	4,629	7,908
Community, social service, legal, arts, design, entertainment, sports, and media	82,419	59,280	18,919	24.2	9,527	5,586	2,036	268	443	1,059	3,597	623
Healthcare practitioners and technicians	32,999	19,574	9,582	32.9	2,596	2,268	4,189	55	122	352	2,210	1,633
Service occupations	139,878	77,668	56,011	41.9	29,001	19,451	4,577	391	1,143	1,448	5,181	1,018
Sales and related occupations	4,600	2,761	1,645	37.3	784	583	155	17	30	76	180	14
Office and administrative support	71,079	40,625	26,479	39.5	10,598	10,157	3,786	180	448	1,310	2,730	1,245
Natural resources, construction, and maintenance	67,993	50,016	15,577	23.7	6,644	6,383	1,250	136	597	567	2,198	202
Production, transportation, and material moving	15,530	10,163	4,743	31.8	2,293	1,704	438	29	140	139	569	55
Females	**2,140,888**	**1,398,169**	**576,551**	**29.2**	**234,493**	**168,146**	**128,935**	**4,619**	**11,442**	**28,916**	**86,516**	**79,652**
Faculty (instruction/research/public service)	765,748	535,522	170,143	24.1	64,534	39,251	52,673	1,687	3,663	8,335	39,007	21,076
Instruction	712,935	506,799	157,245	23.7	61,920	36,686	45,875	1,624	3,448	7,692	36,601	12,290
Research	37,765	18,251	9,084	33.2	1,241	1,776	5,423	45	120	479	1,950	8,480
Public service	15,048	10,472	3,814	26.7	1,373	789	1,375	18	95	164	456	306
Graduate assistants	181,079	87,933	38,086	30.2	9,573	11,235	12,424	267	544	4,043	10,058	45,002
Librarians, curators, and archivists	29,139	22,160	5,981	21.3	2,308	1,502	1,533	45	200	393	816	182
Student and academic affairs and other education services	123,168	81,032	36,532	31.1	16,406	11,531	5,218	415	987	1,975	4,402	1,202
Management	146,415	107,344	34,971	24.6	16,878	9,631	5,838	221	723	1,680	3,477	623
Business and financial operations	156,378	103,999	46,523	30.9	18,445	13,959	10,769	325	807	2,218	4,817	1,039
Computer, engineering, and science	92,991	57,272	27,585	32.5	6,893	6,399	12,495	128	428	1,242	3,007	5,127
Community, social service, legal, arts, design, entertainment, sports, and media	102,231	70,640	27,071	27.7	11,624	8,996	3,785	307	587	1,772	3,818	702
Healthcare practitioners and technicians	76,890	49,580	22,471	31.2	8,752	5,624	6,858	101	277	859	3,372	1,467
Service occupations	101,322	49,468	47,037	48.7	23,459	17,369	3,953	292	776	1,188	3,737	1,080
Sales and related occupations	8,610	5,163	3,107	37.6	1,547	978	305	36	63	178	315	25
Office and administrative support	347,458	222,337	113,792	33.9	52,284	40,716	12,830	769	2,295	4,898	9,324	2,005
Natural resources, construction, and maintenance	6,007	3,721	1,951	34.4	1,017	611	173	13	56	81	223	112
Production, transportation, and material moving	3,452	1,998	1,301	39.4	773	344	81	13	36	54	143	10
Full-time	**2,525,579**	**1,697,742**	**684,618**	**28.7**	**262,617**	**200,901**	**172,490**	**5,114**	**13,833**	**29,663**	**75,420**	**67,799**
Faculty (instruction/research/public service)	821,168	573,560	178,947	23.8	45,427	39,099	82,142	1,200	3,460	7,619	23,439	45,222
Instruction	724,060	524,402	156,986	23.0	42,256	35,132	68,622	1,113	3,202	6,661	19,530	23,142
Research	75,668	34,070	16,765	33.0	1,838	2,824	11,170	60	149	724	3,350	21,483
Public service	21,440	15,088	5,196	25.6	1,333	1,143	2,350	27	109	234	559	597
Graduate assistants	†	†	†	†	†	†	†	†	†	†	†	†
Librarians, curators, and archivists	35,460	27,270	7,033	20.5	2,548	1,963	1,791	44	207	480	899	258
Student and academic affairs and other education services	123,003	81,460	36,572	31.0	16,461	11,387	5,139	466	1,077	2,042	3,766	1,205
Management	253,115	190,001	55,882	22.7	25,962	15,545	10,029	461	1,222	2,663	6,067	1,165
Business and financial operations	200,946	134,719	58,519	30.3	22,769	17,924	13,556	419	1,035	2,816	6,266	1,442
Computer, engineering, and science	216,282	141,774	55,885	28.3	13,574	14,319	23,855	360	963	2,814	6,753	11,870
Community, social service, legal, arts, design, entertainment, sports, and media	149,906	105,359	38,511	26.8	17,708	12,234	4,907	484	839	2,339	5,004	1,032
Healthcare practitioners and technicians	90,729	56,461	27,196	32.5	9,831	6,832	9,025	135	341	1,032	4,801	2,271
Service occupations	199,942	103,558	88,240	46.0	44,926	31,723	7,342	562	1,601	2,086	6,515	1,629
Sales and related occupations	10,756	6,303	4,075	39.3	2,053	1,360	344	47	76	195	357	21
Office and administrative support	339,319	216,464	112,261	34.2	51,746	40,008	12,593	773	2,278	4,863	9,154	1,440
Natural resources, construction, and maintenance	69,686	51,019	16,502	24.4	7,200	6,681	1,321	132	594	574	1,978	187
Production, transportation, and material moving	15,267	9,794	4,995	33.8	2,412	1,826	446	31	140	140	421	57

See notes at end of table.

Table 314.40. Employees in degree-granting postsecondary institutions, by race/ethnicity, sex, employment status, control and level of institution, and primary occupation: Fall 2017—Continued

Sex, employment status, control and level of institution, and primary occupation	Total	White	Black, Hispanic, Asian, Pacific Islander, American Indian/Alaska Native, and Two or more races								Race/ ethnicity unknown	Non-resident alien[2]
			Total	Percent[1]	Black	Hispanic	Asian	Pacific Islander	American Indian/ Alaska Native	Two or more races		
1	2	3	4	5	6	7	8	9	10	11	12	13
Part-time	**1,388,963**	**866,997**	**302,513**	**25.9**	**112,305**	**88,088**	**74,206**	**3,053**	**6,278**	**18,583**	**88,389**	**131,064**
Faculty (instruction/research/public service)	722,401	512,521	146,186	22.2	61,409	38,069	34,252	1,679	3,581	7,196	53,308	10,386
Instruction	700,998	500,276	141,796	22.1	60,255	37,158	32,278	1,645	3,489	6,971	52,154	6,772
Research	13,777	6,931	2,540	26.8	275	553	1,488	19	51	154	808	3,498
Public service	7,626	5,314	1,850	25.8	879	358	486	15	41	71	346	116
Graduate assistants	377,156	170,799	71,084	29.4	15,711	20,773	25,693	657	941	7,309	20,541	114,732
Librarians, curators, and archivists	6,037	4,530	1,174	20.6	474	311	260	19	51	59	287	46
Student and academic affairs and other education services	58,728	38,094	16,602	30.4	6,846	5,872	2,555	178	384	767	3,057	975
Management	6,871	5,242	1,291	19.8	553	319	314	14	26	65	289	49
Business and financial operations	13,515	9,773	2,928	23.1	930	962	788	29	57	162	657	157
Computer, engineering, and science	19,392	12,002	5,342	30.8	1,359	1,676	1,906	34	94	273	883	1,165
Community, social service, legal, arts, design, entertainment, sports, and media	34,744	24,561	7,479	23.3	3,443	2,348	914	91	191	492	2,411	293
Healthcare practitioners and technicians	19,160	12,693	4,857	27.7	1,517	1,060	2,022	21	58	179	781	829
Service occupations	41,258	23,578	14,808	38.6	7,534	5,097	1,188	121	318	550	2,403	469
Sales and related occupations	2,454	1,621	677	29.5	278	201	116	6	17	59	138	18
Office and administrative support	79,218	46,498	28,010	37.6	11,136	10,865	4,023	176	465	1,345	2,900	1,810
Natural resources, construction, and maintenance	4,314	2,718	1,026	27.4	461	313	102	17	59	74	443	127
Production, transportation, and material moving	3,715	2,367	1,049	30.7	654	222	73	11	36	53	291	8
Public 4-year	**1,987,634**	**1,268,832**	**500,998**	**28.3**	**177,464**	**147,011**	**137,921**	**3,581**	**10,603**	**24,418**	**75,914**	**141,890**
Faculty (instruction/research/public service)	654,601	451,513	140,757	23.8	36,512	32,951	61,302	1,070	3,025	5,897	27,560	34,771
Instruction	583,627	413,049	126,770	23.5	34,451	30,187	53,068	990	2,795	5,279	24,029	19,779
Research	54,622	26,136	11,018	29.7	1,146	2,098	7,091	58	147	478	2,936	14,532
Public service	16,352	12,328	2,969	19.4	915	666	1,143	22	83	140	595	460
Graduate assistants	295,783	136,058	54,598	28.6	12,170	16,625	19,026	458	806	5,513	14,919	90,208
Librarians, curators, and archivists	18,397	13,989	3,792	21.3	1,295	1,139	913	21	145	279	475	141
Student and academic affairs and other education services	69,106	45,727	19,890	30.3	8,352	6,507	3,088	254	642	1,047	2,378	1,111
Management	117,602	88,538	26,062	22.7	12,241	7,028	4,770	205	656	1,162	2,357	645
Business and financial operations	127,318	85,899	36,691	29.9	13,547	11,397	9,093	252	711	1,691	3,809	919
Computer, engineering, and science	146,092	97,183	35,506	26.8	7,963	9,412	15,410	214	641	1,866	4,656	8,747
Community, social service, legal, arts, design, entertainment, sports, and media	88,375	60,847	23,579	27.9	10,499	7,824	3,106	246	541	1,363	3,255	694
Healthcare practitioners and technicians	73,122	46,695	20,518	30.5	7,650	4,707	7,006	83	309	763	4,315	1,594
Service occupations	128,423	66,267	56,228	45.9	29,005	19,231	5,195	293	1,087	1,417	4,818	1,110
Sales and related occupations	2,908	1,937	845	30.4	345	302	112	12	27	47	118	8
Office and administrative support	204,688	130,502	67,366	34.0	31,098	24,105	7,566	360	1,441	2,796	5,112	1,708
Natural resources, construction, and maintenance	48,451	35,583	11,051	23.7	4,814	4,282	958	91	453	453	1,635	182
Production, transportation, and material moving	12,768	8,094	4,115	33.7	1,973	1,501	376	22	119	124	507	52
Public 2-year	**577,340**	**400,650**	**152,906**	**27.6**	**65,630**	**52,499**	**22,852**	**1,511**	**4,629**	**5,785**	**19,832**	**3,952**
Faculty (instruction/research/public service)	316,582	236,217	65,105	21.6	27,311	19,603	12,963	670	1,982	2,576	13,230	2,030
Instruction	313,110	233,980	64,063	21.5	26,643	19,413	12,863	667	1,934	2,543	13,121	1,946
Research	109	76	29	27.6	6	9	10	0	3	1	3	1
Public service	3,363	2,161	1,013	31.9	662	181	90	3	45	32	106	83
Graduate assistants	15	10	5	33.3	0	3	1	1	0	0	0	0
Librarians, curators, and archivists	5,211	3,900	1,178	23.2	488	373	215	19	53	30	112	21
Student and academic affairs and other education services	50,072	31,999	16,318	33.8	7,007	5,924	1,991	179	556	661	1,495	260
Management	31,681	22,822	8,123	26.2	4,284	2,448	788	57	275	271	653	83
Business and financial operations	16,797	10,617	5,719	35.0	2,555	1,997	793	43	146	185	364	97
Computer, engineering, and science	15,750	10,589	4,674	30.6	1,504	1,678	1,118	38	128	208	352	135
Community, social service, legal, arts, design, entertainment, sports, and media	23,492	15,033	7,569	33.5	3,718	2,550	651	122	228	300	788	102
Healthcare practitioners and technicians	1,577	1,220	262	17.7	109	74	41	6	15	17	92	3
Service occupations	33,058	18,036	13,733	43.2	6,733	5,305	843	109	413	330	936	353
Sales and related occupations	1,847	1,419	401	22.0	161	134	53	3	26	24	23	4
Office and administrative support	73,879	43,640	27,777	38.9	10,863	11,620	3,241	247	692	1,114	1,615	847
Natural resources, construction, and maintenance	6,050	4,268	1,639	27.7	708	655	119	12	90	55	126	17
Production, transportation, and material moving	1,329	880	403	31.4	189	135	35	5	25	14	46	0
Private nonprofit 4-year	**1,201,512**	**806,364**	**285,028**	**26.1**	**108,499**	**75,859**	**79,261**	**2,526**	**3,984**	**14,899**	**57,349**	**52,771**
Faculty (instruction/research/public service)	482,640	342,758	93,159	21.4	29,010	18,922	38,156	857	1,507	4,707	28,011	18,712
Instruction	438,734	322,146	81,901	20.3	27,430	17,011	31,017	819	1,446	4,178	26,591	8,096
Research	34,608	14,734	8,210	35.8	949	1,258	5,539	21	45	398	1,218	10,446
Public service	9,298	5,878	3,048	34.1	631	653	1,600	17	16	131	202	170
Graduate assistants	80,939	34,493	16,373	32.2	3,498	4,119	6,645	197	134	1,780	5,571	24,502
Librarians, curators, and archivists	16,763	13,125	2,943	18.3	1,124	668	877	19	54	201	554	141
Student and academic affairs and other education services	49,705	34,948	11,862	25.3	5,626	3,077	2,057	145	194	763	2,095	800
Management	99,373	76,045	19,947	20.8	8,689	5,413	4,314	162	271	1,098	2,906	475
Business and financial operations	64,790	44,579	17,114	27.7	6,935	4,822	4,080	132	193	952	2,523	574
Computer, engineering, and science	71,596	44,632	20,324	31.3	5,298	4,655	9,009	136	266	960	2,552	4,088
Community, social service, legal, arts, design, entertainment, sports, and media	67,088	50,709	12,786	20.1	6,006	3,523	1,891	184	229	953	3,066	527
Healthcare practitioners and technicians	34,878	21,046	11,187	34.7	3,552	3,102	3,967	66	72	428	1,144	1,501
Service occupations	77,381	41,765	31,925	43.3	16,262	11,739	2,425	269	398	832	3,058	633
Sales and related occupations	3,898	2,535	1,136	30.9	443	446	137	20	11	79	205	22
Office and administrative support	128,908	83,025	40,331	32.7	19,099	13,175	5,276	283	527	1,971	4,884	668
Natural resources, construction, and maintenance	18,876	13,617	4,515	24.9	2,080	1,822	340	44	98	131	629	115
Production, transportation, and material moving	4,677	3,087	1,426	31.6	877	376	87	12	30	44	151	13

See notes at end of table.

Table 314.40. Employees in degree-granting postsecondary institutions, by race/ethnicity, sex, employment status, control and level of institution, and primary occupation: Fall 2017—Continued

Sex, employment status, control and level of institution, and primary occupation	Total	White	Black, Hispanic, Asian, Pacific Islander, American Indian/Alaska Native, and Two or more races								Race/ ethnicity unknown	Non-resident alien[2]
			Total	Percent[1]	Black	Hispanic	Asian	Pacific Islander	American Indian/ Alaska Native	Two or more races		
1	2	3	4	5	6	7	8	9	10	11	12	13
Private nonprofit 2-year	**7,799**	**4,772**	**2,755**	**36.6**	**1,654**	**651**	**149**	**18**	**135**	**148**	**265**	**7**
Faculty (instruction/research/public service)	3,543	2,483	884	26.3	582	151	66	7	43	35	170	6
Instruction	3,522	2,474	873	26.1	581	151	66	7	33	35	169	6
Research	12	6	5	45.5	1	0	0	0	4	0	1	0
Public service	9	3	6	66.7	0	0	0	0	6	0	0	0
Graduate assistants	7	3	1	25.0	0	1	0	0	0	0	3	0
Librarians, curators, and archivists	111	90	17	15.9	7	4	1	0	4	1	4	0
Student and academic affairs and other education services	1,423	558	832	59.9	480	233	30	3	24	62	33	0
Management	779	546	210	27.8	104	55	26	3	14	8	23	0
Business and financial operations	216	144	71	33.0	27	25	6	1	6	6	1	0
Computer, engineering, and science	132	96	32	25.0	6	11	8	0	5	2	4	0
Community, social service, legal, arts, design, entertainment, sports, and media	206	162	44	21.4	29	10	0	0	2	3	0	0
Healthcare practitioners and technicians	31	29	2	6.5	2	0	0	0	0	0	0	0
Service occupations	195	122	73	37.4	39	19	1	0	12	2	0	0
Sales and related occupations	488	117	366	75.8	245	92	4	3	1	21	5	0
Office and administrative support	597	391	192	32.9	118	41	7	1	17	8	13	1
Natural resources, construction, and maintenance	62	25	28	52.8	14	7	0	0	7	0	9	0
Production, transportation, and material moving	9	6	3	33.3	1	2	0	0	0	0	0	0
Private for-profit 4-year	**112,051**	**68,778**	**33,949**	**33.0**	**15,768**	**9,464**	**5,446**	**412**	**602**	**2,257**	**9,142**	**182**
Faculty (instruction/research/public service)	69,780	43,887	18,981	30.2	9,908	3,993	3,272	215	391	1,202	6,863	49
Instruction	69,689	43,830	18,951	30.2	9,903	3,986	3,255	215	391	1,201	6,861	47
Research	62	37	23	38.3	3	6	14	0	0	0	0	2
Public service	29	20	7	25.9	2	1	3	0	0	1	2	0
Graduate assistants	412	235	107	31.3	43	25	21	1	1	16	48	22
Librarians, curators, and archivists	781	538	206	27.7	76	66	36	3	2	23	36	1
Student and academic affairs and other education services	9,223	5,206	3,295	38.8	1,420	1,119	436	50	33	237	719	3
Management	7,958	5,664	1,944	25.6	783	634	348	33	21	125	340	10
Business and financial operations	4,413	2,767	1,435	34.2	480	463	331	16	29	116	207	4
Computer, engineering, and science	1,880	1,142	610	34.8	134	210	205	5	13	43	64	64
Community, social service, legal, arts, design, entertainment, sports, and media	4,623	2,847	1,528	34.9	636	527	146	21	24	174	246	2
Healthcare practitioners and technicians	174	100	53	34.6	12	7	27	1	3	3	19	2
Service occupations	1,688	703	887	55.8	349	435	53	9	8	33	98	0
Sales and related occupations	2,744	1,327	1,300	49.5	758	357	107	9	18	51	114	3
Office and administrative support	7,821	4,143	3,298	44.3	1,129	1,410	438	44	54	223	358	22
Natural resources, construction, and maintenance	373	133	218	62.1	17	188	5	2	3	3	22	0
Production, transportation, and material moving	181	86	87	50.3	23	30	21	3	2	8	8	0
Private for-profit 2-year	**28,206**	**15,343**	**11,495**	**42.8**	**5,907**	**3,505**	**1,067**	**119**	**158**	**739**	**1,307**	**61**
Faculty (instruction/research/public service)	16,423	9,223	6,247	40.4	3,513	1,548	635	60	93	398	913	40
Instruction	16,376	9,199	6,224	40.4	3,503	1,542	631	60	92	396	913	40
Research	32	12	20	62.5	8	6	4	0	1	1	0	0
Public service	15	12	3	20.0	2	0	0	0	0	1	0	0
Graduate assistants	0	0	0	†	0	0	0	0	0	0	0	0
Librarians, curators, and archivists	234	158	71	31.0	32	24	9	1	0	5	5	0
Student and academic affairs and other education services	2,202	1,116	977	46.7	422	399	92	13	12	39	103	6
Management	2,593	1,628	887	35.3	414	286	97	15	11	64	77	1
Business and financial operations	927	486	417	46.2	155	182	41	4	7	28	19	5
Computer, engineering, and science	224	134	81	37.7	28	29	11	1	4	8	8	1
Community, social service, legal, arts, design, entertainment, sports, and media	866	322	484	60.0	263	148	27	2	6	38	60	0
Healthcare practitioners and technicians	107	64	31	32.6	23	2	6	0	0	0	12	0
Service occupations	455	243	202	45.4	72	91	13	3	1	22	8	2
Sales and related occupations	1,325	589	704	54.4	379	230	47	6	10	32	30	2
Office and administrative support	2,644	1,261	1,307	50.9	575	522	88	14	12	96	72	4
Natural resources, construction, and maintenance	188	111	77	41.0	28	40	1	0	2	6	0	0
Production, transportation, and material moving	18	8	10	55.6	3	4	0	0	0	3	0	0

†Not applicable.
[1]Combined total of staff who were Black, Hispanic, Asian, Pacific Islander, American Indian/Alaska Native, and of Two or more races as a percentage of total staff, excluding race/ethnicity unknown and nonresident alien.
[2]Race/ethnicity not collected.

NOTE: Degree-granting institutions grant associate's or higher degrees and participate in Title IV federal financial aid programs. By definition, all graduate assistants are part time. Race categories exclude persons of Hispanic ethnicity.
SOURCE: U.S. Department of Education, National Center for Education Statistics, Integrated Postsecondary Education Data System (IPEDS), Spring 2018, Human Resources component, Fall Staff section. (This table was prepared November 2018.)

Table 315.10. Number of faculty in degree-granting postsecondary institutions, by employment status, sex, control, and level of institution: Selected years, fall 1970 through fall 2017

Year	Total	Employment status			Sex			Control				Level	
									Private				
		Full-time	Part-time	Percent full-time	Males	Females	Percent female	Public	Total	Nonprofit	For-profit	4-year	2-year
1	2	3	4	5	6	7	8	9	10	11	12	13	14
1970	474,000	369,000	104,000	77.8	—	—	—	314,000	160,000	—	—	382,000	92,000
1971[1]	492,000	379,000	113,000	77.0	—	—	—	333,000	159,000	—	—	387,000	105,000
1972	500,000	380,000	120,000	76.0	—	—	—	343,000	157,000	—	—	384,000	116,000
1973[1]	527,000	389,000	138,000	73.8	—	—	—	365,000	162,000	—	—	401,000	126,000
1974[1]	567,000	406,000	161,000	71.6	—	—	—	397,000	170,000	—	—	427,000	140,000
1975[1]	628,000	440,000	188,000	70.1	—	—	—	443,000	185,000	—	—	467,000	161,000
1976	633,000	434,000	199,000	68.6	—	—	—	449,000	184,000	—	—	467,000	166,000
1977	678,000	448,000	230,000	66.1	—	—	—	492,000	186,000	—	—	485,000	193,000
1979[1]	675,000	445,000	230,000	65.9	—	—	—	488,000	187,000	—	—	494,000	182,000
1980[1]	686,000	450,000	236,000	65.6	—	—	—	495,000	191,000	—	—	494,000	192,000
1981	705,000	461,000	244,000	65.4	—	—	—	509,000	196,000	—	—	493,000	212,000
1982[1]	710,000	462,000	248,000	65.1	—	—	—	506,000	204,000	—	—	493,000	217,000
1983	724,000	471,000	254,000	65.1	—	—	—	512,000	212,000	—	—	504,000	220,000
1984[1]	717,000	462,000	255,000	64.4	—	—	—	505,000	212,000	—	—	504,000	213,000
1985[1]	715,000	459,000	256,000	64.2	—	—	—	503,000	212,000	—	—	504,000	211,000
1986[1]	722,000	459,000	263,000	63.6	—	—	—	510,000	212,000	—	—	506,000	216,000
1987[2]	793,070	523,420	269,650	66.0	529,413	263,657	33.2	552,749	240,321	—	—	547,505	245,565
1989[2]	824,220	524,426	299,794	63.6	534,254	289,966	35.2	577,298	246,922	—	—	583,700	240,520
1991[2]	826,252	535,623	290,629	64.8	525,599	300,653	36.4	580,908	245,344	236,066	9,278	591,269	234,983
1993[2]	915,474	545,706	369,768	59.6	561,123	354,351	38.7	650,434	265,040	254,130	10,910	625,969	289,505
1995[2]	931,706	550,822	380,884	59.1	562,893	368,813	39.6	656,833	274,873	260,900	13,973	647,059	284,647
1997[2]	989,813	568,719	421,094	57.5	587,420	402,393	40.7	694,560	295,253	271,257	23,996	682,650	307,163
1999[2]	1,037,529	593,375	444,154	57.2	608,007	429,522	41.4	718,585	318,944	288,663	30,281	719,256	318,273
2001[2]	1,113,183	617,868	495,315	55.5	644,514	468,669	42.1	771,124	342,059	306,487	35,572	764,172	349,011
2003[2]	1,173,593	630,092	543,501	53.7	663,723	509,870	43.4	791,766	381,827	330,097	51,730	814,289	359,304
2005[2]	1,290,426	675,624	614,802	52.4	714,453	575,973	44.6	841,188	449,238	361,523	87,715	916,996	373,430
2007[2]	1,371,587	703,757	667,830	51.3	744,047	627,540	45.8	876,526	495,061	386,688	108,373	992,385	379,202
2009[2]	1,439,074	729,152	709,922	50.7	761,002	678,072	47.1	913,788	525,286	408,382	116,904	1,038,349	400,725
2011[2]	1,524,469	762,114	762,355	50.0	789,567	734,902	48.2	954,159	570,310	432,630	137,680	1,115,642	408,827
2013[2]	1,545,381	791,378	754,003	51.2	791,971	753,410	48.8	968,734	576,647	449,072	127,575	1,151,638	393,743
2015[2]	1,552,256	807,109	745,147	52.0	789,405	762,851	49.1	970,991	581,265	472,638	108,627	1,180,545	371,711
2016[2]	1,546,081	813,978	732,103	52.6	783,495	762,586	49.3	974,239	571,842	476,872	94,970	1,196,657	349,424
2017[2]	1,543,569	821,168	722,401	53.2	777,821	765,748	49.6	971,183	572,386	486,183	86,203	1,207,021	336,548

—Not available.

[1]Estimated on the basis of enrollment. For methodological details on estimates, see National Center for Education Statistics, *Projections of Education Statistics to 2000*.

[2]Because of revised survey methods, data are not directly comparable with figures for years prior to 1987.

NOTE: Includes faculty members with the title of professor, associate professor, assistant professor, instructor, lecturer, assisting professor, adjunct professor, or interim professor (or the equivalent). Excluded are graduate students with titles such as graduate or teaching fellow who assist senior faculty. Data through 1995 are for institutions of higher education, while later data are for degree-granting institutions. Degree-granting institutions grant associate's or higher degrees and participate in Title IV federal financial aid programs. The degree-granting classification is very similar to the earlier higher education classification, but it includes more 2-year colleges and excludes a few higher education institutions that did not grant degrees. Beginning in 2007, includes institutions with fewer than 15 full-time employees; these institutions did not report staff data prior to 2007. Some data have been revised from previously published figures. Detail may not sum to totals because of rounding.

SOURCE: U.S. Department of Education, National Center for Education Statistics, Higher Education General Information Survey (HEGIS), *Employees in Institutions of Higher Education*, 1970 and 1972, and "Staff Survey" 1976; *Projections of Education Statistics to 2000*; Integrated Postsecondary Education Data System (IPEDS), "Fall Staff Survey" (IPEDS-S:87–99); IPEDS Winter 2001–02 through Winter 2011–12, Human Resources component, Fall Staff section; IPEDS Spring 2014 and Spring 2016 through Spring 2018, Human Resources component, Fall Staff section; and U.S. Equal Employment Opportunity Commission, Higher Education Staff Information Survey (EEO-6), 1977, 1981, and 1983. (This table was prepared November 2018.)

Table 315.20. Full-time faculty in degree-granting postsecondary institutions, by race/ethnicity, sex, and academic rank: Fall 2015, fall 2016, and fall 2017

Year, sex, and academic rank	Total	White	Black, Hispanic, Asian, Pacific Islander, American Indian/Alaska Native, and Two or more races									Race/ ethnicity unknown	Non-resident alien[2]
							Asian/Pacific Islander						
			Total	Percent[1]	Black	Hispanic	Total	Asian	Pacific Islander	American Indian/ Alaska Native	Two or more races		
1	2	3	4	5	6	7	8	9	10	11	12	13	14
2015[3]													
Total	**807,109**	**575,752**	**167,372**	**22.5**	**44,106**	**35,811**	**77,456**	**76,298**	**1,158**	**3,530**	**6,469**	**22,359**	**41,626**
Professors	182,388	147,095	31,171	17.5	6,731	5,957	16,938	16,734	204	599	946	2,486	1,636
Associate professors	158,082	116,754	35,132	23.1	9,090	6,978	17,285	17,067	218	608	1,171	3,070	3,126
Assistant professors	173,409	115,226	40,251	25.9	10,874	7,634	19,432	19,132	300	639	1,672	6,577	11,355
Instructors	99,915	73,052	21,673	22.9	7,264	6,890	5,696	5,467	229	862	961	3,563	1,627
Lecturers	40,894	30,488	7,635	20.0	2,074	2,367	2,690	2,653	37	142	362	1,256	1,515
Other faculty	152,421	93,137	31,510	25.3	8,073	5,985	15,415	15,245	170	680	1,357	5,407	22,367
2016[3]													
Total	**813,978**	**574,515**	**172,618**	**23.1**	**44,466**	**37,406**	**80,004**	**78,855**	**1,149**	**3,543**	**7,199**	**22,370**	**44,475**
Professors	182,604	145,831	32,428	18.2	6,843	6,215	17,737	17,546	191	612	1,021	2,507	1,838
Associate professors	157,586	115,571	35,704	23.6	9,076	7,104	17,695	17,479	216	598	1,231	3,145	3,166
Assistant professors	175,800	115,193	41,984	26.7	11,122	8,130	20,222	19,926	296	622	1,888	6,546	12,077
Instructors	100,688	73,113	22,308	23.4	7,212	7,282	5,841	5,626	215	867	1,106	3,576	1,691
Lecturers	41,401	30,817	7,570	19.7	1,974	2,423	2,569	2,526	43	150	454	1,386	1,628
Other faculty	155,899	93,990	32,624	25.8	8,239	6,252	15,940	15,752	188	694	1,499	5,210	24,075
Males	440,387	309,853	90,021	22.5	19,096	19,022	46,794	46,204	590	1,721	3,388	11,910	28,603
Professors	123,780	98,336	22,292	18.5	4,044	3,957	13,266	13,135	131	376	649	1,726	1,426
Associate professors	86,464	62,971	19,675	23.8	4,307	3,864	10,605	10,495	110	288	611	1,825	1,993
Assistant professors	85,529	54,774	19,832	26.6	4,200	3,956	10,594	10,447	147	274	808	3,395	7,528
Instructors	43,786	32,005	9,285	22.5	2,592	3,270	2,537	2,438	99	430	456	1,585	911
Lecturers	18,494	13,903	3,104	18.3	860	1,013	982	965	17	61	188	677	810
Other faculty	82,334	47,864	15,833	24.9	3,093	2,962	8,810	8,724	86	292	676	2,702	15,935
Females	373,591	264,662	82,597	23.8	25,370	18,384	33,210	32,651	559	1,822	3,811	10,460	15,872
Professors	58,824	47,495	10,136	17.6	2,799	2,258	4,471	4,411	60	236	372	781	412
Associate professors	71,122	52,600	16,029	23.4	4,769	3,240	7,090	6,984	106	310	620	1,320	1,173
Assistant professors	90,271	60,419	22,152	26.8	6,922	4,174	9,628	9,479	149	348	1,080	3,151	4,549
Instructors	56,902	41,108	13,023	24.1	4,620	4,012	3,304	3,188	116	437	650	1,991	780
Lecturers	22,907	16,914	4,466	20.9	1,114	1,410	1,587	1,561	26	89	266	709	818
Other faculty	73,565	46,126	16,791	26.7	5,146	3,290	7,130	7,028	102	402	823	2,508	8,140
2017[3]													
Total	**821,168**	**573,560**	**178,947**	**23.8**	**45,427**	**39,099**	**83,342**	**82,142**	**1,200**	**3,460**	**7,619**	**23,439**	**45,222**
Professors	184,023	145,624	33,895	18.9	6,931	6,518	18,764	18,571	193	631	1,051	2,710	1,794
Associate professors	157,820	114,978	36,492	24.1	9,151	7,241	18,249	18,014	235	569	1,282	3,306	3,044
Assistant professors	178,858	115,706	43,707	27.4	11,505	8,565	20,980	20,700	280	628	2,029	6,875	12,570
Instructors	98,793	71,061	22,506	24.1	7,068	7,430	6,035	5,802	233	851	1,122	3,374	1,852
Lecturers	42,866	31,763	8,054	20.2	1,981	2,693	2,729	2,691	38	153	498	1,480	1,569
Other faculty	158,808	94,428	34,293	26.6	8,791	6,652	16,585	16,364	221	628	1,637	5,694	24,393
Males	440,842	306,914	92,679	23.2	19,423	19,690	48,348	47,759	589	1,689	3,529	12,410	28,839
Professors	123,615	97,303	23,099	19.2	4,125	4,104	13,861	13,733	128	380	629	1,871	1,342
Associate professors	86,158	62,389	19,919	24.2	4,300	3,902	10,805	10,692	113	269	643	1,935	1,915
Assistant professors	86,151	54,381	20,502	27.4	4,344	4,109	10,904	10,771	133	295	850	3,554	7,714
Instructors	42,882	31,062	9,357	23.2	2,585	3,293	2,558	2,458	100	429	492	1,473	990
Lecturers	19,090	14,288	3,300	18.8	838	1,153	1,056	1,038	18	58	195	696	806
Other faculty	82,946	47,491	16,502	25.8	3,231	3,129	9,164	9,067	97	258	720	2,881	16,072
Females	380,326	266,646	86,268	24.4	26,004	19,409	34,994	34,383	611	1,771	4,090	11,029	16,383
Professors	60,408	48,321	10,796	18.3	2,806	2,414	4,903	4,838	65	251	422	839	452
Associate professors	71,662	52,589	16,573	24.0	4,851	3,339	7,444	7,322	122	300	639	1,371	1,129
Assistant professors	92,707	61,325	23,205	27.5	7,161	4,456	10,076	9,929	147	333	1,179	3,321	4,856
Instructors	55,911	39,999	13,149	24.7	4,483	4,137	3,477	3,344	133	422	630	1,901	862
Lecturers	23,776	17,475	4,754	21.4	1,143	1,540	1,673	1,653	20	95	303	784	763
Other faculty	75,862	46,937	17,791	27.5	5,560	3,523	7,421	7,297	124	370	917	2,813	8,321

[1]Combined total of faculty who were Black, Hispanic, Asian, Pacific Islander, American Indian/Alaska Native, and of Two or more races as a percentage of total faculty, excluding race/ethnicity unknown and nonresident alien.
[2]Race/ethnicity not collected.
[3]Only instructional faculty were classified by academic rank. Primarily research and primarily public service faculty, as well as faculty without ranks, appear under "other faculty."
NOTE: Degree-granting institutions grant associate's or higher degrees and participate in Title IV federal financial aid programs. Includes institutions with fewer than 15 full-time employees; these institutions did not report staff data prior to 2007. Race categories exclude persons of Hispanic ethnicity. Some data have been revised from previously published figures.
SOURCE: U.S. Department of Education, National Center for Education Statistics, Integrated Postsecondary Education Data System (IPEDS), Spring 2016 through Spring 2018 Human Resources component, Fall Staff section. (This table was prepared November 2018.)

Table 316.10. Average salary of full-time instructional faculty on 9-month contracts in degree-granting postsecondary institutions, by academic rank, control and level of institution, and sex: Selected years, 1970–71 through 2017–18

Sex and academic year	All faculty	Academic rank: Professor	Associate professor	Assistant professor	Instructor	Lecturer	No rank	Public institutions: Total	4-year	2-year	Private institutions: Total	4-year	2-year
1	2	3	4	5	6	7	8	9	10	11	12	13	14
	Current dollars												
Total													
1970–71	$12,710	$17,958	$13,563	$11,176	$9,360	$11,196	$12,333	$12,953	$13,121	$12,644	$11,619	$11,824	$8,664
1975–76	16,659	22,649	17,065	13,986	13,672	12,906	15,196	16,942	17,400	15,820	15,921	16,116	10,901
1980–81	23,302	30,753	23,214	18,901	15,178	17,301	22,334	23,745	24,373	22,177	22,093	22,325	15,065
1982–83	27,196	35,540	26,921	22,056	17,601	20,072	25,557	27,488	28,293	25,567	26,393	26,691	16,595
1984–85	30,447	39,743	29,945	24,668	20,230	22,334	27,683	30,646	31,764	27,864	29,910	30,247	18,510
1985–86	32,392	42,268	31,787	26,277	20,918	23,770	29,088	32,750	34,033	29,590	31,402	31,732	19,436
1987–88	35,897	47,040	35,231	29,110	22,728	25,977	31,532	36,231	37,840	32,209	35,049	35,346	21,867
1989–90	40,133	52,810	39,392	32,689	25,030	28,990	34,559	40,416	42,365	35,516	39,464	39,817	24,601
1990–91	42,165	55,540	41,414	34,434	26,332	30,097	36,395	42,317	44,510	37,055	41,788	42,224	24,088
1991–92	43,851	57,433	42,929	35,745	30,916	30,456	37,783	43,641	45,638	38,959	44,376	44,793	25,673
1992–93	44,714	58,788	43,945	36,625	28,499	30,543	37,771	44,197	46,515	38,935	45,985	46,427	26,105
1993–94	46,364	60,649	45,278	37,630	28,828	32,729	40,584	45,920	48,019	41,040	47,465	47,880	28,435
1994–95	47,811	62,709	46,713	38,756	29,665	33,198	41,227	47,432	49,738	42,101	48,741	49,379	25,613
1995–96	49,309	64,540	47,966	39,696	30,344	34,136	42,996	48,837	51,172	43,295	50,466	50,819	31,915
1996–97	50,829	66,659	49,307	40,687	31,193	34,962	44,200	50,303	52,718	44,584	52,112	52,443	32,628
1997–98	52,335	68,731	50,828	41,830	32,449	35,484	45,268	51,638	54,114	45,919	54,039	54,379	33,592
1998–99	54,097	71,322	52,576	43,348	33,819	36,819	46,250	53,319	55,948	47,285	55,981	56,284	34,821
1999–2000	55,888	74,410	54,524	44,978	34,918	38,194	47,389	55,011	57,950	48,240	58,013	58,323	35,925
2001–02	59,742	80,792	58,724	48,796	46,959	41,798	46,569	58,524	62,013	50,837	62,818	63,088	33,139
2002–03	61,330	83,466	60,471	50,552	48,304	42,622	46,338	60,014	63,486	52,330	64,533	64,814	34,826
2003–04	62,579	85,333	61,746	51,798	49,065	43,648	47,725	60,874	64,340	53,076	66,666	66,932	36,322
2004–05	64,234	88,158	63,558	53,308	49,730	44,514	48,942	62,346	66,053	53,932	68,755	68,995	37,329
2005–06	66,172	91,208	65,714	55,106	50,883	45,896	50,425	64,158	67,951	55,405	71,016	71,263	38,549
2006–07	68,479	94,649	68,056	57,079	53,272	47,306	52,180	66,443	70,287	57,459	73,358	73,575	41,138
2007–08	71,101	98,595	70,830	59,293	55,356	49,389	54,377	68,988	72,852	59,672	76,169	76,378	43,402
2008–09	73,587	102,336	73,445	61,544	56,918	51,316	56,408	71,236	75,244	61,432	79,191	79,454	43,542
2009–10	74,620	103,682	74,125	62,245	57,791	52,185	56,803	72,178	76,147	62,264	80,379	80,597	44,748
2010–11	75,481	104,961	75,107	63,136	58,003	52,584	56,549	72,715	76,857	62,359	81,897	82,098	45,146
2011–12	76,567	107,090	76,177	64,011	58,350	53,359	56,898	73,496	77,843	62,553	83,540	83,701	47,805
2012–13	77,278	108,074	77,029	64,673	57,674	53,072	58,752	73,877	78,012	62,907	84,932	85,096	44,978
2013–14	78,733	109,998	78,693	66,093	58,240	54,566	59,161	75,491	79,897	63,714	86,178	86,390	44,598
2014–15	80,157	112,825	80,335	67,589	59,208	55,335	58,305	76,811	81,372	64,116	87,605	88,212	38,168
2015–16	82,224	115,539	82,147	69,378	60,911	57,306	60,341	78,869	83,389	66,018	89,867	90,309	31,296
2016–17	84,737	119,159	84,244	71,748	63,613	58,770	61,785	81,392	85,803	67,664	92,458	92,642	53,017
2017–18	86,701	121,764	86,035	73,394	65,351	60,685	62,756	83,211	87,745	68,733	94,818	94,940	57,030
Males													
1975–76	17,414	22,902	17,209	14,174	14,430	13,579	15,761	17,661	18,121	16,339	16,784	16,946	11,378
1980–81	24,499	31,082	23,451	19,227	15,545	18,281	23,170	24,873	25,509	22,965	23,493	23,669	16,075
1982–83	28,664	35,956	27,262	22,586	18,160	21,225	26,541	28,851	29,661	26,524	28,159	28,380	17,346
1984–85	32,182	40,269	30,392	25,330	21,159	23,557	28,670	32,240	33,344	28,891	32,028	32,278	19,460
1985–86	34,294	42,833	32,273	27,094	21,693	25,238	30,267	34,528	35,786	30,758	33,656	33,900	20,412
1987–88	38,112	47,735	35,823	30,086	23,645	27,652	32,747	38,314	39,898	33,477	37,603	37,817	22,641
1989–90	42,763	53,650	40,131	33,781	25,933	31,162	35,980	42,959	44,834	37,081	42,312	42,595	25,218
1990–91	45,065	56,549	42,239	35,636	27,388	32,398	38,036	45,084	47,168	38,787	45,019	45,319	25,937
1991–92	46,848	58,494	43,814	36,969	33,359	32,843	39,422	46,483	48,401	40,811	47,733	48,042	26,825
1992–93	47,866	59,972	44,855	37,842	29,583	32,512	39,365	47,175	49,392	40,725	49,518	49,837	27,402
1993–94	49,579	61,857	46,229	38,794	29,815	34,796	42,251	48,956	50,989	42,938	51,076	51,397	30,783
1994–95	51,228	64,046	47,705	39,923	30,528	35,082	43,103	50,629	52,874	44,020	52,653	53,036	29,639
1995–96	52,814	65,949	49,037	40,858	30,940	36,135	44,624	52,163	54,448	45,209	54,364	54,649	33,301
1996–97	54,465	68,214	50,457	41,864	31,738	36,932	45,688	53,737	56,162	46,393	56,185	56,453	34,736
1997–98	56,115	70,468	52,041	43,017	33,070	37,481	46,822	55,191	57,744	47,690	58,293	58,576	36,157
1998–99	58,048	73,260	53,830	44,650	34,741	38,976	47,610	57,038	59,805	48,961	60,392	60,641	38,040
1999–2000	60,084	76,478	55,939	46,414	35,854	40,202	48,788	58,984	62,030	50,033	62,631	62,905	38,636
2001–02	64,320	83,356	60,300	50,518	48,844	44,519	48,049	62,835	66,577	52,360	67,871	68,100	33,395
2002–03	66,126	86,191	62,226	52,441	50,272	45,469	47,412	64,564	68,322	53,962	69,726	69,976	34,291
2003–04	67,485	88,262	63,466	53,649	50,985	46,214	48,973	65,476	69,248	54,623	72,021	72,250	35,604
2004–05	69,337	91,290	65,394	55,215	51,380	46,929	50,102	67,130	71,145	55,398	74,318	74,540	34,970
2005–06	71,569	94,733	67,654	57,099	52,519	48,256	51,811	69,191	73,353	56,858	76,941	77,143	38,215
2006–07	74,050	98,348	70,077	59,090	55,051	49,487	53,701	71,659	75,890	58,960	79,428	79,599	41,196
2007–08	76,957	102,605	72,943	61,374	57,134	51,795	56,170	74,394	78,671	61,189	82,734	82,903	42,995
2008–09	79,718	106,743	75,633	63,710	58,812	53,935	58,404	76,897	81,394	62,868	86,033	86,231	43,871
2009–10	80,881	108,225	76,400	64,451	59,793	54,947	58,647	77,948	82,423	63,697	87,382	87,546	44,500
2010–11	81,873	109,656	77,429	65,391	59,851	55,457	58,392	78,609	83,279	63,745	89,000	89,160	44,542
2011–12	83,150	112,066	78,560	66,303	60,066	56,367	58,807	79,544	84,444	63,918	90,840	90,976	45,250
2012–13	83,979	113,311	79,423	67,085	59,350	55,759	61,086	80,016	84,700	64,282	92,385	92,530	42,906
2013–14	85,545	115,466	81,178	68,492	59,777	57,218	61,511	81,703	86,646	65,076	93,898	94,065	44,277
2014–15	87,199	118,573	82,954	70,260	60,707	58,441	60,310	83,291	88,393	65,513	95,455	96,041	37,389
2015–16	89,361	121,535	84,781	72,272	62,390	60,428	62,468	85,367	90,464	67,352	98,016	98,466	30,050
2016–17	92,068	125,303	86,943	74,929	65,282	61,466	64,456	88,083	93,062	68,943	100,859	101,034	51,866
2017–18	94,229	128,165	88,841	76,714	67,310	63,487	65,017	90,013	95,157	69,907	103,633	103,721	61,840

See notes at end of table.

Table 316.10. Average salary of full-time instructional faculty on 9-month contracts in degree-granting postsecondary institutions, by academic rank, control and level of institution, and sex: Selected years, 1970–71 through 2017–18—Continued

Sex and academic year	All faculty	Academic rank						Public institutions			Private institutions		
		Professor	Associate professor	Assistant professor	Instructor	Lecturer	No rank	Total	4-year	2-year	Total	4-year	2-year
1	2	3	4	5	6	7	8	9	10	11	12	13	14
Females													
1975–76	14,308	20,308	16,364	13,522	12,572	11,901	14,094	14,762	14,758	14,769	13,030	13,231	10,201
1980–81	19,996	27,959	22,295	18,302	14,854	16,168	20,843	20,673	20,608	20,778	18,073	18,326	13,892
1982–83	23,261	32,221	25,738	21,130	17,102	18,830	23,855	23,892	23,876	23,917	21,451	21,785	15,845
1984–85	25,941	35,824	28,517	23,575	19,362	21,004	26,050	26,566	26,813	26,172	24,186	24,560	17,575
1985–86	27,576	38,252	30,300	24,966	20,237	22,273	27,171	28,299	28,680	27,693	25,523	25,889	18,504
1987–88	30,499	42,371	33,528	27,600	21,962	24,370	29,605	31,215	31,820	30,228	28,621	28,946	21,215
1989–90	34,183	47,663	37,469	31,090	24,320	26,995	32,528	34,796	35,704	33,307	32,650	33,010	24,002
1990–91	35,881	49,728	39,329	32,724	25,534	28,111	34,179	36,459	37,573	34,720	34,359	34,898	22,585
1991–92	37,534	51,621	40,766	34,063	28,873	28,550	35,622	37,800	38,634	36,517	36,828	37,309	24,683
1992–93	38,385	52,755	41,861	35,032	27,700	28,922	35,792	38,356	39,470	36,710	38,460	38,987	25,068
1993–94	40,058	54,746	43,178	36,169	28,136	31,048	38,474	40,118	41,031	38,707	39,902	40,378	26,142
1994–95	41,369	56,555	44,626	37,352	29,072	31,677	38,967	41,548	42,663	39,812	40,908	41,815	22,851
1995–96	42,871	58,318	45,803	38,345	29,940	32,584	41,085	42,871	43,986	41,086	42,871	43,236	30,671
1996–97	44,325	60,160	47,101	39,350	30,819	33,415	42,474	44,306	45,402	42,531	44,374	44,726	30,661
1997–98	45,775	61,965	48,597	40,504	32,011	33,918	43,491	45,648	46,709	43,943	46,106	46,466	30,995
1998–99	47,421	64,236	50,347	41,894	33,152	35,115	44,723	47,247	48,355	45,457	47,874	48,204	31,524
1999–2000	48,997	67,079	52,091	43,367	34,228	36,607	45,865	48,714	50,168	46,340	49,737	50,052	32,951
2001–02	52,662	72,542	56,186	46,824	45,262	39,538	45,003	52,123	53,895	49,290	54,149	54,434	32,921
2002–03	54,105	75,028	57,716	48,380	46,573	40,265	45,251	53,435	55,121	50,717	55,881	56,158	35,296
2003–04	55,378	76,652	59,095	49,689	47,404	41,536	46,519	54,408	56,117	51,591	57,921	58,192	36,896
2004–05	56,926	79,160	60,809	51,154	48,351	42,455	47,860	55,780	57,714	52,566	59,919	60,143	39,291
2005–06	58,665	81,514	62,860	52,901	49,533	43,934	49,172	57,462	59,437	54,082	61,830	62,092	38,786
2006–07	60,926	84,857	65,131	54,909	51,828	45,505	50,814	59,677	61,713	56,121	64,194	64,428	41,099
2007–08	63,357	88,340	67,823	57,102	53,929	47,410	52,809	62,138	64,223	58,346	66,538	66,755	43,670
2008–09	65,662	91,528	70,393	59,291	55,431	49,184	54,663	64,230	66,391	60,195	69,375	69,668	43,344
2009–10	66,647	92,830	71,017	59,997	56,239	49,957	55,206	65,139	67,276	61,047	70,507	70,746	44,892
2010–11	67,473	94,041	72,003	60,888	56,566	50,270	54,985	65,632	67,935	61,193	72,091	72,306	45,518
2011–12	68,468	95,845	73,057	61,763	57,013	50,994	55,299	66,368	68,897	61,417	73,629	73,788	49,382
2012–13	69,124	96,563	73,966	62,321	56,361	50,963	56,777	66,703	69,083	61,774	74,987	75,149	46,407
2013–14	70,589	98,374	75,592	63,782	57,043	52,497	57,196	68,335	71,059	62,597	76,127	76,358	44,789
2014–15	71,792	100,783	77,115	65,009	58,020	52,901	56,616	69,384	72,288	62,971	77,504	78,089	38,841
2015–16	73,850	103,364	78,977	66,603	59,726	54,825	58,562	71,493	74,378	64,924	79,549	79,959	32,495
2016–17	76,199	106,881	81,037	68,701	62,277	56,601	59,568	73,826	76,696	66,616	81,976	82,146	53,866
2017–18	78,051	109,325	82,722	70,264	63,795	58,442	60,908	75,604	78,613	67,768	84,026	84,163	54,319
	Constant 2017–18 dollars[1]												
Total													
1970–71	$79,385	$112,164	$84,718	$69,806	$58,461	$69,931	$77,034	$80,908	$81,958	$78,976	$72,570	$73,855	$54,116
1975–76	74,532	101,335	76,352	62,576	61,172	57,742	67,989	75,801	77,850	70,779	71,231	72,107	48,771
1980–81	66,746	88,088	66,493	54,139	43,475	49,556	63,973	68,014	69,813	63,523	63,283	63,947	43,152
1982–83	68,752	89,846	68,057	55,758	44,496	50,743	64,609	69,490	71,526	64,634	66,722	67,476	41,953
1984–85	71,428	93,236	70,250	57,870	47,459	52,395	64,943	71,895	74,517	65,368	70,168	70,958	43,424
1985–86	73,861	96,380	72,481	59,917	47,698	54,201	66,327	74,677	77,603	67,472	71,603	72,356	44,318
1987–88	76,889	100,757	75,463	62,352	48,681	55,640	67,540	77,604	81,051	68,990	75,073	75,709	46,838
1989–90	78,425	103,197	76,978	63,879	48,912	56,651	67,532	78,978	82,786	69,403	77,117	77,808	48,074
1990–91	78,126	102,906	76,733	63,801	48,789	55,766	67,434	78,407	82,470	68,657	77,426	78,235	44,631
1991–92	78,727	103,110	77,070	64,174	55,503	54,677	67,833	78,349	81,934	69,944	79,668	80,417	46,091
1992–93	77,844	102,345	76,504	63,761	49,615	53,173	65,756	76,944	80,979	67,783	80,056	80,827	45,447
1993–94	78,679	102,920	76,835	63,857	48,920	55,539	68,870	77,925	81,487	69,643	80,547	81,251	48,253
1994–95	78,874	103,449	77,062	63,935	48,937	54,766	68,011	78,248	82,052	69,453	80,407	81,460	42,253
1995–96	79,191	103,651	77,033	63,752	48,733	54,822	69,051	78,432	82,182	69,532	81,048	81,615	51,255
1996–97	79,367	104,085	76,991	63,530	48,706	54,591	69,016	78,545	82,316	69,615	81,370	81,887	50,948
1997–98	80,287	105,440	77,974	64,171	49,779	54,436	69,445	79,217	83,016	70,444	82,901	83,422	51,533
1998–99	81,577	107,553	79,283	65,368	50,998	55,522	69,745	80,404	84,368	71,304	84,419	84,875	52,509
1999–2000	81,913	109,061	79,914	65,923	51,178	55,980	69,457	80,628	84,935	70,704	85,028	85,482	52,653
2001–02	83,188	112,500	81,771	67,946	65,389	58,203	64,845	81,492	86,351	70,789	87,471	87,848	46,145
2002–03	83,563	113,725	82,392	68,879	65,815	58,074	63,137	81,771	86,501	71,301	87,928	88,311	47,451
2003–04	83,440	113,779	82,329	69,065	65,420	58,198	63,635	81,167	85,788	70,769	88,889	89,244	48,429
2004–05	83,145	114,112	82,269	69,002	64,370	57,619	63,350	80,700	85,499	69,809	88,996	89,308	48,319
2005–06	82,511	113,728	81,940	68,712	63,446	57,228	62,875	80,000	84,729	69,085	88,551	88,859	48,067
2006–07	83,235	115,044	82,721	69,379	64,751	57,499	63,423	80,761	85,432	69,840	89,165	89,429	50,003
2007–08	83,334	115,559	83,017	69,494	64,880	57,886	63,732	80,857	85,387	69,939	89,274	89,519	50,870
2008–09	85,060	118,291	84,896	71,139	65,792	59,317	65,203	82,343	86,975	71,011	91,538	91,841	50,330
2009–10	85,428	118,698	84,861	71,260	66,161	59,743	65,030	82,633	87,176	71,283	92,021	92,270	51,229
2010–11	84,713	117,798	84,293	70,858	65,097	59,015	63,465	81,608	86,256	69,986	91,913	92,139	50,667
2011–12	83,485	116,766	83,060	69,795	63,622	58,180	62,039	80,136	84,877	68,205	91,088	91,263	52,125
2012–13	82,881	115,909	82,614	69,362	61,855	56,920	63,012	79,233	83,668	67,468	91,090	91,266	48,239
2013–14	83,143	116,158	83,100	69,794	61,502	57,622	62,474	79,720	84,372	67,282	91,005	91,229	47,096
2014–15	84,034	118,283	84,221	70,859	62,072	58,012	61,126	80,526	85,308	67,218	91,843	92,480	40,015
2015–16	85,624	120,317	85,544	72,247	63,430	59,675	62,836	82,130	86,837	68,748	93,583	94,043	32,590
2016–17	86,648	121,845	86,143	73,365	65,047	60,095	63,178	83,227	87,737	69,190	94,542	94,730	54,212
2017–18	86,701	121,764	86,035	73,394	65,351	60,685	62,756	83,211	87,745	68,733	94,818	94,940	57,030

See notes at end of table.

Table 316.10. Average salary of full-time instructional faculty on 9-month contracts in degree-granting postsecondary institutions, by academic rank, control and level of institution, and sex: Selected years, 1970–71 through 2017–18—Continued

Sex and academic year	All faculty	Academic rank						Public institutions			Private institutions		
		Professor	Associate professor	Assistant professor	Instructor	Lecturer	No rank	Total	4-year	2-year	Total	4-year	2-year
1	2	3	4	5	6	7	8	9	10	11	12	13	14
Males													
1975–76	77,911	102,466	76,993	63,418	64,561	60,754	70,516	79,019	81,074	73,105	75,095	75,817	50,905
1980–81	70,174	89,030	67,172	55,073	44,527	52,364	66,367	71,245	73,067	65,780	67,293	67,797	46,045
1982–83	72,463	90,898	68,919	57,098	45,909	53,657	67,096	72,936	74,984	67,053	71,187	71,745	43,851
1984–85	75,498	94,470	71,299	59,423	49,638	55,264	67,259	75,634	78,224	67,777	75,137	75,723	45,653
1985–86	78,198	97,668	73,589	61,780	49,465	57,548	69,015	78,731	81,600	70,135	76,743	77,299	46,544
1987–88	81,633	102,244	76,730	64,443	50,646	59,229	70,142	82,066	85,459	71,706	80,543	81,002	48,496
1989–90	83,565	104,839	78,421	66,012	50,676	60,894	70,309	83,947	87,612	72,462	82,684	83,235	49,280
1990–91	83,499	104,776	78,261	66,027	50,746	60,028	70,474	83,534	87,394	71,866	83,413	83,969	48,056
1991–92	84,107	105,014	78,660	66,370	59,890	58,964	70,774	83,451	86,895	73,269	85,695	86,250	48,159
1992–93	83,330	104,407	78,090	65,880	51,502	56,601	68,532	82,128	85,989	70,899	86,208	86,763	47,704
1993–94	84,134	104,969	78,449	65,832	50,595	59,047	71,698	83,076	86,527	72,864	86,675	87,219	52,239
1994–95	84,511	105,656	78,699	65,860	50,362	57,874	71,107	83,522	87,225	72,619	86,861	87,493	48,896
1995–96	84,819	105,914	78,754	65,617	49,690	58,033	71,667	83,773	87,444	72,605	87,308	87,766	53,481
1996–97	85,044	106,512	78,785	65,369	49,557	57,667	71,339	83,907	87,694	72,439	87,730	88,148	54,238
1997–98	86,086	108,104	79,835	65,991	50,733	57,499	71,829	84,668	88,585	73,160	89,427	89,861	55,468
1998–99	87,535	110,475	81,174	67,331	52,389	58,774	71,796	86,012	90,185	73,832	91,070	91,445	57,364
1999–2000	88,063	112,091	81,988	68,027	52,550	58,922	71,507	86,451	90,916	73,332	91,796	92,197	56,627
2001–02	89,564	116,070	83,965	70,344	68,013	61,992	66,907	87,495	92,706	72,910	94,508	94,826	46,501
2002–03	90,098	117,437	84,784	71,452	68,496	61,952	64,600	87,970	93,090	73,524	95,003	95,344	46,722
2003–04	89,981	117,684	84,623	71,532	67,980	61,619	65,298	87,302	92,331	72,832	96,030	96,334	47,473
2004–05	89,750	118,166	84,645	71,471	66,506	60,745	64,852	86,893	92,090	71,707	96,197	96,485	45,265
2005–06	89,241	118,124	84,358	71,197	65,487	60,171	64,604	86,275	91,465	70,897	95,939	96,190	47,651
2006–07	90,006	119,540	85,178	71,822	66,913	60,150	65,272	87,100	92,243	71,665	96,543	96,751	50,073
2007–08	90,197	120,258	85,493	71,934	66,964	60,706	65,834	87,194	92,206	71,717	96,969	97,166	50,393
2008–09	92,147	123,386	87,425	73,643	67,982	62,345	67,510	88,886	94,084	72,670	99,447	99,675	50,711
2009–10	92,596	123,900	87,466	73,786	68,453	62,905	67,141	89,237	94,360	72,922	100,038	100,226	50,945
2010–11	91,886	123,068	86,899	73,388	67,171	62,240	65,533	88,222	93,464	71,541	99,885	100,064	49,990
2011–12	90,663	122,191	85,658	72,294	65,493	61,459	64,120	86,731	92,074	69,694	99,048	99,195	49,339
2012–13	90,068	121,526	85,181	71,949	63,653	59,802	65,515	85,817	90,841	68,943	99,083	99,238	46,017
2013–14	90,337	121,933	85,725	72,328	63,125	60,423	64,956	86,279	91,498	68,721	99,157	99,333	46,757
2014–15	91,417	124,308	86,967	73,658	63,644	61,268	63,227	87,320	92,669	68,682	100,072	100,687	39,198
2015–16	93,056	126,561	88,287	75,261	64,970	62,926	65,051	88,898	94,204	70,137	102,069	102,537	31,292
2016–17	94,143	128,127	88,903	76,618	66,753	62,851	65,909	90,069	95,160	70,498	103,132	103,311	53,035
2017–18	94,229	128,165	88,841	76,714	67,310	63,487	65,017	90,013	95,157	69,907	103,633	103,721	61,840
Females													
1975–76	64,014	90,860	73,214	60,499	56,248	53,244	63,058	66,049	66,031	66,077	58,300	59,196	45,638
1980–81	57,276	80,085	63,861	52,424	42,547	46,311	59,702	59,215	59,029	59,516	51,768	52,492	39,792
1982–83	58,804	81,456	65,066	53,417	43,234	47,603	60,306	60,400	60,359	60,463	54,229	55,073	40,057
1984–85	60,857	84,042	66,900	55,306	45,423	49,275	61,112	62,323	62,902	61,399	56,740	57,617	41,230
1985–86	62,879	87,223	69,090	56,928	46,145	50,787	61,956	64,528	65,397	63,146	58,198	59,032	42,193
1987–88	65,328	90,756	71,815	59,118	47,041	52,199	63,412	66,860	68,156	64,746	61,304	62,000	45,441
1989–90	66,798	93,139	73,219	60,753	47,524	52,753	63,564	67,996	69,771	65,086	63,802	64,506	46,903
1990–91	66,481	92,139	72,871	60,632	47,310	52,086	63,327	67,553	69,617	64,331	63,661	64,660	41,847
1991–92	67,385	92,676	73,187	61,153	51,836	51,255	63,953	67,863	69,360	65,560	66,117	66,981	44,314
1992–93	66,825	91,844	72,876	60,989	48,225	50,352	62,311	66,774	68,714	63,910	66,956	67,873	43,641
1993–94	67,978	92,902	73,271	61,377	47,746	52,688	65,289	68,079	69,628	65,684	67,713	68,520	44,362
1994–95	68,246	93,298	73,619	61,619	47,960	52,256	64,283	68,541	70,380	65,677	67,485	68,981	37,697
1995–96	68,851	93,658	73,559	61,582	48,084	52,330	65,982	68,850	70,641	65,984	68,851	69,437	49,258
1996–97	69,210	93,936	73,546	61,443	48,123	52,176	66,321	69,181	70,893	66,410	69,287	69,837	47,876
1997–98	70,223	95,059	74,553	62,136	49,108	52,033	66,719	70,028	71,655	67,413	70,731	71,283	47,550
1998–99	71,509	96,866	75,923	63,175	49,993	52,953	67,441	71,248	72,918	68,548	72,194	72,691	47,537
1999–2000	71,813	98,316	76,348	63,562	50,166	53,654	67,223	71,399	73,530	67,919	72,898	73,360	48,295
2001–02	73,330	101,011	78,237	65,201	63,025	55,055	62,664	72,579	75,047	68,634	75,401	75,798	45,841
2002–03	73,719	102,227	78,640	65,918	63,457	54,862	61,656	72,807	75,103	69,103	76,139	76,517	48,092
2003–04	73,838	102,204	78,795	66,253	63,206	55,382	62,026	72,545	74,824	68,789	77,229	77,590	49,196
2004–05	73,685	102,464	78,711	66,214	62,585	54,954	61,950	72,202	74,705	68,042	77,559	77,849	50,858
2005–06	73,150	101,641	78,380	65,963	61,764	54,782	61,314	71,650	74,113	67,436	77,097	77,424	48,363
2006–07	74,054	103,143	79,166	66,741	62,996	55,311	61,764	72,537	75,011	68,215	78,026	78,311	49,956
2007–08	74,257	103,539	79,492	66,927	63,208	55,567	61,895	72,829	75,273	68,385	77,986	78,241	51,184
2008–09	75,899	105,799	81,368	68,535	64,073	56,853	63,185	74,244	76,742	69,581	80,191	80,530	50,101
2009–10	76,300	106,275	81,302	68,687	64,385	57,193	63,201	74,574	77,020	69,889	80,719	80,993	51,394
2010–11	75,725	105,543	80,810	68,334	63,484	56,418	61,709	73,659	76,244	68,677	80,908	81,149	51,085
2011–12	74,655	104,505	79,658	67,344	62,165	55,601	60,295	72,364	75,122	66,966	80,282	80,455	53,844
2012–13	74,135	103,564	79,329	66,840	60,447	54,658	60,894	71,540	74,092	66,253	80,424	80,598	49,772
2013–14	74,543	103,883	79,826	67,355	60,238	55,438	60,399	72,163	75,039	66,102	80,390	80,634	47,298
2014–15	75,265	105,659	80,846	68,154	60,827	55,460	59,354	72,740	75,784	66,017	81,253	81,866	40,720
2015–16	76,903	107,639	82,243	69,358	62,196	57,092	60,983	74,449	77,454	67,609	82,838	83,265	33,839
2016–17	77,917	109,290	82,864	70,250	63,681	57,877	60,911	75,490	78,425	68,117	83,824	83,998	55,080
2017–18	78,051	109,325	82,722	70,264	63,795	58,442	60,908	75,604	78,613	67,768	84,026	84,163	54,319

[1]Constant dollars based on the Consumer Price Index, prepared by the Bureau of Labor Statistics, U.S. Department of Labor, adjusted to an academic-year basis.

NOTE: Data exclude instructional faculty at medical schools. Data through 1995–96 are for institutions of higher education, while later data are for degree-granting institutions. Degree-granting institutions grant associate's or higher degrees and participate in Title IV federal financial aid programs. Data for 1987–88 and later years include imputations for nonrespondent institutions. Some data have been revised from previously published figures.

SOURCE: U.S. Department of Education, National Center for Education Statistics, Higher Education General Information Survey (HEGIS), "Faculty Salaries, Tenure, and Fringe Benefits" surveys, 1970–71 through 1985–86; Integrated Postsecondary Education Data System (IPEDS), "Salaries, Tenure, and Fringe Benefits of Full-Time Instructional Faculty Survey" (IPEDS-SA:87–99); and IPEDS, Winter 2001–02 through Winter 2011–12 and Spring 2013 through Spring 2018, Human Resources component, Salaries section. (This table was prepared November 2018.)

Table 316.20. Average salary of full-time instructional faculty on 9-month contracts in degree-granting postsecondary institutions, by academic rank, sex, and control and level of institution: Selected years, 1999–2000 through 2017–18

Academic year, control and level of institution	Constant 2017–18 dollars[1]	Current dollars												
		All faculty			Academic rank									
					Professor			Associate professor						
	All faculty, total	Total	Males	Females	Total	Males	Females	Total	Males	Females	Assistant professor	Instructor	Lecturer	No academic rank
1	2	3	4	5	6	7	8	9	10	11	12	13	14	15
1999–2000														
All institutions	$81,913	$55,888	$60,084	$48,997	$74,410	$76,478	$67,079	$54,524	$55,939	$52,091	$44,978	$34,918	$38,194	$47,389
Public	80,628	55,011	58,984	48,714	72,475	74,501	65,568	54,641	55,992	52,305	45,285	35,007	37,403	47,990
4-year	84,935	57,950	62,030	50,168	75,204	76,530	69,619	55,681	56,776	53,599	45,822	33,528	37,261	40,579
Doctoral[2]	91,242	62,253	66,882	52,287	81,182	82,445	74,653	57,744	58,999	55,156	48,190	33,345	38,883	39,350
Master's[3]	77,348	52,773	55,565	48,235	66,588	67,128	64,863	53,048	53,686	51,977	43,396	33,214	34,448	43,052
Other 4-year	70,157	47,867	49,829	44,577	60,360	60,748	59,052	49,567	50,133	48,548	42,306	35,754	36,088	38,330
2-year	70,704	48,240	50,033	46,340	57,806	59,441	55,501	48,056	49,425	46,711	41,984	37,634	40,061	48,233
Nonprofit	85,260	58,172	62,788	49,881	78,512	80,557	70,609	54,300	55,836	51,687	44,423	34,670	40,761	41,415
4-year	85,632	58,425	63,028	50,117	78,604	80,622	70,774	54,388	55,898	51,809	44,502	34,813	40,783	41,761
Doctoral[2]	105,342	71,873	77,214	59,586	95,182	96,768	87,342	62,503	63,951	59,536	52,134	39,721	42,693	45,887
Master's[3]	73,095	49,871	52,642	45,718	62,539	63,603	59,353	50,176	51,470	48,165	41,447	33,991	37,923	44,153
Other 4-year	68,558	46,776	48,847	43,544	60,200	60,757	58,364	46,822	47,135	46,365	38,775	31,574	33,058	35,120
2-year	55,085	37,583	39,933	34,733	39,454	38,431	40,571	36,349	37,342	35,608	31,818	27,696	25,965	40,373
For-profit	43,301	29,543	30,023	28,942	45,505	44,248	49,693	48,469	53,548	43,389	33,043	29,894	‡	27,958
2009–10														
All institutions	85,428	74,620	80,881	66,647	103,682	108,225	92,830	74,125	76,400	71,017	62,245	57,791	52,185	56,803
Public	82,633	72,178	77,948	65,139	99,208	103,746	88,815	73,379	75,687	70,256	62,160	59,310	50,228	55,864
4-year	87,176	76,147	82,423	67,276	103,948	107,191	95,048	75,251	77,282	72,298	63,442	46,028	50,104	54,005
Doctoral[2]	93,705	81,850	89,186	70,307	113,063	115,829	103,793	78,539	80,830	74,963	66,902	44,406	50,313	53,135
Master's[3]	78,127	68,243	71,574	64,239	87,917	88,929	85,883	70,332	71,340	69,036	59,396	44,422	49,746	55,765
Other 4-year	70,067	61,202	63,678	58,349	76,448	79,143	72,073	65,003	66,297	63,338	55,055	54,050	49,432	54,487
2-year	71,283	62,264	63,697	61,047	72,377	74,423	70,429	60,632	61,565	59,852	54,161	65,503	53,548	56,239
Nonprofit	92,259	80,587	87,600	70,676	112,146	116,401	101,119	75,565	77,764	72,502	62,395	47,842	57,508	62,242
4-year	92,432	80,738	87,720	70,834	112,252	116,472	101,290	75,664	77,827	72,642	62,465	47,885	57,520	62,542
Doctoral[2]	109,309	95,480	104,514	80,888	134,776	138,354	123,283	85,864	88,699	81,499	71,973	53,825	58,932	66,634
Master's[3]	75,302	65,776	68,776	62,128	82,516	84,062	79,452	66,524	67,508	65,309	55,469	45,305	53,637	60,591
Other 4-year	73,973	64,614	67,178	61,326	84,869	85,528	83,480	64,747	64,949	64,478	53,130	42,145	52,422	52,775
2-year	52,355	45,731	44,417	46,529	53,063	55,046	51,310	45,768	45,863	45,717	42,706	46,010	32,393	43,562
For-profit	62,785	54,842	56,689	52,925	79,574	81,765	75,817	71,376	72,429	70,199	66,027	41,742	‡	53,705
2016–17														
All institutions	86,648	84,737	92,068	76,199	119,159	125,303	106,881	84,244	86,943	81,037	71,748	63,613	58,770	61,785
Public	83,227	81,392	88,083	73,826	112,823	118,893	101,126	82,984	85,739	79,708	71,632	65,217	56,401	59,984
4-year	87,737	85,803	93,062	76,696	119,052	123,574	108,840	85,287	87,711	82,220	73,608	56,067	56,423	60,793
Doctoral[2]	94,139	92,064	100,435	80,808	128,962	133,014	118,646	89,461	92,111	85,976	77,990	52,210	57,411	61,257
Master's[3]	75,359	73,698	77,084	69,919	93,950	95,341	91,533	76,483	77,552	75,230	65,901	48,444	53,393	57,751
Other 4-year	68,287	66,781	68,402	65,196	79,105	81,771	75,538	68,746	70,074	67,326	59,377	69,412	51,766	60,947
2-year	69,190	67,664	68,943	66,616	77,670	79,278	76,290	66,125	67,004	65,461	59,115	71,324	55,607	59,614
Nonprofit	94,963	92,870	101,320	82,301	131,262	137,139	118,664	86,692	89,289	83,608	72,031	54,933	65,947	71,259
4-year	95,068	92,972	101,406	82,402	131,358	137,207	118,799	86,710	89,303	83,628	72,071	55,043	65,952	71,406
Doctoral[2]	110,861	108,417	119,300	93,292	156,720	162,385	142,293	97,465	100,968	93,073	82,842	60,052	67,213	78,541
Master's[3]	75,191	73,534	76,702	70,052	91,852	92,971	89,933	74,041	75,232	72,707	62,480	51,818	60,475	67,514
Other 4-year	74,971	73,318	75,674	70,711	96,433	96,786	95,846	74,403	74,493	74,302	60,000	46,400	63,368	58,078
2-year	56,697	55,447	53,345	56,637	66,207	64,972	67,158	70,809	67,514	72,250	52,065	48,817	61,460	52,352
For-profit	60,838	59,497	60,324	58,650	79,138	82,347	70,456	69,171	67,517	70,473	58,623	48,241	87,394	61,656
2017–18														
All institutions	86,701	86,701	94,229	78,051	121,764	128,165	109,325	86,035	88,841	82,722	73,394	65,351	60,685	62,756
Public	83,211	83,211	90,013	75,604	115,206	121,473	103,466	84,890	87,722	81,542	73,418	66,728	58,233	60,602
4-year	87,745	87,745	95,157	78,613	121,575	126,327	111,209	87,353	89,835	84,227	75,407	58,648	58,166	61,870
Doctoral[2]	94,224	94,224	102,837	82,877	131,773	136,136	121,098	91,724	94,505	88,104	79,860	53,139	59,217	61,838
Master's[3]	75,387	75,387	78,867	71,543	96,084	97,492	93,701	78,316	79,311	77,140	67,291	49,813	55,529	58,318
Other 4-year	69,221	69,221	71,004	67,480	80,522	83,116	77,053	70,418	71,962	68,734	61,733	74,278	52,801	62,435
2-year	68,733	68,733	69,907	67,768	79,200	80,694	77,921	67,404	68,273	66,749	60,340	72,545	60,610	60,007
Nonprofit	95,194	95,194	104,007	84,373	134,391	140,628	121,389	88,294	91,057	85,034	73,462	58,064	68,197	76,012
4-year	95,282	95,282	104,088	84,454	134,450	140,665	121,479	88,311	91,069	85,053	73,497	58,183	68,204	76,163
Doctoral[2]	110,735	110,735	122,125	95,358	160,220	166,428	145,010	99,182	102,853	94,636	84,079	63,987	69,753	81,822
Master's[3]	74,640	74,640	77,929	71,074	92,541	93,749	90,537	74,409	75,698	72,958	63,318	53,879	62,123	76,162
Other 4-year	74,668	74,668	76,856	72,279	98,123	98,002	98,324	75,517	75,714	75,302	61,131	47,886	63,604	59,106
2-year	57,039	57,039	54,468	58,676	70,019	71,602	68,984	72,127	71,674	72,362	54,995	50,491	62,508	52,523
For-profit	56,155	56,155	59,043	53,543	70,020	69,939	70,218	65,084	62,200	67,616	53,762	49,334	108,443	57,206

‡Reporting standards not met (too few cases).

[1]Constant dollars based on the Consumer Price Index, prepared by the Bureau of Labor Statistics, U.S. Department of Labor, adjusted to an academic-year basis.

[2]Institutions that awarded 20 or more doctor's degrees during the previous academic year.

[3]Institutions that awarded 20 or more master's degrees, but less than 20 doctor's degrees, during the previous academic year. This definition differs from the definition of master's institutions that is used in some *Digest* tables that present postsecondary finance data.

NOTE: Data exclude instructional faculty at medical schools. Degree-granting institutions grant associate's or higher degrees and participate in Title IV federal financial aid programs. Some data have been revised from previously published figures.

SOURCE: U.S. Department of Education, National Center for Education Statistics, Integrated Postsecondary Education Data System (IPEDS), "Salaries, Tenure, and Fringe Benefits of Full-Time Instructional Faculty Survey" (IPEDS-SA:99); and IPEDS, Winter 2009–10, Spring 2017, and Spring 2018, Human Resources component, Salaries section. (This table was prepared November 2018.)

Table 316.30. Average salary of full-time instructional faculty on 9-month contracts in degree-granting postsecondary institutions, by control and level of institution and state or jurisdiction: 2017–18

[In current dollars]

State or jurisdiction	All institutions	Public institutions						Nonprofit institutions						For-profit institutions
		Total	4-year institutions				2-year	Total	4-year institutions				2-year	
			Total	Doctoral[1]	Master's[2]	Other			Total	Doctoral[1]	Master's[2]	Other		
1	2	3	4	5	6	7	8	9	10	11	12	13	14	15
United States	**$86,701**	**$83,211**	**$87,745**	**$94,224**	**$75,387**	**$69,221**	**$68,733**	**$95,194**	**$95,282**	**$110,735**	**$74,640**	**$74,668**	**$57,039**	**$56,155**
Alabama	72,167	74,350	80,468	87,562	64,825	73,236	54,603	58,509	58,509	62,411	53,586	55,169	†	62,270
Alaska	82,491	83,508	83,508	86,189	81,961	†	†	53,368	53,072	†	53,072	†	‡	†
Arizona	84,944	86,332	89,564	90,937	79,561	48,414	68,673	72,489	72,489	†	72,489	†	†	56,578
Arkansas	63,044	63,594	69,379	75,075	57,018	62,597	46,829	59,965	59,952	66,258	62,139	55,791	‡	†
California	105,504	102,910	108,819	119,736	87,358	96,667	92,577	115,245	115,245	125,495	85,778	100,935	†	75,124
Colorado	78,455	75,832	79,255	86,238	62,219	65,951	59,431	91,209	91,209	93,757	87,022	76,947	†	46,960
Connecticut	104,525	95,096	100,316	110,267	89,458	†	77,491	113,554	113,554	121,387	98,588	85,724	†	60,615
Delaware	103,108	103,774	103,774	111,014	†	69,503	†	75,646	82,798	†	82,798	†	46,016	‡
District of Columbia	117,213	82,418	82,418	127,045	76,558	†	†	120,414	120,414	120,970	71,932	†	†	69,876
Florida	81,273	80,278	80,726	94,529	77,483	60,983	58,759	84,379	84,379	98,256	75,572	64,631	†	51,994
Georgia	77,458	76,212	77,474	83,962	63,770	58,418	48,457	81,571	81,722	104,721	69,231	60,661	74,948	65,217
Hawaii	89,453	90,957	98,707	101,800	†	77,607	74,071	78,961	78,961	†	75,446	107,605	†	†
Idaho	67,824	68,382	71,340	72,987	†	54,476	55,620	61,427	61,427	†	56,074	65,728	†	†
Illinois	91,514	84,701	88,393	91,399	74,561	†	78,143	100,240	100,284	116,624	71,178	64,634	40,985	62,203
Indiana	83,119	82,915	87,902	94,677	67,905	54,584	51,614	83,523	83,523	94,512	66,049	72,000	†	†
Iowa	77,927	84,578	94,873	98,490	76,834	†	61,132	66,828	66,828	74,241	59,191	71,708	†	45,761
Kansas	69,327	71,987	78,798	83,846	62,119	†	55,136	52,663	52,663	55,121	56,315	45,571	†	67,506
Kentucky	68,190	70,047	75,573	78,927	60,844	†	52,908	61,119	61,119	65,580	54,261	64,621	†	43,222
Louisiana	68,635	64,852	70,572	79,025	58,695	50,444	44,626	84,378	84,378	92,438	56,637	57,092	†	†
Maine	75,806	72,076	76,967	82,113	62,874	63,854	57,080	81,830	82,260	68,929	54,864	97,924	56,613	†
Maryland	84,268	84,390	89,718	93,146	77,957	†	73,698	83,926	83,926	95,101	74,149	72,564	†	66,673
Massachusetts	109,773	90,244	97,616	105,951	84,570	57,874	67,076	119,052	119,056	131,561	95,763	94,942	‡	57,240
Michigan	92,728	96,327	99,437	102,099	82,411	81,944	78,810	71,040	71,040	90,641	69,142	67,168	†	†
Minnesota	81,488	83,591	91,049	108,231	79,048	65,173	69,919	76,954	76,954	77,055	69,458	80,168	†	33,333
Mississippi	61,964	62,139	68,798	70,522	56,435	†	52,268	60,434	60,434	66,858	60,514	44,844	†	63,980
Missouri	75,869	70,391	73,931	82,229	62,307	†	59,304	85,446	85,446	100,691	65,483	57,593	†	51,716
Montana	67,375	70,148	72,685	77,106	62,930	56,992	52,506	52,417	53,256	†	53,301	53,232	41,696	†
Nebraska	77,331	79,768	83,975	90,248	66,676	†	61,143	69,257	69,257	86,491	57,743	58,526	†	†
Nevada	85,824	86,035	86,834	92,443	†	71,542	75,232	79,781	79,781	‡	74,412	†	†	45,895
New Hampshire	97,902	89,697	96,522	105,622	81,611	85,808	62,159	108,900	108,900	145,214	72,641	75,768	†	†
New Jersey	107,662	104,623	112,573	116,568	102,025	†	76,645	114,824	114,824	131,702	84,187	73,843	†	69,458
New Mexico	67,168	67,170	73,202	78,467	64,529	48,592	53,086	67,849	67,849	†	67,849	†	†	61,125
New York	98,056	87,712	91,405	104,532	85,188	75,902	79,672	107,761	107,841	117,819	81,864	88,874	70,954	44,337
North Carolina	78,963	74,907	86,376	89,657	73,760	75,460	51,478	89,928	90,267	109,878	61,079	65,651	42,569	68,692
North Dakota	69,327	71,386	73,125	80,991	61,730	53,689	57,738	57,066	57,066	60,101	†	50,827	†	†
Ohio	81,193	83,615	87,883	90,598	64,875	68,973	65,386	75,724	75,742	81,757	67,432	74,979	40,000	151,517
Oklahoma	68,554	67,743	72,298	79,771	61,942	47,456	48,985	72,294	72,294	85,181	60,842	38,514	†	44,667
Oregon	79,014	79,411	83,030	87,252	63,868	68,429	71,760	77,630	77,630	79,272	56,188	81,277	†	†
Pennsylvania	92,443	89,525	93,725	101,374	87,179	75,639	65,647	95,588	95,884	110,685	75,680	84,291	51,950	50,768
Rhode Island	100,078	82,132	87,568	94,825	72,578	†	62,747	112,199	112,199	140,137	91,570	†	†	†
South Carolina	70,124	72,497	82,532	95,649	71,070	59,983	49,594	62,584	62,774	66,547	64,893	57,038	51,579	46,219
South Dakota	65,212	66,866	68,923	70,549	69,148	45,856	57,915	57,111	57,111	†	59,170	44,343	†	62,793
Tennessee	77,204	72,901	78,803	80,392	67,113	†	53,309	86,448	86,448	104,949	66,018	50,042	†	66,939
Texas	80,852	78,694	85,913	91,276	69,621	57,656	61,315	91,074	91,190	104,924	72,199	58,253	38,005	59,458
Utah	78,206	78,035	79,854	92,205	69,900	60,352	58,697	81,242	81,242	113,406	72,112	†	†	‡
Vermont	80,432	80,202	80,202	88,888	61,607	58,508	†	80,657	80,657	†	83,755	54,471	†	†
Virginia	84,295	86,577	91,885	95,549	72,808	73,425	64,324	76,845	76,860	85,994	58,814	66,382	‡	47,425
Washington	81,250	81,574	83,190	100,104	83,695	62,688	61,983	80,041	80,041	86,151	65,729	81,343	†	‡
West Virginia	63,854	65,330	68,181	76,127	55,766	56,478	47,252	51,362	51,362	53,394	50,774	50,419	†	†
Wisconsin	77,722	79,299	79,473	91,991	63,065	77,405	78,840	71,345	71,345	79,692	62,643	67,168	†	†
Wyoming	73,473	73,473	86,529	86,529	†	†	58,316	†	†	†	†	†	†	†
U.S. Service Academies	116,438	116,438	116,438	†	†	116,438	†	†	†	†	†	†	†	†
Other jurisdictions	**57,586**	**61,446**	**67,872**	**†**	**74,220**	**48,731**	**35,742**	**34,416**	**34,416**	**40,796**	**37,866**	**16,457**	**†**	**15,547**
American Samoa	30,932	30,932	30,932	†	†	30,932	†	†	†	†	†	†	†	†
Federated States of Micronesia	26,114	26,114	†	†	†	†	26,114	†	†	†	†	†	†	†
Guam	66,961	66,961	71,204	†	71,204	†	56,590	†	†	†	†	†	†	†
Marshall Islands	†	†	†	†	†	†	†	†	†	†	†	†	†	†
Northern Marianas	51,667	51,667	51,667	†	†	51,667	†	†	†	†	†	†	†	†
Palau	†	†	†	†	†	†	†	†	†	†	†	†	†	†
Puerto Rico	59,530	66,093	71,262	†	76,160	54,942	33,512	34,416	34,416	40,796	37,866	16,457	†	15,547
U.S. Virgin Islands	67,458	67,458	67,458	†	67,458	†	†	†	†	†	†	†	†	†

†Not applicable.
‡Reporting standards not met (too few cases).
[1]Institutions that awarded 20 or more doctor's degrees during the previous academic year.
[2]Institutions that awarded 20 or more master's degrees, but less than 20 doctor's degrees, during the previous academic year. This definition differs from the definition of master's institutions that is used in some *Digest* tables that present postsecondary finance data.

NOTE: Data exclude instructional faculty at medical schools. Degree-granting institutions grant associate's or higher degrees and participate in Title IV federal financial aid programs. Data include imputations for nonrespondent institutions.
SOURCE: U.S. Department of Education, National Center for Education Statistics, Integrated Postsecondary Education Data System (IPEDS), Spring 2018, Human Resources component, Salaries section. (This table was prepared November 2018.)

Table 316.50. Average salary of full-time instructional faculty on 9-month contracts in 4-year degree-granting postsecondary institutions, by control and classification of institution, academic rank of faculty, and state or jurisdiction: 2017–18

[In current dollars]

State or jurisdiction	Public doctoral[1]			Public master's[2]			Nonprofit doctoral[1]			Nonprofit master's[2]		
	Professor	Associate professor	Assistant professor	Professor	Associate professor	Assistant professor	Professor	Associate professor	Assistant professor	Professor	Associate professor	Assistant professor
1	2	3	4	5	6	7	8	9	10	11	12	13
United States	**$131,773**	**$91,724**	**$79,860**	**$96,084**	**$78,316**	**$67,291**	**$160,220**	**$99,182**	**$84,079**	**$92,541**	**$74,409**	**$63,318**
Alabama	127,963	90,856	75,108	82,673	68,604	61,421	100,337	72,443	40,898	63,483	56,626	49,023
Alaska	106,345	88,890	73,501	104,446	87,974	69,597	†	†	†	64,878	49,771	46,676
Arizona	130,847	94,930	81,729	131,474	97,006	71,886	†	†	†	102,855	70,699	68,672
Arkansas	107,859	80,126	70,406	72,821	63,958	55,849	80,637	67,795	61,052	71,905	60,683	57,892
California	157,398	107,063	91,776	106,717	90,993	81,007	171,805	108,564	92,503	102,760	81,946	71,902
Colorado	115,388	89,432	76,717	81,100	66,664	57,438	132,631	94,973	83,105	114,440	86,141	66,741
Connecticut	151,296	102,494	83,685	104,568	87,063	69,382	181,457	97,588	86,608	138,079	99,941	82,461
Delaware	147,967	103,107	89,469	†	†	†	†	†	†	100,360	81,706	74,641
District of Columbia	155,545	104,516	97,513	104,665	75,418	62,592	173,091	111,491	91,435	87,320	69,942	68,769
Florida	131,375	92,378	82,227	109,385	85,990	68,717	134,981	94,032	78,552	97,164	79,770	67,048
Georgia	119,699	85,441	74,284	78,536	66,423	59,495	145,659	95,690	85,360	78,808	62,834	54,896
Hawaii	128,644	97,622	85,128	†	†	†	†	†	†	88,534	80,218	72,564
Idaho	94,465	77,181	69,354	†	†	†	†	†	†	65,028	53,955	50,839
Illinois	125,265	88,026	83,950	96,061	77,937	67,823	179,415	102,779	88,936	85,279	71,370	61,549
Indiana	133,168	91,958	82,484	89,351	72,386	64,648	142,812	90,094	73,813	82,727	66,339	56,538
Iowa	135,139	96,032	83,677	92,063	74,385	65,659	90,865	73,290	61,825	69,674	59,679	53,855
Kansas	115,684	82,458	72,060	75,885	65,820	59,130	65,640	53,748	50,240	65,025	59,224	52,881
Kentucky	110,730	79,024	70,024	78,394	66,073	56,327	80,053	64,439	55,239	62,905	55,209	49,231
Louisiana	110,756	77,970	72,734	75,294	62,221	56,855	130,762	83,586	83,056	58,577	58,435	55,342
Maine	107,197	82,956	65,380	77,668	63,024	52,310	94,402	76,102	63,547	67,458	57,908	49,334
Maryland	134,805	96,312	80,993	94,669	76,275	69,760	139,776	100,333	100,010	89,574	72,223	62,298
Massachusetts	147,087	108,171	89,875	101,968	81,056	69,212	187,894	112,953	99,508	125,028	91,110	75,986
Michigan	138,423	96,272	83,290	97,251	83,582	72,314	110,994	88,732	77,298	80,136	68,350	61,349
Minnesota	145,639	97,959	88,853	93,801	78,599	67,629	98,667	78,709	65,050	81,113	67,740	61,630
Mississippi	100,816	76,706	67,330	69,918	61,569	52,390	82,978	67,743	60,965	75,074	60,668	57,678
Missouri	110,036	77,445	69,587	79,598	64,923	56,816	147,955	91,239	78,982	83,260	66,082	57,684
Montana	95,841	74,738	69,213	76,954	68,105	57,828	†	†	†	63,367	52,573	48,494
Nebraska	120,381	87,614	84,981	81,613	67,494	57,686	117,998	84,867	70,194	66,278	57,492	52,192
Nevada	130,632	95,142	74,618	†	†	†	†	†	‡	‡	‡	‡
New Hampshire	133,295	103,394	83,522	96,382	79,452	66,440	190,058	120,522	96,399	91,889	74,796	65,767
New Jersey	160,011	110,435	88,365	126,826	100,460	82,485	194,639	104,405	95,071	102,656	90,177	69,710
New Mexico	104,166	75,615	70,507	77,832	70,460	62,013	†	†	†	‡	‡	38,486
New York	136,296	97,611	83,120	110,336	85,039	72,010	168,067	106,382	88,621	100,633	80,507	69,956
North Carolina	126,889	86,784	78,502	94,385	75,736	68,976	162,917	98,133	75,308	72,081	62,291	56,331
North Dakota	106,453	83,595	71,641	80,945	63,356	55,741	71,134	64,383	55,754	†	†	†
Ohio	123,955	89,065	78,875	77,729	65,037	61,901	111,762	79,992	72,858	80,057	66,151	57,953
Oklahoma	109,542	80,060	73,369	81,130	65,528	57,161	105,174	79,730	76,703	70,498	61,836	54,522
Oregon	125,660	92,971	80,833	79,862	67,892	54,421	102,534	79,796	65,343	64,651	58,340	51,981
Pennsylvania	144,186	100,818	82,896	111,553	90,748	72,485	159,612	100,108	87,310	94,625	77,057	65,536
Rhode Island	124,230	90,450	84,447	82,779	73,051	62,218	181,167	120,354	98,358	118,595	89,048	75,400
South Carolina	133,119	93,900	87,330	89,755	72,439	63,724	69,828	66,204	58,204	81,361	65,849	57,267
South Dakota	95,456	78,771	69,939	91,645	70,306	66,612	†	†	†	68,849	61,866	54,836
Tennessee	109,870	80,751	70,847	83,192	67,464	58,894	148,018	92,959	77,979	81,797	66,043	58,151
Texas	133,214	92,012	78,114	93,992	76,894	67,683	146,520	97,766	86,205	89,628	73,246	62,593
Utah	124,297	87,970	79,559	89,441	72,923	65,367	151,842	108,014	75,936	86,851	76,225	53,748
Vermont	119,777	90,970	76,024	73,468	56,466	49,459	†	†	†	104,727	78,247	71,211
Virginia	134,731	93,926	78,577	91,869	75,410	65,869	116,475	85,452	67,866	72,986	60,238	54,085
Washington	132,222	99,693	91,672	106,057	90,523	78,855	115,080	86,756	71,398	80,141	67,044	62,885
West Virginia	97,879	75,870	67,924	65,943	58,848	50,837	66,654	56,344	49,806	59,998	57,205	47,373
Wisconsin	120,857	82,647	78,930	74,621	63,929	62,503	105,740	82,221	71,965	75,641	63,648	56,714
Wyoming	118,002	82,290	79,942	†	†	†	†	†	†	†	†	†
U.S. Service Academies	†	†	†	†	†	†	†	†	†	†	†	†
Other jurisdictions	**†**	**†**	**†**	**84,828**	**72,306**	**60,962**	**†**	**†**	**49,789**	**†**	**†**	**48,321**
American Samoa	†	†	†	†	†	†	†	†	†	†	†	†
Federated States of Micronesia	†	†	†	†	†	†	†	†	†	†	†	†
Guam	†	†	†	94,653	74,108	57,834	†	†	†	†	†	†
Marshall Islands	†	†	†	†	†	†	†	†	†	†	†	†
Northern Marianas	†	†	†	†	†	†	†	†	†	†	†	†
Palau	†	†	†	†	†	†	†	†	†	†	†	†
Puerto Rico	†	†	†	83,765	72,036	63,110	†	†	49,789	†	†	48,321
U.S. Virgin Islands	†	†	†	87,266	69,755	59,146	†	†	†	†	†	†

†Not applicable.
‡Reporting standards not met (too few cases).
[1]Institutions that awarded 20 or more doctor's degrees during the previous academic year.
[2]Institutions that awarded 20 or more master's degrees, but less than 20 doctor's degrees, during the previous academic year. This definition differs from the definition of master's institutions that is used in some *Digest* tables that present postsecondary finance data.

NOTE: Data exclude instructional faculty at medical schools. Degree-granting institutions grant associate's or higher degrees and participate in Title IV federal financial aid programs. Data include imputations for nonrespondent institutions.
SOURCE: U.S. Department of Education, National Center for Education Statistics, Integrated Postsecondary Education Data System (IPEDS), Spring 2018, Human Resources component, Salaries section. (This table was prepared November 2018.)

Table 316.80. Percentage of degree-granting postsecondary institutions with a tenure system and of full-time faculty with tenure at these institutions, by control and level of institution and selected characteristics of faculty: Selected years, 1993–94 through 2017–18

Selected characteristic and academic year	All institutions	Public institutions						Nonprofit institutions						For-profit institutions
		Total	4-year institutions				2-year	Total	4-year institutions				2-year	
			Total	Doctoral[1]	Master's[2]	Other			Total	Doctoral[1]	Master's[2]	Other		
1	2	3	4	5	6	7	8	9	10	11	12	13	14	15
Percent of institutions with a tenure system														
1993–94	62.6	73.6	92.6	100.0	98.3	76.4	62.1	62.0	66.3	90.5	76.5	58.3	26.1	7.8
1999–2000	55.0	72.8	94.6	100.0	95.5	86.3	60.3	59.0	63.4	81.2	72.6	54.9	14.0	4.0
2003–04	52.7	71.3	90.9	100.0	98.0	70.9	59.4	57.9	61.2	86.6	71.6	49.5	14.4	3.6
2005–06	50.9	71.5	90.9	99.5	98.0	71.6	59.4	56.5	59.8	85.1	67.1	49.2	11.5	2.0
2007–08	49.5	70.7	91.0	100.0	98.6	70.1	57.4	57.5	60.2	81.3	64.2	45.4	13.0	1.4
2009–10	47.8	71.2	90.9	99.6	98.5	71.3	57.7	57.1	59.5	80.6	64.4	44.6	12.9	1.5
2011–12	45.3	71.6	90.8	99.6	98.5	70.5	57.8	55.6	58.6	79.5	64.0	42.7	8.0	1.3
2013–14	49.3	74.6	95.8	99.6	98.1	86.6	58.9	59.7	61.8	79.6	63.2	49.0	12.5	1.2
2015–16	51.9	74.8	95.2	99.6	97.6	85.7	58.9	57.7	60.6	79.8	60.8	47.0	7.5	1.3
2016–17	54.4	74.6	94.6	99.6	97.2	85.0	58.0	58.8	61.5	79.3	61.1	48.8	9.2	1.5
2017–18	55.1	74.7	94.5	99.6	96.8	85.7	57.7	58.3	60.6	80.2	59.4	46.9	7.8	1.6
Faculty with tenure at institutions with a tenure system														
Percent of all full-time faculty[3]														
1993–94	56.2	58.9	56.3	54.5	60.5	51.1	69.9	49.5	49.5	47.6	51.8	50.4	47.9	33.8
1999–2000	53.7	55.9	53.2	50.4	59.1	54.7	67.7	48.2	48.1	43.4	52.3	53.5	59.7	77.4
2003–04	50.4	53.0	50.2	48.9	52.9	51.2	65.2	44.6	44.6	40.1	48.7	51.9	47.7	69.2
2005–06	49.6	51.5	48.7	47.2	52.3	49.1	64.1	45.1	45.1	40.7	49.1	52.5	45.2	69.3
2007–08	48.8	50.5	47.8	45.9	52.7	49.5	63.6	44.7	44.7	41.0	50.5	53.1	41.3	51.3
2009–10	48.7	50.6	47.8	45.7	53.6	51.3	64.1	44.3	44.3	40.4	50.5	54.1	38.5	51.0
2011–12	48.5	50.7	48.0	45.8	54.3	53.4	64.7	43.7	43.7	39.7	50.7	54.3	31.4	31.0
2013–14	48.3	50.4	47.3	44.9	55.4	52.2	67.2	43.8	43.8	39.5	51.7	55.9	31.5	19.8
2015–16	47.2	49.3	46.6	44.2	54.7	53.5	65.0	42.8	42.8	38.6	51.6	55.6	33.9	17.0
2016–17	46.4	48.2	45.8	43.3	53.4	56.9	63.6	42.4	42.4	38.3	51.1	55.4	32.2	17.2
2017–18	45.6	47.3	44.9	42.4	52.7	56.1	63.2	41.8	41.8	37.9	50.7	55.0	27.2	17.6
Percent of full-time instructional faculty only														
2016–17														
Total	48.8	50.7	48.5	46.6	53.6	56.9	63.6	44.9	44.9	41.6	51.1	55.5	32.2	17.2
Male	54.7	56.4	55.1	53.8	59.4	60.3	65.7	51.2	51.3	48.5	56.8	60.9	37.2	20.0
Female	41.7	43.9	40.0	36.9	47.1	53.8	61.8	36.9	37.0	32.2	45.0	49.5	29.4	14.8
Professor	90.2	91.4	91.5	89.9	98.1	96.4	90.8	87.8	87.8	85.2	93.0	96.0	78.8	62.2
Male	90.7	92.0	92.0	90.7	98.1	96.7	92.0	88.2	88.2	86.1	93.0	95.9	84.6	71.1
Female	89.1	90.2	90.3	87.8	97.9	95.9	89.8	86.9	86.9	82.9	92.9	96.3	75.0	51.4
Associate professor	75.8	79.4	79.7	76.8	90.0	87.4	75.4	69.1	69.1	62.8	77.8	87.6	54.7	41.6
Male	76.2	79.9	80.1	77.5	90.0	88.0	77.1	68.9	68.9	63.1	77.7	86.9	75.0	34.3
Female	75.4	78.6	79.1	75.9	89.9	86.7	74.1	69.3	69.4	62.3	77.8	88.3	47.9	47.6
Assistant professor	5.5	7.1	4.0	1.7	8.9	23.3	44.1	2.6	2.6	1.6	5.5	3.9	9.8	‡
Male	5.4	6.7	3.8	1.6	9.0	24.0	47.1	2.9	2.8	1.8	5.8	4.5	11.5	‡
Female	5.7	7.5	4.2	1.8	8.7	22.8	41.9	2.4	2.4	1.3	5.2	3.3	8.6	†
Instructor	26.4	32.4	8.4	0.5	2.0	41.3	56.7	0.2	0.2	0.1	0.1	0.8	†	3.4
Lecturer	1.8	2.3	1.7	1.1	3.5	8.3	25.9	0.2	0.2	0.1	‡	1.5	†	†
No academic rank	29.4	36.9	22.0	1.9	2.6	59.5	65.8	4.8	4.6	1.9	22.0	1.8	34.5	†
2017–18														
Total	48.0	49.7	47.5	45.5	52.9	56.1	63.2	44.4	44.4	41.2	50.7	55.0	27.2	17.6
Male	54.0	55.6	54.2	52.8	58.8	59.5	65.5	50.8	50.8	48.2	56.4	60.5	32.9	20.1
Female	40.9	42.9	39.2	36.0	46.4	52.8	61.3	36.4	36.4	32.0	44.7	49.0	24.0	15.3
Professor	89.7	90.9	90.9	89.1	98.2	96.2	90.6	87.5	87.5	85.0	92.7	95.9	60.9	70.7
Male	90.2	91.4	91.4	90.0	98.1	96.5	91.6	87.9	87.9	85.9	92.7	95.8	77.8	74.5
Female	88.6	89.7	89.6	86.8	98.3	95.7	89.8	86.6	86.6	82.7	92.8	95.9	50.0	65.7
Associate professor	75.0	78.4	78.6	75.6	89.6	86.4	75.1	68.6	68.6	62.5	77.7	87.6	52.7	41.5
Male	75.5	79.1	79.2	76.4	89.8	86.3	77.4	68.6	68.6	63.0	77.7	86.7	71.4	37.5
Female	74.4	77.4	77.9	74.4	89.4	86.5	73.4	68.6	68.7	61.8	77.8	88.6	46.3	45.5
Assistant professor	5.1	6.5	3.5	1.3	8.3	21.9	44.0	2.5	2.5	1.7	5.4	2.8	†	†
Male	5.0	6.3	3.5	1.3	8.6	22.8	47.0	2.6	2.6	1.7	5.7	3.3	†	†
Female	5.2	6.8	3.6	1.4	8.0	21.1	41.7	2.4	2.4	1.6	5.2	2.4	†	†
Instructor	25.6	31.3	9.5	0.6	1.5	45.3	55.5	0.3	0.3	0.2	0.4	1.1	†	3.6
Lecturer	1.7	2.2	1.6	1.0	3.2	5.7	28.2	0.2	0.2	0.1	‡	1.7	†	†
No academic rank	28.4	35.6	21.3	1.2	6.9	56.6	65.3	4.8	4.6	2.1	21.0	1.5	41.4	†

†Not applicable.
‡Reporting standards not met (too few cases).
[1]Institutions that awarded 20 or more doctor's degrees during the previous academic year.
[2]Institutions that awarded 20 or more master's degrees, but less than 20 doctor's degrees, during the previous academic year.
[3]Includes instructional, research, and public service faculty.

NOTE: Degree-granting institutions grant associate's or higher degrees and participate in Title IV federal financial aid programs. Data include imputations for nonrespondent institutions. Some data have been revised from previously published figures.
SOURCE: U.S. Department of Education, National Center for Education Statistics, Integrated Postsecondary Education Data System (IPEDS), "Fall Staff Survey" (IPEDS-S:93–99); and IPEDS Winter 2003–04 through Winter 2011–12 and Spring 2014 through Spring 2018, Human Resources component, Fall Staff section. (This table was prepared November 2018.)

Table 317.10. Degree-granting postsecondary institutions, by control and level of institution: Selected years, 1949–50 through 2017–18

Year	All institutions			Public			Private								
										Nonprofit			For-profit		
	Total	4-year	2-year	Total	4-year	2-year	Total	4-year, total	2-year, total	Total	4-year	2-year	Total	4-year	2-year
1	2	3	4	5	6	7	8	9	10	11	12	13	14	15	16
Excluding branch campuses															
1949–50	1,851	1,327	524	641	344	297	1,210	983	227	—	—	—	—	—	—
1959–60	2,004	1,422	582	695	367	328	1,309	1,055	254	—	—	—	—	—	—
1969–70	2,525	1,639	886	1,060	426	634	1,465	1,213	252	—	—	—	—	—	—
1979–80	2,975	1,863	1,112	1,310	464	846	1,665	1,399	266	—	—	—	—	—	—
1980–81	3,056	1,861	1,195	1,334	465	869	1,722	1,396	326[1]	—	—	—	—	—	—
1981–82	3,083	1,883	1,200	1,340	471	869	1,743	1,412	331[1]	—	—	—	—	—	—
1982–83	3,111	1,887	1,224	1,336	472	864	1,775	1,415	360[1]	—	—	—	—	—	—
1983–84	3,117	1,914	1,203	1,325	474	851	1,792	1,440	352	—	—	—	—	—	—
1984–85	3,146	1,911	1,235	1,329	461	868	1,817	1,450	367	—	—	—	—	—	—
1985–86	3,155	1,915	1,240	1,326	461	865	1,829	1,454	375	—	—	—	—	—	—
Including branch campuses															
1974–75	3,004	1,866	1,138	1,433	537	896	1,571	1,329	242	—	—	—	—	—	—
1975–76	3,026	1,898	1,128	1,442	545	897	1,584	1,353	231	—	—	—	—	—	—
1976–77	3,046	1,913	1,133	1,455	550	905	1,591	1,363	228	1,536	1,348	188	55	15	40
1977–78	3,095	1,938	1,157	1,473	552	921	1,622	1,386	236	—	—	—	—	—	—
1978–79	3,134	1,941	1,193	1,474	550	924	1,660	1,391	269	1,564	1,376	188	96	15	81
1979–80	3,152	1,957	1,195	1,475	549	926	1,677	1,408	269	—	—	—	—	—	—
1980–81	3,231	1,957	1,274	1,497	552	945	1,734	1,405	329[1]	1,569	1,387	182	165	18	147
1981–82	3,253	1,979	1,274	1,498	558	940	1,755	1,421	334[1]	—	—	—	—	—	—
1982–83	3,280	1,984	1,296	1,493	560	933	1,787	1,424	363[1]	—	—	—	—	—	—
1983–84	3,284	2,013	1,271	1,481	565	916	1,803	1,448	355	—	—	—	—	—	—
1984–85	3,331	2,025	1,306	1,501	566	935	1,830	1,459	371	1,616	1,430	186	214	29	185
1985–86	3,340	2,029	1,311	1,498	566	932	1,842	1,463	379	—	—	—	—	—	—
1986–87	3,406	2,070	1,336	1,533	573	960	1,873	1,497	376	1,635	1,462	173	238	35	203
1987–88	3,587	2,135	1,452	1,591	599	992	1,996	1,536	460	1,673	1,487	186	323	49	274
1988–89	3,565	2,129	1,436	1,582	598	984	1,983	1,531	452	1,658	1,478	180	325	53	272
1989–90	3,535	2,127	1,408	1,563	595	968	1,972	1,532	440	1,656	1,479	177	316	53	263
1990–91	3,559	2,141	1,418	1,567	595	972	1,992	1,546	446	1,649	1,482	167	343	64	279
1991–92	3,601	2,157	1,444	1,598	599	999	2,003	1,558	445	1,662	1,486	176	341	72	269
1992–93	3,638	2,169	1,469	1,624	600	1,024	2,014	1,569	445	1,672	1,493	179	342	76	266
1993–94	3,632	2,190	1,442	1,625	604	1,021	2,007	1,586	421	1,687	1,506	181	320	80	240
1994–95	3,688	2,215	1,473	1,641	605	1,036	2,047	1,610	437	1,702	1,510	192	345	100	245
1995–96	3,706	2,244	1,462	1,655	608	1,047	2,051	1,636	415	1,706	1,519	187	345	117	228
1996–97	4,009	2,267	1,742	1,702	614	1,088	2,307	1,653	654	1,693	1,509	184	614	144	470
1997–98	4,064	2,309	1,755	1,707	615	1,092	2,357	1,694	663	1,707	1,528	179	650	166	484
1998–99	4,048	2,335	1,713	1,681	612	1,069	2,367	1,723	644	1,695	1,531	164	672	192	480
1999–2000	4,084	2,363	1,721	1,682	614	1,068	2,402	1,749	653	1,681	1,531	150	721	218	503
2000–01	4,182	2,450	1,732	1,698	622	1,076	2,484	1,828	656	1,695	1,551	144	789	277	512
2001–02	4,197	2,487	1,710	1,713	628	1,085	2,484	1,859	625	1,676	1,541	135	808	318	490
2002–03	4,168	2,466	1,702	1,712	631	1,081	2,456	1,835	621	1,665	1,538	127	791	297	494
2003–04	4,236	2,530	1,706	1,720	634	1,086	2,516	1,896	620	1,664	1,546	118	852	350	502
2004–05	4,216	2,533	1,683	1,700	639	1,061	2,516	1,894	622	1,637	1,525	112	879	369	510
2005–06	4,276	2,582	1,694	1,693	640	1,053	2,583	1,942	641	1,647	1,534	113	936	408	528
2006–07	4,314	2,629	1,685	1,688	643	1,045	2,626	1,986	640	1,640	1,533	107	986	453	533
2007–08	4,352	2,675	1,677	1,685	653	1,032	2,667	2,022	645	1,624	1,532	92	1,043	490	553
2008–09	4,409	2,719	1,690	1,676	652	1,024	2,733	2,067	666	1,629	1,537	92	1,104	530	574
2009–10	4,495	2,774	1,721	1,672	672	1,000	2,823	2,102	721	1,624	1,539	85	1,199	563	636
2010–11	4,599	2,870	1,729	1,656	678	978	2,943	2,192	751	1,630	1,543	87	1,313	649	664
2011–12	4,706	2,968	1,738	1,649	682	967	3,057	2,286	771	1,653	1,553	100	1,404	733	671
2012–13	4,726	3,026	1,700	1,623	689	934	3,103	2,337	766	1,652	1,555	97	1,451	782	669
2013–14	4,724	3,039	1,685	1,625	691	934	3,099	2,348	751	1,675	1,587	88	1,424	761	663
2014–15	4,627	3,011	1,616	1,621	701	920	3,006	2,310	696	1,672	1,584	88	1,334	726	608
2015–16	4,583	3,004	1,579	1,620	710	910	2,963	2,294	669	1,701	1,594	107	1,262	700	562
2016–17	4,360	2,832	1,528	1,623	737	886	2,737	2,095	642	1,682	1,581	101	1,055	514	541
2017–18	4,313	2,828	1,485	1,626	750	876	2,687	2,078	609	1,689	1,590	99	998	488	510

—Not available.
[1]Large increases are due to the addition of schools accredited by the Accrediting Commission of Career Schools and Colleges of Technology.
NOTE: Data through 1995–96 are for institutions of higher education, while later data are for degree-granting institutions. Degree-granting institutions grant associate's or higher degrees and participate in Title IV federal financial aid programs. Changes in counts of institutions over time are partly affected by increasing or decreasing numbers of institutions submitting separate data for branch campuses.

SOURCE: U.S. Department of Education, National Center for Education Statistics, *Education Directory, Colleges and Universities*, 1949–50 through 1965–66; Higher Education General Information Survey (HEGIS), "Institutional Characteristics of Colleges and Universities" surveys, 1966–67 through 1985–86; Integrated Postsecondary Education Data System (IPEDS), "Institutional Characteristics Survey"(IPEDS-IC:86–99); and IPEDS Fall 2000 through Fall 2017, Institutional Characteristics component. (This table was prepared April 2019.)

Table 317.20. Degree-granting postsecondary institutions, by control and classification of institution and state or jurisdiction: 2017–18

State or jurisdiction	Total	All public institutions	Public 4-year institutions							Public 2-year	All nonprofit institutions	Nonprofit 4-year institutions							Nonprofit 2-year	For-profit institutions		
			Total	Research university, very high[1]	Research university, high[2]	Doctoral/research university[3]	Master's[4]	Baccalaureate[5]	Special focus[6]			Total	Research university, very high[1]	Research university, high[2]	Doctoral/research university[3]	Master's[4]	Baccalaureate[5]	Special focus[6]		Total	4-year	2-year
1	2	3	4	5	6	7	8	9	10	11	12	13	14	15	16	17	18	19	20	21	22	23
United States	**4,313**	**1,626**	**750**	**81**	**74**	**38**	**271**	**234**	**52**	**876**	**1,689**	**1,590**	**34**	**30**	**54**	**413**	**462**	**597**	**99**	**998**	**488**	**510**
Alabama	72	40	14	1	4	0	8	1	0	26	21	21	0	0	0	4	12	5	0	11	7	4
Alaska	8	4	4	0	1	0	2	0	1	0	3	2	0	0	0	1	0	1	1	1	0	1
Arizona	78	30	10	2	1	2	2	1	2	20	11	11	0	0	0	2	2	7	0	37	21	16
Arkansas	53	33	11	1	0	1	6	2	1	22	17	13	0	0	0	2	9	2	4	3	2	1
California	441	151	49	8	2	3	18	16	2	102	149	143	3	1	9	31	23	76	6	141	77	64
Colorado	79	28	17	2	3	0	6	6	0	11	15	12	0	1	0	3	3	5	3	36	19	17
Connecticut	43	22	10	1	0	0	4	5	0	12	18	18	1	0	1	8	4	4	0	3	3	0
Delaware	8	3	3	1	0	0	1	1	0	0	4	3	0	0	1	0	1	1	1	1	1	0
District of Columbia	19	2	2	0	0	0	1	0	1	0	12	12	2	3	0	2	0	5	0	5	4	1
Florida	201	43	42	5	2	1	4	30	0	1	70	62	1	2	1	14	21	23	8	88	37	51
Georgia	123	52	29	3	1	4	9	11	1	23	40	36	1	1	1	5	19	9	4	31	12	19
Hawaii	20	10	4	1	0	0	1	2	0	6	6	6	0	0	0	2	3	1	0	4	3	1
Idaho	17	8	4	0	1	2	0	1	0	4	6	6	0	0	0	1	3	2	0	3	2	1
Illinois	171	60	12	2	3	0	7	0	0	48	83	80	2	2	4	19	16	37	3	28	16	12
Indiana	80	15	14	2	2	1	7	2	0	1	41	40	1	0	1	11	16	11	1	24	13	11
Iowa	62	19	3	2	0	0	1	0	0	16	34	34	0	0	0	9	15	10	0	9	7	2
Kansas	69	33	8	2	1	0	4	0	1	25	24	24	0	0	0	6	13	5	0	12	7	5
Kentucky	67	24	8	2	0	0	5	1	0	16	25	25	0	0	2	7	9	7	0	18	10	8
Louisiana	60	32	17	1	2	2	8	1	3	15	14	12	1	0	0	3	4	4	2	14	1	13
Maine	31	15	8	0	1	0	1	6	0	7	13	11	0	0	0	4	6	1	2	3	2	1
Maryland	56	29	13	1	1	2	7	1	1	16	19	19	1	0	0	6	4	8	0	8	3	5
Massachusetts	116	31	15	1	3	0	7	1	3	16	79	77	7	1	4	18	18	29	2	6	3	3
Michigan	94	46	21	3	3	2	6	7	0	25	40	40	0	0	1	10	13	16	0	8	4	4
Minnesota	95	43	12	1	0	0	8	2	1	31	36	35	0	0	2	8	11	14	1	16	14	2
Mississippi	38	23	8	1	3	0	4	0	0	15	9	9	0	0	0	3	4	2	0	6	1	5
Missouri	115	27	13	1	3	0	6	3	0	14	53	51	1	1	2	13	10	24	2	35	16	19
Montana	23	17	7	0	2	0	1	3	1	10	5	4	0	0	0	0	3	1	1	1	0	1
Nebraska	41	16	7	1	0	1	4	0	1	9	19	17	0	0	0	6	6	5	2	6	4	2
Nevada	24	7	6	0	2	0	0	4	0	1	5	4	0	0	0	1	0	3	1	12	5	7
New Hampshire	25	13	6	0	1	0	2	2	1	7	12	11	0	1	0	5	4	1	1	0	0	0
New Jersey	75	32	13	1	2	2	8	0	0	19	31	31	1	1	1	10	2	16	0	12	9	3
New Mexico	42	28	9	1	1	0	4	1	2	19	3	3	0	0	0	2	1	0	0	11	8	3
New York	301	79	43	4	1	1	23	10	4	36	186	173	5	5	7	37	26	93	13	36	22	14
North Carolina	144	75	16	2	4	0	8	1	1	59	50	49	1	1	1	10	24	12	1	19	10	9
North Dakota	20	14	9	0	2	0	1	4	2	5	5	5	0	0	0	1	1	3	0	1	1	0
Ohio	185	60	35	2	7	1	1	21	3	25	74	69	1	1	2	20	22	23	5	51	16	35
Oklahoma	59	30	17	1	1	0	8	5	2	13	14	13	0	1	0	6	3	3	1	15	6	9
Oregon	57	26	9	2	1	0	4	1	1	17	25	24	0	0	0	7	5	12	1	6	4	2
Pennsylvania	239	62	45	3	0	1	16	23	2	17	118	105	2	3	4	33	33	30	13	59	9	50
Rhode Island	13	3	2	0	1	0	1	0	0	1	10	10	1	0	0	5	1	3	0	0	0	0
South Carolina	73	33	13	2	0	0	6	4	1	20	22	21	0	0	0	7	13	1	1	18	8	10
South Dakota	23	12	7	0	2	0	3	0	2	5	7	7	0	0	0	2	2	3	0	4	4	0
Tennessee	100	23	10	1	1	4	3	0	1	13	47	44	1	0	3	13	11	16	3	30	12	18
Texas	261	108	47	7	4	8	16	4	8	61	71	64	1	3	1	18	18	23	7	82	33	49
Utah	32	8	7	1	1	0	3	2	0	1	11	10	0	1	0	3	3	3	1	13	12	1

See notes at end of table.

Table 317.20. Degree-granting postsecondary institutions, by control and classification of institution and state or jurisdiction: 2017–18—Continued

State or jurisdiction	Total	All public institutions	Public 4-year institutions							Public 2-year	All nonprofit institutions	Nonprofit 4-year institutions							Nonprofit 2-year	For-profit institutions		
			Total	Research university, very high[1]	Research university, high[2]	Doctoral/research university[3]	Master's[4]	Baccalaureate[5]	Special focus[6]			Total	Research university, very high[1]	Research university, high[2]	Doctoral/research university[3]	Master's[4]	Baccalaureate[5]	Special focus[6]		Total	4-year	2-year
1	2	3	4	5	6	7	8	9	10	11	12	13	14	15	16	17	18	19	20	21	22	23
Vermont	23	6	5	0	1	0	1	3	0	1	16	16	0	0	0	6	8	2	0	1	1	0
Virginia	122	40	16	4	2	0	7	2	1	24	45	42	0	0	3	6	16	17	3	37	20	17
Washington	80	43	35	2	0	0	6	26	1	8	25	21	0	0	1	10	4	6	4	12	9	3
West Virginia	44	22	13	1	0	0	3	8	1	9	10	10	0	0	0	3	4	3	0	12	3	9
Wisconsin	76	33	16	2	0	0	9	5	0	17	34	34	0	1	2	10	12	9	0	9	7	2
Wyoming	10	8	1	0	1	0	0	0	0	7	2	1	0	0	0	0	1	0	1	0	0	0
U.S. Service Academies	5	5	5	0	0	0	0	5	0	0	†	†	†	†	†	†	†	†	†	†	†	†
Other jurisdictions	**89**	**17**	**9**	**0**	**0**	**0**	**3**	**4**	**2**	**8**	**51**	**46**	**0**	**0**	**3**	**13**	**12**	**18**	**5**	**21**	**11**	**10**
American Samoa	1	1	1	0	0	0	0	1	0	0	0	0	0	0	0	0	0	0	0	0	0	0
Federated States of Micronesia	1	1	0	0	0	0	0	0	0	1	0	0	0	0	0	0	0	0	0	0	0	0
Guam	3	2	1	0	0	0	1	0	0	1	1	1	0	0	0	0	0	1	0	0	0	0
Marshall Islands	1	1	0	0	0	0	0	0	0	1	0	0	0	0	0	0	0	0	0	0	0	0
Northern Marianas	1	1	1	0	0	0	0	1	0	0	0	0	0	0	0	0	0	0	0	0	0	0
Palau	1	1	0	0	0	0	0	0	0	1	0	0	0	0	0	0	0	0	0	0	0	0
Puerto Rico	80	9	5	0	0	0	1	2	2	4	50	45	0	0	3	13	12	17	5	21	11	10
U.S. Virgin Islands	1	1	1	0	0	0	1	0	0	0	0	0	0	0	0	0	0	0	0	0	0	0

†Not applicable.
[1]Research universities with a very high level of research activity.
[2]Research universities with a high level of research activity.
[3]Institutions that award at least 20 research/scholarship doctor's degrees per year, but did not have a high level of research activity.
[4]Institutions that award at least 50 master's degrees and fewer than 20 doctor's degrees per year.
[5]Institutions that primarily emphasize undergraduate education. In addition to institutions that primarily award bachelor's degrees, also includes institutions classified as 4-year in the IPEDS system, but classified as 2-year baccalaureate/associate's colleges in the Carnegie Classification system because they primarily award associate's degrees.
[6]Four-year institutions that award degrees primarily in single fields of study, such as medicine, business, fine arts, theology, and engineering.
NOTE: Branch campuses are counted as separate institutions. Relative levels of research activity for research universities were determined by an analysis of research and development expenditures, science and engineering research staffing, and doctoral degrees conferred, by field. Further information on the research index ranking may be obtained from http://carnegieclassifications.iu.edu/. Degree-granting institutions grant associate's or higher degrees and participate in Title IV federal financial aid programs.
SOURCE: U.S. Department of Education, National Center for Education Statistics, Integrated Postsecondary Education Data System (IPEDS), Fall 2017, Institutional Characteristics component. (This table was prepared October 2018.)

Table 317.40. Number of degree-granting postsecondary institutions and enrollment in these institutions, by enrollment size, control, and classification of institution: Fall 2017

Control and classification of institution	Number of institutions, by enrollment size of institution[1]									
	Total	Under 200	200 to 499	500 to 999	1,000 to 2,499	2,500 to 4,999	5,000 to 9,999	10,000 to 19,999	20,000 to 29,999	30,000 or more
1	2	3	4	5	6	7	8	9	10	11
Total	**4,298**	**687**	**619**	**501**	**822**	**610**	**498**	**340**	**120**	**101**
Research university, very high[2]	115	0	0	0	1	0	4	21	33	56
Research university, high[3]	104	0	0	0	1	3	24	45	23	8
Doctoral/research university[4]	109	0	6	2	10	16	27	29	11	8
Master's[5]	742	14	17	36	173	216	176	84	14	12
Baccalaureate[6]	849	72	117	154	311	108	43	31	6	7
Special-focus[7] 4-year	899	360	216	157	110	40	12	3	1	0
2-year	1,480	241	263	152	216	227	212	127	32	10
Public	1,626	14	39	69	294	357	380	284	106	83
Research university, very high[2]	81	0	0	0	0	0	1	3	26	51
Research university, high[3]	74	0	0	0	0	0	12	34	21	7
Doctoral/research university[4]	38	0	0	0	1	1	5	19	9	3
Master's[5]	271	0	1	0	16	58	105	73	12	6
Baccalaureate[6]	234	0	4	20	65	63	41	29	6	6
Special-focus[7] 4-year	52	3	9	11	14	11	4	0	0	0
Arts, music, or design	2	0	0	0	2	0	0	0	0	0
Business and management	1	0	1	0	0	0	0	0	0	0
Engineering and other technology-related	2	0	0	1	0	1	0	0	0	0
Law	6	1	3	1	1	0	0	0	0	0
Medical schools and centers	25	1	0	5	6	10	3	0	0	0
Other health professions	5	0	3	0	2	0	0	0	0	0
Tribal colleges	10	1	2	4	3	0	0	0	0	0
Other special focus	1	0	0	0	0	0	1	0	0	0
2-year	876	11	25	38	198	224	212	126	32	10
High transfer institutions[8]	336	1	7	5	57	70	99	70	20	7
Mixed transfer/career and technical institutions[9]	302	0	1	16	76	75	77	43	11	3
High career and technical institutions[10]	212	2	4	16	61	79	36	13	1	0
Special-focus[7] 2-year	26	8	13	1	4	0	0	0	0	0
Health professions	5	0	4	0	1	0	0	0	0	0
Tribal colleges	17	8	8	0	1	0	0	0	0	0
Other programs	4	0	1	1	2	0	0	0	0	0
Private nonprofit	1,687	328	248	244	461	229	104	51	11	11
Research university, very high[2]	34	0	0	0	1	0	3	18	7	5
Research university, high[3]	30	0	0	0	1	3	12	11	2	1
Doctoral/research university[4]	54	0	1	1	7	13	20	9	2	1
Master's[5]	413	7	6	27	145	154	62	9	0	3
Baccalaureate[6]	461	23	54	111	232	39	0	1	0	1
Special-focus[7] 4-year	597	258	146	91	73	20	7	2	0	0
Arts, music, or design	57	14	14	13	12	1	2	1	0	0
Business and management	21	6	3	4	3	4	1	0	0	0
Engineering and other technology-related	6	1	2	1	1	0	0	1	0	0
Faith-related	300	190	76	22	9	2	1	0	0	0
Law	21	4	5	8	4	0	0	0	0	0
Medical schools and centers	30	3	2	5	11	9	0	0	0	0
Other health professions	133	30	36	32	31	2	2	0	0	0
Tribal colleges	5	0	2	3	0	0	0	0	0	0
Other special focus	24	10	6	3	2	2	1	0	0	0
2-year	98	40	41	14	2	0	0	1	0	0
High transfer institutions[8]	9	1	1	7	0	0	0	0	0	0
Mixed transfer/career and technical institutions[9]	4	0	1	1	2	0	0	0	0	0
High career and technical institutions[10]	14	5	8	1	0	0	0	0	0	0
Special-focus[7] 2-year	71	34	31	5	0	0	0	1	0	0
Health professions	29	14	11	3	0	0	0	1	0	0
Tribal colleges	2	1	1	0	0	0	0	0	0	0
Other programs	40	19	19	2	0	0	0	0	0	0
Private for-profit	985	345	332	188	67	24	14	5	3	7
Doctoral/research university[4]	17	0	5	1	2	2	2	1	0	4
Master's[5]	58	7	10	9	12	4	9	2	2	3
Baccalaureate[6]	154	49	59	23	14	6	2	1	0	0
Special-focus[7] 4-year	250	99	61	55	23	9	1	1	1	0
Arts, music, or design	63	20	17	18	5	2	0	1	0	0
Business and management	52	27	10	6	5	3	1	0	0	0
Engineering and other technology-related	7	2	2	2	1	0	0	0	0	0
Law	6	2	3	1	0	0	0	0	0	0
Medical schools and centers	2	1	0	1	0	0	0	0	0	0
Other health professions	114	44	27	26	12	4	0	0	1	0
Other special focus	6	3	2	1	0	0	0	0	0	0
2-year	506	190	197	100	16	3	0	0	0	0
High transfer institutions[8]	2	1	1	0	0	0	0	0	0	0
Mixed transfer/career and technical institutions[9]	5	3	1	0	0	1	0	0	0	0
High career and technical institutions[10]	154	56	60	32	5	1	0	0	0	0
Special-focus[7] 2-year	345	130	135	68	11	1	0	0	0	0
Health professions	231	77	91	55	7	1	0	0	0	0
Other programs	114	53	44	13	4	0	0	0	0	0

See notes at end of table.

Table 317.40. Number of degree-granting postsecondary institutions and enrollment in these institutions, by enrollment size, control, and classification of institution: Fall 2017—Continued

Control and classification of institution	Enrollment, by enrollment size of institution									
	Total	Under 200	200 to 499	500 to 999	1,000 to 2,499	2,500 to 4,999	5,000 to 9,999	10,000 to 19,999	20,000 to 29,999	30,000 or more
1	12	13	14	15	16	17	18	19	20	21
Total	**19,765,598**	**71,097**	**206,404**	**363,936**	**1,377,551**	**2,165,922**	**3,548,425**	**4,699,722**	**2,958,258**	**4,374,283**
Research university, very high[2]	3,478,145	0	0	0	2,238	0	28,690	305,673	842,859	2,298,685
Research university, high[3]	1,692,499	0	0	0	1,913	13,126	186,210	651,501	570,530	269,219
Doctoral/research university[4]	1,381,369	0	2,352	1,485	18,509	62,722	205,737	377,915	255,929	456,720
Master's[5]	4,393,610	1,556	5,997	27,740	314,594	768,982	1,228,747	1,134,755	328,783	582,456
Baccalaureate[6]	2,211,990	8,129	39,991	116,254	502,677	371,796	298,389	430,787	155,210	288,757
Special-focus[7] 4-year	666,027	35,988	70,379	110,279	169,759	131,227	81,942	39,354	27,099	0
2-year	5,941,958	25,424	87,685	108,178	367,861	818,069	1,518,710	1,759,737	777,848	478,446
Public	14,560,155	1,864	14,117	54,516	506,686	1,283,877	2,713,802	3,948,751	2,628,244	3,408,298
Research university, very high[2]	2,844,803	0	0	0	0	0	7,674	54,812	675,371	2,106,946
Research university, high[3]	1,366,233	0	0	0	0	0	98,917	506,884	525,547	234,885
Doctoral/research university[4]	628,300	0	0	0	2,213	3,490	42,998	259,326	211,820	108,453
Master's[5]	2,487,434	0	387	0	31,666	215,977	734,506	979,758	282,448	242,692
Baccalaureate[6]	1,433,586	0	1,919	15,312	107,975	224,493	285,004	406,797	155,210	236,876
Special-focus[7] 4-year	93,121	341	3,140	8,326	21,118	34,203	25,993	0	0	0
Arts, music, or design	3,078	0	0	0	3,078	0	0	0	0	0
Business and management	327	0	327	0	0	0	0	0	0	0
Engineering and other technology-related	3,387	0	0	609	0	2,778	0	0	0	0
Law	2,825	195	1,026	576	1,028	0	0	0	0	0
Medical schools and centers	63,586	35	0	4,578	10,150	31,425	17,398	0	0	0
Other health professions	3,621	0	1,242	0	2,379	0	0	0	0	0
Tribal colleges	7,702	111	545	2,563	4,483	0	0	0	0	0
Other special focus	8,595	0	0	0	0	0	8,595	0	0	0
2-year	5,706,678	1,523	8,671	30,878	343,714	805,714	1,518,710	1,741,174	777,848	478,446
High transfer institutions[8]	2,901,287	54	2,444	4,069	102,604	255,000	717,240	1,005,414	482,814	331,648
Mixed transfer/career and technical institutions[9]	1,945,571	0	420	13,356	128,753	261,414	552,519	571,935	270,376	146,798
High career and technical institutions[10]	845,035	210	1,675	12,746	103,670	289,300	248,951	163,825	24,658	0
Special-focus[7] 2-year	14,785	1,259	4,132	707	8,687	0	0	0	0	0
Health professions	3,613	0	1,320	0	2,293	0	0	0	0	0
Tribal colleges	5,700	1,259	2,495	0	1,946	0	0	0	0	0
Other programs	5,472	0	317	707	4,448	0	0	0	0	0
Private nonprofit	4,106,477	33,142	80,865	178,787	771,468	797,620	730,443	680,970	256,580	576,602
Research university, very high[2]	633,342	0	0	0	2,238	0	21,016	250,861	167,488	191,739
Research university, high[3]	326,266	0	0	0	1,913	13,126	87,293	144,617	44,983	34,334
Doctoral/research university[4]	442,414	0	267	957	13,791	50,479	149,966	107,801	44,109	75,044
Master's[5]	1,596,806	773	2,525	20,902	263,446	541,045	425,083	119,428	0	223,604
Baccalaureate[6]	668,707	2,796	19,057	85,140	373,610	124,205	0	12,018	0	51,881
Special-focus[7] 4-year	390,552	25,610	46,192	62,274	112,944	68,765	47,085	27,682	0	0
Arts, music, or design	63,158	1,521	4,675	8,629	19,725	3,648	11,797	13,163	0	0
Business and management	32,130	499	1,062	2,709	5,756	14,233	7,871	0	0	0
Engineering and other technology-related	18,237	98	639	736	2,245	0	0	14,519	0	0
Faith-related	85,020	18,423	23,084	14,219	16,651	6,164	6,479	0	0	0
Law	12,763	484	1,660	6,089	4,530	0	0	0	0	0
Medical schools and centers	53,319	492	532	3,367	16,554	32,374	0	0	0	0
Other health professions	104,345	3,195	12,192	21,905	45,211	6,029	15,813	0	0	0
Tribal colleges	2,557	0	600	1,957	0	0	0	0	0	0
Other special focus	19,023	898	1,748	2,663	2,272	6,317	5,125	0	0	0
2-year	48,390	3,963	12,824	9,514	3,526	0	0	18,563	0	0
High transfer institutions[8]	5,142	47	294	4,801	0	0	0	0	0	0
Mixed transfer/career and technical institutions[9]	4,423	0	265	632	3,526	0	0	0	0	0
High career and technical institutions[10]	4,318	748	2,728	842	0	0	0	0	0	0
Special-focus[7] 2-year	34,507	3,168	9,537	3,239	0	0	0	18,563	0	0
Health professions	24,971	1,403	3,248	1,757	0	0	0	18,563	0	0
Tribal colleges	465	90	375	0	0	0	0	0	0	0
Other programs	9,071	1,675	5,914	1,482	0	0	0	0	0	0
Private for-profit	1,098,966	36,091	111,422	130,633	99,397	84,425	104,180	70,001	73,434	389,383
Doctoral/research university[4]	310,655	0	2,085	528	2,505	8,753	12,773	10,788	0	273,223
Master's[5]	309,370	783	3,085	6,838	19,482	11,960	69,158	35,569	46,335	116,160
Baccalaureate[6]	109,697	5,333	19,015	15,802	21,092	23,098	13,385	11,972	0	0
Special-focus[7] 4-year	182,354	10,037	21,047	39,679	35,697	28,259	8,864	11,672	27,099	0
Arts, music, or design	47,745	1,444	6,145	13,141	8,010	7,333	0	11,672	0	0
Business and management	37,743	2,670	3,281	4,572	8,329	10,027	8,864	0	0	0
Engineering and other technology-related	3,417	222	696	1,372	1,127	0	0	0	0	0
Law	2,147	328	1,255	564	0	0	0	0	0	0
Medical schools and centers	878	99	0	779	0	0	0	0	0	0
Other health professions	88,555	4,906	9,023	18,397	18,231	10,899	0	0	27,099	0
Other special focus	1,869	368	647	854	0	0	0	0	0	0
2-year	186,890	19,938	66,190	67,786	20,621	12,355	0	0	0	0
High transfer institutions[8]	474	117	357	0	0	0	0	0	0	0
Mixed transfer/career and technical institutions[9]	5,329	220	423	0	0	4,686	0	0	0	0
High career and technical institutions[10]	58,369	6,208	20,124	21,502	5,834	4,701	0	0	0	0
Special-focus[7] 2-year	122,718	13,393	45,286	46,284	14,787	2,968	0	0	0	0
Health professions	86,864	7,793	31,336	36,379	8,388	2,968	0	0	0	0
Other programs	35,854	5,600	13,950	9,905	6,399	0	0	0	0	0

See notes at end of table.

Table 317.40. Number of degree-granting postsecondary institutions and enrollment in these institutions, by enrollment size, control, and classification of institution: Fall 2017—Continued

[1]Excludes institutions with no enrollment reported separately from the enrollment of an associated main campus.
[2]Research universities with a very high level of research activity.
[3]Research universities with a high level of research activity.
[4]Institutions that award at least 20 research/scholarship doctor's degrees per year, but did not have a high level of research activity.
[5]Institutions that award at least 50 master's degrees and fewer than 20 doctor's degrees per year.
[6]Institutions that primarily emphasize undergraduate education. In addition to institutions that primarily award bachelor's degrees, also includes institutions classified as 4-year in the IPEDS system, but classified as 2-year baccalaureate/associate's colleges in the Carnegie Classification system because they primarily award associate's degrees.
[7]Institutions that award degrees primarily in single fields of study, such as medicine, business, fine arts, theology, and engineering.
[8]Institutions that award less than 30 percent of their awards in career and technical programs.
[9]Institutions that award 30 to 49 percent of their awards in career and technical programs.
[10]Institutions that award 50 percent or more of their awards in career and technical programs.
NOTE: Degree-granting institutions grant associate's or higher degrees and participate in Title IV federal financial aid programs. Relative levels of research activity for research universities were determined by an analysis of research and development expenditures, science and engineering research staffing, and doctoral degrees conferred, by field. Further information on the research index ranking may be obtained from http://carnegieclassifications.iu.edu/.
SOURCE: U.S. Department of Education, National Center for Education Statistics, Integrated Postsecondary Education Data System (IPEDS), Spring 2018, Fall Enrollment component. (This table was prepared November 2018.)

Table 317.50. Number of degree-granting postsecondary institutions that have closed, by control and level of institution: 1969–70 through 2017–18

Year	All institutions			Public			Private								
							Total			Nonprofit			For-profit		
	Total	4-year	2-year	Total	4-year	2-year	Total	4-year	2-year	Total	4-year	2-year	Total	4-year	2-year
1	2	3	4	5	6	7	8	9	10	11	12	13	14	15	16
1969–70	24	10	14	5	1	4	19	9	10	—	—	—	—	—	—
1970–71	35	10	25	11	0	11	24	10	14	—	—	—	—	—	—
1971–72	14	5	9	3	0	3	11	5	6	—	—	—	—	—	—
1972–73	21	12	9	4	0	4	17	12	5	—	—	—	—	—	—
1973–74	20	12	8	1	0	1	19	12	7	—	—	—	—	—	—
1974–75	18	13	5	4	0	4	14	13	1	—	—	—	—	—	—
1975–76	9	7	2	2	1	1	7	6	1	—	—	—	—	—	—
1976–77	9	6	3	0	0	0	9	6	3	—	—	—	—	—	—
1977–78	12	9	3	0	0	0	12	9	3	—	—	—	—	—	—
1978–79	9	4	5	0	0	0	9	4	5	—	—	—	—	—	—
1979–80	6	5	1	0	0	0	6	5	1	—	—	—	—	—	—
1980–81	4	3	1	0	0	0	4	3	1	—	—	—	—	—	—
1981–82	7	6	1	0	0	0	7	6	1	—	—	—	—	—	—
1982–83	7	4	3	0	0	0	7	4	3	—	—	—	—	—	—
1983–84	5	5	0	1	1	0	4	4	0	—	—	—	—	—	—
1984–85	4	4	0	0	0	0	4	4	0	—	—	—	—	—	—
1985–86	12	8	4	1	1	0	11	7	4	—	—	—	—	—	—
1986–87 and 1987–88	26	19	7	1	0	1	25	19	6	—	—	—	—	—	—
1988–89	14	6	8	0	0	0	14	6	8	—	—	—	—	—	—
1989–90	19	8	11	0	0	0	19	8	11	—	—	—	—	—	—
1990–91	18	6	12	0	0	0	18	6	12	7	5	2	11	1	10
1991–92	26	8	18	1	0	1	25	8	17	8	7	1	17	1	16
1992–93	23	6	17	0	0	0	23	6	17	6	5	1	17	1	16
1993–94	38	11	27	1	0	1	37	11	26	13	10	3	24	1	23
1994–95	15	8	7	2	0	2	13	8	5	8	7	1	5	1	4
1995–96	21	8	13	1	1	0	20	7	13	9	7	2	11	0	11
1996–97	36	13	23	2	0	2	34	13	21	14	10	4	20	3	17
1997–98	5	0	5	0	0	0	5	0	5	1	0	1	4	0	4
1998–99	7	1	6	1	0	1	6	1	5	2	0	2	4	1	3
1999–2000	16	3	13	3	0	3	13	3	10	8	3	5	5	0	5
2000–01	14	9	5	0	0	0	14	9	5	8	8	0	6	1	5
2001–02	14	2	12	0	0	0	14	2	12	1	1	0	13	1	12
2002–03	13	7	6	0	0	0	13	7	6	6	6	0	7	1	6
2003–04	12	5	7	0	0	0	12	5	7	8	5	3	4	0	4
2004–05	3	1	2	0	0	0	3	1	2	1	1	0	2	0	2
2005–06	11	6	5	1	1	0	10	5	5	5	4	1	5	1	4
2006–07	13	4	9	0	0	0	13	4	9	6	4	2	7	0	7
2007–08	26	10	16	0	0	0	26	10	16	9	6	3	17	4	13
2008–09	16	6	10	0	0	0	16	6	10	6	5	1	10	1	9
2009–10	17	11	6	0	0	0	17	11	6	9	9	0	8	2	6
2010–11	20	9	11	0	0	0	20	9	11	7	6	1	13	3	10
2011–12	10	5	5	4	0	4	6	5	1	2	2	0	4	3	1
2012–13	21	3	18	1	1	0	20	2	18	4	2	2	16	0	16
2013–14	20	8	12	1	1	0	19	7	12	4	3	1	15	4	11
2014–15	54	7	47	0	0	0	54	7	47	5	3	2	49	4	45
2015–16	66	24	42	0	0	0	66	24	42	8	5	3	58	19	39
2016–17	112	65	47	0	0	0	112	65	47	20	12	8	92	53	39
2017–18	86	39	47	1	0	1	85	39	46	17	12	5	68	27	41

—Not available.
NOTE: This table indicates the year by which the institution no longer operated (generally it closed at the end of or during the prior year). Data through 1995–96 are for institutions of higher education, while later data are for degree-granting institutions. Degree-granting institutions grant associate's or higher degrees and participate in Title IV federal financial aid programs. The degree-granting classification is very similar to the earlier higher education classification, but it includes more 2-year colleges and excludes a few higher education institutions that did not grant degrees.

SOURCE: U.S. Department of Education, National Center for Education Statistics, *Education Directory, Higher Education*, 1969–70 through 1974–75; *Education Directory, Colleges and Universities*, 1975–76 through 1985–86; 1982–83 *Supplement to the Education Directory, Colleges and Universities*; Integrated Postsecondary Education Data System (IPEDS), "Institutional Characteristics Survey" (IPEDS-IC:86–99); and IPEDS Fall 2000 through Fall 2017, Institutional Characteristics component. (This table was prepared June 2019.)

Table 318.10. Degrees conferred by postsecondary institutions, by level of degree and sex of student: Selected years, 1869–70 through 2028–29

Year	Associate's degrees				Bachelor's degrees				Master's degrees				Doctor's degrees[1]			
	Total	Males	Females	Percent female	Total	Males	Females	Percent female	Total	Males	Females	Percent female	Total	Males	Females	Percent female
1	2	3	4	5	6	7	8	9	10	11	12	13	14	15	16	17
1869–70	—	—	—	—	9,371[2]	7,993[2]	1,378[2]	14.7	0	0	0	—	1	1	0	0.0
1879–80	—	—	—	—	12,896[2]	10,411[2]	2,485[2]	19.3	879	868	11	1.3	54	51	3	5.6
1889–90	—	—	—	—	15,539[2]	12,857[2]	2,682[2]	17.3	1,015	821	194	19.1	149	147	2	1.3
1899–1900	—	—	—	—	27,410[2]	22,173[2]	5,237[2]	19.1	1,583	1,280	303	19.1	382	359	23	6.0
1909–10	—	—	—	—	37,199[2]	28,762[2]	8,437[2]	22.7	2,113	1,555	558	26.4	443	399	44	9.9
1919–20	—	—	—	—	48,622[2]	31,980[2]	16,642[2]	34.2	4,279	2,985	1,294	30.2	615	522	93	15.1
1929–30	—	—	—	—	122,484[2]	73,615[2]	48,869[2]	39.9	14,969	8,925	6,044	40.4	2,299	1,946	353	15.4
1939–40	—	—	—	—	186,500[2]	109,546[2]	76,954[2]	41.3	26,731	16,508	10,223	38.2	3,290	2,861	429	13.0
1949–50	—	—	—	—	432,058[2]	328,841[2]	103,217[2]	23.9	58,183	41,220	16,963	29.2	6,420	5,804	616	9.6
1959–60	—	—	—	—	392,440[2]	254,063[2]	138,377[2]	35.3	74,435	50,898	23,537	31.6	9,829	8,801	1,028	10.5
1969–70	206,023	117,432	88,591	43.0	792,316	451,097	341,219	43.1	213,589	130,799	82,790	38.8	59,486	53,792	5,694	9.6
1979–80	400,910	183,737	217,173	54.2	929,417	473,611	455,806	49.0	305,196	156,882	148,314	48.6	95,631	69,526	26,105	27.3
1980–81	416,377	188,638	227,739	54.7	935,140	469,883	465,257	49.8	302,637	152,979	149,658	49.5	98,016	69,567	28,449	29.0
1981–82	434,526	196,944	237,582	54.7	952,998	473,364	479,634	50.3	302,447	151,349	151,098	50.0	97,838	68,630	29,208	29.9
1982–83	449,620	203,991	245,629	54.6	969,510	479,140	490,370	50.6	296,415	150,092	146,323	49.4	99,335	67,757	31,578	31.8
1983–84	452,240	202,704	249,536	55.2	974,309	482,319	491,990	50.5	291,141	149,268	141,873	48.7	100,799	67,769	33,030	32.8
1984–85	454,712	202,932	251,780	55.4	979,477	482,528	496,949	50.7	293,472	149,276	144,196	49.1	100,785	66,269	34,516	34.2
1985–86	446,047	196,166	249,881	56.0	987,823	485,923	501,900	50.8	295,850	149,373	146,477	49.5	100,280	65,215	35,065	35.0
1986–87	436,304	190,839	245,465	56.3	991,264	480,782	510,482	51.5	296,530	147,063	149,467	50.4	98,477	62,790	35,687	36.2
1987–88	435,085	190,047	245,038	56.3	994,829	477,203	517,626	52.0	305,783	150,243	155,540	50.9	99,139	63,019	36,120	36.4
1988–89	436,764	186,316	250,448	57.3	1,018,755	483,346	535,409	52.6	316,626	153,993	162,633	51.4	100,571	63,055	37,516	37.3
1989–90	455,102	191,195	263,907	58.0	1,051,344	491,696	559,648	53.2	330,152	158,052	172,100	52.1	103,508	63,963	39,545	38.2
1990–91	481,720	198,634	283,086	58.8	1,094,538	504,045	590,493	53.9	342,863	160,842	182,021	53.1	105,547	64,242	41,305	39.1
1991–92	504,231	207,481	296,750	58.9	1,136,553	520,811	615,742	54.2	358,089	165,867	192,222	53.7	109,554	66,603	42,951	39.2
1992–93	514,756	211,964	302,792	58.8	1,165,178	532,881	632,297	54.3	375,032	173,354	201,678	53.8	112,072	67,130	44,942	40.1
1993–94	530,632	215,261	315,371	59.4	1,169,275	532,422	636,853	54.5	393,037	180,571	212,466	54.1	112,636	66,773	45,863	40.7
1994–95	539,691	218,352	321,339	59.5	1,160,134	526,131	634,003	54.6	403,609	183,043	220,566	54.6	114,266	67,324	46,942	41.1
1995–96	555,216	219,514	335,702	60.5	1,164,792	522,454	642,338	55.1	412,180	183,481	228,699	55.5	115,507	67,189	48,318	41.8
1996–97	571,226	223,948	347,278	60.8	1,172,879	520,515	652,364	55.6	425,260	185,270	239,990	56.4	118,747	68,387	50,360	42.4
1997–98	558,555	217,613	340,942	61.0	1,184,406	519,956	664,450	56.1	436,037	188,718	247,319	56.7	118,735	67,232	51,503	43.4
1998–99	564,984	220,508	344,476	61.0	1,202,239	519,961	682,278	56.8	446,038	190,230	255,808	57.4	116,700	65,340	51,360	44.0
1999–2000	564,933	224,721	340,212	60.2	1,237,875	530,367	707,508	57.2	463,185	196,129	267,056	57.7	118,736	64,930	53,806	45.3
2000–01	578,865	231,645	347,220	60.0	1,244,171	531,840	712,331	57.3	473,502	197,770	275,732	58.2	119,585	64,171	55,414	46.3
2001–02	595,133	238,109	357,024	60.0	1,291,900	549,816	742,084	57.4	487,313	202,604	284,709	58.4	119,663	62,731	56,932	47.6
2002–03	634,016	253,451	380,565	60.0	1,348,811	573,258	775,553	57.5	518,699	215,172	303,527	58.5	121,579	62,730	58,849	48.4
2003–04	665,301	260,033	405,268	60.9	1,399,542	595,425	804,117	57.5	564,272	233,056	331,216	58.7	126,087	63,981	62,106	49.3
2004–05	696,660	267,536	429,124	61.6	1,439,264	613,000	826,264	57.4	580,151	237,155	342,996	59.1	134,387	67,257	67,130	50.0
2005–06	713,315	270,139	443,176	62.1	1,485,104	630,502	854,602	57.5	599,862	241,701	358,161	59.7	138,056	68,912	69,144	50.1
2006–07	727,616	275,034	452,582	62.2	1,524,729	649,816	874,913	57.4	610,703	242,213	368,490	60.3	144,694	71,311	73,383	50.7
2007–08	750,166	282,695	467,471	62.3	1,563,734	668,184	895,550	57.3	630,844	250,203	380,641	60.3	149,190	73,340	75,850	50.8
2008–09	787,243	298,066	489,177	62.1	1,601,399	685,422	915,977	57.2	662,082	263,515	398,567	60.2	154,564	75,674	78,890	51.0
2009–10	848,856	322,747	526,109	62.0	1,649,919	706,660	943,259	57.2	693,313	275,317	417,996	60.3	158,590	76,610	81,980	51.7
2010–11	943,506	361,408	582,098	61.7	1,716,053	734,159	981,894	57.2	730,922	291,680	439,242	60.1	163,827	79,672	84,155	51.4
2011–12	1,021,718	393,479	628,239	61.5	1,792,163	765,772	1,026,391	57.3	755,967	302,484	453,483	60.0	170,217	82,670	87,547	51.4
2012–13	1,007,427	389,195	618,232	61.4	1,840,381	787,408	1,052,973	57.2	751,718	301,552	450,166	59.9	175,026	85,080	89,946	51.4
2013–14	1,005,155	391,474	613,681	61.1	1,870,150	801,905	1,068,245	57.1	754,582	302,846	451,736	59.9	177,587	85,585	92,002	51.8
2014–15	1,014,341	396,782	617,559	60.9	1,894,969	812,693	1,082,276	57.1	758,804	306,615	452,189	59.6	178,548	84,922	93,626	52.4
2015–16	1,008,228	392,084	616,144	61.1	1,920,750	821,746	1,099,004	57.2	785,757	320,574	465,183	59.2	178,134	84,240	93,894	52.7
2016–17	1,005,649	394,159	611,490	60.8	1,956,032	836,045	1,119,987	57.3	804,684	326,892	477,792	59.4	181,352	84,646	96,706	53.3
2017–18[3]	981,000	383,000	598,000	61.0	1,963,000	837,000	1,126,000	57.4	814,000	327,000	487,000	59.9	183,000	85,000	99,000	53.8
2018–19[3]	985,000	385,000	600,000	60.9	1,968,000	839,000	1,129,000	57.4	816,000	328,000	489,000	59.9	184,000	85,000	99,000	53.8
2019–20[3]	989,000	386,000	603,000	60.9	1,975,000	842,000	1,133,000	57.4	820,000	329,000	491,000	59.9	184,000	85,000	99,000	53.8
2020–21[3]	991,000	387,000	604,000	60.9	1,976,000	842,000	1,134,000	57.4	821,000	329,000	491,000	59.9	185,000	85,000	99,000	53.8
2021–22[3]	994,000	388,000	606,000	60.9	1,978,000	842,000	1,136,000	57.4	822,000	330,000	492,000	59.9	185,000	85,000	100,000	53.9
2022–23[3]	996,000	389,000	607,000	60.9	1,980,000	843,000	1,137,000	57.4	824,000	330,000	493,000	59.9	185,000	85,000	100,000	53.9
2023–24[3]	1,000,000	390,000	609,000	60.9	1,984,000	844,000	1,140,000	57.4	826,000	331,000	495,000	59.9	186,000	86,000	100,000	53.9
2024–25[3]	1,003,000	392,000	612,000	61.0	1,990,000	847,000	1,143,000	57.4	829,000	332,000	497,000	59.9	186,000	86,000	101,000	53.9
2025–26[3]	1,007,000	393,000	614,000	61.0	1,997,000	850,000	1,147,000	57.5	831,000	333,000	498,000	59.9	187,000	86,000	101,000	53.9
2026–27[3]	1,011,000	395,000	616,000	61.0	2,005,000	853,000	1,152,000	57.4	835,000	334,000	500,000	59.9	188,000	87,000	101,000	53.9
2027–28[3]	1,014,000	396,000	618,000	60.9	2,008,000	855,000	1,153,000	57.4	836,000	335,000	501,000	59.9	188,000	87,000	101,000	53.9
2028–29[3]	1,015,000	396,000	619,000	60.9	2,008,000	855,000	1,153,000	57.4	837,000	335,000	502,000	59.9	188,000	87,000	102,000	53.9

—Not available.
[1]Includes Ph.D., Ed.D., and comparable degrees at the doctoral level. Includes most degrees that were classified as first-professional prior to 2010–11, such as M.D., D.D.S., and law degrees.
[2]Includes some degrees classified as master's or doctor's degrees in later years.
[3]Projected.
NOTE: Data through 1994–95 are for institutions of higher education, while later data are for degree-granting institutions. Degree-granting institutions grant associate's or higher degrees and participate in Title IV federal financial aid programs. Some data have been revised from previously published figures. Detail may not sum to totals because of rounding.

SOURCE: U.S. Department of Education, National Center for Education Statistics, *Earned Degrees Conferred*, 1869–70 through 1964–65; Higher Education General Information Survey (HEGIS), "Degrees and Other Formal Awards Conferred" surveys, 1965–66 through 1985–86; Integrated Postsecondary Education Data System (IPEDS), "Completions Survey" (IPEDS-C:87–99); IPEDS Fall 2000 through Fall 2017, Completions component; and Degrees Conferred Projection Model, 1980–81 through 2028–29. (This table was prepared March 2019.)

Table 318.20. Bachelor's, master's, and doctor's degrees conferred by postsecondary institutions, by field of study: Selected years, 1970–71 through 2016–17

[Standard errors appear in parentheses]

Degree and year	Number of degrees conferred								Percentage distribution of degrees conferred							
	Total degrees	Humanities[1]	Social and behavioral sciences[2]	Natural sciences and mathematics[3]	Computer sciences and engineering[4]	Education	Business	Other fields[5]	Total degrees	Humanities[1]	Social and behavioral sciences[2]	Natural sciences and mathematics[3]	Computer sciences and engineering[4]	Education	Business	Other fields[5]
1	2	3	4	5	6	7	8	9	10	11	12	13	14	15	16	17
Bachelor's degrees																
1970–71	839,730	143,549	193,511	81,916	52,570	176,307	115,396	76,481	100.0	17.1	23.0	9.8	6.3	21.0	13.7	9.1
1975–76	925,746	150,736	176,674	91,596	52,328	154,437	143,171	156,804	100.0	16.3	19.1	9.9	5.7	16.7	15.5	16.9
1980–81	935,140	134,139	141,581	78,092	90,476	108,074	200,521	182,257	100.0	14.3	15.1	8.4	9.7	11.6	21.4	19.5
1985–86	987,823	132,891	134,468	76,228	139,459	87,147	236,700	180,930	100.0	13.5	13.6	7.7	14.1	8.8	24.0	18.3
1990–91	1,094,538	172,485	183,762	70,209	104,910	110,807	249,165	203,200	100.0	15.8	16.8	6.4	9.6	10.1	22.8	18.6
1995–96	1,164,792	193,404	199,895	93,443	102,503	105,384	226,623	243,540	100.0	16.6	17.2	8.0	8.8	9.0	19.5	20.9
2000–01	1,244,171	214,107	201,681	89,772	117,011	105,458	263,515	252,627	100.0	17.2	16.2	7.2	9.4	8.5	21.2	20.3
2005–06	1,485,104	261,666	249,600	105,883	129,108	107,235	318,043	313,569	100.0	17.6	16.8	7.1	8.7	7.2	21.4	21.1
2010–11	1,716,053	288,446	278,075	131,871	136,163	104,008	365,133	412,357	100.0	16.8	16.2	7.7	7.9	6.1	21.3	24.0
2013–14	1,870,150	291,799	290,444	154,951	164,247	98,838	358,132	511,739	100.0	15.6	15.5	8.3	8.8	5.3	19.1	27.4
2014–15	1,894,969	280,956	284,544	161,800	174,691	91,596	363,741	537,641	100.0	14.8	15.0	8.5	9.2	4.8	19.2	28.4
2015–16	1,920,750	274,513	278,658	167,055	188,350	87,221	371,690	553,263	100.0	14.3	14.5	8.7	9.8	4.5	19.4	28.8
2016–17	1,956,032	270,643	275,960	172,100	205,181	85,118	381,353	565,677	100.0	13.8	14.1	8.8	10.5	4.4	19.5	28.9
Master's degrees																
1970–71	235,564	34,510	22,256	17,152	18,535	87,666	26,490	28,955	100.0	14.6	9.4	7.3	7.9	37.2	11.2	12.3
1975–76	317,477	37,079	26,120	15,742	19,403	126,061	42,592	50,480	100.0	11.7	8.2	5.0	6.1	39.7	13.4	15.9
1980–81	302,637	35,130	22,168	13,579	21,434	96,713	57,888	55,725	100.0	11.6	7.3	4.5	7.1	32.0	19.1	18.4
1985–86	295,850	34,834	20,409	14,055	30,216	74,816	66,676	54,844	100.0	11.8	6.9	4.8	10.2	25.3	22.5	18.5
1990–91	342,863	35,984	23,582	13,664	34,774	87,352	78,255	69,252	100.0	10.5	6.9	4.0	10.1	25.5	22.8	20.2
1995–96	412,180	40,795	30,164	16,154	39,422	104,936	93,554	87,155	100.0	9.9	7.3	3.9	9.6	25.5	22.7	21.1
2000–01	473,502	40,625	30,330	15,360	44,098	127,829	115,602	99,658	100.0	8.6	6.4	3.2	9.3	27.0	24.4	21.0
2005–06	599,862	49,590	37,143	19,575	50,581	174,622	146,396	121,955	100.0	8.3	6.2	3.3	8.4	29.1	24.4	20.3
2010–11	730,922	57,160	46,147	23,576	62,695	185,127	187,178	169,039	100.0	7.8	6.3	3.2	8.6	25.3	25.6	23.1
2013–14	754,582	59,834	49,423	28,221	71,857	154,655	189,364	201,228	100.0	7.9	6.5	3.7	9.5	20.5	25.1	26.7
2014–15	758,804	59,181	47,305	29,344	82,916	146,581	185,236	208,241	100.0	7.8	6.2	3.9	10.9	19.3	24.4	27.4
2015–16	785,757	59,067	47,506	31,299	97,843	145,792	186,835	217,415	100.0	7.5	6.0	4.0	12.5	18.6	23.8	27.7
2016–17	804,684	57,839	47,557	32,513	106,799	145,680	187,404	226,892	100.0	7.2	5.9	4.0	13.3	18.1	23.3	28.2
Doctor's degrees[6]																
1970–71	64,998	4,402	5,804	9,126	3,816	6,041	774	35,035	100.0	6.8	8.9	14.0	5.9	9.3	1.2	53.9
1975–76	91,007	5,461	7,314	7,591	3,118	7,202	906	59,415	100.0	6.0	8.0	8.3	3.4	7.9	1.0	65.3
1980–81	98,016	4,827	6,698	7,473	2,860	7,279	808	68,071	100.0	4.9	6.8	7.6	2.9	7.4	0.8	69.4
1985–86	100,280	4,648	6,548	7,668	3,800	6,610	923	70,083	100.0	4.6	6.5	7.6	3.8	6.6	0.9	69.9
1990–91	105,547	4,858	6,944	9,378	6,006	6,189	1,185	70,987	100.0	4.6	6.6	8.9	5.7	5.9	1.1	67.3
1995–96	115,507	6,356	7,901	10,997	7,223	6,246	1,366	75,418	100.0	5.5	6.8	9.5	6.3	5.4	1.2	65.3
2000–01	119,585	6,466	9,021	10,190	6,315	6,284	1,180	80,129	100.0	5.4	7.5	8.5	5.3	5.3	1.0	67.0
2005–06	138,056	6,628	8,835	12,097	8,734	7,584	1,711	92,467	100.0	4.8	6.4	8.8	6.3	5.5	1.2	67.0
2010–11	163,827	8,359	10,241	14,574	10,013	9,642	2,286	108,712	100.0	5.1	6.3	8.9	6.1	5.9	1.4	66.4
2013–14	177,587	8,397	11,358	15,971	12,099	10,929	3,039	115,794	100.0	4.7	6.4	9.0	6.8	6.2	1.7	65.2
2014–15	178,548	8,391	11,411	15,677	12,360	11,772	3,116	115,821	100.0	4.7	6.4	8.8	6.9	6.6	1.7	64.9
2015–16	178,134	8,324	11,246	15,851	12,387	11,838	3,325	115,163	100.0	4.7	6.3	8.9	7.0	6.6	1.9	64.6
2016–17	181,352	8,119	11,408	16,039	12,505	12,687	3,329	117,265	100.0	4.5	6.3	8.8	6.9	7.0	1.8	64.7

[1]Includes degrees in Area, ethnic, cultural, gender, and group studies; English language and literature/letters; Foreign languages, literatures, and linguistics; Liberal arts and sciences, general studies, and humanities; Multi/interdisciplinary studies; Philosophy and religious studies; Theology and religious vocations; and Visual and performing arts.
[2]Includes Psychology; Social sciences; and History.
[3]Includes Biological and biomedical sciences; Mathematics and statistics; and Physical sciences and science technologies.
[4]Includes Computer and information sciences; Engineering; and Engineering technologies.
[5]Includes Agriculture and natural resources; Architecture and related services; Communication, journalism, and related programs; Communications technologies; Family and consumer sciences/human sciences; Health professions and related programs; Homeland security, law enforcement, and firefighting; Legal professions and studies; Library science; Military technologies and applied sciences; Parks, recreation, leisure, and fitness studies; Precision production; Public administration and social services; Transportation and materials moving; and Not classified by field of study.
[6]Includes Ph.D., Ed.D., and comparable degrees at the doctoral level. Includes most degrees that were classified as first-professional prior to 2010–11, such as M.D., D.D.S., and law degrees.

NOTE: Data are for postsecondary institutions participating in Title IV federal financial aid programs. The new Classification of Instructional Programs was initiated in 2009–10. The figures for earlier years have been reclassified when necessary to make them conform to the new taxonomy. To facilitate trend comparisons, certain aggregations have been made of the degree fields as reported in the Integrated Postsecondary Education Data System (IPEDS): "Agriculture and natural resources" includes Agriculture, agriculture operations, and related sciences and Natural resources and conservation; "Business" includes Business, management, marketing, and related support services and Personal and culinary services; and "Engineering technologies" includes Engineering technologies and engineering-related fields, Construction trades, and Mechanic and repair technologies/technicians. Detail may not sum to totals because of rounding. Some data have been revised from previously published figures.
SOURCE: U.S. Department of Education, National Center for Education Statistics, Higher Education General Information Survey (HEGIS), "Degrees and Other Formal Awards Conferred" surveys, 1970–71 through 1985–86; Integrated Postsecondary Education Data System (IPEDS), "Completions Survey" (IPEDS-C:91–96); and IPEDS Fall 2001 through Fall 2017, Completions component. (This table was prepared August 2018.)

Table 318.30. Bachelor's, master's, and doctor's degrees conferred by postsecondary institutions, by sex of student and discipline division: 2016–17

Discipline division	Bachelor's degrees			Master's degrees			Doctor's degrees[1]		
	Total	Males	Females	Total	Males	Females	Total	Males	Females
1	2	3	4	5	6	7	8	9	10
All fields, total	**1,956,032**	**836,045**	**1,119,987**	**804,684**	**326,892**	**477,792**	**181,352**	**84,646**	**96,706**
Agriculture and natural resources	37,719	17,816	19,903	6,844	3,038	3,806	1,561	805	756
Agriculture, agriculture operations, and related sciences	19,664	8,721	10,943	2,949	1,279	1,670	929	514	415
Agriculture, general	2,165	1,132	1,033	311	134	177	29	18	11
Agricultural business and management, general	1,077	689	388	80	44	36	1	0	1
Agribusiness/agricultural business operations	1,917	1,175	742	43	25	18	0	0	0
Agricultural economics	1,573	1,063	510	488	261	227	175	103	72
Farm/farm and ranch management	164	122	42	3	3	0	0	0	0
Agricultural/farm supplies retailing and wholesaling	0	0	0	0	0	0	0	0	0
Agricultural business technology	40	27	13	0	0	0	0	0	0
Agricultural business and management, other	86	53	33	7	4	3	0	0	0
Agricultural mechanization, general	371	347	24	2	0	2	0	0	0
Agricultural mechanics and equipment/machine technology	0	0	0	0	0	0	0	0	0
Agricultural production operations, general	71	50	21	9	1	8	0	0	0
Animal/livestock husbandry and production	185	60	125	4	2	2	0	0	0
Aquaculture	53	29	24	35	21	14	13	9	4
Crop production	66	61	5	0	0	0	0	0	0
Dairy husbandry and production	5	4	1	0	0	0	0	0	0
Horse husbandry/equine science and management	129	10	119	10	0	10	0	0	0
Agroecology and sustainable agriculture	193	86	107	62	18	44	13	9	4
Viticulture and enology	119	66	53	0	0	0	0	0	0
Agricultural and food products processing	90	41	49	0	0	0	0	0	0
Animal training	13	2	11	0	0	0	0	0	0
Equestrian/equine studies	338	15	323	0	0	0	0	0	0
Agricultural and domestic animal services, other	0	0	0	0	0	0	0	0	0
Applied horticulture/horticultural operations, general	92	38	54	11	4	7	3	1	2
Ornamental horticulture	23	14	9	6	3	3	4	2	2
Landscaping and groundskeeping	133	77	56	5	1	4	0	0	0
Plant nursery operations and management	7	3	4	0	0	0	0	0	0
Turf and turfgrass management	100	97	3	7	7	0	0	0	0
Floriculture/floristry operations and management	2	1	1	0	0	0	0	0	0
Applied horticulture/horticultural business services, other	44	31	13	0	0	0	0	0	0
International agriculture	70	21	49	84	26	58	0	0	0
Agricultural and extension education services	65	25	40	71	17	54	9	4	5
Agricultural communication/journalism	446	94	352	14	3	11	0	0	0
Agricultural public services, other	58	26	32	8	0	8	0	0	0
Animal sciences, general	5,595	1,068	4,527	440	141	299	136	74	62
Agricultural animal breeding	0	0	0	5	0	5	2	0	2
Animal health	1	1	0	1	1	0	0	0	0
Animal nutrition	0	0	0	0	0	0	2	2	0
Dairy science	156	40	116	20	6	14	3	2	1
Livestock management	8	4	4	1	0	1	2	2	0
Poultry science	91	33	58	32	18	14	12	7	5
Animal sciences, other	60	8	52	3	1	2	0	0	0
Food science	1,415	406	1,009	441	146	295	162	74	88
Food technology and processing	20	7	13	19	7	12	8	6	2
Food science and technology, other	61	32	29	21	11	10	0	0	0
Plant sciences, general	447	281	166	97	52	45	46	26	20
Agronomy and crop science	694	489	205	225	117	108	138	88	50
Horticultural science	550	287	263	98	49	49	44	20	24
Agricultural and horticultural plant breeding	8	1	7	21	11	10	19	11	8
Plant protection and integrated pest management	92	69	23	39	27	12	3	2	1
Range science and management	119	79	40	34	17	17	7	2	5
Plant sciences, other	25	12	13	50	24	26	34	17	17
Soil science and agronomy, general	216	148	68	102	58	44	48	27	21
Soil chemistry and physics	30	24	6	2	0	2	0	0	0
Soil sciences, other	44	30	14	7	6	1	4	3	1
Agriculture, agriculture operations, and related sciences, other	337	243	94	31	13	18	12	5	7
Natural resources and conservation	18,055	9,095	8,960	3,895	1,759	2,136	632	291	341
Natural resources/conservation, general	1,328	734	594	652	285	367	118	60	58
Environmental studies	5,940	2,665	3,275	861	350	511	103	36	67
Environmental science	6,201	3,015	3,186	927	404	523	181	69	112
Natural resources conservation and research, other	63	37	26	66	30	36	17	8	9
Natural resources management and policy	715	413	302	504	226	278	28	13	15
Natural resource economics	89	53	36	9	2	7	5	5	0
Water, wetlands, and marine resources management	94	53	41	157	63	94	4	2	2
Land use planning and management/development	56	46	10	42	24	18	1	1	0
Natural resource recreation and tourism	44	24	20	42	19	23	2	1	1
Natural resources law enforcement and protective services	25	20	5	0	0	0	0	0	0
Natural resources management and policy, other	247	129	118	41	13	28	0	0	0
Fishing and fisheries sciences and management	403	225	178	72	33	39	11	4	7
Forestry, general	527	388	139	148	75	73	28	16	12
Forest sciences and biology	255	202	53	127	81	46	41	27	14
Forest management/forest resources management	140	115	25	60	39	21	5	1	4
Urban forestry	18	5	13	3	1	2	5	2	3
Wood science and wood products/pulp and paper technology	87	68	19	11	8	3	7	4	3
Forest resources production and management	9	7	2	19	12	7	9	4	5
Forest technology/technician	1	1	0	0	0	0	0	0	0
Forestry, other	48	34	14	12	9	3	6	3	3
Wildlife, fish, and wildlands science and management	1,628	796	832	136	84	52	60	34	26
Natural resources and conservation, other	137	65	72	6	1	5	1	1	0

See notes at end of table.

Table 318.30. Bachelor's, master's, and doctor's degrees conferred by postsecondary institutions, by sex of student and discipline division: 2016–17—Continued

Discipline division	Bachelor's degrees			Master's degrees			Doctor's degrees[1]		
	Total	Males	Females	Total	Males	Females	Total	Males	Females
1	2	3	4	5	6	7	8	9	10
Architecture and related services	8,573	4,585	3,988	7,911	4,014	3,897	291	146	145
Architecture	5,051	2,721	2,330	3,231	1,829	1,402	120	65	55
City/urban, community and regional planning	860	521	339	2,020	937	1,083	130	65	65
Environmental design/architecture	536	303	233	102	30	72	27	10	17
Interior architecture	405	47	358	219	40	179	0	0	0
Landscape architecture	673	380	293	743	268	475	2	1	1
Architectural history and criticism, general	68	26	42	32	16	16	0	0	0
Architectural technology/technician	155	109	46	4	0	4	0	0	0
Architectural and building sciences/technology	670	399	271	1,259	698	561	12	5	7
Real estate development	10	9	1	261	178	83	0	0	0
Architecture and related services, other	145	70	75	40	18	22	0	0	0
Area, ethnic, cultural, gender, and group studies	7,720	2,114	5,606	1,717	594	1,123	349	120	229
African studies	72	14	58	32	10	22	4	1	3
American/United States studies/civilization	1,028	353	675	208	82	126	106	38	68
Asian studies/civilization	668	263	405	91	42	49	3	2	1
East Asian studies	308	120	188	192	85	107	24	9	15
Russian, Central European, East European and Eurasian studies	20	7	13	48	22	26	0	0	0
European studies/civilization	75	20	55	19	12	7	0	0	0
Latin American studies	294	116	178	176	52	124	3	1	2
Near and Middle Eastern studies	173	63	110	158	75	83	30	15	15
Pacific Area/Pacific Rim studies	21	10	11	6	3	3	0	0	0
Russian studies	56	25	31	33	15	18	0	0	0
Scandinavian studies	24	11	13	2	0	2	1	1	0
South Asian studies	11	6	5	15	5	10	3	2	1
Southeast Asian studies	0	0	0	12	4	8	0	0	0
Western European studies	4	2	2	32	11	21	0	0	0
Canadian studies	1	0	1	0	0	0	0	0	0
Slavic studies	1	1	0	3	0	3	1	1	0
Ural-Altaic and Central Asian studies	2	2	0	10	5	5	3	3	0
Regional studies (U.S., Canadian, foreign)	17	0	17	30	7	23	5	1	4
Chinese studies	47	22	25	15	3	12	0	0	0
French studies	45	11	34	17	6	11	4	1	3
German studies	40	14	26	4	4	0	8	4	4
Italian studies	35	5	30	17	5	12	3	1	2
Japanese studies	39	19	20	5	3	2	0	0	0
Korean studies	0	0	0	5	3	2	0	0	0
Spanish and Iberian studies	13	5	8	0	0	0	0	0	0
Irish studies	0	0	0	14	5	9	0	0	0
Latin American and Caribbean studies	50	17	33	18	5	13	0	0	0
Area studies, other	679	194	485	37	15	22	11	5	6
Ethnic studies	130	28	102	14	4	10	3	0	3
African-American/Black studies	671	215	456	66	26	40	32	7	25
American Indian/Native American studies	231	89	142	69	24	45	8	1	7
Hispanic-American, Puerto Rican, and Mexican-American/Chicano studies	406	106	300	32	8	24	19	10	9
Asian-American studies	99	52	47	13	6	7	0	0	0
Women's studies	1,402	107	1,295	155	9	146	28	4	24
Gay/lesbian studies	17	4	13	0	0	0	0	0	0
Folklore studies	16	6	10	30	5	25	11	6	5
Disability studies	31	4	27	30	7	23	8	1	7
Deaf studies	217	39	178	6	3	3	0	0	0
Ethnic, cultural minority, gender, and group studies, other	777	164	613	103	23	80	31	6	25
Biological and biomedical sciences	116,759	45,515	71,244	16,284	6,840	9,444	8,087	3,852	4,235
Biology/biological sciences, general	74,048	27,591	46,457	3,439	1,345	2,094	1,020	484	536
Biomedical sciences, general	4,072	1,596	2,476	2,226	1,049	1,177	535	236	299
Biochemistry	8,745	4,274	4,471	295	147	148	484	269	215
Biophysics	141	97	44	32	19	13	115	77	38
Molecular biology	861	400	461	197	71	126	208	107	101
Molecular biochemistry	354	172	182	99	45	54	54	35	19
Molecular biophysics	0	0	0	1	0	1	19	12	7
Structural biology	0	0	0	1	1	0	3	3	0
Radiation biology/radiobiology	9	1	8	9	5	4	5	4	1
Biochemistry and molecular biology	942	469	473	115	44	71	178	108	70
Biochemistry, biophysics and molecular biology, other	232	121	111	10	4	6	31	12	19
Botany/plant biology	243	121	122	81	36	45	104	53	51
Plant pathology/phytopathology	28	12	16	77	33	44	92	51	41
Plant physiology	0	0	0	5	2	3	13	8	5
Plant molecular biology	0	0	0	0	0	0	12	7	5
Botany/plant biology, other	26	12	14	14	7	7	5	1	4
Cell/cellular biology and histology	372	177	195	38	20	18	124	53	71
Anatomy	472	187	285	211	115	96	37	17	20
Developmental biology and embryology	51	20	31	1	0	1	30	17	13
Cell/cellular and molecular biology	2,550	1,117	1,433	207	92	115	427	203	224
Cell biology and anatomy	7	4	3	36	18	18	42	19	23
Cell/cellular biology and anatomical sciences, other	125	52	73	150	67	83	106	38	68
Microbiology, general	2,049	885	1,164	175	71	104	220	105	115
Medical microbiology and bacteriology	434	171	263	158	55	103	117	61	56
Virology	0	0	0	2	0	2	17	9	8
Parasitology	0	0	0	0	0	0	1	0	1
Immunology	0	0	0	56	22	34	148	70	78
Microbiology and immunology	115	55	60	68	31	37	75	28	47
Microbiological sciences and immunology, other	146	66	80	32	11	21	71	28	43
Zoology/animal biology	1,511	433	1,078	119	36	83	84	34	50
Entomology	105	56	49	150	68	82	119	60	59
Animal physiology	116	42	74	86	35	51	17	5	12
Animal behavior and ethology	140	18	122	24	3	21	5	1	4

See notes at end of table.

Table 318.30. Bachelor's, master's, and doctor's degrees conferred by postsecondary institutions, by sex of student and discipline division: 2016–17—Continued

Discipline division	Bachelor's degrees			Master's degrees			Doctor's degrees[1]		
	Total	Males	Females	Total	Males	Females	Total	Males	Females
1	2	3	4	5	6	7	8	9	10
Wildlife biology	443	185	258	8	4	4	3	2	1
Zoology/animal biology, other	0	0	0	11	4	7	5	3	2
Genetics, general	333	123	210	89	38	51	147	69	78
Molecular genetics	187	64	123	18	7	11	87	39	48
Animal genetics	46	13	33	2	0	2	29	9	20
Plant genetics	9	4	5	5	3	2	14	8	6
Human/medical genetics	0	0	0	157	26	131	90	38	52
Genome sciences/genomics	7	3	4	10	4	6	29	12	17
Genetics, other	0	0	0	4	3	1	11	5	6
Physiology, general	1,562	641	921	731	396	335	147	86	61
Molecular physiology	0	0	0	2	0	2	32	19	13
Cell physiology	0	0	0	39	20	19	25	13	12
Endocrinology	0	0	0	2	1	1	10	4	6
Reproductive biology	2	0	2	3	1	2	2	1	1
Cardiovascular science	0	0	0	7	4	3	8	4	4
Exercise physiology	3,523	1,551	1,972	407	172	235	69	34	35
Vision science/physiological optics	87	20	67	46	17	29	12	5	7
Pathology/experimental pathology	16	3	13	85	34	51	161	68	93
Oncology and cancer biology	0	0	0	30	14	16	115	44	71
Physiology, pathology, and related sciences, other	29	5	24	15	6	9	16	8	8
Pharmacology	73	40	33	181	84	97	214	89	125
Molecular pharmacology	0	0	0	7	3	4	47	19	28
Neuropharmacology	0	0	0	34	14	20	0	0	0
Toxicology	62	19	43	51	19	32	94	41	53
Molecular toxicology	0	0	0	0	0	0	5	2	3
Environmental toxicology	25	6	19	79	35	44	24	14	10
Pharmacology and toxicology	72	37	35	100	39	61	40	23	17
Pharmacology and toxicology, other	18	11	7	13	4	9	7	2	5
Biometry/biometrics	38	20	18	39	17	22	15	7	8
Biostatistics	32	9	23	661	267	394	201	96	105
Bioinformatics	253	131	122	336	178	158	115	69	46
Computational biology	37	16	21	27	16	11	55	33	22
Biomathematics, bioinformatics, and computational biology, other	26	14	12	78	46	32	21	14	7
Biotechnology	765	388	377	1,331	566	765	6	5	1
Ecology	727	283	444	145	75	70	192	94	98
Marine biology and biological oceanography	1,348	411	937	215	68	147	81	34	47
Evolutionary biology	125	42	83	19	8	11	23	11	12
Aquatic biology/limnology	74	31	43	13	6	7	0	0	0
Environmental biology	301	121	180	30	11	19	8	6	2
Population biology	0	0	0	5	2	3	3	2	1
Conservation biology	161	56	105	104	34	70	14	4	10
Systematic biology/biological systematics	0	0	0	1	1	0	10	7	3
Epidemiology	36	11	25	1,284	349	935	288	82	206
Ecology and evolutionary biology	429	164	265	63	26	37	91	45	46
Ecology, evolution, systematics and population biology, other	178	74	104	23	8	15	53	26	27
Molecular medicine	0	0	0	22	9	13	42	17	25
Neuroscience	5,768	2,146	3,622	170	61	109	643	306	337
Neuroanatomy	0	0	0	0	0	0	0	0	0
Neurobiology and anatomy	835	333	502	18	10	8	54	28	26
Neurobiology and behavior	109	32	77	36	12	24	15	8	7
Neurobiology and neurosciences, other	14	5	9	1	0	1	6	3	3
Biological and biomedical sciences, other	1,115	354	761	1,413	666	747	190	79	111
Business, management, marketing, and personal and culinary services	381,353	201,886	179,467	187,404	98,768	88,636	3,329	1,854	1,475
Business, management, marketing, and related support services	380,199	201,444	178,755	187,377	98,765	88,612	3,329	1,854	1,475
Business/commerce, general	25,097	13,444	11,653	8,581	5,205	3,376	231	136	95
Business administration and management, general	138,217	73,593	64,624	104,455	57,862	46,593	1,942	1,131	811
Purchasing, procurement/acquisitions and contracts management	687	384	303	392	220	172	10	6	4
Logistics, materials, and supply chain management	5,128	3,472	1,656	857	578	279	1	1	0
Office management and supervision	391	175	216	52	27	25	0	0	0
Operations management and supervision	3,104	2,026	1,078	605	382	223	8	6	2
Nonprofit/public/organizational management	409	148	261	1,770	576	1,194	6	0	6
Customer service management	56	17	39	9	7	2	0	0	0
E-commerce/electronic commerce	156	83	73	62	28	34	0	0	0
Transportation/mobility management	172	130	42	149	103	46	3	1	2
Research and development management	9	8	1	188	73	115	1	1	0
Project management	509	332	177	925	542	383	12	8	4
Retail management	307	44	263	68	4	64	0	0	0
Organizational leadership	3,927	1,913	2,014	5,120	2,186	2,934	303	148	155
Business administration, management and operations, other	9,120	4,293	4,827	5,680	2,846	2,834	60	34	26
Accounting	50,688	24,778	25,910	19,468	8,731	10,737	42	19	23
Accounting technology/technician and bookkeeping	208	131	77	0	0	0	0	0	0
Auditing	36	8	28	78	25	53	0	0	0
Accounting and finance	719	421	298	948	382	566	0	0	0
Accounting and business/management	1,086	396	690	435	209	226	0	0	0
Accounting and related services, other	165	82	83	179	96	83	1	1	0
Administrative assistant and secretarial science, general	72	24	48	0	0	0	0	0	0
Executive assistant/executive secretary	0	0	0	0	0	0	0	0	0
Business/office automation/technology/data entry	64	37	27	0	0	0	0	0	0
General office occupations and clerical services	0	0	0	0	0	0	0	0	0
Parts, warehousing, and inventory management operations	0	0	0	0	0	0	0	0	0
Traffic, customs, and transportation clerk/technician	17	11	6	0	0	0	0	0	0
Business operations support and secretarial services, other	0	0	0	15	8	7	0	0	0
Business/corporate communications	963	322	641	85	24	61	0	0	0
Business/managerial economics	5,503	3,565	1,938	297	172	125	63	41	22
Entrepreneurship/entrepreneurial studies	2,445	1,595	850	692	420	272	6	4	2
Franchising and franchise operations	2	1	1	0	0	0	0	0	0

See notes at end of table.

Table 318.30. Bachelor's, master's, and doctor's degrees conferred by postsecondary institutions, by sex of student and discipline division: 2016–17—Continued

Discipline division	Bachelor's degrees			Master's degrees			Doctor's degrees[1]		
	Total	Males	Females	Total	Males	Females	Total	Males	Females
1	2	3	4	5	6	7	8	9	10
Small business administration/management	96	60	36	27	16	11	0	0	0
Entrepreneurial and small business operations, other	131	70	61	94	40	54	2	2	0
Finance, general	37,437	26,602	10,835	6,247	3,818	2,429	43	33	10
Banking and financial support services	480	301	179	62	38	24	0	0	0
Financial planning and services	407	288	119	255	164	91	9	6	3
International finance	4	1	3	35	21	14	0	0	0
Investments and securities	111	92	19	150	101	49	0	0	0
Public finance	22	17	5	15	11	4	0	0	0
Finance and financial management services, other	176	125	51	135	86	49	0	0	0
Hospitality administration/management, general	7,811	2,330	5,481	471	153	318	43	17	26
Tourism and travel services management	653	171	482	102	35	67	0	0	0
Hotel/motel administration/management	1,692	599	1,093	99	37	62	9	3	6
Restaurant/food services management	806	312	494	0	0	0	0	0	0
Resort management	293	101	192	0	0	0	0	0	0
Meeting and event planning	543	63	480	2	0	2	0	0	0
Casino management	2	1	1	0	0	0	0	0	0
Hotel, motel, and restaurant management	58	18	40	0	0	0	0	0	0
Hospitality administration/management, other	428	157	271	69	29	40	5	1	4
Human resources management/personnel administration, general	6,951	1,958	4,993	4,471	1,086	3,385	44	13	31
Labor and industrial relations	875	422	453	680	212	468	13	7	6
Organizational behavior studies	2,416	1,052	1,364	1,556	527	1,029	223	88	135
Labor studies	39	17	22	20	9	11	0	0	0
Human resources development	673	134	539	1,029	231	798	27	12	15
Human resources management and services, other	338	82	256	1,102	374	728	0	0	0
International business/trade/commerce	5,543	2,763	2,780	1,877	1,005	872	34	26	8
Management information systems, general	7,838	5,628	2,210	2,140	1,482	658	34	21	13
Information resources management	253	179	74	1,285	956	329	25	15	10
Knowledge management	86	53	33	231	131	100	0	0	0
Management information systems and services, other	150	92	58	216	157	59	0	0	0
Management science, general	3,431	2,037	1,394	3,487	2,033	1,454	41	28	13
Business statistics	306	202	104	720	406	314	0	0	0
Actuarial science	1,387	823	564	471	273	198	0	0	0
Management sciences and quantitative methods, other	520	312	208	1,669	968	701	14	7	7
Marketing/marketing management, general	35,010	16,005	19,005	2,162	826	1,336	27	17	10
Marketing research	37	8	29	174	72	102	2	0	2
International marketing	204	48	156	367	134	233	1	1	0
Marketing, other	923	441	482	216	51	165	8	4	4
Real estate	811	591	220	967	694	273	1	1	0
Taxation	2	0	2	1,547	782	765	0	0	0
Insurance	1,070	707	363	114	64	50	3	1	2
Sales, distribution, and marketing operations, general	1,326	733	593	435	125	310	1	0	1
Merchandising and buying operations	2	1	1	10	1	9	0	0	0
Retailing and retail operations	339	71	268	4	2	2	0	0	0
Selling skills and sales operations	344	225	119	0	0	0	0	0	0
General merchandising/sales/related marketing operations, other	93	29	64	2	2	0	0	0	0
Fashion merchandising	2,954	189	2,765	41	2	39	0	0	0
Apparel and accessories marketing operations	38	2	36	37	5	32	0	0	0
Tourism and travel services marketing operations	35	17	18	0	0	0	0	0	0
Tourism promotion operations	0	0	0	0	0	0	0	0	0
Vehicle and vehicle parts and accessories marketing operations	56	47	9	0	0	0	0	0	0
Business and personal/financial services marketing operations	0	0	0	0	0	0	0	0	0
Special products marketing operations	172	63	109	9	1	8	0	0	0
Hospitality and recreation marketing operations	97	81	16	0	0	0	0	0	0
Specialized merchandising/sales/related marketing operations, other	105	31	74	40	10	30	0	0	0
Construction management	1,925	1,761	164	330	249	81	4	4	0
Telecommunications management	0	0	0	7	5	2	0	0	0
Business/management/marketing/related support services, other	3,443	1,899	1,544	1,088	635	453	27	10	17
Personal and culinary services	1,154	442	712	27	3	24	0	0	0
Funeral service and mortuary science, general	147	43	104	0	0	0	0	0	0
Funeral direction/service	35	11	24	0	0	0	0	0	0
Cosmetology/cosmetologist, general	0	0	0	0	0	0	0	0	0
Cooking and related culinary arts, general	0	0	0	0	0	0	0	0	0
Baking and pastry arts/baker/pastry chef	95	10	85	0	0	0	0	0	0
Culinary arts/chef training	332	138	194	0	0	0	0	0	0
Restaurant, culinary, and catering management/manager	437	198	239	0	0	0	0	0	0
Food service, waiter/waitress, and dining room management	0	0	0	0	0	0	0	0	0
Culinary science/culinology	61	28	33	0	0	0	0	0	0
Culinary arts and related services, other	47	14	33	27	3	24	0	0	0
Personal and culinary services, other	0	0	0	0	0	0	0	0	0
Communication and communications technologies	98,393	35,357	63,036	10,667	3,220	7,447	615	208	407
Communication, journalism, and related programs	93,778	32,478	61,300	10,128	2,943	7,185	615	208	407
Communication, general	9,513	3,146	6,367	970	265	705	71	14	57
Speech communication and rhetoric	34,017	11,654	22,363	1,870	565	1,305	251	83	168
Mass communication/media studies	9,623	3,607	6,016	928	293	635	133	47	86
Communication and media studies, other	1,553	577	976	576	175	401	60	18	42
Journalism	11,481	3,665	7,816	1,314	421	893	25	14	11
Broadcast journalism	974	427	547	22	9	13	0	0	0
Photojournalism	104	28	76	28	12	16	0	0	0
Journalism, other	700	240	460	474	119	355	0	0	0
Radio and television	4,783	2,473	2,310	137	54	83	14	6	8
Digital communication and media/multimedia	3,883	1,708	2,175	836	318	518	29	15	14
Radio, television, and digital communication, other	961	517	444	13	5	8	0	0	0
Public relations, advertising, and applied communication	2,000	509	1,491	285	71	214	0	0	0
Organizational communication, general	1,408	427	981	281	65	216	3	1	2
Public relations/image management	4,811	921	3,890	692	161	531	0	0	0

See notes at end of table.

Table 318.30. Bachelor's, master's, and doctor's degrees conferred by postsecondary institutions, by sex of student and discipline division: 2016–17—Continued

Discipline division	Bachelor's degrees			Master's degrees			Doctor's degrees[1]		
	Total	Males	Females	Total	Males	Females	Total	Males	Females
1	2	3	4	5	6	7	8	9	10
Advertising	4,343	1,460	2,883	214	51	163	7	1	6
Political communication	70	27	43	34	13	21	0	0	0
Health communication	103	19	84	188	36	152	6	2	4
Sports communication	208	145	63	53	38	15	0	0	0
International and intercultural communication	144	30	114	118	29	89	0	0	0
Technical and scientific communication	38	13	25	20	8	12	3	2	1
Public relations, advertising and applied communication, other	1,595	360	1,235	229	61	168	0	0	0
Publishing	8	1	7	191	21	170	0	0	0
Communication, journalism, and related programs, other	1,458	524	934	655	153	502	13	5	8
Communications technologies/technicians and support services	4,615	2,879	1,736	539	277	262	0	0	0
Communications technology/technician	190	152	38	40	17	23	0	0	0
Photographic and film/video technology/technician and assistant	67	42	25	0	0	0	0	0	0
Radio and television broadcasting technology/technician	345	182	163	109	43	66	0	0	0
Recording arts technology/technician	972	848	124	42	31	11	0	0	0
Audiovisual communications technologies/technicians, other	56	49	7	0	0	0	0	0	0
Graphic communications, general	319	128	191	34	10	24	0	0	0
Printing management	110	45	65	0	0	0	0	0	0
Prepress/desktop publishing and digital imaging design	65	27	38	0	0	0	0	0	0
Animation/interactive technology/video graphics/special effects	2,244	1,282	962	306	172	134	0	0	0
Graphic and printing equipment operator, general production	26	13	13	0	0	0	0	0	0
Printing press operator	7	3	4	0	0	0	0	0	0
Graphic communications, other	108	49	59	2	1	1	0	0	0
Communications technologies/technicians and support services, other	106	59	47	6	3	3	0	0	0
Computer and information sciences and support services	71,420	57,766	13,654	46,555	32,173	14,382	1,982	1,538	444
Computer and information sciences, general	18,035	14,896	3,139	11,534	8,442	3,092	603	497	106
Artificial intelligence	11	10	1	183	134	49	17	10	7
Information technology	9,000	7,352	1,648	5,446	3,417	2,029	79	53	26
Informatics	1,078	781	297	394	226	168	25	19	6
Computer and information sciences, other	492	388	104	210	151	59	22	12	10
Computer programming/programmer, general	1,070	929	141	57	41	16	6	3	3
Computer programming, specific applications	441	378	63	18	16	2	0	0	0
Computer programming, vendor/product certification	18	17	1	0	0	0	0	0	0
Computer programming, other	4	4	0	14	6	8	0	0	0
Data processing and data processing technology/technician	107	90	17	1	1	0	0	0	0
Information science/studies	7,244	5,442	1,802	6,863	4,288	2,575	172	86	86
Computer systems analysis/analyst	1,146	912	234	839	570	269	4	3	1
Computer science	22,289	18,484	3,805	14,599	10,474	4,125	981	802	179
Web page, digital/multimedia and information resources design	1,556	854	702	436	175	261	0	0	0
Data modeling/warehousing and database administration	140	101	39	455	290	165	0	0	0
Computer graphics	882	488	394	227	95	132	0	0	0
Modeling, virtual environments and simulation	387	330	57	94	76	18	1	1	0
Computer software and media applications, other	251	161	90	187	123	64	0	0	0
Computer systems networking and telecommunications	1,471	1,315	156	832	607	225	2	2	0
Network and system administration/administrator	429	392	37	68	36	32	0	0	0
System, networking, and LAN/WAN management/manager	164	149	15	32	25	7	0	0	0
Computer and information systems security/information assurance	3,694	3,131	563	2,764	2,163	601	49	37	12
Web/multimedia management and webmaster	171	110	61	10	3	7	0	0	0
Information technology project management	459	371	88	409	245	164	7	5	2
Computer support specialist	8	7	1	0	0	0	0	0	0
Computer/information tech services admin and management, other	612	466	146	604	394	210	0	0	0
Computer and information sciences and support services, other	261	208	53	279	175	104	14	8	6
Education	85,118	16,067	69,051	145,680	33,177	112,503	12,687	4,013	8,674
Education, general	3,698	680	3,018	20,877	4,630	16,247	2,660	727	1,933
Bilingual and multilingual education	150	7	143	347	54	293	10	1	9
Multicultural education	1	0	1	118	20	98	14	3	11
Indian/Native American education	0	0	0	0	0	0	0	0	0
Bilingual, multilingual, and multicultural education, other	0	0	0	91	14	77	4	1	3
Curriculum and instruction	213	46	167	15,179	2,793	12,386	1,422	356	1,066
Educational leadership and administration, general	215	7	208	17,929	6,070	11,859	4,387	1,580	2,807
Administration of special education	0	0	0	76	7	69	58	10	48
Adult and continuing education administration	0	0	0	565	166	399	27	11	16
Educational, instructional, and curriculum supervision	42	11	31	1,114	300	814	128	28	100
Higher education/higher education administration	2	2	0	3,082	871	2,211	555	195	360
Community college education	0	0	0	72	19	53	178	52	126
Elementary and middle school administration/principalship	136	12	124	624	259	365	17	7	10
Secondary school administration/principalship	0	0	0	298	116	182	3	0	3
Urban education and leadership	92	26	66	381	104	277	112	41	71
Superintendency and educational system administration	0	0	0	274	99	175	110	31	79
Educational administration and supervision, other	0	0	0	1,213	352	861	323	126	197
Educational/instructional technology	55	24	31	4,179	1,201	2,978	211	92	119
Educational evaluation and research	0	0	0	89	22	67	135	49	86
Educational statistics and research methods	0	0	0	162	47	115	40	15	25
Educational assessment, testing, and measurement	0	0	0	60	8	52	10	3	7
Learning sciences	306	48	258	108	20	88	11	3	8
Educational assessment, evaluation, and research, other	15	4	11	127	36	91	36	8	28
International and comparative education	38	5	33	287	40	247	11	3	8
Social and philosophical foundations of education	8	5	3	335	83	252	123	38	85
Special education and teaching, general	6,361	672	5,689	11,428	1,884	9,544	201	47	154
Education/teaching of individuals with hearing impairments/deafness	102	3	99	131	8	123	6	2	4
Education/teaching of the gifted and talented	0	0	0	340	35	305	1	0	1
Education/teaching of individuals with emotional disturbances	28	5	23	117	29	88	10	1	9
Education/teaching of individuals with mental retardation	129	12	117	66	13	53	1	0	1
Education/teaching of individuals with multiple disabilities	132	9	123	309	46	263	0	0	0
Education/teaching of individuals with orthopedic/physical health impairments	3	1	2	3	0	3	2	0	2

See notes at end of table.

Table 318.30. Bachelor's, master's, and doctor's degrees conferred by postsecondary institutions, by sex of student and discipline division: 2016–17—Continued

Discipline division	Bachelor's degrees			Master's degrees			Doctor's degrees[1]		
	Total	Males	Females	Total	Males	Females	Total	Males	Females
1	2	3	4	5	6	7	8	9	10
Education/teaching of individuals with vision impairments/blindness	18	1	17	96	18	78	0	0	0
Education/teaching of individuals with specific learning disabilities	210	21	189	308	29	279	0	0	0
Education/teaching of individuals with speech/language impairments	148	6	142	261	5	256	0	0	0
Education/teaching of individuals with autism	0	0	0	836	65	771	0	0	0
Education/teaching of individuals who are developmentally delayed	26	1	25	181	36	145	0	0	0
Education/teaching of individuals in early childhood special educ. programs	588	32	556	971	39	932	0	0	0
Education/teaching of individuals in elementary special educ. programs	432	33	399	1,123	159	964	0	0	0
Education/teaching of individuals in jr. high/middle school special educ. programs	41	6	35	32	7	25	0	0	0
Education/teaching of individuals in secondary special educ. programs	29	10	19	477	154	323	0	0	0
Special education and teaching, other	336	37	299	651	107	544	13	3	10
Counselor education/school counseling and guidance services	0	0	0	11,267	1,939	9,328	353	115	238
College student counseling and personnel services	0	0	0	1,079	263	816	33	9	24
Student counseling and personnel services, other	0	0	0	238	40	198	3	0	3
Adult and continuing education and teaching	53	20	33	1,098	322	776	125	40	85
Elementary education and teaching	28,112	2,350	25,762	7,539	964	6,575	26	1	25
Junior high/intermediate/middle school education and teaching	2,370	581	1,789	683	196	487	1	0	1
Secondary education and teaching	2,979	1,148	1,831	5,325	2,056	3,269	24	3	21
Teacher education, multiple levels	1,467	198	1,269	3,657	934	2,723	15	5	10
Montessori teacher education	12	0	12	158	11	147	0	0	0
Waldorf/Steiner teacher education	0	0	0	0	0	0	0	0	0
Kindergarten/preschool education and teaching	872	43	829	239	14	225	12	1	11
Early childhood education and teaching	12,725	452	12,273	2,957	107	2,850	11	0	11
Teacher education and prof. dev., specific levels and methods, other	148	26	122	3,556	745	2,811	90	26	64
Agricultural teacher education	605	207	398	259	84	175	23	4	19
Art teacher education	866	100	766	633	90	543	27	5	22
Business teacher education	138	63	75	80	26	54	0	0	0
Driver and safety teacher education	0	0	0	11	7	4	0	0	0
English/language arts teacher education	1,818	338	1,480	808	187	621	8	0	8
Foreign language teacher education	68	14	54	183	37	146	14	1	13
Health teacher education	1,240	373	867	465	134	331	46	11	35
Family and consumer sciences/home economics teacher education	230	6	224	74	2	72	1	1	0
Technology teacher education/industrial arts teacher education	246	192	54	424	201	223	1	0	1
Sales and marketing operations/marketing and dist. teacher educ.	11	10	1	0	0	0	0	0	0
Mathematics teacher education	1,448	486	962	1,444	436	1,008	59	31	28
Music teacher education	3,130	1,345	1,785	1,079	468	611	78	37	41
Physical education teaching and coaching	7,043	3,928	3,115	1,663	1,007	656	33	20	13
Reading teacher education	61	2	59	5,599	314	5,285	121	15	106
Science teacher education/general science teacher education	422	162	260	733	264	469	50	21	29
Social science teacher education	451	251	200	88	47	41	0	0	0
Social studies teacher education	1,007	583	424	426	235	191	5	4	1
Technical teacher education	165	81	84	190	82	108	67	22	45
Trade and industrial teacher education	548	325	223	222	86	136	20	10	10
Computer teacher education	72	4	68	154	35	119	1	1	0
Biology teacher education	310	115	195	284	79	205	1	1	0
Chemistry teacher education	86	31	55	65	25	40	1	0	1
Drama and dance teacher education	102	22	80	86	13	73	0	0	0
French language teacher education	33	2	31	19	5	14	0	0	0
German language teacher education	7	3	4	0	0	0	0	0	0
Health occupations teacher education	7	0	7	142	13	129	57	3	54
History teacher education	451	281	170	108	54	54	0	0	0
Physics teacher education	44	26	18	58	46	12	0	0	0
Spanish language teacher education	237	48	189	117	24	93	0	0	0
Speech teacher education	19	4	15	29	4	25	11	2	9
Geography teacher education	2	1	1	1	0	1	0	0	0
Latin teacher education	2	2	0	2	1	1	0	0	0
School librarian/library media specialist	0	0	0	228	25	203	0	0	0
Psychology teacher education	7	2	5	0	0	0	0	0	0
Earth science teacher education	21	11	10	54	20	34	0	0	0
Environmental education	1	1	0	55	14	41	1	0	1
Teacher education and prof. dev., specific subject areas, other	186	67	119	1,336	287	1,049	33	11	22
Teaching English as a second/foreign language/ESL language instructor	289	63	226	3,433	659	2,774	36	15	21
Teaching French as a second or foreign language	0	0	0	0	0	0	0	0	0
Teaching English or French as a second or foreign language, other	13	2	11	5	0	5	0	0	0
Teacher assistant/aide	3	1	2	0	0	0	0	0	0
Adult literacy tutor/instructor	0	0	0	7	1	6	1	0	1
Education, other	1,437	371	1,066	2,403	609	1,794	480	165	315
Engineering and engineering technologies	133,761	106,539	27,222	60,244	45,220	15,024	10,523	8,027	2,496
Engineering	115,640	90,736	24,904	52,841	39,759	13,082	10,371	7,923	2,448
Engineering, general	2,550	1,976	574	2,822	2,190	632	445	360	85
Pre-engineering	35	23	12	0	0	0	0	0	0
Aerospace, aeronautical and astronautical engineering	4,021	3,466	555	1,580	1,336	244	342	304	38
Agricultural engineering	1,063	673	390	316	172	144	137	89	48
Architectural engineering	672	457	215	184	113	71	16	10	6
Bioengineering and biomedical engineering	6,926	3,865	3,061	2,560	1,459	1,101	1,013	607	406
Ceramic sciences and engineering	82	52	30	7	6	1	11	9	2
Chemical engineering	10,759	7,223	3,536	1,771	1,151	620	967	676	291
Chemical and biomolecular engineering	156	85	71	20	11	9	22	16	6
Chemical engineering, other	0	0	0	6	4	2	0	0	0
Civil engineering, general	13,337	10,074	3,263	5,280	3,822	1,458	1,030	728	302
Geotechnicaland geoenvironmental engineering	0	0	0	1	0	1	0	0	0
Structural engineering	233	167	66	231	173	58	22	15	7
Transportation and highway engineering	4	4	0	101	69	32	12	8	4
Water resources engineering	8	5	3	54	31	23	7	4	3
Civil engineering, other	11	9	2	15	9	6	6	6	0
Computer engineering, general	7,290	6,472	818	3,095	2,320	775	356	293	63
Computer hardware engineering	24	18	6	66	56	10	0	0	0

See notes at end of table.

Table 318.30. Bachelor's, master's, and doctor's degrees conferred by postsecondary institutions, by sex of student and discipline division: 2016–17—Continued

Discipline division	Bachelor's degrees			Master's degrees			Doctor's degrees[1]		
	Total	Males	Females	Total	Males	Females	Total	Males	Females
1	2	3	4	5	6	7	8	9	10
Computer software engineering	1,060	930	130	1,847	1,225	622	13	11	2
Computer engineering, other	14	11	3	120	90	30	5	5	0
Electrical and electronics engineering	16,766	14,497	2,269	12,303	9,501	2,802	2,254	1,869	385
Laser and optical engineering	41	29	12	21	20	1	14	12	2
Telecommunications engineering	2	2	0	247	169	78	7	7	0
Electrical, electronics and communications engineering, other	107	92	15	228	181	47	15	13	2
Engineering mechanics	155	134	21	81	71	10	49	43	6
Engineering physics/applied physics	601	509	92	114	85	29	67	57	10
Engineering science	511	351	160	326	257	69	116	102	14
Environmental/environmental health engineering	1,517	748	769	790	426	364	151	80	71
Materials engineering	1,520	1,057	463	1,108	764	344	694	515	179
Mechanical engineering	32,306	27,681	4,625	8,281	7,081	1,200	1,450	1,217	233
Metallurgical engineering	176	134	42	32	18	14	21	16	5
Mining and mineral engineering	288	242	46	77	66	11	14	11	3
Naval architecture and marine engineering	439	380	59	40	28	12	10	10	0
Nuclear engineering	572	475	97	265	216	49	163	143	20
Ocean engineering	206	152	54	88	70	18	14	13	1
Petroleum engineering	2,124	1,759	365	531	421	110	86	70	16
Systems engineering	987	735	252	1,642	1,237	405	125	102	23
Textile sciences and engineering	267	69	198	59	25	34	28	20	8
Polymer/plastics engineering	182	136	46	109	68	41	89	58	31
Construction engineering	442	378	64	296	231	65	0	0	0
Forest engineering	36	25	11	0	0	0	0	0	0
Industrial engineering	5,246	3,494	1,752	3,247	2,514	733	309	210	99
Manufacturing engineering	510	431	79	423	365	58	9	7	2
Operations research	452	283	169	783	479	304	57	50	7
Surveying engineering	39	36	3	8	6	2	4	3	1
Geological/geophysical engineering	233	149	84	170	127	43	16	11	5
Paper science and engineering	16	15	1	8	4	4	4	2	2
Electromechanical engineering	30	28	2	0	0	0	2	1	1
Mechatronics, robotics, and automation engineering	153	132	21	224	191	33	24	20	4
Biochemical engineering	93	52	41	15	8	7	0	0	0
Engineering chemistry	4	4	0	0	0	0	0	0	0
Biological/biosystems engineering	377	236	141	24	14	10	15	8	7
Engineering, other	997	781	216	1,225	879	346	160	112	48
Engineering technologies/construction trades/mechanics and repairers	18,121	15,803	2,318	7,403	5,461	1,942	152	104	48
Engineering technologies and engineering-related fields	17,665	15,383	2,282	7,403	5,461	1,942	152	104	48
Engineering technology, general	1,443	1,310	133	504	370	134	16	6	10
Architectural engineering technology/technician	337	263	74	10	9	1	0	0	0
Civil engineering technology/technician	464	407	57	0	0	0	0	0	0
Electrical/electronic/communications eng. technology/technician	1,428	1,310	118	30	24	6	0	0	0
Laser and optical technology/technician	0	0	0	0	0	0	0	0	0
Telecommunications technology/technician	69	57	12	165	138	27	0	0	0
Electrical/electronic eng. technologies/technicians, other	172	149	23	15	14	1	0	0	0
Biomedical technology/technician	95	74	21	1	1	0	3	2	1
Electromechanical technology/electromechanical eng. technology	133	130	3	3	2	1	0	0	0
Instrumentation technology/technician	27	23	4	0	0	0	0	0	0
Robotics technology/technician	40	38	2	12	8	4	0	0	0
Automation engineer technology/technician	85	80	5	0	0	0	0	0	0
Electromechanical/instrumentation and maintenance technol./tech.	7	6	1	0	0	0	0	0	0
Heating, ventilation, air conditioning and refrig. eng. technol./tech.	1	1	0	0	0	0	0	0	0
Energy management and systems technology/technician	113	95	18	210	159	51	0	0	0
Solar energy technology/technician	0	0	0	12	12	0	0	0	0
Water quality/wastewater treatment management/recycling technol./tech.	0	0	0	0	0	0	0	0	0
Environmental engineering technology/environmental technology	152	111	41	70	38	32	0	0	0
Hazardous materials management and waste technology/technician	0	0	0	0	0	0	0	0	0
Environmental control technologies/technicians, other	10	9	1	72	50	22	0	0	0
Plastics and polymer engineering technology/technician	100	88	12	8	5	3	0	0	0
Industrial technology/technician	1,710	1,518	192	550	421	129	14	12	2
Manufacturing engineering technology/technician	620	570	50	86	76	10	0	0	0
Welding engineering technology/technician	21	21	0	0	0	0	0	0	0
Industrial production technologies/technicians, other	227	193	34	7	5	2	0	0	0
Occupational safety and health technology/technician	1,712	1,385	327	562	420	142	4	3	1
Quality control technology/technician	5	3	2	75	42	33	0	0	0
Industrial safety technology/technician	187	150	37	18	9	9	0	0	0
Quality control and safety technologies/technicians, other	47	37	10	8	4	4	0	0	0
Aeronautical/aerospace engineering technology/technician	164	138	26	42	37	5	0	0	0
Automotive engineering technology/technician	348	331	17	69	64	5	4	4	0
Mechanical engineering/mechanical technology/technician	1,946	1,795	151	14	4	10	0	0	0
Mechanical engineering related technologies/technicians, other	280	265	15	0	0	0	0	0	0
Mining technology/technician	2	2	0	0	0	0	0	0	0
Petroleum technology/technician	59	48	11	0	0	0	0	0	0
Mining and petroleum technologies/technicians, other	0	0	0	0	0	0	0	0	0
Construction engineering technology/technician	1,964	1,805	159	154	123	31	1	1	0
Surveying technology/surveying	129	115	14	4	4	0	2	2	0
Hydraulics and fluid power technology/technician	4	4	0	0	0	0	0	0	0
Engineering-related technologies, other	10	9	1	0	0	0	0	0	0
Computer engineering technology/technician	551	491	60	0	0	0	0	0	0
Computer technology/computer systems technology	212	188	24	280	215	65	2	2	0
Computer hardware technology/technician	0	0	0	0	0	0	0	0	0
Computer software technology/technician	66	60	6	0	0	0	4	3	1
Computer engineering technologies/technicians, other	49	46	3	0	0	0	0	0	0
Drafting and design technologies/technicians, general	125	50	75	53	11	42	0	0	0
CAD/CADD drafting and/or design technology/technician	171	131	40	67	43	24	0	0	0
Architectural drafting and architectural CAD/CADD	30	24	6	34	22	12	0	0	0
Civil drafting and civil engineering CAD/CADD	7	7	0	0	0	0	0	0	0

See notes at end of table.

Table 318.30. Bachelor's, master's, and doctor's degrees conferred by postsecondary institutions, by sex of student and discipline division: 2016–17—Continued

Discipline division	Bachelor's degrees			Master's degrees			Doctor's degrees[1]		
	Total	Males	Females	Total	Males	Females	Total	Males	Females
1	2	3	4	5	6	7	8	9	10
Mechanical drafting and mechanical drafting CAD/CADD	25	16	9	0	0	0	0	0	0
Drafting/design engineering technologies/technicians, other	19	14	5	0	0	0	0	0	0
Nuclear engineering technology/technician	219	191	28	0	0	0	0	0	0
Engineering/industrial management	990	781	209	3,922	2,920	1,002	72	51	21
Engineering design	1	1	0	51	25	26	2	1	1
Packaging science	417	260	157	49	37	12	1	1	0
Engineering-related fields, other	62	42	20	13	7	6	11	4	7
Nanotechnology	10	7	3	56	31	25	16	12	4
Engineering tech. and engineering-related fields, other	600	534	66	177	111	66	0	0	0
Construction trades	153	133	20	0	0	0	0	0	0
Construction trades, general	0	0	0	0	0	0	0	0	0
Mason/masonry	0	0	0	0	0	0	0	0	0
Electrician	0	0	0	0	0	0	0	0	0
Building/property maintenance	0	0	0	0	0	0	0	0	0
Building/construction site management/manager	131	113	18	0	0	0	0	0	0
Building construction technology	0	0	0	0	0	0	0	0	0
Building/construction finishing, mgmt., and inspection, other	22	20	2	0	0	0	0	0	0
Construction trades, other	0	0	0	0	0	0	0	0	0
Mechanic and repair technologies/technicians	303	287	16	0	0	0	0	0	0
Communications systems installation and repair technology	0	0	0	0	0	0	0	0	0
Industrial electronics technology/technician	1	1	0	0	0	0	0	0	0
Heating, air conditioning, ventilation and refrig. main. technician	0	0	0	0	0	0	0	0	0
Heavy equipment maintenance technology/technician	17	17	0	0	0	0	0	0	0
Autobody/collision and repair technology/technician	0	0	0	0	0	0	0	0	0
Automobile/automotive mechanics technology/technician	46	42	4	0	0	0	0	0	0
Diesel mechanics technology/technician	26	25	1	0	0	0	0	0	0
Airframe mechanics and aircraft maintenance technology/technician	47	46	1	0	0	0	0	0	0
Aircraft powerplant technology/technician	96	90	6	0	0	0	0	0	0
Avionics maintenance technology/technician	67	63	4	0	0	0	0	0	0
Vehicle maintenance and repair technologies, other	3	3	0	0	0	0	0	0	0
English language and literature/letters	41,317	12,247	29,070	8,247	2,739	5,508	1,347	519	828
English language and literature, general	33,235	9,595	23,640	4,272	1,365	2,907	1,174	463	711
Writing, general	551	156	395	67	20	47	0	0	0
Creative writing	3,063	966	2,097	2,984	1,067	1,917	10	5	5
Professional, technical, business, and scientific writing	673	208	465	370	108	262	27	10	17
Rhetoric and composition	2,683	1,012	1,671	130	39	91	91	30	61
Rhetoric and composition/writing studies, other	70	24	46	145	54	91	3	0	3
General literature	247	52	195	16	4	12	0	0	0
American literature (United States)	25	6	19	5	1	4	0	0	0
English literature (British and Commonwealth)	205	54	151	99	35	64	5	2	3
Children's and adolescent literature	4	0	4	7	0	7	0	0	0
Literature, other	8	2	6	0	0	0	1	0	1
English language and literature/letters, other	553	172	381	152	46	106	36	9	27
Family and consumer sciences/human sciences	25,077	3,022	22,055	3,295	436	2,859	317	77	240
Work and family studies	0	0	0	1	1	0	0	0	0
Family and consumer sciences/human sciences, general	3,728	426	3,302	552	104	448	41	14	27
Business family and consumer sciences/human sciences	135	48	87	13	8	5	2	1	1
Family and consumer sciences/human sciences communication	21	2	19	0	0	0	0	0	0
Consumer merchandising/retailing management	145	24	121	19	2	17	1	0	1
Family and consumer sciences/human sciences business services, other	6	0	6	0	0	0	0	0	0
Family resource management studies, general	816	251	565	189	37	152	5	0	5
Consumer economics	144	53	91	0	0	0	0	0	0
Consumer services and advocacy	38	16	22	1	0	1	0	0	0
Family and consumer economics and related services, other	317	30	287	4	0	4	9	2	7
Foods, nutrition, and wellness studies, general	2,623	494	2,129	540	75	465	41	11	30
Human nutrition	590	122	468	285	47	238	16	6	10
Food service systems administration/management	903	325	578	18	2	16	0	0	0
Foods, nutrition, and related services, other	57	17	40	60	3	57	0	0	0
Housing and human environments, general	92	23	69	26	14	12	6	5	1
Facilities planning and management	39	37	2	3	3	0	0	0	0
Housing and human environments, other	5	1	4	0	0	0	0	0	0
Human development and family studies, general	8,700	688	8,012	716	68	648	121	22	99
Adult development and aging	13	1	12	133	12	121	0	0	0
Family systems	492	46	446	63	6	57	5	2	3
Child development	1,719	55	1,664	193	9	184	16	2	14
Family and community services	1,091	135	956	248	25	223	21	3	18
Child care and support services management	384	22	362	69	0	69	0	0	0
Child care provider/assistant	40	1	39	0	0	0	0	0	0
Developmental services worker	0	0	0	3	0	3	0	0	0
Human development, family studies, and related services, other	456	39	417	40	6	34	10	2	8
Apparel and textiles, general	2,062	124	1,938	54	5	49	15	5	10
Apparel and textile manufacture	70	10	60	2	2	0	0	0	0
Textile science	4	1	3	0	0	0	2	1	1
Apparel and textile marketing management	332	22	310	52	6	46	6	1	5
Fashion and fabric consultant	11	0	11	0	0	0	0	0	0
Apparel and textiles, other	16	2	14	5	0	5	0	0	0
Family and consumer sciences/human sciences, other	28	7	21	6	1	5	0	0	0
Foreign languages, literatures, and linguistics	17,642	5,561	12,081	3,274	1,170	2,104	1,168	479	689
Foreign languages and literatures, general	1,587	488	1,099	230	67	163	27	7	20
Linguistics	2,060	638	1,422	577	227	350	215	87	128
Language interpretation and translation	41	16	25	200	48	152	3	2	1
Comparative literature	683	206	477	158	64	94	152	65	87
Applied linguistics	29	5	24	58	19	39	5	2	3

See notes at end of table.

Table 318.30. Bachelor's, master's, and doctor's degrees conferred by postsecondary institutions, by sex of student and discipline division: 2016–17—Continued

Discipline division	Bachelor's degrees			Master's degrees			Doctor's degrees[1]		
	Total	Males	Females	Total	Males	Females	Total	Males	Females
1	2	3	4	5	6	7	8	9	10
Linguistic/comparative/related language studies and serv., other	210	53	157	46	12	34	7	3	4
African languages, literatures, and linguistics	3	1	2	4	2	2	2	2	0
East Asian languages, literatures, and linguistics, general	142	65	77	74	28	46	41	13	28
Chinese language and literature	450	197	253	51	12	39	14	6	8
Japanese language and literature	540	233	307	23	8	15	5	3	2
Korean language and literature	67	29	38	5	2	3	2	1	1
East Asian languages, literatures, and linguistics, other	101	49	52	14	6	8	18	8	10
Slavic languages, literatures, and linguistics, general	40	19	21	44	13	31	45	21	24
Russian language and literature	296	152	144	13	5	8	4	2	2
Polish language and literature	4	1	3	0	0	0	0	0	0
Slavic, Baltic, and Albanian languages, literatures, and linguistics, other	0	0	0	0	0	0	1	0	1
Germanic languages, literatures, and linguistics, general	69	40	29	23	10	13	22	8	14
German language and literature	753	369	384	96	48	48	49	13	36
Scandinavian languages, literatures, and linguistics	9	3	6	3	1	2	0	0	0
Danish language and literature	1	1	0	0	0	0	0	0	0
Dutch/Flemish language and literature	2	0	2	0	0	0	0	0	0
Norwegian language and literature	3	0	3	0	0	0	0	0	0
Swedish language and literature	3	1	2	0	0	0	0	0	0
Germanic languages, literatures, and linguistics, other	14	7	7	0	0	0	0	0	0
Modern Greek language and literature	3	3	0	0	0	0	0	0	0
South Asian languages, literatures, and linguistics, general	2	1	1	1	0	1	2	0	2
Sanskrit and classical Indian languages, literatures, and linguistics	0	0	0	1	0	1	0	0	0
Iranian languages, literatures, and linguistics	4	2	2	0	0	0	0	0	0
Romance languages, literatures, and linguistics, general	124	40	84	85	30	55	35	14	21
French language and literature	1,625	430	1,195	265	67	198	85	27	58
Italian language and literature	183	53	130	56	14	42	35	11	24
Portuguese language and literature	41	22	19	17	10	7	5	0	5
Spanish language and literature	6,420	1,704	4,716	740	237	503	171	64	107
Hispanic and Latin American languages, lit., and linguistics, general	113	23	90	18	12	6	13	7	6
Romance languages, literatures, and linguistics, other	64	20	44	55	24	31	44	19	25
American Indian/Native American languages, literatures, and linguistics	4	2	2	1	0	1	1	1	0
Middle/Near Eastern and Semitic languages, lit., and linguistics, general	27	9	18	20	12	8	15	8	7
Arabic language and literature	160	87	73	8	4	4	2	2	0
Hebrew language and literature	5	1	4	8	2	6	6	3	3
Ancient Near Eastern and biblical languages, lit., and linguistics	27	23	4	16	11	5	4	4	0
Middle/Near Eastern and Semitic languages, lit., and linguistics, other	61	28	33	31	13	18	33	24	9
Classics and classical languages, lit., and linguistics, general	856	365	491	167	93	74	77	45	32
Ancient/classical Greek language and literature	14	7	7	1	1	0	0	0	0
Latin language and literature	33	11	22	20	12	8	0	0	0
Classics and classical languages, lit., and linguistics, other	27	14	13	19	11	8	3	1	2
Celtic languages, literatures, and linguistics	2	0	2	0	0	0	2	1	1
Filipino/Tagalog language and literature	5	2	3	0	0	0	0	0	0
Turkish language and literature	0	0	0	0	0	0	0	0	0
Uralic languages, literatures, and linguistics	0	0	0	0	0	0	0	0	0
American sign language (ASL)	129	27	102	27	16	11	0	0	0
Linguistics of ASL and other sign languages	0	0	0	6	2	4	2	0	2
Sign language interpretation and translation	384	41	343	41	5	36	3	1	2
American sign language, other	6	2	4	0	0	0	0	0	0
Foreign languages, literatures, and linguistics, other	216	71	145	52	22	30	18	4	14
Health professions and related programs	238,014	37,758	200,256	119,273	21,982	97,291	77,693	31,845	45,848
Health and wellness, general	14,686	3,512	11,174	921	306	615	236	92	144
Chiropractic	0	0	0	0	0	0	2,521	1,463	1,058
Communication sciences and disorders, general	5,049	254	4,795	1,892	88	1,804	48	12	36
Audiology/audiologist	228	9	219	127	14	113	700	98	602
Speech-language pathology/pathologist	1,360	61	1,299	3,519	141	3,378	45	4	41
Audiology/audiologist and speech-language pathology/pathologist	4,654	196	4,458	2,657	109	2,548	255	41	214
Communication disorders sciences and services, other	51	0	51	105	4	101	13	2	11
Dentistry	0	0	0	0	0	0	6,388	3,328	3,060
Dental clinical sciences, general	0	0	0	326	166	160	17	11	6
Advanced general dentistry	0	0	0	26	14	12	0	0	0
Oral biology and oral maxillofacial pathology	0	0	0	127	71	56	19	4	15
Dental public health and education	0	0	0	8	2	6	7	3	4
Dental materials	0	0	0	0	0	0	0	0	0
Endodontics/endodontology	0	0	0	37	23	14	2	2	0
Oral/maxillofacial surgery	0	0	0	0	0	0	0	0	0
Orthodontics/orthodontology	0	0	0	84	46	38	2	1	1
Pediatric dentistry/pedodontics	0	0	0	22	8	14	1	0	1
Periodontics/periodontology	0	0	0	37	19	18	1	0	1
Prosthodontics/prosthodontology	0	0	0	21	12	9	7	7	0
Advanced/graduate dentistry and oral sciences, other	0	0	0	76	36	40	12	2	10
Dental assisting/assistant	2	0	2	0	0	0	0	0	0
Dental hygiene/hygienist	2,318	109	2,209	81	2	79	0	0	0
Dental laboratory technology/technician	7	1	6	0	0	0	0	0	0
Dental services and allied professions, other	16	0	16	8	1	7	0	0	0
Health/health care administration/management	11,930	2,503	9,427	9,586	2,942	6,644	257	93	164
Hospital and health care facilities administration/management	2,771	429	2,342	1,287	375	912	1	0	1
Health unit manager/ward supervisor	0	0	0	3	1	2	0	0	0
Medical office management/administration	54	5	49	0	0	0	0	0	0
Health information/medical records administration/administrator	1,558	284	1,274	400	120	280	0	0	0
Health information/medical records technology/technician	64	31	33	79	23	56	0	0	0
Medical office assistant/specialist	0	0	0	0	0	0	0	0	0
Medical/health management and clinical assistant/specialist	80	5	75	5	1	4	0	0	0
Medical staff services technology/technician	1	0	1	0	0	0	0	0	0
Long term care administration/management	242	26	216	12	3	9	0	0	0
Clinical research coordinator	9	1	8	89	22	67	0	0	0
Health and medical administrative services, other	695	159	536	207	53	154	14	6	8

See notes at end of table.

Table 318.30. Bachelor's, master's, and doctor's degrees conferred by postsecondary institutions, by sex of student and discipline division: 2016–17—Continued

Discipline division	Bachelor's degrees			Master's degrees			Doctor's degrees[1]		
	Total	Males	Females	Total	Males	Females	Total	Males	Females
1	2	3	4	5	6	7	8	9	10
Medical/clinical assistant	6	0	6	35	10	25	0	0	0
Occupational therapist assistant	8	0	8	0	0	0	0	0	0
Pharmacy technician/assistant	0	0	0	0	0	0	0	0	0
Physical therapy technician/assistant	46	15	31	0	0	0	0	0	0
Veterinary/animal health technology/technician and vet. assistant	499	26	473	0	0	0	0	0	0
Anesthesiologist assistant	0	0	0	205	89	116	0	0	0
Emergency care attendant (EMT ambulance)	3	2	1	0	0	0	0	0	0
Pathology/pathologist assistant	13	2	11	76	15	61	0	0	0
Respiratory therapy technician/assistant	12	5	7	0	0	0	0	0	0
Radiologist assistant	5	2	3	5	4	1	0	0	0
Allied health and medical assisting services, other	480	118	362	148	44	104	0	0	0
Cardiovascular technology/technologist	101	26	75	3	3	0	0	0	0
Electrocardiograph technology/technician	1	0	1	0	0	0	0	0	0
Electroneurodiagnostic/electroencephalographic technology/technologist	6	3	3	0	0	0	0	0	0
Emergency medical technology/technician (EMT paramedic)	295	201	94	11	5	6	0	0	0
Nuclear medical technology/technologist	289	83	206	5	2	3	0	0	0
Perfusion technology/perfusionist	12	3	9	61	25	36	0	0	0
Medical radiologic technology/science radiation therapist	1,163	258	905	73	32	41	0	0	0
Respiratory care therapy/therapist	1,361	410	951	36	12	24	0	0	0
Surgical technology/technologist	19	2	17	0	0	0	0	0	0
Diagnostic medical sonography/sonographer and ultrasound technician	679	97	582	9	1	8	0	0	0
Radiologic technology/science radiographer	1,456	345	1,111	86	38	48	2	1	1
Physician assistant	541	149	392	7,933	2,162	5,771	16	13	3
Athletic training/trainer	3,851	1,498	2,353	825	356	469	40	11	29
Gene/genetic therapy	6	2	4	0	0	0	0	0	0
Cardiopulmonary technology/technologist	5	1	4	0	0	0	0	0	0
Radiation protection/health physics technician	14	3	11	4	4	0	0	0	0
Magnetic resonance imaging (MRI) technology/technician	46	22	24	5	1	4	0	0	0
Allied health diagnostic/intervention/treatment professions, other	541	129	412	25	12	13	68	3	65
Blood bank technology specialist	0	0	0	1	0	1	0	0	0
Cytotechnology/cytotechnologist	40	12	28	11	2	9	0	0	0
Hematology technology/technician	0	0	0	5	3	2	0	0	0
Clinical/medical laboratory technician	160	46	114	0	0	0	0	0	0
Clinical laboratory science/medical technology/technologist	2,868	810	2,058	270	85	185	0	0	0
Histologic technology/histotechnologist	19	6	13	3	1	2	0	0	0
Histologic technician	9	2	7	0	0	0	0	0	0
Cytogenetics/genetics/clinical genetics technology/technologist	31	10	21	11	3	8	0	0	0
Clinical/medical laboratory science and allied professions, other	495	126	369	156	41	115	1	1	0
Pre-dentistry studies	16	7	9	0	0	0	0	0	0
Pre-medicine/pre-medical studies	843	335	508	53	20	33	0	0	0
Pre-pharmacy studies	8	3	5	0	0	0	0	0	0
Pre-veterinary studies	439	70	369	0	0	0	0	0	0
Pre-nursing studies	33	10	23	0	0	0	0	0	0
Pre-occupational therapy studies	84	4	80	0	0	0	0	0	0
Pre-optometry studies	7	0	7	0	0	0	0	0	0
Pre-physical therapy studies	188	73	115	0	0	0	0	0	0
Health/medical preparatory programs, other	1,706	482	1,224	137	55	82	0	0	0
Medicine	0	0	0	0	0	0	18,698	9,834	8,864
Medical scientist	0	0	0	622	278	344	39	21	18
Substance abuse/addiction counseling	472	117	355	386	111	275	3	1	2
Psychiatric/mental health services technician	230	39	191	7	0	7	0	0	0
Clinical/medical social work	179	32	147	955	111	844	8	1	7
Community health services/liaison/counseling	1,468	262	1,206	197	34	163	9	2	7
Marriage and family therapy/counseling	37	4	33	3,086	492	2,594	139	26	113
Clinical pastoral counseling/patient counseling	45	11	34	129	41	88	31	12	19
Psychoanalysis and psychotherapy	0	0	0	9	1	8	4	0	4
Mental health counseling/counselor	9	1	8	5,736	965	4,771	28	10	18
Genetic counseling/counselor	0	0	0	147	13	134	0	0	0
Mental and social health services and allied professions, other	502	56	446	1,684	319	1,365	20	3	17
Optometry	0	0	0	0	0	0	1,630	547	1,083
Ophthalmic technician/technologist	3	0	3	0	0	0	0	0	0
Orthoptics/orthoptist	1	0	1	0	0	0	0	0	0
Ophthalmic/optometric support services/allied professions, other	7	2	5	26	3	23	2	0	2
Osteopathic medicine/osteopathy	0	0	0	0	0	0	6,046	3,287	2,759
Pharmacy	1,031	393	638	1	0	1	14,854	5,659	9,195
Pharmacy admin and pharmacy policy and regulatory affairs	0	0	0	314	121	193	21	9	12
Pharmaceutics and drug design	114	61	53	143	73	70	151	87	64
Medicinal and pharmaceutical chemistry	25	16	9	59	28	31	98	61	37
Natural products chemistry and pharmacognosy	0	0	0	1	1	0	4	3	1
Clinical and industrial drug development	36	8	28	138	46	92	0	0	0
Pharmacoeconomics/pharmaceutical economics	0	0	0	49	24	25	112	55	57
Clinical, hospital, and managed care pharmacy	0	0	0	16	4	12	0	0	0
Industrial and physical pharmacy and cosmetic sciences	9	0	9	44	15	29	0	0	0
Pharmaceutical sciences	749	300	449	183	77	106	145	74	71
Pharmaceutical marketing and management	72	32	40	22	4	18	0	0	0
Pharmacy, pharmaceutical sciences, and administration, other	662	219	443	246	81	165	31	14	17
Podiatric medicine/podiatry	0	0	0	0	0	0	601	364	237
Public health, general	5,671	1,120	4,551	9,419	2,332	7,087	527	153	374
Environmental health	363	169	194	639	192	447	96	32	64
Health/medical physics	37	14	23	104	59	45	39	25	14
Occupational health and industrial hygiene	182	135	47	78	41	37	2	2	0
Public health education and promotion	3,032	572	2,460	877	98	779	79	23	56
Community health and preventive medicine	1,709	297	1,412	242	51	191	25	3	22
Maternal and child health	13	0	13	137	1	136	17	2	15
International public health/international health	131	26	105	539	134	405	19	12	7
Health services administration	1,042	149	893	891	293	598	26	10	16

See notes at end of table.

Table 318.30. Bachelor's, master's, and doctor's degrees conferred by postsecondary institutions, by sex of student and discipline division: 2016–17—Continued

Discipline division	Bachelor's degrees			Master's degrees			Doctor's degrees[1]		
	Total	Males	Females	Total	Males	Females	Total	Males	Females
1	2	3	4	5	6	7	8	9	10
Behavioral aspects of health	296	77	219	89	22	67	30	4	26
Public health, other	1,367	342	1,025	857	216	641	124	34	90
Art therapy/therapist	228	5	223	465	20	445	10	0	10
Dance therapy/therapist	1	0	1	38	0	38	0	0	0
Music therapy/therapist	382	54	328	115	18	97	1	0	1
Occupational therapy/therapist	842	81	761	6,606	731	5,875	740	79	661
Orthotist/prosthetist	14	5	9	216	111	105	0	0	0
Physical therapy/therapist	362	115	247	112	41	71	11,597	4,369	7,228
Therapeutic recreation/recreational therapy	759	92	667	54	8	46	0	0	0
Vocational rehabilitation counseling/counselor	374	55	319	806	175	631	20	4	16
Kinesiotherapy/kinesiotherapist	52	12	40	20	6	14	0	0	0
Assistive/augmentative technology and rehabilitation engineering	0	0	0	51	6	45	1	1	0
Animal-assisted therapy	29	3	26	0	0	0	0	0	0
Rehabilitation science	774	156	618	121	42	79	49	25	24
Rehabilitation and therapeutic professions, other	739	168	571	264	60	204	26	10	16
Veterinary medicine	0	0	0	0	0	0	2,991	596	2,395
Veterinary sciences/veterinary clinical sciences, general	23	6	17	187	39	148	75	32	43
Veterinary physiology	0	0	0	0	0	0	1	1	0
Veterinary microbiology and immunobiology	32	12	20	2	0	2	2	1	1
Veterinary pathology and pathobiology	0	0	0	15	4	11	34	12	22
Large animal/food animal/equine surgery and medicine	0	0	0	1	0	1	0	0	0
Small/companion animal surgery and medicine	0	0	0	5	2	3	0	0	0
Comparative and laboratory animal medicine	0	0	0	39	5	34	1	0	1
Veterinary preventive medicine epidemiology/public health	0	0	0	5	2	3	0	0	0
Veterinary infectious diseases	0	0	0	11	1	10	11	4	7
Medical illustration/medical illustrator	45	11	34	29	7	22	0	0	0
Medical informatics	135	49	86	940	386	554	35	20	15
Medical illustration and informatics, other	0	0	0	28	6	22	0	0	0
Dietetics/dietitian	3,307	418	2,889	496	43	453	2	0	2
Clinical nutrition/nutritionist	191	30	161	548	72	476	7	3	4
Dietetic technician	0	0	0	0	0	0	0	0	0
Dietitian assistant	17	5	12	0	0	0	0	0	0
Dietetics and clinical nutrition services, other	386	69	317	112	9	103	0	0	0
Bioethics/medical ethics	28	5	23	322	128	194	37	17	20
Alternative and complementary medicine and medical systems, general	0	0	0	4	0	4	0	0	0
Acupuncture and oriental medicine	47	16	31	1,296	368	928	417	111	306
Traditional Chinese medicine and Chinese herbology	0	0	0	166	43	123	15	4	11
Naturopathic medicine/naturopathy	0	0	0	0	0	0	335	81	254
Ayurvedic medicine/Ayurveda	0	0	0	8	2	6	0	0	0
Holistic health	246	45	201	39	0	39	0	0	0
Alternative and complementary medicine and medical systems, other	170	32	138	17	0	17	0	0	0
Direct entry midwifery	17	0	17	23	0	23	0	0	0
Alternative and complementary medical support services, other	0	0	0	40	2	38	0	0	0
Massage therapy/therapeutic massage	22	1	21	0	0	0	0	0	0
Asian bodywork therapy	0	0	0	0	0	0	0	0	0
Somatic bodywork and related therapeutic services, other	0	0	0	0	0	0	0	0	0
Movement therapy and movement education	71	23	48	26	1	25	8	5	3
Yoga teacher training/Yoga therapy	0	0	0	27	5	22	0	0	0
Herbalism/herbalist	11	2	9	18	2	16	0	0	0
Energy and biologically based therapies, other	0	0	0	0	0	0	0	0	0
Registered nursing/registered nurse	134,507	17,029	117,478	16,083	1,879	14,204	882	109	773
Nursing administration	726	78	648	6,402	637	5,765	321	37	284
Adult health nurse/nursing	314	37	277	1,583	224	1,359	49	2	47
Nurse anesthetist	0	0	0	1,476	616	860	338	138	200
Family practice nurse/nursing	272	54	218	10,931	1,284	9,647	420	56	364
Maternal/child health and neonatal nurse/nursing	0	0	0	206	6	200	1	0	1
Nurse midwife/nursing midwifery	0	0	0	399	0	399	5	0	5
Nursing science	1,317	150	1,167	1,824	178	1,646	800	72	728
Pediatric nurse/nursing	0	0	0	388	12	376	18	1	17
Psychiatric/mental health nurse/nursing	0	0	0	310	70	240	28	6	22
Public health/community nurse/nursing	198	25	173	294	21	273	1	0	1
Perioperative/operating room and surgical nurse/nursing	0	0	0	133	12	121	0	0	0
Clinical nurse specialist	18	2	16	462	57	405	34	4	30
Critical care nursing	0	0	0	291	56	235	7	0	7
Occupational and environmental health nursing	0	0	0	46	6	40	3	0	3
Emergency room/trauma nursing	0	0	0	18	5	13	0	0	0
Nursing education	16	0	16	1,589	107	1,482	135	9	126
Nursing practice	958	102	856	297	26	271	3,529	394	3,135
Palliative care nursing	1	0	1	4	0	4	0	0	0
Clinical nurse leader	23	2	21	417	58	359	3	2	1
Geriatric nurse/nursing	0	0	0	361	39	322	24	8	16
Women's health nurse/nursing	0	0	0	197	0	197	0	0	0
Reg. nursing, nursing admin., nursing research and clinical nursing, other	1,922	214	1,708	1,438	152	1,286	251	30	221
Licensed practical/vocational nurse training	0	0	0	0	0	0	0	0	0
Practical nursing, vocational nursing and nursing assistants, other	0	0	0	0	0	0	0	0	0
Health professions and related clinical sciences, other	4,765	1,158	3,607	846	284	562	98	34	64
Homeland security, law enforcement, firefighting and related prot. services	59,581	31,585	27,996	10,210	5,177	5,033	177	89	88
Corrections	540	216	324	9	2	7	0	0	0
Criminal justice/law enforcement administration	16,939	9,060	7,879	2,657	1,291	1,366	41	19	22
Criminal justice/safety studies	30,628	15,479	15,149	3,200	1,309	1,891	100	45	55
Forensic science and technology	1,466	410	1,056	573	143	430	1	1	0
Criminal justice/police science	3,160	1,746	1,414	54	19	35	3	2	1
Security and loss prevention services	27	14	13	38	27	11	0	0	0
Juvenile corrections	29	5	24	10	4	6	1	0	1
Criminalistics and criminal science	179	47	132	41	10	31	0	0	0

See notes at end of table.

Table 318.30. Bachelor's, master's, and doctor's degrees conferred by postsecondary institutions, by sex of student and discipline division: 2016–17—Continued

Discipline division	Bachelor's degrees			Master's degrees			Doctor's degrees[1]		
	Total	Males	Females	Total	Males	Females	Total	Males	Females
1	2	3	4	5	6	7	8	9	10
Securities services administration/management	635	386	249	205	163	42	0	0	0
Corrections administration	71	39	32	8	4	4	0	0	0
Law enforcement investigation and interviewing	0	0	0	22	11	11	0	0	0
Cyber/computer forensics and counterterrorism	268	204	64	388	266	122	0	0	0
Financial forensics and fraud investigation	59	29	30	139	54	85	0	0	0
Law enforcement intelligence analysis	11	7	4	5	0	5	0	0	0
Critical incident response/special police operations	0	0	0	0	0	0	0	0	0
Protective services operations	0	0	0	0	0	0	0	0	0
Corrections and criminal justice, other	1,419	635	784	283	104	179	0	0	0
Fire prevention and safety technology/technician	217	197	20	9	6	3	0	0	0
Fire services administration	780	735	45	72	42	30	4	3	1
Fire science/firefighting	333	294	39	5	3	2	0	0	0
Fire/arson investigation and prevention	53	35	18	0	0	0	0	0	0
Fire protection, other	64	53	11	25	22	3	0	0	0
Homeland security	831	637	194	553	354	199	0	0	0
Crisis/emergency/disaster management	913	677	236	807	561	246	15	11	4
Critical infrastructure protection	76	53	23	317	242	75	0	0	0
Terrorism and counterterrorism operations	0	0	0	7	4	3	0	0	0
Homeland security, other	89	73	16	17	10	7	0	0	0
Homeland sec., law enforcement, firefighting and related prot. serv., other	794	554	240	766	526	240	12	8	4
Legal professions and studies	4,272	1,355	2,917	8,674	3,911	4,763	35,123	17,703	17,420
Pre-law studies	233	93	140	19	5	14	0	0	0
Legal studies, general	1,952	655	1,297	316	102	214	5	2	3
Law	0	0	0	0	0	0	34,894	17,579	17,315
Advanced legal research/studies, general	91	43	48	2,245	1,059	1,186	83	51	32
Programs for foreign lawyers	0	0	0	1,387	615	772	13	7	6
American/U.S. law/legal studies/jurisprudence	56	18	38	465	187	278	18	11	7
Banking, corporate, finance, and securities law	0	0	0	306	153	153	1	0	1
Comparative law	0	0	0	55	32	23	0	0	0
Energy, environment, and natural resources law	6	5	1	141	69	72	2	0	2
Health law	0	0	0	252	53	199	4	2	2
International law and legal studies	2	0	2	477	198	279	8	3	5
International business, trade, and tax law	0	0	0	211	106	105	0	0	0
Tax law/taxation	0	0	0	796	492	304	0	0	0
Intellectual property law	0	0	0	135	49	86	0	0	0
Legal research and advanced professional studies, other	0	0	0	826	401	425	13	10	3
Legal administrative assistant/secretary	3	0	3	5	4	1	0	0	0
Legal assistant/paralegal	1,520	374	1,146	79	10	69	0	0	0
Court reporting/court reporter	2	0	2	0	0	0	0	0	0
Legal support services, other	0	0	0	4	3	1	0	0	0
Legal professions and studies, other	407	167	240	955	373	582	82	38	44
Liberal arts and sciences, general studies and humanities	43,841	15,999	27,842	2,485	949	1,536	95	32	63
Liberal arts and sciences/liberal studies	23,921	7,932	15,989	1,448	586	862	8	5	3
General studies	13,964	5,820	8,144	174	67	107	3	1	2
Humanities/humanistic studies	1,904	606	1,298	510	184	326	81	24	57
Liberal arts and sciences, general studies and humanities, other	4,052	1,641	2,411	353	112	241	3	2	1
Library science	109	11	98	4,843	842	4,001	42	13	29
Library and information science	109	11	98	4,554	800	3,754	42	13	29
Children and youth library services	0	0	0	8	0	8	0	0	0
Archives/archival administration	0	0	0	132	22	110	0	0	0
Library science, other	0	0	0	149	20	129	0	0	0
Mathematics and statistics	24,073	14,002	10,071	9,086	5,116	3,970	1,925	1,403	522
Mathematics, general	17,737	10,244	7,493	2,682	1,613	1,069	1,123	856	267
Analysis and functional analysis	1	1	0	0	0	0	0	0	0
Topology and foundations	0	0	0	0	0	0	3	3	0
Mathematics, other	319	154	165	44	22	22	11	7	4
Applied mathematics, general	2,258	1,399	859	981	615	366	255	179	76
Computational mathematics	195	143	52	15	8	7	41	29	12
Computational and applied mathematics	191	124	67	152	107	45	41	35	6
Financial mathematics	276	159	117	1,838	1,022	816	3	2	1
Mathematical biology	30	13	17	0	0	0	0	0	0
Applied mathematics, other	208	122	86	12	8	4	9	7	2
Statistics, general	2,116	1,172	944	3,063	1,588	1,475	397	263	134
Mathematical statistics and probability	224	157	67	152	66	86	13	6	7
Mathematics and statistics	87	57	30	70	31	39	3	2	1
Statistics, other	151	93	58	50	21	29	3	2	1
Mathematics and statistics, other	280	164	116	27	15	12	23	12	11
Military technologies and applied sciences	469	401	68	274	212	62	0	0	0
Intelligence, general	264	230	34	63	41	22	0	0	0
Strategic intelligence	0	0	0	28	19	9	0	0	0
Signal/geospatial intelligence	0	0	0	5	4	1	0	0	0
Cyber/electronic operations and warfare	61	52	9	158	130	28	0	0	0
Intelligence, command control and information operations, other	0	0	0	0	0	0	0	0	0
Military applied sciences, other	49	44	5	0	0	0	0	0	0
Aerospace ground equipment technology	2	2	0	0	0	0	0	0	0
Air and space operations technology	27	18	9	0	0	0	0	0	0
Military systems and maintenance technology, other	15	14	1	0	0	0	0	0	0
Military technologies and applied sciences, other	51	41	10	20	18	2	0	0	0
Multi/interdisciplinary studies	49,658	16,800	32,858	9,234	3,402	5,832	854	358	496
Multi/interdisciplinary studies, general	4,730	1,839	2,891	134	62	72	7	4	3
Biological and physical sciences	2,125	872	1,253	518	238	280	64	35	29

See notes at end of table.

Table 318.30. Bachelor's, master's, and doctor's degrees conferred by postsecondary institutions, by sex of student and discipline division: 2016–17—Continued

Discipline division	Bachelor's degrees			Master's degrees			Doctor's degrees[1]		
	Total	Males	Females	Total	Males	Females	Total	Males	Females
1	2	3	4	5	6	7	8	9	10
Peace studies and conflict resolution	462	161	301	597	221	376	26	10	16
Systems science and theory	300	178	122	228	118	110	17	12	5
Mathematics and computer science	433	318	115	93	61	32	17	8	9
Biopsychology	169	46	123	4	2	2	2	1	1
Gerontology	346	29	317	442	61	381	36	5	31
Historic preservation and conservation	101	39	62	192	49	143	2	0	2
Cultural resource management and policy analysis	0	0	0	41	15	26	0	0	0
Historic preservation and conservation, other	2	0	2	10	4	6	1	0	1
Medieval and renaissance studies	30	9	21	21	8	13	6	3	3
Museology/museum studies	16	1	15	525	74	451	0	0	0
Science, technology and society	875	453	422	147	51	96	35	21	14
Accounting and computer science	8	6	2	5	4	1	0	0	0
Behavioral sciences	3,625	712	2,913	261	36	225	17	7	10
Natural sciences	541	197	344	80	24	56	7	3	4
Nutrition sciences	2,531	426	2,105	1,016	137	879	169	42	127
International/global studies	5,469	1,964	3,505	1,068	561	507	2	0	2
Holocaust and related studies	9	1	8	27	8	19	0	0	0
Ancient studies/civilization	89	27	62	8	7	1	1	1	0
Classical, ancient Mediterranean/Near Eastern studies/archaeology	85	33	52	7	4	3	2	2	0
Intercultural/multicultural and diversity studies	112	33	79	96	31	65	2	2	0
Cognitive science	1,353	512	841	105	34	71	35	24	11
Cultural studies/critical theory and analysis	157	49	108	53	10	43	1	1	0
Human biology	879	257	622	0	0	0	0	0	0
Dispute resolution	0	0	0	312	110	202	40	16	24
Maritime studies	17	8	9	1	0	1	0	0	0
Computational science	38	22	16	311	224	87	15	12	3
Human computer interaction	451	368	83	380	198	182	9	6	3
Marine sciences	114	44	70	62	23	39	22	7	15
Sustainability studies	497	217	280	564	225	339	7	4	3
Multi/interdisciplinary studies, other	24,094	7,979	16,115	1,926	802	1,124	312	132	180
Parks, recreation, leisure, and fitness studies	53,264	27,390	25,874	8,655	4,979	3,676	319	159	160
Parks, recreation and leisure studies	3,131	1,413	1,718	188	84	104	17	7	10
Parks, recreation and leisure facilities management	3,111	1,474	1,637	397	192	205	18	11	7
Golf course operation and grounds management	7	3	4	0	0	0	0	0	0
Parks, recreation and leisure facilities management, other	11	9	2	0	0	0	0	0	0
Health and physical education/fitness, general	10,493	5,089	5,404	1,227	668	559	30	17	13
Sport and fitness administration/management	9,897	7,172	2,725	4,105	2,658	1,447	32	19	13
Kinesiology and exercise science	25,064	11,326	13,738	2,478	1,244	1,234	183	92	91
Physical fitness technician	69	41	28	12	10	2	0	0	0
Sports studies	211	159	52	105	56	49	2	1	1
Health and physical education/fitness, other	959	514	445	86	32	54	30	9	21
Outdoor education	111	67	44	47	26	21	0	0	0
Parks, recreation, leisure, and fitness studies, other	200	123	77	10	9	1	7	3	4
Philosophy and religious studies	9,712	6,008	3,704	1,705	1,108	597	741	507	234
Philosophy and religious studies, general	94	56	38	4	3	1	19	9	10
Philosophy	5,625	3,798	1,827	752	552	200	434	315	119
Logic	8	5	3	9	8	1	2	2	0
Ethics	65	11	54	47	21	26	0	0	0
Applied and professional ethics	20	12	8	18	9	9	0	0	0
Philosophy, other	198	106	92	10	5	5	2	0	2
Religion/religious studies	2,877	1,577	1,300	437	239	198	253	165	88
Buddhist studies	0	0	0	4	2	2	1	1	0
Christian studies	353	220	133	208	142	66	0	0	0
Hindu studies	0	0	0	0	0	0	0	0	0
Islamic studies	12	8	4	17	8	9	6	5	1
Jewish/Judaic studies	180	47	133	91	43	48	9	3	6
Religion/religious studies, other	81	44	37	29	15	14	4	3	1
Philosophy and religious studies, other	199	124	75	79	61	18	11	4	7
Physical sciences and science technologies	31,268	18,860	12,408	7,143	4,418	2,725	6,027	4,072	1,955
Physical sciences	30,720	18,565	12,155	7,093	4,390	2,703	6,024	4,069	1,955
Physical sciences	309	174	135	78	56	22	17	10	7
Astronomy	279	188	91	100	50	50	106	66	40
Astrophysics	214	148	66	42	32	10	56	37	19
Planetary astronomy and science	15	8	7	15	7	8	26	15	11
Astronomy and astrophysics, other	28	16	12	12	10	2	8	5	3
Atmospheric sciences and meteorology, general	449	271	178	204	112	92	135	72	63
Atmospheric chemistry and climatology	5	5	0	0	0	0	0	0	0
Atmospheric physics and dynamics	0	0	0	1	0	1	1	1	0
Meteorology	203	130	73	30	20	10	15	11	4
Atmospheric sciences and meteorology, other	28	12	16	1	0	1	2	1	1
Chemistry, general	14,296	7,265	7,031	2,370	1,315	1,055	2,778	1,699	1,079
Analytical chemistry	5	1	4	23	16	7	4	3	1
Inorganic chemistry	0	0	0	0	0	0	0	0	0
Organic chemistry	0	0	0	3	3	0	14	8	6
Physical chemistry	0	0	0	0	0	0	2	1	1
Polymer chemistry	4	4	0	60	38	22	35	18	17
Chemical physics	31	21	10	7	4	3	13	11	2
Environmental chemistry	8	3	5	1	1	0	5	4	1
Forensic chemistry	152	38	114	1	0	1	0	0	0
Theoretical chemistry	18	6	12	0	0	0	0	0	0
Chemistry, other	440	237	203	29	14	15	36	28	8
Geology/earth science, general	5,606	3,459	2,147	1,387	795	592	463	268	195
Geochemistry	17	11	6	4	4	0	7	5	2

See notes at end of table.

Table 318.30. Bachelor's, master's, and doctor's degrees conferred by postsecondary institutions, by sex of student and discipline division: 2016–17—Continued

Discipline division	Bachelor's degrees			Master's degrees			Doctor's degrees[1]		
	Total	Males	Females	Total	Males	Females	Total	Males	Females
1	2	3	4	5	6	7	8	9	10
Geophysics and seismology	197	134	63	121	85	36	68	45	23
Paleontology	9	7	2	1	0	1	0	0	0
Hydrology and water resources science	50	34	16	89	41	48	18	12	6
Geochemistry and petrology	0	0	0	0	0	0	0	0	0
Oceanography, chemical and physical	215	95	120	166	70	96	108	50	58
Geological and earth sciences/geosciences, other	521	306	215	173	106	67	73	45	28
Physics, general	6,869	5,465	1,404	1,621	1,230	391	1,691	1,395	296
Atomic/molecular physics	0	0	0	13	6	7	4	3	1
Elementary particle physics	0	0	0	1	1	0	0	0	0
Nuclear physics	0	0	0	0	0	0	1	1	0
Optics/optical sciences	23	17	6	73	57	16	49	43	6
Condensed matter and materials physics	1	1	0	2	2	0	9	8	1
Acoustics	17	16	1	16	14	2	5	4	1
Theoretical and mathematical physics	17	17	0	0	0	0	0	0	0
Physics, other	182	141	41	124	99	25	67	52	15
Materials science	190	133	57	224	157	67	151	109	42
Materials chemistry	3	2	1	11	6	5	9	7	2
Materials sciences, other	0	0	0	2	2	0	6	5	1
Physical sciences, other	319	200	119	88	37	51	42	27	15
Science technologies/technicians	548	295	253	50	28	22	3	3	0
Science technologies/technicians, general	46	39	7	0	0	0	0	0	0
Biology technician/biotechnology laboratory technician	36	14	22	0	0	0	3	3	0
Nuclear/nuclear power technology/technician	26	22	4	0	0	0	0	0	0
Nuclear and industrial radiologic technologies/technicians, other	0	0	0	0	0	0	0	0	0
Chemical technology/technician	0	0	0	2	2	0	0	0	0
Physical science technologies/technicians, other	0	0	0	0	0	0	0	0	0
Science technologies/technicians, other	440	220	220	48	26	22	0	0	0
Precision production	32	18	14	14	4	10	0	0	0
Tool and die technology/technician	0	0	0	0	0	0	0	0	0
Welding technology/welder	4	4	0	0	0	0	0	0	0
Furniture design and manufacturing	28	14	14	14	4	10	0	0	0
Psychology	116,861	25,526	91,335	27,542	5,588	21,954	6,702	1,691	5,011
Psychology, general	105,815	23,218	82,597	6,318	1,572	4,746	1,803	537	1,266
Cognitive psychology and psycholinguistics	109	19	90	32	5	27	18	8	10
Comparative psychology	0	0	0	19	4	15	0	0	0
Developmental and child psychology	610	57	553	294	30	264	58	11	47
Experimental psychology	1,615	385	1,230	224	83	141	175	67	108
Personality psychology	13	2	11	10	3	7	10	2	8
Physiological psychology/psychobiology	1,197	331	866	53	20	33	7	3	4
Social psychology	1,131	258	873	36	11	25	45	13	32
Psychometrics and quantitative psychology	2	1	1	13	4	9	12	2	10
Psychopharmacology	0	0	0	16	5	11	0	0	0
Research and experimental psychology, other	2,708	594	2,114	97	33	64	152	52	100
Clinical psychology	201	39	162	2,397	471	1,926	2,440	551	1,889
Community psychology	404	67	337	235	56	179	30	7	23
Counseling psychology	575	99	476	8,588	1,579	7,009	481	115	366
Industrial and organizational psychology	215	51	164	1,338	427	911	191	69	122
School psychology	1	0	1	1,985	251	1,734	348	54	294
Educational psychology	115	6	109	1,269	223	1,046	383	92	291
Clinical child psychology	0	0	0	27	5	22	35	5	30
Environmental psychology	37	17	20	22	8	14	7	3	4
Geropsychology	0	0	0	5	1	4	3	2	1
Health/medical psychology	65	5	60	10	1	9	41	9	32
Family psychology	12	1	11	70	10	60	0	0	0
Forensic psychology	653	112	541	745	117	628	119	10	109
Applied psychology	819	166	653	345	88	257	26	12	14
Applied behavior analysis	161	32	129	1,200	156	1,044	86	22	64
Clinical, counseling and applied psychology, other	46	9	37	304	65	239	75	11	64
Psychology, other	357	57	300	1,890	360	1,530	157	34	123
Public administration and social service professions	35,464	6,238	29,226	45,393	10,799	34,594	1,116	381	735
Human services, general	6,725	879	5,846	1,256	204	1,052	64	12	52
Community organization and advocacy	1,865	411	1,454	349	122	227	6	2	4
Public administration	3,281	1,609	1,672	12,591	5,265	7,326	324	168	156
Public policy analysis, general	1,518	634	884	2,626	1,201	1,425	197	84	113
Education policy analysis	0	0	0	51	15	36	15	6	9
Health policy analysis	98	18	80	60	19	41	17	6	11
International policy analysis	17	4	13	9	4	5	0	0	0
Public policy analysis, other	1	0	1	109	47	62	6	3	3
Social work	21,436	2,551	18,885	27,873	3,788	24,085	433	81	352
Youth services/administration	116	22	94	63	6	57	0	0	0
Social work, other	75	9	66	167	39	128	0	0	0
Public administration and social service professions, other	332	101	231	239	89	150	54	19	35
Social sciences and history	159,099	79,568	79,531	20,015	9,914	10,101	4,706	2,572	2,134
Social sciences	135,041	65,262	69,779	16,579	8,029	8,550	3,781	2,039	1,742
Social sciences, general	7,140	2,597	4,543	671	225	446	17	9	8
Research methodology and quantitative methods	4	2	2	43	21	22	0	0	0
Anthropology	8,223	2,241	5,982	1,082	347	735	538	202	336
Physical and biological anthropology	34	9	25	16	3	13	5	3	2
Medical anthropology	50	7	43	0	0	0	1	0	1
Cultural anthropology	43	6	37	11	3	8	6	1	5
Anthropology, other	41	14	27	13	4	9	11	4	7
Archeology	173	52	121	41	8	33	20	7	13

See notes at end of table.

Table 318.30. Bachelor's, master's, and doctor's degrees conferred by postsecondary institutions, by sex of student and discipline division: 2016–17—Continued

Discipline division	Bachelor's degrees			Master's degrees			Doctor's degrees[1]		
	Total	Males	Females	Total	Males	Females	Total	Males	Females
1	2	3	4	5	6	7	8	9	10
Criminology	7,265	3,380	3,885	715	253	462	51	23	28
Demography and population studies	0	0	0	32	9	23	15	7	8
Economics, general	30,358	20,979	9,379	2,286	1,475	811	901	609	292
Applied economics	493	355	138	327	175	152	28	14	14
Econometrics and quantitative economics	2,280	1,409	871	906	510	396	181	129	52
Development economics and international development	283	82	201	354	125	229	23	12	11
International economics	243	137	106	45	21	24	5	3	2
Economics, other	394	259	135	127	71	56	12	3	9
Geography	3,810	2,327	1,483	612	335	277	263	150	113
Geographic information science and cartography	507	370	137	493	296	197	21	11	10
Geography, other	172	97	75	52	35	17	6	2	4
International relations and affairs	8,467	3,309	5,158	4,164	2,012	2,152	99	58	41
National security policy studies	65	47	18	215	147	68	0	0	0
International relations and national security studies, other	87	42	45	151	86	65	2	1	1
Political science and government, general	33,099	17,533	15,566	1,590	911	679	777	474	303
American government and politics (United States)	144	86	58	147	97	50	0	0	0
Political economy	216	127	89	4	4	0	0	0	0
Political science and government, other	732	367	365	101	57	44	19	9	10
Sociology	27,443	8,127	19,316	1,397	481	916	682	267	415
Urban studies/affairs	957	461	496	413	173	240	46	25	21
Sociology and anthropology	429	121	308	9	2	7	0	0	0
Rural sociology	20	8	12	0	0	0	0	0	0
Social sciences, other	1,869	711	1,158	562	143	419	52	16	36
History	24,058	14,306	9,752	3,436	1,885	1,551	925	533	392
History, general	23,444	13,954	9,490	3,044	1,631	1,413	863	503	360
American history (United States)	37	26	11	51	26	25	4	3	1
European history	16	12	4	2	2	0	0	0	0
History and philosophy of science and technology	117	54	63	32	16	16	30	13	17
Public/applied history	37	17	20	88	31	57	7	1	6
Asian history	2	2	0	0	0	0	0	0	0
Military history	71	69	2	138	119	19	0	0	0
History, other	334	172	162	81	60	21	21	13	8
Theology and religious vocations	9,491	6,619	2,872	13,654	8,865	4,789	1,791	1,361	430
Bible/biblical studies	2,183	1,441	742	639	462	177	40	37	3
Missions/missionary studies and missiology	562	229	333	307	168	139	79	68	11
Religious education	806	417	389	526	226	300	45	29	16
Religious/sacred music	300	170	130	113	72	41	5	2	3
Theology/theological studies	962	669	293	3,954	2,620	1,334	446	345	101
Divinity/ministry	359	279	80	5,216	3,536	1,680	461	345	116
Pre-theology/pre-ministerial studies	171	135	36	2	2	0	0	0	0
Rabbinical studies	3	3	0	115	67	48	9	9	0
Talmudic studies	2,029	2,029	0	486	481	5	18	18	0
Theological and ministerial studies, other	348	201	147	747	458	289	297	231	66
Pastoral studies/counseling	506	347	159	676	292	384	118	82	36
Youth ministry	550	338	212	39	14	25	0	0	0
Urban ministry	27	10	17	26	12	14	15	10	5
Women's ministry	1	0	1	2	0	2	0	0	0
Lay ministry	123	78	45	88	43	45	0	0	0
Pastoral counseling and specialized ministries, other	158	64	94	200	99	101	21	18	3
Theology and religious vocations, other	403	209	194	518	313	205	237	167	70
Transportation and materials moving	4,710	4,136	574	839	672	167	11	10	1
Aeronautics/aviation/aerospace science and technology, general	2,370	2,116	254	570	477	93	11	10	1
Airline/commercial/professional pilot and flight crew	806	717	89	0	0	0	0	0	0
Aviation/airway management and operations	823	682	141	237	177	60	0	0	0
Air traffic controller	123	98	25	0	0	0	0	0	0
Flight instructor	12	10	2	0	0	0	0	0	0
Air transportation, other	38	37	1	26	14	12	0	0	0
Marine science/merchant marine officer	535	473	62	0	0	0	0	0	0
Transportation and materials moving, other	3	3	0	6	4	2	0	0	0
Visual and performing arts	91,262	35,296	55,966	17,523	7,565	9,958	1,774	812	962
Visual and performing arts, general	1,526	541	985	114	50	64	18	6	12
Digital arts	1,153	627	526	169	97	72	0	0	0
Crafts/craft design, folk art and artisanry	125	27	98	19	7	12	0	0	0
Dance, general	2,317	327	1,990	208	47	161	7	1	6
Ballet	39	6	33	0	0	0	0	0	0
Dance, other	40	3	37	0	0	0	0	0	0
Design and visual communications, general	2,699	861	1,838	449	144	305	0	0	0
Commercial and advertising art	1,228	417	811	87	31	56	0	0	0
Industrial and product design	1,758	967	791	207	110	97	0	0	0
Commercial photography	344	96	248	14	6	8	0	0	0
Fashion/apparel design	2,068	226	1,842	198	22	176	1	0	1
Interior design	2,777	278	2,499	338	54	284	0	0	0
Graphic design	5,017	1,702	3,315	199	66	133	0	0	0
Illustration	1,869	542	1,327	173	60	113	0	0	0
Game and interactive media design	1,285	965	320	151	91	60	5	1	4
Design and applied arts, other	589	214	375	250	83	167	13	1	12
Drama and dramatics/theatre arts, general	8,561	3,142	5,419	905	374	531	82	22	60
Technical theatre/theatre design and technology	623	270	353	157	69	88	0	0	0
Playwriting and screenwriting	274	126	148	318	151	167	0	0	0
Theatre literature, history and criticism	27	8	19	10	5	5	2	2	0
Acting	1,059	420	639	193	91	102	0	0	0
Directing and theatrical production	107	45	62	85	29	56	0	0	0
Musical theatre	636	247	389	14	4	10	0	0	0

See notes at end of table.

Table 318.30. Bachelor's, master's, and doctor's degrees conferred by postsecondary institutions, by sex of student and discipline division: 2016–17—Continued

Discipline division	Bachelor's degrees			Master's degrees			Doctor's degrees[1]		
	Total	Males	Females	Total	Males	Females	Total	Males	Females
1	2	3	4	5	6	7	8	9	10
Costume design	22	1	21	7	0	7	0	0	0
Dramatic/theatre arts and stagecraft, other	474	174	300	44	21	23	5	3	2
Film/cinema/video studies	3,659	2,019	1,640	768	432	336	44	16	28
Cinematography and film/video production	4,605	2,869	1,736	916	480	436	9	5	4
Photography	1,376	409	967	284	130	154	0	0	0
Documentary production	13	2	11	34	17	17	0	0	0
Film/video and photographic arts, other	746	414	332	59	21	38	2	0	2
Art/art studies, general	10,842	3,083	7,759	671	264	407	3	0	3
Fine/studio arts, general	9,120	2,732	6,388	1,311	515	796	0	0	0
Art history, criticism and conservation	2,345	339	2,006	828	126	702	228	52	176
Drawing	260	73	187	20	10	10	0	0	0
Intermedia/multimedia	1,151	663	488	55	16	39	0	0	0
Painting	567	163	404	155	56	99	0	0	0
Sculpture	221	78	143	51	20	31	0	0	0
Printmaking	147	38	109	36	11	25	0	0	0
Ceramic arts and ceramics	97	15	82	51	22	29	0	0	0
Fiber, textile and weaving arts	173	12	161	30	3	27	4	1	3
Metal and jewelry arts	113	11	102	34	3	31	0	0	0
Fine arts and art studies, other	611	161	450	275	77	198	2	1	1
Music, general	7,302	3,801	3,501	1,907	1,017	890	544	294	250
Music history, literature, and theory	101	49	52	28	16	12	13	7	6
Music performance, general	4,004	2,102	1,902	2,153	1,103	1,050	448	214	234
Music theory and composition	769	607	162	334	233	101	75	54	21
Musicology and ethnomusicology	46	27	19	59	29	30	58	22	36
Conducting	5	4	1	145	108	37	40	37	3
Keyboard instruments	150	64	86	236	82	154	47	16	31
Voice and opera	354	115	239	263	84	179	26	5	21
Jazz/jazz studies	332	274	58	203	166	37	12	11	1
Stringed instruments	180	68	112	222	96	126	23	12	11
Music pedagogy	54	13	41	65	23	42	16	7	9
Music technology	498	415	83	132	104	28	3	2	1
Brass instruments	32	25	7	45	39	6	3	3	0
Woodwind instruments	47	29	18	59	25	34	6	2	4
Percussion instruments	10	7	3	19	15	4	0	0	0
Music, other	1,236	774	462	254	154	100	10	6	4
Arts, entertainment, and media management, general	526	258	268	312	67	245	0	0	0
Fine and studio arts management	628	138	490	468	73	395	4	2	2
Music management	1,651	946	705	66	24	42	0	0	0
Theatre/theatre arts management	170	49	121	63	16	47	0	0	0
Arts, entertainment, and media management, other	95	37	58	300	179	121	0	0	0
Visual and performing arts, other	409	181	228	303	97	206	21	7	14
Not classified by field of study	0	0	0	0	0	0	0	0	0

[1]Includes Ph.D., Ed.D., and comparable degrees at the doctoral level. Includes most degrees that were classified as first-professional prior to 2010–11, such as M.D., D.D.S., and law degrees.

NOTE: Data are for postsecondary institutions participating in Title IV federal financial aid programs. Aggregations by field of study derived from the Classification of Instructional Programs developed by the National Center for Education Statistics.

SOURCE: U.S. Department of Education, National Center for Education Statistics, Integrated Postsecondary Education Data System (IPEDS), Fall 2017, Completions component. (This table was prepared September 2018.)

Table 318.40. Degrees/certificates conferred by postsecondary institutions, by control of institution and level of degree/certificate: 1970–71 through 2016–17

Year	Public institutions					Private institutions: Total					Private institutions: Nonprofit					Private institutions: For-profit				
	Certificates below the associate's	Associate's degrees	Bachelor's degrees	Master's degrees	Doctor's degrees[1]	Certificates below the associate's	Assciate's degrees	Bachelor's degrees	Master's degrees	Doctor's degrees[1]	Certificates below the associate's	Assciate's degrees	Bachelor's degrees	Master's degrees	Doctor's degrees[1]	Certificates below the associate's	Assciate's degrees	Bachelor's degrees	Master's degrees	Doctor's degrees[1]
1	2	3	4	5	6	7	8	9	10	11	12	13	14	15	16	17	18	19	20	21
1970–71	—	215,645	557,996	151,603	36,927	—	36,666	281,734	83,961	28,071	—	—	—	—	—	—	—	—	—	—
1971–72	—	255,218	599,615	167,075	40,297	—	36,796	287,658	90,126	30,909	—	—	—	—	—	—	—	—	—	—
1972–73	—	278,132	630,899	174,405	44,229	—	38,042	291,463	94,249	35,283	—	—	—	—	—	—	—	—	—	—
1973–74	—	303,188	651,544	184,632	45,018	—	40,736	294,232	97,442	37,573	—	—	—	—	—	—	—	—	—	—
1974–75	—	318,474	634,785	193,804	45,788	—	41,697	288,148	103,741	39,116	—	—	—	—	—	—	—	—	—	—
1975–76	—	345,006	635,161	206,298	47,517	—	46,448	290,585	111,179	43,490	—	—	—	—	—	—	—	—	—	—
1976–77	—	355,650	630,463	208,901	47,573	—	50,727	289,086	114,124	44,157	—	—	—	—	—	—	—	—	—	—
1977–78	—	358,874	627,903	202,099	47,553	—	53,372	293,301	115,888	44,792	—	—	—	—	—	—	—	—	—	—
1978–79	—	346,808	621,666	192,016	48,602	—	55,894	299,724	115,670	46,369	—	—	—	—	—	—	—	—	—	—
1979–80	—	344,536	624,084	187,499	48,550	—	56,374	305,333	117,697	47,081	—	—	—	—	—	—	—	—	—	—
1980–81	—	352,391	626,452	184,384	50,023	—	63,986[2]	308,688	118,253	47,993	—	—	—	—	—	—	—	—	—	—
1981–82	—	366,732	636,475	182,295	50,500	—	67,794[2]	316,523	120,152	47,338	—	—	—	—	—	—	—	—	—	—
1982–83	—	377,817	646,317	176,246	50,943	—	71,803[2]	323,193	120,169	48,392	—	—	—	—	—	—	—	—	—	—
1983–84	—	379,249	646,013	170,693	50,727	—	72,991	328,296	120,448	50,072	—	—	—	—	—	—	—	—	—	—
1984–85	—	377,625	652,246	170,000	51,489	—	77,087	327,231	123,472	49,296	—	—	—	—	—	—	—	—	—	—
1985–86	—	369,052	658,586	169,903	51,001	—	76,995	329,237	125,947	49,279	—	—	—	—	—	—	—	—	—	—
1986–87	—	358,811	659,260	167,797	51,216	—	77,493	332,004	128,733	47,261	—	—	—	—	—	—	—	—	—	—
1987–88	—	354,180	658,491	173,778	51,641	—	80,905	336,338	132,005	47,498	—	—	—	—	—	—	—	—	—	—
1988–89	—	357,001	675,675	179,109	51,963	—	79,763	343,080	137,517	48,608	—	—	—	—	—	—	—	—	—	—
1989–90	—	375,635	700,015	186,104	53,451	—	79,467	351,329	144,048	50,057	—	42,497	344,569	142,681	49,655	—	36,970	6,760	1,367	402
1990–91	—	398,055	724,062	193,057	55,235	—	83,665	370,476	149,806	50,312	—	45,821	360,634	146,161	49,841	—	37,844	9,842	3,645	471
1991–92	—	420,265	759,475	203,398	56,186	—	83,966	377,078	154,691	53,368	—	45,700	370,718	153,291	52,830	—	38,266	6,360	1,400	538
1992–93	—	430,321	785,112	213,843	57,020	—	84,435	380,066	161,189	55,052	—	47,713	373,346	159,562	54,399	—	36,722	6,720	1,627	653
1993–94	—	444,373	789,148	221,428	58,366	—	86,259	380,127	171,609	54,270	—	48,493	371,561	168,718	53,502	—	37,766	8,566	2,891	768
1994–95	—	451,539	776,670	224,152	58,788	—	88,152	383,464	179,457	55,478	—	48,643	373,454	176,485	54,675	—	39,509	10,010	2,972	803
1995–96	307,358	454,291	774,070	227,179	59,398	313,311	100,925	390,722	185,001	56,109	34,259	50,678	379,916	181,142	55,506	279,052	50,247	10,806	3,859	603
1996–97	326,687	465,494	776,677	233,237	61,081	272,237	105,732	396,202	192,023	57,666	35,560	49,168	384,086	186,963	56,864	236,677	56,564	12,116	5,060	802
1997–98	305,910	455,084	784,296	235,922	60,948	246,571	103,471	400,110	200,115	57,787	32,166	47,625	386,455	194,048	57,089	214,405	55,846	13,655	6,067	698
1998–99	304,294	452,616	792,392	238,954	60,028	251,589	112,368	409,847	207,084	56,672	29,402	47,757	394,749	198,481	55,663	222,187	64,611	15,098	8,603	1,009
1999–2000	294,912	448,446	810,855	243,157	60,655	263,217	116,487	427,020	220,028	58,081	28,580	46,337	406,958	209,720	56,972	234,637	70,150	20,062	10,308	1,109
2000–01	309,624	456,487	812,438	246,054	60,820	242,879	122,378	431,733	227,448	58,765	29,336	45,711	408,701	215,815	57,722	213,543	76,667	23,032	11,633	1,043
2001–02	319,291	471,660	841,180	249,820	61,061	264,957	123,473	450,720	237,493	58,602	32,904	45,761	424,322	223,229	57,707	232,053	77,712	26,398	14,264	895
2002–03	355,727	498,279	875,596	265,643	61,611	290,698	135,737	473,215	253,056	59,968	36,926	46,183	442,060	238,069	58,894	253,772	89,554	31,155	14,987	1,074
2003–04	364,053	524,875	905,718	285,138	64,205	323,734	140,426	493,824	279,134	61,882	35,316	45,759	451,518	250,894	60,447	288,418	94,667	42,306	28,240	1,435
2004–05	370,683	547,519	932,443	291,505	67,511	340,190	149,141	506,821	288,646	66,876	35,968	45,344	457,963	253,564	65,278	304,222	103,797	48,858	35,082	1,598
2005–06	370,570	557,366	955,370	293,535	70,036	344,220	155,949	529,734	306,327	68,020	35,909	46,459	467,697	261,203	66,066	308,311	109,490	62,037	45,124	1,954
2006–07	389,244	566,219	975,903	292,073	73,087	339,071	161,397	548,826	318,630	71,607	34,195	43,790	478,053	267,694	69,241	304,876	117,607	70,773	50,936	2,366
2007–08	399,741	578,661	996,769	300,019	75,551	348,613	171,505	566,965	330,825	73,639	33,915	45,014	491,016	275,971	70,473	314,698	126,491	75,949	54,854	3,166
2008–09	428,849	596,391	1,020,521	308,215	77,270	375,771	190,852	580,878	353,867	77,294	31,939	46,930	496,353	290,401	73,583	343,832	143,922	84,525	63,466	3,711
2009–10	472,428	640,265	1,049,179	322,389	78,805	463,291	208,591	600,740	370,924	79,785	35,652	46,673	503,264	300,053	75,172	427,639	161,918	97,476	70,871	4,613
2010–11	519,711	696,884	1,088,722	339,420	82,013	510,766	246,622	627,331	391,502	81,814	36,534	51,967	512,821	313,317	76,595	474,232	194,655	114,510	78,185	5,219
2011–12	525,264	756,484	1,131,885	349,349	84,730	463,797	265,234	660,278	406,618	85,487	32,856	54,347	526,022	325,175	79,498	430,941	210,887	134,256	81,443	5,989
2012–13	545,446	772,978	1,163,616	346,751	86,411	421,768	234,449	676,765	404,967	88,615	30,913	55,651	535,958	327,013	81,543	390,855	178,798	140,807	77,954	7,072
2013–14	576,468	794,925	1,186,742	346,238	88,911	392,810	210,230	683,408	408,344	88,676	30,738	53,127	544,253	333,539	80,894	362,072	157,103	139,155	74,805	7,782
2014–15	602,904	822,218	1,209,464	351,216	90,252	358,242	192,123	685,505	407,588	88,296	46,090	58,613	553,543	336,181	80,093	312,152	133,510	131,962	71,407	8,203
2015–16	615,137	848,081	1,240,423	364,619	90,030	324,154	160,147	680,327	421,138	88,104	40,010	56,595	560,834	350,790	80,067	284,144	103,552	119,493	70,348	8,037
2016–17	630,101	861,859	1,275,756	374,387	91,532	314,839	143,790	680,276	430,297	89,820	35,176	56,563	566,379	360,352	81,545	279,663	87,227	113,897	69,945	8,275

—Not available.
[1]Includes Ph.D., Ed.D., and comparable degrees at the doctoral level. Includes most degrees that were classified as first-professional prior to 2010–11, such as M.D., D.D.S., and law degrees.
[2]Part of the increase is due to the addition of schools accredited by the Accrediting Commission of Career Schools and Colleges of Technology.
NOTE: Data through 1990–91 are for institutions of higher education, while later data are for postsecondary institutions that participate in Title IV federal financial aid programs. Data for associate's degrees and higher awards are for degree-granting institutions. Some data have been revised from previously published figures.

SOURCE: U.S. Department of Education, National Center for Education Statistics, Higher Education General Information Survey (HEGIS), "Degrees and Other Formal Awards Conferred" surveys, 1970–71 through 1985–86; Integrated Postsecondary Education Data System (IPEDS), "Completions Survey" (IPEDS-C:87–99); and IPEDS Fall 2000 through Fall 2017, Completions component. (This table was prepared August 2018.)

Table 318.50. Degrees conferred by postsecondary institutions, by control of institution, level of degree, and field of study: 2016–17

Field of study	All institutions				Public institutions				Private nonprofit institutions				Private for-profit institutions			
	Associate's degrees	Bachelor's degrees	Master's degrees	Doctor's degrees[1]	Associate's degrees	Bachelor's degrees	Master's degrees	Doctor's degrees[1]	Associate's degrees	Bachelor's degrees	Master's degrees	Doctor's degrees[1]	Associate's degrees	Bachelor's degrees	Master's degrees	Doctor's degrees[1]
1	2	3	4	5	6	7	8	9	10	11	12	13	14	15	16	17
All fields, total	**1,005,649**	**1,956,032**	**804,684**	**181,352**	**861,859**	**1,275,756**	**374,387**	**91,532**	**56,563**	**566,379**	**360,352**	**81,545**	**87,227**	**113,897**	**69,945**	**8,275**
Agriculture and natural resources	8,207	37,719	6,844	1,561	7,861	31,571	5,401	1,468	338	5,515	1,332	93	8	633	111	0
Architecture and related services	503	8,573	7,911	291	476	5,933	4,729	220	27	2,551	3,127	71	0	89	55	0
Area, ethnic, cultural, gender, and group studies	420	7,720	1,717	349	415	5,309	1,016	224	5	2,411	701	125	0	0	0	0
Biological and biomedical sciences	5,550	116,759	16,284	8,087	5,458	81,459	9,229	5,325	87	35,062	7,041	2,762	5	238	14	0
Business	122,234	381,353	187,404	3,329	93,700	229,332	69,823	1,049	10,404	116,505	93,693	859	18,130	35,516	23,888	1,421
Communication, journalism, and related programs	7,377	93,778	10,128	615	7,056	67,873	4,195	491	97	24,977	5,603	124	224	928	330	0
Communications technologies	4,305	4,615	539	0	3,397	1,404	51	0	90	1,599	350	0	818	1,612	138	0
Computer and information sciences	31,162	71,420	46,555	1,982	24,682	44,982	25,883	1,326	1,626	17,987	17,831	535	4,854	8,451	2,841	121
Construction trades	5,308	153	0	0	4,528	153	0	0	189	0	0	0	591	0	0	0
Education	16,593	85,118	145,680	12,687	14,815	58,648	72,217	6,299	710	23,117	63,234	4,817	1,068	3,353	10,229	1,571
Engineering	5,915	115,640	52,841	10,371	5,803	90,841	35,541	7,653	27	24,687	17,204	2,718	85	112	96	0
Engineering technologies and engineering-related fields[2]	27,024	17,665	7,403	152	23,467	13,992	3,877	89	1,315	1,888	2,955	63	2,242	1,785	571	0
English language and literature/letters	2,870	41,317	8,247	1,347	2,728	28,282	4,847	994	11	12,344	3,262	353	131	691	138	0
Family and consumer sciences/human sciences	8,881	25,077	3,295	317	8,320	20,218	2,041	258	321	4,336	1,016	47	240	523	238	12
Foreign languages, literatures, and linguistics	2,363	17,642	3,274	1,168	2,344	12,798	2,335	759	19	4,814	939	409	0	30	0	0
Health professions and related programs	186,299	238,014	119,273	77,693	125,480	130,754	46,269	37,931	20,691	75,816	53,755	37,155	40,128	31,444	19,249	2,607
Homeland security, law enforcement, and firefighting	37,361	59,581	10,210	177	30,444	36,366	4,452	115	1,531	14,141	3,743	18	5,386	9,074	2,015	44
Legal professions and studies	6,900	4,272	8,674	35,123	4,988	2,406	2,289	12,780	546	1,261	6,197	21,430	1,366	605	188	913
Liberal arts and sciences, general studies, and humanities	386,658	43,841	2,485	95	375,193	30,797	1,138	47	9,959	12,744	1,291	29	1,506	300	56	19
Library science	158	109	4,843	42	158	73	4,033	39	0	0	810	3	0	36	0	0
Mathematics and statistics	3,454	24,073	9,086	1,925	3,446	16,359	5,496	1,393	8	7,696	3,590	532	0	18	0	0
Mechanic and repair technologies/technicians	20,827	303	0	0	14,561	166	0	0	2,352	137	0	0	3,914	0	0	0
Military technologies and applied sciences	1,093	469	274	0	1,055	165	52	0	0	273	222	0	38	31	0	0
Multi/interdisciplinary studies	30,780	49,658	9,234	854	29,404	34,599	4,636	572	469	11,363	3,962	282	907	3,696	636	0
Parks, recreation, leisure, and fitness studies	5,037	53,264	8,655	319	4,171	39,541	5,728	281	223	13,076	2,699	31	643	647	228	7
Philosophy and religious studies	1,002	9,712	1,705	741	304	4,398	568	295	698	5,261	1,137	445	0	53	0	1
Physical sciences and science technologies	9,223	31,268	7,143	6,027	9,159	22,426	5,368	4,343	64	8,841	1,775	1,684	0	1	0	0
Precision production	5,272	32	14	0	4,664	0	0	0	220	32	14	0	388	0	0	0
Psychology	11,286	116,861	27,542	6,702	10,661	80,098	8,987	2,665	395	34,160	14,738	2,737	230	2,603	3,817	1,300
Public administration and social services	7,591	35,464	45,393	1,116	5,748	23,337	26,715	558	986	9,437	16,486	322	857	2,690	2,192	236
Social sciences and history	21,392	159,099	20,015	4,706	21,248	109,858	10,252	3,074	71	48,359	9,085	1,617	73	882	678	15
Social sciences	19,636	135,041	16,579	3,781	19,546	93,527	8,045	2,493	46	40,894	8,129	1,273	44	620	405	15
History	1,756	24,058	3,436	925	1,702	16,331	2,207	581	25	7,465	956	344	29	262	273	0
Theology and religious vocations	1,619	9,491	13,654	1,791	1	5	0	0	1,602	9,200	13,458	1,784	16	286	196	7
Transportation and materials moving	1,547	4,710	839	11	1,124	2,530	127	3	381	2,179	712	8	42	1	0	0
Visual and performing arts	19,438	91,262	17,523	1,774	15,000	49,083	7,092	1,281	1,101	34,610	8,390	492	3,337	7,569	2,041	1

[1]Includes Ph.D., Ed.D., and comparable degrees at the doctoral level, as well as such degrees as M.D., D.D.S., and law degrees that were classified as first-professional degrees prior to 2010–11.
[2]Excludes "Construction trades" and "Mechanic and repair technologies/technicians," which are listed separately.
NOTE: Data are for degree-granting postsecondary institutions, which are institutions that grant associate's or higher degrees and participate in Title IV federal financial aid programs. To facilitate trend comparisons, certain aggregations have been made of the degree fields as reported in the Integrated Postsecondary Education Data System (IPEDS): "Agriculture and natural resources" includes Agriculture, agriculture operations, and related sciences and Natural resources and conservation; and "Business" includes Business, management, marketing, and related support services and Personal and culinary services.
SOURCE: U.S. Department of Education, National Center for Education Statistics, Integrated Postsecondary Education Data System (IPEDS), Fall 2017, Completions component. (This table was prepared August 2018.)

Table 318.60. Number of postsecondary institutions conferring degrees, by control of institution, level of degree, and field of study: 2016–17

Field of study	All institutions				Public institutions				Private nonprofit institutions				Private for-profit institutions			
	Associate's degrees	Bachelor's degrees	Master's degrees	Doctor's degrees[1]	Associate's degrees	Bachelor's degrees	Master's degrees	Doctor's degrees[1]	Associate's degrees	Bachelor's degrees	Master's degrees	Doctor's degrees[1]	Associate's degrees	Bachelor's degrees	Master's degrees	Doctor's degrees[1]
1	2	3	4	5	6	7	8	9	10	11	12	13	14	15	16	17
All fields, total	**2,701**	**2,445**	**1,924**	**1,016**	**1,234**	**686**	**543**	**350**	**654**	**1,339**	**1,160**	**596**	**813**	**420**	**221**	**70**
Agriculture and natural resources	506	780	234	106	481	343	180	97	24	425	50	9	1	12	4	0
Architecture and related services	71	194	161	42	68	120	106	32	3	71	53	10	0	3	2	0
Area, ethnic, cultural, gender, and group studies	74	470	146	60	71	234	97	40	3	236	49	20	0	0	0	0
Biological and biomedical sciences	292	1,377	507	270	272	539	341	185	19	832	165	85	1	6	1	0
Business	1,765	1,891	1,263	222	1,074	619	443	109	275	956	660	82	416	316	160	31
Communication, journalism, and related programs	318	1,183	363	81	288	464	225	63	18	680	133	18	12	39	5	0
Communications technologies	307	176	24	0	273	55	7	0	9	77	14	0	25	44	3	0
Computer and information sciences	1,272	1,412	549	176	896	535	301	118	95	669	180	55	281	208	68	3
Construction trades	363	6	0	0	325	6	0	0	12	0	0	0	26	0	0	0
Education	710	1,261	1,187	445	616	480	473	239	68	744	649	178	26	37	65	28
Engineering	387	558	339	215	369	302	225	152	10	244	111	63	8	12	3	0
Engineering technologies and engineering-related fields[2]	951	328	189	24	834	234	123	14	40	64	61	10	77	30	5	0
English language and literature/letters	209	1,338	499	153	198	521	324	105	9	808	173	48	2	9	2	0
Family and consumer sciences/human sciences	511	344	165	52	490	206	113	39	11	130	47	12	10	8	5	1
Foreign languages, literatures, and linguistics	205	896	220	98	200	406	164	65	5	488	56	33	0	2	0	0
Health professions and related programs	1,871	1,532	1,122	586	1,055	564	415	257	245	747	565	294	571	221	142	35
Homeland security, law enforcement, and firefighting	1,188	1,003	340	28	857	359	178	24	115	445	127	3	216	199	35	1
Legal professions and studies	568	252	173	217	381	83	66	87	46	122	96	119	141	47	11	11
Liberal arts and sciences, general studies, and humanities	1,388	918	165	15	1,095	391	89	7	284	507	74	7	9	20	2	1
Library science	31	8	63	10	31	7	51	9	0	0	12	1	0	1	0	0
Mathematics and statistics	220	1,187	352	182	216	502	265	129	4	683	87	53	0	2	0	0
Mechanic and repair technologies/technicians	715	18	0	0	636	11	0	0	23	7	0	0	56	0	0	0
Military technologies and applied sciences	10	18	10	0	8	6	3	0	0	10	7	0	2	2	0	0
Multi/interdisciplinary studies	418	991	393	135	386	406	216	96	28	549	163	39	4	36	14	0
Parks, recreation, leisure, and fitness studies	337	864	314	44	297	352	213	39	16	504	94	4	24	8	7	1
Philosophy and religious studies	87	902	230	117	67	316	92	58	20	585	138	58	0	1	0	1
Physical sciences and science technologies	368	1,114	331	221	356	482	245	154	12	631	86	67	0	1	0	0
Precision production	417	5	2	0	392	0	0	0	8	5	2	0	17	0	0	0
Psychology	258	1,476	699	341	220	532	332	166	22	888	335	147	16	56	32	28
Public administration and social services	360	815	565	135	299	363	308	87	33	411	202	46	28	41	55	2
Social sciences and history	302	1,364	471	201	271	535	320	139	19	813	145	61	12	16	6	1
Social sciences	284	1,276	402	186	256	518	268	129	17	744	128	56	11	14	6	1
History	160	1,226	348	142	153	497	273	97	6	723	74	45	1	6	1	0
Theology and religious vocations	116	417	373	158	1	1	0	0	114	413	371	154	1	3	2	4
Transportation and materials moving	106	88	15	3	92	54	7	1	9	33	8	2	5	1	0	0
Visual and performing arts	759	1,435	467	114	602	502	256	76	55	834	195	37	102	99	16	1

[1]Includes Ph.D., Ed.D., and comparable degrees at the doctoral level, as well as such degrees as M.D., D.D.S., and law degrees that were classified as first-professional degrees prior to 2010–11.
[2]Excludes "Construction trades" and "Mechanic and repair technologies/technicians," which are listed separately.
NOTE: Data are for degree-granting postsecondary institutions, which are institutions that grant associate's or higher degrees and participate in Title IV federal financial aid programs. To facilitate trend comparisons, certain aggregations have been made of the degree fields as reported in the Integrated Postsecondary Education Data System (IPEDS): "Agriculture and natural resources" includes Agriculture, agriculture operations, and related sciences and Natural resources and conservation; and "Business" includes Business, management, marketing, and related support services and Personal and culinary services.
SOURCE: U.S. Department of Education, National Center for Education Statistics, Integrated Postsecondary Education Data System (IPEDS), Fall 2017, Completions component. (This table was prepared August 2018.)

Table 319.10. Degrees conferred by postsecondary institutions, by control of institution, level of degree, and state or jurisdiction: 2016–17

State or jurisdiction	Public				Private nonprofit				Private for-profit			
	Associate's degrees	Bachelor's degrees	Master's degrees	Doctor's degrees[1]	Associate's degrees	Bachelor's degrees	Master's degrees	Doctor's degrees[1]	Associate's degrees	Bachelor's degrees	Master's degrees	Doctor's degrees[1]
1	2	3	4	5	6	7	8	9	10	11	12	13
United States	**861,859**	**1,275,756**	**374,387**	**91,532**	**56,563**	**566,379**	**360,352**	**81,545**	**87,227**	**113,897**	**69,945**	**8,275**
Alabama	10,102	24,490	9,687	1,894	194	3,854	880	670	2,746	3,568	2,176	21
Alaska	1,287	1,942	583	56	17	64	50	3	49	0	0	0
Arizona	18,827	29,311	9,214	1,959	209	849	557	742	10,983	26,225	16,503	864
Arkansas	8,153	13,445	5,576	928	383	2,621	536	94	64	41	37	0
California	139,033	152,488	32,244	7,077	1,980	40,549	37,542	9,892	10,330	18,813	9,594	2,367
Colorado	9,800	26,151	8,370	1,856	473	4,089	3,811	567	3,250	4,350	2,631	476
Connecticut	5,590	11,868	3,354	833	1,035	10,513	7,803	1,401	283	984	234	0
Delaware	1,943	4,559	1,077	338	139	2,297	2,843	80	9	17	18	0
District of Columbia	239	387	110	71	249	8,672	11,117	3,372	239	460	832	0
Florida	75,360	72,385	18,375	5,070	11,512	23,014	13,892	3,850	5,883	8,327	2,661	354
Georgia	16,302	39,121	11,500	2,668	1,018	9,965	4,985	1,821	2,022	2,901	2,471	374
Hawaii	3,947	4,735	1,040	482	480	1,723	516		25	354	177	55
Idaho	3,540	6,597	1,667	361	1,587	5,135	249	11	183	27	0	0
Illinois	35,752	33,048	13,428	3,131	921	31,514	25,234	5,350	3,055	11,530	5,112	385
Indiana	11,404	32,899	10,097	2,726	1,487	14,675	5,488	1,179	1,545	390	63	0
Iowa	11,796	13,490	2,714	1,431	342	9,680	2,859	1,321	3,051	4,532	2,742	99
Kansas	9,241	15,470	5,596	1,465	327	3,835	1,483	169	1,194	787	548	0
Kentucky	10,623	18,580	5,616	1,646	276	4,646	3,713	443	1,451	526	373	75
Louisiana	5,801	18,985	5,319	1,633	319	3,480	2,022	838	811	77	26	0
Maine	2,528	4,156	843	143	123	3,300	1,351	527	213	232	37	0
Maryland	16,507	27,680	10,909	1,990	9	6,056	8,324	850	361	414	272	0
Massachusetts	11,900	21,577	6,157	845	1,229	39,841	32,784	7,409	238	292	93	0
Michigan	25,301	48,014	17,352	4,572	2,749	13,055	4,548	1,068	232	272	160	0
Minnesota	15,612	21,453	5,541	1,752	734	11,126	5,407	1,071	1,581	4,202	13,516	2,523
Mississippi	13,213	13,028	3,461	1,115	70	2,178	1,699	306	214	13	16	0
Missouri	12,333	22,445	9,186	1,742	3,259	18,172	13,361	3,335	1,689	573	118	0
Montana	2,078	5,296	1,128	489	159	698	83	0	7	0	0	0
Nebraska	4,727	8,998	3,036	818	182	5,212	2,911	789	158	160	25	0
Nevada	5,638	8,151	1,700	538	66	418	366	553	465	375	121	0
New Hampshire	1,995	5,090	1,229	136	1,704	9,779	6,405	296	0	0	0	0
New Jersey	21,851	32,643	9,815	2,228	157	10,261	7,153	919	1,413	816	111	0
New Mexico	10,048	8,603	3,005	651	0	153	255	0	409	451	48	0
New York	52,161	65,438	18,538	3,019	7,052	70,337	53,257	11,272	6,293	3,961	1,356	1
North Carolina	31,539	39,513	11,909	2,796	982	14,752	6,296	2,342	1,366	682	457	0
North Dakota	2,104	5,737	1,389	458	98	660	293	96	147	30	0	0
Ohio	25,102	49,326	16,693	4,471	3,024	21,592	8,082	1,540	3,248	713	147	2
Oklahoma	10,375	17,225	5,030	1,402	226	3,803	1,631	305	960	113	15	0
Oregon	12,673	18,137	4,350	1,068	60	5,008	4,683	1,055	407	255	60	0
Pennsylvania	16,251	48,571	12,783	3,522	3,626	42,885	25,108	6,904	4,521	1,300	187	0
Rhode Island	1,661	4,778	823	265	1,692	7,384	2,116	479	0	0	0	0
South Carolina	9,954	19,130	4,794	1,491	330	5,754	1,030	169	975	947	369	165
South Dakota	2,069	4,659	1,243	393	67	1,161	320	2	183	248	0	0
Tennessee	11,103	22,330	5,842	1,963	723	12,796	5,944	1,859	1,712	675	394	159
Texas	85,631	107,560	41,250	8,550	1,493	20,735	11,046	2,475	4,517	2,523	751	47
Utah	11,776	16,242	3,716	887	1,324	20,195	9,469	223	603	425	169	167
Vermont	873	3,400	492	222	133	2,966	1,994	130	50	62	0	0
Virginia	18,571	37,944	11,058	3,371	1,547	16,752	11,448	1,949	4,069	3,867	2,152	135
Washington	29,568	26,341	6,482	1,912	141	7,323	3,516	724	508	554	92	6
West Virginia	3,508	9,227	2,875	1,095	139	1,439	393	138	2,809	5,678	3,062	0
Wisconsin	11,777	27,509	5,711	1,771	444	9,410	3,499	957	706	155	19	0
Wyoming	2,692	2,204	475	232	73	3	0	0	0	0	0	0
U.S. Service Academies	0	3,400	5	0	†	†	†	†	†	†	†	†
Other jurisdictions	**2,031**	**2,995**	**621**	**225**	**3,682**	**11,922**	**4,311**	**797**	**3,266**	**2,163**	**492**	**121**
American Samoa	220	8	0	0	0	0	0	0	0	0	0	0
Federated States of Micronesia	241	0	0	0	0	0	0	0	0	0	0	0
Guam	256	446	120	0	7	10	1	0	0	0	0	0
Marshall Islands	103	0	0	0	0	0	0	0	0	0	0	0
Northern Marianas	140	30	0	0	0	0	0	0	0	0	0	0
Palau	102	0	0	0	0	0	0	0	0	0	0	0
Puerto Rico	933	2,283	453	225	3,675	11,912	4,310	797	3,266	2,163	492	121
U.S. Virgin Islands	36	228	48	0	0	0	0	0	0	0	0	0

†Not applicable.
[1]Includes Ph.D., Ed.D., and comparable degrees at the doctoral level. Includes most degrees classified as first-professional prior to 2010–11, such as M.D., D.D.S., and law degrees.

NOTE: Data are for postsecondary institutions participating in Title IV federal financial aid programs.
SOURCE: U.S. Department of Education, National Center for Education Statistics, Integrated Postsecondary Education Data System (IPEDS), Fall 2017, Completions component. (This table was prepared January 2019.)

Table 319.20. Degrees conferred by postsecondary institutions, by level of degree and state or jurisdiction: 2014–15 through 2016–17

State or jurisdiction	2014–15				2015–16				2016–17			
	Associate's degrees	Bachelor's degrees	Master's degrees	Doctor's degrees[1]	Associate's degrees	Bachelor's degrees	Master's degrees	Doctor's degrees[1]	Associate's degrees	Bachelor's degrees	Master's degrees	Doctor's degrees[1]
1	2	3	4	5	6	7	8	9	10	11	12	13
United States	**1,014,341**	**1,894,969**	**758,804**	**178,548**	**1,008,228**	**1,920,750**	**785,757**	**178,134**	**1,005,649**	**1,956,032**	**804,684**	**181,352**
Alabama	13,629	30,060	11,800	2,429	12,882	31,123	12,074	2,432	13,042	31,912	12,743	2,585
Alaska	1,715	1,932	703	49	1,372	1,957	670	53	1,353	2,006	633	59
Arizona	37,703	58,534	27,785	4,368	33,564	56,625	27,353	3,607	30,019	56,385	26,274	3,565
Arkansas	9,095	15,881	4,899	971	8,767	16,019	5,277	1,041	8,600	16,107	6,149	1,022
California	133,600	201,195	74,640	18,308	143,571	203,797	77,468	18,820	151,343	211,850	79,380	19,336
Colorado	13,992	33,626	14,685	2,840	14,027	33,580	14,934	2,969	13,523	34,590	14,812	2,899
Connecticut	7,026	22,344	9,732	2,115	7,320	22,721	10,829	2,052	6,908	23,365	11,391	2,234
Delaware	2,039	6,895	3,112	541	2,064	6,988	3,903	418	2,091	6,873	3,938	418
District of Columbia	741	9,272	11,439	3,384	603	9,337	11,512	3,496	727	9,519	12,059	3,443
Florida	94,738	100,555	33,314	9,210	93,341	101,876	33,785	9,098	92,755	103,726	34,928	9,274
Georgia	19,529	49,863	17,219	4,584	19,815	50,827	18,557	4,751	19,342	51,987	18,956	4,863
Hawaii	4,403	6,966	1,856	624	4,571	6,922	1,917	527	4,452	6,812	1,733	537
Idaho	5,152	10,886	1,957	387	5,588	11,424	1,860	413	5,310	11,759	1,916	372
Illinois	40,187	74,317	40,080	8,757	40,410	75,716	42,129	8,860	39,728	76,092	43,774	8,866
Indiana	17,243	48,082	14,099	3,648	14,703	47,614	14,841	3,609	14,436	47,964	15,648	3,905
Iowa	16,772	28,202	8,298	2,851	15,639	27,761	8,341	2,721	15,189	27,702	8,315	2,851
Kansas	12,043	20,081	7,344	1,698	11,008	20,249	7,480	1,578	10,762	20,092	7,627	1,634
Kentucky	13,055	22,608	9,314	2,095	12,276	23,221	9,503	2,143	12,350	23,752	9,702	2,164
Louisiana	7,146	22,247	7,332	2,509	7,396	22,602	7,508	2,554	6,931	22,542	7,367	2,471
Maine	3,211	7,418	2,046	540	3,103	7,652	2,237	571	2,864	7,688	2,231	670
Maryland	16,919	33,197	18,428	2,994	17,003	33,883	18,829	2,821	16,877	34,150	19,505	2,840
Massachusetts	14,356	59,619	35,957	8,409	13,776	61,053	38,391	8,475	13,367	61,710	39,034	8,254
Michigan	32,572	59,970	20,689	5,875	29,787	60,305	21,675	5,576	28,282	61,341	22,060	5,640
Minnesota	20,141	36,750	22,827	5,092	19,526	36,588	23,884	5,433	17,927	36,781	24,464	5,346
Mississippi	13,320	14,296	5,070	1,294	13,759	14,702	5,029	1,344	13,497	15,219	5,176	1,421
Missouri	18,831	41,161	21,313	4,797	18,305	41,447	22,162	4,700	17,281	41,190	22,665	5,077
Montana	2,477	6,156	1,300	458	2,339	6,011	1,196	430	2,244	5,994	1,211	489
Nebraska	5,712	14,053	5,228	1,583	5,144	14,301	5,506	1,699	5,067	14,370	5,972	1,607
Nevada	6,059	8,519	2,266	1,052	6,097	8,638	2,229	1,016	6,169	8,944	2,187	1,091
New Hampshire	3,034	11,832	5,775	497	3,076	12,527	6,960	468	3,699	14,869	7,634	432
New Jersey	23,154	42,016	15,773	3,021	23,845	42,464	16,970	2,987	23,421	43,720	17,079	3,147
New Mexico	10,533	8,791	3,371	694	9,435	9,183	3,212	656	10,457	9,207	3,308	651
New York	68,302	136,396	70,803	14,524	66,966	139,136	71,571	14,668	65,506	139,736	73,151	14,292
North Carolina	31,876	52,889	17,237	4,835	32,108	53,537	18,162	4,607	33,887	54,947	18,662	5,138
North Dakota	2,309	6,291	1,706	511	2,222	6,298	1,625	569	2,349	6,427	1,682	554
Ohio	33,386	69,631	23,583	6,156	31,494	70,052	24,213	6,046	31,374	71,631	24,922	6,013
Oklahoma	13,047	20,730	6,532	1,626	12,027	21,024	6,576	1,662	11,561	21,141	6,676	1,707
Oregon	13,679	22,656	10,353	1,966	12,955	22,614	10,024	1,973	13,140	23,400	9,093	2,123
Pennsylvania	27,624	92,997	36,579	9,980	25,877	92,353	36,940	10,077	24,398	92,756	38,078	10,426
Rhode Island	3,606	11,730	2,571	724	3,291	11,989	2,676	716	3,353	12,162	2,939	744
South Carolina	11,767	24,823	5,990	1,890	11,517	25,107	6,068	1,892	11,259	25,831	6,193	1,825
South Dakota	2,479	5,638	1,538	407	2,236	6,040	1,538	437	2,319	6,068	1,563	395
Tennessee	12,822	34,197	11,807	3,661	13,225	35,255	11,841	3,670	13,538	35,801	12,180	3,981
Texas	79,409	122,173	48,800	10,987	86,838	126,128	52,585	10,978	91,641	130,818	53,047	11,072
Utah	13,221	32,160	9,982	1,237	13,367	34,118	11,081	1,263	13,703	36,862	13,354	1,277
Vermont	1,156	6,160	2,311	394	1,176	6,222	2,251	347	1,056	6,428	2,486	352
Virginia	25,554	56,878	23,790	5,365	25,123	58,642	24,665	5,258	24,187	58,563	24,658	5,455
Washington	29,998	33,309	9,498	2,584	30,591	33,598	9,750	2,591	30,217	34,218	10,090	2,642
West Virginia	6,497	15,997	6,524	1,055	6,479	16,519	6,244	1,160	6,456	16,344	6,330	1,233
Wisconsin	14,510	37,555	9,082	2,750	13,854	37,493	9,298	2,686	12,927	37,074	9,229	2,728
Wyoming	2,972	2,026	463	222	2,770	2,164	425	216	2,765	2,207	475	232
U.S. Service Academies	0	3,409	4	0	0	3,348	3	0	0	3,400	5	0
Other jurisdictions	**10,278**	**21,135**	**5,272**	**1,420**	**9,635**	**21,422**	**5,642**	**1,476**	**8,979**	**17,080**	**5,424**	**1,143**
American Samoa	245	8	0	0	216	17	0	0	220	8	0	0
Federated States of Micronesia	302	0	0	0	281	0	0	0	241	0	0	0
Guam	217	457	112	0	253	470	112	0	263	456	121	0
Marshall Islands	102	0	0	0	86	0	0	0	103	0	0	0
Northern Marianas	125	26	0	0	120	34	0	0	140	30	0	0
Palau	86	0	0	0	63	0	0	0	102	0	0	0
Puerto Rico	9,143	20,459	5,109	1,420	8,572	20,684	5,486	1,476	7,874	16,358	5,255	1,143
U.S. Virgin Islands	58	185	51	0	44	217	44	0	36	228	48	0

[1]Includes Ph.D., Ed.D., and comparable degrees at the doctoral level. Includes most degrees classified as first-professional prior to 2010–11, such as M.D., D.D.S., and law degrees.

NOTE: Data are for postsecondary institutions participating in Title IV federal financial aid programs. Some data have been revised from previously published figures.

SOURCE: U.S. Department of Education, National Center for Education Statistics, Integrated Postsecondary Education Data System (IPEDS), Fall 2015 through Fall 2017, Completions component. (This table was prepared January 2019.)

Table 320.10. Certificates below the associate's degree level conferred by postsecondary institutions, by length of curriculum, sex of student, institution level and control, and discipline division: 2016–17

Discipline division	Less-than-1-year certificates								1- to less-than-4-year certificates							
		Sex		Institution level		Institution control				Sex		Institution level		Institution control		
	Total	Males	Females	Non-degree-granting (less-than-2-year)[1]	Degree-granting (2-year and 4-year)	Public	Nonprofit	For-profit	Total	Males	Females	Non-degree-granting (less-than-2-year)[1]	Degree-granting (2-year and 4-year)	Public	Nonprofit	For-profit
1	2	3	4	5	6	7	8	9	10	11	12	13	14	15	16	17
Total	**492,653**	**230,044**	**262,609**	**97,922**	**394,731**	**377,195**	**13,351**	**102,107**	**452,287**	**174,669**	**277,618**	**150,999**	**301,288**	**252,906**	**21,825**	**177,556**
Agriculture and natural resources	4,826	2,977	1,849	91	4,735	4,639	44	143	2,467	1,618	849	180	2,287	2,258	130	79
Agriculture, agriculture operations, and related sciences	3,788	2,349	1,439	91	3,697	3,680	23	85	2,261	1,480	781	179	2,082	2,052	130	79
Natural resources and conservation	1,038	628	410	0	1,038	959	21	58	206	138	68	1	205	206	0	0
Architecture and related services	171	91	80	0	171	139	32	0	103	61	42	0	103	90	8	5
Area, ethnic, cultural, gender, and group studies	471	103	368	0	471	445	26	0	119	27	92	0	119	106	13	0
Biological and biomedical sciences	673	212	461	68	605	617	44	12	229	82	147	93	136	174	55	0
Business, management, marketing, and support services	62,013	22,307	39,706	2,039	59,974	56,073	990	4,950	21,158	6,197	14,961	2,378	18,780	18,752	895	1,511
Accounting and related services	11,315	3,381	7,934	498	10,817	10,522	115	678	5,130	1,200	3,930	570	4,560	4,629	350	151
Business/commerce, general	3,100	1,304	1,796	0	3,100	3,099	0	1	1,501	800	701	0	1,501	1,467	6	28
Business administration, management, and operations	18,233	7,381	10,852	76	18,157	16,878	127	1,228	4,449	1,589	2,860	55	4,394	4,305	46	98
Management information systems and services	539	377	162	29	510	413	118	8	109	75	34	33	76	98	0	11
Business operations support and assistant services	8,671	1,999	6,672	843	7,828	7,718	2	951	5,441	859	4,582	1,599	3,842	4,192	218	1,031
Business and management, other	20,155	7,865	12,290	593	19,562	17,443	628	2,084	4,528	1,674	2,854	121	4,407	4,061	275	192
Communication, journalism, and related programs	3,110	1,530	1,580	561	2,549	1,878	56	1,176	1,378	789	589	931	447	516	17	845
Communications technologies	2,572	1,488	1,084	248	2,324	2,233	7	332	2,937	2,163	774	1,347	1,590	1,448	28	1,461
Computer and information sciences and support services	29,309	21,327	7,982	2,065	27,244	24,808	324	4,177	8,951	6,907	2,044	2,015	6,936	7,272	179	1,500
Construction trades	13,395	12,641	754	2,217	11,178	11,558	559	1,278	12,474	11,926	548	3,664	8,810	8,905	831	2,738
Education	7,678	712	6,966	64	7,614	7,082	268	328	3,944	491	3,453	123	3,821	2,800	845	299
Engineering	866	735	131	282	584	670	7	189	333	296	37	109	224	324	9	0
Engineering technologies and engineering-related fields[2]	20,106	17,274	2,832	1,939	18,167	18,353	83	1,670	13,850	12,365	1,485	2,245	11,605	9,720	681	3,449
English language and literature/letters	1,189	419	770	286	903	889	171	129	442	168	274	75	367	135	32	275
Family and consumer sciences/human sciences	15,474	1,145	14,329	900	14,574	15,309	51	114	3,772	181	3,591	197	3,575	3,713	33	26
Foreign languages, literatures, and linguistics	1,560	340	1,220	0	1,560	1,432	128	0	695	143	552	6	689	693	2	0
Health professions and related programs	148,840	29,080	119,760	36,193	112,647	100,265	6,411	42,164	154,259	20,891	133,368	51,166	103,093	62,814	11,657	79,788
Dental assisting	6,124	541	5,583	1,746	4,378	1,423	357	4,344	12,552	1,032	11,520	4,537	8,015	4,007	887	7,658
Emergency medical technician (EMT paramedic)	17,222	10,766	6,456	1,192	16,030	16,796	110	316	5,629	4,097	1,532	383	5,246	5,322	177	130
Clinical/medical lab science	10,129	1,399	8,730	2,488	7,641	6,937	219	2,973	1,836	473	1,363	312	1,524	615	583	638
Medical assisting	11,044	780	10,264	4,851	6,193	2,674	46	8,324	45,899	3,939	41,960	17,147	28,752	5,898	3,631	36,370
Pharmacy assisting	3,199	628	2,571	1,324	1,875	1,541	240	1,418	5,039	1,001	4,038	1,312	3,727	1,577	387	3,075
Other allied health assisting	6,918	2,143	4,775	1,381	5,537	4,684	4	2,230	2,099	240	1,859	569	1,530	1,082	276	741
Nursing and patient care assistant	40,822	5,138	35,684	8,868	31,954	35,813	489	4,520	849	104	745	169	680	313	54	482
Practical nursing	5,031	574	4,457	902	4,129	4,612	0	419	40,537	4,158	36,379	13,900	26,637	27,352	1,189	11,996
Nursing, registered nurse and other	1,369	145	1,224	0	1,369	1,347	22	0	2,585	365	2,220	1,748	837	801	1,483	301
Health sciences, other	46,982	6,966	40,016	13,441	33,541	24,438	4,924	17,620	37,234	5,482	31,752	11,089	26,145	15,847	2,990	18,397
Homeland security, law enforcement, and firefighting	30,453	22,148	8,305	2,504	27,949	29,484	528	441	7,598	5,096	2,502	395	7,203	6,949	104	545
Criminal justice and corrections	22,941	15,660	7,281	1,341	21,600	22,223	397	321	6,369	3,998	2,371	381	5,988	5,769	55	545
Fire control and safety	6,522	5,896	626	1,130	5,392	6,504	0	18	1,082	998	84	14	1,068	1,082	0	0
Homeland security and related protective services, other	990	592	398	33	957	757	131	102	147	100	47	0	147	98	49	0
Legal professions and studies	1,821	339	1,482	48	1,773	1,217	255	349	2,470	388	2,082	381	2,089	1,971	217	282
Liberal arts and sciences, general studies, and humanities	3,795	1,450	2,345	0	3,795	3,787	8	0	63,806	24,910	38,896	0	63,806	63,734	72	0
Library science	203	34	169	0	203	203	0	0	45	5	40	0	45	45	0	0
Mathematics and statistics	195	156	39	0	195	177	18	0	26	21	5	0	26	26	0	0
Mechanic and repair technologies/technicians	36,097	33,970	2,127	3,650	32,447	33,970	290	1,837	47,122	44,940	2,182	21,165	25,957	23,260	2,131	21,731
Military technologies and applied sciences	15	13	2	0	15	1	0	14	2	2	0	0	2	2	0	0
Multi/interdisciplinary studies	2,048	815	1,233	0	2,048	1,739	91	218	1,238	687	551	0	1,238	1,229	9	0

See notes at end of table.

Table 320.10. Certificates below the associate's degree level conferred by postsecondary institutions, by length of curriculum, sex of student, institution level and control, and discipline division: 2016–17—Continued

Discipline division	Less-than-1-year certificates								1- to less-than-4-year certificates							
		Sex		Institution level		Institution control				Sex		Institution level		Institution control		
	Total	Males	Females	Non-degree-granting (less-than-2-year)[1]	Degree-granting (2-year and 4-year)	Public	Nonprofit	For-profit	Total	Males	Females	Non-degree-granting (less-than-2-year)[1]	Degree-granting (2-year and 4-year)	Public	Nonprofit	For-profit
1	2	3	4	5	6	7	8	9	10	11	12	13	14	15	16	17
Parks, recreation, leisure, and fitness studies studies	1,677	846	831	639	1,038	1,020	1	656	670	380	290	134	536	415	20	235
Personal and culinary services	39,879	5,296	34,583	29,251	10,628	11,305	417	28,157	72,114	10,912	61,202	57,022	15,092	13,689	885	57,540
Philosophy and religious studies	64	30	34	0	64	32	32	0	74	29	45	0	74	24	50	0
Physical sciences and science technologies	1,793	847	946	69	1,724	1,793	0	0	1,240	793	447	20	1,220	1,220	0	20
Physical sciences	192	105	87	0	192	192	0	0	27	18	9	0	27	27	0	0
Science technologies/technicians	1,601	742	859	69	1,532	1,601	0	0	1,213	775	438	20	1,193	1,193	0	20
Precision production	29,106	27,000	2,106	3,923	25,183	25,718	420	2,968	18,744	17,570	1,174	5,689	13,055	14,181	1,039	3,524
Psychology	136	20	116	0	136	120	16	0	85	21	64	0	85	85	0	0
Public administration and social services	2,321	455	1,866	1	2,320	1,835	82	404	836	145	691	0	836	734	86	16
Social sciences and history	1,137	623	514	3	1,134	1,038	99	0	460	239	221	0	460	408	52	0
Social sciences	1,114	615	499	3	1,111	1,015	99	0	450	233	217	0	450	400	50	0
History	23	8	15	0	23	23	0	0	10	6	4	0	10	8	2	0
Theology and religious vocations	230	122	108	0	230	3	225	2	895	387	508	395	500	1	894	0
Transportation and materials moving	22,072	20,084	1,988	9,578	12,494	11,254	847	9,971	1,014	947	67	338	676	666	20	328
Visual and performing arts	7,358	3,415	3,943	1,303	6,055	6,109	821	428	6,737	2,892	3,845	931	5,806	4,547	831	1,359
Fine and studio arts	895	326	569	763	132	104	683	108	2,068	742	1,326	8	2,060	2,029	38	1
Music and dance	336	242	94	0	336	274	5	57	549	326	223	166	383	130	183	236
Visual and performing arts, other[3]	6,127	2,847	3,280	540	5,587	5,731	133	263	4,120	1,824	2,296	757	3,363	2,388	610	1,122

[1]Non-degree-granting institutions do not offer accredited 4-year or 2-year programs for degrees at the associate's or higher level, but they may include institutions offering programs 2 years or longer in duration for lower level awards.
[2]Excludes "Construction trades" and "Mechanic and repair technologies/technicians," which are listed separately.
[3]Includes design and applied arts, drama and theatre arts, film and photographic arts, and all other arts not included under "Fine and studio arts" or "Music and dance."

NOTE: Data are for postsecondary institutions participating in Title IV federal financial aid programs. Degree-granting institutions grant degrees at the associate's or higher level, while non-degree-granting institutions grant only awards below that level.
SOURCE: U.S. Department of Education, National Center for Education Statistics, Integrated Postsecondary Education Data System (IPEDS), Fall 2017, Completions component. (This table was prepared March 2019.)

Table 320.20. Certificates below the associate's degree level conferred by postsecondary institutions, by race/ethnicity and sex of student: 1998–99 through 2016–17

Year and sex	Number of certificates conferred to U.S. citizens, permanent residents, and nonresident aliens								Percentage distribution of certificates conferred to U.S. citizens and permanent residents						
	Total	White	Black	Hispanic	Asian/ Pacific Islander	American Indian/ Alaska Native	Two or more races	Non-resident alien	Total	White	Black	Hispanic	Asian/ Pacific Islander	American Indian/ Alaska Native	Two or more races
1	2	3	4	5	6	7	8	9	10	11	12	13	14	15	16
Total															
1998–99	555,883	345,359	92,800	76,833	27,920	7,510	—	5,461	100.0	62.7	16.9	14.0	5.1	1.4	—
1999–2000	558,129	337,546	97,329	81,132	29,361	6,966	—	5,795	100.0	61.1	17.6	14.7	5.3	1.3	—
2000–01	552,503	333,478	99,397	78,528	28,123	6,598	—	6,379	100.0	61.1	18.2	14.4	5.1	1.2	—
2001–02	584,248	352,559	106,647	83,950	27,490	7,430	—	6,172	100.0	61.0	18.4	14.5	4.8	1.3	—
2002–03	646,425	382,289	120,582	95,499	32,981	8,117	—	6,957	100.0	59.8	18.9	14.9	5.2	1.3	—
2003–04	687,787	402,989	129,891	107,216	32,819	8,375	—	6,497	100.0	59.2	19.1	15.7	4.8	1.2	—
2004–05	710,873	415,670	133,601	114,089	32,783	8,150	—	6,580	100.0	59.0	19.0	16.2	4.7	1.2	—
2005–06	714,790	411,919	135,387	118,728	33,848	8,393	—	6,515	100.0	58.2	19.1	16.8	4.8	1.2	—
2006–07	728,315	420,199	139,796	119,375	32,963	8,781	—	7,201	100.0	58.3	19.4	16.6	4.6	1.2	—
2007–08	748,354	429,670	144,982	122,406	35,791	8,548	—	6,957	100.0	58.0	19.6	16.5	4.8	1.2	—
2008–09	804,620	450,562	161,487	138,301	37,941	9,485	—	6,844	100.0	56.5	20.2	17.3	4.8	1.2	—
2009–10	935,719	511,186	191,657	172,015	41,407	12,003	—	7,451	100.0	55.1	20.6	18.5	4.5	1.3	—
2010–11	1,030,477	557,595	207,693	187,433	44,294	11,204	14,999	7,259	100.0	54.5	20.3	18.3	4.3	1.1	1.5
2011–12	989,061	535,621	190,253	187,014	43,048	10,638	14,140	8,347	100.0	54.6	19.4	19.1	4.4	1.1	1.4
2012–13	967,214	524,000	177,006	186,248	44,196	10,824	17,642	7,298	100.0	54.6	18.4	19.4	4.6	1.1	1.8
2013–14	969,278	523,015	177,860	185,677	43,800	10,817	19,971	8,138	100.0	54.4	18.5	19.3	4.6	1.1	2.1
2014–15	961,146	512,077	174,828	187,943	44,707	11,084	21,681	8,826	100.0	53.8	18.4	19.7	4.7	1.2	2.3
2015–16	939,291	496,717	162,367	192,977	43,923	10,558	23,222	9,527	100.0	53.4	17.5	20.8	4.7	1.1	2.5
2016–17	944,940	492,699	158,960	202,602	44,832	10,895	24,681	10,271	100.0	52.7	17.0	21.7	4.8	1.2	2.6
Males															
1998–99	219,872	144,735	29,875	27,719	11,742	3,061	—	2,740	100.0	66.7	13.8	12.8	5.4	1.4	—
1999–2000	226,110	143,634	33,792	30,337	13,082	2,862	—	2,403	100.0	64.2	15.1	13.6	5.8	1.3	—
2000–01	223,951	143,144	34,381	28,685	12,072	2,719	—	2,950	100.0	64.8	15.6	13.0	5.5	1.2	—
2001–02	235,275	152,226	36,482	29,749	10,938	3,226	—	2,654	100.0	65.4	15.7	12.8	4.7	1.4	—
2002–03	254,238	161,001	40,080	33,925	12,930	3,506	—	2,796	100.0	64.0	15.9	13.5	5.1	1.4	—
2003–04	257,138	161,684	40,809	36,157	12,713	3,135	—	2,640	100.0	63.5	16.0	14.2	5.0	1.2	—
2004–05	259,261	161,126	41,644	38,297	12,448	3,068	—	2,678	100.0	62.8	16.2	14.9	4.9	1.2	—
2005–06	259,413	158,719	41,847	40,682	12,575	3,214	—	2,376	100.0	61.7	16.3	15.8	4.9	1.3	—
2006–07	269,470	164,856	44,862	40,932	12,621	3,524	—	2,675	100.0	61.8	16.8	15.3	4.7	1.3	—
2007–08	283,102	172,438	48,013	43,076	13,460	3,431	—	2,684	100.0	61.5	17.1	15.4	4.8	1.2	—
2008–09	302,449	179,813	53,879	47,860	14,427	3,856	—	2,614	100.0	60.0	18.0	16.0	4.8	1.3	—
2009–10	355,381	205,404	65,487	60,771	15,940	5,067	—	2,712	100.0	58.2	18.6	17.2	4.5	1.4	—
2010–11	391,676	223,755	71,867	66,514	16,944	4,760	4,884	2,952	100.0	57.6	18.5	17.1	4.4	1.2	1.3
2011–12	374,086	213,833	65,224	65,838	16,180	4,507	4,952	3,552	100.0	57.7	17.6	17.8	4.4	1.2	1.3
2012–13	375,928	215,432	61,668	67,377	17,352	4,446	6,511	3,142	100.0	57.8	16.5	18.1	4.7	1.2	1.7
2013–14	390,795	223,180	65,595	68,821	17,280	4,731	7,781	3,407	100.0	57.6	16.9	17.8	4.5	1.2	2.0
2014–15	394,707	222,413	64,574	72,020	18,132	4,848	8,836	3,884	100.0	56.9	16.5	18.4	4.6	1.2	2.3
2015–16	396,834	223,269	60,835	76,483	17,667	4,613	9,622	4,345	100.0	56.9	15.5	19.5	4.5	1.2	2.5
2016–17	404,713	224,918	60,022	81,710	18,009	4,965	10,286	4,803	100.0	56.2	15.0	20.4	4.5	1.2	2.6
Females															
1998–99	336,011	200,624	62,925	49,114	16,178	4,449	—	2,721	100.0	60.2	18.9	14.7	4.9	1.3	—
1999–2000	332,019	193,912	63,537	50,795	16,279	4,104	—	3,392	100.0	59.0	19.3	15.5	5.0	1.2	—
2000–01	328,552	190,334	65,016	49,843	16,051	3,879	—	3,429	100.0	58.5	20.0	15.3	4.9	1.2	—
2001–02	348,973	200,333	70,165	54,201	16,552	4,204	—	3,518	100.0	58.0	20.3	15.7	4.8	1.2	—
2002–03	392,187	221,288	80,502	61,574	20,051	4,611	—	4,161	100.0	57.0	20.7	15.9	5.2	1.2	—
2003–04	430,649	241,305	89,082	71,059	20,106	5,240	—	3,857	100.0	56.5	20.9	16.6	4.7	1.2	—
2004–05	451,612	254,544	91,957	75,792	20,335	5,082	—	3,902	100.0	56.9	20.5	16.9	4.5	1.1	—
2005–06	455,377	253,200	93,540	78,046	21,273	5,179	—	4,139	100.0	56.1	20.7	17.3	4.7	1.1	—
2006–07	458,845	255,343	94,934	78,443	20,342	5,257	—	4,526	100.0	56.2	20.9	17.3	4.5	1.2	—
2007–08	465,252	257,232	96,969	79,330	22,331	5,117	—	4,273	100.0	55.8	21.0	17.2	4.8	1.1	—
2008–09	502,171	270,749	107,608	90,441	23,514	5,629	—	4,230	100.0	54.4	21.6	18.2	4.7	1.1	—
2009–10	580,338	305,782	126,170	111,244	25,467	6,936	—	4,739	100.0	53.1	21.9	19.3	4.4	1.2	—
2010–11	638,801	333,840	135,826	120,919	27,350	6,444	10,115	4,307	100.0	52.6	21.4	19.1	4.3	1.0	1.6
2011–12	614,975	321,788	125,029	121,176	26,868	6,131	9,188	4,795	100.0	52.7	20.5	19.9	4.4	1.0	1.5
2012–13	591,286	308,568	115,338	118,871	26,844	6,378	11,131	4,156	100.0	52.6	19.6	20.2	4.6	1.1	1.9
2013–14	578,483	299,835	112,265	116,856	26,520	6,086	12,190	4,731	100.0	52.3	19.6	20.4	4.6	1.1	2.1
2014–15	566,439	289,664	110,254	115,923	26,575	6,236	12,845	4,942	100.0	51.6	19.6	20.6	4.7	1.1	2.3
2015–16	542,457	273,448	101,532	116,494	26,256	5,945	13,600	5,182	100.0	50.9	18.9	21.7	4.9	1.1	2.5
2016–17	540,227	267,781	98,938	120,892	26,823	5,930	14,395	5,468	100.0	50.1	18.5	22.6	5.0	1.1	2.7

—Not available.
NOTE: Includes less-than-1-year awards and 1- to less-than-4-year awards (excluding associate's degrees) conferred by postsecondary institutions participating in Title IV federal financial aid programs. Race categories exclude persons of Hispanic ethnicity. Reported racial/ethnic distributions of students by level of degree, field of degree, and sex were used to estimate race/ethnicity for students whose race/ethnicity was not reported. Some data have been revised from previously published figures. Detail may not sum to totals because of rounding.
SOURCE: U.S. Department of Education, National Center for Education Statistics, Integrated Postsecondary Education Data System (IPEDS), "Completions Survey" (IPEDS-C:99); and IPEDS Fall 2000 through Fall 2017, Completions component. (This table was prepared August 2018.)

Table 321.10. Associate's degrees conferred by postsecondary institutions, by sex of student and discipline division: 2006–07 through 2016–17

Discipline division	2006–07	2007–08	2008–09	2009–10	2010–11	2011–12	2012–13	2013–14	2014–15	2015–16	2016–17		
											Total	Males	Females
1	2	3	4	5	6	7	8	9	10	11	12	13	14
Total	**727,616**	**750,166**	**787,243**	**848,856**	**943,506**	**1,021,718**	**1,007,427**	**1,005,155**	**1,014,341**	**1,008,228**	**1,005,649**	**394,159**	**611,490**
Agriculture and natural resources	5,838	5,738	5,724	5,852	6,430	7,068	6,826	7,057	7,693	7,858	8,207	5,039	3,168
Agriculture, agriculture operations, and related sciences	4,638	4,554	4,525	4,615	4,925	5,400	5,227	5,420	5,975	6,158	6,438	3,836	2,602
Natural resources and conservation	1,200	1,184	1,199	1,237	1,505	1,668	1,599	1,637	1,718	1,700	1,769	1,203	566
Architecture and related services	516	568	605	553	569	593	468	425	491	478	503	332	171
Area, ethnic, cultural, gender, and group studies	164	169	174	199	209	194	271	363	382	419	420	181	239
Biological and biomedical sciences	2,027	2,200	2,337	2,664	3,276	3,834	4,185	4,557	4,883	5,266	5,550	1,749	3,801
Business	116,113	121,221	127,882	133,265	139,994	143,390	134,114	129,957	132,374	128,259	122,234	48,404	73,830
Business, management, marketing, and support services	100,015	104,631	111,524	116,798	121,735	123,014	114,842	113,056	113,681	110,036	108,353	43,299	65,054
Accounting and related services	14,234	15,963	16,707	17,925	20,180	20,270	18,061	17,400	16,080	14,790	13,751	4,027	9,724
Business/commerce, general	12,723	12,496	13,100	14,553	15,083	17,301	17,211	17,372	18,235	18,087	18,293	7,860	10,433
Business administration, management, and operations	43,660	47,910	52,938	46,086	46,253	45,879	49,816	50,121	52,668	52,758	53,927	24,416	29,511
Management information systems and services	2,007	1,232	1,103	1,221	1,244	1,164	1,085	1,176	987	935	954	661	293
Business operations support and assistant services	8,874	7,838	7,550	7,399	8,259	8,977	7,986	7,331	6,570	5,871	5,131	484	4,647
Business and management, other	18,517	19,192	20,126	29,614	30,716	29,423	20,683	19,656	19,141	17,595	16,297	5,851	10,446
Personal and culinary services	16,098	16,590	16,358	16,467	18,259	20,376	19,272	16,901	18,693	18,223	13,881	5,105	8,776
Communication, journalism, and related programs	2,609	2,620	2,722	2,841	3,051	3,495	4,299	4,970	6,034	6,759	7,377	3,202	4,175
Communications technologies	3,068	4,268	4,805	4,418	4,209	5,004	5,028	4,713	4,628	4,569	4,305	2,840	1,465
Computer and information sciences and support services	27,712	28,298	29,912	32,351	37,689	41,250	38,954	37,646	36,420	30,571	31,162	24,816	6,346
Construction trades	3,894	4,309	4,252	4,684	5,402	5,750	5,038	4,837	4,643	4,699	5,308	4,956	352
Education	13,021	13,111	14,123	17,346	20,460	20,762	18,744	17,605	17,178	17,032	16,593	1,882	14,711
Engineering	2,127	2,279	2,170	2,508	2,825	3,382	3,732	4,306	4,875	5,278	5,915	4,995	920
Engineering technologies and engineering-related fields[1]	29,177	29,359	30,441	31,883	35,519	36,642	33,752	31,792	31,958	27,243	27,024	23,278	3,746
English language and literature/letters	1,248	1,402	1,534	1,658	2,019	2,137	2,089	2,082	2,324	2,551	2,870	953	1,917
Family and consumer sciences/human sciences	9,123	8,614	9,035	9,515	8,532	9,506	8,996	8,669	8,750	8,930	8,881	360	8,521
Foreign languages, literatures, and linguistics	1,207	1,258	1,630	1,683	1,888	1,980	2,131	2,284	2,102	2,208	2,363	597	1,766
Health professions and related programs	145,146	155,794	165,015	177,321	202,920	219,491	214,040	208,885	200,018	191,442	186,299	29,779	156,520
Dental assisting	6,295	6,642	6,574	7,063	7,498	7,790	7,823	7,988	7,762	7,584	7,397	399	6,998
Emergency medical technician (EMT paramedic)	2,008	2,140	2,270	2,413	2,895	3,352	3,520	3,521	3,456	3,380	3,452	2,318	1,134
Clinical/medical lab science	2,306	2,316	2,538	2,621	2,811	3,240	3,387	3,517	3,143	3,186	3,062	769	2,293
Medical and other health assisting	23,492	24,291	25,858	29,776	39,277	46,950	41,921	39,126	36,813	34,749	32,285	4,826	27,459
Nursing and patient care assistant	158	329	385	1	33	36	35	38	50	52	56	2	54
Practical nursing	1,509	1,417	1,299	1,973	2,069	2,366	2,361	2,230	1,858	1,404	1,420	125	1,295
Nursing, registered nurse and other	66,578	73,398	77,922	81,281	83,023	84,569	86,380	86,435	82,953	78,577	77,073	10,895	66,178
Health sciences, other	42,800	45,261	48,169	52,193	65,314	71,188	68,613	66,030	63,983	62,510	61,554	10,445	51,109
Homeland security, law enforcement, and firefighting	28,160	29,485	33,012	37,154	44,922	51,318	48,460	45,771	43,041	39,930	37,361	21,010	16,351
Criminal justice and corrections	23,860	25,471	28,998	32,648	40,022	45,971	42,785	40,297	37,820	35,122	32,591	16,729	15,862
Fire control and safety	3,820	3,949	3,947	4,307	4,603	4,779	4,910	4,649	4,525	4,241	4,188	3,860	328
Homeland security and related protective services, other	480	65	67	199	297	568	765	825	696	567	582	421	161
Legal professions and studies	10,385	9,464	9,062	9,999	11,619	12,315	11,862	10,502	9,095	8,017	6,900	1,034	5,866
Liberal arts and sciences, general studies, and humanities	249,981	253,990	263,947	284,954	306,674	336,938	344,171	353,946	367,852	381,202	386,658	147,523	239,135
Library science	84	117	116	112	160	159	181	194	170	146	158	20	138
Mathematics and statistics	827	855	933	1,051	1,644	1,529	1,801	2,148	2,697	3,027	3,454	2,370	1,084
Mechanic and repair technologies/technicians	15,411	15,518	16,059	16,326	19,969	20,715	20,487	20,100	19,984	20,543	20,827	19,401	1,426
Military technologies and applied sciences	781	851	721	668	856	986	1,002	1,084	1,229	1,047	1,093	879	214
Multi/interdisciplinary studies	15,838	16,247	15,472	17,279	23,729	27,263	27,407	28,167	29,139	30,482	30,780	12,873	17,907
Parks, recreation, leisure, and fitness studies	1,251	1,345	1,587	2,006	2,366	3,123	3,455	4,383	4,669	4,771	5,037	2,955	2,082
Philosophy and religious studies	375	458	193	256	283	308	326	435	697	814	1,002	574	428
Physical sciences and science technologies	3,409	3,394	3,650	4,141	5,078	5,827	6,376	6,916	7,568	8,484	9,223	5,457	3,766
Physical sciences	2,019	1,979	2,196	2,378	3,148	3,652	4,083	4,518	5,040	5,528	5,838	3,376	2,462
Science technologies/technicians	1,390	1,415	1,454	1,763	1,930	2,175	2,293	2,398	2,528	2,956	3,385	2,081	1,304
Precision production	1,972	1,967	2,127	2,794	3,254	3,320	3,345	3,903	4,382	4,794	5,272	4,905	367
Psychology	2,213	2,411	3,957	6,582	3,866	4,717	6,122	7,604	8,780	10,603	11,286	2,673	8,613
Public administration and social services	4,340	4,194	4,177	4,522	7,472	9,222	8,788	8,914	8,436	7,988	7,591	1,052	6,539
Social sciences and history	7,080	7,812	9,157	10,649	12,772	14,132	15,668	16,554	17,916	20,056	21,392	7,981	13,411
Social sciences	6,673	7,358	8,670	10,108	12,072	13,321	14,749	15,473	16,631	18,451	19,636	6,880	12,756
History	407	454	487	541	700	811	919	1,081	1,285	1,605	1,756	1,101	655
Theology and religious vocations	608	582	676	613	758	839	881	944	1,135	1,089	1,619	992	627
Transportation and materials moving	1,674	1,550	1,430	1,444	1,698	2,098	2,119	2,102	1,810	1,497	1,547	1,338	209
Visual and performing arts	20,237	18,704	18,606	19,565	21,394	22,431	22,309	21,340	20,988	20,176	19,438	7,759	11,679
Fine and studio arts	1,755	1,706	2,019	2,277	2,414	2,339	2,541	2,699	2,866	3,082	3,315	1,090	2,225
Music and dance	2,288	1,317	1,152	1,335	1,356	1,683	1,743	1,715	1,886	1,989	1,993	1,217	776
Visual and performing arts, other[2]	16,194	15,681	15,435	15,953	17,624	18,409	18,025	16,926	16,236	15,105	14,130	5,452	8,678
Not classified by field of study	0	14	0	0	0	0	0	0	0	0	0	0	0

[1]Excludes "Construction trades" and "Mechanic and repair technologies/technicians," which are listed separately.
[2]Includes design and applied arts, drama and theatre arts, film and photographic arts, and all other arts not included under "Fine and studio arts" or "Music and dance."
NOTE: Data are for degree-granting postsecondary institutions, which are institutions that grant associate's or higher degrees and participate in Title IV federal financial aid programs.

Some data have been revised from previously published figures.
SOURCE: U.S. Department of Education, National Center for Education Statistics, Integrated Postsecondary Education Data System (IPEDS), Fall 2007 through Fall 2017, Completions component. (This table was prepared September 2018.)

Table 321.20. Associate's degrees conferred by postsecondary institutions, by race/ethnicity and sex of student: Selected years, 1976–77 through 2016–17

Year and sex	Number of degrees conferred to U.S. citizens, permanent residents, and nonresident aliens								Percentage distribution of degrees conferred to U.S. citizens and permanent residents						
	Total	White	Black	Hispanic	Asian/ Pacific Islander	American Indian/ Alaska Native	Two or more races	Non-resident alien	Total	White	Black	Hispanic	Asian/ Pacific Islander	American Indian/ Alaska Native	Two or more races
1	2	3	4	5	6	7	8	9	10	11	12	13	14	15	16
Total															
1976–77[1]	404,956	342,290	33,159	16,636	7,044	2,498	—	3,329	100.0	85.2	8.3	4.1	1.8	0.6	—
1980–81[2]	410,174	339,167	35,330	17,800	8,650	2,584	—	6,643	100.0	84.0	8.8	4.4	2.1	0.6	—
1990–91	481,720	391,264	38,835	25,540	15,257	3,871	—	6,953	100.0	82.4	8.2	5.4	3.2	0.8	—
1999–2000	564,933	408,822	60,208	51,563	27,778	6,474	—	10,088	100.0	73.7	10.9	9.3	5.0	1.2	—
2000–01	578,865	411,075	63,855	57,288	28,463	6,623	—	11,561	100.0	72.5	11.3	10.1	5.0	1.2	—
2002–03	634,016	438,261	75,609	66,673	32,629	7,461	—	13,383	100.0	70.6	12.2	10.7	5.3	1.2	—
2003–04	665,301	456,047	81,183	72,270	33,149	8,119	—	14,533	100.0	70.1	12.5	11.1	5.1	1.2	—
2004–05	696,660	475,513	86,402	78,557	33,669	8,435	—	14,084	100.0	69.7	12.7	11.5	4.9	1.2	—
2005–06	713,315	485,481	89,813	80,870	35,215	8,555	—	13,381	100.0	69.4	12.8	11.6	5.0	1.2	—
2006–07	727,616	491,333	91,440	85,275	37,243	8,579	—	13,746	100.0	68.8	12.8	11.9	5.2	1.2	—
2007–08	750,166	501,467	95,566	91,289	38,848	8,827	—	14,169	100.0	68.1	13.0	12.4	5.3	1.2	—
2008–09	787,243	521,834	101,631	98,408	41,364	8,823	—	15,183	100.0	67.6	13.2	12.7	5.4	1.1	—
2009–10	848,856	552,376	113,867	112,403	44,026	10,101	—	16,083	100.0	66.3	13.7	13.5	5.3	1.2	—
2010–11	943,506	604,745	129,044	126,297	45,489	10,180	11,126	16,625	100.0	65.2	13.9	13.6	4.9	1.1	1.2
2011–12	1,021,718	635,755	142,512	151,807	48,861	10,738	14,858	17,187	100.0	63.3	14.2	15.1	4.9	1.1	1.5
2012–13	1,007,427	617,308	135,892	157,989	49,474	10,546	19,383	16,835	100.0	62.3	13.7	15.9	5.0	1.1	2.0
2013–14	1,005,155	601,959	134,621	168,106	50,368	10,338	22,695	17,068	100.0	60.9	13.6	17.0	5.1	1.0	2.3
2014–15	1,014,341	590,616	137,920	180,598	51,767	9,996	25,505	17,939	100.0	59.3	13.8	18.1	5.2	1.0	2.6
2015–16	1,008,228	566,622	134,012	196,044	53,753	9,490	28,933	19,374	100.0	57.3	13.6	19.8	5.4	1.0	2.9
2016–17	1,005,649	551,033	129,874	209,138	55,801	9,268	29,630	20,905	100.0	56.0	13.2	21.2	5.7	0.9	3.0
Males															
1976–77[1]	209,672	178,236	15,330	9,105	3,630	1,216	—	2,155	100.0	85.9	7.4	4.4	1.7	0.6	—
1980–81[2]	183,819	151,242	14,290	8,327	4,557	1,108	—	4,295	100.0	84.2	8.0	4.6	2.5	0.6	—
1990–91	198,634	161,858	14,143	10,738	7,164	1,439	—	3,292	100.0	82.9	7.2	5.5	3.7	0.7	—
1999–2000	224,721	164,317	20,968	20,947	12,009	2,222	—	4,258	100.0	74.5	9.5	9.5	5.4	1.0	—
2000–01	231,645	166,322	22,147	23,350	12,339	2,294	—	5,193	100.0	73.4	9.8	10.3	5.4	1.0	—
2002–03	253,451	179,163	25,591	26,461	14,057	2,618	—	5,561	100.0	72.3	10.3	10.7	5.7	1.1	—
2003–04	260,033	183,819	25,961	27,828	13,907	2,740	—	5,778	100.0	72.3	10.2	10.9	5.5	1.1	—
2004–05	267,536	188,569	27,151	29,658	13,802	2,774	—	5,582	100.0	72.0	10.4	11.3	5.3	1.1	—
2005–06	270,139	190,174	27,618	30,043	14,227	2,777	—	5,300	100.0	71.8	10.4	11.3	5.4	1.0	—
2006–07	275,034	191,487	28,251	31,609	15,502	2,872	—	5,313	100.0	71.0	10.5	11.7	5.7	1.1	—
2007–08	282,695	194,354	29,984	33,852	15,941	2,989	—	5,575	100.0	70.1	10.8	12.2	5.8	1.1	—
2008–09	298,066	202,670	32,004	36,919	17,305	3,075	—	6,093	100.0	69.4	11.0	12.6	5.9	1.1	—
2009–10	322,747	215,977	36,148	42,210	18,268	3,555	—	6,589	100.0	68.3	11.4	13.4	5.8	1.1	—
2010–11	361,408	238,012	41,649	47,911	19,085	3,727	4,197	6,827	100.0	67.1	11.7	13.5	5.4	1.1	1.2
2011–12	393,479	251,964	46,377	57,926	20,537	3,924	5,569	7,182	100.0	65.2	12.0	15.0	5.3	1.0	1.4
2012–13	389,195	243,868	45,458	60,536	21,223	3,638	7,434	7,038	100.0	63.8	11.9	15.8	5.6	1.0	1.9
2013–14	391,474	239,289	45,868	64,658	21,824	3,682	8,969	7,184	100.0	62.3	11.9	16.8	5.7	1.0	2.3
2014–15	396,782	236,381	47,393	69,291	22,377	3,590	9,997	7,753	100.0	60.8	12.2	17.8	5.8	0.9	2.6
2015–16	392,084	226,142	44,777	74,531	23,426	3,335	11,251	8,622	100.0	59.0	11.7	19.4	6.1	0.9	2.9
2016–17	394,159	223,661	43,173	78,464	24,453	3,372	11,676	9,360	100.0	58.1	11.2	20.4	6.4	0.9	3.0
Females															
1976–77[1]	195,284	164,054	17,829	7,531	3,414	1,282	—	1,174	100.0	84.5	9.2	3.9	1.8	0.7	—
1980–81[2]	226,355	187,925	21,040	9,473	4,093	1,476	—	2,348	100.0	83.9	9.4	4.2	1.8	0.7	—
1990–91	283,086	229,406	24,692	14,802	8,093	2,432	—	3,661	100.0	82.1	8.8	5.3	2.9	0.9	—
1999–2000	340,212	244,505	39,240	30,616	15,769	4,252	—	5,830	100.0	73.1	11.7	9.2	4.7	1.3	—
2000–01	347,220	244,753	41,708	33,938	16,124	4,329	—	6,368	100.0	71.8	12.2	10.0	4.7	1.3	—
2002–03	380,565	259,098	50,018	40,212	18,572	4,843	—	7,822	100.0	69.5	13.4	10.8	5.0	1.3	—
2003–04	405,268	272,228	55,222	44,442	19,242	5,379	—	8,755	100.0	68.7	13.9	11.2	4.9	1.4	—
2004–05	429,124	286,944	59,251	48,899	19,867	5,661	—	8,502	100.0	68.2	14.1	11.6	4.7	1.3	—
2005–06	443,176	295,307	62,195	50,827	20,988	5,778	—	8,081	100.0	67.9	14.3	11.7	4.8	1.3	—
2006–07	452,582	299,846	63,189	53,666	21,741	5,707	—	8,433	100.0	67.5	14.2	12.1	4.9	1.3	—
2007–08	467,471	307,113	65,582	57,437	22,907	5,838	—	8,594	100.0	66.9	14.3	12.5	5.0	1.3	—
2008–09	489,177	319,164	69,627	61,489	24,059	5,748	—	9,090	100.0	66.5	14.5	12.8	5.0	1.2	—
2009–10	526,109	336,399	77,719	70,193	25,758	6,546	—	9,494	100.0	65.1	15.0	13.6	5.0	1.3	—
2010–11	582,098	366,733	87,395	78,386	26,404	6,453	6,929	9,798	100.0	64.1	15.3	13.7	4.6	1.1	1.2
2011–12	628,239	383,791	96,135	93,881	28,324	6,814	9,289	10,005	100.0	62.1	15.5	15.2	4.6	1.1	1.5
2012–13	618,232	373,440	90,434	97,453	28,251	6,908	11,949	9,797	100.0	61.4	14.9	16.0	4.6	1.1	2.0
2013–14	613,681	362,670	88,753	103,448	28,544	6,656	13,726	9,884	100.0	60.1	14.7	17.1	4.7	1.1	2.3
2014–15	617,559	354,235	90,527	111,307	29,390	6,406	15,508	10,186	100.0	58.3	14.9	18.3	4.8	1.1	2.6
2015–16	616,144	340,480	89,235	121,513	30,327	6,155	17,682	10,752	100.0	56.2	14.7	20.1	5.0	1.0	2.9
2016–17	611,490	327,372	86,701	130,674	31,348	5,896	17,954	11,545	100.0	54.6	14.5	21.8	5.2	1.0	3.0

—Not available.
[1]Excludes 1,170 males and 251 females whose racial/ethnic group was not available.
[2]Excludes 4,819 males and 1,384 females whose racial/ethnic group was not available.
NOTE: Data through 1990–91 are for institutions of higher education, while later data are for degree-granting postsecondary institutions, which are institutions that grant associate's or higher degrees and participate in Title IV federal financial aid programs. Race categories exclude persons of Hispanic ethnicity. For 1989–90 and later years, reported racial/ethnic distributions of students by level of degree, field of degree, and sex were used to estimate race/ethnicity for students whose race/ethnicity was not reported. Detail may not sum to totals because of rounding. Some data have been revised from previously published figures.
SOURCE: U.S. Department of Education, National Center for Education Statistics, Higher Education General Information Survey (HEGIS), "Degrees and Other Formal Awards Conferred" surveys, 1976–77 and 1980–81; Integrated Postsecondary Education Data System (IPEDS), "Completions Survey" (IPEDS-C:90–99); and IPEDS Fall 2000 through Fall 2017, Completions component. (This table was prepared August 2018.)

Table 321.30. Associate's degrees conferred by postsecondary institutions, by race/ethnicity and field of study: 2015–16 and 2016–17

Field of study	2015–16										2016–17									
					Asian/Pacific Islander										Asian/Pacific Islander					
	Total	White	Black	Hispanic	Total	Asian	Pacific Islander	American Indian/ Alaska Native	Two or more races	Non-resident alien	Total	White	Black	Hispanic	Total	Asian	Pacific Islander	American Indian/ Alaska Native	Two or more races	Non-resident alien
1	2	3	4	5	6	7	8	9	10	11	12	13	14	15	16	17	18	19	20	21
All fields, total	**1,008,228**	**566,622**	**134,012**	**196,044**	**53,753**	**50,498**	**3,255**	**9,490**	**28,933**	**19,374**	**1,005,649**	**551,033**	**129,874**	**209,138**	**55,801**	**52,622**	**3,179**	**9,268**	**29,630**	**20,905**
Agriculture and natural resources	7,858	6,885	124	473	47	43	4	113	170	46	8,207	7,188	127	524	65	56	9	107	153	43
Architecture and related services	478	187	26	212	30	29	1	2	6	15	503	195	26	211	31	31	0	1	17	22
Area, ethnic, cultural, gender, and group studies	419	101	42	106	29	10	19	83	45	13	420	115	47	118	30	19	11	66	37	7
Biological and biomedical sciences	5,266	2,270	451	1,601	618	605	13	57	155	114	5,550	2,213	473	1,783	682	670	12	66	194	139
Business	128,259	66,827	20,774	22,368	8,946	8,521	425	1,365	3,648	4,331	122,234	61,941	18,947	23,188	8,963	8,536	427	1,205	3,430	4,560
Communication, journalism, and related programs	6,759	2,914	702	2,142	469	447	22	29	292	211	7,377	3,035	856	2,433	541	519	22	39	276	197
Communications technologies	4,569	2,492	737	838	181	170	11	44	193	84	4,305	2,384	663	778	169	161	8	31	154	126
Computer and information sciences	30,571	18,483	4,162	3,862	2,169	2,080	89	294	928	673	31,162	18,457	4,037	4,278	2,389	2,280	109	270	947	784
Construction trades	4,699	3,319	500	479	185	165	20	70	135	11	5,308	3,660	519	507	275	230	45	125	198	24
Education	17,032	9,646	2,550	3,524	322	293	29	449	372	169	16,593	9,254	2,442	3,574	400	359	41	365	397	161
Engineering	5,278	2,962	423	993	483	465	18	29	151	237	5,915	3,162	407	1,204	589	582	7	48	152	353
Engineering technologies and engineering-related fields[1]	27,243	18,862	2,841	3,275	990	930	60	282	622	371	27,024	18,694	2,688	3,294	1,001	920	81	257	645	445
English language and literature/letters	2,551	1,087	160	941	184	174	10	17	113	49	2,870	1,154	200	1,110	219	214	5	12	124	51
Family and consumer sciences/human sciences	8,930	4,053	1,647	2,431	428	411	17	94	159	118	8,881	3,776	1,500	2,791	411	392	19	93	187	123
Foreign languages, literatures, and linguistics	2,208	988	96	874	98	95	3	19	90	43	2,363	1,026	106	991	92	88	4	10	84	54
Health professions and related programs	191,442	122,134	27,441	25,484	9,088	8,437	651	1,736	4,449	1,110	186,299	115,545	27,390	26,827	9,130	8,536	594	1,759	4,487	1,161
Homeland security, law enforcement, and firefighting	39,930	20,334	6,375	10,623	1,036	907	129	338	1,031	193	37,361	18,629	5,477	10,836	1,059	923	136	314	881	165
Legal professions and studies	8,017	4,747	1,321	1,464	176	167	9	64	192	53	6,900	4,022	1,071	1,348	160	141	19	64	175	60
Liberal arts and sciences, general studies, and humanities	381,202	210,214	50,191	79,870	18,015	16,833	1,182	3,117	11,515	8,280	386,658	208,656	49,495	85,556	18,676	17,549	1,127	3,147	12,303	8,825
Library science	146	107	4	25	6	6	0	0	3	1	158	109	10	25	7	7	0	2	5	0
Mathematics and statistics	3,027	1,108	104	1,038	496	489	7	14	112	155	3,454	1,221	108	1,149	629	615	14	15	121	211
Mechanic and repair technologies/technicians	20,543	13,749	1,816	3,261	714	606	108	260	536	207	20,827	13,823	1,828	3,469	700	608	92	268	522	217
Military technologies and applied sciences	1,047	648	158	134	45	40	5	14	48	0	1,093	702	144	141	50	43	7	11	45	0
Multi/interdisciplinary studies	30,482	14,624	2,438	8,058	3,471	3,350	121	182	1,119	590	30,780	13,961	2,416	8,875	3,643	3,567	76	153	1,096	636
Parks, recreation, leisure, and fitness studies	4,771	2,376	453	1,271	377	357	20	38	187	69	5,037	2,242	489	1,606	394	366	28	38	188	80
Philosophy and religious studies	814	554	90	106	17	15	2	2	22	23	1,002	719	78	123	31	29	2	4	23	24
Physical sciences and science technologies	8,484	3,948	852	1,930	984	946	38	73	293	404	9,223	4,223	943	2,138	1,036	1,011	25	73	312	498
Precision production	4,794	3,757	231	513	122	112	10	54	100	17	5,272	3,988	257	664	140	125	15	82	129	12
Psychology	10,603	3,691	855	4,665	778	736	42	130	382	102	11,286	3,759	864	5,085	891	844	47	117	446	124
Public administration and social services	7,988	3,690	2,373	1,325	151	143	8	142	244	63	7,591	3,420	2,206	1,475	121	99	22	140	191	38
Social sciences and history	20,056	7,306	1,668	7,694	1,901	1,794	107	190	862	435	21,392	7,467	1,715	8,635	1,973	1,870	103	209	913	480
Social sciences	18,451	6,513	1,615	7,098	1,822	1,718	104	169	806	428	19,636	6,586	1,661	7,983	1,894	1,795	99	199	841	472
History	1,605	793	53	596	79	76	3	21	56	7	1,756	881	54	652	79	75	4	10	72	8
Theology and religious vocations	1,089	680	265	84	12	8	4	11	24	13	1,619	1,144	288	98	29	27	2	16	29	15
Transportation and materials moving	1,497	928	105	225	75	69	6	11	63	90	1,547	948	116	230	107	91	16	10	51	85
Visual and performing arts	20,176	10,951	2,037	4,155	1,110	1,045	65	167	672	1,084	19,438	10,201	1,941	4,074	1,168	1,114	54	151	718	1,185
Other and not classified	0	0	0	0	0	0	0	0	0	0	0	0	0	0	0	0	0	0	0	0

[1]Excludes "Construction trades" and "Mechanic and repair technologies/technicians," which are listed separately.

NOTE: Data are for degree-granting postsecondary institutions, which are institutions that grant associate's or higher degrees and participate in Title IV federal financial aid programs. Race categories exclude persons of Hispanic ethnicity. Reported racial/ethnic distributions of students by level of degree, field of degree, and sex were used to estimate race/ethnicity for students whose race/ethnicity was not reported. To facilitate trend comparisons, certain aggregations have been made of the degree fields as reported in the Integrated Postsecondary Education Data System (IPEDS): "Agriculture and natural resources" includes Agriculture, agriculture operations, and related sciences and Natural resources and conservation; and "Business" includes Business management, marketing, and related support services and Personal and culinary services. Some data have been revised from previously published figures.

SOURCE: U.S. Department of Education, National Center for Education Statistics, Integrated Postsecondary Education Data System (IPEDS), Fall 2016 and Fall 2017, Completions component. (This table was prepared August 2018.)

Table 322.10. Bachelor's degrees conferred by postsecondary institutions, by field of study: Selected years, 1970–71 through 2016–17

Field of study	1970–71	1975–76	1980–81	1985–86	1990–91	1995–96	2000–01	2005–06	2006–07	2008–09	2009–10	2010–11	2011–12	2012–13	2013–14	2014–15	2015–16	2016–17
1	2	3	4	5	6	7	8	9	10	11	12	13	14	15	16	17	18	19
Total	**839,730**	**925,746**	**935,140**	**987,823**	**1,094,538**	**1,164,792**	**1,244,171**	**1,485,104**	**1,524,729**	**1,601,399**	**1,649,919**	**1,716,053**	**1,792,163**	**1,840,381**	**1,870,150**	**1,894,969**	**1,920,750**	**1,956,032**
Agriculture and natural resources	12,672	19,402	21,886	16,823	13,124	21,425	23,370	23,052	23,144	24,982	26,343	28,630	30,972	33,592	35,125	36,278	36,995	37,719
Architecture and related services	5,570	9,146	9,455	9,119	9,781	8,352	8,480	9,515	9,717	10,119	10,051	9,831	9,727	9,757	9,149	9,090	8,825	8,573
Area, ethnic, cultural, gender, and group studies	2,579	3,577	2,887	3,021	4,776	5,633	6,160	7,878	8,196	8,772	8,620	8,955	9,228	8,850	8,275	7,783	7,840	7,720
Biological and biomedical sciences	35,705	54,154	43,078	38,395	39,482	61,014	60,576	70,602	76,809	82,828	86,391	89,984	95,850	100,397	104,657	109,904	113,794	116,759
Business	115,396	143,171	200,521	236,700	249,165	226,623	263,515	318,043	327,850	348,056	358,119	365,133	367,235	360,887	358,132	363,741	371,690	381,353
Communication, journalism, and related programs	10,324	20,045	29,428	41,666	51,650	47,320	58,013	73,658	74,800	77,984	81,280	83,231	83,771	84,818	87,612	90,658	92,551	93,778
Communications technologies	478	1,237	1,854	1,479	1,397	853	1,178	2,987	3,642	5,100	4,782	4,858	4,983	4,987	4,991	5,135	4,824	4,615
Computer and information sciences	2,388	5,652	15,121	42,337	25,159	24,506	44,142	47,702	42,164	37,992	39,593	43,066	47,406	50,961	55,271	59,586	64,402	71,420
Education	176,307	154,437	108,074	87,147	110,807	105,384	105,458	107,235	105,683	101,716	101,287	104,008	105,656	104,698	98,838	91,596	87,221	85,118
Engineering	45,034	38,733	63,642	77,391	62,448	62,168	58,209	66,841	66,875	68,911	72,657	76,356	81,371	85,987	92,169	97,852	106,789	115,640
Engineering technologies	5,148	7,943	11,713	19,731	17,303	15,829	14,660	14,565	14,993	15,493	16,078	16,741	17,283	17,010	16,807	17,253	17,159	18,121
English language and literature/letters	63,914	41,452	31,922	34,083	51,064	49,928	50,569	55,094	55,125	55,465	53,229	52,754	53,765	52,401	50,464	45,851	42,797	41,317
Family and consumer sciences/human sciences	11,167	17,409	18,370	13,847	13,920	14,353	16,421	20,775	21,416	21,906	21,832	22,438	23,441	23,930	24,689	24,584	25,389	25,077
Foreign languages, literatures, and linguistics	20,988	17,068	11,638	11,550	13,937	14,832	16,128	19,393	20,278	21,169	21,507	21,705	21,756	21,647	20,332	19,493	18,436	17,642
Health professions and related programs	25,223	53,885	63,665	65,309	59,875	86,087	75,933	91,973	101,898	120,420	129,623	143,463	163,675	181,149	198,777	216,228	228,907	238,014
Homeland security, law enforcement, and firefighting	2,045	12,507	13,707	12,704	16,806	24,810	25,211	35,319	39,216	41,788	43,613	47,600	54,091	60,264	62,416	62,723	61,159	59,581
Legal professions and studies	545	531	776	1,223	1,827	2,123	1,991	3,302	3,596	3,822	3,886	4,429	4,595	4,425	4,513	4,420	4,243	4,272
Liberal arts and sciences, general studies, and humanities	7,481	18,855	21,643	21,336	30,526	33,997	37,962	44,898	44,268	47,095	46,963	46,717	46,961	46,790	45,281	43,649	43,669	43,841
Library science	1,013	843	375	155	90	58	52	76	82	78	85	96	95	102	127	99	85	109
Mathematics and statistics	24,801	15,984	11,078	16,122	14,393	12,713	11,171	14,760	14,958	15,507	16,029	17,182	18,841	20,449	20,987	21,854	22,778	24,073
Military technologies and applied sciences	357	952	42	255	183	7	21	33	168	55	56	64	86	105	185	276	358	469
Multi/interdisciplinary studies	6,324	13,709	12,986	13,754	17,774	26,885	26,478	30,583	32,118	35,376	37,717	42,473	45,717	47,658	48,392	47,556	48,833	49,658
Parks, recreation, leisure, and fitness studies	1,621	5,182	5,729	4,623	4,315	12,974	17,948	25,489	27,430	31,683	33,332	35,934	38,998	42,628	46,047	49,008	50,912	53,264
Philosophy and religious studies	8,149	8,447	6,776	6,396	7,423	7,541	8,717	11,980	11,973	12,448	12,503	12,830	12,645	12,792	11,999	11,071	10,155	9,712
Physical sciences and science technologies	21,410	21,458	23,936	21,711	16,334	19,716	18,025	20,521	21,295	22,691	23,381	24,705	26,664	28,053	29,307	30,042	30,483	31,268
Precision production	0	0	0	2	2	12	31	55	23	29	29	43	37	36	37	48	51	32
Psychology	38,187	50,278	41,068	40,628	58,655	73,416	73,645	88,132	90,073	94,273	97,215	100,906	109,099	114,446	117,312	117,573	117,447	116,861
Public administration and social services	5,466	15,440	16,707	11,887	14,350	19,849	19,447	21,986	23,147	23,852	25,421	26,799	29,695	31,950	33,483	34,364	34,433	35,464
Social sciences and history	155,324	126,396	100,513	93,840	125,107	126,479	128,036	161,468	164,229	168,517	172,782	177,169	178,534	177,767	173,132	166,971	161,211	159,099
Theology and religious vocations	3,720	5,490	5,808	5,510	4,799	5,292	6,945	8,548	8,696	8,940	8,719	9,073	9,304	9,385	9,642	9,713	9,804	9,491
Transportation and materials moving	0	225	263	1,838	2,622	3,561	3,748	5,349	5,657	5,189	4,998	4,941	4,876	4,661	4,588	4,730	4,531	4,710
Visual and performing arts	30,394	42,138	40,479	37,241	42,186	49,296	61,148	83,292	85,210	89,143	91,798	93,939	95,806	97,799	97,414	95,840	92,979	91,262
Not classified by field of study	0	0	0	0	13,258	1,756	783	0	0	0	0	0	0	0	0	0	0	0

NOTE: Data through 1990–91 are for institutions of higher education, while later data are for postsecondary institutions that participate in Title IV federal financial aid programs. The new Classification of Instructional Programs was initiated in 2009–10. The figures for earlier years have been reclassified when necessary to make them conform to the new taxonomy. To facilitate trend comparisons, certain aggregations have been made of the degree fields as reported in the Integrated Postsecondary Education Data System (IPEDS): "Agriculture and natural resources" includes Agriculture, agriculture operations, and related sciences and Natural resources and conservation; "Business" includes Business, management, marketing, and related support services and Personal and culinary services; and "Engineering technologies" includes Engineering technologies and engineering-related fields, Construction trades, and Mechanic and repair technologies/technicians. Some data have been revised from previously published figures.

SOURCE: U.S. Department of Education, National Center for Education Statistics, Higher Education General Information Survey (HEGIS), "Degrees and Other Formal Awards Conferred" surveys, 1970–71 through 1985–86; Integrated Postsecondary Education Data System (IPEDS), "Completions Survey" (IPEDS-C:91–99); and IPEDS Fall 2000 through Fall 2017, Completions component. (This table was prepared August 2018.)

Table 322.20. Bachelor's degrees conferred by postsecondary institutions, by race/ethnicity and sex of student: Selected years, 1976–77 through 2016–17

Year and sex	Number of degrees conferred to U.S. citizens, permanent residents, and nonresident aliens								Percentage distribution of degrees conferred to U.S. citizens and permanent residents						
	Total	White	Black	Hispanic	Asian/ Pacific Islander	American Indian/ Alaska Native	Two or more races	Non-resident alien	Total	White	Black	Hispanic	Asian/ Pacific Islander	American Indian/ Alaska Native	Two or more races
1	2	3	4	5	6	7	8	9	10	11	12	13	14	15	16
Total															
1976–77[1]	917,900	807,688	58,636	18,743	13,793	3,326	—	15,714	100.0	89.5	6.5	2.1	1.5	0.4	—
1980–81[2]	934,800	807,319	60,673	21,832	18,794	3,593	—	22,589	100.0	88.5	6.7	2.4	2.1	0.4	—
1990–91	1,094,538	914,093	66,375	37,342	42,529	4,583	—	29,616	100.0	85.8	6.2	3.5	4.0	0.4	—
1999–2000	1,237,875	929,102	108,018	75,063	77,909	8,717	—	39,066	100.0	77.5	9.0	6.3	6.5	0.7	—
2000–01	1,244,171	927,357	111,307	77,745	78,902	9,049	—	39,811	100.0	77.0	9.2	6.5	6.6	0.8	—
2002–03	1,348,811	994,616	124,253	89,029	87,964	9,875	—	43,074	100.0	76.2	9.5	6.8	6.7	0.8	—
2003–04	1,399,542	1,026,114	131,241	94,644	92,073	10,638	—	44,832	100.0	75.7	9.7	7.0	6.8	0.8	—
2004–05	1,439,264	1,049,141	136,122	101,124	97,209	10,307	—	45,361	100.0	75.3	9.8	7.3	7.0	0.7	—
2005–06	1,485,104	1,075,471	142,405	107,575	102,371	10,938	—	46,344	100.0	74.7	9.9	7.5	7.1	0.8	—
2006–07	1,524,729	1,100,308	146,767	114,962	105,287	11,463	—	45,942	100.0	74.4	9.9	7.8	7.1	0.8	—
2007–08	1,563,734	1,123,246	152,627	122,770	109,177	11,509	—	44,405	100.0	73.9	10.0	8.1	7.2	0.8	—
2008–09	1,601,399	1,144,628	156,603	129,473	112,581	12,221	—	45,893	100.0	73.6	10.1	8.3	7.2	0.8	—
2009–10	1,649,919	1,167,322	164,789	140,426	117,391	12,405	—	47,586	100.0	72.9	10.3	8.8	7.3	0.8	—
2010–11	1,716,053	1,182,690	172,731	154,450	121,118	11,935	20,589	52,540	100.0	71.1	10.4	9.3	7.3	0.7	1.2
2011–12	1,792,163	1,212,417	185,916	169,736	126,177	11,498	27,234	59,185	100.0	70.0	10.7	9.8	7.3	0.7	1.6
2012–13	1,840,381	1,221,908	191,233	186,677	130,129	11,432	34,128	64,874	100.0	68.8	10.8	10.5	7.3	0.6	1.9
2013–14	1,870,150	1,218,998	191,437	202,425	131,662	10,784	45,422	69,422	100.0	67.7	10.6	11.2	7.3	0.6	2.5
2014–15	1,894,969	1,210,071	192,829	218,098	133,916	10,202	54,215	75,638	100.0	66.5	10.6	12.0	7.4	0.6	3.0
2015–16	1,920,750	1,197,323	194,408	235,190	138,257	9,735	61,584	84,253	100.0	65.2	10.6	12.8	7.5	0.5	3.4
2016–17	1,956,032	1,196,007	196,300	252,166	144,078	9,582	66,526	91,373	100.0	64.1	10.5	13.5	7.7	0.5	3.6
Males															
1976–77[1]	494,424	438,161	25,147	10,318	7,638	1,804	—	11,356	100.0	90.7	5.2	2.1	1.6	0.4	—
1980–81[2]	469,625	406,173	24,511	10,810	10,107	1,700	—	16,324	100.0	89.6	5.4	2.4	2.2	0.4	—
1990–91	504,045	421,290	24,800	16,598	21,203	1,938	—	18,216	100.0	86.7	5.1	3.4	4.4	0.4	—
1999–2000	530,367	402,954	37,029	30,304	35,853	3,463	—	20,764	100.0	79.1	7.3	5.9	7.0	0.7	—
2000–01	531,840	401,780	38,103	31,368	35,865	3,700	—	21,024	100.0	78.7	7.5	6.1	7.0	0.7	—
2002–03	573,258	430,248	41,494	35,101	40,230	3,870	—	22,315	100.0	78.1	7.5	6.4	7.3	0.7	—
2003–04	595,425	445,483	43,851	37,288	41,360	4,244	—	23,199	100.0	77.9	7.7	6.5	7.2	0.7	—
2004–05	613,000	456,592	45,810	39,490	43,711	4,143	—	23,254	100.0	77.4	7.8	6.7	7.4	0.7	—
2005–06	630,502	467,397	48,073	41,805	45,803	4,202	—	23,222	100.0	77.0	7.9	6.9	7.5	0.7	—
2006–07	649,816	480,747	49,715	44,761	47,577	4,508	—	22,508	100.0	76.6	7.9	7.1	7.6	0.7	—
2007–08	668,184	492,360	52,298	47,797	49,535	4,523	—	21,671	100.0	76.2	8.1	7.4	7.7	0.7	—
2008–09	685,422	503,396	53,465	50,596	50,773	4,849	—	22,343	100.0	75.9	8.1	7.6	7.7	0.7	—
2009–10	706,660	513,711	56,136	55,139	53,365	4,879	—	23,430	100.0	75.2	8.2	8.1	7.8	0.7	—
2010–11	734,159	519,992	59,015	60,869	55,321	4,798	8,028	26,136	100.0	73.4	8.3	8.6	7.8	0.7	1.1
2011–12	765,772	532,463	63,736	67,083	57,521	4,476	10,945	29,548	100.0	72.3	8.7	9.1	7.8	0.6	1.5
2012–13	787,408	535,358	67,351	74,067	59,806	4,611	13,834	32,381	100.0	70.9	8.9	9.8	7.9	0.6	1.8
2013–14	801,905	536,009	68,290	80,312	59,844	4,171	18,137	35,142	100.0	69.9	8.9	10.5	7.8	0.5	2.4
2014–15	812,693	530,418	69,316	86,881	61,080	4,061	22,245	38,692	100.0	68.5	9.0	11.2	7.9	0.5	2.9
2015–16	821,746	522,834	69,847	92,989	63,182	3,822	25,157	43,915	100.0	67.2	9.0	12.0	8.1	0.5	3.2
2016–17	836,045	521,421	70,554	99,331	65,398	3,730	27,084	48,527	100.0	66.2	9.0	12.6	8.3	0.5	3.4
Females															
1976–77[1]	423,476	369,527	33,489	8,425	6,155	1,522	—	4,358	100.0	88.2	8.0	2.0	1.5	0.4	—
1980–81[2]	465,175	401,146	36,162	11,022	8,687	1,893	—	6,265	100.0	87.4	7.9	2.4	1.9	0.4	—
1990–91	590,493	492,803	41,575	20,744	21,326	2,645	—	11,400	100.0	85.1	7.2	3.6	3.7	0.5	—
1999–2000	707,508	526,148	70,989	44,759	42,056	5,254	—	18,302	100.0	76.3	10.3	6.5	6.1	0.8	—
2000–01	712,331	525,577	73,204	46,377	43,037	5,349	—	18,787	100.0	75.8	10.6	6.7	6.2	0.8	—
2002–03	775,553	564,368	82,759	53,928	47,734	6,005	—	20,759	100.0	74.8	11.0	7.1	6.3	0.8	—
2003–04	804,117	580,631	87,390	57,356	50,713	6,394	—	21,633	100.0	74.2	11.2	7.3	6.5	0.8	—
2004–05	826,264	592,549	90,312	61,634	53,498	6,164	—	22,107	100.0	73.7	11.2	7.7	6.7	0.8	—
2005–06	854,602	608,074	94,332	65,770	56,568	6,736	—	23,122	100.0	73.1	11.3	7.9	6.8	0.8	—
2006–07	874,913	619,561	97,052	70,201	57,710	6,955	—	23,434	100.0	72.8	11.4	8.2	6.8	0.8	—
2007–08	895,550	630,886	100,329	74,973	59,642	6,986	—	22,734	100.0	72.3	11.5	8.6	6.8	0.8	—
2008–09	915,977	641,232	103,138	78,877	61,808	7,372	—	23,550	100.0	71.9	11.6	8.8	6.9	0.8	—
2009–10	943,259	653,611	108,653	85,287	64,026	7,526	—	24,156	100.0	71.1	11.8	9.3	7.0	0.8	—
2010–11	981,894	662,698	113,716	93,581	65,797	7,137	12,561	26,404	100.0	69.4	11.9	9.8	6.9	0.7	1.3
2011–12	1,026,391	679,954	122,180	102,653	68,656	7,022	16,289	29,637	100.0	68.2	12.3	10.3	6.9	0.7	1.6
2012–13	1,052,973	686,550	123,882	112,610	70,323	6,821	20,294	32,493	100.0	67.3	12.1	11.0	6.9	0.7	2.0
2013–14	1,068,245	682,989	123,147	122,113	71,818	6,613	27,285	34,280	100.0	66.1	11.9	11.8	6.9	0.6	2.6
2014–15	1,082,276	679,653	123,513	131,217	72,836	6,141	31,970	36,946	100.0	65.0	11.8	12.6	7.0	0.6	3.1
2015–16	1,099,004	674,489	124,561	142,201	75,075	5,913	36,427	40,338	100.0	63.7	11.8	13.4	7.1	0.6	3.4
2016–17	1,119,987	674,586	125,746	152,835	78,680	5,852	39,442	42,846	100.0	62.6	11.7	14.2	7.3	0.5	3.7

—Not available.
[1]Excludes 1,121 males and 528 females whose racial/ethnic group was not available.
[2]Excludes 258 males and 82 females whose racial/ethnic group was not available.
NOTE: Data through 1990–91 are for institutions of higher education, while later data are for postsecondary institutions participating in Title IV federal financial aid programs. Race categories exclude persons of Hispanic ethnicity. For 1989–90 and later years, reported racial/ethnic distributions of students by level of degree, field of degree, and sex were used to estimate race/ethnicity for students whose race/ethnicity was not reported. Detail may not sum to totals because of rounding. Some data have been revised from previously published figures.
SOURCE: U.S. Department of Education, National Center for Education Statistics, Higher Education General Information Survey (HEGIS), "Degrees and Other Formal Awards Conferred" surveys, 1976–77 and 1980–81; Integrated Postsecondary Education Data System (IPEDS), "Completions Survey" (IPEDS-C:90–99); and IPEDS Fall 2000 through Fall 2017, Completions component. (This table was prepared August 2018).

Table 322.30. Bachelor's degrees conferred by postsecondary institutions, by race/ethnicity and field of study: 2015–16 and 2016–17

Field of study	2015–16										2016–17									
					Asian/Pacific Islander										Asian/Pacific Islander					
	Total	White	Black	Hispanic	Total	Asian	Pacific Islander	American Indian/ Alaska Native	Two or more races	Non-resident alien	Total	White	Black	Hispanic	Total	Asian	Pacific Islander	American Indian/ Alaska Native	Two or more races	Non-resident alien
1	2	3	4	5	6	7	8	9	10	11	12	13	14	15	16	17	18	19	20	21
All fields, total	**1,920,750**	**1,197,323**	**194,408**	**235,190**	**138,257**	**133,601**	**4,656**	**9,735**	**61,584**	**84,253**	**1,956,032**	**1,196,007**	**196,300**	**252,166**	**144,078**	**139,527**	**4,551**	**9,582**	**66,526**	**91,373**
Agriculture and natural resources	36,995	29,477	1,105	2,922	1,320	1,266	54	212	1,169	790	37,719	29,577	1,180	3,192	1,381	1,315	66	250	1,235	904
Architecture and related services	8,825	4,998	469	1,318	787	772	15	30	273	950	8,573	4,630	466	1,355	742	719	23	23	271	1,086
Area, ethnic, cultural, gender, and group studies	7,840	3,470	1,154	1,602	713	686	27	188	428	285	7,720	3,171	1,142	1,700	701	663	38	163	519	324
Biological and biomedical sciences	113,794	66,584	8,781	12,883	17,563	17,325	238	474	4,262	3,247	116,759	66,725	9,334	14,138	17,920	17,688	232	455	4,688	3,499
Business	371,690	224,640	38,239	42,557	27,215	26,211	1,004	1,847	9,779	27,413	381,353	228,806	38,204	45,609	28,045	27,098	947	1,791	10,590	28,308
Communication, journalism, and related programs	92,551	59,360	10,813	11,598	3,748	3,591	157	341	3,453	3,238	93,778	58,701	11,153	12,500	3,806	3,622	184	296	3,778	3,544
Communications technologies	4,824	2,912	572	586	255	239	16	27	255	217	4,615	2,586	626	647	278	259	19	24	200	254
Computer and information sciences	64,402	37,033	6,004	6,221	8,615	8,411	204	243	2,202	4,084	71,420	39,492	6,391	7,233	10,425	10,238	187	268	2,471	5,140
Construction trades	225	168	5	39	4	4	0	0	6	3	153	103	1	43	1	1	0	0	2	3
Education	87,221	66,992	6,611	7,841	2,140	1,962	178	595	2,100	942	85,118	64,688	6,287	8,277	2,272	2,134	138	552	2,143	899
Engineering	106,789	65,841	4,267	10,502	12,368	12,207	161	315	3,400	10,096	115,640	69,987	4,505	11,871	13,364	13,203	161	301	3,819	11,793
Engineering technologies and engineering-related fields[1]	16,548	11,244	1,519	1,498	806	778	28	122	353	1,006	17,665	11,765	1,522	1,708	778	749	29	119	440	1,333
English language and literature/letters	42,797	29,855	3,456	5,226	1,771	1,700	71	201	1,716	572	41,317	28,424	3,258	5,352	1,804	1,741	63	185	1,720	574
Family and consumer sciences/human sciences	25,389	16,146	3,201	3,269	1,347	1,295	52	137	798	491	25,077	15,305	3,221	3,619	1,388	1,338	50	133	890	521
Foreign languages, literatures, and linguistics	18,436	11,005	913	4,097	1,058	1,039	19	73	786	504	17,642	10,273	859	4,074	1,071	1,051	20	48	781	536
Health professions and related programs	228,907	151,186	26,469	24,113	17,492	16,738	754	1,075	5,943	2,629	238,014	155,670	27,363	26,381	18,290	17,533	757	1,198	6,459	2,653
Homeland security, law enforcement, and firefighting	61,159	33,017	12,056	11,656	1,703	1,448	255	435	1,758	534	59,581	31,302	11,544	12,166	1,697	1,465	232	440	1,829	603
Legal professions and studies	4,243	2,398	720	672	213	207	6	28	148	64	4,272	2,386	659	779	201	194	7	39	156	52
Liberal arts and sciences, general studies, and humanities	43,669	27,129	6,550	5,750	1,567	1,457	110	389	1,408	876	43,841	26,759	6,658	6,117	1,598	1,457	141	359	1,526	824
Library science	85	65	7	9	1	1	0	1	2	0	109	86	7	5	1	0	1	2	8	0
Mathematics and statistics	22,778	13,034	992	2,153	2,441	2,417	24	52	684	3,422	24,073	13,191	1,021	2,320	2,620	2,598	22	59	771	4,091
Mechanic and repair technologies/technicians	386	256	30	27	17	17	0	6	14	36	303	216	25	25	12	12	0	4	9	12
Military technologies and applied sciences	358	270	41	25	5	3	2	4	12	1	469	351	39	40	14	12	2	4	14	7
Multi/interdisciplinary studies	48,833	28,551	6,352	7,472	3,106	2,990	116	282	1,751	1,319	49,658	28,178	6,397	7,945	3,405	3,282	123	269	1,993	1,471
Parks, recreation, leisure, and fitness studies	50,912	34,107	5,844	5,759	2,313	2,196	117	265	1,780	844	53,264	34,468	6,215	6,578	2,555	2,432	123	323	2,072	1,053
Philosophy and religious studies	10,155	6,857	836	1,165	559	528	31	49	389	300	9,712	6,455	791	1,124	570	553	17	40	422	310
Physical sciences and science technologies	30,483	20,408	1,483	2,768	2,948	2,901	47	145	1,119	1,612	31,268	20,447	1,655	3,117	2,934	2,901	33	126	1,200	1,789
Precision production	51	35	1	3	3	3	0	0	1	8	32	24	1	2	4	3	1	0	0	1
Psychology	117,447	67,396	14,718	19,815	7,617	7,347	270	653	4,355	2,893	116,861	65,187	14,807	20,784	7,814	7,520	294	632	4,588	3,049
Public administration and social services	34,433	18,703	7,662	5,265	1,087	976	111	254	1,072	390	35,464	19,018	7,662	5,824	1,106	1,003	103	287	1,140	427
Social sciences and history	161,211	93,924	15,513	23,770	11,264	10,920	344	776	6,104	9,860	159,099	90,393	15,200	25,062	11,176	10,860	316	728	6,373	10,167
Social sciences	135,622	74,729	14,121	20,847	10,469	10,166	303	650	5,251	9,555	135,041	72,601	13,898	22,117	10,419	10,138	281	590	5,537	9,879
History	25,589	19,195	1,392	2,923	795	754	41	126	853	305	24,058	17,792	1,302	2,945	757	722	35	138	836	288
Theology and religious vocations	9,804	7,754	868	556	221	199	22	38	165	202	9,491	7,476	802	558	238	221	17	44	159	214
Transportation and materials moving	4,531	3,214	310	366	171	153	18	19	167	284	4,710	3,306	280	355	204	186	18	25	201	339
Visual and performing arts	92,979	59,294	6,847	11,687	5,819	5,614	205	459	3,732	5,141	91,262	56,861	7,025	11,666	5,663	5,476	187	395	4,059	5,593
Other and not classified	0	0	0	0	0	0	0	0	0	0	0	0	0	0	0	0	0	0	0	0

[1]Excludes "Construction trades" and "Mechanic and repair technologies/technicians," which are listed separately.

NOTE: Data are for postsecondary institutions participating in Title IV federal financial aid programs. Race categories exclude persons of Hispanic ethnicity. Reported racial/ethnic distributions of students by level of degree, field of degree, and sex were used to estimate race/ethnicity for students whose race/ethnicity was not reported. To facilitate trend comparisons, certain aggregations have been made of the degree fields as reported in the Integrated Postsecondary Education Data System (IPEDS): "Agriculture and natural resources" includes Agriculture, agriculture operations, and related sciences and Natural resources and conservation; and "Business" includes Business management, marketing, and related support services and Personal and culinary services. Some data have been revised from previously published figures.

SOURCE: U.S. Department of Education, National Center for Education Statistics, Integrated Postsecondary Education Data System (IPEDS), Fall 2016 and Fall 2017, Completions component. (This table was prepared August 2018.)

Table 323.10. Master's degrees conferred by postsecondary institutions, by field of study: Selected years, 1970–71 through 2016–17

Field of study	1970–71	1975–76	1980–81	1985–86	1990–91	1995–96	2000–01	2005–06	2006–07	2008–09	2009–10	2010–11	2011–12	2012–13	2013–14	2014–15	2015–16	2016–17
1	2	3	4	5	6	7	8	9	10	11	12	13	14	15	16	17	18	19
Total	**235,564**	**317,477**	**302,637**	**295,850**	**342,863**	**412,180**	**473,502**	**599,862**	**610,703**	**662,082**	**693,313**	**730,922**	**755,967**	**751,718**	**754,582**	**758,804**	**785,757**	**804,684**
Agriculture and natural resources	2,457	3,340	4,003	3,801	3,295	4,551	4,272	4,653	4,632	4,878	5,215	5,766	6,390	6,336	6,544	6,426	6,702	6,844
Architecture and related services	1,705	3,215	3,153	3,260	3,490	3,993	4,302	5,743	5,951	6,587	7,280	7,788	8,448	8,095	8,048	8,006	7,991	7,911
Area, ethnic, cultural, gender, and group studies	1,032	993	802	915	1,233	1,652	1,555	2,080	1,699	1,779	1,775	1,913	1,947	1,897	1,844	1,847	1,767	1,717
Biological and biomedical sciences	5,625	6,457	5,766	5,064	4,834	6,593	7,017	8,783	8,898	10,018	10,730	11,324	12,419	13,300	13,964	14,655	15,717	16,284
Business	26,490	42,592	57,888	66,676	78,255	93,554	115,602	146,396	150,213	168,404	177,748	187,178	191,606	188,617	189,364	185,236	186,835	187,404
Communication, journalism, and related programs	1,770	2,961	2,896	3,500	4,123	5,080	5,218	7,106	6,773	7,042	7,630	8,302	9,005	8,760	9,353	9,581	9,676	10,128
Communications technologies	86	165	209	308	204	481	427	521	499	475	463	502	497	577	577	554	491	539
Computer and information sciences	1,588	2,603	4,218	8,070	9,324	10,579	16,911	17,195	16,232	17,907	17,955	19,516	20,925	22,782	24,514	31,475	40,130	46,555
Education	87,666	126,061	96,713	74,816	87,352	104,936	127,829	174,622	176,583	178,538	182,165	185,127	179,047	164,652	154,655	146,581	145,792	145,680
Engineering	16,813	16,472	16,893	21,529	24,454	26,789	25,174	30,845	29,299	34,546	35,133	38,664	40,323	40,420	42,376	46,117	51,646	52,841
Engineering technologies	134	328	323	617	996	2,054	2,013	2,541	2,691	3,462	4,258	4,515	4,793	4,908	4,967	5,324	6,067	7,403
English language and literature/letters	10,441	8,599	5,742	5,335	6,784	7,657	6,763	8,845	8,745	9,262	9,202	9,475	9,938	9,755	9,294	8,928	8,581	8,247
Family and consumer sciences/human sciences	1,452	2,179	2,570	2,011	1,541	1,712	1,838	1,983	2,081	2,453	2,592	2,918	3,155	3,255	3,082	3,148	3,228	3,295
Foreign languages, literatures, and linguistics	5,480	4,432	2,934	2,690	3,049	3,443	3,035	3,539	3,443	3,592	3,756	3,727	3,827	3,708	3,482	3,566	3,407	3,274
Health professions and related programs	5,330	12,164	16,176	18,603	21,354	33,920	43,623	51,492	54,541	62,642	69,112	75,571	84,355	90,933	97,416	103,052	110,350	119,273
Homeland security, law enforcement, and firefighting	194	1,197	1,538	1,074	1,108	1,812	2,514	4,277	4,906	6,125	6,717	7,433	8,420	8,868	9,310	9,643	9,775	10,210
Legal professions and studies	955	1,442	1,832	1,924	2,057	2,751	3,829	4,453	4,486	5,150	5,767	6,475	6,614	7,013	7,654	7,924	8,181	8,674
Liberal arts and sciences, general studies, and humanities	885	2,633	2,375	1,586	2,213	2,778	3,193	3,702	3,634	3,729	3,822	3,997	3,792	3,264	3,002	2,794	2,598	2,485
Library science	7,001	8,037	4,859	3,564	4,763	5,099	4,727	6,448	6,767	7,091	7,448	7,729	7,443	6,983	5,840	5,259	4,926	4,843
Mathematics and statistics	5,191	3,857	2,567	3,131	3,549	3,651	3,209	4,729	4,884	5,211	5,639	5,866	6,246	6,957	7,273	7,589	8,451	9,086
Military technologies and applied sciences	2	0	43	83	0	136	0	0	202	3	0	0	29	32	29	71	152	274
Multi/interdisciplinary studies	924	1,283	2,356	2,869	2,079	2,713	3,413	4,396	4,613	5,225	5,947	6,762	7,746	7,953	8,120	8,100	8,554	9,234
Parks, recreation, leisure, and fitness studies	218	571	643	570	483	1,684	2,354	3,994	4,112	4,825	5,617	6,546	7,047	7,139	7,609	7,654	8,268	8,655
Philosophy and religious studies	1,326	1,358	1,231	1,193	1,471	1,363	1,386	1,739	1,716	1,859	2,045	1,839	2,003	1,934	2,095	1,912	1,756	1,705
Physical sciences and science technologies	6,336	5,428	5,246	5,860	5,281	5,910	5,134	6,063	6,015	5,862	6,066	6,386	6,911	7,014	6,984	7,100	7,131	7,143
Precision production	0	0	0	0	0	8	2	9	5	10	10	5	11	9	15	4	10	14
Psychology	5,717	10,167	10,223	9,845	11,349	15,152	16,539	19,775	21,096	23,415	23,763	25,062	27,052	27,787	27,926	26,772	27,645	27,542
Public administration and social services	7,785	15,209	17,803	15,692	17,905	24,229	25,268	30,492	31,132	33,934	35,740	38,614	41,737	43,591	44,508	45,948	46,754	45,393
Social sciences and history	16,539	15,953	11,945	10,564	12,233	15,012	13,791	17,368	17,666	19,241	20,234	21,085	21,891	21,591	21,497	20,533	19,861	20,015
Theology and religious vocations	7,747	8,964	11,061	11,826	10,498	10,909	9,876	11,758	12,436	12,851	12,848	13,170	13,341	14,275	14,128	14,278	14,352	13,654
Transportation and materials moving	0	0	0	454	406	919	756	784	985	1,048	1,074	1,390	1,702	1,444	1,243	971	911	839
Visual and performing arts	6,675	8,817	8,629	8,420	8,657	10,280	11,404	13,531	13,768	14,918	15,562	16,277	17,307	17,869	17,869	17,756	18,052	17,523
Not classified by field of study	0	0	0	0	8,523	780	528	0	0	0	0	0	0	0	0	0	0	0

NOTE: Data through 1990–91 are for institutions of higher education, while later data are for postsecondary institutions that participate in Title IV federal financial aid programs. The new Classification of Instructional Programs was initiated in 2009–10. The figures for earlier years have been reclassified when necessary to make them conform to the new taxonomy. To facilitate trend comparisons, certain aggregations have been made of the degree fields as reported in the Integrated Postsecondary Education Data System (IPEDS): "Agriculture and natural resources" includes Agriculture, agriculture operations, and related sciences and Natural resources and conservation; "Business" includes Business, management, marketing, and related support services and Personal and culinary services; and "Engineering technologies" includes Engineering technologies and engineering-related fields, Construction trades, and Mechanic and repair technologies/technicians. Some data have been revised from previously published figures.

SOURCE: U.S. Department of Education, National Center for Education Statistics, Higher Education General Information Survey (HEGIS), "Degrees and Other Formal Awards Conferred" surveys, 1970–71 through 1985–86; Integrated Postsecondary Education Data System (IPEDS), "Completions Survey" (IPEDS-C:91–99); and IPEDS Fall 2000 through Fall 2017, Completions component. (This table was prepared August 2018.)

Table 323.20. Master's degrees conferred by postsecondary institutions, by race/ethnicity and sex of student: Selected years, 1976–77 through 2016–17

Year and sex	Number of degrees conferred to U.S. citizens, permanent residents, and nonresident aliens								Percentage distribution of degrees conferred to U.S. citizens and permanent residents						
	Total	White	Black	Hispanic	Asian/ Pacific Islander	American Indian/ Alaska Native	Two or more races	Non-resident alien	Total	White	Black	Hispanic	Asian/ Pacific Islander	American Indian/ Alaska Native	Two or more races
1	2	3	4	5	6	7	8	9	10	11	12	13	14	15	16
Total															
1976–77[1]	322,463	271,402	21,252	6,136	5,127	1,018	—	17,528	100.0	89.0	7.0	2.0	1.7	0.3	—
1980–81[2]	301,081	247,475	17,436	6,534	6,348	1,044	—	22,244	100.0	88.8	6.3	2.3	2.3	0.4	—
1990–91	342,863	265,927	17,023	8,981	11,869	1,189	—	37,874	100.0	87.2	5.6	2.9	3.9	0.4	—
1999–2000	463,185	324,990	36,606	19,379	23,523	2,263	—	56,424	100.0	79.9	9.0	4.8	5.8	0.6	—
2000–01	473,502	324,211	38,853	21,661	24,544	2,496	—	61,737	100.0	78.7	9.4	5.3	6.0	0.6	—
2002–03	518,699	346,003	45,150	25,200	27,492	2,886	—	71,968	100.0	77.5	10.1	5.6	6.2	0.6	—
2003–04	564,272	373,448	51,402	29,806	31,202	3,206	—	75,208	100.0	76.4	10.5	6.1	6.4	0.7	—
2004–05	580,151	383,246	55,330	31,639	33,042	3,310	—	73,584	100.0	75.7	10.9	6.2	6.5	0.7	—
2005–06	599,862	397,519	59,822	32,578	34,302	3,519	—	72,122	100.0	75.3	11.3	6.2	6.5	0.7	—
2006–07	610,703	403,623	63,439	34,962	36,420	3,590	—	68,669	100.0	74.5	11.7	6.5	6.7	0.7	—
2007–08	630,844	413,348	65,912	36,899	37,743	3,775	—	73,167	100.0	74.1	11.8	6.6	6.8	0.7	—
2008–09	662,082	427,713	70,772	39,567	40,510	3,777	—	79,743	100.0	73.4	12.2	6.8	7.0	0.6	—
2009–10	693,313	445,158	76,472	43,603	42,520	3,965	—	81,595	100.0	72.8	12.5	7.1	7.0	0.6	—
2010–11	730,922	462,922	80,742	46,823	43,482	3,946	6,597	86,410	100.0	71.8	12.5	7.3	6.7	0.6	1.0
2011–12	755,967	470,822	86,007	50,994	45,379	3,681	9,823	89,261	100.0	70.6	12.9	7.6	6.8	0.6	1.5
2012–13	751,718	455,896	87,989	52,991	44,906	3,693	11,794	94,449	100.0	69.4	13.4	8.1	6.8	0.6	1.8
2013–14	754,582	444,771	88,606	55,962	44,533	3,512	13,417	103,781	100.0	68.3	13.6	8.6	6.8	0.5	2.1
2014–15	758,804	433,096	87,288	58,752	44,489	3,410	14,628	117,141	100.0	67.5	13.6	9.2	6.9	0.5	2.3
2015–16	785,757	431,885	88,786	63,060	45,921	3,538	16,589	135,978	100.0	66.5	13.7	9.7	7.1	0.5	2.6
2016–17	804,684	433,625	89,577	67,166	47,841	3,396	17,668	145,411	100.0	65.8	13.6	10.2	7.3	0.5	2.7
Males															
1976–77[1]	172,703	144,042	7,970	3,328	3,128	565	—	13,670	100.0	90.6	5.0	2.1	2.0	0.4	—
1980–81[2]	151,602	120,927	6,418	3,155	3,830	507	—	16,765	100.0	89.7	4.8	2.3	2.8	0.4	—
1990–91	160,842	117,993	6,201	4,017	6,765	495	—	25,371	100.0	87.1	4.6	3.0	5.0	0.4	—
1999–2000	196,129	131,221	11,642	7,738	11,299	845	—	33,384	100.0	80.6	7.2	4.8	6.9	0.5	—
2000–01	197,770	128,516	11,878	8,371	11,561	925	—	36,519	100.0	79.7	7.4	5.2	7.2	0.6	—
2002–03	215,172	135,938	13,224	9,389	12,704	1,043	—	42,874	100.0	78.9	7.7	5.4	7.4	0.6	—
2003–04	233,056	146,369	15,027	10,929	14,551	1,137	—	45,043	100.0	77.9	8.0	5.8	7.7	0.6	—
2004–05	237,155	150,076	16,136	11,501	15,238	1,167	—	43,037	100.0	77.3	8.3	5.9	7.8	0.6	—
2005–06	241,701	153,696	17,388	11,738	16,037	1,253	—	41,589	100.0	76.8	8.7	5.9	8.0	0.6	—
2006–07	242,213	154,250	18,340	12,471	16,689	1,275	—	39,188	100.0	76.0	9.0	6.1	8.2	0.6	—
2007–08	250,203	157,622	18,759	13,166	17,480	1,294	—	41,882	100.0	75.7	9.0	6.3	8.4	0.6	—
2008–09	263,515	162,863	20,146	14,314	18,865	1,349	—	45,978	100.0	74.9	9.3	6.6	8.7	0.6	—
2009–10	275,317	170,243	22,121	15,554	19,423	1,419	—	46,557	100.0	74.4	9.7	6.8	8.5	0.6	—
2010–11	291,680	177,786	23,746	17,183	19,918	1,409	2,540	49,098	100.0	73.3	9.8	7.1	8.2	0.6	1.0
2011–12	302,484	183,222	25,284	18,633	20,751	1,298	3,518	49,778	100.0	72.5	10.0	7.4	8.2	0.5	1.4
2012–13	301,552	177,208	26,417	19,441	20,456	1,280	4,472	52,278	100.0	71.1	10.6	7.8	8.2	0.5	1.8
2013–14	302,846	173,303	26,608	20,565	19,955	1,219	4,890	56,306	100.0	70.3	10.8	8.3	8.1	0.5	2.0
2014–15	306,615	168,151	26,295	21,384	19,577	1,223	5,438	64,547	100.0	69.5	10.9	8.8	8.1	0.5	2.2
2015–16	320,574	166,161	27,024	22,749	20,071	1,229	6,129	77,211	100.0	68.3	11.1	9.3	8.2	0.5	2.5
2016–17	326,892	164,719	26,976	23,797	20,705	1,150	6,450	83,095	100.0	67.6	11.1	9.8	8.5	0.5	2.6
Females															
1976–77[1]	149,760	127,360	13,282	2,808	1,999	453	—	3,858	100.0	87.3	9.1	1.9	1.4	0.3	—
1980–81[2]	149,479	126,548	11,018	3,379	2,518	537	—	5,479	100.0	87.9	7.7	2.3	1.7	0.4	—
1990–91	182,021	147,934	10,822	4,964	5,104	694	—	12,503	100.0	87.3	6.4	2.9	3.0	0.4	—
1999–2000	267,056	193,769	24,964	11,641	12,224	1,418	—	23,040	100.0	79.4	10.2	4.8	5.0	0.6	—
2000–01	275,732	195,695	26,975	13,290	12,983	1,571	—	25,218	100.0	78.1	10.8	5.3	5.2	0.6	—
2002–03	303,527	210,065	31,926	15,811	14,788	1,843	—	29,094	100.0	76.5	11.6	5.8	5.4	0.7	—
2003–04	331,216	227,079	36,375	18,877	16,651	2,069	—	30,165	100.0	75.4	12.1	6.3	5.5	0.7	—
2004–05	342,996	233,170	39,194	20,138	17,804	2,143	—	30,547	100.0	74.6	12.5	6.4	5.7	0.7	—
2005–06	358,161	243,823	42,434	20,840	18,265	2,266	—	30,533	100.0	74.4	13.0	6.4	5.6	0.7	—
2006–07	368,490	249,373	45,099	22,491	19,731	2,315	—	29,481	100.0	73.6	13.3	6.6	5.8	0.7	—
2007–08	380,641	255,726	47,153	23,733	20,263	2,481	—	31,285	100.0	73.2	13.5	6.8	5.8	0.7	—
2008–09	398,567	264,850	50,626	25,253	21,645	2,428	—	33,765	100.0	72.6	13.9	6.9	5.9	0.7	—
2009–10	417,996	274,915	54,351	28,049	23,097	2,546	—	35,038	100.0	71.8	14.2	7.3	6.0	0.7	—
2010–11	439,242	285,136	56,996	29,640	23,564	2,537	4,057	37,312	100.0	70.9	14.2	7.4	5.9	0.6	1.0
2011–12	453,483	287,600	60,723	32,361	24,628	2,383	6,305	39,483	100.0	69.5	14.7	7.8	5.9	0.6	1.5
2012–13	450,166	278,688	61,572	33,550	24,450	2,413	7,322	42,171	100.0	68.3	15.1	8.2	6.0	0.6	1.8
2013–14	451,736	271,468	61,998	35,397	24,578	2,293	8,527	47,475	100.0	67.2	15.3	8.8	6.1	0.6	2.1
2014–15	452,189	264,945	60,993	37,368	24,912	2,187	9,190	52,594	100.0	66.3	15.3	9.4	6.2	0.5	2.3
2015–16	465,183	265,724	61,762	40,311	25,850	2,309	10,460	58,767	100.0	65.4	15.2	9.9	6.4	0.6	2.6
2016–17	477,792	268,906	62,601	43,369	27,136	2,246	11,218	62,316	100.0	64.7	15.1	10.4	6.5	0.5	2.7

—Not available.
[1]Excludes 387 males and 175 females whose racial/ethnic group was not available.
[2]Excludes 1,377 males and 179 females whose racial/ethnic group was not available.
NOTE: Data through 1990-91 are for institutions of higher education, while later data are for postsecondary institutions participating in Title IV federal financial aid programs. Race categories exclude persons of Hispanic ethnicity. For 1989–90 and later years, reported racial/ethnic distributions of students by level of degree, field of degree, and sex were used to estimate race/ethnicity for students whose race/ethnicity was not reported. Detail may not sum to totals because of rounding. Some data have been revised from previously published figures.
SOURCE: U.S. Department of Education, National Center for Education Statistics, Higher Education General Information Survey (HEGIS), "Degrees and Other Formal Awards Conferred" surveys, 1976–77 and 1980–81; Integrated Postsecondary Education Data System (IPEDS), "Completions Survey" (IPEDS-C:90–99); and IPEDS Fall 2000 through Fall 2017, Completions component. (This table was prepared August 2018.)

Table 323.30. Master's degrees conferred by postsecondary institutions, by race/ethnicity and field of study: 2015–16 and 2016–17

Field of study	2015–16										2016–17									
					Asian/Pacific Islander										Asian/Pacific Islander					
	Total	White	Black	Hispanic	Total	Asian	Pacific Islander	American Indian/ Alaska Native	Two or more races	Non-resident alien	Total	White	Black	Hispanic	Total	Asian	Pacific Islander	American Indian/ Alaska Native	Two or more races	Non-resident alien
1	2	3	4	5	6	7	8	9	10	11	12	13	14	15	16	17	18	19	20	21
All fields, total	**785,757**	**431,885**	**88,786**	**63,060**	**45,921**	**44,335**	**1,586**	**3,538**	**16,589**	**135,978**	**804,684**	**433,625**	**89,577**	**67,166**	**47,841**	**46,255**	**1,586**	**3,396**	**17,668**	**145,411**
Agriculture and natural resources	6,702	4,644	228	361	200	197	3	32	137	1,100	6,844	4,616	245	392	221	214	7	34	185	1,151
Architecture and related services	7,991	3,908	335	722	480	472	8	12	168	2,366	7,911	3,635	332	703	443	435	8	25	168	2,605
Area, ethnic, cultural, gender, and group studies	1,767	822	160	271	84	80	4	44	61	325	1,717	765	165	222	129	121	8	69	64	303
Biological and biomedical sciences	15,717	8,425	1,072	1,177	2,075	2,062	13	28	437	2,503	16,284	8,505	1,198	1,288	2,162	2,146	16	43	495	2,593
Business	186,835	94,398	26,226	14,535	13,866	13,374	492	772	3,642	33,396	187,404	94,269	25,667	15,354	13,879	13,414	465	737	3,750	33,748
Communication, journalism, and related programs	9,676	5,061	1,243	809	336	320	16	31	257	1,939	10,128	5,121	1,350	942	380	370	10	38	304	1,993
Communications technologies	491	166	35	27	18	18	0	1	9	235	539	197	27	29	33	33	0	3	8	242
Computer and information sciences	40,130	8,018	2,208	1,193	2,909	2,869	40	66	428	25,308	46,555	8,665	2,345	1,275	3,588	3,539	49	78	531	30,073
Construction trades	0	0	0	0	0	0	0	0	0	0	0	0	0	0	0	0	0	0	0	0
Education	145,792	101,747	16,259	14,732	4,706	4,396	310	861	2,992	4,495	145,680	101,781	15,958	15,162	4,562	4,290	272	709	3,071	4,437
Engineering	51,646	14,724	1,174	1,992	3,698	3,675	23	72	711	29,275	52,841	14,862	1,147	2,147	3,744	3,705	39	67	697	30,177
Engineering technologies and engineering-related fields[1]	6,067	2,328	403	257	288	282	6	25	85	2,681	7,403	2,324	394	253	296	290	6	28	82	4,026
English language and literature/ letters	8,581	6,442	498	656	262	256	6	46	301	376	8,247	6,108	483	700	278	272	6	57	270	351
Family and consumer sciences/ human sciences	3,228	1,964	516	324	111	107	4	18	70	225	3,295	2,025	498	318	129	116	13	15	82	228
Foreign languages, literatures, and linguistics	3,407	1,649	87	539	140	135	5	15	86	891	3,274	1,547	81	535	96	96	0	9	95	911
Health professions and related programs	110,350	71,620	14,176	8,435	8,857	8,534	323	562	2,498	4,202	119,273	76,108	15,907	9,733	9,638	9,324	314	588	2,832	4,467
Homeland security, law enforcement, and firefighting	9,775	5,614	2,359	1,031	259	233	26	79	227	206	10,210	5,726	2,438	1,161	295	254	41	65	286	239
Legal professions and studies	8,181	2,095	554	429	244	234	10	51	70	4,738	8,674	2,083	699	494	326	320	6	61	92	4,919
Liberal arts and sciences, general studies, and humanities	2,598	1,735	291	234	51	46	5	20	83	184	2,485	1,668	287	257	63	59	4	25	62	123
Library science	4,926	3,850	238	391	161	155	6	20	184	82	4,843	3,824	256	389	131	125	6	24	146	73
Mathematics and statistics	8,451	2,816	197	294	570	566	4	9	100	4,465	9,086	2,777	188	311	664	659	5	5	132	5,009
Mechanic and repair technologies/ technicians	0	0	0	0	0	0	0	0	0	0	0	0	0	0	0	0	0	0	0	0
Military technologies and applied sciences	152	102	23	5	6	6	0	0	4	12	274	158	67	15	5	5	0	0	3	26
Multi/interdisciplinary studies	8,554	5,065	854	667	532	506	26	36	199	1,201	9,234	5,154	902	809	516	506	10	45	295	1,513
Parks, recreation, leisure, and fitness studies	8,268	5,788	1,046	571	150	139	11	42	197	474	8,655	5,826	1,184	692	202	179	23	31	287	433
Philosophy and religious studies	1,756	1,233	126	124	61	59	2	3	46	163	1,705	1,149	116	144	81	80	1	4	41	170
Physical sciences and science technologies	7,131	3,888	181	378	415	409	6	30	176	2,063	7,143	3,857	187	396	382	376	6	14	159	2,148
Precision production	10	7	0	0	0	0	0	0	0	3	14	4	0	0	1	1	0	0	0	9
Psychology	27,645	17,583	3,790	3,179	1,109	1,045	64	152	744	1,088	27,542	16,975	3,788	3,463	1,199	1,108	91	150	897	1,070
Public administration and social services	46,754	25,469	9,325	5,984	1,776	1,667	109	296	1,336	2,568	45,393	24,290	8,755	6,230	1,896	1,785	111	285	1,295	2,642
Social sciences and history	19,861	11,141	1,467	1,634	852	830	22	71	505	4,191	20,015	10,941	1,431	1,724	892	872	20	74	546	4,407
Social sciences	16,396	8,401	1,314	1,353	788	774	14	58	410	4,072	16,579	8,205	1,313	1,456	827	808	19	63	446	4,269
History	3,465	2,740	153	281	64	56	8	13	95	119	3,436	2,736	118	268	65	64	1	11	100	138
Theology and religious vocations	14,352	9,049	2,476	770	743	721	22	71	243	1,000	13,654	8,756	2,229	689	705	682	23	53	242	980
Transportation and materials moving	911	612	72	49	39	38	1	6	44	89	839	547	98	43	35	33	2	4	43	69
Visual and performing arts	18,052	9,922	1,167	1,290	923	904	19	67	549	4,134	17,523	9,362	1,155	1,296	870	846	24	56	508	4,276
Other and not classified	0	0	0	0	0	0	0	0	0	0	0	0	0	0	0	0	0	0	0	0

[1]Excludes "Construction trades" and "Mechanic and repair technologies/technicians," which are listed separately.

NOTE: Data are for postsecondary institutions participating in Title IV federal financial aid programs. Race categories exclude persons of Hispanic ethnicity. Reported racial/ethnic distributions of students by level of degree, field of degree, and sex were used to estimate race/ethnicity for students whose race/ethnicity was not reported. To facilitate trend comparisons, certain aggregations have been made of the degree fields as reported in the Integrated Postsecondary Education Data System (IPEDS): "Agriculture and natural resources" includes Agriculture, agriculture operations, and related sciences and Natural resources and conservation; and "Business" includes Business management, marketing, and related support services and Personal and culinary services. Some data have been revised from previously published figures.

SOURCE: U.S. Department of Education, National Center for Education Statistics, Integrated Postsecondary Education Data System (IPEDS), Fall 2016 and Fall 2017, Completions component. (This table was prepared August 2018.)

Table 324.10. Doctor's degrees conferred by postsecondary institutions, by field of study: Selected years, 1970–71 through 2016–17

Field of study	1970–71	1975–76	1980–81	1985–86	1990–91	1995–96	2000–01	2005–06	2006–07	2008–09	2009–10	2010–11	2011–12	2012–13	2013–14	2014–15	2015–16	2016–17
1	2	3	4	5	6	7	8	9	10	11	12	13	14	15	16	17	18	19
Total	**64,998**	**91,007**	**98,016**	**100,280**	**105,547**	**115,507**	**119,585**	**138,056**	**144,694**	**154,564**	**158,590**	**163,827**	**170,217**	**175,026**	**177,587**	**178,548**	**178,134**	**181,352**
Agriculture and natural resources	1,086	928	1,067	1,158	1,185	1,259	1,127	1,194	1,272	1,328	1,149	1,246	1,333	1,411	1,407	1,561	1,526	1,561
Architecture and related services	36	82	93	73	135	141	153	201	178	212	210	205	255	247	247	272	245	291
Area, ethnic, cultural, gender, and group studies	143	186	161	156	159	183	216	226	233	239	253	278	302	291	336	312	323	349
Biological and biomedical sciences	3,603	3,347	3,640	3,405	4,152	5,250	5,225	6,162	6,764	7,499	7,672	7,693	7,935	7,939	8,302	8,053	7,939	8,087
Business	774	906	808	923	1,185	1,366	1,180	1,711	2,029	2,123	2,249	2,286	2,538	2,828	3,039	3,116	3,325	3,329
Communication, journalism, and related programs	145	196	171	212	259	338	368	461	479	533	570	577	563	612	611	644	629	615
Communications technologies	0	8	11	6	13	7	2	3	1	2	3	1	4	0	3	0	4	0
Computer and information sciences	128	244	252	344	676	869	768	1,416	1,595	1,580	1,599	1,588	1,698	1,834	1,982	1,998	1,989	1,982
Education	6,041	7,202	7,279	6,610	6,189	6,246	6,284	7,584	8,261	9,028	9,237	9,642	10,118	10,572	10,929	11,772	11,838	12,687
Engineering	3,687	2,872	2,598	3,444	5,316	6,304	5,485	7,243	7,867	7,744	7,706	8,369	8,722	9,356	10,010	10,239	10,265	10,371
Engineering technologies	1	2	10	12	14	50	62	75	61	59	67	56	134	111	107	123	133	152
English language and literature/letters	1,554	1,514	1,040	895	1,056	1,395	1,330	1,254	1,178	1,271	1,334	1,344	1,427	1,377	1,393	1,418	1,402	1,347
Family and consumer sciences/human sciences	123	178	247	307	229	375	354	340	337	333	296	320	325	351	335	335	374	317
Foreign languages, literatures, and linguistics	1,084	1,245	931	768	889	1,020	1,078	1,074	1,059	1,111	1,091	1,158	1,231	1,304	1,230	1,243	1,278	1,168
Health professions and related programs	15,988	25,267	29,595	31,922	29,842	32,678	39,019	45,677	48,945	54,846	57,750	60,221	62,097	64,192	67,447	71,004	73,687	77,693
Homeland security, law enforcement, and firefighting	1	9	21	21	28	38	44	80	85	97	106	131	117	147	152	193	205	177
Legal professions and studies	17,441	32,369	36,391	35,898	38,035	39,919	38,190	43,569	43,628	44,304	44,627	44,853	46,836	47,246	44,169	40,329	37,034	35,123
Liberal arts and sciences, general studies, and humanities	32	162	121	90	70	75	102	84	77	67	96	95	93	98	90	96	105	95
Library science	39	71	71	62	56	53	58	44	52	35	64	50	60	50	52	44	54	42
Mathematics and statistics	1,199	856	728	742	978	1,158	997	1,293	1,351	1,535	1,596	1,586	1,669	1,823	1,863	1,801	1,855	1,925
Multi/interdisciplinary studies	101	156	236	352	306	549	512	600	683	731	631	660	727	730	769	840	849	854
Parks, recreation, leisure, and fitness studies	2	15	42	39	28	104	177	194	218	285	266	257	288	295	317	311	331	319
Philosophy and religious studies	555	556	411	480	464	550	600	578	637	686	667	804	778	794	698	762	750	741
Physical sciences and science technologies	4,324	3,388	3,105	3,521	4,248	4,589	3,968	4,642	5,041	5,237	5,065	5,295	5,370	5,514	5,806	5,823	6,057	6,027
Psychology	2,144	3,157	3,576	3,593	3,932	4,141	5,091	4,921	5,156	5,477	5,540	5,851	5,936	6,326	6,634	6,583	6,540	6,702
Public administration and social services	174	292	362	382	430	499	574	704	726	812	838	851	890	979	1,047	1,123	1,066	1,116
Social sciences and history	3,660	4,157	3,122	2,955	3,012	3,760	3,930	3,914	3,844	4,234	4,238	4,390	4,597	4,610	4,724	4,828	4,706	4,706
Theology and religious vocations	312	1,022	1,273	1,185	1,076	1,517	1,461	1,429	1,573	1,587	2,071	2,374	2,446	2,174	2,103	1,927	1,808	1,791
Transportation and materials moving	0	0	0	3	0	0	0	0	0	0	0	0	0	1	7	5	8	11
Visual and performing arts	621	620	654	722	838	1,067	1,167	1,383	1,364	1,569	1,599	1,646	1,728	1,814	1,778	1,793	1,809	1,774
Not classified by field of study	0	0	0	0	747	7	63	0	0	0	0	0	0	0	0	0	0	0

NOTE: Data through 1990-91 are for institutions of higher education, while later data are for postsecondary institutions that participate in Title IV federal financial aid programs. Includes Ph.D., Ed.D., and comparable degrees at the doctoral level, as well as such degrees as M.D., D.D.S., and law degrees that were classified as first-professional degrees prior to 2010–11. The new Classification of Instructional Programs was initiated in 2009–10. The figures for earlier years have been reclassified when necessary to make them conform to the new taxonomy. To facilitate trend comparisons, certain aggregations have been made of the degree fields as reported in the Integrated Postsecondary Education Data System (IPEDS): "Agriculture and natural resources" includes Agriculture, agriculture operations, and related sciences and Natural resources and conservation; "Business" includes Business, management, marketing, and related support services and Personal and culinary services; and "Engineering technologies" includes Engineering technologies and engineering-related fields, Construction trades, and Mechanic and repair technologies/technicians. Some data have been revised from previously published figures.

SOURCE: U.S. Department of Education, National Center for Education Statistics, Higher Education General Information Survey (HEGIS), "Degrees and Other Formal Awards Conferred" surveys, 1970–71 through 1985–86; Integrated Postsecondary Education Data System (IPEDS), "Completions Survey" (IPEDS-C:91–99); and IPEDS Fall 2000 through Fall 2017, Completions component. (This table was prepared August 2018.)

Table 324.20. Doctor's degrees conferred by postsecondary institutions, by race/ethnicity and sex of student: Selected years, 1976–77 through 2016–17

Year and sex	Number of degrees conferred[1] to U.S. citizens, permanent residents, and nonresident aliens								Percentage distribution of degrees conferred[1] to U.S. citizens and permanent residents						
	Total	White	Black	Hispanic	Asian/ Pacific Islander	American Indian/ Alaska Native	Two or more races	Non-resident alien	Total	White	Black	Hispanic	Asian/ Pacific Islander	American Indian/ Alaska Native	Two or more races
1	2	3	4	5	6	7	8	9	10	11	12	13	14	15	16
Total															
1976–77[1]	91,218	79,932	3,575	1,533	1,674	240	—	4,264	100.0	91.9	4.1	1.8	1.9	0.3	—
1980–81[2]	97,281	84,200	3,893	1,924	2,267	312	—	4,685	100.0	90.9	4.2	2.1	2.4	0.3	—
1990–91	105,547	81,791	4,429	3,210	5,120	356	—	10,641	100.0	86.2	4.7	3.4	5.4	0.4	—
1999–2000	118,736	82,984	7,078	5,042	10,682	708	—	12,242	100.0	77.9	6.6	4.7	10.0	0.7	—
2000–01	119,585	82,321	7,035	5,204	11,587	705	—	12,733	100.0	77.0	6.6	4.9	10.8	0.7	—
2002–03	121,579	82,549	7,537	5,503	12,008	759	—	13,223	100.0	76.2	7.0	5.1	11.1	0.7	—
2003–04	126,087	84,695	8,089	5,795	12,371	771	—	14,366	100.0	75.8	7.2	5.2	11.1	0.7	—
2004–05	134,387	89,763	8,527	6,115	13,176	788	—	16,018	100.0	75.8	7.2	5.2	11.1	0.7	—
2005–06	138,056	91,050	8,523	6,202	13,686	929	—	17,666	100.0	75.6	7.1	5.2	11.4	0.8	—
2006–07	144,694	94,225	9,371	6,576	14,727	917	—	18,878	100.0	74.9	7.4	5.2	11.7	0.7	—
2007–08	149,190	97,701	9,451	6,933	15,170	932	—	19,003	100.0	75.0	7.3	5.3	11.7	0.7	—
2008–09	154,564	101,400	10,188	7,497	15,840	978	—	18,661	100.0	74.6	7.5	5.5	11.7	0.7	—
2009–10	158,590	104,419	10,413	8,085	16,560	952	—	18,161	100.0	74.4	7.4	5.8	11.8	0.7	—
2010–11	163,827	105,990	10,934	8,662	17,078	947	1,251	18,965	100.0	73.2	7.5	6.0	11.8	0.7	0.9
2011–12	170,217	109,365	11,794	9,223	17,896	915	1,571	19,453	100.0	72.5	7.8	6.1	11.9	0.6	1.0
2012–13	175,026	110,759	12,085	10,108	18,406	900	2,440	20,328	100.0	71.6	7.8	6.5	11.9	0.6	1.6
2013–14	177,587	110,157	12,621	10,665	19,118	861	2,966	21,199	100.0	70.4	8.1	6.8	12.2	0.6	1.9
2014–15	178,548	108,914	13,272	11,263	19,186	884	3,670	21,359	100.0	69.3	8.4	7.2	12.2	0.6	2.3
2015–16	178,134	107,235	13,377	11,781	19,614	811	3,782	21,534	100.0	68.5	8.5	7.5	12.5	0.5	2.4
2016–17	181,352	107,445	14,067	12,493	20,344	746	4,166	22,091	100.0	67.5	8.8	7.8	12.8	0.5	2.6
Males															
1976–77[1]	71,709	62,977	2,338	1,216	1,311	182	—	3,685	100.0	92.6	3.4	1.8	1.9	0.3	—
1980–81[2]	68,853	59,574	2,206	1,338	1,589	223	—	3,923	100.0	91.8	3.4	2.1	2.4	0.3	—
1990–91	64,242	48,812	1,991	1,835	3,038	196	—	8,370	100.0	87.4	3.6	3.3	5.4	0.4	—
1999–2000	64,930	45,308	2,762	2,602	5,467	333	—	8,458	100.0	80.2	4.9	4.6	9.7	0.6	—
2000–01	64,171	44,131	2,655	2,564	5,759	346	—	8,716	100.0	79.6	4.8	4.6	10.4	0.6	—
2002–03	62,730	42,569	2,735	2,671	5,683	358	—	8,714	100.0	78.8	5.1	4.9	10.5	0.7	—
2003–04	63,981	43,014	2,888	2,731	5,620	357	—	9,371	100.0	78.8	5.3	5.0	10.3	0.7	—
2004–05	67,257	44,749	2,904	2,863	5,913	370	—	10,458	100.0	78.8	5.1	5.0	10.4	0.7	—
2005–06	68,912	45,476	2,949	2,850	5,977	429	—	11,231	100.0	78.8	5.1	4.9	10.4	0.7	—
2006–07	71,311	46,215	3,223	3,037	6,449	421	—	11,966	100.0	77.9	5.4	5.1	10.9	0.7	—
2007–08	73,340	48,118	3,291	3,139	6,516	447	—	11,829	100.0	78.2	5.4	5.1	10.6	0.7	—
2008–09	75,674	49,880	3,531	3,388	6,914	460	—	11,501	100.0	77.7	5.5	5.3	10.8	0.7	—
2009–10	76,610	50,707	3,609	3,642	7,184	430	—	11,038	100.0	77.3	5.5	5.6	11.0	0.7	—
2010–11	79,672	51,688	3,838	3,990	7,545	454	557	11,600	100.0	75.9	5.6	5.9	11.1	0.7	0.8
2011–12	82,670	53,488	4,121	4,218	7,792	418	701	11,932	100.0	75.6	5.8	6.0	11.0	0.6	1.0
2012–13	85,080	54,196	4,310	4,473	8,190	400	1,085	12,426	100.0	74.6	5.9	6.2	11.3	0.6	1.5
2013–14	85,585	53,374	4,510	4,788	8,270	365	1,297	12,981	100.0	73.5	6.2	6.6	11.4	0.5	1.8
2014–15	84,922	52,069	4,464	5,011	8,330	410	1,678	12,960	100.0	72.4	6.2	7.0	11.6	0.6	2.3
2015–16	84,240	50,694	4,564	5,122	8,632	371	1,718	13,139	100.0	71.3	6.4	7.2	12.1	0.5	2.4
2016–17	84,646	50,003	4,791	5,421	8,906	307	1,780	13,438	100.0	70.2	6.7	7.6	12.5	0.4	2.5
Females															
1976–77[1]	19,509	16,955	1,237	317	363	58	—	579	100.0	89.6	6.5	1.7	1.9	0.3	—
1980–81[2]	28,428	24,626	1,687	586	678	89	—	762	100.0	89.0	6.1	2.1	2.5	0.3	—
1990–91	41,305	32,979	2,438	1,375	2,082	160	—	2,271	100.0	84.5	6.2	3.5	5.3	0.4	—
1999–2000	53,806	37,676	4,316	2,440	5,215	375	—	3,784	100.0	75.3	8.6	4.9	10.4	0.7	—
2000–01	55,414	38,190	4,380	2,640	5,828	359	—	4,017	100.0	74.3	8.5	5.1	11.3	0.7	—
2002–03	58,849	39,980	4,802	2,832	6,325	401	—	4,509	100.0	73.6	8.8	5.2	11.6	0.7	—
2003–04	62,106	41,681	5,201	3,064	6,751	414	—	4,995	100.0	73.0	9.1	5.4	11.8	0.7	—
2004–05	67,130	45,014	5,623	3,252	7,263	418	—	5,560	100.0	73.1	9.1	5.3	11.8	0.7	—
2005–06	69,144	45,574	5,574	3,352	7,709	500	—	6,435	100.0	72.7	8.9	5.3	12.3	0.8	—
2006–07	73,383	48,010	6,148	3,539	8,278	496	—	6,912	100.0	72.2	9.2	5.3	12.5	0.7	—
2007–08	75,850	49,583	6,160	3,794	8,654	485	—	7,174	100.0	72.2	9.0	5.5	12.6	0.7	—
2008–09	78,890	51,520	6,657	4,109	8,926	518	—	7,160	100.0	71.8	9.3	5.7	12.4	0.7	—
2009–10	81,980	53,712	6,804	4,443	9,376	522	—	7,123	100.0	71.8	9.1	5.9	12.5	0.7	—
2010–11	84,155	54,302	7,096	4,672	9,533	493	694	7,365	100.0	70.7	9.2	6.1	12.4	0.6	0.9
2011–12	87,547	55,877	7,673	5,005	10,104	497	870	7,521	100.0	69.8	9.6	6.3	12.6	0.6	1.1
2012–13	89,946	56,563	7,775	5,635	10,216	500	1,355	7,902	100.0	68.9	9.5	6.9	12.5	0.6	1.7
2013–14	92,002	56,783	8,111	5,877	10,848	496	1,669	8,218	100.0	67.8	9.7	7.0	12.9	0.6	2.0
2014–15	93,626	56,845	8,808	6,252	10,856	474	1,992	8,399	100.0	66.7	10.3	7.3	12.7	0.6	2.3
2015–16	93,894	56,541	8,813	6,659	10,982	440	2,064	8,395	100.0	66.1	10.3	7.8	12.8	0.5	2.4
2016–17	96,706	57,442	9,276	7,072	11,438	439	2,386	8,653	100.0	65.2	10.5	8.0	13.0	0.5	2.7

—Not available.
[1]Includes Ph.D., Ed.D., and comparable degrees at the doctoral level, as well as such degrees as M.D., D.D.S., and law degrees that were classified as first-professional degrees prior to 2010–11.
[2]Excludes 500 males and 12 females whose racial/ethnic group was not available.
[3]Excludes 714 males and 21 females whose racial/ethnic group was not available.
NOTE: Data through 1990–91 are for institutions of higher education, while later data are for postsecondary institutions participating in Title IV federal financial aid programs. Race categories exclude persons of Hispanic ethnicity. For 1989–90 and later years, reported racial/ethnic distributions of students by level of degree, field of degree, and sex were used to estimate race/ethnicity for students whose race/ethnicity was not reported. Detail may not sum to totals because of rounding. Some data have been revised from previously published figures.
SOURCE: U.S. Department of Education, National Center for Education Statistics, Higher Education General Information Survey (HEGIS), "Degrees and Other Formal Awards Conferred" surveys, 1976–77 and 1980–81; Integrated Postsecondary Education Data System (IPEDS), "Completions Survey" (IPEDS-C:90–99); and IPEDS Fall 2000 through Fall 2017, Completions component. (This table was prepared August 2018.)

Table 324.25. Doctor's degrees conferred by postsecondary institutions, by race/ethnicity and field of study: 2015–16 and 2016–17

Field of study	2015–16										2016–17									
					Asian/Pacific Islander										Asian/Pacific Islander					
	Total	White	Black	Hispanic	Total	Asian	Pacific Islander	American Indian/ Alaska Native	Two or more races	Non-resident alien	Total	White	Black	Hispanic	Total	Asian	Pacific Islander	American Indian/ Alaska Native	Two or more races	Non-resident alien
1	2	3	4	5	6	7	8	9	10	11	12	13	14	15	16	17	18	19	20	21
All fields, total	**178,134**	**107,235**	**13,377**	**11,781**	**19,614**	**19,283**	**331**	**811**	**3,782**	**21,534**	**181,352**	**107,445**	**14,067**	**12,493**	**20,344**	**20,016**	**328**	**746**	**4,166**	**22,091**
Agriculture and natural resources	1,526	750	43	60	57	57	0	6	17	593	1,561	722	49	56	51	51	0	3	20	660
Architecture and related services	245	84	18	11	27	25	2	0	11	94	291	103	7	15	36	33	3	1	9	120
Area, ethnic, cultural, gender, and group studies	323	156	45	38	17	14	3	7	10	50	349	153	58	42	18	18	0	4	9	65
Biological and biomedical sciences	7,939	4,232	274	446	716	704	12	26	138	2,107	8,087	4,246	303	467	769	758	11	25	210	2,067
Business	3,325	1,535	671	160	220	209	11	14	50	675	3,329	1,412	721	206	238	231	7	14	43	695
Communication, journalism, and related programs	629	368	25	33	23	22	1	0	9	171	615	357	49	30	35	35	0	2	12	130
Communications technologies	4	1	0	0	1	1	0	0	0	2	0	0	0	0	0	0	0	0	0	0
Computer and information sciences	1,989	602	92	44	106	105	1	1	22	1,122	1,982	617	85	54	116	115	1	2	19	1,089
Construction trades	0	0	0	0	0	0	0	0	0	0	0	0	0	0	0	0	0	0	0	0
Education	11,838	7,248	2,268	933	457	425	32	76	168	688	12,687	7,583	2,635	1,009	443	406	37	89	219	709
Engineering	10,265	3,178	207	294	718	715	3	11	121	5,736	10,371	3,076	187	319	749	744	5	12	117	5,911
Engineering technologies and engineering-related fields[1]	133	59	5	6	6	6	0	0	2	55	152	65	13	6	11	11	0	0	0	57
English language and literature/ letters	1,402	1,088	57	63	49	47	2	7	20	118	1,347	994	54	97	49	47	2	10	32	111
Family and consumer sciences/ human sciences	374	182	55	21	18	17	1	1	8	89	317	172	30	18	21	21	0	1	5	70
Foreign languages, literatures, and linguistics	1,278	669	15	126	38	38	0	4	21	405	1,168	604	12	121	50	50	0	4	13	364
Health professions and related programs	73,687	47,242	4,716	4,224	13,063	12,909	154	270	1,793	2,379	77,693	49,286	5,031	4,851	13,715	13,536	179	260	1,949	2,601
Homeland security, law enforcement, and firefighting	205	123	38	15	2	2	0	0	2	25	177	107	30	16	2	2	0	1	0	21
Legal professions and studies	37,034	24,989	3,110	3,872	2,678	2,598	80	293	977	1,115	35,123	23,319	3,006	3,730	2,594	2,537	57	231	1,022	1,221
Liberal arts and sciences, general studies, and humanities	105	79	3	7	4	4	0	0	3	9	95	74	3	5	4	3	1	1	3	5
Library science	54	30	3	1	5	5	0	0	2	13	42	21	4	3	4	3	1	0	0	10
Mathematics and statistics	1,855	723	39	63	111	111	0	4	39	876	1,925	739	22	50	138	138	0	3	30	943
Mechanic and repair technologies/ technicians	0	0	0	0	0	0	0	0	0	0	0	0	0	0	0	0	0	0	0	0
Military technologies and applied sciences	0	0	0	0	0	0	0	0	0	0	0	0	0	0	0	0	0	0	0	0
Multi/interdisciplinary studies	849	496	70	49	40	39	1	3	10	181	854	462	82	40	44	44	0	5	20	201
Parks, recreation, leisure, and fitness studies	331	199	25	22	7	6	1	0	7	71	319	208	20	11	6	6	0	1	7	66
Philosophy and religious studies	750	535	40	37	33	32	1	3	10	92	741	509	42	29	31	31	0	2	18	110
Physical sciences and science technologies	6,057	2,939	121	194	309	307	2	10	84	2,400	6,027	2,910	110	227	327	326	1	14	85	2,354
Precision production	0	0	0	0	0	0	0	0	0	0	0	0	0	0	0	0	0	0	0	0
Psychology	6,540	4,430	618	588	404	385	19	32	143	325	6,702	4,525	623	597	388	373	15	25	162	382
Public administration and social services	1,066	569	200	60	76	75	1	1	15	145	1,116	575	238	67	54	54	0	5	26	151
Social sciences and history	4,706	2,655	210	276	179	178	1	27	54	1,305	4,706	2,564	238	259	215	211	4	19	88	1,323
Social sciences	3,726	1,949	152	209	158	158	0	21	38	1,199	3,781	1,909	197	184	189	185	4	13	71	1,218
History	980	706	58	67	21	20	1	6	16	106	925	655	41	75	26	26	0	6	17	105
Theology and religious vocations	1,808	948	346	62	125	123	2	10	6	311	1,791	949	365	71	143	140	3	4	12	247
Transportation and materials moving	8	2	1	0	0	0	0	0	2	3	11	7	0	0	0	0	0	0	0	4
Visual and performing arts	1,809	1,124	62	76	125	124	1	5	38	379	1,774	1,086	50	97	93	92	1	8	36	404
Other and not classified	0	0	0	0	0	0	0	0	0	0	0	0	0	0	0	0	0	0	0	0

[1]Excludes "Construction trades" and "Mechanic and repair technologies/technicians," which are listed separately.

NOTE: Data are for postsecondary institutions participating in Title IV federal financial aid programs. Race categories exclude persons of Hispanic ethnicity. Reported racial/ethnic distributions of students by level of degree, field of degree, and sex were used to estimate race/ethnicity for students whose race/ethnicity was not reported. To facilitate trend comparisons, certain aggregations have been made of the degree fields as reported in the Integrated Postsecondary Education Data System (IPEDS): "Agriculture and natural resources" includes Agriculture, agriculture operations, and related sciences and Natural resources and conservation; and "Business" includes Business management, marketing, and related support services and Personal and culinary services. Some data have been revised from previously published figures.

SOURCE: U.S. Department of Education, National Center for Education Statistics, Integrated Postsecondary Education Data System (IPEDS), Fall 2016 and Fall 2017, Completions component. (This table was prepared August 2018.)

Table 324.40. Number of postsecondary institutions conferring doctor's degrees in dentistry, medicine, and law, and number of such degrees conferred, by sex of student: Selected years, 1949–50 through 2016–17

Year	Dentistry (D.D.S. or D.M.D.)				Medicine (M.D.)				Law (LL.B. or J.D.)			
	Number of institutions conferring degrees	Number of degrees conferred			Number of institutions conferring degrees	Number of degrees conferred			Number of institutions conferring degrees	Number of degrees conferred		
		Total	Males	Females		Total	Males	Females		Total	Males	Females
1	2	3	4	5	6	7	8	9	10	11	12	13
1949–50	40	2,579	2,561	18	72	5,612	5,028	584	—	—	—	—
1951–52	41	2,918	2,895	23	72	6,201	5,871	330	—	—	—	—
1953–54	42	3,102	3,063	39	73	6,712	6,377	335	—	—	—	—
1955–56	42	3,009	2,975	34	73	6,810	6,464	346	131	8,262	7,974	288
1957–58	43	3,065	3,031	34	75	6,816	6,469	347	131	9,394	9,122	272
1959–60	45	3,247	3,221	26	79	7,032	6,645	387	134	9,240	9,010	230
1961–62	46	3,183	3,166	17	81	7,138	6,749	389	134	9,364	9,091	273
1963–64	46	3,180	3,168	12	82	7,303	6,878	425	133	10,679	10,372	307
1964–65	46	3,108	3,086	22	81	7,304	6,832	472	137	11,583	11,216	367
1965–66	47	3,178	3,146	32	84	7,673	7,170	503	136	13,246	12,776	470
1967–68	48	3,422	3,375	47	85	7,944	7,318	626	138	16,454	15,805	649
1968–69	—	3,408	3,376	32	—	8,025	7,415	610	—	17,053	16,373	680
1969–70	48	3,718	3,684	34	86	8,314	7,615	699	145	14,916	14,115	801
1970–71	48	3,745	3,703	42	89	8,919	8,110	809	147	17,421	16,181	1,240
1971–72	48	3,862	3,819	43	92	9,253	8,423	830	147	21,764	20,266	1,498
1972–73	51	4,047	3,992	55	97	10,307	9,388	919	152	27,205	25,037	2,168
1973–74	52	4,440	4,355	85	99	11,356	10,093	1,263	151	29,326	25,986	3,340
1974–75	52	4,773	4,627	146	104	12,447	10,818	1,629	154	29,296	24,881	4,415
1975–76	56	5,425	5,187	238	107	13,426	11,252	2,174	166	32,293	26,085	6,208
1976–77	57	5,138	4,764	374	109	13,461	10,891	2,570	169	34,104	26,447	7,657
1977–78	57	5,189	4,623	566	109	14,279	11,210	3,069	169	34,402	25,457	8,945
1978–79	58	5,434	4,794	640	109	14,786	11,381	3,405	175	35,206	25,180	10,026
1979–80	58	5,258	4,558	700	112	14,902	11,416	3,486	179	35,647	24,893	10,754
1980–81	58	5,460	4,672	788	116	15,505	11,672	3,833	176	36,331	24,563	11,768
1981–82	59	5,282	4,467	815	119	15,814	11,867	3,947	180	35,991	23,965	12,026
1982–83	59	5,585	4,631	954	118	15,484	11,350	4,134	177	36,853	23,550	13,303
1983–84	60	5,353	4,302	1,051	119	15,813	11,359	4,454	179	37,012	23,382	13,630
1984–85	59	5,339	4,233	1,106	120	16,041	11,167	4,874	181	37,491	23,070	14,421
1985–86	59	5,046	3,907	1,139	120	15,938	11,022	4,916	181	35,844	21,874	13,970
1986–87	58	4,741	3,603	1,138	121	15,428	10,431	4,997	179	36,056	21,561	14,495
1987–88	57	4,477	3,300	1,177	122	15,358	10,278	5,080	180	35,397	21,067	14,330
1988–89	58	4,265	3,124	1,141	124	15,460	10,310	5,150	182	35,634	21,069	14,565
1989–90	57	4,100	2,834	1,266	124	15,075	9,923	5,152	182	36,485	21,079	15,406
1990–91	55	3,699	2,510	1,189	121	15,043	9,629	5,414	179	37,945	21,643	16,302
1991–92	52	3,593	2,431	1,162	120	15,243	9,796	5,447	177	38,848	22,260	16,588
1992–93	55	3,605	2,383	1,222	122	15,531	9,679	5,852	184	40,302	23,182	17,120
1993–94	53	3,787	2,330	1,457	121	15,368	9,544	5,824	185	40,044	22,826	17,218
1994–95	53	3,897	2,480	1,417	119	15,537	9,507	6,030	183	39,349	22,592	16,757
1995–96	53	3,697	2,374	1,323	119	15,341	9,061	6,280	183	39,828	22,508	17,320
1996–97	52	3,784	2,387	1,397	118	15,571	9,121	6,450	184	40,079	22,548	17,531
1997–98	53	4,032	2,490	1,542	117	15,424	9,006	6,418	185	39,331	21,876	17,455
1998–99	53	4,143	2,673	1,470	118	15,566	8,972	6,594	185	38,297	21,102	17,195
1999–2000	54	4,250	2,547	1,703	118	15,286	8,761	6,525	190	38,152	20,638	17,514
2000–01	54	4,391	2,696	1,695	118	15,403	8,728	6,675	192	37,904	19,981	17,923
2001–02	53	4,239	2,608	1,631	118	15,237	8,469	6,768	192	38,981	20,254	18,727
2002–03	53	4,345	2,654	1,691	118	15,034	8,221	6,813	194	39,067	19,916	19,151
2003–04	53	4,335	2,532	1,803	118	15,442	8,273	7,169	195	40,209	20,332	19,877
2004–05	53	4,454	2,505	1,949	120	15,461	8,151	7,310	198	43,423	22,297	21,126
2005–06	54	4,389	2,435	1,954	119	15,455	7,900	7,555	197	43,440	22,597	20,843
2006–07	55	4,596	2,548	2,048	120	15,730	7,987	7,743	200	43,485	22,777	20,708
2007–08	55	4,795	2,661	2,134	120	15,646	7,935	7,711	201	43,588	23,110	20,478
2008–09	55	4,918	2,637	2,281	120	15,987	8,164	7,823	203	44,045	23,860	20,185
2009–10	55	5,062	2,745	2,317	120	16,356	8,468	7,888	205	44,346	23,384	20,962
2010–11	55	5,071	2,764	2,307	120	16,863	8,701	8,162	206	44,421	23,481	20,940
2011–12	55	5,109	2,748	2,361	120	16,927	8,809	8,118	207	46,445	24,576	21,869
2012–13	56	5,219	2,707	2,512	122	17,264	8,976	8,288	209	46,811	25,087	21,724
2013–14	57	5,407	2,839	2,568	124	17,604	9,232	8,372	210	43,772	23,278	20,494
2014–15	60	5,816	3,030	2,786	127	18,302	9,558	8,744	212	40,024	20,810	19,214
2015–16	61	5,951	3,032	2,919	128	18,409	9,852	8,557	214	36,798	18,935	17,863
2016–17	63	6,388	3,328	3,060	131	18,698	9,834	8,864	214	34,894	17,579	17,315

—Not available.
NOTE: Data are for postsecondary institutions participating in Title IV federal financial aid programs. Some data have been revised from previously published figures.
SOURCE: U.S. Department of Education, National Center for Education Statistics, *Earned Degrees Conferred*, 1949–50 through 1964–65; Higher Education General Information Survey (HEGIS), "Degrees and Other Formal Awards Conferred" surveys, 1965–66 through 1985–86; Integrated Postsecondary Education Data System (IPEDS), "Completions Survey" (IPEDS-C:87–99); and IPEDS Fall 2000 through Fall 2017, Completions component. (This table was prepared January 2019.)

Table 326.15. Percentage distribution of first-time, full-time bachelor's degree-seeking students at 4-year postsecondary institutions 6 years after entry, by completion and enrollment status at first institution attended, sex, race/ethnicity, control of institution, and percentage of applications accepted: Cohort entry years 2006 and 2011

Sex, race/ethnicity, control of institution, and percent of applications accepted	Percentage distribution of 2006 entry cohort 6 years after entry						Percentage distribution of 2011 entry cohort 6 years after entry					
		Completed an award at first institution attended		Did not complete an award at first institution				Completed an award at first institution attended		Did not complete an award at first institution		
	Total	Bachelor's degree	Award below bachelor's degree level	Trans-ferred out[1]	Remained enrolled	No longer enrolled, status unknown[2]	Total	Bachelor's degree	Award below bachelor's degree level	Trans-ferred out[1]	Remained enrolled	No longer enrolled, status unknown[2]
1	2	3	4	5	6	7	8	9	10	11	12	13
Total	**100.0**	**59.2**	**0.4**	**9.0**	**2.4**	**29.0**	**100.0**	**60.4**	**0.4**	**11.8**	**2.4**	**25.0**
Sex												
Male	100.0	56.5	0.3	9.0	2.9	31.3	100.0	57.3	0.3	11.8	2.9	27.7
Female	100.0	61.4	0.4	9.0	2.0	27.1	100.0	63.0	0.5	11.8	2.0	22.7
Race/ethnicity												
White	100.0	62.5	0.4	9.1	1.9	26.0	100.0	64.3	0.4	11.5	1.9	21.8
Black	100.0	40.2	0.4	11.5	3.6	44.3	100.0	39.8	0.3	17.4	3.3	39.1
Hispanic	100.0	51.9	0.2	8.6	4.6	34.7	100.0	55.0	0.5	12.3	4.1	28.2
Asian	100.0	70.6	0.1	6.4	2.9	20.0	100.0	74.1	0.1	7.8	3.0	15.0
Pacific Islander	100.0	48.5	0.4	5.4	5.0	40.6	100.0	48.6	1.0	10.6	3.2	36.5
American Indian/Alaska Native	100.0	40.2	0.6	12.6	3.7	42.9	100.0	37.6	1.2	15.6	3.5	42.0
Two or more races	100.0	66.6	0.3	5.3	2.9	25.0	100.0	57.1	0.3	11.4	2.6	28.6
Sex and race/ethnicity												
Male												
White	100.0	59.8	0.3	9.2	2.4	28.3	100.0	61.4	0.3	11.7	2.4	24.2
Black	100.0	35.2	0.4	10.8	3.9	49.7	100.0	34.1	0.3	17.3	3.5	44.7
Hispanic	100.0	47.8	0.2	8.7	5.2	38.0	100.0	50.7	0.3	12.6	4.7	31.6
Asian	100.0	67.8	0.1	6.6	3.5	21.9	100.0	70.7	0.1	8.4	3.8	17.0
Pacific Islander	100.0	46.4	0.2	6.2	5.5	41.6	100.0	44.5	0.9	10.8	4.2	39.5
American Indian/Alaska Native	100.0	37.2	0.6	12.3	4.1	45.8	100.0	36.0	1.1	15.3	3.7	43.9
Two or more races	100.0	64.5	0.2	5.2	3.1	26.9	100.0	53.6	0.2	11.2	3.2	31.8
Female												
White	100.0	64.9	0.5	9.1	1.5	24.1	100.0	66.9	0.5	11.4	1.5	19.7
Black	100.0	43.6	0.4	12.0	3.3	40.6	100.0	43.9	0.3	17.5	3.1	35.1
Hispanic	100.0	54.9	0.3	8.5	4.1	32.2	100.0	58.2	0.5	12.0	3.6	25.6
Asian	100.0	73.1	0.2	6.1	2.3	18.3	100.0	77.1	0.2	7.2	2.4	13.1
Pacific Islander	100.0	50.2	0.6	4.8	4.7	39.8	100.0	52.0	1.2	10.4	2.4	34.1
American Indian/Alaska Native	100.0	42.5	0.7	12.8	3.4	40.7	100.0	38.9	1.4	15.9	3.4	40.5
Two or more races	100.0	68.1	0.3	5.3	2.7	23.6	100.0	59.8	0.3	11.5	2.2	26.2
Control of institution and percent of applications accepted												
Public institutions	100.0	57.2	0.2	11.3	3.2	28.0	100.0	59.7	0.2	13.2	3.2	23.7
Open admissions	100.0	32.2	1.2	16.8	6.0	43.9	100.0	31.3	1.9	19.7	4.6	42.5
90.0 percent or more accepted	100.0	48.1	0.4	14.7	3.6	33.3	100.0	46.2	0.7	18.3	3.9	30.9
75.0 to 89.9 percent accepted	100.0	54.0	0.3	11.8	3.3	30.6	100.0	56.4	0.2	13.8	3.2	26.3
50.0 to 74.9 percent accepted	100.0	60.0	0.1	10.7	3.1	26.1	100.0	61.8	0.2	12.7	3.0	22.3
25.0 to 49.9 percent accepted	100.0	70.0	0.2	8.6	2.5	18.8	100.0	69.1	#	11.3	2.9	16.7
Less than 25.0 percent accepted	100.0	70.4	0.0	4.9	1.9	22.8	100.0	71.3	0.0	5.9	2.9	20.0
Information not available	100.0	37.6	#	9.8	3.5	49.1	100.0	43.4	0.1	12.5	6.4	37.7
Nonprofit institutions	100.0	65.5	0.5	5.2	0.9	27.9	100.0	66.4	0.4	9.6	0.9	22.6
Open admissions	100.0	38.0	1.7	8.9	2.1	49.3	100.0	38.3	2.1	17.4	2.2	40.1
90.0 percent or more accepted	100.0	48.5	0.9	9.1	2.0	39.5	100.0	45.7	1.8	15.5	2.2	34.9
75.0 to 89.9 percent accepted	100.0	61.1	0.9	6.5	0.7	30.8	100.0	62.3	0.4	12.1	1.0	24.1
50.0 to 74.9 percent accepted	100.0	62.3	0.4	5.2	0.9	31.3	100.0	63.2	0.3	10.4	0.8	25.3
25.0 to 49.9 percent accepted	100.0	77.5	0.1	3.9	0.7	17.8	100.0	74.7	0.4	6.7	0.7	17.5
Less than 25.0 percent accepted	100.0	90.6	#	0.9	0.7	7.8	100.0	92.0	#	2.1	0.7	5.2
Information not available	100.0	48.8	2.2	3.7	0.8	44.5	100.0	50.2	0.3	14.1	3.9	31.5
For-profit institutions	100.0	31.5	1.6	1.4	1.9	63.6	100.0	20.8	2.4	6.7	1.8	68.3
Open admissions	100.0	29.9	1.3	0.3	2.4	66.2	100.0	23.2	4.4	3.2	2.0	67.3
90.0 percent or more accepted	100.0	32.4	3.8	1.5	2.1	60.2	100.0	10.8	0.4	24.6	2.0	62.2
75.0 to 89.9 percent accepted	100.0	35.0	1.2	2.4	1.6	59.7	100.0	23.4	3.2	8.1	0.5	64.8
50.0 to 74.9 percent accepted	100.0	35.2	1.9	5.5	0.8	56.7	100.0	27.1	0.9	4.1	0.8	67.2
25.0 to 49.9 percent accepted	100.0	33.2	1.5	1.3	0.9	63.1	100.0	29.9	1.7	2.6	1.6	64.2
Less than 25.0 percent accepted	†	†	†	†	†	†	†	†	†	†	†	†
Information not available	100.0	28.6	1.6	0.3	2.9	66.6	100.0	15.7	0.5	5.0	1.8	77.0

†Not applicable.
#Rounds to zero.
[1]Transfer out data are required to be reported only by those institutions for which preparation for transfers is a substantial part of the institutional mission.
[2]Includes students who dropped out of the reporting institution and students who transferred to another institution without notifying the reporting institution.
NOTE: Data are for first-time full-time bachelor's degree-seeking students at 4-year degree-granting postsecondary institutions participating in Title IV federal financial aid programs.

Detail may not sum to totals because of rounding. Totals include data for persons whose race/ethnicity was not reported. Race categories exclude persons of Hispanic ethnicity.
SOURCE: U.S. Department of Education, National Center for Education Statistics, Integrated Postsecondary Education Data System (IPEDS), Spring 2013 and Winter 2017–18 Graduation Rates component; and IPEDS Fall 2006 and Fall 2011, Institutional Characteristics component. (This table was prepared December 2018.)

Table 326.25. Percentage distribution of first-time, full-time degree/certificate-seeking students at 2-year postsecondary institutions 3 years after entry, by completion and enrollment status at first institution attended, sex, race/ethnicity, and control of institution: Cohort entry years 2009 and 2014

Sex, race/ethnicity, and control of institution	Percentage distribution of 2009 entry cohort 3 years after entry							Percentage distribution of 2014 entry cohort 3 years after entry						
	Total	Completed a program at first institution attended			Did not complete a program at first institution			Total	Completed a program at first institution attended			Did not complete a program at first institution		
		Total, any program	Program of less than 2 years	Program of 2 to 4 years	Transferred out[1]	Remained enrolled	No longer enrolled, status unknown[2]		Total, any program	Program of less than 2 years	Program of 2 to 4 years	Transferred out[1]	Remained enrolled	No longer enrolled, status unknown[2]
1	2	3	4	5	6	7	8	9	10	11	12	13	14	15
Total	**100.0**	**30.9**	**16.6**	**14.3**	**13.5**	**11.0**	**44.6**	**100.0**	**31.6**	**12.6**	**19.0**	**14.7**	**12.4**	**41.2**
Sex														
Male	100.0	27.2	12.9	14.4	14.3	10.7	47.8	100.0	28.7	9.9	18.8	15.3	11.3	44.7
Female	100.0	34.1	19.8	14.3	12.8	11.2	41.9	100.0	34.2	15.0	19.2	14.2	13.5	38.2
Race/ethnicity														
White	100.0	30.1	13.0	17.1	15.4	11.0	43.5	100.0	33.5	10.7	22.8	16.7	11.0	38.8
Black	100.0	26.4	18.6	7.8	13.1	8.0	52.5	100.0	25.3	15.9	9.4	14.9	11.4	48.4
Hispanic	100.0	36.3	25.4	10.9	9.4	13.0	41.2	100.0	30.9	14.1	16.9	11.1	15.4	42.5
Asian	100.0	36.0	13.6	22.4	14.6	16.8	32.6	100.0	37.6	8.7	28.9	15.7	16.7	30.0
Pacific Islander	100.0	25.0	14.9	10.1	14.7	14.7	45.6	100.0	34.6	20.3	14.3	13.2	11.0	41.2
American Indian/Alaska Native	100.0	25.7	14.9	10.7	11.4	10.0	52.9	100.0	28.1	15.0	13.1	11.9	11.3	48.7
Two or more races	100.0	30.5	16.4	14.1	14.1	11.0	44.4	100.0	26.2	8.8	17.5	16.5	11.5	45.8
Sex and race/ethnicity														
Male														
White	100.0	27.8	11.1	16.7	15.6	10.2	46.4	100.0	31.9	9.3	22.6	16.8	9.9	41.3
Black	100.0	22.1	14.8	7.3	14.3	7.5	56.2	100.0	20.8	11.3	9.5	16.4	9.4	53.4
Hispanic	100.0	30.0	19.0	11.1	10.5	13.6	45.8	100.0	26.3	10.7	15.6	11.8	14.9	47.0
Asian	100.0	31.7	9.8	21.9	15.6	18.2	34.5	100.0	33.0	6.2	26.7	16.1	17.8	33.2
Pacific Islander	100.0	21.6	10.5	11.1	15.3	14.4	48.7	100.0	28.9	15.9	13.0	15.6	9.2	46.2
American Indian/Alaska Native	100.0	23.6	13.4	10.2	11.6	8.6	56.1	100.0	23.3	11.5	11.8	12.8	10.5	53.4
Two or more races	100.0	24.6	10.5	14.1	15.7	11.6	48.1	100.0	23.3	6.6	16.7	16.7	11.1	49.0
Female														
White	100.0	32.3	14.8	17.5	15.1	11.8	40.9	100.0	35.0	12.0	23.0	16.5	12.1	36.4
Black	100.0	29.4	21.3	8.1	12.3	8.3	50.0	100.0	28.6	19.2	9.4	13.8	13.0	44.6
Hispanic	100.0	40.9	30.1	10.8	8.7	12.6	37.9	100.0	34.6	16.8	17.8	10.6	15.8	39.0
Asian	100.0	40.3	17.5	22.8	13.6	15.3	30.8	100.0	42.5	11.3	31.2	15.2	15.7	26.7
Pacific Islander	100.0	28.0	18.8	9.2	14.1	15.0	42.9	100.0	39.7	24.2	15.5	11.1	12.5	36.7
American Indian/Alaska Native	100.0	27.3	16.1	11.1	11.2	11.1	50.4	100.0	31.9	17.7	14.2	11.2	11.9	45.0
Two or more races	100.0	35.0	20.9	14.1	12.9	10.5	41.7	100.0	28.8	10.6	18.2	16.3	11.9	43.1
Control of institution														
Public institutions	100.0	19.8	3.8	15.9	17.9	14.5	47.8	100.0	25.1	4.1	21.0	17.6	13.6	43.6
Nonprofit institutions	100.0	62.3	47.2	15.1	4.5	1.9	31.3	100.0	62.2	54.3	7.9	2.6	22.0	13.1
For-profit institutions	100.0	62.7	53.4	9.4	0.4	1.0	35.8	100.0	61.0	50.7	10.3	0.8	2.4	35.8

[1]Transfer out data are required to be reported only by those institutions for which preparation for transfers is a substantial part of the institutional mission.
[2]Includes students who dropped out of the reporting institution and students who transferred to another institution without notifying the reporting institution.
NOTE: Data are for first-time full-time certificate/degree-seeking students at 2-year degree-granting postsecondary institutions participating in Title IV federal financial aid programs. Detail may not sum to totals because of rounding. Totals include data for persons whose race/ethnicity was not reported. Race categories exclude persons of Hispanic ethnicity.
SOURCE: U.S. Department of Education, National Center for Education Statistics, Integrated Postsecondary Education Data System (IPEDS), Spring 2013 and Winter 2017–18 Graduation Rates component. (This table was prepared December 2018.)

Table 326.30. Retention of first-time degree-seeking undergraduates at degree-granting postsecondary institutions, by attendance status, level and control of institution, and percentage of applications accepted: Selected years, 2006 to 2017

Attendance status, level, control, and percent of applications accepted	First-time degree-seekers (adjusted entry cohort),[1] by entry year							Students from adjusted cohort returning in the following year							Percent of first-time undergraduates retained						
	2006	2009	2012	2013	2014	2015	2016	2007	2010	2013	2014	2015	2016	2017	2006 to 2007	2009 to 2010	2012 to 2013	2013 to 2014	2014 to 2015	2015 to 2016	2016 to 2017
1	2	3	4	5	6	7	8	9	10	11	12	13	14	15	16	17	18	19	20	21	22
Full-time students																					
All institutions	**2,170,504**	**2,371,220**	**2,222,696**	**2,222,085**	**2,211,406**	**2,180,675**	**2,176,453**	**1,541,201**	**1,705,242**	**1,620,901**	**1,642,567**	**1,647,295**	**1,640,963**	**1,643,463**	**71.0**	**71.9**	**72.9**	**73.9**	**74.5**	**75.3**	**75.5**
Public institutions	1,522,928	1,732,822	1,637,518	1,646,902	1,639,875	1,619,768	1,619,573	1,071,986	1,222,688	1,168,782	1,193,200	1,200,374	1,198,609	1,203,320	70.4	70.6	71.4	72.5	73.2	74.0	74.3
Nonprofit institutions	466,078	478,755	483,373	483,617	489,834	491,898	491,596	368,783	381,364	388,107	392,080	396,659	399,434	399,154	79.1	79.7	80.3	81.1	81.0	81.2	81.2
For-profit institutions	181,498	159,643	101,805	91,566	81,697	69,009	65,284	100,432	101,190	64,012	57,287	50,262	42,920	40,989	55.3	63.4	62.9	62.6	61.5	62.2	62.8
4-year institutions	1,457,745	1,452,575	1,466,129	1,483,526	1,501,582	1,524,088	1,535,197	1,114,923	1,146,534	1,166,522	1,194,097	1,212,464	1,231,920	1,242,934	76.5	78.9	79.6	80.5	80.7	80.8	81.0
Public institutions	911,509	936,840	957,709	978,041	995,110	1,018,253	1,029,302	711,200	745,703	765,686	790,227	807,687	825,885	836,920	78.0	79.6	79.9	80.8	81.2	81.1	81.3
Open admissions	61,832	45,458	34,897	34,706	31,477	26,888	27,042	38,383	28,675	21,128	21,547	19,618	16,689	16,809	62.1	63.1	60.5	62.1	62.3	62.1	62.2
90.0 percent or more accepted	68,835	63,453	47,775	55,188	60,160	71,117	69,649	49,274	46,280	33,969	40,116	43,559	51,533	50,561	71.6	72.9	71.1	72.7	72.4	72.5	72.6
75.0 to 89.9 percent accepted	244,177	212,573	226,673	261,763	281,422	317,658	288,998	185,457	163,639	174,316	203,517	221,245	251,113	228,226	76.0	77.0	76.9	77.7	78.6	79.1	79.0
50.0 to 74.9 percent accepted	417,093	462,554	469,245	461,551	456,622	435,275	468,263	336,365	376,021	381,576	381,607	376,587	357,438	383,775	80.6	81.3	81.3	82.7	82.5	82.1	82.0
25.0 to 49.9 percent accepted	103,118	131,241	164,067	147,849	145,622	150,981	156,437	88,908	112,209	141,671	127,595	128,568	133,668	139,838	86.2	85.5	86.3	86.3	88.3	88.5	89.4
Less than 25.0 percent accepted	7,716	14,326	8,843	15,315	14,947	15,563	15,951	7,048	13,649	8,357	14,651	14,336	14,959	15,330	91.3	95.3	94.5	95.7	95.9	96.1	96.1
Information not available	8,738	7,235	6,209	1,669	4,860	771	2,962	5,765	5,230	4,669	1,194	3,774	485	2,381	66.0	72.3	75.2	71.5	77.7	62.9	80.4
Nonprofit institutions	457,505	470,795	475,635	476,437	476,823	481,241	484,188	363,459	376,668	383,552	387,685	388,745	392,330	394,215	79.4	80.0	80.6	81.4	81.5	81.5	81.4
Open admissions	26,565	22,613	22,497	12,549	11,792	13,289	13,383	16,019	14,349	14,349	7,653	7,414	8,499	8,799	60.3	63.5	63.8	61.0	62.9	64.0	65.7
90.0 percent or more accepted	13,632	15,135	12,348	22,841	22,225	28,503	23,488	9,543	10,953	8,516	16,881	16,188	20,247	16,811	70.0	72.4	69.0	73.9	72.8	71.0	71.6
75.0 to 89.9 percent accepted	102,358	80,301	79,804	86,040	94,830	80,940	91,351	78,424	62,196	62,184	68,481	74,984	63,872	71,308	76.6	77.5	77.9	79.6	79.1	78.9	78.1
50.0 to 74.9 percent accepted	190,079	218,072	219,709	207,431	199,677	199,442	203,980	148,681	170,232	173,059	162,937	157,866	157,181	162,016	78.2	78.1	78.8	78.5	79.1	78.8	79.4
25.0 to 49.9 percent accepted	93,560	98,312	95,584	98,202	95,164	102,823	98,010	81,880	84,941	81,655	85,484	82,511	89,426	84,290	87.5	86.4	85.4	87.0	86.7	87.0	86.0
Less than 25.0 percent accepted	26,696	32,980	44,735	45,222	48,076	54,573	51,662	25,639	31,790	43,208	43,522	46,054	51,699	49,541	96.0	96.4	96.6	96.2	95.8	94.7	95.9
Information not available	4,615	3,382	958	4,152	5,059	1,671	2,314	3,273	2,207	581	2,727	3,728	1,406	1,450	70.9	65.3	60.6	65.7	73.7	84.1	62.7
For-profit institutions	88,731	44,940	32,785	29,048	29,649	24,594	21,707	40,264	24,163	17,284	16,185	16,032	13,705	11,799	45.4	53.8	52.7	55.7	54.1	55.7	54.4
Open admissions	45,240	16,826	16,799	19,206	21,732	16,511	14,007	18,720	9,260	8,325	10,053	10,827	8,270	6,745	41.4	55.0	49.6	52.3	49.8	50.1	48.2
90.0 percent or more accepted	6,285	3,722	3,337	717	591	770	1,108	3,454	1,311	1,650	509	308	472	559	55.0	35.2	49.4	71.0	52.1	61.3	50.5
75.0 to 89.9 percent accepted	3,703	3,224	1,880	2,920	5,265	3,253	1,174	2,081	1,549	1,224	1,865	3,459	2,159	885	56.2	48.0	65.1	63.9	65.7	66.4	75.4
50.0 to 74.9 percent accepted	12,845	12,061	6,268	3,690	1,489	3,000	4,577	6,536	6,839	3,613	2,472	994	1,973	3,108	50.9	56.7	57.6	67.0	66.8	65.8	67.9
25.0 to 49.9 percent accepted	18,142	6,098	2,908	419	463	1,020	672	8,036	3,423	1,554	293	353	802	363	44.3	56.1	53.4	69.9	76.2	78.6	54.0
Less than 25.0 percent accepted	0	3	0	0	0	8	1	0	2	0	0	0	8	1	†	66.7	†	†	†	100.0	100.0
Information not available	2,516	3,006	1,593	2,096	109	32	168	1,437	1,779	918	993	91	21	138	57.1	59.2	57.6	47.4	83.5	65.6	82.1
2-year institutions	712,759	918,645	756,567	738,559	709,824	656,587	641,256	426,278	558,708	454,379	448,470	434,831	409,043	400,529	59.8	60.8	60.1	60.7	61.3	62.3	62.5
Public institutions	611,419	795,982	679,809	668,861	644,765	601,515	590,271	360,786	476,985	403,096	402,973	392,687	372,724	366,400	59.0	59.9	59.3	60.2	60.9	62.0	62.1
Nonprofit institutions	8,573	7,960	7,738	7,180	13,011	10,657	7,408	5,324	4,696	4,555	4,395	7,914	7,104	4,939	62.1	59.0	58.9	61.2	60.8	66.7	66.7
For-profit institutions	92,767	114,703	69,020	62,518	52,048	44,415	43,577	60,168	77,027	46,728	41,102	34,230	29,215	29,190	64.9	67.2	67.7	65.7	65.8	65.8	67.0
Part-time students																					
All institutions	**461,574**	**545,635**	**515,589**	**490,124**	**470,772**	**429,109**	**412,913**	**190,547**	**229,566**	**222,328**	**213,235**	**205,366**	**192,527**	**187,301**	**41.3**	**42.1**	**43.1**	**43.5**	**43.6**	**44.9**	**45.4**
Public institutions	417,314	497,453	482,851	461,943	445,495	404,279	391,769	170,682	209,164	209,042	202,243	195,147	181,993	178,531	40.9	42.0	43.3	43.8	43.8	45.0	45.6
Nonprofit institutions	14,618	10,359	9,858	9,340	8,885	10,446	8,801	7,027	4,892	3,971	3,883	3,681	4,951	3,895	48.1	47.2	40.3	41.6	41.4	47.4	44.3
For-profit institutions	29,642	37,823	22,880	18,841	16,392	14,384	12,343	12,838	15,510	9,315	7,109	6,538	5,583	4,875	43.3	41.0	40.7	37.7	39.9	38.8	39.5
4-year institutions	81,423	72,046	53,711	49,304	46,606	48,716	46,570	37,988	32,344	23,665	22,269	21,818	23,845	22,712	46.7	44.9	44.1	45.2	46.8	48.9	48.8
Public institutions	47,377	33,327	27,479	26,473	25,833	28,096	29,777	23,337	16,944	13,790	13,862	13,917	15,374	16,050	49.3	50.8	50.2	52.4	53.9	54.7	53.9
Open admissions	19,247	8,356	5,515	5,250	4,605	4,412	5,440	8,004	3,586	1,978	2,098	1,791	1,873	2,151	41.6	42.9	35.9	40.0	38.9	42.5	39.5
90.0 percent or more accepted	3,745	4,004	2,223	2,098	1,951	2,931	2,327	1,909	1,959	1,005	1,063	880	1,382	1,012	51.0	48.9	45.2	50.7	45.1	47.2	43.5
75.0 to 89.9 percent accepted	8,969	6,493	5,226	7,424	6,663	8,722	9,011	4,196	3,268	2,595	3,964	3,591	4,972	4,928	46.8	50.3	49.7	53.4	53.9	57.0	54.7
50.0 to 74.9 percent accepted	11,599	11,254	10,671	9,042	10,343	9,815	10,718	6,766	6,053	5,840	5,065	6,107	5,654	6,462	58.3	53.8	54.7	56.0	59.0	57.6	60.3
25.0 to 49.9 percent accepted	3,373	3,046	2,854	2,553	2,040	2,112	2,103	2,223	1,982	1,774	1,617	1,395	1,433	1,392	65.9	65.1	62.2	63.3	68.4	67.9	66.2
Less than 25.0 percent accepted	65	44	49	51	58	48	65	50	35	38	33	49	38	57	76.9	79.5	77.6	64.7	84.5	79.2	87.7
Information not available	379	130	941	55	173	56	113	189	61	560	22	104	22	48	49.9	46.9	59.5	40.0	60.1	39.3	42.5

See notes at end of table.

Table 326.30. Retention of first-time degree-seeking undergraduates at degree-granting postsecondary institutions, by attendance status, level and control of institution, and percentage of applications accepted: Selected years, 2006 to 2017—Continued

Attendance status, level, control, and percent of applications accepted	First-time degree-seekers (adjusted entry cohort),[1] by entry year							Students from adjusted cohort returning in the following year							Percent of first-time undergraduates retained						
	2006	2009	2012	2013	2014	2015	2016	2007	2010	2013	2014	2015	2016	2017	2006 to 2007	2009 to 2010	2012 to 2013	2013 to 2014	2014 to 2015	2015 to 2016	2016 to 2017
1	2	3	4	5	6	7	8	9	10	11	12	13	14	15	16	17	18	19	20	21	22
Nonprofit institutions	12,861	9,599	9,118	8,501	8,093	9,686	7,938	6,054	4,491	3,603	3,448	3,322	4,612	3,555	47.1	46.8	39.5	40.6	41.0	47.6	44.8
Open admissions	5,419	3,821	4,433	2,434	1,450	1,540	1,615	2,558	1,693	1,400	848	486	673	670	47.2	44.3	31.6	34.8	33.5	43.7	41.5
90.0 percent or more accepted	523	393	915	1,159	494	3,769	1,990	237	199	377	468	204	1,882	887	45.3	50.6	41.2	40.4	41.3	49.9	44.6
75.0 to 89.9 percent accepted	2,459	1,164	1,174	1,332	1,903	874	932	1,047	550	520	622	811	422	463	42.6	47.3	44.3	46.7	42.6	48.3	49.7
50.0 to 74.9 percent accepted	3,131	3,256	1,786	1,515	2,231	1,812	2,293	1,406	1,531	847	701	928	839	1,008	44.9	47.0	47.4	46.3	41.6	46.3	44.0
25.0 to 49.9 percent accepted	853	715	582	606	815	866	602	452	366	276	305	394	381	267	53.0	51.2	47.4	50.3	48.3	44.0	44.4
Less than 25.0 percent accepted	112	93	126	115	136	640	458	86	78	106	101	123	302	238	76.8	83.9	84.1	87.8	90.4	47.2	52.0
Information not available	364	157	102	1,340	1,064	185	48	268	74	77	403	376	113	22	73.6	47.1	75.5	30.1	35.3	61.1	45.8
For-profit institutions	21,185	29,120	17,114	14,330	12,680	10,934	8,855	8,597	10,909	6,272	4,959	4,579	3,859	3,107	40.6	37.5	36.6	34.6	36.1	35.3	35.1
Open admissions	10,514	10,926	9,561	10,395	10,089	8,822	6,432	4,121	4,299	3,909	3,751	3,863	3,183	2,408	39.2	39.3	40.9	36.1	38.3	36.1	37.4
90.0 percent or more accepted	2,212	1,372	360	126	123	246	453	639	375	137	59	30	85	115	28.9	27.3	38.1	46.8	24.4	34.6	25.4
75.0 to 89.9 percent accepted	2,838	3,151	854	1,232	1,794	1,027	109	1,342	1,093	250	353	492	259	29	47.3	34.7	29.3	28.7	27.4	25.2	26.6
50.0 to 74.9 percent accepted	2,774	4,591	1,820	2,471	586	753	812	1,134	2,249	596	756	158	282	328	40.9	49.0	32.7	30.6	27.0	37.5	40.4
25.0 to 49.9 percent accepted	2,033	1,099	2,537	73	9	81	1,043	627	342	727	25	2	45	227	30.8	31.1	28.7	34.2	22.2	55.6	21.8
Less than 25.0 percent accepted	0	0	0	0	0	0	0	0	0	0	0	0	0	0	†	†	†	†	†	†	†
Information not available	814	7,981	1,982	33	79	5	6	734	2,551	653	15	34	5	0	90.2	32.0	32.9	45.5	43.0	100.0	0.0
2-year institutions	380,151	473,589	461,878	440,820	424,166	380,393	366,343	152,559	197,222	198,663	190,966	183,548	168,682	164,589	40.1	41.6	43.0	43.3	43.3	44.3	44.9
Public institutions	369,937	464,126	455,372	435,470	419,662	376,183	361,992	147,345	192,220	195,252	188,381	181,230	166,619	162,481	39.8	41.4	42.9	43.3	43.2	44.3	44.9
Nonprofit institutions	1,757	760	740	839	792	760	863	973	401	368	435	359	339	340	55.4	52.8	49.7	51.8	45.3	44.6	39.4
For-profit institutions	8,457	8,703	5,766	4,511	3,712	3,450	3,488	4,241	4,601	3,043	2,150	1,959	1,724	1,768	50.1	52.9	52.8	47.7	52.8	50.0	50.7

†Not applicable.

[1]Adjusted entry cohort counts exclude students who died or were totally and permanently disabled, served in the armed forces (including those called to active duty), served with a foreign aid service of the federal government (e.g., Peace Corps), or served on official church missions. For 4-year institutions, the adjusted entry cohort is based on first-time bachelor's degree-seeking students.

NOTE: Returning students data for 2-year institutions include returning students, plus students who completed their program. Some data have been revised from previously published figures.

SOURCE: U.S. Department of Education, National Center for Education Statistics, Integrated Postsecondary Education Data System (IPEDS), Spring 2008 through Spring 2018, Fall Enrollment component; and IPEDS Fall 2006 through Fall 2016, Institutional Characteristics component. (This table was prepared October 2018.)

Table 329.10 On-campus crimes, arrests, and referrals for disciplinary action at degree-granting postsecondary institutions, by location of incident, control and level of institution, and type of incident: Selected years, 2001 through 2016

Control and level of institution and type of incident	Number of incidents															
	Total, in residence halls and at other locations													2016		
	2001	2004	2005	2006	2007	2008	2009	2010	2011	2012	2013	2014	2015	Total	In residence halls	At other locations
1	2	3	4	5	6	7	8	9	10	11	12	13	14	15	16	17
All institutions																
Selected crimes against persons and property	41,596	43,555	42,710	44,492	41,829	40,296	34,054	32,097	30,407	29,766	27,236	26,818	27,638	28,406	14,606	13,800
Murder[1]	17	15	11	8	44	12	16	15	16	12	23	11	28	15	3	12
Negligent manslaughter[2]	2	0	2	0	3	3	0	1	1	1	0	2	2	2	0	2
Sex offenses—forcible[3]	2,201	2,667	2,674	2,670	2,694	2,639	2,544	2,927	3,375	4,015	4,977	6,751	8,031	8,906	6,588	2,318
Rape	—	—	—	—	—	—	—	—	—	—	—	4,431	5,125	5,824	4,884	940
Fondling	—	—	—	—	—	—	—	—	—	—	—	2,320	2,906	3,082	1,704	1,378
Sex offenses—nonforcible[4]	461	27	42	43	40	35	65	33	46	46	45	53	63	60	27	33
Robbery[5]	1,663	1,550	1,551	1,547	1,561	1,576	1,409	1,392	1,285	1,368	1,317	1,041	1,048	1,106	208	898
Aggravated assault[6]	2,947	2,721	2,656	2,817	2,604	2,495	2,327	2,221	2,239	2,423	2,044	2,048	2,265	2,205	726	1,479
Burglary[7]	26,904	29,480	29,256	31,260	29,488	28,737	23,083	21,335	19,472	18,183	15,232	13,419	12,386	12,015	6,716	5,299
Motor vehicle theft[8]	6,221	6,062	5,531	5,231	4,619	4,104	3,977	3,441	3,334	3,013	2,971	2,890	3,236	3,499	9	3,490
Arson[9]	1,180	1,033	987	916	776	695	633	732	639	705	627	603	579	598	329	269
Weapons-, drug-, and liquor-related arrests and referrals																
Arrests[10]	40,348	47,939	49,024	50,187	50,558	50,639	50,066	51,519	54,285	52,325	46,975	44,531	40,348	39,049	19,321	19,728
Illegal weapons possession	1,073	1,263	1,316	1,316	1,318	1,190	1,077	1,112	1,023	1,023	1,018	990	1,186	1,211	311	900
Drug law violations	11,854	12,775	13,707	13,952	14,135	15,146	15,871	18,589	20,729	21,212	19,799	19,172	19,466	19,266	9,421	9,845
Liquor law violations	27,421	33,901	34,001	34,919	35,105	34,303	33,118	31,818	32,533	30,090	26,158	24,369	19,696	18,572	9,589	8,983
Referrals for disciplinary action[10]	155,201	196,775	202,816	218,040	216,600	217,526	220,987	230,269	249,694	251,402	244,985	253,315	242,185	231,568	212,497	19,071
Illegal weapons possession	1,277	1,799	1,882	1,871	1,658	1,455	1,275	1,314	1,282	1,404	1,410	1,425	1,434	1,426	971	455
Drug law violations	23,900	25,762	25,356	27,251	28,476	32,469	36,344	42,022	51,562	53,959	53,439	56,575	56,125	56,481	48,888	7,593
Liquor law violations	130,024	169,214	175,578	188,918	186,466	183,602	183,368	186,933	196,850	196,039	190,136	195,315	184,626	173,661	162,638	11,023
Public 4-year																
Selected crimes against persons and property	18,710	19,984	19,582	20,648	19,579	18,695	15,975	15,503	14,675	14,510	13,127	13,346	13,614	14,169	6,865	7,304
Murder[1]	9	8	4	5	42	9	8	9	10	7	10	3	13	8	2	6
Negligent manslaughter[2]	2	0	1	0	2	1	0	0	1	1	0	1	1	2	0	2
Sex offenses—forcible[3]	1,245	1,482	1,398	1,400	1,425	1,317	1,214	1,461	1,638	1,973	2,264	3,211	3,964	4,406	3,204	1,202
Rape	—	—	—	—	—	—	—	—	—	—	—	2,118	2,544	2,933	2,429	504
Fondling	—	—	—	—	—	—	—	—	—	—	—	1,093	1,420	1,473	775	698
Sex offenses—nonforcible[4]	207	16	25	15	23	12	40	15	17	17	18	28	37	30	17	13
Robbery[5]	584	612	696	680	722	750	647	662	612	657	635	550	581	594	111	483
Aggravated assault[6]	1,434	1,269	1,280	1,338	1,258	1,182	1,134	1,076	1,076	1,200	1,000	1,016	1,148	1,158	386	772
Burglary[7]	11,520	13,026	12,935	14,027	13,371	12,970	10,708	10,219	9,373	8,821	7,258	6,678	5,789	5,611	2,946	2,665
Motor vehicle theft[8]	3,072	2,964	2,667	2,662	2,266	2,027	1,824	1,604	1,592	1,406	1,537	1,500	1,774	2,022	2	2,020
Arson[9]	637	607	576	521	470	427	400	457	356	428	405	359	307	338	197	141
Weapons-, drug-, and liquor-related arrests and referrals																
Arrests[10]	31,077	36,746	38,051	39,900	39,570	40,607	40,780	41,992	44,891	43,155	38,073	36,249	32,729	31,596	15,449	16,147
Illegal weapons possession	692	811	878	859	825	759	659	669	629	621	637	619	721	760	215	545
Drug law violations	9,125	9,620	10,606	10,850	10,693	11,714	12,186	14,362	16,323	16,792	15,571	15,119	15,521	15,546	7,677	7,869
Liquor law violations	21,260	26,315	26,567	28,191	28,052	28,134	27,935	26,961	27,939	25,742	21,865	20,511	16,487	15,290	7,557	7,733
Referrals for disciplinary action[10]	79,152	100,588	100,211	107,289	106,148	104,585	108,756	116,029	129,667	132,363	127,155	134,310	127,369	120,467	109,989	10,478
Illegal weapons possession	678	1,001	1,097	972	867	792	669	664	610	644	604	646	571	598	416	182
Drug law violations	13,179	13,658	13,020	13,798	14,458	16,656	18,260	21,451	27,339	28,880	28,259	30,376	30,582	30,164	25,635	4,529
Liquor law violations	65,295	85,929	86,094	92,519	90,823	87,137	89,827	93,914	101,718	102,839	98,292	103,288	96,216	89,705	83,938	5,767
Nonprofit 4-year																
Selected crimes against persons and property	14,844	15,523	15,574	16,864	15,452	14,892	11,964	11,202	10,740	10,790	10,290	9,995	10,514	11,089	6,948	4,141
Murder[1]	5	4	5	3	2	1	6	5	3	2	5	5	2	4	1	3
Negligent manslaughter[2]	0	0	1	0	1	0	0	0	0	0	0	0	1	0	0	0
Sex offenses—forcible[3]	820	1,026	1,088	1,080	1,065	1,083	1,102	1,225	1,431	1,741	2,379	3,105	3,518	3,951	3,177	774
Rape	—	—	—	—	—	—	—	—	—	—	—	2,152	2,370	2,689	2,323	366
Fondling	—	—	—	—	—	—	—	—	—	—	—	953	1,148	1,262	854	408
Sex offenses—nonforcible[4]	113	5	6	10	8	16	11	8	13	10	12	7	15	11	6	5
Robbery[5]	649	577	500	502	460	437	366	319	320	386	373	263	281	327	77	250
Aggravated assault[6]	882	838	744	834	768	754	661	641	631	667	681	655	729	683	262	421
Burglary[7]	10,471	11,426	11,657	13,051	11,941	11,551	8,810	8,138	7,421	7,046	5,999	5,020	4,936	5,067	3,290	1,777
Motor vehicle theft[8]	1,471	1,316	1,248	1,077	984	859	834	641	704	711	667	754	822	834	6	828
Arson[9]	433	331	325	307	223	191	174	225	217	227	174	186	210	212	129	83
Weapons-, drug-, and liquor-related arrests and referrals																
Arrests[10]	6,329	7,722	7,406	6,134	6,732	6,112	5,777	5,459	5,444	5,477	5,642	4,950	4,600	4,511	2,635	1,876
Illegal weapons possession	167	184	150	146	178	158	148	137	129	127	131	129	170	194	68	126
Drug law violations	1,628	1,751	1,691	1,650	1,804	1,883	2,080	2,248	2,425	2,415	2,503	2,258	2,245	2,204	1,297	907
Liquor law violations	4,534	5,787	5,565	4,338	4,750	4,071	3,549	3,074	2,890	2,935	3,008	2,563	2,185	2,113	1,270	843
Referrals for disciplinary action[10]	71,293	90,749	96,646	103,484	103,254	105,289	103,457	104,939	110,607	110,268	109,298	110,150	105,914	102,815	95,708	7,107
Illegal weapons possession	443	608	590	622	545	457	358	393	417	498	535	481	572	576	465	111
Drug law violations	9,688	10,903	11,208	12,114	12,685	14,157	15,845	17,841	21,240	22,168	22,116	23,000	22,237	23,133	20,919	2,214
Liquor law violations	61,162	79,238	84,848	90,748	90,024	90,675	87,254	86,705	88,950	87,602	86,647	86,669	83,105	79,106	74,324	4,782

See notes at end of table.

Table 329.10 On-campus crimes, arrests, and referrals for disciplinary action at degree-granting postsecondary institutions, by location of incident, control and level of institution, and type of incident: Selected years, 2001 through 2016—Continued

Control and level of institution and type of incident	Number of incidents: Total, in residence halls and at other locations: 2001	2004	2005	2006	2007	2008	2009	2010	2011	2012	2013	2014	2015	2016: Total	2016: In residence halls	2016: At other locations
1	2	3	4	5	6	7	8	9	10	11	12	13	14	15	16	17
For-profit 4-year																
Selected crimes against persons and property	505	718	829	641	612	574	525	561	446	364	511	442	317	293	120	173
Murder[1]	0	0	0	0	0	0	0	0	1	0	1	0	0	0	0	0
Negligent manslaughter[2]	0	0	0	0	0	0	0	0	0	0	0	0	0	0	0	0
Sex offenses—forcible[3]	4	5	4	12	12	9	9	22	26	18	18	43	36	35	24	11
Rape	—	—	—	—	—	—	—	—	—	—	—	26	11	18	13	5
Fondling	—	—	—	—	—	—	—	—	—	—	—	17	25	17	11	6
Sex offenses—nonforcible[4]	13	0	1	0	2	0	1	1	0	3	2	2	0	1	1	0
Robbery[5]	64	46	43	25	31	38	86	70	74	51	86	52	25	29	3	26
Aggravated assault[6]	23	38	59	31	31	63	43	51	36	43	58	33	29	40	18	22
Burglary[7]	347	524	607	489	446	385	299	350	249	195	276	251	171	133	73	60
Motor vehicle theft[8]	52	100	110	78	89	79	85	65	58	53	68	59	55	52	1	51
Arson[9]	2	5	5	6	1	0	2	2	2	1	2	2	1	3	0	3
Weapons-, drug-, and liquor-related arrests and referrals																
Arrests[10]	11	41	28	52	28	40	54	165	152	126	74	117	108	110	57	53
Illegal weapons possession	2	5	2	5	3	8	6	13	11	10	12	9	15	11	1	10
Drug law violations	4	12	16	14	16	14	22	66	41	49	48	68	83	80	46	34
Liquor law violations	5	24	10	33	9	18	26	86	100	67	14	40	10	19	10	9
Referrals for disciplinary action[10]	316	298	529	513	519	566	882	760	718	668	1,161	935	885	867	776	91
Illegal weapons possession	11	11	42	13	11	13	23	9	16	23	18	16	15	15	12	3
Drug law violations	92	99	128	138	132	159	231	221	233	254	537	403	371	386	335	51
Liquor law violations	213	188	359	362	376	394	628	530	469	391	606	516	499	466	429	37
Public 2-year																
Selected crimes against persons and property	6,817	6,637	5,981	5,669	5,381	5,464	4,984	4,396	4,141	3,749	3,075	2,845	3,018	2,648	627	2,021
Murder[1]	2	3	2	0	0	2	2	1	2	3	7	3	13	3	0	3
Negligent manslaughter[2]	0	0	0	0	0	0	0	1	0	0	0	1	0	0	0	0
Sex offenses—forcible[3]	118	142	175	167	181	210	205	210	262	263	303	385	495	490	167	323
Rape	—	—	—	—	—	—	—	—	—	—	—	132	197	175	112	63
Fondling	—	—	—	—	—	—	—	—	—	—	—	253	298	315	55	260
Sex offenses—nonforcible[4]	119	6	10	16	7	7	12	8	16	13	11	16	11	18	3	15
Robbery[5]	245	213	248	284	279	285	251	298	262	244	197	148	150	138	16	122
Aggravated assault[6]	545	497	501	546	462	401	431	409	406	437	278	305	334	285	56	229
Burglary[7]	4,132	4,068	3,541	3,261	3,202	3,430	2,920	2,398	2,235	1,964	1,583	1,383	1,414	1,124	383	741
Motor vehicle theft[8]	1,552	1,620	1,428	1,319	1,174	1,059	1,109	1,028	899	776	651	548	542	546	0	546
Arson[9]	104	88	76	76	76	70	54	43	59	49	45	56	59	44	2	42
Weapons-, drug-, and liquor-related arrests and referrals																
Arrests[10]	2,660	3,270	3,416	3,993	4,124	3,764	3,335	3,811	3,723	3,464	3,060	3,121	2,842	2,720	1,138	1,582
Illegal weapons possession	198	255	278	300	304	258	256	282	248	253	230	220	268	222	27	195
Drug law violations	989	1,312	1,326	1,378	1,563	1,490	1,507	1,866	1,892	1,885	1,588	1,671	1,568	1,377	386	991
Liquor law violations	1,473	1,703	1,812	2,315	2,257	2,016	1,572	1,663	1,583	1,326	1,242	1,230	1,006	1,121	725	396
Referrals for disciplinary action[10]	3,529	4,371	4,688	5,897	5,987	6,425	7,241	8,017	8,174	7,586	6,845	7,240	7,292	6,884	5,524	1,360
Illegal weapons possession	127	167	133	238	218	183	210	242	228	224	243	269	271	229	75	154
Drug law violations	761	858	819	908	1,006	1,302	1,745	2,336	2,573	2,468	2,304	2,548	2,626	2,582	1,809	773
Liquor law violations	2,641	3,346	3,736	4,751	4,763	4,940	5,286	5,439	5,373	4,894	4,298	4,423	4,395	4,073	3,640	433
Nonprofit 2-year																
Selected crimes against persons and property	248	166	314	250	258	272	147	120	148	107	66	64	63	92	37	55
Murder[1]	1	0	0	0	0	0	0	0	0	0	0	0	0	0	0	0
Negligent manslaughter[2]	0	0	0	0	0	1	0	0	0	0	0	0	0	0	0	0
Sex offenses—forcible[3]	2	3	8	3	9	16	8	7	11	8	4	3	12	15	14	1
Rape	—	—	—	—	—	—	—	—	—	—	—	2	1	7	6	1
Fondling	—	—	—	—	—	—	—	—	—	—	—	1	11	8	8	0
Sex offenses—nonforcible[4]	2	0	0	1	0	0	0	0	0	0	2	0	0	0	0	0
Robbery[5]	54	22	9	7	2	13	9	5	1	2	3	0	2	8	1	7
Aggravated assault[6]	23	17	22	35	52	66	5	9	53	46	13	27	7	12	2	10
Burglary[7]	142	111	266	187	178	160	120	95	74	47	41	29	32	38	19	19
Motor vehicle theft[8]	23	13	7	14	14	9	4	2	7	4	3	5	8	18	0	18
Arson[9]	1	0	2	3	3	7	1	2	2	0	0	0	2	1	1	0
Weapons-, drug-, and liquor-related arrests and referrals																
Arrests[10]	108	48	76	67	59	93	58	49	52	52	66	39	44	79	34	45
Illegal weapons possession	1	2	5	3	4	3	4	6	5	5	5	5	9	16	0	16
Drug law violations	21	16	32	34	27	33	35	18	34	31	49	28	30	40	12	28
Liquor law violations	86	30	39	30	28	57	19	25	13	16	12	6	5	23	22	1
Referrals for disciplinary action[10]	624	447	514	537	519	413	348	377	360	300	320	448	562	435	414	21
Illegal weapons possession	2	5	12	19	10	6	7	4	1	6	7	11	2	4	2	2
Drug law violations	91	58	47	74	73	85	100	105	109	103	129	155	221	174	159	15
Liquor law violations	531	384	455	444	436	322	241	268	250	191	184	282	339	257	253	4

See notes at end of table.

Table 329.10 On-campus crimes, arrests, and referrals for disciplinary action at degree-granting postsecondary institutions, by location of incident, control and level of institution, and type of incident: Selected years, 2001 through 2016—Continued

Control and level of institution and type of incident	Number of incidents															
	Total, in residence halls and at other locations													2016		
	2001	2004	2005	2006	2007	2008	2009	2010	2011	2012	2013	2014	2015	Total	In residence halls	At other locations
1	2	3	4	5	6	7	8	9	10	11	12	13	14	15	16	17
For-profit 2-year																
Selected crimes against persons and property	472	527	430	420	547	399	459	315	257	246	167	126	112	115	9	106
Murder[1]	0	0	0	0	0	0	0	0	0	0	0	0	0	0	0	0
Negligent manslaughter[2]	0	0	0	0	0	1	0	0	0	0	0	0	0	0	0	0
Sex offenses—forcible[3]	12	9	1	8	2	4	6	2	7	12	9	4	6	9	2	7
Rape	—	—	—	—	—	—	—	—	—	—	—	1	2	2	1	1
Fondling	—	—	—	—	—	—	—	—	—	—	—	3	4	7	1	6
Sex offenses—nonforcible[4]	7	0	0	1	0	0	1	1	0	3	0	0	0	0	0	0
Robbery[5]	67	80	55	49	67	53	50	38	16	28	23	28	9	10	0	10
Aggravated assault[6]	40	62	50	33	33	29	53	35	37	30	14	12	18	27	2	25
Burglary[7]	292	325	250	245	350	241	226	135	120	110	75	58	44	42	5	37
Motor vehicle theft[8]	51	49	71	81	92	71	121	101	74	63	45	24	35	27	0	27
Arson[9]	3	2	3	3	3	0	2	3	3	0	1	0	0	0	0	0
Weapons-, drug-, and liquor-related arrests and referrals																
Arrests[10]	163	112	47	41	45	23	62	43	23	51	60	55	25	33	8	25
Illegal weapons possession	13	6	3	3	4	4	4	5	1	7	3	8	3	8	0	8
Drug law violations	87	64	36	26	32	12	41	29	14	40	40	28	19	19	3	16
Liquor law violations	63	42	8	12	9	7	17	9	8	4	17	19	3	6	5	1
Referrals for disciplinary action[10]	287	322	228	320	173	248	303	147	168	217	206	232	163	100	86	14
Illegal weapons possession	16	7	8	7	7	4	8	2	10	9	3	2	3	4	1	3
Drug law violations	89	186	134	219	122	110	163	68	68	86	94	93	88	42	31	11
Liquor law violations	182	129	86	94	44	134	132	77	90	122	109	137	72	54	54	0

—Not available.
[1]Excludes suicides, fetal deaths, traffic fatalities, accidental deaths, and justifiable homicide (such as the killing of a felon by a law enforcement officer in the line of duty).
[2]Killing of another person through gross negligence (excludes traffic fatalities).
[3]Any sexual act directed against another person forcibly and/or against that person's will.
[4]Includes only statutory rape or incest.
[5]Taking or attempting to take anything of value using actual or threatened force or violence.
[6]Attack upon a person for the purpose of inflicting severe or aggravated bodily injury.
[7]Unlawful entry of a structure to commit a felony or theft.
[8]Theft or attempted theft of a motor vehicle.
[9]Willful or malicious burning or attempt to burn a dwelling house, public building, motor vehicle, or personal property of another.
[10]If an individual is both arrested and referred to college officials for disciplinary action for a single offense, only the arrest is counted.

NOTE: Data are for degree-granting institutions, which are institutions that grant associate's or higher degrees and participate in Title IV federal financial aid programs. Some institutions that report Clery data—specifically, non-degree-granting institutions and institutions outside of the 50 states and the District of Columbia—are excluded from this table. Crimes, arrests, and referrals include incidents involving students, staff, and on-campus guests. Excludes off-campus crimes and arrests even if they involve college students or staff. Some data have been revised from previously published figures.
SOURCE: U.S. Department of Education, Office of Postsecondary Education, Campus Safety and Security Reporting System, 2001 through 2016; and National Center for Education Statistics, Integrated Postsecondary Education Data System (IPEDS), Fall 2002 through Fall 2016, Institutional Characteristics component. (This table was prepared September 2018.)

Table 329.20 On-campus crimes, arrests, and referrals for disciplinary action per 10,000 full-time-equivalent (FTE) students at degree-granting postsecondary institutions, by whether institution has residence halls, control and level of institution, and type of incident: Selected years, 2001 through 2016

Control and level of institution and type of incident	Number of incidents per 10,000 FTE students[1]															
	Total, institutions with and without residence halls													2016		
	2001	2004	2005	2006	2007	2008	2009	2010	2011	2012	2013	2014	2015	Total	Institutions with residence halls	Institutions without residence halls
1	2	3	4	5	6	7	8	9	10	11	12	13	14	15	16	17
All institutions																
Selected crimes against persons and property	35.619	33.580	32.864	33.350	30.559	28.993	22.955	20.869	20.027	19.983	18.461	18.069	18.683	19.203	24.843	5.897
Murder[2]	0.015	0.012	0.008	0.006	0.032	0.009	0.011	0.010	0.011	0.008	0.016	0.007	0.019	0.010	0.013	0.005
Negligent manslaughter[3]	0.002	0.000	0.002	0.000	0.002	0.002	0.000	0.001	0.001	0.001	0.000	0.001	0.001	0.001	0.002	0.000
Sex offenses—forcible[4]	1.885	2.056	2.058	2.001	1.968	1.899	1.715	1.903	2.223	2.695	3.374	4.549	5.429	6.020	8.216	0.842
Rape	—	—	—	—	—	—	—	—	—	—	—	2.985	3.464	3.937	5.540	0.157
Fondling	—	—	—	—	—	—	—	—	—	—	—	1.563	1.964	2.083	2.676	0.686
Sex offenses—nonforcible[5]	0.395	0.021	0.032	0.032	0.029	0.025	0.044	0.021	0.030	0.031	0.031	0.036	0.043	0.041	0.044	0.032
Robbery[6]	1.424	1.195	1.193	1.160	1.140	1.134	0.950	0.905	0.846	0.918	0.893	0.701	0.708	0.748	0.899	0.391
Aggravated assault[7]	2.524	2.098	2.044	2.112	1.902	1.795	1.569	1.444	1.475	1.627	1.385	1.380	1.531	1.491	1.786	0.795
Burglary[8]	23.038	22.728	22.511	23.432	21.543	20.676	15.559	13.872	12.825	12.207	10.325	9.041	8.373	8.122	10.666	2.121
Motor vehicle theft[9]	5.327	4.674	4.256	3.921	3.375	2.953	2.681	2.237	2.196	2.023	2.014	1.947	2.187	2.365	2.693	1.592
Arson[10]	1.010	0.796	0.759	0.687	0.567	0.500	0.427	0.476	0.421	0.473	0.425	0.406	0.391	0.404	0.525	0.120
Weapons-, drug-, and liquor-related arrests and referrals																
Arrests[11]	34.550	36.960	37.722	37.619	36.936	36.435	33.748	33.497	35.755	35.127	31.841	30.004	27.274	26.397	36.155	3.381
Illegal weapons possession	0.919	0.974	1.013	0.986	0.963	0.856	0.726	0.723	0.674	0.687	0.690	0.667	0.802	0.819	0.948	0.513
Drug law violations	10.151	9.849	10.547	10.458	10.327	10.898	10.698	12.086	13.653	14.240	13.420	12.917	13.159	13.024	17.573	2.293
Liquor law violations	23.481	26.137	26.163	26.175	25.647	24.681	22.324	20.687	21.428	20.200	17.730	16.419	13.314	12.555	17.634	0.574
Referrals for disciplinary action[11]	132.899	151.708	156.060	163.438	158.241	156.511	148.959	149.716	164.460	168.772	166.056	170.675	163.711	156.541	221.432	3.474
Illegal weapons possession	1.093	1.387	1.448	1.402	1.211	1.047	0.859	0.854	0.844	0.943	0.956	0.960	0.969	0.964	1.251	0.286
Drug law violations	20.466	19.862	19.511	20.427	20.804	23.362	24.498	27.322	33.961	36.224	36.222	38.118	37.939	38.181	53.711	1.549
Liquor law violations	111.340	130.459	135.101	141.609	136.226	132.103	123.602	121.540	129.654	131.606	128.878	131.597	124.802	117.396	166.469	1.639
Public 4-year																
Selected crimes against persons and property	36.191	35.522	34.295	35.531	32.846	30.535	24.898	23.448	21.958	21.669	19.553	19.545	19.646	19.750	21.295	6.404
Murder[2]	0.017	0.014	0.007	0.009	0.070	0.015	0.012	0.014	0.015	0.010	0.015	0.004	0.019	0.011	0.012	0.000
Negligent manslaughter[3]	0.004	0.000	0.002	0.000	0.003	0.002	0.000	0.000	0.001	0.001	0.000	0.001	0.001	0.003	0.003	0.000
Sex offenses—forcible[4]	2.408	2.634	2.448	2.409	2.391	2.151	1.892	2.210	2.451	2.946	3.372	4.702	5.720	6.141	6.736	1.007
Rape	—	—	—	—	—	—	—	—	—	—	—	3.102	3.671	4.088	4.543	0.161
Fondling	—	—	—	—	—	—	—	—	—	—	—	1.601	2.049	2.053	2.193	0.846
Sex offenses—nonforcible[5]	0.400	0.028	0.044	0.026	0.039	0.020	0.062	0.023	0.025	0.025	0.027	0.041	0.053	0.042	0.047	0.000
Robbery[6]	1.130	1.088	1.219	1.170	1.211	1.225	1.008	1.001	0.916	0.981	0.946	0.805	0.838	0.828	0.871	0.456
Aggravated assault[7]	2.774	2.256	2.242	2.302	2.110	1.931	1.767	1.627	1.610	1.792	1.490	1.488	1.657	1.614	1.688	0.980
Burglary[8]	22.283	23.154	22.654	24.138	22.432	21.184	16.689	15.456	14.025	13.173	10.811	9.780	8.354	7.821	8.484	2.094
Motor vehicle theft[9]	5.942	5.269	4.671	4.581	3.802	3.311	2.843	2.426	2.382	2.100	2.289	2.197	2.560	2.818	2.949	1.692
Arson[10]	1.232	1.079	1.009	0.897	0.788	0.697	0.623	0.691	0.533	0.639	0.603	0.526	0.443	0.471	0.505	0.175
Weapons-, drug-, and liquor-related arrests and referrals																
Arrests[11]	60.113	65.318	66.641	68.660	66.384	66.324	63.558	63.512	67.169	64.447	56.711	53.086	47.230	44.040	48.651	4.243
Illegal weapons possession	1.339	1.442	1.538	1.478	1.384	1.240	1.027	1.012	0.941	0.927	0.949	0.907	1.040	1.059	1.131	0.443
Drug law violations	17.651	17.100	18.575	18.671	17.939	19.133	18.993	21.722	24.424	25.077	23.194	22.142	22.398	21.669	23.790	3.357
Liquor law violations	41.123	46.776	46.529	48.511	47.061	45.952	43.539	40.778	41.804	38.443	32.569	30.038	23.792	21.312	23.730	0.443
Referrals for disciplinary action[11]	153.104	178.800	175.506	184.622	178.077	170.820	169.503	175.490	194.017	197.669	189.403	196.696	183.801	167.913	187.154	1.826
Illegal weapons possession	1.311	1.779	1.921	1.673	1.455	1.294	1.043	1.004	0.913	0.962	0.900	0.946	0.824	0.834	0.901	0.255
Drug law violations	25.492	24.278	22.803	23.744	24.255	27.204	28.459	32.444	40.907	43.129	42.093	44.485	44.132	42.044	46.795	1.034
Liquor law violations	126.301	152.743	150.782	159.206	152.367	142.322	140.001	142.042	152.198	153.578	146.410	151.264	138.845	125.036	139.458	0.537
Nonprofit 4-year																
Selected crimes against persons and property	57.358	54.728	54.165	57.679	52.036	49.337	38.613	35.193	33.154	33.198	31.205	30.156	31.209	32.654	35.151	7.780
Murder[2]	0.019	0.014	0.017	0.010	0.007	0.003	0.019	0.016	0.009	0.006	0.015	0.015	0.006	0.012	0.013	0.000
Negligent manslaughter[3]	0.000	0.000	0.003	0.000	0.003	0.000	0.000	0.000	0.000	0.000	0.000	0.000	0.003	0.000	0.000	0.000
Sex offenses—forcible[4]	3.169	3.617	3.784	3.694	3.586	3.588	3.557	3.848	4.417	5.357	7.214	9.368	10.443	11.635	12.721	0.807
Rape	—	—	—	—	—	—	—	—	—	—	—	6.493	7.035	7.918	8.687	0.258
Fondling	—	—	—	—	—	—	—	—	—	—	—	2.875	3.408	3.716	4.034	0.549
Sex offenses—nonforcible[5]	0.437	0.018	0.021	0.034	0.027	0.053	0.036	0.025	0.040	0.031	0.036	0.021	0.045	0.032	0.036	0.000
Robbery[6]	2.508	2.034	1.739	1.717	1.549	1.448	1.181	1.002	0.988	1.188	1.131	0.793	0.834	0.963	1.017	0.420
Aggravated assault[7]	3.408	2.954	2.588	2.853	2.586	2.498	2.133	2.014	1.948	2.052	2.065	1.976	2.164	2.011	2.048	1.646
Burglary[8]	40.460	40.284	40.542	44.638	40.212	38.269	28.434	25.567	22.908	21.679	18.192	15.146	14.652	14.921	16.114	3.035
Motor vehicle theft[9]	5.684	4.640	4.340	3.684	3.314	2.846	2.692	2.014	2.173	2.188	2.023	2.275	2.440	2.456	2.521	1.808
Arson[10]	1.673	1.167	1.130	1.050	0.751	0.633	0.562	0.707	0.670	0.698	0.528	0.561	0.623	0.624	0.680	0.065

See notes at end of table.

Table 329.20 On-campus crimes, arrests, and referrals for disciplinary action per 10,000 full-time-equivalent (FTE) students at degree-granting postsecondary institutions, by whether institution has residence halls, control and level of institution, and type of incident: Selected years, 2001 through 2016—Continued

Control and level of institution and type of incident	Number of incidents per 10,000 FTE students[1]															
	Total, institutions with and without residence halls													2016		
	2001	2004	2005	2006	2007	2008	2009	2010	2011	2012	2013	2014	2015	Total	Institutions with residence halls	Institutions without residence halls
1	2	3	4	5	6	7	8	9	10	11	12	13	14	15	16	17
Weapons-, drug-, and liquor-related arrests and referrals																
Arrests[11]	24.456	27.225	25.758	20.980	22.670	20.249	18.645	17.150	16.805	16.851	17.110	14.935	13.654	13.284	14.442	1.743
Illegal weapons possession	0.645	0.649	0.522	0.499	0.599	0.523	0.478	0.430	0.398	0.391	0.397	0.389	0.505	0.571	0.603	0.258
Drug law violations	6.291	6.173	5.881	5.643	6.075	6.238	6.713	7.062	7.486	7.430	7.590	6.813	6.664	6.490	7.048	0.936
Liquor law violations	17.520	20.403	19.355	14.837	15.996	13.487	11.454	9.657	8.921	9.030	9.122	7.733	6.486	6.222	6.792	0.549
Referrals for disciplinary action[11]	275.480	319.945	336.127	353.943	347.714	348.824	333.904	329.679	341.437	339.263	331.451	332.331	314.388	302.763	331.140	20.047
Illegal weapons possession	1.712	2.144	2.052	2.127	1.835	1.514	1.155	1.235	1.287	1.532	1.622	1.451	1.698	1.696	1.847	0.194
Drug law violations	37.435	38.440	38.981	41.433	42.718	46.902	51.139	56.050	65.567	68.205	67.068	69.393	66.007	68.120	74.553	4.035
Liquor law violations	236.333	279.362	295.095	310.383	303.161	300.408	281.609	272.395	274.583	269.526	262.761	261.487	246.683	232.946	254.740	15.818
For-profit 4-year																
Selected crimes against persons and property	19.109	13.650	17.049	9.552	8.092	10.334	7.513	6.499	6.003	5.531	8.553	5.763	4.581	4.414	13.423	1.907
Murder[2]	0.000	0.000	0.000	0.000	0.000	0.000	0.000	0.000	0.013	0.000	0.017	0.000	0.000	0.000	0.000	0.000
Negligent manslaughter[3]	0.000	0.000	0.000	0.000	0.000	0.000	0.000	0.000	0.000	0.000	0.000	0.000	0.000	0.000	0.000	0.000
Sex offenses—forcible[4]	0.151	0.095	0.082	0.179	0.159	0.162	0.129	0.255	0.350	0.274	0.301	0.561	0.520	0.527	2.145	0.077
Rape	—	—	—	—	—	—	—	—	—	—	—	0.339	0.159	0.271	1.245	0.000
Fondling	—	—	—	—	—	—	—	—	—	—	—	0.222	0.361	0.256	0.899	0.077
Sex offenses—nonforcible[5]	0.492	0.000	0.021	0.000	0.026	0.000	0.014	0.012	0.000	0.046	0.033	0.026	0.000	0.015	0.069	0.000
Robbery[6]	2.422	0.875	0.884	0.373	0.410	0.684	1.231	0.811	0.996	0.775	1.440	0.678	0.361	0.437	0.830	0.327
Aggravated assault[7]	0.870	0.722	1.213	0.462	0.410	1.134	0.615	0.591	0.485	0.653	0.971	0.430	0.419	0.603	1.868	0.250
Burglary[8]	13.130	9.962	12.484	7.287	5.897	6.931	4.279	4.055	3.351	2.963	4.620	3.273	2.471	2.004	7.058	0.597
Motor vehicle theft[9]	1.968	1.901	2.262	1.162	1.177	1.422	1.216	0.753	0.781	0.805	1.138	0.769	0.795	0.783	1.315	0.636
Arson[10]	0.076	0.095	0.103	0.089	0.013	0.000	0.029	0.023	0.027	0.015	0.033	0.026	0.014	0.045	0.138	0.019
Weapons-, drug-, and liquor-related arrests and referrals																
Arrests[11]	0.416	0.779	0.576	0.775	0.370	0.720	0.773	1.911	2.046	1.915	1.239	1.526	1.561	1.657	6.573	0.289
Illegal weapons possession	0.076	0.095	0.041	0.075	0.040	0.144	0.086	0.151	0.148	0.152	0.201	0.117	0.217	0.166	0.554	0.058
Drug law violations	0.151	0.228	0.329	0.209	0.212	0.252	0.315	0.765	0.552	0.745	0.803	0.887	1.199	1.205	5.189	0.096
Liquor law violations	0.189	0.456	0.206	0.492	0.119	0.324	0.372	0.996	1.346	1.018	0.234	0.522	0.145	0.286	0.830	0.135
Referrals for disciplinary action[11]	11.957	5.665	10.880	7.645	6.862	10.190	12.623	8.804	9.663	10.150	19.433	12.191	12.789	13.062	58.882	0.308
Illegal weapons possession	0.416	0.209	0.864	0.194	0.145	0.234	0.329	0.104	0.215	0.349	0.301	0.209	0.217	0.226	0.830	0.058
Drug law violations	3.481	1.882	2.632	2.056	1.745	2.863	3.306	2.560	3.136	3.860	8.989	5.255	5.361	5.816	26.085	0.173
Liquor law violations	8.060	3.574	7.383	5.394	4.971	7.093	8.988	6.140	6.312	5.941	10.143	6.728	7.211	7.021	31.966	0.077
Public 2-year																
Selected crimes against persons and property	19.867	17.903	16.389	15.430	14.365	13.990	11.745	10.195	9.998	9.379	7.912	7.682	8.417	7.928	14.251	6.227
Murder[2]	0.006	0.008	0.005	0.000	0.000	0.005	0.005	0.002	0.005	0.008	0.018	0.008	0.036	0.009	0.014	0.008
Negligent manslaughter[3]	0.000	0.000	0.000	0.000	0.000	0.000	0.000	0.002	0.000	0.000	0.000	0.003	0.000	0.000	0.000	0.000
Sex offenses—forcible[4]	0.344	0.383	0.480	0.455	0.483	0.538	0.483	0.487	0.633	0.658	0.780	1.040	1.381	1.467	3.249	0.988
Rape	—	—	—	—	—	—	—	—	—	—	—	0.356	0.549	0.524	1.794	0.182
Fondling	—	—	—	—	—	—	—	—	—	—	—	0.683	0.831	0.943	1.455	0.805
Sex offenses—nonforcible[5]	0.347	0.016	0.027	0.044	0.019	0.018	0.028	0.019	0.039	0.033	0.028	0.043	0.031	0.054	0.056	0.053
Robbery[6]	0.714	0.575	0.680	0.773	0.745	0.730	0.591	0.691	0.633	0.610	0.507	0.400	0.418	0.413	0.650	0.350
Aggravated assault[7]	1.588	1.341	1.373	1.486	1.233	1.027	1.016	0.949	0.980	1.093	0.715	0.824	0.932	0.853	1.427	0.699
Burglary[8]	12.042	10.974	9.703	8.876	8.548	8.782	6.881	5.561	5.396	4.914	4.073	3.734	3.944	3.365	7.359	2.291
Motor vehicle theft[9]	4.523	4.370	3.913	3.590	3.134	2.712	2.613	2.384	2.171	1.941	1.675	1.480	1.512	1.635	1.398	1.698
Arson[10]	0.303	0.237	0.208	0.207	0.203	0.179	0.127	0.100	0.142	0.123	0.116	0.151	0.165	0.132	0.099	0.141
Weapons-, drug-, and liquor-related arrests and referrals																
Arrests[11]	7.752	8.821	9.360	10.868	11.009	9.638	7.859	8.838	8.989	8.666	7.874	8.427	7.926	8.143	23.658	3.970
Illegal weapons possession	0.577	0.688	0.762	0.817	0.812	0.661	0.603	0.654	0.599	0.633	0.592	0.594	0.747	0.665	0.847	0.615
Drug law violations	2.882	3.539	3.633	3.751	4.172	3.815	3.551	4.328	4.568	4.716	4.086	4.512	4.373	4.123	9.732	2.614
Liquor law violations	4.293	4.594	4.965	6.301	6.025	5.162	3.704	3.857	3.822	3.317	3.196	3.321	2.806	3.356	13.079	0.741
Referrals for disciplinary action[11]	10.284	11.791	12.846	16.051	15.983	16.451	17.063	18.592	19.735	18.979	17.613	19.549	20.337	20.610	86.738	2.823
Illegal weapons possession	0.370	0.450	0.364	0.648	0.582	0.469	0.495	0.561	0.550	0.560	0.625	0.726	0.756	0.686	1.879	0.365
Drug law violations	2.218	2.314	2.244	2.471	2.686	3.334	4.112	5.417	6.212	6.174	5.928	6.880	7.324	7.730	29.972	1.748
Liquor law violations	7.697	9.026	10.237	12.932	12.715	12.649	12.456	12.614	12.972	12.244	11.059	11.942	12.258	12.194	54.887	0.710

See notes at end of table.

Table 329.20 On-campus crimes, arrests, and referrals for disciplinary action per 10,000 full-time-equivalent (FTE) students at degree-granting postsecondary institutions, by whether institution has residence halls, control and level of institution, and type of incident: Selected years, 2001 through 2016—Continued

Control and level of institution and type of incident	Number of incidents per 10,000 FTE students[1]															
	Total, institutions with and without residence halls													2016		
	2001	2004	2005	2006	2007	2008	2009	2010	2011	2012	2013	2014	2015	Total	Institutions with residence halls	Institutions without residence halls
1	2	3	4	5	6	7	8	9	10	11	12	13	14	15	16	17
Nonprofit 2-year																
Selected crimes against persons and property	63.955	48.535	91.263	81.948	103.794	99.274	55.883	48.448	45.531	35.148	26.993	27.354	16.158	21.663	48.941	12.562
Murder[2]	0.258	0.000	0.000	0.000	0.000	0.000	0.000	0.000	0.000	0.000	0.000	0.000	0.000	0.000	0.000	0.000
Negligent manslaughter[3]	0.000	0.000	0.000	0.000	0.000	0.365	0.000	0.000	0.000	0.000	0.000	0.000	0.000	0.000	0.000	0.000
Sex offenses—forcible[4]	0.516	0.877	2.325	0.983	3.621	5.840	3.041	2.826	3.384	2.628	1.636	1.282	3.078	3.532	14.118	0.000
Rape	—	—	—	—	—	—	—	—	—	—	—	0.855	0.256	1.648	6.588	0.000
Fondling	—	—	—	—	—	—	—	—	—	—	—	0.427	2.821	1.884	7.529	0.000
Sex offenses—nonforcible[5]	0.516	0.000	0.000	0.328	0.000	0.000	0.000	0.000	0.000	0.000	0.818	0.000	0.000	0.000	0.000	0.000
Robbery[6]	13.926	6.432	2.616	2.295	0.805	4.745	3.421	2.019	0.308	0.657	1.227	0.000	0.513	1.884	1.882	1.884
Aggravated assault[7]	5.931	4.970	6.394	11.473	20.920	24.088	1.901	3.634	16.305	15.110	5.317	11.540	1.795	2.826	7.529	1.256
Burglary[8]	36.620	32.454	77.312	61.297	71.610	58.396	45.619	38.354	22.766	15.439	16.768	12.395	8.207	8.948	22.588	4.397
Motor vehicle theft[9]	5.931	3.801	2.035	4.589	5.632	3.285	1.521	0.807	2.154	1.314	1.227	2.137	2.052	4.238	1.882	5.025
Arson[10]	0.258	0.000	0.581	0.983	1.207	2.555	0.380	0.807	0.615	0.000	0.000	0.000	0.513	0.235	0.941	0.000
Weapons-, drug-, and liquor-related arrests and referrals																
Arrests[11]	27.852	14.034	22.089	21.962	23.736	33.943	22.049	19.783	15.998	17.081	26.993	16.669	11.285	18.602	42.353	10.677
Illegal weapons possession	0.258	0.585	1.453	0.983	1.609	1.095	1.521	2.422	1.538	1.642	2.045	2.137	2.308	3.768	3.765	3.768
Drug law violations	5.416	4.678	9.301	11.145	10.862	12.044	13.305	7.267	10.460	10.183	20.040	11.967	7.694	9.419	16.941	6.909
Liquor law violations	22.178	8.771	11.335	9.834	11.264	20.804	7.223	10.093	3.999	5.256	4.908	2.564	1.282	5.416	21.647	0.000
Referrals for disciplinary action[11]	160.920	130.694	149.393	176.025	208.794	150.735	132.294	152.206	110.752	98.545	130.874	191.478	144.140	102.430	405.647	1.256
Illegal weapons possession	0.516	1.462	3.488	6.228	4.023	2.190	2.661	1.615	0.308	1.971	2.863	4.701	0.513	0.942	3.765	0.000
Drug law violations	23.468	16.958	13.660	24.257	29.368	31.023	38.016	42.392	33.533	33.834	52.759	66.248	56.681	40.972	160.941	0.942
Liquor law violations	136.937	112.274	132.244	145.540	175.403	117.523	91.618	108.200	76.911	62.740	75.253	120.528	86.945	60.516	240.941	0.314
For-profit 2-year																
Selected crimes against persons and property	25.385	21.845	17.851	18.237	23.731	14.825	13.033	8.167	7.503	9.325	7.141	6.140	6.280	6.526	14.219	6.071
Murder[2]	0.000	0.000	0.000	0.000	0.000	0.000	0.000	0.000	0.000	0.000	0.000	0.000	0.000	0.000	0.000	0.000
Negligent manslaughter[3]	0.000	0.000	0.000	0.000	0.000	0.037	0.000	0.000	0.000	0.000	0.000	0.000	0.000	0.000	0.000	0.000
Sex offenses—forcible[4]	0.645	0.373	0.042	0.347	0.087	0.149	0.170	0.052	0.204	0.455	0.385	0.195	0.336	0.511	2.031	0.421
Rape	—	—	—	—	—	—	—	—	—	—	—	0.049	0.112	0.113	1.016	0.060
Fondling	—	—	—	—	—	—	—	—	—	—	—	0.146	0.224	0.397	1.016	0.361
Sex offenses—nonforcible[5]	0.376	0.000	0.000	0.043	0.000	0.000	0.028	0.026	0.000	0.114	0.000	0.000	0.000	0.000	0.000	0.000
Robbery[6]	3.603	3.316	2.283	2.128	2.907	1.969	1.420	0.985	0.467	1.061	0.983	1.364	0.505	0.567	0.000	0.601
Aggravated assault[7]	2.151	2.570	2.076	1.433	1.432	1.078	1.505	0.907	1.080	1.137	0.599	0.585	1.009	1.532	2.031	1.503
Burglary[8]	15.704	13.472	10.378	10.638	15.185	8.954	6.417	3.500	3.503	4.170	3.207	2.826	2.467	2.383	6.094	2.164
Motor vehicle theft[9]	2.743	2.031	2.947	3.517	3.991	2.638	3.436	2.619	2.160	2.388	1.924	1.170	1.962	1.532	4.063	1.382
Arson[10]	0.161	0.083	0.125	0.130	0.130	0.000	0.057	0.078	0.088	0.000	0.043	0.000	0.000	0.000	0.000	0.000
Weapons-, drug-, and liquor-related arrests and referrals																
Arrests[11]	8.766	4.643	1.951	1.780	1.952	0.855	1.760	1.115	0.671	1.933	2.565	2.680	1.402	1.873	8.125	1.503
Illegal weapons possession	0.699	0.249	0.125	0.130	0.174	0.149	0.114	0.130	0.029	0.265	0.128	0.390	0.168	0.454	0.000	0.481
Drug law violations	4.679	2.653	1.495	1.129	1.388	0.446	1.164	0.752	0.409	1.516	1.710	1.364	1.065	1.078	3.047	0.962
Liquor law violations	3.388	1.741	0.332	0.521	0.390	0.260	0.483	0.233	0.234	0.152	0.727	0.926	0.168	0.340	5.078	0.060
Referrals for disciplinary action[11]	15.435	13.348	9.465	13.894	7.506	9.215	8.603	3.811	4.905	8.225	8.808	11.305	9.140	5.675	91.408	0.601
Illegal weapons possession	0.861	0.290	0.332	0.304	0.304	0.149	0.227	0.052	0.292	0.341	0.128	0.097	0.168	0.227	2.031	0.120
Drug law violations	4.787	7.710	5.563	9.509	5.293	4.087	4.628	1.763	1.985	3.260	4.019	4.532	4.934	2.383	34.532	0.481
Liquor law violations	9.788	5.347	3.570	4.082	1.909	4.979	3.748	1.996	2.627	4.624	4.661	6.676	4.037	3.064	54.845	0.000

—Not available.

[1]Although crimes, arrests, and referrals include incidents involving students, staff, and campus guests, they are expressed as a ratio to FTE students because comprehensive FTE counts of all these groups are not available.

[2]Excludes suicides, fetal deaths, traffic fatalities, accidental deaths, and justifiable homicide (such as the killing of a felon by a law enforcement officer in the line of duty).

[3]Killing of another person through gross negligence (excludes traffic fatalities).

[4]Any sexual act directed against another person forcibly and/or against that person's will.

[5]Includes only statutory rape or incest.

[6]Taking or attempting to take anything of value using actual or threatened force or violence.

[7]Attack upon a person for the purpose of inflicting severe or aggravated bodily injury.

[8]Unlawful entry of a structure to commit a felony or theft.

[9]Theft or attempted theft of a motor vehicle.

[10]Willful or malicious burning or attempt to burn a dwelling house, public building, motor vehicle, or personal property of another.

[11]If an individual is both arrested and referred to college officials for disciplinary action for a single offense, only the arrest is counted.

NOTE: Data are for degree-granting institutions, which are institutions that grant associate's or higher degrees and participate in Title IV federal financial aid programs. Some institutions that report Clery data—specifically, non-degree-granting institutions and institutions outside of the 50 states and the District of Columbia—are excluded from this table. Crimes, arrests, and referrals include incidents involving students, staff, and on-campus guests. Excludes off-campus crimes and arrests even if they involve college students or staff. Detail may not sum to totals because of rounding. Some data have been revised from previously published figures.

SOURCE: U.S. Department of Education, Office of Postsecondary Education, Campus Safety and Security Reporting System, 2001 through 2016; and National Center for Education Statistics, Integrated Postsecondary Education Data System (IPEDS), Spring 2002 through Spring 2017, Fall Enrollment component. (This table was prepared September 2018.)

Table 329.30. On-campus hate crimes at degree-granting postsecondary institutions, by level and control of institution, type of crime, and category of bias motivating the crime: 2010 through 2016

Type of crime and category of bias motivating the crime[1]	Total, 2010	Total, 2011	Total, 2012	Total, 2013	Total, 2014	2015							2016						
							4-year			2-year				4-year			2-year		
						Total	Public	Non-profit	For-profit	Public	Non-profit	For-profit	Total	Public	Non-profit	For-profit	Public	Non-profit	For-profit
1	2	3	4	5	6	7	8	9	10	11	12	13	14	15	16	17	18	19	20
All on-campus hate crimes	**928**	**761**	**784**	**778**	**794**	**864**	**354**	**350**	**11**	**143**	**0**	**6**	**1,070**	**483**	**395**	**9**	**178**	**0**	**5**
Murder[2]	0	0	0	0	0	0	0	0	0	0	0	0	0	0	0	0	0	0	0
Sex offenses—forcible[3]	7	9	4	7	4	7	3	3	0	1	0	0	8	1	1	0	6	0	0
Race	0	0	1	2	1	0	0	0	0	0	0	0	1	1	0	0	0	0	0
Ethnicity	0	0	0	0	0	0	0	0	0	0	0	0	0	0	0	0	0	0	0
Religion	0	2	0	0	0	1	1	0	0	0	0	0	0	0	0	0	0	0	0
Sexual orientation	4	1	2	1	1	3	2	1	0	0	0	0	1	0	1	0	0	0	0
Gender	3	6	1	4	2	1	0	0	0	1	0	0	5	0	0	0	5	0	0
Gender identity	—	—	—	—	0	2	0	2	0	0	0	0	1	0	0	0	1	0	0
Disability	0	0	0	0	0	0	0	0	0	0	0	0	0	0	0	0	0	0	0
Sex offenses—nonforcible[4]	0	0	0	0	0	0	0	0	0	0	0	0	0	0	0	0	0	0	0
Robbery[5]	2	2	5	1	2	3	3	0	0	0	0	0	2	1	0	0	1	0	0
Aggravated assault[6]	17	13	14	7	18	19	10	2	2	5	0	0	34	25	2	0	7	0	0
Race	6	5	6	5	5	5	1	1	0	3	0	0	8	5	0	0	3	0	0
Ethnicity	1	0	0	1	4	4	3	0	1	0	0	0	15	14	0	0	1	0	0
Religion	1	2	1	0	1	1	1	0	0	0	0	0	1	1	0	0	0	0	0
Sexual orientation	9	6	5	1	7	7	4	0	1	2	0	0	7	5	1	0	1	0	0
Gender	0	0	1	0	1	1	0	1	0	0	0	0	1	0	0	0	1	0	0
Gender identity	—	—	—	—	0	1	1	0	0	0	0	0	2	0	1	0	1	0	0
Disability	0	0	1	0	0	0	0	0	0	0	0	0	0	0	0	0	0	0	0
Burglary[7]	11	8	5	4	28	4	4	0	0	0	0	0	6	0	4	0	2	0	0
Race	7	4	0	1	24	0	0	0	0	0	0	0	1	0	1	0	0	0	0
Ethnicity	0	0	0	0	0	0	0	0	0	0	0	0	0	0	0	0	0	0	0
Religion	0	2	1	1	3	0	0	0	0	0	0	0	0	0	0	0	0	0	0
Sexual orientation	2	1	0	0	1	0	0	0	0	0	0	0	2	0	2	0	0	0	0
Gender	1	1	4	2	0	0	0	0	0	0	0	0	3	0	1	0	2	0	0
Gender identity	—	—	—	—	0	4	4	0	0	0	0	0	0	0	0	0	0	0	0
Disability	1	0	0	0	0	0	0	0	0	0	0	0	0	0	0	0	0	0	0
Motor vehicle theft[8]	0	0	0	0	0	2	0	1	0	0	0	1	0	0	0	0	0	0	0
Arson[9]	0	1	0	0	1	2	1	1	0	0	0	0	2	2	0	0	0	0	0
Simple assault[10]	67	67	79	91	63	81	28	40	0	12	0	1	99	66	25	0	7	0	1
Race	25	22	36	36	14	39	8	25	0	6	0	0	42	28	12	0	2	0	0
Ethnicity	5	10	5	5	11	8	5	3	0	0	0	0	14	10	2	0	2	0	0
Religion	4	8	9	6	2	8	5	2	0	1	0	0	12	9	2	0	1	0	0
Sexual orientation	23	16	21	27	23	18	9	8	0	1	0	0	17	10	5	0	2	0	0
Gender	9	8	5	17	9	2	0	0	0	1	0	1	11	8	2	0	0	0	1
Gender identity	—	—	—	—	3	5	1	2	0	2	0	0	2	1	1	0	0	0	0
Disability	1	3	3	0	1	1	0	0	0	1	0	0	1	0	1	0	0	0	0
Larceny[11]	9	15	9	15	17	25	3	21	0	1	0	0	34	3	15	4	11	0	1
Race	1	2	2	5	5	1	0	1	0	0	0	0	12	1	5	3	2	0	1
Ethnicity	3	3	2	2	1	0	0	0	0	0	0	0	4	0	0	0	4	0	0
Religion	1	2	2	3	3	19	1	18	0	0	0	0	5	2	3	0	0	0	0
Sexual orientation	1	3	3	3	1	1	0	1	0	0	0	0	5	0	4	0	1	0	0
Gender	3	3	0	2	7	3	1	1	0	1	0	0	4	0	0	1	3	0	0
Gender identity	—	—	—	—	0	1	1	0	0	0	0	0	3	0	2	0	1	0	0
Disability	0	2	0	0	0	0	0	0	0	0	0	0	1	0	1	0	0	0	0
Intimidation[12]	260	282	265	296	339	356	142	145	7	58	0	4	421	184	169	1	65	0	2
Race	79	111	120	111	111	141	55	58	1	25	0	2	167	80	60	0	27	0	0
Ethnicity	17	22	22	49	32	38	18	10	0	10	0	0	49	20	22	0	7	0	0
Religion	38	24	28	25	35	47	24	17	1	5	0	0	66	35	22	0	9	0	0
Sexual orientation	87	91	70	68	78	76	30	31	3	12	0	0	84	34	36	1	12	0	1
Gender	37	31	21	37	63	34	9	21	1	1	0	2	27	8	17	0	2	0	0
Gender identity	—	—	—	—	13	12	5	5	0	2	0	0	20	4	11	0	4	0	1
Disability	2	3	4	6	7	8	1	3	1	3	0	0	8	3	1	0	4	0	0
Destruction, damage, and vandalism[13]	555	364	403	357	322	365	160	137	2	66	0	0	464	201	179	4	79	0	1
Race	257	166	186	147	116	151	66	55	0	30	0	0	174	80	56	1	36	0	1
Ethnicity	43	30	34	38	29	25	10	7	1	7	0	0	31	18	11	0	2	0	0
Religion	103	57	70	48	67	109	47	45	0	17	0	0	136	54	53	0	29	0	0
Sexual orientation	135	104	104	108	89	61	27	22	0	12	0	0	66	32	27	2	5	0	0
Gender	17	7	9	14	13	10	7	2	1	0	0	0	36	14	15	1	6	0	0
Gender identity	—	—	—	—	6	8	2	6	0	0	0	0	21	3	17	0	1	0	0
Disability	0	0	0	2	2	1	1	0	0	0	0	0	0	0	0	0	0	0	0

—Not available.
[1]Bias categories correspond to characteristics against which the bias is directed (i.e., race, ethnicity, religion, sexual orientation, gender, gender identity, or disability).
[2]Excludes suicides, fetal deaths, traffic fatalities, accidental deaths, and justifiable homicide (such as the killing of a felon by a law enforcement officer in the line of duty).
[3]Any sexual act directed against another person forcibly and/or against that person's will.
[4]Includes only statutory rape or incest.
[5]Taking or attempting to take anything of value using actual or threatened force or violence.
[6]Attack upon a person for the purpose of inflicting severe or aggravated bodily injury.
[7]Unlawful entry of a structure to commit a felony or theft.
[8]Theft or attempted theft of a motor vehicle.
[9]Willful or malicious burning or attempt to burn a dwelling house, public building, motor vehicle, or personal property of another.
[10]A physical attack by one person upon another where neither the offender displays a weapon, nor the victim suffers obvious severe or aggravated bodily injury involving apparent broken bones, loss of teeth, possible internal injury, severe laceration, or loss of consciousness.
[11]The unlawful taking, carrying, leading, or riding away of property from the possession of another.
[12]Placing another person in reasonable fear of bodily harm through the use of threatening words and/or other conduct, but without displaying a weapon or subjecting the victim to actual physical attack.
[13]Willfully or maliciously destroying, damaging, defacing, or otherwise injuring real or personal property without the consent of the owner or the person having custody or control of it.

NOTE: Data are for degree-granting institutions, which are institutions that grant associate's or higher degrees and participate in Title IV federal financial aid programs. Some institutions that report Clery data—specifically, non-degree-granting institutions and institutions outside of the 50 states and the District of Columbia—are excluded from this table. A hate crime is a criminal offense that is motivated, in whole or in part, by the perpetrator's bias against a group of people based on their race, ethnicity, religion, sexual orientation, gender, gender identity, or disability. Includes on-campus incidents involving students, staff, and on-campus guests. Excludes off-campus crimes and arrests even if they involve college students or staff. Some data have been revised from previously published figures.
SOURCE: U.S. Department of Education, Office of Postsecondary Education, Campus Safety and Security Reporting System, 2010 through 2016. (This table was prepared September 2018.)

Table 330.10. Average undergraduate tuition and fees and room and board rates charged for full-time students in degree-granting postsecondary institutions, by level and control of institution: Selected years, 1963–64 through 2017–18

Year and control of institution	Constant 2017–18 dollars[1]												Current dollars											
	Total tuition, fees, room, and board			Tuition and required fees[2]			Dormitory rooms			Board[3]			Total tuition, fees, room, and board			Tuition and required fees[2]			Dormitory rooms			Board[3]		
	All institutions	4-year	2-year	All institutions	4-year	2-year	All institutions	4-year	2-year	All institutions	4-year	2-year	All institutions	4-year	2-year	All institutions	4-year	2-year	All institutions	4-year	2-year	All institutions	4-year	2-year
1	2	3	4	5	6	7	8	9	10	11	12	13	14	15	16	17	18	19	20	21	22	23	24	25
All institutions																								
1963–64	$10,040	$10,347	$6,238	$4,089	$4,446	$1,378	$2,271	$2,241	$1,683	$3,679	$3,660	$3,178	$1,248	$1,286	$775	$508	$553	$171	$282	$279	$209	$457	$455	$395
1966–67	10,387	10,849	6,978	4,327	4,827	1,615	2,476	2,465	2,110	3,585	3,557	3,252	1,378	1,439	926	574	640	214	328	327	280	476	472	431
1967–68	10,325	10,852	7,178	4,287	4,835	1,694	2,495	2,489	2,199	3,543	3,527	3,286	1,415	1,487	984	588	663	232	342	341	301	486	483	450
1968–69	10,147	10,750	7,325	4,149	4,753	1,742	2,506	2,505	2,274	3,492	3,491	3,309	1,459	1,545	1,053	596	683	250	360	360	327	502	502	476
1969–70	10,247	10,999	7,156	4,238	4,959	1,625	2,557	2,574	2,279	3,453	3,465	3,252	1,560	1,674	1,089	645	755	247	389	392	347	526	528	495
1970–71	10,323	11,145	6,998	4,297	5,083	1,558	2,616	2,635	2,308	3,409	3,427	3,132	1,653	1,784	1,120	688	814	249	419	422	369	546	549	501
1971–72	10,434	11,321	7,065	4,364	5,218	1,512	2,683	2,704	2,357	3,387	3,400	3,196	1,730	1,878	1,172	724	865	251	445	448	391	562	564	530
1972–73	10,632	11,771	7,396	4,402	5,508	1,663	2,827	2,854	2,404	3,403	3,408	3,329	1,834	2,031	1,276	759	950	287	488	492	415	587	588	574
1973–74	10,128	11,161	7,229	4,234	5,240	1,748	2,636	2,660	2,287	3,257	3,261	3,194	1,903	2,097	1,358	796	985	328	495	500	430	612	613	600
1974–75	9,501	10,476	6,858	3,878	4,830	1,570	2,530	2,552	2,205	3,093	3,094	3,084	1,983	2,187	1,432	809	1,008	328	528	533	460	646	646	644
1975–76	9,410	10,536	6,592	3,709	4,801	1,330	2,545	2,577	2,121	3,156	3,157	3,142	2,103	2,355	1,473	829	1,073	297	569	576	474	705	706	702
1976–77	9,619	10,894	6,755	3,907	5,151	1,461	2,551	2,582	2,125	3,161	3,161	3,169	2,275	2,577	1,598	924	1,218	346	603	611	503	748	748	750
1977–78	9,550	10,795	6,748	3,900	5,116	1,498	2,556	2,590	2,079	3,094	3,089	3,171	2,411	2,725	1,703	984	1,291	378	645	654	525	781	780	801
1978–79	9,370	10,567	6,622	3,885	5,059	1,488	2,492	2,519	2,083	2,992	2,988	3,050	2,587	2,917	1,828	1,073	1,397	411	688	696	575	826	825	842
1979–80	8,978	10,122	6,326	3,717	4,836	1,441	2,400	2,427	2,007	2,861	2,860	2,878	2,809	3,167	1,979	1,163	1,513	451	751	759	628	895	895	900
1980–81	8,883	10,024	6,388	3,691	4,808	1,506	2,395	2,423	2,018	2,797	2,792	2,864	3,101	3,499	2,230	1,289	1,679	526	836	846	705	976	975	1,000
1981–82	9,200	10,417	6,527	3,841	5,029	1,554	2,504	2,535	2,090	2,855	2,853	2,883	3,489	3,951	2,476	1,457	1,907	590	950	961	793	1,083	1,082	1,094
1982–83	9,800	11,138	6,860	4,110	5,408	1,705	2,689	2,725	2,208	3,001	3,005	2,946	3,877	4,406	2,713	1,626	2,139	675	1,064	1,078	873	1,187	1,189	1,165
1983–84	10,159	11,573	6,959	4,346	5,713	1,780	2,792	2,833	2,233	3,021	3,027	2,945	4,167	4,747	2,854	1,783	2,344	730	1,145	1,162	916	1,239	1,242	1,208
1984–85	10,704	12,106	7,459	4,657	6,023	1,926	2,973	3,008	2,481	3,074	3,075	3,051	4,563	5,160	3,179	1,985	2,567	821	1,267	1,282	1,058	1,310	1,311	1,301
1985–86[4]	11,138	12,551	7,677	4,973	6,349	2,026	3,051	3,089	2,524	3,113	3,112	3,127	4,885	5,504	3,367	2,181	2,784	888	1,338	1,355	1,107	1,365	1,365	1,372
1986–87	11,612	13,304	7,351	5,157	6,786	2,001	3,133	3,182	2,307	3,322	3,336	3,043	5,206	5,964	3,295	2,312	3,042	897	1,405	1,427	1,034	1,489	1,495	1,364
1987–88	11,769	13,435	6,989	5,265	6,856	1,733	3,186	3,248	2,179	3,318	3,331	3,077	5,494	6,272	3,263	2,458	3,201	809	1,488	1,516	1,017	1,549	1,555	1,437
1988–89	12,015	13,769	7,315	5,441	7,109	2,005	3,224	3,294	2,221	3,350	3,367	3,089	5,869	6,725	3,573	2,658	3,472	979	1,575	1,609	1,085	1,636	1,644	1,509
1989–90	12,130	14,092	7,240	5,548	7,426	1,911	3,201	3,273	2,159	3,381	3,394	3,170	6,207	7,212	3,705	2,839	3,800	978	1,638	1,675	1,105	1,730	1,737	1,622
1990–91	12,158	14,084	7,282	5,589	7,428	2,015	3,230	3,301	2,191	3,339	3,355	3,077	6,562	7,602	3,930	3,016	4,009	1,087	1,743	1,782	1,182	1,802	1,811	1,660
1991–92	12,705	14,789	7,346	5,898	7,873	2,135	3,364	3,449	2,173	3,443	3,467	3,038	7,077	8,238	4,092	3,286	4,385	1,189	1,874	1,921	1,210	1,918	1,931	1,692
1992–93	12,974	15,246	7,325	6,123	8,273	2,221	3,375	3,466	2,159	3,476	3,507	2,945	7,452	8,758	4,207	3,517	4,752	1,276	1,939	1,991	1,240	1,996	2,015	1,692
1993–94	13,459	15,776	7,549	6,495	8,687	2,374	3,491	3,582	2,261	3,474	3,507	2,915	7,931	9,296	4,449	3,827	5,119	1,399	2,057	2,111	1,332	2,047	2,067	1,718
1994–95	13,701	16,048	7,643	6,672	8,893	2,454	3,539	3,628	2,303	3,490	3,526	2,887	8,306	9,728	4,633	4,044	5,391	1,488	2,145	2,200	1,396	2,116	2,138	1,750
1995–96	14,133	16,590	7,588	6,967	9,292	2,445	3,636	3,723	2,365	3,531	3,575	2,778	8,800	10,330	4,725	4,338	5,786	1,522	2,264	2,318	1,473	2,199	2,226	1,730
1996–97	14,374	16,927	7,644	7,127	9,554	2,409	3,693	3,781	2,377	3,554	3,592	2,857	9,206	10,841	4,895	4,564	6,118	1,543	2,365	2,422	1,522	2,276	2,301	1,830
1997–98	14,708	17,300	7,965	7,294	9,742	2,600	3,749	3,846	2,451	3,665	3,712	2,914	9,588	11,277	5,192	4,755	6,351	1,695	2,444	2,507	1,598	2,389	2,419	1,900
1998–99	15,194	17,927	7,979	7,559	10,138	2,602	3,856	3,959	2,437	3,778	3,830	2,940	10,076	11,888	5,291	5,013	6,723	1,725	2,557	2,626	1,616	2,506	2,540	1,950
1999–2000	15,287	18,100	7,943	7,653	10,319	2,532	3,937	4,031	2,596	3,697	3,749	2,815	10,430	12,349	5,420	5,222	7,040	1,728	2,686	2,751	1,771	2,523	2,558	1,920
2000–01	15,333	18,313	7,746	7,620	10,446	2,406	3,998	4,099	2,523	3,714	3,767	2,816	10,820	12,922	5,466	5,377	7,372	1,698	2,821	2,893	1,781	2,621	2,658	1,987
2001–02	15,847	18,992	7,962	7,863	10,842	2,506	4,151	4,261	2,573	3,833	3,889	2,883	11,380	13,639	5,718	5,646	7,786	1,800	2,981	3,060	1,848	2,753	2,793	2,070
2002–03	16,369	19,674	8,519	8,178	11,321	2,593	4,331	4,446	2,830	3,859	3,907	3,095	12,014	14,439	6,252	6,002	8,309	1,903	3,179	3,263	2,077	2,832	2,867	2,272
2003–04	17,272	20,674	8,940	8,811	12,039	2,899	4,479	4,598	2,944	3,982	4,038	3,097	12,953	15,505	6,705	6,608	9,029	2,174	3,359	3,448	2,208	2,986	3,028	2,322
2004–05	17,854	21,370	9,184	9,219	12,563	3,026	4,623	4,740	3,047	4,012	4,067	3,111	13,793	16,510	7,095	7,122	9,706	2,338	3,572	3,662	2,354	3,100	3,142	2,404
2005–06	18,247	21,760	9,022	9,478	12,817	3,014	4,751	4,869	3,006	4,018	4,075	3,003	14,634	17,451	7,236	7,601	10,279	2,417	3,810	3,905	2,411	3,222	3,268	2,408
2006–07	18,822	22,453	9,076	9,837	13,286	3,034	4,884	5,003	3,073	4,101	4,164	2,969	15,486	18,473	7,467	8,093	10,931	2,496	4,019	4,116	2,528	3,374	3,426	2,443
2007–08	19,019	22,696	8,951	9,939	13,426	2,949	4,938	5,059	3,087	4,142	4,211	2,915	16,227	19,364	7,637	8,480	11,455	2,516	4,213	4,317	2,634	3,534	3,593	2,487
2008–09	19,703	23,536	9,500	10,279	13,924	3,025	5,139	5,268	3,216	4,285	4,345	3,260	17,045	20,361	8,219	8,892	12,046	2,617	4,446	4,557	2,782	3,707	3,759	2,820
2009–10	20,206	24,186	9,778	10,458	14,201	3,347	5,333	5,478	3,427	4,416	4,507	3,004	17,650	21,126	8,541	9,135	12,404	2,923	4,658	4,785	2,994	3,857	3,937	2,624
2010–11	20,735	24,773	9,953	10,746	14,529	3,434	5,474	5,634	3,450	4,515	4,611	3,069	18,475	22,074	8,868	9,575	12,945	3,060	4,878	5,020	3,074	4,023	4,108	2,734
2011–12	21,154	25,090	10,191	11,098	14,798	3,537	5,544	5,696	3,490	4,512	4,596	3,163	19,401	23,011	9,347	10,179	13,572	3,244	5,085	5,224	3,201	4,138	4,215	2,901
2012–13	21,700	25,601	10,267	11,455	15,122	3,562	5,680	5,827	3,582	4,565	4,652	3,123	20,233	23,871	9,573	10,681	14,099	3,322	5,296	5,433	3,340	4,256	4,338	2,911
2013–14	22,171	26,084	10,445	11,693	15,378	3,558	5,829	5,970	3,740	4,649	4,736	3,148	20,995	24,701	9,891	11,073	14,563	3,369	5,520	5,654	3,541	4,402	4,484	2,981
2014–15	22,780	26,638	10,644	12,043	15,680	3,553	5,995	6,133	3,832	4,741	4,824	3,259	21,729	25,409	10,153	11,487	14,957	3,389	5,719	5,850	3,655	4,523	4,602	3,109
2015–16	23,367	27,213	10,838	12,352	15,977	3,553	6,160	6,292	4,008	4,855	4,943	3,277	22,439	26,132	10,407	11,862	15,343	3,412	5,915	6,043	3,849	4,662	4,747	3,147
2016–17	23,612	27,192	10,836	12,494	15,861	3,598	6,244	6,371	4,020	4,873	4,959	3,218	23,091	26,592	10,597	12,219	15,512	3,519	6,107	6,231	3,932	4,766	4,850	3,147
2017–18	23,835	27,357	10,704	12,615	15,924	3,539	6,320	6,451	3,926	4,899	4,982	3,240	23,835	27,357	10,704	12,615	15,924	3,539	6,320	6,451	3,926	4,899	4,982	3,240

See notes at end of table.

Table 330.10. Average undergraduate tuition and fees and room and board rates charged for full-time students in degree-granting postsecondary institutions, by level and control of institution: Selected years, 1963–64 through 2017–18—Continued

Year and control of institution	Constant 2017–18 dollars[1]												Current dollars											
	Total tuition, fees, room, and board			Tuition and required fees[2]			Dormitory rooms			Board[3]			Total tuition, fees, room, and board			Tuition and required fees[2]			Dormitory rooms			Board[3]		
	All institutions	4-year	2-year	All institutions	4-year	2-year	All institutions	4-year	2-year	All institutions	4-year	2-year	All institutions	4-year	2-year	All institutions	4-year	2-year	All institutions	4-year	2-year	All institutions	4-year	2-year
1	2	3	4	5	6	7	8	9	10	11	12	13	14	15	16	17	18	19	20	21	22	23	24	25
Public institutions																								
1963–64	7,341	7,471	5,068	1,883	1,958	780	2,009	2,039	1,384	3,449	3,474	2,904	912	929	630	234	243	97	250	253	172	429	432	361
1966–67	7,648	7,907	5,352	2,073	2,279	912	2,195	2,222	1,606	3,380	3,405	2,834	1,015	1,049	710	275	302	121	291	295	213	448	452	376
1967–68	7,701	7,942	5,757	2,065	2,262	1,051	2,264	2,287	1,773	3,373	3,393	2,933	1,055	1,089	789	283	310	144	310	313	243	462	465	402
1968–69	7,732	7,951	6,143	2,052	2,233	1,183	2,324	2,345	1,934	3,356	3,373	3,026	1,112	1,143	883	295	321	170	334	337	278	482	485	435
1969–70	7,860	8,131	6,247	2,122	2,354	1,169	2,404	2,426	2,023	3,334	3,351	3,054	1,197	1,238	951	323	358	178	366	369	308	508	510	465
1970–71	7,970	8,282	6,234	2,192	2,459	1,168	2,482	2,505	2,111	3,296	3,318	2,954	1,276	1,326	998	351	394	187	397	401	338	528	531	473
1971–72	8,122	8,471	6,470	2,267	2,579	1,158	2,567	2,591	2,207	3,288	3,300	3,105	1,347	1,405	1,073	376	428	192	426	430	366	545	547	515
1972–73	8,418	9,004	6,938	2,359	2,913	1,351	2,732	2,761	2,307	3,327	3,330	3,281	1,452	1,553	1,197	407	503	233	471	476	398	574	575	566
1973–74	8,062	8,494	6,780	2,331	2,733	1,458	2,547	2,573	2,177	3,185	3,188	3,145	1,515	1,596	1,274	438	514	274	479	483	409	598	599	591
1974–75	7,479	7,889	6,415	2,070	2,455	1,327	2,420	2,449	2,031	2,990	2,985	3,057	1,561	1,647	1,339	432	512	277	505	511	424	624	623	638
1975–76	7,440	7,962	6,201	1,937	2,426	1,096	2,431	2,469	1,978	3,072	3,067	3,127	1,663	1,780	1,386	433	542	245	543	552	442	687	686	699
1976–77	7,563	8,181	6,302	2,024	2,607	1,198	2,463	2,502	1,965	3,077	3,072	3,138	1,789	1,935	1,491	479	617	283	582	592	465	728	727	742
1977–78	7,478	8,073	6,297	2,027	2,594	1,214	2,460	2,501	1,925	2,991	2,979	3,158	1,888	2,038	1,590	512	655	306	621	631	486	755	752	797
1978–79	7,221	7,769	6,125	1,966	2,491	1,185	2,372	2,405	1,908	2,883	2,873	3,031	1,994	2,145	1,691	543	688	327	655	664	527	796	793	837
1979–80	6,919	7,439	5,822	1,865	2,357	1,134	2,285	2,318	1,834	2,770	2,764	2,854	2,165	2,327	1,822	583	738	355	715	725	574	867	865	893
1980–81	6,798	7,305	5,806	1,819	2,302	1,120	2,288	2,323	1,838	2,692	2,680	2,848	2,373	2,550	2,027	635	804	391	799	811	642	940	936	994
1981–82	7,021	7,569	5,864	1,882	2,398	1,146	2,398	2,440	1,854	2,741	2,731	2,864	2,663	2,871	2,224	714	909	434	909	925	703	1,039	1,036	1,086
1982–83	7,444	8,080	6,041	2,018	2,607	1,196	2,554	2,605	1,909	2,872	2,868	2,936	2,945	3,196	2,390	798	1,031	473	1,010	1,030	755	1,136	1,134	1,162
1983–84	7,694	8,369	6,177	2,173	2,798	1,287	2,650	2,705	1,952	2,871	2,866	2,938	3,156	3,433	2,534	891	1,148	528	1,087	1,110	801	1,178	1,175	1,205
1984–85	7,995	8,637	6,585	2,277	2,881	1,370	2,805	2,854	2,160	2,912	2,902	3,055	3,408	3,682	2,807	971	1,228	584	1,196	1,217	921	1,241	1,237	1,302
1985–86[4]	8,143	8,798	6,797	2,382	3,004	1,462	2,831	2,880	2,189	2,930	2,914	3,147	3,571	3,859	2,981	1,045	1,318	641	1,242	1,263	960	1,285	1,278	1,380
1986–87	8,488	9,230	6,667	2,468	3,153	1,473	2,902	2,950	2,184	3,118	3,126	3,010	3,805	4,138	2,989	1,106	1,414	660	1,301	1,323	979	1,398	1,401	1,349
1987–88	8,675	9,431	6,566	2,609	3,293	1,512	2,952	3,019	2,020	3,114	3,119	3,035	4,050	4,403	3,066	1,218	1,537	706	1,378	1,410	943	1,454	1,456	1,417
1988–89	8,751	9,578	6,516	2,630	3,370	1,495	2,982	3,063	1,975	3,138	3,145	3,047	4,274	4,678	3,183	1,285	1,646	730	1,457	1,496	965	1,533	1,536	1,488
1989–90	8,801	9,722	6,447	2,650	3,478	1,477	2,957	3,043	1,880	3,194	3,202	3,090	4,504	4,975	3,299	1,356	1,780	756	1,513	1,557	962	1,635	1,638	1,581
1990–91	8,814	9,714	6,425	2,694	3,498	1,527	2,987	3,069	1,945	3,133	3,146	2,953	4,757	5,243	3,467	1,454	1,888	824	1,612	1,657	1,050	1,691	1,698	1,594
1991–92	9,225	10,221	6,504	2,923	3,800	1,681	3,107	3,204	1,929	3,195	3,217	2,894	5,138	5,693	3,623	1,628	2,117	936	1,731	1,785	1,074	1,780	1,792	1,612
1992–93	9,364	10,480	6,613	3,102	4,090	1,785	3,057	3,162	1,926	3,205	3,228	2,903	5,379	6,020	3,799	1,782	2,349	1,025	1,756	1,816	1,106	1,841	1,854	1,668
1993–94	9,663	10,801	6,781	3,296	4,305	1,909	3,178	3,282	2,019	3,190	3,215	2,853	5,694	6,365	3,996	1,942	2,537	1,125	1,873	1,934	1,190	1,880	1,895	1,681
1994–95	9,840	11,004	6,824	3,393	4,422	1,967	3,232	3,337	2,032	3,215	3,245	2,825	5,965	6,670	4,137	2,057	2,681	1,192	1,959	2,023	1,232	1,949	1,967	1,712
1995–96	10,047	11,264	6,772	3,499	4,573	1,990	3,304	3,406	2,082	3,244	3,285	2,699	6,256	7,014	4,217	2,179	2,848	1,239	2,057	2,121	1,297	2,020	2,045	1,681
1996–97	10,196	11,452	6,876	3,547	4,664	1,992	3,354	3,457	2,091	3,296	3,331	2,793	6,530	7,334	4,404	2,271	2,987	1,276	2,148	2,214	1,339	2,111	2,133	1,789
1997–98	10,452	11,772	6,918	3,621	4,770	2,016	3,414	3,529	2,149	3,418	3,472	2,753	6,813	7,673	4,509	2,360	3,110	1,314	2,225	2,301	1,401	2,228	2,263	1,795
1998–99	10,717	12,104	6,943	3,665	4,869	2,000	3,513	3,633	2,187	3,539	3,603	2,756	7,107	8,027	4,604	2,430	3,229	1,327	2,330	2,409	1,450	2,347	2,389	1,828
1999–2000	10,711	12,127	6,933	3,669	4,908	1,975	3,576	3,692	2,270	3,465	3,527	2,687	7,308	8,274	4,730	2,504	3,349	1,348	2,440	2,519	1,549	2,364	2,406	1,834
2000–01	10,751	12,263	6,857	3,631	4,961	1,888	3,640	3,761	2,268	3,480	3,541	2,701	7,586	8,653	4,839	2,562	3,501	1,333	2,569	2,654	1,600	2,455	2,499	1,906
2001–02	11,170	12,805	7,154	3,760	5,201	1,921	3,792	3,922	2,398	3,618	3,682	2,834	8,022	9,196	5,137	2,700	3,735	1,380	2,723	2,816	1,722	2,598	2,645	2,036
2002–03	11,583	13,336	7,632	3,955	5,513	2,021	3,992	4,127	2,662	3,637	3,696	2,949	8,502	9,787	5,601	2,903	4,046	1,483	2,930	3,029	1,954	2,669	2,712	2,164
2003–04	12,329	14,233	8,016	4,425	6,115	2,269	4,141	4,283	2,785	3,763	3,834	2,962	9,247	10,674	6,012	3,319	4,587	1,702	3,106	3,212	2,089	2,822	2,876	2,221
2004–05	12,769	14,789	8,252	4,698	6,506	2,393	4,277	4,425	2,814	3,794	3,858	3,045	9,864	11,426	6,375	3,629	5,027	1,849	3,304	3,418	2,174	2,931	2,981	2,353
2005–06	13,036	15,098	8,095	4,830	6,672	2,413	4,421	4,569	2,807	3,785	3,857	2,875	10,454	12,108	6,492	3,874	5,351	1,935	3,545	3,664	2,251	3,035	3,093	2,306
2006–07	13,433	15,557	8,284	4,986	6,887	2,452	4,566	4,714	2,927	3,880	3,956	2,905	11,051	12,799	6,815	4,102	5,666	2,017	3,757	3,878	2,408	3,192	3,255	2,390
2007–08	13,561	15,739	8,178	5,026	6,966	2,413	4,631	4,784	2,936	3,905	3,990	2,829	11,570	13,429	6,977	4,288	5,943	2,058	3,951	4,082	2,505	3,332	3,404	2,414
2008–09	14,112	16,428	8,725	5,215	7,296	2,469	4,843	5,006	3,079	4,054	4,126	3,178	12,209	14,212	7,549	4,512	6,312	2,136	4,190	4,331	2,664	3,507	3,569	2,749
2009–10	14,676	17,214	8,824	5,453	7,689	2,614	5,038	5,225	3,267	4,185	4,299	2,943	12,819	15,036	7,708	4,763	6,717	2,283	4,401	4,564	2,854	3,655	3,755	2,571
2010–11	15,225	17,866	9,067	5,696	8,004	2,739	5,214	5,423	3,317	4,315	4,440	3,011	13,566	15,919	8,079	5,075	7,132	2,441	4,646	4,832	2,955	3,845	3,956	2,683
2011–12	15,656	18,303	9,396	6,066	8,410	2,891	5,288	5,486	3,380	4,302	4,407	3,125	14,359	16,787	8,617	5,563	7,713	2,651	4,849	5,031	3,100	3,946	4,042	2,866
2012–13	16,110	18,742	9,575	6,326	8,655	2,994	5,429	5,621	3,483	4,355	4,465	3,098	15,021	17,475	8,927	5,899	8,070	2,792	5,062	5,241	3,247	4,061	4,163	2,888
2013–14	16,504	19,113	9,803	6,463	8,777	3,042	5,601	5,786	3,641	4,440	4,550	3,120	15,628	18,100	9,283	6,120	8,312	2,881	5,304	5,479	3,448	4,205	4,308	2,955
2014–15	16,971	19,533	10,049	6,678	8,957	3,098	5,771	5,951	3,731	4,522	4,625	3,220	16,188	18,632	9,585	6,370	8,543	2,955	5,504	5,677	3,559	4,313	4,412	3,072
2015–16	17,459	19,998	10,324	6,885	9,141	3,163	5,921	6,092	3,914	4,654	4,765	3,247	16,766	19,204	9,914	6,612	8,778	3,038	5,686	5,850	3,759	4,469	4,576	3,118
2016–17	17,627	19,928	10,318	6,972	9,003	3,228	5,991	6,153	3,909	4,664	4,772	3,181	17,238	19,488	10,090	6,818	8,804	3,156	5,859	6,018	3,823	4,562	4,666	3,111
2017–18	17,797	20,050	10,281	7,054	9,037	3,243	6,060	6,227	3,834	4,683	4,786	3,204	17,797	20,050	10,281	7,054	9,037	3,243	6,060	6,227	3,834	4,683	4,786	3,204

See notes at end of table.

Table 330.10. Average undergraduate tuition and fees and room and board rates charged for full-time students in degree-granting postsecondary institutions, by level and control of institution: Selected years, 1963–64 through 2017–18—Continued

Year and control of institution	Constant 2017–18 dollars[1]												Current dollars											
	Total tuition, fees, room, and board			Tuition and required fees[2]			Dormitory rooms			Board[3]			Total tuition, fees, room, and board			Tuition and required fees[2]			Dormitory rooms			Board[3]		
	All institutions	4-year	2-year	All institutions	4-year	2-year	All institutions	4-year	2-year	All institutions	4-year	2-year	All institutions	4-year	2-year	All institutions	4-year	2-year	All institutions	4-year	2-year	All institutions	4-year	2-year
1	2	3	4	5	6	7	8	9	10	11	12	13	14	15	16	17	18	19	20	21	22	23	24	25
Private nonprofit and for-profit institutions																								
1963–64	14,602	14,559	10,563	8,142	8,132	5,165	2,542	2,516	1,963	3,918	3,912	3,435	1,815	1,810	1,313	1,012	1,011	642	316	313	244	487	486	427
1966–67	16,011	16,046	12,656	9,294	9,357	6,370	2,902	2,876	2,616	3,814	3,813	3,671	2,124	2,129	1,679	1,233	1,241	845	385	382	347	506	506	487
1967–68	16,088	16,223	12,856	9,463	9,610	6,508	2,860	2,848	2,670	3,765	3,765	3,677	2,205	2,223	1,762	1,297	1,317	892	392	390	366	516	516	504
1968–69	16,147	16,391	13,051	9,621	9,859	6,651	2,811	2,814	2,720	3,715	3,718	3,680	2,321	2,356	1,876	1,383	1,417	956	404	405	391	534	534	529
1969–70	16,602	16,807	13,091	10,070	10,259	6,792	2,851	2,861	2,713	3,681	3,687	3,586	2,527	2,559	1,993	1,533	1,562	1,034	434	436	413	560	561	546
1970–71	17,046	17,205	13,136	10,518	10,658	6,927	2,888	2,899	2,711	3,639	3,648	3,498	2,729	2,754	2,103	1,684	1,706	1,109	462	464	434	583	584	560
1971–72	17,500	17,599	13,181	10,974	11,048	7,067	2,928	2,941	2,707	3,599	3,610	3,407	2,902	2,919	2,186	1,820	1,832	1,172	486	488	449	597	599	565
1972–73	17,598	17,918	13,175	11,001	11,293	7,077	3,031	3,053	2,649	3,566	3,572	3,449	3,036	3,091	2,273	1,898	1,948	1,221	523	527	457	615	616	595
1973–74	16,829	17,145	12,825	10,585	10,880	6,934	2,831	2,847	2,570	3,413	3,418	3,321	3,162	3,222	2,410	1,989	2,045	1,303	532	535	483	641	642	624
1974–75	16,232	16,309	12,413	10,142	10,206	6,549	2,769	2,773	2,702	3,321	3,329	3,162	3,388	3,404	2,591	2,117	2,130	1,367	578	579	564	693	695	660
1975–76	16,305	16,414	12,129	10,165	10,251	6,385	2,798	2,812	2,559	3,341	3,350	3,186	3,644	3,669	2,711	2,272	2,291	1,427	625	629	572	747	749	712
1976–77	16,513	16,813	12,560	10,428	10,713	6,730	2,743	2,754	2,568	3,342	3,346	3,262	3,906	3,977	2,971	2,467	2,534	1,592	649	651	607	790	791	772
1977–78	16,473	16,797	12,470	10,394	10,697	6,756	2,766	2,781	2,502	3,314	3,319	3,212	4,158	4,240	3,148	2,624	2,700	1,706	698	702	631	836	838	811
1978–79	16,352	16,697	12,277	10,387	10,714	6,632	2,745	2,757	2,536	3,220	3,225	3,109	4,514	4,609	3,389	2,867	2,958	1,831	758	761	700	889	890	858
1979–80	15,701	16,021	11,990	10,004	10,308	6,590	2,644	2,655	2,449	3,053	3,058	2,951	4,912	5,013	3,751	3,130	3,225	2,062	827	831	766	955	957	923
1980–81	15,668	16,022	12,325	10,019	10,360	6,912	2,628	2,637	2,496	3,020	3,025	2,917	5,470	5,594	4,303	3,498	3,617	2,413	918	921	871	1,054	1,056	1,019
1981–82	16,256	16,689	12,514	10,421	10,845	6,868	2,736	2,738	2,696	3,099	3,106	2,951	6,166	6,330	4,746	3,953	4,113	2,605	1,038	1,039	1,022	1,175	1,178	1,119
1982–83	17,494	18,015	13,561	11,222	11,727	7,604	2,986	2,987	2,976	3,286	3,301	2,980	6,920	7,126	5,364	4,439	4,639	3,008	1,181	1,181	1,177	1,300	1,306	1,179
1983–84	18,304	18,916	13,581	11,825	12,416	7,555	3,115	3,118	3,054	3,365	3,382	2,972	7,508	7,759	5,571	4,851	5,093	3,099	1,278	1,279	1,253	1,380	1,387	1,219
1984–85	19,242	19,825	14,553	12,468	13,034	8,176	3,345	3,345	3,341	3,429	3,446	3,036	8,202	8,451	6,203	5,315	5,556	3,485	1,426	1,426	1,424	1,462	1,469	1,294
1985–86[4]	20,259	21,042	14,849	13,200	13,956	8,373	3,542	3,550	3,420	3,517	3,536	3,055	8,885	9,228	6,512	5,789	6,121	3,672	1,553	1,557	1,500	1,542	1,551	1,340
1986–87	21,584	22,395	14,240	14,089	14,853	8,217	3,699	3,733	2,824	3,797	3,809	3,199	9,676	10,039	6,384	6,316	6,658	3,684	1,658	1,673	1,266	1,702	1,708	1,434
1987–88	22,515	22,831	15,160	14,969	15,242	8,912	3,744	3,770	2,956	3,803	3,819	3,291	10,512	10,659	7,078	6,988	7,116	4,161	1,748	1,760	1,380	1,775	1,783	1,537
1988–89	22,909	23,492	16,311	15,276	15,809	9,863	3,785	3,815	3,153	3,848	3,868	3,295	11,189	11,474	7,967	7,461	7,722	4,817	1,849	1,863	1,540	1,880	1,889	1,609
1989–90	23,485	24,005	16,943	15,921	16,408	10,154	3,758	3,781	3,250	3,806	3,816	3,539	12,018	12,284	8,670	8,147	8,396	5,196	1,923	1,935	1,663	1,948	1,953	1,811
1990–91	23,920	24,526	17,236	16,254	16,828	10,320	3,823	3,849	3,231	3,843	3,849	3,684	12,910	13,237	9,302	8,772	9,083	5,570	2,063	2,077	1,744	2,074	2,077	1,989
1991–92	24,941	25,597	17,293	16,911	17,521	10,330	3,988	4,023	3,211	4,042	4,052	3,752	13,892	14,258	9,632	9,419	9,759	5,754	2,221	2,241	1,788	2,252	2,257	2,090
1992–93	25,476	26,130	17,241	17,308	17,920	10,548	4,088	4,112	3,430	4,081	4,098	3,264	14,634	15,009	9,903	9,942	10,294	6,059	2,348	2,362	1,970	2,344	2,354	1,875
1993–94	26,295	26,988	17,659	17,940	18,586	10,810	4,225	4,253	3,507	4,130	4,149	3,343	15,496	15,904	10,406	10,572	10,952	6,370	2,490	2,506	2,067	2,434	2,445	1,970
1994–95	26,736	27,388	18,428	18,329	18,940	11,406	4,268	4,291	3,685	4,138	4,157	3,337	16,207	16,602	11,170	11,111	11,481	6,914	2,587	2,601	2,233	2,509	2,520	2,023
1995–96	27,637	28,284	18,571	19,054	19,662	11,394	4,397	4,418	3,808	4,186	4,203	3,369	17,208	17,612	11,563	11,864	12,243	7,094	2,738	2,751	2,371	2,606	2,617	2,098
1996–97	28,167	28,797	18,666	19,515	20,113	11,299	4,493	4,511	3,962	4,159	4,172	3,405	18,039	18,442	11,954	12,498	12,881	7,236	2,878	2,889	2,537	2,663	2,672	2,181
1997–98	28,406	29,255	19,822	19,637	20,471	11,451	4,531	4,547	4,100	4,237	4,236	4,272	18,516	19,070	12,921	12,801	13,344	7,464	2,954	2,964	2,672	2,762	2,761	2,785
1998–99	29,207	30,053	20,085	20,249	21,071	11,843	4,636	4,661	3,893	4,321	4,320	4,349	19,368	19,929	13,319	13,428	13,973	7,854	3,075	3,091	2,581	2,865	2,865	2,884
1999–2000	29,626	30,393	20,585	20,666	21,422	12,055	4,743	4,751	4,496	4,217	4,220	4,034	20,213	20,737	14,045	14,100	14,616	8,225	3,236	3,242	3,067	2,877	2,879	2,753
2000–01	30,288	30,973	21,125	21,257	21,923	12,849	4,793	4,807	4,260	4,238	4,242	4,017	21,373	21,856	14,907	15,000	15,470	9,067	3,382	3,392	3,006	2,991	2,993	2,834
2001–02	31,210	31,882	22,036	21,920	22,573	14,031	4,967	4,980	4,339	4,322	4,329	3,667	22,413	22,896	15,825	15,742	16,211	10,076	3,567	3,576	3,116	3,104	3,109	2,633
2002–03	31,802	32,411	24,189	22,322	22,926	14,512	5,112	5,129	4,404	4,368	4,356	5,273	23,340	23,787	17,753	16,383	16,826	10,651	3,752	3,764	3,232	3,206	3,197	3,870
2003–04	32,832	33,427	26,078	23,087	23,685	15,394	5,260	5,270	4,774	4,485	4,472	5,910	24,624	25,070	19,558	17,315	17,763	11,545	3,945	3,952	3,581	3,364	3,354	4,432
2004–05	33,417	33,991	26,273	23,498	24,081	15,691	5,408	5,401	5,793	4,511	4,509	4,789	25,817	26,260	20,297	18,154	18,604	12,122	4,178	4,173	4,475	3,485	3,483	3,700
2005–06	33,552	34,082	26,689	23,520	24,055	15,524	5,486	5,491	5,204	4,545	4,535	5,961	26,908	27,333	21,404	18,862	19,292	12,450	4,400	4,404	4,173	3,645	3,637	4,781
2006–07	34,568	35,151	24,655	24,367	24,938	15,446	5,599	5,607	5,040	4,603	4,607	4,169	28,440	28,919	20,284	20,047	20,517	12,708	4,606	4,613	4,147	3,787	3,790	3,430
2007–08	34,890	35,426	25,417	24,581	25,113	15,387	5,630	5,635	5,256	4,679	4,678	4,775	29,768	30,226	21,686	20,972	21,427	13,128	4,803	4,808	4,484	3,992	3,992	4,074
2008–09	35,561	36,102	26,266	24,939	25,476	15,682	5,809	5,816	5,263	4,813	4,810	5,320	30,764	31,232	22,723	21,575	22,040	13,567	5,025	5,031	4,553	4,164	4,161	4,603
2009–10	35,880	36,459	28,006	24,916	25,495	17,015	6,008	6,009	5,966	4,956	4,956	5,026	31,341	31,847	24,463	21,764	22,269	14,862	5,248	5,248	5,211	4,329	4,329	4,390
2010–11	35,773	36,494	25,926	24,737	25,451	15,361	6,064	6,071	5,543	4,972	4,972	5,022	31,875	32,517	23,101	22,042	22,677	13,687	5,403	5,410	4,939	4,430	4,430	4,475
2011–12	36,045	36,720	25,737	24,915	25,584	15,223	6,130	6,136	5,636	5,000	5,001	4,879	33,058	33,677	23,605	22,850	23,464	13,961	5,622	5,627	5,169	4,586	4,586	4,475
2012–13	36,983	37,614	25,048	25,679	26,301	15,175	6,254	6,260	5,607	5,050	5,054	4,266	34,483	35,071	23,355	23,943	24,523	14,149	5,831	5,837	5,228	4,709	4,712	3,977
2013–14	38,011	38,649	25,207	26,516	27,147	14,964	6,358	6,364	5,796	5,136	5,139	4,447	35,995	36,599	23,870	25,110	25,707	14,170	6,021	6,026	5,489	4,864	4,866	4,211

See notes at end of table.

Table 330.10. Average undergraduate tuition and fees and room and board rates charged for full-time students in degree-granting postsecondary institutions, by level and control of institution: Selected years, 1963–64 through 2017–18—Continued

Year and control of institution	Constant 2017–18 dollars[1]												Current dollars											
	Total tuition, fees, room, and board			Tuition and required fees[2]			Dormitory rooms			Board[3]			Total tuition, fees, room, and board			Tuition and required fees[2]			Dormitory rooms			Board[3]		
	All institutions	4-year	2-year	All institutions	4-year	2-year	All institutions	4-year	2-year	All institutions	4-year	2-year	All institutions	4-year	2-year	All institutions	4-year	2-year	All institutions	4-year	2-year	All institutions	4-year	2-year
1	2	3	4	5	6	7	8	9	10	11	12	13	14	15	16	17	18	19	20	21	22	23	24	25
2014–15	39,232	39,825	25,504	27,448	28,032	14,951	6,522	6,530	5,773	5,262	5,264	4,780	37,422	37,988	24,327	26,182	26,739	14,261	6,221	6,228	5,506	5,019	5,021	4,560
2015–16	40,630	41,168	25,383	28,571	29,097	15,128	6,724	6,732	5,901	5,335	5,340	4,354	39,016	39,534	24,375	27,436	27,942	14,528	6,457	6,464	5,666	5,123	5,128	4,181
2016–17	41,845	42,400	25,449	29,597	30,140	14,918	6,861	6,868	6,083	5,387	5,392	4,448	40,922	41,465	24,888	28,945	29,476	14,589	6,710	6,717	5,949	5,268	5,273	4,350
2017–18	42,681	43,139	25,596	30,282	30,731	14,894	6,961	6,967	6,057	5,437	5,441	4,645	42,681	43,139	25,596	30,282	30,731	14,894	6,961	6,967	6,057	5,437	5,441	4,645
Nonprofit																								
1999–2000	30,763	31,118	17,131	21,854	22,178	10,102	4,696	4,720	3,100	4,214	4,220	3,928	20,989	21,231	11,688	14,911	15,131	6,893	3,204	3,221	2,115	2,875	2,879	2,680
2000–01	31,083	31,417	16,604	22,101	22,407	9,875	4,743	4,769	2,846	4,238	4,242	3,883	21,934	22,170	11,717	15,596	15,811	6,968	3,347	3,365	2,008	2,991	2,993	2,740
2001–02	32,138	32,385	18,060	22,892	23,120	11,316	4,923	4,936	3,208	4,322	4,329	3,536	23,080	23,257	12,970	16,440	16,604	8,126	3,536	3,544	2,304	3,104	3,109	2,540
2002–03	33,077	33,308	19,677	23,652	23,868	12,136	5,072	5,084	3,605	4,353	4,356	3,936	24,276	24,446	14,442	17,359	17,517	8,907	3,723	3,731	2,646	3,195	3,197	2,889
2003–04	34,247	34,471	20,759	24,572	24,779	12,782	5,209	5,220	3,805	4,466	4,472	4,172	25,685	25,853	15,569	18,429	18,584	9,587	3,907	3,915	2,853	3,349	3,354	3,129
2004–05	35,057	35,279	20,589	25,239	25,438	12,827	5,324	5,332	3,792	4,495	4,509	3,970	27,083	27,255	15,906	19,498	19,652	9,910	4,113	4,119	2,929	3,472	3,483	3,067
2005–06	35,562	35,777	20,361	25,646	25,851	12,866	5,381	5,391	3,761	4,535	4,535	3,734	28,520	28,692	16,329	20,568	20,732	10,318	4,315	4,323	3,017	3,637	3,637	2,994
2006–07	36,666	36,854	21,492	26,547	26,733	13,292	5,509	5,515	4,346	4,610	4,607	3,853	30,166	30,321	17,682	21,841	21,994	10,936	4,532	4,537	3,576	3,793	3,790	3,170
2007–08	37,413	37,565	22,101	27,193	27,342	13,817	5,538	5,544	4,449	4,682	4,678	3,835	31,921	32,050	18,857	23,201	23,329	11,789	4,725	4,730	3,796	3,994	3,992	3,272
2008–09	38,879	39,024	23,420	28,323	28,479	14,567	5,730	5,735	4,496	4,826	4,810	4,358	33,635	33,761	20,261	24,503	24,638	12,602	4,957	4,962	3,889	4,175	4,161	3,770
2009–10	39,977	40,118	23,762	29,074	29,234	14,466	5,923	5,928	4,713	4,981	4,956	4,584	34,920	35,042	20,756	25,396	25,535	12,636	5,173	5,178	4,116	4,351	4,329	4,004
2010–11	40,743	40,870	22,549	29,675	29,832	14,218	6,058	6,065	4,466	5,010	4,972	3,865	36,304	36,416	20,092	26,441	26,581	12,668	5,398	5,404	3,980	4,464	4,430	3,444
2011–12	41,112	41,254	24,997	29,923	30,111	15,350	6,136	6,142	4,668	5,053	5,001	4,980	37,705	37,835	22,926	27,443	27,616	14,078	5,628	5,633	4,281	4,634	4,586	4,567
2012–13	42,011	42,149	23,753	30,637	30,827	14,784	6,262	6,268	4,724	5,111	5,054	4,245	39,171	39,299	22,148	28,566	28,743	13,785	5,838	5,844	4,405	4,766	4,712	3,958
2013–14	42,912	43,012	24,289	31,333	31,493	14,787	6,375	6,380	5,061	5,204	5,139	4,441	40,636	40,731	23,001	29,671	29,823	14,003	6,037	6,042	4,793	4,928	4,866	4,206
2014–15	43,999	44,098	24,723	32,124	32,278	14,984	6,551	6,556	5,281	5,324	5,264	4,457	41,969	42,063	23,582	30,641	30,789	14,293	6,249	6,254	5,038	5,078	5,021	4,252
2015–16	44,858	44,989	25,356	32,708	32,884	15,333	6,760	6,765	5,602	5,390	5,340	4,421	43,077	43,202	24,349	31,409	31,578	14,724	6,491	6,497	5,379	5,176	5,128	4,246
2016–17	45,552	45,707	25,838	33,287	33,454	15,646	6,855	6,860	5,741	5,410	5,392	4,450	44,548	44,699	25,268	32,553	32,717	15,301	6,704	6,709	5,615	5,291	5,273	4,352
2017–18	46,014	46,150	26,531	33,605	33,755	15,790	6,950	6,954	6,016	5,459	5,441	4,725	46,014	46,150	26,531	33,605	33,755	15,790	6,950	6,954	6,016	5,459	5,441	4,725
For-profit																								
1999–2000	23,633	24,253	23,060	12,761	12,694	12,848	6,224	6,788	5,733	4,647	4,771	4,479	16,124	16,547	15,734	8,707	8,661	8,766	4,247	4,631	3,912	3,171	3,255	3,056
2000–01	25,065	25,820	24,178	14,444	14,753	14,094	6,387	7,029	5,604	4,235	4,037	4,480	17,688	18,220	17,061	10,192	10,411	9,945	4,507	4,960	3,955	2,988	2,849	3,161
2001–02	25,867	27,532	23,611	15,122	15,413	14,801	6,446	7,514	4,984	4,299	4,605	3,826	18,576	19,772	16,956	10,860	11,069	10,629	4,629	5,396	3,579	3,087	3,307	2,748
2002–03	26,833	27,304	26,439	15,410	15,542	15,163	6,238	7,335	4,809	5,186	4,426	6,466	19,694	20,039	19,404	11,310	11,407	11,129	4,578	5,384	3,530	3,806	3,249	4,746
2003–04	29,096	29,177	29,828	16,371	16,531	16,032	6,789	7,672	5,322	5,935	4,974	8,474	21,822	21,883	22,371	12,278	12,398	12,024	5,092	5,754	3,992	4,451	3,730	6,355
2004–05	29,898	30,309	28,933	16,874	17,083	16,319	7,320	7,589	6,665	5,704	5,637	5,949	23,098	23,415	22,353	13,036	13,197	12,607	5,655	5,863	5,149	4,407	4,355	4,596
2005–06	29,374	28,960	32,009	16,505	16,602	16,158	7,588	8,086	5,956	5,281	4,272	9,895	23,557	23,225	25,670	13,237	13,315	12,959	6,085	6,485	4,776	4,235	3,426	7,935
2006–07	29,180	30,037	25,830	17,354	17,737	15,904	7,542	8,068	5,428	4,285	4,232	4,498	24,007	24,712	21,251	14,277	14,593	13,084	6,205	6,638	4,466	3,525	3,481	3,701
2007–08	29,003	29,398	27,571	16,888	17,163	15,664	7,554	7,948	5,744	4,561	4,288	6,163	24,746	25,083	23,524	14,409	14,643	13,365	6,445	6,781	4,901	3,892	3,658	5,258
2008–09	28,101	28,247	28,491	16,545	16,676	15,872	7,181	7,446	5,687	4,375	4,125	6,932	24,311	24,437	24,648	14,313	14,427	13,731	6,212	6,441	4,920	3,785	3,569	5,997
2009–10	27,612	27,344	29,734	16,061	15,764	17,323	7,146	7,249	6,506	4,405	4,331	5,905	24,118	23,885	25,973	14,029	13,769	15,132	6,242	6,332	5,683	3,847	3,783	5,158
2010–11	25,792	25,672	28,940	15,419	15,405	15,479	6,127	6,149	5,978	4,246	4,118	7,483	22,982	22,875	25,787	13,739	13,727	13,792	5,460	5,479	5,327	3,783	3,669	6,668
2011–12	25,048	24,994	25,608	14,993	14,951	15,204	6,060	6,052	6,135	3,994	3,991	4,269	22,972	22,923	23,486	13,751	13,712	13,944	5,558	5,551	5,627	3,663	3,660	3,915
2012–13	24,845	24,762	25,757	14,769	14,683	15,242	6,157	6,164	6,080	3,920	3,915	4,435	23,165	23,088	24,016	13,770	13,691	14,212	5,740	5,747	5,669	3,655	3,651	4,135
2013–14	24,432	24,338	25,710	14,562	14,482	14,991	6,128	6,119	6,220	3,742	3,736	4,498	23,137	23,047	24,346	13,789	13,714	14,196	5,803	5,795	5,891	3,544	3,538	4,260
2014–15	24,504	24,402	26,869	14,648	14,598	14,945	6,076	6,078	6,059	3,780	3,726	5,865	23,373	23,277	25,629	13,972	13,924	14,256	5,796	5,798	5,780	3,605	3,554	5,594
2015–16	24,760	24,703	25,316	14,780	14,735	15,076	6,091	6,083	6,173	3,889	3,885	4,067	23,777	23,722	24,310	14,193	14,150	14,477	5,849	5,842	5,928	3,735	3,731	3,905
2016–17	26,004	26,107	25,591	14,744	14,748	14,723	7,044	7,154	6,430	4,216	4,206	4,438	25,431	25,531	25,027	14,419	14,423	14,399	6,889	6,996	6,288	4,123	4,113	4,340
2017–18	26,261	26,412	25,065	14,676	14,686	14,605	7,268	7,411	6,102	4,317	4,315	4,357	26,261	26,412	25,065	14,676	14,686	14,605	7,268	7,411	6,102	4,317	4,315	4,357

[1]Constant dollars based on the Consumer Price Index, prepared by the Bureau of Labor Statistics, U.S. Department of Labor, adjusted to an academic-year basis.
[2]For public institutions, in-state tuition and required fees are used.
[3]Data for 1986–87 and later years reflect a basis of 20 meals per week, while data for earlier years are for meals served 7 days a week (the number of meals per day was not specified). Because of this revision in data collection and tabulation procedures, data are not entirely comparable with figures for previous years. In particular, data on board rates are somewhat higher than in earlier years because they reflect the basis of 20 meals per week rather than meals served 7 days a week. Since many institutions serve fewer than 3 meals each day, the 1986-87 and later data reflect a more accurate accounting of total board costs.
[4]Room and board data are estimated.

NOTE: Data are for the entire academic year and are average charges for full-time students. Tuition and fees were weighted by the number of full-time-equivalent undergraduates, but were not adjusted to reflect student residency. Room and board are based on full-time students. Data through 1995-96 are for institutions of higher education, while later data are for degree-granting institutions. Degree-granting institutions grant associate's or higher degrees and participate in Title IV federal financial aid programs. The degree-granting classification is very similar to the earlier higher education classification, but it includes more 2-year colleges and excludes a few higher education institutions that did not grant degrees. Some data have been revised from previously published figures. Detail may not sum to totals because of rounding.

SOURCE: U.S. Department of Education, National Center for Education Statistics, *Projections of Education Statistics to 1986–87*; Higher Education General Information Survey (HEGIS), "Institutional Characteristics of Colleges and Universities" surveys, 1969–70 through 1985–86; "Fall Enrollment in Institutions of Higher Education" surveys, 1963 through 1985; Integrated Postsecondary Education Data System (IPEDS), "Fall Enrollment Survey" (IPEDS-EF:86–99) and "Institutional Characteristics Survey" (IPEDS-IC:86–99); IPEDS Spring 2001 through Spring 2018, Fall Enrollment component; and IPEDS Fall 2000 through Fall 2017, Institutional Characteristics component. (This table was prepared November 2018.)

Table 330.20. Average undergraduate tuition and fees and room and board rates charged for full-time students in degree-granting postsecondary institutions, by control and level of institution and state or jurisdiction: 2016–17 and 2017–18

[In current dollars]

State or jurisdiction	Public 4-year							Private 4-year						Public 2-year, tuition and required fees		
	In-state, 2016–17		In-state, 2017–18				Out-of-state tuition and required fees, 2017–18	2016–17		2017–18						
	Total	Tuition and required fees	Total	Tuition and required fees	Room	Board		Total	Tuition and required fees	Total	Tuition and required fees	Room	Board	In-state, 2016–17	In-state, 2017–18	Out-of-state, 2017–18
1	2	3	4	5	6	7	8	9	10	11	12	13	14	15	16	17
United States	**$19,488**	**$8,804**	**$20,050**	**$9,037**	**$6,227**	**$4,786**	**$25,657**	**$41,465**	**$29,476**	**$43,139**	**$30,731**	**$6,967**	**$5,441**	**$3,156**	**$3,243**	**$7,971**
Alabama	19,052	9,466	19,673	9,827	5,534	4,311	24,939	24,710	15,422	26,164	16,321	4,818	5,025	4,362	4,403	9,133
Alaska	17,370	7,210	18,373	7,221	6,209	4,943	21,284	26,297	19,052	26,887	19,360	3,598	3,929	3,820	†	†
Arizona	21,491	10,057	22,629	10,557	7,081	4,992	26,067	22,559	13,140	22,939	13,487	5,125	4,327	2,129	2,152	8,067
Arkansas	16,871	7,924	17,479	8,187	5,139	4,153	20,061	29,804	21,710	30,828	22,610	4,175	4,043	3,195	3,291	4,762
California	21,356	7,896	22,081	8,020	7,896	6,166	29,173	44,710	31,484	47,410	33,483	7,813	6,113	1,262	1,268	7,504
Colorado	20,943	9,352	21,514	9,540	5,858	6,116	29,846	34,337	22,627	35,152	22,873	7,188	5,092	3,565	3,638	10,354
Connecticut	24,174	11,726	25,182	12,355	7,032	5,795	33,741	53,198	38,975	54,819	40,410	8,227	6,182	4,189	4,312	12,879
Delaware	21,698	9,578	22,371	9,999	7,382	4,990	29,356	25,996	14,383	26,928	15,096	5,911	5,920	†	†	†
District of Columbia	†	5,612	†	5,756	†	†	12,092	55,669	40,618	57,611	41,775	10,288	5,547	†	†	†
Florida	14,806	4,435	14,896	4,455	5,856	4,585	18,241	35,876	24,360	37,336	25,531	6,720	5,084	2,552	2,506	9,111
Georgia	17,353	7,010	17,705	7,206	6,255	4,244	21,957	39,110	27,213	40,414	27,813	6,869	5,731	2,895	2,901	8,090
Hawaii	21,016	9,712	21,201	9,709	5,767	5,725	31,019	28,370	15,937	28,858	16,447	5,693	6,718	3,080	3,080	8,216
Idaho	14,457	7,005	15,455	7,247	3,911	4,297	22,601	13,010	5,925	13,488	5,833	3,275	4,380	3,227	3,282	7,732
Illinois	24,541	13,636	25,089	13,971	6,035	5,084	28,618	43,382	31,298	45,046	32,491	7,264	5,290	3,749	3,891	10,989
Indiana	19,001	8,876	19,297	9,038	5,476	4,783	28,805	41,852	30,928	43,764	32,338	6,029	5,397	4,175	4,255	8,211
Iowa	17,604	8,361	18,426	8,766	5,394	4,266	26,214	35,780	26,742	37,380	27,991	4,584	4,805	4,791	4,923	6,581
Kansas	17,560	8,489	17,963	8,737	4,813	4,414	22,615	28,653	20,198	30,240	21,316	4,319	4,604	3,221	3,382	4,611
Kentucky	19,673	10,014	20,745	10,365	5,889	4,490	24,632	34,895	25,846	35,948	26,719	4,673	4,556	3,962	4,106	13,825
Louisiana	18,319	8,813	18,835	9,165	5,664	4,007	21,632	47,557	35,190	49,452	36,715	7,031	5,706	4,031	4,093	7,057
Maine	19,073	9,219	19,500	9,664	5,028	4,808	26,939	48,107	35,547	49,994	37,043	6,533	6,418	3,673	3,698	6,498
Maryland	20,670	9,094	21,177	9,289	6,821	5,067	24,353	53,775	40,209	55,685	41,859	8,036	5,790	3,983	4,090	9,467
Massachusetts	24,473	12,331	25,229	12,778	7,771	4,680	29,774	57,363	42,655	59,559	44,384	8,835	6,340	4,785	4,991	10,006
Michigan	21,832	11,890	22,665	12,435	5,127	5,103	37,600	33,498	24,058	36,664	26,964	4,949	4,751	3,423	3,469	6,552
Minnesota	19,727	10,883	20,420	11,226	4,983	4,210	20,736	40,939	30,925	42,716	32,416	5,377	4,923	5,310	5,381	6,113
Mississippi	16,843	7,472	17,718	7,980	5,688	4,051	19,691	24,698	16,949	25,774	17,625	4,255	3,895	2,831	3,182	5,626
Missouri	17,639	8,176	18,106	8,387	6,016	3,703	19,519	33,433	23,702	34,623	24,615	5,700	4,308	3,028	3,273	6,157
Montana	15,241	6,503	15,800	6,783	4,184	4,834	23,678	32,375	23,657	33,739	24,953	4,161	4,625	3,381	3,631	8,482
Nebraska	17,379	7,732	18,449	8,188	5,517	4,744	20,555	32,201	23,110	34,598	23,659	4,716	6,223	2,991	3,212	4,101
Nevada	17,145	5,520	16,810	5,920	5,757	5,133	21,176	35,053	21,423	36,163	23,261	6,345	6,557	2,910	3,075	9,853
New Hampshire	26,968	15,491	27,570	15,949	7,047	4,574	28,130	46,533	33,235	47,030	33,322	8,620	5,089	7,002	7,337	15,907
New Jersey	26,070	13,297	26,542	13,633	7,966	4,943	28,649	48,439	35,224	50,321	36,589	8,064	5,668	4,366	4,536	8,049
New Mexico	15,528	6,825	15,803	6,718	4,567	4,518	17,533	32,373	22,535	33,620	23,865	5,655	4,100	1,590	1,666	5,318
New York	21,750	7,709	22,343	7,938	9,260	5,145	21,662	51,791	37,581	53,659	39,007	8,865	5,788	5,122	5,229	9,151
North Carolina	16,635	7,218	17,343	7,354	5,633	4,355	24,274	42,312	30,701	44,050	32,140	6,162	5,747	2,471	2,499	8,496
North Dakota	15,388	7,376	15,998	7,687	3,479	4,832	19,021	20,964	14,290	22,511	15,256	3,077	4,178	4,562	4,700	9,429
Ohio	20,961	9,827	21,674	10,026	6,632	5,017	24,098	40,975	30,291	42,254	31,242	5,742	5,270	3,654	3,672	7,456
Oklahoma	15,755	7,219	16,263	7,623	4,589	4,052	20,200	33,883	24,776	35,542	26,240	4,596	4,706	3,627	3,876	9,059
Oregon	21,324	9,739	22,710	10,363	7,262	5,085	30,487	48,658	37,053	50,617	38,674	6,266	5,677	4,262	4,487	8,503
Pennsylvania	25,331	14,068	25,795	14,534	6,743	4,518	27,129	52,134	39,187	53,239	40,068	7,271	5,900	5,048	5,173	13,679
Rhode Island	23,135	11,386	24,280	12,239	7,538	4,502	29,013	52,874	38,855	54,877	40,361	8,776	5,740	4,266	4,564	12,156
South Carolina	21,508	12,153	22,132	12,579	5,888	3,665	30,919	33,748	24,523	34,421	24,931	4,804	4,686	4,418	4,502	9,480
South Dakota	16,054	8,301	16,421	8,540	3,801	4,080	12,060	30,924	23,146	32,157	24,219	3,943	3,995	5,803	6,026	5,853
Tennessee	18,340	9,287	18,951	9,574	4,988	4,388	25,378	35,928	25,984	37,162	26,939	5,772	4,451	4,048	4,148	16,140
Texas	17,800	8,376	18,271	8,645	5,175	4,451	24,937	41,980	31,010	43,866	32,482	6,368	5,016	2,100	2,209	6,418
Utah	13,709	6,334	14,174	6,557	3,435	4,182	20,168	15,208	7,441	15,389	7,548	3,946	3,894	3,690	3,781	12,020
Vermont	26,786	15,537	27,782	16,103	7,381	4,297	38,968	54,015	41,068	56,172	42,637	7,431	6,105	6,222	6,414	12,678
Virginia	22,567	12,126	23,427	12,637	6,089	4,701	33,428	32,614	22,284	33,658	23,014	5,664	4,980	4,962	5,118	11,275
Washington	18,053	6,903	18,323	6,830	6,146	5,347	28,263	46,667	35,213	48,518	36,807	6,208	5,503	3,848	4,078	5,976
West Virginia	17,096	7,241	17,803	7,619	5,465	4,718	21,032	20,898	12,206	21,300	12,341	4,316	4,643	4,009	4,077	9,410
Wisconsin	16,246	8,419	16,544	8,475	4,864	3,205	23,500	41,503	31,662	43,332	33,156	5,869	4,307	4,292	4,337	6,257
Wyoming	14,354	4,311	14,486	4,443	4,493	5,550	13,731	†	18,021	†	†	†	†	2,987	3,142	7,678

†Not applicable.

NOTE: Data are for the entire academic year and are average charges for full-time students. In-state tuition and fees were weighted by the number of full-time-equivalent undergraduates, but were not adjusted to reflect the number of students who were state residents. Out-of-state tuition and fees were weighted by the number of first-time freshmen attending the institution in fall 2016 from out of state. Institutional room and board rates are weighted by the number of full-time students. Degree-granting institutions grant associate's or higher degrees and participate in Title IV federal financial aid programs. Some data have been revised from previously published figures. Detail may not sum to totals because of rounding.

SOURCE: U.S. Department of Education, National Center for Education Statistics, Integrated Postsecondary Education Data System (IPEDS), Fall 2016 and Fall 2017, Institutional Characteristics component; and Spring 2017 and Spring 2018, Fall Enrollment component. (This table was prepared November 2018.)

Table 330.30. Average undergraduate tuition, fees, room, and board rates for full-time students in degree-granting postsecondary institutions, by percentile of charges and control and level of institution: Selected years, 2000–01 through 2017–18

Control and level of institution, and year	Current dollars										Constant 2017–18 dollars				
	Tuition, fees, room, and board					Tuition and required fees					Tuition and required fees				
	10th percentile	25th percentile	Median (50th percentile)	75th percentile	90th percentile	10th percentile	25th percentile	Median (50th percentile)	75th percentile	90th percentile	10th percentile	25th percentile	Median (50th percentile)	75th percentile	90th percentile
1	2	3	4	5	6	7	8	9	10	11	12	13	14	15	16
Public institutions[1]															
2000–01	$5,741	$6,880	$8,279	$9,617	$11,384	$612	$1,480	$2,403	$3,444	$4,583	$867	$2,097	$3,405	$4,881	$6,495
2005–06	7,700	9,623	11,348	13,543	16,264	990	2,070	3,329	5,322	6,972	1,234	2,581	4,151	6,636	8,693
2010–11	9,889	12,856	15,234	17,860	21,593	1,230	2,626	4,632	7,115	9,420	1,380	2,947	5,198	7,985	10,572
2015–16	13,215	15,947	18,648	21,735	25,180	1,632	3,456	6,452	9,326	11,948	1,699	3,599	6,719	9,712	12,442
2016–17	13,789	16,360	19,346	22,209	25,959	1,632	3,621	6,587	9,574	12,212	1,669	3,703	6,735	9,790	12,487
2017–18	13,965	16,749	19,922	23,093	26,927	1,632	3,726	6,897	9,952	12,700	1,632	3,726	6,897	9,952	12,700
Public 4-year[1]															
2000–01	6,503	7,347	8,468	9,816	11,611	2,118	2,520	3,314	4,094	5,085	3,001	3,571	4,696	5,802	7,206
2005–06	8,863	10,219	11,596	13,830	16,443	3,094	3,822	5,084	6,458	8,097	3,858	4,766	6,339	8,053	10,096
2010–11	12,048	13,604	15,823	18,419	22,191	4,336	5,091	6,779	8,689	11,029	4,866	5,714	7,608	9,752	12,378
2015–16	14,733	16,559	19,217	21,979	25,658	5,360	6,691	8,256	10,509	13,431	5,582	6,968	8,597	10,944	13,986
2016–17	15,292	17,057	19,759	22,515	26,523	4,344	6,737	8,428	10,753	13,539	4,442	6,889	8,618	10,995	13,844
2017–18	15,663	17,461	20,369	23,274	27,283	4,343	6,960	8,738	10,974	14,018	4,343	6,960	8,738	10,974	14,018
Public 2-year[1]															
2000–01	3,321	3,804	4,627	5,750	6,871	310	724	1,387	1,799	2,460	439	1,026	1,966	2,549	3,486
2005–06	4,380	4,822	6,234	7,567	8,993	691	1,109	1,920	2,589	3,100	862	1,383	2,394	3,228	3,865
2010–11	5,347	6,327	7,339	9,370	11,312	700	1,412	2,537	3,315	3,840	786	1,585	2,847	3,720	4,310
2015–16	6,474	7,503	9,337	11,854	14,978	1,182	1,514	3,077	4,115	5,032	1,231	1,577	3,204	4,285	5,240
2016–17	6,650	7,773	9,437	12,269	15,041	1,244	1,632	3,208	4,238	5,154	1,272	1,669	3,280	4,334	5,270
2017–18	6,896	8,355	9,787	12,587	15,400	1,244	1,632	3,304	4,394	5,190	1,244	1,632	3,304	4,394	5,190
Private nonprofit institutions															
2000–01	13,514	17,552	22,493	27,430	32,659	7,800	11,730	15,540	19,600	24,532	11,054	16,623	22,022	27,776	34,765
2005–06	18,243	23,258	29,497	35,918	41,707	9,981	15,375	21,070	26,265	31,690	12,445	19,171	26,272	32,750	39,515
2010–11	23,143	29,884	38,063	47,061	52,235	11,930	19,625	26,920	34,536	40,082	13,389	22,025	30,212	38,760	44,984
2015–16	25,903	36,436	45,951	57,465	63,209	11,900	23,162	32,250	42,270	48,190	12,392	24,120	33,584	44,018	50,183
2016–17	26,798	37,800	47,748	59,514	65,225	12,130	24,130	33,405	43,940	50,022	12,403	24,674	34,158	44,931	51,150
2017–18	28,232	39,206	49,383	61,550	67,643	12,300	24,700	34,470	45,608	51,992	12,300	24,700	34,470	45,608	51,992
Nonprofit 4-year															
2000–01	13,972	17,714	22,554	27,476	32,659	8,450	11,920	15,746	19,730	24,532	11,975	16,892	22,314	27,960	34,765
2005–06	18,350	23,322	29,598	36,028	41,774	10,300	15,560	21,190	26,500	31,690	12,843	19,402	26,422	33,043	39,515
2010–11	23,548	30,042	38,129	47,061	52,235	12,220	19,854	27,100	34,580	40,082	13,715	22,282	30,414	38,809	44,984
2015–16	26,315	36,537	46,094	57,465	63,209	12,240	23,748	32,400	42,288	48,190	12,746	24,730	33,740	44,037	50,183
2016–17	27,233	37,993	47,857	59,514	65,225	12,240	24,427	33,500	43,980	50,063	12,516	24,978	34,255	44,971	51,192
2017–18	28,370	39,206	49,464	61,550	67,643	12,360	25,025	34,600	45,620	52,002	12,360	25,025	34,600	45,620	52,002
Nonprofit 2-year															
2000–01	6,850	6,850	9,995	14,209	20,240	2,430	4,825	7,250	8,266	11,100	3,444	6,838	10,274	11,714	15,730
2005–06	8,030	15,680	16,830	20,829	28,643	4,218	8,640	9,940	12,270	14,472	5,259	10,773	12,394	15,300	18,045
2010–11	10,393	19,718	21,186	27,386	30,758	3,840	9,730	12,000	14,640	18,965	4,310	10,920	13,468	16,430	21,284
2015–16	22,582	23,059	25,696	31,405	53,387	4,904	10,800	14,110	17,346	22,060	5,107	11,247	14,693	18,063	22,972
2016–17	18,431	24,070	25,850	32,311	55,517	4,490	11,170	14,930	17,500	22,760	4,591	11,422	15,267	17,894	23,273
2017–18	18,886	26,265	29,227	33,546	59,560	4,904	9,867	15,022	18,450	23,670	4,904	9,867	15,022	18,450	23,670
Private for-profit institutions															
2000–01	13,396	15,778	19,403	21,400	21,845	6,900	8,202	9,644	12,090	14,600	9,778	11,623	13,667	17,133	20,690
2005–06	17,278	19,098	25,589	26,499	31,903	7,632	10,011	12,450	14,335	17,740	9,516	12,483	15,524	17,875	22,120
2010–11	16,097	16,097	17,484	26,175	31,639	10,194	10,194	13,520	15,750	18,048	11,441	11,441	15,173	17,676	20,255
2015–16	17,407	17,407	26,028	26,405	35,377	10,575	11,003	13,320	17,132	19,286	11,012	11,458	13,871	17,840	20,084
2016–17	24,091	26,218	26,218	28,692	36,414	10,295	11,219	13,567	16,975	21,004	10,527	11,472	13,873	17,358	21,477
2017–18	25,281	26,226	26,226	27,253	37,319	10,935	11,330	13,857	17,002	21,331	10,935	11,330	13,857	17,002	21,331
For-profit 4-year															
2000–01	13,396	15,818	20,417	21,400	21,400	7,206	8,305	9,675	12,800	15,090	10,212	11,769	13,711	18,139	21,384
2005–06	17,383	19,098	25,589	26,499	31,903	7,632	10,418	12,900	14,450	17,735	9,516	12,990	16,085	18,018	22,114
2010–11	16,097	16,097	17,484	26,175	31,639	10,194	10,194	13,560	16,500	18,048	11,441	11,441	15,218	18,518	20,255
2015–16	17,407	17,407	26,028	26,405	35,377	10,607	11,003	12,975	17,132	19,459	11,046	11,458	13,512	17,840	20,264
2016–17	24,091	26,218	26,218	28,692	36,414	9,630	11,219	13,420	17,124	21,252	9,847	11,472	13,723	17,510	21,731
2017–18	25,281	26,226	26,226	27,253	37,319	10,935	11,330	13,654	17,002	23,204	10,935	11,330	13,654	17,002	23,204
For-profit 2-year															
2000–01	15,778	15,778	19,403	21,845	21,845	6,025	7,365	9,644	12,000	14,255	8,538	10,437	13,667	17,005	20,201
2005–06	13,010	18,281	43,425	43,425	43,425	7,870	9,285	11,550	14,196	19,425	9,813	11,578	14,402	17,701	24,221
2010–11	23,687	23,687	25,161	25,161	25,161	10,075	12,049	13,418	15,263	17,918	11,307	13,523	15,059	17,130	20,109
2015–16	25,732	25,732	25,732	25,732	25,732	10,510	12,678	13,975	15,760	18,048	10,945	13,202	14,553	16,412	18,794
2016–17	26,575	26,575	26,575	26,575	26,575	10,496	12,366	14,032	15,550	17,433	10,733	12,645	14,348	15,901	17,826
2017–18	27,356	27,356	27,356	27,356	27,356	10,880	11,580	14,220	15,743	17,614	10,880	11,580	14,220	15,743	17,614

[1]Average undergraduate tuition and fees are based on in-state students only.

NOTE: Data are for the entire academic year and are average charges for full-time students. Student charges were weighted by the number of full-time-equivalent undergraduates, but were not adjusted to reflect student residency. Degree-granting institutions grant associate's or higher degrees and participate in Title IV federal financial aid programs. Some data have been revised from previously published figures.

SOURCE: U.S. Department of Education, National Center for Education Statistics, Integrated Postsecondary Education Data System (IPEDS), Fall 2000 through Fall 2017, Institutional Characteristics component; and Spring 2001 through Spring 2018, Fall Enrollment component. (This table was prepared November 2018.)

Table 330.40. Average total cost of attendance for first-time, full-time undergraduate students in degree-granting postsecondary institutions, by control and level of institution, living arrangement, and component of student costs: Selected years, 2010–11 through 2017–18

Level of institution, living arrangement, and component of student costs	2010–11				2014–15				2015–16				2016–17				2017–18			
	All institutions	Public, in-state	Private Non-profit	Private For-profit	All institutions	Public, in-state	Private Non-profit	Private For-profit	All institutions	Public, in-state	Private Non-profit	Private For-profit	All institutions	Public, in-state	Private Non-profit	Private For-profit	All institutions	Public, in-state	Private Non-profit	Private For-profit
1	2	3	4	5	6	7	8	9	10	11	12	13	14	15	16	17	18	19	20	21
	Current dollars																			
4-year institutions																				
Average total cost, by living arrangement																				
On campus	$27,589	$20,035	$39,676	$31,897	$30,851	$22,599	$45,962	$29,571	$31,726	$23,144	$47,339	$31,223	$32,636	$23,784	$48,866	$31,899	$33,494	$24,320	$50,338	$32,244
Off campus, living with family	20,084	12,554	31,689	22,268	21,785	13,653	36,431	22,289	22,337	13,961	37,530	21,944	22,815	14,129	38,779	22,136	23,377	14,388	39,925	22,414
Off campus, not living with family	29,142	21,324	40,033	31,000	30,940	23,072	45,805	29,265	31,631	23,462	47,154	29,938	32,251	23,857	48,506	29,949	33,018	24,201	50,246	30,419
Component of student costs																				
Tuition and required fees	14,596	7,163	26,637	15,191	16,403	8,282	31,325	15,368	16,963	8,547	32,340	16,275	17,500	8,797	33,511	16,812	18,041	9,044	34,621	17,020
Books and supplies	1,223	1,196	1,221	1,522	1,262	1,269	1,247	1,299	1,257	1,267	1,243	1,208	1,265	1,277	1,250	1,168	1,265	1,276	1,257	1,136
Room, board, and other expenses																				
On campus																				
Room and board	8,912	8,497	9,455	9,304	10,219	9,788	10,852	9,490	10,526	10,077	11,193	9,405	10,823	10,366	11,501	9,691	11,140	10,680	11,826	9,858
Other	2,858	3,179	2,363	5,879	2,967	3,260	2,537	3,414	2,980	3,252	2,563	4,335	3,049	3,344	2,604	4,229	3,047	3,321	2,634	4,231
Off campus, living with family																				
Other	4,265	4,195	3,832	5,554	4,120	4,102	3,858	5,622	4,116	4,147	3,947	4,461	4,051	4,054	4,018	4,156	4,071	4,068	4,047	4,259
Off campus, not living with family																				
Room and board	8,802	8,942	8,202	8,866	9,141	9,595	8,924	8,001	9,123	9,679	8,782	7,603	9,260	9,826	8,870	7,355	9,454	9,952	9,286	7,581
Other	4,521	4,022	3,974	5,421	4,135	3,927	4,308	4,596	4,287	3,969	4,788	4,851	4,227	3,956	4,875	4,614	4,258	3,930	5,082	4,682
2-year institutions																				
Average total cost, by living arrangement																				
On campus	13,777	12,336	25,763	29,179	14,849	13,997	30,488	27,144	15,192	14,335	31,286	27,592	15,547	14,671	31,379	28,334	15,962	15,083	32,452	28,394
Off campus, living with family	8,964	7,843	18,931	19,350	9,234	8,615	22,470	19,943	9,408	8,836	22,454	20,056	9,582	8,993	22,606	19,926	9,757	9,168	23,134	19,909
Off campus, not living with family	16,389	15,153	27,458	27,366	17,315	16,636	30,435	28,418	17,554	16,915	30,827	28,716	17,953	17,317	31,804	28,436	18,362	17,728	32,627	28,651
Component of student costs																				
Tuition and required fees	3,850	2,748	13,832	13,954	3,898	3,297	16,279	14,088	3,985	3,423	16,714	14,180	4,124	3,540	17,030	14,114	4,231	3,642	17,752	14,169
Books and supplies	1,302	1,295	1,153	1,407	1,431	1,434	1,243	1,396	1,447	1,450	1,165	1,454	1,456	1,463	1,129	1,364	1,471	1,482	1,139	1,280
Room, board, and other expenses																				
On campus																				
Room and board	5,654	5,351	7,806	9,961	6,486	6,225	9,950	8,914	6,706	6,405	10,297	9,379	6,898	6,557	10,624	10,047	7,135	6,791	10,926	10,126
Other	2,971	2,941	2,973	3,857	3,035	3,040	3,017	2,745	3,054	3,057	3,110	2,579	3,070	3,111	2,596	2,809	3,125	3,168	2,635	2,820
Off campus, living with family																				
Other	3,812	3,799	3,947	3,989	3,906	3,884	4,949	4,458	3,976	3,963	4,575	4,422	4,002	3,990	4,447	4,448	4,054	4,044	4,243	4,460
Off campus, not living with family																				
Room and board	7,478	7,412	7,999	7,889	8,096	8,091	8,262	8,138	8,204	8,202	8,376	8,199	8,408	8,428	9,006	8,064	8,649	8,683	9,044	8,150
Other	3,759	3,698	4,475	4,117	3,890	3,814	4,652	4,796	3,918	3,840	4,572	4,884	3,965	3,885	4,640	4,894	4,010	3,921	4,692	5,051
	Constant 2017–18 dollars[1]																			
4-year institutions																				
Average total cost, by living arrangement																				
On campus	$30,963	$22,486	$44,528	$35,797	$32,344	$23,692	$48,185	$31,002	$33,038	$24,101	$49,297	$32,514	$33,372	$24,320	$49,967	$32,618	$33,494	$24,320	$50,338	$32,244
Off campus, living with family	22,540	14,090	35,565	24,991	22,839	14,313	38,193	23,367	23,261	14,539	39,082	22,851	23,329	14,447	39,653	22,635	23,377	14,388	39,925	22,414
Off campus, not living with family	32,706	23,931	44,929	34,791	32,437	24,188	48,020	30,680	32,939	24,433	49,104	31,176	32,978	24,394	49,599	30,624	33,018	24,201	50,246	30,419
Tuition and required fees	16,381	8,039	29,894	17,049	17,196	8,682	32,841	16,111	17,665	8,901	33,678	16,948	17,894	8,996	34,266	17,191	18,041	9,044	34,621	17,020
2-year institutions																				
Average total cost, by living arrangement																				
On campus	15,461	13,844	28,913	32,747	15,567	14,674	31,963	28,457	15,820	14,928	32,580	28,733	15,898	15,002	32,086	28,972	15,962	15,083	32,452	28,394
Off campus, living with family	10,060	8,802	21,246	21,716	9,681	9,032	23,557	20,907	9,797	9,202	23,383	20,885	9,798	9,196	23,116	20,375	9,757	9,168	23,134	19,909
Off campus, not living with family	18,393	17,006	30,816	30,713	18,153	17,441	31,908	29,793	18,280	17,615	32,102	29,904	18,358	17,707	32,521	29,077	18,362	17,728	32,627	28,651
Tuition and required fees	4,321	3,084	15,523	15,661	4,087	3,457	17,066	14,770	4,150	3,565	17,405	14,766	4,217	3,620	17,414	14,432	4,231	3,642	17,752	14,169

[1]Constant dollars based on the Consumer Price Index, prepared by the Bureau of Labor Statistics, U.S. Department of Labor, adjusted to an academic-year basis.

NOTE: Excludes students who previously attended another postsecondary institution or who began their studies on a part-time basis. Tuition and fees at public institutions are the lower of either in-district or in-state tuition and fees. Data illustrating the average total cost of attendance for all students are weighted by the number of students at the institution receiving Title IV aid. Detail may not sum to totals because of rounding. Some data have been revised from previously published figures.

SOURCE: U.S. Department of Education, National Center for Education Statistics, Integrated Postsecondary Education Data System (IPEDS), Spring 2011 and Winter 2014–15 through Winter 2017–18, Student Financial Aid component; and Fall 2010 through Fall 2017, Institutional Characteristics component. (This table was prepared November 2018.)

Table 330.50. Average graduate tuition and required fees in degree-granting postsecondary institutions, by control of institution and percentile of charges: 1989–90 through 2017–18

Year	Total	Public institutions[1]	Private institutions			Public institutions,[1] by percentile			Nonprofit institutions, by percentile		
			Total	Nonprofit	For-profit	25th percentile	Median (50th percentile)	75th percentile	25th percentile	Median (50th percentile)	75th percentile
1	2	3	4	5	6	7	8	9	10	11	12
						Current dollars					
1989–90	$4,135	$1,999	$7,881	—	—	—	—	—	—	—	—
1990–91	4,488	2,206	8,507	—	—	—	—	—	—	—	—
1991–92	5,116	2,524	9,592	—	—	—	—	—	—	—	—
1992–93	5,475	2,791	10,008	—	—	—	—	—	—	—	—
1993–94	5,973	3,050	10,790	—	—	—	—	—	—	—	—
1994–95	6,247	3,250	11,338	—	—	—	—	—	—	—	—
1995–96	6,741	3,449	12,083	—	—	—	—	—	—	—	—
1996–97	7,111	3,607	12,537	—	—	—	—	—	—	—	—
1997–98	7,246	3,744	12,774	—	—	—	—	—	—	—	—
1998–99	7,685	3,897	13,299	—	—	—	—	—	—	—	—
1999–2000	8,069	4,042	13,821	$14,123	$9,611	$2,640	$3,637	$5,163	$7,998	$12,870	$20,487
2000–01	8,429	4,243	14,420	14,457	13,229	2,931	3,822	5,347	8,276	13,200	21,369
2001–02	8,857	4,496	15,165	15,232	13,414	3,226	4,119	5,596	8,583	14,157	22,054
2002–03	9,226	4,842	14,983	15,676	9,644	3,395	4,452	5,927	8,690	14,140	22,700
2003–04	10,312	5,544	16,209	16,807	12,542	3,795	5,103	7,063	9,072	15,030	25,600
2004–05	11,004	6,080	16,751	17,551	13,133	4,236	5,663	7,616	9,300	16,060	26,140
2005–06	11,621	6,493	17,244	18,171	13,432	4,608	6,209	7,977	9,745	16,222	26,958
2006–07	12,312	6,894	18,109	19,034	14,421	4,909	6,594	8,341	10,346	17,057	29,118
2007–08	13,001	7,415	18,876	19,896	14,709	5,176	6,990	9,288	10,705	17,647	30,247
2008–09	13,652	7,999	19,245	20,509	14,414	5,612	7,376	9,912	11,340	18,465	30,514
2009–10	14,542	8,763	20,078	21,317	14,512	6,074	7,983	10,658	12,290	19,460	31,730
2010–11	15,017	9,238	20,397	21,993	13,811	6,550	8,788	10,937	12,510	19,586	33,215
2011–12	15,845	9,978	21,230	22,899	14,285	7,506	9,440	11,954	12,936	20,625	34,680
2012–13	16,407	10,408	21,907	23,642	14,418	7,706	9,900	12,590	12,960	21,352	36,820
2013–14	16,948	10,725	22,617	24,482	14,209	7,791	10,242	12,779	13,590	22,018	36,720
2014–15	17,385	10,979	23,263	25,168	14,264	7,914	10,428	12,829	13,868	22,170	38,948
2015–16	17,871	11,306	23,917	25,826	14,432	8,242	10,769	13,193	13,878	22,570	40,670
2016–17	18,417	11,617	24,713	26,555	14,778	8,500	11,097	13,509	13,826	22,913	42,305
2017–18	18,947	11,926	25,442	27,350	14,303	8,776	11,201	13,982	14,460	23,542	43,848
						Constant 2017–18 dollars[2]					
1989–90	$8,080	$3,906	$15,401	—	—	—	—	—	—	—	—
1990–91	8,316	4,087	15,762	—	—	—	—	—	—	—	—
1991–92	9,185	4,531	17,221	—	—	—	—	—	—	—	—
1992–93	9,532	4,859	17,423	—	—	—	—	—	—	—	—
1993–94	10,136	5,176	18,310	—	—	—	—	—	—	—	—
1994–95	10,306	5,362	18,705	—	—	—	—	—	—	—	—
1995–96	10,826	5,539	19,405	—	—	—	—	—	—	—	—
1996–97	11,104	5,632	19,576	—	—	—	—	—	—	—	—
1997–98	11,116	5,744	19,596	—	—	—	—	—	—	—	—
1998–99	11,588	5,876	20,054	—	—	—	—	—	—	—	—
1999–2000	11,827	5,924	20,257	$20,700	$14,087	$3,869	$5,331	$7,567	$11,722	$18,863	$30,027
2000–01	11,946	6,013	20,434	20,487	18,747	4,154	5,416	7,577	11,728	18,706	30,282
2001–02	12,333	6,260	21,117	21,211	18,678	4,492	5,736	7,792	11,952	19,713	30,709
2002–03	12,570	6,597	20,414	21,359	13,140	4,626	6,066	8,076	11,840	19,266	30,929
2003–04	13,749	7,392	21,612	22,410	16,724	5,060	6,804	9,417	12,096	20,040	34,134
2004–05	14,244	7,870	21,683	22,718	17,000	5,483	7,330	9,858	12,038	20,788	33,836
2005–06	14,491	8,096	21,502	22,658	16,749	5,746	7,742	9,947	12,151	20,227	33,614
2006–07	14,965	8,380	22,011	23,136	17,529	5,967	8,015	10,138	12,575	20,732	35,392
2007–08	15,238	8,691	22,124	23,319	17,240	6,067	8,193	10,886	12,547	20,683	35,451
2008–09	15,780	9,246	22,246	23,707	16,662	6,487	8,526	11,457	13,108	21,344	35,272
2009–10	16,648	10,032	22,986	24,405	16,614	6,954	9,139	12,202	14,070	22,279	36,326
2010–11	16,854	10,368	22,891	24,683	15,500	7,351	9,863	12,275	14,040	21,981	37,277
2011–12	17,276	10,880	23,148	24,968	15,576	8,184	10,293	13,034	14,105	22,489	37,813
2012–13	17,597	11,163	23,496	25,356	15,464	8,265	10,618	13,503	13,900	22,900	39,490
2013–14	17,898	11,325	23,884	25,853	15,005	8,227	10,816	13,495	14,351	23,251	38,777
2014–15	18,226	11,510	24,389	26,385	14,954	8,297	10,932	13,450	14,539	23,242	40,832
2015–16	18,610	11,774	24,906	26,894	15,029	8,583	11,214	13,739	14,452	23,503	42,352
2016–17	18,832	11,879	25,270	27,154	15,112	8,692	11,347	13,814	14,138	23,430	43,259
2017–18	18,947	11,926	25,442	27,350	14,303	8,776	11,201	13,982	14,460	23,542	43,848

—Not available.
[1]Data are based on in-state tuition only.
[2]Constant dollars based on the Consumer Price Index, prepared by the Bureau of Labor Statistics, U.S. Department of Labor, adjusted to an academic-year basis.
NOTE: Average graduate student tuition weighted by fall full-time-equivalent graduate enrollment. Excludes doctoral students in professional practice programs. Data through 1995–96 are for institutions of higher education, while later data are for degree-granting institutions. Degree-granting institutions grant associate's or higher degrees and participate in Title IV federal financial aid programs. The degree-granting classification is very similar to the earlier higher education classification, but it includes more 2-year colleges and excludes a few higher education institutions that did not grant degrees. Some data have been revised from previously published figures.
SOURCE: U.S. Department of Education, National Center for Education Statistics, Integrated Postsecondary Education Data System (IPEDS), "Fall Enrollment Survey" (IPEDS-EF:89–99); "Completions Survey" (IPEDS-C:90–99); "Institutional Characteristics Survey" (IPEDS-IC:89–99); IPEDS Fall 2000 through Fall 2017, Institutional Characteristics component; and IPEDS Spring 2001 through Spring 2018, Fall Enrollment component. (This table was prepared April 2019.)

Table 331.10. Percentage of undergraduates receiving financial aid, by type and source of aid and selected student characteristics: 2015–16

[Standard errors appear in parentheses]

Selected student characteristic	Number of undergraduates[1] (in thousands)	Any aid			Grants			Loans			Work study
		Total[2]	Federal[3]	Nonfederal	Total	Federal	Nonfederal	Total[4]	Federal[4]	Nonfederal	Total[5]
1	2	3	4	5	6	7	8	9	10	11	12
All undergraduates	**19,308**	**72.2 (0.22)**	**55.9 (0.14)**	**49.0 (0.31)**	**63.1 (0.23)**	**41.2 (0.11)**	**46.1 (0.33)**	**38.7 (0.11)**	**36.7 (0.09)**	**5.9 (0.11)**	**5.2 (0.14)**
Sex											
Male	8,406	69.1 (0.38)	52.0 (0.33)	47.8 (0.41)	58.9 (0.36)	37.4 (0.31)	44.9 (0.42)	35.4 (0.27)	33.2 (0.25)	5.7 (0.17)	4.8 (0.18)
Female	10,903	74.6 (0.28)	59.0 (0.24)	49.9 (0.39)	66.3 (0.31)	44.1 (0.24)	47.1 (0.41)	41.3 (0.23)	39.3 (0.21)	6.0 (0.17)	5.5 (0.18)
Race/ethnicity											
White	10,276	71.2 (0.42)	53.5 (0.41)	49.3 (0.41)	60.0 (0.40)	34.3 (0.32)	46.0 (0.43)	40.2 (0.37)	37.8 (0.36)	7.1 (0.18)	5.6 (0.17)
Black	3,006	80.0 (0.62)	70.6 (0.71)	45.9 (0.73)	72.4 (0.68)	60.1 (0.70)	43.4 (0.74)	50.8 (0.76)	49.4 (0.76)	4.2 (0.24)	5.2 (0.34)
Hispanic	3,723	71.4 (0.66)	55.6 (0.65)	49.4 (0.75)	65.5 (0.65)	47.1 (0.60)	47.2 (0.76)	30.7 (0.62)	28.9 (0.60)	4.3 (0.26)	4.4 (0.41)
Asian	1,399	62.0 (1.09)	40.5 (1.05)	49.9 (1.11)	56.6 (1.12)	32.1 (1.06)	47.6 (1.09)	23.3 (0.85)	20.9 (0.81)	4.7 (0.41)	5.4 (0.41)
Pacific Islander	83	69.1 (3.97)	54.2 (3.95)	49.8 (4.53)	60.5 (4.50)	42.7 (3.98)	48.1 (4.50)	31.8 (3.49)	30.9 (3.44)	3.1 (0.83)	2.8 ! (1.26)
American Indian/Alaska Native	160	76.7 (3.02)	62.5 (3.34)	44.1 (3.07)	70.8 (2.93)	56.1 (3.16)	42.6 (3.00)	30.9 (2.66)	29.5 (2.64)	2.6 (0.68)	3.3 ! (1.15)
Two or more races	661	76.8 (1.50)	59.9 (1.78)	53.6 (1.46)	67.9 (1.46)	45.9 (1.59)	51.2 (1.40)	42.6 (1.59)	39.9 (1.56)	6.1 (0.65)	4.7 (0.62)
Age											
15 to 23	11,368	74.7 (0.32)	56.4 (0.26)	56.6 (0.41)	65.8 (0.33)	37.6 (0.22)	53.5 (0.43)	40.5 (0.22)	38.1 (0.22)	7.5 (0.15)	7.6 (0.19)
24 to 29	3,536	69.9 (0.63)	58.6 (0.62)	38.5 (0.60)	61.6 (0.66)	50.6 (0.61)	35.9 (0.64)	37.4 (0.53)	35.6 (0.54)	4.0 (0.24)	2.5 (0.24)
30 or older	4,404	67.4 (0.54)	52.7 (0.61)	37.8 (0.64)	57.3 (0.53)	43.0 (0.54)	35.3 (0.65)	35.2 (0.50)	33.9 (0.49)	3.1 (0.19)	1.3 (0.13)
Marital status											
Not married[6]	16,098	73.5 (0.26)	57.0 (0.17)	51.4 (0.34)	64.8 (0.27)	41.2 (0.15)	48.4 (0.36)	40.2 (0.16)	38.0 (0.15)	6.4 (0.13)	6.0 (0.16)
Married	2,940	64.7 (0.67)	49.7 (0.68)	36.8 (0.76)	53.4 (0.69)	39.6 (0.59)	34.4 (0.78)	30.2 (0.53)	28.8 (0.53)	3.0 (0.22)	1.2 (0.18)
Separated	270	75.0 (2.10)	63.6 (2.29)	38.1 (1.90)	68.8 (2.18)	59.1 (2.19)	35.9 (1.87)	41.5 (2.08)	40.6 (2.05)	3.3 (0.75)	2.0 (0.49)
Attendance status[7]											
Full-time, full-year	7,239	86.4 (0.26)	69.8 (0.33)	66.9 (0.40)	76.7 (0.31)	46.3 (0.30)	63.8 (0.41)	54.7 (0.33)	52.5 (0.34)	9.2 (0.21)	10.5 (0.26)
Part-time or part-year	12,069	63.6 (0.33)	47.6 (0.26)	38.2 (0.40)	54.9 (0.33)	38.2 (0.23)	35.5 (0.41)	29.2 (0.23)	27.1 (0.21)	3.9 (0.13)	2.0 (0.15)
Dependency status and family income											
Dependent	9,772	76.9 (0.35)	58.9 (0.28)	59.2 (0.43)	67.1 (0.35)	37.3 (0.24)	56.0 (0.45)	43.2 (0.25)	40.7 (0.24)	8.2 (0.17)	8.3 (0.21)
Less than $20,000	1,713	87.5 (0.72)	80.3 (0.72)	60.9 (0.93)	86.9 (0.75)	79.5 (0.74)	59.2 (0.93)	40.1 (0.83)	38.3 (0.81)	4.1 (0.31)	9.5 (0.50)
$20,000–$39,999	1,644	84.6 (0.75)	76.3 (0.80)	62.4 (0.98)	83.0 (0.76)	74.4 (0.81)	60.8 (0.99)	42.1 (0.81)	40.7 (0.79)	5.3 (0.42)	10.9 (0.56)
$40,000–$59,999	1,281	81.4 (0.96)	68.3 (1.04)	65.1 (1.02)	75.5 (1.00)	56.8 (0.98)	61.8 (1.03)	48.1 (1.11)	45.9 (1.09)	8.2 (0.52)	10.7 (0.65)
$60,000–$79,999	1,157	72.7 (0.98)	50.3 (1.00)	58.4 (1.09)	60.1 (1.03)	19.8 (0.78)	54.9 (1.08)	44.5 (0.92)	42.3 (0.93)	8.6 (0.54)	8.1 (0.52)
$80,000–$99,999	946	69.9 (1.20)	46.3 (1.03)	56.7 (1.26)	53.7 (1.29)	4.9 (0.51)	53.0 (1.28)	45.4 (1.02)	43.1 (0.99)	10.3 (0.67)	8.2 (0.71)
$100,000 or more	3,032	68.6 (0.72)	40.5 (0.57)	55.0 (0.70)	50.7 (0.68)	1.9 (0.17)	50.4 (0.69)	42.2 (0.56)	38.6 (0.54)	11.2 (0.38)	5.3 (0.29)
Independent	9,536	67.3 (0.34)	52.9 (0.31)	38.5 (0.47)	58.9 (0.34)	45.2 (0.29)	36.0 (0.48)	34.2 (0.26)	32.5 (0.24)	3.5 (0.14)	2.0 (0.14)
Less than $10,000	2,909	69.8 (0.64)	56.0 (0.72)	41.0 (0.76)	66.3 (0.69)	53.8 (0.72)	38.7 (0.77)	35.0 (0.58)	33.2 (0.55)	3.6 (0.23)	3.7 (0.26)
$10,000–$19,999	1,783	74.6 (0.86)	64.7 (0.94)	39.9 (0.89)	70.1 (0.90)	61.6 (0.91)	36.8 (0.87)	41.0 (0.79)	38.9 (0.75)	4.3 (0.34)	2.2 (0.24)
$20,000–$29,999	1,372	72.7 (0.96)	58.5 (1.06)	40.6 (1.08)	63.4 (0.96)	48.8 (0.98)	38.2 (1.10)	37.4 (1.04)	36.3 (1.01)	3.1 (0.31)	1.7 (0.21)
$30,000–$49,999	1,467	65.8 (1.00)	53.0 (1.09)	35.3 (1.04)	53.0 (1.02)	40.0 (1.01)	32.8 (1.03)	33.6 (0.81)	32.3 (0.80)	3.2 (0.29)	1.0 (0.24)
$50,000 or more	2,005	54.5 (0.90)	34.1 (0.82)	34.6 (0.85)	39.5 (0.82)	19.7 (0.61)	32.2 (0.86)	25.1 (0.69)	23.2 (0.69)	3.2 (0.33)	0.4 (0.09)
Housing status[8]											
School-owned	2,756	86.8 (0.49)	65.7 (0.63)	76.5 (0.61)	78.6 (0.60)	37.1 (0.62)	73.5 (0.67)	59.5 (0.63)	56.8 (0.64)	12.2 (0.51)	17.1 (0.57)
Off-campus, not with parents	9,926	70.0 (0.39)	54.6 (0.41)	43.4 (0.43)	60.3 (0.36)	42.5 (0.36)	40.3 (0.45)	37.3 (0.36)	35.2 (0.35)	5.0 (0.15)	3.2 (0.15)
With parents	4,749	66.0 (0.57)	49.8 (0.54)	44.3 (0.68)	58.9 (0.58)	39.4 (0.48)	42.0 (0.68)	26.0 (0.52)	24.2 (0.50)	3.9 (0.22)	2.7 (0.24)

!Interpret data with caution. The coefficient of variation (CV) for this estimate is between 30 and 50 percent.
[1]Numbers of undergraduates may not equal figures reported in other tables, since these data are based on a sample survey of students who enrolled at any time during the school year. Includes all postsecondary institutions.
[2]Includes students who reported they were awarded aid, but did not specify the source or type of aid.
[3]Includes Department of Veterans Affairs and Department of Defense benefits.
[4]Includes Parent Loans for Undergraduate Students (PLUS).
[5]Details on federal and nonfederal work-study participants are not available.
[6]Includes students who were single, divorced, or widowed.
[7]Full-time, full-year includes students enrolled full time for 9 or more months. Part-time or part-year includes students enrolled part time for 9 or more months and students enrolled less than 9 months either part time or full time.
[8]Excludes students attending more than one institution.
NOTE: Detail may not sum to totals because of rounding and because some students receive multiple types of aid and aid from different sources. Data include undergraduates in degree-granting and non-degree-granting institutions. Data exclude students attending institutions in Puerto Rico. Race categories exclude persons of Hispanic ethnicity.
SOURCE: U.S. Department of Education, National Center for Education Statistics, 2015–16 National Postsecondary Student Aid Study (NPSAS:16). (This table was prepared June 2018.)

Table 331.20. Full-time, first-time degree/certificate-seeking undergraduate students enrolled in degree-granting postsecondary institutions, by participation and average amount awarded in financial aid programs, and control and level of institution: 2000–01 through 2016–17

Control and level of institution, and year	Number enrolled	Number awarded financial aid	Percent awarded aid	Percent of enrolled students awarded aid: Federal grants	State/local grants	Institutional grants	Student loans[3]	Average award for students in aid programs[1]: Current dollars: Federal grants	State/local grants	Institutional grants	Student loans[3]	Constant 2017–18 dollars[2]: Federal grants	State/local grants	Institutional grants	Student loans[3]
1	2	3	4	5	6	7	8	9	10	11	12	13	14	15	16
All institutions															
2000–01	1,976,600	1,390,527	70.3	31.6	31.2	31.1	40.1	$2,486	$2,039	$4,740	$3,764	$3,524	$2,889	$6,717	$5,334
2001–02	2,050,016	1,481,592	72.3	33.3	32.5	31.5	40.7	2,739	2,057	4,918	3,970	3,814	2,864	6,848	5,528
2002–03	2,135,613	1,553,024	72.7	34.1	30.9	31.5	41.4	2,947	2,189	5,267	4,331	4,015	2,982	7,177	5,901
2003–04	2,178,517	1,610,967	73.9	34.6	31.2	31.9	43.1	2,934	2,226	5,648	4,193	3,911	2,968	7,531	5,591
2004–05	2,260,590	1,689,910	74.8	35.2	31.3	31.7	44.0	2,939	2,343	5,958	4,463	3,804	3,033	7,712	5,776
2005–06	2,309,543	1,731,315	75.0	33.7	30.8	32.7	44.6	2,959	2,441	6,213	4,831	3,690	3,044	7,747	6,024
2006–07	2,426,599	1,766,783	72.8	32.1	30.0	32.2	43.5	3,131	2,526	6,598	5,018	3,806	3,070	8,020	6,099
2007–08	2,528,579	1,911,296	75.6	35.4	30.6	33.6	45.5	3,381	2,586	6,808	6,008	3,962	3,031	7,980	7,041
2008–09	2,542,748	1,974,063	77.6	36.4	31.7	34.6	46.6	3,927	2,706	7,518	6,723	4,539	3,128	8,691	7,771
2009–10	2,855,241	2,323,706	81.4	46.2	28.6	33.3	51.2	4,693	2,771	7,693	7,019	5,373	3,173	8,807	8,035
2010–11	2,648,101	2,179,582	82.3	47.8	31.0	35.8	50.1	4,758	2,843	8,393	6,624	5,340	3,190	9,420	7,434
2011–12	2,571,120	2,140,556	83.3	47.6	30.8	37.9	51.2	4,424	2,912	8,767	6,641	4,824	3,176	9,559	7,241
2012–13	2,510,994	2,077,909	82.8	45.5	31.2	39.8	49.4	4,452	3,051	9,223	6,896	4,775	3,272	9,891	7,396
2013–14	2,505,306	2,077,487	82.9	45.3	32.2	41.4	47.3	4,533	3,101	9,603	7,015	4,786	3,274	10,141	7,408
2014–15	2,471,045	2,062,252	83.5	44.5	32.9	42.8	47.0	4,599	3,214	10,066	6,925	4,822	3,370	10,553	7,260
2015–16	2,458,068	2,031,557	82.6	42.6	32.3	44.3	45.6	4,682	3,375	10,353	6,989	4,876	3,514	10,781	7,278
2016–17	2,491,008	2,063,078	82.8	42.3	31.9	44.7	46.1	4,698	3,460	10,774	7,078	4,804	3,538	11,017	7,238
Public															
2000–01	1,333,236	872,109	65.4	30.0	33.5	22.7	30.7	2,408	1,707	2,275	3,050	3,412	2,419	3,223	4,322
2005–06	1,510,268	1,066,041	70.6	31.1	34.8	25.1	34.2	2,926	2,226	3,162	3,866	3,648	2,776	3,943	4,821
2010–11	1,802,335	1,421,369	78.9	46.0	35.9	27.2	40.2	4,765	2,676	4,160	5,780	5,348	3,004	4,669	6,487
2012–13	1,736,339	1,391,643	80.1	45.1	36.2	31.2	41.4	4,427	2,915	4,696	6,123	4,748	3,126	5,037	6,567
2013–14	1,752,745	1,410,234	80.5	44.9	37.3	32.4	39.8	4,518	2,961	4,950	6,213	4,771	3,126	5,228	6,561
2014–15	1,743,119	1,412,510	81.0	44.2	38.1	34.3	39.6	4,592	3,080	5,165	6,243	4,814	3,229	5,414	6,545
2015–16	1,747,471	1,399,831	80.1	42.2	37.2	35.6	38.1	4,636	3,238	5,322	6,316	4,828	3,372	5,542	6,577
2016–17	1,752,357	1,406,966	80.3	41.6	37.2	37.1	38.2	4,639	3,329	5,499	6,439	4,743	3,404	5,623	6,584
4-year															
2000–01	804,793	573,430	71.3	26.6	36.5	29.6	40.7	2,569	2,068	2,616	3,212	3,641	2,931	3,707	4,551
2005–06	906,948	695,017	76.6	26.6	36.8	34.2	44.4	3,071	2,752	3,573	4,166	3,829	3,432	4,456	5,195
2010–11	1,039,126	858,424	82.6	38.9	38.2	39.6	51.5	4,983	3,469	4,634	6,127	5,593	3,893	5,201	6,876
2012–13	1,056,119	872,932	82.7	37.8	37.3	43.8	50.8	4,506	3,665	5,168	6,576	4,833	3,931	5,543	7,052
2013–14	1,076,356	892,192	82.9	37.9	37.4	45.4	49.5	4,597	3,724	5,435	6,658	4,855	3,933	5,740	7,031
2014–15	1,095,363	915,024	83.5	37.5	37.6	47.2	49.5	4,669	3,842	5,651	6,694	4,895	4,028	5,924	7,018
2015–16	1,144,409	948,342	82.9	36.8	36.8	47.2	47.2	4,707	3,905	5,812	6,710	4,901	4,066	6,053	6,988
2016–17	1,161,575	965,068	83.1	36.4	36.5	48.9	47.1	4,723	3,989	5,997	6,840	4,830	4,079	6,132	6,994
2-year															
2000–01	528,443	298,679	56.5	35.2	28.8	12.1	15.3	2,222	1,009	1,004	2,396	3,149	1,430	1,423	3,395
2005–06	603,320	371,024	61.5	38.0	31.9	11.3	19.0	2,774	1,314	1,297	2,812	3,458	1,639	1,617	3,507
2010–11	763,209	562,945	73.8	55.7	32.8	10.3	24.9	4,557	1,418	1,677	4,802	5,115	1,592	1,882	5,389
2012–13	680,220	518,711	76.3	56.3	34.5	11.5	26.9	4,345	1,653	1,891	4,792	4,660	1,773	2,028	5,139
2013–14	676,389	518,042	76.6	56.0	37.1	11.8	24.4	4,432	1,736	1,983	4,772	4,681	1,833	2,094	5,040
2014–15	647,756	497,486	76.8	55.6	39.0	12.4	22.9	4,504	1,839	2,031	4,595	4,722	1,928	2,129	4,818
2015–16	603,062	451,489	74.9	52.4	38.0	13.5	20.7	4,542	2,010	2,066	4,610	4,730	2,093	2,152	4,800
2016–17	590,782	441,898	74.8	51.9	38.6	14.1	20.8	4,521	2,098	2,111	4,655	4,623	2,146	2,158	4,760
Private nonprofit															
2000–01	439,369	363,044	82.6	28.4	31.8	68.1	57.7	2,879	2,998	7,368	4,019	4,079	4,248	10,441	5,696
2005–06	471,069	401,908	85.3	26.5	31.3	73.8	59.8	3,426	3,117	9,932	5,270	4,272	3,887	12,385	6,571
2010–11	517,831	462,840	89.4	36.4	27.7	78.4	64.3	5,076	3,556	14,324	7,296	5,697	3,991	16,076	8,188
2012–13	515,385	458,633	89.0	33.8	26.1	79.9	61.9	4,663	3,673	15,960	7,886	5,001	3,940	17,117	8,458
2013–14	513,574	458,526	89.3	33.7	26.1	81.1	61.1	4,738	3,760	16,832	8,064	5,003	3,970	17,774	8,516
2014–15	535,142	479,437	89.6	35.0	24.9	78.3	60.1	4,763	3,839	17,705	7,940	4,993	4,025	18,561	8,324
2015–16	540,835	484,705	89.6	35.2	23.8	78.7	61.0	4,998	4,013	18,452	7,925	5,204	4,179	19,215	8,253
2016–17	569,212	511,718	89.9	36.9	22.6	75.7	62.3	5,093	4,125	19,291	8,008	5,208	4,218	19,726	8,188

See notes at end of table.

Table 331.20. Full-time, first-time degree/certificate-seeking undergraduate students enrolled in degree-granting postsecondary institutions, by participation and average amount awarded in financial aid programs, and control and level of institution: 2000–01 through 2016–17—Continued

Control and level of institution, and year	Number enrolled	Number awarded financial aid	Percent awarded aid	Percent of enrolled students awarded aid				Average award for students in aid programs[1]							
								Current dollars				Constant 2017–18 dollars[2]			
				Federal grants	State/local grants	Institutional grants	Student loans[3]	Federal grants	State/local grants	Institutional grants	Student loans[3]	Federal grants	State/local grants	Institutional grants	Student loans[3]
1	2	3	4	5	6	7	8	9	10	11	12	13	14	15	16
4-year															
2000–01	419,499	347,638	82.9	27.4	32.2	70.1	58.1	2,930	3,001	7,458	4,000	4,153	4,253	10,569	5,668
2005–06	460,832	393,429	85.4	26.0	31.2	74.6	59.8	3,437	3,121	10,002	5,264	4,286	3,891	12,472	6,564
2010–11	504,715	451,012	89.4	35.4	27.7	79.6	64.3	5,105	3,574	14,414	7,305	5,729	4,011	16,177	8,198
2012–13	505,079	449,337	89.0	33.1	26.0	80.7	61.9	4,692	3,680	16,070	7,904	5,032	3,947	17,235	8,478
2013–14	504,584	450,228	89.2	33.1	26.1	81.6	61.0	4,758	3,762	16,966	8,069	5,024	3,973	17,917	8,521
2014–15	503,662	450,897	89.5	32.6	25.9	82.3	60.9	4,830	3,838	17,835	7,994	5,064	4,024	18,698	8,380
2015–16	505,549	451,276	89.3	31.9	25.0	82.1	59.2	4,931	4,017	18,826	8,002	5,134	4,183	19,605	8,333
2016–17	508,584	455,063	89.5	31.5	24.9	82.2	59.4	4,924	4,125	19,766	8,176	5,035	4,218	20,211	8,361
2-year															
2000–01	19,870	15,406	77.5	49.2	23.9	25.7	49.5	2,269	2,892	2,168	4,509	3,216	4,099	3,072	6,390
2005–06	10,237	8,479	82.8	51.6	36.1	38.5	55.9	3,176	2,974	3,799	5,531	3,961	3,708	4,737	6,897
2010–11	13,116	11,828	90.2	73.3	26.8	29.8	64.3	4,553	2,835	5,059	6,944	5,109	3,182	5,678	7,793
2012–13	10,306	9,296	90.2	67.1	30.3	37.7	60.6	3,962	3,373	4,347	6,960	4,249	3,617	4,663	7,464
2013–14	8,990	8,298	92.3	70.6	27.3	49.5	65.5	4,216	3,618	4,346	7,818	4,452	3,820	4,590	8,256
2014–15	31,480	28,540	90.7	74.3	8.4	14.4	48.4	4,288	3,881	5,768	6,855	4,495	4,069	6,047	7,187
2015–16	35,286	33,429	94.7	81.8	7.2	30.0	85.8	5,374	3,810	3,770	7,171	5,596	3,967	3,926	7,467
2016–17	60,628	56,655	93.4	81.7	3.7	21.1	86.9	5,641	4,145	3,778	7,041	5,768	4,239	3,863	7,199
Private for-profit															
2000–01	203,995	155,374	76.2	49.3	15.2	6.2	63.5	2,312	2,494	1,540	5,517	3,277	3,534	2,182	7,819
2005–06	328,206	263,366	80.2	55.6	11.4	8.8	70.4	2,725	2,796	1,423	6,454	3,398	3,486	1,775	8,047
2010–11	327,935	295,373	90.1	75.7	9.0	15.5	82.0	4,494	3,028	1,884	8,064	5,044	3,399	2,115	9,050
2012–13	259,270	227,633	87.8	71.9	7.8	18.2	77.3	4,360	3,159	2,343	8,095	4,676	3,388	2,513	8,682
2013–14	238,987	208,727	87.3	72.8	8.2	21.5	73.3	4,394	3,278	2,489	8,336	4,640	3,462	2,628	8,803
2014–15	192,784	170,305	88.3	73.1	8.6	20.7	76.6	4,421	3,571	3,193	7,906	4,634	3,744	3,347	8,289
2015–16	169,762	147,021	86.6	69.9	8.7	25.3	74.4	4,460	3,841	2,860	8,096	4,645	4,000	2,978	8,431
2016–17	169,439	144,394	85.2	67.8	7.6	18.8	73.5	4,355	3,489	3,313	7,870	4,453	3,568	3,387	8,048
4-year															
2000–01	81,075	51,739	63.8	36.1	11.9	8.3	57.7	2,295	2,889	1,616	5,749	3,253	4,094	2,290	8,146
2005–06	157,705	116,237	73.7	46.8	8.9	10.9	67.2	2,490	2,945	1,641	7,046	3,105	3,672	2,047	8,786
2010–11	112,706	102,000	90.5	73.6	11.3	23.6	82.9	4,733	2,950	2,805	8,561	5,312	3,311	3,148	9,608
2012–13	100,555	89,424	88.9	73.5	9.7	26.9	79.1	4,663	2,941	3,028	8,300	5,001	3,154	3,247	8,902
2013–14	90,264	80,686	89.4	72.5	10.5	34.5	78.1	4,624	3,021	3,065	8,581	4,883	3,190	3,237	9,062
2014–15	81,791	73,040	89.3	71.9	9.8	30.9	75.7	4,677	3,262	4,137	8,237	4,903	3,420	4,337	8,636
2015–16	59,269	51,636	87.1	65.5	10.9	38.5	73.4	4,641	3,715	4,128	8,413	4,833	3,869	4,299	8,761
2016–17	57,680	49,044	85.0	63.6	9.9	31.8	71.5	4,646	3,608	4,681	8,328	4,751	3,689	4,787	8,516
2-year															
2000–01	122,920	103,635	84.3	58.0	17.3	4.8	67.3	2,319	2,314	1,453	5,387	3,286	3,279	2,058	7,633
2005–06	170,501	147,129	86.3	63.6	13.7	6.8	73.4	2,885	2,706	1,098	5,951	3,597	3,374	1,370	7,421
2010–11	215,229	193,373	89.8	76.8	7.8	11.3	81.5	4,374	3,088	875	7,799	4,909	3,466	982	8,753
2012–13	158,715	138,209	87.1	70.9	6.6	12.6	76.2	4,160	3,361	1,417	7,961	4,462	3,605	1,520	8,538
2013–14	148,723	128,041	86.1	73.0	6.7	13.6	70.3	4,256	3,523	1,602	8,171	4,494	3,720	1,692	8,629
2014–15	110,993	97,265	87.6	74.0	7.8	13.1	77.2	4,237	3,856	1,556	7,667	4,442	4,042	1,632	8,038
2015–16	110,493	95,385	86.3	72.3	7.5	18.3	75.0	4,373	3,940	1,425	7,930	4,554	4,103	1,484	8,258
2016–17	111,759	95,350	85.3	70.0	6.4	12.1	74.5	4,218	3,394	1,464	7,643	4,313	3,470	1,497	7,816

[1]Average amounts for students participating in indicated programs.
[2]Constant dollars based on the Consumer Price Index, prepared by the Bureau of Labor Statistics, U.S. Department of Labor, adjusted to an academic-year basis.
[3]Includes only loans made directly to students. Does not include Parent Loans for Undergraduate Students (PLUS) and other loans made directly to parents.

NOTE: Degree-granting institutions grant associate's or higher degrees and participate in Title IV federal financial aid programs. Data through 2009–10 are for students receiving aid, while later data are for students awarded aid. Students were counted as receiving aid only if they were awarded and accepted aid and their aid was also disbursed. Some data have been revised from previously published figures.
SOURCE: U.S. Department of Education, National Center for Education Statistics, Integrated Postsecondary Education Data System (IPEDS), Spring 2002 through Spring 2011 and Winter 2011–12 through Winter 2017–18, Student Financial Aid component. (This table was prepared November 2018.)

Table 331.30. Average amount of grant and scholarship aid and average net price for first-time, full-time degree/certificate-seeking students awarded Title IV aid, by control and level of institution and income level: Selected years, 2009–10 through 2016–17

Level of institution and income level	2009–10[1]				2014–15				2015–16				2016–17			
	All institutions	Public	Private		All institutions	Public	Private		All institutions	Public	Private		All institutions	Public	Private	
			Nonprofit	For-profit			Nonprofit	For-profit			Nonprofit	For-profit			Nonprofit	For-profit
1	2	3	4	5	6	7	8	9	10	11	12	13	14	15	16	17
	Current dollars															
4-year institutions																
Grant and scholarship aid[2]																
All income levels	$9,050	$5,980	$15,560	$4,420	$11,280	$6,960	$19,960	$5,610	$11,800	$7,190	$20,900	$5,950	$12,250	$7,370	$21,800	$6,170
$0 to $30,000	10,290	9,080	17,460	5,110	12,430	10,020	21,010	5,930	13,050	10,370	21,890	6,140	13,600	10,710	22,760	6,500
$30,001 to $48,000	11,170	8,330	18,710	4,530	13,530	9,630	23,570	6,110	13,980	9,820	24,580	6,650	14,460	10,140	25,720	6,270
$48,001 to $75,000	9,140	4,910	16,810	2,430	11,770	6,390	22,280	4,770	12,240	6,720	23,200	5,530	12,790	7,090	24,250	5,410
$75,001 to $110,000	7,150	2,270	14,650	1,220	9,580	3,200	19,770	3,470	10,070	3,440	20,730	4,520	10,550	3,700	21,720	4,800
$110,001 or more	6,300	1,590	11,560	1,020	8,650	2,020	16,190	3,270	9,220	2,150	17,270	4,000	9,670	2,270	18,220	5,010
Net price[3]																
All income levels	15,900	11,070	21,780	22,590	17,440	12,890	25,230	21,260	17,750	13,110	25,720	21,760	18,090	13,460	26,240	21,510
$0 to $30,000	12,570	7,720	15,970	21,770	12,690	9,040	19,140	20,360	12,850	9,220	19,500	20,710	12,810	9,300	19,710	20,170
$30,001 to $48,000	13,110	9,260	17,200	23,590	13,730	10,640	19,660	22,050	13,820	10,760	19,860	22,080	13,920	10,950	20,040	21,910
$48,001 to $75,000	16,610	13,290	20,270	26,710	17,400	14,530	22,200	25,170	17,510	14,610	22,550	24,200	17,620	14,700	22,780	24,720
$75,001 to $110,000	19,860	16,410	23,900	29,830	21,410	18,400	25,840	27,480	21,600	18,610	26,080	26,880	21,830	18,810	26,490	26,560
$110,001 or more	24,080	17,880	30,210	32,910	26,600	20,660	33,170	30,190	26,900	20,990	33,490	29,360	27,350	21,400	34,130	28,730
2-year institutions																
Grant and scholarship aid[2]																
All income levels	4,460	4,540	5,180	4,090	4,930	4,970	5,730	4,300	5,070	5,080	6,340	4,450	5,090	5,140	6,490	4,200
$0 to $30,000	5,250	5,450	5,540	4,590	5,750	5,910	5,710	4,690	5,960	6,140	6,110	4,830	5,960	6,180	6,330	4,550
$30,001 to $48,000	4,380	4,520	5,080	3,670	5,270	5,340	6,070	4,020	5,480	5,530	7,570	4,250	5,510	5,600	7,040	4,160
$48,001 to $75,000	2,240	2,250	4,150	1,960	3,170	3,140	5,440	2,640	3,340	3,290	7,210	2,960	3,470	3,440	7,160	2,870
$75,001 to $110,000	800	750	3,240	830	1,150	1,040	5,510	1,070	1,200	1,080	7,830	1,190	1,370	1,250	7,580	1,220
$110,001 or more	610	600	2,940	470	770	650	6,070	670	680	530	6,840	750	1,050	920	7,320	750
Net price[3]																
All income levels	8,930	6,290	16,270	18,360	8,810	7,000	19,670	20,360	9,040	7,060	18,970	20,770	9,410	7,200	21,080	21,330
$0 to $30,000	8,560	5,380	16,500	18,240	8,420	6,040	19,420	20,360	8,700	5,910	18,850	20,780	9,140	6,080	21,230	21,360
$30,001 to $48,000	8,720	6,330	16,620	19,070	8,010	6,650	20,320	20,990	7,940	6,620	19,610	21,330	8,230	6,680	20,910	21,740
$48,001 to $75,000	10,690	8,810	18,650	21,290	9,890	8,930	21,970	22,340	9,930	8,970	20,730	22,630	10,050	8,990	21,640	22,640
$75,001 to $110,000	12,230	10,630	20,760	23,020	12,230	11,270	23,590	23,860	12,380	11,430	23,490	24,540	12,510	11,510	22,880	24,140
$110,001 or more	12,760	10,820	20,930	24,620	12,820	11,770	27,870	25,020	13,160	12,100	27,850	25,010	13,000	11,900	29,300	25,320
	Constant 2017–18 dollars[4]															
4-year institutions																
Grant and scholarship aid[2]																
All income levels	$10,360	$6,840	$17,810	$5,060	$11,830	$7,290	$20,920	$5,890	$12,290	$7,490	$21,760	$6,200	$12,530	$7,540	$22,290	$6,310
$0 to $30,000	11,780	10,390	19,980	5,850	13,040	10,510	22,030	6,220	13,590	10,800	22,790	6,390	13,900	10,950	23,270	6,650
$30,001 to $48,000	12,780	9,540	21,420	5,190	14,180	10,090	24,710	6,410	14,560	10,220	25,590	6,930	14,790	10,370	26,300	6,410
$48,001 to $75,000	10,460	5,620	19,250	2,780	12,330	6,700	23,360	5,000	12,750	7,000	24,160	5,760	13,080	7,250	24,800	5,530
$75,001 to $110,000	8,190	2,600	16,780	1,390	10,050	3,350	20,730	3,630	10,490	3,580	21,590	4,710	10,790	3,780	22,210	4,900
$110,001 or more	7,210	1,820	13,240	1,170	9,060	2,110	16,970	3,420	9,600	2,240	17,990	4,170	9,890	2,330	18,630	5,120
Net price[3]																
All income levels	18,200	12,680	24,940	25,860	18,280	13,510	26,450	22,290	18,480	13,660	26,780	22,660	18,500	13,760	26,840	22,000
$0 to $30,000	14,390	8,840	18,290	24,930	13,300	9,470	20,060	21,350	13,380	9,600	20,310	21,570	13,100	9,510	20,150	20,620
$30,001 to $48,000	15,010	10,600	19,700	27,010	14,390	11,160	20,610	23,120	14,390	11,200	20,680	22,990	14,240	11,200	20,490	22,400
$48,001 to $75,000	19,010	15,210	23,200	30,570	18,240	15,240	23,270	26,380	18,230	15,210	23,480	25,200	18,010	15,030	23,290	25,280
$75,001 to $110,000	22,730	18,780	27,360	34,150	22,440	19,290	27,090	28,810	22,490	19,380	27,160	27,990	22,320	19,240	27,080	27,160
$110,001 or more	27,570	20,470	34,580	37,680	27,890	21,660	34,780	31,650	28,010	21,850	34,880	30,580	27,970	21,880	34,900	29,380

See notes at end of table.

Table 331.30. Average amount of grant and scholarship aid and average net price for first-time, full-time degree/certificate-seeking students awarded Title IV aid, by control and level of institution and income level: Selected years, 2009–10 through 2016–17—Continued

Level of institution and income level	2009–10[1]				2014–15				2015–16				2016–17			
	All institutions	Public	Private Nonprofit	Private For-profit	All institutions	Public	Private Nonprofit	Private For-profit	All institutions	Public	Private Nonprofit	Private For-profit	All institutions	Public	Private Nonprofit	Private For-profit
1	2	3	4	5	6	7	8	9	10	11	12	13	14	15	16	17
2-year institutions																
Grant and scholarship aid[2]																
All income levels	5,100	5,190	5,930	4,690	5,170	5,210	6,000	4,510	5,280	5,290	6,600	4,630	5,210	5,250	6,640	4,300
$0 to $30,000	6,010	6,240	6,350	5,260	6,030	6,200	5,980	4,920	6,200	6,390	6,370	5,030	6,100	6,320	6,480	4,660
$30,001 to $48,000	5,010	5,180	5,810	4,200	5,520	5,600	6,370	4,220	5,710	5,760	7,880	4,430	5,640	5,720	7,200	4,250
$48,001 to $75,000	2,570	2,580	4,760	2,250	3,320	3,300	5,710	2,770	3,470	3,420	7,510	3,080	3,550	3,510	7,330	2,930
$75,001 to $110,000	910	860	3,710	950	1,210	1,090	5,770	1,120	1,250	1,130	8,160	1,240	1,400	1,280	7,750	1,240
$110,001 or more	700	680	3,370	540	810	680	6,360	700	710	560	7,120	780	1,080	940	7,480	770
Net price[3]																
All income levels	10,220	7,200	18,630	21,020	9,230	7,340	20,620	21,340	9,420	7,350	19,750	21,630	9,620	7,370	21,560	21,810
$0 to $30,000	9,800	6,160	18,890	20,880	8,830	6,330	20,360	21,350	9,060	6,150	19,620	21,640	9,350	6,220	21,710	21,840
$30,001 to $48,000	9,980	7,250	19,030	21,830	8,390	6,980	21,300	22,010	8,270	6,900	20,420	22,210	8,410	6,830	21,380	22,230
$48,001 to $75,000	12,240	10,090	21,350	24,380	10,370	9,360	23,030	23,430	10,340	9,340	21,590	23,570	10,280	9,190	22,130	23,150
$75,001 to $110,000	14,000	12,170	23,760	26,360	12,820	11,810	24,730	25,020	12,890	11,900	24,460	25,560	12,790	11,770	23,400	24,680
$110,001 or more	14,610	12,390	23,970	28,190	13,440	12,340	29,220	26,230	13,710	12,610	29,000	26,050	13,290	12,170	29,960	25,900

[1]Data for 2009–10 are for students receiving aid, while later data are for students awarded aid. Students were counted as receiving aid only if they were awarded and accepted aid and their aid was also disbursed.

[2]Grant and scholarship aid consists of federal Title IV grants, as well as other grant or scholarship aid from the federal government, state or local governments, or institutional sources. Title IV grants include Federal Pell Grants, Federal Supplemental Educational Opportunity Grants (FSEOGs), Academic Competitiveness Grants (ACGs), National Science and Mathematics Access to Retain Talent Grants (National SMART Grants), and Teacher Education Assistance for College and Higher Education (TEACH) Grants. The average amount of grant and scholarship aid by income level was calculated based on all students who were awarded any type of Title IV aid, even those students who were awarded zero Title IV aid in the form of grants and were awarded Title IV aid only in the form of work-study aid or loan aid.

[3]Net price is the total cost of attendance minus grant and scholarship aid from the federal government, state or local governments, or institutional sources. However, average net price by income level was calculated based on all students who were awarded any type of Title IV aid, even those who were awarded zero Title IV aid in the form of grants and were awarded Title IV aid only in the form of work-study aid or loan aid.

[4]Constant dollars based on the Consumer Price Index, prepared by the Bureau of Labor Statistics, U.S. Department of Labor, adjusted to an academic-year basis.

NOTE: Excludes students who previously attended another postsecondary institution or who began their studies on a part-time basis. Includes only first-time, full-time students who paid the in-state or in-district tuition rate (if they attended public institutions) and who were awarded Title IV aid. Excludes the approximately 17 percent of students who were not awarded any Title IV aid. Title IV aid includes grant aid, work-study aid, and loan aid. Data are weighted by the number of students at the institution who were awarded Title IV aid. Totals include students for whom income data were not available. Some data have been revised from previously published figures.

SOURCE: U.S. Department of Education, National Center for Education Statistics, Integrated Postsecondary Education Data System (IPEDS), Spring 2011 and Winter 2015–16 through Winter 2017–18, Student Financial Aid component. (This table was prepared November 2018.)

Table 331.35. Percentage of full-time, full-year undergraduates receiving financial aid, and average annual amount received, by type and source of aid and selected student characteristics: Selected years, 1999–2000 through 2015–16

[Standard errors appear in parentheses. Amounts in constant 2017–18 dollars]

Year and selected student characteristic	Number enrolled[1] (in thousands)	Any aid						Grants				Loans[2]	
		Percent receiving			Average amount			Percent receiving		Average amount		Percent receiving	Average amount
		Total[3]	Federal[4]	Nonfederal	Total[3]	Federal[4]	Nonfederal	Total	Pell	Total	Pell		
1	2	3	4	5	6	7	8	9	10	11	12	13	14
1999–2000													
Total	**6,145 (—)**	**71.9 (0.59)**	**56.7 (0.44)**	**52.3 (0.67)**	**$12,410 (146)**	**$8,750 (85)**	**$7,570 (139)**	**58.5 (0.60)**	**28.3 (0.43)**	**$7,470 (118)**	**$3,350 (22)**	**45.6 (0.44)**	**$8,840 (86)**
Sex													
Male	2,687 (—)	69.1 (0.74)	53.9 (0.65)	49.7 (0.79)	12,380 (226)	8,860 (124)	7,600 (217)	53.9 (0.83)	24.5 (0.59)	7,450 (181)	3,280 (31)	43.8 (0.67)	9,030 (151)
Female	3,458 (—)	74.0 (0.73)	59.0 (0.62)	54.3 (0.86)	12,430 (167)	8,660 (98)	7,540 (141)	62.1 (0.75)	31.3 (0.61)	7,490 (124)	3,390 (29)	46.9 (0.64)	8,700 (107)
Race/ethnicity													
White	4,335 (—)	69.9 (0.73)	53.1 (0.59)	52.2 (0.73)	12,540 (196)	8,800 (109)	7,840 (179)	55.2 (0.70)	21.5 (0.53)	7,520 (151)	3,170 (32)	45.3 (0.61)	9,060 (118)
Black	675 (—)	88.0 (1.16)	78.6 (1.49)	54.7 (2.09)	12,170 (423)	9,100 (252)	6,500 (368)	76.2 (1.24)	55.7 (1.38)	7,010 (221)	3,600 (49)	59.2 (2.36)	8,070 (279)
Hispanic	500 (—)	77.1 (1.41)	65.6 (1.84)	53.1 (2.20)	11,350 (443)	8,210 (308)	6,320 (346)	66.7 (1.76)	45.4 (2.10)	6,780 (273)	3,500 (56)	42.7 (1.99)	8,660 (283)
Asian	372 (—)	60.3 (1.65)	47.8 (1.79)	47.9 (1.55)	13,030 (825)	8,570 (321)	7,850 (756)	53.0 (1.67)	31.7 (1.62)	8,650 (681)	3,660 (90)	33.0 (2.03)	8,300 (309)
Pacific Islander	41 (—)	62.3 (6.39)	56.0 (5.70)	48.8 (5.63)	12,810 (1,192)	7,700 (657)	7,500 (1,118)	53.1 (6.29)	31.9 (5.85)	7,680 (884)	3,290 (275)	40.7 (5.58)	9,030 (1,256)
American Indian/Alaska Native	42 (—)	81.5 (4.72)	75.0 (5.05)	61.7 (6.64)	12,790 (1,091)	8,020 (804)	7,140 (1,005)	78.7 (4.73)	50.8 (7.04)	7,830 (709)	3,710 (184)	44.6 (7.94)	8,170 (803)
Two or more races	93 (—)	75.6 (3.00)	60.6 (3.36)	57.1 (3.44)	13,060 (696)	8,390 (424)	8,390 (583)	62.0 (3.22)	34.2 (3.30)	8,850 (629)	3,510 (190)	43.8 (2.76)	8,600 (387)
Other	86 (—)	61.9 (3.54)	45.2 (3.64)	46.9 (4.04)	11,810 (1,070)	7,830 (497)	8,040 (1,062)	51.4 (4.32)	26.0 (3.70)	8,150 (860)	3,180 (238)	29.8 (4.02)	8,660 (909)
Dependency status and family income													
Dependent	4,612 (—)	70.2 (0.65)	53.4 (0.52)	53.7 (0.75)	12,850 (173)	8,410 (98)	8,430 (174)	56.2 (0.70)	21.1 (0.52)	8,160 (144)	3,110 (28)	45.6 (0.50)	8,740 (109)
Low-income[5]	990 (—)	85.4 (0.90)	78.1 (1.03)	65.2 (1.43)	13,150 (234)	8,440 (130)	7,130 (205)	82.3 (0.94)	70.4 (1.12)	8,400 (159)	3,560 (30)	50.5 (1.27)	7,370 (150)
Middle-income[5]	2,383 (—)	70.6 (0.85)	53.4 (0.79)	54.7 (1.01)	12,990 (262)	8,030 (117)	8,910 (258)	54.3 (1.00)	11.6 (0.47)	8,110 (245)	1,990 (51)	49.8 (0.80)	8,610 (126)
High-income[5]	1,238 (—)	57.3 (1.10)	33.7 (0.77)	42.6 (1.07)	12,150 (237)	9,530 (272)	8,830 (192)	38.8 (1.08)	‡ (†)	7,920 (190)	‡ (†)	33.5 (0.72)	10,750 (280)
Independent	1,533 (—)	76.9 (0.88)	66.8 (0.80)	48.1 (1.11)	11,220 (204)	9,550 (134)	4,670 (148)	65.5 (0.84)	50.0 (0.72)	5,690 (117)	3,650 (35)	45.6 (1.17)	9,120 (109)
2003–04													
Total	**7,562 (—)**	**75.3 (0.62)**	**60.3 (0.49)**	**54.9 (0.63)**	**$13,020 (124)**	**$9,340 (80)**	**$7,580 (158)**	**62.2 (0.58)**	**31.4 (0.31)**	**$7,560 (134)**	**$4,060 (24)**	**48.6 (0.42)**	**$9,330 (96)**
Sex													
Male	3,340 (—)	72.8 (0.89)	57.2 (0.83)	53.8 (0.78)	13,170 (164)	9,500 (109)	7,700 (173)	58.6 (0.82)	28.0 (0.62)	7,530 (152)	3,970 (36)	46.8 (0.77)	9,660 (135)
Female	4,222 (—)	77.3 (0.56)	62.7 (0.51)	55.8 (0.70)	12,900 (143)	9,230 (85)	7,490 (180)	65.0 (0.61)	34.2 (0.46)	7,590 (148)	4,120 (28)	50.0 (0.45)	9,090 (98)
Race/ethnicity													
White	5,137 (—)	73.3 (0.86)	56.3 (0.79)	55.2 (0.81)	12,970 (158)	9,320 (92)	7,720 (171)	59.0 (0.79)	23.9 (0.54)	7,390 (157)	3,860 (30)	48.4 (0.68)	9,510 (102)
Black	895 (—)	88.7 (0.90)	81.3 (1.08)	55.5 (1.68)	13,560 (292)	9,930 (198)	7,130 (264)	79.0 (1.27)	61.5 (1.64)	7,740 (244)	4,320 (37)	59.2 (1.90)	8,840 (238)
Hispanic	718 (—)	78.8 (1.09)	67.8 (1.21)	55.0 (1.32)	12,600 (275)	8,970 (171)	7,000 (272)	68.1 (1.15)	46.7 (1.17)	7,690 (196)	4,250 (59)	46.3 (1.19)	8,990 (240)
Asian	459 (—)	65.1 (1.55)	51.4 (1.46)	50.6 (1.70)	13,270 (326)	8,590 (238)	8,360 (279)	54.5 (1.74)	30.6 (1.40)	9,160 (273)	4,300 (76)	35.7 (1.28)	8,740 (310)
Pacific Islander	34 (—)	71.1 (5.10)	61.5 (4.79)	46.2 (4.95)	12,680 (1,241)	9,050 (925)	7,470 (1,210)	53.0 (5.12)	28.1 (4.85)	7,770 (817)	4,320 (304)	45.0 (5.02)	9,800 (1,126)
American Indian/Alaska Native	59 (—)	81.1 (5.18)	66.2 (6.31)	64.5 (4.42)	12,040 (832)	9,160 (483)	5,740 (997)	73.8 (5.79)	43.4 (4.64)	7,240 (783)	3,890 (206)	46.5 (5.70)	8,480 (560)
Two or more races	156 (—)	77.1 (2.12)	61.6 (2.12)	55.9 (2.11)	13,250 (541)	9,700 (380)	7,590 (465)	63.8 (2.18)	31.5 (2.39)	7,450 (395)	4,060 (117)	49.3 (2.34)	9,870 (513)
Other	104 (—)	72.2 (2.56)	56.6 (2.71)	53.2 (2.58)	12,090 (657)	9,090 (438)	6,730 (600)	61.7 (2.89)	35.5 (2.94)	6,950 (420)	4,150 (144)	42.9 (2.65)	9,200 (580)
Dependency status and family income													
Dependent	5,574 (—)	73.3 (0.79)	56.3 (0.68)	57.2 (0.74)	13,460 (155)	8,960 (85)	8,430 (173)	59.6 (0.74)	23.6 (0.39)	8,170 (167)	3,820 (27)	47.5 (0.62)	9,480 (108)
Low-income[5]	1,250 (—)	87.9 (0.70)	77.8 (0.80)	66.6 (1.00)	14,320 (271)	9,590 (126)	7,690 (259)	84.8 (0.80)	70.8 (0.92)	9,390 (220)	4,510 (26)	51.0 (0.91)	7,740 (174)
Middle-income[5]	2,886 (—)	72.7 (1.01)	55.4 (0.89)	58.0 (0.97)	13,180 (183)	8,390 (111)	8,510 (192)	57.2 (0.88)	14.8 (0.42)	7,530 (189)	2,400 (36)	50.4 (0.80)	9,490 (131)
High-income[5]	1,438 (—)	61.6 (0.98)	39.3 (0.82)	47.4 (0.91)	13,070 (228)	9,490 (160)	9,120 (226)	42.5 (1.02)	‡ (†)	7,770 (225)	‡ (†)	38.8 (0.83)	11,440 (200)
Independent	1,988 (—)	80.9 (0.77)	71.5 (0.79)	48.5 (0.91)	11,880 (141)	10,190 (120)	4,790 (132)	69.4 (0.79)	53.5 (0.82)	6,100 (90)	4,360 (32)	51.6 (0.85)	8,960 (119)

See notes at end of table.

Table 331.35. Percentage of full-time, full-year undergraduates receiving financial aid, and average annual amount received, by type and source of aid and selected student characteristics: Selected years, 1999–2000 through 2015–16—Continued

[Standard errors appear in parentheses. Amounts in constant 2017–18 dollars]

Year and selected student characteristic	Number enrolled[1] (in thousands)	Any aid: Percent receiving: Total[3]	Any aid: Percent receiving: Federal[4]	Any aid: Percent receiving: Nonfederal	Any aid: Average amount: Total[3]	Any aid: Average amount: Federal[4]	Any aid: Average amount: Nonfederal	Grants: Percent receiving: Total	Grants: Percent receiving: Pell	Grants: Average amount: Total	Grants: Average amount: Pell	Loans[2]: Percent receiving	Loans[2]: Average amount
1	2	3	4	5	6	7	8	9	10	11	12	13	14
2007–08													
Total	**7,527 (—)**	**80.1 (0.28)**	**63.9 (0.31)**	**63.7 (0.36)**	**$15,220 (115)**	**$9,580 (59)**	**$9,530 (104)**	**64.6 (0.37)**	**32.7 (0.29)**	**$8,500 (83)**	**$3,810 (17)**	**54.8 (0.32)**	**$11,150 (90)**
Sex													
Male	3,277 (—)	77.1 (0.44)	60.0 (0.47)	61.8 (0.49)	15,340 (166)	9,730 (108)	9,690 (128)	60.8 (0.54)	27.7 (0.42)	8,560 (111)	3,770 (26)	52.1 (0.56)	11,380 (137)
Female	4,249 (—)	82.4 (0.36)	66.9 (0.42)	65.2 (0.47)	15,140 (136)	9,470 (66)	9,420 (131)	67.6 (0.47)	36.6 (0.41)	8,460 (99)	3,840 (24)	56.9 (0.43)	11,000 (101)
Race/ethnicity													
White	4,983 (—)	78.1 (0.39)	59.6 (0.44)	63.2 (0.46)	15,220 (147)	9,470 (83)	9,880 (134)	61.1 (0.51)	24.1 (0.37)	8,390 (106)	3,630 (25)	54.0 (0.45)	11,460 (114)
Black	899 (—)	92.1 (0.58)	83.9 (0.86)	67.8 (0.85)	15,890 (195)	10,510 (130)	8,570 (190)	79.6 (0.92)	61.5 (1.06)	8,330 (165)	4,050 (44)	70.3 (0.84)	10,430 (175)
Hispanic	844 (—)	84.3 (0.71)	71.8 (0.88)	65.8 (0.91)	14,460 (228)	9,170 (127)	8,510 (210)	72.0 (0.85)	50.5 (1.02)	8,230 (143)	3,920 (39)	52.0 (0.92)	10,930 (242)
Asian	489 (—)	69.5 (1.35)	53.7 (1.33)	57.6 (1.47)	14,930 (334)	8,760 (211)	9,860 (295)	57.0 (1.61)	32.2 (1.21)	10,360 (282)	4,030 (51)	38.6 (1.29)	10,220 (291)
Pacific Islander	45 (—)	81.4 (3.79)	67.3 (4.93)	64.1 (4.44)	15,890 (1,051)	10,530 (836)	9,140 (860)	69.0 (4.14)	36.1 (4.59)	7,380 (610)	3,700 (246)	53.8 (4.44)	13,090 (816)
American Indian/Alaska Native	50 (—)	85.9 (3.32)	71.3 (3.81)	61.8 (4.53)	12,870 (921)	9,020 (610)	7,480 (756)	76.3 (3.20)	48.3 (4.15)	7,850 (701)	3,850 (197)	48.7 (4.70)	9,500 (701)
Two or more races	199 (—)	83.4 (1.31)	68.1 (1.72)	67.1 (2.01)	16,240 (461)	10,090 (271)	9,940 (411)	67.9 (1.66)	37.6 (1.87)	9,690 (393)	3,910 (102)	59.1 (1.92)	10,490 (401)
Other	17 (—)	79.8 (5.18)	72.9 (5.30)	50.9 (6.42)	14,680 (1,454)	9,240 (697)	9,790 (1,365)	67.3 (5.59)	51.9 (5.87)	8,860 (1,303)	3,690 (279)	54.7 (5.64)	8,600 (870)
Dependency status and family income													
Dependent	5,675 (—)	78.0 (0.34)	59.5 (0.37)	65.1 (0.40)	15,710 (141)	9,260 (76)	10,380 (121)	62.7 (0.44)	25.2 (0.27)	9,310 (102)	3,730 (20)	51.9 (0.38)	11,390 (114)
Low-income[5]	1,203 (—)	92.3 (0.49)	85.9 (0.59)	74.9 (0.62)	16,190 (186)	9,730 (92)	8,790 (153)	89.2 (0.57)	80.9 (0.66)	10,440 (130)	4,370 (19)	56.7 (0.75)	8,820 (167)
Middle-income[5]	2,825 (—)	79.3 (0.41)	59.4 (0.50)	67.1 (0.48)	15,620 (172)	8,690 (100)	10,780 (156)	61.6 (0.50)	16.1 (0.33)	8,850 (136)	2,360 (32)	56.0 (0.50)	11,400 (129)
High-income[5]	1,647 (—)	65.5 (0.66)	40.3 (0.65)	54.4 (0.76)	15,390 (245)	9,960 (222)	11,140 (190)	45.2 (0.84)	‡ (†)	8,750 (175)	‡ (†)	41.4 (0.68)	13,950 (236)
Independent	1,851 (—)	86.4 (0.47)	77.4 (0.59)	59.6 (0.74)	13,880 (140)	10,340 (90)	6,700 (119)	70.5 (0.64)	55.8 (0.64)	6,290 (82)	3,920 (30)	63.6 (0.74)	10,560 (116)
2011–12													
Total	**8,864 (—)**	**84.4 (0.36)**	**72.8 (0.51)**	**56.9 (0.46)**	**$16,910 (116)**	**$11,800 (82)**	**$9,990 (120)**	**72.4 (0.41)**	**47.1 (0.50)**	**$10,070 (100)**	**$4,820 (18)**	**56.7 (0.53)**	**$11,010 (82)**
Sex													
Male	3,868 (—)	82.3 (0.50)	70.1 (0.65)	56.2 (0.61)	17,130 (183)	11,990 (119)	10,140 (189)	68.9 (0.58)	42.9 (0.60)	10,270 (162)	4,800 (26)	53.9 (0.70)	11,100 (122)
Female	4,996 (—)	86.0 (0.42)	74.9 (0.60)	57.5 (0.53)	16,750 (146)	11,660 (95)	9,870 (154)	75.1 (0.46)	50.4 (0.62)	9,920 (119)	4,840 (23)	58.8 (0.58)	10,940 (103)
Race/ethnicity[6]													
White	5,369 (—)	82.6 (0.45)	68.5 (0.63)	57.0 (0.50)	16,770 (159)	11,730 (111)	10,210 (151)	68.8 (0.50)	37.8 (0.57)	9,880 (125)	4,620 (27)	56.4 (0.67)	11,210 (108)
Black	1,209 (—)	94.0 (0.54)	90.7 (0.70)	52.8 (1.24)	17,580 (280)	12,960 (171)	9,010 (327)	84.6 (0.72)	73.5 (1.07)	9,370 (208)	5,050 (29)	71.9 (1.12)	10,900 (182)
Hispanic	1,274 (—)	88.3 (0.74)	79.1 (0.91)	60.4 (1.12)	16,070 (338)	11,110 (171)	8,950 (347)	79.9 (0.84)	62.7 (0.94)	10,120 (292)	5,000 (38)	51.2 (1.09)	10,310 (196)
Asian	603 (—)	71.4 (1.77)	58.5 (1.82)	56.4 (1.60)	17,700 (584)	10,380 (270)	11,650 (558)	63.3 (1.71)	40.8 (1.60)	12,800 (484)	4,970 (69)	38.4 (1.59)	10,340 (436)
Pacific Islander	42 (—)	82.1 (3.87)	71.5 (5.20)	55.0 (4.22)	19,430 (1,809)	12,990 (950)	12,110 (2,039)	67.3 (4.42)	44.6 (4.76)	13,040 (1,858)	5,260 (161)	50.7 (5.38)	11,720 (1,277)
American Indian/Alaska Native	67 (—)	93.0 (2.55)	86.4 (2.44)	57.1 (3.82)	16,090 (1,081)	10,880 (560)	9,740 (1,231)	85.4 (3.24)	69.5 (3.37)	10,190 (856)	4,850 (182)	62.3 (3.60)	8,730 (662)
Two or more races	301 (—)	85.8 (1.46)	76.3 (1.76)	59.6 (2.14)	18,610 (593)	12,530 (321)	10,730 (625)	73.1 (1.71)	49.4 (1.94)	10,980 (453)	4,950 (91)	59.3 (2.06)	11,880 (385)
Age													
15 to 23	6,650 (—)	82.7 (0.39)	68.6 (0.54)	62.4 (0.46)	17,660 (137)	11,400 (99)	10,860 (135)	70.9 (0.43)	39.7 (0.44)	11,280 (122)	4,790 (20)	54.0 (0.53)	11,230 (108)
24 to 29	1,048 (—)	87.5 (0.76)	83.1 (0.91)	43.4 (1.01)	15,390 (262)	12,830 (180)	6,490 (387)	76.7 (0.95)	68.6 (1.11)	7,150 (220)	4,890 (40)	61.9 (1.20)	10,580 (134)
30 or over	1,165 (—)	91.1 (0.72)	87.2 (0.80)	37.8 (1.14)	14,350 (229)	12,670 (158)	5,350 (256)	77.0 (0.90)	70.3 (1.01)	6,330 (136)	4,870 (40)	67.3 (1.08)	10,320 (133)
Marital status													
Not married[7]	7,920 (—)	84.0 (0.37)	71.6 (0.53)	59.1 (0.47)	17,320 (121)	11,790 (86)	10,310 (125)	72.5 (0.41)	45.3 (0.50)	10,480 (106)	4,840 (18)	56.4 (0.54)	11,130 (88)
Married	828 (—)	86.9 (0.90)	80.6 (1.06)	38.4 (1.18)	13,510 (277)	11,770 (194)	5,860 (365)	69.5 (1.15)	59.5 (1.28)	6,530 (204)	4,680 (51)	57.3 (1.16)	10,100 (183)
Separated	117 (—)	97.2 (1.02)	95.9 (1.25)	37.5 (2.73)	14,320 (564)	12,390 (390)	5,420 (891)	88.6 (2.00)	85.0 (2.35)	6,560 (331)	5,060 (80)	71.4 (2.68)	9,760 (342)
Dependency status and family income													
Dependent	6,141 (—)	82.3 (0.39)	67.7 (0.56)	63.3 (0.46)	17,940 (144)	11,450 (104)	11,070 (137)	69.9 (0.43)	37.0 (0.43)	11,530 (128)	4,730 (22)	54.3 (0.55)	11,390 (114)
Low-income[5]	1,361 (—)	94.2 (0.58)	90.6 (0.73)	67.9 (0.94)	18,130 (245)	11,480 (127)	9,840 (292)	93.6 (0.61)	89.2 (0.76)	12,400 (223)	5,680 (17)	56.1 (0.89)	8,780 (144)
Middle-income[5]	3,045 (—)	83.2 (0.50)	69.0 (0.68)	65.8 (0.64)	17,990 (200)	11,020 (121)	11,190 (186)	70.1 (0.59)	34.6 (0.55)	11,190 (176)	3,640 (34)	58.2 (0.70)	11,290 (139)
High-income[5]	1,735 (—)	71.3 (0.73)	47.4 (0.89)	55.4 (0.81)	17,650 (327)	12,520 (275)	12,010 (304)	50.9 (0.83)	0.4 (0.07)	11,100 (295)	3,600 (460)	46.1 (0.92)	14,080 (264)
Independent	2,723 (—)	89.2 (0.54)	84.3 (0.64)	42.5 (0.80)	14,760 (181)	12,420 (113)	6,350 (242)	78.1 (0.67)	70.0 (0.79)	7,110 (129)	4,940 (27)	62.0 (0.86)	10,260 (97)

See notes at end of table.

Table 331.35. Percentage of full-time, full-year undergraduates receiving financial aid, and average annual amount received, by type and source of aid and selected student characteristics: Selected years, 1999–2000 through 2015–16—Continued

[Standard errors appear in parentheses. Amounts in constant 2017–18 dollars]

Year and selected student characteristic	Number enrolled[1] (in thousands)	Any aid: Percent receiving: Total[3]	Any aid: Percent receiving: Federal[4]	Any aid: Percent receiving: Nonfederal	Any aid: Average amount: Total[3]	Any aid: Average amount: Federal[4]	Any aid: Average amount: Nonfederal	Grants: Percent receiving: Total	Grants: Percent receiving: Pell	Grants: Average amount: Total	Grants: Average amount: Pell	Loans[2]: Percent receiving	Loans[2]: Average amount
1	2	3	4	5	6	7	8	9	10	11	12	13	14
Housing status													
School-owned	2,219 (—)	88.2 (0.50)	72.9 (0.66)	76.3 (0.59)	24,220 (273)	13,450 (175)	15,130 (272)	78.1 (0.59)	35.9 (0.67)	15,690 (280)	4,770 (39)	65.9 (0.75)	12,440 (153)
Off-campus, not with parents	3,222 (—)	84.4 (0.63)	74.6 (0.73)	48.9 (0.73)	14,700 (184)	11,760 (123)	7,430 (188)	71.6 (0.63)	53.0 (0.77)	7,840 (134)	4,840 (29)	56.1 (0.74)	10,720 (135)
With parents	2,502 (—)	82.7 (0.69)	72.0 (0.85)	52.0 (0.86)	13,500 (183)	10,420 (107)	7,040 (211)	71.2 (0.73)	52.1 (0.87)	8,000 (154)	4,870 (34)	49.4 (0.88)	10,000 (144)
Attended more than one institution	921 (—)	79.9 (0.74)	68.2 (0.94)	51.5 (0.87)	15,220 (244)	11,640 (156)	8,210 (258)	64.9 (0.90)	40.0 (0.86)	8,520 (199)	4,690 (43)	56.3 (1.00)	10,360 (160)
2015–16													
Total	**7,239 (—)**	**86.4 (0.26)**	**69.8 (0.33)**	**66.9 (0.40)**	**$18,970 (110)**	**$12,280 (61)**	**$11,700 (126)**	**76.7 (0.31)**	**44.0 (0.31)**	**$11,810 (96)**	**$4,870 (16)**	**54.7 (0.33)**	**$11,610 (79)**
Sex													
Male	3,202 (—)	84.2 (0.45)	66.7 (0.56)	65.4 (0.62)	19,330 (177)	12,730 (123)	11,900 (194)	73.3 (0.52)	40.0 (0.58)	11,980 (166)	4,800 (25)	52.0 (0.51)	11,740 (138)
Female	4,037 (—)	88.3 (0.31)	72.3 (0.41)	68.1 (0.51)	18,700 (160)	11,950 (89)	11,550 (163)	79.3 (0.40)	47.2 (0.46)	11,690 (129)	4,920 (22)	56.8 (0.49)	11,510 (114)
Race/ethnicity[6]													
White	4,171 (—)	85.7 (0.42)	66.7 (0.54)	67.6 (0.52)	19,140 (158)	12,260 (93)	12,180 (180)	73.8 (0.48)	34.0 (0.49)	11,680 (130)	4,720 (27)	56.0 (0.52)	12,100 (112)
Black	935 (—)	95.5 (0.42)	88.3 (0.60)	65.9 (1.23)	20,150 (394)	13,780 (226)	10,750 (388)	88.0 (0.66)	71.8 (0.88)	11,650 (299)	5,010 (36)	70.9 (1.08)	11,140 (234)
Hispanic	1,168 (—)	89.0 (0.65)	76.2 (0.81)	67.9 (0.84)	17,550 (342)	11,440 (183)	10,150 (348)	82.4 (0.74)	59.8 (0.90)	11,340 (277)	4,970 (36)	50.1 (0.90)	10,500 (212)
Asian	618 (—)	71.3 (1.30)	49.5 (1.45)	61.1 (1.37)	18,750 (489)	10,850 (287)	13,110 (538)	65.9 (1.35)	36.4 (1.35)	14,150 (440)	5,140 (64)	31.2 (1.26)	10,940 (466)
Pacific Islander	22 (—)	90.1 (3.86)	76.0 (5.62)	71.7 (5.83)	17,930 (1,595)	12,660 (1,222)	9,110 (1,505)	83.5 (4.79)	58.5 (6.28)	10,510 (1,338)	5,150 (224)	52.9 (7.06)	12,560 (1,514)
American Indian/Alaska Native	49 (—)	92.2 (2.28)	77.4 (3.78)	64.5 (4.46)	15,420 (1,515)	9,940 (639)	10,120 (1,753)	87.5 (2.76)	61.6 (4.57)	10,990 (1,503)	4,790 (178)	37.7 (4.26)	9,210 (596)
Two or more races	277 (—)	88.6 (1.39)	70.3 (2.07)	68.5 (1.60)	19,210 (627)	12,670 (450)	11,860 (620)	79.1 (1.59)	48.0 (1.84)	12,210 (506)	4,940 (84)	53.7 (1.95)	11,410 (455)
Age													
15 to 23	5,835 (—)	85.6 (0.28)	66.3 (0.37)	70.5 (0.39)	19,450 (130)	11,560 (64)	12,740 (138)	75.9 (0.34)	38.4 (0.33)	12,930 (117)	4,840 (20)	53.0 (0.37)	11,840 (95)
24 to 29	722 (—)	89.4 (0.73)	84.0 (0.84)	53.6 (1.25)	17,650 (278)	14,520 (203)	6,680 (261)	80.7 (0.86)	69.5 (1.00)	7,970 (168)	4,930 (46)	60.4 (1.01)	10,800 (179)
30 or over	682 (—)	90.7 (0.76)	84.4 (0.90)	50.4 (1.67)	16,430 (240)	14,730 (222)	4,930 (194)	78.9 (1.02)	65.1 (1.07)	6,740 (108)	5,000 (40)	62.3 (1.15)	10,720 (137)
Marital status													
Not married[7]	6,684 (—)	86.4 (0.26)	69.1 (0.34)	68.4 (0.39)	19,170 (114)	12,050 (63)	12,060 (127)	76.9 (0.31)	42.9 (0.32)	12,190 (100)	4,870 (17)	54.8 (0.34)	11,680 (85)
Married	506 (—)	86.6 (1.04)	77.8 (1.25)	48.9 (1.55)	16,410 (317)	14,650 (262)	5,750 (306)	72.4 (1.36)	56.1 (1.34)	6,900 (173)	4,810 (58)	52.0 (1.45)	10,640 (216)
Separated	48 (—)	91.4 (2.46)	87.2 (2.90)	53.2 (4.31)	17,230 (767)	14,930 (640)	5,100 (786)	87.2 (2.79)	80.9 (3.27)	7,830 (460)	5,400 (87)	67.9 (3.86)	10,530 (477)
Dependency status and family income													
Dependent	5,352 (—)	86.7 (0.30)	68.0 (0.37)	71.9 (0.41)	19,690 (132)	11,470 (67)	12,890 (142)	76.5 (0.35)	38.0 (0.35)	13,090 (121)	4,790 (22)	54.8 (0.39)	11,940 (98)
Low-income[5]	1,043 (—)	96.2 (0.40)	91.3 (0.62)	76.7 (0.92)	19,900 (301)	11,720 (155)	11,010 (295)	95.9 (0.41)	90.2 (0.65)	14,080 (256)	5,780 (16)	55.4 (0.95)	9,290 (213)
Middle-income[5]	2,691 (—)	88.2 (0.41)	71.8 (0.51)	74.5 (0.52)	19,530 (189)	10,910 (115)	12,630 (185)	78.9 (0.51)	40.5 (0.59)	12,650 (169)	3,930 (31)	58.4 (0.55)	11,480 (146)
High-income[5]	1,619 (—)	78.0 (0.71)	46.8 (0.77)	64.5 (0.79)	19,820 (300)	12,580 (221)	14,840 (318)	60.0 (0.79)	# (†)	13,030 (292)	‡ (†)	48.6 (0.75)	14,800 (279)
Independent	1,887 (—)	85.7 (0.53)	74.8 (0.63)	52.8 (0.97)	16,900 (192)	14,350 (143)	7,100 (202)	77.2 (0.62)	61.2 (0.68)	8,220 (131)	5,030 (28)	54.1 (0.74)	10,650 (104)
Housing status													
School-owned	2,089 (—)	90.4 (0.45)	69.5 (0.65)	81.2 (0.54)	25,840 (271)	13,560 (156)	17,160 (282)	82.4 (0.57)	35.9 (0.66)	17,240 (251)	4,870 (43)	63.6 (0.71)	13,110 (197)
Off-campus, not with parents	2,794 (—)	85.5 (0.47)	71.3 (0.61)	60.1 (0.72)	16,990 (163)	12,800 (117)	9,000 (164)	74.5 (0.57)	48.3 (0.66)	9,350 (117)	4,910 (25)	55.2 (0.60)	11,220 (112)
With parents	1,502 (—)	83.6 (0.64)	66.4 (0.85)	63.1 (0.93)	13,120 (228)	9,410 (155)	7,490 (179)	75.4 (0.74)	47.8 (0.84)	8,790 (161)	4,860 (37)	39.7 (0.96)	9,810 (220)
Attended more than one institution	855 (—)	84.7 (0.71)	71.6 (0.99)	60.9 (1.07)	17,700 (281)	12,190 (168)	10,280 (395)	72.2 (1.03)	43.4 (1.28)	10,510 (288)	4,770 (42)	57.5 (1.07)	10,940 (178)

—Not available.
†Not applicable.
#Rounds to zero.
‡Reporting standards not met. Either there are too few cases for a reliable estimate or the coefficient of variation (CV) is 50 percent or greater.
[1]Numbers of undergraduates may not equal figures reported in other tables, since these data are based on a sample survey of students who enrolled at any time during the academic year.
[2]Includes Parent Loans for Undergraduate Students (PLUS).
[3]Includes students who reported they were awarded aid but did not specify the source or type of aid as well as students who specified work study, vocational rehabilitation and training, and military education assistance, which are not separately shown.
[4]Includes Department of Veterans Affairs and Department of Defense benefits.
[5]Low-income students have family incomes below the 25th percentile, middle-income students have family incomes from the 25th to the 75th percentile, and high-income students have family incomes above the 75th percentile.
[6]The 2012 and 2016 questionnaires did not offer students the option of choosing an "Other" race category.
[7]Includes students who were single, divorced, or widowed.
NOTE: Full-time, full-year undergraduates are those who were enrolled full time for 9 or more months at one or more institutions. Data include undergraduates in degree-granting and non-degree-granting institutions. Constant dollars based on the Consumer Price Index, prepared by the Bureau of Labor Statistics, U.S. Department of Labor, adjusted to an academic-year basis. Detail may not sum to totals because of rounding and because some students receive multiple types of aid and aid from different sources. Data exclude Puerto Rico. Race categories exclude persons of Hispanic ethnicity. Some data have been revised from previously published figures.
SOURCE: U.S. Department of Education, National Center for Education Statistics, 1999–2000, 2003–04, 2007–08, 2011–12, and 2015–16 National Postsecondary Student Aid Study (NPSAS:2000, NPSAS:04, NPSAS:08, NPSAS:12, and NPSAS:16). (This table was prepared May 2019.)

Table 331.40. Average amount of financial aid awarded to full-time, full-year undergraduates, by type and source of aid and selected student characteristics: 2015–16

[In current dollars. Standard errors appear in parentheses]

Selected student characteristic	Any aid			Grants			Loans			Work study
	Total[1]	Federal[2]	Nonfederal	Total	Federal	Nonfederal	Total[3]	Federal[3]	Nonfederal	Total[4]
1	2	3	4	5	6	7	8	9	10	11
All full-time, full-year undergraduates	**$18,210 (105)**	**$11,790 (58)**	**$11,240 (121)**	**$11,340 (92)**	**$6,190 (57)**	**$10,220 (114)**	**$11,140 (75)**	**$9,810 (48)**	**$10,200 (238)**	**$2,430 (30)**
Sex										
Male	18,560 (170)	12,220 (118)	11,430 (187)	11,510 (159)	7,040 (103)	10,440 (182)	11,270 (133)	9,910 (106)	10,460 (341)	2,450 (51)
Female	17,950 (153)	11,470 (85)	11,090 (156)	11,220 (123)	5,590 (67)	10,050 (151)	11,050 (110)	9,740 (85)	10,010 (326)	2,420 (43)
Race/ethnicity										
White	18,380 (152)	11,770 (89)	11,690 (173)	11,220 (125)	6,370 (86)	10,390 (152)	11,620 (107)	9,900 (73)	10,770 (292)	2,360 (35)
Black	19,350 (378)	13,230 (217)	10,320 (373)	11,180 (287)	5,960 (105)	9,880 (373)	10,700 (225)	10,080 (200)	8,790 (838)	2,450 (98)
Hispanic	16,860 (328)	10,990 (176)	9,750 (334)	10,890 (266)	5,950 (101)	9,100 (327)	10,080 (203)	9,250 (186)	8,630 (697)	2,620 (86)
Asian	18,010 (470)	10,420 (276)	12,580 (517)	13,590 (423)	6,080 (177)	11,900 (481)	10,500 (448)	9,300 (406)	10,120 (992)	2,540 (104)
Pacific Islander	17,220 (1,532)	12,160 (1,174)	8,750 (1,445)	10,090 (1,285)	5,940 (527)	7,990 (1,426)	12,060 (1,454)	10,810 (1,276)	‡ (†)	‡ (†)
American Indian/Alaska Native	14,810 (1,455)	9,540 (614)	9,720 (1,683)	10,560 (1,443)	6,210 (490)	9,420 (1,713)	8,840 (572)	8,450 (544)	‡ (†)	‡ (†)
Two or more races	18,450 (602)	12,170 (432)	11,390 (596)	11,730 (486)	6,630 (315)	10,450 (558)	10,960 (437)	10,060 (393)	8,590 (876)	2,590 (200)
Age										
15 to 23 years old	18,680 (124)	11,100 (61)	12,230 (132)	12,420 (112)	5,330 (51)	11,180 (124)	11,370 (91)	9,860 (57)	10,260 (251)	2,380 (30)
24 to 29 years old	16,950 (267)	13,940 (195)	6,410 (250)	7,660 (162)	8,030 (189)	5,410 (209)	10,370 (172)	9,510 (112)	10,050 (804)	2,780 (149)
30 years old or over	15,780 (231)	14,140 (213)	4,730 (187)	6,470 (104)	8,250 (230)	3,940 (159)	10,290 (132)	9,720 (120)	9,410 (598)	3,430 (257)
Marital status										
Not married[5]	18,410 (110)	11,570 (60)	11,580 (122)	11,710 (96)	5,810 (56)	10,550 (115)	11,220 (82)	9,830 (51)	10,210 (243)	2,420 (30)
Married	15,760 (305)	14,070 (252)	5,520 (294)	6,630 (167)	9,550 (293)	4,640 (256)	10,220 (208)	9,470 (150)	10,350 (911)	2,730 (214)
Separated	16,540 (737)	14,340 (615)	4,890 (754)	7,520 (442)	6,970 (428)	4,450 (757)	10,110 (458)	9,900 (435)	‡ (†)	‡ (†)
Dependency status and family income										
Dependent	18,910 (127)	11,010 (64)	12,380 (137)	12,570 (116)	5,190 (54)	11,300 (128)	11,470 (94)	9,910 (59)	10,240 (250)	2,360 (30)
Less than $20,000	19,080 (352)	11,200 (175)	10,620 (354)	13,570 (306)	5,930 (37)	10,270 (356)	8,810 (235)	8,430 (227)	6,820 (629)	2,460 (83)
$20,000–$39,999	19,360 (369)	11,090 (181)	10,850 (321)	13,420 (281)	5,400 (57)	10,390 (310)	9,160 (224)	8,520 (195)	6,320 (572)	2,510 (80)
$40,000–$59,999	19,210 (396)	10,270 (199)	11,720 (380)	12,130 (333)	3,690 (85)	10,910 (371)	10,390 (245)	9,140 (214)	8,590 (676)	2,470 (89)
$60,000–$79,999	17,730 (413)	9,700 (259)	12,380 (367)	11,360 (338)	2,740 (157)	11,350 (349)	11,150 (317)	9,600 (266)	9,580 (772)	2,250 (101)
$80,000–$99,999	18,810 (481)	11,010 (331)	12,960 (439)	11,440 (429)	6,870 (1,075)	11,320 (430)	12,900 (388)	10,600 (354)	11,270 (671)	2,240 (119)
$100,000 or more	18,910 (266)	11,800 (177)	14,080 (282)	12,420 (261)	13,760 (1,299)	12,440 (264)	13,850 (228)	11,530 (174)	12,030 (394)	2,180 (55)
Independent	16,230 (184)	13,780 (137)	6,810 (194)	7,890 (126)	7,890 (135)	6,010 (189)	10,220 (99)	9,520 (72)	9,970 (526)	2,900 (110)
Less than $10,000	17,120 (307)	13,850 (220)	8,120 (310)	9,630 (230)	7,430 (164)	7,430 (297)	10,100 (167)	9,470 (132)	10,190 (1,082)	2,890 (139)
$10,000–$19,999	15,570 (364)	13,180 (274)	5,780 (318)	7,220 (190)	6,510 (212)	5,110 (278)	9,870 (193)	9,310 (165)	8,220 (677)	2,580 (206)
$20,000–$29,999	16,520 (553)	14,180 (388)	6,120 (585)	6,810 (368)	8,440 (428)	5,320 (557)	10,400 (339)	9,700 (225)	10,690 (1,706)	3,440 (560)
$30,000–$49,999	15,780 (377)	14,210 (331)	5,140 (322)	6,290 (157)	9,770 (390)	4,000 (257)	10,420 (265)	9,580 (199)	10,320 (1,104)	2,850 (256)
$50,000 or more	14,670 (431)	13,710 (414)	6,190 (432)	5,340 (255)	10,760 (704)	4,910 (331)	10,860 (374)	9,850 (222)	10,930 (1,337)	‡ (†)
Housing status										
School-owned	24,820 (260)	13,020 (149)	16,480 (271)	16,550 (241)	5,780 (109)	15,050 (260)	12,590 (189)	10,690 (147)	11,120 (449)	2,300 (38)
Off-campus, not with parents	16,320 (157)	12,290 (113)	8,640 (157)	8,980 (113)	6,810 (98)	7,620 (146)	10,770 (108)	9,610 (89)	10,320 (372)	2,740 (75)
With parents	12,600 (219)	9,040 (148)	7,190 (172)	8,440 (155)	5,260 (81)	6,710 (166)	9,420 (212)	8,670 (202)	7,860 (442)	2,450 (96)
Attended more than one institution	17,000 (270)	11,710 (162)	9,870 (380)	10,100 (277)	6,450 (168)	9,020 (383)	10,510 (171)	9,480 (150)	9,010 (443)	2,290 (71)

†Not applicable.
‡Reporting standards not met. Either there are too few cases for a reliable estimate or the coefficient of variation (CV) is 50 percent or greater.
[1]Includes students who reported they were awarded aid, but did not specify the source or type of aid.
[2]Includes Department of Veterans Affairs and Department of Defense benefits.
[3]Includes Parent Loans for Undergraduate Students (PLUS).
[4]Details on federal and nonfederal work-study participants are not available.
[5]Includes students who were single, divorced, or widowed.

NOTE: Aid averages are for those students who received the specified type of aid. Detail may not sum to totals because of rounding and because some students receive multiple types of aid and aid from different sources. Full-time, full-year undergraduates were enrolled full time for 9 or more months at one or more institutions. Data include undergraduates in degree-granting and non-degree-granting institutions. Data exclude Puerto Rico. Race categories exclude persons of Hispanic ethnicity.
SOURCE: U.S. Department of Education, National Center for Education Statistics, 2015–16 National Postsecondary Student Aid Study (NPSAS:16). (This table was prepared June 2018.)

Table 331.50. Aid status and sources of aid for full-time and part-time undergraduates, by control and level of institution: 2011–12 and 2015–16

[Standard errors appear in parentheses]

Control and level of institution	Number of undergraduates[1] (in thousands)	Aid status (percent of students)											
		Nonaided		Source of aid									
				Any aid[2,3]		Federal[3]		State		Institutional		Other[2]	
1	2	3		4		5		6		7		8	
2011–12													
Full-time, full-year student[4]													
All institutions	**8,864**	**15.6**	**(0.36)**	**84.4**	**(0.36)**	**72.8**	**(0.51)**	**26.5**	**(0.48)**	**31.0**	**(0.45)**	**28.1**	**(0.36)**
Public	5,997	19.6	(0.47)	80.4	(0.47)	68.4	(0.61)	30.2	(0.64)	22.0	(0.52)	24.3	(0.36)
4-year doctoral	2,893	16.1	(0.46)	83.9	(0.46)	70.9	(0.47)	31.2	(0.69)	32.2	(0.90)	28.1	(0.49)
Other 4-year	969	16.5	(0.93)	83.5	(0.93)	72.7	(1.34)	31.3	(1.36)	21.6	(1.32)	27.5	(0.90)
2-year	2,104	25.5	(1.03)	74.5	(1.03)	63.0	(1.24)	28.3	(1.31)	8.3	(0.54)	17.8	(0.57)
Less-than-2-year	31	28.4	(4.50)	71.6	(4.50)	67.8	(4.72)	18.2 !	(6.85)	‡	(†)	18.9	(4.08)
Private, nonprofit	1,875	8.4	(0.55)	91.6	(0.55)	76.1	(0.75)	25.3	(0.87)	73.7	(0.97)	39.6	(0.96)
4-year doctoral	990	9.6	(0.84)	90.4	(0.84)	74.3	(0.94)	23.3	(1.29)	74.5	(1.29)	38.9	(1.50)
Other 4-year	849	6.9	(0.68)	93.1	(0.68)	78.0	(1.20)	28.0	(1.24)	74.3	(1.38)	40.5	(1.08)
Less-than-4-year	36	9.8 !	(4.12)	90.2	(4.12)	78.1	(5.04)	19.5 !	(7.60)	34.5 !	(11.90)	38.4	(4.24)
Private, for-profit	992	5.2	(0.46)	94.8	(0.46)	93.1	(0.51)	6.9	(0.70)	4.8	(0.72)	29.2	(0.89)
2-year and above	859	5.4	(0.53)	94.6	(0.53)	92.8	(0.59)	7.5	(0.78)	5.4	(0.83)	30.7	(0.96)
Less-than-2-year	133	4.1	(0.75)	95.9	(0.75)	95.2	(0.79)	‡	(†)	‡	(†)	19.3	(2.30)
Part-time or part-year students[5]													
All institutions	**14,192**	**37.9**	**(1.05)**	**62.1**	**(1.05)**	**51.1**	**(1.10)**	**14.6**	**(0.51)**	**7.3**	**(0.27)**	**16.4**	**(0.34)**
Public	10,929	44.0	(1.18)	56.0	(1.18)	44.5	(1.22)	16.7	(0.63)	5.6	(0.24)	13.4	(0.36)
4-year doctoral	1,875	33.9	(1.04)	66.1	(1.04)	53.4	(0.81)	15.1	(0.61)	13.4	(0.87)	20.7	(0.73)
Other 4-year	1,477	40.5	(1.46)	59.5	(1.46)	49.7	(1.66)	12.0	(0.74)	6.8	(0.80)	16.9	(0.94)
2-year	7,521	47.3	(1.36)	52.7	(1.36)	41.2	(1.39)	18.0	(0.87)	3.5	(0.25)	10.9	(0.39)
Less-than-2-year	56	29.8	(4.21)	70.2	(4.21)	60.3	(4.47)	19.7	(5.84)	3.1 !	(1.37)	9.2	(2.44)
Private, nonprofit	1,135	22.6	(1.47)	77.4	(1.47)	61.0	(1.61)	13.5	(1.28)	30.2	(1.95)	28.7	(1.58)
4-year doctoral	557	24.0	(1.87)	76.0	(1.87)	57.9	(2.12)	9.5	(1.49)	30.1	(2.15)	28.1	(2.61)
Other 4-year	527	20.8	(2.42)	79.2	(2.42)	64.0	(2.54)	18.6	(2.12)	32.3	(3.36)	30.2	(2.14)
Less-than-4-year	51	25.7	(4.47)	74.3	(4.47)	64.3	(3.22)	‡	(†)	‡	(†)	18.2	(4.18)
Private, for-profit	2,128	14.6	(1.02)	85.4	(1.02)	79.7	(0.83)	4.2	(0.52)	3.7	(0.71)	25.3	(1.09)
2-year and above	1,790	14.7	(1.20)	85.3	(1.20)	78.8	(0.97)	4.2	(0.49)	3.6	(0.68)	27.0	(1.22)
Less-than-2-year	337	14.1	(1.39)	85.9	(1.39)	84.6	(1.40)	‡	(†)	‡	(†)	16.3	(1.71)
2015–16													
Full-time, full-year students[4]													
All institutions	**7,239**	**13.6**	**(0.26)**	**86.4**	**(0.26)**	**69.8**	**(0.33)**	**29.7**	**(0.44)**	**42.8**	**(0.45)**	**28.6**	**(0.36)**
Public	5,023	16.0	(0.34)	84.0	(0.34)	67.7	(0.42)	34.1	(0.55)	32.7	(0.58)	25.8	(0.43)
4-year doctoral	2,849	13.3	(0.38)	86.7	(0.38)	69.4	(0.48)	34.0	(0.61)	42.8	(0.66)	29.0	(0.54)
Other 4-year	765	14.7	(0.78)	85.3	(0.78)	72.6	(0.98)	36.0	(1.61)	29.5	(1.76)	27.5	(1.39)
2-year	1,391	22.2	(0.79)	77.8	(0.79)	61.6	(0.85)	33.4	(1.07)	14.0	(1.22)	18.6	(0.77)
Less-than-2-year	19	18.0 !	(6.98)	82.0	(6.98)	67.0	(8.01)	12.5	(2.54)	23.1 !	(10.82)	9.2 !	(3.31)
Private, nonprofit	1,735	8.3	(0.48)	91.7	(0.48)	70.3	(0.61)	22.6	(0.73)	75.1	(0.82)	37.8	(0.81)
4-year doctoral	1,011	9.0	(0.62)	91.0	(0.62)	67.5	(0.89)	21.4	(0.99)	78.1	(1.07)	39.7	(1.07)
Other 4-year	684	7.1	(0.72)	92.9	(0.72)	73.7	(0.89)	25.1	(1.06)	73.7	(1.46)	36.3	(1.08)
Less-than-4-year	40	13.1	(2.20)	86.9	(2.20)	81.7	(3.76)	‡	(†)	22.3 !	(11.17)	14.0 !	(6.88)
Private, for-profit	481	7.1	(0.59)	92.9	(0.59)	89.4	(0.71)	9.5	(1.01)	30.8	(3.37)	24.3	(0.91)
2-year and above	382	6.4	(0.65)	93.6	(0.65)	89.7	(0.77)	10.2	(1.15)	36.4	(3.98)	26.8	(1.14)
Less-than-2-year	99	9.5	(1.36)	90.5	(1.36)	88.6	(1.74)	7.2	(1.84)	9.1	(2.52)	14.6	(1.55)
Part-time or part-year students[5]													
All institutions	**12,069**	**36.4**	**(0.33)**	**63.6**	**(0.33)**	**47.6**	**(0.26)**	**18.0**	**(0.34)**	**13.9**	**(0.31)**	**17.0**	**(0.30)**
Public	9,468	41.5	(0.39)	58.5	(0.39)	42.0	(0.30)	20.1	(0.43)	9.8	(0.27)	14.9	(0.31)
4-year doctoral	1,825	27.6	(0.74)	72.4	(0.74)	55.5	(0.71)	20.7	(0.80)	24.6	(0.75)	22.2	(0.68)
Other 4-year	1,346	39.7	(1.33)	60.3	(1.33)	44.8	(1.25)	16.9	(0.94)	12.2	(0.93)	18.2	(0.81)
2-year	6,249	45.9	(0.54)	54.1	(0.54)	37.5	(0.38)	20.7	(0.62)	4.9	(0.29)	12.1	(0.40)
Less-than-2-year	48	33.3	(7.04)	66.7	(7.04)	38.4	(2.59)	10.8	(2.31)	23.0	(5.88)	10.8	(3.21)
Private, nonprofit	1,220	21.0	(0.82)	79.0	(0.82)	58.0	(1.03)	12.5	(0.76)	32.6	(1.28)	29.2	(1.19)
4-year doctoral	622	19.9	(1.27)	80.1	(1.27)	53.5	(1.58)	11.9	(0.97)	33.9	(1.89)	34.3	(1.80)
Other 4-year	540	22.1	(0.94)	77.9	(0.94)	61.6	(1.13)	12.8	(1.03)	33.5	(1.81)	24.2	(1.38)
Less-than-4-year	58	21.8	(4.07)	78.2	(4.07)	73.2	(4.47)	15.5 !	(7.70)	10.4	(2.15)	21.4	(5.96)
Private, for-profit	1,381	15.5	(0.48)	84.5	(0.48)	77.0	(0.59)	8.4	(0.75)	25.5	(1.30)	21.2	(0.78)
2-year and above	1,140	14.5	(0.54)	85.5	(0.54)	77.5	(0.67)	9.1	(0.88)	28.9	(1.52)	22.2	(0.70)
Less-than-2-year	240	20.3	(1.47)	79.7	(1.47)	74.6	(1.55)	5.4	(1.18)	9.4	(2.57)	16.5	(3.08)

†Not applicable.
!Interpret data with caution. The coefficient of variation (CV) for this estimate is between 30 and 50 percent.
‡Reporting standards not met. The coefficient of variation (CV) for this estimate is 50 percent or greater.
[1]Numbers of undergraduates may not equal figures reported in other tables, since these data are based on a sample survey of students who enrolled at any time during the academic year.
[2]Includes students who reported that they were awarded aid but did not specify the source of the aid.
[3]Includes Department of Veterans Affairs and Department of Defense benefits.
[4]Full-time, full-year undergraduates are those who were enrolled full time for 9 or more months at one or more institutions.
[5]Part-time or part-year undergraduates include those who were enrolled part time for 9 or more months and those who were enrolled for less than 9 months either part time or full time.
NOTE: Data exclude students whose attendance status was not reported. Data include undergraduates in degree-granting and non-degree-granting institutions. Detail may not sum to totals because of rounding and because some students received multiple types of aid and aid from different sources. Data exclude Puerto Rico.
SOURCE: U.S. Department of Education, National Center for Education Statistics, 2011–12 and 2015–16 National Postsecondary Student Aid Study (NPSAS:12 and NPSAS:16). (This table was prepared July 2018.)

Table 331.60. Percentage of full-time, full-year undergraduates receiving financial aid, by type and source of aid and control and level of institution: Selected years, 1992–93 through 2015–16

[Standard errors appear in parentheses]

Control and level of institution	Any aid: Total[2]	Any aid: Federal[3]	Any aid: Nonfederal	Grants: Total	Grants: Federal	Grants: Nonfederal	Loans: Total[4]	Loans: Federal[4]	Loans: Nonfederal	Work study[1]: Total	Work study[1]: Federal
1	2	3	4	5	6	7	8	9	10	11	12
1992–93, all institutions	**58.2 (0.50)**	**45.0 (0.50)**	**37.9 (0.58)**	**48.3 (0.51)**	**28.6 (0.47)**	**34.9 (0.51)**	**34.0 (0.61)**	**33.1 (0.61)**	**2.7 (0.22)**	**10.3 (0.38)**	**6.8 (0.30)**
Public	52.4 (0.67)	39.8 (0.60)	32.7 (0.69)	42.8 (0.58)	27.4 (0.50)	29.6 (0.64)	27.1 (0.57)	26.3 (0.54)	2.0 (0.27)	6.8 (0.36)	4.2 (0.23)
4-year doctoral	54.0 (0.94)	39.1 (0.80)	34.7 (0.82)	42.2 (0.80)	23.6 (0.65)	31.2 (0.79)	33.1 (0.86)	32.3 (0.86)	2.4 (0.29)	7.1 (0.50)	4.3 (0.34)
Other 4-year	56.5 (1.07)	45.4 (1.19)	36.7 (1.27)	45.4 (1.29)	31.1 (1.24)	32.4 (1.32)	34.4 (0.98)	33.4 (0.93)	2.8 (0.69)	9.7 (0.77)	5.6 (0.57)
2-year	47.2 (1.93)	36.0 (1.70)	27.0 (1.62)	41.9 (1.68)	29.9 (1.43)	25.7 (1.65)	12.7 (1.23)	12.3 (1.17)	0.7 ! (0.28)	4.1 (0.79)	3.0 (0.54)
Less-than-2-year	35.4 (3.60)	31.6 (4.08)	15.7 (4.47)	30.3 (2.53)	26.6 (2.91)	13.3 ! (4.75)	3.0 ! (1.30)	3.0 ! (1.30)	‡ (†)	‡ (†)	‡ (†)
Private, nonprofit	69.5 (1.38)	52.3 (1.42)	58.9 (1.49)	62.0 (1.36)	25.8 (1.59)	55.9 (1.47)	47.6 (1.33)	45.9 (1.40)	5.1 (0.47)	22.5 (1.10)	16.1 (1.00)
4-year doctoral	63.5 (1.65)	44.3 (1.37)	54.7 (1.76)	56.0 (1.61)	17.0 (0.97)	52.7 (1.68)	41.7 (1.27)	39.8 (1.27)	6.1 (0.74)	18.9 (1.33)	13.2 (1.40)
Other 4-year	75.4 (1.91)	59.4 (2.08)	64.3 (2.46)	68.4 (2.11)	33.0 (2.79)	60.6 (2.81)	53.8 (1.88)	52.4 (1.99)	4.3 (0.80)	27.7 (1.75)	20.1 (1.58)
Less-than-4-year	70.7 (3.80)	59.5 (4.15)	44.4 (6.26)	56.6 (4.50)	40.9 (3.70)	39.2 (6.82)	43.5 (5.33)	41.7 (5.08)	2.8 ! (1.17)	4.1 ! (1.90)	2.3 ! (1.00)
Private, for-profit	77.0 (2.18)	72.0 (2.17)	16.8 (2.32)	56.2 (1.75)	49.9 (1.71)	13.6 (2.41)	55.4 (4.82)	55.1 (4.79)	2.2 ! (0.91)	1.9 ! (0.78)	0.7 ! (0.25)
2-year and above	82.2 (4.50)	76.5 (4.35)	24.1 (4.65)	50.3 (4.06)	40.5 (2.52)	21.0 (5.02)	68.5 (5.41)	68.5 (5.41)	‡ (†)	3.6 ! (1.62)	1.4 ! (0.54)
Less-than-2-year	73.2 (2.46)	68.8 (2.64)	11.5 (2.49)	60.4 (2.46)	56.7 (2.31)	8.3 ! (2.53)	46.0 (5.63)	45.4 (5.56)	1.5 ! (0.53)	‡ (†)	0.2 ! (0.09)
1999–2000, all institutions	**71.9 (0.59)**	**56.7 (0.44)**	**52.3 (0.67)**	**58.5 (0.60)**	**29.0 (0.44)**	**49.0 (0.69)**	**45.6 (0.44)**	**44.5 (0.41)**	**6.8 (0.31)**	**11.6 (0.46)**	**8.9 (0.36)**
Public	66.9 (0.73)	51.6 (0.51)	46.4 (0.86)	52.8 (0.68)	29.3 (0.43)	43.0 (0.81)	37.9 (0.50)	36.9 (0.46)	4.4 (0.30)	7.5 (0.47)	5.6 (0.38)
4-year doctoral	71.1 (0.79)	54.4 (0.68)	49.7 (0.77)	53.3 (0.87)	25.1 (0.74)	45.6 (0.68)	49.0 (0.73)	47.9 (0.69)	5.6 (0.41)	8.7 (0.51)	6.1 (0.42)
Other 4-year	75.7 (1.29)	63.0 (1.43)	50.6 (2.13)	57.5 (1.38)	33.7 (1.53)	46.6 (2.10)	51.5 (1.66)	50.7 (1.66)	4.7 (0.45)	11.0 (1.33)	8.1 (1.12)
2-year	55.7 (1.47)	40.5 (1.08)	39.5 (1.51)	49.2 (1.34)	31.9 (0.97)	37.3 (1.49)	14.9 (0.75)	13.9 (0.62)	2.5 (0.40)	3.8 (0.69)	3.5 (0.68)
Less-than-2-year	58.4 (6.03)	45.0 (6.96)	35.0 (5.14)	48.4 (7.50)	39.7 (7.40)	26.4 (6.54)	4.7 ! (2.14)	4.7 ! (2.13)	‡ (†)	‡ (†)	# (†)
Private, nonprofit	84.0 (0.77)	67.3 (0.75)	73.5 (1.37)	74.9 (1.13)	24.2 (1.24)	71.1 (1.42)	62.6 (0.83)	61.2 (0.83)	14.2 (0.89)	25.8 (1.27)	19.8 (0.88)
4-year doctoral	79.0 (1.03)	62.7 (1.22)	71.0 (1.27)	70.4 (1.19)	20.6 (1.22)	68.2 (1.33)	60.0 (1.16)	58.4 (1.19)	16.0 (1.08)	25.7 (1.16)	21.7 (1.05)
Other 4-year	88.7 (1.08)	72.2 (1.31)	76.3 (2.29)	78.9 (1.63)	26.3 (1.80)	74.1 (2.28)	67.4 (1.41)	66.0 (1.45)	13.4 (1.20)	26.7 (2.24)	19.0 (1.55)
Less-than-4-year	77.2 (4.01)	53.3 (2.88)	64.0 (5.11)	72.7 (4.37)	37.0 (3.48)	62.5 (5.62)	27.4 (2.59)	27.3 (2.60)	3.1 (0.62)	13.7 (2.56)	10.0 (2.71)
Private, for-profit	89.9 (1.11)	87.0 (1.39)	33.4 (3.08)	63.5 (2.14)	52.9 (2.59)	26.6 (2.83)	82.7 (1.49)	82.0 (1.50)	7.8 (1.62)	2.2 ! (0.87)	1.9 ! (0.86)
2-year and above	88.6 (1.50)	85.7 (1.77)	37.5 (4.17)	60.8 (2.81)	47.3 (3.29)	32.6 (3.88)	82.9 (2.19)	82.2 (2.19)	6.9 (2.04)	2.9 ! (1.17)	2.5 ! (1.15)
Less-than-2-year	93.7 (1.32)	91.1 (1.88)	20.8 (2.75)	71.9 (2.96)	69.8 (2.97)	8.6 (2.27)	81.9 (3.65)	81.5 (3.64)	10.4 (1.93)	‡ (†)	‡ (0.18)
2007–08, all institutions	**80.1 (0.28)**	**63.9 (0.31)**	**63.7 (0.36)**	**64.6 (0.37)**	**33.1 (0.29)**	**53.6 (0.41)**	**54.8 (0.32)**	**51.0 (0.32)**	**20.5 (0.31)**	**13.8 (0.29)**	**10.6 (0.23)**
Public	75.4 (0.33)	58.7 (0.36)	58.0 (0.39)	59.2 (0.38)	32.3 (0.29)	49.6 (0.40)	46.2 (0.34)	42.7 (0.33)	14.2 (0.25)	9.5 (0.25)	7.1 (0.22)
4-year doctoral	77.8 (0.40)	59.6 (0.48)	62.8 (0.49)	59.9 (0.55)	27.8 (0.38)	53.8 (0.53)	54.7 (0.50)	50.8 (0.50)	17.4 (0.38)	10.2 (0.35)	7.6 (0.32)
Other 4-year	82.5 (0.59)	67.6 (0.68)	62.7 (0.80)	63.2 (0.81)	35.2 (0.66)	52.7 (0.85)	57.5 (0.72)	54.4 (0.72)	16.4 (0.61)	11.5 (0.60)	8.7 (0.45)
2-year	66.9 (0.69)	51.4 (0.73)	47.5 (0.79)	55.5 (0.63)	37.3 (0.65)	41.3 (0.76)	25.5 (0.59)	22.3 (0.57)	7.8 (0.37)	7.1 (0.36)	5.5 (0.29)
Less-than-2-year	69.1 (3.87)	58.6 (3.84)	33.0 (4.74)	56.6 (3.58)	50.0 (3.97)	16.1 (2.88)	26.5 (4.79)	23.6 (4.33)	10.7 (2.75)	# (†)	# (†)
Private, nonprofit	89.5 (0.57)	71.2 (0.62)	83.2 (0.79)	80.9 (0.85)	27.4 (0.67)	77.5 (1.02)	68.1 (0.66)	64.3 (0.61)	30.4 (0.74)	32.2 (1.08)	25.0 (0.86)
4-year doctoral	85.5 (0.93)	67.1 (1.12)	79.4 (1.11)	76.5 (1.18)	23.6 (0.82)	73.6 (1.38)	64.2 (1.21)	60.0 (1.22)	29.7 (1.02)	30.3 (1.10)	24.5 (1.04)
Other 4-year	93.6 (0.74)	75.1 (1.12)	87.5 (1.06)	85.8 (1.11)	31.0 (1.18)	82.1 (1.40)	72.3 (1.18)	68.8 (1.21)	31.2 (1.06)	34.7 (1.88)	26.0 (1.45)
Less-than-4-year	92.0 (2.79)	84.4 (3.65)	61.8 (10.16)	61.3 (4.96)	45.3 (5.77)	48.2 (9.77)	60.2 (7.26)	56.8 (7.31)	26.0 ! (7.94)	5.8 (1.50)	4.7 ! (1.63)
Private, for-profit	92.6 (0.70)	84.6 (1.24)	59.8 (1.60)	65.5 (1.48)	53.0 (1.50)	25.8 (1.66)	86.5 (1.19)	81.2 (1.29)	43.1 (1.67)	1.8 (0.29)	1.6 (0.28)
2-year and above	92.4 (0.79)	84.2 (1.41)	61.7 (1.82)	64.7 (1.69)	50.7 (1.70)	27.8 (1.90)	86.4 (1.36)	81.3 (1.46)	44.1 (1.92)	2.0 (0.34)	1.8 (0.33)
Less-than-2-year	93.6 (0.82)	87.4 (1.74)	47.6 (2.52)	70.8 (2.12)	67.6 (2.14)	13.5 (2.33)	87.2 (1.70)	80.7 (2.44)	36.9 (1.61)	0.7 ! (0.27)	‡ (†)
2011–12, all institutions	**84.4 (0.36)**	**72.8 (0.51)**	**56.9 (0.46)**	**72.4 (0.41)**	**47.4 (0.50)**	**52.6 (0.45)**	**56.7 (0.53)**	**55.5 (0.54)**	**9.2 (0.22)**	**11.9 (0.25)**	**10.5 (0.24)**
Public	80.4 (0.47)	68.4 (0.61)	53.3 (0.58)	67.3 (0.49)	46.1 (0.59)	49.7 (0.56)	48.5 (0.57)	47.4 (0.57)	6.3 (0.19)	6.9 (0.24)	6.2 (0.23)
4-year doctoral	83.9 (0.46)	70.9 (0.47)	61.2 (0.63)	67.8 (0.51)	41.1 (0.40)	56.8 (0.61)	61.6 (0.44)	60.4 (0.43)	8.6 (0.31)	8.3 (0.37)	7.4 (0.37)
Other 4-year	83.5 (0.93)	72.7 (1.34)	54.1 (1.23)	69.2 (0.99)	48.3 (1.10)	50.1 (1.32)	55.5 (1.49)	54.3 (1.51)	7.4 (0.60)	9.3 (0.70)	8.6 (0.61)
2-year	74.5 (1.03)	63.0 (1.24)	42.5 (1.14)	65.7 (1.09)	51.6 (1.30)	40.2 (1.15)	27.5 (0.99)	26.6 (1.00)	2.7 (0.24)	3.9 (0.28)	3.4 (0.28)
Less-than-2-year	71.6 (4.50)	67.8 (4.72)	33.5 (5.54)	68.6 (4.05)	63.7 (4.54)	27.2 (3.90)	20.5 (5.20)	20.2 (5.20)	‡ (†)	1.0 ! (0.46)	‡ (†)
Private, nonprofit	91.6 (0.55)	76.1 (0.75)	83.1 (0.77)	85.4 (0.77)	37.6 (0.65)	80.3 (0.85)	68.4 (0.90)	66.7 (0.88)	15.3 (0.65)	33.1 (0.85)	29.2 (0.81)
4-year doctoral	90.4 (0.84)	74.3 (0.94)	82.9 (1.13)	84.2 (1.17)	34.9 (0.80)	80.4 (1.21)	66.7 (1.08)	65.3 (1.05)	15.0 (0.92)	33.2 (1.27)	30.0 (1.26)
Other 4-year	93.1 (0.68)	78.0 (1.20)	84.2 (0.98)	87.2 (0.92)	40.3 (1.10)	81.3 (1.15)	70.7 (1.41)	68.7 (1.44)	15.8 (0.91)	33.9 (1.22)	29.1 (1.14)
Less-than-4-year	90.2 (4.12)	78.1 (5.04)	60.2 (7.07)	77.8 (6.09)	48.5 (6.54)	51.1 (8.78)	61.2 (5.71)	59.0 (7.42)	12.2 (2.62)	‡ (†)	‡ (†)
Private, for-profit	94.8 (0.46)	93.1 (0.51)	29.3 (1.05)	78.6 (0.76)	73.9 (0.82)	17.4 (0.94)	84.1 (0.85)	83.4 (0.89)	14.8 (0.75)	1.9 (0.21)	1.8 (0.20)
2-year and above	94.6 (0.53)	92.8 (0.59)	30.7 (1.16)	77.4 (0.86)	72.2 (0.92)	18.9 (1.05)	84.2 (0.85)	83.4 (0.89)	15.0 (0.82)	2.2 (0.24)	2.1 (0.23)
Less-than-2-year	95.9 (0.75)	95.2 (0.79)	20.3 (2.64)	86.2 (1.54)	85.4 (1.63)	7.5 (1.82)	83.8 (3.56)	83.0 (3.52)	13.5 (1.58)	‡ (†)	‡ (†)

See notes at end of table.

Table 331.60. Percentage of full-time, full-year undergraduates receiving financial aid, by type and source of aid and control and level of institution: Selected years, 1992–93 through 2015–16—Continued

[Standard errors appear in parentheses]

Control and level of institution	Any aid			Grants			Loans			Work study[1]	
	Total[2]	Federal[3]	Nonfederal	Total	Federal	Nonfederal	Total[4]	Federal[4]	Nonfederal	Total	Federal
1	2	3	4	5	6	7	8	9	10	11	12
2015–16, all institutions	**86.4 (0.26)**	**69.8 (0.33)**	**66.9 (0.40)**	**76.7 (0.31)**	**44.7 (0.31)**	**63.8 (0.41)**	**54.7 (0.33)**	**52.5 (0.34)**	**9.2 (0.21)**	**10.5 (0.26)**	**9.1 (0.25)**
Public	84.0 (0.34)	67.7 (0.42)	63.4 (0.49)	72.5 (0.40)	44.9 (0.39)	60.1 (0.49)	48.5 (0.41)	46.7 (0.41)	6.9 (0.21)	6.6 (0.25)	5.8 (0.24)
4-year doctoral	86.7 (0.38)	69.4 (0.48)	69.8 (0.53)	73.7 (0.47)	41.8 (0.39)	65.8 (0.54)	59.7 (0.43)	57.5 (0.44)	9.1 (0.31)	8.3 (0.36)	7.1 (0.35)
Other 4-year	85.3 (0.78)	72.6 (0.98)	63.3 (1.45)	71.8 (1.18)	45.9 (1.27)	59.6 (1.42)	53.2 (1.29)	51.2 (1.29)	8.3 (0.65)	5.4 (0.68)	5.2 (0.67)
2-year	77.8 (0.79)	61.6 (0.85)	50.6 (1.11)	70.3 (0.86)	50.4 (0.79)	48.9 (1.10)	23.4 (0.62)	22.6 (0.62)	1.9 (0.21)	3.8 (0.44)	3.4 (0.41)
Less-than-2-year	82.0 (6.98)	67.0 (8.01)	36.3 (10.64)	72.2 (7.51)	56.0 (7.26)	34.6 ! (11.07)	25.1 (6.39)	25.1 (6.39)	‡ (†)	‡ (†)	‡ (†)
Private, nonprofit	91.7 (0.48)	70.3 (0.61)	83.1 (0.70)	87.1 (0.59)	36.4 (0.52)	81.1 (0.76)	65.9 (0.61)	62.5 (0.60)	15.9 (0.64)	24.4 (0.82)	21.0 (0.75)
4-year doctoral	91.0 (0.62)	67.5 (0.89)	85.6 (0.84)	87.1 (0.66)	32.9 (0.62)	84.0 (0.88)	62.9 (0.85)	59.3 (0.81)	16.7 (0.87)	23.7 (1.05)	21.3 (1.03)
Other 4-year	92.9 (0.72)	73.7 (0.89)	82.2 (1.20)	87.6 (1.03)	39.3 (0.84)	80.0 (1.37)	69.8 (0.93)	66.7 (0.95)	15.1 (0.95)	26.8 (1.35)	21.7 (1.22)
Less-than-4-year	86.9 (2.20)	81.7 (3.76)	37.5 (10.42)	78.4 (3.61)	72.4 (4.87)	29.3 ! (9.48)	72.9 (5.85)	71.1 (5.79)	8.7 (2.22)	‡ (†)	‡ (†)
Private, for-profit	92.9 (0.59)	89.4 (0.71)	45.4 (2.86)	82.9 (0.97)	72.2 (0.84)	39.9 (3.14)	78.1 (0.77)	76.8 (0.81)	8.9 (0.59)	1.5 (0.23)	1.5 (0.23)
2-year and above	93.6 (0.65)	89.7 (0.77)	50.9 (3.34)	83.5 (1.10)	70.7 (0.97)	45.6 (3.68)	78.4 (0.75)	77.4 (0.79)	9.1 (0.69)	1.6 (0.28)	1.5 (0.28)
Less-than-2-year	90.5 (1.36)	88.6 (1.74)	24.4 (2.72)	80.6 (2.11)	78.0 (2.12)	18.0 (2.87)	76.9 (2.54)	74.7 (2.62)	8.1 (0.94)	‡ (†)	‡ (†)

†Not applicable.
#Rounds to zero.
!Interpret data with caution. The coefficient of variation (CV) for this estimate is between 30 and 50 percent.
‡Reporting standards not met. The coefficient of variation (CV) for this estimate is 50 percent or greater.
[1]Details on nonfederal work-study participants are not available.
[2]Includes students who reported they were awarded aid, but did not specify the source or type of aid.
[3]Includes Department of Veterans Affairs and Department of Defense benefits.
[4]Includes Parent Loans for Undergraduate Students (PLUS).
NOTE: Full-time, full-year undergraduates were enrolled full time for 9 or more months at one or more institutions. Data include undergraduates in degree-granting and non-degree-granting institutions. Detail may not sum to totals because of rounding and because some students receive multiple types of aid and aid from different sources. Data exclude Puerto Rico.
SOURCE: U.S. Department of Education, National Center for Education Statistics, 1992–93, 1999–2000, 2007–08, 2011–12, and 2015–16 National Postsecondary Student Aid Study (NPSAS:93, NPSAS:2000, NPSAS:08, NPSAS:12, and NPSAS:16). (This table was prepared June 2018.)

Table 331.70. Average amount of financial aid awarded to full-time, full-year undergraduates, by type and source of aid and control and level of institution: Selected years, 1992–93 through 2015–16

[Standard errors appear in parentheses]

Control and level of institution	Any aid			Grants			Loans			Work study[1]	
	Total[2]	Federal[3]	Nonfederal	Total[4]	Federal	Nonfederal	Total[5]	Federal[5]	Nonfederal	Total	Federal
1	2	3	4	5	6	7	8	9	10	11	12
	Current dollars										
1992–93, all institutions	**$5,600 (80)**	**$4,320 (54)**	**$3,390 (85)**	**$3,520 (63)**	**$2,000 (17)**	**$3,250 (85)**	**$3,860 (59)**	**$3,750 (54)**	**$2,640 (133)**	**$1,360 (34)**	**$1,280 (38)**
Public	4,030 (39)	3,740 (40)	1,860 (34)	2,420 (28)	1,900 (18)	1,740 (34)	3,350 (42)	3,290 (40)	2,020 (133)	1,380 (48)	1,350 (52)
4-year doctoral	4,720 (60)	4,390 (49)	2,330 (55)	2,750 (45)	1,970 (26)	2,230 (55)	3,660 (46)	3,590 (43)	2,150 (142)	1,440 (57)	1,360 (55)
Other 4-year	4,240 (92)	3,850 (68)	1,710 (47)	2,430 (48)	1,960 (26)	1,530 (52)	3,200 (65)	3,120 (71)	2,150 (198)	1,240 (59)	1,260 (69)
2-year	2,720 (88)	2,640 (87)	1,170 (84)	1,940 (59)	1,760 (42)	1,120 (88)	2,500 (125)	2,530 (112)	‡ (†)	1,500 (179)	1,490 (155)
Less-than-2-year	2,250 (198)	1,950 (192)	1,100! (476)	1,930 (154)	1,760 (60)	880 (154)	3,310 (472)	3,120 (621)	‡ (†)	‡ (†)	‡ (†)
Private nonprofit	9,040 (184)	5,280 (94)	5,880 (206)	6,010 (183)	2,320 (39)	5,600 (171)	4,360 (86)	4,140 (67)	3,350 (274)	1,320 (44)	1,230 (48)
4-year doctoral	10,160 (250)	5,650 (147)	7,060 (225)	6,940 (201)	2,420 (74)	6,590 (200)	4,910 (140)	4,560 (106)	3,750 (411)	1,520 (64)	1,360 (79)
Other 4-year	8,460 (253)	5,120 (130)	5,100 (276)	5,500 (275)	2,290 (56)	4,970 (233)	4,000 (115)	3,880 (103)	2,750 (272)	1,190 (48)	1,140 (51)
Less-than-4-year	4,910 (507)	3,980 (258)	2,490 (434)	2,890 (431)	2,140 (149)	1,940 (427)	3,520 (260)	3,410 (257)	‡ (†)	‡ (†)	‡ (†)
Private for-profit	5,460 (321)	5,130 (301)	2,590 (377)	2,290 (116)	1,950 (47)	2,320 (452)	4,910 (276)	4,840 (254)	2,410 (373)	‡ (†)	‡ (†)
2-year and above	6,670 (296)	6,130 (251)	2,820 (528)	2,780 (265)	2,060 (93)	2,670 (582)	5,590 (291)	5,480 (260)	‡ (†)	‡ (†)	‡ (†)
Less-than-2-year	4,480 (425)	4,330 (416)	2,240 (533)	2,010 (95)	1,890 (68)	1,680 (532)	4,180 (383)	4,150 (372)	‡ (†)	‡ (†)	‡ (†)
1995–96, all institutions	**$6,880 (159)**	**$5,250 (61)**	**$4,000 (163)**	**$3,990 (138)**	**$2,000 (23)**	**$3,710 (162)**	**$4,830 (61)**	**$4,770 (58)**	**$2,790 (232)**	**$1,410 (40)**	**$1,350 (37)**
Public	5,160 (105)	4,670 (77)	2,410 (74)	2,740 (68)	1,920 (23)	2,110 (74)	4,390 (87)	4,370 (81)	2,440 (476)	1,390 (63)	1,350 (63)
4-year doctoral	6,230 (124)	5,490 (122)	3,050 (82)	3,250 (107)	1,920 (35)	2,790 (105)	4,910 (149)	4,850 (140)	2,750 (500)	1,330 (100)	1,290 (89)
Other 4-year	5,440 (235)	4,790 (166)	2,170 (81)	2,720 (81)	1,970 (25)	1,870 (60)	4,100 (139)	4,090 (137)	‡ (†)	1,450 (56)	1,380 (58)
2-year	3,130 (162)	3,110 (101)	1,530 (213)	2,020 (106)	1,900 (53)	1,100 (140)	3,140 (120)	3,210 (137)	‡ (†)	1,430 (254)	1,410 (234)
Less-than-2-year	2,440! (887)	2,040 (267)	2,120! (897)	2,190 (485)	1,650 (127)	2,360! (882)	2,870 (441)	2,870 (441)	‡ (†)	‡ (†)	‡ (†)
Private nonprofit	10,870 (388)	6,470 (137)	6,740 (331)	6,640 (312)	2,280 (75)	6,230 (305)	5,600 (128)	5,470 (126)	3,210 (328)	1,430 (52)	1,350 (45)
4-year doctoral	13,130 (727)	7,160 (176)	8,720 (735)	8,370 (674)	2,350 (63)	8,000 (641)	6,260 (188)	6,120 (160)	3,610 (933)	1,660 (84)	1,550 (63)
Other 4-year	10,220 (453)	6,310 (179)	6,040 (357)	6,090 (349)	2,280 (106)	5,590 (345)	5,340 (162)	5,220 (160)	3,300 (417)	1,320 (40)	1,250 (39)
Less-than-4-year	5,310 (229)	4,150 (229)	3,050 (201)	3,230 (364)	2,060 (159)	2,780 (340)	4,520 (189)	4,480 (181)	‡ (†)	1,260 (81)	1,210 (241)
Private for-profit	6,150 (137)	5,540 (162)	3,010 (188)	2,470 (123)	1,940 (30)	2,350 (211)	4,940 (237)	4,920 (212)	2,300 (210)	‡ (†)	‡ (†)
2-year and above	6,850 (235)	6,110 (310)	3,340 (157)	2,880 (264)	2,010 (40)	2,860 (148)	5,330 (164)	5,250 (200)	‡ (†)	‡ (†)	‡ (†)
Less-than-2-year	5,520 (337)	5,020 (318)	2,700 (284)	2,120 (67)	1,880 (43)	1,520 (264)	4,550 (525)	4,570 (443)	2,080 (160)	‡ (†)	‡ (†)
1999–2000, all institutions	**$8,470 (100)**	**$5,970 (58)**	**$5,160 (95)**	**$5,100 (81)**	**$2,520 (19)**	**$4,590 (92)**	**$6,030 (59)**	**$5,430 (51)**	**$4,870 (155)**	**$1,680 (37)**	**$1,570 (39)**
Public	6,140 (90)	5,260 (60)	2,990 (61)	3,520 (55)	2,490 (22)	2,630 (53)	5,180 (72)	4,870 (55)	3,820 (194)	1,720 (56)	1,630 (69)
4-year doctoral	7,410 (84)	6,180 (65)	3,840 (85)	4,170 (77)	2,530 (33)	3,480 (80)	5,620 (81)	5,300 (68)	3,850 (209)	1,780 (45)	1,680 (42)
Other 4-year	6,190 (175)	5,280 (136)	2,690 (105)	3,270 (91)	2,430 (28)	2,290 (83)	4,770 (179)	4,520 (147)	3,540 (426)	1,670 (148)	1,580 (194)
2-year	3,990 (135)	3,670 (96)	1,860 (96)	2,800 (91)	2,490 (45)	1,560 (80)	4,190 (198)	3,750 (122)	4,090 (841)	1,650 (118)	1,580 (105)
Less-than-2-year	3,490 (383)	3,050 (387)	1,900 (296)	2,930 (234)	2,410 (167)	1,750 (357)	5,090 (950)	5,040 (975)	‡ (†)	‡ (†)	‡ (†)
Private nonprofit	14,050 (307)	7,280 (104)	9,390 (238)	8,710 (235)	2,660 (52)	8,280 (218)	7,460 (117)	6,300 (93)	5,750 (211)	1,620 (41)	1,500 (33)
4-year doctoral	16,060 (359)	7,890 (149)	10,910 (326)	10,140 (302)	2,860 (81)	9,600 (283)	8,240 (156)	6,700 (131)	6,430 (237)	1,810 (51)	1,700 (51)
Other 4-year	12,930 (424)	6,930 (162)	8,480 (318)	7,880 (317)	2,530 (70)	7,490 (291)	6,910 (166)	6,020 (149)	5,070 (312)	1,490 (69)	1,330 (47)
Less-than-4-year	7,700 (780)	5,540 (645)	4,680 (485)	5,070 (459)	2,640 (196)	4,340 (550)	6,010 (186)	5,380 (176)	5,590 (1,440)	950 (96)	850 (63)
Private for-profit	8,730 (285)	7,440 (240)	4,120 (296)	3,380 (144)	2,490 (77)	3,110 (285)	6,590 (285)	6,070 (266)	5,970 (474)	‡ (†)	‡ (†)
2-year and above	9,430 (381)	7,920 (315)	4,190 (375)	3,730 (197)	2,550 (109)	3,240 (321)	7,030 (367)	6,530 (345)	6,620 (663)	‡ (†)	‡ (†)
Less-than-2-year	6,730 (354)	6,080 (330)	3,700 (556)	2,490 (64)	2,370 (63)	1,570 (385)	5,240 (355)	4,670 (319)	4,660 (800)	‡ (†)	‡ (†)
2003–04, all institutions	**$9,760 (93)**	**$7,010 (60)**	**$5,690 (118)**	**$5,670 (101)**	**$3,230 (22)**	**$4,930 (125)**	**$7,000 (72)**	**$6,060 (57)**	**$6,100 (138)**	**$1,940 (36)**	**$1,790 (37)**
Public	7,400 (95)	6,260 (90)	3,620 (45)	4,230 (45)	3,190 (31)	3,110 (45)	6,060 (72)	5,520 (64)	5,100 (114)	2,020 (45)	1,860 (51)
4-year doctoral	8,970 (109)	7,360 (99)	4,500 (70)	4,890 (64)	3,220 (39)	3,930 (63)	6,760 (100)	6,150 (81)	5,510 (160)	2,070 (64)	1,900 (66)
Other 4-year	7,870 (183)	6,440 (146)	3,560 (84)	4,230 (118)	3,150 (64)	2,900 (91)	5,870 (127)	5,280 (112)	5,260 (227)	1,930 (86)	1,820 (100)
2-year	4,690 (130)	4,420 (143)	2,140 (84)	3,330 (64)	3,180 (45)	1,810 (86)	4,170 (146)	3,850 (147)	3,700 (207)	2,010 (100)	1,830 (109)
Less-than-2-year	4,770 (389)	4,490 (368)	2,920 (250)	3,180 (206)	2,800 (157)	2,500 (243)	5,260 (621)	4,740 (402)	4,230 (802)	2,460! (1,180)	‡ (†)
Private nonprofit	16,250 (258)	8,480 (127)	10,270 (234)	9,620 (261)	3,390 (49)	8,860 (250)	8,800 (178)	7,040 (135)	7,430 (273)	1,810 (52)	1,670 (51)
4-year doctoral	17,650 (367)	9,000 (204)	11,590 (383)	10,660 (465)	3,460 (101)	9,950 (466)	9,790 (272)	7,600 (190)	8,220 (333)	2,120 (78)	1,980 (75)
Other 4-year	15,650 (352)	8,260 (161)	9,580 (303)	9,130 (295)	3,340 (57)	8,280 (283)	8,270 (219)	6,740 (161)	6,920 (391)	1,620 (56)	1,470 (52)
Less-than-4-year	8,910 (647)	6,240 (375)	5,160 (534)	5,720 (547)	3,560 (333)	4,600 (607)	6,200 (584)	5,630 (470)	4,460 (774)	1,570! (549)	1,580! (557)
Private for-profit	10,480 (328)	8,550 (222)	5,070 (285)	4,300 (167)	3,230 (72)	3,880 (317)	7,640 (267)	6,580 (190)	5,730 (525)	2,660 (275)	2,730 (328)
2-year and above	11,380 (433)	9,100 (297)	5,330 (349)	4,660 (222)	3,370 (101)	4,030 (369)	8,140 (351)	6,950 (253)	6,050 (657)	2,780 (308)	2,890 (361)
Less-than-2-year	7,810 (139)	6,890 (93)	3,980 (157)	3,210 (102)	2,850 (58)	3,010 (185)	6,050 (140)	5,350 (112)	4,560 (205)	1,760 (129)	1,570 (108)

See notes at end of table.

Table 331.70. Average amount of financial aid awarded to full-time, full-year undergraduates, by type and source of aid and control and level of institution: Selected years, 1992–93 through 2015–16—Continued

[Standard errors appear in parentheses]

Control and level of institution	Any aid			Grants			Loans			Work study[1]	
	Total[2]	Federal[3]	Nonfederal	Total[4]	Federal	Nonfederal	Total[5]	Federal[5]	Nonfederal	Total	Federal
1	2	3	4	5	6	7	8	9	10	11	12
2007–08, all institutions	**$12,990 (98)**	**$8,170 (51)**	**$8,130 (89)**	**$7,250 (71)**	**$3,680 (19)**	**$6,470 (79)**	**$9,520 (77)**	**$7,080 (56)**	**$7,800 (112)**	**$2,270 (26)**	**$2,160 (30)**
Public	9,680 (62)	7,250 (51)	5,240 (50)	5,420 (40)	3,670 (18)	4,080 (43)	7,990 (60)	6,470 (58)	6,520 (108)	2,430 (37)	2,360 (44)
4-year doctoral	11,670 (96)	8,320 (82)	6,550 (83)	6,410 (71)	3,780 (33)	5,170 (67)	8,870 (90)	7,100 (83)	7,130 (156)	2,440 (42)	2,290 (46)
Other 4-year	10,040 (136)	7,430 (110)	5,200 (95)	5,420 (88)	3,690 (32)	4,040 (99)	7,690 (123)	6,240 (95)	6,300 (204)	2,280 (69)	2,110 (81)
2-year	5,750 (68)	5,160 (63)	2,510 (45)	3,750 (44)	3,530 (29)	1,860 (35)	5,450 (91)	4,600 (73)	4,670 (150)	2,560 (107)	2,760 (122)
Less-than-2-year	6,210 (528)	5,200 (441)	3,750 (477)	3,610 (212)	3,320 (153)	2,390 (351)	6,910 (500)	5,550 (387)	4,920 (284)	‡ (†)	‡ (†)
Private nonprofit	21,640 (307)	10,020 (158)	14,700 (221)	12,470 (186)	4,090 (51)	11,570 (176)	12,320 (207)	8,350 (164)	9,930 (224)	2,090 (35)	1,930 (35)
4-year doctoral	22,880 (388)	10,380 (192)	15,850 (289)	13,170 (250)	4,280 (82)	12,320 (231)	13,420 (253)	8,840 (213)	11,140 (351)	2,230 (52)	2,080 (55)
Other 4-year	20,620 (447)	9,720 (224)	13,710 (341)	11,880 (268)	3,920 (60)	10,940 (263)	11,330 (313)	7,920 (223)	8,750 (263)	1,970 (40)	1,780 (43)
Less-than-4-year	12,530 (1,097)	8,340 (1,134)	7,270 (1,107)	6,970 (1,588)	4,710 (935)	4,440 (1,230)	11,310 (613)	8,000 (1,208)	8,740 (1,011)	‡ (†)	‡ (†)
Private for-profit	12,890 (294)	9,160 (176)	6,990 (269)	4,050 (96)	3,200 (60)	3,720 (201)	10,260 (233)	7,040 (133)	7,340 (307)	3,650 (392)	3,840 (385)
2-year and above	13,270 (340)	9,270 (203)	7,220 (303)	4,130 (113)	3,180 (73)	3,810 (216)	10,600 (269)	7,140 (153)	7,610 (350)	3,760 (402)	3,940 (386)
Less-than-2-year	10,540 (234)	8,510 (188)	5,100 (250)	3,590 (86)	3,270 (52)	2,470 (381)	8,150 (215)	6,380 (166)	5,320 (212)	‡ (†)	‡ (†)
2011–12, all institutions	**$15,510 (106)**	**$10,820 (75)**	**$9,160 (110)**	**$9,230 (92)**	**$4,580 (20)**	**$8,590 (115)**	**$10,090 (75)**	**$9,160 (69)**	**$6,980 (187)**	**$2,250 (48)**	**$2,180 (37)**
Public	11,420 (93)	9,400 (71)	5,170 (75)	6,610 (62)	4,560 (22)	4,730 (75)	8,860 (87)	8,300 (81)	5,790 (237)	2,330 (60)	2,290 (60)
4-year doctoral	14,130 (125)	11,000 (106)	6,610 (108)	7,880 (101)	4,610 (27)	6,070 (112)	9,750 (112)	9,040 (109)	6,400 (289)	2,410 (80)	2,320 (79)
Other 4-year	11,730 (229)	9,800 (150)	4,920 (170)	6,440 (133)	4,650 (49)	4,410 (155)	8,790 (186)	8,210 (152)	5,630 (483)	2,020 (106)	2,050 (112)
2-year	7,120 (117)	6,740 (91)	2,480 (76)	4,910 (76)	4,460 (41)	2,320 (74)	6,200 (78)	6,060 (79)	3,380 (208)	2,460 (130)	2,460 (146)
Less-than-2-year	7,300 (989)	6,360 (1,018)	2,740 (813)	5,050 (458)	4,510 (464)	2,170! (676)	7,260 (950)	7,060 (939)	‡ (†)	‡ (†)	‡ (†)
Private nonprofit	27,250 (300)	13,300 (217)	17,870 (265)	17,780 (264)	4,710 (46)	16,720 (266)	12,550 (200)	10,930 (190)	8,460 (437)	2,150 (67)	2,050 (44)
4-year doctoral	29,080 (456)	13,700 (355)	19,410 (383)	19,380 (410)	4,690 (81)	18,260 (396)	13,120 (356)	11,420 (330)	8,700 (728)	2,280 (65)	2,220 (60)
Other 4-year	25,630 (384)	12,870 (216)	16,400 (355)	16,370 (336)	4,720 (46)	15,210 (348)	11,960 (167)	10,430 (172)	8,200 (385)	1,980 (130)	1,830 (69)
Less-than-4-year	16,190 (2,359)	12,830 (1,038)	7,610! (2,474)	7,410 (1,336)	4,870 (140)	6,670! (2,156)	11,600 (1,621)	10,330 (1,239)	8,170! (3,055)	2,750 (478)	2,790 (508)
Private for-profit	15,070 (214)	13,300 (173)	6,480 (205)	5,270 (85)	4,520 (49)	4,600 (257)	10,610 (139)	9,440 (107)	7,170 (211)	3,690 (272)	3,760 (291)
2-year and above	15,520 (219)	13,660 (181)	6,530 (218)	5,310 (85)	4,500 (40)	4,580 (267)	10,960 (151)	9,740 (117)	7,350 (222)	3,750 (281)	3,830 (299)
Less-than-2-year	12,170 (633)	10,990 (483)	5,960 (551)	5,050 (268)	4,670 (230)	4,880 (532)	8,370 (313)	7,510 (211)	5,810 (675)	‡ (†)	‡ (†)
2015–16, all institutions	**$18,210 (105)**	**$11,790 (58)**	**$11,240 (121)**	**$11,340 (92)**	**$4,880 (22)**	**$10,220 (114)**	**$11,140 (75)**	**$9,810 (48)**	**$10,200 (238)**	**$2,430 (30)**	**$2,340 (31)**
Public	13,420 (88)	10,330 (59)	6,740 (83)	8,050 (74)	4,840 (22)	6,100 (77)	9,750 (66)	8,920 (53)	8,160 (222)	2,550 (52)	2,430 (50)
4-year doctoral	16,060 (95)	11,870 (81)	8,140 (96)	9,380 (90)	4,890 (28)	7,390 (90)	10,580 (82)	9,650 (63)	8,510 (268)	2,500 (55)	2,400 (55)
Other 4-year	12,820 (215)	9,610 (135)	6,270 (221)	7,570 (199)	4,750 (82)	5,470 (213)	9,250 (182)	8,270 (143)	8,260 (572)	2,470 (139)	2,410 (135)
2-year	7,820 (135)	7,300 (97)	3,130 (172)	5,520 (120)	4,800 (39)	2,990 (179)	6,080 (104)	5,920 (90)	4,490 (460)	2,820 (195)	2,620 (164)
Less-than-2-year	7,230 (637)	7,110 (655)	3,200! (971)	4,690 (480)	4,130 (250)	3,120! (1,031)	7,630 (1,281)	7,630 (1,281)	‡ (†)	‡ (†)	‡ (†)
Private nonprofit	30,920 (310)	14,380 (130)	21,950 (316)	20,610 (265)	5,120 (71)	19,840 (287)	13,870 (193)	11,380 (98)	12,720 (440)	2,330 (35)	2,250 (40)
4-year doctoral	32,620 (442)	14,630 (173)	23,150 (444)	22,010 (380)	5,170 (122)	20,810 (404)	14,800 (255)	11,950 (137)	13,290 (604)	2,450 (52)	2,380 (58)
Other 4-year	29,450 (460)	14,150 (210)	20,610 (449)	19,360 (416)	5,070 (57)	18,700 (426)	12,960 (250)	10,830 (133)	12,100 (604)	2,180 (51)	2,070 (58)
Less-than-4-year	13,150 (897)	12,550 (571)	3,130! (1,333)	5,600 (469)	5,020 (121)	2,600! (994)	8,470 (624)	8,230 (577)	‡ (†)	‡ (†)	‡ (†)
Private for-profit	18,310 (376)	15,960 (330)	6,030 (415)	6,240 (147)	4,730 (55)	4,420 (316)	11,880 (222)	10,850 (191)	10,560 (653)	3,160 (395)	3,160 (407)
2-year and above	19,750 (471)	17,140 (412)	6,130 (462)	6,500 (173)	4,780 (59)	4,510 (349)	12,700 (263)	11,550 (219)	11,210 (742)	3,410 (400)	3,410 (409)
Less-than-2-year	12,580 (470)	11,380 (414)	5,290 (687)	5,190 (258)	4,550 (121)	3,510 (803)	8,680 (359)	8,090 (355)	7,750 (1,036)	‡ (†)	‡ (†)
	Constant 2017–18 dollars[6]										
All institutions											
1992–93	$9,760 (139)	$7,530 (94)	$5,900 (147)	$6,130 (109)	$3,470 (30)	$5,650 (148)	$6,730 (102)	$6,540 (95)	$4,590 (232)	$2,370 (60)	$2,230 (67)
1995–96	11,040 (256)	8,430 (98)	6,430 (261)	6,400 (222)	3,220 (37)	5,960 (261)	7,760 (98)	7,670 (93)	4,480 (373)	2,260 (64)	2,160 (59)
1999–2000	12,410 (146)	8,750 (85)	7,570 (139)	7,470 (118)	3,700 (27)	6,730 (135)	8,840 (86)	7,950 (74)	7,140 (227)	2,460 (54)	2,300 (58)
2003–04	13,020 (124)	9,340 (80)	7,580 (158)	7,560 (134)	4,310 (30)	6,580 (167)	9,330 (96)	8,080 (76)	8,130 (184)	2,580 (47)	2,380 (50)
2007–08	15,220 (115)	9,580 (59)	9,530 (104)	8,500 (83)	4,310 (22)	7,580 (93)	11,150 (90)	8,300 (65)	9,140 (131)	2,660 (30)	2,530 (35)
2011–12	16,910 (116)	11,800 (82)	9,990 (120)	10,070 (100)	4,990 (22)	9,370 (126)	11,010 (82)	9,990 (75)	7,610 (203)	2,450 (52)	2,370 (40)
2015–16	18,970 (110)	12,280 (61)	11,700 (126)	11,810 (96)	5,080 (22)	10,640 (119)	11,610 (79)	10,210 (50)	10,620 (248)	2,540 (31)	2,440 (32)

†Not applicable.
!Interpret data with caution. The coefficient of variation (CV) for this estimate is between 30 and 50 percent.
‡Reporting standards not met. Either there are too few cases for a reliable estimate or the coefficient of variation (CV) is 50 percent or greater.
[1]Details on nonfederal work-study participants are not available.
[2]Includes students who reported that they were awarded aid but did not specify the source or type of aid.
[3]Includes Department of Veterans Affairs and Department of Defense benefits.
[4]Indicates all grants, scholarships, or tuition waivers received from federal, state, institutional, or private sources, including employers.
[5]Includes Parent Loans for Undergraduate Students (PLUS).
[6]Constant dollars based on the Consumer Price Index, prepared by the Bureau of Labor Statistics, U.S. Department of Labor, adjusted to a school-year basis.
NOTE: Aid averages are for those students who received the specified type of aid. Full-time, full-year students were enrolled full time for 9 or more months from July 1 through June 30. Data exclude Puerto Rico.
SOURCE: U.S. Department of Education, National Center for Education Statistics, 1992–93, 1995–96, 1999–2000, 2003–04, 2007–08, 2011–12, and 2015–16 National Postsecondary Student Aid Study (NPSAS:93, NPSAS:96, NPSAS:2000, NPSAS:04, NPSAS:08, NPSAS:12, and NPSAS:16). (This table was prepared May 2019.)

Table 331.90. Percentage of full-time and part-time undergraduates receiving federal aid, by aid program and control and level of institution: 2011–12 and 2015–16

[Standard errors appear in parentheses]

Control and level of institution	Number of undergraduates[1] (in thousands)	Percent receiving federal aid							
			Selected Title IV programs[2]						
		Any federal aid	Any Title IV aid	Pell	SEOG[3]	CWS[4]	Perkins[5]	Stafford[6]	PLUS[7]
1	2	3	4	5	6	7	8	9	10
2011–12									
Full-time, full-year students									
All institutions	**8,864**	**72.8 (0.51)**	**71.4 (0.54)**	**47.1 (0.50)**	**9.0 (0.24)**	**10.5 (0.24)**	**4.2 (0.18)**	**55.1 (0.54)**	**9.1 (0.23)**
Public	5,997	68.4 (0.61)	67.1 (0.64)	45.8 (0.59)	6.6 (0.26)	6.2 (0.23)	2.7 (0.15)	47.1 (0.57)	7.1 (0.28)
4-year doctoral	2,893	70.9 (0.47)	70.1 (0.48)	40.8 (0.39)	7.1 (0.39)	7.4 (0.37)	4.3 (0.30)	60.0 (0.43)	11.4 (0.45)
Other 4-year	969	72.7 (1.34)	71.4 (1.43)	48.1 (1.07)	6.5 (0.52)	8.6 (0.61)	2.8 (0.35)	54.0 (1.53)	8.1 (0.67)
2-year	2,104	63.0 (1.24)	61.0 (1.29)	51.4 (1.30)	5.9 (0.40)	3.4 (0.28)	0.3 (0.06)	26.5 (0.99)	1.0 (0.11)
Less-than-2-year	31	67.8 (4.72)	66.4 (5.20)	62.4 (5.04)	‡ (†)	‡ (†)	# (†)	19.7 (4.83)	‡ (†)
Private, nonprofit	1,875	76.1 (0.75)	74.9 (0.75)	37.2 (0.64)	12.2 (0.60)	29.2 (0.81)	10.6 (0.61)	66.0 (0.90)	16.5 (0.67)
4-year doctoral	990	74.3 (0.94)	73.4 (0.96)	34.5 (0.77)	11.0 (0.89)	30.0 (1.26)	13.3 (0.97)	64.4 (1.08)	16.7 (1.10)
Other 4-year	849	78.0 (1.20)	76.7 (1.17)	39.8 (1.11)	13.6 (0.74)	29.1 (1.14)	8.0 (0.69)	68.2 (1.48)	16.2 (0.76)
Less-than-4-year	36	78.1 (5.04)	74.6 (5.35)	48.5 (6.54)	13.1 ! (5.38)	‡ (†)	‡ (†)	59.0 (7.42)	13.9 (3.36)
Private, for-profit	992	93.1 (0.51)	90.4 (0.52)	73.8 (0.81)	17.8 (0.87)	1.8 (0.20)	1.4 (0.23)	83.2 (0.90)	7.1 (0.44)
2-year and above	859	92.8 (0.59)	89.7 (0.59)	72.1 (0.91)	15.7 (0.81)	2.1 (0.23)	1.6 (0.27)	83.3 (0.91)	7.3 (0.48)
Less-than-2-year	133	95.2 (0.79)	95.1 (0.80)	85.0 (1.46)	31.4 (4.40)	‡ (†)	‡ (†)	82.9 (3.51)	5.9 (0.77)
Part-time or part-year students									
All institutions	**14,192**	**51.1 (1.10)**	**48.4 (1.09)**	**37.6 (0.85)**	**4.4 (0.19)**	**2.0 (0.12)**	**0.9 (0.08)**	**30.7 (0.44)**	**1.6 (0.10)**
Public	10,929	44.5 (1.22)	42.4 (1.13)	33.4 (0.89)	2.6 (0.14)	1.6 (0.11)	0.5 (0.05)	22.1 (0.43)	1.0 (0.08)
Private, nonprofit	1,135	61.0 (1.61)	56.5 (1.99)	34.8 (1.51)	6.8 (0.66)	7.1 (0.76)	1.9 (0.30)	49.5 (1.57)	4.3 (0.51)
Private, for-profit	2,128	79.7 (0.83)	75.2 (1.16)	60.5 (1.09)	12.8 (0.83)	0.9 (0.14)	2.0 (0.47)	65.3 (0.47)	3.4 (0.32)
2015–16									
Full-time, full-year students									
All institutions	**7,239**	**69.8 (0.33)**	**68.4 (0.34)**	**44.0 (0.31)**	**10.4 (0.22)**	**9.1 (0.25)**	**4.3 (0.17)**	**52.0 (0.34)**	**9.3 (0.18)**
Public	5,023	67.7 (0.42)	66.3 (0.42)	44.3 (0.38)	8.6 (0.25)	5.8 (0.24)	3.3 (0.18)	46.3 (0.40)	7.8 (0.18)
4-year doctoral	2,849	69.4 (0.48)	68.3 (0.48)	41.3 (0.38)	9.4 (0.35)	7.1 (0.35)	4.9 (0.29)	56.9 (0.44)	11.5 (0.28)
Other 4-year	765	72.6 (0.98)	70.9 (1.05)	45.0 (1.20)	7.2 (0.54)	5.2 (0.67)	2.7 (0.49)	50.4 (1.25)	7.3 (0.49)
2-year	1,391	61.6 (0.85)	59.5 (0.86)	50.0 (0.80)	8.0 (0.51)	3.4 (0.41)	0.5 (0.08)	22.6 (0.62)	0.6 (0.10)
Less-than-2-year	19	67.0 (8.01)	64.4 (8.15)	56.0 (7.26)	3.0 ! (1.20)	‡ (†)	‡ (†)	25.1 (6.39)	‡ (†)
Private, nonprofit	1,735	70.3 (0.61)	69.6 (0.59)	35.5 (0.52)	13.9 (0.46)	21.0 (0.75)	8.2 (0.52)	61.9 (0.63)	14.0 (0.43)
4-year doctoral	1,011	67.5 (0.89)	66.8 (0.88)	31.9 (0.61)	13.2 (0.49)	21.3 (1.03)	9.0 (0.71)	58.6 (0.82)	14.2 (0.63)
Other 4-year	684	73.7 (0.89)	73.0 (0.86)	38.7 (0.81)	15.3 (0.82)	21.7 (1.22)	7.4 (0.76)	66.3 (1.00)	14.2 (0.55)
Less-than-4-year	40	81.7 (3.76)	81.0 (3.83)	72.2 (4.88)	‡ (†)	‡ (†)	‡ (†)	70.7 (5.65)	‡ (†)
Private, for-profit	481	89.4 (0.71)	86.7 (0.68)	71.9 (0.85)	15.6 (0.95)	1.5 (0.23)	0.7 (0.16)	76.5 (0.79)	8.0 (0.59)
2-year and above	382	89.7 (0.77)	86.3 (0.74)	70.4 (0.97)	16.2 (0.81)	1.5 (0.28)	0.8 (0.21)	77.2 (0.79)	7.8 (0.48)
Less-than-2-year	99	88.6 (1.74)	88.2 (1.76)	77.5 (2.19)	13.2 (3.37)	1.1 ! (0.54)	‡ (†)	73.9 (2.40)	8.8 (2.05)
Part-time or part-year students									
All institutions	**12,069**	**47.6 (0.26)**	**45.4 (0.24)**	**35.5 (0.20)**	**5.9 (0.16)**	**1.8 (0.15)**	**0.8 (0.07)**	**27.0 (0.21)**	**1.4 (0.08)**
Public	9,468	42.0 (0.30)	40.0 (0.28)	31.4 (0.24)	4.4 (0.16)	1.5 (0.16)	0.6 (0.05)	19.8 (0.21)	0.9 (0.07)
4-year doctoral	1,825	55.5 (0.71)	53.5 (0.73)	34.1 (0.72)	5.5 (0.37)	2.2 (0.26)	2.5 (0.26)	43.4 (0.67)	3.6 (0.32)
Other 4-year	1,346	44.8 (1.25)	42.8 (1.12)	32.9 (0.99)	3.5 (0.42)	1.1 (0.24)	0.4 (0.08)	21.9 (0.75)	1.0 (0.19)
2-year	6,249	37.5 (0.38)	35.5 (0.35)	30.3 (0.30)	4.3 (0.19)	1.4 (0.24)	# (†)	12.6 (0.15)	0.1 (0.02)
Less-than-2-year	48	38.4 (2.59)	35.2 (2.52)	30.0 (2.05)	1.9 ! (0.61)	‡ (†)	‡ (†)	12.4 (2.70)	‡ (†)
Private, nonprofit	1,220	58.0 (1.03)	55.9 (1.03)	37.7 (0.93)	8.0 (0.69)	4.7 (0.63)	2.7 (0.50)	46.7 (0.93)	3.7 (0.40)
4-year doctoral	622	53.5 (1.58)	51.4 (1.55)	32.5 (1.37)	6.5 (0.77)	4.8 (0.98)	3.5 (0.89)	44.7 (1.34)	3.4 (0.52)
Other 4-year	540	61.6 (1.13)	59.5 (1.16)	41.7 (1.18)	9.5 (1.14)	4.9 (0.79)	2.0 (0.46)	48.5 (1.12)	3.9 (0.63)
Less-than-4-year	58	73.2 (4.47)	70.2 (4.96)	56.2 (5.18)	9.0 ! (3.71)	1.1 ! (0.47)	‡ (†)	52.7 (4.60)	3.7 ! (1.39)
Private, for-profit	1,381	77.0 (0.59)	73.5 (0.53)	61.5 (0.57)	14.6 (0.76)	0.9 (0.11)	0.8 (0.19)	58.4 (0.53)	3.0 (0.28)
2-year and above	1,140	77.5 (0.67)	73.6 (0.60)	61.4 (0.60)	15.6 (0.87)	1.0 (0.12)	0.9 (0.22)	59.2 (0.47)	2.9 (0.31)
Less-than-2-year	240	74.6 (1.55)	73.1 (1.41)	61.8 (1.63)	9.9 (1.60)	0.7 ! (0.32)	‡ (†)	54.6 (2.11)	3.5 (0.63)

†Not applicable.
#Rounds to zero.
!Interpret data with caution. The coefficient of variation (CV) for this estimate is between 30 and 50 percent.
‡Reporting standards not met. The coefficient of variation (CV) for this estimate is 50 percent or greater.
[1]Numbers of undergraduates may not equal figures reported in other tables, since these data are based on a sample survey of students who enrolled at any point during the year.
[2]Refers to Title IV of the Higher Education Act.
[3]Supplemental Educational Opportunity Grants.
[4]College Work Study. Prior to October 17, 1986, private for-profit institutions were prohibited by law from spending CWS funds for on-campus work. Includes persons who participated in the program but had no earnings.
[5]Formerly National Direct Student Loans (NDSL).
[6]Formerly Guaranteed Student Loans (GSL).
[7]Parent Loans for Undergraduate Students.
NOTE: Full-time, full-year undergraduates are those who were enrolled full time for 9 or more months. Part-time or part-year undergraduates include those who were enrolled part time for 9 or more months and those who were enrolled for less than 9 months either part time or full time. Excludes students whose attendance status was not reported. Detail may not sum to totals because of rounding and because some students receive multiple types of aid and aid from different sources. Data exclude students attending institutions in Puerto Rico.
SOURCE: U.S. Department of Education, National Center for Education Statistics, 2011–12 and 2015–16 National Postsecondary Student Aid Study (NPSAS:12 and NPSAS:16). (This table was prepared June 2018.)

Table 331.95. Percentage of undergraduate degree/certificate completers who ever received loans and average cumulative amount borrowed, by degree level, selected student characteristics, and institution control: Selected years, 1999–2000 through 2015–16

[Standard errors appear in parentheses]

Degree level, selected student characteristic, and institution control	1999–2000			2011–12				2015–16			
	Loans to students			Loans to students				Loans to students			
	Total loans to students	Federal loan to students	Parent PLUS Loans[1]	Total loans to students	Federal loans to students	Nonfederal loans	Parent PLUS Loans[1]	Total loans to students	Federal loan to students	Nonfederal loans	Parent PLUS Loans[1]
1	2	3	4	5	6	7	8	9	10	11	12
	Percent of completers who ever received loans										
Total, all completers	**52.5 (0.75)**	**50.5 (0.74)**	**7.2 (0.27)**	**61.6 (0.62)**	**58.6 (0.62)**	**24.8 (0.50)**	**10.5 (0.40)**	**61.8 (0.55)**	**59.7 (0.56)**	**10.4 (0.27)**	**10.3 (0.24)**
Certificate below associate's level	**43.5 (2.64)**	**39.6 (2.57)**	**3.3 (0.55)**	**66.3 (1.71)**	**63.8 (1.79)**	**23.4 (1.25)**	**7.9 (0.83)**	**67.7 (1.76)**	**65.9 (1.88)**	**9.2 (0.71)**	**7.2 (0.65)**
Sex											
Male	39.3 (3.48)	35.9 (3.55)	3.4 (0.81)	58.0 (2.93)	55.9 (3.00)	21.5 (2.01)	8.7 (1.67)	57.4 (3.21)	55.9 (3.25)	7.7 (0.86)	8.4 (1.25)
Female	46.7 (3.12)	42.5 (2.95)	3.3 (0.68)	70.0 (1.90)	67.2 (1.96)	24.2 (1.50)	7.6 (0.93)	73.6 (1.75)	71.6 (1.87)	10.0 (0.93)	6.6 (0.76)
Institution control											
Public	27.1 (2.64)	22.2 (2.26)	0.9! (0.39)	36.2 (3.17)	31.8 (3.18)	10.5 (1.81)	1.8! (0.74)	44.6 (2.43)	43.0 (2.47)	4.3 (0.96)	3.4 (0.82)
Private nonprofit	53.2 (7.86)	49.8 (7.91)	9.8! (3.05)	76.1 (5.06)	73.3 (5.80)	23.1 (4.84)	‡ (†)	80.1 (3.50)	76.4 (4.97)	11.9 (2.42)	6.4! (2.07)
Private for-profit	86.3 (1.60)	85.0 (1.75)	8.5 (1.33)	85.9 (1.73)	84.6 (1.92)	32.2 (1.64)	12.0 (1.27)	87.5 (1.58)	85.7 (1.89)	13.3 (1.11)	11.0 (0.98)
Associate's degree	**38.9 (1.59)**	**36.9 (1.65)**	**4.3 (0.54)**	**49.8 (1.09)**	**46.1 (1.03)**	**18.7 (0.83)**	**5.0 (0.44)**	**48.1 (1.04)**	**46.2 (1.04)**	**5.8 (0.46)**	**5.1 (0.42)**
Sex											
Male	37.9 (2.76)	36.0 (2.82)	5.8 (1.28)	46.2 (1.75)	42.1 (1.73)	18.6 (1.05)	6.0 (0.75)	41.9 (1.48)	39.8 (1.46)	5.3 (0.72)	5.4 (0.72)
Female	39.4 (2.04)	37.4 (2.11)	3.5 (0.80)	52.3 (1.41)	48.9 (1.29)	18.9 (1.13)	4.3 (0.47)	52.5 (1.25)	50.8 (1.28)	6.1 (0.58)	4.9 (0.49)
Race/ethnicity											
White	39.5 (2.04)	37.4 (2.03)	4.5 (0.76)	49.2 (1.52)	45.7 (1.54)	19.8 (1.11)	5.0 (0.54)	50.2 (1.60)	48.4 (1.63)	6.4 (0.66)	6.1 (0.67)
Black	44.5 (4.38)	42.3 (4.26)	2.8! (1.06)	66.2 (2.62)	60.8 (2.67)	22.1 (2.06)	3.2 (0.93)	66.7 (2.41)	65.6 (2.48)	5.4 (1.03)	4.2 (0.72)
Hispanic	41.3 (5.26)	39.5 (5.00)	7.2! (2.98)	44.6 (2.34)	40.7 (2.28)	15.8 (1.60)	5.9 (1.18)	35.4 (1.89)	34.0 (1.86)	3.6 (0.70)	4.1 (0.73)
Asian	16.9! (5.79)	16.3! (5.73)	‡ (†)	26.1 (4.11)	23.0 (3.93)	9.9 (2.87)	6.1! (2.18)	26.7 (3.28)	22.1 (3.07)	6.2! (1.95)	2.5! (0.88)
Pacific Islander	‡ (†)	‡ (†)	‡ (†)	‡ (†)	‡ (†)	‡ (†)	‡ (†)	47.3 (11.14)	41.7 (11.28)	‡ (†)	‡ (†)
American Indian/Alaska Native	‡ (†)	‡ (†)	‡ (†)	64.6 (11.14)	64.6 (11.14)	‡ (†)	‡ (†)	67.2 (10.02)	63.3 (10.20)	19.0! (8.22)	‡ (†)
Two or more races	‡ (†)	‡ (†)	‡ (†)	52.1 (6.13)	51.5 (5.97)	21.9 (5.24)	6.2! (2.47)	47.1 (5.10)	45.5 (5.18)	6.4! (2.55)	4.6! (1.95)
Other[2]	‡ (†)	‡ (†)	‡ (†)	† (†)	† (†)	† (†)	† (†)	† (†)	† (†)	† (†)	† (†)
Dependency status											
Dependent	36.7 (2.91)	35.6 (2.89)	8.9 (1.38)	41.3 (1.57)	38.6 (1.54)	16.2 (1.10)	7.9 (0.79)	34.9 (1.57)	33.2 (1.50)	4.4 (0.51)	5.3 (0.59)
Independent	40.1 (1.87)	37.6 (2.04)	1.7 (0.50)	54.7 (1.39)	50.4 (1.34)	20.2 (1.01)	3.3 (0.48)	55.4 (1.29)	53.4 (1.35)	6.5 (0.65)	5.0 (0.59)
Institution control											
Public	32.6 (1.66)	30.6 (1.69)	1.9 (0.48)	42.1 (1.28)	38.1 (1.17)	14.9 (0.87)	3.2 (0.40)	40.9 (1.15)	38.8 (1.15)	4.8 (0.49)	3.9 (0.47)
Private nonprofit	45.7 (5.92)	43.0 (5.63)	11.1! (3.83)	86.9 (5.23)	84.8 (6.80)	43.2 (6.75)	12.5! (4.28)	83.9 (3.01)	83.1 (3.26)	11.9 (3.49)	9.0 (1.99)
Private for-profit	92.5 (1.29)	91.6 (1.20)	22.4 (3.49)	88.3 (1.77)	86.4 (1.87)	37.2 (1.93)	14.1 (1.63)	88.3 (1.16)	87.8 (1.15)	10.6 (0.86)	12.4 (1.02)
Bachelor's degree	**62.2 (0.70)**	**61.0 (0.70)**	**10.2 (0.40)**	**69.0 (0.75)**	**66.3 (0.72)**	**29.8 (0.79)**	**15.5 (0.68)**	**68.9 (0.62)**	**66.7 (0.64)**	**13.8 (0.33)**	**14.6 (0.36)**
Sex											
Male	61.4 (1.00)	60.2 (1.01)	10.6 (0.56)	67.0 (1.39)	63.9 (1.37)	29.4 (1.20)	15.1 (1.00)	65.7 (0.85)	63.3 (0.86)	13.3 (0.53)	14.8 (0.57)
Female	62.8 (0.94)	61.6 (0.92)	9.8 (0.54)	70.5 (0.94)	68.2 (0.92)	30.1 (1.04)	15.9 (0.92)	71.4 (0.71)	69.3 (0.75)	14.2 (0.44)	14.4 (0.46)
Race/ethnicity											
White	60.7 (0.87)	59.5 (0.85)	10.2 (0.45)	67.5 (0.94)	64.8 (0.92)	30.2 (1.03)	16.0 (0.87)	69.4 (0.69)	67.1 (0.70)	15.5 (0.45)	15.7 (0.44)
Black	80.5 (1.81)	80.0 (1.82)	13.9 (1.66)	84.2 (1.78)	82.0 (1.92)	33.2 (2.37)	16.9 (1.83)	84.9 (1.17)	83.8 (1.20)	10.6 (1.03)	16.7 (1.23)
Hispanic	68.7 (1.86)	67.1 (2.00)	11.7 (1.69)	71.9 (2.42)	69.2 (2.32)	30.0 (2.08)	15.1 (1.82)	66.6 (1.57)	64.7 (1.59)	10.2 (0.80)	11.8 (0.94)
Asian	50.2 (2.43)	49.0 (2.55)	4.3 (0.85)	47.2 (3.22)	42.7 (3.02)	20.5 (2.49)	7.8 (1.70)	45.1 (2.04)	41.4 (1.98)	10.6 (1.02)	8.7 (1.19)
Pacific Islander	66.7 (6.35)	66.7 (6.35)	19.1 (5.45)	‡ (†)	‡ (†)	‡ (†)	‡ (†)	89.4 (4.56)	80.7 (8.09)	18.3! (8.05)	14.1! (5.77)
American Indian/Alaska Native	75.2 (6.58)	71.8 (6.80)	3.8! (1.73)	61.5 (11.92)	60.2 (12.04)	19.5! (8.06)	‡ (†)	76.1 (5.87)	69.9 (6.68)	14.4 (4.23)	6.9! (2.22)
Two or more races	55.0 (5.12)	52.7 (5.48)	7.6 (1.95)	81.0 (3.68)	78.7 (3.94)	31.7 (4.43)	21.0 (4.63)	72.9 (2.35)	70.1 (2.60)	17.5 (2.58)	17.1 (2.01)
Other[2]	53.5 (6.22)	53.1 (6.19)	6.3! (2.25)	† (†)	† (†)	† (†)	† (†)	† (†)	† (†)	† (†)	† (†)
Dependency status											
Dependent	59.2 (0.95)	58.0 (0.92)	14.4 (0.63)	64.9 (1.09)	61.6 (1.06)	29.8 (1.02)	21.0 (0.96)	65.9 (0.69)	63.4 (0.70)	15.9 (0.43)	18.9 (0.54)
Independent	65.9 (0.92)	64.8 (0.94)	4.9 (0.34)	74.1 (1.16)	72.2 (1.13)	29.7 (1.19)	8.6 (0.76)	72.6 (0.92)	70.6 (0.97)	11.3 (0.52)	9.3 (0.50)
Institution control											
Public	60.0 (0.80)	58.8 (0.81)	8.3 (0.42)	64.1 (0.89)	61.2 (0.86)	25.9 (0.84)	13.5 (0.69)	66.4 (0.68)	64.1 (0.66)	11.7 (0.40)	13.7 (0.45)
Private nonprofit	66.2 (1.16)	65.2 (1.17)	14.1 (0.93)	73.5 (1.72)	70.7 (1.74)	34.6 (1.83)	21.5 (1.75)	69.2 (0.94)	66.7 (0.96)	17.9 (0.75)	17.0 (0.66)
Private for-profit	77.2 (4.41)	77.0 (4.45)	10.8! (3.55)	87.2 (1.62)	86.3 (1.59)	40.5 (1.76)	10.9 (1.17)	86.5 (1.95)	85.3 (2.43)	15.1 (1.16)	12.7 (1.63)

See notes at end of table.

Table 331.95. Percentage of undergraduate degree/certificate completers who ever received loans and average cumulative amount borrowed, by degree level, selected student characteristics, and institution control: Selected years, 1999–2000 through 2015–16—Continued

[Standard errors appear in parentheses]

Degree level, selected student characteristic, and institution control	1999–2000			2011–12				2015–16			
	Loans to students			Loans to students				Loans to students			
	Total loans to students	Federal loan to students	Parent PLUS Loans[1]	Total loans to students	Federal loans to students	Nonfederal loans	Parent PLUS Loans[1]	Total loans to students	Federal loan to students	Nonfederal loans	Parent PLUS Loans[1]
1	2	3	4	5	6	7	8	9	10	11	12
	Average cumulative loan amount for students with loans (current dollars)[3]										
Total, all completers	**$14,260 (186)**	**$13,540 (162)**	**$12,630 (443)**	**$23,050 (285)**	**$19,510 (208)**	**$11,210 (450)**	**$22,990 (1,197)**	**$24,480 (336)**	**$22,520 (305)**	**$16,160 (439)**	**$27,170 (676)**
Certificate below associate's level	**7,790 (418)**	**7,150 (330)**	**6,850 (1,081)**	**13,280 (374)**	**11,380 (343)**	**6,630 (526)**	**8,900 (612)**	**15,520 (502)**	**14,280 (413)**	**12,080 (1,649)**	**12,920 (1,158)**
Sex											
Male	8,110 (533)	7,550 (544)	8,290 (2,316)	13,370 (743)	10,970 (629)	7,540 (1,314)	10,080 (1,199)	15,380 (1,091)	13,760 (891)	14,630 (3,942)	16,320 (2,136)
Female	7,590 (492)	6,900 (373)	5,720 (941)	13,250 (393)	11,520 (357)	6,280 (510)	8,300 (775)	15,590 (476)	14,520 (423)	10,950 (1,549)	10,450 (1,172)
Institution control											
Public	7,640 (819)	7,540 (623)	‡ (†)	12,420 (1,151)	11,030 (1,095)	9,410 (2,241)	‡ (†)	16,400 (1,080)	15,550 (946)	‡ (†)	‡ (†)
Private nonprofit	11,240 (2,280)	9,880 (1,828)	9,680 (2,443)	15,820 (2,721)	11,850 (1,463)	14,530! (6,937)	‡ (†)	17,110 (2,536)	15,840 (1,951)	13,520! (6,105)	17,470! (6,447)
Private for-profit	7,470 (323)	6,540 (287)	6,260 (1,604)	13,320 (345)	11,430 (329)	5,510 (338)	9,180 (650)	14,880 (434)	13,480 (326)	11,040 (1,616)	11,110 (943)
Associate's degree	**9,490 (334)**	**8,840 (339)**	**7,630 (1,046)**	**17,160 (359)**	**15,130 (305)**	**8,370 (413)**	**14,830 (1,095)**	**18,550 (408)**	**18,060 (392)**	**9,950 (1,136)**	**12,980 (1,148)**
Sex											
Male	9,320 (698)	8,590 (663)	7,860 (2,013)	15,950 (536)	13,930 (418)	8,090 (561)	16,000 (1,696)	17,010 (652)	16,150 (552)	13,220 (2,547)	13,500 (1,712)
Female	9,570 (436)	8,970 (384)	7,430 (803)	17,900 (535)	15,850 (447)	8,570 (621)	13,690 (1,445)	19,420 (492)	19,110 (485)	7,970 (792)	12,580 (1,338)
Race/ethnicity											
White	9,590 (480)	8,910 (433)	8,510 (1,285)	17,110 (485)	14,630 (377)	8,810 (577)	15,400 (1,429)	17,760 (533)	17,100 (486)	10,210 (1,837)	13,350 (1,638)
Black	9,500 (771)	8,590 (659)	‡ (†)	19,280 (922)	17,580 (783)	9,380 (1,321)	15,050 (4,419)	22,300 (834)	21,930 (792)	9,020 (2,182)	11,310 (1,748)
Hispanic	8,840 (2,037)	9,090 (2,124)	‡ (†)	15,170 (912)	14,020 (786)	6,650 (667)	12,220 (1,572)	15,970 (904)	15,590 (928)	9,770 (1,659)	12,440 (1,563)
Asian	‡ (†)	‡ (†)	‡ (†)	13,580 (1,965)	13,400 (1,786)	4,640 (902)	‡ (†)	16,830 (1,772)	17,720 (1,981)	9,340 (2,170)	‡ (†)
Pacific Islander	‡ (†)	‡ (†)	‡ (†)	‡ (†)	‡ (†)	‡ (†)	‡ (†)	‡ (†)	‡ (†)	‡ (†)	‡ (†)
American Indian/Alaska Native	‡ (†)	‡ (†)	‡ (†)	22,330 (3,730)	22,100 (3,720)	‡ (†)	‡ (†)	18,230 (3,431)	17,830 (3,110)	‡ (†)	‡ (†)
Two or more races	‡ (†)	‡ (†)	‡ (†)	17,570 (1,740)	15,260 (1,453)	5,920 (1,367)	‡ (†)	21,790 (2,159)	20,940 (2,134)	‡ (†)	‡ (†)
Other[2]	‡ (†)	‡ (†)	‡ (†)	† (†)	† (†)	† (†)	† (†)	† (†)	† (†)	† (†)	† (†)
Dependency status											
Dependent	8,280 (530)	7,400 (452)	8,830 (1,306)	13,240 (512)	11,200 (391)	7,090 (618)	15,520 (1,739)	12,140 (438)	11,660 (440)	8,340 (1,100)	15,470 (1,677)
Independent	10,120 (479)	9,630 (459)	‡ (†)	18,860 (471)	16,860 (420)	8,960 (534)	13,880 (1,419)	20,780 (474)	20,250 (448)	10,550 (1,504)	11,510 (1,381)
Institution control											
Public	8,060 (431)	7,360 (398)	‡ (†)	13,970 (349)	12,300 (315)	8,080 (538)	12,070 (1,154)	15,640 (511)	15,230 (494)	10,110 (1,639)	11,600 (1,490)
Private nonprofit	11,850 (1,035)	11,950 (999)	‡ (†)	25,310 (2,076)	20,420 (1,564)	10,790 (2,742)	‡ (†)	24,830 (1,159)	23,890 (1,239)	8,180 (2,395)	14,950 (2,567)
Private for-profit	13,440 (685)	12,540 (672)	9,550 (1,804)	24,680 (624)	21,550 (537)	8,550 (486)	17,590 (1,854)	26,420 (512)	25,340 (537)	10,220 (718)	15,740 (1,994)
Bachelor's degree	**17,480 (204)**	**16,530 (180)**	**14,350 (548)**	**29,380 (456)**	**24,400 (295)**	**13,760 (704)**	**27,350 (1,613)**	**29,910 (402)**	**27,050 (384)**	**18,700 (432)**	**32,600 (796)**
Sex											
Male	17,470 (247)	16,530 (232)	14,730 (784)	29,030 (666)	23,740 (451)	14,630 (1,044)	29,780 (3,015)	28,920 (477)	26,120 (429)	18,760 (800)	33,790 (1,296)
Female	17,490 (256)	16,530 (230)	14,050 (627)	29,650 (551)	24,890 (378)	13,090 (857)	25,530 (1,602)	30,610 (451)	27,710 (420)	18,650 (641)	31,660 (967)
Race/ethnicity											
White	17,370 (211)	16,390 (195)	14,720 (591)	29,060 (579)	23,690 (354)	14,050 (766)	27,450 (2,033)	30,090 (346)	26,460 (325)	20,040 (595)	34,370 (1,088)
Black	19,510 (793)	18,760 (718)	10,880 (1,006)	33,020 (1,066)	29,200 (842)	11,620 (1,662)	24,490 (4,344)	34,000 (877)	32,370 (809)	16,450 (1,555)	24,800 (2,009)
Hispanic	17,450 (821)	16,270 (626)	13,810 (1,693)	29,520 (1,584)	23,710 (825)	16,050 (2,820)	26,470 (3,900)	26,820 (774)	25,420 (725)	13,900 (1,028)	29,440 (2,070)
Asian	14,540 (619)	13,990 (545)	20,260 (4,188)	23,130 (1,259)	20,740 (1,041)	10,070 (2,255)	‡ (†)	25,450 (1,094)	22,770 (882)	19,250 (2,191)	34,080 (3,962)
Pacific Islander	18,380 (1,787)	16,850 (1,222)	‡ (†)	‡ (†)	‡ (†)	‡ (†)	‡ (†)	26,520 (3,981)	27,690 (3,236)	‡ (†)	‡ (†)
American Indian/Alaska Native	18,770 (1,553)	18,290 (1,646)	‡ (†)	‡ (†)	‡ (†)	‡ (†)	‡ (†)	26,380 (2,659)	25,550 (2,696)	‡ (†)	‡ (†)
Two or more races	17,720 (1,352)	16,470 (1,229)	‡ (†)	28,050 (1,731)	23,950 (1,427)	12,250 (2,067)	‡ (†)	29,680 (1,097)	27,280 (940)	14,490 (1,605)	40,070 (3,890)
Other[2]	16,210 (1,378)	15,250 (1,361)	‡ (†)	† (†)	† (†)	† (†)	† (†)	† (†)	† (†)	† (†)	† (†)
Dependency status											
Dependent	16,910 (221)	15,620 (177)	15,680 (671)	26,070 (575)	20,370 (285)	14,700 (917)	28,410 (1,566)	26,760 (282)	22,450 (199)	21,340 (575)	36,790 (1,047)
Independent	18,110 (320)	17,540 (300)	9,490 (802)	33,040 (637)	28,740 (481)	12,570 (905)	24,060 (4,374)	33,340 (649)	32,010 (587)	14,230 (634)	22,420 (1,257)
Institution control											
Public	16,210 (233)	15,700 (213)	11,600 (550)	25,640 (454)	22,030 (336)	11,400 (621)	20,460 (1,080)	26,930 (278)	25,000 (235)	15,770 (611)	27,530 (990)
Private nonprofit	19,620 (373)	17,810 (313)	17,950 (810)	32,310 (1,181)	24,610 (594)	18,370 (1,698)	37,130 (3,739)	31,890 (453)	26,670 (331)	23,840 (766)	41,940 (1,853)
Private for-profit	24,040 (1,204)	23,170 (1,160)	‡ (†)	40,040 (798)	34,880 (612)	11,870 (911)	25,650 (2,506)	41,320 (1,592)	39,150 (1,303)	15,460 (1,060)	31,890 (2,316)

See notes at end of table.

Table 331.95. Percentage of undergraduate degree/certificate completers who ever received loans and average cumulative amount borrowed, by degree level, selected student characteristics, and institution control: Selected years, 1999–2000 through 2015–16—Continued

[Standard errors appear in parentheses]

Degree level, selected student characteristic, and institution control	1999–2000			2011–12				2015–16			
	Loans to students			Loans to students				Loans to students			
	Total loans to students	Federal loan to students	Parent PLUS Loans[1]	Total loans to students	Federal loans to students	Nonfederal loans	Parent PLUS Loans[1]	Total loans to students	Federal loan to students	Nonfederal loans	Parent PLUS Loans[1]
1	2	3	4	5	6	7	8	9	10	11	12
	Average cumulative loan amount for students with loans (constant 2017–18 dollars)[3,4]										
Total, all completers	**$20,900 (273)**	**$19,840 (238)**	**$18,510 (649)**	**$25,140 (311)**	**$21,270 (227)**	**$12,230 (490)**	**$25,070 (1,305)**	**$25,500 (350)**	**$23,450 (317)**	**$16,830 (457)**	**$28,290 (704)**
Certificate below associate's level	**11,420 (613)**	**10,490 (484)**	**10,040 (1,584)**	**14,480 (408)**	**12,410 (374)**	**7,230 (574)**	**9,700 (667)**	**16,170 (522)**	**14,870 (430)**	**12,580 (1,717)**	**13,460 (1,206)**
Sex											
Male	11,880 (781)	11,070 (798)	12,150 (3,394)	14,570 (810)	11,960 (686)	8,220 (1,433)	11,000 (1,308)	16,010 (1,136)	14,330 (928)	15,230 (4,105)	17,000 (2,224)
Female	11,130 (722)	10,120 (547)	8,380 (1,379)	14,450 (428)	12,570 (389)	6,850 (556)	9,050 (845)	16,230 (495)	15,120 (440)	11,400 (1,613)	10,890 (1,221)
Institution control											
Public	11,200 (1,200)	11,050 (913)	‡ (†)	13,540 (1,255)	12,030 (1,194)	10,260 (2,443)	‡ (†)	17,080 (1,124)	16,200 (985)	‡ (†)	‡ (†)
Private nonprofit	16,470 (3,341)	14,480 (2,679)	14,190 (3,581)	17,250 (2,967)	12,920 (1,596)	15,840! (7,564)	‡ (†)	17,820 (2,640)	16,490 (2,031)	14,080! (6,358)	18,190! (6,713)
Private for-profit	10,950 (474)	9,590 (420)	9,170 (2,351)	14,530 (376)	12,460 (359)	6,010 (368)	10,010 (709)	15,500 (452)	14,030 (339)	11,500 (1,682)	11,570 (982)
Associate's degree	**13,900 (490)**	**12,960 (497)**	**11,190 (1,532)**	**18,710 (392)**	**16,500 (333)**	**9,130 (450)**	**16,170 (1,194)**	**19,320 (425)**	**18,810 (408)**	**10,360 (1,183)**	**13,520 (1,196)**
Sex											
Male	13,660 (1,023)	12,590 (972)	11,530 (2,950)	17,390 (584)	15,190 (456)	8,820 (611)	17,440 (1,849)	17,710 (678)	16,820 (575)	13,770 (2,653)	14,050 (1,783)
Female	14,030 (639)	13,150 (563)	10,890 (1,176)	19,520 (583)	17,280 (487)	9,350 (677)	14,920 (1,576)	20,220 (512)	19,900 (505)	8,300 (825)	13,100 (1,393)
Race/ethnicity											
White	14,050 (703)	13,050 (635)	12,470 (1,883)	18,660 (529)	15,950 (411)	9,600 (629)	16,790 (1,558)	18,490 (555)	17,810 (506)	10,630 (1,913)	13,900 (1,706)
Black	13,920 (1,130)	12,590 (966)	‡ (†)	21,020 (1,005)	19,170 (853)	10,230 (1,441)	16,410 (4,818)	23,230 (869)	22,840 (824)	9,390 (2,272)	11,780 (1,820)
Hispanic	12,960 (2,985)	13,320 (3,113)	‡ (†)	16,540 (994)	15,290 (857)	7,250 (728)	13,330 (1,714)	16,630 (941)	16,230 (967)	10,170 (1,727)	12,960 (1,628)
Asian	‡ (†)	‡ (†)	‡ (†)	14,810 (2,143)	14,610 (1,947)	5,060 (983)	‡ (†)	17,530 (1,845)	18,450 (2,063)	9,720 (2,260)	‡ (†)
Pacific Islander	‡ (†)	‡ (†)	‡ (†)	‡ (†)	‡ (†)	‡ (†)	‡ (†)	‡ (†)	‡ (†)	‡ (†)	‡ (†)
American Indian/Alaska Native	‡ (†)	‡ (†)	‡ (†)	22,330 (3,730)	22,100 (3,720)	‡ (†)	‡ (†)	18,980 (3,573)	18,570 (3,239)	‡ (†)	‡ (†)
Two or more races	‡ (†)	‡ (†)	‡ (†)	19,160 (1,897)	16,640 (1,584)	6,460 (1,490)	‡ (†)	22,700 (2,248)	21,810 (2,223)	‡ (†)	‡ (†)
Other[2]	‡ (†)	‡ (†)	‡ (†)	† (†)	† (†)	† (†)	† (†)	† (†)	† (†)	† (†)	† (†)
Dependency status											
Dependent	12,140 (777)	10,840 (662)	12,940 (1,914)	14,440 (558)	12,210 (427)	7,740 (674)	16,930 (1,897)	12,640 (456)	12,140 (459)	8,690 (1,145)	16,110 (1,746)
Independent	14,830 (702)	14,110 (673)	‡ (†)	20,560 (514)	18,380 (458)	9,770 (582)	15,140 (1,547)	21,640 (494)	21,090 (466)	10,980 (1,566)	11,980 (1,438)
Institution control											
Public	11,820 (632)	10,790 (584)	‡ (†)	15,230 (380)	13,410 (344)	8,810 (587)	13,170 (1,259)	16,280 (533)	15,860 (514)	10,520 (1,707)	12,080 (1,552)
Private nonprofit	17,360 (1,517)	17,510 (1,464)	‡ (†)	27,600 (2,264)	22,270 (1,706)	11,770 (2,990)	‡ (†)	25,850 (1,207)	24,880 (1,291)	8,520 (2,494)	15,570 (2,673)
Private for-profit	19,700 (1,005)	18,390 (986)	14,000 (2,644)	26,910 (681)	23,490 (586)	9,320 (529)	19,180 (2,022)	27,510 (533)	26,390 (559)	10,640 (748)	16,390 (2,077)
Bachelor's degree	**25,620 (299)**	**24,230 (264)**	**21,040 (803)**	**32,040 (497)**	**26,610 (322)**	**15,000 (768)**	**29,820 (1,759)**	**31,150 (418)**	**28,170 (400)**	**19,470 (450)**	**33,950 (829)**
Sex											
Male	25,600 (362)	24,230 (340)	21,590 (1,149)	31,660 (726)	25,880 (492)	15,950 (1,138)	32,470 (3,287)	30,120 (497)	27,200 (446)	19,540 (834)	35,190 (1,349)
Female	25,630 (375)	24,230 (337)	20,590 (919)	32,330 (601)	27,140 (412)	14,270 (934)	27,840 (1,747)	31,880 (469)	28,860 (437)	19,420 (668)	32,970 (1,007)
Race/ethnicity											
White	25,460 (309)	24,030 (285)	21,570 (867)	31,690 (631)	25,840 (386)	15,320 (835)	29,930 (2,216)	31,340 (360)	27,550 (339)	20,870 (620)	35,790 (1,133)
Black	28,600 (1,163)	27,490 (1,053)	15,940 (1,475)	36,000 (1,162)	31,830 (918)	12,670 (1,812)	26,710 (4,737)	35,410 (913)	33,700 (843)	17,130 (1,620)	25,830 (2,092)
Hispanic	25,570 (1,203)	23,840 (917)	20,250 (2,481)	32,180 (1,727)	25,850 (899)	17,500 (3,075)	28,870 (4,252)	27,930 (806)	26,470 (755)	14,470 (1,070)	30,650 (2,155)
Asian	21,310 (907)	20,500 (799)	29,690 (6,139)	25,230 (1,372)	22,610 (1,135)	10,980 (2,458)	‡ (†)	26,500 (1,139)	23,710 (919)	20,050 (2,281)	35,490 (4,125)
Pacific Islander	26,930 (2,619)	24,700 (1,791)	‡ (†)	‡ (†)	‡ (†)	‡ (†)	‡ (†)	27,610 (4,145)	28,830 (3,370)	‡ (†)	‡ (†)
American Indian/Alaska Native	27,510 (2,276)	26,800 (2,413)	‡ (†)	‡ (†)	‡ (†)	‡ (†)	‡ (†)	27,470 (2,769)	26,610 (2,808)	‡ (†)	‡ (†)
Two or more races	25,960 (1,981)	24,140 (1,801)	‡ (†)	30,590 (1,887)	26,110 (1,556)	13,360 (2,254)	‡ (†)	30,900 (1,142)	28,410 (978)	15,090 (1,671)	41,730 (4,051)
Other[2]	23,750 (2,019)	22,350 (1,995)	‡ (†)	† (†)	† (†)	† (†)	† (†)	† (†)	† (†)	† (†)	† (†)
Dependency status											
Dependent	24,780 (324)	22,900 (259)	22,990 (984)	28,430 (627)	22,210 (311)	16,030 (1,000)	30,980 (1,707)	27,860 (294)	23,380 (208)	22,220 (599)	38,310 (1,090)
Independent	26,550 (469)	25,710 (440)	13,910 (1,175)	36,030 (695)	31,340 (525)	13,710 (986)	26,240 (4,769)	34,720 (676)	33,330 (611)	14,820 (661)	23,350 (1,309)
Institution control											
Public	23,760 (341)	23,010 (312)	17,000 (806)	27,960 (495)	24,020 (366)	12,430 (677)	22,310 (1,177)	28,040 (290)	26,030 (245)	16,420 (636)	28,670 (1,031)
Private nonprofit	28,750 (547)	26,110 (459)	26,300 (1,186)	35,230 (1,288)	26,840 (648)	20,030 (1,852)	40,480 (4,077)	33,210 (472)	27,770 (345)	24,830 (798)	43,680 (1,930)
Private for-profit	35,230 (1,764)	33,960 (1,701)	‡ (†)	43,660 (870)	38,030 (667)	12,940 (993)	27,970 (2,733)	43,030 (1,658)	40,770 (1,357)	16,100 (1,104)	33,210 (2,412)

†Not applicable.
!Interpret data with caution. The coefficient of variation (CV) for this estimate is between 30 and 50 percent.
‡Reporting standards not met. Either there are too few cases for a reliable estimate or the coefficient of variation (CV) is 50 percent or greater.
[1]Parent PLUS Loans are taken out by parents of dependent students and are used toward the students' undergraduate education. Parent PLUS Loans were available through both the William D. Ford Federal Direct Loan Program and the Federal Family Education Loan Program (FFELP) until FFELP was discontinued in 2010. Since then, Parent PLUS Loans have been referred to as Direct PLUS Loans.
[2]The 2012 and 2016 questionnaires did not offer students the option of choosing an "Other" race category.
[3]Average loan amounts were calculated only for students who took out each type of loan (or whose parents took out a PLUS Loan on their behalf).
[4]Constant dollars based on the Consumer Price Index, prepared by the Bureau of Labor Statistics, U.S. Department of Labor, adjusted to a school-year basis.
NOTE: Race categories exclude persons of Hispanic ethnicity. Data exclude students attending institutions in Puerto Rico.
SOURCE: U.S. Department of Education, National Center for Education Statistics, 1999–2000, 2011–12, and 2015–16 National Postsecondary Student Aid Study (NPSAS:2000, NPSAS:12, and NPSAS:16). (This table was prepared November 2018.)

Table 332.10. Amount borrowed, aid status, and sources of aid for full-time, full-year postbaccalaureate students, by level of study and control and level of institution: Selected years, 1992–93 through 2015–16

[Standard errors appear in parentheses]

Level of study, control and level of institution	Cumulative borrowing for undergraduate and graduate education[1]			Aid status (percent of students)					
		Average amount for those who borrowed			Source of aid				
	Percent who borrowed	Current dollars	Constant 2017–18 dollars[2]	Nonaided	Any aid[3]	Federal[4]	State	Institutional	Employer
1	2	3	4	5	6	7	8	9	10
1992–93, all institutions	**— (†)**	**— (†)**	**— (†)**	**30.7 (1.43)**	**69.3 (1.43)**	**44.3 (1.42)**	**6.9 (0.64)**	**40.6 (2.02)**	**5.3 (0.59)**
Master's degree	— (†)	— (†)	— (†)	35.5 (2.54)	64.5 (2.54)	33.8 (1.91)	5.8 (0.79)	42.4 (2.97)	8.3 (1.01)
Public	— (†)	— (†)	— (†)	32.7 (2.40)	67.3 (2.40)	33.9 (2.04)	7.8 (1.10)	44.1 (2.68)	7.6 (1.24)
4-year doctoral	— (†)	— (†)	— (†)	32.4 (2.59)	67.6 (2.59)	32.4 (2.23)	6.7 (0.96)	46.4 (3.19)	7.7 (1.28)
Other 4-year	— (†)	— (†)	— (†)	34.6 (4.38)	65.4 (4.38)	42.5 (5.30)	14.4 (4.13)	30.5 (3.67)	6.8! (2.66)
Private	— (†)	— (†)	— (†)	39.2 (4.74)	60.8 (4.74)	33.7 (3.62)	3.2 (0.89)	40.2 (6.34)	9.4 (1.88)
4-year doctoral	— (†)	— (†)	— (†)	37.4 (4.70)	62.6 (4.70)	34.2 (4.09)	2.9! (1.00)	42.9 (6.75)	8.9 (1.88)
Other 4-year	— (†)	— (†)	— (†)	50.5 (10.60)	49.5 (10.60)	30.5 (7.06)	‡ (†)	22.8! (9.39)	‡ (†)
Doctor's degree	— (†)	— (†)	— (†)	30.1 (2.32)	69.9 (2.32)	28.3 (2.14)	4.4 (0.71)	51.6 (2.70)	3.0 (0.79)
Public	— (†)	— (†)	— (†)	29.9 (2.99)	70.1 (2.99)	22.3 (2.26)	6.5 (1.14)	55.5 (3.01)	3.9 (1.00)
Private	— (†)	— (†)	— (†)	30.4 (3.27)	69.6 (3.27)	37.8 (3.54)	‡ (†)	45.5 (3.52)	‡ (†)
First-professional	— (†)	— (†)	— (†)	22.6 (0.96)	77.4 (0.96)	68.2 (1.54)	9.9 (1.34)	37.0 (1.81)	2.3 (0.52)
Public	— (†)	— (†)	— (†)	20.4 (1.02)	79.6 (1.02)	72.5 (1.29)	13.4 (1.75)	37.7 (1.67)	2.3 (0.59)
Private	— (†)	— (†)	— (†)	24.6 (1.66)	75.4 (1.66)	64.2 (2.42)	6.8 (1.19)	36.4 (3.29)	2.3! (0.70)
Other graduate	— (†)	— (†)	— (†)	38.3 (6.82)	61.7 (6.82)	42.1 (4.26)	6.6 (1.81)	23.0 (4.05)	6.0! (2.98)
1999–2000, all institutions	**69.4 (0.74)**	**$41,920 (863)**	**$61,450 (1,265)**	**18.3 (0.66)**	**81.7 (0.66)**	**52.5 (0.76)**	**6.0 (0.60)**	**49.7 (1.03)**	**6.0 (0.57)**
Master's degree	68.3 (1.12)	31,930 (1,097)	46,800 (1,608)	20.6 (1.15)	79.4 (1.15)	50.6 (1.23)	5.1 (0.66)	45.4 (1.61)	9.2 (1.03)
Public	63.2 (1.60)	28,070 (1,079)	41,140 (1,581)	22.3 (1.52)	77.7 (1.52)	44.8 (1.82)	7.3 (1.14)	49.8 (2.16)	7.0 (1.04)
4-year doctoral	62.5 (1.56)	27,510 (1,234)	40,320 (1,808)	20.2 (1.46)	79.8 (1.46)	43.3 (1.71)	7.0 (1.31)	54.3 (2.02)	7.3 (1.20)
Other 4-year	70.9 (6.04)	31,920 (2,822)	46,790 (4,137)	29.9 (5.08)	70.1 (5.08)	54.7 (6.88)	10.2! (3.32)	27.4 (6.85)	5.1! (1.79)
Private	74.4 (1.55)	35,890 (1,855)	52,610 (2,719)	18.6 (1.59)	81.4 (1.59)	57.8 (1.88)	2.5 (0.63)	40.2 (2.63)	11.8 (1.89)
4-year doctoral	73.3 (1.76)	38,420 (2,521)	56,310 (3,695)	17.1 (1.93)	82.9 (1.93)	58.3 (2.36)	2.9! (0.90)	50.5 (3.22)	8.3 (1.31)
Other[5]	76.9 (3.74)	30,770 (1,850)	45,100 (2,711)	21.8 (2.75)	78.2 (2.75)	56.6 (4.41)	‡ (†)	18.1 (3.91)	19.1 (5.24)
Doctor's degree	56.8 (1.95)	38,990 (3,421)	57,150 (5,014)	12.0 (1.38)	88.0 (1.38)	29.6 (2.80)	2.6 (0.54)	77.4 (1.65)	5.4 (0.64)
Public	54.5 (1.92)	33,600 (1,564)	49,240 (2,293)	11.4 (1.38)	88.6 (1.38)	26.1 (1.86)	3.2 (0.75)	80.0 (1.59)	7.3 (0.88)
Private	60.5 (3.62)	46,680 (7,288)	68,420 (10,682)	13.0 (2.80)	87.0 (2.80)	35.2 (6.26)	‡ (†)	73.2 (3.22)	2.3 (0.55)
First-professional	85.1 (1.14)	60,860 (1,713)	89,200 (2,511)	13.4 (1.18)	86.6 (1.18)	77.1 (1.29)	9.9 (1.65)	41.4 (2.40)	1.7! (0.53)
Public	86.8 (1.70)	52,790 (1,954)	77,380 (2,864)	13.8 (1.82)	86.2 (1.82)	78.3 (2.13)	12.7 (2.57)	38.9 (2.84)	1.8! (0.87)
Private	83.6 (1.63)	67,820 (3,213)	99,400 (4,710)	13.1 (1.49)	86.9 (1.49)	76.1 (1.84)	7.5 (2.11)	43.4 (3.65)	1.7! (0.66)
Other graduate	57.5 (3.81)	27,840 (2,036)	40,800 (2,984)	39.3 (3.68)	60.7 (3.68)	44.9 (3.72)	8.1 (2.37)	25.3 (3.22)	2.8! (1.20)
2007–08, all institutions	**71.3 (1.04)**	**$55,110 (993)**	**$64,590 (1,164)**	**13.1 (0.80)**	**86.9 (0.80)**	**56.6 (1.18)**	**3.8 (0.28)**	**43.9 (1.17)**	**11.6 (0.93)**
Master's degree	71.8 (1.77)	43,250 (1,374)	50,700 (1,610)	15.6 (1.34)	84.4 (1.34)	55.5 (1.93)	2.9 (0.40)	35.5 (1.48)	16.3 (1.76)
Public	66.5 (1.79)	37,770 (1,473)	44,270 (1,727)	13.3 (1.27)	86.7 (1.27)	50.7 (1.91)	4.1 (0.83)	52.2 (2.40)	13.4 (1.49)
4-year doctoral	65.1 (1.95)	38,450 (1,644)	45,070 (1,927)	12.1 (1.34)	87.9 (1.34)	50.1 (2.07)	4.2 (0.93)	56.0 (2.62)	14.5 (1.68)
Other 4-year	77.1 (4.81)	33,440 (2,285)	39,190 (2,678)	22.7 (3.92)	77.3 (3.92)	55.6 (5.96)	‡ (†)	23.5 (4.89)	5.1! (1.92)
Private	75.5 (2.58)	46,590 (1,974)	54,600 (2,313)	17.2 (1.96)	82.8 (1.96)	58.8 (2.81)	2.0 (0.35)	24.0 (1.59)	18.3 (2.79)
4-year doctoral	71.4 (1.85)	46,510 (1,654)	54,510 (1,939)	19.1 (1.45)	80.9 (1.45)	55.1 (1.51)	2.4 (0.50)	36.0 (2.46)	14.4 (1.17)
Other[5]	80.8 (5.13)	46,670 (3,671)	54,710 (4,303)	14.8 (3.91)	85.2 (3.91)	63.6 (5.96)	1.6 (0.43)	8.4 (1.44)	23.4 (6.23)
Doctor's degree	59.8 (1.73)	55,200 (2,108)	64,700 (2,471)	7.1 (0.88)	92.9 (0.88)	38.4 (2.18)	2.9 (0.41)	70.7 (3.03)	7.9 (0.79)
Public	52.3 (2.17)	44,190 (1,604)	51,790 (1,880)	7.9 (1.48)	92.1 (1.48)	29.7 (1.80)	3.6 (0.65)	81.1 (1.89)	7.7 (0.93)
Private	67.8 (2.41)	64,120 (3,123)	75,160 (3,661)	6.2 (1.08)	93.8 (1.08)	47.6 (3.43)	2.2! (0.65)	59.8 (5.02)	8.0 (1.36)
First-professional	84.9 (1.29)	81,400 (1,782)	95,410 (2,088)	11.5 (1.12)	88.5 (1.12)	81.7 (1.35)	7.5 (0.83)	35.7 (1.89)	4.6 (0.75)
Public	84.4 (1.96)	73,230 (2,717)	85,830 (3,185)	11.5 (1.65)	88.5 (1.65)	81.8 (2.12)	10.6 (1.46)	34.0 (2.67)	4.9 (1.44)
Private	85.4 (1.57)	87,800 (2,183)	102,900 (2,559)	11.5 (1.46)	88.5 (1.46)	81.5 (1.67)	5.1 (0.85)	37.0 (2.56)	4.4 (0.72)
Other graduate	62.4 (6.48)	43,740 (3,904)	51,270 (4,576)	30.8 (6.54)	69.2 (6.54)	51.0 (6.62)	‡ (†)	25.5 (5.78)	6.2! (2.33)
2011–12, all institutions	**73.3 (0.90)**	**$74,710 (996)**	**$81,460 (1,086)**	**13.9 (0.77)**	**86.1 (0.77)**	**62.3 (0.93)**	**2.4 (0.34)**	**42.2 (1.19)**	**10.2 (0.48)**
Master's degree	73.5 (1.45)	58,590 (1,142)	63,880 (1,245)	17.4 (1.28)	82.6 (1.28)	63.0 (1.44)	1.8 (0.35)	35.1 (1.53)	8.8 (0.70)
Public	71.8 (2.24)	50,200 (1,816)	54,740 (1,980)	16.2 (1.84)	83.8 (1.84)	58.2 (2.41)	3.7 (0.80)	45.6 (2.35)	10.3 (1.17)
4-year doctoral	70.7 (2.41)	50,620 (2,015)	55,190 (2,197)	16.3 (2.03)	83.7 (2.03)	57.0 (2.60)	4.0 (0.89)	47.1 (2.56)	10.8 (1.28)
Other 4-year	82.2 (3.71)	46,900 (2,538)	51,130 (2,768)	15.4 (4.13)	84.6 (4.13)	69.5 (5.18)	‡ (†)	31.2 (3.46)	5.9 (1.68)
Private	74.8 (1.95)	64,510 (1,456)	70,340 (1,587)	18.2 (1.80)	81.8 (1.80)	66.5 (2.13)	0.4! (0.19)	27.5 (2.09)	7.8 (0.88)
4-year doctoral	70.1 (2.41)	67,130 (2,165)	73,200 (2,361)	19.6 (2.06)	80.4 (2.06)	59.5 (2.45)	‡ (†)	35.2 (2.96)	7.8 (1.23)
Other[5]	81.8 (3.20)	61,140 (1,816)	66,660 (1,980)	16.1 (3.09)	83.9 (3.09)	77.0 (3.66)	‡ (†)	15.9 (2.70)	7.6 (1.04)
Doctor's degree—research/scholarship	50.5 (1.42)	65,090 (2,343)	70,980 (2,555)	6.6 (0.73)	93.4 (0.73)	27.8 (1.19)	1.5! (0.49)	79.8 (1.27)	24.0 (1.25)
Public	47.9 (2.23)	55,500 (2,291)	60,520 (2,498)	5.9 (1.04)	94.1 (1.04)	24.2 (1.41)	2.1! (0.78)	87.2 (1.59)	27.0 (1.93)
Private	54.0 (1.86)	76,180 (4,351)	83,070 (4,744)	7.5 (1.07)	92.5 (1.07)	32.3 (2.30)	‡ (†)	70.1 (2.28)	20.1 (1.06)
Doctor's degree—professional practice and other[6]	88.3 (0.90)	110,570 (1,848)	120,560 (2,015)	9.3 (0.88)	90.7 (0.88)	84.4 (1.03)	4.5 (0.96)	35.1 (1.66)	4.4 (0.51)
Public	88.3 (1.00)	102,220 (2,726)	111,460 (2,973)	8.9 (1.09)	91.1 (1.09)	84.4 (1.31)	8.1 (2.27)	40.6 (2.51)	5.4 (0.82)
Private	88.3 (1.28)	116,000 (2,490)	126,480 (2,715)	9.6 (1.22)	90.4 (1.22)	84.4 (1.50)	2.2 (0.53)	31.5 (2.19)	3.7 (0.62)
Other graduate	74.9 (6.28)	57,540 (5,456)	62,740 (5,948)	29.1 (6.46)	70.9 (6.46)	61.4 (7.24)	‡ (†)	16.9 (4.78)	5.5! (2.47)

See notes at end of table.

Table 332.10. Amount borrowed, aid status, and sources of aid for full-time, full-year postbaccalaureate students, by level of study and control and level of institution: Selected years, 1992–93 through 2015–16—Continued

[Standard errors appear in parentheses]

Level of study, control and level of institution	Cumulative borrowing for undergraduate and graduate education[1]						Aid status (percent of students)											
	Percent who borrowed		Average amount for those who borrowed				Nonaided		Source of aid									
			Current dollars		Constant 2017–18 dollars[2]				Any aid[3]		Federal[4]		State		Institutional		Employer	
1	2		3		4		5		6		7		8		9		10	
2015–16, all institutions	**68.3**	**(0.93)**	**$80,750**	**(2,158)**	**$84,090**	**(2,247)**	**17.0**	**(0.82)**	**83.0**	**(0.82)**	**54.0**	**(0.89)**	**3.3**	**(0.52)**	**46.6**	**(1.25)**	**6.9**	**(0.54)**
Master's degree	66.6	(1.45)	59,100	(1,608)	61,550	(1,674)	20.0	(1.17)	80.0	(1.17)	51.9	(1.48)	3.1	(0.46)	41.6	(1.62)	9.0	(0.75)
Public	63.7	(2.22)	49,450	(2,109)	51,500	(2,197)	21.6	(1.77)	78.4	(1.77)	45.0	(2.10)	5.5	(0.93)	44.4	(2.17)	6.6	(0.89)
4-year doctoral	63.1	(2.34)	49,950	(2,287)	52,010	(2,382)	21.2	(1.86)	78.8	(1.86)	44.2	(2.23)	5.4	(1.00)	46.2	(2.28)	6.6	(0.96)
Other 4-year	71.7	(3.46)	44,240	(2,997)	46,070	(3,121)	25.9	(3.22)	74.1	(3.22)	54.7	(3.65)	5.8!	(1.82)	23.6	(4.31)	6.3!	(2.28)
Private	69.1	(1.74)	66,890	(2,295)	69,660	(2,390)	18.5	(1.52)	81.5	(1.52)	57.9	(1.98)	1.0!	(0.35)	39.1	(2.52)	11.1	(1.14)
4-year doctoral	65.3	(2.35)	67,870	(3,010)	70,680	(3,134)	20.4	(1.97)	79.6	(1.97)	54.3	(2.57)	1.2!	(0.48)	39.7	(3.06)	9.2	(1.44)
Other[5]	78.4	(2.23)	64,910	(2,838)	67,590	(2,955)	14.0	(1.56)	86.0	(1.56)	66.7	(2.52)	0.7!	(0.28)	37.7	(4.15)	15.8	(1.46)
Doctor's degree—research/ scholarship	52.5	(2.13)	74,510	(3,435)	77,590	(3,577)	9.9	(1.05)	90.1	(1.05)	27.9	(1.94)	1.2	(0.31)	71.9	(1.93)	6.2	(0.78)
Public	46.6	(2.93)	61,200	(4,167)	63,730	(4,339)	10.9	(1.82)	89.1	(1.82)	18.3	(2.49)	1.5	(0.44)	78.7	(2.56)	5.0	(0.90)
Private	58.2	(3.11)	84,910	(5,368)	88,420	(5,590)	8.8	(1.18)	91.2	(1.18)	37.3	(2.86)	0.9!	(0.40)	65.2	(3.08)	7.4	(1.24)
Doctor's degree—professional practice and other[6]	80.3	(1.56)	121,940	(6,425)	126,980	(6,691)	14.0	(1.48)	86.0	(1.48)	73.0	(1.54)	4.6!	(1.57)	45.9	(2.17)	2.3	(0.68)
Public	79.8	(2.45)	99,450	(3,685)	103,560	(3,837)	15.9	(2.29)	84.1	(2.29)	71.8	(2.26)	4.5	(1.06)	48.6	(3.18)	2.2!	(0.84)
Private	80.7	(2.02)	138,370	(11,011)	144,090	(11,466)	12.6	(2.00)	87.4	(2.00)	74.0	(2.11)	‡	(†)	43.9	(2.93)	2.5!	(1.04)
Other graduate	70.9	(4.84)	80,210	(8,667)	83,520	(9,026)	20.737	(3.95)	79.3	(3.95)	54.0	(5.41)	‡	(†)	28.2	(5.29)	10.7	(3.09)

—Not available.
†Not applicable.
!Interpret data with caution. The coefficient of variation (CV) for this estimate is between 30 and 50 percent.
‡Reporting standards not met. Either there are too few cases for a reliable estimate or the coefficient of variation (CV) is 50 percent or greater.
[1]Includes all loans ever taken out for both graduate and undergraduate education. Does not include Parent Loans for Undergraduate Students (PLUS) or loans from families and friends.
[2]Constant dollars based on the Consumer Price Index, prepared by the Bureau of Labor Statistics, U.S. Department of Labor, adjusted to a school-year basis.
[3]Includes students who reported they were awarded aid but did not specify the source of aid.
[4]Includes Department of Veterans Affairs and Department of Defense benefits.
[5]Includes nonprofit 4-year nondoctoral institutions and for-profit 2-year-and-above institutions.
[6]Professional practice doctor's degrees include most degrees that were classified as first-professional degrees prior to 2010–11 (such as M.D., D.D.S., and J.D.). "Other" doctor's degrees are those that are neither research/scholarship degrees nor professional practice degrees.
NOTE: Full-time, full-year students are those who were enrolled full time for 9 or more months. Excludes students whose attendance status was not reported. Total includes some students whose level of study or control of institution was unknown. Detail may not sum to totals because of rounding and because some students receive multiple types of aid and aid from different sources. Data exclude students attending institutions in Puerto Rico.
SOURCE: U.S. Department of Education, National Center for Education Statistics, 1992–93, 1999–2000, 2007–08, 2011–12, and 2015–16 National Postsecondary Student Aid Study (NPSAS:93, NPSAS:2000, NPSAS:08, NPSAS:12, and NPSAS:16). (This table was prepared May 2019.)

Table 332.45. Percentage of graduate degree completers with student loan debt and average cumulative amount owed, by level of education funded and graduate degree type, institution control, and degree program: Selected years, 1999–2000 through 2015–16

[Standard errors appear in parentheses]

Graduate degree type, institution control, and degree program	Loans for graduate education only										Total loans (for undergraduate and graduate education)									
	1999–2000		2003–04		2007–08		2011–12		2015–16		1999–2000		2003–04		2007–08		2011–12		2015–16	
1		2		3		4		5		6		7		8		9		10		11
Total	**44.6**	**(1.06)**	**54.6**	**(1.77)**	**54.6**	**(1.18)**	**58.6**	**(1.25)**	**54.2**	**(1.05)**	**51.3**	**(1.00)**	**60.9**	**(1.72)**	**62.9**	**(1.15)**	**64.1**	**(1.23)**	**60.5**	**(1.08)**
Graduate degree type and institution control[1]																				
Postbaccalaureate certificate	35.8	(5.12)	46.3	(7.43)	49.5	(5.02)	39.4	(4.66)	47.6	(4.18)	49.2	(4.72)	53.0	(7.02)	64.1	(4.68)	44.5	(4.53)	55.1	(3.88)
Public	33.4	(6.29)	30.1	(5.25)	45.1	(7.45)	35.5	(6.04)	39.0	(5.78)	51.2	(5.62)	39.9	(6.22)	64.5	(6.95)	41.5	(5.84)	48.7	(5.49)
Private nonprofit	32.8	(9.10)	70.3	(9.55)	54.7	(6.47)	48.0	(7.97)	53.5	(5.99)	40.4	(9.55)	73.1	(9.13)	63.8	(5.82)	50.5	(8.06)	57.8	(6.03)
Private for-profit	‡	(†)	‡	(†)	‡	(†)	‡	(†)	72.5	(4.88)	‡	(†)	‡	(†)	‡	(†)	‡	(†)	78.1	(3.99)
Master's	39.9	(1.30)	52.0	(2.10)	53.8	(1.47)	59.0	(1.50)	52.8	(1.23)	47.2	(1.19)	59.4	(2.03)	62.7	(1.45)	65.2	(1.48)	60.0	(1.28)
Public	35.6	(1.53)	41.6	(2.20)	48.4	(1.79)	53.0	(2.19)	49.1	(1.87)	43.7	(1.57)	50.0	(2.28)	59.1	(1.87)	62.1	(2.14)	57.3	(2.04)
Private nonprofit	44.1	(2.65)	60.8	(3.13)	55.2	(1.69)	60.8	(2.29)	53.0	(1.82)	50.9	(2.46)	67.6	(2.85)	63.3	(1.84)	64.6	(2.38)	59.8	(1.74)
Private for-profit	60.4	(11.61)	76.7	(10.88)	80.3	(6.41)	74.9	(4.97)	67.5	(3.18)	61.6	(10.98)	77.2	(10.76)	83.5	(6.34)	78.6	(4.86)	71.3	(2.74)
Doctor's, research	38.8	(2.92)	45.3	(2.14)	43.1	(2.54)	40.7	(2.33)	43.6	(3.45)	43.6	(3.04)	50.5	(2.28)	49.3	(2.77)	47.5	(2.44)	48.2	(3.51)
Public	34.6	(3.35)	39.6	(2.52)	38.5	(3.12)	35.3	(2.73)	32.7	(3.96)	39.5	(3.52)	45.7	(2.82)	45.0	(3.73)	42.1	(3.04)	36.7	(4.16)
Private nonprofit	46.0	(6.55)	54.5	(4.19)	51.2	(3.39)	39.9	(3.38)	46.8	(6.14)	50.9	(6.29)	58.3	(4.13)	57.2	(3.22)	48.7	(3.30)	54.2	(6.01)
Private for-profit	‡	(†)	‡	(†)	‡	(†)	95.1	(3.45)	75.8	(6.27)	‡	(†)	‡	(†)	‡	(†)	95.1	(3.45)	76.2	(6.26)
Doctor's, professional[2]	79.4	(2.82)	84.8	(2.39)	83.8	(2.09)	84.6	(1.60)	73.5	(2.43)	81.2	(2.77)	84.8	(2.39)	84.9	(1.97)	84.9	(1.65)	74.5	(2.39)
Public	83.6	(4.65)	87.2	(2.82)	82.8	(3.61)	85.9	(2.72)	74.1	(4.18)	84.7	(4.59)	87.2	(2.82)	84.3	(3.28)	85.9	(2.72)	75.9	(4.07)
Private nonprofit	76.7	(4.06)	82.8	(4.21)	84.5	(2.42)	84.2	(2.25)	71.3	(3.40)	79.0	(3.95)	82.8	(4.21)	85.4	(2.34)	84.7	(2.31)	71.9	(3.42)
Private for-profit	‡	(†)	‡	(†)	‡	(†)	94.1	(5.12)	89.5	(1.95)	‡	(†)	‡	(†)	‡	(†)	94.1	(5.12)	90.2	(1.82)
Graduate degree program																				
Postbaccalaureate certificate	35.8	(5.12)	46.3	(7.43)	49.5	(5.02)	39.4	(4.66)	47.6	(4.18)	49.2	(4.72)	53.0	(7.02)	64.1	(4.68)	44.5	(4.53)	55.1	(3.88)
Master of business administration (M.B.A.)	35.7	(2.70)	49.2	(5.05)	54.2	(3.45)	49.4	(4.63)	43.8	(3.41)	41.0	(2.78)	54.8	(4.67)	60.6	(3.29)	57.0	(4.78)	51.0	(3.34)
Master of education (any)	35.7	(2.86)	49.1	(3.14)	55.5	(3.46)	59.7	(3.55)	51.2	(2.83)	45.6	(2.86)	60.2	(3.24)	68.4	(3.13)	67.3	(3.64)	61.9	(3.21)
Other master of arts (M.A.) except in education	46.8	(4.97)	57.7	(5.07)	60.4	(4.04)	62.1	(3.53)	51.9	(4.81)	55.6	(5.09)	62.6	(5.04)	66.6	(3.76)	69.5	(3.50)	58.5	(4.42)
Other master of science (M.S.) except in education	35.9	(2.89)	40.0	(3.85)	45.8	(2.88)	53.6	(2.47)	49.5	(2.42)	41.9	(2.58)	47.1	(4.12)	53.9	(2.83)	59.3	(2.56)	56.1	(2.33)
Theology (M.Div., M.H.L., or B.D.)	‡	(†)	‡	(†)	‡	(†)	‡	(†)	‡	(†)	‡	(†)	‡	(†)	‡	(†)	‡	(†)	‡	(†)
Other master's degree[3]	52.5	(4.06)	69.3	(4.70)	56.3	(2.65)	71.8	(2.61)	65.0	(2.65)	58.4	(3.85)	74.5	(4.33)	62.2	(2.69)	75.0	(2.55)	70.2	(2.53)
Ph.D. except in education	36.3	(3.02)	33.5	(2.01)	31.9	(2.89)	31.6	(2.22)	38.5	(3.41)	43.6	(3.37)	40.3	(2.12)	40.2	(3.52)	40.3	(2.63)	44.7	(3.55)
Education (any doctorate)	33.4	(6.36)	49.7	(4.81)	58.0	(5.68)	72.3	(3.46)	61.4	(6.82)	33.4	(6.36)	51.9	(4.75)	61.4	(5.44)	73.3	(3.33)	63.0	(6.74)
Medicine (M.D. or D.O.)	86.4	(7.18)	91.8	(3.02)	78.3	(4.73)	84.3	(4.12)	80.3	(4.38)	86.4	(7.18)	91.8	(3.02)	79.6	(4.81)	84.3	(4.12)	81.0	(4.34)
Other health science professional practice doctorate[4]	79.1	(6.47)	88.3	(4.13)	86.7	(5.64)	89.5	(3.54)	73.6	(6.22)	80.9	(6.47)	88.3	(4.13)	88.6	(4.54)	89.5	(3.54)	74.6	(5.94)
Law (LL.B. or J.D.)	82.4	(2.69)	86.8	(3.05)	87.3	(2.50)	85.6	(2.46)	68.8	(5.84)	84.6	(2.52)	86.8	(3.05)	87.3	(2.50)	86.3	(2.54)	68.8	(5.84)
Other doctorate (non-Ph.D.)[5]	49.0	(7.64)	66.7	(4.99)	59.6	(4.47)	66.0	(4.09)	65.5	(7.35)	51.5	(7.46)	70.5	(4.56)	62.6	(4.47)	66.7	(4.15)	66.3	(7.42)
	Average cumulative amount owed (current dollars)																			
Total	**$33,300**	**($1,200)**	**$39,500**	**($1,440)**	**$43,700**	**($1,010)**	**$59,400**	**($1,260)**	**$71,000**	**($2,160)**	**$37,900**	**($1,170)**	**$45,600**	**($1,520)**	**$51,700**	**($1,000)**	**$73,100**	**($1,340)**	**$82,800**	**($2,130)**
Graduate degree type and institution control[1]																				
Postbaccalaureate certificate	21,400	(3,250)	20,900	(4,490)	31,400	(3,170)	44,200	(5,080)	54,100	(7,670)	25,500	(2,680)	29,900	(4,290)	38,600	(3,630)	60,800	(5,340)	66,500	(7,950)
Public	‡	(†)	10,300	(1,720)	32,100	(5,330)	40,400	(6,120)	43,300	(8,480)	22,800	(3,110)	19,100	(2,980)	38,700	(4,800)	57,100	(6,200)	50,100	(8,080)
Private nonprofit	‡	(†)	26,900	(5,250)	30,300	(3,870)	48,600	(8,680)	65,700	(18,040)	‡	(†)	37,800	(4,980)	38,200	(6,020)	68,000	(10,010)	80,000	(19,080)
Private for-profit	‡	(†)	‡	(†)	‡	(†)	‡	(†)	61,300	(6,390)	‡	(†)	‡	(†)	‡	(†)	‡	(†)	95,500	(8,530)
Master's	23,500	(970)	29,100	(1,150)	34,300	(1,090)	45,100	(1,250)	50,300	(1,640)	29,400	(1,110)	35,200	(1,330)	43,900	(1,170)	60,000	(1,470)	64,800	(1,690)
Public	19,700	(1,060)	24,800	(1,000)	31,100	(1,100)	35,600	(1,640)	42,300	(2,370)	25,600	(1,100)	31,400	(1,290)	38,800	(1,330)	49,100	(2,180)	53,500	(2,400)
Private nonprofit	27,300	(1,790)	32,300	(1,730)	38,000	(1,370)	50,700	(1,990)	56,400	(2,660)	32,700	(2,090)	37,700	(2,170)	46,800	(1,610)	64,700	(2,170)	70,600	(2,700)
Private for-profit	29,700	(3,680)	‡	(†)	33,900	(6,030)	49,500	(4,430)	62,000	(3,350)	40,900	(6,390)	‡	(†)	54,100	(6,090)	71,900	(3,700)	88,700	(4,060)
Doctor's, research	34,600	(3,720)	52,000	(3,050)	62,700	(3,660)	77,600	(2,760)	101,500	(6,350)	37,300	(3,920)	56,200	(3,210)	65,200	(3,440)	80,300	(3,290)	106,400	(6,550)
Public	28,700	(2,790)	44,500	(2,670)	51,200	(3,470)	60,400	(3,590)	84,800	(9,380)	31,700	(3,040)	48,400	(3,000)	54,000	(3,280)	63,200	(3,980)	90,500	(8,610)
Private nonprofit	42,800	(9,510)	61,300	(5,720)	78,800	(7,050)	84,400	(5,550)	89,400	(13,750)	45,300	(9,650)	66,600	(6,410)	81,400	(6,630)	85,400	(5,400)	92,400	(13,680)
Private for-profit	‡	(†)	‡	(†)	‡	(†)	125,900	(7,660)	144,900	(7,540)	‡	(†)	‡	(†)	‡	(†)	140,300	(7,750)	157,300	(8,520)
Doctor's, professional[2]	61,900	(2,710)	78,800	(3,860)	91,500	(2,900)	132,600	(3,070)	171,700	(9,390)	68,500	(2,990)	90,600	(4,160)	102,600	(3,180)	150,100	(3,650)	183,200	(10,320)
Public	53,500	(2,870)	66,700	(3,000)	81,400	(4,650)	114,600	(3,920)	130,700	(8,470)	60,800	(3,170)	78,000	(3,180)	91,900	(5,140)	130,200	(4,120)	140,100	(9,560)
Private nonprofit	68,900	(4,240)	89,800	(5,750)	97,500	(4,110)	142,600	(4,120)	205,000	(16,330)	74,700	(4,570)	102,300	(6,080)	109,100	(4,640)	160,200	(5,020)	217,800	(18,530)
Private for-profit	‡	(†)	‡	(†)	‡	(†)	175,900	(18,040)	167,400	(5,860)	‡	(†)	‡	(†)	‡	(†)	184,700	(21,610)	186,800	(5,880)

See notes at end of table.

Table 332.45. Percentage of graduate degree completers with student loan debt and average cumulative amount owed, by level of education funded and graduate degree type, institution control, and degree program: Selected years, 1999–2000 through 2015–16—Continued

[Standard errors appear in parentheses]

Graduate degree type, institution control, and degree program	Loans for graduate education only					Total loans (for undergraduate and graduate education)				
	1999–2000	2003–04	2007–08	2011–12	2015–16	1999–2000	2003–04	2007–08	2011–12	2015–16
1	2	3	4	5	6	7	8	9	10	11
Graduate degree program										
Postbaccalaureate certificate	21,400 (3,250)	20,900 (4,490)	31,400 (3,170)	44,200 (5,080)	54,100 (7,670)	25,500 (2,680)	29,900 (4,290)	38,600 (3,630)	60,800 (5,340)	66,500 (7,950)
Master of business administration (M.B.A.)	27,900 (2,860)	36,100 (4,250)	36,400 (3,680)	40,900 (2,880)	50,100 (3,780)	33,100 (2,440)	42,700 (4,540)	47,500 (3,010)	51,400 (3,820)	65,100 (4,180)
Master of education (any)	18,000 (1,240)	25,900 (1,450)	29,900 (1,700)	41,600 (2,510)	41,800 (3,420)	22,500 (1,630)	31,800 (1,930)	39,300 (2,540)	58,700 (3,720)	54,200 (3,410)
Other master of arts (M.A.) except in education	22,900 (1,990)	28,200 (3,720)	36,000 (3,200)	48,900 (3,550)	52,900 (5,160)	30,700 (2,910)	37,400 (3,920)	48,000 (4,170)	66,300 (5,560)	71,500 (5,040)
Other master of science (M.S.) except in education	23,000 (1,620)	29,800 (2,960)	33,600 (2,050)	45,500 (2,670)	48,000 (3,020)	31,300 (2,420)	35,100 (3,100)	42,900 (2,410)	60,900 (3,010)	61,200 (2,950)
Theology (M.Div., M.H.L., or B.D.)	‡ (†)	‡ (†)	‡ (†)	‡ (†)	‡ (†)	‡ (†)	‡ (†)	‡ (†)	‡ (†)	‡ (†)
Other master's degree[3]	26,800 (1,650)	27,200 (1,820)	40,700 (1,880)	49,000 (2,320)	57,300 (3,590)	32,900 (2,180)	32,800 (2,540)	48,800 (2,090)	62,500 (2,570)	73,700 (3,640)
Ph.D. except in education	33,900 (4,150)	41,900 (2,960)	47,900 (2,850)	66,400 (3,270)	96,800 (7,790)	33,700 (4,220)	45,100 (2,770)	49,200 (2,930)	65,100 (3,460)	97,000 (7,870)
Education (any doctorate)	‡ (†)	48,200 (9,270)	58,600 (7,140)	80,900 (6,010)	101,700 (12,690)	‡ (†)	51,600 (8,730)	61,000 (7,030)	93,800 (7,230)	109,900 (13,720)
Medicine (M.D. or D.O.)	78,700 (4,070)	108,100 (8,210)	128,300 (7,370)	166,300 (7,790)	223,100 (24,920)	87,000 (4,320)	118,700 (7,790)	135,500 (7,910)	182,600 (8,000)	241,600 (30,770)
Other health science professional practice doctorate[4]	72,500 (6,420)	79,000 (9,750)	91,700 (8,220)	133,500 (7,020)	190,300 (16,900)	80,600 (6,320)	94,900 (10,230)	108,300 (9,450)	157,700 (7,900)	198,800 (16,400)
Law (LL.B. or J.D.)	51,800 (2,210)	71,300 (3,940)	82,800 (2,640)	126,600 (5,040)	129,300 (10,280)	57,500 (2,540)	82,100 (4,460)	94,400 (3,170)	140,400 (5,880)	142,900 (10,790)
Other doctorate (non-Ph.D.)[5]	36,800 (6,990)	64,100 (5,040)	81,300 (7,120)	105,000 (5,880)	115,500 (12,110)	45,000 (6,840)	71,100 (6,520)	88,900 (7,020)	119,200 (6,600)	129,800 (11,530)
	Average cumulative amount owed (constant 2017–18 dollars)[6]									
Total	**$48,800 ($1,750)**	**$52,600 ($1,920)**	**$51,200 ($1,190)**	**$64,800 ($1,370)**	**$73,900 ($2,240)**	**$55,500 ($1,710)**	**$60,800 ($2,020)**	**$60,600 ($1,170)**	**$79,700 ($1,460)**	**$86,200 ($2,210)**
Graduate degree type and institution control[1]										
Postbaccalaureate certificate	31,400 (4,770)	27,900 (5,990)	36,800 (3,720)	48,200 (5,540)	56,300 (7,990)	37,400 (3,930)	39,900 (5,720)	45,300 (4,260)	66,300 (5,820)	69,300 (8,270)
Public	‡ (†)	13,700 (2,290)	37,600 (6,250)	44,000 (6,670)	45,100 (8,830)	33,400 (4,560)	25,400 (3,970)	45,300 (5,620)	62,200 (6,760)	52,200 (8,410)
Private nonprofit	‡ (†)	35,800 (7,000)	35,500 (4,540)	53,000 (9,470)	68,400 (18,790)	‡ (†)	50,400 (6,640)	44,800 (7,050)	74,100 (10,910)	83,300 (19,870)
Private for-profit	‡ (†)	‡ (†)	‡ (†)	‡ (†)	63,800 (6,660)	‡ (†)	‡ (†)	‡ (†)	‡ (†)	99,400 (8,880)
Master's	34,500 (1,420)	38,700 (1,530)	40,200 (1,280)	49,100 (1,370)	52,400 (1,700)	43,100 (1,620)	47,000 (1,770)	51,400 (1,370)	65,400 (1,600)	67,400 (1,760)
Public	28,900 (1,550)	33,000 (1,330)	36,500 (1,280)	38,800 (1,790)	44,100 (2,470)	37,500 (1,610)	41,900 (1,730)	45,400 (1,560)	53,500 (2,380)	55,700 (2,500)
Private nonprofit	40,000 (2,630)	43,000 (2,300)	44,600 (1,610)	55,300 (2,170)	58,700 (2,770)	48,000 (3,060)	50,300 (2,890)	54,800 (1,880)	70,500 (2,360)	73,500 (2,810)
Private for-profit	43,500 (5,390)	‡ (†)	39,700 (7,070)	54,000 (4,840)	64,600 (3,490)	60,000 (9,370)	‡ (†)	63,400 (7,140)	78,400 (4,040)	92,400 (4,230)
Doctor's, research	50,800 (5,450)	69,400 (4,070)	73,500 (4,290)	84,600 (3,010)	105,700 (6,610)	54,700 (5,750)	74,900 (4,280)	76,400 (4,040)	87,600 (3,590)	110,800 (6,820)
Public	42,100 (4,090)	59,300 (3,560)	60,000 (4,070)	65,900 (3,920)	88,300 (9,770)	46,500 (4,460)	64,600 (4,010)	63,300 (3,840)	68,900 (4,340)	94,300 (8,970)
Private nonprofit	62,700 (13,940)	81,700 (7,630)	92,400 (8,270)	92,000 (6,060)	93,100 (14,320)	66,400 (14,140)	88,700 (8,550)	95,400 (7,770)	93,100 (5,880)	96,200 (14,250)
Private for-profit	‡ (†)	‡ (†)	‡ (†)	137,300 (8,360)	150,900 (7,860)	‡ (†)	‡ (†)	‡ (†)	153,000 (8,450)	163,800 (8,870)
Doctor's, professional[2]	90,800 (3,980)	105,100 (5,140)	107,200 (3,400)	144,600 (3,350)	178,800 (9,770)	100,400 (4,390)	120,800 (5,540)	120,300 (3,730)	163,700 (3,970)	190,800 (10,740)
Public	78,400 (4,210)	89,000 (4,000)	95,500 (5,450)	124,900 (4,280)	136,200 (8,820)	89,200 (4,650)	104,000 (4,240)	107,700 (6,030)	142,000 (4,490)	145,900 (9,960)
Private nonprofit	101,000 (6,220)	119,800 (7,670)	114,300 (4,820)	155,400 (4,490)	213,500 (17,010)	109,500 (6,700)	136,400 (8,100)	127,800 (5,430)	174,700 (5,470)	226,800 (19,300)
Private for-profit	‡ (†)	‡ (†)	‡ (†)	191,800 (19,670)	174,300 (6,100)	‡ (†)	‡ (†)	‡ (†)	201,400 (23,560)	194,500 (6,120)
Graduate degree program										
Postbaccalaureate certificate	31,400 (4,770)	27,900 (5,990)	36,800 (3,720)	48,200 (5,540)	56,300 (7,990)	37,400 (3,930)	39,900 (5,720)	45,300 (4,260)	66,300 (5,820)	69,300 (8,270)
Master of business administration (M.B.A.)	40,900 (4,190)	48,100 (5,670)	42,700 (4,310)	44,600 (3,140)	52,200 (3,940)	48,400 (3,570)	57,000 (6,060)	55,700 (3,530)	56,100 (4,160)	67,800 (4,350)
Master of education (any)	26,400 (1,820)	34,600 (1,930)	35,100 (2,000)	45,400 (2,740)	43,500 (3,560)	32,900 (2,380)	42,400 (2,580)	46,100 (2,980)	64,000 (4,050)	56,400 (3,550)
Other master of arts (M.A.) except in education	33,600 (2,910)	37,600 (4,960)	42,100 (3,750)	53,300 (3,870)	55,100 (5,380)	45,000 (4,270)	49,900 (5,230)	56,200 (4,880)	72,300 (6,070)	74,400 (5,250)
Other master of science (M.S.) except in education	33,700 (2,380)	39,700 (3,950)	39,400 (2,410)	49,600 (2,910)	49,900 (3,150)	45,900 (3,550)	46,900 (4,140)	50,300 (2,830)	66,400 (3,280)	63,700 (3,080)
Theology (M.Div., M.H.L., or B.D.)	‡ (†)	‡ (†)	‡ (†)	‡ (†)	‡ (†)	‡ (†)	‡ (†)	‡ (†)	‡ (†)	‡ (†)
Other master's degree[3]	39,300 (2,420)	36,200 (2,430)	47,700 (2,200)	53,400 (2,530)	59,700 (3,740)	48,300 (3,200)	43,800 (3,380)	57,200 (2,440)	68,100 (2,800)	76,800 (3,790)
Ph.D. except in education	49,600 (6,090)	55,800 (3,950)	56,200 (3,340)	72,500 (3,560)	100,800 (8,110)	49,500 (6,180)	60,100 (3,690)	57,600 (3,440)	71,000 (3,770)	101,000 (8,200)
Education (any doctorate)	‡ (†)	64,300 (12,360)	68,600 (8,370)	88,300 (6,550)	105,900 (13,220)	‡ (†)	68,800 (11,640)	71,500 (8,230)	102,300 (7,890)	114,400 (14,290)
Medicine (M.D. or D.O.)	115,300 (5,960)	144,100 (10,950)	150,300 (8,640)	181,400 (8,490)	232,300 (25,950)	127,500 (6,330)	158,300 (10,390)	158,800 (9,270)	199,100 (8,720)	251,600 (32,040)
Other health science professional practice doctorate[4]	106,200 (9,410)	105,400 (13,010)	107,500 (9,640)	145,600 (7,660)	198,200 (17,600)	118,100 (9,270)	126,500 (13,640)	126,900 (11,080)	171,900 (8,610)	207,000 (17,080)
Law (LL.B. or J.D.)	75,900 (3,230)	95,100 (5,250)	97,000 (3,090)	138,000 (5,500)	134,600 (10,700)	84,300 (3,720)	109,400 (5,950)	110,600 (3,710)	153,100 (6,410)	148,800 (11,230)
Other doctorate (non-Ph.D.)[5]	53,900 (10,240)	85,400 (6,720)	95,300 (8,340)	114,400 (6,420)	120,300 (12,610)	65,900 (10,030)	94,900 (8,690)	104,200 (8,230)	129,900 (7,200)	135,200 (12,010)

†Not applicable.
‡Reporting standards not met. Either there are too few cases for a reliable estimate or the coefficient of variation (CV) is 50 percent or greater.
[1]Individuals who attended more than one institution for graduate studies are included in the subtotals by degree type but excluded from the detail by control of institution.
[2]Includes chiropractic, dentistry, law, medicine, optometry, pharmacy, podiatry, and veterinary medicine.
[3]Includes public administration or policy, social work, fine arts, public health, and other.
[4]Includes chiropractic, dentistry, optometry, pharmacy, podiatry, and veterinary medicine.
[5]Includes science or engineering, psychology, business or public administration, fine arts, theology, and other. Estimates for 2011–12 and 2015–16 also include "other professional practice doctoral degrees," which were not reported as a separate category in previous years.
[6]Constant dollars based on the Consumer Price Index, prepared by the Bureau of Labor Statistics, U.S. Department of Labor, adjusted to a school-year basis.
NOTE: Data refer to students who completed graduate degrees in the academic years indicated. Data are based on the principal balance (excluding interest) as of June 30th of the survey year (e.g., the 2015–16 data are based on the principal balance as of June 30, 2016). Average amounts owed were calculated only for graduate degree completers who had outstanding loans at the level of education indicated. Data include federal and private student loans, but exclude Parent PLUS loans. Direct Subsidized Loans for graduate students were discontinued after academic year 2011–12.
SOURCE: U.S. Department of Education, National Center for Education Statistics, 1999–2000, 2003–04, 2007–08, 2011–12, and 2015–16 National Postsecondary Student Aid Study (NPSAS:2000, NPSAS:04, NPSAS:08, NPSAS:12, and NPSAS:16). (This table was prepared May 2019.)

Table 333.10. Revenues of public degree-granting postsecondary institutions, by source of revenue and level of institution: Selected years, 2007–08 through 2016–17

Level of institution and year	Total revenues	Operating revenue							
		Tuition and fees[1]	Grants and contracts			Sales and services of auxiliary enterprises[1]	Sales and services of hospitals	Independent operations	Other operating revenues[2]
			Federal	State	Local and private				
1	2	3	4	5	6	7	8	9	10
	In thousands of current dollars								
All levels									
2007–08	$273,070,439	$48,068,614	$25,499,038	$7,831,049	$8,699,401	$20,487,684	$25,183,379	$1,174,836	$14,085,890
2010–11	324,473,342	60,268,927	29,821,416	7,019,420	10,110,953	23,605,640	30,998,993	1,330,334	15,758,118
2013–14	353,100,435	70,499,808	27,558,154	7,095,873	11,186,861	25,476,716	37,596,888	1,430,079	18,202,691
2014–15	346,812,800	73,476,374	27,290,446	7,409,069	12,460,665	26,583,777	41,582,927	1,508,778	19,489,191
2015–16	364,349,979	76,603,554	27,677,857	7,779,950	12,979,361	27,585,281	45,956,104	1,537,639	20,825,325
2016–17	390,783,205	79,262,720	28,261,502	8,018,537	13,811,573	28,421,866	50,089,201	1,635,853	21,531,502
4-year									
2007–08	223,530,092	40,083,063	23,500,633	5,715,188	8,106,887	18,507,688	25,183,379	1,174,836	13,112,536
2010–11	266,688,058	51,046,786	27,656,656	5,480,573	9,543,780	21,506,767	30,998,993	1,330,334	14,830,150
2013–14	297,232,858	61,161,200	25,781,989	5,523,623	10,656,706	23,638,690	37,596,888	1,430,079	17,328,388
2014–15	290,239,686	64,152,076	25,570,548	5,578,550	11,912,198	24,830,846	41,582,927	1,508,778	18,615,218
2015–16	308,813,202	67,533,647	26,106,025	6,007,791	12,472,377	25,984,815	45,956,104	1,537,639	19,950,465
2016–17	335,469,510	70,105,960	26,794,644	6,142,873	13,304,061	26,896,974	50,089,201	1,635,853	20,638,734
2-year									
2007–08	49,540,347	7,985,551	1,998,404	2,115,861	592,513	1,979,996	0	0	973,353
2010–11	57,785,284	9,222,142	2,164,760	1,538,848	567,174	2,098,872	0	0	927,968
2013–14	55,867,577	9,338,608	1,776,164	1,572,250	530,155	1,838,026	0	0	874,302
2014–15	56,573,114	9,324,298	1,719,898	1,830,518	548,467	1,752,931	0	0	873,974
2015–16	55,536,777	9,069,907	1,571,832	1,772,158	506,984	1,600,466	0	0	874,859
2016–17	55,313,694	9,156,760	1,466,858	1,875,663	507,512	1,524,892	0	0	892,768
	Percentage distribution								
All levels									
2007–08	100.00	17.60	9.34	2.87	3.19	7.50	9.22	0.43	5.16
2010–11	100.00	18.57	9.19	2.16	3.12	7.28	9.55	0.41	4.86
2013–14	100.00	19.97	7.80	2.01	3.17	7.22	10.65	0.41	5.16
2014–15	100.00	21.19	7.87	2.14	3.59	7.67	11.99	0.44	5.62
2015–16	100.00	21.02	7.60	2.14	3.56	7.57	12.61	0.42	5.72
2016–17	100.00	20.28	7.23	2.05	3.53	7.27	12.82	0.42	5.51
4-year									
2007–08	100.00	17.93	10.51	2.56	3.63	8.28	11.27	0.53	5.87
2010–11	100.00	19.14	10.37	2.06	3.58	8.06	11.62	0.50	5.56
2013–14	100.00	20.58	8.67	1.86	3.59	7.95	12.65	0.48	5.83
2014–15	100.00	22.10	8.81	1.92	4.10	8.56	14.33	0.52	6.41
2015–16	100.00	21.87	8.45	1.95	4.04	8.41	14.88	0.50	6.46
2016–17	100.00	20.90	7.99	1.83	3.97	8.02	14.93	0.49	6.15
2-year									
2007–08	100.00	16.12	4.03	4.27	1.20	4.00	0.00	0.00	1.96
2010–11	100.00	15.96	3.75	2.66	0.98	3.63	0.00	0.00	1.61
2013–14	100.00	16.72	3.18	2.81	0.95	3.29	0.00	0.00	1.56
2014–15	100.00	16.48	3.04	3.24	0.97	3.10	0.00	0.00	1.54
2015–16	100.00	16.33	2.83	3.19	0.91	2.88	0.00	0.00	1.58
2016–17	100.00	16.55	2.65	3.39	0.92	2.76	0.00	0.00	1.61
	Revenue per full-time-equivalent student in constant 2017–18 dollars[3]								
All levels									
2007–08	$32,846	$5,782	$3,067	$942	$1,046	$2,464	$3,029	$141	$1,694
2010–11	33,049	6,139	3,037	715	1,030	2,404	3,157	135	1,605
2013–14	34,855	6,959	2,720	700	1,104	2,515	3,711	141	1,797
2014–15	34,223	7,251	2,693	731	1,230	2,623	4,103	149	1,923
2015–16	35,897	7,547	2,727	767	1,279	2,718	4,528	151	2,052
2016–17	37,797	7,666	2,733	776	1,336	2,749	4,845	158	2,083
4-year									
2007–08	43,719	7,840	4,596	1,118	1,586	3,620	4,925	230	2,565
2010–11	45,104	8,633	4,678	927	1,614	3,637	5,243	225	2,508
2013–14	46,221	9,511	4,009	859	1,657	3,676	5,846	222	2,695
2014–15	44,150	9,758	3,890	849	1,812	3,777	6,325	230	2,832
2015–16	46,137	10,090	3,900	898	1,863	3,882	6,866	230	2,981
2016–17	47,504	9,927	3,794	870	1,884	3,809	7,093	232	2,923
2-year									
2007–08	15,478	2,495	624	661	185	619	0	0	304
2010–11	14,797	2,361	554	394	145	537	0	0	238
2013–14	15,100	2,524	480	425	143	497	0	0	236
2014–15	15,891	2,619	483	514	154	492	0	0	246
2015–16	16,067	2,624	455	513	147	463	0	0	253
2016–17	16,879	2,794	448	572	155	465	0	0	272

See notes at end of table.

Table 333.10. Revenues of public degree-granting postsecondary institutions, by source of revenue and level of institution: Selected years, 2007–08 through 2016–17—Continued

Level of institution and year	Nonoperating revenue: Appropriations: Federal	Appropriations: State	Appropriations: Local	Nonoperating grants: Federal	Nonoperating grants: State	Nonoperating grants: Local	Gifts	Investment return (gain or loss)	Other nonoperating revenues	Other revenues and additions: Capital appropriations	Capital grants and gifts	Additions to permanent endowments	Other
1	11	12	13	14	15	16	17	18	19	20	21	22	23
						In thousands of current dollars							
All levels													
2007–08	$1,849,775	$68,394,962	$9,302,794	$10,045,255	$1,925,994	$177,116	$6,053,147	$5,278,656	$2,234,287	$7,575,827	$3,092,817	$1,151,300	$4,958,618
2010–11	1,946,965	63,063,322	10,023,157	24,231,846	3,404,970	228,055	6,287,358	14,215,863	6,888,955	5,645,126	3,745,699	965,007	4,913,217
2013–14	1,837,494	62,639,192	11,112,241	21,911,740	4,030,058	291,250	8,119,273	20,024,073	6,607,255	5,316,926	3,835,969	1,123,705	7,204,191
2014–15	1,779,758	65,172,431	11,248,036	21,590,392	4,406,434	291,197	8,087,953	1,342,180	5,155,201	6,295,695	3,709,702	1,012,258	6,920,335
2015–16	1,666,978	67,145,689	12,213,323	20,477,681	4,861,395	417,856	8,490,640	3,926,734	5,417,126	6,467,364	3,781,347	1,130,058	7,408,716
2016–17	1,923,743	68,619,833	12,961,692	19,697,099	5,163,737	432,922	8,264,052	15,039,619	7,997,353	6,571,742	3,665,778	1,189,554	8,223,325
4-year													
2007–08	1,776,452	53,268,648	436,856	5,194,645	1,217,818	103,824	5,781,369	4,430,479	1,773,078	5,635,746	2,764,505	1,138,323	4,624,141
2010–11	1,853,109	49,025,814	507,010	11,812,776	2,320,005	130,451	6,061,629	13,781,509	6,061,802	3,884,591	3,249,844	943,748	4,661,730
2013–14	1,732,216	49,142,721	562,506	11,161,457	2,657,000	169,670	7,872,542	19,709,180	5,934,306	3,867,745	3,563,297	1,106,470	6,636,187
2014–15	1,675,671	51,089,552	587,588	11,329,817	2,866,382	158,091	7,767,802	1,194,597	4,464,354	4,632,561	3,383,607	998,211	6,340,310
2015–16	1,617,876	53,067,153	1,051,753	11,522,288	3,008,676	205,597	8,207,812	3,771,368	4,666,805	4,742,620	3,482,369	1,117,698	6,802,323
2016–17	1,884,327	54,698,844	1,400,806	11,400,001	3,227,298	243,196	7,994,260	14,808,960	7,167,064	4,994,242	3,307,490	1,176,695	7,558,027
2-year													
2007–08	73,324	15,126,314	8,865,938	4,850,610	708,176	73,292	271,778	848,177	461,209	1,940,082	328,312	12,978	334,477
2010–11	93,856	14,037,508	9,516,147	12,419,069	1,084,965	97,604	225,730	434,353	827,153	1,760,535	495,855	21,258	251,487
2013–14	105,278	13,496,471	10,549,735	10,750,283	1,373,058	121,580	246,731	314,894	672,949	1,449,181	272,671	17,236	568,004
2014–15	104,087	14,082,879	10,660,448	10,260,575	1,540,052	133,106	320,151	147,583	690,846	1,663,135	326,095	14,047	580,025
2015–16	49,102	14,078,537	11,161,570	8,955,393	1,852,719	212,259	282,827	155,366	750,321	1,724,744	298,979	12,361	606,393
2016–17	39,417	13,920,990	11,560,886	8,297,097	1,936,438	189,726	269,793	230,659	830,289	1,577,500	358,288	12,859	665,298
						Percentage distribution							
All levels													
2007–08	0.68	25.05	3.41	3.68	0.71	0.06	2.22	1.93	0.82	2.77	1.13	0.42	1.82
2010–11	0.60	19.44	3.09	7.47	1.05	0.07	1.94	4.38	2.12	1.74	1.15	0.30	1.51
2013–14	0.52	17.74	3.15	6.21	1.14	0.08	2.30	5.67	1.87	1.51	1.09	0.32	2.04
2014–15	0.51	18.79	3.24	6.23	1.27	0.08	2.33	0.39	1.49	1.82	1.07	0.29	2.00
2015–16	0.46	18.43	3.35	5.62	1.33	0.11	2.33	1.08	1.49	1.78	1.04	0.31	2.03
2016–17	0.49	17.56	3.32	5.04	1.32	0.11	2.11	3.85	2.05	1.68	0.94	0.30	2.10
4-year													
2007–08	0.79	23.83	0.20	2.32	0.54	0.05	2.59	1.98	0.79	2.52	1.24	0.51	2.07
2010–11	0.69	18.38	0.19	4.43	0.87	0.05	2.27	5.17	2.27	1.46	1.22	0.35	1.75
2013–14	0.58	16.53	0.19	3.76	0.89	0.06	2.65	6.63	2.00	1.30	1.20	0.37	2.23
2014–15	0.58	17.60	0.20	3.90	0.99	0.05	2.68	0.41	1.54	1.60	1.17	0.34	2.18
2015–16	0.52	17.18	0.34	3.73	0.97	0.07	2.66	1.22	1.51	1.54	1.13	0.36	2.20
2016–17	0.56	16.31	0.42	3.40	0.96	0.07	2.38	4.41	2.14	1.49	0.99	0.35	2.25
2-year													
2007–08	0.15	30.53	17.90	9.79	1.43	0.15	0.55	1.71	0.93	3.92	0.66	0.03	0.68
2010–11	0.16	24.29	16.47	21.49	1.88	0.17	0.39	0.75	1.43	3.05	0.86	0.04	0.44
2013–14	0.19	24.16	18.88	19.24	2.46	0.22	0.44	0.56	1.20	2.59	0.49	0.03	1.02
2014–15	0.18	24.89	18.84	18.14	2.72	0.24	0.57	0.26	1.22	2.94	0.58	0.02	1.03
2015–16	0.09	25.35	20.10	16.13	3.34	0.38	0.51	0.28	1.35	3.11	0.54	0.02	1.09
2016–17	0.07	25.17	20.90	15.00	3.50	0.34	0.49	0.42	1.50	2.85	0.65	0.02	1.20
						Revenue per full-time-equivalent student in constant 2017–18 dollars[3]							
All levels													
2007–08	$222	$8,227	$1,119	$1,208	$232	$21	$728	$635	$269	$911	$372	$138	$596
2010–11	198	6,423	1,021	2,468	347	23	640	1,448	702	575	382	98	500
2013–14	181	6,183	1,097	2,163	398	29	801	1,977	652	525	379	111	711
2014–15	176	6,431	1,110	2,131	435	29	798	132	509	621	366	100	683
2015–16	164	6,615	1,203	2,018	479	41	837	387	534	637	373	111	730
2016–17	186	6,637	1,254	1,905	499	42	799	1,455	774	636	355	115	795
4-year													
2007–08	347	10,418	85	1,016	238	20	1,131	867	347	1,102	541	223	904
2010–11	313	8,292	86	1,998	392	22	1,025	2,331	1,025	657	550	160	788
2013–14	269	7,642	87	1,736	413	26	1,224	3,065	923	601	554	172	1,032
2014–15	255	7,771	89	1,723	436	24	1,182	182	679	705	515	152	964
2015–16	242	7,928	157	1,721	450	31	1,226	563	697	709	520	167	1,016
2016–17	267	7,746	198	1,614	457	34	1,132	2,097	1,015	707	468	167	1,070
2-year													
2007–08	23	4,726	2,770	1,515	221	23	85	265	144	606	103	4	105
2010–11	24	3,594	2,437	3,180	278	25	58	111	212	451	127	5	64
2013–14	28	3,648	2,851	2,906	371	33	67	85	182	392	74	5	154
2014–15	29	3,956	2,995	2,882	433	37	90	41	194	467	92	4	163
2015–16	14	4,073	3,229	2,591	536	61	82	45	217	499	86	4	175
2016–17	12	4,248	3,528	2,532	591	58	82	70	253	481	109	4	203

[1]After deducting discounts and allowances.
[2]Includes sales and services of educational activities.
[3]Constant dollars based on the Consumer Price Index, prepared by the Bureau of Labor Statistics, U.S. Department of Labor, adjusted to a school-year basis.
NOTE: Degree-granting institutions grant associate's or higher degrees and participate in Title IV federal financial aid programs. Includes data for public institutions reporting data according to either the Governmental Accounting Standards Board (GASB) or the Financial Accounting Standards Board (FASB) questionnaire. Data in this table pertain to institutions' fiscal years that end in the academic year noted. Some data have been revised from previously published figures. Detail may not sum to totals because of rounding.
SOURCE: U.S. Department of Education, National Center for Education Statistics, Integrated Postsecondary Education Data System (IPEDS), Spring 2008 through Spring 2017, Fall Enrollment component; and Spring 2009 through Spring 2018, Finance component. (This table was prepared December 2018.)

Table 333.20. Revenues of public degree-granting postsecondary institutions, by source of revenue and state or jurisdiction: 2016–17

[In thousands of current dollars]

State or jurisdiction	Total revenues	Operating revenue: Total	Operating revenue: Tuition and fees[1]	Operating revenue: Federal grants and contracts	Operating revenue: State, local, and private grants and contracts	Operating revenue: Sales and services of auxiliary enterprises[1]	Operating revenue: Sales and services of hospitals	Operating revenue: Independent operations and other[2]	Nonoperating revenue: Total[3]	Nonoperating revenue: State appro-priations	Nonoperating revenue: Local appro-priations	Other revenues and additions
1	2	3	4	5	6	7	8	9	10	11	12	13
United States	**$390,783,205**	**$231,032,755**	**$79,262,720**	**$28,261,502**	**$21,830,110**	**$28,421,866**	**$50,089,201**	**$23,167,355**	**$140,100,050**	**$68,619,833**	**$12,961,692**	**$19,650,399**
Alabama	8,344,629	5,853,051	1,865,870	688,590	258,785	543,327	2,099,796	396,682	2,352,862	1,397,897	3,005	138,716
Alaska	829,517	391,394	135,096	131,421	63,310	39,705	0	21,862	415,604	333,895	12,356	22,520
Arizona	6,858,333	3,859,365	2,367,290	533,946	299,241	449,585	0	209,303	2,869,109	739,905	874,897	129,859
Arkansas	4,207,496	2,878,718	610,126	210,043	206,084	322,595	1,186,364	343,506	1,279,030	758,090	34,099	49,748
California	59,143,595	33,678,549	7,621,858	3,516,586	3,186,842	2,331,347	11,241,268	5,780,649	23,399,137	10,085,262	3,975,545	2,065,909
Colorado	7,384,698	6,156,205	2,311,052	1,009,997	792,577	620,057	876,298	546,224	940,388	37,332	96,273	288,105
Connecticut	3,911,063	2,069,745	736,404	179,911	115,955	322,249	398,194	317,032	1,433,445	1,185,582	0	407,873
Delaware	1,449,750	930,115	504,262	144,178	80,645	154,039	0	46,991	503,732	243,897	0	15,903
District of Columbia	159,465	59,422	34,424	15,761	5,701	521	0	3,014	90,416	77,671	0	9,627
Florida	12,721,029	6,024,198	2,603,635	1,107,541	1,258,248	891,161	254	163,358	6,067,896	4,040,225	0	628,935
Georgia	8,758,789	5,218,404	2,243,776	881,793	670,897	915,467	221,913	284,558	3,233,159	2,267,964	138	307,226
Hawaii	1,774,938	791,451	270,681	293,913	87,366	103,408	0	36,082	785,813	471,453	0	197,675
Idaho	1,341,067	695,438	356,311	124,105	49,742	113,342	0	51,939	619,499	419,837	30,247	26,130
Illinois	12,938,610	6,264,575	2,569,491	808,544	360,265	881,185	797,636	847,454	6,615,221	1,108,209	1,142,872	58,814
Indiana	7,208,978	4,529,773	2,410,405	587,803	304,060	780,669	0	446,836	2,512,411	1,527,994	4,514	166,794
Iowa	6,072,529	4,487,985	1,018,639	504,831	157,914	583,545	1,846,448	376,608	1,463,636	828,453	147,960	120,908
Kansas	3,756,036	2,188,635	947,098	310,496	193,542	449,801	0	287,698	1,405,040	734,734	296,897	162,361
Kentucky	6,407,593	4,473,617	1,117,141	416,294	253,647	390,297	1,827,453	468,784	1,622,590	885,900	24,906	311,387
Louisiana	4,269,931	2,784,367	1,192,855	285,278	707,518	416,487	49,773	132,456	1,260,943	776,872	0	224,621
Maine	904,988	489,849	229,331	62,299	59,430	88,346	0	50,442	394,810	277,049	0	20,329
Maryland	7,195,545	4,118,660	1,723,127	737,525	463,039	746,374	0	448,594	2,632,019	1,719,050	393,599	444,865
Massachusetts	5,649,992	3,470,830	1,483,177	406,794	286,442	567,145	0	727,273	1,884,873	1,421,967	0	294,288
Michigan	18,359,719	12,496,022	4,296,359	1,534,742	632,032	1,196,632	4,200,081	636,176	5,385,698	1,798,264	559,346	478,000
Minnesota	5,569,283	3,063,459	1,326,125	444,076	462,283	650,813	0	180,161	2,306,218	1,306,661	0	199,606
Mississippi	4,646,323	2,875,358	712,660	335,209	216,082	378,761	1,074,214	158,433	1,524,285	965,054	69,843	246,680
Missouri	5,582,370	3,557,662	1,168,874	222,493	196,855	858,735	944,514	166,191	1,830,295	895,680	157,277	194,413
Montana	1,142,921	722,522	307,948	176,390	43,621	105,942	0	88,621	366,747	243,809	10,799	53,652
Nebraska	2,853,093	1,467,630	479,710	231,398	254,428	346,558	19,902	135,634	1,212,117	721,691	170,110	173,345
Nevada	1,757,768	897,836	417,671	156,784	102,096	91,597	0	129,689	839,523	560,702	0	20,409
New Hampshire	1,084,738	768,123	394,127	68,036	51,626	221,913	0	32,420	222,794	124,775	0	93,821
New Jersey	8,155,910	4,927,652	2,394,590	458,485	454,004	605,348	711,167	304,058	2,790,566	1,591,758	212,472	437,691
New Mexico	3,845,085	2,335,422	303,906	387,284	153,492	101,095	1,191,251	198,395	1,391,814	752,122	264,227	117,849
New York	17,421,958	8,539,132	2,873,885	701,876	1,290,108	716,775	2,722,639	233,849	8,087,404	4,899,793	976,477	795,423
North Carolina	11,753,406	5,272,062	1,990,460	919,978	346,126	1,756,911	0	258,585	6,054,388	3,805,619	242,273	426,957
North Dakota	1,256,710	738,077	324,674	138,065	56,745	110,550	0	108,044	439,509	336,141	5,424	79,123
Ohio	14,934,748	10,407,482	3,755,194	683,901	613,457	1,232,937	3,721,890	400,103	4,142,437	2,107,699	178,479	384,830
Oklahoma	4,453,062	2,891,553	968,530	308,273	339,947	543,269	104,102	627,432	1,373,689	750,534	63,604	187,819
Oregon	7,203,393	5,232,244	1,294,137	663,987	337,831	568,381	2,154,958	212,950	1,709,862	676,660	265,502	261,287
Pennsylvania	15,637,696	12,238,091	4,437,962	1,307,665	694,118	1,099,137	3,930,766	768,443	3,302,621	1,294,264	119,756	96,984
Rhode Island	843,418	532,727	290,107	72,658	29,087	111,188	0	29,688	241,894	172,599	0	68,797
South Carolina	4,840,912	3,379,183	1,618,841	397,598	478,089	531,679	0	352,976	1,310,120	648,894	71,292	151,609
South Dakota	919,147	554,554	261,218	98,585	58,970	75,387	0	60,394	288,155	194,881	0	76,438
Tennessee	4,841,617	2,429,081	1,162,579	280,780	327,264	363,605	0	294,852	2,162,096	1,252,490	6,254	250,440
Texas	41,383,682	17,931,040	5,869,760	2,101,148	2,653,562	1,595,261	2,996,105	2,715,203	16,444,565	5,908,211	2,066,180	7,008,077
Utah	6,710,115	5,079,565	854,947	447,801	159,441	275,377	2,192,329	1,149,670	1,466,388	904,721	0	164,162
Vermont	926,304	747,579	405,807	120,035	67,260	117,249	0	37,228	171,995	69,725	0	6,730
Virginia	11,387,071	7,425,083	2,871,574	878,055	267,533	1,434,820	1,570,246	402,856	3,449,098	1,815,144	3,815	512,890
Washington	10,575,251	7,334,189	1,980,793	1,260,068	892,567	769,298	1,869,238	562,225	2,643,901	1,438,759	0	597,162
West Virginia	1,917,677	1,270,607	615,238	130,872	211,968	250,523	0	62,005	578,526	374,378	601	68,544
Wisconsin	6,607,082	3,922,171	1,434,887	659,398	514,026	477,702	0	836,159	2,473,708	1,286,869	435,592	211,203
Wyoming	960,116	309,959	90,455	59,480	61,613	61,182	0	37,230	549,646	349,444	45,062	100,510
U.S. Service Academies	1,924,054	272,346	7,653	58,733	2,630	62,586	140,403	341	1,558,358	33,258	0	93,350
Other jurisdictions	**1,035,712**	**345,703**	**61,122**	**133,790**	**34,421**	**9,535**	**79,117**	**27,718**	**682,570**	**490,701**	**46,667**	**7,439**
American Samoa	16,399	8,258	1,163	4,717	0	203	0	2,175	8,140	3,000	0	0
Federated States of Micronesia	20,955	9,713	708	3,436	3,880	1,581	0	108	11,243	0	0	0
Guam	135,236	59,583	16,143	30,379	2,326	1,700	0	9,036	75,480	26,134	18,321	172
Marshall Islands	15,047	7,233	641	5,657	0	867	0	68	6,979	2,971	0	835
Northern Marianas	18,080	9,796	2,070	7,316	0	386	0	24	8,284	5,376	0	0
Palau	10,685	5,488	2,551	2,382	0	98	0	456	5,198	2,411	0	0
Puerto Rico	744,590	209,190	23,850	64,316	25,050	1,802	79,117	15,055	532,930	450,809	0	2,470
U.S. Virgin Islands	74,719	36,442	13,997	15,587	3,164	2,898	0	796	34,315	0	28,346	3,961

[1]After deducting discounts and allowances.
[2]Includes sales and services of educational activities.
[3]Includes other categories not separately shown.
NOTE: Degree-granting institutions grant associate's or higher degrees and participate in Title IV federal financial aid programs. Includes data for public institutions reporting data according to either the Governmental Accounting Standards Board (GASB) or the Financial Accounting Standards Board (FASB) questionnaire. Data in this table pertain to institutions' fiscal years that end in the academic year noted. Detail may not sum to totals because of rounding.
SOURCE: U.S. Department of Education, National Center for Education Statistics, Integrated Postsecondary Education Data System (IPEDS), Spring 2018, Finance component. (This table was prepared December 2018.)

Table 333.40. Total revenue of private nonprofit degree-granting postsecondary institutions, by source of funds and level of institution: Selected years: 1999–2000 through 2016–17

Level of institution and year	Total	Student tuition and fees (net of allowances)	Federal appropriations, grants, and contracts[1]	State and local appropriations, grants, and contracts	Private gifts, grants, and contracts: Total	Private gifts, grants, and contracts: Private grants and contracts	Private gifts, grants, and contracts: Private gifts and contributions from affiliated entities	Investment return (gain or loss)	Educational activities	Auxiliary enterprises (net of allowances)	Hospitals	Other
1	2	3	4	5	6	7	8	9	10	11	12	13
	In thousands of current dollars											
All levels												
1999–2000	$120,625,806	$29,651,812	$12,191,827	$1,697,979	$16,488,984	—	—	$37,763,518	$2,865,606	$8,317,607	$7,208,600	$4,439,874
2004–05	140,150,716	41,394,424	19,699,204	1,957,921	16,738,916	—	—	30,431,521	3,595,559	10,823,963	10,377,808	5,131,401
2005–06	152,757,151	44,273,758	19,683,887	2,075,850	18,380,034	—	—	35,636,137	3,716,409	11,600,117	11,536,658	5,854,300
2006–07	182,377,987	47,482,331	20,193,722	2,164,167	20,194,264	—	—	55,907,577	4,104,373	12,291,765	12,636,904	7,402,884
2007–08	139,261,907	50,741,273	20,204,251	2,386,121	20,991,920	—	—	6,261,553	4,848,435	12,930,918	13,298,642	7,598,794
2008–09	69,064,340	53,698,893	21,026,721	2,391,238	17,670,642	—	—	-64,204,943	4,787,360	13,579,506	14,790,231	5,324,691
2009–10	168,688,480	56,386,895	22,913,755	2,193,062	18,019,300	$4,189,574	$13,829,726	28,427,192	4,821,683	14,080,329	16,541,461	5,304,802
2010–11	207,132,349	60,069,691	24,319,663	2,165,584	22,096,853	4,379,206	17,717,647	53,574,169	4,979,595	14,797,601	17,521,091	7,608,102
2011–12	161,843,203	63,010,873	24,147,131	1,964,921	21,619,470	4,446,517	17,172,953	4,538,153	5,082,873	15,500,185	18,658,649	7,320,948
2012–13	202,042,331	65,562,231	23,710,290	1,939,417	22,335,345	4,834,258	17,501,087	38,532,782	5,530,428	15,969,232	19,011,711	9,450,894
2013–14	228,806,876	67,681,378	23,640,029	1,971,815	25,842,976	5,152,784	20,690,192	57,147,772	6,280,766	16,407,013	20,667,484	9,167,642
2014–15	200,395,534	70,181,110	24,186,839	2,113,187	26,932,309	5,520,105	21,412,204	21,274,906	6,702,519	16,883,478	23,880,282	8,240,906
2015–16	182,571,838	72,100,188	23,471,268	2,162,083	28,622,642	5,819,574	22,803,069	-2,735,211	7,042,281	17,608,294	24,107,516	10,192,778
2016–17	242,588,422	73,968,461	25,253,779	2,105,109	28,421,979	6,191,574	22,230,405	48,838,751	7,516,294	18,004,563	26,730,794	11,748,691
4-year												
1999–2000	119,708,625	29,257,523	12,133,829	1,673,707	16,346,616	—	—	37,698,219	2,837,784	8,261,507	7,208,600	4,290,841
2004–05	139,528,763	41,045,608	19,622,002	1,931,021	16,671,017	—	—	30,408,545	3,581,869	10,784,161	10,377,808	5,106,733
2005–06	152,162,678	43,955,298	19,608,453	2,045,814	18,321,593	—	—	35,605,422	3,699,630	11,562,470	11,536,658	5,827,340
2006–07	181,850,660	47,211,942	20,137,197	2,143,146	20,144,883	—	—	55,857,135	4,096,086	12,253,089	12,636,904	7,370,278
2007–08	138,760,610	50,436,622	20,143,562	2,361,744	20,938,758	—	—	6,273,767	4,837,355	12,892,828	13,298,642	7,577,331
2008–09	68,617,705	53,399,912	20,967,794	2,370,169	17,624,319	—	—	-64,172,755	4,781,845	13,542,690	14,790,231	5,313,500
2009–10	168,169,216	56,087,965	22,843,520	2,179,050	17,968,453	4,185,607	13,782,846	28,406,397	4,814,283	14,044,652	16,541,461	5,283,434
2010–11	206,473,105	59,603,541	24,260,568	2,150,124	22,057,300	4,376,381	17,680,919	53,557,782	4,975,158	14,762,888	17,521,091	7,584,652
2011–12	161,246,877	62,571,879	24,098,863	1,953,307	21,580,612	4,444,004	17,136,608	4,532,992	5,079,866	15,471,860	18,658,649	7,298,849
2012–13	201,526,648	65,213,804	23,664,427	1,925,893	22,293,530	4,831,951	17,461,579	38,519,232	5,527,564	15,939,735	19,011,711	9,430,753
2013–14	228,233,305	67,325,986	23,578,760	1,959,405	25,792,211	5,149,819	20,642,392	57,105,397	6,278,456	16,376,022	20,667,484	9,149,584
2014–15	199,546,338	69,519,464	24,127,099	2,102,335	26,895,138	5,518,411	21,376,727	21,267,202	6,696,900	16,840,357	23,880,282	8,217,562
2015–16	181,729,580	71,425,134	23,427,914	2,155,610	28,581,387	5,816,843	22,764,544	-2,736,188	7,037,367	17,562,236	24,107,516	10,168,604
2016–17	241,758,472	73,309,539	25,215,712	2,099,522	28,381,726	6,189,167	22,192,559	48,824,143	7,511,283	17,964,307	26,730,794	11,721,446
2-year												
1999–2000	917,181	394,289	57,998	24,272	142,368	—	—	65,299	27,822	56,100	0	149,033
2004–05	621,953	348,815	77,202	26,900	67,899	—	—	22,976	13,690	39,802	0	24,668
2005–06	594,473	318,460	75,433	30,036	58,441	—	—	30,716	16,778	37,648	0	26,960
2006–07	527,327	270,389	56,525	21,021	49,381	—	—	50,442	8,288	38,675	0	32,606
2007–08	501,297	304,651	60,689	24,377	53,162	—	—	-12,214	11,080	38,091	0	21,462
2008–09	446,635	298,981	58,927	21,069	46,323	—	—	-32,187	5,515	36,816	0	11,191
2009–10	519,264	298,930	70,235	14,012	50,847	3,967	46,880	20,795	7,400	35,677	0	21,368
2010–11	659,244	466,149	59,095	15,460	39,553	2,825	36,727	16,388	4,437	34,712	0	23,450
2011–12	596,326	438,994	48,269	11,614	38,858	2,513	36,345	5,161	3,007	28,325	0	22,099
2012–13	515,683	348,427	45,863	13,524	41,815	2,307	39,508	13,550	2,865	29,498	0	20,140
2013–14	573,571	355,392	61,269	12,409	50,766	2,965	47,800	42,376	2,311	30,991	0	18,058
2014–15	849,197	661,646	59,740	10,852	37,171	1,694	35,477	7,704	5,619	43,121	0	23,344
2015–16	842,258	675,053	43,354	6,473	41,256	2,731	38,525	976	4,913	46,058	0	24,174
2016–17	829,950	658,922	38,068	5,587	40,253	2,407	37,846	14,608	5,012	40,256	0	27,245
	Percentage distribution											
All levels												
1999–2000	100.00	24.58	10.11	1.41	13.67	—	—	31.31	2.38	6.90	5.98	3.68
2004–05	100.00	29.54	14.06	1.40	11.94	—	—	21.71	2.57	7.72	7.40	3.66
2005–06	100.00	28.98	12.89	1.36	12.03	—	—	23.33	2.43	7.59	7.55	3.83
2006–07	100.00	26.04	11.07	1.19	11.07	—	—	30.65	2.25	6.74	6.93	4.06
2007–08	100.00	36.44	14.51	1.71	15.07	—	—	4.50	3.48	9.29	9.55	5.46
2008–09	100.00	77.75	30.45	3.46	25.59	—	—	-92.96	6.93	19.66	21.42	7.71
2009–10	100.00	33.43	13.58	1.30	10.68	2.48	8.20	16.85	2.86	8.35	9.81	3.14
2010–11	100.00	29.00	11.74	1.05	10.67	2.11	8.55	25.86	2.40	7.14	8.46	3.67
2011–12	100.00	38.93	14.92	1.21	13.36	2.75	10.61	2.80	3.14	9.58	11.53	4.52
2012–13	100.00	32.45	11.74	0.96	11.05	2.39	8.66	19.07	2.74	7.90	9.41	4.68
2013–14	100.00	29.58	10.33	0.86	11.29	2.25	9.04	24.98	2.75	7.17	9.03	4.01
2014–15	100.00	35.02	12.07	1.05	13.44	2.75	10.68	10.62	3.34	8.43	11.92	4.11
2015–16	100.00	39.49	12.86	1.18	15.68	3.19	12.49	-1.50	3.86	9.64	13.20	5.58
2016–17	100.00	30.49	10.41	0.87	11.72	2.55	9.16	20.13	3.10	7.42	11.02	4.84
4-year												
1999–2000	100.00	24.44	10.14	1.40	13.66	—	—	31.49	2.37	6.90	6.02	3.58
2004–05	100.00	29.42	14.06	1.38	11.95	—	—	21.79	2.57	7.73	7.44	3.66
2005–06	100.00	28.89	12.89	1.34	12.04	—	—	23.40	2.43	7.60	7.58	3.83
2006–07	100.00	25.96	11.07	1.18	11.08	—	—	30.72	2.25	6.74	6.95	4.05
2007–08	100.00	36.35	14.52	1.70	15.09	—	—	4.52	3.49	9.29	9.58	5.46
2008–09	100.00	77.82	30.56	3.45	25.68	—	—	-93.52	6.97	19.74	21.55	7.74
2009–10	100.00	33.35	13.58	1.30	10.68	2.49	8.20	16.89	2.86	8.35	9.84	3.14
2010–11	100.00	28.87	11.75	1.04	10.68	2.12	8.56	25.94	2.41	7.15	8.49	3.67
2011–12	100.00	38.81	14.95	1.21	13.38	2.76	10.63	2.81	3.15	9.60	11.57	4.53
2012–13	100.00	32.36	11.74	0.96	11.06	2.40	8.66	19.11	2.74	7.91	9.43	4.68
2013–14	100.00	29.50	10.33	0.86	11.30	2.26	9.04	25.02	2.75	7.18	9.06	4.01
2014–15	100.00	34.84	12.09	1.05	13.48	2.77	10.71	10.66	3.36	8.44	11.97	4.12
2015–16	100.00	39.30	12.89	1.19	15.73	3.20	12.53	-1.51	3.87	9.66	13.27	5.60
2016–17	100.00	30.32	10.43	0.87	11.74	2.56	9.18	20.20	3.11	7.43	11.06	4.85

See notes at end of table.

Table 333.40. Total revenue of private nonprofit degree-granting postsecondary institutions, by source of funds and level of institution: Selected years: 1999–2000 through 2016–17—Continued

Level of institution and year	Total	Student tuition and fees (net of allowances)	Federal appropriations, grants, and contracts[1]	State and local appropriations, grants, and contracts	Private gifts, grants, and contracts: Total	Private gifts, grants, and contracts: Private grants and contracts	Private gifts, grants, and contracts: Private gifts and contributions from affiliated entities	Investment return (gain or loss)	Educational activities	Auxiliary enterprises (net of allowances)	Hospitals	Other
1	2	3	4	5	6	7	8	9	10	11	12	13
2-year												
1999–2000	100.00	42.99	6.32	2.65	15.52	—	—	7.12	3.03	6.12	0.00	16.25
2004–05	100.00	56.08	12.41	4.33	10.92	—	—	3.69	2.20	6.40	0.00	3.97
2005–06	100.00	53.57	12.69	5.05	9.83	—	—	5.17	2.82	6.33	0.00	4.54
2006–07	100.00	51.28	10.72	3.99	9.36	—	—	9.57	1.57	7.33	0.00	6.18
2007–08	100.00	60.77	12.11	4.86	10.60	—	—	-2.44	2.21	7.60	0.00	4.28
2008–09	100.00	66.94	13.19	4.72	10.37	—	—	-7.21	1.23	8.24	0.00	2.51
2009–10	100.00	57.57	13.53	2.70	9.79	0.76	9.03	4.00	1.43	6.87	0.00	4.12
2010–11	100.00	70.71	8.96	2.35	6.00	0.43	5.57	2.49	0.67	5.27	0.00	3.56
2011–12	100.00	73.62	8.09	1.95	6.52	0.42	6.09	0.87	0.50	4.75	0.00	3.71
2012–13	100.00	67.57	8.89	2.62	8.11	0.45	7.66	2.63	0.56	5.72	0.00	3.91
2013–14	100.00	61.96	10.68	2.16	8.85	0.52	8.33	7.39	0.40	5.40	0.00	3.15
2014–15	100.00	77.91	7.03	1.28	4.38	0.20	4.18	0.91	0.66	5.08	0.00	2.75
2015–16	100.00	80.15	5.15	0.77	4.90	0.32	4.57	0.12	0.58	5.47	0.00	2.87
2016–17	100.00	79.39	4.59	0.67	4.85	0.29	4.56	1.76	0.60	4.85	0.00	3.28
	Revenue per full-time-equivalent student in constant 2017–18 dollars[2]											
All levels												
1999–2000	$69,635	$17,117	$7,038	$980	$9,519	—	—	$21,800	$1,654	$4,802	$4,161	$2,563
2004–05	63,221	18,673	8,886	883	7,551	—	—	13,727	1,622	4,883	4,681	2,315
2005–06	65,475	18,977	8,437	890	7,878	—	—	15,275	1,593	4,972	4,945	2,509
2006–07	74,853	19,488	8,288	888	8,288	—	—	22,946	1,685	5,045	5,187	3,038
2007–08	53,764	19,589	7,800	921	8,104	—	—	2,417	1,872	4,992	5,134	2,934
2008–09	25,909	20,145	7,888	897	6,629	—	—	-24,086	1,796	5,094	5,548	1,997
2009–10	61,017	20,396	8,288	793	6,518	$1,515	$5,002	10,282	1,744	5,093	5,983	1,919
2010–11	70,769	20,523	8,309	740	7,550	1,496	6,053	18,304	1,701	5,056	5,986	2,599
2011–12	53,257	20,735	7,946	647	7,114	1,463	5,651	1,493	1,673	5,101	6,140	2,409
2012–13	64,654	20,980	7,587	621	7,147	1,547	5,600	12,331	1,770	5,110	6,084	3,024
2013–14	71,991	21,295	7,438	620	8,131	1,621	6,510	17,981	1,976	5,162	6,503	2,884
2014–15	61,680	21,601	7,445	650	8,290	1,699	6,590	6,548	2,063	5,197	7,350	2,536
2015–16	55,384	21,872	7,120	656	8,683	1,765	6,917	-830	2,136	5,342	7,313	3,092
2016–17	71,760	21,881	7,470	623	8,407	1,832	6,576	14,447	2,223	5,326	7,907	3,475
4-year												
1999–2000	70,586	17,252	7,155	987	9,639	—	—	22,229	1,673	4,871	4,251	2,530
2004–05	63,705	18,740	8,959	882	7,612	—	—	13,884	1,635	4,924	4,738	2,332
2005–06	65,930	19,045	8,496	886	7,938	—	—	15,427	1,603	5,010	4,999	2,525
2006–07	75,283	19,545	8,336	887	8,340	—	—	23,124	1,696	5,073	5,231	3,051
2007–08	54,051	19,647	7,846	920	8,156	—	—	2,444	1,884	5,022	5,180	2,952
2008–09	25,960	20,203	7,933	897	6,668	—	—	-24,278	1,809	5,124	5,596	2,010
2009–10	61,329	20,454	8,331	795	6,553	1,526	5,026	10,359	1,756	5,122	6,032	1,927
2010–11	71,300	20,583	8,378	742	7,617	1,511	6,106	18,495	1,718	5,098	6,050	2,619
2011–12	53,587	20,794	8,009	649	7,172	1,477	5,695	1,506	1,688	5,142	6,201	2,426
2012–13	65,033	21,045	7,637	621	7,194	1,559	5,635	12,430	1,784	5,144	6,135	3,043
2013–14	72,391	21,354	7,479	621	8,181	1,633	6,547	18,113	1,991	5,194	6,555	2,902
2014–15	62,241	21,684	7,526	656	8,389	1,721	6,668	6,633	2,089	5,253	7,449	2,563
2015–16	55,797	21,930	7,193	662	8,775	1,786	6,989	-840	2,161	5,392	7,402	3,122
2016–17	72,386	21,950	7,550	629	8,498	1,853	6,645	14,619	2,249	5,379	8,004	3,510
2-year												
1999–2000	25,239	10,850	1,596	668	3,918	—	—	1,797	766	1,544	0	4,101
2004–05	23,380	13,112	2,902	1,011	2,552	—	—	864	515	1,496	0	927
2005–06	23,697	12,694	3,007	1,197	2,330	—	—	1,224	669	1,501	0	1,075
2006–07	25,184	12,913	2,699	1,004	2,358	—	—	2,409	396	1,847	0	1,557
2007–08	21,765	13,227	2,635	1,058	2,308	—	—	-530	481	1,654	0	932
2008–09	19,880	13,308	2,623	938	2,062	—	—	-1,433	245	1,639	0	498
2009–10	23,053	13,271	3,118	622	2,257	176	2,081	923	329	1,584	0	949
2010–11	21,212	14,999	1,901	497	1,273	91	1,182	527	143	1,117	0	755
2011–12	19,977	14,706	1,617	389	1,302	84	1,218	173	101	949	0	740
2012–13	19,731	13,332	1,755	517	1,600	88	1,512	518	110	1,129	0	771
2013–14	22,504	13,944	2,404	487	1,992	116	1,875	1,663	91	1,216	0	709
2014–15	19,788	15,418	1,392	253	866	39	827	180	131	1,005	0	544
2015–16	21,325	17,091	1,098	164	1,045	69	975	25	124	1,166	0	612
2016–17	20,383	16,183	935	137	989	59	929	359	123	989	0	669

—Not available.
[1]Includes independent operations.
[2]Constant dollars based on the Consumer Price Index, prepared by the Bureau of Labor Statistics, U.S. Department of Labor, adjusted to a school-year basis.
NOTE: Degree-granting institutions grant associate's or higher degrees and participate in Title IV federal financial aid programs. Data in this table pertain to institutions' fiscal years that end in the academic year noted. Some data have been revised from previously published figures. Detail may not sum to totals because of rounding.
SOURCE: U.S. Department of Education, National Center for Education Statistics, Integrated Postsecondary Education Data System (IPEDS), "Fall Enrollment Survey" (IPEDS-EF:99); Spring 2001 through Spring 2007, Enrollment component; Spring 2008 through Spring 2017, Fall Enrollment component; and Spring 2001 through Spring 2018, Finance component. (This table was prepared January 2019.)

Table 333.50. Total revenue of private nonprofit degree-granting postsecondary institutions, by source of funds and classification of institution: 2016–17

Classification of institution	Total	Student tuition and fees (net of allowances)	Federal appropriations, grants, and contracts[1]	State appropriations, grants, and contracts	Local appropriations, grants, and contracts	Private grants and contracts	Private gifts and contributions from affiliated entities	Investment return (gain or loss)	Educational activities	Auxiliary enterprises (net of allowances)	Hospitals	Other
1	2	3	4	5	6	7	8	9	10	11	12	13
	In thousands of current dollars											
Total	**$242,588,422**	**$73,968,461**	**$25,253,779**	**$1,581,985**	**$523,124**	**$6,191,574**	**$22,230,405**	**$48,838,751**	**$7,516,294**	**$18,004,563**	**$26,730,794**	**$11,748,691**
4-year	241,758,472	73,309,539	25,215,712	1,576,730	522,792	6,189,167	22,192,559	48,824,143	7,511,283	17,964,307	26,730,794	11,721,446
Research university, very high[2]	121,690,370	18,527,861	19,175,897	817,938	263,810	4,199,132	10,677,511	30,328,783	5,581,792	5,305,664	18,638,707	8,173,274
Research university, high[3]	17,557,800	7,116,771	1,316,478	111,980	30,010	318,161	1,925,863	2,940,274	865,846	1,592,441	523,525	816,451
Doctoral/research[4]	11,130,302	7,187,961	290,063	85,384	5,184	67,157	576,071	1,248,858	55,519	1,235,855	0	378,251
Master's[5]	35,244,228	22,192,470	815,222	255,325	13,763	177,787	2,676,686	3,396,721	204,213	4,697,952	13,151	800,939
Baccalaureate[6]	28,871,168	10,518,230	586,956	101,598	4,054	201,819	4,014,059	8,359,724	128,256	4,265,227	0	691,244
Special-focus institutions[7]	27,264,604	7,766,245	3,031,096	204,505	205,971	1,225,111	2,322,369	2,549,783	675,658	867,168	7,555,411	861,287
Arts, music, or design	2,920,948	1,726,518	38,149	11,577	5,460	22,885	299,340	389,735	16,910	302,188	0	108,187
Business and management	728,645	430,052	28,563	8,982	0	4,982	49,703	105,499	4,473	89,881	0	6,512
Engineering and other technology-related	318,749	174,769	4,367	1,000	0	754	24,305	76,936	1,735	27,236	0	7,647
Faith related	2,296,495	614,544	66,566	2,271	437	44,997	705,344	555,829	9,370	183,834	0	113,303
Law	478,650	335,741	9,187	3,193	372	5,809	25,159	76,788	464	14,349	0	7,588
Medical schools and centers and other heath professions schools	19,737,013	4,119,113	2,704,609	171,187	190,978	1,134,464	1,132,411	1,299,837	628,077	210,516	7,555,411	590,410
Tribal colleges[8]	98,239	9,057	74,179	2,243	234	1,431	1,670	380	962	1,411	0	6,674
Other special focus	685,864	356,452	105,477	4,052	8,491	9,790	84,437	44,779	13,668	37,753	0	20,966
2-year	829,950	658,922	38,068	5,254	332	2,407	37,846	14,608	5,012	40,256	0	27,245
Associate's colleges	812,579	658,733	27,042	4,446	332	1,907	37,176	14,605	5,012	40,027	0	23,298
Tribal colleges[8]	17,371	189	11,025	809	0	500	670	3	0	229	0	3,947
	Percentage distribution											
Total	**100.00**	**30.49**	**10.41**	**0.65**	**0.22**	**2.55**	**9.16**	**20.13**	**3.10**	**7.42**	**11.02**	**4.84**
4-year	100.00	30.32	10.43	0.65	0.22	2.56	9.18	20.20	3.11	7.43	11.06	4.85
Research university, very high[2]	100.00	15.23	15.76	0.67	0.22	3.45	8.77	24.92	4.59	4.36	15.32	6.72
Research university, high[3]	100.00	40.53	7.50	0.64	0.17	1.81	10.97	16.75	4.93	9.07	2.98	4.65
Doctoral/research[4]	100.00	64.58	2.61	0.77	0.05	0.60	5.18	11.22	0.50	11.10	0.00	3.40
Master's[5]	100.00	62.97	2.31	0.72	0.04	0.50	7.59	9.64	0.58	13.33	0.04	2.27
Baccalaureate[6]	100.00	36.43	2.03	0.35	0.01	0.70	13.90	28.96	0.44	14.77	0.00	2.39
Special-focus institutions[7]	100.00	28.48	11.12	0.75	0.76	4.49	8.52	9.35	2.48	3.18	27.71	3.16
Arts, music, or design	100.00	59.11	1.31	0.40	0.19	0.78	10.25	13.34	0.58	10.35	0.00	3.70
Business and management	100.00	59.02	3.92	1.23	0.00	0.68	6.82	14.48	0.61	12.34	0.00	0.89
Engineering and other technology-related	100.00	54.83	1.37	0.31	0.00	0.24	7.63	24.14	0.54	8.54	0.00	2.40
Faith related	100.00	26.76	2.90	0.10	0.02	1.96	30.71	24.20	0.41	8.01	0.00	4.93
Law	100.00	70.14	1.92	0.67	0.08	1.21	5.26	16.04	0.10	3.00	0.00	1.59
Medical schools and centers and other heath professions schools	100.00	20.87	13.70	0.87	0.97	5.75	5.74	6.59	3.18	1.07	38.28	2.99
Tribal colleges[8]	100.00	9.22	75.51	2.28	0.24	1.46	1.70	0.39	0.98	1.44	0.00	6.79
Other special focus	100.00	51.97	15.38	0.59	1.24	1.43	12.31	6.53	1.99	5.50	0.00	3.06
2-year	100.00	79.39	4.59	0.63	0.04	0.29	4.56	1.76	0.60	4.85	0.00	3.28
Associate's colleges	100.00	81.07	3.33	0.55	0.04	0.23	4.58	1.80	0.62	4.93	0.00	2.87
Tribal colleges[8]	100.00	1.09	63.47	4.66	0.00	2.88	3.86	0.01	0.00	1.32	0.00	22.72
	Revenue per full-time-equivalent student in current dollars											
Total	**$70,178**	**$21,398**	**$7,306**	**$458**	**$151**	**$1,791**	**$6,431**	**$14,128**	**$2,174**	**$5,209**	**$7,733**	**$3,399**
4-year	70,791	21,466	7,384	462	153	1,812	6,498	14,296	2,199	5,260	7,827	3,432
Research university, very high[2]	216,430	32,952	34,105	1,455	469	7,468	18,990	53,941	9,927	9,436	33,150	14,536
Research university, high[3]	60,229	24,413	4,516	384	103	1,091	6,606	10,086	2,970	5,463	1,796	2,801
Doctoral/research[4]	31,575	20,391	823	242	15	191	1,634	3,543	157	3,506	0	1,073
Master's[5]	27,494	17,312	636	199	11	139	2,088	2,650	159	3,665	10	625
Baccalaureate[6]	47,352	17,251	963	167	7	331	6,583	13,711	210	6,995	0	1,134
Special-focus institutions[7]	85,942	24,480	9,554	645	649	3,862	7,320	8,037	2,130	2,733	23,816	2,715
Arts, music, or design	50,388	29,783	658	200	94	395	5,164	6,723	292	5,213	0	1,866
Business and management	29,544	17,437	1,158	364	0	202	2,015	4,278	181	3,644	0	264
Engineering and other technology-related	26,503	14,531	363	83	0	63	2,021	6,397	144	2,265	0	636
Faith related	34,288	9,176	994	34	7	672	10,531	8,299	140	2,745	0	1,692
Law	47,922	33,614	920	320	37	582	2,519	7,688	46	1,437	0	760
Medical schools and centers and other heath professions schools	152,158	31,755	20,851	1,320	1,472	8,746	8,730	10,021	4,842	1,623	58,247	4,552
Tribal colleges[8]	41,822	3,856	31,579	955	99	609	711	162	409	601	0	2,841
Other special focus	50,591	26,293	7,780	299	626	722	6,228	3,303	1,008	2,785	0	1,546
2-year	19,933	15,826	914	126	8	58	909	351	120	967	0	654
Associate's colleges	19,730	15,995	657	108	8	46	903	355	122	972	0	566
Tribal colleges[8]	38,432	417	24,392	1,789	0	1,107	1,482	6	0	506	0	8,732

[1]Includes independent operations.
[2]Research universities with a very high level of research activity.
[3]Research universities with a high level of research activity.
[4]Institutions that award at least 20 research/scholarship doctor's degrees per year, but did not have high levels of research activity.
[5]Institutions that award at least 50 master's and fewer than 20 doctor's degrees per year.
[6]Institutions that primarily emphasize undergraduate education. In addition to institutions that primarily award bachelor's degrees, also includes institutions classified as 4-year in the IPEDS system, but classified as 2-year baccalaureate/associate's colleges in the Carnegie Classification system because they primarily award associate's degrees.
[7]Four-year institutions that award degrees primarily in single fields of study, such as medicine, business, fine arts, theology, and engineering.
[8]Tribally controlled colleges, which are located on reservations and are members of the American Indian Higher Education Consortium.

NOTE: Relative levels of research activity for research universities were determined by an analysis of research and development expenditures, science and engineering research staffing, and doctor's degrees conferred, by field. Further information on the Carnegie 2015 classification system used in this table may be obtained from http://carnegieclassifications.iu.edu/. Degree-granting institutions grant associate's or higher degrees and participate in Title IV federal financial aid programs. Data in this table pertain to institutions' fiscal years that end in the academic year noted. Detail may not sum to totals because of rounding.

SOURCE: U.S. Department of Education, National Center for Education Statistics, Integrated Postsecondary Education Data System (IPEDS), Spring 2017, Fall Enrollment component; and Spring 2018, Finance component. (This table was prepared December 2018.)

Table 333.55. Total revenue of private for-profit degree-granting postsecondary institutions, by source of funds and level of institution: Selected years, 1999–2000 through 2016–17

Level of institution and year	Total	Student tuition and fees (net of allowances)	Federal appropriations, grants, and contracts	State and local appropriations, grants, and contracts	Private gifts, grants, and contracts	Investment return (gain or loss)	Educational activities	Auxiliary enterprises (net of allowances)	Other
1	2	3	4	5	6	7	8	9	10
	In thousands of current dollars								
All levels									
1999–2000	$4,321,985	$3,721,032	$198,923	$71,904	$2,151	$18,537	$70,672	$156,613	$82,153
2010–11	28,285,216	25,157,459	1,583,370	157,290	31,272	32,551	402,206	542,622	378,447
2012–13	24,761,608	22,465,786	1,090,992	96,621	14,700	58,243	312,065	484,747	238,453
2013–14	22,645,566	20,481,607	941,363	77,986	12,206	43,032	256,321	482,439	350,611
2014–15	19,665,772	17,705,922	848,223	53,217	15,935	45,317	224,389	434,253	338,516
2015–16	17,049,389	15,493,140	712,642	46,680	14,901	27,484	176,339	312,166	266,036
2016–17	15,779,064	14,429,842	520,794	40,206	12,588	41,453	203,385	247,202	283,595
4-year									
1999–2000	2,381,042	2,050,136	103,865	39,460	1,109	10,340	33,764	102,103	40,266
2010–11	21,690,069	19,483,895	1,113,186	118,054	29,118	28,671	346,786	405,604	164,755
2012–13	19,550,978	17,759,973	809,567	64,261	12,233	49,200	265,836	395,722	194,187
2013–14	17,832,352	16,188,360	709,409	51,830	10,232	36,012	222,841	395,509	218,160
2014–15	15,845,578	14,281,696	626,082	37,570	14,474	37,530	198,393	371,131	278,702
2015–16	13,575,294	12,376,301	519,399	32,097	13,708	21,959	151,174	255,030	205,627
2016–17	12,737,280	11,697,950	368,141	27,872	11,586	34,559	180,132	210,935	206,106
2-year									
1999–2000	1,940,943	1,670,896	95,058	32,444	1,042	8,197	36,908	54,510	41,888
2010–11	6,595,147	5,673,564	470,183	39,236	2,154	3,880	55,420	137,018	213,692
2012–13	5,210,630	4,705,813	281,425	32,361	2,467	9,043	46,230	89,025	44,266
2013–14	4,813,214	4,293,247	231,954	26,157	1,975	7,021	33,480	86,930	132,450
2014–15	3,820,194	3,424,226	222,141	15,647	1,461	7,787	25,996	63,122	59,814
2015–16	3,474,095	3,116,840	193,243	14,583	1,193	5,525	25,166	57,136	60,409
2016–17	3,041,784	2,731,893	152,652	12,334	1,002	6,894	23,253	36,266	77,490
	Percentage distribution								
All levels									
1999–2000	100.00	86.10	4.60	1.66	0.05	0.43	1.64	3.62	1.90
2010–11	100.00	88.94	5.60	0.56	0.11	0.12	1.42	1.92	1.34
2012–13	100.00	90.73	4.41	0.39	0.06	0.24	1.26	1.96	0.96
2013–14	100.00	90.44	4.16	0.34	0.05	0.19	1.13	2.13	1.55
2014–15	100.00	90.03	4.31	0.27	0.08	0.23	1.14	2.21	1.72
2015–16	100.00	90.87	4.18	0.27	0.09	0.16	1.03	1.83	1.56
2016–17	100.00	91.45	3.30	0.25	0.08	0.26	1.29	1.57	1.80
4-year									
1999–2000	100.00	86.10	4.36	1.66	0.05	0.43	1.42	4.29	1.69
2010–11	100.00	89.83	5.13	0.54	0.13	0.13	1.60	1.87	0.76
2012–13	100.00	90.84	4.14	0.33	0.06	0.25	1.36	2.02	0.99
2013–14	100.00	90.78	3.98	0.29	0.06	0.20	1.25	2.22	1.22
2014–15	100.00	90.13	3.95	0.24	0.09	0.24	1.25	2.34	1.76
2015–16	100.00	91.17	3.83	0.24	0.10	0.16	1.11	1.88	1.51
2016–17	100.00	91.84	2.89	0.22	0.09	0.27	1.41	1.66	1.62
2-year									
1999–2000	100.00	86.09	4.90	1.67	0.05	0.42	1.90	2.81	2.16
2010–11	100.00	86.03	7.13	0.59	0.03	0.06	0.84	2.08	3.24
2012–13	100.00	90.31	5.40	0.62	0.05	0.17	0.89	1.71	0.85
2013–14	100.00	89.20	4.82	0.54	0.04	0.15	0.70	1.81	2.75
2014–15	100.00	89.63	5.81	0.41	0.04	0.20	0.68	1.65	1.57
2015–16	100.00	89.72	5.56	0.42	0.03	0.16	0.72	1.64	1.74
2016–17	100.00	89.81	5.02	0.41	0.03	0.23	0.76	1.19	2.55
	Revenue per full-time-equivalent student in constant 2017–18 dollars[1]								
All levels									
1999–2000	$16,470	$14,180	$758	$274	$8	$71	$269	$597	$313
2010–11	19,197	17,075	1,075	107	21	22	273	368	257
2012–13	18,769	17,028	827	73	11	44	237	367	181
2013–14	22,550	20,395	937	78	12	43	255	480	349
2014–15	17,441	15,703	752	47	14	40	199	385	300
2015–16	17,954	16,315	750	49	16	29	186	329	280
2016–17	18,014	16,474	595	46	14	47	232	282	324
4-year									
1999–2000	16,716	14,393	729	277	8	73	237	717	283
2010–11	19,354	17,386	993	105	26	26	309	362	147
2012–13	18,934	17,199	784	62	12	48	257	383	188
2013–14	24,160	21,933	961	70	14	49	302	536	296
2014–15	17,445	15,724	689	41	16	41	218	409	307
2015–16	17,894	16,314	685	42	18	29	199	336	271
2016–17	17,996	16,528	520	39	16	49	255	298	291
2-year									
1999–2000	16,177	13,927	792	270	9	68	308	454	349
2010–11	18,700	16,087	1,333	111	6	11	157	388	606
2012–13	18,175	16,414	982	113	9	32	161	311	154
2013–14	18,085	16,131	872	98	7	26	126	327	498
2014–15	17,425	15,619	1,013	71	7	36	119	288	273
2015–16	18,191	16,320	1,012	76	6	29	132	299	316
2016–17	18,090	16,247	908	73	6	41	138	216	461

[1]Constant dollars based on the Consumer Price Index, prepared by the Bureau of Labor Statistics, U.S. Department of Labor, adjusted to a school-year basis.
NOTE: Degree-granting institutions grant associate's or higher degrees and participate in Title IV federal financial aid programs. Data in this table pertain to institutions' fiscal years that end in the academic year noted. Some data have been revised from previously published figures. Detail may not sum to totals because of rounding.

SOURCE: U.S. Department of Education, National Center for Education Statistics, Integrated Postsecondary Education Data System (IPEDS), "Fall Enrollment Survey" (IPEDS-EF:99); Spring 2011 through Spring 2017, Fall Enrollment component; and selected years, Spring 2001 through Spring 2018, Finance component. (This table was prepared January 2019.)

Table 334.10. Total expenditures of public degree-granting postsecondary institutions, by purpose of expenditure and level of institution: 2009–10 through 2016–17

Level of institution and year	Total	Instruction: Total[3]	Instruction: Salaries and wages	Research	Public service	Academic support	Student services	Institutional support	Auxiliary enterprises[1]	Net grant aid to students[2]	Hospitals	Independent operations	Other
1	2	3	4	5	6	7	8	9	10	11	12	13	14
	In thousands of current dollars												
All levels													
2009–10	$281,390,445	$89,237,995	$51,808,563	$32,270,072	$12,980,154	$22,788,482	$15,661,212	$27,554,886	$25,981,203	$15,494,246	$28,484,978	$1,310,925	$9,626,291
2010–11	296,862,854	93,090,749	53,586,472	33,866,656	13,426,331	23,441,698	16,276,833	29,051,411	27,649,838	17,487,275	29,980,642	1,233,264	11,358,158
2011–12	305,537,590	95,093,836	54,341,187	34,282,999	13,567,337	24,712,457	17,019,195	29,512,479	28,475,340	16,611,881	33,063,066	1,297,507	11,901,492
2012–13	311,421,148	97,716,338	55,555,358	34,634,474	13,495,216	25,725,240	17,679,256	30,850,117	29,002,556	16,227,767	34,208,788	1,320,284	10,561,112
2013–14	323,893,053	101,281,681	57,591,057	34,407,750	13,906,406	27,038,128	18,668,134	32,398,315	30,031,093	15,978,858	36,965,327	1,512,402	11,704,959
2014–15	335,630,086	105,240,912	59,348,073	35,189,410	14,105,428	28,349,420	19,545,937	33,290,396	31,011,138	15,881,788	39,887,678	1,603,180	11,524,799
2015–16	354,775,570	108,299,168	61,715,250	36,125,887	14,756,434	29,627,129	20,278,907	34,475,739	31,449,402	15,518,286	45,053,249	1,688,715	17,502,653
2016–17	371,647,743	111,991,558	63,837,906	37,360,529	15,563,243	31,097,066	21,196,611	35,944,488	33,173,463	15,371,595	49,020,652	1,712,683	19,215,856
4-year													
2009–10	230,212,346	67,643,385	39,032,863	32,246,034	12,071,239	18,517,775	10,439,050	19,637,465	23,267,303	9,103,655	28,484,978	1,310,925	7,490,538
2010–11	242,591,219	70,524,278	40,420,752	33,842,288	12,497,023	19,037,101	10,918,171	20,760,495	24,856,936	10,088,873	29,980,642	1,233,264	8,852,149
2011–12	251,518,494	72,456,621	41,334,687	34,259,475	12,635,035	20,246,241	11,548,269	21,042,773	25,720,831	9,737,295	33,063,066	1,297,507	9,511,380
2012–13	257,550,418	74,836,904	42,537,154	34,613,057	12,608,770	21,150,882	12,114,278	22,151,644	26,335,976	9,823,162	34,208,788	1,320,284	8,386,673
2013–14	269,871,401	78,181,765	44,567,486	34,381,434	13,042,105	22,291,975	12,983,254	23,519,705	27,469,515	9,914,507	36,965,327	1,512,402	9,609,411
2014–15	281,198,453	81,857,112	46,260,575	35,166,043	13,257,351	23,504,976	13,595,835	24,290,848	28,543,769	10,057,062	39,887,678	1,603,180	9,434,598
2015–16	301,270,243	85,962,887	48,769,505	36,100,447	13,954,900	24,946,937	14,449,291	25,621,839	29,213,644	10,403,387	45,053,249	1,688,715	13,874,946
2016–17	317,538,661	89,514,596	50,980,433	37,331,955	14,724,385	26,385,509	15,223,949	26,674,945	30,998,146	10,626,234	49,020,652	1,712,683	15,325,608
2-year													
2009–10	51,178,098	21,594,609	12,775,700	24,038	908,915	4,270,708	5,222,163	7,917,422	2,713,901	6,390,591	0	0	2,135,752
2010–11	54,271,635	22,566,471	13,165,721	24,368	929,308	4,404,597	5,358,662	8,290,916	2,792,902	7,398,402	0	0	2,506,009
2011–12	54,019,096	22,637,215	13,006,500	23,525	932,302	4,466,216	5,470,926	8,469,706	2,754,509	6,874,585	0	0	2,390,112
2012–13	53,870,729	22,879,434	13,018,204	21,417	886,446	4,574,358	5,564,978	8,698,474	2,666,580	6,404,605	0	0	2,174,439
2013–14	54,021,651	23,099,916	13,023,571	26,316	864,300	4,746,153	5,684,879	8,878,610	2,561,577	6,064,351	0	0	2,095,548
2014–15	54,431,633	23,383,800	13,087,499	23,367	848,077	4,844,444	5,950,102	8,999,548	2,467,368	5,824,726	0	0	2,090,201
2015–16	53,505,327	22,336,281	12,945,745	25,440	801,533	4,680,192	5,829,616	8,853,900	2,235,758	5,114,899	0	0	3,627,707
2016–17	54,109,083	22,476,963	12,857,473	28,574	838,859	4,711,556	5,972,662	9,269,542	2,175,317	4,745,362	0	0	3,890,248
	Percentage distribution												
All levels													
2009–10	100.00	31.71	18.41	11.47	4.61	8.10	5.57	9.79	9.23	5.51	10.12	0.47	3.42
2010–11	100.00	31.36	18.05	11.41	4.52	7.90	5.48	9.79	9.31	5.89	10.10	0.42	3.83
2011–12	100.00	31.12	17.79	11.22	4.44	8.09	5.57	9.66	9.32	5.44	10.82	0.42	3.90
2012–13	100.00	31.38	17.84	11.12	4.33	8.26	5.68	9.91	9.31	5.21	10.98	0.42	3.39
2013–14	100.00	31.27	17.78	10.62	4.29	8.35	5.76	10.00	9.27	4.93	11.41	0.47	3.61
2014–15	100.00	31.36	17.68	10.48	4.20	8.45	5.82	9.92	9.24	4.73	11.88	0.48	3.43
2015–16	100.00	30.53	17.40	10.18	4.16	8.35	5.72	9.72	8.86	4.37	12.70	0.48	4.93
2016–17	100.00	30.13	17.18	10.05	4.19	8.37	5.70	9.67	8.93	4.14	13.19	0.46	5.17
4-year													
2009–10	100.00	29.38	16.96	14.01	5.24	8.04	4.53	8.53	10.11	3.95	12.37	0.57	3.25
2010–11	100.00	29.07	16.66	13.95	5.15	7.85	4.50	8.56	10.25	4.16	12.36	0.51	3.65
2011–12	100.00	28.81	16.43	13.62	5.02	8.05	4.59	8.37	10.23	3.87	13.15	0.52	3.78
2012–13	100.00	29.06	16.52	13.44	4.90	8.21	4.70	8.60	10.23	3.81	13.28	0.51	3.26
2013–14	100.00	28.97	16.51	12.74	4.83	8.26	4.81	8.72	10.18	3.67	13.70	0.56	3.56
2014–15	100.00	29.11	16.45	12.51	4.71	8.36	4.83	8.64	10.15	3.58	14.18	0.57	3.36
2015–16	100.00	28.53	16.19	11.98	4.63	8.28	4.80	8.50	9.70	3.45	14.95	0.56	4.61
2016–17	100.00	28.19	16.05	11.76	4.64	8.31	4.79	8.40	9.76	3.35	15.44	0.54	4.83
2-year													
2009–10	100.00	42.20	24.96	0.05	1.78	8.34	10.20	15.47	5.30	12.49	0.00	0.00	4.17
2010–11	100.00	41.58	24.26	0.04	1.71	8.12	9.87	15.28	5.15	13.63	0.00	0.00	4.62
2011–12	100.00	41.91	24.08	0.04	1.73	8.27	10.13	15.68	5.10	12.73	0.00	0.00	4.42
2012–13	100.00	42.47	24.17	0.04	1.65	8.49	10.33	16.15	4.95	11.89	0.00	0.00	4.04
2013–14	100.00	42.76	24.11	0.05	1.60	8.79	10.52	16.44	4.74	11.23	0.00	0.00	3.88
2014–15	100.00	42.96	24.04	0.04	1.56	8.90	10.93	16.53	4.53	10.70	0.00	0.00	3.84
2015–16	100.00	41.75	24.20	0.05	1.50	8.75	10.90	16.55	4.18	9.56	0.00	0.00	6.78
2016–17	100.00	41.54	23.76	0.05	1.55	8.71	11.04	17.13	4.02	8.77	0.00	0.00	7.19

See notes at end of table.

Table 334.10. Total expenditures of public degree-granting postsecondary institutions, by purpose of expenditure and level of institution: 2009–10 through 2016–17—Continued

Level of institution and year	Total	Instruction		Research	Public service	Academic support	Student services	Institutional support	Auxiliary enterprises[1]	Net grant aid to students[2]	Hospitals	Independent operations	Other
		Total[3]	Salaries and wages										
1	2	3	4	5	6	7	8	9	10	11	12	13	14
	Expenditure per full-time-equivalent student in constant 2017–18 dollars[4]												
All levels													
2009–10	$29,976	$9,506	$5,519	$3,438	$1,383	$2,428	$1,668	$2,935	$2,768	$1,651	$3,034	$140	$1,025
2010–11	30,237	9,482	5,458	3,449	1,368	2,388	1,658	2,959	2,816	1,781	3,054	126	1,157
2011–12	30,411	9,465	5,409	3,412	1,350	2,460	1,694	2,937	2,834	1,653	3,291	129	1,185
2012–13	30,978	9,720	5,526	3,445	1,342	2,559	1,759	3,069	2,885	1,614	3,403	131	1,051
2013–14	31,972	9,998	5,685	3,396	1,373	2,669	1,843	3,198	2,964	1,577	3,649	149	1,155
2014–15	33,119	10,385	5,856	3,472	1,392	2,797	1,929	3,285	3,060	1,567	3,936	158	1,137
2015–16	34,954	10,670	6,080	3,559	1,454	2,919	1,998	3,397	3,099	1,529	4,439	166	1,724
2016–17	35,946	10,832	6,174	3,614	1,505	3,008	2,050	3,477	3,209	1,487	4,741	166	1,859
4-year													
2009–10	40,846	12,002	6,926	5,721	2,142	3,286	1,852	3,484	4,128	1,615	5,054	233	1,329
2010–11	41,029	11,928	6,836	5,724	2,114	3,220	1,847	3,511	4,204	1,706	5,071	209	1,497
2011–12	40,725	11,732	6,693	5,547	2,046	3,278	1,870	3,407	4,165	1,577	5,353	210	1,540
2012–13	40,836	11,866	6,745	5,488	1,999	3,354	1,921	3,512	4,176	1,558	5,424	209	1,330
2013–14	41,966	12,157	6,930	5,346	2,028	3,466	2,019	3,657	4,272	1,542	5,748	235	1,494
2014–15	42,774	12,452	7,037	5,349	2,017	3,575	2,068	3,695	4,342	1,530	6,068	244	1,435
2015–16	45,010	12,843	7,286	5,393	2,085	3,727	2,159	3,828	4,365	1,554	6,731	252	2,073
2016–17	44,965	12,676	7,219	5,286	2,085	3,736	2,156	3,777	4,389	1,505	6,942	243	2,170
2-year													
2009–10	13,644	5,757	3,406	6	242	1,139	1,392	2,111	724	1,704	0	0	569
2010–11	13,897	5,778	3,371	6	238	1,128	1,372	2,123	715	1,894	0	0	642
2011–12	13,955	5,848	3,360	6	241	1,154	1,413	2,188	712	1,776	0	0	617
2012–13	14,381	6,108	3,475	6	237	1,221	1,486	2,322	712	1,710	0	0	580
2013–14	14,601	6,244	3,520	7	234	1,283	1,537	2,400	692	1,639	0	0	566
2014–15	15,290	6,569	3,676	7	238	1,361	1,671	2,528	693	1,636	0	0	587
2015–16	15,480	6,462	3,745	7	232	1,354	1,687	2,562	647	1,480	0	0	1,050
2016–17	16,512	6,859	3,924	9	256	1,438	1,823	2,829	664	1,448	0	0	1,187

[1]Essentially self-supporting operations of institutions that furnish a service to students, faculty, or staff, such as residence halls and food services.
[2]Scholarship and fellowship expenses, net of discounts and allowances. Excludes the amount of discounts and allowances that were recorded as a reduction to revenues from tuition, fees, and auxiliary enterprises, such as room, board, and books.
[3]Includes other categories not separately shown.
[4]Constant dollars based on the Consumer Price Index, prepared by the Bureau of Labor Statistics, U.S. Department of Labor, adjusted to a school-year basis.

NOTE: Degree-granting institutions grant associate's or higher degrees and participate in Title IV federal financial aid programs. Includes data for public institutions reporting data according to either the Governmental Accounting Standards Board (GASB) or the Financial Accounting Standards Board (FASB) questionnaire. Data in this table pertain to institutions' fiscal years that end in the academic year noted. Some data have been revised from previously published figures. Detail may not sum to totals because of rounding.
SOURCE: U.S. Department of Education, National Center for Education Statistics, Integrated Postsecondary Education Data System (IPEDS), Spring 2010 through Spring 2017, Fall Enrollment component; and Spring 2011 through Spring 2018, Finance component. (This table was prepared December 2018.)

Table 334.20. Total expenditures of public degree-granting postsecondary institutions, by level of institution, purpose of expenditure, and state or jurisdiction: 2013–14 through 2016–17

State or jurisdiction	Total, 2013–14	Total, 2014–15	Total, 2015–16: All institutions	Total, 2015–16: 4-year institutions	Total, 2015–16: 2-year institutions	2016–17 All institutions: Total[1]	2016–17 All institutions: Instruction	2016–17 4-year institutions: Total[1]	2016–17 4-year institutions: Instruction	2016–17 2-year institutions: Total[1]	2016–17 2-year institutions: Instruction
1	2	3	4	5	6	7	8	9	10	11	12
United States	**$323,893,053**	**$335,630,086**	**$354,775,570**	**$301,270,243**	**$53,505,327**	**$371,647,743**	**$111,991,558**	**$317,538,661**	**$89,514,596**	**$54,109,083**	**$22,476,963**
Alabama	6,762,386	6,961,128	7,306,483	6,594,968	711,515	7,785,726	1,923,520	7,028,015	1,604,931	757,711	318,589
Alaska	852,991	850,928	868,913	851,184	17,729	839,381	255,595	839,381	255,595	0	0
Arizona	5,600,337	5,931,197	6,296,207	4,868,738	1,427,469	6,507,273	2,074,702	5,130,163	1,545,990	1,377,110	528,712
Arkansas	3,704,888	3,800,707	3,934,428	3,475,267	459,160	4,106,519	932,632	3,647,177	751,511	459,342	181,121
California	47,558,693	50,652,807	55,642,923	43,924,762	11,718,161	58,144,991	15,971,067	45,842,517	11,526,790	12,302,474	4,444,277
Colorado	5,698,854	6,109,407	6,587,748	6,053,445	534,303	7,781,063	2,301,843	7,265,477	2,085,437	515,585	216,406
Connecticut	3,295,856	3,496,698	3,662,471	3,144,397	518,073	3,798,052	1,165,155	3,277,990	955,315	520,062	209,840
Delaware	1,153,297	1,190,562	1,247,600	1,247,600	0	1,264,208	562,040	1,264,208	562,040	0	0
District of Columbia	134,230	139,524	147,290	147,290	0	141,861	41,290	141,861	41,290	0	0
Florida	11,087,586	11,511,020	11,822,548	11,617,507	205,040	12,415,119	4,188,647	12,232,102	4,121,108	183,017	67,538
Georgia	7,564,411	7,826,896	8,050,634	7,146,084	904,550	8,496,265	2,579,557	7,570,386	2,174,679	925,880	404,878
Hawaii	1,680,041	1,664,624	1,816,736	1,493,946	322,790	1,847,752	601,583	1,575,966	458,619	271,786	142,964
Idaho	1,188,089	1,203,133	1,255,012	1,051,096	203,916	1,306,760	471,599	1,092,965	386,010	213,794	85,589
Illinois	11,779,510	12,195,375	12,355,733	9,114,775	3,240,958	12,961,076	4,452,819	9,604,390	3,142,088	3,356,686	1,310,731
Indiana	6,395,776	6,372,728	6,563,583	6,001,263	562,320	6,805,880	2,804,268	6,263,480	2,564,925	542,399	239,343
Iowa	5,052,485	5,261,496	5,512,712	4,580,597	932,115	5,789,532	1,255,477	4,842,637	840,859	946,894	414,618
Kansas	3,367,894	3,451,776	3,436,560	2,683,309	753,251	3,498,812	1,251,225	2,748,778	965,265	750,035	285,960
Kentucky	5,235,067	5,547,286	5,873,502	5,256,920	616,582	6,113,027	1,380,733	5,541,058	1,148,243	571,969	232,491
Louisiana	4,010,882	3,910,077	3,883,693	3,398,545	485,149	4,108,399	1,373,504	3,624,253	1,177,457	484,147	196,047
Maine	859,812	864,068	849,532	718,365	131,167	869,566	279,479	738,682	216,058	130,885	63,421
Maryland	6,228,564	6,343,340	6,502,220	5,057,411	1,444,810	6,725,079	2,074,529	5,287,563	1,470,866	1,437,516	603,663
Massachusetts	4,703,032	4,758,073	5,170,474	4,268,644	901,830	5,246,452	1,775,928	4,334,984	1,397,202	911,468	378,727
Michigan	14,155,072	14,627,268	15,327,986	13,839,944	1,488,042	16,259,165	4,377,216	14,803,153	3,725,153	1,456,011	652,063
Minnesota	5,271,821	5,215,646	5,303,793	4,274,251	1,029,542	5,927,210	1,745,469	4,738,233	1,233,452	1,188,977	512,017
Mississippi	4,017,008	4,171,973	4,451,207	3,564,424	886,783	4,623,103	1,166,969	3,675,243	790,117	947,861	376,852
Missouri	4,772,178	4,904,991	5,010,347	4,262,222	748,125	5,175,185	1,565,895	4,420,785	1,233,316	754,400	332,578
Montana	1,012,355	1,022,708	1,046,082	923,655	122,427	1,101,301	328,862	987,966	287,111	113,334	41,750
Nebraska	2,312,160	2,398,348	2,450,500	2,025,782	424,717	2,574,085	858,240	2,146,023	666,148	428,062	192,092
Nevada	1,508,447	1,544,133	1,621,662	1,549,281	72,381	1,701,829	724,989	1,633,648	696,477	68,181	28,512
New Hampshire	963,995	973,796	997,737	846,614	151,123	989,727	332,062	842,941	282,053	146,786	50,009
New Jersey	7,090,602	7,266,925	7,473,275	6,181,807	1,291,468	7,979,452	2,641,775	6,680,061	2,123,485	1,299,391	518,289
New Mexico	3,316,771	3,454,803	3,523,749	2,914,924	608,825	3,786,755	787,624	3,176,827	536,456	609,928	251,168
New York	16,292,947	16,791,853	17,785,235	14,278,920	3,506,315	18,075,297	6,707,552	14,594,521	4,987,013	3,480,775	1,720,540
North Carolina	10,156,317	10,484,190	10,499,040	8,374,516	2,124,525	11,144,591	3,724,035	8,942,833	2,757,537	2,201,758	966,498
North Dakota	1,108,117	1,150,777	1,192,090	1,086,200	105,891	1,194,445	477,978	1,090,829	435,270	103,616	42,708
Ohio	12,303,835	12,534,515	13,257,601	11,873,068	1,384,533	14,314,104	4,162,418	12,875,624	3,530,941	1,438,480	631,477
Oklahoma	4,083,901	4,158,353	4,335,312	3,848,004	487,308	4,364,905	1,397,292	3,884,702	1,205,208	480,203	192,084
Oregon	6,000,874	5,843,944	7,025,969	5,711,518	1,314,451	6,949,056	1,639,944	5,723,589	1,149,606	1,225,467	490,338
Pennsylvania	12,566,618	13,046,794	13,752,080	12,574,953	1,177,126	14,340,017	3,937,336	13,147,338	3,423,120	1,192,679	514,216
Rhode Island	746,067	737,640	775,112	653,967	121,145	792,218	267,875	667,893	204,799	124,325	63,076
South Carolina	4,168,222	4,352,405	4,459,393	3,646,556	812,837	4,658,792	1,759,817	3,839,914	1,383,878	818,877	375,940
South Dakota	777,182	784,051	827,198	715,054	112,144	841,747	298,998	754,648	256,928	87,099	42,070
Tennessee	4,317,495	4,172,603	4,320,721	3,663,379	657,342	4,503,298	1,841,308	3,836,474	1,544,052	666,824	297,256
Texas	29,516,581	31,050,594	33,792,807	28,808,248	4,984,560	35,450,170	10,298,201	30,299,084	8,128,711	5,151,087	2,169,490
Utah	4,995,994	5,349,506	5,700,948	5,493,666	207,282	6,189,020	1,104,524	5,971,621	1,003,765	217,399	100,759
Vermont	853,311	854,406	865,326	832,631	32,694	896,401	277,382	862,132	266,738	34,270	10,644
Virginia	9,099,520	9,540,486	9,896,996	8,742,912	1,154,083	10,253,120	3,165,805	9,125,778	2,615,792	1,127,342	550,013
Washington	8,201,301	8,588,560	9,171,287	8,472,651	698,636	9,892,889	3,025,334	9,472,192	2,857,194	420,697	168,140
West Virginia	1,762,607	1,819,173	1,874,851	1,730,157	144,694	1,889,691	612,504	1,752,931	557,667	136,760	54,837
Wisconsin	6,344,382	6,285,882	6,566,464	5,306,895	1,259,569	6,594,678	2,238,402	5,362,831	1,531,830	1,231,846	706,573
Wyoming	761,062	798,626	878,588	572,717	305,871	877,311	270,211	579,425	170,152	297,886	100,060
U.S. Service Academies	1,501,631	1,662,286	1,805,213	1,805,213	0	1,755,387	538,347	1,755,387	538,347	0	0
Other jurisdictions	**1,699,654**	**1,638,670**	**1,693,441**	**1,599,359**	**94,083**	**981,678**	**256,366**	**885,289**	**225,040**	**96,389**	**31,326**
American Samoa	14,060	13,690	13,952	13,952	0	14,337	4,548	14,337	4,548	0	0
Federated States of Micronesia	27,695	18,324	20,070	0	20,070	20,331	7,089	0	0	20,331	7,089
Guam	136,246	116,302	129,640	90,922	38,717	127,294	30,927	88,902	19,391	38,392	11,536
Marshall Islands	15,117	11,382	13,731	0	13,731	15,022	2,439	0	0	15,022	2,439
Northern Marianas	17,849	19,048	16,502	16,502	0	17,443	2,776	17,443	2,776	0	0
Palau	9,834	10,209	9,425	0	9,425	9,621	3,663	0	0	9,621	3,663
Puerto Rico	1,400,211	1,362,861	1,406,463	1,394,323	12,140	701,403	189,732	688,381	183,132	13,022	6,600
U.S. Virgin Islands	78,643	86,855	83,659	83,659	0	76,227	15,193	76,227	15,193	0	0

[1]Includes other categories not separately shown.
NOTE: Degree-granting institutions grant associate's or higher degrees and participate in Title IV federal financial aid programs. Includes data for public institutions reporting data according to either the Governmental Accounting Standards Board (GASB) or the Financial Accounting Standards Board (FASB) questionnaire. Data in this table pertain to institutions' fiscal years that end in the academic year noted. Some data have been revised from previously published figures. Detail may not sum to totals because of rounding.
SOURCE: U.S. Department of Education, National Center for Education Statistics, Integrated Postsecondary Education Data System (IPEDS), Spring 2015 through Spring 2018, Finance component. (This table was prepared December 2018.)

Table 334.30. Total expenditures of private nonprofit degree-granting postsecondary institutions, by purpose and level of institution: Selected years, 1999–2000 through 2016–17

Level of institution and year	Total	Instruction	Research	Public service	Academic support	Student services	Institutional support	Auxiliary enterprises[1]	Net grant aid to students[2]	Hospitals	Independent operations	Other
1	2	3	4	5	6	7	8	9	10	11	12	13
	In thousands of current dollars											
All levels												
1999–2000	$80,613,037	$26,012,599	$8,381,926	$1,446,958	$6,510,951	$5,688,499	$10,585,850	$8,300,021	$1,180,882	$7,355,110	$2,753,679	$2,396,563
2003–04	104,317,870	33,909,179	12,039,531	1,972,351	8,759,743	7,544,021	13,951,408	10,508,719	1,101,738	8,374,128	4,222,980	1,934,070
2004–05	110,394,127	36,258,473	12,812,857	2,000,437	9,342,064	8,191,737	14,690,328	10,944,342	1,069,591	9,180,775	4,223,779	1,679,741
2005–06	116,821,175	38,451,724	13,242,851	1,937,149	10,225,476	8,925,987	15,668,595	11,790,104	707,411	9,645,428	4,203,523	2,022,926
2006–07	124,558,591	41,224,316	13,704,450	2,036,662	10,881,954	9,591,801	16,831,560	12,449,053	728,200	10,400,055	4,680,393	2,030,146
2007–08	133,501,778	44,227,021	14,474,152	2,182,525	11,883,707	10,361,344	18,366,446	13,317,944	720,764	10,752,821	4,887,609	2,327,446
2008–09	141,363,564	46,456,178	15,264,804	2,298,520	12,585,948	11,016,097	19,403,346	13,713,701	754,752	11,930,840	5,158,480	2,780,898
2009–10	145,115,244	47,566,210	16,221,823	2,090,243	12,953,023	11,422,737	19,438,608	13,890,396	826,379	13,174,405	5,154,851	2,376,569
2010–11	152,501,429	49,759,574	17,362,082	2,255,075	13,601,137	12,198,263	20,214,683	14,460,084	759,683	14,239,347	5,376,016	2,275,486
2011–12	159,831,378	52,163,647	17,483,157	2,333,298	14,215,689	12,881,102	21,175,119	14,948,315	845,525	15,474,737	5,450,038	2,860,752
2012–13	165,515,671	54,296,267	17,597,379	2,317,116	14,924,886	13,692,561	21,766,760	15,349,949	844,435	16,726,819	5,437,783	2,561,716
2013–14	172,529,736	56,711,775	17,736,647	2,459,956	15,454,493	14,555,421	22,623,170	15,984,991	867,482	17,377,766	5,693,990	3,064,047
2014–15	181,419,541	58,769,788	18,310,027	2,636,019	15,557,155	15,421,897	23,845,927	16,358,009	887,495	20,529,450	6,063,555	3,040,219
2015–16	188,689,819	60,227,646	18,386,969	2,730,335	16,011,794	16,061,062	24,829,855	16,723,913	914,001	21,267,887	6,192,792	5,343,565
2016–17	197,222,297	62,147,748	20,975,036	2,877,302	16,165,352	16,771,994	25,693,911	17,232,526	946,226	23,966,117	5,655,027	4,791,058
4-year												
1999–2000	79,699,659	25,744,199	8,376,568	1,438,544	6,476,338	5,590,978	10,398,914	8,228,409	1,162,570	7,355,110	2,752,019	2,176,011
2003–04	103,733,257	33,712,542	12,039,080	1,964,898	8,726,505	7,466,472	13,774,084	10,464,984	1,084,880	8,374,128	4,221,611	1,904,075
2004–05	109,789,731	36,051,084	12,812,326	1,993,767	9,307,600	8,101,214	14,516,197	10,899,456	1,051,216	9,180,775	4,223,779	1,652,317
2005–06	116,250,621	38,235,791	13,242,277	1,927,434	10,185,584	8,854,613	15,525,499	11,745,356	698,715	9,645,428	4,203,523	1,986,402
2006–07	124,062,344	41,057,423	13,703,502	2,028,438	10,850,196	9,523,002	16,694,195	12,412,575	714,459	10,400,055	4,680,393	1,998,105
2007–08	132,965,591	44,041,854	14,473,179	2,176,544	11,847,284	10,284,649	18,218,103	13,280,036	711,180	10,752,821	4,887,609	2,292,334
2008–09	140,866,945	46,289,898	15,264,459	2,294,909	12,544,436	10,947,638	19,261,017	13,676,329	747,586	11,930,840	5,158,480	2,751,352
2009–10	144,624,598	47,400,673	16,221,238	2,085,201	12,910,113	11,353,608	19,303,251	13,855,994	819,196	13,174,405	5,154,851	2,346,068
2010–11	151,878,613	49,550,398	17,361,796	2,252,726	13,547,801	12,111,973	20,048,321	14,430,101	758,318	14,239,347	5,376,016	2,201,817
2011–12	159,245,924	51,959,761	17,482,484	2,331,249	14,164,326	12,795,619	21,024,665	14,924,702	843,453	15,474,737	5,450,038	2,794,891
2012–13	165,015,452	54,115,153	17,597,050	2,315,345	14,885,715	13,624,969	21,628,217	15,323,444	839,753	16,726,819	5,437,783	2,521,204
2013–14	171,974,051	56,513,597	17,736,254	2,458,223	15,405,771	14,462,852	22,499,365	15,953,094	863,119	17,377,766	5,693,990	3,010,020
2014–15	180,583,663	58,497,366	18,309,351	2,633,736	15,460,861	15,226,681	23,669,210	16,323,295	883,309	20,529,450	6,063,555	2,986,850
2015–16	187,829,392	59,962,885	18,386,002	2,728,006	15,907,072	15,846,653	24,654,441	16,684,252	910,455	21,267,887	6,192,792	5,288,945
2016–17	196,362,166	61,892,928	20,973,876	2,875,944	16,061,738	16,556,264	25,506,883	17,195,307	945,046	23,966,117	5,655,027	4,733,035
2-year												
1999–2000	913,378	268,400	5,358	8,415	34,612	97,521	186,936	71,612	18,311	0	1,660	220,553
2003–04	584,612	196,637	451	7,453	33,238	77,549	177,324	43,735	16,859	0	1,369	29,995
2004–05	604,395	207,389	532	6,670	34,464	90,523	174,131	44,886	18,375	0	0	27,425
2005–06	570,554	215,934	574	9,715	39,893	71,374	143,096	44,748	8,696	0	0	36,524
2006–07	496,247	166,893	947	8,224	31,758	68,799	137,366	36,478	13,741	0	0	32,041
2007–08	536,187	185,167	973	5,982	36,423	76,696	148,343	37,908	9,584	0	0	35,112
2008–09	496,620	166,280	345	3,612	41,511	68,459	142,330	37,372	7,165	0	0	29,546
2009–10	490,645	165,538	585	5,041	42,909	69,129	135,357	34,402	7,183	0	0	30,502
2010–11	622,815	209,176	285	2,349	53,336	86,290	166,362	29,983	1,365	0	0	73,669
2011–12	585,454	203,885	673	2,049	51,363	85,483	150,455	23,613	2,072	0	0	65,861
2012–13	500,218	181,113	329	1,771	39,171	67,591	138,543	26,505	4,682	0	0	40,512
2013–14	555,685	198,178	393	1,732	48,722	92,569	123,804	31,897	4,364	0	0	54,027
2014–15	835,878	272,422	677	2,283	96,294	195,216	176,718	34,714	4,186	0	0	53,369
2015–16	860,427	264,761	967	2,329	104,722	214,409	175,414	39,660	3,546	0	0	54,620
2016–17	860,131	254,820	1,160	1,358	103,614	215,729	187,028	37,219	1,180	0	0	58,022
	Percentage distribution											
All levels												
1999–2000	100.00	32.27	10.40	1.79	8.08	7.06	13.13	10.30	1.46	9.12	3.42	2.97
2003–04	100.00	32.51	11.54	1.89	8.40	7.23	13.37	10.07	1.06	8.03	4.05	1.85
2004–05	100.00	32.84	11.61	1.81	8.46	7.42	13.31	9.91	0.97	8.32	3.83	1.52
2005–06	100.00	32.92	11.34	1.66	8.75	7.64	13.41	10.09	0.61	8.26	3.60	1.73
2006–07	100.00	33.10	11.00	1.64	8.74	7.70	13.51	9.99	0.58	8.35	3.76	1.63
2007–08	100.00	33.13	10.84	1.63	8.90	7.76	13.76	9.98	0.54	8.05	3.66	1.74
2008–09	100.00	32.86	10.80	1.63	8.90	7.79	13.73	9.70	0.53	8.44	3.65	1.97
2009–10	100.00	32.78	11.18	1.44	8.93	7.87	13.40	9.57	0.57	9.08	3.55	1.64
2010–11	100.00	32.63	11.38	1.48	8.92	8.00	13.26	9.48	0.50	9.34	3.53	1.49
2011–12	100.00	32.64	10.94	1.46	8.89	8.06	13.25	9.35	0.53	9.68	3.41	1.79
2012–13	100.00	32.80	10.63	1.40	9.02	8.27	13.15	9.27	0.51	10.11	3.29	1.55
2013–14	100.00	32.87	10.28	1.43	8.96	8.44	13.11	9.27	0.50	10.07	3.30	1.78
2014–15	100.00	32.39	10.09	1.45	8.58	8.50	13.14	9.02	0.49	11.32	3.34	1.68
2015–16	100.00	31.92	9.74	1.45	8.49	8.51	13.16	8.86	0.48	11.27	3.28	2.83
2016–17	100.00	31.51	10.64	1.46	8.20	8.50	13.03	8.74	0.48	12.15	2.87	2.43
4-year												
1999–2000	100.00	32.30	10.51	1.80	8.13	7.02	13.05	10.32	1.46	9.23	3.45	2.73
2003–04	100.00	32.50	11.61	1.89	8.41	7.20	13.28	10.09	1.05	8.07	4.07	1.84
2004–05	100.00	32.84	11.67	1.82	8.48	7.38	13.22	9.93	0.96	8.36	3.85	1.50
2005–06	100.00	32.89	11.39	1.66	8.76	7.62	13.36	10.10	0.60	8.30	3.62	1.71
2006–07	100.00	33.09	11.05	1.64	8.75	7.68	13.46	10.01	0.58	8.38	3.77	1.61
2007–08	100.00	33.12	10.88	1.64	8.91	7.73	13.70	9.99	0.53	8.09	3.68	1.72
2008–09	100.00	32.86	10.84	1.63	8.91	7.77	13.67	9.71	0.53	8.47	3.66	1.95
2009–10	100.00	32.77	11.22	1.44	8.93	7.85	13.35	9.58	0.57	9.11	3.56	1.62
2010–11	100.00	32.63	11.43	1.48	8.92	7.97	13.20	9.50	0.50	9.38	3.54	1.45
2011–12	100.00	32.63	10.98	1.46	8.89	8.04	13.20	9.37	0.53	9.72	3.42	1.76

See notes at end of table.

Table 334.30. Total expenditures of private nonprofit degree-granting postsecondary institutions, by purpose and level of institution: Selected years, 1999–2000 through 2016–17—Continued

Level of institution and year	Total	Instruction	Research	Public service	Academic support	Student services	Institutional support	Auxiliary enterprises[1]	Net grant aid to students[2]	Hospitals	Independent operations	Other
1	2	3	4	5	6	7	8	9	10	11	12	13
2012–13	100.00	32.79	10.66	1.40	9.02	8.26	13.11	9.29	0.51	10.14	3.30	1.53
2013–14	100.00	32.86	10.31	1.43	8.96	8.41	13.08	9.28	0.50	10.10	3.31	1.75
2014–15	100.00	32.39	10.14	1.46	8.56	8.43	13.11	9.04	0.49	11.37	3.36	1.65
2015–16	100.00	31.92	9.79	1.45	8.47	8.44	13.13	8.88	0.48	11.32	3.30	2.82
2016–17	100.00	31.52	10.68	1.46	8.18	8.43	12.99	8.76	0.48	12.21	2.88	2.41
2-year												
1999–2000	100.00	29.39	0.59	0.92	3.79	10.68	20.47	7.84	2.00	0.00	0.18	24.15
2003–04	100.00	33.64	0.08	1.27	5.69	13.27	30.33	7.48	2.88	0.00	0.23	5.13
2004–05	100.00	34.31	0.09	1.10	5.70	14.98	28.81	7.43	3.04	0.00	0.00	4.54
2005–06	100.00	37.85	0.10	1.70	6.99	12.51	25.08	7.84	1.52	0.00	0.00	6.40
2006–07	100.00	33.63	0.19	1.66	6.40	13.86	27.68	7.35	2.77	0.00	0.00	6.46
2007–08	100.00	34.53	0.18	1.12	6.79	14.30	27.67	7.07	1.79	0.00	0.00	6.55
2008–09	100.00	33.48	0.07	0.73	8.36	13.78	28.66	7.53	1.44	0.00	0.00	5.95
2009–10	100.00	33.74	0.12	1.03	8.75	14.09	27.59	7.01	1.46	0.00	0.00	6.22
2010–11	100.00	33.59	0.05	0.38	8.56	13.85	26.71	4.81	0.22	0.00	0.00	11.83
2011–12	100.00	34.83	0.11	0.35	8.77	14.60	25.70	4.03	0.35	0.00	0.00	11.25
2012–13	100.00	36.21	0.07	0.35	7.83	13.51	27.70	5.30	0.94	0.00	0.00	8.10
2013–14	100.00	35.66	0.07	0.31	8.77	16.66	22.28	5.74	0.79	0.00	0.00	9.72
2014–15	100.00	32.59	0.08	0.27	11.52	23.35	21.14	4.15	0.50	0.00	0.00	6.38
2015–16	100.00	30.77	0.11	0.27	12.17	24.92	20.39	4.61	0.41	0.00	0.00	6.35
2016–17	100.00	29.63	0.13	0.16	12.05	25.08	21.74	4.33	0.14	0.00	0.00	6.75
	Expenditure per full-time-equivalent student in constant 2017–18 dollars[3]											
All levels												
1999–2000	$46,536	$15,017	$4,839	$835	$3,759	$3,284	$6,111	$4,791	$682	$4,246	$1,590	$1,383
2003–04	49,654	16,140	5,731	939	4,170	3,591	6,641	5,002	524	3,986	2,010	921
2004–05	49,798	16,356	5,780	902	4,214	3,695	6,627	4,937	482	4,141	1,905	758
2005–06	50,072	16,481	5,676	830	4,383	3,826	6,716	5,054	303	4,134	1,802	867
2006–07	51,122	16,920	5,625	836	4,466	3,937	6,908	5,109	299	4,268	1,921	833
2007–08	51,540	17,075	5,588	843	4,588	4,000	7,091	5,142	278	4,151	1,887	899
2008–09	53,031	17,427	5,726	862	4,721	4,133	7,279	5,145	283	4,476	1,935	1,043
2009–10	52,490	17,205	5,868	756	4,685	4,132	7,031	5,024	299	4,765	1,865	860
2010–11	52,103	17,001	5,932	770	4,647	4,168	6,907	4,940	260	4,865	1,837	777
2011–12	52,595	17,165	5,753	768	4,678	4,239	6,968	4,919	278	5,092	1,793	941
2012–13	52,965	17,375	5,631	741	4,776	4,382	6,965	4,912	270	5,353	1,740	820
2013–14	54,284	17,844	5,581	774	4,863	4,580	7,118	5,029	273	5,468	1,792	964
2014–15	55,839	18,089	5,636	811	4,788	4,747	7,340	5,035	273	6,319	1,866	936
2015–16	57,240	18,270	5,578	828	4,857	4,872	7,532	5,073	277	6,452	1,879	1,621
2016–17	58,340	18,384	6,205	851	4,782	4,961	7,601	5,098	280	7,089	1,673	1,417
4-year												
1999–2000	46,995	15,180	4,939	848	3,819	3,297	6,132	4,852	686	4,337	1,623	1,283
2003–04	50,006	16,252	5,804	947	4,207	3,599	6,640	5,045	523	4,037	2,035	918
2004–05	50,127	16,460	5,850	910	4,250	3,699	6,628	4,976	480	4,192	1,928	754
2005–06	50,369	16,567	5,738	835	4,413	3,837	6,727	5,089	303	4,179	1,821	861
2006–07	51,360	16,997	5,673	840	4,492	3,942	6,911	5,139	296	4,305	1,938	827
2007–08	51,794	17,156	5,638	848	4,615	4,006	7,096	5,173	277	4,189	1,904	893
2008–09	53,294	17,513	5,775	868	4,746	4,142	7,287	5,174	283	4,514	1,952	1,041
2009–10	52,742	17,286	5,916	760	4,708	4,140	7,040	5,053	299	4,804	1,880	856
2010–11	52,448	17,111	5,995	778	4,678	4,183	6,923	4,983	262	4,917	1,856	760
2011–12	52,922	17,268	5,810	775	4,707	4,252	6,987	4,960	280	5,143	1,811	929
2012–13	53,251	17,463	5,679	747	4,804	4,397	6,979	4,945	271	5,398	1,755	814
2013–14	54,547	17,925	5,626	780	4,886	4,587	7,136	5,060	274	5,512	1,806	955
2014–15	56,326	18,246	5,711	821	4,822	4,749	7,383	5,091	276	6,403	1,891	932
2015–16	57,670	18,411	5,645	838	4,884	4,865	7,570	5,123	280	6,530	1,901	1,624
2016–17	58,794	18,532	6,280	861	4,809	4,957	7,637	5,149	283	7,176	1,693	1,417
2-year												
1999–2000	25,134	7,386	147	232	952	2,684	5,144	1,971	504	0	46	6,069
2003–04	22,081	7,427	17	282	1,255	2,929	6,698	1,652	637	0	52	1,133
2004–05	22,720	7,796	20	251	1,296	3,403	6,546	1,687	691	0	0	1,031
2005–06	22,743	8,607	23	387	1,590	2,845	5,704	1,784	347	0	0	1,456
2006–07	23,700	7,970	45	393	1,517	3,286	6,560	1,742	656	0	0	1,530
2007–08	23,280	8,039	42	260	1,581	3,330	6,441	1,646	416	0	0	1,524
2008–09	22,105	7,401	15	161	1,848	3,047	6,335	1,663	319	0	0	1,315
2009–10	21,783	7,349	26	224	1,905	3,069	6,009	1,527	319	0	0	1,354
2010–11	20,040	6,730	9	76	1,716	2,776	5,353	965	44	0	0	2,370
2011–12	19,613	6,830	23	69	1,721	2,864	5,040	791	69	0	0	2,206
2012–13	19,140	6,930	13	68	1,499	2,586	5,301	1,014	179	0	0	1,550
2013–14	21,802	7,775	15	68	1,912	3,632	4,857	1,251	171	0	0	2,120
2014–15	19,478	6,348	16	53	2,244	4,549	4,118	809	98	0	0	1,244
2015–16	21,785	6,703	24	59	2,651	5,429	4,441	1,004	90	0	0	1,383
2016–17	21,124	6,258	28	33	2,545	5,298	4,593	914	29	0	0	1,425

[1]Essentially self-supporting operations of institutions that furnish a service to students, faculty, or staff, such as residence halls and food services.
[2]Excludes tuition, fee, and auxiliary enterprise allowances and agency transactions, such as student awards made from contributed funds or grant funds. These exclusions account for the majority of total student grants.
[3]Constant dollars based on the Consumer Price Index, prepared by the Bureau of Labor Statistics, U.S. Department of Labor, adjusted to a school-year basis.
NOTE: Degree-granting institutions grant associate's or higher degrees and participate in Title IV federal financial aid programs. Data in this table pertain to institutions' fiscal years that end in the academic year noted. Some data have been revised from previously published figures. Detail may not sum to totals because of rounding.
SOURCE: U.S. Department of Education, National Center for Education Statistics, Integrated Postsecondary Education Data System (IPEDS), "Fall Enrollment Survey" (IPEDS-EF:99); Spring 2004 through Spring 2007, Enrollment component; Spring 2008 through Spring 2017, Fall Enrollment component; and Spring 2001 through Spring 2018, Finance component. (This table was prepared January 2019.)

Table 334.40. Total expenditures of private nonprofit degree-granting postsecondary institutions, by purpose and classification of institution: 2016–17

Classification of institution	Total	Instruction	Research	Public service	Academic support	Student services	Institutional support	Auxiliary enterprises[1]	Net grant aid to students[2]	Hospitals	Independent operations	Other
1	2	3	4	5	6	7	8	9	10	11	12	13
	In thousands of current dollars											
Total	**$197,222,297**	**$62,147,748**	**$20,975,036**	**$2,877,302**	**$16,165,352**	**$16,771,994**	**$25,693,911**	**$17,232,526**	**$946,226**	**$23,966,117**	**$5,655,027**	**$4,791,058**
4-year	196,362,166	61,892,928	20,973,876	2,875,944	16,061,738	16,556,264	25,506,883	17,195,307	945,046	23,966,117	5,655,027	4,733,035
Research university, very high[3]	95,045,147	28,792,448	16,893,718	1,027,777	6,239,982	3,788,270	8,395,527	6,158,545	658,439	15,989,988	3,872,644	3,227,808
Research university, high[4]	14,716,508	4,920,207	1,402,089	223,406	2,351,698	1,215,873	2,128,440	1,726,696	33,766	490,773	66,534	157,024
Doctoral/research[5]	9,493,609	3,818,916	168,869	119,426	988,389	1,462,596	1,663,595	1,162,757	6,834	0	31,361	70,864
Master's[6]	30,894,260	11,756,019	245,639	228,192	3,078,487	5,303,747	5,919,930	3,822,701	108,008	28,553	113,815	289,168
Baccalaureate[7]	21,664,523	7,686,289	217,793	189,352	1,944,338	3,599,016	4,141,685	3,527,406	67,945	0	45,863	244,835
Special-focus institutions[8]	24,548,119	4,919,047	2,045,766	1,087,792	1,458,844	1,186,762	3,257,706	797,200	70,055	7,456,802	1,524,809	743,336
Arts, music, or design	2,376,064	949,260	975	27,315	302,228	245,181	503,868	252,198	8,309	0	37,201	49,530
Business and management	594,352	152,607	2,235	1,167	70,885	105,271	180,614	73,364	614	0	0	7,594
Engineering and other technology-related	251,085	109,736	3,310	0	21,427	39,357	55,132	18,335	3,789	0	0	0
Faith related	1,901,980	604,501	8,881	61,923	189,842	180,279	501,195	191,821	41,573	0	18,539	103,426
Law	478,224	197,143	3,565	10,525	74,863	64,361	109,507	13,582	1,278	0	0	3,399
Medical schools and centers and other heath professions schools	18,218,889	2,679,880	2,019,529	864,390	745,867	455,560	1,756,406	205,922	12,953	7,456,802	1,469,047	552,532
Tribal colleges[9]	90,896	23,783	1,696	7,814	6,644	13,358	22,633	1,693	970	0	0	12,306
Other special focus	636,629	202,136	5,575	114,657	47,088	83,396	128,352	40,285	569	0	22	14,549
2-year	860,131	254,820	1,160	1,358	103,614	215,729	187,028	37,219	1,180	0	0	58,022
Associate's colleges	843,766	251,016	1	1,144	102,196	213,990	183,215	36,768	206	0	0	55,230
Tribal colleges[9]	16,365	3,804	1,159	214	1,418	1,739	3,814	451	974	0	0	2,792
	Percentage distribution											
Total	**100.00**	**31.51**	**10.64**	**1.46**	**8.20**	**8.50**	**13.03**	**8.74**	**0.48**	**12.15**	**2.87**	**2.43**
4-year	100.00	31.52	10.68	1.46	8.18	8.43	12.99	8.76	0.48	12.21	2.88	2.41
Research university, very high[3]	100.00	30.29	17.77	1.08	6.57	3.99	8.83	6.48	0.69	16.82	4.07	3.40
Research university, high[4]	100.00	33.43	9.53	1.52	15.98	8.26	14.46	11.73	0.23	3.33	0.45	1.07
Doctoral/research[5]	100.00	40.23	1.78	1.26	10.41	15.41	17.52	12.25	0.07	0.00	0.33	0.75
Master's[6]	100.00	38.05	0.80	0.74	9.96	17.17	19.16	12.37	0.35	0.09	0.37	0.94
Baccalaureate[7]	100.00	35.48	1.01	0.87	8.97	16.61	19.12	16.28	0.31	0.00	0.21	1.13
Special-focus institutions[8]	100.00	20.04	8.33	4.43	5.94	4.83	13.27	3.25	0.29	30.38	6.21	3.03
Arts, music, or design	100.00	39.95	0.04	1.15	12.72	10.32	21.21	10.61	0.35	0.00	1.57	2.08
Business and management	100.00	25.68	0.38	0.20	11.93	17.71	30.39	12.34	0.10	0.00	0.00	1.28
Engineering and other technology-related	100.00	43.70	1.32	0.00	8.53	15.67	21.96	7.30	1.51	0.00	0.00	0.00
Faith related	100.00	31.78	0.47	3.26	9.98	9.48	26.35	10.09	2.19	0.00	0.97	5.44
Law	100.00	41.22	0.75	2.20	15.65	13.46	22.90	2.84	0.27	0.00	0.00	0.71
Medical schools and centers and other heath professions schools	100.00	14.71	11.08	4.74	4.09	2.50	9.64	1.13	0.07	40.93	8.06	3.03
Tribal colleges[9]	100.00	26.16	1.87	8.60	7.31	14.70	24.90	1.86	1.07	0.00	0.00	13.54
Other special focus	100.00	31.75	0.88	18.01	7.40	13.10	20.16	6.33	0.09	0.00	#	2.29
2-year	100.00	29.63	0.13	0.16	12.05	25.08	21.74	4.33	0.14	0.00	0.00	6.75
Associate's colleges	100.00	29.75	#	0.14	12.11	25.36	21.71	4.36	0.02	0.00	0.00	6.55
Tribal colleges[9]	100.00	23.24	7.08	1.31	8.67	10.63	23.30	2.76	5.95	0.00	0.00	17.06
	Expenditure per full-time-equivalent student in current dollars											
Total	**$57,054**	**$17,979**	**$6,068**	**$832**	**$4,676**	**$4,852**	**$7,433**	**$4,985**	**$274**	**$6,933**	**$1,636**	**$1,386**
4-year	57,498	18,123	6,141	842	4,703	4,848	7,469	5,035	277	7,018	1,656	1,386
Research university, very high[3]	169,041	51,208	30,046	1,828	11,098	6,738	14,932	10,953	1,171	28,439	6,888	5,741
Research university, high[4]	50,483	16,878	4,810	766	8,067	4,171	7,301	5,923	116	1,684	228	539
Doctoral/research[5]	26,932	10,834	479	339	2,804	4,149	4,719	3,299	19	0	89	201
Master's[6]	24,101	9,171	192	178	2,402	4,137	4,618	2,982	84	22	89	226
Baccalaureate[7]	35,532	12,606	357	311	3,189	5,903	6,793	5,785	111	0	75	402
Special-focus institutions[8]	77,380	15,506	6,449	3,429	4,599	3,741	10,269	2,513	221	23,505	4,806	2,343
Arts, music, or design	40,989	16,375	17	471	5,214	4,230	8,692	4,351	143	0	642	854
Business and management	24,099	6,188	91	47	2,874	4,268	7,323	2,975	25	0	0	308
Engineering and other technology-related	20,877	9,124	275	0	1,782	3,272	4,584	1,524	315	0	0	0
Faith related	28,398	9,026	133	925	2,834	2,692	7,483	2,864	621	0	277	1,544
Law	47,880	19,738	357	1,054	7,495	6,444	10,964	1,360	128	0	0	340
Medical schools and centers and other heath professions schools	140,454	20,660	15,569	6,664	5,750	3,512	13,541	1,588	100	57,486	11,325	4,260
Tribal colleges[9]	38,696	10,125	722	3,326	2,829	5,687	9,635	721	413	0	0	5,239
Other special focus	46,959	14,910	411	8,457	3,473	6,151	9,468	2,972	42	0	2	1,073
2-year	20,658	6,120	28	33	2,489	5,181	4,492	894	28	0	0	1,394
Associate's colleges	20,488	6,095	#	28	2,481	5,196	4,449	893	5	0	0	1,341
Tribal colleges[9]	36,207	8,415	2,565	473	3,138	3,848	8,437	998	2,155	0	0	6,178

#Rounds to zero.
[1]Essentially self-supporting operations of institutions that furnish a service to students, faculty, or staff, such as residence halls and food services.
[2]Excludes tuition, fee, and auxiliary enterprise allowances and agency transactions, such as student awards made from contributed funds or grant funds. These exclusions account for the majority of total student grants.
[3]Research universities with a very high level of research activity.
[4]Research universities with a high level of research activity.
[5]Institutions that award at least 20 research/scholarship doctor's degrees per year, but did not have high levels of research activity.
[6]Institutions that award at least 50 master's and fewer than 20 doctor's degrees per year.
[7]Institutions that primarily emphasize undergraduate education. In addition to institutions that primarily award bachelor's degrees, also includes institutions classified as 4-year in the IPEDS system, but classified as 2-year baccalaureate/associate's colleges in the Carnegie Classification system because they primarily award associate's degrees.
[8]Four-year institutions that award degrees primarily in single fields of study, such as medicine, business, fine arts, theology, and engineering.
[9]Tribally controlled colleges, which are located on reservations and are members of the American Indian Higher Education Consortium.
NOTE: Relative levels of research activity for research universities were determined by an analysis of research and development expenditures, science and engineering research staffing, and doctor's degrees conferred, by field. Further information on the Carnegie 2015 classification system used in this table may be obtained from http://carnegieclassifications.iu.edu/. Degree-granting institutions grant associate's or higher degrees and participate in Title IV federal financial aid programs. Data in this table pertain to institutions' fiscal years that end in the academic year noted. Detail may not sum to totals because of rounding.
SOURCE: U.S. Department of Education, National Center for Education Statistics, Integrated Postsecondary Education Data System (IPEDS), Spring 2017, Fall Enrollment component; and Spring 2018, Finance component. (This table was prepared December 2018.)

Table 334.50. Total expenditures of private for-profit degree-granting postsecondary institutions, by purpose and level of institution: Selected years, 1999–2000 through 2016–17

Year and level of institution	Total	Instruction	Research and public service	Student services, academic and institutional support	Auxiliary enterprises[1]	Net grant aid to students[2]	Other[3]
1	2	3	4	5	6	7	8
			In thousands of current dollars				
All levels							
1999–2000	$3,846,246	$1,171,732	$24,738	$2,041,594	$144,305	$26,278	$437,599
2003–04	7,364,012	1,883,733	8,606	4,592,730	249,472	56,467	573,004
2004–05	8,830,792	2,313,895	7,583	5,693,200	269,883	54,819	491,411
2005–06	10,208,845	2,586,870	8,445	6,575,800	276,108	66,569	695,053
2006–07	12,165,629	2,883,207	6,087	7,776,210	332,887	67,090	1,100,148
2007–08	13,939,251	3,273,627	9,695	9,299,306	421,714	82,072	852,837
2008–09	16,375,034	3,876,258	9,939	11,069,416	396,715	44,440	978,267
2009–10	19,973,034	4,759,300	13,257	13,230,271	466,040	120,032	1,384,134
2010–11	22,632,244	5,656,167	19,327	14,853,799	486,433	87,151	1,529,368
2011–12	22,713,683	5,538,070	42,657	15,111,978	489,409	54,579	1,476,991
2012–13	21,923,722	5,467,671	27,729	14,294,090	467,973	53,555	1,612,705
2013–14	20,644,593	5,536,025	16,447	13,103,182	472,204	36,569	1,480,166
2014–15	18,441,030	4,917,479	20,028	11,624,796	504,091	35,524	1,339,112
2015–16	16,000,640	4,248,320	17,453	10,081,942	399,110	25,277	1,228,537
2016–17	14,704,757	3,927,195	17,018	9,198,033	318,755	26,649	1,217,107
4-year							
1999–2000	2,022,622	595,976	4,393	1,104,001	92,071	11,805	214,377
2003–04	4,821,864	1,143,050	3,705	3,108,697	168,069	32,603	365,740
2004–05	5,989,792	1,430,196	3,513	4,110,514	180,036	38,639	226,894
2005–06	7,218,830	1,680,603	4,065	4,986,009	178,587	54,291	315,276
2006–07	8,850,759	1,856,614	4,303	5,925,855	228,624	56,930	778,433
2007–08	10,422,080	2,184,872	7,682	7,312,117	312,834	71,324	533,252
2008–09	12,409,748	2,585,133	7,629	8,893,714	276,211	33,417	613,644
2009–10	15,286,893	3,268,070	10,726	10,732,002	337,499	72,082	866,514
2010–11	17,141,926	3,925,347	15,582	12,031,073	343,319	74,921	751,684
2011–12	17,407,585	3,928,903	37,912	12,153,860	349,405	51,818	885,687
2012–13	16,759,402	3,939,227	24,432	11,377,216	359,987	46,446	1,012,095
2013–14	16,017,246	4,078,270	15,190	10,545,883	371,018	32,306	974,579
2014–15	14,628,734	3,729,921	17,904	9,617,433	334,087	33,089	896,300
2015–16	12,564,815	3,199,028	15,489	8,199,419	323,247	22,834	804,796
2016–17	11,685,177	2,998,115	15,090	7,595,109	261,582	24,039	791,242
2-year							
1999–2000	1,823,624	575,756	20,345	937,593	52,234	14,473	223,223
2003–04	2,542,148	740,683	4,901	1,484,033	81,403	23,864	207,264
2004–05	2,840,999	883,699	4,070	1,582,687	89,846	16,181	264,517
2005–06	2,990,015	906,267	4,381	1,589,791	97,521	12,278	379,777
2006–07	3,314,870	1,026,592	1,784	1,850,355	104,264	10,160	321,715
2007–08	3,517,171	1,088,755	2,014	1,987,189	108,880	10,747	319,586
2008–09	3,965,287	1,291,124	2,310	2,175,703	120,504	11,023	364,623
2009–10	4,686,142	1,491,230	2,531	2,498,269	128,542	47,950	517,619
2010–11	5,490,318	1,730,820	3,744	2,822,726	143,113	12,230	777,685
2011–12	5,306,098	1,609,167	4,745	2,958,118	140,004	2,761	591,304
2012–13	5,164,320	1,528,444	3,297	2,916,874	107,986	7,109	600,609
2013–14	4,627,347	1,457,755	1,257	2,557,299	101,186	4,263	505,588
2014–15	3,812,297	1,187,558	2,124	2,007,363	170,004	2,435	442,812
2015–16	3,435,825	1,049,292	1,964	1,882,523	75,863	2,443	423,740
2016–17	3,019,580	929,080	1,927	1,602,925	57,173	2,610	425,865
			Percentage distribution				
All levels							
1999–2000	100.00	30.46	0.64	53.08	3.75	0.68	11.38
2003–04	100.00	25.58	0.12	62.37	3.39	0.77	7.78
2004–05	100.00	26.20	0.09	64.47	3.06	0.62	5.56
2005–06	100.00	25.34	0.08	64.41	2.70	0.65	6.81
2006–07	100.00	23.70	0.05	63.92	2.74	0.55	9.04
2007–08	100.00	23.48	0.07	66.71	3.03	0.59	6.12
2008–09	100.00	23.67	0.06	67.60	2.42	0.27	5.97
2009–10	100.00	23.83	0.07	66.24	2.33	0.60	6.93
2010–11	100.00	24.99	0.09	65.63	2.15	0.39	6.76
2011–12	100.00	24.38	0.19	66.53	2.15	0.24	6.50
2012–13	100.00	24.94	0.13	65.20	2.13	0.24	7.36
2013–14	100.00	26.82	0.08	63.47	2.29	0.18	7.17
2014–15	100.00	26.67	0.11	63.04	2.73	0.19	7.26
2015–16	100.00	26.55	0.11	63.01	2.49	0.16	7.68
2016–17	100.00	26.71	0.12	62.55	2.17	0.18	8.28
4-year							
1999–2000	100.00	29.47	0.22	54.58	4.55	0.58	10.60
2003–04	100.00	23.71	0.08	64.47	3.49	0.68	7.59
2004–05	100.00	23.88	0.06	68.63	3.01	0.65	3.79
2005–06	100.00	23.28	0.06	69.07	2.47	0.75	4.37
2006–07	100.00	20.98	0.05	66.95	2.58	0.64	8.80
2007–08	100.00	20.96	0.07	70.16	3.00	0.68	5.12
2008–09	100.00	20.83	0.06	71.67	2.23	0.27	4.94
2009–10	100.00	21.38	0.07	70.20	2.21	0.47	5.67
2010–11	100.00	22.90	0.09	70.19	2.00	0.44	4.39
2011–12	100.00	22.57	0.22	69.82	2.01	0.30	5.09

See notes at end of table.

Table 334.50. Total expenditures of private for-profit degree-granting postsecondary institutions, by purpose and level of institution: Selected years, 1999–2000 through 2016–17—Continued

Year and level of institution	Total	Instruction	Research and public service	Student services, academic and institutional support	Auxiliary enterprises[1]	Net grant aid to students[2]	Other[3]
1	2	3	4	5	6	7	8
2012–13	100.00	23.50	0.15	67.89	2.15	0.28	6.04
2013–14	100.00	25.46	0.09	65.84	2.32	0.20	6.08
2014–15	100.00	25.50	0.12	65.74	2.28	0.23	6.13
2015–16	100.00	25.46	0.12	65.26	2.57	0.18	6.41
2016–17	100.00	25.66	0.13	65.00	2.24	0.21	6.77
2-year							
1999–2000	100.00	31.57	1.12	51.41	2.86	0.79	12.24
2003–04	100.00	29.14	0.19	58.38	3.20	0.94	8.15
2004–05	100.00	31.11	0.14	55.71	3.16	0.57	9.31
2005–06	100.00	30.31	0.15	53.17	3.26	0.41	12.70
2006–07	100.00	30.97	0.05	55.82	3.15	0.31	9.71
2007–08	100.00	30.96	0.06	56.50	3.10	0.31	9.09
2008–09	100.00	32.56	0.06	54.87	3.04	0.28	9.20
2009–10	100.00	31.82	0.05	53.31	2.74	1.02	11.05
2010–11	100.00	31.52	0.07	51.41	2.61	0.22	14.16
2011–12	100.00	30.33	0.09	55.75	2.64	0.05	11.14
2012–13	100.00	29.60	0.06	56.48	2.09	0.14	11.63
2013–14	100.00	31.50	0.03	55.26	2.19	0.09	10.93
2014–15	100.00	31.15	0.06	52.65	4.46	0.06	11.62
2015–16	100.00	30.54	0.06	54.79	2.21	0.07	12.33
2016–17	100.00	30.77	0.06	53.08	1.89	0.09	14.10
	Expenditure per full-time-equivalent student in constant 2017–18 dollars[4]						
All levels							
1999–2000	$14,657	$4,465	$94	$7,780	$550	$100	$1,668
2003–04	15,175	3,882	18	9,464	514	116	1,181
2004–05	14,504	3,800	12	9,351	443	90	807
2005–06	14,136	3,582	12	9,105	382	92	962
2006–07	15,672	3,714	8	10,017	429	86	1,417
2007–08	15,860	3,725	11	10,580	480	93	970
2008–09	15,028	3,557	9	10,159	364	41	898
2009–10	15,348	3,657	10	10,166	358	92	1,064
2010–11	15,361	3,839	13	10,081	330	59	1,038
2011–12	15,363	3,746	29	10,221	331	37	999
2012–13	16,618	4,144	21	10,835	355	41	1,222
2013–14	20,557	5,513	16	13,048	470	36	1,474
2014–15	16,355	4,361	18	10,310	447	32	1,188
2015–16	16,849	4,474	18	10,617	420	27	1,294
2016–17	16,788	4,483	19	10,501	364	30	1,389
4-year							
1999–2000	14,200	4,184	31	7,751	646	83	1,505
2003–04	15,055	3,569	12	9,706	525	102	1,142
2004–05	14,003	3,343	8	9,609	421	90	530
2005–06	13,588	3,163	8	9,385	336	102	593
2006–07	15,278	3,205	7	10,229	395	98	1,344
2007–08	15,476	3,244	11	10,858	465	106	792
2008–09	14,853	3,094	9	10,645	331	40	734
2009–10	15,658	3,347	11	10,993	346	74	888
2010–11	15,296	3,503	14	10,735	306	67	671
2011–12	15,149	3,419	33	10,577	304	45	771
2012–13	16,230	3,815	24	11,018	349	45	980
2013–14	21,701	5,525	21	14,288	503	44	1,320
2014–15	16,106	4,106	20	10,588	368	36	987
2015–16	16,562	4,217	20	10,808	426	30	1,061
2016–17	16,510	4,236	21	10,731	370	34	1,118
2-year							
1999–2000	15,199	4,799	170	7,815	435	121	1,861
2003–04	15,409	4,490	30	8,996	493	145	1,256
2004–05	15,688	4,880	22	8,740	496	89	1,461
2005–06	15,659	4,746	23	8,326	511	64	1,989
2006–07	16,831	5,213	9	9,395	529	52	1,634
2007–08	17,115	5,298	10	9,670	530	52	1,555
2008–09	15,603	5,080	9	8,561	474	43	1,435
2009–10	14,416	4,587	8	7,685	395	148	1,592
2010–11	15,567	4,908	11	8,003	406	35	2,205
2011–12	16,111	4,886	14	8,982	425	8	1,795
2012–13	18,013	5,331	11	10,174	377	25	2,095
2013–14	17,386	5,477	5	9,609	380	16	1,900
2014–15	17,389	5,417	10	9,156	775	11	2,020
2015–16	17,990	5,494	10	9,857	397	13	2,219
2016–17	17,958	5,525	11	9,533	340	16	2,533

[1]Essentially self-supporting operations of institutions that furnish a service to students, faculty, or staff, such as residence halls and food services.
[2]Excludes tuition, fee, and auxiliary enterprise allowances and agency transactions, such as student awards made from contributed funds or grant funds. These exclusions account for the majority of total student grants.
[3]"Other" categories of expenditures include hospitals.
[4]Constant dollars based on the Consumer Price Index, prepared by the Bureau of Labor Statistics, U.S. Department of Labor, adjusted to a school-year basis.
NOTE: Degree-granting institutions grant associate's or higher degrees and participate in Title IV federal financial aid programs. Data in this table pertain to institutions' fiscal years that end in the academic year noted. Some data have been revised from previously published figures. Detail may not sum to totals because of rounding.
SOURCE: U.S. Department of Education, National Center for Education Statistics, Integrated Postsecondary Education Data System (IPEDS), "Fall Enrollment Survey" (IPEDS-EF:99); Spring 2004 through Spring 2007, Enrollment component; Spring 2008 through Spring 2017, Fall Enrollment component; and Spring 2001 through Spring 2018, Finance component. (This table was prepared January 2019.)

CHAPTER 4
Federal Funds for Education and Related Activities

This chapter provides information on federal support for education. The tables include detailed data on funding by specific federal agencies, funding for different levels of education and types of education-related activities, and funding for specific programs. Preceding the tables is a brief chronology of federal education legislation enacted since 1787, which provides historical context for the education funding data.

The data in this chapter primarily reflect outlays and appropriations of federal agencies. The data are compiled from budget information prepared by federal agencies. In contrast, most of the federal revenue data reported in other chapters are compiled by educational institutions or state education agencies and reported to the federal government through standardized survey forms. Tabulations based on institution- or state-reported revenue data differ substantially from federal budget reports because of numerous variations in methodology and definitions. Federal dollars are not necessarily spent by recipient institutions in the same year in which they are appropriated. In some cases, institutions cannot identify the source of federal revenues because they flow through state agencies. Some types of revenues, such as tuition and fees, are reported as revenues from students even though they may be supported by federal student aid programs. Some institutions that receive federal education funds (e.g., Department of Defense overseas and domestic schools, state education agencies, Head Start programs, and federal libraries) are not included in regular surveys, censuses, and administrative data collections conducted by the National Center for Education Statistics (NCES). Thus, the federal programs data tabulated in this chapter are not comparable with figures reported in other chapters. Readers should also be careful about comparing the data on obligations shown in table 402.10 (web only) with the data on outlays and appropriations appearing in other tables in this chapter.

Federal Education Funding

Federal on-budget funding (federal appropriations) for education increased by 404 percent from fiscal year (FY) 1965 to FY 2018, after adjustment for inflation (table D, table 401.10, and figure 20); however, there were periods of decreases during those decades. Federal on-budget funding for education in FY 1975 was 152 percent higher than in FY 1965. However, between FY 1975 and FY 1980, there was a change of less than 1 percentage point, and the FY 1985 amount was 17 percent lower than the amount in FY 1980. Thereafter, federal on-budget funding for education generally increased. From FY 1985 to FY 2000, after adjustment for inflation, federal on-budget funding for education increased by 49 percent. From FY 2000 to FY 2010, federal on-budget funding increased 55 percent. Federal on-budget funding for education in FY 2018 was 3 percent higher than in FY 2010.

Table D. Federal on-budget funding for education, by category: Selected fiscal years, 1965 through 2018

[In billions of constant fiscal year (FY) 2018 dollars]

Fiscal year	Total	Elementary/ secondary	Post-secondary	Other education	Research at educational institutions
1965	$39.7	$14.5	$8.9	$2.8	$13.5
1970	76.2	35.5	20.9	5.9	13.9
1975	100.2	45.7	32.9	6.9	14.7
1980	101.1	47.0	32.5	4.5	17.0
1985	83.9	36.3	24.0	4.5	19.0
1990	95.4	40.6	25.2	6.3	23.3
1995	112.9	53.0	27.8	7.4	24.7
2000	124.6	63.3	21.6	8.4	31.3
2005	188.4	87.7	49.0	9.3	42.5
2010	193.5	85.3	55.7	10.5	42.0
2015	205.4	82.9	78.6	9.9	34.0
2016	195.7	85.6	65.2	10.0	35.0
2017[1]	232.8	83.9	103.5	9.9	35.5
2018	199.8	85.0	69.7	9.6	35.4[2]

[1]The increase in postsecondary expenditures in 2017 resulted primarily from an accounting adjustment.

[2]Estimated.

NOTE: Detail may not sum to totals because of rounding.

SOURCE: U.S. Department of Education, Budget Service and National Center for Education Statistics, unpublished tabulations. U.S. Office of Management and Budget, *Budget of the U.S. Government, Appendix*, various FYs. National Science Foundation, *Federal Funds for Research and Development*, various FYs.

After adjustment for inflation, federal on-budget funding was higher in FY 2010 than in FY 2000 for each of the four major categories reported: postsecondary education (by 158 percent), elementary and secondary education (by 35 percent), research at educational institutions (by 34 percent), and other education (by 25 percent) (table D, table 401.10, and figure 20). In contrast, federal on-budget funding was higher in FY 2018 than in FY 2010 for one of the four programs: for postsecondary education, federal on-budget funding was 25 percent higher in FY 2018 than in FY 2010. Federal funding for research at educational institutions was 16 percent lower in FY 2018 than in FY 2010, after adjustment for inflation. Also, funding for other education was 9 percent lower in FY 2018 than in FY 2010, and funding for elementary and secondary education was less than 1 percent lower.

After adjustment for inflation, off-budget support (federal support for education not tied to appropriations) and nonfederal funds generated by federal legislation (e.g., private loans, grants, and aid) showed an increase of 136 percent between FY 1990 ($20.6 billion in FY 2018 dollars) and FY 2000 ($48.6 billion in FY 2018 dollars) (table 401.10). In FY 2018, these same funds totaled $96.3 billion, an increase of 98 percent over FY 2000.

In current dollars (not adjusted for inflation), federal on-budget funds for education in FY 2017 totaled $227.2 billion (figure 21 and table 401.20). The U.S. Department of Education provided 55 percent ($126.0 billion) of this total. Funds exceeding $2.5 billion also came from the U.S. Department of Health and Human Services ($29.5 billion), the U.S. Department of Agriculture ($25.4 billion), the U.S. Department of Veterans Affairs ($14.4 billion), the U.S. Department of Defense ($7.2 billion), the National Science Foundation ($6.0 billion), the U.S. Department of Labor ($5.0 billion), the U.S. Department of Energy ($3.7 billion), and the National Aeronautics and Space Administration ($2.7 billion).

Chronology of Federal Education Legislation

A capsule view of the history of federal education activities is provided in the following list of selected legislation:

1787 *Northwest Ordinance* authorized land grants for the establishment of educational institutions.

1802 *An Act Fixing the Military Peace Establishment of the United States* established the U.S. Military Academy. (The U.S. Naval Academy was established in 1845 by the Secretary of the Navy.)

1862 *First Morrill Act* authorized public land grants to the states for the establishment and maintenance of agricultural and mechanical colleges.

1867 *Department of Education Act* authorized the establishment of the U.S. Department of Education.[1]

1876 *Appropriation Act*, U.S. Department of the Treasury, established the U.S. Coast Guard Academy.

1890 *Second Morrill Act* provided for monetary grants for support of instruction in the agricultural and mechanical colleges.

1911 *State Marine School Act* authorized federal funds to be used for the benefit of any nautical school in any of 11 specified seaport cities.

1917 *Smith-Hughes Act* provided for grants to states for support of vocational education.

1918 *Vocational Rehabilitation Act* provided for grants for rehabilitation through training of World War I veterans.

[1] The U.S. Department of Education as established in 1867 was later known as the Office of Education. In 1980, under Public Law 96–88, it became a cabinet-level department. Therefore, for purposes of consistency, it is referred to as the "U.S. Department of Education" even in those tables covering years when it was officially the Office of Education.

1920 *Smith-Bankhead Act* authorized grants to states for vocational rehabilitation programs.

1935 *Bankhead-Jones Act* (Public Law 74-182) authorized grants to states for agricultural experiment stations.

Agricultural Adjustment Act (Public Law 74-320) authorized 30 percent of the annual customs receipts to be used to encourage the exportation and domestic consumption of agricultural commodities. Commodities purchased under this authorization began to be used in school lunch programs in 1936. The National School Lunch Act of 1946 continued and expanded this assistance.

1936 *An Act to Further the Development and Maintenance of an Adequate and Well-Balanced American Merchant Marine* (Public Law 74-415) established the U.S. Merchant Marine Academy.

1937 *National Cancer Institute Act* (Public Law 75-244) established the Public Health Service fellowship program.

1941 *Amendment to Lanham Act of 1940* authorized federal aid for construction, maintenance, and operation of schools in federally impacted areas. Such assistance was continued under Public Law 815 and Public Law 874, 81st Congress, in 1950.

1943 *Vocational Rehabilitation Act* (Public Law 78-16) provided assistance to veterans with disabilities.

School Lunch Indemnity Plan (Public Law 78-129) provided funds for local lunch food purchases.

1944 *Servicemen's Readjustment Act* (Public Law 78-346), known as the GI Bill, provided assistance for the education of veterans.

Surplus Property Act (Public Law 78-457) authorized transfer of surplus property to educational institutions.

1946 *National School Lunch Act* (Public Law 79-396) authorized assistance through grants-in-aid and other means to states to assist in providing adequate foods and facilities for the establishment, maintenance, operation, and expansion of nonprofit school lunch programs.

George-Barden Act (Public Law 80-402) expanded federal support of vocational education.

1948 *United States Information and Educational Exchange Act* (Public Law 80-402) provided for the interchange of people, knowledge, and skills between the United States and other countries.

1949 *Federal Property and Administrative Services Act* (Public Law 81-152) provided for donation of surplus property to educational institutions and for other public purposes.

1950 *Financial Assistance for Local Educational Agencies Affected by Federal Activities* (Public Law 81-815 and Public Law 81-874) provided assistance for construction (Public Law 815) and operation (Public Law 874) of schools in federally affected areas.

Housing Act (Public Law 81-475) authorized loans for construction of college housing facilities.

1954 *An Act for the Establishment of the United States Air Force Academy and Other Purposes* (Public Law 83-325) established the U.S. Air Force Academy.

Educational Research Act (Public Law 83-531) authorized cooperative arrangements with universities, colleges, and state educational agencies for educational research.

School Milk Program Act (Public Law 83-597) provided funds for purchase of milk for school lunch programs.

1956 *Library Services Act* (Public Law 84-597) provided grants to states for extension and improvement of rural public library services.

1957 *Practical Nurse Training Act* (Public Law 84-911) provided grants to states for practical nurse training.

1958 *National Defense Education Act* (Public Law 85-864) provided assistance to state and local school systems for instruction in science, mathematics, modern foreign languages, and other critical subjects; state statistical services; guidance, counseling, and testing services and training institutes; higher education student loans and fellowships as well as foreign language study and training; experimentation and dissemination of information on more effective use of television, motion pictures, and related media for educational purposes; and vocational education for technical occupations necessary to the national defense.

Education of Mentally Retarded Children Act (Public Law 85-926) authorized federal assistance for training teachers of the disabled.

Captioned Films for the Deaf Act (Public Law 85-905) authorized a loan service of captioned films for the deaf.

1961 *Area Redevelopment Act* (Public Law 87-27) included provisions for training or retraining of people in redevelopment areas.

1962 *Manpower Development and Training Act* (Public Law 87-415) provided training in new and improved skills for the unemployed and underemployed.

Migration and Refugee Assistance Act of 1962 (Public Law 87-510) authorized loans, advances, and grants for education and training of refugees.

1963 *Health Professions Educational Assistance Act of 1963* (Public Law 88-129) provided funds to expand teaching facilities and for loans to students in the health professions.

Vocational Education Act of 1963 (Public Law 88-210, Part A) increased federal support of vocational education schools; vocational work-study programs; and research, training, and demonstrations in vocational education.

Higher Education Facilities Act of 1963 (Public Law 88-204) authorized grants and loans for classrooms, libraries, and laboratories in public community colleges and technical institutes, as well as undergraduate and graduate facilities in other higher education institutions.

1964 *Civil Rights Act of 1964* (Public Law 88-352) authorized the Commissioner of Education to arrange for support for higher education institutions and school districts to provide inservice programs for assisting instructional staff in dealing with problems caused by desegregation.

Economic Opportunity Act of 1964 (Public Law 88-452) authorized grants for college work-study programs for students from low-income families; established a Job Corps program and authorized support for work-training programs to provide education and vocational training and work experience opportunities in welfare programs; authorized support of education and training activities and of community action programs, including Head Start, Follow Through, and Upward Bound; and authorized the establishment of Volunteers in Service to America (VISTA).

1965 *Elementary and Secondary Education Act of 1965* (Public Law 89-10) authorized grants for elementary and secondary school programs for children of low-income families; school library resources, textbooks, and other instructional materials for school children; supplementary educational centers and services; strengthening state education agencies; and educational research and research training.

Health Professions Educational Assistance Amendments of 1965 (Public Law 89-290) authorized scholarships to aid needy students in the health professions.

Higher Education Act of 1965 (Public Law 89-329) provided grants for university community service programs, college library assistance, library training and research, strengthening developing institutions, teacher training programs, and undergraduate instructional equipment. Authorized insured student loans, established a National Teacher Corps, and provided for graduate teacher training fellowships.

National Foundation on the Arts and the Humanities Act (Public Law 89-209) authorized grants and loans for projects in the creative and performing arts and for research, training, and scholarly publications in the humanities.

National Technical Institute for the Deaf Act (Public Law 89-36) provided for the establishment, construction, equipping, and operation of a residential school for postsecondary education and technical training of the deaf.

School Assistance in Disaster Areas Act (Public Law 89-313) provided for assistance to local education agencies to help meet exceptional costs resulting from a major disaster.

1966 *International Education Act* (Public Law 89-698) provided grants to higher education institutions for the establishment, strengthening, and operation of centers for research and training in international studies and the international aspects of other fields of study.

National Sea Grant College and Program Act (Public Law 89-688) authorized the establishment and operation of Sea Grant Colleges and programs by initiating and supporting programs of education and research in the various fields relating to the development of marine resources.

Adult Education Act (Public Law 89-750) authorized grants to states for the encouragement and expansion of educational programs for adults, including training of teachers of adults and demonstrations in adult education (previously part of Economic Opportunity Act of 1964).

Model Secondary School for the Deaf Act (Public Law 89-694) authorized the establishment and operation, by Gallaudet College, of a model secondary school for the deaf.

1967 *Education Professions Development Act* (Public Law 90-35) amended the Higher Education Act of 1965 for the purpose of improving the quality of teaching and to help meet critical shortages of adequately trained educational personnel.

Public Broadcasting Act of 1967 (Public Law 90-129) established a Corporation for Public Broadcasting to assume major responsibility in channeling federal funds to noncommercial radio and television stations, program production groups, and educational television networks; conduct research, demonstration, or training in matters related to noncommercial broadcasting; and award grants for construction of educational radio and television facilities.

1968 *Elementary and Secondary Education Amendments of 1968* (Public Law 90-247) modified existing programs and authorized support of regional centers for education of children with disabilities, model centers and services for deaf-blind children, recruitment of personnel and dissemination of information on education of children with disabilities; technical assistance in education to rural areas; support of dropout prevention projects; and support of bilingual education programs.

Handicapped Children's Early Education Assistance Act (Public Law 90-538) authorized preschool and early education programs for children with disabilities.

Vocational Education Amendments of 1968 (Public Law 90-576) modified existing programs and provided for a National Advisory Council on Vocational Education and collection and dissemination of information for programs administered by the Commissioner of Education.

1970 *Elementary and Secondary Education Assistance Programs, Extension* (Public Law 91-230) authorized comprehensive planning and evaluation grants to state and local education agencies; provided for the establishment of a National Commission on School Finance.

National Commission on Libraries and Information Science Act (Public Law 91-345) established a National Commission on Libraries and Information Science to effectively utilize the nation's educational resources.

Office of Education Appropriation Act (Public Law 91-380) provided emergency school assistance to desegregating local education agencies.

Environmental Education Act (Public Law 91-516) established an Office of Environmental Education to develop curriculum and initiate and maintain environmental education programs at the elementary/secondary levels; disseminate information; provide training programs for teachers and other educational, public, community, labor, and industrial leaders and employees; provide community education programs; and distribute material dealing with the environment and ecology.

Drug Abuse Education Act of 1970 (Public Law 91-527) provided for development, demonstration, and evaluation of curricula on the problems of drug abuse.

1971 *Comprehensive Health Manpower Training Act of 1971* (Public Law 92-257) amended Title VII of the Public Health Service Act, increasing and expanding provisions for health manpower training and training facilities.

1972 *Drug Abuse Office and Treatment Act of 1972* (Public Law 92-255) established a Special Action Office for Drug Abuse Prevention to provide overall planning and policy for all federal drug-abuse prevention functions; a National Advisory Council for Drug Abuse Prevention; community assistance grants for community mental health centers for treatment and rehabilitation of people with drug-abuse problems; and, in December 1974, a National Institute on Drug Abuse.

Education Amendments of 1972 (Public Law 92-318) established the Education Division in the U.S. Department of Health, Education, and Welfare and the National Institute of Education; general aid for higher education institutions; federal matching grants for state Student Incentive Grants; a National Commission on Financing Postsecondary Education; State Advisory Councils on Community Colleges; a Bureau of Occupational and Adult Education and State Grants for the design, establishment, and conduct of postsecondary occupational education; and a bureau-level Office of Indian Education. Amended current U.S. Department of Education programs to increase their effectiveness and better meet special needs. Prohibited sex bias in admission to vocational, professional, and graduate schools, and public institutions of undergraduate higher education.

1973 *Older Americans Comprehensive Services Amendment of 1973* (Public Law 93-29) made available to older citizens comprehensive programs of health, education, and social services.

Comprehensive Employment and Training Act of 1973 (Public Law 93-203) provided for employment and training opportunities for unemployed and underemployed people. Extended and expanded provisions in the Manpower Development and Training Act of 1962, Title I of the Economic Opportunity Act of 1962, Title I of the Economic Opportunity Act of 1964, and the Emergency Employment Act of 1971 as in effect prior to June 30, 1973.

1974 *Education Amendments of 1974* (Public Law 93-380) provided for the consolidation of certain programs and established a National Center for Education Statistics.

Juvenile Justice and Delinquency Prevention Act of 1974 (Public Law 93-415) provided for technical assistance, staff training, centralized research, and resources to develop and implement programs to keep students in elementary and secondary schools; and established, in the U.S. Department of Justice, a National Institute for Juvenile Justice and Delinquency Prevention.

1975 *Indian Self-Determination and Education Assistance Act* (Public Law 93-638) provided for increased participation of American Indians/Alaska Natives in the establishment and conduct of their education programs and services.

Harry S Truman Memorial Scholarship Act (Public Law 93-642) established the Harry S Truman Scholarship Foundation and created a perpetual education scholarship fund for young Americans to prepare for and pursue careers in public service.

Education for All Handicapped Children Act (Public Law 94-142) provided that all children with disabilities have available to them a free appropriate education designed to meet their unique needs.

1976 *Educational Broadcasting Facilities and Telecommunications Demonstration Act of 1976* (Public Law 94-309) established a telecommunications demonstration program to promote the development of nonbroadcast telecommunications facilities and services for the transmission, distribution, and delivery of health, education, and public or social service information.

1977 *Youth Employment and Demonstration Projects Act of 1977* (Public Law 95-93) established a youth employment training program including, among other activities, promotion of education-to-work transition, literacy training and bilingual training, and attainment of certificates of high school equivalency.

Career Education Incentive Act (Public Law 95-207) authorized the establishment of a career education program for elementary and secondary schools.

1978 *Tribally Controlled Community College Assistance Act of 1978* (Public Law 95-471) provided federal funds for the operation and improvement of tribally controlled community colleges for American Indian/Alaska Native students.

Middle Income Student Assistance Act (Public Law 95-566) modified the provisions for student financial assistance programs to allow middle-income as well as low-income students attending college or other postsecondary institutions to qualify for federal education assistance.

1979 *Department of Education Organization Act* (Public Law 96-88) established a U.S. Department of Education containing functions from the Education Division of the U.S. Department of Health, Education, and Welfare (HEW) along with other selected education programs from HEW, the U.S. Department of Justice, U.S. Department of Labor, and the National Science Foundation.

1980 *Asbestos School Hazard Detection and Control Act of 1980* (Public Law 96-270) established a program for inspection of schools for detection of hazardous asbestos materials and provided loans to assist educational agencies to contain or remove and replace such materials.

1981 *Education Consolidation and Improvement Act of 1981* (Part of Public Law 97-35) consolidated 42 programs into 7 programs to be funded under the elementary and secondary block grant authority.

1983 *Student Loan Consolidation and Technical Amendments Act of 1983* (Public Law 98-79) established an 8 percent interest rate for Guaranteed Student Loans and an extended Family Contribution Schedule.

Challenge Grant Amendments of 1983 (Public Law 98-95) amended Title III of the Higher Education Act of 1965, and added authorization of the Challenge Grant program. The Challenge Grant program provides funds to eligible institutions on a matching basis as an incentive to seek alternative sources of funding.

Education of the Handicapped Act Amendments of 1983 (Public Law 98-199) added the Architectural Barrier amendment (providing funds for altering existing buildings and equipment to make them accessible to those with physical disabilities) and clarified participation of children with disabilities in private schools.

1984 *Education for Economic Security Act* (Public Law 98-377) added new science and mathematics programs for elementary, secondary, and postsecondary education. The new programs included magnet schools, excellence in education, and equal access.

Carl D. Perkins Vocational Education Act (Public Law 98-524) continued federal assistance for vocational education through FY 1989. The act replaced the Vocational Education Act of 1963. It provided aid to the states to make vocational education programs accessible to all people, including disabled and disadvantaged, single parents and homemakers, and the incarcerated.

Human Services Reauthorization Act (Public Law 98-558) created a Carl D. Perkins scholarship program, a National Talented Teachers Fellowship program, a Federal Merit Scholarships program, and a Leadership in Educational Administration program.

1985 *Montgomery GI Bill—Active Duty* (Public Law 98-525), brought about a new GI Bill for individuals who initially entered active military duty on or after July 1, 1985.

Montgomery GI Bill—Selected Reserve (Public Law 98-525), established an education program for members of the Selected Reserve (which includes the National Guard) who enlist, reenlist, or extend an enlistment after June 30, 1985, for a 6-year period.

1986 *Handicapped Children's Protection Act of 1986* (Public Law 99-372) allowed parents of children with disabilities to collect attorneys' fees in cases brought under the Education of the Handicapped Act and provided that the Education of the Handicapped Act does not preempt other laws, such as Section 504 of the Rehabilitation Act.

Drug-Free Schools and Communities Act of 1986 (Part of Public Law 99-570) established programs for drug abuse education and prevention, coordinated with related community efforts and resources, through the use of federal financial assistance.

1988 *Augustus F. Hawkins-Robert T. Stafford Elementary and Secondary School Improvement Amendments of 1988* (Public Law 100-297) reauthorized through 1993 major elementary and secondary education programs, including Chapter 1, Chapter 2, Bilingual Education, Math-Science Education, Magnet Schools, Impact Aid, Indian Education, Adult Education, and other smaller education programs.

Stewart B. McKinney Homeless Assistance Amendments Act of 1988 (Public Law 100-628) extended for 2 additional years programs providing assistance to the homeless, including literacy training for homeless adults and education for homeless youths.

Tax Reform Technical Amendments (Public Law 100-647) authorized an Education Savings Bond for the purpose of postsecondary educational expenses. The bill grants tax exclusion for interest earned on regular series EE savings bonds.

1989 *Childhood Education and Development Act of 1989* (Part of Public Law 101-239) authorized the appropriations to expand Head Start programs and programs carried out under the Elementary and Secondary Education Act of 1965 to include child care services.

1990 *Excellence in Mathematics, Science and Engineering Education Act of 1990* (Public Law 101-589) created a national mathematics and science clearinghouse and created several other mathematics, science, and engineering education programs.

Student Right-To-Know and Campus Security Act (Public Law 101-542) required higher education institutions receiving federal financial assistance to provide certain information about graduation rates of student-athletes and about campus crime statistics and security policies. (The 1990 campus crime and security legislation, along with later acts that amended it, is generally referred to as "the Clery Act.")

Americans with Disabilities Act of 1990 (Public Law 101-336) prohibited discrimination against people with disabilities.

National and Community Service Act of 1990 (Public Law 101-610) increased school and college-based community service opportunities and authorized the President's Points of Light Foundation.

1991 *National Literacy Act of 1991* (Public Law 102-73) established the National Institute for Literacy, the National Institute Board, and the Interagency Task Force on Literacy. Amended various federal laws to establish and extend various literacy programs.

High-Performance Computing Act of 1991 (Public Law 102-194) directed the President to implement a National High-Performance Computing Program. Provided for (1) establishment of a National Research and Education Network; (2) standards and guidelines for high-performance networks; and (3) the responsibility of certain federal departments and agencies with regard to the Network.

Veterans' Educational Assistance Amendments of 1991 (Public Law 102-127) restored certain educational benefits available to reserve and active-duty personnel under the Montgomery GI Bill to students whose courses of studies were interrupted by the Persian Gulf War.

Civil Rights Act of 1991 (Public Law 102-166) amended the Civil Rights Act of 1964, the Age Discrimination in Employment Act of 1967, and the Americans with Disabilities Act of 1990, with regard to employment discrimination. Established the Technical Assistance Training Institute.

1992 *Ready-To-Learn Act* (Public Law 102-545) amended the General Education Provisions Act to establish Ready-To-Learn Television programs to support educational programming and related materials for preschool and elementary school children and their parents, child care providers, and educators.

1993 *Student Loan Reform Act* (Public Law 103-66) reformed the student aid process by phasing in a system of direct lending designed to provide savings for taxpayers and students. Allows students to choose among a variety of repayment options, including income contingency.

National Service Trust Act (Public Law 103-82) amended the National and Community Service Act of 1990 to establish a Corporation for National Service. In addition, provided education grants up to $4,725 per year for 2 years to people age 17 or older who perform community service before, during, or after postsecondary education.

1994 *Goals 2000: Educate America Act* (Public Law 103-227) established a new federal partnership through a system of grants to states and local communities to reform the nation's education system. The Act formalized the national education goals and established the National Education Goals Panel.

School-to-Work Opportunities Act of 1994 (Public Law 103-239) established a national framework within which states and communities can develop School-to-Work Opportunities systems to prepare young people for first jobs and continuing education. The Act also provided money to states and communities to develop a system of programs that include work-based learning, school-based learning, and connecting activities components.

Safe Schools Act of 1994 (Part of Public Law 103-227) authorized the award of competitive grants to local educational agencies with serious crime to implement violence prevention activities such as conflict resolution and peer mediation.

1996 *Contract With America: Unfunded Mandates* (Public Law 104-4) ended the imposition, in the absence of full consideration by Congress, of federal mandates on state, local, and tribal governments without adequate funding, in a manner that may displace other essential governmental priorities; and ensured that the federal government pays the costs incurred by those governments in complying with certain requirements under federal statutes and regulations.

1997 *The Taxpayer Relief Act of 1997* (Public Law 105-34) enacted the Hope Scholarship and Life-Long Learning Tax Credit provisions into law.

Emergency Student Loan Consolidation Act of 1997 (Public Law 105-78) amended the Higher Education Act of 1965 to provide for improved student loan consolidation services.

1998 *Workforce Investment Act of 1998* (Public Law 105-220) enacted the Adult Education and Family Literacy Act, and substantially revised and extended, through FY 2003, the Rehabilitation Act of 1973.

Jeanne Clery Disclosure of Campus Security Policy and Campus Crime Statistics Act (Public Law 105-244) expanded crime categories that must be reported by postsecondary institutions.

Omnibus Consolidated and Emergency Supplemental Appropriations Act, 1999 (Public Law 105-277) enacted the Reading Excellence Act, to promote the ability of children to read independently by the third grade; and earmarked funds to help states and school districts reduce class sizes in the early grades.

Charter School Expansion Act (Public Law 105-278) amended the charter school program, enacted in 1994 as Title X, Part C of the Elementary and Secondary Education Act of 1965.

Carl D. Perkins Vocational and Applied Technology Education Amendments of 1998 (Public Law 105-332) revised, in its entirety, the Carl D. Perkins Vocational and Applied Technology Education Act, and reauthorized the Act through FY 2003.

Assistive Technology Act of 1998 (Public Law 105-394) replaced the Technology-Related Assistance for Individuals with Disabilities Act of 1988 with a new Act, authorized through FY 2004, to address the assistive-technology needs of individuals with disabilities.

1999 *Education Flexibility Partnership Act of 1999* (Public Law 106-25) authorized the Secretary of Education to allow all states to participate in the Education Flexibility Partnership program.

District of Columbia College Access Act of 1999 (Public Law 106-98) established a program to afford high school graduates from the District of Columbia the benefits of in-state tuition at state colleges and universities outside the District of Columbia.

2000 *The National Defense Authorization Act for Fiscal Year 2001* (Public Law 106-398) included, as Title XVIII, the Impact Aid Reauthorization Act of 2000, which extended the Impact Aid programs through FY 2003.

College Scholarship Fraud Prevention Act of 2000 (Public Law 106-420) enhanced federal penalties for offenses involving scholarship fraud; required an annual scholarship fraud report by the Attorney General, the Secretary of Education, and the Federal Trade Commission (FTC); and required the Secretary of Education, in conjunction with the FTC, to maintain a scholarship fraud awareness website.

Consolidated Appropriations Act 2001 (Public Law 106-554) created a new program of assistance for school repair and renovation, and amended the Elementary and Secondary Education Act of 1965 to authorize credit enhancement initiatives to help charter schools obtain, construct, or repair facilities; reauthorized the Even Start program; and enacted the Children's Internet Protection Act.

2001 *50th Anniversary of Brown v. the Board of Education* (Public Law 107-41) established a commission for the purpose of encouraging and providing for the commemoration of the 50th anniversary of the 1954 Supreme Court decision *Brown v. Board of Education.*

2002 *No Child Left Behind Act of 2001* (Public Law 107-110) provided for the comprehensive reauthorization of the Elementary and Secondary Education Act of 1965, incorporating specific proposals in such areas as testing, accountability, parental choice, and early reading.

Education Sciences Reform Act (Public Law 107-279) established the Institute of Education Sciences within the U.S. Department of Education to carry out a coordinated, focused agenda of high-quality research, statistics, and evaluation that is relevant to the educational challenges of the nation.

The Higher Education Relief Opportunities for Students Act of 2001 (Public Law 107-122) provided the Secretary of Education with waiver authority over student financial aid programs under Title IV of the Higher Education Act of 1965, to deal with student and family situations resulting from the September 11, 2001, terrorist attacks.

Public Law 107-139 amended Title IV of the Higher Education Act to establish fixed interest rates for student and parent borrowers.

2003 *The Higher Education Relief Opportunities for Students Act of 2003* (Public Law 108-76) provided the Secretary of Education with waiver authority over student financial aid programs under Title IV of the Higher Education Act of 1965, to deal with student and family situations resulting from wars or national emergencies.

2004 *Assistive Technology Act of 2004* (Public Law 108-364) reauthorized the Assistive Technology program, administered by the Department of Education.

Taxpayer-Teacher Protection Act of 2004 (Public Law 108-409) temporarily stopped excessive special allowance payments to certain lenders under the Federal Family Education Loan (FFEL) Program and increased the amount of loans that can be forgiven for certain borrowers who are highly qualified mathematics, science, and special education teachers who serve in high-poverty schools for 5 years.

Individuals with Disabilities Education Improvement Act of 2004 (Public Law 108-446) provided a comprehensive reauthorization of the Individuals with Disabilities Education Act.

2005 *Student Grant Hurricane and Disaster Relief Act* (Public Law 109-67) authorized the Secretary of Education to waive certain repayment requirements for students receiving campus-based federal grant assistance if they were residing in, employed in, or attending an institution of higher education located in a major disaster area, or their attendance was interrupted because of the disaster.

Natural Disaster Student Aid Fairness Act (Public Law 109-86) authorized the Secretary of Education during FY 2006 to reallocate campus-based student aid funds to institutions of higher learning in Louisiana, Mississippi, Alabama, and Texas, or institutions that had accepted students displaced by Hurricane Katrina or Rita. The law also waived requirements for matching funds that are normally imposed on institutions and students.

Hurricane Education Recovery Act (Public Law 109-148, provision in the Defense Department Appropriations Act for FY 2006) provided funds for states affected by Hurricane Katrina to restart school operations, provide temporary emergency aid for displaced students, and assist homeless youth. The law also permitted the Secretary of Education to extend deadlines under the Individuals with Disabilities Education Act for those affected by Katrina or Rita.

2006 *Higher Education Reconciliation Act of 2005* (Public Law 109-171) made various amendments to programs of student financial assistance under Title IV of the Higher Education Act of 1965.

Public Law 109-211 reauthorized the "ED-FLEX" program (under the Education Flexibility Partnership Act of 1999), under which the Secretary of Education permits states to waive certain requirements of federal statutes and regulations if they meet certain conditions.

Carl D. Perkins Career and Technical Education Improvement Act of 2006 (Public Law 109-270) reauthorized the vocational and technical education programs under the Perkins Act through 2012.

2007 *America COMPETES Act* (or "*America Creating Opportunities to Meaningfully Promote Excellence in Technology, Education, and Science Act*") (Public Law 110-69) created new STEM (science, technology, engineering, and mathematics) education programs in various agencies, including the Department of Education.

College Cost Reduction and Access Act of 2007 (Public Law 110-84) reduced interest rates on student loans and made other amendments to the Higher Education Act of 1965 to make college more accessible and affordable.

Public Law 110-93 made permanent the waiver authority of the Secretary of Education with respect to student financial assistance during a war or other military operation or national emergency.

2008 *Ensuring Continued Access to Student Loans Act of 2008* (Public Law 110-227) provided various authorities to the Department of Education, among other provisions, to help ensure that college students and their parents continue to have access to loans in the tight credit market.

Higher Education Opportunity Act (Public Law 110-315) provided a comprehensive reauthorization of the Higher Education Act of 1965.

2009 *American Recovery and Reinvestment Act of 2009* (Public Law 111-5) provided about $100 billion to state education systems and supplemental appropriations for several Department of Education programs.

Public Law 111-39 made miscellaneous and technical amendments to the Higher Education Act of 1965.

2010 *Health Care and Education Reconciliation Act of 2010* (Public Law 111-152) included, as Title II, the "SAFRA Act" (also known as the "Student Aid and Fiscal Responsibility Act"). The SAFRA Act ended the federal government's role in subsidizing financial institutions that make student loans through the Federal Family Education Loan (FFEL) Program under Part B of Title IV of the Higher Education Act of 1965 (HEA), and correspondingly expanded the Federal Direct Student Loan Program administered by the Department of Education under Part D of Title IV of the HEA.

Public Law 111-226 provided an additional $10 billion to states and school districts, through an "Education Jobs Fund" modeled closely on the State Fiscal Stabilization Fund created by the 2009 Recovery Act, to hire (or avoid laying off) teachers and other educators.

2013 *The Bipartisan Student Loan Certainty Act of 2013* (Public Law 113-28) amended the Higher Education Act of 1965 (HEA) to govern the interest rates on the various categories of student loans under Title IV of the HEA.

Violence Against Women Reauthorization Act of 2013 (Public Law 113-4) amended the Clery Act, increasing the responsibility of postsecondary institutions to prevent, address, and report crimes on campus.

2014 *Workforce Innovation and Opportunity Act* (Public Law 113-128) amended the Workforce Investment Act of 1998 to strengthen the U.S. workforce development system through innovation in, and alignment and improvement of, employment, training, and education programs in the United States, and to promote individual and national economic growth, and for other purposes.

Public Law 113-174 extended the National Advisory Committee on Institutional Quality and Integrity and the Advisory Committee on Student Financial Assistance for 1 year.

2015 *Need-Based Educational Aid Act of 2015* (Public Law 114-44) amended the Improving America's Schools Act of 1994 to extend through FY 2022 the antitrust exemption that allows higher education institutions that admit all students on a need-blind basis to enter or attempt to enter into agreements among themselves regarding the administration of need-based financial aid.

STEM Education Act of 2015 (Public Law 114-59) defined STEM education to include computer science, and provided for continued support for existing STEM education programs at the National Science Foundation.

Every Student Succeeds Act (Public Law 114-95) reauthorized and amended the Elementary and Secondary Education Act of 1965, incorporating provisions to expand state responsibility over schools, provide grants to charter schools, and reduce the federal test-based accountability system of the No Child Left Behind Act.

Federal Perkins Loan Program Extension Act of 2015 (Public Law 114-105) temporarily extended the Federal Perkins Loan program, allowing continued disbursement of loans to current undergraduate borrowers through September 30, 2017.

2016 *National Defense Authorization Act for Fiscal Year 2017* (Public Law 114-328) authorizes appropriations to continue assistance to local educational agencies that benefit dependents of members of the Armed Forces and Department of Defense civilian employees, including assistance to schools with significant numbers of military dependents as well as impact aid for children with severe disabilities.

2017 *Hurricanes Harvey, Irma, and Maria Education Relief Act of 2017* (Public Law 115-64) provides educational relief in areas for which the President has declared a major disaster or an emergency as a result of Hurricanes Harvey, Irma, or Maria or Tropical Storms Harvey, Irma, or Maria.

2018 *National Historic Site Boundary Modification Act of 2018* (Public Law115-117) adjusts the boundary of the Little Rock Central High School National Historic Site in Arkansas to include the 7 residences on South Park Street in Little Rock, which consist of 1.47 acres of specified land.

Bipartisan Budget Act of 2018 (Public Law 115-123) provides disaster-relief funds for Education.

Consolidated Appropriations Act, 2018 (Public Law 115-141) authorizes spending bill for the United States federal government for fiscal year 2018 enacted by the 115th United States Congress and signed into law by the President on March 23, 2018.

National Memorial to Fallen Educators Act (Public Law 115-169) designates a National Memorial to Fallen Educators at the National Teachers Hall of Fame in Emporia, Kansas.

Strengthening Career and Technical Education for the 21st Century Act (Public Law 115-224) brings changes to the $1.2 billion annual federal investment in career and technical education (CTE).

Department of Defense and Labor, Health and Human Services, and Education Appropriations Act, 2019 and Continuing Appropriations Act, 2019 (Public Law 115-245) provides fiscal year 2019 appropriations and continuing appropriations for several federal agencies.

Foundations for Evidence-Based Policymaking Act of 2018 (Public Law 115-435) establishes an Interagency Council on Evaluation Policy to assist the OMB in supporting government-wide evaluation activities and policies.

Figure 20. Federal on-budget funds for education, by level or other educational purpose: Selected years, 1965 through 2018

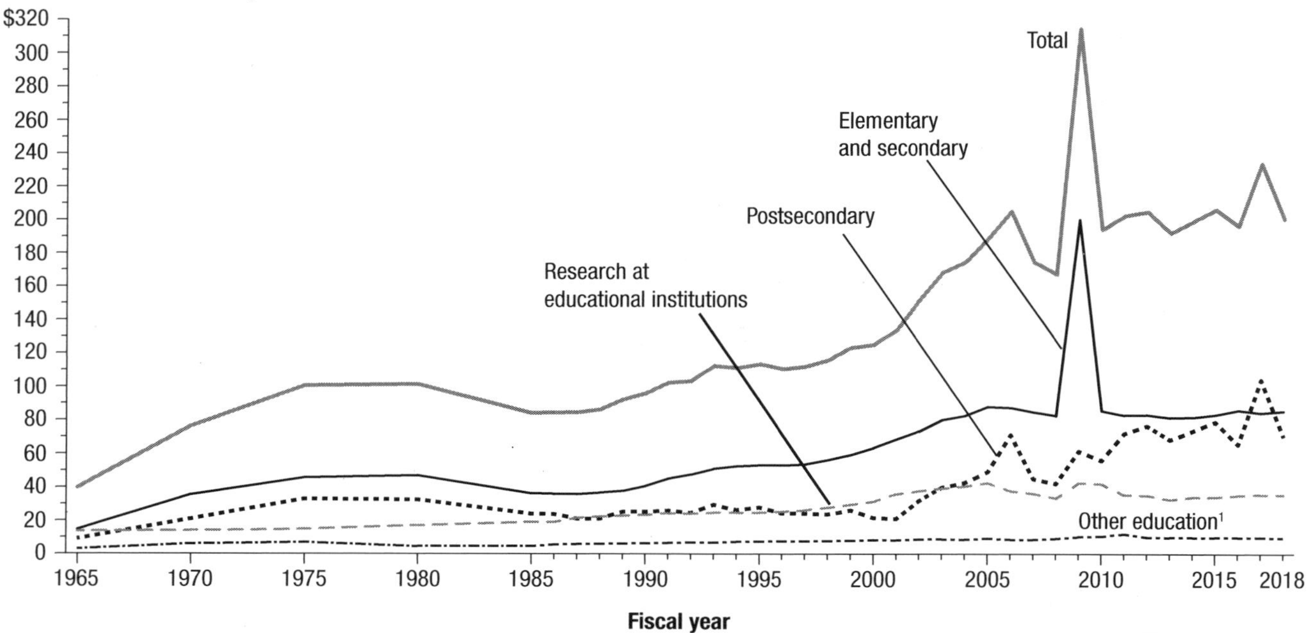

[1]Other education includes libraries, museums, cultural activities, and miscellaneous research.
NOTE: On-budget funds are tied to appropriations for education programs. The increase in postsecondary expenditures in 2006 and 2017 resulted primarily from accounting adjustments. Amounts for 2009 include funds from the American Recovery and Reinvestment Act 2009 (ARRA). Data for research at educational institutions are estimated for 2018.
SOURCE: U.S. Department of Education, Budget Service, unpublished tabulations. U.S. Department of Education, National Center for Education Statistics, unpublished tabulations. U.S. Office of Management and Budget, *Budget of the U.S. Government, Appendix*, fiscal years 1967 through 2019. National Science Foundation, *Federal Funds for Research and Development*, fiscal years 1967 through 2018.

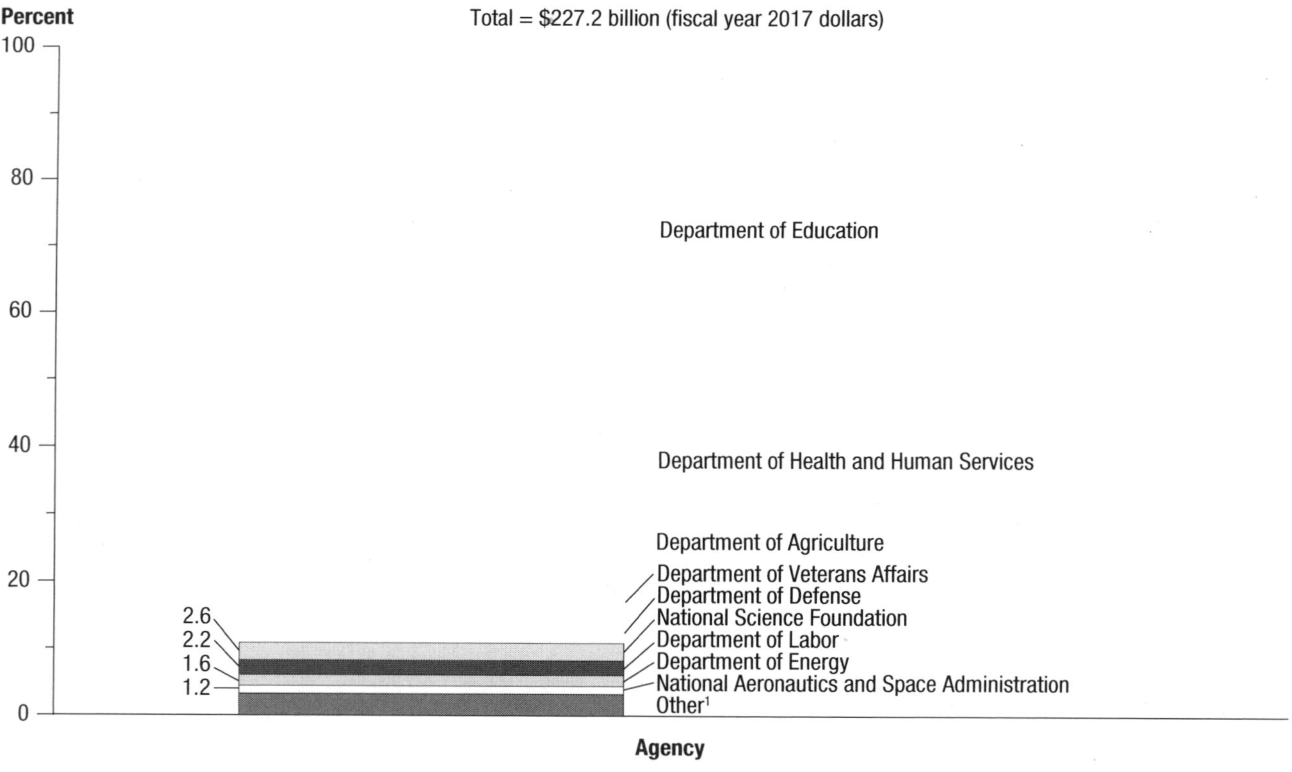

Table 401.10. Federal support and estimated federal tax expenditures for education, by category: Selected fiscal years, 1965 through 2018

[In thousands of dollars]

Fiscal year	Total on-budget support, off-budget support, and nonfederal funds generated by federal legislation	On-budget support[1]					Off-budget support and nonfederal funds generated by federal legislation								Estimated federal tax expenditures for education[2]
								Off-budget support	Nonfederal funds						
		Total	Elementary and secondary	Post-secondary	Other education[3]	Research at educational institutions	Total	Direct Loan Program[4]	Federal Family Education Loan Program[5]	Perkins Loans[6]	Income Contingent Loans[7]	Leveraging Educational Assistance Partnerships[8]	Supplemental Educational Opportunity Grants[9]	Work-Study Aid[10]	
1	2	3	4	5	6	7	8	9	10	11	12	13	14	15	16
							Current dollars								
1965	$5,324,767	$5,331,016	$1,942,577	$1,197,511	$374,652	$1,816,276	-$6,249	†	†	$16,111	†	†	†	-$22,360	—
1970	13,318,909	12,511,079	5,830,442	3,432,277	964,719	2,283,641	807,830	†	$770,000	20,976	†	†	-$30,986	47,840	—
1975	24,412,487	23,288,120	10,617,195	7,644,037	1,608,478	3,418,410	1,124,367	†	1,233,000	35,667	†	$20,000	-39,300	-125,000	$8,605,000
1980	39,273,874	34,465,612	16,027,686	11,087,992	1,548,730	5,801,204	4,808,262	†	4,598,000	31,778	†	76,800	-8,477	110,161	13,320,000
1985	47,642,802	39,027,876	16,901,334	11,174,379	2,107,588	8,844,575	8,614,926	†	8,467,000	21,387	†	76,000	-12,961	63,500	19,105,000
1990	62,748,203	51,593,753	21,984,361	13,620,326	3,383,031	12,606,035	11,154,450	†	10,826,000	15,014	$500	59,181	127,719	126,036	19,040,000
1991	70,349,116	57,599,477	25,418,031	14,707,407	3,698,617	13,775,422	12,749,639	†	12,372,000	17,349	500	63,530	131,115	165,145	18,995,000
1992	74,481,656	60,483,092	27,926,887	14,387,387	3,991,955	14,176,863	13,998,564	†	13,568,000	17,333	542	72,000	175,656	165,033	19,950,000
1993	84,692,869	67,740,617	30,834,326	17,844,015	4,107,193	14,955,083	16,952,252	†	16,524,000	29,255	†	72,429	172,023	154,545	21,010,000
1994	92,724,117	68,254,205	32,304,356	16,177,051	4,483,704	15,289,094	24,469,912	$818,540	23,214,000	52,667	†	72,429	172,000	140,276	22,630,000
1995	95,217,958	71,639,520	33,623,809	17,618,137	4,719,655	15,677,919	23,578,438	4,615,671	18,519,000	52,667	†	63,400	181,000	146,700	24,600,000
1996	96,853,432	71,327,362	34,391,501	15,775,508	4,828,038	16,332,315	25,526,070	8,414,470	16,711,000	31,100	†	31,400	179,000	159,100	26,340,000
1997	103,060,841	73,731,845	35,478,905	15,959,425	5,021,163	17,272,352	29,328,996	9,758,696	19,163,000	52,700	†	50,000	228,200	76,400	28,125,000
1998	107,393,639	76,909,233	37,486,166	15,799,570	5,148,492	18,475,005	30,484,406	10,087,664	20,002,500	45,000	†	25,000	240,950	83,292	29,540,000
1999	113,137,861	82,863,597	39,937,911	17,651,199	5,318,020	19,956,467	30,274,264	9,805,764	20,107,000	33,300	†	25,000	255,900	47,300	37,360,000
2000	119,891,420	86,237,817	43,790,783	14,977,852	5,809,048	21,660,134	33,653,603	10,577,535	22,711,000	33,300	†	50,000	276,743	5,025	39,475,000
2001	130,307,565	94,846,476	48,530,061	14,938,278	5,880,007	25,498,130	35,461,089	10,324,341	24,694,000	25,000	†	80,000	316,655	21,093	41,460,000
2002	149,459,682	109,211,479	52,754,118	22,964,176	6,297,697	27,195,488	40,248,203	11,117,896	28,606,000	25,000	†	104,000	308,811	86,496	—
2003	170,450,390	124,374,489	59,274,219	29,499,694	6,532,502	29,068,074	46,075,901	11,742,063	33,791,000	33,000	†	103,000	304,671	102,167	—
2004	184,648,526	132,420,703	62,653,231	32,432,974	6,576,821	30,757,677	52,227,823	12,448,155	39,266,000	33,000	†	102,000	295,143	83,525	—
2005	204,626,929	148,306,678	69,029,389	38,560,566	7,297,025	33,419,698	56,320,251	12,569,446	43,284,000	0	†	101,000	305,644	60,161	—
2006[11]	226,449,825	166,495,661	70,948,229	57,757,738	7,074,484	30,715,210	59,954,164	12,175,674	47,307,000	0	†	100,000	309,608	61,882	—
2007	209,994,867	145,697,988	70,735,875	37,465,287	7,214,906	30,281,920	64,296,879	12,507,162	51,320,000	0	†	100,000	287,126	82,591	—
2008	219,998,213	144,338,889	71,272,580	36,386,271	7,882,220	28,797,817	75,659,324	17,850,773	57,296,000	0	†	98,000	281,812	132,739	—
2009[12]	367,606,421	271,297,568	172,660,784	53,085,401	8,853,694	36,697,689	96,308,853	28,857,577	66,778,000	0	†	98,000	309,058	266,218	—
2010	271,409,855	170,511,487	75,187,097	49,118,856	9,212,228	36,993,306	100,898,368	80,709,552	19,618,000	0	†	98,000	255,108	217,708	—
2011	292,352,452	182,006,154	74,538,319	64,645,852	10,804,871	32,017,112	110,346,298	109,917,342	0	0	†	0	231,480	197,476	—
2012	292,801,980	187,761,942	76,134,050	70,123,155	9,328,554	32,176,184	105,040,038	104,612,005	0	0	†	0	243,871	184,162	—
2013	280,738,125	178,670,129	75,668,114	63,479,680	9,217,187	30,305,148	102,067,996	101,729,011	0	0	†	0	192,116	146,869	—
2014	287,673,082	188,118,010	77,092,120	69,386,948	9,435,306	32,203,636	99,555,072	99,186,791	0	0	†	0	249,553	118,728	—
2015	291,617,323	195,672,348	78,955,999	74,860,617	9,464,840	32,390,891	95,944,975	95,578,878	0	0	†	0	259,745	106,352	—
2016	282,570,702	187,781,492	82,087,275	62,537,278	9,600,541	33,556,398	94,789,211	94,439,471	0	0	†	0	253,915	95,825	—
2017[11]	320,817,622	227,166,751	81,833,214	101,022,573	9,643,170	34,667,794	93,650,871	93,301,131	0	0	†	0	253,915[13]	95,825[13]	—
2018	296,030,039	199,765,457	85,042,615	69,744,180	9,558,800	35,419,862[13]	96,264,582	95,864,248	0	0	†	0	290,929[13]	109,406[13]	—
							Constant fiscal year 2018 dollars[14]								
1965	$39,624,139	$39,670,641	$14,455,645	$8,911,252	$2,787,965	$13,515,779	-$46,502	†	†	$119,890	†	†	†	-$166,391	—
1970	81,122,229	76,201,933	35,511,801	20,905,163	5,875,868	13,909,101	4,920,296	†	$4,689,882	127,760	†	†	-$188,728	291,382	—
1975	104,989,145	100,153,655	45,660,658	32,874,197	6,917,473	14,701,327	4,835,490	†	5,302,680	153,391	†	$86,013	-169,015	-537,579	$37,006,946
1980	115,059,434	100,972,820	46,955,808	32,484,141	4,537,266	16,995,605	14,086,614	†	13,470,616	93,099	†	224,999	-24,835	322,735	39,023,185
1985	102,386,350	83,872,518	36,321,665	24,014,202	4,529,294	19,007,357	18,513,832	†	18,195,933	45,962	†	163,327	-27,854	136,464	41,057,434
1990	116,020,146	95,395,796	40,648,634	25,183,705	6,255,155	23,308,301	20,624,350	†	20,017,053	27,761	$924	109,424	236,150	233,038	35,204,571
1991	124,505,224	101,940,666	44,985,322	26,029,453	6,545,884	24,380,008	22,564,557	†	21,896,204	30,705	885	112,437	232,050	292,277	33,617,718
1992	126,664,252	102,858,154	47,492,744	24,467,335	6,788,759	24,109,316	23,806,099	†	23,073,877	29,477	922	122,444	298,722	280,657	33,927,170
1993	139,893,782	111,892,432	50,931,448	29,474,344	6,784,169	24,702,471	28,001,350	†	27,293,973	48,323	†	119,637	284,144	255,274	34,703,847
1994	150,507,107	110,788,253	52,435,497	26,258,122	7,277,819	24,816,815	39,718,855	$1,328,631	37,680,294	85,488	†	117,565	279,185	227,692	36,732,362

See notes at end of table.

Table 401.10. Federal support and estimated federal tax expenditures for education, by category: Selected fiscal years, 1965 through 2018—Continued

[In thousands of dollars]

Fiscal year	Total on-budget support, off-budget support, and nonfederal funds generated by federal legislation	On-budget support[1]					Off-budget support and nonfederal funds generated by federal legislation								Estimated federal tax expenditures for education[2]
								Off-budget support	Nonfederal funds						
		Total	Elementary and secondary	Post-secondary	Other education[3]	Research at educational institutions	Total	Direct Loan Program[4]	Federal Family Education Loan Program[5]	Perkins Loans[6]	Income Contingent Loans[7]	Leveraging Educational Assistance Partnerships[8]	Supplemental Educational Opportunity Grants[9]	Work-Study Aid[10]	
1	2	3	4	5	6	7	8	9	10	11	12	13	14	15	16
1995	150,095,642	112,928,065	53,002,472	27,772,131	7,439,769	24,713,692	37,167,577	7,275,856	29,192,195	83,021	†	99,940	285,317	231,249	38,777,903
1996	149,530,036	110,120,858	53,096,336	24,355,485	7,453,909	25,215,128	39,409,178	12,990,929	25,799,772	48,015	†	48,478	276,354	245,631	40,665,788
1997	155,838,311	111,489,933	53,647,657	24,132,249	7,592,501	26,117,526	44,348,378	14,756,125	28,976,375	79,688	†	75,605	345,061	115,524	42,527,816
1998	161,046,020	115,332,025	56,213,737	23,692,817	7,720,608	27,704,863	45,713,995	15,127,322	29,995,473	67,481	†	37,490	361,325	124,904	44,297,777
1999	167,602,510	122,754,194	59,164,051	26,148,499	7,878,119	29,563,525	44,848,316	14,526,265	29,786,525	49,331	†	37,035	379,090	70,070	55,345,131
2000	173,217,212	124,595,023	63,268,225	21,639,762	8,392,820	31,294,216	48,622,190	15,282,254	32,812,491	48,111	†	72,239	399,834	7,260	57,032,850
2001	183,463,331	133,536,763	68,326,706	21,031,981	8,278,611	35,899,465	49,926,568	14,535,902	34,767,310	35,198	†	112,634	445,827	29,697	58,372,587
2002	207,234,493	151,428,032	73,146,636	31,841,158	8,732,121	37,708,117	55,806,461	15,415,605	39,663,873	34,664	†	144,202	428,184	119,932	—
2003	229,803,651	167,683,463	79,914,349	39,771,909	8,807,213	39,189,993	62,120,188	15,830,817	45,557,509	44,491	†	138,866	410,762	137,743	—
2004	242,627,359	174,000,228	82,326,073	42,616,787	8,641,914	40,415,454	68,627,132	16,356,821	51,595,353	43,362	†	134,028	387,817	109,751	—
2005	259,956,062	188,407,362	87,694,265	48,986,968	9,270,069	42,456,059	71,548,700	15,968,102	54,987,573	0	†	128,309	388,287	76,428	—
2006[11]	278,062,175	204,443,283	87,118,720	70,921,858	8,686,897	37,715,808	73,618,892	14,950,749	58,089,192	0	†	122,792	380,174	75,986	—
2007	250,913,748	174,088,199	84,519,226	44,765,645	8,620,778	36,182,551	76,825,549	14,944,265	61,320,040	0	†	119,486	343,074	98,684	—
2008	254,070,594	166,693,478	82,310,972	42,021,621	9,102,985	33,257,900	87,377,116	20,615,424	66,169,759	0	†	113,178	325,458	153,297	—
2009[12]	424,584,830	313,348,258	199,422,930	61,313,553	10,226,002	42,385,772	111,236,572	33,330,456	77,128,484	0	†	113,190	356,961	307,481	—
2010	307,981,207	193,487,202	85,318,246	55,737,418	10,453,538	41,978,001	114,494,004	91,584,829	22,261,444	0	†	111,205	289,483	247,043	—
2011	324,166,839	201,812,433	82,649,730	71,680,745	11,980,679	35,501,279	122,354,406	121,878,770	0	0	†	0	256,670	218,966	—
2012	318,334,313	204,134,784	82,772,939	76,237,894	10,142,003	34,981,948	114,199,529	113,734,172	0	0	†	0	265,137	200,221	—
2013	300,945,069	191,530,432	81,114,547	68,048,815	9,880,621	32,486,450	109,414,637	109,051,253	0	0	†	0	205,944	157,440	—
2014	303,589,764	198,526,403	81,357,555	73,226,063	9,957,353	33,985,433	105,063,361	104,674,703	0	0	†	0	263,361	125,297	—
2015	306,088,389	205,382,290	82,874,071	78,575,461	9,934,519	33,998,239	100,706,099	100,321,835	0	0	†	0	272,634	111,630	—
2016	294,545,415	195,739,250	85,565,949	65,187,467	10,007,391	34,978,443	98,806,165	98,441,604	0	0	†	0	264,676	99,885	—
2017[11]	328,832,769	232,842,172	83,877,694	103,546,471	9,884,090	35,533,917	95,990,598	95,632,120	0	0	†	0	260,259[13]	98,219[13]	—
2018	296,030,039	199,765,457	85,042,615	69,744,180	9,558,800	35,419,862[13]	96,264,582	95,864,248	0	0	†	0	290,929[13]	109,406[13]	—

—Not available.

†Not applicable.

[1]On-budget support includes federal funds for education programs tied to appropriations. Excludes federal support for medical education benefits under Medicare in the U.S. Department of Health and Human Services. Benefits are excluded because data before fiscal year (FY) 1990 are not available. This program has existed since Medicare began but was not available as a separate budget item until FY 1990. Excluded amounts range from an estimated $4,440,000,000 in FY 1990 to an estimated $13,800,000,000 in FY 2018.

[2]Losses of tax revenue attributable to provisions of the federal income tax laws that allow a special exclusion, exemption, or deduction from gross income or provide a special credit, preferential rate of tax, or a deferral of tax liability affecting individual or corporate income tax liabilities.

[3]Other education includes libraries, museums, cultural activities, and miscellaneous research.

[4]The William D. Ford Federal Direct Loan Program (commonly referred to as the Direct Loan Program) provides students with the same benefits they were eligible to receive under the Federal Family Education Loan (FFEL) Program, but provides loans to students through federal capital rather than through private lenders.

[5]The Federal Family Education Loan (FFEL) Program, formerly known as the Guaranteed Student Loan Program, provided student loans guaranteed by the federal government and disbursed to borrowers. Since June 30, 2010, no new FFEL loans have been originated; all new loans are originated through the Direct Loan Program.

[6]Student loans created from institutional matching funds (since 1993, one-third of federal capital contributions). Excludes repayments of outstanding loans.

[7]Student loans created from institutional matching funds (one-ninth of federal contributions). This was a demonstration project that involved only 10 institutions and had unsubsidized interest rates. Program repealed in fiscal year 1992.

[8]Formerly the State Student Incentive Grant Program. Starting in fiscal year 2000, amounts under $30.0 million have required dollar-for-dollar state matching contributions, while amounts over $30.0 million have required two-to-one state matching contributions.

[9]Institutions award grants to undergraduate students, and the federal share of such grants may not exceed 75 percent of the total grant.

[10]Employer contributions to student earnings are generally one-third of federal allocation.

[11]The increases in postsecondary expenditures in 2006 and 2017 resulted primarily from accounting adjustments.

[12]All education funds from the American Recovery and Reinvestment Act of 2009 (ARRA) are included in the FY 2009 row of this table. Most of these funds had a 2-year availability, meaning that they were available for the U.S. Department of Education to obligate during FY 2009 and FY 2010.

[13]Estimated.

[14]Data adjusted by the federal budget composite deflator, as reported in the U.S. Office of Management and Budget's *Budget of the U.S. Government, Historical Tables, Fiscal Year 2020*.

NOTE: To the extent possible, federal education funds data do not represent obligations, but instead represent appropriations or (especially for earlier years) outlays. Negative amounts occur when program receipts exceed outlays. Some data have been revised from previously published figures. Detail may not sum to totals because of rounding.

SOURCE: U.S. Department of Education, Budget Service, unpublished tabulations. U.S. Department of Education, National Center for Education Statistics, unpublished tabulations. U.S. Office of Management and Budget, *Budget of the U.S. Government, Appendix*, fiscal years 1967 through 2019. National Science Foundation, *Federal Funds for Research and Development*, fiscal years 1967 through 2018. (This table was prepared June 2019.)

Table 401.20. Federal on-budget funds for education, by agency: Selected fiscal years, 1970 through 2017

[In thousands of dollars]

Agency	1970	1980	1990[1]	2000[1]	2010[1]	2012[1]	2013[1]	2014[1]	2015[1]	2016[1]	2017[1]
1	2	3	4	5	6	7	8	9	10	11	12
	Current dollars										
Total	**$12,511,079**	**$34,465,612**	**$51,593,753**	**$86,237,817**	**$170,511,487**	**$187,761,942**	**$178,670,129**	**$188,118,010**	**$195,672,348**	**$187,781,492**	**$227,166,751**
Department of Education[2]	4,625,224	13,137,785	23,198,575	34,106,697	80,886,361	98,948,633	88,839,759	95,402,189	100,421,930	88,871,248	125,986,375
Department of Agriculture	960,910	4,562,467	6,260,843	11,080,031	19,719,460	20,578,995	22,354,763	21,739,689	23,855,189	24,712,496	25,388,830
Department of Commerce	13,990	135,561	53,835	114,575	303,000	205,085	235,936	275,521	272,897	272,936	310,300
Department of Defense	821,388	1,560,301	3,605,509	4,525,080	7,686,288	7,400,880	7,036,469	7,297,021	7,006,346	7,194,204	7,230,743
Department of Energy	551,527	1,605,558	2,561,950	3,577,004	3,402,600	2,983,055	2,941,159	3,288,681	3,484,388	3,680,701	3,690,688
Department of Health and Human Services	1,127,521	3,712,930	7,466,197	16,941,831	30,662,472	27,300,826	25,766,013	27,541,095	27,196,167	28,776,948	29,492,380
Department of Homeland Security	†	†	†	†	540,229	333,630	358,580	371,808	372,144	332,266	312,254
Department of Housing and Urban Development	114,709	5,314	118	1,400	400	300	4,500	100	1,100	500	1,200
Department of the Interior	175,555	412,657	599,948	928,939	1,008,316	939,075	873,040	944,214	947,975	1,012,768	1,011,876
Department of Justice	15,728	60,721	99,775	292,859	219,993	224,295	218,994	240,957	233,264	265,780	242,304
Department of Labor	424,494	1,862,738	2,511,380	4,696,100	4,845,735	4,898,863	4,729,187	4,837,010	4,827,861	5,024,580	5,018,397
Department of State	59,742	25,188	51,225	388,349	801,180	741,922	812,957	835,741	870,920	864,395	854,326
Department of Transportation	27,534	54,712	76,186	117,054	160,243	173,888	178,502	168,000	178,050	182,614	188,918
Department of the Treasury	18	1,247,463	41,715	83,000	†	†	†	†	†	†	†
Department of Veterans Affairs	1,032,918	2,351,233	757,476	1,577,374	8,795,010	10,905,455	12,616,616	13,085,173	13,517,156	13,960,336	14,423,386
Other agencies and programs											
ACTION	†	2,833	8,472	†	†	†	†	†	†	†	†
Agency for International Development	88,034	176,770	249,786	332,500	557,900	629,900	603,900	594,039	648,000	657,111	688,243
Appalachian Regional Commission	37,838	19,032	93	7,243	5,070	11,124	13,070	13,073	23,682	39,639	35,712
Barry Goldwater Scholarship and Excellence in Education Foundation	†	†	1,033	3,000	4,000	4,000	4,000	3,000	2,000	3,000	3,000
Corporation for National and Community Service	†	†	†	696,545	857,021	750,252	711,009	756,849	758,349	787,929	736,029
Environmental Protection Agency	19,446	41,083	87,481	98,900	54,700	87,200	73,700	86,100	68,600	56,600	51,500
Estimated education share of federal aid to the District of Columbia	33,019	81,847	104,940	127,127	159,670	151,381	217,160	210,732	147,424	129,091	161,031
Federal Emergency Management Agency	290	1,946	215	14,894	†	†	†	†	†	†	†
General Services Administration	14,775	34,800	†	†	†	†	†	†	†	†	†
Harry S. Truman Scholarship Foundation	†	-1,895	2,883	3,000	2,000	1,200	1,500	1,000	1,000	1,000	1,000
Institute of American Indian and Alaska Native Culture and Arts Development	†	†	4,305	2,000	8,000	9,000	8,000	9,000	9,000	12,000	12,000
Institute of Museum and Library Services	†	†	†	166,000	282,251	231,954	219,821	226,860	227,860	230,000	230,000
James Madison Memorial Fellowship Foundation	†	†	191	7,000	2,000	2,000	2,000	2,000	2,000	2,000	2,000
Japanese-United States Friendship Commission	†	2,294	2,299	3,000	2,000	3,700	3,700	3,000	3,000	3,000	3,000
Library of Congress	29,478	151,871	189,827	299,000	510,877	465,961	442,051	455,760	464,449	469,547	500,915
National Aeronautics and Space Administration	258,366	255,511	1,093,303	2,077,830	1,585,500	2,289,837	2,200,143	2,287,755	2,355,450	2,522,132	2,683,000
National Archives and Records Administration	†	†	77,397	121,879	339,000	391,500	371,022	386,630	381,730	389,073	392,956
National Commission on Libraries and Information Science	†	2,090	3,281	2,000	†	†	†	†	†	†	†
National Endowment for the Arts	340	5,220	5,577	10,048	14,413	16,595	13,910	15,426	13,509	14,364	14,216
National Endowment for the Humanities	8,459	142,586	141,048	100,014	142,654	136,100	114,171	117,533	120,216	121,925	104,533
National Science Foundation	295,628	808,392	1,588,891	2,955,244	5,533,530	5,534,426	5,302,011	5,476,858	5,808,512	5,735,629	5,956,118
Nuclear Regulatory Commission	†	32,590	42,328	12,200	14,500	8,600	5,400	9,400	8,000	8,000	5,900
Office of Economic Opportunity	1,092,410	†	†	†	†	†	†	†	†	†	†
Social Security Administration	669,333	1,901,000	489,814	729,036	1,313,000	1,329,500	1,326,300	1,365,200	1,373,500	1,377,500	1,362,700
Smithsonian Institution	2,461	5,153	5,779	25,764	28,814	28,809	29,986	28,796	29,979	27,779	27,538
U.S. Arms Control and Disarmament Agency	100	661	25	†	†	†	†	†	†	†	†
United States Information Agency	8,423	66,210	201,547	†	†	†	†	†	†	†	†
United States Institute of Peace	†	†	7,621	13,000	49,000	39,000	37,000	37,000	35,000	35,300	37,884
Other agencies	1,421	990	885	300	14,300	5,000	3,800	4,800	5,700	7,100	5,500

See notes at end of table.

Table 401.20. Federal on-budget funds for education, by agency: Selected fiscal years, 1970 through 2017—Continued

[In thousands of dollars]

Agency	1970	1980	1990[1]	2000[1]	2010[1]	2012[1]	2013[1]	2014[1]	2015[1]	2016[1]	2017[1]
1	2	3	4	5	6	7	8	9	10	11	12
	Constant fiscal year 2018 dollars[3]										
Total	**$76,201,933**	**$100,972,820**	**$95,395,796**	**$124,595,023**	**$193,487,202**	**$204,134,784**	**$191,530,432**	**$198,526,403**	**$205,382,290**	**$195,739,250**	**$232,841,147**
Department of Education[2]	28,171,112	38,489,356	42,893,692	49,276,812	91,785,463	107,576,954	95,234,259	100,680,703	105,405,216	92,637,412	129,133,956
Department of Agriculture	5,852,669	13,366,516	11,576,171	16,008,252	22,376,575	22,373,483	23,963,812	22,942,526	25,038,966	25,759,756	26,023,132
Department of Commerce	85,210	397,149	99,540	165,536	343,828	222,968	252,918	290,765	286,439	284,502	318,052
Department of Defense	5,002,874	4,571,165	6,666,513	6,537,763	8,721,983	8,046,237	7,542,939	7,700,758	7,354,025	7,499,078	7,411,392
Department of Energy	3,359,217	4,703,753	4,736,993	5,167,998	3,861,086	3,243,177	3,152,857	3,470,640	3,657,296	3,836,681	3,782,894
Department of Health and Human Services	6,867,456	10,877,654	13,804,845	24,477,287	34,794,113	29,681,458	27,620,597	29,064,918	28,545,736	29,996,451	30,229,203
Department of Homeland Security	†	†	†	†	613,023	362,723	384,390	392,380	390,611	346,347	320,055
Department of Housing and Urban Development	698,665	15,568	218	2,023	454	326	4,824	106	1,155	521	1,230
Department of the Interior	1,069,263	1,208,948	1,109,292	1,342,116	1,144,182	1,020,962	935,879	996,456	995,017	1,055,687	1,037,156
Department of Justice	95,795	177,892	184,482	423,118	249,636	243,854	234,757	254,289	244,840	277,043	248,358
Department of Labor	2,585,490	5,457,205	4,643,490	6,784,850	5,498,678	5,326,044	5,069,584	5,104,637	5,067,436	5,237,510	5,143,774
Department of State	363,874	73,792	94,714	561,080	909,136	806,618	871,472	881,982	914,138	901,026	875,670
Department of Transportation	167,703	160,288	140,866	169,118	181,835	189,051	191,350	177,295	186,885	190,353	193,638
Department of the Treasury	110	3,654,653	77,130	119,917	†	†	†	†	†	†	†
Department of Veterans Affairs	6,291,252	6,888,333	1,400,558	2,278,965	9,980,101	11,856,411	13,524,734	13,809,163	14,187,924	14,551,944	14,783,733
Other agencies and programs											
ACTION	†	8,300	15,665	†	†	†	†	†	†	†	†
Agency for International Development	536,194	517,878	461,849	480,391	633,075	684,827	647,367	626,907	680,156	684,958	705,438
Appalachian Regional Commission	230,462	55,757	172	10,464	5,753	12,094	14,011	13,796	24,857	41,319	36,604
Barry Goldwater Scholarship and Excellence in Education Foundation	†	†	1,910	4,334	4,539	4,349	4,288	3,166	2,099	3,127	3,075
Corporation for National and Community Service	†	†	†	1,006,357	972,501	815,674	762,186	798,725	795,981	821,320	754,418
Environmental Protection Agency	118,441	120,360	161,751	142,889	62,071	94,804	79,005	90,864	72,004	58,999	52,787
Estimated education share of federal aid to the District of Columbia	201,111	239,785	194,032	183,671	181,185	164,581	232,791	222,392	154,740	134,562	165,054
Federal Emergency Management Agency	1,766	5,701	398	21,519	†	†	†	†	†	†	†
General Services Administration	89,991	101,952	†	†	†	†	†	†	†	†	†
Harry S. Truman Scholarship Foundation	†	-5,552	5,331	4,334	2,269	1,305	1,608	1,055	1,050	1,042	†
Institute of American Indian and Alaska Native Culture and Arts Development	†	†	7,960	2,890	9,078	9,785	8,576	9,498	9,447	12,509	12,300
Institute of Museum and Library Services	†	†	†	239,834	320,283	252,180	235,643	239,412	239,167	239,747	235,746
James Madison Memorial Fellowship Foundation	†	†	353	10,113	2,269	2,174	2,144	2,111	2,099	2,085	2,050
Japanese-United States Friendship Commission	†	6,721	4,251	4,334	2,269	4,023	3,966	3,166	3,149	3,127	3,075
Library of Congress	179,543	444,932	350,986	431,990	579,716	506,593	473,869	480,977	487,497	489,445	513,430
National Aeronautics and Space Administration	1,573,644	748,563	2,021,495	3,002,016	1,799,140	2,489,511	2,358,505	2,414,334	2,472,336	2,629,014	2,750,031
National Archives and Records Administration	†	†	143,105	176,089	384,679	425,639	397,727	408,022	400,673	405,561	402,773
National Commission on Libraries and Information Science	†	6,123	6,067	2,890	†	†	†	†	†	†	†
National Endowment for the Arts	2,071	15,293	10,312	14,517	16,355	18,042	14,911	16,280	14,179	14,973	14,571
National Endowment for the Humanities	51,522	417,730	260,795	144,499	161,876	147,968	122,389	124,036	126,182	127,092	107,145
National Science Foundation	1,800,598	2,368,321	2,937,827	4,269,689	6,279,150	6,017,028	5,683,639	5,779,888	6,096,751	5,978,692	6,104,922
Nuclear Regulatory Commission	†	95,478	78,264	17,626	16,454	9,350	5,789	9,920	8,397	8,339	6,047
Office of Economic Opportunity	6,653,603	†	†	†	†	†	†	†	†	†	†
Social Security Administration	4,076,744	5,569,300	905,656	1,053,300	1,489,921	1,445,432	1,421,764	1,440,735	1,441,658	1,435,875	1,396,745
Smithsonian Institution	14,989	15,097	10,685	37,223	32,697	31,321	32,144	30,389	31,467	28,956	28,226
U.S. Arms Control and Disarmament Agency	609	1,937	46	†	†	†	†	†	†	†	†
United States Information Agency	51,302	193,973	372,656	†	†	†	†	†	†	†	†
United States Institute of Peace	†	†	14,091	18,782	55,603	42,401	39,663	39,047	36,737	36,796	38,830
Other agencies	8,655	2,900	1,636	433	16,227	5,436	4,074	5,066	5,983	7,401	5,637

†Not applicable.

[1]Excludes federal support for medical education benefits under Medicare in the U.S. Department of Health and Human Services. Benefits are excluded because data before fiscal year (FY) 1990 are not available. This program has existed since Medicare began but was not available as a separate budget item until FY 1990. Excluded amounts are estimated as follows: $4,440,000,000 in FY 1990, $8,020,000,000 in FY 2000, $9,080,000,000 in FY 2010, $9,800,000,000 in FY 2012, $10,000,000,000 in FY 2013, $11,530,000,000 in FY 2014, $11,800,000,000 in FY 2015, $12,300,000,000 in FY 2016, $13,000,000,000 in FY 2017, and $13,800,000,000 in FY 2018.

[2]The U.S. Department of Education was created in May 1980. It formerly was the Office of Education in the U.S. Department of Health, Education, and Welfare. This table does not include education funds from the American Recovery and Reinvestment Act of 2009 (ARRA) because these funds are included only in tables that show FY 2009. Most of these funds had a 2-year availability, meaning that they were available for the Department of Education to obligate during FY 2009 and FY 2010.

[3]Data adjusted by the federal budget composite deflator, as reported in the U.S. Office of Management and Budget's *Budget of the U.S. Government, Historical Tables, Fiscal Year 2020*.

NOTE: To the extent possible, federal education funds data do not represent obligations but instead represent appropriations or (especially for earlier years) outlays. Negative amounts occur when program receipts exceed outlays. Some data have been revised from previously published figures. Detail may not sum to totals because of rounding.

SOURCE: U.S. Department of Education, National Center for Education Statistics, unpublished tabulations. U.S. Office of Management and Budget, *Budget of the U.S. Government, Appendix*; and supplemental agency budget documents, fiscal years 1972 through 2018. National Science Foundation, *Federal Funds for Research and Development*, fiscal years 1970 through 2017. (This table was prepared June 2019.)

Table 401.60. U.S. Department of Education appropriations for major programs, by state or jurisdiction: Fiscal year 2017

[In thousands of current dollars]

State or jurisdiction	Total	Grants for the disadvan-taged[1]	Block grants to states for school improvement[2]	School assistance in federally affected areas[3]	Career/technical and adult education[4]	Special education[5]	English language acquisition	American Indian education	Student financial assistance[6]	Rehabilitation services[7]
1	2	3	4	5	6	7	8	9	10	11
Total, 50 states and D.C.[8]	**$68,892,638**	**$15,286,845**	**$3,708,864**	**$1,236,287**	**$1,650,273**	**$12,533,386**	**$677,378**	**$100,381**	**$30,553,129**	**$3,146,095**
Total, 50 states, D.C., other activities, and other jurisdictions	**71,222,205**	**15,882,167**	**3,869,443**	**1,254,955**	**1,699,553**	**12,829,607**	**737,400**	**100,381**	**31,593,131**	**3,255,569**
Alabama	1,174,087	253,108	62,207	2,027	28,417	198,684	3,888	1,329	557,879	66,548
Alaska	341,008	57,296	19,751	149,852	5,262	41,397	1,276	14,001	40,924	11,247
Arizona	1,999,059	358,237	71,086	168,082	38,998	218,537	14,269	10,413	1,044,933	74,505
Arkansas	729,072	168,180	42,011	414	16,853	124,470	3,568	144	331,953	41,478
California	8,696,937	1,951,820	411,528	57,523	208,240	1,336,234	149,996	4,759	4,254,080	322,756
Colorado	946,738	158,959	44,273	32,825	23,296	175,989	9,402	667	461,033	40,293
Connecticut	657,649	130,639	35,662	4,163	14,730	145,678	6,475	32	297,063	23,209
Delaware	198,667	51,755	19,401	54	6,405	40,373	1,202	0	67,690	11,786
District of Columbia	274,504	47,518	19,095	0	5,460	21,456	1,166	0	164,004	15,805
Florida	4,075,965	878,803	178,047	7,166	103,061	703,754	43,908	97	1,970,842	190,287
Georgia	2,251,129	548,159	113,723	19,722	57,952	372,566	15,380	0	1,021,238	102,388
Hawaii	270,732	55,985	19,661	41,786	7,716	44,138	3,828	0	83,846	13,773
Idaho	362,697	62,555	22,108	6,126	8,847	62,403	2,134	440	178,442	19,643
Illinois	2,857,785	681,005	155,593	15,271	59,638	552,050	25,938	204	1,252,914	115,171
Indiana	1,479,812	271,008	65,472	84	34,702	284,000	8,622	0	743,494	72,429
Iowa	697,989	99,218	32,978	182	15,581	133,918	4,143	267	379,971	31,731
Kansas	619,056	118,223	35,185	42,438	14,117	118,321	4,491	764	256,829	28,688
Kentucky	972,251	238,929	60,403	373	26,256	178,608	3,807	0	409,482	54,393
Louisiana	1,115,696	320,591	78,862	7,499	30,017	207,081	3,368	879	431,946	35,454
Maine	283,880	55,187	22,572	2,164	7,228	61,022	744	190	117,317	17,457
Maryland	1,010,840	232,467	54,937	5,710	24,922	220,362	10,352	66	416,712	45,312
Massachusetts	1,283,499	247,740	64,503	638	28,079	309,881	14,685	156	565,738	52,079
Michigan	2,143,412	514,107	133,809	4,334	49,521	435,484	11,692	1,937	879,542	112,986
Minnesota	1,087,900	165,907	52,041	22,377	22,635	210,115	9,434	4,009	549,982	51,400
Mississippi	827,020	201,468	54,836	1,968	19,398	131,534	1,514	487	372,151	43,663
Missouri	1,278,480	254,349	70,465	22,929	30,348	247,874	4,993	70	578,541	68,909
Montana	273,646	49,428	24,955	60,701	6,372	42,071	500	3,588	73,069	12,963
Nebraska	386,571	81,314	24,913	19,339	9,310	81,948	3,229	920	146,104	19,493
Nevada	431,364	131,254	25,738	3,335	15,905	83,525	6,773	496	147,173	17,165
New Hampshire	290,435	44,218	21,635	9	7,046	52,624	1,020	0	152,253	11,630
New Jersey	1,680,674	368,275	85,660	16,805	37,615	394,685	19,662	0	694,017	63,954
New Mexico	594,390	120,835	31,847	90,835	12,311	99,818	4,673	7,616	200,651	25,803
New York	4,871,614	1,220,213	279,833	49,209	94,253	839,782	59,665	1,817	2,166,622	160,219
North Carolina	2,001,586	456,848	95,504	13,287	54,639	370,873	14,668	3,431	879,722	112,613
North Dakota	188,434	37,729	20,415	27,676	5,237	33,652	592	2,474	49,426	11,232
Ohio	2,212,642	559,975	140,063	1,481	58,300	476,440	10,630	0	858,086	107,667
Oklahoma	857,834	170,850	54,232	35,240	21,475	162,123	5,340	24,151	341,712	42,712
Oregon	787,009	173,321	40,558	3,280	19,280	141,254	7,167	1,789	354,413	45,947
Pennsylvania	2,482,851	630,677	143,275	1,048	58,731	467,538	15,407	0	1,031,238	134,936
Rhode Island	266,371	53,604	19,557	1,605	7,572	48,899	1,961	0	121,409	11,764
South Carolina	1,003,996	245,568	54,283	1,437	27,035	195,361	4,253	15	411,161	64,883
South Dakota	278,837	47,678	20,979	62,321	5,477	40,168	901	3,978	85,603	11,732
Tennessee	1,328,099	308,397	71,502	2,751	34,869	260,104	5,975	0	583,830	60,671
Texas	6,002,723	1,476,416	323,560	97,529	154,457	1,103,179	112,250	445	2,450,040	284,849
Utah	747,489	89,790	27,407	7,915	16,352	125,496	4,227	1,345	441,771	33,185
Vermont	157,582	35,985	19,349	10	5,143	32,603	500	203	51,900	11,890
Virginia	1,547,776	261,395	68,929	35,025	37,312	312,593	12,743	10	746,102	73,666
Washington	1,188,208	255,339	63,275	53,944	30,105	244,772	16,569	4,077	459,450	60,678
West Virginia	473,339	97,555	30,526	0	11,882	83,059	613	0	221,921	27,783
Wisconsin	1,044,638	210,639	61,418	15,394	26,811	230,643	7,285	2,195	426,008	64,245
Wyoming	158,665	36,327	19,242	20,403	5,102	34,247	500	918	30,902	11,024
Other activities/jurisdictions										
Indian Tribe Set-Aside	292,343	108,184	21,514	0	13,970	100,542	5,000	0	0	43,133
Other nonstate allocations	130,921	16,190	23,481	17,513	2,880	21,400	47,931	0	0	1,526
American Samoa	36,958	18,949	3,787	0	520	6,943	1,110	0	4,506	1,143
Freely Associated States[9]	24,604	1,000	0	0	166	6,579	0	0	16,859	0
Guam	63,668	20,531	6,325	35	1,078	15,611	1,384	0	16,048	2,658
Northern Marianas	25,978	11,454	2,372	0	593	5,307	1,102	0	4,082	1,070
Puerto Rico	1,722,645	409,128	99,309	1,024	29,022	130,071	3,404	0	992,951	57,736
U.S. Virgin Islands	32,450	9,886	3,792	97	1,051	9,769	92	0	5,555	2,208

[1]Title I grants. Includes grants to local education agencies (Basic, Concentration, Targeted, and Education Finance Incentive Grants); School Improvement State Grants; State Agency Program—Migrant Education; and State Agency Program—Neglected and Delinquent Children.

[2]Title VI grants. Includes Supporting Effective Instruction State Grants; Mathematics and Science Partnerships; 21st Century Community Learning Centers; State Assessments; Rural and Low-Income Schools Program; Small, Rural School Achievement Program; and Homeless Children and Youth Education.

[3]Includes Impact Aid—Basic Support Payments; Impact Aid—Payments for Children with Disabilities; and Impact Aid—Construction.

[4]Includes Career and Technical Education State Grants; Adult Basic and Literacy Education State Grants; and English Literacy and Civics Education State Grants.

[5]Includes Special Education—Grants to States; Special Education—Preschool Grants; and Grants for Infants and Families.

[6]Includes Federal Pell Grants; Federal Supplemental Educational Opportunity Grants; Federal Work-Study; and Student Loan Program interest subsidies.

[7]Includes Vocational Rehabilitation State Grants; Client Assistance State Grants; Protection and Advocacy of Individual Rights; Supported Employment State Grants; and Independent Living Services for Older Blind Individuals.

[8]Total excludes other activities and other jurisdictions.

[9]Includes the Marshall Islands, the Federated States of Micronesia, and Palau.

NOTE: Data reflect revisions to figures in the *Budget of the United States Government, Fiscal Year 2019*. Detail may not sum to totals because of rounding.

SOURCE: U.S. Department of Education, Budget Service, retrieved April 2, 2019, from https://www2.ed.gov/about/overview/budget/statetables/index.html; and unpublished tabulations. (This table was prepared April 2019.)

Table 401.70. Appropriations for Title I and selected other programs under the Every Student Succeeds Act of 2015, by program and state or jurisdiction: Fiscal years 2017 and 2018

[In thousands of current dollars]

State or jurisdiction	Title I total, 2017[1]	Title I, 2018: Total[1]	Title I, 2018: Grants to local education agencies[2]	Title I, 2018: State agency programs: Neglected and Delinquent	Title I, 2018: State agency programs: Migrant	Assessing Achievement, 2018	Supporting Effective Instruction State Grants, 2018
1	2	3	4	5	6	7	8
Total, 50 states and D.C.[3]	**$15,286,845**	**$15,595,840**	**$15,185,242**	**$45,847**	**$364,751**	**$360,444**	**$1,965,752**
Total, 50 states, D.C., other activities, and other jurisdictions	**15,882,167**	**16,182,167**	**15,759,802**	**47,614**	**374,751**	**378,000**	**2,055,830**
Alabama	253,108	254,363	251,982	557	1,824	6,097	32,914
Alaska	57,296	59,869	43,993	331	15,545	3,505	9,790
Arizona	358,237	368,734	359,592	1,543	7,600	7,620	35,422
Arkansas	168,180	164,501	159,313	362	4,826	4,985	19,979
California	1,951,820	2,104,943	1,988,156	2,305	114,481	28,444	230,384
Colorado	158,959	159,530	152,700	476	6,354	6,575	23,360
Connecticut	130,639	126,222	125,220	1,001	0	5,165	18,479
Delaware	51,755	51,938	51,200	392	347	3,577	9,790
District of Columbia	47,518	50,996	50,946	49	0	3,307	9,790
Florida	878,803	875,726	853,680	1,556	20,490	14,832	96,873
Georgia	548,159	541,965	533,668	962	7,336	10,161	57,738
Hawaii	55,985	52,114	49,811	95	2,208	3,833	9,790
Idaho	62,555	63,992	59,493	523	3,977	4,262	9,790
Illinois	681,005	681,399	678,373	934	2,092	11,203	81,325
Indiana	271,008	273,351	268,365	583	4,404	7,450	35,890
Iowa	99,218	99,760	97,623	408	1,730	5,058	15,794
Kansas	118,223	108,229	98,754	230	9,244	5,006	15,993
Kentucky	238,929	245,461	238,513	1,027	5,921	5,833	31,896
Louisiana	320,591	342,801	338,910	1,912	1,979	6,075	45,153
Maine	55,187	56,121	55,038	147	937	3,727	9,790
Maryland	232,467	240,867	239,062	1,400	405	6,789	29,196
Massachusetts	247,740	240,813	237,537	1,987	1,289	6,898	35,496
Michigan	514,107	496,235	488,199	1,110	6,926	9,192	76,804
Minnesota	165,907	172,060	169,612	404	2,044	6,643	27,326
Mississippi	201,468	210,779	209,581	369	829	5,033	29,747
Missouri	254,349	246,277	243,692	1,370	1,214	6,895	35,115
Montana	49,428	50,376	48,712	219	1,445	3,640	9,790
Nebraska	81,314	80,833	73,854	367	6,611	4,323	9,988
Nevada	131,254	130,625	129,670	766	189	4,929	11,747
New Hampshire	44,218	40,798	39,758	840	200	3,750	9,790
New Jersey	368,275	366,591	362,319	1,969	2,304	8,628	46,046
New Mexico	120,835	130,195	129,098	360	737	4,390	16,334
New York	1,220,213	1,224,303	1,213,917	2,443	7,943	14,547	157,361
North Carolina	456,848	457,392	451,219	914	5,260	9,537	48,647
North Dakota	37,729	39,166	38,361	105	700	3,470	9,790
Ohio	559,975	559,441	556,646	672	2,123	10,362	75,142
Oklahoma	170,850	189,664	188,010	427	1,228	5,686	24,405
Oregon	173,321	170,229	147,032	1,409	21,788	5,462	19,825
Pennsylvania	630,677	654,535	644,635	1,227	8,673	10,553	80,447
Rhode Island	53,604	53,184	52,883	301	0	3,589	9,790
South Carolina	245,568	246,590	243,788	1,978	824	6,132	27,010
South Dakota	47,678	49,290	48,573	0	717	3,591	9,790
Tennessee	308,397	311,342	309,747	228	1,367	7,244	36,483
Texas	1,476,416	1,560,775	1,511,186	2,432	47,157	23,601	176,878
Utah	89,790	83,789	81,378	935	1,476	5,593	13,851
Vermont	35,985	37,273	36,687	79	507	3,335	9,790
Virginia	261,395	268,436	266,414	1,129	893	8,242	37,196
Washington	255,339	258,176	228,027	2,284	27,866	7,586	33,289
West Virginia	97,555	98,130	97,078	1,052	0	4,047	16,324
Wisconsin	210,639	208,927	207,351	834	742	6,656	32,629
Wyoming	36,327	36,734	35,889	845	0	3,384	9,790
Other activities/jurisdictions							
Indian Tribe Set-Aside	108,184	110,284	110,284	0	0	1,846	10,228
Other nonstate allocations	16,190	16,190	5,000	1,190	10,000	8,900	10,279
American Samoa	18,949	19,323	19,323	0	0	359	2,456
Freely Associated States[4]	1,000	1,000	1,000	0	0	0	0
Guam	20,531	20,936	20,936	0	0	809	3,878
Northern Marianas	11,454	11,680	11,680	0	0	262	1,513
Puerto Rico	409,128	396,833	396,257	576	0	4,965	59,343
U.S. Virgin Islands	9,886	10,081	10,081	0	0	416	2,381

[1]This table does not include funding for School Improvement State Grants because the Every Student Succeeds Act of 2015 did not authorize funding for these grants. For fiscal years prior to FY 2017, School Improvement State Grants had been funded under the No Child Left Behind Act of 2001.
[2]Includes Basic, Concentration, Targeted, and Education Finance Incentive Grants.
[3]Total excludes other activities and other jurisdictions.
[4]Includes the Marshall Islands, the Federated States of Micronesia, and Palau.

NOTE: Data for FY 2017 are revised from previously published figures. Estimates for FY 2018 are preliminary. Detail may not sum to totals because of rounding.
SOURCE: U.S. Department of Education, Budget Service, Elementary, Secondary, and Vocational Education Analysis Division, retrieved April 2, 2019, from https://www2.ed.gov/about/overview/budget/statetables/19stbyprogram.pdf. (This table was prepared April 2019.)

CHAPTER 5
Outcomes of Education

This chapter contains tables comparing educational attainment and workforce characteristics. The data show labor force status, income levels, and occupations of high school dropouts and high school and college graduates. Most of these tables are based on data from the U.S. Census Bureau and the U.S. Bureau of Labor Statistics. Population characteristics are provided for many of the measures to allow for comparisons among various demographic groups. While most of the tables in this chapter focus on labor market outcomes, the chapter ends with several tables on adults' attitudes, skills, and participation in continuing education.

Statistics related to outcomes of education appear in other sections of the *Digest*. For example, statistics on educational attainment of the entire population are in chapter 1. More detailed data on the numbers of high school and college graduates can be found in chapters 2 and 3. Chapter 3 contains trend data on the percentage of high school completers going to college. Chapter 6 includes international comparisons of employment rates by educational attainment. Additional data on earnings by educational attainment may be obtained from the U.S. Census Bureau's Current Population Reports, Series P-60. The U.S. Bureau of Labor Statistics has a series of publications regarding the educational characteristics of the labor force. Further information on survey methodologies can be found in Appendix A: Guide to Sources and in the publications cited in the table source notes.

Labor Force

In 2017, the labor force participation rate—that is, the percentage of people either employed or actively seeking employment—was generally higher for adults with higher levels of educational attainment than for those with less education. Among 25- to 64-year-old adults, 86 percent of those with a bachelor's or higher degree participated in the labor force in 2017, compared with 72 percent of those who had completed only high school and 60 percent of those who had not completed high school (table 501.10). Within each education level, the labor force participation rate also varied by race/ethnicity. For 25- to 64-year-olds who had completed only high school, the 2017 labor force participation rate was highest for Hispanics (77 percent), followed by Asians (73 percent), then Whites (72 percent), then Blacks (68 percent), and then American Indians/Alaska Natives (62 percent). For 25- to 64-year-olds with a bachelor's or higher degree in 2017, the labor force participation rate was highest for Blacks (88 percent), followed by Hispanics and Whites (both at 87 percent), and then American Indians/Alaska Natives (83 percent). The labor force participation rate for Asians with a bachelor's or higher degree (83 percent) was lower than the rates for Blacks, Hispanics, and Whites, but not measurably different from the rate for American Indians/Alaska Natives.

In 2018, the unemployment rate—that is, the percentage of people in the labor force who are not employed and who have made specific efforts to find employment sometime during the prior 4 weeks—was generally higher for people with lower levels of educational attainment than for those with more education. The unemployment rate for 25- to 64-year-old adults who had not completed high school was 7 percent in 2018, compared with 5 percent for those who had completed only high school and 2 percent for those with a bachelor's or higher degree (table 501.80). Within each education level, the unemployment rates for 16- to 19-year-olds and 20- to 24-year-olds tended to be higher than the unemployment rate for 25- to 64-year-olds. For example, among 20- to 24-year-olds who had not completed high school and were not enrolled in school, the 2018 unemployment rate was 19 percent, compared with 7 percent for 25- to 64-year-olds with the same level of educational attainment. Among adults in the 25- to 34-year-old age group, the 2018 unemployment rate was 9 percent for those who had not completed high school, 6 percent for high school completers, and 2 percent for those with a bachelor's or higher degree (table 501.80 and figure 22).

In 2018, the employment to population ratio—that is, the percentage of the population that is employed—was generally higher for people with higher levels of educational attainment than for those with less education. Among 25- to 34-year-olds, for example, 86 percent of those with a bachelor's or higher degree were employed in 2018, compared with 72 percent of those who had completed only high school and 59 percent of those who had not completed high school (table 501.50 and figure 23).

In 2018, about half (52 percent) of all employed people age 25 and over had a postsecondary (i.e., an associate's or higher) degree (table 502.10). Seven percent of employed people age 25 and over had not completed high school.

The relative difficulties that high school dropouts encounter in entering the job market are highlighted by comparing the labor force participation and employment rates of recent high school dropouts with those of recent high school completers who did not immediately enroll in postsecondary education. In October 2017, about 42 percent of 2016–17 dropouts participated in the labor force (i.e., were either employed or looking for work), which was lower than the labor force participation rate for high school completers who were not enrolled in college (67 percent) (table 504.20 and figure 24). Similarly, the employment rate for dropouts (34 percent) was lower than the rate for high school completers who were not enrolled in college (56 percent) (table 504.10 and figure 24). However, the percentages of dropouts and high school completers who were not enrolled in college and who were looking for work were not measurably different.

Earnings

Median annual earnings were generally higher for adults with higher levels of educational attainment than for those with lower levels of educational attainment. Among full-time year-round workers age 25 and over, both males and females who had more education generally earned more than their counterparts of the same sex who had less education. In 2017, for example, males whose highest level of educational attainment was a bachelor's degree earned 70 percent more than males whose highest level of attainment was high school completion, and females who had attained a bachelor's degree earned 63 percent more than females who had only completed high school (table E, table 502.20, and figure 25).

Among full-time year-round workers age 25 and over, the earnings of females were lower than the earnings of males overall, as well as at each education level. For example, median 2017 earnings for full-time year-round workers whose highest level of educational attainment was a bachelor's degree were 37 percent higher for males than for females. Among those who had only completed high school, median 2017 earnings were 32 percent higher for males than for females (table 502.20).

From 1995 to 2017, percentage changes in earnings (after adjustment for inflation) varied by highest level of educational attainment and sex. For male full-time year-round workers age 25 and over who had started but not completed high school, the median annual earnings in 2017 ($34,622) were not measurably different from the earnings in 1995 (table 502.20). The median earnings of males who had completed high school decreased 11 percent from 1995 ($47,470, in constant 2017 dollars) to 2017 ($42,440). For males whose highest level of educational attainment was a bachelor's degree, there was no measurable difference between the median annual earnings in 2017 ($71,990) and in 1995, after adjustment for inflation. For female full-time year-round workers age 25 and over who had started but not completed high school, the median annual earnings in 2017 ($25,450) were not measurably different from the earnings in 1995. In constant 2017 dollars, the median earnings of females who had completed high school were 2 percent lower in 2017 ($32,240) than in 1995 ($32,920). For females whose highest level of attainment was a bachelor's degree, median annual earnings in 2017 ($52,440) were not measurably different from the earnings in 1995.

Table E. Median annual earnings of full-time year-round workers 25 years old and over, by selected levels of educational attainment and sex: Selected years, 1995 through 2017

[In constant 2017 dollars]

Sex and year	Some high school, no completion	High school completion	Bachelor's degree
Males			
1995	$35,690	$47,470	$72,810
2000	35,720	48,830	80,190
2005	34,130	45,560	75,330
2010	33,090	45,030	71,650
2017	34,620	42,440	71,990
Females			
1995	$25,460	$32,920	$51,560
2000	25,510	35,540	57,530
2005	25,260	33,000	52,930
2010	23,470	33,560	53,320
2017	25,450	32,240	52,440

SOURCE: U.S. Department of Commerce, Census Bureau, Current Population Reports, Series P-60, *Money Income in the United States*, 1995 and 2000; and Current Population Survey (CPS), Annual Social and Economic Supplement, 2006, 2011, and 2018.

For 25- to 29-year-old full-time year-round workers with a bachelor's degree, median annual earnings were $50,460 in 2017 (table 505.10 and figure 26). However, the 2017 median annual earnings of 25- to 29-year-old full-time year-round workers with a bachelor's degree varied by degree field. For example, when examining fields in which more than 200,000 25- to 29-year-olds held bachelor's degrees in 2017, median annual earnings were over $60,000 for two fields—computer and information systems ($65,400) and engineering and engineering-related fields ($69,980)—but below $45,000 for the fields of psychology ($40,320), fine and commercial arts ($40,330), English language and literature ($40,420), education ($40,430), and criminal justice and fire protection ($42,310).

Overall, the median annual earnings of 25- to 29-year-old full-time year-round workers with a bachelor's degree did not measurably change between 2010 and 2017, after adjustment for inflation (table 505.10). However, changes in median annual earnings from 2010 to 2017 varied by degree field. For example, inflation-adjusted median annual earnings were lower in 2017 than in 2010 for those with a bachelor's degree in education (6 percent lower), health professions (5 percent lower), and psychology (4 percent lower). There was no measurable change in inflation-adjusted median annual earnings for 25- to 29-year-old full-time year-round workers with a bachelor's degree in business, communications and communications technology, computer and information systems, criminal justice and fire protection, engineering and engineering-related fields, English language and literature, fine and commercial arts, the natural sciences, and the social sciences.

Figure 22. Unemployment rates of persons 25 to 34 years old, by highest level of educational attainment: Selected years, 1990 through 2018

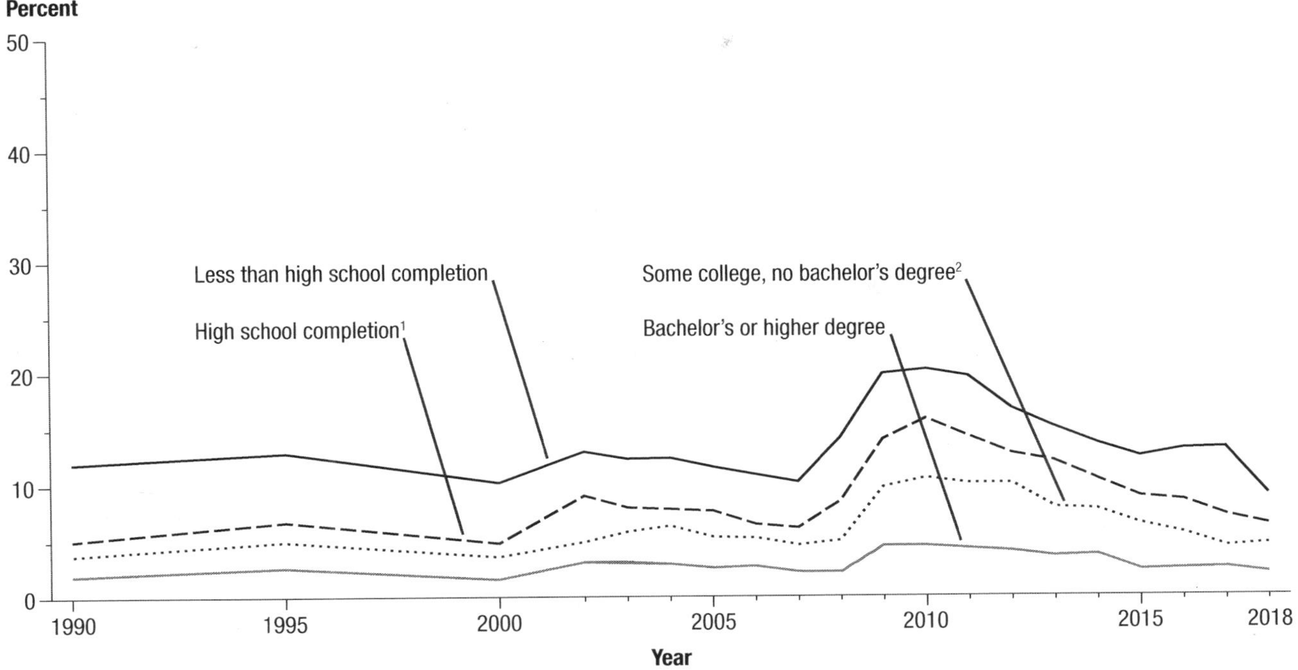

[1]Includes equivalency credentials, such as the GED credential.
[2]Includes persons with no college degree as well as those with an associate's degree.
NOTE: The unemployment rate is the percentage of persons in the civilian labor force who are not working and who made specific efforts to find employment sometime during the prior 4 weeks. The civilian labor force consists of all civilians who are employed or seeking employment.
SOURCE: U.S. Department of Commerce, Census Bureau, Current Population Survey (CPS), Annual Social and Economic Supplement, selected years, 1990 through 2018.

Figure 23. Employment to population ratios of persons 25 to 34 years old, by highest level of educational attainment: Selected years, 1990 through 2018

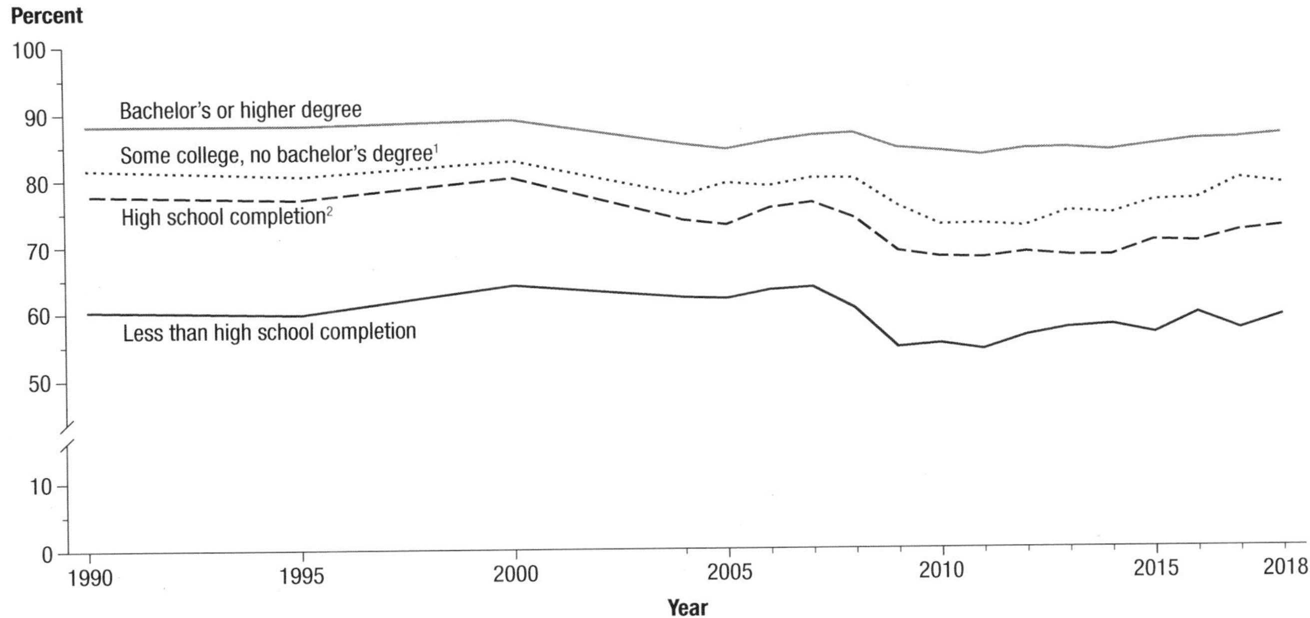

[1]Includes persons with no college degree as well as those with an associate's degree.
[2]Includes equivalency credentials, such as the GED credential.
NOTE: The employment to population ratio is the number of persons employed as a percentage of the civilian population.
SOURCE: U.S. Department of Commerce, Census Bureau, Current Population Survey (CPS), Annual Social and Economic Supplement, selected years, 1990 through 2018.

Figure 24. Percentage distribution of 2016–17 high school dropouts and high school completers not enrolled in college, by labor force status: October 2017

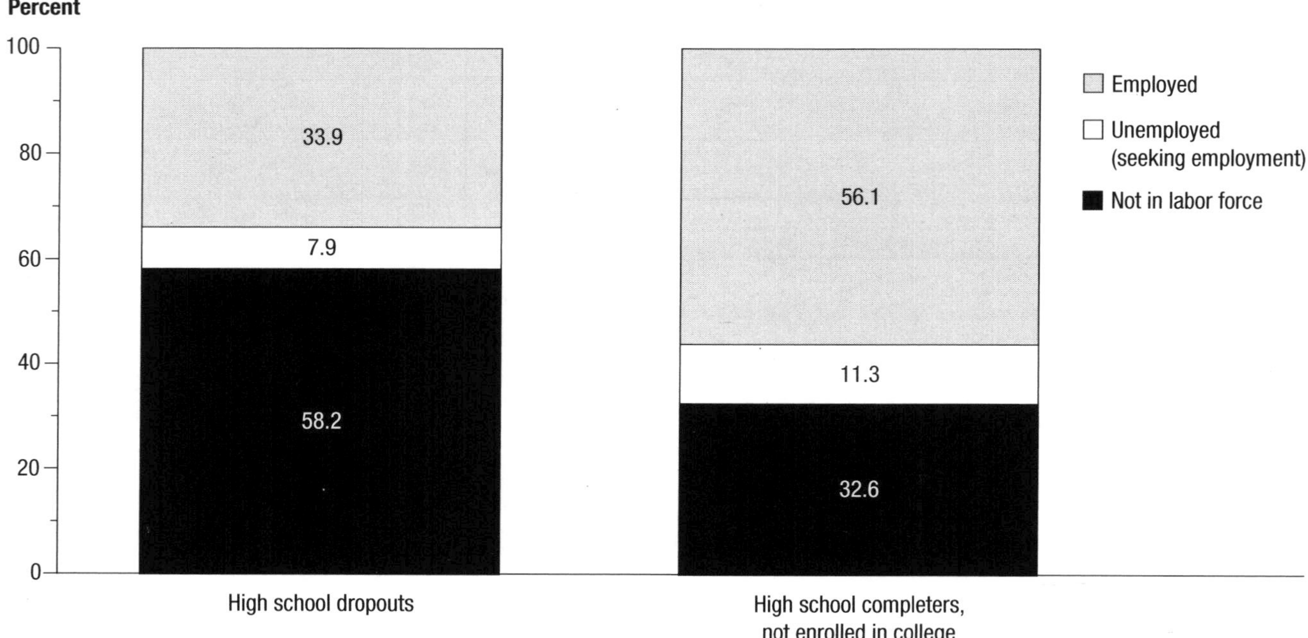

NOTE: Estimates are for 16- to 24-year-olds only. Dropouts are those who left school in the 12-month period ending in October 2017 without completing a high school credential. Completers are those who received either a high school diploma or an equivalency credential between January and October 2017. Excludes persons in the military and persons living in institutions (e.g., prisons or nursing facilities). Graphic display was generated using unrounded data. Detail may not sum to totals because of rounding.
SOURCE: U.S. Department of Commerce, Census Bureau, Current Population Survey (CPS), October 2017.

Figure 25. Median annual earnings of full-time year-round workers 25 to 35 years old, by highest level of educational attainment and sex: 2017

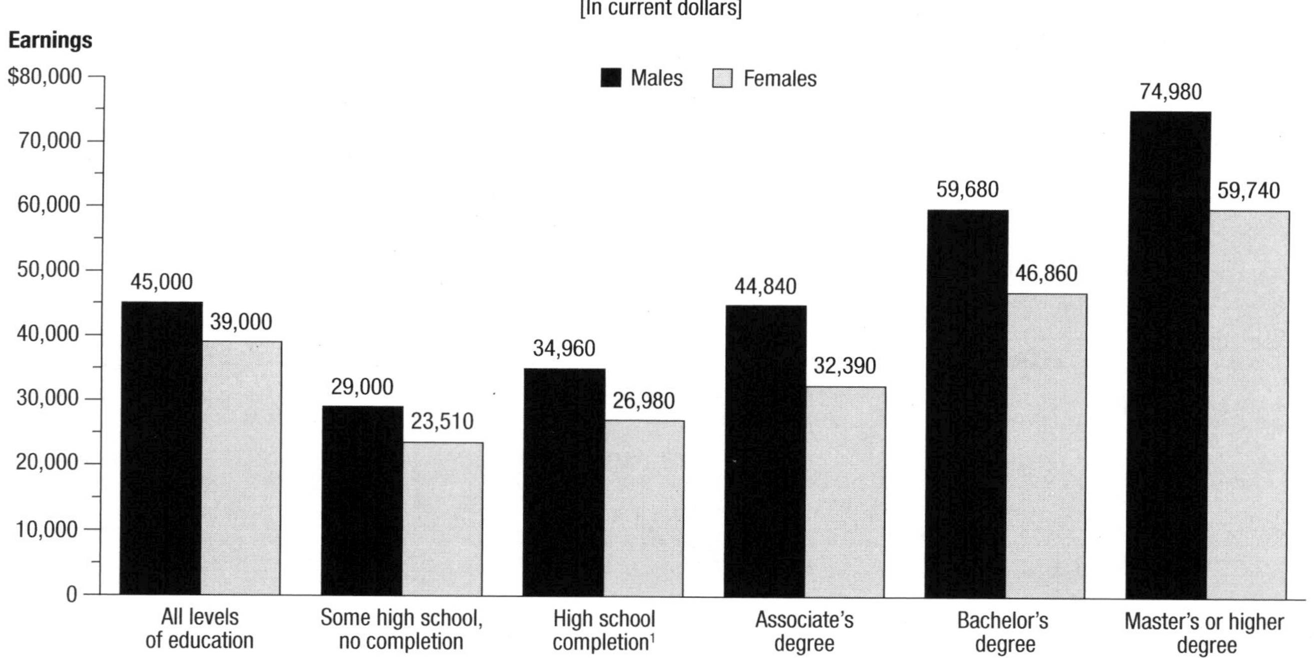

[1]Includes equivalency credentials, such as the GED credential.
SOURCE: U.S. Department of Commerce, Census Bureau, Current Population Survey (CPS), Annual Social and Economic Supplement, 2018.

Figure 26. Median annual earnings of 25- to 29-year-old bachelor's degree holders employed full time, by field of study: 2010 and 2017

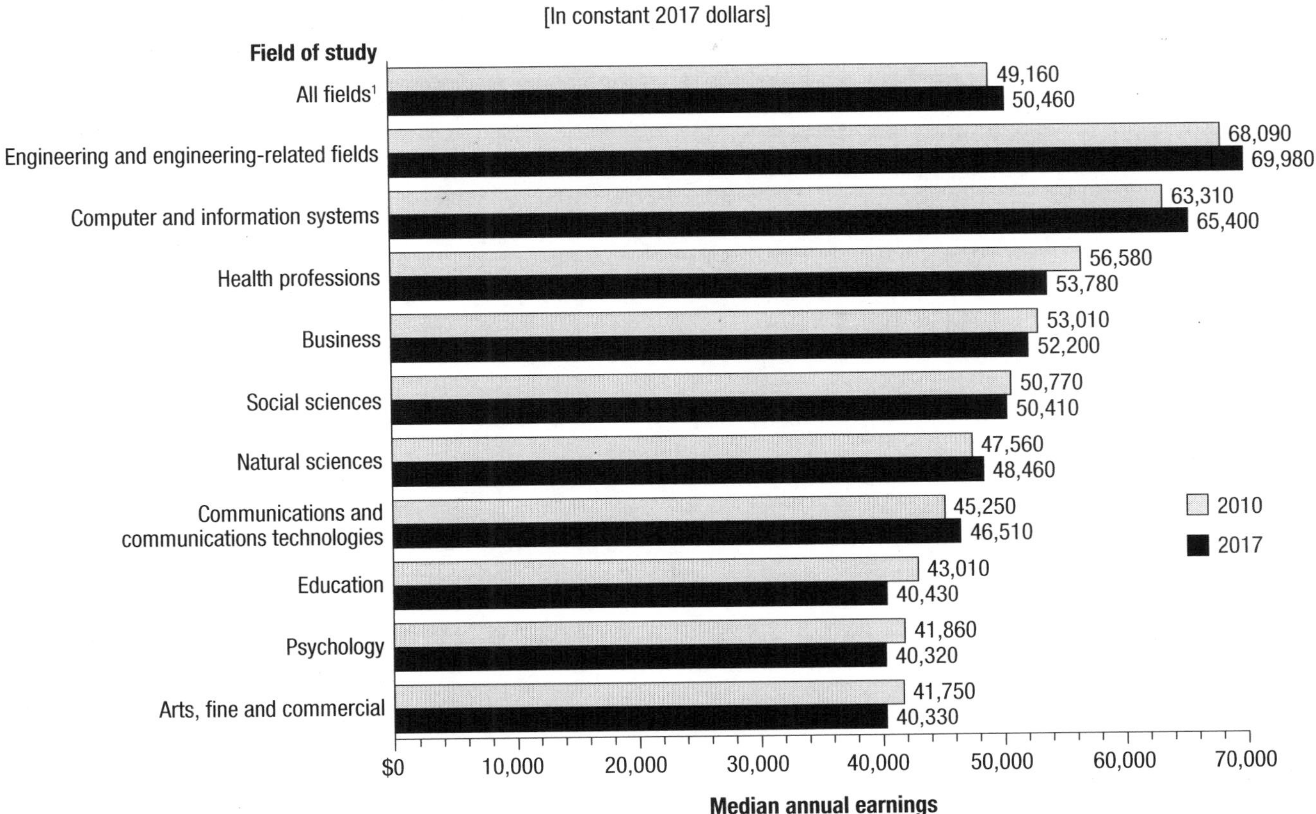

[1]Includes graduates in other fields not separately shown.
SOURCE: U.S. Department of Commerce, Census Bureau, 2010 and 2017 American Community Survey (ACS) Public Use Microdata Sample (PUMS) data.

Table 501.10. Labor force participation, employment, and unemployment of persons 25 to 64 years old, by sex, race/ethnicity, age group, and educational attainment: 2015, 2016, and 2017

[Standard errors appear in parentheses]

Sex, race/ethnicity, age group, and educational attainment	Labor force participation				Employment				Unemployment			
	Labor force participation rate[1]			Number of participants (in thousands)	Employment to population ratio[2]			Number employed (in thousands)	Unemployment rate[3]			Number unemployed (in thousands)
	2015	2016	2017	2017	2015	2016	2017	2017	2015	2016	2017	2017
1	2	3	4	5	6	7	8	9	10	11	12	13
All persons 25 to 64 years old, all education levels	**77.1** (0.04)	**77.3** (0.04)	**77.7** (0.04)	**131,911** (86.9)	**73.1** (0.04)	**73.7** (0.05)	**74.3** (0.04)	**126,239** (88.0)	**5.2** (0.03)	**4.7** (0.02)	**4.3** (0.02)	**5,673** (31.8)
Less than high school completion	60.1 (0.14)	60.2 (0.13)	59.9 (0.14)	11,163 (53.1)	54.3 (0.16)	55.0 (0.14)	55.2 (0.14)	10,271 (51.6)	9.6 (0.12)	8.7 (0.11)	8.0 (0.11)	892 (13.0)
High school completion[4]	71.9 (0.08)	72.0 (0.09)	72.2 (0.09)	31,837 (92.6)	67.0 (0.08)	67.5 (0.09)	68.2 (0.09)	30,056 (88.0)	6.9 (0.06)	6.3 (0.06)	5.6 (0.06)	1,781 (20.6)
Some college, no degree	77.4 (0.09)	77.5 (0.08)	77.8 (0.08)	27,279 (52.0)	73.0 (0.10)	73.5 (0.09)	74.1 (0.08)	25,986 (50.0)	5.6 (0.05)	5.1 (0.05)	4.7 (0.05)	1,294 (15.4)
Associate's degree	81.7 (0.13)	81.5 (0.14)	81.9 (0.11)	12,716 (48.7)	78.3 (0.13)	78.3 (0.14)	79.1 (0.12)	12,280 (48.6)	4.2 (0.08)	3.9 (0.07)	3.4 (0.08)	436 (9.9)
Bachelor's or higher degree	86.0 (0.06)	86.2 (0.06)	86.5 (0.05)	48,916 (133.4)	83.5 (0.06)	83.9 (0.07)	84.2 (0.05)	47,646 (128.1)	2.9 (0.03)	2.7 (0.03)	2.6 (0.03)	1,270 (14.9)
Sex												
Male, all education levels	**82.5** (0.06)	**82.6** (0.05)	**82.9** (0.05)	**69,506** (45.8)	**78.2** (0.06)	**78.7** (0.06)	**79.3** (0.05)	**66,517** (45.2)	**5.2** (0.03)	**4.7** (0.04)	**4.3** (0.03)	**2,989** (20.7)
Less than high school completion	69.5 (0.20)	69.4 (0.18)	69.6 (0.16)	7,094 (38.3)	63.5 (0.21)	64.0 (0.19)	64.6 (0.18)	6,592 (38.2)	8.7 (0.12)	7.7 (0.13)	7.1 (0.13)	501 (9.1)
High school completion[4]	77.9 (0.12)	77.8 (0.12)	78.1 (0.11)	18,689 (57.6)	72.5 (0.12)	72.9 (0.12)	73.7 (0.12)	17,652 (55.5)	6.9 (0.08)	6.3 (0.08)	5.5 (0.08)	1,037 (14.9)
Some college, no degree	82.8 (0.12)	82.8 (0.12)	83.1 (0.11)	14,247 (43.2)	78.3 (0.13)	78.7 (0.12)	79.3 (0.12)	13,604 (42.1)	5.4 (0.08)	4.9 (0.07)	4.5 (0.08)	643 (11.3)
Associate's degree	86.3 (0.17)	86.4 (0.16)	86.8 (0.16)	5,763 (32.6)	82.7 (0.18)	83.0 (0.16)	84.0 (0.18)	5,578 (33.0)	4.1 (0.10)	4.0 (0.10)	3.2 (0.10)	185 (5.6)
Bachelor's or higher degree	91.4 (0.07)	91.4 (0.07)	91.5 (0.07)	23,714 (75.0)	88.8 (0.08)	89.0 (0.09)	89.1 (0.07)	23,091 (71.9)	2.9 (0.05)	2.6 (0.05)	2.6 (0.04)	623 (10.4)
Female, all education levels	**71.8** (0.06)	**72.2** (0.06)	**72.5** (0.06)	**62,405** (63.9)	**68.1** (0.06)	**68.8** (0.06)	**69.4** (0.06)	**59,722** (63.2)	**5.2** (0.04)	**4.7** (0.03)	**4.3** (0.04)	**2,683** (22.6)
Less than high school completion	48.6 (0.17)	49.0 (0.20)	48.3 (0.25)	4,070 (30.1)	43.1 (0.20)	44.0 (0.21)	43.7 (0.23)	3,679 (27.8)	11.3 (0.23)	10.3 (0.19)	9.6 (0.22)	391 (9.5)
High school completion[4]	65.1 (0.12)	65.2 (0.14)	65.2 (0.14)	13,148 (50.9)	60.6 (0.12)	61.2 (0.16)	61.5 (0.14)	12,404 (48.6)	6.9 (0.09)	6.2 (0.09)	5.7 (0.08)	744 (11.7)
Some college, no degree	72.3 (0.13)	72.6 (0.12)	72.7 (0.11)	13,032 (38.8)	68.1 (0.14)	68.6 (0.12)	69.1 (0.12)	12,382 (36.1)	5.9 (0.08)	5.4 (0.08)	5.0 (0.08)	650 (11.0)
Associate's degree	78.4 (0.19)	77.9 (0.19)	78.3 (0.15)	6,953 (29.0)	75.0 (0.17)	74.9 (0.20)	75.5 (0.17)	6,703 (29.6)	4.3 (0.11)	3.8 (0.09)	3.6 (0.10)	251 (6.6)
Bachelor's or higher degree	81.4 (0.08)	81.8 (0.09)	82.2 (0.08)	25,202 (71.8)	79.0 (0.08)	79.5 (0.10)	80.1 (0.08)	24,555 (68.7)	3.0 (0.04)	2.8 (0.04)	2.6 (0.04)	647 (10.8)
Race/ethnicity												
White, all education levels	**78.0** (0.05)	**78.3** (0.05)	**78.5** (0.05)	**81,817** (57.8)	**74.7** (0.05)	**75.2** (0.05)	**75.8** (0.06)	**78,955** (61.2)	**4.3** (0.03)	**3.9** (0.03)	**3.5** (0.02)	**2,862** (19.0)
Less than high school completion	53.2 (0.25)	52.9 (0.27)	52.8 (0.24)	3,258 (24.2)	47.2 (0.26)	47.7 (0.28)	48.1 (0.23)	2,971 (22.9)	11.3 (0.21)	9.8 (0.24)	8.8 (0.20)	287 (7.0)
High school completion[4]	71.8 (0.10)	71.8 (0.11)	71.8 (0.11)	18,917 (59.1)	67.6 (0.11)	68.0 (0.11)	68.3 (0.11)	18,014 (56.6)	5.9 (0.07)	5.3 (0.07)	4.8 (0.07)	903 (14.5)
Some college, no degree	77.1 (0.10)	77.3 (0.10)	77.5 (0.10)	16,912 (43.3)	73.4 (0.11)	73.9 (0.10)	74.4 (0.11)	16,244 (40.7)	4.7 (0.06)	4.4 (0.06)	4.0 (0.06)	668 (11.0)
Associate's degree	81.6 (0.14)	81.7 (0.16)	81.9 (0.13)	8,517 (34.4)	78.7 (0.14)	79.0 (0.15)	79.5 (0.14)	8,266 (34.2)	3.6 (0.08)	3.3 (0.07)	2.9 (0.07)	251 (6.4)
Bachelor's or higher degree	86.3 (0.06)	86.5 (0.07)	86.8 (0.06)	34,212 (91.3)	84.1 (0.07)	84.5 (0.08)	84.9 (0.06)	33,460 (88.5)	2.5 (0.03)	2.4 (0.03)	2.2 (0.03)	752 (10.5)
Black, all education levels	**73.2** (0.12)	**73.4** (0.14)	**73.9** (0.11)	**15,644** (29.3)	**66.3** (0.14)	**67.3** (0.14)	**68.2** (0.13)	**14,433** (31.0)	**9.3** (0.12)	**8.2** (0.10)	**7.7** (0.11)	**1,211** (16.9)
Less than high school completion	46.9 (0.40)	46.9 (0.47)	47.8 (0.44)	1,174 (16.2)	37.4 (0.43)	38.6 (0.43)	39.2 (0.44)	964 (14.8)	20.3 (0.52)	17.6 (0.51)	17.9 (0.48)	210 (6.1)
High school completion[4]	67.8 (0.29)	67.9 (0.27)	68.4 (0.23)	4,562 (29.8)	59.8 (0.30)	60.8 (0.28)	61.8 (0.24)	4,121 (26.3)	11.7 (0.21)	10.5 (0.20)	9.7 (0.22)	441 (11.2)
Some college, no degree	76.9 (0.24)	77.1 (0.23)	77.0 (0.26)	4,129 (28.9)	70.0 (0.26)	71.1 (0.26)	71.1 (0.28)	3,817 (27.8)	9.0 (0.19)	7.9 (0.17)	7.6 (0.16)	312 (6.8)
Associate's degree	82.2 (0.41)	81.5 (0.36)	81.9 (0.39)	1,570 (19.6)	76.9 (0.45)	76.6 (0.39)	77.6 (0.45)	1,489 (18.8)	6.5 (0.29)	6.0 (0.27)	5.1 (0.25)	81 (4.0)
Bachelor's or higher degree	88.2 (0.18)	88.2 (0.17)	88.4 (0.20)	4,209 (27.0)	84.2 (0.20)	84.7 (0.21)	84.9 (0.20)	4,042 (26.0)	4.5 (0.16)	4.0 (0.14)	4.0 (0.13)	167 (5.8)
Hispanic, all education levels	**76.8** (0.10)	**77.0** (0.10)	**77.4** (0.11)	**22,632** (36.9)	**72.4** (0.11)	**72.8** (0.11)	**73.8** (0.11)	**21,555** (37.0)	**5.8** (0.07)	**5.4** (0.08)	**4.8** (0.07)	**1,078** (15.1)
Less than high school completion	69.2 (0.21)	69.6 (0.20)	68.9 (0.22)	5,833 (38.8)	64.6 (0.23)	65.1 (0.21)	65.0 (0.23)	5,502 (38.5)	6.7 (0.14)	6.4 (0.14)	5.7 (0.14)	331 (8.3)
High school completion[4]	76.2 (0.21)	76.1 (0.23)	76.9 (0.19)	6,469 (38.5)	71.4 (0.22)	71.7 (0.25)	73.0 (0.21)	6,145 (38.1)	6.2 (0.12)	5.8 (0.15)	5.0 (0.13)	324 (8.6)
Some college, no degree	80.6 (0.22)	80.2 (0.25)	80.6 (0.25)	4,418 (29.0)	76.0 (0.25)	76.0 (0.27)	76.7 (0.26)	4,207 (29.1)	5.7 (0.15)	5.2 (0.18)	4.8 (0.14)	211 (6.2)
Associate's degree	84.1 (0.38)	82.3 (0.40)	84.1 (0.34)	1,698 (17.4)	80.0 (0.40)	78.3 (0.43)	80.8 (0.40)	1,630 (17.3)	4.9 (0.25)	4.8 (0.23)	4.0 (0.25)	68 (4.3)
Bachelor's or higher degree	86.4 (0.21)	86.7 (0.21)	87.0 (0.20)	4,214 (34.3)	83.0 (0.23)	83.9 (0.22)	84.0 (0.24)	4,071 (34.5)	3.9 (0.13)	3.3 (0.11)	3.4 (0.11)	144 (4.6)
Asian, all education levels	**78.2** (0.17)	**78.4** (0.17)	**78.7** (0.16)	**8,289** (21.2)	**74.7** (0.17)	**75.4** (0.17)	**75.9** (0.18)	**7,994** (22.5)	**4.5** (0.09)	**3.7** (0.10)	**3.6** (0.08)	**294** (6.9)
Less than high school completion	63.3 (0.66)	64.6 (0.54)	63.0 (0.60)	668 (11.1)	59.0 (0.64)	61.5 (0.49)	60.1 (0.62)	637 (10.5)	6.8 (0.42)	4.8 (0.34)	4.6 (0.41)	31 (2.9)
High school completion[4]	73.5 (0.43)	73.6 (0.53)	73.4 (0.54)	1,069 (14.7)	69.1 (0.46)	70.2 (0.50)	70.4 (0.59)	1,025 (14.7)	6.0 (0.33)	4.7 (0.28)	4.1 (0.24)	44 (2.6)
Some college, no degree	77.3 (0.46)	76.4 (0.46)	77.9 (0.51)	939 (13.1)	73.1 (0.50)	72.9 (0.49)	74.6 (0.57)	899 (12.9)	5.3 (0.31)	4.6 (0.28)	4.3 (0.30)	41 (2.8)
Associate's degree	78.4 (0.64)	78.4 (0.65)	79.9 (0.50)	569 (9.4)	74.9 (0.67)	75.1 (0.69)	77.3 (0.53)	550 (9.2)	4.5 (0.37)	4.2 (0.38)	3.3 (0.24)	19 (1.4)
Bachelor's or higher degree	82.4 (0.20)	82.5 (0.19)	82.7 (0.21)	5,043 (23.1)	79.5 (0.22)	79.9 (0.20)	80.0 (0.22)	4,883 (23.0)	3.6 (0.10)	3.1 (0.12)	3.2 (0.10)	160 (4.9)

See notes at end of table.

Table 501.10. Labor force participation, employment, and unemployment of persons 25 to 64 years old, by sex, race/ethnicity, age group, and educational attainment: 2015, 2016, and 2017—Continued

[Standard errors appear in parentheses]

Sex, race/ethnicity, age group, and educational attainment	Labor force participation: Labor force participation rate[1] 2015	2016	2017	Number of participants (in thousands) 2017	Employment: Employment to population ratio[2] 2015	2016	2017	Number employed (in thousands) 2017	Unemployment: Unemployment rate[3] 2015	2016	2017	Number unemployed (in thousands) 2017
1	2	3	4	5	6	7	8	9	10	11	12	13
American Indian/Alaska Native, all education levels	**65.4** (0.61)	**65.5** (0.48)	**65.0** (0.52)	**718** (9.6)	**58.4** (0.60)	**58.2** (0.51)	**58.9** (0.51)	**651** (9.3)	**10.6** (0.37)	**11.1** (0.44)	**9.4** (0.40)	**67** (3.0)
Less than high school completion	44.9 (1.29)	42.1 (1.29)	44.5 (1.35)	75 (3.3)	35.8 (1.11)	34.1 (1.27)	36.3 (1.35)	62 (2.9)	20.3 (1.58)	18.8 (1.51)	18.4 (1.67)	14 (1.4)
High school completion[4]	62.5 (0.96)	63.1 (0.82)	61.7 (0.90)	222 (5.3)	54.0 (1.02)	53.7 (0.86)	54.7 (0.91)	197 (5.0)	13.7 (0.84)	14.9 (0.84)	11.3 (0.85)	25 (2.0)
Some college, no degree	67.8 (1.09)	69.1 (0.94)	68.1 (1.06)	204 (5.4)	60.9 (1.18)	61.9 (1.01)	62.3 (1.03)	186 (5.4)	10.2 (0.87)	10.4 (0.98)	8.5 (0.62)	17 (1.3)
Associate's degree	75.0 (1.58)	74.8 (1.42)	72.2 (1.65)	80 (3.7)	71.8 (1.68)	69.6 (1.57)	68.6 (1.73)	76 (3.6)	4.2 (0.97)	6.9 (1.03)	5.0 (0.73)	4 (0.6)
Bachelor's or higher degree	83.3 (1.13)	82.8 (1.01)	83.0 (0.95)	138 (4.7)	79.8 (1.12)	79.3 (1.05)	78.8 (1.08)	131 (4.8)	4.3 (0.65)	4.2 (0.68)	5.1 (0.62)	7 (0.8)
Age group												
25 to 34, all education levels	**82.0** (0.09)	**82.2** (0.07)	**82.6** (0.08)	**36,766** (41.9)	**76.5** (0.09)	**77.3** (0.08)	**78.1** (0.08)	**34,740** (45.4)	**6.7** (0.06)	**5.9** (0.05)	**5.5** (0.05)	**2,026** (18.2)
Less than high school completion	64.1 (0.30)	63.8 (0.25)	63.4 (0.29)	2,574 (22.7)	55.0 (0.34)	55.9 (0.27)	55.9 (0.32)	2,271 (21.8)	14.2 (0.29)	12.3 (0.26)	11.7 (0.28)	302 (7.4)
High school completion[4]	76.8 (0.17)	76.8 (0.20)	77.2 (0.19)	8,266 (49.2)	69.1 (0.19)	69.9 (0.21)	70.9 (0.20)	7,587 (46.2)	10.0 (0.16)	9.0 (0.13)	8.2 (0.14)	679 (12.2)
Some college, no degree	82.3 (0.18)	82.6 (0.15)	82.7 (0.15)	8,150 (38.6)	76.2 (0.18)	77.2 (0.18)	77.7 (0.18)	7,659 (37.5)	7.3 (0.12)	6.6 (0.11)	6.0 (0.12)	491 (10.0)
Associate's degree	86.7 (0.25)	86.3 (0.23)	87.0 (0.19)	3,481 (23.2)	82.3 (0.27)	82.2 (0.25)	83.3 (0.21)	3,335 (23.1)	5.1 (0.15)	4.7 (0.17)	4.2 (0.16)	146 (5.5)
Bachelor's or higher degree	89.6 (0.11)	89.9 (0.10)	90.0 (0.11)	14,295 (65.5)	86.8 (0.12)	87.4 (0.11)	87.4 (0.11)	13,888 (62.4)	3.1 (0.06)	2.8 (0.05)	2.8 (0.06)	407 (8.5)
35 to 44, all education levels	**82.0** (0.07)	**82.3** (0.08)	**82.3** (0.08)	**33,870** (39.4)	**77.9** (0.08)	**78.4** (0.08)	**78.9** (0.09)	**32,442** (41.1)	**5.0** (0.05)	**4.7** (0.05)	**4.2** (0.04)	**1,429** (13.6)
Less than high school completion	67.0 (0.24)	67.8 (0.26)	66.7 (0.29)	3,185 (25.3)	61.1 (0.26)	62.1 (0.25)	61.4 (0.32)	2,933 (26.0)	8.8 (0.20)	8.4 (0.20)	7.9 (0.21)	252 (6.4)
High school completion[4]	77.2 (0.17)	77.4 (0.21)	77.5 (0.19)	7,535 (40.5)	71.7 (0.18)	72.3 (0.22)	72.9 (0.20)	7,085 (39.4)	7.2 (0.13)	6.6 (0.13)	6.0 (0.12)	450 (9.0)
Some college, no degree	82.6 (0.16)	82.4 (0.17)	82.4 (0.17)	6,647 (30.2)	77.9 (0.20)	78.1 (0.19)	78.5 (0.18)	6,327 (29.8)	5.6 (0.12)	5.3 (0.12)	4.8 (0.10)	321 (6.8)
Associate's degree	86.4 (0.25)	86.1 (0.24)	86.7 (0.22)	3,307 (23.1)	82.8 (0.25)	82.7 (0.27)	83.9 (0.26)	3,199 (23.6)	4.2 (0.15)	4.0 (0.16)	3.3 (0.14)	108 (4.6)
Bachelor's or higher degree	89.2 (0.10)	89.5 (0.08)	89.4 (0.08)	13,197 (41.7)	87.0 (0.11)	87.3 (0.09)	87.4 (0.10)	12,899 (41.4)	2.5 (0.06)	2.5 (0.05)	2.3 (0.06)	298 (7.4)
45 to 54, all education levels	**79.8** (0.08)	**80.2** (0.08)	**80.5** (0.08)	**34,013** (47.9)	**76.1** (0.09)	**76.8** (0.09)	**77.5** (0.09)	**32,740** (48.2)	**4.6** (0.04)	**4.1** (0.04)	**3.7** (0.04)	**1,274** (12.5)
Less than high school completion	62.4 (0.26)	62.7 (0.26)	62.8 (0.28)	3,123 (22.7)	57.2 (0.29)	58.1 (0.29)	58.7 (0.28)	2,916 (21.4)	8.4 (0.20)	7.4 (0.19)	6.7 (0.18)	208 (6.0)
High school completion[4]	75.6 (0.15)	75.7 (0.16)	75.9 (0.16)	8,612 (33.9)	71.2 (0.15)	71.8 (0.15)	72.4 (0.16)	8,219 (33.3)	5.7 (0.09)	5.2 (0.09)	4.6 (0.09)	392 (8.2)
Some college, no degree	80.3 (0.18)	80.6 (0.15)	81.2 (0.17)	6,766 (29.5)	76.5 (0.20)	77.3 (0.17)	78.0 (0.18)	6,498 (28.3)	4.7 (0.10)	4.2 (0.09)	4.0 (0.11)	267 (7.5)
Associate's degree	84.4 (0.21)	84.4 (0.22)	84.5 (0.19)	3,301 (19.8)	81.1 (0.26)	81.4 (0.23)	82.0 (0.21)	3,200 (20.1)	3.9 (0.15)	3.5 (0.12)	3.0 (0.11)	100 (3.6)
Bachelor's or higher degree	88.9 (0.11)	89.1 (0.10)	89.3 (0.10)	12,212 (45.2)	86.4 (0.12)	86.8 (0.11)	87.0 (0.10)	11,906 (42.3)	2.9 (0.06)	2.7 (0.05)	2.5 (0.05)	306 (6.8)
55 to 64, all education levels	**64.2** (0.08)	**64.3** (0.09)	**64.9** (0.09)	**27,262** (37.2)	**61.5** (0.09)	**61.8** (0.09)	**62.6** (0.09)	**26,318** (37.0)	**4.2** (0.04)	**3.8** (0.04)	**3.5** (0.04)	**944** (12.3)
Less than high school completion	46.4 (0.26)	46.6 (0.25)	47.4 (0.30)	2,282 (19.4)	43.3 (0.27)	43.7 (0.26)	44.7 (0.30)	2,151 (19.6)	6.9 (0.22)	6.3 (0.19)	5.7 (0.22)	130 (5.0)
High school completion[4]	59.6 (0.16)	60.0 (0.17)	60.3 (0.17)	7,425 (31.8)	56.9 (0.16)	57.5 (0.17)	58.2 (0.16)	7,165 (31.1)	4.6 (0.09)	4.2 (0.08)	3.5 (0.09)	259 (6.5)
Some college, no degree	64.0 (0.19)	64.2 (0.20)	64.8 (0.17)	5,717 (26.3)	61.2 (0.18)	61.6 (0.20)	62.4 (0.17)	5,502 (25.7)	4.3 (0.11)	4.1 (0.10)	3.7 (0.08)	214 (5.0)
Associate's degree	68.7 (0.29)	68.7 (0.31)	69.2 (0.28)	2,628 (20.2)	66.3 (0.29)	66.5 (0.31)	67.1 (0.28)	2,546 (19.8)	3.6 (0.16)	3.2 (0.12)	3.1 (0.14)	82 (3.7)
Bachelor's or higher degree	74.6 (0.15)	74.5 (0.14)	75.2 (0.15)	9,212 (32.5)	72.2 (0.15)	72.2 (0.14)	73.1 (0.15)	8,953 (32.7)	3.3 (0.07)	3.0 (0.07)	2.8 (0.07)	259 (6.3)

[1]Percentage of the civilian population who are employed or seeking employment.
[2]Number of persons employed as a percentage of the civilian population.
[3]The percentage of persons in the civilian labor force who are not working and who made specific efforts to find employment sometime during the prior 4 weeks.
[4]Includes equivalency credentials, such as the GED credential.

NOTE: Estimates are for the entire civilian population, including persons living in households and persons living in group quarters (e.g., college residence halls, residential treatment centers, or correctional facilities). Race categories exclude persons of Hispanic ethnicity. Totals include racial/ethnic groups not separately shown. Detail may not sum to totals because of rounding.
SOURCE: U.S. Department of Commerce, Census Bureau, American Community Survey (ACS), 2015, 2016, and 2017, unpublished tabulations. (This table was prepared June 2019.)

Table 501.20. Labor force participation, employment, and unemployment of persons 16 to 24 years old who are not enrolled in school, by age group, sex, race/ethnicity, and educational attainment: 2015, 2016, and 2017

[Standard errors appear in parentheses]

Age group, sex, race/ethnicity, and educational attainment	Labor force participation				Employment				Unemployment			
	Labor force participation rate[1]			Number of participants (in thousands)	Employment to population ratio[2]			Number employed (in thousands)	Unemployment rate[3]			Number unemployed (in thousands)
	2015	2016	2017	2017	2015	2016	2017	2017	2015	2016	2017	2017
1	2	3	4	5	6	7	8	9	10	11	12	13
16 to 19 years old												
All persons, all education levels	**64.8** (0.39)	**65.6** (0.41)	**65.3** (0.42)	**1,601** (19.0)	**51.8** (0.45)	**51.8** (0.44)	**52.2** (0.45)	**1,281** (17.0)	**22.6** (0.44)	**21.0** (0.42)	**20.0** (0.42)	**320** (7.6)
Less than high school completion	47.4 (0.81)	48.5 (0.81)	48.4 (0.72)	326 (6.8)	33.2 (0.77)	33.2 (0.73)	35.4 (0.74)	238 (6.1)	30.6 (0.98)	31.4 (1.08)	27.0 (1.03)	88 (3.8)
High school completion[4]	71.4 (0.46)	71.9 (0.50)	70.8 (0.48)	1,042 (13.8)	58.3 (0.56)	58.30 (0.56)	57.0 (0.56)	839 (12.6)	21.7 (0.60)	18.9 (0.53)	19.5 (0.48)	203 (5.4)
At least some college	73.4 (1.19)	76.4 (1.04)	75.9 (1.18)	233 (7.5)	65.0 (1.22)	65.0 (1.17)	66.4 (1.29)	204 (7.3)	15.1 (0.94)	14.9 (1.00)	12.5 (1.11)	29 (2.6)
Male, all education levels	**66.6** (0.56)	**66.5** (0.50)	**66.2** (0.54)	**924** (12.6)	**52.4** (0.61)	**52.4** (0.54)	**52.7** (0.61)	**735** (11.7)	**23.0** (0.56)	**21.2** (0.52)	**20.5** (0.58)	**189** (5.8)
Less than high school completion	50.4 (1.05)	49.9 (0.99)	51.1 (0.99)	209 (6.1)	34.8 (0.93)	34.8 (0.98)	37.3 (0.99)	152 (4.9)	30.1 (1.24)	30.2 (1.45)	27.0 (1.41)	56 (3.6)
High school completion[4]	73.3 (0.69)	73.2 (0.66)	72.1 (0.61)	603 (9.6)	59.2 (0.77)	59.2 (0.75)	58.2 (0.73)	487 (9.4)	21.7 (0.70)	19.1 (0.67)	19.2 (0.67)	116 (4.1)
At least some college	73.9 (1.67)	76.1 (1.54)	75.0 (1.48)	112 (4.6)	63.8 (1.93)	63.8 (1.67)	63.5 (1.56)	95 (4.4)	16.7 (1.66)	16.1 (1.56)	15.3 (1.65)	17 (1.9)
Female, all education levels	**62.5** (0.52)	**64.6** (0.65)	**64.1** (0.69)	**677** (11.6)	**51.2** (0.58)	**51.2** (0.66)	**51.7** (0.70)	**546** (10.4)	**22.1** (0.64)	**20.8** (0.69)	**19.3** (0.68)	**131** (5.2)
Less than high school completion	43.2 (1.23)	46.5 (1.37)	44.4 (1.25)	117 (4.6)	31.0 (1.19)	31.0 (1.16)	32.4 (1.12)	86 (3.8)	31.4 (1.42)	33.3 (1.74)	27.0 (1.60)	32 (2.3)
High school completion[4]	69.0 (0.70)	70.2 (0.83)	69.1 (0.87)	439 (9.7)	57.1 (0.81)	57.1 (0.93)	55.4 (0.88)	352 (8.4)	21.7 (0.83)	18.7 (0.86)	19.9 (0.82)	87 (4.2)
At least some college	72.9 (1.62)	76.7 (1.49)	76.8 (1.54)	120 (5.2)	66.2 (1.61)	66.2 (1.67)	69.2 (1.68)	108 (5.0)	13.5 (1.20)	13.6 (1.30)	9.8 (1.22)	12 (1.5)
White, all education levels	**68.7** (0.60)	**68.3** (0.58)	**69.7** (0.60)	**803** (11.5)	**55.7** (0.72)	**55.7** (0.59)	**57.9** (0.64)	**668** (11.0)	**19.3** (0.58)	**18.6** (0.51)	**16.9** (0.52)	**136** (4.3)
Less than high school completion	49.9 (1.11)	49.6 (1.17)	51.3 (1.25)	156 (5.1)	34.6 (1.03)	34.6 (0.97)	39.3 (1.18)	120 (4.4)	26.3 (1.09)	30.2 (1.23)	23.5 (1.47)	37 (2.6)
High school completion[4]	75.0 (0.67)	74.9 (0.75)	75.2 (0.66)	525 (8.5)	62.8 (0.78)	62.8 (0.76)	62.9 (0.77)	439 (8.0)	18.5 (0.70)	16.2 (0.61)	16.3 (0.64)	86 (3.6)
At least some college	77.7 (1.58)	80.3 (1.19)	81.0 (1.50)	122 (5.0)	70.3 (1.67)	70.3 (1.52)	72.3 (1.61)	109 (4.9)	13.1 (1.28)	12.5 (1.24)	10.8 (1.31)	13 (1.6)
Black, all education levels	**57.3** (1.05)	**60.4** (0.97)	**57.4** (1.14)	**243** (7.8)	**41.0** (1.12)	**41.0** (1.11)	**40.3** (1.22)	**170** (7.0)	**33.6** (1.50)	**32.2** (1.59)	**29.8** (1.29)	**72** (3.4)
Less than high school completion	38.5 (2.10)	43.3 (1.95)	37.9 (1.95)	42 (2.8)	22.2 (1.88)	22.2 (1.60)	21.5 (1.73)	24 (2.1)	51.8 (3.66)	48.7 (3.61)	43.4 (3.34)	18 (1.8)
High school completion[4]	64.4 (1.36)	65.2 (1.34)	63.6 (1.41)	168 (6.7)	46.0 (1.45)	46.0 (1.64)	45.5 (1.53)	120 (6.0)	31.4 (1.78)	29.4 (1.95)	28.5 (1.52)	48 (2.7)
At least some college	65.4 (3.04)	74.3 (3.04)	69.2 (3.32)	32 (2.9)	57.4 (2.96)	57.4 (3.67)	56.1 (3.56)	26 (2.6)	21.2 (2.79)	22.8 (3.16)	19.0 (3.58)	6 (1.3)
Hispanic, all education levels	**64.1** (0.93)	**64.4** (0.77)	**64.5** (0.68)	**441** (7.3)	**52.1** (0.89)	**52.1** (0.81)	**51.7** (0.73)	**353** (6.5)	**22.0** (0.86)	**19.1** (0.81)	**19.9** (0.75)	**88** (3.7)
Less than high school completion	49.9 (1.66)	50.6 (1.47)	52.1 (1.48)	106 (4.3)	38.1 (1.56)	38.1 (1.50)	39.1 (1.45)	80 (3.8)	27.1 (1.97)	24.7 (2.03)	24.9 (1.71)	26 (2.0)
High school completion[4]	70.7 (1.11)	70.7 (0.91)	69.1 (0.76)	278 (6.5)	58.1 (1.13)	58.1 (0.93)	55.6 (0.85)	223 (5.6)	21.5 (1.13)	17.9 (0.99)	19.5 (0.93)	54 (3.0)
At least some college	71.6 (2.62)	70.8 (2.12)	73.2 (1.97)	57 (3.6)	60.8 (2.81)	60.8 (2.16)	64.4 (2.06)	50 (3.3)	13.9 (2.15)	14.1 (1.90)	12.0 (1.74)	7 (1.1)
Asian, all education levels	**59.4** (2.88)	**58.6** (3.14)	**48.9** (3.06)	**25** (2.1)	**50.1** (3.07)	**50.1** (3.25)	**39.2** (2.96)	**20** (1.9)	**19.9** (3.14)	**14.5** (3.17)	**19.8** (3.24)	**5** (0.9)
Less than high school completion	43.7 (5.35)	40.7 (5.06)	29.2 (5.42)	4 (0.8)	33.3 (3.96)	33.3 (5.41)	21.1 (5.17)	3 (0.7)	33.3 (7.37)	18.3! (6.73)	27.8! (8.64)	1! (0.4)
High school completion[4]	67.0 (3.90)	64.0 (3.71)	53.8 (3.98)	14 (1.5)	56.6 (4.37)	56.6 (3.99)	42.7 (4.05)	11 (1.3)	17.2 (3.66)	11.6 (3.44)	20.6 (4.50)	3 (0.7)
At least some college	55.9 (6.56)	66.0 (6.86)	59.2 (7.23)	7 (1.1)	52.7 (7.29)	52.7 (7.22)	51.1 (7.26)	6 (1.0)	14.8! (6.61)	20.2! (7.51)	13.7! (4.97)	1! (0.4)
American Indian/Alaska Native, all education levels	**49.0** (2.55)	**53.6** (3.72)	**52.5** (3.74)	**16** (1.6)	**39.0** (2.28)	**39.0** (3.40)	**39.6** (3.51)	**12** (1.4)	**38.5** (3.73)	**27.3** (3.59)	**24.5** (3.31)	**4** (0.6)
Less than high school completion	35.5 (5.16)	30.8 (4.76)	37.2 (5.79)	4 (0.9)	18.0 (3.52)	18.0 (3.61)	25.3 (5.79)	3 (0.8)	56.5 (9.24)	41.6 (8.34)	32.1 (7.92)	1 (0.3)
High school completion[4]	57.4 (4.05)	65.4 (3.83)	62.4 (4.54)	10 (1.2)	49.0 (3.69)	49.0 (4.27)	48.0 (4.54)	8 (1.0)	33.7 (4.80)	25.0 (4.55)	23.0 (4.67)	2 (0.6)
At least some college	54.3 (9.80)	57.7 (7.60)	59.2 (9.33)	2 (0.4)	45.8 (9.83)	45.8 (7.86)	50.8 (8.91)	2 (0.4)	‡ (†)	20.5! (9.95)	‡ (†)	‡ (†)
20 to 24 years old												
All persons, all education levels	**81.5** (0.15)	**82.2** (0.16)	**82.2** (0.16)	**10,363** (37.3)	**72.9** (0.19)	**72.9** (0.18)	**73.6** (0.19)	**9,281** (36.2)	**12.2** (0.15)	**11.3** (0.14)	**10.4** (0.13)	**1,082** (14.1)
Less than high school completion	64.2 (0.48)	64.4 (0.55)	63.3 (0.55)	918 (14.2)	50.7 (0.52)	50.7 (0.57)	51.3 (0.59)	744 (12.5)	21.4 (0.49)	21.4 (0.56)	19.0 (0.63)	175 (6.6)
High school completion[4]	78.8 (0.27)	79.9 (0.27)	79.2 (0.27)	4,288 (30.5)	69.1 (0.31)	69.1 (0.31)	69.0 (0.29)	3,733 (27.9)	14.5 (0.26)	13.5 (0.25)	12.9 (0.20)	555 (9.5)
Some college, no degree	86.0 (0.25)	86.2 (0.29)	86.6 (0.24)	2,653 (20.4)	78.6 (0.31)	78.6 (0.35)	79.6 (0.27)	2,438 (20.0)	10.3 (0.29)	8.8 (0.24)	8.1 (0.25)	215 (6.8)
Associate's degree	91.6 (0.40)	90.9 (0.57)	90.4 (0.45)	594 (11.3)	85.8 (0.56)	85.8 (0.65)	86.2 (0.55)	566 (11.1)	6.4 (0.48)	5.6 (0.43)	4.7 (0.36)	28 (2.2)
Bachelor's or higher degree	93.4 (0.23)	93.5 (0.24)	94.0 (0.24)	1,911 (19.7)	88.0 (0.32)	88.0 (0.32)	88.6 (0.30)	1,801 (19.1)	6.0 (0.24)	5.9 (0.21)	5.8 (0.21)	110 (4.2)

See notes at end of table.

Table 501.20. Labor force participation, employment, and unemployment of persons 16 to 24 years old who are not enrolled in school, by age group, sex, race/ethnicity, and educational attainment: 2015, 2016, and 2017—Continued

[Standard errors appear in parentheses]

Age group, sex, race/ethnicity, and educational attainment	Labor force participation: Labor force participation rate[1] 2015	Labor force participation rate[1] 2016	Labor force participation rate[1] 2017	Number of participants (in thousands) 2017	Employment: Employment to population ratio[2] 2015	Employment to population ratio[2] 2016	Employment to population ratio[2] 2017	Number employed (in thousands) 2017	Unemployment: Unemployment rate[3] 2015	Unemployment rate[3] 2016	Unemployment rate[3] 2017	Number unemployed (in thousands) 2017
1	2	3	4	5	6	7	8	9	10	11	12	13
Male, all education levels	**83.5 (0.21)**	**83.7 (0.18)**	**83.9 (0.18)**	**5,675 (26.3)**	**73.8 (0.27)**	**73.8 (0.24)**	**74.5 (0.22)**	**5,043 (25.0)**	**12.9 (0.21)**	**11.8 (0.20)**	**11.1 (0.16)**	**632 (9.6)**
Less than high school completion	68.5 (0.55)	68.2 (0.66)	67.1 (0.63)	588 (11.5)	54.8 (0.59)	54.8 (0.69)	55.0 (0.71)	482 (10.2)	20.3 (0.53)	19.8 (0.64)	18.0 (0.75)	106 (4.9)
High school completion[4]	81.9 (0.27)	82.6 (0.31)	82.5 (0.27)	2,598 (22.6)	71.6 (0.39)	71.6 (0.38)	71.8 (0.34)	2,261 (20.9)	14.6 (0.37)	13.3 (0.31)	13.0 (0.25)	337 (7.1)
Some college, no degree	88.6 (0.35)	87.9 (0.34)	88.5 (0.35)	1,396 (14.7)	79.8 (0.44)	79.8 (0.44)	81.3 (0.40)	1,283 (13.6)	10.8 (0.37)	9.2 (0.31)	8.1 (0.36)	113 (5.3)
Associate's degree	94.1 (0.47)	93.7 (0.58)	93.6 (0.56)	283 (7.9)	88.2 (0.86)	88.2 (0.85)	88.5 (0.74)	267 (7.6)	7.2 (0.80)	5.9 (0.63)	5.4 (0.53)	15 (1.5)
Bachelor's or higher degree	94.5 (0.34)	94.1 (0.36)	94.5 (0.36)	810 (12.2)	87.7 (0.50)	87.7 (0.47)	87.4 (0.50)	749 (11.7)	6.9 (0.42)	6.9 (0.35)	7.5 (0.40)	61 (3.4)
Female, all education levels	**79.1 (0.21)**	**80.5 (0.23)**	**80.2 (0.24)**	**4,688 (24.2)**	**71.9 (0.28)**	**71.9 (0.24)**	**72.5 (0.27)**	**4,239 (23.3)**	**11.2 (0.23)**	**10.6 (0.19)**	**9.6 (0.19)**	**450 (9.3)**
Less than high school completion	57.6 (0.87)	58.4 (0.93)	57.6 (0.94)	330 (7.5)	44.1 (0.92)	44.1 (0.95)	45.6 (0.88)	262 (6.7)	23.2 (0.93)	24.4 (1.04)	20.8 (0.91)	69 (3.4)
High school completion[4]	74.3 (0.41)	76.1 (0.40)	74.7 (0.44)	1,689 (16.9)	65.6 (0.42)	65.6 (0.44)	65.1 (0.46)	1,471 (16.3)	14.3 (0.37)	13.7 (0.41)	12.9 (0.33)	218 (5.8)
Some college, no degree	83.2 (0.36)	84.4 (0.42)	84.6 (0.41)	1,257 (15.3)	77.3 (0.46)	77.3 (0.52)	77.8 (0.45)	1,155 (15.4)	9.6 (0.41)	8.4 (0.36)	8.1 (0.35)	101 (4.4)
Associate's degree	89.4 (0.67)	88.6 (0.81)	87.8 (0.68)	311 (7.5)	83.9 (0.78)	83.9 (0.93)	84.2 (0.71)	299 (7.3)	5.7 (0.56)	5.3 (0.59)	4.0 (0.40)	12 (1.3)
Bachelor's or higher degree	92.7 (0.29)	93.0 (0.32)	93.7 (0.28)	1,101 (15.2)	88.2 (0.40)	88.2 (0.41)	89.5 (0.37)	1,052 (14.6)	5.4 (0.29)	5.2 (0.26)	4.5 (0.26)	50 (3.0)
White, all education levels	**84.4 (0.17)**	**84.8 (0.20)**	**85.2 (0.19)**	**5,661 (23.4)**	**77.1 (0.21)**	**77.1 (0.25)**	**77.8 (0.24)**	**5,170 (22.5)**	**9.9 (0.18)**	**9.1 (0.18)**	**8.7 (0.16)**	**492 (9.6)**
Less than high school completion	64.6 (0.79)	65.6 (0.81)	63.8 (0.87)	377 (8.2)	51.1 (0.82)	51.1 (0.96)	51.7 (0.86)	305 (6.9)	21.3 (0.76)	22.1 (1.07)	18.9 (0.85)	71 (3.8)
High school completion[4]	80.7 (0.32)	81.3 (0.36)	82.0 (0.32)	2,212 (20.9)	72.1 (0.36)	72.1 (0.40)	72.6 (0.40)	1,958 (19.9)	12.6 (0.29)	11.3 (0.30)	11.5 (0.28)	254 (6.5)
Some college, no degree	87.6 (0.33)	87.3 (0.35)	88.1 (0.27)	1,375 (14.5)	81.3 (0.38)	81.3 (0.41)	82.5 (0.34)	1,287 (13.9)	7.9 (0.29)	6.9 (0.27)	6.4 (0.28)	88 (4.0)
Associate's degree	93.0 (0.38)	93.0 (0.61)	92.2 (0.51)	388 (8.8)	88.4 (0.64)	88.4 (0.84)	88.6 (0.57)	373 (8.5)	5.1 (0.53)	5.0 (0.56)	3.9 (0.38)	15 (1.6)
Bachelor's or higher degree	95.1 (0.24)	95.0 (0.29)	95.2 (0.27)	1,309 (15.1)	90.4 (0.32)	90.4 (0.37)	90.6 (0.35)	1,246 (14.9)	5.0 (0.23)	4.9 (0.20)	4.8 (0.24)	63 (3.2)
Black, all education levels	**75.8 (0.46)**	**77.1 (0.48)**	**76.0 (0.49)**	**1,501 (18.0)**	**62.9 (0.57)**	**62.9 (0.51)**	**62.2 (0.56)**	**1,228 (16.8)**	**20.8 (0.54)**	**18.5 (0.45)**	**18.2 (0.51)**	**272 (8.2)**
Less than high school completion	52.6 (1.35)	53.5 (1.43)	51.2 (1.41)	128 (5.1)	35.0 (1.28)	35.0 (1.45)	33.8 (1.49)	85 (4.5)	38.4 (1.87)	34.6 (1.82)	34.1 (2.13)	44 (3.2)
High school completion[4]	73.7 (0.68)	76.1 (0.74)	73.7 (0.66)	703 (10.7)	60.0 (0.79)	60.0 (0.91)	58.8 (0.85)	560 (10.9)	23.1 (0.77)	21.1 (0.78)	20.2 (0.79)	142 (5.6)
Some college, no degree	85.0 (0.71)	85.9 (0.76)	84.8 (0.79)	454 (10.9)	74.3 (1.03)	74.3 (0.98)	72.5 (0.86)	388 (9.6)	15.9 (0.90)	13.5 (0.83)	14.6 (0.80)	66 (4.1)
Associate's degree	92.0 (1.29)	84.1 (2.28)	87.5 (1.87)	62 (4.3)	76.1 (2.02)	76.1 (2.48)	79.9 (2.28)	57 (3.9)	10.2 (1.59)	9.5 (1.90)	8.6 (1.78)	5 (1.2)
Bachelor's or higher degree	93.5 (1.01)	92.1 (1.05)	93.1 (0.96)	154 (6.1)	83.8 (1.55)	83.8 (1.25)	84.0 (1.44)	139 (5.6)	11.4 (1.30)	9.0 (1.01)	9.7 (1.15)	15 (1.9)
Hispanic, all education levels	**79.4 (0.35)**	**80.6 (0.34)**	**80.3 (0.28)**	**2,427 (17.3)**	**71.3 (0.38)**	**71.3 (0.39)**	**72.6 (0.32)**	**2,194 (17.0)**	**11.7 (0.29)**	**11.6 (0.31)**	**9.6 (0.26)**	**233 (6.5)**
Less than high school completion	69.7 (0.75)	69.3 (0.85)	69.6 (0.91)	359 (9.4)	58.5 (0.94)	58.5 (0.94)	60.1 (0.91)	310 (7.7)	14.7 (0.77)	15.5 (0.83)	13.6 (0.88)	49 (3.7)
High school completion[4]	78.9 (0.51)	80.6 (0.46)	78.7 (0.49)	1,119 (14.3)	70.5 (0.52)	70.5 (0.56)	70.4 (0.48)	1,001 (13.3)	12.5 (0.43)	12.6 (0.46)	10.5 (0.35)	118 (4.3)
Some college, no degree	84.1 (0.59)	85.1 (0.51)	85.6 (0.59)	623 (10.5)	77.2 (0.68)	77.2 (0.66)	79.1 (0.73)	576 (10.2)	10.1 (0.55)	9.3 (0.59)	7.5 (0.55)	47 (3.6)
Associate's degree	88.7 (1.36)	90.1 (1.09)	88.1 (1.40)	109 (4.9)	84.9 (1.60)	84.9 (1.28)	83.6 (1.66)	103 (4.9)	7.5 (1.03)	5.8 (1.01)	5.2 (0.96)	6 (1.0)
Bachelor's or higher degree	91.5 (0.81)	91.1 (0.93)	93.5 (0.66)	216 (6.7)	83.7 (1.04)	83.7 (1.15)	87.9 (0.88)	203 (6.1)	7.2 (0.83)	8.1 (0.89)	6.0 (0.67)	13 (1.6)
Asian, all education levels	**78.8 (0.83)**	**80.1 (0.91)**	**81.7 (0.73)**	**335 (7.4)**	**72.4 (0.95)**	**72.4 (1.05)**	**74.8 (0.84)**	**307 (7.1)**	**9.8 (0.69)**	**9.6 (0.59)**	**8.4 (0.68)**	**28 (2.4)**
Less than high school completion	69.0 (3.34)	67.9 (2.88)	62.7 (3.54)	20 (1.9)	58.9 (3.60)	58.9 (2.98)	55.5 (3.63)	17 (1.7)	18.0 (3.45)	13.2 (2.70)	11.5! (4.21)	2! (0.9)
High school completion[4]	74.9 (2.14)	76.1 (1.92)	76.6 (1.56)	73 (3.8)	69.3 (2.37)	69.3 (1.99)	68.7 (1.86)	65 (3.8)	11.2 (1.70)	8.9 (1.22)	10.3 (1.29)	7 (0.9)
Some college, no degree	78.8 (1.79)	77.5 (2.04)	80.2 (1.68)	65 (3.8)	68.4 (2.10)	68.4 (2.30)	75.3 (1.90)	61 (3.6)	10.3 (1.66)	11.7 (1.64)	6.1 (1.16)	4 (0.8)
Associate's degree	74.4 (4.19)	77.0 (4.25)	87.8 (3.02)	14 (1.4)	69.4 (4.09)	69.4 (4.32)	85.8 (3.23)	14 (1.5)	6.4! (2.09)	9.8! (3.10)	‡ (†)	‡ (†)
Bachelor's or higher degree	83.5 (1.24)	86.0 (1.21)	87.5 (0.88)	163 (5.2)	78.4 (1.41)	78.4 (1.30)	79.9 (0.95)	149 (5.0)	7.9 (0.81)	8.8 (0.85)	8.7 (0.92)	14 (1.6)
American Indian/Alaska Native, all education levels	**69.7 (1.54)**	**70.0 (1.34)**	**66.4 (1.59)**	**73 (3.0)**	**53.5 (1.89)**	**53.5 (1.57)**	**55.2 (1.89)**	**60 (3.1)**	**23.6 (2.08)**	**23.5 (1.70)**	**16.9 (1.75)**	**12 (1.2)**
Less than high school completion	53.6 (3.78)	55.2 (3.79)	45.1 (4.12)	8 (1.0)	32.3 (3.59)	32.3 (3.86)	32.5 (4.44)	5 (0.9)	30.3 (4.70)	41.6 (5.16)	28.0 (5.48)	2 (0.4)
High school completion[4]	70.0 (2.16)	67.8 (2.10)	66.9 (2.03)	39 (2.3)	49.7 (3.00)	49.7 (2.24)	54.0 (2.22)	31 (2.1)	25.9 (3.24)	26.6 (2.42)	19.2 (2.62)	7 (1.1)
Some college, no degree	77.2 (2.84)	80.7 (3.00)	75.1 (3.05)	20 (1.7)	69.7 (3.60)	69.7 (3.43)	65.9 (3.00)	17 (1.6)	21.7 (3.69)	13.6 (2.55)	12.3 (2.39)	2 (0.5)
Associate's degree	90.1 (4.91)	82.9 (6.08)	76.2 (6.89)	3 (0.6)	82.9 (9.47)	82.9 (6.08)	71.7 (7.75)	3 (0.6)	‡ (†)	‡ (†)	‡ (†)	‡ (†)
Bachelor's or higher degree	92.8 (4.21)	93.4 (4.37)	81.1 (7.52)	4 (0.7)	75.8 (5.07)	75.8 (8.72)	79.0 (7.85)	3 (0.7)	‡ (†)	18.8! (8.63)	‡ (†)	‡ (†)

†Not applicable.
!Interpret data with caution. The coefficient of variation (CV) for this estimate is between 30 and 50 percent.
‡Reporting standards not met. Either there are too few cases for a reliable estimate or the coefficient of variation (CV) is 50 percent or greater.
[1]Percentage of the civilian population who are employed or seeking employment.
[2]Number of persons employed as a percentage of the civilian population.
[3]The percentage of persons in the civilian labor force who are not working and who made specific efforts to find employment sometime during the prior 4 weeks.
[4]Includes equivalency credentials, such as the GED credential.
NOTE: Table excludes persons enrolled in school. Estimates are for all nonenrolled civilians in the given age range, including persons living in households and persons living in group quarters (e.g., residential treatment centers or correctional facilities). Race categories exclude persons of Hispanic ethnicity. Totals include racial/ethnic groups not separately shown. Detail may not sum to totals because of rounding.
SOURCE: U.S. Department of Commerce, Census Bureau, American Community Survey (ACS), 2015, 2016, and 2017, unpublished tabulations. (This table was prepared June 2019.)

Table 501.30. Percentage and number of persons 18 to 24 years old who were neither enrolled in school nor working, by age group, high school completion status, sex, and race/ethnicity: 2006 through 2017

[Standard errors appear in parentheses]

Age group, high school completion status, sex, and race/ethnicity	Percent who were neither enrolled in school nor working: 2006	2007	2008	2009	2010	2011	2012	2013	2014	2015	2016	2017: Number (in thousands): Total, all persons 18 to 24 years old	2017: Number (in thousands): Neither enrolled in school nor working	2017: Percent who were neither enrolled in school nor working
1	2	3	4	5	6	7	8	9	10	11	12	13	14	15
18 to 24 years old, all persons	**15.4 (0.07)**	**15.6 (0.09)**	**15.2 (0.08)**	**17.6 (0.09)**	**17.9 (0.09)**	**17.7 (0.08)**	**17.1 (0.08)**	**16.7 (0.11)**	**15.9 (0.09)**	**14.8 (0.09)**	**14.1 (0.09)**	**30,845 (35.3)**	**4,281 (30.4)**	**13.9 (0.10)**
Male	14.5 (0.10)	14.8 (0.12)	14.8 (0.12)	18.1 (0.15)	18.5 (0.12)	18.3 (0.12)	17.6 (0.11)	17.1 (0.14)	16.1 (0.14)	15.2 (0.13)	14.6 (0.12)	15,827 (21.9)	2,265 (20.4)	14.3 (0.12)
Female	16.4 (0.12)	16.5 (0.13)	15.6 (0.13)	17.0 (0.12)	17.2 (0.12)	17.1 (0.11)	16.6 (0.13)	16.3 (0.14)	15.7 (0.12)	14.5 (0.13)	13.6 (0.12)	15,018 (22.2)	2,015 (19.8)	13.4 (0.13)
White	11.8 (0.08)	11.8 (0.09)	11.7 (0.11)	13.8 (0.11)	14.1 (0.10)	14.1 (0.11)	13.5 (0.10)	13.5 (0.12)	12.9 (0.09)	12.1 (0.11)	11.6 (0.12)	16,492 (11.1)	1,862 (21.6)	11.3 (0.13)
Black	25.3 (0.31)	25.5 (0.31)	25.0 (0.30)	27.3 (0.31)	27.9 (0.29)	27.4 (0.28)	27.2 (0.31)	26.2 (0.29)	24.9 (0.30)	22.6 (0.31)	21.0 (0.29)	4,424 (22.3)	955 (14.1)	21.6 (0.32)
Hispanic	20.9 (0.21)	21.2 (0.23)	20.4 (0.24)	22.8 (0.22)	22.6 (0.23)	22.0 (0.22)	21.2 (0.22)	19.8 (0.26)	18.4 (0.24)	17.5 (0.21)	16.6 (0.22)	6,821 (16.3)	1,098 (13.0)	16.1 (0.18)
Asian	9.1 (0.35)	9.0 (0.34)	7.7 (0.30)	9.9 (0.38)	9.4 (0.30)	9.0 (0.32)	8.6 (0.27)	9.0 (0.31)	8.7 (0.30)	8.2 (0.28)	7.6 (0.26)	1,718 (12.3)	128 (3.9)	7.4 (0.23)
Pacific Islander	19.6 (2.51)	21.1 (2.28)	20.3 (2.69)	21.3 (2.01)	23.8 (2.37)	24.2 (2.32)	24.8 (2.35)	21.3 (2.34)	23.7 (2.65)	16.8 (2.04)	15.5 (1.99)	55 (3.0)	11 (1.5)	19.8 (2.68)
American Indian/Alaska Native	30.2 (1.20)	32.7 (1.30)	29.0 (1.31)	34.0 (1.17)	34.3 (1.15)	33.3 (1.29)	32.7 (1.07)	33.3 (1.06)	32.1 (1.15)	31.0 (1.10)	32.0 (1.01)	221 (5.0)	65 (2.5)	29.2 (1.15)
Some other race	16.4 (1.79)	15.6 (1.74)	15.6 (1.86)	18.5 (1.99)	18.2 (2.22)	20.9 (2.26)	14.5 (1.60)	13.6 (1.73)	14.1 (1.54)	20.1 (2.07)	13.4 (1.82)	93 (5.6)	14 (1.8)	15.0 (1.64)
Two or more races	15.0 (0.55)	17.4 (0.69)	16.3 (0.56)	20.1 (0.64)	18.0 (0.63)	18.5 (0.60)	16.6 (0.55)	15.4 (0.48)	16.6 (0.52)	14.7 (0.54)	13.7 (0.49)	1,022 (16.2)	148 (5.0)	14.4 (0.43)
Race/ethnicity by sex														
Male														
White	11.1 (0.12)	11.1 (0.13)	11.3 (0.14)	14.3 (0.17)	14.9 (0.13)	14.7 (0.15)	13.9 (0.14)	13.9 (0.16)	12.9 (0.16)	12.3 (0.15)	11.9 (0.16)	8,493 (8.9)	980 (15.0)	11.5 (0.17)
Black	28.9 (0.42)	28.3 (0.44)	29.0 (0.43)	31.5 (0.44)	32.5 (0.43)	31.8 (0.37)	31.1 (0.45)	30.3 (0.44)	28.6 (0.51)	26.5 (0.41)	24.5 (0.38)	2,244 (14.8)	568 (11.8)	25.3 (0.52)
Hispanic	15.5 (0.31)	16.6 (0.30)	16.3 (0.28)	20.5 (0.32)	20.3 (0.33)	19.9 (0.29)	19.5 (0.31)	18.1 (0.30)	16.9 (0.34)	15.9 (0.27)	15.3 (0.28)	3,512 (11.9)	531 (8.2)	15.1 (0.23)
Asian	9.0 (0.48)	8.4 (0.47)	6.8 (0.42)	9.2 (0.49)	9.3 (0.43)	8.6 (0.40)	8.1 (0.40)	8.3 (0.34)	8.1 (0.40)	8.0 (0.36)	7.7 (0.36)	876 (8.3)	64 (3.3)	7.3 (0.38)
Pacific Islander	18.0 (3.32)	21.1 (2.96)	17.2 (3.43)	17.4 (2.85)	23.0 (2.89)	19.8 (2.67)	23.6 (3.79)	19.8 (2.85)	17.9 (3.23)	10.4 (1.89)	13.5 (2.56)	29 (2.0)	6 (0.9)	19.0 (3.20)
American Indian/Alaska Native	29.8 (1.63)	33.7 (1.83)	29.0 (1.63)	35.7 (1.89)	36.6 (1.77)	35.2 (1.71)	34.1 (1.50)	34.7 (1.44)	33.0 (1.68)	32.0 (1.46)	34.9 (1.81)	110 (3.2)	31 (2.0)	28.1 (1.76)
Some other race	15.0 (2.32)	15.6 (2.41)	16.1 (2.47)	19.7 (2.91)	19.0 (2.66)	18.1 (2.72)	14.8 (2.17)	16.0 (2.22)	13.0 (2.34)	21.1 (3.11)	16.6 (2.69)	45 (3.4)	7 (1.1)	14.5 (2.10)
Two or more races	15.4 (0.76)	17.6 (0.96)	16.8 (0.85)	21.8 (1.02)	19.4 (0.83)	20.5 (0.83)	18.7 (0.82)	16.1 (0.72)	16.3 (0.74)	15.7 (0.83)	15.2 (0.75)	518 (10.6)	79 (3.6)	15.3 (0.63)
Female														
White	12.5 (0.12)	12.6 (0.14)	12.0 (0.15)	13.2 (0.15)	13.4 (0.15)	13.6 (0.15)	13.0 (0.15)	13.2 (0.17)	13.0 (0.13)	11.9 (0.14)	11.3 (0.14)	7,999 (7.9)	882 (12.7)	11.0 (0.16)
Black	21.6 (0.43)	22.6 (0.41)	20.9 (0.41)	22.9 (0.42)	23.4 (0.39)	23.0 (0.36)	23.3 (0.40)	22.1 (0.39)	21.1 (0.38)	18.6 (0.37)	17.2 (0.37)	2,179 (13.8)	387 (7.6)	17.8 (0.36)
Hispanic	27.3 (0.33)	26.4 (0.36)	24.9 (0.37)	25.4 (0.33)	25.2 (0.30)	24.2 (0.34)	23.1 (0.31)	21.8 (0.40)	20.1 (0.35)	19.2 (0.31)	18.1 (0.30)	3,309 (9.2)	567 (9.6)	17.1 (0.29)
Asian	9.2 (0.47)	9.6 (0.47)	8.7 (0.42)	10.6 (0.51)	9.6 (0.41)	9.4 (0.45)	9.2 (0.41)	9.7 (0.45)	9.3 (0.43)	8.3 (0.40)	7.5 (0.38)	842 (9.1)	64 (2.6)	7.6 (0.30)
Pacific Islander	21.5 (3.59)	21.2 (3.60)	23.5 (3.68)	25.8 (3.18)	24.7 (3.17)	28.6 (3.76)	26.2 (3.11)	23.0 (3.17)	30.6 (4.17)	22.6 (3.27)	17.6 (2.77)	25 (1.9)	5 (0.9)	20.8 (3.29)
American Indian/Alaska Native	30.6 (1.56)	31.6 (1.58)	29.0 (1.76)	32.3 (1.65)	31.9 (1.51)	31.3 (1.65)	31.2 (1.59)	31.9 (1.46)	31.2 (1.53)	30.0 (1.61)	28.9 (1.46)	111 (3.4)	34 (1.7)	30.3 (1.33)
Some other race	18.1 (2.45)	15.6 (2.55)	15.1 (2.84)	17.1 (2.82)	17.5 (3.21)	23.5 (3.24)	14.1 (2.42)	11.4 (2.20)	15.3 (2.36)	19.1 (2.85)	10.2 (2.36)	48 (4.0)	8 (1.4)	15.6 (2.58)
Two or more races	14.6 (0.84)	17.2 (1.00)	15.9 (0.79)	18.3 (0.92)	16.5 (0.88)	16.7 (0.84)	14.5 (0.68)	14.7 (0.61)	16.9 (0.61)	13.8 (0.68)	12.1 (0.63)	504 (9.5)	68 (3.6)	13.5 (0.67)
18 and 19 years old, all persons	**11.8 (0.15)**	**12.4 (0.13)**	**12.1 (0.14)**	**13.8 (0.15)**	**13.9 (0.16)**	**13.5 (0.16)**	**13.0 (0.15)**	**12.5 (0.18)**	**11.6 (0.15)**	**11.1 (0.13)**	**10.5 (0.16)**	**8,817 (26.7)**	**950 (13.9)**	**10.8 (0.15)**
20 to 24 years old, all persons	**16.9 (0.09)**	**17.0 (0.11)**	**16.5 (0.10)**	**19.1 (0.10)**	**19.6 (0.11)**	**19.4 (0.10)**	**18.7 (0.11)**	**18.3 (0.12)**	**17.6 (0.11)**	**16.3 (0.12)**	**15.5 (0.11)**	**22,028 (30.6)**	**3,331 (25.1)**	**15.1 (0.12)**
Male	15.5 (0.13)	15.6 (0.14)	15.7 (0.13)	19.4 (0.17)	20.0 (0.15)	19.6 (0.16)	18.9 (0.14)	18.5 (0.16)	17.4 (0.17)	16.3 (0.17)	15.7 (0.15)	11,309 (21.8)	1,722 (16.8)	15.2 (0.15)
Female	18.4 (0.13)	18.5 (0.17)	17.4 (0.16)	18.9 (0.15)	19.2 (0.16)	19.3 (0.14)	18.5 (0.17)	18.2 (0.16)	17.7 (0.16)	16.2 (0.17)	15.3 (0.14)	10,719 (20.4)	1,609 (16.7)	15.0 (0.16)
White	13.0 (0.10)	13.0 (0.11)	12.8 (0.13)	15.2 (0.14)	15.5 (0.14)	15.6 (0.14)	14.9 (0.13)	15.0 (0.15)	14.3 (0.12)	13.4 (0.12)	12.9 (0.14)	11,848 (14.5)	1,476 (17.9)	12.5 (0.15)
Black	28.0 (0.37)	28.0 (0.39)	27.6 (0.35)	30.1 (0.34)	31.2 (0.37)	30.5 (0.33)	30.1 (0.41)	28.6 (0.37)	27.8 (0.36)	24.9 (0.38)	23.2 (0.32)	3,156 (19.7)	747 (11.7)	23.7 (0.39)
Hispanic	22.4 (0.25)	22.5 (0.28)	21.6 (0.26)	24.3 (0.26)	24.5 (0.25)	23.8 (0.25)	22.8 (0.26)	21.4 (0.31)	19.8 (0.28)	18.8 (0.26)	18.1 (0.27)	4,833 (15.5)	827 (10.8)	17.1 (0.22)
Asian	10.4 (0.43)	10.5 (0.44)	9.1 (0.38)	11.4 (0.47)	10.8 (0.38)	10.3 (0.42)	10.2 (0.32)	10.4 (0.39)	10.1 (0.40)	9.5 (0.36)	9.0 (0.35)	1,247 (11.7)	104 (3.9)	8.3 (0.31)
Pacific Islander	22.2 (2.95)	19.6 (2.59)	22.2 (2.99)	24.5 (2.60)	26.2 (2.88)	27.8 (2.88)	26.5 (2.81)	19.9 (2.59)	22.3 (3.23)	19.8 (2.44)	16.6 (2.52)	38 (2.6)	8 (1.3)	20.2 (3.23)
American Indian/Alaska Native	32.9 (1.54)	37.3 (1.69)	31.9 (1.45)	36.9 (1.32)	37.2 (1.45)	36.4 (1.49)	34.3 (1.25)	37.5 (1.37)	36.5 (1.37)	33.3 (1.41)	35.2 (1.31)	155 (3.9)	49 (2.2)	31.6 (1.52)
Some other race	18.0 (2.26)	17.5 (2.22)	16.8 (2.45)	20.5 (2.71)	18.1 (2.74)	24.7 (2.73)	13.6 (1.85)	13.9 (2.01)	15.5 (1.84)	19.6 (2.39)	14.6 (2.23)	71 (4.9)	11 (1.4)	15.0 (1.63)
Two or more races	16.0 (0.70)	19.4 (0.90)	17.8 (0.71)	23.0 (0.78)	20.9 (0.90)	21.1 (0.80)	18.2 (0.68)	17.6 (0.71)	19.1 (0.72)	16.2 (0.71)	15.0 (0.58)	680 (12.8)	110 (4.8)	16.2 (0.62)
Has completed high school,[1] all persons	13.1 (0.09)	13.2 (0.11)	12.8 (0.11)	15.3 (0.11)	15.8 (0.12)	15.9 (0.09)	15.4 (0.12)	15.2 (0.13)	14.8 (0.11)	13.7 (0.11)	13.1 (0.11)	20,332 (35.0)	2,625 (22.0)	12.9 (0.11)
Male	12.0 (0.14)	12.0 (0.14)	12.1 (0.15)	15.6 (0.17)	16.1 (0.16)	16.2 (0.15)	15.6 (0.15)	15.4 (0.16)	14.7 (0.16)	13.7 (0.15)	13.2 (0.15)	10,296 (22.2)	1,327 (13.3)	12.9 (0.13)
Female	14.2 (0.14)	14.4 (0.17)	13.5 (0.16)	14.9 (0.15)	15.4 (0.16)	15.6 (0.14)	15.2 (0.17)	15.0 (0.16)	14.9 (0.15)	13.8 (0.15)	13.0 (0.15)	10,036 (22.2)	1,298 (15.7)	12.9 (0.16)

See notes at end of table.

Table 501.30. Percentage and number of persons 18 to 24 years old who were neither enrolled in school nor working, by age group, high school completion status, sex, and race/ethnicity: 2006 through 2017—Continued

[Standard errors appear in parentheses]

Age group, high school completion status, sex, and race/ethnicity	Percent who were neither enrolled in school nor working											2017		
												Number (in thousands)		Percent who were neither enrolled in school nor working
	2006	2007	2008	2009	2010	2011	2012	2013	2014	2015	2016	Total, all persons 18 to 24 years old	Neither enrolled in school nor working	
1	2	3	4	5	6	7	8	9	10	11	12	13	14	15
White	10.5 (0.10)	10.5 (0.11)	10.3 (0.13)	12.6 (0.14)	12.9 (0.13)	13.0 (0.13)	12.6 (0.13)	12.8 (0.15)	12.4 (0.11)	11.5 (0.12)	11.0 (0.13)	11,175 (16.3)	1,191 (16.0)	10.7 (0.14)
Black	21.8 (0.41)	21.8 (0.42)	21.6 (0.34)	24.1 (0.35)	25.1 (0.40)	24.8 (0.32)	24.9 (0.41)	23.5 (0.38)	23.4 (0.39)	21.1 (0.40)	19.5 (0.37)	2,849 (20.8)	581 (11.0)	20.4 (0.38)
Hispanic	17.4 (0.26)	17.6 (0.27)	16.4 (0.27)	19.0 (0.27)	19.5 (0.29)	19.8 (0.25)	18.5 (0.27)	17.7 (0.32)	16.4 (0.28)	15.8 (0.25)	15.2 (0.29)	4,235 (18.1)	621 (9.8)	14.7 (0.23)
Asian	9.1 (0.39)	9.1 (0.40)	8.3 (0.40)	10.0 (0.44)	9.4 (0.37)	9.1 (0.41)	8.9 (0.32)	9.5 (0.37)	8.9 (0.37)	8.5 (0.33)	8.2 (0.35)	1,202 (11.3)	90 (3.4)	7.5 (0.28)
Pacific Islander	17.6 (3.08)	17.0 (2.67)	20.4 (3.31)	19.4 (2.61)	24.8 (3.04)	25.0 (2.82)	22.4 (2.72)	18.8 (2.67)	17.6 (3.34)	17.7 (2.36)	15.8 (2.68)	36 (2.6)	7 (1.3)	19.2 (3.40)
American Indian/Alaska Native	25.7 (1.67)	29.4 (2.08)	26.0 (1.45)	29.2 (1.45)	29.6 (1.43)	30.9 (1.71)	29.6 (1.26)	32.9 (1.52)	32.0 (1.40)	27.9 (1.56)	30.8 (1.35)	135 (4.1)	38 (2.0)	28.0 (1.47)
Some other race	13.7 (2.10)	12.6 (1.98)	14.6 (2.53)	17.8 (2.61)	14.2 (2.62)	19.6 (2.59)	12.8 (1.89)	12.2 (1.94)	11.4 (1.80)	17.9 (2.47)	11.9 (1.89)	65 (4.5)	8 (1.2)	12.4 (1.55)
Two or more races	12.7 (0.72)	15.5 (0.94)	14.0 (0.64)	19.6 (0.81)	17.7 (0.93)	17.6 (0.76)	15.6 (0.70)	14.8 (0.69)	16.7 (0.73)	13.6 (0.65)	12.9 (0.57)	636 (12.2)	91 (4.5)	14.2 (0.64)
Has not completed high school, all persons	41.1 (0.37)	43.0 (0.40)	42.8 (0.36)	47.5 (0.35)	47.8 (0.35)	47.9 (0.45)	48.2 (0.39)	46.0 (0.47)	44.8 (0.49)	42.7 (0.48)	42.6 (0.49)	1,696 (19.1)	706 (11.2)	41.6 (0.56)
Male	34.0 (0.48)	36.0 (0.45)	37.0 (0.52)	42.4 (0.47)	43.3 (0.45)	42.3 (0.51)	43.9 (0.58)	41.5 (0.60)	40.3 (0.64)	39.7 (0.55)	39.4 (0.62)	1,013 (14.7)	394 (8.3)	39.0 (0.64)
Female	52.1 (0.65)	53.6 (0.67)	51.5 (0.61)	55.3 (0.56)	55.0 (0.69)	56.3 (0.74)	54.5 (0.71)	52.9 (0.68)	51.4 (0.63)	47.1 (0.87)	47.6 (0.92)	683 (11.7)	311 (7.1)	45.6 (0.87)
White	40.0 (0.50)	42.5 (0.66)	42.6 (0.61)	48.1 (0.67)	49.2 (0.62)	51.0 (0.68)	48.9 (0.66)	46.4 (0.70)	44.5 (0.79)	42.7 (0.69)	43.0 (0.88)	673 (10.7)	285 (7.1)	42.4 (0.79)
Black	58.0 (1.10)	58.9 (0.95)	58.8 (1.02)	62.1 (0.76)	64.6 (0.67)	63.1 (1.00)	63.3 (0.95)	60.0 (1.02)	58.7 (0.93)	55.9 (1.13)	54.2 (1.35)	307 (8.1)	166 (6.1)	54.1 (1.41)
Hispanic	34.3 (0.58)	35.2 (0.73)	35.5 (0.59)	39.3 (0.54)	39.3 (0.56)	38.1 (0.70)	40.5 (0.79)	38.0 (0.78)	37.1 (0.82)	35.6 (0.83)	36.4 (0.83)	597 (11.5)	206 (6.2)	34.5 (0.88)
Asian	36.2 (2.49)	38.2 (3.22)	26.6 (2.48)	38.3 (2.89)	37.8 (2.66)	32.0 (2.27)	37.7 (3.09)	36.4 (3.26)	38.3 (2.73)	31.7 (2.93)	30.4 (2.63)	45 (3.4)	14 (1.7)	30.7 (2.82)
Pacific Islander	49.6 (9.53)	43.1 (10.09)	36.5 (8.89)	58.9 (7.61)	‡ (†)	48.4 (9.11)	49.2 (10.64)	‡ (†)	56.4 (8.67)	‡ (†)	23.6! (7.13)	2 (0.6)	‡ (†)	34.4! (12.22)
American Indian/Alaska Native	58.5 (2.96)	67.5 (3.29)	53.6 (3.82)	66.9 (3.65)	67.1 (3.02)	58.1 (3.66)	57.6 (3.46)	58.0 (3.15)	58.2 (2.89)	56.1 (3.29)	57.5 (3.56)	20 (1.4)	11 (1.1)	56.3 (4.03)
Some other race	43.2 (9.41)	40.4 (6.54)	29.6 (7.61)	41.1 (8.85)	39.8 (7.57)	61.6 (9.79)	23.5! (7.85)	29.2 (8.04)	‡ (†)	39.6 (11.25)	37.7 (10.56)	6 (1.5)	‡ (†)	45.6 (7.32)
Two or more races	48.1 (3.32)	51.1 (3.33)	53.0 (3.29)	56.5 (3.05)	49.4 (3.46)	56.4 (3.09)	47.1 (2.76)	49.7 (3.22)	50.8 (2.55)	55.2 (3.20)	43.1 (3.19)	45 (3.0)	19 (2.0)	43.5 (3.17)

†Not applicable.
!Interpret data with caution. The coefficient of variation (CV) for this estimate is between 30 and 50 percent.
‡Reporting standards not met. Either there are too few cases for a reliable estimate or the coefficient of variation (CV) is 50 percent or greater.
[1]Includes completing high school through equivalency programs, such as a GED program.

NOTE: Data are based on sample surveys of the entire population in the given age range residing within the United States, including both noninstitutionalized persons (e.g., those living in households, college housing, or military housing located within the United States) and institutionalized persons (e.g., those living in prisons, nursing facilities, or other healthcare facilities). Institutionalized persons made up 1 percent of all 18- to 24-year-olds in 2017. Race categories exclude persons of Hispanic ethnicity. Detail may not sum to totals because of rounding.
SOURCE: U.S. Department of Commerce, Census Bureau, American Community Survey (ACS), 2006 through 2017. (This table was prepared October 2018.)

Table 501.40. Percentage distribution of 25- to 34-year-olds with various levels of educational attainment, by labor force status, sex, race/ethnicity, and U.S. nativity and citizenship status: 2017

[Standard errors appear in parentheses]

Sex, race/ethnicity, and U.S. nativity and citizenship status	All 25- to 34-year-olds			Less than high school completion			High school completion[1]			Some college, no bachelor's degree[2]			Bachelor's or higher degree		
	In labor force			In labor force			In labor force			In labor force			In labor force		
	Employed	Unemployed (seeking employment)	Not in labor force	Employed	Unemployed (seeking employment)	Not in labor force	Employed	Unemployed (seeking employment)	Not in labor force	Employed	Unemployed (seeking employment)	Not in labor force	Employed	Unemployed (seeking employment)	Not in labor force
1	2	3	4	5	6	7	8	9	10	11	12	13	14	15	16
Total[3]	**78.1 (0.08)**	**4.6 (0.04)**	**17.4 (0.08)**	**55.9 (0.32)**	**7.4 (0.18)**	**36.6 (0.29)**	**70.9 (0.20)**	**6.3 (0.11)**	**22.8 (0.19)**	**79.4 (0.13)**	**4.6 (0.08)**	**16.0 (0.12)**	**87.4 (0.11)**	**2.6 (0.05)**	**10.0 (0.11)**
Sex															
Male	82.1 (0.10)	4.9 (0.06)	13.0 (0.09)	65.1 (0.39)	7.4 (0.23)	27.5 (0.32)	76.5 (0.25)	6.5 (0.15)	17.1 (0.22)	84.0 (0.19)	4.6 (0.12)	11.4 (0.17)	90.9 (0.16)	2.9 (0.09)	6.2 (0.13)
Female	74.0 (0.12)	4.2 (0.06)	21.8 (0.11)	43.4 (0.47)	7.5 (0.32)	49.1 (0.50)	63.2 (0.33)	6.2 (0.15)	30.6 (0.31)	74.9 (0.21)	4.6 (0.10)	20.5 (0.19)	84.6 (0.15)	2.3 (0.05)	13.1 (0.15)
Race/ethnicity															
White	80.8 (0.11)	3.7 (0.05)	15.4 (0.10)	51.2 (0.60)	8.0 (0.33)	40.8 (0.58)	72.1 (0.26)	5.8 (0.13)	22.1 (0.27)	80.2 (0.16)	3.8 (0.09)	16.0 (0.15)	89.6 (0.13)	2.1 (0.05)	8.3 (0.12)
Black	72.1 (0.28)	8.1 (0.20)	19.8 (0.22)	39.7 (0.96)	13.4 (0.71)	46.9 (0.99)	64.1 (0.54)	10.2 (0.33)	25.7 (0.46)	78.1 (0.37)	7.1 (0.26)	14.8 (0.34)	87.7 (0.41)	4.3 (0.30)	8.0 (0.35)
Hispanic	76.1 (0.19)	4.6 (0.10)	19.3 (0.19)	65.3 (0.44)	5.1 (0.21)	29.6 (0.41)	73.8 (0.36)	4.9 (0.18)	21.3 (0.34)	79.7 (0.34)	4.6 (0.19)	15.7 (0.30)	86.3 (0.37)	3.1 (0.20)	10.6 (0.31)
Asian	75.5 (0.37)	3.5 (0.12)	21.0 (0.33)	57.8 (1.82)	4.7 (0.96)	37.5 (1.76)	70.0 (1.12)	4.1 (0.41)	25.9 (1.04)	75.4 (0.95)	4.3 (0.32)	20.3 (0.86)	77.7 (0.41)	3.1 (0.15)	19.2 (0.38)
Pacific Islander	73.6 (1.99)	4.0 (1.01)	22.4 (1.78)	48.6 (6.52)	‡ (†)	48.9 (6.87)	72.2 (3.59)	3.8! (1.38)	24.0 (3.28)	76.0 (2.81)	6.3! (2.01)	17.6 (2.64)	86.8 (4.33)	‡ (†)	11.9! (4.16)
American Indian/Alaska Native[4]	60.5 (1.13)	9.4 (0.65)	30.0 (1.13)	36.6 (3.03)	12.7 (2.03)	50.7 (3.31)	54.8 (1.87)	10.7 (1.20)	34.4 (1.80)	68.0 (1.71)	8.0 (0.93)	23.9 (1.56)	82.4 (2.17)	6.3 (1.51)	11.3 (1.80)
American Indian	61.2 (1.23)	9.3 (0.66)	29.6 (1.16)	37.1 (3.31)	10.5 (1.67)	52.4 (3.47)	56.2 (2.05)	10.0 (1.22)	33.8 (1.99)	68.0 (1.80)	8.9 (1.09)	23.2 (1.45)	81.0 (2.35)	7.1 (1.72)	11.9 (1.99)
Alaska Native	58.2 (4.57)	20.3 (4.17)	21.5 (2.87)	19.3 (5.43)	42.9 (10.93)	37.8 (8.52)	54.2 (6.22)	21.9 (6.30)	23.9 (4.77)	81.3 (5.78)	6.9! (2.41)	11.8 ! (5.04)	‡ (†)	‡ (†)	‡ (†)
Two or more races	76.5 (0.59)	5.5 (0.29)	18.0 (0.50)	44.9 (3.11)	9.9 (1.64)	45.2 (2.94)	67.8 (1.46)	7.7 (0.69)	24.5 (1.30)	77.4 (0.95)	5.1 (0.53)	17.6 (0.81)	85.5 (0.73)	4.0 (0.39)	10.5 (0.61)
Race/ethnicity by sex															
Male															
White	84.7 (0.13)	4.3 (0.07)	11.1 (0.11)	59.5 (0.75)	8.6 (0.45)	31.8 (0.66)	78.3 (0.29)	6.0 (0.17)	15.6 (0.26)	85.7 (0.21)	4.0 (0.12)	10.3 (0.19)	92.3 (0.14)	2.6 (0.09)	5.2 (0.13)
Black	69.4 (0.42)	8.6 (0.29)	22.0 (0.32)	35.6 (1.27)	13.1 (0.84)	51.3 (1.31)	62.3 (0.80)	10.3 (0.54)	27.4 (0.67)	78.5 (0.65)	7.2 (0.44)	14.3 (0.55)	88.1 (0.68)	5.0 (0.52)	6.9 (0.59)
Hispanic	83.6 (0.22)	4.5 (0.14)	11.9 (0.21)	79.0 (0.52)	4.8 (0.27)	16.2 (0.47)	82.4 (0.46)	4.9 (0.25)	12.7 (0.39)	85.2 (0.39)	4.4 (0.27)	10.5 (0.35)	90.2 (0.51)	3.5 (0.33)	6.2 (0.36)
Asian	84.1 (0.45)	3.4 (0.20)	12.5 (0.38)	72.4 (2.20)	4.1 (1.05)	23.5 (2.09)	78.8 (1.34)	4.0 (0.59)	17.1 (1.25)	79.7 (1.13)	5.0 (0.53)	15.3 (1.03)	87.2 (0.51)	2.7 (0.21)	10.0 (0.44)
Pacific Islander	81.4 (2.38)	3.1! (1.24)	15.5 (2.19)	62.1 (9.31)	‡ (†)	37.9 (9.31)	81.8 (4.02)	‡ (†)	15.8 (3.78)	80.2 (3.88)	6.6! (3.04)	13.3 (3.37)	97.3 (1.82)	‡ (†)	‡ (†)
American Indian/Alaska Native[4]	61.5 (1.72)	9.9 (0.92)	28.6 (1.61)	41.5 (3.76)	10.0 (2.07)	48.5 (4.13)	55.9 (2.58)	11.8 (1.72)	32.2 (2.28)	69.0 (2.52)	8.6 (1.54)	22.4 (2.37)	87.8 (3.16)	7.6! (2.50)	4.6! (1.89)
American Indian	62.5 (1.83)	9.7 (0.95)	27.8 (1.67)	43.5 (4.17)	9.0 (2.04)	47.6 (4.47)	56.7 (2.80)	10.5 (1.71)	32.7 (2.71)	69.8 (2.53)	9.7 (1.80)	20.5 (2.01)	86.8 (3.50)	8.0! (2.74)	5.2! (2.17)
Alaska Native	55.6 (6.43)	19.2! (6.07)	25.2 (3.99)	20.0! (6.82)	31.3! (12.50)	48.7 (10.79)	50.5 (8.66)	23.0! (8.88)	26.5 (6.06)	90.2 (6.51)	‡ (†)	‡ (†)	‡ (†)	‡ (†)	‡ (†)
Two or more races	78.7 (0.79)	5.8 (0.39)	15.5 (0.67)	52.3 (4.35)	10.8 (2.34)	36.9 (4.08)	72.7 (1.76)	7.5 (1.02)	19.8 (1.35)	80.1 (1.16)	4.3 (0.61)	15.6 (1.07)	86.8 (1.11)	5.0 (0.72)	8.2 (0.84)
Female															
White	76.9 (0.16)	3.2 (0.06)	19.8 (0.16)	39.7 (0.82)	7.2 (0.47)	53.1 (0.88)	63.0 (0.44)	5.4 (0.20)	31.6 (0.46)	74.6 (0.26)	3.7 (0.12)	21.7 (0.25)	87.5 (0.19)	1.7 (0.06)	10.8 (0.18)
Black	74.7 (0.39)	7.5 (0.24)	17.8 (0.31)	45.4 (1.54)	13.9 (1.01)	40.7 (1.57)	66.3 (0.68)	10.1 (0.48)	23.6 (0.67)	77.8 (0.56)	7.0 (0.35)	15.1 (0.52)	87.5 (0.48)	3.7 (0.29)	8.8 (0.38)
Hispanic	68.0 (0.33)	4.6 (0.15)	27.4 (0.31)	45.9 (0.70)	5.6 (0.39)	48.4 (0.70)	62.6 (0.59)	4.9 (0.28)	32.5 (0.58)	74.6 (0.59)	4.9 (0.25)	20.6 (0.53)	83.3 (0.48)	2.8 (0.23)	13.9 (0.45)
Asian	67.6 (0.49)	3.6 (0.18)	28.8 (0.47)	44.4 (2.34)	5.3 (1.39)	50.4 (2.40)	61.4 (1.73)	4.2 (0.62)	34.4 (1.72)	70.8 (1.31)	3.5 (0.44)	25.7 (1.22)	69.3 (0.56)	3.4 (0.19)	27.3 (0.57)
Pacific Islander	65.6 (3.23)	4.9 (1.43)	29.4 (2.94)	33.1 (8.36)	‡ (†)	61.6 (9.10)	61.6 (5.25)	5.4! (2.45)	33.0 (4.58)	71.6 (4.07)	6.1! (2.61)	22.3 (4.06)	79.1 (7.34)	‡ (†)	18.8! (7.10)
American Indian/Alaska Native[4]	59.6 (1.54)	8.9 (0.84)	31.5 (1.42)	29.1 (4.51)	16.8 (4.01)	54.2 (4.60)	53.5 (3.10)	9.4 (1.72)	37.1 (2.95)	67.3 (2.29)	7.5 (1.22)	25.2 (2.00)	77.7 (3.26)	5.1! (1.70)	17.2 (3.11)
American Indian	59.7 (1.60)	8.9 (0.85)	31.4 (1.44)	26.6 (5.17)	12.9 (3.03)	60.4 (4.94)	55.5 (3.32)	9.5 (1.91)	35.0 (3.10)	66.5 (2.31)	8.2 (1.43)	25.4 (1.87)	75.6 (3.60)	6.2! (2.05)	18.2 (3.39)
Alaska Native	61.2 (6.85)	21.7 (6.43)	17.1 (4.38)	‡ (†)	‡ (†)	‡ (†)	61.4 (7.24)	19.8! (6.28)	18.8! (6.29)	74.3 (8.05)	8.7! (3.07)	17.0 ! (8.10)	‡ (†)	‡ (†)	‡ (†)
Two or more races	74.3 (0.82)	5.2 (0.39)	20.5 (0.69)	36.8 (3.88)	8.8 (2.26)	54.4 (3.60)	60.4 (2.20)	8.0 (1.01)	31.5 (2.18)	74.6 (1.45)	5.9 (0.76)	19.5 (1.25)	84.5 (0.98)	3.2 (0.41)	12.3 (0.91)
Nativity															
Hispanic															
U.S.-born[5]	76.7 (0.27)	5.1 (0.15)	18.2 (0.24)	55.7 (0.88)	7.8 (0.48)	36.5 (0.78)	73.0 (0.50)	5.8 (0.23)	21.2 (0.46)	79.6 (0.40)	4.9 (0.22)	15.4 (0.35)	88.3 (0.38)	3.1 (0.22)	8.6 (0.32)
Foreign-born	75.1 (0.32)	3.6 (0.12)	21.2 (0.33)	70.5 (0.56)	3.7 (0.24)	25.8 (0.53)	74.9 (0.59)	3.7 (0.26)	21.5 (0.60)	79.9 (0.63)	3.7 (0.30)	16.4 (0.59)	80.9 (0.77)	3.2 (0.36)	15.9 (0.70)
Asian															
U.S.-born[5]	82.1 (0.50)	3.8 (0.20)	14.1 (0.48)	41.0 (4.20)	10.8 (2.59)	48.2 (3.59)	72.7 (1.61)	5.4 (0.70)	21.9 (1.54)	79.7 (1.13)	3.9 (0.48)	16.4 (1.03)	86.5 (0.51)	3.1 (0.25)	10.3 (0.51)
Foreign-born	72.4 (0.47)	3.4 (0.15)	24.3 (0.42)	62.2 (1.86)	3.1 (0.93)	34.7 (1.83)	68.6 (1.35)	3.5 (0.50)	27.8 (1.25)	72.2 (1.22)	4.6 (0.45)	23.2 (1.13)	73.8 (0.53)	3.1 (0.18)	23.1 (0.47)
Citizenship status															
U.S.-born citizen	78.9 (0.08)	4.7 (0.05)	16.4 (0.08)	48.8 (0.44)	9.5 (0.27)	41.7 (0.39)	70.6 (0.22)	6.8 (0.12)	22.7 (0.22)	79.7 (0.13)	4.7 (0.09)	15.6 (0.13)	89.8 (0.11)	2.4 (0.05)	7.8 (0.10)
Naturalized citizen	80.7 (0.33)	3.7 (0.19)	15.6 (0.29)	69.9 (1.57)	4.3 (0.68)	25.8 (1.36)	75.1 (0.82)	4.4 (0.42)	20.5 (0.71)	80.5 (0.73)	3.9 (0.33)	15.6 (0.68)	85.6 (0.45)	3.2 (0.25)	11.2 (0.36)
Noncitizen	70.9 (0.29)	3.7 (0.11)	25.4 (0.29)	68.5 (0.53)	3.8 (0.25)	27.7 (0.49)	71.6 (0.54)	3.9 (0.28)	24.6 (0.51)	73.2 (0.72)	3.8 (0.32)	23.0 (0.66)	71.1 (0.50)	3.5 (0.19)	25.3 (0.46)

†Not applicable.
!Interpret data with caution. The coefficient of variation (CV) for this estimate is between 30 and 50 percent.
‡Reporting standards not met. Either there are too few cases for a reliable estimate or the coefficient of variation (CV) is 50 percent or greater.
[1]Data are for all persons with high school completion as their highest level of education, including those with equivalency credentials, such as the GED credential.
[2]Includes persons with no college degree as well as those with an associate's degree.
[3]Total includes other racial/ethnic groups not shown separately.
[4]Includes persons reporting American Indian alone, persons reporting Alaska Native alone, and persons from American Indian and/or Alaska Native tribes specified or not specified.
[5]Includes those born in the 50 states, the District of Columbia, Puerto Rico, American Samoa, Guam, the U.S. Virgin Islands, and the Northern Marianas, as well as those born abroad to U.S.-citizen parents.
NOTE: Estimates are for the entire civilian population in the given age range, including persons living in households and persons living in group quarters (e.g., college residence halls, residential treatment centers, or correctional facilities). The labor force consists of all employed persons plus those seeking employment. Detail may not sum to totals because of rounding. Race categories exclude persons of Hispanic ethnicity.
SOURCE: U.S. Department of Commerce, Census Bureau, American Community Survey (ACS), 2017. (This table was prepared June 2019.)

Table 501.50. Employment to population ratios of persons 16 to 64 years old, by age group and highest level of educational attainment: Selected years, 1975 through 2018

[Standard errors appear in parentheses]

Age group and highest level of educational attainment	1975	1980	1985	1990	1995	2000	2005	2010	2011	2012	2014	2015	2016	2017	2018
1	2	3	4	5	6	7	8	9	10	11	12	13	14	15	16
16 to 19 years old, all education levels[1]	**— (†)**	**— (†)**	**— (†)**	**60.8 (2.03)**	**58.0 (2.13)**	**62.6 (2.09)**	**53.7 (1.40)**	**43.2 (1.30)**	**44.8 (1.40)**	**45.8 (1.43)**	**51.0 (1.67)**	**49.2 (1.36)**	**50.4 (1.55)**	**56.4 (1.57)**	**55.7 (1.48)**
Less than high school completion	— (†)	— (†)	— (†)	44.2 (3.08)	44.0 (3.13)	52.2 (3.19)	39.4 (2.01)	29.4 (1.83)	31.1 (2.21)	28.5 (2.05)	39.7 (2.63)	35.3 (2.03)	35.6 (2.05)	39.6 (2.27)	40.4 (2.52)
High school completion[2]	— (†)	— (†)	— (†)	74.2 (2.54)	70.1 (2.99)	70.1 (2.92)	65.0 (2.04)	51.1 (1.84)	50.3 (2.01)	53.6 (1.90)	58.5 (2.22)	56.1 (1.83)	58.7 (2.28)	66.4 (1.96)	62.9 (1.96)
At least some college	— (†)	— (†)	— (†)	76.8 (9.32)	71.6 (6.38)	78.2 (6.22)	66.6 (4.54)	57.5 (3.99)	61.5 (3.63)	64.3 (4.07)	60.5 (5.27)	65.7 (3.40)	69.1 (3.66)	69.6 (3.94)	70.9 (3.44)
20 to 24 years old, all education levels[1]	**— (†)**	**— (†)**	**— (†)**	**75.6 (0.90)**	**73.7 (0.93)**	**77.4 (0.93)**	**73.2 (0.66)**	**65.5 (0.72)**	**67.0 (0.59)**	**68.7 (0.67)**	**69.4 (0.74)**	**71.4 (0.66)**	**72.3 (0.59)**	**75.9 (0.64)**	**76.3 (0.59)**
Less than high school completion	— (†)	— (†)	— (†)	54.4 (2.29)	52.7 (2.41)	60.8 (2.43)	55.7 (1.27)	44.4 (1.58)	46.8 (1.71)	47.7 (1.95)	46.6 (2.62)	51.4 (2.17)	48.0 (2.08)	54.5 (2.30)	51.4 (2.25)
High school completion[2]	— (†)	— (†)	— (†)	76.6 (1.26)	72.2 (1.46)	76.5 (1.46)	72.3 (0.91)	61.5 (1.01)	62.9 (1.07)	64.2 (0.99)	63.7 (1.31)	66.9 (1.01)	69.4 (1.03)	72.1 (1.05)	72.4 (0.94)
Some college, no bachelor's degree[3]	— (†)	— (†)	— (†)	85.6 (1.69)	83.6 (1.52)	86.6 (1.49)	80.3 (1.19)	72.9 (1.27)	73.2 (1.01)	75.3 (1.19)	75.0 (1.29)	76.4 (1.03)	76.7 (1.02)	80.3 (0.99)	82.7 (1.07)
Bachelor's or higher degree	— (†)	— (†)	— (†)	93.3 (1.57)	90.9 (1.76)	87.8 (2.07)	89.3 (1.16)	86.5 (1.37)	85.2 (1.41)	87.3 (1.16)	88.1 (1.47)	88.9 (1.05)	88.1 (1.12)	89.3 (1.04)	87.7 (1.28)
25 to 64 years old, all education levels	**65.8 (0.33)**	**70.2 (0.30)**	**71.6 (0.30)**	**75.0 (0.29)**	**75.5 (0.28)**	**77.7 (0.27)**	**75.0 (0.19)**	**71.5 (0.19)**	**71.2 (0.19)**	**71.7 (0.18)**	**72.3 (0.26)**	**73.1 (0.19)**	**73.8 (0.18)**	**74.4 (0.17)**	**74.9 (0.18)**
Less than high school completion	55.3 (0.62)	55.5 (0.66)	53.1 (0.74)	54.9 (0.80)	53.8 (0.85)	57.8 (0.91)	57.2 (0.51)	52.1 (0.60)	51.1 (0.56)	52.9 (0.60)	54.9 (0.78)	54.7 (0.58)	56.6 (0.62)	55.6 (0.65)	56.8 (0.61)
High school completion[2]	65.7 (0.53)	70.4 (0.48)	70.7 (0.48)	74.4 (0.46)	73.3 (0.49)	75.5 (0.49)	71.5 (0.34)	67.0 (0.36)	66.2 (0.39)	66.5 (0.35)	67.0 (0.44)	67.3 (0.37)	67.6 (0.39)	68.4 (0.36)	69.0 (0.36)
Some college, no bachelor's degree[3]	71.7 (0.86)	76.1 (0.70)	77.8 (0.66)	80.2 (0.60)	79.5 (0.51)	80.7 (0.50)	77.7 (0.33)	72.7 (0.30)	72.2 (0.30)	72.2 (0.30)	72.6 (0.44)	74.1 (0.32)	73.9 (0.32)	75.3 (0.30)	75.0 (0.33)
Bachelor's or higher degree	82.5 (0.68)	84.5 (0.55)	85.6 (0.51)	86.7 (0.47)	86.5 (0.44)	86.4 (0.42)	83.7 (0.26)	81.6 (0.24)	81.5 (0.26)	82.1 (0.24)	82.0 (0.34)	82.8 (0.26)	83.5 (0.23)	83.5 (0.25)	83.8 (0.27)
25 to 34 years old, all education levels	**67.7 (0.59)**	**74.5 (0.49)**	**76.2 (0.48)**	**78.6 (0.47)**	**78.5 (0.48)**	**81.6 (0.49)**	**76.8 (0.31)**	**73.2 (0.34)**	**73.0 (0.35)**	**73.8 (0.31)**	**74.5 (0.43)**	**76.0 (0.35)**	**76.8 (0.38)**	**78.1 (0.38)**	**78.7 (0.35)**
Less than high school completion	52.9 (1.43)	58.3 (1.46)	57.0 (1.54)	60.3 (1.50)	59.8 (1.59)	64.1 (1.76)	62.0 (0.95)	55.1 (0.95)	54.2 (1.17)	56.2 (1.14)	57.8 (1.37)	56.5 (1.11)	59.5 (1.30)	57.1 (1.36)	59.1 (1.50)
High school completion[2]	65.5 (0.92)	72.0 (0.81)	74.3 (0.78)	77.7 (0.74)	77.0 (0.84)	80.2 (0.91)	73.1 (0.60)	68.1 (0.72)	67.9 (0.67)	68.7 (0.75)	68.2 (0.73)	70.4 (0.72)	70.1 (0.79)	71.8 (0.70)	72.5 (0.73)
Some college, no bachelor's degree[3]	71.7 (1.33)	77.8 (1.01)	80.1 (0.97)	81.6 (0.96)	80.5 (0.87)	82.8 (0.90)	79.4 (0.54)	72.9 (0.57)	73.0 (0.62)	72.7 (0.68)	74.5 (0.74)	76.4 (0.60)	76.6 (0.65)	79.7 (0.54)	78.9 (0.60)
Bachelor's or higher degree	82.0 (1.04)	85.4 (0.82)	86.6 (0.79)	88.1 (0.76)	88.1 (0.75)	89.0 (0.73)	84.4 (0.52)	84.0 (0.49)	83.4 (0.45)	84.3 (0.45)	84.0 (0.59)	84.8 (0.48)	85.6 (0.49)	85.8 (0.47)	86.4 (0.46)
35 to 44 years old, all education levels	**70.3 (0.66)**	**76.5 (0.58)**	**78.1 (0.54)**	**81.6 (0.48)**	**80.2 (0.46)**	**81.8 (0.45)**	**79.9 (0.26)**	**76.0 (0.30)**	**76.0 (0.35)**	**76.9 (0.35)**	**77.1 (0.40)**	**78.3 (0.31)**	**78.5 (0.33)**	**79.2 (0.31)**	**80.1 (0.30)**
Less than high school completion	61.4 (1.31)	63.4 (1.39)	60.0 (1.58)	62.5 (1.69)	58.6 (1.66)	64.8 (1.64)	64.9 (0.93)	58.2 (1.13)	57.5 (1.04)	59.6 (1.13)	61.3 (1.25)	62.3 (0.84)	64.2 (1.00)	64.0 (1.01)	64.5 (1.13)
High school completion[2]	69.6 (1.02)	76.6 (0.90)	76.6 (0.88)	80.0 (0.80)	78.6 (0.82)	81.0 (0.79)	78.0 (0.52)	72.4 (0.64)	71.8 (0.64)	72.1 (0.68)	72.6 (0.80)	72.5 (0.63)	72.0 (0.76)	73.8 (0.66)	74.4 (0.68)
Some college, no bachelor's degree[3]	74.5 (1.74)	80.9 (1.33)	81.6 (1.15)	85.0 (0.93)	83.3 (0.81)	84.4 (0.80)	82.0 (0.48)	76.9 (0.53)	76.9 (0.62)	78.2 (0.61)	77.3 (0.68)	79.6 (0.53)	79.4 (0.58)	79.7 (0.63)	80.8 (0.55)
Bachelor's or higher degree	84.5 (1.31)	87.1 (1.00)	88.8 (0.80)	89.5 (0.72)	88.5 (0.71)	87.6 (0.74)	85.9 (0.41)	84.7 (0.39)	84.8 (0.43)	85.0 (0.41)	85.0 (0.57)	86.7 (0.39)	86.3 (0.39)	86.1 (0.35)	86.8 (0.37)
45 to 54 years old, all education levels	**68.4 (0.65)**	**71.7 (0.65)**	**73.5 (0.67)**	**77.6 (0.62)**	**78.8 (0.55)**	**81.2 (0.50)**	**78.4 (0.32)**	**74.7 (0.35)**	**74.3 (0.32)**	**74.6 (0.30)**	**76.2 (0.43)**	**75.9 (0.33)**	**77.0 (0.36)**	**77.3 (0.38)**	**77.9 (0.34)**
Less than high school completion	59.8 (1.14)	61.8 (1.24)	58.7 (1.52)	60.7 (1.63)	58.4 (1.79)	60.3 (1.89)	59.0 (1.04)	52.5 (1.05)	51.7 (0.84)	54.7 (1.06)	59.4 (1.50)	56.8 (1.16)	58.8 (1.13)	58.8 (1.22)	59.0 (1.20)
High school completion[2]	68.8 (1.03)	72.0 (1.02)	74.0 (1.03)	77.5 (0.97)	75.9 (1.01)	78.2 (0.95)	75.1 (0.64)	71.0 (0.65)	70.1 (0.58)	70.4 (0.62)	70.7 (0.84)	70.9 (0.63)	71.7 (0.68)	72.2 (0.66)	73.0 (0.67)
Some college, no bachelor's degree[3]	74.7 (1.81)	76.5 (1.72)	79.2 (1.63)	81.9 (1.38)	81.7 (1.03)	83.4 (0.91)	80.4 (0.57)	77.3 (0.54)	76.6 (0.53)	76.2 (0.53)	77.4 (0.76)	77.1 (0.60)	77.2 (0.71)	78.6 (0.61)	78.5 (0.62)
Bachelor's or higher degree	87.1 (1.36)	87.3 (1.21)	87.9 (1.16)	89.4 (0.97)	89.5 (0.78)	89.7 (0.71)	87.5 (0.45)	84.4 (0.45)	84.9 (0.45)	84.7 (0.48)	85.9 (0.54)	85.7 (0.43)	87.1 (0.44)	86.2 (0.46)	86.6 (0.48)
55 to 64 years old, all education levels	**54.6 (0.77)**	**54.1 (0.73)**	**52.1 (0.77)**	**53.4 (0.81)**	**55.0 (0.82)**	**58.1 (0.79)**	**60.8 (0.48)**	**60.6 (0.41)**	**60.2 (0.43)**	**60.6 (0.41)**	**60.9 (0.52)**	**61.9 (0.37)**	**62.6 (0.37)**	**63.0 (0.40)**	**62.9 (0.38)**
Less than high school completion	48.5 (1.11)	43.2 (1.16)	41.8 (1.29)	39.5 (1.46)	38.1 (1.67)	40.4 (1.84)	39.4 (1.13)	40.0 (1.19)	39.4 (1.15)	39.1 (1.08)	39.6 (1.34)	42.4 (1.12)	43.6 (1.27)	42.5 (1.07)	45.4 (1.09)
High school completion[2]	56.5 (1.32)	57.5 (1.19)	52.1 (1.22)	54.0 (1.29)	53.7 (1.34)	55.4 (1.34)	55.3 (0.79)	55.1 (0.71)	54.4 (0.81)	54.6 (0.75)	57.6 (0.90)	56.9 (0.74)	57.7 (0.75)	57.7 (0.73)	58.3 (0.72)
Some college, no bachelor's degree[3]	62.6 (2.48)	62.5 (2.08)	58.9 (2.21)	60.4 (2.12)	62.0 (1.74)	62.4 (1.64)	64.8 (0.90)	61.8 (0.76)	61.2 (0.78)	61.2 (0.70)	60.5 (0.99)	63.2 (0.68)	62.7 (0.68)	63.2 (0.70)	62.2 (0.75)
Bachelor's or higher degree	72.6 (2.34)	71.9 (1.96)	71.3 (1.83)	70.5 (1.79)	70.0 (1.72)	71.9 (1.49)	73.5 (0.74)	72.0 (0.65)	71.8 (0.71)	73.1 (0.66)	71.7 (0.90)	72.3 (0.62)	73.4 (0.60)	74.4 (0.71)	73.6 (0.65)

—Not available.
†Not applicable.
[1]Data for 16- to 19-year-olds and 20- to 24-year-olds exclude persons enrolled in school.
[2]Includes equivalency credentials, such as the GED credential.
[3]Includes persons with no college degree as well as those with an associate's degree.

NOTE: Data are based on sample surveys of the noninstitutionalized population, which excludes persons living in institutions (e.g., prisons or nursing facilities); this table includes only data on the civilian population (excludes all military personnel). For each age group, the employment to population ratio is the number of persons in that age group who are employed as a percentage of the civilian population in that age group.
SOURCE: U.S. Department of Commerce, Census Bureau, Current Population Survey (CPS), Annual Social and Economic Supplement, selected years, 1975 through 2018. (This table was prepared October 2018.)

Table 501.80. Unemployment rates of persons 16 to 64 years old, by age group and highest level of educational attainment: Selected years, 1975 through 2018

[Standard errors appear in parentheses]

Age group and highest level of educational attainment	1975	1980	1985	1990	1995	2000	2005	2010	2011	2012	2014	2015	2016	2017	2018
1	2	3	4	5	6	7	8	9	10	11	12	13	14	15	16
16 to 19 years old, all education levels[1]	**—** **(†)**	**—** **(†)**	**—** **(†)**	**17.0** **(1.83)**	**21.0** **(2.06)**	**17.2** **(1.89)**	**20.9** **(1.63)**	**20.6** **(1.18)**	**31.9** **(1.59)**	**30.6** **(1.57)**	**22.9** **(1.83)**	**22.5** **(1.35)**	**20.2** **(1.37)**	**14.8** **(1.39)**	**15.4** **(1.40)**
Less than high school completion	— (†)	— (†)	— (†)	26.2 (3.54)	30.3 (3.67)	21.4 (3.23)	27.5 (2.90)	25.8 (2.24)	41.7 (3.14)	41.1 (3.01)	22.9 (3.38)	25.6 (2.67)	21.6 (2.39)	21.7 (2.91)	16.3 (2.77)
High school completion[2]	— (†)	— (†)	— (†)	11.7 (2.05)	15.1 (2.59)	15.3 (2.54)	17.6 (2.13)	17.6 (1.43)	29.6 (2.08)	28.7 (2.00)	25.0 (2.32)	23.3 (1.90)	22.0 (2.02)	12.6 (1.44)	16.7 (1.92)
At least some college	— (†)	— (†)	— (†)	‡ (†)	12.4! (5.19)	‡ (†)	12.6! (4.13)	17.7 (3.54)	18.1 (3.65)	19.6 (3.83)	15.1 (4.16)	13.2 (2.96)	11.8 (2.75)	9.2 (2.59)	9.5! (3.19)
20 to 24 years old, all education levels[1]	**—** **(†)**	**—** **(†)**	**—** **(†)**	**8.2** **(0.63)**	**10.7** **(0.72)**	**9.2** **(0.70)**	**11.6** **(0.55)**	**9.3** **(0.46)**	**18.8** **(0.66)**	**15.5** **(0.55)**	**14.9** **(0.70)**	**12.3** **(0.53)**	**10.5** **(0.53)**	**8.1** **(0.43)**	**8.7** **(0.48)**
Less than high school completion	— (†)	— (†)	— (†)	17.4 (2.15)	19.5 (2.37)	16.6 (2.18)	16.0 (1.50)	15.7 (1.34)	32.3 (1.80)	27.6 (2.12)	25.3 (2.75)	19.9 (1.99)	17.3 (2.05)	16.0 (2.10)	19.5 (2.64)
High school completion[2]	— (†)	— (†)	— (†)	7.8 (0.88)	12.0 (1.18)	10.0 (1.12)	13.4 (0.91)	10.4 (0.70)	22.3 (0.95)	18.3 (0.96)	18.9 (1.18)	15.8 (0.92)	12.2 (0.92)	9.7 (0.80)	11.1 (0.85)
Some college, no bachelor's degree[3]	— (†)	— (†)	— (†)	4.8 (1.09)	7.3 (1.13)	5.2 (1.02)	8.6 (0.95)	7.1 (0.68)	14.2 (1.07)	12.7 (0.89)	12.2 (1.16)	9.6 (0.89)	9.9 (0.87)	6.4 (0.75)	5.3 (0.69)
Bachelor's or higher degree	— (†)	— (†)	— (†)	3.1! (1.12)	4.1! (1.26)	5.0 (1.43)	6.7 (1.09)	3.9 (0.72)	7.9 (1.15)	6.0 (0.95)	6.7 (1.09)	5.1 (0.72)	4.9 (0.81)	4.7 (0.76)	5.3 (0.89)
25 to 64 years old, all education levels	**6.8** **(0.21)**	**5.0** **(0.17)**	**6.1** **(0.18)**	**3.6** **(0.14)**	**4.8** **(0.15)**	**3.3** **(0.13)**	**5.1** **(0.11)**	**4.1** **(0.09)**	**9.1** **(0.13)**	**7.4** **(0.11)**	**5.8** **(0.14)**	**4.7** **(0.10)**	**4.4** **(0.09)**	**3.9** **(0.09)**	**3.5** **(0.09)**
Less than high school completion	10.5 (0.49)	8.4 (0.48)	11.4 (0.61)	7.7 (0.55)	10.0 (0.66)	7.9 (0.63)	10.5 (0.50)	8.3 (0.41)	16.8 (0.54)	14.3 (0.49)	10.6 (0.63)	9.2 (0.44)	8.1 (0.42)	8.3 (0.47)	6.6 (0.39)
High school completion[2]	6.8 (0.34)	5.1 (0.27)	6.9 (0.31)	3.8 (0.23)	5.2 (0.28)	3.8 (0.25)	5.9 (0.22)	4.7 (0.16)	12.1 (0.26)	9.2 (0.25)	7.4 (0.29)	6.2 (0.21)	6.1 (0.24)	5.2 (0.18)	4.7 (0.19)
Some college, no bachelor's degree[3]	5.5 (0.50)	4.3 (0.38)	4.7 (0.37)	3.1 (0.29)	4.5 (0.29)	3.0 (0.24)	4.9 (0.21)	3.9 (0.17)	8.8 (0.23)	7.9 (0.24)	6.1 (0.27)	4.9 (0.16)	4.5 (0.17)	3.8 (0.16)	3.7 (0.16)
Bachelor's or higher degree	2.4 (0.30)	1.9 (0.23)	2.4 (0.24)	1.7 (0.19)	2.5 (0.21)	1.5 (0.16)	2.9 (0.15)	2.3 (0.11)	4.7 (0.15)	4.1 (0.14)	3.4 (0.16)	2.4 (0.11)	2.4 (0.12)	2.3 (0.11)	2.2 (0.11)
25 to 34 years old, all education levels	**8.6** **(0.41)**	**6.8** **(0.32)**	**7.3** **(0.33)**	**4.8** **(0.27)**	**5.8** **(0.30)**	**4.0** **(0.27)**	**6.4** **(0.24)**	**5.5** **(0.19)**	**10.8** **(0.28)**	**9.2** **(0.26)**	**7.4** **(0.30)**	**5.9** **(0.20)**	**5.6** **(0.22)**	**4.9** **(0.20)**	**4.3** **(0.17)**
Less than high school completion	17.2 (1.36)	13.7 (1.24)	15.5 (1.38)	12.0 (1.21)	12.9 (1.32)	10.3 (1.33)	12.4 (0.97)	11.0 (0.84)	20.3 (1.02)	16.8 (1.09)	13.7 (1.24)	12.5 (1.01)	13.1 (0.97)	13.2 (1.16)	9.1 (0.98)
High school completion[2]	9.4 (0.67)	7.9 (0.55)	9.1 (0.57)	5.1 (0.44)	6.8 (0.56)	4.8 (0.54)	7.9 (0.50)	6.5 (0.40)	15.9 (0.62)	12.8 (0.57)	10.5 (0.68)	8.9 (0.50)	8.6 (0.52)	7.2 (0.44)	6.4 (0.38)
Some college, no bachelor's degree[3]	6.7 (0.85)	6.0 (0.64)	5.4 (0.60)	3.8 (0.51)	5.0 (0.52)	3.6 (0.49)	6.4 (0.45)	5.3 (0.35)	10.6 (0.44)	10.1 (0.51)	7.8 (0.52)	6.5 (0.39)	5.6 (0.41)	4.4 (0.34)	4.7 (0.34)
Bachelor's or higher degree	2.9 (0.50)	2.5 (0.39)	2.8 (0.41)	1.9 (0.34)	2.7 (0.40)	1.6 (0.31)	2.9 (0.29)	2.8 (0.25)	4.5 (0.28)	4.1 (0.28)	3.7 (0.30)	2.4 (0.20)	2.4 (0.23)	2.5 (0.22)	2.0 (0.19)
35 to 44 years old, all education levels	**6.4** **(0.41)**	**4.3** **(0.31)**	**5.6** **(0.33)**	**3.3** **(0.24)**	**4.6** **(0.27)**	**3.5** **(0.23)**	**5.3** **(0.21)**	**4.1** **(0.17)**	**9.2** **(0.24)**	**7.1** **(0.22)**	**5.7** **(0.24)**	**4.4** **(0.17)**	**4.1** **(0.18)**	**4.0** **(0.16)**	**3.3** **(0.14)**
Less than high school completion	11.2 (1.02)	9.0 (1.00)	12.4 (1.29)	8.3 (1.17)	10.5 (1.28)	8.4 (1.14)	11.1 (0.90)	8.6 (0.70)	17.8 (1.07)	14.1 (0.88)	11.5 (1.08)	8.4 (0.74)	6.2 (0.66)	6.9 (0.61)	5.5 (0.69)
High school completion[2]	5.7 (0.60)	4.2 (0.48)	6.1 (0.55)	3.7 (0.41)	5.1 (0.48)	3.9 (0.43)	6.1 (0.40)	5.1 (0.31)	11.9 (0.51)	9.1 (0.48)	7.4 (0.48)	6.3 (0.41)	6.6 (0.44)	5.7 (0.41)	4.9 (0.36)
Some college, no bachelor's degree[3]	4.6 (0.95)	3.1 (0.64)	4.8 (0.69)	2.8 (0.47)	4.7 (0.49)	3.1 (0.41)	4.9 (0.38)	3.7 (0.32)	9.2 (0.42)	7.4 (0.44)	6.1 (0.49)	4.5 (0.31)	4.5 (0.35)	4.4 (0.35)	3.2 (0.29)
Bachelor's or higher degree	2.3 (0.59)	1.6 (0.41)	2.2 (0.39)	1.6 (0.31)	2.2 (0.34)	1.8 (0.31)	2.8 (0.27)	2.0 (0.19)	4.6 (0.26)	3.6 (0.26)	2.8 (0.30)	2.1 (0.20)	2.0 (0.16)	2.3 (0.21)	2.1 (0.18)
45 to 54 years old, all education levels	**5.9** **(0.39)**	**3.9** **(0.32)**	**5.4** **(0.39)**	**2.5** **(0.26)**	**3.9** **(0.29)**	**2.4** **(0.22)**	**4.3** **(0.20)**	**3.4** **(0.15)**	**8.4** **(0.22)**	**6.8** **(0.18)**	**4.9** **(0.24)**	**4.1** **(0.15)**	**3.7** **(0.17)**	**3.3** **(0.17)**	**3.2** **(0.16)**
Less than high school completion	8.5 (0.81)	6.6 (0.78)	10.2 (1.16)	4.7 (0.89)	7.9 (1.24)	6.1 (1.16)	9.1 (0.99)	5.9 (0.73)	15.6 (0.98)	13.5 (0.92)	8.0 (0.95)	8.6 (0.80)	6.6 (0.65)	6.9 (0.79)	6.5 (0.70)
High school completion[2]	5.6 (0.60)	3.4 (0.48)	5.4 (0.60)	2.3 (0.39)	4.0 (0.53)	2.7 (0.42)	4.9 (0.37)	3.9 (0.30)	11.0 (0.43)	7.8 (0.36)	6.1 (0.50)	5.2 (0.34)	5.0 (0.39)	4.3 (0.32)	3.5 (0.32)
Some college, no bachelor's degree[3]	4.7 (1.00)	3.0 (0.78)	3.2 (0.79)	2.6 (0.62)	3.9 (0.56)	2.4 (0.40)	4.0 (0.35)	3.4 (0.26)	7.6 (0.40)	6.9 (0.36)	4.8 (0.44)	4.1 (0.30)	3.4 (0.33)	2.9 (0.28)	3.3 (0.30)
Bachelor's or higher degree	2.0! (0.61)	1.3! (0.44)	2.1 (0.54)	1.4 (0.38)	2.4 (0.41)	1.3 (0.28)	3.0 (0.28)	2.3 (0.20)	4.8 (0.30)	3.9 (0.27)	3.2 (0.29)	2.2 (0.18)	2.3 (0.24)	2.1 (0.21)	2.2 (0.22)
55 to 64 years old, all education levels	**5.5** **(0.46)**	**3.2** **(0.35)**	**4.6** **(0.44)**	**2.8** **(0.36)**	**3.9** **(0.42)**	**2.8** **(0.35)**	**4.0** **(0.26)**	**2.9** **(0.18)**	**7.3** **(0.25)**	**6.6** **(0.23)**	**5.2** **(0.28)**	**4.2** **(0.20)**	**3.9** **(0.18)**	**3.2** **(0.16)**	**3.3** **(0.18)**
Less than high school completion	7.1 (0.79)	5.2 (0.77)	7.1 (1.01)	3.9 (0.90)	6.7 (1.35)	5.2 (1.28)	7.0 (1.10)	6.0 (0.82)	10.1 (0.99)	11.5 (1.05)	8.2 (1.21)	6.9 (0.84)	6.5 (0.80)	6.0 (0.75)	5.6 (0.71)
High school completion[2]	5.1 (0.76)	2.7 (0.51)	4.5 (0.69)	3.0 (0.59)	3.4 (0.65)	3.1 (0.62)	4.4 (0.49)	2.9 (0.35)	9.3 (0.56)	7.1 (0.50)	5.6 (0.53)	4.4 (0.38)	4.1 (0.41)	3.6 (0.33)	4.0 (0.42)
Some college, no bachelor's degree[3]	4.1! (1.26)	2.0! (0.77)	3.0! (1.00)	2.2! (0.82)	3.2 (0.80)	2.8 (0.70)	3.6 (0.48)	3.1 (0.34)	7.7 (0.52)	7.1 (0.44)	5.5 (0.54)	4.3 (0.40)	4.1 (0.37)	3.2 (0.32)	3.2 (0.33)
Bachelor's or higher degree	1.5! (0.75)	‡ (†)	2.2! (0.70)	1.8! (0.62)	3.3 (0.79)	1.4! (0.46)	3.0 (0.39)	2.0 (0.22)	5.0 (0.34)	4.8 (0.38)	4.0 (0.39)	3.3 (0.30)	3.2 (0.29)	2.4 (0.24)	2.2 (0.23)

—Not available.
†Not applicable.
!Interpret data with caution. The coefficient of variation (CV) for this estimate is between 30 and 50 percent.
‡Reporting standards not met. The coefficient of variation (CV) for this estimate is 50 percent or greater.
[1]Data for 16- to 19-year-olds and 20- to 24-year-olds exclude persons enrolled in school.
[2]Includes equivalency credentials, such as the GED credential.
[3]Includes persons with no college degree as well as those with an associate's degree.

NOTE: Data are based on sample surveys of the noninstitutionalized population, which excludes persons living in institutions (e.g., prisons or nursing facilities); this table includes only data on the civilian population (excludes all military personnel). The unemployment rate is the percentage of persons in the civilian labor force who are not working and who made specific efforts to find employment sometime during the prior 4 weeks. The civilian labor force consists of all civilians who are employed or seeking employment.
SOURCE: U.S. Department of Commerce, Census Bureau, Current Population Survey (CPS), Annual Social and Economic Supplement, selected years, 1975 through 2018. (This table was prepared October 2018.)

Table 502.10. Occupation of employed persons 25 years old and over, by highest level of educational attainment and sex: 2017 and 2018

[Standard errors appear in parentheses]

Sex and occupation	Total employed (in thousands)		Percentage distribution, by highest level of educational attainment: Total	Less than high school completion		High school completion (includes equivalency)		College: Some college, no degree		Associate's degree		Bachelor's degree		Master's or higher degree	
1	2		3	4		5		6		7		8		9	
2017															
All persons	**133,718**	**(362.6)**	**100.0**	**7.0**	**(0.12)**	**25.6**	**(0.25)**	**16.2**	**(0.16)**	**11.2**	**(0.15)**	**24.7**	**(0.20)**	**15.3**	**(0.20)**
Management, professional, and related	57,437	(405.8)	100.0	1.2	(0.07)	9.9	(0.21)	11.0	(0.19)	10.1	(0.21)	37.0	(0.34)	30.8	(0.35)
Management, business, and financial operations	24,172	(253.4)	100.0	2.2	(0.13)	15.0	(0.37)	14.0	(0.33)	8.8	(0.29)	38.6	(0.49)	21.5	(0.43)
Professional and related	33,264	(328.1)	100.0	0.5	(0.06)	6.3	(0.23)	8.8	(0.24)	11.0	(0.30)	35.8	(0.47)	37.6	(0.45)
Education, training, and library	8,897	(149.4)	100.0	0.4	(0.11)	6.3	(0.37)	7.1	(0.44)	5.5	(0.39)	33.8	(0.85)	46.8	(0.87)
Preschool and kindergarten teachers	695	(37.8)	100.0	‡	(†)	14.5	(2.18)	16.5	(2.18)	11.4	(1.96)	38.5	(2.94)	18.5	(2.30)
Elementary and middle school teachers	3,225	(89.0)	100.0	‡	(†)	3.1	(0.48)	2.3	(0.39)	2.3	(0.40)	42.3	(1.32)	50.0	(1.43)
Secondary school teachers	1,034	(47.3)	100.0	‡	(†)	0.7!	(0.30)	0.9!	(0.40)	1.2!	(0.37)	38.4	(2.41)	58.7	(2.50)
Special education teachers	399	(31.8)	100.0	‡	(†)	4.3!	(1.73)	4.1	(1.18)	‡	(†)	37.1	(3.51)	52.8	(3.77)
Postsecondary teachers	1,385	(65.2)	100.0	‡	(†)	1.8!	(0.68)	1.1!	(0.46)	2.8!	(0.89)	15.2	(1.54)	79.0	(1.89)
Other education, training, and library workers	2,160	(68.4)	100.0	1.0!	(0.40)	14.6	(1.02)	18.9	(1.37)	13.0	(1.16)	29.0	(1.64)	23.5	(1.48)
Service occupations	20,759	(222.0)	100.0	14.7	(0.39)	37.6	(0.61)	19.5	(0.42)	12.6	(0.37)	12.6	(0.40)	2.9	(0.18)
Sales and office occupations	27,694	(268.2)	100.0	4.0	(0.17)	29.7	(0.46)	22.7	(0.41)	12.9	(0.31)	24.7	(0.40)	6.0	(0.25)
Natural resources, construction, and maintenance	12,325	(153.0)	100.0	18.8	(0.51)	43.1	(0.73)	17.4	(0.56)	12.1	(0.47)	7.1	(0.39)	1.6	(0.17)
Production, transportation, and material moving	15,504	(211.8)	100.0	14.3	(0.44)	46.1	(0.64)	18.6	(0.48)	9.8	(0.39)	9.1	(0.39)	2.1	(0.19)
Males	**70,824**	**(237.0)**	**100.0**	**8.4**	**(0.16)**	**28.2**	**(0.32)**	**15.9**	**(0.22)**	**9.8**	**(0.18)**	**23.5**	**(0.25)**	**14.1**	**(0.24)**
Management, professional, and related	27,613	(256.8)	100.0	1.6	(0.11)	11.0	(0.31)	10.7	(0.25)	8.2	(0.26)	37.6	(0.46)	30.9	(0.45)
Management, business, and financial operations	13,440	(187.1)	100.0	2.8	(0.21)	15.9	(0.50)	13.4	(0.43)	8.0	(0.39)	39.0	(0.67)	20.9	(0.53)
Professional and related	14,173	(207.7)	100.0	0.5	(0.10)	6.3	(0.37)	8.1	(0.33)	8.4	(0.43)	36.2	(0.66)	40.4	(0.60)
Education, training, and library	2,357	(78.0)	100.0	‡	(†)	4.0	(0.66)	5.0	(0.69)	4.0	(0.63)	29.8	(1.50)	57.1	(1.63)
Service occupations	8,854	(126.4)	100.0	14.8	(0.61)	36.9	(0.93)	19.5	(0.71)	10.9	(0.55)	14.8	(0.64)	3.1	(0.30)
Sales and office occupations	10,633	(158.8)	100.0	3.8	(0.28)	27.3	(0.67)	21.6	(0.73)	10.4	(0.47)	29.2	(0.67)	7.7	(0.47)
Natural resources, construction, and maintenance	11,720	(143.3)	100.0	18.9	(0.53)	43.5	(0.74)	17.4	(0.57)	12.2	(0.48)	6.6	(0.39)	1.4	(0.16)
Production, transportation, and material moving	12,004	(171.5)	100.0	13.1	(0.48)	47.4	(0.73)	18.5	(0.53)	10.0	(0.46)	9.3	(0.46)	1.9	(0.20)
Females	**62,894**	**(241.4)**	**100.0**	**5.5**	**(0.14)**	**22.6**	**(0.26)**	**16.6**	**(0.21)**	**12.7**	**(0.21)**	**25.9**	**(0.29)**	**16.7**	**(0.26)**
Management, professional, and related	29,824	(249.6)	100.0	0.8	(0.08)	8.9	(0.24)	11.3	(0.29)	11.8	(0.30)	36.4	(0.48)	30.7	(0.46)
Management, business, and financial operations	10,733	(145.9)	100.0	1.4	(0.16)	13.8	(0.54)	14.6	(0.53)	9.9	(0.44)	38.0	(0.71)	22.3	(0.70)
Professional and related	19,091	(215.2)	100.0	0.5	(0.08)	6.2	(0.25)	9.4	(0.34)	12.9	(0.38)	35.5	(0.62)	35.5	(0.59)
Education, training, and library	6,540	(122.4)	100.0	0.4!	(0.14)	7.2	(0.42)	7.9	(0.54)	6.1	(0.49)	35.3	(0.95)	43.0	(0.95)
Service occupations	11,905	(164.9)	100.0	14.6	(0.42)	38.1	(0.72)	19.6	(0.49)	13.9	(0.47)	11.1	(0.42)	2.8	(0.24)
Sales and office occupations	17,061	(196.3)	100.0	4.1	(0.22)	31.3	(0.61)	23.3	(0.51)	14.4	(0.45)	21.9	(0.52)	5.0	(0.28)
Natural resources, construction, and maintenance	605	(41.4)	100.0	17.3	(1.99)	35.3	(2.90)	16.8	(2.30)	9.4	(1.68)	16.5	(2.72)	4.7!	(1.45)
Production, transportation, and material moving	3,499	(96.8)	100.0	18.6	(1.01)	41.8	(1.27)	18.9	(1.03)	9.2	(0.76)	8.5	(0.66)	3.0	(0.46)
2018															
All persons	**135,851**	**(365.3)**	**100.0**	**7.0**	**(0.12)**	**25.1**	**(0.24)**	**15.5**	**(0.16)**	**11.1**	**(0.14)**	**25.7**	**(0.25)**	**15.5**	**(0.18)**
Management, professional, and related	59,266	(439.8)	100.0	1.2	(0.07)	9.5	(0.21)	10.5	(0.21)	10.1	(0.20)	37.6	(0.34)	31.1	(0.32)
Management, business, and financial operations	24,827	(277.4)	100.0	2.1	(0.14)	14.2	(0.42)	13.1	(0.33)	9.1	(0.30)	39.8	(0.50)	21.6	(0.42)
Professional and related	34,439	(323.0)	100.0	0.5	(0.06)	6.1	(0.21)	8.7	(0.27)	10.8	(0.29)	36.0	(0.45)	37.9	(0.45)
Education, training, and library	9,187	(175.7)	100.0	0.6	(0.13)	5.8	(0.42)	6.7	(0.42)	5.9	(0.39)	34.4	(0.76)	46.7	(0.90)
Preschool and kindergarten teachers	604	(41.2)	100.0	1.8!	(0.75)	11.3	(1.83)	15.4	(2.47)	13.9	(1.95)	40.2	(2.98)	17.3	(2.68)
Elementary and middle school teachers	3,540	(97.2)	100.0	‡	(†)	2.4	(0.44)	2.7	(0.44)	2.8	(0.41)	44.0	(1.21)	48.1	(1.34)
Secondary school teachers	1,135	(59.4)	100.0	‡	(†)	1.3!	(0.51)	2.6!	(0.84)	1.5!	(0.59)	35.9	(2.33)	58.6	(2.37)
Special education teachers	411	(31.1)	100.0	‡	(†)	3.2!	(1.04)	3.8!	(1.26)	3.4!	(1.28)	30.9	(3.79)	57.8	(4.07)
Postsecondary teachers	1,279	(65.8)	100.0	‡	(†)	‡	(†)	1.9	(0.55)	1.5!	(0.51)	12.2	(1.63)	84.2	(1.79)
Other education, training, and library workers	2,219	(79.2)	100.0	1.8	(0.45)	15.5	(1.22)	16.0	(1.24)	13.8	(1.12)	30.1	(1.57)	22.7	(1.44)
Service occupations	20,719	(221.4)	100.0	14.6	(0.38)	37.2	(0.49)	18.4	(0.41)	12.7	(0.38)	14.2	(0.42)	2.8	(0.18)
Sales and office occupations	27,253	(268.4)	100.0	3.7	(0.18)	29.2	(0.44)	22.5	(0.40)	12.9	(0.33)	26.0	(0.47)	5.7	(0.22)
Natural resources, construction, and maintenance	12,387	(162.3)	100.0	19.4	(0.50)	42.6	(0.74)	16.3	(0.50)	11.8	(0.50)	8.4	(0.47)	1.5	(0.17)
Production, transportation, and material moving	16,226	(213.8)	100.0	14.1	(0.48)	46.7	(0.66)	18.0	(0.49)	9.4	(0.38)	9.7	(0.37)	2.2	(0.18)
Males	**72,248**	**(244.9)**	**100.0**	**8.4**	**(0.16)**	**27.7**	**(0.31)**	**15.5**	**(0.23)**	**9.6**	**(0.18)**	**24.5**	**(0.29)**	**14.2**	**(0.22)**
Management, professional, and related	28,773	(280.9)	100.0	1.5	(0.11)	10.3	(0.29)	11.1	(0.32)	8.0	(0.26)	38.3	(0.44)	30.8	(0.43)
Management, business, and financial operations	13,768	(194.9)	100.0	2.6	(0.20)	15.2	(0.51)	13.3	(0.48)	7.8	(0.37)	39.6	(0.64)	21.4	(0.61)
Professional and related	15,006	(184.7)	100.0	0.5	(0.09)	5.7	(0.34)	9.0	(0.41)	8.2	(0.40)	37.1	(0.64)	39.5	(0.62)
Education, training, and library	2,526	(86.7)	100.0	0.4!	(0.15)	3.6	(0.65)	6.0	(0.79)	4.2	(0.66)	31.1	(1.43)	54.7	(1.59)
Service occupations	8,790	(152.1)	100.0	14.8	(0.62)	36.4	(0.86)	18.2	(0.68)	11.5	(0.58)	16.1	(0.64)	2.9	(0.30)
Sales and office occupations	10,536	(167.7)	100.0	4.2	(0.32)	27.2	(0.66)	21.2	(0.65)	10.3	(0.50)	30.2	(0.78)	6.9	(0.38)
Natural resources, construction, and maintenance	11,814	(159.3)	100.0	19.1	(0.52)	43.3	(0.76)	16.2	(0.51)	11.9	(0.51)	8.0	(0.45)	1.4	(0.17)
Production, transportation, and material moving	12,334	(168.3)	100.0	13.2	(0.50)	47.6	(0.75)	18.4	(0.57)	9.3	(0.43)	9.4	(0.42)	2.2	(0.22)
Females	**63,603**	**(231.6)**	**100.0**	**5.3**	**(0.14)**	**22.2**	**(0.29)**	**15.6**	**(0.21)**	**12.8**	**(0.21)**	**27.1**	**(0.33)**	**17.0**	**(0.23)**
Management, professional, and related	30,493	(260.9)	100.0	0.9	(0.09)	8.8	(0.27)	10.0	(0.28)	12.0	(0.27)	37.0	(0.46)	31.3	(0.40)
Management, business, and financial operations	11,059	(165.8)	100.0	1.6	(0.18)	13.0	(0.55)	12.9	(0.49)	10.7	(0.46)	40.0	(0.78)	21.9	(0.54)
Professional and related	19,434	(218.9)	100.0	0.5	(0.08)	6.4	(0.28)	8.4	(0.33)	12.8	(0.36)	35.2	(0.55)	36.7	(0.54)
Education, training, and library	6,661	(133.0)	100.0	0.7	(0.16)	6.6	(0.51)	6.9	(0.47)	6.5	(0.45)	35.6	(0.92)	43.7	(0.97)
Service occupations	11,929	(149.0)	100.0	14.5	(0.45)	37.8	(0.65)	18.6	(0.54)	13.6	(0.50)	12.8	(0.50)	2.8	(0.23)
Sales and office occupations	16,717	(196.8)	100.0	3.4	(0.21)	30.5	(0.56)	23.3	(0.47)	14.4	(0.44)	23.4	(0.57)	5.0	(0.27)
Natural resources, construction, and maintenance	573	(36.0)	100.0	24.4	(2.64)	27.2	(2.70)	17.0	(2.32)	9.9	(1.79)	17.2	(2.84)	4.3	(1.28)
Production, transportation, and material moving	3,892	(99.7)	100.0	17.0	(0.89)	44.0	(1.25)	16.8	(0.95)	9.6	(0.79)	10.5	(0.86)	2.1	(0.38)

†Not applicable.
!Interpret data with caution. The coefficient of variation (CV) for this estimate is between 30 and 50 percent.
‡Reporting standards not met. Either there are too few cases for a reliable estimate or the coefficient of variation (CV) is 50 percent or greater.

NOTE: Detail may not sum to totals because of rounding. Some data have been revised from previously published figures.
SOURCE: U.S. Department of Commerce, Census Bureau, Current Population Survey (CPS), Annual Social and Economic Supplement, 2018. (This table was prepared June 2019.)

Table 502.20. Median annual earnings, number, and percentage of full-time year-round workers age 25 and over, by highest level of educational attainment and sex: 1990 through 2017

[Standard errors appear in parentheses]

Sex and year	Total	Elementary/secondary			College						
							Bachelor's or higher degree[4]				
		Less than 9th grade	Some high school, no completion[1]	High school completion (includes equivalency)[2]	Some college, no degree[3]	Associate's degree	Total	Bachelor's degree[5]	Master's degree	Professional degree	Doctor's degree
1	2	3	4	5	6	7	8	9	10	11	12
	Current dollars										
Males											
1990	$30,730 (—)	$17,390 (—)	$20,900 (—)	$26,650 (—)	$31,730 (—)	[6] (†)	$42,670 (—)	$39,240 (—)	[6] (†)	[6] (†)	[6] (†)
1995	34,550 (275)	18,350 (545)	22,190 (342)	29,510 (358)	33,880 (517)	35,200 (535)	50,480 (312)	45,270 (510)	55,220 (973)	79,670 (2,582)	65,340 (2,188)
2000	41,060 (156)	20,790 (376)	25,100 (436)	34,300 (457)	40,340 (312)	41,950 (460)	61,870 (303)	56,330 (573)	68,320 (1,506)	99,410 (20,832)	80,250 (2,446)
2001	41,620 (104)	21,360 (235)	26,210 (251)	34,720 (299)	41,050 (214)	42,780 (561)	62,220 (279)	55,930 (335)	70,900 (687)	100,000 (—)	86,970 (3,013)
2002	41,150 (100)	20,920 (213)	25,900 (207)	33,210 (311)	40,850 (195)	42,860 (673)	61,700 (201)	56,080 (385)	67,280 (1,294)	100,000 (—)	83,310 (2,076)
2003	41,940 (90)	21,220 (227)	26,470 (280)	35,410 (168)	41,350 (182)	42,870 (719)	62,080 (187)	56,500 (365)	70,640 (562)	100,000 (—)	87,130 (2,528)
2004	42,090 (89)	21,660 (191)	26,280 (234)	35,730 (148)	41,900 (175)	44,400 (931)	62,800 (798)	57,220 (393)	71,530 (490)	100,000 (—)	82,400 (2,423)
2005	43,320 (367)	22,330 (220)	27,190 (237)	36,300 (141)	42,420 (323)	47,180 (367)	66,170 (356)	60,020 (653)	75,030 (1,229)	100,000 (—)	85,860 (3,061)
2006	45,760 (134)	22,710 (398)	27,650 (573)	37,030 (164)	43,830 (812)	47,070 (390)	66,930 (346)	60,910 (235)	75,430 (859)	100,000 (—)	100,000 (—)
2007	47,000 (130)	23,380 (544)	29,320 (590)	37,860 (406)	44,900 (585)	49,040 (801)	70,400 (241)	62,090 (236)	76,280 (416)	100,000 (—)	92,090 (1,894)
2008	49,000 (339)	24,260 (631)	29,680 (458)	39,010 (399)	45,820 (276)	50,150 (344)	72,220 (236)	65,800 (388)	80,960 (468)	100,000 (—)	100,000 (—)
2009	49,990 (201)	23,950 (394)	28,020 (542)	39,480 (379)	47,100 (347)	50,300 (238)	71,470 (239)	62,440 (707)	79,340 (1,568)	123,240 (2,539)	100,740 (519)
2010	50,360 (93)	24,450 (597)	29,440 (684)	40,060 (237)	46,430 (348)	50,280 (245)	71,780 (267)	63,740 (1,115)	80,960 (453)	115,300 (4,891)	101,220 (653)
2011	50,660 (25)	25,220 (23)	30,420 (300)	40,450 (87)	47,070 (78)	50,930 (212)	73,850 (490)	66,200 (25)	83,030 (755)	119,470 (1,917)	100,770 (192)
2012	50,950 (144)	25,130 (440)	30,330 (430)	40,350 (194)	47,190 (407)	50,960 (329)	75,320 (565)	66,150 (570)	85,120 (1,412)	116,350 (5,632)	106,470 (4,656)
2013	51,120 (149)	26,160 (531)	30,570 (551)	40,290 (227)	47,650 (739)	51,000 (493)	76,110 (485)	67,240 (992)	86,310 (1,429)	126,730 (8,647)	105,280 (4,631)
2014	51,400 (133)	26,580 (382)	30,840 (382)	40,930 (197)	46,900 (429)	51,110 (345)	75,910 (391)	68,160 (1,282)	84,760 (1,988)	121,750 (5,986)	100,710 (852)
2015	52,310 (152)	27,160 (460)	32,140 (320)	41,570 (184)	49,670 (708)	52,070 (352)	79,320 (1,350)	71,390 (420)	86,740 (1,632)	131,190 (7,197)	102,340 (4,801)
2016	53,740 (725)	30,350 (500)	32,490 (1,237)	41,890 (180)	49,240 (784)	52,120 (462)	80,320 (446)	71,630 (383)	88,430 (2,215)	117,550 (7,311)	120,430 (4,017)
2017	55,630 (269)	31,000 (369)	34,620 (1,249)	42,440 (524)	50,850 (274)	54,700 (1,414)	81,390 (321)	71,990 (395)	91,600 (648)	127,230 (5,441)	118,450 (4,152)
Females											
1990	21,370 (—)	12,250 (—)	14,430 (—)	18,320 (—)	22,230 (—)	[6] (†)	30,380 (—)	28,020 (—)	[6] (†)	[6] (†)	[6] (†)
1995	24,880 (160)	13,580 (490)	15,830 (293)	20,460 (162)	24,000 (274)	27,310 (428)	35,260 (313)	32,050 (273)	40,260 (556)	50,000 (2,532)	48,140 (2,373)
2000	30,330 (138)	15,800 (327)	17,920 (434)	24,970 (236)	28,700 (364)	31,070 (307)	42,710 (439)	40,420 (284)	50,140 (735)	58,960 (3,552)	57,080 (2,999)
2001	31,360 (91)	16,690 (255)	19,160 (359)	25,300 (132)	30,420 (186)	32,150 (231)	44,780 (367)	40,990 (231)	50,670 (328)	61,750 (3,976)	62,120 (2,228)
2002	31,010 (83)	16,510 (297)	19,310 (360)	25,180 (121)	29,400 (299)	31,630 (211)	43,250 (568)	40,850 (173)	48,890 (595)	57,020 (2,421)	65,720 (2,268)
2003	31,570 (85)	16,910 (256)	18,940 (327)	26,070 (118)	30,140 (176)	32,250 (241)	45,120 (291)	41,330 (204)	50,160 (454)	66,490 (3,469)	67,210 (2,462)
2004	31,990 (80)	17,020 (241)	19,160 (319)	26,030 (116)	30,820 (135)	33,480 (489)	45,910 (229)	41,680 (172)	51,320 (263)	75,040 (2,436)	68,880 (2,450)
2005	33,080 (242)	16,140 (250)	20,130 (274)	26,290 (134)	31,400 (165)	33,940 (497)	46,950 (232)	42,170 (179)	51,410 (283)	80,460 (2,774)	66,850 (2,490)
2006	35,100 (113)	18,130 (408)	20,130 (270)	26,740 (136)	31,950 (165)	35,160 (376)	49,570 (441)	45,410 (259)	52,440 (561)	76,240 (2,488)	70,520 (1,779)
2007	36,090 (105)	18,260 (461)	20,400 (292)	27,240 (133)	32,840 (415)	36,330 (283)	50,400 (158)	45,770 (262)	55,430 (412)	71,100 (910)	68,990 (2,155)
2008	36,700 (109)	18,630 (494)	20,410 (295)	28,380 (283)	32,630 (355)	36,760 (243)	51,410 (145)	47,030 (237)	57,510 (745)	71,300 (2,859)	74,030 (2,144)
2009	37,260 (107)	18,480 (451)	21,230 (301)	29,150 (273)	34,090 (483)	37,270 (310)	51,880 (169)	46,830 (260)	61,070 (304)	83,910 (3,210)	76,580 (912)
2010	38,290 (272)	18,240 (592)	20,880 (334)	29,860 (260)	33,400 (410)	37,770 (588)	51,940 (159)	47,440 (336)	59,100 (1,021)	76,740 (2,723)	77,390 (2,174)
2011	38,910 (216)	20,100 (250)	21,110 (131)	30,010 (145)	34,590 (512)	39,290 (40)	52,140 (88)	49,110 (103)	60,300 (533)	80,720 (135)	77,460 (21)
2012	39,980 (294)	20,060 (514)	21,390 (285)	30,410 (165)	35,060 (452)	37,320 (455)	53,690 (888)	50,170 (290)	60,930 (464)	94,470 (6,655)	77,900 (3,616)
2013	40,610 (134)	19,840 (502)	22,250 (544)	30,800 (173)	35,240 (312)	37,700 (751)	55,720 (416)	50,750 (341)	61,280 (561)	85,400 (6,196)	75,090 (3,515)
2014	40,830 (151)	20,990 (279)	21,990 (322)	30,650 (151)	34,380 (891)	37,480 (591)	55,940 (333)	51,350 (230)	60,830 (442)	91,810 (8,587)	80,540 (2,875)
2015	41,680 (146)	21,050 (275)	22,670 (714)	31,250 (138)	36,140 (273)	40,190 (437)	57,220 (527)	51,680 (278)	62,380 (1,135)	82,470 (5,049)	82,310 (3,752)
2016	43,010 (617)	22,210 (485)	24,800 (562)	31,540 (152)	36,880 (273)	40,220 (362)	60,060 (483)	52,030 (257)	64,910 (1,091)	92,030 (4,468)	86,370 (4,485)
2017	44,620 (530)	22,360 (533)	25,450 (459)	32,240 (199)	36,620 (259)	40,640 (335)	60,740 (270)	52,440 (601)	68,510 (1,524)	100,180 (4,817)	92,030 (3,137)

See notes at end of table.

Table 502.20. Median annual earnings, number, and percentage of full-time year-round workers age 25 and over, by highest level of educational attainment and sex: 1990 through 2017—Continued

[Standard errors appear in parentheses]

Sex and year	Total	Elementary/secondary			College						
		Less than 9th grade	Some high school, no completion[1]	High school completion (includes equivalency)[2]	Some college, no degree[3]	Associate's degree	Bachelor's or higher degree[4]				
							Total	Bachelor's degree[5]	Master's degree	Professional degree	Doctor's degree
1	2	3	4	5	6	7	8	9	10	11	12
	Constant 2017 dollars[7]										
Males											
1990	$57,700 (—)	$32,630 (—)	$39,210 (—)	$50,000 (—)	$59,530 (—)	[6] (†)	$80,050 (—)	$73,610 (—)	[6] (†)	[6] (†)	[6] (†)
1995	55,580 (442)	29,520 (877)	35,690 (550)	47,470 (576)	54,500 (832)	56,620 (861)	81,200 (502)	72,810 (820)	88,820 (1,565)	128,150 (4,153)	105,100 (3,520)
2000	58,450 (222)	29,590 (535)	35,720 (621)	48,830 (651)	57,420 (444)	59,720 (655)	88,070 (431)	80,190 (816)	97,250 (2,144)	141,510 (29,654)	114,230 (3,482)
2001	57,610 (144)	29,570 (325)	36,280 (347)	48,070 (414)	56,820 (296)	59,220 (777)	86,140 (386)	77,420 (464)	98,150 (951)	138,430 (—)	120,390 (4,171)
2002	56,080 (136)	28,510 (290)	35,300 (282)	45,250 (424)	55,670 (266)	58,400 (917)	84,080 (274)	76,420 (525)	91,690 (1,763)	136,270 (—)	113,520 (2,829)
2003	55,880 (120)	28,270 (302)	35,270 (373)	47,190 (224)	55,100 (243)	57,120 (958)	82,710 (249)	75,290 (486)	94,130 (749)	133,250 (—)	116,100 (3,369)
2004	54,620 (115)	28,110 (248)	34,100 (304)	46,360 (192)	54,370 (227)	57,620 (1,208)	81,490 (1,036)	74,260 (510)	92,830 (636)	129,770 (—)	106,930 (3,144)
2005	54,370 (461)	28,030 (276)	34,130 (297)	45,560 (177)	53,240 (405)	59,220 (461)	83,050 (447)	75,330 (820)	94,170 (1,543)	125,510 (—)	107,770 (3,842)
2006	55,640 (163)	27,610 (484)	33,620 (697)	45,030 (199)	53,300 (987)	57,240 (474)	81,390 (421)	74,060 (286)	91,720 (1,044)	121,590 (—)	121,590 (—)
2007	55,570 (154)	27,630 (643)	34,660 (697)	44,750 (480)	53,080 (692)	57,980 (947)	83,230 (285)	73,400 (279)	90,180 (492)	118,220 (—)	108,870 (2,239)
2008	55,790 (386)	27,610 (718)	33,790 (521)	44,410 (454)	52,170 (314)	57,090 (392)	82,220 (269)	74,910 (442)	92,170 (533)	113,850 (—)	113,850 (—)
2009	57,120 (230)	27,360 (450)	32,020 (619)	45,110 (433)	53,810 (396)	57,470 (272)	81,650 (273)	71,350 (808)	90,650 (1,792)	140,810 (2,901)	115,100 (593)
2010	56,610 (105)	27,490 (671)	33,090 (769)	45,030 (266)	52,200 (391)	56,520 (275)	80,690 (300)	71,650 (1,253)	91,010 (509)	129,610 (5,498)	113,790 (734)
2011	55,200 (27)	27,490 (25)	33,150 (327)	44,080 (95)	51,300 (85)	55,500 (231)	80,480 (534)	72,130 (27)	90,480 (823)	130,190 (2,089)	109,810 (209)
2012	54,400 (154)	26,830 (470)	32,380 (459)	43,080 (207)	50,380 (435)	54,410 (351)	80,410 (603)	70,630 (609)	90,870 (1,507)	124,220 (6,013)	113,670 (4,971)
2013	53,780 (157)	27,530 (559)	32,160 (580)	42,390 (239)	50,140 (778)	53,660 (519)	80,080 (510)	70,750 (1,044)	90,810 (1,504)	133,340 (9,098)	110,780 (4,873)
2014	53,220 (138)	27,520 (396)	31,930 (396)	42,380 (204)	48,560 (444)	52,920 (357)	78,600 (405)	70,570 (1,327)	87,760 (2,058)	126,070 (6,198)	104,270 (882)
2015	54,090 (157)	28,080 (476)	33,240 (331)	42,990 (190)	51,370 (732)	53,850 (364)	82,030 (1,396)	73,830 (434)	89,700 (1,688)	135,670 (7,443)	105,830 (4,965)
2016	54,890 (740)	31,000 (511)	33,190 (1,263)	42,780 (184)	50,280 (801)	53,230 (472)	82,030 (456)	73,160 (391)	90,320 (2,262)	120,050 (7,467)	122,990 (4,103)
2017	55,630 (269)	31,000 (369)	34,620 (1,249)	42,440 (524)	50,850 (274)	54,700 (1,414)	81,390 (321)	71,990 (395)	91,600 (648)	127,230 (5,441)	118,450 (4,152)
Females											
1990	40,090 (—)	22,980 (—)	27,070 (—)	34,370 (—)	41,700 (—)	[6] (†)	56,990 (—)	52,560 (—)	[6] (†)	[6] (†)	[6] (†)
1995	40,010 (257)	21,840 (788)	25,460 (471)	32,920 (261)	38,600 (441)	43,930 (688)	56,720 (503)	51,560 (439)	64,770 (894)	80,430 (4,073)	77,440 (3,817)
2000	43,170 (196)	22,490 (465)	25,510 (618)	35,540 (336)	40,850 (518)	44,230 (437)	60,790 (625)	57,530 (404)	71,370 (1,046)	83,920 (5,056)	81,250 (4,269)
2001	43,410 (126)	23,110 (353)	26,520 (497)	35,030 (183)	42,110 (257)	44,510 (320)	61,980 (508)	56,750 (320)	70,140 (454)	85,480 (5,504)	86,000 (3,084)
2002	42,260 (113)	22,500 (405)	26,310 (491)	34,320 (165)	40,060 (407)	43,100 (288)	58,930 (774)	55,670 (236)	66,620 (811)	77,700 (3,299)	89,550 (3,091)
2003	42,060 (113)	22,530 (341)	25,230 (436)	34,740 (157)	40,160 (235)	42,980 (321)	60,120 (388)	55,070 (272)	66,840 (605)	88,600 (4,622)	89,560 (3,281)
2004	41,510 (104)	22,090 (313)	24,870 (414)	33,780 (151)	39,990 (175)	43,450 (635)	59,580 (297)	54,090 (223)	66,590 (341)	97,380 (3,161)	89,380 (3,179)
2005	41,510 (304)	20,260 (314)	25,260 (344)	33,000 (168)	39,410 (207)	42,600 (624)	58,930 (291)	52,930 (225)	64,530 (355)	100,990 (3,482)	83,910 (3,125)
2006	42,670 (137)	22,050 (496)	24,480 (328)	32,510 (165)	38,850 (201)	42,750 (457)	60,270 (536)	55,210 (315)	63,760 (682)	92,700 (3,025)	85,750 (2,163)
2007	42,660 (124)	21,590 (545)	24,110 (345)	32,200 (157)	38,820 (491)	42,950 (335)	59,580 (187)	54,110 (310)	65,520 (487)	84,050 (1,076)	81,560 (2,548)
2008	41,780 (124)	21,210 (562)	23,230 (336)	32,310 (322)	37,140 (404)	41,850 (277)	58,530 (165)	53,540 (270)	65,480 (848)	81,170 (3,255)	84,280 (2,441)
2009	42,580 (122)	21,110 (515)	24,250 (344)	33,310 (312)	38,950 (552)	42,580 (354)	59,270 (193)	53,510 (297)	69,770 (347)	95,870 (3,668)	87,500 (1,042)
2010	43,050 (306)	20,500 (665)	23,470 (375)	33,560 (292)	37,550 (461)	42,460 (661)	58,390 (179)	53,320 (378)	66,430 (1,148)	86,260 (3,061)	87,000 (2,444)
2011	42,400 (235)	21,910 (272)	23,010 (143)	32,700 (158)	37,700 (558)	42,810 (44)	56,810 (96)	53,510 (112)	65,710 (581)	87,960 (147)	84,410 (23)
2012	42,680 (314)	21,420 (549)	22,830 (304)	32,460 (176)	37,430 (483)	39,840 (486)	57,320 (948)	53,570 (310)	65,050 (495)	100,860 (7,105)	83,170 (3,861)
2013	42,730 (141)	20,880 (528)	23,410 (572)	32,410 (182)	37,080 (328)	39,670 (790)	58,630 (438)	53,390 (359)	64,480 (590)	89,850 (6,520)	79,010 (3,699)
2014	42,270 (156)	21,730 (289)	22,760 (333)	31,730 (156)	35,590 (923)	38,800 (612)	57,920 (345)	53,170 (238)	62,980 (458)	95,060 (8,891)	83,390 (2,977)
2015	43,100 (151)	21,770 (284)	23,450 (738)	32,320 (143)	37,380 (282)	41,560 (452)	59,180 (545)	53,450 (288)	64,510 (1,174)	85,290 (5,222)	85,120 (3,880)
2016	43,920 (630)	22,690 (495)	25,330 (574)	32,210 (155)	37,670 (279)	41,070 (370)	61,340 (493)	53,140 (262)	66,290 (1,114)	93,990 (4,563)	88,210 (4,581)
2017	44,620 (530)	22,360 (533)	25,450 (459)	32,240 (199)	36,620 (259)	40,640 (335)	60,740 (270)	52,440 (601)	68,510 (1,524)	100,180 (4,817)	92,030 (3,137)

See notes at end of table.

Table 502.20. Median annual earnings, number, and percentage of full-time year-round workers age 25 and over, by highest level of educational attainment and sex: 1990 through 2017—Continued

[Standard errors appear in parentheses]

Sex and year	Total	Elementary/secondary			College						
							Bachelor's or higher degree[4]				
		Less than 9th grade	Some high school, no completion[1]	High school completion (includes equivalency)[2]	Some college, no degree[3]	Associate's degree	Total	Bachelor's degree[5]	Master's degree	Professional degree	Doctor's degree
1	2	3	4	5	6	7	8	9	10	11	12
	Number of persons with earnings who worked full time, year round (in thousands)										
Males											
1990	44,406 (268.6)	2,250 (73.9)	3,315 (89.3)	16,394 (188.0)	9,113 (144.6)	[6] (†)	13,334 (171.8)	7,569 (132.6)	[6] (†)	[6] (†)	[6] (†)
1995	48,500 (306.1)	1,946 (72.8)	3,335 (94.9)	15,331 (195.6)	8,908 (152.3)	3,926 (102.8)	15,054 (194.0)	9,597 (157.8)	3,395 (95.7)	1,208 (57.5)	853 (48.4)
2000	54,065 (309.7)	1,968 (68.0)	3,354 (88.4)	16,834 (191.7)	9,792 (148.8)	4,729 (104.7)	17,387 (194.6)	11,395 (159.9)	3,680 (92.6)	1,274 (54.8)	1,038 (49.5)
2001	54,013 (224.8)	2,207 (51.4)	3,503 (64.5)	16,314 (135.4)	9,494 (104.9)	4,714 (74.7)	17,780 (140.9)	11,479 (114.8)	3,961 (68.5)	1,298 (39.5)	1,041 (35.4)
2002	54,108 (225.0)	2,154 (50.7)	3,680 (66.1)	16,005 (134.2)	9,603 (105.5)	4,399 (72.2)	18,267 (142.7)	11,829 (116.5)	4,065 (69.4)	1,308 (39.6)	1,065 (35.8)
2003	54,253 (225.2)	2,209 (51.4)	3,369 (63.3)	16,285 (135.3)	9,340 (104.1)	4,696 (74.5)	18,354 (143.0)	11,846 (116.6)	4,124 (69.9)	1,348 (40.2)	1,037 (35.3)
2004	55,469 (227.0)	2,427 (53.8)	3,468 (64.2)	17,067 (138.3)	9,257 (103.6)	4,913 (76.2)	18,338 (142.9)	11,701 (115.9)	4,243 (70.9)	1,305 (39.6)	1,088 (36.1)
2005	56,717 (228.7)	2,425 (53.8)	3,652 (65.9)	17,266 (139.0)	9,532 (105.1)	5,022 (77.0)	18,820 (144.7)	12,032 (117.4)	4,275 (71.2)	1,369 (40.5)	1,144 (37.1)
2006	58,109 (230.6)	2,361 (53.1)	3,872 (67.8)	17,369 (139.4)	9,493 (104.9)	5,110 (77.7)	19,903 (148.4)	12,764 (120.7)	4,542 (73.3)	1,425 (41.3)	1,172 (37.5)
2007	58,147 (230.7)	2,142 (50.6)	3,451 (64.0)	17,224 (138.9)	9,867 (106.8)	5,244 (78.7)	20,218 (149.5)	12,962 (121.6)	4,800 (75.3)	1,332 (40.0)	1,125 (36.7)
2008	55,655 (227.2)	1,982 (48.7)	3,118 (60.9)	16,195 (135.0)	9,515 (105.0)	5,020 (77.0)	19,825 (148.1)	12,609 (120.0)	4,709 (74.6)	1,388 (40.8)	1,119 (36.7)
2009	52,445 (222.5)	1,561 (43.2)	2,795 (57.7)	15,258 (131.3)	8,609 (100.1)	4,828 (75.5)	19,395 (146.7)	12,290 (118.6)	4,575 (73.6)	1,319 (39.8)	1,212 (38.1)
2010	52,890 (223.2)	1,600 (43.8)	2,615 (55.9)	15,104 (130.7)	8,541 (99.7)	5,042 (77.2)	19,990 (148.7)	12,836 (121.1)	4,670 (74.3)	1,237 (38.5)	1,246 (38.7)
2011	54,279 (225.2)	1,848 (47.0)	2,715 (56.9)	15,335 (131.6)	8,752 (100.9)	5,206 (78.4)	20,423 (150.1)	13,013 (121.8)	4,839 (75.6)	1,300 (39.5)	1,271 (39.0)
2012	55,208 (226.6)	1,793 (46.3)	2,671 (56.4)	15,295 (131.4)	8,974 (102.1)	5,423 (80.0)	21,052 (152.2)	13,315 (123.2)	5,003 (76.9)	1,301 (39.5)	1,433 (41.4)
2013	56,703 (289.3)	1,944 (61.0)	2,910 (74.5)	16,034 (170.0)	8,960 (129.0)	5,605 (102.8)	21,249 (193.4)	13,378 (156.2)	5,146 (98.6)	1,249 (49.0)	1,476 (53.2)
2014	58,435 (256.1)	1,994 (54.0)	3,012 (66.2)	16,429 (150.3)	9,281 (114.7)	5,622 (90.0)	22,098 (172.1)	13,969 (139.3)	5,401 (88.2)	1,359 (44.6)	1,369 (44.8)
2015	59,690 (264.8)	2,008 (54.2)	2,984 (66.0)	16,286 (150.5)	9,445 (116.0)	5,907 (92.3)	23,059 (176.9)	14,469 (142.4)	5,883 (92.2)	1,256 (42.9)	1,451 (46.1)
2016	60,677 (266.4)	1,844 (52.0)	2,828 (64.2)	16,855 (153.0)	9,603 (117.0)	6,091 (93.7)	23,456 (178.3)	14,723 (143.5)	5,975 (92.9)	1,169 (41.4)	1,589 (48.2)
2017	61,794 (268.2)	1,820 (51.6)	2,931 (65.4)	16,997 (153.6)	9,629 (117.1)	6,052 (93.4)	24,365 (181.4)	15,445 (146.8)	6,065 (93.5)	1,188 (41.7)	1,667 (49.4)
Females											
1990	28,636 (234.7)	847 (45.6)	1,861 (67.3)	11,810 (162.8)	6,462 (123.1)	[6] (†)	7,655 (133.3)	4,704 (105.8)	[6] (†)	[6] (†)	[6] (†)
1995	32,673 (268.2)	774 (46.1)	1,763 (69.3)	11,064 (168.6)	6,329 (129.5)	3,336 (94.9)	9,406 (156.3)	6,434 (130.5)	2,268 (78.5)	421 (34.0)	283 (27.9)
2000	37,762 (271.6)	930 (46.8)	1,950 (67.7)	11,789 (162.5)	7,391 (130.0)	4,118 (97.8)	11,584 (161.1)	7,899 (134.3)	2,823 (81.2)	509 (34.7)	353 (28.9)
2001	38,228 (197.0)	927 (33.4)	1,869 (47.3)	11,690 (115.8)	7,283 (92.3)	4,190 (70.5)	12,269 (118.5)	8,257 (98.1)	3,089 (60.6)	531 (25.3)	392 (21.7)
2002	38,510 (197.6)	858 (32.1)	1,841 (46.9)	11,687 (115.8)	7,354 (92.7)	4,285 (71.2)	12,484 (119.5)	8,229 (97.9)	3,281 (62.5)	572 (26.2)	402 (22.0)
2003	38,681 (197.9)	882 (32.6)	1,739 (45.6)	11,587 (115.3)	7,341 (92.6)	4,397 (72.2)	12,735 (120.6)	8,330 (98.5)	3,376 (63.4)	567 (26.1)	462 (23.6)
2004	39,072 (198.7)	917 (33.2)	1,797 (46.4)	11,392 (114.4)	7,330 (92.6)	4,505 (73.0)	13,131 (122.4)	8,664 (100.4)	3,451 (64.0)	564 (26.0)	452 (23.3)
2005	40,021 (200.6)	902 (32.9)	1,740 (45.6)	11,419 (114.5)	7,452 (93.3)	4,751 (74.9)	13,758 (125.1)	9,074 (102.6)	3,591 (65.3)	657 (28.1)	437 (22.9)
2006	41,311 (203.2)	934 (33.5)	1,802 (46.4)	11,652 (115.6)	7,613 (94.3)	4,760 (75.0)	14,549 (128.4)	9,645 (105.7)	3,746 (66.7)	662 (28.2)	497 (24.5)
2007	42,196 (204.9)	823 (31.5)	1,649 (44.4)	11,447 (114.7)	7,916 (96.1)	4,891 (76.0)	15,469 (132.1)	9,931 (107.2)	4,389 (72.1)	666 (28.3)	484 (24.1)
2008	40,979 (202.5)	814 (31.3)	1,568 (43.3)	10,851 (111.8)	7,456 (93.3)	4,955 (76.5)	15,335 (131.6)	9,856 (106.8)	4,176 (70.3)	753 (30.1)	550 (25.7)
2009	40,376 (201.4)	776 (30.5)	1,519 (42.7)	10,467 (109.9)	7,164 (91.6)	4,924 (76.3)	15,526 (132.4)	10,066 (107.9)	4,261 (71.0)	606 (27.0)	592 (26.7)
2010	40,196 (201.0)	732 (29.7)	1,371 (40.5)	10,117 (108.1)	7,150 (91.5)	4,999 (76.8)	15,826 (133.5)	9,903 (107.0)	4,576 (73.6)	622 (27.4)	725 (29.5)
2011	40,885 (202.4)	779 (30.6)	1,380 (40.7)	10,040 (107.7)	6,989 (90.5)	5,131 (77.8)	16,566 (136.4)	10,537 (110.2)	4,700 (74.6)	635 (27.6)	694 (28.9)
2012	41,319 (203.2)	690 (28.8)	1,351 (40.3)	9,870 (106.8)	6,899 (89.9)	5,246 (78.7)	17,263 (139.0)	10,961 (112.3)	4,887 (76.0)	670 (28.4)	745 (29.9)
2013	42,021 (258.8)	788 (38.9)	1,309 (50.1)	9,990 (135.9)	7,070 (115.1)	5,253 (99.6)	17,611 (177.5)	11,124 (143.1)	4,963 (96.9)	793 (39.1)	732 (37.5)
2014	42,957 (228.5)	796 (34.2)	1,356 (44.6)	9,802 (117.7)	7,241 (101.7)	5,426 (88.4)	18,336 (158.1)	11,420 (126.6)	5,310 (87.5)	776 (33.8)	830 (34.9)
2015	44,012 (234.8)	823 (34.8)	1,308 (43.8)	9,739 (117.8)	7,525 (103.9)	5,507 (89.2)	19,109 (162.2)	11,751 (128.9)	5,562 (89.7)	784 (33.9)	1,012 (38.5)
2016	44,968 (236.9)	728 (32.7)	1,382 (45.0)	9,832 (118.3)	7,305 (102.4)	5,764 (91.2)	19,957 (165.5)	12,143 (131.0)	5,997 (93.0)	841 (35.1)	976 (37.9)
2017	45,868 (238.8)	766 (33.5)	1,341 (44.3)	9,783 (118.0)	7,004 (100.4)	5,838 (91.8)	21,136 (170.0)	12,937 (135.0)	6,308 (95.4)	805 (34.4)	1,085 (39.9)

See notes at end of table.

Table 502.20. Median annual earnings, number, and percentage of full-time year-round workers age 25 and over, by highest level of educational attainment and sex: 1990 through 2017—Continued

[Standard errors appear in parentheses]

Sex and year	Total	Elementary/secondary			College						
							Bachelor's or higher degree[4]				
		Less than 9th grade	Some high school, no completion[1]	High school completion (includes equivalency)[2]	Some college, no degree[3]	Associate's degree	Total	Bachelor's degree[5]	Master's degree	Professional degree	Doctor's degree
1	2	3	4	5	6	7	8	9	10	11	12
	Percent of persons with earnings who worked full time, year round[8]										
Males											
2000	81.7 (0.23)	69.2 (1.33)	71.8 (1.01)	80.9 (0.42)	82.2 (0.54)	86.6 (0.71)	84.8 (0.39)	85.6 (0.47)	82.8 (0.87)	85.8 (1.39)	82.5 (1.65)
2001	80.1 (0.17)	69.7 (0.90)	70.9 (0.71)	79.4 (0.31)	80.2 (0.40)	84.1 (0.54)	83.3 (0.28)	83.6 (0.35)	82.4 (0.60)	84.6 (1.01)	82.2 (1.18)
2002	79.4 (0.17)	70.1 (0.91)	71.3 (0.69)	77.8 (0.32)	78.8 (0.41)	81.4 (0.58)	83.9 (0.27)	84.4 (0.34)	82.2 (0.60)	85.7 (0.99)	82.8 (1.16)
2003	79.5 (0.17)	71.5 (0.89)	70.1 (0.73)	78.7 (0.31)	78.8 (0.41)	82.1 (0.56)	83.1 (0.28)	84.0 (0.34)	81.1 (0.60)	84.4 (1.00)	80.3 (1.22)
2004	80.0 (0.17)	74.7 (0.84)	71.2 (0.71)	79.1 (0.30)	79.3 (0.41)	83.6 (0.53)	83.0 (0.28)	83.1 (0.35)	83.1 (0.58)	83.3 (1.03)	81.7 (1.16)
2005	80.3 (0.16)	74.0 (0.84)	73.8 (0.69)	79.5 (0.30)	80.0 (0.40)	82.5 (0.54)	82.9 (0.27)	83.0 (0.34)	82.7 (0.58)	83.7 (1.00)	82.4 (1.12)
2006	81.1 (0.16)	73.6 (0.85)	72.9 (0.67)	79.6 (0.30)	80.1 (0.40)	85.3 (0.50)	84.7 (0.26)	85.2 (0.32)	83.5 (0.55)	85.9 (0.94)	83.4 (1.09)
2007	80.5 (0.16)	71.1 (0.91)	70.8 (0.72)	79.4 (0.30)	79.5 (0.40)	83.3 (0.52)	84.5 (0.26)	85.1 (0.32)	83.5 (0.54)	83.1 (1.03)	83.5 (1.11)
2008	77.0 (0.17)	66.3 (0.95)	64.6 (0.76)	74.6 (0.32)	76.5 (0.42)	79.4 (0.56)	82.6 (0.27)	83.2 (0.33)	80.9 (0.57)	82.4 (1.02)	83.1 (1.12)
2009	73.9 (0.18)	56.2 (1.03)	61.8 (0.79)	70.1 (0.34)	73.4 (0.45)	77.9 (0.58)	80.8 (0.28)	79.9 (0.35)	82.0 (0.56)	85.1 (0.99)	81.2 (1.11)
2010	74.8 (0.18)	58.8 (1.04)	61.6 (0.82)	71.9 (0.34)	72.9 (0.45)	78.2 (0.56)	81.4 (0.27)	81.8 (0.34)	80.0 (0.58)	81.4 (1.10)	82.2 (1.08)
2011	76.6 (0.17)	67.2 (0.98)	64.2 (0.81)	74.2 (0.33)	75.2 (0.44)	78.0 (0.56)	82.0 (0.27)	82.1 (0.33)	82.3 (0.55)	81.6 (1.07)	81.0 (1.09)
2012	76.5 (0.17)	65.4 (1.00)	64.4 (0.82)	74.5 (0.33)	73.7 (0.44)	78.8 (0.54)	82.1 (0.26)	82.5 (0.33)	80.8 (0.55)	84.4 (1.01)	81.4 (1.02)
2013	78.1 (0.21)	69.3 (1.21)	68.9 (0.99)	76.5 (0.41)	76.2 (0.55)	79.6 (0.67)	82.4 (0.33)	82.6 (0.41)	82.5 (0.67)	83.2 (1.34)	79.7 (1.30)
2014	79.2 (0.18)	72.2 (1.03)	69.4 (0.85)	78.3 (0.35)	76.7 (0.47)	79.9 (0.58)	83.3 (0.28)	83.7 (0.35)	82.7 (0.57)	83.5 (1.12)	81.2 (1.15)
2015	79.3 (0.18)	72.2 (1.03)	71.1 (0.85)	77.7 (0.35)	77.2 (0.46)	80.6 (0.56)	83.0 (0.27)	83.5 (0.34)	82.7 (0.54)	82.1 (1.19)	80.0 (1.14)
2016	80.1 (0.18)	72.3 (1.08)	71.5 (0.87)	78.8 (0.34)	78.4 (0.45)	81.1 (0.55)	83.4 (0.27)	83.8 (0.34)	82.8 (0.54)	82.3 (1.23)	83.5 (1.03)
2017	80.4 (0.17)	74.3 (1.07)	72.2 (0.85)	79.5 (0.34)	79.1 (0.45)	81.8 (0.54)	83.0 (0.27)	83.1 (0.33)	82.7 (0.54)	83.7 (1.19)	82.0 (1.03)
Females											
2000	64.6 (0.30)	53.5 (1.84)	56.5 (1.30)	64.1 (0.54)	65.3 (0.69)	66.6 (0.92)	66.5 (0.55)	66.7 (0.67)	64.9 (1.11)	70.6 (2.61)	71.5 (3.13)
2001	64.3 (0.22)	54.0 (1.32)	55.3 (0.94)	63.5 (0.39)	65.1 (0.49)	65.8 (0.65)	66.6 (0.38)	66.6 (0.47)	65.6 (0.76)	70.3 (1.83)	70.9 (2.12)
2002	64.1 (0.22)	52.6 (1.36)	55.5 (0.95)	63.2 (0.39)	65.0 (0.49)	65.6 (0.65)	66.5 (0.38)	65.9 (0.47)	66.1 (0.74)	74.3 (1.73)	73.8 (2.07)
2003	64.4 (0.21)	56.5 (1.38)	53.8 (0.96)	64.4 (0.39)	64.2 (0.49)	65.6 (0.64)	66.4 (0.37)	65.8 (0.46)	66.3 (0.73)	72.3 (1.75)	71.9 (1.95)
2004	64.5 (0.21)	56.3 (1.35)	56.1 (0.96)	64.5 (0.40)	64.2 (0.49)	64.6 (0.63)	66.7 (0.37)	66.3 (0.45)	66.3 (0.72)	71.5 (1.77)	71.2 (1.97)
2005	65.3 (0.21)	56.5 (1.36)	54.5 (0.97)	65.1 (0.40)	63.5 (0.49)	67.2 (0.61)	68.2 (0.36)	68.0 (0.44)	68.3 (0.70)	71.2 (1.64)	67.3 (2.02)
2006	66.2 (0.21)	58.5 (1.35)	56.0 (0.96)	65.6 (0.39)	65.9 (0.48)	67.3 (0.61)	68.6 (0.35)	68.4 (0.43)	67.5 (0.69)	73.6 (1.61)	74.0 (1.86)
2007	66.7 (0.21)	56.8 (1.43)	55.3 (1.00)	65.7 (0.39)	66.7 (0.48)	67.3 (0.60)	69.3 (0.34)	68.4 (0.42)	70.6 (0.63)	74.1 (1.60)	71.2 (1.91)
2008	64.4 (0.21)	51.6 (1.38)	52.8 (1.01)	62.4 (0.40)	64.7 (0.49)	65.5 (0.60)	67.9 (0.34)	67.8 (0.43)	66.9 (0.65)	74.0 (1.51)	70.0 (1.80)
2009	64.3 (0.21)	52.0 (1.42)	54.5 (1.04)	62.4 (0.41)	63.9 (0.50)	64.5 (0.60)	68.0 (0.34)	68.3 (0.42)	67.5 (0.65)	66.4 (1.72)	68.3 (1.74)
2010	64.4 (0.21)	51.7 (1.46)	52.4 (1.07)	62.6 (0.42)	63.3 (0.50)	64.3 (0.60)	68.5 (0.34)	67.7 (0.42)	68.5 (0.62)	73.9 (1.66)	76.3 (1.51)
2011	65.0 (0.21)	52.2 (1.42)	49.1 (1.04)	63.0 (0.42)	62.9 (0.50)	66.3 (0.59)	69.6 (0.33)	69.4 (0.41)	69.0 (0.62)	72.8 (1.65)	73.6 (1.58)
2012	64.8 (0.21)	50.0 (1.48)	51.1 (1.07)	62.3 (0.42)	61.7 (0.50)	64.7 (0.58)	70.0 (0.32)	70.6 (0.40)	68.0 (0.60)	73.2 (1.61)	73.9 (1.52)
2013	65.6 (0.26)	56.0 (1.84)	52.3 (1.07)	63.8 (0.46)	63.4 (0.62)	65.1 (0.79)	69.6 (0.40)	70.4 (0.50)	67.4 (0.82)	73.9 (1.86)	69.4 (1.97)
2014	66.1 (0.23)	53.5 (1.57)	54.1 (1.21)	63.6 (0.47)	64.3 (0.55)	66.5 (0.63)	70.0 (0.34)	70.3 (0.44)	69.2 (0.64)	73.8 (1.65)	68.1 (1.62)
2015	66.3 (0.22)	54.9 (1.56)	51.5 (1.20)	64.1 (0.47)	65.4 (0.54)	65.6 (0.63)	70.1 (0.34)	70.3 (0.43)	68.3 (0.63)	75.9 (1.62)	74.5 (1.44)
2016	67.2 (0.22)	55.4 (1.66)	56.0 (1.21)	63.7 (0.47)	65.7 (0.55)	67.7 (0.62)	71.0 (0.33)	70.6 (0.42)	71.1 (0.60)	75.8 (1.56)	71.3 (1.48)
2017	68.0 (0.22)	57.3 (1.64)	55.1 (1.22)	64.5 (0.47)	65.5 (0.56)	68.0 (0.61)	72.2 (0.32)	71.9 (0.41)	72.4 (0.58)	75.6 (1.60)	71.8 (1.41)

—Not available.
†Not applicable.
[1]Includes 1 to 3 years of high school for 1990.
[2]Includes 4 years of high school for 1990.
[3]Includes 1 to 3 years of college and associate's degrees for 1990.
[4]Includes 4 or more years of college for 1990.
[5]Includes 4 years of college for 1990.
[6]Not reported separately for 1990.
[7]Constant dollars based on the Consumer Price Index, prepared by the Bureau of Labor Statistics, U.S. Department of Labor.
[8]Data not available for 1990 through 1995.
NOTE: Detail may not sum to totals because of rounding.
SOURCE: U.S. Department of Commerce, Census Bureau, Current Population Reports, Series P-60, *Money Income of Households, Families, and Persons in the United States* and *Income, Poverty, and Valuation of Noncash Benefits*, 1990; Series P-60, *Money Income in the United States*, 1995 through 2002; and Current Population Survey (CPS), Annual Social and Economic Supplement, 2004 through 2018. Retrieved January 9, 2019, from https://www.census.gov/data/tables/time-series/demo/income-poverty/cps-pinc/pinc-03.html. (This table was prepared January 2019.)

Table 502.40. Annual earnings of persons 25 years old and over, by highest level of educational attainment and sex: 2017

[Standard errors appear in parentheses]

Sex and earnings	Total	Elementary/secondary			College						
							Bachelor's or higher degree				
		Less than 9th grade	Some high school, no completion	High school completion (includes equivalency)	Some college, no degree	Associate's degree	Total	Bachelor's degree	Master's degree	Professional degree (e.g., M.D., D.D.S., or J.D.)	Doctor's degree (e.g., Ph.D. or Ed.D.)
1	2	3	4	5	6	7	8	9	10	11	12
Number of persons (in thousands)	**219,820 (306.3)**	**8,722 (113.7)**	**13,682 (141.2)**	**62,668 (275.7)**	**35,457 (218.7)**	**22,372 (177.9)**	**76,919 (296.3)**	**48,218 (248.9)**	**21,053 (172.9)**	**3,179 (69.3)**	**4,471 (82.0)**
With earnings	144,454 (340.7)	3,779 (75.5)	6,523 (98.7)	36,558 (221.6)	22,883 (179.7)	15,977 (152.0)	58,734 (269.0)	36,626 (221.8)	16,050 (152.3)	2,502 (61.5)	3,557 (73.2)
For persons with earnings											
Percentage distribution, by total annual earnings[1]	100.0 (†)	100.0 (†)	100.0 (†)	100.0 (†)	100.0 (†)	100.0 (†)	100.0 (†)	100.0 (†)	100.0 (†)	100.0 (†)	100.0 (†)
$1 to $4,999 or loss[2]	3.9 (0.06)	6.0 (0.48)	6.9 (0.39)	4.1 (0.13)	5.1 (0.18)	4.2 (0.20)	2.7 (0.08)	2.9 (0.11)	2.3 (0.15)	2.1 (0.36)	1.9 (0.28)
$5,000 to $9,999	3.7 (0.06)	5.9 (0.47)	7.3 (0.40)	4.9 (0.14)	4.2 (0.16)	3.3 (0.17)	2.4 (0.08)	2.6 (0.10)	2.4 (0.15)	1.0 (0.25)	2.1 (0.30)
$10,000 to $14,999	5.0 (0.07)	11.8 (0.65)	9.4 (0.45)	6.8 (0.16)	5.1 (0.18)	4.8 (0.21)	2.9 (0.09)	3.2 (0.11)	2.7 (0.16)	2.4 (0.38)	1.7 (0.27)
$15,000 to $19,999	5.5 (0.07)	12.8 (0.67)	10.5 (0.47)	7.6 (0.17)	6.6 (0.20)	5.5 (0.22)	2.6 (0.08)	3.1 (0.11)	2.0 (0.14)	0.9 (0.23)	2.3 (0.31)
$20,000 to $24,999	7.2 (0.08)	16.2 (0.74)	15.2 (0.55)	10.0 (0.19)	8.0 (0.22)	7.2 (0.25)	3.6 (0.09)	4.2 (0.13)	3.0 (0.17)	1.4 (0.29)	1.3 (0.24)
$25,000 to $29,999	6.8 (0.08)	11.5 (0.64)	9.8 (0.46)	9.6 (0.19)	8.2 (0.22)	7.6 (0.26)	3.6 (0.10)	4.5 (0.13)	2.4 (0.15)	1.6 (0.31)	1.5 (0.26)
$30,000 to $34,999	7.3 (0.08)	9.8 (0.60)	9.7 (0.45)	9.4 (0.19)	9.4 (0.24)	8.7 (0.28)	4.3 (0.10)	5.1 (0.14)	3.2 (0.17)	1.9 (0.34)	2.1 (0.30)
$35,000 to $39,999	6.3 (0.08)	6.2 (0.49)	6.5 (0.38)	7.9 (0.17)	7.5 (0.21)	7.8 (0.26)	4.4 (0.10)	5.4 (0.15)	3.1 (0.17)	1.9 (0.34)	1.8 (0.28)
$40,000 to $49,999	11.3 (0.10)	8.0 (0.55)	9.2 (0.44)	12.3 (0.21)	11.9 (0.26)	13.1 (0.33)	10.3 (0.15)	12.1 (0.21)	8.3 (0.27)	4.2 (0.50)	4.5 (0.43)
$50,000 to $74,999	20.5 (0.13)	8.4 (0.56)	10.3 (0.47)	17.9 (0.25)	20.3 (0.33)	21.9 (0.40)	23.6 (0.22)	24.2 (0.28)	24.9 (0.42)	16.8 (0.92)	16.8 (0.77)
$75,000 to $99,999	9.4 (0.09)	2.3 (0.30)	3.0 (0.26)	5.2 (0.14)	7.0 (0.21)	8.8 (0.28)	14.3 (0.18)	12.8 (0.22)	17.5 (0.37)	13.3 (0.84)	16.3 (0.76)
$100,000 or more	13.3 (0.11)	1.0 (0.20)	2.1 (0.22)	4.2 (0.13)	6.6 (0.20)	7.1 (0.25)	25.2 (0.22)	19.9 (0.26)	28.2 (0.44)	52.3 (1.23)	47.6 (1.03)
Median annual earnings[1]	$42,230 (127)	$23,760 (564)	$25,200 (308)	$32,350 (163)	$36,540 (242)	$40,360 (274)	$61,260 (215)	$54,600 (760)	$70,330 (628)	$101,250 (903)	$95,700 (3,238)
Number of males (in thousands)	**105,851 (222.5)**	**4,264 (79.5)**	**6,956 (100.7)**	**31,297 (194.8)**	**16,981 (151.8)**	**9,652 (117.5)**	**36,701 (206.2)**	**23,079 (172.9)**	**9,240 (115.1)**	**1,785 (51.9)**	**2,598 (62.4)**
With earnings	76,850 (241.3)	2,442 (60.6)	4,104 (78.1)	21,350 (167.4)	12,154 (130.7)	7,378 (103.5)	29,422 (190.4)	18,606 (157.9)	7,355 (103.4)	1,425 (46.4)	2,036 (55.4)
For males with earnings											
Percentage distribution, by total annual earnings[1]	100.0 (†)	100.0 (†)	100.0 (†)	100.0 (†)	100.0 (†)	100.0 (†)	100.0 (†)	100.0 (†)	100.0 (†)	100.0 (†)	100.0 (†)
$1 to $4,999 or loss[2]	2.7 (0.07)	3.9 (0.48)	4.8 (0.41)	2.9 (0.14)	3.6 (0.21)	3.1 (0.25)	1.7 (0.09)	1.9 (0.12)	1.4 (0.17)	2.0 (0.45)	1.4 (0.32)
$5,000 to $9,999	2.8 (0.07)	3.6 (0.47)	5.6 (0.44)	3.5 (0.15)	3.2 (0.20)	2.2 (0.21)	1.8 (0.10)	1.8 (0.12)	2.1 (0.21)	‡ (†)	1.8 (0.36)
$10,000 to $14,999	3.6 (0.08)	9.0 (0.72)	5.8 (0.45)	4.8 (0.18)	3.6 (0.21)	3.1 (0.25)	2.1 (0.10)	2.3 (0.13)	1.8 (0.19)	1.5 (0.40)	1.8 (0.36)
$15,000 to $19,999	4.1 (0.09)	10.1 (0.75)	7.8 (0.52)	5.1 (0.19)	4.6 (0.23)	3.8 (0.27)	2.2 (0.11)	2.7 (0.15)	1.4 (0.17)	1.3 (0.37)	1.4 (0.32)
$20,000 to $24,999	6.2 (0.11)	16.9 (0.94)	14.6 (0.68)	8.2 (0.23)	6.6 (0.28)	5.3 (0.32)	2.7 (0.12)	3.0 (0.16)	2.6 (0.23)	1.0! (0.32)	1.3 (0.31)
$25,000 to $29,999	6.0 (0.11)	11.9 (0.81)	10.8 (0.60)	8.8 (0.24)	6.4 (0.27)	5.6 (0.33)	2.8 (0.12)	3.4 (0.16)	2.0 (0.20)	1.5 (0.39)	1.3 (0.31)
$30,000 to $34,999	6.5 (0.11)	10.8 (0.77)	10.5 (0.59)	9.2 (0.24)	7.8 (0.30)	6.5 (0.36)	3.2 (0.13)	3.7 (0.17)	2.6 (0.23)	1.2 (0.36)	2.0 (0.38)
$35,000 to $39,999	6.0 (0.11)	7.1 (0.64)	7.7 (0.51)	8.0 (0.23)	7.2 (0.29)	6.8 (0.36)	3.6 (0.13)	4.3 (0.18)	2.8 (0.24)	1.5 (0.39)	1.8 (0.37)
$40,000 to $49,999	11.2 (0.14)	11.0 (0.78)	11.9 (0.62)	13.4 (0.29)	12.5 (0.37)	13.7 (0.49)	8.3 (0.20)	10.4 (0.28)	5.3 (0.32)	3.3 (0.58)	3.2 (0.48)
$50,000 to $74,999	21.9 (0.18)	11.2 (0.79)	13.4 (0.66)	22.4 (0.35)	24.7 (0.48)	25.9 (0.63)	21.5 (0.30)	23.4 (0.38)	19.7 (0.57)	15.2 (1.18)	14.6 (0.97)
$75,000 to $99,999	11.0 (0.14)	3.2 (0.44)	4.4 (0.39)	7.5 (0.22)	9.9 (0.33)	12.7 (0.48)	15.2 (0.26)	14.6 (0.32)	18.0 (0.55)	11.4 (1.04)	13.3 (0.93)
$100,000 or more	17.9 (0.17)	1.3 (0.28)	2.9 (0.32)	6.0 (0.20)	10.0 (0.34)	11.4 (0.46)	34.9 (0.34)	28.5 (0.41)	40.3 (0.71)	59.6 (1.61)	56.1 (1.36)
Median annual earnings[1]	$50,370 (145)	$26,700 (417)	$30,210 605	$39,240 (672)	$45,020 (1052)	$49,920 (907)	$75,080 (1,499)	$65,690 (538)	$82,450 (2,392)	$120,200 (8,359)	$105,290 (4,507)

See notes at end of table.

Table 502.40. Annual earnings of persons 25 years old and over, by highest level of educational attainment and sex: 2017—Continued

[Standard errors appear in parentheses]

Sex and earnings	Total	Elementary/secondary			College						
							Bachelor's or higher degree				
		Less than 9th grade	Some high school, no completion	High school completion (includes equivalency)	Some college, no degree	Associate's degree	Total	Bachelor's degree	Master's degree	Professional degree (e.g., M.D., D.D.S., or J.D.)	Doctor's degree (e.g., Ph.D. or Ed.D.)
1	2	3	4	5	6	7	8	9	10	11	12
Number of females (in thousands)	**113,969 (238.8)**	**4,458 (81.4)**	**6,726 (99.3)**	**31,371 (197.5)**	**18,476 (158.5)**	**12,720 (134.0)**	**40,218 (216.4)**	**25,139 (180.8)**	**11,813 (129.5)**	**1,394 (45.9)**	**1,873 (53.2)**
With earnings	67,604 (249.1)	1,337 (45.0)	2,419 (60.3)	15,208 (145.3)	10,729 (123.8)	8,599 (111.6)	29,312 (192.3)	18,020 (156.8)	8,695 (112.2)	1,077 (40.4)	1,521 (48.0)
For females with earnings											
Percentage distribution, by total annual earnings[1]	100.0 (†)	100.0 (†)	100.0 (†)	100.0 (†)	100.0 (†)	100.0 (†)	100.0 (†)	100.0 (†)	100.0 (†)	100.0 (†)	100.0 (†)
$1 to $4,999 or loss[2]	5.2 (0.11)	9.9 (1.01)	10.5 (0.77)	5.8 (0.23)	6.8 (0.30)	5.2 (0.30)	3.6 (0.14)	4.1 (0.18)	3.1 (0.23)	2.2 (0.56)	2.7 (0.51)
$5,000 to $9,999	4.8 (0.10)	9.9 (1.01)	10.1 (0.76)	6.8 (0.25)	5.4 (0.27)	4.3 (0.27)	3.1 (0.12)	3.4 (0.17)	2.7 (0.21)	1.9 (0.51)	2.5 (0.49)
$10,000 to $14,999	6.5 (0.12)	16.9 (1.27)	15.6 (0.91)	9.5 (0.29)	6.8 (0.30)	6.3 (0.32)	3.7 (0.14)	4.1 (0.18)	3.3 (0.24)	3.6 (0.70)	1.6 (0.40)
$15,000 to $19,999	7.0 (0.12)	17.9 (1.29)	15.2 (0.90)	11.1 (0.32)	8.9 (0.34)	7.0 (0.34)	3.1 (0.12)	3.4 (0.17)	2.5 (0.21)	‡ (†)	3.4 (0.57)
$20,000 to $24,999	8.3 (0.13)	14.9 (1.20)	16.2 (0.93)	12.4 (0.33)	9.6 (0.35)	8.8 (0.38)	4.5 (0.15)	5.5 (0.21)	3.3 (0.24)	1.9 (0.52)	1.4 (0.37)
$25,000 to $29,999	7.7 (0.13)	10.8 (1.05)	8.3 (0.69)	10.7 (0.31)	10.4 (0.36)	9.4 (0.39)	4.4 (0.15)	5.6 (0.21)	2.7 (0.21)	‡ (†)	1.8 (0.43)
$30,000 to $34,999	8.1 (0.13)	8.2 (0.92)	8.3 (0.69)	9.6 (0.30)	11.2 (0.38)	10.6 (0.41)	5.4 (0.16)	6.6 (0.23)	3.8 (0.25)	2.9 (0.63)	2.3 (0.47)
$35,000 to $39,999	6.6 (0.12)	4.6 (0.71)	4.4 (0.52)	7.9 (0.27)	7.8 (0.32)	8.6 (0.37)	5.2 (0.16)	6.5 (0.23)	3.4 (0.24)	2.5 (0.59)	1.8 (0.43)
$40,000 to $49,999	11.4 (0.15)	2.5 (0.53)	4.8 (0.54)	10.8 (0.31)	11.2 (0.38)	12.5 (0.44)	12.3 (0.24)	13.9 (0.32)	10.9 (0.41)	5.4 (0.85)	6.4 (0.77)
$50,000 to $74,999	18.8 (0.19)	3.3 (0.60)	5.1 (0.55)	11.6 (0.32)	15.3 (0.43)	18.4 (0.52)	25.8 (0.32)	25.0 (0.40)	29.2 (0.60)	19.0 (1.48)	19.7 (1.26)
$75,000 to $99,999	7.6 (0.13)	0.7! (0.28)	0.6! (0.20)	2.1 (0.14)	3.8 (0.23)	5.4 (0.30)	13.3 (0.25)	10.8 (0.29)	17.1 (0.50)	15.7 (1.37)	20.2 (1.27)
$100,000 or more	8.0 (0.13)	0.5! (0.24)	0.8 (0.22)	1.6 (0.13)	2.8 (0.20)	3.5 (0.24)	15.5 (0.26)	11.0 (0.29)	18.0 (0.51)	42.7 (1.86)	36.2 (1.52)
Median annual earnings[1]	$36,270 (162)	$18,510 (554)	$19,410 (596)	$26,390 (198)	$30,610 (218)	$33,510 (730)	$51,890 (196)	$46,880 (341)	$60,520 (402)	$85,650 (4,132)	$80,580 (1,621)

†Not applicable.
!Interpret data with caution. The coefficient of variation (CV) for this estimate is between 30 and 50 percent.
‡Reporting standards not met. Either there are too few cases for a reliable estimate or the coefficient of variation (CV) is 50 percent or greater.
[1]Excludes persons without earnings.
[2]A negative amount (a net loss) may be reported by self-employed persons.
NOTE: Detail may not sum to totals because of rounding and suppression of data that do not meet reporting standards.
SOURCE: U.S. Department of Commerce, Census Bureau, Current Population Survey (CPS), Annual Social and Economic Supplement, 2017; retrieved May 19, 2019, from https://www.census.gov/data/tables/time-series/demo/income-poverty/cps-pinc/pinc-03.html. (This table was prepared June 2019.)

Table 503.10. Percentage of high school students age 16 and over who were employed, by age group, sex, race/ethnicity, family income, nativity, and hours worked per week: Selected years, 1970 through 2017

[Standard errors appear in parentheses]

Year	Total	Age group: 16 and 17 years old	Age group: 18 years old and over	Sex: Male	Sex: Female	Race/ethnicity: White	Race/ethnicity: Black	Race/ethnicity: Hispanic	Family income[1]: Low income	Family income[1]: Middle income	Family income[1]: High income	Nativity: U.S.-born	Nativity: Foreign-born
1	2	3	4	5	6	7	8	9	10	11	12	13	14
						Percent employed[2]							
1970	31.9 (0.88)	30.8 (0.93)	39.7 (2.55)	35.2 (1.24)	28.3 (1.22)	— (†)	— (†)	— (†)	22.0 (2.51)	31.5 (1.12)	35.9 (1.64)	— (†)	— (†)
1975	33.2 (0.85)	32.9 (0.91)	34.9 (2.40)	35.0 (1.19)	31.2 (1.22)	38.0 (1.00)	13.9 (1.63)	21.8 (3.59)	18.4 (2.22)	31.8 (1.10)	40.4 (1.59)	— (†)	— (†)
1980	35.6 (0.87)	34.9 (0.94)	39.6 (2.28)	36.9 (1.22)	34.2 (1.24)	41.2 (1.03)	15.0 (1.64)	24.1 (3.65)	19.4 (2.10)	35.2 (1.15)	42.3 (1.59)	— (†)	— (†)
1985	31.6 (0.93)	30.8 (1.00)	36.1 (2.47)	32.1 (1.29)	31.0 (1.33)	37.9 (1.15)	15.0 (1.85)	17.6 (2.63)	14.7 (1.85)	31.0 (1.23)	41.1 (1.81)	— (†)	— (†)
1990	32.3 (0.98)	31.2 (1.08)	37.1 (2.33)	33.1 (1.37)	31.3 (1.39)	37.8 (1.24)	17.3 (2.05)	26.4 (2.86)	21.4 (2.16)	33.1 (1.29)	36.8 (1.97)	— (†)	— (†)
1995	33.6 (0.92)	32.7 (1.02)	37.5 (2.19)	33.1 (1.26)	34.2 (1.35)	40.8 (1.18)	18.0 (1.91)	22.2 (2.41)	17.4 (1.82)	34.4 (1.23)	42.1 (1.88)	34.9 (0.97)	20.1 (2.65)
2000	34.1 (0.93)	33.3 (1.03)	37.7 (2.15)	33.2 (1.28)	35.1 (1.36)	41.3 (1.20)	21.3 (2.14)	20.9 (2.18)	22.0 (2.11)	34.1 (1.22)	40.7 (1.85)	35.1 (0.99)	24.4 (2.74)
2001	32.4 (0.86)	31.1 (0.95)	37.8 (1.99)	30.6 (1.17)	34.5 (1.27)	38.9 (1.11)	18.7 (1.85)	23.6 (2.23)	21.4 (2.04)	33.3 (1.12)	36.1 (1.70)	33.3 (0.90)	23.0 (2.64)
2002	30.6 (0.84)	29.2 (0.93)	35.9 (1.92)	28.0 (1.13)	33.4 (1.24)	37.5 (1.11)	16.9 (1.81)	21.1 (1.94)	18.4 (1.83)	31.4 (1.11)	35.3 (1.64)	31.6 (0.89)	21.3 (2.34)
2003	27.0 (0.79)	25.3 (0.86)	34.6 (1.97)	26.7 (1.09)	27.3 (1.15)	33.3 (1.07)	15.2 (1.68)	18.8 (1.82)	14.3 (1.64)	27.8 (1.05)	31.8 (1.57)	28.0 (0.84)	17.7 (2.17)
2004	27.2 (0.80)	25.6 (0.87)	34.7 (2.03)	26.2 (1.09)	28.3 (1.17)	32.9 (1.08)	15.1 (1.71)	21.2 (1.92)	12.0 (1.55)	27.5 (1.05)	34.4 (1.64)	27.8 (0.85)	20.8 (2.43)
2005	26.4 (0.77)	25.2 (0.84)	32.2 (1.95)	25.3 (1.05)	27.6 (1.14)	31.8 (1.05)	13.7 (1.63)	19.4 (1.78)	14.8 (1.61)	26.9 (1.03)	31.7 (1.55)	26.8 (0.81)	21.7 (2.49)
2006	27.6 (0.79)	26.0 (0.86)	34.1 (1.87)	26.5 (1.08)	28.8 (1.16)	33.6 (1.08)	20.1 (1.85)	17.5 (1.72)	17.8 (1.72)	27.5 (1.04)	33.5 (1.59)	27.9 (0.82)	23.9 (2.64)
2007	26.2 (0.78)	24.8 (0.85)	32.2 (1.87)	25.0 (1.06)	27.6 (1.14)	31.3 (1.06)	15.1 (1.68)	21.1 (1.83)	17.3 (1.74)	25.9 (1.01)	32.1 (1.62)	26.0 (0.81)	28.5 (2.64)
2008	22.6 (0.74)	21.0 (0.80)	29.5 (1.83)	20.0 (0.99)	25.4 (1.10)	27.7 (1.04)	15.5 (1.69)	15.1 (1.54)	13.5 (1.54)	22.6 (0.96)	28.4 (1.59)	23.1 (0.78)	18.0 (2.35)
2009	17.0 (0.67)	15.2 (0.72)	23.8 (1.65)	16.0 (0.91)	18.1 (0.98)	21.5 (0.96)	10.5 (1.43)	11.9 (1.39)	9.7 (1.33)	16.3 (0.85)	23.5 (1.51)	17.0 (0.70)	16.9 (2.32)
2010	16.2 (0.55)	15.0 (0.59)	20.8 (1.52)	14.0 (0.78)	18.5 (0.86)	20.9 (0.86)	9.6 (1.28)	10.4 (1.18)	8.5 (1.01)	16.5 (0.80)	20.9 (1.31)	16.4 (0.60)	13.4 (2.20)
2011	16.9 (0.67)	16.4 (0.77)	18.7 (1.28)	14.7 (0.76)	19.4 (1.09)	22.2 (1.07)	10.2 (1.43)	11.3 (1.11)	10.2 (1.29)	17.5 (0.83)	19.6 (1.39)	17.3 (0.74)	12.4 (1.91)
2012	18.0 (0.71)	16.0 (0.75)	24.5 (1.88)	16.6 (0.83)	19.4 (1.13)	23.2 (0.97)	12.7 (2.17)	11.4 (1.23)	13.0 (1.42)	16.4 (0.88)	24.9 (1.55)	18.6 (0.76)	12.0 (2.01)
2013	17.9 (0.65)	15.8 (0.69)	24.7 (1.73)	17.6 (0.89)	18.3 (0.94)	23.3 (0.99)	11.8 (1.42)	14.0 (1.19)	9.7 (1.26)	16.9 (0.90)	25.4 (1.69)	17.8 (0.66)	19.0 (2.67)
2014	19.2 (0.70)	17.3 (0.71)	25.5 (1.63)	18.1 (0.90)	20.3 (1.03)	23.2 (1.00)	14.0 (1.65)	14.7 (1.47)	12.6 (1.52)	19.3 (0.88)	23.2 (1.54)	19.2 (0.75)	18.8 (2.20)
2015	19.0 (0.73)	17.2 (0.79)	25.8 (1.70)	18.1 (0.92)	20.0 (1.23)	22.2 (1.05)	15.0 (2.03)	15.7 (1.42)	13.7 (1.87)	18.8 (0.93)	22.3 (1.47)	19.0 (0.78)	19.2 (2.20)
2016	18.3 (0.70)	16.5 (0.79)	24.9 (1.80)	15.8 (0.88)	20.9 (1.16)	22.9 (0.95)	9.3 (1.54)	15.0 (1.38)	8.1 (1.17)	18.9 (0.98)	22.8 (1.58)	18.7 (0.77)	14.0 (2.13)
2017	20.3 (0.73)	17.7 (0.72)	29.5 (1.88)	18.1 (0.89)	22.7 (1.08)	24.8 (1.01)	15.7 (1.73)	15.9 (1.53)	13.3 (1.60)	19.9 (0.92)	25.0 (1.57)	20.4 (0.74)	19.4 (2.75)
						Percent working less than 15 hours per week[3]							
1970	13.6 (0.64)	14.5 (0.71)	7.5 (1.37)	12.3 (0.85)	14.9 (0.97)	— (†)	— (†)	— (†)	9.9 (1.81)	12.6 (0.80)	16.8 (1.28)	— (†)	— (†)
1975	13.4 (0.62)	14.0 (0.67)	8.8 (1.43)	12.5 (0.82)	14.3 (0.92)	15.5 (0.75)	5.3 (1.05)	6.6! (2.15)	6.8 (1.44)	12.3 (0.78)	17.4 (1.23)	— (†)	— (†)
1980	14.0 (0.63)	14.9 (0.70)	8.9 (1.33)	13.7 (0.87)	14.2 (0.91)	16.4 (0.77)	4.6 (0.96)	9.4 (2.49)	7.7 (1.41)	13.2 (0.82)	17.7 (1.23)	— (†)	— (†)
1985	12.3 (0.65)	12.8 (0.72)	9.5 (1.51)	11.7 (0.89)	12.9 (0.96)	15.2 (0.85)	6.2 (1.25)	3.0! (1.18)	3.6 (0.97)	11.8 (0.86)	17.5 (1.40)	— (†)	— (†)
1990	11.7 (0.67)	12.9 (0.78)	6.8 (1.21)	11.3 (0.92)	12.2 (0.98)	14.7 (0.90)	6.0 (1.28)	4.8 (1.39)	5.9 (1.24)	11.5 (0.88)	15.6 (1.48)	— (†)	— (†)
1995	11.9 (0.63)	13.1 (0.73)	6.8 (1.14)	11.1 (0.84)	12.9 (0.96)	14.8 (0.85)	6.5 (1.22)	6.5 (1.42)	4.4 (0.98)	11.3 (0.82)	18.1 (1.47)	12.6 (0.68)	5.1 (1.46)
2000	11.9 (0.64)	12.9 (0.73)	7.8 (1.19)	11.2 (0.86)	12.6 (0.94)	15.4 (0.88)	6.3 (1.27)	3.7 (1.01)	5.4 (1.15)	11.3 (0.82)	16.5 (1.40)	12.6 (0.68)	5.2 (1.42)
2001	11.6 (0.59)	12.6 (0.68)	7.7 (1.10)	9.8 (0.75)	13.7 (0.91)	15.0 (0.82)	4.3 (0.96)	6.1 (1.26)	5.7 (1.15)	10.8 (0.74)	16.4 (1.31)	12.2 (0.63)	5.5 (1.43)
2002	11.1 (0.57)	12.1 (0.66)	7.2 (1.04)	9.7 (0.74)	12.7 (0.87)	15.0 (0.82)	4.5 (1.00)	3.6 (0.89)	6.0 (1.12)	10.0 (0.72)	16.1 (1.26)	11.9 (0.62)	4.1 (1.13)
2003	9.6 (0.52)	10.0 (0.59)	7.8 (1.11)	9.0 (0.70)	10.2 (0.78)	12.4 (0.75)	4.5 (0.96)	5.5 (1.06)	4.8 (1.00)	9.1 (0.67)	13.1 (1.14)	10.2 (0.57)	3.7 (1.07)
2004	10.4 (0.55)	10.9 (0.62)	8.4 (1.18)	9.9 (0.74)	11.0 (0.82)	14.0 (0.80)	4.9 (1.03)	4.4 (0.96)	3.5 (0.87)	8.5 (0.66)	18.1 (1.33)	11.0 (0.59)	5.2 (1.33)
2005	10.1 (0.53)	10.7 (0.60)	7.2 (1.08)	8.9 (0.69)	11.4 (0.81)	13.4 (0.77)	3.7 (0.89)	5.0 (0.99)	3.7 (0.85)	9.9 (0.69)	13.9 (1.16)	10.6 (0.56)	4.6 (1.26)
2006	9.9 (0.53)	10.7 (0.61)	6.4 (0.97)	8.8 (0.69)	11.0 (0.80)	12.8 (0.76)	5.2 (1.03)	4.2 (0.91)	3.7 (0.85)	9.2 (0.67)	14.7 (1.20)	10.5 (0.56)	3.0! (1.06)
2007	10.6 (0.54)	11.4 (0.63)	7.0 (1.02)	9.5 (0.72)	11.7 (0.82)	14.2 (0.80)	3.0 (0.80)	6.0 (1.06)	6.1 (1.10)	9.6 (0.68)	15.3 (1.25)	11.1 (0.58)	5.7 (1.36)
2008	9.2 (0.51)	9.9 (0.59)	6.1 (0.96)	8.1 (0.68)	10.3 (0.77)	12.4 (0.77)	3.2 (0.82)	4.1 (0.85)	3.1 (0.78)	9.1 (0.66)	13.0 (1.18)	9.6 (0.54)	4.6 (1.28)
2009	7.6 (0.47)	8.0 (0.54)	6.2 (0.94)	6.8 (0.62)	8.4 (0.71)	10.1 (0.71)	3.6 (0.86)	4.7 (0.91)	3.6 (0.83)	6.9 (0.58)	11.8 (1.15)	7.8 (0.50)	5.2 (1.38)

See notes at end of table.

Table 503.10. Percentage of high school students age 16 and over who were employed, by age group, sex, race/ethnicity, family income, nativity, and hours worked per week: Selected years, 1970 through 2017—Continued

[Standard errors appear in parentheses]

Year	Total		Age group: 16 and 17 years old		Age group: 18 years old and over		Sex: Male		Sex: Female		Race/ethnicity: White		Race/ethnicity: Black		Race/ethnicity: Hispanic		Family income[1]: Low income		Family income[1]: Middle income		Family income[1]: High income		Nativity: U.S.-born		Nativity: Foreign-born	
1	2		3		4		5		6		7		8		9		10		11		12		13		14	
2010	7.3	(0.42)	7.5	(0.49)	6.8	(0.94)	6.3	(0.50)	8.4	(0.69)	9.5	(0.65)	4.1	(0.82)	4.5	(0.79)	3.0	(0.63)	7.1	(0.54)	10.9	(1.01)	7.7	(0.45)	3.4!	(1.21)
2011	7.3	(0.40)	8.1	(0.50)	4.4	(0.71)	5.8	(0.51)	9.0	(0.66)	11.0	(0.66)	2.2	(0.60)	2.7	(0.54)	3.7	(0.81)	7.0	(0.55)	10.2	(0.94)	7.7	(0.44)	2.8!	(0.98)
2012	8.2	(0.46)	8.5	(0.53)	7.3	(0.95)	7.1	(0.57)	9.4	(0.73)	12.2	(0.73)	3.7	(0.92)	2.4	(0.58)	4.2	(0.89)	7.2	(0.53)	13.3	(1.27)	8.8	(0.50)	2.4!	(0.75)
2013	7.9	(0.50)	8.2	(0.54)	6.8	(0.99)	6.9	(0.61)	8.9	(0.77)	12.2	(0.81)	2.6	(0.71)	3.4	(0.62)	2.9	(0.78)	7.0	(0.54)	13.1	(1.38)	8.1	(0.50)	5.5!	(1.75)
2014	7.8	(0.43)	8.4	(0.49)	5.7	(0.85)	6.5	(0.54)	9.1	(0.67)	10.7	(0.67)	3.5	(0.91)	3.5	(0.65)	3.8	(0.90)	7.6	(0.57)	10.9	(1.04)	8.2	(0.46)	3.7!	(1.14)
2015	8.5	(0.48)	8.7	(0.54)	7.8	(1.07)	7.8	(0.70)	9.3	(0.75)	10.9	(0.75)	7.0	(1.49)	5.3	(0.97)	5.0	(1.07)	7.7	(0.60)	12.2	(1.18)	9.1	(0.53)	3.4	(1.00)
2016	8.1	(0.48)	8.4	(0.57)	7.0	(1.12)	6.5	(0.58)	9.8	(0.85)	10.8	(0.73)	2.4!	(0.81)	5.0	(0.81)	2.6	(0.70)	7.5	(0.63)	12.4	(1.18)	8.5	(0.51)	4.5	(1.33)
2017	7.7	(0.50)	7.6	(0.55)	8.0	(1.01)	6.4	(0.58)	9.2	(0.73)	10.9	(0.79)	3.3	(0.84)	3.9	(0.80)	3.3	(0.74)	6.3	(0.59)	13.1	(1.19)	8.1	(0.54)	3.1!	(1.19)
Percent working 15 or more hours per week[3]																										
1970	17.5	(0.71)	15.6	(0.73)	30.8	(2.41)	22.1	(1.08)	12.6	(0.90)	—	(†)	—	(†)	—	(†)	10.6	(1.87)	18.4	(0.93)	18.1	(1.32)	—	(†)	—	(†)
1975	19.2	(0.71)	18.2	(0.75)	25.7	(2.20)	21.7	(1.03)	16.4	(0.97)	21.8	(0.85)	8.3	(1.30)	14.7	(3.08)	11.3	(1.81)	19.0	(0.93)	22.1	(1.34)	—	(†)	—	(†)
1980	20.5	(0.73)	19.0	(0.77)	29.4	(2.12)	22.1	(1.05)	18.9	(1.02)	23.5	(0.89)	10.1	(1.39)	14.3	(2.99)	11.4	(1.69)	21.0	(0.98)	23.1	(1.36)	—	(†)	—	(†)
1985	18.4	(0.77)	17.2	(0.81)	25.5	(2.24)	19.5	(1.09)	17.3	(1.09)	21.7	(0.97)	8.4	(1.44)	13.7	(2.37)	10.0	(1.57)	18.4	(1.03)	22.6	(1.54)	—	(†)	—	(†)
1990	19.7	(0.83)	17.5	(0.88)	29.1	(2.19)	21.0	(1.19)	18.3	(1.16)	22.1	(1.06)	10.6	(1.67)	21.5	(2.66)	15.0	(1.88)	20.8	(1.11)	20.2	(1.64)	—	(†)	—	(†)
1995	20.5	(0.79)	18.4	(0.84)	29.7	(2.07)	20.8	(1.09)	20.2	(1.14)	24.5	(1.03)	10.9	(1.55)	15.1	(2.07)	12.7	(1.60)	21.9	(1.07)	22.5	(1.59)	21.1	(0.83)	14.9	(2.35)
2000	21.1	(0.80)	19.2	(0.86)	28.8	(2.01)	21.1	(1.11)	21.0	(1.16)	24.6	(1.05)	13.8	(1.80)	16.3	(1.98)	15.6	(1.85)	21.5	(1.06)	23.1	(1.59)	21.3	(0.84)	19.0	(2.50)
2001	19.4	(0.73)	17.1	(0.77)	28.3	(1.85)	19.6	(1.01)	19.1	(1.05)	22.2	(0.95)	13.4	(1.62)	17.0	(1.97)	14.6	(1.76)	20.9	(0.97)	18.4	(1.37)	19.6	(0.76)	16.9	(2.35)
2002	18.5	(0.71)	16.1	(0.75)	27.9	(1.80)	17.5	(0.95)	19.7	(1.04)	21.4	(0.94)	11.9	(1.57)	16.8	(1.78)	12.3	(1.55)	20.7	(0.97)	17.4	(1.30)	18.7	(0.75)	16.5	(2.12)
2003	16.4	(0.66)	14.3	(0.69)	25.9	(1.82)	16.8	(0.92)	16.0	(0.94)	19.5	(0.90)	10.4	(1.42)	13.1	(1.57)	9.1	(1.35)	17.6	(0.89)	17.7	(1.29)	16.7	(0.70)	13.6	(1.95)
2004	16.0	(0.66)	13.8	(0.68)	26.2	(1.88)	15.5	(0.90)	16.6	(0.97)	17.8	(0.88)	10.2	(1.45)	16.6	(1.75)	8.1	(1.30)	18.3	(0.91)	15.2	(1.24)	16.1	(0.69)	15.2	(2.15)
2005	15.2	(0.63)	13.4	(0.66)	23.5	(1.77)	15.5	(0.88)	14.8	(0.90)	17.0	(0.84)	9.6	(1.40)	13.6	(1.55)	10.8	(1.40)	15.9	(0.85)	16.1	(1.23)	15.1	(0.66)	16.5	(2.24)
2006	17.0	(0.66)	14.4	(0.69)	27.0	(1.75)	16.8	(0.91)	17.1	(0.96)	19.5	(0.90)	14.5	(1.63)	13.3	(1.54)	13.8	(1.55)	17.7	(0.89)	17.3	(1.27)	16.6	(0.68)	20.8	(2.51)
2007	15.0	(0.63)	12.8	(0.66)	24.2	(1.72)	14.8	(0.87)	15.2	(0.92)	16.2	(0.85)	11.4	(1.49)	14.9	(1.59)	10.9	(1.44)	15.6	(0.83)	15.8	(1.27)	14.3	(0.65)	22.2	(2.43)
2008	12.8	(0.59)	10.3	(0.60)	22.7	(1.68)	11.4	(0.79)	14.1	(0.88)	14.3	(0.82)	11.9	(1.51)	10.6	(1.32)	9.9	(1.34)	12.8	(0.77)	14.4	(1.23)	12.7	(0.62)	13.0	(2.06)
2009	8.7	(0.50)	6.4	(0.49)	17.3	(1.47)	8.4	(0.69)	9.1	(0.73)	10.4	(0.71)	6.5	(1.15)	7.2	(1.11)	5.9	(1.06)	8.9	(0.66)	9.9	(1.07)	8.4	(0.52)	11.7	(1.99)
2010	8.3	(0.45)	6.9	(0.47)	13.4	(1.24)	7.2	(0.62)	9.4	(0.70)	10.5	(0.67)	5.3	(1.01)	5.6	(0.84)	5.3	(0.88)	9.0	(0.58)	8.7	(1.16)	8.1	(0.46)	9.6	(1.83)
2011	9.0	(0.52)	7.7	(0.56)	13.6	(1.10)	8.4	(0.63)	9.8	(0.78)	10.5	(0.77)	7.4	(1.30)	8.4	(1.06)	6.3	(1.10)	10.0	(0.69)	8.5	(0.94)	9.0	(0.55)	9.6	(1.84)
2012	8.9	(0.55)	6.7	(0.51)	16.5	(1.62)	8.4	(0.62)	9.5	(0.84)	10.0	(0.69)	8.2	(1.97)	8.4	(1.04)	8.3	(1.22)	8.7	(0.68)	9.9	(1.30)	8.9	(0.59)	9.6	(1.76)
2013	9.7	(0.56)	7.3	(0.53)	17.4	(1.57)	10.3	(0.85)	9.1	(0.67)	10.6	(0.81)	9.1	(1.37)	10.6	(1.10)	6.7	(1.19)	9.7	(0.82)	11.7	(1.12)	9.4	(0.60)	13.4	(2.15)
2014	10.7	(0.55)	8.2	(0.48)	19.3	(1.49)	10.8	(0.72)	10.6	(0.81)	11.6	(0.75)	9.4	(1.52)	11.0	(1.30)	8.6	(1.34)	11.1	(0.73)	11.1	(1.25)	10.2	(0.56)	15.1	(2.12)
2015	9.7	(0.54)	7.8	(0.53)	17.2	(1.50)	9.7	(0.66)	9.7	(0.86)	10.5	(0.75)	7.3	(1.31)	9.8	(1.11)	8.2	(1.41)	10.2	(0.72)	9.7	(1.05)	9.2	(0.57)	15.0	(2.08)
2016	9.7	(0.55)	7.6	(0.58)	17.3	(1.54)	8.8	(0.65)	10.6	(0.87)	11.6	(0.79)	6.9	(1.32)	9.0	(1.16)	5.5	(1.01)	10.8	(0.72)	9.8	(1.13)	9.7	(0.60)	9.0	(1.69)
2017	11.6	(0.58)	9.1	(0.55)	20.5	(1.62)	11.0	(0.75)	12.3	(0.90)	12.4	(0.77)	12.4	(1.61)	11.6	(1.33)	9.7	(1.47)	12.7	(0.67)	10.5	(1.17)	11.3	(0.58)	15.7	(2.54)

—Not available.
†Not applicable.
!Interpret data with caution. The coefficient of variation (CV) for this estimate is between 30 and 50 percent.
[1]Low income refers to the bottom 20 percent of all family incomes; high income refers to the top 20 percent of all family incomes; and middle income refers to the 60 percent in between.
[2]Percent employed includes those who were employed but not at work during the survey week.
[3]Hours worked per week refers to the number of hours the respondent worked at all jobs during the survey week. The estimates of the percentage of high school students age 16 and over who worked less than 15 hours per week or 15 or more hours per week exclude those who were employed but not at work during the survey week. Therefore, detail may not sum to total percentage employed.
NOTE: Race categories exclude persons of Hispanic ethnicity. Totals include racial/ethnic groups not shown separately. Prior to 2010, standard errors were computed using generalized variance function methodology rather than the more precise replicate weight methodology used in later years.
SOURCE: U.S. Department of Commerce, Census Bureau, Current Population Survey (CPS), October, 1970 through 2017. (This table was prepared April 2019.)

Table 503.20. Percentage of college students 16 to 24 years old who were employed, by attendance status, hours worked per week, and control and level of institution: Selected years, October 1970 through 2017

[Standard errors appear in parentheses]

Control and level of institution and year	Full-time students								Part-time students							
	Percent employed[1]		Hours worked per week[2]						Percent employed[1]		Hours worked per week[2]					
			Less than 20 hours		20 to 34 hours		35 or more hours				Less than 20 hours		20 to 34 hours		35 or more hours	
1	2		3		4		5		6		7		8		9	
Total, all institutions																
1970	33.8	(0.88)	19.0	(0.73)	10.4	(0.57)	3.7	(0.35)	82.1	(1.81)	5.0	(1.03)	15.9	(1.72)	60.1	(2.31)
1975	35.3	(0.83)	18.0	(0.67)	12.0	(0.56)	4.6	(0.36)	80.8	(1.55)	6.0	(0.94)	19.4	(1.56)	52.6	(1.97)
1980	40.0	(0.84)	21.3	(0.70)	14.0	(0.59)	3.9	(0.33)	84.7	(1.38)	7.9	(1.04)	22.5	(1.60)	52.7	(1.91)
1985	44.2	(0.88)	21.7	(0.73)	17.3	(0.67)	4.3	(0.36)	85.9	(1.41)	5.7	(0.94)	26.9	(1.80)	52.2	(2.03)
1990	45.7	(0.89)	20.6	(0.73)	19.3	(0.71)	4.8	(0.38)	83.7	(1.50)	4.0	(0.80)	26.0	(1.78)	52.7	(2.03)
1991	47.2	(0.88)	20.9	(0.72)	19.8	(0.70)	5.6	(0.41)	85.9	(1.45)	8.2	(1.15)	25.4	(1.82)	51.0	(2.09)
1992	47.2	(0.87)	20.3	(0.70)	20.3	(0.70)	5.5	(0.40)	83.4	(1.50)	7.5	(1.06)	27.2	(1.79)	47.8	(2.01)
1993	46.3	(0.89)	20.8	(0.72)	19.5	(0.71)	5.1	(0.39)	84.6	(1.43)	8.5	(1.10)	31.4	(1.84)	43.7	(1.96)
1994	48.6	(0.87)	20.1	(0.70)	21.7	(0.72)	5.8	(0.41)	86.3	(1.28)	9.8	(1.10)	31.1	(1.72)	43.8	(1.84)
1995	47.2	(0.87)	19.1	(0.69)	20.3	(0.70)	6.5	(0.43)	82.9	(1.45)	8.6	(1.08)	30.4	(1.77)	42.3	(1.90)
1996	49.2	(0.88)	18.2	(0.68)	22.3	(0.74)	7.0	(0.45)	84.8	(1.47)	8.3	(1.13)	27.5	(1.83)	48.0	(2.05)
1997	47.8	(0.86)	18.3	(0.67)	21.4	(0.71)	7.4	(0.45)	84.4	(1.46)	9.4	(1.17)	26.2	(1.77)	47.7	(2.01)
1998	50.2	(0.86)	20.2	(0.69)	20.6	(0.70)	8.0	(0.47)	84.1	(1.45)	7.0	(1.01)	26.8	(1.76)	49.3	(1.98)
1999	50.4	(0.86)	19.0	(0.68)	22.3	(0.72)	7.8	(0.46)	82.3	(1.55)	6.2	(0.98)	28.8	(1.85)	45.9	(2.03)
2000	52.0	(0.86)	20.1	(0.69)	21.7	(0.71)	8.9	(0.49)	84.9	(1.38)	8.6	(1.08)	27.8	(1.73)	47.5	(1.93)
2001	47.1	(0.80)	17.4	(0.61)	20.6	(0.65)	7.9	(0.43)	84.4	(1.29)	8.0	(0.97)	25.8	(1.56)	48.9	(1.78)
2002	47.8	(0.78)	17.3	(0.59)	20.9	(0.64)	8.5	(0.44)	78.9	(1.51)	8.7	(1.04)	25.3	(1.61)	43.4	(1.84)
2003	47.7	(0.78)	17.1	(0.59)	20.7	(0.63)	8.8	(0.44)	79.0	(1.44)	7.8	(0.95)	27.2	(1.58)	42.8	(1.75)
2004	49.0	(0.76)	17.7	(0.58)	21.6	(0.62)	8.6	(0.43)	81.5	(1.44)	8.5	(1.04)	27.4	(1.66)	44.1	(1.84)
2005	49.1	(0.75)	17.8	(0.58)	21.1	(0.61)	9.0	(0.43)	85.0	(1.30)	10.2	(1.10)	27.1	(1.62)	47.1	(1.82)
2006	46.5	(0.76)	15.1	(0.55)	22.0	(0.63)	8.1	(0.42)	81.0	(1.41)	7.3	(0.94)	27.6	(1.61)	45.5	(1.80)
2007	45.5	(0.74)	15.4	(0.54)	20.7	(0.60)	8.7	(0.42)	81.2	(1.39)	6.8	(0.90)	27.2	(1.59)	45.9	(1.78)
2008	45.3	(0.72)	15.6	(0.53)	20.1	(0.58)	8.7	(0.41)	79.4	(1.51)	9.3	(1.09)	24.7	(1.61)	44.4	(1.86)
2009	40.6	(0.69)	15.6	(0.51)	17.6	(0.54)	6.2	(0.34)	76.2	(1.57)	10.1	(1.11)	27.5	(1.65)	36.9	(1.78)
2010	39.8	(1.01)	14.9	(0.57)	17.2	(0.77)	6.6	(0.46)	73.4	(2.03)	10.7	(1.24)	28.3	(1.92)	32.8	(2.19)
2011	41.3	(0.94)	15.8	(0.67)	17.4	(0.66)	7.0	(0.44)	75.5	(1.93)	9.7	(1.21)	28.4	(1.99)	35.5	(2.16)
2012	41.0	(0.83)	15.1	(0.72)	17.8	(0.71)	7.2	(0.44)	71.7	(2.07)	9.0	(1.27)	29.5	(2.09)	32.1	(2.07)
2013	39.5	(1.00)	14.0	(0.67)	18.5	(0.77)	6.6	(0.50)	75.7	(2.06)	10.5	(1.44)	28.7	(1.76)	35.4	(2.11)
2014	41.3	(0.97)	15.6	(0.69)	17.9	(0.80)	6.6	(0.48)	80.3	(1.81)	13.8	(1.58)	26.9	(2.33)	38.5	(2.36)
2015	39.5	(0.98)	15.6	(0.77)	16.1	(0.75)	6.7	(0.56)	75.3	(2.33)	10.5	(1.48)	32.2	(2.67)	31.7	(2.15)
2016	39.7	(0.99)	15.5	(0.71)	16.6	(0.72)	6.6	(0.55)	79.2	(2.18)	10.8	(1.55)	31.4	(2.35)	36.0	(2.21)
2017	41.1	(1.10)	15.6	(0.76)	17.2	(0.81)	7.1	(0.54)	82.2	(1.78)	11.0	(1.45)	34.3	(2.19)	35.8	(2.32)
Public 4-year institutions																
1990	43.0	(1.18)	19.8	(0.95)	18.6	(0.93)	3.7	(0.45)	87.4	(2.25)	4.2!	(1.37)	27.9	(3.05)	54.7	(3.39)
1995	48.8	(1.16)	19.4	(0.92)	22.6	(0.97)	5.6	(0.53)	86.7	(2.08)	9.6	(1.80)	30.8	(2.83)	45.0	(3.05)
2000	50.5	(1.15)	19.1	(0.90)	21.5	(0.94)	9.0	(0.66)	87.3	(1.91)	8.5	(1.60)	26.4	(2.53)	50.9	(2.87)
2005	49.6	(0.99)	17.8	(0.76)	22.7	(0.83)	8.0	(0.54)	86.3	(1.90)	9.0	(1.58)	26.8	(2.45)	49.7	(2.76)
2010	40.8	(1.27)	15.2	(0.88)	18.0	(0.93)	6.6	(0.64)	70.4	(3.58)	10.5	(2.04)	26.9	(2.82)	32.1	(3.59)
2012	41.0	(1.13)	14.9	(0.95)	18.6	(0.99)	6.7	(0.57)	77.6	(3.20)	9.9	(2.41)	28.0	(3.44)	38.8	(3.36)
2013	40.1	(1.31)	13.9	(0.88)	19.2	(0.98)	6.6	(0.63)	78.8	(2.88)	9.8	(1.94)	26.6	(2.80)	41.1	(3.84)
2014	41.1	(1.31)	14.6	(0.91)	18.4	(0.99)	6.9	(0.69)	83.4	(2.86)	12.2	(2.61)	28.4	(3.69)	42.3	(3.81)
2015	39.5	(1.32)	14.9	(0.98)	16.5	(1.01)	6.6	(0.73)	76.9	(3.39)	10.1	(2.01)	30.4	(3.84)	34.8	(3.38)
2016	39.7	(1.27)	15.0	(0.81)	16.8	(0.95)	6.9	(0.72)	81.9	(3.00)	11.6	(2.10)	32.6	(3.67)	36.7	(3.33)
2017	39.8	(1.28)	14.7	(0.81)	16.3	(0.91)	7.4	(0.69)	85.1	(2.21)	8.8	(1.97)	37.2	(3.24)	38.0	(3.47)
Private 4-year institutions																
1990	38.1	(1.89)	24.0	(1.66)	9.9	(1.17)	3.5	(0.72)	89.9	(4.27)	‡	(†)	31.9	(6.62)	53.1	(7.09)
1995	38.6	(1.78)	21.6	(1.51)	10.7	(1.13)	4.6	(0.77)	80.1	(4.85)	14.9	(4.32)	26.8	(5.38)	36.5	(5.84)
2000	45.8	(1.88)	23.6	(1.60)	14.9	(1.34)	5.4	(0.85)	78.0	(5.36)	‡	(†)	18.5	(5.02)	52.6	(6.46)
2005	42.3	(1.64)	20.1	(1.33)	13.8	(1.15)	7.0	(0.85)	88.5	(3.32)	10.6!	(3.20)	34.5	(4.94)	43.2	(5.15)
2010	35.6	(2.37)	15.7	(1.63)	12.2	(1.52)	6.0	(1.08)	78.6	(7.00)	‡	(†)	23.4!	(7.49)	45.6	(9.01)
2012	40.4	(2.39)	19.9	(1.80)	12.2	(1.40)	6.7	(1.13)	84.4	(5.35)	9.5!	(4.53)	33.9	(6.58)	36.9	(7.38)
2013	34.0	(2.27)	14.9	(1.55)	12.8	(1.33)	5.6	(1.13)	86.9	(4.71)	21.9	(6.40)	29.8	(7.01)	35.2	(6.56)
2014	37.8	(2.29)	18.7	(1.72)	12.0	(1.62)	5.3	(1.00)	77.1	(6.82)	12.9!	(4.92)	13.5!	(5.59)	50.8	(8.76)
2015	32.8	(2.49)	18.5	(1.86)	8.3	(1.40)	5.7	(1.20)	73.8	(8.30)	10.4!	(4.68)	17.8!	(5.73)	45.6	(8.91)
2016	34.8	(2.20)	17.2	(1.73)	11.0	(1.20)	5.4	(0.94)	75.6	(8.00)	‡	(†)	13.4!	(5.72)	53.3	(8.65)
2017	37.7	(2.41)	19.7	(2.09)	12.4	(1.69)	4.7	(1.09)	78.3	(7.39)	‡	(†)	29.5	(7.41)	41.5	(9.13)
Public 2-year institutions																
1990	61.2	(1.94)	19.1	(1.57)	31.2	(1.85)	9.2	(1.15)	81.5	(2.17)	4.1	(1.12)	24.9	(2.42)	51.1	(2.80)
1995	52.9	(1.97)	15.6	(1.43)	25.3	(1.72)	10.9	(1.23)	81.1	(2.21)	6.1	(1.35)	32.5	(2.64)	40.5	(2.77)
2000	63.9	(1.79)	20.6	(1.51)	29.9	(1.71)	11.9	(1.21)	85.5	(2.09)	9.9	(1.77)	30.0	(2.72)	44.9	(2.95)
2005	54.2	(1.69)	15.6	(1.23)	24.2	(1.46)	13.4	(1.16)	82.0	(2.20)	10.8	(1.77)	25.8	(2.50)	44.8	(2.84)
2010	40.6	(1.90)	14.0	(1.20)	19.1	(1.50)	6.8	(0.78)	74.7	(2.51)	11.6	(1.93)	30.1	(2.86)	31.0	(3.08)
2012	41.2	(1.76)	12.0	(1.17)	19.8	(1.44)	8.4	(0.95)	66.1	(2.98)	8.3	(1.60)	30.0	(2.70)	26.9	(2.79)
2013	41.8	(1.89)	13.8	(1.37)	20.5	(1.55)	7.1	(1.05)	71.1	(3.02)	8.8	(1.92)	29.8	(2.85)	31.2	(3.09)
2014	45.0	(2.28)	15.9	(1.57)	21.3	(1.82)	6.9	(0.91)	77.5	(2.64)	15.2	(2.35)	28.3	(3.35)	32.4	(3.58)
2015	44.9	(2.08)	15.1	(1.44)	21.8	(1.64)	7.5	(1.08)	75.1	(3.03)	11.4	(2.54)	36.6	(3.66)	26.7	(3.20)
2016	45.6	(2.01)	15.4	(1.51)	22.4	(1.70)	7.5	(1.14)	78.2	(3.23)	10.7	(2.31)	33.0	(3.46)	33.4	(3.33)
2017	46.8	(2.30)	14.9	(1.47)	22.9	(1.91)	7.9	(1.22)	81.0	(2.85)	14.0	(2.46)	33.0	(3.47)	32.7	(3.47)

†Not applicable.
!Interpret data with caution. The coefficient of variation (CV) for this estimate is between 30 and 50 percent.
‡Reporting standards not met. Either there are too few cases for a reliable estimate or the coefficient of variation (CV) is 50 percent or greater.
[1]Includes those who were employed but not at work during the survey week.
[2]Excludes those who were employed but not at work during the survey week; therefore, detail may not sum to total percentage employed. "Hours worked per week" refers to the number of hours worked at all jobs during the survey week.

NOTE: Students were classified as full time if they were taking at least 12 hours of classes (or at least 9 hours of graduate classes) during an average school week and as part time if they were taking fewer hours. Prior to 2010, standard errors were computed using generalized variance function methodology rather than the more precise replicate weight methodology used in later years.
SOURCE: U.S. Department of Commerce, Census Bureau, Current Population Survey (CPS), October, selected years, 1970 through 2017. (This table was prepared April 2019.)

Table 504.10. Labor force status of recent high school completers, by college enrollment status, sex, and race/ethnicity: October 2015, 2016, and 2017

[Standard errors appear in parentheses]

College enrollment status, sex, and race/ethnicity	Total number of high school completers (in thousands)	Percent of high school completers: Separately for those enrolled in college vs. those not enrolled[3]	Percent of high school completers: For all high school completers	Percentage distribution of all high school completers: Employed	Percentage distribution of all high school completers: Unemployed (seeking employment)	Percentage distribution of all high school completers: Not in labor force	Labor force participation rate of all high school completers[1]	High school completers in civilian labor force[2]: Number (in thousands): Total, all completers in labor force	Number (in thousands): Employed	Number (in thousands): Unemployed (seeking employment)	Unemployment rate	High school completers not in labor force (in thousands)
1	2	3	4	5	6	7	8	9	10	11	12	13
2015 high school completers[4]												
Total	**2,965 (87.5)**	**† (†)**	**100.0 (†)**	**39.5 (1.68)**	**7.8 (0.90)**	**47.3 (1.72)**	**47.3 (1.72)**	**1,401 (61.3)**	**1,171 (57.7)**	**230 (26.9)**	**16.4 (1.81)**	**1,563 (73.0)**
Male	1,448 (64.6)	† (†)	48.8 (1.43)	43.4 (2.07)	7.8 (1.24)	51.2 (2.27)	51.2 (2.27)	742 (46.8)	628 (41.3)	114 (18.5)	15.3 (2.20)	706 (45.4)
Female	1,516 (56.6)	† (†)	51.2 (1.43)	35.8 (2.39)	7.7 (1.23)	43.5 (2.32)	43.5 (2.32)	659 (42.1)	543 (41.5)	116 (18.8)	17.7 (2.79)	857 (48.1)
White	1,748 (64.3)	† (†)	59.0 (1.58)	41.2 (2.11)	5.6 (1.00)	46.8 (2.25)	46.8 (2.25)	818 (49.1)	720 (46.8)	98 (17.2)	11.9 (2.00)	930 (52.3)
Black	370 (36.5)	† (†)	12.5 (1.13)	39.3 (5.07)	11.5! (3.80)	50.7 (5.43)	50.7 (5.43)	188 (29.3)	145 (25.1)	‡ (†)	22.6! (6.81)	182 (24.9)
Hispanic	589 (46.7)	† (†)	19.9 (1.40)	36.8 (3.90)	12.8 (2.83)	49.6 (4.01)	49.6 (4.01)	293 (31.7)	217 (25.3)	‡ (†)	25.9 (5.26)	297 (34.3)
Enrolled in college, 2015	2,053 (75.1)	100.0 (†)	69.2 (1.54)	31.4 (2.09)	4.5 (0.76)	36.0 (2.09)	36.0 (2.09)	738 (49.8)	645 (48.4)	93 (15.8)	12.6 (2.10)	1,314 (65.2)
Male	953 (51.9)	46.4 (1.86)	32.1 (1.43)	31.7 (2.66)	6.2 (1.41)	37.9 (2.86)	37.9 (2.86)	361 (33.6)	302 (30.6)	‡ (†)	16.3 (3.44)	592 (41.9)
Female	1,100 (55.2)	53.6 (1.86)	37.1 (1.58)	31.2 (2.78)	3.1 (0.82)	34.3 (2.75)	34.3 (2.75)	377 (35.6)	343 (34.8)	‡ (†)	9.0 (2.41)	723 (47.0)
2-year	748 (48.4)	36.5 (1.92)	25.2 (1.48)	40.7 (3.78)	6.6 (1.79)	47.3 (3.64)	47.3 (3.64)	354 (34.8)	305 (33.9)	‡ (†)	14.0 (3.79)	394 (37.9)
4-year	1,304 (61.3)	63.5 (1.92)	44.0 (1.61)	26.1 (2.29)	3.3 (0.77)	29.5 (2.37)	29.5 (2.37)	384 (36.7)	341 (34.8)	‡ (†)	11.3 (2.53)	920 (51.5)
Full-time students	1,880 (72.6)	91.6 (1.23)	63.4 (1.60)	28.7 (2.20)	4.2 (0.78)	32.9 (2.20)	32.9 (2.20)	619 (46.6)	540 (45.5)	‡ (†)	12.8 (2.40)	1,262 (65.2)
Part-time students	172 (26.1)	8.4 (1.23)	5.8 (0.87)	61.2 (6.57)	‡ (†)	69.3 (6.10)	69.3 (6.10)	119 (21.2)	106 (20.4)	‡ (†)	11.7! (5.74)	‡ (†)
White	1,247 (51.9)	60.7 (1.76)	42.1 (1.42)	33.1 (2.76)	3.6 (0.95)	36.7 (2.89)	36.7 (2.89)	458 (41.6)	413 (39.7)	‡ (†)	9.9 (2.47)	789 (47.1)
Black	206 (25.9)	10.0 (1.18)	6.9 (0.85)	28.1 (6.15)	‡ (†)	32.2 (6.46)	32.2 (6.46)	‡ (†)	‡ (†)	‡ (†)	‡ (†)	140 (22.8)
Hispanic	406 (37.6)	19.8 (1.56)	13.7 (1.14)	29.8 (4.23)	8.3! (2.62)	38.1 (4.48)	38.1 (4.48)	155 (22.0)	121 (18.1)	‡ (†)	21.7 (6.30)	251 (31.0)
Not enrolled in college, 2015	912 (53.5)	100.0 (†)	30.8 (1.54)	57.7 (2.97)	15.0 (2.34)	72.7 (2.94)	72.7 (2.94)	663 (46.1)	526 (40.1)	137 (22.7)	20.7 (3.01)	249 (31.2)
Male	495 (40.9)	54.3 (2.96)	16.7 (1.23)	65.9 (4.09)	11.0 (2.63)	76.9 (3.64)	76.9 (3.64)	381 (35.7)	326 (33.3)	‡ (†)	14.3 (3.38)	114 (20.6)
Female	416 (35.2)	45.7 (2.96)	14.0 (1.16)	47.9 (4.55)	19.8 (4.06)	67.7 (4.30)	67.7 (4.30)	282 (29.0)	199 (24.6)	‡ (†)	29.3 (5.53)	135 (21.6)
White	501 (37.4)	55.0 (3.15)	16.9 (1.18)	61.3 (3.74)	10.4 (2.27)	71.7 (3.76)	71.7 (3.76)	360 (31.2)	307 (29.8)	‡ (†)	14.5 (3.02)	142 (22.6)
Black	164 (28.9)	18.0 (2.77)	5.5 (0.94)	53.2 (8.70)	20.8! (7.6)	74.0 (7.66)	74.0 (7.66)	121 (25.3)	‡ (†)	‡ (†)	28.1! (9.64)	‡ (†)
Hispanic	184 (26.2)	20.1 (2.64)	6.2 (0.87)	52.2 (7.52)	23.0 (6.23)	75.2 (6.84)	75.2 (6.84)	138 (22.9)	96 (17.6)	‡ (†)	30.6 (7.81)	‡ (†)
2016 high school completers[4]												
Total	**3,137 (102.3)**	**† (†)**	**100.0 (†)**	**42.3 (1.64)**	**6.4 (0.85)**	**48.7 (1.75)**	**48.7 (1.75)**	**1,526 (72.2)**	**1,327 (66.1)**	**199 (27.1)**	**13.1 (1.63)**	**1,610 (77.4)**
Male	1,517 (70.6)	† (†)	48.3 (1.47)	45.2 (2.62)	8.3 (1.33)	53.4 (2.62)	53.4 (2.62)	811 (52.5)	685 (48.9)	126 (20.9)	15.5 (2.42)	706 (53.2)
Female	1,620 (66.7)	† (†)	51.7 (1.47)	39.6 (2.18)	4.6 (1.00)	44.2 (2.37)	44.2 (2.37)	716 (48.4)	642 (45.4)	‡ (†)	10.3 (2.12)	904 (53.2)
White	1,714 (66.9)	† (†)	54.6 (1.65)	47.6 (2.20)	4.6 (0.89)	52.2 (2.30)	52.2 (2.30)	895 (55.0)	816 (51.8)	79 (15.5)	8.8 (1.64)	819 (48.2)
Black	364 (35.6)	† (†)	11.6 (1.02)	41.7 (5.07)	20.4 (4.19)	62.1 (5.30)	62.1 (5.30)	226 (29.8)	152 (23.0)	‡ (†)	32.8 (6.10)	138 (23.0)
Hispanic	742 (50.8)	† (†)	23.7 (1.32)	35.5 (3.53)	4.2 (1.23)	39.7 (3.69)	39.7 (3.69)	295 (32.3)	264 (31.0)	‡ (†)	10.7 (2.95)	447 (42.8)
Enrolled in college, 2016	2,188 (93.4)	100.0 (†)	69.8 (1.64)	35.3 (1.94)	3.1 (0.63)	38.4 (2.03)	38.4 (2.03)	840 (57.2)	773 (54.3)	‡ (†)	8.0 (1.58)	1,348 (72.5)
Male	1,023 (57.8)	46.8 (1.86)	32.6 (1.36)	37.0 (3.07)	4.5 (1.06)	41.5 (3.21)	41.5 (3.21)	425 (38.0)	379 (35.8)	‡ (†)	10.8 (2.45)	599 (49.9)
Female	1,165 (66.2)	53.2 (1.86)	37.1 (1.72)	33.9 (2.56)	1.8! (0.67)	35.7 (2.64)	35.7 (2.64)	416 (40.0)	394 (38.9)	‡ (†)	5.2! (1.83)	749 (50.8)
2-year	744 (56.3)	34.0 (2.12)	23.7 (1.56)	47.0 (3.39)	4.9 (1.29)	51.8 (3.58)	51.8 (3.58)	386 (38.3)	349 (35.7)	‡ (†)	9.4 (2.38)	359 (39.1)
4-year	1,444 (76.1)	66.0 (2.12)	46.0 (1.85)	29.4 (2.20)	2.1! (0.66)	31.5 (2.27)	31.5 (2.27)	455 (40.6)	424 (39.4)	‡ (†)	6.8 (2.03)	989 (61.5)
Full-time students	1,992 (88.1)	91.0 (1.30)	63.5 (1.80)	31.7 (1.92)	2.9 (0.64)	34.6 (1.98)	34.6 (1.98)	689 (49.7)	632 (47.1)	‡ (†)	8.4 (1.79)	1,303 (70.2)
Part-time students	196 (30.1)	9.0 (1.30)	6.3 (0.91)	72.3 (7.83)	‡ (†)	77.1! (7.67)	77.1 (7.67)	151 (23.4)	142 (22.7)	‡ (†)	‡ (†)	‡ (†)
White	1,194 (59.5)	54.6 (1.93)	38.1 (1.56)	39.7 (2.63)	2.9 (0.83)	42.6 (2.72)	42.6 (2.72)	509 (41.7)	475 (40.7)	‡ (†)	6.8 (1.88)	685 (46.2)
Black	209 (31.9)	9.5 (1.36)	6.7 (0.97)	40.5 (7.07)	7.7! (2.90)	48.2 (6.96)	48.2 (6.96)	‡ (†)	‡ (†)	‡ (†)	‡ (†)	108 (21.1)
Hispanic	534 (44.6)	24.4 (1.60)	17.0 (1.22)	28.0 (3.98)	2.6! (1.09)	30.6 (4.11)	30.6 (4.11)	163 (25.3)	149 (24.2)	‡ (†)	8.5! (3.47)	371 (38.5)
Not enrolled in college, 2016	948 (56.3)	100.0 (†)	30.2 (1.64)	58.4 (2.69)	14.0 (2.17)	72.3 (2.65)	72.3 (2.65)	686 (46.2)	554 (38.6)	132 (22.5)	19.3 (2.81)	262 (30.4)
Male	493 (39.1)	52.0 (2.98)	15.7 (1.17)	62.0 (4.06)	16.2 (3.09)	78.3 (3.25)	78.3 (3.25)	386 (33.0)	306 (29.2)	80 (16.9)	20.7 (3.89)	107 (18.8)
Female	455 (40.5)	48.0 (2.98)	14.5 (1.26)	54.4 (4.02)	11.5 (3.07)	65.9 (4.23)	65.9 (4.23)	300 (33.3)	248 (28.8)	‡ (†)	17.5 (4.31)	155 (23.1)
White	520 (46.0)	54.8 (3.50)	16.6 (1.45)	65.6 (3.45)	8.5 (2.13)	74.2 (3.17)	74.2 (3.17)	386 (37.2)	341 (32.3)	‡ (†)	11.5 (2.81)	134 (20.6)
Black	156 (25.0)	16.4 (2.49)	5.0 (0.78)	43.3 (8.12)	37.4 (8.29)	80.7! (6.97)	80.7 (6.97)	126 (23.9)	‡ (†)	‡ (†)	46.4 (9.29)	‡ (†)
Hispanic	208 (27.2)	21.9 (2.60)	6.6 (0.85)	54.8 (6.14)	8.5! (3.34)	63.3 (6.30)	63.3 (6.30)	132 (21.5)	114 (20.2)	‡ (†)	13.4! (5.02)	‡ (†)

See notes at end of table.

Table 504.10. Labor force status of recent high school completers, by college enrollment status, sex, and race/ethnicity: October 2015, 2016, and 2017—Continued

[Standard errors appear in parentheses]

College enrollment status, sex, and race/ethnicity	Total number of high school completers (in thousands)	Percent of high school completers: Separately for those enrolled in college vs. those not enrolled[3]	Percent of high school completers: For all high school completers	Percentage distribution of all high school completers: Employed	Percentage distribution of all high school completers: Unemployed (seeking employment)	Percentage distribution of all high school completers: Not in labor force	Labor force participation rate of all high school completers[1]	High school completers in civilian labor force[2]: Number (in thousands): Total, all completers in labor force	Number (in thousands): Employed	Number (in thousands): Unemployed (seeking employment)	Unemployment rate	High school completers not in labor force (in thousands)
1	2	3	4	5	6	7	8	9	10	11	12	13
2017 high school completers[4]												
Total	**2,870 (95.9)**	**† (†)**	**100.0 (†)**	**42.5 (1.95)**	**6.5 (0.88)**	**49.0 (1.87)**	**49.0 (1.87)**	**1,407 (72.4)**	**1,221 (70.4)**	**186 (25.7)**	**13.2 (1.80)**	**1,463 (70.8)**
Male	1,345 (60.2)	† (†)	46.9 (1.58)	44.9 (2.48)	8.0 (1.40)	52.9 (2.41)	52.9 (2.41)	712 (44.4)	604 (41.8)	108 (19.4)	15.2 (2.57)	633 (43.8)
Female	1,525 (71.3)	† (†)	53.1 (1.58)	40.5 (2.71)	5.1 (1.14)	45.6 (2.73)	45.6 (2.73)	695 (51.5)	617 (49.2)	‡ (†)	11.2 (2.46)	830 (57.9)
White	1,601 (64.5)	† (†)	55.8 (1.57)	42.8 (2.41)	5.5 (1.10)	48.3 (2.37)	48.3 (2.37)	774 (49.1)	686 (47.2)	88 (18.0)	11.4 (2.24)	827 (50.3)
Black	402 (35.5)	† (†)	14.0 (1.19)	38.4 (5.44)	8.2! (2.53)	46.6 (5.14)	46.6 (5.14)	187 (25.2)	154 (24.7)	‡ (†)	17.6! (5.58)	214 (29.1)
Hispanic	597 (52.0)	† (†)	20.8 (1.62)	47.9 (4.36)	8.4 (2.34)	56.3 (4.19)	56.3 (4.19)	336 (38.4)	286 (35.9)	‡ (†)	15.0 (4.11)	261 (33.8)
Enrolled in college, 2017	1,915 (80.6)	100.0 (†)	66.7 (1.68)	35.8 (2.32)	4.1 (0.82)	39.8 (2.32)	39.8 (2.32)	763 (54.4)	685 (53.1)	‡ (†)	10.2 (2.06)	1,152 (65.9)
Male	822 (53.1)	42.9 (2.06)	28.7 (1.62)	36.8 (3.23)	4.4! (1.35)	41.2 (3.24)	41.2 (3.24)	339 (34.1)	303 (33.0)	‡ (†)	10.6! (3.20)	483 (41.3)
Female	1,093 (59.8)	57.1 (2.06)	38.1 (1.60)	35.0 (3.15)	3.8! (1.21)	38.8 (3.21)	38.8 (3.21)	424 (41.2)	382 (39.4)	‡ (†)	9.9! (3.07)	669 (51.5)
2-year	648 (45.9)	33.8 (2.11)	22.6 (1.50)	53.5 (3.75)	4.9! (1.68)	58.4 (3.66)	58.4 (3.66)	378 (33.9)	346 (33.6)	‡ (†)	8.4! (2.83)	269 (31.7)
4-year	1,267 (70.3)	66.2 (2.11)	44.2 (1.83)	26.7 (2.63)	3.6 (0.92)	30.3 (2.81)	30.3 (2.81)	384 (43.4)	338 (39.9)	‡ (†)	11.9 (2.87)	883 (57.3)
Full-time students	1,764 (80.2)	92.1 (1.23)	61.5 (1.74)	32.5 (2.37)	4.4 (0.89)	36.9 (2.39)	36.9 (2.39)	651 (51.4)	574 (49.5)	‡ (†)	11.9 (2.39)	1,113 (65.7)
Part-time students	150 (23.6)	7.9 (1.23)	5.2 (0.83)	74.0 (6.68)	‡ (†)	74.0 (6.68)	74.0 (6.68)	111 (20.8)	111 (20.8)	‡ (†)	‡ (†)	‡ (†)
White	1,106 (54.9)	57.8 (2.06)	38.5 (1.61)	35.7 (2.88)	3.2! (1.07)	38.9 (2.89)	38.9 (2.89)	431 (38.3)	395 (37.3)	‡ (†)	8.3! (2.69)	675 (46.2)
Black	239 (30.0)	12.5 (1.48)	8.3 (1.01)	28.4 (6.37)	‡ (†)	33.5 (6.66)	33.5 (6.66)	‡ (†)	‡ (†)	‡ (†)	‡ (†)	159 (25.7)
Hispanic	364 (42.4)	19.0 (1.98)	12.7 (1.40)	45.1 (5.78)	7.8! (2.69)	52.8 (5.62)	52.8 (5.62)	193 (29.5)	164 (28.4)	‡ (†)	14.7! (5.13)	172 (29.3)
Not enrolled in college, 2017	955 (57.1)	100.0 (†)	33.3 (1.68)	56.1 (3.07)	11.3 (1.94)	67.4 (2.80)	67.4 (2.80)	644 (47.4)	536 (44.4)	108 (19.2)	16.8 (2.83)	311 (32.1)
Male	523 (39.5)	54.8 (3.03)	18.2 (1.30)	57.6 (3.78)	13.8 (2.67)	71.3 (3.34)	71.3 (3.34)	373 (33.3)	301 (30.0)	‡ (†)	19.3 (3.66)	150 (20.5)
Female	432 (41.4)	45.2 (3.03)	15.1 (1.33)	54.3 (4.92)	8.4! (2.57)	62.7 (4.68)	62.7 (4.68)	271 (32.6)	235 (31.7)	‡ (†)	13.3! (4.08)	161 (25.8)
White	495 (39.4)	51.8 (2.86)	17.2 (1.26)	58.8 (4.10)	10.6 (2.51)	69.4 (3.79)	69.4 (3.79)	343 (33.2)	291 (30.4)	‡ (†)	15.3 (3.54)	151 (22.1)
Black	163 (22.6)	17.1 (2.18)	5.7 (0.80)	52.9 (7.65)	12.9! (5.02)	65.8 (7.14)	65.8 (7.14)	107 (19.2)	‡ (†)	‡ (†)	19.6! (7.46)	‡ (†)
Hispanic	233 (28.6)	24.4 (2.61)	8.1 (0.94)	52.3 (6.10)	9.4! (3.98)	61.7 (5.84)	61.7 (5.84)	144 (23.4)	122 (21.2)	‡ (†)	15.3! (6.28)	‡ (†)

†Not applicable.
!Interpret data with caution. The coefficient of variation (CV) for this estimate is between 30 and 50 percent.
‡Reporting standards not met (too few cases for a reliable estimate).
[1]The labor force participation rate is the percentage of persons who are either employed or seeking employment.
[2]The labor force includes all employed persons plus those seeking employment. The unemployment rate is the percentage of persons in the labor force who are not working and who made specific efforts to find employment sometime during the prior 4 weeks.
[3]Column 3 does not present any percentages that apply to all high school completers. Instead, it presents one set of percentages for only those completers who were enrolled in college and a second set of percentages for only those completers who were not enrolled in college.
[4]Includes 16- to 24-year-olds who completed high school between January and October of the given year. Includes recipients of equivalency credentials as well as diploma recipients.
NOTE: Data are based on sample surveys of the civilian noninstitutionalized population, which excludes persons in the military and persons living in institutions (e.g., prisons or nursing facilities). Data are for October of a given year. Standard errors were computed using replicate weights. Totals include race categories not separately shown. Race categories exclude persons of Hispanic ethnicity. Detail may not sum to totals because of rounding.
SOURCE: U.S. Department of Commerce, Census Bureau, Current Population Survey (CPS), October 2015, 2016, and 2017. (This table was prepared April 2019.)

Table 504.20. Labor force status of recent high school dropouts, by sex and race/ethnicity: Selected years, October 1980 through 2017

[Standard errors appear in parentheses]

Year, sex, and race/ethnicity	Number of dropouts (in thousands)	Percent of all dropouts	Percentage distribution of dropouts: Employed	Percentage distribution of dropouts: Unemployed (seeking employment)	Percentage distribution of dropouts: Not in labor force	Labor force participation rate of dropouts[1]	Dropouts in civilian labor force[2]: Number (in thousands): Total	Dropouts in civilian labor force[2]: Number (in thousands): Unemployed (seeking employment)	Dropouts in civilian labor force[2]: Unemployment rate	Dropouts not in labor force (in thousands)
1	2	3	4	5	6	7	8	9	10	11
					Estimates for individual years					
All dropouts										
1980	738 (44.0)	100.0 (†)	43.8 (2.97)	20.0 (2.37)	36.2 (2.87)	63.8 (2.87)	471 (35.2)	148 (19.5)	31.4 (3.44)	267 (26.5)
1990	412 (36.0)	100.0 (†)	46.3 (4.37)	21.6 (3.57)	32.2 (4.09)	67.8 (4.09)	279 (29.7)	89 (16.6)	31.8 (4.90)	132 (20.4)
2000	515 (28.5)	100.0 (†)	48.7 (2.77)	19.2 (3.01)	32.0 (2.59)	68.0 (2.59)	350 (23.5)	99 (17.2)	28.1 (4.16)	165 (16.2)
2005	407 (35.3)	100.0 (†)	38.3 (4.22)	18.9 (3.42)	42.8 (3.32)	57.2 (4.30)	233 (26.7)	77 (15.4)	32.9 (5.42)	174 (17.9)
2010[3]	340 (29.0)	100.0 (†)	30.9 (4.24)	23.0 (4.29)	46.1 (4.78)	53.9 (4.78)	183 (21.5)	78 (16.0)	42.7 (6.67)	157 (21.9)
2016[3]	513 (40.6)	100.0 (†)	34.7 (4.01)	16.2 (3.00)	49.1 (3.72)	50.9 (3.72)	261 (29.9)	83 (16.7)	31.9 (5.65)	252 (25.3)
2017[3]	530 (42.6)	100.0 (†)	33.9 (3.53)	7.9 (2.06)	58.2 (3.66)	41.8 (3.66)	222 (23.4)	‡ (†)	18.9 (4.59)	308 (34.2)
					3-year moving averages[4]					
All dropouts										
1980	748 (44.3)	100.0 (†)	44.4 (1.70)	19.9 (1.38)	35.7 (1.27)	64.3 (1.64)	481 (35.6)	149 (19.9)	30.9 (1.99)	267 (20.5)
1990	413 (36.1)	100.0 (†)	43.5 (2.50)	21.5 (2.08)	35.0 (1.86)	65.0 (2.41)	268 (29.1)	89 (16.8)	33.1 (2.96)	144 (16.5)
2000	515 (41.8)	100.0 (†)	44.1 (2.33)	19.0 (1.85)	36.9 (1.75)	63.1 (2.27)	325 (33.2)	98 (18.3)	30.1 (2.72)	190 (19.7)
2005	449 (37.1)	100.0 (†)	36.8 (2.30)	17.7 (1.83)	45.5 (1.84)	54.5 (2.38)	245 (27.4)	79 (15.7)	32.5 (3.04)	205 (19.4)
2010	365 (33.4)	100.0 (†)	28.7 (2.39)	23.7 (2.26)	47.6 (2.04)	52.4 (2.64)	191 (24.2)	87 (16.4)	45.2 (3.65)	174 (17.8)
2016	521 (27.4)	100.0 (†)	35.1 (2.31)	11.0 (1.67)	53.8 (2.32)	46.2 (2.32)	241 (17.7)	57 (9.7)	23.9 (3.37)	281 (18.8)
2017	522 (29.6)	100.0 (†)	34.3 (2.76)	12.0 (1.85)	53.7 (2.68)	46.3 (2.68)	241 (19.9)	63 (10.3)	25.9 (3.80)	280 (20.7)
Sex										
Male										
1980	393 (31.6)	52.6 (1.69)	55.5 (2.31)	19.5 (1.84)	25.0 (2.01)	75.0 (2.01)	295 (27.4)	77 (14.0)	25.9 (2.35)	98 (15.8)
1990	216 (25.7)	52.3 (2.48)	50.9 (3.44)	25.2 (2.98)	23.9 (2.93)	76.1 (2.93)	164 (22.4)	55 (12.9)	33.1 (3.71)	52 (12.6)
2000	279 (30.3)	54.1 (2.30)	49.8 (3.14)	19.6 (2.49)	30.7 (2.90)	69.3 (2.90)	193 (25.2)	55 (13.4)	28.2 (3.39)	85 (16.8)
2005	254 (27.4)	56.5 (2.33)	40.0 (3.06)	19.0 (2.45)	41.0 (3.07)	59.0 (3.07)	150 (21.1)	48 (12.0)	32.2 (3.80)	104 (17.6)
2010	196 (24.1)	53.6 (2.60)	32.1 (3.32)	22.4 (2.97)	45.5 (3.54)	54.5 (3.54)	107 (17.8)	44 (11.4)	41.2 (4.74)	89 (16.3)
2016	298 (20.3)	57.1 (2.35)	39.4 (3.15)	13.0 (2.39)	47.6 (3.11)	52.4 (3.11)	156 (13.9)	39 (7.8)	24.9 (4.24)	142 (13.5)
2017	306 (23.3)	58.7 (2.80)	41.0 (3.79)	13.5 (2.54)	45.6 (3.57)	54.4 (3.57)	167 (16.2)	41 (8.2)	24.7 (4.47)	139 (15.6)
Female										
1980	354 (29.1)	47.4 (1.63)	32.1 (2.21)	20.4 (1.91)	47.5 (2.37)	52.5 (2.37)	186 (21.1)	72 (13.1)	38.9 (3.19)	168 (20.0)
1990	197 (23.7)	47.7 (2.40)	35.4 (3.33)	17.4 (2.64)	47.2 (3.48)	52.8 (3.48)	104 (17.2)	34 (9.9)	33.0 (4.51)	93 (16.3)
2000	236 (27.0)	45.9 (2.23)	37.4 (3.19)	18.3 (2.55)	44.3 (3.28)	55.7 (3.28)	132 (20.1)	43 (11.6)	32.9 (4.15)	105 (18.0)
2005	196 (23.3)	43.5 (2.25)	32.6 (3.23)	16.0 (2.52)	51.4 (3.44)	48.6 (3.44)	95 (16.2)	31 (9.3)	32.9 (4.64)	101 (16.7)
2010	169 (21.7)	46.4 (2.51)	24.9 (3.20)	25.1 (3.21)	50.0 (3.70)	50.0 (3.70)	85 (15.3)	43 (10.9)	50.2 (5.23)	85 (15.3)
2016	224 (16.5)	42.9 (2.35)	29.5 (3.19)	8.4 (1.93)	62.2 (3.26)	37.8 (3.26)	85 (9.6)	‡ (†)	22.1 (4.82)	139 (12.4)
2017	216 (18.3)	41.3 (2.80)	24.8 (3.96)	10.0 (2.54)	65.2 (4.32)	34.8 (4.32)	75 (11.3)	‡ (†)	28.6 (6.67)	141 (15.0)
Race/ethnicity										
White										
1980	494 (36.0)	66.0 (1.62)	50.9 (2.11)	17.6 (1.61)	31.5 (1.52)	68.5 (1.96)	338 (29.8)	87 (15.2)	25.7 (2.24)	156 (15.7)
1990	240 (27.5)	58.0 (2.49)	51.4 (3.31)	19.3 (2.63)	29.3 (2.33)	70.7 (3.02)	170 (23.1)	46 (12.1)	27.3 (3.53)	70 (11.5)
2000	279 (30.8)	54.1 (2.34)	48.3 (3.19)	18.7 (2.50)	33.0 (2.32)	67.0 (3.00)	187 (25.2)	52 (13.4)	27.8 (3.51)	92 (13.7)
2005	215 (25.7)	48.0 (2.38)	41.6 (3.40)	14.2 (2.42)	44.2 (2.64)	55.8 (3.42)	120 (19.2)	31 ! (9.7)	25.5 (4.04)	95 (13.2)
2010	164 (22.4)	45.0 (2.63)	32.7 (3.70)	20.8 (3.22)	46.4 (3.04)	53.6 (3.93)	88 (16.4)	34 ! (10.3)	38.9 (5.28)	76 (11.8)
2016	246 (15.0)	47.2 (2.34)	45.9 (3.25)	8.6 (1.66)	45.5 (3.12)	54.5 (3.12)	134 (12.2)	‡ (†)	15.8 (3.02)	112 (9.3)
2017	257 (18.8)	49.3 (2.95)	42.0 (3.67)	10.7 (2.18)	47.3 (3.65)	52.7 (3.65)	135 (14.1)	‡ (†)	20.3 (3.99)	122 (12.4)
Black										
1980	154 (21.3)	20.6 (1.47)	21.0 (3.27)	28.3 (3.62)	50.6 (4.01)	49.4 (4.01)	76 (15.0)	44 (11.4)	57.4 (5.65)	78 (15.2)
1990	96 (18.5)	23.3 (2.27)	27.1 (4.93)	29.0 (5.04)	43.9 (5.51)	56.1 (5.51)	54 (13.8)	28 ! (10.0)	51.7 (7.41)	42 (12.3)
2000	102 (19.7)	19.8 (1.98)	28.0 (5.03)	22.2 (4.65)	49.8 (5.60)	50.2 (5.60)	51 (14.0)	‡ (†)	44.2 (7.85)	51 (13.9)
2005	88 (17.4)	19.5 (2.01)	21.5 (4.71)	27.7 (5.13)	50.9 (5.73)	49.1 (5.73)	43 (12.2)	‡ (†)	56.3 (8.11)	45 (12.4)
2010	70 (15.6)	19.3 (2.22)	22.4 (5.33)	30.4 (5.88)	47.2 (6.38)	52.8 (6.38)	37 ! (11.3)	‡ (†)	57.5 (8.69)	33 ! (10.7)
2016	89 (10.7)	17.0 (1.79)	27.6 (5.38)	16.0 (5.14)	56.4 (6.50)	43.6 (6.50)	39 (7.6)	‡ (†)	36.7 (9.74)	50 (8.1)
2017	83 (12.6)	15.9 (2.16)	28.3 (6.43)	12.6 (5.44)	59.1 (7.58)	40.9 (7.58)	‡ (†)	‡ (†)	‡ (†)	49 (10.1)
Hispanic										
1980	84 (18.7)	11.3 (1.36)	48.2 (6.40)	19.5 (5.07)	32.3 (5.99)	67.7 (5.99)	57 (15.4)	‡ (†)	28.8 (7.05)	27 ! (10.6)
1990	66 (15.3)	15.9 (1.96)	39.3 (6.56)	19.9 (5.36)	40.8 (6.60)	59.2 (6.60)	39 ! (11.8)	‡ (†)	33.5 (8.24)	27 ! (9.8)
2000	113 (20.8)	21.9 (2.06)	50.4 (5.32)	17.7 (4.06)	31.9 (4.96)	68.1 (4.96)	77 (17.1)	‡ (†)	26.0 (5.66)	36 ! (11.7)
2005	125 (20.8)	27.9 (2.27)	39.2 (4.68)	16.1 (3.52)	44.7 (4.77)	55.3 (4.77)	69 (15.4)	‡ (†)	29.1 (5.86)	56 (13.9)
2010	102 (18.8)	28.0 (2.52)	25.8 (4.64)	24.3 (4.55)	49.9 (5.30)	50.1 (5.30)	51 (13.3)	25 ! (9.3)	48.4 (7.49)	51 (13.3)
2016	140 (14.7)	26.8 (2.20)	22.5 (3.83)	13.0 (2.81)	64.5 (3.97)	35.5 (3.97)	50 (7.9)	‡ (†)	36.6 (7.25)	90 (10.5)
2017	137 (15.3)	26.4 (2.48)	24.7 (4.94)	13.7 (3.46)	61.6 (5.12)	38.4 (5.12)	53 (8.8)	‡ (†)	35.6 (8.26)	85 (12.1)

†Not applicable.

!Interpret data with caution. The coefficient of variation (CV) for this estimate is between 30 and 50 percent.

‡Reporting standards not met. Either there are too few cases for a reliable estimate or the coefficient of variation (CV) is 50 percent or greater.

[1]The labor force participation rate is the percentage of persons who are either employed or seeking employment.

[2]The labor force includes all employed persons plus those seeking employment. The unemployment rate is the percentage of persons in the labor force who are not working and who made specific efforts to find employment sometime during the prior 4 weeks.

[3]Beginning in 2010, standard errors for the individual year estimates were computed using replicate weights in order to produce more precise values. This methodology can only be used for these estimates. For all other estimates in the table, standard errors were computed using generalized variance function methodology.

[4]A 3-year moving average is the arithmetic average of the year indicated, the year immediately preceding, and the year immediately following. For example, the estimates shown for 2000 reflect an average of 1999, 2000, and 2001. Use of a moving average increases the sample size, thereby reducing the size of sampling errors and producing more stable estimates. For the final year of available data, a 2-year moving average is used; thus, the estimates for 2017 reflect the average of 2016 and 2017.

NOTE: Data are based on sample surveys of the civilian noninstitutionalized population, which excludes persons in the military and persons living in institutions (e.g., prisons or nursing facilities). Data are for October of a given year. Dropouts are considered persons 16 to 24 years old who dropped out of school in the 12-month period ending in October of years shown. Includes dropouts from any grade, including a small number from elementary and middle schools. Totals include race categories not separately shown. Race categories exclude persons of Hispanic ethnicity. Detail may not sum to totals because of rounding.

SOURCE: U.S. Department of Commerce, Census Bureau, Current Population Survey (CPS), selected years, October 1979 through 2017. (This table was prepared May 2019.)

Table 505.10. Number, percentage distribution, unemployment rates, and median earnings of 25- to 29-year-old bachelor's degree holders and percentage of degree holders among all 25- to 29-year-olds, by field of study and science, technology, engineering, or mathematics (STEM) status of field: 2010 and 2017

[Standard errors appear in parentheses]

Field of study and STEM status of field	2010: 25- to 29-year-old bachelor's degree holders: Number, in thousands	Percentage distribution	Unemployment rate for the civilian labor force	Median annual earnings of full-time year-round workers: Current dollars	Constant 2017 dollars[1]	Percent of all 25- to 29-year-olds with degree in specific field	2017: 25- to 29-year-old bachelor's degree holders: Number, in thousands	Percentage distribution	Unemployment rate for the civilian labor force	Median annual earnings of full-time year-round workers	Percent of all 25- to 29-year-olds with degree in specific field
1	2	3	4	5	6	7	8	9	10	11	12
Total, all bachelor's degrees	**6,366 (30.5)**	**100.0 (†)**	**5.6 (0.13)**	**$43,730 (684)**	**$49,160 (769)**	**30.5 (0.14)**	**7,890 (42.2)**	**100.0 (†)**	**3.1 (0.08)**	**$50,460 (448)**	**34.3 (0.18)**
Agriculture	59 (2.8)	0.9 (0.04)	3.8 (0.99)	40,150 (424)	45,140 (477)	0.3 (0.01)	75 (3.5)	0.9 (0.04)	1.4! (0.45)	45,440 (1,599)	0.3 (0.02)
Architecture	47 (2.5)	0.7 (0.04)	13.8 (2.49)	44,300 (2,686)	49,800 (3,020)	0.2 (0.01)	54 (3.6)	0.7 (0.05)	4.2 (1.19)	50,140 (462)	0.2 (0.02)
Area, ethnic, and civilization studies	28 (1.9)	0.4 (0.03)	5.2! (1.61)	41,250 (3,100)	46,380 (3,485)	0.1 (0.01)	31 (2.3)	0.4 (0.03)	3.7! (1.40)	41,730 (1,726)	0.1 (0.01)
Arts, fine and commercial	334 (7.0)	5.3 (0.11)	6.8 (0.55)	37,140 (803)	41,750 (873)	1.6 (0.03)	444 (9.7)	5.6 (0.12)	4.1 (0.34)	40,330 (141)	1.9 (0.04)
Fine arts	245 (5.4)	3.8 (0.08)	6.1 (0.69)	36,170 (888)	40,650 (998)	1.2 (0.03)	330 (8.2)	4.2 (0.10)	4.0 (0.42)	40,080 (408)	1.4 (0.04)
Commercial art and graphic design	89 (3.9)	1.4 (0.06)	8.6 (1.09)	38,860 (1,799)	43,680 (2,022)	0.4 (0.02)	113 (3.7)	1.4 (0.05)	4.3 (0.79)	44,420 (1,463)	0.5 (0.02)
Business	1,252 (13.9)	19.7 (0.19)	5.5 (0.24)	47,160 (1,004)	53,010 (1,091)	6.0 (0.07)	1,381 (17.4)	17.5 (0.19)	2.8 (0.19)	52,200 (225)	6.0 (0.08)
Business, general	222 (5.5)	3.5 (0.09)	5.7 (0.66)	45,960 (1,425)	51,670 (1,602)	1.1 (0.03)	261 (8.4)	3.3 (0.11)	3.3 (0.64)	50,440 (41)	1.1 (0.04)
Accounting	194 (5.7)	3.0 (0.09)	5.8 (0.68)	50,100 (141)	56,320 (158)	0.9 (0.03)	223 (6.5)	2.8 (0.08)	2.2 (0.42)	57,660 (1,348)	1.0 (0.03)
Business management and administration	339 (7.2)	5.3 (0.11)	6.5 (0.57)	43,200 (1,200)	48,560 (1,349)	1.6 (0.03)	335 (8.5)	4.2 (0.10)	3.4 (0.40)	50,480 (627)	1.5 (0.04)
Marketing and marketing research	187 (5.5)	2.9 (0.08)	4.6 (0.57)	44,250 (765)	49,740 (860)	0.9 (0.03)	195 (5.9)	2.5 (0.07)	1.6 (0.37)	50,360 (70)	0.8 (0.03)
Finance	170 (5.5)	2.7 (0.09)	4.9 (0.61)	52,620 (1,865)	59,150 (2,097)	0.8 (0.03)	166 (6.0)	2.1 (0.07)	2.9 (0.49)	63,680 (2,125)	0.7 (0.03)
Management information systems and statistics	23 (1.6)	0.4 (0.03)	3.4! (1.12)	55,020 (1,939)	61,850 (2,180)	0.1 (0.01)	25 (2.0)	0.3 (0.03)	‡ (†)	65,600 (4,674)	0.1 (0.01)
Business, other and medical administration	118 (3.7)	1.9 (0.06)	4.5 (0.57)	44,400 (720)	49,920 (810)	0.6 (0.02)	176 (4.9)	2.2 (0.06)	3.2 (0.61)	50,540 (121)	0.8 (0.02)
Communications and communications technologies	373 (8.2)	5.9 (0.12)	6.4 (0.45)	40,260 (18)	45,250 (20)	1.8 (0.04)	427 (7.8)	5.4 (0.10)	3.2 (0.34)	46,510 (978)	1.9 (0.03)
Computer and information systems	249 (6.2)	3.9 (0.10)	5.6 (0.55)	56,320 (1,809)	63,310 (2,034)	1.2 (0.03)	318 (8.6)	4.0 (0.11)	3.7 (0.58)	65,400 (665)	1.4 (0.04)
Construction/electrical/transportation technologies	35 (2.6)	0.5 (0.04)	4.8! (1.64)	49,720 (1,595)	55,890 (1,793)	0.2 (0.01)	43 (3.2)	0.5 (0.04)	2.8! (1.21)	58,700 (1,833)	0.2 (0.01)
Criminal justice and fire protection	140 (4.7)	2.2 (0.07)	6.2 (0.74)	39,300 (1,458)	44,170 (1,639)	0.7 (0.02)	209 (6.4)	2.6 (0.08)	3.5 (0.57)	42,310 (452)	0.9 (0.03)
Education	573 (8.0)	9.0 (0.12)	3.4 (0.31)	38,260 (80)	43,010 (87)	2.7 (0.04)	559 (10.0)	7.1 (0.12)	1.5 (0.25)	40,430 (15)	2.4 (0.04)
General education	151 (5.3)	2.4 (0.09)	4.7 (0.80)	39,350 (1,076)	44,230 (1,210)	0.7 (0.03)	163 (6.5)	2.1 (0.08)	1.0 (0.28)	40,340 (716)	0.7 (0.03)
Early childhood education	32 (2.0)	0.5 (0.03)	1.2! (0.58)	36,820 (1,808)	41,390 (2,032)	0.2 (0.01)	41 (2.6)	0.5 (0.03)	2.0! (0.92)	37,190 (1,918)	0.2 (0.01)
Elementary education	181 (5.0)	2.8 (0.08)	3.2 (0.53)	38,150 (938)	42,890 (1,055)	0.9 (0.02)	138 (4.6)	1.8 (0.06)	1.6! (0.57)	40,380 (23)	0.6 (0.02)
Secondary teacher education	19 (1.4)	0.3 (0.02)	2.5! (1.08)	36,140 (976)	40,630 (1,097)	0.1 (0.01)	17 (1.5)	0.2 (0.02)	‡ (†)	42,320 (3,103)	0.1 (0.01)
Education, other	190 (4.8)	3.0 (0.07)	2.9 (0.45)	38,480 (940)	43,260 (1,057)	0.9 (0.02)	199 (5.3)	2.5 (0.07)	1.8 (0.45)	41,930 (912)	0.9 (0.02)
Engineering and engineering-related fields	474 (8.8)	7.4 (0.13)	5.0 (0.41)	60,580 (748)	68,090 (813)	2.3 (0.04)	679 (9.9)	8.6 (0.12)	3.5 (0.31)	69,980 (523)	2.9 (0.04)
General engineering	63 (3.0)	1.0 (0.05)	4.3! (1.44)	60,100 (324)	67,560 (364)	0.3 (0.01)	74 (3.8)	0.9 (0.05)	3.9! (1.43)	62,140 (3,245)	0.3 (0.02)
Chemical engineering	28 (2.2)	0.4 (0.03)	4.4! (1.42)	65,580 (3,098)	73,710 (3,482)	0.1 (0.01)	50 (3.1)	0.6 (0.04)	2.6! (0.96)	69,240 (3,332)	0.2 (0.01)
Civil engineering	46 (2.9)	0.7 (0.05)	6.6 (1.69)	58,910 (1,276)	66,220 (1,434)	0.2 (0.01)	67 (3.2)	0.9 (0.04)	2.6! (1.00)	62,660 (2,804)	0.3 (0.01)
Computer engineering	45 (2.8)	0.7 (0.04)	7.1 (1.50)	65,320 (842)	73,430 (947)	0.2 (0.01)	61 (3.4)	0.8 (0.04)	4.0 (1.12)	75,430 (1,921)	0.3 (0.01)
Electrical engineering	86 (4.3)	1.3 (0.07)	5.1 (1.13)	65,060 (685)	73,130 (770)	0.4 (0.02)	115 (4.7)	1.5 (0.06)	3.0 (0.70)	72,630 (2,458)	0.5 (0.02)
Mechanical engineering	86 (3.9)	1.3 (0.06)	3.7 (0.77)	61,620 (1,428)	69,270 (1,605)	0.4 (0.02)	136 (4.7)	1.7 (0.06)	3.8 (0.77)	71,580 (1,011)	0.6 (0.02)
Engineering, other	78 (3.6)	1.2 (0.06)	4.9 (1.01)	59,850 (600)	67,280 (674)	0.4 (0.02)	122 (4.1)	1.6 (0.05)	3.7 (0.82)	69,780 (1,990)	0.5 (0.02)
Engineering technologies	42 (2.5)	0.7 (0.04)	4.7 (1.17)	55,890 (2,180)	62,820 (2,451)	0.2 (0.01)	52 (3.1)	0.7 (0.04)	3.6 (1.06)	60,270 (711)	0.2 (0.01)
English language and literature	194 (5.2)	3.0 (0.08)	7.6 (0.73)	38,100 (1,100)	42,820 (1,236)	0.9 (0.02)	217 (6.2)	2.8 (0.08)	3.4 (0.46)	40,420 (651)	0.9 (0.03)
Family and consumer sciences	55 (3.1)	0.9 (0.05)	3.9 (0.97)	36,060 (1,375)	40,530 (1,545)	0.3 (0.01)	69 (3.5)	0.9 (0.04)	3.7! (1.24)	38,040 (2,736)	0.3 (0.02)
Health professions	378 (8.2)	5.9 (0.12)	3.3 (0.39)	50,330 (20)	56,580 (21)	1.8 (0.04)	618 (8.2)	7.8 (0.10)	1.7 (0.23)	53,780 (1,085)	2.7 (0.04)
General medical and health services	200 (6.5)	3.1 (0.10)	3.6 (0.54)	46,290 (1,500)	52,040 (1,686)	1.0 (0.03)	312 (6.5)	4.0 (0.08)	1.8 (0.33)	50,190 (110)	1.4 (0.03)
Nursing	179 (5.5)	2.8 (0.08)	3.0 (0.57)	53,350 (1,366)	59,970 (1,535)	0.9 (0.03)	305 (6.9)	3.9 (0.08)	1.6 (0.32)	57,310 (1,117)	1.3 (0.03)
History	138 (4.5)	2.2 (0.07)	8.4 (0.77)	41,060 (1,385)	46,150 (1,557)	0.7 (0.02)	155 (4.7)	2.0 (0.06)	3.8 (0.58)	41,720 (944)	0.7 (0.02)
Liberal arts and humanities	76 (3.4)	1.2 (0.05)	7.2 (1.19)	40,130 (1,161)	45,110 (1,305)	0.4 (0.02)	85 (3.6)	1.1 (0.05)	5.8 (1.21)	38,960 (2,621)	0.4 (0.02)
Linguistics and comparative language and literature	68 (3.5)	1.1 (0.05)	8.6 (1.73)	38,130 (1,373)	42,860 (1,544)	0.3 (0.02)	75 (2.8)	1.0 (0.04)	2.2 (0.64)	44,670 (953)	0.3 (0.01)

See notes at end of table.

Table 505.10. Number, percentage distribution, unemployment rates, and median earnings of 25- to 29-year-old bachelor's degree holders and percentage of degree holders among all 25- to 29-year-olds, by field of study and science, technology, engineering, or mathematics (STEM) status of field: 2010 and 2017—Continued

[Standard errors appear in parentheses]

Field of study and STEM status of field	2010: 25- to 29-year-old bachelor's degree holders: Number, in thousands	2010: Percentage distribution	2010: Unemployment rate for the civilian labor force	2010: Median annual earnings of full-time year-round workers: Current dollars	2010: Median annual earnings: Constant 2017 dollars[1]	2010: Percent of all 25- to 29-year-olds with degree in specific field	2017: 25- to 29-year-old bachelor's degree holders: Number, in thousands	2017: Percentage distribution	2017: Unemployment rate for the civilian labor force	2017: Median annual earnings of full-time year-round workers	2017: Percent of all 25- to 29-year-olds with degree in specific field
1	2	3	4	5	6	7	8	9	10	11	12
Mathematics	78 (3.8)	1.2 (0.06)	4.6 (1.04)	50,120 (781)	56,350 (878)	0.4 (0.02)	107 (3.9)	1.4 (0.05)	3.9 (0.98)	55,230 (1,713)	0.5 (0.02)
Multi/interdisciplinary studies	55 (2.6)	0.9 (0.04)	5.4 (0.96)	39,770 (922)	44,700 (1,037)	0.3 (0.01)	93 (3.7)	1.2 (0.05)	2.9 (0.81)	45,000 (1,031)	0.4 (0.02)
Natural sciences	586 (9.2)	9.2 (0.14)	5.2 (0.38)	42,300 (787)	47,560 (856)	2.8 (0.04)	791 (13.3)	10.0 (0.15)	3.0 (0.32)	48,460 (655)	3.4 (0.06)
Biology	364 (8.1)	5.7 (0.13)	4.9 (0.50)	43,300 (927)	48,680 (1,042)	1.7 (0.04)	507 (10.1)	6.4 (0.12)	2.6 (0.33)	49,450 (1,563)	2.2 (0.04)
Environmental science	42 (2.8)	0.7 (0.04)	9.7 (1.98)	39,960 (1,549)	44,920 (1,741)	0.2 (0.01)	66 (3.2)	0.8 (0.04)	3.6 (0.79)	45,340 (842)	0.3 (0.01)
Physical sciences	180 (4.8)	2.8 (0.08)	4.7 (0.76)	42,210 (1,545)	47,450 (1,737)	0.9 (0.02)	218 (6.9)	2.8 (0.09)	3.7 (0.68)	48,280 (1,337)	0.9 (0.03)
Physical fitness, parks, recreation and leisure	101 (3.6)	1.6 (0.06)	3.5 (0.68)	40,250 (27)	45,240 (30)	0.5 (0.02)	169 (5.5)	2.1 (0.07)	3.7 (0.63)	42,320 (1,762)	0.7 (0.02)
Philosophy and religious studies	53 (2.3)	0.8 (0.04)	7.8 (1.56)	40,280 (1,419)	45,280 (1,595)	0.3 (0.01)	51 (2.8)	0.6 (0.04)	4.9 (1.35)	41,970 (3,354)	0.2 (0.01)
Psychology	378 (7.9)	5.9 (0.12)	5.9 (0.48)	37,240 (532)	41,860 (598)	1.8 (0.04)	482 (8.9)	6.1 (0.11)	3.5 (0.36)	40,320 (68)	2.1 (0.04)
Public administration and public policy	12 (1.6)	0.2 (0.02)	‡ (†)	50,090 (6,667)	56,300 (7,494)	0.1 (0.01)	16 (1.7)	0.2 (0.02)	‡ (†)	45,450 (5,270)	0.1 (0.01)
Social sciences	519 (8.6)	8.2 (0.13)	6.9 (0.43)	45,160 (528)	50,770 (574)	2.5 (0.04)	588 (10.6)	7.4 (0.12)	3.7 (0.31)	50,410 (35)	2.6 (0.05)
Anthropology and archeology	33 (2.0)	0.5 (0.03)	4.5 (1.14)	37,950 (2,738)	42,660 (3,078)	0.2 (0.01)	48 (2.8)	0.6 (0.04)	5.9 (1.49)	40,500 (1,589)	0.2 (0.01)
Economics	126 (4.4)	2.0 (0.07)	8.2 (1.00)	52,380 (2,049)	58,880 (2,304)	0.6 (0.02)	157 (5.6)	2.0 (0.07)	4.1 (0.68)	65,050 (1,287)	0.7 (0.02)
Geography	15 (1.7)	0.2 (0.03)	9.2! (3.53)	43,580 (2,973)	48,990 (3,342)	0.1 (0.01)	24 (1.9)	0.3 (0.02)	6.9! (2.43)	47,620 (3,066)	0.1 (0.01)
International relations	23 (2.0)	0.4 (0.03)	7.1! (2.75)	49,080 (1,756)	55,170 (1,974)	0.1 (0.01)	33 (2.3)	0.4 (0.03)	4.0! (1.50)	50,000 (2,196)	0.1 (0.01)
Political science and government	173 (4.8)	2.7 (0.08)	5.9 (0.70)	45,220 (108)	50,830 (121)	0.8 (0.02)	169 (5.2)	2.1 (0.06)	2.7 (0.45)	50,400 (346)	0.7 (0.02)
Sociology	116 (4.3)	1.8 (0.07)	7.6 (1.15)	38,200 (1,253)	42,940 (1,408)	0.6 (0.02)	119 (4.3)	1.5 (0.05)	3.8 (0.76)	42,110 (976)	0.5 (0.02)
Miscellaneous social sciences	32 (2.0)	0.5 (0.03)	5.3 (1.38)	40,250 (798)	45,250 (897)	0.2 (0.01)	39 (2.9)	0.5 (0.04)	1.9! (0.86)	42,110 (2,411)	0.2 (0.01)
Social work and human services	59 (2.8)	0.9 (0.04)	5.6 (1.38)	35,020 (138)	39,370 (155)	0.3 (0.01)	100 (4.3)	1.3 (0.06)	1.6 (0.34)	38,400 (588)	0.4 (0.02)
Theology and religious vocations	28 (2.0)	0.4 (0.03)	3.9! (1.88)	32,790 (1,349)	36,870 (1,516)	0.1 (0.01)	31 (2.1)	0.4 (0.03)	‡ (†)	34,950 (513)	0.1 (0.01)
Other fields	26 (2.0)	0.4 (0.03)	9.0 (2.31)	36,660 (2,542)	41,210 (2,858)	0.1 (0.01)	26 (2.0)	0.3 (0.03)	5.6! (1.87)	40,150 (2,094)	0.1 (0.01)
STEM status of field[2]											
STEM field	1,345 (13.7)	21.1 (0.21)	5.0 (0.26)	53,150 (967)	59,750 (1,087)	6.4 (0.07)	1,828 (19.2)	23.2 (0.21)	3.3 (0.19)	60,490 (35)	7.9 (0.08)
Non-STEM field	5,021 (29.4)	78.9 (0.21)	5.7 (0.14)	41,660 (692)	46,830 (778)	24.0 (0.14)	6,063 (35.9)	76.8 (0.21)	3.0 (0.10)	46,430 (562)	26.3 (0.15)

†Not applicable

!Interpret data with caution. The coefficient of variation (CV) for this estimate is between 30 and 50 percent.

‡Reporting standards not met. Either there are too few cases for a reliable estimate or the coefficient of variation (CV) is 50 percent or greater.

[1]Constant dollars based on the Consumer Price Index, prepared by the Bureau of Labor Statistics, U.S. Department of Labor.

[2]STEM fields include biological and biomedical sciences, computer and information sciences, engineering and engineering technologies, mathematics and statistics, and physical sciences and science technologies.

NOTE: The first bachelor's degree major reported by respondents was used to classify their field of study, even though they were able to report a second bachelor's degree major and may possess advanced degrees in other fields. Median earnings are for full-time employees working 35 or more hours per week. Data are based on sample surveys of the entire population residing within the United States, including both noninstitutionalized persons (e.g., those living in households, college housing, or military housing located within the United States) and institutionalized persons (e.g., those living in prisons, nursing facilities, or other healthcare facilities). Detail may not sum to totals because of rounding. Some data have been revised from previously published figures.

SOURCE: U.S. Department of Commerce, Census Bureau, 2010 and 2017 American Community Survey (ACS) Public Use Microdata Sample (PUMS) data. (This table was prepared October 2018.)

Table 507.15. Average literacy and numeracy scale scores and percentage distribution of 25- to 65-year-olds, by proficiency level and selected characteristics: 2012/2014

[Standard errors appear in parentheses]

Selected characteristic	Literacy						Numeracy					
	Average scale score[1]	Percentage distribution, by proficiency level[2]					Average scale score[1]	Percentage distribution, by proficiency level[2]				
		Below level 1	Level 1	Level 2	Level 3	Level 4/5		Below level 1	Level 1	Level 2	Level 3	Level 4/5
1	2	3	4	5	6	7	8	9	10	11	12	13
Total	**271 (1.0)**	**4.8 (0.50)**	**13.6 (0.64)**	**31.8 (0.94)**	**36.0 (1.02)**	**13.9 (0.75)**	**258 (1.2)**	**8.5 (0.53)**	**18.7 (0.75)**	**32.7 (0.97)**	**29.5 (1.01)**	**10.6 (0.76)**
Sex												
Male	273 (1.2)	4.5 (0.60)	13.9 (1.10)	31.3 (1.63)	35.0 (1.41)	15.2 (1.06)	266 (1.4)	6.7 (0.67)	16.7 (1.08)	30.5 (1.36)	31.5 (1.33)	14.6 (1.04)
Female	270 (1.3)	5.0 (0.70)	13.3 (0.79)	32.2 (1.18)	36.9 (1.34)	12.6 (0.90)	250 (1.4)	10.2 (0.84)	20.5 (0.99)	34.7 (1.45)	27.7 (1.23)	7.0 (0.83)
Age												
25 to 34	281 (1.8)	2.9 (0.49)	10.2 (1.02)	29.8 (1.40)	39.5 (1.66)	17.6 (1.51)	267 (1.9)	5.7 (0.72)	16.0 (1.25)	32.0 (1.60)	33.2 (1.75)	13.0 (1.35)
35 to 44	275 (1.8)	3.6 (0.86)	12.6 (1.49)	31.6 (2.19)	35.7 (1.81)	16.5 (1.59)	261 (1.6)	7.2 (0.91)	18.9 (1.48)	31.7 (1.72)	30.0 (1.66)	12.1 (1.31)
45 to 54	267 (1.7)	6.4 (0.95)	14.7 (1.41)	31.4 (1.71)	35.4 (1.90)	12.2 (1.06)	253 (2.1)	10.8 (1.19)	19.4 (1.58)	32.7 (1.97)	27.1 (2.09)	10.0 (1.28)
55 to 65	262 (1.5)	6.1 (0.98)	16.9 (1.67)	34.3 (1.81)	33.2 (1.83)	9.4 (1.23)	252 (1.8)	10.0 (1.11)	20.4 (1.69)	34.1 (1.80)	27.9 (1.85)	7.5 (1.08)
Race/ethnicity												
White	285 (1.1)	1.5 (0.29)	8.1 (0.58)	30.2 (1.19)	42.3 (1.32)	17.9 (0.96)	273 (1.3)	2.9 (0.45)	13.5 (0.81)	34.0 (1.08)	36.0 (1.15)	13.7 (1.04)
Black	245 (2.4)	7.5 (1.44)	26.3 (2.45)	39.3 (2.28)	23.4 (2.33)	3.6 (0.99)	217 (3.0)	21.3 (2.42)	34.0 (2.34)	32.4 (2.61)	10.8 (1.78)	1.4 ! (0.62)
Hispanic	229 (3.4)	19.1 (2.58)	28.1 (2.55)	31.6 (2.53)	17.6 (2.39)	3.6 ! (1.09)	218 (4.2)	25.2 (2.76)	29.9 (2.51)	27.1 (2.93)	14.8 (2.37)	2.9 ! (0.99)
Asian/Pacific Islander	271 (4.5)	4.9 ! (1.85)	15.0 (3.06)	31.1 (4.18)	34.1 (3.89)	14.9 (3.11)	267 (5.6)	6.0 ! (2.18)	16.8 (3.27)	30.7 (4.75)	32.2 (4.92)	14.4 (3.23)
Other[3]	268 (6.1)	‡ (†)	15.8 ! (5.24)	39.8 (7.24)	30.6 (5.42)	11.3 ! (3.80)	252 (6.2)	8.5 ! (3.65)	25.4 (5.82)	33.7 (6.10)	22.8 (4.79)	9.7 ! (3.55)
Nativity												
Born in United States	278 (1.0)	2.5 (0.33)	11.5 (0.67)	32.3 (1.02)	38.6 (1.15)	15.2 (0.82)	263 (1.2)	6.2 (0.53)	17.5 (0.79)	33.7 (1.01)	31.4 (1.11)	11.2 (0.83)
Not born in United States	238 (3.1)	17.1 (2.29)	24.7 (2.30)	29.3 (2.38)	22.1 (1.84)	6.8 (1.19)	232 (3.7)	20.7 (2.42)	24.7 (2.15)	27.3 (2.36)	19.8 (1.95)	7.5 (1.33)
Educational attainment												
Less than high school completion	209 (2.7)	26.1 (2.81)	35.7 (2.76)	30.2 (2.48)	7.5 (1.34)	# (†)	194 (2.6)	35.9 (2.59)	35.6 (3.07)	23.8 (2.96)	4.3 (1.24)	# (†)
High school completion[4]	260 (1.3)	3.9 (0.59)	17.3 (1.03)	41.2 (1.52)	31.4 (1.33)	6.3 (0.76)	245 (1.6)	8.9 (0.83)	24.6 (1.23)	39.4 (1.43)	22.7 (1.60)	4.4 (0.70)
Associate's degree	284 (2.5)	‡ (†)	6.7 (1.73)	31.6 (2.84)	47.8 (3.20)	12.9 (2.20)	268 (2.9)	2.8 ! (1.23)	13.6 (2.41)	38.8 (3.23)	36.4 (3.33)	8.5 (1.59)
Bachelor's degree or higher	304 (1.6)	0.6 ! (0.27)	3.1 (0.52)	17.9 (1.22)	48.3 (1.70)	30.0 (1.96)	295 (1.8)	1.1 ! (0.33)	5.9 (0.75)	23.2 (1.56)	45.8 (1.76)	24.1 (1.94)
Employment[5]												
Full-time[6]	278 (1.2)	3.9 (0.47)	11.0 (0.78)	29.0 (1.22)	39.8 (1.28)	16.3 (1.02)	267 (1.4)	6.2 (0.61)	15.5 (0.91)	31.6 (1.19)	33.6 (1.20)	13.1 (0.95)
Part-time[7]	274 (2.5)	3.2 (0.82)	12.3 (1.87)	33.3 (2.72)	37.5 (2.59)	13.7 (1.74)	259 (3.0)	7.1 (1.24)	18.5 (1.85)	35.4 (2.43)	28.6 (2.29)	10.3 (1.74)
Unemployed	257 (2.4)	5.2 (1.14)	20.3 (2.34)	39.5 (3.28)	28.3 (2.70)	6.7 (1.48)	237 (2.5)	11.7 (2.07)	29.9 (2.84)	35.7 (2.84)	18.4 (2.09)	4.4 (1.08)
Not in labor force	251 (2.3)	9.1 (1.72)	21.6 (2.00)	37.8 (2.05)	23.8 (1.81)	7.7 (1.06)	233 (2.3)	16.7 (1.57)	26.4 (2.00)	32.9 (2.24)	19.4 (1.69)	4.6 (0.86)
Annual earnings[8]												
Bottom quintile	262 (3.6)	6.2 (1.48)	17.0 (2.75)	34.6 (3.44)	32.1 (3.49)	10.2 (2.25)	244 (3.8)	12.1 (1.89)	23.8 (2.70)	33.9 (2.90)	23.7 (3.23)	6.6 (1.65)
Fourth quintile	255 (2.5)	8.5 (1.57)	17.5 (2.02)	36.9 (2.40)	29.5 (2.17)	7.5 (1.26)	241 (2.5)	13.6 (2.01)	23.9 (2.33)	35.3 (3.15)	21.4 (2.11)	5.9 (1.12)
Third quintile	270 (2.0)	3.6 (0.91)	13.5 (1.58)	34.2 (2.88)	37.8 (2.61)	11.0 (1.54)	257 (2.1)	5.6 (1.05)	20.0 (1.75)	37.4 (2.66)	29.5 (2.35)	7.4 (1.67)
Second quintile	287 (1.9)	‡ (†)	6.7 (1.24)	30.2 (2.67)	46.4 (2.48)	16.2 (1.82)	275 (2.0)	1.5 ! (0.59)	11.8 (1.87)	36.6 (2.52)	38.2 (2.60)	11.9 (1.62)
Top quintile	303 (2.2)	1.7 ! (0.65)	3.6 (0.96)	16.9 (2.30)	46.3 (3.04)	31.4 (2.49)	297 (2.5)	2.4 ! (0.72)	5.3 (1.18)	20.5 (2.08)	44.2 (2.34)	27.7 (2.31)

†Not applicable.
#Rounds to zero.
!Interpret data with caution. The coefficient of variation (CV) for this estimate is between 30 and 50 percent.
‡Reporting standards not met. Either there are too few cases for a reliable estimate or the coefficient of variation (CV) is 50 percent or greater.
[1]Scale ranges from 0 to 500.
[2]Proficiency levels 4 and 5 are combined for reporting purposes. The proficiency levels correspond to the score ranges shown in parentheses: below level 1 (0–175), level 1 (176–225), level 2 (226–275), level 3 (276–325), and level 4/5 (326–500). For details about the proficiency levels as well as specific examples of tasks at each level, see appendix B of *Skills of U.S. Unemployed, Young, and Older Adults in Sharper Focus: Results from the Program for the International Assessment of Adult Competencies (PIAAC) 2012/2014* (NCES 2016-039rev), available at http://nces.ed.gov/pubs2016/2016039rev.pdf.
[3]Includes persons of all other races and those of Two or more races.
[4]Includes completion through an equivalency program, such as a GED program.
[5]Excludes those who were employed but did not report the number of hours worked per week.
[6]Full-time employment is defined as working 35 hours or more per week.
[7]Part-time employment is defined as working less than 35 hours per week.
[8]Annual earnings were calculated based on monthly earnings, which include bonuses and self-employment income. Excludes those who reported no earnings.
NOTE: Results in this table are based on combined data from two rounds of U.S. data collection. The first round, completed in 2012, was the main data collection. The second round, completed in 2014, was a supplemental round, conducted to expand the sample of U.S. adults, allowing for more in-depth analysis. Race categories exclude persons of Hispanic ethnicity. Detail may not sum to totals because of rounding.
SOURCE: U.S. Department of Education, National Center for Education Statistics, Program for the International Assessment of Adult Competencies (PIAAC), U.S. PIAAC 2012/2014, retrieved May 9, 2017, from the PIAAC International Data Explorer (https://nces.ed.gov/surveys/piaac/ideuspiaac/). (This table was prepared May 2017.)

Table 507.30. Participation of employed persons, 17 years old and over, in career-related adult education during the previous 12 months, by selected characteristics of participants: 1995, 1999, and 2005

[Standard errors appear in parentheses]

Characteristic of employed person	1995: Percent of adults participating in career- or job-related courses		1995: Number of career- or job-related courses taken, per employed adult		1999: Percent of adults participating in career- or job-related courses		1999: Number of career- or job-related courses taken, per employed adult		2005: Employed persons, in thousands		2005: Percent of adults participating: In career- or job-related courses[1]		2005: Percent of adults participating: In apprenticeship programs		2005: Percent of adults participating: In personal interest courses		2005: Percent of adults participating: In informal learning activities for personal interest		2005: Number of career- or job-related courses taken[1]: In thousands	2005: Number of career- or job-related courses taken[1]: Per employed adult	
1	2		3		4		5		6		7		8		9		10		11	12	
Total	**31.1**	**(0.54)**	**0.8**	**(0.02)**	**30.5**	**(1.14)**	**0.7**	**(0.03)**	**133,386**	**(1,508.1)**	**38.8**	**(0.83)**	**1.4**	**(0.24)**	**21.8**	**(0.94)**	**73.5**	**(1.01)**	**108,443**	**0.8**	**(0.03)**
Sex																					
Male	29.0	(0.72)	0.7	(0.02)	28.3	(1.15)	0.6	(0.03)	71,754	(934.7)	31.7	(1.22)	2.0	(0.37)	18.5	(1.30)	73.4	(1.52)	44,512	0.6	(0.03)
Female	33.4	(0.83)	0.9	(0.03)	32.9	(1.14)	0.8	(0.03)	61,632	(1,219.3)	47.1	(1.43)	0.8	(0.23)	25.8	(1.23)	73.6	(1.37)	63,931	1.0	(0.05)
Age																					
17 through 24 years old	18.6	(1.01)	0.4	(0.02)	19.1	(1.91)	0.4	(0.06)	15,027	(1,030.4)	26.4	(3.01)	3.0 !	(1.03)	25.2	(3.37)	71.4	(3.15)	8,024	0.5	(0.09)
25 through 29 years old	31.2	(1.46)	0.8	(0.05)	34.3	(2.44)	0.8	(0.08)	14,555	(918.4)	36.1	(2.94)	3.1 !	(1.12)	24.5	(3.66)	70.9	(4.49)	9,493	0.7	(0.06)
30 through 34 years old	31.6	(1.30)	0.8	(0.04)	34.4	(2.50)	0.8	(0.08)	15,250	(977.2)	41.0	(3.06)	2.7 !	(1.10)	23.7	(2.63)	74.0	(2.54)	12,681	0.8	(0.07)
35 through 39 years old	35.1	(1.02)	0.9	(0.03)	29.2	(2.15)	0.7	(0.07)	15,286	(922.4)	41.7	(4.16)	1.0 !	(0.46)	21.6	(3.15)	77.7	(3.00)	13,807	0.9	(0.14)
40 through 44 years old	36.6	(1.29)	0.9	(0.04)	36.4	(2.44)	0.8	(0.07)	18,141	(946.3)	39.8	(2.73)	‡	(†)	23.3	(2.60)	71.2	(3.15)	15,586	0.9	(0.07)
45 through 49 years old	39.6	(1.94)	1.0	(0.06)	30.4	(2.42)	0.7	(0.06)	18,149	(842.5)	45.0	(2.15)	0.7 !	(0.29)	19.0	(2.09)	73.5	(2.68)	16,809	0.9	(0.06)
50 through 54 years old	34.4	(1.69)	0.9	(0.04)	34.7	(2.57)	0.8	(0.07)	14,624	(732.1)	42.6	(2.49)	0.7 !	(0.32)	19.5	(1.92)	76.3	(2.27)	14,881	1.0	(0.10)
55 through 59 years old	26.7	(1.86)	0.7	(0.06)	30.3	(2.83)	0.6	(0.08)	10,522	(676.0)	44.7	(2.98)	‡	(†)	18.3	(1.93)	73.0	(2.95)	9,901	0.9	(0.09)
60 through 64 years old	21.1	(2.41)	0.5	(0.06)	27.2	(3.80)	0.7	(0.15)	6,021	(498.8)	38.9	(3.97)	‡	(†)	23.4	(3.52)	73.0	(4.22)	4,919	0.8	(0.10)
65 years old and over	13.7	(1.86)	0.4	(0.06)	20.3	(4.21)	0.4	(0.08)	5,812	(493.3)	21.6	(3.48)	#	(†)	17.4	(3.13)	74.2	(3.75)	2,343	0.4	(0.07)
65 through 69	13.1	(2.28)	0.4	(0.08)	—	(†)	—	(†)	3,385	(415.5)	19.1	(4.05)	#	(†)	20.9	(4.88)	75.4	(5.18)	1,102	0.3	(0.08)
70 and over	14.6	(2.85)	0.4	(0.09)	—	(†)	—	(†)	2,427	(282.3)	25.1	(5.81)	#	(†)	12.6	(2.93)	72.6	(6.11)	1,241	0.5	(0.14)
Race/ethnicity																					
White	33.2	(0.61)	0.8	(0.02)	32.8	(0.98)	0.6	(0.03)	94,881	(1,538.6)	41.3	(0.93)	1.2	(0.25)	22.2	(1.11)	75.3	(1.17)	82,511	0.9	(0.03)
Black	26.2	(1.46)	0.7	(0.04)	28.1	(2.34)	1.0	(0.07)	13,773	(533.2)	39.2	(3.82)	1.7 !	(0.83)	23.5	(3.04)	66.9	(3.02)	10,311	0.7	(0.11)
Hispanic	18.1	(1.00)	0.4	(0.02)	16.4	(1.83)	0.5	(0.05)	15,741	(681.1)	25.0	(2.66)	2.9	(0.85)	16.2	(2.31)	65.8	(3.39)	8,786	0.6	(0.11)
Asian	—	(†)	—	(†)	—	(†)	—	(†)	3,770	(520.7)	36.9	(7.00)	‡	(†)	32.3	(7.26)	81.1	(5.88)	2,207	0.6	(0.12)
Pacific Islander	—	(†)	—	(†)	—	(†)	—	(†)	‡	(†)	‡	(†)	‡	(†)	‡	(†)	‡	(†)	‡	‡	(†)
Asian/Pacific Islander	25.5	(2.69)	0.6	(0.07)	32.8	(4.84)	0.4 !	(0.15)	—	(†)	—	(†)	—	(†)	—	(†)	—	(†)	—	—	(†)
American Indian/Alaska Native	34.0	(6.32)	0.9	(0.20)	29.5 !	(11.52)	‡	(†)	‡	(†)	‡	(†)	‡	(†)	‡	(†)	‡	(†)	‡	‡	(†)
Two or more races	—	(†)	—	(†)	—	(†)	—	(†)	3,786	(562.7)	39.1	(6.85)	‡	(†)	22.6	(6.34)	77.6	(8.40)	3,083	0.8	(0.15)
Other races	25.3	(2.99)	0.7	(0.09)	—	(†)	—	(†)	‡	(†)	‡	(†)	‡	(†)	‡	(†)	‡	(†)	‡	‡	(†)
Highest level of education completed																					
Less than high school completion	8.8	(1.05)	0.1	(0.02)	7.9	(2.29)	0.4	(0.05)	16,627	(838.2)	10.4	(2.11)	2.4 !	(0.90)	8.8	(1.54)	57.0	(3.76)	2,592	0.2	(0.03)
8th grade or less	6.1 !	(2.00)	0.1 !	(0.04)	—	(†)	—	(†)	5,016	(599.7)	2.7	(1.12)	‡	(†)	3.8 !	(1.71)	46.7	(7.11)	197	#	(†)
9th through 12th grade, no completion	10.0	(1.27)	0.2	(0.02)	—	(†)	—	(†)	11,610	(792.8)	13.7	(2.99)	‡	(†)	11.0	(2.06)	61.5	(4.05)	2,396	0.2	(0.04)
High school completion	20.9	(0.79)	0.4	(0.02)	21.4	(1.45)	0.8	(0.03)	34,121	(1,147.2)	24.7	(1.76)	1.3 !	(0.46)	17.1	(1.89)	63.4	(2.55)	16,640	0.5	(0.05)
Some vocational/technical	32.3	(2.50)	0.8	(0.07)	28.7	(5.76)	0.9	(0.17)	3,744	(393.1)	48.2	(5.92)	‡	(†)	25.5	(4.61)	74.0	(5.54)	3,802	1.0	(0.17)
Some college	29.9	(0.91)	0.7	(0.03)	29.0	(1.78)	0.7	(0.06)	24,479	(1,067.7)	39.9	(2.36)	1.9 !	(0.69)	25.2	(2.50)	79.8	(2.04)	18,437	0.8	(0.05)
Associate's degree	39.2	(1.58)	1.0	(0.05)	39.7	(3.07)	0.9	(0.09)	9,943	(730.7)	50.4	(3.71)	2.3 !	(0.84)	19.1	(2.86)	78.4	(3.88)	14,224	1.4	(0.21)
Bachelor's degree	44.6	(1.33)	1.2	(0.04)	43.8	(2.01)	1.0	(0.06)	26,475	(902.7)	53.1	(1.88)	‡	(†)	29.0	(1.77)	78.7	(1.94)	28,099	1.1	(0.06)
Some graduate work (or study)	50.2	(1.63)	1.4	(0.05)	46.8	(4.17)	1.2	(0.14)	17,998	(735.4)	61.1	(2.16)	‡	(†)	28.6	(2.01)	88.8	(1.16)	24,649	1.4	(0.07)
No degree	44.3	(3.18)	1.2	(0.10)	54.2	(4.94)	1.2	(0.14)	2,125	(227.9)	53.8	(5.79)	‡	(†)	39.3	(6.05)	75.0	(5.64)	2,412	1.1	(0.16)
Master's	50.5	(1.99)	1.4	(0.06)	45.3	(2.97)	1.1	(0.11)	11,330	(614.7)	62.7	(2.98)	‡	(†)	28.2	(2.27)	90.5	(1.40)	15,394	1.4	(0.09)
Doctor's	40.4	(6.42)	1.0	(0.16)	34.4	(4.79)	0.7	(0.12)	1,600	(227.2)	49.0	(5.80)	‡	(†)	28.8	(4.76)	87.8	(4.35)	2,204	1.4	(0.36)
Professional	67.6	(3.89)	2.0	(0.15)	67.6	(6.98)	1.9	(0.31)	2,943	(382.7)	66.5	(6.39)	‡	(†)	22.1	(5.05)	92.9	(2.21)	4,639	1.6	(0.21)

See notes at end of table.

Table 507.30. Participation of employed persons, 17 years old and over, in career-related adult education during the previous 12 months, by selected characteristics of participants: 1995, 1999, and 2005—Continued

[Standard errors appear in parentheses]

Characteristic of employed person	1995: Percent of adults participating in career- or job-related courses	1995: Number of career- or job-related courses taken, per employed adult	1999: Percent of adults participating in career- or job-related courses	1999: Number of career- or job-related courses taken, per employed adult	2005: Employed persons, in thousands	2005: Percent of adults participating: In career- or job-related courses[1]	2005: Percent of adults participating: In apprenticeship programs	2005: Percent of adults participating: In personal interest courses	2005: Percent of adults participating: In informal learning activities for personal interest	2005: Number of career- or job-related courses taken[1]: In thousands	2005: Number of career- or job-related courses taken[1]: Per employed adult
1	2	3	4	5	6	7	8	9	10	11	12
Locale[2]											
City	— (†)	— (†)	— (†)	— (†)	39,283 (1,391.3)	39.6 (1.67)	2.2 (0.60)	23.1 (1.43)	74.0 (1.77)	34,327	0.9 (0.05)
Suburban	— (†)	— (†)	— (†)	— (†)	48,452 (1,555.0)	41.1 (1.87)	1.2 (0.32)	23.3 (1.38)	74.2 (1.49)	39,802	0.8 (0.04)
Town	— (†)	— (†)	— (†)	— (†)	17,616 (1,060.7)	36.0 (2.64)	‡ (†)	19.6 (2.83)	71.7 (3.02)	12,947	0.7 (0.07)
Rural	— (†)	— (†)	— (†)	— (†)	27,847 (885.2)	35.4 (2.14)	1.4 ! (0.58)	19.0 (2.19)	72.7 (2.22)	21,135	0.8 (0.06)
Occupation											
Executive, administrative, or managerial occupations	42.9 (1.49)	1.2 (0.05)	40.6 (2.06)	1.0 (0.07)	14,596 (707.6)	53.6 (2.79)	‡ (†)	29.5 (2.89)	77.7 (2.87)	16,567	1.1 (0.09)
Engineers, surveyors, and architects	44.2 (4.46)	1.1 (0.12)	52.1 (6.96)	1.0 (0.16)	1,987 (244.9)	56.3 (5.68)	‡ (†)	30.5 (6.36)	81.0 (4.73)	2,323	1.2 (0.16)
Natural scientists and mathematicians	59.7 (3.97)	1.7 (0.15)	46.0 (6.61)	0.8 (0.14)	4,130 (445.4)	51.5 (5.64)	‡ (†)	31.2 (4.83)	85.3 (5.44)	3,693	0.9 (0.11)
Social scientists and workers, religious workers, and lawyers	59.5 (2.61)	1.8 (0.11)	56.9 (5.66)	1.7 (0.24)	4,697 (480.9)	66.8 (4.48)	‡ (†)	28.3 (3.81)	88.6 (2.95)	7,822	1.7 (0.29)
Teachers, elementary/secondary	53.9 (2.23)	1.5 (0.08)	52.1 (3.53)	1.2 (0.11)	7,085 (568.5)	67.7 (4.16)	‡ (†)	31.5 (3.93)	83.0 (2.79)	12,233	1.7 (0.13)
Teachers, postsecondary and counselors, librarians, and archivists	41.6 (4.57)	1.0 (0.15)	35.6 (5.85)	0.7 (0.14)	2,393 (420.9)	53.1 (8.63)	‡ (†)	17.7 (4.91)	90.9 (3.97)	2,122	0.9 (0.09)
Health diagnosing and treating practitioners	68.6 (5.85)	2.0 (0.23)	65.2 (11.99)	1.5 ! (0.50)	978 (208.8)	78.9 (7.10)	‡ (†)	27.4 ! (9.60)	86.6 (5.37)	1,951	2.0 (0.25)
Registered nurses, pharmacists, dieticians, therapists, and physician's assistants	72.8 (3.02)	2.2 (0.14)	72.2 (5.04)	1.8 (0.21)	2,794 (238.8)	79.7 (4.60)	‡ (†)	29.4 (4.17)	84.3 (3.70)	4,984	1.8 (0.15)
Writers, artists, entertainers, and athletes	23.4 (2.89)	0.5 (0.07)	30.6 (6.21)	0.6 (0.18)	2,969 (405.2)	29.9 (5.69)	‡ (†)	31.8 (6.15)	88.9 (4.39)	1,865	0.6 (0.15)
Health technologists and technicians	50.0 (4.08)	1.4 (0.12)	41.8 (6.00)	1.0 (0.19)	3,060 (436.7)	70.6 (7.31)	‡ (†)	27.8 (6.48)	77.5 (6.40)	4,473	1.5 (0.18)
Technologists and technicians, except health	43.8 (2.67)	1.1 (0.10)	37.6 (4.87)	1.0 (0.15)	1,774 (336.5)	29.4 (8.10)	‡ (†)	5.3 ! (2.02)	75.2 (8.98)	1,015	0.6 (0.17)
Marketing and sales occupations	25.2 (1.26)	0.6 (0.03)	21.1 (2.27)	0.4 (0.06)	14,845 (971.9)	32.3 (3.17)	‡ (†)	20.8 (2.64)	70.5 (3.53)	7,724	0.5 (0.05)
Administrative support occupations, including clerical	30.8 (1.15)	0.7 (0.03)	27.4 (2.02)	0.6 (0.05)	21,167 (1,179.4)	36.1 (2.95)	0.8 ! (0.40)	28.2 (2.28)	72.9 (2.37)	15,443	0.7 (0.10)
Service occupations	22.6 (1.25)	0.6 (0.04)	21.0 (2.15)	0.5 (0.07)	17,180 (1,033.7)	33.7 (3.13)	1.1 ! (0.36)	16.2 (2.31)	69.0 (2.74)	13,029	0.8 (0.10)
Agriculture, forestry, and fishing occupations	12.4 (2.47)	0.3 (0.07)	12.2 ! (4.09)	0.2 ! (0.07)	2,522 (423.8)	22.4 ! (7.61)	‡ (†)	23.0 ! (11.03)	62.9 (11.04)	960	0.4 ! (0.12)
Mechanics and repairers	29.1 (2.62)	0.7 (0.08)	15.0 (3.40)	0.3 (0.09)	5,241 (521.6)	28.3 (4.47)	4.0 ! (1.44)	12.6 (3.24)	69.3 (4.36)	2,669	0.5 (0.09)
Construction and extractive occupations	18.6 (2.33)	0.3 (0.04)	13.2 (3.16)	0.2 (0.06)	6,827 (647.1)	12.4 (3.04)	5.3 ! (2.26)	7.8 (1.88)	69.0 (5.25)	2,323	0.3 ! (0.13)
Precision production[3]	25.6 (4.04)	0.6 (0.12)	18.3 ! (6.52)	0.4 ! (0.12)	10,483 (839.3)	23.5 (3.79)	‡ (†)	14.0 (3.34)	64.9 (3.74)	4,904	0.5 (0.07)
Production workers	14.8 (1.13)	0.3 (0.02)	23.0 (3.17)	0.5 (0.08)	— (†)	— (†)	— (†)	— (†)	— (†)	—	— (†)

See notes at end of table.

Table 507.30. Participation of employed persons, 17 years old and over, in career-related adult education during the previous 12 months, by selected characteristics of participants: 1995, 1999, and 2005—Continued

[Standard errors appear in parentheses]

Characteristic of employed person	1995: Percent of adults participating in career- or job-related courses	1995: Number of career- or job-related courses taken, per employed adult	1999: Percent of adults participating in career- or job-related courses	1999: Number of career- or job-related courses taken, per employed adult	2005: Employed persons, in thousands	2005: Percent of adults participating: In career- or job-related courses[1]	2005: Percent of adults participating: In apprenticeship programs	2005: Percent of adults participating: In personal interest courses	2005: Percent of adults participating: In informal learning activities for personal interest	2005: Number of career- or job-related courses taken[1]: In thousands	2005: Number of career- or job-related courses taken[1]: Per employed adult
1	2	3	4	5	6	7	8	9	10	11	12
Transportation and material moving	15.8 (1.83)	0.3 (0.04)	18.4 (3.62)	0.3 (0.06)	7,858 (742.5)	15.2 (2.81)	‡ (†)	10.5 (3.10)	62.5 (5.32)	1,935	0.2 (0.05)
Handlers, equipment cleaners, helpers, and laborers	11.7 (2.77)	0.2 (0.06)	‡ (†)	‡ (†)	— (†)	— (†)	— (†)	— (†)	— (†)	—	— (†)
Miscellaneous occupations	38.8 (3.50)	1.0 (0.11)	14.2 ! (4.62)	0.3 ! (0.08)	801 (189.4)	17.2 ! (6.87)	‡ (†)	8.7 ! (4.31)	48.3 (13.96)	409	‡ (†)
Annual household income											
$10,000 or less	12.6 (1.31)	0.2 (0.03)	9.5 ! (3.09)	0.2 ! (0.05)	4,425 (444.8)	16.7 (4.35)	‡ (†)	26.2 ! (7.96)	69.7 (5.72)	1,556	0.4 ! (0.12)
$5,000 or less	8.7 (1.91)	0.1 (0.03)	— (†)	— (†)	1,635 (252.7)	19.1 (6.52)	‡ (†)	22.9 ! (7.91)	60.9 (8.84)	850	‡ (†)
$5,001 to $10,000	15.1 (1.62)	0.3 (0.04)	— (†)	— (†)	2,791 (454.1)	15.3 (5.68)	‡ (†)	28.1 ! (12.27)	74.8 (6.88)	706	0.3 ! (0.10)
$10,001 to $15,000	15.1 (1.71)	0.4 (0.04)	8.3 (1.88)	0.1 (0.03)	4,814 (633.4)	22.2 (5.77)	‡ (†)	17.3 ! (5.25)	64.5 (7.57)	2,189	0.5 (0.12)
$15,001 to $20,000	20.1 (1.36)	0.4 (0.03)	16.3 (2.75)	0.3 (0.05)	4,515 (398.8)	18.2 (3.09)	5.7 ! (2.71)	11.5 (1.96)	60.4 (5.11)	1,322	0.3 (0.05)
$20,001 to $25,000	20.4 (1.52)	0.5 (0.05)	18.8 (2.79)	0.4 (0.08)	5,593 (490.2)	23.8 (4.02)	1.1 ! (0.51)	13.3 (3.21)	71.5 (4.11)	2,817	0.5 (0.10)
$25,001 to $30,000	24.7 (1.34)	0.5 (0.03)	22.2 (2.73)	0.5 (0.07)	7,444 (680.4)	31.4 (4.88)	‡ (†)	16.7 (3.77)	73.5 (3.91)	4,322	0.6 (0.11)
$30,001 to $40,000	30.2 (1.13)	0.8 (0.03)	26.6 (2.82)	0.6 (0.07)	13,123 (928.5)	35.1 (3.45)	1.5 ! (0.65)	21.7 (3.71)	69.1 (3.55)	8,224	0.6 (0.06)
$40,001 to $50,000	34.7 (1.30)	0.8 (0.04)	32.3 (2.34)	0.7 (0.07)	13,647 (1,058.4)	31.5 (3.01)	1.8 ! (0.72)	20.1 (3.32)	73.5 (2.78)	10,072	0.7 (0.10)
$50,001 to $75,000	40.0 (1.18)	1.0 (0.04)	36.6 (1.86)	0.9 (0.06)	33,665 (1,430.4)	42.7 (1.80)	1.2 ! (0.51)	20.9 (2.10)	71.3 (2.55)	28,991	0.9 (0.06)
More than $75,000	45.2 (1.40)	1.3 (0.04)	42.5 (1.79)	1.0 (0.06)	46,160 (1,263.3)	48.1 (1.57)	1.3 ! (0.39)	26.0 (1.37)	79.2 (1.55)	48,951	1.1 (0.05)

—Not available.
†Not applicable.
#Rounds to zero.
!Interpret data with caution. The coefficient of variation (CV) for this estimate is between 30 and 50 percent.
‡Reporting standards not met. The coefficient of variation (CV) for this estimate is 50 percent or greater.
[1]The 2005 estimates on participation in career- or job-related courses were based on responses to multiple questions. Specifically, respondents were first asked what courses they had taken, and then whether each course was career- or job-related. In contrast, 1995 and 1999 respondents were asked a single, general question about whether they had participated in any career- or job-related courses. Therefore, 2005 results may not be comparable to results from the earlier years.
[2]Detail may not sum to totals due to missing locale information.
[3]For 2005, figures include "Production workers" occupations data.
NOTE: Data do not include persons enrolled in high school or below. Race categories exclude persons of Hispanic ethnicity. Detail may not sum to totals because of rounding.
SOURCE: U.S. Department of Education, National Center for Education Statistics, Adult Education Survey (AE-NHES:1995, AE-NHES:1999, and AE-NHES:2005) of the National Household Education Surveys Program. (This table was prepared October 2010.)

Table 507.40. Participation rate of persons, 17 years old and over, in adult education during the previous 12 months, by selected characteristics of participants: Selected years, 1991 through 2005

[Standard errors appear in parentheses]

Characteristic of participant	Percent taking any program, class, or course					Percent taking specific programs, classes, or courses, 2005						Percent doing informal learning activities for personal interest, 2005
	1991	1995	1999	2001	2005	Basic skills/ General Educational Development (GED) classes	English as a second language (ESL) classes	Part-time post-secondary education[1]	Career- or job-related courses	Apprenticeship programs	Personal-interest courses	
1	2	3	4	5	6	7	8	9	10	11	12	13
Total	**33.0 (0.68)**	**40.2 (0.48)**	**44.5 (0.77)**	**46.4 (0.55)**	**44.4 (0.74)**	**1.3 (0.22)**	**0.9 (0.17)**	**5.0 (0.29)**	**27.0 (0.63)**	**1.2 (0.18)**	**21.4 (0.71)**	**70.5 (0.79)**
Sex												
Male	32.6 (1.09)	38.2 (0.65)	41.7 (1.15)	43.1 (0.83)	41.0 (1.20)	1.4 (0.41)	0.9 ! (0.29)	5.0 (0.44)	24.5 (0.99)	1.7 (0.31)	18.3 (1.08)	70.8 (1.10)
Female	33.2 (0.97)	42.1 (0.59)	47.1 (1.02)	49.5 (0.78)	47.5 (1.01)	1.2 (0.19)	0.9 (0.15)	5.1 (0.37)	29.2 (0.95)	0.7 (0.15)	24.2 (0.88)	70.2 (1.03)
Age												
17 to 24 years old	37.8 (1.46)	47.0 (1.12)	49.9 (2.34)	52.8 (2.04)	52.8 (2.79)	6.0 (1.48)	1.7 ! (0.61)	11.5 (1.34)	21.3 (2.22)	2.7 (0.76)	26.3 (2.60)	69.2 (2.54)
25 to 29 years old	40.0 (2.33)	49.6 (1.31)	56.5 (2.53)	52.9 (2.60)	51.6 (3.82)	1.8 (0.48)	3.3 ! (1.48)	9.1 (1.50)	29.5 (2.48)	3.2 ! (1.06)	20.9 (2.78)	66.8 (3.75)
30 to 34 years old	37.6 (2.88)	47.3 (1.41)	56.2 (2.57)	53.7 (2.18)	52.7 (2.52)	1.9 ! (0.66)	1.6 ! (0.64)	8.4 (1.28)	33.8 (2.71)	2.5 ! (0.89)	23.2 (2.23)	73.8 (2.22)
35 to 39 years old	42.1 (2.71)	47.7 (1.15)	50.1 (2.43)	54.0 (1.71)	48.6 (3.21)	0.4 ! (0.16)	0.7 ! (0.26)	6.1 (0.90)	32.6 (3.29)	0.9 ! (0.36)	20.7 (2.67)	75.5 (2.69)
40 to 44 years old	49.2 (3.28)	50.9 (1.15)	50.5 (2.43)	53.5 (1.88)	48.9 (2.43)	0.8 ! (0.31)	0.6 ! (0.23)	4.7 (0.77)	34.8 (2.30)	0.9 ! (0.42)	23.4 (2.29)	71.5 (2.62)
45 to 49 years old	40.0 (2.43)	48.7 (1.66)	49.8 (2.69)	55.4 (2.02)	49.0 (2.09)	‡ (†)	0.6 ! (0.25)	3.2 (0.48)	37.7 (1.83)	0.5 ! (0.23)	19.3 (1.88)	71.6 (2.52)
50 to 54 years old	26.8 (3.31)	42.5 (1.38)	47.2 (2.51)	51.1 (2.22)	46.6 (2.36)	‡ (†)	0.3 ! (0.15)	4.5 (0.75)	35.2 (2.25)	0.6 ! (0.28)	20.3 (1.64)	75.6 (1.89)
55 to 59 years old	29.0 (3.74)	32.2 (1.66)	38.0 (2.60)	44.1 (1.98)	42.2 (2.78)	‡ (†)	‡ (†)	1.9 (0.43)	31.9 (2.39)	‡ (†)	18.0 (1.63)	69.5 (2.56)
60 to 64 years old	17.4 (1.90)	23.7 (1.89)	31.4 (2.83)	30.8 (2.18)	37.9 (3.00)	‡ (†)	‡ (†)	0.9 ! (0.36)	20.9 (2.07)	‡ (†)	24.1 (2.40)	71.4 (3.04)
65 to 69 years old	14.2 (2.97)	18.1 (1.46)	25.4 (2.54)	20.5 (1.74)	26.2 (2.67)	‡ (†)	‡ (†)	0.5 ! (0.22)	8.1 (1.36)	‡ (†)	20.9 (2.41)	67.6 (2.52)
70 years old and over	8.6 (1.25)	13.8 (1.09)	15.0 (1.38)	21.7 (1.37)	21.5 (1.44)	‡ (†)	‡ (†)	‡ (†)	4.0 (0.78)	‡ (†)	17.9 (1.33)	62.9 (1.82)
Racial/ethnic group												
White	34.1 (0.82)	41.5 (0.54)	44.4 (0.89)	47.4 (0.59)	45.6 (0.84)	0.9 (0.23)	0.2 ! (0.08)	4.9 (0.35)	29.1 (0.70)	0.9 (0.17)	22.1 (0.87)	73.0 (0.92)
Black	25.9 (2.23)	37.0 (1.45)	46.3 (2.30)	43.3 (1.50)	46.4 (2.81)	1.9 (0.49)	‡ (†)	5.4 (0.97)	27.0 (2.53)	1.5 ! (0.73)	23.7 (2.11)	65.3 (2.02)
Hispanic	31.4 (2.63)	33.7 (1.18)	41.3 (2.51)	41.7 (2.28)	37.8 (2.43)	2.6 (0.72)	5.6 (1.22)	5.7 (1.55)	16.9 (1.72)	2.2 (0.63)	15.4 (1.75)	57.5 (2.86)
Asian	— (†)	— (†)	— (†)	— (†)	48.3 (5.39)	‡ (†)	2.6 ! (1.03)	7.6 ! (2.62)	27.2 (4.70)	‡ (†)	26.5 (5.06)	81.1 (4.10)
Pacific Islander	— (†)	— (†)	— (†)	— (†)	‡ (†)	‡ (†)	‡ (†)	‡ (†)	‡ (†)	‡ (†)	‡ (†)	‡ (†)
Asian/Pacific Islander	35.9 (5.55)	39.7 (2.92)	51.1 (4.63)	49.5 (3.81)	‡ (†)	‡ (†)	‡ (†)	‡ (†)	‡ (†)	‡ (†)	‡ (†)	‡ (†)
American Indian/Alaska Native	29.3 ! (11.55)	38.8 (4.85)	36.3 (9.16)	50.2 (8.28)	36.3 (10.17)	‡ (†)	‡ (†)	4.4 ! (1.82)	23.0 ! (8.51)	‡ (†)	13.0 ! (6.16)	70.6 (9.18)
Two or more races	— (†)	— (†)	— (†)	— (†)	39.4 (4.94)	5.1 ! (2.17)	‡ (†)	3.2 ! (1.07)	23.8 (4.06)	1.3 ! (0.59)	21.0 (4.13)	77.6 (5.28)
Highest level of education completed												
8th grade or less	7.7 (1.44)	10.0 (1.10)	14.7 (2.92)	19.7 (2.84)	15.5 (2.47)	1.9 (0.57)	4.3 ! (1.70)	‡ (†)	1.7 ! (0.55)	‡ (†)	7.3 (1.24)	38.1 (3.27)
9th through 12th grade, no completion	15.8 (2.25)	20.2 (1.38)	25.6 (2.55)	25.5 (1.53)	27.2 (2.40)	7.9 (1.69)	1.1 ! (0.41)	2.1 (0.57)	7.6 (1.44)	1.5 ! (0.61)	12.5 (1.53)	55.7 (2.52)
High school completion	24.1 (1.10)	30.7 (0.84)	34.8 (1.37)	33.9 (1.07)	33.0 (1.62)	0.5 ! (0.24)	0.7 ! (0.24)	2.5 (0.36)	17.2 (1.18)	1.1 ! (0.35)	16.8 (1.27)	63.6 (1.93)
Some vocational/technical	34.2 (3.80)	41.9 (2.16)	41.1 (3.97)	50.7 (3.51)	43.3 (4.30)	‡ (†)	‡ (†)	4.5 ! (1.42)	28.3 (3.71)	‡ (†)	23.2 (3.09)	77.6 (3.98)
Some college	41.4 (1.67)	49.3 (0.92)	51.1 (1.76)	57.4 (1.29)	51.1 (1.79)	‡ (†)	‡ (†)	8.6 (1.06)	28.8 (1.54)	1.4 ! (0.47)	26.8 (1.80)	79.8 (1.52)
Associate's degree	49.2 (5.82)	56.1 (1.85)	56.6 (2.93)	62.5 (2.15)	56.5 (3.64)	‡ (†)	1.1 ! (0.51)	6.6 (1.42)	40.8 (3.27)	1.9 ! (0.66)	20.1 (2.48)	75.9 (3.70)
Bachelor's degree	51.1 (2.46)	56.9 (1.20)	60.3 (1.84)	64.5 (1.39)	59.8 (1.56)	‡ (†)	0.4 ! (0.17)	6.3 (0.82)	44.1 (1.61)	0.4 ! (0.17)	28.6 (1.55)	79.3 (1.72)
Some graduate work (or study)	55.1 (2.90)	59.9 (1.55)	63.6 (1.96)	68.9 (1.64)	66.3 (1.99)	‡ (†)	‡ (†)	8.7 (0.86)	49.3 (2.15)	‡ (†)	30.7 (1.77)	88.0 (1.06)
No degree	— (†)	62.2 (2.67)	64.7 (4.39)	64.2 (3.54)	65.3 (4.84)	‡ (†)	‡ (†)	14.5 (2.55)	40.5 (4.68)	‡ (†)	38.7 (4.81)	78.2 (4.34)
Master's	— (†)	59.1 (1.88)	65.7 (2.64)	70.7 (2.10)	67.5 (2.59)	‡ (†)	‡ (†)	8.9 (1.31)	51.4 (2.81)	‡ (†)	30.6 (2.04)	88.8 (1.33)
Doctor's	— (†)	54.0 (6.99)	53.1 (4.73)	63.7 (3.98)	58.0 (4.94)	‡ (†)	‡ (†)	10.1 ! (3.14)	34.0 (4.53)	‡ (†)	31.4 (3.95)	90.3 (3.26)
Professional	— (†)	65.9 (3.91)	72.5 (5.75)	72.8 (3.79)	68.2 (5.77)	‡ (†)	‡ (†)	‡ (†)	59.0 (6.35)	‡ (†)	23.9 (4.35)	91.6 (2.15)
Urbanicity												
City	— (†)	— (†)	— (†)	— (†)	45.8 (1.46)	1.4 (0.31)	1.6 (0.38)	5.7 (0.59)	26.3 (1.24)	1.8 (0.43)	22.5 (1.10)	69.2 (1.39)
Suburban	— (†)	— (†)	— (†)	— (†)	46.9 (1.33)	0.9 (0.23)	0.9 ! (0.36)	5.8 (0.55)	29.7 (1.26)	0.9 (0.22)	23.4 (1.16)	73.4 (1.28)
Town	— (†)	— (†)	— (†)	— (†)	41.8 (2.33)	2.7 ! (1.16)	0.4 ! (0.14)	4.2 (0.87)	25.6 (1.74)	0.5 ! (0.21)	18.5 (1.96)	70.5 (2.43)
Rural	— (†)	— (†)	— (†)	— (†)	39.5 (2.04)	0.8 (0.22)	‡ (†)	3.3 (0.59)	24.2 (1.38)	1.2 ! (0.40)	18.3 (1.76)	67.6 (1.76)
Labor force status												
In labor force	40.7 (0.96)	49.8 (0.69)	52.1 (0.94)	— (†)	52.3 (0.93)	1.4 (0.32)	0.8 (0.19)	6.4 (0.39)	37.1 (0.83)	1.5 (0.24)	21.9 (0.91)	73.0 (0.94)
Employed	42.0 (1.00)	50.7 (0.53)	52.5 (0.96)	— (†)	53.4 (0.94)	1.1 (0.31)	0.7 (0.20)	6.5 (0.39)	38.8 (0.83)	1.4 (0.24)	21.8 (0.94)	73.5 (1.01)
Unemployed	26.0 (3.24)	36.6 (1.91)	44.9 (4.60)	— (†)	37.8 (4.26)	5.8 (1.60)	1.9 ! (0.79)	5.2 (1.37)	13.5 (2.16)	‡ (†)	22.1 (3.99)	66.7 (3.80)
Not in labor force	15.7 (0.91)	21.3 (0.69)	24.9 (1.17)	— (†)	27.6 (1.18)	1.1 (0.24)	1.3 (0.36)	2.3 (0.45)	5.7 (0.55)	0.6 ! (0.22)	20.5 (0.97)	65.2 (1.27)

See notes at end of table.

Table 507.40. Participation rate of persons, 17 years old and over, in adult education during the previous 12 months, by selected characteristics of participants: Selected years, 1991 through 2005—Continued

[Standard errors appear in parentheses]

Characteristic of participant	Percent taking any program, class, or course					Percent taking specific programs, classes, or courses, 2005						Percent doing informal learning activities for personal interest, 2005
	1991	1995	1999	2001	2005	Basic skills/ General Educational Development (GED) classes	English as a second language (ESL) classes	Part-time post-secondary education[1]	Career- or job-related courses	Apprenticeship programs	Personal-interest courses	
1	2	3	4	5	6	7	8	9	10	11	12	13
Occupation												
Executive, administrative, or managerial occupations	49.3 (3.45)	55.8 (1.92)	57.0 (2.11)	66.2 (1.61)	64.1 (2.73)	‡ (†)	‡ (†)	6.0 (1.10)	51.8 (2.82)	‡ (†)	28.8 (2.89)	78.6 (2.71)
Engineers, surveyors, and architects	62.6 (7.85)	65.5 (4.18)	79.8 (6.01)	68.1 (4.46)	71.2 (5.68)	‡ (†)	‡ (†)	9.3 ! (3.21)	55.6 (5.60)	‡ (†)	31.4 (6.19)	81.1 (4.63)
Natural scientists and mathematicians	48.2 (9.86)	72.3 (3.52)	60.5 (6.74)	74.0 (4.46)	69.1 (4.63)	‡ (†)	‡ (†)	9.2 (2.49)	49.6 (5.27)	‡ (†)	30.2 (4.53)	85.5 (5.16)
Social scientists and workers, religious workers, and lawyers	55.6 (6.01)	76.6 (2.61)	79.3 (4.35)	83.5 (3.05)	77.7 (4.11)	‡ (†)	‡ (†)	12.8 (3.16)	64.3 (4.42)	‡ (†)	29.2 (3.52)	89.4 (2.78)
Teachers, elementary/secondary	56.0 (4.20)	54.8 (4.64)	66.5 (5.61)	79.9 (2.95)	79.7 (2.59)	‡ (†)	‡ (†)	8.3 ! (3.16)	65.0 (3.99)	‡ (†)	31.7 (3.78)	83.8 (2.62)
Teachers: college, university, postsecondary institutions	45.5 (8.31)	76.7 (1.98)	78.4 (3.11)	69.4 (4.60)	61.3 (6.96)	‡ (†)	‡ (†)	‡ (†)	49.0 (8.50)	‡ (†)	19.5 (4.98)	91.7 (3.58)
Health diagnosing and treating practitioners	67.1 (13.73)	71.1 (5.78)	79.8 (9.02)	78.5 (6.38)	88.8 (5.59)	‡ (†)	‡ (†)	15.4 (2.47)	79.5 (6.59)	‡ (†)	31.9 (9.15)	84.5 (5.63)
Registered nurses, pharmacists, dieticians, therapists, and physician's assistants	59.6 (6.69)	86.7 (2.47)	85.4 (4.10)	82.7 (3.83)	85.4 (4.05)	‡ (†)	‡ (†)	7.9 (2.17)	78.2 (4.89)	‡ (†)	27.4 (3.73)	83.1 (3.92)
Writers, artists, entertainers, and athletes	42.9 (6.63)	49.9 (4.37)	50.0 (6.93)	46.8 (6.03)	52.5 (6.59)	‡ (†)	‡ (†)	5.4 ! (2.16)	27.8 (5.02)	‡ (†)	35.3 (6.42)	88.2 (3.89)
Health technologists and technicians	68.6 (10.03)	74.8 (3.64)	66.9 (6.16)	85.6 (3.25)	72.1 (8.37)	‡ (†)	‡ (†)	6.0 ! (2.11)	63.2 (8.67)	‡ (†)	24.6 (5.91)	75.6 (7.26)
Technologists and technicians, except health and engineering	53.0 (6.49)	64.3 (2.84)	59.6 (5.07)	70.2 (3.32)	33.8 (8.53)	‡ (†)	‡ (†)	7.1 ! (3.19)	29.1 (7.68)	‡ (†)	6.2 ! (2.14)	76.0 (8.80)
Marketing and sales occupations	34.4 (2.38)	44.2 (1.34)	44.4 (2.73)	51.1 (2.10)	45.7 (3.00)	1.7 ! (0.59)	‡ (†)	4.5 (0.88)	30.2 (2.77)	‡ (†)	21.5 (2.43)	68.9 (3.37)
Administrative support occupations, including clerical	29.9 (1.74)	51.7 (1.25)	50.1 (2.29)	58.7 (1.72)	54.6 (2.70)	1.1 ! (0.53)	‡ (†)	6.6 (0.98)	33.5 (2.70)	‡ (†)	27.7 (2.18)	73.8 (2.33)
Service occupations	25.2 (1.82)	46.5 (1.38)	50.9 (2.74)	49.3 (2.24)	44.7 (2.47)	1.6 (0.39)	1.9 ! (0.88)	6.8 (1.42)	28.5 (2.64)	1.4 ! (0.57)	17.5 (2.10)	65.4 (2.71)
Agriculture, forestry, and fishing occupations	14.3 ! (5.19)	26.4 (3.55)	34.3 (7.16)	46.4 (6.80)	44.4 (9.02)	‡ (†)	‡ (†)	‡ (†)	20.3 ! (6.92)	‡ (†)	21.6 ! (10.05)	64.0 (10.03)
Mechanics and repairers	32.1 (4.72)	47.6 (2.70)	42.2 (5.44)	35.1 (3.40)	40.1 (5.10)	‡ (†)	‡ (†)	6.0 ! (1.89)	27.4 (4.26)	3.8 ! (1.38)	12.7 (3.18)	69.3 (4.27)
Construction and extractive occupations	21.9 (3.38)	38.0 (2.45)	34.5 (4.78)	32.3 (3.19)	27.6 (3.73)	‡ (†)	1.1 ! (0.49)	3.2 ! (1.08)	12.3 (2.54)	5.2 ! (1.89)	11.4 (2.72)	72.3 (4.48)
Precision production[2]	31.2 (6.09)	43.0 (4.32)	38.3 (8.48)	35.1 (6.19)	33.0 (3.98)	‡ (†)	0.4 ! (0.16)	4.2 ! (1.42)	22.2 (3.41)	‡ (†)	13.3 (2.99)	63.9 (3.46)
Production workers	21.1 (2.31)	30.7 (1.29)	38.0 (3.47)	39.4 (2.82)	— (†)	— (†)	— (†)	— (†)	— (†)	— (†)	— (†)	— (†)
Transportation, material moving	20.7 (4.69)	28.4 (2.32)	33.3 (4.25)	30.4 (3.29)	34.6 (5.27)	‡ (†)	‡ (†)	‡ (†)	14.7 (2.63)	3.2 ! (1.57)	11.2 (2.85)	60.8 (4.98)
Handler, equipment, cleaners, helpers, and laborers	20.8 (3.49)	25.1 (2.70)	19.6 (4.56)	18.2 (3.20)	— (†)	— (†)	— (†)	— (†)	— (†)	— (†)	— (†)	— (†)
Miscellaneous occupations	— (†)	56.6 (3.61)	43.0 (7.98)	64.9 (7.07)	39.2 (11.25)	‡ (†)	‡ (†)	‡ (†)	15.7 ! (5.81)	‡ (†)	7.8 ! (3.63)	52.2 (12.32)
Annual household income												
$5,000 or less	13.6 (1.70)	21.3 (1.59)	21.0 (3.22)	25.1 (2.92)	35.9 (4.83)	‡ (†)	‡ (†)	3.6 ! (1.52)	13.7 (4.00)	‡ (†)	17.2 (3.59)	52.9 (4.97)
$5,001 to $10,000	17.5 (2.14)	23.9 (1.37)	24.5 (3.39)	28.0 (2.74)	29.6 (4.49)	2.4 ! (0.92)	1.5 ! (0.71)	1.7 ! (0.81)	8.4 (2.11)	‡ (†)	21.8 (4.75)	61.0 (3.75)
$10,001 to $15,000	22.8 (2.60)	26.7 (1.61)	22.8 (2.45)	28.6 (2.30)	25.0 (3.41)	2.4 (0.69)	0.8 ! (0.33)	3.3 ! (1.17)	11.3 (2.52)	‡ (†)	15.5 (3.14)	58.6 (4.43)
$15,001 to $20,000	21.9 (2.35)	31.8 (1.55)	31.4 (2.75)	30.2 (2.48)	24.3 (2.54)	1.0 ! (0.38)	‡ (†)	3.3 ! (1.19)	10.1 (1.37)	2.6 ! (1.20)	12.9 (2.00)	61.1 (3.17)
$20,001 to $25,000	26.7 (3.20)	31.4 (1.27)	35.8 (2.81)	35.2 (2.27)	28.2 (2.51)	1.7 ! (0.78)	1.9 ! (0.62)	4.4 (1.26)	12.8 (2.04)	1.1 ! (0.50)	13.6 (1.88)	63.2 (3.11)
$25,001 to $30,000	32.1 (2.51)	37.9 (1.47)	36.7 (2.61)	38.3 (2.43)	38.6 (3.63)	‡ (†)	1.3 ! (0.61)	6.8 ! (2.09)	20.2 (3.37)	‡ (†)	18.4 (2.52)	71.0 (3.38)
$30,001 to $40,000	35.6 (1.84)	42.7 (0.86)	45.2 (2.05)	44.6 (1.54)	42.7 (2.65)	1.9 ! (0.65)	1.0 ! (0.49)	3.7 (0.68)	22.8 (2.27)	1.1 ! (0.39)	23.0 (2.49)	68.7 (2.36)
$40,001 to $50,000	44.8 (1.84)	46.8 (1.39)	47.9 (2.31)	49.1 (1.93)	41.4 (2.92)	1.6 ! (0.53)	‡ (†)	2.9 (0.55)	22.4 (2.00)	1.5 ! (0.56)	20.5 (2.47)	71.9 (2.62)
$50,001 to $75,000	46.6 (2.03)	52.0 (0.94)	55.1 (1.80)	55.7 (1.48)	47.7 (1.74)	0.4 ! (0.19)	‡ (†)	5.8 (0.69)	33.0 (1.37)	0.9 ! (0.36)	20.5 (1.67)	70.6 (2.15)
More than $75,000	48.7 (3.15)	58.0 (1.27)	56.9 (1.66)	— (†)	— (†)	— (†)	— (†)	— (†)	— (†)	— (†)	— (†)	— (†)
$75,001 to $100,000	— (†)	— (†)	— (†)	59.7 (1.91)	56.4 (2.28)	‡ (†)	‡ (†)	7.5 (0.89)	38.6 (2.26)	1.8 ! (0.64)	25.3 (1.51)	75.0 (1.97)
More than $100,000	— (†)	— (†)	— (†)	59.3 (1.82)	58.4 (2.11)	‡ (†)	‡ (†)	6.1 (0.70)	39.4 (1.80)	‡ (†)	28.2 (1.62)	81.2 (1.68)

—Not available.
†Not applicable.
!Interpret data with caution. The coefficient of variation (CV) for this estimate is between 30 and 50 percent.
‡Reporting standards not met. Either there are too few cases for a reliable estimate or the coefficient of variation (CV) is 50 percent or greater.
[1]Includes college and university degree programs, post-degree certificate programs, and vocational certificate programs.
[2]For 2005, figures include "Production workers" occupations data.
NOTE: Adult education is defined as all education activities, except full-time enrollment in higher education credential programs. Data do not include persons enrolled in high school or below. Race categories exclude persons of Hispanic ethnicity.
SOURCE: U.S. Department of Education, National Center for Education Statistics, Adult Education Survey (AE-NHES:1991, AE-NHES:1995, AE-NHES:1999, and AE-NHES:2005) and Adult Education and Lifelong Learning Survey (AELL-NHES:2001) of the National Household Education Surveys Program. (This table was prepared November 2010.)

This page intentionally left blank.

CHAPTER 6
International Comparisons of Education

This chapter offers a broad perspective on education across the nations of the world. It also provides an international context for examining the condition of education in the United States. Insights into the educational practices and outcomes of the United States are obtained by comparing them with those of other education systems. Most of the education systems represent countries; however, some of the tables in this chapter also include data for subnational entities with separate education systems, such as Hong Kong. The National Center for Education Statistics (NCES) carries out a variety of activities to provide statistical data for international comparisons of education.

This chapter presents data drawn from materials prepared by the United Nations Educational, Scientific, and Cultural Organization (UNESCO), the Organization for Economic Cooperation and Development (OECD), and the International Association for the Evaluation of Educational Achievement (IEA). Basic summary data on enrollments and enrollment ratios, teachers, educational attainment, and finances are synthesized from data published by the OECD in the Online Education Database, as well as from data collected by UNESCO. Even though these tabulations are carefully prepared, international data users should be cautioned about the many problems of definition and reporting involved in the collection of data about the education systems of the world, which vary greatly in structure from country to country (see the UNESCO entry at the end of Appendix A: Guide to Sources).

Also presented in this chapter are data from two international assessments of student achievement that are carried out under the aegis of IEA and supported by NCES. The Trends in International Mathematics and Science Study (TIMSS), formerly known as the Third International Mathematics and Science Study, assesses the mathematics and science knowledge and skills of fourth- and eighth-graders every 4 years. The Progress in International Reading Literacy Study (PIRLS) measures the reading knowledge and skills of fourth-graders every 5 years.

This chapter includes additional information from two OECD assessments supported by NCES. The Program for International Student Assessment (PISA) provides performance scores of 15-year-olds in the areas of reading, mathematics, and science literacy; it also measures general, or cross-curricular, competencies such as learning strategies. The Program for the International Assessment of Adult Competencies (PIAAC) assesses the cognitive skills of adults in the areas of literacy, numeracy, and problem solving in technology-rich environments. PIAAC measures relationships between adults' skills in these areas and their educational background, workplace experiences, occupational attainment, and use of information and communication technology. While PISA and PIAAC focus on OECD countries, data from some non-OECD education systems are also provided.

Further information on survey methodologies is in Appendix A: Guide to Sources and in the publications cited in the table source notes.

Population

Among reporting OECD countries, Mexico had the largest percentage of its population made up of young people ages 5 to 14 (19 percent) in 2016, followed by Israel (18 percent) and Turkey (16 percent) (*web-only table 601.30*). OECD countries with the smallest percentages of people in this age group were Lithuania, Italy, the Republic of Korea, Germany, and Japan (all at 9 percent) and Spain, the Czech Republic, Poland, the Slovak Republic, Latvia, Greece, Portugal, Hungary, Switzerland, Slovenia, and Austria (all at 10 percent). In the United States, 13 percent of the population was 5 to 14 years old, which was higher than the percentages in most other OECD countries.

Enrollments

In 2016, about 1.5 billion students were enrolled in schools around the world (table 601.10). Of these students, 737 million were in elementary programs, 588 million were in secondary programs, and 220 million were in postsecondary programs.

From 2000 to 2016, enrollment changes varied from region to region. Elementary enrollment in 2016 was 71 percent higher in Africa, 34 percent higher in Oceania, and 2 percent higher in Asia than it was in 2000 (table F, table 601.10, and figure 27). In contrast, elementary enrollment in 2016 was 9 percent lower in Central and South America (including Latin America and the Caribbean), 6 percent lower in Europe, and less than 1 percent lower in Northern America (including Bermuda, Canada, Greenland, St. Pierre and Miquelon, and the United States) than it was in 2000. At the secondary level, enrollment in 2016 was 101 percent higher in Africa, 38 percent higher in Asia,

20 percent higher in Oceania, 13 percent higher in Central and South America, and 9 percent higher in Northern America than it was in 2000. In contrast, secondary enrollment in Europe was 17 percent lower in 2016 than it was in 2000. At the postsecondary level, enrollment in all major areas of the world was higher in 2016 than it was in 2000. Postsecondary enrollment in 2016 was 205 percent higher in Asia, 138 percent higher in Central and South America, 134 percent higher in Africa, 71 percent higher in Oceania, 45 percent higher in Northern America, and 14 percent higher in Europe than it was in 2000.

Table F. Population and enrollment at different levels in major areas of the world: 2000 and 2016

[In millions]

Area of the world	Population	Enrollment		
		Elementary	Secondary	Post-secondary
World total				
2000	6,084.7	657.1	452.5	99.9
2016	7,345.8	736.6	588.2	220.0
Africa				
2000	805.9	109.4	38.4	6.2
2016	1,205.8	187.2	77.1	14.5
Asia				
2000	3,686.1	405.2	258.3	41.0
2016	4,372.2	414.7	356.9	126.0
Europe				
2000	730.5	41.7	70.5	25.5
2016	746.3	39.2	58.6	29.2
Central and South America				
2000	518.5	70.2	57.0	11.5
2016	625.0	64.0	64.4	27.3
Northern America				
2000	313.4	27.4	25.1	14.4
2016	358.9	27.3	27.4	20.9
Oceania				
2000	30.4	3.1	3.2	1.3
2016	37.6	4.2	3.9	2.2

SOURCE: United Nations Educational, Scientific, and Cultural Organization, unpublished tabulations; and U.S. Department of Commerce, Census Bureau, International Data Base.

Across OECD countries in 2016, the average enrollment rate of 5- to 14-year-olds was 98 percent, and this enrollment rate was at least 93 percent in all 36 of the OECD countries that reported data (table 601.35). In the United States, the enrollment rate for 5- to 14-year-olds was 99 percent. Among the 35 OECD countries that reported data for 15- to 19-year-olds, 9 countries had rates of at least 90 percent and 2 countries had rates of 70 percent or lower (table 601.40). The U.S. enrollment rate for 15- to 19-year-olds was 83 percent, which was lower than the OECD average of 85 percent. Among the 35 countries that reported data for 20- to 29-year-olds, 4 countries had rates of at least 40 percent, and 1 country had a rate of 15 percent or lower. The U.S. enrollment rate for 20- to 29-year-olds was 25 percent, which was lower than the OECD average of 29 percent.

In all 35 OECD countries that reported secondary and postsecondary enrollment data in 2016, a higher percentage of 17-year-olds were enrolled at the secondary level than at the postsecondary level (table 601.40). For older students, however, patterns of enrollment at the secondary and postsecondary levels varied across OECD countries. For example, 14 countries had a higher percentage of their 19-year-olds enrolled at the secondary level than at the postsecondary level, while 21 countries had a higher percentage enrolled at the postsecondary level than at the secondary level. The percentage of 19-year-olds enrolled at the secondary level was at least 5 times higher than the percentage enrolled at the postsecondary level in 3 countries. At the other end of the spectrum, the percentage of 19-year-olds enrolled at the postsecondary level was at least 5 times higher than the percentage enrolled at the secondary level in 6 countries, including the United States (52 vs. 5 percent). For 20-year-olds, although only 4 OECD countries reported a higher enrollment rate at the secondary level than at the postsecondary level, there were 13 countries that reported a secondary enrollment rate of at least 15 percent. For the 20- to 29-year-old age group, there were no countries that reported a higher enrollment rate at the secondary level than at the postsecondary level, and all secondary enrollment rates were below 15 percent. At the postsecondary level, only 3 OECD countries reported an enrollment rate below 15 percent for this age group, and 10 countries reported a rate that was at least 25 percent. The U.S. postsecondary enrollment rate for 20- to 29-year-olds was 23 percent, which was the same as the OECD average for this age group.

Achievement

Mathematics and Science at Grades 4 and 8

The 2015 Trends in International Mathematics and Science Study (TIMSS) assessed students' mathematics and science performance at grades 4 and 8. Mathematics performance was assessed in 43 countries at grade 4 and in 34 countries at grade 8. Science performance was assessed in 42 countries at grade 4 and in 34 countries at grade 8. TIMSS Advanced data were also collected by 9 countries from students in their final year of secondary school (grade 12 in the United States). At grades 4 and 8, in addition to countries, several subnational entities also participated in TIMSS as separate education systems. Examples of subnational participants include the cities of Hong Kong and Chinese Taipei, the U.S. state of Florida, the Canadian provinces of Ontario and Quebec, England and Northern Ireland within the United Kingdom, and the Flemish community in Belgium. In the following paragraphs, comparisons of the United States to other countries do not include the subnational participants. Results for Florida are based on public school students only, while U.S. national results are based on both public and private school students. TIMSS is curriculum based, and the assessments of fourth- and eighth-graders measure what students have actually learned against the subject matter that is expected to be taught by the end of grades 4 and 8, as described in the TIMSS mathematics and science frameworks, which guide assessment development. TIMSS Advanced is designed to broadly align with the advanced mathematics and physics curricula in the participating countries. At all three grades, TIMSS scores are reported on a scale of 0 to 1,000, with a fixed scale centerpoint of 500.

In 2015, the average mathematics scores of U.S. fourth-graders (539) and eighth-graders (518) were higher than the TIMSS scale centerpoint of 500 (tables 602.20 and 602.30). At grade 4, the average U.S. mathematics score was higher than the average score in 30 of the 42 other countries participating at grade 4, lower than the average score in 6 countries, and not measurably different from the average score in the remaining 6 countries (table 602.20). The 6 countries that outperformed the United States in fourth-grade mathematics were Ireland, Japan, the Republic of Korea, Norway, the Russian Federation, and Singapore. At grade 8, the average U.S. mathematics score was higher than the average score in 21 of the 33 other participating countries, lower than the average score in 5 countries, and not measurably different from the average score in the remaining 7 countries (table 602.30). The 5 countries that outperformed the United States in eighth-grade mathematics were Canada, Japan, the Republic of Korea, the Russian Federation, and Singapore.

Florida, the only U.S. state participating in the 2015 TIMSS as a separate education system, had an average mathematics score for public schools at grade 4 (546) that was higher than the TIMSS scale centerpoint but was not measurably different from the U.S. national average score in mathematics (table 602.20). At grade 8, Florida had a public school average score (493) that was not measurably different from the TIMSS scale centerpoint but was lower than the U.S. national average in mathematics (table 602.30).

The average science scores of both U.S. fourth-graders (546) and U.S. eighth-graders (530) were higher than the TIMSS scale centerpoint of 500 in 2015 (tables 602.20 and 602.30). The average U.S. fourth-grade science score was higher than the average score in 30 of the 41 other countries participating at grade 4, lower than the average score in 5 countries, and not measurably different from the average score in the remaining 6 countries (table 602.20). The 5 countries that outperformed the United States in fourth-grade science were Finland, Japan, the Republic of Korea, the Russian Federation, and Singapore. At grade 8, the average U.S. science score was higher than the average score in 23 of the 33 other countries participating at grade 8, lower than the average score in 5 countries, and not measurably different from the average score in the remaining 5 countries (table 602.30). The 5 countries that outperformed the United States in eighth-grade science were Japan, the Republic of Korea, the Russian Federation, Singapore, and Slovenia.

Public schools in Florida had an average fourth-grade science score (549) that was higher than the TIMSS scale centerpoint but was not measurably different from the U.S. national average (table 602.20). At grade 8, Florida had a public school average score (508) that was not measurably different from the TIMSS scale centerpoint but was lower than the U.S. national average in science (table 602.30).

The TIMSS Advanced assessment measures the advanced mathematics and physics achievement of students in their final year of secondary school who are taking or have taken advanced courses (table 602.35). On TIMSS Advanced in 2015, the U.S. average advanced mathematics score (485) and physics score (437) were both lower than the TIMSS Advanced scale centerpoint of 500.

Reading Literacy at Grade 4

The Progress in International Reading Literacy Study (PIRLS) conducted international assessments of fourth-grade reading literacy in 2001, 2006, 2011, and 2016. In 2016, PIRLS participants consisted of 43 countries as well as several subnational education systems. Examples of subnational participants include the cities of Hong Kong and Chinese Taipei, the Canadian provinces of Ontario and Quebec, England and Northern Ireland within the United Kingdom, and the Flemish and French communities in Belgium. PIRLS scores are reported on a scale of 0 to 1,000, with a fixed scale centerpoint of 500.

On the 2016 PIRLS, U.S. fourth-graders had an average reading literacy score of 549 (table 602.10). The U.S. average score in 2016 was 7 points lower than in 2011 but 10 points higher than in 2006. In all 4 assessment years, the U.S. average score was higher than the PIRLS scale centerpoint.

In 2016, the average reading literacy score of fourth-graders in the United States was higher than the average score in 24 of the 42 other participating countries, lower than the average score in 7 countries, and not measurably different from the average score in the remaining 11 countries. The 7 countries that outperformed the United States on the 2016 PIRLS were Finland, Ireland, Latvia, Norway, Poland, the Russian Federation, and Singapore.

Reading, Mathematics, and Science Literacy at Age 15

The Program for International Student Assessment (PISA) assesses 15-year-old students' application of reading, mathematics, and science literacy to problems within a real-life context. In 2015, PISA assessed students in the 35 OECD countries as well as several other education systems. Some subnational entities participated as separate education systems, including the U.S. states of Massachusetts and North Carolina. Results for individual U.S. states are based on public school students only, while U.S. national results are based on both public and private school students. PISA scores are reported on a scale of 0 to 1,000.

On the 2015 PISA assessment, U.S. 15-year-olds' average score in reading literacy was 497, which was not measurably different from the OECD average score of 493 (table 602.50). The average reading literacy score in the

United States was lower than the average score in 11 of the 34 other OECD countries, higher than the average score in 13 OECD countries, and not measurably different from the average score in 10 OECD countries. The average reading literacy score of public school students in Massachusetts (527) was higher than both the U.S. average score and the OECD average score, while the average score in North Carolina (500) was not measurably different from either the U.S. average score or the OECD average score. In all participating education systems, females outperformed males in reading literacy (table 602.40). The U.S. gender gap in reading (20 points) was not measurably different from the OECD average gap but was smaller than the gaps in 12 other OECD countries.

In mathematics literacy, U.S. 15-year-olds' average score of 470 on the 2015 PISA assessment was lower than the OECD average score of 490 (table 602.60). The average mathematics literacy score in the United States was lower than the average score in 27 of the 34 other OECD countries, higher than the average score in 4 OECD countries, and not measurably different from the average score in 3 OECD countries. The average mathematics literacy score of public school students in Massachusetts (500) was higher than the U.S. average score but was not measurably different from the OECD average score, while the average score in North Carolina (471) was not measurably different from the U.S. average score but was lower than the OECD average score. In 18 OECD countries, including the United States, males outperformed females in mathematics literacy (table 602.40). The U.S. gender gap in favor of males in mathematics (9 points) was not measurably different from the OECD average gap.

In science literacy, U.S. 15-year-olds' average score of 496 on the 2015 PISA assessment was not measurably different from the OECD average score of 493 (table 602.70). The average science literacy score in the United States was lower than the average score in 12 of the 34 other OECD countries, higher than the average score in 10 OECD countries, and not measurably different from the average score in 12 OECD countries. The average science literacy score of public school students in Massachusetts (529) was higher than both the U.S. average score and the OECD average score. The average score in North Carolina (502) was not measurably different from either the U.S. average score or the OECD average score. In 15 OECD countries, including the United States, males outperformed females in science literacy. In 4 OECD countries, females outperformed males in science literacy. The U.S. gender gap in favor of males in science (7 points) was not measurably different from the OECD average gap.

Educational Attainment

In 2017, the percentage of 25- to 64-year-olds who had completed high school varied among the 34 reporting OECD countries (table 603.10). The OECD country reporting the highest percentage of 25- to 64-year-olds who had completed high school was the Czech Republic (94 percent). High school completers made up at least 80 percent of 25- to 64-year-olds in 21 other OECD countries, including the United States (91 percent). The OECD country reporting the lowest percentage of 25- to 64-year-olds who had completed high school was Mexico (38 percent).

In 2017, the percentage of 25- to 64-year-olds with a postsecondary degree (i.e., any degree at the associate's level or higher) also varied among the 35 OECD countries reporting data for this level of educational attainment (table 603.20). The OECD country reporting the highest percentage of 25- to 64-year-olds with a postsecondary degree was Canada (57 percent). Forty-six percent of 25- to 64-year-olds in the United States attained a postsecondary degree, and an additional 20 OECD countries reported that more than 35 percent of their 25- to 64-year-olds had a postsecondary degree. The OECD country reporting the lowest percentage of 25- to 64-year-olds with a postsecondary degree was Mexico (17 percent).

Among younger adults (those 25 to 34 years old) in the 35 OECD countries reporting data, the percentage with a postsecondary degree also varied in 2017 (table 603.20 and figure 28). The OECD country reporting the highest percentage of younger adults with a postsecondary degree was the Republic of Korea (70 percent). More than 35 percent of younger adults had a postsecondary degree in 27 other OECD countries, including the United States (48 percent). Nine countries reported percentages of younger adults with a postsecondary degree that were higher than the percentage in the United States. In 4 countries (Norway, Israel, Iceland, and Sweden), the percentages of younger adults with a postsecondary degree were not measurably different from the percentage in the United States. In contrast, 21 countries reported percentages of younger adults with a postsecondary degree that were lower than the percentage in the United States. The OECD country reporting the lowest percentage of younger adults with a degree was Mexico (23 percent).

Degrees

In 2016, more than half of all postsecondary degrees (i.e., any degree at the associate's level or higher) were awarded to women in 32 of the 34 OECD countries reporting a total percentage awarded to women (*web-only table 603.60*). For example, in the United States, 58 percent of all postsecondary degrees were awarded to women. However, the percentage of degrees awarded to women varied by field. Thirty-three countries reported data for the field of education; in 32 of these countries, including the United States, at least 70 percent of education degrees were awarded to women. In contrast, in 16 of the 33 countries reporting data for the combined field of engineering, manufacturing, and construction, less than 25 percent of these degrees were awarded to women. In the United States,

20 percent of degrees in engineering, manufacturing, and construction were awarded to women.

In 2016, the percentage of bachelor's degrees awarded in science and mathematics, information technologies, and engineering fields—including natural science, mathematics, statistics, information and communication technologies, engineering, manufacturing, and construction—varied across the 36 OECD countries reporting these data (*web-only table 603.70*). Two of the reporting OECD countries awarded 30 percent or more of their bachelor's degrees in science and mathematics, information technologies, and engineering fields: Germany (36 percent) and the Republic of Korea (32 percent). Three countries awarded 15 percent or less of their bachelor's degrees in science and mathematics, information technologies, and engineering fields: Norway, Luxembourg, and the Netherlands (all at 15 percent). The United States awarded 20 percent of its bachelor's degrees in science and mathematics, information technologies, and engineering fields, which was lower than the OECD average (23 percent).

The percentages of graduate degrees awarded in science and mathematics, information technologies, and engineering fields varied widely across OECD countries in 2016. In all but 1 of the 35 OECD countries reporting data on both master's and doctor's degrees, a higher percentage of degrees were awarded in these fields at the doctoral level than at the master's level. The exception was Japan, which had a higher percentage of degrees awarded in these fields at the master's level than at the doctoral level. At the master's level, 5 of the 36 OECD countries reporting data at this level awarded 30 percent or more of their degrees in science and mathematics, information technologies, and engineering fields: Japan (42 percent), Germany (35 percent), Portugal (34 percent), Estonia (32 percent), and Sweden (31 percent). The United States awarded 16 percent of its master's degrees in science and mathematics, information technologies, and engineering fields, which was lower than the OECD average (22 percent). However, 5 of the reporting OECD countries awarded 15 percent or less of their master's degrees in these fields: Luxembourg (13 percent), Israel (12 percent), Iceland (12 percent), Mexico (10 percent), and Chile (7 percent). At the doctoral level, 9 of the 35 OECD countries reporting data at this level awarded at least half of their degrees in science and mathematics, information technologies, and engineering fields: France (63 percent), Israel (58 percent), Estonia (56 percent), Chile (55 percent), Luxembourg (55 percent), Sweden (52 percent), Canada (52 percent), Switzerland (51 percent), and Austria (50 percent). Two OECD countries reported awarding less than 30 percent of their doctor's degrees in science and mathematics, information technologies, and engineering fields: Slovenia (25 percent) and Mexico (17 percent). The United States awarded 42 percent of its doctor's degrees in science and mathematics, information technologies, and engineering fields, which was lower than the OECD average of 44 percent.

Skills of Adults

The Program for the International Assessment of Adult Competencies (PIAAC) assesses the cognitive skills of adults in three areas—literacy, numeracy, and problem solving in technology-rich environments—that are considered key to facilitating the social and economic participation of adults in advanced economies. The discussion below focuses on the areas of literacy and numeracy. PIAAC 2012 results are available for adults in 24 participating countries and regions, including 22 that belong to the OECD. Participating countries and regions are referred to collectively as "education systems" in the *Digest*. The education systems that participated in the 2012 assessment were primarily countries but also included 3 subnational education systems: Northern Ireland and England within the United Kingdom and the Flemish community in Belgium. PIAAC literacy and numeracy scores are reported on a scale of 0 to 500.

In 2012, average scores on the PIAAC literacy scale for adults ages 25 to 65 ranged from 249 in Italy and 250 in Spain to 296 in Japan (table 604.10). U.S. 25- to 65-year-olds had an average PIAAC literacy score of 269, which was not measurably different from the OECD average score of 271. Across education systems, adults' average literacy scores generally increased with higher levels of educational attainment. In the United States, for example, 25- to 65-year-olds whose highest level of educational attainment was high school completion had an average literacy score of 259, compared with an average score of 302 for those who had a bachelor's or higher degree. The literacy score for U.S. 25- to 65-year-olds who had completed only high school was lower than the OECD average score of 268 for those who had completed only high school, while the literacy score for U.S. 25- to 65-year-olds with a bachelor's or higher degree was not measurably different from the OECD average score of 302 for those with a bachelor's or higher degree.

On the PIAAC numeracy scale, 2012 average scores for adults ages 25 to 65 ranged from 245 in Spain and 246 in Italy to 289 in Japan. U.S. 25- to 65-year-olds had an average PIAAC numeracy score of 254, which was lower than the OECD average score of 268. Across education systems, adults' average numeracy scores generally increased with higher levels of educational attainment. In the United States, for example, 25- to 65-year-olds whose highest level of attainment was high school completion had an average numeracy score of 241, compared with an average score of 293 for those who had a bachelor's or higher degree. The numeracy score for U.S. 25- to 65-year-olds who had completed only high school was lower than the OECD average score of 265 for those who had completed only high school. Likewise, the average numeracy score of U.S. 25- to 65-year-olds with a bachelor's or higher degree was lower than the OECD average score of 303 for those with a bachelor's or higher degree.

Finances

In 2015, expenditures per full-time-equivalent (FTE) student (expressed in current U.S. dollars) varied by level of education and across OECD countries. At the combined elementary and secondary level of education, expenditures per FTE student were $12,400 in the United States, which was higher than the OECD average of $9,300 (table 605.10). In addition to the United States, 8 of the 32 other OECD countries that reported data at the combined elementary and secondary level had expenditures of at least $11,000 per FTE student: Luxembourg ($20,500), Norway ($14,400), Austria ($13,900), Belgium ($11,900), the Republic of Korea ($11,700), Iceland ($11,200), Sweden ($11,100), and the United Kingdom ($11,000). At the higher education level, the United States spent $30,000 per FTE student, which was higher than the OECD average of $15,600. In addition to the United States, 6 of the 33 other OECD countries that reported higher education finance data had expenditures of over $20,000 per FTE student: Luxembourg ($48,900), the United Kingdom ($26,300), Sweden ($24,400), Canada ($21,800), Norway ($21,000), and Australia ($20,300). These expenditures were adjusted to U.S. dollars using the purchasing-power-parity (PPP) index. This index is considered more stable and comparable than indexes using currency exchange rates; for more information, see Appendix B: Definitions.

Total government and private expenditures on education institutions as a percentage of gross domestic product (GDP) varied across the 34 reporting OECD countries in 2015, ranging from 3.5 percent in Ireland and Luxembourg to 6.4 percent in Norway (table 605.20 and figure 29). In the United States, total expenditures on education institutions amounted to 6.1 percent of GDP, which was higher than the OECD average of 5.0 percent. A comparison of government expenditures on education institutions as a percentage of GDP shows that public investment in education ranged from 2.9 percent in Japan to 6.3 percent in Norway. In the United States, the government expenditure on education institutions as a percentage of GDP was 4.1 percent. The OECD average government expenditure on education institutions was also 4.1 percent of GDP.

Figure 27. Percentage change in enrollment, by major areas of the world and level of education: 2000 to 2016

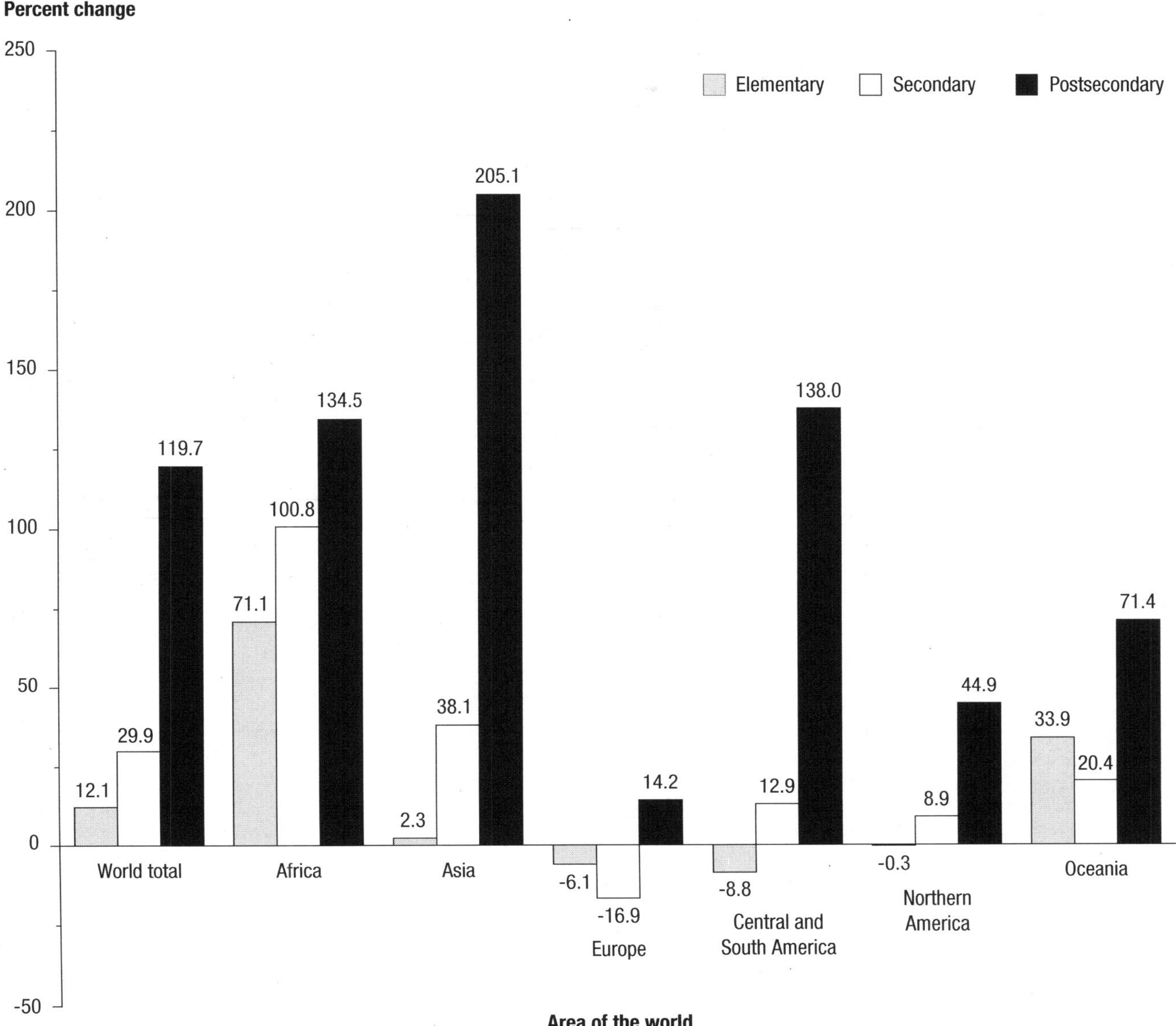

NOTE: Europe includes all countries of the former Union of Soviet Socialist Republics (U.S.S.R.) except Armenia, Azerbaijan, Georgia, Kazakhstan, Kyrgyzstan, Tajikistan, Turkmenistan, and Uzbekistan, which are included in Asia. Asia also includes Turkey, the Arab states (except those located in Africa), and Israel. Central and South America includes Latin America and the Caribbean. Northern America includes Bermuda, Canada, Greenland, St. Pierre and Miquelon, and the United States. Data include imputed values for nonrespondent countries. Graphic display was generated using unrounded data.
SOURCE: United Nations Educational, Scientific, and Cultural Organization (UNESCO), unpublished tabulations; U.S. Department of Commerce, Census Bureau, International Data Base (March 2019).

Figure 28. Percentage of the population 25 to 34 years old with an associate's or higher degree, by country: 2017

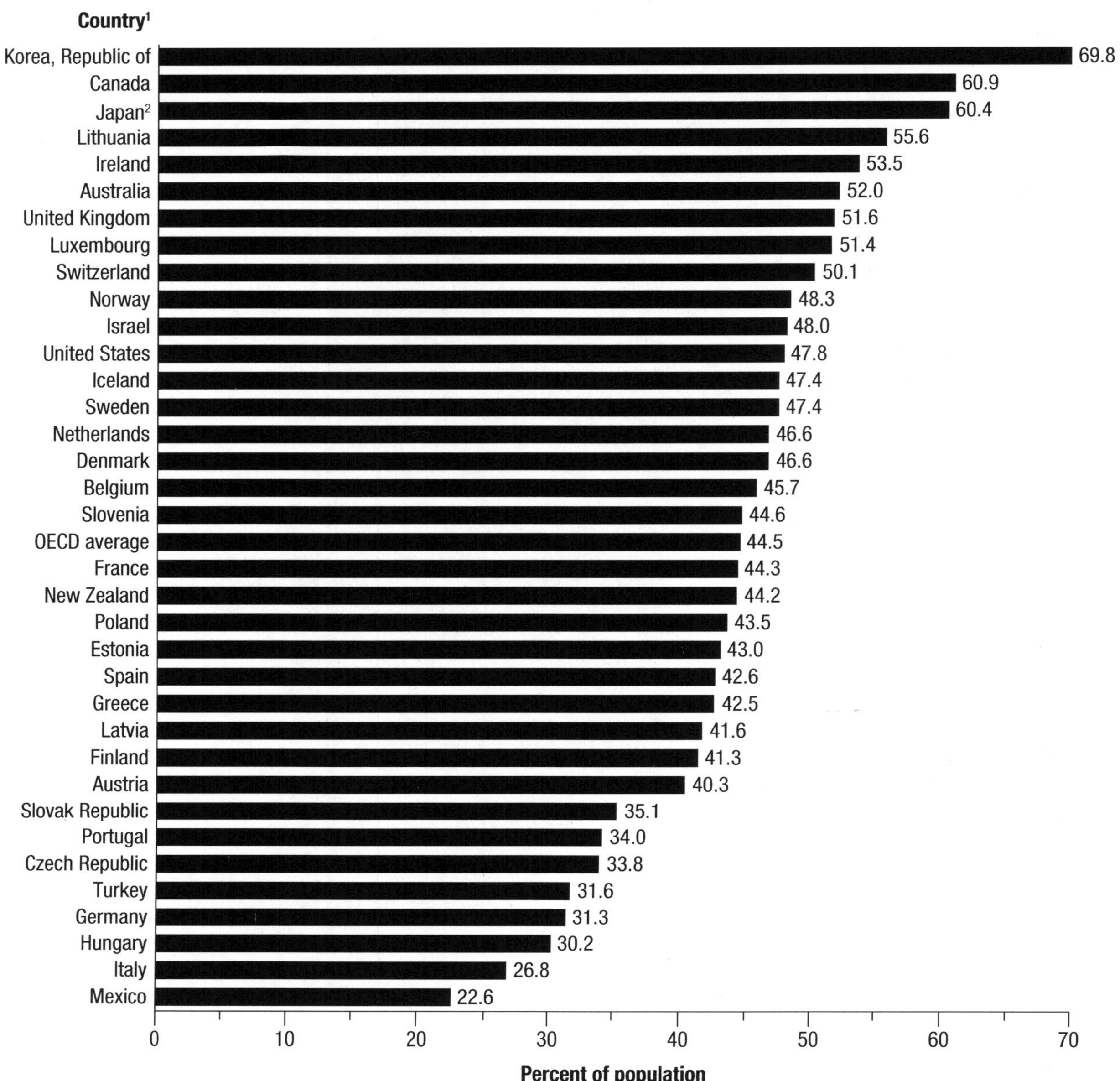

[1]All the countries shown in this figure are members of the Organization for Economic Cooperation and Development (OECD).
[2]Data include some upper secondary and postsecondary nontertiary awards (i.e., awards that are below the associate's degree level).
NOTE: All data in this figure were calculated using International Standard Classification of Education (ISCED) 2011. The data refer to tertiary degrees, which correspond to all degrees at the associate's level and above in the United States and include the following ISCED 2011 levels: level 5 (corresponding to the associate's degree in the United States), level 6 (bachelor's or equivalent degree), level 7 (master's or equivalent degree), and level 8 (doctoral or equivalent degree). Graphic display was generated using unrounded data.
SOURCE: Organization for Economic Cooperation and Development (OECD), Online Education Database, retrieved September 19, 2018, from http://stats.oecd.org/Index.aspx.

Figure 29. Government and private expenditures on education institutions as a percentage of gross domestic product (GDP), by country: 2015

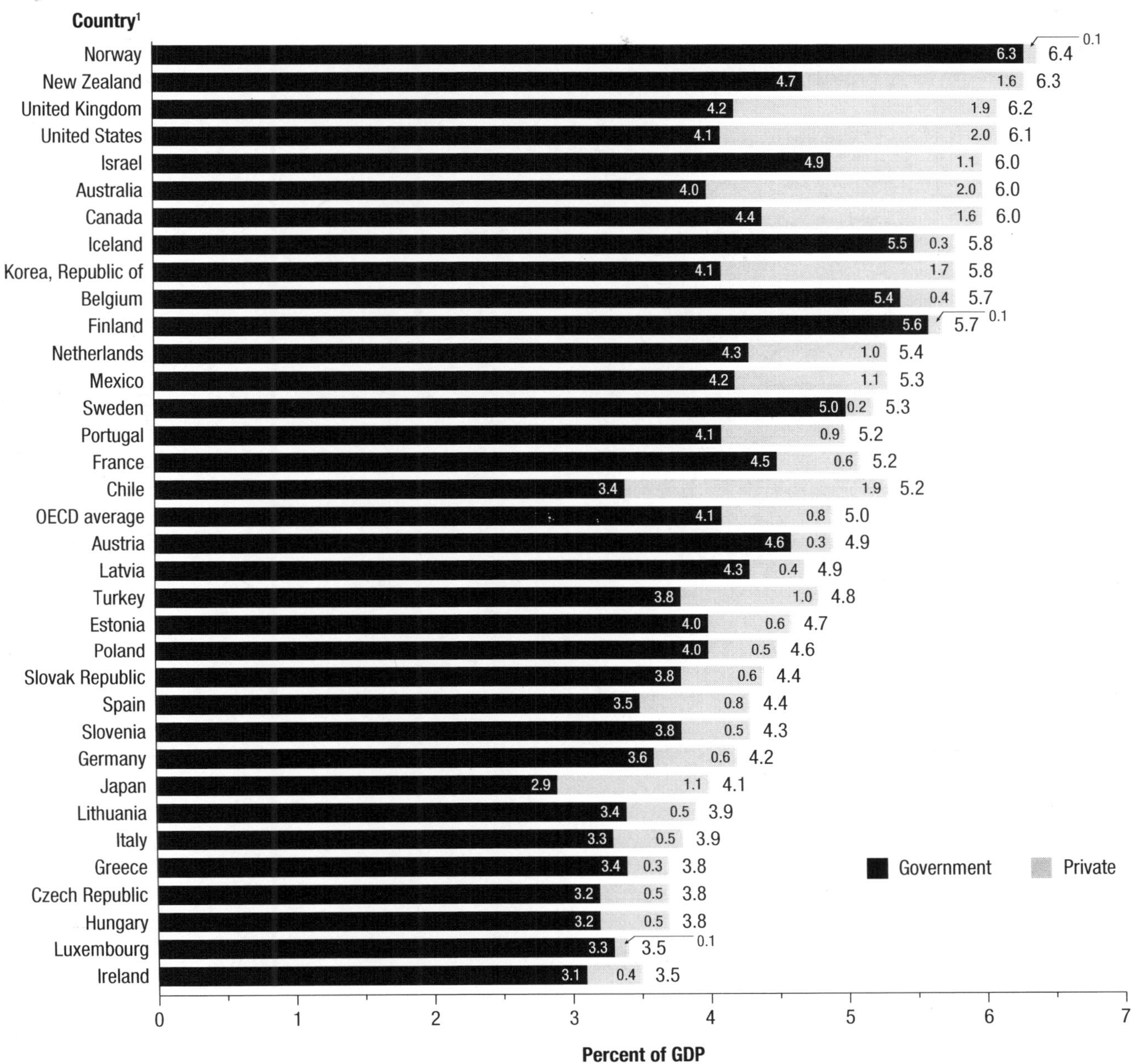

[1]All the countries shown in this figure are members of the Organization for Economic Cooperation and Development (OECD).

NOTE: Includes government and private expenditures on all levels of education institutions. Government expenditures include both amounts spent directly by governments to hire education personnel and to procure other resources, and amounts provided by governments to public or private institutions. Government subsidies used by households for payments to education institutions are counted as government expenditures, not private expenditures. Graphic display was generated using unrounded data. Detail may not sum to totals because of rounding. In addition, totals include expenditures not shown separately because the originating source could not be separately identified.

SOURCE: Organization for Economic Cooperation and Development (OECD), Online Education Database, retrieved November 28, 2018, from https://stats.oecd.org/Index.aspx.

Table 601.10. Population, school enrollment, and number of teachers, by major areas of the world and level of education: Selected years, 1980 through 2016

[In thousands]

Year and selected characteristic	World total[1,2]	Major areas of the world					
		Africa	Asia[2,3]	Europe[3]	Central and South America[4]	Northern America[4]	Oceania
1	2	3	4	5	6	7	8
1980							
Population, all ages[5]	4,445,386	479,432	2,637,685	695,225	358,579	251,929	22,534
Enrollment, all levels	872,107	77,988	495,321	134,782	98,268	60,543	5,205
Elementary[6]	525,219	61,303	333,888	47,694	56,791	22,893	2,649
Secondary[7]	296,795	14,987	148,054	70,240	36,673	24,695	2,145
Postsecondary[8]	50,093	1,698	13,378	16,847	4,803	12,956	411
Teachers, all levels	40,148	2,373	19,587	2,505	4,577	2,124	277
Elementary[6]	18,528	1,676	10,729	2,505	1,871	—	134
Secondary[7]	17,650	605	7,664	—	2,321	1,309	112
Postsecondary[8]	3,970	91	1,194	—	384	815	31
1990							
Population, all ages[5]	5,286,811	631,684	3,184,509	725,798	440,874	277,533	26,412
Enrollment, all levels	988,220	107,082	563,363	132,634	117,812	61,543	5,786
Elementary[6]	576,865	78,042	361,386	45,161	65,041	24,629	2,607
Secondary[7]	343,466	26,205	178,765	68,866	45,534	21,534	2,562
Postsecondary[8]	67,889	2,836	23,213	18,607	7,237	15,380	617
Teachers, all levels	48,326	3,692	24,667	8,402	5,779	3,938	314
Elementary[6]	22,005	2,330	12,924	2,608	2,396	1,608	139
Secondary[7]	21,227	1,223	9,955	5,794	2,781	1,340	135
Postsecondary[8]	5,094	140	1,787	—	602	991	41
2000							
Population, all ages[5]	6,086,149	807,188	3,686,112	730,427	518,614	313,388	30,421
Enrollment, all levels	1,209,991	153,985	705,005	137,714	138,656	66,968	7,664
Elementary[6]	657,128	109,443	405,225	41,717	70,177	27,435	3,131
Secondary[7]	452,703	38,374	258,492	70,477	57,007	25,117	3,236
Postsecondary[8]	100,160	6,167	41,288	25,520	11,472	14,416	1,297
Teachers, all levels	57,250	4,990	29,651	10,719	6,823	4,650	155
Elementary[6]	24,976	2,899	14,616	2,741	2,760	1,806	155
Secondary[7]	25,512	1,807	12,540	6,104	3,186	1,682	—
Postsecondary[8]	6,762	285	2,496	1,875	877	1,163	—
2010							
Population, all ages[5]	6,872,671	1,039,861	4,127,141	740,240	587,253	343,230	34,946
Enrollment, all levels	1,425,360	233,184	828,197	129,054	150,345	75,233	9,347
Elementary[6]	697,049	159,488	403,500	36,749	67,190	26,565	3,556
Secondary[7]	546,102	62,318	333,471	58,629	61,100	26,809	3,776
Postsecondary[8]	182,209	11,378	91,227	33,676	22,055	21,859	2,014
Teachers, all levels	72,185	7,661	39,869	10,555	8,139	5,464	175
Elementary[6]	28,669	4,139	16,853	2,673	2,908	1,920	175
Secondary[7]	32,355	3,051	18,177	5,470	3,542	1,898	—
Postsecondary[8]	11,161	471	4,840	2,412	1,689	1,646	—
2015							
Population, all ages[5]	7,267,035	1,177,295	4,332,060	745,332	618,928	356,273	37,147
Enrollment, all levels	1,521,003	272,630	882,468	125,592	154,839	75,254	10,221
Elementary[6]	720,228	182,538	403,431	38,485	64,580	27,094	4,101
Secondary[7]	583,316	76,019	354,816	57,462	64,042	27,063	3,913
Postsecondary[8]	217,459	14,072	124,221	29,645	26,217	21,097	2,207
Teachers, all levels	77,694	9,741	42,820	10,430	8,742	5,435	195
Elementary[6]	31,185	5,237	18,197	2,724	2,985	1,847	195
Secondary[7]	33,528	3,898	18,374	5,328	3,907	1,803	—
Postsecondary[8]	12,981	607	6,249	2,377	1,850	1,786	—
2016							
Population, all ages[5]	7,345,786	1,205,830	4,372,158	746,316	625,003	358,903	37,576
Enrollment, all levels	1,544,819	278,750	897,605	126,892	155,682	75,578	10,312
Elementary[6]	736,616	187,228	414,680	39,168	64,007	27,342	4,191
Secondary[7]	588,197	77,061	356,944	58,570	64,372	27,353	3,897
Postsecondary[8]	220,006	14,461	125,981	29,155	27,303	20,883	2,223
Teachers, all levels	78,844	9,809	43,729	10,533	8,828	5,421	199
Elementary[6]	31,386	5,344	18,215	2,796	2,967	1,864	199
Secondary[7]	34,319	3,846	19,159	5,367	3,914	1,822	—
Postsecondary[8]	13,139	619	6,355	2,370	1,947	1,735	—

—Not available.
[1]The world total includes estimations for missing data on teachers.
[2]Enrollment and teacher data for the world total and Asia exclude Taiwan.
[3]Europe includes all countries of the former Union of Soviet Socialist Republics (U.S.S.R.) except Armenia, Azerbaijan, Georgia, Kazakhstan, Kyrgyzstan, Tajikistan, Turkmenistan, and Uzbekistan, which are included in Asia. Asia also includes Turkey, the Arab states (except those located in Africa), and Israel.
[4]Central and South America includes Latin America and the Caribbean. Northern America includes Bermuda, Canada, Greenland, St. Pierre and Miquelon, and the United States.
[5]Estimate of midyear population.
[6]This level generally corresponds to grades 1–6 in the United States.
[7]Includes general education, teacher training (at the secondary level), and technical and vocational education. This level generally corresponds to grades 7–12 in the United States.
[8]Includes college and university enrollment, and technical and vocational education beyond the secondary level.
NOTE: Detail may not sum to totals because of rounding and missing teacher data. Data include imputed values for nonrespondent countries. Enrollment and teacher data exclude several island countries or territories with small populations (less than 150,000). Some data have been revised from previously published figures.
SOURCE: United Nations Educational, Scientific, and Cultural Organization (UNESCO), unpublished tabulations. U.S. Department of Commerce, Census Bureau, International Data Base, retrieved March 27, 2019, from https://www.census.gov/programs-surveys/international-programs/about/idb.html. (This table was prepared March 2019.)

Table 601.35. Percentage of 3- and 4-year-olds and 5- to 14-year-olds enrolled in school, by country: 2000 through 2016

Country	Percent of 3- and 4-year-olds enrolled					Percent of 5- to 14-year-olds enrolled																
	2012	2013	2014	2015	2016	2000	2001	2002	2003	2004	2005	2006	2007	2008	2009	2010	2011	2012	2013	2014	2015	2016
1	2	3	4	5	6	7	8	9	10	11	12	13	14	15	16	17	18	19	20	21	22	23
OECD average[1]	**76.4**	**80.9**	**80.4**	**81.0**	**81.9**	**97.8**	**98.1**	**98.3**	**98.0**	**98.0**	**98.2**	**98.3**	**98.5**	**98.7**	**98.5**	**98.8**	**98.6**	**98.4**	**98.3**	**98.1**	**98.2**	**98.1**
Australia	46.6	72.1	77.3	79.2	77.0	100.0	100.1	99.3	98.2	98.5	99.1	99.6	99.3	99.3	99.3	99.2	99.4	101.1	100.0	100.0	100.0	100.0
Austria	77.8	81.4	82.3	83.7	84.2	98.2	98.7	98.9	98.5	98.5	98.4	98.1	98.3	98.5	98.4	98.4	98.2	98.2	98.4	98.4	98.5	97.9
Belgium	98.6	98.3	98.1	98.2	98.2	99.1	100.2	100.1	100.3	100.4[2]	99.6[2]	99.4	99.3	99.1	98.9	98.6	98.5	98.5	98.2	98.3	98.2	98.2
Canada	—	—	—	—	—	97.1	97.2	—	—	—	—	—	—	—	98.7	98.8	98.9	99.9	99.9	100.0	100.0	100.0
Chile	62.1	67.3	69.3	71.2	71.3	93.6	—	92.1	90.8	89.5	88.3	91.2	96.1	96.1	93.2	95.1	94.3	93.9	97.3	97.5	97.7	97.8
Czech Republic	70.3	70.9	76.1	81.5	84.3	99.8	99.8	99.3	99.8	99.7	99.8	99.9	99.8	98.7	98.7	98.1	97.7	98.6	98.1	97.7	97.7	97.5
Denmark	97.5	96.9	96.9	97.5	97.3	99.2	97.2	99.1	99.1	98.0	97.1	97.4	98.0	97.6	97.6	99.1	99.4	99.3	99.4	99.3	99.3	99.2
Estonia	88.9	89.2	88.4	88.7	89.4	—	—	—	—	—	104.6	102.2	100.4	100.4	100.0	96.4	95.7	95.2	95.6	96.5	96.4	96.6
Finland	55.1	71.4	71.1	71.5	76.1	91.6	93.5	94.4	94.6	95.1	95.1	95.1	95.3	95.5	95.5	95.5	95.7	95.7	96.8	96.7	96.5	97.2
France	99.1	100.0	100.0	100.0	100.0	99.8	101.0	101.1	101.4	101.6	101.3	101.0	100.9	100.7	99.8	99.6	99.4	99.1	99.0	99.0	99.0	99.1
Germany	93.3	94.5	94.6	95.0	93.7	99.4	100.1	97.5	97.6	97.9	98.3	98.8	99.2	99.3	99.4	99.4	98.5	99.4	99.2	98.9	98.9	98.1
Greece	25.6	—	58.7	46.6	46.8	99.8	98.1	96.3	96.7	97.2	97.5	98.1	97.7	98.9	100.1	100.7	100.0	99.2	—	95.7	97.7	97.3
Hungary	83.6	84.3	86.6	88.2	90.1	99.9	99.4	100.3	100.4	100.5	100.3	100.3	99.8	99.6	98.9	98.5	98.1	97.6	97.1	96.6	95.9	95.5
Iceland	96.1	96.4	96.6	96.9	96.7	98.5	98.9	98.5	98.8	98.8	98.9	98.8	98.3	98.5	98.2	98.5	98.6	98.8	98.5	98.6	98.7	98.9
Ireland	69.1	73.0	73.0	68.3	75.7	100.5	100.6	101.4	100.4	100.9	101.1	101.2	102.6	101.5	101.7	102.1	101.1	100.9	100.0	100.0	100.0	100.0
Israel	89.1	100.0	97.9	100.0	100.0	96.6	96.9	96.1	96.8	96.6	96.0	95.8	96.1	95.7	96.2	97.8	96.8	97.8	98.3	97.8	97.5	97.4
Italy	94.2	96.5	94.1	93.9	94.1	99.7	99.4	101.7	101.9	101.6	101.2	100.7	100.3	100.3	99.8	99.5	99.0	98.6	100.0	98.2	97.8	97.6
Japan	85.9	88.2	88.4	87.0	89.6	101.2	101.0	100.8	100.7	100.7	100.7	100.7	100.5	100.7	101.0	101.5	101.1	101.3	101.4	101.6	101.7	101.5
Korea, Republic of	86.3	93.6	91.4	91.5	94.9	92.3	92.6	92.7	93.2	93.5	94.1	94.9	95.7	95.1	95.7	99.7	99.1	98.8	98.1	98.2	98.4	97.5
Latvia	83.4	86.1	88.3	89.1	90.5	—	—	—	—	—	—	—	—	—	—	—	—	98.2	97.8	97.7	97.6	98.0
Lithuania	—	77.7	80.6	81.3	81.3	—	—	—	—	—	—	—	—	—	—	—	—	—	98.5	98.9	99.4	100.0
Luxembourg	85.4	85.1	83.1	80.4	80.2	95.3	92.2	93.4	96.7	96.4	96.7	96.2	95.9	95.8	95.6	95.8	96.0	97.9	97.1	97.1	97.0	97.0
Mexico	63.3	66.1	66.0	67.6	67.9	94.8	95.0	95.7	96.9	97.7	99.9	100.9	102.1	103.4	104.6	106.1	107.7	100.2	100.0	100.0	100.0	100.0
Netherlands	91.4	91.5	88.4	89.5	91.2	99.4	99.3	99.3	99.7	99.6	99.0	99.6	99.5	99.6	99.5	99.5	99.8	99.8	99.5	99.4	99.8	99.8
New Zealand	90.7	91.6	90.2	91.9	90.7	99.0	99.3	99.5	100.1	100.5	100.9	101.0	99.7	100.2	100.6	100.9	101.0	100.7	100.0	98.5	98.7	99.0
Norway	96.1	96.2	96.1	96.2	96.4	97.4	97.6	97.9	98.1	98.3	98.4	98.8	99.2	99.5	99.5	99.5	99.6	99.5	99.5	99.4	99.3	99.1
Poland	58.0	60.0	64.7	72.5	78.1	93.6	94.3	94.4	94.2	94.5	94.6	94.5	94.5	94.0	94.1	94.9	95.3	95.5	95.9	95.6	95.3	95.4
Portugal	84.9	84.2	83.6	84.6	85.2	105.2	107.0	106.0	105.3	104.1	103.9	103.8	104.2	104.1	103.1	102.4	102.1	102.1	100.0	99.7	98.9	98.3
Slovak Republic	67.5	68.1	68.9	67.7	69.1	—	97.9	98.1	97.3	97.3	97.1	96.8	96.8	96.6	96.1	95.8	95.5	94.5	94.2	93.7	93.4	93.3
Slovenia	87.1	86.7	85.8	86.1	86.8	—	—	—	—	—	96.5	96.4	96.2	96.8	97.1	97.1	97.1	97.4	97.1	97.0	97.4	97.1
Spain	96.1	96.2	96.5	96.2	96.3	104.4	103.6	103.8	102.5	101.8	101.4	101.0	100.7	100.4	100.1	99.5	99.0	97.8	97.5	97.2	97.1	97.1
Sweden	93.4	93.7	93.9	92.2	92.9	97.8	98.1	98.2	98.6	99.1	99.5	98.8	100.3	99.3	98.7	98.5	97.4	99.0	98.5	98.2	98.5	99.0
Switzerland	21.6	22.2	23.5	24.8	25.1	98.8	98.7	98.6	99.3	99.6	99.6	100.3	100.4	100.2	100.0	100.1	99.5	99.3	99.6	99.8	99.8	99.7
Turkey	12.0	21.7	20.0	20.8	21.1	80.2	83.5	—	82.0	81.2	81.8	82.9	84.3	91.9	91.3	94.1	94.9	95.2	96.3	95.9	95.8	94.9[3]
United Kingdom	95.5	96.3	90.7	100.0	100.0	98.9	98.7	98.9	100.5	100.4	101.0	100.7	99.3	101.5	101.4	103.1	100.7	98.0	98.2	98.4	98.4	98.5
United States	53.5	53.7	54.7	54.4	52.7	99.3	102.1	96.9	97.1	97.3	97.7	98.0	98.3	98.6	97.1	96.8	96.2	97.3	96.9	97.2	98.0	99.2
Other reporting countries																						
China	—	—	—	—	—	79.6	81.7	80.7	85.9	—	—	—	—	—	—	—	—	[4]	—	—	—	—
Russian Federation	73.4	75.8	80.5	81.6	81.4	—	83.3	84.6	94.2	90.4	81.5	—	—	93.8	93.5	93.1	92.1	92.7	93.2	93.5	94.8	96.1

—Not available.

[1]Refers to the mean of the data values for all reporting Organization for Economic Cooperation and Development (OECD) countries, to which each country reporting data contributes equally. The average includes all current OECD countries for which a given year's data are available, even if they were not members of OECD in that year.

[2]Excludes the German-Speaking Community of Belgium.

[3]Includes 15- to 17-year-olds enrolled in primary education.

[4]Percentage suppressed due to apparent data quality or comparability issues.

NOTE: For each country, this table shows the number of persons in each age group who are enrolled in that country as a percentage of that country's total population in the specified age group. However, some of a country's population may be enrolled in a different country, and some persons enrolled in the country may be residents of a different country. Enrollment rates may be underestimated for countries such as Luxembourg that are net exporters of students and may be overestimated for countries that are net importers. If a country enrolls many residents of other countries, the country's total population in the specified age group can be smaller than the total number enrolled, resulting in enrollment estimates exceeding 100 percent. Some data have been revised from previously published figures.

SOURCE: Organization for Economic Cooperation and Development (OECD), *Education at a Glance*, 2002 through 2014; and Online Education Database, retrieved November 7, 2018, from https://stats.oecd.org/Index.aspx. (This table was prepared November 2018.)

Table 601.40. Percentage of 15- to 29-year-olds enrolled in school, by selected levels of education, age, and country: 2016

Country	All levels of education[1]		Secondary education[2]								Total tertiary education (postsecondary degree programs)[3]							
			15 to 19 years old						20 to 29 years old					20 to 29 years old				
	15 to 19 years old	20 to 29 years old	Total	15 years old	16 years old	17 years old	18 years old	19 years old	Total	20 years old	17 years old	18 years old	19 years old	Total	20 years old	21 year old	22 years old	23 to 29 years old
1	2	3	4	5	6	7	8	9	10	11	12	13	14	15	16	17	18	19
OECD average[4]	**84.9**	**28.6**	**72.4**	**97.4**	**95.0**	**89.7**	**56.5**	**25.5**	**4.5**	**12.2**	**1.5**	**18.1**	**34.0**	**22.6**	**39.3**	**39.3**	**35.1**	**16.6**
Australia	91.4	43.3	69.9	101.0	101.7	90.4	39.4	21.8	10.5	18.5	5.8	37.9	50.7	28.8	51.1	47.0	41.0	21.9
Austria	78.0	25.8	61.9	93.8	89.2	72.8	42.5	19.3	2.3	8.7	13.4	29.4	31.0	22.6	30.9	31.0	29.3	19.5
Belgium	92.9	29.9	73.4	98.0	97.7	95.8	50.5	27.2	6.0	13.6	1.1	37.8	51.2	21.6	54.0	49.2	40.0	11.5
Canada	78.4	21.6	61.1	101.3	99.4	82.9	23.5	8.5	1.7	4.3	3.1	35.2	43.2	19.9	42.5	39.7	32.2	12.4
Chile	81.4	29.4	64.6	97.0	92.8	92.0	34.3	11.3	1.7	4.5	0.2	30.0	48.3	27.7	50.6	47.8	42.7	20.0
Czech Republic	90.8	24.5	85.5	99.6	97.6	95.4	87.8	48.0	2.9	14.3	0.2	1.7	24.1	21.6	41.4	40.6	38.0	15.2
Denmark	86.4	43.8	84.7	98.8	94.8	90.6	85.0	55.6	12.4	27.9	#	0.6	7.6	31.3	21.5	35.9	43.9	30.2
Estonia	88.8	26.0	82.1	97.7	96.6	94.3	88.0	36.5	3.8	14.9	0.1	1.4	27.3	19.8	34.5	36.2	31.9	15.4
Finland	86.9	41.1	83.5	98.3	95.9	96.0	95.0	35.3	12.9	19.7	0.1	1.0	14.9	27.8	27.3	35.4	39.5	25.1
France	85.3	21.4	65.9	96.3	93.9	88.0	34.6	12.4	1.6	5.6	2.8	41.8	50.9	19.6	47.5	41.0	34.7	10.7
Germany	86.2	33.3	75.8	97.4	93.5	87.9	65.1	38.6	5.8	21.5	0.5	7.4	19.3	22.7	27.5	30.4	30.5	20.3
Greece	84.0	35.9	60.8	95.7	91.8	92.9	15.6	8.7	1.7	5.3	1.0	48.2	54.3	30.5	55.9	54.1	43.6	22.3
Hungary	83.9	22.9	73.3	96.3	93.5	88.0	67.7	27.9	2.6	10.8	0.4	4.9	20.7	17.2	28.7	29.5	28.4	12.4
Iceland	86.8	36.0	86.0	99.0	95.9	88.6	81.2	66.9	11.6	30.8	0.0	0.2	3.3	23.7	18.2	30.6	33.1	22.1
Ireland	93.5	27.1	68.5	101.6	100.4	89.9	41.6	4.6	0.6	1.5	3.3	28.1	55.4	21.3	55.7	50.2	35.3	10.8
Israel	66.2	20.4	61.6	96.9	96.1	91.5	16.0	1.9	0.1	0.9	0.6	8.7	13.7	20.2	15.0	15.9	18.8	21.8
Italy	83.4	22.0	76.2	97.3	94.3	91.7	77.8	20.4	1.3	6.8	#	2.5	32.9	20.8	37.1	36.6	31.8	15.1
Japan	—	—	57.8	96.9	96.5	93.0	2.7	0.8	0.0	0.0	0.0	—	—	—	—	—	—	—
Korea, Republic of	86.9	30.3	58.6	100.9	95.9	96.0	9.3	0.3	#	0.1	0.6	61.0	72.9	30.3	68.7	64.4	50.9	16.5
Latvia	92.5	27.7	83.2	97.9	96.2	97.3	88.6	36.5	3.0	12.6	0.4	4.1	37.2	23.4	46.6	46.5	41.1	16.6
Lithuania	93.9	30.0	79.8	100.5	100.1	98.2	83.4	21.7	2.1	6.1	0.4	9.2	49.4	24.8	54.0	53.6	43.1	14.9
Luxembourg	75.9	13.0	75.2	92.3	90.1	82.5	71.7	41.2	5.6	24.9	#	0.6	2.2	6.8	7.7	8.7	10.7	6.0
Mexico	59.3	16.7	49.2	82.0	72.0	57.4	23.0	11.1	3.7	5.8	3.1	20.3	26.7	13.0	27.8	26.4	20.8	7.4
Netherlands	93.1	35.2	79.0	99.6	98.9	89.7	63.0	42.7	8.8	27.9	7.5	25.4	38.3	26.4	44.1	44.8	41.3	19.4
New Zealand	80.8	26.1	62.4	97.9	97.8	85.5	26.7	8.7	2.9	4.8	2.1	31.5	40.7	20.5	42.4	37.3	28.4	13.9
Norway	87.2	31.4	82.9	100.0	94.9	92.9	89.9	38.5	5.2	20.0	0.1	0.4	19.9	25.8	35.8	41.7	38.9	20.6
Poland	92.9	29.2	83.6	95.1	95.3	94.5	92.9	44.0	2.2	10.2	1.2	2.4	34.9	23.6	46.5	46.5	44.3	15.6
Portugal	88.5	23.0	74.4	96.0	97.0	97.0	52.8	26.2	3.7	12.5	0.5	28.2	38.0	18.9	40.3	38.2	32.0	11.4
Slovak Republic	83.6	19.0	76.6	96.9	92.2	88.4	75.7	32.9	1.0	5.8	0.2	3.1	21.7	17.2	34.3	34.3	32.7	11.3
Slovenia	93.3	34.4	81.6	97.3	96.9	96.2	90.6	30.0	7.8	17.0	0.0	2.2	53.6	26.6	57.3	55.8	49.8	16.8
Spain	87.2	31.7	70.3	96.2	95.7	89.5	42.8	25.9	6.4	16.9	#	37.2	46.7	24.9	49.3	49.0	40.5	16.9
Sweden	87.5	34.4	83.6	101.2	101.0	98.6	94.7	26.2	9.4	16.4	0.2	0.9	15.2	20.7	22.8	28.2	29.4	18.2
Switzerland	85.1	26.9	81.4	97.6	92.8	90.5	79.4	49.3	5.9	24.8	0.3	3.6	11.2	20.3	20.7	26.9	29.9	18.2
Turkey	71.0	40.3	59.4	90.4	83.0	76.8	34.0	10.9	5.6	9.5	0.5	18.0	40.4	34.7	49.2	50.1	47.7	28.4
United Kingdom	85.3	23.6	69.1	99.9	99.5	91.6	38.5	21.6	9.3	15.0	2.3	32.7	42.4	14.3	43.1	31.2	19.2	7.6
United States	82.5	24.5	63.7	100.3	97.5	86.5	29.6	4.8	0.0	0.0	1.1	37.4	51.6	23.3	46.6	42.4	33.5	16.0
Other reporting countries																		
China	—	—	—	—	—	—	—	—	—	—	3.5	21.8	35.0	8.1	36.3	28.7	17.4	2.0
Russian Federation[5]	84.1	17.7	36.3	84.7	54.9	38.6	3.1	0.1	#	#	40.2	64.8	63.1	17.2	54.3	46.0	32.8	9.6

—Not available.
#Rounds to zero.
[1]In addition to secondary and tertiary education, may include enrollment in the following International Standard Classification of Education (ISCED) 2011 education levels that are not shown separately: level 1 (primary or elementary education) and level 4 (nontertiary education that typically corresponds to postsecondary vocational programs below the associate's degree level in the United States).
[2]Refers to ISCED 2011 level 2 (lower secondary education) and level 3 (upper secondary education). Secondary education generally corresponds to grades 7–12 in the United States.
[3]Total tertiary education corresponds to all postsecondary programs leading to associate's and higher degrees in the United States. Tertiary education includes ISCED 2011 level 5 (corresponding to U.S. programs at the associate's degree level), level 6 (bachelor's or equivalent level), level 7 (master's or equivalent level), and level 8 (doctoral or equivalent level). Enrollment rates may not be directly comparable across countries due to differing definitions of tertiary education and the age at which it begins.
[4]Refers to the mean of the data values for all reporting Organization for Economic Cooperation and Development (OECD) countries, to which each country reporting data contributes equally.
[5]Data for total tertiary education include some vocational education programs at the upper secondary level (ISCED 2011 level 3).
NOTE: For each country, this table shows the number of persons at a given age who are enrolled in that country as a percentage of that country's total population at the specified age. If a country enrolls many residents of other countries, the country's total population at the specified age can be smaller than the total number enrolled, resulting in enrollment estimates exceeding 100 percent. Conversely, if a country has many residents who are enrolled outside of the country, the country's enrollment rates may be underestimated. Enrollment estimates can also be affected if population and enrollment data were collected at different times. Includes both full-time and part-time students.
SOURCE: Organization for Economic Cooperation and Development (OECD), Online Education Database, retrieved October 2, 2018, from http://stats.oecd.org/Index.aspx. (This table was prepared October 2018.)

Table 601.50. Pupil/teacher ratios in public and private elementary and secondary schools, by level of education and country: 2013 through 2016

Country	Elementary school (primary)				Junior high school (lower secondary)				Senior high school (upper secondary)			
	2013	2014	2015	2016	2013	2014	2015	2016	2013	2014	2015	2016
1	2	3	4	5	6	7	8	9	10	11	12	13
OECD average[1]	**14.9**	**14.9**	**15.1**	**14.9**	**13.0**	**12.8**	**12.8**	**12.6**	**13.2**	**13.1**	**13.3**	**12.8**
Australia	15.6	15.6	15.4	15.2	—	—	—	—	12.0[2,3]	—	12.3[2,3]	12.1[2,3]
Austria	11.9	12.0	11.8	11.6	9.0	8.8	8.7	8.6	9.9	10.0	10.1	10.1
Belgium	12.7	12.7	12.8	12.8	9.3	9.2	9.5	9.0	9.9	9.9	9.9	9.8
Canada	16.5[4,5]	16.6[4,5]	17.0[4,5]	16.9[4,5]	—	—	—	—	13.8	12.8	13.0	12.2
Chile	22.5	21.3	20.9	20.3	24.3	22.8	21.9	21.1	25.1	23.9	23.0	22.1
Czech Republic	18.8	18.7	19.0	19.1	11.2	11.9	11.8	12.0	11.1	11.7	11.1	11.0
Denmark	—	11.9	—	—	—	11.0	—	—	—	13.1	—	—
Estonia	13.0	12.9	13.3	13.2	9.8	9.9	9.5	10.1	14.1[6]	14.6[6]	15.2	15.3
Finland	13.2	13.3	13.6	13.3	9.0	8.9	9.0	9.0	16.0	16.2	16.5	17.2
France	19.3	19.4	18.7[7]	19.4	15.4	15.4	14.6[7]	14.7	10.1	10.4	10.0[7]	11.3
Germany	15.6	15.4	15.4	15.3	13.6	13.4	13.3	13.2	13.2	13.1	13.0	12.9
Greece	9.5	9.4	—	—	7.3	7.8	—	—	8.1	—	—	—
Hungary	10.6	11.5	11.2	11.0	10.4	10.9	10.6	10.3	12.0	12.5	11.5	11.1
Iceland	10.4	—	10.7	10.8	10.5	—	10.5	10.2	—	—	—	—
Ireland	16.4[7]	16.3[7]	16.2[7]	16.0	—	—	—	—	13.9[2,7]	13.9[2,7]	13.9[2,7]	13.8
Israel	15.3	15.5	15.4	15.4	13.5	12.1	11.8	11.8	10.7[7]	10.6	10.8[7]	10.9
Italy	12.3	12.4	12.4	11.4	11.7	11.6	11.5	10.9	13.0[7]	12.5	12.5	10.4
Japan	17.4	17.1	16.9	16.6	13.9	13.8	13.6	13.4	11.7[6]	11.9[6]	12.0	11.8
Korea, Republic of	17.3	16.9	16.8	16.5	17.5	16.6	15.7	14.7	15.1	14.5	14.1	13.8
Latvia	11.2	11.2	11.6	11.4	7.8	7.6	7.7	7.8	10.2	10.0	9.7	9.8
Lithuania	10.2	10.2	10.3	10.5	7.6	7.4	7.3	7.3	8.0	8.1	8.1	7.7
Luxembourg	8.8	8.9	10.7	10.5	11.2	10.9	11.0	10.7	7.1	8.9	10.8	9.0
Mexico	27.7	27.4	26.9	26.7	32.2	33.0	33.6	33.9	27.3	20.6	20.0	20.0
Netherlands	16.6[7]	16.6	16.6	16.8	16.0[7]	16.2	16.0	16.1	18.6[7]	19.2[7]	18.0	17.9
New Zealand	16.4	16.4	16.5	16.6	16.4	16.2	16.3	16.4	13.3	13.1	12.8	12.6
Norway	10.3	10.3	10.4[7]	10.1	9.8	9.7	9.6[7]	9.1	10.3[6,8]	10.3[6,8]	10.3	10.2
Poland	11.1	11.0	11.1	11.4	9.9	10.4	9.7	9.6	11.0	10.9	10.3	10.2
Portugal	13.2	14.0	13.7	13.1	10.4	10.1	10.0	9.8	8.4[6]	8.9[6]	9.7	9.6
Slovak Republic	16.9	17.2	17.2	17.1	12.5	12.5	11.6	12.3	13.6	13.5	13.5	13.5
Slovenia	16.0	15.9	15.9	14.3	8.2	8.3	8.5	6.1	13.5	13.7	13.4	14.2
Spain	13.8	13.5	13.7	13.6	11.6	11.8	11.9	11.7	11.0	11.3	11.1	10.7
Sweden	12.7	12.7	12.8	13.1	12.0	12.2	12.3	12.4	12.8	13.8	14.4	13.7
Switzerland	13.8	13.8	15.6[7]	15.5	10.9	10.8	11.9[7]	11.8	—	—	—	12.3[7]
Turkey	19.8	19.3	18.4	17.7	19.3	18.4	16.8	15.3	15.6	14.8	14.1	12.6
United Kingdom	20.7	19.6	18.4	16.9	18.5	15.0	14.3	14.8	18.5	16.3	26.1	16.5
United States	15.3	15.4	15.4	15.2	15.4	15.5	15.4	15.3	15.4	15.5	15.4	15.5
Other reporting countries												
Argentina	—	—	—	—	—	—	—	—	—	—	—	—
Brazil	21.2	20.9	24.8	24.4	18.5	17.8	25.0	24.9	15.7	15.4	23.6	24.1
China	16.9	16.2	16.3	16.5	13.4	12.6	12.5	12.3	17.5	16.5	15.6	15.1
Colombia	25.0	24.3	23.8	24.2	26.6	26.3	26.3	26.2	22.9	21.9	23.9	25.6
Costa Rica	13.3	13.2	12.7	12.0	14.1	14.4	14.0	12.8	13.8	14.3	13.9	12.6
India	32.3	31.3	31.5	35.2	29.8	30.5	30.5	27.0	32.1	33.3	33.0	30.3
Indonesia	16.1	16.6	—	14.0	14.4	14.7	—	13.9	16.9	16.6	—	14.4
Russian Federation	20.3	20.2	20.6	21.0	8.9[9]	8.8[9]	10.4[9]	10.6[9]	—	—	—	—
Saudi Arabia	10.5	10.8	10.9	11.7	10.4	10.6	—	—	11.2	11.4	—	—
South Africa	32.0	32.8	30.3	30.3	—	—	—	—	—	—	17.1[2]	17.1[2]

—Not available.
[1]Refers to the mean of the data values for all reporting Organization for Economic Cooperation and Development (OECD) countries, to which each country reporting data contributes equally. The average includes all current OECD countries for which a given year's data are available, even if they were not members of OECD in that year.
[2]Junior high school data are included with the senior high school data.
[3]Includes only general programs; data on vocational programs are not available.
[4]Preprimary data are included with the elementary school data.
[5]Junior high school data are included with the elementary school data.
[6]Postsecondary non-higher-education data are included with the senior high school data.
[7]Public institutions only.
[8]Short-cycle higher education data are included with the senior high school data.
[9]Senior high school data are included with the junior high school data.
NOTE: The pupil/teacher ratio is the number of full-time-equivalent students divided by the number of full-time-equivalent teachers, including teachers for students with disabilities and other special teachers. All data in this table were calculated using International Standard Classification of Education (ISCED) 2011. In this table, elementary school corresponds to ISCED 2011 level 1 (U.S. grades 1 through 6), junior high school corresponds to ISCED 2011 level 2 (U.S. grades 7 through 9), and senior high school corresponds to ISCED 2011 level 3 (U.S. grades 10 through 12).
SOURCE: Organization for Economic Cooperation and Development (OECD), Online Education Database, retrieved August 1, 2019, from https://stats.oecd.org/Index.aspx. (This table was prepared August 2019).

Table 602.10. Average reading literacy scale scores of fourth-graders and percentage distribution, by international benchmark level and country or other education system: Selected years, 2001 through 2016

[Standard errors appear in parentheses]

Country or other education system[1]	Average reading literacy scale score[2]								Percentage distribution, by international benchmark level (score range), 2017[3]							
	2001		2006		2011		2016		Low (400–474) and below[4]		Intermediate (475–549)		High (550–624)		Advanced (625 and above)	
1	2		3		4		5		6		7		8		9	
Scale centerpoint[2] or median percentage[5]	**500**	**(†)**	**500**	**(†)**	**500**	**(†)**	**500**	**(†)**	**18**	**(†)**	**31**	**(†)**	**36**	**(†)**	**10**	**(†)**
Australia	—	(†)	—	(†)	527	(2.2)	544	(2.5)	19	(1.0)	30	(1.0)	35	(1.0)	16	(1.0)
Austria	—	(†)	538	(2.2)	529	(2.0)	541[6]	(2.4)	16[6]	(1.1)	37[6]	(0.9)	39[6]	(1.3)	8[6]	(0.8)
Azerbaijan[7]	—	(†)	—	(†)	462[6]	(3.3)	472[8]	(4.2)	46[8]	(2.0)	36[8]	(1.5)	16[8]	(1.0)	2[8]	(0.3)
Bahrain	—	(†)	—	(†)	—	(†)	446	(2.3)	59	(1.0)	27	(0.8)	12	(0.6)	2	(0.3)
Belgium (Flemish)	—	(†)	—	(†)	—	(†)	525	(1.9)	20	(1.3)	45	(1.1)	31	(1.1)	4	(0.4)
Belgium (French)	—	(†)	500	(2.6)	506[6,9]	(2.9)	497[6]	(2.6)	35[6]	(1.4)	42[6]	(1.1)	20[6]	(1.1)	3[6]	(0.4)
Bulgaria	550	(3.8)	547	(4.4)	532	(4.1)	552	(4.2)	17	(1.6)	28	(1.3)	35	(1.3)	19	(1.3)
Canada	—	(†)	—	(†)	548[6]	(1.6)	543[6,10]	(1.8)	17[6,10]	(0.9)	33[6,10]	(0.8)	37[6,10]	(0.8)	13[6,10]	(0.7)
Chile	—	(†)	—	(†)	—	(†)	494	(2.5)	39	(1.5)	36	(1.4)	22	(1.2)	3	(0.4)
Chinese Taipei	—	(†)	535	(2.0)	553	(1.9)	559	(2.0)	10	(0.7)	31	(1.1)	44	(1.2)	14	(1.1)
Colombia	422	(4.4)	—	(†)	448	(4.1)	—	(†)	—	(†)	—	(†)	—	(†)	—	(†)
Croatia	—	(†)	—	(†)	553[6]	(1.9)	—	(†)	—	(†)	—	(†)	—	(†)	—	(†)
Czech Republic	537	(2.3)	—	(†)	545	(2.2)	543	(2.1)	15	(0.9)	36	(1.0)	39	(1.0)	10	(0.7)
Denmark	—	(†)	546	(2.3)	554[6]	(1.7)	547[6]	(2.1)	14[6]	(1.0)	34[6]	(1.0)	41[6]	(1.1)	11[6]	(1.0)
Egypt	—	(†)	—	(†)	—	(†)	330[11]	(5.6)	89[11]	(1.2)	9[11]	(1.0)	2[11]	(0.3)	‡[11]	(†)
England (United Kingdom)	553[6,9]	(3.4)	539	(2.6)	552[9]	(2.6)	559	(1.9)	14	(0.7)	28	(0.9)	37	(1.1)	20	(0.9)
Finland	—	(†)	—	(†)	568	(1.9)	566	(1.8)	9	(0.8)	29	(1.0)	44	(1.1)	18	(0.8)
France	525	(2.4)	522	(2.1)	520	(2.6)	511	(2.2)	28	(1.2)	42	(1.2)	26	(1.1)	4	(0.6)
Georgia[7]	—	(†)	471[6,10]	(3.1)	488[10]	(3.1)	488[10]	(2.8)	40[10]	(1.6)	38[10]	(1.4)	20[10]	(1.1)	2[10]	(0.4)
Germany	539	(1.9)	548	(2.2)	541	(2.2)	537	(3.2)	19	(1.4)	34	(1.0)	36	(1.1)	11	(0.8)
Hong Kong (China)	528	(3.1)	564	(2.4)	571[12]	(2.3)	569[6,9]	(2.7)	7[6,9]	(0.9)	27[6,9]	(1.4)	47[6,9]	(1.5)	18[6,9]	(1.3)
Hungary	543	(2.2)	551	(3.0)	539	(2.9)	554	(2.9)	15	(1.0)	30	(1.2)	39	(1.1)	17	(1.2)
Indonesia	—	(†)	405	(4.1)	428	(4.2)	—	(†)	—	(†)	—	(†)	—	(†)	—	(†)
Iran, Islamic Republic of	414	(4.2)	421	(3.1)	457	(2.8)	428[13]	(4.0)	63[13]	(1.3)	26[13]	(1.0)	9[13]	(0.5)	1[13]	(0.2)
Ireland	—	(†)	—	(†)	552	(2.3)	567	(2.5)	11	(0.9)	28	(1.2)	40	(1.3)	21	(1.2)
Israel	509[14]	(2.8)	512[14]	(3.3)	541[12]	(2.7)	530[12]	(2.5)	25[12]	(1.0)	29[12]	(1.0)	33[12]	(1.1)	13[12]	(0.9)
Italy	541	(2.4)	551	(2.9)	541	(2.2)	548	(2.2)	13	(1.0)	35	(1.3)	41	(1.7)	11	(0.8)
Kazakhstan	—	(†)	—	(†)	—	(†)	536	(2.5)	16	(1.5)	42	(1.3)	35	(1.4)	7	(0.8)
Kuwait	—	(†)	—	(†)	—	(†)	393[11]	(4.1)	78[11]	(1.5)	16[11]	(1.2)	5[11]	(0.8)	‡[11]	(†)
Latvia	—	(†)	—	(†)	—	(†)	558[6]	(1.7)	10[6]	(0.8)	33[6]	(1.3)	43[6]	(1.4)	14[6]	(1.0)
Lithuania	543[10]	(2.6)	537[10]	(1.6)	528[6,10]	(2.0)	548[15]	(2.6)	14[15]	(1.1)	34[15]	(1.3)	40[15]	(1.2)	12[15]	(0.9)
Macao (China)	—	(†)	—	(†)	—	(†)	546	(1.0)	14	(0.5)	36	(0.8)	41	(0.9)	10	(0.6)
Malta (Maltese)	—	(†)	—	(†)	457	(1.5)	452[6]	(1.8)	55[6]	(1.1)	32[6]	(1.1)	12[6]	(0.8)	‡[6]	(†)
Morocco	350[16]	(9.6)	323	(5.9)	310[17]	(3.9)	358[13]	(3.9)	86[13]	(0.8)	11[13]	(0.7)	3[13]	(0.4)	‡[13]	(†)
Netherlands[9]	554	(2.5)	547	(1.5)	546	(1.9)	545	(1.7)	12	(0.9)	39	(1.3)	40	(1.1)	8	(0.6)
New Zealand	529	(3.6)	532	(2.0)	531	(1.9)	523	(2.2)	27	(1.0)	32	(1.0)	30	(1.0)	11	(0.6)
Northern Ireland (United Kingdom)	—	(†)	—	(†)	558[9]	(2.4)	565	(2.2)	13	(0.8)	26	(1.0)	38	(1.0)	22	(1.4)
Norway (grade 5)[18]	—	(†)	—	(†)	—	(†)	559	(2.3)	10	(0.9)	32	(1.4)	43	(1.4)	15	(0.9)
Oman	—	(†)	—	(†)	391[19]	(2.8)	418	(3.3)	68	(1.3)	22	(0.9)	8	(0.7)	2	(0.3)
Poland	—	(†)	519	(2.4)	526	(2.1)	565	(2.1)	11	(0.7)	28	(1.1)	41	(1.1)	20	(1.1)
Portugal	—	(†)	—	(†)	541	(2.6)	528[6]	(2.3)	21[6]	(1.3)	42[6]	(1.1)	31[6]	(1.2)	7[6]	(0.9)
Qatar	—	(†)	353	(1.1)	425[6]	(3.5)	442	(1.8)	58	(1.1)	25	(1.1)	14	(0.6)	3	(0.3)
Romania	512	(4.6)	489	(5.0)	502	(4.3)	—	(†)	—	(†)	—	(†)	—	(†)	—	(†)
Russian Federation	528[6]	(4.4)	565[6]	(3.4)	568	(2.7)	581	(2.2)	6	(0.6)	23	(1.0)	44	(1.0)	26	(1.2)
Saudi Arabia	—	(†)	—	(†)	430	(4.4)	430	(4.2)	65	(1.7)	24	(1.3)	9	(1.0)	1	(0.4)
Singapore	528	(5.2)	558	(2.9)	567[6]	(3.3)	576[12]	(3.2)	11[12]	(1.0)	23[12]	(1.1)	38[12]	(1.5)	29[12]	(1.6)
Slovak Republic	518	(2.8)	531	(2.8)	535	(2.8)	535	(3.1)	19	(1.3)	33	(1.1)	37	(1.3)	10	(0.8)
Slovenia	502	(2.0)	522	(2.1)	530	(2.0)	542	(2.0)	17	(0.9)	34	(0.9)	38	(1.1)	11	(0.8)
South Africa	—	(†)	—	(†)	—	(†)	320[11]	(4.4)	92[11]	(1.0)	6[11]	(0.7)	2[11]	(0.4)	‡[11]	(†)
Spain	—	(†)	513	(2.5)	513	(2.3)	528	(1.7)	20	(1.0)	41	(0.8)	33	(0.9)	6	(0.4)
Sweden	561	(2.2)	549	(2.3)	542	(2.1)	555	(2.4)	12	(0.9)	31	(1.1)	43	(1.7)	14	(1.4)
Trinidad and Tobago	—	(†)	436	(4.9)	471	(3.8)	479	(3.3)	45	(1.7)	31	(1.3)	20	(1.1)	4	(0.5)
United Arab Emirates	—	(†)	—	(†)	439	(2.2)	450	(3.2)	57	(1.4)	23	(0.7)	15	(0.8)	5	(0.3)
United States	542[6,9]	(3.8)	540[9]	(3.5)	556[6]	(1.5)	549[9]	(3.1)	17[9]	(1.2)	31[9]	(1.1)	37[9]	(1.4)	16[9]	(1.3)

See notes at end of table.

Table 602.10. Average reading literacy scale scores of fourth-graders and percentage distribution, by international benchmark level and country or other education system: Selected years, 2001 through 2016—Continued

[Standard errors appear in parentheses]

Country or other education system[1]	Average reading literacy scale score[2]								Percentage distribution, by international benchmark level (score range), 2017[3]							
	2001		2006		2011		2016		Low (400–474) and below[4]		Intermediate (475–549)		High (550–624)		Advanced (625 and above)	
1	2		3		4		5		6		7		8		9	
Benchmarking education systems																
Abu Dhabi (United Arab Emirates)	—	(†)	—	(†)	424	(4.7)	414	(4.7)	69	(1.7)	20	(1.1)	9	(0.9)	2	(0.4)
Alberta (Canada)	—	(†)	560[6]	(2.4)	548[6]	(2.9)	—	(†)	—	(†)	—	(†)	—	(†)	—	(†)
Andalusia (Spain)	—	(†)	—	(†)	515	(2.3)	525	(2.1)	22	(1.2)	41	(0.9)	32	(1.1)	5	(0.5)
Bueno Aires (Argentina)	—	(†)	—	(†)	—	(†)	480	(3.1)	45	(1.5)	34	(1.1)	18	(1.0)	3	(0.4)
Dubai (United Arab Emirates)	—	(†)	—	(†)	476	(2.0)	515	(1.9)	31	(0.9)	30	(0.9)	29	(0.8)	11	(0.6)
Florida (United States)[21]	—	(†)	—	(†)	569[9,14]	(2.9)	—	(†)	—	(†)	—	(†)	—	(†)	—	(†)
Madrid (Spain)	—	(†)	—	(†)	—	(†)	549[6]	(2.0)	11[6]	(0.9)	38[6]	(1.1)	42[6]	(1.1)	9[6]	(0.7)
Malta (English)	—	(†)	—	(†)	477	(1.4)	—	(†)	—	(†)	—	(†)	—	(†)	—	(†)
Moscow City (Russian Federation)	—	(†)	—	(†)	—	(†)	612	(2.2)	2	(0.3)	14	(0.9)	41	(1.2)	43	(1.5)
Norway (grade 4)[18]	499	(2.9)	498[20]	(2.6)	507[16]	(1.9)	517	(2.0)	26	(1.1)	40	(1.1)	29	(1.0)	5	(0.6)
Ontario (Canada)	548[6]	(3.3)	555[6]	(2.7)	552[6]	(2.6)	544	(3.2)	18	(1.4)	32	(1.1)	37	(1.4)	14	(1.5)
Quebec (Canada)	537	(3.0)	533	(2.8)	538	(2.1)	547[22]	(2.8)	13[22]	(1.5)	37[22]	(1.5)	39[22]	(1.6)	11[22]	(1.2)

—Not available.
†Not applicable.
‡Reporting standards not met (too few cases for a reliable estimate).
[1]Most of the education systems represent complete countries, but some represent subnational entities; examples include the Flemish and French communities of Belgium, two components of the United Kingdom (England and Northern Ireland), a few individual cities (such as Abu Dhabi within the United Arab Emirates), and the U.S. state of Florida.
[2]Progress in International Reading Literacy Study (PIRLS) scores are reported on a scale from 0 to 1,000, with the scale centerpoint set at 500 and the standard deviation set at 100.
[3]PIRLS international benchmarks group achievement into four levels, providing a way to interpret scale scores and to understand how student proficiency varies at different points on the scale. The score range for each benchmark level (i.e., the lowest and highest score in that level) is shown in parentheses. The score cut-points (i.e., lowest scores) that define the beginning of each level were selected to be as close as possible to the standard percentile cut-points (i.e., the 25th, 50th, 75th, and 90th percentiles). Descriptions of the skills associated with each level can be found at https://nces.ed.gov/surveys/pirls/pirls2016/tables/pirls2016_exhibit02.asp.
[4]This column combines students who are in the Low level (scores of 400 to 474) with students who are below the Low level (scores of less than 400).
[5]International median percentages are shown in columns 6 through 9 of this row. Half the education systems have a percentage of students equal to or higher than the international median and half have a percentage of students below the median. The median includes only the education systems shown in the top part of this table, which are members of the International Association for the Evaluation of Educational Achievement (IEA). "Benchmarking" education systems are not members of the IEA and are therefore not included in the median.
[6]National Defined Population covers 90 to 95 percent of National Target Population.
[7]Exclusion rates for Azerbaijan and Georgia are slightly underestimated as some conflict zones were not covered and no official statistics were available for 2011.
[8]In 2016, Azerbaijan expanded its sample to include students taught in Russian. All 2016 data shown in this table are based on the expanded sample and therefore are not comparable with data for previous years.
[9]Met guidelines for sample participation rates only after replacement schools were included.
[10]National Target Population does not include all of the International Target Population.
[11]Administered PIRLS Literacy instead of the standard PIRLS assessment. PIRLS Literacy is a less difficult version of PIRLS designed to assess foundational reading skills.
[12]National Defined Population covers less than 90 percent of National Target Population (but at least 77 percent).
[13]Administered both the standard PIRLS assessment and PIRLS Literacy, a less difficult version of PIRLS that is designed to assess foundational reading skills. Results are based on an average of both assessments.
[14]National Defined Population covers less than 80 percent of National Target Population.
[15]In 2016, Lithuania expanded its sample to include students taught in Polish and Russian. All 2016 data shown in this table are based on the expanded sample and therefore are not comparable with data for previous years.
[16]Nearly satisfied guidelines for sample participation rates after replacement schools were included.
[17]The TIMSS & PIRLS International Study Center has reservations about the reliability of the average achievement score because the percentage of students with achievement too low for estimation exceeds 25 percent.
[18]In PIRLS cycles prior to 2016, Norway assessed only students in grade 4, which is similar to grade 3 in many other countries because grade 1 in Norway is considered the equivalent of kindergarten rather than the first year of primary school. For PIRLS 2016, Norway started assessing students in grade 5. For purposes of comparing results across years, however, Norway also continued to collect grade 4 data in 2016. This table includes the grade 5 results in the top part of the table and the grade 4 results under "Benchmarking education systems."
[19]The TIMSS & PIRLS International Study Center has reservations about the reliability of the average achievement score because the percentage of students with achievement too low for estimation exceeds 15 percent, though it is less than 25 percent.
[20]Data are available for at least 70 percent but less than 85 percent of students.
[21]All data for Florida are based on public schools only.
[22]Did not satisfy guidelines for sample participation rates.
SOURCE: International Association for the Evaluation of Educational Achievement (IEA), Progress in International Reading Literacy Study (PIRLS), 2001, 2006, 2011, and 2016. (This table was prepared November 2017).

Table 602.20. Average fourth-grade scores and annual instructional time in mathematics and science, by country or other education system: 2015

[Standard errors appear in parentheses]

Country or other education system[1]	Total instructional hours per year		Mathematics: Average score[2]		Mathematics: Instructional time in mathematics: Hours per year		Mathematics: Instructional time in mathematics: As a percent of total instructional hours		Science: Average score[2]		Science: Instructional time in science: Hours per year		Science: Instructional time in science: As a percent of total instructional hours	
1	2		3		4		5		6		7		8	
International average[3]	**888**	**(2.0)**	**500**	**(†)**	**155**	**(0.5)**	**17**	**(0.1)**	**500**	**(†)**	**76**	**(0.4)**	**9**	**(#)**
Australia	1,014[4]	(8.4)	517	(3.1)	202[4]	(3.5)	20	(0.4)	524	(2.9)	57[4]	(1.5)	6	(0.2)
Bahrain[5]	976	(0.6)	451	(1.6)	159[4]	(2.9)	16	(0.3)	459	(2.6)	103[4]	(0.6)	11	(0.1)
Belgium (Flemish)[6]	955[4]	(11.6)	546	(2.1)	218[4]	(3.2)	23	(0.4)	512	(2.3)	—	(†)	—	(†)
Bulgaria	707[4]	(27.3)	524	(5.3)	105	(2.9)	15	(0.7)	536	(5.9)	42	(2.3)	6	(0.4)
Canada[5,6,7,8]	951	(4.1)	511	(2.3)	196[4]	(3.2)	21	(0.3)	525	(2.6)	81[4]	(2.0)	9	(0.2)
Chile	1,094[4]	(16.9)	459	(2.4)	206[9]	(6.4)	19	(0.7)	478	(2.7)	93[9]	(2.5)	9	(0.3)
Chinese Taipei	969	(14.4)	597	(1.9)	128[4]	(4.3)	13	(0.5)	555	(1.8)	91	(1.9)	9	(0.2)
Croatia	778	(21.6)	502	(1.8)	124	(1.8)	16	(0.5)	533	(2.1)	82	(1.5)	11	(0.4)
Cyprus	827[4]	(12.4)	523	(2.7)	161[4]	(5.5)	19	(0.7)	481	(2.6)	48[4]	(0.9)	6	(0.1)
Czech Republic	771	(10.4)	528	(2.2)	125	(4.1)	16	(0.6)	534	(2.4)	38	(2.0)	5	(0.3)
Denmark[5,6]	1,051[4]	(11.2)	539	(2.7)	150[9]	(3.1)	14	(0.3)	527	(2.1)	80[9]	(2.3)	8	(0.2)
England (United Kingdom)	994	(9.9)	546	(2.8)	189[4]	(4.5)	19	(0.5)	536	(2.4)	61[4]	(2.2)	6	(0.2)
Finland	737	(8.9)	535	(2.0)	115	(2.2)	16	(0.4)	554	(2.3)	82	(1.8)	11	(0.3)
France	858[4]	(8.2)	488	(2.9)	193[4]	(3.9)	22	(0.5)	487	(2.7)	56[4]	(1.8)	7	(0.2)
Georgia[8]	743[4]	(19.5)	463	(3.6)	138[4]	(2.1)	19	(0.6)	451	(3.7)	80	(1.4)	11	(0.3)
Germany	820[4]	(9.1)	522	(2.0)	147[4]	(2.0)	18	(0.3)	528	(2.4)	61[9]	(3.8)	7	(0.5)
Hong Kong[6] (China)	999	(13.1)	615	(2.9)	159	(4.7)	16	(0.5)	557	(2.9)	‡	(†)	—	(†)
Hungary	784	(11.8)	529	(3.2)	129	(2.5)	16	(0.4)	542	(3.3)	63	(1.7)	8	(0.2)
Indonesia	1,095[4]	(20.9)	397	(3.7)	149[4]	(5.0)	14	(0.5)	397	(4.8)	116[4]	(4.0)	11	(0.4)
Iran, Islamic Republic of	645[4]	(6.4)	431	(3.2)	112[4]	(2.3)	17	(0.4)	421	(4.0)	87[4]	(3.0)	13	(0.5)
Ireland	854	(#)	547	(2.1)	165	(2.4)	19	(0.3)	529	(2.4)	32	(0.7)	4	(0.1)
Italy[5]	1,061	(20.5)	507	(2.6)	231[4]	(4.5)	22	(0.6)	516	(2.6)	76	(1.6)	7	(0.2)
Japan	903	(3.7)	593	(2.0)	151	(1.1)	17	(0.1)	569	(1.8)	91	(0.5)	10	(0.1)
Jordan	931	(14.2)	388	(3.1)	133	(3.3)	14	(0.4)	—	(†)	—	(†)	—	(†)
Kazakhstan	813	(16.2)	544	(4.5)	132	(3.8)	16	(0.6)	550	(4.4)	58	(2.9)	7	(0.4)
Korea, Republic of	712	(8.9)	608	(2.2)	100	(1.4)	14	(0.3)	589	(2.0)	76	(1.0)	11	(0.2)
Kuwait[10]	912[9]	(27.9)	353	(4.6)	128[9]	(4.4)	14	(0.6)	337	(6.2)	77[9]	(3.5)	8	(0.5)
Lithuania[5]	629	(5.5)	535	(2.5)	111	(1.6)	18	(0.3)	528	(2.5)	53	(1.0)	8	(0.2)
Morocco	1,054[4]	(18.8)	377	(3.4)	172[4]	(2.8)	16	(0.4)	352[10]	(4.7)	54[4]	(0.9)	5	(0.1)
Netherlands[6]	1,073[9]	(16.2)	530	(1.7)	‡	(†)	—	(†)	517	(2.7)	‡	(†)	—	(†)
New Zealand	923	(5.5)	491	(2.3)	163[4]	(2.3)	18	(0.3)	506	(2.7)	43[4]	(2.0)	5	(0.2)
Northern Ireland[11] (United Kingdom)	962[4]	(10.2)	570	(2.9)	215[9]	(6.5)	22	(0.7)	520	(2.2)	38[9]	(2.1)	4	(0.2)
Norway[12]	817	(8.7)	549	(2.5)	117[4]	(2.4)	14	(0.3)	538	(2.6)	59[4]	(1.7)	7	(0.2)
Oman	962[4]	(11.7)	425	(2.5)	148[9]	(4.5)	15	(0.5)	431	(3.1)	123[9]	(3.1)	13	(0.4)
Poland	752[4]	(6.9)	535	(2.1)	112[4]	(1.1)	15	(0.2)	547	(2.4)	84[4]	(1.1)	11	(0.2)
Portugal[5]	864	(8.5)	541	(2.2)	275[4]	(4.0)	32	(0.6)	508	(2.2)	111[4]	(3.8)	13	(0.5)
Qatar	1,056[4]	(16.1)	439	(3.4)	185[4]	(4.6)	18	(0.5)	436	(4.1)	125[4]	(4.4)	12	(0.5)
Russian Federation	661	(6.9)	564	(3.4)	106	(1.4)	16	(0.3)	567	(3.2)	49	(0.9)	7	(0.2)
Saudi Arabia	1,080[4]	(19.6)	383[10]	(4.1)	148[9]	(4.5)	14	(0.5)	390	(4.9)	77[4]	(3.7)	7	(0.4)
Serbia[13]	737	(16.2)	518	(3.5)	154	(1.6)	21	(0.5)	525	(3.7)	75	(3.5)	10	(0.5)
Singapore[5]	986	(#)	618	(3.8)	201	(1.6)	20	(0.2)	590	(3.7)	85	(1.4)	9	(0.1)
Slovak Republic	759	(8.1)	498	(2.5)	129	(2.1)	17	(0.3)	520	(2.6)	52	(2.0)	7	(0.3)
Slovenia	716[4]	(7.2)	520	(1.9)	144[4]	(1.2)	20	(0.3)	543	(2.4)	86[4]	(1.3)	12	(0.2)
Spain[5]	864	(10.2)	505	(2.5)	161	(2.3)	19	(0.3)	518	(2.6)	124[4]	(2.6)	14	(0.3)
Sweden[5]	839[4]	(10.6)	519	(2.8)	110[4]	(2.3)	13	(0.3)	540	(3.6)	79	(1.8)	9	(0.2)
Turkey	847	(18.0)	483	(3.1)	120	(3.3)	14	(0.5)	483	(3.3)	83	(1.7)	10	(0.3)
United Arab Emirates	1,009[4]	(4.6)	452	(2.4)	162[9]	(2.4)	16	(0.2)	451	(2.8)	111[9]	(2.1)	11	(0.2)
United States[5,6]	1,088	(9.2)	539	(2.3)	216[4]	(4.1)	20	(0.4)	546	(2.2)	100[4]	(3.7)	9	(0.3)
Benchmarking education systems														
Abu Dhabi[5] (United Arab Emirates)	1,025[4]	(11.1)	419[10]	(4.7)	163[9]	(4.5)	16	(0.5)	415	(5.6)	116[9]	(4.3)	11	(0.4)
Buenos Aires (Argentina)	951[9]	(31.3)	432	(2.9)	‡	(†)	—	(†)	418	(4.7)	‡	(†)	—	(†)
Dubai (United Arab Emirates)	996[4]	(0.4)	511	(1.4)	160[9]	(1.4)	16	(0.1)	518	(1.8)	110[4]	(1.2)	11	(0.1)
Florida[14] (United States)	1,075[4]	(21.6)	546	(4.7)	212[9]	(11.1)	20	(1.1)	549	(4.8)	105[9]	(5.8)	10	(0.6)
Ontario (Canada)	953	(6.2)	512	(2.3)	195[4]	(3.2)	20	(0.4)	530	(2.5)	88[4]	(3.1)	9	(0.3)
Quebec[15] (Canada)	910	(8.0)	536	(4.0)	221	(8.9)	24	(1.0)	525	(4.1)	43	(2.9)	5	(0.3)

—Not available.
†Not applicable.
#Rounds to zero.
‡Reporting standards not met. Either data are available for less than 50 percent of students or the coefficient of variation (CV) is 50 percent or greater.
[1]Most of the education systems represent complete countries, but some represent subnational entities; examples include the Flemish community of Belgium, two components of the United Kingdom (England and Northern Ireland), a few individual cities (such as Abu Dhabi within the United Arab Emirates), and the U.S. state of Florida.
[2]Trends in International Mathematics and Science Study (TIMSS) scores are reported on a scale from 0 to 1,000, with the scale centerpoint set at 500 and the standard deviation set at 100.
[3]The international average includes only education systems that are members of the International Association for the Evaluation of Educational Achievement (IEA), which develops and implements TIMSS at the international level. "Benchmarking" education systems are not members of the IEA and are therefore not included in the average.
[4]Data are available for at least 70 percent but less than 85 percent of students.
[5]National Defined Population covers 90 to 95 percent of National Target Population.
[6]Met guidelines for sample participation rates only after replacement schools were included.
[7]Data for Canada include only students from the provinces of Alberta, Manitoba, Newfoundland, Ontario, and Quebec.
[8]National Target Population does not include all of the International Target Population.
[9]Data are available for at least 50 percent but less than 70 percent of students.
[10]The TIMSS & PIRLS International Study Center has reservations about the reliability of the average achievement score because the percentage of students with achievement too low for estimation exceeds 15 percent, though it is less than 25 percent.
[11]Nearly satisfied guidelines for sample participation rates after replacement schools were included.
[12]Norway collected data from students in their fifth year of schooling rather than in grade 4 because year 1 in Norway is considered the equivalent of kindergarten rather than the first year of primary school.
[13]National Defined Population covers less than 90 percent of National Target Population (but at least 77 percent).
[14]U.S. state-level data are based on public school students only.
[15]Did not satisfy guidelines for sample participation rates.
NOTE: Countries and other education systems were required to draw probability samples of students who were nearing the end of their fourth year of formal schooling (counting the first year of primary school as year 1), provided that the mean age at the time of testing was at least 9.5 years. Instructional times shown in this table are actual or implemented times (as opposed to intended times prescribed by the curriculum). Principals reported total instructional hours per day and school days per year. Total instructional hours per year were calculated by multiplying the number of school days per year by the number of instructional hours per day. Teachers reported instructional hours per week in mathematics and science. Instructional hours per year in mathematics and science were calculated by dividing weekly instructional hours by the number of school days per week and then multiplying by the number of school days per year.
SOURCE: International Association for the Evaluation of Educational Achievement (IEA), Trends in International Mathematics and Science Study (TIMSS), 2015; International Results in Mathematics and Science, retrieved from Boston College, TIMSS & PIRLS International Study Center website (http://timssandpirls.bc.edu/timss2015/international-results/). (This table was prepared December 2016.)

Table 602.30. Average eighth-grade scores and annual instructional time in mathematics and science, by country or other education system: 2015

[Standard errors appear in parentheses]

Country or other education system[1]	Total instructional hours per year		Mathematics: Average score[2]		Mathematics: Instructional time in mathematics: Hours per year		Mathematics: Instructional time in mathematics: As a percent of total instructional hours		Science: Average score[2]		Science: Instructional time in science[3]: Hours per year		Science: Instructional time in science[3]: As a percent of total instructional hours	
1	2		3		4		5		6		7		8	
International average[4]	**1,013**	**(2.1)**	**500**	**(†)**	**136**	**(0.5)**	**13**	**(0.1)**	**500**	**(†)**	**144**	**(0.7)**	**14**	**(0.1)**
Australia	1,011[5]	(6.3)	505	(3.1)	139[5]	(2.0)	14	(0.2)	512	(2.7)	126[6]	(1.6)	12	(0.2)
Bahrain	1,032	(1.0)	454	(1.4)	153	(2.3)	15	(0.2)	466	(2.2)	125[5]	(10.2)	12	(1.0)
Canada[7,8,9]	949[5]	(4.9)	527	(2.2)	168[5]	(2.9)	18	(0.3)	526	(2.1)	97[6]	(2.2)	10	(0.2)
Chile	1,127[5]	(18.0)	427[10]	(3.2)	192[6]	(5.8)	17	(0.6)	454	(3.1)	113[6]	(5.0)	10	(0.5)
Chinese Taipei	1,132	(9.7)	599	(2.4)	160	(2.4)	14	(0.2)	569	(2.1)	144	(2.3)	13	(0.2)
Egypt	1,099	(21.2)	392[10]	(4.1)	132	(3.3)	12	(0.4)	371	(4.3)	114	(2.9)	10	(0.3)
England (United Kingdom)	1,009[5]	(8.3)	518	(4.2)	126[5]	(3.4)	12	(0.4)	537	(3.8)	97[6]	(3.8)	10	(0.4)
Georgia[8,11]	864[5]	(16.7)	453	(3.4)	122[5]	(4.0)	14	(0.5)	443	(3.1)	241[6]	(6.8)	28	(1.0)
Hong Kong (China)	995	(11.7)	594	(4.6)	139	(3.1)	14	(0.4)	546	(3.9)	102	(2.8)	10	(0.3)
Hungary	842	(10.3)	514	(3.8)	113	(2.3)	13	(0.3)	527	(3.4)	201	(5.4)	24	(0.7)
Iran, Islamic Republic of	971	(16.9)	436[10]	(4.6)	131	(4.6)	13	(0.5)	456	(4.0)	120	(3.1)	12	(0.4)
Ireland	963[5]	(3.2)	523	(2.7)	109	(0.8)	11	(0.1)	530	(2.8)	90[5]	(0.9)	9	(0.1)
Israel[12]	1,133[5]	(15.5)	511	(4.1)	153[5]	(2.2)	14	(0.3)	507	(3.9)	129[5]	(3.5)	11	(0.3)
Italy[11]	1,047[5]	(9.6)	494	(2.5)	149	(2.9)	14	(0.3)	499	(2.4)	71[5]	(1.3)	7	(0.1)
Japan	1,036	(6.1)	586	(2.3)	106	(1.5)	10	(0.2)	571	(1.8)	131	(1.7)	13	(0.2)
Jordan	976	(12.5)	386[13]	(3.2)	132	(2.3)	14	(0.3)	426	(3.3)	131	(2.3)	13	(0.3)
Kazakhstan	933	(19.4)	528	(5.3)	129	(3.4)	14	(0.5)	533	(4.4)	239	(5.4)	26	(0.8)
Korea, Republic of	947	(6.0)	606	(2.6)	114	(1.2)	12	(0.1)	556	(2.3)	94	(2.1)	10	(0.2)
Kuwait	997[5]	(18.6)	392[10]	(4.6)	136[5]	(3.5)	14	(0.4)	411	(5.2)	117[5]	(3.0)	12	(0.4)
Lebanon	945[5]	(14.8)	442	(3.6)	158[5]	(5.0)	17	(0.6)	398	(5.3)	243[5]	(10.7)	26	(1.2)
Lithuania[11]	856	(10.2)	511	(2.8)	115	(1.7)	13	(0.3)	519	(2.8)	205	(4.2)	24	(0.6)
Malaysia	1,172[5]	(15.6)	465	(3.6)	135	(4.1)	12	(0.4)	471	(4.1)	130[5]	(4.0)	11	(0.4)
Malta	964	(0.3)	494	(1.0)	127[5]	(0.1)	13	(#)	481	(1.6)	311[5]	(1.0)	32	(0.1)
Morocco	1,364	(25.8)	384[13]	(2.3)	152[5]	(2.4)	11	(0.3)	393	(2.5)	160[5]	(4.5)	12	(0.4)
New Zealand[9]	966[5]	(6.9)	493	(3.4)	144[5]	(2.5)	15	(0.3)	513	(3.1)	133[5]	(2.5)	14	(0.3)
Norway[14]	895	(8.8)	512	(2.3)	105[5]	(2.2)	12	(0.3)	509	(2.8)	81[5]	(1.5)	9	(0.2)
Oman	980[5]	(14.5)	403[10]	(2.4)	166[6]	(2.7)	17	(0.4)	455	(2.7)	143[5]	(3.1)	15	(0.4)
Qatar	1,085[5]	(1.9)	437[10]	(3.0)	157[5]	(2.8)	14	(0.3)	457	(3.0)	155[5]	(2.6)	14	(0.2)
Russian Federation	884	(9.4)	538	(4.7)	145	(3.1)	16	(0.4)	544	(4.2)	219[5]	(2.9)	25	(0.4)
Saudi Arabia	1,112	(18.7)	368[13]	(4.6)	155[5]	(4.3)	14	(0.5)	396	(4.5)	130	(5.7)	12	(0.5)
Singapore[11]	1,065	(#)	621	(3.2)	129	(1.3)	12	(0.1)	597	(3.2)	106	(1.4)	10	(0.1)
Slovenia	867[5]	(10.3)	516	(2.1)	114[5]	(1.3)	13	(0.2)	551	(2.4)	221[5]	(4.7)	25	(0.6)
Sweden	921	(8.6)	501	(2.8)	99	(1.5)	11	(0.2)	522	(3.5)	122	(4.1)	13	(0.5)
Thailand	1,209	(6.8)	431	(4.8)	111	(1.7)	9	(0.1)	456	(4.2)	110	(1.7)	9	(0.1)
Turkey	983	(22.6)	458	(4.7)	117	(2.7)	12	(0.4)	493	(4.0)	112	(3.0)	11	(0.4)
United Arab Emirates	1,016[5]	(6.4)	465	(2.0)	159[6]	(2.7)	16	(0.3)	477	(2.3)	115[6]	(4.3)	11	(0.4)
United States[9]	1,135	(8.8)	518	(3.1)	155[5]	(3.9)	14	(0.4)	530	(2.8)	144[6]	(2.4)	13	(0.2)
Benchmarking education systems														
Abu Dhabi (United Arab Emirates)	1,024[5]	(11.0)	442	(4.7)	166[6]	(5.2)	16	(0.5)	454	(5.6)	122[6]	(6.6)	12	(0.7)
Buenos Aires[9] (Argentina)	1,164[6]	(46.7)	396[13]	(4.2)	‡	(†)	—	(†)	386	(4.2)	‡	(†)	—	(†)
Dubai (United Arab Emirates)	1,010[5]	(1.3)	512	(2.1)	152[5]	(1.7)	15	(0.2)	525	(2.0)	115[6]	(3.5)	11	(0.3)
Florida[8,15] (United States)	1,155[6]	(39.9)	493	(6.4)	146[6]	(9.0)	13	(0.9)	508	(6.0)	‡	(†)	—	(†)
Ontario (Canada)	970[5]	(6.0)	522	(2.9)	179[5]	(3.8)	18	(0.4)	524	(2.5)	91[6]	(3.3)	9	(0.3)
Quebec[16] (Canada)	906	(7.0)	543	(3.9)	149	(4.2)	16	(0.5)	530	(4.4)	98[5]	(2.7)	11	(0.3)

—Not available.
†Not applicable.
#Rounds to zero.
‡Reporting standards not met. Either data are available for less than 50 percent of the students or the coefficient of variation (CV) is 50 percent or greater.
[1]Most of the education systems represent complete countries, but some represent subnational entities; examples include two Canadian provinces (Ontario and Quebec), a component of the United Kingdom (England), the U.S. state of Florida, and a few individual cities (such as Abu Dhabi within the United Arab Emirates).
[2]Trends in International Mathematics and Science Study (TIMSS) scores are reported on a scale from 0 to 1,000, with the scale centerpoint set at 500 and the standard deviation set at 100.
[3]General/integrated science instructional time is shown for the 27 participating countries that teach science as a general or integrated subject at eighth grade. For the 10 participating countries that teach the sciences as separate subjects (biology, chemistry, etc.) at eighth grade, total instructional time across science subjects is shown.
[4]The international average includes only education systems that are members of the International Association for the Evaluation of Educational Achievement (IEA), which develops and implements TIMSS at the international level. "Benchmarking" education systems are not members of the IEA and are therefore not included in the average.
[5]Data are available for at least 70 percent but less than 85 percent of students.
[6]Data are available for at least 50 percent but less than 70 percent of students.
[7]Data for Canada include only students from the provinces of Manitoba, Newfoundland, Ontario, and Quebec.
[8]National Target Population does not include all of the International Target Population.
[9]Met guidelines for sample participation rates only after replacement schools were included.
[10]The TIMSS & PIRLS International Study Center has reservations about the reliability of the average achievement score because the percentage of students with achievement too low for estimation exceeds 15 percent, though it is less than 25 percent.
[11]National Defined Population covers 90 to 95 percent of National Target Population.
[12]National Defined Population covers less than 90 percent of the National Target Population (but at least 77 percent).
[13]The TIMSS & PIRLS International Study Center has reservations about the reliability of the average achievement score because the percentage of students with achievement too low for estimation exceeds 25 percent.
[14]Norway collected data from students in their ninth year of schooling rather than in grade 8 because year 1 in Norway is considered the equivalent of kindergarten rather than the first year of primary school.
[15]U.S. state-level data are based on public school students only.
[16]Did not satisfy guidelines for sample participation rates.
NOTE: Countries and other education systems were required to draw probability samples of students who were nearing the end of their eighth year of formal schooling (counting the first year of primary school as year 1), provided that the mean age at the time of testing was at least 13.5 years. Instructional times shown in this table are actual or implemented times (as opposed to intended times prescribed by the curriculum). Principals reported total instructional hours per day and school days per year. Total instructional hours per year were calculated by multiplying the number of school days per year by the number of instructional hours per day. Teachers reported instructional hours per week in mathematics and science. Instructional hours per year in mathematics and science were calculated by dividing weekly instructional hours by the number of school days per week and then multiplying by the number of school days per year.
SOURCE: International Association for the Evaluation of Educational Achievement (IEA), Trends in International Mathematics and Science Study (TIMSS), 2015; International Results in Mathematics and Science, retrieved from Boston College, TIMSS & PIRLS International Study Center website (http://timssandpirls.bc.edu/timss2015/international-results/). (This table was prepared December 2016.)

Table 602.35. Average advanced mathematics and physics scores of high school seniors who had taken advanced courses in these subjects, seniors who had taken such courses as a percentage of their age cohort, and instructional time in such courses, by country: 2015

[Standard errors appear in parentheses]

Country	Advanced mathematics									Physics								
	Total instructional hours per year (includes all subjects)[1]		Average score[2]		Percent of age cohort taking advanced mathematics courses[3,4]	Instructional time in advanced mathematics: Hours per year		Instructional time in advanced mathematics: As a percent of total instructional hours		Total instructional hours per year (includes all subjects)[1]		Average score[2]		Percent of age cohort taking physics courses[3,5]	Instructional time in physics: Hours per year		Instructional time in physics: As a percent of total instructional hours	
1	2		3		4	5		6		7		8		9	10		11	
International average[6]	**1,027**	**(5.8)**	**500**	**(†)**	**†**	**171**	**(1.5)**	**17**	**(0.2)**	**1,023**	**(6.2)**	**500**	**(†)**	**†**	**133**	**(1.8)**	**13**	**(0.2)**
France	1,340	(22.5)	463	(3.1)	21.5	222[7]	(4.3)	17	(0.4)	1,340	(22.5)	373	(4.0)	21.5	116[7]	(4.2)	9	(0.3)
Italy	1,036[7]	(9.6)	422	(5.3)	24.5	130	(2.1)	13	(0.2)	1,018[7]	(8.2)	374	(6.9)	18.2	102[7]	(1.7)	10	(0.2)
Lebanon[8]	931	(11.2)	532	(3.1)	3.9	242	(7.8)	26	(0.9)	932	(11.2)	410	(4.5)	3.9	200	(3.1)	21	(0.4)
Norway	1,033[7]	(19.8)	459	(4.6)	10.6	149[7]	(5.7)	14	(0.6)	991[7]	(14.1)	507	(4.6)	6.5	139[7]	(3.0)	14	(0.4)
Portugal	1,073[7]	(32.3)	482[9]	(2.5)	28.5	186	(3.6)	17	(0.6)	1,046[7]	(37.1)	467	(4.6)	5.1	120	(6.2)	11	(0.7)
Russian Federation (intensive courses)[10]	942[7]	(14.4)	540	(7.8)	1.9	207	(4.2)	22	(0.6)	†	(†)	†	(†)	†	†	(†)	†	(†)
Russian Federation	914	(8.9)	485	(5.7)	10.1	178	(2.1)	19	(0.3)	920	(8.7)	508	(7.1)	4.9	133	(2.0)	14	(0.3)
Slovenia	902	(10.6)	460	(3.4)	34.4	131	(1.8)	15	(0.3)	902	(5.9)	531	(2.5)	7.6	115	(1.0)	13	(0.1)
Sweden	901	(12.9)	431	(4.0)	14.1	141	(4.2)	16	(0.5)	920	(13.8)	455	(5.9)	14.3	106	(3.0)	12	(0.4)
United States[8]	1,111	(13.3)	485	(5.2)	11.4	156[7]	(4.3)	14	(0.4)	1,132[7]	(22.5)	437	(9.7)	4.8	162[11]	(13.3)	14	(1.2)

†Not applicable.
[1]Because countries may have used two different school samples—one for advanced mathematics and one for physics—the total number of instructional hours per year for a particular country may be different in column 2 (based on the advanced mathematics sample) than in column 7 (based on the physics sample).
[2]Trends in International Mathematics and Science Study (TIMSS) Advanced scores are reported on a scale from 0 to 1,000, with the scale centerpoint set at 500 and the standard deviation set at 100.
[3]Columns 4 and 9 show final-year secondary school students who have taken or are taking the specified courses as a percentage of the age cohort that corresponds to the final year of secondary school in their country. The age cohort represents the entire population of the country that is about the same age as the average age of final-year secondary students (approximately 18 or 19 years old, depending on the country). In the United States, the cohort consists of the total population of 18-year-olds. For the United States, therefore, columns 4 and 9 show the percentage of all 18-year-olds who have taken the specified courses.
[4]Includes advanced mathematics courses covering topics in geometry, algebra, and calculus. In the United States, includes Advanced Placement (AP) calculus, International Baccalaureate (IB) mathematics, and state- and school-specific calculus courses.
[5]Includes physics courses covering topics in mechanics and thermodynamics, electricity and magnetism, and wave phenomena and atomic/nuclear physics. In the United States, includes AP physics, IB physics, and state- and school-specific second-year physics courses.
[6]The international average includes only education systems that are members of the International Association for the Evaluation of Educational Achievement (IAE), which develops and implements TIMSS at the international level. All nine of the education systems that participated in TIMSS Advanced are countries that are members of IAE.
[7]Data are available for at least 70 percent but less than 85 percent of students.
[8]Did not satisfy guidelines for sample participation rates.
[9]Met guidelines for sample participation rates only after replacement schools were included.
[10]Intensive courses are advanced mathematics courses that involve 6 or more hours per week. Results for students in these courses are reported separately from the results for other students from the Russian Federation taking courses that involve 4.5 hours per week.
[11]Data are available for at least 50 percent but less than 70 percent of students.
NOTE: Countries were required to draw probability samples of students in their final year of secondary school; in the United States, samples of 12th-graders were drawn. Instructional times shown in this table are actual or implemented times (as opposed to intended times prescribed by the curriculum). Principals reported total instructional hours per day and school days per year. Total instructional hours per year were calculated by multiplying the number of school days per year by the number of instructional hours per day. Teachers reported instructional hours per week in advanced mathematics and physics. Instructional hours per year in advanced mathematics and physics were calculated by dividing weekly instructional hours by the number of school days per week and then multiplying by the number of school days per year.
SOURCE: International Association for the Evaluation of Educational Achievement (IEA), Trends in International Mathematics and Science Study (TIMSS) Advanced, 2015. (This table was prepared January 2017.)

Table 602.40. Average reading literacy, mathematics literacy, and science literacy scores of 15-year-old students, by sex and country or other education system: 2009, 2012, and 2015

[Standard errors appear in parentheses]

Country or other education system	Reading literacy					Mathematics literacy					Science literacy				
			2015					2015					2015		
	2009	2012	Total	Male	Female	2009	2012	Total	Male	Female	2009	2012	Total	Male	Female
1	2	3	4	5	6	7	8	9	10	11	12	13	14	15	16
OECD average[1]	**493 (0.5)**	**496 (0.5)**	**493 (0.5)**	**479 (0.6)**	**506 (0.5)**	**496 (0.5)**	**494 (0.5)**	**490 (0.4)**	**494 (0.6)**	**486 (0.5)**	**501 (0.5)**	**501 (0.5)**	**493 (0.4)**	**495 (0.5)**	**491 (0.5)**
Australia	515 (2.3)	512 (1.6)	503 (1.7)	487 (2.3)	519 (2.3)	514 (2.5)	504 (1.6)	494 (1.6)	497 (2.1)	491 (2.5)	527 (2.5)	521 (1.8)	510 (1.5)	511 (2.1)	509 (1.7)
Austria	470 (2.9)	490 (2.8)	485 (2.8)	475 (4.3)	495 (3.7)	496 (2.7)	506 (2.7)	497 (2.9)	510 (3.8)	483 (3.6)	494 (3.2)	506 (2.7)	495 (2.4)	504 (3.6)	486 (3.1)
Belgium	506 (2.3)	509 (2.3)	499 (2.4)	491 (3.1)	507 (2.9)	515 (2.3)	515 (2.1)	507 (2.4)	514 (3.1)	500 (2.8)	507 (2.5)	505 (2.2)	502 (2.3)	508 (3.1)	496 (2.7)
Canada	524 (1.5)	523 (1.9)	527 (2.3)	514 (2.6)	540 (2.5)	527 (1.6)	518 (1.8)	516 (2.3)	520 (2.9)	511 (2.6)	529 (1.6)	525 (1.9)	528 (2.1)	528 (2.5)	527 (2.3)
Chile	449 (3.1)	441 (2.9)	459 (2.6)	453 (3.4)	465 (2.9)	421 (3.1)	423 (3.1)	423 (2.5)	432 (3.1)	413 (3.0)	447 (2.9)	445 (2.9)	447 (2.4)	454 (3.1)	440 (2.7)
Czech Republic	478 (2.9)	493 (2.9)	487 (2.6)	475 (3.6)	501 (2.9)	493 (2.8)	499 (2.9)	492 (2.4)	496 (3.3)	489 (2.8)	500 (3.0)	508 (3.0)	493 (2.3)	497 (3.3)	488 (2.5)
Denmark	495 (2.1)	496 (2.6)	500 (2.5)	489 (2.8)	511 (3.4)	503 (2.6)	500 (2.3)	511 (2.2)	516 (2.5)	506 (2.8)	499 (2.5)	498 (2.7)	502 (2.4)	505 (2.6)	499 (3.2)
Estonia	501 (2.6)	516 (2.0)	519 (2.2)	505 (2.9)	533 (2.3)	512 (2.6)	521 (2.0)	520 (2.0)	522 (2.7)	517 (2.3)	528 (2.7)	541 (1.9)	534 (2.1)	536 (2.7)	533 (2.3)
Finland	536 (2.3)	524 (2.4)	526 (2.5)	504 (3.0)	551 (2.8)	541 (2.2)	519 (1.9)	511 (2.3)	507 (2.6)	515 (2.6)	554 (2.3)	545 (2.2)	531 (2.4)	521 (2.7)	541 (2.6)
France	496 (3.4)	505 (2.8)	499 (2.5)	485 (3.3)	514 (3.3)	497 (3.1)	495 (2.5)	493 (2.1)	496 (2.9)	490 (2.6)	498 (3.6)	499 (2.6)	495 (2.1)	496 (2.7)	494 (2.7)
Germany	497 (2.7)	508 (2.8)	509 (3.0)	499 (3.7)	520 (3.1)	513 (2.9)	514 (2.9)	506 (2.9)	514 (3.5)	498 (3.0)	520 (2.8)	524 (3.0)	509 (2.7)	514 (3.2)	504 (2.8)
Greece	483 (4.3)	477 (3.3)	467 (4.3)	449 (5.1)	486 (4.2)	466 (3.9)	453 (2.5)	454 (3.8)	454 (4.7)	454 (3.6)	470 (4.0)	467 (3.1)	455 (3.9)	451 (4.6)	459 (3.9)
Hungary	494 (3.2)	488 (3.2)	470 (2.7)	457 (3.7)	482 (3.1)	490 (3.5)	477 (3.2)	477 (2.5)	481 (3.6)	473 (3.0)	503 (3.1)	494 (2.9)	477 (2.4)	478 (3.4)	475 (2.9)
Iceland	500 (1.4)	483 (1.8)	482 (2.0)	460 (2.8)	502 (2.6)	507 (1.4)	493 (1.7)	488 (2.0)	487 (2.9)	489 (2.4)	496 (1.4)	478 (2.1)	473 (1.7)	472 (2.6)	475 (2.1)
Ireland	496 (3.0)	523 (2.6)	521 (2.5)	515 (3.2)	527 (2.7)	487 (2.5)	501 (2.2)	504 (2.1)	512 (3.0)	495 (2.4)	508 (3.3)	522 (2.5)	503 (2.4)	508 (3.2)	497 (2.6)
Israel	474 (3.6)	486 (5.0)	479 (3.8)	467 (5.4)	490 (4.6)	447 (3.3)	466 (4.7)	470 (3.6)	474 (5.4)	466 (4.0)	455 (3.1)	470 (5.0)	467 (3.4)	469 (4.7)	464 (4.1)
Italy	486 (1.6)	490 (2.0)	485 (2.7)	477 (3.5)	493 (3.6)	483 (1.9)	485 (2.0)	490 (2.8)	500 (3.5)	480 (3.4)	489 (1.8)	494 (1.9)	481 (2.5)	489 (3.1)	472 (3.6)
Japan	520 (3.5)	538 (3.7)	516 (3.2)	509 (4.2)	523 (3.3)	529 (3.3)	536 (3.6)	532 (3.0)	539 (3.8)	525 (3.1)	539 (3.4)	547 (3.6)	538 (3.0)	545 (4.1)	532 (2.9)
Korea, Republic of	539 (3.5)	536 (3.9)	517 (3.5)	498 (4.8)	539 (4.0)	546 (4.0)	554 (4.6)	524 (3.7)	521 (5.2)	528 (3.9)	538 (3.4)	538 (3.7)	516 (3.1)	511 (4.6)	521 (3.3)
Latvia	484 (3.0)	489 (2.4)	488 (1.8)	467 (2.3)	509 (2.4)	482 (3.1)	491 (2.8)	482 (1.9)	481 (2.6)	483 (2.5)	494 (3.1)	502 (2.8)	490 (1.6)	485 (2.0)	496 (2.2)
Luxembourg	472 (1.3)	488 (1.5)	481 (1.4)	471 (1.9)	492 (2.2)	489 (1.2)	490 (1.1)	486 (1.3)	491 (2.0)	480 (2.0)	484 (1.2)	491 (1.3)	483 (1.1)	487 (1.7)	479 (1.5)
Mexico	425 (2.0)	424 (1.5)	423 (2.6)	416 (2.9)	431 (2.9)	419 (1.8)	413 (1.4)	408 (2.2)	412 (2.7)	404 (2.4)	416 (1.8)	415 (1.3)	416 (2.1)	420 (2.6)	412 (2.3)
Netherlands	508 (5.1)	511 (3.5)	503 (2.4)	491 (3.0)	515 (2.9)	526 (4.7)	523 (3.5)	512 (2.2)	513 (2.6)	511 (2.5)	522 (5.4)	522 (3.5)	509 (2.3)	511 (2.9)	507 (2.5)
New Zealand	521 (2.4)	512 (2.4)	509 (2.4)	493 (3.3)	526 (3.0)	519 (2.3)	500 (2.2)	495 (2.3)	499 (3.4)	491 (2.7)	532 (2.6)	516 (2.1)	513 (2.4)	516 (3.2)	511 (2.7)
Norway	503 (2.6)	504 (3.2)	513 (2.5)	494 (3.1)	533 (2.9)	498 (2.4)	489 (2.7)	502 (2.2)	501 (2.9)	503 (2.3)	500 (2.6)	495 (3.1)	498 (2.3)	500 (2.7)	497 (2.7)
Poland	500 (2.6)	518 (3.1)	506 (2.5)	491 (2.9)	521 (2.8)	495 (2.8)	518 (3.6)	504 (2.4)	510 (2.8)	499 (2.8)	508 (2.4)	526 (3.1)	501 (2.5)	504 (2.9)	498 (2.8)
Portugal	489 (3.1)	488 (3.8)	498 (2.7)	490 (3.1)	507 (2.8)	487 (2.9)	487 (3.8)	492 (2.5)	497 (3.0)	487 (2.7)	493 (2.9)	489 (3.7)	501 (2.4)	506 (2.9)	496 (2.6)
Slovak Republic	477 (2.5)	463 (4.2)	453 (2.8)	435 (3.3)	471 (3.5)	497 (3.1)	482 (3.4)	475 (2.7)	478 (3.0)	472 (3.6)	490 (3.0)	471 (3.6)	461 (2.6)	460 (3.0)	461 (3.3)
Slovenia	483 (1.0)	481 (1.2)	505 (1.5)	484 (2.3)	528 (2.1)	501 (1.2)	501 (1.2)	510 (1.3)	512 (1.9)	508 (2.2)	512 (1.1)	514 (1.3)	513 (1.3)	510 (1.9)	516 (1.9)
Spain	481 (2.0)	488 (1.9)	496 (2.4)	485 (3.0)	506 (2.8)	483 (2.1)	484 (1.9)	486 (2.2)	494 (2.4)	478 (2.8)	488 (2.1)	496 (1.8)	493 (2.1)	496 (2.5)	489 (2.5)
Sweden	497 (2.9)	483 (3.0)	500 (3.5)	481 (4.1)	520 (3.5)	494 (2.9)	478 (2.3)	494 (3.2)	493 (3.8)	495 (3.3)	495 (2.7)	485 (3.0)	493 (3.6)	491 (4.1)	496 (3.7)
Switzerland	501 (2.4)	509 (2.6)	492 (3.0)	480 (3.4)	505 (3.4)	534 (3.3)	531 (3.0)	521 (2.9)	527 (3.2)	515 (3.5)	517 (2.8)	515 (2.7)	506 (2.9)	508 (3.1)	502 (3.5)
Turkey	464 (3.5)	475 (4.2)	428 (4.0)	414 (4.5)	442 (4.8)	445 (4.4)	448 (4.8)	420 (4.1)	423 (4.6)	418 (4.9)	454 (3.6)	463 (3.9)	425 (3.9)	422 (4.5)	429 (4.4)
United Kingdom	494 (2.3)	499 (3.5)	498 (2.8)	487 (2.9)	509 (3.5)	492 (2.4)	494 (3.3)	492 (2.5)	498 (2.9)	487 (3.1)	514 (2.5)	514 (3.4)	509 (2.6)	510 (2.9)	509 (3.3)
United States	500 (3.7)	498 (3.7)	497 (3.4)	487 (3.7)	507 (3.9)	487 (3.6)	481 (3.6)	470 (3.2)	474 (3.6)	465 (3.4)	502 (3.6)	497 (3.8)	496 (3.2)	500 (3.7)	493 (3.4)
Non-OECD education systems															
Albania	385 (4.0)	394 (3.2)	405 (4.1)	376 (4.8)	435 (3.8)	377 (4.0)	394 (2.0)	413 (3.4)	409 (4.2)	418 (3.5)	391 (3.9)	397 (2.4)	427 (3.3)	415 (4.0)	439 (3.0)
Algeria	— (†)	— (†)	350 (3.0)	335 (2.9)	366 (3.5)	— (†)	— (†)	360 (3.0)	356 (3.1)	363 (3.6)	— (†)	— (†)	376 (2.6)	369 (3.0)	383 (3.1)
Beijing, Shanghai, Jiangsu, Guangdong (China)	— (†)	— (†)	494 (5.1)	486 (5.0)	503 (5.8)	— (†)	— (†)	531 (4.9)	534 (4.8)	528 (5.7)	— (†)	— (†)	518 (4.6)	522 (4.5)	513 (5.3)
Brazil	412 (2.7)	410 (2.1)	407 (2.8)	395 (3.1)	419 (3.0)	386 (2.4)	391 (2.1)	377 (2.9)	385 (3.2)	370 (3.0)	405 (2.4)	405 (2.1)	401 (2.3)	403 (2.5)	399 (2.4)
Buenos Aires (Argentina)	398 (4.6)	396 (3.7)	475 (7.2)	468 (8.1)	483 (7.8)	388 (4.1)	388 (3.5)	456 (6.9)	467 (8.0)	446 (7.8)	401 (4.6)	406 (3.9)	475 (6.3)	483 (7.2)	468 (7.1)

See notes at end of table.

Table 602.40. Average reading literacy, mathematics literacy, and science literacy scores of 15-year-old students, by sex and country or other education system: 2009, 2012, and 2015—Continued

[Standard errors appear in parentheses]

Country or other education system	Reading literacy					Mathematics literacy					Science literacy				
	2009	2012	2015			2009	2012	2015			2009	2012	2015		
			Total	Male	Female			Total	Male	Female			Total	Male	Female
1	2	3	4	5	6	7	8	9	10	11	12	13	14	15	16
Bulgaria	429 (6.7)	436 (6.0)	432 (5.0)	409 (5.8)	457 (5.0)	428 (5.9)	439 (4.0)	441 (4.0)	440 (4.8)	442 (4.3)	439 (5.9)	446 (4.8)	446 (4.4)	438 (5.3)	454 (4.4)
Chinese Taipei	— (†)	523 (3.0)	497 (2.5)	485 (3.7)	510 (3.4)	— (†)	560 (3.3)	542 (3.0)	545 (4.7)	539 (4.1)	— (†)	523 (2.3)	532 (2.7)	535 (4.1)	530 (3.8)
Colombia	413 (3.7)	403 (3.4)	425 (2.9)	417 (3.6)	432 (3.2)	381 (3.2)	376 (2.9)	390 (2.3)	395 (3.3)	384 (2.4)	402 (3.6)	399 (3.1)	416 (2.4)	421 (3.1)	411 (2.4)
Connecticut[2] (USA)	— (†)	521 (6.5)	— (†)	— (†)	— (†)	— (†)	506 (6.2)	— (†)	— (†)	— (†)	— (†)	521 (5.7)	— (†)	— (†)	— (†)
Costa Rica	— (†)	441 (3.5)	427 (2.6)	420 (3.1)	435 (2.9)	— (†)	407 (3.0)	400 (2.5)	408 (2.8)	392 (3.0)	— (†)	429 (2.9)	420 (2.1)	429 (2.5)	411 (2.2)
Croatia	476 (2.9)	485 (3.3)	487 (2.7)	473 (3.3)	500 (3.0)	460 (3.1)	471 (3.5)	464 (2.8)	471 (3.7)	458 (3.4)	486 (2.8)	491 (3.1)	475 (2.5)	478 (3.2)	473 (2.8)
Cyprus	— (†)	449 (1.2)	443 (1.7)	417 (2.0)	469 (2.1)	— (†)	440 (1.1)	437 (1.7)	435 (2.1)	440 (2.2)	— (†)	438 (1.2)	433 (1.4)	424 (1.7)	441 (1.9)
Dominican Republic	— (†)	— (†)	358 (3.1)	342 (3.5)	373 (3.1)	— (†)	— (†)	328 (2.7)	326 (3.2)	330 (2.8)	— (†)	— (†)	332 (2.6)	332 (3.2)	331 (2.6)
Florida[2] (USA)	— (†)	492 (6.1)	— (†)	— (†)	— (†)	— (†)	467 (5.8)	— (†)	— (†)	— (†)	— (†)	485 (6.4)	— (†)	— (†)	— (†)
Georgia	— (†)	— (†)	401 (3.0)	374 (4.1)	432 (2.8)	— (†)	— (†)	404 (2.8)	398 (3.9)	411 (2.5)	— (†)	— (†)	411 (2.4)	403 (3.3)	420 (2.3)
Hong Kong (China)	533 (2.1)	545 (2.8)	527 (2.7)	513 (3.4)	541 (3.6)	555 (2.7)	561 (3.2)	548 (3.0)	549 (3.6)	547 (4.3)	549 (2.8)	555 (2.6)	523 (2.5)	523 (3.1)	524 (3.4)
Indonesia	402 (3.7)	396 (4.2)	397 (2.9)	386 (3.4)	409 (3.3)	371 (3.7)	375 (4.0)	386 (3.1)	385 (3.5)	387 (3.7)	383 (3.8)	382 (3.8)	403 (2.6)	401 (3.0)	405 (2.8)
Jordan	405 (3.3)	399 (3.6)	408 (2.9)	372 (4.3)	444 (3.4)	387 (3.7)	386 (3.1)	380 (2.7)	373 (4.0)	387 (3.6)	415 (3.5)	409 (3.1)	409 (2.7)	389 (3.9)	428 (3.6)
Kosovo	— (†)	— (†)	347 (1.6)	329 (2.2)	365 (2.0)	— (†)	— (†)	362 (1.6)	366 (2.2)	357 (2.1)	— (†)	— (†)	378 (1.7)	374 (2.0)	383 (2.1)
Lebanon	— (†)	— (†)	347 (4.4)	339 (5.4)	353 (4.7)	— (†)	— (†)	396 (3.7)	408 (4.4)	386 (3.9)	— (†)	— (†)	386 (3.4)	388 (4.0)	386 (3.7)
Liechtenstein	499 (2.8)	516 (4.1)	— (†)	— (†)	— (†)	536 (4.1)	535 (4.0)	— (†)	— (†)	— (†)	520 (3.4)	525 (3.5)	— (†)	— (†)	— (†)
Lithuania	468 (2.4)	477 (2.5)	472 (2.7)	453 (3.1)	492 (3.0)	477 (2.6)	479 (2.6)	478 (2.3)	478 (2.8)	479 (2.5)	491 (2.9)	496 (2.6)	475 (2.7)	472 (3.3)	479 (2.8)
Macao (China)	487 (0.9)	509 (0.9)	509 (1.3)	493 (1.9)	525 (1.6)	525 (0.9)	538 (1.0)	544 (1.1)	540 (1.7)	548 (1.5)	511 (1.0)	521 (0.8)	529 (1.1)	525 (1.5)	532 (1.5)
Macedonia, Republic of	— (†)	— (†)	352 (1.4)	330 (2.3)	376 (1.8)	— (†)	— (†)	371 (1.3)	368 (2.2)	375 (1.8)	— (†)	— (†)	384 (1.2)	374 (1.6)	394 (1.8)
Malta	— (†)	— (†)	447 (1.8)	426 (2.7)	468 (2.2)	— (†)	— (†)	479 (1.7)	477 (2.4)	481 (2.4)	— (†)	— (†)	465 (1.6)	460 (2.5)	470 (2.2)
Massachusetts[2] (USA)	— (†)	527 (6.1)	527 (6.0)	518 (5.9)	536 (7.3)	— (†)	514 (6.2)	500 (5.5)	505 (5.7)	496 (6.5)	— (†)	527 (6.0)	529 (6.6)	534 (6.5)	524 (7.9)
Moldova, Republic of	— (†)	— (†)	416 (2.5)	390 (2.7)	442 (3.0)	— (†)	— (†)	420 (2.5)	419 (2.9)	421 (3.1)	— (†)	— (†)	428 (2.0)	425 (2.4)	431 (2.4)
Montenegro, Republic of	408 (1.7)	422 (1.2)	427 (1.6)	410 (2.0)	444 (2.3)	403 (2.0)	410 (1.1)	418 (1.5)	418 (2.1)	418 (2.0)	401 (2.0)	410 (1.1)	411 (1.0)	409 (1.7)	414 (1.3)
North Carolina[2] (USA)	— (†)	— (†)	500 (5.4)	487 (5.7)	513 (6.0)	— (†)	— (†)	471 (4.4)	474 (4.8)	468 (5.3)	— (†)	— (†)	502 (4.9)	503 (5.1)	502 (5.7)
Peru	370 (4.0)	384 (4.3)	398 (2.9)	394 (3.4)	401 (3.6)	365 (4.0)	368 (3.7)	387 (2.7)	391 (3.0)	382 (3.2)	369 (3.5)	373 (3.6)	397 (2.4)	402 (2.8)	392 (2.9)
Puerto Rico[2] (USA)	— (†)	— (†)	410 (7.1)	395 (8.3)	425 (7.0)	— (†)	— (†)	378 (5.6)	375 (6.8)	382 (5.2)	— (†)	— (†)	403 (6.1)	398 (7.5)	407 (5.9)
Qatar	372 (0.8)	388 (0.8)	402 (1.0)	376 (1.3)	429 (1.4)	368 (0.7)	376 (0.8)	402 (1.3)	397 (1.8)	408 (1.8)	379 (0.9)	384 (0.7)	418 (1.0)	406 (1.4)	429 (1.3)
Romania	424 (4.1)	438 (4.0)	434 (4.1)	425 (4.4)	442 (4.4)	427 (3.4)	445 (3.8)	444 (3.8)	444 (4.2)	444 (4.1)	428 (3.4)	439 (3.3)	435 (3.2)	432 (3.7)	438 (3.4)
Russian Federation	459 (3.3)	475 (3.0)	495 (3.1)	481 (3.4)	507 (3.5)	468 (3.3)	482 (3.0)	494 (3.1)	497 (4.0)	491 (3.2)	478 (3.3)	486 (2.9)	487 (2.9)	489 (3.6)	485 (3.1)
Serbia, Republic of	442 (2.4)	446 (3.4)	— (†)	— (†)	— (†)	442 (2.9)	449 (3.4)	— (†)	— (†)	— (†)	443 (2.4)	445 (3.4)	— (†)	— (†)	— (†)
Shanghai (China)	556 (2.4)	570 (2.9)	— (†)	— (†)	— (†)	600 (2.8)	613 (3.3)	— (†)	— (†)	— (†)	575 (2.3)	580 (3.0)	— (†)	— (†)	— (†)
Singapore	526 (1.1)	542 (1.4)	535 (1.6)	525 (1.9)	546 (2.3)	562 (1.4)	573 (1.3)	564 (1.5)	564 (2.1)	564 (1.7)	542 (1.4)	551 (1.5)	556 (1.2)	559 (1.8)	552 (1.7)
Thailand	421 (2.6)	441 (3.1)	409 (3.3)	392 (4.3)	423 (3.2)	419 (3.2)	427 (3.4)	415 (3.0)	414 (3.7)	417 (3.4)	425 (3.0)	444 (2.9)	421 (2.8)	416 (3.6)	425 (2.9)
Trinidad and Tobago	416 (1.2)	— (†)	427 (1.5)	401 (2.1)	452 (2.2)	414 (1.3)	— (†)	417 (1.4)	408 (2.1)	426 (2.0)	410 (1.2)	— (†)	425 (1.4)	414 (2.1)	435 (1.9)
Tunisia	404 (2.9)	404 (4.5)	361 (3.1)	348 (3.9)	373 (3.0)	371 (3.0)	388 (3.9)	367 (3.0)	370 (3.4)	364 (3.2)	401 (2.7)	398 (3.5)	386 (2.1)	388 (2.4)	385 (2.2)
United Arab Emirates	— (†)	442 (2.5)	434 (2.9)	408 (3.9)	458 (3.3)	— (†)	434 (2.4)	427 (2.4)	424 (3.9)	431 (2.9)	— (†)	448 (2.8)	437 (2.4)	424 (3.4)	449 (3.0)
Uruguay	426 (2.6)	411 (3.2)	437 (2.5)	424 (3.4)	448 (2.7)	427 (2.6)	409 (2.8)	418 (2.5)	425 (3.6)	412 (2.5)	427 (2.6)	416 (2.8)	435 (2.2)	440 (3.1)	431 (2.2)
Vietnam	— (†)	508 (4.4)	487 (3.7)	474 (4.0)	499 (3.8)	— (†)	511 (4.8)	495 (4.5)	493 (4.7)	496 (4.8)	— (†)	528 (4.3)	525 (3.9)	523 (4.0)	526 (4.2)

—Not available.
†Not applicable.
[1]Refers to the mean of the data values for all Organization for Economic Cooperation and Development (OECD) countries, to which each country contributes equally regardless of the absolute size of the student population of each country.
[2]Results are for public school students only.
NOTE: Program for International Student Assessment (PISA) scores are reported on a scale from 0 to 1,000.
SOURCE: Organization for Economic Cooperation and Development (OECD), Program for International Student Assessment (PISA), 2009, 2012, and 2015. (This table was prepared January 2017.)

Table 602.50. Average reading literacy scores of 15-year-old students and percentage attaining reading literacy proficiency levels, by country or other education system: 2015

[Standard errors appear in parentheses]

Country or other education system	Average reading literacy score[1]	Percentage attaining reading literacy proficiency levels[2]									
		Below level 2				At level 2	At level 3	At level 4	At or above level 5		
		Total below level 2	Below level 1b	At level 1b	At level 1a				Total at or above level 5	At level 5	At level 6
1	2	3	4	5	6	7	8	9	10	11	12
OECD average[3]	**493 (0.5)**	**20.1 (0.17)**	**1.3 (0.04)**	**5.2 (0.09)**	**13.6 (0.13)**	**23.2 (0.15)**	**27.9 (0.15)**	**20.5 (0.14)**	**8.3 (0.11)**	**7.2 (0.09)**	**1.1 (0.04)**
Australia	503 (1.7)	18.1 (0.55)	1.2 (0.16)	4.8 (0.24)	12.0 (0.47)	21.4 (0.63)	27.5 (0.58)	22.0 (0.58)	11.0 (0.51)	9.0 (0.46)	2.0 (0.20)
Austria	485 (2.8)	22.5 (1.04)	1.7 (0.25)	6.5 (0.67)	14.3 (0.76)	23.5 (0.86)	27.0 (1.07)	19.7 (0.74)	7.2 (0.57)	6.4 (0.52)	0.8 (0.18)
Belgium	499 (2.4)	19.5 (0.90)	1.0 (0.20)	5.3 (0.39)	13.2 (0.62)	21.1 (0.68)	26.8 (0.77)	23.2 (0.68)	9.3 (0.56)	8.4 (0.50)	1.0 (0.16)
Canada	527 (2.3)	10.7 (0.63)	0.4 (0.10)	2.1 (0.26)	8.2 (0.46)	19.0 (0.55)	29.7 (0.69)	26.6 (0.68)	14.0 (0.74)	11.6 (0.58)	2.4 (0.29)
Chile	459 (2.6)	28.4 (1.16)	1.3 (0.29)	7.4 (0.59)	19.8 (0.86)	29.9 (1.22)	27.0 (0.89)	12.4 (0.78)	2.3 (0.29)	2.2 (0.28)	0.1! (0.05)
Czech Republic	487 (2.6)	22.0 (1.10)	1.3 (0.28)	6.0 (0.62)	14.7 (0.69)	23.3 (0.80)	27.5 (1.01)	19.3 (0.90)	7.9 (0.55)	6.9 (0.49)	1.0 (0.16)
Denmark	500 (2.5)	15.0 (0.81)	0.5 (0.14)	3.3 (0.35)	11.2 (0.65)	24.1 (0.84)	32.4 (0.76)	22.0 (0.85)	6.5 (0.61)	5.9 (0.56)	0.6! (0.17)
Estonia	519 (2.2)	10.6 (0.72)	‡ (†)	2.1 (0.31)	8.4 (0.66)	21.6 (0.73)	31.4 (0.86)	25.4 (0.95)	11.0 (0.65)	9.7 (0.61)	1.4 (0.24)
Finland	526 (2.5)	11.1 (0.75)	0.6 (0.15)	2.6 (0.31)	7.8 (0.52)	17.6 (0.77)	29.7 (0.91)	27.9 (0.96)	13.7 (0.72)	11.7 (0.62)	2.0 (0.26)
France	499 (2.5)	21.5 (0.91)	2.3 (0.43)	6.5 (0.57)	12.7 (0.52)	19.0 (0.80)	24.5 (0.91)	22.5 (0.79)	12.5 (0.74)	10.5 (0.68)	2.0 (0.23)
Germany	509 (3.0)	16.2 (0.93)	0.9 (0.20)	4.1 (0.46)	11.2 (0.69)	21.0 (0.97)	27.6 (0.91)	23.5 (0.85)	11.7 (0.70)	9.7 (0.65)	1.9 (0.29)
Greece	467 (4.3)	27.3 (1.79)	2.3 (0.51)	7.8 (0.96)	17.2 (0.96)	25.3 (0.97)	27.2 (1.08)	16.1 (0.92)	4.0 (0.47)	3.8 (0.45)	0.3! (0.09)
Hungary	470 (2.7)	27.5 (1.12)	1.4 (0.29)	8.1 (0.78)	18.0 (0.92)	24.5 (0.85)	27.0 (1.01)	16.8 (0.75)	4.3 (0.45)	3.9 (0.40)	0.4! (0.11)
Iceland	482 (2.0)	22.1 (0.98)	1.8 (0.32)	6.0 (0.52)	14.3 (0.90)	26.0 (1.09)	27.3 (0.93)	18.0 (0.75)	6.6 (0.60)	5.8 (0.54)	0.8! (0.24)
Ireland	521 (2.5)	10.2 (0.80)	‡ (†)	1.7 (0.30)	8.3 (0.67)	21.0 (0.87)	31.8 (1.06)	26.4 (0.78)	10.7 (0.65)	9.4 (0.58)	1.3 (0.23)
Israel	479 (3.8)	26.6 (1.25)	3.3 (0.47)	8.1 (0.65)	15.2 (0.83)	21.7 (0.97)	24.0 (0.85)	18.5 (0.89)	9.2 (0.74)	7.7 (0.64)	1.4 (0.25)
Italy	485 (2.7)	21.0 (1.03)	1.0 (0.24)	5.4 (0.45)	14.5 (0.77)	25.4 (0.95)	28.8 (0.81)	19.2 (0.86)	5.7 (0.48)	5.1 (0.41)	0.6 (0.15)
Japan	516 (3.2)	12.9 (0.98)	0.6 (0.18)	3.0 (0.40)	9.2 (0.67)	19.8 (0.92)	30.5 (0.87)	26.0 (1.02)	10.8 (0.90)	9.5 (0.81)	1.3 (0.25)
Korea, Republic of	517 (3.5)	13.7 (0.98)	0.7 (0.19)	3.4 (0.48)	9.5 (0.72)	19.3 (0.95)	28.9 (1.03)	25.5 (1.16)	12.7 (0.96)	10.8 (0.83)	1.9 (0.31)
Latvia	488 (1.8)	17.7 (0.93)	0.4! (0.17)	3.8 (0.40)	13.4 (0.78)	27.2 (0.83)	32.1 (0.88)	18.7 (0.82)	4.3 (0.47)	4.0 (0.44)	0.3! (0.13)
Luxembourg	481 (1.4)	25.6 (0.58)	1.9 (0.28)	7.8 (0.49)	15.9 (0.67)	22.0 (0.84)	24.7 (0.65)	19.4 (0.73)	8.1 (0.45)	7.0 (0.39)	1.2 (0.19)
Mexico	423 (2.6)	41.7 (1.28)	2.0 (0.29)	11.4 (0.79)	28.4 (0.90)	34.2 (1.00)	19.5 (0.91)	4.2 (0.51)	0.3! (0.12)	0.3! (0.12)	‡ (†)
Netherlands	503 (2.4)	18.1 (1.03)	1.1 (0.20)	4.4 (0.45)	12.6 (0.80)	21.8 (0.88)	26.6 (1.05)	22.7 (0.79)	10.9 (0.63)	9.5 (0.58)	1.4 (0.28)
New Zealand	509 (2.4)	17.3 (0.85)	1.0 (0.18)	4.8 (0.55)	11.5 (0.71)	20.6 (0.74)	26.5 (0.93)	22.0 (0.91)	13.6 (0.87)	11.0 (0.73)	2.6 (0.37)
Norway	513 (2.5)	14.9 (0.82)	0.8 (0.18)	3.6 (0.39)	10.6 (0.60)	20.4 (0.74)	28.5 (0.79)	23.9 (0.83)	12.2 (0.67)	10.1 (0.61)	2.1 (0.36)
Poland	506 (2.5)	14.4 (0.78)	0.5! (0.17)	3.2 (0.41)	10.8 (0.64)	22.5 (0.84)	31.4 (0.82)	23.5 (0.88)	8.2 (0.70)	7.5 (0.63)	0.7 (0.20)
Portugal	498 (2.7)	17.2 (0.88)	0.6 (0.13)	3.9 (0.39)	12.7 (0.67)	23.2 (0.83)	30.2 (0.92)	21.9 (0.98)	7.5 (0.58)	6.9 (0.59)	0.6 (0.18)
Slovak Republic	453 (2.8)	32.1 (1.14)	4.4 (0.53)	9.4 (0.57)	18.3 (0.79)	25.7 (0.78)	24.8 (0.88)	14.0 (0.65)	3.5 (0.40)	3.2 (0.37)	0.2! (0.11)
Slovenia	505 (1.5)	15.1 (0.58)	0.5 (0.10)	3.4 (0.34)	11.2 (0.52)	22.5 (0.90)	30.3 (0.89)	23.1 (0.78)	8.9 (0.68)	8.0 (0.68)	1.0! (0.36)
Spain	496 (2.4)	16.2 (0.85)	0.7 (0.16)	3.5 (0.37)	12.0 (0.69)	24.4 (0.80)	32.3 (0.97)	21.6 (0.85)	5.5 (0.53)	5.1 (0.51)	0.4 (0.10)
Sweden	500 (3.5)	18.4 (1.09)	1.5 (0.28)	4.8 (0.46)	12.2 (0.84)	21.7 (0.84)	27.5 (0.77)	22.5 (0.98)	10.0 (0.79)	8.5 (0.74)	1.5 (0.28)
Switzerland	492 (3.0)	20.0 (1.10)	1.2 (0.26)	5.2 (0.56)	13.5 (0.74)	23.2 (0.87)	28.1 (0.96)	20.9 (0.94)	7.8 (0.65)	6.9 (0.60)	0.9 (0.20)
Turkey	428 (4.0)	40.0 (2.00)	2.3 (0.32)	10.9 (0.96)	26.8 (1.38)	32.6 (1.48)	21.1 (1.41)	5.7 (0.88)	0.6! (0.23)	0.6! (0.22)	‡ (†)
United Kingdom	498 (2.8)	17.9 (0.86)	0.8 (0.16)	4.0 (0.37)	13.1 (0.70)	24.3 (0.85)	28.4 (0.73)	20.3 (0.75)	9.2 (0.64)	7.7 (0.51)	1.5 (0.22)
United States	497 (3.4)	19.0 (1.14)	1.1 (0.24)	4.8 (0.53)	13.0 (0.77)	22.9 (0.90)	28.0 (0.95)	20.5 (0.87)	9.6 (0.74)	8.2 (0.64)	1.4 (0.23)
Non-OECD education systems											
Albania	405 (4.1)	50.3 (1.92)	7.4 (0.70)	15.9 (1.06)	27.0 (1.25)	27.3 (1.08)	16.3 (1.05)	5.1 (0.68)	1.0 (0.23)	0.9 (0.21)	‡ (†)
Algeria	350 (3.0)	79.0 (1.55)	11.0 (1.02)	31.2 (1.17)	36.8 (1.20)	17.0 (1.23)	3.7 (0.55)	0.3! (0.12)	‡ (†)	‡ (†)	# (†)
Beijing, Shanghai, Jiangsu, Guangdong (China)	494 (5.1)	21.9 (1.51)	2.1 (0.44)	6.2 (0.64)	13.5 (0.84)	20.9 (1.06)	25.4 (1.11)	20.9 (1.19)	10.9 (1.29)	9.1 (0.97)	1.8 (0.45)
Brazil	407 (2.8)	51.0 (1.13)	7.1 (0.47)	17.4 (0.65)	26.5 (0.61)	25.0 (0.66)	16.2 (0.57)	6.4 (0.46)	1.4 (0.25)	1.3 (0.21)	‡ (†)
Buenos Aires (Argentina)	475 (7.2)	21.8 (2.29)	1.5! (0.54)	5.8 (1.09)	14.5 (1.66)	28.2 (2.10)	30.1 (1.98)	16.2 (2.03)	3.8 (1.09)	3.5 (1.00)	0.3! (0.21)
Bulgaria	432 (5.0)	41.5 (1.99)	7.7 (0.93)	14.3 (1.16)	19.5 (0.98)	22.0 (1.04)	21.2 (1.26)	11.7 (0.97)	3.6 (0.47)	3.2 (0.40)	0.4! (0.13)
Chinese Taipei	497 (2.5)	17.2 (0.82)	1.0 (0.16)	4.4 (0.37)	11.8 (0.59)	22.4 (0.77)	31.3 (1.00)	22.1 (0.86)	6.9 (0.77)	6.3 (0.66)	0.6 (0.19)
Colombia	425 (2.9)	42.8 (1.49)	3.2 (0.47)	13.6 (1.00)	26.1 (0.95)	29.2 (0.92)	19.9 (0.93)	7.0 (0.51)	1.0 (0.16)	0.9 (0.17)	‡ (†)
Costa Rica	427 (2.6)	40.3 (1.44)	1.7 (0.28)	10.3 (0.72)	28.3 (1.00)	34.6 (1.04)	19.2 (1.05)	5.2 (0.57)	0.7 (0.18)	0.6 (0.17)	‡ (†)
Croatia	487 (2.7)	19.9 (1.14)	0.6 (0.14)	4.5 (0.45)	14.8 (0.86)	26.6 (0.91)	28.6 (0.99)	19.0 (0.93)	5.9 (0.54)	5.4 (0.55)	0.5 (0.14)

See notes at end of table.

Table 602.50. Average reading literacy scores of 15-year-old students and percentage attaining reading literacy proficiency levels, by country or other education system: 2015—Continued

[Standard errors appear in parentheses]

Country or other education system	Average reading literacy score[1]	Percentage attaining reading literacy proficiency levels[2]: Below level 2: Total below level 2	Below level 2: Below level 1b	Below level 2: At level 1b	Below level 2: At level 1a	At level 2	At level 3	At level 4	At or above level 5: Total at or above level 5	At or above level 5: At level 5	At or above level 5: At level 6
1	2	3	4	5	6	7	8	9	10	11	12
Cyprus	443 (1.7)	35.6 (0.85)	4.4 (0.38)	11.4 (0.56)	19.8 (0.96)	27.0 (0.73)	23.0 (0.84)	11.3 (0.58)	3.1 (0.34)	2.8 (0.33)	0.2! (0.09)
Dominican Republic	358 (3.1)	72.1 (1.46)	13.1 (1.06)	28.2 (1.24)	30.8 (1.23)	19.5 (1.06)	7.0 (0.72)	1.3 (0.29)	‡ (†)	‡ (†)	# (†)
Georgia	401 (3.0)	51.7 (1.27)	9.5 (0.65)	16.4 (0.80)	25.8 (0.80)	25.4 (0.91)	16.1 (0.76)	5.7 (0.54)	1.1 (0.23)	1.1 (0.21)	‡ (†)
Hong Kong (China)	527 (2.7)	9.3 (0.76)	0.3! (0.12)	2.0 (0.28)	7.0 (0.61)	18.1 (0.93)	32.1 (1.07)	29.0 (0.97)	11.6 (0.86)	10.4 (0.82)	1.1 (0.21)
Indonesia	397 (2.9)	55.4 (1.49)	3.8 (0.65)	16.8 (1.07)	34.8 (1.05)	30.9 (1.13)	11.7 (0.78)	1.9 (0.32)	‡ (†)	‡ (†)	‡ (†)
Jordan	408 (2.9)	46.3 (1.40)	7.4 (0.70)	13.7 (0.76)	25.2 (0.92)	30.7 (0.76)	18.7 (0.94)	4.1 (0.39)	0.3! (0.10)	0.3! (0.10)	‡ (†)
Kosovo	347 (1.6)	76.9 (0.89)	14.6 (0.74)	28.0 (0.95)	34.2 (1.13)	19.4 (0.93)	3.6 (0.43)	‡ (†)	# (†)	# (†)	# (†)
Lebanon	347 (4.4)	70.4 (1.63)	24.1 (1.51)	24.5 (1.32)	21.7 (1.11)	15.8 (1.00)	9.4 (0.85)	3.6 (0.49)	0.8 (0.25)	0.7! (0.25)	‡ (†)
Lithuania	472 (2.7)	25.1 (0.93)	1.3 (0.24)	6.7 (0.51)	17.1 (0.72)	27.1 (0.81)	26.7 (0.91)	16.7 (0.90)	4.4 (0.51)	4.1 (0.46)	0.4! (0.11)
Macao (China)	509 (1.3)	11.7 (0.45)	0.3! (0.10)	2.1 (0.26)	9.3 (0.50)	23.1 (0.83)	34.2 (0.91)	24.4 (0.87)	6.7 (0.55)	6.2 (0.53)	0.5 (0.14)
Macedonia, Republic of	352 (1.4)	70.7 (0.73)	18.8 (0.68)	24.1 (0.82)	27.7 (0.91)	19.3 (0.76)	8.1 (0.56)	1.7 (0.24)	‡ (†)	‡ (†)	‡ (†)
Malta	447 (1.8)	35.6 (0.84)	7.5 (0.48)	11.1 (0.75)	17.0 (0.93)	22.5 (0.84)	22.5 (0.84)	13.9 (0.71)	5.6 (0.42)	4.7 (0.45)	0.9 (0.24)
Massachusetts[4] (USA)	527 (6.0)	11.3 (1.28)	0.5! (0.22)	2.3 (0.52)	8.5 (1.15)	17.9 (1.56)	29.7 (1.58)	26.7 (1.78)	14.5 (1.63)	11.9 (1.51)	2.5 (0.61)
Moldova, Republic of	416 (2.5)	45.8 (1.14)	5.9 (0.47)	14.7 (0.68)	25.1 (0.92)	27.7 (0.85)	18.7 (0.76)	6.6 (0.56)	1.2 (0.23)	1.1 (0.21)	‡ (†)
Montenegro, Republic of	427 (1.6)	41.9 (0.73)	4.1 (0.32)	13.0 (0.66)	24.9 (0.81)	28.6 (0.74)	20.2 (0.58)	7.9 (0.45)	1.4 (0.28)	1.3 (0.27)	‡ (†)
North Carolina[4] (USA)	500 (5.4)	18.0 (1.44)	0.6! (0.28)	3.8 (0.66)	13.6 (1.24)	23.4 (1.63)	28.0 (1.51)	21.0 (1.79)	9.6 (1.05)	8.5 (0.99)	1.2! (0.35)
Peru	398 (2.9)	53.9 (1.49)	6.4 (0.57)	19.2 (0.95)	28.3 (1.13)	27.3 (0.91)	15.0 (0.81)	3.5 (0.50)	0.3! (0.10)	0.3! (0.10)	‡ (†)
Puerto Rico (USA)	410 (7.1)	50.4 (3.21)	5.8 (1.37)	16.6 (2.25)	28.0 (1.84)	25.8 (1.97)	16.4 (1.83)	6.2 (1.23)	1.2! (0.39)	1.1! (0.38)	‡ (†)
Qatar	402 (1.0)	51.6 (0.49)	11.1 (0.32)	17.7 (0.44)	22.8 (0.61)	22.7 (0.50)	16.8 (0.49)	7.4 (0.33)	1.6 (0.17)	1.4 (0.16)	0.1! (0.04)
Romania	434 (4.1)	38.7 (1.86)	3.7 (0.55)	11.6 (0.88)	23.4 (1.19)	29.5 (1.18)	21.3 (1.23)	8.4 (0.85)	2.0 (0.39)	1.8 (0.37)	0.2! (0.07)
Russian Federation	495 (3.1)	16.2 (1.20)	0.3! (0.10)	3.2 (0.42)	12.8 (0.99)	27.1 (0.98)	30.7 (1.12)	19.3 (1.00)	6.6 (0.60)	5.9 (0.59)	0.8 (0.17)
Singapore	535 (1.6)	11.1 (0.52)	0.3! (0.12)	2.5 (0.24)	8.3 (0.42)	16.9 (0.54)	26.2 (0.74)	27.4 (0.73)	18.4 (0.70)	14.7 (0.66)	3.6 (0.35)
Thailand	409 (3.3)	50.0 (1.76)	2.8 (0.43)	15.1 (1.07)	32.1 (1.03)	31.1 (0.97)	15.0 (0.98)	3.7 (0.54)	0.3! (0.12)	0.3! (0.12)	# (†)
Trinidad and Tobago	427 (1.5)	42.5 (0.90)	5.7 (0.52)	14.3 (0.67)	22.5 (0.85)	25.6 (1.00)	20.3 (0.88)	9.2 (0.63)	2.4 (0.30)	2.2 (0.30)	0.2! (0.09)
Tunisia	361 (3.1)	71.6 (1.28)	11.1 (1.13)	26.6 (1.08)	33.9 (1.17)	21.0 (1.10)	6.5 (0.59)	0.8 (0.22)	‡ (†)	‡ (†)	# (†)
United Arab Emirates	434 (2.9)	40.4 (1.20)	5.4 (0.44)	13.2 (0.65)	21.8 (0.67)	25.4 (0.63)	20.5 (0.79)	10.7 (0.60)	3.0 (0.35)	2.7 (0.31)	0.3 (0.08)
Uruguay	437 (2.5)	39.0 (1.11)	3.0 (0.33)	12.5 (0.74)	23.5 (0.84)	27.8 (0.81)	21.3 (0.84)	9.3 (0.58)	2.5 (0.40)	2.3 (0.37)	0.2! (0.09)
Vietnam	487 (3.7)	13.8 (1.45)	‡ (†)	1.7 (0.38)	12.1 (1.32)	32.5 (1.47)	35.2 (1.33)	15.8 (1.19)	2.7 (0.71)	2.5 (0.65)	‡ (†)

†Not applicable.
#Rounds to zero.
!Interpret data with caution. The coefficient of variation (CV) for this estimate is between 30 and 50 percent.
‡Reporting standards not met. The coefficient of variation (CV) for this estimate is 50 percent or greater.
[1]Program for International Student Assessment (PISA) scores are reported on a scale from 0 to 1,000.
[2]To reach a particular proficiency level, a student must correctly answer a majority of items at that level. Students were classified into reading literacy levels according to their scores. Exact cut scores are as follows: below level 1b (a score less than 262.04); level 1b (a score of at least 262.04 but less than 334.75); level 1a (a score of at least 334.75 but less than 407.47); level 2 (a score of at least 407.47 but less than 480.18); level 3 (a score of at least 480.18 but less than 552.89); level 4 (a score of at least 552.89 but less than 625.61); level 5 (a score of at least 625.61 but less than 698.32); and level 6 (a score of at least 698.32).
[3]Refers to the mean of the data values for all Organization for Economic Cooperation and Development (OECD) countries, to which each country contributes equally, regardless of the absolute size of the student population of each country.
[4]Results are for public school students only.
NOTE: Detail may not sum to totals because of rounding.
SOURCE: Organization for Economic Cooperation and Development (OECD), Program for International Student Assessment (PISA), 2015. (This table was prepared December 2016.)

Table 602.60. Average mathematics literacy scores of 15-year-old students and percentage attaining mathematics literacy proficiency levels, by country or other education system: 2015

[Standard errors appear in parentheses]

Country or other education system	Average mathematics literacy score[1]		Percentage attaining mathematics literacy proficiency levels[2]																	
			Below level 2												At or above level 5					
			Total below level 2		Below level 1		At level 1		At level 2		At level 3		At level 4		Total at or above level 5		At level 5		At level 6	
1	2		3		4		5		6		7		8		9		10		11	
OECD average[3]	**490**	**(0.4)**	**23.4**	**(0.18)**	**8.5**	**(0.12)**	**14.9**	**(0.13)**	**22.5**	**(0.15)**	**24.8**	**(0.15)**	**18.6**	**(0.14)**	**10.7**	**(0.13)**	**8.4**	**(0.10)**	**2.3**	**(0.06)**
Australia	494	(1.6)	22.0	(0.61)	7.6	(0.43)	14.4	(0.45)	22.6	(0.70)	25.4	(0.61)	18.7	(0.54)	11.3	(0.62)	8.6	(0.48)	2.7	(0.28)
Austria	497	(2.9)	21.8	(1.08)	7.8	(0.71)	13.9	(0.68)	21.3	(0.82)	24.6	(0.85)	19.9	(0.85)	12.5	(0.87)	9.7	(0.69)	2.7	(0.40)
Belgium	507	(2.4)	20.1	(0.96)	7.2	(0.61)	12.9	(0.61)	18.8	(0.82)	23.4	(0.73)	21.8	(0.70)	15.9	(0.67)	12.3	(0.51)	3.6	(0.35)
Canada	516	(2.3)	14.4	(0.70)	3.8	(0.35)	10.5	(0.50)	20.4	(0.60)	27.1	(0.65)	23.0	(0.74)	15.1	(0.76)	11.4	(0.56)	3.7	(0.34)
Chile	423	(2.5)	49.4	(1.28)	23.0	(1.09)	26.3	(0.99)	25.5	(0.78)	17.4	(0.88)	6.4	(0.54)	1.4	(0.21)	1.3	(0.21)	#	(†)
Czech Republic	492	(2.4)	21.7	(1.07)	7.4	(0.68)	14.3	(0.76)	23.3	(0.95)	26.2	(0.84)	18.4	(0.74)	10.4	(0.78)	8.1	(0.63)	2.2	(0.30)
Denmark	511	(2.2)	13.6	(0.85)	3.1	(0.33)	10.5	(0.73)	21.9	(0.97)	29.5	(0.90)	23.4	(0.86)	11.7	(0.73)	9.8	(0.67)	1.9	(0.33)
Estonia	520	(2.0)	11.2	(0.71)	2.2	(0.31)	9.0	(0.67)	21.5	(0.94)	28.9	(0.84)	24.2	(0.72)	14.2	(0.81)	11.3	(0.66)	2.9	(0.41)
Finland	511	(2.3)	13.6	(0.83)	3.6	(0.48)	10.0	(0.65)	21.8	(0.80)	29.3	(0.79)	23.7	(0.98)	11.7	(0.70)	9.5	(0.68)	2.2	(0.30)
France	493	(2.1)	23.5	(0.93)	8.8	(0.71)	14.7	(0.69)	20.7	(0.88)	23.8	(0.77)	20.6	(0.71)	11.4	(0.69)	9.5	(0.61)	1.9	(0.27)
Germany	506	(2.9)	17.2	(1.00)	5.1	(0.57)	12.1	(0.76)	21.8	(0.94)	26.8	(0.74)	21.2	(0.94)	12.9	(0.78)	10.1	(0.64)	2.9	(0.36)
Greece	454	(3.8)	35.8	(1.77)	15.1	(1.33)	20.7	(0.97)	26.0	(0.89)	22.1	(1.00)	12.3	(0.85)	3.9	(0.48)	3.4	(0.44)	0.5	(0.14)
Hungary	477	(2.5)	28.0	(1.15)	11.3	(0.83)	16.6	(0.78)	23.1	(1.01)	24.5	(0.97)	16.3	(0.81)	8.1	(0.64)	6.7	(0.49)	1.5	(0.26)
Iceland	488	(2.0)	23.6	(1.01)	8.4	(0.59)	15.2	(0.88)	23.7	(1.13)	24.8	(1.10)	17.5	(0.87)	10.3	(0.78)	8.1	(0.71)	2.2	(0.34)
Ireland	504	(2.1)	15.0	(0.89)	3.5	(0.46)	11.5	(0.65)	24.1	(0.89)	30.0	(0.89)	21.2	(0.71)	9.8	(0.58)	8.3	(0.51)	1.5	(0.22)
Israel	470	(3.6)	32.1	(1.37)	15.0	(0.99)	17.1	(0.78)	21.1	(0.98)	21.7	(0.99)	16.1	(0.79)	8.9	(0.89)	7.1	(0.65)	1.9	(0.32)
Italy	490	(2.8)	23.3	(1.06)	8.3	(0.64)	14.9	(0.78)	23.3	(0.85)	24.7	(0.80)	18.3	(0.87)	10.5	(0.80)	8.1	(0.60)	2.4	(0.34)
Japan	532	(3.0)	10.7	(0.81)	2.9	(0.40)	7.8	(0.57)	17.2	(0.90)	25.8	(0.87)	25.9	(0.91)	20.3	(1.26)	15.0	(0.90)	5.3	(0.73)
Korea, Republic of	524	(3.7)	15.5	(1.06)	5.4	(0.63)	10.0	(0.74)	17.2	(0.78)	23.7	(0.81)	22.7	(0.94)	20.9	(1.33)	14.3	(0.87)	6.6	(0.68)
Latvia	482	(1.9)	21.4	(1.01)	5.7	(0.63)	15.8	(0.81)	28.3	(0.91)	28.8	(0.95)	16.3	(0.74)	5.2	(0.42)	4.5	(0.40)	0.6	(0.14)
Luxembourg	486	(1.3)	25.8	(0.69)	8.8	(0.49)	17.0	(0.71)	22.5	(0.69)	23.6	(0.96)	18.0	(0.67)	10.0	(0.52)	7.8	(0.41)	2.2	(0.30)
Mexico	408	(2.2)	56.6	(1.31)	25.5	(1.11)	31.1	(0.92)	26.9	(0.92)	12.9	(0.76)	3.2	(0.36)	#	(†)	#	(†)	#	(†)
Netherlands	512	(2.2)	16.7	(0.89)	5.2	(0.50)	11.5	(0.70)	19.8	(0.75)	24.9	(0.88)	23.0	(0.83)	15.5	(0.78)	12.3	(0.68)	3.2	(0.33)
New Zealand	495	(2.3)	21.6	(1.02)	7.1	(0.54)	14.6	(0.83)	22.6	(0.99)	25.3	(1.01)	19.0	(0.79)	11.4	(0.71)	8.6	(0.66)	2.8	(0.37)
Norway	502	(2.2)	17.1	(0.77)	4.8	(0.48)	12.3	(0.65)	23.6	(0.89)	27.7	(0.82)	21.0	(1.02)	10.6	(0.67)	8.7	(0.62)	1.9	(0.27)
Poland	504	(2.4)	17.2	(1.00)	4.5	(0.52)	12.7	(0.75)	22.9	(0.96)	27.1	(0.78)	20.6	(0.89)	12.2	(0.88)	9.3	(0.64)	2.9	(0.46)
Portugal	492	(2.5)	23.8	(0.95)	8.7	(0.61)	15.1	(0.73)	21.6	(0.71)	23.9	(0.78)	19.2	(0.77)	11.4	(0.70)	8.9	(0.62)	2.5	(0.33)
Slovak Republic	475	(2.7)	27.7	(1.19)	11.6	(0.79)	16.1	(0.74)	23.5	(1.02)	24.3	(0.87)	16.7	(0.71)	7.8	(0.64)	6.6	(0.50)	1.3	(0.26)
Slovenia	510	(1.3)	16.1	(0.58)	4.4	(0.40)	11.7	(0.63)	21.4	(0.80)	26.8	(0.75)	22.3	(0.84)	13.5	(0.68)	10.4	(0.59)	3.0	(0.36)
Spain	486	(2.2)	22.2	(0.97)	7.2	(0.49)	15.0	(0.80)	24.9	(0.83)	27.5	(0.98)	18.1	(0.70)	7.2	(0.62)	6.3	(0.52)	1.0	(0.20)
Sweden	494	(3.2)	20.8	(1.20)	7.0	(0.68)	13.8	(0.83)	23.3	(0.96)	26.1	(1.10)	19.4	(0.93)	10.4	(0.86)	8.4	(0.65)	2.0	(0.38)
Switzerland	521	(2.9)	15.8	(1.03)	4.9	(0.54)	10.9	(0.78)	18.1	(0.81)	23.6	(0.89)	23.3	(0.83)	19.2	(1.05)	14.0	(0.80)	5.3	(0.54)
Turkey	420	(4.1)	51.4	(2.17)	22.9	(1.54)	28.4	(1.36)	25.3	(1.14)	16.3	(1.24)	5.9	(0.93)	1.1!	(0.36)	1.0!	(0.33)	0.1!	(0.08)
United Kingdom	492	(2.5)	21.9	(1.01)	7.7	(0.63)	14.1	(0.73)	22.7	(0.76)	26.0	(0.77)	18.8	(0.83)	10.6	(0.69)	8.3	(0.57)	2.3	(0.32)
United States	470	(3.2)	29.4	(1.44)	10.6	(0.81)	18.8	(1.01)	26.2	(1.00)	23.8	(0.89)	14.7	(0.80)	5.9	(0.70)	5.0	(0.61)	0.9	(0.20)

See notes at end of table.

Table 602.60. Average mathematics literacy scores of 15-year-old students and percentage attaining mathematics literacy proficiency levels, by country or other education system: 2015—Continued

[Standard errors appear in parentheses]

Country or other education system	Average mathematics literacy score[1]	Percentage attaining mathematics literacy proficiency levels[2]: Below level 2: Total below level 2	Below level 2: Below level 1	Below level 2: At level 1	At level 2	At level 3	At level 4	At or above level 5: Total at or above level 5	At or above level 5: At level 5	At or above level 5: At level 6
1	2	3	4	5	6	7	8	9	10	11
Non-OECD education systems										
Albania	413 (3.4)	53.3 (1.92)	26.3 (1.49)	27.0 (1.54)	25.4 (1.18)	14.8 (0.96)	5.4 (0.62)	1.1 (0.25)	1.0 (0.26)	‡ (†)
Algeria	360 (3.0)	81.0 (1.34)	50.6 (1.69)	30.4 (0.92)	14.2 (0.96)	4.0 (0.53)	0.8 (0.23)	‡ (†)	‡ (†)	‡ (†)
Beijing, Shanghai, Jiangsu, Guangdong (China)	531 (4.9)	15.8 (1.21)	5.8 (0.71)	10.0 (0.85)	16.3 (0.95)	20.5 (0.94)	21.8 (0.95)	25.6 (1.90)	16.6 (1.08)	9.0 (1.09)
Brazil	377 (2.9)	70.3 (1.22)	43.7 (1.34)	26.5 (0.79)	17.2 (0.70)	8.6 (0.54)	3.1 (0.36)	0.9 (0.21)	0.8 (0.17)	‡ (†)
Buenos Aires (Argentina)	456 (6.9)	34.1 (3.20)	13.8 (2.09)	20.2 (2.36)	27.0 (1.97)	22.3 (1.92)	12.5 (1.79)	4.0 (1.09)	3.5 (0.96)	‡ (†)
Bulgaria	441 (4.0)	42.1 (1.80)	20.8 (1.49)	21.2 (1.08)	23.7 (1.00)	19.3 (0.98)	10.6 (0.82)	4.4 (0.63)	3.6 (0.47)	0.8! (0.25)
Chinese Taipei	542 (3.0)	12.7 (0.73)	4.4 (0.41)	8.3 (0.51)	14.6 (0.68)	21.2 (0.85)	23.3 (0.90)	28.1 (1.25)	18.0 (0.65)	10.1 (0.92)
Colombia	390 (2.3)	66.3 (1.18)	35.4 (1.28)	30.9 (0.77)	21.5 (0.82)	9.5 (0.57)	2.4 (0.25)	# (†)	# (†)	‡ (†)
Costa Rica	400 (2.5)	62.5 (1.51)	27.4 (1.16)	35.1 (0.98)	25.8 (1.01)	9.4 (0.77)	2.0 (0.35)	# (†)	# (†)	‡ (†)
Croatia	464 (2.8)	32.0 (1.37)	11.5 (0.92)	20.5 (0.80)	26.3 (0.86)	23.0 (0.83)	13.1 (0.77)	5.6 (0.54)	4.6 (0.47)	1.0 (0.18)
Cyprus	437 (1.7)	42.6 (0.80)	20.2 (0.72)	22.4 (0.73)	25.8 (0.82)	18.9 (0.85)	9.5 (0.49)	3.2 (0.41)	2.8 (0.40)	# (†)
Dominican Republic	328 (2.7)	90.5 (1.04)	68.3 (1.61)	22.2 (1.15)	7.7 (0.79)	1.5 (0.39)	‡ (†)	‡ (†)	‡ (†)	# (†)
Georgia	404 (2.8)	57.1 (1.18)	31.2 (1.36)	25.9 (0.98)	22.8 (0.82)	13.4 (0.71)	5.2 (0.53)	1.6 (0.40)	1.4 (0.34)	‡ (†)
Hong Kong (China)	548 (3.0)	9.0 (0.77)	2.5 (0.42)	6.4 (0.56)	13.6 (0.86)	23.4 (0.94)	27.4 (1.05)	26.5 (1.14)	18.8 (0.89)	7.7 (0.71)
Indonesia	386 (3.1)	68.6 (1.56)	37.9 (1.68)	30.7 (1.12)	19.6 (1.01)	8.4 (0.72)	2.7 (0.38)	0.7 (0.19)	0.6 (0.17)	‡ (†)
Jordan	380 (2.7)	67.5 (1.31)	38.9 (1.28)	28.7 (0.90)	20.9 (0.90)	9.2 (0.64)	2.1 (0.30)	# (†)	# (†)	‡ (†)
Kosovo	362 (1.6)	77.7 (1.05)	48.7 (1.00)	29.0 (1.26)	16.5 (0.95)	5.1 (0.60)	0.7! (0.23)	‡ (†)	‡ (†)	‡ (†)
Lebanon	396 (3.7)	60.2 (1.58)	36.6 (1.73)	23.6 (1.21)	19.5 (0.91)	12.3 (0.93)	5.9 (0.58)	2.0 (0.33)	1.7 (0.30)	# (†)
Lithuania	478 (2.3)	25.4 (1.07)	8.5 (0.75)	16.9 (0.82)	26.4 (1.08)	25.4 (1.04)	15.9 (0.90)	6.9 (0.66)	5.8 (0.58)	1.1 (0.22)
Macao (China)	544 (1.1)	6.6 (0.52)	1.3 (0.20)	5.3 (0.46)	15.1 (0.64)	27.3 (0.84)	29.1 (0.74)	21.9 (0.62)	16.9 (0.67)	5.0 (0.54)
Macedonia, Republic of	371 (1.3)	70.2 (0.77)	45.1 (0.74)	25.1 (0.83)	17.3 (0.92)	8.6 (0.59)	3.1 (0.39)	0.8 (0.19)	0.7 (0.17)	‡ (†)
Malta	479 (1.7)	29.1 (0.81)	14.7 (0.61)	14.4 (0.75)	20.0 (0.86)	21.6 (0.69)	17.5 (0.76)	11.8 (0.67)	8.9 (0.59)	3.0 (0.32)
Massachusetts[4] (USA)	500 (5.5)	17.2 (1.84)	5.4 (0.99)	11.8 (1.55)	22.6 (1.82)	29.6 (1.66)	20.6 (1.63)	10.0 (1.34)	8.5 (1.25)	1.5! (0.49)
Moldova, Republic of	420 (2.5)	50.3 (1.25)	24.8 (1.05)	25.5 (0.97)	25.0 (1.12)	16.3 (0.77)	6.7 (0.57)	1.7 (0.25)	1.5 (0.24)	# (†)
Montenegro, Republic of	418 (1.5)	51.9 (0.95)	25.0 (0.74)	26.9 (0.80)	24.9 (0.97)	15.7 (0.72)	6.1 (0.42)	1.5 (0.22)	1.4 (0.21)	# (†)
North Carolina[4] (USA)	471 (4.4)	28.8 (2.08)	9.9 (1.28)	18.9 (1.64)	26.0 (1.48)	24.7 (1.64)	15.0 (1.18)	5.5 (0.89)	4.9 (0.86)	0.7! (0.25)
Peru	387 (2.7)	66.2 (1.41)	37.7 (1.18)	28.4 (0.86)	21.0 (0.89)	9.8 (0.71)	2.7 (0.38)	# (†)	# (†)	# (†)
Puerto Rico (USA)	378 (5.6)	72.6 (3.66)	41.6 (3.11)	31.0 (1.92)	17.7 (2.11)	7.2 (1.27)	2.2! (0.82)	‡ (†)	‡ (†)	‡ (†)
Qatar	402 (1.3)	58.7 (0.70)	34.7 (0.54)	24.0 (0.56)	19.9 (0.57)	12.8 (0.38)	6.4 (0.32)	2.2 (0.19)	1.9 (0.18)	# (†)
Romania	444 (3.8)	39.9 (1.84)	16.2 (1.26)	23.7 (1.21)	27.4 (1.08)	20.1 (1.11)	9.3 (0.85)	3.3 (0.53)	2.8 (0.44)	# (†)
Russian Federation	494 (3.1)	18.9 (1.17)	5.1 (0.67)	13.9 (0.89)	25.5 (0.93)	27.5 (0.93)	19.3 (0.96)	8.8 (0.74)	7.3 (0.62)	1.5 (0.24)
Singapore	564 (1.5)	7.6 (0.39)	2.0 (0.20)	5.5 (0.40)	12.4 (0.63)	20.0 (0.74)	25.1 (0.88)	34.8 (0.77)	21.7 (0.84)	13.1 (0.67)
Thailand	415 (3.0)	53.8 (1.62)	24.2 (1.20)	29.6 (1.13)	26.1 (0.90)	13.8 (0.89)	4.8 (0.56)	1.4 (0.35)	1.2 (0.29)	‡ (†)
Trinidad and Tobago	417 (1.4)	52.3 (0.83)	28.3 (0.76)	23.9 (0.91)	22.1 (0.84)	15.6 (0.75)	7.5 (0.55)	2.5 (0.31)	2.2 (0.29)	# (†)
Tunisia	367 (3.0)	74.8 (1.24)	47.4 (1.46)	27.4 (1.06)	16.4 (0.88)	6.4 (0.63)	1.8 (0.42)	0.5! (0.23)	# (†)	‡ (†)
United Arab Emirates	427 (2.4)	48.7 (1.21)	24.4 (0.99)	24.4 (0.72)	23.2 (0.76)	15.9 (0.70)	8.5 (0.50)	3.7 (0.34)	3.1 (0.31)	0.6 (0.10)
Uruguay	418 (2.5)	52.4 (1.23)	25.4 (1.22)	27.0 (1.02)	24.4 (0.89)	15.3 (0.77)	6.2 (0.48)	1.7 (0.37)	1.5 (0.32)	0.2! (0.09)
Vietnam	495 (4.5)	19.1 (1.67)	4.5 (0.77)	14.6 (1.16)	26.4 (1.19)	27.0 (1.31)	18.2 (1.08)	9.3 (1.34)	7.2 (0.85)	2.1! (0.66)

†Not applicable.
#Rounds to zero.
!Interpret data with caution. The coefficient of variation (CV) for this estimate is between 30 and 50 percent.
‡Reporting standards not met. The coefficient of variation (CV) for this estimate is 50 percent or greater.
[1]Program for International Student Assessment (PISA) scores are reported on a scale from 0 to 1,000.
[2]To reach a particular proficiency level, a student must correctly answer a majority of items at that level. Students were classified into mathematics literacy levels according to their scores. Exact cut scores are as follows: below level 1 (a score less than 357.77); level 1 (a score of at least 357.77 but less than 420.07); level 2 (a score of at least 420.07 but less than 482.38); level 3 (a score of at least 482.38 but less than 544.68); level 4 (a score of at least 544.68 but less than 606.99); level 5 (a score of at least 606.99 but less than 669.30); and level 6 (a score of at least 669.30).
[3]Refers to the mean of the data values for all Organization for Economic Cooperation and Development (OECD) countries, to which each country contributes equally, regardless of the absolute size of the student population of each country.
[4]Results are for public school students only.
NOTE: Detail may not sum to totals because of rounding.
SOURCE: Organization for Economic Cooperation and Development (OECD), Program for International Student Assessment (PISA), 2015. (This table was prepared December 2016.)

Table 602.70. Average science literacy scores of 15-year-old students and percentage attaining science literacy proficiency levels, by country or other education system: 2015

[Standard errors appear in parentheses]

Country or other education system	Average science literacy score[1]	Percentage attaining science literacy proficiency levels[2] — Below level 2: Total below level 2	Below level 2: Below level 1b	Below level 2: At level 1b	Below level 2: At level 1a	At level 2	At level 3	At level 4	At or above level 5: Total at or above level 5	At or above level 5: At level 5	At or above level 5: At level 6
1	2	3	4	5	6	7	8	9	10	11	12
OECD average[3]	**493 (0.4)**	**21.2 (0.17)**	**0.6 (0.03)**	**4.9 (0.08)**	**15.7 (0.13)**	**24.8 (0.14)**	**27.2 (0.15)**	**19.0 (0.13)**	**7.7 (0.09)**	**6.7 (0.08)**	**1.1 (0.03)**
Australia	510 (1.5)	17.6 (0.56)	0.6 (0.09)	4.3 (0.26)	12.8 (0.48)	21.6 (0.53)	27.3 (0.51)	22.3 (0.53)	11.2 (0.45)	9.2 (0.42)	2.0 (0.22)
Austria	495 (2.4)	20.8 (0.96)	0.5! (0.16)	4.5 (0.47)	15.8 (0.82)	23.9 (0.77)	28.1 (0.83)	19.5 (0.79)	7.7 (0.55)	6.8 (0.49)	0.9 (0.18)
Belgium	502 (2.3)	19.8 (0.90)	0.5 (0.12)	4.9 (0.42)	14.4 (0.62)	21.9 (0.63)	26.8 (0.74)	22.5 (0.65)	9.0 (0.43)	8.0 (0.41)	1.0 (0.13)
Canada	528 (2.1)	11.1 (0.53)	# (†)	1.8 (0.19)	9.1 (0.44)	20.2 (0.58)	30.3 (0.54)	26.1 (0.69)	12.4 (0.61)	10.4 (0.52)	2.0 (0.21)
Chile	447 (2.4)	34.8 (1.18)	1.0 (0.21)	8.9 (0.57)	25.0 (0.91)	31.0 (0.98)	23.8 (0.91)	9.1 (0.66)	1.2 (0.19)	1.2 (0.19)	‡ (†)
Czech Republic	493 (2.3)	20.7 (1.00)	# (†)	4.3 (0.48)	16.1 (0.80)	25.9 (0.81)	27.7 (0.89)	18.4 (0.74)	7.3 (0.51)	6.3 (0.45)	0.9 (0.17)
Denmark	502 (2.4)	15.9 (0.83)	# (†)	3.0 (0.29)	12.5 (0.70)	25.9 (0.90)	31.1 (1.05)	20.2 (0.80)	7.0 (0.63)	6.1 (0.55)	0.9 (0.19)
Estonia	534 (2.1)	8.8 (0.65)	‡ (†)	1.2 (0.23)	7.5 (0.60)	20.1 (0.73)	30.7 (0.91)	26.9 (0.94)	13.5 (0.73)	11.6 (0.68)	1.9 (0.26)
Finland	531 (2.4)	11.5 (0.69)	# (†)	2.3 (0.33)	8.9 (0.56)	19.1 (0.73)	29.2 (0.79)	26.0 (0.83)	14.3 (0.65)	11.9 (0.58)	2.4 (0.28)
France	495 (2.1)	22.1 (0.86)	0.9 (0.18)	5.8 (0.48)	15.3 (0.63)	22.0 (0.86)	26.5 (0.78)	21.4 (0.75)	8.0 (0.53)	7.2 (0.52)	0.8 (0.15)
Germany	509 (2.7)	17.0 (0.95)	0.4! (0.14)	3.8 (0.41)	12.8 (0.69)	22.7 (0.81)	27.7 (0.80)	22.0 (0.80)	10.6 (0.61)	8.8 (0.56)	1.8 (0.20)
Greece	455 (3.9)	32.7 (1.88)	1.2 (0.31)	9.1 (0.99)	22.4 (1.07)	28.4 (1.11)	25.2 (1.10)	11.6 (0.86)	2.1 (0.31)	2.0 (0.29)	# (†)
Hungary	477 (2.4)	26.0 (1.04)	0.8 (0.19)	6.8 (0.63)	18.4 (0.86)	25.5 (0.85)	27.3 (0.88)	16.6 (0.77)	4.6 (0.47)	4.3 (0.41)	# (†)
Iceland	473 (1.7)	25.3 (0.87)	0.8 (0.23)	5.8 (0.51)	18.7 (0.86)	29.0 (1.00)	27.3 (0.93)	14.6 (0.80)	3.8 (0.39)	3.5 (0.37)	# (†)
Ireland	503 (2.4)	15.3 (0.96)	# (†)	2.7 (0.38)	12.4 (0.78)	26.4 (0.94)	31.1 (0.87)	20.1 (0.82)	7.1 (0.47)	6.3 (0.41)	0.8 (0.16)
Israel	467 (3.4)	31.4 (1.36)	2.1 (0.37)	9.5 (0.75)	19.9 (0.88)	24.4 (0.82)	23.3 (0.98)	15.0 (0.82)	5.8 (0.46)	5.1 (0.45)	0.7 (0.14)
Italy	481 (2.5)	23.2 (1.02)	0.6 (0.17)	5.4 (0.55)	17.2 (0.79)	27.1 (0.95)	28.6 (1.04)	17.0 (0.75)	4.1 (0.38)	3.8 (0.36)	# (†)
Japan	538 (3.0)	9.6 (0.70)	‡ (†)	1.7 (0.28)	7.7 (0.57)	18.1 (0.80)	28.2 (0.87)	28.8 (0.93)	15.3 (1.04)	12.9 (0.80)	2.4 (0.40)
Korea, Republic of	516 (3.1)	14.4 (0.91)	# (†)	2.9 (0.36)	11.1 (0.70)	21.7 (0.95)	29.2 (0.92)	24.0 (1.00)	10.6 (0.80)	9.2 (0.71)	1.4 (0.25)
Latvia	490 (1.6)	17.2 (0.75)	‡ (†)	2.6 (0.30)	14.5 (0.68)	29.8 (0.81)	31.7 (0.82)	17.4 (0.77)	3.8 (0.36)	3.5 (0.36)	# (†)
Luxembourg	483 (1.1)	25.9 (0.71)	0.5 (0.14)	6.4 (0.48)	18.9 (0.59)	24.8 (0.74)	25.1 (0.72)	17.3 (0.63)	6.9 (0.40)	6.0 (0.39)	0.9 (0.17)
Mexico	416 (2.1)	47.8 (1.29)	1.1 (0.27)	11.7 (0.74)	35.0 (1.00)	34.7 (0.89)	15.1 (0.89)	2.3 (0.29)	# (†)	# (†)	# (†)
Netherlands	509 (2.3)	18.5 (0.97)	# (†)	4.0 (0.45)	14.3 (0.73)	21.8 (0.88)	26.1 (0.86)	22.4 (0.80)	11.1 (0.58)	9.5 (0.53)	1.6 (0.23)
New Zealand	513 (2.4)	17.4 (0.90)	# (†)	4.0 (0.37)	13.0 (0.77)	21.6 (0.78)	26.3 (0.79)	21.8 (0.79)	12.8 (0.70)	10.1 (0.63)	2.7 (0.37)
Norway	498 (2.3)	18.7 (0.81)	0.6 (0.15)	4.1 (0.40)	14.0 (0.68)	24.6 (0.76)	29.1 (0.81)	19.6 (0.78)	8.0 (0.53)	6.9 (0.49)	1.1 (0.18)
Poland	501 (2.5)	16.3 (0.85)	# (†)	2.6 (0.36)	13.3 (0.70)	26.6 (0.93)	29.9 (0.93)	19.9 (0.78)	7.3 (0.63)	6.3 (0.55)	1.0 (0.19)
Portugal	501 (2.4)	17.4 (0.92)	# (†)	3.2 (0.37)	14.0 (0.85)	25.4 (0.77)	28.8 (0.84)	21.0 (0.81)	7.4 (0.51)	6.7 (0.46)	0.7 (0.15)
Slovak Republic	461 (2.6)	30.7 (1.10)	2.1 (0.31)	8.9 (0.73)	19.7 (0.81)	27.6 (0.79)	24.8 (0.72)	13.3 (0.64)	3.6 (0.37)	3.3 (0.34)	# (†)
Slovenia	513 (1.3)	15.0 (0.50)	# (†)	2.8 (0.29)	11.9 (0.51)	23.3 (0.72)	29.1 (0.87)	22.1 (0.84)	10.6 (0.57)	9.1 (0.58)	1.5 (0.29)
Spain	493 (2.1)	18.3 (0.80)	# (†)	3.7 (0.42)	14.3 (0.70)	26.5 (0.71)	31.3 (0.73)	18.9 (0.73)	5.0 (0.38)	4.7 (0.37)	# (†)
Sweden	493 (3.6)	21.6 (1.15)	0.9 (0.18)	5.7 (0.53)	15.0 (0.91)	24.0 (0.86)	26.8 (0.88)	19.0 (0.87)	8.5 (0.72)	7.2 (0.61)	1.3 (0.24)
Switzerland	506 (2.9)	18.5 (1.06)	0.5! (0.16)	4.0 (0.48)	13.9 (0.79)	22.8 (0.82)	26.3 (1.08)	22.7 (1.02)	9.8 (0.65)	8.6 (0.62)	1.1 (0.22)
Turkey	425 (3.9)	44.5 (2.10)	1.1 (0.25)	11.8 (0.98)	31.6 (1.47)	31.3 (1.32)	19.1 (1.38)	4.8 (0.86)	# (†)	# (†)	‡ (†)
United Kingdom	509 (2.6)	17.4 (0.80)	# (†)	3.4 (0.30)	13.6 (0.68)	22.6 (0.72)	27.5 (0.70)	21.6 (0.69)	10.9 (0.67)	9.1 (0.60)	1.8 (0.23)
United States	496 (3.2)	20.3 (1.07)	0.5 (0.14)	4.3 (0.47)	15.5 (0.78)	25.5 (0.78)	26.6 (0.89)	19.1 (0.93)	8.5 (0.64)	7.3 (0.55)	1.2 (0.22)
Non-OECD education systems											
Albania	427 (3.3)	41.7 (1.68)	1.6 (0.29)	10.3 (0.77)	29.8 (1.23)	34.5 (0.99)	18.9 (1.31)	4.5 (0.58)	# (†)	# (†)	‡ (†)
Algeria	376 (2.6)	70.8 (1.42)	3.9 (0.50)	24.1 (1.04)	42.8 (1.01)	22.7 (1.07)	5.6 (0.62)	0.9 (0.22)	‡ (†)	‡ (†)	‡ (†)
Beijing, Shanghai, Jiangsu, Guangdong (China)	518 (4.6)	16.2 (1.29)	0.6! (0.19)	3.8 (0.50)	11.8 (0.91)	20.7 (1.08)	25.8 (1.06)	23.8 (1.12)	13.6 (1.38)	11.5 (1.08)	2.1 (0.47)
Brazil	401 (2.3)	56.6 (1.08)	4.4 (0.31)	19.9 (0.63)	32.4 (0.62)	25.4 (0.59)	13.1 (0.60)	4.2 (0.40)	0.7 (0.13)	0.6 (0.13)	‡ (†)
Buenos Aires (Argentina)	475 (6.3)	22.7 (2.41)	‡ (†)	4.8 (0.88)	17.2 (1.78)	30.8 (1.87)	29.0 (1.86)	14.9 (1.81)	2.7 (0.77)	2.6 (0.73)	‡ (†)
Bulgaria	446 (4.4)	37.9 (1.88)	2.7 (0.41)	12.4 (1.01)	22.8 (1.08)	25.2 (1.12)	22.6 (1.17)	11.4 (0.91)	2.9 (0.44)	2.7 (0.39)	‡ (†)
Chinese Taipei	532 (2.7)	12.4 (0.79)	# (†)	2.7 (0.35)	9.4 (0.63)	18.1 (0.63)	27.0 (0.92)	27.1 (0.80)	15.4 (1.08)	12.7 (0.76)	2.7 (0.47)
Colombia	416 (2.4)	49.0 (1.32)	1.7 (0.32)	14.5 (0.91)	32.8 (0.89)	30.6 (0.92)	15.9 (0.71)	4.1 (0.36)	# (†)	# (†)	‡ (†)
Costa Rica	420 (2.1)	46.4 (1.23)	0.7 (0.19)	10.1 (0.64)	35.6 (0.99)	35.5 (0.83)	15.2 (0.87)	2.7 (0.36)	‡ (†)	‡ (†)	‡ (†)
Croatia	475 (2.5)	24.6 (1.18)	# (†)	5.1 (0.48)	19.2 (1.00)	29.5 (0.85)	27.5 (0.99)	14.4 (0.74)	3.9 (0.39)	3.6 (0.38)	# (†)

See notes at end of table.

Table 602.70. Average science literacy scores of 15-year-old students and percentage attaining science literacy proficiency levels, by country or other education system: 2015—Continued

[Standard errors appear in parentheses]

Country or other education system	Average science literacy score[1]	Percentage attaining science literacy proficiency levels[2]									
		Below level 2							At or above level 5		
		Total below level 2	Below level 1b	At level 1b	At level 1a	At level 2	At level 3	At level 4	Total at or above level 5	At level 5	At level 6
1	2	3	4	5	6	7	8	9	10	11	12
Cyprus	433 (1.4)	42.1 (0.82)	2.3 (0.28)	12.9 (0.56)	26.9 (0.82)	28.6 (0.77)	19.6 (0.68)	8.1 (0.43)	1.6 (0.23)	1.5 (0.25)	‡ (†)
Dominican Republic	332 (2.6)	85.7 (1.12)	15.8 (1.03)	39.6 (1.28)	30.4 (1.31)	11.3 (0.85)	2.6 (0.48)	0.3! (0.14)	‡ (†)	‡ (†)	# (†)
Georgia	411 (2.4)	50.8 (1.28)	4.2 (0.44)	16.0 (0.93)	30.5 (1.07)	28.2 (1.02)	15.2 (0.69)	4.9 (0.49)	0.9 (0.21)	0.8 (0.20)	‡ (†)
Hong Kong (China)	523 (2.5)	9.4 (0.75)	‡ (†)	1.6 (0.29)	7.8 (0.63)	19.7 (0.87)	36.1 (0.91)	27.4 (1.08)	7.4 (0.65)	6.9 (0.64)	# (†)
Indonesia	403 (2.6)	56.0 (1.65)	1.2! (0.36)	14.4 (1.11)	40.4 (1.47)	31.7 (1.26)	10.6 (0.82)	1.6 (0.30)	‡ (†)	‡ (†)	# (†)
Jordan	409 (2.7)	49.8 (1.44)	4.2 (0.51)	15.2 (0.89)	30.4 (0.85)	30.9 (0.97)	16.1 (0.85)	3.1 (0.37)	# (†)	# (†)	# (†)
Kosovo	378 (1.7)	67.7 (1.08)	4.0 (0.48)	24.4 (0.98)	39.3 (1.12)	24.4 (1.02)	7.2 (0.68)	0.7 (0.18)	‡ (†)	‡ (†)	# (†)
Lebanon	386 (3.4)	62.6 (1.74)	6.8 (0.74)	23.6 (1.30)	32.3 (1.23)	22.0 (1.17)	11.6 (0.94)	3.3 (0.43)	# (†)	# (†)	‡ (†)
Lithuania	475 (2.7)	24.7 (1.07)	0.5 (0.13)	5.4 (0.49)	18.9 (0.85)	29.7 (0.87)	26.3 (0.71)	15.1 (0.70)	4.2 (0.50)	3.9 (0.47)	# (†)
Macao (China)	529 (1.1)	8.1 (0.41)	‡ (†)	1.1 (0.21)	6.9 (0.42)	20.6 (0.65)	34.2 (0.90)	28.0 (0.75)	9.2 (0.48)	8.3 (0.52)	0.9 (0.22)
Macedonia, Republic of	384 (1.2)	62.9 (0.76)	6.8 (0.49)	22.3 (0.81)	33.8 (0.90)	24.6 (0.72)	10.3 (0.54)	2.0 (0.31)	# (†)	# (†)	‡ (†)
Malta	465 (1.6)	32.5 (0.77)	3.9 (0.40)	10.6 (0.67)	18.0 (0.86)	23.4 (0.81)	21.7 (0.90)	14.8 (0.89)	7.6 (0.48)	6.1 (0.40)	1.6 (0.26)
Massachusetts[4] (USA)	529 (6.6)	12.0 (1.38)	‡ (†)	2.2 (0.55)	9.6 (1.26)	19.2 (1.78)	29.3 (1.78)	25.3 (1.89)	14.2 (1.68)	11.4 (1.52)	2.8 (0.72)
Moldova, Republic of	428 (2.0)	42.2 (1.11)	2.3 (0.31)	11.8 (0.61)	28.2 (0.82)	31.5 (1.20)	19.7 (0.91)	5.9 (0.56)	0.7 (0.16)	0.7 (0.15)	‡ (†)
Montenegro, Republic of	411 (1.0)	51.0 (0.66)	3.1 (0.27)	15.8 (0.49)	32.1 (0.69)	29.0 (0.62)	15.1 (0.51)	4.4 (0.33)	# (†)	# (†)	‡ (†)
North Carolina[4] (USA)	502 (4.9)	18.0 (1.60)	‡ (†)	3.4 (0.67)	14.3 (1.45)	25.4 (1.51)	27.0 (1.35)	20.5 (1.54)	9.2 (0.97)	8.2 (0.91)	1.0! (0.34)
Peru	397 (2.4)	58.5 (1.40)	2.8 (0.35)	19.0 (0.82)	36.7 (1.02)	27.9 (0.97)	11.5 (0.74)	2.0 (0.30)	# (†)	# (†)	# (†)
Puerto Rico (USA)	403 (6.1)	55.3 (3.01)	3.6 (0.90)	19.5 (2.17)	32.3 (1.88)	26.7 (2.00)	13.5 (1.74)	4.1 (0.85)	‡ (†)	‡ (†)	# (†)
Qatar	418 (1.0)	49.8 (0.47)	3.9 (0.25)	17.9 (0.47)	28.0 (0.64)	24.6 (0.45)	16.4 (0.49)	7.5 (0.30)	1.7 (0.16)	1.6 (0.14)	# (†)
Romania	435 (3.2)	38.5 (1.81)	0.9 (0.24)	9.3 (0.87)	28.4 (1.39)	35.0 (1.35)	19.9 (1.04)	5.9 (0.71)	0.7 (0.19)	0.7 (0.19)	‡ (†)
Russian Federation	487 (2.9)	18.2 (1.12)	‡ (†)	2.9 (0.43)	15.2 (0.98)	31.2 (0.90)	30.9 (0.86)	16.0 (0.85)	3.7 (0.40)	3.5 (0.38)	# (†)
Singapore	556 (1.2)	9.6 (0.40)	# (†)	2.0 (0.22)	7.5 (0.46)	15.1 (0.46)	23.4 (0.62)	27.7 (0.65)	24.2 (0.60)	18.6 (0.67)	5.6 (0.42)
Thailand	421 (2.8)	46.7 (1.48)	1.1 (0.21)	11.9 (0.75)	33.7 (1.07)	32.2 (0.90)	16.0 (0.82)	4.6 (0.61)	# (†)	# (†)	‡ (†)
Trinidad and Tobago	425 (1.4)	45.8 (0.80)	2.9 (0.46)	15.0 (0.71)	27.9 (0.92)	27.1 (0.82)	18.3 (0.65)	7.3 (0.54)	1.4 (0.23)	1.3 (0.24)	‡ (†)
Tunisia	386 (2.1)	65.9 (1.26)	1.6 (0.31)	20.0 (1.06)	44.2 (1.06)	26.6 (1.15)	6.8 (0.63)	0.7! (0.26)	‡ (†)	‡ (†)	# (†)
United Arab Emirates	437 (2.4)	41.8 (1.11)	2.6 (0.29)	13.0 (0.61)	26.1 (0.71)	26.9 (0.62)	19.0 (0.66)	9.5 (0.53)	2.8 (0.21)	2.5 (0.20)	# (†)
Uruguay	435 (2.2)	40.8 (1.13)	1.2 (0.23)	11.2 (0.78)	28.4 (0.93)	30.3 (0.83)	20.3 (0.76)	7.4 (0.54)	1.3 (0.23)	1.2 (0.21)	‡ (†)
Vietnam	525 (3.9)	5.9 (0.76)	‡ (†)	‡ (†)	5.7 (0.73)	25.3 (1.41)	36.6 (1.21)	23.9 (1.22)	8.3 (1.22)	7.1 (0.84)	1.2! (0.46)

†Not applicable.
#Rounds to zero.
!Interpret data with caution. The coefficient of variation (CV) for this estimate is between 30 and 50 percent.
‡Reporting standards not met. The coefficient of variation (CV) for this estimate is 50 percent or greater.
[1]Program for International Student Assessment (PISA) scores are reported on a scale from 0 to 1,000.
[2]To reach a particular proficiency level, a student must correctly answer a majority of items at that level. Students were classified into science literacy levels according to their scores. Exact cut scores are as follows: below level 1b (a score less than 260.54); level 1b (a score of at least 260.54 but less than 334.94); level 1a (a score of at least 334.94 but less than 409.54); level 2 (a score of at least 409.54 but less than 484.14); level 3 (a score of at least 484.14 but less than 558.73); level 4 (a score of at least 558.73 but less than 633.33); level 5 (a score of at least 633.33 but less than 707.93); and level 6 (a score of at least 707.93).
[3]Refers to the mean of the data values for all Organization for Economic Cooperation and Development (OECD) countries, to which each country contributes equally, regardless of the absolute size of the student population of each country.
[4]Results are for public school students only.
NOTE: Detail may not sum to totals because of rounding.
SOURCE: Organization for Economic Cooperation and Development (OECD), Program for International Student Assessment (PISA), 2015. (This table was prepared December 2016.)

Table 603.10. Percentage of the population 25 to 64 years old who completed high school, by age group and country: Selected years, 2000 through 2017

[Standard errors appear in parentheses]

Country	2000		2005		2010		2015		2016		2017				
	Total, 25 to 64 years old	25 to 34 years old	Total, 25 to 64 years old	25 to 34 years old	Total, 25 to 64 years old	25 to 34 years old	Total, 25 to 64 years old	25 to 34 years old	Total, 25 to 64 years old	25 to 34 years old	Total, 25 to 64 years old	25 to 34 years old	35 to 44 years old	45 to 54 years old	55 to 64 years old
1	2	3	4	5	6	7	8	9	10	11	12	13	14	15	16
OECD average[1]	**65.7**	**75.8**	**71.2**	**79.5**	**75.0 (0.06)**	**81.7 (0.12)**	**77.6 (0.03)**	**83.8 (0.07)**	**78.8 (0.03)**	**84.3 (0.06)**	**79.3 (0.03)**	**84.8 (0.06)**	**82.5 (0.06)**	**78.0 (0.06)**	**71.0 (0.07)**
Australia	58.8	68.3	65.0	78.6	73.2 (—)	84.8 (—)	79.0 (0.25)	88.1 (0.39)	79.9 (0.24)	88.6 (0.38)	81.0 (0.23)	89.4 (0.36)	87.1 (0.39)	77.0 (0.49)	67.5 (0.58)
Austria[2]	—	—	76.9	85.6	82.4 (0.12)	87.8 (0.23)	84.6 (0.12)	90.0 (0.22)	84.5 (0.12)	88.6 (0.22)	85.0 (0.11)	88.5 (0.22)	87.7 (0.22)	84.2 (0.21)	79.4 (0.25)
Belgium	58.5	75.3	66.1	80.9	70.5 (—)	82.1 (—)	74.7 (0.19)	82.5 (0.35)	75.1 (0.19)	82.8 (0.35)	76.8 (0.15)	83.4 (0.29)	83.0 (0.27)	76.6 (0.28)	64.2 (0.32)
Canada[2,3]	80.7	88.3	85.2	90.8	88.3 (0.12)	92.1 (0.19)	90.4 (0.11)	93.3 (0.17)	90.6 (0.11)	93.1 (0.17)	91.1 (0.12)	93.5 (0.18)	93.8 (0.17)	91.0 (0.22)	86.3 (0.24)
Chile	—	—	—	—	— (†)	— (†)	64.9 (0.13)	83.2 (0.20)	— (†)	— (†)	— (†)	— (†)	— (†)	— (†)	— (†)
Czech Republic	85.9	92.4	89.9	93.9	91.9 (—)	94.2 (—)	93.2 (0.07)	93.7 (0.16)	93.4 (0.07)	93.4 (0.17)	93.8 (0.07)	94.0 (0.16)	95.6 (0.12)	94.6 (0.13)	90.4 (0.17)
Denmark	79.8	86.9	81.0	87.4	75.6 (—)	79.6 (—)	80.4 (0.17)	83.6 (0.36)	80.7 (0.18)	83.4 (0.38)	81.3 (0.18)	83.3 (0.37)	85.7 (0.34)	81.8 (0.33)	74.6 (0.36)
Estonia[2]	85.2	91.4	88.7	87.3	89.1 (0.30)	86.5 (0.73)	88.6 (0.28)	87.7 (0.60)	88.9 (0.27)	87.5 (0.60)	88.7 (0.26)	87.2 (0.57)	86.9 (0.54)	92.0 (0.42)	88.8 (0.50)
Finland[2]	73.2	86.3	78.8	89.4	83.0 (—)	90.8 (—)	87.2 (0.21)	89.5 (0.42)	87.9 (0.13)	90.1 (0.24)	88.1 (0.13)	90.2 (0.25)	91.1 (0.23)	88.7 (0.25)	82.9 (0.28)
France[2]	62.2	76.4	66.8	81.5	70.8 (—)	83.8 (—)	77.5 (0.08)	86.5 (0.15)	78.1 (0.08)	86.7 (0.15)	78.4 (0.08)	86.2 (0.15)	84.1 (0.15)	77.1 (0.16)	66.7 (0.18)
Germany	81.7	84.9	83.1	84.1	85.8 (—)	86.5 (—)	86.8 (0.06)	87.3 (0.12)	86.5 (0.05)	87.0 (0.11)	86.5 (0.05)	86.9 (0.11)	85.8 (0.12)	87.2 (0.10)	86.1 (0.10)
Greece	49.3	68.7	57.7	74.4	62.7 (0.12)	75.5 (0.22)	70.2 (0.13)	83.6 (0.24)	71.7 (0.13)	84.5 (0.24)	72.7 (0.13)	85.7 (0.24)	79.4 (0.22)	70.1 (0.24)	55.8 (0.26)
Hungary[2]	69.2	81.3	76.4	85.0	81.3 (—)	86.3 (—)	83.2 (0.10)	86.0 (0.21)	83.4 (0.11)	85.5 (0.23)	84.0 (0.11)	86.0 (0.23)	86.2 (0.20)	84.1 (0.21)	79.5 (0.22)
Iceland[2]	—	—	68.2	70.9	70.7 (0.48)	73.6 (0.91)	74.7 (0.47)	75.2 (0.96)	78.0 (0.46)	80.0 (0.94)	77.1 (0.49)	80.7 (0.98)	79.7 (0.94)	77.5 (0.94)	69.7 (1.03)
Ireland	57.3	73.0	64.5	81.1	72.8 (—)	85.6 (—)	79.8 (0.13)	90.8 (0.19)	— (†)	— (†)	82.0 (0.14)	91.9 (0.22)	88.3 (0.22)	78.7 (0.29)	64.9 (0.36)
Israel	—	—	78.9	85.5	82.1 (—)	88.1 (—)	85.5 (—)	91.2 (—)	86.8 (0.09)	91.8 (0.14)	87.4 (0.09)	92.4 (0.13)	89.2 (0.15)	85.1 (0.19)	80.2 (0.22)
Italy	42.1	56.4	50.1	65.9	55.2 (—)	71.0 (—)	59.9 (0.09)	74.4 (0.19)	60.1 (0.09)	73.9 (0.19)	60.9 (0.09)	74.8 (0.19)	66.7 (0.18)	55.4 (0.17)	49.7 (0.18)
Japan	—	—	—	—	— (†)	— (†)	— (†)	— (†)	— (†)	— (†)	— (†)	— (†)	— (†)	— (†)	— (†)
Korea, Republic of[4]	68.2	93.2	75.6	97.3	80.9 (—)	97.9 (—)	85.8 (—)	98.3 (—)	86.8 (0.17)	98.3 (0.12)	87.6 (0.17)	98.0 (0.13)	97.7 (0.14)	90.5 (0.28)	63.5 (0.61)
Latvia[2]	83.2	88.7	84.4	80.4	88.6 (0.23)	83.7 (0.57)	87.8 (0.23)	84.9 (0.56)	88.7 (0.22)	86.7 (0.52)	87.6 (0.22)	85.4 (0.54)	83.1 (0.53)	92.3 (0.34)	89.4 (0.38)
Lithuania	84.2	91.8	87.5	86.8	91.9 (0.14)	88.3 (0.41)	91.4 (0.16)	89.7 (0.43)	92.5 (0.15)	92.2 (0.38)	92.8 (0.14)	92.9 (0.35)	87.5 (0.39)	95.4 (0.20)	94.8 (0.21)
Luxembourg	60.9	68.2	65.9	76.5	77.7 (—)	84.0 (—)	74.6 (0.33)	84.5 (0.59)	78.8 (0.39)	86.6 (0.73)	76.7 (0.36)	87.3 (0.65)	81.7 (0.68)	70.7 (0.70)	63.0 (0.82)
Mexico[2]	29.1	37.1	28.2	33.7	32.1 (0.11)	38.3 (0.20)	35.7 (0.11)	45.0 (0.21)	36.6 (0.11)	46.7 (0.21)	37.7 (0.11)	48.1 (0.21)	36.5 (0.21)	33.8 (0.22)	27.0 (0.25)
Netherlands[4]	64.9	74.3	71.8	81.3	73.0 (—)	82.7 (—)	76.4 (—)	85.6 (—)	77.1 (0.20)	85.8 (0.40)	78.4 (0.09)	86.7 (0.17)	83.2 (0.18)	77.4 (0.16)	67.2 (0.18)
New Zealand	—	—	—	—	— (†)	— (†)	74.7 (—)	81.0 (—)	76.6 (0.31)	83.7 (0.57)	78.9 (0.30)	85.0 (0.55)	83.0 (0.56)	75.9 (0.61)	70.7 (0.68)
Norway[2]	—	—	77.2	83.5	80.6 (—)	82.9 (—)	82.4 (0.17)	81.3 (0.35)	82.2 (0.16)	81.2 (0.35)	82.0 (0.16)	80.7 (0.34)	85.6 (0.30)	82.1 (0.31)	79.1 (0.35)
Poland[4]	79.9	89.4	85.1	92.0	88.5 (—)	93.6 (—)	90.8 (—)	93.9 (—)	91.3 (0.07)	94.2 (0.12)	92.1 (0.07)	94.5 (0.12)	94.3 (0.11)	92.5 (0.14)	87.1 (0.15)
Portugal[2]	19.4	31.8	26.5	42.8	31.9 (—)	52.1 (—)	45.1 (0.17)	66.7 (0.39)	46.9 (0.17)	69.5 (0.40)	48.0 (0.17)	69.6 (0.41)	58.6 (0.33)	40.3 (0.31)	26.6 (0.29)
Slovak Republic	83.8	93.7	87.9	92.8	91.0 (—)	94.1 (—)	91.3 (0.25)	92.8 (0.49)	91.7 (0.24)	93.4 (0.48)	91.3 (0.26)	91.3 (0.57)	93.3 (0.46)	91.8 (0.50)	88.4 (0.53)
Slovenia[4]	74.8	85.4	80.3	91.2	83.3 (—)	93.5 (—)	86.8 (0.18)	94.1 (0.27)	87.3 (0.18)	94.1 (0.27)	87.7 (0.17)	94.4 (0.27)	93.2 (0.28)	83.9 (0.37)	78.7 (0.40)
Spain[2]	38.6	55.6	48.8	64.5	52.9 (0.08)	65.3 (0.16)	57.4 (0.08)	65.6 (0.19)	58.3 (0.08)	65.3 (0.19)	59.1 (0.08)	66.2 (0.20)	67.2 (0.16)	57.0 (0.16)	44.4 (0.16)
Sweden	77.6	87.3	83.6	90.6	86.3 (0.08)	90.8 (0.14)	82.0 (0.10)	82.3 (0.20)	82.7 (0.10)	83.1 (0.20)	83.0 (0.10)	83.0 (0.20)	85.1 (0.18)	85.6 (0.17)	77.7 (0.21)
Switzerland	83.9	89.8	85.2	89.8	85.0 (0.12)	87.8 (0.26)	87.3 (0.11)	91.0 (0.24)	87.4 (0.12)	91.4 (0.24)	87.8 (0.12)	91.9 (0.23)	88.6 (0.22)	86.8 (0.21)	83.7 (0.26)
Turkey[4]	23.3	27.7	28.1	36.8	31.2 (—)	42.2 (—)	37.0 (—)	52.1 (—)	38.5 (0.10)	54.7 (0.21)	39.3 (0.10)	55.5 (0.19)	40.9 (0.18)	26.2 (0.17)	23.3 (0.18)
United Kingdom[5]	62.6	66.8	66.8	73.1	75.1 (—)	82.9 (—)	79.6 (0.18)	86.2 (0.33)	80.7 (0.18)	87.5 (0.32)	81.2 (0.18)	87.5 (0.32)	85.0 (0.33)	78.9 (0.36)	72.4 (0.40)
United States[2,6]	87.4	88.2	87.8	86.7	89.0 (0.10)	88.4 (0.19)	89.5 (0.10)	90.5 (0.18)	90.1 (0.10)	91.5 (0.18)	90.6 (0.09)	92.1 (0.17)	90.0 (0.19)	90.1 (0.19)	90.3 (0.20)
Other reporting countries															
China[2]	—	—	—	—	24.5 (—)	35.7 (—)	— (†)	— (†)	— (†)	— (†)	— (†)	— (†)	— (†)	— (†)	— (†)
Russian Federation[2]	—	—	—	—	93.9 (—)	94.0 (—)	94.8 (—)	95.0 (—)	94.9 (—)	95.0 (—)	— (†)	— (†)	— (†)	— (†)	— (†)

—Not available.
†Not applicable.
[1]Refers to the mean of the data values for all reporting Organization for Economic Cooperation and Development (OECD) countries, to which each country reporting data contributes equally. The average includes all current OECD countries for which a given year's data are available, even if they were not members of OECD in that year. Standard errors for the OECD average were estimated by the National Center for Education Statistics (NCES).
[2]Although all data for years prior to 2015 were originally calculated using the 1997 version of the International Standard Classification of Education (ISCED), the footnoted countries revised earlier years' data to align with the 2011 version of ISCED, which is the most recent. Most of these countries revised all of their data for years prior to 2015. The exceptions are Mexico (which revised only 2005 and 2010 data) and Spain (which revised only 2010 data).
[3]All standard errors shown for Canada were calculated by Statistics Canada.
[4]For 2016 and 2017, standard errors were estimated by NCES using population estimates provided by Eurostat.
[5]Data include some persons who completed a sufficient number of certain types of programs, any one of which individually would be classified as a program that only partially completes the high school (or upper secondary) level of education.
[6]All standard errors shown for the United States were calculated by NCES.
NOTE: The International Standard Classification of Education (ISCED) was revised in 2011. Unless otherwise noted, all data for years prior to 2015 were calculated using the previous version, ISCED 1997. ISCED 2011 was used to calculate all data for 2015 and later years. Except where otherwise noted, data in this table refer to degrees classified under ISCED 2011 as completing level 3 (upper secondary education) or to comparable degrees under ISCED 1997. For more information on OECD and NCES estimation methodology used for this table, see the "Online Education Database" section of the entry for OECD in Appendix A: Guide to Sources. Standard errors for 2000 and 2005 have been excluded due to limited data availability. Some data have been revised from previously published figures.
SOURCE: Organization for Economic Cooperation and Development (OECD), Online Education Database, retrieved September 13, 2018, from http://stats.oecd.org/Index.aspx. Eurostat, unpublished tabulations on population by age group. (This table was prepared September 2018.)

Table 603.20. Percentage of the population 25 to 64 years old who attained any postsecondary degree, by age group and country: Selected years, 2000 through 2017

[Standard errors appear in parentheses]

Country	2000		2005		2010		2015		2016		2017				
	Total, 25 to 64 years old	25 to 34 years old	Total, 25 to 64 years old	25 to 34 years old	Total, 25 to 64 years old	25 to 34 years old	Total, 25 to 64 years old	25 to 34 years old	Total, 25 to 64 years old	25 to 34 years old	Total, 25 to 64 years old	25 to 34 years old	35 to 44 years old	45 to 54 years old	55 to 64 years old
1	2	3	4	5	6	7	8	9	10	11	12	13	14	15	16
OECD average[1]	**22.3**	**26.4**	**26.5**	**32.4**	**30.6 (0.07)**	**37.7 (0.16)**	**34.7 (0.04)**	**42.2 (0.10)**	**35.8 (0.04)**	**43.4 (0.09)**	**36.9 (0.04)**	**44.5 (0.09)**	**42.1 (0.08)**	**33.4 (0.07)**	**27.2 (0.07)**
Australia	27.5	31.4	31.7	38.1	37.6 (—)	44.4 (—)	42.9 (0.30)	48.5 (0.60)	43.7 (0.30)	49.3 (0.59)	45.4 (0.30)	52.0 (0.59)	51.2 (0.58)	42.0 (0.58)	33.8 (0.58)
Austria[2]	—	—	24.6	30.6	27.7 (0.14)	33.9 (0.33)	30.6 (0.15)	38.6 (0.35)	31.4 (0.15)	39.7 (0.34)	32.4 (0.15)	40.3 (0.34)	36.8 (0.32)	29.3 (0.26)	23.4 (0.26)
Belgium	27.1	36.0	31.0	40.6	35.0 (—)	43.8 (—)	36.9 (0.21)	43.1 (0.45)	37.5 (0.21)	44.3 (0.46)	40.3 (0.17)	45.7 (0.38)	46.6 (0.35)	38.4 (0.33)	30.5 (0.31)
Canada[2,3]	40.1	48.4	46.0	53.7	50.3 (0.22)	56.2 (0.43)	55.2 (0.20)	59.2 (0.37)	56.3 (0.20)	60.6 (0.38)	56.7 (0.22)	60.9 (0.40)	63.1 (0.35)	56.6 (0.37)	46.5 (0.37)
Chile[2]	—	—	—	—	— (†)	— (†)	22.5 (0.11)	29.9 (0.24)	— (†)	— (†)	— (†)	— (†)	— (†)	— (†)	— (†)
Czech Republic	11.0	11.2	13.1	14.2	16.8 (—)	22.6 (—)	22.2 (0.12)	31.0 (0.31)	23.0 (0.13)	32.6 (0.32)	23.9 (0.13)	33.8 (0.32)	25.7 (0.25)	18.8 (0.23)	16.6 (0.21)
Denmark	25.8	29.3	33.5	39.8	33.3 (—)	37.6 (—)	37.1 (0.21)	44.5 (0.49)	38.2 (0.22)	45.9 (0.51)	39.2 (0.22)	46.6 (0.50)	45.0 (0.48)	35.7 (0.41)	30.6 (0.38)
Estonia[2]	28.7	28.7	33.0	32.9	35.4 (0.46)	38.0 (1.03)	38.0 (0.42)	40.5 (0.89)	38.8 (0.42)	41.0 (0.89)	39.7 (0.39)	43.0 (0.85)	41.9 (0.80)	36.9 (0.75)	36.4 (0.76)
Finland[2]	32.6	38.7	34.6	37.5	38.1 (—)	39.2 (—)	42.7 (0.30)	40.5 (0.68)	43.6 (0.19)	41.1 (0.40)	44.3 (0.20)	41.3 (0.41)	51.5 (0.40)	46.6 (0.39)	38.5 (0.36)
France[2]	21.6	31.4	25.4	39.8	29.0 (—)	42.9 (—)	34.1 (0.09)	44.7 (0.22)	34.6 (0.09)	44.0 (0.22)	35.2 (0.09)	44.3 (0.22)	43.7 (0.20)	30.8 (0.17)	22.8 (0.16)
Germany	23.5	22.3	24.6	22.5	26.6 (—)	26.1 (—)	27.6 (0.07)	29.6 (0.16)	28.3 (0.07)	30.5 (0.16)	28.6 (0.07)	31.3 (0.15)	30.5 (0.16)	26.9 (0.13)	26.3 (0.13)
Greece	17.7	23.9	21.5	25.7	24.7 (0.11)	31.2 (0.24)	29.1 (0.13)	40.1 (0.32)	30.2 (0.13)	41.0 (0.32)	31.0 (0.13)	42.5 (0.34)	31.8 (0.26)	28.8 (0.24)	22.0 (0.22)
Hungary[2]	14.0	14.7	17.1	19.6	20.1 (—)	26.0 (—)	24.2 (0.12)	32.1 (0.29)	23.7 (0.12)	30.4 (0.29)	24.1 (0.12)	30.2 (0.30)	27.2 (0.25)	21.1 (0.24)	17.7 (0.21)
Iceland[2]	—	—	29.5	34.5	32.6 (0.50)	36.2 (0.99)	38.8 (0.53)	40.1 (1.08)	40.5 (0.55)	43.3 (1.16)	42.4 (0.57)	47.4 (1.24)	49.0 (1.16)	41.2 (1.11)	30.3 (1.03)
Ireland	21.6	29.8	29.1	40.7	37.6 (—)	48.3 (—)	42.8 (0.16)	52.0 (0.34)	— (†)	— (†)	45.7 (0.18)	53.5 (0.40)	53.2 (0.34)	41.9 (0.35)	29.9 (0.35)
Israel	—	—	43.0	42.9	45.6 (—)	44.2 (—)	48.8 (—)	45.9 (—)	49.9 (0.13)	47.4 (0.25)	50.9 (0.13)	48.0 (0.25)	56.1 (0.24)	50.6 (0.27)	48.1 (0.28)
Italy	9.4	10.4	12.2	16.1	14.8 (—)	20.7 (—)	17.5 (0.07)	25.1 (0.19)	17.7 (0.07)	25.6 (0.19)	18.7 (0.07)	26.8 (0.20)	22.1 (0.15)	14.8 (0.12)	12.8 (0.12)
Japan[4,5]	33.6	47.8	39.9	53.2	44.8 (—)	56.7 (—)	49.5 (—)	59.6 (—)	50.5 (0.19)	60.1 (0.40)	51.4 (0.19)	60.4 (0.40)	56.4 (0.37)	48.7 (0.42)	41.1 (0.45)
Korea, Republic of[4]	23.8	36.8	31.6	50.9	39.0 (—)	61.4 (—)	45.4 (—)	68.9 (—)	46.6 (0.25)	69.9 (0.45)	47.7 (0.25)	69.8 (0.45)	62.1 (0.45)	39.6 (0.47)	21.3 (0.52)
Latvia[2]	18.2	17.3	20.3	21.7	26.9 (0.32)	34.7 (0.74)	31.6 (0.32)	39.9 (0.76)	33.4 (0.32)	42.1 (0.76)	33.9 (0.32)	41.6 (0.75)	38.5 (0.70)	28.5 (0.58)	27.1 (0.55)
Lithuania	41.8	39.7	26.5	36.9	32.4 (0.25)	46.3 (0.63)	38.7 (0.27)	54.8 (0.71)	39.7 (0.27)	54.9 (0.70)	40.3 (0.26)	55.6 (0.67)	46.0 (0.59)	32.1 (0.44)	29.5 (0.43)
Luxembourg	18.3	22.9	26.5	37.0	35.5 (—)	44.2 (—)	39.8 (0.37)	49.9 (0.82)	42.9 (0.47)	51.4 (1.07)	40.3 (0.42)	51.4 (0.98)	48.1 (0.88)	34.0 (0.73)	22.5 (0.71)
Mexico[2]	14.6	17.5	12.7	14.9	14.7 (0.08)	17.7 (0.16)	16.3 (0.08)	20.8 (0.17)	16.8 (0.09)	21.8 (0.17)	17.4 (0.09)	22.6 (0.18)	16.9 (0.16)	14.5 (0.17)	13.4 (0.19)
Netherlands[4]	23.4	26.6	30.1	35.4	32.4 (—)	40.8 (—)	35.3 (—)	45.1 (—)	36.0 (0.23)	45.2 (0.58)	37.2 (0.10)	46.6 (0.25)	42.4 (0.23)	33.2 (0.18)	27.9 (0.17)
New Zealand	—	—	—	—	— (†)	— (†)	34.0 (—)	39.1 (—)	36.3 (0.35)	43.4 (0.76)	37.7 (0.36)	44.2 (0.76)	42.0 (0.74)	34.3 (0.67)	29.5 (0.68)
Norway[2]	—	—	32.7	40.9	37.3 (—)	47.3 (—)	42.7 (0.21)	48.1 (0.45)	43.0 (0.21)	48.6 (0.45)	43.2 (0.21)	48.3 (0.43)	49.5 (0.42)	40.6 (0.39)	33.2 (0.40)
Poland[4]	11.4	14.2	16.9	25.5	22.5 (—)	37.1 (—)	27.7 (—)	43.2 (—)	28.7 (0.11)	43.5 (0.25)	29.9 (0.11)	43.5 (0.26)	37.7 (0.24)	21.3 (0.21)	15.1 (0.16)
Portugal[2]	8.8	12.9	12.8	19.1	15.4 (—)	24.8 (—)	22.9 (0.14)	33.1 (0.39)	23.8 (0.15)	35.0 (0.41)	24.0 (0.15)	34.0 (0.42)	30.8 (0.31)	19.5 (0.25)	13.2 (0.22)
Slovak Republic	10.4	11.2	14.0	16.3	17.3 (—)	24.0 (—)	21.1 (0.36)	31.3 (0.88)	22.0 (0.37)	33.4 (0.91)	23.1 (0.38)	35.1 (0.96)	23.7 (0.77)	16.0 (0.67)	15.7 (0.60)
Slovenia[4]	15.7	19.3	20.2	24.7	23.7 (—)	31.3 (—)	30.2 (0.25)	40.8 (0.57)	30.7 (0.25)	43.0 (0.57)	34.3 (0.25)	44.6 (0.58)	39.1 (0.53)	35.1 (0.49)	19.7 (0.39)
Spain[2]	22.7	34.0	28.5	40.7	31.0 (0.08)	40.3 (0.17)	35.1 (0.08)	41.0 (0.19)	35.7 (0.08)	41.0 (0.20)	36.4 (0.08)	42.6 (0.20)	43.9 (0.16)	33.6 (0.15)	24.2 (0.14)
Sweden	30.1	33.6	29.6	37.3	33.9 (0.11)	42.2 (0.23)	39.8 (0.12)	46.4 (0.26)	41.1 (0.13)	47.2 (0.26)	41.9 (0.13)	47.4 (0.26)	50.8 (0.26)	37.3 (0.24)	31.1 (0.23)
Switzerland	24.2	25.6	28.8	31.0	33.9 (0.16)	37.4 (0.39)	39.8 (0.17)	46.5 (0.41)	41.2 (0.17)	48.8 (0.42)	42.6 (0.17)	50.1 (0.42)	47.8 (0.35)	39.6 (0.31)	32.4 (0.33)
Turkey[4]	8.3	8.9	10.2	12.5	13.1 (—)	17.4 (—)	18.0 (—)	27.5 (—)	19.4 (0.08)	30.5 (0.20)	20.0 (0.08)	31.6 (0.18)	19.6 (0.15)	11.8 (0.13)	9.8 (0.13)
United Kingdom[5]	25.7	28.9	29.7	35.3	38.2 (—)	46.0 (—)	44.2 (0.23)	49.9 (0.48)	45.8 (0.23)	51.8 (0.48)	45.7 (0.23)	51.6 (0.49)	51.2 (0.46)	42.6 (0.43)	36.9 (0.44)
United States[2,6]	36.5	38.1	39.1	39.4	41.7 (0.15)	42.3 (0.30)	44.6 (0.16)	46.5 (0.31)	45.7 (0.16)	47.5 (0.32)	46.4 (0.16)	47.8 (0.32)	50.3 (0.31)	45.4 (0.32)	42.0 (0.34)
Other reporting countries															
China	—	—	—	—	9.7 (—)	17.9 (—)	— (†)	— (†)	— (†)	— (†)	— (†)	— (†)	— (†)	— (†)	— (†)
Russian Federation	—	—	—	—	50.4 (0.06)	52.5 (0.13)	52.4 (0.06)	56.3 (0.13)	53.1 (0.06)	57.6 (0.13)	— (†)	— (†)	— (†)	— (†)	— (†)

—Not available.
†Not applicable.
[1]Refers to the mean of the data values for all reporting Organization for Economic Cooperation and Development (OECD) countries, to which each country reporting data contributes equally. The average includes all current OECD countries for which a given year's data are available, even if they were not members of OECD in that year. Standard errors for the OECD average were estimated by the National Center for Education Statistics (NCES).
[2]Although all data for years prior to 2015 were originally calculated using the 1997 version of the International Standard Classification of Education (ISCED), the footnoted countries revised earlier years' data to align with the 2011 version of ISCED, which is the most recent. Most of these countries revised all of their data for years prior to 2015. The exceptions are Mexico (which revised only 2005 and 2010 data) and Spain (which revised only 2010 data).
[3]All standard errors shown for Canada were calculated by Statistics Canada.
[4]For 2016 and 2017, standard errors were estimated by NCES using population estimates provided by Eurostat.
[5]Data for all years include some postsecondary nontertiary awards (i.e., awards that are below the associate's degree level).
[6]All standard errors shown for the United States were calculated by NCES.
NOTE: Data in this table include all tertiary degrees, which correspond to all degrees at the associate's level and above in the United States. The International Standard Classification of Education (ISCED) was revised in 2011. Unless otherwise noted, all data for years prior to 2015 were calculated using the previous version, ISCED 1997. ISCED 2011 was used to calculate all data for 2015 and later years. Under ISCED 2011, tertiary degrees are classified at the following levels: level 5 (corresponding to an associate's degree in the United States), level 6 (a bachelor's or equivalent degree), level 7 (a master's or equivalent degree), and level 8 (a doctoral or equivalent degree). For more information on OECD and NCES estimation methodology used for this table, see the "Online Education Database" section of the entry for OECD in Appendix A: Guide to Sources. Standard errors for 2000 and 2005 have been excluded due to limited data availability. Some data have been revised from previously published figures.
SOURCE: Organization for Economic Cooperation and Development (OECD), Online Education Database, retrieved September 19, 2018 from http://stats.oecd.org/Index.aspx. Eurostat, unpublished tabulations on population by age group. (This table was prepared September 2018.)

Table 603.30. Percentage of the population 25 to 64 years old who attained a postsecondary degree, by highest degree attained, age group, and country: 2017

[Standard errors appear in parentheses]

Country	Associate's degree (short-cycle tertiary)					Bachelor's or equivalent degree				
	Total, 25 to 64 years old	25 to 34 years old	35 to 44 years old	45 to 54 years old	55 to 64 years old	Total, 25 to 64 years old	25 to 34 years old	35 to 44 years old	45 to 54 years old	55 to 64 years old
1	2	3	4	5	6	7	8	9	10	11
OECD average[1]	**7.4 (0.02)**	**8.0 (0.04)**	**8.0 (0.04)**	**8.2 (0.04)**	**7.1 (0.04)**	**17.0 (0.03)**	**23.2 (0.07)**	**19.0 (0.06)**	**14.1 (0.05)**	**11.3 (0.05)**
Australia	11.5 (0.19)	11.5 (0.38)	11.7 (0.38)	12.5 (0.39)	10.3 (0.38)	25.6 (0.26)	31.3 (0.55)	29.4 (0.53)	22.4 (0.49)	17.6 (0.47)
Austria	15.4 (0.11)	15.8 (0.25)	16.6 (0.25)	16.0 (0.21)	13.2 (0.21)	3.7 (0.06)	9.8 (0.21)	3.0 (0.11)	1.5 (0.07)	0.8 (0.06)
Belgium	0.5 (0.02)	0.5 (0.05)	0.5 (0.05)	0.4 (0.04)	0.5 (0.05)	22.5 (0.15)	24.7 (0.33)	24.9 (0.31)	22.2 (0.28)	18.1 (0.26)
Canada[2,3]	25.5 (0.17)	24.7 (0.31)	27.1 (0.33)	26.3 (0.30)	24.1 (0.30)	21.2 (0.17)	25.9 (0.36)	24.1 (0.34)	20.3 (0.31)	14.8 (0.26)
Chile[2,4]	7.9 (0.07)	8.7 (0.15)	9.0 (0.16)	8.1 (0.14)	5.4 (0.13)	13.3 (0.09)	20.0 (0.21)	14.2 (0.19)	8.6 (0.15)	9.3 (0.17)
Czech Republic	0.1 (0.01)	0.1 (0.02)	0.1 (0.02)	0.1 (0.02)	0.1 (0.02)	5.8 (0.07)	12.6 (0.22)	6.4 (0.14)	2.5 (0.09)	1.6 (0.07)
Denmark	4.9 (0.10)	5.1 (0.22)	5.3 (0.22)	5.2 (0.19)	4.0 (0.16)	20.6 (0.18)	23.3 (0.42)	21.6 (0.39)	19.2 (0.34)	18.7 (0.32)
Estonia	6.4 (0.20)	0.2! (0.07)	5.6 (0.37)	8.5 (0.43)	12.1 (0.51)	12.2 (0.26)	26.0 (0.75)	13.2 (0.55)	6.5 (0.38)	1.7 (0.20)
Finland	11.5 (0.13)	‡ (†)	5.8 (0.19)	19.5 (0.31)	20.0 (0.29)	16.9 (0.15)	27.0 (0.37)	24.1 (0.35)	10.5 (0.24)	7.1 (0.19)
France	14.2 (0.07)	14.1 (0.16)	18.2 (0.16)	13.9 (0.13)	10.6 (0.12)	9.7 (0.06)	12.0 (0.15)	12.4 (0.13)	8.9 (0.11)	5.7 (0.09)
Germany	0.5 (0.01)	0.3 (0.02)	0.4 (0.02)	0.7 (0.02)	0.6 (0.02)	15.2 (0.06)	16.5 (0.12)	14.8 (0.12)	14.9 (0.10)	14.6 (0.11)
Greece	1.8 (0.04)	1.1 (0.07)	1.1 (0.06)	2.2 (0.08)	2.7 (0.08)	25.6 (0.12)	36.5 (0.33)	25.6 (0.24)	23.4 (0.22)	17.8 (0.20)
Hungary	1.3 (0.03)	2.7 (0.11)	1.3 (0.06)	0.8 (0.05)	0.4 (0.03)	13.2 (0.10)	14.6 (0.23)	15.4 (0.20)	12.0 (0.19)	10.6 (0.17)
Iceland	2.7 (0.19)	1.5 (0.31)	2.4 (0.35)	3.5 (0.42)	3.6 (0.42)	21.3 (0.48)	27.2 (1.11)	24.5 (1.00)	18.8 (0.88)	13.5 (0.77)
Ireland	9.8 (0.11)	8.3 (0.22)	11.3 (0.22)	10.7 (0.22)	8.3 (0.21)	24.7 (0.16)	32.3 (0.37)	27.5 (0.30)	21.4 (0.29)	15.5 (0.28)
Israel	14.3 (0.09)	11.9 (0.16)	14.0 (0.17)	15.5 (0.19)	16.7 (0.21)	23.3 (0.11)	28.2 (0.23)	26.5 (0.22)	19.0 (0.21)	16.7 (0.21)
Italy	# (†)	# (†)	‡ (†)	— (†)	— (†)	4.3 (0.04)	11.1 (0.14)	4.0 (0.07)	2.1 (0.05)	1.5 (0.04)
Japan[5,6,7]	21.2 (0.16)	20.2 (0.33)	24.8 (0.33)	22.4 (0.35)	16.7 (0.34)	30.2 (0.18)	40.2 (0.40)	31.5 (0.35)	26.3 (0.37)	24.3 (0.39)
Korea, Republic of[5,7]	13.5 (0.17)	21.4 (0.40)	19.8 (0.37)	9.2 (0.28)	4.3 (0.26)	34.2 (0.24)	48.3 (0.49)	42.3 (0.46)	30.3 (0.45)	17.0 (0.48)
Latvia	3.0 (0.12)	5.7 (0.35)	3.1 (0.25)	2.1 (0.18)	1.2 (0.13)	18.5 (0.26)	24.2 (0.65)	21.2 (0.58)	15.1 (0.46)	13.7 (0.43)
Lithuania	† (†)	† (†)	† (†)	† (†)	† (†)	25.8 (0.23)	39.9 (0.66)	31.2 (0.55)	18.9 (0.37)	15.3 (0.34)
Luxembourg	2.8 (0.14)	1.8 (0.26)	3.2 (0.31)	3.8 (0.29)	2.4 (0.26)	11.7 (0.28)	16.7 (0.73)	12.6 (0.58)	9.3 (0.45)	6.9 (0.43)
Mexico	0.5 (0.02)	0.6 (0.03)	0.5 (0.03)	0.5 (0.03)	0.3 (0.03)	15.4 (0.08)	20.7 (0.17)	14.6 (0.15)	12.3 (0.15)	11.6 (0.18)
Netherlands[5]	2.2 (0.03)	1.4 (0.06)	2.5 (0.07)	2.6 (0.06)	2.4 (0.06)	21.3 (0.09)	27.4 (0.22)	24.1 (0.20)	18.2 (0.15)	16.4 (0.14)
New Zealand	4.0 (0.15)	3.7 (0.29)	3.2 (0.26)	4.0 (0.28)	5.1 (0.33)	27.9 (0.33)	34.9 (0.73)	32.0 (0.70)	24.2 (0.61)	19.4 (0.59)
Norway	11.8 (0.14)	12.7 (0.29)	12.0 (0.27)	12.1 (0.26)	10.2 (0.26)	19.0 (0.17)	21.0 (0.35)	22.0 (0.35)	17.5 (0.30)	15.3 (0.31)
Poland[5]	0.1 (0.01)	# (†)	0.1 (0.02)	0.1 (0.02)	0.2 (0.02)	6.7 (0.06)	12.5 (0.17)	7.4 (0.13)	3.7 (0.10)	2.5 (0.07)
Portugal	‡ (†)	‡ (†)	‡ (†)	‡ (†)	— (†)	6.1 (0.08)	16.3 (0.33)	4.8 (0.14)	3.1 (0.11)	2.4 (0.10)
Slovak Republic	0.2 (0.04)	‡ (†)	0.2! (0.08)	‡ (†)	0.2! (0.07)	2.6 (0.14)	6.0 (0.48)	2.1 (0.26)	1.2 (0.20)	0.8 (0.14)
Slovenia[5]	7.5 (0.14)	7.4 (0.30)	7.1 (0.28)	7.7 (0.27)	7.8 (0.26)	7.0 (0.13)	11.1 (0.37)	8.9 (0.31)	5.1 (0.22)	2.7 (0.16)
Spain	11.2 (0.05)	13.2 (0.14)	14.1 (0.12)	10.9 (0.10)	6.1 (0.08)	9.8 (0.05)	13.0 (0.14)	11.2 (0.10)	8.2 (0.09)	7.3 (0.09)
Sweden	9.8 (0.08)	11.1 (0.16)	8.5 (0.14)	9.4 (0.14)	10.1 (0.15)	17.0 (0.10)	22.6 (0.22)	20.5 (0.21)	13.8 (0.17)	10.3 (0.15)
Switzerland[8]	[8] (†)	[8] (†)	[8] (†)	[8] (†)	[8] (†)	21.0 (0.14)	27.0 (0.37)	22.2 (0.29)	19.1 (0.25)	15.5 (0.25)
Turkey[5]	5.5 (0.05)	8.4 (0.11)	4.8 (0.08)	3.5 (0.07)	3.9 (0.08)	12.4 (0.07)	20.4 (0.16)	12.3 (0.12)	6.8 (0.10)	5.0 (0.10)
United Kingdom	10.0 (0.14)	7.6 (0.26)	9.4 (0.27)	11.6 (0.28)	11.7 (0.29)	22.6 (0.19)	29.5 (0.44)	25.8 (0.41)	19.0 (0.34)	15.5 (0.33)
United States[9]	10.9 (0.10)	10.5 (0.20)	10.8 (0.19)	11.2 (0.20)	11.0 (0.21)	22.5 (0.14)	25.7 (0.28)	24.0 (0.27)	21.1 (0.26)	19.1 (0.27)

See notes at end of table.

Table 603.30. Percentage of the population 25 to 64 years old who attained a postsecondary degree, by highest degree attained, age group, and country: 2017—Continued

[Standard errors appear in parentheses]

Country	Master's or equivalent degree										Doctoral or equivalent degree									
	Total, 25 to 64 years old		25 to 34 years old		35 to 44 years old		45 to 54 years old		55 to 64 years old		Total, 25 to 64 years old		25 to 34 years old		35 to 44 years old		45 to 54 years old		55 to 64 years old	
1		12		13		14		15		16		17		18		19		20		21
OECD average[1]	**12.5**	**(0.03)**	**14.5**	**(0.07)**	**15.2**	**(0.06)**	**11.3**	**(0.05)**	**8.9**	**(0.05)**	**1.1**	**(0.01)**	**0.8**	**(0.02)**	**1.4**	**(0.02)**	**1.2**	**(0.02)**	**1.0**	**(0.02)**
Australia	6.9	(0.15)	8.3	(0.33)	8.7	(0.33)	5.5	(0.27)	4.4	(0.25)	1.3	(0.07)	0.8	(0.11)	1.5	(0.14)	1.7	(0.15)	1.5	(0.15)
Austria	12.2	(0.10)	14.0	(0.24)	15.8	(0.24)	10.7	(0.18)	8.5	(0.17)	1.1	(0.03)	0.8	(0.06)	1.5	(0.08)	1.2	(0.06)	1.0	(0.06)
Belgium	16.6	(0.13)	20.1	(0.31)	19.9	(0.28)	15.1	(0.24)	11.4	(0.21)	0.7	(0.03)	0.5	(0.06)	1.2	(0.08)	0.6	(0.05)	0.6	(0.05)
Canada[2,3]	10.0	(0.14)	10.3	(0.27)	11.9	(0.29)	10.0	(0.23)	7.6	(0.20)	[2]	(†)	[2]	(†)	[2]	(†)	[2]	(†)	[2]	(†)
Chile[2,4]	1.3	(0.03)	1.2	(0.06)	1.7	(0.07)	1.2	(0.06)	0.9	(0.06)	[2]	(†)	[2]	(†)	[2]	(†)	[2]	(†)	[2]	(†)
Czech Republic	17.3	(0.11)	20.6	(0.27)	18.2	(0.22)	15.8	(0.22)	14.3	(0.20)	0.7	(0.02)	0.5	(0.05)	1.1	(0.06)	0.5	(0.04)	0.5	(0.04)
Denmark	12.5	(0.15)	17.3	(0.38)	15.9	(0.35)	10.0	(0.26)	7.3	(0.22)	1.1	(0.05)	0.8	(0.09)	2.1	(0.14)	1.2	(0.09)	0.6	(0.06)
Estonia	20.4	(0.32)	16.2	(0.63)	22.3	(0.67)	21.2	(0.64)	22.0	(0.66)	0.6	(0.06)	0.6	(0.13)	0.7	(0.14)	0.7	(0.13)	0.6	(0.12)
Finland	14.7	(0.14)	14.0	(0.29)	20.0	(0.32)	15.3	(0.28)	9.9	(0.22)	1.2	(0.04)	0.3	(0.04)	1.7	(0.10)	1.3	(0.09)	1.5	(0.09)
France	10.4	(0.06)	17.6	(0.17)	12.1	(0.13)	6.9	(0.09)	5.7	(0.09)	0.9	(0.02)	0.6	(0.04)	1.0	(0.04)	1.0	(0.04)	0.8	(0.03)
Germany	11.5	(0.05)	13.6	(0.11)	13.4	(0.12)	9.9	(0.09)	9.7	(0.09)	1.4	(0.02)	0.8	(0.03)	1.9	(0.05)	1.4	(0.03)	1.4	(0.04)
Greece	3.1	(0.05)	4.6	(0.14)	4.4	(0.11)	2.6	(0.08)	1.0	(0.05)	0.5	(0.02)	0.3	(0.04)	0.7	(0.05)	0.6	(0.04)	0.6	(0.04)
Hungary	8.9	(0.08)	12.4	(0.22)	9.9	(0.17)	7.5	(0.15)	6.1	(0.13)	0.6	(0.02)	0.4	(0.04)	0.7	(0.05)	0.9	(0.05)	0.5	(0.04)
Iceland	17.1	(0.44)	18.2	(0.96)	21.4	(0.96)	17.4	(0.86)	10.7	(0.69)	1.2	(0.13)	0.4!	(0.16)	0.7	(0.20)	1.4	(0.27)	2.5	(0.35)
Ireland	10.1	(0.11)	12.1	(0.26)	12.9	(0.23)	8.8	(0.20)	5.2	(0.17)	1.0	(0.04)	0.8	(0.07)	1.5	(0.08)	1.0	(0.07)	0.8	(0.07)
Israel	12.0	(0.08)	7.6	(0.13)	14.3	(0.17)	14.4	(0.19)	12.7	(0.18)	1.3	(0.03)	0.4	(0.03)	1.4	(0.06)	1.8	(0.07)	2.0	(0.08)
Italy	13.9	(0.06)	15.3	(0.16)	17.3	(0.14)	12.3	(0.11)	11.1	(0.11)	0.5	(0.01)	0.4	(0.03)	0.9	(0.03)	0.4	(0.02)	0.2	(0.02)
Japan[5,6,7]	[7]	(†)	[7]	(†)	[7]	(†)	[7]	(†)	[7]	(†)	[7]	(†)	[7]	(†)	[7]	(†)	[7]	(†)	[7]	(†)
Korea, Republic of[5,7]	[7]	(†)	[7]	(†)	[7]	(†)	[7]	(†)	[7]	(†)	[7]	(†)	[7]	(†)	[7]	(†)	[7]	(†)	[7]	(†)
Latvia	12.0	(0.22)	11.4	(0.48)	13.9	(0.49)	11.0	(0.40)	11.8	(0.40)	0.3	(0.04)	0.3	(0.08)	0.4	(0.09)	0.3	(0.07)	0.4	(0.08)
Lithuania	13.8	(0.18)	15.1	(0.48)	13.9	(0.41)	12.8	(0.32)	13.5	(0.32)	0.6	(0.04)	0.6	(0.10)	0.8	(0.11)	0.4	(0.06)	0.7	(0.08)
Luxembourg	23.8	(0.37)	31.3	(0.91)	30.0	(0.81)	18.7	(0.60)	11.3	(0.54)	2.0	(0.12)	1.6	(0.25)	2.3	(0.26)	2.1	(0.22)	1.9	(0.24)
Mexico	1.5	(0.03)	1.2	(0.05)	1.7	(0.06)	1.7	(0.06)	1.4	(0.06)	0.1	(0.01)	0.0	(0.01)	0.1	(0.01)	0.1	(0.01)	0.1	(0.02)
Netherlands[5]	13.0	(0.07)	17.4	(0.19)	14.9	(0.17)	11.8	(0.12)	8.6	(0.10)	0.6	(0.02)	0.4	(0.03)	0.9	(0.05)	0.7	(0.03)	0.5	(0.03)
New Zealand	4.8	(0.16)	5.0	(0.33)	5.5	(0.34)	4.9	(0.31)	3.7	(0.28)	1.0	(0.08)	0.6	(0.12)	1.2	(0.17)	1.1	(0.15)	1.2	(0.17)
Norway	11.3	(0.13)	14.1	(0.30)	14.1	(0.29)	9.6	(0.24)	6.9	(0.22)	1.1	(0.04)	0.6	(0.07)	1.4	(0.10)	1.4	(0.10)	0.8	(0.08)
Poland[5]	22.6	(0.10)	30.8	(0.24)	29.3	(0.22)	17.0	(0.20)	11.9	(0.15)	0.5	(0.02)	0.3	(0.03)	0.8	(0.04)	0.5	(0.04)	0.5	(0.03)
Portugal	17.2	(0.13)	17.3	(0.34)	25.2	(0.29)	15.3	(0.23)	10.3	(0.20)	0.7	(0.03)	‡	(†)	0.7	(0.06)	1.1	(0.07)	0.5	(0.05)
Slovak Republic	19.7	(0.36)	28.1	(0.90)	20.6	(0.74)	14.2	(0.64)	14.3	(0.58)	0.7	(0.07)	0.9	(0.19)	0.9	(0.17)	0.4	(0.12)	0.4	(0.11)
Slovenia[5]	16.2	(0.20)	21.8	(0.48)	18.5	(0.42)	17.8	(0.39)	7.8	(0.26)	3.6	(0.10)	4.2	(0.23)	4.6	(0.23)	4.6	(0.21)	1.4	(0.11)
Spain	14.5	(0.06)	16.1	(0.15)	17.8	(0.13)	13.6	(0.11)	10.0	(0.10)	0.7	(0.01)	0.4	(0.03)	0.9	(0.03)	0.8	(0.03)	0.8	(0.03)
Sweden	13.5	(0.09)	13.0	(0.18)	19.4	(0.20)	12.0	(0.16)	9.4	(0.15)	1.6	(0.03)	0.7	(0.04)	2.4	(0.08)	1.9	(0.07)	1.4	(0.06)
Switzerland[8]	18.6	(0.14)	20.9	(0.34)	21.3	(0.28)	17.6	(0.24)	14.3	(0.25)	3.0	(0.06)	2.3	(0.12)	4.3	(0.14)	3.0	(0.11)	2.6	(0.11)
Turkey[5]	1.7	(0.03)	2.5	(0.06)	2.0	(0.05)	1.0	(0.04)	0.5	(0.03)	0.4	(0.01)	0.2	(0.02)	0.6	(0.03)	0.5	(0.03)	0.3	(0.02)
United Kingdom	11.8	(0.15)	13.6	(0.33)	14.4	(0.33)	10.5	(0.27)	8.4	(0.25)	1.3	(0.05)	0.9	(0.09)	1.6	(0.12)	1.4	(0.10)	1.4	(0.10)
United States[9]	11.2	(0.10)	10.0	(0.19)	13.3	(0.21)	11.2	(0.20)	10.2	(0.21)	1.8	(0.04)	1.5	(0.08)	2.2	(0.09)	1.9	(0.09)	1.7	(0.09)

—Not available.
†Not applicable.
#Rounds to zero.
!Interpret data with caution. The coefficient of variation (CV) for this estimate is between 30 and 50 percent.
‡Reporting standards not met.
[1]Refers to the mean of the data values for all reporting Organization for Economic Cooperation and Development (OECD) countries, to which each country reporting data contributes equally. Standard errors for the OECD average were estimated by the National Center for Education Statistics (NCES).
[2]Doctoral or equivalent degree data are included in columns for master's or equivalent degree.
[3]Standard errors were calculated by Statistics Canada.
[4]Data are from 2015.
[5]Standard errors were estimated by NCES using population estimates provided by Eurostat.
[6]Associate's degree data include postsecondary nontertiary awards (i.e., awards that are below the associate's degree level).
[7]Master's or equivalent degree data and doctoral or equivalent degree data are included in columns for bachelor's or equivalent degree.
[8]Associate's degree data are included in columns for bachelor's or equivalent, master's or equivalent, and doctoral or equivalent degrees.
[9]Standard errors were calculated by NCES.
NOTE: All data in this table were calculated using the International Standard Classification of Education (ISCED) 2011 classification of tertiary degrees. Includes degrees at ISCED 2011 level 5 (short-cycle tertiary, which corresponds to the associate's degree in the United States), level 6 (bachelor's or equivalent degree), level 7 (master's or equivalent degree), and level 8 (doctoral or equivalent degree). For more information on OECD and NCES estimation methodology, see the "Online Education Database" section of the entry for OECD in Appendix A: Guide to Sources.
SOURCE: Organization for Economic Cooperation and Development (OECD), Online Education Database, retrieved September 20, 2018, from http://stats.oecd.org/Index.aspx. Eurostat, unpublished tabulations on population by age group. (This table was prepared September 2018.)

Table 603.90. Employment to population ratios of 25- to 64-year-olds, by sex, highest level of educational attainment, and country: 2017

[Standard errors appear in parentheses]

Country	Total population, 25 to 64 years old				Male				Female			
	All levels of education	Less than high school completion	High school completion	Associate's or higher degree	All levels of education	Less than high school completion	High school completion	Associate's or higher degree	All levels of education	Less than high school completion	High school completion	Associate's or higher degree
1	2	3	4	5	6	7	8	9	10	11	12	13
OECD average[1]	**75.8 (0.18)**	**57.5 (0.52)**	**75.5 (0.28)**	**85.0 (0.26)**	**82.2 (0.23)**	**67.4 (0.70)**	**82.0 (0.34)**	**89.5 (0.34)**	**69.5 (0.27)**	**47.4 (0.75)**	**68.4 (0.43)**	**80.9 (0.37)**
Australia	77.1 (0.25)	58.9 (0.66)	78.2 (0.41)	84.0 (0.33)	83.4 (0.32)	66.7 (0.93)	85.1 (0.47)	89.2 (0.42)	71.1 (0.37)	51.8 (0.92)	69.0 (0.69)	79.8 (0.47)
Austria	76.4 (0.13)	54.1 (0.41)	76.6 (0.18)	86.4 (0.19)	81.0 (0.18)	60.6 (0.67)	80.4 (0.24)	89.2 (0.25)	71.9 (0.20)	49.9 (0.52)	72.5 (0.27)	83.6 (0.30)
Belgium	71.9 (0.16)	46.5 (0.35)	73.3 (0.26)	85.2 (0.20)	77.0 (0.21)	55.2 (0.50)	79.8 (0.32)	88.3 (0.27)	66.8 (0.23)	37.2 (0.49)	65.9 (0.40)	82.6 (0.28)
Canada	77.2 (—)	55.6 (—)	74.2 (—)	82.4 (—)	81.1 (—)	63.7 (—)	79.4 (—)	85.9 (—)	73.4 (—)	44.5 (—)	67.3 (—)	79.6 (—)
Chile[2]	71.2 (0.12)	62.2 (0.21)	71.8 (0.19)	84.4 (0.23)	86.3 (0.14)	83.6 (0.23)	85.9 (0.22)	91.0 (0.26)	58.4 (0.18)	43.9 (0.29)	59.6 (0.29)	78.8 (0.34)
Czech Republic	81.2 (0.12)	50.5 (0.58)	82.2 (0.14)	86.0 (0.23)	88.9 (0.14)	61.7 (0.95)	89.2 (0.16)	93.9 (0.23)	73.2 (0.19)	43.2 (0.72)	74.4 (0.22)	78.9 (0.36)
Denmark	79.4 (0.18)	62.1 (0.55)	81.0 (0.27)	85.9 (0.24)	82.8 (0.25)	70.9 (0.71)	84.1 (0.35)	88.4 (0.35)	75.9 (0.27)	51.2 (0.81)	77.4 (0.43)	83.9 (0.34)
Estonia	80.0 (0.32)	65.4 (1.09)	78.8 (0.46)	85.7 (0.46)	83.5 (0.43)	70.6 (1.32)	82.9 (0.58)	91.1 (0.64)	76.5 (0.47)	55.5 (1.86)	73.5 (0.74)	82.5 (0.62)
Finland	76.3 (0.17)	52.7 (0.57)	74.1 (0.26)	84.9 (0.21)	78.0 (0.23)	58.6 (0.71)	76.6 (0.34)	87.7 (0.30)	74.6 (0.24)	42.5 (0.92)	70.9 (0.40)	82.8 (0.29)
France	72.9 (0.09)	52.7 (0.20)	73.0 (0.13)	85.2 (0.12)	77.2 (0.12)	60.7 (0.29)	76.8 (0.18)	88.3 (0.17)	68.8 (0.13)	45.5 (0.27)	68.9 (0.20)	82.6 (0.18)
Germany	80.7 (0.06)	60.0 (0.21)	81.6 (0.08)	88.6 (0.09)	85.1 (0.08)	68.4 (0.30)	85.0 (0.10)	91.7 (0.11)	76.2 (0.09)	52.8 (0.29)	78.3 (0.12)	84.7 (0.16)
Greece	60.6 (0.14)	49.6 (0.25)	59.3 (0.22)	71.8 (0.24)	71.2 (0.18)	62.9 (0.34)	72.1 (0.29)	78.1 (0.33)	50.1 (0.20)	35.4 (0.33)	46.5 (0.31)	66.4 (0.35)
Hungary	75.8 (0.12)	55.1 (0.32)	77.6 (0.15)	85.1 (0.24)	83.8 (0.15)	66.0 (0.47)	84.8 (0.18)	92.4 (0.28)	68.1 (0.19)	46.9 (0.42)	69.3 (0.25)	79.6 (0.35)
Iceland	88.2 (0.38)	77.0 (1.01)	89.5 (0.61)	93.1 (0.46)	91.3 (0.47)	82.1 (1.33)	92.6 (0.67)	95.9 (0.57)	84.9 (0.58)	71.5 (1.49)	84.5 (1.13)	91.1 (0.65)
Ireland	74.0 (0.16)	50.9 (0.42)	71.9 (0.27)	84.9 (0.20)	80.9 (0.21)	62.3 (0.54)	81.6 (0.34)	89.5 (0.25)	67.5 (0.24)	35.2 (0.61)	62.5 (0.41)	81.0 (0.29)
Israel	77.8 (0.11)	52.5 (0.36)	73.6 (0.19)	87.1 (0.12)	82.9 (0.14)	68.6 (0.48)	78.4 (0.24)	90.8 (0.16)	72.9 (0.16)	35.4 (0.49)	67.7 (0.29)	84.2 (0.18)
Italy	65.3 (0.09)	51.8 (0.15)	71.0 (0.13)	80.7 (0.17)	75.9 (0.11)	66.7 (0.19)	81.0 (0.16)	85.7 (0.24)	55.0 (0.13)	35.5 (0.20)	60.8 (0.19)	77.1 (0.24)
Japan[3]	81.6 (—)	— (—)	— (—)	84.0 (—)	91.3 (—)	— (—)	— (—)	94.1 (—)	71.9 (—)	— (—)	— (—)	74.2 (—)
Korea, Republic of	74.2 (—)	65.8 (—)	73.0 (—)	77.4 (—)	86.0 (—)	77.3 (—)	84.4 (—)	88.9 (—)	62.1 (—)	58.3 (—)	61.7 (—)	63.8 (—)
Latvia	76.4 (0.29)	61.4 (0.89)	72.9 (0.40)	87.6 (0.41)	78.6 (0.41)	67.6 (1.09)	77.0 (0.54)	89.9 (0.66)	74.4 (0.40)	50.6 (1.47)	68.4 (0.60)	86.3 (0.51)
Lithuania	78.8 (0.22)	52.1 (1.02)	73.4 (0.31)	90.7 (0.26)	79.2 (0.32)	54.0 (1.30)	76.5 (0.43)	91.4 (0.42)	78.5 (0.30)	48.7 (1.63)	70.0 (0.46)	90.2 (0.33)
Luxembourg	76.1 (0.37)	60.4 (0.81)	74.8 (0.60)	86.3 (0.50)	80.0 (0.49)	68.7 (1.13)	76.7 (0.81)	89.8 (0.64)	72.0 (0.54)	52.2 (1.14)	72.7 (0.89)	82.9 (0.77)
Mexico	68.5 (0.11)	64.6 (0.14)	70.6 (0.23)	80.0 (0.21)	89.0 (0.11)	89.0 (0.14)	89.6 (0.23)	88.4 (0.23)	50.6 (0.16)	43.8 (0.20)	54.5 (0.34)	71.6 (0.33)
Netherlands	79.3 (—)	61.3 (—)	80.1 (—)	88.8 (—)	85.2 (—)	73.5 (—)	85.4 (—)	91.7 (—)	73.4 (—)	49.5 (—)	74.6 (—)	86.0 (—)
New Zealand	82.8 (0.28)	72.9 (0.69)	82.6 (0.44)	88.6 (0.39)	89.1 (0.34)	81.3 (0.87)	89.9 (0.49)	92.9 (0.48)	76.9 (0.43)	64.6 (1.03)	74.9 (0.71)	85.1 (0.58)
Norway	80.3 (0.17)	61.1 (0.49)	79.7 (0.27)	88.8 (0.20)	82.4 (0.23)	66.9 (0.66)	82.8 (0.34)	89.6 (0.29)	78.1 (0.25)	54.5 (0.72)	75.7 (0.43)	88.2 (0.28)
Poland	73.0 (—)	41.8 (—)	69.6 (—)	88.1 (—)	80.3 (—)	52.9 (—)	78.9 (—)	93.3 (—)	65.7 (—)	30.5 (—)	58.7 (—)	84.6 (—)
Portugal	76.0 (0.15)	68.4 (0.21)	81.8 (0.29)	86.8 (0.25)	80.2 (0.20)	75.9 (0.28)	84.0 (0.40)	87.9 (0.40)	72.3 (0.21)	60.3 (0.32)	79.8 (0.41)	86.2 (0.33)
Slovak Republic	73.8 (0.40)	39.1 (1.46)	75.4 (0.47)	82.0 (0.76)	79.8 (0.52)	45.4 (2.34)	80.9 (0.59)	88.6 (0.95)	67.7 (0.59)	34.3 (1.83)	69.0 (0.72)	77.1 (1.10)
Slovenia	72.8 (—)	45.9 (—)	70.1 (—)	86.6 (—)	74.1 (—)	52.0 (—)	71.7 (—)	88.0 (—)	71.6 (—)	41.4 (—)	68.2 (—)	85.7 (—)
Spain	68.1 (0.08)	55.5 (0.13)	70.2 (0.17)	80.9 (0.11)	74.5 (0.11)	65.1 (0.17)	77.0 (0.22)	85.0 (0.15)	61.7 (0.12)	44.7 (0.19)	63.4 (0.25)	77.5 (0.16)
Sweden	84.2 (0.09)	66.8 (0.29)	86.0 (0.14)	89.5 (0.12)	86.3 (0.12)	72.9 (0.38)	88.3 (0.17)	90.4 (0.18)	82.0 (0.14)	60.0 (0.45)	82.9 (0.22)	88.8 (0.16)
Switzerland	82.8 (0.13)	67.2 (0.49)	81.8 (0.21)	88.3 (0.17)	88.0 (0.17)	75.1 (0.70)	86.7 (0.27)	92.0 (0.19)	77.5 (0.20)	60.8 (0.66)	77.5 (0.29)	83.5 (0.29)
Turkey	58.9 (—)	52.3 (—)	62.5 (—)	75.2 (—)	78.9 (—)	75.7 (—)	81.6 (—)	84.4 (—)	36.5 (—)	29.3 (—)	34.0 (—)	63.6 (—)
United Kingdom[4]	79.6 (0.19)	62.6 (0.50)	81.0 (0.30)	85.5 (0.24)	85.2 (0.24)	71.2 (0.68)	86.4 (0.38)	90.0 (0.30)	74.1 (0.28)	54.5 (0.71)	75.3 (0.47)	81.3 (0.36)
United States	74.1 (0.14)	55.6 (0.51)	70.0 (0.22)	81.8 (0.18)	79.7 (0.19)	66.5 (0.68)	75.9 (0.29)	87.0 (0.24)	68.7 (0.21)	43.1 (0.73)	63.6 (0.33)	77.5 (0.27)
Other reporting countries												
Argentina	73.0 (—)	65.3 (—)	73.8 (—)	85.5 (—)	86.5 (—)	82.8 (—)	87.6 (—)	92.9 (—)	60.8 (—)	46.3 (—)	61.2 (—)	80.8 (—)
Brazil[2]	70.8 (0.10)	65.0 (0.15)	73.9 (0.17)	83.4 (0.22)	83.5 (0.12)	80.6 (0.18)	85.8 (0.20)	89.9 (0.29)	59.2 (0.16)	49.1 (0.23)	63.7 (0.26)	78.9 (0.32)
Colombia	75.4 (0.07)	71.8 (0.11)	75.2 (0.12)	83.0 (0.12)	88.9 (0.08)	89.2 (0.12)	88.2 (0.13)	89.3 (0.15)	62.7 (0.11)	54.0 (0.18)	63.0 (0.19)	78.0 (0.17)
Costa Rica	68.6 (0.41)	63.8 (0.52)	69.1 (1.03)	80.8 (0.82)	85.5 (0.46)	84.4 (0.56)	87.2 (1.11)	87.5 (1.08)	51.8 (0.60)	42.0 (0.74)	52.7 (1.50)	74.9 (1.18)
Indonesia	74.7 (—)	73.0 (—)	74.1 (—)	85.1 (—)	91.2 (—)	91.3 (—)	90.8 (—)	91.9 (—)	58.4 (—)	56.7 (—)	52.4 (—)	78.5 (—)
Russia[2]	75.5 (0.05)	51.1 (0.26)	71.5 (0.09)	81.3 (0.07)	81.0 (0.07)	58.4 (0.34)	78.5 (0.11)	87.3 (0.09)	70.7 (0.08)	42.1 (0.38)	63.1 (0.14)	77.4 (0.09)
Saudi Arabia[5]	65.1 (—)	59.7 (—)	65.2 (—)	75.4 (—)	92.8 (—)	91.4 (—)	92.9 (—)	95.2 (—)	21.9 (—)	16.4 (—)	14.7 (—)	43.1 (—)
South Africa	55.9 (0.14)	43.3 (0.27)	57.7 (0.18)	84.7 (0.41)	63.2 (0.21)	51.1 (0.39)	65.3 (0.25)	89.2 (0.53)	48.8 (0.20)	35.6 (0.35)	50.4 (0.25)	80.7 (0.61)

—Not available.

[1]Refers to the mean of the data values for all reporting Organization for Economic Cooperation and Development (OECD) countries, to which each country reporting data contributes equally.

[2]Data are for 2015 instead of 2017.

[3]Associate's or higher degree data include some persons (less than 5 percent of the total) whose highest level of education was high school completion or a postsecondary program below the associate's degree level.

[4]High school completion data include some persons (17 percent of the total) who have completed a sufficient volume and standard of programs, any one of which individually would be classified as a program that only partially completes the high school (or upper secondary) level of education.

[5]Data are for 2014 instead of 2017.

NOTE: All data in this table were calculated using International Standard Classification of Education (ISCED) 2011. High school completion refers to completion of ISCED 2011 level 3 (upper secondary education); programs classified under ISCED 2011 as only partially completing level 3 are not included in the high school completion data except where otherwise noted. In this table, persons completing ISCED 2011 level 4 are also considered to have high school completion as their highest level of educational attainment. ISCED level 4 typically corresponds to postsecondary vocational programs below the associate's degree level in the United States. Associate's or higher degrees include ISCED 2011 level 5 (corresponding to the associate's degree in the United States), level 6 (bachelor's or equivalent degree), level 7 (master's or equivalent degree), and level 8 (doctoral or equivalent degree). For each country, the employment to population ratio of 25- to 64-year-olds is the number of persons in this age group who are employed as a percentage of the total civilian population in this age group.

SOURCE: Organization for Economic Cooperation and Development (OECD), Online Education Database, retrieved May 28, 2019, from https://stats.oecd.org/Index.aspx. (This table was prepared May 2019.)

Table 604.10. Average literacy and numeracy scale scores of 25- to 65-year-olds, by sex, age group, highest level of educational attainment, and country or other education system: 2012

[Standard errors appear in parentheses]

Country or other education system[1]	Total population of 25- to 65-year-olds	Sex		Age group				Highest level of educational attainment[2]			
		Male	Female	25 to 34	35 to 44	45 to 54	55 to 65	Less than high school completion	High school completion	Associate's degree	Bachelor's or higher degree
1	2	3	4	5	6	7	8	9	10	11	12
	Literacy scale score[3]										
OECD average[4]	**271 (0.2)**	**273 (0.3)**	**270 (0.2)**	**284 (0.4)**	**279 (0.3)**	**268 (0.3)**	**255 (0.3)**	**235 (0.5)**	**268 (0.3)**	**286 (0.5)**	**302 (0.3)**
Austria	268 (0.8)	270 (1.1)	266 (1.0)	280 (1.5)	275 (1.7)	266 (1.4)	250 (1.6)	239 (2.1)	268 (0.9)	282 (2.2)	305 (1.7)
Canada	273 (0.6)	274 (0.9)	271 (0.9)	285 (1.3)	279 (1.4)	268 (1.3)	260 (1.1)	219 (2.1)	265 (1.1)	278 (1.2)	300 (1.0)
Czech Republic	273 (1.0)	274 (1.3)	271 (1.5)	287 (1.8)	275 (2.0)	266 (1.7)	262 (2.0)	242 (3.4)	269 (1.0)	293 (4.6)	303 (2.5)
Denmark	270 (0.7)	270 (1.1)	269 (0.9)	282 (1.7)	281 (1.6)	266 (1.4)	252 (1.1)	234 (2.1)	264 (1.2)	286 (1.3)	298 (1.5)
England (UK)	274 (1.1)	275 (1.4)	273 (1.4)	280 (2.1)	279 (1.6)	271 (1.8)	265 (2.0)	241 (1.6)	273 (1.5)	283 (2.4)	302 (1.9)
Estonia	273 (0.8)	273 (1.2)	274 (0.9)	286 (1.7)	278 (1.2)	269 (1.4)	261 (1.5)	244 (2.0)	267 (1.0)	276 (1.5)	298 (1.4)
Finland	286 (0.8)	284 (1.4)	287 (1.2)	309 (1.7)	299 (2.1)	284 (1.8)	260 (1.4)	245 (2.8)	276 (1.4)	294 (1.5)	318 (1.6)
Flanders (Belgium)	274 (0.9)	277 (1.1)	270 (1.1)	291 (1.8)	282 (1.6)	272 (1.6)	255 (1.6)	232 (2.0)	265 (1.2)	294 (1.6)	313 (1.7)
France	259 (0.6)	260 (0.9)	259 (0.8)	278 (1.4)	267 (1.3)	254 (1.2)	242 (1.3)	224 (1.3)	258 (0.9)	287 (1.4)	297 (1.2)
Germany	268 (1.0)	271 (1.2)	265 (1.3)	281 (1.8)	275 (1.6)	264 (1.7)	254 (1.7)	220 (3.0)	262 (1.1)	280 (2.3)	301 (1.6)
Ireland	266 (1.0)	267 (1.3)	264 (1.2)	276 (1.5)	271 (1.8)	259 (2.1)	251 (1.8)	232 (1.8)	266 (1.5)	279 (1.9)	301 (1.7)
Italy	249 (1.1)	249 (1.6)	248 (1.4)	260 (2.2)	253 (1.9)	249 (1.8)	233 (2.2)	231 (1.6)	263 (1.3)	‡ (†)	282 (1.6)
Japan	296 (0.7)	297 (1.0)	294 (1.0)	309 (1.7)	307 (1.0)	297 (1.5)	273 (1.6)	260 (2.6)	287 (1.0)	304 (1.4)	320 (1.1)
Korea, Republic of	269 (0.6)	273 (0.9)	264 (0.9)	290 (1.2)	278 (1.2)	259 (1.4)	244 (1.4)	230 (1.7)	265 (1.0)	282 (1.4)	297 (1.3)
Netherlands	282 (0.8)	286 (1.2)	278 (1.0)	298 (2.0)	294 (1.8)	277 (1.7)	261 (1.6)	246 (1.7)	283 (1.3)	293 (3.4)	312 (1.3)
Northern Ireland (UK)	268 (2.1)	271 (2.7)	265 (2.0)	278 (2.9)	274 (2.3)	262 (2.6)	255 (3.2)	239 (2.6)	270 (2.6)	280 (3.3)	303 (2.9)
Norway	279 (0.7)	281 (1.1)	277 (1.1)	289 (1.8)	288 (1.6)	277 (1.5)	262 (1.5)	251 (1.8)	271 (1.4)	288 (3.1)	303 (1.1)
Poland	264 (0.7)	260 (1.1)	267 (1.0)	277 (1.5)	268 (1.9)	259 (1.7)	249 (1.7)	227 (2.6)	254 (1.0)	— (†)	297 (1.3)
Slovak Republic	273 (0.7)	273 (1.0)	274 (0.9)	278 (1.4)	278 (1.4)	270 (1.3)	266 (1.3)	238 (1.9)	275 (0.9)	— (†)	295 (1.4)
Spain	250 (0.8)	253 (1.1)	248 (1.2)	263 (1.5)	260 (1.3)	248 (1.5)	227 (1.9)	225 (1.3)	258 (1.4)	266 (2.1)	288 (1.3)
Sweden	278 (0.8)	280 (1.2)	276 (1.2)	290 (1.9)	287 (1.8)	276 (1.7)	262 (1.3)	238 (2.2)	277 (1.2)	294 (2.4)	309 (1.4)
United States	269 (1.1)	270 (1.3)	269 (1.4)	275 (2.0)	273 (1.8)	266 (1.7)	263 (1.5)	211 (2.7)	259 (1.4)	282 (2.8)	302 (1.7)
Non-OECD education systems											
Cyprus[5]	269 (0.9)	269 (1.3)	270 (1.1)	275 (1.7)	270 (1.5)	270 (1.7)	261 (1.6)	248 (1.9)	266 (1.2)	273 (2.0)	290 (1.5)
Russian Federation[6]	275 (3.0)	274 (3.3)	277 (3.1)	273 (4.1)	278 (3.9)	277 (3.7)	275 (3.9)	248 (7.5)	272 (4.2)	276 (2.8)	282 (3.1)
	Numeracy scale score[3]										
OECD average[4]	**268 (0.2)**	**275 (0.3)**	**262 (0.3)**	**279 (0.4)**	**275 (0.4)**	**266 (0.4)**	**253 (0.4)**	**227 (0.5)**	**265 (0.3)**	**283 (0.9)**	**303 (0.4)**
Austria	274 (0.9)	281 (1.3)	267 (1.1)	282 (1.7)	281 (2.0)	274 (1.7)	257 (1.7)	237 (2.3)	276 (1.1)	292 (2.6)	315 (1.8)
Canada	265 (0.8)	273 (1.0)	257 (1.0)	276 (1.4)	272 (1.5)	260 (1.4)	251 (1.4)	206 (2.5)	255 (1.2)	271 (1.5)	295 (1.0)
Czech Republic	275 (1.0)	280 (1.5)	270 (1.4)	288 (1.8)	277 (1.8)	272 (2.2)	263 (2.0)	235 (3.3)	271 (1.0)	287 (6.1)	313 (2.5)
Denmark	279 (0.8)	285 (1.4)	273 (1.0)	287 (1.9)	290 (1.6)	277 (1.6)	265 (1.2)	241 (2.4)	275 (1.3)	295 (1.4)	309 (1.8)
England (UK)	263 (1.1)	270 (1.4)	256 (1.6)	267 (2.2)	269 (1.9)	259 (1.9)	257 (1.9)	226 (1.9)	262 (1.5)	271 (3.0)	295 (2.2)
Estonia	272 (0.6)	276 (1.0)	269 (0.9)	284 (1.7)	275 (1.1)	269 (1.4)	259 (1.3)	236 (1.8)	265 (0.9)	275 (1.4)	300 (1.3)
Finland	282 (0.8)	286 (1.3)	277 (1.2)	302 (2.1)	292 (2.2)	279 (2.0)	260 (1.3)	244 (2.8)	271 (1.3)	291 (1.6)	314 (1.7)
Flanders (Belgium)	280 (0.9)	289 (1.2)	271 (1.3)	295 (1.9)	289 (1.8)	280 (1.9)	260 (1.6)	235 (1.9)	272 (1.2)	300 (1.5)	323 (1.8)
France	252 (0.7)	258 (1.0)	247 (1.0)	269 (1.5)	262 (1.6)	246 (1.4)	234 (1.5)	208 (1.3)	251 (1.0)	287 (1.7)	299 (1.4)
Germany	271 (1.1)	280 (1.4)	262 (1.4)	282 (1.8)	279 (2.0)	268 (1.9)	256 (1.9)	210 (3.4)	264 (1.2)	287 (2.5)	310 (1.7)
Ireland	255 (1.0)	261 (1.4)	249 (1.3)	266 (1.7)	260 (1.7)	250 (2.1)	238 (2.3)	218 (2.2)	254 (1.6)	274 (2.1)	294 (1.9)
Italy	246 (1.1)	253 (1.6)	240 (1.4)	262 (2.3)	251 (1.9)	244 (2.0)	229 (2.2)	225 (1.5)	265 (1.5)	‡ (†)	280 (2.1)
Japan	289 (0.8)	296 (1.2)	282 (1.1)	297 (1.6)	297 (1.3)	291 (1.7)	273 (1.6)	247 (2.5)	281 (1.3)	291 (1.3)	319 (1.2)
Korea, Republic of	260 (0.7)	266 (1.0)	254 (1.1)	281 (1.4)	271 (1.5)	251 (1.4)	232 (1.7)	215 (1.9)	256 (1.0)	275 (1.6)	293 (1.5)
Netherlands	279 (0.8)	288 (1.3)	270 (1.1)	293 (1.8)	287 (2.1)	277 (1.7)	262 (1.7)	243 (1.9)	281 (1.2)	292 (3.5)	310 (1.3)
Northern Ireland (UK)	258 (1.8)	265 (2.2)	251 (2.0)	268 (2.9)	266 (2.4)	252 (2.1)	245 (3.1)	225 (2.9)	261 (2.1)	273 (3.0)	298 (2.4)
Norway	280 (0.9)	288 (1.3)	272 (1.2)	285 (2.0)	289 (1.9)	280 (1.7)	265 (1.7)	246 (2.2)	273 (1.5)	296 (3.7)	306 (1.3)
Poland	258 (1.0)	259 (1.5)	257 (1.0)	270 (1.5)	262 (2.2)	254 (2.1)	244 (1.9)	216 (3.1)	250 (1.2)	— (†)	290 (1.5)
Slovak Republic	275 (0.9)	277 (1.2)	274 (1.1)	279 (1.6)	281 (1.7)	275 (1.6)	265 (1.6)	226 (2.4)	278 (1.0)	— (†)	306 (1.5)
Spain	245 (0.7)	251 (1.1)	238 (1.1)	257 (1.3)	255 (1.3)	242 (1.6)	221 (1.7)	217 (1.3)	254 (1.5)	264 (2.4)	283 (1.3)
Sweden	279 (1.0)	286 (1.5)	272 (1.2)	288 (2.0)	286 (2.0)	276 (2.3)	268 (1.7)	237 (2.6)	277 (1.4)	297 (2.6)	311 (1.5)
United States	254 (1.2)	262 (1.3)	246 (1.5)	260 (2.2)	258 (1.9)	250 (2.1)	247 (1.8)	185 (3.1)	241 (1.5)	266 (3.1)	293 (1.7)
Non-OECD education systems											
Cyprus[5]	265 (0.9)	270 (1.2)	260 (1.3)	273 (2.0)	269 (1.6)	265 (1.8)	250 (1.8)	230 (2.3)	264 (1.4)	270 (2.1)	292 (1.6)
Russian Federation[6]	269 (2.8)	268 (3.3)	271 (3.0)	269 (4.2)	270 (3.6)	272 (3.2)	267 (3.9)	234 (8.5)	265 (4.0)	268 (2.6)	280 (3.0)

—Not available.
†Not applicable.
‡Reporting standards not met (too few cases).
[1]Most of the education systems represent complete countries, but three of them represent subnational entities: England (which is part of the United Kingdom), Flanders (which is part of Belgium), and Northern Ireland (which is part of the United Kingdom).
[2]High school completion includes International Standard Classification of Education (ISCED) 1997 levels 3 and 4, with the exception of ISCED level 3C short programs. ISCED 3C short programs do not correspond to high school completion in the United States and are included in the "less than high school completion" column in this table. The associate's degree data in this table refer to degrees classified as ISCED 1997 level 5B. The data for bachelor's or higher degree refer to degrees classified as ISCED 1997 level 5A and as level 6.
[3]Scale scores range from 0 to 500.
[4]Refers to the mean of the data values for all reporting Organization for Economic Cooperation and Development (OECD) countries and subnational education systems, to which each country or subnational education system reporting data contributes equally, with the exception of England (UK) and Northern Ireland (UK), which contribute to the mean as a combined entity, England/Northern Ireland (UK).
[5]Cyprus includes only the population under the effective control of the Government of the Republic of Cyprus. For the educational attainment data (columns 9 through 12), the item response rate for Cyprus is below 85 percent; missing data have not been explicitly accounted for.
[6]The Russian Federation does not include the population of the Moscow municipal region.
SOURCE: Organization for Economic Cooperation and Development (OECD), Program for the International Assessment of Adult Competencies (PIAAC), 2012. (This table was prepared May 2016.)

Table 604.20. Percentage distribution of 25- to 65-year-olds, by literacy proficiency level, numeracy proficiency level, selected levels of educational attainment, and country or other education system: 2012

[Standard errors appear in parentheses]

Country or other education system[1]	Total population of 25- to 65-year-olds				Highest level of educational attainment[2]							
					High school completion				Bachelor's or higher degree			
	At or below level 1	At level 2	At level 3	At level 4 or level 5	At or below level 1	At level 2	At level 3	At level 4 or level 5	At or below level 1	At level 2	At level 3	At level 4 or level 5
1	2	3	4	5	6	7	8	9	10	11	12	13
	Percentage distribution, by literacy proficiency level											
OECD average[3]	**16.6 (0.15)**	**34.0 (0.21)**	**37.6 (0.21)**	**11.8 (0.13)**	**15.1 (0.23)**	**39.7 (0.34)**	**38.0 (0.33)**	**7.2 (0.18)**	**4.0 (0.16)**	**18.7 (0.35)**	**49.5 (0.45)**	**27.8 (0.40)**
Austria	16.3 (0.70)	39.0 (1.06)	36.7 (1.04)	8.0 (0.47)	14.3 (0.86)	41.9 (1.38)	37.9 (1.40)	5.9 (0.60)	2.5! (0.79)	16.8 (1.99)	52.9 (2.47)	27.8 (2.03)
Canada	17.3 (0.47)	31.9 (0.70)	36.7 (0.74)	14.2 (0.55)	18.2 (0.85)	39.0 (1.05)	35.4 (1.13)	7.5 (0.80)	5.9 (0.49)	21.3 (0.88)	44.1 (1.20)	28.7 (1.20)
Czech Republic	12.5 (0.87)	38.5 (1.87)	40.9 (1.76)	8.1 (0.77)	12.4 (1.11)	43.4 (2.34)	39.5 (1.97)	4.8 (0.73)	1.9! (0.89)	17.1 (3.16)	57.2 (3.80)	23.8 (3.21)
Denmark	16.7 (0.58)	33.9 (0.83)	39.4 (0.81)	10.0 (0.57)	16.6 (1.01)	41.7 (1.48)	36.3 (1.46)	5.4 (0.64)	5.8 (0.69)	17.0 (1.20)	51.9 (1.86)	25.2 (1.87)
England (UK)	16.1 (0.77)	32.8 (0.97)	36.7 (1.01)	14.4 (0.89)	14.4 (1.36)	35.4 (1.81)	39.2 (1.58)	11.0 (1.07)	5.5 (1.06)	18.1 (1.55)	46.2 (2.37)	30.1 (2.26)
Estonia	14.3 (0.62)	35.5 (0.68)	39.3 (0.93)	10.9 (0.67)	16.0 (0.95)	40.4 (1.11)	37.2 (1.07)	6.5 (0.65)	4.4 (0.70)	22.8 (1.42)	48.4 (1.94)	24.5 (1.65)
Finland	11.6 (0.57)	27.5 (0.90)	39.2 (0.92)	21.7 (0.61)	13.3 (0.99)	33.8 (1.65)	39.6 (1.55)	13.2 (1.03)	2.9 (0.66)	11.0 (1.23)	39.7 (2.01)	46.4 (1.74)
Flanders (Belgium)	15.8 (0.66)	32.0 (0.96)	39.4 (1.06)	12.8 (0.65)	16.7 (1.13)	41.7 (1.53)	35.9 (1.76)	5.7 (0.68)	2.1! (0.65)	10.3 (1.62)	51.1 (2.84)	36.5 (2.44)
France	23.6 (0.55)	36.6 (0.77)	32.5 (0.69)	7.3 (0.39)	20.4 (0.95)	45.2 (1.08)	31.1 (0.96)	3.4 (0.44)	5.1 (0.71)	20.2 (1.40)	52.2 (1.56)	22.5 (1.51)
Germany	18.7 (0.86)	35.3 (1.12)	35.9 (1.00)	10.2 (0.64)	19.9 (1.13)	41.6 (1.55)	32.8 (1.33)	5.7 (0.73)	4.2 (0.90)	19.1 (1.66)	50.6 (1.84)	26.2 (1.80)
Ireland	18.5 (0.87)	37.2 (0.91)	35.6 (0.89)	8.8 (0.62)	14.7 (1.18)	42.3 (1.62)	37.6 (1.78)	5.3 (0.90)	3.0 (0.71)	20.7 (1.64)	52.2 (1.96)	24.2 (1.87)
Italy	29.2 (1.18)	42.5 (1.01)	25.1 (1.01)	3.2 (0.34)	16.6 (1.30)	44.6 (1.55)	34.9 (1.77)	3.9 (0.73)	9.2 (1.27)	30.9 (2.28)	48.2 (2.63)	11.7 (1.72)
Japan	5.3 (0.43)	23.4 (0.90)	48.4 (1.06)	22.9 (0.75)	5.8 (0.78)	30.1 (1.42)	51.1 (1.45)	13.0 (1.03)	1.1! (0.35)	8.2 (0.96)	46.2 (2.06)	44.5 (1.93)
Korea, Republic of	14.9 (0.60)	39.6 (0.92)	38.5 (0.96)	6.9 (0.43)	13.0 (0.92)	48.0 (1.67)	35.4 (1.74)	3.6 (0.50)	2.1 (0.56)	22.8 (1.48)	57.6 (1.66)	17.5 (1.30)
Netherlands	13.4 (0.56)	27.5 (0.82)	41.1 (0.84)	18.0 (0.74)	8.9 (0.96)	30.9 (1.47)	46.5 (1.56)	13.8 (1.04)	2.7 (0.59)	12.7 (1.09)	47.5 (1.52)	37.0 (1.56)
Northern Ireland (UK)	18.4 (1.29)	37.0 (1.71)	34.7 (1.76)	9.9 (0.78)	13.8 (1.97)	41.1 (2.91)	37.6 (3.61)	7.5 (1.21)	3.2! (0.99)	17.8 (2.14)	51.6 (2.26)	27.5 (2.55)
Norway	12.5 (0.67)	30.1 (0.90)	42.6 (0.86)	14.9 (0.67)	13.1 (1.26)	37.7 (1.62)	41.5 (1.47)	7.7 (0.95)	4.5 (0.57)	16.3 (1.09)	50.1 (1.44)	29.0 (1.26)
Poland	20.7 (0.73)	37.5 (1.09)	32.7 (1.05)	9.0 (0.60)	24.0 (1.08)	43.6 (1.39)	28.6 (1.15)	3.8 (0.53)	4.4 (0.77)	24.5 (1.53)	48.1 (2.05)	23.0 (1.68)
Slovak Republic	11.9 (0.69)	36.7 (1.18)	44.0 (1.02)	7.4 (0.53)	8.7 (0.68)	39.2 (1.53)	46.1 (1.48)	6.0 (0.60)	2.7! (0.84)	23.3 (2.01)	57.4 (2.04)	16.6 (1.85)
Spain	29.2 (0.84)	39.1 (0.84)	27.0 (0.76)	4.8 (0.43)	21.0 (1.42)	46.1 (1.96)	29.5 (1.81)	3.5 (0.82)	5.8 (0.90)	29.3 (1.76)	50.1 (2.15)	14.8 (1.40)
Sweden	14.1 (0.71)	29.0 (1.13)	40.5 (0.99)	16.4 (0.62)	11.7 (0.96)	32.9 (1.71)	44.9 (1.83)	10.5 (0.90)	4.9 (0.64)	13.2 (1.35)	44.5 (1.78)	37.4 (1.90)
United States	19.2 (0.88)	32.8 (1.15)	35.5 (1.08)	12.5 (0.79)	22.0 (1.32)	41.7 (1.83)	30.8 (1.38)	5.5 (0.79)	3.7 (0.68)	18.9 (1.28)	49.6 (1.79)	27.8 (2.02)
Non-OECD education systems												
Cyprus[4]	14.4 (0.73)	39.7 (1.31)	38.7 (1.18)	7.1 (0.53)	14.5 (1.20)	43.1 (2.24)	37.5 (2.17)	4.8 (0.79)	4.6 (0.94)	29.9 (2.42)	49.3 (2.27)	16.2 (1.45)
Russian Federation[5]	12.9 (1.63)	34.7 (1.92)	41.5 (2.17)	10.9 (1.93)	15.0 (2.46)	35.8 (2.59)	39.9 (3.68)	9.4! (2.87)	9.8 (1.85)	31.2 (3.01)	45.3 (3.29)	13.7 (2.60)
	Percentage distribution, by numeracy proficiency level											
OECD average[3]	**19.8 (0.16)**	**33.1 (0.20)**	**34.3 (0.20)**	**12.8 (0.14)**	**18.4 (0.25)**	**38.8 (0.33)**	**34.6 (0.33)**	**8.2 (0.19)**	**5.0 (0.18)**	**19.6 (0.35)**	**45.3 (0.45)**	**30.1 (0.40)**
Austria	15.0 (0.72)	34.2 (0.96)	37.0 (1.05)	13.8 (0.66)	11.7 (0.90)	37.1 (1.27)	39.6 (1.41)	11.5 (0.88)	2.5! (0.94)	12.9 (1.90)	44.6 (2.56)	40.0 (2.33)
Canada	23.3 (0.57)	31.8 (0.65)	32.2 (0.76)	12.7 (0.50)	26.8 (1.21)	38.0 (1.25)	29.2 (1.17)	6.0 (0.58)	8.3 (0.67)	23.5 (1.12)	42.0 (1.58)	26.2 (1.23)
Czech Republic	13.2 (0.87)	35.4 (1.31)	39.9 (1.24)	11.5 (0.81)	12.7 (1.02)	40.1 (1.72)	40.7 (1.76)	6.6 (0.84)	1.1! (0.44)	13.5 (2.52)	50.0 (3.70)	35.4 (3.22)
Denmark	14.3 (0.58)	29.7 (0.78)	38.3 (0.82)	17.7 (0.56)	12.8 (1.07)	35.4 (1.41)	39.8 (1.37)	12.0 (0.95)	5.5 (0.64)	14.0 (1.36)	41.9 (1.70)	38.7 (1.91)
England (UK)	24.1 (1.04)	32.8 (1.15)	30.7 (1.08)	12.3 (0.85)	22.4 (1.43)	37.1 (1.79)	31.8 (2.03)	8.8 (1.35)	8.1 (1.61)	23.2 (1.95)	42.1 (2.07)	26.6 (1.92)
Estonia	15.0 (0.55)	36.6 (0.71)	37.4 (0.63)	11.0 (0.46)	16.5 (0.95)	42.3 (1.15)	34.6 (1.07)	6.5 (0.60)	4.2 (0.64)	21.4 (1.48)	49.0 (2.02)	25.5 (1.55)
Finland	13.5 (0.58)	29.3 (0.70)	37.5 (0.91)	19.7 (0.66)	16.4 (0.98)	35.7 (1.27)	36.0 (1.39)	11.8 (1.04)	3.3 (0.67)	13.5 (1.38)	41.9 (1.94)	41.3 (1.89)
Flanders (Belgium)	14.7 (0.68)	29.2 (0.83)	37.8 (1.03)	18.3 (0.78)	15.0 (1.04)	37.1 (1.55)	38.0 (1.57)	10.0 (1.06)	1.7! (0.63)	8.4 (1.45)	41.4 (2.45)	48.4 (2.52)
France	29.9 (0.69)	33.5 (0.79)	28.3 (0.59)	8.4 (0.37)	26.8 (1.02)	43.0 (1.16)	26.8 (0.99)	3.4 (0.42)	5.9 (0.79)	20.0 (1.13)	48.2 (1.40)	25.9 (1.37)
Germany	19.1 (0.79)	31.5 (0.91)	34.9 (0.90)	14.5 (0.68)	19.7 (1.05)	38.7 (1.30)	33.4 (1.42)	8.1 (0.74)	3.4 (0.88)	15.6 (1.65)	45.5 (1.71)	35.5 (1.86)
Ireland	25.8 (0.94)	37.7 (0.96)	28.7 (0.89)	7.8 (0.66)	23.8 (1.57)	43.6 (1.58)	28.1 (1.37)	4.5 (0.72)	5.2 (0.89)	26.8 (1.74)	46.5 (2.31)	21.5 (2.14)
Italy	32.4 (1.13)	39.0 (1.15)	24.1 (1.03)	4.6 (0.37)	17.4 (1.38)	40.7 (1.92)	35.3 (1.81)	6.6 (0.75)	11.8 (1.65)	31.7 (2.32)	42.3 (2.59)	14.2 (1.80)
Japan	8.2 (0.55)	27.7 (0.92)	44.4 (0.94)	19.7 (0.70)	8.6 (1.01)	34.0 (1.56)	46.3 (1.61)	11.0 (1.10)	1.0! (0.41)	10.4 (0.99)	45.0 (1.86)	43.5 (1.76)
Korea, Republic of	21.3 (0.64)	40.3 (0.98)	32.1 (0.89)	6.3 (0.52)	20.3 (1.14)	49.4 (1.34)	27.5 (1.40)	2.8 (0.56)	3.3 (0.67)	26.4 (1.65)	53.3 (2.00)	17.0 (1.55)
Netherlands	14.5 (0.60)	28.6 (0.85)	39.3 (1.00)	17.6 (0.72)	10.5 (1.13)	32.4 (1.78)	43.3 (1.93)	13.8 (1.10)	2.8 (0.64)	15.6 (1.14)	46.8 (1.78)	34.9 (1.78)
Northern Ireland (UK)	26.0 (1.54)	36.1 (1.36)	29.4 (1.34)	8.5 (0.74)	20.4 (2.01)	42.9 (2.24)	30.9 (2.52)	5.8 (1.19)	4.8 (1.10)	21.5 (2.20)	49.2 (2.74)	24.5 (2.32)
Norway	14.4 (0.62)	28.1 (0.89)	38.3 (0.96)	19.1 (0.73)	15.0 (1.19)	34.8 (1.58)	38.3 (1.46)	11.8 (1.24)	5.4 (0.61)	15.8 (1.07)	44.2 (1.57)	34.5 (1.46)
Poland	24.9 (0.88)	37.5 (1.03)	29.4 (1.10)	8.1 (0.63)	28.2 (1.11)	42.7 (1.52)	25.3 (1.25)	3.9 (0.62)	7.3 (1.00)	28.0 (1.77)	44.7 (2.28)	20.0 (1.63)
Slovak Republic	14.1 (0.65)	32.5 (0.96)	40.8 (1.07)	12.6 (0.72)	9.9 (0.71)	36.0 (1.21)	44.0 (1.32)	10.2 (0.93)	2.0! (0.65)	18.1 (1.58)	51.0 (2.49)	28.9 (2.12)
Spain	32.1 (0.72)	39.6 (0.97)	24.2 (0.78)	4.1 (0.37)	22.8 (1.63)	46.9 (2.07)	26.8 (1.88)	3.6 (0.73)	7.0 (0.88)	33.7 (1.85)	47.4 (2.18)	11.9 (1.35)
Sweden	15.2 (0.79)	27.9 (1.08)	37.5 (1.02)	19.4 (0.76)	13.1 (1.02)	31.5 (1.70)	40.9 (1.90)	14.5 (1.16)	4.9 (0.68)	14.0 (1.69)	40.8 (1.85)	40.2 (2.00)
United States	29.8 (0.93)	32.9 (1.05)	27.7 (0.90)	9.6 (0.66)	36.4 (1.34)	39.3 (1.69)	20.6 (1.58)	3.7 (0.67)	7.5 (0.73)	24.1 (1.56)	45.9 (1.82)	22.6 (1.82)
Non-OECD education systems												
Cyprus[4]	18.9 (0.81)	38.6 (1.17)	33.9 (1.17)	8.7 (0.62)	17.4 (1.30)	42.1 (1.93)	34.1 (1.99)	6.4 (1.08)	5.6 (0.96)	28.5 (2.07)	46.1 (2.26)	19.9 (1.62)
Russian Federation[5]	14.4 (1.66)	39.8 (1.95)	38.1 (1.74)	7.7 (1.44)	17.1 (3.00)	41.5 (3.33)	35.5 (3.59)	5.9 (1.74)	8.5 (1.59)	36.7 (2.84)	42.9 (2.56)	11.9 (2.27)

!Interpret data with caution. The coefficient of variation (CV) for this estimate is between 30 and 50 percent.

[1]Most of the education systems represent complete countries, but three of them represent subnational entities: England (which is part of the United Kingdom), Flanders (which is part of Belgium), and Northern Ireland (which is part of the United Kingdom).

[2]High school completion includes International Standard Classification of Education (ISCED) 1997 levels 3 and 4, with the exception of ISCED level 3C short programs. ISCED 3C short programs do not correspond to high school completion in the United States and are not included in the high school completion columns in this table. The data for bachelor's or higher degree refer to degrees classified as ISCED 1997 level 5A and as level 6.

[3]Refers to the mean of the data values for all reporting Organization for Economic Cooperation and Development (OECD) countries and subnational education systems, to which each country or subnational education system reporting data contributes equally, with the exception of England (UK) and Northern Ireland (UK), which contribute to the mean as a combined entity, England/Northern Ireland (UK).

[4]Cyprus includes only the population under the effective control of the Government of the Republic of Cyprus. For the educational attainment data (columns 6 through 13), the item response rate for Cyprus is below 85 percent; missing data have not been explicitly accounted for.

[5]The Russian Federation does not include the population of the Moscow municipal region.

NOTE: In this table, scores below level 1 and scores at level 1 are combined into the "at or below level 1" reporting category; scores at level 4 and scores at level 5 are combined into the "at level 4 or level 5" reporting category. For both literacy and numeracy, the proficiency-level reporting categories correspond to the score ranges shown in parentheses: at or below level 1 (0–225.9), at level 2 (226.0–275.9), at level 3 (276.0–325.9), at level 4 or level 5 (326.0–500.0).

SOURCE: Organization for Economic Cooperation and Development (OECD), Program for the International Assessment of Adult Competencies (PIAAC), 2012. (This table was prepared May 2016.)

Table 604.30. Employment rates and mean monthly earnings of 25- to 65-year-olds, by literacy proficiency level, numeracy proficiency level, and country or other education system: 2012

[Standard errors appear in parentheses]

Country or other education system[1]	Total population of 25- to 65-year-olds: Employment rate of labor force[3]	Total population of 25- to 65-year-olds: Mean monthly earnings (in current dollars)[4]	Proficiency level[2] At or below level 1: Employment rate of labor force[3]	At or below level 1: Mean monthly earnings (in current dollars)[4]	At level 2: Employment rate of labor force[3]	At level 2: Mean monthly earnings (in current dollars)[4]	At level 3: Employment rate of labor force[3]	At level 3: Mean monthly earnings (in current dollars)[4]	At level 4 or level 5: Employment rate of labor force[3]	At level 4 or level 5: Mean monthly earnings (in current dollars)[4]
1	2	3	4	5	6	7	8	9	10	11
					Literacy					
OECD average[5]	**93.7 (0.08)**	**$2,930 (9)**	**89.7 (0.36)**	**$2,170 (24)**	**93.1 (0.19)**	**$2,580 (16)**	**95.1 (0.16)**	**$3,140 (16)**	**96.4 (0.30)**	**$3,740 (36)**
Austria	96.2 (0.38)	— (†)	92.9 (1.54)	— (†)	96.0 (0.79)	— (†)	97.2 (0.60)	— (†)	97.8 (1.28)	— (†)
Canada	95.9 (0.22)	— (†)	93.7 (0.92)	— (†)	95.4 (0.55)	— (†)	96.7 (0.46)	— (†)	97.3 (0.61)	— (†)
Czech Republic	94.2 (0.20)	1,620 (22)	91.3 (2.62)	1,320 (66)	92.6 (0.93)	1,470 (43)	95.6 (0.87)	1,720 (43)	97.7 (1.39)	2,030 (96)
Denmark	94.5 (0.38)	4,090 (28)	90.8 (1.45)	3,210 (84)	94.5 (0.75)	3,730 (53)	95.0 (0.62)	4,390 (58)	96.4 (1.44)	4,850 (139)
England (UK)	94.0 (0.08)	3,180 (43)	87.5 (1.65)	2,140 (108)	92.5 (0.91)	2,610 (91)	96.2 (0.55)	3,440 (96)	97.3 (0.79)	4,380 (151)
Estonia	93.4 (0.34)	1,750 (25)	89.5 (1.48)	1,420 (75)	92.1 (0.75)	1,560 (42)	94.5 (0.53)	1,820 (41)	97.4 (0.74)	2,260 (87)
Finland	95.5 (0.39)	3,250 (18)	92.5 (2.04)	2,670 (120)	95.3 (0.84)	2,920 (56)	95.8 (0.59)	3,330 (43)	96.1 (0.63)	3,590 (56)
Flanders (Belgium)	98.0 (0.21)	3,650 (35)	96.5 (0.93)	2,790 (106)	97.4 (0.55)	3,220 (67)	98.6 (0.40)	3,860 (69)	98.9 (0.68)	4,470 (151)
France	92.9 (0.19)	2,490 (17)	89.4 (1.08)	1,910 (39)	92.9 (0.66)	2,340 (33)	94.3 (0.64)	2,760 (33)	95.0 (1.39)	3,270 (84)
Germany	95.2 (0.40)	— (†)	91.1 (1.53)	— (†)	94.9 (0.84)	— (†)	96.3 (0.63)	— (†)	98.3 (0.73)	— (†)
Ireland	89.2 (0.53)	3,410 (52)	83.6 (1.95)	2,370 (106)	86.7 (1.12)	2,950 (68)	92.0 (1.02)	3,820 (90)	95.8 (1.36)	4,610 (206)
Italy	87.7 (0.66)	2,510 (36)	84.1 (1.91)	2,290 (103)	87.2 (1.30)	2,360 (68)	90.8 (1.34)	2,800 (75)	93.5 (3.39)	3,140 (248)
Japan	97.6 (0.22)	3,000 (37)	98.9 (1.01)	2,210 (199)	99.1 (0.63)	2,540 (84)	97.5 (0.45)	3,000 (60)	96.2 (0.83)	3,550 (100)
Korea, Republic of	96.8 (0.27)	3,000 (32)	97.4 (0.86)	2,180 (86)	97.0 (0.53)	2,820 (60)	96.7 (0.59)	3,290 (63)	95.5 (1.71)	3,960 (133)
Netherlands	95.8 (0.41)	3,490 (30)	91.5 (2.00)	2,350 (117)	94.7 (0.93)	2,930 (75)	97.0 (0.59)	3,640 (63)	96.8 (0.88)	4,230 (90)
Northern Ireland (UK)	94.7 (0.49)	2,750 (42)	90.6 (2.03)	1,820 (90)	94.4 (0.96)	2,330 (96)	95.9 (1.01)	3,070 (92)	96.0 (2.10)	3,870 (188)
Norway	97.1 (0.31)	4,090 (30)	93.6 (1.66)	2,910 (110)	96.8 (0.74)	3,630 (66)	97.6 (0.45)	4,340 (56)	98.8 (0.65)	4,850 (99)
Poland	91.9 (0.49)	1,610 (22)	88.0 (1.75)	1,260 (56)	90.8 (1.08)	1,430 (52)	93.9 (0.89)	1,780 (56)	95.5 (1.56)	2,190 (90)
Slovak Republic	90.7 (0.48)	1,570 (25)	79.6 (2.60)	1,060 (63)	90.4 (1.06)	1,380 (39)	92.5 (0.80)	1,700 (46)	93.3 (2.09)	2,110 (150)
Spain	82.7 (0.63)	2,390 (32)	75.1 (1.60)	1,910 (55)	82.5 (1.32)	2,260 (48)	87.4 (1.19)	2,680 (61)	92.1 (2.30)	3,280 (157)
Sweden	94.9 (0.44)	— (†)	85.3 (2.21)	— (†)	94.2 (1.01)	— (†)	96.3 (0.69)	— (†)	98.4 (0.73)	— (†)
United States	92.5 (0.44)	4,260 (80)	89.0 (1.53)	2,730 (150)	90.8 (1.13)	3,480 (110)	93.8 (0.85)	4,740 (148)	97.1 (0.72)	6,310 (323)
Non-OECD education systems										
Cyprus[6]	92.0 (0.64)	2,860 (38)	87.3 (2.50)	2,490 (149)	91.8 (1.22)	2,660 (73)	93.1 (1.03)	3,010 (73)	93.9 (2.04)	3,440 (197)
Russian Federation[7]	94.9 (1.02)	840 (25)	95.0 (2.53)	790 (55)	95.9 (1.48)	770 (31)	95.0 (1.33)	870 (36)	91.7 (2.82)	1,000 (61)
					Numeracy					
OECD average[5]	**93.7 (0.08)**	**$2,930 (9)**	**88.8 (0.36)**	**$2,110 (21)**	**93.2 (0.20)**	**$2,560 (16)**	**95.5 (0.17)**	**$3,180 (18)**	**97.0 (0.27)**	**$3,940 (38)**
Austria	96.2 (0.38)	— (†)	92.7 (1.56)	— (†)	95.9 (0.79)	— (†)	97.0 (0.56)	— (†)	97.6 (0.88)	— (†)
Canada	95.9 (0.22)	— (†)	93.0 (0.83)	— (†)	95.7 (0.57)	— (†)	96.8 (0.54)	— (†)	98.4 (0.58)	— (†)
Czech Republic	94.2 (0.20)	1,620 (22)	87.3 (2.81)	1,280 (56)	92.8 (0.92)	1,460 (38)	95.9 (0.69)	1,690 (43)	97.9 (1.82)	2,060 (86)
Denmark	94.5 (0.38)	4,090 (28)	89.4 (1.72)	3,100 (84)	93.2 (1.02)	3,580 (66)	95.6 (0.60)	4,210 (64)	96.8 (0.77)	4,980 (98)
England (UK)	94.0 (0.08)	3,180 (43)	87.6 (1.25)	2,120 (90)	94.1 (0.83)	2,690 (81)	96.5 (0.74)	3,650 (102)	97.6 (0.87)	4,530 (179)
Estonia	93.4 (0.34)	1,750 (25)	87.6 (1.53)	1,250 (65)	92.2 (0.76)	1,520 (46)	94.9 (0.58)	1,850 (45)	98.0 (0.73)	2,470 (83)
Finland	95.5 (0.39)	3,250 (18)	90.8 (2.06)	2,510 (89)	94.9 (0.94)	2,880 (57)	96.3 (0.58)	3,320 (47)	96.8 (0.62)	3,830 (73)
Flanders (Belgium)	98.0 (0.21)	3,650 (35)	96.8 (0.99)	2,640 (96)	97.4 (0.62)	3,100 (65)	98.5 (0.39)	3,740 (57)	98.5 (0.51)	4,650 (129)
France	92.9 (0.19)	2,490 (17)	89.1 (0.87)	1,850 (31)	92.4 (0.75)	2,300 (32)	95.5 (0.84)	2,860 (37)	95.7 (1.42)	3,440 (87)
Germany	95.2 (0.40)	— (†)	89.8 (1.52)	— (†)	94.5 (0.89)	— (†)	96.4 (0.65)	— (†)	98.8 (0.58)	— (†)
Ireland	89.2 (0.53)	3,410 (52)	84.1 (1.85)	2,340 (96)	88.2 (1.12)	3,030 (85)	92.1 (1.17)	3,970 (113)	94.9 (1.77)	4,990 (281)
Italy	87.7 (0.66)	2,510 (36)	82.5 (1.91)	2,260 (105)	88.0 (1.28)	2,330 (60)	90.8 (1.28)	2,770 (84)	95.0 (2.64)	3,290 (205)
Japan	97.6 (0.22)	3,000 (37)	98.8 (0.95)	1,980 (141)	96.9 (0.83)	2,420 (85)	97.6 (0.54)	2,990 (66)	98.1 (0.64)	4,030 (99)
Korea, Republic of	96.8 (0.27)	3,000 (32)	96.4 (0.85)	2,210 (72)	96.8 (0.52)	2,880 (61)	96.9 (0.61)	3,370 (68)	97.1 (1.17)	4,040 (145)
Netherlands	95.8 (0.41)	3,490 (30)	90.1 (1.95)	2,280 (116)	95.5 (0.92)	2,900 (79)	96.9 (0.57)	3,650 (70)	97.2 (0.96)	4,470 (106)
Northern Ireland (UK)	94.7 (0.49)	2,750 (42)	91.2 (1.54)	1,810 (81)	94.5 (1.19)	2,400 (70)	96.4 (1.06)	3,230 (107)	96.0 (2.39)	3,990 (213)
Norway	97.1 (0.31)	4,090 (30)	92.9 (1.65)	2,880 (119)	96.6 (0.77)	3,480 (69)	97.9 (0.45)	4,250 (61)	98.5 (0.56)	5,110 (101)
Poland	91.9 (0.49)	1,610 (22)	86.5 (1.75)	1,260 (53)	91.8 (1.15)	1,430 (38)	94.0 (0.86)	1,800 (49)	96.4 (1.47)	2,290 (107)
Slovak Republic	90.7 (0.48)	1,570 (25)	75.3 (2.92)	1,030 (62)	89.5 (1.12)	1,320 (52)	93.4 (0.77)	1,660 (43)	94.9 (1.41)	2,090 (94)
Spain	82.7 (0.63)	2,390 (32)	74.2 (1.59)	1,830 (51)	82.7 (1.45)	2,270 (53)	88.9 (1.51)	2,800 (68)	93.3 (2.70)	3,300 (170)
Sweden	94.9 (0.44)	— (†)	86.2 (2.24)	— (†)	93.9 (1.33)	— (†)	96.5 (0.68)	— (†)	98.2 (0.63)	— (†)
United States	92.5 (0.44)	4,260 (80)	88.2 (1.36)	2,760 (94)	91.3 (1.13)	3,690 (120)	95.6 (0.92)	5,110 (157)	98.1 (0.71)	6,780 (370)
Non-OECD education systems										
Cyprus[6]	92.0 (0.64)	2,860 (38)	86.6 (2.24)	2,250 (112)	91.7 (1.26)	2,630 (75)	93.4 (1.04)	3,050 (74)	95.9 (1.57)	3,640 (163)
Russian Federation[7]	94.9 (1.02)	840 (25)	96.3 (2.04)	750 (55)	95.5 (1.41)	780 (35)	94.9 (1.53)	890 (38)	90.5 (3.89)	990 (68)

—Not available.
†Not applicable.
[1]Most of the education systems represent complete countries, but three of them represent subnational entities: England (which is part of the United Kingdom), Flanders (which is part of Belgium), and Northern Ireland (which is part of the United Kingdom).
[2]In this table, scores below level 1 and scores at level 1 are combined into the "at or below level 1" reporting category; scores at level 4 and scores at level 5 are combined into the "at level 4 or level 5" reporting category. For both literacy and numeracy, the proficiency-level reporting categories correspond to the score ranges shown in parentheses: at or below level 1 (0–225.9), at level 2 (226.0–275.9), at level 3 (276.0–325.9), at level 4 or level 5 (326.0–500.0).
[3]The employment rate is the percentage of the labor force that is employed. The labor force consists of those who are employed as well as those who are unemployed but actively looking for work.
[4]Mean monthly earnings for those who are employed. Data adjusted to U.S. dollars using the purchasing power parity (PPP) index.
[5]Refers to the mean of the data values for all reporting Organization for Economic Cooperation and Development (OECD) countries and subnational education systems, to which each country or subnational education system reporting data contributes equally, with the exception of England (UK) and Northern Ireland (UK), which contribute to the mean as a combined entity, England/Northern Ireland (UK).
[6]Cyprus includes only the population under the effective control of the Government of the Republic of Cyprus.
[7]The Russian Federation does not include the population of the Moscow municipal region.
SOURCE: Organization for Economic Cooperation and Development (OECD), Program for the International Assessment of Adult Competencies (PIAAC), 2012. (This table was prepared March 2016.)

Table 605.10. Gross domestic product per capita and expenditures on education institutions per full-time-equivalent (FTE) student, by level of education and country: Selected years, 2005 through 2015

Country	Gross domestic product per capita						Elementary and secondary education expenditures per FTE student[1]						Higher education expenditures per FTE student[1]					
	2005	2010	2012	2013	2014	2015	2005	2010	2012	2013	2014	2015	2005	2010	2012	2013	2014	2015
1	2	3	4	5	6	7	8	9	10	11	12	13	14	15	16	17	18	19
	Current dollars																	
OECD average[2]	**$28,852**	**$34,788**	**$37,278[3]**	**$38,853[3]**	**$39,973[3]**	**$41,259[3]**	**$6,079**	**$8,195**	**$8,901**	**$9,009**	**$9,232**	**$9,258**	**$9,749**	**$12,882**	**$14,565**	**$15,032**	**$15,359**	**$15,611**
Australia	35,545	42,740	43,810	47,679	47,551	47,273	6,891	10,325	9,560	10,318	10,319	10,766	14,172	16,326	16,003	18,253	19,494	20,344
Austria	35,025	42,018	46,478	47,937	48,814	49,954	—	—	12,481	13,391	13,454	13,931	—	—	16,476	16,900	16,868	17,555
Belgium	33,331	40,050	42,585	43,746	44,720	45,729	7,583	10,467	11,280	11,719	11,866	11,856	12,286	15,464	15,953	16,697	17,002	17,320
Canada[4,5]	36,213	40,012	42,145	44,101	45,520	44,407	—	9,950	10,398	10,536	10,502	10,468	—	—	20,987[6]	21,474[6]	21,458[6]	21,848[6]
Chile	12,668	18,129	21,447	22,353	22,692	22,601	2,140	3,284	4,534	4,376	4,167	4,227	5,969	7,171	8,354	7,974	7,813	6,677
Czech Republic	21,907	27,555	29,051	30,496	32,265	33,701	4,051	5,768	6,482	6,639	6,887	7,075	6,572	7,961	10,422	10,308	10,490	10,891
Denmark	34,153	43,005	44,809	46,743	47,905	49,071	8,942	11,760	11,477	11,808	12,827	—	14,867	19,571	14,746[6]	15,698	15,626	—
Estonia	16,466	21,552	25,973	27,450	28,937	29,260	3,706	6,219	6,534	6,897	6,436	6,663	3,838	6,756	8,490	11,798	11,965	12,867
Finland	31,993	38,737	40,620	41,293	41,463	42,144	6,637	8,835	9,448	9,659	9,769	10,025	12,332	17,189	18,046	18,018	17,875	17,591
France	30,504	35,909	37,684	39,529	40,145	40,833	7,483	9,265	9,312	9,778	9,918	9,897	11,220	15,160	15,392	16,234	16,354	16,145
Germany	32,414	39,916	43,564	45,232	47,190	47,979	7,061	9,203	9,821	10,300	10,779	10,863	13,056	17,309	17,143	16,949	17,144	17,036
Greece[4]	25,577	28,148	25,284[7]	26,098[7]	26,839[7]	26,902[7]	5,354	—	6,006	6,277	6,192	6,191	6,320	—	3,811[6]	3,713[6]	3,881[6]	4,095[6]
Hungary	17,082	21,535	23,094	24,464	25,518	26,356	3,555	—	4,452	4,642	5,552	5,852	5,522	—	9,039	10,374	8,647	8,761
Iceland	37,338	39,582	41,928	44,153	45,713	48,730	8,962[8]	8,806	9,241	9,757	10,599	11,207	9,665[8]	8,945	10,898	11,200	11,418	12,671
Ireland	40,437	43,296	46,304	48,006	51,250	69,050	6,481	9,751	10,071	9,434	9,170	8,671	10,582	16,350	15,622	12,993	13,702	13,229
Israel	24,700	28,840	31,738	34,193	34,278	35,527	4,579	5,696	6,765	7,215	7,302	—	9,952	10,340	11,681	13,592	13,103	11,003[4]
Italy[4]	29,938	34,685	35,757	35,885	36,071	36,836	7,103	8,170	8,609	8,840	8,727	8,996	7,274	10,064	10,669	11,303	11,439	11,257
Japan[8]	31,668	34,994	37,214	39,008	39,183	40,457	7,452	8,886	9,564	9,802	10,022	10,167	13,915	17,399	18,828	19,724	19,547	19,289
Korea, Republic of	24,196	30,365	32,097	32,616	33,587	35,761	5,696	9,123	10,344	10,524	10,804	11,688	7,736	11,018	11,391	11,402	11,711	10,109
Latvia	13,848	17,561	21,260	22,675	23,802	24,726	3,033	4,758	5,098	5,968	6,631	6,824	4,270	5,859	7,411	8,051	8,974	10,137
Lithuania	14,526	20,091	24,658	26,661	28,174	28,910	—	4,539	4,803	5,212	5,383	5,292	4,496	7,182	8,964	9,147	10,049	9,657
Luxembourg	68,141	85,515	91,527	95,246	100,934	102,817	—	—	19,943	18,758	20,939	20,451	—	—	34,761[6]	41,995[6]	45,801[6]	48,907[6]
Mexico	12,522	15,239	17,195	17,437	18,143[3]	18,414[3]	2,025	2,547	2,826	2,925	3,033	2,998	6,225	8,138	8,188	7,693	8,901	8,170
Netherlands	37,632	45,050	47,280	49,255	49,239	50,329	7,760	9,899	10,338	10,995	10,674	10,960	15,411	17,617	18,758	19,588	19,234	19,286
New Zealand	25,590	31,165	32,912	36,074	37,083	37,341	—	—	8,360	8,770	9,064	9,266	—	—	13,603	14,234	15,109	15,166
Norway	47,775	57,969	65,442	67,051	66,018	60,492	9,793	12,945	13,508[9]	14,396[9]	14,194	14,353	—	18,873	20,052[9]	21,179[9]	21,009	20,973
Poland	13,898	20,789	23,542	24,423	25,298	26,529	3,181	5,585	6,362	6,608	6,824	6,725	4,774	7,136	7,731	8,423	8,793	9,687
Portugal	22,740	27,308	26,454	27,899	28,747	29,685	5,620	—	8,232[8]	9,514[8]	9,411[8]	8,533[8]	9,636	10,270	9,798[8]	11,094[8]	11,788[8]	11,766[8]
Slovak Republic	16,572	24,785	26,654	27,900	28,928	29,700	2,770	5,282	5,382	5,929	6,369	6,747	5,846	7,198	9,282	10,225	11,234	15,874
Slovenia	23,941	27,736	28,906	29,803	30,857	31,627	6,972	8,676	8,838	8,950	8,875	8,406	7,936	8,991	10,015	9,865	10,037	10,208
Spain	27,696	31,933	31,993	32,623	33,728	35,055	6,329	8,371	7,963	7,753	7,814	8,189	9,924	13,204	12,083	12,699	12,524	12,605
Sweden	34,006	41,633	44,774	45,722	46,573	48,437	7,672	10,106	10,860	11,061	11,007	11,052	15,550	20,654	23,142	23,817	24,509	24,417
Switzerland	40,327	52,860	57,850	60,109	61,902	63,939	—	—	16,862	—	—	—	—	—	24,848	—	—	—
Turkey	11,773	17,264	20,549[3]	22,314[3]	24,159[3]	25,986[3]	—	—	2,977	3,203	3,560	3,715	—	—	10,116	10,298	10,393	8,901
United Kingdom	32,486	36,016	37,908	39,519	40,878	42,055	7,698	9,432	9,967	11,487	11,875	11,028	—	—	24,112	25,614	24,346	26,320
United States	44,044	48,394	51,521	53,016	54,935	56,701	9,775	11,815	11,743	11,881	12,176	12,424	23,637	25,681	27,527	27,579	29,328	30,003

See notes at end of table.

Table 605.10. Gross domestic product per capita and expenditures on education institutions per full-time-equivalent (FTE) student, by level of education and country: Selected years, 2005 through 2015—Continued

Country	Gross domestic product per capita						Elementary and secondary education expenditures per FTE student[1]						Higher education expenditures per FTE student[1]					
	2005	2010	2012	2013	2014	2015	2005	2010	2012	2013	2014	2015	2005	2010	2012	2013	2014	2015
1	2	3	4	5	6	7	8	9	10	11	12	13	14	15	16	17	18	19
	Constant 2017 dollars																	
OECD average[2]	**$36,813**	**$38,819**	**$39,498[3]**	**$40,552[3]**	**$41,273[3]**	**$42,368[3]**	**$7,730**	**$9,117**	**$9,389**	**$9,396**	**$9,529**	**$9,520**	**$12,318**	**$14,295**	**$15,470**	**$15,754**	**$15,905**	**$16,063**
Australia	47,626	49,444	48,211	51,215	49,837	48,810	9,233	11,945	10,521	11,083	10,815	11,116	18,988	18,887	17,610	19,606	20,431	21,005
Austria	43,707	47,900	50,054	50,613	50,724	51,448	—	—	13,442	14,139	13,981	14,348	—	—	17,744	17,843	17,528	18,080
Belgium	41,709	45,309	45,248	45,969	46,834	47,623	9,489	11,842	11,985	12,315	12,427	12,347	15,374	17,494	16,950	17,546	17,805	18,038
Canada[4,5]	44,151	44,807	45,176	46,833	47,435	45,760	—	11,142	11,146	11,188	10,943	10,787	—	—	22,496[6]	22,804[6]	22,361[6]	22,514[6]
Chile	18,965	22,724	25,254	25,823	25,111	23,968	3,204	4,117	5,339	5,055	4,611	4,483	8,936	8,989	9,838	9,212	8,646	7,081
Czech Republic	27,926	30,549	30,597	31,663	33,385	34,763	5,163	6,395	6,827	6,893	7,126	7,298	8,378	8,827	10,976	10,702	10,854	11,234
Denmark	41,219	46,718	46,261	47,880	48,796	49,758	10,792	12,776	11,849	12,095	13,066	—	17,943	21,260	15,224[6]	16,079	15,917	—
Estonia	24,034	24,883	27,483	28,260	29,822	30,305	5,410	7,181	6,914	7,101	6,633	6,901	5,602	7,801	8,983	12,146	12,331	13,327
Finland	38,583	42,611	42,026	42,100	41,837	42,613	8,004	9,718	9,775	9,848	9,857	10,137	14,872	18,908	18,670	18,370	18,036	17,787
France	35,144	38,374	38,682	40,229	40,649	41,331	8,621	9,901	9,559	9,951	10,043	10,018	12,927	16,201	15,800	16,521	16,559	16,341
Germany	38,313	43,622	45,722	46,769	48,356	49,049	8,346	10,058	10,308	10,650	11,045	11,106	15,433	18,916	17,993	17,525	17,568	17,415
Greece[4]	30,296	28,447	24,363[7]	25,381[7]	26,448[7]	26,979[7]	6,342	—	5,787	6,104	6,102	6,208	7,486	—	3,673[6]	3,611[6]	3,824[6]	4,106[6]
Hungary	25,418	24,647	24,072	25,065	26,204	27,082	5,290	—	4,640	4,756	5,701	6,013	8,217	—	9,422	10,629	8,880	9,003
Iceland	67,894	48,273	46,743	47,388	48,079	50,429	16,295[8]	10,739	10,302	10,472	11,148	11,598	17,574[8]	10,909	12,149	12,021	12,009	13,113
Ireland	45,622	45,495	46,652	48,122	51,280	69,291	7,312	10,246	10,147	9,457	9,175	8,701	11,939	17,180	15,739	13,024	13,710	13,276
Israel	29,927	30,685	32,092	34,046	33,969	35,419	5,548	6,061	6,841	7,184	7,236	—	12,058	11,002	11,811	13,534	12,985	10,970[4]
Italy[4]	35,776	37,708	36,705	36,393	36,493	37,253	8,488	8,882	8,837	8,965	8,830	9,098	8,692	10,941	10,952	11,463	11,573	11,384
Japan[8]	32,790	36,381	38,812	40,544	39,631	40,598	7,716	9,238	9,975	10,188	10,137	10,203	14,408	18,088	19,636	20,500	19,770	19,357
Korea, Republic of	31,750	34,328	34,135	34,241	34,817	36,810	7,474	10,314	11,001	11,049	11,200	12,031	10,152	12,456	12,114	11,970	12,140	10,406
Latvia	21,279	19,466	22,081	23,558	24,577	25,487	4,661	5,274	5,295	6,200	6,847	7,034	6,562	6,494	7,698	8,365	9,266	10,448
Lithuania	21,070	22,631	25,874	27,686	29,227	30,258	—	5,113	5,040	5,413	5,585	5,538	6,522	8,090	9,406	9,499	10,425	10,107
Luxembourg	84,642	95,275	96,052	98,252	103,468	104,901	—	—	20,929	19,350	21,464	20,865	—	—	36,480[6]	43,320[6]	46,951[6]	49,898[6]
Mexico	20,252	19,841	20,795	20,315	20,320[3]	20,077[3]	3,275	3,316	3,418	3,408	3,396	3,269	10,068	10,596	9,902	8,963	9,969	8,908
Netherlands	45,088	50,024	50,071	50,886	50,378	51,185	9,298	10,992	10,948	11,359	10,921	11,147	18,464	19,562	19,865	20,237	19,679	19,615
New Zealand	32,541	34,485	34,641	37,543	38,125	38,278	—	—	8,799	9,127	9,319	9,498	—	—	14,317	14,813	15,533	15,546
Norway	61,251	66,403	73,501	73,745	71,156	63,814	12,556	14,828	15,171[9]	15,833[9]	15,299	15,142	—	21,619	22,521[9]	23,293[9]	22,644	22,125
Poland	17,537	22,793	23,910	24,561	25,427	26,900	4,014	6,123	6,461	6,645	6,859	6,819	6,025	7,824	7,852	8,470	8,838	9,823
Portugal	27,052	29,811	27,110	28,512	29,460	30,274	6,686	—	8,436[8]	9,723[8]	9,645[8]	8,703[8]	11,463	11,211	10,041[8]	11,338[8]	12,081[8]	11,999[8]
Slovak Republic	20,923	27,162	27,130	28,006	29,060	29,933	3,497	5,789	5,478	5,951	6,398	6,800	7,381	7,888	9,447	10,264	11,285	15,999
Slovenia	29,617	29,789	29,724	30,113	31,116	32,062	8,625	9,318	9,089	9,043	8,950	8,521	9,818	9,656	10,298	9,968	10,121	10,348
Spain	33,739	34,608	32,797	32,978	34,147	35,668	7,709	9,072	8,163	7,837	7,911	8,332	12,090	14,310	12,386	12,837	12,679	12,826
Sweden	39,063	44,335	45,902	46,894	47,852	49,791	8,813	10,762	11,133	11,345	11,310	11,361	17,862	21,995	23,724	24,428	25,182	25,100
Switzerland	41,404	51,944	57,111	59,471	61,253	64,001	—	—	16,647	—	—	—	—	—	24,531	—	—	—
Turkey	31,280	30,207	31,012[3]	31,328[3]	31,159[3]	31,128[3]	—	—	4,493	4,497	4,591	4,450	—	—	15,267	14,458	13,404	10,662
United Kingdom	42,387	41,413	40,910	41,692	42,519	43,569	10,044	10,845	10,756	12,118	12,352	11,425	—	—	26,021	27,022	25,323	27,268
United States	55,281	54,400	55,005	55,784	56,881	58,639	12,269	13,281	12,537	12,502	12,607	12,849	29,668	28,869	29,388	29,019	30,367	31,029

—Not available.
[1]Includes both government and private expenditures. Includes expenditures on both public and private institutions unless otherwise noted.
[2]Refers to the mean of the data values for all reporting Organization for Economic Cooperation and Development (OECD) countries, to which each country reporting data contributes equally. The average includes all current OECD countries for which a given year's data are available, even if they were not members of OECD in that year.
[3]Estimated value.
[4]Education expenditures exclude postsecondary non-higher-education.
[5]Elementary and secondary education expenditures include preprimary education (for children ages 3 and older).
[6]Includes public institutions only.
[7]Provisional value; data subject to revision.
[8]Postsecondary non-higher-education included in both secondary and higher education.
[9]Short-cycle tertiary education corresponding to that offered at the vocational associate's degree level in the United States is included in elementary and secondary education instead of in higher education.
NOTE: All education expenditure data in this table were calculated using International Standard Classification of Education (ISCED) 2011. Expenditures for International Standard Classification of Education (ISCED) level 4 (postsecondary non-higher-education) are included in elementary and secondary education unless otherwise noted. Data adjusted to U.S. dollars using the purchasing power parity (PPP) index. Constant dollars based on national Consumer Price Indexes, available on the OECD database cited in the SOURCE note below. Some data have been revised from previously published figures. This table includes only data that had been validated for consistency and accuracy by OECD and the relevant country as of January 11, 2019.
SOURCE: Organization for Economic Cooperation and Development (OECD), Online Education Database, retrieved January 11, 2019, from https://stats.oecd.org/Index.aspx. (This table was prepared January 2019.)

Table 605.20. Government and private expenditures on education institutions as a percentage of gross domestic product, by level of education and country: Selected years, 2005 through 2015

Country	All institutions[1]								Elementary and secondary institutions								Higher education institutions							
	Government expenditures					All expenditures, 2015			Government expenditures					All expenditures, 2015			Government expenditures					All expenditures, 2015		
	2005	2010	2012	2013	2014	Government	Private	Total	2005	2010	2012	2013	2014	Government	Private	Total	2005	2010	2012	2013	2014	Government	Private	Total
1	2	3	4	5	6	7	8	9	10	11	12	13	14	15	16	17	18	19	20	21	22	23	24	25
OECD average[2]	**4.2**	**4.5**	**4.3**	**4.3**	**4.3**	**4.1**	**0.8**	**5.0**	**3.3**	**3.4**	**3.3**	**3.3**	**3.2**	**3.1**	**0.3**	**3.5**	**1.0**	**1.0**	**1.0**	**1.0**	**1.0**	**1.0**	**0.5**	**1.5**
Australia	3.9	4.6	4.0[3]	4.0	3.9	4.0	2.0	6.0	3.2	3.8	3.3	3.3	3.2	3.2	0.7	3.9	0.7	0.8	0.7[3]	0.7	0.7	0.8	1.3	2.0
Austria	—	—	4.7	4.7	4.6	4.6	0.3	4.9	—	—	3.0	3.1	3.0	3.0	0.1	3.1	—	—	1.7	1.6	1.6	1.6	0.1	1.7
Belgium	4.9	5.3	5.4	5.5	5.4	5.4	0.4	5.7	3.9	4.1	4.2	4.2	4.2	4.1	0.1	4.3	1.1	1.2	1.2	1.3	1.3	1.2	0.2	1.5
Canada	4.2	4.8	4.5	4.4	4.3	4.4	1.6	6.0	2.9	3.3	3.2[4,5]	3.2[4,5]	3.1[4,5]	3.2[4,5]	0.3[4,5]	3.5[4,5]	1.3	1.5	1.3	1.2	1.2	1.2	1.2	2.4
Chile	2.8	3.2	3.5	3.5	3.3	3.4	1.9	5.2	2.5	2.7	2.9	2.6	2.5	2.6	0.5	3.2	0.3	0.5	0.6	0.8	0.9	0.7	1.3	2.0
Czech Republic	3.3	3.3	3.5	3.3	3.2	3.2	0.5	3.8	2.5	2.5	2.5	2.4	2.4	2.4	0.2	2.6	0.8	0.9	1.0	0.9	0.8	0.8	0.2	1.2
Denmark	5.9	6.2	6.0	6.0	6.2	—	—	—	4.3	4.6	4.5	4.4	4.7	—	—	—	1.6	1.7	1.5	1.5	1.6	—	—	—
Estonia	4.2	4.8	4.1	4.3	4.0	4.0	0.6	4.7	3.4	3.8	3.1	3.1	2.7	2.7	0.2	3.0	0.8	1.0	0.9	1.2	1.4	1.3	0.4	1.8
Finland	5.3	5.7	5.7	5.6	5.6	5.6	0.1	5.7	3.7	3.9	3.9	3.9	3.9	4.0	#	4.0	1.6	1.8	1.8	1.7	1.7	1.6	0.1	1.7
France	4.6	4.8	4.6	4.6	4.6	4.5	0.6	5.2	3.5	3.6	3.4	3.4	3.4	3.4	0.3	3.7	1.1	1.2	1.1	1.1	1.1	1.1	0.3	1.5
Germany	3.7	3.9	3.7	3.7	3.7	3.6	0.6	4.2	2.8	2.9	2.7	2.7	2.7	2.6	0.4	3.0	0.9	1.0	1.0	1.0	1.0	1.0	0.2	1.2
Greece	3.9	—	3.4	3.3	3.3	3.4	0.3	3.8	2.5	—	2.6	2.7	2.7	2.7	0.2[5]	2.9[5]	1.4	—	0.7	0.6	0.6	0.7	0.1	1.0
Hungary	4.1	3.6	3.1	3.1	3.3	3.2	0.5	3.8	3.2	2.7	2.4	2.3	2.7	2.7	0.2	2.9	0.8	0.8	0.7	0.8	0.7[3]	0.6	0.3	0.9
Iceland	6.1[5]	5.5[5]	5.5	5.5	5.6	5.5	0.3	5.8	5.0[5]	4.5[5]	4.4	4.3	4.5	4.4	0.2	4.5	1.1	1.1	1.1	1.1	1.1	1.1	0.1	1.3
Ireland	4.0	5.4	5.3	4.7	4.3	3.1	0.4	3.5	3.1	4.3	4.1	3.8	3.5	2.5	0.1	2.7	0.9	1.2	1.1	0.9	0.8	0.6	0.2	0.8
Israel	4.4	4.5	4.7	4.7	4.7	4.9	1.1	6.0	3.5	3.7	3.9	3.9	3.9	4.0	0.5	4.5	0.8	0.8	0.8	0.8	0.8	0.9	0.6	1.5
Italy	3.6	3.6	3.4	3.5	3.4	3.3	0.5	3.9	3.0	3.0	2.8	2.8	2.8	2.8	0.2	3.0	0.6	0.6	0.6	0.6	0.6	0.6	0.3	0.9
Japan[6]	2.9	3.2	3.1	3.1	3.0	2.9	1.1	4.1	2.5	2.6	2.6	2.5	2.5	2.5	0.2	2.7	0.5	0.5	0.5	0.5	0.5	0.5	0.9	1.4
Korea, Republic of	3.5	4.2	4.4	4.4	4.3	4.1	1.7	5.8	2.9	3.5	3.7	3.6	3.5	3.5	0.5	4.0	0.5	0.7	0.7	0.7	0.8	0.7	1.2	1.8
Latvia	3.9	4.0	3.6	3.9	4.3	4.3	0.4	4.9	3.1	3.2	2.8	3.0	3.2	3.3	0.1	3.3	0.8	0.7	0.8	0.9	1.0	1.1	0.3	1.5
Luthuania	3.9	4.4	4.0	3.8	3.7	3.4	0.5	3.9	3.0	3.3	2.7	2.6	2.5	2.3	0.1	2.4	0.8	1.1	1.3	1.2	1.2	1.1	0.4	1.5
Luxembourg	—	—	3.5	3.3	3.3	3.3	0.1	3.5	3.7	3.5	3.1	2.8	2.9	2.8	0.1	2.9	—	—	0.4	0.5	0.5	0.5	#	0.5
Mexico	4.0	4.2	4.1	4.1	4.2	4.2	1.1	5.3	3.2	3.2	3.2	3.2	3.2	3.2	0.7	3.9	0.8	0.9	0.9	0.8	1.0	1.0	0.4	1.4
Netherlands	4.2	4.4	4.4	4.5	4.4	4.3	1.0	5.4	3.1	3.3	3.3	3.3	3.2	3.2	0.5	3.6	1.0	1.1	1.2	1.2	1.2	1.2	0.5	1.7
New Zealand	—	—	4.9	4.7	4.7	4.7	1.6	6.3	—	—	3.9	3.8	3.8	3.8	0.8	4.5	—	—	0.9	0.9	0.9	0.9	0.9	1.8
Norway	6.6	6.4	6.1	6.2	6.1	6.3	0.1	6.4	4.9	4.9	4.6	4.7[7]	4.5	4.6	#	4.6	1.7	1.6	1.5	1.5[7]	1.6	1.7	0.1	1.7
Poland	4.8[5]	4.4[5]	4.1	4.1	4.1	4.0	0.5	4.6	3.6[5]	3.4[5]	3.1	3.1	3.0	2.9	0.3	3.2	1.2	1.0	1.0	1.1	1.0	1.1	0.2	1.4
Portugal[6]	4.4	4.6	4.2	4.5	4.4	4.1	0.9	5.2	3.6	3.7	3.5	3.8	3.6	3.4	0.4	3.9	0.8	0.9	0.7	0.7	0.8	0.7	0.4	1.3
Slovak Republic	3.1	3.3	3.1	3.2	3.3	3.8	0.6	4.4	2.4	2.6	2.3	2.4	2.5	2.6	0.3	2.9	0.7	0.6	0.7	0.8	0.8	1.2	0.3	1.6
Slovenia	4.7	4.5	4.4	4.3	4.1	3.8	0.5	4.3	3.7	3.5	3.4	3.3	3.2	3.0	0.3	3.3	0.9	1.0	1.0	1.0	0.9	0.9	0.1	1.0
Spain	3.5	4.0	3.7	3.6	3.5	3.5	0.8	4.4	2.7	2.9	2.7	2.7	2.6	2.7	0.4	3.1	0.8	1.0	0.9	0.9	0.9	0.9	0.4	1.3
Sweden	5.3	5.2	5.2	5.2	5.1	5.0	0.2	5.3	4.0	3.8	3.7	3.7	3.7	3.6	†	3.6	1.3	1.5	1.4	1.5	1.4	1.4	0.2	1.6
Switzerland	4.7	4.4[5]	4.6	4.6	4.6	4.5	—	—	3.5	3.2[5]	3.4	3.4	3.4	3.2	—	—	1.3	1.2	1.2	1.2	1.3	1.3	—	—
Turkey	2.7	3.3	3.9	3.9	3.9	3.8	1.0	4.8	1.9	2.4	2.6	2.6	2.6	2.5	0.6	3.1	0.7	0.9	1.3	1.3	1.3	1.2	0.4	1.7
United Kingdom	—	—	4.6	4.9	4.6	4.2	1.9	6.2	3.3	3.3	3.6	3.9	4.1	3.8	0.6	4.4	—	—	1.0	1.0	0.5	0.5	1.3	1.9
United States	4.5[5]	4.7[5]	4.4	4.2	4.1	4.1	2.0	6.1	3.5[5]	3.6[5]	3.3	3.2	3.2	3.2	0.3	3.5	1.0	1.1	1.0	1.0	0.9	0.9	1.7	2.6
Other reporting countries																								
Russian Federation	2.5	2.7	2.8	2.9	2.8	2.6	0.5	3.1	1.7	1.8	2.0	2.0	1.9	1.8	0.1	1.9	0.7	0.9	0.8	0.8	0.8	0.7	0.4	1.1

—Not available.
†Not applicable.
#Rounds to zero.
[1]Includes expenditures that could not be reported by level of education.
[2]Refers to the mean of the data values for all reporting Organization for Economic Cooperation and Development (OECD) countries, to which each country reporting data contributes equally. The average includes all current OECD countries for which a given year's data are available, even if they were not members of OECD in that year.
[3]Includes expenditures on education institutions from international sources.
[4]Includes preprimary education.
[5]Excludes postsecondary non-higher-education.
[6]Postsecondary non-higher-education included in both secondary and higher education.
[7]Short-cycle tertiary education corresponding to that offered at the vocational associate's degree level in the United States is included in elementary and secondary education instead of in higher education.

NOTE: Government expenditures on education include both amounts spent directly by governments to hire education personnel and to procure other resources, and amounts provided by governments to public or private institutions. Types of expenditures may include direct expenditures, research and development activities, ancillary expenditures, and capital expenditures. Government expenditures may also include subsidies to households for payments to education institutions. Private expenditures exclude government subsidies that are used for payments to education institutions. All data in this table were calculated using International Standard Classification of Education (ISCED) 2011. Expenditures for ISCED level 4 (postsecondary non-higher-education) are included in elementary and secondary education unless otherwise noted. Detail may not sum to totals because of rounding. Some data have been revised from previously published figures. This table includes only data that had been validated for consistency and accuracy by OECD and the relevant country as of November 28, 2018.
SOURCE: Organization for Economic Cooperation and Development (OECD), Online Education Database, retrieved November 28, 2018, from https://stats.oecd.org/Index.aspx. (This table was prepared December 2018.)

This page intentionally left blank.

CHAPTER 7
Libraries and Use of Technology

This chapter presents statistics on elementary and secondary school libraries, college and university libraries (including institution-level information for the 60 largest college libraries in the country), and public libraries. It contains data on library collections, staff, and expenditures, as well as library usage. The tables on libraries in educational institutions are based on National Center for Education Statistics (NCES) data, while the table on public libraries is based on Institute of Museum and Library Sciences data. Also included in this chapter are tables on access to and use of computers and the Internet among children and adults of various racial/ethnic groups, age groups, educational attainment levels, and income levels. These tables are based on data from the U.S. Census Bureau. Other chapters also provide information on use of computers and technology. Chapter 2 includes tables on use of computers and the Internet by elementary and secondary students and schools. Chapter 3 includes tables on distance and online education at the postsecondary level.

Libraries

Among public schools that had a library in 2011–12, the average number of library staff per school was 1.8, including 0.9 certified library/media specialists (*web-only table 701.10*). On average, public school libraries had larger numbers of books on a per student basis in 2011–12 (2,188 per 100 students) than in 1999–2000 (1,803 per 100 students), 2003–04 (1,891 per 100 students), and 2007–08 (2,015 per 100 students). In 2011–12, public elementary school libraries had larger holdings on a per student basis than did public secondary school libraries (2,570 books per 100 students, compared with 1,474 books per 100 students).

In 2016–17, there were libraries at 91 percent of degree-granting postsecondary institutions overall, 96 percent of public institutions, 95 percent of private nonprofit institutions, and 77 percent of private for-profit institutions (table 701.40). The calculations of library operating expenditures and number of books per full-time-equivalent (FTE) student in the following paragraph include both institutions with libraries and those without libraries.

At degree-granting postsecondary institutions, library operating expenditures per FTE student were 1 percent higher in 2001–02 than in 1991–92, after adjustment for inflation (table 701.40). Library operating expenditures per FTE student dropped by 25 percent from 2001–02 to 2011–12 (in inflation-adjusted dollars), but then rose by 17 percent from 2011–12 to 2016–17, resulting in a net decrease of 12 percent between 2001–02 and 2016–17. In 2016–17, library operating expenditures per FTE student averaged $551 (in current dollars) across all degree-granting institutions. The amount varied widely by institution control, however: library operating expenditures averaged $457 per FTE student attending a public institution in 2016–17, compared with $959 per FTE student attending a private nonprofit institution and $94 per FTE student attending a private for-profit institution. In 2016–17, the average number of books (including physical and electronic books) per FTE student also differed for public institutions (84 books), private nonprofit institutions (185 books), and private for-profit institutions (134 books). Across all degree-granting institutions, the average number of books per FTE student in 2016–17 was 111.

In 2016, there were 9,057 public libraries in the United States with a total of 732 million books and serial volumes (table 701.60). The annual number of visits per capita—that is, per resident of the areas served by the libraries—was 4.4, the annual number of reference transactions per capita was 0.8, and the annual number of uses of public-access internet computers per capita was 0.9.

Computer and Internet Use

Ninety-seven percent of all 3- to 18-year-old children had some type of computer or smartphone in their household in 2017 (table 702.10). A higher percentage of 3- to 18-year-old children lived in a household with a smartphone (94 percent) than in a household with a desktop or laptop (83 percent) or in a household with a tablet or other portable wireless computer (78 percent).

The percentages of children ages 3 to 18 with various types of devices in their household differed by race/ethnicity in 2017. For example, 94 percent of Asian children had a desktop or laptop in their household, compared with 90 percent of White children, 87 percent of children of Two or more races, 74 percent of Hispanic children, 73 percent of Pacific Islander children, 72 percent of Black children, and 65 percent of American Indian/Alaska Native children (table 702.10). The percentages of children who lived in a household with a smartphone were higher for Asian children (97 percent), children of Two or more races

(96 percent), and White children (96 percent) than for Hispanic children (93 percent), Black children (91 percent), Pacific Islander children (90 percent), and American Indian/Alaska Native children (84 percent).

In 2017, the percentages of children ages 3 to 18 who lived in households with desktops or laptops, smartphones, and tablets or other portable wireless computers were generally higher for those with higher family incomes than for those with lower family incomes. For example, the percentage of children living in a household with a desktop or laptop computer was highest for children with family incomes of over $100,000 (97 percent) and lowest for children with family incomes of less than $10,000 (55 percent) (table 702.10). The percentages of children who lived in a household with a smartphone and who lived in a household with a tablet or other portable wireless computer were also highest for children with family incomes of over $100,000 (98 and 92 percent, respectively) and lowest for children with family incomes of less than $10,000 (84 and 53 percent, respectively).

In 2017, the percentages of children who lived in households with various types of devices were generally higher for children whose parent(s) had higher levels of educational attainment than for those whose parent(s) had lower levels of educational attainment (table 702.10 and figure 30). For example, the percentage of children with a desktop or laptop in their household was higher for those who had a parent with a bachelor's or higher degree (97 percent) than for those who had a parent whose highest level of education was an associate's degree (90 percent), some college (82 percent), a high school diploma or equivalent (69 percent), and less than high school (55 percent). The percentage of children with a smartphone in their household was higher for those who had a parent with a bachelor's or higher degree (98 percent) than for those who had a parent whose highest level of education was an associate's degree (96 percent), some college (95 percent), a high school diploma or equivalent (91 percent), and less than high school (85 percent).

Seventy-eight percent of the U.S. population age 3 and over used the Internet in 2017, up from 70 percent in 2011 (table 702.30). Internet usage differed by various demographic characteristics in 2017. For example, the percentage of internet users was higher for persons age 3 and over who were of Two or more races (82 percent), White (80 percent), and Asian (79 percent) than for those who were Black (73 percent) and Hispanic (72 percent). The percentage of internet users who were American Indian/Alaska Native (63 percent) was lower than the percentages for all other racial/ethnic groups. The percentage of the population age 3 and over who used the Internet was generally higher for those with higher family incomes than for those with lower family. For example, about 86 percent of persons with family incomes of $100,000 to $149,000 used the Internet, compared with 68 percent of persons with family incomes of $20,000 to $29,999. Among persons age 25 and over, the percentage of internet users tended to be higher for those with higher levels of educational attainment (table 702.30 and figure 31). For example, the percentage of persons age 25 and over who used the Internet was higher for those whose highest level of education was a bachelor's or higher degree (89 percent) than for those whose highest level of education was an associate's degree (86 percent), some college (83 percent), a high school diploma or equivalent (70 percent), and less than high school (51 percent).

Figure 31. Percentage of persons age 25 and over who used the Internet anywhere, at home, and at the workplace, by highest level of educational attainment: 2011 and 2017

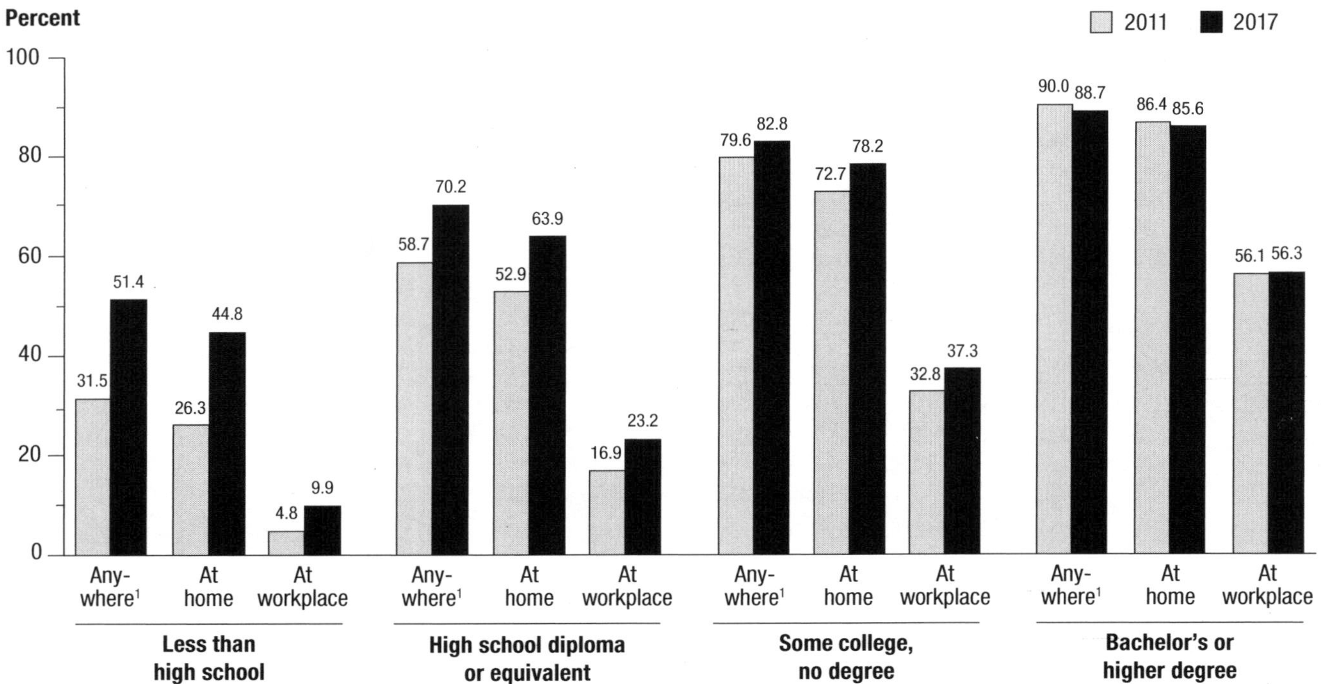

[1]Includes all persons who use the Internet at any location.
NOTE: Data are based on sample surveys of the civilian noninstitutionalized population, which excludes persons in the military and persons living in institutions (e.g., prisons or nursing facilities).
SOURCE: U.S. Department of Commerce, Census Bureau, Current Population Survey (CPS), July 2011 and November 2017.

Table 701.15. Number and percentage of public schools with libraries/media centers and average number of staff per library/media center, by staff type and employment status and school level, enrollment size, and locale: 2015–16

[Standard errors appear in parentheses]

School level, enrollment size, and locale	Schools with libraries/ media centers				Average number of staff per library/media center											
					Librarians or library media specialists				Library media center instructional aides				Library media center noninstructional aides			
	Number		Percent		Full time		Part time		Full time		Part time		Full time		Part time	
1	2		3		4		5		6		7		8		9	
Total, all public schools[1]	**82,300**	**(440)**	**91.0**	**(0.43)**	**0.7**	**(0.01)**	**0.2**	**(0.01)**	**0.3**	**(0.01)**	**0.1**	**(0.01)**	**0.1**	**(#)**	**0.1**	**(#)**
Elementary schools	**59,500**	**(350)**	**95.4**	**(0.39)**	**0.6**	**(0.01)**	**0.2**	**(0.01)**	**0.3**	**(0.01)**	**0.1**	**(0.01)**	**0.1**	**(#)**	**0.1**	**(0.01)**
Enrollment size																
Less than 150 students	3,200	(300)	81.4	(3.88)	0.2	(0.03)	0.4	(0.05)	0.1 !	(0.03)	0.2	(0.04)	‡	(†)	0.1 !	(0.03)
150 to 499 students	28,700	(560)	95.1	(0.49)	0.6	(0.01)	0.3	(0.01)	0.2	(0.01)	0.2	(0.01)	0.1	(0.01)	0.1	(0.01)
500 to 749 students	18,600	(480)	97.8	(0.42)	0.7	(0.01)	0.2	(0.01)	0.3	(0.02)	0.1	(0.01)	0.1	(0.01)	0.1	(0.01)
750 or more students	9,000	(340)	97.8	(0.61)	0.8	(0.02)	0.2	(0.02)	0.3	(0.02)	0.1	(0.02)	0.1	(0.02)	0.1	(0.01)
Locale																
City	16,500	(210)	92.0	(0.92)	0.6	(0.02)	0.2	(0.02)	0.2	(0.02)	0.1	(0.01)	0.1	(0.01)	0.1	(0.01)
Suburban	21,100	(190)	97.0	(0.60)	0.7	(0.02)	0.2	(0.02)	0.2	(0.01)	0.2	(0.01)	0.1	(0.01)	0.1	(0.01)
Town	7,600	(280)	97.1	(0.69)	0.6	(0.02)	0.2	(0.02)	0.3	(0.02)	0.1	(0.02)	0.1	(0.01)	0.1	(0.01)
Rural	14,300	(320)	96.4	(0.82)	0.6	(0.02)	0.2	(0.02)	0.3	(0.02)	0.1	(0.02)	#	(†)	0.1	(0.01)
Secondary schools	**16,300**	**(410)**	**82.0**	**(1.46)**	**0.8**	**(0.02)**	**0.1**	**(0.01)**	**0.3**	**(0.02)**	**0.1**	**(0.01)**	**0.2**	**(0.01)**	**0.1**	**(0.01)**
Enrollment size																
Less than 150 students	1,400	(200)	46.0	(5.28)	0.2	(0.06)	0.2	(0.05)	‡	(†)	‡	(†)	‡	(†)	‡	(†)
150 to 499 students	4,600	(260)	77.4	(2.60)	0.6	(0.04)	0.2	(0.03)	0.2	(0.02)	0.1	(0.02)	0.1	(0.02)	0.1	(0.01)
500 to 749 students	2,600	(180)	89.6	(2.22)	0.8	(0.04)	0.2	(0.03)	0.2	(0.03)	0.2	(0.04)	0.1	(0.02)	0.1	(0.02)
750 or more students	7,600	(290)	96.5	(0.81)	1.1	(0.02)	0.1	(0.01)	0.4	(0.03)	0.1	(0.02)	0.3	(0.02)	0.1	(0.01)
Locale																
City	4,200	(220)	79.2	(2.51)	0.8	(0.04)	0.1	(0.02)	0.2	(0.03)	0.1	(0.01)	0.2	(0.03)	#	(†)
Suburban	4,800	(210)	80.9	(2.84)	1.0	(0.03)	0.1	(0.02)	0.3	(0.04)	0.1	(0.03)	0.2	(0.03)	0.1	(0.02)
Town	2,900	(180)	82.9	(3.24)	0.8	(0.03)	0.2	(0.03)	0.3	(0.03)	0.1	(0.02)	0.2	(0.03)	0.1	(0.02)
Rural	4,400	(230)	85.6	(2.42)	0.8	(0.04)	0.2	(0.03)	0.3	(0.03)	0.1	(0.02)	0.1	(0.02)	#	(†)

†Not applicable.
#Rounds to zero.
!Interpret data with caution. The coefficient of variation (CV) for this estimate is between 30 and 50 percent.
‡Reporting standards not met. Either there are too few cases for a reliable estimate or the coefficient of variation (CV) is 50 percent or greater.

[1]Total includes combined elementary/secondary schools, which are not separately shown.
NOTE: Detail may not sum to totals because of rounding.
SOURCE: U.S. Department of Education, National Center for Education Statistics, National Teacher and Principal Survey (NTPS), "Public School Data File," 2015–16. (This table was prepared May 2018.)

Table 701.40. Collections, staff, and operating expenditures of degree-granting postsecondary institution libraries: Selected years, 1991–92 through 2016–17

Collections, staff, and operating expenditures	1991–92	2001–02	2011–12	2014–15	2015–16				2016–17			
					Total	Public	Private nonprofit	Private for-profit	Total	Public	Private nonprofit	Private for-profit
1	2	3	4	5	6	7	8	9	10	11	12	13
Number of libraries	3,274	3,568	3,793	4,134	3,999	1,558	1,611	830	3,944	1,559	1,612	773
Percentage of institutions with libraries	—	85.0	80.6	90.2	91.7	96.0	95.8	78.7	91.4	95.9	95.4	77.5
Number of circulation transactions (in thousands)	—	189,248	154,409	917,510	778,357	450,032	229,091	99,235	768,383	473,808	211,565	83,010
Physical transactions (includes serials)	—	—	—	81,182	67,796	41,240	25,504	1,053	58,244	34,691	22,855	699
Electronic transactions (does not include serials)	—	—	—	836,328	710,561	408,792	203,587	98,182	710,139	439,117	188,710	82,311
Number of circulation transactions per full-time-equivalent (FTE) student	—	16	10	60	52	43	67	93	51	45	61	91
Enrollment (in thousands)												
Total enrollment[1]	14,359	15,928	20,994	20,209	19,988	14,573	4,066	1,349	19,847	14,586	4,079	1,182
Full-time-equivalent (FTE) enrollment[1]	10,361	11,766	15,886	15,263	15,079	10,570	3,441	1,068	14,938	10,572	3,454	912
Collections (in thousands)												
Total number of physical and electronic materials (books, media, and databases)	—	—	—	2,128,233	1,985,142	1,078,659	716,292	190,191	2,209,958	1,188,603	839,164	182,191
Number of books	—	—	—	1,711,851	1,573,341	854,394	594,267	124,681	1,651,471	888,869	640,484	122,118
Physical books	—	—	—	1,036,223	824,767	508,288	312,466	4,013	799,263	485,998	309,346	3,918
Electronic books	—	10,318	252,599	675,629	748,575	346,106	281,801	120,668	852,208	402,871	331,138	118,200
Number of media (includes audiovisual materials)	—	—	—	411,822	410,274	223,725	121,376	65,172	557,541	299,421	198,393	59,727
Physical media	—	—	—	253,826	190,049	135,924	53,580	545	194,634	130,051	64,135	448
Electronic media	—	—	—	157,996	220,225	87,801	67,797	64,627	362,907	169,370	134,258	59,279
Number of databases (electronic only)	—	—	—	4,560	1,527	540	649	338	946	313	288	345
Number of volumes at end of year	749,429	954,030	1,099,951	—	—	—	—	—	—	—	—	—
Number of volumes added during year	20,982	24,574	27,605	—	—	—	—	—	—	—	—	—
Number of serials at end of year[2]	6,966	9,855	—	—	222,010	124,399	75,307	22,303	290,224	112,429	85,801	91,994
Microform units at end of year	—	1,143,678	1,044,521	—	—	—	—	—	—	—	—	—
Number of volumes per full-time-equivalent (FTE) student	72	81	69	—	—	—	—	—	—	—	—	—
Number of books per full-time-equivalent (FTE) student	—	—	—	112	104	81	173	117	111	84	185	134
Full-time-equivalent (FTE) library staff												
Total staff in regular positions[3]	67,166	69,526	65,242	—	—	—	—	—	—	—	—	—
Librarians and professional staff	26,341	32,053	34,423	—	—	—	—	—	—	—	—	—
Other paid staff	40,421	37,473	30,819	—	—	—	—	—	—	—	—	—
Contributed services	404	—	—	—	—	—	—	—	—	—	—	—
Student assistants	29,075	25,305	20,509	—	—	—	—	—	—	—	—	—
FTE student enrollment per FTE staff member	154	169	243	—	—	—	—	—	—	—	—	—
Library operating expenditures[4]												
Total operating expenditures (in thousands of current dollars)	$3,648,654	$5,416,716	$7,008,114	$7,957,153	$8,085,556	$4,749,633	$3,248,421	$87,502	$8,233,469	$4,835,333	$3,312,472	$85,664
Salaries and wages[5]	1,889,368	2,753,404	3,443,831	3,422,050	3,455,940	2,127,768	1,290,595	37,577	3,499,591	2,168,144	1,295,935	35,512
Fringe benefits	—	—	—	745,195	759,363	467,031	288,499	3,833	780,980	486,278	290,912	3,789
Computer hardware/software	—	155,791	143,660	—	—	—	—	—	—	—	—	—
Bibliographic utilities/networks/consortia	—	92,242	123,650	—	—	—	—	—	—	—	—	—
Information resources	1,240,419	1,990,989	2,790,039	3,016,495	3,083,854	1,753,092	1,292,472	38,290	3,126,353	1,766,804	1,322,388	37,161
Books, serial backfiles, and other materials	—	—	—	604,100	614,389	312,052	297,454	4,883	606,196	298,142	304,108	3,947
Books and serial backfiles—paper	—	563,007	503,851	—	—	—	—	—	—	—	—	—
Books and serial backfiles—electronic	—	44,792	180,570	—	—	—	—	—	—	—	—	—
Audiovisual materials	23,879	37,041	37,022	—	—	—	—	—	—	—	—	—
Ongoing commitments to subscriptions	—	—	—	2,217,573	2,287,252	1,338,496	918,941	29,816	2,349,849	1,375,453	943,571	30,824
Current serials—paper	—	926,105	487,265	—	—	—	—	—	—	—	—	—
Current serials—electronic	—	297,657	1,436,671	—	—	—	—	—	—	—	—	—
Preservation	43,126	46,499	26,838	32,339	42,353	27,142	15,095	115	28,459	14,642	13,740	78
Other materials/services expenditures	—	—	—	162,484	139,860	75,401	60,982	3,477	141,848	78,567	60,969	2,312
Document delivery/interlibrary loan	—	22,913	32,490	—	—	—	—	—	—	—	—	—
Other collection expenditures	1,173,414	52,976	85,334	—	—	—	—	—	—	—	—	—
Other library operating expenditures	518,867	424,290	506,934	773,413	786,399	401,743	376,854	7,802	826,546	414,106	403,237	9,202
Operating expenditures per full-time-equivalent (FTE) student												
In current dollars	352	460	441	521	536	449	944	82	551	457	959	94
In constant 2017–18 dollars[6]	632	641	481	547	558	468	983	85	564	468	981	96
Information resource expenditures per FTE student												
In current dollars	120	169	176	198	205	166	376	36	209	167	383	41
In constant 2017–18 dollars[6]	215	236	191	207	213	173	391	37	214	171	391	42
Operating expenditures (percentage distribution)	100.0	100.0	100.0	100.0	100.0	100.0	100.0	100.0	100.0	100.0	100.0	100.0
Salaries and wages[5]	51.8	50.8	49.1	43.0	42.7	44.8	39.7	42.9	42.5	44.8	39.1	41.5
Fringe benefits	—	—	—	9.4	9.4	9.8	8.9	4.4	9.5	10.1	8.8	4.4
Preservation	1.2	0.9	0.4	0.4	0.5	0.6	0.5	0.1	0.3	0.3	0.4	0.1
Information resources	32.8	35.9	39.4	37.5	37.6	36.3	39.3	43.6	37.6	36.2	39.5	43.3
Other[7]	14.2	12.4	11.0	9.7	9.7	8.5	11.6	8.9	10.0	8.6	12.2	10.7
Library operating expenditures as a percent of total institutional expenditures for educational and general purposes	3.0	—	—	—	—	—	—	—	—	—	—	—

—Not available.
[1]Fall enrollment for the academic year specified.
[2]For 2001–02 and later years, includes electronic serials. If a single title comes in both paper and electronic formats, it counts as two serials.
[3]Excludes student assistants.
[4]Excludes capital outlay. Expenditure data are reported only by degree-granting institutions with total expenditures over $100,000.
[5]Includes student hourly wages.
[6]Constant dollars based on the Consumer Price Index, prepared by the Bureau of Labor Statistics, U.S. Department of Labor, adjusted to a school-year basis.
[7]Includes computer hardware/software, bibliographic utilities/networks/consortia, and "other library operating expenditures" not individually listed.

NOTE: Data through 1995 are for institutions of higher education, while later data are for degree-granting institutions. Degree-granting institutions grant associate's or higher degrees and participate in Title IV federal financial aid programs. The degree-granting classification is very similar to the earlier higher education classification, but it includes more 2-year colleges and excludes a few higher education institutions that did not grant degrees. Detail may not sum to totals because of rounding.
SOURCE: U.S. Department of Education, National Center for Education Statistics, Integrated Postsecondary Education Data System (IPEDS), "Academic Libraries Survey" (IPEDS-L:92) and "Fall Enrollment Survey" (IPEDS-EF:92); Academic Libraries Survey (ALS), 2000 through 2012; IPEDS Spring 2015 through Spring 2017, Fall Enrollment component; and IPEDS Spring 2015 through Spring 2017, Academic Libraries component. (This table was prepared July 2019.)

Table 701.60. Number of public libraries, number of books and serial volumes, and per capita usage of selected library services per year, by state: Fiscal years 2015 and 2016

State	Number of public libraries[1]		Number of books and serial volumes				Per capita[2] usage of selected services per year							
			In thousands		Per capita[2]		Number of library visits[3]		Circulation (number of materials lent)		Reference transactions[4]		Uses of public-access internet computers	
	2015	2016	2015	2016	2015	2016	2015	2016	2015	2016	2015	2016	2015	2016
1	2	3	4	5	6	7	8	9	10	11	12	13	14	15
United States	**9,068**	**9,057**	**750,249**	**732,240**	**2.4**	**2.4**	**4.5**	**4.4**	**7.3**	**7.2**	**0.8**	**0.8**	**1.0**	**0.9**
Alabama	219	219	9,227	9,007	2.0	2.0	3.5	3.4	4.3	4.3	0.9	0.9	0.9	0.8
Alaska	80	71	2,354	2,048	3.6	3.2	4.8	5.4	6.9	7.4	0.5	0.7	1.2	0.9
Arizona	90	90	8,196	7,663	1.2	1.1	3.9	3.7	6.5	6.6	0.6	0.9	1.1	1.0
Arkansas	58	59	6,371	5,722	2.4	2.3	3.9	4.0	5.4	5.2	0.9	0.8	0.7	0.6
California	184	184	63,676	62,770	1.6	1.6	4.2	4.0	5.6	5.4	0.5	0.6	0.8	0.8
Colorado	113	114	9,943	10,526	1.9	2.0	6.1	6.0	12.0	11.8	0.7	0.8	1.4	1.2
Connecticut	182	182	13,577	13,103	4.0	4.0	6.1	6.0	8.3	8.1	0.9	1.0	1.2	1.2
Delaware	21	21	1,646	1,532	1.8	1.6	4.4	4.4	6.5	6.6	0.5	0.5	0.7	0.7
District of Columbia	1	1	1,863	1,863	2.8	2.7	6.2	5.8	6.0	6.5	1.2	1.2	1.7	1.4
Florida	80	80	30,794	29,261	1.6	1.5	3.7	3.5	5.7	5.5	1.2	1.2	0.8	0.8
Georgia	63	63	16,522	16,839	1.6	1.6	2.8	2.7	3.6	3.7	0.7	0.8	1.1	1.2
Hawaii	1	1	3,197	2,967	2.3	2.1	3.5	3.1	4.5	4.4	0.4	0.5	0.5	0.6
Idaho	102	102	4,342	4,289	3.2	3.1	6.3	6.2	11.4	10.9	0.9	0.8	1.4	1.2
Illinois	622	621	42,366	40,487	3.6	3.4	6.0	5.7	9.5	9.1	0.9	0.9	1.2	1.1
Indiana	237	236	23,210	22,693	3.8	3.7	5.7	5.5	12.7	12.2	0.7	0.7	1.1	1.1
Iowa	534	534	11,934	11,749	3.9	3.9	5.9	5.9	8.9	8.8	0.6	0.6	1.0	1.0
Kansas	320	321	9,113	8,972	3.6	3.6	5.6	5.5	10.0	9.9	0.8	0.8	1.2	1.2
Kentucky	119	119	9,171	9,051	2.1	2.1	4.2	4.1	6.9	6.8	1.0	1.0	1.0	1.0
Louisiana	68	68	11,833	11,746	2.5	2.5	4.3	4.3	4.5	4.6	1.1	1.1	1.1	1.1
Maine	228	227	5,981	5,903	5.2	5.2	5.8	5.9	7.7	7.6	0.6	0.6	1.0	0.9
Maryland	24	24	11,922	10,459	2.0	1.8	4.8	4.6	9.9	9.8	1.4	1.5	1.0	0.9
Massachusetts	368	368	30,857	30,276	4.6	4.5	6.1	6.1	9.2	9.3	0.7	0.7	1.0	0.9
Michigan	392	396	31,818	29,473	3.2	3.0	4.9	4.7	8.3	7.9	0.9	0.9	1.0	1.0
Minnesota	137	137	14,363	14,339	2.6	2.6	4.4	4.4	9.6	9.3	0.7	0.7	0.9	0.9
Mississippi	52	52	5,704	5,599	1.9	1.9	3.0	3.0	2.6	2.5	0.5	0.5	0.8	0.8
Missouri	149	147	16,288	16,019	3.0	2.9	5.2	4.9	10.0	9.8	0.6	0.6	1.1	1.0
Montana	82	82	2,622	2,627	2.7	2.7	4.3	4.4	6.1	6.1	0.5	0.5	1.2	1.2
Nebraska	247	237	5,733	5,555	3.7	3.6	5.3	5.1	8.2	8.2	0.5	0.5	1.3	1.2
Nevada	22	22	4,116	4,149	1.4	1.4	3.5	3.4	7.3	6.9	0.5	0.5	0.9	0.9
New Hampshire	219	222	5,818	5,619	5.0	4.4	6.4	5.5	8.6	7.9	0.7	0.8	0.8	0.6
New Jersey	282	282	27,177	26,513	3.1	3.1	5.0	4.9	6.4	6.3	0.8	0.8	1.0	1.0
New Mexico	87	88	4,232	4,128	2.6	2.5	4.5	4.4	5.5	5.7	0.6	0.9	1.2	1.1
New York	756	756	69,313	68,858	3.6	3.6	5.4	5.3	6.9	6.8	1.4	1.4	1.1	0.9
North Carolina	80	81	16,021	15,584	1.6	1.6	3.6	3.3	5.2	5.0	0.6	0.7	0.7	0.7
North Dakota	72	74	2,173	2,173	3.2	3.2	3.3	3.3	5.9	6.3	0.7	0.8	0.9	0.9
Ohio	251	251	41,024	40,060	3.6	3.5	6.8	6.4	15.9	16.0	1.6	1.6	1.7	1.4
Oklahoma	119	119	7,093	7,351	2.2	2.3	4.2	4.1	6.9	7.0	0.6	0.6	1.1	1.1
Oregon	131	131	9,805	9,497	2.6	2.7	5.5	5.8	15.0	15.5	0.6	0.6	1.0	1.0
Pennsylvania	455	454	25,298	24,617	2.0	2.0	3.6	3.6	5.2	5.1	0.6	0.6	0.6	0.6
Rhode Island	48	48	4,241	3,561	4.0	3.4	5.6	5.5	6.4	6.1	0.6	0.6	1.2	1.0
South Carolina	42	42	9,108	8,962	2.0	1.9	3.7	3.4	5.7	5.4	0.6	0.6	0.9	0.8
South Dakota	112	112	2,768	2,755	3.7	3.6	4.9	4.9	7.6	7.8	0.5	0.6	1.5	1.4
Tennessee	185	186	11,722	11,648	1.8	1.8	3.0	2.9	4.1	4.1	0.5	0.5	0.8	0.7
Texas	549	544	39,660	39,600	1.5	1.6	2.7	2.8	4.2	4.6	0.5	0.5	0.6	0.6
Utah	72	72	6,627	6,494	2.3	2.2	6.0	5.4	12.6	12.0	0.9	1.0	1.0	0.9
Vermont	159	162	2,791	2,586	4.8	4.7	6.2	6.3	7.4	7.6	0.8	0.9	1.1	1.0
Virginia	91	92	17,210	17,097	2.1	2.1	4.6	4.3	8.8	8.2	0.8	0.8	0.9	0.9
Washington	62	62	13,261	12,825	1.9	1.8	5.7	5.5	12.0	12.1	0.5	0.6	1.3	1.1
West Virginia	97	97	5,005	4,917	2.7	2.7	2.9	2.8	3.4	3.5	0.3	0.3	0.5	0.5
Wisconsin	381	381	18,781	18,401	3.3	3.2	5.5	5.5	10.1	9.9	0.7	0.7	1.0	0.9
Wyoming	23	23	2,384	2,311	4.1	3.9	6.1	6.0	8.4	8.2	0.7	0.8	1.5	1.5

[1]Refers to the number of administrative entities that are legally established under local or state law to provide public library service to the population of a local jurisdiction. A public library (administrative entity) may have a single outlet that provides direct service to the public, or it may have multiple service outlets. In 2015, a total of 16,560 stationary service outlets (8,891 central libraries and 7,669 branch libraries) were open to the public; 647 additional service outlets were bookmobiles. In 2016, a total of 16,568 stationary service outlets (8,884 central libraries and 7,684 branch libraries) were open to the public; 659 additional service outlets were bookmobiles.

[2]Per capita (or per person) data are based on unduplicated populations of the areas served by public libraries.

[3]Includes only the number of physical visits (entering the library for any purpose). The survey does not collect data on the number of online visits.

[4]A reference transaction is an information contact that involves the knowledge, use, recommendations, interpretation, or instruction in the use of one or more information sources by a member of the library staff.

NOTE: Data include imputations for nonresponse. Detail may not sum to totals because of rounding.

SOURCE: Institute of Museum and Library Services, Public Libraries Survey, fiscal years 2015 and 2016, retrieved June 26, 2018, from https://www.imls.gov/research/public_libraries_in_the_united_states_survey.aspx. (This table was prepared June 2018.)

Table 702.10. Percentage of children ages 3 to 18 living in households with a computer, by type of computer and selected child and family characteristics: Selected years, 2010 through 2017

[Standard errors appear in parentheses]

Selected child or family characteristic	2010	2013	2015	2016					2017				
					Desktop, laptop, tablet, or other portable wireless computer					Desktop, laptop, tablet, or other portable wireless computer			
	Total, any computer or smartphone	Total, any computer or smartphone	Total, any computer or smartphone	Total, any computer or smartphone[1]	Total[1]	Desktop or laptop	Tablet or other portable wireless computer	Smartphone	Total, any computer or smartphone[1]	Total[1]	Desktop or laptop	Tablet or other portable wireless computer	Smartphone
1	2	3	4	5	6	7	8	9	10	11	12	13	14
Total	**85.3 (0.37)**	**92.6 (0.08)**	**94.5 (0.06)**	**96.6 (0.05)**	**89.5 (0.09)**	**83.3 (0.13)**	**73.7 (0.15)**	**90.9 (0.05)**	**97.3 (0.04)**	**89.9 (0.11)**	**83.3 (0.13)**	**77.9 (0.16)**	**94.3 (0.05)**
Sex													
Male	85.0 (0.44)	92.5 (0.08)	94.4 (0.07)	96.5 (0.06)	89.4 (0.11)	83.1 (0.14)	73.4 (0.17)	90.8 (0.07)	97.3 (0.05)	89.8 (0.12)	83.2 (0.14)	77.7 (0.18)	94.3 (0.06)
Female	85.5 (0.45)	92.6 (0.10)	94.5 (0.07)	96.7 (0.05)	89.6 (0.11)	83.4 (0.14)	74.1 (0.17)	91.0 (0.07)	97.4 (0.05)	90.0 (0.11)	83.4 (0.14)	78.0 (0.17)	94.4 (0.06)
Race/ethnicity													
White	92.4 (0.34)	95.9 (0.07)	97.0 (0.06)	97.9 (0.05)	94.2 (0.09)	90.1 (0.12)	79.8 (0.16)	92.1 (0.08)	98.2 (0.04)	94.3 (0.08)	89.9 (0.12)	84.3 (0.15)	95.6 (0.06)
Black	72.8 (1.30)	87.1 (0.25)	90.2 (0.21)	94.0 (0.20)	81.4 (0.28)	72.3 (0.31)	63.1 (0.36)	87.8 (0.22)	94.9 (0.16)	82.1 (0.32)	72.0 (0.36)	66.9 (0.39)	90.8 (0.20)
Hispanic	74.3 (0.90)	87.2 (0.20)	90.7 (0.16)	94.8 (0.12)	82.5 (0.22)	73.0 (0.25)	65.2 (0.24)	89.4 (0.16)	96.5 (0.10)	83.9 (0.23)	73.8 (0.26)	68.8 (0.30)	93.2 (0.14)
Asian	93.5 (1.18)	97.9 (0.13)	98.3 (0.14)	98.9 (0.11)	97.0 (0.18)	94.8 (0.23)	80.8 (0.34)	93.7 (0.25)	98.9 (0.12)	96.6 (0.19)	94.0 (0.24)	85.1 (0.38)	96.9 (0.18)
Pacific Islander	83.9 (7.10)	87.8 (2.10)	90.9 (1.55)	94.3 (1.50)	77.8 (2.31)	69.3 (2.56)	60.7 (2.71)	85.9 (2.21)	94.0 (1.37)	81.7 (2.28)	72.6 (2.64)	64.3 (3.30)	90.2 (1.66)
American Indian/Alaska Native	72.4 (4.70)	79.0 (0.73)	83.7 (0.82)	87.3 (0.62)	75.6 (0.81)	64.7 (1.01)	61.1 (1.04)	80.3 (0.73)	90.2 (0.61)	75.4 (0.84)	64.7 (0.96)	61.9 (1.03)	84.4 (0.76)
Two or more races	85.2 (2.09)	95.8 (0.19)	97.1 (0.18)	98.5 (0.12)	92.9 (0.28)	86.8 (0.37)	79.3 (0.44)	93.0 (0.25)	98.7 (0.11)	93.1 (0.25)	87.0 (0.35)	83.8 (0.39)	96.1 (0.19)
Age													
3 and 4	81.0 (0.76)	90.4 (0.15)	93.1 (0.15)	96.0 (0.10)	86.6 (0.22)	79.0 (0.24)	71.5 (0.27)	91.2 (0.13)	96.9 (0.08)	87.4 (0.19)	79.1 (0.24)	75.8 (0.26)	94.3 (0.11)
5 to 10	83.9 (0.52)	91.8 (0.09)	93.8 (0.09)	96.2 (0.06)	88.3 (0.12)	80.8 (0.16)	74.0 (0.16)	90.6 (0.07)	97.2 (0.06)	89.1 (0.13)	81.0 (0.14)	78.5 (0.18)	94.1 (0.07)
11 to 14	87.3 (0.59)	93.5 (0.10)	95.1 (0.08)	96.9 (0.07)	90.8 (0.12)	85.4 (0.15)	75.4 (0.18)	90.8 (0.10)	97.5 (0.06)	91.1 (0.13)	85.2 (0.17)	79.3 (0.19)	94.4 (0.09)
15 to 18	87.7 (0.49)	93.9 (0.10)	95.4 (0.08)	97.2 (0.06)	91.3 (0.11)	87.0 (0.14)	72.8 (0.21)	91.3 (0.10)	97.6 (0.06)	91.2 (0.15)	86.7 (0.16)	76.6 (0.21)	94.5 (0.08)
Metropolitan status[2]													
Metropolitan[3]	85.7 (0.40)	— (†)	— (†)	— (†)	— (†)	— (†)	— (†)	— (†)	— (†)	— (†)	— (†)	— (†)	— (†)
Nonmetropolitan[4]	82.8 (0.94)	— (†)	— (†)	— (†)	— (†)	— (†)	— (†)	— (†)	— (†)	— (†)	— (†)	— (†)	— (†)
Highest level of education attained by either parent[5]													
Less than high school	57.0 (1.77)	75.7 (0.40)	81.3 (0.35)	87.9 (0.27)	67.4 (0.34)	54.1 (0.38)	48.5 (0.37)	80.8 (0.30)	90.4 (0.28)	68.4 (0.44)	54.8 (0.43)	50.8 (0.43)	85.0 (0.33)
High school diploma or equivalent	76.1 (0.91)	87.3 (0.22)	90.2 (0.18)	94.1 (0.13)	80.6 (0.26)	69.6 (0.30)	61.4 (0.26)	87.4 (0.17)	95.3 (0.12)	81.3 (0.24)	69.2 (0.29)	65.1 (0.28)	90.9 (0.13)
Some college	88.7 (0.73)	94.3 (0.13)	95.8 (0.12)	97.5 (0.09)	90.5 (0.15)	83.0 (0.21)	73.3 (0.27)	92.4 (0.13)	98.1 (0.07)	90.5 (0.18)	82.0 (0.22)	77.1 (0.25)	95.4 (0.10)
Associate's degree	91.5 (0.67)	96.7 (0.14)	97.7 (0.12)	98.7 (0.09)	94.9 (0.18)	90.1 (0.24)	79.4 (0.28)	93.9 (0.16)	98.9 (0.08)	95.0 (0.15)	89.9 (0.19)	83.4 (0.27)	96.5 (0.12)
Bachelor's or higher degree	96.8 (0.28)	99.0 (0.04)	99.2 (0.03)	99.6 (0.03)	98.5 (0.05)	97.0 (0.08)	86.6 (0.12)	94.9 (0.07)	99.6 (0.02)	98.4 (0.04)	96.8 (0.06)	90.8 (0.10)	98.1 (0.05)
Bachelor's degree	95.9 (0.40)	98.6 (0.06)	99.0 (0.05)	99.4 (0.04)	98.0 (0.07)	95.9 (0.11)	85.1 (0.17)	94.7 (0.10)	99.5 (0.03)	97.8 (0.07)	95.6 (0.10)	88.9 (0.16)	97.9 (0.08)
Master's or higher degree	98.0 (0.35)	99.4 (0.04)	99.5 (0.04)	99.7 (0.03)	99.1 (0.06)	98.3 (0.08)	88.4 (0.17)	95.0 (0.12)	99.7 (0.03)	99.1 (0.05)	98.2 (0.07)	93.0 (0.13)	98.3 (0.07)
Family income (in current dollars)													
Less than $10,000	53.9 (1.90)	76.4 (0.40)	82.1 (0.42)	87.7 (0.40)	67.1 (0.52)	54.5 (0.50)	49.0 (0.49)	79.5 (0.44)	90.3 (0.29)	68.3 (0.52)	55.1 (0.55)	52.8 (0.57)	84.5 (0.37)
$10,000 to $19,999	68.4 (1.35)	81.2 (0.34)	85.7 (0.31)	90.6 (0.26)	72.4 (0.44)	59.3 (0.44)	52.7 (0.45)	82.7 (0.33)	92.5 (0.24)	73.0 (0.47)	59.4 (0.48)	55.7 (0.51)	86.8 (0.28)
$20,000 to $29,999	75.4 (1.34)	86.9 (0.32)	89.2 (0.29)	93.8 (0.25)	79.0 (0.40)	67.3 (0.40)	58.6 (0.43)	86.4 (0.31)	94.9 (0.20)	78.9 (0.41)	65.8 (0.42)	61.6 (0.45)	90.3 (0.23)
$30,000 to $39,999	84.9 (1.05)	90.6 (0.22)	92.8 (0.22)	95.4 (0.20)	83.7 (0.38)	74.2 (0.47)	64.0 (0.44)	88.7 (0.27)	96.2 (0.16)	84.6 (0.32)	73.6 (0.39)	67.2 (0.42)	91.9 (0.22)
$40,000 to $49,999	91.1 (0.98)	93.3 (0.22)	94.2 (0.26)	96.5 (0.16)	88.5 (0.28)	80.0 (0.36)	69.3 (0.36)	90.2 (0.25)	97.1 (0.17)	87.8 (0.30)	78.8 (0.36)	71.9 (0.38)	93.2 (0.20)
$50,000 to $74,999	92.4 (0.71)	95.7 (0.14)	96.6 (0.12)	97.9 (0.08)	92.6 (0.18)	86.6 (0.24)	75.5 (0.28)	92.2 (0.15)	98.2 (0.07)	92.2 (0.17)	85.4 (0.22)	78.2 (0.26)	95.1 (0.11)
$75,000 to $99,999	95.2 (0.59)	97.5 (0.12)	98.0 (0.09)	98.6 (0.08)	95.9 (0.13)	92.2 (0.19)	81.0 (0.29)	93.6 (0.14)	98.9 (0.09)	95.5 (0.17)	91.2 (0.23)	84.7 (0.29)	96.5 (0.14)
$100,000 or more	98.3 (0.29)	99.0 (0.04)	99.1 (0.04)	99.4 (0.04)	98.4 (0.06)	96.9 (0.08)	87.7 (0.13)	95.2 (0.09)	99.4 (0.03)	98.4 (0.06)	96.6 (0.08)	92.0 (0.11)	98.2 (0.05)
$100,000 to $149,999	98.0 (0.44)	98.8 (0.06)	98.8 (0.07)	99.2 (0.07)	97.8 (0.10)	95.7 (0.13)	85.5 (0.21)	94.8 (0.13)	99.3 (0.05)	97.8 (0.08)	95.3 (0.13)	89.9 (0.17)	97.8 (0.08)
$150,000 or more	98.8 (0.36)	99.3 (0.05)	99.4 (0.05)	99.6 (0.04)	99.0 (0.05)	98.1 (0.08)	90.0 (0.16)	95.7 (0.11)	99.5 (0.03)	98.9 (0.06)	98.0 (0.09)	94.2 (0.13)	98.6 (0.06)

—Not available.
†Not applicable.
[1]Households indicating they had the types of computers/devices listed in more than one survey question were counted only once in the total. Therefore, the total is less than the sum of the categories. In addition to the types of computers/devices specified, the total includes a small percentage (less than 1 percent) of children whose households had "some other type of computer" not listed in the survey questions.
[2]Children living in areas whose metropolitan status was not identified are excluded from this analysis. In 2010, less than 1 percent of children ages 3 to 18 lived in an area with nonidentified metropolitan status.
[3]Refers to metropolitan statistical areas, which contain at least one urbanized area with a population of 50,000 or more.
[4]Refers to areas that are outside of metropolitan statistical areas.
[5]Highest education level of any parent residing with the child (including an adoptive or stepparent). Includes only children who resided with at least one of their parents.

NOTE: Data are based on children living in households and exclude children living in institutions (e.g., prisons or nursing facilities). The surveys asked about "computers" or "types of computer" (including smartphones) in the household. Percentages refer to children whose household members owned or used at home any computers/devices listed in the survey questions or "some other type of computer" that was not listed. Estimates for 2010 may not be comparable to those for later years because the 2010 estimates are based on the Current Population Survey, while those for later years are based on the American Community Survey (ACS). Estimates for 2016 and 2017 may not be comparable to those for 2013 and 2015 because the wording of the ACS computer questions was revised as of 2016. Race categories exclude persons of Hispanic ethnicity.
SOURCE: U.S. Department of Commerce, Census Bureau, Current Population Survey (CPS), October 2010; and American Community Survey (ACS), 2013, 2015, 2016, and 2017. (This table was prepared January 2019.)

Table 702.30. Percentage of persons age 3 and over who use the Internet anywhere and who use the Internet at selected locations, by selected characteristics: 2011 and 2017

[Standard errors appear in parentheses]

Selected characteristic	Percent using the Internet, 2011								Percent using the Internet, 2017							
	Anywhere[1]		At home		At school		At workplace		Anywhere[1]		At home		At school		At workplace	
1		2		3		4		5		6		7		8		9
Total	**69.7**	**(0.22)**	**64.1**	**(0.24)**	**17.6**	**(0.17)**	**23.9**	**(0.15)**	**77.7**	**(0.24)**	**71.9**	**(0.25)**	**15.6**	**(0.14)**	**29.2**	**(0.17)**
Sex																
Male	69.4	(0.26)	64.0	(0.28)	17.1	(0.20)	24.8	(0.19)	77.5	(0.27)	71.5	(0.27)	15.4	(0.17)	30.1	(0.23)
Female	70.1	(0.23)	64.1	(0.26)	18.0	(0.19)	23.1	(0.19)	77.9	(0.26)	72.2	(0.29)	15.7	(0.17)	28.3	(0.20)
Race/ethnicity																
White	75.0	(0.25)	70.5	(0.27)	16.9	(0.18)	28.0	(0.20)	80.2	(0.27)	75.2	(0.29)	14.0	(0.18)	33.1	(0.21)
Black	60.2	(0.67)	51.0	(0.77)	18.8	(0.49)	16.6	(0.40)	73.4	(0.54)	65.3	(0.64)	16.0	(0.40)	23.6	(0.49)
Hispanic	54.4	(0.66)	46.6	(0.72)	18.2	(0.41)	13.3	(0.35)	72.1	(0.59)	64.5	(0.62)	18.6	(0.34)	19.4	(0.34)
Asian	73.6	(0.83)	70.8	(0.91)	18.9	(0.63)	26.9	(0.75)	79.4	(0.98)	74.9	(0.99)	17.3	(0.63)	33.3	(0.77)
Pacific Islander	67.3	(3.76)	60.6	(4.16)	18.3	(2.54)	23.3	(2.95)	75.9	(3.85)	70.9	(3.83)	14.3	(2.13)	30.2	(3.17)
American Indian/Alaska Native	59.7	(2.62)	49.4	(3.47)	18.3	(1.69)	14.6	(1.31)	62.7	(2.27)	51.5	(2.41)	13.9	(1.41)	17.6	(1.54)
Two or more races	72.6	(1.26)	64.2	(1.41)	27.3	(1.30)	17.1	(0.98)	82.5	(1.13)	76.5	(1.30)	31.0	(1.32)	23.8	(1.03)
Age																
3 and 4	25.9	(0.85)	24.1	(0.85)	10.0	(0.57)	†	(†)	51.0	(1.18)	45.1	(1.16)	14.8	(0.83)	†	(†)
5 to 10	51.3	(0.63)	47.1	(0.66)	33.7	(0.59)	†	(†)	69.3	(0.68)	57.5	(0.70)	44.2	(0.67)	†	(†)
11 to 14	73.0	(0.73)	66.6	(0.78)	55.8	(0.81)	†	(†)	77.0	(0.71)	68.0	(0.75)	56.1	(0.87)	†	(†)
15 to 18	85.2	(0.54)	76.9	(0.61)	62.4	(0.70)	3.2	(0.23)	84.9	(0.58)	77.6	(0.71)	59.6	(0.74)	4.8	(0.28)
19 to 24	83.1	(0.53)	73.5	(0.69)	39.0	(0.72)	18.9	(0.42)	85.3	(0.55)	79.3	(0.62)	32.2	(0.74)	28.2	(0.56)
25 to 29	81.5	(0.55)	72.8	(0.64)	12.8	(0.42)	38.4	(0.71)	85.6	(0.52)	81.4	(0.60)	11.1	(0.41)	47.6	(0.72)
30 to 39	80.9	(0.39)	74.4	(0.42)	9.3	(0.29)	42.3	(0.43)	85.5	(0.42)	80.7	(0.46)	5.8	(0.24)	49.4	(0.47)
40 to 49	79.6	(0.40)	74.6	(0.45)	7.6	(0.23)	42.8	(0.43)	84.9	(0.43)	80.2	(0.48)	4.5	(0.21)	49.7	(0.50)
50 to 59	71.9	(0.44)	67.3	(0.46)	5.1	(0.22)	36.0	(0.43)	79.7	(0.40)	73.9	(0.45)	2.3	(0.13)	44.3	(0.44)
60 to 69	64.4	(0.54)	60.3	(0.56)	3.3	(0.20)	19.9	(0.38)	75.8	(0.43)	70.4	(0.46)	1.5	(0.13)	26.2	(0.42)
70 or older	38.5	(0.55)	35.0	(0.56)	0.9	(0.10)	3.9	(0.20)	57.1	(0.52)	53.6	(0.56)	0.7	(0.09)	6.4	(0.24)
Highest level of education attained by persons age 25 and over																
Less than high school	31.5	(0.58)	26.3	(0.57)	1.2	(0.15)	4.8	(0.28)	51.4	(0.72)	44.8	(0.73)	1.8	(0.19)	9.9	(0.45)
High school diploma or equivalent	58.7	(0.38)	52.9	(0.38)	1.9	(0.10)	16.9	(0.28)	70.2	(0.41)	63.9	(0.44)	1.9	(0.12)	23.2	(0.33)
Some college	79.6	(0.42)	72.7	(0.42)	7.7	(0.26)	32.8	(0.47)	82.8	(0.43)	78.2	(0.46)	4.8	(0.21)	37.3	(0.51)
Associate's degree	82.6	(0.48)	76.4	(0.52)	7.3	(0.34)	39.9	(0.60)	85.5	(0.45)	80.7	(0.52)	4.0	(0.26)	44.5	(0.66)
Bachelor's or higher degree	90.0	(0.22)	86.4	(0.26)	12.1	(0.27)	56.1	(0.34)	88.7	(0.27)	85.6	(0.31)	5.7	(0.18)	56.3	(0.37)
Bachelor's degree	89.1	(0.28)	85.2	(0.31)	9.6	(0.31)	53.1	(0.41)	87.8	(0.31)	84.5	(0.37)	5.2	(0.21)	53.9	(0.48)
Master's or higher degree	91.6	(0.32)	88.6	(0.39)	16.6	(0.48)	61.5	(0.58)	90.4	(0.41)	87.5	(0.45)	6.7	(0.30)	60.6	(0.55)
Metropolitan status[2]																
Metropolitan[3]	71.0	(0.24)	65.5	(0.27)	18.0	(0.18)	25.0	(0.18)	78.5	(0.25)	72.8	(0.26)	15.8	(0.16)	30.0	(0.20)
Nonmetropolitan[4]	62.8	(0.69)	55.9	(0.71)	15.2	(0.38)	18.5	(0.42)	72.9	(0.67)	65.4	(0.70)	14.1	(0.41)	23.9	(0.50)
Family income (in current dollars)																
Less than $10,000	48.9	(0.82)	36.5	(0.89)	15.3	(0.56)	6.3	(0.36)	62.8	(1.07)	52.7	(1.12)	17.0	(0.82)	9.4	(0.51)
$10,000 to $19,999	48.2	(0.67)	38.7	(0.70)	13.1	(0.43)	7.8	(0.29)	59.7	(0.86)	51.4	(0.82)	12.7	(0.53)	10.2	(0.37)
$20,000 to $29,999	55.6	(0.62)	47.5	(0.69)	13.4	(0.38)	11.4	(0.32)	67.7	(0.71)	59.9	(0.76)	13.4	(0.50)	15.2	(0.43)
$30,000 to $39,999	62.0	(0.70)	54.8	(0.73)	15.2	(0.44)	15.8	(0.39)	71.3	(0.70)	64.3	(0.69)	13.5	(0.45)	19.9	(0.45)
$40,000 to $49,999	70.3	(0.72)	64.8	(0.76)	16.2	(0.48)	21.3	(0.47)	78.0	(0.72)	72.2	(0.79)	14.0	(0.48)	24.7	(0.60)
$50,000 to $74,999	77.6	(0.43)	73.8	(0.47)	18.0	(0.36)	27.8	(0.40)	81.4	(0.44)	75.8	(0.49)	14.4	(0.34)	30.7	(0.38)
$75,000 to $99,999	83.6	(0.37)	80.6	(0.42)	20.9	(0.48)	36.0	(0.47)	84.8	(0.51)	80.3	(0.54)	16.7	(0.47)	37.2	(0.51)
$100,000 or more	86.6	(0.36)	84.5	(0.43)	23.2	(0.39)	42.5	(0.41)	86.3	(0.35)	82.3	(0.39)	18.5	(0.28)	43.9	(0.33)
$100,000 to $149,999	86.9	(0.45)	84.7	(0.50)	23.1	(0.48)	41.3	(0.56)	85.7	(0.47)	81.5	(0.52)	17.7	(0.40)	42.0	(0.47)
$150,000 or more	86.2	(0.54)	84.2	(0.66)	23.4	(0.61)	44.1	(0.61)	87.0	(0.54)	83.2	(0.57)	19.5	(0.44)	46.1	(0.50)

†Not applicable.

[1]Includes all persons who use the Internet at any location.

[2]Persons living in areas whose metropolitan status was not identified are excluded from this analysis. In 2011 and 2017, less than 1 percent of persons lived in an area with non-identified metropolitan status.

[3]Refers to metropolitan statistical areas, which contain at least one urbanized area with a population of 50,000 or more.

[4]Refers to areas that are outside of metropolitan statistical areas.

NOTE: Data are based on sample surveys of the civilian noninstitutionalized population, which excludes persons in the military and persons living in institutions (e.g., prisons or nursing facilities). Race categories exclude persons of Hispanic ethnicity.

SOURCE: U.S. Department of Commerce, Census Bureau, Current Population Survey (CPS), July 2011 and November 2017. (This table was prepared March 2019.)

This page intentionally left blank.

APPENDIX A

Guide to Sources

The information presented in the *Digest of Education Statistics* was obtained from many sources, including federal and state agencies, private research organizations, and professional associations. The data were collected using many research methods, including surveys of a universe (such as all colleges) or of a sample, compilations of administrative records, and statistical projections. Brief descriptions of the information sources, data collections, and data collection methods that were used to produce this report are presented below, grouped by sponsoring organization. Additional details about many of these and other data sets can be found on the Department of Education's Data Inventory website (https://datainventory.ed.gov/).

National Center for Education Statistics (NCES)

Baccalaureate and Beyond Longitudinal Study

The Baccalaureate and Beyond Longitudinal Study (B&B) is based on the National Postsecondary Student Aid Study (NPSAS) and provides information concerning education and work experience after completing a bachelor's degree. A special emphasis of B&B is on those entering teaching. B&B provides cross-sectional information 1 year after bachelor's degree completion (comparable to the information that was provided in the Recent College Graduates study), while at the same time providing longitudinal data concerning entry into and progress through graduate-level education and the workforce, income, and debt repayment. This information has not been available through follow-ups involving high school cohorts or even college-entry cohorts, because these cohorts have limited numbers who actually complete a bachelor's degree and continue their graduate education. Also, these cohorts are not representative of all bachelor's degree recipients.

B&B followed NPSAS baccalaureate degree completers for a 10-year period after completion, beginning with NPSAS:93. About 11,000 students who completed their degrees in the 1992–93 academic year were included in the first B&B cohort (B&B:93). The first follow-up of this cohort (B&B:93/94) occurred 1 year later. In addition to collecting student data, B&B:93/94 collected postsecondary transcripts covering the undergraduate period, which provided complete information on progress and persistence at the undergraduate level. The second follow-up of this cohort (B&B:93/97) took place in spring 1997 and gathered information on employment history, family formation, and enrollment in graduate programs. The third follow-up (B&B:93/03) occurred in 2003 and provided information concerning graduate study and long-term employment experiences after degree completion.

The second B&B cohort (B&B:2000), which was associated with NPSAS:2000, included 11,700 students who completed their degrees in the 1999–2000 academic year. The first and only follow-up survey of this cohort was conducted in 2001 (B&B:2000/01) and focused on time to degree completion, participation in postbaccalaureate education and employment, and the activities of newly qualified teachers.

The third B&B cohort (B&B:08), which is associated with NPSAS:08, included 18,000 students who completed their degrees in the 2007–08 academic year. The first follow-up took place in 2009 (B&B:08/09), and the second follow-up took place in 2012 (B&B:08/12). The report *Baccalaureate and Beyond: A First Look at the Employment Experiences and Lives of College Graduates, 4 Years On (B&B:08/12)* (NCES 2014-141) presents findings based on data from the second follow-up. It examines bachelor's degree recipients' labor market experiences and enrollment in additional postsecondary degree programs through the 4th year after graduation. In addition, *2008/12 Baccalaureate and Beyond Longitudinal Study (B&B:08/12) Data File Documentation* (NCES 2015-141) describes the universe, methods, and data collection procedures used in the second follow-up. A third and final follow-up (B&B:08/18) to the third B&B cohort was conducted in 2018 and early 2019.

Further information on B&B may be obtained from

Aurora D'Amico
Ted Socha
Longitudinal Surveys Branch
Sample Surveys Division
National Center for Education Statistics
550 12th Street SW
Washington, DC 20202
aurora.damico@ed.gov
ted.socha@ed.gov
https://nces.ed.gov/surveys/b&b

Beginning Postsecondary Students Longitudinal Study

The Beginning Postsecondary Students Longitudinal Study (BPS) provides information on persistence, progress, and attainment for 6 years after initial time of entry into postsecondary education. BPS includes traditional and nontraditional (e.g., older) students and is representative of all beginning students in postsecondary education in a given year. Initially, these individuals are surveyed in the National Postsecondary Student Aid Study (NPSAS) during the year in which they first begin their postsecondary education. These same students are surveyed again 2 and 5 years later through the BPS. By starting with a cohort that has already entered postsecondary education and following it for 6 years, the BPS can determine the extent to which students who start postsecondary education at various ages differ in their progress, persistence, and attainment, as well as their entry into the workforce. The first BPS was conducted in 1989–90, with follow-ups in 1992 (BPS:90/92) and 1994 (BPS:90/94). The second BPS was conducted in 1995–96, with follow-ups in 1998 (BPS:96/98) and 2001 (BPS:96/01). The third BPS was conducted in 2003–04, with follow-ups in 2006 (BPS:04/06) and 2009 (BPS:04/09).

The fourth BPS was conducted in 2012, with follow-ups in 2014 (BPS:12/14) and 2017 (BPS:12/17). In the base year, 1,690 institutions were sampled, of which all were confirmed eligible to participate. In addition, 128,120 students were sampled, and 123,600 were eligible to participate in the NPSAS:12 study. In the first follow-up (BPS:12/14), of the 35,540 eligible NPSAS:12 sample students, 24,770 responded, for an unweighted student response rate of 70 percent and a weighted response rate of 68 percent.

Further information on BPS may be obtained from

Aurora D'Amico
David Richards
Longitudinal Surveys Branch
Sample Surveys Division
National Center for Education Statistics
550 12th Street SW
Washington, DC 20202
aurora.damico@ed.gov
david.richards@ed.gov
https://nces.ed.gov/surveys/bps/

Common Core of Data

The Common Core of Data (CCD) is NCES's primary database on public elementary and secondary education in the United States. It is a comprehensive, annual, national statistical database of all public elementary and secondary schools and school districts containing data designed to be comparable across all states. This database can be used to select samples for other NCES surveys and provide basic information and descriptive statistics on public elementary and secondary schools and schooling in general.

The CCD collects statistical information annually from approximately 100,000 public elementary and secondary schools and approximately 18,000 public school districts (including supervisory unions and regional education service agencies) in the 50 states, the District of Columbia, the Department of Defense Education Activity (DoDEA), the Bureau of Indian Education (BIE), Puerto Rico, American Samoa, Guam, the Northern Mariana Islands, and the U.S. Virgin Islands. Three categories of information are collected in the CCD survey: general descriptive information on schools and school districts, data on students and staff, and fiscal data. The general school and district descriptive information includes name, address, and phone number; the data on students and staff include selected demographic characteristics; and the fiscal data pertain to revenues and current expenditures.

The ED*Facts* data collection system is the primary collection tool for the CCD. NCES works collaboratively with the Department of Education's Performance Information Management Service to develop the CCD collection procedures and data definitions. Coordinators from state education agencies (SEAs) submit the CCD data at different levels (school, agency, and state) to the ED*Facts* collection system. Prior to submitting CCD files to ED*Facts*, SEAs must collect and compile information from their respective local education agencies (LEAs) through established administrative records systems within their state or jurisdiction.

Once SEAs have completed their submissions, the CCD survey staff analyzes and verifies the data for quality assurance. Even though the CCD is a universe collection and thus not subject to sampling errors, nonsampling errors can occur. The two potential sources of nonsampling errors are nonresponse and inaccurate reporting. NCES attempts to minimize nonsampling errors through the use of annual training of SEA coordinators, extensive quality reviews, and survey editing procedures. In addition, each year SEAs are given the opportunity to revise their state-level aggregates from the previous survey cycle.

The NCES Education Demographic and Geographic Estimate (EDGE) program develops annually updated point locations (latitude and longitude) for public elementary and secondary schools included in the CCD database. The estimated location of schools and agency administrative offices is primarily derived from the physical address reported in the CCD directory files. The NCES EDGE program collaborates with the U.S. Census Bureau's EDGE Branch to develop point locations for schools reported in the annual CCD directory file. For more information about NCES school point data, please see https://nces.ed.gov/programs/edge/Geographic/SchoolLocations.

The CCD survey consists of five components: The Public Elementary/Secondary School Universe Survey, the Local Education Agency (School District) Universe Survey, the State Nonfiscal Survey of Public Elementary/Secondary Education, the National Public Education Financial Survey (NPEFS), and the School District Finance Survey (F-33).

Public Elementary/Secondary School Universe Survey

The Public Elementary/Secondary School Universe Survey includes all U.S. public schools providing education services to prekindergarten, kindergarten, grade 1–13, and ungraded students.

The Public Elementary/Secondary School Universe Survey includes data for variables such as NCES school ID number, state school ID number, name of the school, name of the agency that operates the school, mailing address, physical location address, phone number, school type, operational status, county number, county name, full-time-equivalent (FTE) classroom teacher count, low/high grade span offered, school level, students eligible for free lunch, students eligible for reduced-price lunch, total students eligible for free and reduced-price lunch, and student totals and detail (by grade, by race/ethnicity, and by sex). The survey also contains flags indicating whether a school is Title I eligible, schoolwide Title I eligible, a magnet school, a charter school, a shared-time school, or a BIE school, as well as which grades are offered at the school.

Local Education Agency (School District) Universe Survey

The coverage of the Local Education Agency Universe Survey includes all school districts and administrative units providing education services to prekindergarten, kindergarten, grade 1–13, and ungraded students.

The Local Education Agency Universe Survey includes the following variables: NCES agency ID number, state agency ID number, agency name, phone number, mailing address, physical location address, agency type code, supervisory union number, American National Standards Institute (ANSI) state and county code, county name, core based statistical area (CBSA), metropolitan/micropolitan code, metropolitan status code, locale code, congressional district, operational status code, BIE agency status, low/high grade span offered, agency charter status, number of schools, number of full-time-equivalent teachers, number of ungraded students, number of PK–13 students, number of special education/Individualized Education Program students, number of English language learner students, instructional staff fields, support staff fields, and LEA charter status.

State Nonfiscal Survey of Public Elementary/Secondary Education

The State Nonfiscal Survey of Public Elementary/Secondary Education provides state-level, aggregate information about students and staff in public elementary and secondary education. This survey covers public school student membership by grade, race/ethnicity, and state or jurisdiction and covers number of staff in public schools by category and state or jurisdiction. Beginning with the 2006–07 school year, the number of diploma recipients and other high school completers were no longer included in the State Nonfiscal Survey of Public Elementary/Secondary Education File. These data are now published in the public-use CCD State Dropout and Completion Data File.

National Public Education Financial Survey

The purpose of the National Public Education Financial Survey (NPEFS) is to provide district, state, and federal policymakers, researchers, and other interested users with descriptive information about revenues and expenditures for public elementary and secondary education. The data collected are useful to (1) chief officers of state education agencies; (2) policymakers in the executive and legislative branches of federal and state governments; (3) education policy and public policy researchers; and (4) the public, journalists, and others.

Data for NPEFS are collected from SEAs in the 50 states, the District of Columbia, Puerto Rico, American Samoa, Guam, the Northern Mariana Islands, and the U.S. Virgin Islands. The data file is organized by state or jurisdiction and contains revenue data by funding source; expenditure data by function (the activity being supported by the expenditure) and object (the category of expenditure); average daily attendance data; and total student membership data from the CCD State Nonfiscal Survey of Public Elementary/Secondary Education.

School District Finance Survey

The purpose of the School District Finance Survey (F-33) is to provide finance data for all LEAs that provide free public elementary and secondary education in the United States. National and state totals are not included (national- and state-level figures are presented, however, in the National Public Education Financial Survey).

NCES partners with the U.S. Census Bureau in the collection of school district finance data. The Census Bureau distributes Census Form F-33, Annual Survey of School System Finances, to all SEAs, and representatives from the SEAs collect and edit data from their LEAs and submit data to the Census Bureau. The Census Bureau then produces two data files: one for distribution and reporting by NCES and the other for distribution and reporting by the Census Bureau. The files include variables for revenues by source, expenditures by function and object, indebtedness, assets, and student membership counts, as well as identification variables.

The coverage of the F-33 survey is different from the coverage of the NPEFS survey, as NPEFS includes special state-run and federal-run school districts that are not included in the F-33. In addition, variances in data availability between the two surveys may occur in cases where some data are available at the state level but not at the district level, and this might result in state-aggregated district totals from F-33 differing from the state totals in NPEFS. When states submit NPEFS and F-33 data in their own financial accounting formats instead of the NCES-requested format, variances in the state procedures may result in variances in the data. In these instances, Census Bureau analysts design and implement a crosswalk system to conform state-formatted data to the format for variables in the F-33. Also, differences between the two surveys in the reporting of expenditures for similar data items can occur when there are differences in the methodology that the state respondents use to crosswalk their NPEFS or F-33 data. Finally, the imputation and editing processes and procedures of the two surveys can vary. For further detail on imputations and data editing in the F-33 and NPEFS surveys, please see the FY 16 NCES F-33 (Cornman, Ampadu, and Hanak 2019 [NCES 2019-304]) and NPEFS (Cornman et al. 2019 [NCES 2019-302]) survey documentation.

The following text table lists the CCD file versions used in the current edition of the *Digest of Education Statistics*:

Further information on the nonfiscal CCD data may be obtained from

Patrick Keaton
Elementary and Secondary Branch
Administrative Data Division
National Center for Education Statistics
550 12th Street SW
Washington, DC 20202
patrick.keaton@ed.gov
https://nces.ed.gov/ccd

Further information on the fiscal CCD data may be obtained from

Stephen Cornman
Elementary and Secondary Branch
Administrative Data Division
National Center for Education Statistics
550 12th Street, SW
Washington, DC 20202
stephen.cornman@ed.gov
https://nces.ed.gov/ccd

Table G. Common Core of Data (CCD) file versions used in the current edition of the *Digest of Education Statistics*: 1986–87 through 2016–17

Year	State Nonfiscal Survey of Public Elementary and Secondary Education	NCES CCD State Dropout and Completion Data	National Public Education Financial Survey	Local Education Agency Universe Survey	School District Finance Survey	Public Elementary/ Secondary School Universe File
1986–87 (FY 1987)	v.1c	†	v.1b–Revised	v.1	†	v.1
1987–88 (FY 1988)	v.1c	†	v.1b–Revised	v.1	†	v.1
1988–89 (FY 1989)	v.1c	†	v.1b–Revised	v.1	†	v.1
1989–90 (FY 1990)	v.1c	†	v.1b–Revised	v.1	v.1a–Final[1]	v.1
1990–91 (FY 1991)	v.1c	†	v.1b–Revised	v.1	†	v.1
1991–92 (FY 1992)	v.1c	†	v.1b–Revised	v.1	v.1a–Final1	Revised
1992–93 (FY 1993)	v.1c	†	v.1b–Revised	v.1	†	v.1
1993–94 (FY 1994)	v.1b	†	v.1b–Revised	v.1	†	Revised
1994–95 (FY 1995)	v.1b	†	v.1b–Revised	Revised	v.1d–Revised[1]	Revised
1995–96 (FY 1996)	v.1b	†	v.1b–Revised	v.1	v.1b–Revised[1]	v.1
1996–97 (FY 1997)	v.1c	†	v.1b–Revised	v.1	v.1a–Final[1]	v.1
1997–98 (FY 1998)	v.1c	†	v.1b–Revised	v.1	v.1e–Revised[1]	v.1
1998–99 (FY 1999)	v.1b	†	v.1b–Revised	v.1c	v.1c–Revised[1]	v.1c
1999–2000 (FY 2000)	v.1b	†	v.1b–Revised	v.1b	v.1d–Revised[1]	v.1b
2000–01 (FY 2001)	v.1c	†	v.1b–Revised	v.1a	v.1d–Revised[1]	v.1a
2001–02 (FY 2002)	v.1c	†	v.1c–Revised	v.1a	v.1c–Revised[1]	v.1a
2002–03 (FY 2003)	v.1b	†	v.1b–Revised	v.1a	v.1b–Revised[1]	v.1a
2003–04 (FY 2004)	v.1b	†	v.1b–Revised	v.1b	v.1b–Revised[1]	v.1a
2004–05 (FY 2005)	v.1f	†	v.1b–Revised	v.1c	v.1c–Revised[1]	v.1b
2005–06 (FY 2006)	v.1b	v.1b	v.1b–Revised	v.1a	v.1a–Final[1]	v.1a
2006–07 (FY 2007)	v.1c	v.1a	v.1b–Revised	v.1c	v.1a–Final[1]	v.1c
2007–08 (FY 2008)	v.1b	v.1a	v.1a–Final	v.1b	v.1a–Final[1]	v.1b
2008–09 (FY 2009)	v.1c	v.1a	v.1b–Revised	v.1a	v.1a–Final[1]	v.1b
2009–10 (FY 2010)	v.1b	v.1a	v.1a– Provisional	v.2a	v.1a–Provisional[1]	v.2a
2010–11 (FY 2011)	v.1a	v.1a–Provisional[1]	v.1a–Preliminary	v.2a	v.1a–Provisional[1]	v.2a
2011–12 (FY 2012)	v.1a	v.1a–Preliminary	v.1a– Provisional	v.1a	v.1a–Provisional	v.1a
2012–13 (FY 2013)	v.1a	—	v.1a–Provisional	v.1a	v.1a–Provisional	v.1a
2013–14 (FY 2014)	v.1a	—	v.1–Provisional	v.1a	v.1a–Provisional	v.1a
2014–15 (FY 2015)	v.1a	—	v.1a–Provisional	v.1a	v.1a–Provisional	v.1a
2015–16 (FY 2016)	v.1a	—	v.1a–Provisional	v.1a	v.1a–Provisional	v.2a
2016–17 (FY 2017)	v.1a	—	—	v.1a	—	v.1a

—Not available.
†Not applicable. Survey not conducted.
[1]Data not used in current edition of *Digest of Education Statistics*.
NOTE: Preliminary data have been edited but are subject to further NCES quality control procedures. Provisional data have undergone all NCES data quality control procedures. NCES releases a final data file after a publication using provisional data has been released. If NCES receives revised data from states or discovers errors in the final data file, a revised data file is released.
SOURCE: U.S. Department of Education, National Center for Education Statistics, Common Core of Data (CCD), retrieved June 5, 2019, from https://nces.ed.gov/ccd/ccddata.asp. (This table was prepared June 2019.)

Early Childhood Longitudinal Study, Birth Cohort

The Early Childhood Longitudinal Study, Birth Cohort (ECLS-B) was designed to provide policymakers, researchers, child care providers, teachers, and parents with nationally representative information about children's early learning experiences and their transition to child care and school. From the time the ECLS-B children were infants until they entered kindergarten, their cognitive and physical development was measured using standardized assessments, and information about their care and learning experiences at home, in early care and education settings, and at school was collected through interviews with adults in the children's lives.

Data were collected from a sample of about 14,000 children born in the United States in 2001, representing a population of approximately 4 million. The children participating in the study came from diverse socioeconomic and racial/ethnic backgrounds, with oversamples of Chinese, other Asian and Pacific Islander, and American Indian/Alaska Native children. There were also oversamples of twins and of children born with moderately low and very low birthweight. Children, their parents (including nonresident and resident fathers), their child care and early education providers, and their kindergarten teachers provided information on children's cognitive, social, emotional, and physical development. Information was also collected about the children's experiences across multiple settings (e.g., home, child care, and school).

Information about the ECLS-B children was collected when they were approximately 9 months old (2001–02), 2 years old (2003–04), and 4 years old/preschool age (2005–06). Additionally, in the fall of 2006, data were collected from all participating sample children, approximately 75 percent of whom were in kindergarten or higher. In the fall of 2007, data were collected from the approximately 25 percent of participating sample children who had not yet entered kindergarten or higher in the previous collection, as well as children who were repeating kindergarten in the 2007–08 school year.

In every round of data collection, children participated in assessment activities and parent respondents (usually the mothers of the children) were asked about themselves, their families, and their children. Resident fathers were asked about themselves and their role in the ECLS-B children's lives in the 9-month, 2-year, and preschool collections. Similar information was collected from nonresident biological fathers in the 9-month and 2-year collections. In addition, beginning when the children were 2 years old, their child care and early education providers were asked to provide information about their own experience and training and their setting's learning environment. At 2 years and at preschool, observations were conducted in the regular nonparental care and education arrangements of a subsample of children in order to obtain information about the quality of the arrangements. When the ECLS-B children were in kindergarten, their teachers were asked to provide information about the children's early learning experiences and their school and classroom environments. Also, the before- and after-school care and education providers of children in kindergarten were asked to provide information about their own experience, their training, and their setting's learning environment. School-level data, taken from other NCES datasets (the Common Core of Data and the Private School Universe Survey), and residential ZIP codes collected at each wave are also available.

Further information on the ECLS-B may be obtained from

Gail Mulligan
Jill McCarroll
Longitudinal Surveys Branch
Sample Surveys Division
National Center for Education Statistics
550 12th Street SW
Washington, DC 20202
ecls@ed.gov
https://nces.ed.gov/ecls/birth.asp

Early Childhood Longitudinal Study, Kindergarten Class of 1998–99

The Early Childhood Longitudinal Study, Kindergarten Class of 1998–99 (ECLS-K) was designed to provide detailed information on children's school experiences throughout elementary school and into middle school. The study began in the fall of 1998. A nationally representative sample of about 21,300 children enrolled in 940 kindergarten programs during the 1998–99 school year was selected to participate in the ECLS-K. The children attended both public and private kindergartens and full- and part-day programs. The sample included children from different racial/ethnic and socioeconomic backgrounds and oversamples of Asian and Pacific Islander children and private school kindergartners.

In the kindergarten year (1998–99), base-year data were collected in the fall and spring. In the first-grade year (1999–2000), data were collected again in the fall and spring. In the 3rd-grade (2002), 5th-grade (2004), and 8th-grade (2007) years, data were collected in the spring. The fall 1999 collection drew from a 30 percent subsample of schools; all other collections drew from the full sample of schools.

From kindergarten to 5th grade, the ECLS-K included a direct child cognitive assessment that was administered one on one with each child in the study. The assessment used a computer-assisted personal interview (CAPI) approach and a two-stage adaptive testing methodology. In the 8th grade, a two-stage adaptive paper-and-pencil assessment was administered in small groups. In kindergarten and first grade, the assessment included three cognitive domains: reading, mathematics, and general knowledge. General knowledge was replaced by science in the 3rd, 5th, and 8th grades. Children's height and weight were measured at each data collection point, and a direct measure of children's psychomotor development was administered in the fall of the kindergarten year only. In addition to these measures, the ECLS-K collected information about children's social skills and academic achievement through teacher reports in every grade and through student reports in the 3rd, 5th, and 8th grades.

A computer-assisted telephone interview with the children's parents/guardians was conducted at each data collection point. Parents/guardians were asked to provide key information about the children in the ECLS-K sample on subjects such as family structure (e.g., household members and composition), family demographics (e.g., family members' age, relation to the child being studied, and race/ethnicity), parent involvement, home educational activities (e.g., reading to the child), child health, parental education and employment status, and the social skills and behaviors of their children.

Data on the schools that children attended and their classrooms were collected through self-administered questionnaires completed by school administrators and classroom teachers. Administrators provided information about their schools' populations, programs, and policies. At the classroom level, data were collected from teachers on the composition of the classroom, teaching practices, curriculum, and teacher qualifications and experience. In addition, special education teachers and related services staff provided reports on the services received by children with an Individualized Education Program (IEP).

Further information on the ECLS-K may be obtained from

Gail Mulligan
Jill McCarroll
Longitudinal Surveys Branch
Sample Surveys Division
National Center for Education Statistics
550 12th Street SW
Washington, DC 20202
ecls@ed.gov
https://nces.ed.gov/ecls/kindergarten.asp

Early Childhood Longitudinal Study, Kindergarten Class of 2010–11

The Early Childhood Longitudinal Study, Kindergarten Class of 2010–11 (ECLS-K:2011) provides detailed information on the school achievement and experiences of students throughout their elementary school years. The students who participated in the ECLS-K:2011 were followed longitudinally from the kindergarten year (the 2010–11 school year) through the spring of 2016, when most of them were expected to be in 5th grade. This sample of students was designed to be nationally representative of all students who were enrolled in kindergarten or who were of kindergarten age and being educated in an ungraded classroom or school in the United States in the 2010–11 school year, including those in public and private schools, those who attended full-day and part-day programs, those who were in kindergarten for the first time, and those who were kindergarten repeaters. Students who attended early learning centers or institutions that offered education only through kindergarten were included in the study sample and represented in the cohort if those institutions were included in NCES's Common Core of Data or Private School Survey universe collections.

The ECLS-K:2011 placed emphasis on measuring students' experiences within multiple contexts and development in multiple domains. The design of the study included the collection of information from the students, their parents/guardians, their teachers, and their schools. Information was also collected from their before- and after-school care providers in the kindergarten year.

A nationally representative sample of approximately 18,170 children from about 1,310 schools participated in the base-year administration of the ECLS-K:2011 in the 2010–11 school year. The sample included children from different racial/ethnic and socioeconomic backgrounds. Asian/Pacific Islander students were oversampled to ensure that the sample included enough students of this race/ethnicity to make accurate estimates for the group as a whole. Nine data collections were conducted: fall and spring of the children's kindergarten year (the base year), fall 2011 and spring 2012 (the 1st-grade year), fall 2012 and spring 2013 (the 2nd-grade year), spring 2014 (the 3rd-grade year), spring 2015 (the 4th-grade year), and spring 2016 (the 5th-grade year). Although the study refers to later rounds of data collection by the grade the majority of children were expected to be in (that is, the modal grade for children who were in kindergarten in the 2010–11 school year), children were included in subsequent data collections regardless of their grade level.

A total of approximately 780 of the 1,310 originally sampled schools participated during the base year of the study. This translates to a weighted unit response rate (weighted by the base weight) of 63 percent for the base year. In the base year, the weighted child assessment unit response rate was 87 percent for the fall data collection and 85 percent for the spring collection, and the weighted parent unit response rate was 74 percent for the fall collection and 67 percent for the spring collection.

Fall and spring data collections were conducted in the 2011–12 school year, when the majority of the children were in the 1st grade. The fall collection was conducted within a 33 percent subsample of the full base-year sample, and the spring collection was conducted within the full base-year sample. The weighted child assessment unit response rate was 89 percent for the fall data collection and 88 percent for the spring collection, and the weighted parent unit response rate was 87 percent for the fall data collection and 76 percent for the spring data collection.

In the 2012–13 data collection (when the majority of the children were in the 2nd grade) the weighted child assessment unit response rate was 84.0 percent in the fall and 83.4 percent in the spring. In the 2014 spring data collection (when the majority of the children were in the 3rd grade), the weighted child assessment unit response rate was 79.9 percent. In the 2015 spring data collection (when the majority of the children were in the 4th grade), the weighted child assessment unit response rate was 77.3 percent; in the 2016 spring data collection (when the majority of the children were in the 5th grade), the weighted child assessment unit response rate was 72.4 percent.

Further information on ECLS-K:2011 may be obtained from

Gail Mulligan
Jill McCarroll
Longitudinal Surveys Branch
Sample Surveys Division
National Center for Education Statistics
550 12th Street SW
Washington, DC 20202
ecls@ed.gov
https://nces.ed.gov/ecls/kindergarten2011.asp

ED*Facts*

ED*Facts* is a centralized data collection through which state education agencies (SEAs) submit PK–12 education data to the U.S. Department of Education (ED). All data in ED*Facts* are organized into "data groups" and reported to ED using defined file specifications. Depending on the data group, SEAs may submit aggregate counts for the state as a whole or detailed counts for individual schools or school districts. ED*Facts* does not collect student-level records. The entities that are required to report ED*Facts* data vary by data group but may include the 50 states, the District of Columbia, the Department of Defense Education Activity, the Bureau of Indian Education, Puerto Rico, American Samoa, Guam, the Northern Mariana Islands, and the U.S. Virgin Islands. More information about ED*Facts* file specifications and data groups can be found at https://www2.ed.gov/about/inits/ed/edfacts/index.html.

ED*Facts* is a universe collection and is not subject to sampling error, although nonsampling errors such as nonresponse and inaccurate reporting may occur. The U.S. Department of Education attempts to minimize nonsampling errors by training data submission coordinators and reviewing the quality of state data submissions. However, anomalies may still be present in the data.

Differences in state data collection systems may limit the comparability of ED*Facts* data across states and across time. To build ED*Facts* files, SEAs rely on data that were reported by their schools and school districts. The systems used to collect these data are evolving rapidly and differ from state to state.

In some cases, ED*Facts* data may not align with data reported on SEA websites. States may update their websites on schedules different from those they use to report data to ED. Furthermore, ED may use methods for protecting the privacy of individuals represented within the data that could be different from the methods used by an individual state.

ED*Facts* data on homeless students enrolled in public schools are collected in data group 655 within file 118. ED*Facts* data on English language learners enrolled in public schools are collected in data group 678 within file 141. ED*Facts* four-year adjusted cohort graduation rate (ACGR) data are collected in data group 695 within file 150 and in data group 696 within file 151. ED*Facts* data on students in incidents involving firearms are collected in data group 596 within file 086. ED*Facts* data on students being removed from school due to disciplinary action are collected in data group 523 within file 030. ED*Facts* collects these data groups on behalf of the Office of Elementary and Secondary Education.

For more information about ED*Facts*, please contact

ED*Facts*
Elementary/Secondary Branch
Administrative Data Division
National Center for Education Statistics
550 12th Street SW
Washington, DC 20202
EDFacts@ed.gov
https://www2.ed.gov/about/inits/ed/edfacts/index.html

Education Longitudinal Study of 2002

The Education Longitudinal Study of 2002 (ELS:2002) is a longitudinal survey that is monitoring the transitions of a national probability sample of 10th-graders in public, Catholic, and other private schools. Survey waves follow both students and high school dropouts and monitor the transition of the cohort to postsecondary education, the labor force, and family formation.

In the base year of the study, of 1,200 eligible contacted schools, 750 participated, for an overall weighted school participation rate of approximately 68 percent (62 percent unweighted). Of 17,600 selected eligible students, 15,400 participated, for an overall weighted student response rate of approximately 87 percent. (School and student weighted response rates reflect use of the base weight [design weight] and do not include nonresponse adjustments.) Information for the study is obtained not just from students and their school records, but also from the students' parents, their teachers, their librarians, and the administrators of their schools.

The first follow-up was conducted in 2004, when most sample members were high school seniors. Base-year students who remained in their base schools were resurveyed and tested in mathematics. Sample freshening was conducted to make the study representative of spring 2004 high school seniors nationwide. Students who were not still at their base schools were all administered a questionnaire. The first follow-up weighted student response rate was 89 percent.

The second follow-up, conducted in 2006, continued to follow the sample of students into postsecondary education, the workforce, or both. The weighted student response rate for this follow-up was 82 percent. The third follow-up, which had a weighted student response rate of 78 percent, was conducted in 2012; the data were released in January 2014.

The postsecondary transcript data collection was conducted in 2013–14. Postsecondary transcripts were requested for each of the ELS:2002 sample members who reported attending an IPEDS postsecondary institution. Transcripts were obtained for 11,623 of 12,549 eligible sample members for a weighted response rate of 77 percent. For more information on the postsecondary transcript data collection, see *Education Longitudinal Study of 2002 (ELS:2002): A First Look at the Postsecondary Transcripts of 2002 High School Sophomores* (NCES 2015-034).

Further information on ELS:2002 may be obtained from

Elise Christopher
Longitudinal Surveys Branch
Sample Surveys Division
National Center for Education Statistics
550 12th Street SW
Washington, DC 20202
elise.christopher@ed.gov
https://nces.ed.gov/surveys/els2002/

Fast Response Survey System

The Fast Response Survey System (FRSS) was established in 1975 to collect issue-oriented data quickly, with a minimal burden on respondents. The FRSS, whose surveys collect and report data on key education issues at the elementary and secondary levels, was designed to meet the data needs of Department of Education analysts, planners, and decision makers when information could not be collected quickly through NCES's large recurring surveys. Findings from FRSS surveys have been included in congressional reports, testimony to congressional subcommittees, NCES reports, and other Department of Education reports. The findings are also often used by state and local education officials.

Data collected through FRSS surveys are representative at the national level, drawing from a sample that is appropriate for each study. The FRSS collects data from state education agencies and national samples of other educational organizations and participants, including local education agencies, public and private elementary and secondary schools, elementary and secondary school teachers and principals, and public libraries and school libraries. To ensure a minimal burden on respondents, the surveys are generally limited to three pages of questions, with a response burden of about 30 minutes per respondent. Sample sizes are relatively small (usually about 1,000 to 1,500 respondents per survey) so that data collection can be completed quickly.

Further information on the FRSS may be obtained from

Chris Chapman
Sample Surveys Division
National Center for Education Statistics
550 12th Street SW
Washington, DC 20202
chris.chapman@ed.gov
https://nces.ed.gov/surveys/frss/

Condition of Public School Facilities in the United States

Condition of America's Public School Facilities: 1999 (NCES 2000-032) is a report that presents national data about the condition of public schools in 1999. It provides results from the survey "Condition of Public School Facilities, 1999" (FRSS 73), which was conducted by NCES using its Fast Response Survey System (FRSS). The survey collected information about the condition of school facilities and the costs of bringing them into good condition; school plans for repairs, renovations, and replacements; the age of public schools; and overcrowding and practices used to address overcrowding. The results presented in this report are based on questionnaire data for 900 public elementary and secondary schools in the United States. The responses were weighted to produce national estimates that represent all regular public schools in the United States.

In 2013, NCES conducted "Condition of Public School Facilities: 2012–13" (FRSS 105), an FRSS survey covering most of the same topics. The First Look report *Condition of America's Public School Facilities: 2012–13* (NCES 2014-022) is based on results from this FRSS survey.

Further information on these FRSS reports and surveys may be obtained from

Chris Chapman
Sample Surveys Division
National Center for Education Statistics
550 12th Street SW
Washington, DC 20202
chris.chapman@ed.gov
https://nces.ed.gov/surveys/frss/

Public School Principals Report on Their School Facilities: Fall 2005

This report (NCES 2007-007) presents information on the extent of the match between the enrollment and the capacity of school buildings, environmental factors that can affect the use of classrooms and school buildings, the extent and ways in which schools use portable buildings and the reasons for using them, the availability of dedicated rooms for particular subject areas (such as science labs or music rooms), and the cleanliness and maintenance of student restrooms.

Results from the FRSS survey "Public School Principals' Perceptions of Their School Facilities: Fall 2005" (FRSS 88) form the basis of the report. The survey was mailed to school principals, who were asked to complete it themselves. The sample included 1,205 public schools in the 50 states and the District of Columbia. The sample was selected from the 2002–03 Common Core of Data (CCD) Public Elementary/Secondary School Universe File, the most current available at the time of selection. Of the 1,205 schools surveyed, 47 were determined to be ineligible. Of the remaining 1,158 schools, responses were received from 1,045. Data have been weighted to yield national estimates of public elementary/secondary schools. The unweighted response rate was 90 percent, and the weighted response rate was 91 percent.

Further information on this report may be obtained from

Chris Chapman
Sample Surveys Division
National Center for Education Statistics
550 12th Street SW
Washington, DC 20202
chris.chapman@ed.gov
https://nces.ed.gov/surveys/frss/

Internet Access in U.S. Public Schools and Classrooms: 1994–2005

This report (NCES 2007-020) is based on data collected in the FRSS survey "Internet Access in U.S. Public Schools, Fall 2005" (FRSS 90). The survey was designed to assess the federal government's commitment to assist every school and classroom in connecting to the Internet by the year 2000.

In 1994, NCES began surveying approximately 1,000 public schools each year regarding their access to the Internet, access in classrooms, and, since 1996, their type of internet connections. Later administrations of this survey were expanded to cover emerging issues. The 2003 survey (FRSS 86) was designed to update the questions in the 2002 survey (FRSS 83) and covered the following topics: school connectivity, student access to computers and the Internet, school websites, technologies and procedures to prevent student access to inappropriate websites, and teacher professional development on how to incorporate the Internet into the curriculum.

In 2005, respondents were asked about the number of instructional computers with access to the Internet, the types of internet connections, the technologies and procedures used to prevent student access to inappropriate material on the Internet, and the availability of handheld and laptop computers for students and teachers. Respondents also provided information on teacher professional development in integrating the use of the Internet into the curriculum and using the Internet to provide opportunities and information for teaching and learning.

Use of Educational Technology in Public Schools

In 2008, the NCES survey on educational technology use in public schools was redesigned and expanded to a set of three surveys (i.e., a school-level, a district-level, and a teacher-level survey). The three surveys provide complementary information and together cover a broader range of topics than would be possible with one survey alone. The set of surveys collected data on availability and use of a range of educational technology resources, such as district and school networks, computers, devices that enhance the capabilities of computers for instruction, and computer software. They also collected information on leadership and staff support for educational technology within districts and schools.

Educational Technology in U.S. Public Schools: Fall 2008 (NCES 2010-034) is based on the school-level survey, "Education Technology in U.S. Public Schools: Fall 2008" (FRSS 92); *Educational Technology in Public School Districts: Fall 2008* (NCES 2010-003) is based on the district-level school technology survey, "Educational Technology in Public School Districts, Fall 2008" (FRSS 93); and *Teachers' Use of Educational Technology in U.S. Public Schools: 2009* (NCES 2010-040) is based on the teacher-level school technology survey, "Teachers' Use of Educational Technology in U.S. Public Schools, 2009" (FRSS 95).

Further information on internet access and technology use in public schools and classrooms may be obtained from

Chris Chapman
Sample Surveys Division
National Center for Education Statistics
550 12th Street SW
Washington, DC 20202
chris.chapman@ed.gov
https://nces.ed.gov/surveys/frss/

Distance Education for Public Elementary and Secondary School Students

The report *Technology-Based Distance Education Courses for Public Elementary and Secondary School Students: 2002–03 and 2004–05* (NCES 2008-008) presented data collected in the FRSS survey "Distance Education Courses for Public Elementary and Secondary School Students, 2004–05" (FRSS 89, 2005). The report included national estimates of the prevalence and characteristics of technology-based distance education courses in public schools nationwide in school year 2004–05. The report also compared those data with the baseline data that were collected in the FRSS survey "Distance Education Courses for Public Elementary and Secondary School Students: 2002–03" (FRSS 84, 2003) and provided longitudinal analysis of change in the districts that responded to both the 2002–03 and 2004–05 surveys.

Distance education courses were defined as credit-granting courses offered to elementary and secondary school students enrolled in the district in which the teacher and student were in different locations. These courses could be delivered via audio, video (live or prerecorded), or Internet or other computer technologies.

Distance Education Courses for Public Elementary and Secondary School Students: 2009–10 (NCES 2012–008) presents national estimates about student enrollment in distance education courses in public school districts. The estimates are based on a district survey, "Distance Education Courses for Public Elementary and Secondary School Students: 2009–10" (FRSS 98, 2010), about distance education courses offered by the district or by any of the schools in the district during the 12-month 2009–10 school year. Distance education courses were defined as courses offered to elementary and secondary school students regularly enrolled in the district that were (1) credit granting; (2) technology delivered; and (3) had the instructor in a different location than the students and/or had course content developed in, or delivered from, a different location than that of the students.

Further information on FRSS reports on distance education may be obtained from

Chris Chapman
Sample Surveys Division
National Center for Education Statistics
550 12th Street SW
Washington, DC 20202
chris.chapman@ed.gov
https://nces.ed.gov/surveys/frss

School Safety and Discipline

The FRSS survey "School Safety and Discipline: 2013–14" (FRSS 106, 2014) collected nationally representative data on public school safety and discipline for the 2013–14 school year. The topics covered included specific safety and discipline plans and practices, training for classroom teachers and aides related to school safety and discipline issues, security personnel, frequency of specific discipline problems, and number of incidents of various offenses.

The survey was mailed to approximately 1,600 regular public schools in the 50 states and the District of Columbia. Recipients were informed that the survey was designed to be completed by the person most knowledgeable about safety and discipline at the school. The unweighted survey response rate was 86 percent, and the weighted response rate using the initial base weights was 85 percent. The survey weights were adjusted for questionnaire nonresponse, and the data were then weighted to yield national estimates that represent all eligible regular public schools in the United States. The report *Public School Safety and Discipline: 2013–14* (NCES 2015-051) presents selected findings from the survey.

Further information on this FRSS survey may be obtained from

Chris Chapman
Sample Surveys Division
National Center for Education Statistics
550 12th Street SW
Washington, DC 20202
chris.chapman@ed.gov
https://nces.ed.gov/surveys/frss

Federal Support for Education

NCES prepares an annual compilation of federal funds for education for the *Digest of Education Statistics*. Data for U.S. Department of Education programs come from the *Budget of the United States Government*. Budget offices of other federal agencies provide information for all other federal program support except for research funds, which are obligations reported by the National Science Foundation in *Federal Funds for Research and Development*. Some data are estimated, based on reports from the federal agencies contacted and the *Budget of the United States Government*.

Except for money spent on research, outlays are used to report program funds to the extent possible. Some *Digest of Education Statistics* tables report program funds as obligations, as noted in the title of the table. Some federal program funds not commonly recognized as education assistance are also included in the totals reported. For example, portions of federal funds paid to some states and counties as shared revenues resulting from the sale of timber and minerals from public lands have been estimated as funds used for education purposes. Parts of the funds received by states (in 1980) and localities (in all years) under the General Revenue Sharing Program are also included, as are portions of federal funds received by the District of Columbia. The share of these funds allocated to education is assumed to be equal to the share of general funds expended for elementary and secondary education by states and localities in the same year, as reported by the U.S. Census Bureau in its annual publication, *Government Finances*.

The share of federal funds assigned to education for the District of Columbia is assumed to be equal to the share of the city's general fund expenditures for each level of education.

For the job training programs conducted by the Department of Labor, only estimated sums spent on classroom training have been reported as educational program support.

During the 1970s, the Office of Management and Budget (OMB) prepared an annual analysis of federal education program support. These were published in the *Budget of the United States Government, Special Analyses*. The information presented in this report is not, however, a continuation of the OMB series. A number of differences in the two series should be noted. OMB required all federal agencies to report outlays for education-related programs using a standardized form, thereby assuring agency compliance in reporting. The scope of education programs reported in the

Digest of Education Statistics differs from the scope of programs reported in the OMB reports. Off-budget items such as the annual volume of guaranteed student loans were not included in OMB's reports. Finally, while some mention is made of an annual estimate of federal tax expenditures, OMB did not include them in its annual analysis of federal education support. Estimated federal tax expenditures for education are the difference between current federal tax receipts and what these receipts would be without existing education deductions to income allowed by federal tax provisions.

Recipients' data are estimated based on *Estimating Federal Funds for Education: A New Approach Applied to Fiscal Year 1980* (Miller, V., and Noell, J., 1982, Journal of Education Finance); *Federal Support for Education*, various years; and the *Catalog of Federal Domestic Assistance* (https://beta.sam.gov/). The recipients' data are estimated and tend to undercount higher education institutions, students, and local education agencies. This is because some of the federal programs have more than one recipient receiving funds. In these cases, the recipients were put into a "mixed recipients" category, because there was no way to disaggregate the amount each recipient received.

Further information on federal support for education may be obtained from

Tom Snyder
Annual Reports and Information Staff
National Center for Education Statistics
550 12th Street SW
Washington, DC 20202
tom.snyder@ed.gov
https://nces.ed.gov/surveys/AnnualReports/federal.asp

High School and Beyond Longitudinal Study

The High School and Beyond Longitudinal Study (HS&B) is a nationally representative sample survey of individuals who were high school sophomores and seniors in 1980. As a large-scale, longitudinal survey, its primary purpose is to observe the educational and occupational plans and activities of young people as they pass through the American educational system and take on their adult roles. The study contributes to the understanding of the development of young adults and the factors that determine individual education and career outcomes. The availability of this longitudinal data encourages research in such areas as the strength of secondary school curricula, the quality and effectiveness of secondary and postsecondary schooling, the demand for postsecondary education, problems of financing postsecondary education, and the adequacy of postsecondary alternatives open to high school students.

The HS&B survey gathered data on the education, work, and family experiences of young adults for the pivotal years during and immediately following high school. The student questionnaire covered school experiences, activities, attitudes, plans, selected background characteristics, and language proficiency. Parents were asked about their educational aspirations for their children and plans for how their postsecondary education would be financed. Teachers were surveyed regarding their assessments of their students' futures. The survey also collected detailed information, from complete high school transcripts, on courses taken and grades achieved.

The base-year survey (conducted in 1980) was a probability sample of 1,015 high schools with a target number of 36 sophomores and 36 seniors in each school. A total of 58,270 students participated in the base-year survey. Substitutions were made for nonparticipating schools—but not for students—in those strata where it was possible. Overall, 1,120 schools were selected in the original sample and 810 of these schools participated in the survey. An additional 200 schools were drawn in a replacement sample. Student refusals and absences resulted in an 82 percent completion rate for the survey.

Several small groups in the population were oversampled to allow for special study of certain types of schools and students. Students completed questionnaires and took a battery of cognitive tests. In addition, a sample of parents of sophomores and seniors (about 3,600 for each cohort) was surveyed.

HS&B first follow-up activities took place in the spring of 1982. The sample for the first follow-up survey included approximately 30,000 individuals who were sophomores in 1980. The completion rate for sample members eligible for on-campus survey administration was about 96 percent. About 89 percent of the students who left school between the base-year and first follow-up surveys (e.g., dropouts, transfer students, and early graduates) completed the first follow-up sophomore questionnaire.

As part of the first follow-up survey of HS&B, transcripts were requested in fall 1982 for an 18,150-member subsample of the sophomore cohort. Of the 15,940 transcripts actually obtained, 12,120 transcripts represented students who had graduated in 1982 and thus were eligible for use in the overall curriculum analysis presented in this publication. All courses in each transcript were assigned a 6-digit code based on the Classification of Secondary School Courses (a coding system developed to standardize course descriptions; see https://nces.ed.gov/surveys/hst/courses.asp). Credits earned in each course are expressed in Carnegie units. (The Carnegie unit is a standard of measurement that represents one credit for the completion of a 1-year course. To receive credit for a course, the student must have received a passing grade—"pass," "D," or higher.) Students who transferred from public to private schools or from private to public schools between their sophomore and senior years were eliminated from public/private analyses.

In designing the senior cohort first follow-up survey, one of the goals was to reduce the size of the retained sample while still keeping sufficient numbers of various racial/ethnic groups to allow important policy analyses. A total of about 11,230 of the 12,000 individuals subsampled

(93.6 percent) completed the questionnaire. Information was obtained about the respondents' school and employment experiences, family status, and attitudes and plans.

The samples for the second follow-up, which took place in spring 1984, consisted of about 12,000 members of the senior cohort and about 15,000 members of the sophomore cohort. The completion rate for the senior cohort was 91 percent, and the completion rate for the sophomore cohort was 92 percent.

HS&B third follow-up data collection activities were performed in spring 1986. Both the sophomore and senior cohort samples for this round of data collection were the same as those used for the second follow-up survey. The completion rates for the sophomore and senior cohort samples were 91 percent and 88 percent, respectively.

HS&B fourth follow-up data collection activities were performed in 1992 but only covered the 1980 sophomore class. These activities included examining aspects of these students' early adult years, such as enrollment in postsecondary education, experience in the labor market, marriage and child rearing, and voting behavior. In the postsecondary transcript update conducted in 1993, transcripts were collected based on student reports of enrollment in postsecondary education.

An NCES series of technical reports and data file user's manuals, available electronically, provides additional information on the survey methodology.

Further information on HS&B may be obtained from

Aurora D'Amico
Longitudinal Surveys Branch
Sample Surveys Division
National Center for Education Statistics
550 12th Street SW
Washington, DC 20202
aurora.damico@ed.gov
https://nces.ed.gov/surveys/hsb/

High School Longitudinal Study of 2009

The High School Longitudinal Study of 2009 (HSLS:09) is a nationally representative, longitudinal study of approximately 21,000 9th-grade students in 944 schools who will be followed through their secondary and postsecondary years. The study focuses on understanding students' trajectories from the beginning of high school into postsecondary education, the workforce, and beyond. The HSLS:09 questionnaire is focused on, but not limited to, information on science, technology, engineering, and mathematics (STEM) education and careers. It is designed to provide data on mathematics and science education, the changing high school environment, and postsecondary education. This study features a new student assessment in algebra skills, reasoning, and problem solving and includes surveys of students, their parents, math and science teachers, and school administrators, as well as a new survey of school counselors.

The HSLS:09 base year took place in the 2009–10 school year, with a randomly selected sample of fall-term 9th-graders in more than 900 public and private high schools that had both a 9th and an 11th grade. Students took a mathematics assessment and survey online. Students' parents, principals, and mathematics and science teachers and the school's lead counselor completed surveys on the phone or online.

The HSLS:09 student questionnaire includes interest and motivation items for measuring key factors predicting choice of postsecondary paths, including majors and eventual careers. This study explores the roles of different factors in the development of a student's commitment to attend college and then take the steps necessary to succeed in college (the right courses, courses in specific sequences, etc.). Questionnaires in this study have asked more questions of students and parents regarding reasons for selecting specific colleges (e.g., academic programs, financial aid and access prices, and campus environment).

The first follow-up of HSLS:09 occurred in the spring of 2012, when most sample members were in the 11th grade. A between-round postsecondary status update survey took place in the spring of students' expected graduation year (2013). It asked respondents about college applications, acceptances, and rejections, as well as their actual college choices. In the fall of 2013 and the spring of 2014, high school transcripts were collected and coded.

A full second follow-up took place in 2016, when most sample members were 3 years beyond high school graduation. Additional follow-ups are planned, to at least age 30.

Further information on HSLS:09 may be obtained from

Elise Christopher
Longitudinal Surveys Branch
Sample Surveys Division
National Center for Education Statistics
550 12th Street SW
Washington, DC 20202
hsls09@ed.gov
https://nces.ed.gov/surveys/hsls09/

High School Transcript Studies

High school transcript studies have been conducted since 1982 in conjunction with major NCES data collections. The studies collect information that is contained in a student's high school record—courses taken while attending secondary school, information on credits earned, when specific courses were taken, and final grades.

A high school transcript study was conducted in 2004 as part of the Education Longitudinal Study of 2002 (ELS:2002/2004). A total of 1,550 schools participated in the request for transcripts, for an unweighted participation rate of approximately 79 percent. Transcript information was received on 14,920 members of the student sample (not just graduates), for an unweighted response rate of 91 percent.

Similar studies were conducted on the coursetaking patterns of 1982, 1987, 1990, 1992, 1994, 1998, 2000, 2005, and 2009 high school graduates. The 1982 data are based on approximately 12,000 transcripts collected by the High School and Beyond Longitudinal Study (HS&B). The 1987 data are based on approximately 25,000 transcripts from 430 schools obtained as part of the 1987 NAEP High School Transcript Study, a scope comparable to that of the NAEP transcript studies conducted in 1990, 1994, 1998, and 2000. The 1992 data are based on approximately 15,000 transcripts collected by the National Education Longitudinal Study of 1988 (NELS:88/92). The 2005 data, from the 2005 NAEP High School Transcript Study, come from a sample of over 26,000 transcripts from 640 public schools and 80 private schools. The 2009 data are from the 2009 NAEP High School Transcript Study, which collected transcripts from a nationally representative sample of 37,700 high school graduates from about 610 public schools and 130 private schools.

Because the 1982 HS&B transcript study used a different method for identifying students with disabilities than was used in NAEP transcript studies after 1982, and in order to make the statistical summaries as comparable as possible, all the counts and percentages in this report are restricted to students whose records indicate that they had not participated in a special education program. This restriction lowers the number of 1990 graduates represented in the tables to 20,870.

Further information on NAEP high school transcript studies may be obtained from

Linda Hamilton
International Assessment Branch
Assessments Division
National Center for Education Statistics
550 12th Street SW
Washington, DC 20202
linda.hamilton@ed.gov
https://nces.ed.gov/surveys/hst/

Integrated Postsecondary Education Data System

IPEDS consists of 12 interrelated survey components that provide information on postsecondary institutions and academic libraries at these institutions, student enrollment, student financial aid, programs offered, retention and graduation rates, degrees and certificates conferred, and the human and financial resources involved in the provision of institutionally based postsecondary education. Prior to 2000, the IPEDS survey had the following subject-matter components: Institutional Characteristics; Total Institutional Activity (these data were moved to the Institutional Characteristics component in 1990–91, then to the Fall Enrollment component in 2000–01); Fall Enrollment; Fall Staff; Salaries, Tenure, and Fringe Benefits of Full-Time Faculty; Completions; Finance; Academic Libraries (in 2000, the Academic Libraries component separated from the IPEDS collection); and Graduation Rates. Since 2000, IPEDS survey components occurring in a particular collection year have been organized into three seasonal collection periods: fall, winter, and spring. The Institutional Characteristics and Completions components first took place during the fall 2000 collection. The Employees by Assigned Position (EAP); Salaries, Tenure, and Fringe Benefits of Full-Time Faculty; and Fall Staff components first took place during the winter 2001–02 collection. The Fall Enrollment, Student Financial Aid, Finance, and Graduation Rates components first took place during the spring 2001 collection. In the winter 2005–06 data collection, the EAP; Fall Staff; and Salaries, Tenure, and Fringe Benefits of Full-Time Faculty components were merged into the Human Resources component. During the 2007–08 collection year, the Fall Enrollment component was broken into two components: 12-Month Enrollment (taking place in the fall collection) and Fall Enrollment (taking place in the spring collection). In the 2011–12 IPEDS data collection year, the Student Financial Aid component was moved to the winter data collection to aid in the timing of the net price of attendance calculations displayed on the College Navigator (https://nces.ed.gov/collegenavigator/). In the 2012–13 IPEDS data collection year, the Human Resources component was moved from the winter data collection to the spring data collection, and in the 2013–14 data collection year, the Graduation Rates and Graduation Rates 200 Percent components were moved from the spring data collection to the winter data collection. In the 2014–15 data collection year, a new component (Admissions) was added to IPEDS and a former IPEDS component (Academic Libraries) was reintegrated into IPEDS. The Admissions component, created out of admissions data contained in the fall collection's Institutional Characteristics component, was made a part of the winter collection. The Academic Libraries component, after having been conducted as a survey independent of IPEDS between 2000 and 2012, was reintegrated into IPEDS as part of the spring collection. Finally, in the 2015–16 data collection year, the Outcome Measures survey component was added to IPEDS.

Beginning in 2008–09, the first-professional degree category was combined with the doctor's degree category. However, some degrees formerly identified as first-professional that take more than 2 full-time-equivalent academic years to complete, such as those in Theology (M.Div, M.H.L./Rav), are included in the master's degree category. Doctor's degrees were broken out into three distinct categories: research/scholarship, professional practice, and other doctor's degrees.

The collection of race/ethnicity data also changed in 2008–09. IPEDS now collects a count of students who identify as Hispanic and counts of non-Hispanic students who identify with each race category. The "Asian" race category is now separate from the "Native Hawaiian or Other Pacific Islander" category, and a new category of "Two or more races" has been added.

The degree-granting institutions portion of IPEDS is a census of colleges that award associate's or higher degrees and are eligible to participate in Title IV financial aid programs. Prior to 1993, data from technical and vocational institutions were collected through a sample survey. Beginning in 1993, all data are gathered in a census of all postsecondary institutions. Beginning in 1997, the survey was restricted to institutions participating in Title IV programs. The tabulations developed for editions of the *Digest of Education Statistics* from 1993 forward are based on lists of all institutions and are not subject to sampling errors.

The classification of institutions offering college and university education changed as of 1996. Prior to 1996, institutions that either had courses leading to an associate's or higher degree or that had courses accepted for credit toward those degrees were considered higher education institutions. Higher education institutions were accredited by an agency or association that was recognized by the U.S. Department of Education or were recognized directly by the Secretary of Education. The newer standard includes institutions that award associate's or higher degrees and that are eligible to participate in Title IV federal financial aid programs. Tables that contain any data according to this standard are titled "degree-granting" institutions. Time-series tables may contain data from both series, and they are noted accordingly. The impact of this change on data collected in 1996 was not large. For example, tables on faculty salaries and benefits were only affected to a very small extent. Also, degrees awarded at the bachelor's level or higher were not heavily affected. The largest impact was on private 2-year college enrollment. In contrast, most of the data on public 4-year colleges were affected to a minimal extent. The impact on enrollment in public 2-year colleges was noticeable in certain states, such as Arizona, Arkansas, Georgia, Louisiana, and Washington, but was relatively small at the national level. Overall, total enrollment for all institutions was about one-half of 1 percent higher in 1996 for degree-granting institutions than for higher education institutions.

Prior to the establishment of IPEDS in 1986, the Higher Education General Information Survey (HEGIS) acquired and maintained statistical data on the characteristics and operations of higher education institutions. Implemented in 1966, HEGIS was an annual universe survey of institutions accredited at the college level by an agency recognized by the Secretary of the U.S. Department of Education. These institutions were listed in NCES's *Education Directory, Colleges and Universities*.

HEGIS surveys collected information on institutional characteristics, faculty salaries, finances, libraries, fall enrollment, student residence and migration, and earned degrees. Since these surveys, like IPEDS, were distributed to all higher education institutions, the data presented are not subject to sampling error. However, they are subject to nonsampling error, the sources of which varied with the survey instrument.

The NCES Taskforce for IPEDS Redesign recognized that there were issues related to the consistency of data definitions as well as the accuracy, reliability, and validity of other quality measures within and across surveys. The IPEDS redesign in 2000 provided institution-specific web-based data forms. While the new system shortened data processing time and provided better data consistency, it did not address the accuracy of the data provided by institutions.

Beginning in 2003–04 with the Prior Year Data Revision System, prior-year data have been available to institutions entering current data. This allows institutions to make changes to their prior-year entries either by adjusting the data or by providing missing data. These revisions allow the evaluation of the data's accuracy by looking at the changes made.

NCES conducted a study (NCES 2005-175) of the 2002–03 data that were revised in 2003–04 to determine the accuracy of the imputations, track the institutions that submitted revised data, and analyze the revised data they submitted. When institutions made changes to their data, NCES accepted that the revised data were the most accurate, correct, and "true" data. The data were analyzed for the number and type of institutions making changes, the type of changes, the magnitude of the changes, and the impact on published data.

Because NCES imputes for missing data, imputation procedures were also addressed by the Redesign Taskforce. For the 2003–04 assessment, differences between revised values and values that were imputed in the original files were compared (i.e., revised value minus imputed value). These differences were then used to provide an assessment of the effectiveness of imputation procedures. The size of the differences also provides an indication of the accuracy of imputation procedures. To assess the overall impact of changes on aggregate IPEDS estimates, published tables for each component were reconstructed using the revised 2002–03 data. These reconstructed tables were then compared to the published tables to determine the magnitude of aggregate bias and the direction of this bias.

Since the 2000–01 data collection year, IPEDS data collections have been web based. Data have been provided by "keyholders," institutional representatives appointed by campus chief executives, who are responsible for ensuring that survey data submitted by the institution are correct and complete. Because Title IV institutions are the primary focus of IPEDS and because these institutions are required to respond to IPEDS, response rates for Title IV institutions have been high (data on specific components are cited below). More details on the accuracy and reliability of IPEDS data can be found in the *Integrated Postsecondary Education Data System Data Quality Study* (NCES 2005-175).

Further information on IPEDS may be obtained from

Samuel Barbett
Postsecondary Branch
Administrative Data Division
National Center for Education Statistics
550 12th Street SW
Washington, DC 20202
samuel.barbett@ed.gov
https://nces.ed.gov/ipeds/

Fall (12-Month Enrollment)

The 12-month period during which data are collected is July 1 through June 30. Data are collected by race/ethnicity, gender, and level of study (undergraduate or postbaccalaureate) and include unduplicated headcounts and instructional activity (contact or credit hours). These data are also used to calculate a full-time-equivalent (FTE) enrollment based on instructional activity. FTE enrollment is useful for gauging the size of the educational enterprise at the institution. Prior to the 2007–08 IPEDS data collection, the data collected in the 12-Month Enrollment component were part of the Fall Enrollment component, which is conducted during the spring data collection period. However, to improve the timeliness of the data, a separate 12-Month Enrollment survey component was developed in 2007. These data are now collected in the fall for the previous academic year. The response rate for the 12-Month Enrollment component of the fall 2017 data collection was nearly 100 percent. Data from 5 of the 6,635 Title IV institutions that were expected to respond to this component were imputed due to unit nonresponse.

Further information on the IPEDS 12-Month Enrollment component may be obtained from

Tara Lawley
Postsecondary Branch
Administrative Data Division
National Center for Education Statistics
550 12th Street SW
Washington, DC 20202
tara.lawley@ed.gov
https://nces.ed.gov/ipeds/

Fall (Completions)

This survey was part of the HEGIS series throughout its existence. However, the degree classification taxonomy was revised in 1970–71, 1982–83, 1991–92, 2002–03, and 2009–10. Collection of degree data has been maintained through IPEDS.

Degrees-conferred trend tables arranged by the 2009–10 classification are included in the *Digest of Education Statistics* to provide consistent data from 1970–71 through the most recent year. Data in this edition on associate's and other formal awards below the baccalaureate degree, by field of study, cannot be made comparable with figures from years prior to 1982–83. The nonresponse rate does not appear to be a significant source of nonsampling error for this survey. The response rate over the years has been high; for the fall 2017 Completions component, it rounded to 100 percent. Data from 3 of the 6,642 Title IV institutions that were expected to respond to this component were imputed due to unit nonresponse. Imputation methods for the fall 2017 IPEDS Completions component are discussed in the *2017–18 Integrated Postsecondary Education Data System (IPEDS) Methodology Report* (NCES 2018-195).

Further information on the IPEDS Completions component may be obtained from

Tara Lawley
Postsecondary Branch
Administrative Data Division
National Center for Education Statistics
550 12th Street SW
Washington, DC 20202
tara.lawley@ed.gov
https://nces.ed.gov/ipeds/

Fall (Institutional Characteristics)

This survey collects the basic information necessary to classify institutions, including control, level, and types of programs offered, as well as information on tuition, fees, and room and board charges. Beginning in 2000, the survey collected institutional pricing data from institutions with first-time, full-time, degree/certificate-seeking undergraduate students. Unduplicated full-year enrollment counts and instructional activity are now collected in the 12-Month Enrollment survey. Beginning in 2008–09, the student financial aid data collected include greater detail.

In the fall 2017 data collection, the response rate for Title IV entities on the Institutional Characteristics component rounded to 100 percent. Of the 6,715 Title IV entities that were expected to respond to this component, 2 responses were missing, and these data were imputed. In addition, some data were imputed for 2 institutions that partially responded to the Institutional Characteristics component.

Further information on the IPEDS Institutional Characteristics component may be obtained from

Moussa Ezzeddine
Postsecondary Branch
Administrative Data Division
National Center for Education Statistics
550 12th Street SW
Washington, DC 20202
moussa.ezzeddine@ed.gov
https://nces.ed.gov/ipeds/

Winter (Student Financial Aid)

This component was part of the spring data collection from IPEDS data collection years 2000–01 to 2010–11, but it moved to the winter data collection starting with the 2011–12 IPEDS data collection year. This move assists with the timing of the net price of attendance calculations displayed on College Navigator (https://nces.ed.gov/collegenavigator/).

Financial aid data are collected for undergraduate students. Data are collected regarding federal grants, state and local government grants, institutional grants, and loans. The collected data include the number of students receiving each type of financial assistance and the average amount of aid received by type of aid. Beginning in 2008–09, student financial aid data collected includes greater detail on types of aid offered.

In the winter 2017–18 data collection, the Student Financial Aid component collected data about financial aid awarded to undergraduate students, with particular emphasis on full-time, first-time degree/certificate-seeking undergraduate students awarded financial aid for the 2016–17 academic year. In addition, the component collected data on undergraduate and graduate students receiving benefits for veterans and members of the military service. Finally, student counts and awarded aid amounts were collected to calculate the net price of attendance for two subsets of full-time, first-time degree/certificate-seeking undergraduate students: those awarded any grant aid, and those awarded Title IV aid.

The response rate for the Student Financial Aid component in 2017–18 was nearly 100 percent. Of the 6,544 Title IV institutions that were expected to respond, responses were missing for 28 institutions, and these missing data were imputed. Additionally, data from 2 institutions that responded to the Student Financial Aid component contained item nonresponse, and these missing items were imputed.

Further information on the IPEDS Student Financial Aid component may be obtained from

Tara Lawley
Postsecondary Branch
Administrative Data Division
National Center for Education Statistics
550 12th Street SW
Washington, DC 20202
tara.lawley@ed.gov
https://nces.ed.gov/ipeds/

Winter (Graduation Rates and Graduation Rates 200 Percent)

In IPEDS data collection years 2012–13 and earlier, the Graduation Rates and Graduation Rates 200 Percent components were collected during the spring collection. In the IPEDS 2013–14 data collection year, however, the Graduation Rates and Graduation Rates 200 Percent collections were moved to the winter data collection.

The 2017–18 Graduation Rates component collected counts of full-time, first-time degree/certificate-seeking undergraduate students beginning their postsecondary education in the specified cohort year and their completion status as of 150 percent of normal program completion time at the same institution where the students started. If 150 percent of normal program completion time extended beyond August 31, 2017, the counts as of that date were collected. Four-year institutions used 2011 as the cohort year, while less-than-4-year institutions used 2014 as the cohort year. Four-year institutions also report for full-time, first-time bachelor's degree-seeking undergraduate students.

Starting with the 2016–17 Graduation Rates component, two new subcohort groups—students who received Pell Grants and students who received a subsidized Direct loan and did not receive Pell Grants—were added.

Of the 5,908 institutions that were expected to respond to the Graduation Rates component, responses were missing for 26 institutions, and these missing data were imputed. Additionally, data from 1 institution that responded contained item nonresponse, and these missing items were imputed.

The 2017–18 Graduation Rates 200 Percent component was designed to combine information reported in a prior collection via the Graduation Rates component with current information about the same cohort of students. From previously collected data, the following counts were obtained: the number of students entering the institution as full-time, first-time degree/certificate-seeking students in a cohort year; the number of students in this cohort completing within 100 and 150 percent of normal program completion time; and the number of cohort exclusions (such as students who left for military service). Then the number of additional cohort exclusions and additional program completers between 151 and 200 percent of normal program completion time was collected. Four-year institutions reported on bachelor's or equivalent degree-seeking students and used cohort year 2009 as the reference period, while less-than-4-year institutions reported on all students in the cohort and used cohort year 2013 as the reference period. Of the 5,500 institutions that were expected to respond to the Graduation Rates 200 Percent component, responses were missing for 22 institutions, and these missing data were imputed.

Further information on the IPEDS Graduation Rates and Graduation Rates 200 Percent components may be obtained from

Andrew Mary
Postsecondary Branch
Administrative Data Division
National Center for Education Statistics
550 12th Street SW
Washington, DC 20202
andrew.mary@ed.gov
https://nces.ed.gov/ipeds/

Winter (Admissions)

In the 2014–15 survey year, an Admissions component was added to the winter data collection. This component was created out of the admissions data that had previously been a part of the fall Institutional Characteristics component. Situating these data in a new component in the winter collection enables all institutions to report data for the most recent fall period.

The Admissions component collects information about the selection process for entering first-time degree/certificate-seeking undergraduate students. Data obtained from institutions include admissions considerations (e.g., secondary school records, admission test scores), the number of first-time degree/certificate-seeking undergraduate students who applied, the number admitted, and the number enrolled. Admissions data were collected only from institutions that do not have an open admissions policy for entering first-time students. Data collected for the IPEDS winter 2017–18 Admissions component relate to individuals applying to be admitted during the fall of the 2017–18 academic year (the fall 2017 reporting period). Of the 2,048 Title IV institutions that were expected to respond to the Admissions component, responses were missing for 2 institutions, and these missing data were imputed.

Further information on the IPEDS Admissions component may be obtained from

Moussa Ezzeddine
Postsecondary Branch
Administrative Data Division
National Center for Education Statistics
550 12th Street SW
Washington, DC 20202
moussa.ezzeddine@ed.gov
https://nces.ed.gov/ipeds/

Winter (Outcome Measures)

First administered in the winter 2015–16 data collection, the Outcome Measures component is designed to provide measures of student success for traditional college students, as well as for nontraditional college students, including those who are part-time students and transfers.

Starting with the winter 2015–16 data collection, the Outcome Measures component collected data from 2- and 4-year degree-granting institutions on the award and enrollment status for these four cohorts of degree/certificate-seeking undergraduates:

- First-time, full-time entering students;
- First-time, part-time entering students;
- Non-first-time (or "transfer-in"), full-time entering students; and
- Non-first-time, part-time entering students.

Starting with the 2017–18 collection, two new subcohort groups—students who received Pell Grants and students who did not receive Pell Grants—have also been added to each of the four main cohorts in the Outcome Measures component, resulting in a total of eight undergraduate subcohorts.

The cohorts that were a part of the winter 2017–18 data collection consisted of all entering students who began their studies between July 1, 2009, and June 30, 2010. Student completion status was collected as of August 31 at 4 years, 6 years, and 8 years after students entered the institution (e.g., 4-year completion status was measured on August 31, 2013). For students within the cohorts who did not receive a degree or certificate, the Outcome Measures component collected the enrollment status as of 8 years after they entered the reporting institution (August 31, 2017).

The response rate for the Outcome Measures component of the winter 2017–18 collection was nearly 100 percent. Of the 3,959 institutions that were expected to respond, 20 responses were missing, and these data were imputed. Additionally, data from 1 institution that responded to the Outcome Measures component contained item nonresponse, and these missing items were imputed.

Further information on the IPEDS Outcome Measures component may be obtained from

Tara Lawley
Postsecondary Branch
Administrative Data Division
National Center for Education Statistics
550 12th Street SW
Washington, DC 20202
tara.lawley@ed.gov
https://nces.ed.gov/ipeds/

Spring (Academic Libraries)

From 1966 to 1988, the Academic Libraries Survey was conducted on a 3-year cycle as part of HEGIS. From 1988 to 1998, the survey was a part of IPEDS and conducted on a 2-year cycle. It remained on a 2-year cycle from 2000 to 2012, but during that period it was conducted independently of IPEDS. In 2014, the survey was reincorporated into IPEDS as the Academic Libraries component, with data collection occurring annually.

The Academic Libraries component collects information from degree-granting institutions on library collections, circulations, expenditures, and services. Institutions answer a screening question in the IPEDS Institutional Characteristics component to determine whether they should also respond to the Academic Libraries component. The component consists of two sections, one for institutions reporting any library expenditures and one for institutions reporting total library expenditures greater than $100,000. Of the 4,286 institutions that were expected to respond to the Academic Libraries component in the IPEDS spring 2018 data collection, 22 responses were missing, and these data were imputed.

Further information on the IPEDS Academic Libraries component may be obtained from

Samuel Barbett
Postsecondary Branch
Administrative Data Division
National Center for Education Statistics
550 12th Street SW
Washington, DC 20202
samuel.barbett@ed.gov
https://nces.ed.gov/ipeds/

Spring (Fall Enrollment)

This survey has been part of the HEGIS and IPEDS series since 1966. Response rates have been relatively high, generally exceeding 85 percent. Beginning in 2000, with web-based data collection, higher response rates were attained. In the spring 2018 data collection, in which the Fall Enrollment component covered student enrollment in fall 2017, the response rate was greater than 99 percent. Of the 6,617 institutions that were expected to respond, 33 institutions did not respond, and these data were imputed. Additionally, data from 8 institutions that responded contained item nonresponse, and these missing items were imputed. Data collection procedures for the Fall Enrollment component of the spring 2018 data collection are presented in *Enrollment and Employees in Postsecondary Institutions, Fall 2017; and Financial Statistics and Academic Libraries, Fiscal Year 2017: First Look (Provisional Data)* (NCES 2019-021rev).

Beginning with the fall 1986 survey and the introduction of IPEDS (see above), a redesign of the survey resulted in the collection of data by race/ethnicity, gender, level of study (i.e., undergraduate and graduate), and attendance status (i.e., full-time and part-time). Other aspects of the survey include allowing (in alternating years) for the collection of age and residence data. The Fall Enrollment component also collects data on first-time retention rates, student-to-faculty ratios, and student enrollment in distance education courses. Finally, in even-numbered years, four-year institutions provide enrollment data by level of study, race/ethnicity, and gender for nine selected fields of study or Classification of Instructional Programs (CIP) codes. (The CIP is a taxonomic coding scheme that contains titles and descriptions of primarily postsecondary instructional programs.)

Beginning in 2000, the survey collected instructional activity and unduplicated headcount data, which are needed to compute a standardized, full-time-equivalent (FTE) enrollment statistic for the entire academic year. As of 2007–08, the timeliness of the instructional activity data has been improved by collecting these data in the fall as part of the 12-Month Enrollment component instead of in the spring as part of the Fall Enrollment component.

Further information on the IPEDS Fall Enrollment component may be obtained from

Tara Lawley
Postsecondary Branch
Administrative Data Division
National Center for Education Statistics
550 12th Street SW
Washington, DC 20202
tara.lawley@ed.gov
https://nces.ed.gov/ipeds/

Spring (Finance)

This survey was part of the HEGIS series and has been continued under IPEDS. Substantial changes were made in the financial survey instruments in fiscal year (FY) 1976, FY 1982, FY 1987, FY 1997, and FY 2002. While these changes were significant, a considerable effort has been made in this report to present only comparable information on trends and to note inconsistencies. The FY 1976 survey instrument contained numerous revisions to earlier survey forms, which made direct comparisons of line items very difficult. Beginning in FY 1982, Pell Grant data were collected in the categories of federal restricted grant and contract revenues and restricted scholarship and fellowship expenditures. The introduction of IPEDS in the FY 1987 survey included several important changes to the survey instrument and data processing procedures. Beginning in FY 1997, data for private institutions were collected using new financial concepts consistent with Financial Accounting Standards Board (FASB) reporting standards, which provide a more comprehensive view of college finance activities. The data for public institutions continued to be collected using the older survey form. The data for public and private institutions were no longer comparable and, as a result, no longer presented together in analysis tables. In FY 2001, public institutions had the option of either continuing to report using Government Accounting Standards Board (GASB) standards or using the new FASB reporting standards. Beginning in FY 2002, public institutions could use either the original GASB standards, the FASB standards, or the new GASB Statement 35 standards (GASB35). Beginning in FY 2004, public institutions could no longer submit survey forms based on the original GASB standards. Beginning in FY 2008, public institutions could submit their GASB survey forms using a revised structure that was modified for better comparability with the IPEDS FASB finance forms, or the institutions could use the structure of the prior forms used from FY 2004 to FY 2007. Similarly, in FY 2008, private nonprofit institutions and public institutions using the FASB form were given an opportunity to report using the forms that had been modified to improve comparability with the GASB forms, or they could use forms with a structure that was consistent with the prior years. In FY 2010, the use of the forms with the older structure was discontinued, and all institutions used either the GASB and FASB forms that had been modified for comparability. Also, in FY 2010, a new series of forms was introduced for non-degree-granting institutions that included versions for for-profit, FASB, and GASB reporting institutions. From FY 2000 through FY 2013, private for-profit institutions used a version of the FASB form with much less detail than the FASB form used by private nonprofit institutions. As of FY 2014, however, private for-profit institutions have been required to report the same level of detail as private nonprofit institutions.

Possible sources of nonsampling error in the financial statistics include nonresponse, imputation, and misclassification. The unweighted response rate has been about 85 to 90 percent for most of the years these data appeared in the *Digest of Education Statistics*; however, in more recent years, response rates have been much higher because Title IV institutions are required to respond. Since 2002, the IPEDS data collection has been a full-scale web-based collection, which has improved the quality and timeliness of the data. For example, the ability of IPEDS to tailor online data entry forms for each institution based on characteristics such as institutional control, level of institution, and calendar system and the institutions' ability to submit their data online are aspects of full-scale web-based collections that have improved response.

The response rate for the FY 2017 Finance component was greater than 99 percent: Of the 6,695 institutions and administrative offices that were expected to respond, 47 did not respond, and these missing data were imputed. Of the institutions that provided data, items were missing for 2 institutions, and these missing items were imputed. Data collection procedures for the FY 2017 component are discussed in *Enrollment and Employees in Postsecondary Institutions, Fall 2017; and Financial Statistics and Academic Libraries, Fiscal Year 2017: First Look (Provisional Data)* (NCES 2019-021rev).

Further information on the IPEDS Finance component may be obtained from

Samuel Barbett
Postsecondary Branch
Administrative Data Division
National Center for Education Statistics
550 12th Street SW
Washington, DC 20202
samuel.barbett@ed.gov
https://nces.ed.gov/ipeds/

Spring (Human Resources)

The Human Resources component was part of the IPEDS winter data collection from data collection years 2000–01 to 2011–12. For the 2012–13 data collection year, the Human Resources component was moved to the spring 2013 data collection in order to give institutions more time to prepare their survey responses.

IPEDS Collection Years, 2012–13 to Present

In 2012–13, new occupational categories replaced the primary function/occupational activity categories previously used in the IPEDS Human Resources component. This change was required in order to align the IPEDS Human Resources categories with the 2010 Standard Occupational Classification (SOC) system. In tandem with the change in 2012–13 from using primary function/occupational activity categories to using the new occupational categories, the sections making up the IPEDS Human Resources component (which previously had been Employees by Assigned Position, Fall Staff, and Salaries) were changed to Full-Time Instructional Staff, Full-time Noninstructional Staff, Salaries, Part-Time Staff, and New Hires.

The webpages "Archived Changes—Changes to IPEDS Data Collections, 2012–13" (https://nces.ed.gov/ipeds/InsidePages/ArchivedChanges?year=2012-13) and "2012–13 IPEDS Human Resources (HR) Occupational Categories Compared with 2011–12 IPEDS HR Primary Function/Occupational Activity Categories" (https://nces.ed.gov/ipeds/resource/download/IPEDS_HR_2012-13_compared_to_IPEDS_HR_2011-12.pdf) provide information on the redesign of IPEDS Human Resources component initiated in the 2012–13 data collection year. The survey materials for the spring 2018 Human Resources component provide a crosswalk comparing the IPEDS occupational categories for the 2017–18 data collection year to the 2010 Standard Occupational Classification (SOC) occupational categories. (The crosswalk can be found at https://nces.ed.gov/ipeds/UseTheData/ArchivedSurveyMaterialPdf?year=2017&fileName=package_1_43.pdf, in the "2017–18 Survey Materials, Instruction" section.

Of the 6,692 institutions and administrative offices that were expected to respond to the spring 2018 Human Resources component, 31 institutions did not respond, and these missing data were imputed. Of the institutions that provided data, items were missing for 2 institutions, and these missing items were imputed. Data collection procedures for this component are presented in *Enrollment and Employees in Postsecondary Institutions, Fall 2017; and Financial Statistics and Academic Libraries, Fiscal Year 2017: First Look (Provisional Data)* (NCES 2019-021rev).

IPEDS Collection Years Prior to 2012–13

In collection years before 2001–02, IPEDS conducted a Fall Staff survey and a Salaries survey; in the 2001–02 collection year, the Employees by Assigned Position (EAP) survey was added to IPEDS. In the 2005–06 collection year, these three surveys became sections of the IPEDS "Human Resources" component.

Data gathered by the EAP section categorized all employees by full- or part-time status, faculty status, and primary function/occupational activity. Institutions with M.D. or D.O. programs were required to report their medical school employees separately. A response to the EAP was required of all 6,858 Title IV institutions and administrative offices in the United States and other jurisdictions for winter 2008–09, and 6,845, or 99.8 percent unweighted, responded. Of the 6,970 Title IV institutions and administrative offices required to respond to the winter 2009–10 EAP, 6,964, or 99.9 percent, responded. Of the 7,256 Title IV institutions and administrative offices required to respond to the EAP for winter 2010–11, about 99.9 percent responded. In the original winter 2010–11 data collection, 7,252 responded to the EAP and data for the 4 nonrespondents were imputed; the next year, 1 of the nonrespondents whose data were imputed submitted a revision.

The main functions/occupational activities of the EAP section were primarily instruction, instruction combined with research and/or public service, primarily research, primarily public service, executive/administrative/managerial, other professionals (support/service), graduate assistants, technical and paraprofessionals, clerical and secretarial, skilled crafts, and service/maintenance.

All full-time instructional faculty classified in the EAP full-time non-medical school part as either (1) primarily instruction or (2) instruction combined with research and/or public service were included in the Salaries section, unless they were exempt.

The Fall Staff section categorized all staff on the institution's payroll as of November 1 of the collection year by employment status (full time or part time), primary function/occupational activity, gender, and race/ethnicity. Title IV institutions and administrative offices were only required to respond to the Fall Staff section in odd-numbered reporting years, so they were not required to respond during the 2008–09 Human Resources data collection. However, of the 6,858 Title IV institutions and administrative offices in the United States and other jurisdictions, 3,295, or 48.0 percent unweighted, did provide data in the Fall Staff section that year. During the 2009–10 Human Resources data collection, when all 6,970 Title IV institutions and administrative offices were required to respond to the Fall Staff section, 6,964, or 99.9 percent, did so. A response to the Fall Staff section of the 2010–11 Human Resources collection was optional, and 3,364 Title IV institutions and administrative offices responded that year (a response rate of 46.3 percent).

The Salaries section collected data for full-time instructional faculty (except those in medical schools in the EAP section, described above) on the institution's payroll as of November 1 of the collection year by contract length/teaching period, gender, and academic rank. The reporting of data by faculty status in the Salaries section was required from 4-year degree-granting institutions and above only. Salary outlays and fringe benefits were also collected for full-time instructional staff on 9/10- and 11/12-month contracts/teaching periods. This section was applicable to degree-granting institutions unless exempt.

Between 1966–67 and 1985–86, this survey differed from other HEGIS surveys in that imputations were not made for nonrespondents. Thus, there is some possibility that the salary averages presented in this report may differ from the results of a complete enumeration of all colleges and universities. Beginning with the surveys for 1987–88, the IPEDS data tabulation procedures included imputations for survey nonrespondents. The unweighted response rate for the 2008–09 Salaries survey section was 99.9 percent. The response rate for the 2009–10 Salaries section was 100.0 percent (4,453 of the 4,455 required institutions responded), and the response rate for 2010–11 was 99.9 percent (4,561 of the 4,565 required institutions responded). Imputation methods for the 2010–11 Salaries survey section are discussed in *Employees in Postsecondary Institutions, Fall 2010, and Salaries of Full-Time Instructional Staff, 2010–11* (NCES 2012-276).

Further information on the Human Resources component may be obtained from

Samuel Barbett
Postsecondary Branch
Administrative Data Division
National Center for Education Statistics
550 12th Street SW
Washington, DC 20202
samuel.barbett@ed.gov
https://nces.ed.gov/ipeds/

Library Statistics

In the past, NCES collected library data through the Public Libraries Survey (PLS), the State Library Agencies (StLA) Survey, the Academic Libraries Survey (ALS), and the Library Media Centers (LMC) Survey. On October 1, 2007, the administration of the Public Libraries Survey (PLS) and the State Library Agencies (StLA) Survey was transferred to the Institute of Museum and Library Services (IMLS) (see below).

NCES administered the Academic Libraries Survey (ALS) on a 3-year cycle between 1966 and 1988. From 1988 through 1999, ALS was a component of the Integrated Postsecondary Education Data System (IPEDS) and was on a 2-year cycle. Beginning in the year 2000, ALS began collecting data independent from the IPEDS data collection, but it remained on a 2-year cycle. ALS provided data on approximately 3,700 academic libraries. In aggregate, these data provided an overview of the status of academic libraries nationally and statewide. The survey collected data on the libraries in the entire universe of degree-granting institutions. Beginning with the collection of FY 2000 data, ALS changed to web-based data collection. ALS produced descriptive statistics on academic libraries in postsecondary institutions in the 50 states, the District of Columbia, and the outlying areas. *Academic Libraries: 2012* (NCES 2014-038) presented tabulations for the 2012 survey. In 2014, ALS was reincorporated into the IPEDS collection. Since then, it has been collected annually, as the Academic Libraries component, in the IPEDS spring data collection.

School library data were collected on the School and Principal Surveys of the 1990–91 Schools and Staffing Survey (SASS). The School Library Media Centers (LMC) Survey became a component of SASS with the 1993–94 administration of the survey. Thus, readers should refer to the section on the Schools and Staffing Survey, below, regarding data on school libraries. Data for the 2011–12 LMC Survey are available on the NCES website at https://nces.ed.gov/surveys/sass/index.asp.

Further information on library statistics may be obtained from

Christopher Cody
Postsecondary Branch
Administrative Data Division
National Center for Education Statistics
550 12th Street SW
Washington, DC 20202
christopher.cody@ed.gov
https://nces.ed.gov/surveys/libraries/

National Adult Literacy Survey

The National Adult Literacy Survey (NALS), funded by the U.S. Department of Education and 12 states, was created in 1992 as a new measure of literacy. The aim of the survey was to profile the English literacy of adults in the United States based on their performance across a wide array of tasks that reflect the types of materials and demands they encounter in their daily lives.

To gather information on adults' literacy skills, trained staff interviewed a nationally representative sample of nearly 13,600 individuals ages 16 and over during the first 8 months of 1992. These participants had been randomly selected to represent the adult population in the country as a whole. Black and Hispanic households were oversampled to ensure reliable estimates of literacy proficiencies and to permit analyses of the performance of these subpopulations. In addition, some 1,100 inmates from 80 federal and state prisons were interviewed to gather information on the proficiencies of the prison population. In total, nearly 26,000 adults were surveyed.

Each survey participant was asked to spend approximately an hour responding to a series of diverse literacy tasks, as well as to questions about his or her demographic characteristics, educational background, reading practices, and other areas related to literacy. Based on their responses to the survey tasks, adults received proficiency scores along three scales that reflect varying degrees of skill in prose, document, and quantitative literacy. The results of the 1992 survey were first published in *Adult Literacy in America: A First Look at the Findings of the National Adult Literacy Survey* (NCES 93-275), in September 1993. See the section on the National Assessment of Adult Literacy (below) for information on later adult literacy surveys.

Further information on NALS may be obtained from

Emmanuel Sikali
Reporting and Dissemination Branch
Assessments Division
National Center for Education Statistics
550 12th Street SW
Washington, DC 20202
emmanuel.sikali@ed.gov
https://nces.ed.gov/naal/nals_products.asp

National Assessment of Adult Literacy

The 2003 National Assessment of Adult Literacy (NAAL) was conducted to measure both English literacy and health literacy. The assessment was administered to 19,000 adults (including 1,200 prison inmates) age 16 and over in all 50 states and the District of Columbia. Components of the assessment included a background questionnaire; a prison component that assesses the literacy skills of adults in federal and state prisons; the State Assessment of Adult Literacy (SAAL), a voluntary survey given in conjunction with NAAL; a health literacy component; the Fluency Addition to NAAL (FAN), an oral reading assessment; and the Adult Literacy Supplemental Assessment (ALSA). ALSA is an alternative to the main NAAL for those with very low scores on seven core screening questions. NAAL assesses literacy directly through the completion of tasks that covered quantitative literacy, document literacy, and prose literacy. Results were reported using the following achievement levels: *Below Basic*, *Basic*, *Intermediate*, and *Proficient*.

Results from NAAL and NALS can be compared. NALS offers a snapshot of the condition of literacy of the U.S. population as a whole and among key population subgroups in 1992. NAAL provides a picture of adult literacy skills in 2003, revealing changes in literacy over the intervening decade.

Further information on NAAL may be obtained from

Emmanuel Sikali
Reporting and Dissemination Branch
Assessments Division
National Center for Education Statistics
550 12th Street SW
Washington, DC 20202
emmanuel.sikali@ed.gov
https://nces.ed.gov/naal/

National Assessment of Educational Progress

The National Assessment of Educational Progress (NAEP) is a series of cross-sectional studies initially implemented in 1969 to assess the educational achievement of U.S. students and monitor changes in those achievements. In the main national NAEP, a nationally representative sample of students is assessed at grades 4, 8, and 12 in various academic subjects. The assessment is based on frameworks developed by the National Assessment Governing Board (NAGB). It includes both multiple-choice items and constructed-response items (those requiring written answers). Results are reported in two ways: by average score and by achievement level. Average scores are reported for the nation, for participating states and jurisdictions, and for subgroups of the population. Percentages of students performing at or above three achievement levels (*Basic*, *Proficient*, and *Advanced*) are also reported for these groups.

Main NAEP Assessments

From 1990 until 2001, main NAEP was conducted for states and other jurisdictions that chose to participate. In 2002, under the provisions of the No Child Left Behind Act of 2001, all states began to participate in main NAEP, and an aggregate of all state samples replaced the separate national sample. (School district-level assessments—under the Trial Urban District Assessment [TUDA] program—also began in 2002.)

Results are available for the mathematics assessments administered in 2000, 2003, 2005, 2007, 2009, 2011, 2013, 2015, and 2017. In 2005, NAGB called for the development of a new mathematics framework. The revisions made to the mathematics framework for the 2005 assessment were intended to reflect recent curricular emphases and better assess the specific objectives for students at each grade level.

The revised mathematics framework focuses on two dimensions: mathematical content and cognitive demand. By considering these two dimensions for each item in the assessment, the framework ensures that NAEP assesses an appropriate balance of content, as well as a variety of ways of knowing and doing mathematics.

Since the 2005 changes to the mathematics framework were minimal for grades 4 and 8, comparisons over time can be made between assessments conducted before and after the framework's implementation for these grades. The changes that the 2005 framework made to the grade 12 assessment, however, were too drastic to allow grade 12 results from before and after implementation to be directly compared. These changes included adding more questions on algebra, data analysis, and probability to reflect changes in high school mathematics standards and coursework; merging the measurement and geometry content areas; and changing the reporting scale from 0–500 to 0–300. For more information regarding the 2005 mathematics framework revisions, see https://nces.ed.gov/nationsreportcard/mathematics/frameworkcomparison.asp.

Results are available for the reading assessments administered in 2000, 2002, 2003, 2005, 2007, 2009, 2011, 2013, 2015, and 2017. In 2009, a new framework was developed for the 4th-, 8th-, and 12th-grade NAEP reading assessments.

Both a content alignment study and a reading trend, or bridge, study were conducted to determine whether the new reading assessment was comparable to the prior assessment. Overall, the results of the special analyses suggested that the assessments were similar in terms of their item and scale characteristics and the results they produced for important demographic groups of students. Thus, it was determined that the results of the 2009 reading assessment could still be compared to those from earlier assessment years, thereby maintaining the trend lines first established in 1992. For more information regarding the 2009 reading framework revisions, see https://nces.ed.gov/nationsreportcard/reading/whatmeasure.asp.

In spring 2013, NAEP released results from the NAEP 2012 economics assessment in *The Nation's Report Card: Economics 2012* (NCES 2013-453). First administered in 2006, the NAEP economics assessment measures 12th-graders' understanding of a wide range of topics in three main content areas: market economy, national economy, and international economy. The 2012 assessment is based on a nationally representative sample of nearly 11,000 students in the 12th grade.

In *The Nation's Report Card: A First Look—2013 Mathematics and Reading* (NCES 2014-451), NAEP released the results of the 2013 mathematics and reading assessments. Results can also be accessed using the interactive graphics and downloadable data available at the online Nation's Report Card website (https://nationsreportcard.gov/reading_math_2013/).

The Nation's Report Card: A First Look—2013 Mathematics and Reading Trial Urban District Assessment (NCES 2014-466) provides the results of the 2013 mathematics and reading TUDA, which measured the reading and mathematics progress of 4th- and 8th-graders from 21 urban school districts. Results from the 2013 mathematics and reading TUDA can also be accessed using the interactive graphics and downloadable data available at the online TUDA website (https://nationsreportcard.gov/reading_math_tuda_2013/).

The online interactive report *The Nation's Report Card: 2014 U.S. History, Geography, and Civics at Grade 8* (NCES 2015-112) provides grade 8 results for the 2014 NAEP U.S. history, geography, and civics assessments. Trend results for previous assessment years in these three subjects, as well as information on school and student participation rates and sample tasks and student responses, are also presented.

In 2014, the first administration of the NAEP Technology and Engineering Literacy (TEL) Assessment asked 8th-graders to respond to questions aimed at assessing their knowledge and skill in understanding technological principles, solving technology and engineering-related problems, and using technology to communicate and collaborate. The online report *The Nation's Report Card: Technology and Engineering Literacy* (NCES 2016-119) presents national results for 8th-graders on the TEL assessment.

The Nation's Report Card: 2015 Mathematics and Reading Assessments (NCES 2015-136) is an online interactive report that presents national and state results for 4th- and 8th-graders on the NAEP 2015 mathematics and reading assessments. The report also presents TUDA results in mathematics and reading for 4th- and 8th-graders. The online interactive report *The Nation's Report Card: 2015 Mathematics and Reading at Grade 12* (NCES 2016-018) presents grade 12 results from the NAEP 2015 mathematics and reading assessments.

Results from the 2015 NAEP science assessment are presented in the online report *The Nation's Report Card: 2015 Science at Grades 4, 8, and 12* (NCES 2016-162). The assessment measures the knowledge of 4th-, 8th-, and 12th-graders in the content areas of physical science, life science, and Earth and space sciences, as well as their understanding of four science practices (identifying science principles, using science principles, using scientific inquiry, and using technological design). National results are reported for grades 4, 8, and 12, and results from 46 participating states and one jurisdiction are reported for grades 4 and 8. Since a new NAEP science framework was introduced in 2009, results from the 2015 science assessment can be compared to results from the 2009 and 2011 science assessments, but cannot be compared to the science assessments conducted prior to 2009.

NAEP is in the process of transitioning from paper-based assessments to technology-based assessments; consequently, data are needed regarding students' access to and familiarity with technology, at home and at school. The Computer Access and Familiarity Study (CAFS) is designed to fulfill this need. CAFS was conducted as part of the main administration of the 2015 NAEP. A subset of the grade 4, 8, and 12 students who took the main NAEP were chosen to take the additional CAFS questionnaire. The main 2015 NAEP was administered in a paper-and-pencil format to some students and a digital-based format to others, and CAFS participants were given questionnaires in the same format as their NAEP questionnaires.

The online Highlights report *2017 NAEP Mathematics and Reading Assessments: Highlighted Results at Grades 4 and 8 for the Nation, States, and Districts* (NCES 2018-037) presents an overview of results from the NAEP 2017 mathematics and reading reports. Highlighted results include key findings for the nation, states/jurisdictions, and 27 districts that participated in the Trial Urban District Assessment (TUDA) in mathematics and reading at grades 4 and 8.

Results from the NAEP 2018 TEL Assessment are contained in the online report *The Nation's Report Card: Highlighted Results for the 2018 Technology and Engineering Literacy (TEL) Assessment at Grade 8* (NCES 2019-068). The digitally based assessment (participants took the assessment via laptop) was taken by approximately 15,400 eighth-graders from about 600 schools across the nation. Results were reported in terms of average scale scores (on a 0 to 300 scale) and in relation to the NAEP achievement levels *NAEP Basic*, *NAEP Proficient*, and *NAEP Advanced*.

NAEP Long-Term Trend Assessments

In addition to conducting the main assessments, NAEP also conducts the long-term trend assessments. Long-term trend assessments provide an opportunity to observe educational progress in reading and mathematics of 9-, 13-, and 17-year-olds since the early 1970s. The long-term trend reading assessment measures students' reading comprehension skills using an array of passages that vary by text types and length. The assessment was designed to measure students' ability to locate specific information in the text provided; make inferences across a passage to provide an explanation; and identify the main idea in the text.

The NAEP long-term trend assessment in mathematics measures knowledge of mathematical facts; ability to carry out computations using paper and pencil; knowledge of basic formulas, such as those applied in geometric settings; and ability to apply mathematics to skills of daily life, such as those involving time and money.

The Nation's Report Card: Trends in Academic Progress 2012 (NCES 2013-456) provides the results of 12 long-term trend reading assessments dating back to 1971 and 11 long-term trend mathematics assessments dating back to 1973.

Further information on NAEP may be obtained from

Daniel McGrath
Reporting and Dissemination Branch
Assessments Division
National Center for Education Statistics
550 12th Street SW
Washington, DC 20202
daniel.mcgrath@ed.gov
https://nces.ed.gov/nationsreportcard

National Education Longitudinal Study of 1988

The National Education Longitudinal Study of 1988 (NELS:88) was the third major secondary school student longitudinal study conducted by NCES. The two studies that preceded NELS:88—the National Longitudinal Study of the High School Class of 1972 (NLS:72) and the High School and Beyond Longitudinal Study (HS&B) in 1980—surveyed high school seniors (and sophomores in HS&B) through high school, postsecondary education, and work and family formation experiences. Unlike its predecessors, NELS:88 began with a cohort of 8th-grade students. In 1988, some 25,000 8th-graders, their parents, their teachers, and their school principals were surveyed. Follow-ups were conducted in 1990 and 1992, when a majority of these students were in the 10th and 12th grades, respectively, and then 2 years after their scheduled high school graduation, in 1994. A fourth follow-up was conducted in 2000.

NELS:88 was designed to provide trend data about critical transitions experienced by young people as they develop, attend school, and embark on their careers. It complements and strengthens state and local efforts by furnishing new information on how school policies, teacher practices, and family involvement affect student educational outcomes (i.e., academic achievement, persistence in school, and participation in postsecondary education). For the base year, NELS:88 included a multifaceted student questionnaire, four cognitive tests, a parent questionnaire, a teacher questionnaire, and a school questionnaire.

In 1990, when most of the students were in 10th grade, students, school dropouts, their teachers, and their school principals were surveyed. (Parents were not surveyed in the 1990 follow-up.) In 1992, when most of the students were in 12th grade, the second follow-up conducted surveys of students, dropouts, parents, teachers, and school principals. Also, information from the students' transcripts was collected. The 1994 survey data were collected when most sample members had completed high school. The primary goals of the 1994 survey were (1) to provide data for trend comparisons with NLS:72 and HS&B; (2) to address issues of employment and postsecondary access and choice; and (3) to ascertain how many dropouts had returned to school and by what route. The 2000 follow-up examined the educational and labor market outcomes of the 1988 cohort at a time of transition. Most had been out of high school for 8 years; many had completed their postsecondary educations, were embarking on first or even second careers, and were starting families. For those who had attended postsecondary institutions after high school, student transcript data were collected from the institutions attended.

Further information on NELS:88 may be obtained from

Elise Christopher
Longitudinal Surveys Branch
Sample Surveys Division
National Center for Education Statistics
550 12th Street SW
Washington, DC 20202
elise.christopher@ed.gov
https://nces.ed.gov/surveys/nels88

National Household Education Surveys Program

The National Household Education Surveys Program (NHES) is a data collection system that is designed to address a wide range of education-related issues. Surveys have been conducted in 1991, 1993, 1995, 1996, 1999, 2001, 2003, 2005, 2007, 2012, and 2016. NHES targets specific populations for detailed data collection. It is intended to provide more detailed data on the topics and populations of interest than are collected through supplements to other household surveys.

The 2007 and earlier administrations of NHES used a random-digit-dial sample of landline phones and computer-assisted telephone interviewing to conduct interviews. However, due to declining response rates for all telephone surveys and the increase in households that only or mostly use a cell phone instead of a landline, the data collection method was changed to an address-based sample survey for NHES:2012. Because of this change in survey mode, readers should use caution when comparing NHES:2012 estimates to those of prior NHES administrations.

The topics addressed by NHES:1991 were early childhood education and adult education. About 60,000 households were screened for NHES:1991. In the Early Childhood Education Survey, about 14,000 parents/guardians of 3- to 8-year-olds completed interviews about their children's early educational experiences. Included in this component were participation in nonparental care/education; care arrangements and school; and family, household, and child characteristics. In the NHES:1991 Adult Education Survey, about 9,800 people 16 years of age and over, identified as having participated in an adult education activity in the previous 12 months, were questioned about their activities. Data were collected on programs and up to four courses, including the subject matter, duration, sponsorship, purpose, and cost. Information on the household and the adult's background and current employment was also collected.

In NHES:1993, nearly 64,000 households were screened. Approximately 11,000 parents of 3- to 7-year-olds completed interviews for the School Readiness Survey. Topics included the developmental characteristics of preschoolers; school adjustment and teacher feedback to parents for kindergartners and primary students; center-based program participation; early school experiences; home activities with family members; and health status. In the School Safety and Discipline Survey, about 12,700 parents of children in grades 3 to 12 and about 6,500 youth in grades 6 to 12 were interviewed about their school experiences. Topics included the school learning environment, discipline policy, safety at school, victimization, the availability and use of alcohol/drugs, and alcohol/drug education. Peer norms for behavior in school and substance use were also included in this topical component. Extensive family and household background information was collected, as well as characteristics of the school attended by the child.

In NHES:1995, the Early Childhood Program Participation Survey and the Adult Education Survey were similar to those fielded in 1991. In the Early Childhood component, about 14,000 parents of children from birth to 3rd grade were interviewed out of 16,000 sampled, for a completion rate of 90.4 percent. In the Adult Education Survey, about 24,000 adults were sampled and 82.3 percent (20,000) completed the interview.

NHES:1996 covered parent and family involvement in education and civic involvement. Data on homeschooling and school choice also were collected. The 1996 survey screened about 56,000 households. For the Parent and Family Involvement in Education Survey, nearly 21,000 parents of children in grades 3 to 12 were interviewed. For the Civic Involvement Survey, about 8,000 youth in grades 6 to 12, about 9,000 parents, and about 2,000 adults were interviewed. The 1996 survey also addressed public library use. Adults in almost 55,000 households were interviewed to support state-level estimates of household public library use.

NHES:1999 collected end-of-decade estimates of key indicators from the surveys conducted throughout the 1990s. Approximately 60,000 households were screened for a total of about 31,000 interviews with parents of children from birth through grade 12 (including about 6,900 infants, toddlers, and preschoolers) and adults age 16 or older not enrolled in grade 12 or below. Key indicators included participation of children in nonparental care and early childhood programs, school experiences, parent/family involvement in education at home and at school, youth community service activities, plans for future education, and adult participation in educational activities and community service.

NHES:2001 included two surveys that were largely repeats of similar surveys included in earlier NHES collections. The Early Childhood Program Participation Survey was similar in content to the Early Childhood Program Participation Survey fielded as part of NHES:1995, and the Adult Education and Lifelong Learning Survey was similar in content to the Adult Education Survey of NHES:1995. The Before- and After-School Programs and Activities Survey, while containing items fielded in earlier NHES collections, had a number of new items that collected information about what school-age children were doing during the time they spent in child care or in other activities, what parents were looking for in care arrangements and activities, and parent evaluations of care arrangements and activities. Parents of approximately 6,700 children from birth through age 6 who were not yet in kindergarten completed Early Childhood Program Participation Survey interviews. Nearly 10,900 adults completed Adult Education and Lifelong Learning Survey interviews, and parents of nearly 9,600 children in kindergarten through grade 8 completed Before- and After-School Programs and Activities Survey interviews.

NHES:2003 included two surveys: the Parent and Family Involvement in Education Survey and the Adult Education for Work-Related Reasons Survey (the first administration). Whereas previous adult education surveys were more general in scope, this survey had a narrower focus on occupation-related adult education programs. It collected in-depth information about training and education in which adults participated specifically for work-related reasons, either to prepare for work or a career or to maintain or improve work-related skills and knowledge they already had. The Parent and Family Involvement Survey expanded on the first survey fielded on this topic in 1996. In 2003, screeners were completed with 32,050 households. About 12,700 of the 16,000 sampled adults completed the Adult Education for Work-Related Reasons Survey, for a weighted response rate of 76 percent. For the Parent and Family Involvement in Education Survey, interviews were completed by the parents of about 12,400 of the 14,900 sampled children in kindergarten through grade 12, yielding a weighted unit response rate of 83 percent.

NHES:2005 included surveys that covered adult education, early childhood program participation, and after-school programs and activities. Data were collected from about 8,900 adults for the Adult Education Survey, from parents of about 7,200 children for the Early Childhood Program Participation Survey, and from parents of nearly 11,700 children for the After-School Programs and Activities Survey. These surveys were substantially similar to the surveys conducted in 2001, with the exceptions that the Adult Education Survey addressed a new topic—informal learning activities for personal interest—and the Early Childhood Program Participation Survey and After-School Programs and Activities Survey did not collect information about before-school care for school-age children.

NHES:2007 fielded the Parent and Family Involvement in Education Survey and the School Readiness Survey. These surveys were similar in design and content to surveys included in the 2003 and 1993 collections, respectively. New features added to the Parent and Family Involvement Survey were questions about supplemental education services provided by schools and school districts (including use of and satisfaction with such services), as well as questions that would efficiently identify the school attended by the sampled students. New features added to the School Readiness Survey were questions that collected details about TV programs watched by the sampled children. For the Parent and Family Involvement Survey, interviews were completed with parents of 10,680 sampled children in kindergarten through grade 12, including 10,370 students enrolled in public or private schools and 310 homeschooled children. For the School Readiness Survey, interviews were completed with parents of 2,630 sampled children ages 3 to 6 and not yet in kindergarten. Parents who were interviewed about children in kindergarten through 2nd grade for the Parent and Family Involvement Survey were also asked some questions about these children's school readiness.

NHES:2012 included the Parent and Family Involvement in Education Survey and the Early Childhood Program Participation Survey. The Parent and Family Involvement in Education Survey gathered data on students age 20 or younger who were enrolled in kindergarten through grade 12 or who were homeschooled at equivalent grade levels. Survey questions that pertained to students enrolled in kindergarten through grade 12 requested information on various aspects of parent involvement in education (such as help with homework, family activities, and parent involvement at school) and survey questions pertaining to homeschooled students requested information on the student's homeschooling experiences, the sources of the curriculum, and the reasons for homeschooling.

The 2012 Parent and Family Involvement in Education Survey questionnaires were completed for 17,563 (397 homeschooled and 17,166 enrolled) children, for a weighted unit response rate of 78.4 percent. The overall estimated unit response rate (the product of the screener unit response rate of 73.8 percent and the Parent and Family Involvement in Education Survey unit response rate) was 57.8 percent.

The 2012 Early Childhood Program Participation Survey collected data on the early care and education arrangements and early learning of children from birth through the age of 5 who were not yet enrolled in kindergarten. Questionnaires were completed for 7,893 children, for a weighted unit response rate of 78.7 percent. The overall estimated weighted unit response rate (the product of the screener weighted unit response rate of 73.8 percent and the Early Childhood Program Participation Survey unit weighted response rate) was 58.1 percent.

NHES:2016 used a nationally representative address-based sample covering the 50 states and the District of Columbia. The 2016 administration of NHES included a screener survey and three topical surveys: The Parent and Family Involvement in Education Survey, the Early Childhood Program Participation Survey, and the Adult Training and Education Survey. The screener survey questionnaire identified households with children under age 20 and adults ages 16 to 65. A total of 206,000 households were selected based on this screener, and the screener response rate was 66.4 percent. All sampled households received initial contact by mail. Although the majority of respondents completed paper questionnaires, a small sample of cases was part of a web experiment with mailed invitations to complete the survey online.

The 2016 Parent and Family Involvement in Education Survey, like its predecessor in 2012, gathered data about students age 20 or under who were enrolled in kindergarten through grade 12 or who were being homeschooled for the equivalent grades. The 2016 survey's questions also covered aspects of parental involvement in education similar to those in the 2012 survey. The total number of completed questionnaires in the 2016 survey was 14,075 (13,523 enrolled and 552 homeschooled children), representing a population of 53.2 million students either homeschooled or enrolled in a public or private school in 2015–16. The survey's weighted unit response rate was 74.3 percent, and the overall response rate was 49.3 percent.

The 2016 Early Childhood Program Participation Survey collected data about children from birth through age 6 who were not yet enrolled in kindergarten. The survey asked about children's participation in relative care, nonrelative care, and center-based care arrangements. It also requested information such as the main reason for choosing care, factors that were important to parents when choosing a care arrangement, the primary barriers to finding satisfactory care, activities the family does with the child, and what the child is learning. Questionnaires were completed for 5,844 children, representing a population of 21.4 million children from birth through age 6 who were not yet enrolled in kindergarten. The Early Childhood Program Participation Survey weighted unit response rate was 73.4 percent, and the overall estimated weighted unit response rate (the product of the screener weighted unit response rate and the Early Childhood Program Participation Survey weighted unit response rate) was 48.7 percent.

The third topical survey of NHES:2016 was a new NHES survey, the Adult Training and Education Survey. The survey collected information from noninstitutionalized adults ages 16 to 65 not enrolled in high school—it also collected information from adults living at residential addresses associated with educational institutions such as colleges (thus, it collected information from enrolled college students). One of the main goals of the Adult Training and Education Survey is to capture the prevalence of nondegree credentials, including estimates of adults with occupational certifications or licenses, as well as to capture the prevalence of postsecondary educational certificates. A further goal is to learn more about work experience programs. The survey's data, when weighted, were nationally representative of noninstitutionalized adults ages 16 to 65, not enrolled in grades 12 or below. The total number of completed questionnaires was 47,744, representing a population of 196.3 million. The survey had a weighted response rate of 73.1 percent and an overall response rate of 48.5 percent.

Data for the three topical surveys in the 2016 administration of NHES are available in *Parent and Family Involvement in Education: Results From the National Household Education Surveys Program of 2016* (NCES 2017-102); *Early Childhood Program Participation, Results From the National Household Education Surveys Program of 2016* (NCES 2017-101); and *Adult Training and Education: Results From the National Household Education Surveys Program of 2016* (NCES 2017-103rev). In addition, public-use data for the three 2016 surveys are available at https://nces.ed.gov/nhes/dataproducts.asp.

Further information on NHES may be obtained from

Sarah Grady
Andrew Zukerberg
Sample Surveys Division
National Center for Education Statistics
550 12th Street SW
Washington, DC 20202
sarah.grady@ed.gov
andrew.zukerberg@ed.gov
https://nces.ed.gov/nhes/

National Longitudinal Study of the High School Class of 1972

The National Longitudinal Study of the High School Class of 1972 (NLS:72) began with the collection of base-year survey data from a sample of about 19,000 high school seniors in the spring of 1972. In each of the years 1973, 1974, 1976, 1979, and 1986, a follow-up survey of these students was conducted. NLS:72 was designed to provide the education community with information on the transitions of young adults from high school through postsecondary education and the workplace.

In addition to the follow-ups, a number of supplemental data collection efforts were made. For example, a Postsecondary Education Transcript Study (PETS) was conducted in 1984; in 1986, the fifth follow-up included a supplement for those who became teachers.

The sample design for NLS:72 was a stratified, two-stage probability sample of 12th-grade students from all schools, public and private, in the 50 states and the District of

Columbia during the 1971–72 school year. During the first stage of sampling, about 1,070 schools were selected for participation in the base-year survey. As many as 18 students were selected at random from each of the sample schools. The sizes of both the school and student samples were increased during the first follow-up survey. Beginning with the first follow-up and continuing through the fourth follow-up, about 1,300 schools participated in the survey and slightly fewer than 23,500 students were sampled. The unweighted response rates for each of the different rounds of data collection were 80 percent or higher.

Sample retention rates across the survey years were quite high. For example, of the individuals responding to the base-year questionnaire, the percentages who responded to the first, second, third, and fourth follow-up questionnaires were about 94, 93, 89, and 83 percent, respectively. The fifth follow-up took its sample from students who had participated in at least one of the prior surveys. In all, 91.7 percent of participants had responded to at least five of the six surveys, and 62.1 percent had responded to all six.

Further information on NLS:72 may be obtained from

Aurora D'Amico
Longitudinal Surveys Branch
Sample Surveys Division
National Center for Education Statistics
550 12th Street SW
Washington, DC 20202
aurora.damico@ed.gov
https://nces.ed.gov/surveys/nls72/

National Postsecondary Student Aid Study

The National Postsecondary Student Aid Study (NPSAS) is a comprehensive nationwide study of how students and their families pay for postsecondary education. Data gathered from the study are used to help guide future federal student financial aid policy. The study covers nationally representative samples of undergraduates, graduates, and first-professional students in the 50 states, the District of Columbia, and Puerto Rico, including students attending less-than-2-year institutions, community colleges, and 4-year colleges and universities. Participants include students who do not receive aid and those who do receive financial aid. Since NPSAS identifies nationally representative samples of student subpopulations of interest to policymakers and obtains baseline data for longitudinal study of these subpopulations, data from the study provide the base-year sample for the Beginning Postsecondary Students (BPS) longitudinal study and the Baccalaureate and Beyond (B&B) longitudinal study.

Originally, NPSAS was conducted every 3 years. Beginning with the 1999–2000 study (NPSAS:2000), NPSAS has been conducted every 4 years. NPSAS:08 included a new set of instrument items to obtain baseline measures of the awareness of two new federal grants introduced in 2006: the Academic Competitiveness Grant (ACG) and the National Science and Mathematics Access to Retain Talent (SMART) grant.

The first NPSAS (NPSAS:87) was conducted during the 1986–87 school year. Data were gathered from about 1,100 colleges, universities, and other postsecondary institutions; 60,000 students; and 14,000 parents. These data provided information on the cost of postsecondary education, the distribution of financial aid, and the characteristics of both aided and nonaided students and their families.

NPSAS:90 included a stratified sample of approximately 69,000 eligible students (about 47,000 of whom were undergraduates) from about 1,100 institutions. For each of the students included in the NPSAS sample, there were up to three sources of data. First, institution registration and financial aid records were extracted. Second, a Computer Assisted Telephone Interview (CATI) designed for each student was conducted. Finally, a CATI designed for the parents or guardians of a subsample of students was conducted. The purpose of the parent survey was to obtain detailed information on the family and economic characteristics of dependent students who did not receive financial aid, especially first-time, first-year students. In keeping with this purpose, parents of financially independent students who were over 30 years of age and parents of graduate/first-professional students were excluded from the sample. Data from these three sources were synthesized into a single system with an overall response rate of 89 percent.

For NPSAS:93, information on 77,000 undergraduates and graduate students enrolled during the school year was collected at 1,000 postsecondary institutions. The sample included students who were enrolled at any time between July 1, 1992, and June 30, 1993. About 66,000 students and a subsample of their parents were interviewed by telephone. NPSAS:96 contained information on more than 48,000 undergraduate and graduate students from about 1,000 postsecondary institutions who were enrolled at any time during the 1995–96 school year. NPSAS:2000 included nearly 62,000 students (50,000 undergraduates and almost 12,000 graduate students) from 1,000 postsecondary institutions. NPSAS:04 collected data on about 80,000 undergraduates and 11,000 graduate students from 1,400 postsecondary institutions. For NPSAS:08, about 114,000 undergraduate students and 14,000 graduate students who were enrolled in postsecondary education during the 2007–08 school year were selected from more than 1,730 postsecondary institutions.

NPSAS:12 sampled about 95,000 undergraduates and 16,000 graduate students from approximately 1,500 postsecondary institutions.

NPSAS:16 sampled about 89,000 undergraduate and 24,000 graduate students attending approximately 1,800 Title IV eligible postsecondary institutions in the 50 states, the District of Columbia, and Puerto Rico. The sample represents approximately 20 million undergraduate and 4 million graduate students enrolled in postsecondary education at Title IV eligible institutions at any time between July 1, 2015, and June 30, 2016. Public access to the data is available online through PowerStats (http://nces.ed.gov/datalab/).

Further information on NPSAS may be obtained from

Aurora D'Amico
Tracy Hunt-White
Longitudinal Surveys Branch
Sample Surveys Division
National Center for Education Statistics
550 12th Street SW
Washington, DC 20202
aurora.damico@ed.gov
tracy.hunt-white@ed.gov
https://nces.ed.gov/surveys/npsas/

National Study of Postsecondary Faculty

The National Study of Postsecondary Faculty (NSOPF) was designed to provide data about faculty to postsecondary researchers, planners, and policymakers. NSOPF is the most comprehensive study of faculty in postsecondary education institutions ever undertaken.

The first cycle of NSOPF (NSOPF:88) was conducted by NCES with support from the National Endowment for the Humanities (NEH) in 1987–88 with a sample of 480 colleges and universities, over 3,000 department chairpersons, and over 11,000 instructional faculty. The second cycle of NSOPF (NSOPF:93) was conducted by NCES with support from NEH and the National Science Foundation in 1992–93. NSOPF:93 was limited to surveys of institutions and faculty, but with a substantially expanded sample of 970 colleges and universities and 31,350 faculty and instructional staff. The third cycle, NSPOF:99, included 960 degree-granting postsecondary institutions and approximately 18,000 faculty and instructional staff. The fourth cycle of NSOPF was conducted in 2003–04 and included 1,080 degree-granting postsecondary institutions and approximately 26,000 faculty and instructional staff.

There are no plans to repeat the study. Rather, NCES plans to provide technical assistance to state postsecondary data systems and to encourage the development of robust connections between faculty and student data systems so that key questions concerning faculty, instruction, and student outcomes—such as persistence and completion—can be addressed.

Further information on NSOPF may be obtained from

Aurora D'Amico
Longitudinal Surveys Branch
Sample Surveys Division
National Center for Education Statistics
550 12th Street SW
Washington, DC 20202
aurora.damico@ed.gov
https://nces.ed.gov/surveys/nsopf/

National Teacher and Principal Survey (NTPS)

The National Teacher and Principal Survey is a set of related questionnaires that collect descriptive data on the context of elementary and secondary education. Data reported by schools, principals, and teachers provide a variety of statistics on the condition of education in the United States that may be used by policymakers and the general public. The NTPS system covers a wide range of topics, including teacher demand, teacher and principal characteristics, teachers' and principals' perceptions of school climate and problems in their schools, teacher and principal compensation, district hiring and retention practices, general conditions in schools, and basic characteristics of the student population.

The NTPS was first conducted during the 2015–16 school year. The survey is a redesign of the Schools and Staffing Survey (SASS), which was conducted from the 1987–88 school year to the 2011–12 school year. Although the NTPS maintains the SASS survey's focus on schools, teachers, and administrators, the NTPS has a different structure and sample than SASS. In addition, whereas SASS operated on a 4-year survey cycle, the NTPS operates on a 2-year survey cycle.

The school sample for the 2015–16 NTPS was based on an adjusted public school universe file from the 2013–14 Common Core of Data (CCD), a database of all the nation's public school districts and public schools. The NTPS definition of a school is the same as the SASS definition of a school—an institution or part of an institution that provides classroom instruction to students, has one or more teachers to provide instruction, serves students in one or more of grades 1–12 or the ungraded equivalent, and is located in one or more buildings apart from a private home.

The 2015–16 NTPS universe of schools is confined to the 50 states plus the District of Columbia. It excludes the Department of Defense dependents schools overseas, schools in U.S. territories overseas, and CCD schools that do not offer teacher-provided classroom instruction in grades 1–12 or the ungraded equivalent. Bureau of Indian Education schools are included in the NTPS universe, but these schools were not oversampled, and the data do not support separate BIE estimates.

The NTPS includes three key components: school questionnaires, principal questionnaires, and teacher questionnaires. NTPS data are collected by the U.S. Census Bureau through mail and online questionnaires with telephone and in-person field follow-up. The school and principal questionnaires were sent to sampled schools, and the teacher questionnaire was sent to a sample of teachers working at sampled schools. The NTPS school sample consisted of about 8,300 public schools; the principal sample consisted of about 8,300 public school principals; and the teacher sample consisted of about 50,000 public school teachers.

The school questionnaire asks knowledgeable school staff members about grades offered, student attendance and enrollment, staffing patterns, teaching vacancies, programs and services offered, curriculum, and community service requirements. In addition, basic information is collected about the school year, including the beginning time of students' school days and the length of the school year. The weighted unit response rate for the 2015–16 school survey was 72.5 percent.

The principal questionnaire collects information about principal/school head demographic characteristics, training, experience, salary, goals for the school, and judgments about school working conditions and climate. Information is also obtained on professional development opportunities for teachers and principals, teacher performance, barriers to dismissal of underperforming teachers, school climate and safety, parent/guardian participation in school events, and attitudes about educational goals and school governance. The weighted unit response rate for the 2015–16 principal survey was 71.8 percent.

The teacher questionnaire collects data from teachers about their current teaching assignment, workload, education history, and perceptions and attitudes about teaching. Questions are also asked about teacher preparation, induction, organization of classes, computers, and professional development. The weighted response rate for the 2015–16 teacher survey was 67.8 percent.

Further information about the NTPS is available in *User's Manual for the 2015–16 National Teacher and Principal Survey, Volumes 1–4* (NCES 2017-131 through NCES 2017-134).

For additional information about the NTPS program, please contact

Maura Spiegelman
Cross-Sectional Surveys Branch
Sample Surveys Division
National Center for Education Statistics
550 12th Street SW
Washington, DC 20202
maura.spiegelman@ed.gov
https://nces.ed.gov/surveys/ntps/

Principal Follow-up Survey

The Principal Follow-up Survey (PFS), originally a component of the Schools and Staffing Survey (SASS) and currently a component of the National Teacher and Principal Survey (NTPS), was created in order to provide attrition rates for principals in K–12 schools. It assesses, from one year to the year following, how many principals are principals at the same school, how many are principals at a different school, and how many are no longer working as principals.

The 2012–13 PFS sample consisted of schools who had returned a completed 2011–12 SASS principal questionnaire. Schools that had returned the completed SASS questionnaire were mailed the 2012–13 PFS form in March 2013. The 2012–13 PFS sample included about 7,500 public schools and 1,700 private schools; it was made up of only one survey item and had a response rate of nearly 100 percent.

The 2016–17 PFS sample consisted of schools who had returned a completed 2015–16 NTPS principal questionnaire. Schools that had returned the completed NTPS questionnaire were mailed the 2016–17 PFS form in March 2017. The 2016–17 PFS sample included about 5,700 public schools. (The 2016–17 PFS did not include private schools because these schools were not included in the 2015–16 NTPS.) The survey was made up of only one item and had a response rate of about 95 percent.

Further information on the PFS may be obtained from

Isaiah O'Rear
Cross-Sectional Surveys Branch
Sample Surveys Division
National Center for Education Statistics
550 12th Street SW
Washington, DC 20202
isaiah.orear@ed.gov
https://nces.ed.gov/surveys/sass/

Private School Universe Survey

The purposes of the Private School Universe Survey (PSS) data collection activities are (1) to build an accurate and complete list of private schools to serve as a sampling frame for NCES sample surveys of private schools and (2) to report data on the total number of private schools, teachers, and students in the survey universe. Since its inception in 1989, the survey has been conducted every 2 years. Selected findings from the 2015–16 PSS are presented in the First Look report *Characteristics of Private Schools in the United States: Results From the 2015–16 Private School Universe Survey* (NCES 2017-073).

The PSS produces data similar to that of the Common Core of Data for public schools and can be used for public-private comparisons. The data are useful for a variety of policy- and research-relevant issues, such as the growth of religiously affiliated schools, the number of private high school graduates, the length of the school year for various private schools, and the number of private school students and teachers.

The target population for this universe survey is all private schools in the United States that meet the PSS criteria of a private school (i.e., the private school is an institution that provides instruction for any of grades K through 12, has one or more teachers to give instruction, is not administered by a public agency, and is not operated in a private home).

The survey universe is composed of schools identified from a variety of sources. The main source is a list frame initially developed for the 1989–90 PSS. The list is updated regularly by matching it with lists provided by nationwide private school associations, state departments of education, and other national guides and sources that list private schools. The other source is an area frame search in approximately 124 geographic areas, conducted by the U.S. Census Bureau.

Of the 40,302 schools included in the 2009–10 sample, 10,229 were found ineligible for the survey. Those not responding numbered 1,856, and those responding numbered 28,217. The unweighted response rate for the 2009–10 PSS survey was 93.8 percent.

Of the 39,325 schools included in the 2011–12 sample, 10,030 cases were considered as out-of-scope (not eligible for the PSS). A total of 26,983 private schools completed a PSS interview (15.8 percent completed online), while 2,312 schools refused to participate, resulting in an unweighted response rate of 92.1 percent.

There were 40,298 schools in the 2013–14 sample; of these, 10,659 were considered as out-of-scope (not eligible for the PSS). A total of 24,566 private schools completed a PSS interview (34.1 percent completed online), while 5,073 schools refused to participate, resulting in an unweighted response rate of 82.9 percent.

The 2015–16 PSS included 42,389 schools, of which 12,754 were considered as out-of-scope (not eligible for the PSS). A total of 22,428 private schools completed a PSS interview and 7,207 schools failed to respond, which resulted in an unweighted response rate of 75.7 percent.

Further information on the PSS may be obtained from

Steve Broughman
Cross-Sectional Surveys Branch
Sample Surveys Division
National Center for Education Statistics
550 12th Street SW
Washington, DC 20202
stephen.broughman@ed.gov
https://nces.ed.gov/surveys/pss/

Projections of Education Statistics

Since 1964, NCES has published projections of key statistics for elementary and secondary schools and higher education institutions. The latest report is *Projections of Education Statistics to 2027* (NCES 2019-001). The *Projections of Education Statistics* series provides national data for elementary and secondary enrollment, high school graduates, elementary and secondary teachers, expenditures for public elementary and secondary education, enrollment in postsecondary degree-granting institutions, and postsecondary degrees conferred. The report also provides state-level projections for public elementary and secondary enrollment and public high school graduates. These models are described in the report's appendix on projection methodology.

Differences between the reported and projected values are, of course, almost inevitable. In *Projections of Education Statistics to 2027*, an evaluation of past projections revealed that, at the elementary and secondary level, projections of public school enrollments have been quite accurate: mean absolute percentage differences for enrollment in public schools ranged from 0.3 to 1.2 percent for projections from 1 to 5 years in the future, while those for teachers in public schools were 3.2 percent or less. At the higher education level, projections of enrollment have been fairly accurate: mean absolute percentage differences were reported as 5.9 percent or less for projections from 1 to 5 years into the future in *Projections of Education Statistics to 2026* (NCES 2018-019). (*Projections of Education Statistics to 2027* did not report mean absolute percentage errors for institutions at the higher educational level because enrollment projections were calculated using a new model.)

Further information on *Projections of Education Statistics* may be obtained from

William Hussar
Annual Reports and Information Staff
National Center for Education Statistics
550 12th Street SW
Washington, DC 20202
william.hussar@ed.gov
https://nces.ed.gov/pubs2019/2019001.pdf

Recent College Graduates Study

Between 1976 and 1991, NCES conducted periodic surveys of baccalaureate and master's degree recipients 1 year after graduation with the Recent College Graduates (RCG) Study. The RCG Study—which was replaced by the Baccalaureate and Beyond Longitudinal Study (B&B) in 1993 (see listing above)—concentrated on those graduates entering the teaching profession. The study linked respondents' major field of study with outcomes such as whether the respondent entered the labor force or was seeking additional education. Labor force data collected included employment status (unemployed, employed part time, or employed full time), occupation, salary, career potential, relation to major field of study, and need for a college degree. To obtain accurate results on teachers, NCES oversampled graduates with a major in education. The last two studies oversampled education majors and increased the sampling of graduates with majors in other fields.

For each of the selected institutions, a list of graduates by major field of study was obtained, and a sample of graduates was drawn by major field of study. Graduates in certain major fields of study (e.g., education, mathematics, and physical sciences) were sampled at higher rates than were graduates in other fields. Roughly 1 year after graduation, the sample of graduates was located, contacted by mail or telephone, and asked to respond to the questionnaire.

The locating process was more detailed than that in most surveys. Nonresponse rates were directly related to the time, effort, and resources used in locating graduates, rather than to graduates' refusals to participate. Despite the difficulties in locating graduates, RCG response rates are comparable to studies that do not face problems locating their sample membership.

The 1976 study of 1974–75 college graduates was the first, and smallest, of the series. The sample consisted of about 210 institutions, of which 200 (96 percent) responded. Of the approximately 5,850 graduates in the sample, 4,350 responded, for a response rate of 79 percent.

The 1981 study was somewhat larger than the 1976 study, covering about 300 institutions and 15,850 graduates. Responses were obtained from 280 institutions, for an institutional response rate of 95 percent, and from 9,310 graduates (about 720 others were found not to meet eligibility requirements), for a response rate of 74 percent.

The 1985 study sampled about 400 colleges and 18,740 graduates, of whom 17,850 were found to be eligible. Responses were obtained from 13,200 graduates, for a response rate of 78 percent. The response rate for colleges was 98 percent. The 1987 study sampled 21,960 graduates. Responses were received from 16,880, for a response rate of nearly 80 percent.

The 1991 study sampled about 18,140 graduates of 400 bachelor's and master's degree-granting institutions, including 16,170 bachelor's degree recipients and 1,960 master's degree recipients receiving diplomas between July 1, 1989, and June 30, 1990. Random samples of graduates were selected from lists stratified by field of study. Graduates in education, mathematics, and the physical sciences were sampled at a higher rate, as were graduates of various racial/ethnic groups, to provide a sufficient number of these graduates for analysis purposes. The graduates included in the sample were selected in proportion to the institution's number of graduates. The unweighted institutional response rate was 95 percent, and the unweighted graduate response rate was 83 percent.

Further information on the RCG Study may be obtained from

Aurora D'Amico
Longitudinal Surveys Branch
Sample Surveys Division
National Center for Education Statistics
550 12th Street SW
Washington, DC 20202
aurora.damico@ed.gov
https://nces.ed.gov/surveys/b&b/

School Survey on Crime and Safety (SSOCS)

The School Survey on Crime and Safety (SSOCS) is the only recurring federal survey that collects detailed information on the incidence, frequency, seriousness, and nature of violence affecting students and school personnel, as well as other indicators of school safety from the schools' perspective. SSOCS is conducted by the National Center for Education Statistics (NCES) within the U.S. Department of Education and collected by the U.S. Census Bureau. Data from this collection can be used to examine the relationship between school characteristics and violent and serious violent crimes in primary, middle, high, and combined schools. In addition, data from SSOCS can be used to assess what crime prevention programs, practices, and policies are used by schools. SSOCS has been conducted in school years 1999–2000, 2003–04, 2005–06, 2007–08, 2009–10, 2015–16, and 2017–18.

The sampling frame for SSOCS:2016 was constructed from the 2013–14 Public Elementary/Secondary School Universe data file of the Common Core of Data (CCD), an annual collection of data on all public K–12 schools and school districts. The SSOCS sampling frame was restricted to regular public schools (including charter schools) in the United States and the District of Columbia. Other types of schools from the CCD Public Elementary/Secondary School Universe file were excluded from the SSOCS sampling frame. For instance, schools in Puerto Rico, American Samoa, the Commonwealth of the Northern Mariana Islands, Guam, and the U.S. Virgin Islands, as well as Department of Defense dependents schools and Bureau of Indian Education schools, were excluded. Also excluded were special education, alternative, vocational, virtual, newly closed, ungraded, and home schools, and schools with the highest grade of kindergarten or lower.

The SSOCS:2016 universe totaled 83,600 schools. From this total, 3,553 schools were selected for participation in the survey. The sample was stratified by instructional level, type of locale (urbanicity), and enrollment size. The sample of schools in each instructional level was allocated to each of the 16 cells formed by the cross-classification of the four categories of enrollment size and four types of locale. The target number of responding schools allocated to each of the 16 cells was proportional to the sum of the square roots of the total student enrollment over all schools in the cell. The target respondent count within each stratum was then inflated to account for anticipated nonresponse; this inflated count was the sample size for the stratum.

Data collection began in February 2016 and ended in early July 2016. Questionnaire packets were mailed to the principals of the sampled schools, who were asked to complete the survey or have it completed by the person at the school who is most knowledgeable about school crime and policies for providing a safe school environment. A total of 2,092 public schools submitted usable questionnaires, resulting in an overall weighted unit response rate of 62.9 percent.

Further information about SSOCS may be obtained from

Rachel Hansen
Cross-Sectional Surveys Branch
Sample Surveys Division
National Center for Education Statistics
550 12th Street SW
Washington, DC 20202
rachel.hansen@ed.gov
https://nces.ed.gov/surveys/ssocs/

Schools and Staffing Survey

The Schools and Staffing Survey (SASS) was a set of related questionnaires that collected descriptive data on the context of public and private elementary and secondary education. Data reported by districts, schools, principals, and teachers provided a variety of statistics on the condition of education in the United States that may be used by policymakers and the general public. The SASS system covered a wide range of topics, including teacher demand, teacher and principal characteristics, teachers' and principals' perceptions of school climate and problems in their schools, teacher and principal compensation, district hiring and retention practices, general conditions in schools, and basic characteristics of the student population.

SASS data were collected through a mail questionnaire with telephone and in-person field follow-up. SASS was conducted by the Census Bureau for NCES beginning with the first administration of the survey, which was conducted during the 1987–88 school year. Subsequent SASS administrations were conducted in 1990–91, 1993–94, 1999–2000, 2003–04, 2007–08, and 2011–12.

SASS was designed to produce national, regional, and state estimates for public elementary and secondary schools, school districts, principals, teachers, and school library media centers and national and regional estimates for public charter schools, as well as principals, teachers, and school library media centers within these schools. For private schools, the sample supported national, regional, and affiliation estimates for schools, principals, and teachers.

From its inception, SASS had four core components: school questionnaires, teacher questionnaires, principal questionnaires, and school district (prior to 1999–2000, "teacher demand and shortage") questionnaires. A fifth component, school library media center questionnaires, was introduced in the 1993–94 administration and was included in every subsequent administration of SASS. School library data were also collected in the 1990–91 administration of the survey through the school and principal questionnaires.

School questionnaires used in SASS included the Public and Private School Questionnaires; teacher questionnaires included the Public and Private School Teacher Questionnaires; principal questionnaires included the Public and Private School Principal (or School Administrator) Questionnaires; and school district questionnaires included the School District (or Teacher Demand and Shortage) Questionnaires.

Although the four core questionnaires and the school library media questionnaires remained relatively stable over the various administrations of SASS, the survey was changed to accommodate emerging issues in elementary and secondary education. Some questionnaire items were added, some were deleted, and some were reworded.

During the 1990–91 SASS cycle, NCES worked with the Office of Indian Education to add an Indian School Questionnaire to SASS, and it remained a part of SASS through 2007–08. The Indian School Questionnaire explored the same school-level issues that the Public and Private School Questionnaires explored, allowing comparisons among the three types of schools. The 1990–91, 1993–94, 1999–2000, 2003–04, and 2007–08 administrations of SASS obtained data on Bureau of Indian Education (BIE) schools (schools funded or operated by the BIE), but the 2011–12 administration did not obtain BIE data. SASS estimates for all survey years presented in this report exclude BIE schools, and as a result, estimates in this report may differ from those in previously published reports.

School library media center questionnaires were administered in public, private, and BIE schools as part of the 1993–94 and 1999–2000 SASS. During the 2003–04 administration of SASS, only library media centers in public schools were surveyed, and in 2007–08 only library media centers in public schools and BIE and BIE-funded schools were surveyed. The 2011–12 survey collected data only on school library media centers in traditional public schools and in public charter schools. School library questions focused on facilities, services and policies, staffing, technology, information literacy, collections and expenditures, and media equipment. New or revised topics included access to online licensed databases, resource availability, and additional elements on information literacy. The Student Records and Library Media Specialist/Librarian Questionnaires were administered only in 1993–94.

As part of the 1999–2000 SASS, the Charter School Questionnaire was sent to the universe of charter schools in operation in 1998–99. In 2003–04 and in subsequent administrations of SASS, there was no separate questionnaire for charter schools—charter schools were included in the public school sample instead. Another change in the 2003–04 administration of SASS was a revised data collection procedure using a primary in-person contact within the school intended to reduce the field follow-up phase.

The SASS teacher surveys collected information on the characteristics of teachers, such as their age, race/ethnicity, years of teaching experience, average number of hours per week spent on teaching activities, base salary, average class size, and highest degree earned. These teacher-reported data may be combined with related information on their school's characteristics, such as school type (e.g., public traditional, public charter, Catholic, private other religious, and private nonsectarian), community type, and school enrollment size. The teacher questionnaires also asked for information on teacher opinions regarding the school and teaching environment. In 1993–94, about 53,000 public school teachers and 10,400 private school teachers were sampled. In 1999–2000, about 56,300 public school teachers, 4,400 public charter school teachers, and 10,800 private school teachers were sampled. In 2003–04, about 52,500 public school teachers and 10,000 private school teachers were sampled. In 2007–08, about 48,400 public school teachers and 8,200 private school teachers were sampled. In 2011–12, about 51,100 public school teachers and 7,100 private school teachers were sampled. Weighted overall response rates in 2011–12 were 61.8 percent for public school teachers and 50.1 percent for private school teachers.

The SASS principal surveys focused on such topics as age, race/ethnicity, sex, average annual salary, years of experience, highest degree attained, perceived influence on decisions made at the school, and hours spent per week on all school activities. These data on principals can be placed in the context of other SASS data, such as the type of the principal's school (e.g., public traditional, public charter, Catholic, other religious, or nonsectarian), enrollment, and percentage of students eligible for free or reduced-price lunch. In 2003–04, about 10,200 public school principals were sampled, and in 2007–08, about 9,800 public school principals were sampled. In 2011–12, about 11,000 public school principals and 3,000 private school principals were sampled. Weighted response rates in 2011–12 for public school principals and private school principals were 72.7 percent and 64.7 percent, respectively.

The SASS 2011–12 sample of schools was confined to the 50 states and the District of Columbia and excluded the other jurisdictions, the Department of Defense overseas schools, the BIE schools, and schools that did not offer teacher-provided classroom instruction in grades 1–12 or the ungraded equivalent. The SASS 2011–12 sample included 10,250 traditional public schools, 750 public charter schools, and 3,000 private schools.

The public school sample for the 2011–12 SASS was based on an adjusted public school universe file from the 2009–10 Common Core of Data, a database of all the nation's public school districts and public schools. The private school sample for the 2011–12 SASS was selected from the 2009–10 Private School Universe Survey (PSS), as updated for the 2011–12 PSS. This update collected membership lists from private school associations and religious denominations, as well as private school lists from state education departments. The 2011–12 SASS private school frame was further augmented by the inclusion of additional schools that were identified through the 2009–10 PSS area frame data collection.

The NCES data product 2011–12 Schools and Staffing Survey (SASS) Restricted-Use Data Files (NCES 2014-356) contains eight files (Public School District, Public School Principal, Public School, Public School Teacher, Public School Library Media Center, Private School Principal, Private School, and Private School Teacher) in multiple formats. It also contains a six-volume User's Manual, which includes a codebook for each file. (Information on how to obtain a restricted-use data license is located at https://nces.ed.gov/pubsearch/licenses.asp.)

Further information on SASS may be obtained from

Maura Spiegelman
Cross-Sectional Surveys Branch
Sample Surveys Division
National Center for Education Statistics
550 12th Street SW
Washington, DC 20202
maura.spiegelman@ed.gov
https://nces.ed.gov/surveys/sass/

Teacher Follow-up Survey

The Teacher Follow-up Survey (TFS) is a follow-up survey of selected elementary and secondary school teachers who participate in the NCES Schools and Staffing Survey (SASS). Its purpose is to determine how many teachers remain at the same school, move to another school, or leave the profession in the year following a SASS administration. It is administered to elementary and secondary teachers in the 50 states and the District of Columbia. The TFS uses two questionnaires, one for teachers who left teaching since the previous SASS administration and another for those who are still teaching either in the same school as last year or in a different school. The objective of the TFS is to focus on the characteristics of each group in order to answer questions about teacher mobility and attrition.

The 2008–09 TFS is different from any previous TFS administration in that it also serves as the second wave of a longitudinal study of first-year teachers. Because of this, the 2008–09 TFS consists of four questionnaires. Two are for respondents who were first-year public school teachers in the 2007–08 SASS and two are for the remainder of the sample.

The 2012–13 TFS sample was made up of teachers who had taken the 2011–12 SASS survey. The 2012–13 TFS sample contained about 5,800 public school teachers and 1,200 private school teachers. The weighted overall response rate using the initial basic weight for private school teachers was notably low (39.7 percent), resulting in a decision to exclude private school teachers from the 2012–13 TFS data files. The weighted overall response rate for public school teachers was 49.9 percent (50.3 percent for current and 45.6 percent for former teachers). Additional information about the 2012–13 TFS, including the analysis of unit nonresponse bias, is available in the First Look report *Teacher Attrition and Mobility: Results From the 2012–13 Teacher Follow-up Survey* (NCES 2014-077).

Further information on the TFS may be obtained from

Isaiah O'Rear
Cross-Sectional Surveys Branch
Sample Surveys Division
National Center for Education Statistics
550 12th Street SW
Washington, DC 20202
isaiah.orear@ed.gov
https://nces.ed.gov/surveys/sass/

Other Department of Education Agencies

National Center for Special Education Research

The National Center for Special Education Research (NCSER) was created as part of the reauthorization of the Individuals with Disabilities Education Act (IDEA). NCSER sponsors a program of special education research designed to expand the knowledge and understanding of infants, toddlers, and children with disabilities. NCSER funds programs of research that address its mission. In order to determine which programs work, as well as how, why, and in what settings they work, NCSER sponsors research on the needs of infants, toddlers, and children with disabilities and evaluates the effectiveness of services provided through IDEA.

Further information on NCSER may be obtained from

Joan McLaughlin
Commissioner
National Center for Special Education Research
550 12th Street SW
Washington, DC 20202
joan.mclaughlin@ed.gov
https://ies.ed.gov/ncser/

The National Longitudinal Transition Study-2

Funded by NCSER, the National Longitudinal Transition Study-2 (NLTS-2) was a follow-up of the original National Longitudinal Transition Study conducted from 1985 through 1993. NLTS-2 began in 2001 with a sample of students who received special education services, were ages 13 through 16, and were in at least 7th grade on December 1, 2000. The study was designed to provide a national picture of these youths' experiences and achievements as they transition into adulthood. Data were collected from parents, youth, and schools by survey, telephone interviews, student assessments, and transcripts.

NLTS-2 was designed to align with the original NLTS by including many of the same questions and data items, thus allowing comparisons between the NLTS and NLTS-2 youths' experiences. NLTS-2 also included items that have been collected in other national databases to permit comparisons between NLTS-2 youth and the general youth population. Information was collected over five waves, beginning in 2001 and ending in 2009.

Further information on NLTS-2 may be obtained from

Jacquelyn Buckley
Office of the Commissioner
National Center for Special Education Research
550 12th Street SW
Washington, DC 20202
jacquelyn.buckley@ed.gov
https://nlts2.sri.com/

Office for Civil Rights

Civil Rights Data Collection

The U.S. Department of Education's Office for Civil Rights (OCR) has surveyed the nation's public elementary and secondary schools since 1968. The survey was first known as the OCR Elementary and Secondary School (E&S) Survey; in 2004, it was renamed the Civil Rights Data Collection (CRDC). The survey collects data on school discipline, access to and participation in high-level mathematics and science courses, teacher characteristics, school finances, and other school characteristics. These data are reported by race/ethnicity, sex, and disability.

Data in the survey are collected pursuant to 34 C.F.R. Section 100.6(b) of the Department of Education regulation implementing Title VI of the Civil Rights Act of 1964. The requirements are also incorporated by reference in Department regulations implementing Title IX of the Education Amendments of 1972, Section 504 of the Rehabilitation Act of 1973, and the Age Discrimination Act of 1975. School, district, state, and national data are currently available. Data from individual public schools and districts are used to generate national and state data.

The CRDC has generally been conducted biennially in each of the 50 states plus the District of Columbia. The 2009–10 CRDC was collected from a sample of approximately 7,000 school districts and over 72,000 schools in those districts. It was made up of two parts: part 1 contained beginning-of-year "snapshot" data and part 2 contained cumulative, or end-of-year, data.

The 2011–12 and 2013–14 CRDC were surveys of all public school schools and school districts in the nation. The 2011–12 survey collected data from approximately 16,500 school districts and 97,000 schools; the 2013–14 survey collected data from approximately 16,800 school districts and 95,500 schools.

Further information on the Civil Rights Data Collection may be obtained from

Office for Civil Rights
U.S. Department of Education
400 Maryland Avenue SW
Washington, DC 20202
OCR@ed.gov
https://www2.ed.gov/about/offices/list/ocr/data.html

Office of Federal Student Aid

Cohort Default Rate Database

A school's cohort default rate is the percentage of the school's borrowers who enter repayment on certain Federal Family Education Loan (FFEL) program or William D. Ford Federal Direct Loan (Direct Loan) program loans during a particular federal fiscal year and default within the cohort default period. The 2-year cohort default period is the period that begins on October 1 of the fiscal year when the borrower enters repayment and ends on September 30 of the following fiscal year. The 3-year cohort default period is the period that begins on October 1 of the fiscal year when the borrower enters repayment and ends on September 30 of second fiscal year following the fiscal year in which the borrower entered repayment.

The Office of Federal Student Aid's cohort default rate database can be accessed at https://nslds.ed.gov/nslds/nslds_SA/defaultmanagement/search_cohort_2015_CY.cfm.

Further information about cohort default rates produced by the Office of Federal Student Aid may be obtained from

https://www2.ed.gov/offices/OSFAP/defaultmanagement/schooltyperates.pdf
https://www2.ed.gov/offices/OSFAP/defaultmanagement/cdr.html
https://ifap.ed.gov/DefaultManagement/CDRGuideMaster.html

Office of Special Education Programs

Annual Report to Congress on the Implementation of the Individuals with Disabilities Education Act

The Individuals with Disabilities Education Act (IDEA) is a law ensuring services to children with disabilities throughout the nation. IDEA governs how states and public agencies provide early intervention, special education, and related services to more than 6.9 million eligible infants, toddlers, children, and youth with disabilities.

IDEA, formerly the Education of the Handicapped Act (EHA), requires the Secretary of Education to transmit, on an annual basis, a report to Congress describing the progress made in serving the nation's children with disabilities. This annual report contains information on children served by public schools under the provisions of Part B of IDEA and on children served in state-operated programs for persons with disabilities under Chapter I of the Elementary and Secondary Education Act.

Statistics on children receiving special education and related services in various settings and school personnel providing such services are reported in an annual submission of data to the Office of Special Education Programs (OSEP) by the 50 states, the District of Columbia, the Bureau of Indian Education schools, Puerto Rico, American Samoa, Guam, the Northern Mariana Islands, the U.S. Virgin Islands, the Federated States of Micronesia, Palau, and the Marshall Islands. The child count information is based on the number of children with disabilities receiving special education and related services on December 1 of each year. Count information is available from https://ideadata.org/.

Since all participants in programs for persons with disabilities are reported to OSEP, the data are not subject to sampling error. However, nonsampling error can arise from a variety of sources. Some states only produce counts of students receiving special education services by disability category because Part B of the EHA requires it. In those states that typically produce counts of students receiving special education services by disability category without regard to EHA requirements, definitions and labeling practices vary.

Further information on this annual report to Congress may be obtained from

Office of Special Education Programs
Office of Special Education and Rehabilitative Services
U.S. Department of Education
400 Maryland Avenue SW
Washington, DC 20202
https://www2.ed.gov/about/reports/annual/osep/index.html
https://sites.ed.gov/idea/
https://ideadata.org/

Office of Career, Technical, and Adult Education, Division of Adult Education and Literacy

Enrollment Data for State-Administered Adult Education Programs

The Division of Adult Education and Literacy (DAEL) promotes programs that help American adults get the basic skills they need to be productive workers, family members, and citizens. The major areas of support are Adult Basic Education, Adult Secondary Education, and English Language Acquisition. These programs emphasize basic skills such as reading, writing, math, English language competency, and problem solving. Each year, DAEL reports enrollment numbers in state-administered adult education programs for these major areas of support for all 50 states, the District of Columbia, American Samoa, the Federated States of Micronesia, Guam, the Marshall Islands, the Northern Mariana Islands, Palau, Puerto Rico, and the U.S. Virgin Islands.

Further information on DAEL may be obtained from

Office of Career, Technical, and Adult Education
Division of Adult Education and Literacy
U.S. Department of Education
400 Maryland Avenue SW
Washington, DC 20202
https://www2.ed.gov/about/offices/list/ovae/pi/AdultEd/index.html

Other Governmental Agencies and Programs

Bureau of Economic Analysis

National Income and Product Accounts

The National Income and Product Accounts (NIPAs), produced by the Bureau of Economic Analysis, are a set of economic accounts that provide information on the value and composition of output produced in the United States during a given period. NIPAs represent measures of economic activity in the United States, including production, income distribution, and personal savings. NIPAs also include data on employee compensation and wages. These estimations were first calculated in the early 1930s to help the government design economic policies to combat the Great Depression. Most of the NIPA series are published quarterly, with annual reviews of estimates from the three most recent years conducted in the summer.

Revisions to the NIPAs have been made over the years to create a more comprehensive economic picture of the United States. For example, in 1976, consumption of fixed capital (CFC) estimates shifted to a current-cost basis. In 1991, NIPAs began to use gross domestic product (GDP) instead of gross national product (GNP) as the primary measure of U.S. production. (At that time, virtually all other countries were already using GDP as their primary measure of production.) In the 2003 comprehensive revision, a more complete and accurate measure of insurance services was adopted. The incorporation of a new classification system for personal consumption expenditures (PCE) was among the changes contained in the 2009 comprehensive revision. The comprehensive revision of 2013 included the treatment of research and development expenditures by business, government, and nonprofit institutions serving households as fixed investment. The 2017 annual update of the NIPA accounts contained estimates that reflected the incorporation of newly available and revised source data and the adoption of improved estimating methods. Previews of the 2018 comprehensive update and of the 2019 annual update of the NIPA accounts are available at https://apps.bea.gov/scb/2018/04-april/pdf/0418-preview-2018-comprehensive-nipa-update.pdf and https://www.bea.gov/information-updates-national-income-and-product-accounts, respectively.

NIPAs are slowly being integrated with other federal account systems, such as the federal account system of the Bureau of Labor Statistics.

Further information on NIPAs may be obtained from

U.S. Department of Commerce
Bureau of Economic Analysis
https://www.bea.gov/

Bureau of Labor Statistics

Consumer Price Indexes

The Consumer Price Index (CPI) represents changes in prices of all goods and services purchased for consumption by urban households. Indexes are available for two population groups: a CPI for All Urban Consumers (CPI-U) and a CPI for Urban Wage Earners and Clerical Workers (CPI-W). Unless otherwise specified, data in this report are adjusted for inflation using the CPI-U. These values are generally adjusted to a school-year basis by averaging the July through June figures. Price indexes are available for the United States, the four Census regions, size of city, cross-classifications of regions and size-classes, and 23 local areas. The major uses of the CPI include as an economic indicator, as a deflator of other economic series, and as a means of adjusting income.

Also available is the Consumer Price Index research series using current methods (CPI-U-RS), which presents an estimate of the CPI-U from 1978 to the present that incorporates most of the improvements that the Bureau of Labor Statistics has made over that time span into the entire series. The historical price index series of the CPI-U does not reflect these changes, though these changes do make the present and future CPI more accurate. The limitations of the CPI-U-RS include considerable uncertainty surrounding the magnitude of the adjustments and the several improvements in the CPI that have not been incorporated into the CPI-U-RS for various reasons. Nonetheless, the CPI-U-RS can serve as a valuable proxy for researchers needing a historical estimate of inflation using current methods. This series has not been used in NCES tables.

Further information on consumer price indexes may be obtained from

Bureau of Labor Statistics
U.S. Department of Labor
2 Massachusetts Avenue NE
Washington, DC 20212
https://www.bls.gov/cpi/

Employment and Unemployment Surveys

Statistics on the employment and unemployment status of the population and related data are compiled by the Bureau of Labor Statistics (BLS) using data from the Current Population Survey (CPS) (see below) and other surveys. The CPS, a monthly household survey conducted by the U.S. Census Bureau for the Bureau of Labor Statistics, provides a comprehensive body of information on the employment and unemployment experience of the nation's population, classified by age, sex, race, and various other characteristics.

Further information on unemployment surveys may be obtained from

Bureau of Labor Statistics
U.S. Department of Labor
2 Massachusetts Avenue NE
Washington, DC 20212
cpsinfo@bls.gov
https://www.bls.gov/bls/employment.htm

Census Bureau

American Community Survey

The Census Bureau introduced the American Community Survey (ACS) in 1996. Fully implemented in 2005, it provides a large monthly sample of demographic, socioeconomic, and housing data comparable in content to the Long Forms of the Decennial Census up to and including the 2000 long form. Aggregated over time, these data serve as a replacement for the Long Form of the Decennial Census. The survey includes questions mandated by federal law, federal regulations, and court decisions.

Since 2011, the survey has been mailed to approximately 295,000 addresses in the United States and Puerto Rico each month, or about 3.5 million addresses annually. A larger proportion of addresses in small governmental units (e.g., American Indian reservations, small counties, and towns) also receive the survey. The monthly sample size is designed to approximate the ratio used in the 2000 Census, which requires more intensive distribution in these areas. The ACS covers the U.S. resident population, which includes the entire civilian, noninstitutionalized population; incarcerated persons; institutionalized persons; and the active duty military who are in the United States. In 2006, the ACS began collecting data from the population living in group quarters. Institutionalized group quarters include adult and juvenile correctional facilities, nursing facilities, and other health care facilities. Noninstitutionalized group quarters include college and university housing, military barracks, and other noninstitutional facilities such as workers and religious group quarters and temporary shelters for the homeless.

National-level data from the ACS are available from 2000 onward. The ACS produces 1-year estimates for jurisdictions with populations of 65,000 and over and 5-year estimates for jurisdictions with smaller populations. The 1-year estimates for 2017 used data collected between January 1, 2017, and December 31, 2017, and the 5-year estimates for 2013–2017 used data collected between January 1, 2013, and December 31, 2017. The ACS produced 3-year estimates (for jurisdictions with populations of 20,000 or over) for the periods 2005–2007, 2006–2008, 2007–2009, 2008–2010, 2009–2011, 2010–2012, and 2011–2013. Three-year estimates for these periods will continue to be available to data users, but no further 3-year estimates will be produced.

Further information about the ACS is available at https://www.census.gov/programs-surveys/acs/.

Annual Survey of State and Local Government Finances

The Census Bureau conducts an Annual Survey of State and Local Government Finances as authorized by law under Title 13, United States Code, Section 182. Periodic surveys of government finances have been conducted since 1902 and have been conducted annually since 1952. This survey covers the entire range of government finance activities: revenue, expenditure, debt, and assets. Revenues and expenditures comprise actual receipts and payments of a government and its agencies, including government-operated enterprises, utilities, and public trust funds. The expenditure-reporting categories comprise all amounts of money paid out by a government and its agencies, with the exception of amounts for debt retirement and for loan, investment, agency, and private trust transactions.

State government finances are based primarily on the Census Bureau Annual Survey of State and Local Government Finances. Census Bureau analysts compile figures from official records and reports of the state governments for most of the state financial data. States differ in the ways in which they administer activities; they may fund such activities directly, or they may disburse the money to a lower level government or government agency. Therefore, caution is advised when attempting to make a direct comparison between states regarding their state fiscal aid data.

The sample of local governments is drawn from the periodic Census of Governments (which is conducted in years ending in "2" and "7") and consists of certain local governments sampled with certainty plus a sample below the certainty level. Finance data for all school districts are collected on an annual basis and released through the NCES Common Core of Data system. A new sample is usually selected every 5 years (in years ending in "4" and "9").

The statistics in Government Finances that are based wholly or partly on data from the sample are subject to sampling error. State government finance data are not subject to sampling error. Estimates of major U.S. totals for local governments are subject to a computed sampling variability of less than one-half of 1 percent. The estimates are also subject to the inaccuracies in classification, response, and processing that would occur if a complete census had been conducted under the same conditions as the sample.

Further information on government finances may be obtained from

Governments Division
Census Bureau
U.S. Department of Commerce
4600 Silver Hill Road
Washington, DC 20233
https://www.census.gov/econ/overview/go0400.html

Local government
ewd.local.finance@census.gov

State government
govs.statefinance@census.gov
https://www.census.gov/govs/

Census of Population—Education in the United States

Some NCES tables are based on a part of the decennial census that consisted of questions asked of a 1 in 6 sample of people and housing units in the United States. This sample was asked more detailed questions about income, occupation, and housing costs, as well as questions about general demographic information. This decennial census "long form" has been discontinued and has been replaced by the American Community Survey (ACS).

School enrollment. People classified as enrolled in school reported attending a "regular" public or private school or college. They were asked whether the institution they attended was public or private and what level of school they were enrolled in.

Educational attainment. Data for educational attainment were tabulated for people ages 15 and over and classified according to the highest grade completed or the highest degree received. Instructions were also given to include the level of the previous grade attended or the highest degree received for people currently enrolled in school.

Poverty status. To determine poverty status, answers to income questions were used to make comparisons to the appropriate poverty threshold. All people except those who were institutionalized, people in military group quarters and college dormitories, and unrelated people under age 15 were considered. If the total income of each family or unrelated individual in the sample was below the corresponding cutoff, that family or individual was classified as "below the poverty level."

Further information on the 1990 and 2000 Census of Population may be obtained from

Population Division
Census Bureau
U.S. Department of Commerce
4600 Silver Hill Road
Washington, DC 20233
https://www.census.gov/main/www/cen1990.html
https://www.census.gov/main/www/cen2000.html

Current Population Survey

The Current Population Survey (CPS) is a monthly survey of about 54,000 households conducted by the U.S. Census Bureau for the Bureau of Labor Statistics. The CPS is the primary source of labor force statistics on the U.S. population. In addition, supplemental questionnaires are used to provide further information about the U.S. population. The March supplement (also known as the Annual Social and Economic [ASEC] supplement) contains detailed questions on topics such as income, employment, and educational attainment; additional questions, such as items on disabilities, have also been included. In the July supplement, items on computer and internet use are the principal focus. The October supplement also contains some questions about computer and internet use, but most of its questions relate to school enrollment and school characteristics.

CPS samples are initially selected based on results from the decennial census and are periodically updated to reflect new housing construction. The current sample design for the main CPS, last revised in July 2015, includes about 74,000 households. Each month, about 54,000 of the 74,000 households are interviewed. Information is obtained each month from those in the household who are 15 years of age and over, and demographic data are collected for children 0–14 years of age. In addition, supplemental questions regarding school enrollment are asked about eligible household members age 3 and over in the October CPS supplement.

In January 1992, the CPS educational attainment variable was changed. The "Highest grade attended" and "Year completed" questions were replaced by the question "What is the highest level of school . . . has completed or the highest degree . . . has received?" Thus, for example, while the old questions elicited data for those who completed more than 4 years of high school, the new question elicited data for those who were high school completers, i.e., those who graduated from high school with a diploma as well as those who completed high school through equivalency programs, such as a GED program.

A major redesign of the CPS was implemented in January 1994 to improve the quality of the data collected. Survey questions were revised, new questions were added, and computer-assisted interviewing methods were used for the survey data collection. Further information about the redesign is available in *Current Population Survey, October 1995: (School Enrollment Supplement) Technical Documentation* at https://www.census.gov/prod/techdoc/cps/cpsoct95.pdf.

Caution should be used when comparing data from 1994 through 2001 with data from 1993 and earlier. Data from 1994 through 2001 reflect 1990 census-based population controls, while data from 1993 and earlier reflect 1980 or earlier census-based population controls. Changes in population controls generally have relatively little impact on summary measures such as means, medians, and percentage distributions; they can, however, have a significant impact on population counts. For example, use of the 1990 census-based population controls resulted in about a 1 percent increase in the civilian noninstitutional population and in the number of families and households. Thus, estimates of levels for data collected in 1994 and later years will differ from those for earlier years by more than what could be attributed to actual changes in the population. These differences could be disproportionately greater for certain subpopulation groups than for the total population.

Beginning in 2003, the race/ethnicity questions were expanded. Information on people of Two or more races were included, and the Asian and Pacific Islander race category was split into two categories—Asian and Native

Hawaiian or Other Pacific Islander. In addition, questions were reworded to make it clear that self-reported data on race/ethnicity should reflect the race/ethnicity with which the responder identifies, rather than what may be written in official documentation.

The estimation procedure employed for monthly CPS data involves inflating weighted sample results to independent estimates of characteristics of the civilian noninstitutional population in the United States by age, sex, and race. These independent estimates are based on statistics from decennial censuses; statistics on births, deaths, immigration, and emigration; and statistics on the population in the armed services. Generalized standard error tables are provided in the Current Population Reports; methods for deriving standard errors can be found within the CPS technical documentation at https://www.census.gov/programs-surveys/cps/technical-documentation/complete.html. The CPS data are subject to both nonsampling and sampling errors.

Standard errors were estimated using the generalized variance function prior to 2005 for March CPS data and prior to 2010 for October CPS data. The generalized variance function is a simple model that expresses the variance as a function of the expected value of a survey estimate. Standard errors were estimated using replicate weight methodology beginning in 2005 for March CPS data and beginning in 2010 for October CPS data. Those interested in using CPS household-level supplement replicate weights to calculate variances may refer to *Estimating Current Population Survey (CPS) Household-Level Supplement Variances Using Replicate Weights* at https://thedataweb.rm.census.gov/pub/cps/supps/HH-level_Use_of_the_Public_Use_Replicate_Weight_File.doc.

Further information on the CPS may be obtained from

Associate Directorate for Demographic Programs—Survey Operations
Census Bureau
U.S. Department of Commerce
4600 Silver Hill Road
Washington, DC 20233
(301) 763-3806
dsd.cps@census.gov
https://www.census.gov/programs-surveys/cps.html

Computer and Internet Use

The Current Population Survey (CPS) has been conducting supplemental data collections regarding computer use since 1984. In 1997, these supplemental data collections were expanded to include data on internet access. More recently, data regarding computer and internet use were collected in October 2010, July 2011, October 2012, July 2013, July 2015, and November 2017.

In the July 2011, 2013, and 2015 supplements, as well as in the November 2017 supplement, the sole focus was on computer and internet use. In the October 2010 and 2012 supplements questions on school enrollment were the principal focus, and questions on computer and internet use were less prominent. Measurable differences in estimates taken from these supplements across years could reflect actual changes in the population; however, differences could also reflect any unknown bias from major changes in the questionnaire over time due to rapidly changing technology. In addition, data may vary slightly due to seasonal variations in data collection between the July, October, and November supplements. Therefore, caution should be used when making year-to-year comparisons of CPS computer and internet use estimates.

The most recent computer and internet use supplement, conducted in November 2017, collected household information from all eligible CPS households, as well as information from individual household members age 3 and over. Information was collected about the household's computer and internet use and the household member's use of the Internet from any location in the past year. Additionally, information was gathered regarding a randomly selected household respondent's use of the Internet.

For the November 2017 basic CPS, the household-level nonresponse rate was 14.3 percent. The person-level nonresponse rate for the computer and internet use supplement was an additional 23.0 percent. Since one rate is a person-level rate and the other a household-level rate, the rates cannot be combined to derive an overall rate.

Further information on the CPS Computer and Internet Use Supplement may be obtained from

Associate Directorate for Demographic Programs—Survey Operations
Census Bureau
U.S. Department of Commerce
4600 Silver Hill Road
Washington, DC 20233
(301) 763-3806
dsd.cps@census.gov
https://www.census.gov/programs-surveys/cps.html

Dropouts

Each October, the Current Population Survey (CPS) includes supplemental questions on the enrollment status of the population age 3 years and over as part of the monthly basic survey on labor force participation. In addition to gathering the information on school enrollment, with the limitations on accuracy as noted below under "School Enrollment," the survey data permit calculations of dropout rates. Both status and event dropout rates are tabulated from the October CPS. Event rates describe the proportion of students who leave school each year without completing a high school program. Status rates provide cumulative data on dropouts among all young adults within a specified age range. Status rates are higher than event rates because they include all dropouts ages 16 through 24, regardless of when they last attended school.

In addition to other survey limitations, dropout rates may be affected by survey coverage and exclusion of the institutionalized population. The incarcerated population has increased and has a high dropout rate. Dropout rates for the total population might be higher than those for the noninstitutionalized population if the prison and jail populations were included in the dropout rate calculations. On the other hand, if military personnel, who tend to be high school graduates, were included, it might offset some or all of the impact from the theoretical inclusion of the jail and prison populations. Tables on status dropout rates based on the American Community Survey do include the institutionalized population and are also included in the *Digest of Education Statistics*.

Another area of concern with tabulations involving young people in household surveys is the relatively low coverage ratio compared to older age groups. CPS undercoverage results from missed housing units and missed people within sample households. Overall CPS undercoverage for October 2017 is estimated to be about 11 percent.

CPS coverage varies with age, sex, and race. Generally, coverage is larger for females than for males and larger for non-Blacks than for Blacks. This differential coverage is a general problem for most household-based surveys. Further information on CPS methodology may be found in the technical documentation at https://www.census.gov/programs-surveys/cps.html. Tables on status dropout rates based on the American Community Survey do include the institutionalized population and are also included in the *Digest of Education Statistics*.

Further information on the calculation of dropouts and dropout rates may be obtained from the *Trends in High School Dropout and Completion Rates in the United States* report at https://nces.ed.gov/programs/dropout/index.asp or by contacting

Joel McFarland
Annual Reports and Information Staff
National Center for Education Statistics
550 12th Street SW
Washington, DC 20202
joel.mcfarland@ed.gov

Educational Attainment

Reports documenting educational attainment are produced by the Census Bureau using the March Current Population Survey (CPS) supplement (Annual Social and Economic supplement [ASEC]). Currently, the ASEC supplement consists of approximately 70,000 interviewed households. Both recent and earlier editions of *Educational Attainment in the United States* may be downloaded at https://www.census.gov/topics/education/educational-attainment/data/tables.All.html.

In addition to the general constraints of CPS, some data indicate that the respondents have a tendency to overestimate the educational level of members of their household. Some inaccuracy is due to a lack of the respondent's knowledge of the exact educational attainment of each household member and the hesitancy to acknowledge anything less than a high school education.

Further information on educational attainment data from CPS may be obtained from

Associate Directorate for Demographic Programs—Survey Operations
Census Bureau
U.S. Department of Commerce
4600 Silver Hill Road
Washington, DC 20233
(301) 763-3806
dsd.cps@census.gov
https://www.census.gov/programs-surveys/cps.html

School Enrollment

Each October, the Current Population Survey (CPS) includes supplemental questions on the enrollment status of the population age 3 years and over. Currently, the October supplement consists of approximately 54,000 interviewed households, the same households interviewed in the basic Current Population Survey. The primary sources of nonsampling variability in the responses to the supplement are those inherent in the main survey instrument. The question of current enrollment may not be answered accurately for various reasons. Some respondents may not know current grade information for every student in the household, a problem especially prevalent for households with members in college or in nursery school. Confusion over college credits or hours taken by a student may make it difficult to determine the year in which the student is enrolled. Problems may occur with the definition of nursery school (a group or class organized to provide educational experiences for children) where respondents' interpretations of "educational experiences" vary.

For the October 2017 basic CPS, the household-level nonresponse rate was 13.8 percent. The person-level nonresponse rate for the school enrollment supplement was an additional 9.9 percent. Since the basic CPS nonresponse rate is a household-level rate and the school enrollment supplement nonresponse rate is a person-level rate, these rates cannot be combined to derive an overall nonresponse rate. Nonresponding households may have fewer persons than interviewed ones, so combining these rates may lead to an overestimate of the true overall nonresponse rate for persons for the school enrollment supplement.

Although the principal focus of the October supplement is school enrollment, in some years the supplement has included additional questions on other topics. In 2010 and 2012, for example, the October supplement included additional questions on computer and internet use.

Further information on CPS methodology may be obtained from https://www.census.gov/programs-surveys/cps.html.

Further information on the CPS School Enrollment Supplement may be obtained from

Associate Directorate for Demographic Programs—Survey Operations
Census Bureau
U.S. Department of Commerce
4600 Silver Hill Road
Washington, DC 20233
(301) 763-3806
dsd.cps@census.gov
https://www.census.gov/programs-surveys/cps.html

Decennial Census, Population Estimates, and Population Projections

The decennial census is a universe survey mandated by the U.S. Constitution. It is a questionnaire sent to every household in the country, and it is composed of seven questions about the household and its members (name, sex, age, relationship, Hispanic origin, race, and whether the housing unit is owned or rented). The Census Bureau also produces annual estimates of the resident population by demographic characteristics (age, sex, race, and Hispanic origin) for the nation, states, and counties, as well as national and state projections for the resident population. The reference date for population estimates is July 1 of the given year. With each new issue of July 1 estimates, the Census Bureau revises estimates for each year back to the last census. Previously published estimates are superseded and archived.

Census respondents self-report race and ethnicity. The race questions on the 1990 and 2000 censuses differed in some significant ways. In 1990, the respondent was instructed to select the one race "that the respondent considers himself/herself to be," whereas in 2000, the respondent could select one or more races that the person considered himself or herself to be. American Indian, Eskimo, and Aleut were three separate race categories in 1990; in 2000, the American Indian and Alaska Native categories were combined, with an option to write in a tribal affiliation. This write-in option was provided only for the American Indian category in 1990. There was a combined Asian and Pacific Islander race category in 1990, but the groups were separated into two categories in 2000.

The census question on ethnicity asks whether the respondent is of Hispanic origin, regardless of the race option(s) selected; thus, persons of Hispanic origin may be of any race. In the 2000 census, respondents were first asked, "Is this person Spanish/Hispanic/Latino?" and then given the following options: No, not Spanish/Hispanic/Latino; Yes, Puerto Rican; Yes, Mexican, Mexican American, Chicano; Yes, Cuban; and Yes, other Spanish/Hispanic/Latino (with space to print the specific group). In the 2010 census, respondents were asked "Is this person of Hispanic, Latino, or Spanish origin?" The options given were No, not of Hispanic, Latino, or Spanish origin; Yes, Mexican, Mexican Am., Chicano; Yes, Puerto Rican; Yes, Cuban; and Yes, another Hispanic, Latino, or Spanish origin—along with instructions to print "Argentinean, Colombian, Dominican, Nicaraguan, Salvadoran, Spaniard, and so on" in a specific box.

The 2000 and 2010 censuses each asked the respondent "What is this person's race?" and allowed the respondent to select one or more options. The options provided were largely the same in both the 2000 and 2010 censuses: White; Black, African American, or Negro; American Indian or Alaska Native (with space to print the name of enrolled or principal tribe); Asian Indian; Japanese; Native Hawaiian; Chinese; Korean; Guamanian or Chamorro; Filipino; Vietnamese; Samoan; Other Asian; Other Pacific Islander; and Some other race. The last three options included space to print the specific race. Two significant differences between the 2000 and 2010 census questions on race were that no race examples were provided for the "Other Asian" and "Other Pacific Islander" responses in 2000, whereas the race examples of "Hmong, Laotian, Thai, Pakistani, Cambodian, and so on" and "Fijian, Tongan, and so on," were provided for the "Other Asian" and "Other Pacific Islander" responses, respectively, in 2010.

The census population estimates program modified the enumerated population from the 2010 census to produce the population estimates base for 2010 and onward. As part of the modification, the Census Bureau recoded the "Some other race" responses from the 2010 census to one or more of the five OMB race categories used in the estimates program (for more information, see https://www.census.gov/programs-surveys/popest/technical-documentation/methodology.html).

Further information on the decennial census may be obtained from https://www.census.gov/

Small Area Income and Poverty Estimates

Small Area Income and Poverty Estimates (SAIPE) are produced for school districts, counties, and states. The main objective of this program is to provide updated estimates of income and poverty statistics for the administration of federal programs and the allocation of federal funds to local jurisdictions. Estimates for 2017 were released in November 2018. These estimates combine data from administrative records, postcensal population estimates, and the decennial census with direct estimates from the American Community Survey to provide consistent and reliable single-year estimates. These model-based single-year estimates are more reflective of current conditions than multiyear survey estimates.

Further information on the SAIPE program may be obtained from

Small Area Estimates Branch
Census Bureau
U.S. Department of Commerce
sehsd.saipe@census.gov
https://www.census.gov/programs-surveys/saipe/about/contact.html

Centers for Disease Control and Prevention

Morbidity and Mortality Weekly Report: Summary of Notifiable Diseases

The Summary of Notifiable Diseases, a publication of the Morbidity and Mortality Weekly Report (MMWR), contains the official statistics, in tabular and graphical form, for the reported occurrence of nationally notifiable infectious diseases in the United States. These statistics are collected and compiled from reports sent by U.S. state and territory, New York City, and District of Columbia health departments to the National Notifiable Diseases Surveillance System (NNDSS), which is operated by the Centers for Disease Control and Prevention (CDC) in collaboration with the Council of State and Territorial Epidemiologists.

For more information on the MMWR: Summary of Notifiable Diseases, see https://www.cdc.gov/mmwr/mmwr_nd/.

National Vital Statistics System

The National Vital Statistics System (NVSS) is the method by which data on vital events—births, deaths, marriages, divorces, and fetal deaths—are provided to the National Center for Health Statistics (NCHS), part of the Centers for Disease Control and Prevention (CDC). The data are provided to NCHS through the Vital Statistics Cooperative Program (VSCP). In 1984 and earlier years, the VSCP included varying numbers of states that provided data based on a 100 percent sample of their birth certificates. Data for states not in the VSCP were based on a 50 percent sample of birth certificates filed in those states. Population data used to compile birth rates are based on special estimation procedures and are not actual counts.

Race and Hispanic ethnicity are reported separately in the NVSS. Data are available for non-Hispanic Whites and non-Hispanic Blacks for 1990 and later; however, for 1980 and 1985, data for Whites and Blacks may include persons of Hispanic ethnicity. For all years, Asian/Pacific Islander and American Indian/Alaska Native categories include persons of Hispanic ethnicity.

For more information on the NCHS and the NVSS, see https://www.cdc.gov/nchs/nvss/index.htm.

School-Associated Violent Death Surveillance System

The School-Associated Violent Death Surveillance System (SAVD-SS) is an epidemiological study developed by the Centers for Disease Control and Prevention in conjunction with the U.S. Department of Education and the U.S. Department of Justice. SAVD-SS seeks to describe the epidemiology of school-associated violent deaths, identify common features of these deaths, estimate the rate of school-associated violent death in the United States, and identify potential risk factors for these deaths. The study includes descriptive data on all school-associated violent deaths in the United States, including all homicides, suicides, or legal intervention in which the fatal injury occurred on the campus of a functioning elementary or secondary school; while the victim was on the way to or from regular sessions at such a school; or while attending or on the way to or from an official school-sponsored event. Victims of such incidents include nonstudents, as well as students and staff members. SAVD-SS includes descriptive information about the school, event, victim(s), and offender(s). The study has collected data since July 1, 1992.

SAVD-SS uses a four-step process to identify and collect data on school-associated violent deaths. Cases are initially identified through a search of the LexisNexis newspaper and media database. Then law enforcement officials are contacted to confirm the details of the case and to determine if the event meets the case definition. Once a case is confirmed, a law enforcement official and a school official are interviewed regarding details about the school, event, victim(s), and offender(s). A copy of the full law enforcement report is also sought for each case. The information obtained on schools includes school demographics, attendance/absentee rates, suspensions/expulsions and mobility, school history of weapon-carrying incidents, security measures, violence prevention activities, school response to the event, and school policies about weapon carrying. Event information includes the location of injury, the context of injury (while classes were being held, during break, etc.), motives for injury, method of injury, and school and community events happening around the time period. Information obtained on victim(s) and offender(s) includes demographics, circumstances of the event (date/time, alcohol or drug use, number of persons involved), types and origins of weapons, criminal history, psychological risk factors, school-related problems, extracurricular activities, and family history, including structure and stressors.

Some 105 school-associated violent deaths were identified from July 1, 1992, to June 30, 1994 (Kachur et al., 1996, School-Associated Violent Deaths in the United States, 1992 to 1994, *Journal of the American Medical Association, 275*: 1729–1733). A more recent report from this data collection identified 253 school-associated violent deaths between July 1, 1994, and June 30, 1999 (Anderson et al., 2001, School-Associated Violent Deaths in the United States, 1994–1999, *Journal of the American Medical Association, 286*: 2695–2702). Other publications from this study have described how the number of events change during the school year (Centers for Disease Control and Prevention, 2001, Temporal Variations in School-Associated Student Homicide and Suicide Events—United States, 1992–1999, *Morbidity and Mortality Weekly Report, 50*: 657–660), the source of the firearms used in these events (Reza et al., 2003, Source of Firearms Used by Students in

School-Associated Violent Deaths—United States, 1992–1999, *Morbidity and Mortality Weekly Report, 52*: 169–172), and suicides that were associated with schools (Kauffman et al., 2004, School-Associated Suicides—United States, 1994–1999, *Morbidity and Mortality Weekly Report, 53*: 476–478). The most recent publication describes trends in school-associated homicide from July 1, 1992, to June 30, 2006 (Centers for Disease Control and Prevention, 2008, School-Associated Student Homicides—United States, 1992–2006, *Morbidity and Mortality Weekly Report 2008, 57*: 33–36). The interviews conducted on cases between July 1, 1994, and June 30, 1999, achieved a response rate of 97 percent for police officials and 78 percent for school officials.

For several reasons, all data for years from 1999 to the present are flagged as preliminary. For some recent data, the interviews with school and law enforcement officials to verify case details have not been completed. The details learned during the interviews can occasionally change the classification of a case. Also, new cases may be identified because of the expansion of the scope of the media files used for case identification. Sometimes other cases not identified during earlier data years using the independent case finding efforts (which focus on nonmedia sources of information) will be discovered. Also, other cases may occasionally be identified while the law enforcement and school interviews are being conducted to verify known cases.

Further information on SAVD-SS may be obtained from

Kristin Holland
Principal Investigator & Behavioral Scientist
School-Associated Violent Death Surveillance System
Division of Violence Prevention
National Center for Injury Control and Prevention
Centers for Disease Control and Prevention
1600 Clifton Road
Atlanta, GA 30329
imh1@cdc.gov

Web-Based Injury Statistics Query and Reporting System Fatal

Web-Based Injury Statistics Query and Reporting System (WISQARS) Fatal is an interactive online database that provides mortality data related to injury. The mortality data reported in WISQARS Fatal come from death certificate data reported to the National Center for Health Statistics (NCHS), Centers for Disease Control and Prevention. Data include causes of death reported by attending physicians, medical examiners, and coroners and demographic information about decedents reported by funeral directors, who obtain that information from family members and other informants. NCHS collects, compiles, verifies, and prepares these data for release to the public. The data provide information about unintentional injury, homicide, and suicide as leading causes of death, how common these causes of death are, and whom they affect. These data are intended for a broad audience—the public, the media, public health practitioners and researchers, and public health officials—to increase their knowledge of injury.

WISQARS Fatal mortality reports provide tables of the total numbers of injury-related deaths and the death rates per 100,000 U.S. population. The reports list deaths according to cause (mechanism) and intent (manner) of injury by state, race, Hispanic origin, sex, and age groupings.

Further information on WISQARS Fatal may be obtained from

National Center for Injury Prevention and Control
Centers for Disease Control and Prevention
1600 Clifton Road
Atlanta, GA 30329
https://wwwn.cdc.gov/dcs/ContactUs/Form
https://www.cdc.gov/injury/wisqars/fatal_help/data_sources.html

Youth Risk Behavior Surveillance System

The Youth Risk Behavior Surveillance System (YRBSS) is an epidemiological surveillance system developed by the Centers for Disease Control and Prevention (CDC) to monitor the prevalence of youth behaviors that most influence health. The YRBSS focuses on priority health-risk behaviors established during youth that result in the most significant mortality, morbidity, disability, and social problems during both youth and adulthood. The YRBSS includes a national school-based Youth Risk Behavior Survey (YRBS), as well as surveys conducted in states and large urban school districts.

The national YRBS uses a three-stage cluster sampling design to produce a nationally representative sample of students in grades 9–12 in the United States. The target population consists of all public and private school students in grades 9–12 in the 50 states and the District of Columbia. The first-stage sampling frame includes selecting primary sampling units (PSUs) from strata formed on the basis of urbanization and the relative percentage of Black and Hispanic students in the PSU. These PSUs are either counties; subareas of large counties; or groups of smaller, adjacent counties. At the second stage, schools were selected with probability proportional to school enrollment size.

The final stage of sampling consists of randomly selecting, in each chosen school and in each of grades 9–12, one or two classrooms from either a required subject, such as English or social studies, or a required period, such as homeroom or second period. All students in selected classes are eligible to participate. In surveys conducted before 2013, three strategies were used to oversample Black and Hispanic students: (1) larger sampling rates were used to select PSUs that are in high-Black and high-Hispanic strata; (2) a modified measure of size was used that increased the probability of selecting schools with a disproportionately high minority enrollment; and (3) two classes per grade, rather than one, were selected in schools with a high percentage of combined Black, Hispanic, Asian/Pacific Islander, or American Indian/Alaska Native enrollment. In 2013, only selection of two classes per grade was needed to achieve an adequate precision with minimum variance. Approximately 16,300 students participated in the 1993 survey, 10,900 students participated in the 1995 survey, 16,300 students participated in the 1997 survey, 15,300 students participated in 1999, 13,600 students participated in 2001, 15,200 students participated in 2003, 13,900 participated in 2005, 14,000 participated in 2007, 16,400 participated in 2009, 15,400 participated in 2011, 13,600 participated in 2013, 15,600 participated in 2015, and 14,700 participated in 2017.

The overall response rate was 70 percent for the 1993 survey, 60 percent for the 1995 survey, 69 percent for the 1997 survey, 66 percent in 1999, 63 percent in 2001, 67 percent in 2003, 67 percent in 2005, 68 percent in 2007, 71 percent in 2009, 71 percent in 2011, 68 percent in 2013, 60 percent in 2015, and 60 percent in 2017. NCES standards call for response rates of 85 percent or greater for cross-sectional surveys, and bias analyses are required by NCES when that percentage is not achieved. For YRBS data, a full nonresponse bias analysis has not been done because the data necessary to do the analysis are not available. The weights were developed to adjust for nonresponse and the oversampling of Black and Hispanic students in the sample. The final weights were constructed so that only weighted proportions of students (not weighted counts of students) in each grade matched national population projections.

State-level data were downloaded from the Youth Online: Comprehensive Results web page (https://nccd.cdc.gov/Youthonline/App/Default.aspx). Each state and district school-based YRBS employs a two-stage, cluster sample design to produce representative samples of students in grades 9–12 in their jurisdiction. All except a few state samples, and all district samples, include only public schools, and each district sample includes only schools in the funded school district (e.g., San Diego Unified School District) rather than in the entire city (e.g., greater San Diego area).

In the first sampling stage in all except a few states and districts, schools are selected with probability proportional to school enrollment size. In the second sampling stage, intact classes of a required subject or intact classes during a required period (e.g., second period) are selected randomly. All students in sampled classes are eligible to participate. Certain states and districts modify these procedures to meet their individual needs. For example, in a given state or district, all schools, rather than a sample of schools, might be selected to participate. State and local surveys that have a scientifically selected sample, appropriate documentation, and an overall response rate greater than or equal to 60 percent are weighted. The overall response rate reflects the school response rate multiplied by the student response rate. These three criteria are used to ensure that the data from those surveys can be considered representative of students in grades 9–12 in that jurisdiction. A weight is applied to each record to adjust for student nonresponse and the distribution of students by grade, sex, and race/ethnicity in each jurisdiction. Therefore, weighted estimates are representative of all students in grades 9–12 attending schools in each jurisdiction. Surveys that do not have an overall response rate of greater than or equal to 60 percent and that do not have appropriate documentation are not weighted and are not included in this report.

In the 2017 YRBS, 39 states and 21 large urban districts had weighted data. (For information on the location of the districts, please see https://www.cdc.gov/healthyyouth/data/yrbs/participation.htm.) In 26 states and 13 large urban school districts, weighted estimates are representative of all students in grades 9–12 attending regular public schools; in 13 states and 8 large urban school districts, weighted estimates are representative of regular public school students plus students in grades 9–12 in other types of public schools (e.g., public alternative, special education, or vocational schools or Bureau of Indian Education schools). The student sample sizes ranged from 1,273 to 51,087 across the states and from 805 to 10,191 across the large urban school districts. Among the states, the school response rates ranged from 68 percent to 100 percent, student response rates ranged from 66 percent to 90 percent, and overall response rates ranged from 60 percent to 82 percent. Among the large urban school districts, the school response rates ranged from 84 percent to 100 percent, student response rates ranged from 63 percent to 89 percent, and overall response rates ranged from 61 percent to 89 percent.

For the 2015 YRBS, data from 37 states and 19 large urban districts were weighted. In 36 states and all large urban school districts, weighted estimates are representative of all students in grades 9–12 attending public schools in each jurisdiction. In one state (South Dakota), weighted estimates are representative of all students in grades 9–12 attending public and private schools. Student sample sizes ranged from 1,313 to 55,596 across the states and from 1,052 to 10,419 across the large urban school districts. Among the states, school response rates ranged from 70 percent to 100 percent, student response rates ranged from 64 percent to 90 percent, and overall response rates ranged from 60 percent to 84 percent. Among the large urban school districts, school response rates ranged from 90 percent to 100 percent, student response rates ranged from 66 percent to 88 percent, and overall response rates ranged from 64 percent to 88 percent.

In 2013, a total of 42 states and 21 districts had weighted data. Not all of the districts were contained in the 42 states. For example, California was not one of the 42 states that obtained weighted data, but it contained several districts that did. In sites with weighted data, the student sample sizes for the state and district YRBS ranged from 1,107 to 53,785. School response rates ranged from 70 to 100 percent, student response rates ranged from 60 to 94 percent, and overall response rates ranged from 60 to 87 percent.

Readers should note that reports of these data published by the CDC and in this report do not include percentages for which the denominator includes fewer than 100 unweighted cases.

In 1999, in accordance with changes to the Office of Management and Budget's standards for the classification of federal data on race and ethnicity, the YRBS item on race/ethnicity was modified. The version of the race and ethnicity question used in 1993, 1995, and 1997 was

How do you describe yourself?

a. White—not Hispanic
b. Black—not Hispanic
c. Hispanic or Latino
d. Asian or Pacific Islander
e. American Indian or Alaskan Native
f. Other

The version used in 1999, 2001, 2003, and in the 2005, 2007, and 2009 state and local district surveys was

How do you describe yourself? (Select one or more responses.)

a. American Indian or Alaska Native
b. Asian
c. Black or African American
d. Hispanic or Latino
e. Native Hawaiian or Other Pacific Islander
f. White

In the 2005 national survey and in all 2007, 2009, 2011, 2013, and 2015 surveys, race/ethnicity was computed from two questions: (1) "Are you Hispanic or Latino?" (response options were "Yes" and "No"), and (2) "What is your race?" (response options were "American Indian or Alaska Native," "Asian," "Black or African American," "Native Hawaiian or Other Pacific Islander," or "White"). For the second question, students could select more than one response option. For this report, students were classified as "Hispanic" if they answered "Yes" to the first question, regardless of how they answered the second question. Students who answered "No" to the first question and selected more than one race/ethnicity in the second category were classified as "More than one race." Students who answered "No" to the first question and selected only one race/ethnicity were classified as that race/ethnicity. Race/ethnicity was classified as missing for students who did not answer the first question and for students who answered "No" to the first question but did not answer the second question.

CDC has conducted two studies to understand the effect of changing the race/ethnicity item on the YRBS. Brener, Kann, and McManus (*Public Opinion Quarterly, 67*: 227–226, 2003) found that allowing students to select more than one response to a single race/ethnicity question on the YRBS had only a minimal effect on reported race/ethnicity among high school students. Eaton, Brener, Kann, and Pittman (*Journal of Adolescent Health, 41*: 488–494, 2007) found that self-reported race/ethnicity was similar regardless of whether the single-question or a two-question format was used.

Further information on the YRBSS may be obtained from

Laura Kann
Division of Adolescent and School Health
National Center for HIV/AIDS, Viral Hepatitis, STD, and TB Prevention
Centers for Disease Control and Prevention
1600 Clifton Road
Atlanta, GA 30329
lkk1@cdc.gov
https://wwwn.cdc.gov/dcs/ContactUs/Form
https://www.cdc.gov/healthyyouth/data/yrbs/index.htm

Department of Defense

Defense Manpower Data Center

The Statistical Information Analysis Division of the Defense Manpower Data Center (DMDC) maintains the largest archive of personnel, manpower, and training data in the Department of Defense (DoD). The DMDC's statistical activities include the personnel survey program, an enlistment testing program to support screening of military applicants, and a client support program to provide statistical support to the Office of the Secretary of Defense. The DMDC collects DoD contract information in support of national economic tables and the Small Business Competitiveness Demonstration Program; it also produces statistics on DoD purchases from educational and nonprofit institutions and from state and local governments.

For more information on the DMDC, see https://www.dmdc.osd.mil.

Department of Justice

Bureau of Justice Statistics

A division of the U.S. Department of Justice Office of Justice Programs, the Bureau of Justice Statistics (BJS) collects, analyzes, publishes, and disseminates statistical information on crime, criminal offenders, victims of crime, and the operations of the justice system at all levels of government and internationally. It also provides technical and financial support to state governments for development of criminal justice statistics and information systems on crime and justice.

For information on the BJS, see https://www.bjs.gov/.

National Crime Victimization Survey

The National Crime Victimization Survey (NCVS), administered for the U.S. Bureau of Justice Statistics (BJS) by the U.S. Census Bureau, is the nation's primary source of information on crime and the victims of crime. Initiated in 1972 and redesigned in 1992 and 2016, the NCVS collects detailed information on the frequency and nature of the crimes of rape, sexual assault, robbery, aggravated and simple assault, theft, household burglary, and motor vehicle theft experienced by Americans and American households each year. The survey measures both crimes reported to the police and crimes not reported to the police.

NCVS estimates presented may differ from those in previous published reports. This is because a small number of victimizations, referred to as series victimizations, are included using a new counting strategy. High-frequency repeat victimizations, or series victimizations, are six or more similar but separate victimizations that occur with such frequency that the victim is unable to recall each individual event or describe each event in detail. As part of ongoing research efforts associated with the redesign of the NCVS, BJS investigated ways to include high-frequency repeat victimizations, or series victimizations, in estimates of criminal victimization. Including series victimizations results in more accurate estimates of victimization. BJS has decided to include series victimizations using the victim's estimates of the number of times the victimizations occurred over the past 6 months, capping the number of victimizations within each series at a maximum of 10. This strategy for counting series victimizations balances the desire to estimate national rates and account for the experiences of persons who have been subjected to repeat victimizations against the desire to minimize the estimation errors that can occur when repeat victimizations are reported. Including series victimizations in national rates results in rather large increases in the level of violent victimization; however, trends in violence are generally similar regardless of whether series victimizations are included. For more information on the new counting strategy and supporting research, see *Methods for Counting High-Frequency Repeat Victimizations in the National Crime Victimization Survey* at https://www.bjs.gov/content/pub/pdf/mchfrv.pdf.

Readers should note that in 2003, in accordance with changes to the Office of Management and Budget's standards for the classification of federal data on race and ethnicity, the NCVS item on race/ethnicity was modified. A question on Hispanic origin is now followed by a new question on race. The new question about race allows the respondent to choose more than one race and delineates Asian as a separate category from Native Hawaiian or Other Pacific Islander. An analysis conducted by the Demographic Surveys Division at the U.S. Census Bureau showed that the new race question had very little impact on the aggregate racial distribution of the NCVS respondents, with one exception: There was a 1.6 percentage point decrease in the percentage of respondents who reported themselves as White. Due to changes in race/ethnicity categories, comparisons of race/ethnicity across years should be made with caution.

There were changes in the sample design and survey methodology in the 2006 NCVS that may have affected survey estimates. Caution should be used when comparing the 2006 estimates to estimates of other years. Data from 2007 onward are comparable to earlier years. Analyses of the 2007 estimates indicate that the program changes made in 2006 had relatively small effects on NCVS estimates. For more information on the 2006 NCVS data, see *Criminal Victimization, 2006*, at https://www.bjs.gov/content/pub/pdf/cv06.pdf; the NCVS 2006 technical notes, at https://bjs.ojp.usdoj.gov/content/pub/pdf/cv06tn.pdf; and *Criminal Victimization, 2007*, at https://bjs.ojp.usdoj.gov/content/pub/pdf/cv07.pdf.

The NCVS sample was redesigned in 2016 in order to account for changes in the U.S. population identified through the 2010 Decennial Census and to make it possible to produce state- and local-level victimization estimates for the largest 22 states and specific metropolitan areas within those states. This redesign resulted in a historically large number of new households and first-time interviews in the sample and produced challenges in comparing 2016 to prior data years. In order to allow for year-to-year comparisons between 2016 and other data years, BJS worked with the U.S. Census Bureau to create a revised 2016 NCVS data file. For more information on the revised 2016 NCVS data file, see *Criminal Victimization, 2016:* Revised, at https://www.bjs.gov/content/pub/pdf/cv16re.pdf. (For the original release of the 2016 NCVS data, see *Criminal Victimization, 2016*, at https://www.bjs.gov/content/pub/pdf/cv16_old.pdf.)

The number of NCVS-eligible households in the 2017 NCVS sample was about 146,000. Households were selected using a stratified, multistage cluster design. In the first stage, the primary sampling units (PSUs), consisting of counties or groups of counties, were selected. In the second stage, smaller areas, called Enumeration Districts (EDs), were selected from each sampled PSU. Finally, from selected EDs, clusters of four households, called segments, were selected for interview. At each stage, the selection was done proportionate to population size in order to create a self-weighting sample. The final sample was augmented to account for households constructed after the decennial census. Within each sampled household, the U.S. Census Bureau interviewer attempts to interview all household members age 12 and over to determine whether they had been victimized by the measured crimes during the 6 months preceding the interview.

The first NCVS interview with a housing unit is conducted in person. Subsequent interviews are conducted by telephone, if possible. Households remain in the sample for 3 years and are interviewed seven times at 6-month intervals. Since the survey's inception, the initial interview at each sample unit has been used only to bound future interviews to establish a time frame to avoid duplication of crimes uncovered in these subsequent interviews. Beginning in 2006, data from the initial interview have been adjusted to account for the effects of bounding and have been included in the survey estimates. After a household has been interviewed its seventh time, it is replaced by a new sample household. In 2017, the household response rate was about 76 percent and the completion rate for persons within households was about 84 percent. Weights were developed to permit estimates for the total U.S.

population 12 years and older. For more information on the 2017 NCVS, see https://www.bjs.gov/content/pub/pdf/cv17.pdf.

Further information on the NCVS may be obtained from

Rachel E. Morgan
Victimization Statistics Branch
Bureau of Justice Statistics
rachel.morgan@usdoj.gov
https://www.bjs.gov/

School Crime Supplement

Created as a supplement to the NCVS and codesigned by the National Center for Education Statistics and Bureau of Justice Statistics, the School Crime Supplement (SCS) survey has been conducted in 1989, 1995, and biennially since 1999 to collect additional information about school-related victimizations on a national level. This report includes data from the 1995, 1999, 2001, 2003, 2005, 2007, 2009, 2011, 2013, 2015, and 2017 collections. The 1989 data are not included in this report as a result of methodological changes to the NCVS and SCS. The SCS was designed to assist policymakers, as well as academic researchers and practitioners at federal, state, and local levels, to make informed decisions concerning crime in schools. The survey asks students a number of key questions about their experiences with and perceptions of crime and violence that occurred inside their school, on school grounds, on the school bus, or on the way to or from school. Students are asked additional questions about security measures used by their school, students' participation in after-school activities, students' perceptions of school rules, the presence of weapons and gangs in school, the presence of hate-related words and graffiti in school, student reports of bullying and reports of rejection at school, and the availability of drugs and alcohol in school. Students are also asked attitudinal questions relating to fear of victimization and avoidance behavior at school.

The SCS survey was conducted for a 6-month period from January through June in all households selected for the NCVS (see discussion above for information about the NCVS sampling design and changes to the race/ethnicity variable beginning in 2003). Within these households, the eligible respondents for the SCS were those household members who had attended school at any time during the 6 months preceding the interview, were enrolled in grades 6–12, and were not homeschooled. In 2007, the questionnaire was changed and household members who attended school sometime during the school year of the interview were included. The age range of students covered in this report is 12–18 years of age. Eligible respondents were asked the supplemental questions in the SCS only after completing their entire NCVS interview. It should be noted that the first or unbounded NCVS interview has always been included in analysis of the SCS data and may result in the reporting of events outside of the requested reference period.

The prevalence of victimization for 1995, 1999, 2001, 2003, 2005, 2007, 2009, 2011, 2013, 2015, and 2017 was calculated by using NCVS incident variables appended to the SCS data files of the same year. The NCVS type of crime variable was used in the SCS to classify student victimizations into the categories "serious violent," "violent," and "theft." The NCVS variables asking where the incident happened (at school) and what the victim was doing when it happened (attending school or on the way to or from school) were used to ascertain whether the incident happened at school. Only incidents that occurred inside the United States are included.

In 2001, the SCS survey instrument was modified. In 1995 and 1999, "at school" had been defined for respondents as meaning in the school building, on the school grounds, or on a school bus. In 2001, the definition of at "school" was changed to mean in the school building, on school property, on a school bus, or going to and from school. The change to the definition of "at school" in the 2001 questionnaire was made in order to render the definition there consistent with the definition as it is constructed in the NCVS. This change to the definition of "at school" has been retained in subsequent SCS collections. Cognitive interviews conducted by the U.S. Census Bureau on the 1999 SCS suggested that modifications to the definition of "at school" would not have a substantial impact on the estimates.

A total of about 9,700 students participated in the 1995 SCS, and 8,400 students participated in both the 1999 and 2001 SCS. In 2003, 2005, 2007, 2009, 2011, 2013, 2015, and 2017, the numbers of students participating were 7,200, 6,300, 5,600, 5,000, 6,500, 5,700, 5,500, and 7,100, respectively.

In the 1995, 1999, 2001, 2003, 2005, 2007, 2009, 2011, 2013, 2015, and 2017 SCS collections, the household completion rates were 95 percent, 94 percent, 93 percent, 92 percent, 91 percent, 90 percent, 92 percent, 91 percent, 86 percent, 82 percent, and 76 percent, respectively, and the student completion rates were 78 percent, 78 percent, 77 percent, 70 percent, 62 percent, 58 percent, 56 percent, 63 percent, 60 percent, 58 percent, and 52 percent, respectively. The overall SCS unit response rate (calculated by multiplying the household completion rate by the student completion rate) was about 74 percent in 1995, 73 percent in 1999, 72 percent in 2001, 64 percent in 2003, 56 percent in 2005, 53 percent in 2007, 51 percent in 2009, 57 percent in 2011, 51 percent in 2013, 48 percent in 2015, and 40 percent in 2017. (Prior to 2011, overall SCS unit response rates were unweighted; starting in 2011, overall SCS unit response rates are weighted.)

There are two types of nonresponse: unit and item nonresponse. NCES requires that any stage of data collection within a survey that has a unit base-weighted response rate of less than 85 percent be evaluated for the potential magnitude of unit nonresponse bias before the data or any analysis using the data may be released (NCES Statistical Standards, 2002, at https://nces.ed.gov/statprog/2002/std4_4.asp). Due to the low unit response rate in 2005, 2007, 2009, 2011, 2013, 2015, and 2017, a unit nonresponse bias analysis was done. Unit response rates indicate how many sampled units have completed interviews. Because interviews with students could only be completed after households had responded to the NCVS, the unit completion rate for the SCS reflects both the household interview completion rate and the student interview completion rate. Nonresponse can greatly affect the strength and application of survey data by leading to an increase in variance as a result of a reduction in the actual size of the sample and can produce bias if the nonrespondents have characteristics of interest that are different from the respondents. In order for response bias to occur, respondents must have different response rates and responses to particular survey variables. The magnitude of unit nonresponse bias is determined by the response rate and the differences between respondents and nonrespondents on key survey variables. Although the bias analysis cannot measure response bias since the SCS is a sample survey and it is not known how the population would have responded, the SCS sampling frame has several key student or school characteristic variables for which data are known for respondents and nonrespondents: sex, age, race/ethnicity, household income, region, and urbanicity, all of which are associated with student victimization. To the extent that there are differential responses by respondents in these groups, nonresponse bias is a concern.

In 2005, the analysis of unit nonresponse bias found evidence of bias for the race, household income, and urbanicity variables. White (non-Hispanic) and Other (non-Hispanic) respondents had higher response rates than Black (non-Hispanic) and Hispanic respondents. Respondents from households with an income of $35,000–$49,999 and $50,000 or more had higher response rates than those from households with incomes of less than $7,500, $7,500–$14,999, $15,000–$24,999, and $25,000–$34,999. Respondents who live in urban areas had lower response rates than those who live in rural or suburban areas. Although the extent of nonresponse bias cannot be determined, weighting adjustments, which corrected for differential response rates, should have reduced the problem.

In 2007, the analysis of unit nonresponse bias found evidence of bias by the race/ethnicity and household income variables. Hispanic respondents had lower response rates than respondents of other races/ethnicities. Respondents from households with an income of $25,000 or more had higher response rates than those from households with incomes of less than $25,000. However, when responding students are compared to the eligible NCVS sample, there were no measurable differences between the responding students and the eligible students, suggesting that the nonresponse bias has little impact on the overall estimates.

In 2009, the analysis of unit nonresponse bias found evidence of potential bias for the race/ethnicity and urbanicity variables. White students and students of other races/ethnicities had higher response rates than did Black and Hispanic respondents. Respondents from households located in rural areas had higher response rates than those from households located in urban areas. However, when responding students are compared to the eligible NCVS sample, there were no measurable differences between the responding students and the eligible students, suggesting that the nonresponse bias has little impact on the overall estimates.

In 2011, the analysis of unit nonresponse bias found evidence of potential bias for the age variable. Respondents 12 to 17 years old had higher response rates than did 18-year-old respondents in the NCVS and SCS interviews. Weighting the data adjusts for unequal selection probabilities and for the effects of nonresponse. The weighting adjustments that correct for differential response rates are created by region, age, race, and sex, and should have reduced the effect of nonresponse.

In 2013, the analysis of unit nonresponse bias found evidence of potential bias for the age, region, and Hispanic origin variables in the NCVS interview response. Within the SCS portion of the data, only the age and region variables showed significant unit nonresponse bias. Further analysis indicated that only the age 14 and the west region categories showed positive response biases that were significantly different from some of the other categories within the age and region variables. Based on the analysis, nonresponse bias seems to have little impact on the SCS results. In 2015, the analysis of unit nonresponse bias found evidence of potential bias for age, race, Hispanic origin, urbanicity, and region in the NCVS interview response. For the SCS interview, the age, race, urbanicity, and region variables showed significant unit nonresponse bias. The age 14 group and rural areas showed positive response biases that were significantly different from other categories within the age and urbanicity variables. The northeast region and Asian race group showed negative response biases that were significantly different from other categories within the region and race variables. These results provide evidence that these subgroups may have a nonresponse bias associated with them. In 2017, the analysis of unit nonresponse bias found that the race/ethnicity and census region variables showed significant differences in response rates between different race/ethnicity and census region subgroups. Respondent and nonrespondent distributions were significantly different for the race/ethnicity subgroup only. However, after using weights adjusted for person nonresponse, there was no evidence that these response differences introduced nonresponse bias in the final victimization estimates. Response rates for SCS survey items in all survey years were high—typically over 95 percent of all eligible respondents, meaning there is little potential for item nonresponse bias for most items in the survey. The weighted data permit inferences about the eligible student population who were enrolled in schools in all SCS data years.

Further information about the SCS may be obtained from

Rachel Hansen
Cross-Sectional Surveys Branch
Sample Surveys Division
National Center for Education Statistics
550 12th Street SW
Washington, DC 20202
rachel.hansen@ed.gov
https://nces.ed.gov/programs/crime/

Federal Bureau of Investigation

The Federal Bureau of Investigation (FBI) collects statistics on crimes from law enforcement agencies throughout the country through the Uniform Crime Reporting (UCR) Program. The UCR Program was conceived in 1929 by the International Association of Chiefs of Police to meet a need for reliable, uniform crime statistics for the nation. In 1930, the FBI was tasked with collecting, publishing, and archiving those statistics. Today, several annual statistical publications, such as the comprehensive *Crime in the United States* (CIUS), are produced from data provided by over 18,000 law enforcement agencies across the United States. CIUS is an annual publication in which the FBI compiles the volume and rate of crime offenses for the nation, the states, and individual agencies. This report also includes arrest, clearance, and law enforcement employee data.

For more information on the UCR Program, see https://ucr.fbi.gov/ucr.

Studies of Active Shooter Incidents

The Investigative Assistance for Violent Crimes Act of 2012, which was signed into law in 2013, authorizes the attorney general, upon the request of an appropriate state or local law enforcement official, to "assist in the investigation of violent acts and shootings occurring in a place of public use and in the investigation of mass killings and attempted mass killings." The attorney general delegated this responsibility to the FBI.

In 2014, the FBI initiated studies of active shooter incidents in order to advance the understanding of these incidents and provide law enforcement agencies with data that can inform efforts toward preventing, preparing for, responding to, and recovering from them.

Data on active shooter incidents at educational institutions come from the FBI reports *A Study of Active Shooter Incidents in the United States Between 2000 and 2013, Active Shooter Incidents in the United States in 2014 and 2015*, and *Active Shooter Incidents in the United States in 2016 and 2017*, which can be accessed at https://www.fbi.gov/about/partnerships/office-of-partner-engagement/active-shooter-resources.

Further information about FBI resources on active shooter incidents may be obtained from

Active Shooter Resources
Office of Partner Engagement
Federal Bureau of Investigation
U.S. Department of Justice
935 Pennsylvania Avenue NW
Washington, DC 20535
https://www.fbi.gov/about/partnerships/office-of-partner-engagement/active-shooter-resources

Supplementary Homicide Reports

Supplementary Homicide Reports (SHR) are a part of the Uniform Crime Reporting (UCR) program of the Federal Bureau of Investigation (FBI). These reports provide incident-level information on criminal homicides, including situation type (e.g., number of victims, number of offenders, and whether offenders are known); the age, sex, and race of victims and offenders; the weapon used; circumstances of the incident; and the relationship of the victim to the offender. The data are provided monthly to the FBI by local law enforcement agencies participating in the UCR program. The data include murders and nonnegligent manslaughters in the United States; thus, negligent manslaughters and justifiable homicides have been eliminated from the data.

About 90 percent of homicides are included in the SHR program. However, adjustments can be made to the weights to correct for missing victim reports. Estimates from the SHR program used in this report were generated by the Bureau of Justice Statistics (BJS).

Further information on the SHR program may be obtained from

Criminal Justice Information Services Division
Federal Bureau of Investigation
Module D3
1000 Custer Hollow Road
Clarksburg, WV 26306
(304) 625-4995
crimestatsinfo@fbi.gov

Institute of Museum and Library Statistics

On October 1, 2007, the administration of the Public Libraries Survey (PLS) and the State Library Agencies (StLA) Survey was transferred from the National Center for Education Statistics to the Institute of Museum and Library Statistics (IMLS).

IMLS Library Statistics

Public library statistics are collected annually using the PLS and disseminated annually through the Federal-State

Cooperative System (FSCS) for Public Library Data. Descriptive statistics are produced for over 9,000 public libraries. The PLS includes information about staffing; operating income and expenditures; type of governance; type of administrative structure; size of collection; and service measures such as reference transactions, public service hours, interlibrary loans, circulation, and library visits. In the FSCS, respondents supply the information electronically, and data are edited and tabulated in machine-readable form.

PLS respondents are public libraries identified by state administrative library agencies in the 50 states, the District of Columbia, and certain U.S. territories. At the state level, FSCS is administered by State Data Coordinators, who are appointed by the chief officer of each state library agency. The State Data Coordinator collects the requested data from local public libraries. The 50 states, District of Columbia, and territories submit data for individual public libraries, which are aggregated to state and national levels.

Further information on these library surveys can be obtained from

Institute of Museum and Library Services
Office of Policy, Planning, Research, and Communication
Research and Statistics Division
955 L'Enfant Plaza North SW
Washington, DC 20024-2135
imlsinfo@imls.gov
https://www.imls.gov/

National Institute on Drug Abuse

Monitoring the Future Survey

The National Institute on Drug Abuse of the U.S. Department of Health and Human Services is the primary supporter of the long-term national study "Monitoring the Future: A Continuing Study of American Youth," conducted by the University of Michigan Institute for Social Research. One component of this national sample survey deals with student drug abuse, and its results have been published annually since 1975.

In this study, 8th-, 10th-, and 12th-graders complete self-administered questionnaires given to them in their classrooms by University of Michigan personnel (12th-graders have participated since the beginning of the study, and 8th- and 10th-graders began participating in 1991). The 8th- and 10th-grade surveys are anonymous, while the 12th-grade survey is confidential. In addition, beginning with the class of 1976, a randomly selected sample from each senior class has been followed in the years after high school on a continuing basis.

The annual sample for each grade is made up of roughly 16,000 students in 140 public and private schools, for a total of about 50,000 students in 420 public and private secondary schools. In 2018, the survey involved about 44,500 8th-, 10th-, and 12th-graders in 392 public and private secondary schools nationwide, and about 89 percent of the 8th-graders, 86 percent of the 10th-graders, and 81 percent of the 12th-graders surveyed participated in the study.

Understandably, there is some reluctance to admit illegal activities. In addition, students who are out of school on the day of the survey are nonrespondents, and the survey does not include high school dropouts. The inclusion of absentees and dropouts would tend to increase the proportion of individuals who had used drugs. A 1983 study found that the inclusion of absentees could increase some of the drug usage estimates by as much as 2.7 percentage points. (Details on that study and its methodology were published in *Drug Use Among American High School Students, College Students, and Other Young Adults*, by L.D. Johnston, P.M. O'Malley, and J.G. Bachman, available from the National Clearinghouse on Drug Abuse Information, 5600 Fishers Lane, Rockville, MD 20857.)

The first published results of the 2018 survey were presented in *Monitoring the Future, National Results on Drug Use, 1975–2018: Overview, Key Findings on Adolescent Drug Use*, at http://www.monitoringthefuture.org.

Further information on the Monitoring the Future drug abuse survey may be obtained from

National Institute on Drug Abuse
Division of Epidemiology, Services and Prevention Research
6001 Executive Boulevard
Rockville, MD 20852
mtfinformation@umich.edu
http://www.monitoringthefuture.org

National Science Foundation

Survey of Federal Funds for Research and Development

The annual Survey of Federal Funds for Research and Development is the primary source of information about federal funding for research and development in the United States. It is used by policymakers in the executive and legislative branches of the federal government in determining policies, laws, and regulations affecting science; it is also used by those who follow science trends in every sector of the economy, including university administrators and professors, economic and political analysts, research and development managers inside and outside the government, the science press, and leading members of the science community in the United States and around the world.

The survey's target population consists of the federal agencies that conduct research and development programs, which are identified from information in the President's budget submitted to Congress. In the survey cycle for data collection on fiscal years 2015–17, a total of 28 federal agencies (15 federal departments and 13 independent agencies) reported research and development data. Because multiple subdivisions of a federal department were requested to complete the survey in some cases, there were 74 individual respondents.

Federal funds data, as collected, span 3 government fiscal years: the fiscal year just completed, the current fiscal year, and the next fiscal year. Actual data are collected for the year just completed; estimates are obtained for the current fiscal year and the next fiscal year.

The data are collected and managed online; this system was designed to help improve survey reporting by offering respondents direct online reporting and editing.

The federal funds survey has an unweighted response rate of 100 percent with no known item nonresponse. The information included in this survey has been stable since fiscal year 1973, when federal obligations for research to universities and colleges by agency and detailed science and engineering fields were added to the survey.

Further information on federal funds for research and development may be obtained from

Christopher Pece
Project Officer
Research and Development Statistics Program
National Center for Science and Engineering Statistics
National Science Foundation
2415 Eisenhower Avenue
Alexandria, VA 22314
cpece@nsf.gov
https://www.nsf.gov/statistics/srvyfedfunds/

Survey of Earned Doctorates

The Survey of Earned Doctorates (SED) has collected basic statistics from the universe of doctoral recipients in the United States each year since 1957. It is supported by six federal agencies: the National Science Foundation, National Institutes of Health, U.S. Department of Education, U.S. Department of Agriculture, National Endowment for the Humanities, and National Aeronautics and Space Administration.

With the assistance of institutional coordinators at each doctorate-awarding institution, a survey form or web link is distributed to each person completing the requirements for a research doctorate. Of the 54,664 persons receiving research doctorates granted in 2017, approximately 91 percent responded to the survey. The survey questionnaire obtains information on sex, race/ethnicity, marital status, citizenship, disabilities, dependents, specialty field of doctorate, educational institutions attended, time spent in completion of doctorate, financial support, education debt, postgraduation plans, and educational attainment of parents.

Further information on the Survey of Earned Doctorates may be obtained from

Kelly Kang
Project Officer
Human Resources Statistics Program
National Center for Science and Engineering Statistics
National Science Foundation
2415 Eisenhower Avenue
Alexandria, VA 22314
kkang@nsf.gov
https://www.nsf.gov/statistics/srvydoctorates/

Survey of Graduate Students and Postdoctorates in Science and Engineering

The Survey of Graduate Students and Postdoctorates in Science and Engineering, also known as the graduate student survey (GSS), is an annual survey of all U.S. academic institutions granting research-based master's degrees or doctorates in science, engineering, or selected health fields. Sponsored by the National Science Foundation and the National Institutes of Health, the survey collects counts of enrolled graduate students, postdoctoral researchers, and other doctorate-holding nonfaculty researchers at these institutions by demographics and other characteristics, such as source of financial support. Results are used to assess shifts in graduate enrollment, postdoctoral researcher and nonfaculty researcher appointments, and trends in financial support.

Data collection for the 2017 GSS began in fall 2017. The 2017 survey universe consisted of 399 doctorate-granting and 304 master's-granting institutions, for a total of 703 institutions. There were 814 schools affiliated with these institutions: 509 at doctorate-granting institutions and 305 at master's-granting institutions.

New procedures to improve coverage of GSS-eligible units were introduced in the 2007 survey cycle and were continued in subsequent cycles. Increased emphasis was given to updating the unit list by providing an exhaustive list of GSS-eligible programs within existing GSS fields. In previous years, only a representative list was provided for each GSS field, which may have resulted in not reporting all eligible units. The set of GSS-eligible fields was also modified. Due to these changes, data for 2007 and later years are not directly comparable with data from previous years.

More recently, the survey universe was modified in 2014 to include 151 new institutions and exclude 2 for-profit institutions; these changes were the result of a comprehensive frame evaluation study conducted from 2010 to 2013 and the annual frame evaluation conducted in the 2013–14 cycle. In 2015 and 2016, some institutions became newly eligible for GSS, some became ineligible, some changed GSS degree-granting status, and some merged. As a result of these changes, the total number of institutions included in the GSS increased from 706 in 2014 to 714 in 2016. In the 2017 GSS, the number of institutions that became ineligible was greater than the number of new institutions that were added; thus. the total number of institutions decreased to 703.

Further information on the Survey of Graduate Students and Postdoctorates in Science and Engineering may be obtained from

Mike Yamaner
Project Officer
Human Resources Statistics Program
National Center for Science and Engineering Statistics
National Science Foundation
2415 Eisenhower Avenue
Alexandria, VA 22314
myamaner@nsf.gov
https://www.nsf.gov/statistics/srvygradpostdoc/

Substance Abuse and Mental Health Services Administration

National Survey on Drug Use and Health

Conducted by the federal government since 1971 (annually since 1991), the National Survey on Drug Use and Health (NSDUH) is a survey of the civilian, noninstitutionalized population of the United States age 12 or older. It is the primary source of information on the prevalence, patterns, and consequences of alcohol, tobacco, and illegal drug use and abuse. The survey collects data by administering questionnaires to a representative sample of the population (since 1999, the NSDUH interview has been carried out using computer-assisted interviewing). NSDUH collects information from residents of households, noninstitutional group quarters, and civilians living on military bases. The main results of the NSDUH present national estimates of rates of use, numbers of users, and other measures related to illicit drugs, alcohol, and tobacco products.

Prior to 2002, the survey was called the National Household Survey on Drug Abuse (NHSDA). The 2002 update of the survey's name coincided with improvements to the survey. In light of these improvements, NSDUH data from 2002 and later should not be compared with NHSDA data from 2001 and earlier as a method of assessing changes in substance use over time.

The 2005 NSDUH was the first in a coordinated 5-year sample design providing estimates for all 50 states and the District of Columbia for the years 2005 through 2009. Because the 2005 design enables estimates to be developed by state, states may be viewed as the first level of stratification, as well as a reporting variable.

In the 2017 NSDUH, screening was completed at 138,061 addresses, and 68,032 completed interviews were obtained: 17,033 interviews from adolescents ages 12 to 17 and 50,999 interviews from adults age 18 and over. Weighted response rates for household screening and for interviewing were 75.1 and 67.1 percent, respectively, for an overall response rate of 50.4 percent for persons age 12 and over. The weighted interview response rates were 75.1 percent for adolescents and 66.3 percent for adults.

Further information on the NSDUH may be obtained from

SAMHSA
Center for Behavioral Health Statistics and Quality
5600 Fishers Lane
Rockville, MD 20857
https://www.samhsa.gov/data/

Other Organization Sources

ACT

ACT assessment

The ACT assessment is designed to measure educational development in the areas of English, mathematics, social studies, and natural sciences. The assessment is taken by college-bound high school students. The test results are used to predict how well students might perform in college.

Prior to the 1984–85 school year, national norms were based on a 10 percent sample of the students taking the test. Since then, national norms have been based on the test scores of all students taking the test. Beginning with 1984–85, these norms have been based on the most recent ACT scores available from students scheduled to graduate in the spring of the year. Duplicate test records are no longer used to produce national figures.

Separate ACT standard scores are computed for English, mathematics, science reasoning, and, as of October 1989, reading. ACT standard scores are reported for each subject area on a scale from 1 to 36. In 2018, the national composite score (the simple average of the four ACT standard scores) was 20.8, with a standard deviation of 5.8. The tests emphasize reasoning, analysis, problem solving, and the integration of learning from various sources, as well as the application of these proficiencies to the kinds of tasks college students are expected to perform.

It should be noted that graduating students who take the ACT assessment are not necessarily representative of graduating students nationally. Students who live in the Midwest, Rocky Mountains, Plains, and South are overrepresented among ACT-tested students as compared to graduating students nationally. Students in these areas often aspire to public colleges and universities, which in these jurisdictions require the ACT assessment more often than the SAT test.

Further information on the ACT may be obtained from

ACT
500 ACT Drive
Iowa City, IA 52243
(319) 337-1270
https://www.act.org/

The College Board

Advanced Placement Exam

The Advanced Placement (AP) program is a curriculum sponsored by the College Board that offers high school students the opportunity to take college-level courses in a high school setting. A student taking an AP course in high school can earn college credit for participation by attaining a certain minimum score on the AP exam in that subject area.

The AP program offers 38 courses and exams. In most cases, the College Board does not require students to take an AP course before taking an AP exam. AP exams are given in the first two weeks in May. Most of the exams take 2 to 3 hours to complete. The scores for all AP exams range from 1 to 5, with 5 being the highest score.

SAT

The Admissions Testing Program of the College Board is made up of a number of college admissions tests, including the Preliminary Scholastic Assessment Test (PSAT) and the Scholastic Assessment Test, now known as the SAT. High school students participate in the testing program as sophomores, juniors, or seniors—some more than once during these three years. If they have taken the tests more than once, only the most recent scores are tabulated. The PSAT and SAT report subscores in the areas of mathematics and verbal ability.

Each year, approximately 2 million students take the SAT examination. SAT results are not representative of high school students or college-bound students nationally, however, since the sample is self-selected (i.e., taken by students who need the results to apply to a particular college or university). In addition, public colleges in many states—particularly those in the Midwest, parts of the South, and the West—require ACT scores rather than SAT scores; thus, the proportion of students taking the SAT in these states is very low and is inappropriate for comparison. The current version of the SAT, which includes an optional writing component among other content, format, and scoring changes, was first administered in March 2016.

Further information on AP and the SAT may be obtained from

The College Board National Office
250 Vesey Street
New York, NY 10281
https://www.collegeboard.org/

Commonfund Institute

Higher Education Price Index

Commonfund Institute took over management of the Higher Education Price Index (HEPI) in 2005 from Research Associates of Washington, which originated the index in 1961. HEPI is an inflation index designed specifically to track the main cost drivers in higher education. It measures the average relative level of prices in a fixed basket of goods and services purchased each year by colleges and universities through current fund educational and general expenditures, excluding research.

The main components of HEPI are faculty salaries; administrative salaries; clerical salaries; service employee salaries; fringe benefits; miscellaneous services; supplies and materials; and utilities. These represent the major items purchased for current operations by colleges and universities. Prices for these items are obtained from salary surveys conducted by the American Association of University Professors, the College and University Professional Association for Human Resources, and the Bureau of Labor Statistics (BLS), as well as from price series for components of BLS's Consumer Price Index (CPI), Employment Cost Index (ECI), and Producer Price Index (PPI).

HEPI measures price levels from a designated reference year in which budget weights are assigned. This base year is FY 1983 and is assigned a price value of 100.0 for index compilation. An index value of 115.0, for example, represents a 15 percent price increase over 1983 values.

Further information on HEPI may be obtained from

Commonfund Institute
15 Old Danbury Road
Wilton, CT 06897
https://www.commonfund.org/commonfund-institute/higher-education-price-index-hepi

Council for Aid to Education

Survey of Voluntary Support of Education

The Council for Aid to Education, Inc. (CAE) is a nonprofit corporation funded by contributions from businesses. CAE largely provides consulting and research services to corporations and information on voluntary support services to education institutions. Each year, CAE conducts a survey of colleges and universities and private elementary and secondary schools to obtain information on the amounts, sources, and purposes of private gifts, grants, and bequests received during the academic year.

The annual Voluntary Support of Education (VSE) survey consistently captures about 85 percent of the total voluntary support to colleges and universities in the United States. Institutional reports of voluntary support data from the VSE survey are more comprehensive and detailed than the related data in the Integrated Postsecondary Education Data System (IPEDS) Finance survey conducted by NCES.

The VSE survey is conducted online. All accredited higher education institutions are eligible to participate, and about a quarter of these institutions fill out a survey each year. CAE reviews the survey forms for internal consistency, queries institutions whose data appear out of line with national trends or their own historical data and makes an effort to clean the data before preparing a computerized database of the results.

Individual institutions and several state systems of higher education use the VSE data to monitor and analyze their fundraising results. CAE uses the data to develop national estimates of giving to education and to report in detail on private support of education. Results from the VSE survey are available by subscription to VSE Data Miner, an online interactive database; they are also published in the annual report *Voluntary Support of Education*, which may be purchased from CAE.

Further information on the VSE survey may be obtained from

Ann Kaplan
Council for Aid to Education
215 Lexington Avenue
16th Floor
New York, NY 10016
vse@cae.org
https://cae.org/

Council of Chief State School Officers

State Education Indicators

The Council of Chief State School Officers (CCSSO) is a nonpartisan, nationwide, nonprofit organization of the public officials who head departments of public education in the 50 states, the District of Columbia, the Department of Defense Education Activity, the Bureau of Indian Education, Puerto Rico, American Samoa, Guam, the Northern Mariana Islands, and the U.S. Virgin Islands. The CCSSO State Education Indicators project provides leadership in developing a system of state-by-state indicators of the condition of K–12 education. Indicator activities include collecting and reporting statistical indicators by state, tracking state policy changes, assisting with accountability systems, and conducting analysis of trends in education. *Key State Education Policies on PK–12 Education* is one of the publications issued by the State Education Indicators project. It is intended to inform policymakers and educators about the current status of key education policies that define and shape elementary and secondary education in the nation's public schools. State education staff reported on current policies through a survey, and CCSSO staff collected additional assessment information through state websites.

Further information on CCSSO publications may be obtained from

State Education Indicators Program
Standards, Assessment, and Accountability
Council of Chief State School Officers
1 Massachusetts Avenue NW
Suite 700
Washington, DC 20001
https://ccsso.org/

Editorial Projects in Education

Education Week

Editorial Projects in Education is an independent, nonprofit publisher of *Education Week* and other print and online products on K–12 education.

Further information on Editorial Projects in Education publications may be obtained from

Editorial Projects in Education
6935 Arlington Road
Bethesda, MD 20814
https://www.edweek.org/info/about/

Education Commission of the States

StateNotes

Education Commission of the States (ECS) regularly issues compilations, comparisons, and summaries of state policies—enacted or pending—on a number of education issues, including high school graduation requirements and school term information. ECS monitors state education activities for changes in education policies and updates ECS state information accordingly.

Further information on ECS StateNotes may be obtained from

Education Commission of the States
700 Broadway, #810
Denver, CO 80203-3442
ecs@ecs.org
https://www.ecs.org/

GED Testing Service

GED Testing Service is a joint venture, begun in 2011, between the American Council on Education (ACE) and Pearson. A GED credential documents high school-level academic skills. The test was first administered to World War II veterans in 1942 and was subsequently administered to civilians beginning in 1947. The first four generations of the GED test were the original GED test released in 1942, the 1978 series, the 1988 series, and the 2002 series. In 2014, a new test was implemented. A comparison of the 2014 GED test and the 2002 series test is available at https://files.eric.ed.gov/fulltext/ED578900.pdf.

The annual *GED Testing Program Statistical Report* provides information on those who take the GED, performance statistics of GED test takers, and some historical background on the GED testing program.

It is important to note that attempting to make comparisons in GED testing across jurisdictions is problematic, since each jurisdiction manages its own GED testing program. Thus, each jurisdiction develops its own policies, and these policies are reflected in a jurisdiction's testing program outcomes (its pass rates, for instance).

Further information on the GED may be obtained from

GED Testing Service
1850 M Street NW
Washington, DC 20036
https://ged.com/

Graduate Record Examinations Board

GRE tests

Graduate Record Examinations (GRE) tests are taken by individuals applying to graduate or professional school. GRE offers two types of tests, the GRE General Test and Subject Tests. The GRE General Test, which is mainly taken via computer, measures verbal, quantitative, and analytical writing skills. The analytical writing section (which replaced the analytical reasoning section on the GRE General Test in 2002) consists of two analytical writing tasks. The Subject Tests measure achievement in biochemistry, cell and molecular biology, biology, chemistry, literature in English, mathematics, physics, and psychology. Each graduate institution (or institution division) determines which GRE tests are required for admission.

Individuals may take GRE tests more than once. Score reports only reflect scores earned within the past 5-year period.

Further information on the GRE may be obtained from

GRE-ETS
Educational Testing Service
P.O. Box 6000
Princeton, NJ 08541
https://www.ets.org/gre

Institute of International Education

Open Doors

Each year, the Institute of International Education (IIE) conducts a survey of the number of foreign students studying in American colleges and universities and U.S. students studying abroad. The results of these surveys are reported in the publication *Open Doors*. All of the regionally accredited institutions in NCES's Integrated Postsecondary Education Data System (IPEDS) are surveyed by IIE. The foreign student enrollment data presented in the *Digest of Education Statistics* are drawn from IIE surveys that ask U.S. institutions for information on enrollment of foreign students, as well as student characteristics such as country of origin. For the 2016–17 survey, 62.3 percent of the 2,821 institutions surveyed reported data. For 2017–18, 62.3 percent of the 2,812 institutions surveyed reported data.

Surveys on the flows of U.S. college students studying abroad have been conducted since 1985–86. Surveys are sent to U.S. institutions asking them to provide information on the number and characteristics of the students to whom they awarded credit for study abroad during the previous academic year. For the 2015–16 academic year, data were obtained from 1,204, or 65.9 percent, of the 1,826 institutions surveyed; for the 2016–17 academic year, data were obtained from 1,242, or 67.9 percent, of the 1,830 institutions surveyed.

Additional information may be obtained from the publication *Open Doors* or by contacting

Institute of International Education
809 United Nations Plaza
New York, NY 10017
(212) 883-8200
opendoors@iie.org
https://www.iie.org/en/Research-and-Insights/Open-Doors

International Association for the Evaluation of Educational Achievement

The International Association for the Evaluation of Educational Achievement (IEA) is composed of governmental research centers and national research institutions around the world whose aim is to investigate education problems common among countries. Since its inception in 1958, the IEA has conducted more than 30 research studies of cross-national achievement. The regular cycle of studies encompasses learning in basic school subjects. Examples are the Trends in International Mathematics and Science Study (TIMSS) and the Progress in International Reading Literacy Study (PIRLS). IEA projects also include studies of particular interest to IEA members, such as the TIMSS 1999 Video Study of Mathematics and Science Teaching, the Civic Education Study, and studies on information technology in education.

The international bodies that coordinate international assessments vary in the labels they apply to participating education systems, most of which are countries. IEA differentiates between IEA members, which IEA refers to as "countries" in all cases, and "benchmarking participants." IEA members include countries such as the United States and Ireland, as well as subnational entities such as England and Scotland (which are both part of the United Kingdom), the Flemish community of Belgium, and Hong Kong (a Special Administrative Region of China). IEA benchmarking participants are all subnational entities and include Canadian provinces, U.S. states, and Dubai in the United Arab Emirates (among others). Benchmarking participants, like the participating countries, are given the opportunity to assess the comparative international standing of their students' achievement and to view their curriculum and instruction in an international context.

Some IEA studies, such as TIMSS and PIRLS, include an assessment portion, as well as contextual questionnaires for collecting information about students' home and school experiences. The TIMSS and PIRLS scales, including the scale averages and standard deviations, are designed to remain constant from assessment to assessment so that education systems (including countries and subnational education systems) can compare their scores over time as well as compare their scores directly with the scores of other education systems. Although each scale was created to have a mean of 500 and a standard deviation of 100, the subject matter and the level of difficulty of items necessarily differ by grade, subject, and domain/dimension. Therefore, direct comparisons between scores across grades, subjects, and different domain/dimension types should not be made.

Further information on the International Association for the Evaluation of Educational Achievement may be obtained from https://www.iea.nl/.

Trends in International Mathematics and Science Study

The Trends in International Mathematics and Science Study (TIMSS, formerly known as the Third International Mathematics and Science Study) provides data on the mathematics and science achievement of U.S. 4th- and 8th-graders compared with that of their peers in other countries. TIMSS collects information through mathematics and science assessments and questionnaires. The questionnaires request information to help provide a context for student performance. They focus on such topics as students' attitudes and beliefs about learning mathematics and science, what students do as part of their mathematics and science lessons, students' completion of homework, and their lives both in and outside of school; teachers' perceptions of their preparedness for teaching mathematics and science, teaching assignments, class size and organization, instructional content and practices, collaboration with other teachers, and participation in professional development activities; and principals' viewpoints on policy and budget responsibilities, curriculum and instruction issues, and student behavior. The questionnaires also elicit information on the organization of schools and courses. The assessments and questionnaires are designed to specifications in a guiding framework. The TIMSS framework describes the mathematics and science content to be assessed and provides grade-specific objectives, an overview of the assessment design, and guidelines for item development.

TIMSS is on a 4-year cycle. Data collections occurred in 1995, 1999 (8th grade only), 2003, 2007, 2011, and 2015. TIMSS 2015 consisted of assessments in 4th-grade mathematics; numeracy (a less difficult version of 4th-grade mathematics, newly developed for 2015); 8th-grade mathematics; 4th-grade science; and 8th-grade science. Students in Bahrain, Indonesia, Iran, Kuwait, Jordan, Morocco, and South Africa as well as Buenos Aires participated in the 4th-grade mathematics assessment through the numeracy assessment. In addition, TIMSS 2015 included the third administration of TIMSS Advanced since 1995. TIMSS Advanced is an international comparative study that measures the advanced mathematics and physics achievement of students in their final year of secondary school (the equivalent of 12th grade in the United States) who are taking or have taken advanced courses. The TIMSS 2015 survey also collected policy-relevant information about students, curriculum emphasis, technology use, and teacher preparation and training.

Progress in International Reading Literacy Study

The Progress in International Reading Literacy Study (PIRLS) provides data on the reading literacy of U.S. 4th-graders compared with that of their peers in other countries. PIRLS is on a 5-year cycle: PIRLS data collections have been conducted in 2001, 2006, 2011, and 2016. In 2016, a total of 58 education systems, including both IEA members and IEA benchmarking participants, participated in the survey. Sixteen of the education systems participating in PIRLS also participated in ePIRLS, an innovative, computer-based assessment of online reading designed to measure students' approaches to informational reading in an online environment.

PIRLS collects information through a reading literacy assessment and questionnaires that help to provide a context for student performance. Questionnaires are administered to collect information about students' home and school experiences in learning to read. A student questionnaire addresses students' attitudes toward reading and their reading habits. In addition, questionnaires are given to students' teachers and school principals in order to gather information about students' school experiences in developing reading literacy. In countries other than the United States, a parent questionnaire is also administered. The assessments and questionnaires are designed to specifications in a guiding framework. The PIRLS framework describes the reading content to be assessed and provides objectives specific to 4th grade, an overview of the assessment design, and guidelines for item development.

TIMSS and PIRLS Sampling and Response Rates

2016 PIRLS

As is done in all participating countries and other education systems, representative samples of students in the United States are selected. The sample design that was employed by PIRLS in 2016 is generally referred to as a two-stage stratified cluster sample. In the first stage of sampling, individual schools were selected with a probability proportionate to size (PPS) approach, which means that the probability is proportional to the estimated number of students enrolled in the target grade. In the second stage of sampling, intact classrooms were selected within sampled schools.

PIRLS guidelines call for a minimum of 150 schools to be sampled, with a minimum of 4,000 students assessed. The basic sample design of one classroom per school was designed to yield a total sample of approximately 4,500 students per population. About 4,400 U.S. students participated in PIRLS in 2016, joining 319,000 other student participants around the world. Accommodations were not provided for students with disabilities or students who were unable to read or speak the language of the test. These students were excluded from the sample. The IEA requirement is that the overall exclusion rate, of which exclusions of schools and students are a part, should not exceed more than 5 percent of the national desired target population.

In order to minimize the potential for response biases, the IEA developed participation or response rate standards that apply to all participating education systems and govern whether or not an education system's data are included in the TIMSS or PIRLS international datasets and the way in which its statistics are presented in the international reports. These standards were set using composites of response rates at the school, classroom, and student and teacher levels. Response rates were calculated with and without the inclusion of substitute schools that were selected to replace schools refusing to participate. In the 2016 PIRLS administered in the United States, the unweighted school response rate was 76 percent, and the weighted school response rate was 75 percent. All schools selected for PIRLS were also asked to participate in ePIRLS. The unweighted school response rate for ePIRLS in the final sample with replacement schools was 89.0 percent and the weighted response rate was 89.1 percent. The weighted and unweighted student response rates for PIRLS were both 94 percent. The weighted and unweighted student response rates for ePIRLS were both 90 percent.

2015 TIMSS and TIMSS Advanced

TIMSS 2015 was administered between March and May of 2015 in the United States. The U.S. sample was randomly selected and weighted to be representative of the nation. In order to reliably and accurately represent the performance of each country, international guidelines required that countries sample at least 150 schools and at least 4,000 students per grade (countries with small class sizes of fewer than 30 students per school were directed to consider sampling more schools, more classrooms per school, or both, to meet the minimum target of 4,000 tested students). In the United States, a total of 250 schools and 10,029 students participated in the grade 4 TIMSS survey, and 246 schools and 10,221 students participated in the grade 8 TIMSS (these figures do not include the participation of the state of Florida as a subnational education system, which was separate from and additional to its participation in the U.S. national sample).

TIMSS Advanced, also administered between March and May of 2015 in the United States, required participating countries and other education systems to draw probability samples of students in their final year of secondary school—ISCED Level 3—who were taking or had taken courses in advanced mathematics or who were taking or had taken courses in physics. International guidelines for TIMSS Advanced called for a minimum of 120 schools to be sampled, with a minimum of 3,600 students assessed per subject. In the United States, a total of 241 schools and 2,954 students participated in advanced mathematics, and 165 schools and 2,932 students participated in physics.

In TIMSS 2015, the weighted school response rate for the United States was 77 percent for grade 4 before the use of substitute schools (schools substituted for originally sampled schools that refused to participate) and 85 percent with the inclusion of substitute schools. For grade 8, the weighted school response rate before the use of substitute schools was 78 percent, and it was 84 percent with the inclusion of substitute schools. The weighted student response rate was 96 percent for grade 4 and 94 percent for grade 8.

In TIMSS Advanced 2015, the weighted school response rate for the United States for advanced mathematics was 72 percent before the use of substitute schools and 76 percent with the inclusion of substitute schools. The weighted school response rate for the United States for physics was 65 percent before the use of substitute schools and 68 percent with the inclusion of substitute schools. The weighted student response rate was 87 percent for advanced mathematics and 85 percent for physics. Student response rates are based on a combined total of students from both sampled and substitute schools.

Further information on the TIMSS study may be obtained from

Stephen Provasnik
International Assessment Branch
Assessments Division
National Center for Education Statistics
550 12th Street SW
Washington, DC 20202
(202) 245-6442
stephen.provasnik@ed.gov
https://nces.ed.gov/timss/
https://www.iea.nl/timss

Further information on the PIRLS study may be obtained from

Sheila Thompson
International Assessment Branch
Assessments Division
National Center for Education Statistics
550 12th Street SW
Washington, DC 20202
(202) 245-8330
sheila.thompson@ed.gov
https://nces.ed.gov/surveys/pirls/
https://www.iea.nl/pirls

National Association of State Directors of Teacher Education and Certification

NASDTEC Manual/KnowledgeBase

The National Association of State Directors of Teacher Education and Certification (NASDTEC) was organized in 1928 to represent professional standards boards and commissions and state departments of education that are responsible for the preparation, licensure, and discipline of educational personnel. Currently, NASDTEC's membership includes all 50 states, the District of Columbia, the U.S. Department of Defense Education Activity, U.S. territories, and Canadian provinces and territories.

The NASDTEC Manual on the Preparation and Certification of Educational Personnel was printed between 1984 and 2004, when it was replaced by an online publication, KnowledgeBase. KnowledgeBase is an expanded version of the Manual and is recognized as a comprehensive source of state-by-state information pertaining to the preparation, certification, and fitness of teachers and other school personnel in the United States and Canada.

Further information on KnowledgeBase may be obtained from

Phillip S. Rogers
Executive Director
NASDTEC
1629 K Street NW
Suite 300
Washington, DC 20006
philrogers@nasdtec.com
https://www.nasdtec.net/default.aspx

National Catholic Educational Association

The United States Catholic Elementary and Secondary Schools

The National Catholic Educational Association (NCEA) has been providing leadership and service to Catholic education since 1904. NCEA began to publish *The United States Catholic Elementary and Secondary Schools: Annual Statistical Report on Schools, Enrollment and Staffing* in 1970 in order to fill a need for educational data on the private sector. The report is based on data gathered by all of the archdiocesan and diocesan offices of education in the United States. These data enable NCEA to present information on school enrollment patterns, regional geographic trends, types and locations of schools, student and staffing demographic characteristics, and student participation in selected education programs.

Further information on *The United States Catholic Elementary and Secondary Schools: Annual Statistical Report on Schools, Enrollment, and Staffing* may be obtained from

Sister Dale McDonald, PBVM
National Catholic Educational Association
1005 North Glebe Road
Suite 525
Arlington, VA 22201
mcdonald@ncea.org
https://www.ncea.org/

National Education Association

Estimates of School Statistics

The National Education Association (NEA) publishes *Estimates of School Statistics* annually as part of the report *Rankings of the States & Estimates of School Statistics. Estimates of School Statistics* presents projections of public school enrollment, employment and personnel compensation, and finances, as reported by individual state departments of education. The state-level data in these estimates allow broad assessments of trends in the above areas. These data should be looked at with the understanding that the state-level data do not necessarily reflect the varying conditions within a state on education issues.

Data in *Estimates of School Statistics* are provided by state and District of Columbia departments of education and by other, mostly governmental, sources. Surveys are sent to state departments of education requesting estimated data for the current year and revisions to 4 years of historical data, as necessary. NEA submits current-year estimates of education statistics to each state's department of education for verification or revision each year. The estimates are generated using regression analyses; these regression-generated figures are only used in the report in cases where a state does not provide current data.

Further information on *Estimates of School Statistics* may be obtained from

NEA Rankings & Estimates Team—NEA Research
1201 16th Street NW
Washington, DC 20036
http://www.nea.org

Organization for Economic Cooperation and Development

The Organization for Economic Cooperation and Development (OECD) publishes analyses of national policies and survey data in education, training, and economics in OECD and partner countries. Newer studies include student survey data on financial literacy and on digital literacy.

Education at a Glance

To highlight current education issues and create a set of comparative education indicators that represent key features of education systems, OECD initiated the Indicators of Education Systems (INES) project and charged the Centre for Educational Research and Innovation (CERI) with developing the cross-national indicators for it. The development of these indicators involved representatives of the OECD countries and the OECD Secretariat. Improvements in data quality and comparability among OECD countries have resulted from the country-to-country interaction sponsored through the INES project. The most recent publication in this series is *Education at a Glance 2018: OECD Indicators*.

Education at a Glance 2018 features data on the 36 OECD countries (Australia, Austria, Belgium, Canada, Chile, the Czech Republic, Denmark, Estonia, Finland, France, Germany, Greece, Hungary, Iceland, Ireland, Israel, Italy, Japan, the Republic of Korea, Latvia, Lithuania, Luxembourg, Mexico, the Netherlands, New Zealand, Norway, Poland, Portugal, the Slovak Republic, Slovenia, Spain, Sweden, Switzerland, Turkey, the United Kingdom, and the United States) and a number of partner countries, including Argentina, Brazil, China, Colombia, Costa Rica, India, Indonesia, the Russian Federation, Saudi Arabia, and South Africa.

The *OECD Handbook for Internationally Comparative Education Statistics: Concepts, Standards, Definitions and Classifications* provides countries with specific guidance on how to prepare information for OECD education surveys; facilitates countries' understanding of OECD indicators and their use in policy analysis; and provides a reference for collecting and assimilating educational data. Chapter 6 of the *OECD Handbook for Internationally Comparative Education Statistics* contains a discussion of data quality issues. Users should examine footnotes carefully to recognize some of the data limitations.

Further information on international education statistics may be obtained from

Andreas Schleicher
Director for the Directorate of Education and Skills and Special Advisor on Education Policy to the OECD's Secretary General
OECD Directorate for Education and Skills
2 rue André Pascal
75775 Paris CEDEX 16
France
andreas.schleicher@oecd.org
https://www.oecd.org/

Online Education Database (OECD.Stat)

The statistical online platform of the OECD, OECD.Stat, allows users to access OECD's databases for OECD member countries and selected nonmember economies. A user can build tables using selected variables and customizable table layouts, extract and download data, and view metadata on methodology and sources.

Data for educational attainment in this report are pulled directly from OECD.Stat. (Information on these data can be found in chapter A, indicator A1 of annex 3 in *Education at a Glance 2018* and accessed at https://www.oecd-ilibrary.org/education/education-at-a-glance-2018/sources-methods-and-technical-notes_eag-2018-36-en.) However, to support statistical testing for NCES publications, standard errors for some countries had to be estimated and therefore may not be included on OECD.Stat. Standard errors for 2017 for the Republic of Korea, the Netherlands, Poland, Slovenia, and Turkey, as well as standard errors for the 2017 postsecondary educational attainment data for Japan, were estimated by NCES using a simple random sample assumption. These standard errors are likely to be lower than standard errors that take into account complex sample designs. Lastly, NCES estimated the standard errors for the OECD average using the sum of squares technique.

OECD.Stat can be accessed at https://stats.oecd.org/. A user's guide for OECD.Stat can be accessed at https://stats.oecd.org/Content/themes/OECD/static/help/WBOS%20User%20Guide%20(EN).pdf.

Program for International Student Assessment

The Program for International Student Assessment (PISA) is a system of international assessments organized by the Organization for Economic Cooperation and Development (OECD), an intergovernmental organization of industrialized countries, that focuses on 15-year-olds' capabilities in reading literacy, mathematics literacy, and science literacy. PISA also includes measures of general, or cross-curricular, competencies such as learning strategies. PISA emphasizes functional skills that students have acquired as they near the end of compulsory schooling.

PISA is a 2-hour exam. Assessment items include a combination of multiple-choice questions and open-ended questions that require students to develop their own response. PISA scores are reported on a scale that ranges from 0 to 1,000, with the OECD mean set at 500 and a standard deviation set at 100. In 2015, literacy was assessed in science, reading, and mathematics through a computer-based assessment in the majority of countries, including the United States. Education systems could also participate in optional pencil-and-paper financial literacy assessments and computer-based mathematics and reading assessments. In each education system, the assessment is translated into the primary language of instruction; in the United States, all materials are written in English.

Forty-three education systems participated in the 2000 PISA; 41 education systems participated in 2003; 57 (30 OECD member countries and 27 nonmember countries or education systems) participated in 2006; and 65 (34 OECD member countries and 31 nonmember countries or education systems) participated in 2009. (An additional nine education systems administered the 2009 PISA in 2010.) In PISA 2012, 65 education systems (34 OECD member countries and 31 nonmember countries or education systems), as well as the states of Connecticut, Florida, and Massachusetts, participated. In the 2015 PISA, 73 education systems (35 OECD member countries and 31 nonmember countries or education systems), as well as the states of Massachusetts and North Carolina and the territory of Puerto Rico, participated.

To implement PISA, each of the participating education systems scientifically draws a nationally representative sample of 15-year-olds, regardless of grade level. In the PISA 2015 national sample for the United States, about 5,700 students from 177 public and private schools were represented. Massachusetts, North Carolina, and Puerto Rico also participated in PISA 2015 as separate education systems. In Massachusetts, about 1,400 students from 48 public schools participated; in North Carolina, about 1,900 students from 54 public schools participated; and in Puerto Rico, about 1,400 students in 47 public and private schools participated.

The intent of PISA reporting is to provide an overall description of performance in reading literacy, mathematics literacy, and science literacy every 3 years, and to provide a more detailed look at each domain in the years when it is the major focus. These cycles will allow education systems to compare changes in trends for each of the three subject areas over time. In the first cycle, PISA 2000, reading literacy was the major focus, occupying roughly two-thirds of assessment time. For 2003, PISA focused on mathematics literacy as well as the ability of students to solve problems in real-life settings. In 2006, PISA focused on science literacy; in 2009, it focused on reading literacy again; and in 2012, it focused on mathematics literacy. PISA 2015 focused on science, as it did in 2006.

Further information on PISA may be obtained from

Patrick Gonzales
International Assessment Branch
Assessments Division
National Center for Education Statistics
550 12th Street SW
Washington, DC 20202
patrick.gonzales@ed.gov
https://nces.ed.gov/surveys/pisa/

Program for the International Assessment of Adult Competencies

The Program for the International Assessment of Adult Competencies (PIAAC) is a cyclical, large-scale study that aims to assess and compare the broad range of basic skills and competencies of adults around the world. Developed under the auspices of the Organization for Economic Cooperation and Development (OECD), it is the most comprehensive international survey of adult skills ever undertaken. Adults were surveyed in 24 participating countries in 2012 and in an additional 9 countries in 2014.

PIAAC focuses on what are deemed basic cognitive and workplace skills necessary to adults' successful participation in 21st-century society and in the global economy. Skills assessed include literacy, numeracy, problem solving in technology-rich environments, and basic reading skills. PIAAC measures the relationships between these skills and other characteristics such as individuals' educational background, workplace experiences, and occupational attainment. PIAAC was administered on laptop computers or in paper-and-pencil format. In the United States, the background questionnaire was administered in both English and Spanish, and the cognitive assessment was administered only in English.

The 2012 PIAAC assessment for the United States included a nationally representative probability sample of households. This household sample was selected on the basis of a four-stage, stratified area sample: (1) primary sampling units (PSUs) consisting of counties or groups of contiguous counties; (2) secondary sampling units (referred to as segments) consisting of area blocks; (3) housing units containing households; and (4) eligible persons within households. Person-level data were collected through a screener, a background questionnaire, and the assessment.

Based on the screener data, 6,100 U.S. respondents ages 16 to 65 were selected to complete the 2012 background questionnaire and the assessment; 4,898 actually completed the background questionnaire. Of the 1,202 respondents who did not complete the background questionnaire, 112 were unable to do so because of a literacy-related barrier—either the inability to communicate in English or Spanish or a mental disability. Twenty others were unable to complete the questionnaire due to technical problems. The final response rate for the background questionnaire, which included respondents who completed it and respondents who were unable to complete it because of a language problem or mental disability, was 82.2 percent weighted. The overall person-weighted response rate for the household sample—the product of the component response rates—was 70.3 percent.

The 2014 PIAAC supplement repeated the 2012 administration of PIAAC to an additional sample of U.S. adults in order to enhance the 2012 sample. It included a sample of participants from different households in the PSUs from the 2012 sample.

Key to PIAAC's value is its collaborative and international nature. In the United States, NCES has consulted extensively with the Department of Labor in the development of the survey, and staff from both agencies are co-representatives of the United States in PIAAC's international governing body. Internationally, PIAAC has been developed through the collaboration of OECD staff and participating countries' representatives from their ministries or departments of education and labor. Through this cooperative effort, all participating countries follow the quality assurance guidelines set by the OECD consortium and closely follow all agreed-upon standards set for survey design, assessment implementation, and reporting of results.

Further information on PIAAC may be obtained from

Holly Xie
International Assessment Branch
Assessments Division
National Center for Education Statistics
550 12th Street SW
Washington, DC 20202
holly.xie@ed.gov
https://nces.ed.gov/surveys/piaac/
https://www.oecd.org/skills/piaac/

United Nations Educational, Scientific, and Cultural Organization

Statistical Yearbook and Global Education Digest

The United Nations Educational, Scientific, and Cultural Organization (UNESCO) conducts annual surveys of education statistics of its member countries. Data from official surveys are supplemented by information obtained by UNESCO through other publications and sources. Each year, more than 200 countries reply to the UNESCO surveys. In some cases, estimates are made by UNESCO for particular items, such as world and continent totals. While great efforts are made to make them as comparable as possible, the data still reflect the vast differences among the countries of the world in the structure of education. While there is some agreement about the reporting of primary and secondary data, tertiary-level data (i.e., postsecondary education data) present numerous substantive problems. Some countries report only university enrollment, while other countries report all postsecondary enrollment, including enrollment in vocational and technical schools and correspondence programs. A very high proportion of some countries' tertiary-level students attend institutions in other countries. The member countries that provide data to UNESCO are responsible for their validity. Thus, data for particular countries are subject to nonsampling error as well as possible sampling error. Users should examine footnotes carefully to recognize some of the data limitations. UNESCO publishes the data in reports such as the *Statistical Yearbook* and the *Global Education Digest*.

Further information on the *Statistical Yearbook* and the *Global Education Digest* may be obtained from

UNESCO Institute for Statistics
C.P. 6128 Succursale Centre-Ville
Montreal, Quebec, H3C 3J7
Canada
http://uis.unesco.org/
https://en.unesco.org/

This page intentionally left blank.

APPENDIX B
Definitions

Academic support This category of college expenditures includes expenditures for support services that are an integral part of the institution's primary missions of instruction, research, or public service. It also includes expenditures for libraries, galleries, audio/visual services, academic computing support, ancillary support, academic administration, personnel development, and course and curriculum development.

Achievement gap See Gap.

Achievement levels, NAEP Specific achievement levels for each subject area and grade to provide a context for interpreting student performance. At this time they are being used on a trial basis.

> ***Basic***—denotes partial mastery of the knowledge and skills that are fundamental for *proficient* work at a given grade.
>
> ***Proficient***—represents solid academic performance. Students reaching this level have demonstrated competency over challenging subject matter.
>
> ***Advanced***—signifies superior performance.

Achievement test An examination that measures the extent to which a person has acquired certain information or mastered certain skills, usually as a result of specific instruction.

ACT The ACT (formerly the American College Testing Program) assessment program measures educational development and readiness to pursue college-level coursework in English, mathematics, natural science, and social studies. Student performance on the tests does not reflect innate ability and is influenced by a student's educational preparedness.

Administrative support staff Staff whose activities are concerned with support of teaching and administrative duties of the office of the principal or department chairpersons, including clerical staff and secretaries.

Advanced Placement (AP) A program of tertiary-level courses and examinations, taught by specially qualified teachers, that provides opportunities for secondary school students to earn undergraduate credits for university courses. The schools and teachers offering AP programs must meet College Board requirements and are monitored by the College Board.

Agriculture Courses designed to improve competencies in agricultural occupations. Included is the study of agricultural production, supplies, mechanization and products, agricultural science, forestry, and related services.

Alternative school A public elementary/secondary school that serves students whose needs cannot be met in a regular, special education, or vocational school; may provide nontraditional education; and may serve as an adjunct to a regular school. Although alternative schools fall outside the categories of regular, special education, and vocational education, they may provide similar services or curriculum. Some examples of alternative schools are schools for potential dropouts; residential treatment centers for substance abuse (if they provide elementary or secondary education); schools for chronic truants; and schools for students with behavioral problems.

Appropriation (federal funds) Budget authority provided through the congressional appropriation process that permits federal agencies to incur obligations and to make payments.

Appropriation (institutional revenues) An amount (other than a grant or contract) received from or made available to an institution through an act of a legislative body.

Associate's degree A degree granted for the successful completion of a sub-baccalaureate program of studies, usually requiring at least 2 years (or equivalent) of full-time college-level study. This includes degrees granted in a cooperative or work-study program.

Autism See Disabilities, children with.

Autocorrelation Correlation of the error terms from different observations of the same variable. Also called Serial correlation.

Auxiliary enterprises This category includes those essentially self-supporting operations which exist to furnish a service to students, faculty, or staff, and which charge a fee that is directly related to, although not necessarily equal to, the cost of the service. Examples are residence halls, food services, college stores, and intercollegiate athletics.

Average daily attendance (ADA) The aggregate attendance of a school during a reporting period (normally a school year) divided by the number of days school is in session during this period. Only days on which the pupils are under the guidance and direction of teachers should be considered days in session.

Average daily membership (ADM) The aggregate membership of a school during a reporting period (normally a school year) divided by the number of days school is in session during this period. Only days on which the pupils are under the guidance and direction of teachers should be considered as days in session. The ADM for groups of schools having varying lengths of terms is the average of the ADMs obtained for the individual schools. Membership includes all pupils who are enrolled, even if they do not actually attend.

Averaged freshman graduation rate (AFGR) A measure of the percentage of the incoming high school freshman class that graduates 4 years later. It is calculated by taking the number of graduates with a regular diploma and dividing that number by the estimated count of incoming freshman 4 years earlier, as reported through the NCES Common Core of Data (CCD). The estimated count of incoming freshman is the sum of the number of 8th-graders 5 years earlier, the number of 9th-graders 4 years earlier (when current seniors were freshman), and the number of 10th-graders 3 years earlier, divided by 3. The purpose of this averaging is to account for the high rate of grade retention in the freshman year, which adds 9th-grade repeaters from the previous year to the number of students in the incoming freshman class each year. Ungraded students are allocated to individual grades proportional to each state's enrollment in those grades. The AFGR treats students who transfer out of a school or district in the same way as it treats students from that school or district who drop out.

Bachelor's degree A degree granted for the successful completion of a baccalaureate program of studies, usually requiring at least 4 years (or equivalent) of full-time college-level study. This includes degrees granted in a cooperative or work-study program.

Books Nonperiodical printed publications bound in hard or soft covers, or in loose-leaf format, of at least 49 pages, exclusive of the cover pages; juvenile nonperiodical publications of any length found in hard or soft covers.

Breusch-Godfrey serial correlation LM test A statistic testing the independence of errors in least-squares regression against alternatives of first-order and higher degrees of serial correlation. The test belongs to a class of asymptotic tests known as the Lagrange multiplier (LM) tests.

Budget authority (BA) Authority provided by law to enter into obligations that will result in immediate or future outlays. It may be classified by the period of availability (1-year, multiple-year, no-year), by the timing of congressional action (current or permanent), or by the manner of determining the amount available (definite or indefinite).

Business Program of instruction that prepares individuals for a variety of activities in planning, organizing, directing, and controlling business office systems and procedures.

Capital outlay Funds for the acquisition of land and buildings; building construction, remodeling, and additions; the initial installation or extension of service systems and other built-in equipment; and site improvement. The category also encompasses architectural and engineering services, including the development of blueprints.

Career/technical education (CTE) In high school, encompasses occupational education, which teaches skills required in specific occupations or occupational clusters, as well as nonoccupational CTE, which includes family and consumer sciences education (i.e., courses that prepare students for roles outside the paid labor market) and general labor market preparation (i.e., courses that teach general employment skills such as word processing and introductory technology skills).

Carnegie unit The number of credits a secondary student received for a course taken every day, one period per day, for a full year; a factor used to standardize all credits indicated on secondary school transcripts across studies.

Catholic school A private school over which a Roman Catholic church group exercises some control or provides some form of subsidy. Catholic schools for the most part include those operated or supported by a parish, a group of parishes, a diocese, or a Catholic religious order.

Central cities The largest cities, with 50,000 or more inhabitants, in a Metropolitan Statistical Area (MSA). Additional cities within the metropolitan area can also be classified as "central cities" if they meet certain employment, population, and employment/residence ratio requirements.

Certificate A formal award certifying the satisfactory completion of a postsecondary education program. Certificates can be awarded at any level of postsecondary education and include awards below the associate's degree level.

Charter school A school providing free public elementary and/or secondary education to eligible students under a specific charter granted by the state legislature or other appropriate authority, and designated by such authority to be a charter school.

City school See Locale codes.

Class size The membership of a class at a given date.

Classification of Instructional Programs (CIP) The CIP is a taxonomic coding scheme that contains titles and descriptions of primarily postsecondary instructional programs. It was developed to facilitate NCES's collection and reporting of postsecondary degree completions by major field of study using standard classifications that capture the majority of reportable program activity. It was originally published in 1980 and was revised in 1985, 1990, 2000, and 2010.

Classification of Secondary School Courses (CSSC) A modification of the Classification of Instructional Programs used for classifying high school courses. The CSSC contains over 2,200 course codes that help compare the thousands of high school transcripts collected from different schools.

Classroom teacher A staff member assigned the professional activities of instructing pupils in self-contained classes or courses, or in classroom situations; usually expressed in full-time equivalents.

Coefficient of variation (CV) Represents the ratio of the standard error to the estimate. For example, a CV of 30 percent indicates that the standard error of the estimate is equal to 30 percent of the estimate's value. The CV is used to compare the amount of variation relative to the magnitude of the estimate. A CV of 30 percent or greater indicates that an estimate should be interpreted with caution. For a discussion of standard errors, see Appendix A: Guide to Sources.

Cohort A group of individuals who have a statistical factor in common, for example, year of birth.

Cohort-component method A method for estimating and projecting a population that is distinguished by its ability to preserve knowledge of an age distribution of a population (which may be of a single sex, race, and Hispanic origin) over time.

College A postsecondary school that offers general or liberal arts education, usually leading to an associate's, bachelor's, master's, or doctor's degree. Junior colleges and community colleges are included under this terminology.

Combined school A school that encompasses instruction at both the elementary and the secondary levels; includes schools starting with grade 6 or below and ending with grade 9 or above.

Combined school (2007–08 Schools and Staffing Survey) A school with at least one grade lower than 7 and at least one grade higher than 8; schools with only ungraded classes are included with combined schools.

Combined Statistical Area (CSA) A combination of Core Based Statistical Areas (see below), each of which contains a core with a substantial population nucleus as well as adjacent communities having a high degree of economic and social integration with that core. A CSA is a region with social and economic ties as measured by commuting, but at lower levels than are found within each component area. CSAs represent larger regions that reflect broader social and economic interactions, such as wholesaling, commodity distribution, and weekend recreation activities.

Computer science A group of instructional programs that describes computer and information sciences, including computer programming, data processing, and information systems.

Constant dollars Dollar amounts that have been adjusted by means of price and cost indexes to eliminate inflationary factors and allow direct comparison across years.

Consumer Price Index (CPI) This price index measures the average change in the cost of a fixed market basket of goods and services purchased by consumers. Indexes vary for specific areas or regions, periods of time, major groups of consumer expenditures, and population groups. The CPI reflects spending patterns for two population groups: (1) all urban consumers and urban wage earners and (2) clerical workers. CPIs are calculated for both the calendar year and the school year using the U.S. All Items CPI for All Urban Consumers (CPI-U). The calendar year CPI is the same as the annual CPI-U. The school year CPI is calculated by adding the monthly CPI-U figures, beginning with July of the first year and ending with June of the following year, and then dividing that figure by 12.

Consumption That portion of income that is spent on the purchase of goods and services rather than being saved.

Control of institutions A classification of institutions of elementary/secondary or postsecondary education by whether the institution is operated by publicly elected or appointed officials and derives its primary support from public funds (public control) or is operated by privately elected or appointed officials and derives its major source of funds from private sources (private control).

Core Based Statistical Area (CBSA) A population nucleus and the nearby communities having a high degree of economic and social integration with that nucleus. Each CBSA includes at least one urban area of 10,000 or more people and one or more counties. In addition to a "central county" (or counties), additional "outlying counties" are included in the CBSA if they meet specified requirements of commuting to or from the central counties.

Credit The unit of value, awarded for the successful completion of certain courses, intended to indicate the quantity of course instruction in relation to the total requirements for a diploma, certificate, or degree. Credits are frequently expressed in terms such as "Carnegie units," "semester credit hours," and "quarter credit hours."

Current dollars Dollar amounts that have not been adjusted to compensate for inflation.

Current expenditures (elementary/secondary) The expenditures for operating local public schools, excluding capital outlay and interest on school debt. These expenditures include such items as salaries for school personnel, benefits, student transportation, school books and materials, and energy costs. Beginning in 1980–81, expenditures for state administration are excluded.

Instruction expenditures Includes expenditures for activities related to the interaction between teacher and students. Includes salaries and benefits for teachers and instructional aides, textbooks, supplies, and purchased services such as instruction via television, webinars, and other online instruction. Also included are tuition expenditures to other local education agencies.

Administration expenditures Includes expenditures for school administration (i.e., the office of the principal, full-time department chairpersons, and graduation expenses), general administration (the superintendent and board of education and their immediate staff), and other support services expenditures.

Transportation Includes expenditures for vehicle operation, monitoring, and vehicle servicing and maintenance.

Food services Includes all expenditures associated with providing food to students and staff in a school or school district. The services include preparing and serving regular and incidental meals or snacks in connection with school activities, as well as the delivery of food to schools.

Enterprise operations Includes expenditures for activities that are financed, at least in part, by user charges, similar to a private business. These include operations funded by sales of products or services, together with amounts for direct program support made by state education agencies for local school districts.

Current expenditures per pupil in average daily attendance Current expenditures for the regular school term divided by the average daily attendance of full-time pupils (or full-time equivalency of pupils) during the term. See also Current expenditures and Average daily attendance.

Current-fund expenditures (postsecondary education) Money spent to meet current operating costs, including salaries, wages, utilities, student services, public services, research libraries, scholarships and fellowships, auxiliary enterprises, hospitals, and independent operations; excludes loans, capital expenditures, and investments.

Current-fund revenues (postsecondary education) Money received during the current fiscal year from revenue which can be used to pay obligations currently due, and surpluses reappropriated for the current fiscal year.

Deaf-blindness See Disabilities, children with.

Default rate The percentage of loans that are in delinquency and have not been repaid according to the terms of the loan. According to the federal government, a federal student loan is in default if there has been no payment on the loan in 270 days. The Department of Education calculates a 3-year cohort default rate, which is the percentage of students who entered repayment in a given fiscal year (from October 1 to September 30) and then defaulted within the following 2 fiscal years. For example, the 3-year cohort default rate for fiscal year (FY) 2009 is the percentage of borrowers who entered repayment during FY 2009 (any time from October 1, 2008, through September 30, 2009) and who defaulted by the end of FY 2011 (September 30, 2011).

Degree An award conferred by a college, university, or other postsecondary education institution as official recognition for the successful completion of a program of studies. Refers specifically to associate's or higher degrees conferred by degree-granting institutions. See also Associate's degree, Bachelor's degree, Master's degree, and Doctor's degree.

Degree/certificate-seeking student A student enrolled in courses for credit and recognized by the institution as seeking a degree, certificate, or other formal award. High school students also enrolled in postsecondary courses for credit are not considered degree/certificate-seeking. See also Degree and Certificate.

Degree-granting institutions Postsecondary institutions that are eligible for Title IV federal financial aid programs and grant an associate's or higher degree. For an institution to be eligible to participate in Title IV financial aid programs, it must offer a program of at least 300 clock hours in length, have accreditation recognized by the U.S. Department of Education, have been in business for at least 2 years, and have signed a participation agreement with the Department.

Degrees of freedom The number of free or linearly independent sample observations used in the calculation of a statistic. In a time series regression with t time periods and k independent variables including a constant term, there would be t minus k degrees of freedom.

Department of Defense (DoD) dependents schools Schools that are operated by the Department of Defense Education Activity (a civilian agency of the U.S. Department of Defense) and provide comprehensive prekindergarten through 12th-grade educational programs on military installations both within the United States and overseas.

Dependency status A designation of whether postsecondary students are financially dependent on their parents or financially independent of their parents. Undergraduates are assumed to be dependent unless they meet one of the following criteria: are age 24 or older, are married or have legal dependents other than a spouse, are veterans, are orphans or wards of the court, or provide documentation that they are self-supporting.

Dependent variable A mathematical variable whose value is determined by that of one or more other variables in a function. In regression analysis, when a random variable, y, is expressed as a function of variables $x1$, $x2$, ... xk, plus a stochastic term, then y is known as the "dependent variable."

Developmental delay See Disabilities, children with.

Disabilities, children with Those children evaluated as having any of the following impairments and who, by reason thereof, receive special education and related services under the Individuals with Disabilities Education Act (IDEA) according to an Individualized Education Program (IEP), Individualized Family Service Plan (IFSP), or a services plan. There are local variations in the determination of disability conditions, and not all states use all reporting categories.

Autism Having a developmental disability significantly affecting verbal and nonverbal communication and social interaction, generally evident before age 3, that adversely affects educational performance. Other characteristics often associated with autism are engagement in repetitive activities and stereotyped movements, resistance to environmental change or change in daily routines, and unusual responses to sensory experiences. A child is not considered autistic if the child's educational performance is adversely affected primarily because of an emotional disturbance.

Deaf-blindness Having concomitant hearing and visual impairments that cause such severe communication and other developmental and educational problems that the student cannot be accommodated in special education programs solely for deaf or blind students.

Developmental delay Having developmental delays, as defined at the state level, and as measured by appropriate diagnostic instruments and procedures in one or more of the following cognitive areas: physical development, cognitive development, communication development, social or emotional development, or adaptive development. Applies only to 3- through 9-year-old children.

Emotional disturbance Exhibiting one or more of the following characteristics over a long period of time, to a marked degree, and adversely affecting educational performance: an inability to learn that cannot be explained by intellectual, sensory, or health factors; an inability to build or maintain satisfactory interpersonal relationships with peers and teachers; inappropriate types of behavior or feelings under normal circumstances; a general pervasive mood of unhappiness or depression; or a tendency to develop physical symptoms or fears associated with personal or school problems. This term does not include children who are socially maladjusted, unless they also display one or more of the listed characteristics.

Hearing impairment Having a hearing impairment, whether permanent or fluctuating, that adversely affects the student's educational performance. Also reported in this category is deafness, a hearing impairment so severe that the student is impaired in processing linguistic information through hearing (with or without amplification).

Intellectual disability Having significantly subaverage general intellectual functioning, existing concurrently with defects in adaptive behavior and manifested during the developmental period, that adversely affects the child's educational performance.

Multiple disabilities Having concomitant impairments (such as intellectually disabled-blind, intellectually disabled-orthopedically impaired, etc.), the combination of which causes such severe educational problems that the student cannot be accommodated in special education programs solely for one of the impairments. This term does not include deaf-blind students.

Orthopedic impairment Having a severe orthopedic impairment that adversely affects a student's educational performance. The term includes impairment resulting from congenital anomaly, disease, or other causes.

Other health impairment Having limited strength, vitality, or alertness due to chronic or acute health problems—such as a heart condition, tuberculosis, rheumatic fever, nephritis, asthma, sickle cell anemia, hemophilia, epilepsy, lead poisoning, leukemia, or diabetes—that adversely affect the student's educational performance.

Specific learning disability Having a disorder in one or more of the basic psychological processes involved in understanding or in using spoken or written language, which may manifest itself in an imperfect ability to listen, think, speak, read, write, spell, or do mathematical calculations. The term includes such conditions as perceptual disabilities, brain injury, minimal brain dysfunction, dyslexia, and developmental aphasia. The term does not include children who have learning problems that are primarily the result of visual, hearing, motor, or intellectual disabilities, or of environmental, cultural, or economic disadvantage.

Speech or language impairment Having a communication disorder, such as stuttering, impaired articulation, language impairment, or voice impairment, that adversely affects the student's educational performance.

Traumatic brain injury Having an acquired injury to the brain caused by an external physical force, resulting in total or partial functional disability or psychosocial impairment or both, that adversely affects the student's educational performance. The term applies to open or closed head injuries resulting in impairments in one or more areas, such as cognition; language; memory; attention; reasoning; abstract thinking; judgment; problem-solving; sensory, perceptual, and motor abilities; psychosocial behavior; physical functions; information processing; and speech. The term does not apply to brain injuries that are congenital or degenerative or to brain injuries induced by birth trauma.

Visual impairment Having a visual impairment that, even with correction, adversely affects the student's educational performance. The term includes partially seeing and blind children.

Discipline divisions Degree programs that include breakouts to the 6-digit level of the Classification of Instructional Programs (CIP). See also Fields of study.

Disposable personal income Current income received by people less their contributions for social insurance, personal tax, and nontax payments. It is the income available to people for spending and saving. Nontax payments include passport fees, fines and penalties, donations, and tuitions and fees paid to schools and hospitals operated mainly by the government. See also Personal income.

Distance education Education that uses one or more technologies to deliver instruction to students who are separated from the instructor and to support regular and substantive interaction between the students and the instructor synchronously or asynchronously. Technologies used for instruction may include the following: Internet; one-way and two-way transmissions through open broadcasts, closed circuit, cable, microwave, broadband lines, fiber optics, and satellite or wireless communication devices; audio conferencing; and DVDs and CD-ROMs, if used in a course in conjunction with the technologies listed above.

Doctor's degree The highest award a student can earn for graduate study. Includes such degrees as the Doctor of Education (Ed.D.); Doctor of Juridical Science (S.J.D.); Doctor of Public Health (Dr.P.H.); and Doctor of Philosophy (Ph.D.) in any field, such as agronomy, food technology, education, engineering, public administration, ophthalmology, or radiology. The doctor's degree classification encompasses three main subcategories—research/scholarship degrees, professional practice degrees, and other degrees—which are described below.

Doctor's degree—research/scholarship A Ph.D. or other doctor's degree that requires advanced work beyond the master's level, including the preparation and defense of a dissertation based on original research, or the planning and execution of an original project demonstrating substantial artistic or scholarly achievement. Examples of this type of degree may include the following and others, as designated by the awarding institution: the Ed.D. (in education), D.M.A. (in musical arts), D.B.A. (in business administration), D.Sc. (in science), D.A. (in arts), or D.M (in medicine).

Doctor's degree—professional practice A doctor's degree that is conferred upon completion of a program providing the knowledge and skills for the recognition, credential, or license required for professional practice. The degree is awarded after a period of study such that the total time to the degree, including both preprofessional and professional preparation, equals at least 6 full-time-equivalent academic years. Some doctor's degrees of this type were formerly classified as first-professional degrees. Examples of this type of degree may include the following and others, as designated by the awarding institution: the D.C. or D.C.M. (in chiropractic); D.D.S. or D.M.D. (in dentistry); L.L.B. or J.D. (in law); M.D. (in medicine); O.D. (in optometry); D.O. (in osteopathic medicine); Pharm.D. (in pharmacy); D.P.M., Pod.D., or D.P. (in podiatry); or D.V.M. (in veterinary medicine).

Doctor's degree—other A doctor's degree that does not meet the definition of either a doctor's degree—research/scholarship or a doctor's degree—professional practice.

Double exponential smoothing A method that takes a single smoothed average component of demand and smoothes it a second time to allow for estimation of a trend effect.

Dropout The term is used to describe both the event of leaving school before completing high school and the status of an individual who is not in school and who is not a high school completer. High school completers include both graduates of school programs as well as those completing high school through equivalency programs such as the GED program. Transferring from a public school to a private school, for example, is not regarded as a dropout event. A person who drops out of school may later return and graduate but is called a "dropout" at the time he or she leaves school. Measures to describe these behaviors include the event dropout rate (or the closely related school persistence rate), the status dropout rate, and the high school completion rate.

Durbin-Watson statistic A statistic testing the independence of errors in least squares regression against the alternative of first-order serial correlation. The statistic is a simple linear transformation of the first-order serial correlation of residuals and, although its distribution is unknown, it is tested by bounding statistics that follow R.L. Anderson's distribution.

Early childhood school Early childhood program schools serve students in prekindergarten, kindergarten, transitional (or readiness) kindergarten, and/or transitional first (or prefirst) grade.

Econometrics The quantitative examination of economic trends and relationships using statistical techniques, and the development, examination, and refinement of those techniques.

Education specialist/professional diploma A certificate of advanced graduate studies that advance educators in their instructional and leadership skills beyond a master's degree level of competence.

Educational and general expenditures The sum of current funds expenditures on instruction, research, public service, academic support, student services, institutional support, operation and maintenance of plant, and awards from restricted and unrestricted funds.

Educational attainment The highest grade of regular school attended and completed.

Educational attainment (Current Population Survey) This measure uses March CPS data to estimate the percentage of civilian, noninstitutionalized people who have achieved certain levels of educational attainment. Estimates of educational attainment do not differentiate between those who graduated from public schools, those who graduated from private schools, and those who earned a GED; these estimates also include individuals who earned their credential or completed their highest level of education outside of the United States.

1972–1991 During this period, an individual's educational attainment was considered to be his or her last fully completed year of school. Individuals who completed 12 years of schooling were deemed to be high school graduates, as were those who began but did not complete the first year of college. Respondents who completed 16 or more years of schooling were counted as college graduates.

1992–present Beginning in 1992, CPS asked respondents to report their highest level of school completed or their highest degree received. This change means that some data collected before 1992 are not strictly comparable with data collected from 1992 onward and that care must be taken when making comparisons across years. The revised survey question emphasizes credentials received rather than the last grade level attended or completed. The new categories include the following:

- High school graduate, high school diploma, or the equivalent (e.g., GED)
- Some college but no degree
- Associate's degree in college, occupational/vocational program
- Associate's degree in college, academic program (e.g., A.A., A.S., A.A.S.)
- Bachelor's degree (e.g., B.A., A.B., B.S.)
- Master's degree (e.g., M.A., M.S., M.Eng., M.Ed., M.S.W., M.B.A.)
- Professional school degree (e.g., M.D., D.D.S., D.V.M., LL.B., J.D.)
- Doctor's degree (e.g., Ph.D., Ed.D.)

Elementary education/programs Learning experiences concerned with the knowledge, skills, appreciations, attitudes, and behavioral characteristics that are considered to be needed by all pupils in terms of their awareness of life within our culture and the world of work, and that normally may be achieved during the elementary school years (usually kindergarten through grade 8 or kindergarten through grade 6), as defined by applicable state laws and regulations.

Elementary school A school classified as elementary by state and local practice and composed of any span of grades not above grade 8.

Elementary/secondary school Includes only schools that are part of state and local school systems, and also most nonprofit private elementary/secondary schools, both religiously affiliated and nonsectarian. Includes regular, alternative, vocational, and special education schools. U.S. totals exclude federal schools for American Indians, and federal schools on military posts and other federal installations.

Emotional disturbance See Disabilities, children with.

Employees in degree-granting institutions Persons employed by degree-granting institutions, who are classified into the following occupational categories in this publication:

Executive/administrative/managerial staff Employees whose assignments require management of the institution or of a customarily recognized department or subdivision thereof. These employees perform work that is directly related to management policies or general business operations and that requires them to exercise discretion and independent judgment.

Faculty (instruction/research/public service) Employees whose principal activities are for the purpose of providing instruction or teaching, research, or public service. These employees may hold such titles as professor, associate professor, assistant professor, instructor, or lecturer. Graduate assistants are not included in this category. The aggregated "faculty (instruction/research/public service)" category includes faculty reported in four separate Integrated Postsecondary Education System (IPEDS) occupational categories: "primarily instruction," "research," "public service," and "instruction combined with research and/or public service." These categories are based on the types of assignments that employees formally spend the majority of their time doing. "Instruction combined with research and/or public service" includes those who provide instruction but "for whom it is not possible to differentiate between instruction or teaching, research, and public service because each of these functions is an integral component of their regular assignment." For purposes of presentation in the *Digest of Education Statistics*, "instruction" faculty include those reported in the "instruction combined with research and/or public service" category as well as those reported in the "primarily instruction" category.

Graduate assistants Graduate-level students who are employed on a part-time basis for the primary purpose of assisting in classroom or laboratory instruction or in the conduct of research.

Nonprofessional staff Employees whose primary activities can be classified as one of the following: technical and paraprofessional work (which generally requires less formal training and experience than required for professional status); clerical and secretarial work; skilled crafts work; or service/maintenance work.

Other professional staff Employees who perform academic support, student service, and institutional support and who need either a degree at the bachelor's or higher level or experience of such kind and amount as to provide a comparable background.

Professional staff Employees who are classified as executive/administrative/managerial staff, faculty, graduate assistants, or other professional staff.

Employment Includes civilian, noninstitutional people who (1) worked during any part of the survey week as paid employees; worked in their own business, profession, or farm; or worked 15 hours or more as unpaid workers in a family-owned enterprise; or (2) were not working but had jobs or businesses from which they were temporarily absent due to illness, bad weather, vacation, labor-management dispute, or personal reasons whether or not they were seeking another job.

Employment (Current Population Survey) According to the October Current Population Survey (CPS), employed persons are persons age 16 or older who, during the reference week, (1) did any work at all (at least 1 hour) as paid employees or (2) were not working but had jobs or businesses from which they were temporarily absent because of vacation, illness, bad weather, child care problems, maternity or paternity leave, labor-management dispute, job training, or other family or personal reasons, whether or not they were paid for the time off or were seeking other jobs.

Employment status A classification of individuals as employed (either full or part time), unemployed (looking for work or on layoff), or not in the labor force (due to being retired, having unpaid employment, or some other reason).

Endowment A trust fund set aside to provide a perpetual source of revenue from the proceeds of the endowment investments. Endowment funds are often created by donations from benefactors of an institution, who may designate the use of the endowment revenue. Normally, institutions or their representatives manage the investments, but they are not permitted to spend the endowment fund itself, only the proceeds from the investments. Typical uses of endowments would be an endowed chair for a particular department or for a scholarship fund. Endowment totals tabulated in this book also include funds functioning as endowments, such as funds left over from the previous year and placed with the endowment investments by the institution. These funds may be withdrawn by the institution and spent as current funds at any time. Endowments are evaluated by two different measures, book value and market value. Book value is the purchase price of the endowment investment. Market value is the current worth of the endowment investment. Thus, the book value of a stock held in an endowment fund would be the purchase price of the stock. The market value of the stock would be its selling price as of a given day.

Engineering Instructional programs that describe the mathematical and natural science knowledge gained by study, experience, and practice and applied with judgment to develop ways to utilize the materials and forces of nature economically. Includes programs that prepare individuals to support and assist engineers and similar professionals.

English A group of instructional programs that describes the English language arts, including composition, creative writing, and the study of literature.

English language learner (ELL) An individual who, due to any of the reasons listed below, has sufficient difficulty speaking, reading, writing, or understanding the English language to be denied the opportunity to learn successfully in classrooms where the language of instruction is English or to participate fully in the larger U.S. society. Such an individual (1) was not born in the United States or has a native language other than English; (2) comes from environments where a language other than English is dominant; or (3) is an American Indian or Alaska Native and comes from environments where a language other than English has had a significant impact on the individual's level of English language proficiency.

Enrollment The total number of students registered in a given school unit at a given time, generally in the fall of a year. At the postsecondary level, separate counts are also available for full-time and part-time students, as well as full-time-equivalent enrollment. See also Full-time enrollment, Full-time-equivalent (FTE) enrollment, and Part-time enrollment.

Estimate A numerical value obtained from a statistical sample and assigned to a population parameter. The particular value yielded by an estimator in a given set of circumstances or the rule by which such particular values are calculated.

Estimating equation An equation involving observed quantities and an unknown that serves to estimate the latter.

Estimation Estimation is concerned with inference about the numerical value of unknown population values from incomplete data, such as a sample. If a single figure is calculated for each unknown parameter, the process is called point estimation. If an interval is calculated within which the parameter is likely, in some sense, to lie, the process is called interval estimation.

Executive/administrative/managerial staff See Employees in degree-granting institutions.

Expenditures, Total For elementary/secondary schools, these include all charges for current outlays plus capital outlays and interest on school debt. For degree-granting institutions, these include current outlays plus capital outlays. For government, these include charges net of recoveries and other correcting transactions other than for retirement of debt, investment in securities, extension of credit, or as agency transactions. Government expenditures include only external transactions, such as the provision of perquisites or other payments in kind. Aggregates for groups of governments exclude intergovernmental transactions among the governments.

Expenditures per pupil Charges incurred for a particular period of time divided by a student unit of measure, such as average daily attendance or fall enrollment.

Exponential smoothing A method used in time series analysis to smooth or to predict a series. There are various forms, but all are based on the supposition that more remote history has less importance than more recent history.

Expulsion Removing a student from his or her regular school for an extended length of time or permanently for disciplinary purposes.

Extracurricular activities Activities that are not part of the required curriculum and that take place outside of the regular course of study. They include both school-sponsored (e.g., varsity athletics, drama, and debate clubs) and community-sponsored (e.g., hobby clubs and youth organizations like the Junior Chamber of Commerce or Boy Scouts) activities.

Faculty (instruction/research/public service) See Employees in degree-granting institutions.

Family A group of two or more people (one of whom is the householder) related by birth, marriage, or adoption and residing together. All such people (including related subfamily members) are considered as members of one family.

Family income Includes all monetary income from all sources (including jobs, businesses, interest, rent, and Social Security payments) over a 12-month period. The income of nonrelatives living in the household is excluded, but the income of all family members age 15 or older (age 14 or older in years prior to 1989), including those temporarily living outside of the household, is included. In the October Current Population Survey, family income is determined from a single question asked of the household respondent.

Federal funds Amounts collected and used by the federal government for the general purposes of the government. The major federal fund is the general fund, which is derived from general taxes and borrowing. Other types of federal fund accounts include special funds (earmarked for a specific purpose other than a business-like activity), public enterprise funds (earmarked for a business-like activity conducted primarily with the public), and intragovernmental funds (earmarked for a business-like activity conducted primarily within the government).

Federal sources (postsecondary degree-granting institutions) Includes federal appropriations, grants, and contracts, and federally funded research and development centers (FFRDCs). Federally subsidized student loans are not included.

Fields of study The primary field of concentration in postsecondary certificates and degrees. In the Integrated Postsecondary Education Data System (IPEDS), refers to degree programs that are broken out only to the 2-digit level of the Classification of Instructional Programs (CIP). See also Discipline divisions.

Financial aid Grants, loans, assistantships, scholarships, fellowships, tuition waivers, tuition discounts, veteran's benefits, employer aid (tuition reimbursement), and other monies (other than from relatives or friends) provided to students to help them meet expenses. Except where designated, includes Title IV subsidized and unsubsidized loans made directly to students.

First-order serial correlation When errors in one time period are correlated directly with errors in the ensuing time period.

First-professional degree NCES no longer uses this classification. Most degrees formerly classified as first-professional (such as M.D., D.D.S., Pharm.D., D.V.M., and J.D.) are now classified as doctor's degrees—professional practice. However, master's of divinity degrees are now classified as master's degrees.

First-time student (undergraduate) A student who has no prior postsecondary experience (except as noted below) attending any institution for the first time at the undergraduate level. Includes students enrolled in the fall term who attended college for the first time in the prior summer term, and students who entered with advanced standing (college credits earned before graduation from high school).

Fiscal year A period of 12 months for which accounting records are compiled. Institutions and states may designate their own accounting period, though most states use a July 1 through June 30 accounting year. The yearly accounting period for the federal government begins on October 1 and ends on the following September 30. The fiscal year is designated by the calendar year in which it ends; e.g., fiscal year 2006 begins on October 1, 2005, and ends on September 30, 2006. (From fiscal year 1844 to fiscal year 1976, the federal fiscal year began on July 1 and ended on the following June 30.)

Forecast An estimate of the future based on rational study and analysis of available pertinent data, as opposed to subjective prediction.

Forecasting Assessing the magnitude that a quantity will assume at some future point in time, as distinct from "estimation," which attempts to assess the magnitude of an already existent quantity.

Foreign languages A group of instructional programs that describes the structure and use of language that is common or indigenous to people of a given community or nation, geographical area, or set of cultural traditions. Programs cover such features as sound, literature, syntax, phonology, semantics, sentences, prose, and verse, as well as the development of skills and attitudes used in communicating and evaluating thoughts and feelings through oral and written language.

For-profit institution A private institution in which the individual(s) or agency in control receives compensation other than wages, rent, or other expenses for the assumption of risk.

Free or reduced-price lunch See National School Lunch Program.

Full-time enrollment The number of students enrolled in postsecondary education courses with total credit load equal to at least 75 percent of the normal full-time course load. At the undergraduate level, full-time enrollment typically includes students who have a credit load of 12 or more semester or quarter credits. At the postbaccalaureate level, full-time enrollment includes students who typically have a credit load of 9 or more semester or quarter credits, as well as other students who are considered full time by their institutions.

Full-time-equivalent (FTE) enrollment For postsecondary institutions, enrollment of full-time students, plus the full-time equivalent of part-time students. The full-time equivalent of the part-time students is estimated using different factors depending on the type and control of institution and level of student.

Full-time-equivalent (FTE) staff Full-time staff, plus the full-time equivalent of the part-time staff.

Full-time-equivalent teacher See Instructional staff.

Full-time instructional faculty Those members of the instruction/research staff who are employed full time as defined by the institution, including faculty with released time for research and faculty on sabbatical leave. Full-time counts exclude faculty who are employed to teach less than two semesters, three quarters, two trimesters, or two 4-month sessions; replacements for faculty on sabbatical leave or those on leave without pay; faculty for preclinical and clinical medicine; faculty who are donating their services; faculty who are members of military organizations and paid on a different pay scale than civilian employees; those academic officers whose primary duties are administrative; and graduate students who assist in the instruction of courses.

Full-time worker In educational institutions, an employee whose position requires being on the job on school days throughout the school year for at least the number of hours the schools are in session. For higher education, a member of an educational institution's staff who is employed full time, as defined by the institution.

Function A mathematical correspondence that assigns exactly one element of one set to each element of the same or another set. A variable that depends on and varies with another.

Functional form A mathematical statement of the relationship among the variables in a model.

Gap Occurs when an outcome—for example, average test score or level of educational attainment—is higher for one group than for another group, and the difference between the two groups' outcomes is statistically significant.

GED certificate An award that is received following successful completion of the GED test. The GED program—sponsored by the GED Testing Service (a joint venture of the American Council on Education and Pearson)—enables individuals to demonstrate that they have acquired a level of learning comparable to that of high school graduates. See also High school equivalency certificate.

GED program Academic instruction to prepare people to take the high school equivalency examination. Formerly known as the General Educational Development program. See also GED recipient.

GED recipient A person who has obtained certification of high school equivalency by meeting state requirements and passing an approved exam, which is intended to provide an appraisal of the person's achievement or performance in the broad subject matter areas usually required for high school graduation.

General administration support services Includes salary, benefits, supplies, and contractual fees for boards of education staff and executive administration. Excludes state administration.

General program A program of studies designed to prepare students for the common activities of a citizen, family member, and worker. A general program of studies may include instruction in both academic and vocational areas.

Geographic region One of the four regions of the United States used by the U.S. Census Bureau, as follows:

Northeast	*Midwest*
Connecticut (CT)	Illinois (IL)
Maine (ME)	Indiana (IN)
Massachusetts (MA)	Iowa (IA)
New Hampshire (NH)	Kansas (KS)
New Jersey (NJ)	Michigan (MI)
New York (NY)	Minnesota (MN)
Pennsylvania (PA)	Missouri (MO)
Rhode Island (RI)	Nebraska (NE)
Vermont (VT)	North Dakota (ND)
	Ohio (OH)
	South Dakota (SD)
	Wisconsin (WI)

South	*West*
Alabama (AL)	Alaska (AK)
Arkansas (AR)	Arizona (AZ)
Delaware (DE)	California (CA)
District of Columbia (DC)	Colorado (CO)
Florida (FL)	Hawaii (HI)
Georgia (GA)	Idaho (ID)
Kentucky (KY)	Montana (MT)
Louisiana (LA)	Nevada (NV)
Maryland (MD)	New Mexico (NM)
Mississippi (MS)	Oregon (OR)
North Carolina (NC)	Utah (UT)
Oklahoma (OK)	Washington (WA)
South Carolina (SC)	Wyoming (WY)
Tennessee (TN)	
Texas (TX)	
Virginia (VA)	
West Virginia (WV)	

Government appropriation An amount (other than a grant or contract) received from or made available to an institution through an act of a legislative body.

Government grant or contract Revenues received by a postsecondary institution from a government agency for a specific research project or other program. Examples are research projects, training programs, and student financial assistance.

Graduate An individual who has received formal recognition for the successful completion of a prescribed program of studies.

Graduate assistants See Employees in degree-granting institutions.

Graduate enrollment The number of students who are working toward a master's or doctor's degree and students who are in postbaccalaureate classes but not in degree programs.

Graduate Record Examination (GRE) Multiple-choice examinations administered by the Educational Testing Service and taken by college students who intend to attend certain graduate schools. There are two types of testing available: (1) the general exam which measures critical thinking, analytical writing, verbal reasoning, and quantitative reasoning skills, and (2) the subject test which is offered in eight specific subjects and gauges undergraduate achievement in a specific field. The subject tests are intended for those who have majored in or have extensive background in that specific area.

Graduation Formal recognition given to an individual for the successful completion of a prescribed program of studies.

Gross domestic product (GDP) The total national output of goods and services valued at market prices. GDP can be viewed in terms of expenditure categories that include purchases of goods and services by consumers and government, gross private domestic investment, and net exports of goods and services. The goods and services included are largely those bought for final use (excluding illegal transactions) in the market economy. A number of inclusions, however, represent imputed values, the most important of which is rental value of owner-occupied housing.

Group quarters Living arrangements where people live or stay in a group situation that is owned or managed by an entity or organization providing housing and/or services for the residents. Group quarters include such places as college residence halls, residential treatment centers, skilled nursing facilities, group homes, military barracks, correctional facilities, and workers' dormitories.

> ***Noninstitutionalized group quarters*** Include college and university housing, military quarters, facilities for workers and religious groups, and temporary shelters for the homeless.
>
> ***Institutionalized group quarters*** Include adult and juvenile correctional facilities, nursing facilities, and other health care facilities.

Handicapped See Disabilities, children with.

Head Start A local public or private nonprofit or for-profit entity authorized by the Department of Health and Human Services' Administration for Children and Families to operate a Head Start program to serve children age 3 to compulsory school age, pursuant to section 641(b) and (d) of the Head Start Act.

Hearing impairment See Disabilities, children with.

High school A secondary school offering the final years of high school work necessary for graduation. A high school is usually either a 3-year school that includes grades 10, 11, and 12 or a 4-year school that includes grades 9, 10, 11, and 12.

High school (2007–08 Schools and Staffing Survey) A school with no grade lower than 7 and at least one grade higher than 8.

High school completer An individual who has been awarded a high school diploma or an equivalent credential, including a GED certificate.

High school diploma A formal document regulated by the state certifying the successful completion of a prescribed secondary school program of studies. In some states or communities, high school diplomas are differentiated by type, such as an academic diploma, a general diploma, or a vocational diploma.

High school equivalency certificate A formal document certifying that an individual has met the state requirements for high school graduation equivalency by obtaining satisfactory scores on an approved examination and meeting other performance requirements (if any) set by a state education agency or other appropriate body. One particular version of this certificate is the GED test. The GED test is a comprehensive test used primarily to appraise the educational development of students who have not completed their formal high school education and who may earn a high school equivalency certificate by achieving satisfactory scores. GEDs are awarded by the states or other agencies, and the test is developed and distributed by the GED Testing Service (a joint venture of the American Council on Education and Pearson).

High school program A program of studies designed to prepare students for employment and postsecondary education. Three types of programs are often distinguished—academic, vocational, and general. An academic program is designed to prepare students for continued study at a college or university. A vocational program is designed to prepare students for employment in one or more semiskilled, skilled, or technical occupations. A general program is designed to provide students with the understanding and competence to function effectively in a free society and usually represents a mixture of academic and vocational components.

Higher education Study beyond secondary school at an institution that offers programs terminating in an associate's, bachelor's, or higher degree.

Higher education institutions (basic classification and Carnegie classification) See Postsecondary institutions (basic classification by level) and Postsecondary institutions (Carnegie classification of degree-granting institutions).

Higher Education Price Index A price index that measures average changes in the prices of goods and services purchased by colleges and universities through current-fund education and general expenditures (excluding expenditures for sponsored research and auxiliary enterprises).

Historically black colleges and universities Accredited higher education institutions established prior to 1964 with the principal mission of educating Black Americans. Federal regulations (20 USC 1061 (2)) allow for certain exceptions of the founding date.

Hours worked per week According to the October Current Population Survey, the number of hours a respondent worked in all jobs in the week prior to the survey interview.

Household All the people who occupy a housing unit. A house, an apartment, a mobile home, a group of rooms, or a single room is regarded as a housing unit when it is occupied or intended for occupancy as separate living quarters, that is, when the occupants do not live and eat with any other people in the structure, and there is direct access from the outside or through a common hall.

Housing unit A house, an apartment, a mobile home, a group of rooms, or a single room that is occupied as separate living quarters.

Income tax Taxes levied on net income, that is, on gross income less certain deductions permitted by law. These taxes can be levied on individuals or on corporations or unincorporated businesses where the income is taxed distinctly from individual income.

Independent operations A group of self-supporting activities under control of a college or university. For purposes of financial surveys conducted by the National Center for Education Statistics, this category is composed principally of federally funded research and development centers (FFRDC).

Independent variable In regression analysis, a random variable, y, is expressed as a function of variables x1, x2, ... xk, plus a stochastic term; the x's are known as "independent variables."

Individuals with Disabilities Education Act (IDEA) IDEA is a federal law enacted in 1990 and reauthorized in 1997 and 2004. IDEA requires services to children with disabilities throughout the nation. IDEA governs how states and public agencies provide early intervention, special education, and related services to eligible infants, toddlers, children, and youth with disabilities. Infants and toddlers with disabilities (birth–age 2) and their families receive early intervention services under IDEA, Part C. Children and youth (ages 3–21) receive special education and related services under IDEA, Part B.

Inflation A rise in the general level of prices of goods and services in an economy over a period of time, which generally corresponds to a decline in the real value of money or a loss of purchasing power. See also Constant dollars and Purchasing Power Parity indexes.

Institutional support The category of higher education expenditures that includes day-to-day operational support for colleges, excluding expenditures for physical plant operations. Examples of institutional support include general administrative services, executive direction and planning, legal and fiscal operations, and community relations.

Instruction (colleges and universities) That functional category including expenditures of the colleges, schools, departments, and other instructional divisions of higher education institutions and expenditures for departmental research and public service that are not separately budgeted; includes expenditures for both credit and noncredit activities. Excludes expenditures for academic administration where the primary function is administration (e.g., academic deans).

Instruction (elementary and secondary) Instruction encompasses all activities dealing directly with the interaction between teachers and students. Teaching may be provided for students in a school classroom, in another location such as a home or hospital, and in other learning situations such as those involving co-curricular activities. Instruction may be provided through some other approved medium, such as the Internet, television, radio, telephone, and correspondence.

Instructional staff Full-time-equivalent number of positions, not the number of different individuals occupying the positions during the school year. In local schools, includes all public elementary and secondary (junior and senior high) day-school positions that are in the nature of teaching or in the improvement of the teaching-learning situation; includes consultants or supervisors of instruction, principals, teachers, guidance personnel, librarians, psychological personnel, and other instructional staff, and excludes administrative staff, attendance personnel, clerical personnel, and junior college staff.

Instructional support services Includes salary, benefits, supplies, and contractual fees for staff providing instructional improvement, educational media (library and audiovisual), and other instructional support services.

Intellectual disability See Disabilities, children with.

Interest on debt Includes expenditures for long-term debt service interest payments (i.e., those longer than 1 year).

International baccalaureate (IB) A recognized international program of primary, middle, and secondary studies leading to the International Baccalaureate (IB) Diploma. This diploma (or certificate) is recognized in Europe and elsewhere as qualifying holders for direct access to university studies. Schools offering the IB program are approved by the International Baccalaureate Organization (IBO) and their regional office and may use IBO instructional materials, local school materials, or a combination.

International finance data Include data on public and private expenditures for educational institutions. Educational institutions directly provide instructional programs (i.e., teaching) to individuals in an organized group setting or through distance education. Business enterprises or other institutions that provide short-term courses of training or instruction to individuals on a "one-to-one" basis are not included. Where noted, international finance data may also include publicly subsidized spending on education-related purchases, such as school books, living costs, and transportation.

Public expenditures Corresponds to the nonrepayable current and capital expenditures of all levels of the government directly related to education. Expenditures that are not directly related to education (e.g., cultures, sports, youth activities) are, in principle, not included. Expenditures on education by other ministries or equivalent institutions (e.g., Health and Agriculture) are included. Public subsidies for students' living expenses are excluded to ensure international comparability of the data.

Private expenditures Refers to expenditures funded by private sources (i.e., households and other private entities). "Households" means students and their families. "Other private entities" includes private business firms and nonprofit organizations, including religious organizations, charitable organizations, and business and labor associations. Private expenditures are composed of school fees, the cost of materials (such as textbooks and teaching equipment), transportation costs (if organized by the school), the cost of meals (if provided by the school), boarding fees, and expenditures by employers on initial vocational training.

Current expenditures Includes final consumption expenditures (e.g., compensation of employees, consumption of intermediate goods and services, consumption of fixed capital, and military expenditures); property income paid; subsidies; and other current transfers paid.

Capital expenditures Includes spending to acquire and improve fixed capital assets, land, intangible assets, government stocks, and nonmilitary, nonfinancial assets, as well as spending to finance net capital transfers.

International Standard Classification of Education (ISCED) Used to compare educational systems in different countries. ISCED is the standard used by many countries to report education statistics to the United Nations Educational, Scientific, and Cultural Organization (UNESCO) and the Organization for Economic Cooperation and Development (OECD). ISCED was revised in 2011.

ISCED 2011 ISCED 2011 divides educational systems into the following nine categories, based on eight levels of education.

ISCED Level 0 Education preceding the first level (early childhood education) includes early childhood programs that target children below the age of entry into primary education.

ISCED Level 01 Early childhood educational development programs are generally designed for children younger than 3 years.

ISCED Level 02 Pre-primary education preceding the first level usually begins at age 3, 4, or 5 (sometimes earlier) and lasts from 1 to 3 years, when it is provided. In the United States, this level includes nursery school and kindergarten.

ISCED Level 1 Education at the first level (primary or elementary education) usually begins at age 5, 6, or 7 and continues for about 4 to 6 years. For the United States, the first level starts with 1st grade and ends with 6th grade.

ISCED Level 2 Education at the second level (lower secondary education) typically begins at about age 11 or 12 and continues for about 2 to 6 years. For the United States, the second level starts with 7th grade and typically ends with 9th grade. Education at the lower secondary level continues the basic programs of the first level, although teaching is typically more subject focused, often using more specialized teachers who conduct classes in their field of specialization. The main criterion for distinguishing lower secondary education from primary education is whether programs begin to be organized in a more subject-oriented pattern, using more specialized teachers conducting classes in their field of specialization. If there is no clear breakpoint for this organizational change, lower secondary education is considered to begin at the end of 6 years of primary education. In countries with no clear division between lower secondary and upper secondary education, and where lower secondary education lasts for more than 3 years, only the first 3 years following primary education are counted as lower secondary education.

ISCED Level 3 Education at the third level (upper secondary education) typically begins at age 15 or 16 and lasts for approximately 3 years. In the United States, the third level starts with 10th grade and ends with 12th grade. Upper secondary education is the final stage of secondary education in most OECD countries. Instruction is often organized along subject-matter lines, in contrast to the lower secondary level, and teachers typically must have a higher-level, or more subject-specific, qualification. There are substantial differences in the typical duration of programs both across and between countries, ranging from 2 to 5 years of schooling. The main criteria for classifications are (1) national boundaries between lower and upper secondary education and (2) admission into educational programs, which usually requires the completion of lower secondary education or a combination of basic education and life experience that demonstrates the ability to handle the subject matter in upper secondary schools. Includes programs designed to review the content of third level programs, such as preparatory courses for tertiary education entrance examinations, and programs leading to a qualification equivalent to upper secondary general education.

ISCED Level 4 Education at the fourth level (postsecondary nontertiary education) straddles the boundary between secondary and postsecondary education. This program of study, which is primarily vocational in nature, is generally taken after the completion of secondary school and typically lasts from 6 months to 2 years. Although the content of these programs may not be significantly more advanced than upper secondary programs, these programs serve to broaden the knowledge of participants who have already gained an upper secondary qualification.

ISCED Level 5 Education at the fifth level (short-cycle tertiary education) is noticeably more complex than in upper secondary programs giving access to this level. Programs at the fifth level typically provide practically based, occupationally specific content and prepare students to enter the labor market. However, the fifth level may also provide a pathway to other tertiary education programs (the sixth or seventh level). Short-cycle tertiary programs last for at least 2 years, and usually for no more than 3. In the United States, this level includes associate's degrees.

ISCED Level 6 Education at the sixth level (bachelor's or equivalent level) is longer and usually more theoretically oriented than programs at the fifth level, but may include practical components. Entry into these programs normally requires the completion of a third or fourth level program. They typically have a duration of 3 to 4 years of full-time study. Programs at the sixth level do not necessarily require the preparation of a substantive thesis or dissertation.

ISCED Level 7 Education at the seventh level (master's or equivalent level) has significantly more complex and specialized content than programs at the sixth level. The content at the seventh level is often designed to provide participants with advanced academic and/or professional knowledge, skills, and competencies, leading to a second degree or equivalent qualification. Programs at this level may have a substantial research component but do not yet lead to the award of a doctoral qualification. In the United States, this level includes professional degrees such as J.D., M.D., and D.D.S., as well as master's degrees.

ISCED Level 8 Education at the eighth level (doctoral or equivalent level) is provided in graduate and professional schools that generally require a university degree or diploma as a minimum condition for admission. Programs at this level lead to the award of an advanced, postgraduate degree, such as a Ph.D. The theoretical duration of these programs is 3 years of full-time enrollment in most countries (for a cumulative total of at least 7 years at the tertiary level), although the length of the actual enrollment is often longer. Programs at this level are devoted to advanced study and original research.

ISCED 1997 ISCED 1997 divides educational systems into the following seven categories, based on six levels of education.

ISCED Level 0 Education preceding the first level (early childhood education) usually begins at age 3, 4, or 5 (sometimes earlier) and lasts from 1 to 3 years, when it is provided. In the United States, this level includes nursery school and kindergarten.

ISCED Level 1 Education at the first level (primary or elementary education) usually begins at age 5, 6, or 7 and continues for about 4 to 6 years. For the United States, the first level starts with 1st grade and ends with 6th grade.

ISCED Level 2 Education at the second level (lower secondary education) typically begins at about age 11 or 12 and continues for about 2 to 6 years. For the United States, the second level starts with 7th grade and typically ends with 9th grade. Education at the lower secondary level continues the basic programs of the first level, although teaching is typically more subject focused, often using more specialized teachers who conduct classes in their field of specialization. The main criterion for distinguishing lower secondary education from primary education is whether programs begin to be organized in a more subject-oriented pattern, using more specialized teachers conducting classes in their field of specialization. If there is no clear breakpoint for this organizational change, lower secondary education is considered to begin at the end of 6 years of primary education. In countries with no clear division between lower secondary and upper secondary education, and where lower secondary education lasts for more than 3 years, only the first 3 years following primary education are counted as lower secondary education.

ISCED Level 3 Education at the third level (upper secondary education) typically begins at age 15 or 16 and lasts for approximately 3 years. In the United States, the third level starts with 10th grade and ends with 12th grade. Upper secondary education is the final stage of secondary education in most OECD countries. Instruction is often organized along subject-matter lines, in contrast to the lower secondary level, and teachers typically must have a higher-level, or more subject-specific, qualification. There are substantial differences in the typical duration of programs both across and between countries, ranging from 2 to 5 years of schooling. The main criteria for classifications are (1) national boundaries between lower and upper secondary education and (2) admission into educational programs, which usually requires the completion of lower secondary education or a combination of basic education and life experience that demonstrates the ability to handle the subject matter in upper secondary schools.

ISCED Level 4 Education at the fourth level (postsecondary nontertiary education) straddles the boundary between secondary and postsecondary education. This program of study, which is primarily vocational in nature, is generally taken after the completion of secondary school and typically lasts from 6 months to 2 years. Although the content of these programs may not be significantly more advanced than upper secondary programs, these programs serve to broaden the knowledge of participants who have already gained an upper secondary qualification.

ISCED Level 5 Education at the fifth level (first stage of tertiary education) includes programs with more advanced content than those offered at the two previous levels. Entry into programs at the fifth level normally requires successful completion of either of the two previous levels.

ISCED Level 5A Tertiary-type A programs provide an education that is largely theoretical and is intended to provide sufficient qualifications for gaining entry into advanced research programs and professions with high skill requirements. Entry into these programs normally requires the successful completion of an upper secondary education; admission is competitive in most cases. The minimum cumulative theoretical duration at this level is 3 years of full-time enrollment. In the United States, tertiary-type A programs include first university programs that last approximately 4 years and lead to the award of a bachelor's degree and second university programs that lead to a master's degree or a first-professional degree such as an M.D., a J.D., or a D.V.M.

ISCED Level 5B Tertiary-type B programs are typically shorter than tertiary-type A programs and focus on practical, technical, or occupational skills for direct entry into the labor market, although they may cover some theoretical foundations in the respective programs. They have a minimum duration of 2 years of full-time enrollment at the tertiary level. In the United States, such programs are often provided at community colleges and lead to an associate's degree.

ISCED Level 6 Education at the sixth level (advanced research qualification) is provided in graduate and professional schools that generally require a university degree or diploma as a minimum condition for admission. Programs at this level lead to the award of an advanced, postgraduate degree, such as a Ph.D. The theoretical duration of these programs is 3 years of full-time enrollment in most countries (for a cumulative total of at least 7 years at levels five and six), although the length of the actual enrollment is often longer. Programs at this level are devoted to advanced study and original research.

Interpolation See Linear interpolation.

Junior high school A separately organized and administered secondary school intermediate between the elementary and senior high schools. A junior high school is usually either a 3-year school that includes grades 7, 8, and 9 or a 2-year school that includes grades 7 and 8.

Labor force People employed (either full time or part time) as civilians, unemployed but looking for work, or in the armed services during the survey week. The "civilian labor force" comprises all civilians classified as employed or unemployed. See also Unemployed.

Lag An event occurring at time $t + k$ ($k > 0$) is said to lag behind an event occurring at time t, the extent of the lag being k. An event occurring k time periods before another may be regarded as having a negative lag.

Land-grant colleges The First Morrill Act of 1862 facilitated the establishment of colleges through grants of land or funds in lieu of land. The Second Morrill Act in 1890 provided for money grants and for the establishment of land-grant colleges and universities for Black Americans in those states with dual systems of higher education.

Lead time When forecasting a statistic, the number of time periods since the last time period of actual data for that statistic used in producing the forecast.

Level of school A classification of elementary/secondary schools by instructional level. Includes elementary schools, secondary schools, and combined elementary and secondary schools. See also Elementary school, Secondary school, and Combined school.

Limited English proficient Refers to an individual who was not born in the United States and whose native language is a language other than English, or who comes from an environment where a language other than English has had a significant impact on the individual's level of English language proficiency. It may also refer to an individual who is migratory, whose native language is a language other than English, and who comes from an environment where a language other than English is dominant; and whose difficulties in speaking, reading, writing, or understanding the English language may be sufficient to deny the individual the ability to meet the state's proficient level of achievement on state assessments as specified under the Every Student Succeeds Act (2015), the ability to successfully achieve in classrooms where the language of instruction is English, or the opportunity to participate fully in society. See also English language learner.

Linear interpolation A method that allows the prediction of an unknown value if any two particular values on the same scale are known and the rate of change is assumed constant.

Local education agency (LEA) See School district.

Locale codes A classification system to describe a type of location. The "Metro-Centric" locale codes, developed in the 1980s, classified locations based on their proximity to a Metropolitan Statistical Area (MSA) and their population size and density. In 2006, the "Urban-Centric" locale codes were introduced. These locale codes are based on an address's proximity to an urbanized area. For more information see https://nces.ed.gov/ccd/CCDLocaleCodeDistrict.asp.

Pre-2006 Metro-Centric Locale Codes (used in *Digest of Education Statistics* tables that reference "urbanicity"). The eight urbanicity subcategories are often collapsed into three major categories—urban, suburban, and rural—as shown below.

Urban

Large City: A central city of a consolidated metropolitan statistical area (CMSA) or MSA, with the city having a population greater than or equal to 250,000.

Mid-size City: A central city of a CMSA or MSA, with the city having a population less than 250,000.

Suburban

Urban Fringe of a Large City: Any territory within a CMSA or MSA of a Large City and defined as urban by the Census Bureau.

Urban Fringe of a Mid-size City: Any territory within a CMSA or MSA of a Mid-size City and defined as urban by the Census Bureau.

Rural (not within a CMSA or MSA)

Large Town: An incorporated place or Census-designated place with a population greater than or equal to 25,000 and located outside a CMSA or MSA.

Small Town: An incorporated place or Census-designated place with a population less than 25,000 and greater than or equal to 2,500 and located outside a CMSA or MSA.

Rural, Outside MSA: Any territory designated as rural by the Census Bureau that is outside a CMSA or MSA of a Large or Mid-size City.

Rural, Inside MSA: Any territory designated as rural by the Census Bureau that is within a CMSA or MSA of a Large or Mid-size City.

2006 Urban-Centric Locale Codes (used in *Digest of Education Statistics* tables that reference "locale"). The 12 locale subcategories are often collapsed into 4 major categories—city, suburban, town, and rural—as shown below.

City

City, Large: Territory inside an urbanized area and inside a principal city with population of 250,000 or more.

City, Midsize: Territory inside an urbanized area and inside a principal city with population less than 250,000 and greater than or equal to 100,000.

City, Small: Territory inside an urbanized area and inside a principal city with population less than 100,000.

Suburban

Suburb, Large: Territory outside a principal city and inside an urbanized area with population of 250,000 or more.

Suburb, Midsize: Territory outside a principal city and inside an urbanized area with population less than 250,000 and greater than or equal to 100,000.

Suburb, Small: Territory outside a principal city and inside an urbanized area with population less than 100,000.

Town

Town, Fringe: Territory inside an urban cluster that is less than or equal to 10 miles from an urbanized area.

Town, Distant: Territory inside an urban cluster that is more than 10 miles and less than or equal to 35 miles from an urbanized area.

Town, Remote: Territory inside an urban cluster that is more than 35 miles from an urbanized area.

Rural

Rural, Fringe: Census-defined rural territory that is less than or equal to 5 miles from an urbanized area, as well as rural territory that is less than or equal to 2.5 miles from an urban cluster.

Rural, Distant: Census-defined rural territory that is more than 5 miles but less than or equal to 25 miles from an urbanized area, as well as rural territory that is more than 2.5 miles but less than or equal to 10 miles from an urban cluster.

Rural, Remote: Census-defined rural territory that is more than 25 miles from an urbanized area and is also more than 10 miles from an urban cluster.

Magnet school or program A special school or program designed to reduce, prevent, or eliminate racial isolation and/or to provide an academic or social focus on a particular theme.

Mandatory transfer A transfer of current funds that must be made in order to fulfill a binding legal obligation of a postsecondary institution. Included under mandatory transfers are debt service provisions relating to academic and administrative buildings, including (1) amounts set aside for debt retirement and interest and (2) required provisions for renewal and replacement of buildings to the extent these are not financed from other funds.

Margin of error The range of potential true or actual values for a sample survey estimate. The margin of error depends on several factors such as the amount of variation in the responses, the size and representativeness of the sample, and the size of the subgroup for which the estimate is computed. The magnitude of the margin of error is represented by the standard error of the estimate.

Master's degree A degree awarded for successful completion of a program generally requiring 1 or 2 years of full-time college-level study beyond the bachelor's degree. One type of master's degree, including the Master of Arts degree, or M.A., and the Master of Science degree, or M.S., is awarded in the liberal arts and sciences for advanced scholarship in a subject field or discipline and demonstrated ability to perform scholarly research. A second type of master's degree is awarded for the completion of a professionally oriented program, for example, an M.Ed. in education, an M.B.A. in business administration, an M.F.A. in fine arts, an M.M. in music, an M.S.W. in social work, and an M.P.A. in public administration. Some master's degrees—such as divinity degrees (M.Div. or M.H.L./Rav), which were formerly classified as "first-professional"—may require more than 2 years of full-time study beyond the bachelor's degree.

Mathematics A group of instructional programs that describes the science of numbers and their operations, interrelations, combinations, generalizations, and abstractions and of space configurations and their structure, measurement, transformations, and generalizations.

Mean absolute percentage error (MAPE) The average value of the absolute value of errors expressed in percentage terms.

Mean test score The score obtained by dividing the sum of the scores of all individuals in a group by the number of individuals in that group for which scores are available.

Median earnings The amount that divides the income distribution into two equal groups, half having income above that amount and half having income below that amount. Earnings include all wage and salary income. Unlike mean earnings, median earnings either do not change or change very little in response to extreme observations.

Middle school A school with no grade lower than 5 and no grade higher than 8.

Migration Geographic mobility involving a change of usual residence between clearly defined geographic units, that is, between counties, states, or regions.

Minimum-competency testing Measuring the acquisition of competence or skills to or beyond a certain specified standard.

Model A system of postulates, data, and inferences presented as a mathematical description of a phenomenon, such as an actual system or process. The actual phenomenon is represented by the model in order to explain, predict, and control it.

Montessori school A school that provides instruction using Montessori teaching methods.

Multiple disabilities See Disabilities, children with.

National Assessment of Educational Progress (NAEP) See Appendix A: Guide to Sources.

National School Lunch Program Established by President Truman in 1946, the program is a federally assisted meal program operated in public and private nonprofit schools and residential child care centers. To be eligible for free lunch, a student must be from a household with an income at or below 130 percent of the federal poverty guideline; to be eligible for reduced-price lunch, a student must be from a household with an income between 130 percent and 185 percent of the federal poverty guideline.

Newly qualified teachers People who (1) first became eligible for a teaching license during the period of the study referenced or who were teaching at the time of survey, but were not certified or eligible for a teaching license; and (2) had never held full-time, regular teaching positions (as opposed to substitute) prior to completing the requirements for the degree that brought them into the survey.

Non-degree-granting institutions Postsecondary institutions that participate in Title IV federal financial aid programs but do not offer accredited 4-year or 2-year degree programs. Includes some institutions transitioning to higher level program offerings, though still classified at a lower level.

Nonprofessional staff See Employees in degree-granting institutions.

Nonprofit institution A private institution in which the individual(s) or agency in control receives no compensation other than wages, rent, or other expenses for the assumption of risk. Nonprofit institutions may be either independent nonprofit (i.e., having no religious affiliation) or religiously affiliated.

Nonresident alien A person who is not a citizen of the United States and who is in this country on a temporary basis and does not have the right to remain indefinitely.

Nonsectarian school Nonsectarian schools do not have a religious orientation or purpose and are categorized as regular, special program emphasis, or special education schools. See also Regular school, Special program emphasis school, and Special education school.

Nonsupervisory instructional staff People such as curriculum specialists, counselors, librarians, remedial specialists, and others possessing education certification, but not responsible for day-to-day teaching of the same group of pupils.

Nursery school An instructional program for groups of children during the year or years preceding kindergarten, which provides educational experiences under the direction of teachers. See also Prekindergarten and Preschool.

Obligations Amounts of orders placed, contracts awarded, services received, or similar legally binding commitments made by federal agencies during a given period that will require outlays during the same or some future period.

Occupied housing unit Separate living quarters with occupants currently inhabiting the unit. See also Housing unit.

Off-budget federal entities Organizational entities, federally owned in whole or in part, whose transactions belong in the budget under current budget accounting concepts, but that have been excluded from the budget totals under provisions of law. An example of an off-budget federal entity is the Federal Financing Bank, which provides student loans under the Direct Loan Program.

On-budget funding Federal funding for education programs that is tied to appropriations. On-budget funding does not include the Direct Loan Program, under which student loans are provided by the Federal Financing Bank, an off-budget federal entity. See also Off-budget federal entities.

Operation and maintenance services Includes salary, benefits, supplies, and contractual fees for supervision of operations and maintenance, operating buildings (heating, lighting, ventilating, repair, and replacement), care and upkeep of grounds and equipment, vehicle operations and maintenance (other than student transportation), security, and other operations and maintenance services.

Ordinary least squares (OLS) The estimator that minimizes the sum of squared residuals.

Organization for Economic Cooperation and Development (OECD) An intergovernmental organization of industrialized countries that serves as a forum for member countries to cooperate in research and policy development on social and economic topics of common interest. In addition to member countries, partner countries contribute to the OECD's work in a sustained and comprehensive manner.

Orthopedic impairment See Disabilities, children with.

Other health impairment See Disabilities, children with.

Other professional staff See Employees in degree-granting institutions.

Other religious school Other religious schools have a religious orientation or purpose, but are not Roman Catholic. Other religious schools are categorized according to religious association membership as Conservative Christian, other affiliated, or unaffiliated.

Other support services Includes salary, benefits, supplies, and contractual fees for business support services, central support services, and other support services not otherwise classified.

Other support services staff All staff not reported in other categories. This group includes media personnel, social workers, bus drivers, security, cafeteria workers, and other staff.

Outlays The value of checks issued, interest accrued on the public debt, or other payments made, net of refunds and reimbursements.

Parameter A quantity that describes a statistical population.

Part-time enrollment The number of students enrolled in postsecondary education courses with a total credit load less than 75 percent of the normal full-time credit load. At the undergraduate level, part-time enrollment typically includes students who have a credit load of less than 12 semester or quarter credits. At the postbaccalaureate level, part-time enrollment typically includes students who have a credit load of less than 9 semester or quarter credits.

Pass-through transaction A payment that a postsecondary institution applies directly to a student's account. The payment "passes through" the institution for the student's benefit. Most private institutions treat Pell grants as pass-through transactions. At these institutions, any Pell grant funds that are applied to a student's tuition are reported as tuition revenues. In contrast, the vast majority of public institutions report Pell grants both as federal revenues and as allowances that reduce tuition revenues.

Personal income Current income received by people from all sources, minus their personal contributions for social insurance. Classified as "people" are individuals (including owners of unincorporated firms), nonprofit institutions serving individuals, private trust funds, and private noninsured welfare funds. Personal income includes transfers (payments not resulting from current production) from government and business such as social security benefits and military pensions, but excludes transfers among people.

Physical plant assets Includes the values of land, buildings, and equipment owned, rented, or utilized by colleges. Does not include those plant values that are a part of endowment or other capital fund investments in real estate; excludes construction in progress.

Postbaccalaureate certificate An award that requires completion of an organized program of study beyond the bachelor's. It is designed for persons who have completed a bachelor's degree, but does not meet the requirements of a master's degree.

Postbaccalaureate enrollment The number of students working toward advanced degrees and of students enrolled in graduate-level classes but not enrolled in degree programs. See also Graduate enrollment.

Postsecondary education The provision of formal instructional programs with a curriculum designed primarily for students who have completed the requirements for a high school diploma or equivalent. This includes programs of an academic, vocational, and continuing professional education purpose, and excludes avocational and adult basic education programs.

Postsecondary institutions (basic classification by level)

4-year institution An institution offering at least a 4-year program of college-level studies wholly or principally creditable toward a baccalaureate degree.

2-year institution An institution offering at least a 2-year program of college-level studies that terminates in an associate degree or is principally creditable toward a baccalaureate degree. Data prior to 1996 include some institutions that have a less-than-2-year program, but were designated as higher education institutions in the Higher Education General Information Survey.

Less-than-2-year institution An institution that offers programs of less than 2 years' duration below the baccalaureate level. Includes occupational and vocational schools with programs that do not exceed 1,800 contact hours.

Postsecondary institutions (2005 Carnegie classification of degree-granting institutions)

Doctorate-granting Characterized by a significant level and breadth of activity in commitment to doctoral-level education as measured by the number of doctorate recipients and the diversity in doctoral-level program offerings. These institutions are assigned to one of the three subcategories listed below based on level of research activity (for more information on the research activity index used to assign institutions to the subcategories, see http://carnegieclassifications.iu.edu/):

Research university, very high Characterized by a very high level of research activity.

Research university, high Characterized by a high level of research activity.

Doctoral/research university Awarding at least 20 doctor's degrees per year, but not having a high level of research activity.

Master's Characterized by diverse postbaccalaureate programs but not engaged in significant doctoral-level education.

Baccalaureate Characterized by primary emphasis on general undergraduate, baccalaureate-level education. Not significantly engaged in postbaccalaureate education.

Special focus Baccalaureate or postbaccalaureate institution emphasizing one area (plus closely related specialties), such as business or engineering. The programmatic emphasis is measured by the percentage of degrees granted in the program area.

Associate's Institutions conferring at least 90 percent of their degrees and awards for work below the bachelor's level. In NCES tables, excludes all institutions offering any 4-year programs leading to a bachelor's degree.

Tribal Colleges and universities that are members of the American Indian Higher Education Consortium, as identified in IPEDS Institutional Characteristics.

Poverty (official measure) The U.S. Census Bureau uses a set of money income thresholds that vary by family size and composition. A family, along with each individual in it, is considered poor if the family's total income is less than that family's threshold. The poverty thresholds do not vary geographically and are adjusted annually for inflation using the Consumer Price Index. The official poverty definition counts money income before taxes and does not include capital gains and noncash benefits (such as public housing, Medicaid, and food stamps). See also Supplemental Poverty Measure (SPM).

Prekindergarten Preprimary education for children typically ages 3–4 who have not yet entered kindergarten. It may offer a program of general education or special education and may be part of a collaborative effort with Head Start.

Preschool An instructional program enrolling children generally younger than 5 years of age and organized to provide children with educational experiences under professionally qualified teachers during the year or years immediately preceding kindergarten (or prior to entry into elementary school when there is no kindergarten). See also Nursery school and Prekindergarten.

Primary school A school with at least one grade lower than 5 and no grade higher than 8.

Private institution An institution that is controlled by an individual or agency other than a state, a subdivision of a state, or the federal government; that is usually supported primarily by other than public funds; and the operation of whose program rests with other than publicly elected or appointed officials.

Private nonprofit institution An institution in which the individual(s) or agency in control receives no compensation other than wages, rent, or other expenses for the assumption of risk. These include both independent nonprofit institutions and those affiliated with a religious organization.

Private for-profit institution An institution in which the individual(s) or agency in control receives compensation other than wages, rent, or other expenses for the assumption of risk (e.g., proprietary schools).

Private school Private elementary/secondary schools surveyed by the Private School Universe Survey (PSS) are assigned to one of three major categories (Catholic, other religious, or nonsectarian) and, within each major category, one of three subcategories based on the school's religious affiliation provided by respondents.

Catholic Schools categorized according to governance, provided by Catholic school respondents, into parochial, diocesan, and private schools.

Other religious Schools that have a religious orientation or purpose but are not Roman Catholic. Other religious schools are categorized according to religious association membership, provided by respondents, into Conservative Christian, other affiliated, and unaffiliated schools. Conservative Christian schools are those "Other religious" schools with membership in at least one of four associations: Accelerated Christian Education, American Association of Christian Schools, Association of Christian Schools International, and Oral Roberts University Education Fellowship. Affiliated schools are those "Other religious" schools not classified as Conservative Christian with membership in at least 1 of 11 associations—Association of Christian Teachers and Schools, Christian Schools International, Evangelical Lutheran Education Association, Friends Council on Education, General Conference of the Seventh-Day Adventist Church, Islamic School League of America, National Association of Episcopal Schools, National Christian School Association, National Society for Hebrew Day Schools, Solomon Schechter Day Schools, and Southern Baptist Association of Christian Schools—or indicating membership in "other religious school associations." Unaffiliated schools are those "Other religious" schools that have a religious orientation or purpose but are not classified as Conservative Christian or affiliated.

Nonsectarian Schools that do not have a religious orientation or purpose and are categorized according to program emphasis, provided by respondents, into regular, special emphasis, and special education schools. Regular schools are those that have a regular elementary/secondary or early childhood program emphasis. Special emphasis schools are those that have a Montessori, vocational/technical, alternative, or special program emphasis. Special education schools are those that have a special education program emphasis.

Professional staff See Employees in degree-granting institutions.

Program for International Student Assessment (PISA) See Appendix A: Guide to Sources.

Projection In relation to a time series, an estimate of future values based on a current trend.

Property tax The sum of money collected from a tax levied against the value of property.

Proprietary (for profit) institution A private institution in which the individual(s) or agency in control receives compensation other than wages, rent, or other expenses for the assumption of risk.

Public school or institution A school or institution controlled and operated by publicly elected or appointed officials and deriving its primary support from public funds.

Pupil/teacher ratio The enrollment of pupils at a given period of time, divided by the full-time-equivalent number of classroom teachers serving these pupils during the same period.

Purchasing Power Parity (PPP) indexes PPP exchange rates, or indexes, are the currency exchange rates that equalize the purchasing power of different currencies, meaning that when a given sum of money is converted into different currencies at the PPP exchange rates, it will buy the same basket of goods and services in all countries. PPP indexes are the rates of currency conversion that eliminate the difference in price levels among countries. Thus, when expenditures on gross domestic product (GDP) for different countries are converted into a common currency by means of PPP indexes, they are expressed at the same set of international prices, so that comparisons among countries reflect only differences in the volume of goods and services purchased.

R^2 The coefficient of determination; the square of the correlation coefficient between the dependent variable and its ordinary least squares (OLS) estimate.

Racial/ethnic group Classification indicating general racial or ethnic heritage. Race/ethnicity data are based on the *Hispanic* ethnic category and the race categories listed below (five single-race categories, plus the *Two or more races* category). Race categories exclude persons of Hispanic ethnicity unless otherwise noted.

White A person having origins in any of the original peoples of Europe, the Middle East, or North Africa.

Black or African American A person having origins in any of the black racial groups of Africa. Used interchangeably with the shortened term *Black*.

Hispanic or Latino A person of Cuban, Mexican, Puerto Rican, South or Central American, or other Spanish culture or origin, regardless of race. Used interchangeably with the shortened term *Hispanic*.

Asian A person having origins in any of the original peoples of the Far East, Southeast Asia, or the Indian subcontinent, including, for example, Cambodia, China, India, Japan, Korea, Malaysia, Pakistan, the Philippine Islands, Thailand, and Vietnam. Prior to 2010–11, the Common Core of Data (CCD) combined Asian and Pacific Islander categories.

Native Hawaiian or Other Pacific Islander A person having origins in any of the original peoples of Hawaii, Guam, Samoa, or other Pacific Islands. Prior to 2010–11, the Common Core of Data (CCD) combined Asian and Pacific Islander categories. Used interchangeably with the shortened term *Pacific Islander*.

American Indian or Alaska Native A person having origins in any of the original peoples of North and South America (including Central America), and who maintains tribal affiliation or community attachment.

Two or more races A person identifying himself or herself as of two or more of the following race groups: White, Black, Asian, Native Hawaiian or Other Pacific Islander, or American Indian or Alaska Native. Some, but not all, reporting districts use this category. "Two or more races" was introduced in the 2000 Census and became a regular category for data collection in the Current Population Survey in 2003. The category is sometimes excluded from a historical series of data with constant categories. It is sometimes included within the category "Other."

Region See Geographic region.

Regression analysis A statistical technique for investigating and modeling the relationship between variables.

Regular school A public elementary/secondary or charter school providing instruction and education services that does not focus primarily on special education, vocational/technical education, or alternative education.

Related children Related children in a family include own children and all other children in the household who are related to the householder by birth, marriage, or adoption.

Remedial education Instruction for a student lacking those reading, writing, or math skills necessary to perform college-level work at the level required by the attended institution.

Resident population Includes civilian population and armed forces personnel residing within the United States; excludes armed forces personnel residing overseas.

Retention in grade Retaining a student in the same grade from one school year to the next.

Revenue All funds received from external sources, net of refunds, and correcting transactions. Noncash transactions, such as receipt of services, commodities, or other receipts in kind are excluded, as are funds received from the issuance of debt, liquidation of investments, and nonroutine sale of property.

Revenue receipts Additions to assets that do not incur an obligation that must be met at some future date and do not represent exchanges of property for money. Assets must be available for expenditures.

Rho A measure of the correlation coefficient between errors in time period *t* and time period *t* minus 1.

Rural location See Locale codes.

Salary The total amount regularly paid or stipulated to be paid to an individual, before deductions, for personal services rendered while on the payroll of a business or organization.

Sales and services Revenues derived from the sales of goods or services that are incidental to the conduct of instruction, research, or public service. Examples include film rentals, scientific and literary publications, testing services, university presses, and dairy products.

Sales tax Tax imposed upon the sale and consumption of goods and services. It can be imposed either as a general tax on the retail price of all goods and services sold or as a tax on the sale of selected goods and services.

SAT An examination administered by the Educational Testing Service and used to predict the facility with which an individual will progress in learning college-level academic subjects. It was formerly called the Scholastic Assessment Test.

Scholarships and fellowships This category of college expenditures applies only to money given in the form of outright grants and trainee stipends to individuals enrolled in formal coursework, either for credit or not. Aid to students in the form of tuition or fee remissions is included. College work-study funds are excluded and are reported under the program in which the student is working.

School A division of the school system consisting of students in one or more grades or other identifiable groups and organized to give instruction of a defined type. One school may share a building with another school or one school may be housed in several buildings. Excludes schools that have closed or are planned for the future.

School administration support services Includes salary, benefits, supplies, and contractual fees for the office of the principal, full-time department chairpersons, and graduation expenses.

School climate The social system and culture of the school, including the organizational structure of the school and values and expectations within it.

School district An education agency at the local level that exists primarily to operate public schools or to contract for public school services. Synonyms are "local basic administrative unit" and "local education agency."

Science The body of related courses concerned with knowledge of the physical and biological world and with the processes of discovering and validating this knowledge.

Secondary enrollment The total number of students registered in a school beginning with the next grade following an elementary or middle school (usually 7, 8, or 9) and ending with or below grade 12 at a given time.

Secondary instructional level The general level of instruction provided for pupils in secondary schools (generally covering grades 7 through 12 or 9 through 12) and any instruction of a comparable nature and difficulty provided for adults and youth beyond the age of compulsory school attendance.

Secondary school A school comprising any span of grades beginning with the next grade following an elementary or middle school (usually 7, 8, or 9) and ending with or below grade 12. Both junior high schools and senior high schools are included.

Senior high school A secondary school offering the final years of high school work necessary for graduation.

Serial correlation Correlation of the error terms from different observations of the same variable. Also called Autocorrelation.

Serial volumes Publications issued in successive parts, usually at regular intervals, and as a rule, intended to be continued indefinitely. Serials include periodicals, newspapers, annuals, memoirs, proceedings, and transactions of societies.

Social studies A group of instructional programs that describes the substantive portions of behavior, past and present activities, interactions, and organizations of people associated together for religious, benevolent, cultural, scientific, political, patriotic, or other purposes.

Socioeconomic status (SES) The SES index is a composite of often equally weighted, standardized components, such as parental education and occupations, and family income. The terms high, middle, and low SES refer to ranges of the weighted SES composite index distribution.

Special education Direct instructional activities or special learning experiences designed primarily for students identified as having exceptionalities in one or more aspects of the cognitive process or as being underachievers in relation to general level or model of their overall abilities. Such services usually are directed at students with the following conditions: (1) physically disabled; (2) emotionally disabled; (3) culturally different, including compensatory education; (4) intellectually disabled; and (5) students with learning disabilities. Programs for the mentally gifted and talented are also included in some special education programs. See also Disabilities, children with.

Special education school A public elementary/secondary school that focuses primarily on special education for children with disabilities and that adapts curriculum, materials, or instruction for students served. See also Disabilities, children with.

Special program emphasis school A science/mathematics school, a performing arts high school, a foreign language immersion school, and a talented/gifted school are examples of schools that offer a special program emphasis.

Specific learning disability See Disabilities, children with.

Speech or language impairment See Disabilities, children with.

Standard error of estimate An expression for the standard deviation of the observed values about a regression line. An estimate of the variation likely to be encountered in making predictions from the regression equation.

Standardized test A test composed of a systematic sampling of behavior, administered and scored according to specific instructions, capable of being interpreted in terms of adequate norms, and for which there are data on reliability and validity.

Standardized test performance The weighted distributions of composite scores from standardized tests used to group students according to performance.

Status dropout rate The percentage of individuals within a given age range who are not enrolled in school and lack a high school credential, regardless of when they dropped out.

Status dropout rate (Current Population Survey) The percentage of civilian, noninstitutionalized young people ages 16–24 who are not in school and have not earned a high school credential (either a diploma or equivalency credential such as a GED certificate). The numerator of the status dropout rate for a given year is the number of individuals ages 16–24 who, as of October of that year, have not completed a high school credential and are not currently enrolled in school. The denominator is the total number of individuals ages 16–24 in the United States in October of that year. Status dropout rates count the following individuals as dropouts: those who never attended school and immigrants who did not complete the equivalent of a high school education in their home country.

Status dropout rate (American Community Survey) Similar to the status dropout rate (Current Population Survey), except that institutionalized persons, incarcerated persons, and active duty military personnel living in barracks in the United States may be included in this calculation.

STEM fields Science, Technology, Engineering, and Mathematics (STEM) fields of study that are considered to be of particular relevance to advanced societies. In current *Digest of Education Statistics* tables, STEM fields include biological and biomedical sciences, computer and information sciences, engineering and engineering technologies, mathematics and statistics, and physical sciences and science technologies. STEM occupations include computer scientists and mathematicians; engineers; life and physical scientists; and managers of STEM activities.

Student An individual for whom instruction is provided in an educational program under the jurisdiction of a school, school system, or other education institution. No distinction is made between the terms "student" and "pupil," though "student" may refer to one receiving instruction at any level while "pupil" refers only to one attending school at the elementary or secondary level. A student may receive instruction in a school facility or in another location, such as at home or in a hospital. Instruction may be provided by direct student-teacher interaction or by some other approved medium such as television, radio, telephone, and correspondence.

Student membership Student membership is an annual headcount of students enrolled in school on October 1 or the school day closest to that date. The Common Core of Data (CCD) allows a student to be reported for only a single school or agency. For example, a vocational school (identified as a "shared time" school) may provide classes for students from a number of districts and show no membership.

Student support services Includes salary, benefits, supplies, and contractual fees for staff providing attendance and social work, guidance, health, psychological services, speech pathology, audiology, and other support to students.

Study abroad population U.S. citizens and permanent residents, enrolled for a degree at an accredited higher education institution in the United States, who received academic credit for study abroad from their home institutions upon their return. Students studying abroad without receiving academic credit are not included, nor are U.S. students enrolled for a degree overseas.

Suburban location See Locale codes.

Supervisory staff Principals, assistant principals, and supervisors of instruction; does not include superintendents or assistant superintendents.

Supplemental Poverty Measure (SPM) An alternative measure of poverty that supplements the U.S. Census Bureau's official poverty measure by adding to family income the value of benefits—including nutritional assistance, housing subsidies, and home energy assistance—from many government programs designed to assist those with low incomes, subtracting taxes and necessary expenses such as child care costs (for working families) and out-of-pocket medical expenses, and adjusting poverty thresholds for geographic differences in housing costs. See also Poverty (official measure).

Suspension Temporarily removing a student from his or her regular classroom (an in-school suspension) or from his or her regular school (an out-of-school suspension), generally for disciplinary purposes.

Tax base The collective value of objects, assets, and income components against which a tax is levied.

Tax expenditures Losses of tax revenue attributable to provisions of the federal income tax laws that allow a special exclusion, exemption, or deduction from gross income or provide a special credit, preferential rate of tax, or a deferral of tax liability affecting individual or corporate income tax liabilities.

Teacher see Instructional staff.

Technical education A program of vocational instruction that ordinarily includes the study of the sciences and mathematics underlying a technology, as well as the methods, skills, and materials commonly used and the services performed in the technology. Technical education prepares individuals for positions—such as draftsman or lab technician—in the occupational area between the skilled craftsman and the professional person.

Three-year moving average An arithmetic average of the year indicated, the year immediately preceding, and the year immediately following. Use of a 3-year moving average increases the sample size, thereby reducing the size of sampling errors and producing more stable estimates.

Time series A set of ordered observations on a quantitative characteristic of an individual or collective phenomenon taken at different points in time. Usually the observations are successive and equally spaced in time.

Time series analysis The branch of quantitative forecasting in which data for one variable are examined for patterns of trend, seasonality, and cycle.

Title I school A school designated under appropriate state and federal regulations as a high-poverty school that is eligible for participation in programs authorized by Title I of the Reauthorization of the Elementary and Secondary Education Act, P.L. 107-110.

Title IV Refers to a section of the Higher Education Act of 1965 that covers the administration of the federal student financial aid program.

Title IV eligible institution A postsecondary institution that meets the criteria for participating in federal student financial aid programs. An eligible institution must be any of the following: (1) an institution of higher education (with public or private, nonprofit control), (2) a proprietary institution (with private for-profit control), and (3) a postsecondary vocational institution (with public or private, nonprofit control). In addition, it must have acceptable legal authorization, acceptable accreditation and admission standards, eligible academic program(s), administrative capability, and financial responsibility.

Total expenditure per pupil in average daily attendance Includes all expenditures allocable to per pupil costs divided by average daily attendance. These allocable expenditures include current expenditures for regular school programs, interest on school debt, and capital outlay. Beginning in 1980–81, expenditures for state administration are excluded and expenditures for other programs (summer schools and designated subsidies for community colleges and private schools) are included.

Town location See Locale codes.

Traditional public school Publicly funded schools other than public charter schools. See also Public school or institution and Charter school.

Transcript An official list of all courses taken by a student at a school or college showing the final grade received for each course, with definitions of the various grades given at the institution.

Traumatic brain injury See Disabilities, children with.

Trust funds Amounts collected and used by the federal government for carrying out specific purposes and programs according to terms of a trust agreement or statute, such as the Social Security and unemployment trust funds. Trust fund receipts that are not anticipated to be used in the immediate future are generally invested in interest-bearing government securities and earn interest for the trust fund.

Tuition and fees A payment or charge for instruction or compensation for services, privileges, or the use of equipment, books, or other goods. Tuition may be charged per term, per course, or per credit.

Type of school A classification of public elementary and secondary schools that includes the following categories: regular schools, special education schools, vocational schools, and alternative schools. See also Regular school, Special education school, Vocational school, and Alternative school. "School type" can also refer to whether the public school attended by a student was assigned to the student by the school district or chosen by the student's family in a district that allows school choice.

Unadjusted dollars See Current dollars.

Unclassified students Students who are not candidates for a degree or other formal award, although they are taking higher education courses for credit in regular classes with other students.

Undergraduate students Students registered at an institution of postsecondary education who are working in a baccalaureate degree program or other formal program below the baccalaureate, such as an associate's degree or a vocational or technical program.

Unemployed Civilians who had no employment but were available for work and (1) had engaged in any specific job-seeking activity within the past 4 weeks; (2) were waiting to be called back to a job from which they had been laid off; or (3) were waiting to report to a new wage or salary job within 30 days.

Ungraded student (elementary/secondary) A student who has been assigned to a school or program that does not have standard grade designations.

Urban location See Locale codes.

U.S. Service Academies These higher education institutions are controlled by the U.S. Department of Defense and the U.S. Department of Transportation. The 5 institutions counted in the NCES surveys of degree-granting institutions include: the U.S. Air Force Academy, U.S. Coast Guard Academy, U.S. Merchant Marine Academy, U.S. Military Academy, and the U.S. Naval Academy.

Variable A quantity that may assume any one of a set of values.

Visual and performing arts A group of instructional programs that generally describes the historic development, aesthetic qualities, and creative processes of the visual and performing arts.

Visual impairment See Disabilities, children with.

Vocational education Organized educational programs, services, and activities that are directly related to the preparation of individuals for paid or unpaid employment, or for additional preparation for a career, requiring other than a baccalaureate or advanced degree.

Vocational school A public school that focuses primarily on providing formal preparation for semiskilled, skilled, technical, or professional occupations for high school-age students who have opted to develop or expand their employment opportunities, often in lieu of preparing for college entry.

Years out In forecasting by year, the number of years since the last year of actual data for that statistic used in producing the forecast.

This page intentionally left blank.